The Schoolmaster, and Edinburgh Weekly Magazine, Conducted by J. Johnstone - Primary Source Edition

Anonymous

Nabu Public Domain Reprints:

You are holding a reproduction of an original work published before 1923 that is in the public domain in the United States of America, and possibly other countries. You may freely copy and distribute this work as no entity (individual or corporate) has a copyright on the body of the work. This book may contain prior copyright references, and library stamps (as most of these works were scanned from library copies). These have been scanned and retained as part of the historical artifact.

This book may have occasional imperfections such as missing or blurred pages, poor pictures, errant marks, etc. that were either part of the original artifact, or were introduced by the scanning process. We believe this work is culturally important, and despite the imperfections, have elected to bring it back into print as part of our continuing commitment to the preservation of printed works worldwide. We appreciate your understanding of the imperfections in the preservation process, and hope you enjoy this valuable book.

THE Schoolmaster,
AND
EDINBURGH WEEKLY MAGAZINE.

CONDUCTED BY JOHN JOHNSTONE.

THE SCHOOLMASTER IS ABROAD.—LORD BROUGHAM.

No. 1.—Vol. I.   SATURDAY, AUGUST 4, 1832.   Price Three-Halfpence

NOTICE TO THE NEW EDITION OF THE SCHOOLMASTER.

This little Periodical, the object of which is explained below, has now been in course of publication for above two months. Without puffing, fudgifying, or effort of any kind, it has been received throughout Scotland as a welcome, well-timed, cheap publication. Through friendly advice, and repeated invitation, the SCHOOLMASTER is now induced to make his appearance across the Border. Though his lucubrations are printed in Edinburgh, it will be seen that his objects are as extensive as British society, or as humanity itself. For their encouragement and furtherance, we venture to solicit the kindness of all liberal and intelligent Englishmen and Irishmen; and it is confidently hoped that the favour and protection of his own countrymen, abroad as at home, will not be withheld from the SCHOOLMASTER while he shall continue to deserve their countenance. For his honesty of purpose and earnest endeavour, we can undertake, and that thus far at least he will not disgrace their kindness.
ST. JAMES'S SQUARE,
October 12, 1832.

₊ This work is published in Weekly Numbers, price Three-Halfpence; and in Monthly Parts, stitched in a neat wrapper, with JOHNSTONE'S MONTHLY REGISTER OF PUBLIC EVENTS AND SCOTTISH LISTS, price Sevenpence when consisting of four numbers, and Ninepence when consisting of five numbers, with an enlarged Register. For the convenience of those who take the Weekly Numbers, the Register and Cover may be had separately, price One Penny.

ADDRESS.

This little periodical publication owes its existence to the non-removal of the Taxes on Knowledge. In January, 1831, I, in common with every one connected with the newspaper press, exulted in the prospect of an immediate and large reduction of the duty on newspapers as among the first fruits of a liberal Administration. This hope, delayed for a time to be renewed in the present year, has been at length completely frustrated; and the failure of the late generous attempt made by MR. BULWER, leads me to despair of it ever being effected till the measure is wrung from the legislature by the increase of the unstamped periodicals. I have long had the present Miscellany in contemplation, and have spoken of it from time to time; but as a periodical of this kind can never be of equal value with a newspaper, nor at all supply its place, I still hoped that a change in the law would permit those alterations, and that reduction in price, which is all that is wanted to make newspapers sweep away all other kinds of cheap publications. To the month of April of the present year I looked forward as the era of reduced prices and improved form; and on the 14th January I noticed this expectation in the Edinburgh Weekly Chronicle. Mr. BULWER's recent defeat, however, settles a question which, I fear, the state of the revenue—if that be the only real obstacle—will for a long time prevent being agitated with any hope of a successful termination. The appearance of the Penny Magazine, almost under the sanction of Ministers, indicates the course to be pursued with the newspapers, and also the sort of reading which even a liberal go.. vernment approves for the people. It is evidently thought better that they should read of the growth of the tea-plant, than watch the progress of legislation, or inquire into rights of industry; and learn of the ostrich and the giraffe, than jealously scrutinize the conduct of their rulers. Both kinds of reading are good; but the knowledge which teaches men how they may increase the comforts of their home and hearth is immeasurably the most important. It is, therefore, the avowed purpose of this publication to be political, in so far as the science of politics is connected with social wellbeing :—in short, to be as political as the existing laws permit, and to approach, as closely as is possible, to the character of what I conceive a really useful newspaper. We must not tell what passes in Parliament, nor at public meetings; but, if restricted in details, the fundamental principles of all good government are surely open to discussion; and the complicated phenomena of social life present endless subjects for speculation and popular disquisition. What must not be attempted by a relation of facts, may be accomplished by illustrations; and we have high authority for shadowing forth in parable that which a Pharisaical jealousy of the freedom of discussion does not permit to appear in the direct form of naked truth. As an exemplification of the principle, I refer to the Tale, and the Observations given in the present week on a subject which at present occupies much of the public attention—Military Flogging. THE SCHOOLMASTER, therefore, besides being as political as the laws allow, will embrace as wide a range of intelligence, scientific and literary, as is permitted to the Weekly Reviews and Literary Journals. It will require a few more statutes to define the exact limits which the unstamped publications may not trespass; and it may soon be found wiser to abrogate a pernicious law, which there is uch strong temptation to evade, than by farther pains and penalties to struggle to maintain what is unworthy of longer protection.

Such being the origin and purpose of THE SCHOOLMASTER, I have now briefly to detail its exact plan. The main object will be the cheap and universal diffusion of really useful information of every kind,—of such snatches and foretastes of all kinds of knowledge, as may stimulate to more extended inquiries, and supply ELEMENTS OF THOUGHT in all departments of mind. *Mechanical Inventions*, and the progress of discovery in the physical sciences, but above all in what are truly called the *Useful Arts*, will, so far as space permits, be attended to with the degree of interest due to their importance, as the chief instruments, under the guidance of a gracious Providence, of all the civilization and improvement which mark the highest condition of the human family. The mariner's compass and the steam-engine have already done more for the world than all the conquerors that ever carried "arts and arms" into barbarous regions. The printing press has done more for mankind than all the law-makers that ever lived. What has it still to accomplish!—It shall be the constant, as it is the highest aim of this Miscellany to accelerate its progress and extend its power. To the young, THE SCHOOLMASTER will study to supply, along with useful information and subjects for intellectual exercise, snatches of that graceful and humanizing light literature with which contemporary times abound.

As this small Miscellany is intended for the *Many*—for the great mass of the *People*—that mighty class from which in every country the greatest men have arisen,—from which in our island, and almost in our own day, have sprung a BURNS, a CULLEN, a COOK, a FERGUSON, a WATT,—as almost without any exception all great men have arisen from among the people, we shall, in catering for them, address ourselves at once as if to the best order of capacities; and with "milk for babes" that will yet be men, furnish food "for strong men," believing that our world is now old enough to relish the fitting nourishment of masculine intellects. If this plan shall be less immediately popular than pitching our tone in a lower key, we shall still deem it more wise, as well as more respectful, to endeavour to raise all our audience to the level, which, for a great part of it, may still be found too humble. The price at which THE SCHOOLMASTER is sold is so low as only to be afforded on the expectation of considerable sales. It is such as could scarcely be lessened by any reduction of taxation, and only by improvements in the manual operations of printing which are not at present anticipated. It has not been undertaken without due consideration, nor without securing the means, by the assistance of practised writers, to make it worthy of the patronage which is solicited for it. It is for time and chance to determine the degree in which it may deserve encouragement. Though late in the field, the boundaries are every day extending:—there is room for all.

With this explanation of motives and purposes, and without farther preface or profession, I leave this undertaking to speak henceforth for itself. All that can be claimed for it, or that ought to be desired, is a fair field and no favour,—with a trial deliberate enough to enable the judges to make a sound and true deliverance.

JOHN JOHNSTONE.

CHEAP PERIODICALS

CHEAP PERIODICALS are in Britain of rather ancient, and of most respectable lineage. They are older, by half, than two-thirds of the House of Peers, and all of them are the descendants of great men. The first, *The Review*, was projected by De Foe. It appeared three times a-week. The next Penny Paper was the *Tatler*—projected by Steele, and supported by the contributions of Addison and Swift, and the greatest *Wits* (as they were termed) of that day. It was followed by the *Spectator* and the *Guardian*. The *Tatler* sold at a penny; but was not, in 1709, nearly half the size which the *Schoolmaster* is, more than a century later, and was very inferior in appearance. The effect of these *great little* works was prodigious, as may be gathered from contemporary writers, and especially from Swift's Journal. Of the *Spectator*, 20,000 were occasionally sold; which, it would be no exaggeration to say, was more for that time than a half million of penny papers would be now, when the population of London has increased so prodigiously, and readers in a much larger proportion; while steam, and canals, and coaches have connected with the Metropolis all those hives of industry in Lancashire, Yorkshire, Warwickshire, and the West of Scotland.

After a lapse of thirty years, Johnson, in 1750, commenced the *Rambler*. It appears to have been sold at twopence, and was published every Monday and Saturday for two years. The number sold was only 500! The property belonged to a bookseller, who paid the writer four guineas a-week. To make amends for this tardy success, Johnson lived to see ten editions of the collected work printed and sold. Had the *Rambler* been allowed to go by post, at a small charge, at least ten times the number must have been sold then. Two years after its decease, Johnson undertook the *Idler*, which also existed two years; the natural limit, it would seem, of the cheap periodicals of those days. *Franklin* is to be enrolled among the ancestors of the cheap periodicals. His *Poor Richard's Almanack* was, in its own land and day, among the most valuable of these publications. Upwards of fifty years ago, the *Mirror* was begun in this city. The principal papers were contributed by Henry Mackenzie, the Man of Feeling. It had some sale in England; but no very great success anyway, in point of numbers. It has, however, often been reprinted. The *Mirror* was followed by the *Lounger*, which was supported by the same writers. The *Bee*, a *utilitarian* small periodical, was conducted by Dr. Anderson, in Edinburgh, and contained many good papers. About twenty years ago, Mr. James Hogg projected the *Spy*, and has humorously recorded its fortune. Within the last seven years, many little periodicals have risen and flourished for a time, and then been forgotten. But good they must have done, even the humblest of them; and their effects, though they may never become visible or tangible, are no doubt beneficially felt in some quarter or other. The cause of failure, generally speaking, has been the want of some presiding mind to give the little work tone and consistency of purpose. They were generally some third or fourth-rate bookseller's temporary speculation, who employed some poor literary wight, who *cut* with the scissors, right and left, without either judgment or discrimination, as long as any one would buy.

HOLYDAY RAMBLES ROUND EDINBURGH.

BY ZACHARY ZIGZAG, ESQ.

No. I.—THE RAIL-WAY.

No city like to thee, our own dear and venerable Mother! whether in variety, beauty, or scope of scenery. Youth, gaiety, and fashion are promenading in thy most princely Prince's Street—love and romance strolling in thy parks and gardens—bravery and hoar tradition are enthroned on all thy encircling hills! What picturesque outstepping, —round the fringed, breezy brow of thy Corstorphine, looking smiling down on the blue smoke of quiet Craigcruik!—round the coroneted front of thy stately Salisbury, or the crest of thy couchant Lion, thy peerless, noble Arthur! Well do we know all thy beauties; and fondly and reverently could we expatiate on them, and the delights they have yielded us, since at four we could just toddle over the *stiles*, and tumble our short length into the daisied lap thou spreadest for thy children in thy King's Park—

Speering no bold Baron's leave—

till the bold Saturday school-boy ventures, of reckless twelve, explored thy remoter and more hidden charms—proudly drew the minnow, and named it trout, from Braid's Burn; rifled, monster-like, the linnet's nest, on the "uncultured breast" of Blackford, sought our rural or silvan prey throughout all the land of Egypt, extending a traveller's right of conquest over Canaan, meditating spoils in the gardens of Goshen, taking personal possession of all the fair domains of St. Cuthbert, and extending our rambling dominion where the scarlet coat of postman not yet illumines the solitude, and where only the persevering foot of *Chronicle deliverer*—slow but sure, dilatory, but the more welcome—makes its adventurous way. But from these *old familiar places* we must stoically turn. We are bound on higher hests; and our very starting post is at the distance of a Sabbath-day's journey of our simpler years.

It is not without reason we choose the Rail-way Waggon. We like the quiet unexpensive pleasures which "after no repenting draws." As we propose being the guide of as many of the SCHOOLMASTER's pupils as will put themselves under our care in this excursion, we recommend them to breakfast with what appetite they may; and, "according to their several circumstances," make preparation for the creature-comforts of the day, whether in hunting-pouch, fishing-basket, or the neat willowy reticule borne by more delicate fingers.—And now we stride off, all through Lady Nicolson's Park, and down the Cross-Causey:—the Castle of Clouts' towers in sight, Gibbet Toll, "that was," in the distance. There are many things here to awaken boyish reminiscences. There *were* bickers in those days! Under the auspices of St. Catherine of Sienna, the patroness of skirmishing, how often has *our side* beat them back from the sacred precincts named for her, which stocking-weavers call the Sciennes, and march-of-intellect men, not quiet perfect in their orthography, Science Street.—But these glories are all past: their memory we leave in charge of J——— S———, best of local antiquaries—the modest, unknown Ashmole of Edina; and the new streets and feus to the care of Mr. Grubb and the Improvements' Commission; for we are now at the Depot, in the midst of coal cabinets, coal *bings*, coal carters, black, grey, and red, and waggons of every form and hue,—where, some five years back, we could sit under trees, or in hop-vine bowers, sucking honey-*blobs*, and green Gascoignes; another sense regaled all the while by the profuse fragrance of Mr. Bachelor,—gentlest name, of gentlest culler of simples for the maidens and matrons of Edinburgh. But here comes the Waggon; and as the eyes of the world are on us, we must now act, if possible, like a rational creature. We are snugly dove-tailed, about sixteen Christian souls in the space allotted to ten bodies; but good-humour is a first-rate bundler:—so off we go!—The rolling down the Tunnel* is not quite the MOUNTAINS at Paris; but it is a much finer thing in its way. Still finer is it to

---

* Mr. Fox, we understand, denies the breaking down of any part of the *Whig* administration in the Tunnel, and we must believe what we wish true.

emerge from its gloom, with the giant iron Ribs of Sampson, two hundred feet almost sheer overhead, and neighbouring them the fretted rock-work of the breechless western hip of Arthur. The scene here is indeed striking. The beautiful grounds of Prestonfield, or Priestfield, on the right, and on the other hand, the upward magnificent sweep of Arthur's Seat, leading on by the little placid Loch, to the romantic village church of Duddingstone, and the plantations of Lord Abercorn. We might pause here, but could not get beyond the city of the bone-bridges of antiquity, and of the " roaring curlers" of modern times, for this week, were the temptation not manfully resisted :—so turn we to willowy Pepper or Peffer Mill, with its cool cattle-pool and natural meadows, finer to our thinking than any young upstart villa of its acquaintance. The Railway here is most enviously shut up by high dead stone walls. The same spirit has been at work, which has demolished the stiles, and shut up the old pleasant path leading across the meadows to Duddingstone. Say, ye Road Trustees, whither has it vanished ?—that sweet path "traversed so oft in life's morning march." With the recollection of its delicious freshness the veteran L———— had cooled himself in the burning plains of India. When he returned three years ago, and found this haunt of boyhood for ever gone, the echoes of Arthur prolonged the *Soldier's malison*,—which we must not repeat, lest Mr Thomson, who, from yon distant upper window of the Manse, is doubtless making a sketch of the Waggon, might overhear the somewhat profane denunciation of all heartless, fanciless, brainless Road Trustees. The sketch, which we shall perhaps see in the Exhibition next spring, if " nobody buys" before then, comprehends *Our Waggon*, sweeping through the thick foliage— Craigmillar Castle in the distance—Priestfield in the middle distance, and here and there, a chance-bedropt tree ;—storied Craigmillar, where " beauteous Mary" bathed in wine, saith tradition, and became more beautiful even in the cruel languishment of her imprisonment!

It is only now that we find time to look round on our travelling companions. A respectable young shopkeeper, his wife, and three children ; Peggy, the lass, too, her hands full enough with the baby and the basket. There is a younger sister also, and a young man, likely enough, if things go well, by the diligent culture of five years, to ripen into a sober lover. It is a family holyday. That old lady in the dark shawl, her smile of quiet excitement only now taking place of the rigid horrors of the tunnel, goes but as far as Lugton-Path, to see an old neighbour, and obtain change of air for her grandchild, the sickly, pale little girl who leans on her. She has not been this way since her daughter (" the lassie's mother") married ; but " this is so reasonable ;" and she speaks of the Railway Waggon affectionately as of an obliging living female creature, and the " power of good *she* would do the bairns."

Opposite me is a sturdy, square-set, 'sponsible-looking person of fifty, or, by're lady, inclining to threescore. The swell of his breast-pocket shews a well-stuffed pocketbook, under the broad-skirted pepper-and-salt coat, and bodes corn exchanges in the market-place of Dalkeith, before the dinner hour, with the farmers of Ford, Crichton, Borthwick, Temple, or Newbattle parishes. He is a middle-man, between the granaries of the Lothians and the devouring maw of the manufactories of the West. He is a stanch Radical, I find, on every point save the Corn Laws ; of that only he is " not clear." This may account for his observations to my inquiring neighbour the matron, as, waving his umbrella-staff abroad, like a magician's wand—paying his way, and careless of who hears, he cries :—" Ay, all that good corn-land, every rig, from *his* gate in the high street of Dalkeith, down to Inveresk Kirk—the manors o' Smeaton and Castlesteads—or were they baronies ? locked into *his* park ; and two running waters *keppt* in't for *his* pleasure. What a sight o' mills and engines that stretch o' ground might support ! what a bee-hive of industry, and nest of comfortable homes for hundreds on hundreds o' puir bodies, and their bits o' bairns !"

" What a quantity of oatmeal they would consume !" cried a somewhat waggish youth on my right, whose japanned case boded botanical research, though a small copy of Grahame's Birds of Scotland starting from the waistcoat pocket, spoke of something else on an idling holyday.

" Ay, just sae," said the man of meal—the champion of productive industry—quite satisfied with this ironical crowning of his climax ; but my matron neighbour put in a woman's word for " the Duke." She had seen " the Park in auld Deuke Henry's time, and in the time o' the auld Duchess ; and a beautifu' sight it was,—with the hairy man, [orang-outang,] the hermitage, and the creatures o' deers—hundreds o' them, like sheep."

" And would five hundred, or, as John Storie has calculated, nearer five thousand, men, wives, and bairns, with their bits o' snug cot-houses and kail-yards about the banks and holms ; their rose-bushes, grozerts, and apple-renzie, as ye see in the West ; and may-be a *pig* and a bees' skep or twa— no been as bonny a sight, think ye, gudewife, whether taking their stoup o' wholesome ale, after their labours were over on a Saturday night, or praising their Maker in the Kirk on a Sabbath ?" said my friend, who, spite of his comfortable contours, and good *cleeding*, I now suspected of inveterate radicalism.

" That's the sight I ne'er saw there," replied the matron meekly ; " so I cannot say. But the auld Duchess was a kind woman to beast and body. And what this man has is his *own*, surely ?"

" Ay, so it is, mistress ; but how came it to be sae—sae muckle o't ?—can ye tell me that ?"

" From his forbears, I daur-to-say ; and I hope he remembers who is the *Giver* of all, and is a kind man to the poor, and to his tenantry."

" And where got they—the forbears, I mean—

where got they it, gudewife?" demanded my friend triumphantly.

"Deed, gudeman, ye have overly mony questions for a simple body like me. I wish ye binna like our Rob: there's ower mony of your kind in the warld, at this same time. Where should the auld Buccleuchs get their heritage and their prey, but as Jacob did,—wi' their sword, and wi' their bow!"

This ingenious Scriptural parrying of the question amused my botanical neighbour and me not a little; though it evidently excited the contempt of our honest man of meal, who took a persevering pinch of "The Chancellor," and looked rather at fault. I diverted the discourse into the different channels of the rich flat valley through which we now rolled, veined with rail-ways, branching off, right and left, to the several coal-works—to Edmonstone, Newton, "Sir John's," &c. &c. The hay harvest was in full luxuriance around us, a richer mining harvest below; and sometimes the apparition of a "bonny bruckit lassie" crossed our line of vision—till we obtained a glimpse of the neat, clean, pretty town of Dalkeith, where a popular canvass was going forward on this day—the first in the memory of man!—and that too with the odds of burgher against Duke! But we have no taste for politics.—At the crossing of the Dalkeith road we dropped a quantity of our live lumber, besides matron and meal-monger, and in a few minutes had reached the lofty bridge which crosses the North Esk and the valley at Elgin Haugh. Let the *Waggoneer* look round now. The view here is superb. The high, undulating, and finely-wooded slopes of the Esk, "Melville's beechy groves," and, in the distance, a splendid sweep of the Pentlands, which, whatever be their private reason, certainly turn their most lumpish side to Edinburgh. Here they spread out, light, aerial at once and magnificent. Dalkeith is seen rising to the left again; its church-spire over and among banks, trees, and the garden slopes of suburban villas—if the whole town be not suburban—which will be just so much the better.

But now a wider, wilder range of country opens before the fast-whirling Waggon. From the Pentlands on the south-west, our glance may sweep round and along the browner and more distant ridge of the Moorfoot Hills; and over hills, and holts, and ridges, enclosing a vast and wavy expanse of country, from the rich, umbrageous foreground of Newbattle Abbey, stretching on to Dalhousie, with its handsome church-tower, up and onwards to the misty sources of the Esk and the Gala. A beautiful near prospect, indeed, here opens to us; for the Waggon has stopped at the magnificent viaduct the Marquis of Lothian has lately thrown over the vale of Newbattle. At *Dalhousie Mains* we get out, and all part company, save those who voluntarily tarry the guidance of the *Schoolmaster's* deputy, *Ourself*. Let us follow them. Yon blithe, bonny lass, who, long before the lark was abroad this morning, was on her way to Edinburgh, with her butter and eggs, in that same basket, made by the blind old soldier, in which she now carries back some *trios* of Imitation Finnans, as good as the real, and three yards of bobbin net, which she wonders the weaver could work at 1½d., or rather her wise mother, a political economist, wonders; for Phemie only guesses how it will look in Borthwick Kirk on Sabbath, under the bit of pink twopenny ribbon, garlanding her face—fair though freckled—the nearest landmark I can give you to the homestead of Phemie, is the *Shank*, on before us, about two miles, on that gradually rising ground, and almost the centre object,—the old howlet-haunted biggin of the "bloody Mackenzie" of persecuted Scotland—the true high-priest of tyrany—conscienceless, remorseless; but a man of fine taste withal—full of graceful amenities!—in the refinements of life much in advance of his age, of which he was the thorough-bred Tory Attorney-General and Chief Justice. The lime-tree avenues, bowling-green, and desolation of the ancient garden, surrounding these ruins of a "blood-cemented house," are worth going to see some day that you make a waggon excursion,—but not to-day. When you do go, do not fail to have pointed out to you the ruined cottage that was once that of Grahame's Kilgour. Contrast the peasant's reputation, as it survives in the honest page of the poet, with that of the man thus apostrophized:—

Perfidious minion of a sceptred priest!
The huge enormity of crime on crime,
Accumulated high, but ill conceals
The reptile meanness of thy dastard soul;
Whose favourite art was *lying* with address,
Whose hollow promise helped the princely hand
To screw confessions from the tortured lips.
Base hypocrite! thy character, pourtrayed
By modern history's too lenient touch,
Truth loves to blazon!

You, Waggon-ashamed young companion of the youth of the botanic japanned case! you, whom the black gown has just blest with visions—fair though distant—of Depute-advocateships, Sheriff-ships, or the Deanship itself, look on this other picture: *Time* has set his seal on both.

Better far Truth loves to paint yon house
Of humbler wall, half stone, half turf, with roof
Of mended thatch, the sparrow's warm abode;
The wisp-wound chimney, with its rising wreath,
The sloping garden filled with useful herbs,
Yet not without its rose; the patch of corn
Upon the brow; the blooming, vetchy ridge.
But most the aged man, now wandering forth,
I love to view; for, 'neath yon homely guise,
Dwell worth, and simple dignity, and sense,
Politeness natural, that puts to shame
The world's grimace, and kindness crowning all.
Why should the falsely great, the glittering names
Engross the Muse's praise? My humble voice
They ne'er engrossed, and never shall; I claim
The title of the Poor Man's bard; I dare
To celebrate an unambitious name;
And thine, KILGOUR, may yet some few years live,
When low these reverend locks mix with the mould.

They will not have made an idle or profitless waggon-jaunt who contemplate with feelings like these the dismantled walls of the prosperous, base man of worldly ambition, contrasted with the dwelling of " the poor man." Within a short distance is sweet Kirkhill, and the favourite residence of this most amiable of the poets:—but it shall not tempt us to-day, for, have we not promised to act as guide to the travelling pupils of the *Schoolmaster?*

The Waggon stops at " the Mains," but suppose we walk a few hundred yards along that magnificent viaduct, and view how the land lies. The first sight of this work of art alone, viewed from beneath, and especially from the eastern, or Newbattle side, is worth ten times the journey we have made this morning. Look up from a respectful distance to those lofty but light arches, the masses of wood and umbrage hanging on the slopes beyond, and filling up their graceful circumference. Look up and down the valley of the Esk, by " copse-wood steep, or dingle deep," and say which is the more beautiful! The groves of Newbattle more rich beyond a doubt. But now many fathoms above that slender river, and perched upon the central arch of the viaduct, we look about us.—Yonder, five miles off, lies Temple, *up the water:*—but the best of the fishing season is past, and the near woods of Dalhousie promise a banquet to the botanist, and his friend the black-robed sketcher. They leave us, and, guided by *our* finger, steal down to the high-way. There they are no bigger each than a crow—" choughs that wing the midway air." We positively forbid any divergence to the smith's. A caulker of unmingled Esk, may do the feat with their young spirits;—besides, they have, ready concocted, the basis, the sherbet of Glasgow Punch: ten waters, we counsel. They advance a few paces on the Dalhousie road, and plunge down a winding high-banked lane on the left, which leads to certain stepping-stones of a burn that falls into the Esk, below the little Paper-mill. It is a lovely rural spot altogether; like all fords, the small as well as the great. One may now begin to herbalize, the other to sketch forthwith. If they push over, a few steps place them beside a clover field, running along a high bank of the Esk, skirted by an old oak coppice, mingled with hazel, and white-thorn, and black-thorn, and tangled with wild plants and creepers innumerable; an aviary of warblers, with the hares and leverets scudding across the open track every other minute. The opposite banks of the river, equally well-wooded, rise yet higher; and across its entire breadth the Marquis of Lothian has lately constructed a dam-head, which, after a spate, when the Esk, like a salmon taking the leap with its tail in its mouth, launches over its whole impetuous volume, makes to untravelled folks no contemptible *Terni.* There are many fine points of view around you, though they are somewhat confined; and the magnificent viaduct becomes the more imposing the farther you recede from it.

The mavis and blackbird, and all the woodland choir will be in full *bravura:* they don't take their *siesta* till about eleven. Plants here are so many and various, that were you a Nebuchadnezzar, they would satisfy your appetite. You will probably already have admired the taste of the " My Lord Marquis" of the *Viaduct* and the *Terni.* There is every where a good deal of what is rough, and shaggy, and untidy about him; but it is like the flowing untrimmed mane of the Arab courser, snuffing the gale, and tossing abroad his wavy *undocked* tail.

At the end of this open path you come upon the wrong side of the walls of Dalhousie gardens, and a warning board: but it can have no reference to you; pass on through the nettles quietly. You emerge in a short time on the highway; cross it, and enter freely by the first green gate you find: —there is nothing of the cold spirit of aristocracy about the keeping of these two noblemen's grounds, either up or down the river—no tremendous walls, nor jealous fastenings. You are now in the Earl of Dalhousie's park. Keep the castle on your right, follow the path for some time—then wheel back and pass under the arch of the bridge. We leave you in one of the loveliest scenes in nature. If you be not a goose you need no further guidance, —if you be, we can do little more for you:— wander and worship, or straddle and gape. You will assuredly find your way across a rustic bridge, and up the steep path which leads to all that is left of "the good and the great" Laird of Cockpen. The house was lately levelled, but a few stones still indicate its site. The Dalhousie grounds, lying on both sides of the Esk, abound in natural beauty, to which the hand of Art has done her part, and nothing more. In the *haugh* or holm are some stately limes, coeval, apparently, with those of the Shank. There is also a romantic narrow Pass blasted through the living rock, rich in plants —its sides a thick enwoven tracery of leaf, leaflet, stem, and tendril. If, haply, after spending your day in the woods, you *cut* the waggon, Lasswade lies before you, and the outside of the stage; and we warrant you know something of Muir's. Having thus comfortably bestowed you, we return to our small family party—still standing exalted on the viaduct. No wonder that they turn longing eyes eastward to sweet, sequestered, silvan Newbattle, nestling in its pomp of groves—fitting haunt of Pan and the Dryads. We descend, and passing under the arches on which we lately stood, follow that rural, kirk-going path down the river's bank, and then skirt the meadow we call Robin Hood's meadow, for want of a better name. The turf stretches out on one side; on the other are wood and water blending, of which we hear the liquid murmurs, but cannot perceive the flow for the tangling brushwood. Let Edinburgh folks who would know how glorious a thing a tree may be, now enter a swing gate at the end of this meadow, surrounded on two sides by the greenwood. Dotting its bosom, are many fine trees, under which the cattle now pant away their lazy noon; but none equal to those of the avenue we bid you enter. Immediately inside the gate is a Druid grove—dark, mysterious—a silvan entanglement of all sorts of cultivated timber,—stately horse-chestnuts, and the tallest hollies we ever beheld, conspicuous among the sycamores and ashes. In the avenue, which leads straight down to the street of the village, and opens exactly opposite the old massive stone-work and truly baronial gateway of the Abbey, there are some of the most beautiful beeches in the world. No! the round globe with all that beautifies it of woodland or primeval forest, cannot hold finer trees than those, there where they stand, side by side, erect, majestic; like Indian warriors, with their stately naked stems, and plumed heads, making tree-worship a not incredible thing.—Back to the Robin-Hood meadow again:—the oak copse on one hand, the gamekeeper's cottage in a corner, snug but not picturesque: groups of reposing cattle, and single trees break its surface. They are chiefly oaks, with "one in eminence above the rest," bow-houghed, knarled, and tough, breaking into two strong stems at less than two feet from the ground. Such is the GOW CHROM of a hamadryad of our acquaintance, who in other days might often be found kneeling about its sturdy trunk, and old fantastic roots, a believer in tree-worship. GOW CHROM is now very properly paled in, to prevent the too near approaches of the cattle.

In the neighbouring grounds of Newbattle and Dalhousie, a tree-fancier may see many fair specimens of the various sorts once *fashionable*. At Dalhousie, yew and arbor-vitæ, and near Newbattle house one slender, graceful, yellow-haired acacia, rare in this country of such growth. The same park abounds in fine timber-trees of immense growth, ashes, beeches, chestnuts, horse-chestnuts, and that beautiful tree, the walnut, in its full perfection.

We now resume the path from which we deviated when we left the meadow. It leads by the *mill-dam*, overhung with elder and bordered by copse and gardens on one hand, and strawberry beds on the other,—down to the old dilapidated village, which of itself, spite of all its silvan beauty of glade and grove, and luxuriance of orchard bloom, is as fully qualified to form part of the dower of the Owl's daughter in the Vizier's tale, as any inhabited spot we know. The tumble-down dwellings cannot have been touched since the Reformation laid its destructive hands upon the fair Abbacy. The people stick to their old sheds like barnacles, and the proprietor lets them have their own way. Very pretty stories could be told about this, but we won't give to Fame what was never intended for her trumpet. The village is a long narrow street, to which from both approaches, one descends by a steep path. We, as you know, struck down into its centre by the by-path. On one side of the street is the abbey wall, high and gloomy, overhung with old sycamores, pear-trees and elder bushes, probably coeval with the monks. Since we remember, there was here a flourishing rookery; and the sign of the Sun flamed opposite that fine baronial gate-way, with its turrets and postern doors, and the *jougs* frowning in terror by its side. These things are all vanished, every third house is a ruin, the church exteriorly not much better—garden patches, and dismantled gables alternate all along the street. The Park, properly so called, is in the finest style of English monastic places,—the river gliding serenely and peacefully through the freshest verdure,—steep wooded banks rising on the right side, and the level ground stretching away in far perspective,—glades and vistas opening to the left, formed by those old "patrician trees." The mansion is an object of inferior consideration. It stands apart, finely enough, and does not interfere to mar the prospects of the park,—to the sweet, soothing serenity of which, nothing seems wanting but the figures of the old monks stealing across the intersecting paths, or musing, as they must often have done, under the over-arching melancholy boughs, by that placid and gentle river. How delicious this retreat—which we could pity the lazy friars for being forced to abandon!

But we have another duty on hand. Our family group is on the grass in the Robin-Hood meadow, through which we passed; and Peggy, having with some difficulty kept the boys out of the *mill-dam*, when poking up the eels from under the roots and stumps, and pelting the water-rats, spreads the contents of her basket for a joyous repast, young and old mingled round the same roomy board. It is not yet one o'clock, and I have still to guide the strong-limbed of the party, four in number, to the Roman Camp, whence a new world, bounded by its own horizon, will open to them. But the events of that excursion must be deferred till another week. Now we leave the children with their mother, and the whole under the protection of GOW CHROM: there they are, wild with the delights of this new and beautiful world of birds and flowers, wood and water—exhaustless in novelty and wonder—no fear of want of amusement till papa returns:—the river is singing its first-heard madrigals.

    Robin and little Jenny wren,
  The Queen of the Fairies' cock and hen,
are fluttering about. Some of the prettier of the wild flowers are past—the hyacinth and primrose with which these banks are yearly covered,—the chestnut flower, the white bird-cherry, the elder bloom, and the May, are all faded,—the butter-cups have vanished from the meadow; but the gowan and the meadow-queen are still found, and the little forget-me-not, the speedwell, and the eye-bright, are scarce gone yet. Then Jack can have a tumble on the yellow ladies' bed-straw, and Jane decorate her bonnet with the blue-bells dear to Scotland. From the deepwooded glades the wood-pigeon is croodling; and the cuckoo is heard for the first time; for he seldom comes near the King's Park, nor yet Newhaven. In the avenue one may see a squirrel, and a pheasant or two for certain; and in the oak belt bounding the meadow, and dividing it from the dam and the river, there are innumerable

song-birds. It will go hard if Peggy does not strip off her "woman's blacks," and give the youngest children a cooling dip up near the bridge; while the elder boys tuck their trousers, and wade down the dam in the wake of Admiral Drake, who has just left the Paper-mill, or thereabouts, at the head of a small fleet, on a voyage of discovery, which he finds it necessary to bring to a close by a homeward journey overland. By the time that we rejoin the still untired groups, a whole basketful of green acorns, manufactured into *cups and ladles*, and of wild flowers, peebles, and forfeited nests, have been collected; and all are stowed into the waggon, which is now waiting us, at six precisely. Again from the Roman grandeur of our elevation on the viaduct we look fondly back on the woods and meadows; and with a sweeping farewell glance at the expanse of charming country we are about to leave, hurry on to where we pick up our matron of the morning and her little grandchild; both looking healthier and happier for their day of pleasure; both, too, loaded with dairy and garden produce; armfuls of roses and sweet-williams in the maiden's close embrace; and butter and eggs tenderly handled by the old lady; who assures us, besides its being a penny a pound dearer, town's butter never has the flavour of country butter.

It was her son, that at his breakfast-hour, had put them into the waggon; but now every domestic duty sped, the daughter-in-law, *rede* up, and with a merry bevy of children, her own and her neighbour's, has wandered out as far as the Wells-o'-Weary, "to see grandmother and Mary sitting in the waggon." A joyful shout of recognition greeted our appearance from these urchins, posted on the rocks above, as we hurried on below, and vanished in the tunnel, leaving them to run back through the park and overtake us as they could.

Next week shall find us posted at the ROMAN CAMP, which we uphold as the first station for a *coup d'œil* in the three Lothians. Till then,—*Vale!*

ELEMENTS OF THOUGHT.

HINTS TO THE OPERATIVE CLASSES.
BY GEORGE COMBE, ESQ.

IN Manchester and other towns in the manufacturing districts of England, the operatives have been forming societies for the purpose of preventing a reduction of wages; they are also bent upon accomplishing a restriction of the hours of labour. The restriction of labour, which some of them actually carry into effect, is devoting one day in the week to idleness and drunkenness, in addition to Sunday, which probably they spend in a similar manner. We are strenuous advocates for restricting the hours of labour and ameliorating the condition of the working classes; but we wish to see these ends accomplished according to the principles of reason, and the constitution of human nature.

The great question is,—Whether man is intended by the Creator to reap his chief enjoyment on earth from his appetites, or from the faculties which constitute his rational nature? If from the former, then society is essentially constituted at present on a right basis; the lives of the lower and middle classes are dedicated to the production and accumulation of wealth as their proper business, and those of the higher classes to the enjoyment of wealth already acquired. If, however, man is destined to derive happiness chiefly from his rational nature, a great change remains to be accomplished in the institutions and practices of society; and we entreat of the operatives to consider what these changes must be, in order to produce real and permanent benefit to themselves and society at large.

If man shall ever assume the station of a rational being on earth, the business of his life must be to study the works and the will of his Creator, to frame his institutions in conformity with them, and to act in harmony with the designs which these reveal to his understanding. One requisite to enable him to follow pursuits referrible to these principles, is provision for the wants of his animal nature; namely, food, raiment, and comfortable lodging. It is clear that muscular power, intellect, and mechanical skill, have been conferred on man with the design that he should build houses, plough fields, and fabricate commodities, because his nature requires the aid of the articles produced by these means. But the question is, whether ought his whole life and energies, aided by all his discoveries, be dedicated to these ends, as his proper business, to the neglect of the study of the works and will of the Creator? Has man been permitted to discover the steam-engine and apply it in propelling ships on the ocean and carriages on rail-ways, in spinning, weaving, and forging iron,—and has he been gifted with intellect to discover the astonishing power of physical agents, such as are revealed by chemistry and mechanics, only that he may be enabled to build more houses, weave more webs, and forge more iron utensils, without any direct regard to his moral and intellectual improvement? If an individual, unaided by animal or mechanical power, has wished to travel from Manchester to Liverpool, a distance of thirty miles, he would have required to devote ten or twelve hours of time, and considerable muscular energy, to the task. When roads and carriages were constructed, and horses trained, he could, by their assistance, have accomplished the same end in four hours with little fatigue; and now, when rail-ways and steam-engines have been successfully completed, he may travel that distance, without any bodily exertion whatever, in an hour and a half. We ask for what purpose has Providence bestowed the nine hours which are thus set free as spare time to the individual? We humbly answer for the purpose of *cultivating his rational nature*. Again, before steam-engines were applied to spinning and weaving, a human being would have required to labour, say for a month, in order to produce linen, woollen, and cotton cloth necessary to cover his own person for a year; in other words, the twelfth part of the time of each individual would have required to be spent in making raiment for himself, or in case of a division of labour, a twelfth part of the population would have required to be constantly engaged in this employment: by the application of steam, the same ends may be gained in a day. We repeat our inquiry, For what purpose has Providence bestowed the twenty-nine days out of the month, set free by the invention of the steam-engine and machinery? These proportions are not stated as statistically correct, but as mere illustrations of our proposition, that every discovery in natural science, and invention in mechanics, has for its direct tendency to increase to man the command of time, and to enable him to provide for his physical wants with less laborious exertion. The grand question constantly recurs, Whether, in thus favouring the human race, the object of Providence be to enable them to cultivate and enjoy their rational faculties, or merely to reap more enjoyment from their propensities, by accumulating wealth, and all that it commands, in greater and more superfluous abundance? We again answer,—That the former is the object of the Creator, because He is wise and good, and because He has bestowed on man intellectual and moral faculties which cannot be contented to grub for ever in the mine of mere wealth.

SOCIETY IN BRITAIN.
BY GEORGE COMBE, ESQ.

SOCIETY in Britain is constituted at present on essentially erroneous principles. If we survey the lives of men in this country, we shall find that the effect of all the discoveries that have been made in arts and sciences has been to render the great mass of the people more busy, and more unremittingly occupied in pursuits that bear reference chiefly to the support and gratification of the animal portion of human nature. Instead of every individual in society enjoying more leisure, and devoting more time than formerly to the cultivation of his moral and intellectual powers, and the enjoyment of his rational nature, the great body of the people are greater slaves to toil than formerly; the only effect being an increase in the number of persons who live independently of all labour, and in the wealth and luxury diffused through society at large. The portion who have been rendered independent of labour, do not generally devote themselves to the improvement of the species as a business, but seek gratification to their individual feelings in such a way as best pleases themselves; so that society has not improved in its moral and intellectual aspects in a due proportion to its advance in ingenuity, mechanical skill, and industry. The great change, therefore, that remains to be accomplished, is, that society at large should recognize man's rational nature as a divine institution, and practically allot time for its due cultivation and enjoyment. This can be accomplished only by masters and operatives uniting in abridging the hours of labour *every day*, and forming social arrangements by which the hours gained may be devoted to the acquisition of knowledge, and the exercise of the moral feelings. This ought to be practicable, if man be really a rational being: and to any one who declares the proposal to be Utopian, enthusiastic, and absurd, we answer, that by maintaining such opinions he really degrades man into a mere labouring animal, and sets at nought his boasted adaptation for an immortal existence in a moral and intellectual sphere.

The *effects of a limitation of labour* of this kind would be to raise wages, to render trade more steady, and above all, to increase the power, and elevate the aspirations, of the moral and intellectual faculties, by which means society would become capable of viewing its real position and estimating fairly and dispassionately the proper value of its different pursuits. The real standard by which to estimate value, is the adaptation of any object to promote human happiness; and if happiness consists in the gratification of our rational powers, then it is clear that society is at present engaged in a blind pursuit of wealth, for its own sake, and that it misses enjoyment in consequence of neglecting moral and intellectual cultivation.

FLOGGING IN THE ARMY.

Stripes, that Mercy, with a bleeding heart,
Weeps when she sees inflicted on a brute.

FLOGGING is a punishment of torture which not only degrades the man who suffers it, and makes the chances of moral improvement less than before, but it is often fatal to life. Let us imagine a soldier—whose breast is, perhaps, scarred with honourable wounds—tied up to the halberts for some violation of military law; his back stripped, and that instrument of torture applied by a vigorous arm, every stroke of which cuts into the flesh; let us imagine the surgeon* standing by, and occasionally feeling his pulse, to ascertain how much more of this exquisite torture he can bear, before the effects of the agony and mutilation inseparably break in upon the sources of life; let us suppose that the scientific calculator upon the capacity of the sufferer to endure the protracted torture, makes a mistake, and estimates his powers of endurance a little beyond what they really are;—let us suppose him sinking exhausted under the repeated infliction, and carried away to linger in the dreadful anguish that closes but in the grave. By imagining such a scene of punishment, and such a result, we only figure to ourselves what has often in reality happened under the existing system of military torture.

If it were proposed, that, whether in peace or war, the sleeping sentinel should actually suffer death, there are perhaps few persons capable of reflection, and not of sickly sensibility, who would not accede to an evil so sanctioned by necessity; but then it must not be death by torture. The lash fills the mind of an Englishman with abhorrence; that death should follow its infliction would even render it somewhat less appalling. The scourge is infamy as well as cruelty. It sinks into the soul of a warrior—it breaks down the man—it is extinction of pride, and hope, and honour. The physical agony is but a small part (however dreadful) of what the wretch endures. Shoot him, rather: for mercy, shoot him!

How does it happen that the French army can be brought to the highest state of discipline without being subjected to such degrading and inhuman punishment? The most completely organized and powerful army which, perhaps, the world ever saw—that which Napoleon marched into Russia, and which the resistless powers of the elements only vanquished—knew nothing of military torture, by the lash, or in any other shape. If the British soldier be less amenable to moral discipline, and less susceptible of feelings of honour and shame than the French, it can only be attributed to the man-degrading effects of the barbarous cat-o'-nine-tails upon the mind and character of the former.

Such things cannot go on in England; already they have remained too long. The age is against them, and the state of the world: the frame of society in this land may be unhinged by their prolongation.

THE STORY-TELLER.

THE FLOGGED SOLDIER.

BY MRS. JOHNSTONE.

EVERY one acquainted with the two countries, must have remarked a strong resemblance between a certain class of old Irish families, and those families to whom Scotland owes her bravest officers: both are alike poor, gallant, well born, and possessed of the pride of birth. Young Irishmen of this description formerly found honourable employment in the service of foreign princes; but these times were gone, and lamentable prejudices had now fated them to an inactivity as pernicious to themselves, as alarming to their country. While the Highlander entered life with the most inspiring hopes, and directed the energies of youthful ambition to the promotion of his country's welfare, mutual distrust and aversion condemned the unfortunate Irishman to find happiness in carousing with the ragged peasants who acknowledged his imaginary superiority; to employ his talents in cultivating the arts of vulgar popularity; and to place his ambition in heading brawls at fairs and funerals. Nothing but wisdom and conciliation can, for any length of time, be "retentive of the strength of spirit;" and it is not very surprising that such persons sometimes displayed their prowess in enterprises even more desperate than beating excisemen and tithe-proctors, and carrying off young women.

Roderick Bourke lived in the province of Connaught, in a decayed house, which, by the courtesy of Ireland, was called Castle Bourke. The heir to a barren sceptre, he was accustomed to hear himself addressed by his loving kernes, in a style which the Herald's office decrees to a very different person. The same devoted people had often ventured life and limb in his service; and Roderick, who had the true spirit of an Irish prince, could not, in requital, do less than spend his last acre in regaling them with whisky and tobacco. Roderick died, after a short and tumultuous, but, on the whole, a glorious reign, and was splendidly buried by voluntary contribution; and his only son, whose immediate ancestors had been general officers in the service of all the Catholic princes in Europe, was now a private soldier in the regiment of Sir Archibald Gordon.

The young Irishman had entered the army at the age of seventeen; in three quarters of the globe he had proved his bravery; he was now in his twenty-seventh year, and in all the pride and strength of manhood. Gaiety of temper, drollery of manner, genuine Irish humour, and an exquisite talent for mimickry, extending to mind as well as manner, rendered him the favourite of the whole camp. The drunken sailor, swaggering officer, strutting martinet, and awkward recruit of Phelim Bourke, were the highest comic treat to the soldiers who gathered round him; and the officers of the different regiments, when over their wine, often sent for the graceful buffoon, delighted with his jovial *chanson à boire*, and the brilliancy of his repartee. Phelim also played finely on several instruments, and, in manly exercise, excelled all his companions. These fine qualities were all heightened by a warm and open spirit of military comradeship, and set off to the best advantage by a figure uncommonly handsome, even in Ireland; a gay, gallant air, and a countenance so intelligent, in its saucy

* The *Algometer* of our Tale.

archness, that no one could look on it without being tempted to smile, even at its quietest expression. Every man was the friend of Phelim, and Phelim was the friend of every *Irishman*; every woman admired "handsome Bourke," and Phelim adored the whole sex.

Such did Phelim Bourke appear to the dullest observer whom his wit quickened, or his gaiety enlivened. But to the watchful scrutiny of Norman Macalbin, a young Scotch volunteer, he presented something far more striking :—a mind of the loftiest order, dallying with its own conscious powers, and mocking at its petty purposes—hanging loose on life, and turning, in half-affected scorn, from that high prize of virtuous achievement, which it despaired of attaining. Norman could perceive that the laughing Carlini of the camp had very serious moments; at which times he treated those who depended for amusement on his wit, or his scenic excellence, with caprice equal to any spoiled actress of them all. It could not be doubted but that, with the blood of his ancestors, he inherited that proud hate which, for centuries, they had cherished against those whom boyish folly had made his masters;—circumstances alone could reveal, whether this principle was extinguished, or only smothered in his bosom. But, in his darkest moods, if the trumpet sounded, or woman smiled, the intruding phantoms fled, and glory and gaiety reclaimed their slave.

The careless laugh of this young Irishman, and his frank and graceful salutation, had ever been peculiarly exhilarating to the spirits of Norman, for whom he performed many little offices of kindness, and whom he treated with all the respect a nature so gay and so familiar could shew to any one, especially since he understood that Norman was neither a prince of the blood, nor of the half blood, but, like himself, "an unfortunate gentleman." They spent many of their leisure hours together, with much pleasure, and some improvement.

At this time, there was a little black-eyed girl, a kind of toast among the heroes of the camp, to whom Phelim was paying his *devoirs*, and who had also attracted the regards of his colonel. That a soldier should presume to rival his colonel, was a thing almost unexampled in military annals; and for some time Sir Archibald was lost in astonishment. But when Phelim, though well apprised of the intentions of his superior, showed no inclination to give up the pursuit, a favourite sergeant was sent to admonish him of his duty. Phelim would not believe that the articles of war forbade him to make love to Dora Tracey; so he laughed at the messenger, ridiculed the message, and was more than ever determined on conquest. Sir Archibald was equally resolved. His vanity and other bad passions, were now powerfully excited; from a lover by proxy, he condescended to woo in person; and both officers and soldiers anxiously watched the progress of the contending rivals.

Nature and habit had conspired to accomplish Phelim for enterprizes of this kind ;—his gallantry had ever been found resistless, but he now also contended for the honour of victory,—and he proved the happy conqueror. Phelim was not altogether insensible to his triumph; some of the officers ventured to rally Sir Archibald on his disappointment; and all saw the tempest grow darker and darker round the head of the thoughtless soldier.

A portentous week passed over; and Phelim, who neither foresaw, nor dreaded danger, had forgotten every hostile feeling, and even the occasion of animosity. On a fine summer's evening, he sat by the door of his tent, with some of his comrades, gaily tossing off bumpers to " Love and War," and carolling his last new song in

"Such is the love of a true Irishman,
That he loves all the lovely, he loves all he can,
With his slips of shillelah," &c.

Sir Archibald happened to pass. It was the anniversary of the battle of ——; and the officers had taken a holyday to themselves, and given a fête to as many of the soldiers as had been engaged in that affair. Sir Archibald knew nothing about this battle; but he felt his heart boiling with ungovernable rage against Phelim Bourke, whom he instantly assailed with a torrent of military rhetoric, commanding him to remove from the spot where he sat, and threatening punishment for the excess he had already committed. Phelim disdained to answer; and some of the men having explained the occasion of the festivity, Sir Archibald thought proper to walk on. " I see I'm a prodigious favourite," said Phelim, smiling scornfully, and continuing his song. In a few minutes, the drum beat for evening parade, and Phelim hastened to his place. He had been under arms all the morning; the day had been remarkably sultry, and he was still warm and fatigued. When standing at ease, as it is called, Phelim took off his grenadier cap, and began to fan himself; and, as he was expected to do nothing like sober people, in performing this operation, he displayed all the coquetry and languishing airs of an affected lady. Sir Archibald Gordon was now walking along the line, and, the more enraged that he durst not vent his anger, he sternly commanded the soldier to put on his cap, enforcing his command with the usual accompaniment of oaths, and Phelim obeyed; but, still supporting his assumed character, threw into his fine features so exquisite an expression of mawkish languishment, that his companions burst into stifled laughter. This was throwing the last drop into the cup of Sir Archibald's wrath. Transported with mingled anger and mortification, he repeatedly struck the soldier; while as fast, and as coherently as he could, he cursed what he was pleased to call his " damned Irish impudence." It was not easy for Bourke to bear a *national* reflection from this man; yet he stood with the coolest indifference, till he saw himself struck a second time. Phelim was a saucy, privileged offender; his birth, and his fascinating qualities, had almost dispensed him from the slavish subordination of a soldier. He still, however, moved neither limb nor tongue to defend himself; but, with a look of withering contempt, slightly blew on his arm, as if to puff away the puny strokes. The full force of that emphatic look fell on the exasperated spirit of the baronet, and again he furiously showered his blows on the soldier. Phelim had, on this occasion, great command of temper; he also knew the pains and penalties of his condition; yet thus provoked, he haughtily bowed to Sir Archibald, saying, " Thank you, brave sir; this is the more generous as you well know I cannot pay you back these eight good years." The rage of Sir Archibald was, if possible, redoubled,—he rushed upon the soldier; and Bourke being a large and very powerful man, grasped him firmly in his arms, threw him down, and spurned him with his foot !

The officers immediately gathered round; Phelim was surrounded, disarmed, and escorted to prison by a guard of Englishmen, and followed by many of his countrymen.

" What has he done, Pat Leary?—What has he done?" was the universal cry. " What the devil has he done, think ye?" answered the Irishman who was following Phelim; " Sure it was no great matter to forget he was an English soldier and remember he was an Irish gentleman." ——" But, Bourke, they say you put off your Irish impudence to the Colonel," cried another soldier. " Pray, what sort of impudence may that be?"——" Pat will tell you," replied Phelim ; " he has had most experience."——" Ay, do tell us," cried all the soldiers laughing aloud. " Is it me?" said Pat; " Why, faith, I fancy, it's much the same as *your* Scottish soberness, and not very different from *your English sincerity*."——" Right, Paddy," cried Phelim, smiling in his turn; " all national virtues! Poor Ireland has her *impudence!* Well, England calls her sister;—*the sister kingdom!*"

Pat, who had been anxiously watching his opportunity, pressed up to Phelim, as they drew near the prison-door, whispering, " Phelim, jewel, if you would take leg bail for it now, we make you as welcome as ever you was to your mother's milk !—White be the place of her rest !—By the Holy !—it's ourselves would compass our ould shister's boys, and by the same token we have done it before. Don't ye mind them." Phelim thanked his countryman, but he scorned to fly: and, besides, he had more good principle, than to purchase his own safety by the horror and blood which so wild a scheme might have occasioned to its good-hearted, though inconsiderate projectors. When they had seen him lodged in prison, they gave him a farewell cheer, in which they were joined by both the Scottish and English soldiers, to the great joy of Pat Leary, and the infinite indignation of Sir Archibald Gordon.

Bourke was a great and general favourite; but, in a military court, the colonel of a regiment must needs be fearful odds against a private soldier.

The sentence of a general court-martial condemned Bourke to expiate his offence by suffering four hundred lashes! His cheerful and manly spirit was at first completely overwhelmed by the idea of an ignominious punishment; he reminded the court of his birth,—he pleaded for honourable death. But he soon appeared to have recovered his customary gaiety; and when Norman visited him in prison, on the evening after his trial, and previous to his suffering, he found him gaily whistling, and caricaturing Sir Archibald Gordon, who at this moment was seen from the window, exercising the drum-boys in flogging a large stone. Bourke was working on the prison walls with a piece of red chalk, which he had ingeniously fixed in his *handcuffs*; the figures he had sketched possessed great spirit and force of expression, and the explanatory sentences all the points of Phelim's wit, when in his happiest vein.

"You are a universal genius, Bourke," said Norman, looking with sincere admiration on this bold caricature; "but this display of your talents will do no good, so you must pardon me if I efface it;" and he began to rub out the lines with his handkerchief, while Phelim looked on smiling. "Mr. Macalbin," said he at length, in a grave and earnest tone, "you are most kind; I have ever found you all the soldier and the gentleman, and with my whole heart I love and honour you. Were it not for these damned bracelets," and he clashed his *handcuffs* together, "I hope you will permit me, condemned as I am, to shake your hand, and to bid you think kindly of me, when all is over with me!" Norman clasped the fettered hands within his own, saying, "That shall not thwart our purpose." He perceived the sunny eyes of Phelim glisten for a moment;—but he again began to whistle, with his usual thoughtless hilarity, and Norman ventured to allude to his punishment. "I am not only happy, but proud to see you bear yourself so manfully," said he; "you know how much you are beloved,—you may count on every possible indulgence." Phelim made an involuntary start,— his features changed with fearful celerity, and he replied, "Yes, I know that I am beloved,—I have a stout heart too,—yet many a stouter has dishonour broken,—mine, I trust, will bear me out bravely!"—and he struck his fettered hands on the seat of that manly heart; and then, as if ashamed of his emotion, added, laughingly, "I am sometimes obliged to knock it up, and ask it how it does."

In a few minutes Norman left him; and, when locked up for the night, he was still whistling and caricaturing.

Next morning Norman heard, with indescribable concern, that Phelim had attempted suicide during the night, by opening the jugular vein; but that he had been discovered, and that strong hopes were entertained of his recovery. Night and day he was watched,—and he did recover.

At this time Colonel Grant, an old Scotch officer, returned to the camp, much dispirited by the result of a certain trial on which he had been witnessing. Norman knew his abhorrence of that horrid species of punishment, which is alike disgraceful to those who decree, and to those who suffer; and he ventured to plead for Phelim, as he knew a second court-martial was to be held, at which the Colonel was likely to be present. Colonel Grant knew the temper of Sir Archibald Gordon too well to give Norman much hope; he also knew, that vulgar minds cannot separate the idea of authority from the person in whom it is vested. To render the one contemptible, was to degrade the other. "Poor Bourke must suffer," said he; and Norman withdrew in bitterness of spirit.

On the day of the second trial, if it may be so called, he hovered round the tent in which it was held, with Phelim's young mistress and her father, a veteran sergeant belonging to his own regiment. When Colonel Grant left the court, the old man accosted him, saying, "Is there any hope for that poor fellow?"——"None, Tracey, none!" cried the Colonel, in great agitation! "We have ordered him an additional hundred for his second sally;"—and he hastily passed on. The poor girl fell into the arms of her father; and Norman hastened to the sea-shore to vent his feelings in solitude.

Phelim was now declared able to bear the punishment he would have died a thousand deaths to avoid; and, as the day drew near, Colonel Grant sent him a private message by Norman, bidding him be of good heart, as his punishment would be very lenient. "Does he think it is pain that *I* fear?" cried Phelim, indignantly tearing open his waistcoat and exposing his honourable scars. When this was reported to Colonel Grant, his features suffered a sudden contraction; and when the hour arrived which was to expose the lacerated and bleeding back of Phelim to the eyes of his countrymen, the Colonel contrived to be absent himself, though he could not extend the same kindness to Norman. He was compelled to attend. He saw the man, for whom his soul was in agony, brought out heavily ironed, more dead than alive, and brutally stripped to undergo the most horrid of punishments. Nothing could make him witness more of this revolting spectacle. He closed his eyes, but he still heard the soldiers muttering around him:—"That is the wound he got in Egypt," said one. "I tell you no," whispered another, "it is the sabre cut he got defending the colours at Maida!" Though sights of this kind are unfortunately too common to be much regarded, an awful stillness marked the strong sensation experienced by every individual in the little army when the signal was at last given, and when the *leaden bullet*,[*] which he indignantly rejected, was offered to Phelim Bourke. A death-like coldness crept through the veins of Norman; he leaned heavily on his musket;—in the next moment the rocks of the sea-shore were resounding to the strokes of the lash!—he became dizzy and sick, and heard and saw no more.

When he recovered he found himself supported in the arms of a soldier, and at a distance from the circle. "Bourke is taken down, sir," said the man, who was pleased to see so great sensibility to the sufferings of a soldier; "he had got two hundred, and the *flogometer* said he must get the rest afterwards."——"What mean you?" said Norman. "Oh, the surgeon who holds a man's pulse, to see how many lashes he can take at a time, sir; poor Bourke invented that name for him. Well, thank God, he never uttered one groan, nor shrunk a bit. Had he shrieked, we never could have borne it,—he was always such a merry fellow."——"What! do they then 'shriek?" cried Norman. "Dreadfully, sir, dreadfully!" replied the soldier, evidently shocked by personal recollections; "can you doubt but they must?"

At this moment some soldiers were seen bearing the mangled and almost inanimate body of Phelim Bourke across the field to the hospital tent. A few days back, and Norman had seen the gallant fellow, so wild with life, so full of talent and enjoyment!—"My friend, I am faint again!" said he to the soldier, and he hid his face in the grass.

For three succeeding days Phelim shrouded his head in the bed-clothes, refusing to look on the light which had witnessed his disgrace, and obstinately rejecting food. While in this condition Norman knelt by his bed-side, imploring that he would speak to him, and take nourishment and comfort; but Phelim continued inflexibly silent. Only once did Norman catch a glimpse of his face; and, oh! how changed the once fine features and radiant eyes

---

[*] In suffering this punishment, a leaden bullet is sometimes kept in the mouth, that the strong exertion of the teeth on this substance may deaden the sensation of excrutiating pain; and perhaps to keep the soldier from biting through his own tongue in his agony.

of Phelim! He sadly recollected of Captain Drummond of his regiment holding a dispute with the daughter of Colonel Grant, on the colour of Bourke's eyes, and of that young lady saying, "They were the colour of gladness."

Norman, though somewhat astonished to find any thing make so deep, and, above all, so lasting an impression on his light and joyous nature, still persisted in attending Phelim, and in attempting to sooth a noble mind, writhing under unmerited dishonour. One evening, after having exhausted every argument to console the poor sufferer, who continued dumb and sullen, his head wrapt in the bed-clothes, Norman tried to work on his generous temper by reproach and upbraiding.

"This cannot be that gay good-natured Bourke," said he, "whom every one loved. He would not thus sullenly reject the sympathy of his friends."

"Oh, no, no!" exclaimed Phelim, in a heart-piercing tone, "I am not that happy soldier!—A dishonoured wretch,—insulted degraded,—mangled by a scourge,—all that is man in me brutally violated. Why, then, should I live? Why, if you love me, do you look on me?" He immediately relapsed into silence, sullenly turned round, and told Norman to be gone. Recommending him to a Catholic priest, who kindly attended him, Norman withdrew, much grieved, and even alarmed at the strange perverseness and ferocity which a brutal punishment had wrought in the generous mind of this gallant Irishman.

Next morning, Phelim Bourke was missing. The whole encampment was, for some hours, in dismay and confusion; but the unfortunate soldier was never heard of. His comrades concluded that he had thrown himself into the sea,—a catastrophe which had sometimes happened in similar cases. At high water, Norman wandered along the shore, with Pat Leary, and some kind-hearted Connaught-men, in hopes of finding the dead body of their friend. The sea rolled in with a heavy wave, but nothing was to be seen. "Ah!" sighed Norman, "many a brave heart lies under thee.—Poor Phelim!"

When he returned from wandering on the shore, the glories of a resplendent sunset were streaming over the picturesque encampment, and flashing, in a thousand radiant lines from rows of flickering spears. Every soft and every martial form, caught new grace or grandeur from the rich tints of the evening. Groups of females and of military were every where gliding around; and children, born to war, frolicked about with the airy grace of their happy age. At a considerable distance a body of men under arms were still performing their evolutions, and sometimes marching across the plain, in motion measured by a lofty strain of martial music. In its pause was heard the round, full-toned voice of the commander, or that soothing hum of mingled sounds which fluctuates on a summer air in a still evening. Norman gazed on this fine picture with a cold practised eye; and of all the sounds that wooed his ear, he heard only the sullen murmur of the heavy wave which rolled over Phelim Bourke.

"'Tis a disenchanted scene!" thought he, as he leaned on the entrance of his tent. "Will they drill these poor fellows all night, because they presumed to lament their countryman? to play the march he loved too,—cruel!"

He stood wrapt in musing sadness, when darkness had come on, and when the camp-fires ruddied the field, which was still graced by female, and enlivened by infant beauty. His comrades, gathered around these fires, were enjoying the passing hour with all the happy, and thrice happy thoughtlessness of their profession.

"Who would wish a soldier to be a thinking creature!" sighed Norman. "Poor Phelim! already is he forgotten! How was he wont to fling round his jests at an hour like this!"

"'Tis a disenchanted scene!" Again the enthusiast began to ruminate bitter fancies. "Poor fellows! defenders of their country! How dearly is its defence purchased, if this be the price? A soldier,—a being degraded below the level of humanity,—a man who has surrendered the high privileges of his nature, and placed his freedom in another's power;—a solitary part of a vast machine, estimated only by its aggregate force,—subservient to every impulse of perverted power,—the blind instrument of pitiful intrigue, or lawless ambition;—an unfortunate, thrust beyond the pale of social life, almost prescribed the intercourse of his species;—the limits which separate him from the citizen so obtrusively pointed out, so rigidly maintained;—a creature placed beyond the influence of those salutary restraints imposed by the customs of society, and the observing eye of the world,—with personal responsibility losing all chance, all desire of acquiring the esteem of his fellow-men. Poor fellow: cruelty and force alone employed in enforcing that blind submission, and in exciting that animal ferocity, which seem to comprehend the whole of his duties,—duties which are perhaps incompatible with moral influence, since I never, never saw it tried!"

It was some three or four years after this that Norman, the young Scot, accompanied the memorable retreat of Sir John Moore to Corunna. During that miserable period, he was often employed on foraging parties, and in reconnoitring, for which his education, and the habits of a Highlander had peculiarly fitted him.

On an expedition of this latter kind, he was despatched to some heights on the banks of the Minho, the same morning that the troops left Lugo. He rode, and Pat Leary, generally a straggler, wandered after him, espying a cottage smoke, round which cottage some fowls might be straying. At this period, Leary was by no means delicate or confined in his notions of property; he had no scruple in thrusting into his pouch whatever *ammunition* he could find,—fowls,—bread,—indeed food of any kind,—clothing,—or even money. Macalbin said *stealing*—Leary said *lifting*,—and on this point they differed, about terms, like other philosophers. "Sure we came to *sarve* them, the souls," said Pat indignantly. "And if we did, shall we rob them," said Macalbin; "I command you not to approach that house."—Macalbin had gained the heights, and Leary was scrambling after him, when both were suddenly alarmed by a party of the enemy's cavalry, dashing down the opposite heights, while, before the rest, one man furiously pursued an English officer. He soon far outstripped the speed of his fellows, and gained fast on the fugitive.

"That is Colonel Gordon, I have *knowed* him by that stump of an ostrich feather ever since we left Salamanca. The Frenchman will give his plumes a *tussel* any way." Careless of personal safety, Leary, with delight he sought neither to suppress nor conceal, enjoyed the probability of Sir Archibald being made prisoner, while Norman eagerly looked round for some bridge, some ford on the rapid river; but seeing no marks of either, spurred down the steeps, and plunged into the stream, struggled with its violence, and, at the risk of life, reached the opposite bank, saw the sabre of the French officer descending on the head of Gordon, and joined the cry he set up for quarter—mercy! That voice seemed to arrest the death-stroke that hung over Gordon. The Frenchman, however, unhorsed him, tossed his sword into the river, and exclaimed, "You are the prisoner of France." All this passed in the twinkling of an eye, and before Norman, recollecting for the first time that he was in danger of being surrounded by a party of French dragoons, knew which way to turn. Yet to his prostrate countryman he instinctively turned and alighted. At this moment the officer on whom he had not yet looked, sprang from his horse, dashed sabre and helmet on the frozen snow, and leaped forward, exclaiming—

"*Look on me, Macalbin! I am* BOURKE*! I am a man again!*"

"Gracious God!" cried Norman, receding one step, overcome with astonishment to find, not only in life, but in an officer of the French Imperial Guard, apparently of high rank, and decorated with the splendid insignia of the Legion of Honour, his lamented comrade, "Phelim Bourke."

"Yes, I am that Bourke whom the English,—for whom I fought and bled,—insulted, degraded, mangled with brutal stripes.—Coward and slave," and he turned fiercely to Gordon, "you shrink beneath me now!—I am that

Bourke, whose country, kindred, family, and faith, have for six hundred years suffered at the hands of the English every species of cruelty, indignity, and oppression; massacred in hot, murdered in cold blood,—proscribed,—exiled,—tortured! I am that Bourke who shed my blood for the destroyers of my race! whose heart lacked gall to make oppression bitter, till their chains corroded my individual soul!"

It would neither be agreeable, nor perhaps very prudent to relate that story of country and family which Bourke rapidly and vehemently sketched; and still less so to detail all those motives and imaginary necessities by which he lulled his better genius to sleep, and fortified himself in error. Yet, let it not be imagined that he thought himself a traitor. He said, he vowed, that his heart glowed with love to Ireland, of which those who live in her bosom can have but a faint perception; and perverted as was that love, Norman could not doubt of its existence. This passion seemed even more ardent than the burning hatred which made him pant to avenge his own and her wrongs on those whom, in bitterness of soul, he termed "*the English.*"

Macalbin had much to say, and to inquire; but the trampling of the horses' feet of that party whom Bourke had out-rode, was now heard rapidly advancing, though the steep banks of the river still screened them from view.

"Hark!" cried Bourke,—"Fly, Macalbin!—cross the river!—It will not be known that it is practicable. Fly! or I cannot save you!" He eagerly waved his hand. Norman leaped on horseback, exclaiming as he went—"I have left a friend in Astorga, the wife of Colonel Monro, in the convent of ———. See her, protect her, tell her that her husband is well."——"I will,—I swear I will. Fly, Macalbin!—that is a vile word,—gallop though."

Macalbin plunged into the stream, and got over before the party came up.

AUGUST.—NOTES OF THE MONTH,
AND POPULAR ANTIQUITIES.

AUGUST, the eighth month of the year, is so named in compliment to the Roman Emperor Augustus. By the *Saxons* and old English (who were Saxons) it was named *Arn*, or *Barn-moneth*, as this with them, was then as now the month of general harvest. In our end of the island harvest is from a fortnight to three weeks later than in England, as the tardy Spring does not permit so early sowing. Barley harvest, however, is generally completed in Scotland before the middle of this month, and all CORN, in favourable situations, is in progress of reaping. "It is a gladdening sight," says Howitt, in his late pleasing book of the Seasons, " to stand upon some eminence and behold the yellow hues of harvest amid the dark relief of hedges and trees, to see the *shocks* standing thickly in a land of peace; the partly reaped fields, and the clear cloudless sky shedding over all its lustre * * *." The wheat crops shine on the hills and slopes, as Wordsworth expresses it, "like golden shields cast down from the sun." This is a sight which may now be enjoyed in high perfection from every eminence in and around the city. This, in Scotland, is the abundant month of fruits—the small fruits, are at its commencement still plentiful, and apples, pears, plums, peaches, apricots, and nectarines, become common, and grapes cheaper. The summer flowers disappear, but others not less beautiful succeed them. The passion-flower in favoured situations, the tamarisk, the trumpet-flower, and the clematis, are coming into blossom; and all the heathy mountains and moors of Scotland are waving purple with the heather-bells. The grouse are now strong on the wing, and the joyous 12th gives the signal for the commencement of the animating work of destruction. This is the chief month of insects, and all kind of flies, from the bloated blue-bottle, against whose approaches the careful housewife guards, "to the gay motes which people the sunbeam." The Highlanders name August the *Worm month*.

Change may already be perceived in the woodlands. The foliage, impaired by the fervid heats of July, now turns dry, rugged, and faintly sallow. The birds have ceased to sing; but the young broods, every where abroad, pleasingly supply the woodland melody. The starlings now congregate in vast flocks, and some of the swallow tribes begin to think of migrating, and may be seen wheeling over head, "as if exercising their wings, and preparing for their long aerial journey." The pre-eminent flowers of this month in Scotland are *blue-bells* and *heather-bells*. In the gardens are the capsicum, or Indian cress, African marigold, hollyhocks, golden rods, Guernsey lily, sunflower, common balsams, convolvuluses, the common amaranth, varieties of pinks, several of the finer annuals, and the poetical flower—*Love-lies-bleeding*. This is the month, when school holydays, too long deferred, commence in good earnest, and when every one hurries to the seacoast, for the healthful enjoyment of bathing, with sailing, paddling, marine weed-picking, and shell-gathering,—pleasures for every age.

THE GLOW-WORM, the star of the earth, is often seen in August. In some situations the glow-worms lie as thick on the banks of hedgerows as stars in the sky. This insect has afforded the poets many fine images. Like the more brilliant luminous insects of warmer regions, as the lantern-fly of the West Indies, and the flying *lucciola* of Italy, its lustre is lost by day :—as morning dawns the glow-worm begins to "pale its ineffectual fires." The luminous flies form beautiful objects in the black profound night of the forests of the West Indian settlements. We have read of a female naturalist there, who imprisoned as many lantern-flies in a small cage, as afforded her light to sketch their own pictures.

Lammas-day—Lammas-tide, the most memorable calendar day in August, is presumed to be derived from *Lamb-Mass*, on which certain kirk tenants paid their quit-rents by a live *lamb*. Some derive it from *Loaf-Mass*, i. e. *Bread-Mass*, a feast of thanksgiving for the first-fruits of the corn.

Lambs-wool is a kind of beer or sweetened liquor, supposed to be so named from its softness.—But we have *Yule-ale*, Whitsun-ale, why not *Lammas-ale?*—easily corrupted into *Lambs-wool*. Rains are frequent and heavy about this time, and are expected by the name of " the Lammas flood."

MEMORABILIA.—The 15th of August, 1769, was the birth-day of Napoleon. On the 11th, the *Dog-days*, which commence on the 3d July, end. On the 12th of August, 1762, George IV. was born. The 15th is the festival of the Assumption of the Virgin, to which festival that elegant creeper, the clematis, which shoots up rapidly, and flowers at this season, is dedicated by the name of *Virgin's Bower*. The 24th, St. Bartholomew's Day, will long be memorable for the most sanguinary scene of atrocity ever perpetrated in the abused name of Christianity. Ten thousand Protestants were massacred in Paris alone, and ninety thousand in the provinces, in consequence of a plan deliberately concerted by the Court, and the higher churchmen, and remorselessly followed up.

THE GLORIOUS TWELFTH OF AUGUST.

Glorious 12th! Mountain holyday! ushered in by a running *feu-de-joie* from " Lord Reay's country" even down to Lanark Moor, and the heights of Ettrick. But we must draw upon other pens rightly to describe the 12th. Take first the unfavourable side of the picture from a gentle limner :—

To man, bird, beast, *man* is the deadliest foe—
"Tis he who wages universal war.
Soon as his murderous law gives leave to wound
The heathfowl, dweller on the mountain wild,
The sportsman, anxious watching for the dawn,
Lies turning, while his dog in happy dreams,
With feeble bark anticipates the day.
Some, ere the dawn steals o'er the deep blue lake,
The hill ascend. Vain is their eager haste—
The dog's quick breath is heard, panting around—
But neither dog, nor springing game is seen
Amid the floating mist; short interval
Of respite to the trembling dewy wing.

> Ah! many a bleeding wing, ere mid-day hour,
> Shall vainly flap the purple-bending heath.
> Fatigued, at noon the spoiler seeks the shade
> Of some lone oak, fast by the rocky stream—
> The hunter's rest in days of other years.

Let us now reverse the picture:

> High life of a hunter! he meets on the hill
> The new-ushered daylight, so bright and so still!
> And feels, as the clouds of the morning unroll,
> The silence, the splendour ennoble his soul.
> 'Tis his on the mountains to stalk like a ghost,
> Enshrouded in mist, in which nature is lost;
> Till he lifts up his eyes, and flood, valley, and height,
> In one moment all swim in an ocean of light;
> While the sun, like a glorious banner unfurled,
> Seems to wave o'er a now more magnificent world.
> * * * * *
> As his eyes in the sunshiny solitude close,
> 'Neath a rock of the desert, in dreaming repose,
> He sees in his slumbers such visions of old
> As wild Gaelic songs to his infancy told.
> O'er the mountains a thousand plumed hunters are borne,
> And he starts from his dream at the blast of the horn!

So far Wilson's *Wild Deer*. This is different sport from the wholesale unmanly *battue* in the aristocratic preserve, where the only glory is the number of birds slaughtered.

THE SCHOOLMASTER'S REVIEW.

TAIT'S MAGAZINE, No. V.—*August.*

Mr. Tait has just produced his best, or, at all events, his most brilliant number. There is, however, still a due mixture of the *solid* and *utilitarian*. The opening article, an exceedingly just and able one, is on the most momentous topic that can at present be discussed; the qualities and training requisite to fit men for Parliamentary representatives. We would recommend its careful perusal to every elector. With the copious contents of this number we know not where to begin; nor among so much that is good, how to make choice. Suppose we give the poets precedence:—the number is absolutely rich in verse. A jubilee song on *the passing of the Bill*, by the author of the "Corn Law Rhymes," is not equal to some of the productions of this extraordinary and gifted person, who might himself be made the subject of a most interesting and edifying article, but it is a vigorous strain, nevertheless; and for the sake of those living Scotch Patriarchs of reform, who may see the *Schoolmaster* and not the *Magazine*, we quote one verse from the Sheffield workman,—from Ebenezer Elliot—who, in intellectual and poetical power, far distances—immeasurably far, all our rhyming Lords and Esquires put together.

> Oh! could the wise, the brave, the just,
> Who suffered—died, to break our chains—
> Could Muir, could Palmer from the dust,
> Could murdered Gerald hear our strains!
> Death would see, and souls in bliss,
> Unborn ages blessed in this!

The Magazine boasts a pretty song enough, by Mrs. Gore; and also a much higher strain, probably from the same source,—*Stanzas written in Windsor Chapel*—a piece of truly noble musing and moralizing on the vain shows and shadows of a life too high to be happy.—*Stanzas to the Madonna Alla Seggiola* is a gem, steeped in the softest dews of the morn of English poetry. It breathes the tender piety, the sweetness and purity of the muse of Crashaw; and is almost worthy of the divine painting, a copy of which has suggested it—a homage worthy of those "*calm-brooding eyes.*" Those who have not seen the picture, or any copy of it, to understand the poem, should be told that the Infant St. John forms one of that heavenly group. Poetry is not done yet, for *Auri Panegyricon* is also a poetical piece, and a composition of a very high order and energetic character—a noble and dignified flow of sentiment, sustained by powerful thought. We shall all owe Tait's Magazine a debt of gratitude if it proceed *unburrowing* minds like that which has poured forth these verses:—

> "Most lovely Earth! and was it to sustain
> This pismire toil; which, bending o'er a heap
> Of shining dust and pebbles, straws and grain,
> Makes for a shrine the mud where it doth creep;
> And blind to broader paths or fairer views,
> Crawls, dull and grovelling, to its last poor sleep—
> Thy countless stores of scents, and sounds, and hues,
> Gush forth, and sing, and glow? was *this* their noblest use?
> * * * * * Sacred Dead! whose words
> In Memory's solemn pages shine enrolled!
> Was this the spell that taught your thrilling chords
> Their deathless tones, their poet-numbers bold?
> Did drossy streams defile the liquid springs
> Wherewith your eyeballs sprinkled did behold
> Riches of endless space and angel wings,
> Covering the face of Heaven! were such *your* precious things?

At the risk of differing with all the admirers of pretty verses in periodicals, we call this *poetry*; and hope that if any Magazine reader feel it too strong for him just yet, he will learn to like it better by-and-by. There are more good verses in this number; but, like wise men, we stick to the *best* and pass the *bonniest*. And now for other matters:—A Tale by the Author of the O'Hara Tales—*The Family of the Cold Feet*, with their great progenitor *Tony Nugent*, a gentleman every way worthy of the pen that sketched the *Nowlans*.—It is interesting, as if every thing which proceeds from Mr. Banim; but somewhat inconclusive. The writer appears to falter in his stern purpose, and bungles his story, because he has not the heart to make a woman a fiend.—Tony, himself, is a peerless laird's brother:—not that any thing exactly like him is ever seen in this country, till one crosses the Highland line, some twenty miles. Among the other lighter pieces a "*A 'Squire, and a Whole 'Squire*" is a happy hit-off. But the flower of *The Family of the Light Wits* in this month is beyond all peradventure *Paddy Foorhane's Fricassee*. Dear reader, if you at all value humour, or have any perception of Irish humour,—not the vulgar blunders and brogue, and bulls, uncouth words, and perverted orthography, so nick-named; but rich, *quiet*, genuine Irish humour,—true wit, with Irish mannerism,—do peruse *Paddy Foorhane*, the brief story of a party of "good boys," who, after a funeral take refuge in a *shebeen* house, "because grief is dry;" and after a long bout at cards and whisky, are at midnight suddenly seized with that horror, the *devil twist*. There is not a morsel of pig meat nor any sort of meat in the house, and the ravenous guests are not the boys, nor yet in the humour, to be trifled with. In this desperate strait the ready-wit of Paddy Foorhane suggests his immortal *Fricassee*. But it is sin to spoil this precious bit which the *Schoolmaster* may yet make his own.

Among the grave articles, one on Lord Mahon's *War of the Succession*, contains an estimate of the moral and intellectual character of the modern British nobility, which they would do well to lay to heart. *British Taxation and Expenditure* is a plain political sermon, of which the *Black Book* furnishes the text;—even down, hard hitting the nail on the head,—every sentence a new fact, and every fact an argument. There is also a good article on *Death Punishments*—one on *Louis Philippe*, who, we hope, is not quite so bad as he is here called;—and another short sensible paper on the *Bank Charter* follows up those of Sir H. Parnell on the same subject in former numbers. We have also another chapter of the Late History of the *Bull Family*, and a *Johannic*, shewing John's present dangers, from his natural weaknesses of character, and tuft-hunting propensities. To-day we cannot dip farther, and in this number things are passed over which would have formed the praise of ordinary months. No one, we presume, will doubt the success of the New Edinburgh Magazine now; nor, what some few will be more prone to question, its claims to success. It has only to keep up to its own standard.

. We propose giving such brief notices of new publications, and particularly of the periodicals, which now embody the very spirit of the time, as may prove both *useful* and amusing to general readers. But this cannot be done till our fourth week, in a Monthly Retrospect of Current Literature.

IRISH HUMOUR—POWER OF THE PRIESTS.

This, besides being a true story, is one of the most genuinely *Irish* we ever met with; and we pretend to some knowledge of Ireland, to which we hope the SCHOOLMASTER will yet bear testimony.—Mr. O'Dwyer of Waterford, being sadly annoyed by his nephew wedding a low and inferior person, resolved to punish his heir-presumptive by taking a wife to himself. He judiciously fixed upon a young lady whose father had much influence in the county, and was, moreover, to receive a *real* fortune of a thousand guineas on her wedding-day. The ceremony over, bride and bridegroom prepared to depart for their abode, which had been " illigantly fitted up." The thousand guineas, which were literally told down, were thrown, *à l'Irlandaise*, into an ancient trunk, amongst other sundries appertaining to Mr. and Mrs. Dermot O'Dwyer. This trunk was strapped at the back of a nondescript gig, (rather an uncomfortable machine of the " make-shift" species,) two fine spirited horses were harnessed to it, and so the fair bride was conveyed to her future dwelling. The next morning the bridegroom, wanting some money, thought he would go to his black trunk for it; but, on counting the sum over—not of his own free will, but by the advice of his servant Dennis O'Hay—into what he called his cash-box, he was dismayed at the discovery that the sum was minus three hundred and sixty guineas! " Plaze ye'r honour," says Dennis, " that's no way strange, seeing that the mice, or may-be the rats, the beasts! have, by way of employment, eat as good as seven or eight holes in the heart's blood o' the thrunk, bad cess to 'em for a pack o' Tories!" It was quite true—plenty of holes there certainly were; and now nothing could be done, except trying to get the money back again. In those days there was but one way of effecting this—sending for Father Dillon, the kind but illiterate parish priest, and inducing him to " speak of it from the altar."—" And sure I'll do that same, honey, with all the veins of my heart," he said, " there's not one of them shall dare even to drink a drop of it this warm weather. I'm glad I heard it before the confessions; for in them we're bound, ye understand." Next Sunday Father Dillon from the altar made the following proclamation!—" Good people—(though upon my conscience, that's more nor I can say to ye all)—but good, bad and indifferent, then—just as you stand before me—(Mrs. Dacy, ma'am, stuff something in that child's mouth, to hinder him from kicking up such a bobbery)—as I was saying, just as ye are, I want to discourse ye. My good friend and parishioner, Dermot O'Dwyer, Esq., who has lived man and boy in the one place for more than three hundred years, without ever spending cross or coin—(Jerry, Jerry Fingan, agra! just clap ye'r wig into the broken pane that's at the back o' my head; Tim Dooly, you that call yerself glazier, it's astonishing to me, coming to this holy house as ye do every Sunday, that ye havn't had the grace to stick a bit of glass in the window for the love of God and yer priest)—cross or coin, as I said, in foreign parts, but spends every farthing he has, and ten to the back of them, amongst you—(ye unruly pack of devil-serving creatures)—like a gentleman as he is, seeing he could not be otherwise. Well, Mr. O'Dwyer has had the misfortune to drop out of a blackguard hole in his thrunk a matter of about—but the sum's no consarn of yours—*I know what it is*; and what's more, *I know who's got it*; and if every farthing o' the money isn't returned by to-morrow morning, either to me or to his honour, I'll publish ye, and penance ye, and excommunicate ye;—and it's the devil 'll have nice pickings then, when none *dare say*, God save, or God speed ye! And sure it's the black shame has come over me, to think that the minute ye see the temptation the Ould Boy threw in yer way, ye didn't come straight to me, and let me know the rights of it. Oh, you in the blue clock [about sixty women wore no other garb] 'twas ill luck took ye so soon from yer own hearth stone last Tuesday!—but if ye repent and return the money, I'll contrive a penance that will clear ye once more, for yer poor souls' sake. O! O! O! to think how busy the Ould One was in my parish—easy knowing I was sleeping at the same time. There's fresh holy water at the door—take plenty of it—sure I never begrudged ye; for, God save us! poor ignorant craythurs like you can't see how the very air is full of evil spirits—things that go buzzing about like blue-bottles, and whisper ye to forget yer God, and yer duty, and yer priest. (Martin Doyle! is the horse gone lame, that ye never sent a sod o' turf to my poor place, and yer own rick built up as high as the hill o' Howth!' Oh! Martin, Martin, yer a bitter sinner, and so was yer father before ye.) And in regard, as I said, of Mr. O'Dwyer's money: look to it, I say, directly; or else—(and ye'll have reason to think o' my words)—every guinea will be changed into a torch o' fire and brimstone to scorch the flesh of yer bones!—look to it, I say, once more—FOR IF YOU DON'T —— there, be off with yerself, every mother's son of ye; and no blessing from me 'll any of ye have this day :—take care, you with the white stockings and bran new beaver, how you got them! Pack, I say." It is no less true than extraordinary, as showing the power possessed by an illiterate but truly honest priest, that before the next morning dawned the money was returned, with the exception of ten or twelve guineas, which were doubtless lost, as some heavy rain had fallen during the night.

TEMPORARY BAD EFFECTS OF MACHINERY.

MANUFACTURING machines may assuredly be detrimental to the labourers whom they throw out of employ. But as they produce a greater profit and a greater demand for the article, they add to the mass of wealth and of capital, the only source whence employment, wages, food, population, are derived. They are, therefore, beneficial to the nation, because the ultimate effect is a balance of good. To the work-people thus thrown out of employment they are undoubted evils. It is easy for a speculating political economist to say, these discharged work-people will turn their attention to some other means of employment. How are they to live in the mean time, if they have neglected to save when full employment enabled them? Their wages do little more than furnish them and their families with food from day to day in such a country as Britain. A week's want will bring them on the parish. Moreover, the books of political economy do not sufficiently consider the " time" is one of the elements that should always be taken into consideration. It is not easy to move twenty-thousands pounds from one branch of manufacture to another, or to convert a man, whose life has been employed in spinning cotton, making pins, into a seaman or a farmer.

The introduction and improvement of machinery, then, appears to be always productive of more or less misery among the poor for a time. But we are not to legislate upon every case where the imperfection of human arrangements is productive of some portion of unavoidable evil. If the clear result of the improvement be a balance of good, we ought to be content. Good, pure and unmixed, is not to be expected in the course of human affairs. Moreover why is an ingenious and industrious man to be prohibited from exercising his ingenuity and industry, when they give him an advantage over his less capable, less skilful, or less energetic neighbour? Are we to make laws for the protection of imbecility? or to put a weight on the shoulders of a strong man, that he may be brought down to the level of performance of his weaker competitor? If the introduction of machinery adds to profit, adds to the demand for the article, adds to the perfection of the article, adds to the wealth of the manufacturer, and thereby to the wealth of the nation, and thereby to capital, and by capital to employment, by employment to wages and food, and by them to the mass of healthy population—if articles before scarce and dear, and confined to the few, are brought within the purchase of the many, and the comforts, conveniences and pleasures of life made procurable at a cheaper rate, it is enough. We ought to be contented with such a result, although it be attended for a short time with a large amount of evil. The permanent advantages of machinery will form another article, next week.

ORIGIN OF TWO GREAT ENGLISH FAMILIES, THE PEELS AND THE JENNIES.

In a tour through England, Sir Richard Phillips at Manchester was introduced to the indigent daughters of Hargreave, the inventor of the spinning-jenny, the moving crank, &c. &c. They were poor aged women, living on parochial charity in Salford. "My father and mother," said the eldest of them, "were spinners by hand like all the villagers at that time in Lancashire, of whom thousands abounded through the country. They had many children, but they sent each, as soon as it had the use of fingers, to assist in spinning; but our joint earnings were so scanty, that my father, who was very studious and ingenious, began to consider how he could multiply our earnings. Early and late he used to be making trials, and often was reproved by my mother as a foolish schemer; but at length he produced a machine, which he called by her name, Jenny, and set it to work in her bed-room, where I and my sister, by its means, spun as much as five or six could do, and finer and more even work. He worked for a Mr. Peel, then a little master in Blackburn, and beginning very soon to carry home more work in a week, and more uniform in quality than others, Mr. P. often marvelled at his industry and cleverness. My father then made another machine, and keeping it a profound secret, he augmented the surprise of Master Peel; and he so teased my father about it, that at length he told him he had a bit of a contrivance to multiply the powers of the common wheel. Master Peel then teased him to let him see it, but my father refused again and again. At length Master Peel so worretted him, that he consented to let him see it, provided he told no one, and gave his word of honour not to imitate it. And sure enough," said the poor woman, "one morning, for I remember it as though it was but yesterday, my father brought in Master Peel and his partner, Mr. Yates, while I and my sister were working away at Jenny* in the chamber, I was much flustered, but after they had seen it work, and asked many questions, Master Peel dropt sixpence on the floor for me, and went away. The folk now began to talk about father's machine; and as he soon began to get money, and was better off than many, a great uproar was made about his machine: and one day when my father was from home, a great mob assembled, broke into the house, destroyed the two Jennies, all our furniture, windows, and every thing in the house. I shall never forget my poor father's coming home, and not having a chair to sit upon, nor any room which had windows left. He was almost ruined; and being pointed at and jeered by every body, he could no longer bear the neighbourhood, so he and all of us set out for Nottingham; and there my father went into partnership with Dick Arkwright, who had been used to shave my father at Bolton; and they went on in the spinning, my father inventing the moving crank, and making all kinds of improvements. But the partnership was out before much was got, and then my father went on making machines for others, till he died in the year 1788, and we buried him, poor anxious soul, at Nottingham.—He left my mother and seven or eight of us; and as she could not make machines, others stole my father's inventions; and my mother fell into trouble after trouble, and her children into poverty. My brothers afterwards upset Arkwright and Strutt's patent to serve others, not themselves; and we have lived to see thousands raised to wealth by our poor father's invention; but they never thought of us. We did hope that Mr. Peel, (the father of the Secretary of State), might do something for us, and Mr. Brotherton of Salford, kindly wrote to him, but he did not even vouchsafe an answer, which I and my sisters thought hard; because, when my father left Blackburn and went to Nottingham, he was the first to imitate what my father had shewn him, and made his fortune by our jennies and their improvement. Dick Arkwright used to claim my father's invention as his own, and therefore would do nothing for poor mother; and when our evidence upset his patent, he never forgave the family. Mother once applied to *Bobby Peel*, as we used to call him when I was a girl; but like his father, the Secretary did nothing for us. I am therefore content with the 3s. 6d. per week, which the good man Mr. Brotherton gets for me from a charity."—This poor old woman died in 1829, but two of her sisters were then, and may still be alive, *unpensioned* even with 3s. 6d. a-week, to prove the immense difference there is between the legitimate daughters of a most ingenious and meritorious man, and undoubted benefactor of his species, and —— the reader may fill up the blank.   D. D.

* A *bon mot*, which it was said the Peels never forgave, is attributed to George IV. On hearing of the marriage of one of the Peels, to a Lady Jane Something, he laughed, and said, "Ah, those Peels!—They'll ever be after the Jennies."

COLUMN FOR YOUTH.

DUTIES OF CHILDREN TO THEIR PARENTS.
Channing, an Eminent American Preacher.

You are required to view and treat your parents with respect. Your tender inexperienced age requires that you think of yourselves with humility, and conduct yourselves with modesty; that you respect the superior age, and wisdom, and improvements of your parents; and observe towards them a submissive deportment. Nothing is more unbecoming in you, nothing will render you more unpleasant in the eyes of others, than forward or contemptuous conduct towards your parents. There are children, and I wish I could say there are only a few, who speak to their parents with rudeness, grow sullen at their rebukes, behave in their presence as if they deserved no attention, hear them speak without noticing them, and rather ridicule than honour them.

Beware, my young friends, lest you grow up with an assuming and selfish spirit. Regard your parents as kindly given you by God, to support, direct, and govern you in your present state of weakness and inexperience. Express your respect for them in your manner and conversation. Do not neglect those outward signs of dependence and inferiority which suit your age; you are young, and should therefore take the lowest place, and rather retire than thrust yourselves forward into notice. You have much to learn, and should therefore hear instead of seeking to be heard. You are dependent, and should therefore *ask* instead of *demanding* what you desire, and you should receive every thing from your parents as a favour and not as a debt. I do not mean to urge on you a slavish fear of your parents. Love them and love them ardently, but mingle a sense of their superiority with your love. Feel a confidence in their kindness, but let not this confidence make you rude and presumptuous, and lead to indecent familiarity; talk to them with openness and freedom, but never contradict with violence, never answer with passion or contempt.

VERSES FOR AN ALBUM.
BY FRANCIS JEFFREY, LORD ADVOCATE OF SCOTLAND.

Why write my name midst songs and flowers
  To meet the eye of lady gay?
I have no voice for lady's bowers,
  For page like this no fitting lay.

Yet though my heart no more must bound
  At witching call of sprightly joys,
Mine is the brow that never frowned
  On laughing lips or sparkling eyes.

No—though behind me now is closed
  The youthful paradise of love,
Yet I can bless with soul composed,
  The lingerers in that happy grove.

Take then, fair girls, my blessing take,
  Where'er amid its charms you roam,
Or where by western hill or lake,
  You brighten a serener home.

Edinburgh: Printed by and for John Johnstone, 19, St. James's Square.—Published by John Anderson, Jun., Bookseller, 55, North Bridge Street, Edinburgh; by John Macleod, and Atkinson & Co. booksellers, Glasgow; and sold by all Booksellers and Venders of Cheap Periodicals.

THE Schoolmaster,
AND
EDINBURGH WEEKLY MAGAZINE.

CONDUCTED BY JOHN JOHNSTONE.

THE SCHOOLMASTER IS ABROAD.—LORD BROUGHAM.

No. 2.—Vol. I.   SATURDAY, AUGUST 11, 1832.   Price Three-Halfpence.

HOLYDAY RAMBLES ROUND EDINBURGH.
BY ZACHARY ZIGZAG, ESQ.

No. II.—THE ROMAN CAMP—BY THE RAILWAY.

*Hill, brook, nor dell, nor rock, nor stone,
Lie in the path, to me unknown.*

The Roman Camp was announced last Saturday, as the most expansive and commanding point of view in the three Lothians. The easiest and best mode of approach is to go along the viaduct, and then keeping to the left, follow the rail-way leading to the Marquis of Lothian's coal works on the face of the extensive ridge it crowns. The distance from where the waggon stops to the extreme point, or Roman Camp, may be about two miles and a half, estimated distance on a hot day. The country is quite open, and a plantation crowning the ridge makes an unerring landmark, though there is no danger of straying. The mineralogist will find objects of his own, with which we, a popular guide, have nothing to do. Though this long ridge is no obstinate hill, every foot is an ascent, more or less gentle, for the full two miles which the Camp rises above the level of New-battle valley on the side we are ascending; and above the valley of the Tyne, or of Crichton Castle, on the other.

At every advancing step, the view, looking backward, becomes wider and more varied, though we see yet but the half of the grand panorama of from 40 to 60 miles in diameter, which the summit gives us entirely. To the Schoolmaster Abroad, one of the most interesting objects on the way, is about half way up—a new Parochial School-house, and the handsomest structure of the kind we have seen in any country parish in Scotland,—where the apparent object of some heritors is, how they may most dexterously evade the law for building and maintaining school-houses, which they seem to consider a flagrant encroachment on their purses. This edifice, which may be mistaken for a farm-house of the better class, or a factor's residence, is situated at a central point of the parish, among the coal mines, though there is no population in the immediate neighbourhood. The new school is, we understand, well attended, and well taught. Its structure and arrangements ought to be a pattern to Scottish heritors. Let the pedestrian breathe a blessing on it, there where it stands, a star on the hill-side, long to effuse the blessings of light and intelligence, and pass quietly on to West-Houses, a small collier hamlet immediately under the Roman Camp. It commands a splendid view, and is remarkable for a sprinkling of those old ash trees, which our rustic ancestors admired so much, that, save a few alders, and mountain-ashes, to ward off witch-craft, and make spindles, they planted no other timber; so that the ash with its graceful branchery, and deep green foliage, still forms the principal ornament of our most primeval farm-touns and hill-side tafts. Here, at the spring, you may lay in water for the remainder of your outward voyage, as you will find none in higher latitudes. Here also you may Rest and be thankful, under the last tree, and look round you at your ease on the magnificent prospect opening far down the Firth of Forth, and sweeping round through West Lothian, and terminating in the farthest western point of the Pentland ridge.

As one ascends, the view gradually expands, till standing near the summit, the enlarged line of prospect sweeps from the Bass-Rock out to sea, along the hills of Fife, the Lomonds, and the Ochils, round to the Pentlands, the Moorfoot, and part of the Soutra hills; and towering behind, and over the Pentlands far in the South-west, to the shadowy top of Tintoc and the other mountains in the Upper Ward of Clydesdale, and about the bordering sources of the Tweed and the Nith. The fairest portion of Mid-Lothian lies at your feet. Along the courses of both the hidden Esks the eye travels eastward, passing many a lovely nook, wooded slope, and ripening corn-field, from Woodhouselee and the Bush lying warmly in the lap of the Pentlands, down all the way to the Bay of Preston. In the prospect Edinburgh Castle and the picturesque ridge of the old city keep their pre-eminence, though taken thus at Roman 'vantage. So does Arthur's Seat,—which, rising isolated in solitary majesty, occupying its full place in the champaign, unelbowed and unshouldered, exhibits from all points more of the mountain sublime, than heights of far greater real altitude. The seats of the aristocracy of Mid-Lothian are in general only indicated by the wood which surrounds them; so *domestically* are their sites chosen. That of the Duke of Buccleuch, from this point, shews merely a flat amplitude of well-wooded park. Dalhousie Castle is however finely conspicuous; and the Drum, the old residence of the noble family of Somerville, so completely lost to travellers in its vicinity, becomes an imposing object viewed four miles off from this sloping ridge. But it is my purpose merely to indicate, not to expatiate, on the objects to be seen—to open up, not forestall the pleasures of this ramble. To those familiar with many of the spots in view, there is one unfailing effect, after long absence. The poet expresses it—

> By thousand petty fancies I was crost,
> To see the trees that I had thought so tall,
> Mere dwarfs, the brooks so narrow, fields so small:—
> A juggler's balls old Time about him tossed.

And now we are at the Camp. Its exact site is covered with plantation, and enclosed. The prying eye of the antiquary is not required in tracing its lines. They are distinctly visible to the most unpractised spectator. Since the MASTERS OF THE WORLD abandoned this commanding station, it cannot have had many tenants, though some of them have been rather singular personages. A hut was erected here for the use of the military attendants, during the alarm of French invasion, when the Roman Camp was a signal post. Twenty years back this habitation was abandoned and dilapidated, and in this condition taken possession of by—

CAMP MEG,—

a mysterious female, who kept this mountain hermitage till her death, which happened about four years ago. We have heard twenty editions of her history, each more romantic or more incredible than the other. A century earlier Meg might have graced a tar-barrel on the Major's Knowe.* There still were doubts about a woman who came from no one knew where, and lived no one knew how, being altogether *cannie;* but they never took a definite or dangerous form. Instead of turning her off the estate as an interloper or *squatter*, the noble proprietor protected this "kindly tenant,"— her solitary habitation was repaired, and, besides obtaining occasional *awmouses* in meal, or other necessaries, she was allowed to raise a few vegetables, and cut the coarse grass in the Camp, with which she reared a colt or two, which she generally sold at Gifford Fair. Visiters to the Camp were mindful of her wants; and fox-hunters extended their protection to Meg, as a variety among the wild animals. This singular female was conjectured by her nearest neighbours, with whom she held as little intercourse as possible, to be a native of Ireland,—a compliment too readily paid in this country, to every sturdy vagrant; nor could anything short of a conscience haunted by the commission of some horrible crime account to many of them for her strange anti-social habits, and kirk-going antipathy. Her independent, self-relying character, was quite overlooked; and the qualities of a mind too strong or too stubborn to be bent down to the mean or petty miseries of a life, which had driven her in preference to take refuge in this roofless hut. For aught that is accurately known of the female hermit, she remains a fresh untouched property for the poets and romance writers, and may flourish in the Annuals of the year. The probability is, that Meg was neither more nor less than a wandering princess of the gipsies; who, as youth receded, began to feel that lying "in kilns and barns" was even more miserable than this solitary abode, in which her condition improved, and to which she naturally grew every year more attached. Peace be with her mysterious memory!

And now we enter the Camp from her house end, and a few yards of walking, and crossing the opposite enclosure, suddenly places before us the other half of the panorama, now become a cosmorama; our own legs the pivot on which it turns. Now looking southward, as before we did northward, the prospect again extends from the ocean by the Bass Rock and North Berwick Law, along the Lammermoor ridge, on to the Soutra hills, and the heights of Moorfoot. The valley of the Tyne, which stream here in its infancy, is at this season but a languid rill, lies below us; crowning the opposite banks stand Crichton Castle and Crichton church; an expanse of flat and upland moor swells behind this parish, and that of Borthwick, rising on to Fala parish. Borthwick Castle and church though close at hand, are hidden from us by intervening banks; to the right are uplands, plantations, and high-lying farms rising to the hill-ridges, and to the left the most beautiful division of—

EAST LOTHIAN.

The view this way though neither so rich nor varied as that to be seen from the southern side of the ridge is still of great beauty; and to most sight-seers from Edinburgh, or the west, it must possess more novelty and attraction. The view of East Lothian from Arthur's Seat is distant, and obstructed in the best points by the ridge on which we stand. The spectator will now naturally walk eastward, skirting the plantation:—we defy him to do otherwise. At every new step the view changes and expands, till it takes in a wide sweep of the sea, the coasts of Fife, bays, and headlands, and islands, which may make the eastern point of this ridge the favourite station with many persons. For a resting-place, one, however, prefers the southern stile of the Camp enclosure, with Vogrie and Newland-rigg below us, and Crichton directly opposite, its grey towers rising among pastoral banks, steep, but not abrupt, broken, and diversified, and partially clothed with furze and brushwood. Seen at this distance nothing exteriorly is

---

* A square in the High Street of Dalkeith, so named, from the famous or infamous Major Weir, who either lived or had some possession in this town.

changed, since Lord Marmion might have made it his place of sojourn. A herd tending a few sheep and young cattle, must indeed supply the place of the men-at-arms, and the attendants of the feudal lord; an adventurous calf or stirk the warder on the wall. We cannot find a better guide than Sir Walter,

<blockquote>
To trace against the Tyne,
</blockquote>

through the country expanding before us.

<blockquote>
The green-sward way was smooth and good,
Through Humbie's and through Saltoun's wood,
A forest glade, which varying still,
Here gave a view of dale and hill,
There narrower closed, till overhead
A vaulted screen the branches made.
</blockquote>

Among the more attractive features of the eastward part of the valley of Tyne, one distinguishes the tower of Cranston Church, Oxenforde Castle, almost buried in stately old woods; and nearer, the handsome new bridge opened the other day at Ford. But the most beautiful peculiarity of the landscape here is wood,—not the solemn old forests around the mansions, but that sprinkled over the whole face of this fertile country; the single trees, and clumps of three or four, and the lines in the hedge-rows, now of stately growth, with which the prescient taste of the proprietors has ornamented their farms and home-steads. They are seen to much advantage at this season, contrasting with the fast-ripening grain; which is again finely contrasted with the soft green of the turnip fields, and the yet sweeter green of the clover. Two months hence, when the woodland has put on the gorgeous apparel of autumn, when the rich brown fallows are lying intersecting the fields of after grass, with a quiet low October sky brooding overall, the landscape from this chosen station will be yet more harmonious and enchanting. But this spot, like every other, has its drawbacks, man's not Nature's: she is ever as faultless as she is fair. On the southern slope of this ridge there are several coal mines, wrought on so small a scale, that the few persons seen about them look more like swart goblins than regular work people. Among them are girls almost children. This may be no fault of either proprietor or miner, but a cruel necessity of the latter,—and we are far from blaming any one. There must, however, be something wrong, where, in a Christian land, human beings of tender age are condemned to such unsuitable employment, with its unfailing consequences, a dwarfed mind, if not a stunted and diseased frame—a wretched physical existence, and a degraded moral one—the certain inheritance of unremitting toil and its sure attendant, ignorance. In the bill for regulating the work hours of children in factories, those miserable female children who bear coals—worse off even than the climbing boys—should not be forgotten. This is a painful subject for a Holyday Ramble.

The rambler having now transferred to his memory the best county map to be had, and, moreover, feasted his eyes and imagination, has the choice of either returning through Newbattle, first descending by the route he came, and then through a path, the old road to the South, which may now be called a wooded glade;—or striking Eastward till he join the Dalkeith road leading South into Lauderdale, he may return by that town. There is yet a third and more romantic route, which the pedestrian who starts early may easily accomplish.—To this we shall next week be his guide.

MAID-SERVANTS.

THE worldly condition of *servant lasses* has improved more within the last fifty years of change than that of any other class of useful *labourers*; yet it may be questioned if this increased prosperity is not more in show than substance. Certain it is, that, with wages doubled, and in many cases quadrupled, if not more, they enter the married state much worse *provided* than their predecessors, at a pound of penny-fee in the year. About a century ago, the money wages of maid-servants, in the North of Scotland, were so low as seven-and-sixpence a-year, with some allowance for shoes. Even now in Shetland, Orkney, and Caithness, the wages of female servants is exceedingly low, two pounds being about the maximum. While domestic manufactures were carried on, many maid-servants were kept, whose time was occupied in spinning, either for home consumption or for sale; yarn and cloth sent to market being no unimportant part of the household revenue. With some difference of wages in favour of London, the condition of female servants, in most considerable towns, is now pretty much the same. Their condition in 1730 and in 1830 affords an amusing and favourable contrast for the lasses of the time being. We take our first picture from the North of Scotland, then at a very low ebb in the encouragement given to female domestics; and conclude with what is a fair representation of every part of the country now. We quote from an ancient but competent authority.

"They have not a great deal of household work to do; but when that little is done, they are kept to spinning, by which some of their mistresses are chiefly maintained. Sometimes there are two or three of them in a house of no greater number of rooms, at the wages of three half-crowns a-year each, a peck of oatmeal for a week's diet; and happy she that can get the skimming of a pot to mix with her oatmeal for better commons. To this allowance is added a pair of shoes or two, for Sundays, when they go to kirk.

"These are such as are kept at board-wages. In larger families, I suppose, their standing wages is not much more, because they make no better appearance than the others.

"All these generally lie in the kitchen, a very improper place, one would think, for a lodging, especially of such who have not wherewithal to keep themselves clean.

"They do several sorts of work with their feet. I have already mentioned their washing at the river. When they wash a room, which the English lodgers require to be sometimes done, they likewise do it with their feet.

"First, they spread a wet cloth upon part of the floor; then, with their coats tucked up, they stand upon the cloth and shuffle it backward and forward with their feet; then they go to another part and do the same, till they have gone all over the room. After this, they wash the cloth, spread it again, and draw it along in all places, by turns, till the whole work is finished. This last operation draws away all the remaining foul water. I have seen this likewise done at my lodgings, within a quarter of a mile of Edinburgh.

"When I first saw it, I ordered a mop to be made, and the girls to be shown the use of it; but, as it is said of the Spaniards, there was no persuading them to change their old method.

"I have seen women by the river-side washing parsnips, turnips, and herbs, in tubs, with their feet; and, since that, upon inquiry, I have been told it is a common thing.

"They hardly ever wear shoes, as I said before, but on a Sunday; and then, being unused to them, when they go to church they walk very awkwardly: or, as we say, like a cat shod with walnut-shells.

"When they go abroad, they wear a blanket over their heads, as the poor women do, something like the pictures you may have seen of some bare-footed order among the Romish priests.

"And the same blanket that serves them for a mantle by day, is made a part of their bedding at night, which is generally spread upon the floor; this, I think, they call a *shakedown*."

Such was the very *worst* condition of female servitude viewed by an Englishman. The maid-servants of those times, as least those in rural service, had many little advantages not noticed in this statement, and probably unknown to the author. They were often, indeed till very lately, allowed a certain quantity of flax, and wool, and time for spinning for themselves; and no young woman was conceived worthy of the honours of the married state, who did not largely contribute to the household gear, in blankets, coarse linen, and things of this useful description. Their own home-made coarse linen shifts, checked aprons, striped petticoats, and linseywoolsey gowns, were often, considering the enduring texture of the cloth, in sufficient quantity, when the lass married, to last her half her life-time. We have her picture, as she existed twenty years back, in many of Hogg's tales, and in the sketches of Allan Cunningham.—When she got " a house of her own " she entered it fortified by prudence and steady habits of industry. Her guiding household maxim was " A woman's work is never done," and her only variety was in change of occupation. Her favourite *wheel*, which stood always ready, was her recreation. She spun by snatches, at odd ends of time; and hank on hank was gathered, till the WEB was prepared for the country weaver, and the burn-side bleach-green; where, early as the lark in a cold clear March morning, she might be seen, and late, as the *corn-craik* on the shortening evenings of September, at her homely industry, spreading, or watering, or lifting " *the bit claith*," the in-door glory of her year. Without entering on the question, it may at once be conceded, that prices are much reduced by the employment of machinery. But all is not solid gain that so seems. A stout enduring fabric at 2s. 6d. per ell is, in fact, cheaper than one at 1s. 3d. which will not wear half the time; the trouble of twice purchasing, and the double expense of twice making-up, being subtracted from the apparently high first cost. But, laying aside the general question, any one who remembers the lively *birr* of the little wheel, and the soothing, drowsy hum of the great wool-wheel, cannot help regretting their gradual disappearance from the cot-house, and the farmer's ingle-neuk. The in-door picture is incomplete without them, especially since nothing has taken their place in the vacant hours of female employment. A very clever woman, speaking of the sexes, said, " A woman hems a pocket-handkerchief, and so does not go mad." Now the wife and daughters of the *hynd*, or small farmer, drew in the wheel, and spun, and *sung*,—and so did not weary, and yawn, and *make bad tea*, which their husbands and fathers could not afford.

(To be continued.)

CANVASSING—AN OLD-FASHIONED MEMBER OF PARLIAMENT.

Hot work canvassing, especially if it fall upon the tail of the Dog-Days. But nothing can conquer the perseverance, good-humour, patience, zeal, and forbearance of a thorough-trained parliamentary candidate, who must be all things to all men, and moreover to all women; must take rebuffs with cheerfulness, and return rudenesses with courtesy. Personal canvassing is new in Scotland, and candidates are not likely to be exposed to the gruff incivilities sometimes offered by honest John Bull. The danger lies on the other side. No Scottish elector, or at least no Scotch elector's wife or daughter, will ever be able to say *No* to any smiling, well-dressed gentleman, with a good orthodox family name, who takes the trouble to solicit in person for such a trifle as a vote. Not that they may exactly approve him, nor even feel the necessity of keeping the promise made. " But who could turn a good-looking, *discreet* gentleman from the door with a sore heart?" No one seems yet to have imagined, that there can be any thing really wrong in canvassing; or that soliciting a voter, is precisely the same thing in principle as soliciting a juryman or a judge. The practice of *canvassing* judges was once as openly carried on as the canvassing of voters is now. In one of her letters, Madame Sevigné mentions, as a matter of course, her formal round of solicitation, and of meeting her fair-litigious rival in the ante-chamber of the Judge come on the same errand with herself. So late as the celebrated *Douglas Cause*, it was at least said that solicitation from certain quarters had weight with the Scotch Judges. Now, any attempt made by the parties, even to *talk to* a judge of a case that is to be decided by him, would be considered an insult; and jurymen are understood to be equally scrupulous. With a voter it still is different; and indeed the only thing that can be said for canvassing is the perfect openness and unconsciousness of wrong with which it is practised. The ballot, or the progress of public opinion, must, however, soon finish this illegitimate means of obtaining votes. Candidates will come to be judged by their previous public and private character and conduct; and a mode of procedure will be abandoned, which gives the bustling, and forward such unfair advantage of modest worth and ability.

Cowper, in one of his delightful letters, gives the following humorous account of a candidate going his rounds:—

"As when the sea is uncommonly agitated, the water finds its way into creeks and holes of rocks, which in its calmer state it never reaches, in like manner the effect of these turbulent times is felt even at Orchard-side, where in general we live as undisturbed by the political element, as shrimps or cockles that have been accidentally deposited in some hollow beyond the water mark, by the usual dashing of the waves. We were sitting yesterday after dinner, the two ladies and myself, very composedly, and without the least apprehension of any such intrusion in our snug parlour, one lady knitting, the other netting, and the gentleman winding worsted, when, to our unspeakable surprise a mob appeared before the window; a smart rap was heard at the door, the boys halloo'd, and the maid announced Mr. G——. Puss * was unfortunately let out of her box, so that the candidate, with all his good friends at his heels, was refused admittance at the grand entry, and referred to the back door, as the only possible way of approach.

Candidates are creatures not very susceptible of affronts, and would rather I suppose climb in at a window, than be absolutely excluded. In a minute, the yard, the kitchen, and the parlour were filled. Mr. G—— advancing toward me shook me by the hand with a degree of cordiality that was extremely seducing. As soon as he and as many as could find chairs were seated, he began to open the intent of his visit. I told him I had no vote, for which he readily gave me credit. I assured him I had no influence, which he was not equally inclined to believe, and the less, no doubt, because Mr. A——, addressing himself to me at that moment, informed me that I had a great deal. Supposing that I could not be possessed of such a treasure without knowing it, I ventured to confirm my first assertion, by saying, that if I had any I was utterly at a loss to imagine where it could be, or wherein it consisted. Thus ended the conference. Mr. G—— squeezed me by the hand again, kissed the ladies, and withdrew. He kissed likewise the maid in the kitchen, and seemed upon the whole a most loving, kissing, kind-hearted gentleman. He is very young, genteel, and handsome. He has a pair of very good eyes in his head, which not being sufficient as it should seem for the many nice and difficult purposes of a senator, he has a third also, which he wore suspended by a riband from his button-hole. The boys halloo'd, the dogs barked, Puss scampered, the hero with his long train of obsequious followers, withdrew. We made ourselves very merry with the adventure, and in a short time settled into our former tranquillity, never probably to be thus interrupted more. I thought myself however happy in being able to affirm truly that I had not that influence for which he sued; and for which, had I been possessed of it, with my present views of the dispute between the Crown and the Commons, I must have refused him, for he is on the side of the former."

ANDREW MARVEL.

While so much is said about the *fortune* and *status* required for a *Parliament man*, we take leave to revive the memory of one of the best members that ever appeared in the Honourable House.

Andrew Marvel, the knight-errant of British patriots, was born at Hull in 1620. His father, who was a clergyman in that place, he had the misfortune to lose early in life in a way of which this singular story is told. The old gentleman embarked on the Humber with a young pair, whom he was to marry in Lincolnshire. The weather was fine when the wedding party entered the boat; but Mr. Marvel expressed a presentiment of danger by throwing his cane ashore, and crying out, "Ho! for heaven!" A storm came on, and the whole company perished.

The father of the unfortunate bride adopted young Marvel, who in consequence received a better education than his father could have afforded him. After travelling for improvement, he was appointed secretary to the English embassy at Constantinople. On his return it is probable that he found no suitable employment; but he assisted Milton for a time as Latin secretary to the Protector.

After the Restoration, Marvel was elected one of the members of Parliament for his native town of Hull; and he continued to represent that place till his death, regularly receiving the salary allowed to Parliamentary representatives. Trained in the school of Milton, he was through life the zealous friend of constitutional freedom, and as pure-minded a public man as ever lived. Marvel kept up *an uninterrupted* correspondence with his constituents, and daily gave them a faithful and minute account of all public transactions before he either ate or slept. His attendance in his place was unremitting; and, though he was no exhibiting orator, the influence which he acquired from his character, principles, and talents, was very great in both Houses. Many interesting anecdotes are told of his simplicity of manners and inflexible integrity. Though constantly in Opposition, he was a favourite with the King, who, with all his faults, had nothing of the bitterness of a partisan in his nature. His Majesty had met Marvel in private society, and found him so agreeable that he thought him worth gaining over. A person, uniting elegant and complacent manners with incorruptible integrity, was probably a variety of the human species unknown to Charles; and it is related, that he one day sent his lord-treasurer, Danby, to prove the honesty of the patriot. After groping his way up several dark staircases to a very mean lodging, situated in a court in the Strand, Danby found his man, who said, in some surprise, "He believ'd his lordship had mistaken his way."—" Not if I have found Mr. Marvel," was the courtly reply. "I come from the king, to know what he can do to serve Mr. Marvel." Marvel told the Lord-treasurer that "he had no need of his Majesty's assistance;" and good-humouredly put an end to the conference by calling his servant to testify that he had for the last three days dined off one shoulder of mutton. Marvel's mutton is quite as admirable in its way as are the turnips of Cincinnatus. The patriotic member for Hull then gave the king's minister a rational and manly explanation of his principles, declined the royal bounty and favour, and borrowed a guinea from a friend for his immediate exigencies. It is stated that a thousand guineas were proffered to him by Danby at this interview; but it ought to be recollected that Charles the Second seldom had a thousand guineas to send a-begging. It is enough that Marvel would have declined the largess had it been tendered. But the Member for Hull was not always thus inflexible: he often accepted a barrel of ale as a present from his grateful constituents. He died in 1678; and the corporation of Hull voted a sum for his funeral expenses. When will there be such another member of the honourable house?

This accomplished man and inflexible patriot was not less valued for his learning and acuteness in controversial writing, than for the warmth and elegance of his poetry. "He was," says Mr. Campbell, "the champion of Milton's living reputation, and the victorious supporter of free principles against Bishop Parker, when that venerable apostate to bigotry, promulgated, in his ecclesiastical polity, that it is more necessary to set a severe government over men's consciences than over their vices and immoralities.— The humour and eloquence of Marvel's prose tracts were admired, and probably imitated by Swift. In playful exuberance of thought he sometimes resembles Burke. For consistency of principles it is not easy to find his parallel!"—*Johnstone's Specimens and Biographical Notices of the Poets.*

---

* His tame hare.

FUNDAMENTAL PRINCIPLES OF THE BRITISH CONSTITUTION.

In Britain the supreme government,—that is the power of making and enforcing laws,—is divided into two branches, the one LEGISLATIVE, consisting of King, Lords, and Commons; the other EXECUTIVE, consisting of the King alone.

For the maintenance and security of the rights of the people, and the preservation and enforcement of the laws, the King is invested with certain Prerogatives; and the Legislature as a collective body, and also in its separate estates, possesses various privileges:—for the Prerogatives of the Crown, and the Privileges of Parliament, are, in substance and effect, *The Rights of the People.*

In England the Executive or Regal office is hereditary on certain conditions; but the right of inheritance may be changed or limited by act of Parliament. The principal duty of the King is, to govern the people according to the laws: " but although the King is the fountain of Justice, and is intrusted with the whole executive power of the law, yet he hath no power to change or alter the laws which have been received and established in these Kingdoms, and are the birthright of every subject; for it is by those very laws that he is to govern."* The King owns no superior but God and the Laws.

It is a maxim of the Constitution, that the King in his political capacity can do NO WRONG, because he acts only by officers responsible to the law, called the MINISTRY or CABINET. The King NEVER DIES; that is, the Executive authority never ceases to exist. The King is head of the Church; but he cannot alter the established religion. He is also Generalissimo of all the Forces; but he cannot raise an army without the consent of Parliament, nor can he maintain it without that consent being renewed from year to year. He has the power of coining money; but he cannot alter the standard. He is the sole representative of his people with foreign States, having the power of sending Ambassadors, concluding treaties of alliance, and making peace or war. The King has the power of summoning, proroguing, or dissolving the Parliament; but he is bound to summon a new Parliament at least every seven years. He is also bound to administer justice in the established course in his Courts of Law, not as a free gift but as the right of the people. The King is the fountain of Mercy,—he alone can pardon all public offences, either absolutely or conditionally; and of Honour, as the Constitution has intrusted him with the sole power of conferring titles, dignities and honours. He is also intrusted with the immense patronage of the Church, the Army, the Navy, the Excise, and the Colonies. He has the power of erecting and disposing of new offices, and in short, the entire disposal of an enormous public revenue. As first Magistrate of a great and free people he is invested with many other splendid marks of regal dignity and pre-eminence, " all intended by the Constitution to be employed for the good of the People, none to their detriment, nor can any prerogative be legally so employed."†

The LEGISLATIVE authority is vested in a Parliament consisting of the King, the Lords Spiritual and Temporal, and the Commons.

The House of Lords consists of the two Archbishops and twenty-four Bishops, and of all the Peers of the realm who are entitled to a seat either by inheritance, creation, or election. Since the union with Ireland, an Archbishop and three Bishops represent the Irish Church in Parliament.

The House of Commons consists at present of six hundred and fifty-eight persons, who are returned by the counties, cities, and boroughs, possessing the right of election. Of these, five hundred and thirteen are returned by England, a hundred by Ireland, and forty-five by Scotland.‡ Though delegated by particular places, they are bound as members of Parliament to act for the general good of the country. Their principal duties are to check and reform abuses of the Administration—to redress public and private grievances—to watch over the public expenditure—to enforce by their power of inquiry and impeachment a pure administration of justice in all departments—to assist in framing wise laws—and, finally, *to preserve and promote, by every constitutional means, the freedom and prosperity of the great body of the people.*

The powers and privileges of this part of the Legislature, are commensurate to its great importance in the government. The Commons hold the sinews of war, for they are the keepers of the public purse; all grants, subsidies, and taxes must originate with them; for it is a constitutional maxim, *that taxation and representation go hand in hand,* and that the people only have a right to tax themselves. By the power of withholding supplies, they have a strong control over the Executive; and, by the Constitution, they enjoy all the privileges necessary to their dignity and independence, and the unbiassed discharge of their high functions.

Though new laws may be proposed by any member of either House, the consent of all the three constituent parts of the Legislature is necessary to make them binding on the subject; and though any part of the Legislature may, by withholding its consent, prevent the enactment of a law, it requires the agreement of all the three to repeal an existing statute.

" Thus the true excellence of the British Government consists in all its parts forming a mutual check upon each other. The Legislature cannot abridge the Executive power of any rights which it now has by law, without its own consent. The People are a check upon the Nobility; and the Nobility are a check upon the people, by the mutual privilege of rejecting what the other has resolved: while the King is a check upon both; which preserves the Executive power from encroachment. And this very Executive power is again checked, and kept within due bounds, by the two Houses, through the privilege they have of inquiring into, impeaching, and punishing the conduct, not indeed of the King, (which would destroy his constitutional independence,) but which is more beneficial to the public, of his evil and pernicious counsellors."§

The same laws that secure to the King his crown and prerogative, secure to the meanest subjects those rights, which are emphatically styled *the birthright of Britons.* These are principally, the right of personal SECURITY, of personal LIBERTY, and of private PROPERTY. They are asserted, first by the GREAT CHARTER obtained, sword in hand, from King John, and afterwards confirmed in Parliament by Henry III. Next, by a multitude of corroborating statutes; and, after a long interval, by the PETITION OF RIGHT, the HABEAS CORPUS act, and the BILL OF RIGHTS. And lastly, these liberties were again asserted in the same act (the Act of Settlement) that limits the crown to the present royal family. The Great Charter declaratory of these rights, states, " That no freeman shall be taken or imprisoned but by the lawful judgment of his equals, or the law of the land:" and the Petition of Rights, " That no person shall be imprisoned or detained without cause shewn, to which he may answer according to law." What has just passed under our own eyes, I am not yet at liberty to describe.

The Constitution has established certain other auxiliary subordinate rights of the subject, which serve principally as outworks or barriers, to protect and maintain inviolate the three great primary rights of *personal security, personal liberty,* and *personal property.* One of these is, that of applying to courts of Justice for redress of injuries. Since the law is in England the supreme Arbiter of every man's life, liberty and property, Courts of justice must at all times be open to the subject, and the law duly administered therein.

As the sole executive power is vested in the King, all

---

* Bacon. † Bacon.
‡ The Reform Act will make a change which this publication dare not now notice.
§ Blackstone.

Courts are derived from the crown; and justice is administered by judges of its appointment. The principal judicatures are,

The COURT OF COMMON PLEAS, which takes cognizance of all civil suits between subject and subject. It is composed of the Lord Chief Justice of the Common Pleas and three other judges. From its judgment appeal may be made to the Court of King's Bench.

The COURT OF KING'S BENCH determines in criminal causes; and also in many merely civil. In it four judges preside; the first of whom is called the Lord Chief Justice of England, in consequence of the jurisdiction of his court over all subordinate tribunals and civil corporations. Appeals from the decisions of the King's Bench are made to the Court of Exchequer Chamber, or to the House of Peers.

The COURT OF EXCHEQUER was originally established to manage the revenues of the Crown. It is inferior to the two former Courts in its jurisdiction, though it has the power of determining causes, either according to law or equity. Here preside the Chief Baron of the Exchequer, and three inferior Barons.

The COURT OF CHANCERY is so called from the Lord Chancellor, who presides there as sole judge. In this Court are two tribunals; the one determining causes by the Common law, the other in Equity, to provide for cases the existing laws do not meet; to moderate, in peculiar circumstances, the rigour of strict law; to defend the unprotected from oppression; and to extend relief in cases of accident, fraud, and breach of trust. To the Lord Chancellor belongs the appointment of all the Justices of the peace; he is the general guardian of infants, idiots, and lunatics; and has also a general superintendence of all public charities. Appeals from his decisions lie to the House of Peers.

The COURT OF EXCHEQUER CHAMBER has no original jurisdiction, but is only a Court of Appeal to correct the errors of other Courts. In appealed cases, this Court consists of all the judges except those of the court from whence the appeal is made. Into it also, are sometimes adjourned from the other Courts, such causes as the judges find upon argument, to be of great weight and difficulty. It then consists of all the judges of the King's Bench, Common Pleas, and Court of Exchequer; and sometimes also the Lord Chancellor. The judgments then pronounced are those of the TWELVE JUDGES of England. But even from their decision a writ of error lies to,—

The HOUSE of PEERS, which is the supreme Court of Judicature in this United Kingdom. From it there can be no appeal; and to its judgment every subordinate tribunal must conform.

These Courts are all held in Westminster; but for the expeditious and due administration of justice, the judges hold Assizes in most county towns twice a-year, and in every county once a-year.

Such are the principal Courts, "where every subject, for injury done to him in goods, person, or estate, by any other subject without exception, may take his remedy in course of law; and have justice and right, for the injury done to him, freely, without fail; fully, without any denial; and, speedily, without any delay."† And such in substance are the rights of British Subjects; maintained against the encroachments of power by a Free Press, Freedom of Speech, and the Trial by Jury; an institution which is justly venerated as the chief guardian of the lives, liberties, and properties of the people, since it provides, That no man shall answer to the King for any criminal offence, unless upon the preparatory accusation of at least twelve of his fellow-subjects, (called the Grand Jury) and, that the truth of every accusation shall afterwards be confirmed by the unanimous suffrages of twelve of his equals and neighbours, indifferently chosen, and superior to all suspicion.

"To preserve these rights from violation, it is necessary that the constitution of Parliament be supported in its full vigour, and limits certainly known be set to the royal prerogative. And to vindicate them when actually violated or attacked, the subjects of England are entitled, in the first place, to the regular administration, and free course of justice in the Courts of Law; next, to the right of petitioning the King, and Parliament for redress of grievances; and lastly, to the right of having and using arms for self-preservation and defence."†

Such is a brief exposition of the fundamental principles of the British Constitution, as it theoretically exists: it would take a volume to point out the abuses that have crept into it; and the many insidious ways in which its best constituents have been corrupted and warped. J. J.

COLUMN FOR YOUTH.

WHAT MEN HAVE DONE.

The school of ———— got its summer holydays before our schools; and last week William Martin and his little sister came by the steam-boat to Edinburgh, for the first time, to spend a fortnight with their aunt. Every day after breakfast was over, either their aunt or uncle, or some kind friend, took them to *see sights*, which might amuse and instruct them. They were taken to the University *Museum*, where they saw what to them seemed an infinity of beautiful birds, shells, and minerals. And where were they to be got? for both William and Anne would have liked much to have some. Their aunt could not tell. "It was *men*—men who sent, or brought them, from all corners of the earth; who had searched land and sea for them." They visited the Botanic Garden. What a variety of beautiful plants! Where were they brought from? "*Men*—men," was ever the answer—men had discovered and selected them, in India, Japan, America—throughout the whole world, civilized or barbarous—*men* had sailed over the widest seas and brought them to Scotland;—*men* were rearing and tending them; investigating their properties and healing uses." They visited the Advocates' Library one morning—Whence had come all these books?—The aunt's answer was ever the same—*Men—men*—these wonderful creatures, had written, printed, bound, arranged them; made the shelves, and placed the volumes upon them. On their walks they saw some of the finest of the new churches and chapels, and the New High School. Who had planned these fine edifices? There certainly never was any lady so much at fault in her proper names—for *men* was still the answer of the kind aunt; she did not even say *gentlemen*. "Men," she said, "who had spent years in studying architecture, or the art of building. "You will yet see beautiful statues, exquisitely chiselled by *men*—who have made their names famous in sculpture, and painting, engraving, mechanical contrivances, the printing press, the steam-engine, and many more beautiful and useful things than I can even name; and for all of them we are indebted to *men*—to human genius, and human industry. A little boy who is capable of reflection, will think when he sees the productions of genius, or of industry—of the Fine or the *Useful Arts*—" Like the makers of these, I am the beginning of a man; they have got before me, but like them, I may be able to do something, for which I shall be honourably remembered among *men*;—once they were all little boys, the smallest beginnings of *men*. Thus, William, even your holyday walks and plays may be useful to you; you may learn that MEN, to which class you belong, are more wonderful creatures than either ants, or bees, or any other living thing."

THE GIRAFFE—THE GAZELLE.

FROM remote antiquity the GIRAFFE has excited wonder and curiosity, and been the subject of many marvellous tales. The form and habits of this remarkable animal are now, however, well ascertained, principally from the observations of the enthusiastic and indefatigable naturalist Le Vaillant. Travelling in Great Mamaqua-land, he saw a hut entirely covered with what he knew to be the skin of a cameleopard, as the giraffe is often termed. He had soon after the satisfaction of seeing a living specimen. One of the guides made this discovery so welcome to Le Vaillant; the animal was standing under a mimosa tree, on the leaves of which it was browsing; by the time he reached the spot on horseback, the animal was trotting away across the plain.

After a pursuit of giraffes, continued for days under many difficulties and hardships, his hopes were at last realized. Specimens have since been seen in France; and a female lived for some time, about three years ago, at Windsor, where it increased in size to thirteen feet from the hoof to the top of the head. After this the animal gradually pined and died.

There is a fine specimen, in excellent preservation, in the museum of the Edinburgh University. The giraffe, though a beautiful and graceful animal, is no favourite with the Bedouin Arabs, who in this case prefer utility to beauty. They say it can neither carry like a horse, give flesh and milk like a goat, or hair for spinning like a camel.

The GAZELLE is the most elegant and beautiful of the antelope tribe. One in the menagerie at Windsor, which died in 1827, was only twenty inches in height, and in length twenty-two. Its skin was beautifully soft and sleek, its body extremely graceful, its head peculiarly light, its ears flexible, its eyes, which have afforded the Arabian poets their finest comparisons for the eyes of beautiful women, most brilliant and glancing, its legs as slender as a reed.

The SPRINGBOK, so frequently seen near the Cape of Good Hope, in the Bushman territory, is another interesting species of antelope. They are scattered in herds over great part of Southern Africa. They receive their name from the extraordinary springs or leaps they make. Though looking like other deer when at feed, they will, if pursued, bound into the air to the height of eight feet, as if they were about to fly. Sometimes when driven from the wilderness by long-continued droughts, they pour upon the settlements in vast herds, and with all the destructive consequences of the locusts, devouring every thing they can find. When the rains fall they immediately retire. Herds of nearly thirty thousand have been seen scattered over one vast plain. When taken young, the springbok, like other species of deer, is easily tamed; and it is often seen, as deer are in America, and even in the Highlands of Scotland, as a pet about farm-houses, and a playmate of the children; living in peace and amity among dogs, goats, and poultry. The writer of this sketch remembers a tame deer, that had been brought when newly dropt, from the hills to a farm-house near Inverness, which grew up in such perfect familiarity with the house dog, that the latter constituted itself its protector, and not only defended it from all attacks, but would at night-fall go to the neighbouring brushwood to seek out its friend and bring it home. C.I.J.

ELEMENTS OF THOUGHT.

THE PEOPLE.

It is the populace which compose the bulk of mankind: those which are not in this class are so few in number, that they are hardly worth notice. Man is the same creature in every state; therefore that which is the most numerous ought to be the most respected. To a man capable of reflection, all civil distinctions are nothing. He observes the same passions, the same feelings, in the clown and the man of quality. The principal distinction between them consists in the language they speak; in a little refinement of expression. But if there be any distinction, it is certainly to the disadvantage of the least sincere. The common people appear as they really are, and they are often not amiable. If those in high life were equally undisguised, their appearance would make us shudder with horror. There is, say our philosophers, an equal allotment of happiness and misery to every rank of men; a maxim as dangerous as it is absurd. If all mankind are equally happy, it would be ridiculous to give ourselves any trouble to promote their felicity. Let each remain in his situation. Let the slave endure the lash, the lame his infirmity, and let the beggar perish, since they would gain nothing by a change of situation. The same philosophers enumerate the pangs of the rich, and expatiate on the vanity of their pleasures. Was there ever so palpable a sophism. The pangs of a rich man are not essential to riches, but to the abuse of them. If he were even more wretched than the poor, he would deserve no compassion, because he is the creator of his own misery, and happiness was in his power. But the sufferings of the indigent are the natural consequences of his state; he feels the weight of his hard lot; no length of time nor habit, can ever render him insensible to fatigue and hunger. Neither wisdom, nor good-humour, can annihilate the evils which are inseparable from his situation. What avails it in Epictetus to foresee that his master is going to break his leg? Doth that prevent the evil? On the contrary, his foreknowledge added greatly to his misfortune. If the populace were really as wise as we suppose them stupid, how could they act otherwise than as they do?—*Rousseau.*

EQUALITY OF CONDITIONS.

It is one of the most important objects of government, to prevent an extreme inequality of fortunes; not by taking away the wealth of the possessors, but in depriving them of the means to accumulate them; not by building hospitals for the poor, but by preventing the citizens from becoming poor. The term equality, does not mean that individuals should all absolutely possess the same degree of wealth and power; but only that, with respect to the latter, it should never be exercised contrary to good order and the laws; and with respect to the former, that no citizen should be rich enough to buy another, and that none should be so poor as to be obliged to sell himself. This supposes a moderation of possessions and credit on the side of the great; and a moderation of desires and covetousness on the part of the small. Would you give consistency and strength to a state, prevent the two extremes as much as possible; let there be no rich persons, nor beggars. These two conditions, naturally inseparable, are equally destructive to the commonwealth. The one furnishes tyrants, the other the supporters of tyranny. It is by such the traffic of public liberty is carried on; the one buying, the other selling it. This equality, they tell us, is a mere speculative chimera, which cannot exist in practice. But though abuses are inevitable, does it thence follow they are not to be corrected? It is for the very reason that things always tend to destroy this equality, that the laws should be calculated to preserve it.—*Rousseau.*

EQUALITY AMONG CITIZENS.

A too great disproportion of wealth among citizens weakens any state. Every person, if possible, ought to enjoy the fruits of his labour, in a full possession of all the necessaries, and many of the conveniences of life. No one can doubt but such equality is most suitable to human nature, and diminishes much less from the happiness of the rich, than it adds to that of the poor. It also augments the power of the state, and makes very extraordinary taxes, or impositions, be paid with more cheerfulness. Where the riches are engrossed by a few, these must [ought to] contribute very largely to supplying public necessities. But when the riches are dispersed among multitudes, the burden feels light on every shoulder; and the taxes make not a sensible difference on any one's mode of living.* Add to this, that where the riches are in few hands, these must enjoy all the power, and will readily conspire to lay all the burden on the poor, and oppress them still farther, to the discouragement of all industry.—*Hume.*

HUNTING, OR WINTER SHOES.—A pound of boiled linseed oil, two ounces of coarse bees wax, two of spirit of turpentine, and one of Burgundy pitch; melt slowly, and rub into the leather before the fire with sponge, again and again giving a fresh layer, till the leather will absorb no more. The shoes or boots are not only impervious to wet, but will wear much longer. N. B.—In America, Indian rubber is now used for *clogs*, an effectual preventive of moisture.

* Written half a century ago.—What follows looks like prophecy.

THE STORY-TELLER.

It is intended that the STORY-TELLER shall remain a permanent department in this Miscellany; and that every week there shall be a *Tale*, either moral, domestic, romantic, or biographical; and also that these Tales shall be of the *best kind*. There would be no great difficulty in giving an original story every week,—and an original story will occasionally be given; but while English, French, German, and American Literature, abound with materials of *first-rate excellence*, it is conceived that, in a little work of this kind, time and pains will be better bestowed in abridging, translating, and adapting these to our purpose, than in fabricating commodities which must often be so far inferior in value. It is meant, in short, to do here, on a small scale, for Tales, what the *Libraries* are doing for Voyages, Travels, Memoirs, and Histories; to select and condense, and bring within reasonable compass what neither ordinary purses nor ordinary leisure can reach; to do, at a humble distance, for Novels and Stories what Mr. Lamb has done for Shakspeare's Plays. This comparison is made in no vain assumption; but to give a clear notion of what is intended. To her task, the writer to whom this department of the SCHOOLMASTER is entrusted, brings a well-stored memory, and some experience of the art of narration. The first story may serve as a specimen of the plan.

MARY LAWSON:
A STORY FOR YOUNG WOMEN.

Condensed and adapted to the *Schoolmaster*, by Mrs. JOHNSTONE.

(From the Canterbury Tales.)

"Where, Mary, will you find a character?"

MRS. DIXON, the good-hearted and respectable maiden landlady of a Weymouth lodging house, sat one evening, poring over a large volume, when Mr. Atkinson entered her parlour. Though he had but very lately become her boarder, they were, from particular circumstances, already on a footing of easy intimacy. "You are a great reader of your Bible," said Mr. Atkinson, as his landlady laid aside her spectacles. "Heaven forbid I should not," replied Mrs. Dixon; "but this, to my shame, is not my Bible." It was, in fact, a *story-book* in manuscript; and the story which I am now about to tell from it, in the *Schoolmaster* was that of *Crazy Mary Lawson*, Mrs. Dixon's old servant, or helper. In doing so, I shall use her own words as often as is possible. I could find none half so appropriate.

"She was not always old!" said the landlady: "no truly—nor always crazed; nay, for that matter, she is not so old now! but poor thing she has had enough to craze her! Mary Lawson, sir, was, within my memory, one of the best looking girls in Weymouth, not but that there were different opinions concerning her. Many of our lodgers used to say, that she would be pretty enough if she would open her eyes; but to my thinking there was something soft and sorrowful in them when half closed, as they generally were, that was quite out of the common way. Mary was born in a village upon the banks of the Dee, not very far from the neighbourhood of Wrexham. Her father, though he held only a small farm, lived in a very reputable way, and Mary's education was therefore not neglected.

At fourteen Mary lost her mother; nor was that the greatest of her misfortunes; for her father soon married again, and as his second wife was a careless idling sort of body, the charge of a young family, which quickly came on, was left almost entirely to his eldest daughter. "I did not at that time love children," said Mary afterwards to me, "I thought them all noisy and troublesome alike. Oh, Mrs. Dixon, who could have persuaded me, young and giddy as I then was, that to sit by the cradle of a sick baby, to listen to its little moans, and to give it the bread that I wanted myself, would be a more pleasing employment to me than all the pleasures of the whole world besides! But I then thought there were a great many people and things to love in the world; and perhaps too fine folks there may be: *my* lot was different; but my sins began with children, and so did my punishment."

This was only the poor girl's talk, sir, for I could never gather that she did any harm at that time, only, I suppose, was a little heedless, like those of her age. However, her mother-in-law and she did not agree. So the father bethought himself of an expedient that pleased both parties, though Mary was best pleased of the two. An aunt of hers was settled at Bristol in the haberdashery line. Her shop drove no mighty trade; but she was an infirm single woman, and therefore not unwilling to take her niece in, as an assistant. Mary was accordingly fitted out with two new gowns; great doings, as she said, for those days, and I know not how many different ribands.

For a short time she thought Bristol the finest and happiest place in the whole globe. Her aunt was not unkind to her; she herself was naturally of a gay and cheerful character, and all the new scenes around made her gayer still. But by-and-by this novelty began to fade a little; and after being familiar with busy streets and close-packed houses, she could not help calling to mind the green lanes and clear river of her native place. Her greatest delight was to walk on a fine Sunday to a village not far distant, called Clifton, and to sit on the brow of the rocks.

These walks, however, proved very unlucky for her. A regiment was at that time quartered at Bristol, and one of the officers took particular notice of Mary. There are strawberry gardens, it seems in that neighbourhood, sir, where common folks, and sometimes gentry, go to eat fruit. It was at one of these that Captain Mandeville contrived to make a sort of acquaintance with the poor girl. He was at that time about eight-and-twenty; a very fine-looking man, as I understand, (for Heaven knows he was strangely altered when I saw him,) and had all the dashing air that gentlemen of the army affect. Mary's eyes were treacherous ones; for they played her heart false, and showed her this gay young officer in his best colours. He was not wanting to himself, it was very easy to find out where she resided; and Captain Mandeville soon became a great customer for ribands and feathers, which he pretended were bestowed upon recruits. Never did man enlist so many in so short a time; for by-and-by there was hardly a yard of riband left in the shop. In the meanwhile, vows, promises, letters, and presents were lavished upon Mary, though in an underhand way, you may be sure. The poor girl loved him, and he had discernment enough to perceive it; nevertheless she was innocent and well-disposed.—I do not want to excuse her fault, sir,—it was a great one:—the greater, as she herself in bitterness of heart acknowledged, because she had not been brought up in ignorance of her duty. But what is to be said to this man, sir, who saw she was no bold, nor forward creature, ready to throw herself in his way: for she has affirmed to me, and I will pledge my life she spoke truly, that she has many times shut herself up in the back shop, and avoided her accustomed walks in order to struggle with her own weak heart, and endeavour to forget him. What is to be said to him, I ask? Only what he has been obliged since to say to himself: you will hear it, sir.—All Mary's efforts, however, would not do. To be short, sir, it was *his* day of triumph, and the poor girl became his victim.

Melancholy was the change that succeeded. Captain Mandeville must have been a hard man, though Mary's partiality made her think otherwise. His heart, his pleasures, his fortune, except when he had some great object in view, *were all for himself*. He had no care for others; nor, for aught I could learn, had he really any for her, when his first passion had subsided. He was one of those rattling sparks, sir, who dash on in life without looking to the right or the left, through a long lane of the maimed and the blind, whom they have made so.

All seemed now at the worst with Mary. She was ruined, neglected, and had reason to suppose herself in a situation that would soon render her disgrace apparent. Sometimes, as she told me, she thought with horror of being a mother. At others, the recollection of the infantine caresses of her little brothers and sisters, and of the pleasure their parents used to take in them, came to her heart; till, between that, and conscience, which began every way to afflict her, it nearly burst. To expiate the sin of having wished to leave her family, and to be sure that was but a fancied sin, she had almost resolved to make a voluntary sacrifice of herself, and carry back her shame and her penitence to her father's house, quitting for ever all sight of the man who had wronged her; when another idea more flattering to her passion suddenly came across her mind; for poor Mary's remorse was, I fear, as you will see, sir, only love in disguise.

Captain Mandeville had a very fine estate and house in Northumberland. It was a family mansion, and his mother, as his serjeant, from whom alone Mary got any information concerning him, had told her, resided in it. The wild project of fixing herself somewhere in the neighbourhood of Mandeville Park, occurred to the poor girl. Yet the great effort still remained to be made; which was to resolve on separating herself for ever from the only man on earth whom she loved; and to convince him, by so doing, that though she had been frail, she was not vicious, nor would consent to continue the disgraceful correspondence, which, more from habitual libertinism than any particular fondness, he still would have preserved.

It was a long journey to Newcastle, in the neighbourhood of which lay Mandeville Park. When the poor unhappy girl first saw its outward paling, her heart, she often declared to me, died within her, as though she had at the same moment foreseen all the guilt and the sorrow that was to arise from thence.

At length she came within view of the house: and, "Oh," said she, "how great did *he* seem, and how little did I!"

"What, Mary," said I, "were you not yet cured then of judging by appearances?—Was it because he was gay and handsome, and had magnificent houses, and large parks, that he was in reality *better* than you? or how were you sure that in the end he would be happier?"

"Most true," she replied; "but I had sinned against my conscience, and every living being seemed greater and happier than I was at that time."

No wonder Mary was dazzled, however, sir; for I have been told since that it is a very fine house. The hall had grand marble statues in it: there was a shrubbery of I can't tell you how many acres extent, and grounds without end. A stately lawn was in front, and vast quantities of deer feeding under the trees. Then there was a library, worth I know not how much money, with painted glass windows, and curious busts. What a pity, sir, that these rich gentlemen *who set up the heads of so many good and wise folks, can't get a little of their hearts!* For my share, I never saw the Captain, and heard talk of his fine seats, without calling to mind the parable of Nathan and the lamb. How can it be that those who are able to command so many pleasures, can, for a temporary gratification, deprive another of their only comfort!

Under pretence of indisposition, though indeed it could hardly be called a pretence, Mary was set down at a decent house, in the neighbourhood of the great estate. And here, what with agitation of mind and fatigue of body, she found herself really so ill as to be obliged to go to bed. Sleep, however, she could not. So after a restless night full of melancholy reflections, she was up with the lark, and once more on foot. I need not tell, you, sir, which way she turned her steps. It was a clear fresh morning. The dew lay on the grass; birds were singing on every tree, and at a little distance was a fine piece of water, with a hanging wood on one side of it, that dipped its branches in the stream. The village where she was born, and all her girlish days, came at once to the recollection of poor Mary; so leaning her head on one of the outer green gates, she relieved her over-charged heart with a flood of tears. In this situation she was seen by a young woman, who observing her, I suppose, to make a respectable appearance, for she was in mourning for her aunt, and interested, perhaps, by her condition, very good-naturedly invited her to rest herself in a house hard by. This woman was the park-keeper's wife, and the house to which she invited her was that in which they lived. A pretty place, with a fine honeysuckle curling all over the windows, but no comfort did the sight of it give to Mary, though it was as neat as a palace. There was a baby in a cradle, and a breakfast set for the husband, who was just returning home: they were young people, sir, and had not been married above a twelve-month, which no doubt made them so fond of each other: and to be sure the father did so caress and dandle the child! Mary's heart was ready to burst. Every thing she saw put her in mind of some happiness that was past, or which she could never hope to enjoy; and she began to cry more bitterly than before.

Well! with much ado she made out, between whiles, the story of her soldier husband, and supposed widowhood; blushing and trembling all the while with the consciousness of deceit. But the good folks took it all for gospel.

In the course of the morning two fine ladies, one old the other young, sauntered in; and superciliously questioned her, and listened to her feigned story from the park-keeper's wife. Mary knew that one was the mother, the other might be the sister of Mandeville, and she buoyed herself up with vain hopes of kindness from them. Having gratified their curiosity they withdrew as haughtily as they had entered.

And here, sir, was an end at once to all the hopes that Mary had entertained from the fortune, the fine education, and the tender heart of a great lady!—" I did flatter myself," said she, "that seeing me look sorrowful and sick, and having nothing to do but to comfort the sick and the sorrowful, she would have taken some little compassion upon me. I was a young creature then: she had no reason to think that I was a wicked one, and I was in circumstances when a woman ought to feel for a woman; yet, like the Priest and the Levite, she passed over to the other side, and left me to the poor Samaritan; and this was done both by the elder and the younger lady; yet they gave a great deal of money, I am told, to different charities at Newcastle; but they would neither tax their time nor their feelings."—"To my thinking Mrs. Mandeville looks very sick," said the woman to her husband, when they were gone.—"Much as usual," replied he; "she is always so pale since my knowledge."—"She has Madam Selborne's own complexion," returned the other.—"And who is Madam Selborne?" said Mary, who had concluded the stranger to be Mr. Mandeville's sister.—"Why my lady's own mother. Bless you, you did not take the *elderly* gentlewoman for his honour's wife, to be sure;—the *young* one is Mrs. Mandeville."

The good folks were sitting at their breakfast, and did not look at Mary as they spoke, for she was standing behind them, near the cradle. Lucky it was that things were so disposed; for she had time to lean her head down, and recover herself from this last stroke; which, although her presumptuous heart had never whispered to her would be any new affliction, yet seemed to double all that she had before felt. She now perceived the extent of Captain Mandeville's art.

Mrs. Mandeville was with child, and near her time; poor Mary was also near her confinement, which a fright, which she got from seeing Mrs. Mandeville in danger of an accident, prematurely hastened. "Oh, Mrs. Dixon," said she to me, "imagine what my sufferings were, when, after a long and painful trial, the first thing I distinctly saw was my own dear baby dead: the first feelings that entered my heart were those of a mother, and of a mother without a child! to have been lodged in the cold grave, where I imagined Mrs. Mandeville, would have been happiness to what I endured."

I am afraid poor Mary never knew what she did endure. Her child did not come dead into the world, however; but it went off, almost immediately in convulsions. She had nevertheless an excellent constitution; and God, sir, could never intend that women should die, just when it is most necessary that they should live.

"Well," said Mary's landlady one morning, "God Almighty don't send burdens to common folk alone! there's the young 'Squire, as the servants say, wont live neither. His mother won't suckle him; and the dry-nurse, as come from Durham, can't manage to make him keep life and soul together, with all her fine silver boats and new-fashioned ways. Old Madam Selborne says, that for self-willedness he is his father's own son, for nothing will he swallow: so you may comfort yourself that you are not the only poor soul as loses a child."—"Oh that I could save one!" said Mary, and a thought glanced across her mind. "Will he live if he is suckled, do you say?" added she, impatiently? Is it Captain Mandeville's child of which you speak? Is *he* born?"—and then the recollection of her own words, is it *Captain Mandeville's child*, as though no other than the heir could be his, put her into a second agony of tears. The child had indeed been born several days before, but it was in no way to live. It was a sickly little thing. The mother never intended to nurse it herself; and if she had had the will, the doctors said she would not have the power; so the poor babe, as they could not rear him with dry-nursing, which they had all along intended to do, was like not to be reared at all. Well, sir, it does not signify going round about the bush: by the recommendation of the park-keeper's wife, the babe was put to Mary's bosom. With many a bitter heartache, and many a tear, did she receive it. The poor little thing began from that day to gain strength, and its first smiles, its first looks were Mary's. His mother saw him not, or very rarely.

Mrs. Mandeville, who was of a fretful temper, and a sickly habit, became soon after this seriously ill, and her husband was sent for in haste, however he made none in coming: and before he arrived another express was despatched to inform him that his wife was dead. He stopped short at York, and wrote from thence to Mrs. Selborne, requesting that she would undertake to order every thing that was suitable on the occasion, and informing her that he would be at Mandeville Park within a certain time.

This was a dreadful interval for Mary. She could not resolve to stay; much less could she resolve to depart. The baby's very life seemed to depend upon her care; and neither night nor day had she ceased to watch it; and if there was a moment when she remembered with sorrow that it was not her own, she at the same time called to mind that it was Captain Mandeville's. None but a woman, sir, can tell how closely the infant creeps into your heart that lies at your bosom; and, if in common cases this is daily proved, what wonder that Mary's fondness exceeded all common measure! It had even no longer a mother to excite her jealousy, or share her attentions; and the early loss which it sustained seemed to point out a particular providence in the manner by which that loss was supplied. In short, sir, love, maternal love, I think we may call it, conquered fear, shame, and every other feeling. Mary, therefore, at length resolved to stay, and encounter the man, whom, in any other circumstances, she had determined to fly to the world's end to avoid.

Captain Mandeville arrived within the time appointed, just after the evening had closed. Mary heard the clattering of the horse's feet, and soon after his well-known voice and step. The many—many occasions when she had listened to them with a beating heart, interesting as they had been, were all, she thought, nothing to this. He staid some little time below with Mrs. Selborne, and then the feet of both were to be heard on the staircase.

"Now," exclaimed Mary, with a palpitating heart, "now comes the trial!"—and she turned to the infant that was sleeping sweetly in its cradle.—"Oh, if it were my child that he was coming to look at," she softly whispered—" but mine sleeps sounder still!"

Mr. Mandeville came in; he neither cast his eyes to the right nor the left, but, with a candle in his hand, walked straight to the cradle, and stooping down to see the baby, kissed its little hand.

"Will he wake, do you think?" said he to Mrs. Selborne, motioning to kiss its cheek.—" Oh, no, no, no," murmured Mary, pursuing, in the anguish of her heart, nothing but her own recollections, "mine will never wake again." Mr. Mandeville started at the voice, indistinctly as it reached him, and turned towards the speaker; but she was at a remote end of the room, and the single candle which he held did not enable him to discern her features. "Who is that person," exclaimed he hastily to Mrs. Selborne, "and what is she saying?"— "She says that you will not disturb the child; it never wakes, I believe, at this hour." They then talked together in a low voice of its health, its age, and its mother. "You will probably recollect the young woman who nurses him," concluded Mrs. Selborne, after saying something which Mary did not distinctly hear. "She is the widow of a private who served under you; she owes the place to your recommendation." The abashed and unfortunate girl leaned against the chimney; her eyes, which she raised only for a single moment, swimming in tears.

Mr. Mandeville staid but two days longer at the Park, during which time Mary, by substituting in her own place, at certain hours, a girl who was sometimes employed as under nursery-maid, contrived that they should meet no more. She learned, however, that by means of this girl Mr. Mandeville had satisfied himself that her child was dead; and she had reason to hope that he had gathered enough information as to what related to her, to be assured that she must on this occasion have purposely shunned him.

And now, after Mary had been so heavily beaten by the storm, an interval of tranquillity seemed to succeed in her life.

The infant was not robust, but it daily grew stronger, and to her daily more precious. It was her care, her pleasure, her employment: it engrossed her whole soul, and by degrees, filled up all those fond affections of her heart which had no other object they could venture to dwell upon. The very circumstance of not being a strong child made it only the dearer, by furnishing a perpetual succession of hopes and fears: both were already in some sort rewarded. He began to distinguish her; would crow when she appeared; "and stretch its little arms as it would fly," when hers opened to receive him. The range of Mandeville House, with the beautiful grounds, pleasure-garden, and country adjoining, were in themselves sources both of health and delight. She enjoyed almost undisturbed possession of the whole. "What more could I gain, had I been born in a rank to have become its mistress," would she sometimes say to herself, "except an ungrateful man!" Tears then would fill her eyes. "But this baby would indeed have been mine.—Well—and could I have loved him better?" The recollection that

had she been his mother she need never have feared parting with him, would again agitate her heart, and unsettle her spirits.

Just in the beginning of autumn, when every thing looked full of happiness and beauty, and Mary's heart was daily more light on seeing her nursling prosper in the way he did,—dear Sir, would you believe it? One night Mr. Mandeville alighted at his own door! his coming was quite unexpected on all hands.

Mary's happy days were now at an end. The woman that does wrong must, I fear, remember, sir, that she will always be exposed to suspicion. Captain Mandeville, it was plain, had no faith in after-virtue, when he had found it failing in the first instance; and although a decent respect for circumstances, or accidental indifference, had induced him to take no notice of her during his first visit to the Park, these motives had ceased to operate, and she even perceived that he suspected her of placing herself voluntarily within his reach. Humbled by this opinion, which she was unable to remove; finding all remonstrances vain, and all efforts to avoid him useless, her life now became as miserable as it had before been tranquil. To complete her affliction, Mrs. Selborne soon suspected that some particular pursuit detained her son-in-law at Mandeville Park, and she quickly guessed its object. How Mary passed her days in consequence of all this, you may judge, sir. Mr. Mandeville finding solicitation and allurement vain, grew insolent and troublesome; the servants sneered; the park-keeper's wife avoided her; there was no security from persecution either in the house or the grounds; and, in short, of all that had soothed or comforted her poor heart, nothing remained the same but the baby.

Mary's mind began, I fear to undergo a strange revolution about this time. She grew desperate, as it were; and she has acknowledged to me that she sometimes debated with herself whether she should not accept his fine offers; for, rather than be crossed in his inclination, he did offer her liberally, sir; at others, she determined to tell the whole story to Mrs. Selborne, and throw herself upon her mercy; but against one temptation there was remorse, and a thousand other painful feelings, resulting from her experience of the selfishness and cruelty of the man; against the other, stood the severe temper and unfeeling character of the woman. Shame, too, at the thought of being exposed and degraded in the eyes of the neighbourhood, for she feared they would judge hardly of her, made her resolve, whatever might be the consequence, to keep her own secret. No third project then remained but that of quitting the family altogether; and this she so nearly determined upon, as to collect all her little savings; so that if driven to extremities, either by the persecution of Mr. Mandeville or Mrs. Selborne, she might be able to leave the house at a moment's warning; but how was she to leave the child?—The thought of doing so was little less than a death-stroke.

Well, things continued in this way till near the time when Mrs. Selborne was to quit the Park: the day was anxiously expected by Mary. On the last but one preceding it, she had the ill-fortune to encounter Mr. Mandeville, as she was returning to the nursery from her dinner. He insisted on talking with her; which she positively refused; but finding that he prepared to follow her up stairs, she thought it better to listen to him where she was. Mrs. Selborne was abroad. All that Mr. Mandeville could offer or say on such an occasion, for it was his purpose to engage her to remain at the Park with him, may, as one should think, be easily imagined; but you would not easily imagine, sir, that, finding all other efforts fail, he should, before they parted, strive to alarm the fears of the poor girl, by indirectly threatening to publish her former misconduct. I cannot think so ill of him, or of any man, as to believe that he was in earnest; but Mary's agitated heart and distempered fancy gave credit to the worst. With what little eloquence she was mistress of, she endeavoured, it seems, to represent to him the great disadvantage her loss would prove to his child; but he treated it as a matter of no consequence. "The infant was nearly weaned, and any old woman in the parish might nurse it," he said. Driven to the last extremity, she then positively declared her resolution to quit the country, and find a situation elsewhere.

"And where will you find a character?" said Mr. Mandeville, with a sneer; he had little time for more, as the old lady's chariot drove up at that moment to the door. "Remember, Mary, what I say to you;" a hint from me to Mrs. Selborne dismisses you with disgrace from the house; where, I say, will you then find a character?"

It was not necessary to bid her remember the words; they were engraved in letters of fire, as it seemed to Mary, both on her heart and her brain.

"Where, Mary, will you find a character?" exclaimed

she, as she ran up into the nursery, and mechanically took the child in her arms; for it was her hour of walking with him. "Where will you find a character?" she continued repeating to herself, as she hurried on, without exactly knowing whither; tears, caresses, and every thing that was afflicting succeeded this tumult of resentment.—I cannot give you an exact account of what followed, sir; she could never give me one herself: but certain it is, that she continued to walk till she reached the mouth of the river; and there, meeting by ill-fortune with a small vessel bound for London, and in the very act of sailing, she got directly on board, and still carrying with her the precious child, was in a few hours many leagues out at sea.—Now comes the fearful part of Mary's life! now comes the time when she strove to whiten by comparison: to use her little knowledge and experience in justifying a wicked action, and to say to herself, "Why should I alone be upright in a worthless and cruel world!" Mr. Mandeville, sir, could no longer tempt, but his influence had corrupted her, and left her exposed to the temptation within. Mary and the child escaped without detection, and she buried herself in London.

What Mary's feelings or thoughts were during the period that succeeded, it would be difficult precisely to ascertain. She was not without money; but she had neither friends nor connexion. Industry, sir, is nevertheless a trusty auxiliary, and either finds or makes its way. By giving security, which her stock of money enabled her to do, she contrived to get employment in a small but creditable shop, not unlike that in which she had lived with her aunt: her readiness and good qualities rendered her valuable wherever she had an opportunity of making them known, as she very quickly did. Her wants were few: she had neither vanity nor pleasure but in the child; and he, little fellow, grew and did well; while her excessive fondness for him made it impossible for any one to suspect that she was not its mother. He was no longer, indeed, at Mandeville Park, the heir of a fine estate, and waited upon by a numerous train of servants; but he had still one servant more anxious, more devoted than any he had left there; he had also the best of everything, however plain: all her leisure was employed, as he grew older, in teaching him the little she knew either of writing, reading, or accounts; his health was still tender and uncertain; she watched him with the care of a mother and the fatigue of a nurse. No thought like self-reproach, I believe, ever crossed her mind, with respect to his father; her heart was quite hardened towards Mr. Mandeville, and she was persuaded that Mrs. Selborne would grieve but little for the child when it was once out of her sight. She shut her eyes deliberately to the past and the future, and determined to think only of the present day.

Such was her own account of her life in London; and I never had reason to doubt its truth.

I saw Mary for the first time about eighteen years ago; she was then nine-and-twenty. It was in the beginning of summer, and a very sultry day; I was sitting during the forenoon at work, with my parlour windows open, when a young woman, holding a little boy by the hand, walked past the house and returned. She did this more than once without my taking any particular notice of her, though she, as I afterwards found, took a great deal of me; at last she made a little stop close by the window.

"Did you want an industrious person to assist you in needlework, madam?" said she.

[Mrs. Dixon related at some length all her doubts and perplexities, but she said Mary conquered them at last.]

"Your little boy," said I, "seems sickly." Tears flowed down her cheeks in a moment.—"He has had a fever," she replied; "but thank God he is now likely to do well. The doctor tells me that bathing in the sea will recruit his strength, and I have therefore brought him here for that purpose." I know not what there was so taking in her and the child, but for my life I could not turn them from the door.

It was now all plain sailing, sir, and she knew it: for I presently discovered that my industry and usefulness, on which I valued myself, were nothing to her ingenuity. She did so cut out and contrive! "And this, Mrs. Dixon," said she, "is just the right pattern for such a thing: and that will do for another. She was like a good fairy."

Mary's character was a mystery to Mrs. Dixon; but her conduct was unexceptionable: her melancholy and her varying moods wore off in time; her conscience was lulled, as her heart had been seared; her only weakness now was excessive fondness for her little boy.

He was, continued the landlady, about eight, when she brought him to Weymouth; the sea air agreed with him wonderfully, and he was never sickly from that time; but grew so arch, so sprightly, so diverting, that *little Bob* was the universal favourite. He was, withal, very proud; although nobody could tell of what: it could not be of his birth or his great estate, poor child! for, alas, he knew nothing of either! but in spite of his humble situation, Bob was a great *hoper*, and was always talking of the mighty things he would do when he should grow to be a man:—I beg your pardon, sir—my eyes will fill with tears at the recollection. His mother encouraged this folly in him.

"Mary," said I to her one day, "you will totally ruin that boy."—"Oh, no, no," returned she impatiently.—"You will make his mind a great deal too high."—"*I* do not make it," said she;—"it makes itself.'—" But ought it to make itself? Consider he is growing a great lad." "Don't talk to me, Mrs. Dixon. I cannot control his spirit. If you knew how dearly I bought him——' "At what price *did* you buy him?" returned I. She started, and looked at me very earnestly for a moment, but said nothing. I cannot but own that I had my private thoughts.

Time wore on. Bob was now twelve years old. No longer a delicate small-limbed child, but a fine well-grown boy; with a manly and open countenance, a forward and proud spirit; full of frolic, but without any mischief. He had beaten a neighbour's son much bigger than himself, who persisted in calling him *little Bob*; so he was now Robert; and it was laughable to see the vehemence with which he insisted upon this claim. All our acquaintance blamed us for keeping such a great boy at home, without any occupation, and I began secretly to be a little ashamed of the weakness myself, for, to say truth, sir, I was nearly as weak as Mary on that subject. The child was never idle either, nor was it in his nature to be so; he made himself useful ten thousand ways. There was nothing so low that he disdained to do for those he loved; he has cleaned knives, and gone on errands. Good God, little did I think who it was that was so employed! It was not with Mary's approbation, however, that he did this; but she could not prevent him; he undertook it all as if it were sport—" all for his dear little granny Dixon," as he used to call me. Think of his making me his grandmother, sir!—I was then a young woman; but it was his playful way. The fact was, that he had an inexhaustible stock of health and spirits to spare, and having neither companion nor employment, was fain to spend both as he could. Every one, however, that came to the house noticed and spoiled him. "Gads my life, Mrs. Dixon," said one of our actor gentlemen, who was drinking tea with me, while Bob, in tip-top spirits, handed us the tea kettle, "this is a fellow of whom the world may say that ' he will ride a bay trotting horse over a four inched bridge, and course his own shadow for a traitor.'"* To be sure, sir, Bob was too fond of riding strange horses; but how the child's foible came to be so generally known was what I never could guess.

Bob's own mind was quite made up as to his future destination. "He would be a soldier," he said, "like his father."—"*Like his father!*' said Mary, and tears came into her eyes. The soldiers took to him mightily. The master, seeing how fond he was of horses, taught him to ride; which Mary did not object to. They looked upon him as one of themselves, and acted very kindly by him. But still they were men, and he was only a boy; so that, without meaning it, they made him forward and presuming.

The interval between this time and his fifteenth birth-day was the most melancholy we had ever passed since we lived together. He was almost beyond our control; yet we knew no harm of him; but he kept growing very handsome and very tall: every day, therefore, told us that something must be done with him. A dreadful gloom came over Mary. She was no longer the same creature she had been. No sleep did she get at night; no quiet in the day.

About this time, Mary heard of her father, who was become very old and feeble; and in the despair of parting with her boy, to which conscience now urged her, she turned to her own family. I believe she soothed her conscience with the hope of attending her father's age, and watching his death-bed. In short, she found it absolutely necessary to hope, if she meant to live; and this was all she *could* hope.

I tell you merely my own conjectures; for her restlessness, her total loss of appetite, and the long fits of absence that now grew very remarkable in her, were the only symptoms by which I could guess that she was privately forming some resolution. I had no clew at that time to her inmost thoughts; but by after events I could trace them. Her health suffered too much to

---

* Shakspeare.

permit me to ask many questions, for I really could not guess what their effect upon her might prove. At length she fixed her determination; but, like a drowning person catching at straws, she could not prevail on herself to take the great step till she had settled everything that concerned her besides. And so, sir, this new delay in entering upon the path of justice and uprightness was the cause of all the melancholy story that followed.

Mary was to be away three weeks, and Bob formed the delight of Mrs. Dixon in her absence, "going and coming," she said, "and asking what he could do for me, this and the other." At this time Mrs. Dixon's lodgings were taken for the season, for a gentleman with a large establishment of servants.—It was Mr. Mandeville!

Yes—it was Mr. Mandeville himself! but not that Mr. Mandeville who had robbed Mary of her heart, in all the bloom and fire of eight-and-twenty; free-living, and the years that had passed over his head, had left strong traces on his features. He had a fixed redness in his face, and had lost the slightness of his person. One might indeed see that he had been handsome, for he had a manly character of countenance: and I could afterwards recollect that his son greatly resembled him in this: but such was then the wide difference in their age and appearance, that nothing of the sort occurred to me. How indeed should it?

Mr. Mandeville's profusion and vices were imitated by every servant he had; and if they strove a little to conceal this from him, they only added hypocrisy to every other fault: but they did not endeavour to conceal it, sir; or in a very trifling degree. His own man openly professed to follow his master's example in all things. The butler was several years older, but he was insolent, unfeeling, and extravagant. The other servants did not fall short of these models: but oh, sir! a worse grief than all remained behind, though I did not immediately know its extent: the groom whom I had been obliged to place with my poor innocent boy, was a very ill-disposed lad; and the bad effects of his society were too soon visible in the latter, though sooner to others than to me.

The loss of Mary's assistance threw a vast load upon my spirits and time. In truth, where servants were so disorderly and ill-managed, I had hardly a moment to spare from my domestic concerns, or to call my own. Occupied, as I was, however, I observed that some alteration had taken place in Bob. He affected to be the man more than I thought became him; and began to be very nice in his linen and appearance. He had been hitherto a fine rough boy, ten thousand times more manly than the groom that he admired; yet the latter was a personable lad too; but there was something of native fire and character about Bob, or I fancied so, that was much above his degree: it could not be fancy either, for every body that saw him used to say the same thing."

In the meantime Mary wrote, saying she would soon return; and make some hearts happy, and then there would be some chance for her; but she did not appear, and Mrs. Dixon grew uneasy, both on her account and that of her son. My warnings to him she said to break off the intimacy which he had so lately formed were not attended to, and I had no power to enforce them. Nor could I send either lad out of my house. They were constantly together. They rode matches on the sands, or elsewhere. Their companions betted upon them: they betted themselves; and I was convinced that Bob lost. I taxed him with it. Nothing spoils the temper, sir, like the consciousness of doing wrong. This boy, this child as I may call him, formerly so complying and open, was capable of being rude and sullen: quite at a loss what to do, I desired him to write to his mother, and hasten her return. He obeyed me, though not with a good grace: but she came not, nor did we receive any answer, and I repented that I had not written myself; but I was not a ready pen woman, and had much occupation.—I thought that I was now quite miserable!—I did not know how much more miserable I was to be. Every possible way did I turn over in my mind to remedy the mischief I had so innocently caused: but the mischief was doing, sir, past all remedy:—it was done, as I may say, even while I was considering.

Of what nature the extravagance might be of these two boys I cannot tell, but they had been very extravagant. Bob's means were scanty indeed; the other threw money about like dirt; but I have much reason to believe that he was as ready to take as to part with it. At last neither of them had any left, and both grievously wanted it. My boy would have stopped short; but the wicked one with whom he associated had other ways of proceeding. The old butler was, in private, his constant theme of aversion and ridicule: and more, as he made it appear, in sport than in wickedness; but it *was* wickedness, I am persuaded: he now proposed to secrete several valuable articles that were in this man's possession, on which, he assured Bob, he could raise money, and return them without difficulty in the course of two days; declaring that should it in the interim be discovered they were missing, he would easily face it out for a joke. Robert was, as he confessed, in debt: he had besides contracted a thousand wants, and a thousand wishes, during his intercourse with the worthless crew around him; and too proud to own to any but his immediate companion that he had no resources, he fell into the snare which folly, vice, and ill-fortune prepared for him. The butler, however, was either more subtle, or more watchful, than they had believed him to be. He discovered the fact a very few hours after it was committed; nor did he fail to guess at the culprits. Thomas was first secured, and his evidence criminated Bob. The latter was with me when they came to fetch him. Never to the latest moment of my life, sir, shall I forget *that!* There was no need of accusation nor proof; his countenance told all, and both lads were thrown into prison.

I pass over the trial, but cannot pass the tender pleading of Mrs. Dixon, with the selfish, unconscious father, who harshly blamed poor Bob for corrupting his favourite groom : " Not his fellow left in the stable," he said ; " I would rather he robbed me every day in the year than have lost him." " If you would take the trouble to examine into the rights of the case, sir," said Mrs. Dixon. " A man cannot spend his life in examining your rights and your wrongs, Mrs. Dixon." " I beg your pardon, sir ; I thought that members of Parliament, and rich gentlemen, did spend their lives—" " You take great liberties," said Mandeville, " justice must have its course ; justice *must* and *will* be executed." And so it was. Mrs. Dixon turned from the dissolute and selfish father, to the condemned cell of her only child. " To be sure," she continued, " it was a dismal sight ! so promising a boy !—and not yet sixteen ! Ah, sir, was this, as I afterwards thought, the little fellow that had been fondled and caressed at Mandeville Park, and for whom so much had been expected !—But is not every infant fondled and caressed ?—The poorest outcast that ever went in irons to finish his miserable life, as Bob did, in a distant country, has been pressed to some maternal heart, more tenderly perhaps than ever he was."

" I have been considering, Mrs. Dixon," said the dear fellow, " how it happens that all this evil and wickedness have fallen upon me ; and I think I have found out the cause."—" And what is that, my dear Bob ?" said I, for I was still accustomed to call him so, and he never took it ill of me, though he would not suffer any body else to do it : it was the name I used to him when he was a bit of a child on my knee, and I loved it for that reason. " What is that, my dear Bob ?" said I.—" Why it comes from my having no father. My mother, to be sure, was very good ; but then she was only my mother : and you were very good too ; but I was a boy, and I often thought that to myself, that boys should not be governed by women ; and her hand was as gentle as her heart : so I grew up without any other guide than my own proud thoughts, and easily fell a prey to the wicked suggestions of others.—Now, if I had had a father, Mrs. Dixon, you see I should have been saved from all this; for if he had been a rich man I should not have fallen into the way of temptation ; and if he had been poor and industrious, I should have early learned not to be ashamed of poverty, and his example might have made me industrious too : for indeed I was not naturally wicked ; but God," added he, laying his finger on the Testament, which the chaplain left with him, " as his book assures me, will be a father to the fatherless; and although I have none to apply to in this world, I will put my trust in Him."—I thought my heart must have broken : for, with his finger between the leaves of the book, he dropped on his knees, and hid his face over it ; and when he raised it again, on hearing my sobs, there was something so sweet in his eyes that mine were quite blind with tears. Oh, what, have I since thought, had not Mary to answer for ! Dreadfully, sir, *did* she answer for it ! Yet, had Bob been Mr. Mandeville's son by her, would not his fate have been the same ! for where, even in that case, would he have found a father ?

The boy was now on the sea, and on his way to his place of exile ;—and where was Mary ? " I was sitting," said Mrs. Dixon, " one night very sorrowfully alone with the newspaper in my hand, waiting for the tea-kettle to boil, and examining, as I constantly did, whether I could find any tidings about the vessel that was to carry away poor Bob, when suddenly a voice that was more like the shriek of a ghost than any human tongue, called me by my name. I looked up, and standing in the doorway beheld Mary. It was horrible to see her. She was not merely white but livid. Her figure, which was slight, and generally somewhat drooping, was unnaturally stiff and erect. Her eyes were wider open than usual, and seemed quite glassy; in a word, she looked exactly like an untended corpse placed upright.

"Lord have mercy on us, Mary!" said I, starting and dropping my spectacles, "when did you arrive?"

"Where is Mr. Mandeville?" said she, in the same hurried and frightful tone as before, without taking her eyes off me, or the smallest notice of my question.

"Why, what signifies where he is?" replied I, much alarmed, though I did not exactly know at what.

"Where is Mr. Mandeville?" again repeated she with great violence, and with a gesture as though she would have seized hold of me.

"I do not know—I cannot tell," cried I, holding back in prodigious perturbation.—"William, where is your master?" I added, to a servant who was passing the door.

"In the drawing-room, madam, playing with the Major."

"Tell him, Mary Lawson must see him this moment," said she, addressing herself to the man in the same extraordinary tone. What he thought of her, I know not; but he seemed startled; so without farther delay he ran up stairs, and opened the drawing-room door. Sure enough we heard the rattle of the dice, and the two gentlemen laughing: Mr. Mandeville in particular; for he had a loud and noisy laugh that one could not mistake: it was his last, however, for many a long day!—I suppose the man delivered his message exactly, for the laughter ceased as it were all at once.

"Mary Lawson!" exclaimed Mr. Mandeville with great vehemence, "and where the devil does she come from?"

He had no time to say a word more: for Mary, who had run like a wild thing up stairs, in spite of all my efforts to prevent her, heard his voice, and burst into the room.

"Your child—your own child, Mr. Mandeville, save your child!" was all she could say.

He shook her off roughly, for she had snatched hold of the sleeve of his coat: but he changed colour, and looked very earnestly in her face.

"I call God to witness," said she, in a faltering, but very distinct voice, "that Robert Innis is your own lawful son. He is *Robert Mandeville*." A pistol bullet could not have taken a more sudden effect than these few words; it was a frightful sight, sir, to see this great strong man drop dead like a stone at her feet: it was because he was so strong that the surprise thus acted upon him.

A surgeon came, sent for by the major of the regiment, a particular friend of Mr. Mandeville's. The major shortly after came in search of Mary, whom he sternly questioned, "but he had no need," said Mrs. Dixon, "for out at once came the whole tale."

"Woman," said he, resentfully, when she had finished, "you have ruined Mr. Mandeville!"—Mary looked up at him, but not a word did she utter.

"You have robbed him of what was as dear to him as his life!"—Mary looked again; to my thinking they were speaking looks, but not a syllable did she say. I thought the Major seemed embarrassed by them, however.

"This cursed connexion," continued he, turning half to me, only, I really believe, to avoid looking at her again, "will cost him both his credit and his happiness."

"It cost me both," said Mary.

"Circumstances were very different," replied he angrily.

"Very!—for *I* had nothing else to lose!"

I am sure he was moved, for he was a good-natured man, sir; but he did not care to show it,—" The boy—the poor unfortunate boy," said he to himself. "What has become of him!"—This was touching the tender string with Mary; and off she went again, into something between madness and hysterics: so that finding he had obtained all the information that he could, he charged me to keep the girl close from observation, and returned to his wicked companion.

And now, sir, if a ship freighted with gold could have redeemed the poor lad, his father would have thought it too little.

Poor Bob! little did he think how many great folks who would not once have looked at him, were busy for him now—his father racked between hopes and fears counting the hours. To increase his chagrin, the business could not be kept so quiet but that all his own friends, and great numbers besides, talked of it openly; and various falsehoods were circulated, of the early wickedness and bad disposition of the boy; so that it seemed as if that cruel speech of Mr. Mandeville's, which drove Mary to desperation, "Where will you find a character?" was now to be verified in the person of his more innocent, and no less friendless child.

The boy died as the ship crossed the line, and from that hour Mary's head was never right again. It would have broken anybody's heart, sir, to hear her talk continually of her boy, and of going to Newcastle to find him; for in her rambling fits she confounded her own first unhappy voyage and his last together, and nothing could persuade her that he was not there.

As to Mr. Mandeville, he lives on in a miserable way; infirm of body, and very sick I believe, in mind. The tide of public opinion had changed before he left Weymouth; and I am told that, great and rich as he is, he too, in advanced life, knows what it is to want a character—for respectability at least. He has been wounded by cold looks and private whispers; nor, while suffering under the double penalty inflicted by a reproaching world and a reproaching conscience, has he even the same poor consolation which Mary finds, when she fancies, in her rambling fits, that Bob is a great man, and lives in a palace. Alas! poor Mary!†

HENRY OF NAVARRE.

BY MR. MACAULAY, M. P. FOR CALNE.

Now glory to the Lord of Hosts, from whom all glories are!
And glory to our Sovereign Leige, King Henry of Navarre!
Now let there be the merry sound of music and of dance,
Through thy corn-fields green, and sunny vines, O pleasant land of France!
And thou, Rochelle, our own Rochelle, proud city of the waters,
Again let rapture light the eyes of all thy mourning daughters.
As thou wert constant in our ills, be joyous in our joy,
For cold, and stiff, and still are they who wrought thy walls annoy.
Hurrah! hurrah! a single field hath turn'd the chance of war,
Hurrah! hurrah! for Ivry, and Henry of Navarre.

O! how our hearts were beating, when, at the dawn of day,
We saw the army of the League drawn out in long array;
With all its priest-led citisens, and all its rebel peers,
And Appenzel's stout infantry, and Egmont's Flemish spears.
There rode the brood of false Lorraine, the curses of our land;
And dark Mayenne was in the midst, a truncheon in his hand:
And, as we looked on them, we thought of Seine's empurpled flood,
And good Coligni's hoary hair all dabbled with his blood;
And we cried unto the living God, who rules the fate of war,
To fight for his own holy name, and Henry of Navarre.

The king is come to marshal us, in all his armour drest,
And he has bound a snow-white plume upon his gallant crest.
He looked upon his people, and a tear was in his eye;
He looked upon the traitors, and his glance was stern and high.
Right graciously he smiled on us, as roll'd from wing to wing,
Down all our line, a deafening shout, "God save our Lord the King!"
" And if my standard-bearer fall, as fall full well he may,
For never saw I promise yet of such a bloody fray,
Press where ye see my white plume shine, amidst the ranks of war,
And be your Oriflamme to-day the helmet of Navarre."

Huwah! the foes are moving. Hark to the mingled din
Of fife, and steed, and trump, and drum, and roaring culverin.
The fiery Duke is pricking fast across Saint Andre's plain,
With all the hireling chivalry of Guelders and Almayne.
Now by the lips of those we love, fair gentlemen of France,
Charge for the golden lilies,—upon them with the lance.
A thousand spurs are striking deep, a thousand spears in rest,
A thousand knights are pressing close behind the snow-white crest;
And in they burst, and on they rushed, while, like a guiding star,
Amidst the thickest carnage blazed the helmet of Navarre.

Now, God be praised, the day is ours. Mayenne hath turned his rein.
D'Aumale hath cried for quarter. The Flemish Count is slain.
Their ranks are breaking like thin clouds before a Biscay gale;
The field is heaped with bleeding steeds, and flags, and cloven mail.
And then we thought on vengeance, and, all along our van,
"Remember St. Bartholomew," was pass'd from man to man.
But out spake gentle Henry, "No Frenchman is my foe:
Down, down, with every foreigner, but let your brethren go."
Oh! was there ever such a knight, in friendship or in war,
As our Sovereign Lord, King Henry, the soldier of Navarre.

Ho! maidens of Vienna; ho! matrons of Lucerne;
Weep, weep, and rend your hair for those who never shall return.
Ho! Philip, send, for charity, thy Mexican pistoles,
That Antwerp monks may sing a mass for thy poor spearmen's souls.
Ho! gallant nobles of the League, look that your arms be bright;
Ho! burghers of Saint Genevieve, keep watch and ward to night.
For our God hath crush'd the tyrant, our God hath rais'd the slave,
And mocked the counsel of the wise, and the valour of the brave.
Then glory to his Holy name, from whom all glories are;
And glory to our Sovereign Lord, King Henry of Navarre.

† A Cheap handsome edition of the Canterbury Tales was lately published by Colburn and Co.

PERMANENT ADVANTAGES OF MACHINERY.

NEEDLES are not so cheap as pins, because the material of which they are made is more expensive, and the processes cannot be executed so completely by machinery. But without machinery, how could that most beautiful article, a fine needle, be sold at the rate of six for a penny? As in the case of pins, machinery is at work at the first formation of the material. Without the tilt hammer, which beats out the bar of steel, first at the rate of 10 strokes a minute, and lastly at that of 500, how could that bar be prepared for needle making at any thing like a reasonable price? In all the processes of needle making, labour is saved by contrivance and machinery. What human touch would be exquisite enough to make the eye of the finest needle, through which the most delicate silk is with difficulty passed? Needles are made in large quantities, so that it is even important to save the time of the child who lays them all one way when they are completed. Mr. Babbage, who is equally distinguished for his profound science, and his mechanical ingenuity, has described this process as an example of one of the simplest contrivances which can come under the denomination of a tool. "It is necessary to separate the needles into two parcels, in order that their points may be all in one direction. This is usually done by women and children. The needles are placed sideways in a heap on a table, in front of each operator. From five to ten are rolled towards this person by the fore-finger of the left hand; this separates them a very small space from each other, and each in its turn is pushed lengthways to the right or to the left hand, according as its eye is on the right or the left hand. This is the usual process, and in it every needle passes individually under the finger of the operator. A small alteration expedites the process considerably; the child puts on the fore-finger of its right hand a small cap or finger-stall, and rolling from the heap from 6 to 12 needles, it keeps them down by the fore-finger of the left hand; whilst it presses the fore-finger of the right hand gently against the ends of the needles, those which have their points towards the right hand stick into the finger-stall; and the child removing the finger of the left hand, allows the needles sticking into the cloth to be slightly raised, and then pushes them towards the left side. Those needles which had their eyes on the right hand do not stick into the finger cover, and are pushed to the heap on the right side previous to the repetition of this process. By means of this simple contrivance, each movement of the finger, from one side to the other, carries five or six needles to their proper heap; whereas, in the former method, frequently only one was moved, and rarely more than two or three were transported at one movement to their place."

We have selected this description of a particular process in needle making, to show that great saving of labour may be effected by what is not popularly called machinery. In modern times, whatever work is carried on upon a large scale, the division of labour is applied, by which one man attending to one thing, learns to perform that one thing more perfectly than if he had attended to many things. He thus saves a considerable portion of the whole amount of labour. Every skilful workman has some mode of working peculiar to himself, by which he lessens his labour. An expert blacksmith, for instance, will not strike one more blow upon the anvil than is necessary to produce the effect he desires. A compositor or printer, who arranges the types, is a swift workman when he makes no unnecessary movement of his arm or fingers in lifting a single type into what is called his composing stick, where the types are arranged in lines. There is a very simple contrivance to lessen the labour of the compositor, by preventing him putting the type into his composing stick the wrong side outwards. It is a nick or two nicks on the side of the type which corresponds with the lower side of the face of the letter. By this nick or nicks he is enabled to see by one glance of his eye on which side the letter is first to be grasped, and then to be arranged. If the nick were not there he would have to look at the face of every letter before he could properly place it. Now, if the printers as a body, were to resolve to perform their work in a difficult instead of an easy way—if they were to resolve, that the labour employed in printing were desirable to be doubled, they might effect their unwise resolution by the simplest proceeding in the world. They might refuse to work upon types which had any nicks. In that case two compositors would certainly be required to do the work of one; and the price of printing would consequently be greatly raised, if the compositors were paid at the present rate for their time. But would the compositors, who thus rejected one of the most obvious natural aids to their peculiar labour, be benefited by this course? No. For the price of books would rise in the same proportion that the labour required to produce them was doubled in its quantity, by being lessened one-half in its efficiency. And the price of books rising, and that rise lessening purchasers, thousands of families would be deprived of a livelihood;—not only those of compositors, but those of paper-makers, type-founders, and many other trades connected with books.

COLUMN FOR THE LADIES.

LADY MORGAN AND HER NIECES.

"I spent a very pleasant evening to-day at Lady M―――'s. The company was small, but amusing, and enlivened by the presence of two very pretty friends of our hostess, who sang in the best Italian style. I talked a great deal with Lady M―――― on various subjects, and she has talent and feeling enough always to excite a lively interest in her conversation. On the whole, I think I did not say enough in her favour in my former letter; at any rate, I did not then know one of her most charming qualities,—that of possessing two such pretty relatives.

" 'But in Heaven's name,' replied I, 'how can a woman of sense, like you,—forgive me,—utter such nonsense?' 'Ah, I know well enough all that you can say on that subject,' said she; 'certainty no man can give me.' This obscurity in a most acute mind was unintelligible to me, even in a woman. ('Ne vous en fachez pas, Julie!')

"My last and longest visit this morning was to the sweet girls I met at Lady M―――'s. I took them some Italian music, which they sang like nightingales, and with a total absence of all pretension and all affectation. Their father is a distinguished physician; and like most of the 'doctors' of eminence here, a 'Baronet' or 'Knight,' a title which is not esteemed a mark of nobility in England, although some families of great antiquity and consideration bear it. There are, however, Creti and Pleti, as among our lower nobility. A Baronet is generally called not by his family, but by his Christian, name; as Sir Charles, Sir Anthony: as in Vienna they say, Graf Tinterle, Kurst Muckerle, and so on. The medical Knight of whom I now speak, received his title in consequence of the establishment of excellent baths, and is a very interesting man. His wife seemed to me still more remarkable for talent. She is very superior to her celebrated relative in accurate tact and judgment, and possesses an extraordinary power of mimicry, whose comic bent does not always spare her own family. The daughters, though perfectly different, are both very original; the one in the gentle, the other in the wild 'genre.' I always call her Lady M―――'s 'wild Irish girl.' All three have a characteristic nationality, and indeed have never quitted Ireland.

"I spend a great deal of my time with the little nightingales, see Lady M―――― frequently, and avoid general society as much as I can. The young ladies keep a burlesque journal, in which they write a chronicle of their daily 'fata,' illustrated with the most extravagant drawings, which is infinitely diverting. After that, we sing, talk, or act pictures, in which the mother, with her talent for the drama, contrives admirable dresses out of the most heterogeneous materials. You would have laughed if you had seen the 'wild Irish girl,' with moustaches and whiskers marked with charcoal, pocket-handkerchief and stick in her hand, come in as my caricature. These girls have an inexhaustible fund of grace and vivacity, extremely un-English, but truly Irish.

"The eldest, who is eighteen, has brown eyes, and hair of a most singular kind and expression: the latter has a sort of deep golden hue without being red, and in the former is a tranquil humid glow, over which comes at times a perfectly red light like that of fire; but yet it always remains only an intense glow, not a lightning-flash like that which often glances from the eyes of the little wild girl. With her, all is flame; and under her maidenly blushes there often breaks out the determination and high spirit of a boy. Indiscreet, and carried away by the impulse of the moment, she sometimes gives way to too great vivacity, which however, from her sweet simplicity and inimitable grace, does but enhance the charm which distinguishes her. To-day, when my carriage was announced, I exclaimed with a sigh, 'Ah, que cette voiture vient mal à propos!' 'Eh bien,' cried she, with the perfect air of a little hussar (she was still in male costume), 'envoyez la au diable.' A very severe and reproving look from her mamma, and one of terror from her gentle sister, covered all of her little face, that was not concealed by her disguise, over and over with scarlet; she cast down her eyes ashamed, and looked indescribably pretty.

"Lady M—— received me to-day in her authoress-boudoir, where I found her writing, not without some view to effect, elegantly dressed, and with a mother-of-pearl and gold pen in her hand. She was employed on a new book, for which she had invented a very good title, 'Memoirs of Myself and for Myself.' She asked me whether she should put 'of myself' or 'for myself' first. I decided for the former as the more natural order; for I observed she must *write*, before she can *have written*. Upon this we fell into a sportive contest, in which she reproached me with my German pedantry, and maintained that hitherto 'bonnet blanc' and 'blanc bonnet' had been the same; the justice of which I was obliged to admit. The motto she had chosen was from Montaigne, 'Je n'enseigne pas, je raconte.' She read me some passages, which I thought very good. This woman, who appears so superficial, is quite another being when she takes the pen in her hand.

"She told me that she intended to go next winter to Paris, and wished to go on into Germany, but that she had a great dread of the Austrian police. I advised her to go to Berlin. 'Shall not I be persecuted there?' said she. 'God forbid!' rejoined I; 'in Berlin talent is worshipped, only I advise you to take at least one of your pretty young friends, who is fond of dancing and dances well, so that you may be invited to the balls at court, and may thus have an opportunity of becoming acquainted with our amiable and accomplished young military men: they are well worth knowing, and you may not find any other way of being introduced to them.' At this moment her husband entered, and begged me to get his philosophical work translated into German, that he might not figure there only as aid-de-camp to his wife, but fly with his own wings. I promised all he wished; but observed that a new prayer-book would have a better chance of success at the present day than a new system of philosophy, of which we had enough already.

"I dined at Lady M——'s. She had invited me by a note, such as I have received a dozen of during my stay here:—I must mention them as characteristic, for I never in my life saw worse calligraphy, or a more negligent style from a lady's pen. The aim of the great authoress was manifest;—to announce the most perfect 'insouciance,' the most entire 'abandon,' in the affairs of ordinary life; just as the great solo dancers in Paris affect to walk with their toes turned in, that they may not betray the dancer by profession. At table Lady M——, with her aid-de-camp K. Cl——, 'faisoient les frais d'esprit obligé.' Mr. Shiel, too, appeared in the character of an agreeable man of the world. The most amusing part of the entertainment, however, was the acting of proverbs by Lady M—— and her sister, who both extemporized admirably in French. Among others, they performed 'Love me, love my dog.'—*Tour of a German Prince.*

THE JUBILEE GLEE.
FOR "THE SCHOOLMASTER."

Come, boys, sit jollily round the can,
Let each take a pull, till he's twice a man,—
Drink till his heart and his brains are clear,
Draughts of bluff Berwick's stout brown beer?
Leave griping claret, and French champagne
To fellows who try to be men in vain;
And take your turns at the tankard warm,
Draining it dry "To the great Reform!"

What care we, who boldly think,
What the Clerks, the Melvilles, or Buccleuchs drink;
Jolly boys, what care we a jot
Whether Blair's professions are false or not:—
So that the tankard is foaming full,
And that we are able to take a pull—
So that our hearts are stout and warm
To the cause of "An honest and just Reform!"

We don't want to demolish the State,
Nor to steal their tags from the "titled great,"
Garter nor ribbon, nor sash nor cord;—
The Devil for us may be dubbed "a lord."
The jobber may swallow the gold he's got,—
We want but enough to boil the pot;
And to keep out the cold, and the starving storm,
And quietly live 'neath "A true Reform."

Let us have friends who may tell our tale,
And argue it out with the Tories pale—
Our free chosen Members to represent
Our *rights* and our *wrongs* in Parliament.—
Then will we readily meet and bear,
Hardships, taxes, toil, and care,
Taking our chance for the sun and storm,
So it be under "A true Reform!"

Here's a health to MURRAY and ABERCROMBY!
May they both do double the good they say:—
To fine little Jeffrey—He's not big—
But he'll batter down Croker, and Peel the prig;
To the SCHOOLMASTER Brougham! when he begins,
He'll *palmie* the Tories, and crack their shins;
And flog in the Bishops (a terrible swarm,)
Yea give Sugden a brush till he bawl "Reform!"

RULES FOR CHESS.
BY A LADY.

Alas—that it should be my fate to sing
The small dominion of the wretched King!
One single move from LEFT to RIGHT he makes,
Another then from RIGHT to LEFT he takes:
One single move; and can he do no more?
Ah no! 'tis true, the sov'reign pow'r is o'er.
Not so his consort; mark her gen'ral sway,
She—unrestrained, can move in every way,
The sex's softness banish'd from the scene—
She aims at all: oh, blush, presumptuous QUEEN!
The MITRED heroes next must join the throng;
Diagonally—suits but ill with song,
Else would I tell thee—thus each move they make,
Just *entre nous*—for opposition sake.

CONTENTS OF NO. II.

	Page
Holyday Rambles Round Edinburgh, No. II.—The Roman Camp, by the Railway	17
Maid-Servants	19
Canvassing—An Old-Fashioned Member of Parliament	20
Fundamental Principles of the British Constitution	22
COLUMN FOR YOUTH—What Men have done—The Giraffe—The Gazelle	23
ELEMENTS OF THOUGHT—The People—Equality of Conditions—ROUSSEAU. Equality among Citizens—HUME	24
THE STORY TELLER—MARY LAWSON: Story for Young Women	25
Henry of Navarre—A Poem, by Mr. Macaulay, M.P.	30
Permanent Advantages of Machinery	31
COLUMN FOR THE LADIES—Lady Morgan and her Nieces	31
THE JUBILEE GLEE.	

EDINBURGH: Printed by and for JOHN JOHNSTONE, 19, St. James's Square.—Published by JOHN ANDERSON, Jun., Bookseller, 55, North Bridge Street.

THE Schoolmaster,
AND
EDINBURGH WEEKLY MAGAZINE.

CONDUCTED BY JOHN JOHNSTONE.

THE SCHOOLMASTER IS ABROAD.—LORD BROUGHAM.

No. 3.—Vol. I.   SATURDAY, AUGUST 18, 1832.   Price Three-Halfpence

CONDITION OF OPERATIVE MANUFACTURERS.

"God sends meat, but the Devil sends cooks," says the adage; and the saying is applicable to many things besides boiling and roasting. The man that should sit down at this time of day, to doubt of the immense advantages society *ought* permanently to gain from the late great improvements in machinery, and the application of the discoveries of science to manufactures and agriculture, must, if not actually mad, be strangely prejudiced; but equally prejudiced, and more mad must he be, who, looking stedfastly at the actual condition of the mass of the manufacturing population, does not confess, that 'All is not gold that glisters,'—that the cooks are somehow spoiling the good meat which Heaven sends us. Instead of marching, hand in hand, mutually aiding each other, *Labour and Capital* are too often seen running an antagonist race, in which the latter, always the stronger party, enjoys fearful odds. A struggle is continually going on, of *man* against *machine*, till that which should be the staff in the hands of the human being is converted into the instrument of his degradation and torture. In the words of Mr. Combe, in our first number, "Has man been permitted to discover the steam-engine, and apply it in propelling ships on the ocean and carriages on railways, in spinning, weaving, and forging iron; and has he been gifted with intellect to discover the astonishing power of physical agents, such as are revealed by chemistry and mechanics, *only that he may be enabled to build more houses, weave more webs, and forge more iron utensils, without any direct regard to his moral and intellectual improvement?*" And Mr. Combe might have added—In the employment of those newly-revealed agencies, must he lead a more degraded and wretched life, than before these powers of science and mechanism were ever heard of,—" spending his strength for that which is not bread, and his labour for that which satisfieth not?"

To ascertain the nature and full extent of an evil is the first sure step towards the remedy. The few strong facts we have to state do not comprehend half the evil; but they are sufficient to stimulate the *many* to inquiry, and to set them on looking for redress where alone it may be obtained, in the exertion of their own physical and intellectual energies; and also to show the *few* the dangers of the crater, on the brink of which they are lulling themselves into a selfish and stupid repose. We are enabled to do this effectually from a little work by Dr. Kay of Manchester, which, in a few pages, gives us a sketch of the wretched circumstances of an immense body of the people of Britain; for Glasgow, Paisley, and many of the populous manufacturing towns differ, in few respects, from Manchester, which he describes. It is a heart-breaking, and to many it will be a repulsive exhibition, this of the helots of our wealthy commercial society; and yet, Thou Most Gracious and Benevolent Being! who callest all of us into existence, and who, gifting each with like capacities, lookest upon all alike, these, our degraded, suffering, fellow-creatures, number hundreds for the tens of the comfortable and well-sustained in this favoured land.—After some general preliminary observations, Dr. Kay enters early on that great admitted evil, and standing reproach of artisans, the *Gin Shop*, and those habits of improvidence which act at once as cause and effect in aggravating the miseries of the manufacturing poor.—And who are the manufacturing poor? Nearly every one, it appears, connected with manufacturing operations, is now included in this sweeping phrase. All are *the poor*, and most the wretchedly poor. After considering the actual circumstances of this numerous class, the writer has the humanity to make generous allowance for even their worst faults. "No wonder," he says, "that the wretched victim, invited by those haunts of misery and crime—the gin-shop and the tavern—as he passes to his daily labour, should endeavour to cheat his suffering of a few moments, by the false excitement procured by ardent spirits; or that the exhausted artisan, driven by *ennui* and discomfort from his squalid home, should strive, in the delirious dreams of a continued debauch, to forget the remembrance of his reckless improvidence—of the destitution, hunger, and uninterrupted toil, which threaten to destroy the remaining energies of his enfeebled constitution." This is a faithful picture of the gaunt, famine-struck, ragged man, whom more in sorrow than in anger one meets at the turning of every crowded thoroughfare of a manufacturing town. Let us now look into his home. "The houses, in such situations, (in Manchester,) are uncleanly, ill-provided with furniture; an air of discomfort, if not of squalid and loathsome wretchedness, pervades them; they are often dilapidated, badly drained, and damp; and the habits of their tenants are gross. They are ill-fed, ill-clothed, and uneconomical; at once spendthrifts and destitute; denying themselves the comforts of life, in order that they may wallow in the unrestrained licence of animal appetite. An intimate connexion subsists among the poor, between the cleanliness of the street and that of the house and person. Uneconomical habits and dissipation are almost inseparably allied: and they are so frequently connected with uncleanliness, that we cannot consider their concomitance as altogether accidental. The first step to recklessness may often be traced in a neglect of that self-respect, and of the love of domestic enjoyments, which are indicated by personal slovenliness, and discomfort of the habitation—hence the importance of providing, by police regulations or general enactment, against those fertile sources, alike of disease and demoralization, presented by the gross neglect of the streets and habitations of the poor."

Police regulations are, however, but
"The hangman's whip to haud the wretch in order;"
and nothing should ever reconcile any class of the British people to the regular domiciliary visits of police in their habitations, nor justify such an encroachment on personal rights, save the direst necessity. They are at best a painful palliative of a small part of the evil; not the remedy which can ever have a lasting, sanative operation even against uncleanliness. Take this other picture of the human ant-hill, where a few grow to enormous wealth on the toils, and amid the miseries of the many. "In Manchester, in the divisions numbered 1, 2, 3, 4, 7, 10, 13, and 14, which contain a large proportion of the poor, we find 579 streets, 243 of which are altogether unpaved; and 307 containing heaps of refuse, deep ruts, stagnant pools, &c. Replies to the tabular inquiries relating to dwellings, afford equally remarkable, if not more disgusting results: suffice it to say, that out of 6951 houses examined, 2565 wanted whitewashing, 1435 were reported as damp, and 2221 entirely wanting necessary conveniences. In one street, called Parliament Street, there appears only one for 380 inhabitants, and this built in a narrow passage, which must, consequently, prove a fertile source of contagion and disease." Such is the accommodation of thousands on thousands in the great metropolis of the commercial system. Nor have we yet seen the worst. In the miseries of a manufacturing town there are lower deeps. "Unwilling," says Dr. Kay, "to weary the patience of the reader by extending these disgusting details, it may suffice to refer generally to the wretched state of the habitations of the poor, especially throughout the whole of the districts, Nos. 1, 2, 3, 4: the houses, too, generally built back to back, having, therefore, only one outlet—no yard, no privy—and no receptacle for refuse. Consequently, the narrow, unpaved streets, in which mud and water stagnate, become the common receptacles of offal and ordure; often low, damp, ill-ventilated cellars exist beneath the houses. The streets in the districts where the poor reside are generally unsewered, and the drainage is consequently superficial.

"Much less can we obtain satisfactory statistical results concerning the want of furniture, especially of bedding, and of food, clothing, and fuel. In these respects, the habitations of the Irish are most destitute:—they can scarcely be said to be furnished. They contain one or two chairs, a mean table, the most scanty culinary apparatus, and one or two beds loathsome with filth. A whole family is often accommodated on a single bed; and sometimes a heap of filthy straw, and a covering of old sacking, hide them in one undistinguished heap, debased alike by penury, want of economy, and dissolute habits. A family are often crowded into one room, or damp cellar, in whose pestilential atmosphere from twelve to sixteen persons are huddled." Dr. Kay gives a rather more favourable account of the condition, and consequently of the character, of the cotton-spinners, than of the hand-loom weavers; they may earn, he says, from 9s. to 12s. a-week. From the evidence of Mr. Foster, an intelligent practical man, we learn, that in Glasgow and Paisley, there are, even in moderately good times, about 11,000 hand-loom weavers, toiling at all times for fourteen hours a-day, at a rate of wages of which the average may be 5s. 6d. a-week! Dr. Kay makes the rate vary from 5s. to 8s., which gives a higher average. In Manchester the hand-loom weavers are chiefly Irish; the poorest, wherever they are found, and in every way the most wretched of the manufacturing population. The Doctor forgets his own apology for these heirs of toil and misery, and again returns to the gin-shops and the beer-houses,—now converting into a cause what he had almost admitted to be a consequence. "Some idea may be formed of the influence of these establishments on the health and morals of the people," says Dr. Kay, "from the following statement, drawn up by Mr. Braidley, the boroughreeve:—He observed the number of persons entering a gin-shop in five minutes, during eight successive Saturday evenings, and at various periods, from seven o'clock until ten. The average result was 112 men and 163 women, or 275 in forty minutes, which is equal to 412 per hour." This is bad enough.

Dr. Kay concludes with Mr. M'Culloch's prescription, which has been written out at least some ten thousand times now. Full time some attempt were made to administer it. "If," says M'Culloch, "we would really improve the condition of the lower classes, if we would give them better habits, as well as make them better workmen, we ought to endeavour to make them acquainted with the principles that must determine their condition in life. The poor ought to be taught that they are in a great measure the architects of their own fortune; that what others can do for them is trifling indeed compared with what they can do for themselves; that they are infinitely more interested in the preservation of the public tranquillity than any other class of society; that mechanical inventions and discoveries *are always supremely advantageous to them;* and that their real interests can only be effectually promoted by their displaying greater prudence and forethought."—" *Ought to be supremely advantageous,*" M'Culloch should have said—and will yet be so, we fervently trust; though, in the meantime, the inmates of the wretched abodes described by Dr. Kay, instead of laying to heart the, to them, somewhat abstract truth, that " they are infinitely more interested in the preservation of the public tranquillity than any other class of society," are more likely, in their desperate circumstances, to join the Highland reaver's prayer, " Lord turn the world upside down, that honest folk may make bread out of it!"

BOOKS OF THE SOCIETY FOR THE DIFFUSION OF USEFUL KNOWLEDGE.

It was fondly expected that the labours of this Society were to regenerate the operative classes, enlighten their dark minds, teach them their duty, and purify and strengthen their moral natures. Disappointment has hitherto attended the Society's efforts, and latterly grumbling. Under the sanction of the Society there came out lately a well-written small volume, entitled the WORKMAN'S COMPANION—*Rights of Industry*, which has strongly moved the spleen of the better-informed of the artisans, from the ingenious, but, as they think, specious, attempt made to persuade them that their condition, from improvements in machinery, and the extension of commerce, is so much better than they feel it to be,—that they are far happier men than their barbarous ancestors of the fourteenth and fifteenth centuries. They readily acknowledge that the country has improved immensely—that vast accumulations of capital have been made; but they add, that they, the producers, have no portion, or a very small one in these good things. The author of the *Rights of Industry*, they say, in his elaborate comparison of the state of this island five hundred years ago and now, forgets entirely to enter the hovels of the woollen manufacturers, the cellars of the hand-loom weavers of Manchester; and completely overlooks that in those barbarous times the condition of one class, in domestic accommodation, was nearly that of every class. When the nobility lay on flock beds, the labourer had no great cause to complain of his bag of rushes. When Lochiel's pillow was not even a snow-ball, the clansman would have been a whining poltroon who had grumbled at a couch in the heather; but the *producers*, the many, sunk, or kept in abject poverty, while the few are luxuriously accommodated, presents a very different state of things,— and the shrewd artisans laugh, bitterly laugh, in the faces of those who gravely tell them they ought to rejoice over their condition; for that the great Earl of Northumberland, three hundred years ago, ate off pewter or wooden trenchers, whereas they have all more or less of crockeryware and some glass vessels—while the real question with them is, how any kind or quality of vessel of theirs is to be filled; and not that their barbarous ancestors had fresh meat only in summer, and were condemned to salted wild hog's flesh all winter. How would the families of Almondbury have rejoiced over those coarse commons! The nobility were rather scanty of linen, and had no glass to their windows, and the Scotch soldiers at Bannockburn were nearly naked. The change now may be a happy one for the nobility and the military, but the labourers at Manchester, in their quantity of linen, and completeness of glazing and accoutrements, are still in much the old state. These unhappy ancestors of ours had no turnip or cabbage to eat to their meat, but the complaint of their modern descendants is, that they have no meat to eat to their cabbage. They were liable to periodical visitations of the plague, occasioned, we are told by filth and want; but to what are Typhus and Cholera now attributed? The former plague lurking among the manufacturing poor, at all times, peculiar to them, or nearly so—the latter in all probability about to establish itself among them. We shall quote a few pertinent remarks on the Working Man's Companion; though from a hardship unknown to the 14th century, and to the 15th, and 16th, and 17th centuries, we are not at liberty to tell their origin:—

" If the poor of the reigns of the Edwardses slept on straw, the rich did little better. There was, in fact, not so great a disparity then as now.[*] Fortescue, however, a writer of the 15th century, spoke highly of the actual *comforts* of the labourers; comforts which even now, would well deserve the name. Colquhoun, in 1812, stated that the sum of L.430,000,000 sterling was annually produced by the working classes of this country, or L.54 per annum for each man, woman, or child; while in fact each individual of these producers did not receive, on average, so much as L.11 annually, or one-fifth of his share. Was this equitable? The author also declared that " capital was always ready to be exchanged for labour." On the contrary, Mr. P. M'Queen has stated not long ago, that a large number of persons were confined in Bedford jail, who were known as men of general good character, but who were actually forced and driven to crime by the pressure of want. Such statements, then, were either errors of ignorance, or cruel mockeries of the poor. Again, to quote once more the often-cited phrase ' Become Capitalists.' Labourers now *could not* become Capitalists.'[†] Neither would a reduction of taxation, a revision of the Corn Laws, and the consequent fall of prices, really serve the working classes—for at each such reduction—or what was the same thing—at

[*] A striking observation was made in Parliament by Mr. R. Grant some months ago. We cannot recollect his apt words, but the substance was, that the higher and lower classes were every day approaching closer in intellect, in power of thinking, and falling more widely asunder in affection and external circumstances.

[†] Certainly those of Dr. Kay's districts of Manchester and the manufacturers of Almondbury, to whom we shall advert next week, could not.

each reduction of comforts which the labourers had consented to, the master had pounced upon them to claim a reduction in wages; and such was the over-supply of labour that they always succeeded. But there was nothing of this in the Society's books. The working men of the 15th century might be badly off, but they were not *Sold by Auction*, as at present; they did not *wheel sand* 22 *miles* a-day for fourteen-pence. They were not forbidden to marry, nor driven to emigration."

The country might be full of glory, and its prosperity might be ever so well displayed by the Society, but this display was of little use to the starving population. The way really to serve such persons, was to show them how to obtain and secure a competence.

The following eloquent description of the state of the labouring classes in England, at the time the Society commenced its labours, will show how much need there was for their instruction, and the *Utility* of that which has been offered them:—

"Consider the condition, mental and physical, of a labouring weaver in 1826. Remember that he knew of scholastic education little more than reading and writing; perhaps he was able to add a few figures together, and that formed the sum total of his arithmetic. This man, reduced to distress, seeks for the means of relief; he contemplates the various circumstances around him, and endeavours to learn what of those circumstances have an influence on his well-being, what of those circumstances he can control, so that his well-being may be secured. Rude, ignorant, seeing only a few, a very few, of the many intricate workings of society, he mistakes (is it wonderful?) the real cause of his misery. Driven to desperation, he clamours against the existence of machinery, he accuses the government of creating his distress. In the midst of his doubts and his misery, he hears that a society of really benevolent men have combined together, for the purpose not of conveying to him immediate relief, but of enlightening his mind, of giving him forethought and useful knowledge—knowledge by which he will eventually be enabled to set a guardupon his well-being, and ward off the attacks of poverty, and its long train of miseries. He, with his friends, subscribes a sixpence, and buys the Society's first Treatise. He finds it headed—Hydrostatics!"

EDINBURGH A CENTURY AGO—GOLDSMITH THE POET.

The Letters from the North of Scotland to a Friend in London have lately acquired considerable celebrity, from the frequent reference made to them by Sir Walter Scott, in elucidating the manners and customs of the Highlanders. Their author was a Captain Burt, an officer of engineers, who, exactly a century back, was sent to Scotland by Government for surveys, and public business. The letters are highly amusing and interesting, particularly those from Inverness, where the Captain long had his head quarters. Like Pennant, he was struck with the height of the Edinburgh houses. "At a distance" says Pennant, " they strike with wonder; their own loftiness, improved by their almost aerial situation, gives them a look of magnificence not to be found in any other part of Great Britain." Captain Burt, though not addicted to flatter; and in truth a very " pock-pudding" stuffed full of cockney notions, and English prejudice, and measuring, and comparing every object he beheld by the standard of England, says—" When I first came into the High Street of the City, I thought I had never seen any thing of the kind more magnificent; the extreme height of the houses, which are for the most part built of stone, and well sashed; the breadth and length of the street, and (it being dry weather) a cleanness made by the high winds * * * * Being a stranger, I was invited to sup in a tavern. The cook was too filthy an object to be described; only another English gentleman whispered me, and said, he believed if the fellow were to be thrown against the wall *he would stick*.—Twisting round and round his hand a greasy towel, he stood waiting to know what we would have for supper, and mentioned several things himself; among the rest, a *duke*, a *fool*, a *meer fool*." Burt's modern editor notices " that had it been dinner, he might also have recommended a *bubbly-jock*, a *pully*, a *bawd* (hare) and *rabbits*, under names which might have led a gay young *militaire* completely astray; with a *tappet-hen* of ale (or claret?) to wash all down." In fact, Burt and his friends after faring in *substantials* as well as they could do to-day in Gibb's or Steventon's at five times the cost, " drank good French claret, and were very merry till the clock struck ten, the hour when every body is at liberty by beat of the city drum to throw their filth out at the windows. * * * " Being in my retreat," he says, " to pass through a long narrow *wynde* or alley, to go to my new lodgings, a guide was assigned me, who went before me to prevent my disgrace, crying out all the way with a loud voice, *hud your haunds*." The throwing up a sash, or otherwise opening a window made me tremble. * * * * Eight, ten, and even twelve stories have each a particular family, and perhaps a separate proprietor; and there, any thing so expensive as a conveyance from the uppermost floor could never be agreed on."

To the disgrace of the successive civic rulers of Edinburgh, this fine street remains, in point of the means of domestic cleanliness, much where Captain Burt left it in 1726. Even then it seems the New Town had been contemplated; but was discountenanced for jobbing reasons.——Captain Burt commemorates the ingenuity of our *cannie* ancestors in guarding against *cabbaging*. The cloth was weighed out to the tailor, and the clothes when brought home weighed again with all the odd bits and clippings.—His account of the ladies is more gratifying, " The *plaid* is the undress of the ladies; and to a genteel woman, who adjusts it with a good air, is a becoming veil. But as I am pretty sure you never saw one of them in England, I shall employ a few words to describe it to you. It is made of silk or fine worsted, chequered with various lively colours, two breadths wide, and three yards in length; it is brought over the head, and may hide or discover the face according to the woman's fancy or occasion. It reaches to the waist behind:—one corner falls as low as the ancle on one side, and the other part in folds hangs down from the opposite arm. I have been told that the ladies in Edinburgh distinguish their political principles, whether *Whig* or *Tory*, by the manner of wearing their plaids: that is, one of them reverses the old fashion, but which it is I do not remember [the Whigs no doubt.] I assure you we have here (Inverness) among the better sort, a full proportion of pretty women, as indeed there is all over Scotland. The men have more regard to the comeliness of their posterity, than in those countries where a large fortune serves to soften the hardest features, and even to make the crooked straight: and indeed their definition of a fine woman seems chiefly directed to that purpose; for after speaking of her face they say "She's a fine, healthy, straight, strong, strapping lassie." I was once commending to a lady of fortune in London, the upright, firm, yet easy manner of the ladies walking in Edinburgh; and when I had done, she fluttered her fan; and with a kind of disdain mixed with jealousy to hear them commended, she said, "Mr. Burt, I do not at all wonder at that—*they are used to walk.*"

Among other changes Mr. Burt, could he look up, would now, we fear, find the motives to matrimony considerably changed in Scotland. About twenty years after this, Goldsmith the poet was studying medicine in Edinburgh; and we have his lively account of the Scotch, and of the ladies of our city; in which, according to him, balls were conducted in the very same way they are now in the United States, if we may believe *Mrs. Trollope*, the last Tory traveller in America. Goldsmith's letter is otherwise very characteristic. One sees in it the germ of some of his best occasional papers in after periods:—

"The Scotchman," he says, (not, dear reader, the newspaper now so named) is one of the proudest things alive—the poor have pride ever ready to relieve them—if mankind should happen to despise them they are masters of their own admiration, and that they can plentifully bestow on themselves. From their pride and poverty, as I take it, results one advantage this country enjoys, namely the gentlemen are much better bred than amongst us. No such character here as our fox-hunters; and they have expressed great surprise when I informed them that some men in Ireland of a thousand pounds a-year spend their whole lives in running after a hare, drinking to be drunk, and getting every girl that will let them with child; and truly, if such a being, equipped in his hunting dress, came among a circle of Scotch gentry, they would behold him with the same astonishment that a countryman would King George on horseback. The men have generally high cheek bones, and are lean and swarthy, fond of action, and dancing in particular. Though now I have mentioned dancing, let me say something of their balls, which are very frequent here. When a stranger enters the dancing-hall,* he sees one end of the room taken up with the ladies, who sit, dismally, in a group by themselves; on the other end stand their pensive partners, that are to be; but no more intercourse between the sexes than there is between two countries at war. The ladies, indeed may ogle and the gentlemen sigh, but an embargo is laid on any closer commerce. At length, to interrupt hostilities, the lady-directress, or intendant, or what you will, pitches on a gentleman and lady to walk a minuet, which they perform with a formality that approaches despondence. After five or six couple have thus walked the gauntlet, all stand up to country dances, each gentleman furnished with a partner from the aforesaid lady-directress; so they dance much, and say nothing, and thus concludes our assembly. I told a Scotch gentleman that such profound silence resembled the ancient procession of the Roman matrons in honour of Ceres; and the Scotch gentleman told me (and faith I believe he was right) that I was a very great pedant for my pains. Now I am come to the ladies; and to show that I love Scotland, and every thing that belongs to so charming a country, I insist on it, and will give him leave to break my head that denies it, that the Scotch ladies are ten thousand times handsomer and finer than the Irish.—To be sure, now, I see your sisters Betty and Peggy vastly surprised at my partiality; but tell them flatly, I don't value them, or their fine skins, or eyes, or good sense, a potato; for I say it, and will maintain it; and as a convincing proof (I'm in a very great passion) of which I assert, the Scotch ladies say it themselves. But to be less serious, where will you find a language so pretty, become a pretty mouth, as the broad Scotch?—and the women here speak it in its highest purity. For instance, were one of your young ladies to pronounce "Whaur will I gong"—with a becoming wideness of mouth, I'll lay my life they will wound every hearer. We have no such character here as a coquet; but alas! how many envious prudes! Some days ago, I walked into my Lord Kilcoubry's* (don't be surprised, my lord is but a glover,) when the Duchess of Hamilton (that fair who sacrificed her beauty to her ambition, and her inward peace to a title and gilt equipage) passed by in her chariot; her battered husband, or, more properly, the guardian of her charms, sat by her side. Straight envy began, in the shape of no less than three ladies who sat with me, to find faults in her faultless form. "For my part," says the first, "I think, what I always thought, that the Duchess has too much red in her complexion." "Madam, I am of your opinion," says the second; "and I think her face has a palish cast, too much on the delicate order." "And let me tell you," adds the third lady, whose mouth was puckered up to the size of an issue, "that the Duchess has fine lips, but she wants a mouth;"—at this every lady drew up her mouth, as if she was going to pronounce the letter P. But how ill, my Bob, does it become me to ridicule women with whom I have scarce any correspondence! There are, 'tis certain, handsome women here; and 'tis as certain there are handsome men to keep them company. An ugly and a poor man is society for himself; and such society the world lets me enjoy in great abundance. Fortune has given you circumstances, and nature a person, to look charming in the eyes of the fair world. Nor do I envy, my dear Bob, such blessings, while I may sit down and laugh at the world, and at myself, the most ridiculous object in it—but I begin to grow splenetic; and perhaps the fit may continue till I receive an answer to this. I know you can't send news from B. Mahon, but, such as it is, send it all; everything you write will be agreeable and entertaining to me. Has George Conway put up a sign yet; or John Finecly left off drinking drams; or Tom Allan got a new wig? But I leave to your own choice what to write. While Oliver Goldsmith lives, know you have a friend!

P.S.—Give my sincerest regards (not compliments, do you mind) to your agreeable family; and give my service to my mother, if you see her; for, as you express it in Ireland, I have a sneaking kindness for her still.

Direct to me—Student in Physic, in Edinburgh.

TWO WENT UP INTO THE TEMPLE.
Two went up to pray. Oh, rather say,
One went to brag, the other to pray;
One stands up close, and treads on high,
Where the other dares not send his eye;
One nearer to God's altar trode,
The other to the altar's God.

---

* This must have been the rooms in THE OLD ASSEMBLY CLOSE!

* This *lord*, the *glover*, is Mrs. Trollope or Captain Basil Hall all over; save that they are serious, and Goldsmith in jest. The Duchess was his fair countrywoman Elizabeth, the elder of the beautiful Miss Gunnings, who afterwards married the Duke of Argyle; and who, in 1773 was Dr. Johnson's "Duchess of Two-tails"—the mother of the Lady Charlotte Bury—and the present Duke of Argyle. At the time when "poor Goldy" wrote there was a Mr. Maclellan a claimant for the title of Lord Kirkcudbright, who may have sold gloves.—Louis Philippe taught Mathematics. His son twenty years afterwards established the claim, and enjoyed the title.

THE SPINNING-WHEEL.

Burns has dedicated one of his sweetest songs "to Bessie and her spinning wheel;" the author of Anster Fair, one of his liveliest poems to the same *romantic* implement. A philosophic poet, Wordsworth, has taken the same view of the value of the wheel to the cottage maid or matron, that the lady whom we quoted last week, did of hemming pocket-handkerchiefs, which, of course, includes netting-purses, working collars, and twisting tape into garnishing for petticoats. Not to mention the cheerful looks of the blithe lass driving at her small wheel, there was something stately and imposing in the matron pacing with solemn, measured steps before that more respectable machine, whose very size gave her labour an air of dignity. We give Wordsworth's sonnet, as less generally accessible than the songs of our countrymen.

> Grief, thou hast lost an ever ready friend,
> Now that the cottage spinning-wheel is mute,
> And care a comforter, that best could suit
> Her froward mood, and softliest reprehend;
> And love, a charmer's voice, that used to lend,
> More efficaciously than ought that flows
> From harp or lute, kind influence to compose
> The throbbing pulse,—else troubled without end;
> Even joy could tell, joy craving truce and rest
> From her own overflow, what power sedate
> On those revolving motions did await
> Assiduously, to sooth her aching breast;
> And—to a point of just relief—abate
> The mantling triumphs of a day too blest.

It will be worth while to inquire whether the catastrophe of poisoning or drowning for love be on the increase among young women, since the wheel became obsolete. We turn now to a sketch by a master-hand—the modern Servant-Lass.

THE MAID-SERVANT.

The maid-servant, in her apparel, is either slovenly or fine by turns, and dirty always; or she is at all times snug and neat, and dressed according to her station. In the latter case, her ordinary dress is black stockings, a stuff gown, a cap, and neck-handkerchief pinned corner-wise behind. If you want a pin, she just feels about her, and has always one to give you. On Sundays and holydays, and perhaps of afternoons, she changes her black stockings for white, puts on a gown of a better texture and fine pattern, sets her cap and her curls jauntily, and lays aside the neck-handkerchief for a high body, which, by the way, is not half so pretty. There is something very warm and latent in the handkerchief,—something easy, vital, and genial. A woman in a high-bodied gown, made to fit her like a case, is by no means more modest, and is much less tempting. She looks like a figure at the head of a ship. We could almost see her chucked out of doors into a cart with as little remorse as a couple of sugar-loaves. The tucker is much better, as well as the handkerchief, and is to the other what the young lady is to the servant. The one always reminds us of the Sparkler in the 'Guardian;' the other of Fanny in 'Joseph Andrews.' But to return:— The general furniture of her ordinary room, the kitchen, is not so much her own as her master's and mistress's, and need not be described; but in a drawer of the dresser of the table, in company with a duster and a pair of snuffers, may be found some of her property, such as a brass thimble, a pair of scissars, a thread-case, a piece of wax candle much wrinkled with the thread, an odd volume of 'Pamela,' and perhaps a sixpenny play, such as 'George Barnewell,' or Mrs. Behn's 'Oroonoko.' There is a piece of looking-glass also in the window. The rest of her furniture is in the garret, where you may find a good looking-glass on the table, and in the window a Bible, a comb, and a piece of soap. Here stands also, under stout lock and key, the mighty mystery—the box,—containing among other things her clothes, two or three song-books, consisting of nineteen for the penny; sundry tragedies at a halfpenny the sheet; the 'Whole Nature of Dreams laid Open;' together with the 'Fortune-Teller,' and the 'Account of the Ghost of Mrs. Veal;' 'the Story of the beautiful Zoa, who was cast away on a desert island, showing how,' &c.; some half-crowns in a purse, including pieces of country money, with the good Countess of Coventry on one of them riding naked on the horse; a silver penny wrapped up in cotton by itself; a crooked sixpence, given her before she came to town, and the giver of which has either forgotten her or been forgotten by her, she is not sure which; two little enamel boxes, with looking-glass in the lids, one of them a fairing, the other 'a trifle from Glasgow;' and lastly, various letters, square and ragged, and directed in all sorts of spelling, chiefly with little letters for capitals. One of them, written by a girl who went to a day-school with her, is directed 'miss.' In her manners, the maid-servant sometimes imitates her young mistress; she puts her hair in papers, cultivates a shape, and occasionally contrives to be out of spirits. But her own character and condition overcome all sophistications of this sort; her shape, fortified by the mop and scrubbing-brush, will make its way; and exercise keeps her healthy and cheerful. From the same cause her temper is good; though she gets into little heats when a stranger is over saucy, or when she is told not to go so heavily down stairs, or when some unthinking person goes up her wet stairs with dirty shoes, or when she is called away often from dinner; neither does she much like to be seen scrubbing the street-door steps of a morning; and sometimes she catches herself saying, 'drat that butcher,' but immediately adds, 'God forgive me.' Thus pass the mornings between working, and singing, and giggling, and grumbling, and being flattered. If she takes any pleasure unconnected with her office before the afternoon, it is when she runs up the area-steps, or to the door to hear and purchase a new song, or to see a troop of soldiers go by; or when she happens to thrust her head out of a chamber window at the same time with a servant at the next house, when a dialogue infallibly ensues, stimulated by the imaginary obstacles between. If the maid-servant is wise, the best part of her work is done by dinner-time, and nothing else is necessary to give perfect zest to the meal. She tells us what she thinks of it, when she calls it 'a bit o' dinner.' There is the same sort of eloquence in her other phrase, 'a cup o' tea;' but the old ones, and the washerwomen, beat her at that. After tea in great houses, she goes with the other servants to hot cockles, or What-are-my-thoughts like, and tells Mr. John to 'have done then;' or if there is a ball given that night, they throw open all the doors, and make use of the music up stairs to dance by. In smaller houses, she receives the visit of her country cousin; and sits down alone, or with a fellow maid-servant, to work; talks of her young master, or mistress, Mr. Ivins (Evans); or else she calls to mind her own friends in the country, where she thinks the cows and 'all *that*' beautiful, now she is away. Meanwhile, if she is lazy, she snuffs the candle with her scissars; or if she has eaten more heartily than usual, she sighs double the usual number of times, and thinks that tender hearts were born to be unhappy. Such being the maid-servant's life in-doors, she scorns, when abroad, to be any thing but a creature of sheer enjoyment. The maid-servant, the sailor, and the schoolboy, are the three beings that enjoy a holyday beyond all the rest of the world; and all for the same reason—because their inexperience, peculiarity of life, and habit of being with persons, or circumstances, or thoughts above them, give them all, in their way, a cast of the romantic. The most active of money-getters is a vegetable compared with them. The maid-servant, when she first goes to the play-house, thinks she is in heaven. A theatre is all pleasure to her, whatever is going forward, whether the play, or the music, or the waiting which makes others impatient, or the munching of apples and gingerbread nuts, which she and her party commence almost as soon as they have seated themselves. She prefers tragedy to comedy, because it is grander, and less like what she meets with in general; and because she thinks it more in earnest also, especially in the love scenes. Her favourite play is 'Alexander the Great, or the Rival Queens.' Another great delight is in going a-shopping. She loves to look at the patterns in the windows, and the fine things labelled with those corpulent numerals of 'only 7s.'—'only 6s. 6d.' She has also, unless born and bred in London, been to see My Lord Mayor, the fine people coming out of court, and the 'beasties' in the Tower; and at all events she has been to Astley's and the Circus, from which she comes away equally smitten with the rider, and sore with laughing at the clown. But it is difficult to say what pleasure she enjoys most. One of the completest of all is the fair, where she walks through an endless round of noise, and toys, and gallant apprentices, and wonders. Here she is invited in by courteous, well-dressed people, as if she were the mistress. Here also is the conjuror's booth, where the operator himself, a most stately and genteel person, all in white, calls her 'ma'am;' and says to John by her side, in spite of his laced hat, 'Be good enough, sir, to hand the card to the lady.' Ah! may her cousin turn out as true as he says he is; or may she get home soon enough, and smiling enough, to be as happy again next time."

CAUSES OF THE BAD EFFECTS OF THE EAST WINDS.

THERE never were so many persons in this locality affected with colds, hoarseness, rheumatism, &c. &c., from the east winds, in the month of August, as last week. We find the following theory of these troublesome effects of this detested wind, in our Commonplace Book, but cannot at present refer to the author:—The ill effects of the east wind on health have always been noticed. It is well known that air, as it grows warmer, becomes capable of holding in solution (or drinking up) a greater quantity of moisture; a current of cold air rushing into a place which is warmer, will therefore dry up a great deal of wet. For this reason damp clothes in winter, placed in the open window of a warm room, dry uncommonly fast. Now it is well known that nothing is more pernicious to the health than a sudden drying up of the perspiration. Whether this be owing merely to the cold caused on the skin by the evaporation of so much moisture, or to the derangement of some other link in the animal economy, need not be asked; it is sufficient that the fact is so. For this reason, exposure to any current of air which is acquiring heat, and is therefore becoming drier, is uncommonly prejudicial. Every one has observed how disagreeable are currents of air in warm rooms: in fact, the warmer the room, and the nearer we are to the fire place, so much the more annoying is a draught from any of its crannies. Such a current, increasing in heat as it passes from the cold of the external air to the warmth of a room, will absorb double its former moisture, and of course will dry the perspiration on the body faster than it can be supplied, causing, by that means, rheumatism in all its forms, toothach, headach, &c. Now it is evident that the same reason which causes a draught from the open air into a room to be disagreeable, will cause any wind blowing from a cold region into one that is warmer, to have exactly the same effects. The east wind is in this predicament; it blows from a colder continent, which retains the cold of winter longer than the marine tract on which we are situated, the temperature of which is more equal, and at such times warmer. Damp or misty winds are also proverbially hurtful, and the injurious effects seem to arise from the moisture continually deposited by them on the body, which is evaporated by the natural heat, and causes in that process an unusual and hurtful degree of cold, or diminution of the animal temperature.

ENGLISH JUSTICE.

THE following story was lately told in a large company:—'A man had his pocket handkerchief stolen in the street. He seized the thief; and, being the stronger, held him fast, though not without receiving many violent blows; and at length gave him into the charge of a police officer who came up. The transaction was perfectly clear, and passed in the presence of many witnesses; and the delinquent, if prosecuted, would have been transported. His wife went to the gentleman, and begged for mercy on her knees; the thief himself, who was not an uneducated man, wrote the most moving letters;—and who will wonder that he at length found pity? On the appointed day the prosecutor staid away, and the criminal was accordingly acquitted. The gentleman paid dearly enough for his ill-timed compassion. A fortnight after this transaction, he was prosecuted by the very man that picked his pocket, for an assault, which was proved by the testimony of several witnesses. The defendant replied that it was certainly true that he had seized the man, but that he had done so only because he had caught him in the act of picking his pocket. But as the criminal had already been acquitted of this, and no man can be tried twice for the same offence, no notice was taken of the justification. In short, it cost the too generous sufferer about a hundred pounds, which he had to pay partly to the man who robbed him, and partly to the Court.' The whole company thought this sort of justice monstrous; but an old Englishman defended it with great warmth and pertinacity. 'I think,' exclaimed he earnestly, 'that the incident just related, exactly goes to illustrate the wisdom of our laws in the most striking manner. All laws and judicial authorities are instituted for the sole purpose of preventing crime. This is also the sole end of punishment. The receiver of stolen goods is, therefore, in the eye of the law, nearly as guilty as the thief; and he who knowingly tries to rescue a criminal from the grasp of the law, is almost as pernicious to the community as the criminal himself. That man who, perhaps, began his career in crime with the stealing of this pocket-handkerchief, and therefore ought to have been withdrawn from society for penitence and amendment, now, emboldened by success, is probably planning a larger theft,—perhaps a murder.— Who ought to bear the blame? This very gentleman,— who has been deservedly punished for his illegal pity. He who thrusts his hand uncalled for and inconsiderately between the wheels of a useful machine, must not wonder if he break his fingers.'

SAGE CHEESE.—This is made by steeping one night, in a proper quantity of milk, two parts of sage, one part of marigold leaves, and a little parsley, after they have been bruised. On the following morning the *greened* milk is strained off, and mixed with about one-third of the whole quantity intended to be run or coagulated. The green and white milks are run separately, the two curds being kept apart until they be ready for vatting; these may be mixed either evenly and intimately, or irregularly and fancifully, according to the pleasure of the manufacturer.

STILTON CHEESE.—This delicious cheese may be made by the following simple process:—To the new milk of the cheese-making morning add the cream from that of the preceding evening, together with the rennet, watching the full separation of the curd, which must be removed from the whey without breaking, and placed into a sieve, until of such consistence as to bear being lifted up and placed in a hoop that will receive it without much pressure. The cheese, as it dries, will shrink up, and must, therefore, be placed from time to time in a tighter hoop, and turned daily, until it acquires the proper degree of consistence for use or keeping.

DEBT.—If you boast of a contempt for the world, avoid getting into debt. It is giving unto gnats the fangs of vipers.

SYMPATHY IN WATCHES.—It has been found that in a watchmaker's shop the time-pieces or clocks, connected with the same wall or shelf, have such a sympathetic effect in keeping time, that they stop those which beat in irregular time; and if any are at rest, set a-going those which beat accurately.

ELEMENTS OF THOUGHT.

PATIENCE OF THE BRITISH PEOPLE.

The people of this country have always borne extreme oppression for a long time, before there has appeared any danger of a general insurrection against the Government. What a series of encroachments did even the feudal barons, whose number was not very considerable, and whose power was great, bear from William the Conqueror, before they broke into actual rebellion, on that account; as in the reigns of King John, and Henry III. And how much were the poor Commons trampled on till a much later period. After the people had begun to acquire property, independence, and an idea of their natural rights, how long did they bear a load of old and new oppressions under the Tudors, but more especially under the Stuarts, before they broke out into what the friends of arbitrary power affect to call the grand rebellion! And how great did that long civil war shew the power of the King to be, notwithstanding the most intolerable abuse of it. At the close of 1642 it was more probable that the King would have prevailed than the Parliament; and his success would have been certain, if his conduct had not been as weak as it was wicked. So great was the power of the Crown, that after the Restoration, Charles II. was tempted to act the same part as his father, and actually did it in a great measure with impunity, till he was at last even able to reign without Parliaments; and if he had lived much longer, he would probably have been as arbitrary as the King of France. His brother James had nearly subverted both the civil and religious liberties of his country in the short space of four years; and might have done it completely, had he been content to proceed with more cunning and caution. In our own days the Ministers Castlereagh, and Sidmouth, suspended * * *
We must not go farther, lest we get involved in *news.*

DIFFERENCE BETWEEN A FREE AND A DESPOTIC GOVERNMENT.

The difference consists in the manner in which that whole mass of power, which, taken together, is supreme, is, in a free state divided among the several ranks of persons who are sharers in it:—in the source from whence their titles to it are successively derived; in the frequent and easy changes of condition between the governors, and governed; whereby the interests of one class are more or less undistinguishably blended with those of the other; *in the responsibility of the governors;* or the right a subject has of having the reasons publicly assigned and canvassed, of every act of power exercised over him;—*in the liberty of the press;* or the security with which every man, be he of the one class or the other, may make known his complaints and remonstrances to the whole community:—in the liberty *of public associations;* or the security with which mal-contents may communicate their sentiments, concert their plans, and practise every mode of opposition, short of actual revolt, before the executive power can be justified in disturbing them.—*Bentham.*

WHEN RESISTANCE TO A GOVERNMENT BECOMES JUSTIFIABLE.

It is then, and not till then, allowable, if not incumbent, on every man, as well on the score of duty as of interest, to enter into measures of resistance, when according to the best calculations he can make, the probable mischiefs of resistance (speaking with respect to the community in general) appear less to him than the probable mischiefs of submission. This is the *juncture of resistance :* By what sign shall it be known? By what common signal, alike conspicuous to all. A common sign there is none. Every man must therefore be determined, by his own internal persuasion of a balance of utility upon the side of resistance; for *utility* is the test and measure of loyalty. Utility is the test and measure of all government; and the obligation of governors of every denomination to minister to general happiness, is an obligation superior to, and inclusive of every other * * * Rank, privileges, and prerogatives in a state, are constituted for the good of the state; and those who enjoy them, whether they be called Kings, senators, or nobles, or by whatever names or titles they be distinguished, are, to all intents and purposes, the servants of the public, and accountable to the people for the discharge of their respective offices. If such magistrates abuse their trust, in the people lies the power of *deposing* them, and consequently of punishing them. And the only reason why abuses which have crept into offices have been connived at, is, that the correcting them, by having recourse to first principles, is far from being easy, except in small states, so that the remedy would often be worse than the disease * * * With respect to large societies, it is very improbable that the people should be too soon alarmed, so as to be driven to extremities; and so obvious are the difficulties that lie in the way of procuring redress of grievances by force of arms, that I think we may say, without exception, that in all cases of hostile opposition to government, the people must have been in the right; and that nothing but very great oppression could drive them to such desperate measures. The bulk of a people seldom so much as complain without reason, because they never think of complaining till they feel; so that in all cases of dissatisfaction with government, it is most probable that the people are injured.—*Priestley.*

BOUNDLESSNESS OF THE CREATION.

About the time of the invention of the telescope, another instrument was formed, which laid open a scene no less wonderful, and rewarded the inquisitive spirit of man. This was the microscope. The one led me to see a system in every star; the other leads me to see a world in every atom. The one taught me that this mighty globe, with the whole burden of its people and its countries, is but a grain of sand on the high field of immensity; the other teaches me that every grain of sand may harbour within it the tribes and the families of a busy population. The one told me of the insignificance of the world I tread upon; the other redeems it from all its insignificance; for it tells me, that in the leaves of every forest, and in the flowers of every garden, and in the waters of every rivulet, there are worlds teeming with life, and numberless are the glories of the firmament. The one has suggested to me, that beyond and above all that is visible to man, there may be fields of creation which sweep immeasurably along, and carry the impress of the Almighty's hand to the remotest scenes of the universe; the other suggests to me, that within and beneath all that minuteness which the aided eye of man has been able to explore, there may be a region of invisibles; and that, could we draw aside the mysterious curtain which shrouds it from our senses, we might see a theatre of as many wonders as astronomy has unfolded, a universe within the compass of a point so small as to elude all the powers of the microscope, but where the wonder-working God finds room for the exercise of all his attributes, where he can raise another mechanism of worlds, and fill and animate them all with the evidence of his glory.—*Chalmers.*

WANT OF SENSIBILITY TO NATURAL BEAUTY.

"It is unfortunate," says Foster, "I have thought within these few minutes, while looking out on one of the most enchanting nights of the most interesting season of the year, the calm sky, the beautiful stripes of clouds, the stars, and waning moon just risen, to hear the voices of a company to whom, I can perceive, these things are not in the least more interesting than the walls, ceiling, and candle-light of a room."

"The sweet shady side of Pall Mall" is to many far before the finest rural scene in the world. "Is not this very fine?" said Johnson to Boswell, in Greenwich Park. Boswell, who owns that he preferred "the busy hum of men" to any thing else, said it was, "but Fleet Street was finer." "Sir, you are right," replied the Sage, the Philosopher of streets and lanes.

THE STORY-TELLER.

THE THREE WESTMINSTER BOYS.*
BY MRS. JOHNSTONE.

THE Magic Lantern, which belonged to Mr. Dodsley, was elegantly and ingeniously formed. He chose to exhibit its wonders himself; and story, and picture, aiding and illustrating each other, agreeably occupied several

NIGHTS OF THE ROUND-TABLE.

"Peep, and tell us what you see, Charles," said the Reverend showman to our old friend Charles Herbert.—"An old building, forms, desks, a lofty large room, many boys and youths, and three apart and prominent."—"Let me look," cried Sophia,—"Westminster school, I declare! and those three boys!—one very noble and graceful; the next dark, thoughtful, resolute, with keen eyes, and compressed lips; and the third—O! how gently, yet brightly he smiles, dear bashful boy, as his dark, bold companion extends his arm, haranguing and pointing forward to some high distant object!—A picture is it,—a figure in state robes?—or is it to the insignia blazoned on that desk?—Nay, I daresay he wishes to be head-master."

"Have you all seen the three school-fellows?" asked Mr. Dodsley; "look at them well, for here they part on the path of life, never to meet again. Presto! change:—What see you now, Sophia?"—"Still the dark stern youth, and the gentle timid one—they are older now, but I know them well. The noble-looking boy has disappeared. The scene seems chambers in the Temple. Through an open window I have a glimpse of gardens: piles of huge books are lying on tables, floors, and shelves. The dark resolute youth pores on a black-letter folio, and makes as it were notes or extracts. The other leans by the window, gazing over the gardens, a small open volume fluttering in his relaxed hand. Ha! I read on it 'Thomson's Seasons.'"—"Yes, Sophia, your gentle law-student is an idle rogue; he has been seduced into the 'primrose paths of poesy'—let us see the result;—meanwhile here is another picture."—"Beautiful! beautiful!" cried the admiring girl, "A large ship?"—"An outward-bound Indiaman," said Mr. Dodsley.—"All her sails set," continued Sophia. "How proudly, how stately she ploughs her way, breasting the waters like a swan. And there, on her deck, that noble gentleman, the third Westminster boy,—and yet not he,—walking so proudly as if in accordance with the majestic motion of the brave ship. I am glad to meet him again:—and all those military attendants—the gaudily dressed musical band,—the plumed officers,—and he the centre of all! What a great man he must be, and how well honour becomes him!"

"Shall we follow his progress to the East, or return to yonder gloomy, sombre chamber in the Temple?"—"Both," cried several young eager voices; "we must trace them all,—all the three school-fellows."

The next view was of a large Oriental city, its architectural splendour and magnificence of outline glittering in the dazzling, but uncertain brilliance of the morning sun; domes and minarets, Mahomedan mosques, and Indian pagodas, fountains, and palaces, and stately dwellings, sparkling in the out-pouring of the increasing flood of intense and golden light. Over this scene were grouped and scattered Mussulmans, Arab warriors, Brahmins and Sepoys,—all in diversified and picturesque costumes,—ornamented palanquins, European officers richly dressed, and mounted on beautiful horses; elephants prancing in their splendid trappings; females and children, their dark skins and silky hair, and large black eyes, contrasting with their white and gaudily spangled dresses; dancing girls, and marabouts,—all, in short, that could compose a picture of Oriental beauty and splendour; and that princely man, now of middle age, on the large white elephant, still the centre of all.

The scene changed slightly, and discovered the interior of the magnificent saloon of a residence that appeared royal, where the noble figure, whom Sophia still rightly declared the third boy of Westminster school, received, in Oriental state, homage, paid with the lowliest prostrations of the East, from a long train of nawaubs, rajahs, and envoys, illustrious captives or princely tributaries, whom his policy or his prowess had subdued to the dominion of England. Royal and magnificent was all about him; his aspect grave, dignified, and elate, his step and air majestic; yet the shadow of deep, anxious thought, of heart-struck care, at times darkened his embrowned visage. Whence then had fled the generous, sunny, open smile, that lightened the grey walls of Westminster school?—the noble, free expression of the younger man, who so proudly trode the deck of the outward-bound Indiaman?

"Alas! what change!" said Sophia; "I almost dread, yet long to follow him farther."

Dim, troubled, misty scenes next flitted by; battles hid in smoke and obscurity; the wide plain of Hindostan flooded or desolate,—naked huddled millions,—signs of disaster, famine, and misery; and in the foreground still that princely man, his features ploughed with care, knitting his brows in fierce anger and disdain, stamping on the ground, while his eastern slaves cowered around him, as he hastily perused letters and despatches, his English secretary, attendants, and aids-de-camp standing back, anxiously scanning his looks, and reading his troubled mind in his working and eloquent features.

This scene passed, and he was next seen in an English ship, more stately if possible than the former vessel, freighted with all the rich and rare productions of the East; but the bright look had waxed dim, the buoyant step of the outward-bound voyager was now heavy and slow. Anon, and he lay reclined on a couch on the deck, under a silken and gold awning. A physician felt his pulse; black servants in splendid costumes fanned him; others approached with profound salams, bearing perfumes, and offering service, as they might have done to a divinity. Indifferent to all, his eye remained riveted on one paper, on a few cabalistic words, which, like the damned blood-spot on the hand of Lady Macbeth, would not out, could not sweeten.

"Turn we again to England," said Mr. Dodsley, shifting the scene, "to our stern, ambitious, iron-minded man, of invincible purpose, of unconquerable perseverance, and, let me add, of strong intellect, and yet stronger ambition:—there you see him, the slough of the Temple cast, in the King's Bench, in the Court of Chancery, in the Commons House of Parliament, every energy of his mind in perpetual activity, already surrounded by satellites, the ministers or slaves of his will, subdued by that mighty and resistless will to its own purposes of selfish aggrandizement, of intrigue and political ambition, and, it may occasionally be, of pure patriotism. And now every obstacle overcome, undermined, or boldly trampled under foot, see him make one grand spring to reach the height at which every act of his life has aimed; while all men, the stronger as well as the feebler spirits, give way to his resistless progress, or cheer him on to the spot where lie the coveted rich robes, the patents, and the purses, and by these the mighty insignia of the Lord High Chancellor of England."

"I begin to long for a glimpse of our gentle boy now," said Sophia, "dreaming over his 'Thomson's Seasons.' Has he been borne down by the torrent which has carried his bold and daring companion so high and far?—Our gentle interesting boy!—has he been cast away like a weed, or has he cast away himself?"—"You shall judge," said Mr. Dodsley,—"Here is our lost one——" And there he was, the very boy, developed in the thin, melancholy, wo-worn man, sitting lonely on a tombstone, under the elms of a country church-yard.—"He is curate of that church," said Sophia; "and I daresay he has lost his wife or his child. How refined and how expressive are his faded features; a look of meek resignation, stealing over the traces of some deep mysterious affliction."

"He never was in orders, nor yet had wife or child, my sprightly guesser," said Mr. Dodsley. "Mental blight, dark and fearful trial, and the utter desolation of worldly prospects, have all passed over him; but he is, as you see,

---

* From "Nights of the Round Table," published by Oliver & Boyd.

better now,—there is even an occasional flash of humour kindling over those placid features,—of which, however, gentle kindness, deep, holy submission, is the fixed and habitual expression."

"It makes my heart ache to see him so far thrown out," said Sophia ; "for even at Westminster I liked him best." —"He was my boy too," cried Fanny. This was not quite correct, for Sophia had expressed strong sympathy with the "noble boy," as she called him, and great admiration of the Oriental Vice-king ; but Mr. Dodsley accepted her own interpretation of her altered feelings, and said "He was 'a stricken deer that left the herd'—nor was he free from blame ; but his dark hour is past. Shall we follow him to his humble abode, not far from those churchyard elms, or return to those scenes of splendour, of grandeur, of substantial wealth, of real power, in which his early compeers preside, guiding or wielding the energies and the destinies of nations ?"

"Follow him, sir," said Sophia ; and the boys, though anxious for more stirring pictures of life, politely yielded to her wish. The quickly shifting scenes exhibited a dull, dingy, and even mean-looking house, in the centre of a small fifth-rate market town, and again a low-roofed parlour in that house, very plainly furnished with things neither fine nor new, and still less fashionable. Here sat an elderly, but comely gentlewoman knitting ; and before her stood a plain tea equipage, waiting, as the next scene shewed, the arrival of the loiterer under the churchyard elms, whom she seemed to welcome with the placid smile of long-tried affection. This scene looked brighter than the former. The old window curtain was let down, the old sofa wheeled in, the tea-kettle was steaming,—and it was singing also, no doubt, if pictures could give out sounds ; the shadows of a blazing fire of wood were dancing and quivering on walls and roof, and shining on all the polished surfaces of the furniture ; and a couple of hares at a touch were seen in another scene, leaping from a box. They gamboled and wheeled on the well-brushed carpet, their benevolent master and protector looking on their sports, and caracoles, and gambades, with pleased, affectionate, and even interested eyes.

"How lively those scenes—they are nature itself, Mr. Dodsley," said Miss Jane Harding—"Your magic lantern is the finest mimic representation of life I ever saw."

"I know whereabouts we are now," cried Sophia, in a low, earnest, yet delighted tone of voice. "Olney ! Cowper ! Mrs. Unwin !—Ah ! sulky Tiney, and Mistress Bess the vaulter !"—"Let me see, let me see," cried the younger children ; and Sophia had now a much stronger object of interest than the pictured scene, which she left to Fanny and Charles, and the other little ones.

"But the studious, thoughtful youth, who pored over the folio in the Temple," she cried,—"the dark-browed, stern man of the Chancery Court, Cowper's early friend— who was he ?"

"Edward Thurlow, Lord High Chancellor of England." —"And that other boy—the noble boy—the Westminster scholar ?" said Sophia.

"Warren Hastings, Governor-General of India. These three youths started from the same point.—In birth, Cowper was certainly the most distinguished of the three ;—of their respective talents we will not now speak—great men they all were—good men too, let us hope. The lot was cast into the lap. All started for the prize :—by routes how different did each gain the appointed place where all human travellers meet ! What then were their gains ?— which was happiest in his course of life ?—But we must follow them farther : true is the Italian proverb, which says that no man can be pronounced happy till he is dead ! Which of the three Westminster boys became the best man ? Which most nobly fulfilled his duties to his God, his country, and his kind ? Which—now that they all are gone to their reward—enjoys the widest, the purest, the highest fame ? Which remains the best model to the youth of England ?—Not one of the three faultless, without doubt ; but which of these three great men comes nearest the mark at which you, my boys, would aim ?"

"I suppose Lord Thurlow was Chancellor before Henry VII.'s time," said Fanny Herbert ; and Charles added in explanation, "Our history of England only begins then, so we don't know Lord Thurlow. Sir Thomas More, you remember, Fanny ?—he was a merry, kind man that Chancellor."

"Your history goes back to a decently remote period," said Mr. Dodsley, smiling at the observation of the young historians. "Lord Thurlow held this high office at a very recent date, in the reign of George III., at the same time that Mr. Hastings exercised the mighty government of the East, and Mr. Cowper lived in neglect, and obscurity, composing his poetry."

"If we were to judge by our little audience," said Mrs. Herbert, "one of your questions, nay, perhaps two, are already answered. The modest poet, living apart in that nameless obscurity, already enjoys not only a higher, but a more universal fame than either of his youthful compeers. All our good little folks here know him, less or more, in his daily life, as well as in his beautiful verse ; they read him, and quote him, and love him, and, by daily draughts from his stores of wisdom and of love, nourish their moral and intellectual nature to a strength and stature it might never otherwise have attained."

"I fear you are a confirmed Cowperite," said Miss Harding, to her sister. "But what say you, young gentlemen ?"

"Hastings for me !" cried Mr. Frank Consadine, the Irish youth. "Hastings, Prince and Conqueror !" "And for me the woolsack," cried George Herbert. "I would rather, I think, just now, but I may change my mind, be High Chancellor of England, than England's Sovereign : to the one a prince is born, the other a *man* must achieve."

"If," said Norman Gordon, the Scottish youth, "one could be an Eastern Vice-king, or English-Chancellor, and author of the ' Task' at the same time, one would be at no loss to decide ;" and he half-laughed at the profound silliness of his own cautious conclusion.

"You would unite impossibilities, Mr. Norman," said the Curate. "Cowper's poetry required not only an original cast or bias of mind, but a preparatory course of life, and a mental discipline quite peculiar—very different, indeed, from that of a lawyer and politician, or Eastern legislator and conqueror. We must take our three school-boys and men exactly as we find them ; and determine the claims, and estimate the happiness of each on his own merits, nor think of what might have been."

The younger children liked pictures better than discussion, so the whole group solicited Mr. Dodsley to proceed with his exhibition, which he did, still adhering to the original idea.

"To afford you wider grounds for forming your opinions, my little friends, you shall see each of our heroes by his own fireside, and also in more active and distinguished scenes. This first, is the Lords' House of Parliament, solemn and antique, with its Gothic, tag-rag decorations.

"It is the day of a trial. These are the peers of Britain,—yonder the judges and prelates of the land,— there some of the young princes of the blood-royal, honoured in being created members of this House. Taken all in all, the scene before you represents the most august tribunal in the world ; and before that tribunal is arraigned Warren Hastings, the victim of a triumphant faction, the object of much ignorant clamour, and of popular hatred, which one can yet hardly condemn, as it sprung from the best feelings of humanity. You see the long perspective of counsel, and clerks, and ushers, and reporters. That is Burke, who, with the lightnings of his eloquence, blights and withers the once flourishing and princely Hastings. And there stands Sheridan, ready to pounce on his victim, —to hold up the proud-minded vice-king to the abhorrence and execration of the world, as a monster of rapacity, cruelty, and tyranny, swollen with wealth and bloated with crime, the desolator of the fairest portion of the east, the wholesale, cold-blooded murderer of millions of Asiatics.

"The partisan orator may be half-conscious of the falsehood of many of his representations, and entirely so of their artificial gloss and high-colouring; but candour and truth are not the object of the party man; he vehemently proceeds in his statements, boldly makes his charges, and eloquently supports them.

"We shall now presume the House adjourned, and follow Hastings to his retirement. Where now, Sophia, is the gay Westminster boy, the gallant, ambitious, high-minded statesman and soldier of the east? Can you trace him in that sallow, drooping, arraigned criminal, whose spirit is chafed almost to madness. In public he folds up his arms in self-supporting disdain; he tries to smooth his care-worn brow, and to teach his quivering lip to curl in contempt of his open accusers, and more rancorous secret enemies. But, alas! contempt and disdain of our fellow-men are not calm, much less are they happy feelings. The persecuted, if not yet degraded man, is sick at his very soul; his heart is bursting with the indignant anguish which will break it at last. There may have been, and in this still hour of self-communion conscience so whispers, things faulty and blame-worthy in his bold and illustrious career. Nor is he free of guilt; for his station was one of great difficulty, and loaded with responsibility which might make even the strongest and best-hearted man tremble. Images of long-acted, painful scenes rise before him in his solitude; actions justified, in their passing, by the plea of a strong necessity, which he dislikes and dreads to think of now. And here, the world shut out, surrounded as he is with all the wealth and luxury of the eastern and western hemispheres, the hootings of the London rabble, and the hissings of the adder-tongues of his enemies, still ring in his ears; and to these envenomed sounds conscience in his own bosom returns a faint, yet an undying echo. Perhaps he may wish, in this anguished hour, that his lot, though less splendid, had been more safe.

"To beguile an hour of care he takes up a volume of the poetry of his old school-fellow, the lost William Cowper. He has little leisure for literature, but a lingering taste remains for what engrossed so many of the happy hours of happier days. He turns up one passage after another; and the map and history of Cowper's life lie before him. Are his feeling those of pity or of envy? Probably they are a strangely-entangled mixture of both. His eye is riveted on a passage in the poem of Expostulation; he reads on and on; and, as if spell-urged, pronounces aloud,

> ' Hast thou, though suckled at fair Freedom's breast,
> Exported slav'ry to the conquered East?
> Pulled down the tyrants India served with dread,
> And raised thyself a greater in their stead?
> Gone thither armed and hungry, returned full,
> Fed from the richest veins of the Mogul,
> A despot big with power, obtained by wealth,
> And that obtained by rapine and by stealth?'

Hastings can read no farther. This passage could not, did not apply to himself; in his proud integrity of heart he felt assured of this. The opinions too were those of ignorance. What could Cowper know of the east. And then he wonders at the latitude of discussion, and the licentiousness of the press in England. He dips again; his fortune may be better this time; for in these rich volumes he perceives that there is much poetic beauty. He is more fortunate now, for he opens at the admired description of the coming in of the Post. How fine an opening; and he read aloud—

> Hark! 'tis the twanging horn * * *
> * * * * *
> But oh! the important budget! ushered in
> With such heart-shaking music, who can say
> What are its tidings?—have our troops awaked?
> Or do they still, as if with opium drugged,
> Snore to the murmurs of the Atlantic wave?
> Is INDIA FREE? and does she wear her plumed
> And jewelled turban with a smile of peace,
> Or do we grind her still?'——

"The heart-struck but fascinated reader proceeds on, in spite of himself, till he finishes the finest passages of the poem, those which unveil the habits and amiable character of his early friend. If there were some stir and bitterness in his spirit on the first perusal of offensive strictures, that is past now. He lays down the book with a quiet sigh; and, striving to fix his mind upon all that has been most brilliant in his fortunes, can only remember how many years have elapsed since he was a Westminster school-boy; and that both he and William Cowper have long since passed the meridian of life.

"Are you not yet tired, Miss Fanny, of gazing on that gorgeous bed-chamber," said the curate; "the bed of carved ivory and gold, the silken draperies, and couches of crimson and gold curiously worked; the silver-framed mirrors, the rich porcelain vases and foot-baths; the splendid toilette, with its jewelled ornaments; the ivory and ebony cabinets, richly inlaid with gold, and in the highest style of eastern decoration, exhibiting groups exquisitely executed; religious processions, festivals, marriages, in short, a series of gorgeous pictures of eastern manners. Those caskets on the toilette contain some of the rarest jewels of the east. That large emerald is to be sent to-morrow morning to a certain lady of questionable fame, but of great influence; for the proud Hastings must stoop to make friends, at this crisis, by arts he would once have spurned, and still loathes. That gold bed, preserved with such care in his own chamber, is intended for a gift or tribute to the Queen of England."

The children were not yet satisfied with gazing; and Mrs. Herbert said, "I fear, my dears, if thus fascinated by grandeur, you will ill bear a transition to the dull, low-roofed parlour at Olney." "No: were it a dungeon with such inmates," cried Sophia, resolutely turning from the beautiful picture of the interior of Mr. Hastings' bed-chamber.—"Well said, Sophia, if you stand to it," returned her mother—"But I see Charles and Mr. Norman long for another peep of those Eastern weapons suspended over the chimney."—"That most beautiful scimitar, the handle studded and blazing with jewels!" cried the peeping boy,—"and those exquisite pistols! how was it possible to paint them so truly? And that—Damascus blade, did you call it?"

"Lest the transition to sad, sombre, puritanic Olney, be too violent, we will first, if you please, visit the Lord Chancellor," said Mr. Dodsley.—"Presto! There he is at the head of the state council-board; these are his colleagues—his party friends, his rivals, his flatterers, his underminers, ranged on each side of him; and he knows them all well: they may injure, but they cannot deceive him. He looks grim, and stern, and unhealthy. Even now there is spasm upon him; a youth of hard sedentary study, a manhood of incessant labour, and latterly, a weight of public and of private cares, have weighed and broken down Lord Thurlow. He looks old before his time. His temper, even his friends allow, has become rugged, boisterous, arrogant,—almost brutal. But they know not the secret pangs that torture him, or they might bear with patience, or pardon with gentleness, those fierce ebullitions of rage that will not acknowledge sickness nor infirmity. Even in the death-gripe, he will clutch those magic seals. But now he presides at that Board, where the subject of discussion is the glory and safety of the Empire,—the weal or wo of millions yet unborn. If the feeling of bodily languor for an instant overpower his intellectual energies, alarmed ambition stings his mind into preternatural strength, for he penetrates the arts of a wily rival, who, affecting to acquiesce in his measures, secretly labours to thwart them, and to undermine him in the favour and confidence of his sovereign. He puts forth all his strength, tramples the reptile in the dust, and seats himself at the head of empire more firmly and securely than ever. Is he happy now? He thinks he should be so, but he thinks little of it; he has leisure for nothing, heart for nothing, memory for nothing, save his high function, and the arts necessary to maintain himself in it. He has no time, and indeed no wish to ascertain his own state either of body or mind. If he has no leisure to attend to his health, how can he be supposed to have time for self-examination, or for serious thought. He once had many schemes, the growth of his strong and even enlarged mind, for the welfare of the State, and the happiness of his old private friends,—but they must be delayed. And now he loses even the wish for their accomplishment; his heart, never either very kind or soft, has become narrowed as well as callous; his temper waxes more and more hard, and gloomy, and repulsive; his private friends fall off, disgusted by his neglect, and surly, arrogant haughtiness. They have no longer any common sympathies with Edward, Lord Thurlow. He stalks through his magnificent house alone; he writes, erases, burns, knits his brows over communications and despatches which offend him,—and many things offend him, —he sits up half the night plunged in business; the surgeon who of late sleeps in his house administers a sleeping draught, and he will try to obtain a few hours of troubled repose. Had pride allowed him, he could almost have addressed the obsequious medical man in the well-remembered words of Macbeth,—

'Canst thou not minister to a mind diseased?'

Many, many years ago, he had seen Garrick play that character and many others, when William Cowper, of the Inner Temple, was his companion to Drury Lane. They had spouted the favourite passages together fifty times, after returning home to sup, now in Cowper's chambers, now in Thurlow's. Of rhetoric and declamation Edward Thurlow was ever an admirer; young Cowper relished more the intense passion, or the deep pathos of the scene.

"The memory of his old fellow-student and companion had been revived on this night, by the arrival of a volume, just published, of Cowper's poetry. With a feeling bordering on contempt, Lord Thurlow threw it from him unopened. Now another scene of our magic glass, and behold the High Chancellor lays his throbbing but ever clear head on a downy pillow, and sets his alarum-watch to an early hour; for, sick or well, he must be at Windsor by ten to-morrow. He, however, leaves orders, that at whatever hour his private secretary, who is waiting the issue of an important debate in the House of Commons, shall return, he be admitted to him;—Lord Thurlow has an impression, that, though he may stretch his limbs on that bed of state, sleep will not visit him till he learn the fortune of the day,—hears how the vote has gone. It was a debate on the African slave-trade. He first inquired the vote—it was favourable. He glanced over the reports of the leading speeches:—the vote was his,—but the feeling, the spirit of the night was strongly against him. There was the speech of Charles Fox; and he had quoted Cowper!—a beautiful apostrophe to Freedom, cheered by all the members on both sides of the House, forced to admire, vote afterwards as they might.

"Lord Thurlow now sets himself to sleep in good earnest, and his strong will is omnipotent even here. But over the empire of dreams the Lord High Chancellor had no power,—Fancy is not a ward of Chancery. His visions were gloomy and distempered. His youth, his manhood, his present life are all fantastically, but vividly blended. Sometimes the spirit that haunts him is the Prince of Wales, then it becomes Charles Fox, and anon it changes to William Cowper, and again back to Fox. But his hour comes, the alarum wakes him, and he is almost glad of the relief."

"Would you choose to see the Chancellor's dressing-room, Fanny, and his anti-chamber, and the persons met in levee there, thus early, in a chill, foggy, winter's morning?" Fanny chose to do so.

And there was seen the plain chamber of the English Minister, lights burning dimly in the cold, heavy air,—a fire choked with smoke.

"Ah, poor old gentleman," cried Fanny, "there he is, so cold, I am sure, and so very cross he looks,—the poor servant that shaves him looks so terribly frightened. Well, considering how late he was of getting to bed, and all, I don't think, brother George, it is very pleasant to be a High Chancellor—at least in winter; particularly when the King wishes to see him so early at Windsor, to scold him perhaps."

"O, you silly child," said her sister.

"Not so silly, Miss Sophia," said the Curate. "To be sure, there is no great hardship visible here, still I could have wished the Lord Chancellor a longer and sounder sleep; and it is very wise, Fanny, to learn young, 'that all is not gold which glisters.' But now we shall suppose the Chancellor shaved and booted, his hasty cup of coffee swallowed—as the Jews did the Passover—standing, his loins girt; for he too is bound for the wilderness. In short, he detests Windsor interviews. A secretary bears his portfolio; his carriage is at the door; he hurries through the circle of adulators, solicitors of his patronage, understrappers of all kinds, that wait his appearance,— the whole herd hateful to him, and he to them; and he is not a man of glozing words or feigning courtesy. No man in England can say '*No*' more gruffly or decidedly. A few indispensable words uttered, he hurries on. Near the door you note a young clergyman, his fine features 'sicklied o'er with the pale cast of thought.' His profile strikingly resembles that of William Cowper, and Lord Thurlow recals his dream, and Charles Fox's quotation; and, with his old accurate Temple habits, takes the port-folio himself, and directs his secretary to return and bring him a volume 'lying on the third shelf of a certain cabinet in his business-room, between a pamphlet on India affairs, and that something about Lord George Gordon.' He now perfectly recollected—for his memory was tenacious of every thing,—that Cowper had lost his paltry sort of appointment, —had gone deranged,—was always *swainish*,—and now piped in some rural shades or other, sunk into *nobody*, with probably not political interest sufficient to influence the election of the neighbouring borough-reeve. There had been a degree of impertinence in sending such a book to him; or it was, at least, an act of silliness, and shewed small knowledge of life. But Fox had quoted it; so once beyond the smoke of London, Thurlow turns over the leaves. The carriage rolls on, post-haste, to the audience of Majesty; but habit has enabled the Lord Chancellor to read even in the most rapid whirling motion. He dips at random in search of Fox's passage, and stumbles on that splendid one—'All flesh is grass.' 'Cowper should have been in the church,' thought he; 'a dignified churchman he is unfit for, but he might have made a tolerable parish priest, if he would steer clear of Methodistical nonsense.'—He dips again—'One sheltered hare;' 'whining stuff! or is he mad still?' His eye falls on that passage beginning—'How various his employments whom the world calls idle;' and he reads on, not with the natural feelings of Hastings, but yet not wholly unmoved, till he got to the words, 'Sipping calm the fragrant lymph which neatly she prepares,' when, throwing down the book, the man, strong in the spirit of this world's wisdom, mutters to himself, 'piperly trash!—and is it this Charles Fox quotes? The devil quotes scripture for his use, and Fox would quote the devil for his.' Lord Thurlow then plunges into that red portfolio which engrosses so much of his time —so much of his soul.

"And now 'the proud keep of Windsor' rises on the ambitious, and prosperous, and proud statesman:—he smooths his brow; his sovereign welcomes him graciously; his audience passes off well; he hastens back to London, where a thousand affairs await to occupy and torture though they cannot distract him. He snatches a morsel of cold meat; swallows a glass of wine: and off to the House of Peers, to be baited for six long hours by the bull-dogs of Opposition."

"And what has the poor gentleman for all this?" said little Fanny. "I am sure he has hard work of it."

"How idly you do talk, Fanny; is he not Lord Chancellor of England?" cried her sister.

"And fills high—I may say, the highest place; has immense patronage; is the maker of bishops, and deans, and judges, and every thing," said George.

"And has immense revenues," added the Curate; "estates, mansions,—all that money can command."

"Poor old gentleman," said Fanny, "I am glad he has also that wool-sack to rest himself on, for I am sure he must be sadly tired and worried."

"Turn we to Olney—to that dwelling in the very heart

of that shabby, but now honoured town—to Cowper's abode:—no poet's fabled retirement, embowered in sylvan solitudes, by wild wandering brook or stately river's brink, skirted with hanging woods, or vine-clad steeps, or towering mountains.—Here is the parlour."—"But pray stop, sir," cried Sophia, "that dull house had its pleasant accessories; have you forgot the greenhouse, the plants, the goldfinches; that pleasant window, looking over the neighbour's orchard?—and what so beautiful as an orchard, when the white plum-blossom has come full out, and the pink apple flowers are just budding!"

"And Beau, and Tiney," cried Fanny.

"I have forgot none of these things, my dears, said Mr. Dodsley. Only I fear that to see them, as Cowper saw them, we must have a poet's glass; an instrument of higher powers than a Claude Lorraine glass, and clothing every object with softer, or warmer, or sunnier hues than even that pretty toy:—where could that be bought, Fanny?"

"Indeed, sir, I don't know," said Fanny.

"We may borrow one for a day, or a few hours or so," said Sophia, smiling intelligently.

"It is but fair to use Mr. Cowper's glass in viewing his own pictures,—and Mrs. Unwin's spectacles, in judging of her domestic comforts," said the Curate. "There is the parlour;—it looks doubly snug to-night. Now you are to recollect ladies and gentlemen, that this scene passes on a night when Mr. Hastings' *trial* is proceeding; and while Lord Thurlow is busy and distracted in his bureau. Tea is over—the hares are asleep on the rug.—Beau, the spaniel, lies in the bosom of Bess, the maukin. On the table lie some volumes of voyages, which Mrs. Hill has this day sent from London to Mr. Cowper, with a few rare, West India seeds for his greenhouse, as he calls it. There is a kind but short letter from her husband, Cowper's old friend;—for he too, is a busy man in the courts, though not Lord Chancellor—and there is a polite note from herself. There has also been a letter from Mr. Unwin this evening, a very kind one, filial and confidential. Mr. Cowper's cumbrous writing apparatus is on the table, for he has not yet got his neat, handy, writing-desk from Lady Hesketh. His former writing-table had become crazy, and paralytic in its old limbs; but to-night, he has, by a happy thought of Mrs. Unwin's got that forgotten card-table lugged down from the lumber garret, and he shakes it, finds it steady, and rejoices over it. And now the fire is trimmed for the evening; the candles are snuffed; they shew a print of Mr. Newton, and a few prints of other rather ugly, grim-looking, evangelical ministers, and black profile shades of some of Mrs. Unwin's friends. Yet all looks comfortable and feels pleasant to the inmates—for this is their home. O! that magic, transfiguring word! but this home is indeed a peaceful and a happy one.

"Mr. Cowper relates to his companion the events of his long, morning ramble,—a rambling narrative; simple, descriptive, somewhat pathetic too, nor unrelieved by a few delicate touches of Cowper's peculiar humour. And she listens all benevolent smiles to his ventures, happened in meadow and mire—' o'er hills, through valleys, and by rivers' banks;' and, in her turn, tells him of two poor persons distressed in mind, and pinched in circumstances, who had called at their house; and mentions what she had done for them, and consults what farther deed of mercy or charity she and her friend may jointly accomplish before that day closed. And now Sam, Mr. Cowper's excellent and attached servant, or rather humble friend, who in adversity had cleaved to him, enters the room. Sam knew nothing of London life or London wages, or official bribes, or perquisites; but I should like to know if ever Lord Thurlow had such a servant as Mr. Cowper's Sam; for this is no inconsiderable item in a man's domestic happiness. And unless we know all these little matters, how can we pronounce a true deliverance."

"We may guess, that honest Sam and his qualities would have been of little utility, and of small value to Edward, Lord Thurlow, any way," said Mrs. Herbert; "and so throw the attached servant out of his scale altogether."

"I fear so:—Well Sam, civilly, but rather formally, neither like a footman of parts nor of figure, mentions that John Cox, the parish clerk of All Saints' Parish, Northampton, waits in the kitchen for those obituary verses engrossed with the annual bill of mortality, which Mr. Cowper had for some years furnished on his solicitation.

"'Ay, Sam,—say I will be ready for him in a few minutes, and give the poor man a cup of beer,' said the courteous poet. 'I must first read the verses to you, Mary,' continued he, as Sam left the parlour; 'you are my critic, my Sam Johnson, and Monthly Reviewer:'—and he reads those fine verses beginning, 'He who sits from day to day.'

"'I like them, Mr. Cowper,' said his calm friend; and that was praise enough.—John Cox was ushered in, brushed his eye hastily over the paper, scraped with his feet, and said he dared to say these lines might do well enough. The gentleman he employed before was so learned, no one in the parish understood him. And Cowper smiles, and says, 'If the verses please, and are not found too learned, he hopes Mr. Cox will employ him again.'

"And now the postboy's horn is heard, and Sam hies forth. Mr. Cowper is not rich enough to buy newspapers; but his friends don't forget him, nor his tastes. Whenever any thing likely to interest his feelings occurs in the busy world, some kind friend addresses a paper to Olney. Thus he keeps pace with the world, though remote from its stir and contamination. He reads aloud another portion of the trial of Hastings, most reluctant as friend and as Christian to believe his old school-fellow the guilty blood-dyed oppressor that he is here described. He reads the heads of a bill brought in by the Lord Chancellor to change, to extend rather, the criminal code of the country; and says, passionately, 'Will they never try preventive means? There is no flesh in man's obdurate heart, it doth not feel for man.' He skims the motley contents of the 'little folio of four pages,' gathering the goings on of the great Babel, as food for future rumination; and he would have read the speech of the Chancellor, had not more important concerns carried him away,—for old John Queeney, the shoemaker in the back street, longs to see Mr. Cowper by his bed-side. Mr. Newton, John's minister, is in London; and though John and Mr. Cowper are in nowise acquainted, saving seeing each other in church, there are dear ties and blessed hopes common to both; so Cowper goes off immediately. But since Mrs. Unwin insists that it is a cold damp night, he takes his great-coat, though only to please her, and Sam marches before with the lantern. John Queeney has but one poor room, Sam would be an intruder there; and as it is harsh to have him wait in the street, like the attendant or horses of a fine lady, Sam is sent home by his amiable master.

"When, in an hour afterwards, Mr. Cowper returns, he tells that John Queeney is dying, and will probably not see over the night; that he is ill indeed, but that the King and the nobles of England might gladly exchange states with that poor shoemaker, in the back street of Olney:—his warfare was accomplished! Mrs. Unwin understands him; she breathes a silent inward prayer, for her dying fellow-creature, and fellow-Christian; and no more is said on this subject. Cowper, now in a steady and cheerful voice, reads the outline of a petition he has drawn out in name of the poor lace-workers of Olney, against an intended duty on candles. On them such a tax would have fallen grievously. 'My dear Mr. Cowper, this is more like an indignant remonstrance than an humble petition,' said his friend, with her placid smile.

"'Indeed and I fear it is. How could it well be otherwise? But this must be modified; the poet's imprudence must not hurt the poor lace-workers' cause.'

"And now Sam brings in supper—a Roman meal, in the day's of Rome's heroic simplicity; and when it is withdrawn, Hannah, the sole maid-servant, comes in to say she has carried one blanket to Widow Jennings, and another to Jenny Hibberts; and that the shivering children had actually danced round, and hugged, and kissed the comfortable night-clothing, for lack of which they perished; and that the women themselves shed tears of thankfulness, for this well-timed, much-wanted supply.

"' And you were sure to tell them they came not from us,' said the poet. Hannah replied that she had, and withdrew.

"' These blankets cannot cost the generous Thornton above ten shillings a-piece, Mr. Cowper,' says Mrs. Unwin. 'Oh! how many a ten-shillings that would, in this severe season, soften the lot of the industrious poor, are every night lavished in the city he inhabits! How many blankets would the opera-tickets of this *one* night purchase! And can any *one* human creature have the heart or the right thus to lavish, yea, though not sinfully, yet surely not without blame, while but *one* other of the same great family perishes of hunger, or of cold?'

"And they speak of their poor neighbours by name; they know many of them, their good qualities, their faults, and their necessities. And fireside discourse flows on in the easy current of old, endeared, and perfect intimacy; and Cowper is led incidentally to talk of dark passages in his earlier life; of the Providence which had guided and led him to this resting-place ' by the green pastures and still waters;' of the mercy in which he had been afflicted; of a great deliverance suddenly wrought; of the ARM which had led him into the wilderness, while ' the banner over him was love.' And then the talk ebbs back to old friends, now absent; to domestic cares, and little family concerns and plans; the garden, or the greenhouse, matter ' fond and trivial,' yet interesting, and clothed in the language of a poet, and adorned by a poet's fancy.

"I must again ask, had the Lord High Chancellor ever gained to his heart any one intelligent and affectionate woman, to whom he could thus unbend his mind—pour forth his heart of hearts—in the unchilled confidence of a never-failing sympathy: This I shall consider—the possession of this friend—an immense weight in Cowper's scale, when we come to adjust the balance," said Mr. Dodsley.

"' I must now read you the fruits of my morning's study, ma'am,' says our poet, after a pause; ' I had well-nigh forgot that.'—And he reads his sublime requiem on the loss of the Royal George.

"' I am mistaken if this be not wonderfully grand, Mr. Cowper,' says his ancient critic. ' But hark! our cuckoo clock. It must be regulated—you forget your duties, sir—Tiney must be put up, and'—

"' You must just allow me, Mary, to give one puff of the bellows to the greenhouse embers. The air feels chilly to-night—my' precious' orange-tree.' And Mrs. Unwin smiles over his fond care, as the gentleman walks off with the bellows under his arm.

"And now it is the stated hour of family worship. Sam and Hannah march forward in decent order. But I shall not attempt to describe the pious household rites, where the author of the Task is priest and worshipper. Affectionate ' Goodnights,' close the scene. And this is the order of the evenings at Olney.

"Cowper regulates the cuckoo clock; for though he has no alarum watch, or impending audience of Majesty, he lays many duties on himself, lowly, yet not ignoble; so about the same hour that the Chancellor rolls off for Windsor, Cowper, also alert in duty, is penning his fair copy of the lace-worker's petition to Parliament, or despatching one of his playful, affectionate epistles to his cousin, Lady Hesketh, or acknowledging the bounty of the benevolent Thornton to the poor of Olney. And now, body and mind refreshed, the blessings of the night remembered, and the labours of the day dedicated in short prayer and with fervent praise, and he is in his greenhouse study, chill though it be, for it is quiet and sequestered. See here, Fanny—our last picture. But so minutely has the poet described his favourite retreat that this sketch may be deemed superfluous labour. Yet this is and will ever be a cherished spot; for here many of his virtuous days were spent.

"Why, pursue the theme farther," continued the Curate, "you all know the simple tenor of his life :—

'Thus did he travel on life's common way,
In cheerful godliness.'

The visitations to which his delicately-organized mind was liable, I put out of view. They were a mystery beyond his mortal being—far beyond our limited human intelligence. And tell me now, my young friends, which, at the close of his memorable life, may be pronounced the best, and, by consequence, the happiest man of our Three Westminster Boys? Each was ' sprung of earth's first blood;' and though I do not assert that any one of the three is a faultless model, it is a fair question to ask, which has your suffrage?—He who, by the force of his intellect and ambition, the hardihood and energy of his character, took his place at the head of the councils of this mighty empire,—he, the conqueror of so fair a portion of the East, who, by arms and policy, knit another mighty empire to this,—or he—' the stricken deer,' who sought the shades, the arrow rankling in his side—who dwelt apart, in ' blest seclusion from a jarring world,' and who, as his sole memorial and trophy, has left us

'This single volume paramount.'"

And Mr. Dodsley lifted Sophia's small and elegant copy of Cowper's works, and gave it into the hand of the youth next him.

An animated discussion now arose; and when Miss Harding collected the votes, she found the young gentlemen were equally divided between Hastings and Thurlow. The young ladies were, however, unanimous for Cowper; and the Curate gave his suffrage with theirs, repeating,

"Blessings be with them, and eternal praise,
Who gave us nobler loves and nobler cares—
The poets—who, on earth have made us heirs
Of truth, and pure delight, by heavenly lays,"

DIRGE OF WALLACE.

They lighted a taper at the dead of night,
  And chanted their holiest hymn;
But her brow and her bosom were damp with affright,
  Her eye was all sleepless and dim!
And the lady of Elderslie wept for her Lord,
  When a death-watch beat in her lonely room,
When her curtain had shook of its own accord,
  And the raven had flapp'd at her window-board,
  To tell of her warrior's doom!

" Now sing you the death-song, and loudly pray
  " For the soul of my knight so dear;
" And call me a widow this wretched day,
  " Since the warning of God is here!
" The nightmare rides on my strangled sleep :—
  " The lord of my bosom is doom'd to die;
" His valorous breast they have wounded deep;
" And the blood-red tears shall his country weep,
  " For Wallace of Elderslie!"

Yet knew not his country that ominous hour,
  Ere the loud matin-bell was rung,
That a trumpet of death on an English tower,
  Had the dirge of her champion sung!
When his dungeon-light looked dim and red
  On the high-born blood of a martyr slain,
No anthem was sung at his holy death-bed—
No weeping there was when his bosom bled,
  And his heart was rent in twain!

Yet bleeding and bound, though her Wallace wight,
  For his long-loved country die,
The bugle ne'er sung to a braver knight
  Than Wallace of Elderslie!
But the day of his glory shall never depart,
  His head unentombed shall with glory be palmed,
From its blood-streaming altar his spirit shall start;
Though the raven has fed on his mouldering heart,
  A nobler was never embalmed!

Campell.

COLUMN FOR THE LADIES.

DOMESTIC ECONOMY.

A flourishing nation is living evidence of the wisdom, sagacity and statesmanship of Benjamin Franklin. But the nicest points of domestic economy did not escape his attention; for these he justly regarded as the main foundation of national economy. The letter which we to-day submit to the ladies, was sent from Paris to his daughter, a married woman with a family, who, while her father at Paris retained all his republican simplicity of character and manners, was beginning to be, like most ladies, a little too ambitious of *fashion.* "I was charmed," he says, "with the account you give me of your industry; the table-cloths of your own spinning, &c., but your sending for long black pins, and lace, and feathers, dissolved the charm, and disgusted me as much, as if you had put salt into my strawberries. The spinning, I see, is laid aside, and you are to be dressed for the ball. You seem not to know, my dear daughter, that of all dear things, idleness is the dearest in the world, except mischief. When I began to read your account of the high prices of goods, 'a pair of gloves seven dollars, a yard of gauze twenty-four dollars, and that it required a fortune to maintain a family in a very plain way,' I expected you would conclude with telling me that every woman, as well as yourself, was grown frugal and industrious; and I could scarce believe my eyes in reading on, 'that there was never so much dressing and pleasure going forward;' and that you yourself wanted feathers, and black pins, from France—to appear, as I suppose, in the mode. This leads me to imagine that perhaps it is not so much the goods that are grown dear, as that the money is grown cheap, as every thing else will do, when excessively plenty; and that people are still nearly as easy in their circumstances as when a pair of gloves might be had for half a crown."

And now Franklin's elevated patriotism comes into action. The war in which America was engaged he thought a *just* and *necessary* war. He says, "to support the war may make our frugality necessary; and as I am always preaching this doctrine, I cannot in conscience, or in decency, encourage the contrary, by my example, in furnishing my children with foolish modes and luxuries. I therefore send all the articles you desire that are useful, and omit the rest; for, as you say, you should have great pleasure in wearing every thing I send you, and showing it as your father's, I must avoid giving you an opportunity of doing that with either lace or feathers. If you wear cambric ruffles, and take care not to mend the holes, they will come in time to be lace; and feathers, my dear daughter, may be had in America from every cock's tail. If you happen to see General Washington assure him of my great and sincere respect, and write often, my dear child."

Be it remembered that this *thinking* and this *writing* is that of a man laying, in *frugality*, the stable foundation of a mighty empire. He bids women abridge or give up their lace and feathers, that there might be funds for *war*—for a struggle which conquered independence and freedom to their posterity; but many causes dictate the same virtue to women, in all places, and in all seasons.

FEMALE DRESS.—FRENCH WOMEN.

BY LADY MORGAN.

"Let me off to Lafayette now, and you shall find me very tractable another time," said she. "I am well enough dressed for the organiser of two great revolutions, and the founder and commander-in-chief of the National Guards."

"You put me out of all patience," burst forth Madame de ———, in a fit of petulance that makes a French woman so awful, or so amusing. "Because a man founds, or destroys an empire, is he, therefore, to have no eyes, no judgment? Your General is a great man, I allow; but he is *Français avant tout;* and with a Frenchman, though it were St. Denis himself, an old fashion is ever a ridicule."

"Well," I said, endeavouring in vain to pitch my voice as high as hers, "it does not signify talking, I must go now; for my illustrious friend expects me: but, to please you, we will stop on our road, and buy a fashionable bonnet."

"Stop, and buy a bonnet! *Ah! j'en mourirai*," and she almost laughed herself into a convulsion; then suddenly drawing up, and drying her eyes, she continued: " So, you think then that to be well dressed, one has only to stop and buy a bonnet. You suppose that I will take you to the Rue Vivienne, and empty some shop window of its *chapeau d'affiche*, and order it into the carriage, as one does an ice; and then fit you out with a robe *à prix fixe*, in the Passage de Lorme, and send you with the price-ticket fastened to your skirts, into the *salon* of General Lafayette, for the special amusement of his elegant relation, Madame de T., one of the best-dressed women of France. No, no, stay at home for this day, and amuse yourself by looking out of the window, and seeing the fashionables going into the gardens at the hour of promenade; and that will give you a general idea of the toilette of the day. Meantime, I will go to Victorine and Herbaut, and see what can be done for you."

"What can be done for me!"

"To be sure: I will get their earliest day and hour; and *faire inscrire votre nom sur leur livre rouge.*"

"Take their day and hour! take *mine*, you mean."

"By no means. Were you Sappho herself, you must wait their leisure. When the Duchess de Berri sent her *dame d'honneur* to Victorine, the other day, to desire she would come and take her orders at the *Pavillon Marson*, she replied that she would be happy of having the honour of dressing her Royal Highness, who would find her at home on such a day, at such an hour."

"And how did the Duchess bear this?"

"Bear it! What could she do? There are princesses everywhere: there is but one Victorine on earth, as there was formerly but one Le Roi, and one Bertin. The throne and the altar have been shaken and overthrown in France,—the toilet never!"

At this moment my servant brought in a card, for a diplomatic ball. Madame de ——— read it with all the delight with which Signore Mai would feel in a newly discovered manuscript of Cicero.

"*Voila qui est bien*," she said, "I must not lose a minute in making interest for you. It would be impossible for you to go to a diplomatic ball, without being *habillée par Victorine et berretée par Herbaut. Il vous faut leur cachet.* Your beautiful countrywoman, Lady C———, by neglecting to keep her appointment with the latter, never recovered her *ton* during the season of her *début.* But *fiez vous à moi;* if I cannot get these two great sovereigns to dress you, you shall have some of their school; and I will write you my success to-night; so *a demain n'est ce pas;*" and away fluttered this friendliest and most frivolous of Frenchwomen; leaving me the most mortified and desolate of Irishwomen; for I was too late for my appointment and found Lafayette, as I expected, gone to the Chamber. This certainly was "*le plus beau jour de ma vie;*" so having the fear of my bonnet before my eyes, I returned to finish the morning, as I had begun it, and seated myself at the window,—as Madame de ——— had desired me,—to take that general view of the *beau monde*, which the comings and goings of the walkers in the Tuileries were calculated to give me."

Lady Morgan's distress reminds us of an adventure which befel another English lady; Lady Davy, which is at once ludicrous and serious. It happened in 1813, when Sir. H. Davy was allowed by Buonaparte to visit Paris:—While he was at the meeting of the Institute, her ladyship, attended by her maid, walked into the Tuileries garden. She wore a very small hat, of a simple cockle-shell form, such as was fashionable at that time in London, while the Parisian ladies wore bonnets of most voluminous dimensions. It happened to be a saint's day, on which the shops being closed, the citizens repaired in crowds to the garden. On seeing the diminutive bonnet of Lady Davy, the Parisians felt little less surprised than did the inhabitants of Brobdignag on beholding the hat of Gulliver; and a crowd of persons soon assembled around the unknown exotic; in consequence of which, one of the inspectors of the garden immediately presented himself and informed her Ladyship that no cause of *rassemblement* could be suffered, and therefore requested her to retire. Some officers of the Imperial Guard, to whom she appealed, replied, that however much they might regret the circumstance, they were unable to afford her any redress, as the order was peremptory. She then requested that they would conduct her to her carriage; an officer immediately offered his arm; but the crowd had by this time so greatly increased, that it became necessary to send for a corporal's guard; and the party quitted the garden surrounded by fixed bayonets."

SCIENTIFIC NOTICES.

CAOUTCHOUC, or what has been commonly called India-rubber, which has for some time past been manufactured into various useful articles of wearing apparel, impervious to wet, &c. is the subject of an article in a recent number of the "Journal des Connaissances Usuelles et Pratiques," in which it is observed that the caoutchouc is formed from the juice of two plants growing in the Indies, namely the Jahopha Elastica, and the Ecvea Caoutchou, which the natives by means of moulds form into various shapes, and especially make of it a species of bottles, on which various designs are executed. To dry it, they expose it to the flame of resinous wood, the black smoke of which gives it the dark colour which is generally observed in it. M. de Humboldt brought to Europe some of the juice of the Ecvea Caoutchou, from which white caoutchouc was produced, as it would all be, were it not for the process already mentioned. It appears, however, that the mode of manufacturing it in England, of an apparently uniform consistency, has not been hitherto discovered in France, where in the attempts made for similar purposes, it was found that the places of junction of the different pieces of caoutchouc were discoverable in the manufactured article, whilst, as already observed, the articles made in England presented an uniform texture, and the points of juncture were not discernible. But it is now thought that the secret has been discovered, and that by carrying on the whole process under water, of separating the lamina of caoutchouc (which the French writer compares, as to its mass, with Gruyere cheese,) the object may be achieved of obtaining lamina or strips, which may be joined together in the manufacturing of various articles without the points of juncture being discernible. And it is stated that strips thus obtained become so solid at the point of junction, that they could be more easily torn or fractured at any other part than that. Tubes have been thus prepared which, from their imperviability and the facility of employing them, have been found of the greatest service in chemistry.

IMPROVED RAW SUGAR.—We are indebted to a correspondent for the following notice, and submit it without at all pledging ourselves for its accuracy:—"A sample of native raw sugar, prepared by the improved process of concentrating the cane juice in vacuo, has been introduced into the market, and has excited great interest in every person connected with this important branch of our commercial and colonial prosperity. It is raw sugar, obtained in perfect, pure, transparent granular crystals, developing the form of the crystal of the sugar, and being wholly free from any portion of uncrystallizable sugar, molasses, or colouring matter."—*Athenæum*.

[The correspondent is quite correct. The good folks here in Edinburgh have been using this *elegant* preparation for some time; for coffee always, for tea or toddy occasionally.

IMPROVEMENT IN THE STEAM ENGINE.

The "Sheffield Iris" states that a great improvement in the steam-engine has been recently made by Mr. George Rennoldson, of South Shields. This engine has three cylinders from one boiler, with the connecting rods on a triangular crank, so that while one piston is moving upwards another is going down, and another passing the centre, the pistons following each other in a regular division of time, and completely balancing each other as far as weight and pressure are concerned, the slides of course moving upon a smaller triangular crank. This engine has nearly as complete an equability and uniformity of motion as it is possible to procure from a rotatory engine. The necessity of a fly-wheel is altogether superseded. It is so steady in its motion, indeed, as hardly to affect the frame in which it stands, and makes so little noise that it would scarcely be known to be at work, were it not seen to be so. Such an engine must necessarily be of great use in steam-boats, in cotton-factories, and in those manufactories at Birmingham and Sheffield where fine metal-work is wrought. An engine of this description will go in less bounds than those of the ordinary construction.

WONDERS OF MECHANISM.—Those young people who may lately have visited *Thiodon's* Mechanical Theatre in any of the towns of Scotland, where its marvels were exhibited, will be prepared for the *curiosity* we have to describe.—VAUCANSON'S DUCK. This duck exactly resembles the living animal in size and appearance. It executed accurately all its movements and gestures; it ate and drank with avidity, performed all the quick motions of the head and throat which are peculiar to the living animal, as did Thiodon's swan; and like the duck it muddled the water which it drank with its bill. It produced also the sound of quacking in the most natural manner. In the anatomical structure of the duck, the artist exhibited the highest skill, now Thiodon's animals were entirely for stage effect. Every bone in the real duck had its representative in the automaton, and its wings were anatomically exact. Every cavity, apophysis, and curvature was imitated, and each bone executed its proper movements. When corn was thrown down before it, the duck stretched out its neck to pick it up; it swallowed it, digested it, and discharged it in a digested condition. The process of digestion was effected by chemical solution, and not by trituration, and the food digested in the stomach was conveyed away by tubes to the place of its discharge.

SUPERSTITION OF THE URISK.—The dedication of groves, in particular the grottoes and caves in their most retired recesses, to sacred purposes, was, it is well known, a practice common to the theology and demonology of every ancient nation. In this respect the Druids do not appear to have been professors of a system, or observers of rites peculiar to themselves, but to have been participators along with other heathen priests, in observances which are spoken of in the sacred writings, as corruptions of purer institutions. Almost every divinity had his or her favourite tree, from which they gave out their oracles; and it is at least a curious coincidence, that while the sacred temple of the true worshipper had its *Urim* (the *lights* or emanations from the breastplate by which responses were given,) the leafy temple of the idolater had its *Urisk*, (Urisk or Uritz, in the same language, signifying *light from the tree*.)—A Skye terrier, of the small light coloured peculiar breed, known only in the Hebrides, belonging to Sir Walter Scott, received the appropriate name of *Urisk*, and has made some figure both in literature and painting. We believe *Urisk* has shared the fate of *Maida*, Sir Walter's stag hound—gone to his rest.

Besides appearing in WEEKLY NUMBERS, the SCHOOLMASTER will be published in MONTHLY PARTS, which, stitched in a neat cover, will contain as much letter-press, of good execution, as any of the large Monthly Periodicals: A Table of Contents will be given at the end of the year; when, *at the weekly cost of three-halfpence*, a handsome volume of 532 pages, super-royal size, may be bound up, containing much matter worthy of preservation.

CONTENTS OF NO. III.

	Page
Condition of Operative Manufacturers,	33
Books of the Society for the Diffusion of Useful Knowledge	35
Edinburgh a Century Ago—Goldsmith the Poet	36
The Spinning-Wheel	38
The Maid-Servant	38
Causes of the Bad Effects of the East Wind	39
English Justice	39
Sage Cheese—Stilton Cheese, &c.	39
ELEMENTS OF THOUGHT—Patience of the British People—Difference between a Free and a Despotic Government—When Resistance to a Government becomes justifiable—Boundlessness of the Creation—Want of Sensibility to Natural Beauty	40
THE STORY-TELLER—The Three Westminster Boys	41
Dirge of Wallace	46
COLUMN FOR THE LADIES—Domestic Economy—Female Dress—French Women, by Lady Morgan	47
SCIENTIFIC NOTICES—Caoutchouc—Improved Raw Sugar—Improved Steam Engine—Wonders of Mechanism Superstition of the Urisk	48

EDINBURGH: Printed by and for JOHN JOHNSTONE, 19, St. James's Square.—Published by JOHN ANDERSON, Jun., Bookseller, 55, North Bridge Street, Edinburgh; by JOHN MACLEOD, and ATKINSON & Co., booksellers, Glasgow; and sold by all Booksellers and Venders of Cheap Periodicals.

THE Schoolmaster,
AND
EDINBURGH WEEKLY MAGAZINE.

CONDUCTED BY JOHN JOHNSTONE.

THE SCHOOLMASTER IS ABROAD.—LORD BROUGHAM.

No. 4.—Vol. I.   SATURDAY, AUGUST 25, 1832.   Price Three-Halfpence.

MANUFACTURING OPERATIVES.

SCHOOLMASTER AND FRIEND—A MORSEL OF DIALOGUE.

Friend. Monstrously radical last Saturday, Mr. Schoolmaster! Could you not very safely leave the attack on the *Society for the Diffusion of Useful Knowledge* to the "Westminster" on the one hand, and "Blackwood" on the other?—the former decrying, the latter ridiculing its labours.

Schoolmaster. You labour under a great mistake, my Friend, if you imagine the *Schoolmaster* meant to *attack* the Society, in simply expressing the discontent generally felt among the best-informed operatives at the line it is pursuing,—at its giving, after its own fashion, every sort of knowledge, but that which, in the words of the text to which you object, may enable the poor man to gain a competency, and secure it to himself. The artisans undoubtedly presume that the Society view with increasing jealousy attempts made to disseminate *cheaply* the sort of knowledge which they no longer deem it advisable to promulgate themselves.

Friend. Political knowledge, you mean, now; but that they do not pretend to teach: you need not blame them for not doing what they never proposed.

Schoolmaster. Here again, my Friend, you mistake. The operatives who are grumbling at the Society, ask nothing but what was voluntarily promised by its own original plan. Will you give me leave to read you a short passage from what may be termed the Society's preliminary discourse, written by no less distinguished a member than Lord Brougham. Unfortunately, the Society's publications must have got into less liberal guidance; for than his Lordship's views expounded in 1825, nothing can be more deserving the approbation of the people. But hear his doctrine of

CHEAP POLITICAL PUBLICATIONS.

"Why," says Mr. Brougham, "should not political, as well as all other works, be published in a cheap form, and in numbers? That history, the nature of the constitution, the doctrines of political economy, may safely be disseminated in this shape, no man now-a-days will be hardy enough to deny. Popular tracts, indeed, on the latter subject, ought to be much more extensively circulated for the good of the working classes, as well as of their superiors. The interests of both are deeply concerned in sounder views being taught them. I can hardly imagine, for example, a greater service being rendered to the men, than expounding to them the true principles and mutual relations of population and wages; and both they and their masters will assuredly experience the effects of the prevailing ignorance upon such questions, as soon as any interruption shall happen in the commercial prosperity of the country, if, indeed, the present course of things, daily tending to lower wages as well as profits, and set the two classes in opposition to each other, shall not of itself bring on a crisis. To allow, or rather to induce the people to take part in these discussions, is, therefore, not merely safe, but most wholesome for the community, and yet some points connected with them are matter of pretty warm contention in the present times; but these may be freely handled, it seems, with safety; indeed, unless they are so handled, such subjects cannot be discussed at all Why, then, may not every topic of politics, party as well as general, be treated of in cheap publications? It is highly useful to the community, that the true principles of the constitution, ecclesiastical and civil, should be well understood by every man who lives under it. The great interests of civil and religious liberty are mightily promoted by such wholesome instruction; but the good order of society gains to the full as much by it. The peace of the country, and the stability of the government, could not be more effectually secured than by the universal diffusion of this kind of knowledge."

What say you to this, my Friend? But I must crave your attention to another sentence—"The abuses," says Mr. Brougham, "which through time have crept into the practice of the constitution, the errors committed in its administration, and the improvements which a change of circumstances require, even in its principles, may *most fitly* be expounded in the same manner. And if any man, or set of men, deny the existence of such abuses, see no error in the conduct of those who administer the government, and regard all innovation upon its principles as pernicious, they may propagate their doctrines through the like channels. Cheap works being furnished, the choice may be left to the readers—assuredly a country which tolerates every kind, even the most unmeasured of daily and weekly discussion in the newspapers, can have nothing to dread from the diffusion of political doctrines in a form less desultory." This I call a manly and complete recognition of *cheap political* publications.

Friend. I confess I was not aware—few persons are— one cannot remember every thing—that the Society had ever proposed such scope for their labours. But all prospectuses, you know—the thing is proverbial—You have the Society on the hip, I own. Yet surely there is no good in parading that shocking picture of the actual state of the manufacturing poor—ministering to the worst passions of the mob!

Schoolmaster. A serious charge, my Friend, were it a just one. The Schoolmaster's descriptions, however, were only taken at second hand; and moreover, from untroubled and unpolluted, and, I presume, irreproachable sources—from statistical tables and deliberate reports. Nothing was either exaggerated or over-coloured in pictures which humanity requires to be kept constantly before the public eye—brought forward week after week, and day after day, till the evil is arrested, and the remedy found. But you shall hear, if you please, what the *Schoolmaster* has to say in the present week on this momentous subject; perhaps you may find it less objectionable; it is, at all events, from a quarter *you* must respect. *Reads—*

HAPPY ENGLAND.

[You are to understand that this was written in Manchester, twenty-four years before Dr. Kay's pamphlet, and in the character of a Spanish traveller in England.]

"We (the Spanish) purchase English cloth, English muslins, English buttons, &c., and admire the excellent skill with which they are fabricated, and wonder that from such a distance they can be afforded at so low a price, and think what a happy country is England! A happy country indeed it is for the higher orders; nowhere have the rich so many enjoyments, nowhere have the ambitious so fair a field, nowhere have the ingenious such encouragement, nowhere have the intellectual such advantages. But to talk of English happiness, is like talking of Spartan freedom—*the helots are overlooked.* In no other country can such riches be acquired by commerce; but it is the *one* who grows rich by the labour of the *hundred.* The hundred, human beings like himself, as wonderfully fashioned by nature, gifted with the like capacities, and equally made for immortality, are sacrificed, body and soul. Horrible as it must needs appear, the assertion is true to the very letter. They are deprived in infancy of all instruction, and all enjoyment; of the sports in which childhood instinctively indulges; of fresh air by day, and natural sleep by night. Their health, physical and moral, is alike destroyed; they die of diseases, induced by unremitting task-work, by confinement in the impure air of crowded rooms, by the particles of metallic or vegetable dust they are continually inhaling; or they live to grow up without decency, without comfort, and without hope; without morals, without religion, and without shame; and bring forth slaves like themselves, to tread in the same paths of misery. The dwellings of the labouring manufacturers are in narrow streets and lanes, blocked up from light and air, not as in our country, (Spain) to exclude an insupportable sun, but crowded together, because every inch of the land is of such value, that room for light and air cannot be afforded them. Here, in Manchester, a great proportion of the poor lodge in cellars, damp and dark, where every kind of filth is suffered to accumulate, *because no exertions of domestic care can ever make such homes decent.* These places are so many hot-beds of infection; and the poor in large towns are rarely or never without an infectious fever among them—a plague of their own, which leaves the habitations of the rich, like a Goshen of cleanliness and comfort, unvisited. Wealth flows into the country; but how does it circulate there? Not equally and healthfully through the whole system; it sprouts into wens and tumours, and collects in aneurisms, which starve and palsy the extremities. The government, indeed, raises millions now as easily as it raised thousands in the reign of Elizabeth. The metropolis is six times the size which it was a century ago. It has nearly doubled during the present reign. A thousand carriages drive about the streets of London, where three generations ago there were not a hundred. A thousand hackney coaches are licenced in the same city, where at the same distance of time there was not one. They whose grandfathers dined at noon, from wooden trenchers, and upon the produce of their own farms, sit down by the light of waxen tapers, to be served upon silver, and to partake of the delicacies of the four quarters of the globe. *But the numbers of the poor, and the sufferings of the poor, have continued to increase.* The price of every thing they consume has always been advancing; and the price of labour, the only thing they have to dispose, remains the same. Work-houses are erected in one place, and infirmaries in another; the poor-rates increase in proportion to the taxes; and in times of dearth the rich even prepare food, and retail it to them at a reduced price, or supply them with it gratuitously; still every year adds to their number."

What say you to this, my Friend? Can you lay your hand upon your heart, and pronounce this painful description a false one?

Friend. Why, this is worse and worse. This fellow is more inflammatory than your worshipful self. You never can publish this stuff.

Schoolmaster. And yet it is written by a chief of the conservative party—one of the best and ablest of them—Mr. Southey.

Friend. Mr. Southey Well, I suppose we must not call him an incendiary, and pander to the basest passions of the mob. 'Tis a shocking state we are got into, that is certain; but, after all, least said is soonest mended. It may last our time.—*Exit Friend, shrugging his shoulders.*

THE LABOURING CLASSES.—THE WOOLLEN MANUFACTURERS.

"One half of the world does not know how the other lives," is a common saying; "One half does not *care* how the other lives is a true one." Last week we gave the state of the manufacturers of cottons. Agricultural labourers, persons engaged in mining, and at the potteries, are often in nearly as bad a condition. Let us then turn to the woollen manufacture of Yorkshire. It is rightly supposed, less liable to fluctuation and sudden depression than the cotton-trade of Lancashire. We quote at large from a careful report drawn up last year, after deliberate investigation. The sum of it may first be given in few words: "On diligent inquiry, it was ascertained that the average support of members of families at Almondbury* and the adjoining hamlets was *twopence per day!* and that there were hundreds of adult persons who have not tasted butchers' meat for many months, some of whom have not even tasted bread nor tea, but lived upon potatoes."

How thankful would these poor starving creatures have been for the hardest fare of their rude ancestors, with whom their happy condition is so often contrasted.

Mr. Geo. Beaumont, one of the committee appointed to ascertain the state of the poor, said, the cases were not *selected*, but taken from door to door. The first case was that of a widow, with six children, whose weekly income was 6s. When visited, they were in a state of actual starvation; the youngest child was ill of the typhus fever, of which disease its father died some months before. At the time of his decease, there was not a farthing or a farthing's worth of food in the house, nor the least bit of soap to wash their few rags—nor any means of getting any. The second case was that of a family of three persons, whose income amounted to three shillings, who lived upon potatoes, and sometimes a litle oatmeal. This poor man was 18s. in arrear with his rent, for which his landlord sold his jenny, which cost him 3*l.*, so that if the man had work, he had no means of working. The next case

---

* Near Huddersfield.

a family of ten persons, whose weekly income was 6s., who, when visited in the evening, were found breaking their fasts with coarse bread and mint tea, without ***. The mother was crying over her distressed offspring. *** the fourth :—a family of five persons; weekly income 3s. ; the wife had been in the typhus fever ten weeks ; a family lived chiefly on potatoes and salt, balm tea, without sugar ; and they had had only four ounces of *** during four weeks. Case the fifth :—a family of ***, whose weekly income for the last twelve months was ***; they lived upon potatoes mixed with salt and water—sometimes an onion to savour this unsavoury food. Case sixth :—a family of seven, all without work, and had not *** more than a pound of animal food during the last four ***. The seventh case was a family of seven, who had *** more than 7s. a week for the last three months. These unfortunate beings had not tasted animal food for eighteen weeks; they lived chiefly upon oatmeal porridge ; and, when visited, they had not a morsel of food in the house ; *** were all pining for want. This was on a Tuesday, and they had not had any food since the previous Friday, *** a little that they borrowed. Case eighth :— family of seven ; weekly income 10s. ; they had not *** animal food for many weeks, and had not had a gill of beer in the house for two years. They knew not how *** lived ; *they were tired of living*. The ninth case *** a family of five; weekly income, for the last six months, 7s. ; all the furniture had been taken for rent ; *** a table or chair left. When visited they had no animal ***, no bread, no beer, no tea, no nothing. They had neither tea nor sugar in the house, but lived upon potatoes and oatmeal porridge when it could be procured. The *** was a family of five, whose weekly income was 7s. One of these poor creatures had to work all the night before he (Beaumont) took his statement, to finish the work in his loom, for the purpose of saving the rest from dying of actual starvation, as the whole family had not had more than sixpennyworth of food for the three preceding days.

At Scammoden in that same neighbourhood, in Yorkshire, the richest agricultural county in the world perhaps, the results of investigation were yet more distressing—of thirty-eight cases selected we give nine.

1. A family of three—income 1s. 9d. per week ; they sleep in a corner of the loom-shop, upon straw, strewn upon the floor, without any covering except the old clothing which they wore in the day time. 2. A family of four—weekly income 5s. ; they lived on potatoes and thin water porridge ; no milk, as they could not pay for it; no bread, no meat ; had woven 160 yards, and travelled 48 miles, for 16s. 4d. 3. A widow and four children with a weekly income of 4s. 6d. ; they lived upon oatmeal porridge, without milk, treacle, or any thing else ; no furniture ; their bed was not worth a penny ; indeed, they were perishing for want of food. 4. A family of nine, whose weekly income was 7s. ; the whole of them lay on a bed of straw, in a corner of a wretched hovel, not fit for one of the brute creation to inhabit. They had no bed clothes or other covering, except a dirty coarse wrapper. In this family misery reigned in silent triumph. 5. A family of nine, with a weekly income of 8s. ; they laboured fourteen hours per day ; they had three beds, and but one blanket for the three, and that was nine years old. These miserable creatures, when visited, were getting their breakfast ; the mother had a gill of milk, which she measured out by spoonfuls to their thin water porridge, being only two spoonfuls and a half each. 6. A family of ten, whose weekly income was 10s. ; they had only one straw bed for the whole family, they had no bed-clothes, but slept in those which they wore during the day. This family lived chiefly on potatoes, but sometimes had a pound of suet ; they had not had a pound of bread in the house, excepting two or three penny cakes, during the last three years. 7. A family consisting of a widow and three children ; they are employed in weaving woollen ends at 1s. 4d. per score ; she scoured her own weft, for doing which she had nothing allowed, and took her work to Huddersfield. There was neither meat, drink, nor money in the house, when visited. 8. A family of three ; weekly income, 1s. 8d. ; no bed, excepting some straw, with an old bag for covering. It was so long since this family had any animal food that they did not recollect the time. They had not had any bread in the house for the last five years. The old woman is seventy years of age, and *has long been praying for death to relieve her from her misery*. 9. A family of four, whose weekly income was 3s. ; they could not tell when they had any animal food, and it was two years since they had tasted bread. This was the state of men in middle age, and in the prime of life—of young men and women ; what, then, was the state of their aged parents? If they searched the workhouse and poor books, they would find that they had so much allowed them as would keep them alive, and keep them miserable or pining in workhouses.

And this is England ! rich, glorious, prosperous England ! We shall not dare to look at Ireland, nor our own country, though the latter cannot be worse than wealthier England, and in fact is, on the whole, better, how long to continue no one can tell.

BOOKS OF THE MONTH.

THOUGH the length of the Parliamentary Session has made this a long publishing season, few original works have appeared that promise abiding interest. Yet there are some to be *bought*, a *few* to be borrowed, and a considerable number to be glanced over, if they fall easily into one's way.

To be *bought*, at least, by all Book-clubs and Subscription Libraries is—The ECONOMY of MACHINERY and MANUFACTURES, by Charles Babbage, Esq., Mathematical Professor, Cambridge—a thorough master of the details of this multifarious subject. The work opens with a discussion on the value of Machinery and Manufactures and their various capabilities of converting worthless substances into useful products—of saving human labour, and time, and gaining many additional powers. We give one small specimen of the writer's manner:—

"The force of vapour is a fertile source *of moving power* ; but even in this case it cannot be maintained that power is created. Water is converted into elastic vapour by the combustion of fuel. The chemical changes which thus take place are constantly increasing the atmosphere by large quantities of carbonic acid and other gases noxious to animal life. The means by which nature decomposes or reconverts these elements into a solid form, are not sufficiently known ; but if the end could be accomplished by mechanical force, it is almost certain that the power necessary to produce it would at least equal that which was generated by the original combustion. Man, therefore, does not create power ; but, availing himself of his knowledge of nature's mysteries, he applies his talents to diverting a small and limited portion of her energies to his own wants: and, whether he employs the regulated action of steam, or the more rapid and tremendous efforts of gunpowder, he it only producing on a small scale compositions and decompositions which nature is incessantly at work in reversing, for the restoration of that equilibrium which we cannot doubt is constantly maintained throughout even the remotest limits of our system."

Of Time gained, or saved by contrivance, we have this familiar illustration from the printing press:—

" In the old method of inking types, by large hemispherical

balls stuffed and covered with leather, [sheep-skin] the printer, after taking a small portion of ink from the ink-block, was continually rolling them in various directions against each other, in order that a thin layer of ink might be uniformly spread over their surface. This he again transferred to the type by a kind of rolling action. In such a process, even admitting considerable skill in the operator, it could not fail to happen that a large quantity of ink should get near the edges of the balls, which not being transferred to the type became hard and useless, and was taken off in the form of a thick black crust. Another inconvenience also arose,—the quantity of ink spread on the block not being regulated by measure, and the number and direction of the transits of the inking-balls over each other depending on the will of the operator, and being irregular, it was impossible to place on the type a uniform layer of ink, of exactly the quantity sufficient for the impression. The introduction of cylindrical rollers of an elastic substance, formed by the mixture of glue and treacle, superseded the inking-balls, and produced considerable saving in the consumption of ink; but the most perfect economy was only to be produced by mechanism. When printing-presses moved by the power of steam, were introduced, the action of these rollers was found well adapted to the performance of the machine; and a reservoir of ink was formed, from which one roller regularly abstracted a small quantity at each impression. From three to five other rollers spread this portion uniformly over a slab (by most ingenious contrivances varied in almost each kind of press,) and another travelling roller, having fed itself on the slab, passed and repassed over the type just before it gave the impression to the paper."

Every one connected with the construction of machinery, or with manufactures and trade, should read this laborious digest. The moral consequences of the manufacturing system lie out of the author's road. He is, moreover, an economist out and out, a Pharisee of the Pharisees, save in the Truck system, which we are glad to find Mr. Babbage reprobates. When we can obtain a Government of angels, or of angel-men, to apply the strict principles of political economy, for the good of the whole human race, we shall all be economists as rigid. Till then the hearts of many will misgive and shrink from some of the palpable consequences of the system, *well as it works* in theory and for some in practice.

EMIGRANT BOOKS.—STATISTICAL SKETCH OF UPPER CANADA. BY A BACKWOODSMAN.—CANADAS. BY A. PICKEN.

BOTH works may be read with advantage by persons meditating emigration. The latter work is a compilation from many late volumes, with useful tables, maps, &c., &c. The author of the first work broaches as original the plan of what he calls *Infant Emigration*, which is only a revival of *indenting* or *selling* children to the colonies. The idea will be eagerly grasped at by churchwardens in England; and revolting as the plan is, infant bond-servants may be as comfortably placed in the Canadas, as are parish apprentices at home, and have besides a speedier prospect of emancipation; as they could, and no doubt would, if they found it convenient, decamp across the frontier as soon as their legs would bear them. This writer gives encouragement to weavers and persons of trades for which there is no demand, to emigrate; by the assurance that they may make very good American farmers though not trained to agricultural labour. Those linen weavers who are accustomed to throw the shuttle with both hands, make capital wood-choppers, as they can wield the axe with either hand, to the help of both. Emigrants whose object is New South Wales or Van Diemen's Land, may peruse with benefit "AUTHENTIC INFORMATION about *New South Wales*, by Mr. Busby;" and also the "*Van Diemen's Land Almanack*," which gives a good and recent history of the colony.

EXCURSIONS IN INDIA. BY CAPTAIN SKINNER.

A PLEASANT, companionable book, into which, if found lying in an inn window, or on a steam-boat table, we may dip at random, and be sure to bring up such lively passages as this, describing a ride through the streets of Delhi:—

" Riding through the town requires much management, and some skill. It is necessary to shout, push, and kick the whole way to warn the multitude to get out of the road. Occasionally you have to squeeze past a string of loaded camels, or start away from a train of elephants; and if your horse be frightened at these last animals, which is frequently the case, it needs some ingenuity to avoid being plunged into the caldrons which simmer on each side of the way, in front of the cooks' shops. The fear is mutual very often; and the elephants, in attempting to escape from the approach of a horseman, may well be supposed to throw the whole street into a fine confusion. In one of my strolls through the city on horseback, I was nearly swept away by a species of simoom, caused by the progress, through the dusty town, of some important personage travelling in state.

" When overtaken by such a storm, it is a long time before you can recover either your sight or position. The idle cause of all this tumult was reposing quietly in a shining, yellow palanquin, tricked out with gilt moulding in every possible direction. He was preceded by a large retinue of strange-looking beings, mounted on horses and dromedaries and dressed in the most fantastic style. The animals were covered with scarlet bousings, bound by gold lace, their bridles studded with shells; round their necks were collars of gold or silver, with little drops hanging to them, that kept time most admirably with their jogging measure. The camels were likewise adorned with bells."

The source of the Ganges, the river of Indian worship, was thus first seen by the retinue of Captain Skinner.

" After emerging from a grove of reeds, (many of them broken and strewed on the ground, which gave a variety to the cause of our slipping, though the effect was much the same,) we found ourselves on the point of a projecting crag that ' beetled o'er its base,' and gave us the first glimpse of the Ganges, which was rapid and broad, but dark and sandy as it flows through the plains. If the sound of *Jumsoons* excited my followers to a high pitch, at merely the commencement of their pilgrimage, how much more so would the thrice welcome shout of *Gunga Jee!* when they had at length gained it, after a painful journey of more than thirty days. *Gunga Jee!* was the universal cry for some minutes; and *Gunga Jee!* was echoed by the woods and hills around, till it reached the ears of the slowest of my stragglers, when, calling upon its name long before they saw it, they endeavoured to rush forward, and enjoy the sight they had been so long toiling to obtain. The Hindoos salaam'd and muttered its name over and over again; and even the unbending Mahometan seemed in some way softened by the scene. I sat on one side, to allow full scope to their feelings, affected by the beauty of the picture as much as they were by the veneration of the river."

MIRABEAU'S LETTERS FROM ENGLAND.

OF the authenticity of these letters, written in the scape-grace days of Mirabeau, there are some doubts. The name of their author is the chief attraction, and the introduction of such names as Romilly, then a young barrister, and Chatham in the noon of his fame. Many of the passages in these letters do look like after thoughts, though the probability is in favour of their authenticity.

CHARACTERISTICS OF WOMEN. BY MRS. JAMIESON.

THE book for drawing-room tables in the autumn of 1832. It is elegantly embellished. The sketches of Shakspeare's heroines, Rosalind, Beatrice, Imogene, and Miranda are written with a fine feeling of the beautiful in their characters. Thus of Rosalind:—

"Everything about Rosalind breathes of youth's prime. She is fresh as the morning, sweet as the dew-awakened blossoms, and light as the breeze that plays among them. She is as witty, as voluble, as sprightly as Beatrice: but in a style altogether distinct. In both, the wit is equally unconscious; but in Beatrice it plays about us like the lightning, dazzling, but also alarming; while the wit of Rosalind bubbles up and sparkles like the living fountain refreshing all around. Her volubility is like the bird's song; it is the outpouring of a heart filled to overflowing with life, love, and joy, and all sweet and affectionate impulses. She has as much tenderness as mirth, and in her most petulant raillery there is a touch of softness— 'By this hand it will not hurt a fly!'"

LETTERS ON NATURAL MAGIC. BY SIR D. BREWSTER,

Is a book to delight boys, and a guide to juvenile experiments. It contains explanations of the arts of necromancy, phantasmagoria, mysterious writings on the wall, &c., &c., &c., spectral illusions, echoes, ventriloquism, aerial spectres, jugglers' tricks, the Invisible girl, Automaton chess-player, and, in brief, many curious things put together in a long course of peculiar reading. As a specimen of the work we select *The Art of Breathing Fire*, an art which is still practised to the wonderment of many. This is an ancient feat, but the old method is not exactly known. Now, according to Sir David—

"This art is performed more simply by the modern juggler. Having rolled together some flax or hemp, so as to form a ball the size of a walnut, he sets it on fire, and allows it to burn till it is nearly consumed: he then rolls round it while burning some additional flax, and by these means the fire may be retained in it for a considerable time. At the commencement of his exhibition he introduces the ball into his mouth, and while he breathes through it the fire is revived, and a number of burning sparks are projected from his mouth. These sparks are too feeble to do any harm, provided he inhales the air through his nostrils."

This volume is to be among the last of *Murray's Family Library*, which has it seems turned out a bad concern. Of THE EDINBURGH CABINET LIBRARY, The 3d volume of *the History of India* has appeared, and completes this useful portion of a well-conducted series.

WILDERSPIN ON INFANT TUITION

Is merely mentioned here as a work recently published. The subject of Infant Education deserves an article to itself, of which this book must be the text.

In Poetry there are several small volumes lately published. The 8th volume of the cheap edition of Byron contains the whole of Childe Harold, with a few additional vituperative stanzas, which neither add to the beauty of the poem, nor do any honour to the memory of the poet.

THE WESTERN GARLAND

Is a Glasgow publication: "Original melodies;"—The words are by Mr. Atkinson, the most versatile and copious of western writers. Beautiful, or at least, fresh young lips may be singing at this hour under the shadow of the Argyleshire hills, or on the shores of Bute, the sweet little song, "One hour with thee," of which this is a stanza:—

O! fleetly sped my gallant Grey
Like wild bird o'er the hill;
Full well it knew the love-ward way,
And guessed its master's will!
With swifter pace my wishings flew,
My heart leaped yet more free;
It well the priceless value knew
Of one fond hour with thee.

"Barry Cornwall's Songs" will not add much to his fame as a poet, though some of them are rather pretty. He is becoming *Radical*, even imitative, at humble distance, of the author of Corn-Law Rhymes. The *Leveller* is but one production of this sort, which we can give out of many.

THE LEVELLER.

The King he reigns on a throne of gold,
 Fenced round by his "power divine;"
The Baron he sits in his castle old,
 Drinking his ripe red wine:
But below, below, in his ragged coat,
 The beggar he tuneth a hungry note,
And the spinner is bound to his weary thread,
And the debtor lies down with an aching head.

 So the world goes!
 So the stream flows!
 Yet there is a fellow whom nobody knows,
 Who maketh all free
 On land and sea,
 And forceth the rich like the poor to flee!

The lady lies down in her warm white lawn,
 And dreams of her pearled pride;
The milk-maid sings, to the wild-eyed dawn,
 Sad songs on the cold hill side:
And the Saint he leaves (while he prattles of faith)
Good deeds to the Sinner, as scandal saith,
And the scholar he bows to the face of brass,
And the wise man he worships a golden ass!
 So the world goes, &c.

"*The Blue Bag*" is a collection of political parodies on popular songs, which without much point are amusing enough.—Croker-go-bragh sets out with—

To London there came a poor lawyer from Erin,
Ah! heavy the mud on his brogues old and thin,
Through his threadbare green coat, his red elbows were peering,
Nor had he a stocking to cover his shin.

NEW NOVELS.

There is generally a second crop of novels about this season, to appear spick and span new at the watering places; two belong to Scotland, "The *Highland Smuggler*," by Mr. Fraser, author of Kuzzilbash, which we have not yet read but see noticed with approbation in the reviews: and "*Clarenswold*, or Tales of the North," a neat volume in its outward shew, and of fair promise otherwise, if the author be, as we understand, still very young.

THE HEIDENMAUER, by the American author of the Spy, Pioneers, Pilot, &c. &c. will prove a disappointment and a provocation to many. It is a romantic story, laid in Germany. Mr. Cooper must keep to Sea, or to his own side of the Atlantic, and to his own *line*, in which he is unapproachable.

CONTARINI FLEMING, by the author of Vivian Grey, or at least universally attributed to that gentleman, has been bandied about among the weekly critics like a shuttle-cock the excessive praise of the one, drawing forth the sneers of another; the book exhibits some power, alloyed with much absurdity, and wilful perversion, both of taste and judgment.—Enough, and too much of books merely to be *glanced at* if they fall in one's way.

EARLE'S RESIDENCE IN NEW ZEALAND will be perused with interest by those who already know something of the character of the manly and energetic race depicted

Mr. Earle's anticipations of the rapid civilization of the New Zealanders appears sanguine to us who cannot see with his eyes. It would, however, be as presumptuous in us to pronounce them wholly unfounded, as it is rash in him, to assert that the labours of the Missionaries in New Zealand have been worse than useless. If the constant practice of cannibalism among the New Zealanders had not been previously sufficiently established, Mr. Earle's direct testimony might settle the point; to satisfy his curiosity he visited a chief while the process of baking a young runaway female slave was going on.

" Atoi received us in his usual manner; and his handsome open countenance could not be imagined to belong to so savage a monster as he proved himself to be. I shuddered at beholding the unusual quantity of potatoes his slaves were preparing to eat with this infernal banquet. We talked coolly with him on the subject; for as we could not prevent what had taken place, we were resolved to learn, if possible, the whole particulars. Atoi at first tried to make us believe he knew nothing about it, and that it was only a meal for his slaves; but we had ascertained it was for himself and his favourite companions. After various endeavours to conceal the fact, Atoi frankly owned that he was only waiting till the cooking was completed to partake of it. He added, that, knowing the horror we Europeans held these feasts in, the natives are always most anxious to conceal them from us, and he was very angry that it had come to our knowledge; but, as he had acknowledged the fact, he had no objection to talk about it. He told us that human flesh required a greater number of hours to cook than any other; that if not done enough, it was very tough, but when sufficiently cooked it was as tender as paper. He held in his hand a piece of paper which he tore in illustration of his remark. He said the flesh then preparing would not be ready till next morning; but one of his sisters whispered in my ear, that her brother was deceiving us, as they intended feasting at sunset.

We inquired why and how he had murdered the poor girl. He replied, that running away from him to her own relations was her only crime. He then took us outside his village, and showed us the post to which she had been tied, and laughed to think how he had cheated her—" For," said he, " I told her I only intended to give her a flogging; but I fired, and shot her through the heart!" My blood ran cold at this relation, and I looked with feelings of horror at the savage while he related it. Shall I be credited when I again affirm, that he was not only a handsome young man, but mild and genteel in his demeanour? He was a man we had admitted to our table, and was a general favourite with us all; and the poor victim to his bloody cruelty was a pretty girl of about sixteen years of age!"

This is sorry progress in civilization.

HISTORY OF THE HIGHLANDS AND CLANS.

This is the first approach that has been made to anything like a regular history of that singular portion of the Scottish people, which has, for a half century, fixed the attention of the rest of Europe. The History of the Clans could not have fallen into better hands than those of Dr. Browne, from private and personal considerations even more than ability and literary qualification. His former writings evinced that warm and enthusiastic feeling towards the Highlanders, and intimate acquaintance with their characteristic peculiarities, without which other requisites would have been comparatively a dead letter. Part I., which appears in a shape worthy of the permanent place to which the work is entitled in Scotchmen's libraries, is devoted to the early history, antiquities, manners, language, poetry and music of the *Gael*, and to their wars with the Danes. It gets over a great deal of curious ground, and clears the way for the prowess and achievements of particular Clans, which will prove yet more interesting.

CHAUNTS OF THE PEOPLE.

As we wish our pages to reflect as closely as possible the image of the time, we cannot pass over without notice what is called the mob poetry, when it appears in the vigorous and definite shape of these *Chaunts*. Barry Cornwall's songs reflect a softened resemblance of " the spirit bitterer than aught in books," but it is merely the shadow of the stern and rugged substance which we find here. Who is the author of these effusions composed evidently with purpose prepense?

THE POOR MAN'S SONG.

I'll sing a song, and such a song
  As men will weep to hear—
A sorrowing song, of right and wrong,
  So brethren, lend an ear.

God said to man, " This pleasant land
  I make it wholly thine."
I look and say on this sad day,
  There's not one furrow mine.

God said to man, " Increase, enjoy,
  Build, till, and sow your seed ;"
But through the land the Lord gave me,
  My children beg their bread.

The north belongs unto the crown,
  The south to the divine ;
And east and west Wealth holds her hands,
  And says the rest is mine.

God said to man, " All winged fowl,
  The finned fish of the flood,
The heathcock on his desert hills,
  The wild deer of the wood—

Take them and live." The strong man came,
  As came the fiend of yore
To Paradise—put forth his hand,
  And they are mine no more.

I saw the rulers of the land,
  In chariots bright with gold
Roll on—I gazed my babes and I,
  In hunger and in cold.

I saw a prelate, sleek and proud,
  Drawn by four chargers, pass :
How much he seemed like Jesus meek,
  When he rode on an ass!

A trinket of a Lord swept by
  With all his rich array,
And waved me off, my babes and I,
  As things of coarser clay.

There followed close a hideous throng
  Of pert and pensioned things—
Muck-worms, for whom our sweat and blood
  Must furnish gilded wings.

I will not tell you what I thought,
  Nor for my burning looks
Find words ; but they were bitterer far
  Than aught that's writ in books.

I'll set my right foot to a stone,
  And 'gainst a rock my back—
Stretch thus my arm, and sternly say,
  " Give me my birthright back."

WHISTLEBINKIE

We must not forget ; a snug little collection of capital songs just published in Glasgow, for the daily and hourly consumption of a merry or a pensive public. But we defer individual merits for the present.

DRINKING.—Lime applied to trees makes them put forth leaves, and flourish, and produce food early ; but then it kills them! Wine cheers and stimulates men, and makes them put forth flowers of wit; but then there is no doubt it shortens life.

AMERICAN MODES OF THINKING.
FROM A RAMBLE THROUGH THE UNITED STATES.
BY S. A. FERRALL. JUST PUBLISHED.

"Near Mountpleasant, I stopped to dine at the house of a Dutchman by descent. After dinner, the party adjourned, as is customary, to the bar-room, where divers political and polemical topics were canvassed with the usual national warmth. An account of his late Majesty's death was inserted in a Philadelphia paper, and happened to be noticed by one of the politicians present, when the landlord asked me how we elected our king in England. I replied that he was not elected, but that he became king by birthright, &c. A Kentuckian observed, placing his leg on the back of the next chair, " That's a kind of unnatural." An Indianian said, " I don't believe in that system myself." A third—" Do you mean to tell me, that because the last king was a smart man, and knew his duty, that his son or his brother should be a smart man, and fit for the situation?" I explained that we had a premier, minister, &c.; when the last gentlemen replied, " Then you pay half-a-dozen men to do one man's business. Yes, yes, that may do for Englishmen very well! but I guess it would not go down here: no, no, Americans are a little more enlightened than to stand that kind of wiggery." During this conversation a person had stepped into the room, and had taken his seat in silence. I was about to reply to the last observations of my antagonist, when this gentleman opened out with " Yes! that may do for Englishmen very well." He was an Englishman, I knew at once by his accent, and I verily believe, the identical radical who set the village of Bracebridge by the ears, and pitched the villagers to the devil, on seeing them grin through a horse-collar, when they should have been calculating the interest of the national debt, or conning over the list of sinecure placemen. He held in his hand, instead of *Cobbett's Register*, the *Greenville Republican*: he had substituted for his short-sleeved coat " a round-about;" he seemed to have put on flesh, and looked somewhat more contented. " Yes, yes," he says " that may do for Englishmen very well, but it won't do here. Here we make our own laws, and we keep them too. It may do for Englishmen very well, to have *the liberty* of paying taxes for the support of the nobility—to have *the liberty* of being incarcerated in a jail for shooting the wild animals of the country—to have *the liberty* of being seized by a press-gang, torn away from their wives and families, and flogged at the discretion of my Lord Tom, Dick, or Harry's bastard." At this the Kentuckian gnashed his teeth, and instinctively grasped his hunting-knife; an old Indian doctor, who was squatting in one corner of the room, said, slowly and emphatically, as his eyes glared, his nostrils dilated, and his lip curled with contempt, " The Englishman is a dog;" while a Georgian slave, who stood behind his master's chair, grinned and chuckled with delight, as he said, " Poor Englishman, him meaner man den black nigger." " To have," continued the Englishman, " *the liberty* of being transported for seven years for being caught learning the use of the sword or the musket. To have the tenth lamb, and the tenth sheaf seized, or the blanket torn from off his bed, to pay a bloated, a plethoric bishop or parson; to be kicked and cuffed about by a parcel of ' Bourbon *gendarmerie*'—Liberty!—why hell sweat." Here I slipped out at the side door into the water-melon patch. As I receded, I heard the whole party burst out into an obstreperous fit of laughter. A few broken sentences from the Kentuckian and the radical reached my ear, such as " backed out"—" damned aristocratic." I returned in about half an hour to pay my bill, when I could observe one or two of those doughty politicians who remained, leering at me most significantly. However, I—" smiled and said nothing."

" There are two things eminently remarkable in America; the one is, that every American, from the highest to the lowest, thinks the Republican form of government *the best*; and the other, that the seditious and rebellious of all countries become there the most peaceable and contented citizens."

HORSE SELLING.

A SCENE AT TATTERSALL'S.—" Gentlemen, what can you hesitate about? Only look at her! She is one of the most beautiful creatures that I have ever had the honour of submitting to your notice! So gentle in her paces—indeed so safe a goer that a child might ride her. Her pedigree is excellent —she is thorough-bred from her ear to her hoof; and the Heralds College could not produce a more sound and satisfactory one. She comes from a good house, I pledge my word. Gentlemen. My Lord Duke, will you allow me to say L.250 for your Grace? She will, notwithstanding the excellence of your Grace's stud, be an ornament to it. She is a picture—complete to a shade; in fact, I could gaze upon her for ever, and always be struck with some new beauty she possesses. Thank you, my Lord Duke, I was certain your Grace would not let such an opportunity pass. There is not a horse-dealer in the kingdom who can show such a fine creature! She is above competition—I may say she is matchless! The Regent's Park might be betted to a mole-hill with safety that she has no paragon. Sir Henry, let me call your attention to Cleopatra! She is like her namesake in the olden times—but beautiful without paint? She is pure Nature, and no vice! Her action, Sir Henry—yes, her action—I could dilate upon it for a quarter of an hour—but *puffing* is out of the question—you shall judge for yourself. Run her down, John—The Graces, I am sure, *Sir Harry*, were they to behold her movements, would be out of temper with her captivating excellence! *Taglioni*, I must admit, can perform wonders with her pretty feet; but *Cleopatra*, my Lord Duke, can *distance* the whole of them put together; and positively leave the Opera House, with all its talent, in the back ground. In fact, I am deficient in words to display her immense capabilities—L.300 *Going!*—*Going!* L.310. Thank you, my Lord Duke, she must be yours. For the last time, going at L.310; but I will do the handsome thing, I will allow you five minutes to compose your mind.—I am well aware that such unparalleled beauty is very dazzling—therefore, before you lose sight of this handsome creature, I do impress upon you to remember that the opportunity once lost—L.320; Sir Harry, I am obliged to you—the world has always acknowledged you as a man of great taste in matters of this kind; and, without flattery, you have never shown it more than in the present instance—according to the poet—" Beauty unadorned is adorned the most!" *Going!*—Cleopatra, my Lord Duke, will be in other hands if your Grace does not make up your mind in your usual princely style of doing things—a good bidding will make Cleopatra your own for ever; therefore, now's the time to put on the *distancing* power, and your Grace will win the race in a canter! L.340. My Lord Duke, I can only express my gratitude to say, that you have done me honour—*Going!* —*going!*—in fact, gentlemen, I am like an artist in this case, I do not like to leave such a delightful picture, and I could *dwell* upon the qualities of Cleopatra to the echo that applauds again —but most certainly I have given you all a fair chance—Cleopatra is on the go—are you all silent?—*going* for L.340 after all. What is that sum for one of the greatest English beauties ever submitted to the inspection of the public! L.350—thank you, Sir Charles—worth your money at any price. I have witnessed your notice of Cleopatra for some time past—she will bear looking at again and again! Charming Cleopatra! I am glad to see she has so many suitors for her *hand*—I beg pardon, gentlemen—a slip will happen to the best of us—her *feet*, I should have said, but, nevertheless, I am happy to see she has a host of admirers. I cannot *bid* myself, or else I would " make play," and Cleopatra should become a noble prize. L.370 Bravo! my Lord Duke! for L.370 positively, yes positively, 'pon my honour, positively the last time—or else the beautiful Cleopatra goes into the *keeping* of my Lord Duke. You are sure, gentlemen, that you have all done? Don't blame me, blame yourselves! Going, *once!* Going, *twice!* Going, *three times!* [*The auctioneer, after a long pause, and numerous flourishes with his hammer*, in hopes to obtain another bidding, but the 'cock would not fight,' exclaimed] Gone!!! Cleopatra belongs to the Duke.—*Egan's Book of Sports.*

NATIONAL CHARACTER.—The Regent Duke of Orleans once asked a stranger, what were the different characters and distinctions of the various nations in Europe. " The only manner in which I can answer your Royal Highness is, to repeat to you the first questions which are asked among the several nations in regard to a stranger who comes among them. In Spain, they ask, is he a nobleman of the first rank? In Germany, can he be admitted into the Chapters? In France, is he in favour at courts? In Holland how much money has he? And in England, who is that man?

ELEMENTS OF THOUGHT.

POWER OF BEING USEFUL TO MANKIND.

For this neither splendid talents, nor profound learning, nor great wealth, are required. A well-informed man of good sense, filled with the resolution to obtain for the great body of his fellow-creatures that high improvement, which both their understandings and their morals are, by nature, fitted to receive, may labour in this good work with the certainty of success, if he have only that blessing of leisure, for the sake of which riches are chiefly to be coveted. Such a one, however averse by taste or habit, to the turmoil of public affairs, or the more ordinary strifes of the world, may in all quiet and innocence, enjoy the noblest gratification of which the most aspiring nature is susceptible; he may influence by his single exertions the character and fortunes of a whole generation, and thus wield a power to be envied even by vulgar ambition, for the extent of its dominion—to be cherished by virtue itself for the unalloyed blessings it bestows.—*Brougham.*

SYMPATHY—FORBEARANCE.

The wisest and best men have always been the most indulgent. It has been finely said, "that indulgence is a justice which frail humanity has a right to expect from wisdom. Nothing has a greater tendency to dispose us to indulgence, to close our hearts against hatred, and to open them to the principles of a humane and mild morality, than a profound knowledge of the human heart. In this view, Wordsworth's rambling poem of *Peter Bell* is worth a volume of ethics. The wisest men have, accordingly always been the most indulgent. It was the saying of Plato, "Live with your inferiors and domestics, as with unfortunate friends." "Must I always," says an Indian philosopher, "hear the rich crying out, 'Lord destroy all who take from us the least part of our possessions;' while the poor man, with a plaintive voice and eyes lifted up to Heaven, cries, 'Lord! give me a small part of the goods dealt out in profusion to the rich;' if others less fortunate deprive me of a portion, instead of imprecating Thy vengeance, I shall consider these thefts in the same manner as in seed time we see the doves ranging over the fields in quest of their food."

LONDON—FROM ST. PAUL'S.

Few objects are so sublime—if by sublimity we understand that which completely fills the imagination, to the utmost measure of its powers—as the view of a huge city thus seen at once. It was a sight which awed me and made me melancholy. I was looking down upon the habitations of a million of human beings; upon the single spot whereon were crowded together more wealth, more splendour, more ingenuity, more wordly wisdom, and, alas! more worldly blindness, poverty, depravity, dishonesty, and wretchedness than upon any other spot in the whole habitable earth!—*Southey.*

UNIVERSITIES AND SCHOOLS.

The institutions of men grow old, like men themselves, and, like women, they are always the last to perceive their own decay. When Universities were the only schools of learning, they were of great and important utility; as soon as there were others, they ceased to be the best, because their forms were prescribed, and they could adopt no improvement till long after it was generally acknowledged.—*Ibid.*

DISHONEST WEALTH.

It is not wealth that is the evil; it is the habit of dishonesty that wealth has got into. The moment a man gets wealth, he begins to cast about for the means of getting more by the plunder of his neighbours; and the government of the country, from the memory of living men to the late accession of the Whig and Radical dynasty, has been one great joint-stock committee of management, for the organization of the plans of individuals upon this point into an operative whole. Once or oftener has the resistance to it been put down, by the skill of the plunderers in confounding the attack on unjust wealth with attacks on wealth in the abstract, and the awkwardness of the assailants in leaving pegs for the fallacy to hang upon. But honest men, as well as the devil, may grow wiser than of yore; and on no point have they attained more light, than on the distinction between that kind of wealth and property which society is united to defend, and that which it is united to pull down.—*Westminster Review.*

MOTIVES TO MUTUAL CHARITY.

If three children, born four months ago, were to be brought up in separate apartments in a hermitage, entirely shut out from all the world and taught nothing, only fed and kept clean by a dumb man, dressed unlike any creature on the earth,—let them be brought out and examined at 21 years of age—each of them would have a yelp, a groan, or sigh, peculiar to man—none of them could speak, or understand any thing—they would not know a man, beast, bird, plant or tree—they would have no idea of God, angels, devils, heaven, or hell—they would not even *know that they themselves must die;* such is the state of untaught man! Again,—If three children were born, four months ago, of Protestant parents—one by the wife of an Aristocrat; one by the wife of a beggar; one by the wife of a tradesman,—send the first to be brought up and educated by a Mahometan, in Turkey; the second to be brought up and educated by a Roman Catholic, in Spain; the third to be brought up and educated by a Jew, in Amsterdam. Let these meet in London when they are 21 years of age. The Aristocrat's son will be a Mahometan; the beggar's son a Roman Catholic; the tradesman's son a Jew. Now mark, all these were born of Christian parents, professing the Protestant religion; and if they had been brought up and educated by their parents, they would all have been Protestant Christians instead of a Mahometan, a Roman Catholic, and a Jew. No man that ever reasoned will believe, that any responsibility can possibly attach to the belief or religion of any of these three young men; and, if so, no reasonable being can believe that any responsibility can attach to himself for his belief, whether it be true or false: therefore, there neither can be merit or demerit for any man's religious belief. Now, it is evident from this, that every sect should have kind feelings for each other, and should esteem each other, as if they all believed alike. Each man has only to say to himself, "If I had been brought up and educated as my friend has been, who professes a religion different from mine, I should believe as he now does." These facts of nature must speak conviction to every unprejudiced mind: by them all the sects in the world may learn how to be undeceived, and to "love one another."

ARTIFICIAL MAN.

The following passage has been pronounced by Wordsworth, the poet, "one of the finest in the English language." It forms a note to the Poem of the Hurricane. Milton might have owned it with pride. "A man is supposed to improve by going out into the *world*, by visiting London: *Artificial man* does; he extends with his sphere; but, alas! the sphere is microscopic; it is formed of minutiæ, and he surrenders his genuine vision to the artist in order to embrace it in his ken. His bodily senses grow acute even to barren and inhuman pruriency, while his mental become proportionally obtuse. The reverse is the Man of Mind: he who is placed in the sphere of Nature and of God might be a mock at Tattersall's and Brooke's, and a sneer at St. James's; he would certainly be swallowed alive by the first *Pizarro* that crossed him:— but when he walks along the River of Amazons; when he rests his eye on the unrivalled Andes; when he measures the long and watered Savannah; or contemplates from a sudden promontory the distant, vast, Pacific; and feels himself a free man in this vast theatre, and commanding each ready-produced fruit of this wilderness, and each progeny of this stream, his exaltation is not less than imperial. He is as gentle too as he is great; his emotions of tenderness keep pace with his elevation of sentiment; for he says these were made by a good Being, who unsought by me, placed me here to enjoy them. He becomes at once a child and a king. His mind is in himself; from hence he argues, and from hence he acts; and he argues unerringly, and acts magisterially; his mind in himself is also in his God, and therefore he loves, and therefore he soars.

THE STORY TELLER.

ELIZABETH VILLIERS.
A TALE FOR THE YOUNG.

My father is the curate of a village church, about five miles from Amwell. I was born in the parsonage house, which joins the church-yard. The first thing I can remember was my father teaching me the alphabet from the letters on a tombstone that stood at the head of my mother's grave. I used to tap at my father's study-door: I think I now hear him say, "Who is there? What do you want, little girl?" "Go and see mamma. Go and learn pretty letters." Many times in the day would my father lay aside his books and his papers to lead me to this spot, and make me point to the letters, and then set me to spell syllables and words. In this manner the epitaph on my mother's tomb being my primer and spelling-book, I learned to read.

I was one day sitting on a step placed across the church-yard stile, when a gentleman passing by, heard me distinctly repeat the letters which formed my mother's name, and then say, *Elizabeth Villiers*, with a firm tone, as if I had performed some great matter. This gentleman was my uncle James, my mother's brother: he was a lieutenant in the navy, and had left England a few weeks after the marriage of my father and mother, and now returned home from a long sea-voyage, he was coming to visit my mother; no tidings of her decease having reached him, though she had been dead more than a twelvemonth.

When my uncle saw me sitting on the stile, and heard me pronounce my mother's name, he looked earnestly in my face, and began to fancy a resemblance to his sister, and to think I might be her child. I was too intent on my employment to observe him, and went spelling on. "Who has taught you to spell so prettily, my little maid?" said my uncle. "Mamma," I replied; for I had an idea that the words on the tomb-stone were somehow a part of mamma, and that she had taught me. "And who is mamma?" asked my uncle. "Elizabeth Villiers," I replied; and then my uncle called me his dear little niece, and said he would go with me to mamma; he took hold of my hand, intending to lead me home, delighted that he had found out who I was, because he imagined it would be such a pleasant surprise to his sister to see her little daughter bringing home her long lost sailor uncle.

I agreed to take him to mamma, but we had a dispute about the way thither. My uncle was for going along the road which led directly up to our house: I pointed to the church-yard, and said, that was the way to mamma. Though impatient of any delay, he was not willing to contest the point with his new relation, therefore he lifted me over the stile, and was then going to take me along the path to a gate he knew was at the end of our garden; but no, I would not go that way neither; letting go his hand, I said, "You do not know the way; I will shew you;" and making what haste I could among the long grass and thistles, and jumping over the low graves, he said, as he followed what he called my *wayward steps* "What a positive soul this little niece of mine is! I knew the way to your mother's house before you were born, child." At last I stopped at my mother's grave, and pointing to the tombstone said, "Here is mamma!" in a voice of exultation, as if I had now convinced him that I knew the way best; I looked up in his face to see him acknowledge his mistake; but, oh! what a face of sorrow did I see! I was so frightened, that I have but an imperfect recollection of what followed. I remember I pulled his coat, and cried, "Sir, sir!" and tried to move him. I knew not what to do; my mind was in a strange confusion; I thought I had done something wrong, in bringing the gentleman to mamma to make him cry so sadly; but what it was I could not tell. This grave had always been a scene of delight to me. In the house my father would often be weary of my prattle, and send me from him; but here he was all my own. I might say anything, and be as frolicksome as I pleased here; all was cheerfulness and good humour in our visits to mamma, as we called it. My father would tell me how quietly mamma slept there, and that he and his little Betsy would one day sleep beside mamma in that grave; and when I went to my bed, as I laid my little head on the pillow, I used to wish I was sleeping in the grave with my papa and mamma; and in my childish dreams I used to fancy myself there; and it was a place within the ground, all smooth, and soft, and green. I never made out any figure of mamma, but still it was the tombstone, and papa, and the smooth green grass, and my head resting upon the elbow of my father.

How long my uncle remained in this agony of grief I know not; to me it seemed a very long time. At last he took me in his arms, and held me so tight that I began to cry, and ran home to my father, and told him that a gentleman was crying about mamma's pretty letters.

No doubt it was a very affecting meeting between my father and my uncle. I remember that it was the very first day I ever saw my father weep; that I was in sad trouble, and went into the kitchen, and told Susan, our servant, that papa was crying; and she wanted to keep me with her, that I might not disturb the conversation; but I would go back to the parlour to *poor papa*, and I went in softly, and crept between my father's knees. My uncle offered to take me in his arms, but I turned sullenly from him, and clung closer to my father, having conceived a dislike to my uncle, because he made my father cry.

Now I first learned that my mother's death was a heavy affliction; for I heard my father tell a melancholy story of her long illness, her death, and what he had suffered from her loss. My uncle said, what a sad thing it was for my father to be left with such a young child; but my father replied, his little Betsy was all his comfort, and that, but for me, he should have died with grief. How I could be any comfort to my father struck me with wonder. I knew I was pleased when he played and talked with me; but I thought that was all goodness and favour done to me, and I had no notion how I could make any part of his happiness. The sorrow I now heard he had suffered, was as new and strange to me. I had no idea that he had ever been unhappy; his voice was always kind and cheerful; I had never before seen him weep, or shew any such signs of grief as those in which I used to express my little troubles. My thoughts on these subjects were confused and childish; but from that time I never ceased pondering on the sad story of my dead mamma.

The next day I went by mere habit to the study door, to call papa to the beloved grave; my mind misgave me, and I could not tap at the door. I went backwards and forwards between the kitchen and the study, and what to do with myself I did not know. My uncle met me in the passage, and said, "Betsy, will you come and walk with me in the garden?" This I refused, for this was not what I wanted, but the old amusement of sitting on the grave, and talking to papa. My uncle tried to persuade me, but still I said, "No, no," and ran crying into the kitchen. As he followed me in there, Susan said, "This child is so fretful to-day, I do not know what to do with her." "Aye," said my uncle, "I suppose my poor brother spoils her, having but one." This reflection on my papa made me quite in a little passion of anger, for I had not forgot that with this new uncle, sorrow had first come into our dwelling: I screamed loudly, till my father came out to know what it was all about. He sent my uncle into the parlour, and said, he would manage the little wrangler by himself. When my uncle was gone, I ceased crying; my father forgot to lecture me for my ill humour, or to enquire into the cause, and we were soon seated by the side of the tombstone. No lesson went on that day; no talking of pretty mamma sleeping in the green grave; no jumping from the tombstone to the ground; no merry jokes or pleasant stories. I sat upon my father's knee, looking up in his face, and thinking, "*How sorry papa looks*," till, having been fatigued with crying, and now oppressed with thought, I fell fast asleep.

My uncle soon learned from Susan, that this place was our constant haunt; she told him she did verily believe her master would never get the better of the death of her mistress, while he continued to teach the child to read at the tombstone; for, though it might soothe his grief, it kept it for ever fresh in his memory. The sight of his sister's grave had been such a shock to my uncle, that he readily entered into Susan's apprehensions; and concluding, that if I were set to study by some other means, there would no longer be a pretence for these visits to the grave; away my kind uncle hastened to the nearest market-town to buy me some books.

I heard the conference between my uncle and Susan, and I did not approve of his interfering in our pleasure. I saw him take his hat and walk out, and I secretly hoped he was gone *beyond seas again*, from whence Susan had told me he had come. Where *beyond seas* was I could not tell; but I concluded it was somewhere a great way off. I took my seat on the church-yard stile, and kept looking down the road, and saying, "I hope I shall not see my uncle again. I hope my uncle will not come from *beyond seas* any more:" but I said this very softly, and had a kind of notion that I was in a perverse ill-humoured fit. Here I sat till my uncle returned from the market-town with his new purchases. I saw him come walking very fast with a parcel under his arm. I was very sorry to see him, and I frowned, and tried to look very cross. He untied his parcel, and said, "Betsy, I have brought you a pretty book." I turned my head away, and said, "I don't want a book;" but I could not help peeping again to look at it. In the hurry of opening the parcel, he had scattered all the books upon the ground, and there I saw fine gilt-covers and gay pictures all fluttering about. What a fine sight!—All my resentment vanished, and I held up my face to kiss him, that being my way of thanking my father for any extraordinary favour.

My uncle had brought himself into rather a troublesome office; he had heard me spell so well, that he thought there was nothing to do but to put books into my hand, and I should read; yet, notwithstanding I spelt tolerably well, the letters in my new library were so much smaller than I had been accustomed to, they were like Greek characters to me; I could make nothing at all of them. The honest sailor was not to be discouraged by this difficulty; though unused to play the schoolmaster, he taught me to read the small print, with unwearied diligence and patience; and whenever he saw my father and me look as if we wanted to resume our visits to the grave, he would propose some pleasant ramble; and if my father said it was too far for the child to walk, he would set me on his shoulder, and say, "Then Betsey shall ride;" and in this manner has he carried me many, many miles.

In these pleasant excursions my uncle seldom forgot to make Susan furnish him with a luncheon, which, though it generally happened every day, made a constant surprise to my papa and me, when, seated under some shady tree, he pulled it out of his pocket, and began to distribute his little store; and then I used to peep into the other pocket, to see if there were not some currant wine there, and the little bottle of water for me; if, perchance, the water was forgot, then it made another joke,—that poor Betsy must be forced to drink a little drop of wine. These are childish things to tell of; and, instead of my own silly history, I wish I could remember the entertaining stories my uncle used to relate of his voyages and travels, while we sat under the shady trees, eating our noon-tide meal.

The long visit my uncle made us was such an important event in my life, that I fear I shall tire your patience with talking of him, but when he is gone, the remainder of my story will be but short.

The summer months passed away, but not swiftly;—the pleasant walks, and the charming stories of my uncle's adventures, made them seem like years to me; I remember the approach of winter by the warm great coat he bought for me, and how proud I was when I first put it on; and that he called me Little Red Riding Hood, and bade me beware of wolves; and that I laughed, and said there were no such things now: then he told me how many wolves, and bears, and tigers, and lions, he had met with in uninhabited lands, that were like Robinson Crusoe's island. O these were happy days!

In the winter our walks were shorter and less frequent.

My books were now my chief amusement, though my studies were often interrupted by a game of romps with my uncle, which too often ended in a quarrel, because he played so roughly; yet long before this I dearly loved my uncle, and the improvement I made while he was with us was very great indeed. I could now read very well, and the continual habit of listening to the conversation of my father and my uncle, made me a little woman in understanding; so that my father said to him, "James, you have made my child quite a companionable little being."

My father often left me alone with my uncle; sometimes to write his sermons, sometimes to visit the sick, or give counsel to his poor neighbours; then my uncle used to hold long conversations with me, telling me how I should strive to make my father happy, and endeavour to improve myself when he was gone;—now I began justly to understand why he had taken such pains to keep my father from visiting my mother's grave, that grave which I often stole privately to look at; but now never without awe and reverence; for my uncle used to tell me what an excellent lady my mother was, and I now thought of her as having been a real mamma, which before seemed an ideal something, no way connected with life. And he told me that the ladies from the Manor-house, who sate in the best pew in the church, were not so graceful, and the best women in the village were not so good, as was my sweet mamma; and that if she had lived, I should not have been forced to pick up a little knowledge from him, a rough sailor, or to learn to knit and sew of Susan, but that she would have taught me all lady-like fine works, and delicate behaviour, and perfect manners, and would have selected for me proper books, such as were most fit to instruct my mind, and of which he nothing knew. If ever in my life I shall have any proper sense of what is excellent or becoming in the womanly character, I owe it to these lessons of my rough unpolished uncle; for, in telling me what my mother would have made me, he taught me what to wish to be; and when, soon after my uncle left us, I was introduced to the ladies at the Manor-house, instead of hanging down my head with shame, as I should have done before my uncle came, like a little village rustic, I tried to speak distinctly, with ease, and a modest gentleness, as my uncle had said my mother used to do: instead of hanging down my head abashed, I looked upon them, and thought what a pretty sight a fine lady was, and how well my mother must have appeared, since she was so much more graceful than these high ladies were; and when I heard them compliment my father on the admirable behaviour of his child, and say how well he had brought me up, I thought to myself, "Papa does not much mind my manners, if I am but a good girl; but it was my uncle that taught me to behave like mamma." I cannot now think my uncle was so rough and unpolished as he said he was, for his lessons were so good and so impressive, that I shall never forget them, and I hope they will be of use to me as long as I live: he would explain to me the meaning of all the words he used, such as grace and elegance, modest diffidence and affectation, pointing out instances of what he meant by those words, in the manners of the ladies and their young daughters who came to our church; for besides the ladies of the Manor-house, many of the neighbouring families came to our church, because my father preached so well.

It must have been early in the spring when my uncle went away, for the crocuses were just blown in the garden, and the primroses had begun to peep from under the young budding hedge-rows. I cried as if my heart would break, when I had the last sight of him through a little opening among the trees, as he went down the road. My father accompanied him to the market-town, from whence he was to proceed in the stage-coach to London. How tedious I thought all Susan's endeavours to comfort me were. The stile where I first saw my uncle, came into my mind, and I thought I would go and sit there, and think about that day; but I was no sooner seated there, than I remembered how I had frightened him, by taking him so foolishly to my mother's grave, and then again how naughty I had been when I sate muttering to myself at this same stile, wishing that he, who had gone so far to buy me books, might never come back any more: all my little quarrels with my uncle came into my mind, now that I could never play with him again, and it almost broke my heart. I was forced to run into the house to Susan, for that consolation I had just before despised.

Some days after this, as I was sitting by the fire with my father, after it was dark, and before the candles were lighted, I gave him an account of my troubled conscience at the church-stile, when I remembered how unkind I had been to my uncle when he first came, and how sorry I still was, whenever I thought of the many quarrels I had had with him.

My father smiled, and took hold of my hand, saying, " I will tell you all about this, my little penitent. This is the sort of way in which we all feel, when those we love are taken from us. When our dear friends are with us, we go on enjoying their society, without much thought or consideration of the blessing we are possessed of, nor do we too nicely weigh the measure of our daily actions;—we let them freely share our kind or our discontented moods: and, if any little bickerings disturb our friendship, it does but the more endear us to each other when we are in a happier temper. But these things come over us like grievous faults when the object of our affection is gone for ever. Your dear mamma and I had no quarrels; yet in the first days of my lonely sorrow, how many things came into my mind, that I might have done to have made her happier. It is so with you, my child. You did all a child could do to please your uncle, and dearly did he love you; and these little things which now disturb your tender mind, were remembered with delight by your uncle; he was telling me in our last walk, just perhaps as you were thinking about it with sorrow, of the difficulty he had in getting into your good graces when he first came: he will think of these things with pleasure when he is far away. Put away from you this unfounded grief; only let it be a lesson to you, to be as kind as possible to those you love; and remember, when they are gone from you, you will never think you had been kind enough. Such feelings as you have now described, are the lot of humanity. So you will feel when I am no more, and so will your children feel when you are dead. But your uncle will come back again, Betsy, and we will now think of where we are to get the cage to keep the talking parrot in, he is to bring home; and go and tell Susan to bring the candles, and ask her if the nice cake is almost baked, that she promised to give us for our tea.

[I have heard this beautiful story attributed to *Elia*, to the sister of *Elia*, and also to other female writers.—I cannot say to whom its authorship belongs; nor is this of much consequence.]

ROBERT BURNS.
BORN 1758—DIED 1796.

The leading circumstances of the life of Burns are so familiarly known to every class of readers, that it seems superfluous to go over them, unless in a manner very different from what can be attempted in this limited publication. His own eloquent and energetic letters, wherever his genuine feelings guided his pen, afford the truest insight into his manly, and, in many points, noble character, as a man and a man of genius. His single letter to Dr. Moore is one of the most precious morsels of autobiography that the world possesses. Yet there is pleasure in enumerating the important circumstances of the life of Burns however cursorily, for they are all such as do honour to his memory.

Robert Burns was the eldest son of William Burness or Burns, and Agnes Brown, a couple in almost the lowest class of rural life in what was at that time a poor country. They were one of those excellent and virtuous pairs to whom Scotland owes her high moral and religious character among the nations of Europe. The father was a person of uncommon worth and intelligence, but not one of those whose portion is of this world.*

The school education of Robert Burns was scanty and precarious, though his father made great exertions to educate all the family. At an age when boys more prosperously situated are dividing their time between learning and amusement, Burns was exerting himself above his strength to assist his father and his father's family—at the age of a boy doing a man's work—ill-fed, and probably not very well-clothed; and, worse than all, feeling, with all the torturing sensibility of genius, the miseries arising to himself and those he loved from great poverty and unavoidable misfortune. The pity that is felt for his misfortunes in after-life may be alloyed by blame of his conduct, but our sympathy for Burns and his virtuous relatives, during this season of his early hardships, is an unmingled and a holy feeling. What generous young person ever perused the following passage of Burns' celebrated letter to Dr. Moore, without feeling his heart overflow with tenderness, and his spirit burn with indignation!

" My father was advanced in life when he married; I was the eldest of seven children; and he, worn out by early hardships, was unfit for labour. My father's spirit was soon irritated, but not easily broken. There was a freedom in his lease in two years more; and to weather these we retrenched our expenses. We lived very poorly. I was a dexterous ploughman for my age; and the next eldest to me was a brother (Gilbert), who could drive very well, and help me to thrash the corn. A novel-writer might perhaps have viewed these scenes with some satisfaction; but so did not I. My indignation yet boils at the recollection of the s———l factor's insolent threatening letters, which used to set us all in tears."

In this manner the last years of the boyhood of B rns, and the first of his youthful manhood, were passed, sustained by nothing save the warmth of his affections and the strength of his good spirit. If it were possible for penury, neglect, and misfortune, to depress and to extinguish genius, the mind of Burns must have been early crushed into dulness; but, as is said of another vivifying principle, " Many strong waters cannot quench it, neither can the fire consume it."

At the age of twenty-four, his younger brothers being now able to assist their father in the management of their unlucky farm, Robert tried to establish himself as a flax-dresser in Irvine. This project failed; by an accident his premises took fire; and, in conjunction with his brother Gilbert, he took a small farm. In his letters, Burns often jocularly speaks of his own early imprudence and want of thought, and probably over-rates his faults.

* None of the biographers of Burns mention his mother, save as an excellent wife and mother in her rank of life. I have heard a gentleman—himself a poet and a man of feeling and genius—who had opportunities of seeing this venerable matron in her latter years, say, that the mother was the poetical ancestor of Burns. This old lady certainly possessed something of her son's magical power of eloquence. In describing to my informant the localities of their residence near Alloway Kirk, the birth-place of the poet, she talked quite naturally of their hearing on dark nights " the sea roaring on the shore, and the scaighs yowling," in language more bold and figurative than ever cottage matron used before.—EDITOR.

The grave world appears always to take him at his own light and reckless estimate, and as a much more heedless youth than he really was. It was about the time he occupied this farm, on which he had entered with his brother, that they might provide a home for the rest of the family, now deprived of their father, that Burns formed that connexion with Jean Armour his future wife, which, as a man of good feeling and true honour, does him more credit than may at first sight be imagined. When most anxious to repair the injury in which this young woman had been involved by what was certainly a mutual imprudence, he was prevented from establishing his marriage by those forms which the laws of Scotland sanction, in consequence of the harsh and unjustifiable interference of her relatives, and no doubt in some degree by her own acquiescence. A disgraced daughter appeared better than the wife of an honest man in circumstances so hopeless and desperate as were those of Burns. His anguish on the occasion is expressed with great feeling in one of his poems. Shortly after this it is well known how bright " a change came o'er the spirit of his dream." His poems were published in Edinburgh; after he had come to the metropolis of his country, and met such a reception as no rustic author ever met before, nor ever will again. The tide of prosperity flowed for the time as high as even the hopes of a poet could have risen; and, caressed and applauded by the gay and the great, the fair and the learned, by men of rank and women of elegance, Burns returned home comparatively a rich man, and finally formed that matrimonial connexion which is a trait in his character that none of his biographers have sufficiently appreciated. This step, we are warranted in believing, he at last took from the highest and purest motives. How many prudent mothers, virtuous sisters, and honourable friends—even Miss Chalmers and Mrs. Dunlop—would not only have pardoned his abandonment of his future wife, but even have anxiously desired to see him form a connexion more suitable to a man of his changed prospects, and, above all, to one of his extraordinary endowments. Burns himself ascribes his marriage to necessity; but it was a necessity which ninety-nine out of a hundred young men—" all honourable men," chivalrous spirits—would have thought it quite justifiable to evade. One of the most generous sentiments that any man ever uttered, contains the true reason of this sacrifice to a high-minded integrity. In writing to Mrs. Dunlop, Burns says of the marriage he had formed,—" The happiness of a once much-loved and still loved fellow-creature was in my power, and I durst not trifle with so sacred a rust."

Burns had brought five hundred pounds from Edinburgh, the honourable reward of his abilities. Of this sum he lent or gave two hundred pounds* to his brother Gilbert, for his own use, and the use of the rest of the family. He then settled with his wife at the farm of Ellisland, near Dumfries, and entered the Excise. The rest of his story may be soon told. His conduct was not wise, nor was his life happy. Could we unveil all the struggles of remorse, pride, shame, and despair, in that heart so essentially noble, all the agony, in the latter years of life, of that mind so indefeasibly great, what a lesson it were of wisdom and warning!

> Look on that brow!—the laurel-wreath
> Beam'd on it like a wreath of fire!
> * * * * * *
> Look on that brow!—the lowest slave,
> The veriest wretch of want and care,
> Might shudder at the lot that gave
> *His* genius, glory and despair!

Burns died on the 21st of July, 1796, at his house in Dumfries, in his thirty-eighth year, having, beyond any preceding Scotsman, extended and refined the intellectual pleasures of his country. His fame will ever remain an illustrious portion of her literary honours—his misfortunes an indelible disgrace to some of her institutions.—" A life of literary leisure," he says in one of his letters—and he often repeated the same thing—" with a decent competence, is the summit of my wishes." This he never found; and his notions of competence were certainly far from extravagant.

When the faults of Burns are dwelt upon with a seeming zest even by the warmest admirers of his genius, it ought ever to be kept in remembrance, that the boy who did a man's office for his parents, and the man who divided his little fortune with his brother, lived with his infant family, and with all his imputed reckless improvidence, on an income varying from fifty to eighty pounds a-year, and died without once incurring the burden of pecuniary obligation, or owing any man a shilling! His manly, independent spirit, and almost savage pride, prevented him at least from the debasing consequences which pecuniary involvement entails on the finest minds; from all the pitiful shifts, subterfuges, expedients, and complicated meannesses which degrade a man in the eyes of his fellows, while they corrode his own heart, and ultimately destroy all delicacy of character, and completely undermine that self-respect which is the prop of so many virtues. The faults of Burns have often been held out in warning to young men of talent. They were great and lamentable, though none of them were those of a cold, an ostentatious, or a mean nature. Let the warning be coupled with his example in this important point. Neither vanity, nor self-indulgence, nor that contempt of future consequences, which

---

* I have much pleasure in recording the following circumstance:—Mr. Gilbert Burns, a man of considerable literary ability, and in all respects one " of the excellent of the earth," died lately in East Lothian, where he had long lived as the factor of Lord Blantyre. The mother of the poet, who many years survived her illustrious son, lived till her death with Gilbert Burns, who had a large family of his own. This debt of L.200 to his brother—for such he seems to have considered it—necessarily stood over. The exertions of Dr. Currie, and of the other friends and admirers of Burns, had placed his widow far above the fear of want, and every member of the family was respectably settled in life. It seems to have been almost the romance of integrity which induced Mr. Gilbert Burns to devote to the repayment of this loan a sum of money which he received from the booksellers shortly before his death for revising his brother's works. Had Burns survived, it would have gone hard with him before he had taken back this money.

is sometimes senselessly arrogated as matter of poetical privilege and the mark of a high spirit, betrayed him, surrounded as he ever was with manifold temptation, into the dishonesty and meanness of living beyond his scanty income. In some points of pecuniary interest he indeed showed a spirit of poetic chivalry which his critics are well entitled, if they please, to call Quixotic. While a herd of inferior writers, noble or gentle, are every day gaining hundreds and thousands by their productions, Burns declined receiving any remuneration whatever for his unrivalled lyrics! But a few years have passed since it was thought *shabby* for a gentleman in Scotland to sell the fruits of his garden, or to farm out the game on his estate; and Burns probably had the idea, that to sell songs was equally discreditable to the honour of the Muses." " A nation of shopkeepers" has very properly dismissed this superstition. There is no disgrace now except in getting too little.

(To be continued.)

THE SCHOOLMASTER AT HOME IN IRELAND.

" Pierce Mahon, come up wid your multiplication. Pierce, multiply four hundred by two—put it down—that's it,

400
By 2

" Twicet nought is one." (Whack, whack.) " Take that as an illustration—is that one?" " Faith, masther, that's one an' one any how; but, Sir, is not wanst nought, nothin'; now, masther, sure there can't be less than nothin'." " Very good, Sir." " If wanst nought be nothin', then twicet nought must be somethin', for its double what wanst nought is—see how *I'm sthruck* for *nothin'*, an' me knows it—hoo! hoo! hoo! hoo!" " Get out, you Esculapian; but I'll give you *somethin'* by-and-by, just to make you remember that you know *nothin'*—off wid ye to your sate, you spalpeen you—to tell me there can't be less than nothin', when it's well known that sportsman Squire O'Canter is a thousand pounds worse than nothin'."

" Paddy Doran, come up to your ' Inthrest.' Well, Paddy, what's the inthrest of a hundred pound at five per cent? Boys, some of you let a *fox pass* there—manners, you thieves you."

" Do you mane, masther, *per cent per annum?*"

" To be sure I do—how do you state it?"

" I'll say, as a hundhred pound is to one year, so is five per cent per annum."

" Hum—why—what's the number of the sum, Paddy?" " 'Tis No. 84, Sir." (The master steals a glance at the Key to Gray.) " I only want to look at it in the Gray, you see Paddy—an' how dare you give me such an answer, you big-headed dunce you—go off an' study it, you rascally Lilliputian—off wid you, and don't let me see your ugly mug till you know it."

" Now, *gintlemen*, for the Classics; and first for the Latinarians—Larry Cassidy, come up wid your Asop. Larry, you're a year at Latin, an' I don't think you know Latin for *frise*, what your own coat is made of, Larry. But, in the first place, Larry, do you know what a man that taches classics is called?" " A schoolmaster, Sir." (Whack, whack, whack.) " Take that for your ignorance, you wooden-headed goose, you—(whack, whack)—and that to the back of it—ha! that'll tache you—to call a man that taches classics a schoolmaster, indeed! 'tis a Profissor of Humanity itself, he is—(whack, whack, whack,)—ha! you ringleader, you; you're as bad as Dick O'Connell, that no masther in the county could get any good of, in regard that he put the whole school together by the ears, wherever he'd be, though the spalpeen wouldn't stand fight himself. Hard fortune to you! to go to put such an affront upon me, an' me a Profissor of Humanity. What's Latin for breeches!" " Fem—fem—femina." " No, it's not, Sir; that's Latin for a woman." " Femora—" " Can you do it?" " Don't strike me, Sir; don't strike me, Sir, an' I will." " I say, can you do it?" " Femorali"—(whack, whack, whack,)—" *Ah*, Sir! *ah*, Sir! 'tis fermorali—*ah*, Sir! 'tis fermorali—*ah*, Sir!" " This thratement to a Profissor of Humanity—(whack, whack, whack, whack, kick, kick, kick, thump, thump, thump, cuff, cuff, cuff—drives him head over heels to his seat.)—Now, Sir, maybe you'll have Latin for breeches again, or, by my sowl, if you don't, you must strip and I'll tache you what a Profissor of Humanity is!"

THE SICILIAN VESPERS.

IN the notes on the month of August was mentioned that foul stain on humanity, *the Massacre of St. Bartholomew*. Along with it is often coupled another diabolical enormity, named the *Sicilian Vespers*. There was here no preconcert, though in the progress of these horrible transactions men seem, under the excitement of remembered wrongs and brutal passions, to have become demons.—The inhabitants of Palermo, according to ancient custom, resorted to the church of Sante Espiritu, outside the walls of the city, to celebrate the solemnization of Easter. On the way they were watched by the French, who were always jealous of their assembling. Among them was a lady, Nymphia by name, the wife of Rogero of Mastrangelo, whose beauty made an impression on one of the ministers, Droghet. Under the pretext of ascertaining whether she had arms (which the Sicilians had been forbidden to carry) concealed under her garments, he approached her, and was guilty of such disgusting rudeness, that the lady swooned away in the arms of her husband. The insult fired all who were present at the procession; but none had courage to avenge it, until a young man, whose name history has concealed, but whose memory will ever be dear to his patriotic countrymen, seized the sword of Droghet, and plunged it into the lewd owner's heart. A shout of exultation was immediately raised by the multitude; who, in the excitement of the moment, swore to exterminate the odious strangers. As they had no arms at hand, they seized stones and other missiles, which they hurled with such effect at the heads of the Frenchmen, that the ground was soon covered with dead bodies. The citizens of Palermo rose as one man, and destroyed every Frenchman on whom they could lay hands. Their example was followed by other towns—by none more heartily than Messina; so that scarcely a Frenchman was left alive from one extremity of the island to another. This indiscriminate butchery occupied a full month. The church was no asylum for the proscribed victims; nor, as we are told, though upon authority somewhat apocryphal, was much mercy shown to the Sicilian women who had married them.

HINT FOR INVALIDS.—" It is worthy of particular remark, that it is not in the lungs only that the blood exerts an action on atmospherical air, for a similar function appears to belong to the skin, over the whole body. If the hand is confined in a portion of atmospherical air, or oxygen gas, it is found that the oxygen disappears, and is replaced by a portion of carbonic acid. At the same time, a considerable quantity of watery fluid transpires, and may be collected by a proper apparatus. This fact gives us an insight into one grand source of benefit arising from full exposure to the open air."—*Dr. Graham's Chemical Catechism*.

A GOLDEN RULE.—Industry will make a man a purse, and frugality will find him strings for it. Neither the purse nor the strings will cost him any thing. He who has it should only draw the strings as frugality directs, and he will be sure always to find a useful penny at the bottom of it. The servants of industry are known by their livery; it is always *whole* and *wholesome*. Idleness travels very leisurely, and poverty soon overtakes him. Look at the *ragged slaves* of *idleness*, and judge which is the best master to serve—*industry* or *idleness*.

COLUMN FOR THE LADIES.

BISHOP HEBER'S WIDOW.—THE WRITING WIDOWS.—Our women are all heroines now; the newspapers say, that Lady Harcourt, whose noble husband could hardly have been consigned to the earth when the late king was buried, sent for *twelve tickets* to St George's Chapel. A snug funeral party this. Of course they all got tickets, and were well entertained. No doubt her ladyship was very much at her ease, and has continued so ever since. Yet it is not so much by women of rank, who are bred up to this stony-heartedness as a part of their education, and think much the same of a dead husband as of a cast-off gown, that our indignation has been excited of late. It is with the "weeping widows," the "undone and bereaved of all their souls held dear," the walking hearses of a husband's beloved memory, black and tragic from top to toe—the *writing widows*—those sorrowing authoresses, who, in insatiable fondness for the dear dead-and-gone, and "in a holy desire to give the world some knowledge of the virtues and various perfections of him whom they shall never cease to deplore, whose image they treasure in their heart of hearts, and whom they day and night implore heaven that they may soon rejoin in the grave; make books and sell them for the highest price they can get; blustered up by puffery of all kinds, demands on the "recollections of college friends," or, "the sympathy of sorrowing relations," and on the *humbugability* of the public in general. These are the true Widow-of-Ephesus tribe; and, we will confess, it would not seriously afflict our souls to see them thrown into public scorn, or hear the first application for assistance, the first presentation of the prospectus of "The Recollections and Remains of the late lamented Honourable Reverend Charles Montague Antonio Belville, with fac-similes of his writing, and his billets doux and epigrams in the magazines, carefully collected, with notes, by his affectionate and disconsolate widow, the Honourable Amelia Antoinetta Isabinda Seymour" answered in every instance by "Madam, you are an impostor! No woman who cared for a husband's memory, would make such an exhibition of him. You only want to parade yourself before the public, and get money and a second husband as fast as you can."—There is not one of the scribbling widows that has not "changed her condition" with the greatest alertness possible. The latest candidate on the list has been poor Heber's widow; this lady was the widow *par excellence*, all devotedness, all sublime, all the mother of the Gracchi. But nobody better knew what she was about, when softening the "sentimental reader" was the question. With an alacrity worthy of an undertaker, she collected every fragment of the dead that she could turn into money, enlisted every friend he had in the scheme, made a Jew's bargain with a bookseller, and out came the quarto:—The late Bishop Heber's Travels in India," &c. "with sketches, engravings, vignettes," and, she ought to have added, in justice to the sentimental reader, with a variety of weak correspondence and of childish and unepiscopal verses: but the whole tenderly blazoned "with notes by his widow!" Now, to those who have hearts in their bosoms, and have known the loss of any for whom they felt even common regard, the idea of hunting over their papers, conning their letters, gathering every scrap that fell from their hands, recalling the familiar penmanship, the familiar phrase, till almost the familiar voice is in the ear, and the dead seems to stand before them; is one of the most repulsive thoughts that can come into the mind; in fact, those who have any heart at all, shrink from it wholly and cannot prevail upon themselves to go near any object which calls back the image; and if they make any exertion, it is to avoid all recurrence to sensations which cannot return without great pain. But not so with the she-editor. The Widow of Ephesus first looks to the market, considers how much better books will sell if they are taken in time; and then before the breath is well out of the husband's body, she is neck-deep in his trunks, turning out his portfolios, cutting extracts out of his books, and inditing circulars to all his friends for every fragment of his letters; then comes, without a moment's delay, the "Proposal for publishing the Life and Remains, with Notes by his *Widow !*" The book is published; sympathy with some, shame with others, common charity with the rest, make a considerable sum of money; which the world, of course, conceive that they are contributing for the support of a worthy man's children, and giving into the hands of a worthy widow. But the money is scarcely lodged, when, lo! the widow is a wife; some gay lounger of St. James's air has caught her taste, and wooed her to be his, by virtue of his knowledge of her subscription; or she has been charmed by the grin and guitar of some exquisite, who, though figuring as a peruquier in the sunny south, figures as a Marquis in foggy England; or the moustachios of some half Turk have charms for her, and she wends her way—La Condesa Catapulta Cavatina—to the lovely land where all above is moonshine, and all below is heroism and piracy. Thus goes the world of widows. Without knowing or caring what kind of match Heber's masculine and managing widow may have carved out for her tender fancies, it is enough for us to know that she has made eleven thousand pounds by his "Remains," and is now worrying the public again with his "Life and Travels." But we should be sorry to impede the progress of the lady's prosperity, or the goodness of the catch which the man of moustaches has made in her, and we recommend its purchase to all those who patronize the Widow of-Ephesus class of marriageable dames above forty-five.—*Whitaker's Monthly Magazine.*

[It is scarce necessary to say, that since this clever though severe paper was written, the widow of the amiable and excellent Heber has *wedded* and *separated* from the Greek adventurer, to whom it was believed she was secretly married when the last of Heber's works was played off against public credulity and sympathy. On the subject of these letters a late No. of the Edinburgh Review observes "About some feelings of a domestic nature, which allow the veil only to be lifted upon solemn occasions, and with a trembling hand. Among those letters, one is, we perceive, endorsed ' to my dear wife, in case of my death.' It requests her to be ' comforted concerning him, to bear his loss patiently, and to trust in the Almighty to raise up friends, and give food and clothing to herself and her children.' " Any one who had seen an advertisement to this effect must surely have exclaimed " an enemy hath done this!—or, would interpret the notice into a scandalous expedient for extorting money by purchasing suppression.]

THREE FEMALE DANCERS.—The *Schoolmaster* has nothing to do with dancers or singers, and only gives the subjoined bit of playful raving for the sake of the striking moral to be appended to it.

"The names of the three Poetesses of Motion, whom it is the good fortune of rich and luxurious England to possess at this season, are inscribed above. Of Brugnoli we have spoken before,—she is the impossible Grace; Heberle is the goddess of elegance and art; Taglioni of elastic joy—of grace in ecstacy. None can equal Brugnoli, for her muscles are at once composed of ivory and Indian-rubber—she is a creature of vegetable gum and elephant's tooth; prior muscle never had its equal either in energy or rigour.

Heberle is a creature of the most refined art : her exquisite powers seem to transcend mortality; and yet we fancy we can discover their origin, progress, perfection, in the traces left behind. But it is like looking in the Pyramids for marks of masonry Attitude is the forte of the divine Heberle: she is great, too—ye gods, how great!—in the graceful exertion of power: she seems to do those exquisite movements that dazzle while they delight, simply as if they were specimens only of the gifts that had been given to her.

Could an apothecary so commingle essences, that he might make up our prescription for mental disease, we should say—*Recipe*, the power, and the grace, and the form of Heberle : mix them in some vase of witchery: let lights innumerable, odours inexpressible, and tunes inconceivable, fill the air and impregnate it with delight; and at some favourable moment of returning spirit, draw up the curtain. Such a vision floating behind it! If music can cure the bite of a tarantula, then is Heberle a specific for the Cholera."

The sister of the young foreigner thus bepraised, died of Cholera in two hours illness, before this paragraph could have travelled the rounds. Heberle fled in horror. This incident may teach a better style of joking to theatrical critics.

DAHLIAS.

The Dahlia was a flower unknown in Europe within the last twenty years; it is a native of the marshes of Peru; it was called after Dahl, the famous Swedish botanist. Its varieties at present amount to nearly 500. The most beautiful flowering time of the dahlia is from the beginning of August to the middle of October; a temperature of ten or twelve degrees appears to be the most favourable for them. The dahlia is multiplied by seeds and parting the roots; the French say, by slips and grafts; but they are so easily increased by the two first methods, that the others need not be adopted even if practicable. The double varieties, that flower first in the time, are those whose time of florescence soonest terminates, while the latter plants, whose first blossoms are lovely, generally furnish the finest flowers, on the approach of winter.

THE LIVERPOOL RAILWAY.

MECHANISM AND ITS MARVELS.—This is the age of mechanical invention, and we have no doubt, that before its course is run out, we shall have made a prodigious advance in the power of man over nature. The railway system is of itself a great triumph. We are not to be discouraged by the accidents which from time to time occur in its use, for in every instance of those accidents the misfortune has been fairly earned by the folly or rashness of the sufferer. Two or three things of this kind have lately happened on the Liverpool Railway. But what is to be expected, if a clown who thinks he can outrun a vehicle flying thirty miles an hour, is crushed in consequence. Another fellow gets drunk, and will choose no place to sleep off his drunkenness but the middle of the railway; the engine comes, with the rapidity of a shaft of lightning, and before the engineer can see that there is any thing before him but the sky, the body is cut in two. Another clown chooses to hang on the engine, at full speed, as he would hang on the shafts of his cart; warning is of no use to him; he drops off, and is ground into powder at the moment. But those are no more impeachments of the system than the possibility of breaking one's neck by a fall from a first-floor window is an argument for living on the ground. Even the more serious doubt, whether the railway be in reality the cheaper, as it is decidedly the more rapid and powerful mode, vanishes before just consideration. The expense of the Liverpool railway has been heavy, and like all commencements, there have been errors, and even some unnecessary expenditures in the undertaking. A railway, too, on which the chief articles of carriage must be the bulky products of manufacture, or the still bulkier raw material, must have dimensions that can scarcely be required for the usual intercourse of the country. There may have also been a rather ostentatious attention to magnificence in the design, which, however laudable and even fitting in a great national monument, is not required in a mere instrument of connexion between two trading towns in a remote part of the kingdom. But this is of all faults the most venial. We hope that no London railway will be constructed without a view to the national honour. It is a nobler monument than all the triumphal arches of Rome. We say, then, that the Liverpool railway is an *experiment* no longer; that it has fully succeeded. The profits may be less than the sanguineness of speculation imagine. But the facts are ascertained that a steam-engine can carry weights to which no animal power is equal, with a rapidity that sets all animal speed at defiance; and that it can do this without intermission, without regard to night or day, frost or sunshine, the height of summer, or the depth of the most inclement season of the year. If the Liverpool railway were not to pay its own expenses, all that could be rationally said would be: ' There has been some rashness or clumsiness in the details, but you have got all that an inventive people can require. You have got a new and mighty power of nature; such things are not vouchsafed for nothing; and your business is now to bring to it the observation and ingenuity with which you have been furnished by Providence for such purposes, and to bring this noble principle, this new revelation in mechanics, into the active and manageable employment of man.

TRANSMISSION OF ARTICULATE SOUNDS.—One of the curious results of the railway will probably be some improvement in the communication of sound. Every body knows the contrivance, which has now become so common in the shops of workmen and tradesmen, the tin tube by which a message is conveyed through all parts of the house, at the moment, and which of course saves the delay and trouble of sending a servant. Those tubes are capable of much more general application, and might be very conveniently applied to every house. The principle is now to be tried on a large scale. It is proposed, by means of a small tube throughout the length of the Liverpool and Manchester railway, to convey information as quickly as in conversation. The length of the longest tunnel of the Liverpool and Manchester railway is about 6,600 feet, but it is thought that articulate sounds could be transmitted not only through the tunnels, but along the whole length of the railway. Its convenience on the railway would be obvious, as by a few men stationed at regular distances several miles apart, warning could be instantly given through the speaking-pipe of any obstruction or accident. But the probability is, that it will be discovered that not only can the words of a speaker at Liverpool be transmitted to Manchester, but that they can be transmitted through any distance however great, and with an almost instantaneous rapidity. The progress of sound through the air is well known to be 1142 feet in a second, and it is a singular fact that the feeblest sound travels as rapidly as the loudest; thus a whisper has the speed of a burst of thunder. But by all the experiments on tubes it appears that the transmission of sound is infinitely more rapid than in the open air, or actually occupies no time whatever. A series of experiments made a few years ago by M. Biot and other French mathematicians when the iron pipes were laying down for conveying water to Paris, seems to promise an unbounded power of transmission. They joined long ranges of those pipes to each other, so as to make a continued tube of several miles. The results were, that the lowest whisper at one end of the tube was heard with the most perfect distinctness at the other, and that it was heard instantaneously. The moment the speaker at one end was seen to apply his lips to the tube, his words were heard at the other. If this discovery should be substantiated by the railway tube, man will possess another power over nature of the most curious and the most useful kind. The telegraph, admirable an invention as it is, would be a toy to an instrument by which a public order or any other piece of intelligence could be conveyed at its full length from the seat of government to a seaport, or any other important spot of the kingdom, equally in fog and clear weather, night and day, and without even the delay that occurs by the telegraph. The sailing and triumph of a fleet, the surprise of an enemy, a stroke that might decide the fate of a nation, might be the consequence of this simple invention. And its value would be still enhanced, if in the course of time, it could be turned to the individual use of the community; if a system could be established allowing every body to avail himself of this mode of communication; like the Post Office, the intercourse of which was originally established only for the uses of the state and monarchs, but is now turned to the service of every man who desires to write a letter.

MR. COULTHURST, THE AFRICAN TRAVELLER.—It is with feelings of deep regret that we have to announce the death of this young and enterprising traveller—another victim added to the long and melancholy catalogue of men of spirit and talent who have fallen a sacrifice to their enthusiasm on the subject of African discovery. Mr. Coulthurst had, it appears, made a fortnight's journey from the Old Calabar river into the interior, when, for reasons unknown at present, he returned to that place, and embarked on board the Agnes, a Liverpool vessel bound for Fernando Po. It was during this voyage that this intelligent and amiable man breathed his last, on the 15th of April.

THE AFRICAN EXPEDITION.—The expedition will probably leave Liverpool in a day or two. The steam-boats, one of which is composed of iron, are two of the neatest and most elegant construction, and have been very generally admired.

THE IRISH WIDOW'S FAREWELL TO HER INFANT.

O, where is thy father, my own *lanna-bawn*,*
Who kissed the fresh balm of thy lip, as with dawn
He rose, and with eyes raised to Heaven in prayer,
Sought blessings for thee and his wedded love there?

From thence, 'till the day-star sank tired in the west,
He toiled with delight for the pair he loved best;
Then homeward, though wearied, he hastened to twine
His heart in pure fondness with yours, babe, and mine.

Wo, wo to the day, when a blood-thirsting band
Came to levy the *tithe* and arrears of our land;
Its morn saw thy father young, beauteous, and bold,
Its noontide beheld him pale, gory, and cold.

Redeemer of man! didst thou grant, for one hour,
To thine own chosen priesthood the right or the power
To go in robed state to thy temple and pray,
Then take from distress its last morsel away?

They have taken our blanket—our last one—and where
Shall I shelter my darling? My bosom is bare
And withered; and ah, such a chill's in my heart,
That the grave of thy father more warmth would impart.

I could live for thee, doat on thee, beg through the world,
Nor repine, though by want, ay, even misery unfurled;
But grief for thy parent, and terror for thee,
Have dried up the source of existence for me.

I leave thee, my *lanna*, all helpless and lorn;
Were it lawful, I'd wish that thou never wert born,
Or rather the tithe-bullet pierced thy young breast,
Then sweetly with thee and my love I would rest.

* My fair-haired babe.

THE GLEANER.

HUMBUG.—Every body is not acquainted with the etymology of the word humbug, which is now very generally applied to cholera. It is a corruption of 'Hamburgh,' and originated in the following manner:—During a period when war prevailed on the continent, so many false reports and lying bulletins were fabricated at Hamburgh, that at length, when any one would signify his disbelief of a statement, he would say, 'You had that from Hamburgh; and thus, 'That is Hamburgh,' or 'humbug,' became a common expression of incredulity."

AN OUT-AND-OUT SKITTLE-PLAYER.—In an imperial city, lately, a criminal was condemned to be beheaded, who had a singular itching to play at nine-pins. While his sentence was pronouncing, he had the temerity to offer a request to be permitted to play once more at his favourite game, at the place of execution; and then, he said, he should submit without a murmur. As the last prayer of a dying man, his request was granted. When arrived at the solemn spot, he found everything prepared, the pins being set up and the bowl being ready. He played with no little earnestness; but the Sheriff, at length, seeing that he shewed no inclination to desist, privately ordered the executioner to strike the fatal blow as he stooped for the bowl. The executioner did so, and the head dropped into the culprit's hand, as he raised himself to see what had occurred: he immediately aimed at the nine, conceiving it was the bowl which he grasped. All nine falling, the head exclaimed, "By—, I have won the game."

INEFFICACY OF GOVERNMENT RESTRICTIONS ON COMMERCE.—It is the policy of many of the states of Italy rigidly to exclude British manufactured goods from their territories. Yet as we annually take from them merchandize, principally raw silk, to the value of two millions sterling, and as no exportation of the precious metals is made in payment for the same, it became a question in what shape and by what channels the Italian merchants obtained returns for their produce. Upon investigation, it appeared that the foreign traders took their remuneration in bills of exchange drawn upon London merchants, by far the largest portion of which were remitted to Manchester and Glasgow from Austria and the German states, in return for those products of British industry against which the Italian governments so strictly closed their ports.—*Cabinet Cyclopædia.*

A life of contemplation is not unfrequently a miserable one; a man should be active, think less, and not watch life too closely.—*Mirabeau's Letters.*

THE DUTIES OF THE GREAT.—When a prince or prelate, a noble and a rich person, hath reckoned all his immunities and degrees of innocence from those evils that are incident to inferior persons, or the worse sort of their own order, they do 'the work of the Lord,' and their own too, 'very deceitfully,' unless they account correspondences of piety to all their powers and possibilities; they are to reckon and consider concerning what oppressions they have relieved, what widows and what fatherless they have defended, how the word of God and of religion, of justice and charity, hath thrived in their hands.—*Jeremy Taylor an eminent English Divine.*

SERVILITY is a sort of bastard envy. We heap our whole stock of involuntary adulation on a single prominent figure, to have an excuse for withdrawing our notice from all other claims (perhaps juster and more galling ones) and in the hope of sharing a part of the applause as train bearers.

BEING CONTENT.—It is a very right thing to be content; scripture and reason teach us the same; that is, we ought to be content with what we have, when we have done the best for ourselves, but not before. If a man is content with dirt, poverty, and rags, when he might by care and industry better his condition, he is a fool to be content. I have seen a mud cabin or cot in Ireland, where they were content to have the pig, the ass, the ducks and fowls, all in the kitchen with the children: and it is said they often burn a stair at a time to save the trouble of getting wood.—In Savoy, the people have a hole in each mattress to move its contents, that they may not be musty; and accordingly if a fire is to be lighted the lazy Savoyard immediately resorts to his store-house of straw and shavings. In our own country we frequently see a puddle of water close to the door into which all who enter the cottage must step, and dirty the house, yet an hour's work would draw it off.—In the mountains of Scotland a very poor tract of country, if you ask, why do you not open the window, or cure the smoky chimney! they answer, "It's a' weel eneuch"*—an answer fit for a slave, but not for a freeman.—*Working Man's Companion.*

* They don't say, "It's a' weel eneuch;" they have more sense; but they say "There's nae reek in the laverock's nest." The smoke helps to warm the hut, and where fuel is always scarce, is the preference in a choice of evils.

EXTRAORDINARY INSTANCE OF STRENGTH AND SPEED.—One of the most extraordinary instances of strength combined with speed that we ever recollect to have heard of, took place lately in Manchester. In a warehouse in Dale Street, a conversation lately took place about running between a young man employed there and a porter, belonging to the Railway Company, who was waiting at the warehouse for some packages that had to be forwarded by the Railway, when the Railway porter, whose name is Darlington, said he could run 120 yards with a certain package upon his back whilst the warehouse porter ran 200 without load. This package contained 120 pieces of prints, weighing about 3½lbs. each, and had been packed in an hydraulic press. A wager was made for 5s., half in ale and half in money, and preparations were instantly made for the race. The package was lowered on the shoulders of the man, and when properly balanced off they started, when to the utter astonishment of several who witnessed the exploit, the man carrying this ponderous load finished his 120 yards, when the other, who is, by the bye an excellent runner, was eight yards from home.

A DRAKE BETTER THAN A DUKE.—The Duke of Leeds was very affable with his tenants and people; one of them came up to him one day when he was riding, and told him he had a great favour to beg of him. The Duke asked him what it was. The man replied, after some hesitation, that he had a little boy who plagued him day and night to let him see the Duke, and that as his Grace was now close to his cottage, he would perhaps do him the great favour to let his son look at him. The Duke readily consented, and rode laughing to the cottage, where the delighted father ran in and fetched his child. The boy stood amazed, looking at the middle-aged gentleman of not very commanding exterior before him, of whose greatness and power he heard so much; and suddenly asked "Can you swim?'—"No, my good boy," said the Duke." "Can you fly?"—"No, I can't fly neither." "Then I like father's Drake better, for he can do both."

TO CORRESPONDENTS.

The hint, regarding Public Institutions, will be attended to. We should be glad to see the College Museum on such a footing that a popular guide to it would become desirable. But while 2s 6d. must be paid at each visit, by child, as well as adult, its treasures are so far sealed.

We are indebted to several correspondents for pieces of poetry of merit; but our narrow limits forbid the insertion of original compositions of this kind.

CONTENTS OF NO. IV.

	Page
Manufacturing Operatives,	49
The Labouring Classes—The Woollen Manufacturers,	50
BOOKS OF THE MONTH; Economy of Machinery; Emigrant Books,—Statistical Sketch of Upper Canada—Canada, by A. Picken; Excursions in India; Mirabeau's Letters from England; Characteristics of Women; Letters on Natural Magic; Wilderspin on Infant Tuition; The Western Garland; The Heidenmauer; Contarini Fleming; Earle's Residence in New Zealand; History of the Highlands and Clans —Chaunts of the People, &c.	51 to 54
American Modes of Thinking; Horse Selling—A Scene at Tattersall's	55
ELEMENTS OF THOUGHT—Power of being Useful to Mankind; Sympathy; Forbearance; Motives to Mutual Charity; Artificial Man, &c., &c.	56
THE STORY-TELLER—Elizabeth Villiers, a Tale for the Young	57
ROBERT BURNS	59
The Sicilian Vespers; Hints to Invalids; A Golden Rule; The Schoolmaster at Home in Ireland	61
COLUMN FOR THE LADIES—Bishop Heber's Widow; Three Female Dancers; The Irish Widow's Farewell to her Infant	62
THE GLEANER	64

BESIDES appearing in WEEKLY NUMBERS, the SCHOOLMASTER will be published in MONTHLY PARTS, which, stitched in a neat cover, will contain as much letter-press, of good execution, as any of the large Monthly Periodicals: A Table of Contents will be given at the end of the year; when, *at the weekly cost of three-halfpence*, a handsome volume of 832 pages, super-royal size, may be bound up, containing much matter worthy of consideration.

PART I. for August, containing the first four Numbers, with JOHNSTONE'S MONTHLY REGISTER, will be ready for delivery on Monday next.

EDINBURGH: Printed by and for JOHN JOHNSTONE, 19, St. James's Square.—Published by JOHN ANDERSON, Jun., Bookseller, 55, North Bridge Street, Edinburgh; by JOHN MACLEOD, and ATKINSON & Co. booksellers, Glasgow; and sold by all Booksellers and Venders of Cheap Periodicals.

THE Schoolmaster,
AND
EDINBURGH WEEKLY MAGAZINE.

CONDUCTED BY JOHN JOHNSTONE.

THE SCHOOLMASTER IS ABROAD.—LORD BROUGHAM.

No. 5.—Vol. I.   SATURDAY, SEPTEMBER 1, 1832.   Price Three-Halfpence.

YOUNG NAPOLEON.

The *true story* of the younger Napoleon, the Duke de Reichstadt, is more wonderful than any romance extant. But it is romance inverted. The brilliant fortune is all crowded into the opening scenes; and the King in his cradle, whose playthings were crowns and sceptres, and whose lacqueys were princes, runs his brief career, a deserted orphan; and closes it, a secluded, jealously-watched dependant,—without having tasted either the innocent delights of a happy childhood, or the free pleasures of a joyous youth. The history is full of instruction. Never did retribution more visibly follow the heels of error, than in the fortunes of the father of this young victim of abortive ambition.

Napoleon the elder, the greatest soldier of the last thousand years, at an early period of his career, married Josephine, the widow of Count Beauharnois, an amiable woman, to whom he long remained fondly and even passionately attached. She possessed the entire confidence of her husband, shared his sorrows with his successes, and more than repaid his affection. With his own hand he crowned the faithful companion of his fortunes, Empress of France. Up to this period, and for ten more years, the history of Josephine reads like a fairy tale, or the wildest romance; but in her case also it was romance inverted. Let us see her fortune at its highest flow:—

"On the 2d of December," says her affectionate historian, "all was stir in Paris and the Tuileries, from an early hour. On this morning, which was to witness the completion of her greatness, Josephine rose about eight o'clock, and immediately commenced the weighty concerns of the toilet. The body drapery of the Empress was of white satin, beautifully embroidered in gold, and on the breast ornamented with diamonds. The mantle was of crimson velvet, lined with white satin and ermine, studded with golden bees, and confined by an aigrette of diamonds. The coronation jewels consisted of a crown, a diadem, and a ceinture. The first, used for the actual crowning, and worn only on state occasions, consisted of eight branches, four wrought in palm, and four in myrtle leaves of gold incrusted with diamonds; round the circle ran a corded fillet, set with eight very large emeralds; and the bandeau which immediately enclosed the head, shone with resplendent amethysts. The diadem worn before the coronation, and on the more ordinary state occasions, was composed of four rows of pearls of the finest water, interlaced with foliage of diamonds, the workmanship of which equalled the materials; in front were several brilliants, the largest weighing one hundred and forty-nine grains. The ceinture was of gold so pure as to be quite elastic, enriched with thirty-nine rose-coloured diamonds. What a change from the time of her first marriage, when, as Josephine, with her wonted simplicity, used to relate, she carried the few trinkets presented by Beauharnois (her first husband) for several days in the large pockets which ladies were then accustomed to wear, shewing them to every acquaintance, and hearing them pronounced the wonder of all eyes!

"On the throne, hung with crimson velvet, under a canopy of the same, appeared Napoleon, with Josephine on his left, attended by the princesses of the empire, and, on his right, his two brothers, with the arch-chancellor and arch-treasurer. The religious ceremony continued nearly four hours, enlivened by music composed for the occasion chiefly by Paesiello, and sung by upwards of three hundred performers. Napoleon took the crown destined for the Empress, and first putting it for an instant on his own, placed it upon his consort's brow, as she knelt before him on the platform of the throne. The appearance of Josephine was at this moment most touching. Even then she had not forgot that she was once 'an obscure woman;' tears of deep emotion fell from her eyes; she remained for a space kneeling, with hands crossed upon her bosom, then, slowly and gracefully rising, fixed upon her husband a look of gratitude and tenderness. Napoleon returned the glance. It was a silent but conscious interchange of the hopes, the promises, and the memories of years."

Vain hopes! faithless promises! bitter memories! The conqueror of Europe pressed forward in his extraordinary career, till, every other obstacle overcome, the wife of his youth appeared in his perverted sight, the only remaining barrier between his selfish ambition, and the consummation of his unchastised and mad desire to transmit the crown of France to his offspring. The sacrifice was soon resolved on; but the slave of ambition and headlong will was not altogether a monster; and it cost him some pangs to plant an Austrian princess on the throne he had raised for Josephine, and to give to one to whom he was a stranger, and indifferent, the place she had held in his heart for twenty-three years. The cruel resolution once taken, was not long concealed.

"On returning," says Bourrienne, his schoolfellow, secretary, and afterwards his memorialist, "from the last Austrian campaign, Napoleon, as already mentioned, stopped at Fontainbleau, and Josephine there joined him. For the first time, the communication which had previously united his own with his wife's apartments was shut up, by his order. While I lived as one of the household, their domestic arrangements had been still more direct; Bonaparte's bed-chamber, as the reader knows, having been only an apartment of ceremony. Josephine did not deceive herself as to the fatal prognostics to be deduced from this conjugal separation. Duroc having been sent for one day, found her alone, and in tears.—' I am undone,' said she, in a tone, the recollection of which still moved Duroc; ' I am undone! all is now over with me! How hide my shame? You, Duroc, you have always been my friend,—you and Rapp: it is neither of you who has advised him to separate from me: my enemies have done this,—Savary, Junot, and others: alas! they are still more his enemies than mine. And, my poor Eugene! what will become of him when he knows I am repudiated by an ingrate? Yes, Duroc, ungrateful he is. My God! my God! what shall we do?' Josephine sobbed convulsively, while speaking thus to Duroc; and I myself witnessed the tears which she still wept over the separation.

Bourrienne, who had lived many years in the family of Bonaparte, and who sincerely loved and esteemed her whom he ever names " the excellent Josephine, thus describes her melancholy condition:—

" On entering, Josephine held out her hand to me, pronouncing only these words, ' Well, my friend!' But the tone was one of such profound emotion, that, to this moment, the sounds vibrate upon my heart: tears prevented her saying more. Seating herself on an ottoman, placed on the left of the fire, she motioned me to take my seat beside her; and I saw Hortense still standing, leaning against the mantel-piece, vainly endeavouring to hide her tears.

" Josephine had taken one of my hands, which she held pressed between both her own, and for a long time wept in silence, unable to utter a single word; at length recovering a little empire over herself, she said, ' My good Bourrienne, I have suffered the full extent of my misfortune. He has cast me off—abandoned me: the empty title of Empress conferred by him has only rendered my disgrace the more public. Ah! how truly did we estimate him! I never deluded myself as to my fate; for whom would he not sacrifice to his ambition? You, my good Bourrienne, were for years a witness of what passed between us—you saw all, knew all, heard all; you are aware that I never had a secret from you, but confided to you my sad forebodings. He accomplished his resolution, too, with a cruelty of which you can form no idea. I have now played, to its end, my part of wife in this world. I have endured all, and am resigned.' At these words, one of these melancholy smiles wandered across Josephine's countenance, which tell only of woman's suffering, and are so inexpressibly affecting.—' In what self-constraint did I pass those days in which, though no longer his wife, I was obliged to appear so to all eyes! What looks, my friend, are those which courtiers allow to fall upon a divorced wife! In what stupor, in what uncertainty, more cruel than death, did I live, from that period to the fatal day in which he avowed to me the thoughts I had so long read in his countenance: it was the 30th of November. What an expression he wore that day; and how many sinister things appeared in his looks! We dined together as usual; I struggled with my tears, which, despite of my efforts, overflowed from my eyes. I uttered not a single word during that sorrowful meal, and he broke silence but once, to ask one of the attendants about the weather. My sunshine I saw had passed away; the storm was coming, and it burst quickly. Immediately after coffee, Bonaparte dismissed every one, and I remained alone with him. What an expression, Bourrienne! what a look he had! I beheld in the alteration of his features the struggle which was in his soul; but at length I saw that my hour had come. His whole frame trembled; and I felt a shuddering horror come over mine. He approached, took my hand, placed it on his heart, gazed upon me for a moment, without speaking, then at last let fall these dreadful words—' Josephine! my excellent Josephine! thou knowest if I have loved thee! To thee—to thee alone do I owe the only moments of happiness which I have enjoyed in this world. Josephine! my destiny overmasters my will. My dearest affections must be silent before the interests of France.' ' Say no more,' I had still strength sufficient to reply; ' I was prepared for this; I understand you; but the blow is not the less mortal. More I could not utter,' pursued Josephine: ' I cannot tell what passed within me; I believe my screams were loud; I thought reason had fled; I remained unconscious of every thing; and, on returning to my senses, found I had been carried to my chamber. Your friend, Corvisart, will tell you, better than I can, what afterwards occurred; for, on recovering, I perceived that he and my poor daughter were with me. Bonaparte returned to visit me in the evening. No, Bourrienne, you cannot imagine the horror with which the sight of him, at that moment, inspired me; even the interest which he affected to take in my sufferings, seemed to me additional cruelty. Oh! my God! how justly had I reason to dread ever becoming an Empress!"

The account given of these painful events by Dr. Memes is fuller, and somewhat different. The scene is so deeply tragic, that it would be injurious to give it, but in his own language:—

" Formerly, in their days of happiness, their intercourse had thus been free even amid the restraints of a court; Napoleon would surprise Josephine in her boudoir, and she steal upon his moments of relaxation in his cabinet. But all was now reversed; the former never entered, but knocked when he would speak to the latter, who hardly dared to obey the signal, the sound of which caused such violent palpitations of the heart, that she had to support herself by leaning against the walls or furniture, as she tottered towards the little door, on the other side of which Napoleon waited her approach. From these conferences, Josephine returned so exhausted, and with eyes so swollen with weeping, as to give ground for the belief that her lord used violence to constrain her consent to their separation. Her own words also, ' He accomplished his resolution with a cruelty of which no idea can be formed,' might at first seem to countenance this supposition. But justice is to be done; the violence and the cruelty, great as they both were, consisted solely in the act itself, and in coldly withstanding all claims of affection, and of gentle entreaty, urged by the being who had loved him so well, and at length tendered a voluntary sacrifice of her love and happiness.* During their private conferences, previous to the direct announcement of his determination, Napoleon endeavoured to persuade Josephine of the political necessity and advantages of a separation, at first rather hinting at than disclosing the measure. His true object was, as much to effect his wish with the least possible pain to the Empress, as to lead her to a resignation of her state; for though she could not have successfully resisted a despotic enactment, the deed would thereby have been rendered doubly odious to all France. This, indeed, was but too obviously a preparation for an event, though future, yet certain; and Josephine, regarding it as such, defended her claims sometimes with a strength of argument which it was difficult to answer, and, at others, by tears, supplications, and appeals, or by the calm resignation of self-devotedness to his will, against which the heart of Napoleon, had he possessed the feelings of a man, ought never to have been proof. Meanwhile, ' in what stupor,' the words are Josephine's own, ' in what uncertainty, more cruel than death, did I live during these discussions, until the fatal day in which he avowed the resolution which I had so long read in his countenance.' Sometimes, however, rallying amid her sorrows and resignation, she assumed a commanding attitude, on those mysterious principles, by which he deemed his career to be regulated, that for a space awed even the spirit of Napoleon. One night, Josephine, in tears and silence, had listened for some time to these overtures and discussions, when, with a sudden energy, she started up, drew Napoleon to the window, and, point-

* It is amusing to be so gravely told that the Emperor did not actually beat his refractory wife.

ing to the heavens, whose lights seemed in placid sweetness to look down upon her distress, with a firm yet melancholy tone, said, 'Bonaparte, behold that bright star; it is mine! And remember, to mine, not to thine, has sovereignty been promised; separate, then, our fates, and your star fades!'

"But 'the fatal day' was not to be averted. The 30th of November arrived, which Napoleon appears to have destined for declaring his final determination to Josephine. She had wept all day; they were to dine together as usual, and, to conceal her tears, the Empress wore a large white hat, fastened under the chin, which, with its deep front, shaded the whole of the upper part of the face. Napoleon, also, had shown marks of the strongest agitation; he scarcely spoke to any one, but, with arms folded, continued, at intervals, to pace his library alone; from time to time, a convulsive movement, attended with a hectic flush, passed for an instant across his features; and at table, when he raised his eye, it was only to look by stealth upon the Empress, with an expression of the deepest regret. The dinner was removed untouched; neither tasted a morsel, and the only use to which Napoleon turned his knife, was to strike mechanically upon the edge of his glass, which he appeared to do unconsciously, and like one whose thoughts were painfully pre-occupied. Every thing during this sad repast seemed to presage the impending catastrophe. The officers of the court, even, who were in attendance, stood in motionless expectancy, like men who look upon a sight they feel portends evil, though what they know not; not a sound was heard beyond the noise of placing and removing the untasted viands, and the monotonous tinkling already noticed; for the Emperor spoke only once to ask a question, without giving any attention to the reply. 'We dined together, as usual,' says Josephine; 'I struggled with my tears, which, notwithstanding every effort, overflowed from my eyes. I uttered not a single word during that sorrowful meal, and he broke silence but once, to ask an attendant about the weather. My sunshine, I saw, had passed away; the storm burst quickly. Directly after coffee, Bonaparte dismissed every one, and I remained alone with him. We have already described the manner of Napoleon's taking coffee after dinner; the change which on this day first took place seemed to indicate to Josephine that her cares were no longer indispensable to the happiness of her husband. She had risen as usual from table with Napoleon, whom she slowly followed into the saloon, and with a handkerchief pressed upon her mouth, to restrain the sobbing, which, though inaudible, shook her whole frame. Recovering, by an effort, her self-command, Josephine prepared to pour out the coffee, when Napoleon, advancing to the page, performed the office for himself, casting upon her a regard, remarked even by the attendants, and which seemed to fall with stunning import, for she remained as if stupified. The Emperor having drunk, returned the cup to the page, and, by a sign, indicated his wish to be alone, shutting, with his own hand, the door of the saloon. In the dining-room, separated by this door, there remained only the Count de Beaumont, chief chamberlain, who continued to walk about in silence, and the favourite personal attendant of the Emperor, both expecting some terrible event,—an apprehension which was but too speedily confirmed by loud screams from the saloon.

"When Josephine thus fainted, Napoleon hastily opened the door of the saloon, and called to the two individuals who remained in the dining-room. The opening of the door allowed them to see the Empress on the floor, insensible, yet still speaking in broken murmurs—'Oh, no! you cannot surely do it!—you would not kill me!' M. de Beaumont entered on a sign from his master, and lifted in his arms the hapless Josephine, now perfectly unconscious of all that was passing.

"'On recovering,' says Josephine, 'I perceived that Corvisart was in attendance, and my poor daughter weeping over me. No, no! I cannot describe the horror of my situation during that night. Even the interest which *he* affected to take in my sufferings, seemed to me additional cruelty. Oh, my God! how justly had I reason to dread becoming an Empress!'

"The following is a letter addressed by Josephine to her husband, a few days after these events, less in the hope of withdrawing him from his resolution, than with the intention of proving her resignation to an arrangement proceeding from him:—

"'My presentments are realized. You have pronounced the word which separates us; the rest is only a formality. Such is the reward, I will not say of so many sacrifices, (they were sweet because made for you,) but of an attachment unbounded on my part, and of the most solemn oaths on yours. But the state, whose interests you put forward as a motive, will, it is said, indemnify me, by justifying you! These interests, however, to which you feign to immolate me, are but a pretext; your ill-dissembled ambition, as it has been, so it will ever continue, the guide of your life; a guide which has led you to victories and to a throne, and which now urges you to disasters and to ruin.

"'You speak of an alliance to contract—of an heir to be given to your empire—of a dynasty to be founded! But with whom do you contract that alliance? With the natural enemy of France—that insidious house of Austria, which detests our country from feeling, system, and necessity.'

"'The fatal day' at length arrived. On the 15th of December, the imperial council of state was convened, and, for the first time, officially informed of the intended separation. On the morrow, the whole of the imperial family assembled in the grand saloon in the Tuileries. All were in grand costume. Napoleon's was the only countenance which betrayed emotion, but ill concealed by the drooping plumes of his hat of ceremony. He stood motionless as a statue, his arms crossed upon his breast, without uttering a single word. The members of his family were seated around, shewing, in their expression, less of sympathy with so painful a scene, than of satisfaction that one was to be removed who had so long held influence, gently exercised as it had been, over their brother. In the centre of the apartment was placed an arm chair, and before it a small table, with a writing apparatus of gold. All eyes were directed to that spot, when a door opened, and Josephine, pale, but calm, appeared, leaning on the arm of her daughter, whose fast-falling tears shewed that she had not attained the resignation of her mother. Both were dressed in the simplest manner. Josephine's dress of white muslin, exhibited not a single ornament. All rose on her entrance. She moved slowly, and with wonted grace, to the seat prepared for her, and, her head supported on her hand, with the elbow resting on the table, listened to the reading of the act of separation. Behind her chair stood Hortense, whose sobs were audible, and a little farther on, towards Napoleon, Eugene, trembling, as if incapable of supporting himself. Josephine heard, in composure, but with tears coursing each other down her cheeks, the words that placed an eternal barrier between her and greatness, and bitterer still, between affection and its object. This painful duty over, the Empress appeared to acquire a degree of resolution from the very effort to resign with dignity the realities of title for ever. Pressing for an instant the handkerchief to her eyes, she rose; and with a voice which, but for a slight tremor, might have been called firm, pronounced the oath of acceptance; then, sitting down, she took the pen from the hand of Count St. Jean-d'Angely, and signed. The mother and daughter now retired as they had entered, followed immediately by Eugene, who appears to have suffered most severely of the three; for he had no sooner gained the space between the folding doors, which opened into the private cabinet, than he fell lifeless on the floor, and was recovered, not without difficulty, by the attentions of the usher of the cabinet, and his own aides-de-camp.

"The sad interests of the day had not yet been exhausted. Josephine had remained unseen, sorrowing in her chamber, till Napoleon's usual hour of retiring to rest. He had just placed himself in bed, silent and melancholy, while his favourite attendant waited only to receive orders, when suddenly the private door opened, and the Empress appeared, her hair in disorder, and her face swollen with weeping. Advancing with a tottering step, she stood, as if irresolute, about a pace from the bed, clasped her hands, and burst into an agony of tears. Delicacy—a feeling as if she had now no right to be there—seemed at first to have arrested her progress; but forgetting every thing in the fulness of her grief, she threw herself on the bed, clasped her husband's neck, and sobbed as if her heart had been breaking. Napoleon also wept, while he endeavoured to console her, and they remained for some time locked in each other's arms, silently mingled their tears together, until the Emperor, perceiving Constant in waiting, dismissed him to the anti-chamber. After an interview of about an hour, Josephine parted for ever with the man whom she had so long and so tenderly loved."

Such were the cruel scenes which paved the way for the second nuptials of Napoleon; such the sin and sorrow which preceded that final small event, scarce claiming a passing sigh, which adds a new heap of dust to the funeral vault of the Austrian princes, and reads a solemn lesson to ambition. Brief as is the space, how much has intervened since Napoleon thus laid the foundation of his subsequent misfortunes. A few more years were still to be added to his measured term of prosperity. A few more drops were yet to be poured into the cup, ere it was tasted, and found to be only mingled blood and ashes.

Bourrienne still frequently visited the Ex-Empress at Malmaison.

" Although more than a year had passed since the separation, sorrow was ever new in Josephine's heart, for every thing contributed to augment it. ' Think, my friend,' she would often say, ' of all the tortures which I must have endured since that fatal day; I cannot conceive how I have not sunk under them. Can you imagine punishment greater than for me every where to see descriptions of fetes for *his* marriage! And the first time he came to see me, after having wedded another,—what an interview! How many tears did it cause me to shed! Still, the days when he comes here are, to me, days of suffering, for he has no regard to my feelings, or, if you will, weaknesses. With what cruelty does he converse about the child he is to have! You can understand, Bourrienne, how all that afflicts me. Far better be exiled a thousand leagues from hence. Yet, (as if her kindly heart reproached her) yet some friends have remained faithful to me: those are now my only consolation."

And now behold the most ambitious hopes of Napoleon fulfilled by the birth of the poor boy whose death has just closed a joyless life. The birth of the King of Rome was proclaimed to all expectant France, by the voice of cannon, and welcomed by the Continental Sovereigns, with the most hypocritical and courtly felicitations. It had been previously settled that a certain number of cannon shots were to announce the birth of a female child. When they were given, Paris hung in breathless suspense on the next sound. There was a pause, as if by sound or silence a world was about to be created, or annihilated. And when the shot came!—Well may it be said, " Vain capital! Vain people!" " Pleased with a rattle, tickled with a straw." With humiliation, and almost contempt, one looks back to the rapturous welcome given to the heir of that dynasty which the same people had repudiated, before this worshipped " King of the Romans" was well out of leading-strings. How can one ever forget the ecstasy of the French nation when the King of Rome cut his first tooth! Among those most eager to congratulate the Emperor on the event which crowned his prosperity, was Josephine; nor is there room to doubt of the sincerity of her sentiments, so exalted was the nature of her attachment to her ungrateful husband, now that her personal feelings were subdued, and the bitterness of her sacrifice past. Bonaparte had still sufficient generosity of character to estimate the genuine feelings of the woman he had so cruelly wronged. When her son, Eugene, went to visit the Ex-Empress, he said, " You are going to see your mother; tell her that I am sure she will rejoice more than any one at my good fortune. This evening I will write to Josephine."

Josephine did not long outlive the downfall of her husband. The " King of Rome," stripped of his mock title, went, by the grace of the Allied Powers, to Vienna with his mother.—The Empress Maria Louise, become Archduchess of Parma, separated by state policy, and soon by inclination, from her husband, obtained the reputation of being the mistress of her Chamberlain, the Count de Neippperg; and, in 1825, confessed with him all the marriage a Princess of Germany may contract with a subject. Her imputed indifference to and desertion of her son, would be a fault less pardonable; and now that we hear of her sorrow for his death, nature and charity bid us believe the tale, though a tardy display of maternal feeling cannot soften the fate of Young Napoleon.

From his fourth year, the boy lived a hostage of the Holy Alliance; and as he advanced in life, almost as a state prisoner. His education was retarded, and his mind moulded to the objects of Metternich. It is alleged that he was kept ignorant of all recent history, and that the school-boy in Europe, who, for good or for evil, knew least of Bonaparte, the artillery officer who became Emperor of France, was his own son. This is scarcely possible. The birds of the air would have carried to him the story of his father's exploits.

Young Napoleon, when seen by strangers at the theatre and other public places, became an object of eager and melancholy scrutiny. He inherited something of the Italian beauty, and classic delicacy of feature which distinguished all his father's family; and those who rested the forlorn hope of Italian liberty upon him, and were kept aloof by a jealous policy, sought to read his character in his countenance. One of the latest of those observers remarks, " from the varying expression of his face during the representation of some of Schiller's spirit-stirring plays, —of Tell, for instance, and Wallenstein, I could not help feeling persuaded that young Napoleon would have made but an indifferent cardinal—a vocation to which he is said to have been formerly devoted. So gay and animated is his real disposition, that he is sent for whenever his illustrious grandsire becomes tired of feeding his pigeons and scraping his violoncello, in order to dispel the *ennui*, the evil spirit, of the imperial Saul!"

It is reported that Young Napoleon made a will, which he endeavoured to transmit to his cousin, the son of the Duchess St. Leu. This young man was lately involved in the insurrection in Italy; and with him, it is said, the son of Napoleon maintained a constant secret correspondence; a thing not very probable, considering how he had been educated, and how he was surrounded. To this gallant cousin he bequeathed his father's sword. From the humble tomb of Josephine in the village church of Ruel,—the willows that shadow Napoleon's grave in St. Helena,—the newly tenanted burial vault of the young Duke de Reichstadt,—what lessons may be read!—

"We are such stuff as dreams are made on—
And our little life is rounded by a sleep."

ROBERT BURNS.
BORN 1758—DIED 1796.
(Continued from page 61.)

THE social eloquence of Burns—his conversational talents, and power over the feelings of those with whom he associated—have often been described as more astonishing than even the written records of his genius; and this appears to have been true. He obtained an influence for the time which we hear of nothing resembling, save some few moments of the life of Rousseau, when Parisian saloons were deluged with genuine tears. One of the most eminent of his critics attributes the bold development of the genius of Burns to the lowness of his origin. However this may be, it is fair to suppose, that a young man, trained in the frigid circles of *persiflage* and civil sneer, however great his genius and vehement his natural sensibility, would have been scared from the betrayal of his feelings, where the rustic gave his impetuous impulses unbounded sway, with consequences which startle belief.

"It was in female circles," says a generous admirer and excellent judge, "that his powers of expression displayed their utmost fascination. In such, where the respect demanded by rank was readily paid as due to beauty or accomplishment, where he could resent no insult, and vindicate no claim of superiority, his conversation lost all its harshness, and often became so energetic and impressive, as to dissolve the whole circle into tears. The traits of sensibility which, told of another, would sound like instances of gross affectation, were so native to the soul of this extraordinary man, and burst from him so involuntarily, that they not only obtained full credence as the genuine feelings of his own heart, but melted into unthought-of sympathy all who witnessed them. In such a mood they were often called forth by the slightest and most trifling occurrences; an ordinary engraving, the wild turn of a simple Scottish air, a line in an old ballad, were, like 'the field mouse's nest,' and 'the uprooted daisy,' sufficient to excite the sympathetic feelings of Burns. And it was wonderful to see those, who, left to themselves, would have passed over such trivial circumstances without a moment's reflection, sob over the picture, when its outline had been filled up by the magic art of his eloquence."

Reflections on the life and fortunes of this extraordinary man, must, for a long while to come, be mingled with pain and indignation; but in passing to his works all is nearly unmixed pleasure. He has produced a few poems of equivocal tendency, and some of a trivial wit; but they are comparatively few; and so rich was the ore of his vein, that even in the rubbish thrown carelessly out, the pure metal is continually glancing forth. If Burns has not reached the highest heaven of invention, it may have been because he has never aimed his flight thither; for whatever he fairly attempted he has done better than any other man. His songs, the species of composition to which he gave most attention, are, taken as a whole, the finest in the world—in spirit—in nationality—in beauty—in simplicity—and in the most exquisite tenderness. It has become fashionable of late, even in Scotland, to compare Burns with more polished lyrists: all such comparison is as senseless as invidious. In the wide dominion of imagination and poetry there is room for all adventurers, and even for a few *squatters*, with questionable charter; nor need they with such ample verge encroach on the domains of each other; or, like the petty German principalities, contend which shall be paramount. A singer, with a nicely-cultivated ear and fine taste, must occasionally use a little ungraceful force in drilling the refractory syllables of Burns and Sir Walter Scott, and in bending their stubborn sense to certain musical pauses and cadences; but we can have no unmixed good, and this fault most frequently arises when the verse, as it were, o'er-informs the music, and the sound has not body sufficient to sustain the sentiment; like richly-freighted vessels which draw too much water, and lag ungracefully, where the little, airy, nicely-trimmed bark will swim like a halcyon. Besides, many of those polished strains which go so "softly, sweetly" to the music, are in fact, in reading, more rugged to the ear than the worst adapted lines of Burns. In the modern popular lyrics, the music and the verse reflect and support each other;—they mutually perform, as it were, a waltz to the ear, dancing on together, gracefully intertwined, throughout their light and airy, or languid and voluptuous movements. With the harsher and worse accented strains of our national bard, the music may lag and lose in expression, but the tears gush forth—the touched heart murmurs it low under-song.

The love-verses of Burns, by those who bring no objection to their lack of musical smoothness, are charged with the want of that tone of gallantry which distinguishes the productions of higher-born men. It is certain that his manly mind knew nothing of feelings merely factitious, however elevated; and it does not appear to have been his hard fortune ever to encounter "stony-hearted maidens." He never dreamt of extolling the charms of his mistress from vain-glory in their brilliancy. He poured forth the praises of the fair idols of his fancy from the exuberant delight with which their real or ideal charms enraptured his own spirit. Like Julie's lover, the fair being he admired became exalted above humanity by the prerogatives of his passion and his genius; and her nominal rank in life had no power over those precious immunities. But if Burns' songs want the tone of chivalry, the same fault may be found with the finest writers of love-verses in the language. Surrey—for the authenticity of whose passion it would not be very safe to swear—is indeed very doleful; but the love-strains of Sydney show no puling sentiment nor sophisticated feeling of any kind. If they want the beauty and tenderness of the love-songs of Burns, they equal them in nature and in warmth. This is their praise. The love-verses of Herrick, Carew, Ben Jonson, Shakspeare, and Suckling, have nothing of this "tone of chivalry." Those of Lovelace have an exquisite delicacy and sweetness peculiar to themselves; but their sentiment is as natural as it is refined. It is not easy to tell where we are to look for the tone of chivalry in love-songs, unless in such inditings as those of Harrington—" To a most stony-hearted maiden, who did most cruelly use the knight, my good friend;" or, " To the Lady Isabella when I first saw her look forth of a window at Court, and thought her beautiful;" or, " To the divine Saccharissa." The love of Burns was neither that of a knight-errant nor a sylph. It could neither subsist on sighs nor essences; but it was composed of those feelings which have imparted delicacy and elegance to the untutored strains of the rude Laplander and the Russ. Who shall say its effusions want refinement? Burns was undoubtedly impatient of suing seven years for a smile; for he possessed the sympathetic art of winning " the dear angel-smile" with wondrous facility. Instead of catching the descending tear on a cushion of rose-leaves, or preserving it in " an urn of emerald," or crystallizing " the pearly treasure," he gathered it, as it trembled on the eyelash, with his own glowing lip, and devoutly drunk in it, a new essence of being. Thus, if his verses want the character of chivalrous gallantry, they possess something far better in that purified natural tenderness, of which gallantry is at best but the substitute or the counterfeit. His notions of the female character appear throughout quite *Shaksperian*: his women are all gentleness, and softness, and tenderness. The idea of a lofty, predominating, high-souled, and capricious beauty, such as is pictured in the old romances—ennobling to female character in a general view, yet a most chilling and repulsive individuality—never appears to have entered his imagination. The utmost extent of his belief in female cruelty is, that—

> A thought ungentle canna be
> The thought o' Mary Morrison.

The poems of Burns are so generally diffused, that copious specimens are the less necessary. " The Cottar's Saturday Night"—part of " The Vision"—" The Twa Dogs"—the " Address to the De'il"—" Tam o' Shanter"—two-thirds of the songs, and especially " Highland Mary"—" Poortith cauld"—" Bonny was yon rosy brier"—" A man's a man for a' that"—" The bonny lad that's far awa' "—" Gae, bring to me a pint o' wine"—and that exquisite song which does indeed contain the essence of a thousand love-stories—

> Had we never lov'd sae kindly,
> Had we never lov'd sae blindly,
> Never met, or never parted,
> We had ne'er been broken-hearted.
>
> Fare thee weel, thou first and fairest!
> Fare thee weel, thou best and dearest!
> Thine be ilka joy and treasure,
> Peace, enjoyment, love and pleasure!

I have said, that so rich was the ore of the vein of Burns, that it often breaks forth where it could least be expected. Among his neglected songs is a ditty called " Bessy and her Spinning-wheel," which, for pure and felicitous moral sentiment, and scenic description, such as only Burns could have given, is worthy of being oftener noticed. In a neglected song called " The Posy," among many fine stanzas is this exquisite one—

> The hawthorn I will pu',
> Wi' his locks o' siller grey,
> Where, like an aged man,
> He stands at break o' day;
> But the songster's nest within the bush
> I winna tak' away;
> And it's a' to make a posy to my ain dear May.

In the song called " The Auld Man," the first stanza, describing the return of Spring, is no way remarkable; the second is strikingly fine and pathetic—

> But my white pow, nae kindly thowe
>   Shall melt the snaws of age;
> My trunk of eild, but buss or bield,
>   Sinks in time's wintry rage.
> Oh! age has weary days,
>   And nights o' sleepless pain!
> Thou golden time o' youthfu' prime,
>   Why com'st thou not again?

There is another song called " The Waefu' Heart," little noticed, though it must be admired by every mind of feeling, which has this exclamation breathed by bereaved affection and pious resignation—

> This waefu' heart lies low with his
>   Whose heart was only mine;—
> And, oh! what a heart was that to lose!—
>   But I maun nae repine.

In a few rather trivial verses, in which Burns is speaking of his filial regard for Scotland in his boyhood, is this fine incidental burst of nationality—

> The rough bur-thistle spreading wide
>   Among the bearded bear,
> I turn'd my weeding hook aside,
>   And spared the symbol dear.

There is no doubt that this stanza records a real fact; and that the young enthusiastic husbandman may have spared the noxious weed for the sake of the cherished sentiment.—*Johnstone's Specimens of the Poets.*

ON THE CHURCH OF KRISUVIK IN ICELAND.

"There was nothing so sacred in the appearance of this church as to make us hesitate to use the altar as our dining-table."—MACKENZIE's *Travels in Iceland*. The levity of the traveller is thus apostolically reproved:—

> Though gilded domes, and splendid fanes,
> And costly robes, and choral strains,
>   And altars richly drest,
> And sculptur'd saints, and sparkling gems,
> And mitred heads, and diadems,
>   Inspire with awe the breast;
>
> The soul enlarged—devout—sincere,
> With equal piety draws near
>   The holy House of God,
> That rudely rears its rustic head,
> Scarce higher than the peasant's shed,
>   By peasant only trod.
>
> 'Tis not the pageantry of show,
> That can impart devotion's glow,
>   Nor sanctify a pray'r:
> Then why th' Icelandic Church disdain,
> Or why its sacred walls profane,
>   As though God dwelt not there?
>
> The contrite heart—the pious mind—
> The christian—to that spot confined,
>   Before its altar kneels!
> There breathes his hopes—there plights his vows—
> And there, with low submission, bows,
>   And to his God appeals.
>
> Oh! scorn it not because 'tis poor,
> Nor turn thee from its sacred door,
>   With contumelious pride;
> But entering in—that Power adore,
> Who gave thee, on a milder shore,
>   In safety to reside.
>
> Let no presumptuous thoughts arise,
> That thou art dearer in his eyes
>   Than poor Icelandic swain;
> Who bravely meets the northern wind,
> With brow serene—and soul resign'd
>   To penury and pain.
>
> Where much is given—more is required;
> Where little—less is still desired;
>   Enjoy thy happier lot
> With trembling awe, and chasten'd fear;
> *Krisuvik's Church to God is dear,*
>   *And will not be forgot.*

FAREWELL TO FIFE.

> Adieu to thee, delightful land!
>   Ages have o'er thee past,
> And round each mould'ring tower of thine,
>   Their hoary mantle cast.
>
> I've lov'd thee with the love of one,
>   Whose home was far away,
> And through thy verdant vales my feet,
>   In youth, rejoiced to stray.
>
> But now we part, and it may be,
>   That years shall wing their flight,
> Ere thou again wilt cheer my eye,
>   Or burst upon my sight.
>
> Then fare thee well! in other days,
>   In after years of life,
> On Fancy's wing I'll turn to thee,
>   And bless the land of Fife!   ANON.

MILITARY FLOGGING.—" The offender is sometimes sentenced to receive a thousand lashes; a surgeon stands by to feel his pulse during the execution, and determine how long the flogging can be continued without killing him. When human nature can sustain no more, he is remanded to prison; his wound—for from the shoulder to the loins it leaves him one wound——is dressed; and as soon as it is sufficiently healed, to be laid open again in the same manner, he is brought out to undergo the remainder of his sentence. And this is repeatedly and openly practised in a country, where they read in their churches, and in their houses that Bible, which saith, " Forty stripes may the judge inflict upon the offender *and not exceed*." We recommend this to conservative legislators—it is the opinion of Dr. Southey.

ADVANTAGES OF FREE TRADE.

A change has lately been made for the better in the American Tariff. Our government has met this relaxation, and step on the right side, by a corresponding relaxation, which must ultimately benefit every body; and in the first place the distressed manufacturers of coarse woollen goods in the counties of York, Lancashire, Cumberland, &c., &c., to whose condition we adverted last week. We dare not tell what those wise changes are, because this is an *unstamped publication*; and to do so would be *news*; but *pat* to the occasion we quote Franklin, whose sayings ought to be no *news*, and then look back to the history of American restrictions. " Suppose," says Franklin, "a country, X, with three manufactures, as *cloth, silk,* and *iron,* supplying three other countries, A, B, C, but desirous of increasing the vent, and raising the price of cloth in favour of her own clothiers. In order to this she forbids the importation of foreign cloth from A.

A, in return, forbids silks from X.
Then the silk workers complain of a decay of trade.
And X, to content them, forbids silks from B.
B in return forbids iron ware from X.
Then the iron workers complain of decay.
And X forbids the importation of iron from C.
C in return forbids cloth from X.
What is got by all these prohibitions?
ANSWER.—All four find their common stock of the enjoyments and conveniences of life diminished."

So intimately has commerce connected nations, that the repeal of a duty across the Atlantic is as sensible an advantage to us as the repeal of a tax in our own country. The taxes on each side of the Atlantic go into different treasuries, but both press alike on the same people—on the community of industrious producers on both sides of the water, whose wealth ought to consist in the unrestricted exchange of each other's commodities. We tax American produce—and the American farmer cannot purchase English clothing; the Americans tax our manufactures, and the English weaver cannot buy food. The Americans reap a harvest of heartburnings and contention; the English a standing army, a crippled revenue, famine, muttered rebellion, and poor rates.

The American restrictive duties were imposed originally as a measure of self-protection. The measure was not a wise one, but it was a natural one. Before the separation of the two countries, our commerce with our colonies was esteemed more valuable than that with all the world besides. After the separation, the Americans desired that the intercourse should continue on the old terms. Jefferson was sent over to negociate a treaty to that effect. He failed. George the Third had conceived the idea, that, by shutting up all intercourse with the colonies, he could produce such a state of distress as would compel them to submit to his own terms. Henceforward the two countries treated each other as foreign states. Restrictions multiplied. We prohibited their spirits, their wood, their sugar, their corn. Then tobacco, and cotton, and potashes were taxed to the utmost, and nothing but absolute famine would make us admit even of a few barrels of their flour. They retaliated; and finally to put a stop to the drain of silver and gold, which our refusal to take their goods for ours occasioned, and to encourage their own manufactures, they passed the famous Tariff, imposing prohibitory duties on the importation of any goods they could manufacture themselves.

The relaxation of this tariff is the consequence of the diffusion throughout the world of commercial knowledge, and of the liberal aspect which the policy of Great Britain has latterly assumed. It must be met, on our side, in a similar spirit. And it will be so met. Both Englishmen and Americans are now too wise to be persuaded by factious knaves and brawling fools, that there is either safety or prosperity in setting at defiance the first law of social existence, which teaches men to enjoy all the comforts of life, by the reciprocal exchange of each other's superfluities.

NOTES OF THE MONTH.
SEPTEMBER.

This month was called *Gerst-monath* by our Saxon ancestors, from a kind of barley which was reaped during it, from which *beer* was made, from which sort of beer is derived *beerlegh*, barley. It is called September, from being the seventh month of the Roman year. It is the *harvest month* of Scotland, on the average of years, and the vintage of England; *cider* and *perry* being now manufactured in all the orchard counties. It is the season of picnics and nutting excursions, which should go hand in hand. *Saffron* is now gathered—a production never raised in our country, though golden fields of it may still be seen near Saffron Walden, in Essex, and on towards Cambridge. The forest trees are now taking the rich and varied hues of autumn; and in the pleasant rustling winds for which this month is distinguished, wherever nipt by early evening frosts, they begin to shed their leaves. In the meadows, and among old pastures, one may now frequently encounter the mushroom-gatherer, and children collecting beech mast, or acorns for the nurseryman; bramble berries are fast ripening on the banks and by the wayside, and nuts in the copses. The deep orange berries of the mountain ash, and the hips and haws are glowing in every hedge. In the vale of Clyde, and wherever there are orchards, fruit is gathered, sorted, and stored. The swallow now again "knows her time," and begins in earnest to take leave of us, till Spring returns. The rural dainties of fruit and honey are daily arriving from the country to our markets—at their best. But reaping is still the grand concern. "The farmer," says William Howitt, "is in the field, like a rural king among his people." The labourer old and young is there; the dame has left her wheel and her shady cottage, and with sleeve-defended arms, scorns to be behind the best of them; the blooming damsel is there, adding her sunny beauty to that of universal nature; the boy cuts down the stalks which overtop his head; children glean among the shocks, and even the infant sits, propt with sheaves, and plays with the stubble, and "with all its twined flowers."—The reaping-hook is almost the only implement which has descended from the olden time in its pristine simplicity. It is the same now as it was in those scenes of rural beauty which the Scripture history, without any laboured description, often by a single stroke, presents so livingly to the imagination; as it was when tender thoughts passed

> Through the sad heart of Ruth, when sick for home,
> She stood in tears amid the alien corn;

when the minstrel-king wandered through the solitudes of Paran, and the fields reposing at the feet of Carmel; or, "as it fell on a day that the child of the Shunamite went out to his father, to the reapers." Let us look on the September reapers in another light,—presented to us by Grahame:—

> At sultry hour of noon, the reaper-band
> Rest from their toil, and in the lusty *stook*
> Their sickles hang. Around their simple fare,
> Upon the stubble spread, blythesome they form
> A circling group, while humble waits behind
> The wistful dog; and with expressive look,
> And pawing foot, implores his little share.
> * * * * *
> The gleaners wandering with the morning ray,
> Spread o'er the new-reaped field. Tottering old age
> And lisping infancy are there, and she
> Who better days has seen.

ENJOYMENTS OF THE POOR.

Let no one say this is not a season of happiness to the toiling peasantry; I know that it is. In the days of boyhood I have partaken of their harvest labours, and listened to the overflowing of their hearts, as they sate amid the sheaves beneath the fine blue sky, or among the rich herbage of some green headland, beneath the shade of a tree, while the cool keg plentifully replenished the horn; and sweet, after exertion, were the contents of the basket. I know that the poor harvesters are amongst the most thankful contemplators of the bounty of Providence, though so little of it falls to their share. To them harvest comes as an annual festivity. To their healthful frames the heat of the open fields, which would oppress the languid and relaxed, is but an exhilarating and pleasant glow. The inspiration of the clear sky above, and of the scenes of plenty around them; and the very circumstance of their being drawn at this bright season from their homes, opens their hearts, and gives a life to their memories.—*Howitt.*

An interesting feature of our Scottish harvest is the annual migration and return of the Highlanders, and latterly of the poor Irish, who, at this season, pour out upon the Lothians like locusts. Fewer have appeared this year than usual, from alarm of cholera.

THE HIGHLAND REAPER'S SONG.

> Such have I heard in Scottish land,
> Rise from the busy harvest-band,
> When falls before the mountaineer,
> On Lowland plains, the ripened ear.
> Now one shrill voice the notes prolong,
> Now a wild chorus swells the song.
> Oft have I listened and stood still,
> As it came softened up the hill,
> And deemed it the lament of men
> Who languished for their native glen;
> And thought how sad would be the sound
> On Susquehana's swampy ground,
> Kentucky's wood-encumbered brake,
> Or wild Ontario's boundless lake,
> Where heart-sick exiles, in the strain,
> Recalled fair Scotland's hills again.
> *Sir Walter Scott.*

THE HARVEST-MOON.

"Two peculiarities of the moon, which occasion a good deal of speculation among those who are ignorant of the causes, are, "the harvest-moon," in September, and "the hunters' moon," in March; the former of which, when near the full, rises for several nights at nearly the same hour; and the latter, at the same age, is equally remarkable for the difference between the times of its rising. The moon moves nearly to the same distance from the sun every day, but it moves in a path the one half of which is much nearer the north than the other; and this is the case also with the apparent annual path of the sun, that luminary appearing much nearer to the north in summer than in winter. Thus, when the moon is moving northward at the most rapid rate, it escapes from the horizon northward, and rises earlier; and when it moves southward at the most rapid rate, it approaches to the horizon, and sets earlier. The full moon can be in the former position only in September or October, and in the latter in March or April; and thus the harvest and hunters' moons are occasioned.

So much for science. But the HARVEST-MOON is also one of the most beautiful objects in the visible creation. "At its rising," says the amiable Howitt, "it has a character so peculiarly its own, that the more a person is accustomed to expect and observe it, the more it strikes him with astonishment. * * * The warmth and balmy serenity of the atmosphere at that season, the sounds of voices borne from distant fields, the freshness which comes with the evening, combines to make the twilight walks delicious; and scarcely has the sun departed in the west, when the moon in the east rises from beyond some solitary hill, or from behind the dark foliage of the trees, and sails up into the still and transparent air, in the full magnificence of a world. It comes not as in common, a fair but flat disc on the face of the sky,—we behold it suspended in the crystal air in its greatness and rotundity; we perceive the distance beyond it as sensibly as that before it; and its apparent size is magnificent."

MEMORABILIA OF THE MONTH.

ON the 3d, partridge-shooting commences, as the fields are now supposed to be cleared of grain, though in Scotland it is often a full fortnight later. The 8th is a high festival of the Romish Church, the nativity of the Virgin. The 14th was *Rood-day*, or the Exaltation of the Cross. Fairs wont to be held on all holidays; and among others we have still the *Rood Fair* at Dumfries. Schoolboys were anciently treated with a *nutting* on *Holy-Rood Day*; the Catholic clergy never being inattentive to the pleasures and amusements of the people. *Michaelmas* day, the 29th, is one of the terms still observed for the election of magistrates, from "The Lord Mayor of London," downward to the most insignificant burgh bailie in Scotland.—Stubble geese are now in perfection, having in England had six weeks feeding; and the goose is accordingly, by prescription at any rate, dedicated to St. Michael. A roast goose is universally the appropriate dinner-dish of Michaelmas day in England. In Scotland the goose belongs of right to Christmas. In Denmark it is the supper of St. Martin's Eve, the 11th November. It is said that the custom of eating goose on Michaelmas day arose from Queen Elizabeth having dined on one with the Governor of the Tower on the 29th September, and while at dinner receiving intelligence of the defeat of the Spanish Armada; but the custom is certainly much older than the reign of Elizabeth. The festival of St. Michael was long observed in Skye, where, "after a procession," the *St. Michael's bannock* was solemnly baked, of which every one partook. In Ireland, a sheep was killed, wherever it could be afforded, and in part given to the poor, in commemoration of St. Michael.

THE SWALLOW—is one of my favourite birds. He is the joyous prophet of the year, the harbinger of the best season; he lives a life of enjoyment amongst the loveliest forms of nature; winter is unknown to him, and he leaves the green meadows of England in autumn, for the myrtle and orange groves of Italy, and for the palms of Africa. He has always objects of pursuit, and his success is secure. Even the beings selected for his prey are poetical, beautiful, and transient. The ephemerae are saved by his means from a slow and lingering death in the evening, and killed in a moment when they have known nothing of life but pleasure. He is the constant destroyer of insects, the friend of man; and, with the stork and the ibis, may be regarded as a sacred bird. He is now taking his leave.

JEWISH HARVEST-HOME.—The Feast of Pentecost was an annual offering of gratitude to Jehovah for having blessed the land with increase. It took place fifty days after the Passover, and hence the origin of its name in the Greek version of our Scriptures. Another appellation was applied to it—the Feast of Weeks. * * * This was a very suitable celebration in an agricultural society, where joy is always experienced upon the gathering in of the fruits of the earth. The Hebrews were especially desired on that happy occasion to contrast their improved condition, as freemen reaping their own lands, with the miserable state from which they had been rescued by the good providence of Jehovah. The month of May witnessed the harvest-home of all Palestine in the days of Moses, as well as in the present times; and no sooner was the pleasant toil of filling their barns completed, than all the males repaired to the holy city with the appointed tribute in their hands, and the song of praise in their mouths. Jewish antiquaries inform us, that there was combined with eucharistical service a commemoration of the wonders which took place at Mount Sinai when the Lord condescended to pronounce his law in the ears of his people.—*Cabinet Library*.

THE STORY-TELLER.

THE GHAIST O' KININVIE.
A TRUE STORY.
(For the Schoolmaster.)

ABOUT the year 1750, a drover returning with his pockets well lined from an Aberlour market, took up his quarters for the night in a farm-house on the small estate of Kininvie, near the romantic and beautiful scenery of the Bridge of Fiddich. He started next morning for the south; and, as he was never afterwards heard of, it was generally believed that he had been murdered. At this period there resided at Hillockhead of Kininvie, William Reid, a stanch old Presbyterian, and member of the Kirk Session of Mortlach—a believer so strong in faith that, as he himself was wont to say—" Wi' my Bible i' my pouch i'll neither fear ghaist nor deil." But soon alas! had poor Willie to tell another tale. One night as Willie was steering his course homewards from Mortlach Manse, a road he oft had measured both early and late, he had just reached the lonesome Brig o' Park, when a large black dog came up to him, barking and howling—stared him in the face—went often round about—and kept him company till near his well known door at Hillockhead.

Willie was so frightened that he almost lost his seven senses; he told far and near of the Ghaist—how it appeared like a black dog, and grew by degrees as big as a horse; and whenever the elder ventured out at night-fall, the Ghaist appeared, and kept him in such a state of alarm that he was soon reduced to a skeleton. The Ghaist persevered in his visits for many a night, to the terror not only of the elder, but of the whole country-side. At last, however, as if wearied of enacting a dumb character, one night when very late, it met Willie on his homeward path, and announced itself as the ghost of him who murdered the drover, ordering him to follow it to a certain spot where evidence of that deed of darkness would be found. The supposed murder immediately presented itself to Willie's mind, he felt convinced of the truth of what he had heard concerning the mysterious disappearance of the drover; and notwithstanding this dread of the Ghaist, and his horror at these recollections, he was constrained by an ungovernable impulse, to accompany his mysterious guide. When he had nearly reached the house of Tininver,—"There," says the Ghaist, pointing to a green spot with a cross hollowed out, "there is the very turf that conceals the remains of the drover;—to-morrow take them up and bury them in consecrated ground. Then I shall have rest and will never trouble you again." After these words, and just as the clock struck twelve, the Ghaist disappeared, with a yell which the rocks of Tininver reverberated in such tremendous echoes, that the ground on which Willie stood seemed to quiver beneath his feet. As soon as day broke, Willie went to the minister of Mortlach, and gave him a faithful account of what he had seen and heard on the preceding night. The good-natured pastor lost no time in collecting a large number of his parishioners, with whom he proceeded, under the elder's guidance, to the celebrated spot pointed out by the Ghaist. After digging to the depth of about four feet, they found some large bones, which they at first supposed to have been those of a sturdy Highlander who had been buried about the same place many years before; but they soon changed their opinion, and were convinced that they had discovered the bones of the murdered drover. The skull, however, was awanting; but as there was no remedying this, they carefully collected all the bones they could find, and deposited them in the churchyard of Mortlach. The minister rewarded Willie for his conduct in this interesting affair, and congratulated him on being relieved from the Ghaist o' Kininvie. Willie left the manse and trudged homewards with a light and happy heart; but on coming to the Brig o' Park, who should appear but the black Ghaist again. It ordered him to go next day to a certain spot at Tininver, where he would find the drover's head, and to bury it with the rest of his bones, which Willie, assisted by the minister and his parishioners, honestly and carefully performed.

The Ghaist o' Kininvie, after that time, no doubt slept sound enough, although thousands who crossed the Brig o' Park afterwards, did so with fear and trembling.

Lately, upon a dreary winter's night, I formed one of a rural party, composed of young and old, and seated as usual before a blazing fire, listening to the tales and gossip which even still have their power to wile away the darkness of a dismal night in the country. The story of the Ghaist o' Kininvie was told in the manner I have now related it, when an old man, with hoary locks, made the following statement:—

When a boy I herded the cows in the woods of Tininver; and oft have I trembled to pass the celebrated spot where it was said the Ghost directed the bones to be lifted. One night in particular, being obliged to pass by the place on my way home, I got a most terrible fright. The darkness was but feebly penetrated, by here and there a wreath of snow which had not yielded to the thaw, although it was now the beginning of March. The wind was up, and the woods of Tininver moaning to the passing gale, conspired to heighten the terror of the hour. This is a dreary place, said I to myself, and oh! but this is a dismal night! Should the Ghost appear to me, I am sure I should die on the spot. Just as I had uttered these words, a rustling noise among some bushes behind me made my head crouch between my shoulders, and my hair stand on end. As I ventured a glance towards the place—oh! horrible!—a thing like a dog was ready to leap upon my back.—I screamed aloud—mercy! mercy!—and fled with the utmost precipitation; but, the object of my terror kept close at my heels until I reached my father's house. The innocent prattle of my sisters—"Eh! Geordy, whar got ye colley?"—Colley, said I,—"Ay, colley," said they—"he's been awa a' day,"—scarcely prevented me from fainting; while it half convinced me that what I had been so much afraid of was nothing more than my father's old dog, which had run into the wood that day after a hare. "Where's my father?" inquired I, rather hastily. "Ben the house wi' a stranger man," was the reply. Thither I went; when my father seeing me so much agitated, inquired what was the matter?—while he at the same time, Scotsman-like, answered his own questions, by saying,—"Ho! ho! ye've been fear'd coming through the wood." "What made you afraid, my man?" said the stranger. "Nothing," said I, sheepishly. "Oh! he's been fear'd for the Ghaist," said my father. —"What Ghaist?" inquired the stranger. "Oh, by the by," he immediately added, "The Ghaist o' Kininvie—I recollect now—Faith that was a well played game. Is that story still believed to be true?" "True," said my father, "ay, as sure as you are Charlie M'Intosh. Though I'm nae fear'd for't mysel', I believe it to be as true as the Bible." "It was just as much a ghaist as I am one," said Charlie, giving proof that he himself was no spirit, by gulping a glass of mountain dew that graced the table, in company with a wooden trencher well plenished with bannocks and cheese.—"I'll tell you the true way of the story," continued he, at the same time setting down the glass, in the hope of its being again filled, which was done more than once during the course of his narration.

The old Laird of Tininver was a merry fellow, as you well know. One of the servant girls had a child to him, of which he was very fond, and was of course anxious to have it christened. Although it was a bastard, he was so intimate with the minister (for many a hearty glass they used to have together) that he imagined there could be little difficulty in obtaining baptism. To his confusion and disappointment however, a William Reid who was a stanch member of the church, became so obstreperous in his opposition to the measure, as to vow he would make the case known to the Presbytery, should the minister attempt to baptize the infant. This menace so operated on the minister and the other members of the session, that it was resolved by a majority to refuse the baptism unless the laird made satisfaction according to the usual forms of the church. The minister announced his resolution to the laird, informing him at the same time, that it was Reid who had influenced the votes against him. This intelligence highly enraged the laird, who but a short time before had saved Reid from ruin by coming to his relief when his creditors were about to roup his all; and from that moment he determined on vexing and punishing the ungrateful elder.

The laird had a man who was "fu' o' tricks," to whom he told what had happened, and who readily and cheerfully agreed to be the instrument for accomplishing his purposes. Accordingly, next time Reid was in Mortlach attending the session, the laird's man waylaid him at a lonely place near the Brig o' Park, and having previously fitted two or three black dogs' skins to his body, got upon all fours, and by barking and howling, succeeded in frightening poor Reid almost out of his wits. Next day it was spread through the whole country-side that William Reid, the elder, had seen a ghost in the shape of a big black dog, which had barked at him, and had threatened to appear again. Prayer meetings were held in Reid's house, and every means tried that could be thought of to "lay" the spirit, but in vain; for the elder was continually visited in the same way. At last the man in dog-skin getting wearied of so many nights' excursions, told the laird that it was necessary the business should be brought to an end in some way or other. Having recollected the spot where a *calf* had been buried many years before, the head of which had been previously cut off, in order to terrify a timorous old woman, he proposed to make Reid believe that its bones were those of a murdered man, and cause him lift and bury them in the churchyard. The laird approved of this plan. The Ghaist appeared again to Reid in one of his nocturnal journeyings from the manse, and declared himself to be the ghost of a man who had murdered a drover, desiring the elder to come along with him that he might shew him where he had buried the body, and promising that, if he would lift the bones and bury them in consecrated ground, he would trouble him no more. Reid was rejoiced at the rospect of bidding an eternal farewell to so frightful an apparition, and gladly allowed himself at the dark hour of midnight, to be led to the calf's grave, when the ghost, after again renewing his charge anent the lifting of the bones, vanished with a hideous howl into an adjoining thicket, while poor Reid was left to escape from his terrible situation the best way he could. Next day he reported the circumstance to the minister, who, with the elders, and almost all the other parishioners, proceeded to lift the bones, which they, with due solemnity, removed and buried in the churchyard. Both the laird and his man were present, and saw and heard what passed, with no small satisfaction at the success of their stratagem. All the bones except the shanks were decayed, having been buried many years. The minister said, " He had been a strong man," and added, " but the strongest may be overpowered." " I wonder," said one of the elders, " how the skull is not to be seen, for I have known the skull to be quite whole when no other bone was to the fore; surely his head has been made away with." " No," said William Reid; " for the ghaist told me he was brought down by the help of a dog, and then murdered with a stick." The murmurings about the absence of the skull raised a fear in the minds of the laird and his man, that the whole affair would be discovered to be an imposture; and to prevent this, they, on the same day, procured a skull from the kirkyard, and laid it down near the place whence the bones were lifted. The Ghaist again appeared that night to Reid, and told him that a bone had been left, which, for his future peace, he must go back and find. Accordingly next day the skull was found, and laid beside the bones of the calf in the kirkyard of Mortlach.

When Charlie had finished his story, my father exclaimed, " Weel, if that be true, mony a' ane has been frightened for naething." " There is no fear of it's being true," said Charlie, " for Sandy Roy told it to me the night before he went to Germany with the 42d regiment, and from whom could you hear it better than from the Ghaist himself?"

MOUSTACHE,* A BIOGRAPHICAL SKETCH.

ARMA CANEMQUE CANO!

MOUSTACHE was Born at Falaise, in Normandy, as nearly as can be ascertained, in or about the month of September, 1799. The family being numerous, he was sent, at the age of six months, to Caen to push his own fortunes, and was received into the house of an eminent grocer, where he was treated in the kindest manner.

But, strolling about the town one day, not long after his arrival, he happened to come upon the parade of a company of grenadiers who had just received the route for Italy. They were brilliantly equipped,—their spirits were high,—and their drums loud. Moustache was fired on the instant with a portion of their fine enthusiasm. He cut the grocer for ever, slunk quietly out of the town, and joined the grenadiers ere they had marched an hour.

He was dirty—he was tolerably ugly—but there was an intelligence, a sparkle, a brightness about his eye that could not be overlooked. " We have not a single dog in the regiment," said the petit tambour, " and, at any rate, he looks as if he could forage for himself." The drum-major, having his pipe in his mouth, nodded assent; and Moustache attached himself to the band.

The recruit was soon found to be possessed of considerable tact, and even talent. He already fetched and carried to admiration. Ere three weeks were over he could not only stand with as erect a back as any private in the regiment, but shoulder his musket, act sentinel, and keep time in the march. He was a gay soldier, and of course lived from paw to mouth; but, long ere they reached the Alps, Moustache had contrived to cultivate a particular acquaintance with the messman of his company,—a step which he had no occasion to repent.

He endured the fatigues of Mont St. Bernard with as good grace as any veteran in the army, and they were soon at no great distance from the enemy. Moustache by this time had become quite familiar with the sound not only of drums, but of musketry; and even seemed to be inspired with new ardour as he approached the scene of action.

The first occasion on which he distinguished himself was this :—His regiment being encamped on the heights above Alexandria, a detachment of Austrians, from the vale of Belbo, were ordered to attempt a surprise, and marched against them during the night. The weather was stormy, and the French had no notion any Austrians were so near them. Human suspicion, in short, was asleep, and the camp in danger. But Moustache was on the alert; walking his rounds, as usual, with his nose in the air, he soon detected the greasy Germans. Their knapsacks, full of sourcrout and rancid cheese, betrayed them to his sagacity. He gave the alarm, and these foul feeders turned tail immediately,—a thing Moustache never did.

Next morning it was resolved, nem. con. that Moustache had deserved well of his country. The Greeks would have voted him a statue; the Romans would have carried him in triumph, like the geese of the Capitol. But Moustache was hailed with a more sensible sort of gratitude. He would not have walked three yards, poor fellow, to see himself cast in plaster; and he liked much better to tread on his own toes than to be carried breast high on the finest hand-barrow that ever came out of the hands of the carpenter. The colonel put his name on the roll—it was published in a regimental order, that he should henceforth receive the ration of a grenadier per diem—and Moustache was " le plus heureux des chiens." †

He was now cropped à la militaire,—a collar, with the name of the regiment, was hung round his neck, and the barber had orders to comb and shave him once a-week.

From this time Moustache was certainly a different animal. In fact he became so proud, that he could scarcely pass any of his canine brethren without lifting his leg.

In the mean time, a skirmish occurred, in which Moustache had a new opportunity of shewing himself. It was here that he received his first wound,—it, like all the rest, was in front. He received the thrust of a bayonet in his left shoulder, and with difficulty reached the rear. The regimental surgeon dressed the wound which the Austrian steel had inflicted. Moustache suffered himself to be treated secundum artem, and remained in the same attitude, during several entire days, in the Infirmary.

He was not yet perfectly restored when the great battle of Marengo took place. Lame as he was, he could not keep away from so grand a scene. He marched, always keeping close to the banner, which he had learned to recognize among a hundred; and, like the fifer of the great Gustavus, who whistled all through the battle of Lutzen, Moustache never gave over barking until evening closed upon the combatants of Marengo.

The sight of the bayonets was the only thing that kept him from rushing personally upon the Austrians; but his good fortune at last presented him with an occasion to do something. A certain German corporal had a large pointer with him, and this rash animal dared to shew itself in advance of the ranks. To detect him—to jump upon him—and to seize him by the throat—all this was, on the part of Moustache, only a mouvement à la Française. The German, being strong and bulky, despised to flinch, and a fierce struggle ensued. A musket-ball interrupted them; the German dog fell dead on the spot; and Moustache, after a moment of bewilderment, put up his paw, and discovered that he had lost an ear. He was puzzled for a little, but soon regained the line of his regiment; and Victory having soon after shewn herself a faithful goddess, ate his supper among his comrades with an air of satisfaction that spoke plainer than words,—" When posterity talk of Moustache, it will be said, That dog also was at Marengo."

I think it has already been observed, that Moustache owned no particular master, but considered himself as the dog of the whole regiment. In truth, he had almost an equal attachment for every one that wore the French uniform, and a sovereign contempt to boot for every thing in plain clothes. Trades-people and their wives were dirt in his eyes, and whenever he did not think himself strong enough to attack a stranger, he ran away from him.

He had a quarrel with his grenadiers, who, being in garrison, thought fit to chain Moustache to a sentry-box. He could not endure this, and took the first opportunity to escape to a body of chasseurs, who treated him, with more respect.

" The sun of Austerlitz" found him with his chasseurs. In the heat of the action he perceived the ensign who bore the colours of his regiment surrounded by a detachment of the enemy. He flew to his rescue—barked like ten furies—did everything he could to encourage the young officer—but all in vain. The gentleman sunk, covered with a hundred wounds; but not before, feeling himself about to fall, he had wrapt his body in the folds of the standard. At that moment the cry of

* This story, published in JANUS, is taken, but not translated, from the Anecdotes du dix-neuvième siècle.

† The happiest of dogs.

victory reached his ear: he echoed it with his last breath, and his generous soul took its flight to the abode of heroes. Three Austrians had already bit the dust under the sword of the ensign, but five or six still remained about him, resolved not to quit it until they had obtained possession of the colours he had so nobly defended. Moustache, meanwhile, had thrown himself on his dead comrade, and was on the point of being pierced with half-a-dozen bayonets when the fortune of war came to his relief. A discharge of grape-shot swept the Austrians into oblivion. Moustache missed a paw, but of that he thought nothing. The moment he perceived that he was delivered from his assailants, he took the staff of the French banner in his teeth, and endeavoured all he could to disengage it. But the poor ensign had griped it so fast in the moment of death, that it was impossible for him to get it out of his hands. The end of it was, that Moustache tore the silk from the cane, and returned to the camp. limping, bleeding, and laden with this glorious trophy.

Such an action merited honours; nor were they denied. The old collar was taken from him, and General Lannes ordered a red ribbon to replace it, with a little copper-medal, on which were inscribed these words:—" Il perdit une jambe à la bataille d'Austerlitz, et sauva le drapeau de son regiment."* On the reverse:—" Moustache, chien Français: qu'il soit partout respecté et cheri comme un brave." Meantime it was found necessary to amputate the shattered limb. He bore the operation without a murmur, and limped with the air of a hero.

As it was very easy to know him by his collar and medal, orders were given, that at whatever mess he should happen to present himself, he should be welcomed en camarade; and thus he continued to follow the army. Having but three paws and one ear, he could lay small claims to the name of a beauty; nevertheless, he had his little affairs of the heart. Faithful in every thing to the character of a French soldier, Moustache was volatile, and found as many new mistresses as quarters.

At the battle of Essling, he perceived a vidette of his own species; it was a poodle. Moustache rushed to the combat; but O, tender surprise! the poodle was a ————. More happy than Tancred, who had not wit enough to recognise his Clorinda, Moustache in a single instant found his martial ardour subside into transports of another description. In a word, he seduced the fair enemy, who deserted with him to the French camp, where she was received with every consideration.

This attachment lasted the best part of a year. Moustache appeared before his comrades in the new capacity of a father; and the Moll Flagons of the regiment took great care of his offspring. Moustache seemed to be happy. His temper was acquiring a softer character. But one day a chasseur, mistaking his dog no doubt, hit him a chance blow with the flat side of his sabre. Moustache, piqued to the heart, deserted, abandoning at once his regiment and his family. He attached himself to some dragoons, and followed them into Spain.

He continued to be infinitely useful in these new campaigns. He was always first up and first dressed. He gave notice the moment any thing struck him as suspicious; he barked at the least noise, except during night-marches, when he received a hint that secrecy was desirable. At the affair of the Sierra-Morena, Moustache gave a signal proof of his zeal and skill, by bringing home in safety to the camp the horse of a dragoon who had had the misfortune to be killed. How he had managed it no one could tell exactly; but he limped after him into the camp; and the moment he saw him in the hands of a soldier, turned and flew back to the field.

Moustache was killed by a cannon-ball, on the 11th of March, 1811, at the taking of Badajos. He was buried on the scene of his last glories, collar, medal, and all. A plain stone served him for a monument; and the inscription was simply,—

"CY GIT LE BRAVE MOUSTACHE."

ORIGINAL ANECDOTE OF HENRY BROUGHAM.
For the Schoolmaster.

In the year 18—, as Wull, or William Hall, then overseer of the farm of Sunderland, in Selkirkshire, Scotland, the labours of the day being over, was leaning against the dyke of the farm yard, a young gentleman of genteel appearance came up to him, wished him good evening, and observed that the country here looked beautiful. The two getting into conversation, Hall, who was a talkative lad, after a few observations, asked him " where he was ga'in?" He said he intended going to Jedburgh; " And what business hae ye at Jeddart?" says Wull. "Oh," says the gentleman, "I am going to attend the Circuit Court; but my feet have failed me on the road." And observing a pony in the farm-yard, he said " That's a bit nice pony of your's;—is it to sell?—would ye like to part with it?" " A wad'na' care," Wull says; " but ma brother Geordy, he's the farmer; and he's at Selkirk the day. But if we could get a guid price for't, a daresay we might part wi't." " What do you ask for it?" says the stranger. " Ma brother," quoth Wull, " says it's a thing we hae nae use for, and if we could get ought of a wiselike price for't, it would be as weel to let it gang."

There were only two words to the bargain, the gentleman and Wull agreed. Says the gentleman, " By the way, I cannot pay you to-night, but if you have any hesitation about me, my name is HENRY BROUGHAM, and I refer you to the Earl of Buchan, or Mr. George Currie of Greenhead, who will satisfy you:"—It will be observed that the places of residence of this nobleman, and Henry's brother advocate, Mr. Currie, were in the neighbourhood. On this reference, without making any inquiry, honest Wull immediately gave the gentleman the pony with the necessary trappings.

Wull being a man of orderly habits, went early to bed; and next morning when the business of the farm called him and Geordy together, says Wull to Geordy, " Ye was unco late in coming hame last night;—Aw selt the powny."
" And wha did you sell it to?" says Geordy. " Oh, to a young gentleman." " And what did ye get for't?" Wull having mentioned the price,—" My faith," says Geordy, " ye hae selt it weel." " But," says Wull, " a did na' get the siller." " You d————d idiot, ye did na' gie away the powny without getting the siller for't; wha was he?" " Oh, he ca'd himsel' Henry Brougham, and he said if a had any jealousin' about him, that the Earl of Buchan, or George Currie, advocate, Greenhead, would say he was guid enough for the money. Oh, he was an honest-looking lad; a could hae trusted ony thing in his hand." Geordy's temper became quite ungovernable at Wull's simplicity. After the whole Southern Circuit was finished, there was no word of payment, and Wull's life became quite miserable at Geordy's incessant grumbling and taunting; the latter ever and anon repeating, " What a d————d idiot Wull was to gie the beast without the money till a man he kend naething about;" and the other as pertinaciously insisting, " that he (the gentleman) was an honest looking man, there was nae fear o' him." In the course of six weeks an order came for the payment of the steed. " L————d," says Wull, " did na a tell ye he was an honest man, a kend by the look o' him."

From that moment Wull stood eminently high in Geordy's eyes; and while the one chuckled at his penetration of character, the other was no less humbled at having called his superior judgment in question.

William Hall is still alive, and there is not a prouder man in Britain's Isle, than he is, when he relates the little incident in his life, of which the present LORD CHANCELLOR of Great Britain forms the hero.

A SCOTCH GENTLEMAN AND REPUBLICAN.—Laing the historian has celebrated the character of Fletcher of Saltoun, which is thus dashed off in a few masterly strokes by Mackay:—" He is a gentleman steady in his principles; of nice honour; brave as the sword he wears, and bold as a lion; would lose his life readily to serve his country, and would not do a base thing to save it."

---

* He lost a leg in the battle of Austerlitz; and saved the colours of his regiment.

HYDROPHOBIA.

(From a Paper in the Westminster Review.)

Hydrophobia in man is of rare occurrence. During the last thirty years only six or eight cases have been known at Bartholomew's Hospital, and among twenty persons, who at one time were bitten, only one had the disease; so that the exceptions from the effects of this supposed virulent poison, here seem to form the rule, whilst the observance of the usual laws of cause and effect, if the received theory of hydrophobia be a true one, are very rare; not more frequent than one in twenty! It is said, that there are ten animals besides the human species, that are susceptible of this disease. They are the dog, wolf, fox, and the cat; the horse, ass, mule, cow, sheep, and pig. The first four only as it is pretended, have the power of communicating it. The mysterious and capricious agency with which, among the human species, hydrophobia has hitherto appeared to select its victims, has been one fearful adjunct in the catalogue of its horrors. It has set at defiance all the laws by which we reason, either from experience or analogy. By some unknown spell it has seemed to seize upon its unhappy choice, and to have exerted its baneful influence peculiarly over the powers of his mind. But on a short examination, the solution of the enigma presented itself. As far as we know, it has never occurred to any one to suppose, that the cause of this direful malady originates in the nature and shape of the wound, and not from any virulent matter injected into it. A wound made with a pointed instrument, a nail for instance, in the hand or foot, has not unfrequently been followed by tetanus; and the same consequences have succeeded a wound where the nerve has been injured, without being divided. It deserves particular notice, that the only four animals that are said to have the power of communicating this malady have teeth of a similar form. They would make a deeply-punctured wound, which is precisely the kind of wound which more often than any other is the herald of tetanus. Though the symptoms of hydrophobia have hitherto been considered somewhat to differ from tetanus, they agree in their principal characteristics; in being spasmodic, in peculiarly affecting the muscles of the throat, and, in short, in producing the same great excitement in the whole nervous system. A more attentive examination of the subject will perhaps show, that the symptoms of each disease are more exactly similar than has hitherto been imagined; and that they have been modified only by the peculiar constitution of the patient. All that is meant here to be asserted, is, that there is nothing in the symptoms of the one disease which has not, in its general character, been found in the symptoms of the other. Immense quantities of opium can be borne by those labouring under either disease without the usual effects. Excision is said to be the only remedy in both diseases; and in each it is equally powerless after the nervous excitement has once commenced. The horrible custom is said not to be yet entirely exploded of smothering the unhappy sufferer between two feather beds, from the fear that he may communicate the disease by biting those around him. It has sometimes happened, that under the influence of extreme terror, the poor wretch has, in his agony, begged to be prevented from injuring his attendants; but we have never known of any instance where an inclination to bite has been exhibited. Hydrophobia is no more the necessary consequence of a bite than blindness is. One word on the hydrophobia of animals, and particularly as it appears in the dog; he is more often the subject of the disease, and his domestic habits bring him more under our observation. There seems to be scarcely the slightest resemblance between any of the symptoms of the hydrophobia of man and those of the brute creation. The dog, under the influence of his disease, generally appears dull and out of spirits, and snaps at any person or thing near him. His aversion to fluids is by no means universal—he has very frequently been known to drink a short time before death; so that the horror of water does not form a characteristic symptom of his malady. It applies much more properly to that of the human species, where even the sight of fluids often produces violent spasms in the throat; the contraction has been so great that it has been found impossible to swallow, notwithstanding the earnest wish of the patient to do so. That a dog should be called mad in consequence of having the symptoms referred to above, is a sad error of language, and leads to the many absurd opinions which depend upon this term; we must consider, however, that the moment such an idea enters into the head of any person (who has a tongue also), the alarm of a mad dog is echoed far and wide; the poor animal is hunted about till its frightened condition gives it the appearance of wildness or madness. There are few people who have not, at one time of their lives, felt the terror inspired by either seeing or hearing of such an animal in their neighbourhood. Men may call a certain disease canine madness if they will; our position is, that this disease is not to be communicated to other animals by a bite, but by the usual manner in which other diseases that are called infectious are communicated. It may be as infectious among animals, as the disease called the distemper among dogs is considered to be; or, possibly, it may be an epidemic: either supposition will account for the fact, that dogs in the same neighbourhood have frequently had this disease, when there has been an almost, if not an absolute certainty that they have not been bitten. In conclusion, we state, that the saliva of the so-called rabid animal has no poisonous quality. The disease named hydrophobia in man is caused by the injury of a nerve. When fatal effects occur, there are accidental circumstances attending the wound; and as they more frequently follow punctured wounds than others, the teeth of a dog are as likely to produce them as any thing else, and the reason why every bite is not succeeded by the same consequences is, because no nerve is injured so as to produce the appalling nervous excitement that has received the name of hydrophobia. A witch! the plague! and a mad dog! behold the trinity which long held the dominion of fear over mankind. The days of the first person in this trio are at an end: scarcely can any one be found to pay her homage. The plague, though no trifle, is viewed with less horror, because its nature is better understood, and it may be, at all events, avoided by not entering the fatal locality. A mad dog still exercises a fearful influence over almost all the thinking as well as unthinking portions of society; but the star of his ascendancy may be on the decline, and perhaps the little that has been here said on the subject may contribute to hasten his sinking below our horizon. How much of anguish—how much of apprehension—may be disposed of by the removal of unfounded fears; and in this effort to dispel them, we anticipate the cordial co-operation of others.

Regimental Soup.—The village where Lord Townsend's brigade was quartered on this occasion, had been occupied two days before by the French as an hospital; and it appeared, that to expedite the interment of their dead, they had thrown them into the well of the village. When the soup was served up, a universal complaint was made of its horrid taste; and, although soldiers on a march have seldom an opportunity of indulging in gastronomic fancies, it was agreed on this occasion that some inquiry should be made into the cause which made their meal so unpalatable, when it was speedily traced to the corrupted state of the water in the well. The discovery was sufficient to stay the appetite of most of the company; but among the number present was old Major Hume, of the 25th Foot, then known as the Edinburgh regiment, who had been a soldier from his infancy, and had served with distinction at Fontenoy and Dettingen. After so many campaigns, he had no doubt often been exposed to fare on viands not perhaps the most delicate; and when the company had broken up in a most admired disorder, he proceeded with characteristic indifference to finish his dinner, exclaiming with an oath, that the soup was good, and that it would have been better if the whole French army had been in it.—*Campbell's Memoirs.*

COLUMN FOR THE LADIES.

FEMALE DRESS.

About a century ago Rousseau was preaching to women on this subject of dress, in almost the words of the Phrenological Journal now. There was an *interregnum* in the reign of stays for about the first twenty years of this century, but the restoration seems to be followed, like other restorations, with greater tyranny than before. " It is well known," says Rousseau, " that a loose and easy dress contributes much to give both sexes those fine proportions of body, which are observable in the Grecian statues, and which serve as models to our present artists; nature being too much disfigured among us to afford them any such. The Greeks knew nothing of those Gothic shackles, that multiplicity of ligatures, and bandages, with which our bodies are compressed. Their women were ignorant of the use of whalebone stays, by which ours distort their shape, instead of displaying it. This practice, carried to so great length as it is in England, must in time degenerate the species, and is an instance of bad taste. Can it be a pleasing sight to behold a woman cut in two in the middle, as it were like a wasp?" On the contrary, it is as shocking to the eye, as painful to the imagination. A fine shape like the limbs, hath its due size and proportion; a diminution of which is certainly a defect. Such a deformity also would be shocking in a naked figure; wherefore then should it be esteemed a beauty in one that is dressed!" Rousseau may be content with having emancipated the limbs of infancy from Gothic trammels and ligatures, and may leave the ladies in peace to scold Janet Macdonald for not having tougher stay-laces. Lately some young men in America resolved that they would not marry the wasp-waisted girls, and were very properly answered, that when they left off drinking and smoking, the ladies would not longer insist upon becoming " small" by such rapid degrees. Admiration of the wasp-waist is confined, like that for a fine gown, to the sex themselves. Men at most forgive a blemish, which staymakers' apprentices only can consider as a beauty.

MISS WRIGHT,† THE POLITICAL APOSTLE.

From Ferrall's Ramble in the United States.

The person of Frances Wright is tall and commanding; her features are rather masculine, and the melancholy cast which her countenance ordinarily assumes, gives it rather a harsh appearance; her dark chestnut hair hangs in long graceful curls about her neck; and when delivering her lectures, her appearance is romantic and unique.

She is a speaker of great eloquence and ability, both as to the matter of her orations and the manner of her delivery. The first sentence she utters rivets your attention; and, almost unconsciously, your sympathies are excited, and you are carried on by the reasonings and the eloquence of this disciple of the Gardens. The impression made on the audience assembled on that occasion was really wonderful. Once or twice, when I could withdraw my attention from the speaker, I regarded the countenances of those around me, and certainly never witnessed any thing more striking. The high-wrought interest depicted in their faces, added to the breathless silence that reigned throughout the building, made the spectacle the most imposing I ever beheld. She was the Cumæan Sybil delivering oracles and labouring under the inspiration of the God of Day. This address was chiefly of a political character; and she took care to flatter the prejudices of the Americans, by occasionally recurring to the advantages their country possessed over European states—namely, the absence of country gentlemen and of a church establishment; for to the absence of these the Americans attribute a large portion of the very great degree of comfort they enjoy. If I understand this lady's principles correctly, they are strictly epicurean. She contends, that mankind have nothing whatever to do with any but this tangible world; that the sole and only legitimate pursuit of man, is terrestrial happiness; that looking forward to an ideal state of existence, diverts his attention from the pleasures of this life, destroys all real sympathy towards his fellow-creatures, and renders him callous to their sufferings. However different the *theories* of other systems may be, she contends that the *practice* of the world, in all ages and generations, shows that this is the *effect* of their inculcation. These are alarming doctrines; and when this lady made her *debût* in public, the journals contended that their absurdity was too gross to be of any injury to society, and that in a few months, if she continued lecturing, it would be to empty benches.

The editor of *The New York Courier and Enquirer* and she have been in constant enmity, and have never failed denouncing each other when opportunity offered. Miss Wright sailed from New York for France, where she still remains in the month of July, 1830: and previous to her departure delivered an address, on which the *New York Enquirer* makes the following observations:—

" The parting address of Miss Wright at the Bowery Theatre, on Wednesday evening, was a singular *mélange* of politics and impiety, eloquence and irreligion, bold invective and electioneering slang. The theatre was very much crowded, probably three thousand persons being present; and what was the most surprising circumstance of the whole, is the fact, that about *one half of the audience were females—respectable females*.

" When Fanny first made her appearance in this city as a lecturer on the ' new order of things,' she was very little visited by respectable females. At her first lecture in the Park Theatre, about half-a-dozen appeared; but these soon left the house."

Mr. Ferrall notices, that this lady had organized in New York, associations similar to our *Trades Unions*. These held different doctrines, some being much the same as our own Spenceans. Some of the objects sought are unexceptionable. A just compensation for labour. Abolishing imprisonment for debt. A general system of education; including food, clothing, and instruction, equal for all, at the public expense, *without separation of children from parents*. Exemption from sale, by execution, of mechanics' tools and implements, sufficiently extensive to enable them to carry on business.

The *New York Enquirer* appears to have suffered great alarm from her invasion. It says her doctrines, and opinions, and philosophy, appear to have made much greater progress in the city than we ever dreamt of. Her fervid eloquence— her fine action—her *soprano-toned* voice—her bold and daring attacks upon all the present systems of society—and particularly upon priests, politicians, bankers, and aristocrats, as she calls them, have raised a party around her of considerable magnitude, and of much fervour and enthusiasm."

* * * * *

" The present state of things in this city, says the Enquirer, to say the least of it, is very singular. A bold and eloquent woman lays siege to the very foundations of society, inflames and excites the public mind, declaims with vehemence against everything religious and orderly. She avows that her object is a thorough and radical reform and change in every relation of life—even the dearest and most sacred. Father, mother, husband, wife, son, and daughter, in all their delicate and endearing relationships, are to be swept away equally with clergymen, churches, banks, parties, and benevolent societies. Hundreds and hundreds of respectable families, by frequenting her lectures, give countenance and currency to these startling principles and doctrines."

It is probable that Miss Wright is already forgotten by

---

* We also have the variety *sand-glass*,—made by the squeezing in of stout girls, to whom nature has denied the power of waspifying.

† This lady, originally from Glasgow, or educated there, made a considerable noise in this country before going to America. Extremes meet. She was the friend or patroness of Mrs. Trollope. Hazlitt, in speaking of Edward Irving, gives the true key to what is called success in such eccentric courses as that adopted by Frances Wright. Had Mr. Irving, he says, been a little man, with a thin small voice, and a wig, or lanky hair in small quantity, no one would have looked at him a second time.

all but a remnant of her disciples. There is an immense ballasting of sober sense and sound principle in Britain and America. The apostle generally long outlives the influence of his creed.

TINCTURE OF ROSES.—Take the leaves of the common rose, or cabbage rose, place them, without pressing them, in a bottle, pour some good spirits of wine upon them, close the bottle, and let it stand until it is required for use. This tincture will keep for years and yield a perfume, little inferior to attar of roses; a few drops of it will suffice to impregnate the atmosphere of a room with a delicious odour. Common vinegar is greatly improved by a very small quantity being added to it.

METHOD OF DRYING CORN IN SHEAVES IN SWEDEN.

THE weather has been showery, and may continue so, which induces us, for the benefit of all whom it may concern, to publish the following method, communicated by Mr. Stevens of this city, to the Journal of Agriculture:—

"The simplest method for securing the crop after cutting it down, from being damaged by standing long in stooks on the ground, is that universally practised by the agriculturists in the woody parts of Sweden and Norway, and which never fails in completely protecting at least nine-tenths of the grain from growing in the sheaf, as well as the straw, from any serious injury.

"In those districts, every farmer provides as many "*sädes stör,*" corn stakes (i. e. stakes for drying the grain on,) as will be necessary for the quantity of his growing crop. They are generally made of young white pines, 8 feet long, about 1½ inch diameter at the top, and 4 inches at the bottom. The upper end is pointed, to admit the sheaf passing easily down over it, and the lower end is likewise pointed to facilitate its being fixed in the ground.

"When a field of grain is ready for the sickle, the stakes are conveyed to the spot, and, as the reapers proceed with their work, the stakes are put up in rows behind them, in the same manner, and at the same distance from each other, as is common in stooking the crop. A man, with the assistance of an iron, crow, or spit, will set up five hundred of these in a day. The next operation is to put the sheaves on the stakes. This is performed by raising the first sheaf up to the top of the stake, and passing it with the root-ends downwards to the ground, the stake being kept as nearly as possible in the middle of the sheaf; the sheaf thus stands perpendicular, and round the stake. The second sheaf is fixed on the stake in an inclined position with the grain-end sloping a little downwards, the stake passing through the sheaf at the band in a transverse manner, and in that position it is pressed down to the first sheaf, and thus forms a covering to it. All the other sheaves are threaded on the stake in a similar way as the sheaf last put on, keeping them all one above another, with the root-ends facing the south-west, to receive as much of the sunshine as possible, on account of the greater quantity of grassy substance which they contain at that end. As each sheaf thus acts as a complete covering to the one beneath it, and as there is only one which can touch the ground, rain cannot at any time penetrate through them, and it is very rare that any single heads of grain on a stake are injured.

"I have witnessed these operations performed with as much expedition as actually attends the common way of setting the crop in the field in stooks. The number of sheaves put upon each stake is generally fifteen or sixteen.

"The advantages arising from the above simple manner of protecting the crop are many, exclusive of the consideration of the grain and straw being preserved in a wholesome state. The farmer by it is enabled to commence reaping early in the morning while the dew is yet on the grain. Partial rainy weather does not prevent his operations; he can employ all his people in cutting down the crop before carrying home any part of it; and when he does commence carrying it home, not the least particle is shaken out; for instead of throwing a single sheaf into the corn cart, or waggon, at a time (by which much grain is frequently lost,) the stake, with the whole of its contents, is taken up, put into the cart and carried to the barn-yard.

"When the crop is all carried home, the stakes are collected and laid aside to be similarly applied the succeeding year; and when they are carefully kept during the period they are not in use, they will last twenty or thirty years. I have known many farmers residing in the plains of Sweden, where wood is extremely scarce, who rather than be without such preservatives of their crop, choose to purchase them at a dear rate, and transport them thirty or forty miles to their possessions. Indeed the practice of staking the grain is there so general, and so beneficial, that the number of stakes used is often taken notice of when a lot of land is offered for sale."

THE GLEANER.

FOX AND GOOSE.—The Duchess of Marlborough, at her evening conversations, occasionally covered her head with a handkerchief, and was then supposed to be asleep. She was in that state one evening, at a time which she was much displeased with her grandson, then Mr. John Spencer, for acting, as she conceived, under the influence of Mr. Fox, whose name being mentioned, she exclaimed, "Is that the Fox that stole my Goose?"

In one of the latest days of Fox, the conversation turned on the comparative wisdom of the French and English character. "The Frenchman," it was observed, "delights himself with the present; the Englishman makes himself anxious about the future. Is not the Frenchman the wiser?" "He may be the *merrier*," said Fox; "but did you ever hear of a savage who did not buy a *mirror* in preference to a *telescope?*"

USE OF PERIWIGS.—A barber of Northamptonshire had on his sign this inscription:—"Absolam, hadst thou worn a periwig thou hadst not been hanged;" which a brother of the craft versified:—

Oh, Absolam, oh, Absolam!
Oh, Absolam my son!
If thou hadst worn a periwig
Thou hadst not been undone!

THE DRAYMAN AND THE SOLDIER.—A few days ago a drayman was brutally lashing one of his horses. A Life Guardsman interfered. "Arn't you ashamed," said he, "to lash the animal? You have no right to whip him in that manner!" "Why that's true," replied the fellow, "for the beast isn't paid a shilling a day to be whipped as you are!" The Life-Guardsman walked on.—*Asmodeus in London.*

It is an extraordinary fact, that chalk has not yet been discovered in any part of the vast continent of North America.

A POETICAL IDEA.—Mr. Jones, the Indian chief, at a Missionary Meeting in London, related several amusing anecdotes of the early intercourse of the Indians with the Whites. He said that when whisky and rum were first tasted by his red brethren, they cried out, 'Oh, how sweet and delicious it is! I wish my throat had been two miles long, that I might have tasted it all the way.'

SHEEP-FARMING.—Throughout, the season has been favourable for sheep; for, though the spring was bleak and late, the flocks, for months continuously, had a comfortable bite, and are at present in high condition. The lambing season was got well over; doublets were very common, and the mortality, we believe, lighter than usual. The clip, too, was a good one, and the loss of the fleece, to the animal itself, a benefit rather than a drawback, amid the heat of the dog-days.

CATTLE.—In some districts the disease called the red-water has prevailed to a considerable extent. A simple remedy for this consists in bleeding freely, and in giving a full grown animal about an English pint of common salt, dissolved in 2 quarts of warm water. If this is attended to in the first stage of the disorder, it generally passes away in 24 hours; but if unobserved or neglected, strong purgatives and injections should then be tried, though they often prove unavailing.

BRITISH INCOME AND TAXATION.

A question is often asked, what proportion of a man's income is taken from him in taxes? Now, the total income of the people of Great Britain may be estimated on data, which we have not room to specify, at L.250,000,000.

That of Ireland we may assume at L.50,000,000,—making in the whole for the United Kingdom L.300,000,000. Of this sum more than one-sixth is drawn directly by Government. But that is not the whole. The local taxes amount to a very large sum. The poor's rates in England exceed L.8,000,000. Other local taxes and contributions probably amount to L.10,000,000 more. Then, as we have already explained, the higher and richer classes are exempted in a great measure from contributing their proper share of the national taxation. When these different circumstances are taken into view, it will hardly be disputed that one-third part of every man's income, in the middle and lower classes of society, is taken away by the tax collector. Every man who works nine hours a-day is employed during three of these hours to enable him to pay his taxes.—*Tait's Magazine.*

THE DUKE OF WELLINGTON'S POLICY.—His Grace's habit was never to encourage discussion, or to indulge himself in argument. It was the general observation in the Peninsula that on dining at head-quarters nothing was ever learnt, but that the whole conversation was trifling—a display either of dandyism or buffoonery from the aides-de-camp, or "the gentleman's sons." This system was understood to have been adopted upon a principle of military prudence that no indiscreet remarks should be made, no false interpretations drawn from any casual observation which might escape the commander-in chief. When Sir Thomas Picton arrived at head-quarters, it always produced a sensation; and, as he was a highly intellectual person, an amiable young officer of the guards, who played the part of a very amusing buffo, was always sent for as a check to all serious conversation. Force has always been his means, servility his attendant. While in command in Paris, his table never feasted any of the enlightened men of Europe; the conversation was ever frivolous, a noise with empty words. At Cambrai, the same system was pursued—no one ever presumed to contradict his Grace, or to propose any subject of interest as a matter of conversation.—*From a sketch of the Duke.*

HEALTH OF SHOPKEEPERS.—They are generally temperate in their diet. They injure health, not by direct attacks, not by the introduction of injurious agents, but by witholding the pabulum of life—a due supply of that pure fluid, which nature designed as food for the constitution. Be it remembered that man subsists upon the air, more than upon his meat and drink. Numerous instances might be adduced of persons existing for months and years on a very scanty supply of aliment, but it is notorious that no one can exist for an hour without a copious supply of air. The atmosphere which shopkeepers breathe is contaminated and adulterated; air, with its vital principles so diminished, that it cannot fully decarbonize the blood, nor fully excite the nervous system. Hence shopkeepers are pale, dyspeptic, and subject to affections of the head. They often drag on a sickly existence, die before the proper end of human life, and leave a progeny like themselves.—*Thackrah's Effects of Arts and Trades.*

THE MERCHANT AND MANUFACTURER.—Of the causes of disease, anxiety of mind is one of the most frequent and important. When we walk the streets of large commercial towns, we can scarcely fail to remark the hurried gait and care-worn features of the well-dressed passengers. Some young men, indeed, we may see, with countenances possessing natural cheerfulness and colour; but these appearances rarely survive the age of manhood. Cuvier closes an eloquent description of animal existence and change, with the conclusion that "Life is a state of force." What he would urge in a physical view, we may more strongly urge in a moral. Civilization has changed our character of mind as well as of body. We live in a state of unnatural excitement;—unnatural, because it is partial, irregular, and excessive. Our muscles waste for *want* of action, our nervous system is worn out by *excess* of action. Vital energy is drawn from the operations for which nature designed it, and devoted to operations which nature never contemplated. If we cannot adopt the doctrine of a foreign philosopher, "That a thinking man is a depraved animal," we may without hesitation affirm, "That inordinate application of mind, the cares, anxieties, and disappointments of commercial life, greatly impair the physical powers.—*Ibid.*

ULTIMATE EFFECTS OF STEAM CONVEYANCE.— There seems little doubt that steam-carriages and rail-roads, will, in less than fifty years, have entirely superseded the present means of conveyance. The obvious consequence is the greater rapidity of travelling, as well as greater security; but there are others of an important character. The diminution of the cost of carriage will equalize the value of land and its produce in every part of the country; no one will go into Wales for economy, for prices will be as low at Hampstead. The capital is considered to have a market extending in a circle round it, whose radius is from fifty to sixty miles; the circle will be multiplied in some directions sevenfold, so that the *town* will cease to be a curse. The general produce of the country will also be greatly increased by the easy conveyance of appropriate manures; and all those heaps of articles, of which it is often remarked they are not worth carriage, will suddenly rise into great value. Treasures will start up under the feet of some men. A fishery, perhaps, that was not worth L.3, may become worth L.3000. In steam conveyance, the safety of the passenger is the only limit of speed; what, then, will be the rate of travelling for a cargo that runs no risk? mackerel, for instance: we may expect mackerel from Brighton in an hour, the cart returns with a load of sugar, salt, soot, or slate, in the same time. Farmers, who are the most timid of God's people, and about the most short-sighted, cry out that horses will cease to be wanted; that is very dubious—they may be in still greater demand —but should draught horses cease to be, what then? fewer oats will be wanted, and more wheat may be grown for men, or more turnips for sheep.—*New Monthly Mag.*

VERSES BY AN OLD POET.

In going to my naked bed, as one that would have slept,
I heard a wife sing to her child, that long before had wept;
She sighed sore, and sung full sweet, to bring her babe to rest,
That would not cease, but cried still, in sucking at her breast.
She was full weary of her watch, and grieved with her child;
She rocked it, she rated it, till that on her it smiled;
Then kissed she her little babe, and swore by God above,
The falling out of faithful friends renewing is of love.

BESIDES appearing in WEEKLY NUMBERS, the SCHOOLMASTER will be published in MONTHLY PARTS, which, stitched in a neat cover, will contain as much letter-press, of good execution, as any of the large Monthly Periodicals: A Table of Contents will be given at the end of the year; when, *at the weekly cost of three-halfpence,* a handsome volume of 832 pages, super-royal size, may be bound up, containing much matter worthy of preservation.

PART I. for August, containing the first four Numbers, with JOHNSTONE'S MONTHLY REGISTER, may be had of all the Booksellers. Price 7d. For the accommodation of weekly readers, the Monthly Register and Cover may be had separately at the different places of sale.

CONTENTS OF NO. V.

Young Napoleon..65
Robert Burns..69
Lines on the Church of Krisuvik in Iceland......................71
Farewell to Fife...71
Military Flogging..71
Advantages of Free Trade..71
NOTES OF THE MONTH, &c.—Enjoyments of the Poor—The Highland Reaper's Song; The Harvest Moon; Memorabilia of the Month; The Swallow; The Jewish Harvest Home......72, 73
THE STORY TELLER—The Ghaist o' Kininvie, a True Story, 73; Moustache, a Biographical Sketch, 73; Original Anecdote of Henry Brougham...76
Hydrophobia..77
COLUMN FOR THE LADIES..78
Female Dress; Miss Wright, the Political Apostle.............78
Method of Leaving Corn in Sheaves in Sweden...................78
THE GLEANER..79-80

EDINBURGH: Printed by and for JOHN JOHNSTONE, 19, St. James's Square.—Published by JOHN ANDERSON, Jun., Bookseller, 55, North Bridge Street, Edinburgh; by JOHN MACLEOD, and ATKINSON & Co., Booksellers, Glasgow; and sold by all Booksellers and Venders of Cheap Periodicals.

THE Schoolmaster,
AND
EDINBURGH WEEKLY MAGAZINE.

CONDUCTED BY JOHN JOHNSTONE.

THE SCHOOLMASTER IS ABROAD.—LORD BROUGHAM.

No. 6.—Vol. I. SATURDAY, SEPTEMBER 8, 1832. Price Three-Halfpence.

JEREMY BENTHAM.

The year 1832 will long be memorable for the disappearance of the greatest among those spirits "that had on earth been sojourning,"—Goethe, Bentham, Cuvier, and—by an eclipse as total as death, and far more mournful—Walter Scott. In the same season, Crabbe, the poet, whose worth we seem only to appreciate in his loss, has been gathered home, a ripe sheaf; Wordsworth, declined into the vale of years, is, in approaching blindness, completing his resemblance to Milton, in life as in spirit. To the condition of Coleridge, if we may judge of him from his latest published effusion,* it is painful to advert. In the words of one gone but a little before, and worthy to twinkle as a lesser star even in this glorious constellation—" They have gone out, one by one, like evening lights."— Though some of our readers will scruple to place Mr. Bentham in this lofty category, and though many of them can know of him only as a name, his own disciples, who are now neither few nor inconsiderable persons, will scarcely be contented with the rank we have assigned their venerable apostle, who still remains, with the generality of persons, more glorified in their zeal, than in his own character and pretensions. Mr. Bentham is understood to be the founder of a sect in philosophy, or in morals and legislation, the name signifies the less, as in a few significant and easily intelligible words, his creed,—the basis, the object of his system, is defined, to be

THE GREATEST POSSIBLE HAPPINESS OF THE GREATEST NUMBER.

The principles of this, THE UTILITARIAN SYSTEM, Mr. Bentham has been expounding to the world for a half century, from the calm obscurity of philosophic retirement. It is now perhaps better understood over the continent of Europe than in Britain. Mr. Bentham, who was born, lived, and at a very advanced age, lately died in London, belonged to two great epochs in literature and in politics. He was bred a barrister, but early renounced the law as a profession. Its intricacies, delays, and injustice, observes the New Monthly Magazine, " soon disgusted one, whose vital principle seems to have been benevolence, joined with an intense love of justice ; and as soon as a very moderate income was opened to him, he retired to amend those proceedings he had learned only to lament over. It is not meant that he shut himself up, and lived like a hermit; on the contrary, he loved society, and admitted many to his table— but only such as he himself solicited, and never in number above two or three at a time. In this manner, singly, at his hospitable board, have sat a succession of the greatest men in Europe, for thirty years. He husbanded his time with the most avaricious care ; and it was only during the period devoted to refection and relaxation that he saw any body ; this was during and after his dinner hour, which was as late as seven or eight o'clock. " Mr Bentham," observes the True Sun, in an article written probably by Leigh Hunt, " was an old man, with venerable white locks, social and cheerful, robust in body, and promising a still longer life; but it is always impossible to say, in highly intellectual men, how far the spirit of life is kept up by the mere vivacity of the brain, and subject to abrupt extinction from causes of accident or weather. His appearance, both in the amplitude of his look, the flow of his reverend hair, and the habitual benevolence of his smile, had a striking likeness to Franklin ; and, on a hasty glance, the busts of the two might be confounded. He had all the practical wisdom of one of the sages of good sense ; took exercise as long as he could, both abroad and at home ; indulged in reasonable appetite ; and, notwithstanding the mechanical-mindedness with which his Utilitarianism has been charged, and the suspicious jokes he could crack against fancy and the poets, could quote his passages out of Virgil, ' like a proper Eton boy.' He also played upon the organ, which looked the more poetical in him, because he possessed, on the border of his garden, a house in which Milton had lived, and had set up a bust against it in honour of the great bard, himself an organ-player. Emperors, as well as other Princes, have sought to do him honour, but he was too wise to encourage their advances beyond what was good for mankind. The Emperor Alexander, who was afraid of his legislation, sent him a diamond ring, which the philosopher, to his immortal

* Sonnets in a late Number of Blackwood

honour, returned, saying (or something to that effect) that his object was not to receive rings from Princes, but to do good to the world."

Such was the philosopher, the sum of whose doctrines we now give in his own words:—

THE PRINCIPLE OF UTILITY.

By the principle of utility, is meant that principle which approves or disapproves of every action whatsoever, according to the tendency which it appears to have to augment or diminish the happiness of the party whose interest is in question: or, what is the same thing in other words, to promote or to oppose that happiness. I say of every action whatsoever; and therefore not only of every action of a private individual, but of every measure of government.

By utility is meant that property in any object, whereby it tends to produce benefit, advantage, pleasure, good, or happiness (all this in the present case comes to the same thing); or (what comes again to the same thing,) to prevent the happening of mischief, pain, evil, or unhappiness to the party whose interest is considered: if that party be the community in general, then the happiness of the community; if a particular individual, then the happiness of that individual.

The interest of the community is one of most general expressions that occur in the phraseology of morals: no wonder that the meaning of it is often lost. When it has a meaning, it is this: The community is a fictitious body, composed of the individual persons who are considered as constituting as it were its members. The interest of the community then is,—what? the sum of the interests of the several members who compose it.

It is in vain to talk of the interest of the community, without understanding what is the interest of the individual. A thing is said to promote the interest, or to be for the interest of an individual, when it tends to add to the sum total of his pleasures; or, what comes to the same thing, to diminish the sum total of his pains.

An action then may be said to be conformable to the principle of utility, or, for shortness sake, of utility (meaning with respect to the community at large), when the tendency it has to augment the happiness of the community is greater than any it has to diminish it.

A measure of government, (which is but a particular kind of action, performed by a particular person or persons), may be said to be conformable to or dictated by the principle of utility, when in like manner the tendency which it has to augment the happiness of the community is greater than any which it has to diminish it.

Of an action that is conformable to the principle of utility, one may always say, either that it is one that ought to be done, or at least that it is not one that ought not to be done. One may say also, that it is right it should be done; at least, that it is not wrong it should be done: that it is a right action; at least, that it is not a wrong action. When thus interpreted, the words *ought*, and *right*, and *wrong*, and others of that stamp, have a meaning: when otherwise, they have none.

When a man attempts to combat the principle of utility, it is with reasons drawn, without his being aware of it, from that very principle itself. His arguments, if they prove any thing, prove, not that the principle is *wrong*, but that according to the applications he supposes to be made of it, it is *misapplied*. Is it possible for a man to move the earth? Yes; but he must first find out another earth to stand upon.

To disprove the propriety of it by arguments is impossible; but, from the causes that have been mentioned, or from some confused or partial view of it, a man may happen to be disposed not to relish it. Where this is the case, if he thinks the settling of his opinions on such a subject worth the trouble, let him take the following steps, and at length perhaps he may come to reconcile himself to it.

1. Let him settle with himself, whether he would wish to discard this principle altogether; if so, let him consider what it is that all his reasonings, (in matters of politics especially,) can amount to?

2. If he would, let him settle with himself, whether he would judge and act without any principle, or whether there is any other he would judge and act by?

3. If there be, let him examine and satisfy himself, whether the principle he thinks he has found is really any separate intelligible principle; or whether it be not a mere principle in words, a kind of phrase, which at bottom expresses neither more nor less than the mere averment of his own unfounded sentiments; that is, what in another person he might be apt to call caprice?

4. If he is inclined to think that his own approbation or disapprobation, annexed to the idea of an act, without any regard to its consequences, is a sufficient foundation for him to judge and act upon, let him ask himself, whether his sentiment is to be a standard of right and wrong with respect to every other man, or whether every man's sentiment has the same privilege of being a standard to itself?

5. In the first case, let him ask himself, whether his principle is not despotical, and hostile to all the rest of the human race?

6. In the second case, whether it is not anarchical; and whether at this rate there are not as many different standards of right and wrong as there are men? And whether, even to the same man, the same thing which is right to-day may not (without the least change in its nature,) be wrong to-morrow? and whether the same thing is not right and wrong in the same place at the same time? and in either case, whether all argument is not an end? and whether, when two men have said, " I like this," and " I do not like it," they can (upon such a principle) have any thing more to say?

7. If he should have said to himself, No: for that the sentiment which he proposes as a stand-

and must be grounded on reflection; let him say on what particulars the reflection is to turn? If on particulars having relation to the utility of the act, then let him say, whether this is not deserting his own principle, and borrowing assistance from that very one in opposition to which he sets it up: Or, if not on those particulars, on what other particulars?

8. If he should be for compounding the matter, and adopting his own principle in part, and the principle of utility in part, let him say how far he will adopt it?

9. When he has settled with himself where he will stop, then let him ask himself, how he justifies to himself the adopting it so far? and why he will not adopt it any further?

10. Admitting any other principle than the principle of utility to be a right principle, a principle that it is right for a man to pursue; admitting (what is not true) that the word *right* can have a meaning without reference to utility; let him say, whether there is any such thing as a *motive* that a man can have to pursue the dictates of it? If there is, let him say what that motive is, and how it is to be distinguished from those which enforce the dictates of utility? If not, then, lastly, let him say, what it is this other principle can be good for?

We have somewhere heard, or read, that Mr. Bentham wished he might be permitted to complete the one-half of his earthly pilgrimage five hundred years hence, that he might be enabled to contemplate the happy effects obtained for mankind by his doctrines; a very natural wish for the founder of a system, though too surely, could it have been accomplished, pregnant with deep disappointment. How many new systems will rise and fall within the next five hundred years! How small progress in eighteen hundred years have the principles of that Divine system made, which, once fairly acted on, should supersede, and make void and useless every other!

A SHETLAND PARSON, OR GOOD LUCK AT LAST.

IN 1775, Mr. Andrew Dishington, the assistant of an old minister in the Orkneys, at a salary of £20 a-year, for which he preached in two islands, came up to Edinburgh to solicit the survivancy of his charge, the incumbent being old, and in bad health. The poor helper was disappointed. He had got his travel, or his sail, for his pains; but before going back to his family, he made a visit to an old familiar of early days, Mr. Hepburn, then the minister of Athelstoneford, East Lothian, and so friendly and good a man to poor probationers, that "his house was known to all the black-coat train." Saturday night came in Athelstone Manse. Many a happy "Saturday at e'en" must have brightened what has been successively the dwelling of Home, the author of "Douglas," and of Robertson, the historian. And this was to lead to many happy ones in Shetland; for it brought a letter to Mr. Hepburn, from a friend on his way to Athelstoneford to preach next day, who had fallen from his horse and injured himself, and now solicited, that if any preacher happened to be in the neighbourhood, such reverend person might be sent to officiate in his parish. In this emergency the unsuccessful Orkney solicitor was dispatched early on Sunday morning. His appearance in the pulpit drew forth the following letter, addressed by Sir Hew Dalrymple, to Sir Laurence Dundas:—

Dalzell, *May* 24, 1775.

DEAR SIR,

Having spent a long life in pursuit of pleasure and health, I am now retired from the world in poverty, and with the gout; so joining with Solomon, that "all is vanity and vexation of spirit," I go to church and say my prayers. I assure you, that most of us religious people reap some little satisfaction in hoping, that you, wealthy voluptuaries, have a fair chance of being damned to all eternity.

* * * *

Now, Sir, that doctrine being laid down, I wish to give you, my friend, a loop-hole to creep through. Going to church last Sunday as usual, I saw an unknown face in the pulpit, and rising up to prayers as others, I began to look round the church, to find out if there were any pretty girls there, when my attention was attracted by the foreign accent of the parson. I gave him my attention, and had my devotion awakened by the most pathetic prayer I ever heard. This made me all attention to the sermon. A finer discourse never came from the lips of a man. I returned in the afternoon, and heard the same preacher exceed his morning work, by the finest chain of reasoning, conveyed by the most eloquent expressions. I immediately thought of what Agrippa said to Paul,—" Almost thou persuadest me to be a Christian."—I sent to ask the man of God to honour my roof, and dine with me. I asked him of his country, and what not, and even asked him if his sermons were his own composition, which he affirmed they were. I assured him I believed it, for never man spoke or wrote so well. "My name is Dishington," said he; "I am assistant to an old minister in the Orkneys, who enjoys a fruitful benefice of L.50 a-year, out of which I am allowed L.20, for preaching, and instructing 1200 people who live in two separate islands; out of this I pay L.1 5s. a-year to the boatman who transports me from the one to the other. I should be happy, if I could continue in that terrestrial paradise; but we have a great lord who has many little people soliciting him, for many little things that he can do, and that he cannot do; and if my minister dies, his succession is too great a prize not to raise up many powerful rivals to baulk my hopes of preferment." I asked him if he possessed no other wealth. "Yes," says he, " I married the prettiest girl in the island, and she has blessed me with three children; and as we are both young, we may expect more. Besides, I am so beloved in the island, that I have all my peats brought home carriage free."—This is my story—now to the prayer of my petition. I never before envied you the possession of the Orkneys which I now do, only to provide for this eloquent, innocent apostle. The sun has refused your barren isles his kindly influence; do not deprive them of so pleasant a preacher; let not so great a treasure be for ever lost to that damned inhospitable country; for I assure you, were the Archbishop of Canterbury to hear him, or hear of him, he would not do less that make him an Archdeacon. The man has but one weakness, that of preferring the Orkneys to all the earth. This way and no other you have a chance for salvation. Do this man good, and he will pray for you. This will be a better purchase than your Irish estate, or the Orkneys."

The conclusion of Sir Hew's friendly letter is

not quite in modern good taste. His application was successful. Sir Laurence wrote him:—

"Sir Hew, your man shall get the first vacancy; and to show you that I am fixed in this matter, I will tell you that the Princess Amelia (sister of George III.) desired the favour of me to give my first kirk to a young man of her recommendation. I told her I was sorry I was pre-engaged. She asked to whom? I replied, to you, and she said it was well, for that it was for your man she was applying."

But Mr. Dishington's troubles were not yet over. He obtained the presentation of Mid and South Yell, but so tardily, that he was in danger of losing all benefit from it, the six months being about expired from the death of the last incumbent, and the right of presenting consequently lapsing to the presbytery. It was now the depth of winter, and at that season of the year there is usually no communication between Shetland and Orkney; but when the unlucky presentee had given up all for lost, a small vessel came into Papa Sound, in Orkney, very near the manse, where he then resided; and on inquiring, he rejoiced to hear that it was the Shetland packet on her way from Leith to Shetland. Here was a stroke of good fortune; for this packet has never been known, before nor after, to put into Orkney. Mr. Andrew lost no time in packing up his best black suit, and kissing his children; he made good his landing in time, and became the rejoicing pastor of South Yell, for ever confirmed in his belief of a special Providence, and as devoutly quoting Cicero as if he had achieved a fat Deanery in Lincolnshire. "*Nec vero universo generi humano solum, sed etiam singulis, Deus consuli et provideri solet*"—quoth good Mr. Andrew.

By 1790 the three original olive branches, the only plants that grow to any size in Orkney or Shetland, had increased to 10 in number, and the apostle's means had thriven with them. A manse and offices built at the original expense of L.50, had been repaired for him. A handsome augmentation left the miscellaneous stipend in the following hopeful way: *Butter* 178 *lispunds;* 70 lambs, and 5-12ths of a lamb, and four merks wool with each; 211 *ling*, and the ¼ of a ling; 503 cans, and a ½ can of oil; and L.175 15s. Scots in money, and L.40 Scots for communion elements: altogether L.17, 17s. 7d. English money.

A SHETLAND FLOCK.

The primitive flock of this primitive pastor deserve a passing notice. Their condition is one which political economists, of a certain description, would condemn in the lump. They united the business of fishermen and cultivators, the arable land being divided into small portions. They married early; delved their little farms with the spade, and had no need, their minister tells, of any great stock of goods to begin life. All that was required was a cow, a pot, a spade, a *tusker*, a *buthie*, fishing-rods, and a rug or blanket. Of course the wealthy might have half-a-dozen cows, and as many blankets. They had abundance of peats, and fish in immense quantities. Mr. Dishington says his parishioners of both sexes, made "a very decent and genteel appearance on Sundays;" most of them could read pretty well, and many write; all the women spun wool, and knitted the *Shetland hose*, once so famous; now so scarce. This was a branch of industry their minister did not patronize. The knitter's labours yielded only about 1½d per day; and for this wool was consumed, which, if manufactured into good cloth of all sorts, might, says Mr. Dishington, "serve all ranks for clothing, and put a stop to the pernicious rage they have for foreign fopperies;" such, no doubt, as corduroys, printed shawls, hats, and coloured calicoes; and certainly cotton frame-knit stockings.

Crabbe the poet would have admired the management of the poor in Yell. There was, of course, no workhouse—those dens of human suffering or languishment being still unknown to rural Scotland. The poor of Mr. Dishington's flock were clothed from the kirk funds, and each had liberty to seek his *awmous*, his weekly or monthly dole, in an alloted district of the parish.

THE OLD BEGGAR.
The aged man had placed his staff across
A broad smooth stone, and from a bag
All white with meal, the dole of village dames,
He drew his scraps and fragments, one by one;
And scanned them with a fixed and serious look
Of idle computation. * * * *
While on he creeps
From door to door, the villagers in him
Behold a record which together binds
Past deeds and offices of charity,
Else unremembered, and so keep alive
The kindly mood in hearts, which lapse of years,
And that half-wisdom, half-experience gives
Makes slow to feel.
Among the farms and solitary huts,
Hamlets, and thinly-scattered villages,
The mild necessity of use compels
To acts of love; and habit does the work
Of reason. * * * * *

Some there are
By their good works exalted, lofty minds
And meditative, authors of delight
And happiness, which, to the end of time
Will live, and spread, and kindle; minds like these
In childhood, from the solitary Beggar
The helpless wanderer, have perchance received
(A thing more precious far than all that books
Or the solicitude of love can do!)
The first mild touch of sympathy and thought,
In which they found their kindred with a world
Where want and sorrow were.

LESSONS TO BE LEARNED FROM THE WANDERING BEGGAR.
The easy man
Who sits at his own door—and like the pear
Which overhangs his head from the green wall,
Feeds in the sunshine; the robust and young,
The prosperous and unthinking, they who live
Sheltered, and flourish in a little grove
Of their own kindred—all behold in him
A silent monitor, which, on their minds
Must needs impress a transitory thought
Of self-congratulation, to the heart of each
Recalling his peculiar boons,
His charters and exemptions.
Man is dear to man;—the poorest poor
Long for some moments in a weary life,

When they can know and feel that they have been
Themselves the fathers and the dealers-out
Of some small blessings; have been kind to such
As needed kindness; for this single cause,
That we have all of us *one human heart*.
—Such pleasure is, to one kind Being known,
My Neighbour, when with punctual care each week
Duly as Friday comes, though prest herself
By her own wants, she from her chest of meal
Takes one unsparing handful for the scrip
Of the old mendicant; and from her door
Returning with exhilarated heart,*
Sits by her fire and builds her hope in heaven.

THEODOR KÖRNER.

BORN 31ST SEPT., 1791. KILLED IN A SKIRMISH WITH THE FRENCH TROOPS ON THE 20TH AUGUST, 1813, WHILE FIGHTING, A VOLUNTEER AND PATRIOT-SOLDIER, FOR THE LIBERTIES OF GERMANY.

An interesting account of this heroic person appears in the last number of TAIT'S MAGAZINE, from which we give the following extract; to this is subjoined THE GRAVE OF KÖRNER, by Mrs. HEMANS.

Two hours before the conflict, while bivouacking in the wood, he had composed the last and most remarkable of his war-songs, the celebrated " Lay of the Sword," and read it to a comrade, from the leaf of his pocket-book, on which he had transcribed it in pencil. It was found upon his person after his decease. We must attempt to present to our readers this noble, yet nearly untranslateable lyric, although we feel that no version can approach the power and wild beauty of the original. The startling boldness of the metaphor, the fiery brevity of the language, and a certain tone of stern joy, which distinguish this remarkable strain, absolutely mock the efforts of a translator. At the close of each strophe, the fierce " Hurra !" was to be accompanied by the clang of sabres; it is, indeed, a song such as could not be composed but by one with the very breath of war in his nostrils.

SWORD SONG.

Thou sword beside me ringing!
What means the wild joy springing
　　From those glad looks, and free,
　　That fill my soul with glee?
　　　　Hurra!

" I am borne by a gallant rider,
Therefore my glance is brighter;
　　I am a free man's choice;
　　This makes a sword rejoice."
　　　　Hurra!

Yes! free I am; and prize thee,
Dear sword, with love that eyes thee,
　　As though the marriage-vows
　　Had pledged thee for my spouse.
　　　　Hurra!

" To thee did I surrender
My life of iron splendour;
　　Ah! were the band but tied!
　　When wilt thou fetch thy bride?"
　　　　Hurra!

For the bridal-night red glowing,
The trumpets' call is blowing:
　　At the first cannon's peal,
　　I'll clasp my bridal steel.
　　　　Hurra!

* * * * * * * *

Why in thy scabbard shivering,
Thou iron-gladness quivering?
　　So hot with battle-thirst;
　　Say, bright one, why thou stir'st?
　　　　Hurra!

" Yes! in the sheath I rattle,
With longings keen for battle:—
　　I gasp with war's hot thirst;
　　My bonds I yearn to burst!"
　　　　Hurra!

Yet keep thy narrow cover,—
What wouldst thou yet, wild rover?
　　Rest in thy little home,
　　My lov'd one! soon I come!
　　　　Hurra!

" Now free me! break my prison!
O for Love's fields Elysian,
　　With rose-buds gory red,
　　And glowing wreaths of dead!"
　　　　Hurra!

Then quit the sheath, and pleasure
Thine eyes, thou soldier's treasure!
　　Come forth, bright sabre, come!
　　Now will I bear thee home!
　　　　Hurra!

" Ah! the free air's entrancing,
'Midst the marriage-revellers dancing!
　　How gleams in sun-rays bright,
　　Thy steel with bridal light!"
　　　　Hurra!

Now on! ye valiant fighters!
Now on! ye Almain riders!
　　And, feel your hearts but cold,
　　Let each his love enfold!
　　　　Hurra!

Once, at your left hand prisoned,
Her stolen glance but glistened;
　　Now at her lord's right side
　　God consecrates the bride!
　　　　Hurra!

So to the bright steel yearning
With bridal-transports burning,
　　Be your fond lips applied,—
　　Accursed! who quits his bride!
　　　　Hurra!

Now raise the marriage-chorus,
Till the red sparks lighten o'er us!—
　　The nuptial dawn spreads wide—
　　Hurra! thou Iron-bride!
　　　　Hurra!

On the high road from Gadebusch to Schwerin, in Mecklenburg, hardly two miles from the hamlet of Rosenburg, the affray began. The French, after a short struggle, fell back upon a wood not far distant, hotly pursued by Lutzow's cavalry. Among the foremost of these was Theodor Körner; and here it was that a glorious death overtook him. A ball passing through the neck of his charger lodged in his body, and robbed him at once of speech and consciousness. He was instantly surrounded by his comrades, and borne to an adjacent wood; where every expedient that skill or affection could devise was employed to preserve his life: but in vain. The spirit of the singer and warrior had arisen to its native heaven!

Beside the highway, as you go from Lubelow to Dreycrug, near the village of Wobbelin, in Mecklenburg, was his body lovingly laid to rest, by his companions in arms, beneath an oak; the favourite tree of his country, which he had ever desired to mark the place of his sepulchre. A

---

* In our remote parishes even the solitary maiden, whose sole breadwinner was the spinning wheel, would have fancied her exemption from the customary dole, to " the old remembered beggar" an injury or slight to her free condition; and it may be still observed by mistresses of families in towns, that when they get a young country servant, the tender heart of the maiden conceives it harsh, if not sinful to turn away an old beggar unserved. It takes an apprenticeship to town life to make her suspect imposition in piteous tales; and a long time to convince her that they are often wholly false and deceitful. The duty which falls to the mistress of enlightening the rustic eyes, and hardening the tender heart, is often no pleasing task.

monument has since been raised on the spot. It is a plain, square, pillar of stone, one side of which bears the device of a lyre and sword, with the brief inscription, from one of his own poems, *Vergiss die treuen Todten nicht:*—" Forget not the faithful dead!" a strong, and not a vain appeal!—for surely, so long as the excellence of generous sacrifice, and bright genius, and warm feelings, and whatever else is brave, and pure, and lovely, shall be held in esteem amongst men, this faithful Dead shall not be forgotten; but his tomb will be a place of pilgrimage, and a sanctuary of deep and holy emotions, in all time henceforward. Nor is the sepulture sanctified by his ashes alone. A fair young sister is sleeping there, by the side of the poet-soldier;—his dearest sister, who survived but to complete a last labour of love, his portrait, and then passed away, to rejoin in the grave the object of her undying affection. Their fellowship had been too intimate and entire for death to disturb. A memory of the loving girl will for ever accompany the name of the chief tenant of that tomb, and adorn it with another and more beautiful association.

THE GRAVE OF KORNER.

Green wave the Oak for ever o'er thy rest!
Thou that beneath its crowning foliage sleepest,
And, in the stillness of thy Country's breast,
Thy place of memory, as an altar, keepest!
Brightly thy spirit o'er her hills was poured,
Thou of the Lyre and Sword!

Rest, Bard! rest, Soldier!—By the Father's hand,
Here shall the Child of after-years be led,
With his wreath-offering silently to stand
In the hushed presence of the glorious dead,
Soldier and Bard!—For thou thy path hast trod
With Freedom and with God!

The Oak waved proudly o'er thy burial-rite,
On thy crowned bier to slumber warriors bore thee;
And with true hearts, thy brethren of the fight
Wept as they veiled their drooping banners o'er thee;
And the deep guns with rolling peal gave token,
That Lyre and Sword were broken!

Thou hast a hero's tomb!—A lowlier bed
Is hers, the gentle girl, beside thee lying,
The gentle girl, that bowed her fair young head,
When thou wert gone, in silent sorrow dying.
Brother! true friend! the tender and the brave!
She pined to share thy grave.

Fame was thy gift from others—but for her
To whom the wide earth held that only spot—
—*She* loved thee!—lovely in your lives ye were,
And in your early deaths divided not!
Thou hast thine Oak—thy trophy—what hath she?
Her own blest place by thee.

THE MOST IMPORTANT MARRIAGE EVER CELEBRATED IN SCOTLAND.

THE marriage of our Scottish monarch James IV. with Margaret, daughter of King Henry VII. of England, has merited, from its consequences, the title of *most important*, because it united, in those descended from it, the royal families of the two kingdoms, and terminated thereby the bloody wars which had so long desolated both of them; and it was the remote means of introducing and fostering all the arts of peace, and of raising Great Britain to a degree of power and happiness, which the countries of which it consisted would never have otherwise enjoyed. James V., the son of that marriage, it will be remembered, was the father of Queen Mary; and she was the mother of James VI. In this way that prince succeeded to the *Scottish* crown. On the death of Queen Elizabeth he got also that *of England*, as the descendant of Margaret, Henry the Seventh's daughter, just mentioned; and thus in his person were joined the sovereignties of both kingdoms.

The marriage between James IV. and Margaret took place in the year 1503, above three hundred years ago,—the bride being fifteen, and the bridegroom twenty-nine years old. The following circumstances of the bride's journey to Scotland, her arrival at Edinburgh, and the celebration of her nuptials at Holycross (Holyrood), cannot fail to be not a little interesting to us all, when we reflect what might have been our condition at this day but for the consequences of that marriage,—the gay and happy events connected with which are now to be shortly detailed.

King Henry himself conducted his daughter through Northamptonshire, and then consigned her to the care of the Earls of Surrey and Northumberland. Margaret travelled leisurely, never commencing her ride till noon, nor continuing it beyond five o'clock, when she reached the castle or palace prepared for her reception during the night. Wherever she appeared she was greeted kindly: fair dames and gallant cavaliers followed in her train; and every day produced a repetition of pageantry and jubilee. After a week's progress she reached Berwick, where the Earl of Northumberland gave up his fair charge to the Scottish lords whom James had appointed to receive her. From Berwick she departed in regal state, attired and attended as future Queen of Scotland. To use the language of an old writer—" She was arrayed and crowned with gold and precious stones, sitting in her litter richly appointed; her footmen nigh; her palfrey following after, led by Sir James Wortley, master of the horse. Next came her ladies and gentlemen, mounted on fair palfreys, with their harness rich in apparel; then followed her chariot, and, after that, gentlemen on horseback."

In that manner, attended by two thousand horsemen, she approached *Lamber-church*[*] (or *Lamberterche*, as the old writers call it), where King James's party were waiting for her in a pavilion which had been erected there for the purpose.

" When she was come there," says the same ancient writer, " the Earl of Morton advanced, and kneeling to the ground, made the receiving; and after this she was brought to the pavilion appointed for recreation, and *helped down and kissed by the said lord*. After the receiving done, each put himself in order, and the Queen mounted on horseback. The said Lord of Northumberland made his devoir, at the departing, of *gambades and leaps with his horse*, as did likewise the Lord Scroop, his father, and many others that took charge."

The number of the Scots at this junction was estimated at one thousand persons. Passing through Haddington, the bridal party proceeded to the castle of the Earl of Morton, at Dalkeith, which for the present was to be the bourne of Margaret's pilgrimage. At the gate of the castle she was met by the Countess of Morton, and by her conducted to the state-chamber, where King James, accompanied by a few select courtiers, arrived to welcome her to Scotland. The language of Somerset, the ancient journalist, regarding this meeting, is so *naïve*, that I give his own words. Alluding to the happy pair, he says, " *Having made each other great reverences, his head being uncovered, they kissed together; and in likewise kissed the ladies, and others also*. Then the Queen and he went aside, and communed for lang space; she held good *maners*, and he bareheaded." After this courtly introduction, continues the same author, " they washed their hands in humble reverence, and after set them down togeder. The table being cleared, *the minstrels began to blow*, when danced the Queen, accompanied by my Lady Surrey. This doon, the King took licence of her, for it was late, and went to his bed at Edinburgh, very well content of so fair meeting."

On the young Queen's departure from Dalkeith, she was superbly dressed. She was seated in her wheeled carriage, which had been brought with her from England, and which was the first of the kind that ever had been seen north of the Tweed;[†] and, with a magnificent retinue, she was conveyed towards Edinburgh. When she had proceeded a few miles on the road she was met by James, who, vaulting from his steed, walked for some time by her side; then exchanging his own horse for her more gentle palfrey, he invited her *to mount behind him*; and in this manner they made their entry into Edinburgh. Never, perhaps

---

[*] This is Lamberton, a few miles north of Berwick, where there is a toll-bar. It is the first village in Scotland after leaving Berwick circuit, and, among the country people, is almost as busiest for the irregular marriages celebrated there on the eastern part of the border, as Gretna Green is for those in the west. The people in the neighbourhood have a particular respect for *Lamerton Toll* as a marriage place, saying, that a king and queen were once married there.

[†] That carriage remained in Muthven Castle.—*See Bell's Life of Queen Mary.*

were royal nuptials more sportively solemnized, and never were bridal pair attended by a more numerous and merry cavalcade. The Scots are said to have outshone the English in the superb housings of their steeds, their brilliant armour, and their accoutrements. On approaching the church of the "*Holy Cross,*" (Holyrood) each cavalier leaped from his horse; and James, putting his arm round Margaret's waist, carried her to the altar, at which they were canonically united.

EMIGRATION.
WHO SHOULD GO TO AMERICA.

IT cannot be worth any man's while, who has a means of living at home, to expatriate himself, in hopes of obtaining a profitable office in America. Much less is it advisable for a person to go thither, who has no other quality to recommend him but *his birth.* In Europe it has, indeed, its value; but it is a commodity that cannot be carried to a worse market than to that of America, where people do not inquire concerning a stranger, *What is he?* but, *What can he do?* If he has any useful art, he is welcomed; and if he exercises it, and behaves well, he will be respected by all that know him; but a mere man of quality, who, on that account, wants to live upon the public by some office or salary, will be disappointed, despised, and disregarded. The husbandman is in honour there, and even the mechanic, because their employments are useful. The people have a saying, that God Almighty is himself a mechanic, the greatest in the universe; and he is respected and admired more for the variety, ingenuity, and utility of handy-works, than for the antiquity of his family. They are pleased with the observation of a negro, and frequently mention it, that Boccarora (meaning the white man) make de black man workee, make de horse workee, make de ox workee, make ebry ting workee, only de hog. He, de hog, no workee; he eat, he drink, he walk about, he go to sleep when he please, he libb like a gentleman. According to these opinions of the Americans, one of them would think himself more obliged to a genealogist, who could prove for him, that his ancestors and relations for ten generations had been ploughmen, smiths, carpenters, turners, weavers, tanners, or even shoemakers, and, consequently, that they were useful members of society, than if they could only prove that they were gentlemen, doing nothing of value, but living idly on the labour of others, mere *fruges consumere nati,** and otherwise *good for nothing,* till by their death their estates, like the carcass of the negro's Gentleman hog, come to be cut up.

With regard to encouragements for strangers from government, they are really only what are derived from good laws and liberty. Strangers are welcome, because there is room enough for them all, and therefore the old inhabitants are not jealous of them; the laws protect them sufficiently, so that they have no need of the patronage of great men; and every one will enjoy securely the profits of his industry. *America is the land of labour,* and by no means what the English call Lubberland, and the French *Pays de Cocagne,* where the streets are said to be paved with half-peck loaves, the houses tiled with pancakes, and where the fowls fly about already roasted, crying, *Come eat me!*

Who then are the kind of persons to whom an emigration to America may be advantageous? And what are the advantages they may reasonably expect? Land being cheap in that country, from the vast forests still void of inhabitants, and not likely to be occupied in an age to come, hearty young labouring men, who understand the husbandry of corn and cattle, which is nearly the same in that country as in Europe, may easily establish themselves there. First, they must engage as labourers, and a little money saved of the good wages they receive there, while they work for others, enables them in time to buy the land and begin their plantation, in which they are assisted by the good will of their neighbours, and some credit. Multitudes of poor people from England, Ireland, Scotland,

*——————— born
Merely to eat up the corn.

and Germany, have by this means in a few years become wealthy farmers, who, in their own countries, where all the lands are fully occupied, and the wages of labour low, could never have emerged from the mean condition wherein they were born.

Next week,—or in an early week,—we shall give extracts of letters from Canada, and the United States, which may be useful to intending emigrants.

WITCHCRAFT AND ITS BELIEVERS.—When Lord Chief Justice Holt was on the Oxford Circuit, a woman was put on her trial for witchcraft; having done many injuries to her neighbours, their houses, goods, and cattle, by means of having in her possession a ball of black worsted, which she had received from a person, who *told* her that it had *certain properties.* The poor old woman did not deny the possession of the said ball, but said that she had never done any one *harm* with it, but on the contrary, *good;* and that they only envied her having such an important thing in her possession. "Well," says the judge, "you seem to admit having used the ball as a charm; now, will you tell me how long you have had it, and from whom you had it?" The poor woman answered, that she kept a small public house, near to Oxford, about forty years ago; and one day, a party of young men belonging to the University came to her house, and ate and drank what they liked to call for, but had no money among them wherewith to pay for what they devoured; and that one of the young men gave her, in lieu of it, the said ball, which he assured her would do wonders for her, as it possessed surprising powers; and the youth looked so grave and wise, that she believed him; and she had no occasion to repent of it, for it had really done a great deal of good to her and others. "Well, my good woman," said his Lordship, "did the young man say any thing about unwinding the ball?" "O yes, my Lord, he told me, that if I should do so, the charm would be gone; and here it is (producing it) in the same state I had it forty years ago." The judge having requested her to hand it up to him for his inspection, he thus addressed the jury:—"Gentlemen, I believe it is known to some of you that I was educated at the University of Oxford; and it is now about forty years ago. Like some of my companions, I joined in youthful frolics, which riper judgment taught me were wrong. On one occasion about that period, I recollect of going to the house, which it appears this woman then kept; neither I nor any of my companions having any money, I thought of this expedient in order to satisfy her claim upon us. I produced a ball of black worsted, and having written a few Hebrew characters on a slip of paper, I put it inside, telling her, that in that consisted a charm that would do wonders for her and others: seeing she believed in the deception, we quietly took our departure, but not before I had enjoined her never to undo the said ball. Now, gentlemen, in order to prove to your minds the folly of those who believe in, and persecute, such deluded and silly creatures as this woman, now arraigned *as a witch,* I will undo this ball before your eyes, and I have no doubt will find the characters I wrote on a slip of paper forty years ago." The judge soon unwound the ball, and produced the identical paper, with the Hebrew characters; which so convinced the jury of the folly and absurdity of the then general belief, that the woman was immediately pronounced NOT GUILTY, and discharged.

ORGANIC DEFECTS.—Professor Rudolphi, in a memoir read before the Berlin Academy of Sciences, remarks, that the intermarriage of parties who labour under defective organs, is not a matter of such little moment as many apprehend. "It fell under our observation," says he, "that here, in Berlin, a deaf person having married a person who could hear, the male offspring of this marriage are all deaf and dumb, whilst the females have their hearing perfect. It has been also communicated from North America, that, in one family several members for various generations have been struck with blindness at a certain age. Block mentions, that, in the family of a Berliner, a severing of the iris and a central cataract are hereditary; and I am acquainted with a girl, who is one of the youngest of that family, and is afflicted with these evils in both eyes. Indeed, we may observe the absence of the black pigment of the eye in more animals than the white mouse and rabbit."

ELEMENTS OF THOUGHT.

MIND.

Mind has, by its own native energy, won for itself its proper station in the affairs of the external world. Not only has it given laws to nature, but it is now exerting supreme dominion over the great heart of society. The spirit of the age is of its begetting; the march of intellect is but its going-forth. The age of reason long ago commenced. In its infancy, by the mere novelty of its appearance, it startled the state " from its propriety :" then came its non-age,—the period between puberty and manhood,—during which its character was felt to be doubtful, as at such seasons character always is. But the fixed time awaited it; the inevitable years advanced, and its manhood appeared in the attributes of resolution. Such is the attitude which it has now assumed; the free daring of its mien is not to be cowed. It wakes, glorious in its strength, as the sun when he rises, like a giant rejoicing to run his course. But shall its setting come also at last? Nay, what has mind to do with rising or setting, or with day and night? Chance and change approach not the pure element which it inhabiteth; time is but the motion of its thoughts, and space only the intuition of its feelings. Let but its fiat be uttered, and the universe shall shake to its foundations, or a new world start from the ruins of the old.

GREAT MEN.

In the more enlightened classes of individuals, some now and then rise up, who, through a singular force and elevation of soul, obtain a sway over men's minds to which no limits can be prescribed. They speak with a voice which is heard by distant nations, and which goes down to future ages. Their names are repeated with veneration by millions, and millions read in their lives and writings, a quickening testimony to the greatness of the mind, to its moral strength, to the reality of disinterested virtue. These are the true sovereigns of the earth. They share in the royalty of Jesus Christ. They have a greatness which will be more and more felt. The time is coming, its signs are visible, when this long-mistaken attribute of greatness will be seen to belong eminently, if not exclusively, to those, who, by their character, deeds, sufferings, writings, leave imperishable and ennobling traces of themselves on the human mind.

ORTHODOXY.

Orthodoxy* is a Greek word, which signifies *a right opinion*, and hath been used by churchmen as a term to denote a soundness of doctrine or belief with regard to all points and articles of faith. But as there have been among those churchmen several systems of doctrine or belief, they all assert for themselves that they *only* are *orthodox*, and in the right, and that all others are heterodox, and in the wrong. What is orthodoxy at Constantinople, is heterodoxy, or heresy, at Rome. What is orthodoxy at Rome, is heterodoxy at Geneva, London, and many other places. What was orthodoxy here in the reign of Edward VI., became heresy in the reign of his sister Mary; and in Elizabeth's time things changed their names again. Various was the fate of those poor words in the reigns of our succeeding kings, as the currents of Calvinism, Arminianism, and Popery ebbed and flowed.—*Dr. Robertson.*

* The definition given by a Loanhead weaver to a Gilmerton carter, is as complete, and more brief—" I say, David, you that kens a' thing, the minister was telling us yesterday about orthodoxy and *heterodoxy*—now, what's that?"—" I'll soon tell ye that, Jock.—When your doxy and my doxy 'gree, ye observe—well, that's orthodoxy; but when your doxy and my doxy differ—that's heterodoxy."—No definition could be more complete.

THE PETTICOAT KIRK.

Patronage is the most absurd and unreasonable bondage ever inflicted upon men. One great apology for its exercise is, that the presentee must every way be fit for those upon whom he is forced, for the Presbytery have licensed him. Now, observe this reasoning. The college of physicians license a professional man, but of all whom they license they allow me to make my choice. Not so the patron and the Presbytery :—here is the man, and a whole congregation must take him to be their pastor. How shamefully absurd! I can choose the man to care for my body, but I cannot choose the man to care for my soul!! The same holds with respect to a lawyer :—he has been licensed by the faculty of advocates, but I may take my choice of any one I think best :—thus I may choose the man to whom I commit my character or my worldly fortune; but the patron and the Presbytery will force me to commit my spiritual comfort and eternal welfare to any man they please. Now, I have a word for the patron. He has a beautiful daughter, and an accomplished young lady she is. I say to her father, the patron of the kirk, I mean to present a husband to your daughter, and she must marry him whether she will or not. It is true, he is not well behaved, and he will spend her fortune!!! What an outcry the father, and mother, and daughter would make. You will ruin my daughter's comfort all her life. What, then, I reply, you will ruin my comfort in this life, and in the life that is to come. Which is the most to be pitied—your daughter or me? Let the affair of patronage be fairly examined, and you will perceive the colouring of the picture is not overcharged. But patronage takes other cunning ways to effect the same purpose. The young preacher makes up to the patron's daughter, for he knows well that in any other way he will never get a kirk. And now the patron's daughter must be provided with a husband, at the expense of the feeling, comfort, and edification, of a whole parish, during his incumbency. Now, a kirk that is disposed of in this way is, in every sense of the word, a *petticoat kirk*. But if the preacher has money or friends, ways and means may be taken secretly to buy the living. And this is sometimes resorted to. In this case, we may safely call the kirk secrectly bought, a *penny kirk*. Another way may be open for the disposal of a kirk, and that is in the case of an election. The patron may say to an elector, if you vote for me or my friend you shall have the vacant kirk! A kirk disposed of in this way may be called a *political kirk.* The words sound harmoniously—A petticoat kirk—a penny kirk—a political kirk !—*Dr. Kidd of Aberdeen.*

MANUFACTURES.

Manufactures are founded in poverty. It is the multitude of poor without land in a country, and who must work for others at low wages, or starve, that enables undertakers to carry on a manufacture, and to afford it cheap enough to prevent the importation of the same kind from abroad, and to bear the expense of its own exportation. But no man who can have a piece of land of his own, sufficient by his labour to subsist his family in plenty, is *poor enough* to be a manufacturer, and to work for a master. Hence, while there is land enough in a country sufficient for the people, upon easy terms, there can be no manufactures to any amount or value. It is an observation founded upon facts, that the natural livelihood of the thin inhabitants of a forest country is hunting; that of a greater number pasturage; and that of a middling population agriculture; and that of the greatest, manufactures; which last must subsist the bulk of the people in a full country, or they must be subsisted by charity, or perish.—*Franklin.*

THE ORGAN.—Two Highlandmen, kilted in primitive order, dropped inadvertently into St. Paul's Chapel, York Place, on a Sunday, and seated themselves in a respectable pew. Having never been in an Episcopal chapel before, their astonishment cannot be described on a beautiful symphony being struck up by the organist. At that instant a gentleman came to take possession of the seat, and civilly laid his hand on the shoulder of one of them, and pointed to the door. " Hout tout!" cried the Highlander, " tak' out Donald there, he be a far better dancer than me."

THE STORY-TELLER.
TO-MORROW.
Abridged from Miss Edgeworth.

"Oh, this detestable *To-morrow!*—a thing always expected, yet never found." — Johnson.

It has long been my intention to write my own history; and I am determined to begin it to-day; for half the good intentions of my life have been frustrated by my unfortunate habit of putting things off till to-morrow.

When I was a young man, I used to be told that this was my only fault; I believed it; and my vanity or laziness persuaded me that this fault was but small, and that I should easily cure myself of it in time.

That time, however, has not yet arrived; and at my advanced time of life, I must give up all thoughts of amendment, hoping, however, that sincere repentance may stand instead of reformation.

My father was an eminent London bookseller: he happened to be looking over a new biographical dictionary on the day when I was brought into the world; and at the moment when my birth was announced to him, he had his finger upon the name *Basil*; he read aloud—"Basil, canonized bishop of Cæsarea, a theological, controversial, and moral writer."

"My boy," continued my father, "shall be named after this great man, and I hope and believe that I shall live to see him either a celebrated theological, controversial, and moral author, or a bishop. I am not so sanguine as to expect that he should be both these good things."

I was christened Basil, according to my father's wishes; and his hopes of my future celebrity and fortune were confirmed, during my childhood, by instances of wit and memory, which were not perhaps greater than what could have been found in my little contemporaries, but which appeared to the vanity of parental fondness extraordinary, if not supernatural.

When I was sent to a public school, I found among my companions so many temptations to idleness, that, notwithstanding the quickness of my parts, I was generally flogged twice a-week. As I grew older, my reason might perhaps have taught me to correct myself, but my vanity was excited to persist in idleness by certain imprudent sayings or whisperings of my father.

When I came home from school at the holydays, and when complaints were preferred against me in letters from my schoolmaster, my father, even while he affected to scold me for my negligence, flattered me in the most dangerous manner by adding—*aside* to some friend of the family—

"My Basil is a strange fellow; can do anything he pleases—all his masters say so; but he is a sad idle dog—all your men of genius are so; puts off business always to the last moment—all your men of genius do so. For instance there is —— whose third edition of odes I have just published—what an idle dog he is. Yet who makes such a noise in the world as he does?—puts off everything till *to-morrow*, like my Basil; but can do more at the last moment than any man in England—that is, if the fit seizes him; for he does nothing but by fits; has no application —none; says it would 'petrify him to a dunce.' I never knew a man of genius who was not an idle dog."

Not a syllable of such speeches was lost upon me; the ideas of a man of genius and of an idle dog were soon so firmly joined together in my imagination, that it was impossible to separate them, either by my own reason or by that of my preceptors.

Basil's father got time to change his notions as the son proceeded in the old course. He obtained a patron in a learned prelate, and was educated for the church with good hopes of preferment. He says,—My patron, who seemed to like me the better the oftener I dined with him, gave me reason to hope that he would provide for me handsomely. I was not yet ordained, when a living of four hundred per annum fell into his gift; he held it over for some months, as it was thought, on purpose for me.

In the mean time, he employed me to write a charity sermon for him, which he was to preach, as it was expected, to a crowded congregation. None but those who are themselves slaves to the habit of procrastination, will believe that I could be so foolish as to put off writing this sermon till the Saturday evening before it was wanted. Some of my young companions came unexpectedly to sup with me; we sat late; in the vanity of a young author, who glories in the rapidity of composition, I said to myself that I could finish my sermon in an hour's time. But, alas! when my companions at length departed, they left me in no condition to complete a sermon. I fell fast asleep, and was wakened in the morning by the bishop's servant. The dismay I felt is indescribable; I started up—it was nine o'clock; I began to write; but my hand and my mind trembled, and my ideas were in such confusion, that I could not, great genius as I was, produce a beginning sentence in a quarter of an hour.

I kept the bishop's servant forty minutes by his watch; wrote and re-wrote two pages, and walked up and down the room; tore my two pages; and at last, when the footman said he could wait no longer, was obliged to let him go with an awkward note, pleading sudden sickness for my apology. It was true that I was sufficiently sick at the time when I penned this note; my head ached terribly; and I kept my room, reflecting upon my own folly, the whole of the day. I foresaw the consequences; the living was given away by my patron the next morning, and all hopes of future favour were absolutely at an end.

Basil's next adventure was in the suite of Lord Macartney to China, for which voyage he made immense preparations, but unfortunately lost his ship; and did not recover it till at Sumatra. His resolution was now taken to write a history of China, which should make his own fortune, and delight his father; but when at Pekin, he found his note-books had been left in his bed on ship-board, and his remarks, written down on scraps of paper, were mislaid, long before he came to require them. Through negligence, Basil got into disagreeable adventures, and finally returned home, neither richer nor wiser than when he left England. Besides his imperfect notes, he found his great work on China forestalled by a more prompt and industrious writer, probably of very inferior ability. That he might be able to redeem lost time, Basil set off to an uncle Lowe, who, he says, lived in the country, in a retired part of England. He was a farmer, a plain, sensible, affectionate man; and, says Basil, as he had often invited me to come and see him, I made no doubt that I should be an agreeable guest. I had intended to have written a few lines the week before I set out, to say that I was coming; but I put it off till at last I thought that it would be useless, because I should get there as soon as my letter.

I had soon reason to regret that I had been so negligent; for my appearance at my uncle's, instead of creating that general joy which I had expected, threw the whole house into confusion. It happened that there was company in the house, and all the beds were occupied. While I was taking off my boots, I had the mortification to hear my aunt Lowe say, in a voice of mingled distress and reproach, "Come! is he?—My goodness! What shall we do for a bed? How could he think of coming without writing a line before-hand? My goodness! I wish he was a hundred miles off, I'm sure."

My uncle shook hands with me, and welcomed me to old England again, and to his house; which, he said, should always be open to all his relations. I saw that he was not pleased; and, as he was a man who, according to the English phrase, scorned *to keep a thing long upon his mind*, he let me know, before he had finished his first glass of ale to my good health, that he was *inclinable to take it very unkind indeed*, that, after all he had said about my writing a letter now and then, just to say how I did, and how I was going on, I had never put pen to paper to answer one of his letters, since the day I first promised to write, which was the day I went to Eton school, till this present time of speaking. I had no good apology to make for myself, but I attempted all manner of excuses; that I had put off writing from day to day, and from year to year, till I was ashamed to write at all; that it was not from want of affection, &c.

My uncle took up his pipe and puffed away, while I spoke; and, when I had said all that I could devise, I sat silent; for I saw, by the looks of all present, that I had not mended the matter. My aunt pursed up her mouth, and "wondered, if she must tell the plain truth, that so great a scholar as Mr. Basil could not, when it must give him so little trouble to indite a letter, write a few lines to an uncle, who had begged it so often, and who had ever been a good friend."

"Say nothing of that," said my uncle:—"I scorn to have that put into account. I loved the boy, and all I could do was done of course; that's nothing to the purpose; but the longest day I have to live, I'll never trouble him with begging a letter from him no more. For now I see he does not care a fig for me; and of course I do not care a fig for he. Lucy, hold up your head, girl; and don't look as if you were going to be hanged."

My cousin Lucy was the only person present who seemed to have any compassion for me; and, as I lifted up my eyes to look at her when her father spoke, she appeared to me quite beautiful. I had always thought her a pretty girl, but she never struck me as any thing very extraordinary till this moment. I was very sorry that I had offended my uncle; I saw he was seriously displeased, and that his pride, of which he had a large portion, had conquered his affection for me.

"'Tis easier to lose a friend than gain one, young man," said he; "and, take my word for it, as this world goes, it is a foolish thing to lose a friend for want of writing a letter or so. Here's seven years I have been begging a letter now and then, and could not get one. Never wrote a line to me before you went to China; should not have known a word about it but for my wife, who met you by mere chance in London, and gave you some little commissions for the children, which it seems you forgot till it was too late. Then after you came back, never wrote to me."

"And even not to write a line to give one notice of his coming here to-night," added my aunt.

"Oh, as to that," replied my uncle, "he can never find our larder at a nonplus; we have no dishes for him dressed Chinese fashion; but as to roast beef of old England, which, I take it, is worth all the foreign meats, he is welcome to it, and to as much of it as he pleases. I shall always be glad to see him as an acquaintance, and so forth, as a good Christian ought, but not as the favourite he used to be— that it is out of the question; for things cannot be both done and undone, and time that's past cannot come back again, that is clear; and cold water thrown on a warm heart puts it out; and there's an end of the matter. Lucy, bring me my night-cap."

Lucy, I think, sighed once, and I am sure I sighed above a dozen times; but my uncle put on his red night-cap, and heeded us not. I was in hopes that the next morning he would have been better disposed toward me, after having slept off his anger. The moment that I appeared in the morning, the children, who had been in bed when I arrived the preceding night, crowded round me; and one cried,

"Cousin Basil, have you brought me the tumbler you promised me from China?"

"Cousin Basil, where's my boat?"

"Oh, Basil, did you bring me the the calibash box that you promised me?"

"And pray," cried my aunt, "did you bring my Lucy the fan that she commissioned you to get?"

"No, I'll warrant," said my uncle. "He that cannot bring himself to write a letter in the course of seven years, to his friends, will not be apt to trouble his head about their foolish commissions, when he is in foreign parts."

Though I was abashed and vexed, I summoned sufficient courage to reply that I had not neglected to execute the commissions of any of my friends; but that, by an unlucky accident, the basket into which I had packed all their things was washed overboard.

"Hum!" said my uncle.

"And pray," said my aunt, "why were they all packed in a basket? Why were not they put into your trunks, where they might have been safe?"

I was obliged to confess that I had delayed to purchase them till after we left Pekin; and that the trunks were put on board before they were all procured at Canton. My vile habit of procrastination! How did I suffer for it at this moment! Lucy began to make excuses for me, which made me blame myself the more; she said, that as to her fan, it would have been of little or no use to her; that she was sure she should have broken it before it had been a week in her possession; and that, therefore, she was glad that she had it not. The children were clamorous in their grief for the loss of the boat, the tumbler, and the calibash boxes; but Lucy contrived to quiet them in time, and to make my peace with all the younger part of the family. To reinstate me in my uncle's good graces was impossible; he would only repeat to her,—"The young man has lost my good opinion; he will never do any good. From a child upwards, he has always put off doing every- thing he ought to do. He will never do any good; he will never be any thing."

My aunt was not my friend, because she suspected that Lucy liked me; and she thought her daughter might do much better than marry a man who had quitted the profession to which he was bred, and was, as it seemed, little likely to settle to any other. My pretensions to genius and my literary qualifications were of no advantage to me, either with my uncle or my aunt; the one being *only* a good farmer, and the other *only* a good housewife. They contented themselves with asking me, coolly, what I had ever made by being an author? And, when I was forced to answer, *nothing*, they smiled upon me in scorn. My pride was roused, and I boasted that I expected to receive at least £600 for my Voyage to China, which I hoped to complete in a few weeks. My aunt looked at me with astonishment; and, to prove to her that I was not passing the bounds of truth, I added that one of my travelling companions had, as I was credibly informed, received a thousand pounds for his narrative, to which mine would certainly be far superior.

"When it is done, and when you have the money in your hand to show us, I shall believe you," said my aunt; "and then, and not till then, you may begin to think of my Lucy."

"He shall never have her," said my uncle; "he will never come to good. He shall never have her."

During my stay at my uncle's, I received several letters from my father, inquiring how my work went on, and urging me to proceed as rapidly as possible, lest another Voyage to China, which it was reported was now composing by a gentleman of high reputation, should come out and preclude mine for ever. I cannot account for my folly; the power of habit is imperceptible to those who submit passively to its tyranny. From day to day I continued procrastinating and sighing, till at last the fatal news came that "Sir George Staunton's History of the Embassy to China," in two volumes quarto, was actually published.

And now two melancholy, idle, years passed over Basil, who all the while deplored that he could not marry Lucy, and every day resolved to begin one of his thousand schemes of advancing himself *to-morrow*. At this time his father died, and left Basil, though sorrowing and repenting, richer than he either expected or deserved; and though Farmer Lowe persisted in refusing his consent to his daughter marrying a man of a *putting off* temper, Lucy's mother was softened on hearing of the inheritance, and she promised to befriend him, if for one six months he would attend to business, and *show that he could come to good*. With this motive Basil persevered; and at the end of his term claimed the reward. But Farmer Lowe was not yet convinced of the durability of this wonderful and sudden reformation. He would not give his consent, nor would Lucy marry without it.——It was in vain, says Basil, that I combated her resolution: I alternately resented and deplored the weakness which induced Lucy to sacrifice her own happiness and mine to the obstinate prejudices of a father; yet I could not avoid respecting her the more for her adhering to what she believed to be her duty. The sweetness of temper, gentleness of disposition, and filial piety, which she showed on this trying occasion, endeared her to me beyond expression.

Her father, notwithstanding his determination to be as immoveable as a rock, began to manifest symptoms of internal agitation; and one night, after breaking his pipe, and throwing down the tongs and poker twice, which Lucy twice replaced, he exclaimed, " Lucy, girl, you are a fool! and, what is worse, you are growing into a mere shadow. You are breaking my heart. Why I know this man, this Basil, this cursed nephew of mine, will never come to good. But cannot you marry him without my consent?"

Upon this hint Lucy's scruples vanished; and, a few days afterward, we were married. Prudence, virtue, pride, love, every strong motive which can act upon the human mind, stimulated me to exert myself to prove that I was worthy of this most amiable woman. A year passed away, and my Lucy said that she had no reason to repent of her choice. She took the most affectionate pains to convince her father that she was perfectly happy, and that he had judged of me too harshly. His delight, at seeing his daughter happy, vanquished his reluctance to acknowledge that he had changed his opinion. I never shall forget the pleasure I felt at hearing him confess that he had been too positive, and that his Lucy had made a good match for herself.

Alas! when I had obtained this testimony in my favour, when I had established a character for exertion and punctuality, I began to relax in my efforts to deserve it: I indulged myself in my old habits of procrastination. My customers and country correspondents began to complain that their letters were unanswered, and that their orders were neglected. Their remonstrances became more and more urgent in process of time; and nothing but actually seeing the dates of their letters could convince me that they were in the right, and I was in the wrong. An old friend of my father's, a rich gentleman, who loved books and bought all that were worth buying, sent me, in March, an order for books to a considerable amount. In April he wrote to remind me of his first letter.

April 3.
'My dear Sir,—Last month I wrote to request that you
'would send me the following books:—I have been much
'disappointed by not receiving them; and I request you
'will be so good as forward them *immediately*.—I am, my
'dear Sir, yours sincerely, J. C.'

In May he wrote to me again.

'Dear Sir,—I am much surprised at not having yet re-
'ceived the books I wrote for last March—beg to know
'the cause of this delay; and am, dear Sir, yours, &c. J. C.'

This reprimand had little effect upon me, because, at the time when I received it, I was intent upon an object, in comparison with which the trade of a bookseller appeared absolutely below my consideration. I was inventing a set of new taxes for the minister, for which I expected to be liberally rewarded. Like many men of genius, I was always disposed to think that my fortune was to be made by some extraordinary exertion of talent, instead of the vulgar means of daily industry. I was ever searching for some *short cut* to the temple of Fame, instead of following the beaten road.

I was a publisher, as well as a bookseller, and was assailed by a tribe of rich and poor authors. The rich complained continually of delays that affected their fame; the poor of delays that concerned their interest, and sometimes their very existence. I was cursed with a compassionate as well as with a procrastinating temper; and I frequently advanced money to my poor authors, to compensate for my neglect to settle their accounts, and to free myself from the torment of their reproaches.

About this time Basil put a helping hand to his disastrous fortune by losing a MSS., which the author valued at L.500, and for which he accordingly prosecuted the loser, and obtained that sum as damages. His wife's relations, who saw the trial in the newspapers, were enraged at this occurrence; but her patience and kindness continued unexhausted, and her gentle influence was ever exerted to dissuade her husband from his various schemes, and to give his attention to his proper business. Her advice Basil would have taken if he had been able, but habit was powerful, and before applying again to business, he had to finish a pamphlet against government, which was to make his fortune, and bring all the Whigs to his shop. And thus time passed, business was more and more neglected, and Basil abandoning his involved affairs in despair, was declared a bankrupt, and thrown into the King's Bench. We must now adopt his own words. My wife's relations refused to give me any assistance; but her father offered to receive her and her little boy, on condition that she would part from me, and spend the remainder of her days with them. This she positively refused; and I never shall forget the manner of her refusal. Her character rose in adversity. With the utmost feminine gentleness and delicacy, she had a degree of courage and fortitude which I have seldom seen equalled in any of my own sex. She followed me to prison, and supported my spirits by a thousand daily instances of kindness. During eighteen months that she passed with me in a prison, which we then thought must be my abode for life, she never, by word or look, reminded me that I was the cause of our misfortunes: on the contrary, she drove this idea from my thoughts with all the address of female affection. I cannot, even at this distance of time, recall these things to my memory without tears.

What a woman, what a wife had I reduced to distress! I never saw her, even in the first months of our marriage, so cheerful and so tender as at this period. She seemed to have no existence but in me, and in our little boy; of whom she was doatingly fond. He was at this time just able to run about and talk; his playful caresses, his thoughtless gaiety, and at times a certain tone of compassion for *poor papa* were very touching. Alas! he little foresaw * * *

But let me go on with my history, if I can, without anticipation.

Among my creditors was a Mr. Nun, a paper-maker, who, from his frequent dealings with me, had occasion to see something of my character and of my wife's; he admired her, and pitied me. He was in easy circumstances, and delighted in doing all the good in his power. One morning my Lucy came into my room with a face radiant with joy.

"My love," said she, "here is Mr. Nun below, waiting to see you; but he says he will not see you till I have told you the good news. He has got all our creditors to enter into a compromise, and to set you at liberty."

I was transported with joy and gratitude: our benevolent friend was waiting in a hackney-coach to carry us away from prison. When I began to thank him, he stopped me with a blunt declaration that I was not a bit obliged to him; for that, if I had been a man of straw, he would have done just the same for the sake of my wife, whom he looked upon to be one or other the best woman he had ever seen, Mrs. Nun always excepted.

He proceeded to inform me how he had settled my affairs, and how he had obtained from my creditors a small allowance for the immediate support of myself and family. He had given up the third part of a considerable sum due to himself. As my own house was shut up, he insisted upon taking us home with him: "Mrs. Nun," he said, "had provided a good dinner; and he must not have her ducks and green pease upon the table, and no friends to eat them."

Never were ducks and green pease more acceptable; never was a dinner eaten with more appetite, or given with more good-will. I have often thought of this dinner, and compared the hospitality of this simple-hearted man with the ostentation of great folks, who give splendid entertainments to those who do not want them. In trifles and in matters of consequence this Mr. Nun was one of the most liberal and unaffectedly generous men I ever knew; but the generous actions of men in middle life are lost in obscurity. No matter. They do not act from the love of fame; they act from a better motive, and they have their reward in their own hearts.

As I was passing through Mr. Nun's warehouse, I was thinking of writing something on this subject; but whether it should be a poetic effusion, in the form of "*An Ode to him who least expects it*," or a prose work, under the title of "*Modern Parallels*," in the manner of Plutarch, I had not decided, when I was roused from my reverie by my wife, who pointing to a large bale of paper that was directed to "*Ezekiel Croft, merchant, Philadelphia*," asked me if I knew that this gentleman was a very near relation of her mother? "Is he, indeed?" said Mr. Nun. "Then I can assure you that you have a relation of whom you have no occasion to be ashamed: he is one of the most respectable merchants in Philadelphia."

"He was not very rich when he left this country about six years ago," said Lucy.

"He has a very good fortune now," answered Mr. Nun.

"And has he made this very good fortune in six years?" cried I. "My dear Lucy, I did not know that you had any relations in America. I have a great mind to go over there myself."

"Away from all our friends!" said Lucy.

"I shall be ashamed," replied I, "to see them after all that has happened. A bankrupt cannot have many friends. The best thing that I can possibly do is to go over to a new world, where I may establish a new character, and make a new fortune."

My Lucy consented to accompany me. She spent a week in the country with her father and friends, by my particular desire; and they did all they could to prevail upon her to stay with them, promising to take the best possible care of her and her little boy during my absence; but she steadily persisted in her determination to accompany her husband. I was not too late in going on ship-board this time; and, during the whole voyage, I did not lose any of my goods; for, in the first place, I had very few goods to lose, and, in the next, my wife took entire charge of those few.

And now behold me safely landed at Philadelphia, with one hundred pounds in my pocket—a small sum of money; but many, from yet more trifling beginnings, have grown rich in America. My wife's relation, Mr. Croft, had not so much, as I was told, when he left England. Many passengers, who came over in the same ship with me had not half so much. Several of them were, indeed, wretchedly poor.

Among others, there was an Irishman, who was known by the name of Barny, a contraction, I believe, for Barnaby. As to his surname he could not undertake to spell it; but he assured me there was no better. This man, with many of his relatives, had come to England, according to their custom, during harvest time, to assist in reaping, because they gain higher wages than in their own country. Barny heard that he should get still higher wages for labour in America, and accordingly he, and his two sons, lads of eighteen and twenty, took their passage for Philadelphia. A merrier mortal I never saw. We used to hear him upon deck, continually singing or whistling his Irish tunes; and I should never have guessed that this man's life had been a series of hardships and misfortunes.

When we were leaving the ship I saw him, to my great surprise, crying bitterly; and, upon inquiring what was the matter, he answered that it was not for himself, but for his sons, he was grieving, because they were to be made *Redemption men.*—That is, they were to be bound to work, during a certain time, for the captain, or for whomever he pleased, till the money due for their passage should be paid. Though I was somewhat surprised at any one's thinking of coming on board a vessel without having one farthing in his pocket, yet I could not forbear paying the money for this poor fellow. He dropped down on the deck upon both his knees as suddenly as if he had been shot, and, holding up his hands to Heaven, prayed, first in Irish, and then in English, with fervent fluency, that "I and mine might never want; that I might live long to reign over him; that success might attend my honour wherever I went; and that I might enjoy for evermore all sorts of blessings and crowns of glory." As I had an English prejudice in favour of silent gratitude, I was rather disgusted by all this eloquence; I turned away abruptly, and got into the boat which waited to carry me to shore.

As we rowed away I looked at my wife and child, and reproached myself with having indulged in the luxury of generosity perhaps at their expense.

My wife's relation, Mr. Croft, received us better than she expected, and worse than I hoped. He had the face of an acute money-making man; his manners were methodical; caution was in his eye, and prudence in all his motions. In our first half hour's conversation he convinced me that he deserved the character he had obtained, of being upright and exact in all his dealings. His ideas were just and clear, but confined to the objects immediately relating to his business; as to his heart, he seemed to have no notion of general philanthropy, but to have perfectly learned by rote his duty to his neighbour. He appeared disposed to do charitable and good-natured actions from reason, and not from feeling; because they were proper, not merely because they were agreeable. I felt that I should respect, but never love him; and that he would never either love or respect me, because the virtue which he held in the highest veneration was that in which I was most deficient—punctuality.

But I will give, as nearly as I can, my first conversation with him; and from that a better idea of his character may be formed than I can afford by any description.

I presented to him Mr. Nun's letter of introduction, and mentioned that my wife had the honour of being related to him. He perused Mr. Nun's letter very slowly. I was determined not to leave him in any doubt respecting who and what I was; and I briefly told him the particulars of my history. He listened with immovable attention; and when I had finished he said, "You have not yet told me what your views are in coming to America."

I replied, "that my plans were not yet fixed."

"But of course," said he, "you cannot have left home without forming some plan for the future. May I ask what line of life you mean to pursue?"

I answered, "that I was undetermined, and meant to be guided by circumstances."

"Circumstances!" said he; "May I request you to explain yourself more fully? for I do not precisely understand to what circumstances you allude."

I was provoked with the man for being so slow of apprehension; but, when driven to the necessity of explaining, I found that I myself did not understand what I meant.

I changed my ground; and, lowering my tone of confidence, said that, as I was totally ignorant of the country, I should wish to be guided by the advice of better-informed persons; and that I begged leave to address myself to him, as having had the most successful experience.

After a considerable pause, he replied, it was a hazardous thing to give advice; but that, as my wife was his relation, and he held it a duty to assist his relations, he should not decline giving me—all the advice in his power.

I bowed, and felt chilled all over by his manner.

"And not only my advice," continued he; "but my assistance—in reason."

I said, "I was much obliged to him."

"Not in the least, young man; you are not in the least obliged to me yet, for I have done nothing for you."

This was true, and not knowing what to say I was silent.

"And that which I may be able to do for you in future must depend as much upon yourself as upon me. In the first place, before I can give you any advice, I must know what you are worth in the world?"

My worth in money, I told him, with a forced smile, was but very trifling indeed. With some hesitation I named the sum.

"And you have a wife and child to support!" said he, shaking his head. "And your child is too young and your wife too delicate to work. They will be sad burdens upon your hands; these are not the things for America. Why did you bring them with you? But, as that is done, and cannot be mended," continued he, "we must make the best of it, and support them. You say you are ignorant of the country. I must explain to you then how money is to be made here, and by whom. The class of labourers make money readily, if they are industrious; because they have high wages and constant employment; artificers and mechanics, carpenters, shipwrights, wheelwrights, smiths, bricklayers, masons, get rich here, without difficulty, from the same causes; but all these things are out of the question for you. You have head, not hands, I perceive. Now, mere head, in the line of bookmaking or bookselling, brings in but poor profit in this country. The sale for imported books is extensive; and our printers are doing something by subscription here, in Philadelphia, and in New York, they tell me. But London is the place for a good bookseller to thrive; and you come from London, where you tell me you were a bankrupt. I would not advise you to have anything more to do with bookselling or bookmaking. Then, as to becoming a planter—Our planters, if they are skilful and laborious, thrive well; but you have not capital sufficient to clear land and build a house; or hire servants to do the work for which you are not sufficiently robust. Besides, I do not imagine that you know much of agricultural concerns, or country business; and even to oversee and guide others, experience is necessary. The life of a back settler I do not advise, because you and your wife are not equal to it. You are not accustomed to live in a log house, or to feed upon racoons and squirrels; not to omit the constant dread, if not imminent danger, of being burnt in your beds, or scalped by the Indians with whom you would be surrounded. Upon the whole, I see no line of life that promises well for you but that of a merchant; and I see no means of your getting into this line, without property and without credit, except by going into some established house as a clerk. You are a good penman and a ready accountant, I think you tell me; and I presume you have a sufficient knowledge of bookkeeping. With sobriety, diligence, and honesty, you may do well in this way; and may look forward to being a partner, and in a lucrative situation some years hence. This is the way I managed and rose myself by degrees to what you see. It is true, I was not at first encumbered with a wife and young child. In due time I married my master's daughter, which was a great furtherance to me; but then, on the other hand, your wife is my relation; and to be married to the relation of a rich merchant is next best to not being married at all, in your situation. I told you I thought it my duty to proffer assistance as well as advice: so take up your abode with me for a fortnight: in that time I shall be able to judge whether you are capable of being a clerk; and, if you and I should suit, we will talk farther. You understand that I enter into no engagement, and make no promise; but shall be glad to lodge you, and your wife, and little boy, for a fortnight: and it will be your own fault, and must be your own loss, if the visit turns out waste of time. I cannot stay to talk to you any longer at present," added he, pulling out his watch, "for I have business, and business waits for no man. Go back to your inn for my relation, and her little one. We dine at two precisely."—(*To be concluded next week.*)

SHORT-HAND WRITING AND THE PRESS.

The Romans invented short or abridged writing, which enabled their secretaries to collect the speeches of orators, however rapidly delivered. The characters used by such writers were called notes. They did not consist in letters of the alphabet, but certain marks, one of which often expressed a whole word, and frequently a phrase. The same description of writing is known at the present day by the words stenography, tachygraphy, and echography. From notes came the word notary, which was given to all who professed the art of quick writing. The system of note writing was not suddenly brought to perfection—it only came into favour when the professors most accurately reported an excellent speech which Cato pronounced in the Senate. The orators, the philosophers, the dignitaries, and nearly all the rich patricians, then took for secretaries notawriters, to whom they allowed handsome pay. It was usual to take from their slaves all who had intellect to acquire a knowledge of that art. Gruterus has preserved, for our information, the notes of Tyro, the freed-man of Cicero. The republic and the Government of cities also maintained at their expense these secretaries. It is not necessary here to detail the history of the notaries in Europe, who succeeded the *tabelliona* of Rome. The intention is only to throw some light on the origin of short-hand-writing, and to prove the great estimation in which the art was held by ancient statesmen and orators.

Next to the art of printing, short-hand writing claims the admiration of mankind; it may be called the triumph of human intellect. The wisdom of the senate, the principles of legislation, and the *dicta* of legal tribunals, are now diffused over the British islands with the rapidity of the eagle's wing. The learning, taste, and reasoning of the most distinguished men, taken, as it were, from the lips of the speakers, and conveyed daily and hourly by the press of Great Britain, must produce light and knowledge among the people, which no other system of education can impart. The advantages derived from short-hand writing are not only great in a public point of view, but privately the art is useful. The student who attends lectures may bring away the very words of the lecturer, and impress upon the mind at leisure the correct ideas of a speaker, in a way that can never lead to error. The art, some years ago, was not applied to any useful purpose in England. The debates in the British Parliament were reported, but the writers conveyed no valuable information to the public. The speeches reported were too often the mere composition of reporters, who wrote from memory. We have now, so far as the limits of newspapers will allow, the emphatic words of the leaders in Parliament, upon all important subjects. It is true inaccuracy will sometimes occur, but every one who has attended the House of Commons, and the other branch of the legislature, must know that errors are occasioned by the want of proper facilities to report. The distance at which strangers or writers are placed from the speakers in the House of Lords and House of Commons is too great. It is impossible to hear persons who speak in a low tone of voice, and it is almost unnecessary to observe that a reporter cannot report accurately that which he does not distinctly hear, and clearly understand. We are enabled to make what may be considered a bold assertion, but it is nevertheless true, namely, that a short-hand writer, placed in a situation where he can hear, may commit to paper, if necessary, every word uttered by a speaker. The skill evinced daily in the art of reporting, must be considered one of the great foundations of public liberty; and every friend to the British Constitution should stand forward the advocate of reporters, who have done much within the last twenty years to promote the liberty of the subject, the blessings of the British Constitution, and the morals of the people.

It would not be difficult to prove that the present system of reporting is advantageous to domestic peace, and the stability of Government. The people of England are the best subjects in the world, provided they find in their rulers due regard for the principles of that constitution which their best blood has been so often and so nobly shed to defend. Expose fairly the sentiments of the representatives in Parliament, who discuss the measures of Government, and there will be no disposition to form plans of conspiracy, treason, and disaffection, which have generally been the result of false or mistaken views of the measures of Governments. The public press is now a stream of light and information, flowing through the United Kingdom, and should any Government be weak enough to arrest its progress, the obstruction must produce consequences fatal indeed to public peace and tranquillity. Let the press be unshackled, and its licentiousness, which seems to be an inseparable vice, stand restrained by wise legislative enactments. Experience has proved that no Government can expect to prosper without a free press. The great Republic of Venice, established upon a system of secrecy, fell a victim to that very principle. The measures of its council, though intended to promote the public interest, were dark and mysterious. The people kept in ignorance, and naturally suspicious of all rulers, engaged in plots against the State, and at last the army itself, on which the Senate most relied for protection, became the destroyer of the Republic. Had Venice in the plenitude of her greatness, possessed a free press, and not the false policy of concealment, the government of that once powerful commercial state might have existed to this day. Events of more recent date have proved, that an attempt to keep down the spirit of the age by restraint upon the Press must excite universal disgust, and kindle the flame of revolution; that flame which drove Charles X. from the throne of the Bourbons. Happily there is no apprehension that the liberty of the press can be suppressed in this country; whilst short-hand writing gives to the reporter the invaluable power of spreading truth and information over the land, the people may boast of advantages unknown to surrounding nations.

SCOTTISH TEA-PARTY,
FROM WHISTLE BINKIE.

Now let's sing how Miss M'Wharty,
T'other evening had a party,
To have a cup of tea;
And how she had collected
All the friends that she respected,
All as merry as merry could be.
Dames and damsels came in dozens,
With two-three country cousins,
In their lily-white so gay;
Just to sit and chitter-chatter,
O'er a cup of scalding water,
In the fashion of the day.

(*Spoken in different female voices.*) Dear me, how hae ye been this lang time, Mem? Pretty weel, I thank ye, mem. How hae ye been yoursel'? O mem, mem, I've been verra ill wi' the rheumatisms, and though I was your tippet, I couldna be fu'er o' *stitches* than I am ; but whan did you see Mrs. Pinkerton, mem? O mem, I hae na seen her this lang time. Did ye no hear that Mrs. Pinkerton and I hae had a difference? No, mem, I did na hear. What was't about, mem? I'll tell you what it was about, mem. I gaed o'er to ca' upon her yae day, and when I gaes in, ye see, she's sitting feeding the parrot, and I says tae her, Mrs. Pinkerton, how d'ye do mem? and she never let on she heard me ; and I says again, Mrs. Pinkerton, how d'ye do, I says? and wi' that she turns about and says, says she, Mrs. M'Saunter, I'm really astonished you should come and ask me how I do, considering the manner you've ridiculed me and my husband in public companies! Mrs Pinkerton, quo' I, what's that ye mean, mem? and then she began and gied me a' the ill-mannered abuse you can possibly conceive. And I just says to her, quo' I, that's no what I came to hear, and if that's the way ye intend tae gae on, quo' I, I wish ye gude morning; so I comes awa'. Now I'll tell ye what a' this is about. Ye see, it was just about the term time, ye ken, they flitted aboon us, and I gaed up the term morning tae see if they wanted a kettle boiled or ony thing o' that kind; and when I gaes in, Mr. Pinkerton, he's sitting in the middle o' the floor, and the barber's shaving him, and the barber had laid a' his face round wi' the *white* saip, and Mr. Pinkerton, ye ken, has a vera *red* nose, and the red nose sticking through the white saip, just put me in mind o' a *carrot* sticking through a *collyflower*; and I very innocently happened tae mention this in a party where I had been dining, and some officious body's gane and tell't Mrs. Pinkerton, and Mrs. Pinkerton's tane this wonderfully amiss.—What d'ye think o' Mrs. Pinks? Deed mem, she's no worth your while; but did you hear what happened to Mrs. Clapperton the ither day? No mem. You see, she was coming down Montrose-Street, and she had on a red pelisse, and a white muff, and there's a bubbly-jock coming out o' the brewery, and whether the red pelisse had ta'en the beast's eye or no, I dinna ken, but the bubbly-jock rins after Mrs. Clapperton, and Mrs. Clapperton ran puir body, and the bubbly-jock after her, and in crossing the causey, ye see, her fit slipped, and the muff flew frae her, and there's a cart gaes ower the muff, and yae gentleman rins and lifts Mrs Clapperton, and a anither lifts the muff, and when he looks intae the muff, what's there but a wee bit broken bottle, wi' a wee soup brandy in't ; and the gentlemen fell a looking and laughing tae ane anither, and they're gaun about tae their dinner parties and their supper parties, and telling about Mrs. Clapperton wi' the bubbly-jock and the bottle o' brandy. Now it's very ill done o' the gentlemen tae do any thing o' the kind, for Mrs. Clapperton was just like tae drap down wi' perfect vexation, for she's a body o' that kind o' laithfu' kind o' disposition, she would just as soon take aquafortis as she would take brandy in ony clandestine kind o' manner.

Thus to sit and chitter-chatter,
O'er a cup of scalding water,
Is the fashion of the day!
Each gemman at his post now,
In banding tea or toast now,
Is striving to outshine ;
While keen to find a handle
To *tip* a little scandal,
The ladies all combine.
Of this one's dress or carriage,
Or t'other's death or marriage,
The dear chit-chat's kept up ;
While the lady from the table,
Is calling while she's able—
"Will you have another cup?"

Dear me, your no done, mem—you'll take another cup, mem—take out your spoon, mem. Oh no, mem, I never take mair than yae cup upon ony occasion. Toots, sic nonsense. You may toots awa, but its true sense, mem. And whan did you see Mrs Peticraw, mem? 'Deed, mem, I hae nae seen her this lang time, and I'm no wanting to see her, she's a body o' that kind, she just gangs frae house tae house gatherin clashes, and gets her tea here and her tea there, and tells in your house what she bears in mine, and when she begins, she claver clavers on and on, and the claver just comes frae her as if it cam' aff a *clew*, and there's nae end o' her. O you maun excuse her puir body, ye ken she's lost a' her *teeth*, and her tongue *wearies* in her mouth wantin' company. 'Deed they may excuse her that wants her, for it's no me. Oh! ladies, did ye hear what's happened in Mr M'Farlane's family? there's an awfu' circumstance happened in that family; Mr. and Mrs. M'Farlane hae na spoken to yin anither for this fortnight, and I'll tell ye the reason o't. Mrs. M'Farlane, puir body, had lost ane o' her teeth, and she gaed awa' to the dentist to get a tooth put in, and the dentist showed her twa-three kinds o' them, and among the rest he showed her a Waterloo yin, and she thought she would hae a Waterloo yin, puir body. Weel the dentist puts in yin tae her, and the tooth running in her head a' day, and when she gangs tae her bed at nicht, as she tells me, but I'm certain she must hae been dreaming—just about yin or twa o'clock o' the morning, mem, just about yin or twa o'clock in the morning, when she looks out o' her bed, there's a *great lang* sodger standing at the bed-side ; and quo' she, man, what are ye wanting? she says. Quo' he, Mrs. M'Farlane, that's my tooth that ye've got in your mouth. Your tooth!! quo' she, the very teeth that I bought the day at the dentist's. It does na matter for that, quo he, I lost it at Waterloo. Ye lost it at Waterloo! sic nonsense. Weel, wi' that he comes foret to pit his finger into Mrs. M'Farlane's mouth tae tak the teeth out o' her mouth, and she gies a snap and catched him by the finger, and he gied a great scraich, and took her a gowf i' the side o' the head, and that waukened her, and when she waukens, what has she gotten but Mr. M'Farlane's finger atween her teeth, and him roaring like to gae 'out o' his judgment!! Now Mr. M'Farlane has been gaun about wi' his thumb in a clout, and looking as surly as a bear, for he thinks Mrs. M'Farlane had done it out o' spite, because he wadna let her buy a sofa at a sale the other day ; noo its vera ill done o' Mr. M'Farlane tae think ony thing o' that kind, as if ony woman wad gang and *bite* her ain *flesh* and *blood* if she *kent o't*.

So thus to sit and chitter-chatter, &c.

STANZAS TO A DAUGHTER.
By David Vedder.

When the lunar light is leaping
On the streamlet and the lake ;
When the winds of Heaven are sleeping,
And the nightingale awake ;—
While mirrored in the ocean
The bright orbs of Heaven appear,—
'Tis an hour for deep devotion—
Lift thy soul to Heaven in prayer.

When the autumn breeze is sighing,
Through the leafless forest wide ;
And the flowers are dead, or dying,
Once the sunny garden's pride ;—
When the yellow leaves in motion,
Are seen whirling on the air,
'Tis an hour for deep devotion—
Lift thy soul to Heaven in prayer.

On His power and greatness ponder,
When the torrent, and the gale,
And the cataract, and thunder,
In *one* fearful *chorus swell* ;
Amidst nature's wild emotion
Is thy soul oppressed with care ?
'Tis the hour for deep devotion—
Lift thy soul to Him in prayer.

In sorrow, and in sickness,
And in poverty, and pain ;
And in vigour, or in weakness,
On the mountain or the plain ;
In the desert, on the ocean,
To the Throne of Love repair ;
All are hours for deep devotion—
Lift thy soul to Heaven in prayer.

MEDICAL SELECTIONS. NO. I.

PREMATURE INTERMENT.

A French paper, after enumerating the many cases which have occurred of persons attacked with cholera having been buried before they were really dead, in the haste to dispose of the bodies, enumerates various signs by which to discover whether life is really extinct. It, however, excuses this precipitation, on the ground that persons attacked with this fatal disorder are, in some instances, in a state of lethargy, which may be easily confounded with death. Whenever a cholera patient exhibits the peculiar character of the countenance, cold extremities, cramps, and the other unequivocal symptoms, and if in spite of the usual means employed, those symptoms increase, and particularly if after three, four, six, or twenty-four hours, the cholera signs on the countenance become more marked, the livid circle of the eyes is more prominent, and the livid state of the hands and feet more perceptible; if joined to these phenomena, the pulse almost ceases to beat, the oppression becomes greater, and the agitation arrives at its height—then there can no longer be any doubt that at the cessation of these symptoms the calm which succeeds is the calm of death. In cases of this nature, the whole chain of phenomena of the disorder, of which the termination is necessarily death, has been closely watched, and the most common cause of death in these cases is found to be suffocation. It sometimes happens that without going through this progressive augmentation of the symptoms, the patient suddenly falls into a state of absolute immovability, and dares not breathe, or the breath is scarcely perceptible, without any pulse, and becomes like ice, and in short is apparently dead. The suddenness of this change should excite the greatest distrust among persons who would otherwise be inclined to imagine that all was over with the patient. A case lately occurred where a child was affected exactly as we describe. It was given up for dead, but a skilful surgeon fortunately suspecting that it was not so, covered the surface of the body with sinapisms, and administered a strong narcotic. A few hours afterwards the child revived from its lethargic state.

THE SPASMODIC CHOLERA which devastated Europe in the fourteenth century, would, with but little change, serve for a description of the disease which still holds its course through it now. This plague, originating among the Hyperborean Scythians, spread over all the maritime coasts of the habitable world, and destroyed a vast number of people. For it not only passed through Pontus, Thrace, Macedon, Greece Proper, and Italy, but also all the islands, Egypt, Libya, Judæa, and Syria, and wandered over almost the entire circuit of the globe. But so incurable was the disease, that neither any system of dietetics, nor any strength of body, could resist it; for it prostrated all bodies alike, the weak as well as the strong; and those who were attended with the utmost care died, as well as those who were wholly neglected. That year, indeed, was remarkably free from other diseases; but if any person had been previously indisposed, his sickness assumed the type and character of this disease. The entire art of medicine was found unavailing. Nor did it similarly attack all; for some holding out but for a little brief space, died the very same day, some the very same hour. But those who held out for two or three days were first attacked by acute fever; the disease then ascending to the head, they became dumb and insensible to all occurrences, and so dropped off as into a profound slumber.

TEMPERANCE.—A much greater number of diseases originate from irregularities in eating than in drinking; and we commit more errors with regard to the quantity than in the quality of our aliment. When the intestines are in a relaxed state, we should instantly begin to be more moderate in eating. There are three kinds of appetite.—1.) The natural appetite, which is equally stimulated and satisfied with the most simple dish. 2. The artificial appetite, or that produced by elixirs, liquors, pickles, digestive salts, &c., and which remains only as long as the operation of these stimulants continues. 3. The habitual appetite, or that by which we accustom ourselves to take victuals at certain hours, without a desire of eating. If after dinner we feel ourselves as cheerful as before it, we may be assured that we have taken a dietical meal; for if the proper measure has been exceeded, torpor and relaxation is the necessary consequence, our faculty of digestion will be impaired, and a variety of complaints be gradually induced. Weakly individuals ought to eat frequently but little at a time. There is no instance on record of any person having injured his health or endangered his life by drinking water with his meals; but wine, beer, and spirits have generated a much greater number and diversity of patients than would fill all the hospitals in the world. It is a vulgar prejudice, that water disagrees with many constitutions, and does not promote digestion so well as wine, beer, or spirits. On the contrary, pure water is greatly preferable to all brewed and distilled liquors, both with a view of bracing the digestive organs, and preventing complaints which arise from acrimony or fullness of the blood. It is an observation no less important than true, that by attending merely to a proper diet, a phlegmatic habit may frequently be changed into a sanguine one, and the hypochondriac may be so far converted as to become a cheerful and contented member of society.—*Dr. Willich on Diet and Regimen.*

EFFECT OF THE PASSIONS ON HEALTH.—The passions are to be considered, in a medical point of view, as a part of our constitution, which are to be examined with the eye of a natural historian, and the spirit and impartiality of a philosopher. The passions stimulate the mind, as the food and drink do the body. Employed occasionally and in moderation, both may be of use to us, and are given to us by nature for this purpose; but when urged to excess, they throw the system off its healthy balance, raise it by excitement, or depress it by exhaustion, and weaken the sensorial vessels by the wear and tear they produce. The temperate action of the vital influence through every part of the system constitutes the perfection of health. The mind, undisturbed by any violent emotions, agitations, or depressions of a corporeal nature, is able to exercise its noblest powers with a tranquil vigour. The body continues in a regular discharge of its proper functions, without the least sensation of difficulty and embarrassment. Respiration is free and easy, neither checked nor excessive. Aliments are sought with appetite, enjoyed with relish, and digested with facility. Every secretion and excretion is duly performed. The body is perfectly free from pain, oppression, and every species of uneasiness; and a certain vivacity and vigour, not to be described, reign through the system. "The bodily machine disordered," says Cheyne, "will sink, debase, blunt, and confound the operations of the spirit; and the spirit violently agitated, or too closely confined, will disturb the economy of the bodily functions; and the perfect state of health and the last perfection of all intelligent creatures, consisting of an intelligent spirit and a material machine, depend on the perfect sanity and harmony of both united.—*Month. Gaz.*

FRICTION AND COLD WASHING.—An inattention to the condition of the surface of the body is a fruitful source of stomach ailment; and one of the principles upon which exercise proves beneficial to the dyspeptic is, that of its tendency to preserve the excretions from the skin in good condition. Friction of the surface ought to be enjoined as one of the most useful remedies for indigestion. This should be had recourse to every morning immediately on rising from bed; and with it should be combined a sort of shower bath by a sponge. I have not been so satisfied, in my own case, with any single article of preventive management as the one I now refer to. It is preventive both of stomach derangement, and of that inordinate susceptibility to cold which is usually a concomitant of stomach weakness; and I have no hesitation in saying, that it ought to be employed by all whose nerves and digestive organs are in any degree disposed to be out of order. Of cold, since I have adopted the practice, I am comparatively careless, and my digestive energies are improved, to say the least, in an equal proportion. It is a practice in my mind, far superior to the plunging in the cold bath.—*Dr. Unwin on Indigestion.*

A FACTORY CHILD'S TALE.—" I work at Bradley-mills, near Huddersfield. A few days since I had three 'wretched cardings,' about two inches long. The slubber, Joseph Riley, saw them, showed them to me, and asked me if this was good work. I said 'No.' He then, in the billy gait, took a thick, round leathern thong, and wailed me over the head and face, for, I think a quarter of an hour, and for all my cheek and lips were bleeding, he wailed me on, then sent me to my work again, and I worked till a quarter past seven. I went to the mill at half-past five in the morning: he wailed me a bit past one in the afternoon. I worked in my blood—as I worked, *the blood dropped all in the piecening gait!* My right cheek was torn open, swelled very much, and was black. *My lips were very much torn;* and each of them was as *thick as three lips.* He lashed me very hard over my back, too, in all directions; but the skin was not torn because I had my clothes on. He has many a time strapped me before till I have been black; he has often struck me over the head, with the billy roller, and raised great lumps upon it. At one time, when I had thrice 'little flyings,' which I could not help, he took me out of the billy gait, lifted me into the window, tied a rope round my body, and hung me up to a long pole that was sticking out of the wall, and there he left me hanging about five feet from the floor. I cried very much, and so in about ten minutes he took me down."

ANT POLITICAL HISTORY.

The ant history is more especially delightful, inasmuch as it so closely images the habits of mankind; man has been recommended to go to the ant, and to learn foresight and industry, but already they have learned of us, or we of them; the resemblance is too close to be accidental. For instance, ants have their battle fields on which hundreds and thousands contend for victory, the reward of the victor being an ant-hill the more; their soldiers, like ours, are useful for no other purpose but fighting: the ants, in fact, keep up a large standing army, the soldiers of which, consider every thing beneath them but killing and slaying, and will not even feed themselves; the ants called the workers, are even obliged to produce meat for them from their own bowels, which they squeeze out for their sustenance, and absolutely insert it into the mouths of these indolent and overfed warriors, with their poor hard-working mandibles, which, though they have been all day carpentering and masoning with never-ceasing industry, yet find time for this supposed duty. But the resemblance does not end here—the ants keep slaves; yes, some of the more aristocratic societies absolutely keep slaves—mostly prisoners of war, who do the duty of Helots or negroes, by which name they are termed by naturalists. The negroes do all the work of the community, while the rest of a finer and nobler species, at least so they think, consider themselves entitled to exact the hardest labour from the foreign ants, while they themselves sit in the sun or the shelter, as it may happen, to receive and enjoy the results of the exertions made by their inferiors.

Some ants may be considered a pastoral people; and are in possession of a numerous stock of cattle, from which they draw their sole subsistence. These cattle are an insect tribe, termed by naturalists aphides. These aphides are able to exude from their mouths, a drop of honeyed liquor or milk, in which the ants greatly delight, and on which they gladly subsist. A community of ants will get possession of great numbers of these aphides, carry them in their mandibles to green pastures, sedulously attend their young, and hatch their eggs: and when a fine old milch aphides is well full of his honey-wine, the cunning ant will stroke her on the back, and pat her on the neck, in order to persuade her to give up the precious drop—which she soon yields, and moreover places it in the very mouth of the cunning rogue. All this, it must be allowed, is very human; they seem only to want speech. The younger Huber has discovered, indeed, that they possess a sort of dumb language—a language of signs and strokes with the antennae, to which he has given the name of the *antennal*: by very minute observation, he was enabled to interpret some of the principal signs, such as those of alarm, departure, encouragement, &c. But it would be an endless business, even to indicate the many points of resemblance between the Ant and the Man; we must refer to the works of Huber, Latreille, and others, or to this work, where the principal facts are noted: we shall, however, give an abridged account of the Ant Waterloo, greatly celebrated by insect historians, and of which the consequences are supposed to have been unusually important. Myriads of ants died on this heroic field, and it is believed that the victors got possession of a very finely built ant-city, belonging to their antagonists, sacked great numbers of larvae, and wholly destroyed one large Ant state. Huber is the Despatch writer.—*Examiner.*

AN ANT WATERLOO.

I observed two of the largest ant-hills engaged in arms against each other. I cannot say what might have kindled the torch of discord between these republics. They were of the same species, similar as to size and population, and situated at a hundred paces distant from each other. Two mighty empires do not possess a greater number of combatants. Figure to yourself a prodigious crowd of these insects filling all the space which separate the two ant-hills, and occupying a breadth of two feet. The armies met half way from their respective habitations, and there gave battle. Thousands of ants, mounted on the natural projections of the soil, struggled two by two, holding by their mandibles, and opposite to each other. A greater number were brought out, attacked, and dragged along as prisoners. The latter made vain efforts to escape, as if they had foreseen that when they arrived at the hostile ant-field, they would experience a cruel fate.

The field of battle was two or three feet square. A penetrating odour was inhaled from all quarters. A number of ants was to be seen there dead, and covered with poison; others composing groups and chains, were hooked together by their feet or pincers, and dragging each other by turns in opposite directions. These groups were formed successively. The struggle had begun between two ants, who squeezed each other by the mandibles, raised themselves on their legs, to let the belly pass in front, and mutually spouted venom against the adversary. They squeezed so close that they tumbled on the side, and fought for a long time in the dust; they soon arose again, and tugged away at each other, each endeavouring to drag off its antagonist. But, when their strength was equal, these athletae remained motionless and crooked to the ground, until a third ant came up to decide the advantage. Most frequently one and the other received assistance at the same time; then all the four, holding by one foot, or one antennae, again made vain efforts to gain the victory; others united themselves to the former, and sometimes these were again seized in their turn by new comers. In this manner were formed chains of six, eight, or ten ants, all hooked to each other. The equilibrium was broken only when several warriors belonging to the same republic advanced at once. They forced those that were enchained to let go, and the private combatants were recommenced.

At the approach of night each party re-entered gradually into the city, which served as an asylum; and the ants which were killed or taken prisoners not being replaced by others the number of combatants diminished, until, at last, no more remained. But the ants returned to the fight with the dawn of the day,—the groups were formed, the carnage commenced with increased fury, and the place of encounter was six feet in depth, and two abreast.—*Griffith's Animal Kingdom.*

SIMPLE MEAT-SAFE.—Meat may be preserved from putrefaction by the following contrivance:—To a wooden or cloth safe, placed in the shade, and directed as much as possible towards the north, adapt a ventilating wheel of considerable diameter, the axle projecting inwards. To the part of the axle thus projecting inwards attach fans; the effect will be that a current of air is constantly kept up, inasmuch as the fans are put into motion by the slightest action of the external wheel. In windy weather the wheel may of course be fixed.

BESIDES appearing in WEEKLY NUMBERS, the SCHOOLMASTER will be published in MONTHLY PARTS, which, stitched in a neat cover, will contain as much letter-press, of good execution, as any of the large Monthly Periodicals: A Table of Contents will be given at the end of the year; when, *at the weekly cost of three-halfpence*, a handsome volume of 832 pages, super-royal size, may be bound up, containing much matter worthy of preservation.

PART I. for August, containing the first four Numbers, with JOHNSTONE'S MONTHLY REGISTER, may be had of all the Booksellers. Price 7d. For the accommodation of weekly readers, the Monthly Register and Cover may be had separately at the different places of sale.

TO CORRESPONDENTS.

Several communications are received, and will be attended to. As the numbers are printed early, to be despatched to distant places, we cannot even notice the receipt of communications, till long after they have come to hand.

CONTENTS OF NO. VI.

Jeremy Bentham—The Principle of Utility..........................81
A Shetland Parson, or Good Luck at last..........................83
Theodor Korner, the Volunteer Patriot............................85
The Most Important Marriage ever celebrated in Scotland........86
Emigration..87
Witchcraft and its Believers....................................ib.
ELEMENTS OF THOUGHT.—Mind; Great Men; Orthodoxy................88
The Petticoat Kirk;—Manufactures, &c............................88
THE STORY TELLER.—To Morrow.....................................89
Short Hand Writing and the Press................................93
Scottish Tea Party..94
Stanzas to a Daughter; by D. Vedder.............................ib.
MEDICAL SELECTIONS.—Premature Interment; Effect of the Passions on Health; The Spasmodic Cholera, &c.......................95
Political Ant History; and an Ant Waterloo......................96

EDINBURGH: Printed by and for JOHN JOHNSTONE, 19, St. James's Square.—Published by JOHN ANDERSON, Jun., Bookseller, 55, North Bridge Street, Edinburgh; by JOHN MACLEOD, and ATKINSON & Co., Booksellers, Glasgow; and sold by all Booksellers and Venders of Cheap Periodicals.

THE Schoolmaster,
AND
EDINBURGH WEEKLY MAGAZINE.

CONDUCTED BY JOHN JOHNSTONE.

THE SCHOOLMASTER IS ABROAD.—LORD BROUGHAM.

No. 7.—Vol. I. SATURDAY, SEPTEMBER 15, 1832. Price Three-Halfpence.

MEMOIR OF WILLIAM COBBETT.

This is a name which properly belongs to the history of the last forty years; yet it is neither as a public man, nor as a political journalist, that Mr. Cobbett is introduced into these pages. The Cobbett for the Schoolmaster is the self-educated youth, the soldier, the lover, husband, father, and the able writer on matters of daily life and practical utility. As this celebrated character is to make his long-promised visit to Scotland next week, the time is appropriate.

William Cobbett was born at Farnham, in Surrey, about 1765-6, in that humble rank of the rural population, to be sprung from which, he seems to consider as almost essential to the formation of a healthy body, and an energetic mind.

The man, known only to our fine ladies and gentlemen as the Dragon of Botley, or the Bear of Kensington, and some other things which we shall not describe, is, after all, tolerably human, sometimes really amiable when speaking of women, children, and rural affairs; as, for example, of the class among which he was born and bred:—" The poor mother is frequently compelled, in order to help to get bread for her children, to go to a distance from home, and leave the group, baby and all, to take care of the house and themselves. * * * * In summer time you see the little groups rolling about on the green, or amongst the heath, not far from the cottage, and at a mile perhaps from any other dwelling, the dog their only protector. And what fine, and straight, and healthy, and fearless, and acute persons they become! It used to be remarked in Philadelphia, when I lived there, that there was not a single man, of any eminence, whether doctor, lawyer, merchant, trader, or any thing else, that had not been born and bred in the country, and of parents in a low state of life. Examine London, and you will find it much about the same. From their very childhood they are *from necessity intrusted with the care of something valuable.*" It was thus the subject of our memoir was trained.

With whatever Cobbett had been previously intrusted, from eleven he had the care of himself, and away from his parents led a scrambling sort of hard-working life, till at eighteen he was tall and strong enough to be a soldier. He enlisted in the 54th regiment of foot, then commanded by the Duke of Kent, and went to British America; in which the whole of his military life, of about eight years, was passed, as private, corporal, and serjeant-major. He already possessed the rudiments of what he considers a useful education, " distinct reading, plain and neat writing, and arithmetic." To these acquirements, while a private soldier, he added the grammar of his own language—we need not say how thoroughly; but we must tell *how* it was acquired, for things of this sort are the main object of this sketch.

" I learned grammar, says Cobbett, when I was a private soldier on the pay of sixpence a-day. The edge of my birth, or that of the guard-bed, was my seat to study in; my knapsack was my book-case; a bit of board, lying on my lap, was my writing table; and the task did not demand any thing like a year of my life. I had no money to purchase candle or oil; in winter time it was rarely that I could get any evening-light but that of *the fire,* and only my *turn* even of that. And, if I, under such circumstances, and without parent or friend to advise or encourage me, accomplished this undertaking, what excuse can there be for *any youth,* however poor, however pressed with business, or however circumstanced as to room or other conveniences? To buy a pen or a sheet of paper I was compelled to forego some portion of food, though in a state of half-starvation; I had no moment of time that I could call my own; and I had to read and to write amidst the talking, laughing, singing, whistling and brawling of at least half a score of the most thoughtless of men, and that, too, in the hours of their freedom from all control. Think not lightly of the *farthing* that I had to give, now and then, for ink, pen, or paper! That farthing was, alas! a *great sum* to me! I was as tall as I am now; I had great health and great exercise. The whole of the money, not expended for us at market, was *two pence a-week* for each man. I remember, and well I may! that, upon one occasion I, after all absolutely necessary expenses, had, on a Friday, made shift to have a half-penny in reserve, which I had destined for the purchase of a *red-herring* in the morning; but, when I pulled off my clothes at night, so hungry then as to be hardly able to endure life, I found that I had *lost my half-penny!* I buried my head under the miserable sheet and rug, and cried like a child! And, again I say, if I, under circumstances like these, could encounter and overcome this task, is there, can there be, in the whole world, a youth to find an excuse for the non-performance? What youth, who shall read this, will not be ashamed to say, that he is not able to find time and opportunity for this most essential of all the branches of book-learning?

"I press this matter with such earnestness, because a knowledge of grammar is the foundation of all literature; and because without this knowledge opportunities for writing and speaking are only occasions for men to display their unfitness to write and speak. How many false pretenders to erudition have I exposed to shame merely by my knowledge of grammar! How many of the insolent and ignorant great and powerful have I pulled down and made little and despicable!"

The rules and precepts which COBBETT lays down for young men are those which he practised in youth. They are *Vivre de peu*—that is, *Live upon little*, which is the only foundation of independence, *Toujours prêt—Always ready*—or, in the words of our countrymen's motto, *Ready, aye ready*, as the only certain condition of advancement in life, for the young man who has no friends save his own head and hands. And the example follows the rule.

"I was *always ready*: if I had to mount guard at *ten* I was ready at *nine*: never did any man, or any thing, wait one moment for me. Being, at an age *under twenty years*, raised from Corporal to Sergeant-Major *at once*, over the heads of thirty sergeants, I naturally should have been an object of envy and hatred; but this object of early rising and of rigid adherence to the precepts which I have given you, really subdued these passions; because every one felt, that what I did he had never done, and never could do. Before my promotion, a clerk was wanted to make out the morning report of the regiment. I rendered the clerk unnecessary; and, long before any other man was dressed for the parade, my work for the morning was all done, and I myself was on the parade, walking, in fine weather, for an hour perhaps. My custom was this: to get up in summer at day-light, and in winter at four o'clock; shave, dress, even to the putting of my sword belt over my shoulder, and having my sword lying on the table before me, ready to hang by my side. Then I ate a bit of cheese or pork, and bread. Then I prepared my report, which was filled up as fast as the companies brought in the materials. After this I had an hour or two to read, before the time came for any duty out of doors, unless, when the regiment or part of it went out to exercise in the morning. When this was the case, and the matter was left to me, I always had it on the ground in such time as that the bayonets glistened in the *rising sun*, a sight which gave me delight, of which I often think, but which I should in vain endeavour to describe. If the *officers* were to go out, eight or ten o'clock was the hour, sweating the men in the heat of the day, breaking in upon the time for cooking their dinner, putting all things out of order and all men out of humour. When I was commander, the men had a long day of leisure before them: they could ramble into the town or into the woods; go to get raspberries, to catch birds, to catch fish, or to pursue any other recreation, and such of them as chose, and were qualified, to work at their trades. So that here, arising solely from the early habits of one very young man, were pleasant and happy days given to hundreds."

The virtues which COBBETT must have practised at this time, and to which he eloquently exhorts young men, are obedience, frugality, industry, temperance, husbanding of time, perseverance, cleanliness, civil manners, promptitude, *early rising*; and, as connected with these, a manly contempt of "table-enjoyments," gluttony, drunkenness, gambling, and debasing sensuality of every kind; moreover, to eschew, as deadly poison, all "kettle slops," and to shave with cold water!

The study of GEOGRAPHY and HISTORY succeeded Grammar, while COBBETT remained in the army; and he had always been a rapacious miscellaneous reader. We remember him somewhere saying that he exhausted—probably for want of something better—all the novels of a country-town library, at that time supplied in its staple from the Minerva press. His amusing incidental, but ever recurring abuse of Shakspeare and Milton, and, indeed, of all the poets, discovers, as does his general writings, very considerable intimacy with their works; though the effect of that intimacy has been to steel him against their beauties.

Men, from twenty and upwards, are very apt, a fair occasion presented, to fall in love; and " the hoary demagogue of Kensington," strange as it may appear, some fifty years ago, proved no exception to the rule. There is much natural tenderness and beauty, yea there is true romance in COBBETT's history of the rise, progress, and happy termination of his single love. Here it is in his own words:

"When I first saw my wife she was *thirteen years old*, and I was within about a month of *twenty-one*. She was the daughter of a sergeant of artillery, and I was the sergeant-major of a regiment of foot, both stationed in forts near the city of St. John, in the province of New Brunswick. I sat in the same room with her for about an hour, in company with others, and I made up my mind, that she was the very girl for me. That I thought her beautiful is certain, for that I had always said should be an indispensable qualification; but I saw in her what I deemed marks of that sobriety of *conduct* of which I have said so much, and which has been by far the greatest blessing of my life. It was now dead of winter, and, of course, the snow several feet deep on the ground, and the weather piercing cold. It was my habit, when I had done my morning's writing, to go out at break of day to take a walk on a hill at the foot of which our barracks lay. In about three mornings after I had first seen her, I had, by an invitation to breakfast with me, got up two young men to join me in my walk; and our road lay by the house of her father and mother. It was hardly light, but she was out on the snow, scrubbing out a washing-tub. "That's the girl for me," said I, when we had got out of her hearing. One of these young men came to England soon afterwards; and he, who keeps an inn in Yorkshire, came over to Preston, at the time of the election, to verify whether I were the same man. When he found that I was, he appeared surprised; but what was his surprise, when I told him that those tall young men, whom he saw around me, were the *sons* of that pretty little girl that he and I saw scrubbing out the washing-tub on the snow in New Brunswick, at day-break in the morning!

"From the day that I first spoke to her, I never had a thought of her ever being the wife of any other man, more than I had a thought of her being transformed into a chest of drawers; and I formed my resolution at once, to marry her as soon as we could get permission, and to get out of the army as soon as I could. So that this matter was, at once, settled as firmly as if written in the book of fate. At the end of about six months, my regiment, and I along with it, were removed to Fredericton, a distance of a *hundred miles* up the river of St. John; and, which was worse, the artillery were expected to go off to England a year or two before our regiment! The artillery went, and she along with them; and now it was that I acted a part becoming a real and sensible lover. I was aware, that, when she got to that gay place, Woolwich, the house of her father and mother, necessarily visited by numerous persons not the most select, might become unpleasant to her, and I did not like, besides, that she should continue to *work hard*. I had saved a *hundred and fifty guineas*, the earnings of my early hours, in writing for the paymaster, the quartermaster, and others, in addition to the savings of my own pay. *I sent her all my money*, before she sailed; and wrote to her to beg of her, if she found her home uncomfortable, to hire a lodging with respectable people: and, at any rate, not to spare the money, by any means, but to buy herself good clothes, and to live without hard work, until I arrived in England; and I, in order to induce her to lay out the money, told her that I should get plenty more before I came home.

"As the malignity of the devil would have it, we were kept abroad *two years longer* than our time, Mr. Pitt (England not being so tame then as she is now) having knocked up a dust with Spain about Nootka Sound. Oh, how I cursed Nootka Sound, and poor bawling Pitt too, I am afraid! At the end of *four years*, however, home I came; landed at Portsmouth, and got my discharge from the army by the great kindness of poor Lord Edward Fitzgerald, who was then the Major of my regiment. I found my little girl *a servant of all work* (and hard work it was), at *five pounds a year*, in the house of a Captain Brisac; and, without hardly saying a word about the matter, she put into my hands *the whole of my hundred and fifty guineas unbroken!*

"Need I tell the reader what my feelings were? Need I tell kind-hearted English parents what effect this anecdote must have produced on the minds of our children?"

COBBETT went to France, where he perfected his knowledge of the French language; and from thence to Philadelphia, with his wife, where he became a teacher of English to Frenchmen, and composed his "famous grammar" for teaching French people English. He also commenced THE PORCUPINE, the most furious Anti-Jacobin Journal that has ever appeared. But this is a difficult subject, and on this Saturday the 15th Sept. 1832, it might be an invidious one. It is enough, that this vigorous, vehement, and reckless writer, if he did desert his original standard, apostatized to the true side, left the cause of authority, and in many essential points embraced that of right. The true key to his character as a political writer, is, that his Guardian Genius, his own robust mind, originally whispered him, "BE BOLD, BE BOLD, BE BOLD,—*You cannot be too bold.*—The mass of mankind, like the women,

Born to be controlled,
Stoop to the forward and the BOLD."

On such promptings and calculations COBBETT has acted throughout, and with success which justifies their sagacity, if nothing more. But while thus occupied in Philadelphia in lauding the Bourbons, and denouncing Jacobins and revolutionists, with all the fiery vehemence, and more than the coarseness and personal scurrility of his writings on the other side, COBBETT was also rocking the cradle, and nursing the baby; and from the desk of the fierce political writer we turn with pleasure to the fireside, and *The Porcupine* with his quills sheathed. "I began my young marriage days," he says, "in and near Philadelphia." His wife kept no servant, which, on principle and calculation, he approves, and recommends to all young couples, where there is but one young child,—the second specimen of the womankind, in the young beginner's household, being, according to him, a more expensive article than the wife herself; and in the circumstances described, his reasoning is sound, and his estimates are correct. For the sake of wives, we must be somewhat liberal of extracts here; but first, for the exhortation to the husband, to follow his example *in keeping at home.*

"Let the new-married husband resolve *never to spend an hour from home*, unless business or some necessary or rational purpose demand it. Where ought he to be? What *other company* ought he to deem so good and so fitting, as that of the person whom he himself hath chosen to be his partner for life. * * * * With whom else can he so pleasantly spend his hours of leisure and relaxation? Besides, if he quit her, to seek company more agreeable, is she not set at large by that act of his? What justice is there in confining her at home without any company at all, while he rambles forth in search of company more gay than he finds at home?

"Let the young married man try the thing: let him resolve not to be seduced from his home; let him never go, in one single instance, unnecessarily, from his own fire-side. *Habit* is a powerful thing; and if he begin right, the pleasure that he will derive from it will induce him to continue right. This is not being 'tied to the apron-strings,' which means quite another matter, as I shall show by-and-by. It is being at the husband's place, whether he have children or not. And is there any want of matter for conversation between a man and his wife? Why not talk of the daily occurrences to her, as well as to any body else, and especially to a company of tippling and noisy men? If you excuse yourself by saying that you go *to read the newspaper*, I answer, *buy the newspaper*, if you must read it: the cost is not half of what you spend per day at the pot-house; and then you have it your own, and may read it at your leisure, and your wife can read it as well as yourself, if read it you must. And, in short, what must that man be made of, who does not prefer sitting by his own fireside, with his wife and children, reading to them, or hearing them read, to hearing the gabble and balderdash of a club or a pot-house company!"

So far precept and exhortation, and now for example.

"Few men have been more frequently taken from home by business, or by a necessity of some sort, than I have; and I can positively assert, that, as to my return, I never once disappointed my wife in the whole course of our married life. If the time of return was contingent, I never failed to keep her informed *from day to day*: if the time was fixed, or when it became fixed, my arrival was as sure as my life. Going from London to Botley, once, with Mr. Finnerty, whose name I can never pronounce without an expression of my regard for his memory, we stopped at Alton, to dine with a friend, who, delighted with Finnerty's talk, as every body else was, kept us till ten or eleven o'clock, and was proceeding to *the other bottle*, when I put in my protest, saying, 'We must go, my wife will be frightened.' 'Blood, man,' said Finnerty, 'you do not mean to go home to-night!' I told him I did; and then sent my son, who was with us, to order out the post-chaise. We had twenty-three miles to go, during which we debated the question, whether Mrs. Cobbett would be up to receive us, I contending for the affirmative, and he for the negative. She was up, and had a nice fire for us to sit down at. She had not committed the matter to a servant; her servants and children were all in bed; and she was up to perform the duty of receiving her husband and his friend. 'You did not expect him?' said Finnerty. 'To be sure I did,' said she; 'he never disappointed me in his life.'

"Now, if all young men knew how much value women set upon this species of fidelity, there would be fewer unhappy couples than there are. If men have appointments with *lords* they never dream of breaking them; and I can assure them that wives are as sensitive in this respect as lords."

And now for a little wholesome counsel to the wives; but first the chapter of servants.

"The oppression is most heavy on those least able to bear it; and particularly on clerks and such like people, whose wives seem to think that because the husband's work is of a genteel description, they should be kept like *ladies*. Poor fellows! their work is not hard and rough to be sure; but it is *work*, and work for many hours too, and painful enough; and as to their income, it scarcely exceeds, on an average, the double, at any rate, of that of a journeyman carpenter, bricklayer, or tailor.

"Besides, the man and wife will live on cheaper diet and drink than a servant will live. Thousands, who would never have had beer in their house, have it for the servant, who will not live without it. However frugal your wife, her frugality is of little use, if she have one of these inmates to provide for. Many a hundred thousand times has it happened that the butcher and the butter-man have been applied to solely because there was a servant to satisfy. You cannot, with this clog everlastingly attached to you, be frugal, if you would: you can save nothing against the days of expense, which are, however, pretty sure to come. And why should you bring into your house a trouble like this; an absolute annoyance; a something for your wife to watch, to be a constraint upon her, to thwart her in her best intentions, to make her uneasy, and to sour her temper? Why should you do this foolish thing? Merely to comply with corrupt fashion; merely from false shame and false and contemptible pride? If a young man were, on his marriage, to find any difficulty in setting this ruinous fashion at defiance, a very good way would be, to count down to his wife, at the end of every week, the amount of the expense of a servant for that week, and request her to deposit it in her drawer. In a short time she would find the sum so large, that she would be frightened at the thoughts of a servant; and would never dream of one again, except in case of absolute necessity, and then for as short a time as possible.

"But the wife may not be *able* to do all the work to be done in the house. Not *able!* A young woman not able to cook and wash, and mend and make, and clean the house, and make the bed for one young man and herself, and that young man her husband too, who is quite willing (if he be worth a straw) to put up with cold dinner, or with a crust; to get up and light her fire; to do any thing that the mind can suggest to spare her labour, and to conduce to her convenience! Not *able* to do this! Then, if she brought no fortune, and be had none, she ought not to have been *able to marry*: and, let me tell you, young man, a *small fortune* would not put a servant-keeping wife upon an equality with one who required no such inmate.

"If, indeed, the work of a house were *harder* than a young woman could perform without pain, or great fatigue; if it had a tendency to impair her health or deface her beauty; then you might hesitate: but it is not too hard, and it tends to preserve health, to keep the spirits buoyant, and, of course, to preserve beauty. You often hear girls, while scrubbing or washing, singing till they are out of breath; but never while they are at what they call *working* at the needle. The American wives are most exemplary in this respect. They have none of that false pride which prevents thousands in England from doing that which interest, reason, and even their own inclination, would prompt them to do. They work, not from necessity; not from compulsion of any sort; for their husbands are the most indulgent in the whole world. In the towns they go to the market, and cheerfully carry home the result: in the country, they not only do the work in the house, but extend their labours to the garden, plant, and weed, and hoe, and gather and preserve the fruits and the herbs; and this, too, in a climate far from being so favourable to labour as that of England; and they are amply repaid for these by those gratifications which their excellent economy enables their husbands to bestow upon them, and which it is their universal habit to do with a liberal hand.

"But, did I *practise* what I am here preaching? Ay, and to the full extent. Till I had a second child, no servant ever entered my house, though well able to keep one: and never in my whole life did I live in a house so clean, in such trim order; and never have I eaten or drunk, or slept or dressed, in a manner so perfectly to my fancy as I did then. I had a great deal of business to attend to, that took me a great part of the day from home; but, whenever I could spare a minute from business, the child was in my arms; I rendered the mother's labour as light as I could; any bit of food satisfied me: when watching was necessary, we shared it between us; and that famous GRAMMAR for teaching French people English, which has been for thirty years, and still is, the great work of this kind, throughout all America, and in every nation of Europe, was written by me, in hours not employed in business, and, in great part during my share of the night watchings over a sick, and then only child, who, after lingering many months, died in my arms.

"This was the way that we went on; this was the way that we *began* the married life."

In another place, in exhorting to *moderation in expense*, our Oracle says, "When children come, there must at times be some foreign aid; but until then, what need can the wife of a young tradesman, or even farmer, (unless the family be great,) have of a servant? The wife is young, and why is she not to work as well as the husband? What justice is there in wanting him to keep two women instead of one? You have not married them both in form; but if they be inseparable, you have married them in substance; and if you are free from the crime of bigamy, you have the far most burdensome part of its consequences." Sensible, thoughtful, young husbands will read this extract with attention; and some will become grave over it; but it is proper, that when they hear of the wisdom of discarding the servant, they should see the substitute—the help, as the Americans name it.

Mrs. Cobbett being a patriot and far from home, assured her neighbours in Philadelphia that all English husbands were as kind and *helpful* as her own. Let the reader judge:—" I had business to occupy the whole of my time, Sundays and week days, except sleeping hours; but I used to make time to assist her in taking care of her baby, and in all sort of things; get up, light her fire, boil her tea-kettle (!) carry her up warm water in cold weather, take the child while she dressed herself and got breakfast ready; then breakfast; get her in water and wood for the day; then dress myself neatly, and sally forth to my business. The moment that was over I used to hasten back to her again; and I no more thought of spending a moment away from her, unless business compelled, than I thought of quitting the country and going to sea."—This is true gallantry; and we foresee that Mr. COBBETT will be a prodigious favourite among the ladies of Scotland. He relates once watching a whole night, barefooted, driving away the dogs which kept his wife from sleep most necessary to her health; and tells, that as she was afraid of thunder, however engaged he used always to hasten home if he saw a storm approaching—" Scores of times have I, first and last, run on this errand in the streets of Philadelphia! The Frenchmen, who were my scholars, used to laugh at me exceedingly on this account; and sometimes when I was making an appointment with them, they would say, with a smile and bow, ' *Sauve la tonnere toujours, Monsieur Cobbett,*' [" *Always excepting a thunder-storm, Mr. Cobbett.*']

Now all this is very aimable and useful, and leads us to pass lightly over the extreme bad odour in which the author of *The Porcupine* was, at this time, with the friends of liberty, both in Britain and America, and that libel on the excellent Dr. Rush, which caused a prosecution and fine; and led COBBETT back to England, reviling America, the Americans and their institutions, at least as heartily as on further knowledge and increased experience he has since extolled them. He returned in 1800, and was received as a God-send by the Pitt Administration. As a powerful, unscrupulous partisan-writer, he had no equal; and they hoped to find him as ductile, truckling, and subservient, as higher-born men had been. There is much doubt and contradiction about the offers and promises made to COBBETT at this time; but there need be none in believing that a government so corrupt would have gone any safe length to secure so powerful an instrument—secrecy and fidelity, and an implicit surrender of principle and opinion, being their measure of safety and of usefulness in a hireling writer. But laying aside the political writer, just settled in London, and about to open his trenches anew, we have here a delightful retrospective glimpse of the man. It is found in his " Year's Residence in America."

"When I returned to England in 1800, after an absence from the country parts of it, of sixteen years, the trees, the hedges, even the parks and woods seemed so *small!* It made me laugh to hear little gutters that I could jump over, called *rivers!*—the Thames was but a *creek;* but when in about a month after my arrival in London I went to Farnham, the place of my birth, what was my surprise! Every thing was become so pitifully small. I had to cross in my post-chaise the long and dreary heath of Bagshot; then at the end of it to mount a hill called Hungry Hill; and from that hill I knew I could look down into the beautiful and fertile vale of Farnham. My heart fluttered with impatience, mixed with a sort of fear, to see all the scenes of my childhood; for I had learned before of the death of my father and mother. There is a hill not far above the town called *Crooksbury* hill, which rises up out of a flat, in the form of a cone, and is planted with Scotch fir trees. Here I used to take the eggs and young ones of crows and magpies. This hill was a famous object in the neighbourhood. It served as a superlative degree of height. ' As high as *Crooksbury hill* ' meant with us the utmost degree of height. Therefore the first object that my eyes sought was this hill. I could not believe my eyes! Literally speaking, I thought the famous hill removed, and a little heap put in its stead; for I had seen in New Brunswick, a single rock, or hill of solid rock ten times as big, and four times as high! The post-boy going down hill, and not a bad road, whisked me in a few minutes to the Bush Inn, from the garden of which I could see the prodigious *sand hill* where I had begun my gardening works. What a *nothing!* But now came rushing into my mind, all at once, my pretty little garden, my little blue smock-frock, my little nailed shoes, my pretty pigeons that I used to feed out of my hand, and the last kind words and tears of my gentle, and tender-hearted, and affectionate mother. I hastened back into the room. If I had looked a moment longer I should have dropt. When I came to reflect, *What a change!* I looked down at my dress. What a change! What scenes I had gone through! How altered my state! I had dined the day, before at a Secretary of State's in company with *Mr. Pitt!* and had been waited upon by men in gaudy liveries! I had nobody to assist me in the world. No teachers of any sort. Nobody to shelter me from the consequences of bad, and no one to counsel me to good behaviour. I felt proud! The distinctions of rank, birth, and wealth, all became nothing in my eyes; and from that moment, (less than a month after my arrival in England,) I resolved never to bend before them!"

The change, if from this time it began to work, was not immediately visible. The *Political Register,* when commenced, promised to be a worthy successor of *The Porcupine;* but by-and-by, whatever were the reasons, strange, discordant, bold, startling opinions began to peer forth in the Anti-Jacobin periodical, till in fine, in six years, Mr. COBBETT avowed nearly all the opinions he has since so eloquently and powerfully supported by his writings, and assisted in propagating beyond any other individual. He now began to proclaim the corruption of Parliament, to denounce placemen and pensioners, to advocate frequent elections, to revile the followers of the Heaven-born Minister, and to laud among the former objects of his unwearied abuse—Sir Francis Burdett! Mr. COBBETT should not have been astonished, and much less offended, at people seeing inconsistency in this, and indulging in doubts of the integrity and inflexibility of his principles; especially when, instead of frankly owning previous error, he continued boldly to maintain that he had always been in the right, and that Time and Truth might change, but not the infallible WILLIAM COBBETT. When, for example, he could sit down and gravely write, " For the last fourteen years, alarms, referring to the French Revolution, have from time to time been played off upon this nation, and that too with *disgraceful success;*" gay people laughed, and grave ones shook their heads; and blunt, commonplace honest men inquired, " And who, pray, most successfully played them off, Mr. COBBETT?" But when, again, he went on and wrote, " To these alarms, artfully excited and kept up, the country owes almost the whole of her present difficulties; for, had it not been for the fear men entertained of the overthrow of all order, law, and religion, Pitt never could have held so long that power, by the exercise of which, he has entailed such a train of curses on us." When he wrote in this strain the temptation was irresistible, to say, " And who so active in exciting these alarms?" If Mr. COBBETT would have manfully avowed, " I did so in my days of defective knowledge, or defective public principle," a satisfactory end would have been put to the matter at once, and the friends of liberty would have hailed their new auxiliary and champion; and have welcomed, as a patriot-volunteer, the man whom many of the best of them, even yet mistakingly reckon but as a suspicious mercenary, useful to the cause, but not worthy of the confidence of its leaders. This equivocal political *status* Mr. COBBETT owes to certain qualities of his mind, with which we do not mean to quarrel; as we could not, if we would, remove them, without destroying the whole structure. To keep him right with the mass of the world, he should have had either more hypocrisy, or more real magnanimity and candour; and then, in either case, a little occasional coarseness and scurrility, verbal injustice and egotistical balderdash, would easily have been overlooked in a man of his acuteness, activity, and power. The hypocrisy he is as far above, as the candour exceeds him. It is a quality not yet naturalized, if it has ever been met with, in the regions of his individual experience, whether as a Pittite and admirer of the Bourbons, or as a democrat, and something of a demagogue. But this is a long digression. —— By 1809 COBBETT had become the most popular political writer that had ever appeared in England. We need not enumerate, how; besides his standing topics, he was successively occupied, for years, with the trial of Lord Melville—the Cintra Convention,—the investigation concerning the Duke of York—the political and private adventures of Sir Francis Burdett; and also in making a fortune. His income, from the Register alone, is calculated, at this time, to have been about £60 a-week—pretty well from an original fortune of 6d. a-day; and a proof that it may, sometimes, be even more profitable to serve the people somewhat honestly, than the Crown very corruptly.

COBBETT had now retired to Botley, in Hampshire, a farm which he purchased and actively improved.—And here, domesticated with his wife and four children, his life was, in all respects, commendable and happy; and from hence he weekly despatched Registers to the press,—the eye of power and the grasp of the law ever upon him.

In the act which first laid Mr. COBBETT under the mercy of that scourge of bad government, the libel-law, there is nothing equivocal. Every circumstance about this affair does honour to the head and heart which brought him into trouble. In 1809, some English Local Militiamen were flogged at the Isle of Ely, in Cambridgeshire, *under a guard of foreign soldiers—of Hanoverians!* and COBBETT denounced the infamy in the generous spirit of a free-born Englishman, and with warmth of language not—certainly not—unsuitable to the atrocity of the transaction. After being tortured, for many months, by the minions of Government for the time being, he was brought to trial, sentenced to two years imprisonment in Newgate, to pay a fine of a thousand pounds to the King, and be held to bail for seven years, under heavy penalties. This was, no doubt of it, intended to annihilate the offender; and it did injure him very deeply, and would for ever have ruined any man of less bodily and intellectual enegy. Among its other effects, this excessive punishment converted a hearty, honest hater, into an exasperated and furious one. With an exultation almost fiendish in the eyes of some sober Scotch Christians, Mr. COBBETT has, ever since, exulted in the discomfiture or misery of his persecutors of those days—and not on public, but, avowedly, on private and personal grounds. His expressions of triumph over Lord Castlereagh's suicide can never be forgotten. In America, to which he retired from another storm, he says, "I am happy to tell you, that Ellenborough and Gibbs have retired! Ill health is the *pretence*. I never yet knew ill health induce such fellows to loosen their grasp of the public purse. But, be it so; *then I feel pleasure on that account.* To all the other pangs of the body and mind, let them add that of knowing that WILLIAM COBBETT, whom they thought they had put down for ever, if not killed, lives *to rejoice at their pains and their death; to trample on their graves; and to hand down their names for the just judgment of posterity.*" This is not going about the bush, at any rate. But we must enter a little more into this business. It is an essential part of COBBETT's history. After describing his happiness in the midst of his family at Botley, which, in his picturing, seems a domestic paradise, he proceeds :—

"In this happy state we lived, until the year 1810, when the Government laid its merciless fangs upon me, dragged me from these delights, and *crammed me into a jail amongst felons*; of which I shall have to speak more fully, when, in the last Number, I come to speak of the duties of the Citizen. This added to the difficulties of my task of *teaching*; for now I was snatched away from the *only* scene in which it could, as I thought, properly be executed. But even these difficulties were got over. The blow was, to be sure, a terrible one; and, Oh God! how was it felt by these poor children! It was in the month of July when the horrible sentence was passed upon me. My wife, having left her children in the care of her good and affectionate sister, was in London, waiting to know the doom of her husband. When the news arrived at Botley, the three boys, one eleven, another nine, and the other seven, years old, were hoeing cabbages in that garden which had been the source of so much delight. When the account of the savage sentence was brought to them, the youngest could not, for some time, be made to understand what a *jail* was; and, when he did, he, all in a tremor, exclaimed, 'Now I'm sure, William, that Papa is not in a place *like that!*' The other, in order to disguise his tears and smother his sobs, fell to work with the hoe, and *chopped about like a blind person.* This account, when it reached me, affected me more, filled me with deeper resentment, than any other circumstance. And, oh! how I despise the wretches who talk of my *vindictiveness;* of my *exultation* at the confusion of those who inflicted those sufferings! How I despise the base creatures, the crawling slaves, the callous and cowardly hypocrites, who affect to be '*shocked*' (tender souls!) at my expressions of *joy*, and at the death of Gibbs, Ellenborough, Perceval, Liverpool, Canning, and the rest of the tribe that I have already seen out, and at the fatal workings of *that system*, for endeavouring to check which I was thus punished? How I despise these wretches, and how I, above all things, enjoy their ruin, and anticipate their utter beggary! What! I am to forgive, am I, injuries like this; and that, too, without any *atonement?* Oh, no! I have not so read the Holy Scriptures; I have not, from them, learned that I am not to rejoice at the fall of unjust foes; and it makes a part of my happiness to be able *to tell millions of men* that I do thus rejoice, and that I have the means of calling on so many just and merciful men to rejoice along with me."

In Newgate, Mr. COBBETT, to be free of jail society, at the monstrous expense of twelve guineas a-week, hired apartments in the keeper's house, kept some of his elder children with him, and maintained a constant intercourse, by letter, with his family. A hamper, with a lock and two keys, was always upon the road, coming or going.

"It brought me *a journal of labours, proceedings*, and *occurrences*, written on paper of shape and size uniform, and so contrived, as to margins, as to admit of binding. The journal used, when my son was the writer, to be interspersed with drawings of our dogs, colts, or any thing that he wanted me to have a correct idea of. The hamper brought me plants, bulbs, and the like, that I might *see the size* of them ; and always every one sent his or her *most beautiful flowers* ; the earliest violets, and primroses, and cowslips, and blue-bells ; the earliest twigs of trees : and, in short, every thing that they thought calculated to delight me. The moment the hamper arrived, I, casting aside every thing else, set to work to answer *every question*, to give new directions, and to add anything likely to give pleasure at Botley. *Every* hamper brought one "*letter*," as they called it, if not more, from every child ; and to *every letter*, I wrote *an answer*, sealed up and sent to the party, being sure that that was the way to produce other and better letters ; for, though they could not read what I wrote, and though their own consisted at first of mere *scratches*, and afterwards, for a while, of a few words written down for them to imitate, I always thanked them for their '*pretty letter* ;' and never expressed any wish to see them *write better* ; but took care to write in a very neat and plain hand *myself*, and to do up my letter in a very neat manner.

"Thus, while the ferocious tigers thought I was doomed to incessant mortification, and to rage that must extinguish my mental powers, I found in my children, and in their spotless, and courageous, and most affectionate mother, delights to which the callous hearts of those tigers were strangers. ' Heaven first taught letters for some wretch's aid.' How often did this line of Pope occur to me when I opened the little *spuddling* 'letters' from Botley ? This correspondence occupied a good part of my time : I had all the children with me, turn and turn about ; and, in order to give the boys exercise, and to give the two eldest an opportunity of beginning to learn French, I used, for a part of the two years, to send them a few hours of the day to an Abbé, who lived in Castle Street, Holborn. All this was a great relaxation to my mind ; and, when I had to return to my literary labours, I returned *fresh* and cheerful, full of vigour, and *full of hope*, of finally seeing my unjust and merciless foes at my feet, and that, too, without caring a straw on whom their fall might bring calamity, so that my own family were safe ; because, say what any one might, the *community, taken as a whole*, had *suffered this thing to be done unto us*."

Pregnant words these—and plainly spoken.

Evil times again drew on ; and COBBETT had not yet recovered the ruinous effects of his long imprisonment. He had quarrelled with his friend, Sir Francis Burdett; the Crown-lawyers and stamp-officers were ever on the watch to pounce upon him ; and, tired of longer maintaining the vexatious strife, he sought, in America, an asylum from an arbitrary government. Into the merits of the case, between him and Sir Francis Burdett, we do not intend to enter ; but Mr. COBBETT has had close opportunities of looking into the character of the Baronet, and subsequent events rather go to confirm parts of his report. Be this as it may, COBBETT's sophisms and moral fallacies, in the affair of the debt, shocked and alienated many of his admirers in England. He may, indeed, have taken new ground, but he has certainly never fully recovered what he lost then.

In America COBBETT continued as active and indefatigable as ever, and employed his time to good purpose ; but his heart, his hopes, and, we may add, his interest, pointed back to England. His flight was, on the whole, a rash step ; and he came home lowered in popularity.

In the subsequent years,—though from this time vanity, which is at times perfectly ludicrous, egotism, and personal resentments, mingle to an offensive degree in every paper he has written,—COBBETT has done the State, not the Government, some service. The Manchester Massacre, the Trial of the Queen, Ireland, the Currency Question, Tithes, and many other topics of passing interest, have been his themes in these years, during which, however, his influence and reputation seemed to languish ; till the Reform Bill, and all that hung on it, restored him in his original force. The readers of COBBETT, or any who ever heard of his name, need not be told of his detestation of the established clergy. In the war of man and yeoman against priest, the side which the Farnham boy would take, could not be doubtful. He likewise makes war to the knife's point with Dr. Malthus and the political economists—" The Scotch feelosophers," as he contemptuously names them ; and there are many, even among the Scotch, who think he has often the best of it. The Jews, or great capitalists, whether nominally Jew or Christian, are also especial objects of his hatred :—so are the Whigs as a party, and his brother journalists in general ; and all and each he abuses in a style which might have excited the envy of a sculler on the Thames some fifty years back. His running a-muck at the greatest names in English literature, his extravagant eulogiums on hog's flesh, and furious crusade against potatoes, his contempt of our own " filthy, lick-spittle, itch-covered nation,"[*] and other eccentricities, and perhaps affectations, are more amusing than any thing else. Besides, Mr. COBBETT has often told us, he in his heart thinks handsomely of us Scotch, though he occasionally indulges in a little coarse invective at our expense ; and we believe he does, and think handsomely, and moreover justly of him ; allow that some of his censures are deserved, laugh at the rest, and thus, in disappointing his humour, secure our revenge.

Whatever difference of opinion may exist on some points of Mr. COBBETT's character, as a benefactor of his country, there are others on which all, but the most bigoted and narrow-minded, will cordially agree. He has given an interesting and helpless class of the population a new branch of industry—*Cobbett's Plat* ; and even if his Corn[†]

---

[*] The *Scotsman* thinks it will be necessary for us to wear gloves before we venture to put forth the right hand of fellowship to Mr. Cobbett, when he visits us. We believe he has now got over his dread of cutaneous contagion.

[†] The SCHOOLMASTER may not at all times be sufficiently full and explicit for the younger pupils, or those of the *lower forms*. It may therefore be proper to explain here, that *Cobbett's Plat* is plat for working ladies' bonnets, the same as those called Tuscan, or Leghorn, and is now extensively made by young females in this country. Cobbett discovered the proper kind of straw, or rather grass, and also its proper mode of culture, and in fact created this useful branch of home manufacture. *Cobbett's corn* is the maize, or Indian corn, grown in America and other places, which he has zealously attempted to naturalize in Britain. In some seasons fine specimens of this beautiful plant have been produced, but on the whole the experiment has not succeeded, though no one can foretell what careful acclimation may yet do.

should not succeed,—and we trust it may,—we owe his vigilance and patriotism gratitude for the attempt to introduce it. He has given us several excellent elementary works on education—his GRAMMAR especially;—and a valuable treatise on household economy, (Cobbett's Cottage Economy;) and in the ADVICE TO YOUNG MEN, with certain trifling allowances, a manual of sound practical sense, and of philosophy bearing on the daily business and important relations of social life. These are not trifling benefits, nor have they been thanklessly received. These, however, may not be considered by Mr. COBBETT's admirers as his most important works. We have his RESIDENCE IN AMERICA, a book full of interest and beauty; and his RURAL RIDES, the production which makes us most in love with the writer, of all the volumes he has published,—a work intensely and beautifully English.—" When I was a very little boy," says Cobbett, " I was, in the barley-sowing season, going along by the side of a field near WAVERLEY Abbey; the primroses and blue-bells* bespangling the banks on both sides of me; a thousand linnets singing in a spreading oak over my head, while the jingle of the traces, and the whistling of the ploughboys saluted my ear from over the hedge; and as it were to snatch me from the enchantment, the hounds, at that instant, having started a hare in the hanger (our Scottish *shaw*) on the other side of the field, came up scampering over it in full cry, taking me after them many a mile: I was not then eight years old." This was the very man to take, and to describe RURAL RIDES in England.—Mr. Cobbett has written a bulky work, which has made him very popular with the Catholics. It contains much that is true, and much that is strong; but must, nevertheless, be received *cum grano salis.*†

Mr. COBBETT, who is now upwards of 66, enjoys a vigorous and robust green old age, and appears to take and court exertion as freely as when twenty years younger. From a political tournament, held at Birmingham, in which his antagonist was Mr. Attwood, he comes among us like a giant refreshed with mighty ale. For the particulars of this *passage-of-arms*, we must of course refer to the newspapers—we dare not meddle with it.

There have been innumerable likenesses and caricatures of this remarkable man—pencil, and pen-and-ink sketches. Of his appearance now, many of our readers will be able to judge for themselves; of how he looked some dozen or more years back, they may form some notion from the subjoined portrait, which we confidently ascribe to a high Tory writer whom COBBETT seems absolutely to fascinate, and one of the most eminent and gifted of their number, Mr. JOHN LOCKHART, of the Quarterly Review.

---

* To Scotch readers who understand wild flowers, this may seem impossible. The blue-bell and primrose do not blossom at the same season; but our wild blue hyacinth is the blue-bell of the English banks.

† A whole peck.—*Editor.*

" It was at a county meeting in Hampshire. * * * * He is perhaps the very man whom I would select from all I have ever seen, if I wished to show a foreigner the *beau-ideal* of an English yeoman. He was then, I suppose, at least fifty, but plump and fresh as possible. His hair was worn smooth on his forehead, and displayed a few curls, nut-brown then, but probably greyish by this time, about his ears. There is something very stately about his step and port; at least, there was so in those days. You could see the sergeant blended with the farmer in every motion of his body. His eye is small, grey, quiet and good tempered—perfectly mild. You say, ' There is a sweet old boy —butter would not melt in his mouth.' He was dressed, the day I saw him, in brown coat, waistcoat and breeches, all of the same piece,—a scarlet under-waistcoat, a drab greatcoat hanging wide, and fastened before by a ' flying strap,' top-boots of a true work-like pattern, and not new, but well cleaned, (another relic probably of his camp habits); he had strong grey worsted gloves and a stout ash plant in his hand. If he had not been pointed out to me by one who knew him, I should probably have passed him over as one of the innocent bacon-eaters of the New Forest; but when I knew that it was COBBETT, you may believe I did not allow his placid, easy eye and smile, to take me in."

Having entered a shaft, in this rich mine, we shall probably work it a little deeper. COBBETT, on the points of a good wife,—on training children, and also pigs,—on baking, brewing, " kettle-slops," " tea-tackle," education, literature, and the formation of manly and independent character, is quite the writer for the SCHOOLMASTER.

LORD BROUGHAM AND VAUX.

Some of the newspapers have got a custom of late of twitting the Lord Chancellor with the assumption of airs of aristocracy and of high birth—or claims of high descent. However this absurdity is attached to his name, it assuredly belongs not to the man. At his election dinner, when, so honourably chosen for Yorkshire, two years ago—so it is no news now.—Mr. Brougham, among the many patriotic and grateful sentiments expressed in his speech of thanks, adverted to himself in the following terms: "Though I have been in courts often, and in senates, and in malls, and in assemblies of all kinds, I never was in one, not only where I was so much pleased, but where I felt it so difficult to account for my being there, as I do on the present occasion; and the more I consider of it, the more I am puzzled and perplexed. Gentlemen, there are three principal grounds on which persons who aspire to the representation of a county usually rely—*high birth, extensive landed possessions, and great local and personal influence*. Now of all these, the usual causes of success, I am totally destitute. I have no property in this county —and not much anywhere; *I have no sort of aristocratic pretensions, though my forefathers ranked in the class of esquires, and I myself am of that class;* I am totally without patronage; and I have no local influence in the county whatever; nay, I am not even a Yorkshireman, and what is more, I am not likely ever to become one," &c. &c. &c. This should surely clear his lordship.

THE STORY-TELLER.

TO-MORROW.
(Concluded from our last Number.)

I LEFT Mr. Croft's house with a vague, indescribable feeling of dissatisfaction and disappointment; but when I arrived at my inn, and repeated all that had passed to my wife, she seemed quite surprised and delighted by the civil and friendly manner in which this gentleman had behaved. She tried to reason the matter with me; but there is no reasoning with imagination.

The fact was, Mr. Croft had destroyed certain vague and visionary ideas, that I had indulged, of making, by some unknown means, a rapid fortune in America; and to be reduced to real life, and sink into a clerk in a merchant's counting-house, was mortification and misery. Lucy in vain dwelt upon the advantage of having found, immediately upon my arrival in Philadelphia, a certain mode of employment, and a probability of rising to be a partner in one of the first mercantile houses, if I went on steadily for a few years. I was forced to acknowledge that her relation was very good; that I was certainly very fortunate, and that I ought to think myself very much obliged to Mr. Croft. But after avowing all this, I walked up and down the room in melancholy reverie for a considerable length of time. My wife reminded me repeatedly that Mr. Croft said he dined precisely at two o'clock; that he was a very punctual man; that it was a long walk, as I had found it, from the inn to his house; that I had better dress myself for dinner; and that my clean shirt and cravat were ready for me. I still walked up and down the room in reverie till my wife was completely ready, had dressed the child, and held up my watch before my eyes to show me that it wanted but ten minutes of two. I then began to dress in the greatest hurry imaginable; and, unluckily, as I was pulling on my silk stocking, I tore a hole in the leg, or, as my wife expressed it, a stitch dropped, and I was forced to wait while she repaired the evil. Certainly this operation of *taking up a stitch*, as I am instructed to call it, is one of the slowest operations in nature; or rather, one of the most tedious and teazing manœuvres of art. Though the most willing and the most dexterous fingers that ever touched a needle were employed in my service, I thought the work would never be finished.

At last, I was hosed and shod, and out we set. It struck a quarter past two as we left the house; we came to Mr. Croft's in the middle of dinner. He had a large company at table; every body was disturbed; my Lucy was a stranger to Mrs. Croft, and was to be introduced; and nothing could be more awkward and embarrassing than our *entrée* and introduction. There were such compliments and apologies, such changing of places, such shuffling of chairs, and running about of servants, that I thought we should never be seated.

In the midst of the bustle my little chap began to roar most horribly, and to struggle to get away from a black servant, who was helping him up on his chair. The child's terror at the sudden approach of the negro could not be conquered, nor could he by any means be quieted. Mrs. Croft, at last, ordered the negro out of the room, the roaring ceased, and nothing but the child's sobs were heard for some instants.

The guests were all silent, and had ceased eating; Mrs. Croft was vexed because *every thing was cold*; Mr. Croft looked much discomfited, and said not a syllable more than was absolutely necessary, as master of the house. I never ate, or rather I was never at, a more disagreeable dinner. I was in pain for Lucy, as well as for myself; her colour rose up to her temples. I cursed myself a hundred times for not having gone to dress in time.

At length, to my great relief, the cloth was taken away; but even when we came to the wine after dinner, the cold formality of my host continued unabated, and I began to fear that he had taken an insurmountable dislike to me, and that I should lose all the advantages of his protection and assistance; advantages which rose considerably in my estimation, when I apprehended I was upon the point of losing them.

Soon after dinner, a young gentleman, of the name of Hudson, joined the company; his manners and appearance were prepossessing; he was frank and well-bred; and the effect of his politeness was soon felt, as if by magic, for every body became at their ease. His countenance was full of life and fire; and though he said nothing that showed remarkable abilities, every thing he said pleased. As soon as he found that I was a stranger, he addressed his conversation principally to me. I recovered my spirits, exerted myself to entertain him, and succeeded. He was delighted to hear news from England, and especially from London; a city which he said he had an ardent desire to visit. When he took leave of me in the evening, he expressed very warmly the wish to cultivate my acquaintance, and I was the more flattered and obliged by this civility, because I was certain that he knew exactly my situation and circumstances, Mrs. Croft having explained them to him very fully even in my hearing.

In the course of the ensuing week, young Mr. Hudson and I saw one another almost every day; and our mutual liking for each other's company increased. He introduced me to his father, who had been a planter; and, having made a large fortune, came to reside at Philadelphia to enjoy himself, as he said, for the remainder of his days. He lived in what the sober Americans called a most luxurious and magnificent style. The best company in Philadelphia met at his house; and he delighted particulary in seeing those who had convivial talents, and who would supply him with wit and gaiety, in which he was naturally rather deficient.

On my first visit, I perceived that his son had boasted of me as one of the best companions in the world; and I determined to support the character that had been given of me: I told two or three good stories, and sung two or three good songs. The company were charmed with me; old Mr. Hudson was particularly delighted; he gave me a pressing general invitation to his house, and most of the principal guests followed his example. I was not a little elated with this success. Mr. Croft was with me at this entertainment; and I own I was peculiarly gratified by feeling that I at once became conspicuous, by my talents, in a company where he was apparently of no consequence, notwithstanding all his wealth and prudence.

As we went home together, he said to me very gravely, "I would not advise you, Mr. Basil Lowe, to accept of all these invitations; nor to connect yourself intimately with young Hudson. The society at Mr. Hudson's is very well for those who have made a fortune, and want to spend it; but for those who have a fortune to make, in my opinion, it is not only useless but dangerous."

I was in no humour, at this moment, to profit by this sober advice; especially as I fancied it might be dictated, in some degree, by envy of my superior talents and accomplishments. My wife, however, supported his advice by many excellent and kind arguments. She observed that these people, who invited me to their houses as a good companion, followed merely their own pleasure, and would never be of any real advantage to me; that Mr. Croft, on the contrary, showed, from the first hour when I applied to him, a desire to serve me; that he had pointed out the means of establishing myself; and that, in the advice he gave me, he could be actuated only by a wish to be of use to me; that it was more reasonable to suspect him of despising than of envying talents, which were not directed to the grand object of gaining money.

Good sense, from the lips of a woman whom a man loves, has a mighty effect upon his understanding, especially if he sincerely believe that the woman has no desire to rule. This was my singular case. I promised Lucy I would refuse all invitations for the ensuing fortnight, and devote myself to whatever business Mr. Croft might devise. No one could be more assiduous than I was for ten days, and I perceived that Mr. Croft, though it was not his custom to praise, was well satisfied with my diligence. Unluckily, on the eleventh day, I put off in the morning making out an invoice, which he left for me to do, and I was persuaded in the evening to go out with young Mr. Hudson. I had expressed, in conversation with him, some curiosity about the American *frog-concerts*; of which I had read, in modern books of travels, extraordinary accounts.

Mr. Hudson persuaded me to accompany him to a swamp, at some miles distant from Philadelphia, to hear one of these concerts. The performance lasted some time, and it was late before we returned to town: I went to bed tired, and waked in the morning with a cold, which I had caught by standing so long in the swamp. I lay an hour after I was called, in hopes of getting rid of my cold: when I was at last up and dressed, I recollected my invoice, and resolved to do it the first thing after breakfast, but, unluckily, I put it off till I had looked for some lines in Homer's "Battle of the Frogs and Mice." There was no Homer, as you may guess, in Mr. Croft's house, and I went to a bookseller's to borrow one: he had Pope's Iliad and Odyssey, but no Battle of the Frogs and Mice. I walked over half the town in search of it; at length I found it, and was returning in triumph, with Homer in each pocket, when at the door of Mr. Croft's house I found half-a-dozen porters, with heavy loads upon their backs.

"Where are you going, my good fellows?" said I.

"To the quay, sir, with the cargo for the Betsey."

"My God!" cried I, "stop. Can't you stop a minute? I thought the Betsey was not to sail till to-morrow. Stop one minute."

"No, sir," said they, "that we can't; for the Captain bade us make what haste we could to the quay to load her."

I ran into the house; the Captain of the Betsey was bawling in the hall with his hat on the back of his head; Mr. Croft on the landing-place of the warehouse stairs, with open letters in his hand, and two or three of the under-clerks were running different ways with pens in their mouths.

"Mr. Basil! the invoice!" exclaimed all the clerks at once, the moment I made my appearance.

"Mr. Basil Lowe, the invoice and the copy, if you please," repeated Mr. Croft. "We have sent three messengers after you. Very extraordinary to go out at this time of day, and not even to leave word where you were to be found. Here's the Captain of the Betsey has been waiting this half-hour for the invoice. Well, sir! will you go for it now? and at the same time bring me the copy, to enclose in this letter to our correspondent by post."

I stood petrified.—" Sir, the invoice, sir!—Good Heavens! I forgot it entirely."

"You remember, it now, sir, I suppose. Keep your apologies till we have leisure. The invoices if you please."

"The invoices! My God, sir! I beg ten thousand pardons! They are not drawn out."

"Not drawn out! Impossible!" said Mr. Croft.

"Then I'm off!" cried the captain, with a tremendous oath. "I can't wait another tide for any clerk breathing."

"Send back the porters, Captain, if you please," said Mr. Croft coolly. "The whole cargo must be unpacked. I took it for granted, Mr. Basil, that you had drawn the invoice, according to order, yesterday morning; and of course the goods were packed in the evening. I was certainly wrong in taking it for granted that you would be punctual. A man of business should take nothing for granted. This is a thing that will not occur to me again as long as I live."

I poured forth expressions of contrition; but apparently unmoved by them, and without anger or impatience in his manner, he turned from me as soon as the porters came back with the goods, and ordered them all to be unpacked and replaced in the warehouse. I was truly concerned.

"I believe you spent your evening yesterday with young Mr. Hudson?" said he, returning to me.

"Yes, sir,—I am sincerely sorry———"

"Sorrow in these cases does no good, sir," interrupted he. "I thought I had sufficiently warned you of the danger of forming that intimacy. Midnight carousing will not for men of business."

"Carousing, sir!" said I. "Give me leave to assure you that we were not carousing. We were only at a *frog-concert*."

Mr. Croft, who had at least suppressed his displeasure till now, looked absolutely angry; he thought I was making a joke of him. When I convinced him that I was in earnest, he changed from anger to astonishment, with a large mixture of contempt in his nasal muscles.

"A frog-concert!" repeated he. "And is it possible that any man could neglect any invoice merely to go to hear a parcel of frogs croaking in a swamp? Sir, you will never do in a mercantile house." He walked off to the warehouse, and left me half mortified, and half provoked.

From this time all hopes from Mr. Croft's friendship was at an end. He was coldly civil to me during the few remaining days of the fortnight that we staid at his house. He took the trouble, however, of looking out for a cheap and tolerably comfortable lodging for my wife and boy; the rent of which he desired to pay for his relation, he said, as long as I should remain in Philadelphia, or till I should find myself in some eligible situation. He seemed pleased with Lucy, and said she was a very properly conducted, well-disposed, prudent young woman, whom he was not ashamed to own for a cousin. He repeated at parting, that he should be happy to afford me every assistance *in reason*, toward pursuing any feasible plan of advancing myself; but it was his decided opinion that I could never succeed in a mercantile line.

I never liked Mr. Croft; he was much too *punctual*, too much of an automaton, for me; but I should have felt more regret at leaving him, and losing his friendship, and should have expressed more gratitude for his kindness to Lucy and my boy, if my head had not at the time been full of young Hudson. He professed the warmest regard for me, congratulated me from getting free from old Croft's mercantile clutches, and assured me that such a man as I was could not fail to succeed in the world by my own talents and the assistance of friends and good connexions.

I was now almost every day at his father's house, in company with numbers of rich and gay people, who were all *my friends*. I was the life of society, was invited everywhere, and accepted every invitation, because I could not offend Mr. Hudson's intimate acquaintance.

From day to day, from week to week, from month to month, I went on in this style. I was old Hudson's grand favourite, and every body told me he could do anything he pleased for me. I had formed a scheme, a bold scheme, of obtaining from government a large tract of territory in the ceded lands of Louisiana, and of collecting subscriptions in Philadelphia, among *my friends*, to make a settlement there; the subscribers to be paid by instalments, so much the first year, so much the second, and so onward, till the whole should be liquidated. I was to collect hands from the next ships, which were expected to be full of emigrants from Ireland and Scotland. I had soon a long list of subscribers, who gave me their names always after dinner or after supper. Old Hudson wrote his name at the head of the list, with an ostentatiously large sum opposite to it.

In this way poor Basil hangs on for a whole twelvemonth, ere he can be persuaded that old Hudson was a boaster and a *fabulist*; and it takes another to convince him that he is, as well as indolent and obstinate, the most selfish of human beings. Young Hudson was, however, still the friend. He had expectations of money, and made large promises, and with him Basil continued to shoot and skait, and remain a miserable dependant.

Many a desperately cold winter's day, he says, I have submitted to be driven in his sledge, when I would much rather, I own, have been safe and snug by my own fireside, with my wife.

Poor Lucy spent her time in a disagreeable and melancholy way during these three years; for, while I was out almost every day, and all day long, she was alone in her lodging for numberless hours. She never repined, but always received me with a good-humoured countenance when I came home, even after sitting up half the night to wait for my return from Hudson's suppers. It grieved me to the heart to see her thus seemingly deserted; but I comforted myself with the reflection that this way of life would last but for a short time; that my friend would soon be of age, and able to fulfil all his promises; and that we should then all live together in happiness. I assured Lucy that the present idle, if not dissipated manner in which I spent my days, was not agreeable to my taste; that I was often extremely melancholy, even when I was forced to appear in the highest spirits; and that I often longed to be quietly with her when I was obliged to sacrifice my time to friendship.

It would have been impossible that she and my child could have subsisted all this time independently, but for her steadiness and exertions. She would not accept of any pecuniary assistance, except from her relation, Mr. Croft, who regularly paid the rent of her lodgings. She undertook to teach some young ladies, whom Mrs. Croft introduced to her, various kinds of fine needle-work, in which she excelled; and for this she was well paid. I know that she never cost me one farthing during the three years and three months that we lived in Philadelphia. But even for this I do not give her so much credit as for her sweet temper, during these trials, and her great forbearance in never reproaching or disputing with me. Many wives, who are called excellent managers, make their husbands pay tenfold in suffering what they save in money. This was not my Lucy's way; and, therefore, with my esteem and respect, she ever had my fondest affections. I was in hopes that the hour was just coming when I should be able to prove this to her, and when we should no longer be doomed to spend our days asunder. But, alas, her judgment was better than mine.

My friend Hudson was now within six weeks of being of age, when unfortunately there arrived in Philadelphia a company of players from England. Hudson, who was eager for everything that had the name of pleasure, insisted upon my going with him to their first representation. Among the actresses there was a girl of the name of Marion, who seemed to be ordinary enough, just fit for a company of strolling players, but she danced passably well, and danced a great deal between the acts that night. Hudson clapped his hands till I was quite out of patience. He was in raptures; and the more I depreciated, the more he extolled the girl. I wished her in Nova Zembla, for I saw he was falling in love with her, and had a kind of presentiment of all that was to follow. To tell the matter briefly, for what signifies dwelling upon past misfortunes, the more young Hudson's passion increased for this dancing girl, the more his friendship for me declined, for I had frequent arguments with him upon the subject, and did all I could to open his eyes. I saw that the damsel had art, that she knew the extent of her power, and that she would draw her infatuated lover in to marry her. He was headstrong and violent in all his passions; he quarrelled with me, carried the girl off to Jamaica, married her the day he was of age, and settled upon his plantation. There was an end of all my hopes about the ceded territory.

Lucy, who was always my resource in misfortune, comforted me by saying I had done my duty in combating my friend's folly at the expense of my own interest; and that, though he had quarrelled with me, she loved me the better for it. All things considered, I would not have exchanged feelings and situations with him.

Reflecting upon my own history and character, I have often thought it a pity that, with certain good qualities, and, I will add, talents, which deserved a better fate, I should have never succeeded in anything I attempted, because I could not conquer one seemingly slight defect in my disposition, which had grown into a habit. Thoroughly determined by Lucy's advice to write to Mr. Croft, to request he would give me another trial, I put off sending the letter till the next day; and that very morning Mr. Croft set off on a journey to a distant part of the country, to see a daughter who was newly married.

By an accident, seconded by Basil's procrastinating temper, he, at this time drew upon himself the suspicion of having attempted to poison old Hudson and a party of gentlemen, by laying in the cook's way a dangerous herb. Out of this affair he is extricated with some difficulty; but his former friends looked coldly upon him. Mr. Croft was still absent from town, and he had not money sufficient to leave America, which was become in every way disagreeable, without selling his watch and trinkets.

I was not, says Basil, accustomed to such things, and I was ashamed to go to the pawnbroker's, lest I should be met and recognized by some of my friends. I wrapped myself up in an old surtout, and slouched my hat over my face.

As I was crossing the quay, I met a party of gentlemen walking arm in arm. I squeezed past them, but one stopped to look after me; and, though I turned down another street to escape him, he dodged me unperceived. Just as I came out of the pawnbroker's shop, I saw him posted opposite to me: I brushed by; I could with pleasure have knocked him down for his impertinence. By the time that I had reached the corner of the street, I heard a child calling after me. I stopped, and a little boy put into my hands my watch, saying, "Sir, the gentleman says you left your watch and these thingumbobs by mistake."

"What gentleman?"

"I don't know, but he was one that said I looked like an honest chap, and he'd trust me to run and give you the watch. He is dressed in a blue coat. He went toward the quay. That's all I know."

On opening the paper of trinkets, I found a card with these words:—

"*Barny*—with kind thanks."

"Barny! poor Barny! An Irishman whose passage I paid coming to America three years ago. Is it possible?"

I ran after him the way which the child directed, and was so fortunate as just to catch a glimpse of the skirt of his coat as he went into a neat, good-looking house. I walked up and down some time, expecting him to come out again; for I could not suppose that it belonged to Barny. I asked a grocer, who was leaning over his hatch door, if he knew who lived in the next house?

"An Irish gentleman of the name of O'Grady."

"And his Christian name?"

"Here it is in my books, sir—Barnaby O'Grady."

I knocked at Mr. O'Grady's door, and made my way into the parlour; where I found him, his two sons, and his wife, sitting very sociably at tea. He and the two young men rose immediately, to set me a chair.

"You are welcome, kindly welcome, sir," said he. "This is an honour I never expected any way. Be pleased to take the seat near the fire. 'Twould be hard indeed if you *would** not have the best seat that's to be had in this house, where we none of us never should have sat, nor had seats to sit upon, but for you."

The sons pulled off my shabby great coat, and took away my hat, and the wife made up the fire. There was something in their manner, altogether, which touched me so much that it was with difficulty I could keep myself from bursting into tears. They saw this, and Barny (for I shall never call him anything else,) as he thought that I should like better to hear of public affairs than to speak of my own, began to ask his sons if they had *seen the day's* papers, and what news there were?

As soon as I could command my voice, I congratulated this family upon the happy situation in which I found them; and asked by what lucky accident they had succeeded so well?

"The luckiest accident ever *happened me* before or since I came to America," said Barny, "was being on board the same vessel with such a man as you. If you had not given me the first lift, I had been down for good and all, and trampled under foot long and long ago. But after that first lift, all was as easy as life. My two sons here were not taken from me—God bless you; for I never can bless you enough for that. The lads were left to work for me and with me; and we never parted, hand or heart, but just kept working on together, and put all our earnings, as fast as we got them, into the hands of that good woman, and lived

---

* Should.

hard at first, as we were born and bred to do, thanks be to heaven. Then we swore against drink of all sorts entirely. And, as I had occasionally served the masons, when I lived a labouring man in the county of Dublin, and knew something of that business, why, whatever I knew I made the most of, and a trowel felt no ways strange to me; so I went to work, and had higher wages at first than I deserved. The same with the two boys: one was as much of a blacksmith as would shoe a horse: and t'other a bit of a carpenter; and the one got plenty of work in the forges, and t'other in the dock-yards, as a ship-carpenter. So early and late, morning and evening, we were all at the work, and just went this way struggling on even for a twelvemonth, and found, with the high wages and constant employ we had met, that we were getting greatly better in the world. Besides, the wife was not idle. When a girl, she had seen baking, and had always a good notion of it, and just tried her hand upon it now, and found the loaves went down with the customers, and the customers coming faster and faster for them; and this was a great help. Then I grew master mason, and had my men under me, and took a house to build by the job, and that did; and then on to another and another; and, after building many for the neighbours, 'twas fit and my turn, I thought, to build one for myself, which I did out of theirs, without wronging them of a penny. And the boys grew master-men, in their line; and when they got good coats, nobody could say against them, for they had come fairly by them, and became them well perhaps for that rason. So, not to be tiring you too much, we went on from good to better, and better to best; and if it pleased God to question me how it was we got on so well in the world, I should answer, Upon my conscience, myself does not know; except it be that we never made Saint Monday, nor never put off till the morrow what we could do the day."

I believe I sighed deeply at this observation, notwithstanding the comic phraseology in which it was expressed.

"But all this is no rule for a gentleman born," pursued the good-natured Barny, in answer, I suppose, to the sigh which I uttered; "nor is it any disparagement to him if he has not done as well in a place like America, where he had not the means, not being used to bricklaying, and slaving with his hands, and striving as we did. Would it be too much liberty to ask you to drink a cup of tea, and to taste a slice of my good woman's bread and butter? And happy the day we see you eating it, and only wish we could serve you in any way whatsoever."

I verily believe the generous fellow forgot, at this instant, that he had redeemed my watch and wife's trinkets. He would not let me thank him as much as I wished, but kept pressing upon me fresh offers of service. When he found I was going to leave America, he asked what vessel we should go in? I was really afraid to tell him, lest he should attempt to pay for my passage. But for this he had, as I afterward found, too much delicacy of sentiment. He discovered, by questioning the captains, in what ship we were to sail; and, when we went on board, we found him and his sons there to take leave of us, which they did in the most affectionate manner; and, after they were gone, we found in the state cabin, directed to me, every thing that could be useful or agreeable to us, as sea-stores for a long voyage.

How I wronged this man, when I thought his expressions of gratitude were not sincere, because they were not made exactly in the mode and with the accent of my own countrymen! I little thought that Barny and his sons would be the only persons who would bid us a friendly adieu when we were to leave America.

We had not exhausted our bountiful provision of sea-stores when we were set ashore in England. We landed at Liverpool; and I cannot describe the melancholy feelings with which I sat down, in the little back parlour of the inn, to count my money, and to calculate whether we had enough to carry us to London. Is this, thought I, as I looked at the few guineas and shillings spread on the table —is this all I have in this world—I, my wife and child. And is this the end of three years' absence from my native country? As the negroes say of a fool who takes a voyage in vain, I am come back, "*with little more than the hair upon my head.*" Is this the end of all my hopes, and all my talents? What will become of my wife and child? I ought to insist upon her going home to her friends, that she may at least have the necessaries and comforts of life, till I am able to maintain her.

The tears started from my eyes; they fell upon an old newspaper, which lay upon the table under my elbow. I took it up to hide my face from Lucy and my child, who just then came into the room; and, as I read without well knowing what, I came among the advertisements to my own name.

"If Mr. Basil Lowe, or his heir, will apply to Mr. Gregory, attorney, No. 34, Cecil Street, he will hear of something to his advantage."

I started up with an exclamation of joy, wiped my tears from the newspaper, put it into Lucy's hand, pointed to the advertisement, and ran to take places in the London coach for the next morning. Upon this occasion, I certainly did not delay. Nor did I, when we arrived in London, put off one moment going to Mr. Gregory's, No. 34, Cecil Street. Upon application to him, I was informed that a very distant relation of mine, a rich miser, had just died, and had left his accumulated treasures to me, "because I was the only one of his relations who had never cost him a single farthing." Other men have to complain of their ill fortune, perhaps with justice; and this is a great satisfaction, which I have never enjoyed: for I must acknowledge that all my disasters have arisen from my own folly. Fortune has been uncommonly favourable to me. Without any merit of my own, or rather, as it appeared, in consequence of my negligent habits, which prevented me from visiting a rich relation, I was suddenly raised from the lowest state of pecuniary distress to the height of affluent prosperity.

I took possession of a handsome house in an agreeable part of the town, and enjoyed the delight of sharing all the comforts and luxuries which wealth could procure, with the excellent woman who had been my support in adversity. I must do myself the justice to observe, that I did not become dissipated or extravagant; affection and gratitude to my Lucy filled my whole mind, and preserved me from the faults incident to those who rise suddenly from poverty to wealth. I did not forget my good friend, Mr. Nun.

I was now placed in a situation where the best parts of my character appeared to advantage, and where the grand defect of my disposition was not apparently of any consequence. I was not now obliged, like a man of business, to be punctual; and delay, in mere engagements of pleasure, was a trifling offence, and a matter of raillery among my acquaintance. My talents in conversation were admired, and if I postponed letter-writing, my correspondents only tormented me a little with polite remonstrances. I was conscious that I was not cured of my faults; but I rejoiced that I was not now obliged to reform, or in any danger of involving those I loved in distress by my negligence.

For one year I was happy, and flattered myself that I did not waste my time; for, at my leisure I read with attention all the ancient and modern works upon education. I resolved to select from them what appeared most judicious and practicable; and so to form, from the beauties of each, a perfect system for the advantage of my son. He was my only child; he had lived with me eighteen months in prison; he was the darling of his mother, whom I adored, and he was thought to be in mind and person a striking resemblance of myself.—How many reasons had I to love him!—I doated upon the child. He certainly shewed great quickness of intellect, and gave as fair a promise of talents as could be expected at his age. I formed hopes of his future excellence and success in the world, as sanguine as those which my poor father had early formed of mine. I determined to watch carefully over his temper, and to guard him particularly against that habit of procrastination, which had been the bane of my life.

One day, while I was alone in my study, leaning on my elbow, and meditating upon the system of education which I designed for my son, my wife came to me and said, "My dear, I have just heard from our friend, Mr. Nun, a circumstance that alarms me a good deal. You know little Harry Nun was inoculated at the same time with our Basil, and by the same person. Mrs. Nun, and all the family, thought he had several spots, just as much as our boy had, and that that was enough; but two years afterward, while we were in America, Harry Nun caught the small pox in the natural way and died. Now, it seems the man who inoculated him was quite ignorant; for two or three other children, whom he attended, have caught the disease since, though he was positive that they were safe. Don't you think we had better have our boy inoculated again immediately, by some proper person?"

"Undoubtedly, my dear, undoubtedly, but I think we had better have him vaccined. I am not sure, however, but I will ask Dr. ———'s opinion this day, and be guided by that; I shall see him at dinner; he has promised to dine with us."

Some accident prevented him from coming, and I thought of writing to him the next day, but afterwards put it off.— Lucy came again into my study where she was sure to find me in the morning. "My dear," said she, "do you recollect that you desired me to defer inoculating our little boy till you could decide whether it be best to inoculate him in the common way or the vaccine?"

"Yes, my dear, I recollect it perfectly well. I am much inclined to the vaccine. My friend, Mr. L—, has had all his children vaccined, and I just wait to see the effect."

"Oh, my love!" said Lucy, "do not wait any longer; for you know we run a terrible risk of his catching the small pox every day, every hour."

"We have run that risk, and escaped for these three years past," said I; "and, in my opinion, the boy has had the small-pox."

"So Mr. and Mrs. Nun thought, and you see what has happened. Remember our boy was inoculated by the same man. I am sure, ever since Mr. Nun mentioned this, I never take little Basil out to walk, I never see him in a shop, I never have him in the carriage with me without being in terror. Yesterday a woman came to the coach with a child in her arms, who had a breaking out on his face. I thought it was the small-pox and was so terrified that I had scarcely strength or presence of mind enough to draw up the glass. Our little boy was leaning out of the door to give a half-penny to the child. My God! if that child had the small-pox!"

"My love," said I, "do not alarm yourself so terribly; the boy shall be inoculated to-morrow."

"To-morrow! Oh, my dearest love, do not put it off till to-morrow," said Lucy; "let him be inoculated to day."

"Well, my dear, only keep your mind easy, and he shall inoculated to-day, if possible; surely you must know that I love the boy as well as you do, and am as anxious about him as you can be."

"I am sure of it, my love," said Lucy.—"I meant no reproach. But, since you have decided that the boy shall be vaccined, let us send directly for the surgeon, and have it done, and then he will be safe."

She caught hold of the bell-cord to ring for a servant.— I stopped her.

"No, my dear, don't ring," said I; "for the men are both out. I have sent one to the library for the new Letters on Education, and the other to the rational toy-shop for some things I want for the child."

"Then, if the servants are out, I had better walk to the surgeon's, and bring him back with me."

"No, my dear," said I; "I must see Mr. L——'s children first. I am going out immediately; I will call upon them: they are healthy children; we can have the vaccine infection from them, and I will inoculate the boy myself."

Lucy submitted. I take a melancholy pleasure in doing her justice, by recording every argument that she used, and every persuasive word that she said to me, upon this occasion. I am anxious to shew that she was not in the least to blame. I alone am guilty! I alone ought to have been the sufferer. It will scarcely be believed—I can hardly believe it myself, that, after all Lucy said to me, I delayed two hours, and stayed to finish making an extract from Rousseau's Emilius before I set out. When I arrived at Mr. L——'s, the children were just gone out to take an airing, and I could not see them. A few hours may sometimes make all the difference between health and sickness, happiness and misery! I put off till the next day the inoculation of my child!

In the meantime a coachman came to me to be hired: my boy was playing about the room, and, as I afterward collected, went close up to the man, and, while I was talking, stood examining a greyhound upon his buttons. I asked the coachman many questions, and kept him for some time in the room. Just as I agreed to take him into my service, he said he could not come to live with me till the next week, because *one of his children was ill of the small-pox.*

These words struck me to the heart. I had a dreadful presentiment of what was to follow. I remember starting from my seat, and driving the man out of the house with violent menaces. My boy, poor innocent victim, followed, trying to pacify me, and holding me back by the skirts of my coat. I caught him up in my arms.—I could not kiss him; I felt as if I was his murderer. I set him down again; indeed I trembled so violently that I could not hold him. The child ran for his mother.

I cannot dwell on these things;—our boy sickened the next week—and the week afterward died in his mother's arms!

Her health had suffered much by the trials which she had gone through since our marriage. The disapprobation of her father, the separation from all her friends, who were at variance with me, my imprisonment, and then the death of her only child, were too much for her fortitude. She endeavoured to conceal this from me, but I saw that her health was rapidly declining. She was always fond of the country; and, as my sole object now in life was to do whatsoever I could to console and please her, I proposed to sell our house in town, and to settle somewhere in the country. In the neighbourhood of her father and mother there was a pretty place to be let, which I had often heard her mention with delight; I determined to take it; I had secret hopes that her friends would be gratified by this measure, and that they would live upon good terms with us. Her mother had seemed, by her letters, to be better disposed toward me since my rich relation had left me his fortune. Lucy expressed great pleasure at the idea of going to live in the country, near her parents; and I was rejoiced to see her smile once more. Being naturally of a sanguine disposition, hope revived in my heart: I flattered myself that we might yet be happy; that my Lucy would recover her peace of mind and her health; and that perhaps Heaven might bless us with another child.

I lost no time in entering into treaty for the estate in the country, and I soon found a purchaser for my excellent house in town. But my evil genius prevailed. I had neglected to renew the insurance of my house; the policy was out but nine days, when a fire broke out in one of my servant's rooms at midnight, and, in spite of all the assistance we could procure, the house, was burnt to the ground. I carried my wife out senseless in my arms; and, when I had deposited her in a place of safety, returned to search for a portfolio, in which was the purchase-money of the country estate, all in bank notes. But whether this portfolio was carried off by some of the crowd, which had assembled round the ruins of my house, or whether it was consumed in the flames, I cannot determine. A more miserable wretch than I was could now scarcely be found in the world; and, to complete my misfortunes, I felt the consciousness that they were all occasioned by my own folly.

I am now coming to the most extraordinary and the most interesting part of my history. A new and surprising accident happened.

* * * * * *

NOTE BY THE EDITOR.—What this accident was can never be known; for Basil put off finishing his history till TO-MORROW. This fragment was found in an old escrutoire, in an obscure lodging in Swallow Street.

COLUMN FOR THE YOUNG.

He serves the Muses erringly and ill,
Whose aim is pleasure light and fugitive.—WORDSWORTH.

A SMALL division of the SCHOOLMASTER is appropriated every week to verse, intended chiefly for the young. It is therefore desirable that this department be conducted on some understood principle and regular plan. One short piece, or extract, which shall merit to be preserved, and which, by very young readers, may occasionally be committed to memory, as a household lesson, will be given each week, reserving the remaining space allotted to verse, for poetry recommended by novelty, or any temporary interest. This, with occasional illustrative quotations and extracts from new works, is all the verse to which we can afford space.

MOTIVES TO FORBEARANCE AND CHARITY.
Inscription for a Column at Newbury.

Art thou a Patriot, Traveller? On this field
Did FALKLAND fall, the blameless and the brave,
Beneath a tyrant's banners. Dost thou boast
Of loyal ardour—HAMPDEN perished here—
The Rebel HAMPDEN, at whose glorious name
The heart of every honest Englishman
Beats high with conscious pride. Both uncorrupt,
Friends to their common country both, they fought,
They died in adverse armies. Traveller!
If with thy neighbour thou should'st not accord
In charity, remember these good men,
And quell all angry and injurious thoughts.

Southey.

The PATRIOT HAMPDEN died in July 1643, of wounds received in a skirmish with the royalist troops, in Chalgrave Field, near Oxford, while fighting nobly for the cause of freedom and his country, in the army of the Parliament. Until the country rose in arms to repel the tyranny of Charles I., Hampden either lived as a private gentleman on his estate, or discharged his duties as an independent and patriotic member of Parliament. Single-handed, he resisted the payment of an impost named *ship-money*, illegally levied by the king, without the sanction of the representatives of the people; and was from that time considered by them as their champion. His death struck his own party with momentary consternation, and delighted the royalists. Lord Falkland was rather entangled into the service of the King, than there of choice. He was a high and pure-minded man, a devoted lover of his country, and therefore, ever desirous of peace. He fell at the battle of Newbury, about two months after the death of Hampden. "From the commencement of the war," says Hume the historian, "his natural cheerfulness and vivacity became clouded." He became negligent of his dress, but on the morning of the battle in which he fell, he showed some care in equipping himself; and gave, for a reason, that the enemy should not find his body in any slovenly, indecent situation. "I am weary," he said, "of the times, and foresee much misery to my country; but I believe I shall be out of it ere night." His presentiment was verified. He died at the age of thirty-four. These are the "good men" for whom Mr. Southey wrote the above inscription. They fell, victims alike to the ambition of the King, and to his determination not only to resist the just demands of the people, but arbitrarily to encroach on their ancient liberties

COLUMN FOR THE LADIES.

THE PHILOSOPHY OF OLD MAIDISM.—If any share of independence be the lot of woman, it falls to the wealthy old maid. The policy of man has made old maidism the bugbear of the sex. They have judiciously levelled against it the whole artillery of ridicule, the squibs and crackers of which are vastly more fearful than the two-edged sword of satire; the first hurts a woman's fine vanities—it falls upon her flounces and furbelows; the latter only cuts her vices; and though the wound it makes be sore, it is probably unseen; and she heals it, and says nothing about it.

WOMAN, THE SOURCE OF EVIL!—It is an article of faith with the orthodox in the east, that no evil can take place of which a woman is not the first cause. "Who is she?" a rajah was always in the habit of asking, whenever a calamity was related to him, however severe, or however trivial. His attendants reported to him one morning, that a labourer had fallen from a scaffold when working at his palace and had broken his neck. "Who is she?" immediately demanded the rajah. "A man, no woman, great prince!" was the reply. "Who is she?" repeated with increased anger, was all the rajah deigned to utter. In vain did the servant assert the manhood of the labourer. "Bring me instant intelligence what woman caused this accident, or wo upon your heads!" exclaimed the prince! In an hour the active attendants returned, and prostrating themselves cried out, "O wise and powerful prince!" "Well, who is she?" interrupted he. "As the ill-fated labourer was working on the scaffold he was attracted by the beauty of your Highness's damsels, and, gazing upon them, lost balance, and fell to the ground."—"You hear, now," said the Prince, "no accident can happen without a woman in some way being an instrument."

MADAME AND HER "BUSK."—Poor dear Madame de Staël, I shall never forget seeing her one day, at table with a large party, when the busk (I believe you ladies call it) of her corset forced its way through the top of the corset, and would not descend though pushed by all the force of both hands of the wearer, who became crimson from the operation. After fruitless efforts, she turned in despair to the valet de chambre behind her chair, and requested him to draw it out, which could only be done by his passing his hand from behind over her shoulder, and across her chest, when with a desperate effort, he unsheathed the busk. Had you seen the faces of some of the English ladies of the party, you would have been, like me, almost convulsed; while Madame remained perfectly unconscious that she had committed any solecism on *la decence Anglaise*.—Lady Blessington gives this anecdote in the New Monthly, as related to her by Lord Byron.

WOMEN.—It is much the custom of writers who write about the talkers, to limit the programme of their dissertations, to "MEN AND THINGS." In these our times, this is manifestly an impertinence, for the WOMEN are just now unquestionably the busiest moiety of the creation; and as to the BOOKS, we would ask whether advertisements of new works abound not far more than paragraphs of new measures? It is a *woman* (Miss Boaden) who has translated the new piece so ably for the Haymarket; and a *woman* (Miss Taylor) who renders it so effective. It is a *woman* (Mrs. Waylett) who crams the Strand Theatre, night after night, as close as a pottle of strawberries; and a *woman* (Mrs. Fitzwilliam) who, cholera notwithstanding, draws mobs of spectators to Sadler's Wells—the well-spring of whose attractions had been so long dried up. It is a *woman* (Mrs. Jameson) who has rendered Kit North for once mild and mellifluous as the sweet south; it is a *woman* (Mrs. Trollope) who has invited the leathery Jonathan into a passion. It is a *woman* (Mrs. Norton) who, in her periodical, commands a majority of the Lords; it is a *woman* (Fanny Kemble) who, having ruled the waves of a stormy pit, for the sake of her family, is about to brave those of the Atlantic. It is a *woman* (Miss Sharpe) whose exquisite picture of Brunetta raises a rival flag, in Pall-mall, to Wilkie's in the Strand. It is a *woman* (Miss Bagster) who has defied a whole college of mad doctors to drive her out of her senses. The gossip of the young *ladies* in the gallery of St. Stephen's, overpowers the patter of the elderly gentlemen below; the fancy fairs of the charitable *ladies* have rendered their stalls more productive than those of Tattersall. Of all the constitutions of Europe, the one ruled at Almack's, by a female Cabinet, has alone withstood the shock of modern revolutions; and we are convinced, that had the Reform Bill been dedicated to *fairer* hands, bishops would not have been burnt in effigy, nor Bristol in reality. Women! WOMEN against the world.—*Court Journal.*

USEFUL ARTS.

ARITHMETICAL RODS.—This is a very useful invention, by which the teaching of arithmetic both to the tutor and pupil is much facilitated. Every one knows that much time is occupied by writing down the figures to be summed, multiplied, &c.; but Mr. P. B. Templeton of Preston has invented a set of rods, by which all the labour of setting or preparing the question is avoided. These rods are four-sided, on three of which figures are stamped, and when a question in addition, for instance, is to be solved, it is only necessary to place under each other any number of rods, which may be thought necessary, and then the figures are summed up by the pupil. Questions in subtraction, division, &c. are managed in a similar manner. There is a key to the rods which contains the answers, so that a person may examine fifty pupils at a time. The rods may also be used as an amusement for children, the key enabling the parent, nurse, or governess to prove the accuracy of the answers. The invention has been approved of by some of the first literary and scientific men in the kingdom, and by several of our professors and clergymen from whom Mr. Templeton has letters. It has also been examined, and much commended by most of the respectable teachers in this city, and has already been introduced into George Watson's Hospital, Heriot's Hospital, and some other schools. The invention has indeed only to be seen and understood to secure its universal adoption. The rods, which are in sets of different sizes, cost only a few shillings, and will last many years.

THE NEW FORM OF SUGAR.—Further trial has been made of the sugar, of which we gave an account in No. 3. It is in perfect, pure, transparent granular crystals, developing the true crystalline form of the sugar, and being entirely free from the least portion of uncrystallizable sugar, molasses, or colouring matter, consequently stands in no need of any subsequent process of decolourization or refining for all purposes of domestic economy and the table. In solution it is not apt to become acescent, and it is a purer sweet, and of a more mellifluous taste, than even the best refined sugar. In the manufacture of rum from the molasses, which are separated during the process of the operation, there is no danger of deterioration in the production of empyreuma, an almost unavoidable attendant when ordinary molasses are employed. The improved process is now in successful operation on eight estates in Demerara. This sugar, which is on our table every morning, will soon be on every breakfast table in the country where sugar is used.

ORNAMENTAL YARNS, COTTONS, &c.—The "Repertory of Arts" details the nature of a patent granted to Mr. Pierrepont Greaves of Lancaster, for making ornamental or fancy cotton yarns and threads, applicable to the making, sewing, or embroidering of cotton and other fabrics. The skilful combination of the primary colours, so as to produce new shades or self-colours, has proved a puzzling point for the dyer; nay, it is held impossible by a mixture of dyes to produce certain tints on cotton. It is of some importance that this difficulty should be got over; silk embroidery and worsted tapestry have long been foster-sisters to painting. This discovery is therefore not only ingenious and useful, but it is capable of an easy explanation, and may be made clear in a few words, with little trouble to the understanding. Mr Greaves procures a quantity of cotton-wool, dyed as usual, in each of the primary colours; and without the aid of any machinery, without the slightest additional expense, with no more than the common quantity of labour, he produces his novel and variegated store. He uses the wool as a painter would do the earths, which are called colours, from the colours they bear. He takes, for instance, a portion of blue wool of a deeper or a lighter shade, and a portion of pink wool, and mingles these together until the mass becomes purple, adding red or blue according to the tone he seeks. If he wish to produce a delicate green, he uses a proportionate quantity of blue and yellow.

ADVANTAGES OF RAILWAYS.—A railroad is the river of art; it is the nearest approach to creation that man has yet arrived at. We have made loans to carry on war; we have turned our gold into iron often enough in the shape of muskets—why not of trams? we have winged the bullet, messenger of death, on credit—why not borrow a little for the speedy promulgation and the wide dispersion of the means of life? The debt, unlike most debts, would prove a source of wealth.

It is estimated with tolerable correctness that the annual consumption of fat bullocks in the metropolis amounts to 150,000, and that the average distance each beast is brought to Smithfield market is 100 miles, and the loss of value from the fatigue of the journey is at least 40s. per head, that is, 300,000*l*. per annum.

The number of sheep brought is 1,500,000, the average loss on each from the same cause is 5s. per head, which amounts to 375,000*l*.: thus here is entirely lost of animal food 675,000*l*. per annum by an imperfect mode of conveyance; and injured as much in quality as it is reduced in quantity.

London, which is now the dearest, would become the cheapest market in England; provisions would not cost more than one farthing per pound carriage to the markets. The greatest part of the cattle and sheep would be killed in the country, and sent in dead meat to the metropolis, superior in quality, and undiminished in quantity; and that which would remain from the offal, as good manure in the country, would no longer be brought to the great slaughter houses in London, spreading pestilence around so far as its noxious influence extended.

These are important considerations; but it is not a mere affair of butcher's meat. It is whether the whole country shall beat with one uniform pulse, feel its whole strength, and rise to a state of equal and universally diffused prosperity. It is now hamstrung: its ligaments are loose and broken: it is out of joint:—one part is labouring under repletion—another of starvation: the fluids in one part are stagnant—at another raging and racing at the heat of fever.—*New Monthly Magazine for September.*

THE EXHUMATION OF BURNS.

THE original resting-place of the poet was an humble spot in the northern corner of St. Michael's Church-yard, Dumfries, in no way distinguished from the tombs which contained the "nameless ashes" of hundreds around him; and it was not till about 1814, eighteen years after his decease, that public attention became generally directed to the erection of a suitable monument to " Coila's Bard." An humble " head-stone," placed there by the poet's widow out of her own limited resources, had hitherto been the sole land-mark to point out the spot to the inquiring pilgrim. At the above-mentioned period, subscriptions were entered into, and a sum raised sufficient for the purpose of erecting a monument suited to his fame. An elegant design by Mr. Hunt of London was at last fixed upon, and in September 1815, the erection was so far advanced as to be ready for the reception of the remains of the Poet. The spot where he was originally interred being too confined for the erection of the monument, it had been found necessary to choose out a more advantageous site, to which the remains were of course removed. The following account of the exhumation is by Mr. Grierson, under whose superintendence it was performed:—

" Mrs. Burns, on being informed that the situation where the body was interred was not convenient, and did not contain sufficient space for the mausoleum, very kindly agreed that the committee might remove the remains, but expressed a wish that it should be done in as private a manner as possible. I therefore undertook the management, and, at an early hour in the morning, having procured the necessary workmen, the grave was opened, and the coffin was found entire,—a shell had been provided to receive the remains,—the coffin was removed into it with all possible care, but on being moved, and coming to the air, it fell in pieces, and exposed the remains; the skull in particular was in good preservation."

It may be added, that though the time chosen for the removal was before sunrise, and though the proceeding was kept a secret, yet ere it could be completed, a considerable number of spectators had gathered round the church-yard gate, all eager to snatch a glance even of the illustrious dead.

What an impression does it convey of the hold which the genius of Burns has taken of the minds of his countrymen. I use this word in its most extended sense—that while the rank grass and the " charnel weed" luxuriate round the " narrow homes" of his fellow slumberers, the track which leads to his monument exhibits a beaten pathway, worn bare by the " frequent feet" of those who crowd around to gaze on the spot which contains the mortal remains of the Peasant Bard!

SCRAPS.
Original and Selected.

POACHING.—It is known that the effectual way to cure the sweet tooth of a grocer's young apprentice, is to allow him a surfeit of sugar bowls, candy, and currants; and we are told by Macgregor, that those who have at home been noted poachers, if left with the free range of the Canadian forests, seldom think of handling a gun,—a fact full of instruction to our legislators, could they profit by it. Some one has observed, how much natives of America must be puzzled when reading the proceedings of our parliament. In America, where light, air, and water are free to all, a native could as well believe that the moon was a Queen Ann's farthing, and a grant of the Crown to a lady of the bed-chamber, as understand that a man living by the side of a river could be prevented catching the fish, because some feudal king or lord had granted the river to somebody else for ever. Fortunately, Jonathan is not an heir to any such wisdom of ancestry, or he might have found the Mississippi, or the Chesapeake, and the St. Lawrence, granted in fee-simple, or in perpetuity, to some Jeremiah or Timothy of old, by virtue of constitutional charters. The bequests of the wisdom of our ancestors are very numerous.

CHARACTER OF MEN OF SPIRIT.

I am reputed by some of my acquaintence to want *spirit*, and it is for no other reason but that I do not live above my income. I have *spirit* enough to keep out of debt, and endeavour to make all my friends welcome when they visit me; but, when I make any entertainment, they exclaim, it is not done with *spirit*, though it is always as elegant as my circumstances will allow. I know several of these men of *spirit*, who are *mean-spirited* enough to borrow money of me. Our jails swarm with men of *spirit*, and our streets are crowded by children whose parents were persons of *spirit*. There are men of *spirit*, of all degrees, from the peer in his chariot to the porter with his ropes, who ridicule frugality and all economy which prevents superfluous expense. By these persons a man that is frugal is said to be miserable; and economy is despised as the want of *spirit*. I am convinced that, if men of *spirit* were to become a litttle less vain and ostentatious, it would be of great advantage, not only to themselves, but to the community; for it is notorious that they too often keep up their *spirit* at the expense of the public; and it does not appear to me that they are influenced by a good *spirit*, when they ruin a tradesmen by getting into his debt for superfluities, or when they take in a friend for their surety to keep up their credit. I know men of *spirit* who wear the *tailors'* clothes. I am often blamed by these people for not appearing oftener at public diversions; but I can divert myself and family without going to the Theatre every other evening in winter, and to the gardens in summer four or five times a-week. Though I am condemned by these *gentlemen* as a *mean-spirited* and *unpolished* niggard, yet my conduct enables me to provide for my family all the necessaries of life, and for myself a perpetual succession of peaceful pleasures, without the risk of my independence, my virtue, my health, or my fortune, all of which are continually attacked by the man of *spirit*.

THE SCOTCH CHURCH, LONDON.—It is supposed that there are about 100,000 Scotchmen in the metropolis, yet there are in communion with the Church of Scotland, only six congregations viz. :—The Scotch Church, London-wall; the Scotch Church, Swallow Street; St. Andrew's Scotch Church; Scotch Church, Chadwell Street; Verulam Scotch Church, Lambeth; and the National Scotch Church, Regent Square.

EPIGRAM ON AN EDITOR.
To dot an I, to cross a T,
Scratch out a comma, add a colon,
All day would fussy Cr—k—r be,
And wiser think himself than Solon.

FIGHTING FAMILIES.—There yet survives the Battle of Waterloo, three families, with three brothers in each, who greatly distinguished themselves on that memorable day—three Somersets, three Hills, and three Wildmans.

HOW NAMES DIE OUT.—In the times of James the Second, there were no fewer than twelve Knights, of the name of Macklellan,—the head of which was William Earl Kircndbright. There are more Baronets of the name of Gordon (Elevin,) than any other.

The County of Ayr is more prolific of Baronets of one name, than any other in England, or Scotland, namely Sir William Cunningham of Robertland, Sir William of Caprington, Sir Richard of Auchinharves, Sir William of Milncraig, and Sir James Cunningham of Corsehill, Bart.

HONOURABLE CONDUCT.—Lord Mornington's father dying L.5,000 more in debt than his effects would pay, the present Lord Mornington, father of the Marquis Wellesley, Lord Maryborough, the Duke of Wellington, and Lord Cowley, summoned the creditors together, and promised them payment in three years, which, much to his honour, his Lordship has fulfilled to the last shilling.—*Morning Chronicle*, Sept. 10, 1787.

A LONG BREAKFAST.—A farmer observing his servant a long time at breakfast, said, "John, you make a long breakfast!" "Master!" answered John, "a cheese of this size is not so soon eaten as you would think."

GREATEST GOOD.—In a company of young men, of whom Paley was one, arose a discussion concerning the *summum bonum*: the argument was carried on by the different speakers with due seriousness and gravity; and several opinions, both ancient and modern, were sifted and examined in relation to this most important topic; at length Paley cried out, "You are mistaken: I will tell you in what consists the *summum bonum* of human life—it consists in reading Tristram Shandy, in blowing with a pair of bellows into your shoes in hot weather, and roasting potatoes under the grate in cold."

IRISH CON BY CROKER.—Why are the Tories like certain small fish out of the water?—Because they are *dead bait* (beat).

A CUT BETWEEN FRIENDS.—Sir Robert Peel is reported to have said on the case of Somerville, that "soldiers ought not to be allowed to become politicians." This is another sly cut for his *quondam* colleague Wellington.

FIRES IN LONDON.—From a register of fires kept for one year in London, it appears that there were 360 alarms of fire, attended with very little damage, 31 serious fires, and 151 fires, occasioned by chimneys being on fire, amounting in all to 542 accidents.

A WHISTLE-BINKIE.—A French musical amateur has challenged all the whistlers in Europe to make as much noise with one instrument as he can make with his mouth. He has been engaged by the Director of the French Theatre in London.

COTTON.—The first cost of a year's cotton manufactured in England, is estimated at L.6,000,000, sterling, the wages paid to 833,000 persons employed in its manufacture, in various ways, is L.20,000,000, sterling; the profit of the manufacturers may be estimated at L.6,000,000, at least.

BESIDES appearing in WEEKLY NUMBERS, the SCHOOLMASTER will be published in MONTHLY PARTS, which, stitched in a neat cover, will contain as much letter-press, of good execution, as any of the large Monthly Periodicals: A Table of Contents will be given at the end of the year; when, *at the weekly cost of three-halfpence*, a handsome volume of 832 pages, super-royal size, may be bound up, containing much matter worthy of preservation.

PART I. for August, containing the first four Numbers, with JOHNSTONE'S MONTHLY REGISTER, may now be had of the Booksellers, and dealers in cheap Periodicals.

CONTENTS OF NO. VII.
MEMOIR OF WILLIAM COBBETT	97
LORD BROUGHAM AND VAUX	103
THE STORY-TELLER—TO-MORROW	105
COLUMN FOR THE YOUNG	110
COLUMN FOR THE LADIES	110
USEFUL ARTS	111
THE EXHUMATION OF BURNS	111
SCRAPS—Poaching—Character of Men of Spirit, &c	112

EDINBURGH: Printed by and for JOHN JOHNSTONE, 19, St. James's Square.—Published by JOHN ANDERSON, Jun., Bookseller, 55, North Bridge Street, Edinburgh; by JOHN MACLEOD, and ATKINSON & Co., Booksellers, Glasgow; and sold by all Booksellers and Venders of Cheap Periodicals.

THE Schoolmaster,
AND
EDINBURGH WEEKLY MAGAZINE.

CONDUCTED BY JOHN JOHNSTONE.

THE SCHOOLMASTER IS ABROAD.—LORD BROUGHAM.

No. 8.—Vol. I. SATURDAY, SEPTEMBER 22, 1832. PRICE THREE-HALFPENCE.

HOLYDAY RAMBLES ROUND EDINBURGH.
No. III.
CRICHTON CASTLE—THE VALE OF BORTHWICK.—
BY THE RAILWAY.

WE have shewn too much *adhesiveness* to the ROMAN CAMP, and, bound on further quests, must make short work of our promised third and romantic route homeward to Edinburgh.

Suppose the Rambler, blessed with healthful limbs and good spirits, to have reached our central station by half-past ten, there is still a long day before him, and work for it. Let him descend towards the new bridge, where it will not be amiss to take a second breakfast, and cutting across the valley, wheel to the west, properly south-west, and coursing against the Tyne, though far above its bed, held on by Crichton Church and Crichton Castle, to the valley of Borthwick, till he join the post-road at Fushie-Bridge. A pedestrian only can make out this route, for in the finest part of it, there is not even a bridle track.

In the early part of the ramble, some of the objects formerly indicated, will be more immediately under inspection. Others of humbler pretension, though of infinitely greater utility, should not be forgotten. Let the young traveller remember that, in the village of Ford, lived

JAMES SMALL,

a country cart-wright, whose improvements on the plough have been of far more benefit to mankind than all the warlike deeds of all the Hepburns, and Crichtons, and Borthwicks, and other feudal barons, who, for five hundred years, lorded it over this valley. This ingenious man was indefatigable in improving the most important of agricultural implements; and from his humble village workshop, he at last sent forth five hundred ploughs a-year, to all parts of the three kingdoms.

Though this part of the parish of Crichton does not boast the rich, exuberant fertility of the vicinity, through which the *waggoneer* and pedestrian has already passed, once arrived among the clumps, holts, and stripes of plantation, in the neighbourhood of the Church, the Manse, and the Castle, the scenery is of a highly pleasing character; the opposite banks are fine and picturesque; the Church itself is a venerable and enduring structure—old, but staunch. The Castle is, however, the most attractive feature of the landscape. It stands on a pre-eminent, but not immediately steep bank, among open natural pastures, the ground breaking on every side into slopes and *baulks;* and swelling into knolls and small heights, sprinkled with underwood, gorse, and fern. The Notes to Marmion afford the best description we know of Crichton Castle: they are Pennant extended by Scott, and we copy them almost implicitly, remarking, by the way, that Sir Walter surely means Scots measure when he calls Crichton only seven miles from Edinburgh. It is full twelve.

CRICHTON CASTLE.

CRICHTON! though now thy miry court
But pens the lazy steer and sheep,
Thy turrets rude, and tottered Keep,
Have been the minstrels' lov'd resort :
Oft have I traced within thy fort
  Of mouldering shields, the mystic sense,
  'Scutcheons of honour or pretence,
Quartered in old armorial sort,
  Remains of rude magnificence.

But a prose guide is safer than a poetical one for the young student in architectural and Heraldic antiquities. Crichton Castle was built at different times, "and," says Sir Walter, "with a very different regard to splendour and accommodation. The oldest part of the building is a narrow keep or tower, such as formed the mansion of the lesser Scottish baron; but so many additions have been made to it, that there is now a large court yard, surrounded by buildings of different ages. The eastern front is raised above the portico, and decorated with entablatures bearing anchors. All the stones of this front are cut into diamond facets, the angular protections of which have an uncommonly rich appearance. The inside of this part of the building appears to have contained a gallery of great length and uncommon elegance. Access was given to it by a magnificent staircase, now quite destroyed. The soffits are ornamented with twining cordage and rosettes; and the whole seems to have been far more splendid than was usual in Scottish castles."

Crichton was the habitation of the Chancellor Crichton, the joint guardian with the Earl of Callander, of James II., and the determined and politic enemy of the turbulent and ambitious house of Douglas. During the life of the Chancellor, it was besieged, taken, and levelled by the Earl of Douglas, who imputed to Crichton the betrayal and beheading, in Edinburgh Castle, of Earl William, his predecessor. "It was garrisoned, (we again quote Sir Walter) by Lord Crichton in 1483 against James III. whose displeasure he had incurred by seducing his sister Margaret, in revenge, it is said, for the Monarch having dishonoured his bed." It would have been worth a day's travel to have seen Crichton on the days of siege. From the Crichton family this Castle passed to the Hepburns, Earls of Bothwell; and when the forfeitures of the last Earl of Bothwell, or Stewart, were divided, this share fell to the Earl of Buccleuch. It latterly passed to other families. *Pennant* describes the architecture of Crichton as of uncommon elegance. The Castle had that indispensable requisite to the feudal lord, a dungeon, or *Massy More*.

There is no road, we said, between Crichton and Borthwick, though the distance from church to church cannot be above two miles. The foot or sheep-track meanders delightfully through natural pastures and rushy meadows, among dwarf hazel and alder and black-thorn bushes, broom, and brackens, till walled in by a nearly impenetrable wilderness of furze, roughly clothing the bank. The waters divide hereabouts—the infant Tyne running eastward, while the Borthwick burn, here a considerable stream, descending from the southward heights, flows west, till it falls into the Esk. To townsfolk, or such as have only looked on the rich and cultivated landscapes around Edinburgh, the country here will be of quite a new character; far more wild and rustic; a charming mixture of sylvan and pastoral scenery. Leaving Crichton Castle behind, which is soon hidden by the juttings and bulgings of the steep banks, the valley of Borthwick opens on us, and its lordly tower rises abruptly, and with a far bolder effect than the larger and more ornate feudal hold we have left. With a tolerably extensive personal acquaintance among the glens, valleys, and broad straths of Highland and Lowland Scotland, we cannot, at this moment, recall a more pleasant valley of its peculiar kind, than this of Borthwick, clipt closely in by its own green heights, kept in perennial freshness by its own clear stream,—sober, peaceful, sequestered, and exquisitely rural—a spot where, to the chafed spirit, repose might come without the pains of wooing it, where the heart is invited to commune with itself and be still, and where the disease of the city,—the perpetual wearing mind-fever of busy life, might intermit, and gradually subside into tranquillity and healthfulness. The feudal lords, who like the eagles lived apart, rarely built their nests so near each other, as they have done here. But the eyries of Borthwick and Crichton, though close together, were not in sight, and the one opened into the east, the other into the west, with considerable natural bulwarks and obstacles between them.

BORTHWICK TOWER

Shews nothing of the rich architecture and elaborate elegance of its neighbour, Crichton Castle, but is on the whole more in harmony with the country and age to which it properly belonged. Stately in height, rising from the bank to about 100 feet, and massive in structure, this ancient edifice is still so entire, as to give a perfect idea of a baronial residence exposed to frequent attacks. The walls formed of the most substantial and complete masonry, from 13 feet of thickness, which they are in the lower storeys, taper into 6 feet. Borthwick keep had the usual defences of flanking towers, and where the ground is not itself a defence, a moat. In the place on which you are looking Queen Mary and Bothwell found refuge before the battle of Carberry-hill. Borthwick Castle submitted to the summons of Cromwell, without a single soldier showing himself for King Charles.—It is well worth a half hour's inspection, were it only from the highest point to which one can scramble to enjoy the view "over dale and down." The farm-houses, cottages, and better sort of small homesteads in this quiet valley, and in sight of the old castle and the church, are in complete harmony with its prevailing character. None are fine, or modern, or even show too obtrusive a glare of freshness. The site of the church, placed high on a green bank, and upward and downward overlooking the vale, is well chosen; and the edifice itself is built in much better taste than the common run of presbyterian country churches. It is with this, of full age to harmonize in colouring with the wonted church accessories of stiles, foot-paths, ancient trees, and mouldering and mossy gravestones. The village is tolerably well screened off by hedgerows and trees; and the old long manse, beyond the church and the village—originally pitched on one of the green billows of the valley, and commanding the openings of some of the small dells and the depths of others—is to the passing rambler a much finer object than the more ambitious ecclesiastical edifices of later years, built since "handsome augmentations" have made extended household accommodation and appliances desirable. It is one of those modest dwellings which bespeak little or no first cost, over which the hand of Time has passed lightly and caressingly, and which seems to have unfolded into grace and beauty under the same happy influences which have formed the characters of the inmates of so peaceful and sweet an abiding place. To the Manse of Borthwick belongs a more profound interest. Under this roof Robertson the historian was born. The scene of the first wanderings of him who traced the discoveries of Columbus and the conquests of Pizarro, were the braes and burns of Borthwick valley. It was on brooding in a still summer's eve, on this quiet heart of a truly Scottish rural parish, that the author of the SABBATH breathed his most ambitious aspiration.*

* It is related by one of Grahame's friends, in an interesting little notice of his life, that some time before he left the bar, looking, in a fine summer evening, with delighted complacency, on the little kirk of Borthwick, not far from his retirement on the Esk, he said, "I wish such a place had fallen to my lot;" and when it was remarked, that retirement might become wearisome, "O, no," he replied, "it would be delightful to live a life of usefulness among a simple people, unmolested with cares and ceremonies!" The reader of THE SABBATH and the BIRDS OF SCOTLAND must be convinced that these were his genuine sentiments; nor is it easy to imagine a picture of human beatitude more touching and complete than the author of THE SABBATH, "the Poor Man's Bard," living surrounded by his family, the pastor of "a simple people," in one of the glens of his own romantic land.—*Johnstone's Specimens of the Poets*.

More recently, within this same sanctuary of piety and peace, was filled up and finished the design of a dedicated mental labour ;* bread cast upon the waters to nourish man's inner life, and to be found after many days. Many will place these among the feelings and remembrances which give a holiday ramble vitality and abiding interest. They enable one, looking back through long, dim, and it may be, troubled years, upon the Borthwick water, or the Esk water, or any of the thousand lovely streams of Scotland, ever to say with swelling consciousness—

<blockquote>The eternal spirit of one happy day,
Lingers upon its marge, in vision pure!</blockquote>

Descending the bank from the church and tower, and crossing the streamlet, the traveller merrily holds on his way by its side along the church path-way, (the carriage road, with which we have nothing to do, is on the opposite side,) to Fushie-Bridge. This point may still be distant three miles from the rail-way Waggon, to which one has the option of returning either by the post-road, passing Arniston and Kirkhill gates; or through the village of Gore Bridge: the distance is much the same either way, and we rather advise the latter route. It lies higher; and Arniston gate, and grounds may be apt, like those of the " purple Mackenzie," the adjoining Shank, to beget jarring remembrances of a time worse than even the age of the lords of Crichton and Borthwick, that which has just received its death-blow, though it is still writhing—*the age of corrupt influence.*

To give the devil his due, there was in the personal character of the GREAT MAN of the House of Arniston, Henry Dundas, to wit, the first Lord Melville, something so bold-faced, hearty, and genial, that one half-pardons his fawning or grateful eulogists, and only wishes them better informed in what love of country really consists. The most corrupt and unprincipled of modern Scottish statesmen, the deadly enemy, and remorseless destroyer of all public spirit, the hardened disbeliever in all political virtue, whose conscience never once rebuked him in his *bad* career, is pictured and monumented as the truest and most patriotic of *Countrymen*; because—and for this alone—that in the general plunder he always struggled manfully for a full share of the spoil to his own immediate tools, of both sexes, and their dependents; and never scrupled gracefully and frankly to confer a personal kindness, if it were only at the expense of justice and the nation. The unblushing political profligacy of the Scottish leader, and his open contempt of public morality, were revolting even to the better order of Tories in England; and would have disgusted and alienated them from the bosom friend of Pitt, save that they generally forgot there existed a country called Scotland, forming an integral part of the kingdom of Great Britain, and represented in Parliament by the delegates of Mr. Dundas. But we have passed the gates of Arniston,—We are in a new world—step into the Waggon.—CA IRA!

PRESBYTERIAN NOTION OF A BISHOP.

A Bishop among us, is generally supposed to be a stately and pompous person, clothed in purple and fine linen, and faring sumptuously every day—somewhat obsequious to persons in power, and somewhat haughty and imperative to those who are beneath him—with more authority in his tone and manner, than solidity in his learning; and yet, with much more learning, than humility and charity—very fond of being called my Lord, and driving about in a chariot, with mitres on the panels; but little addicted to visiting the sick and fatherless, or earning for himself the blessing of those who are ready to perish—

<blockquote>Familiar with a round
Of ladyships—a stranger to the poor;</blockquote>

decorous in his manners, but no foe to luxurious indulgences,—rigid in maintaining discipline among his immediate dependents, and in exacting the homage due to his dignity, from the undignified mob of his brethren; but perfectly willing to leave to them the undivided privileges of comforting, and of teaching their people, and of soothing the sins and sorrows of their erring flocks,—scornful, if not openly hostile, upon all occasions, to the claims of the people from whom he is generally sprung,—and presuming every thing in favour of the royal will and prerogative by which he has been exalted; setting, indeed, in all cases, a much higher value on the privileges of the few, than the rights that are common to all, and exerting himself strenuously, that the former may ever prevail; caring more accordingly for the interests of his order, than the general good of the church and far more for the church, than the religion it was established to teach; hating dissenters still more bitterly than infidels, but combating both, rather with obloquy and invocation of civil penalties, than with the artillery of a powerful reason, or the reconciling influences of a humble and holy life; uttering, now and then, haughty professions of humility, and regularly bewailing, at fit seasons, the severity of those episcopal labours which sadden, and even threaten to abridge a life, which, to all other eyes, appears to flow on in an almost unbroken leisure, and continued indulgence. —*Edinburgh Review.*

---

* PLAN OF A LIVING TEMPLE, of which the reverend author thus speaks impersonally :—" No length of days can ever efface from his mind the remembrance of that bright summer noon, made more bright, and infinitely more affecting by the thought that such brightness might be seen but for a little, when, being incapable of more active exertion, he sketched with his pencil in the open air, and amidst the blossoms and overshadowing foliage of that "cottage garden," which had been dear to him from infancy, the whole series of views and principles which, in a more finished form, but with no alteration whatever of their original design, he now submits to the public, with the solemn belief that they are in accordance with the purest truth, and that their adoption, as rules of conduct, would indeed make man " a Living Temple;" or, to use the words of the divine teacher, would bring the " Kingdom of Heaven upon Earth."

ON THE MORAL TRAINING OF CHILDREN.

To the Editor of the Schoolmaster.

SIR,—The object of these observations is chiefly to convey (through the medium of your instructive miscellany) some salutary hints to parents; particularly such as are desirous to discharge their duty as they ought, but who are at a loss to know how, so as to train up their offspring in the way they should go. My object also is, to arouse still more, if possible, the attention of people in general to the vast importance of the subject.

Great, indeed, is the responsibility of parents, and not less the vigilance necessary in the management of their children. But the lively sensibility of fond parents, whilst it awakens many fears of failure on their part, operates also as a powerful stimulus, not only to the faithful and diligent discharge of their duty to their children, but to be strictly watchful over themselves, that their own conduct and example should not be at variance with their precepts. Thus they will endeavour, for their children's sake, to keep themselves as much as possible under self-government, from a conviction that every dereliction of duty in that respect, has the tendency not only to injure the temper, but also to weaken that influence which they ever ought to be careful of maintaining over the minds of their children.

The necessity of early restraint, as well as culture, must be evident to every judicious and enlightened parent; but to obtain that ascendancy over the minds of their children, which is so necessary to keep them under proper restraint, care must be taken to avoid all fond indulgence on the one hand, and all harsh severity on the other; both being alike calculated to frustrate their endeavours.

When a child is capable of being reasoned with, it ought certainly to be treated as a rational being; though it is well known that long before a child can be reasoned with, habits of obedience and submission may be formed. The first endeavour which it makes is to gratify the impulse of its will, and therefore the first step in the process of education ought to be, to bring the will under subjection, at least to a certain extent, which is perfectly practicable, even with the infant at the breast, if it is gone about in a proper manner. For instance, an infant will stretch out its hand to take something improper for it to have; but if its hand is withheld, and the parent, unmoved by its cries or struggles, shows by his countenance and manner that he refuses the indulgence, the child will soon learn to yield; and by uniformly experiencing similar treatment whenever its wishes ought not to be gratified, submission will soon become familiar and easy.

As children advance in age, parents, by a simple and affectionate manner of conversing with them, acquire almost unbounded influence over their young minds, which being quite in a ductile or pliable state, may be made to receive almost whatever impressions the parent pleases; and indeed such as will never afterwards be effaced. If, therefore, parents were only sufficiently careful during this interesting period, to impress the minds of their children with correct ideas of right and wrong, to check their unruly passions, to keep their wills under proper subjection, but above all, to set before them a proper example, seeking at the same time a divine blessing on their humble endeavours, they would seldom or ever be disappointed in seeing them grow up all that their hearts could desire.

But the great object in the first instance undoubtedly is, to secure their implicit obedience and respect, without which nothing can be done in the way of improvement. As soon, therefore, as a child is capable of comprehending what is said to him, he should in a mild, gentle, but firm manner, be informed of his duty, and what his parents shall expect of him; and among other things, that he will never obtain what he wants by ill-humour or crying; but that if he asks pleasantly for what is suitable it will be granted. This method, if steadily pursued, will tend greatly to prevent that fretting, crying, importuning disposition, which we often see in children, who have been accustomed in this manner to obtain what they want. But when they find that tears and murmurs have no effect, they soon become manageable, and acquire a habitual command over themselves. On the contrary, a child accustomed to have what he cries for, will sometimes cry for things a parent may not choose to give, and persevere in crying till he exhausts the patience of the parent, and then he is whipped. Thus people first indulge children, and then chastise them for the natural consequence of that indulgence; and it is perhaps difficult to say which injures the temper most. Don't touch this! don't do that! are frequent injunctions of a parent, who, nevertheless, permits both to be done with impunity, till at length some petty mischief is done, though the child was not able to make the distinction; and then he is again whipped; and to this whipping do parents sometimes appeal as a testimony that they do not spoil their children. By an early habit of implicit obedience, and a fixed determination not to grant a child what he cries for to prevent his crying—the occasion of all this whipping—would not both the parent and child be much happier! Persevering yet gentle firmness begun in infancy establishes proper discipline, procures respect and obedience, and prevents the necessity of almost all punishment; while, on the contrary, by improper indulgence, the will becomes incorrigible, and then the rod is resorted to as the only means of bringing it into subjection, though the effect in general is only to make it still more obdurate.

By diminishing temptations to do wrong, we act more humanely than by multiplying restraints and punishments; hence the propriety of but few prohibitions, and these judicious and decisive, such as we can steadily persevere to enforce. If we are not exact in requiring obedience, we shall never obtain it, either by persuasion or authority. The parent's word should be considered a law; and when made so from early infancy, it will not often be controverted. The will of the child will be habitually subordinate to the will of the parent, and obedience rendered natural and easy. But this requires steadiness and self-command, without which there is very little hope that the education of a child will ever be conducted upon consistent principles.

The following anecdote, as related by a female writer on education, well exemplifies the happy effects of early obedience:—" One morning," she states, " as I entered the drawing-room of my friend, I found the little group of cherubs at high play around their fond mother, who was encouraging their sportive vivacity, which was at that time noisy enough; but which, on my entrance, she hushed into silence by a single word. No bad humour followed; but as the spirits which had been elevated by the preceding amusement could not at once sink into a state of acquiescence, the judicious mother did not require what she knew could not without difficulty be complied with; but calmly addressing them, gave the choice of remaining in the room without making any noise, or going to their own apartment. The eldest and youngest of the four preferred the former, while the two others went to the nursery. Those who staid with us, amused themselves by cutting paper in a corner, without giving any interruption to our conversation. I begged to know by what art she attained such a perfect government of her childrens' wills and actions? " By no art, returned this excellent parent, but that of teaching from the cradle an implicit obedience. Having never once been permitted to disobey me, they have no idea of attempting it. But you see, I always give them a choice, when it can be done with propriety; if it cannot, whatever I say, they know to be a law, like that of the Medes and Persians, which altereth not."

How widely different, and how much more advantageous to children, as well as comfortable to parents, is this mode of treatment from that of rigid strictness, which only produces slavish fear; or that unwarrantable indulging the humours of children, which deprives parents of all control over them. Pure and genuine affection is so directed to the real happiness of the child, as to guard against both of these extremes. For while it endeavours by kindness to prevent any thing like forced obedience, it also guards against that kind of liberty by which it loses its authority.

By the wise provision of Providence, the fond endearment of parental love produces a reciprocal attachment in the breast of the child. A judicious parent will take advantage of this circumstance, to lay a foundation for that entire freedom which ought to exist between parents and their children. If confidence has been early invited by endearing affability, and prudently managed, reserve in children will seldom have to be complained of in maturer age. And when they are thus accustomed to unbosom themselves to their parental friend, who is most interested in their welfare, what advantages must result to them, and what pleasure to the parent! Nor is there any fear of losing respect by such familiarity; on the contrary, as it more firmly establishes the affection of children, it at the same time, and in the same degree, secures their respect, the one being a necessary consequence of the other.

Young people who have been thus treated by judicious and communicative parents, are seldom addicted to degrading practices. They will even forego many indulgences to avoid displeasing them, or giving them pain. And as they can freely open their minds and tell their schemes to their liberal-minded parents, how often must these have it in their power to caution them against indiscretions, and thus be the means of saving them from much harm! And there are few young people so void of gratitude or sense, as not to avail themselves of parental advice and experience when thus proffered them. But let it be remembered, that if we would have our children make us their confidants, and freely unbosom their thoughts to us, they must not be discouraged by the coldness or distance of our deportment towards them, but rather be studiously invited by kindness and condescension.

The subject, Mr. Editor, on which this letter treats, I doubt not, you will agree with me, is one of the very highest importance, as it respects the future welfare not only of the rising generation, but of society at large, and is one on which volumes may be written without exhausting the subject; wherefore you will not be surprised when I inform you that I have still something farther to say.——Meanwhile, I am, &c.

A FRIEND TO EARLY EDUCATION.
Edinburgh, Sept. 1, 1832.

EMIGRATION,
THE UNITED STATES——CANADA.

The following extracts from letters written by a gentleman, who in September last emigrated from Bristol to America with his family, will doubtless prove interesting to many of our readers. The letters are addressed to his sister.

"NEWARK, STATE OF OHIO, *Nov. 30th,* 1831.—The English appearance of every thing at New York exceedingly delighted us, and, though we have journeyed many hundred miles since, we can even now scarcely believe we are in America; all we want to make this England to us, is the presence of our English friends, and some trifling alteration in the Americans. In New York, and through all the country we have passed, we have had a settled conviction that the standard of *morals* in America is *much above* that of England. This opinion is formed from a thousand little incidents which must strike an Englishman. In walking the streets of New York, we see goods are left about the shop doors to a late hour, and such goods as may be easily removed, and would be removed very quickly in Bristol, by some of the hundreds of thieves who are always on the look out. I was full a week, or nearly so, in getting clear of the Custom House, which was a very toilsome business indeed, chiefly from my having so *many packages,* and arranged with too much *order,* so as to give them the appearance of merchandise. But the toil was rendered not merely *bearable* but even *agreeable,* by the *kind* and *gentlemanly* conduct of *all the Officers,* whether at the ship, the public store, or the Custom House; nothing like rapacity on the one hand, or obsequiousness or insolence on the other. The churches in New York, and throughout all that state, are very numerous and handsome; which proves there is no need of supporting religion by acts of parliament, but that it prospers most when left to its own resources. The steam packets are splendid indeed. The people evince a power and ingenuity of mind which every Englishman must admire. * * * * All persons who come here with high notions of teaching the Americans, will find their mistake by merely making use of their eyes on their ships, buildings, or manufactories. For example, in the town of Lowell, Massachusets, there have been built in the last eight years, 31 woollen and cotton manufactories, 155 feet long, 60 feet wide, and 5 stories high, where from 3000 to 4000 respectable females are employed. We have had most ample opportunities of noticing the disposition of the people, which is uniformly *easy, kind,* and *affable;* they evidently respect the English, but are not disposed to think too highly of any, nor the rich more than others. In New York men and women dress well, generally genteelly; but in the country (as well in the State of New York as this) the men of all classes dress slovenly. They have nurseries in the neighbourhood of New York, but certainly with that exception nothing that deserves the name of garden, though it must be noticed this is not the time of year to look out for them. It is not possible to conceive the existence of a more easy, contented, and happy people than the Americans. *They all* speak well of their Government; any thing like grumbling about hard times, or the difficulty of getting a living, we have not heard of; on the contrary, every one says, any man may support himself a week by two days' labour—genteelly by three days. The land yields its increase, and farmers rarely work more than two or three days in a week. Those who are industrious always get wealthy; any industrious man who rents a farm could buy that farm in *three years.* This State (Ohio) is no doubt, the best for farmers; the canals being now open they have a better price for their produce. I wish I could present America to your view, you would be surprised to find everything so much like dear England—the soil, the weeds, the grass, the clover, the trees, the rivers, the rocks, the canals, the houses, with some additional varieties. We have passed through tens of thousands of acres of woods. The trees in general are not large—few so large as those in the grove of Sir R. Vaughan, near Bristol. Except on the Hudson, the prospects are greatly confined by woods; though you are surprised to find so much land cleared, and towns springing up every where, so that the idea of living in the woods seems to vanish. I was greatly pleased with the county of Coshocton; it is, as brother Powell says, more like Herefordshire than any other part we have yet been through. The English I have met with in the United States do well, and are fully satisfied with the change. The most disagreeable thing is, at first, to get a house, a home, or even apartments, nothing scarcely to be let, though it is easy to buy a house any where, as the Americans are fond of selling and beginning again."

"WORTHINGTON, STATE OF OHIO, *26th Dec.* 1831.—We are all very comfortable, and often meet together, and discuss, contrast, and compare things in America with those in England: on some points we agree, in our likes and dislikes, and on some differ very widely. On all material points, however, we fully agree, that *this is* the best *poor man's country;* the best in which to bring up and launch out a family; the best for persons of small incomes, (if they can accommodate themselves to circumstances, and depend upon their own resources). Servants ("Helps") may be had here, *board* and wages both considered, at an expense but little more than in England; but then the maid is about as good as her mistress, the man as his master, though in respectable families they rarely take their meals together, except in farm houses. * * * * Though, to parents coming out here, if they have the common feelings of our nature, it must be a sacrifice of the pleasures of friendship, and at first an endurance of several inconveniences, yet their children will bless them for their self-denial, and I believe, in ninety-nine cases out of a hundred, parents will feel thankful they had sufficient nerve to come to this country. Parents have no difficulty in bringing up their children, and placing them out in business; nor need they fear their future prosperity. Here, also, there is far less temptation to vice of every kind—sobriety and good order prevail in a way unknown in England. The direct and indirect effects of Temperance Societies are truly astonishing. It is true happiness may be found in England; and so the Christian may find it everywhere; for wherever he goes, his God is with him; but I believe the sum of happiness is infinitely greater here than in England. The chief cause of sorrow and distress in England is *unknown here!* Here there is *not* the *garb* of poverty nor the *look* of distress. I knew a farmer, an industrious and honest man, not far from West Park, Bristol, who has walked his fields in distress for hours together, not having wherewith to pay his taxes!! * * * It was a beautiful morning; I walked five miles before breakfast, on a very good tow path, with the canal on my right and the Mohawk river on my left, with a pretty fertile country, and varied scenery. It reminded me strongly of the Hay, my native place. We met a very agreeable English gentleman on the aqueduct over the Mohawk. He had travelled extensively through the States, and was then on hi return to England, with a view of bringing his family over. He was highly pleased with the country and the people, and said, "The English will never believe America to be so happy and prosperous a country, unless they see for themselves." This reminded me of what an English gentleman at New York said to me. He inquired if I intended to send a full account home of what I saw. 'Certainly,' was my reply. 'And do you,' he said, 'expect they will believe you?' 'Surely they will.' 'Take my word for it,' he said, 'they will not believe the one half of what *even you* say.' * * * We arrived at Shenectady about two o'clock. It is a pretty good town. Here we laid in more provisions. There is a railroad from Albany to this place, for steam coaches, which go fourteen miles an hour. Wednesday morning, at daylight, we came in sight of Utica. This is a very handsome town, abounding with well-built churches, of the various denominations with spires. I do not know in England so regular and so good a town—not the semblance of poverty or poor houses. The oxen are fine large beasts for labour. Self-supporting, or manual labour schools, are already established in many parts of the Union.

(*To be continued occasionally.*)

MEDICAL SELECTIONS. NO. II.
EFFECTS OF DIFFERENT PROFESSIONS AND TRADES ON HEALTH.*

THE *Literary Gazette* lately gave an analysis of Mr. Thackrah's volume on health; his second division treats of Dealers. *Shopkeepers* suffer from want of air and exercise. They are "pale, dyspeptic, and subject to affections of the head. They drag on a sickly existence, die before the proper end of human life, and leave a progeny like themselves." *Commercial Travellers* are compelled to take more liquor daily than nature requires; and the consequence is, in spite of their active employments, that few of them bear the wear and tear for thirty years; the majority not twenty. For the drinker, if he "be not suddenly taken off by apoplexy, or other affection of the brain, he merges into dropsy, and the bloated mass sinks into an early grave." The third division of the work before us refers to merchants and master-manufacturers: These are affected by the general principles applicable to other classes. If not too much confined, or exposed to injurious dusts, or effluvia from manufactures, or so hurried as to swallow their meals in a hasty manner, their lives are of a fair proportion. But, truly adds the author, "of all agents of disease and decay, the most important is anxiety of mind. When we walk the streets of large commercial towns, we must be struck with the hurried gait and care-worn features of the well-dressed passengers. Some young men, indeed, we may remark, with countenances possessing natural cheerfulness and colour, but these appearances rarely survive the age of manhood. * * * The physical evils of commercial life would be considerably reduced, if men reflected, that the success of business may be prevented by the very means used to promote it. Excessive application and anxiety, by disordering the animal economy, weaken the mental powers. Our opinions are affected by states of the body, and our judgment often perverted. If a clear head be required in commercial transactions, a healthy state of the body is of the first importance; and a healthy state of the body is incompatible with excessive application of mind, the want of exercise and fresh air. But subjects like these find no entry in the books of our merchants. Intent on their avocations, they strangely overlook the means necessary for pursuing them with success. They find, too late, that they have sacrificed the body to the mind." Mr. Thackrah allows for the pleasures of the table; but goes into details, enough to frighten the most resolute *bon vivants*, who exceed, and make a god of their belly. The worshippers of *venter Deus*, who build houses as if they were immortal, and feast as if they meant to live only for a very short time, are denounced as the sure consummaters of the latter purpose. But we need not insist on the evils which attend those who will indulge their appetites; all that we can do is to suggest the use of an improvement of our own day for their benefit; we allude to the stomach-pump! The Romans, we know, had some not very delicate modes of prolonging and repeating gastronomic enjoyments; had they been enlightened with the knowledge of this machine, how happy it must have made

* Mr. Thackrah's work has just appeared in a *second edition*—we are glad to see it so well appreciated.

them! But, leaving both Roman and English epicures, we approach the fourth, the last, and not the least interesting of Mr. Thackrah's divisions—professional men, and persons engaged in literature: those who work by mind more than by body. Some have mental application conjoined or alternating, with considerable exercise in the open air. Civil engineers, surveyors, and architects, belong to this division. Though confined to the desk occasionally, yet they travel frequently through the country, and thus enjoy fresh air and muscular exertion. They are, indeed, occasionally exposed to wet and cold; but these agents seldom injure persons in motion. Few individuals in this department are unhealthy, except those who are irregular in their habits, and addicted to high living. Ministers of religion have a similar alternation of study and exercise. The latter, however, is too gentle or restricted for muscular men. Their situation, and the ideas attached to it, unfortunately prevent their joining in sports or amusements which produce a full circulation of the blood, and a full action of the viscera. Hence, congestion of the venous system of the bowels is a frequent occurrence. The individuals of this class who are hard students may be referred to the section of literary men. *Clergymen* who preach long, frequently, or with vehemence, as well as orators, actors, public singers, and persons who play much on wind instruments, are subject to pains in the chest, spitting of blood, and diseases of the larynx. Practitioners of medicine and surgery. "Night calls," says Mr. T., "are generally thought to be very injurious. I think the evil less than the public and the profession suppose; for, if we observe those who have for thirty or forty years been much engaged as accoucheurs, we shall find them as robust as others. Anxiety of mind does more, I conceive, to impair health, than breach of sleep, nocturnal exposure, or irregularity in meals." As a profession, the medical is by no means healthy; and there is an extraordinary mortality among the students. We have next to refer to persons who have much mental application, without adequate exercise of the body: *Clerks, Book-keepers, Accountants*, &c. suffer from confined atmosphere and a fixed position. Though urgent disease is not generally produced, yet a continuance of the employment in its full extent never fails to impair the constitution, and render the individual sickly for life. The profession of the law, in most of its branches, is sedentary. Solicitors' and other clerks are kept, from morning to night, in a bad position, with the limbs fixed, and the trunk bent forward. But, leaving the lawyers to take care of themselves, which they very well know how to do in this world, we have now arrived at the last class of society, persons who live in a bad atmosphere, maintain one position most of the day, take little exercise, and are frequently under the excitement of ambition. This class includes individuals from the several professions, as well as the men devoted to science and literature. And on this subject we cannot but quote the first observation feelingly:—"The position of the student is obviously bad. Leaning forward, he keeps most of the muscles wholly inactive, breathes imperfectly, and often irregularly, and takes a full inspiration only when he sighs!"

CONTAGIOUS AND EPIDEMIC DISEASES.

How much crude nonsense, and scarcely intelligible jargon has lately been spoken by professional and non-professional persons on this subject of contagion. As soon as some new disease is imported from abroad, or arises in some spot at home, from which it spreads through the community, discussions and contentions arise on all sides as to its having simply an *epidemical* character, or one that is *contagious*, or both. These discussions are important, and the contention of men and discrepancy of facts are so great, that we should be perplexed indeed, did not a simple reflection occur to solve the difficulty. The contagious, as well as the malignant character of diseases, depends mostly, if not entirely, upon the degree of vital energy, and the narrowness of the space, &c. within which those who suffer from it are confined. At Madeira, in the south of France and elsewhere, consumption is deemed contagious, on account of the number of sufferers that resort to those parts. Authors have enumerated many other complaints which we deem non-contagious, as contagious under similar circumstances. For instance, Dr. Cleghorn and Dr. Fordyce, both physicians of high authority in medical science, have considered the ague as contagious, &c. &c. Therefore it would appear that epidemics, like the cholera, may be *conditionally* contagious. In the narrow streets, in the dark blind alleys, and small rooms, where human beings are found, of immoral and filthy habits, ground down, moreover, by poverty, labour, and misfortune—by every thing, in a word, that affects vitality—in such places it is that epidemics first appear, and then grow into *contagion*. If persons who can command comforts and conveniences are attacked by the invading disease, its contagious character disappears, or no longer betrays itself, and then it is rashly pronounced *only* an epidemic, or disease from local miasmata, or influences.

WORMS IN SPRING WATER.—The common opinion of medical men that the worms found in the stomach and human intestines are introduced by drinking water containing such worms, and the vulgar opinion that they are introduced by eating fruit, are both easily refuted by the simple experiment of exposing the worms found in water or fruits to a heat equal to that of the human bowels; namely, 98° fahr., when it will be found (as was shown by experiment) that such worms will instantly die. The knowledge of this simple experiment may often prevent unfounded alarms—such as when a family are induced to abandon a country house, from their physician finding small worms in the spring water of their well, and which he erroneously concludes to be ascarides.

ELEMENTS OF THOUGHT.

DISTINCTION OF CLASSES INJURIOUS TO VIRTUE.

Virtue and wisdom may have an inspired prophet or two always upon earth. But, for the body of mankind, a certain approach to a recognized equality seems requisite as a guarantee for virtues which are to be as extensive as mankind, instead of virtues limited to, and estimated by, their effect upon a particular class or order. The barons of Magna Charta stipulated only for the *liber homo*, and thought as little about the rights of a villien, as a Jamaica planter about codifying for negroes...... There is little check upon ordinary consciences, wherever the want of a social feeling, and a common interest between the parties, fails to bring home to the bosoms of the principal in the transaction its general consequences to society. England continues to be, in this sense, much more aristocratical, than many European nations, far behind it in general spirit and refinement. Only our line of aristocracy, and consequently of demarcation, falls far lower than the House of Peers; and thus, from want of being embodied in one uniform set of facts, or denounceable in one short denomination, it attracts less invidious attention. But the actual separation produces its natural effects. As strong instances as any in modern civilization, of the perilous length to which exemption from the cause may run, when once administered into practice, exist in some anomalous proceedings long made compatible with the political morality of the gentlemen of England. Purchasers of game in London, they have had no remorse, in what goes by the name of their justice-room in the country, to send to jail their unknown accomplice—the wretched poacher, whom, perhaps, their own money may have bribed—certainly their own participation had seduced—into the commission of the offence. A member of Parliament, sitting there by no title but that of corruption, does not feel the least scruple in joining the recommendation of a committee, that the uttermost pennyworth of penalty under the bribery acts should be enforced against some insignificant freeman, not a hundredth part as guilty as himself. The proceedings on committees for private bills, we will not enlarge on. Our observations might be a breach of the privileges of that honourable house. But we have heard a lawyer, as much employed in this line of practice as any man of his time, and afterwards upon the bench, describe these committees as tribunals, where gentlemen of the same rank of life met to compliment each other at the expense of the property of strangers. His picture was that of dens of injustice, where men—who, in cases not under the protection of one of those artificial exceptions, would shrink from the suspicion of wrong—are parties to transactions for which juries would have been attainted, their houses ploughed into the ground, and salt sown on the foundations, in ancient times."—*Edinburgh Review.*

THE MORAL SENSE.

The moral sense is formed by time, and experience. So are all the natural senses, not one of which is born with us: they are all created, some instantaneously, others in a little time, some in a long time, but all by experience. The moral sense differs from a natural one, as much as the effect of reflection differs from simple feeling. But the conformation given by nature and education may be so exquisitely just in some men, that they may be said to judge of actions and principles by a kind of instantaneous sensation, which may be very properly termed a moral sense. The eye, as a sense, is formed by the experience of many years; but when it is formed, it judges of distances and magnitude, of beauty and deformity, apparently by an immediate sensation; but in fact by a process which is the effect of experience. The mind is in the same state as to moral: it has judged of causes by effects on all natural occasions. It has so associated virtue with pleasure, and vice with pain, that when actions and principles under these denominations present themselves, they seem to act on the mere sense, not as virtues or vices, but as pleasure or pain.

STRENGTH OF MIND.

All men are equally desirous of happiness, but few are successful in the pursuit. One chief cause is the want of *strength of mind*, which might enable them to resist the temptation of present ease or pleasure, and carry them forward in the desire of more distant profit and enjoyment * * * *. However poets may employ their wit and eloquence in celebrating present pleasure, and rejecting all distant views to fame, health, or fortune, it is obvious that this practice is the source of all dissoluteness and disorder, repentance, and misery. A man of strong determined temper, adheres tenaciously to his general resolutions, and is neither seduced by the allurements of pleasure, nor terrified by the menaces of pain; but keeps still in view those distant pursuits, by which he at once ensures his happiness and his honour.

HUME.

If we must pray for special favour, let it be for a sound mind, in a sound body. Let us pray for fortitude, that we may think the labours of Hercules, and all his sufferings preferable to a life of luxury, and the soft repose of Sardanapalus; this is a blessing within the reach of every man. This we can give ourselves. It is virtue, and virtue only that can make us happy.

JUVENAL.

TESTIMONY OF ROUSSEAU TO THE DIVINE PERFECTION OF THE CHARACTER OF THE SAVIOUR.

The Majesty of the Scriptures strikes me with admiration, as the purity of the gospel has its influence on my heart. Peruse the works of our philosophers, with all their pomp of diction; how mean, how contemptible are they, compared with the Scriptures! Is it possible a book at once so simple and so sublime should merely be the work of man? What prepossession, what blindness, it must be to compare the son of Sophroniscus to the Son of Mary! What an infinite disproportion is there between them! Socrates, dying without pain r ignominy, easily supported his character to the last; and if his death, however easy, had not crowned his life, it might be doubted if Socrates, with all his wisdom, was any thing more than a vain sophist. He invented, it is said, the theory of morals. Others, however, had before put them in practice; he had therefore only to say what they had done, and to reduce their examples to precept. But where could Jesus learn among his contemporaries that pure and sublime morality, of which he only has given us both precept and example? The death of Socrates peacefully philosophizing with his friends, appears the most agreeable that could be wished for: that of Jesus expiring in the midst of agonizing pains, abused, insulted, and accused by a whole nation is the most horrible that could be found. Socrates, in receiving the cup of poison, blessed the weeping executioner who administered it; but Jesus, in the midst of excruciating tortures, prayed for his merciless tormentors. Yes! if the life and death of Socrates were those of a philosopher, the life and death of Jesus were those of a God.—*Emilius.*

USEFUL NOTICES.

STEAM CARRIAGES.—A short time back Mr. Walter Hancock, of Stratford, made the first public experiment with his new steam-carriage. Several scientific gentlemen attended from London, and sixteen of them took their seats in the two bodies. The carriage, guided by Mr. Hancock in front, was put in motion by his turning a lever connected with the steam-cock of the boiler, and proceeded through Stratford, up the hill, to the Green Man, on the Forest, at a steady pace of eight miles an hour. He then turned short, and returned to the factory within forty minutes, after running about seven miles in the pleasantest manner, and with a perfect sense of security to every one in the carriage. In fact, the experiment was successful, and we may henceforward look to the rapid introduction of a safe and greatly improved mode of travelling, leading to a very important revolution in the domestic economy of nations. The carriage in question has two bodies for sixteen passengers, and two seats for outside ones. This double body occupies a length of ten feet, and the engine-house and apparatus about eight feet in the rear. The quantity of fuel consumed during this trip was about 2½ bushels of coke, the fire being fed behind. The stock of water converted into steam was about three barrels, or 100 gallons. The height of the vehicle is nine feet, and it stands three feet eight inches from the ground. The boiler is of the description called *tubular*, and in this engine it consists of twelve chambers, each distinct, and formed of the best charcoal iron, so that no explosion is probable, and if any took place, it could only be one of the chambers, and unconsequential. This carriage is built for the Greenwich road, and it will perform that journey in half an hour. The facility of stopping is perfect, and its traverses on a crowded road are effected with a far greater surety than in any carriages drawn even by the best-trained horses. It turns in the shortest compass, and, in fact, possesses all the best qualities of a modern-built carriage. Other carriages, with omnibus bodies, to carry fourteen passengers, are now building, of somewhat lighter construction, which are intended to travel about twelve miles an hour. As the engine is placed in the rear of the carriage, and the boiler and fire at the extremity, no inconvenience is experienced by the passengers from noise, heat, or smoke, and the sensation is precisely that of travelling in any other carriage.

NEW COMET.—Professor Harding of Gottingen, discovered a comet in the head of the serpent on the 29th of July. It is different from any of those announced this year. It is without a train.

USEFUL INSTRUCTION REGARDING THE MILKING OF COWS.—The operation of milking is performed differently in various parts of the country. In some, the dairy-maid dips her hand into a little milk, and by successively stripping the teat between her finger and thumb, unloads the udder. The plan, however, is attended with the disadvantage of irritating more or less the teat, and rendering it liable to cracks and chops, which are followed by inflammation, extending to the rest of the quarter. This accounts for the disease occurring more frequently among the cows under the charge of one milker than it does in those which are under the charge of another; and, as this practice is more common in some parts of the country than in others, it also accounts for the disease being more common in these parts. This plan of milking where the irritation is not sufficient to excite the extent of inflammation to which I have alluded, frequently produces a horny thickening of the teat, a consequence of the cracks and chops, which renders it more difficult to milk than when in its natural state; and, at the same time, predisposed to inflammation, when any cause occurs to set it up. These effects may be, and are almost entirely avoided by the more scientific plan of milking adopted in other parts of the country, where, instead of drawing down or stripping the teat between the thumb and fingers, the dairy-maid follows more closely the principles which instinct has taught the calf. (The calf jerks its nose into the udder, and forces down the milk.) She first takes a slight hold of the teat with her hand, by which she merely encircles it; then lifts her hand up, so as to press the body of the udder upwards, by which the milk escapes into the teat, or if (as is generally the case when some hours have elapsed between milking times,) the teat is full, she grasps the teat close to its origin with her thumb and her fore finger, so as to prevent the milk which is in the teat from escaping upwards; then making the rest of the fingers to close from above downwards in succession, forces out what milk may be contained in the teat through the opening of it. The hand is again pressed up and closed as before, and thus, by repeating this action, the udder is completely emptied, without that coarse tugging and tearing of the teat which is so apt to produce disease.—*Quarterly Journal of Agriculture.*

SONG OF THE RHENISH PROVINCES.
(FROM TAIT'S MAGAZINE.)

The Rhine is born in the winter storm
  Upon a bed of snow;
He's suckled by the avalanche
  Dissolved in summer's glow;
He's cradled on the iron ledge
  Of Constance' craggy wall,
And rocked to sleep on the roaring steep
  Of wild Schauffhausen's fall.
With such a sire—what wonder then
  Our maids are fair, our sons are men.

Like a proud conqueror advancing,
  Triumphantly he rolls,
The flood his chariot, and the waves,
  His steeds of foam, controls.
Before his brow the forests bow:
  Attendant on his state,
On either hand a giant band,
  The chained mountains wait,
Like captive kings—their sentinels
A thousand crested citadels.

Johannisberg and Rudesheim,
  With grape-besmeared hand,
All reeking from their fragrant toil,
  His proud cupbearers stand;
The tribute of a thousand keels
  He takes with high disdain,
And borne before his rushing wheels,
  He sweeps it to the main.
Such are thy triumphs, Father Rhine!
Who dare to boast such glorious line?

The Switzer on thy native mountains,
  Thine eldest born is he;
He drinks thy first free-bubbling fountains;
  He drinks and he is free.
Would that thine after ampler waters,
  Descending to the plain,
If such their first ennobling spirit,
  Like virtue could retain;
'Tis pity sure thy boundless waves
Should e'er be soiled by lips of slaves.

Slaves! who are slaves? bring me my sword!
  Have we not fought and bled?
Yes: triumphed too 'gainst freedom's foes—
  Behold our wounds are red!
This blade—what dims it to the hilt?
  Life blood—'tis of the Frank—
We rose and burst their yoke accurst,
  And gained—that sullen clank—
Could it be chains? Say, hath our aid
In Freedom's cause been thus repaid?

Rhine, I would pledge thee in a cup
  Of thine own native growth;
But my hand trembles as I raise
  The goblet to my mouth;
It seems as if by fettered limbs
  The wine-press had been trod;
To me at least it has the taste
  Of friends', of brothers' blood,
And broken faith.—In such curst wine,
I may not, dare not, pledge thee, Rhine!

Sweep on, thou dark majestic river!
  Ten thousand years thy roar
Has swelled as now; and shall for ever
  Till time shall be no more.
If then the hand that first designed
  And sent thee on thy course,
In depth of thy sublimity,
  Recall thee to thy source,
Thine earthly race of glory run,—
Tell not the deeds thy kings have done.

In one of the imperial towns in Germany it is customary to address the Mayor as "Your Wisdom." A party, who had consumed hour after hour in a bootless chase after the sapient functionary, having at last fallen in with him, very innocently hailed him, ejaculating, "I have been rummaging every nook and corner the whole day long, but deuce a bit could I find out your wisdom."

THE STORY-TELLER.

ANDREW HOWIE—A MAN OF THE WEST.
(Written for the Schoolmaster.)

It was a day of public rejoicing in Glasgow; and Mr. Mathewson, one of the most respectable, if not the largest of the manufacturers of the town, had taken charge of his own warehouse, that his son and two young clerks, with sundry inferior assistants, who usually officiated there, might have an opportunity of witnessing and sharing in the gaieties of the holyday. Already had Mr. Mathewson himself, by what was thought an extraordinary degree of condescension, viewed, examined, and paid for several pieces of cloth, brought in by hand-loom workers. He was going through the same process with an exhausted, broken-down workman, yet one who in years seemed scarce in the prime of life, when an elderly, small, thin man, of poor but decent appearance, entered on the same errand, was saluted with more than ordinary attention, and desired to sit down on the bench. The old man nodded, and obeyed; wiped the perspiration from his thin temples and bald forehead, and then fixed a keen, hollow, grey eye on the speakers before him. He who stood in the place of workman was making a low, but earnest expostulation, to which the master answered at first calmly; and then, with a show of impatience, he whipped up a bundle of cotton yarn, saying aloud, "Do ye think we would wrong ye, Robert? If ye are not pleased with what we can give, ye are welcome to take your change. This is a land of liberty;—we can find weavers, and ye are just as free to look out for another warehouse." The poor man laid his emaciated, eager fingers upon the bundle—" Say no more about it, sir. Weel do ye ken I *must* take it."

This poor man had brought in the fruits of his own and his neighbour's fortnight's labour from his cottage, five miles off in the country, that he might have a stolen sight of the grand procession. With thanks he had accepted wages reduced a full half below the prices of former years. These diminutions he had met by gradually retrenching and, in many instances, entirely surrendering the little comforts of his home, and at the same time eking out his hours of labour;—but to hear of farther reduction, which lowered the price of his labour to three-eighths of what had been given for the same kind and quantity of work twenty years before, and to be told that in this sort of barter between *capital* and *labour*, the manufacturer and the workman are on equal terms, wrung forth a hasty expression of impatience which he afterwards regretted. "Ay, ay, Mr. William," said the old man, as the poor weaver sung dumb, "so he is quite free to seek another warehouse; only where will the poor fellow find it, when every master has a third mair hands hanging on, than he can fully employ. So he is to jump o'er the brig as he gangs hame; and may-be, in a sense, that would be the best thing he could do, only he would rin a chance o' drownin', and o' leavin' an orphan family to hale starve, instead o' half starving,—and also o' committin' a deadly sin. Had a war been going on, and the king needed soldiers, he might have left his family and ta'en the bounty. This is all the real choice he has between working for what ye think best—or starving, and seeing them suffer who can worse bear hardship. Ye ken, sir, better than I can tell ye, it's little a weaver can turn his hand to. But I am far from blaming you, sir. When I see your full shelves, I ken weel ye are mair to be pitied than blamed. But oh there's something sair wrang among us ———." With this lecture the weaver, having now carefully knotted up his yarn in his ragged *Monteith handkerchief*, left the warehouse. "An' how is a' with you, Andrew?" said Mr. Mathewson to the old man, when they were left alone. "A man o' sense, like you, is no doubt surprised to hear half their unreasonable nonsense. Ye may all know that in the present state of the market, our house, and too many others in this same town, are stuffing our warehouses with goods, for which there is neither demand nor likelihood of demand; and dipping rashly into our capitals, rather than throw our hands all at once idle. Remunerating prices, such as we once got, need never be looked for again; and how, then, can men be so unjust as to expect the same wages."

"It may be sae, sir," said the old man. "And it might be better for us all if there were less *labour*, and less *stuffing* up of the white goods; but oh, Mr. William, dinna go to aggravate (exasperate) a poor worn-out, half-starved workman, by telling him he is as free to refuse work as ye are to refuse him employment. I canna thole to hear that even from you, sir.—So were ye, when a bairn boarding wi' the gudewife—and a dour loonie ye were—to tarry* at your porridge; but ye ken weel that in an hour or twa afterwards ye were fain to draw to your bicker."

Mr. Mathewson smiled—" And how, Andrew, is my kind old nurse? You should remember (for the sake of poor weavers) that if I *persevered*, she would at last give the porridge a tempting dash of more milk, and coax me to eat."

"It will be lang ere you masters pour cream on our cogs, or coax huz to eat, Mr. William," said the old man, smiling grimly. "Where saw ye ever, for twenty years bygane, in town or country, in this land, masters in any calling that could not find hands,—ay, and double, and triple hands. In the back woods of America there may sometimes be lack of labourers, but seldom at our door-cheek,—and in our trade never; and never again will be, I jalouse. It will be fine times for the workman when he is able, for any length of time, to refuse an ill-paid job, Mr. William."

Andrew's business was now despatched, and the conversation became more general. Mr. Mathewson inquired about lodgings, which he wished to procure in his native air, and in Andrew's neighbourhood. Something had disgusted him with his handsome villa on the Ayrshire coast, which he was trying to sell; and his health required change of air.

"Ye are looking, like myself, thin, auld-like, and yellow enough, sir," said Andrew, with compassionate interest.

"It's but a thin, yellow, hungry trade grown, this of ours, Andrew, compared with what we have both seen it," replied the manufacturer, smiling at Andrew's homely compliment to his complexion. "There is a change of times since I wont to come out on the top of the yarn in my uncle's caravan on a Saturday afternoon, to get an afternoon's fishing with your laddies, and a capital *four-hours* of tea and bacon, or burn trouts, from my old nurse, while the overseer went about among ye. Those were happy days."

"Ye let us come to you now, sir. Ay, a weaver's wife could gie a bairn a piece, or a friend a *four-hours* then.

---

* Take the pet at—refuse.—*See Jamieson.*

Weel, weel!"—The old man's sigh filled up the sentence.— "But I am wae to hear ye need country quarters for health, sir; and there is ane at hame will be much concerned. What is like the matter?"

"No great matter, Andrew—something and nothing. The docter says air, the pony, and ease of mind, will soon make all right; but the last is a commodity become right scarce among us."

"With a' those shelfs, and bales, and muckle books, sir, and so many poor folk about ye, I can weel understand that," replied Andrew, glancing over the array of desks, and on through the long perspective of the deep and well-stored warehouse, room after room retiring from view. Mr. Mathewson's complaint was that of hundreds of commercial men in these times. He was nervous—he was dyspeptic—his sleep was broken—his appetite uncertain. Then he became almost quite well again, or much better, or nothing particular; and again there was a sense of languor, oppression, and exhaustion, or irritation; and the physician saw something was going wrong, but could neither tell what, nor yet confess ignorance. His most distinct fear was for water on the chest; and "the pony, and ease of mind," were his universal prescription for all men in business. "If it's to be got ony where, it will be found about ———— side, by me, Andrew; so make the gudewife look for some bit room—no fine place—and I'll try to get out on Saturday; and now for your news."

"Yours it maun be, sir—The BILL is to do us a' a power of good, nae doubt? But what's come ower the Factory Bill?—the wives will a' be at me for news about that. Whatever comes of us auld, doited, weaver bodies, it would be heartsome to see the bits o' bairns, poor, dowie, spiritless, dwining, decrepit things, eased of their lang hours. I wonder what the manufacturing tribe will crine and dwindle into, sir, in a generation or twa."

"If the wives would take care o' their bairns themselves, Andrew, that would be better than ten bills. There has been a deal of senseless clamour about this same story. The Government have more wit than interfere with the entire freedom of all contracts between capitalists and labourers. The Factory Bill will get the go-bye, ye'll see."

"Entire freedom!—how can ye ca' it sae, sir? Its a' delusion and mockery to tell even huz, that's grown men, that we have entire freedom of working at ony price. But freedom of contract for children! Na, na. Can they manage for themselves? Are they free? Alack, alack!"

"They have their parents, and friends, Andrew, to take charge of their engagements. May they not be safely left to them?"

"No, sir, they cannot—ye see they *cannot*. In a cot-house on a moor, with a kail-yard and potatoes enow, I would leave, cheerfully, a bairn to its ain mother; but in this weary town of yours, wi' a man thrown clean out-of work, or brought down to the starving point in wages, hunger and cauld pinching, and a mill open for bairns, be the hours short, or those of black niggers, be the place healthy or murderous, we are come to that state, that fathers and mothers *maun* sell their bairns' labour. Necessity has no law,—the poor thing of eight maun slave for the sister of two and three. Ye have read in our auld Josephus o' mothers so bested as to eat the very fruit of their bodies."

"And now we may hear of them *drinking* it, Andrew," said the manufacturer.

"I'm no denying *our* faults, sir: would we were in a way to mend them, or had encouragement thereto. But it's plain to be seen that we are far, far departed frae the natural state, in whilk things might be left to themselves, and *ourselves* to *ourselves*. But think ye it right to meddle or make only to scathe us? If you protect your corn, and your whisky, and your what not, by laws and statutes, and fines and felonies, why no protect ours and our bairns' wearied limbs and exhausted bodies, as weel as at our cost the bread which should nourish us?"

"I have nothing to say for the Corn laws, Andrew; yet I cannot see that one bad law should be an apology for another useless one. These are difficult complicated questions, and we have scarce leisure for them,—but you will surely own the world is much more prosperous than when you first saw it, sixty years back?"

"Indeed, and I'll no be rash there," cried Andrew, briskly; "but I freely own its a *brawer* warld; and plenty changes in it, too, whilk young folk say are lightsome. Changes especially in our *line*; and, as far as machinery goes, changes for the better, I'll not dispute,—sair as machines have borne on me in my ain peculiar.——But oh, we have surely made an ill use o' these marvellous inventions Providence has permitted us to make. They have no been blessed to us, sir, in the use. We are making man's master o' the dumb creations of iron and timber should be man's servants."

"A little of the old leaven still, Andrew," said Mr. Mathewson, smiling. "But hark, the music of our lads, and the procession."

"Then I must be off to get a sight of their daft doings. It's aye some good THE BILL has done, when it gives them a play-day or two, and causes a brushing up among lads and lasses for a walk in the air. But I would like to argue out the point with you, too, sir; for I'm sure I could convince ye."

The honest man showed such divided inclination between witnessing the Reform Procession and expounding his opinions, that his old foster-child, or boarder, compassionately suggested the adjournment of the question, to be resumed on ———— banks, or in Andrew's garden seat, under the bourtrees. The old man's eye brightened. As he took a glass of medicated port, kept in the warehouse, because prescribed for the manufacturer at this noon-day hour, he pledged to his better health, and shook his head with earnest gesticulation, saying, "O'd, but Mr. William, this o' ours should be a better warld if we kenned but right how to manage 't. I'm not just sure if the birkies up bye yonder,"—and he pointed over his shoulder towards London,— "ken a' the rights and wrangs o't, or the real outs and ins; but howsomever, I hope they're honest men this new set; and, wi' the aid of Divine wisdom"—["And our good advising," interrupted the smiling manufacturer,]—"they may make some small beginning to set us in the right way. I could leave the warld in peace, if I but saw it since in the right way."

"In which for forty years ye have been shewing it how to walk."——

"I'll no deny—it would be fause shame,—that since Mr. Muir's day, I may have been ettling at that," replied the hilosopher of Spindleton; "It's a man's duty, sir,—and though but a poor man and a weaver, I would be loath to forget 'A man's a man for a' that.'" But here the musical instruments attending an Irish detachment of the procession, now just at hand, poured forth "St. Patrick's Day," so loudly, that it was only by signs the friends took leave; and thus ended the first *idle*, leisurely talk that had taken place in that busy warehouse for months or years, at least when the master was present.

By Saturday evening Mr. Mathewson and his youngest daughter were settled in the small rural lodging near Spindleton which Mrs. Howie had engaged for them in a gardener's house. His lady and elder daughters were reported to be prodigiously fine people, but in manners and simplicity of character, though his habits had become more luxurious, Mathewson himself was the same man as when an under clerk in the establishment to which he had succeeded, and which he had so much extended. Yet he had in many things gone with the stream which he now fancied it his duty to oppose, at least, in the instance of his own thoughtless family. He deferred his visit to his foster-mother till Monday; but saw, with satisfaction, the decent, quiet couple in their old back pew in the church, from which Andrew's grey eye ever and anon shot a challenge to renewal of their argument.

Andrew Howie, for a hand-loom weaver of 1832, might be considered a comfortable man; his good fortune was the fruit of his own good conduct. His cottage, the looms in one end, the dwelling in the other, was, together with the garden, his own property, on paying twenty-five shillings a-year of feu. His long-used furniture was still in sufficient quantity, and well-kept. Fuel was cheap here. He had long since put "a little to the fore." It was, indeed, very little, but still something; and for the sake of a kind and dutiful daughter, Andrew would have suffered any hardship, save the humiliation of receiving parish aid, before he had touched it. This fund, of L.23, 17s., was deposited in a Glasgow bank, for Andrew's prudent wife would not trust this treasure even to her foster-child. "There were so many ups and downs," she said wisely, "amang the great masters." Two benefit societies to which he sometimes grudged having paid for forty years, without being above three times sick, placed Andrew above the dread of destitution in illness, or of wanting decent and Christian burial, which always supposes expense; and the membership of a book-club which he had mainly established, and of a newspaper-club which originally took in the Gazetteer! supported his social importance in the neighbourhood. He kept his seat in the church, though that too was felt a heavy cess in bad times, and having surmounted the evil political fame of his youth, he was now on the new Minister's leet for an elder. It was indeed suspected that Mr. Draunt the clergyman, had done this as a stroke of policy, at a time when a rumour of building a Seceder Meeting-house arose in the village. Andrew had at one time kept a couple of apprentices; but this source of profit was stopt; he however let his loom stances, and was often not paid. His own gains were little indeed; not above 4s. 6d. a week on the average; but somehow he contrived to maintain his place as patriarch of the village. The only aid he received was from his daughter, who kept him clear of arrears with his societies; and who once, when in a desperate fit of necessary economy, he gave up both his clubs which cost a shilling a quarter each, entered him anew. Deprived of the distinction of having the newspaper directed, as for forty years, to "Mr Andrew Howie, Manufacturer, Spindleton," the old man became spiritless and insignificant in his own esteem. What is life deprived of life's enjoyments! Restored to his club, he read, expounded, and rehearsed with greater zest than before; and was again the village oracle.

Andrew Howie, though not an idler, was on principle not keenly industrious. Constant *slavery* at the loom, as he called the modern long hours, was against his creed and his habits; and though the old man toiled only ten hours a day, where his poor neighbours worked fourteen, and sixteen, he never ceased to maintain, that his own hours were much too long, and the necessity for such continued labour, owing to a bad constitution of society. Man was intended, Andrew loftily affirmed, for something better than perpetual monotonous drudgery.

Long before Mr. Owen, or Spence, or any of those apostles, or their new systems were heard of, Andrew's benevolent speculations had wandered into forms, to which some of his neighbours looked with interest, and others with amusement. His visionary Societies, and manufacturing villages, were to be centres of domestic comfort, leisure, instruction, health, happiness for all—

For the young who labour, and the old who rest.

He, however, differed entirely from Mr. Owen in one essential particular. Every household in Andrew's town, was to have its own sacred fire-side. If more extravagant in politics, Andrew Howie was more strictly religious than many of his younger neighbours. The spirit of Christianity entered fully into his weaving Utopia, and mingled with all his visions of the social Millennium of Spindleton.

When the old couple returned from afternoon service, on the Sunday after Mr. Mathewson's arrival, the conversation naturally turned on their former boarder, and as naturally reverted to their own changed condition. Sunday was now the only day of the week, in which they indulged in the extravagance of that thin *blue* dilution, which they, perhaps from habit, named tea; and which a weekly slice of wheaten bread, and a sprinkling of treacle, which Andrew thought good for his elocution, accompanied. Yet it ill becomes me to speak thus slightingly of the beverage which the philosophic weaver sucked up like a leviathan, even to the sixth or seventh maceration of the bitter many-coloured leaves.

Though curtailed at his board, Andrew enjoyed many little comforts and great blessings unknown to his brethren in "yon weary town." He retained, after all his losses, the blessings—how great!—of fresh air, free space, his garden, his good bed and useful furniture, the *leisure* which he took, preferring it, in a balance of comfort, to what others might have reckoned necessaries; though he thus forfeited the trifle of more wages, at which men with families greedily grasped, at the expense of weary limbs, exhausted spirits, and finally of ruined health. He also enjoyed, to the full, his own importance in his ancient neighbourhood, and the superiority he ever maintained in argument and conversation. Though his wages were scarcely a third of what he had once earned, his kitchen in a cold night was almost as snug as ever, his bed as warm, his church seat as sacred. How few old weavers could boast of as much!

"That's a dish of prime tea, gudewife," said Andrew, breathing hard, from gulping down the fifth filling—the last three without sugar; "Whate'er Mr. COBBETT may say—and he is a wonderful man—I wad na' care, in my auld days now, to take as much every night; he's a strong stamacket man o' his nature, I reckon Mr. COBBETT, and does na ken the wants o' sedentary callings."

"And sair do I wish Andrew, joe, I could gee ye a dish ilka evening, after toiling at that weary loom for six lang hours frae dinner to supper, upon may-be potatoes and salt."

"And under a good dispensation o' civil government, I ken not, Tibby, what should forbid. I told you how kindly Mr. William bore in mind the hearty Saturday *four-hours* ye wont to give him, and the laddies langsyne."

"We durst na bid him to a dish o' tea now; and it's the less matter, as we have it not to offer. Then I had baith a bit sweet butter and loaf sugar for a stranger. But oh! he looks wan, and defaite, poor man—muckle worse than ye let on to me. That extravagant family is breaking his heart. They say, Andrew, his wife and tawpie daughters ne'er entered the kirk door six times in the same gown. They say Dr. Chalmers since gledged off the book, and glowered braid at them ae day they rustled in."

"Hout lass, ye ken little about it—It's no a woman's gown, or fifty o' them—gude kens they're ower cheap—could have played *phew!* on a trade like his. It's the trade itsel, Tibby, that's ruined. The losses in South America, and the crosses in North America, and Botany, and Van Diemen's. Shops fu' o' finished goods rotting in the faulds of the hydraulic press, or roupit abroad for far below the first cost."

"Poor man! I wot nae, Andrew, but auld Geordie Mathewson's trade, though sma', was, when a' comes to a', a surer calling than this high-flying o' Mr. William's; wi' a' their new-fangled tackle, throwing greedy grips to the ends of the Earth, and spreading out gauze duds to bring hame midges."

"Partly right, but far mair wrang, Tibby, as the women-folk generally are," said Tibby's apostle. "Mr. William and his neighbours have done good and ill baith to themselves, and to huz weavers. But this jabbering about temporalities, is scarce Sabbath-e'ening discourse—so ye'll rinse up your tea-tackle, as Mr. COBBETT ca's it, and let's get in the BOOKS, my woman."

Mr. Mathewson, on this night, was also at his *books*, brought out on the previous day in his gig-box; and as a first draught of the prescribed ease of mind, in his rural abode, he dwelt upon them, comparing the fair and glittering array of figures in the ledger, shewing what ought to be the profits of the year, with what he feared they might eventually turn out, till Andrew Howie was awakened after his tea-supper, out of his long refreshing first sleep, by the twittering of the swallows in the eaves of his cottage.

All next day Andrew hung over his loom, full-primed, and at half-cock, prepared for a vigorous discharge of argument and eloquence upon the manufacturer. It was evening before Mr. Mathewson paid his visit; and then he appeared fonder of a fire-side chat with Tibby, than political discussion. But *ben* came Andrew, his Kilmarnock nightcap in one hand, a bunch of well-thumbed pamphlets in the other, consisting of a few select numbers of Cobbett's Register, a stray Carpenter's Political Magazine, some old *Examiners*, and the last Trades' Advocate. Without loss of time or ceremony he opened his broadside.

"Think ye still, sir," said he, following the eye of his visiter round the apartment, which, as contrasted with the memory of former years, shewed few tokens of increasing national prosperity; "Think ye still this a better world than that of the last generation? Have we mair meat, mair leisure to make ourselves wiser and better men; mair peace of mind, mair comfort at the fireside, and in our families than the auld folk ye remember here?"

"There's more, and merrier of you any way," said the manufacturer smiling, as a squad of children scoured yelling past the door.

"Granted, sir,—and mair work too,—far mair production,—and if we could warm ourselves with brass and metal trinkrums, and eat crockery ware and our ain saft goods, it would be a brave world this coming up among us:—the lady has her two silken gowns, and the lass her three printed ones, o' *Peel's rotten cottons*, as Mr. Cobbett ca's them, for one langsyne; but does that, sir, make up to you and me for our long weary work hours, our anxious minds, and outlay of siller.—If four gowns, and a dozen needles, or candlesticks, bring huz labourers no more bread than the half o' them did long ago, it will be ill to make me believe our world is the gainer by our reduced wage and lengthened hours. A' thing has thriven but the meat and the mense* Mr. William."

"The mouths have thriven pretty well too, Andrew. Do ye reckon for nothing the immense increase of the manufacturing population? enough of itself to account for the reduction of wages."

"Scarce enough, sir, when we have fifty times more production.—But something I own:—the wives had a saying in my young day, 'God never sends the mouth, but He sends the meat with it.' But we must give up that—and adopt the new and unhappily ower true doctrine, that with the numerous mouths come the famine and the pestilence."

"Well, well, Andrew, when the BILL gets us down the meal and the bread, this will be half-mended—for I fear it will be but half even then.—If we could only get these Chinese and Hindoo creatures, to make or grow some useful product, to send us in return for the goods we can furnish them, we could then pay ye, and content ye better."

"I own that, sir—and Tibby there for one, would be glad to get a reasonable hold of a little more of their tea and sugar, among other good things.——— But ye are not altogether right about the number of mouths producing so great a glut of labour—for, compared with our young days, every single hand-loom hand is now equal to a man and a-fifth."—"A man and a-fifth, what do ye mean by that?" "Our Andrew has sic droll similitudes," said the admiring Tibby; and Andrew with a suppressed exulting chuckle of which vanity he was ashamed in an affair so serious, replied, "The long hours—the long, exhausting, weary hours of toil, make every man's labour now-a-days equal to a man and a fifth of former times.—And if frail nature would sustain eighteen hours work out of the twenty-four, we would soon see such hours—and if the cold form of religion subsisting among us, permitted Sabbath work, we would have that too, and the poor folks in three months no a bawbee the better of it."

"Operatives are quite as free to restrict their hours of work, as to make their own price."

---

* Mense,—manners, and something more: menseful includes discretion, and propriety of conduct.

"Now, sir, that's no like you," cried Andrew hastily. Dinna provoke a starving man, by telling him he may eat he likes, and shewing him bread and meat locked-up in an iron cage far beyond his grip.—But you masters I grant re not without your ain share in the miseries of these times.—And for what is't a'!—That the lady may have two shawls, and the laird two coats, where their father and mother had but one—that the mistress may have three sets of china tea-tackle, where one served her goodmother. This hree to be bought with a prodigiously increased quantity of our labour."

"Of my capital, or profits, Andrew."

"We shall not dispute about words, sir,—yours and ours together—and what ought to be your profits. You great folks, the Cotton Lords as Mr. Cobbett ca's ye, are far from free of troubles and anxieties.—And what for incurred? Twa or three gold seals with coats o' arms dangling at the gold watch, give unco little comfort, aboon the auld clumsey clicking turnip, if the chief business is to remind the owner that the fatal hour is drawing nigh and little to meet Maister Carrick's peremptor demand." Mr. Mathewson gave a half-smile which Andrew construed into assent or perhaps approbation.

"I may be speaking ower long, sir; but looking on this nation as one family and fellowship, and B, the cotton spinner or weaver, as equally the child of the commonwealth with C, ye observe, the landed man, or *great* farmer,—the question with our rulers—or stewards rather—for the people maun rule themselves,—stewards I say who fear the Lord, and understand their duty, is this—if what C suffers or sacrifices shall not be met by more than an equivalent, in what B gains."—But here, when Andrew had almost foundered at any rate, Tibby, with woman's tact perceiving symptoms of weariness in her visiter broke in with—" Sic a man!—bothering Mr. William wi' his B's and C's—when Andrew gets to the B's he is as wud as ever was Johnnie Waldie, reading the 10th of Nehemiah—ye mind auld John Waldie, sir? He died only last Michaelmas."

Andrew turned eyes of stern reproof upon his helpmate, who however bore his rebuke with great *sang froid*. "It is not for the mere conveniences of life I speak," he said, " but something far mair lasting and precious, lost sight of—made shipwreck of altogether.—By-and-by we must alter our Single Book, and make the answer to the question ' What's the chief end of man?'—at least of manufacturing man—to be—" To work fourteen or fifteen hours out of the twenty-four, fabricating, half the time, trash worth no rational body's buying; and half starving while he is about it."

"There is much truth and much error in what you say, Andrew," replied Mr. Mathewson. "But how do you system-mongers, and state-tinkers propose mending your condition—would ye advise a Strike."

"Na, sir; I'm for nae Strike—unless it were better managed than ever I saw a strike yet. If the yearthen vesshel smite itself against the vesshel of iron, where will lie the pot-sherds? But if ye would give up underselling each other, sir."

"And I may retort, if ye would give up your underworking, Andrew—and overworking, and long hours, and diminish your numbers."

"I showed you how it could not be, sir,—situate as *we* are; entangled every limb and power o' us, in that weary loom."

"And how do you know that we are not equally entangled—Reckon ye for nought all our mills, machinery, goods, debts; binding us hand and foot as firmly as the necessity of daily supplying the daily meal does you—character, capital and credit, are with us all at stake ;—ye should be considerate in your judgments of us, Andrew."

"Ay that they should; and that's what I aye tell them," put in Tibby.—" It would be wiser like, Andrew Howie, if you, that's a man of knowledge and experience, gave Mr. William a gude advice." Tibby had unlimited faith in the wisdom of her head.

"Then I could caution you masters, sir, how ye build mair mills, and machinery; though we may have a spurt of better trade shortly."

"And try ye, Andrew, and advise your neighbours to make at least three out of every five of their boys, some other trade than weavers, though brisk times should come."

"We must have down the peck too, sir—and that shortly; but how are we to keep it down if ye go on at this same rate,—ye may cover all the hills in America, with Paisley shawls, and the plains of India with ginghams and mull muslins, and hang yarns on ilka buss o' the wilderness; but what the better would we be?—Cheap bread itself, the blessing we are all craving, will last but for a short time, if we manage no a' the better. If by underselling, and over-producing, we learn the agriculturist, by small degrees, to get six ells for his bushel instead o' three, what the richer, better fed I mean, will us poor operatives be, in the long run? Till we can make the field yield its increase as rapidly as the machine does its products, or limit those products, it makes little odds whether the loaf is nominally a 6d. or a 1s. It will still be aboon our hand."

"Na, Andrew Howie, ye are surely gaen clean daft now!" cried Tibby. " My certes! a sixpence or a shilling! There's an unco odds."

Andrew looked from his half-closed eyelids with a sort of pitying contempt of the weaker vessel, which was irresistible to Mr. Mathewson, low as his spirits were; laughing heartily, he declared that Tibby had the best of it.

Her delight was complete, and Andrew himself was much gratified when rising, the manufacturer requested his old fosterer to cook for him the well remembered supper of his simple childhood, the only dish he could now fancy for his early rural supper.

"Sowens! Sowens!" cried Tibby, with glowing eyes— " eh, sir! and do ye think ye could sup sowens yet! at weel ye'se no want them." Mr. Mathewson believed he was thus undegenerate,—Master Manufacturer, and great Cotton Lord, as he had so long been.

Andrew putting on his night-cap to ward off the night air, and still carrying his printed documents, convoyed the visiter to the end of the village, adding " line upon line." "That's Mathewson the great manufacturer," was whispered among the lounging groups in the village street. " He's had great losses lately they say, and is come out here to seek his health. I'll wager Andrew Howie has been gi'in him a hecklin.—I see it in Andrew's eyne." Nor could Andrew, beset by friends on his return, deny the honourable impeachment. " It will be twa days, lads, ere Mr. William, say again, *man* and *master* meet on equal terms in this country." But we leave Andrew to the glory of fighting his battle over again, till Tibby had three times summoned him to his water-gruel supper.

If any courteous reader shall imagine that in ANDREW HOWIE, he recognizes an old acquaintance, we trust that be will like our hero none the worse for such recollection of another honest man.

PETER JONES'S OPINION OF ENGLISH MANNERS.

The following extracts, from a letter written by Peter Jones, whose original name was Kahkewaquonaby, a chief of the Chippeway Indians in British America, to the editor of the Christain Guardian newspaper, published in Canada, will be perused with interest and amusement by many of our readers. They will perceive from this reverberating echo of his sentiments, the estimation in which we are held by this unsophisticated observer of English manners and modes of life:—

"London, England, Dec. 30th, 1831.

"My Dear Brother,—I take up my pen for the purpose of sending you a little *paper talk*, that you may know how I am, and what I have seen in this land of light. I am happy to inform you that my health is much improved since I wrote to you last, for which I desire to thank our Heavenly Father, from whom cometh every good and perfect gift. I rejoice also to state, that my soul still follows hard after the Good Spirit, in whose service I find much joy and comfort in my heart, while wandering in a foreign land, and in the midst of strangers—strangers they are in one sense, but brothers and sisters in Christ, for such they have been to me ever since I landed upon their shores.

"I have visited many cities and towns in this country, for the purpose of attending missionary meetings; and I am happy to say, that all who love the Lord Jesus Christ have received me and my talk with open arms, and their hearts have been made very glad when they heard of the conversion of my poor perishing countrymen in the woods of Canada.

"The British and Foreign Bible Society have printed a thousand copies of the translation of the Gospel of St. John into the Chippeway language, which will be forwarded to Canada early in the spring. I have made arrangements with this Society to proceed on in translating the Gospel of St. Luke, the Acts, and some of the Epistles, into the Chippeway.

"I have thought you would be glad to hear my remarks, as an Indian traveller, on the customs and manners of the English people, and therefore send you the following brief remarks made from actual observation:—The English in general are a noble, generous-minded people—free to act, and free to think—they pride themselves very much in their civil and religious privileges, in their learning, generosity, manufactures, and commerce, and they think that no other nation is equal to them in respect to these things. I have found them very open and friendly, always ready to relieve the wants of the poor and needy when properly brought before them. No nation, I think, can be more fond of novelties or new things than the English are; they will gaze and look upon a foreigner as if he had just dropped down from the moon; and I have often been amused in seeing what a large number of people, a monkey riding upon a dog will collect in the streets of London, where such things may be seen almost every day. When my Indian name, (Kahkewaquonaby) is announced to attend any public meeting, so great is their curiosity, that the place is always sure to be filled; and it would be the same if notice was given that a man with his toes in his mouth, would address a congregation in such a place and on such a day; the place without fail would be filled with English hearers. They are truly industrious, and in general very honest and upright in their dealings. Their close attention to business, I think, rather carries them too much to a worldly-mindedness, and hence many forget to think about their souls and their God, and are entirely swallowed up in the cares of the world: their motto seems to be, 'Money, money, get money—get rich and be a gentleman.' With this sentiment they all fly about in every direction like a swarm of bees in search of that treasure which lies so near their hearts. This remark refers more particularly to the men of the world, and of such there are not a few. The English are very fond of good living, and many who live on roasted beef, plum-pudding, and turtle-soup, get very fat and round as a toad. Roasted beef to an Englishman is as sweet as bear's meat to an old Indian hunter, and plum-pudding as a beaver's tail.

"They eat four times a-day: breakfast at eight or nine in the morning, which consists of coffee or tea, with bread and butter, and sometimes a little fried bacon, fish, or eggs; dinner at about two p. m., when every thing that is good and strong is spread before the eater, and winds up with fruit, nuts, and a few glasses of wine; tea at six in the evening, with bread and butter, and sometimes a little sweet cakes. Supper at about nine or ten, when the leavings of the dinner again make their appearance, and upon which John Bull makes a sound, hearty meal to go to bed upon at midnight. The fashion in dress varies and changes so often that I am unable to describe it—I will only say, that the ladies of fashion wear very curious bonnets, which look something like a farmer's scoop shovel; and when they walk in the tiptoe style, they put me in mind of the little snipes that run along the shores of the lakes and rivers in Canada. They also wear sleeves as big as bushel bags, which make them appear as if they had three bodies with one head. Yet with all their big bonnets and sleeves, the English ladies, I think, are the best of women.

"If you should see any of my Indian brethren, I would thank you to tell them that I pray for them every day, that the Great Spirit through Christ may keep them in the good way. I often have longing desires to be in the midst of my friends and brethren in Upper Canada. We expect to leave England for America about the month of May next."

When the above letter was written, it is scarcely probable that Mr. Jones had any idea of its ever being returned to England in print, before he bade adieu to this country. It is therefore just to infer, that in this epistle his real and unvarnished sentiments are fairly expressed. At many public meetings, the editor has heard him with much pleasure; and perhaps few speakers ever excited, in a listening audience, a more intense or lively interest. The time of his departure, we apprehend, is now nearly at hand; but we feel assured, that when the intervention of the Atlantic shall separate him from our view, he will be remembered with the utmost respect by the multitudes whom he delighted with his talk.—*Imperial Magazine.*

THE COMPOSITOR.

Let not the compositor be confounded with the printer or pressman. These two agents of a most marvellous art, are separated by an immense interval in typographical importance. The one presides over the first transformation which speech undergoes—the other only directs the machine, which repeats it in a thousand echoes. Mechanism already begins to deprive the latter of his occupation; without his assistance the ink is now spread over the types; without his aid the paper is placed upon the form, slid under the press, and given forth, by the mute instrument, with the stamp of thought and the voice of genius. Thus the pressman finds his department invaded by a workman more laborious than himself, and not, like him, subject to hunger, fatigue, and sleep. The compositor is beyond such competition; he may defy the power of matter to supply the place of his intellectual activity. There can exist no subtle combination of springs and wheels to enable the fingers of an automaton to seize the characters which correspond with the written word, and arrange them in a composing stick; for, to do this, the automaton must be able to read. See the compositor in action, his eyes fixed upon the manuscript, and scarcely paying attention to the motion of his fingers—and you readily infer, from the intelligence of his look, and the expression of his countenance, that in him the mind alone is at work, whilst his right hand, which goes from the case to the composing stick and back again to the case, seems but to follow the poise of his body. To read well is a very important part of the compositor's duties, and is the more difficult, because the literati and men of science who intrust their works to him, neglect, for the most part, to write legibly. I speak not here of those who leave to him the care of punctuation, sometimes even that of correcting their violations of grammar and orthography. What service does he not render to ungraceful authors, who repay them in calumny, and impose upon him in their *errata* the responsibility of their own blunders, which they term typographical errors, or negligence of the corrector? If his vanity had likewise the resource of *errata*, how many correct sentences might he not claim, substituted in the proof for the original solecism? It may readily be imagined, that the compositor must come to his first apprenticeship in typography, with a mind stored with all the elementary knowledge necessary for any literary profession. He must be grammatically acquainted with his own language, and, according to the kind of work, be has to do, must be conversant with, at least, the nomenclature of the science treated of in the manuscript before him. More than one compositor, it is true, has learned whilst composing, as more than one author has done whilst writing. A printing-office is a school of universal knowledge; it was there Beranger felt the first throb of poetic inspiration, and he learned orthography in the exercise of a calling which was the first occupation of Franklin. Such are the general outlines of a compositor's life; but in this calling, as in every other, there are exceptions and individualities. I could name the man who reads his manuscript without understanding it, without seizing the idea expressed by the characters which his fingers have assembled, like the tapestry workmen at the Gobelins, who does not see the masterpiece he is producing. I could indicate another whom I could vouch for as prudent, economical, and of regular habits—he is upwards of thirty, and has a wife and children: he is preparing to become a corrector and foreman.—*Translation from the French, in the Athenæum.*

COLUMN FOR THE LADIES.

THE CONVENT AT YORK.

Many of our fair readers are probably acquainted with the fact that a Convent with a Lady Abbess, and a numerous sisterhood of Nuns, exists in the heart of England, and that the conventual regulations are as strictly observed, and the fair votaries as much secluded from the world, as in romantic Italy—or more Catholic Spain. Near the Micklegate Bar, in the ancient city of York, stands a large mansion, which has for many years been occupied by those religious ladies. An old gentleman, a friend of the writer's, who had a young girl consigned to his protection by her parents on the Continent, wished to place her in this establishment, and for that purpose waited upon the Abbess, who is styled the Rev. Mother by the community.—Being a Catholic of good family, he was readily admitted, and fortunately for the curiosity of our readers, we were permitted to accompany him.

The Superior's parlour is a handsome apartment, hung with pictures by various foreign masters, but scarcely had we time to examine them before she made her appearance. It is impossible to convey to our readers the impression which this elegant woman made when we first beheld her in her monastic habit; the costume was so picturesque though simple, that we could fancy ourselves removed, at least, three centuries back, when the cowl of the Friar and the veil of the Nun were as common in merry England, as buff and jerkin; a full flowing dress of black cloth quilted round the waist, gave an air of dignity to her person; her face was shrouded in the close white cap, which comes down over the brow and is continued round the chin, something like that worn by widows, and over her head hung the ample black veil of the order,—a rosary of beads and a cross completed the picture. With the easy dignity of one who had mingled with the world, she returned our salutations, and entered at once into the subject of the interview. From my friend's letters of introduction and well-known connexions, little hesitation was made, terms satisfactory to both parties were arranged, and in reply to some questions, relative to the regulations of the establishment, the Abbess invited us to visit the different schools, chapel, and buildings of the Convent. The first apartment into which we were shown was the dining-room, which adjoins the kitchen, and the food is conveyed by means of the turning board so common in religious houses on the Continent; by this means all intercourse between the pupils and servants is avoided. The girls are divided into four classes, each under its superintendent; when we entered the different rooms, the nuns and children stood up to receive us, while some opening large folding doors at the extreme end of the apartment discovered an oratory; each room in this respect being furnished alike. Amongst the number of children presented to us, was a niece of Cardinal Weld, and several Spanish girls, whose parents had been driven from their own country by the political disturbances of the times.—The chapel, to which we were next conducted, is a building of elegant proportions, neatly fitted up for the purpose of devotion. Its prevailing colours are white and gold; the altar is plain, but ornamented by a valuable painting. Here again our imaginations were powerfully appealed to—the greater part of the sisterhood were assembled at their devotions, and knelt in rows before the altar, as fixed and unmoved as statues; amongst them was a beautiful girl, of eighteen, who had just commenced her noviciate; her plain white dress, contrasted with the sombre black garb of the nuns, produced a curious effect. The Abbess informed us that the sum presented to the establishment, on a nun's taking the veil, was six hundred pounds, which went towards the fund for their general support. The exercise ground, which lies at the back of the establishment, adjoins the burial place; both are unfortunately overlooked by the old city wall, and many persons frequently assemble to watch them taking their mid-day walk. The burial ground resembles a garden more than a spot set aside for the interment of the dead; the graves are marked by stones—those of the superiors by a cross. There is attached to this retired spot, an oratory, exquisitely fitted up. Here the sisterhood may indulge in their contemplations of the past, or breathe their hopes for the future. The writer and his friend took their leave of the worthy Abbess with feelings of respect for her unaffected piety and politeness, and could not avoid expressing regret that one, whose manners appeared so calculated to form all that was amiable in domestic life, should voluntarily have retired from it.

LORD AND LADY CONYNGHAM.—Lady Conyngham, since become so celebrated in England, was then in the full bloom of her charms. In this respect, she was entitled to a brilliant reputation; but, I confess, I could never admire beauty so totally devoid of expression. I am not surprised at the Venus de Medicis not returning my smile, because she is a statue, and nothing but marble; but when I approach a beautiful woman, I expect a look and expression of animated nature. This was not to be found in Lady Conyngham. She was very elegant, took great care of her beauty, dressed well, and carried the care of her person so far as to remain in bed the whole day until she dressed to go to a ball. She was of opinion that this preserved the freshness of her complexion, which she said was always more brilliant when she did not rise till nine at night. She was a beautiful idol, and nothing more. Lord Conyngham, her husband, might be called ugly. The Duchess of Gordon, who, in her frightful language, sometimes uttered smart things, said of Lord Conyngham, that he was like a comb, all teeth and back.—*Memoirs of the Duchess of Abrantes, lately Published.*

A PERTINENT QUESTION.—A little girl, on hearing her mamma say she intended changing her dress for half-mourning, replied, looking up in her face with great archness, "Pray, dear Ma, are any of your relations *half dead?*"

GLENCO.—Of the many romantic valleys which wind among the rugged and tempest-beaten mountains of Scotland, there is none, excepting Coruisk in Skye, that can vie with Glenco. Entering it from the dreary moor on which the King's house is situated, the traveller is struck with astonishment and awe as the great mountain masses, which form the southern side, burst successively upon his view. As he advances, new objects of admiration present themselves in the vast ravines between the huge cliffs down which the torrents are seen pouring with headlong impetuosity, the varying appearance of the tremendous dark rocks rent and shattered by the convulsions of nature, and the broken and jagged summits of the mountains rising among the mists to the height of 3000 feet. The northern side is less irregular, being a continuous ridge of deeply fissured and broken rock, from whose chasms the winter torrents have swept thousands of fragments, which lie heaped at the base of the rocks, and along the sides of the diminutive rills which, in summer, mark the place of the impetuous streams which are collected from the rains of winter. At the base of a lofty mountain which rises in broken precipices to a height of several thousand feet, and in the bottom of the glen is a lake of clear water; and near it is the little green pasturage which this scene of sterile grandeur affords. Considered individually, this part, which may be called the upper valley, is inferior in grandeur to none in Britain. Coruisk, in the bosom of the Cuillin mountains in Skye, a scene less known, because more remote, and in a very secluded situation, is the only rival of Glenco. Passing the lake in the latter, the traveller finds the valley continued in an easterly direction, nearly at a right angle to the upper glen. Here the scenery is changed. The mountains are less majestic, and several of them are covered with verdure. Woods, corn fields, pastures, and huts are seen along the course of the wild stream that flows from the lake. Further on Loch Leven, an arm of the sea, but joining to the advantage of having a direct communication with the ocean, many of the agreeable qualities of a fresh water lake, comes into view. Here again new scenes present themselves; villages, woods, and fields, the whole enlivened by the busy hands occupied in the slate quarries, and the appearance of a vessel or two in the loch. The latter has a very narrow outlet, and the tide rushes through it with such impetuosity, that at Ballychulish, the ferrying place, one fancies himself on the banks of a large and rapid river.

COLUMN FOR THE YOUNG.

It is with a feeling of deep awe and reverence that we, in the passing week, select our lesson for the young from the works of Sir Walter Scott.

THE LAST JUDGMENT.

That day of wrath, that dreadful day,
When heaven and earth shall pass away,
What power shall be the sinner's stay?
How shall he meet that dreadful day?
When, shrivelling like a parched scroll,
The flaming heavens together roll;
When louder yet, and yet more dread,
Swells the high trump that wakes the dead!

Oh! on that day, that wrathful day,
When man to judgment wakes from clay,
Be God the trembling sinner's stay,
Though heaven and earth shall pass away.

TIME.

"Why sitt'st thou by that ruin'd hall,
Thou aged carle so stern and grey?
Dost thou its former pride recall,
Or ponder how it passed away?"—

"Know'st thou not me!" the deep voice cried;
So long enjoyed, so oft misused—
Alternate, in thy fickle pride,
Desired, neglected, and accused?

"Before my breath, like blazing flax,
Man and his marvels pass away;
And changing empires wane and wax,
Are founded, flourish, and decay.

"Redeem mine hours—the space is brief—
While in my glass the sand-grains shiver,
And measureless thy joy or grief,
When Time and thou shalt part for ever!"

SCRAPS.
Original and Selected.

POLITICAL CONTEMPT.—Or in other words, political ridicule, is a compensation which the powerful leave to the weak. It is like the wooden sword of harlequin—used with vigour and wielded with force; but the blows make a great noise and do little injury; he upon whom they fall, is scarcely aware that he is struck.

DILATORY AND OVER CAREFUL PEOPLE.—It is loss in business to be too full of respects, or to be too curious in observing times and opportunities. Solomon saith, "He that considereth the wind shall not sow, and he that looketh to the clouds shall not reap." A wise man will make more opportunities than he finds. Men's behaviour should be like their apparel; not too strait or point device, but free for exercise or motion.

CHOLERA.—Bassora, which is situated at the Persian Gulf, on the River Uphrates, and contains about 60,000 inhabitants, is the great market for Asiatic produce destined for the Ottoman empire. The cholera lasted fourteen days in this city, in which time it carried off from 15,000 to 18,000 persons, or nearly one-fourth of the inhabitants. From Bassora it was carried by the boats navigating the Tigris, as far as Bagdad, and there it destroyed one-third of the population.

A pilgrim, says the fable, met the plague going into Smyrna. What are you going for?—To kill three thousand people answered the plague. Some time after they met again. But you killed thirty thousand says the pilgrim. No! answered the plague, I killed three thousand—*it was fear killed the rest.*

SALARY OF THE CHANCELLOR 700 YEARS SINCE.—The salary of the Chancellor, as fixed by Henry I., amounted to 5s. per diem, and a livery of provisions.—*Mirror.*

EXTRAORDINARY SEDUCTION.—The *Morning Post* of Friday contains the following extraordinary piece of intelligence: "The Duchess of Kent, with her suite, were seduced to remain a whole day at Llangollen, in consequence of George Robins's sale of Lady Eleanor Butler and Miss Ponsonby being in progress." (Any stranger to the circumstances would naturally infer that her Royal Highness felt a desire to purchase one or both of the above-mentioned ladies, and that George Robins was commissioned to knock them down instead of their collection of curiosities.)

A GOOD REASON.—"What is the reason," asked a junior on Circuit the other day of Charles Phillips, "that delicate, modest, and sensitive women will allow themselves to be brought forward as evidence in actions for breach of promise of marriage, seduction, &c.?" "'Pon my conscience, I can't say," said Sir Charles, "unless they mean to shew how much they wish to bring their quondam sweethearts into *Court* again."

BENTHAM.—The *Edinburgh Review*, talking of Bentham and the parties of flatterers and detractors which he had during his life time, says—"He will now have judges—posterity will pronounce its calm and impartial decision; and that decision will, we firmly believe, place in the same rank with Galileo and Locke, the man who had found jurisprudence a gibberish, and left it a science."

FALL OF THE WIGS.—It is a curious fact, that, except York and Canterbury, not one of the Bishops at present wears a wig—all walk about *incog.* Ravenscroft, of Lincoln's Inn, London, the principal wig-maker, said the other day, that he had lost half his business, he having hitherto made wigs for all the Bishops. Poor Ravenscroft is, of course, a Tory, and may be excused, for, unlike some *other barbers*, he honestly confesses his motives, and very naturally hates a *Wig Reform?*

STORY TOLD BY LUTHER.—A monk who had introduced himself to the bedside of a dying Nobleman, who was at that time in a state of insensibility, continued crying out, "My Lord, will you make the grant of such and such a thing to our monastery?" The sick man, unable to speak, nodded his head. The monk turned round to the son, "You see, Sir, that my Lord your father gives his consent to my request." The son immediately exclaimed, "Father, is it your will that I should kick this monk down stairs?" The usual nod was given. The young man immediately rewarded the assiduities of the monk by sending him with great precipitation out of the house.

M. de Lennox of Paris, who failed in a former attempt to inflate a colossal balloon in the form of a whale, succeeded lately in filling one of somewhat smaller dimensions, and ascended, accompanied by Mad. de Lennox and M. Berrier, a physician. They were furnished with oars of a peculiar construction, with a view of making an experiment as to the possibility of directing the balloon in its course through the air. The ascent was at first made with difficulty, but after some of the ballast was thrown out it became more rapid and gained a very high elevation, passing over Paris in a southern direction.

BESIDES appearing in WEEKLY NUMBERS, the SCHOOLMASTER is published in MONTHLY PARTS, which, stitched in a neat cover, will contain as much letter-press, of good execution, as any of the large Monthly Periodicals: A Table of Contents will be given at the end of the year; when, *at the weekly cost of three-halfpence*, a handsome volume of 832 pages, super-royal size, may be bound up, containing much matter worthy of preservation.

PART I. for August, containing the first four Numbers, with JOHNSTONE'S MONTHLY REGISTER, may now be had of the Booksellers, and dealers in cheap Periodicals.

TO CORRESPONDENTS.

We have received several communications which will be attended to.

CONTENTS OF NO. VIII.

HOLYDAY RAMBLES ROUND EDINBURGH. No. III.—Crichton Castle—The Vale of Borthwick—by the Railway.....................113
Presbyterian Notion of a Bishop................................115
On the Moral Training of Children.............................116
EMIGRATION—United States; Canada............................117
MEDICAL SELECTIONS.—Effects of Different Professions and Trades on Health—Contagious and Epidemic Diseases.........118
ELEMENTS OF THOUGHT.—Distinction of Classes injurious to Virtue—The Moral Sense—Strength of Mind—Testimony of Rousseau to the Divine Perfection of the Character of the Saviour..........119
USEFUL NOTICES.—Steam Carriages, &c.........................120
Song of the Rhenish Provinces.................................120
THE STORY TELLER.—Andrew Howie, a Man of the West......121
Peter Jones' Opinion of English Manners; The Compositor.....126
COLUMN FOR LADIES.—The Convent at York; Glenco, &c.......127
COLUMN FOR THE YOUNG.—Last Judgment; Time..............128
SCRAPS.—Political Contempt; Cholera, &c.....................128

EDINBURGH: Printed by and for JOHN JOHNSTONE, 19, St. James's Square.—Published by JOHN ANDERSON, Jun., Bookseller, 55, North Bridge Street, Edinburgh; by JOHN MACLEOD, and ATKINSON & Co., Booksellers, Glasgow; and sold by all Booksellers and Venders of Cheap Periodicals.

THE Schoolmaster,
AND
EDINBURGH WEEKLY MAGAZINE.

CONDUCTED BY JOHN JOHNSTONE.

THE SCHOOLMASTER IS ABROAD.—LORD BROUGHAM.

No. 9.—Vol. I. SATURDAY, SEPTEMBER 29, 1832. Price Three-Halfpence.

DEATH OF SIR WALTER SCOTT.

Sir Walter Scott died at Abbotsford, on the afternoon of Friday the 21st curt., about half-past one o'clock. No form of words could express our deep and emphatic sense of the event we are called upon to announce—and we employ the simplest. It was the will of God that the spark of the Divine Essence should return whence it had emanated,—and a painful preparation had taught us all to acquiesce. We do not lament Sir Walter Scott's decease. The Great—the Good—the Gifted, is taken from us only when it was no longer desirable that the ruined earthy tenement should imprison its immortal tenant. We forbear dwelling upon the few trifling details that have reached us.—The event itself comprehends all. Amidst the homage and regret of millions he passes from our Earth, who never had an enemy on its surface. No death that can befal, not in our country alone, but in the whole civilized world, could be so universally felt. Kings may bow their heads, and Mighty men pass away unregarded, if not unnoticed; but the death of Sir Walter Scott comes strongly home to the sympathies of every Human being that ever heard of his name, and understood but the least part of what that immortal name signified. Such are the claims and the triumphs of Genius, when united as in his instance, with the finest spirit of humanity that ever attempered human clay, and made goodness visible.

ON THE POLITICAL TENDENCY OF SIR WALTER SCOTT'S WRITINGS.

In this brief notice, we neither intend to write history, nor criticise the works of Sir Walter Scott, neither to indulge in laudation nor gossip. His works are in every man's hands; and if ever there was an author who needed no commentator, so dangerous to interpret between him and the human heart, it is the author of *Waverley*. All the tongues and tribes of Europe at once understood his broadest Scotch, because it spoke of things which were common to all, long before the confusion of Babel. His life, like his character, was simple and open; and, until it shall be written by one of three persons whom we shall name, there is little can be known which curiosity or impertinence has not dragged to light a thousand times already. These three gentlemen are, Sir Walter's son-in-law, Mr Lockhart; his Secretary, Mr William Laidlaw, his intimate friend from before the time that his genius dawned upon the world till his eyes were closed; and Mr James Ballantyne, also his friend from schoolboy days, and his literary associate through life. We can receive no acceptable life of the author of the Waverley novels save from one or all of these gentlemen; until some master-mind shall arise, who, commanding all the lesser lights which they shall bring to bear on one point, may, in the memoirs of Sir Walter Scott, embody the Philosophy of Humanity, and the spirit of our own national history, with that finer spirit, expansive as Life, and enduring as Time, which pervades all that he has written. If he has left memoirs of himself, that will be better than all. Dreading, therefore, the tattle, gossip, indelicacy, and obtrusiveness ready to be poured forth on this subject, and disliking all needless exhibition, even though made in an affectionate and reverential spirit, we shall not follow the example we deprecate, either in personal anecdote, in superficial criticism, or hackneyed laudation of works so universally familiarized, so deeply sunk and fast-rooted in the hearts of all readers. We propose a different task, which, however ill it may be performed, has at least the merit of honest purpose.

Convinced that in heart and mind, in principle and affection, and (with a few incidental and casual aberrations into which he was hurried or betrayed) in conduct also, this illustrious person belonged to no state party, we would fain redeem his venerable and beloved name from the political party which claims it—and sound to a Crusade which should " conquer his tomb from the infidels." If Shakspeare deserve the epithet of the myriad-minded, to Sir Walter Scott belongs that of the myriad-hearted; and, with this large natural character, it will not be difficult to shew that he essentially belonged to the *People*—to *Mankind*; and that the tendency of all his writings has been to enlighten and expand the minds of men, by enlarging their affections; by making them neither Whig nor Tory, but something infinitely better than both. Of the perpetual, and undeviating tendency of Sir WALTER SCOTT's writings, to exalt humanity at the expense of high *castes*, he may, and, we believe, often must have been unconscious. That signifies little. His mind was formed to sympathize with the true, the pure, and the noble; and the stream of truth bore him triumphantly onward, in spite of all the little eddies, and cross currents, and stones, and rubbish, which prejudice, and habit, and time, and circumstance, threw in his way. He could neither long resist, nor ever once conquer that power which struggled in his understanding, and triumphed in his heart, and made him what he is, always a *Liberal*, and often a *Radical* writer, differing only in shadows and modes from many who are avowedly so.

One sentence will suffice for narrative before we commence our task.

All the world knows that Sir WALTER SCOTT was born in Edinburgh, and received his learned and professional education there. The better part of his early education was gathered here and there, through all Scotland, in huts and halls; in ancient battle fields and at old covenanting stations; from gipsies at fairs, and Highland chieftains on their hills; from legendary Jacobite ladies, and grayhaired Cameronian farmers; from the rudest ballad, recording the exploits of the Border reaver, to the sublimity of the Hebrew Scriptures. No young mind ever fed on more varied elements, or turned them all to healthier aliment. The father of Sir WALTER was that well known character in Edinburgh, a W.S., and a thriving one. He was also a Whig and Presbyterian; but Whiggery was, in his young days, the thriving side. Like every other imaginative man, born in the last century, his son, Sir WALTER, was *poetically* a Jacobite. There was nothing remarkable about the Author of Waverley, as a youth, save a huge frame, great fondness for old stories and solitary rambling, modesty, and invincible good temper. How soon he began to pore on the musty and neglected volumes of the Advocates' and College Library, no one, save himself, could tell. But readers in the same track, and they alone, will often perceive to what felicitous use he has turned strange and apparently worthless materials. "Industry and patience," says the eastern proverb, "change the mulberry leaf to satin;" but it is industry and patience applied by a creature of peculiar and wonderful instincts.

The time in which the world opened upon Sir WALTER SCOTT was critical. His vivid youthful mind had just taken strong hold on the past, flitting rapidly away, with its long train of broken but gorgeous images, when the crash of the French Revolution opened the dark chasm, revealing the mighty *future*, and discovering the conflict already commenced between the old and the new order of things. His imagination, already occupied and filled with the past, has ever belonged to that period: his understanding stretching boldly forward into the *future*, is often seen sporting with the heraldic tags and silken fetters, which yet hung so lightly and gracefully about him, that no one wished to see him cast them off. This is nearly the key to the character of Sir WALTER SCOTT as a writer. Had he not in youth been previously a Jacobite, he would assuredly have been, with SOUTHEY and CAMPBELL, COLERIDGE and MOORE, a *Jacobin*, or at least a *Bonapartist*—which he half was at any rate, —until in manhood he had fallen back on that universal and catholic faith in which he lived and died, whatever little sect may think to number him as of its votaries. Sir WALTER SCOTT was in nothing precocious. Good sense and innate modesty preserved him in youth, as through life, from the manifold absurdities, pretensions, vanities, and presumptions of authorship. His first literary attempt was a translation from Goethe; this was followed by the *Border Minstrelsy*, in which, in the secondary rank of editor, he imped his wings for a bolder flight. The LAY OF THE LAST MINSTREL was decisive of his reputation. We shall not speak of the *sensation* it made, nor of the censure and praise, alike foolish, senseless, ignorant, or purely idiotical, that was heaped upon so "strange a poem." Sir WALTER SCOTT was by this time Sheriff of Selkirkshire, a married man, and by courtesy, and the ordinary understanding in these affairs, allied to the Tory or Dundas party in Scotland. His other poems followed in rapid succession; and his poetical reputation rose like "a rocket and fell like the stick." One can easily understand how *The Lay* and *The Lady of the Lake* should have been exceedingly popular; but only on the false principles of fashionable fame can we explain why *Rokeby* and the *Lord of the Isles* should have been decried or disregarded. The true key-note to which every breast must respond, had not yet been struck; and the *Town*, the ladies and gentlemen, had, in Lord Byron, found a newer and more attractive idol. In *Waverley* Sir WALTER SCOTT appealed to a more just tribunal,—to a wider and wiser audience. The true key-note was struck at last; accidentally it is said—and in this sense everything is accident.—But this is wandering from our specific purpose, which is to shew that the tendency of all the writings of this,—shall we say *soi-disant*—Tory, is *Liberal*. Shall we begin with his gallery of kings? The character of Charles I. is the very touchstone and shibboleth of an educated Tory. This Sir WALTER has evaded, though all true Tories, even when they have ostensibly given up the *jus divinum*, stickle here, and let out their rooted prepossessions most significantly when talking of this party idol. But how has Sir WALTER dealt with kings? He has prudently steered clear of all contemporary portraiture; but from what he has sketched, are we not warranted to believe, that a hundred years hence his picture of the luxurious, effeminate, cold, selfish, unloving and unloved George the Fourth, would have been as faithful to the true character of the man, as that which he has traced, in *Quentin Durward*, of that laughing hyena—the cruel, rapacious, superstitious, and basely deceitful Louis XI.; or, in *Ivanhoe*, of the weak, cowardly, perfidious, profligate, and despicable royal poltroon, Prince John. Need we instance that yet uglier blot on the escutcheons of monarchy, and truer portraiture of a modern king, the gossiping, prying, prating pedant—the buffoon and old wife conjoined—the uncouth, awkward, cowardly James,* who made king-craft as contemptible, as till then it had been hateful, and who certainly loses nothing in Sir WALTER SCOTT's hands. These, with the virago Elizabeth, and Queen Mary, to whom Sir WALTER perhaps does injustice, in representing her as a spiteful abigail, studying all pitiful and waspish means of petty annoyance, forgetting the self-respect due by a rational creature to herself, and laying aside the dignity ascribed to princes—these are the royal personages whose portraits this Tory writer, the imagined champion of his party, has drawn with astonishing accuracy and fidelity; and has bequeathed to the study and judgment of his countrymen, when they shall come to weigh the merits and demerits of monarchy. Has the railing of the most violent Radical, or the strongest arguments of Paine, struck a more fatal blow at monarchy than the popular narratives of Scott?

Let us turn to his *Peers*, to the *higher orders* generally, as they are depicted in his works. Is it on his masterly delineations of the cruel ambition of Leicester, the profligacy of Buckingham, the atrocity of Morton, the cunning brutality and utter baseness of Lauderdale, that we are to found our admiration of the aristocracy? Is there not one worthy, or honest, or strictly honourable man to be found in the living catalogue,—that Sir WALTER is forced to create, when he would picture a truly generous and patriotic nobleman, in histories embracing centuries? It did not suit Sir WALTER to meddle with "My Lords, the Bishops," and the Buck Parsons, as they have descended to our happy times; but we have in Friar Tuck and Prior Aylmer a fair prototype of the best among them—those who are least hypocrites. The Prior was "a free and jovial priest, who loved the wine-cup and the bugle-horn better than book or bell," and was as delicate a critic on the points of a fine damosel or a good horse, as any churchman that ever haunted Windsor Castle or the Pavilion, from 1825 to 1830. What a scene for the pen of Sir WALTER SCOTT, had he lived a century later, the sycophant, court-haunting churchmen, courtiers, and harridans of the latter years of the late reign!

The law, as a profession generally, at least as a profession in Scotland, is the butt of the constant sly hits and direct thrusts of this *universal leveller*. No man understood lawyers better; no one has described them, from the pettifogging attorney to the corrupt judge, with half the truth and severity, veiled, as it may be, under humour and jest. The mass of corruption, intrigue, selfish ambition, sycophancy, cruelty, arrogance, perfidy, and loathsome baseness which he has exposed among churchmen, but especially statesmen, in courts and cabinets, and among those that hang on or lurk in their purlieus, is sufficient to turn the world *Radical* without further argument. Nor has this Tory writer spared the Bench. The seat of justice is shewn to be the stronghold of oppression. We need not instance the monstrous iniquities of Lauderdale and his coadjutors, in the reign of Charles II., but let us contemplate the Scotch Judges in the *Bride of Lammermoor*. Was ever satire so keen as the truth we have here. The smooth, plausible, supple, wary, and calmly ambitious Lord Keeper, is, in part, a creation of fancy; but the originals of the other "reverend seniors" may be found in a less distant day. The parallel of *Turntippet*, shrewd, brutal, bigoted, and time-serving, may be found without looking farther back than that dark and foul period in the annals of the political justice of Scotland, with which the early manhood of Sir WALTER SCOTT was contemporary.

To the modern country gentry, the lower ranks of the rural aristocracy, and the worshipful members of the county quorum, he shows little more mercy. We have the ignorant and blackguard Balmawhapple, the shallow and pompous Sir Arthur Wardour, the ruffianly, blasphemous elder Dumbiedykes, and the half-idiot, harmless junior of that Ilk; the modern variety of Conservative *Goose* in Sir Robert Hazlewood of Hazlewood,* and the fierce, reckless, ruthless, turbulent Scottish baron in old Redgauntlet. As if such delineations of kings, peers, statesmen, judges, and gentry, were not enough, he has drawn nearly all his *noble* or perfect characters from the great storehouse of humanity, and from the basis classes. It is among them, the poor or the unregarded, that we are taught to look for shrewdness, intelligence, generosity, fidelity, disinterested attachment, religion that is not hypocrisy or mummery, and patriotism which is not ambition in flimsy disguise. We have from among the very offscourings of the degraded *castes*, spae-

* We have often wondered how a sensible Tory Lord Chamberlain could ever have licensed a play, which burlesques monarchy more egregiously than *Tom Thumb the Great*—as *Gentle King Jowie* is a real royal personage. This piece was exceedingly popular, solely from the grotesque figure, and absurd character of the King.

* How can we forget his speech,—or that inimitable scene between the Conservative Baronet and Mr. Gilbert Glossin. "These are dreadful days, indeed, my worthy neighbour; days when the bulwarks of society are shaken to their mighty base; and that rank which forms, as it were, its highest grace and ornament, is mingled and confused with the viler part of the architecture. O, my good Mr. Gilbert Glossin! in my time, sir, &c. &c. But now, sir, the clouted shoe of the peasant galls the kibe of the courtier. The lower ranks, sir, have their quarrels, sir, and their points of honour, and their revenges, &c. &c. But well, well, it will last my time!" This we call the best refutation of Burke's Alarm that ever was written. There are still better things of this sort in the *Antiquary*, among the town-council of Fair-Port.

wives and gaberlunzies, who, by the grandeur of their elementary character, their generosity, eloquence, and enthusiasm, make gentles and nobles look small in the comparison. There is no need to run over the catalogue of poor schoolmasters, post-boys, fish-wives, idiots, and such? tag-rag, whose prepossessing qualities, steady, virtues, and redeeming points, it is the study and delight of this truthful writer to bring out. We might travel over all these novels one by one for proofs of our assertion.—Who, for example, is the hero—the really noble fellow of *Guy Mannering?*—Dandy Dinmont for certain, the princely yeoman of Liddisdale,—the frank, loyal, brave, and generous. In this work even poor Dominie Sampson, though his wits are always wool-gathering, is surely a very superior being to his patron, the worthy and far-descended successor of the Bold Bertrams; and with Meg Merrilies, the " commoner of air," and gipsy vagrant, what fine lady shall cope withal?—If Sir WALTER SCOTT has gone to his grave in the belief that he is a Tory writer, no man was ever the dupe of so gross self-delusion. Where next shall we look for proofs of Toryism? In *Old Mortality*, where we have worthy Tory Lady Bellenden, with her high-flown and fantastic loyalty, and her " Throne," contrasted with the old blind widow, sitting, like her of Zareptha, alone by the wayside, to warn the people of God from the snares of the oppressor,—she who had seen both her sons fall in defence of the purity of the Church of Christ, and of the independence of Scotland,—she, from whose aged eyes, dazzled by the flash of the shot which struck down her last child, light had gradually faded, yet who possessed her soul in patience, sustained by the love and the hope of that Cause in which her all had perished. If all this be evidence of Toryism, it is the Toryism after our own hearts. Here, too, we have honest Mause Headrigg, " that precious woman," who, with her really noble sentiments and inflexible principles, requires only a Spartan name, and a little better keeping, to equal in dignity a Spartan matron. We smile at Don Quixote, and the Baron of Bradwardine, even while we dearly love their persons, and feel their enthusiasm. But the illusions of chivalry, and loyalty, and feudalism, are naught, weighed in the balance against the high spirit of Covenanted Scotland;—and we are prouder of our country, that in her hour of trial and peril, she could send a *Mause Headrigg* from the cot-house to " testify," than a *Vich Ian Vhor* from his halls, to draw his sword for his Prince. It had not been given to any writer to conceive the character of Mause Headrigg, had its nobler points, and the nobler points of his land's history, not deeply touched his own heart. One may blamelessly laugh at our favourite Mause, as one does at the humorous absurdities of a venerated grandmother, or dearest old aunt; but they must be of cold or shallow natures who can only laugh, and never once rise to sympathy with her heroic patriotism and sustaining faith, conquering the strongest affections of nature, in obedience to an ennobling sense of duty, and sending forth, and exhorting her beloved Cuddie, " to fight the good fight, to remain faithful unto the death, and not to sully his wedding garment." We have lingered too long on Mause, who has undeservedly,. as we think, drawn much censure on him who presented her to us. This censure is ridiculous and overstrained. The Tory party have quite as much reason to resent Lady Bellenden as the old Whigs have to think Mause Headrigg a burlesque.

It would be idle to run through all Sir WALTER SCOTT's characters. Take Jeanie Deans, the simple sublime of moral virtue,—or her father; and which of all the great personages delineated in these works, will, in the qualities which, when driven to the wall, all men acknowledge to be the alone sterling and enduring—which will take place before David Deans, the cow-feeder of St. Leonards? We remember when the *Heart of Mid-Lothian* appeared, of an Edinburgh lady, a great admirer of Sir WALTER SCOTT—as who was not—an excellent and sensible person besides, saying, with much appearance of grief and disappointment—and of real disgust too, " He is at these *low creatures* again—cow-feeders!" Now *cow-feeder* was the last step of low life then, when we had very few *Irish* helots among us; and in *Guy Mannering*, Sir WALTER had recently given " proper people" serious alarm about vulgarity and a grovelling taste. It is not quite certain if some of these *low* propensities smelt altogether sweetly in the nostrils of the Edinburgh Review. Many of its Whig disciples loathed them, and would have been at some loss to settle whether Dandy Dinmont and Davy Deans were entitled to the honour of dining at ————.

But how, asks the reader, could Sir WALTER SCOTT, if a *Radical* or levelling writer, be so very popular with the Tories? Why, many of the nominal or accidental adherents of that party were no more Tories *in grain* than Sir WALTER himself. Others, like those of the higher nobility of France, who, up to the Revolution, countenanced and supported the more distinguished individuals among the men of letters—the economists and philosophers—from the spirit of contradiction, thought it all a good joke. Dandy Dinmont and Bailie Jarvie were capital, honest fellows—to laugh at; and Jeanie Deans was " a good creature," and really deserved the patronage of the Duke of Argyle; but that such scenes and characters did more to spread true *Liberalism* (that which has its foundation in sound moral sentiment, and pure and warm affections) than the most elaborate discourses of the Whig teachers, no one ever dreamed.

If we shall ever have any opportunity to resume this subject, it shall be, with the moral tendency of Sir WALTER SCOTT's writings. In an age prone to deep and vehement emotion, arising from whatever polluted source; and surrounded by popular writers, whose pleasure and pride it was to awaken false and dangerous sympathies, *his* works, without the slightest exception, and with perfect contempt of cant, prudery and false delicacy, have been *safe*, corrective, or directly stimulative of all manly virtues and qualities:—to women they have throughout been ennobling! And here, in concluding this rambling article, it may be remarked, in proof of our original position, that Sir WALTER's heroines are all Revolutionists, or in the Opposition. *Flora MacIvor* wishes to overturn the Hanoverian line. *Minna Troil* is bewildered into a dangerous maze, by a grand but visionary scheme of revolutionizing the isles of Zetland. *Edith Bellenden* is in love with a fugitive leader of the party of the Covenant. *Rebecca*, the high-souled Jewess, is the alone, and eloquent, and bold defender of her oppressed race, against the rapacious and dissolute aristocracy of that dark and tyrannical age.

SIR WALTER SCOTT'S CHILDHOOD.

The following interesting particulars have just reached us from a source which guarantees their authenticity:—

The Grandfather of SIR WALTER SCOTT was ROBERT SCOTT,* a distant relation of SCOTT of Harden, from whom he held the farm of Sandy Knowe, a short distance from the family residence, Mertoun House, in Berwickshire. He was a man of singular activity and energy, and was highly respected; and held, beside Sandy Knowe, large sheep farms in Eskdale. His son WALTER, was bred a Writer to the Signet. Sir WALTER SCOTT was born in George's Square. He was a very weak, puny child, and, owing to a fall from his keeper's arms, became lame. His mother was a daughter of the celebrated Dr. RUTHERFORD, Physician in Edinburgh, and his great-grandfather, the Doctor's father, was minister of Yarrow, and died there in 1707. Sir WALTER was sent to reside at Sandy Knowe with his grandfather, with very small hopes of his recovery. He used to be carried out in a fine day, and laid on a plaid on the brae, that he might enjoy the air and the sun. The view from this situation is one of the finest—

> The Lady sat in mournful mood,
> Looked over hill and dale;
> O'er Tweed's fair flood, and Mertoun's wood,
> And all down Teviotdale.

The boy was now under the watchful care of a maiden aunt,† who used to sing old ballads to sooth him to sleep in his illness, and to amuse him in the confinement unsuitable to his infant years.

When he was fit to attend school, he resided for some time with his uncle, Capt. ROBERT SCOTT, at Rosebank, close by Kelso; and there JAMES and JOHN BALLANTYNE were among his companions.

When he had gained sufficient health to be trusted at the High School, he was brought to Edinburgh; but he spent his vacations always with his grandfather at Sandy Knowe, or at Rosebank with his uncle.

There was hardly a sheep farmer in Teviotdale, Liddisdale, or Selkirkshire, in whose house he had not been at one time or other a most welcome guest.

* Many of our readers will recollect an incidental notice of this "grandsire" in Marmion, which contains frequent allusions to the author's boyhood.
† His aunt Jenny, whom he held in tender and grateful remembrance.

I cannot help saying, that the ruling *trait* in Sir WALTER SCOTT's character was his great benevolence and kindheartedness, not only towards all around him, but to every living thing, of which many beautiful instances could be given. Nothing could induce him to give way to angry or unpleasant feelings towards any of his neighbours.

It may be right to inform some of our readers that Sir WALTER SCOTT, who was born on the 15th August, 1771, died in his sixty-second year; and that his death was caused by a paralytic affection, and probably hastened by anxiety of mind, and the fatigue of foreign travel in pursuit of health. He had been for several years a widower, and has left two sons and two daughters.

MORAL AND PHYSICAL CONDITION OF THE MIDDLE AND LOWER CLASSES.

BY A BENTHAMITE.

UNDER similar titles, in a recent number, you favoured the public with two valuable extracts on the above subject; and without detracting from the merit or philanthropy of such endeavours, it is much to be lamented, no *popular* information is anywhere to be had on the subject of their intellectual disease; the which, in truth, is the prime cause of nearly all disease. This is also chargeable upon the true pabulum of its health being withheld—a due supply of that mental aliment so profusely everywhere spread around us, evidently designed by nature as food for the constitution of the mind. By the title of this article I mean the *labouring* parts of the professions. These may more properly be briefly treated of separately.

For the most part, lads who go to shop-keeping as apprentices, are the children of those in the most difficult sphere of life—in that grade where respectable appearance is considered indispensable from the society in which the parents necessarily mix, where "a decent outside" must be supported, in deference to the ruinous, though current policy of concealing narrow circumstances, by a forced appearance of means. Doubtless there are others, but this class forms a large majority; and, as may be naturally supposed, the pressure of this vulgar error, with which gentility is attempted to be nursed, affords but a very limited period for the education of the poor, because ignorant, offspring of the "shabby genteeel," who, from twelve years of age, are trammelled by the shackles of a five year's bondage, of from 14 to 16 hours a-day servitude, in preference to other occupations of shorter duration, for the sake of empty shew. During this period, the little education (under the existing system information is scarcely comprised in this term) obtained in their boyhood, has nearly left them, except, indeed, that only staple part embraced by this highsounding term, viz. reading, writing, and the simple rules of Arithmetic; and, as to read or improve the mind in the hours of idleness, is so "unbusiness-like" as to be almost criminal in the eyes of masters, at the close of their apprenticeship, the lads are set out into the world, nearly quite ignorant of the first principles upon which their success depends, and total strangers to the more valuable knowledge of which, as moral agents, they ought to be possessed. This is the general rule; the exception is, where he for whom "it is well his father was before him," enters upon this era in search of further mercantile knowledge, merely that, in the field of business, he may apply the longer scholastic and more intricate arithmetical tuition which it has been his good fortune to obtain, to the accumulation of what the world calls riches, without one grain of that precious wealth which feels for the situation of others. In these two classes, it is to be observed, intellectual starvation prevails to an incredible extent, concealed in a great measure by the frothy loquacity, professionally attained, which, coupled with the little information derived from the necessarily few minutes they can devote to reading periodicals, enables them to skim the surface of an occasionally leading topic of every-day talk, and thereby hide from the galling inquisition of knowledge, *the deep-felt ignorance and painful vacuum of their minds.*

Now all these desiderata, and that too in much more aggravated forms and degrees, generally attend the actual manufacturer or operative. Driven by necessity to work at a very early age, for the simple elements of nutrition, he enters upon a life of close and laborious duration, without even that manual instruction which renders knowledge accessible; and the lamentable state which society consequently presents, although so loud and universal in its groans as to be heard in every corner of the mechanical world, is yet so unheeded or misunderstood as, until even now, scarcely to have produced one responding sympathy from sleeping humanity, or called forth one effective step towards its amelioration. The exceptions are those, who, from some happier circumstances in their situation, have been permitted to obey the natural laws of their constitution, by availing themselves of those antidotes to such a state, disseminated by Mechanics' Institutions, Schools of Arts, and Libraries, the which appear to be destined ultimately to grow from the real "Balm in Gilead," to the "Physician there," or, in other words, from the salve to the saving agency of application. But it is unnecessary to inquire further into the various other grades or genera of these orders, as our present purpose more particularly is to proclaim the fact, that both these call loudly for change—a sweeping reform in the false policy by which their hours, we might say lives, of unintermitting labour are meted out. From the present system of employment, it is clear that little or no time can be applied to the cultivation of the mind; for, goaded by the parsimony of others, or the attendant necessities of a starving home, the latest hours available to avarice on the one part, and on the other sustenable by human nature, are exacted for labour, or merely animal operations; and to this treasonable system alone of continued ignorance, is to be attributed the debased passions of nature thus degraded, so appalling and injurious to the commonweal of man, and disturbative and ruinous to the true interests of society. In short, the order of both classes forces upon the mind of humanity *the great necessity of abridging the hours of labour;* its eye is disgusted with the practice, which proceeds as if man were mere animate mechanism, and revolts at the principle which governs as if the Great Creator and Ruler of the Universe had constituted the world with relation only to physical and animal operations and feelings, while He has peopled it with moral and intellectual beings,—as if His moral policy were subversive of His holy law, and, by the fixed order of things, His characteristic and infinite benevolence and justice were shown forth in the golden but false security of those few callous victims of sordid sensuality, who, for the sake of "the things which perish," daily sacrifice upon the altar of preclusion, the best present and eternal interests of thousands,—depriving them of all those opportunities and means of improving their stewardship,—shutting them out from every employment of those "talents" which shall be required again "with increase,"—and in fact crowding into their own criminal line of conduct, and setting an example to others to do so, not only every selfish act of despite to the golden rule, but also to the every divine institution of our nature, and moral precept which He taught who commanded us to "love one another," all of which, as professing Chistians, they have sworn to observe.

Let all masters, then, of whatever profession or branch of trade, which excludes time for study, remember that it is written, "Man shall not live by bread alone, but by every word which proceedeth out of the mouth of God;" and that it is therefore their duty to themselves and others, by a considerable abridgment of the hours of ill-paid employment, to lend their hitherto-abused influence and power to the spoliators of those forts of immorality, reckless wretchedness, and mental apathy, which, by protracted and exclusive labour, have been reared upon deplorable *ignorance* and misery, and by affording the employed opportunity to increase their knowledge, build upon their ruins that enlightened economy, social dependence, and general intelligence, which are clearly the divinely-instituted principles of that moral structure, which has been inscribed "the temple of the living God." This most certainly can be effected only by an extended intimacy with those eternal relations, dependencies, and principles of divine truth, which, by expanding the mind, fit us for the reception, cultivation, and more extensive enjoyment of the inexhaustible pleasures of the present, and those spiritual delights of the future, which "it hath not entered into the heart of man to conceive." Expositions of these principles everywhere pervade the wide field of Divine Knowledge around us. Time exclusively for such a purpose is indispensable to a survey of an extent and variety so unmeasured, as every-day's experience goes to establish the doctrine in abstract, "that those precepts which learned men have committed to writing, transcribing them from the common reason and common feelings of our nature, are to be accounted as not less divine than those contained in the Tables given to Moses;" as "it could not be the intention of our Maker to supersede, by a law graven upon stone, that which is written with his own finger on the table of the heart."

THE WISDOM OF OUR ANCESTORS.

It is amusing to look into the statute-book—at least that of this ancient kingdom of Scotland—and to observe with how much gravity enactments are made, on the most ridiculous and unimportant occasions, and the singular juxtaposition of statutes on the most opposite and contradictory subjects. An act appointing certain days for the "lepperfolk" to enter within burgh, and particular stations where they are to be "tholed to thig;"—for restraining the propensity for fine dress, by which the state "is greatumlie pured;"—"that na woman cum to the kirk mussellled" [masked;]—"that all beggars sald begge within their awin paroch, and have the mark thereof;"—"that na man ride bot in sober maner;"—and "that nane be foundin in tauernis, after nine houris,"—will be found side by side with one "for observing trewes [truce] on the borders:"—"for planting of wooddes, forests, and orchardis;"—for the institution of the College of Justice; and others on subjects of the last importance to the well-being of the community. Our ancestors, indeed—and we believe the observation will be found to hold true of all communities little advanced in civilization—seem to have imagined that not only was it necessary to legislate on subjects of importance, but that the most trivial abuse should be met by a special enactment.

Such a record, indeed, as the ancient code of laws of a kingdom—the very source of history, as it may be called—throws much light not only on the public transactions, but also on the social habits and domestic condition of its inhabitants. As it is to the latter only that we wish at present to direct the attention of our readers, we will confine the extracts of some of the more curious old laws of Scotland, while it was yet a separate and independent kingdom, which we intend to transfer to our pages, to such as involve either of these subjects. It may be proper to premise, that we quote from President Balfour's Practicks of Scots Law.

Will the reader believe that in 1494, so little was education attended to—the Schoolmaster, it appears, was not them even "at home"—that it was found necessary to pass an act requiring that "all baronnes and freeholders of substance sould put their airis to the schulis," under a penalty of "twentie pound." Yet in 1579, nearly a century later, an act for what nowadays may be deemed even a more singular purpose, received the sanction of James VI., "and his thre estatis,"—to wit, that,—

"All gentilmen, houshaldaris, and utheris, worth 300 markis of zeirlie rent or aboue, and all substantious zemen or burgessis, likewise houschaldaris, estemit worth 500 pundis in landis or gudis, be haldin to have ane bybill and psalme buik in vulgair language in their housis, for the better instructioun of thameselfis, and thair familiis, in the knawledge of God, within zeir and day efter the dait heirof, ilk persoun under the pane of ten pundis."

The old system of "burrow lawis," as we have them digested by the President, presents many curious particulars. The bakers and brewers seem to have been under the special surveillance of the law:—

"Gif ony Baxter in baiking of the breid, or ony brouster in brewing of the aill, committis ony fault, na persoun sould mell thairwith bot the Provest and Baillies; and gif ony of thame failzeis twyse, thay sall be twyse correctit thairfoir; and gif thay faill the third time, they sall suffer punishment in thair bodie: that is, the Baxter sall be put to the pillorie, and the Brouster upon the tumbrell or cokstuill."

At a time when the necessaries of life were scarce, and the supply uncertain, it would seem that a greater punishment than a pecuniary loss was necessary for the government of those to whom the supplying of the citizens was intrusted.

The very number of assistants which a baker should employ at his oven was rigidly laid down. We fear, in the present day, more than the legal number of *knaves* are too frequently allowed.

"Gif a man hes ane oyne (oven) of his awin, he sall keip in the samin the King is lawis maid thairanent be the the honest and wyse men of the burgh, viz. he sall not hald ma servandis nor four, viz. ane maister, twa servandis, and ane knaive. The maister or lord of the oyne sall have for his oyne, at ilk tyme, ane peny; the twa servandis, ane peny; and the knaive ane farding."

On the subject of a wife's dowery, "the wisdom of our ancestors" seems to have taken a very common-sense view. In an act passed to oblige "ilk husband to give ane reasonable dowrie and tierce to his wife," it is declared that "the quhilk [that is the dowery] is gevin to the wife, to the effect that gif it happen hir husband to deceis before her scho may the mair easilie be maryit with ane uther man." We presume a modern dower is ostensibly given for a different purpose. A very singular enactment was made in the reign of William, with regard to the damage or "skaith" done to the property of *ane* person by the hens, geese, or goats of another. Does not the provision regarding the goat point out that it must at that time have been a much more common animal in Scotland than at present? The object in "stikking the nose in the zeird," [earth] we can scarce comprehend :—

"Gif ony man findis and apprehendis ane uther man's hennis, geis or gait, doand him harm and skaith, he may tak and cut off the heid of the geis and of the hennis, and stikth the nose in the zeird, and may tak and eit the bodies thairof, gif he plessis; and the gait may be eschete be him, swa that he may slay and eit the samin at his plessour."

The doing skaith to a man's dog seems to have been a very serious matter :—

"*Item*, It is statute and ordanit, gif ony man of set purpois, and aganis the law, slayis ane uther man's dog, he sall walk his midding [dunghill] be the space of xij monethis, and ane day, or than sall content and pay to him all his skaithis sustenit be him within that xij monethis and day, for want of his hound or dog."

With how much gravity is the following case put! Yet it is tameness itself when compared with that which immediately follows, and which the worthy President, in a marginal note, justly entitles, "a merrie questioun anent the burning of a miln."

"Gif ony persoun havand na burding nor uther thing, is haldand ane horse, or uther beist, in his hand, or leidand the samin on ane brig, or ony strait passage, or ony uther perillous or dangerous place, meitis and rancounteris ony uther persoun, calland or drivand twa or ma horse or beistis befoir him, or leidand in his hand ane horse, or uther beist, chargit with ane laid or burding, upon the samin brig or place, in the quhilk, throw the straitness of the passage, the ane may not pass by the uther without dammage and skaith; in this cais, he quha has na uther thing bot ane horse, or uther beist, sould return back agane, and give place to the uther to come fordwart quha is drivand the said horsis or beistis, or the said laidnit horse or beist: And gif he dois not return, bot cumis fordwardt, and thairthrow ony harm or skaith happinis to be done, he is haldin of the law to amend and repair the samin; because he quha is chargit with ane beist allanerlie, sould saif himself, and give place to him quha has care of divers beistis, or of ane beist laidnit with ony thing."

"Gif it happin that ony man be passand in the King's gait or passage, drivand befoir him twa sheip festnit and knit togidder, be clinace ane horse, havand ane sair bak, is lying in the said gait, and ane of the sheep passis be the ane side of the horse, and the uther sheep be the uther side, swa that the band quhairwith they are bund tuich or kittle his sair bak, and he thairby movit dois arise, and carryis the said scheip with him heir and thair, untill at last he cumis and enteris in ane mile havand ane fire, without ane keipar, and skatteris the fire, quhairby the miln, horse, sheep, and all, is brunt : *Quæritur*, Quha sall pay the skaith? *Respondetur*, The awner of the horse sall pay the sheip, because his horse sould not have been lying in the King's hie street, or commoun passage; and the miller sall pay for the miln, and the horse, and for all uther damage and skaith, because he left ane fire in the miln, without ane keipar."

How strongly does the following enactment resemble the barbarous policy practised toward the poor negro in our slave colonies in the present day!

"Gif ony man is fund within the King's land, havand na proper lord or master, he sall have the space of xv. dayis to get him a maister: And gif he, within the said time, findis na lord nor master, be sall give ane unlaw of viij ky to the King's Justice: And, mairover, the King's Justice sall put his persoun in presoun, and keip him to the King's behove, till he get ane lord and master."

A man from whom it was possible to levy a fine of eight cows might have passed, one would think, pretty well for his own master.

Shade of Croker—the land-surveyor, we mean, *not* the Secretary—with how much ingenuity is the passage to be allowed at the centre of a stream, marked out in the following enactment! The idea is excellent. We question if the Boundary Commissioners—the fabricators of schedule M of the great charter of our liberties—were aware of such a mode of admeasurement.

"It is statute and ordanit be King *Alexander* at *Perth* on *Thursday*, befoir the feist of Sanct *Margaret*, with consent of the Erlis, Baronis, and Judges of *Scotland*, that the midst of the water sall be fre, in sa mekill that ane swine of thre zeir auld and weill fed, is of leuth, and may turn him within it, in sic ane maner, that nather his grunzie [mouth] nor his tail tuich ony of the sides of the cruives that ar biggit on ilk side of the water."

The "Chalmerlane of Scotland" in the "Air," (or circuit court?) which he is directed to hold, is enjoined to summon before him the various functionaries connected with the burgh, and to "challenge them on particulars which are set forth at length. From the challenge which he is directed to make, as well as from various enactments in the course of the statute-book, it appears that there were persons appointed as "gusteris and tasteris," and "prysouris," to see that the "baxters," "brouster-wiffis," and "fleshouris" not only offered for sale goods of proper quality, but that they (the prysouris) should also fix the price at which such articles were to be sold, and to which price the traders were obliged to agree "under the pane of ane unlaw." The sign or signal by which the "brouster-wiffis" gave notice to the "gusteris and tasteris of aill that they come and taist it," appears to have been a stick or staff denominated an "aill wand," which they were obliged to display whenever their ale was ready for the inspection of the "guster." The "guster and taster" was then bound to repair to the said "brousteris," and to remain on the "midstreit," and send ane of his company into the house along with "thair serjand to elect and cheise the barrel or pitcher quhairof they will taist." From the form of challenge, it appears to have been matter of complaint against the "gusteris" that "they drank in ilk hous quhair they sould bot anis taist, quhairthrow they tine their gust and ar maid drunke." The particular manner by which the "baxteris" and fleshouris" gave notice to the "prysour" is not mentioned.

As a specimen of the "challenges," it may perhaps be sufficient to select that of the tailors, shoemakers, and weavers.

CHALLENGE OF TAILZEOURIS.

In the first, thay mak refuse and skreidis in men's claith, sumtimes for haist, and sometimes for ignorance. *Item*, That thay tak pieces and skreidis to sleives, and uther small thingis. *Item*, That thay mak men's garmentis and claethis utherwayis than men biddis thame. *Item*, That they sew with false threid and graith.

Item, That thay keip not thair day to ilk man.

Item, That thay mak thame masteris or thay can knaw the craft, in greit skaithing of the King and pepill.

Item, That thay work on haly-dayis, aganis the law of God.

CHALLENGE OF SOUTERIS.

In the first, that thay bark and mak schoone utherwayis than law will; that is, thay buy not sic hides as has the horn and the eare of equal lenth.

Item, That thay mak schoone, butes, or uther graith, of the ledder befoir it be barkit.

Item, That thay sew with false and rotten threid, throw the quhilk the schoone ar tint befoir thay be half worn.

Item, That quhair thay sould give thair ledder gude oyle or taulch, thay give it but water and salt.

Item, That thay mak schoone and work of it or it be wrocht or curreit, in greit prejudice of the King's lieges.

CHALLENGE OF WEBSTARIS.

In the first, that thay mak over lang thrumis, in skaithing of the pepil.

Item, That quhair thay tak in with weichtis, quhen thay give out the claith thay mak it donk and wet, castand water on it, and uther thingis, to cause it to wey, and thairthrow haldand to thameselfis ane greit quantitie out of it.

Item, That thay tak ane man's zairn, and puttis in ane uther man's web for haist.

Tailors have been long proverbial for the fidelity of their promises; but we were not aware that it dated so far back. The object in making it illegal for shoemakers to buy such hides as had the horns and ears of unequal length, we are at a loss to divine. To such as are curious in the old laws we recommend the perusal of the curious and well-known collection of Murray of Glendook:—they will there find much to amuse. It is unfortunate, however, that his collection begins only at the reign of James I. For the many curious enactments previous to that reign, should the inquirer wish to push his researches farther, it will be necessary to refer to such compilations as that to which we have been indebted for the above extracts. "Ane admonition tuiching the buikes contenand the lawes of this Realme" will be found at the end of Skene's "Exposition of the termes and difficill wordes conteined in the foure buikes of Regiam Majestatem."

STATISTICAL VERSES.

The following verses were sent to Sir John Sinclair by the eccentric, benevolent, and pious minister of Lochcarron on the west coast of Ross-shire: a man of whom many droll stories are told, and who is most affectionately remembered by his parishioners by the name of "The Good Mr. Lauchlan." After stoutly resisting the "Whig Ministers," as the Evangelical preachers were long called by Highlanders, this parish submitted, about the middle of the last century, or rather earlier, to an apostle militant, named Eneas Sage; whom, after attempting to burn, they came almost to worship. He attacked the vices of his parishioners with *the arm of flesh*; fought Seaforth's factor on a Sunday with claymore and dirk, and put him to flight; and expelled, with the strong hand, the mistress whom Malcolm Roy, another of his flock, kept in the house with his wife. He was very passionate, but made his parishioners "*warm Christians*." His successor, the eccentric poet we are about to quote, says quaintly of the people,—"They have a strong attachment to religion, yet would be the better for a little more. They are hospitable, charitable, engaging and obliging; but it must be owned, very few of them would refuse a dram." Mr. Lauchlan was at deadly feud with female neck-frills, and with the combs with which the girls began to tuck up their hair, instead of the primitive snood.

> This same statistical account
> Is sent to please Sir John,
> And if it be not elegant,
> Let critics throw a stone.
>
> We have not fine materials,
> And our account is plain;
> Our purling streams are well enough,
> But we have too much rain.
>
> In Humbay there's a harbour fine,
> Where ships their course may steer;
> Such as are building villages
> Might build a village there.
>
> From Castle Strom there is a road
> Straight down to Kessock Ferry,[*]
> And by this road the men of Skye
> Do all their whisky carry.
>
> Our girls are dressed in cloak and gown,
> And think themselves right bonny;
> Each comes on Sunday to the Kirk,
> In hopes to see her Johnny.
>
> A drover, when the sermon's done,
> Will ask the price of cows,
> But the good, honest Christian
> Will stick to Gospel news.
>
> We call for *tea* when we are sick,
> When we want *salt* we grumble;
> When drovers' offers are not brisk,
> It makes our hopes to tumble.
>
> The parson has no horse nor farm,
> Nor goat, nor watch, nor wife:
> Without an augmentation,[†] too,
> He leads a happy life.
>
> Now, good Sir John, it was for you
> I gathered all this news;
> But you will say that I forgot
> To count the sheep and cows.
>
> Of these we have a number, too;
> But then, 'twixt you and I,
> The number they would never tell,
> For fear the beasts should die.[‡]

[*] Kessock, the Ferry at Inverness, from whence a Parliamentary road goes across the island to Lochcarron.
[†] The stipend of Lochcarron was then worth little more than L.50, with a glebe reckoned at L.3 or L.4.
[‡] This superstition is common to Highlanders, and to other people.

THE STORY TELLER.

A FEMALE MONSTER.
EFFECTS OF IGNORANCE AND SUPERSTITION.

GESCHE MARGARETHE GOTTFRIED, living in Bremen, was, in March, 1828, accused of having caused the death of a number of persons by poison. Before this accusation, she had lived in apparently easy circumstances in the middle ranks of life; her house was elegantly furnished, and her dress and demeanour that of a lady; her reputation was untainted; and the frequent deaths which occurred in her house were ascribed to heavy visitations of God.

Her father was a tailor in Bremen; active and industrious, but stingy, selfish, and inclined to superstition. His religion was of a kind that influenced him as long as its practice did not interfere with his own interests; and he attended church only when he had no work to do at home. Gesche Margarethe, and her twin brother, were born in March, 1783. These were the only children of their father, and, when about four years old, were both sent to school, where they remained till they were nearly twelve. The commencement of Gesche's career in sin may be dated from her seventh year, and was partly owing to the avarice of her parents. Being allowed no pocket-money, she was unable to appear on an equal footing with her school companions, and she began to steal from her mother small sums at first, but afterwards to a larger amount. This did not remain long concealed from her mother, who, however, ascribed it to the son, who was of a silent bashful disposition, rather than to the daughter, whose manners were frank; and although the mother had afterwards occasion to suspect her daughter, still she could not be certain, so artfully were the crimes concealed. Her father was accustomed to sing a hymn every morning before commencing work, and it frequently happened that his daughter was moved to tears by it. She was, however, of a very contradictory spirit, and her mother had frequent occasion to complain of her conduct. As she became older, she was sent to learn dancing, an accomplishment in which she greatly delighted. She also attended a French class, where, to appear the first of her class, she employed a young man, one of her acquaintances, to write her lessons for her, which she then copied and passed for her own.

Thus her life passed on with little variety till she was twenty years of age, although, when sixteen, she had already received three offers of marriage, which she, or rather her father, declined. She was beautiful, and almost everywhere beloved and well received.

When about twenty, she received an offer of marriage from a saddler, of the name of Miltenberg, which she was induced to accept. This marriage proved far from happy. Miltenberg had formerly been married to a woman who rendered his house a scene of misery and discord, and to avoid her society he always took refuge in the taverns, and so acquired a propensity to liquor which he could never overcome. He was induced to marry again chiefly by his father; for he had been so thoroughly disgusted with marriage by his former experience, that he had little desire to enter into another contract, and frequent quarrels took place between him and his father on the subject. Gesche had evinced no great love towards him, but the riches of the suitor had a powerful influence over the mind of her father, who prevailed on her to accept of the offer.

Miltenberg, however, loved his wife, and the more he had been ashamed of his former wife the more he seemed to doat upon this one; but he still frequented the taverns, and she was often left without his society or guidance.

They had been four months married when Gesche met Gottfried, her future husband, at a ball; and from that day all her wishes were directed towards him. She now began to colour her cheeks with rouge; hours were spent before her glass; and from her toilet she hurried to her kitchen window, and remained there to see him pass to his counting-room; but Gottfried took no notice of her.

It was about this period, namely, in September, 1807, that her first child was born. About the same time Miltenberg became acquainted with one Kassou, who used very frequently to visit him, and who soon conceived a liking for his wife, which Gesche did not leave unreturned. Their intimacy always continued to increase, and presents passed between them. Gesche was desirous to present to Kassou a breast-pin enclosing a lock of her hair, but did not well know how to express a note which she wished to send along with it. She, therefore, applied to Miltenberg, telling him that she wished to make a present to one of her female friends, and requesting him to write a note to be sent along with it, which he accordingly did. This she copied and sent to Kassou along with the pin.

In 1808 she had a still-born child, and after her confinement, began, on account of her thin appearance, to wear not fewer than thirteen pairs of stays, to improve her form. This was not discovered till her arrestment. She now began to be tired of Miltenberg; calumniating him to her parents, and directing her passions sometimes to Gottfried and sometimes towards Kassou. She was obliged to sell several articles of household furniture to pay some of her secret debts, telling her husband she wanted the money to send to her brother, who was then a soldier in the army of Napoleon, and representing to her mother that her husband had sold them.

In 1810 she had another child, and had no sooner recovered from her confinement, than, being short of money, she resolved to open her husband's desk. To accomplish this she pretended to have lost one of her own keys, and sent for a smith to get the desk opened; she observed narrowly how he proceeded, and after he was gone went and opened it and abstracted ten dollars. Not content with this, she proceeded afterwards to open the desk of a gentleman who lodged in her house, and took away ninety dollars. She remained, however, unsuspected, and a favourite with all her acquaintances; and was for some time cured of stealing by a fright which she got by a very narrow search being made on the desks being broken open.

Her passion for Gottfried increased more and more, and the habits and sickness of her husband gave them many opportunities of meeting. Her husband was intimate with Gottfried, and used to have him very often at his house. But her passion was not confined to Gottfried, it extended also to Kassou; and the necessity of keeping her love for the one concealed from the other brought her into many petty scrapes. Her fourth child was born in 1813.

Miltenberg was still in her way. She had never loved him, and now that he crossed her path, she began to wish him dead, that she might give free vent to her passion for Gottfried. Miltenberg's father had lately died, and she had observed nothing particularly fearful in death, so that by degrees she accustomed herself to the thought of Miltenberg dying. As he was always in bad health, she began to think that, as his life was only an encumbrance to himself, and an impediment to her, it would be no great sin to help him out of the world. In this state of mind she went to a fortune-teller, who prophesied that her whole family would die before her. She knew that her mother had some arsenic which she kept for poisoning mice. She accordingly went to her, and saying that she was troubled with mice in her house, asked if she knew of any means of destroying them, pretending that she knew nothing of poison. Her mother put some arsenic on bread, and placed it in the room said to be infested with the mice, warning her daughter at the same time to keep the apartment locked for fear of mischief to the children. A day or two after this, Gesche went into the room and took away the poison, which she scratched from the bread as if the mice had taken it, with the intention of giving it to Miltenberg. Some time afterwards her mother said that she would go and see if the mice had taken the poison. "Oh yes!" exclaimed the daughter, "pray bring me some more;" which her mother did.

She was now in possession of the means of death, but could not for several weeks bring herself to the resolution of administering it to her husband.

At last she gave him some, one morning, to breakfast, and afterwards another dose in some water-gruel. She could not, however, approach the bed of the sick man; it appeared to her as if he knew that she was his murderer;

but this was far from being the case, as he recommended her to Gottfried before he died. The corpse was dreadfully swollen, but no suspicion was excited.

After Miltenberg's death, she received an offer of marriage; but her thoughts being directed to Gottfried, she refused it. Her parents suspecting this to be the cause of her refusal, told her that her marriage with Gottfried should never take place with their consent. Gottfried loved her, but did not wish to marry a person with children. She now again consulted a fortune-teller, and received the same answer. Thus, although she had got quit of her husband, there still remained serious obstacles to her union with Gottfried; first her father and mother, and then her children. She hoped also to get possession, by the death of her children, of a legacy of about 650 dollars, left them by old Miltenberg.

In April 1815, her mother was rather unwell, and came to live in her house, when she (Gesche) happening to light upon the packet of arsenic, part of which she had saved and locked up, it immediately occurred to her to poison her mother. As her mother seemed likely to recover, she gave her the poison in her favourite beverage of lemonade; and while mixing it, she burst into loud laughter, so that she shuddered at herself; but it instantly occurred to her, that God made her laugh as a sign that her mother would soon be laughing in heaven. A witness afterwards said that she appeared happy at her mother's death.

Death now followed death with fearful rapidity. The very first day after her mother's burial, Gesche was sitting in a room with her second youngest child on her knee; the thought of poisoning it occurred to her, and without hesitating a moment, she administered to the child some arsenic on a piece of the cake which had been presented at the burial of its grandmother. This was on the 10th of May, and on the 18th, without the least remorse, she poisoned her eldest child. In the agony of death, it clasped its arms round the mother's neck, but Gesche remained unmoved. Two weeks afterwards, she poisoned her father. About ten weeks after these events, while her son was sitting on her knee, he asked her why God took away all her children? This pierced her to the heart, and she immediately resolved that he also should die.

Thus, in the short interval between May and September, she murdered both her parents and her children. But the death of so many in so short a space of time, naturally excited some suspicion, and to silence this, she was advised by her friends to have the body of the child opened. This she readily consented to, and the child was declared to have died of inflammation of the bowels.

In this manner, as she thought, was every obstacle to her marriage with Gottfried removed; but Gottfried himself did not show any particular desire to marry her, although he liked her company; and so the winter of 1815-16 passed free from murder. It was on a Saturday in May 1816, that her brother returned home a cripple and in rags, having lost the use of his feet in the Russian campaign. Here, then, might be another obstacle to her marriage; at all events, he must share her father's property with her. This was motive enough for his death. As already mentioned, he arrived on Saturday, or, as some say, on Friday, after a long absence; he was poisoned on Sunday, and, to avoid suspicion, she passed a great part of the time at his bedside. On every occasion, she had the precaution to employ a different physician. Seldom or never did any of them attend two of her patients.

Another obstacle, however, arose; Gottfried would not marry her. But this also she overcame, by the interest of some of his friends. His original refusal had hurt her, and she began to dislike him, and came to the resolution of poisoning him also. But she thought him rich, and therefore determined at all events first to marry him, in order to be made his heir, and then to execute her purpose. One Monday morning, she and Gottfried had resolved to make a pleasure party to a little distance out of town; and she seized this opportunity of poisoning him, that his sickness might appear the more unexpected. While he was on his deathbed, she sent for a priest to marry them, so that she might make sure of the property. Thus had she poisoned father, mother, brother, and children, in order to be put in possession of Gottfried, and at length we find him also in the list of her victims.

She seemed now to delight in murder, and the slightest cause was sufficient to decide upon the life or death of any of her relations. She was disappointed, however, as to Gottfried's riches, for, instead of wealth, he left her debt, and it required all her secretiveness to conceal her disappointment.

Now that she was alone, she occasionally felt severely the loss of her children; often when she thought of them, she shut herself up in her garret, and wept bitterly. She carefully avoided schools, and every place where children were to be met; and seemed to be particularly conscientious in paying off the debts of Gottfried. She loved money, not so much for its own sake, as because it afforded her the means of making a figure among her acquaintances, and so of gratifying her vanity.

Yet, in spite of all these murders, she was not unhappy; she became acquainted with H——— (the name is not given,) and in his company forgot all her sins, and, in her own words, believed herself the happiest in the world. She rejoiced in her reputation, especially as, after the death of Gottfried, she again immediately received an offer of marriage, which she refused. She had one child by Gottfried, begotten before marriage. We find at this period another instance of her hypocrisy; some one requested from her the loan of sermons, which she delivered, with the request that great care of them should be taken, as they were the only means by which she was able to sustain so many judgments. She never read any of them. Whenever she attempted to read the Bible, she thought the perusal of it of no use, and immediately closed the book.

She was now often ill supplied with money, but always found means of borrowing; often obtaining it from one in order to pay another. After the death of Gottfried, she seems to have rested for some years from her murders, and during that time to have had little to occupy her mind except the care of preserving her reputation untainted. In 1822 she went to Stade to spend a few weeks with some friends. Here, before she was aware, her money failed her; she was too proud to own it, and could get none from home; she knew no person from whom she might borrow, and had recourse to falsehood. She broke the key of her drawer in the lock, threw it away, and then raised an alarm that somebody had stolen her money out of the drawer. The drawer was forced open, and no money appeared, and nothing could be more obvious than that she had been robbed. Being obliged to take an oath before a magistrate that this was the case, she did not scruple to commit perjury; after which she got a supply of money from her friends.

From time to time she received offers of marriage, all of which she turned to good account, by extorting money from her admirers. She was reputed rich, and in this belief her admirers readily yielded to her requests.

One of them, named Zimmermann, was thus induced to advance her very considerable sums, which she repaid with a great shew of tenderness. She was betrothed to him, but he too was doomed to swell the list of her victims; after extracting all the booty in her power, she poisoned him by degrees, that she might have an opportunity of shewing her tenderness to him during his sickness, and thus lull suspicion. By his death she was free of the money due to him, which he had advanced on her word alone, without taking a legal obligation.

She now began to poison her acquaintances, without any visible motive:—a child came to congratulate her on her birth-day, and received a dose on a piece of biscuit: a friend called one forenoon, and also received a dose; and she tried the strength of her poison on another of her friends, on whose face it caused blotches to appear.

She gave a dose to one of her lodgers, that, during his sickness, she might plunder his pantry. Zimmermann had a cousin named Kleine, in Hanover, from whom she succeeded in borrowing 800 dollars, but he became impatient her repayment, and she had only 300 to give him. In this predicament she set out for Hanover, with the intention of poisoning Kleine, thinking by his death to gain delay. She accomplished her end, and after his death affirmed that she had given him a double Louis d'or the day before he died; but the whole story was a falsehood. She committed also several other murders for purely selfish ends, but the soul sickens in reporting them.

She was now often in want of money, and therefore could not keep up a large establishment, so that she was obliged to sell her house to a person named Rumpff, at the same time reserving a room or two for herself. Rumpff was fond of her, and used to call her aunt, but he had not been more than eight weeks in the house when his wife died, and he himself fell into bad health. He could do nothing but run about searching the whole house, from the garret to the cellar, for the cause of his trouble.

It chanced that he kept a pig; and wishing to have it killed, he sent for a butcher for that purpose. The butcher, with the view of pleasing him, brought to his room a choice bit of the pork, of which Rumpff partook, putting the remainder into his pantry. On the morrow he went to cut a slice from it, but he was surprised to find it in a different position from that in which he had left it the day before, and he perceived also that it was covered with a white powder. This excited his suspicions; he had the substance examined, and detected poison. Gesche's motive for this crime was to endeavour to regain possession of her house. She was arrested on suspicion.

The work before us, from which these particulars have been derived, gives no account of the trial or execution, which, as we are informed, is reserved for a separate publication; but it mentions that, in prison, she was tormented by dreams, in which she saw her victims sitting in the churchyard and beckoning to her; and she was often so much afraid, that, immediately on awakening, she could not remain longer in bed.

The following judgment was pronounced by the High Court of Bremen, on 17th September, 1830:—

"The Court of Justice, in terms of the law, and after the inquiries have been conducted according to the decree of the 22d May last, find the widow of Michael Christopher Gottfried, Gesche Margarethe, formerly Timm, accused of poisoning, and of several other offences, to be guilty of the following crimes, as proven, besides several robberies, frauds, and perjuries, and attempted abortion of her offspring, viz.

"1. To have poisoned both her parents, her three children, her first and second husbands, her suitor Paul Thomas Zimmermann, Anne Lucie Meyerholtz, Johann Mosses, the wife of Johann Rumpff otherwise Mentz, the wife of Frederic Schmidt otherwise Cornelius, and Frederic Kleine of Hanover; and also to have caused the death of Eliza, the daughter of the said Schmidt, by poison, although this is not proven to have been intentional.

"2. Several times to have given poison to the said Johann Rumpff, with the intention of killing him, and thereby causing to him a severe illness:

"3. To have given poison to several other individuals, without any proven intention, but which was more or less injurious to their health.

"The Court of Justice, therefore, according to the penal code, Art. 130, and taking into consideration the milder principles of the present usages of the law, condemn the accused, the widow of Michael Christopher Gottfried, as her well-merited punishment, and to serve as a warning to others, to death by the sword, and intrusts to the criminal court the execution and publication of the sentence, and also the adoption of all necessary measures: all the expenses caused by the inquiries, judgment and punishment, to be paid from the funds which she leaves, so far as they shall be sufficient."

[For these strange particulars, we are indebted to the *Phrenological Journal.*]

A correspondent of the *Athenæum*, an admirable literary Paper, in mentioning this woman, says, "that her case presents the most unprecedented riddle on record. Though the offender stands accused with the poisoning of both her parents, three children, one brother, two husbands, one suitor, two pregnant women, friends male and female, helpless children, and domestic companions; though accused of adultery, false-witnessing, perjury, theft, calumny, and swindling, she seems endued with a singular mildness of temper, appears to possess a decided inclination to kind and benevolent acts, and betrays outward susceptibility for what is noble and generous." The article from which we have copied solves this riddle on the principles of the Phrenologists; but for the solution we must refer to the Journal itself, No. XXXII.

BIOGRAPHIC SKETCH OF
HELEN WALKER, A GENTLEWOMAN OF HEAVEN'S MAKING.

HELEN WALKER was the daughter of a small farmer, or labourer at Dalwhairn, in the parish of Irongray. From whence her parents came is not known, but it is generally believed that they were what are called "incomers" into the parish of Irongray, and were in no way connected with the Walkers of Clouden, a race alike distinguished for respectability and longevity, and who have flourished time out of mind upon the fertile banks of the Cairn. At her father's death, his widow, who was then well stricken in years, became dependant for support on the industry of her daughters, Nelly and Tibby Walker. But this the former was far from viewing in the light of a hardship—she who was so rich in sisterly, could not be deficient in filial affection—and I have been informed by Elizabeth Grierson, housekeeper to Mr. Stott, optician, Dumfries, who, when a "lassie," knew Helen well, that though sometimes constrained to dine on dry bread and water, rather than pinch her poor old mother, she consoled herself with the idea that a blessing flowed from her virtuous abstinence, and that "she was as clear in the complexion, and looked as like her meat and work as the best of them." Helen Walker at this time,—that is at least "sixty years since,"—was much, as the phrase goes, about Elizabeth's father's house; nursed her mother during her confinement, and even acted as the leading gossip at all the christenings; was respected as a conscientious auxiliary in the harvest, and uniformly invited to share the good things of rural life, when the *mart* happened to be killed, or a *melder* of corn was brought from the mill. Her conversational powers were of a high order, considering her humble situation in life; her language most correct, ornate, and pointed; her deportment sedate and dignified in the extreme. Many of the neighbours regarded her as "a little *pensy body*"—that is conceited or proud; but at the same time they bore willing testimony to her exemplary conduct and unwearied attendance on the duties of religion. Wet or dry, she appeared regularly at the parish church, and even when at home, delighted in searching the Scriptures daily. On a small round table the "big ha' Bible" usually lay open, and though "household affairs would often call her hence," it was observed by her visitors that when she lacked leisure to read continuously, she sometimes glanced at a single verse, and then appeared to ponder the subject deeply. A thunder storm, which appals most females, had on her quite an opposite effect. While the elemental war continued, it was her custom to repair to the door of her cottage, the knitting gear in hand, and well-coned Bible open before her, and when questioned on the subject by her wondering neighbours, she replied, "That she was not afraid of thunder, and that the Almighty, if such were his divine pleasure, could smite in the city as well as in the field." Helen, though a woman of small stature, had been rather well-favoured in her youth. On one occasion she told Elizabeth Grierson that she should not do as she had done, but "winnow the corn when the wind blew in the barn-door." By this she meant that she should not hold her head too high, by rejecting the offer of a husband when it came in her way; and when joked on the subject of matrimony herself, she confessed, though reluctantly, that she once had a sweetheart—a youth she esteemed, and by whom she imagined she was respected in turn; that her lover, at a fair time, overtook her on horseback, and that when she asked him to take her up, answered gaily, "That I will, Helen, if you can ride an inch behind the tail." The levity of this answer offended her greatly, and from that moment she cast the recreant from her heart, and never, as she confessed, loved again.

I regret that I am unable to fix the exact date of the principal incident in Helen Walker's life. I believe, however, that it occurred a few years previous to the more lenient law *anent* child murder, which was passed in 1736. At this time her sister Tibby, who was considerably younger, and a comely girl, resided in the same cottage; and it is not improbable that their father, a worthy man, was also alive. Isabella was courted by a youth of the name of Waugh, who had the character of being rather wild, fell a victim to his snares, and became pregnant, though she obstinately denied the fact to the last. The neighbours, however, suspected that a child had been born, and repeatedly urged her to confess her fault. But she was deaf to their entreaties, and denied all knowledge of a dead infant, which was found shortly after in the Cairn, or Clouden. The circumstance was soon bruited abroad, and by the directions of the Rev. Mr. Guthrie, of Irongray, the suspected person, and *corpus delicti*, were carried before the authorities for examination. The unnatural mother was committed to prison, and confined in what was called the "thief's hole," in the old jail of Dumfries—a grated room on the ground floor, whither her seducer sometimes repaired and conversed with her through the grating. When the day of trial arrived, Helen was told that "a single word of her mouth would save her sister, and that she would have time to repent afterwards;" but trying, as was the ordeal, harassing the alternative, nothing could shake her noble fortitude, her enduring and virtuous resolution. Sleep for nights fled from her pillow: most fervently she prayed for help and succour in the time of need; often she wept till the tears refused to flow, and her heart seemed too large for her body; but still no arguments, however subtle—no entreaties, however agonizing—could induce her to offend her Maker by swerving from the truth.

Her sister was tried, condemned, and sentenced to be executed at the termination of the usual period of six weeks. The result is well known, and is truly as powerfully set forth in the novel. Immediately after the conviction, Helen Walker borrowed a sum of money, procured one or more letters of recommendation, and, without any other guide than the public road, began to wend her way to the City of London—a journey which was then considered more formidable than a voyage to America is in our day. Over her best attire she threw a plaid and hood, walked barefooted the whole way, and completed the distance in fourteen days. Though her feet were "sorely blistered," her whole frame exhausted, and her spirits sadly jaded, she found it impossible to rest until she had inquired her way to the residence of John, Duke of Argyle. As she arrived at the door, his Grace was just about to step into his carriage, and as the moment was too critical to be lost, the heroic pilgrim presented her petition, fell upon her knees, and urged its prayer with a degree of earnestness and natural eloquence, that more than realized the well-known saying of "snatching a grace beyond the reach of art." Here again the result is well known; a pardon was procured and despatched to Scotland, and the pilgrim, after her purse had been replenished, returned home, gladdened and supported by the consoling thought, that she had done her duty without violating her conscience. Touching this great chapter in her history, she was always remarkably shy and reserved; but there is one person still alive who has heard her say, that it was through "the Almighty's strength" that she was enabled to meet the Duke at the most critical moment—a moment which, if lost, never might have been recalled in time to save her sister's life.

Tibby Walker, from the stain cast on her good name, retired to England, and afterwards became united to the man that had wronged her, and with whom, as is believed, she lived happily for the greater part of half a century. Her sister resumed her quiet rural employments, and after a life of unsullied integrity, died in Nov. or Dec. 1791, at the age of nearly fourscore. My respectable friend, Mr. Walker, found her residing as a cottier on the farm of Clouden, when he entered it, upwards of forty years ago, was exceedingly kind to her when she became frail, and even laid her head in the grave. Up to the period of her last illness, she corresponded regularly with her sister, and received every year from her a cheese and "pepper cake," portions of which she took great pleasure in presenting to her friends and neighbours. The exact spot in which she was interred was lately pointed out in Irongray churchyard—a romantic cemetery on the banks of the Cairn—and though, as a country woman said, there was nothing to distinguish it "but a stane ta'en aff the dyke."

This, some of our readers need not be told, is the original JEANIE DEANS: a character too noble to be invented: it belongs to nature and religion; and Sir Walter Scott has done himself great honour in adopting and embellishing it. For the particulars of her story, given above, we are indebted to Mr. M'Diarmid of Dumfries. A few more incidents we may take from the letter of Mrs. Goldie to Sir Walter. The Christian heroism of this poor woman's character had so powerfully struck this lady, that she anonymously communicated to the Baronet the facts of which he has made such admirable use.

Her communication was in these words:

"I had taken for summer lodgings a cottage near the old Abbey of Lincluden. It had formerly been inhabited by a lady who had pleasure in embellishing cottages, which she found perhaps homely and even poor enough; mine, therefore, possessed many marks of taste and elegance unusual in this species of habitation in Scotland, where a cottage is literally what its name declares.

"From my cottage door I had a partial view of the old Abbey before mentioned; some of the highest arches were seen over, and some through, the trees scattered along the land which led down to the ruin, and the strange fantastic shapes of almost all those old ashes accorded wonderfully well with the building they at once shaded and ornamented.

"The Abbey itself from my door was almost on a level with the cottage; but on coming to the end of the lane, it was discovered to be situated on a high perpendicular bank, at the foot of which run the clear waters of the Cluden, where they hasten to join the sweeping Nith,

"Whose distant roaring swells and fa's."

As my kitchen and parlour were not very far distant, I one day went in to purchase some chickens from a person I heard offering them for sale. It was a little rather stout-looking woman, who seemed to be between seventy and eighty years of age; she was almost covered with a tartan plaid, and her cap had over it a black silk hood, tied under the chin, a piece of dress still much in use among elderly women of that rank of life in Scotland; her eyes were dark, and remarkably lively and intelligent. I entered into conversation with her, and began by asking how she maintained herself, &c.

"She said that in winter she footed stockings, that is, knit feet to country people's stockings, which bears about the same relation to stocking-knitting that cobbling does to shoemaking, and is of course both less profitable and less dignified; she likewise taught a few children to read, and in summer she whiles reared a few chickens.

"I said I could venture to guess from her face she had never been married. She laughed heartily at this, and said, 'I maun hae the queerest face that ever was seen, that ye could guess that. Now, do tell me, madam, how ye cam to think sae?' I told her it was from her cheerful disengaged countenance. She said, 'Mem, have ye na far mair reason to be happy than me, wi' a gude husband and a fine family o' bairns, and plenty o' every thing? for me, I'm the puirest o' a' puir bodies, and can hardly contrive to keep mysel' alive in a' the wee bits o' ways I hae tell't ye.' After some more conversation, during which I was more and more pleased with the old woman's sensible conversation, and the *naiveté* of her remarks, she rose to go away, when I asked her name. Her countenance suddenly clouded, and she said gravely, rather colouring, 'My name is Helen Walker; but your husband kens weel about me.'

"In the evening I related how much I had been pleased, and inquired what was extraordinary in the history of the poor woman. Mr. —— said, there were perhaps few more remarkable people than Helen Walker. She had been left an orphan, with the charge of her sister considerably younger than herself, and who was educated and maintained by her exertions. Attached to her by so many ties, therefore, it will not be easy to conceive her feelings, when she found that this only sister must be tried by the laws of her country for child-murder, and upon being called as principal witness against her. The counsel for the prisoner told Helen, that if she could declare that her sister had made any preparations, however slight, or had given her any intimation on the subject, that such a statement would save her sister's life, as she was the principal witness against her. Helen said, 'It is impossible for me to swear to a falsehood; and, whatever may be the consequence, I will give my oath according to my conscience.'"

The sequel is already known.

Mrs. Goldie endeavoured to collect further particulars of Helen Walker, particularly concerning her journey to London, but found this nearly impossible; as the natural dignity of her character, and a high sense of family respectability, made her so indissolubly connect her sister's disgrace with her own exertions, that none of her neighbours durst ever question her upon the subject. One old woman, a distant relation of Helen's, and who is still living, says she worked a harvest with her, but that she never ventured to ask her about her sister's trial, or her journey to London; 'Helen,' she added, 'was a lofty body, and used a high style o' language.' The same old woman says, that every year Helen received a cheese from her sister, who lived at Whitehaven, and that she always sent a liberal portion of it to herself or to her father's family. This fact, though trivial in itself, strongly marks the affection subsisting between the two sisters, and the complete conviction on the mind of the criminal, that her sister had acted solely from high principle, not from any want of feeling, which another small but characteristic trait will further illustrate. A gentleman, a relation of Mrs. Goldie's, who happened to be travelling in the north of England, on coming to a small inn, was shown into the parlour by a female servant, who, after cautiously shutting the door, said, 'Sir, I'm Nelly Walker's sister!'—thus practically showing that she considered her sister as better known by her high conduct, than even herself by a different kind of celebrity.

Mrs. Goldie was extremely anxious to have a tombstone and an inscription upon it, erected in Irongray churchyard. This Sir Walter did before he went abroad.

THE PUIR MAN'S BAIRN.

The puir man's bairn—the puir man's bairn,
 She has muckle in her lifetime to thole and to learn;
She maun bruick—she maun cruick—like the larch on the lea;
 But God's blessing on the head o' the puir man's bairn.

The puir thing had an e'e, like an angel's, meek and mild,
 But when feeling lit it up, it would glisten like the Erne;
When I censured, she was frozen, but I praised her and she smiled—
 Oh, blessings on the head o' the puir man's bairn.

Oh, she had a cheek wad ha'e charm'd even a saint,
 And a look wad ha'e softened the hard heart o' airn;
And Virtue, the whole she could spare her, had lent,
 And Beauty kiss'd the cheek of the puir man's bairn.

The puir man's bairn bides the scorn and the scaith,
 And her wee bit penny fee taks a lang time to earn;
She has little to expect frae our cauld hearts aneath—
 There's a better place aboon for the puir man's bairn.

VERSES FOR THE YOUNG.

THE WOOD MOUSE.
BY MARY HOWITT—A QUAKERESS.

"D'ye know the little wood-mouse?
 That pretty little thing,
That sits among the forest leaves,
 Or by the forest spring?
Its fur is red, like the red chestnut,
 And it is small and slim;
It leads a life most innocent,
 Within the forest dim.

'Tis a timid, gentle creature,
 And seldom comes in sight;
It has a long and wiry tail.
 And eyes both black and bright.
It makes its bed of soft, dry moss,
 In a hole that's deep and strong;
And there it sleeps secure and warm,
 The dreary winter long.

And though it keeps no calendar,
 It knows when flowers are springing;
And it waketh to its summer life,
 When the nightingale is singing.
Upon the bows the squirrel plays,
 The wood-mouse plays below;
And plenty of food he finds for himself,
 Where the beech and chestnut grow.

He sits in the hedge-sparrow's nest,
 When its summer brood is fled;
And picks the berries from the bow
 Of the hawthorn overhead.
And I saw a little wood mouse once,
 Like Oberon, in his hall;
With the green, green moss beneath his feet,
 Sit under a mushroom tall.

I saw him sit, and his dinner eat,
 All under the forest tree,—
His dinner of chestnut ripe and red;
 And he ate it heartily.
I wish you could have seen him there;
 It did my spirit good.
To see the small thing God had made
 Thus eating in the wood.

I saw that God regardeth them,
 Those creatures weak and small;
Their table in the wild is spread
 By Him who cares for all."

THE WEAVER'S SONG.
BY BARRY CORNWALL.

Weave, brothers, weave!—Swiftly throw
 The shuttle athwart the loom,
And show us how brightly your flowers grow,
 That have beauty, but no perfume!
Come, show us the rose, with a hundred dyes,
 The lily, that hath no spot;
The violet, deep as your true love's eyes,
 And the little Forget-me-not!
  Sing,—sing, brothers! weave and sing!
   'Tis good both to sing and to weave;
  'Tis better to work than live idle:
   'Tis better to sing than grieve.

Weave, brothers, weave! Weave, and bid
 The colours of sunset glow!
Let grace in each gliding thread be hid!
 Let beauty about you blow!
Let your skein be long, and your silk be fine,
 And your hands both firm and sure,
And time nor chance shall your work entwine;
 But all,—like a truth,—endure!—
  So,—sing, brothers, &c.

Weave, brothers, weave!—Toil is ours;
 But toil is the lot of men;
One gathers the fruit, one gathers the flowers,
 One soweth the seed again.
There is not a creature, from England's King,
 To the peasant that delves the soil,
That knows half the pleasures the seasons bring
 If he have not his share of toil!
  So,—sing, brothers, &c.

COLUMN FOR THE LADIES.

STAGNATION OF MARRIAGES.

Looking around this town, and recalling days of "auld lang syne," who can fail of being struck with the number of lovely women that year after year have passed through the ordeal of a season without advancing one step towards the hymneneal altar? And who, seeing these things, can fail of being convinced that society, as at present constituted, is not what it ought, or what it was intended to be? In former days our homely ancestors sought the bosom of their families for that recreation which modern youth roam abroad in quest of. Marriage then was a necessary, now it is a luxurious—I might almost say—an artificial state. So in former days, our hardy ancestors took the field, to provide by the precarious toils of the chase, for the maintenance of themselves and families until, by degrees, that which at first was an act of necessity, gradually mellowed down into a luxurious and expensive pastime. If there is one fault more unpardonable than another in a huntsman, it is not allowing the hounds to hunt for themselves; and if there is one that tends more frequently to the marring of matches than another, it is the short-sighted interference of our knowing mothers. I have had much experience in these matters, Mr. Editor—experience that none but men can gain; and if your fair readers will bear with my sporting phraseology, I will endeavour to point out the safest mode of pursuing the biped, as also those errors into which they generally fall. The first chapter is on the "kennel management," the latter of which words is strangely comprehensive of what many old comprehensive mammas do at and pride themselves on not a little. Then comes suggestions on names—a very material point, for what man would fall in love with the barbarously-named Barbara? who would woo the soft, tender, pincushioned Emily? The third was on rounding ears, which might very appropriately be applied for boring them for ear-rings. But what struck my fancy most was, on *entering puppies*—a proceeding so much in favour with the ladies as to require a little eulogy from me, but whereon some useful hints might well be offered.—" Taking your hounds often by way of making them bandy," answers to our balls and rout, which rub off any little rust or *gaucherie*; and " enticing young hounds to the chase," of course, is the same as "young ladies entering life or looking for husbands. "The description of a fox-chase" would do well for the description of a flirtation, and would combine an immensity of information, and give rise to much subsequent reflection. Placing hounds advantageously is commented upon, and very proper information it is; nor ought drafting hounds to be overlooked, for taking too many daughters out to a ball is a very bad thing. "When a huntsman should be after his time," might stand in the place of telling an old Dowager not to come down too early to breakfast, and, "long drags" and "long courtships" are synonimous.—I am, Sir, &c.

BYRON'S OPINION OF BEAUTY.—I do not talk of mere beauty (continued Byron) of feature or complexion, but of expression, that looking out of the soul through the eyes, which, in my opinion, constitutes true beauty. Women have been pointed out to me as beautiful, who never could have interested my feelings, from their want of countenance, or expression, which means countenance; and others, who were little remarked, have struck me as being captivating, from the force of countenance. A woman's face ought to be like an April day—susceptible of change and variety; but sunshine should often gleam over it, to replace the clouds and showers that may obscure its lustre—which, poetical description apart, (said Byron,) in sober prose, means that good-humoured smiles ought to be ready to chase away the expression of pensiveness or care, that sentiment or earthly ills call forth. Women were meant to be the exciters of all that is finest in our natures, and the soothers of all that is turbulent and harsh. Of what use, then, can a handsome automaton be, after one has got acquainted with a face that knows no change, though it causes many? This is a style of looks I could not bear the sight of for a week; and yet such are the looks that pass in society for pretty, handsome, and beautiful.

THE POLISH HEROINE.

Claudia Potocka, daughter of the Senator Palatine Count Xavier Dzialynski, was born at Konarzew, in Great Poland, the cradle of the Polish nation, now the Grand Duchy of Posen, in 1808, and was married, in 1824, to Count Bernard Potocki.

Descended from one of the most ancient houses of Poland, and bred in the strictest principles of virtue, the young Claudia imbibed the germ of patriotism, hereditary in her family. When she entered into the married state, she found her husband animated by the same sentiments, and the same examples prevailed.

Previous to the great political convulsion which imposed other duties upon her, life glided happy and cheerfully on, in the midst of youthful pleasures, and those serious studies towards which her taste inclined; but the explosion of the 29th Nov. 1830, disturbed this quiet and uniform existence. Claudia Potocka was then residing in the Grand Duchy of Posen. The first appeal of their native country was received by the youth of this ancient province, with a universal burst of enthusiastic sympathy. Notwithstanding the threats of the King of Prussia, and in defiance of the Ukases of the Muscovites, thousands of courageous citizens passed the frontiers to the support of their brethren in arms. Foremost in the ranks of these patriotic emigrants were Count Bernard and his young spouse.

Although, on reaching Warsaw, Claudia Potocka did not join those intrepid heroines who were seen, like true Amazons, with well-poised lances, charging pulks of Cossacks, or seizing the standards of the enemy, yet her services in the national cause were neither less useful nor less perilous. The hospitals of Warsaw were the scene of her heroic devotion; there, accompanied by many distinguished associates, and surrounded by wounded warriors and those stricken with malignant cholera, she sacrificed every thing to the duties she had undertaken.— Seated by the couches of the sick, during seven successive months, she was constantly occupied in dressing their wounds and alleviating their sufferings. Neither the sight of hideous gashes, nor the fear of contagion, deterred her from her course of persevering charity. The daughter of Dzialynski and the wife of Potocki became the humble and attentive nurse of Poland's brave sons. Such modest and unostentatious devotion is as truly heroic, and perhaps more profound, than that displayed in the field of battle.

When the day of adversity came, Countess Claudia accompanied the Polish army in its retreat to Modlin; when, in the midst of general confusion, she once with great difficulty procured a truss of straw, on which to repose her wearied head, but relinquished it in favour of a sick officer who accidentally caught her eye. Having, as a female, more facility in obtaining a passport, she availed herself of it for the purpose of saving, at great risk and peril, several patriots deeply compromised during the revolution. By this means, disguised in the costume of her domestics, Count Vincent Tyzkiewicz, Captain Tanski, young Wladimir Potocki, and others, were enabled to traverse Prussia undiscovered. Her friend Miss Saczaniecka, accompanied her on this sad journey, disguised as a waiting-maid. On one occasion the proscribed band was placed in imminent danger; at Thorn the Prussian police seemed disposed to imprison some of its members; but the Countess declared that she would be responsible for all; she offered the whole of her possessions as a guarantee, and by this generous act again preserved them.

On quitting Prussia, the Countess Potocka took up her abode at Dresden, there to deplore in solitude the misfortunes of her country. She, however, consented, at the solicitation of her compatriots, to join a ladies' committee, formed in the first instance under the auspices of the late Madame Dobrsycka, and which still continues to watch over the fate of unfortunate refugees. The remains of her fortune, her influence, her care, even her personal exertions, are entirely at the disposal of the unfortunate. A lady of her acquaintance, having one day made inquiries for a person to copy a voluminous manuscript, the Countess offered to provide one; under this pretext she obtained possession of the work, and laboured at it herself day and night, in order to deposit the proceeds of her industry in the funds of the society.

In the month of February last, General Bem arrived in Dresden, from the Prussian frontiers, for the purpose of explaining to the committee the deplorable situation of the Polish soldiers who had sought refuge in the Prussian territory. Without provisions and without clothes, in the depth of a severe winter, these unhappy men resolved rather to perish of cold and hunger, or even to face the fire of the Prussians, than to return to a land henceforth under the despotism of Russia.

The members of the committee were affected even to tears at the recital of such heroism and suffering; but funds were wanting, and they were at a loss how to afford the required assistance, when our young heroine, more ready or more devoted than the rest, hit upon an expedient for obviating the difficulty. She still possessed some jewels and cachemires which the foreign police had not succeeded in depriving her of; these she instantly pledged, and the following day the sum of 40,000 florins was counted into the hands of General Bem for its pious destination. It was in honour of this noble action, that the Poles assembled at Dresden recently presented to their virtuous countrywoman a bracelet, with an inscription commemorative of the act, and pointing it out for national gratitude.

The bracelet was closed by a plate of gold, surmounted by the arms of Poland and Lithuania, with the following inscription: Wdzięczni Polacy zgromadzeni w Dreźnie, 1832. R : 18 Marca. The grateful Poles assembled at Dresden, 18th March, 1832.

A FAREWELL TO ABBOTSFORD.
BY MRS. HEMANS.

Home of the gifted ! fare thee well,
   And a blessing on thee rest ;
While the heather waves its purple bell
   O'er moss and mountain crest ;
While stream to stream around thee calls,
   And banks with broom are drest,
Glad be the harping in thy halls—.
   A blessing on thee rest !

While the high voice, from thee sent forth,
   Bids rocks and cairn reply,
Wakening the spirits of the North,
   Like a chieftain's gathering cry ;
While its deep master-tones hold sway,
   As a king's, o'er every breast,
Home of the Legend and the Lay !
   A blessing on thee rest.

Joy to thy hearth, and board, and bower !
   Long honours to thy line !
And hearts of proof, and hands of power,
   And bright names worthy thine !
By the merry steps of childhood still
   May thy free sward be prest !—
While one proud pulse in the land can thrill,
   A blessing on thee rest !

OUR CLUB, AND OUR TOWN.

Our Whist club is going of, Some of the members go on so ; two of em are perpetualy quareling like anything but double dummies, for one plays like Hoyle, and the other like Vinegar. The young men have interduced Shorts, but I doant think they'le Last long. They are all so verry Sharp at the Pints, and as for drinking, I never se sich Liqverish Chaps in my life. They are al ways laying ods, even at Super, when they'le Bet about the age of a Roosted foul, wich they cal Chicken hazzard, or about the Wait of a Curran py, wich they cal the Currency question. They al so smoke a grate manny seagars, but they cant Put the old man's pipe out, wich it Wood be a Burning shame if they did. I am sorry to say politicks has Crept in ; Sum is al for reform, and sum is al for none at al, and the only thing they agre in is, that the land Lord shant bring in no Bil. There is be sides grate dis-cushions as to the new game laws, sum entertaining douts wen sum people go out a shooting wether even acts of Parliament will enable them to shute anny game. The cricket Club is going on uncomon wel. They are 36 members with out reckoning the byes ; our best man at Wicket is Captin Batty—he often gets four notches running ; and our best boler is Uae Ball, tho we sumtims get Dr. Bilby to bolus. As for the cricket Bal, it is quit wore out, wich the gals say they are very Sorry for it, as they took a grate interest in our matches. My lads are boath of an em marred, wich mayhap you have Herd, —and if the gals are not, I Beleve its no falt of theres. They hope youle cum to the Wake, wich is next Sunday week, for they Say there will be High fun, al tho I think it is Rather Low. The only use of waking that I can See, is to prevent folkes Sleeping, and as for there jumping and throwing up there Heals, I see no Pleasur in it. If they had the Roomatis as Bad as I have, they woudent be for Dancing there fandangoes at that rat, and Kicking for partners.—Hood.

SCRAPS.
Original and Selected.

TREATMENT OF HORSES.—The learned and benevolent Burbequius, who was ambassador at Constantinople in the 17th century, gives the following account of the Turkish horses. Our grooms, and their masters, too, may learn a lesson of wisdom and humanity from his words :—" There is no creature so gentle as a Turkish horse, nor more respectful to his master, or the groom that dresses him. The reason is, because they treat their horses with great lenity. This makes them great lovers of mankind ; and they are so far from kicking, wincing, or growing untractable by this gentle usage, that you will hardly find a masterless horse amongst them. But, alas ! our Christian grooms' horses go on at another rate. They never think them rightly curried till they thunder at them with their voices, and let their clubs and horsewhips, as it were, dwell on their sides. This makes some horses even tremble when their keepers come into the stable, so that they hate and fear them too. But the Turks love to have their horses so gentle, that at the word of command they fall on their knees, and in this position receive their riders. They will take up a staff or club upon the road with their teeth, which their rider has let fall, and hold it up to him again. I saw some horses, when their master was fallen from the saddle, stand stock still without wagging a foot, till he got up again. Once I saw some horses, when their master was at dinner with me, prick up their ears to hear his voice, and when they did so, they neighed for joy.

SUBSTITUTE FOR TEA.—A patent was granted in February last to a tea dealer, " for a new mode of preparing the leaf of a British plant for producing a healthy beverage by infusion." According to the specification, the British plant in question is the Hawthorn, from which the leaves may be taken from the month of April to September inclusive ; they are first to be carefully picked and cleansed, then to be well rinced in cold water and drained ; and whilst in the damp state they are to be put into a common culinary steamer, where they are to be subjected to the action of the vapour until they change from a green to an olive colour ; the leaves are then to be taken out and dried upon a " hot plate well heated," and to be continually stirred up and turned over until they are thoroughly dry, in which state they may be preserved for use. When required for that purpose, an infusion is to be made in the same manner as tea, and sugar and cream are to be added to suit the taste of the drinker.

AMERICAN INVENTIONS.—A New York paper gives the following account of a steam coach, recently built at Cincinnati, which, it says, promises to surpass every thing of the kind in other countries :—" This engine, independent of the boiler, is made so compact, that a box two feet long, one foot wide, and one foot deep, would contain it if taken to pieces ! and yet such is its power, it will overcome a rise of forty-five feet in the mile without any essential variation in its velocity. We rode in the carriage propelled by it at the rate of fourteen to sixteen miles an hour, on a circular road : the same force would propel the same weight twenty miles an hour, and, more, on a straight line, there being so much less friction. Another great improvement consists in the mode of applying the power, and another in the construction of the boiler, which is perfectly novel. Add to which the consumption of fuel does not exceed one-fourth a cord a week, to run from nine in the morning to nine in the evening. It appears, in fact, to have been reserved for a citizen of Cincinnati to bring this great improvement in travelling so near perfection."—*Literary Gazette.*

THE HIGHEST MOUNTAIN IN SCOTLAND.—Ben Nevis has, till very lately, been considered the monarch of Scottish mountains, but it now appears, from the trigonometrical survey lately made by order of government, that he must yield the palm to Ben Macdui, a mountain in Aberdeenshire, who o'ertops him by about twenty feet. The height of Ben Nevis is 4370 feet ; of Ben Macdui, 4390 feet. Thus Ben Macdui is the loftiest mountain, not only in Scotland but in Great Britain.

JACK MITFORD, A CHARACTER.—In St. Giles's workhouse, expired some time back the well-known Jack Mitford, perhaps the most eccentric character of his day. He was originally in the navy, and fought under Hood and Nelson; he was born at Mitford Castle, Northumberland; the authoress of "Rienzi," and the author of "The History of Greece," were his cousins: he was also related to Lord Redesdale. His name will be long remembered in connexion with Lady Perceval, in the Blackheath affair, for his share in which he was tried and acquitted. For many years Mitford has lived by chance, and slept three nights in the week in the open air when his finances did not admit of his paying 3d. for a den in St. Giles's. Though formerly a nautical fop, for the last fourteen years he was ragged and loathsome; he never thought but of the moment. Having had a handsome pair of Wellington boots presented to him, he sold them for 1s. The fellow who bought them went and put them in pawn for 15s. and came back in triumph with the money. "Ah!" said Jack, "but you went out in the cold for it." He was the author of "Johnny Newcombe in the Navy," the publisher of which gave him a shilling a day until he finished it. Incredible as it may appear, he lived the whole of the time in Bayswater fields, making a bed at night of grass and nettles; two pennyworth of bread and cheese and an onion were his daily food; the rest was expended in gin. He thus passed 43 days, washing his shirt and stockings himself in a pond, when he required clean linen. A hundred efforts were made to reclaim him, but without avail. At the time of his death he was editing a penny production. He wrote the popular modern song "The King is a true British sailor," and sold it to seven different publishers. Notwithstanding his habits he was employed by some religious publishers. This miserable man was buried by Mr. Green, of Will's coffee house, Lincoln's Inn Fields, who had formerly been his shipmate. He has left a wife and family, but they were provided for by Lord R———. Jack Mitford was a respectable classic, and a man of varied attainments; yet for fourteen years "he had not where to lay his head." He had been heard to say, "if his soul was placed on one table and a bottle of gin on another, he would sell the former to taste the latter."

DESCENT OF THE BISHOPS.—The present amiable and respected primate of all England, chances to be the son of a poor country clergyman. The Bishop of London derives his descent from a schoolmaster in Norwich. The father of the Bishop of Durham was nothing more than a shopkeeper in London. The Bishops of Winchester and Chester boast of no nobler lineage than belongs to the sons of an under-master at Harrow. Bishop Burgess, as all the world knows, is the son of that illustrious citizen with whose excellent fish-sauce civilized men are generally well acquainted; while his Lordship of Exeter dates his parentage through a long line of hereditary innkeepers in the town of Gloucester. Besides these, we have the Bishop of Bristol, the son of a silver-smith in London; the Bishop of Bangor, the son of a schoolmaster in Wallingford; the Bishop of Llandaff, whose father was a country clergyman; with many others, whom it were superfluous to enumerate. Lincoln, St. Asaph, Ely, Peterborough, Gloucester, all spring from the middling classes of society.—*Fraser's Magazine.*

DIALECT—*Edinburgh v. Aberdeen.*—A gentleman from Aberdeen was awoke one night lately in a Hotel in Prince's Street, Edinburgh, by an alarm of fire. Upon going to the window, he called out "Vautchman, far eist?" The watchman thanked him and went towards the Register Office, where he found he was going in the wrong direction, and returned. On repassing the Hotel, he was again called to by the Aberdonian, who bauled out, "Vautchman, far was't?" On looking up to him the watchman replied, "Ye're a d——d leein sconnril; ye first tell'd me it was far east, an' noo ye say its far wast; but I tell ye it's nither e' tane or e' tither, 'cause its oure i' e' Coogate."

TABLE LUXURIES OF THE ROMANS.—The meats used by the Greeks did not materially differ from those approved by the Romans. Some of the luxuries of the latter are less esteemed at the present day, such as puppies, and the large white worm found in rotten wood, which is now extensively used, we believe, in New Holland. The snail was another of their dishes which has now lost favour, except in Germany, notwithstanding an attempt to revive it, made by two men of science in Edinburgh half a century ago. The supper of Pliny consisted of a barley cake, lettuce, two eggs, three snails, with a due proportion of wine.

CHRISTIAN FORGIVENESS.—When Mary de Medicis lay on her death-bed, she was asked by her confessor if she freely forgave all her enemies, and in particular Cardinal Richelieu.—"Madame, as a token, will you send him your bracelet?" "Nay, that is going too far," said the lady, lying back.

LITERARY PARTIES.—A person who liked the glory of entertaining authors, arranged them at table according to the size and thickness of their published volumes, the folios taking precedence of the quartos, and the 32mos occupying the lowest place.

EPITAPH ON THOMAS MUIR.
By the Author of the Corn Law Rhymes.

Thy earth, Chantilly, boasts the grave of Muir,
The wise, the loved, the murdered, and the pure;
While in his native land the murderers sleep,
Where marble forms in mockery o'er them weep.
His sad memorials tell to future times,
How Scotchmen honour worth, and gibbet crimes.

TO CORRESPONDENTS.

To several Correspondents we are indebted for valuable hints and advices, and beg to return thanks; to many for good wishes, and an expression of kindness, for our work's sake, which we gratefully feel and acknowledge.

Our monthly notices of books are unavoidably delayed till next week.

☞ Orders for copies and Parts of the SCHOOLMASTER, have in numerous cases been delayed from the numbers being out of print. This we are striving to supply; and complete copies may be had soon at all the publishers and salesmen. But many orders for single copies, we are sorry that we cannot execute, as it is impossible to send so small a work every week, or even every month, to places off the line of the towns to which Booksellers' parcels go. When such orders are sent, we beg that specific directions may be given as to the manner in which the work is to be transmitted.

All orders must be addressed to Mr. Anderson, the Publisher, 55 North Bridge Street.

BESIDES appearing in WEEKLY NUMBERS, the SCHOOLMASTER is published in MONTHLY PARTS, which, stitched in a neat cover, contain as much letter-press, of good execution, as any of the large Monthly Periodicals: A Table of Contents will be given at the end of the year; when, at the weekly cost of three halfpence, a handsome volume of 832 pages, super-royal size, may be bound up, containing much matter worthy of preservation.

PART II. for September, containing Five Numbers of the SCHOOLMASTER, with JOHNSTONE'S MONTHLY REGISTER, consisting this month of Eight pages, will be published on Monday. Price Ninepence. It may be had of all the Booksellers and dealers in Cheap Periodicals.

CONTENTS OF NO. IX.

Death of Sir Walter Scott................................129
On the Political Tendency of Sir Walter Scott's Writings.....ib.
Sir Walter Scott's Childhood............................133
Moral and Physical Condition of the Middle and Lower Classes..ib.
The Wisdom of our Ancestors............................136
Statistical Verses......................................136
THE STORY TELLER.—A Female Monster..................137
      Helen Walker.....................................139
The Puir Man's Bairn...................................141
The Wood Mouse..ib.
The Weaver's Song.....................................ib.
COLUMN FOR THE LADIES.—Stagnation of Marriages.........142
      The Polish Heroine................................ib.
      A Farewell to Abbotsford..........................143
      Our Club and our Town.............................ib.
SCRAPS.—Original and Selected..........................ib.

EDINBURGH: Printed by and for JOHN JOHNSTONE, 19, St. James's Square.—Published by JOHN ANDERSON, Jun., Bookseller, 55 North Bridge Street, Edinburgh; by JOHN MACLEOD, and ATKINSON & Co., Booksellers, Glasgow; and sold by all Booksellers and Vendors of Cheap Periodicals.

THE Schoolmaster,
AND
EDINBURGH WEEKLY MAGAZINE.

CONDUCTED BY JOHN JOHNSTONE.

THE SCHOOLMASTER IS ABROAD.—LORD BROUGHAM.

No. 10.—Vol. I.   SATURDAY, OCTOBER 6, 1832.   Price Three-Halfpence.

NOTES OF THE MONTH.

OCTOBER.

The year is now in the Fall. The days, already drawn short, are still rapidly " creeping in." The woods are falling into the " sere and yellow leaf," and towards the middle of the month, shew all the variegated shades of reds, warm browns, russets, and yellows, with greater diversity of greens than is seen in the vernal months. This is often a charming, tranquil season. The Americans speak with rapture of the Fall, or *Indian Summer* in their country; when the gorgeous hues of their vast and magnificent forests become glorious. In the Hebrides and Orcades, the few weeks of fine, serene weather, which frequently occur at this season are endearingly called, *The Little Summer*. October is, however, often blustering and plashy, and the season of high winds and devastating floods. The husbandman is still busily occupied in ploughing the fallows, and preparing the fields for new productions; and the planter and gardener have their hands full. The last lingering young broods of the swallow tribe disappear. Even the twitter of the martlet, which, more snugly sheltered than its congeners, lingers the longest, is, on some soft morning, missed from the eaves. The Royston crow, the teal, and the first " Baltic fleets" of the woodcock, begin to arrive. The squirrels in the woods are yet busy completing their winter hoards, and storing their garners. Many of these spruce, brisk, perkish, lively, and nimble creatures may be seen at this season in the woods on the South Esk, springing from branch to branch, more easily detected than when the trees are leafy.——That

Sweet Bird! that ever in the haunch of Winter sings—

The Robin Redbreast—may now be heard in every quiet, rural scene, trilling his plaintive hymn to the departing year.

At this season, the squire and yeoman, the laird and tenant, wont to brew the " stout October" beer, the beverage so congenial to the British Islands, which impolitic and cruel taxation has almost banished from the fireside of the poor, and completely knocked up as a home manufacture,[*] substituting an expensive, insalubrious, or deleterious mixture, for the sound, wholesome, and potent home-brewed of our ancestors.

HARVEST-HOME—THE KIRN—THE MAIDEN.

It is often far on in October before this festival of the husbandman is celebrated with us. Though this has been a fortunate year, we not unfrequently find, that

> The harvest had been cauld and wat,
>   And corn was unco green;
> And aye a rantin' kirn we gat,
>   Though just on Hallow-e'en
>   It fell that night.

This feast of fat things is known by as many different observances as names; though in substantials it is much the same; everywhere attended by mirth, good cheer, hilarity, and gratitude for the barn-yard stored—the bounty of the year secured. It is the *Saturnalia* of the Christian world, uniting master and man, mistress and maiden, in the enjoyment of common blessings. There is, we are sorry to understand, symptoms of this venerable custom falling into desuetude in certain quarters. In others, it is perverted from its true and best use, by being converted into a *genteel* ball and supper, with which the farmer entertains his city friends. No one should be allowed to partake of the Kirn who does not go to its celebration in the good old spirit, contented to be for one night (under the superintending eye of the master and mistress of the feast,) " hail fellow, well met," with every rustic lad and lass assembled in the barn.

[*] The Malt Tax.—The amount of this tax, including the expense of collection, is about six millions a-year. Now, mark: when the barley is four shillings a-bushel, the malt would be four shillings a bushel, if there were no tax; because the increase during the malting pays for the malting. As things now stand, when barley is four shillings a bushel, malt is nine shillings, though the tax is only two and sixpence. The other two and sixpence goes to the maltster to pay for the capital, which he is obliged to employ in the advance of duties, to compensate him for the various injuries he receives from the excise restrictions, and to guarantee him against the perils amidst which he is continually placed by the pains and penalties which surround him: so that this malt-tax, which nominally amounts to six millions a-year, amounts in reality to thirteen millions and a-half a-year.—*Cobbett.*

MEMORABILIA OF THE MONTH.

This month was named by the Saxons *Wyn Monath, Wine Month*, and also *Winter-futteth*. Antiquaries say, that although they made no wine, they procured it at this season of the closing vintage, from neighbouring countries. Is it not as probable that it was so named from their *Barley-wine*—their stout OCTOBER. The 25th of the month is St. Crispin's Day, ever memorable as that on which the Battle of Agincourt was fought, in 1415; when the English beat the French, *six to one!*

> He, that shall live this day and see old age,
> Will yearly on the vigil, feast his friends,
> And say,—" To-morrow is St. Crispian !"
> Then will he strip his sleeve and shew his scars.
> Old men forget, yet shall not all forget;
> But they'll remember with advantage,
> What feats they did that day. Then shall our names,
> Familiar in their mouths as household words,
> Harry the King, Bedford, and Exeter, Salisbury and Gloster,
> *Be in their flowing cups freshly remembered.*
> This story shall the good man teach his son :
> And CRISPIN CRISPIAN shall ne're go bye
> From this day to the ending of the world.

N.B.—In this month 'Squires run mad after foxes.

THE WOODS OF OCTOBER.

The glory of this month, is the gorgeous splendour of wood-scenery. Woods have, in all ages, vividly impressed the human mind: they possess a majesty and sublimity, which strike and charm the eye. Their silence and obscurity affect the imagination with a meditative awe. They sooth the spirit by their grateful seclusion, and delight it by glimpses of their wild inhabitants; by their novel cries, and by odours and beautiful phenomena peculiar to themselves. In remote ages, their fearful solitudes, and ever-brooding shadows fostered superstition, and peopled them with satyrs, fauns, dryads, hamadryads, and innumerable spirits of dubious natures. The same cause consecrated them to religious rites. It was from the mighty and ancient oak of Dodona that the earliest oracles of Greece were pronounced. The Syrians had their groves dedicated to Baal, and Ashtorath the Queen of Heaven; and infected the Israelites with their idolatrous customs. In the heart of the woods the Druid cut down the bough of misletoe, and performed the horrible ceremonies of his religion, The philosophers of Greece resorted to groves, as spots the most august and befitting the delivery of their sublime precepts. In the depths of the woods did Anchorites seek to forget the world, and to prepare their hearts for the purity of heaven. To lovers and poets, they have ever been favourite haunts; and the poets, by making them the scenes of their most beautiful fictions and descriptions, have added to their native charms a thousand delightful associations. Ariosto, Tasso, Spencer, Shakspeare, and Milton, have sanctified them to the hearts of all generations. What a world of magnificent creations comes swarming upon the memory as we wander in the woods! The gallant knights and beautiful dames, the magical castles, and hippogrifs of the Orlando: the enchanted Forest, the Armida, and Erminia of the Gerusalemma Liberata. Fair Una, with her milk-white Lamb, Pan, and the Satyrs, Archimages, the fair Florimels, and false Duessas of the Fairy Queen; Ariel and Caliban, Jaques and his motley fool in Ardennes, the fairies of the Midsummer Nights Dream, Oberon, Titania, and that pleasantest of all mischief-makers, Puck—the noble spirits of the immortal Comus. With such company, woods are to us any thing but solitudes, they are populous and inexhaustible worlds.

TREES.

What can be more beautiful than trees? Their lofty trunks august in their simplicity, asserting to the most inexperienced eye, their infinite superiority over the imitative pillars of man's pride; their graceful play of wide-spreading branches; and all the delicate and glorious machinery of buds, leaves, flowers, and fruit, that with more than magical effect burst forth from naked and rigid twigs, with all the rich, brilliant, and unimaginably varied colours under heaven; breathing delectable odours, pure and fresh, and animating; pouring out spices and medicinal essences; and making music from the softest and the most melancholy undertones, to the full organ-peal of the tempest. I wonder not that trees have commanded the admiration of men in all nations, and periods of the world.—*Howitt*.

RATIONALE OF THE COLOURING OF THE WOODS IN OCTOBER.

It is at the end of summer, or in the course of autumn, that the leaves change their colour. However varied the tints may be which they present, they may, with a small number of exceptions, be reduced to shades of yellow or red. The change is by no means sudden. In general the green colour gradually disappears in the leaf. Many leaves, however, begin to grow yellow here and there in spots. In others, there long remain dots of a beautiful green on the orange or yellow ground of the leaves. Some begin to change at their edges, and especially at the tip. The nerves seem to retain the green colour longest. The leaves whose green is deep assume the red colour, and those whose green is pale the yellow or yellowish tint. Most of the leaves, however, which become red, pass through the yellow as an intermediate tint. The action of light exercises a great influence upon the autumnal change of the colour of the leaves. In darkness all change of colour is prevented, and the leaf falls off green. It is well known that the green parts of plants absorb oxygen during the night, and expire a certain proportion of that gas when exposed to the sun in spring water. Leaves already coloured do not disengage oxygen on being exposed to the sun's light. Leaves when coloured in part, or on the point of changing colour, from that moment cease to give out oxygen in the sun. On arriving at the point where the tendency to autumnal colouring commences, they continue to inspire oxygen during the night, and in a quantity always decreasing as the colouring advances; from which it may be concluded that it is to the fixation of the oxygen in the colouring matter of the leaf that the change of tint is owing. The colouring principle of the leaf is a substance which is named *chromule*. If a yellow leaf is allowed to remain some time in potassa, it becomes of a beautiful green. Ammonia and all the alkalies produce the same effect. On the other hand, when a green leaf is left in an acid, it becomes yellow or red, and potash restores the green colour. As the green chromule is frequently seen to pass through the yellow hues, before arriving at the red, it might naturally be concluded that the latter is at a higher degree of oxygenation. The autumnal change in the colour of the chromule might therefore depend upon the fixation of new doses of oxygen, which would continue to be absorbed without being exhaled. This would account for the phenomena presented by certain leaves which exhibit the three colours, red, yellow, and green at once.

BOOKS OF THE MONTH.

AUGUST and SEPTEMBER are proverbially the heaviest months of the year for books. They are few and far between; and the great *hits* are reserved for what is technically called the publishing season. Periodicals, accordingly, form the staple of the dead months; for works publishing in a *series* or in *numbers* are only matter of concernment to those unfortunate persons who are too generally wondering if that Encyclopedia, that Dictionary, or that Biographical or Historical work, is to have any end.

MAGAZINES FOR SEPTEMBER.

THE NEW MONTHLY contains nothing by the Great Editor, Mr. Bulwer, save, perhaps, a short introductory political article. Lady Blessington's Recollections of Lord Byron are continued in this number. They are acute, penetrative, and written in a just but kindly spirit. We fear that this most impatient of all worlds is beginning to tire even of his Lordship, and to feel his memory somewhat of a bore. There is at present Lord Byron in the New Monthly, Lord Byron in Murray's New Edition, Lord Byron in the *Athenæum*, and altogether too much Lord Byron. The business part of the *New Monthly* is always well, and most industriously managed. Nothing is forgotten which may enable the superficial to talk, and the thoughtful to learn, about whatever is going forward in Literature, Art, Science, and Inventions.

BLACKWOOD is chiefly remarkable for two things; a *Noctes* without a Shepherd, and a Number without one line from the prolific pen of Christopher North. Yet it is a fair number, of the ordinary staple.

FRASER, which steers the same course in politics as Blackwood, contains one good paper—*The Schoolmaster in Newgate*—a shocking picture, and, we fear, too correct a one, of the way in which the cruel criminal law of England is made more cruel by haste and injustice in the administration. Fraser's Magazine has discovered that the way the Press is so universally inimical to the Church, is, that the wicked lives of editors and newspaper writers are reproved by the sanctity of the clergy! We give it credit for the discovery.

THE BRITISH MAGAZINE.—This is a recent publication got up to prop the Church, and take its defence, in these awful times, out of the profane and rough hands of such friends as *Blackwood* and *Fraser*. Well-meaning people seem to be connected with it; but hitherto it is, in a literary view, a wishy-washy concern. The Church would do well to retain her old corners in her old sinful organs, if she wish to have her voice heard through the Press in any tone above the *cheep* of a sick chicken.

TAIT'S Magazine for September is especially welcome to us, for the re-appearance of John Galt in a Scottish periodical. *The Howdie* could not have been written by any one save the author of the Annals of the Parish, and the Ayrshire Legatees. This new *autobiography* exhibits all his quaint humour and rich, homely pathos. We are glad to see that it is to be a series. The adventures of the Howdie must be an exhaustless subject: all life lies before her. Of the politics of this Magazine we need not speak. They are those of *Radical* reformers, (reform to the root,) and able, bold, and uncompromising. This number contains the second part of the article on *Parliamentary Candidates*, to which we gave such unqualified praise last month. It is written, we have reason to believe, by a favourite liberal candidate, who, we hope, will soon, in Parliament, act on the doctrines he here lays down. We should be glad to see this paper reprinted in a cheap form, and distributed by tens of thousands among electors. Sir H. Parnell's papers on *Financial Reform* and the *Bank Charter* are worthy of him who is the ablest writer of the day on practical Political Economy. From *The Life and Writings of Korner* we formerly made a quotation. It is one of those splendid articles which form the glory of modern periodical literature.

Tait is the only October* Magazine we have yet seen. The October Number supports the high station this periodical at once took, and so skilfully maintains. *The Ministry and the People* speak out severe but necessary truths. In *Rousseau* and *Shelley* we have literature and philosophy combined. *Rose Blanche* is a tale of high-toned chivalry. *Night-Burial at Sea*, a wild and romantic *Coleridgian* poem; and in the *Elegy of the King of the Gipsies*, whose death we announced last week, a piece of fresh, spirited, and stirring verse. In poetry, it is not a little remarkable, that the *Utilitarian Magazine* has, since its commencement, immeasurably outstripped all the elder periodicals. It has contained the first sprightly runnings of several young and gifted minds.

POETRY.

About this still autumnal season, the minor bards are heard chirruping like as many grasshoppers; like them also to disappear with the first frost. Save the NATURAL SON, the first part of a strange story in verse, there is nothing lately worthy of notice in this way.

NEW NOVELS.

The NEW GIL BLAS is written by Mr. Henry David Inglis, the author of Travels in Spain, &c. The New Gil Blas is a rascally modern Spaniard, who runs away from his native village, wanders about a few years, meets with a variety of improbable adventures, and, his wild oats being sown, returns home with his plunder, marries and settles for life. We get over three volumes without knowing much more about Spain, or of men or women any where, than when we begin. The book is nearly a string of episodes; and though never very interesting, is never tedious. The hero is a paltry rogue, tricky and selfish, a disgrace to the ancient family of Blas of Santillane.

ZOHRAB THE HOSTAGE is a Persian historical novel. Persian tales were given up thirty years since. Persian novels have little more attraction for British people now, unless they can let us deeper into the Persian character and manners than does *Zohrab*.

---

* We print in advance to be able to supply distant places.

OUR VILLAGE, was so pleasant, really so charming, that one regrets seeing it run to the lees in this new and *last* volume. It is one *got up* of shreds and patches, from annuals, &c., and shows us that even Miss Mitford's sprightly fancy has its seamy side, and fag end. We are glad that she is to break cover in new ground. This volume is not worthy the authoress of *Ellen*, which we give to-day.

THE REFORMER is a novel written to expose the awful dangers of reforming tenets. This is done by the original plan of the author painting Radicals either as wild visionaries, or ruffians and infidels. This candid manner of describing political opponents, is now so familiar among the Tories that it requires no exposure from us.

The DOUBLE TRIAL is a book composed by some right-hearted, if not quite right-headed, old person of the noble gender, who, twenty years ago, would have called those lucubrations Essays, which here he interweaves with a story, which, after all, does not connect them together very neatly. Novel-readers of the elderly and patient cast will find this book amusing. It abounds in material of one kind or other.

LEGENDS OF THE RHINE: BY THE AUTHOR OF HIGH WAYS AND BYE WAYS, &c. &c.

WE always liked Mr. Grattan's books, his early ones especially; and, in this, differ from learned critics; but with the public on our side, which is better. Those who have read his Heiress of Bruges, may have a better idea of the pleasure the Legends will afford them than any description we can give could convey. We have the same sort of characters, and strain of sentiment, with almost the same scenes. With thorough novel-readers, this will be the favourite romance of the present autumn.

MEMOIRS OF THE DUCHESS OF ABRANTES.

ANOTHER volume of Madame Junot's Memoirs has appeared, and is on the whole less interesting than the former. Still a work that has Napoleon for a hero, and is written by a clever Frenchwoman, who possessed such opportunities of close observation of the First Consul and Emperor, and all the leading men and women of his Court and Camp, cannot want entertainment. To us it is truly wonderful how tenacious the memories of ladies are, when they sit down to write domestic histories. They might almost tempt one to believe also, that the curious faculty of second-sight cannot be exclusively confined to the Highlands of Scotland. It would, however, be ungracious to quarrel with a power which makes their writings so much more amusing than they would otherwise be.—After the Memoirs of the Duchess comes

PRIVATE CORRESPONDENCE OF A WOMAN OF FASHION.

WHETHER this work be spurious or genuine, written by lady or gentlewoman, makes not much difference. It includes a portion of the domestic history of England for seven years, beginning with the victory of Waterloo, gained by the Duke of Wellington, and ending with the victory of the British nation gained by Mr. Brougham seven years afterwards in the House of Peers, and at the trial of Queen Caroline. These affairs are related, as if by an eye witness, and in a lively, gossiping, pleasing style. Whether the original letters bear any post mark, either of Brussels, London, or Brighton, we have strong doubts.

LIVES OF EMINENT MISSIONARIES. BY J. CARNE.

To small Book Clubs in the country we should imagine this a desirable volume. It forms part of the SELECT LIBRARY, and is to be followed by more volumes on the same subject. This one contains the Memoirs of Eliot, the American evangelist; of Swartz, the Indian apostle; the history of the Moravian Mission to Greenland; and of some other missions. The great fault to us in this volume is, that, save Eliot, we have no British missionary. Some of the sketches may be drawn rather *en beau*; but simple, unadorned truth has lost its relish. We have read the volume with interest and pleasure, and can safely say, it is calculated both to delight and edify. It is adorned with a portrait of Swartz, and a picture of an interview between Eliot and the Indians, to whom he first addressed himself as a preacher.

LIFE OF ANDREW MARVELL.

A LIFE of this pure patriot and useful Member of Parliament, appeared in the second number of the SCHOOLMASTER. Here we have the same facts in a fuller form, and numerous extracts from both the prose and verse of the man who first deserved the name of "representative of the people." As a specimen of his humour, which was piquant, though delicate—the flavour of the fresh-gathered lemon, instead of the vinegar of ordinary, vulgar satire—we give his happy parody of a royal speech of Charles II. It might appear as a gem even in this refined age,—not that there is much reason to compliment the present age on the delicacy of the prevailing style of irony and satire.

"MY LORDS AND GENTLEMEN,

"I told you at our last meeting, the winter was the fittest time for business; and truly I thought so, till My Lord Treasurer assured me the spring was the best season for salads and subsidies. I hope, therefore, that April will not prove so unnatural a month, as not to afford some kind showers on my parched exchequer, which gapes for want of them. Some of you, perhaps, will think it dangerous to make me too rich; but I do not fear it; for I promise you faithfully, whatever you give me I will always want; and although in other things my word may be thought a slender authority, yet in that, you may rely on me I will never break it."

"MY LORDS AND GENTLEMEN,

"I can bear my straits with patience; but My Lord Treasurer[*] does protest to me, that the revenue, as it now stands, will not serve him and me too. One of us must pinch for it, if you do not help me. I must speak freely to you; I am in bad circumstances, for besides my harlots in service, my *reformado* concubines lie heavy upon me. I have a passable good estate, I confess; but God's-fish, I have a great charge upon it. Here is my Lord Treasurer can tell, that all the money designed for next summer's guards must, of necessity, be applied to the next year's craddles and swaddling clothes. What shall we do for ships then? I hint this only to you, it being your business, not mine; I know, by experience, I can live without ships. I lived ten years abroad without and never had my health better in my life; but how *you* will be without, I leave to yourselves to judge, and therefore hint this only by the bye: I do not insist upon it. There is another thing I must press more earnestly, and that is this: it seems a good part

---

[*] "The person," says Burnett, "who was appointed to succeed Lord Clifford as treasurer, was Sir Thomas Osborn, a gentleman of Yorkshire, whose estate was sunk. He was a very plausible speaker, but too copious, and could not easily make an end of his discourse. He had been always among the high cavaliers; and missing preferment, he opposed the court much, and was one of Lord Clarendon's bitterest enemies. He gave himself great liberties in discourse, and did not seem to have any regard for truth, or so much as to the appearances of it; and was an implacable enemy; but he had a peculiar way to make his friends depend on him, and to believe he was true to them.

of my revenue will expire in two or three years, except you will be pleased to continue it. I have to say for it; pray, why did you give me so much as you have done, unless you resolve to give on as fast as I call for it? The nation hates you already for giving so much, and I will hate you too, if you do not give me more. So that, if you stick not to me, you will not have a friend in England. On the other hand, if you will give me the revenue I desire, I shall be able to do those things for your religion and liberty, that I have had long in my thoughts, but cannot effect them without a little more money to carry me through. Therefore look to't, and take notice, that if you do not make me rich enough to undo you, it shall lie at your doors. For my part, I wash my hands on it. But that I may gain your good opinion, the best way is to acquaint you what I have done to deserve it, out of my royal care for your religion and your property. For the first, my proclamation is a true picture of my mind. He that cannot, as in a glass, see my zeal for the Church of England, does not deserve any farther satisfaction, for I declare him wilful, abominable, and not good. Some may, perhaps, be startled, and cry, how comes this sudden change? To which I answer, I am a changeling, and that is sufficient, I think. But to convince men farther, that I mean what I say, there are these arguments.

"First, I tell you so,—and you know I never break my word.

"Secondly, My Lord Treasurer says so,—and he never told a lie in his life."

The press was as hateful to a certain party after the Restoration as now. "The doleful evils" it brought upon the country are thus happily lamented:—

"The *press*, (that villainous engine) invented much about the same time with the Reformation, hath done more mischief to the discipline of our church than the doctrine can make amends for. It was a happy time, when all learning was in manuscript, and some little officer, like our author, did keep the keys of the library. When the clergy needed no more knowledge than to read the liturgy, and the laity no more clerkship than to save them from hanging. But now, since printing came into the world, such is the mischief that a man cannot write a book, but presently he is answered. Could the Press but at once be conjured to obey only an *imprimatur*, our author might not disdaine, perhaps, to be one of its most zealous patrons. There have been wayes found out to banish ministers, to find not only the people, but even the grounds and fields where they assembled, in conventicles; but no art yet could prevent these seditious meetings of letters. Two or three *brawny* fellows in a corner, with meer ink, and elbow grease, do more harm than a hundred systematical divines, with their sweaty preaching. And, what is a strange thing, the very spunges, which one would think should rather deface and blot out the whole book, and were anciently used for that purpose, are become now the instruments to make them legible. Their ugly printing letters, which look but like so many rotten tooth-drawers; and yet these rascally operators of the press have got a trick to fasten them again in a few minutes, that they grow as firm a set, and as biting and talkative as ever. O, printing! how hast thou disturbed the peace of mankind! that lead, when moulded into *bullets*, is not so mortal as when formed into *letters!* There was a mistake, sure, in the story of *Cadmus*; and the serpent's teeth which he sowed, were nothing else but the letters which he invented. The first essay that was made towards this art, was in single characters upon iron, wherewith, of old, they stigmatized slaves, and remarkable offenders; and it was of good use, sometimes, to brand a schismatic; but a bulky Dutchman diverted it quite from its first institution, and contriving those innumerable *syntagmes* of alphabets, hath pestered the world ever since, with the gross bodies of their German divinity. One would have thought in reason, that a Dutchman might have contented himself only with the wine-press."

MEMOIRS OF LA FAYETTE AND OF THE REVOLUTION OF 1830. By M. Sarrans, Secretary to La Fayette.—This work is exciting some interest in the political world. Portions of it have been translated, and the whole is to appear in an English garb forthwith. It is severe, and it may be just, on Louis Philippe, who is neither increasing in favour at home nor abroad.

MEMOIR OF AN EDINBURGH TRADESMAN.

WE like the teaching which is given by living example; and therefore conceive ourselves fortunate in being able to produce one so excellent, and greatly obliged to the respectable tradesman, who, in compliance with our request, has furnished us with the subjoined history. The name we do not publish, from motives that will be easily intelligible; but it is no secret, and we vouch for the authenticity of a narrative which enables us emphatically to say to the young of the same numerous class, "*Go ye and do likewise.*" The story, and we wish it had been more circumstantially told, is given in the simple words of the writer:—

"I was born in 1770, in the north part of the kingdom, of very poor parents, who came to reside in Edinburgh about 1774–5. My father soon lost his health by living in a town; of my three elder brothers, one went to sea and two into the army, and therefore could give no assistance to our father and mother. In December 1780, I was put apprentice to a most respectable tradesman, who finding that my education had been entirely neglected, did what he could to remedy this defect; taught me partly to read and to write, and kindly lent me books, by which I became somewhat acquainted with the general history of mankind. Until I reached my 13th year, I made very little progress in the knowledge of my business, but having attained this age I had become a very strong lad, and being very handy, my good tutor took care to reward me for my exertions, and placed me over my fellow apprentices, who were much elder boys. Thus encouraged, I could at the age of 15 or 16 perform fully as much work as is usually performed by ordinary workmen. This was soon spread abroad by my *most worthy* instructor, and drew from my shop-mates some ill will and many advices, such as, "Why do you work so hard? Why turn out so much work? I who do not do the one-half, will just get as much thanks as you who fight so much." This I met with, "I do not care for thanks. I wish to be an expert workman and able to earn money." In this I was so successful, that by the time I reached my 22d year, I was able to make 18s., 20s., 30s. or even £2 per week. It was fortunate that I early turned my attention to practising speedy methods of proceeding with my work, as in my 17th year, I unluckily became acquainted with a very handsome young woman. We were unluckily so well pleased with each other, that at last we were advised to marry. I was 17, and she wanted three months of that age. Thus, without experience, we were placed together, I an apprentice at 5s. per week; my worthy teacher made it a shilling more, and in this way I made out my time. I then had 9s. per week, but this was not nearly sufficient to answer all our purposes. I therefore fell upon an expedient which nearly doubled my income, by working at home. In this way I worked from 8 at night till 12, and up again at 5 in the morning. I thus made good wages, and was enabled to help my father and mother, until I succeeded in keeping them in competence and comfort for a considerable number of years. And all this was accomplished without in the least diminishing my own comforts. In a short time I was able to save as much money as enabled me to procure a good stock of tools, and at the age of 26, I was farther able to set up in trade for myself, and soon gathered a good stock of goods. Finding that my want of scientific knowledge was a sad drawback to me in my trade, I resolved to attend the lectures of Professor ———— in the University of Edinburgh. This most excellent man did all he could to encourage me in my studies, and I soon found that

KNOWLEDGE IS POWER.

I was now able to undertake work of a much more profitable kind than what I could have done, before I received the instructions of that most excellent Professor, who also did all in his power to recommend me as a tradesman to his acquaintances. By these means I soon made as much as enabled me to retire from all concern with business.

Let me add that feasting, drinking, gaming, or company-keeping were never included in my pursuits. I therefore at an advanced age enjoy excellent health and spirits, and walk about at my ease. All these advantages are within the reach of every workman, if he will only abstain from ale, porter, whisky, &c. What a contrast this is to the generality of workmen when age overtakes them. Even at 40 or 50, do we not find them generally useless for any good purpose. Both body and mind enfeebled by the almost constant use of that accursed beverage, whisky. I beg to add, that while I was a journeyman, I was made to suffer all the petty persecution possible from my shop-mates, because I would not join them in their debasing pursuits. I am now the only one alive out of 23 journeymen who were in that work in 1788–9. Thus I have had a good reward for having in time avoided that vile practice of drinking and idling; and having accustomed myself to hard labour when young, I found as I advanced in life that it was no hardship at the age of 60 to do the hardest work in my line.

THE CORN LAWS, alias THE BREAD TAX.

Besides prohibiting duties, there are the Corn Laws, for the protection of what is called the agricultural interest, or, in plain parlance, for swelling the rental of the landlord. It appears from the resolutions submitted to the House of Commons by Lord Milton, that the average price of wheat in England, in the year ending February, 1830, had been 64s. 2d. per quarter. The average price on the Continent and in America, during the same period, had been 46s. 3d. per quarter. Now, if there were no restrictions on the importation of corn, the price in England would be nearly the same as in Poland or the United States; but, in consequence of the boroughmongering tax, the price is about 20s. per quarter higher: so that if the annual consumption of corn by the community be 48 millions of quarters, they pay exactly so many pounds additional taxes, in order to swell the rents of the landowners. This tax, be it observed, is chiefly borne by those who are least able to bear it— by that class which has been so long disfranchised, and whose consequent poverty now prevents them from availing themselves of the privileges with which the Reform Bill would otherwise invest them. It has been often and justly observed, that a tax upon bread is the most oppressive and unjust that could be imposed upon the industrious classes. The hard-working mechanic, that slaves from morning to night for a scanty support, consumes as much bread, individually, as the Marquess of Westminster, or the Duke of Buccleuch, with his 130,000l. per annum; and the tradesman's family, when he can support them, eat more bread than the same number in the family of the wealthiest peer.

How Vanity Quickeneth the Sense of Hearing.—An old naval officer, had lost the hearing of one ear by the bursting of a cannon near him during an action, yet would the faintest echo of an encomium, designed for himself, strike upon the drum of the other, and awaken his attention as acutely as the sound of a salute from the port-guns of a foreign power.

PROGRESS OF SCOTCH AGRICULTURE.

During the first half of the last century agriculture was in the most miserable state throughout Scotland; but after the Union many of the most active spirits of the country being relieved from political turmoils, and their ambitious schemes of aggrandisement brought to an end by that event, turned their attention to agriculture. Among these Fletcher of Saltoun and Lord Belhaven, both of whom had eagerly opposed the Union, distinguished themselves by their example and by their writings. In 1733 the society of improvers was formed in Edinburgh, who exerted themselves to introduce the modes of culture then practised in the Low Countries and in England. The turnip husbandry, the first and most important of the improvements in modern agriculture, had been introduced into Norfolk by Lord Townsend from Hanover, whither he had accompanied George I. But the unsettled state of Scotland, the discontents about the malt tax, which broke out into open insurrection in 1725, and the rebellions of 1715 and 1745, impeded all the efforts of the society. Although, therefore, the practice of draining, enclosing, the cultivation of artificial grasses, turnips, and potatoes had been introduced by the middle of the last century to a limited extent in the south-east part of the kingdom, on the estates of some of the land proprietors who paid attention to agriculture, their example was not followed by the tenantry generally, who laboured under a great deficiency of capital, and who were unwilling to adopt changes till they saw them succeed when tried by men in their own rank. Green crops being almost unknown, fresh animal food could not be obtained during one half of the year. Each family salted in October or November its supply of beef till Whitsunday. If the cattle were alive in the spring, and able to go to the pastures without assistance, it was thought sufficient. In the west of Scotland agriculture was in a still more backward state. When Wight visited Wigtonshire, he found, as late as 1777, that the rotation of crops, and the beneficial effects of the intervention of green crops among those of corn, were utterly unknown. The system there practised was to raise crops of oats and bear in perpetual succession; or, in order to avoid the thirlage on oats, from which the bear was exempted, one crop of oats, and three or four crops of bear were raised in succession. In Dumfries-shire there was only one road in 1774, that from Dumfries to Portpatrick, which had been made for military purposes fifteen years before that period. Wheat was then little cultivated: it was very rare in many districts well fitted for its cultivation, as Clackmannanshire, Forfarshire, &c. In the county of Kirkcudbright bear was grown on the same land in perpetual succession. On the outfield land a return of three for one was considered a fair crop of oats, and three bolls of oats only produced one boll of meal. The barley was so mixed with the seeds of noxious weeds, that the ale made from it produced a narcotic effect on persons not accustomed to drink it. Ayrshire, where the management of the dairy is at present so well understood, is thus described, in 1750: "The farm-houses are mere hovels, having an open hearth, a fire place in the middle of the floor, the dunghills at the door, the cattle starving, the people wretched. There are no fallows, no green crops, no artificial grass, no carts, or waggons, and hardly a potato or esculent root." When the late Mr. Barclay succeeded to the estate of Ury, in Kincardineshire, in 1760, there was no road upon it, and consequently, neither carts nor wheel carriages in use. The use of lime, as a manure, was unknown. In the Highland districts, matters were still worse. The land was scourged by a repetition of grain-crops, till it refused to bear any longer. Weeds and natural grasses were then allowed to accumulate for a number of years, till the ground gained such heart, as fitted it for a renewal of the former exhausting process. The natural pastures, which were free to all the community, were, at the same time, overstocked with cattle, and numerous deaths were thus occasioned every winter. Farms were let to the whole body of tenants in each town or village in run-rig. The subdivisions or ridges of the farm passing into the hands of the joint tenants in succession, each person had only a temporary interest in the portion which he happened to hold, and had no prospective benefit to induce him to ameliorate it. Agriculture, in short, was unknown, and a few black cattle roamed over extensive districts which now bring ample revenues to their proprietors. Troops of banditti infested the Highland districts, and the counties adjoining. It was usual to pay a sum of money annually to the leaders of these bands for the protection which the government was too weak to afford. The exacting of blackmail, for so the payment was called, was soon converted into a means of extortion and rapine; and though an act existed rendering the paying as well as taking of it a capital crime, yet the practice continued. There is still extant a contract of Blackmail, dated as late as June, 1741, drawn out on stamped paper, in good formal style, and attested with all the solemnities of law, between James and John Grahame, elder and younger of Glengyle, and ten gentlemen of the counties of Perth, Stirling, and Dumbarton. By this deed the Grahames engage, on receiving notice of the theft or robbery of any cattle, within 48 hours after the robbery, and in consideration of an annual payment of L.4 for every L.100 of the valued rents of the lands subscribed for, either to restore the cattle within six months, or to pay their value to the owners. The deed is drawn with much precision, and the manner of giving intimation of the thefts, and the places where it is to be given, are distinctly specified. It was, however, only intended to provide against robberies on the great scale, for it is provided that the Grahames were not to be liable for *pickeries*, and the distinction between a *theft* and a *pickery* is accurately defined. "Declaring that one horse or black cattle stolen within or without doors, or any number of sheep *above six*, shall be construed to be a theft and not pickery."

Meantime, various attempts had been made to encourage industry, and to furnish the capital necessary for its successful exertion; but some of these attempts had, at first, an injurious effect. The Royal Bank was established in 1727, but the disputes which immediately arose between it and the Bank of Scotland were attended with the most disastrous consequences. Duncan Forbes of Culloden, then Lord Advocate, in writing to the Duke of Newcastle, 26th June, 1728, says, "At present, credit is run so low by a struggle between the two banks, that money can scarcely be found to go to market with." In 1731 another attempt was made by the Bank of Scotland to settle branches at Aberdeen, Dundee, Glasgow, and Berwick, but they were all recalled in 1733. Such was the miserable state of manufactures and commerce, that imperfect as the state of agriculture was, Scotland then exported corn, and the exportation increased from 23,000 quarters in 1707 to 50,000 quarters in 1743. This fact shews that the cultivation of the soil had been somewhat improved; for the population of the country had increased about one-fifth, and the price of corn had rather fallen. The fall in the price of grain may, however, also be accounted for by a rise in the value of the precious metals during the first half of the last century, as supposed by Dr. Adam Smith; who shows that a fall in the price of grain had taken place in other countries, where no improvement in agriculture appears to have been made.

The rebellion of 1745, though attended with much immediate evil, proved ultimately of great benefit to Scotland. Before that event the English statesmen had overlooked Scotland, despising it as a poor barren country, hardly worthy of their attention. The Rebellion showed, that it at least contained materials of a highly dangerous nature, which it was absolutely necessary to watch narrowly, and attention was thus directed to the means of turning the energies of the country to useful purposes. Among the evils which it was necessary speedily to eradicate, was the great power exercised over the lower orders by the proprietors of land. This is a circumstance remarked by many of the English travellers in the early part of the last century; and it was occasioned by the remains of the feudal system, and by many of the nobility and gentry possessing heritable jurisdictions, by which they were enabled, under colour of law, to oppress the lower orders. After much hesitation and opposition these jurisdictions were abolished in 1747; but not until their owners had exacted L.150,000 sterling from the public revenue, for giving up their right. At present it is necessary to pay judges to administer the law, and we may judge what was the nature of the justice dealt out by these hereditary judges, when they considered their tribunals an object of emolument. Order being now restored throughout the country, and justice impartially administered in every district by the King's judges, a change rapidly took place in the moral character of the people. The laziness, the want of industry, and of business habits of the Scotch, are remarked by the English travellers at the end of the 17th century. Things seem to have been much in the same state as they are in Ireland at present. The industry, perseverance, and many of the other good qualities for which the Scotch character is now distinguished, only date from the middle of the last century. The chief cause of the beneficial change of character, must be principally sought in the establishment of parochial schools. The first effectual provision for that object had been made during the usurpation by a statute in the year 1646. It authorized a compulsory assessment on the heritors of each parish, for the building of a school-house, and the providing of a salary to a Schoolmaster. On the restoration, however, this excellent statute was repealed, together with all the other laws passed during the Commonwealth, and it was not until the year 1696, that it was re-enacted. Its effects on the national character may be considered to have commenced at the union, though it was nearly half a century later till its beneficial influence was fully felt. The seeds of agricultural prosperity had been already sown by the Society of Improvers, and only required cultivation. This was not long wanting. Many Scotch officers had served in the army under the Duke of Cumberland, in the low countries, and had there an opportunity of learning improved modes of agriculture. On their return home after the peace of 1748, many of them betook themselves to farming, an art with which some of them had been acquainted before entering the army; and they introduced the improved system. Their example was followed much more readily than when it had been given by the landed proprietors. But the tenantry had not the stimulus which an increasing price of corn is so much calculated to bestow. For a century and a half, the prices had been singularly uniform. We have accurate accounts of the prices of corn in Scotland, since the year 1627, when the Sheriff Fiars, a system of judicially ascertaining the average prices for the year, by the examination of witnesses, before the Sheriff of the county, and a jury, was introduced. The prices so ascertained, are called the Fiars. From the year 1627, to the year 1699, a period of 73 years, the average fiar price of wheat, in East Lothian, was 15s. 6¾d. per boll, containing almost exactly half a Winchester quarter. From the year 1700, to the year 1735, the average is 14s. 5½d. From 1736, to 1770, 14s. 6¾d. The account of the prices at the Windsor market exhibit a similar result, the fall from the year 1646 to 1770, amounting to about 20 per cent. The rents of land did not, therefore, increase in any appreciable degree, during the first half of the last century. "As an example, I have access to know that one large farm in the Lothians, was let in the year 1728, at a rent payable in victual, with L.100 Scots, or L.8. 6s. 8d. of money; and converting the former at the prices of these times, the whole amounted to L.430, a large rent in those days. In 1748, the lease was renewed with an addition to the money rent of L.2 12s. 6d., but with no other addition; and lastly, on the expiry of this lease, without any increase of rent whatever; and many other instances to the same effect might be given."

Between the years 1760 and 1777, however, it appears from Wight's Agricultural Surveys, that most of the improvements of the Norfolk and Flemish Husbandry had been introduced into the south-eastern counties. From the great demand for agricultural produce occasioned by the increase of our population, and of the wealth, and consequently of the consumption of the country, poorer soils were brought into cultivation, and the amount of the rental of the southern counties, and probably of the other parts of the kingdom, doubled in the period between 1774 and 1794.

This increase of the rents of land could only be occasioned by the great improvement of cultivation, for the rise in the price of grain was very inconsiderable. Thus the average price of wheat at Windsor market in the ten years ending with 1775 was L.2 11s. 3½d. per quarter; and in the ten years ending with 1795, only 3s. higher. It will be observed this great rise took place before the passing of the Bank Restriction Act in 1797. It is well to remark this fact, because many writers now hold out, that the Restriction Act, by enabling the Bank of England to issue their notes in great quantities and depreciate the currency, and consequently to raise the prices of grain, was the great cause of the rapid progress of agriculture. After this period the price of corn continued rapidly to increase,—wheat rose repeatedly in England to L.6 per quarter, and the average of the eight years, ending with 1813, is L.5, 1s. 9d. In consequence of this great rise, combined with the improvements of agriculture, the rent of land continued rapidly to increase. This increase, in the sixteen years ending with 1811, cannot, in the corn counties, be estimated at less than 100 per cent. upon the rental of 1795. Thus the rental of Berwickshire, which was estimated at L.112,000 in 1795, appeared from the property tax returns, to be L.231,973 in 1811. The county of Renfrew had advanced from L.67,000, to L.127,068; Edinburghshire, from L.184,575, to L.277,827. We thus see that in less than forty years, the rental of the farms in Scotland had been augmented fourfold. "On one of the largest estates in East Lothian, extensive farms, of a very mixed quality, which had been let on lease, at a rack-rent in 1793, were re-let in 1812 on leases of 21 years, and the rule by which the new rents were fixed, was 2½ of the old." In six years, from 1806, to 1813, the rental of Kirkcudbrightshire, rose from L.167,125, to above L.206,000, or 25 per cent. But the increase of the value of stock farms, was still more extraordinary. The rental of Argyleshire was under L.20,000 in 1751. It had risen to L.89,000 in 1798, and to L.192,000 in 1811. In Caithness there were many instances of farms bringing, in 1809, eight times the rent they had yielded in 1762. In Dumbartonshire, the increase on many farms was tenfold. In the period between 1667, when the valued rent of Scotland was taken, and 1811, the land rental of the whole kingdom increased fifteen fold; but the rental of Inverness, in the same period, was augmented thirty fold. Mr. Smith, in his Agricultural Survey of Galloway, published about twenty years ago, asserts, "that a variety of instances might be adduced, where the present rents of farms are equal to the prices paid for them in the memory of persons still living."

The great increase in the value of stock farms arose in a great degree from the introduction of sheep instead of the rearing of black cattle. The rental of the estate of Chisholm in Strathglass was L.700 in 1783, and in 1827, L.5000. The rental of the Glengary estates increased from L.800 in 1788 to L.6000 or L.7000 in 1827. The improvements in agriculture, and the large capitals which had been acquired by the tenantry, by enabling them to farm in the best manner, and to ameliorate the soil, greatly contributed to the increase of rents. The bank restriction also, by continually raising the prices of grain, and by enabling the bankers to lend large sums of money to the tenantry, had a great effect. The value of estates, particularly in the Highlands, rose enormously. In 1779, the estate of Castlebill, in Inverness-shire, was sold judicially for L.9900. In 1804 it brought L.60,000. In 1787, the barony of Lentran was sold for L.2500—in 1802, for L.20,000. In 1781, the rental of the estate of Glenelg, in Inverness-shire, was L.600;—it was exposed, towards the close of the last century, at L.30,000. In 1811, it was sold for L.100,000. In 1789, the lands of Ardnagrask were purchased at a judicial sale for L.1200, the rental then being L.30; in 1825, they were sold for L.6000. The estate of Fairburn, in Ross shire, in 1787, yielded a rental of only L.700 sterling; between 1791 and 1824, it was sold in lots, and brought in all L.80,000 sterling. In 1790, the property of Redcastle, in the same county, was sold by judicial sale for L.25,000, the rental being L.1000: in 1824, it was purchased by Sir William Fettes, Baronet, for L.135,000 sterling.—There was no district, however wild, which did not participate in the improvement, and the rental of the remote isles of Orkney, has increased from L.19,704 in 1798 to L.65,000 at present.

The following account of the change in the south-west counties of Scotland, is from the pen of a very competent judge in such matters, Mr. Loudon, the author of the Encyclopedia of Agriculture:—"The progress which the tract in question has made since we passed through it in 1805, is no less gratifying than it is astonishing. Good lines of road are now formed, where the roads were formerly hilly, circuitous, and always in bad order. Extensive tracts of country which, in 1805, were open waste; for instance, about Lochmaben, in Dumfries-shire, Castle Douglas, in Kirkcudbrightshire, and Galston, in Ayrshire, are now enclosed, drained, sheltered by plantations, studded with farm-houses, and cottages, and subjected to a regular rotation of crops. Many thousands of acres of rocky surface have been planted, and of the steep sides of hills, where aration could not be practised, we think we may safely state, that for every ten acres of plantation, which existed in 1805, there are a thousand in 1831. Almost all the farm-houses and farm-yards of the country have been renewed since the former period, and these now present a most regular and comfortable appearance. A great many of the labourers' cottages have also been rebuilt in a more substantial style, though not, as we shall hereafter show, with that attention to the comfort, decency, and cleanliness of the inhabitants, which has taken place in farm-houses. Next to the improvement which has taken place in the agriculture of the country, is that which has been effected on the country-seats of the landed proprietors. Almost every gentleman's house has been enlarged or rebuilt; new kitchen gardens have been formed, and the pleasure grounds altered; the number of hot-houses is increased, at least a hundred fold, and lodges, winding approaches, and scattered timber-trees are now substituted for common-place roads, gates, and grass fields; the latter either naked, or displaying only a few round clumps. All the towns have been more or less increased in size; the new buildings are larger, of an improved architecture, and the streets are wider."* In consequence of these improvements, the quantity of grain must have been greatly increased, but we have no means either of estimating the increase accurately, or the quantity of land brought into cultivation.

(To be continued.)

THE SEA SERPENT.

SOLUTION.—The public were amused for some time, a few years ago, by the tales of brother Jonathan, respecting the huge sea serpent. Without at all disputing the existence of creatures of that nature in the ocean, I have little doubt that a sight I witnessed, in a voyage to the West Indies, was precisely such as some of the Americans had construed into a "sea serpent, a mile in length," agreeing, as it did, with one or two of the accounts given. This was nothing more than a tribe of black porpoises in one line, extending fully a quarter of a mile, fast asleep! The appearance, certainly, was a little singular, not unlike a raft of puncheons, or a ridge of rocks; but the moment it was seen some one exclaimed (I believe the Captain), "Here is a solution of Jonathan's enigma!" and the resemblance to his "sea serpent" was at once striking. A good many years ago, an account appeared in the newspapers of a *veritable* sea serpent, seen between Coll and Eigg, by the Rev. Niell Maclean, minister of Small Isles. This imagined monster of the deep may be often seen in the Hebridean seas, if a congregation of grampuses pass for him. A voyager, who committed no mistake, gives the following account of a herd: "In the summer of 1821, in sailing from the island of Lewis to the opposite coast of Ross-shire, we passed through an immense drove of grampuses, passing slowly southwards into the Minch. These animals, of which there were probably two hundred, were scattered over an extent of about a square mile. They were of all sizes, from about 30 to 10 feet in length. The sea was smooth, with a slight breeze, and the sun shone gloriously on the waters. The gambols of these monsters of the deep were of the most interesting, I shall not say ludicrous, description. Sometimes one of them suddenly rushed up from the deep, raising himself, bolt upright in the air, until three-fourths of his length were above the surface, and then fell with a noise like thunder, splashing the foam around to a great distance. Some of them even leapt entirely out of the water, as one often sees a salmon do. Sometimes two or three of them would chase each other at the surface, with astonishing velocity. At other times they would almost all disappear of a sudden, and their rise again was marked by a hundred jets of steam, which they emit from their blow-holes. These animals are of a dark colour, and at a distance, on emerging from the water, they seem jet black. The sun glancing upon their polished sides as they rose in promiscuous succession, had a most singular effect."

MAGIC OF A NAME.—SIR WALTER SCOTT.—Perhaps the finest compliment ever paid Sir Walter Scott, was at the time of the late coronation. The streets were crowded so densely, that he could not make his way from Charing-cross down to Rose's, in Abingdon Street, though he elbowed ever so stoutly. He applied for help to a serjeant of the Scotch Greys, whose regiment lined the streets. "Countryman," said the soldier, "I am sorry I cannot help you," and made no exertion. Scott whispered his name—the blood rushed to the soldier's brow—he raised his bridle-hand, and exclaimed—"Then, Sir, you shall go down—Corporal Gordon, here—see this gentleman safely to Abingdon Street, come what will!" It is needless to say how well the order was obeyed.

* Loudon's Magazine, January, 1832.

THE STORY-TELLER.

ELLEN.

BY MISS MITFORD.

CHARLOTTE and ELLEN PAGE were the twin daughters of the Rector of N., a small town in Dorsetshire. They were his only children, having lost their mother shortly after their birth; and as their father was highly connected, and still more highly accomplished, and possessed good church preferment, with a considerable private fortune, they were reared and educated in the most liberal and expensive style. Whilst mere infants, they had been uncommonly beautiful, and as remarkably alike, as occasionaly happens with twin sisters, distinguished only by some ornament of dress. Their very nurse, as she used to boast, could hardly tell her pretty "couplets" apart, so exactly alike were the soft blue eyes, the rosy cheeks, the cherry lips, and the curly light hair. Change the turquoise necklace for the coral, and nurse herself would not know Charlotte from Ellen. This pretty puzzle, this inconvenience, of which mammas, and aunts, and grandmammas love to complain, did not last long. Either from a concealed fall, or from original delicacy of habit, the little Ellen faded and drooped almost into deformity. There was no visible defect in her shape, except a slight and almost imperceptible lameness when in quick motion; but there was the marked and peculiar look in the features, the languor and debility, and above all, the distressing consciousness attendant upon imperfect formation; and, at the age of twenty years, the contrast between the sisters was even more striking than the likeness had been at two.

Charlotte was a fine, robust, noble-looking girl, rather above the middle height. Her eyes and complexion sparkled and glowed with life and health, her rosy lips seemed to be made for smiles, and her glossy brown hair played in natural ringlets round her dimpled face. Her manner was a happy mixture of the playful and the gentle: frank, innocent, and fearless, she relied with a sweet confidence on every body's kindness, was ready to be pleased, and secure of pleasing. Her artlessness and *naïveté* had great success in society, especially as they were united with the most perfect good-breeding, and considerable quickness and talent. Her musical powers were of the most delightful kind; she sang exquisitely, joining, to great taste and science, a life, and freedom, and buoyancy, quite unusual in that artificial personage, a young lady. Her clear and ringing notes had the effect of a milk-maid's song, as if a mere ebullition of animal spirits; there was no resisting the contagion of Charlotte's glee. She was a general favourite, and, above all, a favourite at home,—the apple of her father's eye, the pride and ornament of his house, and the delight and comfort of his life. The two children had been so much alike, and born so nearly together, that the precedence in age had never been definitively settled; but that point seemed very early to decide itself. Unintentionally, as it were, Charlotte took the lead, gave invitations, received visiters, sate at the head of the table, became, in fact and in name Miss Page, while her sister continued Miss Ellen.

Poor Ellen! she was short, and thin, and sickly, and pale, with no personal charm but the tender expression of her blue eyes and the timid sweetness of her countenance. The resemblance to her sister had vanished altogether, except when, very rarely, some strong emotion of pleasure, a word of praise, or a look of kindness from her father, would bring a smile and a blush at once into her face, and lighten it up like a sunbeam. Then for a passing moment, she was like Charlotte, and even prettier,—there was so much of mind, of soul, in the transitory beauty. In manner she was unchangeably gentle, and distressingly shy, shy even to awkwardness. Shame and fear clung to her like her shadow. In company she could neither sing, nor play, nor speak, without trembling, especially when her father was present; her awe of him was inexpressible. Mr. Page was a man of considerable talent and acquirement, of polished and elegant manners, and great conversational power,—quick, ready, and sarcastic. He never condescended to cold there; but was something very formidable in the keen glance and the cutting jest, to which poor Ellen's want of presence of mind frequently exposed her,—something from which she shrank into the very earth. He was a good man, too, and a kind father,—at least he meant to be so,—attentive to her health and comfort, strictly impartial in favours and presents, in pocket-money and amusements, making no difference between the twins, except that which he could not help, the difference in his love. But, to an apprehensive temper, and an affectionate heart, that was everything; and, whilst Charlotte flourished and blossomed like a rose in the sunshine, Ellen sickened and withered like the same plant in the shade.

Mr. Page lost much enjoyment by this unfortunate partiality; for he had taste enough to have particularly valued the high endowments which formed the delight of the few friends to whom his daughter was intimately known. To them not only her varied and accurate acquirements, but her singular richness of mind, her grace and propriety of expression, and fertility of idea, joined to the most perfect ignorance of her own superiority, rendered her an object of as much admiration as interest. In poetry, especially, her justness of taste and quickness of feeling were almost unrivalled. She was no poetress herself, never, I believe, even ventured to compose a sonnet; and her enjoyment of high literature was certainly the keener for that wise abstinence from a vain competition. Her admiration was really worth having. The tears would come into her eyes, the book would fall from her hand, and she would sit lost in ecstacy over some noble passage, till praise, worthy of the theme, would burst in unconscious eloquence from her lips.

But the real charm of Ellen Page lay in the softness of her heart, and the generosity of her character; no human being was ever so free from selfishness in all its varied and clinging forms. She literally forgot herself in her pure and ardent sympathy with all whom she loved, or all to whom she could be useful. There were no limits to her indulgence, no bounds to her candour. Shy and timid as she was, she forgot her fears to plead for the innocent, or the penitent, or even the guilty. She was the excuser-general of the neighbourhood, turned every speech and action the sunny side without, and often, in her good-natured acuteness, hit on the real principle of action, when the cunning, and the wordly-wise, and the cynical, and such as look only for bad motives, had failed. She had, too, that rare quality, a genuine sympathy, not only with the sorrowful, (there is a pride in that feeling, a superiority,—we have all plenty of that,) but with the happy. She could smile with those who smiled, as well as weep with those who wept, and rejoice in a success to which she had not contributed, protected from every touch of envy no less by her noble spirit than by her pure humility: she never thought of herself.

So constituted, it may be imagined that she was, to all who really knew her, an object of intense admiration and love. Servants, children, poor people, all adored Miss Ellen. She had other friends in her own rank of life, who had found her out—many; but her chief friend, her principal admirer, she who loved her with the most entire affection, and looked up to her with the most devoted respect, was her sister. Never was the strong and lovely tie of twin-sisterhood more closely knit than in these two charming young women. Ellen looked on her favoured sister with a pure and unjealous delight that made its own happiness, a spirit of candour and of justice that never permitted her to cast a shade of blame on the sweet object of her father's partiality: she never indeed blamed him, it seemed to her so natural that every one should prefer her sister. Charlotte, on the other hand, used all her influence for Ellen, protected and defended her, and was half-tempted to murmur at an affection which she would have valued more, if shared equally with that dear friend. Thus they lived in peace and harmony, Charlotte's bolder temper and higher spirits leading and guiding in all common points, whilst, on the more important, she implicitly yielded to Ellen's judgment. But, when they had reached their twenty-first year, a great evil threatened one of the sisters, arising (strange to say) from the other's happiness. Charlotte, the reigning *bells* of an extensive and affluent neighbourhood, had had almost as many suitors as Penelope; but, light-hearted, happy at home, constantly busy and gay, she had taken no thought of love, and always struck me as a very likely subject for an old maid: yet her time came at last. A young man, the very reverse of herself, pale, thoughtful, gentlemanlike, and melancholy, wooed and won our fair Euphrosyne. He was the second son of a noble house, and bred to the church; and it was agreed between the fathers, that, as soon as he should be ordained, (for he still wanted some months of the necessary age,) and settled in a family-living held for him by a friend, the young couple should be married.

In the meanwhile Mr. Page, who had recently succeeded to some property in Ireland, found it necessary to go thither for a short time; and, unwilling to take his daughters with him, as his estate lay in the disturbed districts, he indulged us with their company during his absence. They came to us in the bursting spring-time, on the very same day with the nightingale; the country was new to them, and they were delighted with the scenery and with our cottage life. We, on our part, were enchanted with our young guests. Charlotte was certainly the most amiable of enamoured damsels, for love with her was but a more sparkling and smiling form of happiness;—all that there was of care and fear in this attachment, fell to Ellen's lot; but even she, though sighing at the thought of parting, could not be very miserable whilst her sister was so happy.

A few days after their arrival, we happened to dine with our accomplished neighbours, Colonel Falkner and his sister. Our young friends of course accompanied us; and a similarity of age, of liveliness, and of musical talent, speedily recommended Charlotte and Miss Falkner to each other. They became immediately intimate, and were soon almost inseparable. Ellen at first hung back. "The house was too gay, too full of shifting company, of titles, and of strange faces. Miss Falkner was very kind; but she took too much notice of her, introduced her to lords and ladies, talked of her drawings, and pressed her to sing:—she would rather, if I pleased, stay with me, and walk in the coppice, or sit in the arbour, and one might read Spenser whilst the other worked—that would be best of all. Might she stay?"—" Oh surely! But Colonel Falkner, Ellen, I thought you would have liked him?"—" Yes!"—" That *yes* sounds exceedingly like *no*."—" Why, is he not almost too clever, too elegant, too grand a man? Too mannered, as it were? Too much like what one fancies of a prince— of George the Fourth for instance—too high and too condescending? These are strange faults," continued she laughing; " and it is a curious injustice that I should dislike a man merely because he is so graceful, that he makes me feel doubly awkward—so tall, that I am in his presence a conscious dwarf—so alive and eloquent in conversation, that I feel more than ever puzzled and unready. But so it is. To say the truth, I am more afraid of him than of any human being in the world, except one. I may stay with you—may I not? and read of Una and of Britomart—that prettiest scene where her old nurse sooths her to sleep? I may stay?" And for two or three mornings she did stay with me; but Charlotte's influence and Miss Falkner's kindness speedily drew her to Holly-grove, at first shily and reluctantly, yet so with an evident, though quiet enjoyment; and we, sure that our young visitors could gain nothing but good in such society, were pleased that they should so vary the humble home-scene.

Colonel Falkner was a man in the very prime of life, of that happy age which unites the grace and spirit of youth with the firmness and vigour of manhood. The heir of a large fortune, he had served in the peninsular war, fought in Spain and France, and at Waterloo, and, quitting the army at the peace, had loitered about Germany and Italy and Greece, and only returned on the death of his father, two or three years back, to reside on the family estate, where he had won " golden opinions from all sorts of people." He was, as Ellen truly described him, tall and graceful, and well-bred almost to a fault; reminding her of that *beau idéal* of courtly elegance, George the Fourth, and me, (pray, reader, do not tell!) me, a little, a very little, the least in the world, of Sir Charles Grandison. He certainly did excel rather too much in the mere forms of politeness, in clokings and bowings, and handings down stairs; but then he was, like both his prototypes, thoroughly imbued with its finer essence—considerate, attentive, kind, in the most comprehensive sense of that comprehensive word. I have certainly known men of deeper learning and more original genius, but never any one whose powers were better adapted to conversation, who could blend more happily the most varied and extensive knowledge with the most playful wit and the most interesting and amiable character. *Fascinating* was the word that seemed made for him. His conversation was entirely free from trickery and display— the charm was (or seemed to be) perfectly natural: he was an excellent listener: and when he was speaking to any eminent person—orator, artist, or poet—I have sometimes seen a slight hesitation, a momentary diffidence, as attractive as it was unexpected. It was this astonishing evidence of fellow-feeling, joined to the gentleness of his tone, the sweetness of his smile, and his studied avoidance of all particular notice or attention, that first reconciled Ellen to Colonel Falkner. His sister, too, a charming young woman, as like him as Viola to Sebastian, began to understand the sensitive properties of this shrinking and delicate flower, which, left to itself, repaid their kind neglect by unfolding in a manner that surprised and delighted us all. Before the spring had glided into summer, Ellen was as much at home at Holly-grove as with us; talked and laughed and played and sang as freely as Charlotte. She would indeed break off, if visibly listened to, either when speaking or singing; but still the ice was broken; that rich, low, mellow voice, unrivalled in pathos and sweetness, might be heard every evening, even by the Colonel, with little more precaution, not to disturb her by praise or notice, than would be used with her fellow-warbler the nightingale.

She was happy at Holly-grove, and we were delighted; but so shifting and various are human feelings and wishes, that, as the summer wore on, before the hay-making was over in its beautiful park, whilst the bees were still in its lime-trees, and the golden beetle lurked in its white rose, I began to lament that she had ever seen Holly-grove, or known its master. It was clear to me, that, unintentionally on his part, unwittingly on hers, her heart was gone, —and, considering the merit of the unconscious possessor, probably gone for ever. She had all the pretty marks of love at that happy moment when the name and nature of the passion are alike unsuspected by the victim. To her there was but one object in the whole world, and that one was Colonel Falkner: she lived only in his presence; hung on his words; was restless, she knew not why, in his absence; adopted his tastes and opinions, which differed from hers as those of clever men so frequently do from those of clever women; read the books he praised, and praised them too, deserting our old idols, Spenser and Fletcher, for his favourites, Dryden and Pope; sang the songs he loved as she walked about the house; drew his features instead of Milton's, in a portrait which she was copying for me of our great poet—and finally wrote his name on the margin. She moved as in a dream—a dream as innocent as it was delicious!— but oh, the sad, sad waking! It made my heart ache to think of the misery to which that fine and sensitive mind seemed to be reserved. Ellen was formed for constancy and suffering—it was her first love, and it would be her last. I had no hope that her affection was returned. Young men, talk as they may of mental attractions, are commonly the slaves of personal charms. Colonel Falkner, especially, was a professed admirer of beauty. I had even sometimes fancied that he was caught by Charlotte's, and had therefore taken an opportunity to communicate her engagement to his sister. Certainly he paid our fair and blooming guest extraordinary attention; any thing of gallantry or compliment was always addressed to her, and so for the most part was his gay and captivating conversation; whilst his manner to Ellen, though exquisitely soft and kind, seemed rather that of an affectionate brother. I had no hopes.

Affairs were in this posture, when I was at once grieved and relieved by the unexpected recall of our young visiters. Their father had completed his business in Ireland, and was eager to return to his dear home, and his dear children; Charlotte's lover, too, was ordained, and was impatient to possess his promised treasure. The intended bridegroom was to arrive the same evening to escort the fair sisters, and the journey was to take place the next day. Imagine the revulsion of feeling produced by a short note, a bit of folded paper—the natural and redoubled ecstasy of Charlotte, the mingled emotions of Ellen. She wept bitterly: at first she called it joy—joy that she should again see her dear father; then it was grief to lose her Charlotte; grief to part from me; but, when she threw herself in a farewell embrace on the neck of Miss Falkner, whose brother happened to be absent for a few days on business, the truth appeared to burst upon her at once, in a gush of agony that seemed likely to break her heart. Miss Falkner was deeply affected; begged her to write to her often, very often; loaded her with the gifts of little price, the valueless tokens which affection holds so dear, and stole one of her fair ringlets in return. "This is the curl which William used to admire," said she; "have you no message for poor William?"—Poor Ellen! her blushes spoke, and the tears which dropped from her downcast eyes; but she had no utterance. Charlotte, however, came to her relief with a profusion of thanks and compliments; and Ellen, weeping with a violence that would not be controlled, at last left Holly-grove.

The next day we, too, lost our dear young friends. Oh, what a sad day it was! how much we missed Charlotte's bright smile, and Ellen's sweet complacency! We walked about desolate and forlorn, with the painful sense of want and insufficiency, and of that vacancy in our home, and at our board, which the departure of a cherished guest is sure to occasion. To lament the absence of Charlotte, the dear Charlotte, the happiest of the happy, was pure selfishness; but of the aching heart of Ellen, my dearer Ellen, I could not bear to think—and yet I could think of nothing else, could call up no other image than her pale and trembling form, weeping and sobbing as I had seen her at Holly-grove: she haunted even my dreams.

Early the ensuing morning I was called down to the Colonel, and found him in the garden. He apologized for his unseasonable intrusion; talked of the weather, then of the loss which our society had sustained; blushed and hesitated; had again recourse to the weather; and at last, by a mighty effort, after two or three sentences begun and unfinished, contrived, with an embarrassment more graceful and becoming than all his polished readiness, to ask me to furnish him with a letter to Mr. Page. "You must have seen," said he, colouring and smiling, "that I was captivated by your beautiful friend: and I hope——I could have wished to have spoken first to herself, to have made an interest—but still if her affections are disengaged—tell me, you who must know, you who are always my friend, have I any chance? Is she disengaged?" "Alas! I have sometimes feared this; but I thought you had heard—your sister at least was aware." "Of what? It was but this very morning—aware of what?"—"Of Charlotte's engagement." "Charlotte! it is of Ellen, not her sister, that I speak and think! Of Ellen, the pure, the delicate, the divine! That whitest and sweetest of flowers, the jasmine, the myrtle, the tuberose among women," continued he, elucidating his similes by gathering a sprig of each plant, as he paced quickly up and down the garden walk—"Ellen, the fairest and the best; your darling and mine! Will you give me a letter to her father? And will you wish me success?" "Will I! O how sincerely! My dear Colonel, I beg a thousand pardons for undervaluing your taste—for suspecting you of preferring a damask rose to a blossomed myrtle; I should have known you better." And then we talked of Ellen, dear Ellen, talked and praised till even the lover's heart was satisfied. I am convinced that he went away that morning, persuaded that I was one of the cleverest women, and the best judges of character that ever lived.

And now my story is over. What need to say, that the letter was written with the warmest zeal, and received with the most cordial graciousness—or that Ellen, though shedding sweet tears, bore the shock of joy better than the shock of grief,—or that the twin sisters were married on the same day, at the same altar, each to the man of her heart, and each with every prospect of more than common felicity.

ELEMENTS OF THOUGHT.

RICH AND POOR.

OUR rich and our very poor are almost equally ignorant, and equally enslaved by prejudice. The one class have their minds occupied with notions of fashion, ancestry, power, distinction, and separation from the rest of mankind, whom they look upon, not as intellectual and moral beings, but, as a sort of inheritance, to be turned, like their estates, to their own account; while the other look upon all above them, not as holders of capital, without which there would be no useful employment beyond that of picking up the few natural productions of the soil, but as a sort of natural enemies, leagued together to enslave and coerce all below them. Which is most in the right? The idle classes occupy the highest stations of society, and are looked up to with respect and reverence. Whatever they do is necessarily imitated. As all their natural wants are supplied, they have nothing to do but fancy "low, unreal" wants. Their imaginations are racked to hunt up new gratifications. They indulge in all sorts of expensive vanities; and, setting the fashion, what they indulge in out of idleness and whim, is also sought after by all below them.

THE INFERIOR GENTRY—EFFECTS OF TAXATION.—The gentry of small fortune have disappeared. The American war bore hard upon them, but the last has crushed them. Inheriting what to their forefathers had been an ample subsistence, they have found themselves step by step curtailed of the luxuries, and at last of the comforts of life, without a possibility of helping themselves. For those who were arrived at manhood, it was too late to enter into any profession, and to embark what they possessed in trade was hazarding all, and putting themselves at the mercy of a partner. Meantime, year after year, the price of every article of necessary consumption has increased with accelerating rapidity; education has become more costly, and, at the same time, more indispensable; and taxation, year after year, falls heavier, while the means of payment becomes less. In vain does he whose father has lived in opulence, and whom the villagers, with hereditary respect, still address hat in hand—in vain does he put down the carriage, dismiss the footman, and block up windows even in the house front. There is no escape. Wine disappears from his side-board, there is no longer a table ready for his friend. The priest is no longer invited after service—all will not do. *Southey.*

If you do not like Dr. Southey's picture, take a sketch by a different hand, more brief, but equally conclusive, and written after several years had added their melancholy sum of experience to the original statement. "This island exhibits the melancholy spectacle of millions of men toiled to the extremity of human endurance for a pittance scarcely sufficient to sustain life; weavers labouring for fourteen or sixteen hours a-day for eightpence, frequently unable to procure work even on these terms; other artisans exhausted almost to death by laborious drudgery, who, if better recompensed, seek compensation and enjoyment in the grossest sensual debauchery, drunkenness, and gluttony; master traders and manufacturers anxiously labouring for wealth, now gay in the fond hope that all their expectations will be realized, then sunk in deep despair by the breath of ruin having passed over them; landlords and tenants now reaping unmeasured returns from their properties, then pining in penury amidst an overflow of every species of produce; the Government cramped by an overwhelming debt, and the prevalence of ignorance and selfishness on every side, so that it is impossible for it to follow with a bold step the most obvious dictates of reason and justice, owing to the countless prejudices and imaginary interests which everywhere obstruct the path of improvement."—*Combe's Constitution of Man.*

All the ideas that man can form of the ways of Providence, and of the employment of angels and of spirits, must ever fall short of the reality; but still it is right to think of them. What can have a more exalting influence on the earthly life, than in those first days of our existence to make ourselves conversant with the lives of the blessed; with the happy spirits whose society we shall hereafter enjoy? We should accustom ourselves to consider the spirits of heaven always around us; observing and witnessing our most secret actions. Whoever is become familiar with these ideas will find the most solitary spot peopled with the best society.—*Klopstock.*

He who, by an intellectual and moral energy, awakens kindred energy in others, touches springs of infinite might, gives impulse to faculties to which no bound can be prescribed—begins an action which will never end. One great and kindling thought from a retired and obscure man may live when thrones are fallen, and the memory of those who filled them obliterated; and, like an undying fire, may illuminate and quicken all future generations.

WHALE FISHERY OF NEW SOUTH WALES.

An extraordinary impulse has been given of late to the sperm and black whale fisheries, from the port of Sydney. Two years ago five sperm vessels constituted the whole of the shipping employment in that trade. Of these one has been lost, and another despatched to England; while nine new sperm and four black whalers have been added to the list, making in all sixteen sail, measuring 3304 tons, and navigated by 464 men, while arrangements are in progress forthwith to increase the sperm list by nine new vessels. Each vessel (both sperm and black whale,) is provided with four boats, and manned with twenty-nine men. Six men, five harpoons, three lances, and two whale lines of one hundred and twenty fathoms each, are furnished to every boat; also three drogues, to one of which a flag is attached from a pole through its centre. The drogues are simply square floats of timber, serving as buoys to three of the boat harpoons, and are only used after the two line harpoons have been struck into whales, a line of eight fathoms securing the harpoon to the drogue, which though pulled under water by the whale on diving, quickly bobs up again on the latter approaching the surface to blow, and thus points out the whale's position. Each whaler has two iron boilers on deck of 220 gallons, and two copper coolers of 378 gallons, the oil being boiled in the iron boilers, and then drawn off into the coolers, to allow the sediment to settle previous to being put into the barrels. The fuel consists of the refuse of the blubber from the boiler, 90 gallons per hour being the average quantity of oil boiled, which is barrelled up hot, and rolled to the after part of the ship to cool. Every sperm vessel is victualled for 15 months, about 30 months being the average of two voyages (including stoppages in harbour to discharge or refresh), when no material repairs are required, and 180 tons of oil, the average fishing of each vessel for a single voyage. The following provisions constitute the 15 months' supply for one vessel:—9000lbs. of beef, 9000lbs. of pork, 6 tons of flour, 6 tons of biscuit, 200 bushels of pease, 259 gallons of rum, 300 gallons of molasses, and twelve cwt. of sugar. The crew have no wages, being paid by shares of the proceeds, called lays, after deducting rather more than two-thirds of the proceeds for the owner. The captain has a twelfth, the chief mate a twenty-eighth, the second mate a forty-eighth, the third mate an eightieth, the cooper and carpenter an eighty-fifth, and seamen each a hundredth lay. The largest whales seldom exceed sixty feet in length, or furnish more than eighty barrels of oil and spermaceti of thirty-one and a half gallons each, the spermaceti or head matter, as it is called, averaging one-third of the above quantity; eight barrels being a tun, consequently the largest whales seldom furnish more than ten tuns of oil and head matter. The two principal sperm grounds are the coasts of Japan and Solomon Islands, the fishing at the former commencing in April and ending in September, and at the latter commencing in September and ending in April, so that, when the ships commence at Japan, they conclude the voyage at the Solomons, and *vice versa.* The whales are all large on the Japan ground, few being under thirty barrels, whereas, at the Solomons, seldom more than two large whales are seen in a shoal, however numerous.

The black whales are taken in the bays of New Zealand and Van Diemen's Land, and also of New South Wales, to the southward of Sydney, the vessels lying at anchor during the time, and boiling the oil like the sperm whalers. The black whale season commences in April and ends in September, the whales entering the bays at that period for the purpose of calving. Black oil sells only at about half the price of the sperm oil; but the fishery being so nigh, and consequently attended with so much less expense, is found to be a very profitable concern. Many boats, indeed, are employed in this fishery both at New South Wales and Van Diemen's Land, towing their fish on shore, flinching them, and boiling the blubber there. The twelve sperm vessels now from Sydney, at 180 tuns of oil and spermaceti per vessel, thus realise in the gross 2160 tuns, which at L.70 per tun, amounts to L.151,200 for each voyage; and when the nine others now arranged for are added, the proceeds of the whole (including the black whalers) will reach to about L.250,000 per annum,—a tolerable sum added to the exports of a colony in the course of a few years, whose population, according to the last census, does not at present much exceed 40,000 souls.

EUROPEAN POPULATION.—A German periodical (*Hesperus*) contains some very fanciful speculations on the causes which affect population, from which we have selected the following particulars:—The increase and decrease of marriages in a country are naturally influenced by great events, such as peace and war, public prosperity and public calamities, famine and disease; but here we are told that political feelings exercise an influence. Thus, in Prussia, the number of marriages was greatly increased after the expulsion of the French. During the years 1817, 1818, and 1819, when the political prospects of that country were in their zenith, 1 person was married in 98; in the subsequent years the numbers again fell to 1 in 108, 1 in 111, and 1 in 118. In France, from the year 1815 to 1822, the number of marriages was much less than before the revolution, although the population was greater by several millions. After 1817 the number of annual marriages increased by about 8000, and continued stationary at that rate till 1821; but in 1822, after the evacuation of the country by foreign troops, the number quickly rose by 20,000, and, in the ensuing year, even by 40,000. But it again declined during the obnoxious administration of Villele, and again increased after the overthrow of his Ministry. Even in Russia from 70 to 80,000 couples less than usual were married in 1812. The proportion of deaths among children under five years is also remarkable, as it seems to keep pace with the degree of education and comfort of the inhabitants. It is smallest in the large towns, and would be smaller still if it were not for those who die in workhouses and hospitals, deserted by their parents. The degree of fertility of marriages seems to vary between 3500 and 5500 children to 1000 couples. The author, from an average of more than 77 millions of births, and 17 millions of marriages, all extending over a period of several years, comes to some results, from which we shall extract two or three of the most interesting.—To a thousand marriages there were born in the

Kingdom of the Two Sicilies	5546 children
In France	4148
In England	3565
In Zealand	3439

the Two Sicilies and Zealand being the extremes. Marriages appear to be less prolific as the countries lie nearer to the north. A fourth point of importance in these investigations is the growing excess of males over females since the general peace, which, if correctly stated, is not a little alarming, and seems to make a periodical return of war an indispensable evil. Thus, in Russia, the increase of males over females, in 15 years, was 804,453; in France, 347,254; in Prussia, 69,764; in Naples, 25,796; in Bavaria, 8398; in Bohemia, 69,172; in Sweden, 15,195; in Wurtemberg, 6877; in Hesse, 3361; in Nassau, 6484;—briefly, in a total population of 101,707,212, an excess of 1,356,754 males. If this proportion be applied to all Europe, with a population of 215 millions, the excess of the males would amount, in the same period of peace, to 2,700,000. In the southern provinces of Russia, near the Caucasus, in the two Americas, and the Cape of Good Hope, the disproportion is still greater.

COLUMN FOR THE LADIES.

LINES SET TO A BEAUTIFUL WELSH AIR.
BY BISHOP HEBER.

I mourn not the forest whose verdure is dying;
I mourn not the summer whose beauty is o'er;
I weep for the hopes that for ever are flying;
I sigh for the worth that I slighted before;
And sigh to bethink me how vain is my sighing,
For love, once extinguished, is kindled no more.

The spring may return with his garland of flowers,
And wake to new rapture the bird on the tree;
The summer smile soft through his chrystalline bowers;
The blessings of autumn wave brown o'er the lea;
The rock may be shaken—the dead may awaken,
But the friend of my bosom returns not to me.

KISSING OFF SAILORS.

Halifax is a charming, hospitable place. Its name is associated with so many pleasing recollections, that it never fails to extort another glass from the bottle which, having been gagged, was going to pass the night in the cellaret. But only say "Halifax!" and it is like "open sesame!"—out flies the cork, and down goes a bumper to the "health of all good lasses!" An Irish Guineaman had been fallen in with by one of our cruisers, and the commander of his Majesty's sloop, the Humming-bird, made a selection of some thirty or forty stout Hibernians to fill up his own complement, and hand over the surplus to the admiral. Short-sighted mortals we all are, and captains of men-of-war are not exempted from human imperfection! How much, also, drop between the cup and the lip! There chanced to be on board of the same trader two very pretty Irish girls of the better sort of bourgeoisie; they were going to join their friends at Philadelphia. The name of the one was Judy, and of the other Maria. No sooner were the poor Irishmen informed of their change of destination, than they set up a howl loud enough to make the scaly monsters of the deep seek their dark caverns. They rent the hearts of the poor-hearted girls; and when the thorough bass of the males was joined by the sopranos and trebles of the women and children, it would have made Orpheus himself turn round and gaze. "Oh, Miss Judy! Oh, Miss Maria! would ye be so cruel as to see us poor craturs dragged away to a man-of-war, and not for to go and spake a word for us? A word to the captain wid your own pretty mouths, no doubt he would let us off." The young ladies, though doubting the powers of their own fascinations, resolved to make the experiment. So, begging the Lieutenant of the sloop to give them a passage on board to speak with his Captain, they added a small matter of finery to their dress, and skipped into the boat like a couple of mountain kids, caring neither for the exposure of legs nor the spray of the salt water, which, though it took the curls out of their hair, added a bloom to their cheeks, which, perhaps, contributed in no small degree to the success of their project. There is something in the sight of a petticoat at sea that never fails to put a man into a good humour, provided he be rightly constructed. When they got on board the Humming-bird, they were received by the Captain. "And pray, young ladies," said he, "what may have procured me the honour of this visit?" "It was to beg a favour of your honour," said Judy. "And his honour will grant it too," said Maria; "for I like the look of him." Flattered by this little shot of Maria's, the Captain said that nothing ever gave him more pleasure than to oblige the ladies; and if the favour they intended to ask was not utterly incompatible with his duty, that he would grant it. "Well, then," said Judy, "will your honour give me back Pat Flannagan, that you have pressed just now?" The Captain shook his head. "He's no sailor, your honour; but a poor bog-trotter; and he will never do you any good." The Captain again shook his head. "Ask me any thing else," said he, "and I will give it you." "Well then," said Maria, "give us Felim O'Shaughnessy?" The Captain was equally inflexible. "Come, come, your honour," said Judy, we must not stand upon trifles now-a-days. I'll give you a kiss, if you'll give me Pat Flannagan." "And I another," said Maria, "for Felim." The Captain had one seated on each side of him; his head turned like a dog-vane in a gale of wind; he did not know which to begin with; the most ineffable good-humour danced in his eyes, and the ladies saw at once the day was their own. Such is the power of beauty, that this lord of the ocean was fain to strike to it. Judy laid a kiss on his right cheek; Maria matched it on his left; the Captain was the happiest of mortals. "Well then," said he, "you have your wish; take your two men, for I am in a hurry to make sail." "Is it sail ye are after making; and do ye mane to take all these pretty cratura away wid ye? No, faith, another kiss, *and another man.*" I am not going to relate how many kisses these lovely girls bestowed on this envied Captain. If such are Captains' perquisites, who would not be a Captain? Suffice it to say, they released the whole of their countrymen, and returned on board in triumph. The Lord Chancellor used to say, he always laughed at the settlement of pin-money, as ladies were generally either kicked out of it, or kissed out of it; but his Lordship, in the whole course of his legal practice, never saw a Captain of a man-of-war kissed out of forty men by two pretty Irish girls. After this, who would not shout "Erin go bragh!"

WEDDING PRESENTS.—It is the custom of the continent for a bridegroom to present to his bride, on the eve of their union, a collection of jewels, contained in what is called a *corbeille de noces*. The *corbeille* presented by King Leopold to the Princess Louise, consisted of a Gothic chest of ebony, inlaid with silver, in a damask pattern, and studded with oriental pearls. Its contents were a magnificent suite of diamonds, consisting of a necklace, comb, and wreath of wheat-ears, the latter made so as to take to pieces, and become applicable in various other forms; besides a variety of brooches, intended for looping up the drapery of court dresses, and clasping on bouquets. A complete suite of different coloured stones, mounted in gold so lightly that the setting was invisible, and a great variety of wheat-ears in emerald, chrysophrase, jacinths, topazes, chrysolites, and other stones, representing wheat in every shade of its growth. A set of Neapolitan shells, and another of antique cameos, richly set in gold, besides a great variety of gold chains—some light, others very massive. Two studs for night-dresses of large single diamonds. Eight cachemere shawls, four being square, and four long. Scarfs in every variety of lace, viz. Alençon and Brussels point, Lisle, Mechlin, Valenciennes, Chantilly; besides some curious varieties in cachemere, embroidered with gold, silver, and pearls. A dress of silk muslin (one of the new French stuffs), embroidered in bunches of grapes, of which the fruit was composed of amethysts. A dress of Chinese silk, painted in bouquets of flowers by the hands of the first artist; enclosed in a case of Japan, painted in flowers *a la chinoise*, and richly gilt. A great variety of what are called *cadeaux de corbeille*, accompanied this beautiful chest. Among others, a set of chimney ornaments, *a la Francaise*, consisting of clocks, candelabra, and vases; a breakfast service to match, with a beautiful plateau of the same; another breakfast service of silver gilt; a dressing-case, work-box, and writing-desk, *en suite*, of crystal and gold, lined with rich velvet; several beautiful cases of oriental Japan, filled with birds of Paradise, heron's feathers, marabout and ostrich feathers, and the richest plumes, in all their varieties; several pieces of velvet, brocade, blonde, gold and silver stuffs, and rich silks of every description; besides an infinite variety of trinkets and ornaments for the embellishment of a dressing-room or boudoir, each contained in a travelling-case of the richest kind. The wedding-clothes presented by Louis Philippe to his daughter, were of corresponding magnificence.

MOORE.—Moore is very sparkling in a choice or chosen society, (said Byron;) with lord and lady listeners he shines like a diamond, and thinks that, like that precious stone, his brilliancy should be preserved *pour le beau monde*. Moore has a happy disposition, his temper is good, and he has a sort of firefly imagination, always in movement, and in each evolution displaying new brilliancy. He has not done justice to himself in living so much in society; much of his talents are frittered away in display, to support the character of "a man of wit about town," and Moore was meant for something better. Society and genius are incompatible, and the latter can rarely, if ever, be in close or frequent contact with the former, without degenerating; it is otherwise with wit and talent, which are excited and brought into play by the friction of society, which polishes and sharpens both. I judge from personal appearance.—*Lady Blessington's Memoirs.*

IMPORTANCE OF A VOTE.—I hope to see the day when an Englishman will think it as great an affront to be courted and fawned upon in his capacity of elector as in his capacity of a juryman. In the polling-booth, as in a jury-box, he has a great trust confided to him—a sacred duty to discharge. He would be shocked at the thought of finding an unjust verdict because the plaintiff or the defendant had been very civil and pressing; and, if he would but reflect on this, he would, I think, be equally shocked at the thought of voting for a candidate for whose public character he felt no esteem, merely because that candidate had called upon him, and begged very hard, and had shaken his hand very warmly.—*T. B. Macaulay, Esq.*

MR. BABBAGE'S CALCULATING-MACHINE.

Of all the machines which have been constructed in modern times, the calculating-machine is doubtless the most extraordinary. Pieces of mechanism for performing particular arithmetical operations have been long ago constructed, but these bear no comparison either in ingenuity or in magnitude to the grand design conceived, and nearly executed, by Mr. Babbage. Great as the power of mechanism is known to be, yet we venture to say, that many of the most intelligent of our readers will scarcely admit it to be possible that astronomical and navigation tables can be accurately computed by machinery; that the machine can itself correct the errors which it may commit; and that the results of its calculations, when absolutely free from error, can be printed off, without the aid of human hands, or the operation of human intelligence. All this, however, Mr. Babbage's machine can do; and as I have had the advantage of seeing it actually calculate, and of studying its construction with Mr. Babbage himself, I am able to make the above statement on personal observation. The calculating machine, now constructing under the superintendence of the inventor, has been executed at the expense of the British Government, and is, of course, their property. It consists essentially of two parts, a calculating part, and a printing part, both of which are necessary to the fulfilment of Mr. Babbage's views, for the whole advantage would be lost if the computations made by the machines were copied by human hands and transferred to types by the common process. The greater part of the calculating machinery is already constructed, and exhibits workmanship of such extraordinary skill and beauty that nothing approaching to it has been witnessed. In order to execute it, particularly those parts of the apparatus which are dissimilar to any used in ordinary mechanical constructions, tools and machinery of great expense and complexity have been invented and constructed; and in many instances contrivances of singular ingenuity have been resorted to, which cannot fail to prove extensively useful in various branches of the mechanical arts. The drawings of this machinery, which form a large part of the work, and on which all the contrivance has been bestowed, and all the alterations made, cover upwards of 400 square feet of surface, and are executed with extraordinary care and precision. In so complex a piece of mechanism, in which interrupted motions are propagated, simultaneously, along a great variety of trains of mechanism, it might have been supposed that obstructions would arise, or even incompatibilities occur, from the impracticability of foreseeing all the possible combinations of the parts; but this doubt has been entirely removed, by the constant employment of a system of mechanical notation, invented by Mr. Babbage, which places distinctly in view, at every instant the progress of motion through all the parts of this or any other machine, and by writing down in tables the times required for all the movements, this method renders it easy to avoid all risk of two opposite actions arriving at the same instant at any part of the engine. In the printing part of the machine less progress has been made in the actual execution than in the calculating part. The cause of this is the greater difficulty of its contrivance, not for transferring the computations from the calculating part to the copper or other plate destined to receive it, but for giving to the plate itself that number and variety of movements which the forms adopted, in printed tables, may call for in practice. The practical object of the calculating engine is to compute and print a great variety and extent of astronomical and navigation tables, which could not be done without enormous intellectual and manual labour, and which, even if executed by such labour, could not be calculated with the requisite accuracy. Mathematicians, astronomers, and navigators do not require to be informed of the real value of such tables; but it may be proper to state, for the information of others, that seventeen large folio volumes of logarithmic tables alone were calculated at an enormous expense by the French Government, and that the British Government regarded these tables to be of such national value that they proposed to the French Board of Longitude to print an abridgement of them at the joint expense of the two nations, and offered to advance 5000l. for that purpose. Besides logarithmic tables, Mr. Babbage's machine will calculate tables of the powers and products of numbers, and all astronomical tables for determining the positions of the sun, moon, and planets; and the same mechanical principles have enabled him to integrate innumerable equations of finite differences that is, when the equation of differences is given, he can, by setting an engine, produce at the end of a given time, any distant term which may be required, or any succession of terms commencing at a distant point. Besides the cheapness and celerity with which this machine will perform its work, the absolute accuracy of the printed results deserves especial notice. By peculiar contrivances, any small error produced by accidental dust, or by any slight inaccuracy in one of the wheels, is corrected as soon as it is transmitted to the next, and this is done in such a manner as effectually to prevent any accumulation of small errors, from producing an erroneous figure in the result.—*Sir David Brewster's Treatise on Natural Magic.*

OF CUTS.—Generally speaking, all that is necessary to be done in case of incised wounds or cuts, is to clear away the surrounding blood, with all extraneous substances, and then to bring the lips of the ground close together, retaining them in that position by slips of adhesive plaster, spread on linen; and if the cut be deep and extensive, supporting it and the surrounding parts by proper bandages. In large grounds, small openings should be carefully left between each of the slips of plaster, to facilitate the escape of secret matter, or effused blood. The first dressing should remain on untouched for three or four days; and if much pain or inflammation follow the accident, a little opening physic ought to be taken. The bleeding consequent upon wounds may generally be stopped by pressure. The application of a quantity of cobweb may, however, be resorted to, and is sometimes useful in obstinate bleedings from cuts. Formerly it was the practice of surgeons to sew up long or deep wounds with the needle, but it is now rarely done, and should always be avoided if possible. The lips of the most severe cuts can generally be retained in contact much better, and with far less irritation, by means of adhesive plaster and bandages than by ligatures. In cuts which nearly separate any particular member of the body, as a finger, for example, a union by the foregoing means ought to be invariably attempted, and will usually succeed if the attempt be made without delay. It is well known that even the nose, after being nearly or quite separated from the face, has been perfectly united to it again by means of strips of plaster.—*The Doctor.*

THE TEMPLE OF NATURE.
BY DAVID VEDDER.

Talk not of temples, there is one
Built without hands, to mankind given;
Its lamps are the meridian sun,
    And all the stars of heaven;
Its walls are the cerulean sky;
Its floor the earth so green and fair;
The dome is vast immensity—
    All nature worships there!

The Alps arrayed in stainless snow,
The Andean ranges yet untrod,
At sunrise and and at sunset glow,
    Like altar-fires, to God.
A thousand fierce volcanoes blaze,
As if with hallow'd victims rare,
And thunder lifts its voice in praise—
    All nature worships there!

The ocean heaves resistlessly,
And pours his glittering treasure forth;
His waves, the priesthood of the sea,
    Kneel on the shell gemmed earth,
And there emit a hollow sound,
As if they murmured praise and prayer;
On every side 'tis holy ground—
    All nature worships there!

The grateful earth her odour yields
In homage, MIGHTY ONE, to thee;
From herbs and flowers in all the fields,
    From fruit on every tree:
The balmy dew at morn and even
Seems, like the penitential tear,
Shed only in the sight of heaven—
    All nature worships there!

The cedar and the mountain pine,
The willow on the fountain's brim,
The tulip and the eglantine,
    In reverence bend to Him.
The song-birds pour their sweetest lays,
From tower, and tree, and middle air;
The rushing river murmurs praise—
    All nature worships there!

AUTOBIOGRAPHY OF AN UNHAPPY OBJECT.

My life is shortly told. My first impression was the sensation of a tremendous squeeze, which instantly awoke me into life and thought. I was now spread out to the light, and a glow of intelligence completely pervaded me. My ideas were at first new, multifarious, and confused. Nations, politics, courts, wars, speeches, fightings, feasts, merchandize, marriages, deaths, ditties, &c. &c. made up my thoughts, which were various and mixed, and I lay in a silent state of wonder and amazement. I soon found that I was but one of a large family, that was ushered into the world at the same time, from the same prolific mother. Our whole litter was laid in regular order in a pile;—my situation being one of the first born, was particularly oppressed, damp and uncomfortable, I had a silent, intuitive longing wish to get into the world, which was at length gratified. Saturday morning came and I was carefully folded, and laid, Moses like, in a basket, by an urchin who was called the deliverer, and borne into the street. The said deliverer I soon found was an object of interest and desire. He was soon accosted by an elderly looking man, with threadbare rusty breeches :—' Have you a spare paper this morning, my boy?' 'No Sir,' was the short reply, and he trudged on with us, muttering "not as you know on, Old Gripe; you are the same chap that promised me some coppers for a paper the other morning and ha'nt paid me yet; you are too stingy to take the paper, but wont get another from me." My brethren were now fast leaving me, being deposited at their proper destinations; at length my turn came, and I was tucked into the crevice of a shop door in Leith. The first sample of the kind was not at all prepossessing. I had not been long in my new situation, when a reluctantly early apprentice, swinging a key on his hand, wistfully eyed me; and casting a look about him, feloniously seized, and thrust me into his pocket. My rightful owner being in sight, hailed and arrested the pilferer, and with threats compelled him to relinquish his prize. He entered his shop, and I soon found that I was the first object of interest. After hastily drying me by the fire, in which progress I narrowly escaped conflagration, he ran over me, and fixed his eyes upon sales at auction, advertisements, &c. I was then more particularly examined, and dismissed with condemnation. ' Nothing but foreign news, Parliament and Cabinet—love stories and accidents by flood and field; a newspaper should be a commercial report—one side at least should be devoted to prices current.' I was then pettishly thrown upon the counter, but was soon in requisition. A bare-headed boy made his appearance, with a "Please to lend mamma your paper a few minutes, just to look at the ship news." The request was reluctantly granted, with something about the plague of paper borrowing, and a determination to stop it. I was soon borne to a neighbouring house. The good old woman, whose husband was at sea, eagerly sought the ship news, but was disappointed in her search. "How negligent and careless these printers are," said she, "not a word of intelligence of the Jumping Jenny; they print of Poland, and poetry, and fill their papers with advertisements, and that stuff, is all they care about." Miss now took her turn. She sought the stories, the poetry, and marriages, which in half an hour were all devoured; with "the wonder that they put any thing else in the paper." An elderly lady now took me, who, adjusting her spectacles, surveyed me a little while, and declared me a "terribly uninteresting paper: hardly a column of deaths, and not more than fifteen or twenty murders and accidents." In this way I passed through all hands of the family, and after being well soiled and somewhat torn by the little ones, was sent home. For three whole days I had no rest, but was continually borrowed and abused. At the end of this period, I was supplanted by a new face, and was then discarded and thrown aside like all servants, when they have become useless. I was, however, again resuscitated, and employed as a wrapper to some merchandise, and sent into the country. There, again, I became an object of interest, went the rounds of the neighbourhood, and was a "nine days wonder." I am now quietly hanging up in a shattered condition in a Kirkaldy kitchen, from which I have written this brief memoir. I have seen much of the world, and have learned that mankind are unreasonable and ungrateful, and that in a world of great variety of taste and wishes it is impossible to please all.

SCRAPS.
Original and Selected.

CHARACTER OF THE LATE SIR SAMUEL ROMILLY.—Romilly, always so quiet and measured in his motions, is yet a man of unceasing activity. He does not lose even minutes. He devotes himself in earnest to whatever he is doing; and, like the hand of a clock, never stops, although his motions are so equal as to be scarcely perceptible.—*Dumont.*

NATIONAL CHARACTERISTICS.—The most certain way of ascertaining the real character of a people, is to view them in the most populous states, and that part of the nation who have the least interest in disguising themselves. If, in China, you see two porters jostle against each other in a narrow street, they will take the loads off their backs, and make a thousand excuses to each other for the accident occasioned, and on their knees will ask pardon for the offence. On the contrary, in London or Paris, two porters on such an occasion would quarrel, and exercise upon each other the *fistic* powers. A Frenchman is continually talking about his *mistress*,—the inseparable companion of an Englishman is his *umbrella*,—and the watchman is not happy without his *pipe*—nor an Italian without his *fiddle*.

A LEARNED BODY-SERVANT.—CURIOUS ADVERTISEMENT.—The following amusing advertisement lately appeared. The advertiser seems to be a sort of "Admirable Crichton" in his own estimation :—" A man of thirty years of age, born at the foot of the Grampian Mountains, in Scotland, self-taught, has a strong propensity for studying nature and nature's law, men and manners, barbarous and refined; capable of bearing the severity of the frigid or the intensity of the torrid zone; has a general knowledge of astronomy, geography, history, metaphysical reasoning, with the elements of poetical and musical composition naturally; plays several musical instruments; has a pleasant tenor voice, with a compass of eighteen notes; a slow but a distinct reader; of sober habits; who would be happy to meet an intelligent person, where he would make himself generally useful; and a pleasant companion in the capacity of body-servant. Letters, post paid, addressed, " J. P. coach-office," &c. &c.

PANDERING TO ARISTOCRATICAL FEELINGS.—Individuals may be trustworthy above others, but classes cannot be pointed out as at all peculiarly entitled to confidence. This assertion is diametrically opposed to the prevalent opinion of the day. Riches, station, and high birth are supposed, to a certain extent, to be guarantees for good conduct. The testimony of experience is, that neither riches, nor station, nor high birth, deserve consideration, as unconnected with a given individual. The temptations to error are as potent in the case of the rich as the poor man; the man of high, as of humble, station; of exalted, as of obscure, lineage. The ruling party hold these opinions peculiarly obnoxious; and so strong is the sentiment prevalent on this head, that all the biographers, both of Mr. Canning and Mr. Huskisson, for example, laboured hard to make out a gentleman's ancestry for the one, and for the other. It was thought by the aristocracy the very height of presumption, in these "new men," to pretend to the situation of Premier. "He is nobody," was the potent exclamation. "His father was this, his mother was that." The son of an actress, Prime Minister of England! The idea is monstrous . it is the portentous offspring of the French Revolution; "of the large and liberal cant of the day," [a phrase, be it remembered, coined by Mr. Canning himself,] and deserves to be considered as one of the most horrid atrocities of that atrocious commotion.—*Tait's Edinburgh Magazine.*

"A house-going minister," says Dr. Chalmers, "wins for himself church-going people; and his week-day attentions and their Sabbath attendance go hand in hand."

INTRODUCTION OF GAS LIGHT INTO DUMFRIES.—"Na, the like o' that!" said Jenny Bryden.—"I wonder what the world 'll come to at last. Gas light they ca't, but *elf light* wad be a better name. My certy! but there's an unco difference atween a low that needs neither oil, tallow, nor wick, an' a bawbee cannel, an auld cruizie, or a bit fir stick ta'en oot o' the moss. My mither, honest woman! was weel eneuch pleased wi' sic a taper; and am doubtin' whether she wad hae been unco fond o' reading her Bible at a witch-light. Puir spunkie! am maist wae for him. His bit dancin' light was cheerie as well as eerie whan twa war thegither, an' no that far frae hame; but he may douce his glim an' gang his wa's hame whene'er be likes, if it be true that the man at the gas-wark can mak' ten thousand spunkies at ae brewin'. A' things hae changed noo." —"Ay," said Betty Cameron, "if it's no enchantment, it's unco like it. In place o' being fashed with weeks and creesh, ye just turn about a bit spigot thing, an' oot spoots a light like soor milk out o' a barrel. Changed times indeed! Atween Liverpool an' Manchester the coaches rin their lane; an' noo we hae a boony clear light, ta'en like water in pipes under the grund, that'll spoot up at ony part ye like, if ye only bore a hole no muckle bigger than a preen-head. Weel, weel, I wish them muckle luck o't; but it'll be a while afore the gudeman catches me darnin' his stockings wi' a witch-taper at the chumley lug. The brownies langayne war very helpfu'; but we've nae use for brownie, noo. The Yediter, as they ca' him, says the only salamander kent noo's the spark bred in the blacksmith's throat, and the only brownie a steam-engine, sic as they hae in the Infirmary at Liverpool, that pumps water, kirns the kirn, washes claes, minches turnips, champs potatoes, and wad even mak' the bed wi' its iron arms if they wad let it. Everything's dune wi' machinery that can be dune, an' a great deal mair than should be done—that's what I say."—*M'Diarmid's Picture of Dumfries.*

THE SCOTTISH THISTLE.—This ancient emblem of Scottish pugnacity, with its motto *Nemo me impune lacessit*, is represented of various species in royal bearings, coins, and coats of armour, so that there is some difficulty in saying which is the genuine original thistle. The origin of the national badge itself is thus handed down by tradition:—When the Danes invaded Scotland, it was deemed unwarlike to attack an enemy in the pitch darkness of night, instead of a pitched battle by day; but on one occasion the invaders resolved to avail themselves of this stratagem; and in order to prevent their tramp from being heard, they marched barefooted. They had thus neared the Scottish force unobserved, when a Dane unluckily stepped with his naked foot upon a superbly prickled thistle, and instinctively uttered a cry of pain, which discovered the assault to the Scots, who ran to their arms, and defeated the foe with a terrible slaughter. The thistle was immediately adopted as the insignia of Scotland.—*Literary Gazette.*

LORDS ELDON AND STOWELL.—John Scott, Lord Eldon, was born at Newcastle upon-Tyne, and is the third son of William Scott, of that town. His father was by trade what in the language of the place is called a "fitter," or agent for the sale and shipment of coals. He had, by industry and habits of close saving, accumulated rather considerable means from small beginnings. Beyond this he was a man of great shrewdness and knowledge of the world, and quickly perceiving the strong, and what was better, marketable talents of his younger boys, William and John, he wisely gave them an education in accordance with their mental endowments. It is said that the singular variety in the talent of these two remarkable youths was manifested at a very early age. When asked to "give an account of the sermon," which was a constant Sabbath custom of their father, William, the eldest (now Lord Stowell), gave at once a condensed and lucid digest of the general argument and points of the discourse, if it had the good fortune to possess any smack of qualities so rarely to be found in sermons. John, on the other hand, would go into all the *minutiæ* of the harangue, whether long or short; but failed in producing the lucid general view embodied in half the number of words by his brother. And thus were their characters through life; so true to nature is the admirable aphorism of Wordsworth: "The boy's the father of the man." William was from the beginning destined for the study of the law. John, however, was at first intended for the church, a destination which his early marriage was the unfortunate means of changing; and he, together with his brother, set out to fight his way in the world as a young lawyer. The issue of the encounter was not long doubtful; for not only were his education and character, but every previous incident of his life, admirably calculated to fit him for the scenes in which he was destined to act a part.—*Tait's Magazine.*

SHARP ENOUGH ALREADY.—A solicitor, who was remarkable for the length and sharpness of his nose, once told a lady, that if she did not immediately settle a matter in dispute, he would file a bill against her. "Indeed, sir," said the lady, "there is no necessity for you to *file* your *bill*, for I am sure it is sharp enough already."

NATIONAL PARADOXES.—Somebody once remarked, that the Englishman is never happy but when he is miserable; the Scotchman is never at home but when he is abroad; and the Irishman is never at peace but when he is fighting.

NAPOLEON AND THE TWELVE APOSTLES.—The *Cabinet de Lecture* gives the following anecdote of Napoleon, without pledging itself for its authenticity—if not so, it is at all events very characteristic:—" Napoleon having entered one of the cities of Italy, the churchwardens recommended to him the reliques of their church. 'Sire, will you deign to take our Apostles under your protection?' 'Your Apostles! are they of wood? 'No, sire.' 'Of what are they, then?' 'Of silver, sire—of solid silver.' 'Solid silver!' replied Napoleon quickly, ' Yes, I shall help them to fulfil their mission; it has been ordained that they should go throughout the world, and they shall.' Having said so, the Emperor sent the twelve Apostles to the Mint at Paris."

TO DETERMINE THE ECONOMY OF A COW.—The annual consumption of food per cow, if turned to grass, is from one acre to an acre and a half in summer, and from a ton to a ton and a half of hay in the winter. A cow may be allowed two pecks of carrots per day. The grass being cut and carried, will economize it full one-third. The annual product of a good fair dairy cow, during several months after calving, and either summer or winter, if duly fed and kept in the latter season, will be an average of seven pounds of butter per week, from five to three gallons per day. Afterwards a weekly average of three or four pounds of butter from barely half the quantity of milk. It depends upon the constitution of the cow, how nearly she may be milked to the time of her calving, some giving good milk until within a week or two of that period, others requiring to be dried eight or nine weeks previously.

Besides appearing in WEEKLY NUMBERS, the SCHOOLMASTER is published in MONTHLY PARTS, which stitched in a neat cover, contains as much letter-press, of good execution, as any of the large Monthly Periodicals: A Table of Contents will be given at the end of the year; when, *at the weekly cost of three-halfpence*, a handsome volume of 832 pages, super-royal size, may be bound up, containing much matter worthy of preservation.

PART II., containing the five September Numbers, with JOHN. STONE'S MONTHLY REGISTER, may be had of all the Booksellers. Price 9d. For the accommodation of weekly readers, the Monthly Register and Cover may be had separately at the different places of sale. Price One Penny.

CONTENTS OF NO. X.

OCTOBER.—Notes of the Month; Harvest-home; the Kirn; the Maiden; the Woods of October; Rationale of the Colouring of the Woods.................................146
BOOKS OF THE MONTH.—The Magazines; New Novels; Life of Andrew Marvell, &c.................................147 to 149
MEMOIR OF AN EDINBURGH TRADESMAN.................................149
The Corn Laws, *alias* The Bread Tax.................................150
Progress of Scotch Agriculture.................................150
The Sea Serpent—solved.................................152
THE STORY TELLER—Ellen.................................153
ELEMENTS OF THOUGHT—Rich and Poor; The Inferior Gentry, &c.................................155
Whale Fishery of New South Wales.................................156
European Population.................................156
COLUMN FOR THE LADIES—Kissing off Sailors—Wedding Presents, &c.................................157
Mr. Babbage's Calculating Machine.................................158
The Temple of Nature by David Vedder.................................ib.
Autobiography of an Unhappy Object.................................159
SCRAPS—Original and Selected.................................ib.

EDINBURGH: Printed by and for JOHN JOHNSTONE, 19, St. James's Square.—Published by JOHN ANDERSON, Jun., Bookseller, 55, North Bridge Street, Edinburgh; by JOHN MACLEOD, and ATKINSON & Co., Booksellers, Glasgow; and sold by all Booksellers and Venders of Cheap Periodicals.

The Schoolmaster,

AND

EDINBURGH WEEKLY MAGAZINE.

CONDUCTED BY JOHN JOHNSTONE.

THE SCHOOLMASTER IS ABROAD.—LORD BROUGHAM.

No. 11.—Vol. I.   SATURDAY, OCTOBER 13, 1832.   Price Three-Halfpence.

IMPORTANCE OF THE STUDY OF SCIENCE.

Although, in our preliminary address, we stated that one of our chief objects in conducting the Schoolmaster, would be to give as much political information as the state of the laws affecting the press would allow, yet we were fully aware of the great importance of diffusing a knowledge of the Sciences, in general, among the people, and, of course, had no intention of excluding them from our pages. We consider it, however, to be one of man's first duties to make himself acquainted with the political affairs of the world at large, and particularly with those of his own country, and, as a necessary accompaniment, with the general doctrines of *Political Economy*. Our reason for wishing information of this kind extensively diffused, is, that the people, having a correct knowledge of their situation, may exercise an intelligent and moral influence over their rulers; and that thus the affairs of the nation may be conducted on just, rational, and equitable principles; because experience tells us that, unless this wholesome influence is exercised, government will be carried on in an unjust, irrational, and oppressive manner.

He, however, who limits his studies to politics, and especially to the mere politics of the day, stops very far short of that degree of intelligence which a person living in the nineteenth century ought to possess. A mere violent, babbling politician, ignorant of every thing else, is a being infinitely inferior to one who, with a competent knowledge of political science, lends his influence, founded on such knowledge, to ameliorate the condition of society, and has, at the same time, a general knowledge of the sciences in general; or, in other words, of the works of the Almighty:—such a being is indeed worthy of the name and Godlike form of man. In the words of Dr. Arnott, " He whose view is bounded by the limits of one or two small departments, will probably *have very false ideas even of them*, but he certainly will, of other parts, and of the whole, so as to be constantly exposed to commit errors hurtful to himself or to others. His mind, compared to the well-ordered mind of a properly educated man, is what the crooked and misshapen body of the mechanic, confined to certain actions and attitudes, is to the Godlike form of the most perfect specimen of human nature." We entreat our readers, therefore, that, while they take every proper means to increase their political information, they neglect no opportunity of acquiring a knowledge of general science. The interest, indeed, which belongs to political discussions, is often temporary and dependent on circumstances, and may therefore be exhausted,—as, for example, who would *now* take any interest in discussing the reasonableness of the system of Parliamentary representation happily " now no more?" But the gratification and improvement to be derived from inquiring into the ways of nature, are like a mine which is not only inexhaustible, but which grows richer and richer the farther we proceed in our excavations. For example, we may take great delight in observing the annual growth and decay of the flowers of the fields, even though almost entirely ignorant of their economy. But let us proceed to inquire into their nature and habits, the structure of their organs, and the means by which they appropriate the juices of the earth and convert them into their own substance; and who will doubt that the gratification derived from such plants will be infinitely increased? In like manner, no one can behold the powerful movements of a steam-engine without gratification, though ignorant of its principles and structure. But when he learns that the power which causes all the wonderful movements before him is nothing but common steam—when he comes to understand the simplicity of what at first appeared complex—with what an increased feeling of delight will he then gaze on the object before him! And this will be found to be the same to whatever province of nature's works we direct our attention;—our gratification and improvement will just be in proportion to our knowledge.

When we speak of acquiring a knowledge of the various sciences, we mean, in other words, a general knowledge of the laws of the Almighty. He who possesses a complete knowledge of the various sciences which relate to matter, has a complete knowledge of the laws to which matter has been subjected by the Creator. Water, for instance, has certain properties inherent in it; and it possesses these properties by a law, or laws, of the Almighty. One of its properties is, that it runs from a higher to a lower level; hence we have rivers. Another property is, that when heated to a certain degree, it passes into that wonderful aeriform matter called steam. In like manner, the two metals, copper and zinc, have distinctive qualities; but when combined together in certain proportions, their distinctive qualities cease, and they form that useful and beautiful metal, *brass*. And this, too, proceeds from laws of the Almighty. The study of science, therefore, is the study of the laws of God; and the investigation of these laws is a duty which we owe, not only to ourselves, but to their divine author.

In the Scriptures we have much important information conveyed to us, rules of morality laid down, and the will of God revealed, in regard to matters of which, if left to our unaided faculties, we must have for ever remained ignorant. Now, surely no one will deny the benefit to be derived from studying the will of God, as made known to us in the Scriptures; and we conceive that the benefit to be in like manner derivable from studying His will, or laws, as made known to us by science, is only secondary in importance to the other. In both cases, we acquire a knowledge of the Divine will—in the former case conveyed to us in direct terms, because our faculties are too weak to have otherwise made the acquirement—in the latter case we are left to discover them of ourselves, because they are within the reach of our faculties. Some people who fancy themselves very pious and devout, either do, or fain would, interdict from their shelves all books except such as are strictly termed religious; little fancying, in the depths of their ignorance, that they are thus shewing a contempt for, and a dislike to, the works of their Creator—those of his works, namely, which are revealed to us by science. We think that the habit of studying science, with a reference to the Divine Author of the objects we are investigating, is too much neglected; and that we ought never to forget that, while engaged in the pursuit of science, we are *investigating the works of God*. We conceive, therefore, that it is eminently the duty of the clergy to convey to the people a knowledge of the Divine laws, revealed to us by science, as well as of those which are revealed to us in the Scriptures; and as eminently the duty of the people to spare no labour in acquiring such knowledge;— the latter, indeed, is the peculiar province of the Sabbath—the former of the week days.

But the benefits derivable from possessing a knowledge of science do not stop here; but, what may perhaps have more influence on many than any other considerations, *profit*, also follows in their train. The most unthinking must be aware of the benefits which even our present limited knowledge of science has conferred on us in our manufactures, agriculture, &c. The steam-engine is indeed of itself a host. Let it suffice, that it is the knowledge of science, of the laws to which the numerous substances in nature have been subjected by the Almighty, and the power of applying our knowledge to the improvement of our condition, which has placed this country in its present proud situation among the nations of the earth. "A man," says Lord Brougham, "having only a pot to boil, is sure to learn from science reasons which will enable him to cook his morsel better, save his fuel, and both vary his dish and improve it." We have read of some savages, who, when they were first discovered, did not know even how to "boil their pot," and when they saw their visitors proceed to kindle a fire, and to "boil their pot," the poor savages ran off in terror. These men were therefore almost in total ignorance of nature's laws, and they lived in a state of the extremest poverty and wretchedness. But under the head of *profit*, we may include the benefits which accrue to us in the shape of *health*, from knowing and obeying God's laws. The enjoyment of health depends to a very great extent on the attention we pay certain laws of our Maker. Many of these yet remain to be discovered—as, for example, the laws which, when obeyed, will make that disease—frightful in the present state of our knowledge—Cholera, turn harmless from our doors. But many of the laws of health are habitually neglected, as in the daily recurring scenes of dissipation, neglecting proper exercise, ventilation, &c., not because they positively are not known, but because we have not a sufficiently extensive acquaintance with the laws of nature in general, and have not attained that all-relying confidence in their invariableness, which a more extensive knowledge of them can alone create.

This ignorance—this contracted view of the works of nature, is the cause of the many absurd notions so prevalent in society. It is this which causes us rashly and presumptuously to conceive that we can improve on the works of nature— which causes ladies to imagine that they can improve their beauty by contracting their waists one-half, and which causes gentlemen to conceive they can improve the appearance of their horses by cutting away their tails! The circumference of ladies' waists, and the length of horses' tails, were not, however, given without a purpose; and he or she who presumes, with cord or scissors, to improve the one or the other, must infallibly work mischief. It was at one time the custom to cut trees into various fantastic shapes by way of improving their appearance, but this notion has passed away as a knowledge of nature increased; and we hope to see the day when ladies' waists and horses' tails will in like manner be allowed to grow to their natural dimensions. These deviations from Nature do not, however, as those acquainted with the invariable workings of the Almighty's laws would have anticipated, escape the consequences. Medical men tell us that diseases in the spine are rapidly increasing among females, and this in consequence of tight lacing! And we have somewhere seen it stated, that at the commencement of a summer campaign, the horses in the British cavalry used always to be in better condition than those of other countries, but that ere the campaign was half done, they were in the worst condition, and this from want of their tails to drive away the flies!

We have thus attempted to show that we ought vigorously to investigate science, 1st, Because we will derive much gratification and improvement from the study; 2dly, Because the study of science is the study of the works of God, and that therefore we are bound in duty and gratitude to make it the subject of our anxious investigation; and, 3dly, Because a knowledge of science will enable us to better our condition. We have only then to add, that we shall occasionally devote a column of the *Schoolmaster* to investigations in science; and we need hardly add, our explanations shall at all times be of the most popular description, and level to the minds of the least-educated reader.

CONDITION OF THE POOR OF ENGLAND.

"THE VILLAGE POOR-HOUSE." BY A COUNTRY CURATE.*

WE conceive ourselves happy in an opportunity of introducing to Scotch readers a poem which the *Schoolmaster* thinks the most striking publication of the season, both in subject and execution. It had, we understand, been out of print, before it was even heard of at this end of the island, where, however, it was noticed cursorily, but with high praise, in *Tait's Magazine* for August. It will make its own speedy way to extensive popularity. The writer, in a neatly turned dedication to Lord BROUGHAM, describes his poem as "an attempt to illustrate the state of feeling amidst the pauper population." A portentous state of feeling that must needs be, if, as we dare not doubt, his descriptions are accurate and faithful. In an introductory epistle to a friend, he says:—

"Five years' experience as a country curate, has taught me many painful lessons and many bitter truths. It has shown me a degraded and besighted peasantry, and convinced me that all the descriptions of country life, which we admire in the poets, are *only* poetical. 'God made the country, and man made the town.' Alas! God made both, and man defaces both. But when we turn from the representations of rural life to its reality, we are startled to find the virtues as much banished from the groves as from the crowded alley; and, I grieve to say it, a stronger line drawn between the extremes of society—or, at least, a wider gap between its connecting links, than even in great cities. Was the rural population once happy and contented, as we find them described in books? or was it the surface only that presented this appearance, while misery and discontent lurked unseen below? Men are becoming progressively enlightened, and acquire a power of feeling their miseries, and of expressing them. My neighbours here—charitable, kind-hearted and benevolent on all other subjects—have an apathy about the sufferings of the poor which surprises me. They tell me that, thirty years ago, when all the articles of consumption were dearer, their wages were less,—and still that there were no complaints while the Tories were in power. I am not old enough to know whether this be true or not, from my own observation; but if it be true that their misery was greater and their complaints unuttered, I can only hail it as a '*specimen melioris ævi*,' that the poor are beginning to have their claims advocated, and their sufferings attended to."

The author then contends for educating the poor, and modestly concludes:—

"With regard to the following verses, if they attract any attention to the actual present state of feeling amongst the poor, I shall be quite satisfied. As to the *poetry* of the performance, the less said the better; poetry is too high a word to be applied to any composition of mine."

* Smith and Elder, London. Pp. 61.

The poetry, notwithstanding this modest disclamature, is of no ordinary merit, but *truth* is the soul of the performance, presented in vivid and stirring forms. The poem opens with this pleasing description of *The Village*:—

Our village has a pleasant look,
 A happy look as e'er was seen—
Right through the valley flows a brook,
 Which winds in many a flow'ry nook,
  And freshens all the green.
On either side, so clean and white,
 A row of cottages you see—
And jessamine is clustered o'er
The humble trellis of each door,
 Then left to clamber free,
And shake its blossoms far and wide
O'er all the white-wash'd cottage side.
As dying evening sinks away,
The old church tower, erect and grey,
Catches far up the parting light,
And half grows holy to the sight.

The picture of the church is wound up to point the contrast between the "pensive sinner" and the comfortable Rector. It is

Calm, silent, shaded, and serene,
Some blessed spot where God has been.
Here might the pensive sinner creep
 To mourn his wicked courses:
Here, o'er his "youth's fond errors" weep—
What matter though the Rector keep
 His carriage and four horses?
Weep on! thou man of sin and tears!—
But trouble not the Rector's ears.
 The Rectory stands all aloof,
 And rears its proudly slated roof
 In middle of a stately park,
  (Five acres and a perch.)
 The porter's lodge, where lives the clerk,
 Gives entrance by an iron gate
 Wide-opened upon days of state,
  When my lady drives from Church;
For my lady's knees are so stiff with kneeling,
And her nerves so strain'd with devotional feeling,
That she sends for the carriage and takes a drive,
And comes home to dinner at half-past five.

We have next the spruce dwelling of the thriving Attorney, which, besides its plaster front, verandah, and pilasters, has a gravelled drive, and a high-railed wall; for, the worthy inmate

—— could not endure that his windows should lie
Exposed to every vulgar eye—
The principal gate is always barr'd,
But a door leads through the stable-yard,—
And see!—just over the wall, you can get
A view of the roof of his barouchette,
Blazon'd and gilt for his lady's rides;
And he keeps a green gig for himself besides.
A thriving village—fair to see—
 Admired by each new comer,
And leaves are out on every tree,
The birds sing loud, the birds fly free,—
 'Tis now the height of summer.
Oh, blessed God! who o'er the earth,
The air, the sea, hast scatter'd mirth,
The blessed mirth that cheers the heart,
When happiness and joy must rise
From every sight that charms the eyes—
How good, how bountiful thou art!
Oh, what has man to think of more
Than bless thy goodness and adore?

The gloomy *Village Poor-house* comes next, with its miserable inmates,

Men—young, and sinewy, and strong,
Condemn'd to see, day after day,
 Their moments creep along
In sloth—for they have nought to do,
And—start ye not—in *hunger* too!

From the picture of these gnawing miseries, and the black despair of the men and women of the work-house, we have this rapid transition:—

There's a wit at the Parson's board to-day,
How fast he speaks, and the party how gay
The gentlemen roar—at a College joke,
The ladies blush—at an equivoque—

> And ever as livelier leaps the champaigne,
> Still merrier grows the jester's strain.
> Ha! ha! how his puns would fall flat and dead
> If his auditor's souls were faint for bread;
> How shudderingly from his quips they'd start
> If hunger and thirst were gnawing the heart!
> > Music!—a lady's jewell'd finger
> > Fondly seems to love to linger
> > O'er the harp's enamour'd string
> > Ere she opes her lips to sing
> > Roses—posies—bliss, and kiss.
> > Every hand is raised in praise
> > Of the sentimental lays,
> > And tears,—ay, tears,—are seen to pour
> > O'er the mock miseries of Moore!

Back again to a wretched room of the work-house, where we listen to the song of Will Somers, a pauper, whose misery is, even now, hurrying into crime; and who, taxed beyond human endurance, is resolute to revenge the evils of his condition in the Squire's covers. Some stanzas of beautiful description lead us to the *modern* Farmer, whose work

> ———— is over and done,
> And merrily now, as sinks the sun,
> He quaffs the brown ale till his heart grows kind,
> And he sups as if he had never dined;
> And a village pauper comes creeping up,
> Who envies his mutton and envies his cup,
> And the Farmer hears his complaint with a frown,
> And looses the mastiff to tear him down.
> This farmer is a yeoman bold
> Of the right *modern* English mould;
> To Rector and Squire, with countenance sad,
> He says tithes are heavy and times are bad.
> The Rector and Squire at his tale relent,
> And take off from the tithes and diminish the rent.
> Ho! ho! shouts the farmer, and jingles his purse,
> The tithes might be higher, the times might be worse,
> But the Rector and Squire are a couple of sages—
> I'll take sixpence a-week from my workmen's wages,
> For the indolent rogues are much overfed—
> And I'll buy little Jane a piano instead.

Again we return to the work-house to have another pauper history and song; impassioned, powerful, and painful—a pauper domestic tragedy. The deep misery of Jack Morley, brutalized by the extreme of want, and the degradation of his un-wedded bride, whom we see but in her grave, are contrasted with the joyous nuptials of that happy pair of industrious persons, the butler and the lady's-maid. The village bells are, on a balmy morning, playing the triple bob-major in honour of a ceremony not opposed by "the prudential restraint."

> Well, I declare! 'tis a beautiful sight—
> Six pretty maidens dress'd trimly in white,
> And see, all stiffen'd with velvet and silk,
> The Bride, in a bonnet as spotless as milk.
> Louder and louder, the bells ring out,
> And a crowd has collected all round about,
> And off in four gigs sweeps the cavalcade,—
> The Butler has wedded the Lady's-Maid.
>
> The Butler has two score and ten pounds a-year,
> The key of the cellar and cook of the beer,
> A hard-working man you may solemnly swear,
> For he stands every day at his master's chair,
> And, after such labour, how hard is his fate,
> He must lock up the bottles and count the plate;
> Ah! truth to say, he's the worst used of men.
> His pounds should be double of two score and ten.
>
> The Lady's-maid! *she's* to be pitied too,
> She has twenty pounds, and so much to do,
> To curl up her mistress's hair night and morning—
> It leaves *so* little time for her own adorning;—
> And just when dear Jenkins is saying sweet things,
> To be off in the midst, if her lady's bell rings!
> In short, she's surrounded with toils and woes,
> And wears all her mistress's cast-off clothes,
>
> Besides tinging her cheek with rouges and plaster,
> And listening nonsensical-tales from her master;—
> With labour and cares her position abounds,
> And all for a trifle of twenty pounds!
> Rumour asserts, but then Rumour's a liar,
> That the Butler's first-born will resemble the Squire.

In this way the poem proceeds. Part II. opens with the description of a well-fed, pompous, and slyly sensual clerical magistrate riding to Quarter Sessions, to officiate as Chairman, when his horse is startled in passing the village work-house door—and

> It seems so strange to a Magistrate's steed
> That a pauper should sing, that he's startled indeed;
> And the clerical Justice has some thoughts of bringing
> An action against the low wretches for singing;
> Impertinent dogs!

The song is that of Martha Green, an aged female pauper, who sings her yesternight's dreams of her cottage home, and early maternal happiness. This song is replete with pathos and beauty.

> ———— It was a blessed dream,
> Methought I saw a fair young child, a cottage, and a stream,—
> A fair young child beside the stream, a cottage clean and white;
> Methought my heart leapt up, to see so beautiful a sight.
> And soon from forth the cottage came, with many a merry noise,
> A playful group of children fair, of happy girls and boys,
> Four fair-hair'd boys, four blue-eyed maids,—my heart leapt up to see
> A careful mother watching them beneath a spreading tree.
>
> I look'd and look'd, and as I gazed on each fair boy and girl,
> My bosom heaved with many thoughts, my mind was in a whirl.
> Oh, God! the truth flash'd forth at once, the dream was a sign,—
> *I* was that mother 'neath the tree, those little ones were mine!
>
> Eight girls and boys were there, I ween,—where are the darlings now?

We can follow the fate of only one of this offspring of virtuous and suffering poverty—the widow's last son:—

> My stately James, my pensive boy, so thoughtful and sedate,
> What fault is theirs who stung thy soul, and spurn'd thee into hate!
> All, all at once, his nature changed—a man of savage mood,
> A ravening savage—demon-sold—despairingly he stood.
>
> What was his crime they never told, yet afterwards I heard,
> He spread a net, and caught in it some curious kind of bird—
> Some silly bird. They took my James and bound him as he slept,
> No word he spoke, but scowl'd severe, and scorn'd me as I wept.
>
> I saw my James, my gallant James;—one night when, all alone,
> I shiver'd at the fireless hearth, and made to God my moan,
> A man rush'd in, all spent with haste, with wild and blood-shot eye,
> "Mother, I come to see you once,—once more, before I die!
>
> "Nay, doubt me not, I'm yours indeed, your James in very truth,
> Not the same silent, soul-less James you knew me in my youth,—
> A man—though they have trampled me, and stamp'd with felon brand,
> A man—for I've had vengeance now! there's murder on my hand!"

Take, in opposition to the tragedy of poor Martha Green, this grave congregation of "Learned Fellows."

> > Six massive men in sable suit,
> > Of mighty bulk, and hanging brows,
> > Are darkly sitting, foot to foot,
> > Enjoying a carouse,—
> All learned men, and fill'd with knowledge,
> Six Senior Fellows of a College.
> How grave they sit! how wise they look!
> Each portly face is as a book,
> Where ye may read triangle and line,
> Cube root, parallelogram, circle, and sign,
> And a very particular judgment in wine!
> Wise Senior Fellows are they all,
> Steady as clock-work in chapel and hall;
> Six mighty parsons devoted to heaven,
> All looking out for a college living.
> Twenty years have they wasted their breath,
> In praying for murder and sudden death,—
> But the jolly incumbents, whose death would delight them,
> Live on, as if merely on purpose to spite them :—
> Twenty years they have all been engaged,
> And their mistresses now have grown "certainly aged."
> Oh! how they wade through the Morning Post,
> In hopes the old Rector has yielded the ghost,
> That he's broken his neck by a fall from his horse,
> Or gone off in a fit in the second course,
> Providentially choked by the bone of a cod,
> Or some morning found "Dead,—by the finger of God;"—
> Ah! Senior Fellowships always give birth
> To "Glory to God and good will upon earth."

Though thus lavish in quotation, we can give our readers no adequate idea of the force, point, and beauty of this poem—full of rapid and brilliant transitions—its shifting lights brought broadly out by the dark depths of its massive shadows. As a relief to the scenes we have passed, we would like to dwell on the benevolent speculations of the Curate, and upon his Church Reform; but he hurries back to his cantatory paupers, and we follow him to hear Tom Perkins, the old soldier's song of the glories of Waterloo. It is bitter enough; and after the clerical gallop is interrupted by what may truly be called kindred sounds.

Clang! clang! goes the village bell again,
And the Rector, red and hot,
Has rattled along, without slacking his rein,
All through the village, and up the church lane,
At an Osbaldiston trot:
Wiping his brow, and panting for breath,
He's afraid he will scarcely be in at the death.
Faintly, wearily, tolls the bell;
Clang! clang! clang! 'tis a pauper's knell,
A poor old man with silver hair,
Broken by seventy years of care.
The panting steed is tied to the gate,
And the Rector goes into church, in state;
Soon you will see him, in robes of snow,
Forth from the church's portal go,
A holy man, devout and sincere,
And much underpaid with two thousand a-year!

The pauper funeral is a description in the finest manner of CRABBE. The rites are huddled over:—

Seventy years of want and sin
Sleep that narrow cell within,—
And the earth is shovell'd in!
Jarringly, with accent drear,
The parting knell grates on the ear.
The boys are gone, the bearers fled,
The women in their cloaks of red;
There's no one 'neath the yew-trees cold,
Save the sexton, stamping down the mould.
The Rector awakens the silent street,
With the quick sounds of galloping feet;
The sky is bright, the flowers are out,
The school is let loose with a joyous shout;
There's gladness in each light wind's breath.
Tush!—We have said too much of death!

Would it not be much better to dispense altogether in the case of the English poor, with a solemnity which is so often converted into a mockery or indecency.

We have compared the writer with CRABBE; and the comparison holds in many points, besides the general strain of sentiment and tone of colouring; but he gains another power from greater rapidity of transition, and liveliness of fancy.

Part III opens with a sweet description of evening, and the village workman's return; but his, alas! is no Cottar's Saturday Night. Copious as our extracts have been, we must give this in-door picture of our English labourer's home, and of the dens from which Swing issues forth. He is crossing the stile to his cottage, bearing his spade on his shoulder:—

Hark! is he singing?—no such thing,
His heart is much too full to sing.
Is he weary?—thirsty?—cold?
All day long, since morning's peep,
He's been ditching in the mould,
In mud and water ancle deep.
Home that happy man's returning—
Doubtless there's a bright fire burning;
Thirsty from his toil severe—
Doubtless there's some home-brew'd beer.
Happy man! how blest is he!
How much more happy than the bee!
A fire?—No wood has he to burn—
No tankard foams at his return;
Off to his pallet let him creep,
And sink reality in sleep.
But, e'er to slumber he is past,
What's the sound that meets him last?
Is it children's gentle voices?
(To father's ear most bless'd of noises,)
Children laughing loud and long,
Or bursting into joyful song?
Laughing they are not—nor singing,
Yet their voices loud are ringing;
They have gathered round his bed,
They have been but scant'ly fed,—
They are asking him for bread.
Oh, lullaby, supremely blest!
What dreams must beautify his rest?

These dreams—the night-mare, in which he struggles with the Parson and the Overseer—we hasten over, that we may contrive to sweeten the reader's imagination, ere we part, with a stanza of the Pauper Emigrant's Song. Bill Harvey, who looks to another country for the means of subsistence, denied him for his willing labour in England, or in his native village, sings thus,

The shaded savannah has pestilent brakes;
The wood has its tigers, the swamp has its snakes.
He fears no savannah who's toil'd in a drain,
The snake on the pauper glares fearful in vain;
From priest, squire, and farmer but let me go free,
The tiger and serpent are welcome to me!

Oh give me the wood where the axe never swung,
Where man never entered, and voice never rung,
A hut made of logs, and a gun by my side,
The land for my portion, and Jane for my bride,
That hut were a palace, a country for me,—
Dash on, thou proud ship, o'er the wide-rolling sea!

Were it practicable we would like to present our readers with the surgeon who physics three hundred paupers in this, and the neighbouring parishes, by wholesale. He hurries off from the dying bed of a beautiful and lost woman, undone by the strong temptations of poverty, but, first shakes his head, then shakes it again,

For, with seventeen pounds, and his patients so many,
Two shakes is all he can waste upon any.

The picture of true and counterfeit Charity is among the best things in the volume; the one, holy, pure, pitying; the other—but for the benefit of our fair readers we shall give False Charity at full length, having long suspected that many need their ideas of charity expanded and rectified. Here she is,

A little French Milliner fill'd with grimace,
Takes Charity's name and stands forth in her place.
Flaunting abroad in a furbelow'd gown
She's the wonder and pride, and the belle of the town:—
O how she sighs at a story of wo!
A sigh so becoming to bosom of snow—
Oh! how she begs, looking pretty the while,
Till hearts, and subscriptions are gain'd by her smile;
She sits in her parlour, surrounded by beaux,
And looks so divine making poor people's clothes,
And fans of goose feathers, and shoes made of scraps,
And fire-screens, and needle-books, babies and caps,—
She's so tender and busy,—she levies a war
'Gainst the gentlemen's hearts at a Fancy Bazaar.
Oh! Charity flaunts it in feather and plume,
And smiles like an angel—in rouge and perfume
She flirts at her booth—she's the gayest of belles,
And hardly she bargains, and dearly she sells;
And customers wonder, that lady so free,
So kind to the poor, and so tender should be;
A truce to your wonder—she heeds not the poor—
If once she is married she's tender no more.
Ah, me! that such labour, such feeling and care,
Should all be bestowed upon Vanity Fair,—
And deeper the error, and darker the shame,
That this is transacted in Charity's name!

We must not linger on the Pauper Dirge, nor yet on the midnight moralizing of the Curate on the Village, and those solemn thoughts which wind up a subject pregnant with the weal or wo of unborn millions. The subject, we confess, has engrossed us more than the mode in which it is managed; and we have spoken of this poem as a Schoolmaster, not as a critic. It is a production which any poet might be proud to own; yet its purpose is a higher merit, and fervently do we wish that the object of the author may be accomplished in rousing attention "to the actual state of feeling among the poor." For the sake of suffering humanity we are glad the Village Work-house has been written, and for the sake of Scotland, we are proud to understand that we may claim this CRABBE REDIVIVUS as a strayed countryman. He has caught the honoured mantle of the author of the Parish Register as it fell—long may he wear it!

THE NEW MONTHLY MAGAZINE.

THE October number is a pleasant one, and of considerable variety. *Lady Blessington's Recollections; Shelley at Oxford; Private* (smart) *Hints to a Young Physician*, quite as applicable to the beginning practitioner in Edinburgh, Bath or Dublin, as London; a little *moderate* politics, a few peppery paragraphs in the *Monthly Commentary*; and some eloquent, generous, and touchingly beautiful remarks on the DEATH OF SIR WALTER SCOTT, by the Author of Pelham, and Eugene Aram, are the main articles. MR. BULWER'S opinion of the character of Scott's writings so entirely meets the hasty view taken of them in the SCHOOLMASTER of the 29th ult., that we really feel proud of the coincidence, and gratified in believing that this opinion, which only does justice to the illustrious Dead, may be much more general than we had imagined. We give one short passage, which is as beautiful in language, as true and noble in feeling.

"But this power to charm and to beguile is not that moral excellence to which we refer. Scott has been the first great genius—Fielding alone excepted—who invited our thorough and uncondescending sympathy to the wide mass of the human family—who has *stricken* (for in this artificial world it requires an effort) into our hearts a love and a respect for those chosen from the people. Shakspeare has not done this—Shakspeare paints the follies of the mob with a strong and unfriendly hand. Where, in Shakespeare, is there a Jeanie Deans? Take up which you will of those numerous works which have appeared, from "Waverley" to the "Chronicles of the Canongate,"—open where you please, and you will find portraits from the people—and your interest keeping watch beside the poor man's hearth. Not, in Scott, as they were in the dramatists of our language, are the peasant, the artificer, the farmer, dragged on the stage merely to be laughed at for their brogue, and made to seem ridiculous because they are useful.

"He paints them, it is true, in their natural language, but the language is subservient to the character; he does not bow the man to the phrase, but the phrase to the man. Neither does he flatter on the one hand, as he does not slight on the other. Unlike the maudlin pastoralists of France, he contents himself with the simple truth—he contrasts the dark shadows of Meg Merrilies, or of Edie Ochiltree, with the holy and pure lights that redeem and sanctify them—he gives us the poor, even to the gipsy and the beggar, as they really are—contented, if our interest is excited, and knowing that nature is sufficient to excite it. From the palaces of kings, from the tents of warriors, he comes—equally at home with man in all aspects—to the cottar's hearth;—he bids us turn from the pomp of the Plantagenets to bow the knee to the poor Jew's daughter—he makes us sicken at the hollowness of the royal Rothsay, to sympathize with the honest love of Hugh the smith. No, never was there one—not even Burns himself—who forced us more intimately to acknowledge, or more deeply to feel, that

'The rank is but the guinea stamp,
The man's the gowd for a' that.'

"And is this being, to whom intellect taught philanthropy, to be judged by ordinary rules?—are we to guage and mete his capacities of good, by the common measure we apply to common men?—No! there was in him a large and catholic sympathy with all classes, all tempers, all conditions of men; and this it was that redeemed his noble works from all the taint of party, and all the leaven of sectarianism; this it was that made him, if the Tory in principle, the all-embracing leader in practice. Compare with what *he* has done for the people—in painting the people—the works of poets called Liberal by the *doctrinaires*—compare the writings of Scott with those of Byron—which have really tended the most to bind us to the poor?—The first has touched the homely strings of our real heart—the other has written fine vague stanzas about freedom. Lara, the Corsair, Childe Harolde, Don Juan, these are the works—we will not say of the misanthrope—at least of the aristocrat. Are Scott's so? Yet Byron was a Liberal, and Scott a Tory. Alas, the sympathy with humanity is the true republicanism of a writer of fiction. Liberal and Tory are words which signify nothing out of the sphere of the politics of the day. Who shall we select from the Liberal poets of our age who has bound us to the people like Scott—Shelley, with his metaphysical refinings?—Moore, with his elaborate floridity of patriotism?—No! we feel at once that Nature taught Scott more of friendship with all mankind, than the philosophy of the one or the fancy of the other. *Out of print, Scott might belong to a party—in print, mankind belonged to him. Toryism, which is another name for the spirit of monopoly, forsook him at that point where his inquiries into human nature began.* He is not, then, we apprehend, justly liable to the charge of wanting a sound moral—even a great *political* moral—(and political morals are the greatest of all)—in the general tenor of works which have compelled the highest classes to examine and respect the lowest. In this, with far less learning, far less abstract philosophy than Fielding, he is only exceeded by him in one character—(and that, indeed, the most admirable in English fiction)—the character of Parson Adams. Jeanie Deans is worth a thousand such as Fanny Andrews."

COLUMN FOR THE LADIES.
ADVENTURE OF A FEMALE INDIAN.

ON Hearne's return from the mouth of the Coppermine, an incident occured strikingly characteristic of savage life: The Indians came suddenly on the track of a strange snow-shoe, and following it to a wild part of the country, remote from any human habitation, they discovered a hut, in which a young Indian woman was sitting alone. She had lived for the last eight moons in absolute solitude, and recounted, with affecting simplicity, the circumstances by which she had been driven from her own people: She belonged, she said, to the tribe of the Dog-ribbed Indians, and in an inroad of the Athabasca nation, in the summer of 1770, had been taken prisoner. The savages, according to their invariable practice, stole upon the tents in the night, and murdered before her face her father, mother, and husband, whilst she and other three young women were reserved from the slaughter, and made captive. Her child, four or five months old, she contrived to carry with her, concealed among some clothing; but on arriving at the place where the party had left their wives, her precious bundle was examined by the Athabasca women, one of whom tore the infant from its mother, and killed it on the spot. In Europe, an act so inhuman would, in all probability, have been instantly followed by the insanity of the parent; but in North America, though maternal affection is equally intense, the nerves are more sternly strung. So horrid a cruelty, however, determined her, though the man whose property she had become was kind and careful of her, to take the first opportunity of escaping, with the intention of returning to her own nation; but the great distance, and the numerous winding rivers and creeks she had to pass, caused her to lose the way, and winter coming on, she had built a hut in the secluded spot. When discovered she was in good health, well fed, and, in the opinion of Hearne, one of the finest Indian women he had ever seen. Five or six inches of hoop made into a knife, and the iron shank of an arrow-head which served as an awl, were the only implements she possessed; and with these she made snow-shoes and other useful articles. For subsistence she snared partridges, rabbits, and squirrels, and had killed two or three beavers and some porcupines. After the few deer-sinews she had brought with her were expended in making snares and sewing her clothing, she supplied their place with the sinews of rabbits' legs, which she twisted together with great dexterity. Thus occupied, she not only became reconciled to her desolate situation, but had found time to amuse herself by manufacturing little pieces of personal ornament. Her clothing was formed of rabbit-skins sewed together: the materials, though rude, being tastefully disposed, so as to make her garb assume a pleasing though desert-bred appearance. The singular circumstances under which she was found, her beauty and useful accomplishments, occasioned a contest among the Indians as to who should have her for a wife; and the matter being decided, she accompanied them in their journey.—[The above adventure is from the ninth number of *Oliver and Boyd's Cabinet Library*. The subject of this volume, of which Mr. Patrick Fraser Tytler is the author, is *Discoveries on the Northern Coasts of America*, from the earliest periods down to Beechey's voyage. It is one of great interest.]

LOVE! LOVE!—Verbatim copy of a love-letter lately sent by an enamoured swain to his beloved in Leeds. The lady, not having partaken of the march of intellect, handed it over to her master, who deciphered it for her; and we publish it as a model for Yorkshire Corydons:—

"Dear Bessy,—A I do loike thee—My Love is stroner than iver—I nivir had a wink of sleep sin I wor at Leeds—Sun may melt mountains—and sea may run wick before I can change my love agin—I loike Poy better nor onght but I loike thee better than Poy—therefore thou may make up thee mind to let me put spurrings in—and we will be wed and gang home in a chaise at Martinmas."

FERRONIERE.*—These ornaments are universally worn in Paris. They were very much in vogue about fifteen years since, and were reproduced by the celebrated hair-dresser Nardin, at the commencement of the present season, in compliment to a lady of high rank in Paris, who is disfigured by a mole in the centre of the forehead, and who brought back the fashion by means of a beautiful diamond ferroniere, which was found a considerable improvement to her countenance. Jewel-boxes are now made to contain six ferronieres, without which no fashionable toilette is complete; two for morning use, fastened by a cameo and antaglio of antique workmanship; two with engraved coral and amethyst clasps, for dinner dress; one with diamonds, and one with mixed stones. These are united by chains of gold, hair, or pearls, so that they can also be worn on the neck.

WILLIAM COBBETT.

The following remarks by two excellent judges, Mr. Hazlitt and the *Examiner*, will in this quarter be read with interest at present:—

"Cobbett is not only unquestionably the most powerful political writer of the day, but one of the best writers in the language. He speaks and thinks plain, broad, downright English.

"He might be said to have the clearness of Swift, the naturalness of De Foe, and the picturesque satirical description of Mandeville; if all such comparisons were not impertinent.

"The late Lord Thurlow used to say that Cobbett was the only writer who deserved the name of a political reasoner.

"His episodes, which are numerous as they are pertinent, are striking, interesting, full of life and *naiveté*, minute, double measure running over, but never tedious. He is one of those writers who can never tire us, not even of himself; and the reason is, he is always ' full of matter.' He never runs to lees, never gives us the vapid leavings of himself, is never ' weary, stale, and unprofitable,' but always setting out afresh on his journey, clearing away some old nuisances, and turning up new mould. His egotism is delightful, for there is no affectation in it. He does not talk of himself for lack of something to write about, but because some circumstance that has happened to himself is the best possible illustration of the subject, and he is not the man to shrink from giving the best possible illustration of the subject from a squeamish delicacy. He writes himself plain William Cobbett, strips himself quite as naked as any body would wish—in a word, his egotism is full of individuality, and has room for very little vanity in it. We feel delighted, rub our hands, and draw our chair to the fire, when we come to a passage of this sort; we know it will be something new and good, manly and simple, not the same insipid story of self over again.

"Mr. Cobbett speaks almost as well as he writes. The only time I ever saw him, he seemed to me a very pleasant man—easy of access, affable, clear-headed, simple, and mild in his manner, deliberate and unruffled in his speech, though some of his expressions were not very qualified. His figure is tall and portly. He has a good sensible face, rather full, with little grey eyes, a hard, square forehead, a ruddy complexion, with hair grey or powdered; and had on a scarlet broad-cloth waistcoat, with the flaps of the pockets hanging down, as was the custom for gentlemen-farmers in the last century, or as we see it in the pictures of Members of Parliament in the reign of George I. I certainly did not think less favourably of him for seeing him.

"As a political partisan, no one can stand against him. With his brandished club, like Giant Despair in the Pilgrim's Progress, he knocks out their brains; and not only no individual, but no corrupt system could hold out against his powerful and repeated attacks, but with the same weapon, swung round like a flail, that he levels his antagonists, he lays his friends low, and puts his own party *hors de combat*. This is a bad propensity and a worse principle in political tactics, though a common one. If his blows were straight-forward and steadily directed to the same object, no unpopular minister could live before him; instead of which he lays about right and left, impartially and remorselessly, makes a clear stage, has all the ring to himself, and then runs out of it, just when he should stand his ground. He throws his head into his adversary's stomach, and takes away from him all inclination for the fight, hits fair or foul, strikes at every thing, and as you come up to his aid or stand ready to pursue his advantage, trips up your heels, or lays you sprawling, and pummels you when down as much to his heart's content, as ever the Sanguesian carriers belaboured Rosinante with their pack staves.

"Mr. Cobbett has no comfort in fixed principles; as soon as any thing is settled in his own mind, he quarrels with it. He has no satisfaction but in the chase after truth, runs a question down, worries and kills it, then quits it like vermin, and starts some new game, to lead him a new dance, and give him a fresh breathing through bog and brake, with the rabble yelping at his heels, and the leaders perpetually at fault. This he calls sport royal. He thinks it as good as cudgel-playing, or single-stick, or any thing that has life in it. He likes the cut and thrust, the falls, bruises, and dry blows of an argument: as to any good or useful results that may come of the amicable settling of it, any one is welcome to them for him. The amusement is over, when the matter is once fairly decided."

"Whatever Mr. Cobbett takes in hand he takes to heart, and he not only shapes his works of instruction with the exactest attention to the uses, but delights in availing himself of all the opportunities for agreeable illustration and appropriate embellishment. It is his art, when treating on the most familiar subject, to touch the reader with a new sense of it; this he effects partly by the rare zest with which he writes, and partly by producing all the little circumstances, and setting upon them their just value. Cobbett is a fine critic—he has an eye for beauty, and an excellent faculty for picking out the right point of view—his tastes are simple, but eager, and glow with the flush of health.

"Analysis is his great power, and as he is earnest himself upon every part he touches, he communicates his earnestness to the reader. No man has the faculty of seeing so much of the good and so much of the bad of any subject, and his inconsistencies are referable to his capricious division of their powers.

"Until Cobbett has praised or abused a thing, it is hardly known what may be said for and against it. When his rancour is not excited, when his singular powers are employed in instruction, in adding to the conveniences and comforts of society, or the inculcation of moral principles, they work to unmixed advantage, and with such a pervading tone of benevolence, and so nice an apprehension of every good that is passingly touched on, that a stranger to other performances could hardly suppose the author capable of an uncharitable purpose, or an uncharitable enjoyment."
—*Examiner*.

PASSAGES FROM COBBETT'S EARLY LIFE. WRITTEN BY HIMSELF.

"At *eleven* years of age, my employment was clipping off box-edgings and weeding beds of flowers in the garden of the Bishop of Winchester, at the castle of Farnham, my native town. I had always been fond of beautiful gardens; and a gardener, who had just come from the King's gardens at Kew, gave such a description of them as made me instantly resolve to work in these gardens. The next morning, without saying a word to any one, off I set, with no clothes

---
* An ornament worn on the forehead

except those upon my back, and with thirteen half-pence in my pocket. I found that I must go to Richmond, and I accordingly went on, from place to place, enquiring my way thither. A long day (it was in June) brought me to Richmond in the afternoon. Two-penny worth of bread and cheese, and a penny-worth of small beer, which I had on the road, and one half-penny that I had lost somehow or other, left three-pence in my pocket. With this for my whole fortune, I was trudging through Richmond, in my blue smock frock, and my red garters tied under my knees, when, staring about me, my eye fell upon a little book, in a bookseller's window, on the outside of which was written, "TALE OF A TUB; PRICE 3d." The title was so odd, that my curiosity was excited. I had the 3d., but then I could have no supper. In I went, and got the little book, which I was so impatient to read, that I got over into a field, at the upper corner of Kew gardens, where there stood a hay-stack. On the shady side of this I sat down to read. The book was so different from any thing that I had ever read before: it was something so new to my mind that, though I could not at all understand some of it, it delighted me beyond description; and it produced what I have always considered a sort of birth of intellect. I read on till it was dark, without any thought about supper or bed. When I could see no longer, I put my little book in my pocket and tumbled down by the side of the hay-stack, where I slept till the birds in Kew gardens awaked me in the morning; when off I started to Kew, reading my little book. The singularity of my dress, the simplicity of my manner, my confident and lively air, and, doubtless, his own compassion besides, induced the gardener, who was a Scotchman, I remember, to give me victuals, find me lodging, and set me to work. And, it was during the period that I was at Kew, that the present king and two of his brothers laughed at the oddness of my dress, while I was sweeping the grass plat round the foot of the pagoda. The gardener, seeing me fond of books, lent me some gardening books to read; but these I could not relish after my *Tale of a Tub*, which I carried about with me wherever I went, and when I, at about twenty years old, lost it in a box that fell overboard in the Bay of Fundy in North America, the loss gave me greater pain than I have ever felt at losing thousands of pounds.

"This circumstance, trifling as it was, and childish as it may seem to relate it, has always endeared the recollection of *Kew* to me. About five weeks ago, I had occasion to go from Cheltenham to Twickenham with my two eldest sons: I brought them back through Kew, in order *to show them the place where the hay-stack stood*, having frequently related to them what I have now related to you * * * *.

"You have how, and at what age, I started in the world. Those of you who are *mothers*, will want nothing but the involuntary impulse of your own hearts to carry your minds back to the alarm, the fears and anxieties of my most tender mother. But if I am "an *extraordinary* man," as I have been called by some persons, who ought to have found out a different epithet, I was a still more extraordinary *boy*. For though I never returned home for any length of time, and never put my parents to a farthing in expense after the time above mentioned, I was always a most dutiful son, never having, in my whole life, wilfully and deliberately disobeyed either my father or my mother. I carried in my mind their precepts against *drinking* and *gaming*; and I have never been drunk, and have never played at any game in my life. When in the army, I was often tempted to take up the cards, but the words of my father came into my mind and rescued me from the peril. Exposed as you must well know to all sorts of temptations; young, strong, adventurous, uncommonly gay, and greatly given to talk; still I never in my whole life was brought before a magistrate either as defendant or complainant. And even up *to this hour*, about *five oaths* are all that I have ever taken, notwithstanding the multitude and endless variety of affairs in which I have been engaged. I entered the army at *sixteen*, and quitted it at *twenty-five*. I never was once even *accused* of a fault of any sort. At *nineteen* I was promoted to *Serjeant-Major* from a Corporal over the heads of nearly fifty serjeants. While my regiment was abroad, I received the public and official thanks of the Governor of the province for my zeal in the king's service; while no officer of the regiment received any thanks at all. Many years after this, this same Governor (General Carleton) came to see me, and to claim the pleasure of my acquaintance. When I quitted the army at Portsmouth, I had a discharge bearing on it, that I had been discharged at my own request, *and in consequence of the great services I had rendered the king's service in that regiment*. During this part of my life I lived amongst, and was compelled to associate with, the most beastly of drunkards, where liquor was so cheap, that even a soldier might be drunk every day; yet I never, during the whole time, even *tasted* of any of that liquor. My father's, and more especially my mother's precepts were always at hand to protect me.

"In 1792 I went to the United States of America. There I became a *writer*. I understood little at that time; but the utmost of my ability was exerted on the side of my *country*, though I had been greatly disgusted with the trick that had been played me in England, with regard to a court-martial, which I had demanded upon some officers. I forgot every thing when the honour of England was concerned. The King's minister in America made me offers of reward. I refused to accept of any thing, in any shape whatever. Reward was offered me when I came home. I always refused to take one single penny from the government. If I had been to be *bought*, judge you, my countrywomen, how *rich*, and even how *high*, I might have been at this day! But I value the present received from the females of Lancashire a million times higher than all the money and all the titles which ministers and kings have to bestow.

* * * *

"These cowardly and brutal men (the libellers of the London press) have represented me as being a harsh, tyrannical, passionate, merciless, and even greedy man. I have said before, that, in the whole course of my life, I never was once before a magistrate in any criminal case, either as accuser or accused, and that is a great deal to say, at the end of fifty-three years, and having no one to protect or advise me since I was eleven years old. Very few men can say as much. There is hardly a Quaker that can say as much, though he be much younger than I am. I never, in the whole course of my life, brought an action against any man for debt, though I have lost thousands of pounds by not doing it. Where is there a man, so long engaged in business of various sorts, as I have been, who can say as much? I know of no such man. I never could find in my heart to oppress any man merely because he had not the ability to pay. I lose money by acting thus; but I did not lose my good opinion of myself, and that was far more valuable than money. Nor have I ever had an action brought against me for debt, in all my lifetime, until since my last return from America; when an attorney at Bishop's Waltham, in Hampshire, had a writ served upon me, *without any notice—without even writing to me for the money*. The debt was for about £30; a thing which I had totally forgotten—the malt having been served during the year before I went to America * * * *

"I have seven children, the greater part of whom are fast approaching the state of young men and young women. *I never struck one of them in anger in my life*; and I recollect *only one single instance in which I have ever spoke to one of them in a really angry tone and manner*. And, when I had so done, it appeared as if my heart was gone out of my body. It was but once; and I hope it will never be again. Are there many men who can say as much as this? To my servants I have been the most kind and indulgent of masters; and I have been repaid, in general, by their fidelity and attachment. Two *consumate* villains I have met with. But their treachery, though of the blackest dye, will by no means tend to make me distrustful or ill-tempered. The attachment and devotion which I have experienced from others, exceeds even the perfidy of these two blackhearted men, who, besides, have yet to be rendered as notorious as they are infamous.

THE STORY-TELLER.

LITTLE DAVY—A JUVENILE TALE.

THE Minister of ———, one of the best livings, in point of *chalders*, in the synod of Dumblane, was one autumn evening, towards the close of the last century, riding leisurely along by the foot of the green Ochils, homeward-bound from a presbytery dinner at Stirling, but diverging something from his course, to pass a day or two with a landed proprietor, the friend of his patron, and former pupil. This gentleman had lately married the sister of our minister's pupil, and had just settled on his estate in this part of the country. Whether the reverend divine merely wished to pay his respects to the lady, whom he had not seen since her childhood, or to ascertain the precise state of the "cough and defluxion," which had threatened all spring to carry off the aged incumbent of the parish—in which the manse and glebe were some L.15 per annum better than his own; —and whether his sitting-down cold still hung about the incumbent, or if these causes all combined produced the actuating motive which led him so far out of his course, it is not to tell, certain only it is, that as night began to fall, coming to a point where the road divided, he found it prudent to question the elder of two boys, who were slowly driving the cows they herded homeward, down a green loaning. "Can you direct me, my man, the road to T———?" said our divine; and with more frankness, and better breeding than is usual in his age and calling, the elder boy gave copious directions. "I have been there a hundred times," said he, "going to Menstrie Fair. Do you see the Fir Park yonder?—the park where the cushat's nest is?— Weel, ye'll just haud down a'blow that, and pass the bour-trees, and next Brownie's well, and then ye come to the stepping-stanes. But maybe ye would like to take the New Brig? That's the way little Pate and I went to gather *reddans** yesternight—may be ye would like some?" And here the boy hastily and hospitably produced the delicacy, which, however our divine, in his days of herding, might have relished, had no attractions to a seventeen years' thriving incumbent, who had now for twice seventeen years "sat at good men's feasts." But he remembered having very lately heard Colonel Thornton, no mean authority, recommend a conserve of *rowans* as a better condiment with either mutton or venison than the Cockney's currant jelly, usually employed for the same meats; and he accordingly stuffed the gift into his pockets, meditating experiment. "You're a good boy, Davy—is it Davy they call ye?—I think I know my way now.—But *where's your bonnet?* —and a Minister speaking to ye?" For, though humble in his own person, our divine liked to support the dignity of the Kirk. "Where's my bonnet?" quoth Davy, rubbing his eyes as the minister rode off.—"He must be blind, or he would have seen my bonnet, just where it should be, on my ain head. If he could not see it, he'll never see the bour-trees, and the stepping-stanes, and the road to T———. Tent Hawkey, Pate, and I'll run after the gentleman, and set him right." The minister was to-night in a very gracious humour, and when Davy, out of breath, overtook him, and explained his purpose of becoming his guide, with his reasons, the clergyman smiled at the simplicity of the boy, and now carefully informed him, that by saying *where's your bonnet?* he meant, where is your bow? which, he instructed

* Berries of the mountain-ash.

Davy, should always be promptly ready for his *superiors*, and especially for ministers. "Thank you, sir," said Davy, now taking off his bonnet; "neither the gudeman, nor the gudewife, ever fash with that; and our ministeris a Seceder, and only targes us on the *Carritch*. And I have nobody to learn me manners now, since the Almighty took my poor mother. She would ay say to me, 'Be a civil obliging laddie, David, and every body will like you; and no fear but ye get a good master.' I kent I should take off my bonnet to the laird, and the minister, but after this I will take it off to all gentlemen when I ken them, and ladies too; I ay ken them by their handing up their gowds,* and ga'en on their taes; thank you, sir, for bidding me," —"And what's your name, my little man?"—"Davy, sir, just Davy."—"That I know already, but what besides? what was your father called?"—"My father is dead too— he was dead before Peter, that is my little brother, was born—the gudeman, the gudewife, and all the men and lasses just call me Davy, at your service; and so does the minister." Our divine bestowed a penny on his guide, and in the course of the next forenoon, he related his adventure to his young hostess, who had a kind and generous heart. "The little boys, with broad blue bonnets, herding two black and white cows," she said, she had seen the boys frequently in her walks; their mother, who was one of the best poor women in the country side, had formerly been laundress in the family of which she was now the mistress, and it was one of her husband's tenants, who, at her request, gave employment and shelter to the orphans. Our minister revolved a generous act. He needed an intelligent boy about the age of Davy, who could clean knives, brush shoes, rub down and water the pony, and go an errand occasionally to Dunfermline or Alloa when letters were looked for, or wheaten bread, or fresh meat required. "It will be an act of great charity," said the lady, delighted to get Davy into such a comfortable home; and she sent for him immediately, and introduced him to the minister. "I know him very well already," said Davy; "it is the gentleman that asked, 'Where's your bonnet?'" Davy's bonnet was in his hand now. "And you will be pleased to go home with him, and do what he bids you till you are strong and big enough for other work."—"Surely!" cried Davy; "if he send me to school, like the gudeman, and let me see little Peter on the Saturday."—"Certainly, my little man; Girzy and myself will give you a lesson every day in the Bible and your catechism."

Davy longed for the happy day which was to take him to the *manse*, fifteen miles off, and make him the "minister's little man;"—but this did not place him in Goshen. Little drudges about a kitchen or stable, "the servants of servants," are seldom the most fortunate of children. The minister was naturally of a selfish and harsh temper, which long waiting for a *kirk*, and celibacy, had not softened,— and Girzy was only like too many of the ancient housekeepers of old bachelors. That poor Davy could either feel or reflect, more than the three-foot stool on which he sat cleaning knives, never seemed to enter into their minds; for they cuffed and kicked him about as readily as that piece of furniture. He was, among his many employments, sent t weed the garden, and if he drew a new-sprung plant in place of a weed, though it was next to impossible for him to know the difference, a thrashing was his sure reward. When

* Parasols.

sent an errand in the worst weather, wind and rain, and bad roads, if he staid a few minutes beyond the time which Girzy and the minister, fixed for his return by the cuckoo clock, or the watch, "he is diverting himself with his blackguard companions," Girzy would cry maliciously; and a slap in the face would welcome his return, while the minister considered it his duty to chastise him with the horsewhip.

The minister had no roasting jack in his kitchen, and one of Davy's most frequent jobs was to turn on the spit, meat of which he was never to have nearer knowledge than by smell. Nothing made his master more angry than the roast not being nicely done. A good beating was always promised for this offence, of often falsely imputed negligence; and the minister never forfeited his word. If Davy was promised half a dozen lashes, he was generally paid with a round dozen; and in short, no minister's little man had ever been so wretched as poor Davy. It happened one Saturday, that the lady who recommended the orphan to this service, sent the minister a present of a sucking-pig, a favourite morsel with him; and informed him at the same time that an old friend of theirs was to come to sermon at his church next day, and would afterwards take pot-luck with him. His chops watered at sight of the pig, for he was naturally gluttonous, and by long habit, good eating was become his favourite solitary enjoyment;—he would have gone a day's journey at any time for a bit of the stuffing, and the nice crisp skin, well basted with a faggot of sage, dipped in butter, salt, and water. The church was almost adjoining the manse; and Girzy, having made every preparation for dinner, put the pig to the fire, believing Davy had now experience enough to turn the spit, and baste the roast by himself, without her superintendence. She was just gone, when the servant who attended his guest, brought the minister two small bottles from the same lady who had sent the pig. He had only time to place them on the kitchen window shelf, as the bell for church was just ringing in. He cast a last anxious look on the pig, which was now making slow revolutions round and round, under the steady guiding hand of Davy, and already beginning to exhale a savoury odour. "It will just be ready when sermon is over," thought the minister; and he said aloud, "If you roast it *well*, I will not forget it to you; but if you dare to burn it, you had as good be sleeping: I'll certainly kill you." Davy, who had never known his master fail in fulfilling his threats of punishment, promised to be careful to keep up the fire, and to baste diligently; and thanks to the sage and onions, and Girzy's odoriferous stuffing, a most tempting flavour to a hungry boy was soon spread through the kitchen from the pig; which became as golden brown as a chestnut. It has often been said, and the maxim is still as true as ever, that nothing is worse for young persons than evil example. This was the first pig ever Davy had roasted. Neither hen, nor goose, nor lamb, hare, nor turkey, had ever smelt so temptingly; and he was all alone. He manfully resisted the first stirrings of temptation. "No," said he, "though I am certain if I managed like Girzy, that the minister could not find it out, I won't taste it." But the more turns of the spit Davy made, and the nearer his nose approached the savour that arose from his frequent bastings, the more powerful the temptation grew; and now the bad consequences of evil example were seen. He had often, when turning the spit, laden with pork, veal, beef, or mutton, seen Girzy dexterously slice out a piece horizontally, and by a layer of dusted-in flour, and frequent basting, and holding to the fire, raise a fictitious appearance of skin, that deceived even the keen-eyed minister. It was of this trick, the unhappy Davy, now, in an evil hour, made use. He could no longer resist. He hastily seized a knife, and cut off a morsel of crisp skin, which tasted so deliciously, that he returned to the charge, again and again, in a kind of frenzy of appetite, till the whole *crackling* was devoured! and then——vain attempt!—to conceal the fraud, he had recourse to Girzy's device, which ended in the skinless pig being scorched black in many places.——"What shall I do! what shall I do!" cried Davy; "the minister will kill me—and I deserve it." And for the first time, Davy felt that he had merited the punishment, which he often received for no fault at all. He was too candid and conscientious to blame the evil example of Girzy, which had led him into this snare. "Oh, I deserve all that he can do to me—and he will kill me! he will kill me! Lord have mercy upon me!" In this extremity Davy turned his eyes on the two small bottles standing in the window, which, as was mentioned in his hurry, the minister had left there, hastily charging the boy, for his life, not to touch them, as they contained poison. Davy had not hitherto thought of this injunction, but now it darted on his mind—"As good be poisoned, as killed with the horse-whip," he cried; and abandoning the pig to burn to a cinder at its leisure, he eagerly swallowed the contents of one of the bottles at a draught. It was marked *Maraschino*, which Davy took for granted was, as well as the Curaçoa written on the label of the other, some potent, deadly poison. He now sat down on his little stool to die. "I will soon die," thought Davy; "and when the minister and Girzy come from the kirk I will be lying there dead, and he wont kick me then." But death approached very slowly. Davy heard the church clock strike three, and knew the minister would return in a few minutes more. In a frenzy of despair, he rushed upon the other bottle, and despatched it also; and now he was sure death could not be far off. In the meantime, in waiting its arrival, Davy fell into a deep sleep, and sunk on the kitchen floor. It was Girzy who entered first, as the minister had to put off his gown. The bad smell of the burnt pig met her outside the door. "Come here, minister, and see your bonny Davy," cried the malicious jade; and the minister entered in a fury. "Where is my whip! where is my whip?—rascal, I will kill you!" cried he. Davy roused himself at this threat. He crawled to the feet of the minister, who had returned with the lash, and cried for mercy, though he was hardly able to articulate, for the poison had now begun to operate. Davy exhibited every symptom of a drunk man a boy can shew, except a drunk man's gaiety. "Do not kill me, minister," he cried. "There's no need, I have swallowed the two little bottles of poison you left in the window. I must soon die now." Imagine the rage of the minister, when, turning to the window, he saw the two *liqueur* bottles empty! He brought the lash several times about the boy's shoulders; but, perceiving that he was nearly dead drunk, he delayed his punishment till next day, and ordered Girzy to throw the young vagabond on his bed in the stable, resolving that Davy should get his dues with interest. The sight of the empty place on the table, which the sucking-pig should have occupied—one of the finest, fat, delicate, sucking-pigs he had ever seen!—did not soften the minister's resentment. The pig run in his head all day and all night.

On Monday morning, Davy awoke, after a sleep of eighteen hours, with a dreadful headach, and a consuming thirst. "It is the effect of the poison," thought he. "I thought I would die sooner; and my master would not then kill me. It will be hard to be poisoned and killed too. It was a great sin to poison myself—Lord pardon me for it." He again fell asleep, and when the minister saw him still deprived of sense and motion, he left him without striking him. "I'm surprised at your patience with the young rascal," cried Girzy, "that you have not thrashed him within an inch of his life."—"No," said her master; "he could not feel what he gets now; I'll give him such a flogging as he will have cause to remember for the rest of his life. He'll be seeking his breakfast by and by, and before he get that he shall have all his dues, *quod justum*, as he richly deserves."

In the afternoon, Davy awoke once more—not yet dead! His headach was, indeed, rather better, and he was famishing of hunger, having tasted nothing save the pilfered *crackling*, from breakfast time on Sunday. But he durst not venture into the house to ask for food. All the horror of his crimes, theft and self-murder, now appeared before him. But the dread of punishment was yet more appalling. "What will become of me?" cried the miserable Davy;—and they must be cruel and inconsiderate persons, indeed, who rashly drive a boy, at his thoughtless years, to such painful extremity. They may be the authors of all his future misfortunes; and of crimes he never would otherwise have committed. He thought of running to sea, which he had heard of boys doing; of going to a cotton-mill, and of a coal pit. For a soldier he was far too little. Happily he wanted courage for any of these exploits; and he finally resolved to run back to the GUDEMAN's. "I do not know the way," thought Davy; "but the Lord will guide me. Pate is not so well off as *me*—the minister's little man—but Pate is not scolded and cuffed by Girzy, and thrashed by the minister, every day, whether he be a good boy or a bad boy, all the same. Yes, when night comes, I will bolt the stable-door, and creep out by the loft-window. I will ask the road first to Tillicoultry; I have a gude Scotch tongue in my head, as the gudeman used to say. If I once get to Tillicoultry, I'll soon find the road to the gudeman's." Davy wore a sort of clerical livery that Girzy and the tailor of the village had provided for him, out of an old suit of the minister's. He knew the clothes did not belong to him; so he dressed himself in his old *harren* shirt, and tattered breeches, and without shoes, stockings, or bonnet, made his escape, in a terrible fright, repeating the Lord's Prayer as he ran, and in mortal dread of the minister pursuing, overtaking, and killing him. This was not very likely; but Davy was not yet the close, acute reasoner he afterwards became. The effects of deadly fear which impeded his breathing, prevented him from making much way; till at last he began to think,—"The minister will never break open the door, and Girzy cannot climb to the window. They'll just wait till the morn, thinking me poisoned; and then Davy Dibble will come to bury me." With such thoughts for his companions, Davy marched the whole of the long, dark night; but luckily, as his sensible mother had never told him of fairies, nor let him hear of ghosts, he had no fear of them. And now an unexpected stroke of good fortune awaited him, for at day-dawn, he joyfully beheld the farm of which he was in search, and which he well knew, though he was a stranger to the road to it. "The gudewife will give me my breakfast," cried he; "and then I'll get a good sleep in Pate's bed. O! but I am tired!"

No one was yet stirring about the farm-house; and as Davy sat musing on the stile, till the ha' door would open, his heart began to fail. "They'll be angry at me. O! I wish I had staid and been thrashed or killed. But I must tell what I did—that I ate the pig's skin, and then let it burn, and then poisoned myself. That was a great sin. The gudewife will be angry. The gudeman will maybe thrash me—but I deserve that—I dinna ken what to do. Lord have mercy upon me!" And Davy again said the Lord's Prayer, and repeated every psalm he knew. The door was now opened, and he crept into a corner of the porch, but feared to enter, or let himself be seen. It was the gudewife herself saw him first, as she went out to the byre to milk the cows. "Is it you, Davy! where have ye been all night, my man? What for have ye left the manse, bairn?"—"I durst not stay at the manse," sobbed Davy, "the minister was going to kill me."—"What do you mean, my bairn?" cried the compassionate gudewife,—"tell me Davy all has happened ye." And Davy told his whole story, most ingenuously, and with the strictest observance of truth; for he had not been long enough under the cruel discipline of Girzy and the Minister to have acquired the slave's vice of lying, and concealing a small fault by committing a greater. The gudewife laughed in her sleeve when Davy described his unfortunate imitation of Girzy's trick of making fresh skin to a roast; but when he gravely informed her that he had swallowed two bottles of poison under dread of the lash, the honest woman shrieked out, and her maid, half dressed, and her husband, came running to her help. "The poor bairn Davy," she cried, "he is poisoned, gudeman :—for fear of being lashed on Sabbath last, for spoiling the minister's roast pig, he has swallowed as much poison as would kill a horse."—"Lord be about us!" cried the maid. "Tell me how it's wi' you, Davy, my man," said the gudeman, hoping there was some mistake; as Davy, though ragged, dirty, and tired, did not look like one at the point of death. "Tell me about this poison?"—"It was in two little bottles about the length of that," said Davy, shewing his hand, which was not a large one.—"The minister said to me, 'Davy, for your life, dinna touch these bottles; they are poison:' but when the pig was burnt, kennin' the minister would kill me when he came in from the kirk, I just swallowed first one, and then the other. The one was as red as blood and very sweet, and the other was as yellow as a gowan; I fell asleep after that; and I have done a great sin in trying to put hand to mysell, I ken that." The gudeman had a shrewd guess what the minister's bottles of poison, that had thrown Davy into so long a sleep, might be. He bade his wife compose herself. "You'll no die this time, Davy, my man; but ye must take better care how ye swallow poison again. Mary must gie ye some breakfast; and then you must go to bed." Davy did not require two invitations to breakfast; and the gudeman and the gudewife consulted about what was to be done with him. They had had children of their own, and did not like to hear of punishment, the terror of which drove little orphan boys to poison themselves, and run off from their homes. The gudeman sat down and wrote to the minister, to inquire, in the first place, into the truth of this extraordinary story, and how, in so short a period, Davy's character and conduct had changed so far for the worse, that it was necessary to punish him so harshly every day. The minister, whom conscience upbraided for severity to the poor little orphan lad, was, at the same time, exceedingly offended that the culprit had not been sent back to his tender mercies. Girzy was accordingly ordered to make up the few goods and chattels of our small hero into a bundle, which was sent to the gudeman with a message, saying, " The minister hoped never to see the wicked ungrateful little rascal's face again." " You never shall," said the angry gudeman.

Good fortune often springs from the darkest sources— Davy's poisoning and thrashings were the beginning of his. The lady who had sent him to the manse now put him to school, where in two years, he was able to assist the master. From thence he went to Edinburgh, and to the office of the agent of his patroness; where he made such good use of his time and talents, that, in ten years afterwards, he was a partner in the business, and his brother Peter one of the clerks. In after life, as often as Mr. David heard of little boys rebelling, playing truant, or running away from home, he remembered his poisoning, and said there were probably more persons in fault than the runaway; and he would inquire into the affair, and see justice done to the offender.

⁂ As soon as the SCHOOLMASTER can find space, he will give the *Sequel* to the TALE OF LITTLE DAVY, in MEMOIRS OF MR DAVID BROWN, W. S.

ELEMENTS OF THOUGHT.

KINGS, THEIR USE.—A King is a thing men have made for *their own sakes*, for quietness' sake. Just as in a family one man is appointed to buy the meat; if every man should buy, or if there were many buyers, they would never agree; one would buy what the other liked not, or what the other had already bought, and so there would be a confusion. But that charge being committed to one, he, according to his discretion, pleases all: the word King diverts our eyes. Suppose it had been Consul or Dictator. To think all Kings alike, is the same folly as if a Consul of Aleppo or Smyrna should claim to himself the same power with a Consul of Rome. Kings are all individuals: this, or that King; there is no species of Kings: A King that claims privileges in his own country, because they have them in another, is just as a cook that claims fees in one lord's house because such are allowed in another. If the master of the house will yield them, well and good. The text, " render unto Cæsar the things that are Cæsar's," makes as much against King's as for them; for it says plainly, some things are not Cæsar's. But divines make choice of it, first in flattery, and then because of the other part adjoined to it, " render unto God the things that are God's," whereby they bring in the Church.—*Selden.*

THE COMMON CENTRE.—*An old Radical.*

Euclid was beaten in Boccaline, for teaching his scholars a mathematical figure, whereby he showed that all the lives both of Princes and private men tended to one centre, *con gentilezza*, handsomely to get money out of other men's pockets, and put it into their own. " In all times," says Selden, " The Princes of England have done something illegal to get money; but then came a Parliament, and all was well; the people and the Prince kissed, and were friends; and so things were quiet for a while. Afterwards there was a new trick found out to get more money; and after they had got it, another Parliament was called to set all right, &c. But now they have so outrun the Constable, &c. &c.

LEARNING.

No man is the wiser for his learning. It may administer matter to work upon; but wit and wisdom are born with a man. Most men's learning is nothing but history, duly taken up.

JEWS.—Talk what we will of the Jews, they thrive wherever they come; they are able to oblige the Prince of the country by lending him money; none of them beg; they keep together, and for their being hated, my life for yours, Christians hate one another as much.

PUNISHMENTS.

THE intent of punishments is not to torment a sensible being, nor to undo a crime already committed. Is it possible that torments and useless cruelty, the instruments of furious fanaticism, or of the impotency of tyrants, can be authorized by a political body; which, so far from being influenced by passion, should be the cool moderator of the passions of individuals. Can the groans of a tortured wretch recal the time past, or reverse the crime he committed?—the end of punishment, therefore, is no other than to prevent the criminal from doing farther injury to society, and to prevent others from committing the like offence. Such punishments therefore should be chosen, and such modes of inflicting them, as will make the strongest, and most lasting impression on the minds of others, with the least torment to the body of the criminal.—*Beccaria.*

The frequency of executions is always a sign of the weakness or indolence of governments. There is no malefactor who might not be made good for something; nor ought any to be put to death, even by way of example, unless such as could not be preserved without endangering the community. When a state is on the decline, the multiplicity of crimes occasions their impunity. Under the Roman republic, neither the senate nor the councils ever attempted to grant pardons; even the people never did this, though they sometimes recalled their own sentences.—*Rousseau.*

If punishments be very severe, men are naturally led to the perpetration of other crimes to conceal the first. A murder conceals a theft. In proportion also, as punishments became more cruel, the minds of men, as a fluid rises to the same height with that which surrounds it, grow hardened or insensible; and the force of the passions still continuing in the space of an hundred years, the wheel terrifies no more than formerly the prison. That a punishment may produce the effect required, it is sufficient that the evil it occasions should exceed the good expected from the crime; including in the calculation the *certainty* of the punishment, and the privation of the expected advantage. All severity beyond this is superfluous, and therefore tyrannical * * * Severe punishments also occasion impunity. Human nature is limited, no less in evil than in good. Excessive barbarity can never be more than temporary.—*Beccaria.*

A great part of the intemperate and vindictive spirit of the English law, is to be ascribed to the practice of our legislators acting upon some temporary excitement, or, as Lord Bacon describes it, on " the spur of the occasion." It will suffice to illustrate this by one or two examples. There was a statute passed in the reign of Henry VIII., by which it was enacted, that persons convicted of poisoning should be *boiled to death.* It must be admitted that, atrocious and malignant as the crime of poisoning is, it does not become the character of justice, even if it be right to exterminate the offender, to take a fiend-like pleasure in protracting the agonies of death, and to display a horrid ingenuity in torturing the wretch whom she cuts off from mankind. It is surely enough that he dies, without his death being made the occasion of exhibiting the cruel and revengeful feelings of the legislator, by examples which teach cruelty to the people. In the present instance, we cease to wonder at the eccentric barbarity of the statute, when we find that it was made under the impulse of strong public indignation, in consequence of the atrocious crime of a person named Roos, who was cook to the Bishop of Rochester, and who by putting poison into a pot of broth, part of which was served up to the Bishop's family, and the remainder to the poor of the parish, destroyed several lives; though we by no means vouch for the cogency of the proof, on which the charge of so enormous a crime was sustained. We know that sometimes families have been poisoned by accident; as, for instance, by an ill-cleaned copper vessel. However this may be, no doubt of the man's guilt was entertained. The novel and dreadful sort of punishment which he underwent, was inflicted by a special statute, passed for the occasion, and of course subsequently to the commission of the crime; and the *boiling to death* was intended to be a sort of retaliation, because the crime had been effected by *boiling!* He suffered the punishment by a retrospective operation of the act. This statute, however, did not long exist, to convert the proceedings of a court of justice into a sort of culinary process; for, in the first year of Edward VI., it was repealed. Only think of a British Parliament sitting in consultation upon a proposition of boiling a human being to death, and that by a law made after the crime had been committed! They could only have surpassed this by being actually present at the execution of their own sentence, and by taking care that the lingering torments of the diabolical cookery were not abridged by any merciful rapidity of operation on the part of the person whom the sheriff appointed to stir the fire, and preside over the horrors of the judicial cauldron. The sentence was executed in Smithfield. There was the fire lit—the cauldron raised—and the man boiled, by act of Parliament, to the great edification of the people; who, if they learned nothing else from it, learned, at least, that atrocious cruelty was a legislative virtue, which the vulgar might not, therefore, be ashamed to practise. It is bad enough in a legislative body to become ridiculous by its follies, but it is still worse to deserve the abhorrence of all enlightened minds by its inhumanity. If any thing could diminish the public indignation against the culprit who was convicted of so heinous a crime, it was the greater enormity of having recourse to such a mode of punishing it. We may fairly infer, that the deliberate and shocking cruelty of the legislature excited disgust even in that rude time, when we find that one of the first acts of the popular reign of Edward VI., a few years after, was to erase the monstrous penalty of " boiling to death" for ever from the criminal law of England.—*Tait's Magazine.*

USEFUL NOTICES.

EXPLOSION OF STEAM BOILERS.

THE following remarks on the causes of these explosions, are by Mr. Jacob Perkins, a gentleman who has devoted almost the whole of his life to the study of the nature and properties of steam :—

It appears to be a well-established fact, that the caloric of steam, at a given density, is a constant quantity when in contact with water. This is undoubtedly the case, if the steam is properly generated; but if any part of the boiler, which contains the steam, is suffered to get at a higher temperature than the water contained in it, from want of a sufficient supply of water, the steam will receive an excess of caloric, and become supersaturated steam, without adding any available power thereto. In some recent experiments I have heated steam to a temperature (viz. 1200) that would have given to it all the power which steam is capable of exerting (viz. nearly 60,000lbs to the square inch), if it had had its full quantum of water. Yet the indicator showed a pressure of less that five atmospheres. Having satisfied myself, by repeated experiments, as to the certainty of this curious fact, the thought struck me, that if heated water was injected suddenly into this mass of supersaturated steam, the effect would be instantly to form highly elastic steam—the strength of which would depend upon the temperature of the supersaturated steam, and the temperature and quantity of water injected. To ascertain the truth of the theory, I made the following experiments :—The generator was filled with water, and heated to about 500 degrees. The pressure valve being loaded at 70 atmospheres, it prevented the water from expanding into steam. The receiver, which was destitute of both water and steam, being heated to about 1200 degrees, a small quantity of water was injected into the generator with the forcing pump, which forced out from under a pressure valve of the generator, into the receiver, a corresponding quantity; and this instantly flashed into steam, which, from its having ignited the hemp that covered the steam-pipe ten feet from the generator, must have been at a temperature of at least 800 degrees; but from want of water to give it its necessary density, the indicator shewed a pressure of only about five atmospheres. Whether the pressure of the steam which was rushing through the steam-pipe, was at five or one hundred atmospheres, the steam-pipe kept up at the high temperature before mentioned; undoubtedly, owing to the steam being supersaturated with caloric. The pump was now made to inject a much larger quantity of heated water; and the indicator, in an instant, showed a pressure of from 50 to 60 atmospheres. It soon expanded (the throttle-valve being partially opened) to the former pressure of about five atmospheres. The water was injected again; and again the indicator was observed to oscillate, at each stroke of the pump, from 4 to between 40 and 100 atmospheres, according to the quantity of water injected—clearly showing that, at the reduced pressure, there was a great redundance and loss of heat, with little elastic force. It soon occurred to me, that here may be traced the true cause of the tremendous explosions which suddenly take place, in low as well as high pressure boilers. There are many instances where an instant before one of these terrific explosions had taken place, the engine laboured—showing evidently a decrease of power in the steam. To illustrate the theory of sudden explosions, let us suppose the feed-pipe, or pump of a boiler, to be choked. In this case the water would soon get below some parts of the boiler, which should be constantly covered with water, thus leaving them to become heated to a much higher temperature than the water; the steam being now in contact with the heated metal, readily takes up the heat, and becomes supercharged with caloric. Since caloric will not descend in water it cannot be taken up by it when above its surface. The steam thus supersaturated, will heat the upper surface of the boiler, in some cases, red-hot; and ignite coals or any other combustible matter which may be in contact with it. Now if steam, in this state, could be supplied with heated water, as was the case in the experiment before-mentioned, the result may be readily anticipated. Let the same cause continue which cut off the supply of water from the boiler, until it shall no longer be able, from its diminished quantity, to lay on the bottom of the boiler, then, all at once, like the boiling over of an over-heated pot, the heated water will rush up into, and be immediately taken up by, this mass of supersaturated steam. Thus, having suddenly acquired a sufficient density, by the addition of heated water, it will become steam of immense power, and will as suddenly explode—no safety-valve being calculated to guard against this rapid generation of high steam.

In converting cast into wrought iron, a mass of metal of about one hundred weight is heated almost to a white heat, and placed under a heavy hammer moved by water or steam power. This is raised by a projection on a revolving axis; and if the hammer derived its momentum only from the space through which it fell, it would require a considerable greater time to give a blow. But as it is important that the softened mass of red-hot iron should receive as many blows as possible before it cools, the form of the cam or projection on the axis is such, that the hammer, instead of being lifted to a small height, is thrown up with a jerk, and almost the instant after it strikes against a large beam, which acts as a powerful spring, and drives it down on the iron with such velocity that by these means about double the number of strokes can be made in a given time. In the smaller tilt-hammers, this is carried still further; by striking the tail of the tilt-hammer forcibly against a small steel anvil, it rebounds with such velocity, that from three to five hundred strokes are made in a minute. In the manufacture of scythes, the length of the blade renders it necessary that the workman should move readily, so as to bring every part on the anvil in quick succession. This is effected by placing him in a seat suspended by ropes from the ceiling; so that he is enabled, with little bodily exertion, by pressing his feet against the block which supports the anvil, to vary his distance to any required extent. In the manufacture of anchors, an art in which this contrivance is of still greater importance, it has only been recently applied.—*Babbage on Machinery and Manufactures.*

ON OILING RAIL-WAY CARRIAGES, BY MR. J. L. SULLIVAN, CIVIL ENGINEER, BALTIMORE.

(*From the Journal of an American Society.*)

THERE is no difficulty in oiling axles continually, but to do it so as not to waste a drop of oil, has not been done, I believe, till the latest improvements in the friction-saving carriage of the Baltimore rail-road, where very accurate experiments have been making by Mr. George Brown, one of the principal proprietors of that work; the result of which, he informs me, is, that one quart of oil will be sufficient for 2000 miles' run of a carriage, which, with its load, weighs 3 tons. He informs me, at the same time, that he has ascertained that the Lehigh railway carriages consume 4 quarts in running 321 miles with 1 ton. This, it will be perceived, is nearly 80 times as much.— The manner of oiling the Winan's waggon is peculiar to its construction as now improved. The secondary wheels now run in a cast-iron case, the top of which is formed so as to affix to the under surface of the side timbers of the frame of the waggon. Its sides sustain the axle, and are supported or joined by an intermediate part or bottom, which forms a tight case, into which the oil is put, so that the friction wheel dips into it, and its rim carries up a little of it continually to the rubbing and rolling surfaces, returning it to the reservoir; thus oiling its own axle, where all the rubbing is situated, and the rolling-axle, and no more is consumed than evaporates. Its enclosure keeps clean. I need not remind the reader that the use of oil on axles is not only to keep the surfaces from actual contact, and grinding together, but to keep them cool, and this is better done by the successive application of new portions of oil than by keeping the same oil on the axle as long as it will last, partaking of the heat the axle requires, and therefore evaporating the faster. This method must therefore be of consequence when great velocity is to be given to heavy loads.

We extract the following additional observations on the subject from the minutes of a monthly meeting of the Franklin Institute:—

"Geo. W. Smith, Esq., to whom was referred the question, 'What is the best unguent, and the most economical mode of its application, to diminish the friction of rail-way cars, locomotive engines, and other machinery of similar construction?' stated, that the result of several experiments which have recently been made, have led to the conclusion, that the finest quality of sperm oil most effectually relieves machinery from the effects of friction.

"Professor A. D. Bache remarked, that Mr. Wood's experiments on the friction of railway carriages had shown the fact to be in that case, as stated by Mr. Smith; and that those of Rennie led to the conclusion, that the nature of the unguent should bear some relation to the weights to be supported, or resistances to be overcome, *the more fluid unguents applying best to light loads.*

"After which Mr. J. M'Ilvaine stated, that in using the various kinds of unguents on this machinery, he had come to the same conclusion as that stated by Mr. S., that the best quality of sperm oil was the most beneficial; having considered it as a question of much importance, he had devoted a considerable time to the subject, and was very particular in making his observations. He further remarked, that the oil should be carefully cleansed, and deprived of those parts which water could ove."

DR. HENRY'S DISINFECTING PROCESS.—An apparatus for the disinfection of clothes, bedding, &c., on the plan proposed by Dr. Henry, has been erected at Lancaster Castle (at an expense of only L.10;) and another is also about to be put up at the New Bailey, Manchester. The apparatus consists simply of two cast-iron pans—the inner one 3 feet 6 inches diameter, and 2 feet 2 inches deep; the outer one 3 feet 8 inches diameter, and 2 feet 4 inches deep. They are united at the flanches. The shape, however, is of no consequence, provided the clothes are only sufficiently heated. Neither has steam any advantages over hot air, except in so far as it may secure linen or woollen articles from being burned. A hot closet, so constructed as that the heat should not rise above from 212 to 220 degrees, would doubtless answer the purpose.

REMEDY FOR THE FOOT-ROT IN SHEEP.—The following remedy is suggested by a correspondent of the *Essex Independent*, for the prevention and cure of the foot-root in sheep, which disease has this season been more than usually prevalent. He recommends it from experience, having found it decidedly harmless as well as efficacious. His plan is this; about once a month, whether the sheep be affected or not, sprinkle some fresh lime on some dry place about an inch thick; and while sloaking, put the sheep upon it, making them walk over it some few minutes; this cauterising the foot renders it bad, and still less to be affected by the above baneful as well as highly contagious disease. Should the foot be previously diseased, the parts affected had better be removed by a sharp knife, and the above plan, without any other application, be adopted.

A GENTLEMAN.—In St Constant's Sketches of London and English manners, it is asserted that the nurse of James I., having followed him from Edinburgh to London, entreated him to make her son a gentleman. "My good woman," said the King, "I might make him a laird, but I could never make him a gentleman."

DECLINE OF SCOTTISH AGRICULTURE.
Continued from Number 10.

With the return of peace in 1814, a severe depression took place in agriculture, and a fall in the price of produce of the soil of all kinds. The crop of 1811 was bad, but those of 1812 and 1813 had been very good in England. The average prices of wheat for the two last years, were 125s. 5d. and 108s. 9d. The great importations of foreign grain began in 1813. In the years 1811 and 1812, the value of grain, the flour, &c. imported, was from foreign countries, L.2,306,651; and from Ireland, L.2,478,509. In the next two years, grain, &c. to the value of £.5,007,911, was imported from foreign countries, and to the amount of L.4,445,827, from Ireland. The quantities imported in the latter years are nearly one-third greater than the respective values would indicate, for the value was estimated at the average market prices, which were about one-third lower in 1813 and 1814, than in 1811 and 1812. In consequence of these large importations, and on account of the crop 1814 and 1815 being also abundant in most parts of Britain, the average prices of wheat fell in 1814 to 73s. 11d., and in 1815 to 64s. Other grain fell in the same proportion. To add to the misfortunes of the Scotch agriculturists, the quality of their wheat in 1815 and 1816, was very indifferent, so much so, that it sold for a third less than English wheat, though the prices in the three prior years had differed little; and in some of these years, Scotch wheat had been superior to English. In 1815 the average price of wheat in Scotland was only 53s. 6d. This state of matters produced great distress and alarm. It appears from a variety of evidence, that all parties had calculated that wheat would bring 80s. or 84s. a-quarter; and leases for several years preceding, had been entered into, with the most perfect reliance on the permanence of a price of at least 90s. Nor was this estimate at all exaggerated, as far as data then existed. Mr. Turnbull, a very intelligent farmer, near Dunbar, stated in his examination before the committee of the House of Commons, on agricultural distress in 1814, that his sales of wheat for crops, 1805-1813, gave an average of 94s. per quarter. No reduction of rents was, however, given. The distress was considered merely temporary, and farms continued to be taken at high rents during the years 1814, 1815, and 1816. The Corn Law of 1815, by prohibiting all importation, till wheat reached 80s. it was very generally supposed, would have the effect of keeping that grain near that price, and landlords and tenants acted for several years on that supposition. This law proved most injurious to British agriculture, and the protection it held out was a mere delusion. In the meanwhile, a cause of misfortune, generally unexpected, though ultimately inevitable, appeared. The evils necessarily attending the restriction of cash payments by the Bank of England, without any provision to limit within proper bounds the issues of paper, shewed themselves in a new form. This proceeding had hitherto operated to defraud annuitants, stockholders, and other persons, living on the interest of capital, of a third, or fourth of their property by raising the price of commodities to that extent, while their receipts remained unchanged. But now the time had come when debtors were to be defrauded, and creditors enriched. The over-issues of the Bank of England had led to an equal over-issuing by the English country banks. Bills were discounted almost without limitation. In many counties the agriculturists, or those depending on them, were their principal debtors; and as the fall in the value of agricultural produce rendered it impossible for them to discharge their engagements, the banks failed in great numbers. It has been estimated, that of 699 country banks in England and Wales, in 1814, 240 either became utterly bankrupt or stopped payment before the end of the year 1816; nor did the mischief cease here. The currency was not only diminished by the sudden withdrawing of the notes of the insolvent banks, but the issues of all the rest were very greatly contracted. The Board of Agriculture estimated, that in the county of Lincoln only, above three millions of bank paper had, in the course of eighteen months, been withdrawn from circulation, and in a variety of other extensive districts in England, and in the south of Ireland, no money was to be found in circulation, credit was totally annihilated; and so great was the panic, that even the notes of the Bank of England would hardly pass current except at a discount. These failures were the more distressing and calamitous, as they chiefly affected the industrious classes, and frequently swallowed up in an instant the fruits of a long life of laborious and unremitting exertions. That support on which too many of the agriculturists and manufacturers rested, suddenly gave way at the moment when it was most necessary. Prices instantly fell; and thousands who, but a moment before, considered themselves affluent, found they were destitute of all real property, and sunk, as if by enchantment, and without any fault of their own, into the abyss of poverty. The late Mr. Horner, the accuracy and extent of whose information on such subjects cannot be called in question, stated in his place in the House of Commons, " that the destruction of English country bank paper in 1814 and 1815 had given rise to a universality of wretchedness and misery, which had never been equalled, except perhaps by the breaking up of the Mississippi scheme in France." (Article " Money" in Supp. Encycl. Britt. by Prof. MacCulloch.) Agricultural produce became unsaleable. It was not merely that prices fell, but purchasers were not to be found at any price. Bank paper, which, when compared with gold, had been, at its greatest depreciation, upwards of 25 per cent in 1814, rose very nearly to par before the end of 1816. In October of that year the discount was only, L.1, 8s. 7d. Such were the consequences of the Bank Restriction Act, a measure for which Mr. Pitt is now lauded by some writers, and held up as the benefactor of his country! It may safely be asserted that there never was a more pernicious scheme adopted in any country. Admitting that the measure was necessary in 1797, and without inquiring whether that necessity was not caused by the improper management of the affairs of the bank, why were not means devised to prevent the degradation of the currency by over issues of paper, and where was the necessity of continuing the Restriction for so long a period?

The Scotch Banks, resting on a more stable basis than the English Provincial Banks, and avoiding the speculations in which the latter so often and so improperly engaged, withstood the storm, but were under the necessity of greatly limiting the accommodation they had hitherto afforded. From the successes which had hitherto attended their exertions, and the ease with which money was to be had, many agriculturists had engaged in speculations more extensive than their capital warranted, and being called on by the banks for payment of the loans, necessarily became bankrupt. In a few years, the profits which had been made during the war were lost, and in many instances the original capital besides. In proportion generally as a farmer had been fortunate, were his speculations extensive; and the more extensive his concerns, the greater and more rapid his loss. Money could not be had at the legal rate of interest. Any amount might have been lent out in Edinburgh in 1816, 1817, and 1818, on the best landed security at 12 and 15 per cent, and higher interest even was paid. The money had of course to be borrowed on annuity to avoid the laws against usury, and many instances could be pointed out in which the creditor received 10 per cent clear, and the debtor had also to pay 4 or 5 per cent more, as the annual premium to secure the creditor in re-payment of the principal sum, at the death of the person on whose life the annuity was payable. In 1817 wheat rose in England to 94s., and in 1818 it was 84s. per quarter; but the crops were deficient, foreign grain, to the enormous amount of 14 millions and a half in value, having been entered for home consumption in these two years. The average price of wheat in Scotland, for the years 1819, 1820, and 1821, was under 60s. per quarter. The proceedings before the Committee of the House of Commons, on the depression of agriculture in 1821, furnishes us with much valuable information. It appears from the evidence then adduced, that the fall upon all the produce of the soil, and on sheep and wool, as compared with the prices from 1800 to 1813, amounted to 31 per cent, and those on which the farmer has most to depend on to 40 per cent, while in England, the taxes had increased 75 per cent, the poor's rates, 82 per cent., and the price of labour had fallen only 12½ per cent. It further appeared that in England the soil had been much deteriorated by over-cropping since 1818, by the quantity of stock kept in farms being greatly diminished. The greatest distress prevailed among the tenantry, and the rents of the preceding year, where not in arrear, had been generally paid from the capital of the tenantry. Only two Scotch farmers were examined, both from East Lothian. Their evidence is of importance even at present, because it will be shown that agriculture must necessarily be more depressed now than it was at that time, as the price of agricultural produce is lower in the 10 years since that investigation, than it was between 1813 and 1821. Mr. John Brodie of Scoughall, stated that he had taken a farm of 670 Scotch acres,* in the year 1812, at a rent of L.2900, that rent being more than double what the preceding tenant had paid. He expended L.5000 in putting a proper stock on it, and L.3000 more in buildings, his lease being for 21 years. Since 1814 his losses has been very considerable, though a great proportion of the farm was fine land, and the loss on such land was not so great as on that of inferior quality. There had

* The Scotch acre is a fifth larger than the English.

not been one penny of profit notwithstanding the great outlay, and no return from the money expended on the farm. He had received no reduction of rent from his landlord. The farmers in East Lothian were living on their capital, and great arrears of rent were understood to exist. The prices which he considered necessary to remunerate the farmer were 84s. per quarter for wheat, and 32s. for oats. The average price in East Lothian of wheat for 1821 and two preceding years, was only 60s., of oats, 22s. He was of opinion that without paying any rent, wheat could not be produced on the very best land, such as brought L.6 per acre during the war, under 36s. a-quarter; on land worth L.3 at the same period, the raising of wheat would cost 50s. to 54s.; and on land worth L.1 per acre, 70s. He thought the best land would require a reduction of rent of 20 or 25 per cent; middling land, 30 or 35; inferior soils fully 50 per cent. Mr. John Brodie of West Fenton concurred with the former witness in most particulars. His farm having been taken in 1801, had not been a losing concern for the preceding five or six years; but loss would have been sustained, had not a great deal of capital been laid out on it. For one article, he had brought from Leith and Edinburgh upwards of L.3000 worth of manure, and he estimated the carriage at L.1000 more. The tenantry in East Lothian, though they had not suffered so much as in other districts, had for some years been paying their rents out of their capital.

Now it will be found that the average prices of British grain for the six years 1815-1820 were, wheat, 76s. 3d.; barley, 40s. 11d.; oats, 27s. 8d. per Winchester quarter; while the average of the ten years since 1821-1830 per imperial quarter, which is about two per cent larger than the Winchester, are only for wheat, 59s. 4d.; barley, 32s. 6d.; oats, 23s. 6d.; being a fall of about 20 per cent. If the witnesses examined before the committee were, therefore, correct in estimating the reduction on rents, which ought generally to have been made to enable the tenantry to cultivate their farms at 30 per cent, it is obvious that a still greater reduction from the rents paid during the war would now be necessary to attain the same object. But it is well known that in very few instances, indeed, have reductions to the amount of 30 per cent been made. Indeed, in most cases, reductions have not been given so long as it was possible to recover the rent from the tenant. In this manner his capital has been exhausted, his means for the proper cultivation of his farm diminished, and the soil greatly deteriorated. When the reduction of rent was, therefore, given, it has very generally turned out inadequate, for in the period which had elapsed between the demand and the complying with the request, the farm had decreased greatly in value by the deterioration of the soil, and the exhausted circumstances of the tenant, did not enable him to bring his farm to its proper state of fertility.

The outgoings of the farmer have not diminished in a proportional degree since 1813. Their servants are paid their wages in grain, and the quantity given to them has not been diminished, while the charges of the saddler, blacksmith, and wright are not much lower than they were during the war. These tradesmen contend that there is no room for lessening their charges, as they allege that their charges did not rise previously, in any proportion, to the increase of the price of food. On sheep farms, again, there has been no saving whatever in the outgoings, as the shepherds are, it is believed, universally paid in stock.

In Scotland, pastoral districts are of more than usual importance. The total extent of the kingdom is nineteen millions of English acres, of which little more than five are under cultivation, and of these, one half is estimated to be in pasture or hay. In the Committee of the House of Commons on the wool trade in 1828, it was said that more than one half of Scotland was occupied in the rearing of Cheviot and black-faced sheep, but the proportion is probably much more considerable. The distress in such districts can easily be understood. On sheep farms, it is expected that the wool should pay the rent, leaving the carcase to discharge the other expenses, and for profit on the capital employed; but between the years 1813 and 1827, Cheviot tarred wool had fallen fully one half in value, and other wool in nearly the same proportion. The value of sheep and lambs had also fallen nearly to the same extent. Lord Napier has extensive sheep farms in Ettrick Forest, which he managed for many years himself, and he stated in his evidence before the Committee on Wool, that the produce of a farm which, on the average from 1806 to 1817, yielded L.490 per annum, only brought L.240 in 1827. He was asked " Are the Committee then to understand from your lordship, that the produce of at least half of Scotland, and from which half of the rent is paid, has fallen 50 per cent in value?"— " Certainly." The value of black cattle fell also considerably, but never reached so great a depression as the produce of sheep farms, the average price of the last 15 years compared with the war prices, shewing a fall of about 30 per cent. Since 1827 or 1828, the value of sheep and wool has risen considerably, and now approaches within 30 per cent of the war prices.

Next week we shall give the present state of Scotch Agriculture.

SCRAPS.
ORIGINAL AND SELECTED.

Edinburgh has been often praised, but seldom so successfully as in the following sonnet, translated from the Latin of Arthur Johnstone:—

Install'd on Hills, her Head near starrye bowres,
Shines Edinburgh, proud of protecting powers:
Justice defendes her heart; Religion east
With temples; Mars with towres doth guard the west:
Fresh Nymphes and Ceres seruing, waite upon her,
And Thetis, tributarie, doth her honour.
The Sea doth Venice slake, Rome Tiber beates,
Whilst she bot scornes her vassall watteres threats.
For scepters so where standes a Towne more fitt,
Nor place where Toune, World's Queene, may fairer sitt.
Bot this thy praise is, aboue all, most braue,
No man did e're diffame thee bot a slaue.

TRIBUTES.*—It would require a volume to describe all the curiosities, ancient and modern, living and dead, which are here gathered together. I say living, because a menagerie might be formed out of birds and beasts, sent as presents from distant lands. A friend told me he was at Abbotsford one evening, when a servant announced, "A present from"—I forget what chieftain in the North. "Bring it in," said the poet. The sound of strange feet were soon heard, and in came two beautiful Shetland ponies, with long manes and uncut tails, and so small, that they might have been sent to Elfland to the Queen of the Faries herself. One poor Scotsman, to show his gratitude for some kindness Scott, as Sheriff, had shown him, sent two kangaroos from New Holland; and Washington Irving lately told me, that some Spaniard or other, having caught two young wild Andalusian boars, consulted him how he might have them sent to the Author of "The Vision of Don Roderick."

LONDON SPARROWS.—At a late lecture on animal and vegetable life in London, delivered by Dr. J. Mitchell at the London Literary and Scientific Institution, he stated that the London sparrows were often as sooty and black as chimney-sweepers. Their favourite abode for building their nests is within the foliage of the capitals of Corinthian columns and pilasters. He stated that they also build within the mouth of the lion on the top front of Northumberland-house. The benevolence of some, and the cruelty of others, placed pots on the sides of houses for their reception. Dr. Johnson marks with his abhorrence one man who did this. The sparrows, not knowing the character of the man with whom they had to deal, built their nests in his pots. It was disgusting to hear the fellow express his delight at the prospect of making pies of their young.

BEGGARY.—There is a saying among country-people, that many insects in spring is a sign of many birds in summer. Begging keeps pace, or slackens, with the disposition to give, or withhold, alms. In a former age, the rich dispensed liberally to the poor, and poverty itself could afford to relieve indigence. Then, beggar joined company with beggar, and troops of mendicants, swarming from towns, overspread the country, and fattened on gleanings which, in the midst of plenty, were scarcely missed. The demands outgrew the supplies. So early as the reign of Henry VII., there is a statute directing that every impotent beggar should resort to the hundred where he has dwelt, was best known, or was born, and there remain, upon pain of being set in the stocks for three days and nights, with only bread and water, and then sent out of the town. In the next reign, when Henry VIII. dissolved the monasteries and nunneries "with good incomes and warm kitchens," whence provisions were daily distributed to the needy, the helpless poor wandered far and wide, and so troubled the kingdom for sustenance, that parliament authorised the justices of every county to grant licenses to indigent, aged, and impotent beggars, to beg within a certain district.

* Account of a Visit to Abbotsford.

DRINKING "BY INFERENCE."—Of Mirza Abu Taleb Khan, the well-known Persian Ambassador, Sinclair relates:—"At one of the dinners I gave to the Mirza, the celebrated Dr. Watson, Bishop of Llandaff, was present. The Bishop observed that the Persian took wine very freely; upon which he said to him, "Mirza, how comes this? Is not drinking wine prohibited by the Koran?" Upon which the Persian said, "I take it *by inference*. In the Koran it is said that we may take whatever is good for our health. I am informed, that taking wine in this country is good for the health, *therefore, I infer*, that I may take it consistently with the precepts of the Koran."

Mr. Locke was asked how he had contrived to accumulate a mine of knowledge so rich, yet so extensive and deep. He replied, that he attributed what little he knew, to the not having been ashamed to ask for information; and to the rule he had laid down, of conversing with all descriptions of men, on those topics chiefly that formed their own peculiar professions or pursuits.

An Irishman, some years ago, when he was studying at Edinburgh, asked a celebrated teacher of the German flute on what terms he would give him a few lessons. The answer was, "I charge two guineas for the first month, and one guinea for the second."—"Then, by my soul," said the Hibernian, "I'll come the second month first."

A very old lady died lately in a *certain* country town, and was greatly lamented by a contemporary, though they had not been the best of friends before. "Why do you lament her so grievously?" said a friend. "Don't you know?—was she not the only person left between me and death?"

TO CORRESPONDENTS.

Various poetical tributes to the memory of Sir Walter Scott are received for the *Schoolmaster* and the *Chronicle*. As we cannot adopt them *all*, we must resolve on omitting all, as it is unfair to make invidious distinctions.

☞ Our good friend in Forfarshire appears entirely to misunderstand the gist of Dr. Kidd's argument. His reply is, besides, far too long.

We gave the theory of the *East Wind*, mentioning that we did not recollect whence we obtained it. If not satisfactory, and we admit it is not, let our polite pupil send the *Schoolmaster* a better if he can, and we shall be glad to give his exercises publicity.

☞ We feel deeply obliged by the amiable letter of T. S. M.

The weather may henceforth be unfavourable for *rambling* till the return of spring; though we may before then resume our excursions, directing them to favourite portions of the "rich store of scenery" to which he alludes. In the meanwhile, we shall be glad if he, or any one of congenial tastes, shall indicate their own peculiar paths to those

"Fresh fields and pastures new."

Besides appearing in WEEKLY NUMBERS, the SCHOOLMASTER is published in MONTHLY PARTS, which stitched in a neat cover, contains as much letter-press, of good execution, as any of the large Monthly Periodicals: A Table of Contents will be given at the end of the year; when, *at the weekly cost of three-halfpence*, a handsome volume of 832 pages, super-royal size, may be bound up, containing much matter worthy of preservation.

PART II., containing the five September Numbers, with JOHNSTONE'S MONTHLY REGISTER, may be had of all the Booksellers. Price 9d. For the accommodation of weekly readers, the Monthly Register and Cover may be had separately at the different places of sale. Price One Penny.

CONTENTS OF NO. XI.

IMPORTANCE OF THE STUDY OF SCIENCE...................161
Condition of the Poor in England.........................163
The New Monthly Magazine................................166
COLUMN FOR THE LADIES.—Adventures of a Female Indian...ib.
William Cobbett..167
THE STORY TELLER.—Little Davy...........................169
ELEMENTS OF THOUGHT—Kings, their use.—The Common
  Centre.—Learning—Punishments, &c....................172
USEFUL NOTICES.—Explosion of Steam Boilers.—On Oiling
  Rail-way Carriages.—Dr. Henry's Disinfecting Process,
  &c...173
Decline of Scottish Agriculture..........................174
SCRAPS, Original and Selected,...........................176

EDINBURGH: Printed by and for JOHN JOHNSTONE, 19, St. James's Square.—Published by JOHN ANDERSON, Jun., Bookseller, 55, North Bridge Street, Edinburgh; by JOHN MACLEOD, and ATKINSON & Co. Booksellers, Glasgow; and sold by all Booksellers and Venders of Cheap Periodicals.

THE Schoolmaster,
AND
EDINBURGH WEEKLY MAGAZINE.

CONDUCTED BY JOHN JOHNSTONE.

THE SCHOOLMASTER IS ABROAD.—LORD BROUGHAM.

No. 12.—VOL. I. SATURDAY, OCTOBER 20, 1832. PRICE THREE-HALFPENCE.

ORIGINAL LETTER OF BURNS—POLITICAL MARTYRS OF THE END OF LAST CENTURY.

How we wish some one qualified in intellect and spirit would write their history! Muir, Gerald, Palmer, Skirving, and many others; nor last nor least, among the illustrious band—ROBERT BURNS. His political sentiments are well known. The letter we publish to-day merely confirms them, without adding at all to their force. It was addressed to Captain JOHNSTON, the proprietor of the Gazetteer, upon perusing the prospectus of that "Revolutionary print." We regret that we cannot procure a copy of the prospectus, though there may still be one among the archives of the Sheriff's Chambers, to which, we believe, the types, paper, files, &c. &c. of that obnoxious paper, were, by an *ordonnance,* carried *en masse.* It must, however, have been a pithy document. Burns writes,—

SIR,
    I have just read your prospectus of the Edinburgh Gazetteer. If you go on in your paper with the same spirit, it will, beyond all comparison, be the first composition of the kind in Europe. I beg leave to insert my name as a subscriber; and if you have already published any papers, please send me them from the beginning. Point out your own way of settling payments in this place, or I shall settle with you through the medium of my friend, Peter Hill, bookseller in Edinburgh.

Go on, sir! Lay bare, with undaunted heart and steady hand, that horrid mass of corruption called Politics and State-craft. Dare to draw in their native colours, these—

"Calm-thinking villains, whom no faith can fix"—

whatever be the shibboleth of their pretended party.

The address, to me at Dumfries, will find,
    Sir,
        Your very humble Servant,
            ROBERT BURNS.
Dumfries, 13th November, 1792.

This sin of Burns, it is probable, was never known till now; though the Scotch Post Office* was in those days as subservient to Mr. Dundas, as ever was the Parisian bureau of letters to FOUCHE. But Burns had committed other overt acts of a dangerous tendency; such as demurring to the health—not of his Majesty, but of his Majesty's "Heaven-born War Minister," Mr. Pitt! It is even alleged that his atrocity amounted to the height of leaving a room in displeasure, when some of the party refused to drink the health of George Washington, which he wished to substitute as that "of a greater and better man." "I suppose," says Mr. Lockhart, in his life of the Poet, "the warmest admirers of Mr. Pitt's talents and politics would hardly venture *nowadays* to dissent substantially from Burns's estimate of the comparative merits of these two great men." We rather believe they would. But on this point, the Editor of the Quarterly may consult the writers of its American articles, Mrs. Trollope and Captain Hall inclusive. Burns had been persecuted and ruined before he sealed his fate, and committed another unpardonable overt act, by drinking, in a public company, *"May our success in the present war be equal to the justice of our cause."* To this ruinous and most disastrous war, into which Mr. Pitt, in despite of his own better judgment, precipitated the country, that, by gratifying the Tories, he might retain place, Burns, in common with nine-tenths of the nation, was decidedly hostile. Meetings had been held, and declarations and petitions adopted over all the country against a war with the French Republic. Much ignorance seems to prevail now on this point. As Sheridan said at the time, "No one liked the war save those who were to share in the taxes raised to support it," nor was it ever endurable, till the alarm of invasion roused the spirit of the country.

Burns had committed another great indiscretion. He chanced to capture a smuggling brig, and at the sale of the condemned effects, purchased four carronades, which (before war was declared) he presented to the French Convention, accompanied by a letter expressive of his respect and admiration of the new government of France. This present was intercepted at Dover, and the Poet became a marked man. His memorable letter to Mr. Grahame of Fintry was written in the month following the above letter to the Editor of the *Gazetteer,* and immediately on his being informed, that "Mr. Mitchell, an excise collector, had received an order to inquire into his political conduct." The subsequent history of Burns' martyrdom we shall give in the exact words of Tory writers, that the testimony may be less questionable. "The exact result of the Excise Board's investigation is hidden," says Lockhart, "in obscurity; nor is it at all likely that the

---

* At that period, the Earl of Buchan, who, as the brother of Thomas Erskine, aimed at the glory of being "a suspicious character," always sent his letters to the post-office unsealed.

cloud will be withdrawn hereafter. A general impression, however, appears to have gone forth, that the affair terminated in something which Burns himself considered tantamount to the destruction of all hope of future promotion in his profession * * *. In a word, the early death of Burns has been (by implication at least) ascribed mainly to the circumstances in question." This Sir Walter Scott seems to have believed. In an article on Burns, written in 1809,* in the height of Sir Walter's partisanship, if he might ever be called a partisan, he says, " That the poet should have chosen the side on which high talents were most likely to procure celebrity; that he, to whom the fastidious distinctions of society were always odious, should have listened with complacence to the voice of French philosophy, which denounced them as usurpations on the rights of man, was precisely the thing to be expected. Yet we cannot but think, that if his superiors in the Excise department had tried the experiment of soothing, rather than irritating his feelings, they might have spared themselves the *disgrace* of rendering desperate the possessor of such uncommon talents. For *it is but* too certain, that from the moment his hopes of promotion were *utterly blasted*, his tendency to dissipation hurried him precipitately into those excesses which shortened his life." Here is the martyrdom of Burns distinctly stated; and we shall not stop to remark that Sir Walter Scott might at once have " placed the saddle on the right horse," as he could not but know that the same creatures, who, in the insolence of office, crushed the mighty spirit of Burns, or broke the heart where they were powerless wholly to crush the spirit, would have crawled and licked the dust in his path, had this course been imagined acceptable to the faction for which they acted, and which then, unhappily, governed this country. On the subject of BURNS's martyrdom, we must quote one more Tory writer. Mr. Wilson, alias Christopher North, says, " Burns gave great offence to that fine and delicate abstraction, the *Board of Excise;* and at one time there seems to have been some danger of his losing his splendid situation—no *sinecure*—of something less than a supervisor of the district, with an annual salary of L.70. The Excise rebuked him for ' *thinking*'†—a vice to which, from infancy, he had been sadly addicted, as well as to the kindred, and even more dangerous one of feeling; and Burns, we believe, came under a sort of half-and-half promise and threat to do what he could to wean himself from that habit; but he made no promise at all *not to feel;* and feel he did, till his heart bled at every pore with indignation, shame and grief—a state in which he must have been found an easier prey to the evils which beset him from other quarters, and to those social seductions to which, in the heroism of his hard-working youth, he had so often shown himself superior." All this is truly and well said. But why blame the wretched Board of Excise, and it alone, when the justice seat was equally culpable, if not in the individual case of Burns, yet in many as flagrantly oppressive. The Excise had but one political victim—the tribunals a hecatomb.

WHAT HAVE YOU TO DO WITH POLITICS?

A letter of BURNS to Mr. Erskine of Mar, which Dr. Currie has but very partially quoted, places this question in the true light, and is so intimately connected with the affair noticed above, that we cannot forbear giving a fuller extract of it than would otherwise suit our limits. His letter to Mr. Grahame of Fintray, disclaiming the foul imputations which the servile creatures of the period attempted to cast upon him, and avowing his real sentiments as a REFORMER, gave, as has been stated, " great offence" to that pure and august body, the Board of Excise. " One of our supervisors general," BURNS writes, " was instructed to inquire on the spot, and to document me—' that my business was to act, *not to think:* and that whatever might be men or measures, it was for me to be *silent* and *obedient.*'

" Mr. Corbet was my steady friend; so between Mr. Graham and him, I have been partly forgiven; only I understand that all hopes of my getting officially forward, are blasted.

" Now, sir, to the business in which I would more immediately interest you. The partiality of my COUNTRYMEN has brought me forward as a man of genius, and has given me a character to support. In the POET I have avowed manly and independent sentiments, which I trust will be found in the MAN. Reasons of no less weight than the support of a wife and family have pointed out as the eligible, and, situated as I was, the only eligible line of life for me, my present occupation. Still my honest fame is my dearest concern; and a thousand times have I trembled at the idea of those *degrading* epithets that malice or misrepresentation may affix to my name. I have often, in blasting anticipation, listened to some future hackney scribbler, with the heavy malice of savage stupidity, exulting in his hireling paragraphs—' BURNS, notwithstanding the *fanfaronade* of independence to be found in his works, and after having been held forth to public view, and to public estimation as a man of some genius, yet, quite destitute of resources within himself to support his borrowed dignity, he dwindled into a paltry exciseman, and slunk out the rest of his insignificant existence in the meanest of pursuits, and among the vilest of mankind.'

" In your illustrious hands, sir, permit me to lodge my disavowal and defiance of these slanderous falsehoods. BURNS was a poor man from birth, and an exciseman by necessity; but *I will* say it! the sterling of his honest worth, no poverty could debase, and his independent British mind, oppression might bend, but could not subdue. Have not I, to me, a more precious stake in my country's welfare than the richest dukedom in it?—I have a large family of children, and the prospect of many more. I have three sons who, I see already, have brought into the world souls ill qualified to inhabit the bodies of slaves. Can I look tamely on, and see any machination to wrest from them the birth-right of my boys,—the little independent Britons, in whose veins run my own blood? No! I will not! should my heart's blood stream around my attempt to defend it!

" Does any man tell me that my full efforts can be of no service; and that it does not belong to my humble station to meddle with the concerns of a nation?

" I can tell him, that it is on such individuals as I that a nation has to rest, both for the hand of support and the eye of intelligence."

HOW TO PLEASE YOUR FRIENDS.—Go to India, stay there twenty years, work hard, get money, save it, come home—bring with you a store of wealth, and a diseased liver; visit your friends, make a will, provide for them all —then die—what a prudent, good, generous, kind-hearted soul you will be!

---

* Published in the Quarterly Review.

† " He was admonished that it was his business to act, not to think."—*Lockhart's Life of Burns.*

PRICE OF JUSTICE.

REMARKS ON THE COURT OF SESSION, AND THE EXPENSE ATTENDING CAUSES BROUGHT BEFORE IT.

The courts of law and equity in every country ought to be open to all classes at little expense. In fact, justice should be administered freely, and without delay.

The Court of Session, which is the Supreme Court of Scotland, is now composed of thirteen Judges, including a President. These are divided into two Divisions, which form distinct Courts, called the First and Second Divisions. The Lord President is chairman, and has the casting-vote in the First Division, and the Lord Justice Clerk in the Second. These are again divided into the Outer and Inner House, each having four Judges composing the Inner House, and two, who act as Lords Ordinary, in the Outer House. The junior Judge is common to both Divisions.

The Judges of the Inner House compose what is properly called the *Court,* and act both in a judicial and ministerial capacity. They review the judgments pronounced by the Lords Ordinary, which are brought before them by a reclaiming note, at the instance of the party who considers himself aggrieved. The Lords Ordinary sit in the Outer House, and all cases, except summary applications, and a few others, come before them in the first place; and it is only when a party is dissatisfied with the judgment of the Lord Ordinary, that he takes the opinion of the Court. Appended to the reclaiming note, which requires to be printed, there must be a full record of the proceedings before the Ordinary, together with the proof or documents founded upon; all which must also be printed.

From such a number of Judges, and such machinery, one might suppose that justice would flow like a stream, and that a law-suit could not be long in dependence. But experience has taught us, that even from this Court justice comes forth with tardy steps. The existing forms are not so complex, neither do they admit of such delay as formerly; but still under them a case can seldom be brought to a conclusion in less than two years; and a much longer period is often occupied in the discussion than three or even four years. A part of the delay may, and often does arise in consequence of the conduct of the agent; but the chief cause of it is in the long vacations, which take up nearly seven months out of the twelve; and in the consequent arrears of cases before the Ordinaries and the Court.

As to the expense attending the procedure, it is so great, that it often acts as a barrier in the way of justice; for, in consequence, many a man will rather, and often does suffer oppression, than attempt to vindicate his rights by an appeal to the laws of his country. Many persons cannot comprehend how this expense is incurred. Now, as we wish to put the saddle upon the right back, we shall briefly show how this expense in general arises.

It is a common opinion, though an erroneous one, that the agents are chiefly instrumental in incurring a long string of charges; and that the greater part of a law-business account goes to the lining of their pockets. But upon examining an account, one will find that the greater proportion of charges is for outlay, or cash advanced in the course of the proceedings. To account for this it is only necessary to attend to the following facts:—

Every step of procedure, excepting the first, and ofttimes even that, requires, by the forms of Court, to be drawn by counsel, whose fees are paid beforehand, and rather in the shape of an honorary, than a remuneration for the work to be done. These fees vary from two to five guineas in ordinary cases, exclusive of a fee of 7s. 6d. to their clerks. Again, upon every step of a process there must be paid, before it can be received by the Clerk of Court, a sum of from 5s. to 30s., in name of *fee-fund dues;* and then there comes the clerk's dues, which amount to 2s., and often more, upon every paper. At every borrowing up of the process, there must be paid a sum varying from 2s. to 6s., and 1s. at every returning. Before a case can be moved before the Lord Ordinary, a fee of 5s. must be paid for enrolling. In fact, nothing can be done without the hand of the agent being continually in his pocket. No wonder, then, that an account of charges soon swells up, and that a client should grumble at the sum total. Two-thirds of a business account, as taxed by the Auditor of Court, is for pure outlay, which has in the first place to be advanced by the agent, and often at the risk of losing the whole. No doubt the agent's fees are high, and we shall say far too high; but it is the dues paid to the fee-fund, which go to the payment of the public officers, to clerks, and for printing, &c., that bear so heavily upon the shoulders of litigants.

Even if a person should be so fortunate as to gain his case, he frequently comes off a loser; for, although he may get his expenses allowed him, these are generally taxed by the Auditor at a sum which does not nearly cover the actual amount incurred by him to his agent; as many items of charge for business, which was indispensably requisite for the due conduct of the case, are disallowed by that officer.

We hope we have succeeded in showing our readers where the rock lies; and as we like to call every thing by its proper name, (which is one of the principal duties of the *Schoolmaster,*) we have endeavoured to clear professional men from a great deal of unjust opprobrium, which has been attached to them on the score of expense. In doing so, however, we must not be understood as defending their scale of charges. On the contrary, we also consider the agent's fees capable of much reduction, and of being put upon a better footing; and we hope that a reformed Parliament will repeal the attorney tax, which bears hard upon the agents, and do away with the abominable fee-fund; that the fees of all public officers will be reduced; and the business put upon a footing which will enable the practitioner to make moderate charges, and the public to get a cheap and efficient administration of justice.

HYDROSTATIC BED.

AMONGST the numerous and important uses to which water has been applied, that of a comfortable bed is one, which, to say the least, does not naturally present itself to the mind. A watery bed, and a watery grave, have hitherto been held to be synonymous, or convertible terms; and we would as soon have thought of lying down in the *Grotto del Can,* as in a trough filled with water. For, not being gifted with the power possessed by amphibious animals, of living equally well in water, as on land we would not have hazarded so dangerous an experiment; yet, true it is, that in the progress of knowledge, this discovery has been made, and not, it is observed, accidentally, as many valuable discoveries have been, but by reflection on well-ascertained facts, by a mind capable of grasping these facts, and of applying them to practical purposes.

It is well known that "the support of water to a floating body is so uniformly diffused, that every thousandth part of an inch of the inferior surface has, as it were, its own separate liquid pillar, and no one part bears the load of its neighbour." Reflecting on this fact, Dr. Arnott was led to infer, that if a person were laid upon the surface of a bath, over which a large sheet of the waterproof India rubber-cloth was previously thrown, the pressure would be so uniform over the whole body, that no one part could possibly suffer more than any other part, and consequently that one who had already suffered from inequality of pressure, as always happens to bed-ridden people, especially when the constitution has been debilitated from whatever cause, would, on being placed on such a couch, be immediately relieved of the pains and other disagreeable consequences of long confinement to even the softest bed; and the result showed the correctness of his reasoning. A lady who, after her confinement, had passed through a combination of diseases, low fever, jaundice, &c., rested so long in one posture that mortification came on, sloughs formed, inflammation also occurred, terminating in the formation of abscesses. She was watched with the most affectionate assiduity, and every expedient adopted for her comfort that could be devised. She was placed upon the bed contrived for invalids by Mr. Earl, with pillows of down and air, and out of the mattress of which portions were cut opposite to the sloughing parts. In spite, however, of all endeavours, the mischief advanced, the chief slough enlarged, another slough and a new abscess were produced, and her life was in imminent danger. No sooner, however, was she laid upon the Hydrostatic Bed, than "she was instantly relieved; sweet sleep came to her; she awoke refreshed; she passed the next night much better than usual; and on the following day all the sores had assumed a healthy appearance. The healing from that time went on rapidly, and no new sloughs were formed: the down pillows were needed no more."

Such is the account given by Dr. Arnott of the wonderful effects produced by the Hydrostatic Bed. Nor are they at all exaggerated. The bed has been introduced into St Bartholomew's and St George's Hospitals, and elsewhere; and in the Medical and Surgical Journal for the present month, we have an account of its employment by Dr. Spittal, in the case of an old lady of 70, who had been confined constantly to bed for upwards of six weeks, during the last few of which, she had suffered much from restlessness and want of sleep. She was unable to turn herself in bed, and mortification seemed coming on. Two hours after being placed in the hydrostatic bed, she fell asleep, and slept for seven hours, being the longest sleep she had enjoyed for weeks, and she continued to enjoy long and refreshing sleep. The condition of the mortified parts amended, and she became altogether improved. It is worthy of remark, that this lady was not made acquainted with the nature of the bed—she was not aware she was lying on water—but when asked how she liked it, when compared with her former bed, she replied that she liked it better, for it was much softer. It is impossible, indeed, to convey an idea of the comfortable support afforded by means of this bed to those who have not experienced it. So strongly did this impress the mind of an able and pious clergyman, that he was led to remark, "How great is the goodness of God, that puts it into the hearts of men to provide such comforts for his creatures!!" But though we cannot communicate the feeling of comfort to our readers, we can easily give them a description of the bed itself, and recommend them to make a trial of it. Let them imagine, then, an ordinary bed—on which is laid a wooden trough, a foot deep, lined with zinc or lead, the same size as the bed, filled with water to the depth of about 6 inches, over which is placed a sheet of the India rubber cloth, upon which again is placed a suitable mattress, ready to receive its pillow and bed-clothes—and they will have a tolerable idea of what is meant by a hydrostatic bed, the only difference between it and a common bed being the substitution of water for the canvass or spars on which the mattress is usually placed. It will naturally suggest itself to every individual, that some plan must be adopted in order to prevent the water escaping from under the India rubber cloth. This is effected, by merely fixing it very firmly to the edges of the trough all round, nailing it, and filling up all the crevices by means of white lead, or other cement. The cloth being of such a size as would suffice to line the trough were it empty, leaves ample room for free and easy motion when half filled with water, which is done through an aperture near the top—the water being again drawn off when required by a stop-cock at the lower extremity. The trough, instead of being placed upon an ordinary bed, may be, and in fact has hitherto been, made the bed itself, resting on four supports, one at each corner, like an ordinary bed;—and in this state it may be seen at Mr. Sibbald's, Ironmonger, South Bridge.

Singular and unfounded fears have been entertained respecting this bed. "Oh! I shudder," says one, "at the very thoughts of it—is there no chance of being drowned?" —Another again, apparently with more reason, asks,— "Will the person not catch cold lying on water?"— How many have done so, when, through ignorance, or from dire necessity, they have slept in a damp bed, or on a watery spot? Both these ideas are quite erroneous—the first ludicrously so,—the second equally erroneous, though certainly not equally ludicrous. The bed is, in short, as dry as a bed can be, for the India rubber cloth is quite impenetrable to water; and as Dr. Arnott remarks, "The bed is a warm bed, owing to water being nearly an absolute non-conductor of heat from above, downwards, and owing to its allowing no passage of cold air from below."

The advantages of this bed, not merely to the bed-ridden from chronic distempers, but also in cases of accidents, injured spine, &c. are very great. It is not, however, our province to enter at large into this point; we leave it to our medical friends to illustrate them, which, we have no doubt, they will soon have ample opportunity to do, as we cannot doubt its introduction into our hospitals, as well as its employment by the private practitioner—nay, we would not be at all surprised at its introduction amongst the luxuries of the great.

RISE, PROGRESS, AND PRESENT STATE OF THE SECESSION CHURCH.

As a very considerable proportion of our readers are connected with the Secession Church, it may not be uninteresting to them, as well as to the public in general, at the close of the first century from its commencement, to present them with the following abstract of the rise, progress, and present state of that respectable body of Presbyterians, as furnished us by one of our correspondents.

The more immediate cause of the origin of the Secession, was the delivery of a sermon at Perth by the Rev. Ebenezer Erskine, minister at Stirling, on the 10th October 1732, at the opening of the Provincial Synod of Perth and Stirling. In the sequel, that rev. gentleman took the liberty of reflecting somewhat freely on the conduct of the judicatories of the Established Church, in reference, among other evils and corruptions, to the undue countenance given by them, in a number of instances, to the violent settlement of ministers on reclaiming parishes, under the anti-scriptural and tyrannical law of lay patronage. Upon the Synod's proceeding to censure Mr. Erskine for the manly freedom he had taken, he forthwith protested, in which he was immediately adhered to by the Rev. William Wilson, Perth; Alexander Moncrieff, Abernethy; and James Fisher, Kinclaven. These four brethren, who have since been justly designated as the Fathers of the Secession, after having given in to the General Assembly and its Commission a number of farther remonstrances and protestations, instead of obtaining any redress of their grievances, were loosed from their respective charges by the Assembly's Commission, on the 16th November 1733, and on the 6th of December following they constituted themselves into a Presbytery, afterwards known by the appellation of the Associate Presbytery. In May 1734, the General Assembly, apprehensive of the disagreeable consequences which were likely to ensue to the Church on account of their secession, passed an act restoring them to their former charges; but as the Assembly in this act appeared to view them more in the character of delinquents, to whom they were willing to extend the boon of pardon, than as conscientious individuals, who had been unjustly aggrieved for faithfully discharging their duty in their judicial and ministerial capacities, neither their honour nor their consciences would allow them to take the benefit of it. On the 3d December 1736, they agreed upon, and shortly afterwards published, their Act, Declaration, and Testimony, for the Doctrine, Worship, Discipline, and Government of the Church of Scotland. In 1737 they were joined by other three ministers, viz. the Rev. Ralph Erskine, Dunfermline; Thomas Mair, Orwell; and Thomas Nairn, Abbotshall; and in 1738, by another, viz. the Rev. James Thomson, Burntisland; making in all now eight ministers, all of whom had seceded from the Established Church. In 1739 the whole of these eight brethren, in the capacity of a constituted Presbytery, appeared at the bar of the General Assembly, to which they had been previously summoned, to answer for the line of conduct which they had adopted, when their moderator, Mr Mair, read and then gave in a paper termed their Declinature, in which they declined all authority and jurisdiction of that court over them. Thus was their connexion with the Established Church totally and finally broken up.

In some subsequent years, they were engaged, in their Presbyterial capacity, in passing a number of acts in defence of several important doctrines closely connected with evangelical truth, in opposition to the errors of the times, as also in support of Scotland's Covenanted Work of Reformation, together with a Declaration of their Principles concerning the authority of the present Civil Government, in opposition to what they conceived the anti-scriptural and anarchical notions on that subject held by the M'Millanites, to whom one of their number, viz. Mr. Nairn, had gone over. In October 1744, finding that the number of their congregations had increased to 41, of which 16 were vacant, they came to the resolution of disjoining themselves into three Presbyteries, afterwards to meet collectively under the designation of the Associate Synod. The first meeting of this new ecclesiastical body accordingly took place at Stirling on the first Tuesday of March 1745, a year which will be long remembered in the civil history of our country, as having given rise to the last Rebellion. While here, it may not be unnecessary to remark, that their political principles, which had been grossly misrepresented by some high-flying churchmen, were now fairly put to the test. The result was, that not a single individual connected with the Secession body was to be found either to favour the cause, or to join the ranks of the Pretender, while, on the contrary, numbers of them voluntarily took up arms in defence of Government, in which several actually lost their lives.

But to return. No sooner had the arrangements above alluded to been carried into effect, than did the well-known question regarding the lawfulness of those individuals in connexion with the Secession swearing the religious clause of some burgess oaths, come under their considerations at the first meeting of the Associate Synod. This question unfortunately led the members, who were about equally divided on the subject, into a painful and protracted controversy, which, on the 9th of April 1747, was followed up by a complete and final rupture of the parties, who were afterwards known by the designations of Burghers and Antiburghers—the former being in favour of the religious clause of the burgess oaths, and the latter against it. Each of these divisions, as might have been expected, claimed to its own members the powers and authority of the Associate Synod, and henceforth continued to act in their official and judicial capacities independently of each other. It is altogether foreign to our present object to enter into any discussion on the merits of this unhappy controversy. Suffice it to say, that whatever opinions may have been formed of the conduct of the parties involved, the whole matter was so far over-ruled by the Great King and Head of his Church, who "maketh the very wrath of man to praise him," as ultimately not only to conduce to the greater extension of a knowledge of the principles and designs of the Secession by the emulation between the two bodies which it excited, but also—and what is of far more importance—it greatly contributed to the farther diffusion of evangelical truth, and consequently of true practical piety.

Having now erected themselves into separate and rival associations, both of the parties, in their distinct capacities, nevertheless continued to preach the same doctrines, maintain the same church polity, and to increase in numbers much in the same proportion. Nor were their labours merely confined to our own land. They were likewise extended to Ireland, and even America, where they succeeded to such a degree, that in process of time, in both of these countries, the congregations which they had organized became so numerous, as to be erected into independent, though sister Synods. We are not in possession of sufficient data so as to be able to state when these erections took place, but they must have been some time posterior to 1773, when we find that the Antiburgher Synod was divided into 11 Presbyteries, viz. 8 in Scotland, 2 in Ireland, and 1 in America, comprehending in all about 100 ministers. Assuming the Burgher Synod at that period to consist of the same number, and making allowance in both for vacancies, which were then much more numerous in proportion than at present, there must have been at this time about 250 congregations under the inspection of both Synods, including those in Ireland and America, as formerly adverted to.

Matters thus went on with little interruption in the case of both bodies, till about the end of the last and beginning of the present century, when a new controversy arose, first in the Burgher, and then in the Antiburgher Synod, respecting the power of the civil magistrate in matters of religion, the obligation of our National Covenants, and the nature of Public Covenanting in general. The result was, that a few ministers and congregations broke off from each Synod, claiming to themselves the designations of Original Burghers and Original Antiburghers, but perhaps better known at the time by the appellation of Old Lights, in contradistinction from the two larger bodies which they had left, who, on account of the more liberal principles which they had adopted, were also denominated New Lights. Thus was the Secession now split up into four distinct associations, two larger and two smaller ones, in which state it continued till the memorable union which took place on the 8th of September 1820, in Bristo Street Chapel, Edinburgh, the same spot on which they had separated 73 years and five months before. The bodies which composed this union, were the whole of the ministers and congregations—in number about 300—of the two larger branches of the Secession above alluded to, with the exception of a small number of protesters on the Antiburgher side, who having thus left their present brethren, in a few years afterwards connected themselves with their old friends, the Original Antiburghers, or Constitutional Presbytery, as they called themselves. It is rather a curious fact, that the Burghers and Antiburghers in Ireland and America, who were originally only branches of the Secession churches in Scotland, were the first to set the example of union to their respective mother churches, they having united some time previously.

The state of the different bodies composing at present the Secession in Great Britain and Ireland, at the close of 1831, according to the Edinburgh Almanack for this year, is as under, viz.

	Presbyteries	Ministers	Congregations
United Associate Synod in Scotland, including three Presbyteries in England.	23	316	343
Synod of Ireland, connected with the above,	9	95	96
Original Antiburgher Synod in Scotland, including one congregation in Ireland,	4	30	33
Original Burgher Synod in Scotland, including one Presbytery in Ireland,	5	46	56
Total connected with the Secession in Britain and Ireland,	41	487	528

To the above a number of new congregations, during the present year, have been added, not to mention those in America, of which we have no account, though there is not the smallest doubt but that they must also be pretty numerous in that country. We may also state, that besides the above 343 congregations under the inspection of the United Associate Synod of Scotland, there are likewise a considerable number of missionary stations in the more unenlightened parts of both Scotland and England, which are occasionally supplied with sermon by its probationers, the expenses of which are defrayed from the Synod fund, in aid of which a collection from each of its congregations is asked annually. The Synod has also lately established a separate fund for the support of foreign missions, under its own immediate inspection, to which additional collections are also made by its congregations, independently of their occasionally contributing, along with their brethren of other denominations, for Missionary and Bible Societies, as well as for other philanthropical and charitable purposes.—*Fife Herald.*

PORTRAITS BY A LADY—TAKEN IN THE VENTILATOR OF THE HOUSE OF COMMONS.

SIR ROBERT PEEL.

There are many attributes of a statesman about Sir R. Peel, and yet some wanting. He has formed his style of speaking entirely in the House of Commons, and has seldom addressed any other assembly of men; and although he began with what I have just complained of, a set speech, seconding the address in 1810, afterwards he spoke in debate, and with a determination to become a useful member of Parliament. He neither has now, nor, as I have heard from his contemporaries, ever *had*, the faculty of attachment. His countenance and manner are distant and suspicious. His eye appears rather to avoid than confront the person with whom he converses; but this alters in speaking. His manner is bold, though not gallant. His spirit is cramped by the stiffness of his figure, and the vulgarity of his address. I feel that these criticisms are rather feminine, or will be called so, but they tell strangely in a popular assembly, and I must vindicate my sex by saying that they often discover with their microscopic observation, the real *cause* of what every one acknowledges as an *effect*. His attention to every thing said in a debate is extreme and undivided, as well to the worst as the best speakers, and this was thought and said by Mr. Fox to be of great use in debate. I watched him particularly the other evening throughout a debate, from the moment he entered the House, walking on his heels, and throwing his coat aside to his seat, and then listening most attentively, and occasionally, as any thing said appeared to excite or embarrass him, passing his small delicate hand along his nose; and when George Dawson, or any one in whom he took interest, said what he disliked, or ventured upon dangerous ground, pulling down his neckcloth, and fidgetting his fingers about his face, which is itself singularly inexpressive. At length he rose to speak himself, and very soon animated the House by the *warmth* of his manner. His speech was impressive, full of sense, and well worded, with much appearance of literature and historical reading. There was great variety in his tone and manner, sometimes familiar and expostulatory, at others important and impressive; but the impression remained rather than the language of it. There was no very eloquent expression which captivated your taste, as well as convinced your judgment; none of those splendid sentences that carry your reason off by storm, like the energetic periods of Brougham, or the vigorous condensation of argument and knowledge in Plunkett; but he seemed to command the House, to understand its temper, and to be fearless of who was to come after him. He was evidently " cunning of fence," but more from experience than ability, and more from conviction of the weakness of his adversaries than confidence in his allies. —*Court Magazine.*

MR. STANLEY.

I observed opposite to him, while speaking, a younger man who seemed restlessly attentive to what he said; now taking up a spy-glass to look at him, and then bending his body down quite between his legs, and twisting the same glass round and round with an impatient gesture. He took no notes, as some of the members did, and his whole attitude was unquiet; that I should have said he rather wanted to get away than to speak, but for the frequent observations he appeared to be making to his friends on what was going forward, sometimes angrily, sometimes peevishly, but always impetuously, as I could see by his very brilliant eye, set in otherwise ordinary features. At last Peel sat down amidst thunders of applause from his party, showered on a very fine peroration on the present state and future prospects of this country. There seemed, during his last sentence, some conversation and consultations on the ministerial bench, as to who should answer him, which my young friend perceiving, gave a sort of hurried wave with his hand, and dashing of his hat, presented himself to the House. A general cry from his party, of " Stanley!—Stanley!" informed me who he was. Mr. Stanley began by complaining of the unfair introduction of so many topics by Sir Robert; he then took advantage of that unfairness to reply to every one of them. The excessive animation of his manner; the pitch of his voice, not strong but stirring; the action, so agreeable for its perfect nature and utter inattention to graceful forms, which made it so easy, that you forgot, or rather had not time to think, whether it was graceful. His uninterrupted language, as if he was " too warm on picking work to dwell," the audacity of his tone and presence, not only carried you along with him, but humiliated you if you did not agree with him. The readiness of every reply, the abundance of his illustrations, made him in power, force, and fancy, by far the most lively effective speaker I had yet heard. I have not called him eloquent, because I reserve that word for men like Lord Brougham and Lord Plunkett, whose sentences ring in my ear like favourite music. Now, though I listened with breathless attention—indeed his rapid eagerness almost took away my breath—to Mr. Stanley; though he left nothing unanswered, and would certainly have gained my vote; though his diamond eye kept dancing before me long after I had left the dark Ventilator, yet I could not, by any effort of memory, repeat a single sentence he had uttered.—*Court Magazine for September.*

LORD ALTHORP.

The two present leaders of the House of Commons, Sir Robert Peel and Lord Althorp, are both men of sense, but the former is seldom, and the latter never, eloquent. And yet of him we may say that he is a more striking example of the tone of the times than any that could be given. He has foiled enemies that the wit of Canning could not have lashed into order; he has managed a House, whose turbulence Pitt could scarcely have controlled—and by what powers of speech?—None. But by candour, integrity, and simplicity. His manner is completely without ornament, but polished by his own kindness of heart; his unirritable temper has defeated the malice of his enemies; and his plain perseverance has assuaged the irritation of his friends. His good humour is so universally acknowledged, that the singularity of having made an illnatured observation upon him has been reserved exclusively for the two O'Connells, father and son, and for them once only when they were put down by acclamation. Lord Althorp seems to want all the talents that make great leaders of parties, and yet to possess enough of what they have none of them had, to make a capital one. He is laughed at by the political dandies, and become a jest among Parliamentary coxcombs. There is not a more offensive coxcomb than the Parliamentary one. I detest a young man who talks of " our House," and lards his lean conversation with second readings and committees, and sends his neglected speeches to the Mirror of Parliament. These are the men the Chancellor of the Exchequer hopes to be rid of in a Reformed Parliament. I was rather led into this strain, by hearing a young fop, who introduced a lady to the Ventilator, say, I am afraid you ladies will bear little to captivate you in Lord Althorp. He was mistaken, however, and avowed himself so at last. At that moment a rapturous cheer was heard through the whole Ministerial side of the house, such as had never perhaps greeted a resigning minister, for it seemed wrung from their hearts. The girl who had just seated herself put her head forward, and exclaimed, " Oh, it is Lord Althorp coming in; but why is he always in black?" " He has never been out of it since his wife died; he was passionately fond of her, and is now as kind to her mother." " Indeed!" said the young lady, looking down at him again " Oh, one must say that for him; a truer hearted man does not exist; he may speak bluntly, and look gruffly; but I doubt if Althorp ever offended the most fastidious man alive." " Nor dog either," said another in a half-laughing whisper. " Don't you remember Pytchley?" I was rather interested, and asked the second gentleman, whom I knew, to explain. " Oh," he said, " it was only that he and I were out at the early forest hunting, and I remember in one of the most beautiful mornings in August, when the early sun was breaking upon the foliage, which was waving over the green glades of the forest, one of the red-jackets galloping down the riding, seized up a young hound, tied it to a tree, and was lashing it most severely, when a weather-beaten keeper, looking askance at him, said, " My lord would never have allowed that." " What lord?" " Why, Lord Althorp, the kindest and best master that ever kept hounds—and the worst rider to them, said my companion;—but I could not help recollecting that I had just left his pack in the House of Commons, where he had kept the same character." After this, I saw him at his election. There his voice is strong and loud, and his whole manner eager and unhesitating. Accustomed to express their sentiments more openly and more simply than is usual in the upper classes—unused to the " eloquence of lies," because less called upon to conceal their feelings on some occasions, and affect what they do *not* feel on others—that class commonly called " the people," distinguish instantly, and, as it were, intuitively, the language of the head from that of the heart, and invariably give the preference to the latter; borne down by a torrent of words, they still remain unconvinced, and grumble even while they yield; but appealed to, as Lord Althorp appeals to them,

" And lo! their eager hearts outrun his own."

THE COMET.

INFECTIOUS CHARACTER OF SUPERSTITION.

A great many persons have, it seems, been in alarm at news of the *Comet*, though the present Comet has been already proved among the most innocent and harmless of all celestial strangers; and is, in truth, an old familiar friend of our Earth, and not a rare visitant either. The vague feeling of alarm entertained only by those totally unacquainted with the laws of nature which regulate the return of Comets, was considerably increased, when on the night of Sunday, the 7th, the following phenomena were visible in this quarter: "About nine, the moon was surrounded by a broad halo, and threw a strange brassy hue over a third part of the firmament. On getting behind a dense black cloud, her disc was still visible through the gloom, but tinged with elastic vapours, presenting something like the appearance created by cool air moving upon a surface of molten brass. The northern sky was at this time clothed with dark massive clouds, through the interstices of which luminous matter was seen playfully disporting, and enacting the most fantastic metamorphoses. At times the streamers shot up to the zenith with great velocity, forming large fluted pillars against the sky, and outshining the light of the moon. At other times they formed something like banks of willows hanging over a lake, then castellated towers, then ranges of mountains, and innumerable other figures, which at once suggested themselves to the imagination, without taxing the powers of fancy. These sublime and interesting appearances continued for some hours, and arrested the attention of thousands of spectators. To similar phenomena we are indebted for all the marvellous traditionary stories of armies fighting in the heavens, bloody swords, &c. In these legends in the low country of Scotland, the warriors latterly have been all Highlanders; though in those of older date, and in the North of England, the celestial combatants wore the military garb of Germany, or of the *Mounseys*, (*i. e.* Monsieurs.) Sir Walter Scott relates one of those marvels, which is as well authenticated, and minutely remembered as any of them. He gives it as an instance of the "*Infectious nature of superstition.*"

"There can be little doubt," he says, "that it refers, in its first origin, to some uncommon appearance of the aurora borealis, or the northern lights, which do not appear to have been seen in Scotland so frequently as to be accounted a common and familiar atmospherical phenomenon until the beginning of the eighteenth century. The passage is striking and curious; for the narrator, Peter Walker, though an enthusiast, was a man of credit, and does not even affect to have seen the wonders, the reality of which he unscrupulously adopts on the testimony of others, to whose eyes he trusted rather than to his own. The conversion of the sceptical gentleman of whom he speaks, is highly illustrative of popular credulity, carried away into enthusiasm, or into imposture, by the evidence of those around, and at once shows the imperfection of such a general testimony, and the ease with which it is procured, since the general excitement of the moment impels even the more cold-blooded and judicious persons present to catch up the ideas, and echo the exclamations of the majority, who, from the first, had considered the heavenly phenomenon as a supernatural weapon-schaw, held for the purpose of a sign and warning of civil wars to come.

"'In the year 1686, in the months of June and July,' says the honest chronicler, 'many yet alive can witness, that about the Crossford Boat, two miles beneath Lanark, especially at the Mains, on the water of Clyde, many people gathered together for several afternoons, where there were showers of bonnets, hats, guns, and swords, which covered the trees and the ground; companies of men in arms marching in order upon the water side; companies meeting companies, going all through other, and then all falling to the ground and disappearing; other companies immediately appeared, marching the same way. I went there three afternoons together, and as I observed there were two-thirds of the people that were together saw, and a third that saw not, and *though I could see nothing*, there was such a fright and trembling on those that did see, that was discernible to all from those that saw not. There was a gentleman standing next to me, who spoke as too many gentlemen and others speak, who said, ' A pack of damned witches and warlocks that have the second sight ! the devil ha't do I see;' and immediately there was a discernible change in his countenance. With as much fear and trembling as any woman I saw there, he called out, ' All you that do not see, say nothing ; for I persuade you it is matter of fact, and discernible to all that is not stone-blind.' And those who did not see told what works (*i. e.* locks) the guns had, and their length and wideness, and what handles the swords had, whether small or three-barr'd, or Highland guards, and the closing knots of the bonnets, black or blue; and those who did see them there, whenever they went abroad, saw a bonnet and a sword drop in the way.'

"This singular phenomenon, in which a multitude believed, although only two-thirds of them saw what must, if real, have been equally obvious to all, may be compared with the exploit of a humorist, who planted himself in an attitude of astonishment, with his eyes riveted on the well-known bronze lion that graces the front of Northumberland-house in the Strand; and having attracted the attention of those who looked at him by muttering, ' By Heaven, it wags !—it wags again !' contrived in a few minutes to blockade the whole street with an immense crowd, some conceiving that they had absolutely seen the lion of Percy wag his tail, others expecting to witness the same phenomenon."

VERSES FOR THE YOUNG.

The following verses, the composition of an American gentleman, Mr. Washington Allston, well deserve a place in the memory of the young.

AMERICA AND ENGLAND.

Though ages long have past,
　Since our fathers left their home,
Their pilot in the blast,
　O'er untravelled seas to roam,
Yet lives the blood of England in our veins;
　And shall we not proclaim
　That blood of honest fame
　Which no tyranny can tame
　　　By its chains?

While the language free and bold
　Which the bard of Avon sung,
In which our Milton told
　How the vault of Heaven rung,
When Satan, blasted, fell with all his host;
　While these with reverence meet,
　Ten thousand echoes greet,
　And from rock to rock repeat,
　　　Round our coast.

While the manners, while the arts,
　That mould a nation's soul
Still cling around our hearts,
　Between, let ocean roll,
Our joint communion breaking with the sun;
　Yet still from either beach
　The voice of blood shall reach,
　More audible than speech,
　　　We are One!

COMET.—In this month a comet of six and a half years duration will make its re-appearance. It has been ascertained, by the most distinguished astronomers in France, that it will, when nearest the earth, be at the distance of sixteen millions of leagues. The comet of 1811, when nearest the earth, was one hundred and forty-four millions of miles distant; it will therefore be sixty-six millions of miles nearer the earth than the one which appeared in 1811.

ELEMENTS OF THOUGHT.

THE PRESS.

They who conceive that our newspapers are no restraint upon bad men, or impediment to the execution of bad measures, know nothing of this country. In that state of abandoned servility, to which the undue influence of the Crown has reduced the other branches of the Legislature, our ministers and magistrates have in reality little punishment to fear, and few difficulties to contend with, beyond the censure of the press, and the spirit of resistance which it excites among the people.—*Junius.*

JUDGMENTS.

Who can tell what is a judgment of God? It is presumption to take upon us to know. In time of plague we know we want health; and therefore we pray to God to give us health. In time of war we know we want peace; and therefore we pray to God to give us peace. Commonly we say a judgment falls upon a man for something in him we cannot abide. An example of this we have in King James, concerning the murder of Henry IV. of France. He was killed for keeping so many mistresses, said one. He was killed for changing his religion, said another. "No, he was killed," said King James, a constitutional coward, who turned pale at the sight of a drawn sword, "for permitting duels in his kingdom."

> Let not this weak unknowing hand
> Presume thy bolts to throw,
> Nor deal damnation round the land,
> On each I deem thy foe.

We single out particulars, and apply God's Providence to them. Thus, when two persons are married, and have undone one another, they cry "It was God's Providence we should come together."—*Selden.*

THE PEOPLE.—TRIENNIAL PARLIAMENTS.

It always gives us pleasure to quote Edmund Burke. With all the inconsistencies and backslidings which attended his latter life, he was in mind the first man of his party. Probably he did not admire triennial Parliaments himself, though triennial Parliaments was a fundamental principle of the English constitution; but looking deeper into the very first principles of all society, he distinctly recognises the *power of the people*, on this as on every public question. "I most heartily wish," he says, "that the deliberate sense of the kingdom on this great subject should be known. When it is known it *must* be prevalent. It would be dreadful, indeed, if there were any power in the nation capable of resisting its unanimous desire, or even the desire of any great and decided majority of the people. The people may be deceived in their choice of an object; but I can scarcely conceive any choice they can make to be so very mischievous as the existence of any force capable of resisting it. It will certainly be the duty of every man, in the situation to which God has called him, to give his best opinion and advice upon the matter: it will not be his duty, let him think what he will, to use any violent or fraudulent means of counteracting the general wish, or even of employing the legal and conclusive organ of expressing the *people's sense* against the sense they actually do entertain."

COLUMN FOR THE LADIES.

Governesses.—There is a lady in Paris whose only employment consists in examining the registers of young women desirous of being admitted into the faculty of teachers, and in afterwards questioning them as to the extent of their attainments; she is thence enabled to certify to the individuals composing the jury of public instruction, that Miss A or Miss Z is qualified to pass her examination; and in this event the latter makes her appearance before one or two of this jury, notes the questions put to her, and replies to them to the best of her ability. Three species of diplomas are granted; the first is that of *mistresses of studies* and *mistresses of schools*; the qualification required is, the having made extracts from the Scriptures, grammar, and arithmetic, and given pertinent answers on these three subjects. Armed with this diploma, a female may venture upon opening a class for children or an elementary school. The second degree is somewhat more respectable; the additional qualification required is, the History of France and Geography; and the female possessed of a corresponding diploma may inscribe the words "Boarding School" (*pension*) on the door of her establishment, and undertake to board and instruct young persons: but the *ne plus ultra* of diplomas is that of governesses (*instructrices.*) It does not fall to the lot of all who seek the distinction; for she who would obtain it must possess sound information, and have gone through a course of long and extensive study; it is not mere phrases, but real attainments, which she must have at command; and I know many a young man, who has turned the corner of his rhetoric and pored over philosophy, that would find no little difficulty in answering the questions which the aspirant after a governess's diploma is expected to solve. She must be familiar with the history of ancient times and the middle ages, as well as every modern annal; is expected to be versed in French and foreign literature; to be as conversant with cosmography as M. Azais and to dispute with Condillac, were he still in the land of the living, on logic and rhetoric. Whenever a lady provided with this rank of diploma offers to teach your daughters, you need not fear entrusting them to her care; she will inevitably be found well informed. Mademoiselle A. F., one of my pupils, obtained a governess's degree at the early age of sixteen: she is the youngest hitherto entered on the register; nor do I mention the circumstance with a view of gratifying any personal vanity. The lady in possession of such a passport as this has nothing to do but to turn it to account.

THE BRIDE.
BY SAMUEL ROGERS.

Then she is blest indeed; and swift the hours
Till her young sisters wreathe her hair in flowers,
Kindling her beauty—while, unseen, the least
Twitches her robe, then runs behind the rest,
Known by her laugh that will not be suppressed.
Then before all they stand—the holy vow
And ring of gold, no fond illusions now,
Bind her as his. Across the threshold led,
And every tear kissed off as soon as shed,
His house she enters, there to be a light
Shining within, when all without is night;
A guardian-angel o'er his life presiding.
Doubling his pleasures, and his cares dividing!
How oft her eyes read his; her gentle mind
To all his wishes, all his thoughts inclined;
Still subject ever on the watch to borrow
Mirth of his mirth, and sorrow of his sorrow.
The soul of music slumbers in the shell,
Till waked to rapture by the master's spell;
And feeling hearts—touch them but rightly—pour
A thousand melodies unheard before!
And laughing eyes and voices fill
Their halls with gladness. She, when all are still,
Comes and undraws the curtain as they lie,
In sleep how beautiful!

Nor many moons o'er hill and valley rise,
Ere to the gate with nymph like step she flies,
And their first-born holds forth, their darling boy,
With smiles how sweet, how full of love and joy,
To meet him coming; theirs through every year
Pure transports, such as each to each endear!

THE STORY-TELLER.

THE OLD WHITE HAT—AND THE OLD GREY MARE.

I COULD write a volume upon this old white hat, and upon the eccentric but excellent being that once wore it.— Poor Frank Chilvers! thou wert my chosen one, in whom I had much joy; my Lycidas, with whom at morn and dewy eve I have wandered over woodland, hill, and dale; and shalt thou go down into the darkness and corruption of the great mother, without the " meed of one melodious tear?"

Frank Chilvers was a younger son of that respectable family, which has for many ages been settled at Fordham, in Nottinghamshire; and as he objected, upon those peculiar and fastidious notions which formed his character, to the army, navy, and church, all of which had been submitted to his adoption with reasonable prospects of advancement, his parents gave him his portion, which was not inconsiderable, and, at his own request, left him to select his own occupation and mode of life. His first speculation was to establish a brewery in the country, upon the novel principle of consuming malt and hops, and excluding quassia, coculus indicus, " poppy, mandragora, and all the drowsy syrups of the East;" but the knowing rustics did not understand being defrauded of their full allowance. They had been accustomed to clammy, warming, and soporific compound, and they did not comprehend why a gentleman's son should come into the place and introduce a new liquor, not half so comforting and drowsy as the old.— He calmly assured them that it was no new liquor of his invention, but of the very same quality with that barley wine which Xenophon brewed and gave to his troops, in the memorable retreat of the ten thousand. But they shook their heads; tapping their foreheads to one another, to insinuate that his wits were not quite right; and as no one would venture upon a beverage brewed by a madman, he sold off his stock and his business, retiring from the concoction of Utopian beer, with about one-half the property he had embarked in the concern. He made a bad pun upon the occasion, which was one of his inveterate habits, and thought no more of his loss.

Virgil's well-known line, "O fortunatæ agricolæ," &c. determined his next choice, which was the occupation of a farmer; almost the only one, he observed, in which a man can honourably and independently maintain himself by contributing to the support of others. The latter part of this opinion he exemplified more practically than the former; for as he was quite certain that his labourers could not exist upon the common wages, he instantly doubled them; and as, in many instances, he was aware that his customers could not afford to pay the regular price for his produce, he sold it under the market rate; both which modes of farming, co-operating with the bad times, eventually impoverished him, and procured him, from those who had benefited by his ruin, the title of the silly gentleman-farmer. Various were the methods to which he now had recourse for his maintenance, for he disdained all application to friends or relations. At one time he was an usher; at another, he supported himself, like Rousseau, by copying music, in which he was a proficient; now he translated for the booksellers; and for some time he was in the situation of a banker's clerk. It were useless to recapitulate the manifold employments in which he was engaged, or the variform difficulties he had to encounter: but it is not useless to record, that in all his trials he invariably preserved the same philosophical equanimity, nor ever suffered his reiterated disappointments to cool his philanthropic ardour, or diminish his favourable opinion of mankind. Many men, of restless and inquiring minds, are perpetually running backwards and forwards, between the past and the future, those two impassable boundaries of human knowledge; and in their inability to escape from this narrow range, content themselves, like the squirrel in his cage, with repeating the unprofitable rotations which afford exercise to their faculties without advancing their progress a single step. Chilvers built up the level of his mind, and prevented himself from sinking into the Slough of Despond, by drawing materials from those two terminal mounds; making the past contribute its rich store of historic and poetical recollections, and extracting from the future those sweet and soothing assurances, of whose truth he found daily and delicious confirmation in the beauty, accordance, and benevolent ordinations of nature. Thus he lived on, often in great poverty, but never discontented with his lot, until nearly his sixtieth year, when the death of an old bachelor cousin suddenly placed him in a state of actual independence, and comparative affluence. He immediately quitted London and retired to C—— Row, a village about eleven miles distant from the metropolis, where he purchased a beautiful cottage, and where the writer of this memoir first had the happiness of his acquaintance.

A natural modesty, and the perfect content he found in his own reflections and occupations, gave him a disposition to segregate himself from that class of formal and heartless visitors, whose invasions of your house originate in curiosity, and are continued by ceremony; but as the world, however little disposed to liberality upon other occasions, is seldom deficient in magnifying any sudden accession of fortune, and had exhibited its usual powers of multiplication in the present instance, he found it somewhat difficult to repress the eager advances of his neighbours, when they had regularly ascertained that Mr. Jackson, the rich city grocer, had sanctioned their visits, by first leaving his card. A blind, stupid, and crawling deference to wealth, if it be not peculiar to the English nation, certainly attains its maximum of intensity among those idolatrous worshippers of the golden calf; of which the reader may be convinced, if he will walk along Cheapside with any civic Crœsus, and observe the sycophantic homage and cringing servility with which he will be saluted. Let him travel with such a man in any part of the island, and as he clatters into a country town with his outriders and gay equipage, contemplate the awe-struck look of the natives, and the fawning alacrity of host, hostlers, and waiters, and he will not be surprised that Mr. Jackson, with three stars at the India House, and the best portion of a plum in bank stock, should be deemed a little monarch in his own village. Nobody rode in such a gorgeous equipage; and when he went to church to abjure pomps and vanities, nobody's servant followed, with a gilt prayer-book, in a finer livery or more flaming shoulder knot: of course, nobody could be so proper to decide, whether the philosophic Chilvers was a visitable person or not. Miss Briggs, an elderly maiden relation, and an inmate in the family, decided this important question in his favour, when it was very near being negatived, by declaring, that his being undoubtedly a person of property was quite sufficient; that she dared to say, he was a very good sort of man, in spite of his little oddities; and that, in her opinion, he ought to be visited even in spite of his old white hat.

Chilvers was so elemental in his views, as generally to overlook all conventional modes and forms; and thus, without affectation of singularity, he often fell into somewhat grotesque peculiarities. One summer he purchased a white hat, and once ventured to tie it down under his chin, on account of a face ach. The ridicule and laughter of the rustics first made him sensible that he had presumed to deviate from customary fashions; but as he felt benefit from that which he had adopted, and had a perfect contempt for vulgar or polite raillery, he adhered to his hat as religiously as a Quaker; and partly from habit, partly from obstinacy, constantly wore it, even within doors. The giggling, sneers, and whispering of the visitors, when the irruption formally broke in upon his quiet cottage, suggested to him the idea of checking their unwelcome invitations, by going to their houses in his old white hat, and giving them to understand that he never took it off. Even this expedient failed. A rich man without children, or apparent relations, has too much to leave to be left alone, and cards and visits rather increased than diminished, in spite of the old white hat.

Accident, however, effected what this inseparable appendage could not accomplish. A female cousin of Chilvers, about thirty years of age, had been left a widow, with a little girl of five years old, in a state of utter destitution; and so soon as she learnt his accession of fortune, very naturally applied to him for assistance. Upon occasions of benevolence he was not in the habit of calculating appearances, or balancing surmises, so he tied down his old white hat, got into a glass coach, drove to his relation's, and in less than twelve hours from the receipt of her letter, had established her, with her child, in his cottage, giving up his bed-room for her use, "Because," as he said, "young women liked to be cheerful, and from the corner window she could see all the company on the great Romford road." When the dust allowed any object to be discerned at that distance, it is certain that a glimpse might occasionally be caught of a drove of oxen, or a cart laden with calves for Whitechapel market; but Chilvers had been told that his window commanded this great thoroughfare, and had never been at the pains to ascertain the nature of its command. Such as it was, there the widow had her habitation, her kinsman little dreaming that, in following the dictates of his kind heart, he had at last hit upon an expedient for effectually clearing his house of ceremonious, card-leaving, and card-playing annoyances.

However liberal the world may be in measuring a man's fortune, they seldom extend the same generous estimate to his actions and morals, but are exceedingly prone to deduct from his honour and honesty, at least as much as they have added to his wealth. So it fared with Chilvers. They were willing to overlook his whims and caprices, and even tolerate his old white hat, but there was really no shutting their eyes to the improper nature of the connexion with this pretended widow, this Mrs. Hall, or Ball, or whatever he called her; and, indeed, it was obviously an old affair, for the brat of a child was the very picture of him. He might, at least, have concealed the creature, and not have brought her into his own house, and under the very noses of such universally allowed-to-be-respectable people as the inhabitants of C—— Row. Miss Briggs again took the lead on this momentous abomination; and although, but a very few days before, she had been heard to pronounce him remarkably good-looking for a middle-aged man, she now, with a toss of ineffable anger and disdain, most energetically termed him a good-for-nothing nasty old fellow; and the obsequious village re-echoed the assertion. Footmen, boys, and maids, no longer lifted his latch with cards and invitations; and the females of the place were suddenly seized with an unaccountable obliquity of vision, when they saw him approaching with the unconscious author of this revolution leaning upon his arm. The outrageous puritans instantly crossed over the road, regardless of mud or puddle; some looked steadily at a signpost, on the opposite side of the way; others gazed upon the heavens, or contemplated the earth: while a few summoned a whole Pandemonium of outraged chastity into their countenances, and passed him with a fling of ineffable scorn; but he was too absent and heedless to be even conscious of the cut direct and insolent, still less of the cut oblique and embarrassed. He was too happy in the quiet repossession of his house, and resumption of his studies, to be solicitous about the cause; and as to the poor widow, her time and thoughts were so exclusively occupied with little Fanny, her daughter, that she required not the attentions of her neighbours.

Nothing could exceed the amazement of Chilvers when I explained to him the meaning of this estrangement. "Why, she is not thirty," he exclaimed, "and I am sixty; what disproportion will secure a man from scandal?" With his usual philanthropy, however, he soon began to find excuses for the world, and as he was highly sensitive to any imputations thrown upon his relative, though utterly callous to them in his own person, he consulted me as to what conduct he could adopt, so as to silence calumny, and yet afford the shelter of his roof to this destitute widow. "None," I replied, "but by marrying her."—"With all my heart," he rejoined, "if Mrs. Ball will give her consent." Already deeply impressed with gratitude and esteem, weary with struggling with misfortune, and anxious to secure a protector for her little portionless daughter, this simple-minded and kind-hearted woman did not hesitate in accepting his hand; the marriage took place, and Chilvers, who was before an old rogue, and an old sinner, was instantly converted, in the village vocabulary, into an old fool and an old dotard. This union, dictated solely by benevolence on one side, by gratitude and maternal solicitude on the other, without a particle of love on either, was, without exception, the happiest and most undisturbed that has ever fallen within my observation. And yet there was no intellectual congruity between them; she was an uneducated simple woman; he was a profound, original, and elemental philosopher. But there was affinity and sympathy in their kind and generous hearts; he had found an object for the overflowings of his benevolent bosom, and she looked up to her benefactor with a mixture of filial and conjugal affection. This case may have been an exception to the general rule, but it certainly affords a proof that disproportion of age is not necessarily incompatible with married happiness. Theirs was unbroken except by death; and he, alas! unlike Miss Briggs, came but too soon to visit the cottage, in spite of the imputed mistress, and even of the old white hat.

Chilvers had a mortal antipathy to all interference in parochial affairs, deeming them the infallible foes of neighbourly concord, and the bitter springs of jealousy, bickering, and ill will. During the war, when the militia papers were left at his house, he regularly inserted in the column of exemptions—"old, lame, and a coward,"—and returned it to the proper officer, generally within an hour of his having seen it. Once he was appointed overseer for the poor, in the very natural supposition that from his indolent and sequestrated habits he would appoint a deputy, for which office several applicants accordingly presented themselves; but he detected the motive of his nomination, determined to punish his annoyers, and to the amazement of the whole village declared his intention of acting. His first step was to abolish the quarterly dinners, and other indulgences and perquisites, which his coadjutors had been in the long established habit of enjoying;—his second was to compel them to the performance of those duties which for an equally lengthened period they had been accustomed to neglect; and the result was precisely what he wished—they never troubled him in future. Upon only one other occasion was he moved to enter into the parochial arena, and as it occurred but shortly before his death, of which indeed it was the ultimate cause, and was productive of a little scene of which I was an eyewitness, I shall proceed to relate it.

About half way down Loughton Lane, a footpath strikes off across a large field, and coming out opposite the free school considerably shortens the way to church. I say *considerably* in a relative sense, as to those who principally availed themselves of it—the lame, and the feeble, and the crutch-supported old men and women who toddled out of the alms-houses in the lane, and were duly seen on a Sunday morning creeping across it, as if they could never complete their journey, though they were always sure to be in their places before the bell had done tolling. In point of fact, the distance saved was not above two hundred yards; but a footpath had existed, not only in Farmer Blunt's day, who had owned the field for the last forty years, but time out of mind before him. Farmer Blunt's time, however, was up; he was deposited in the churchyard; and the property having been sold at his death, fell into the hands of a Mr. Martindale, who had lately returned from Calcutta, so saturated with gold, that it had completely tinged his face, and converted half his liver into bile. Visiting his new purchase with a worthy successor of Capability Browne, it was pointed out to him that Farmer Blunt's house, though uninhabitable at present, offered singular advantages for the construction of a mansion worthy of its new proprietor. A very little rebuilding and alteration would convert it into an admirable wing, and there would then be nothing in the world to do, but to run up a centre and another wing in order to complete the edifice; while the fields, naturally picturesque, by simply grubbing up the hedges, and planting a few trees, would spontaneously assume a parkish appearance. Such palpable facilities were not to be neglected; the old farm-house was tortured and transmogrified to qualify it for acting the part of a wing; a park paling speedily encircled the field, and a board at each extremity of the abolished footpath informed the world, that " trespassers would be punished with the utmost severity of the law." After church, on the following Sunday, the aforesaid old alms-women of both sexes assembled in a body, under this obnoxious notice, where they spent an hour or two in debating how long they had respectively remembered the thoroughfare; complained bitterly of the alteration; and though they were all comfortably maintained upon charity, unanimously agreed that nobody cared for the poor now-a-days. The rest of the parishioners, who were either uninterested in the question, or had not the remotest idea of quarreling with a rich man, took no notice of the occurrence, although two or three, who had left cards at the nabob's temporary residence, and not had their visits returned, were heard to declare it was a scandalous proceeding—quite contrary to law, and, for their parts, they wondered the matter was not taken up by somebody. Although every body wishes to be thought somebody, nobody seemed desirous of assuming the character upon the present occasion. My friend having been prevented going to church by illness, his wife staid at home to nurse him for two successive Sundays, and though she was present on the third, and passed the board with the usual conclave of superannuated malcontents under it, she was just then so busy in calculating the cost of Mrs. Palmer's new puce velvet pelisse with fur trimmings, which she was sure she could not afford, and had no right to wear, that she saw nothing on her way home but the shameful sum of nine pounds fifteen shillings, "without reckoning the lining;" which latter words she repeated to herself in a graduated tone of increasing amazement as she recapitulated her calculation, and arrived at the same startling conclusion. Owing thus to his own sickness, and Mrs Palmer's new velvet pelisse, nearly a month elapsed before the nabob's innovation came to the knowledge of the owner of the old white hat.

With his usual scepticism he would not trust to the reports of others, but in spite of a recent sickness, and the expostulations of his wife, tied his old hat under his chin, sallied into Loughton Lane, and not content with reading the placard in that direction, skirted the new paling, till he came in front of the free school, where he perused the duplicate, notwithstanding the mud with which some indignant urchins had bespattered it. His resolution was instantly formed. " How can we expect the poor," said he, " who so fearfully outnumber us, to leave us in quiet possession of our fortunes and luxuries, if we are to look coldly on and see them deprived of their humble rights. Reciprocal forbearance and protection are the upholding principles of the social compact, and the best security for the continuance of the former is the scrupulous exercise of the latter." " They may take the law," said a neighbour to whom he thus expressed himself. " They may take Okehamhall," said Chilvers, " for it has been to let these three years, but how are they to pay for it? I wouldn't have gone to law for myself if he had blocked up my hall door, and compelled me get in at the top of my house, like Robinson Crusoe; but though I might compromise my own rights, I do not feel at liberty to sacrifice those of the poor, so I'll just step on and call upon Mr. Clinch."

Mr. Clinch was a brisk little lawyer, who, by a smirking industry, and technical knowledge of legal quibbles and subtleties, had bustled himself into a thriving business, though he knew no more of the leading principles upon which the noble palladium of the law was built, or of its great expositors, than the rat which is conversant with all the holes, flaws, and hiding places under St. Paul's, knows of architecture and Sir Christopher Wren. He had lately settled in the neighbourhood, having bought a small brick house at the confluence of three roads, on the top of which he had built a fantastical wooden tower, where he occasionally took his wine and the dust; and upon the strength of this castellated superstructure, and two little brass cannons on the lawn, which were always fired when he set off for London at the commencement of term, he gave his residence the very consistent name of Castle-cottage. The rustics called it the Lawyer's Folly;—Chilvers denominated the tower, Mr. Clinch's Coke upon Littleton, and the guns his Term Reports. At this interview hostilities were resolved on, and the man of law having learnt, in the course of his inquiries, that old Adam Wright remembered when there was not even a stile at the thoroughfare in question, and had rode through it scores of times on horseback, wrote to my friend, requesting he would order the fellow to step up to C—— Row, and he would come over, take his bit of mutton with him, and examine the rustic after dinner. Old Adam Wright was a pensioner of Squire Tilson, in whose lodge he resided; and as Chilvers knew him to be infirm, as well as old, his method of ordering the fellow to step up was to send over a chaise-cart for him, with a civil message requesting an interview. I was in the parlour when he arrived, and could not help smiling at his rueful looks, when he saw Mr. Clinch at table with paper before him and pen in hand. Standing close to the door as if fearful of advancing, he cast a most suspicious glance from his little grey eyes, which, from the bend of his body, he was obliged to turn upwards, while a sudden blush reddened his wrinkled forehead, and even tinged his bald head. " Sit down, Mr. Wright," said my friend, at the same time pouring him out a bumper of wine, which the old man tossed off at one gulp with a dexterity worthy of his younger days. The lawyer stared; Adam Wright sate timidly down—drew up his breath, and again gazed round him suspiciously, but upon learning the object of his examination, presently recovered his composure. " I understand, good man," said Mr. Clinch, " that you have rode through this field when it was open, scores of times?"—" Never but once," was the reply. " Only once! why then did you say you had?"—" I never did say so."—" Hem!" said Clinch, " a shy bird."—" Behold the exaggeration of village gossips," said Chilvers; " but you did once ride through it, Mr. Wright; will you have the goodness to relate to us what you recollect of the circumstances?"—" I recollect them all," replied Adam, " as well as if it happened yesterday, though I was only nine years old at the time. Mayhap, sir, you might know strait-haired Jack, as they called him, that drove the Cambridge?" Chilvers regretted that he never had that honour. " Well, sir, I was then apprenticed to his own father, old Harrison, that kept the farrier's shop at the lower common."—" How was it bounded on the north?" interrupted Clinch. " The Lord knows how," resumed Adam. " That must be ascertained, however," quoth Clinch, laying down his pen. " It can't be done no how," said Adam, " for the great stack of chimneys has fallen in, right where I used to stand and blow the bellows. God preserve us! Thank heaven there's only a low chimney to our lodge."—" See how an old man clings to life," whispered Chilvers; " he never troubled his head about chimneys when he was young."—" Well, sir," said Wright, in continuation, " old Harrison (I called him *master* then) had been trumpeter or horse-doctor in the Greys"—— " Which was he?" again interrupted Clinch—" he must have been one or the other."—" No, sir, he wasn't, for I believe he was both."—" Ay, that will do—go on."—" Well, he served in the Greys, I don't know how many years, and when he was discharged superannuated, they allowed him to buy his grey mare that he always rode; and how old she was, God knows, for the mark was out of her mouth afore ever she came to him, and he rode her twelve years in the army. Upon this mare he used to go about for orders, attending the gentlemen's hunters round the country, and what not; but never suffered any body to mount her without it was himself. He had only to call out Polly, and she would come running up to him directly, and would follow him up and down town, just like a dog without ever a bridle, no nor so much as a halter.—Well, master never breakfasted at home;—the first thing in the morning, he used to put some soft gingerbread into his pocket, for his teeth were knocked out at some great battle, and go down to the King's Head, and there, if you passed the bow window, you would be sure to see him in his cocked hat sitting behind a half pint of purl. On the morning I was telling you of"——

"You have told us of no morning yet," cried Clinch. "I mean the morning when I rode through the field in the afternoon:—on that morning I took Polly down to the King's Head, according to orders, as master was going over to Romford to look at Squire Preston's hunter that was took ill; but it seems that just as he got to Woodly-end, down came Polly, and a terrible fall by all accounts it was. However, master wasn't much hurt, but we saw something had happened by his coming home without Polly, though he never said a word, but desired us all, for he kept three men besides me, to leave off work, take spades and dig a great hole in the yard, while he broke up the ground for us with a pickaxe. To work we went, and in three hours we had made a rare pit, all wondering what it could mean. 'Adam,' said he to me, when we had done, 'go to the paddock at the upper common where you will find Polly; bring her here, but don't offer to get upon her back, and don't go faster than a walk.'—So I took a halter"—
"Was it leather or rope?" inquired Clinch. Adam could not tell, so he proceeded. "When I got to the paddock, there was Polly, sure enough, with her knees all bloody; but as I saw she wasn't lame at all, and seemed in good spirits, I put the halter in her mouth, and going back a little, so as to get a short run, I put my hand upon her shoulder, and jumped upon her back."—"Jumped upon her back!" echoed Clinch, looking incredulously at the decrepit object before him. "Lord love you," continued Adam, "I was then as nimble as a squirrel, and as lissome as a withy. So I rode her across this here field, for there wasn't even a stile then, nor any sign of one, and got off when we reached the high road for fear of being seen, and led her into our yard, where master was sitting in his cocked hat, and the men all whispering together up in a corner. As soon as I came in, he called out to our big foreman, 'Sam,' says he, 'step up into my room, and bring me down the horse-pistols that I took from the French officer at the battle of'—— I forget what place he said, but I know it ended with a *quet*, or a *narde*, or some such sound; so, I can't be much out. They glittered as he took them out of their cases, for he always cleaned them every Sunday morning, and as I stared first at master, as he proceeded to load them, putting two bullets in each—then at the great hole in the ground, then at the men all looking solemn-like, and then at poor Polly, gazing in master's face, while her knees and legs were covered with blood, I felt my heart beat, and was all over in a fluster. When he had finished loading the pistols, he went and stood in front of the mare. 'Polly,' said he, 'I have rode thee these sixteen years over road and river, through town and country, by night and by day, through storm and sunshine, and thou never made a bolt or boggle with me till now. Thou hast carried me over five thousand dead bodies before breakfast, and twice saved my life; once when the allies left us in the lurch, and we were obliged to scamper for it; once when our company fell into an ambush, and only thirty men escaped. We must both die soon, and should I go first, which I may quickly do if you give me such another tumble, it will be a bad day's work for thee. Thou wouldst not wish to be starved, and mauled, and worked to death, and thy carcase given over to the nackers, wouldst thou?' Polly put down her head, and rubbed it against him, and while she was doing so, he tied a handkerchief over her eyes, and kissing her first on one side of the face and then on the other, he said : ' Polly, God bless thee ;' and instantly fired one of his pistols right into her ear. She fell down, gave one kick, and never moved nor moaned afterwards; but I remember the tears gushed out of my eyes just as if a Christian had been shot, and even big Sam looked ready to cry as he stood over her, and said ' Poor Polly !' We buried her in the hole, and master told us we had worked enough for one day, and might spend the afternoon where we liked, and he was just going to fire his other pistol in the air, when he saw a crow on the top of the weathercock ; and, sure enough he brought her down, for he was a rare shot. After all, it was a cruel thing to use a poor dumb beast in that way only for tumbling with him; and no one could tell why he buried her in the yard, when the Squire's gamekeeper would have given a fair price for the carcase to feed the hounds. But old Harrison was an odd one. Ah ! we've got a mort of regular doctors in the parish now, besides the poticary, and I dare say they may do well enough for Christians, and such like, but I reckon there's ne'er a one of 'em could stop the glanders in a horse like Mr. Harrison."

Adam having finished his narrative, Clinch proceeded to question him again upon the more recent occurrences of his life, and finding his recollection much impaired upon these points, he very unceremoniously gave him his dismissal, but not before Chilvers had slipped something into his hand. "Here's a pretty rascal," said the man of law; "he has heard that we wanted evidence, and has trumped up this circumstantial tale in the hope of a reward; but did you observe how neatly I detected the old rogue when I began to cross-question him? Will any one believe that he could so minutely detail an occurrence of sixty or seventy years ago, in which, by his own account, he was no way interested, when he cannot recollect much more recent and important particulars of his own life ?"—" The importance of these matters," said Chilvers, "is not to be considered abstractedly but relatively; at the time of poor Polly's death, Adam had never witnessed any exhibition more solemn and affecting; probably had never been present at the death of a large animal. You seem to forget that the tablet of the memory, like certain stones, though sufficiently soft at first to receive deep and distinct impressions, hardens with age; and that this very induration fixes and indelibly preserves the characters first engraved, while it prevents any future incisions, unless of a very superficial and evanescent nature. You may scratch or write upon it, and this answers the temporary wants of age, you can no longer chisel or stamp any durable impress upon its stubborn substance. This seeming inconsistency is, in my opinion, a forcible confirmation of old Adam's veracity."—" A jury won't think so," retorted Clinch, " and that's the only thing to look to."

I have given this dialogue, and old Adam Wright's examination, circumstantially, because every particular is deeply fixed in my own recollection, by the fatal results of which the affair was speedily productive. Chilvers, as I have mentioned, had been ill when he sallied forth to read the placard announcing the shutting up of the footpath. Upon that occasion he got wet—he sat some time at Mr. Clinch's: his complaint, which was the gout, was driven into his stomach, and in spite of immediate medical advice, and the unremitted self-devotion of his wife, who never quitted his side, he expired in ten days. Death-bed descriptions are productive of no good to counteract their painful details; they prove nothing; for whatever may be gained in the sincerity of the dying person, is balanced by the diseased state which the mind generally participates with the body. A man's opinions are worth nothing unless they emanate from a vigorous intellect and sound frame, uninfluenced by immediate hopes or fears. Suffice it to say, that Chilvers died as he lived—a philanthropist and a philosopher.

After the melancholy ceremonies of the funeral, which I took upon myself to direct, I accompanied my wife to the cottage, where we meant to reside for some little time, to offer our consolations to his relict, now a second time a widow. I have never been more forcibly impressed with the vanity of human learning, and the vain glory of philosophy, than in the instance of this uneducated female, who, from an innate principle, or instinct of religion, although utterly ignorant of all theological points, possessed a mastery over her mind, and a consolation under afflictions, which the most profound adept in the schools of worldly wisdom would in vain attempt to rival. Conscious that the death of her husband was a dispensation of Providence, under which it was perhaps guilty to repine, she set resolutely about the suppressing of her grief, beginning by carefully locking up and concealing all those articles of his dress and daily use, which, by recalling him suddenly and forcibly to her recollection, might upset her pious resolutions; so that upon our arrival, we found her in a frame of mind much more calm and resigned than we had anticipated. Though Chilvers never killed a bird, or caught a fish in his life, he had a favourite spaniel, called Juno, almost as inseparable a companion as his old white hat; the partaker of his morning rambles, and the invariable residuary of his crusts at tea-time. This faithful animal his widow could not resolve to dismiss; but with this exception she imagined she had so disposed of every personal memorial, as to be secure from too frequent a renewal of her griefs by the sight of external objects. She was, however, mistaken. We were all seated in the parlour, myself and my wife endeavouring to divert the widow's thoughts from the past, by directing them to the future management of her little girl, and flattering ourselves that we had infused into her mind a more than usual serenity, when our attention was aroused by a barking and laughing without, the door was thrown open, and in scampered Juno with the old white hat tied upon her head, while little Fanny followed, shouting behind, delighted with the success of her frolic!—" O, Fanny! Fanny!" cried the agonised mother; why did they suffer"—— she could not utter a word more; but, overcome by her feelings, rushed out of the room, and locked herself into her own chamber. The child, it seems, had seized the old white hat in the first confusion of her father's death, and concealed it in a closet of the nursery, whence she had now withdrawn it to fasten upon Juno's head, quite unconscious of the distress she was preparing. Young as she was, I endeavoured to impress upon her mind the loss of her papa, for so she always called him, and the necessity of refraining from all mention of his name, or allusion to his death, in the presence of her mother. She appeared to understand, and promised to obey my directions. Fortified and composed by the consolations she never failed to draw from her solitary religious exercises, the widow shortly returned to the parlour, and a tranquillity, though somewhat embarrassed, was again established in our little circle; when Fanny, ready to burst with the possession of what she considered a mystery, kept hovering about her mother; and at last, taking her hand, and looking up in her face with an affectionate importance, she lisped out hesitatingly, " I know something. Papa's dead, but I mustn't tell you, because it's a great secret, and you'll be angry if I do." The poor widow hid her face in her handkerchief with one hand, and with the other covered the child's mouth, as if to silence her; but as the little urchin seemed disposed to expostulate, I took her by the hand, led her out of the room, and directed the maid to put her to bed.

On re-entering the parlour, I once more found the mother in a state of comparative serenity, and calculated on passing the evening without further outrage to her feelings. The child was asleep, the old white hat was locked up, and it was settled that after tea I was to read a sermon, which I had selected for the purpose, as the best adapted to pour balm and peace into her wounded bosom. The equipage was already set out, and I recalled that simple but exquisite picture of fire-side enjoyment, which Chilvers was so fond of quoting :

The hearth was swept—the fire was bright,
The kettle on for tea, &c.

when my attention was called to Juno, who, instead of basking leisurely before the fire, as was her wont, kept searching round the room, smelling to every individual, and occasionally planting herself close to the door, with an earnest air, as if expecting the arrival of some one else. After waiting some time, she betook herself to the rug, with an appearance of disappointment, whence she presently started with a short bark, and expression of alacrity towards the door. It was Patty entering with the urn. Now, if Juno had been in a frame of mind to be easily pleased, she could not have muttered such a discontented growl at the sight of Patty, whose fair complexion, auburn hair, red arms, and somewhat substantial figure, constituted her a pleasing specimen of the rural English, or rather Saxon beauty; while her manner and attire rendered her a worthy counterpart to Milton's " neat handed Philis." Juno, however, who had no eyes except for her poor master, whom she was never to see more, returned grumbling to the rug. Exactly the same eager excitement and surly disappointment occurred, when the maid returned with the toast; but the dog, instead of contenting herself with the rug upon this occasion, stood before her mistress, looked wistfully in her face and whined, as if inquiring for her master. I exchanged glances with my wife, and saw at once that we mutually understood what was passing in Juno's mind, as well as her mistress's. Poor widowed sufferer! who shall describe her agony? The gush of passion overpowered all the barriers of resolution and religion,— the woman predominated over the Christian, and her emotions flowed more vehemently from the previous control to which they had been subjected. Convulsive and hysterical sobs for some time choaked her utterance, and when she was able to articulate, as if anxious to excuse the violence of her grief by the virtue of its object, she turned towards me, and exclaimed :—" Wasn't he a kind creature—everybody loved him, and even Juno, you see, cannot forget him. O! sir, you dont know half the kind, generous, and charitable things he did in private." Her feelings again overpowered her; she sunk her head upon Juno's, who by this time had leaped into her lap, and I shall never forget her wo-stricken look when she raised it, and sobbed out— (Psha! where is my handkerchief—my tears are blotting the paper)—when she sobbed out—

Gentle reader, forgive me; my heart and my eyes are both too full; I cannot write a word more.

SAILORS AND MARINES.
BEAUTIES OF FLOGGING.

THE words marine and mariner differ by one small letter only; but no two races of men, I had well said no two animals, differ from one another more completely than the "Jollies" and the "Johnnies." The marines, as I have before mentioned, are enlisted for life, or for long periods, as in the regular army, and when not employed afloat, are kept in barracks, in such constant training, under the direction of their officers, that they are never released for one moment of their lives from the influence of strict discipline and habitual obedience. The sailors, on the contrary, when their ship is paid off, are turned adrift, and so completely scattered abroad, that they generally lose, in the riotous dissipation of a few weeks, or it may be days, all they have learned of good order during the previous three or four years. Even when both parties are placed on board of ship, and the general discipline maintained in its fullest operation, the influence of regular order and exact subordination is at least twice as great over the marines as it ever can be over the sailors. Many, I may say most of their duties are entirely different. It is true, both the marines and the seamen pull and haul at certain ropes leading along the quarter-deck; both assist in scrubbing and washing the decks; both eat salt junk, drink grog, sleep in hammocks, and keep watch at night; but in almost every other thing they differ. As far as the marines are concerned, the sails would never be let fall, or reefed, or rolled up. There is even a positive Admiralty order against their being made to go aloft; and, accordingly, a marine in the rigging is about as ridiculous and helpless an object, as a sailor would prove if thrust into a tight, well pipe-clayed pair of pantaloons, and barrel round the throat with a stiff stock.

In short, without going further, it may be said, that the colour of their clothing, and the manner in which it is put on, do not differ more from one another than the duties and habits of the marines and sailors. Jack wears a blue jacket, and Johnny wears a red one. Jack would sooner take a round dozen than be seen with a pair of braces across his shoulders; while the marine, if deprived of his suspensors, would speedily be left sans culotte. A thorough-going, barrack bred, regular-built marine in a ship of which the sergeant-major truly loves his art has, without any exaggerated metaphor, been compared to a man who has swallowed a set of fire-irons; the tongs representing the legs, the poker the backbone, and the shovel the neck and head. While, on the other hand, your sailor-man is to be likened to nothing, except one of those delicious figures in the fantoccini show-boxes, where the legs, arms, and head are flung loosely about to the right and left, no one bone apparently having the slightest organic connexion with any other; the whole being an affair of strings, and universal joints!

The marines live, day and night, in the after part of the ship, close to the apartments of the officers; their arms-chest is placed on the quarter-deck; their duties, even in the cases where they are most mixed up with those of the seamen, group them well aft. The marines are exclusively planted as sentries at the cabin doors of the captain and officers; and even the look-out men on the quarters, at night, are taken from the royal corps. To all this it may be added, that the marines furnish the officers with such small service, in the way of attendance, as they may require, and generally wait at table.

In a well-known instance of mutiny on board a frigate, the operation of these principles was shown in a most striking manner. The captain was one of that class of officers, now happily extinct, whose chief authority consisted of severity. To such an excess was this pushed, that his ship's company, it appears, were at length roused to actual revolt, and proceeded in a tumultuous, but apparently resolute body, to the quarter-deck. It is extremely curious to remark, that the same stern system of discipline which had driven the seamen into revolt, had likewise been applied to the marines without weakening their paramount sense of duty under any circumstances. Such, at all events, was the force of habit and discipline, that when the captain ordered them to fall in, they formed instantly, as a matter of course, across the deck. At his farther orders, they loaded their muskets with ball, and screwed on their bayonets. Had the corps now proved traitors, all must have been lost; but the captain, who with all his faults of temper and system, was yet a great, and gallant, and clever-headed officer, calculated with good reason upon a different result. Turning first to the mutineers, he called out,

"I'll attend to you directly!"

And then addressing the soldiers, he said with a tone of such perfect confidence of manners and so slightly interrogative as to furnish its own answer.

"You'll stand by your king and country?"

The marines, thus appealed to, said nothing, but grasped their firearms with an air of fixed resolution. It was exactly one of those occasions when silence gives the most expressive of all consents; and the captain, assured that if he were now only true to himself, the soldiers would be true to their duty, exclaimed,

"Then royal and loyal marines, we don't care a damn for the blue jackets!"

And, stepping forward, he seized the principal ringleaders by the throat, one with each hand, and calling out, in a voice like thunder, to the rest, instantly to move off the quarter-deck, he consigned the astonished and deserted culprits to the master at arms, by whom they were speedily and quietly placed in double irons—and the whole mutiny was at an end!

The successful issue of the recent mutiny, and his well grounded confidence in his own resources, had taught him to believe that he could command the services of his people, not only on ordinary occasions, but at moments of utmost need. Here was his grand mistake. The obedience he exacted at the point of the lash had no heartiness in it; and when the time came that the argument of force could no longer be used, and when the bayonets of the marines had lost their terrors, there was read to him, and in letters of blood, the bitterest lesson of retributive justice that perhaps was ever pronounced to any officer since the beginning of the naval service.

The frigate under command of this energetic officer, when in company with another ship, chased two French frigates off the Isle of France. As his ship sailed much faster than her consort, he soon outstripped her, and closed with the enemy single-handed. The Frenchmen, seeing only one ship near them, and the other far astern, shortened sail, and prepared for the attack, which, however, they could hardly suppose would be undertaken by one ship. In this expectation, however, they underrated the gallant spirit of her commander, who, unquestionably, was one of the bravest officers in the service. It is said, also, that he deemed himself, at this critical moment of his fate, one of the most fortunate of men, to possess such an opportunity for distinction. Seeing the enemy's frigate within his reach, and well knowing what his men could execute if they chose,—never dreaming for a moment that they would fail him at this pinch,—he exclaimed, in the greatest rapture, "We shall take them both! steer right for them! and now, my brave lads, stand to your guns, and show what you are made of!"

This was the last order he ever gave! The men obeyed, and stood to their guns, like gallant fellows as they were; but they stood there only to be shot to death. They folded their arms, and neither loaded nor fired a single shot in answer to the pealing broadsides which the unresisted and astonished enemy were pouring fast upon them! Now had arrived the dreadful moment of revenge for them—as their captain, who was soon struck down like the rest, lived only long enough to see the cause of his failure, and to witness the shocking sight of his gallant self-devoted crew cut to pieces, *rather than more their hands to fire one gun to save the credit of their commander—all consideration for their own lives, or for the honour of their country, appearing to be absorbed in their desperate determination to prove at last how completely they had it in their power to show their sense of the unjust treatment they had received.*—*Hall's Fragments.*

OLD FOOT-PATHS.

Stiles and foot-paths are vanishing everywhere. There is nothing upon which the advance of wealth and population has made so serious an inroad.* As land has increased in value, wastes and heaths have been parcelled out and enclosed, but seldom have foot-paths been left. The poet and the naturalist, who before had, perhaps, the greatest real property in them, have had no allotment. They have been totally driven out of the promised land. Goldsmith complained in his day, that

The man of wealth and pride
Takes up a space that many poor supplied;
Space for his lake, his park's extended bounds,
Space for his horses, equipage, and hounds;
The robe that wraps his limbs in silken sloth
Has robb'd the neighbouring fields of half their growth:
His seat, where solitary sports are seen,
Indignant spurns the cottage from the green.

And it is but too true that the pressure of contiguous pride has driven farther, from that day to this, the public from the rich man's lands. "They make a solitude and call it peace." Even the quiet and picturesque foot-path that led across his fields, or stole along his wood-side, giving to the poor man with his burden a cooler and nearer cut to the village, is become a nuisance. One would have thought that the rustic labourer, with his sithe on his shoulder, or his bill-hook and hedging mittens in his hand, the cottage-dame in her black bonnet and scarlet cloak, the neat village maiden, in the sweetness of health and simplicity, or the boy strolling along full of life and curiosity, might have had sufficient interest in themselves, for a cultivated taste not merely to tolerate, but to welcome—passing occasionally at a distance across the park or wood, as objects agreeably enlivening the stately solitude of the hall. But they have not; and what is more, *they* are commonly the most jealous of pedestrian trespassers, who seldom visit their own estates, but permit the seasons to scatter their charms around their villas and rural possessions without the heart to enjoy, or even the presence to behold them. How often have I myself been arrested in some long-frequented dale,—in some spot endeared by its own beauties and the fascinations of memory—by a board exhibiting in giant characters, "STOPPED BY AN ORDER OF SESSIONS," and denouncing the terrors of the law upon trespassers! This is a little too much. I would not be querulous for the poor against the rich. I would not teach them to look with an envious and covetous eye upon their villas, lawns, cattle, and equipage; but when the path of immemorial usage is closed, when the little streak, almost as fine as a mathematical line, along the wealthy man's ample field, is grudgingly erased, it is impossible not to feel indignation at the pitiful monopoly. Is there no village champion to be found, bold enough to put in his protest against these encroachments,—to assert the public right?—for a right it is, as authentic as that by which the land is itself held, and as clearly acknowledged by the laws. Is there no local "Hampden, with dauntless breast," to "withstand the petty tyrants of the fields," and to save our good old foot-paths? If not, we shall in a few years be doomed to the highways and the hedges; to look, like Dives, from a sultry region of turnpikes, into a pleasant one of verdure and foliage which we may not approach. Already, the stranger, if he lose his way, is in jeopardy of falling into the horrid fangs of a steel trap; the botanist enters a wood to gather a

---

* For six or eight miles around Edinburgh especially. The Earl of Rosslyn is unpopular at present; and we do not affect to be better pleased with his conduct than our neighbours; but he deserves the praise of *not* shutting up his grounds on the banks of the Esk, while the newer proprietors seem afraid their possessions will run away unless they are kept close caged.

flower, and is shot with a spring-gun; death hunts our dells and copses, and the poet complains, in regretful notes, that he

> Wanders away to the field and glen,
> Far as he may for the gentlemen.—HOWITT.

FIELD-PATHS.
BY THE AUTHOR OF CORN-LAW RHYMES.

Path of the quiet fields! that oft of yore
Call'd me at morn, on Shenstone's page to pore;
Oh poor man's footpath! where, " at evening's close,"
He stopp'd to pluck the woodbine and the rose,
Shaking the dew-drops from the wild-brier bowers,
That stoop'd beneath their load of summer flowers,
Then ey'd the west, still bright with fading flame,
As whistling homeward by the wood he came;
Sweet, dewy, sunny, flowery footpath, thou
Art gone for ever, like the poor man's cow!
No more the wandering townsman's *Sabbath smile;*
No more the hedger, waiting on the stile
For tardy Jane; no more the muttering bard,
Startling the heifer, near the lone farm-yard;
No more the pious youth, with book in hand,
Spelling the words he fain would understand,
Shall bless thy mazes, *when the village bell*
Sounds o'er the river, soften'd up the dell,
But from the parlour of the loyal inn,
The Great Unpaid, who cannot err or sin,
Shall see, well pleas'd, the pomp of Lawyer Ridge,
And poor Squire Grubb's starv'd maids, and dandy bridge,
Where youngling fishers, in the grassy lane,
Purloin'd their tackle from the brood-mare's mane,
And truant urchins, by the river's brink,
Caught the fledged throstle as it stoop'd to drink,
Or with the ramping colt, all joyous, play'd,
Or scar'd the owlet in the *blue belled shade.*

USEFUL NOTICES.

BEER FROM SUGAR.—For making excellent ale or table beer, it is not absolutely necessary to use malt. To conceive this subject rightly, we must consider that it is the sugar of the malt which undergoes fermentation, and that any other sugar will ferment just as well, although no other sugar is so cheap. Economy and long habit have established malt-sugar as a brewing material, but cane-sugar will afford an excellent drink. To persons residing in the country, and far from breweries, as well as those who do not choose the great trouble of managing malt, this is a valuable fact. Another advantage of cane-sugar is, that the apparatus necessary for converting it into beer is much more simple; all that is required. is a cask which has no bung-hole, or has it well stopped up. This is to be set standing on either of its ends; a cock is to be fixed in one of the staves, about an inch above the bottom chimb, so that in drawing off the liquor, the sediment cannot also run. In the centre of the top of the cask, that is, in the centre of its other end, a hole is to be bored, of such size as will admit a large bottle-cork. Let us suppose that the cask holds 10 gallons, and the drink is to be tolerably strong ale. The proper quantity of hops required for 10 gallons of ale, in this process, will be about 1¼lb. On this quantity, contained in any convenient vessel, pour on 11 gallons of boiling water; or, what is much better, boil the hops in the water for about five minutes, and no more; then strain off the hops; in the strained liquor dissolve 14lbs. of sugar, and mix in a pint of yeast of the best quality. Pour the whole into the cask; it will soon begin to ferment; it will throw up its yeast through the cork-hole at the top, and, this being retained within the external rim of the chimb, it will, for the most part, fall back into liquor, and run back into the cask. It will require, at the ordinary temperature of summer, so much as three weeks or a month to complete the fermentation. For the last fortnight the cork may be generally kept in the hole; but should, once every two days be removed, to give vent to the fixed air, and then replaced. When the fermentation appears at an end, the taste of the sugar will almost entirely have disappeared, it will be barely perceptible. The cork may then be permanently driven in, and in four days the ale will be fit for draught, or for bottling. As to the quality of the sugar, it is a matter of little consequence; white sugar will afford an ale scarcely coloured; brown sugar will impart proportionate colour, and not quite so pure a flavour. Should colour be an object, it may be communicated by the raspings of an over-baked loaf, or by scorched treacle; but this is matter of little moment. The drink will spontaneously fine itself. To persons who have acquired an inveterate predilection for the abominable and varied flavours which the skill of the brewer enables him to communicate, this pure and simple drink may be less pleasing; but it is singular how soon the consumer acquires a high relish for it, and prefers it to every other. There is a purity of taste belonging to it quite different from the indescribable jumble of tastes so perceptible in common ales, and a light sharpness, combined with tenuity, which is much more agreeable than the glutinous or mucilaginous softness of even the best ales. But it has one advantage which places it above all competition, and that is its lightness on the stomach; this, when compared with the sickly heaviness of malt-ale, is really remarkable. The whiter the sugar the lighter will be the ale; and age greatly conduces to the same end, provided that the drink is sound, which is best insured by bottling. Hops are not the only bitter which may be made use of for preparing and flavouring such ales; others can much more conveniently be procured in certain situations. Mixtures, in various proportions, of wormwood, powdered bitter oranges, gentian root, and rind of Seville oranges, will afford an excellent bitter, perhaps more wholesome than hops, and, if skilfully combined, to the full as palatable; in this position the *brewers cannot refuse to bear me out,* for reasons with which many of them are acquainted. Gentian, and particularly quassia, must be used sparingly; for the bitterness of these is of so lasting and penetrating a kind, that much of it is sure to be disagreeable. It has been shown by M. Dubrunfaut, that a good beer can be procured from potatoes; the potatoes are to be grated to a pulp; this is to be well mixed with boiling water, and ground barley-malt is to be added. The liquid being drawn off, is to be hopped in the usual way. yeast added, and the fermentation induced. The beer thus produced, after being bottled, was found greatly to resemble Paris beer. In certain parts of Ireland an excellent beer is brewed from parsnips, by a process somewhat like the foregoing, except that no malt is used; the bitter employed is hops. In short, malt is by no means necessary to the production of wholesome and agreeable beers.—*Lardner's Cyclopædia; Domestic Economy.*

THE USES OF THE BRAMBLE.—The shrub which we are in the habit of despising, and which is only used by the chance passenger occasionally plucking its fruit, possesses, however, several advantages which deserve our attention. It is now to be found in every bank and ditch. About the *braes* opposite Hawthornden, and by the side of the path by the river-side, so iniquitously shut up, bramble-berries wont to be found in profusion; but in the vale of Clyde, between Lanark and Hamilton, this becomes a *rich fruit.* Its roots, when dried in the shade, cut into small fragments, and, taken in the shape of a weak infusion, form one of the best specifics against obstinate coughs. Its long branches can, in cases of need, be used as cords; and its fruit produces an excellent wine, the mode of making which is as follows:—Five measures of the ripe fruit, with one of honey and six of wine, are taken and boiled; the froth is skimmed off, the fire removed, and the mixture being passed through a linen cloth, is left to ferment. It is then boiled anew, and allowed to ferment in a suitable cask. In Provence, bramble-berries are used to give a deep colour to particular wines.

ODE TO FREEDOM.
BY DAVID VEDDER.

In youth I adored thee, and knelt at thy shrine;
In manhood I worship thee, Spirit divine:
When my last pulse shall throb, when my last sigh is sighing,
If thy presence is there, there is bliss even in dying.

Thy fanes have been thronged, in days that are past,
With ardent adorers in multitudes vast;
The priests at thine altar have ministered well,
Leonidas, Washington, Wallace, and Tell!

Enrobed in thy vestments in Bannock's red field,
Thy patriot sons made Plantagenet yield;
With the flesh of his minions the eagles were gorged,
And he writhed and blasphemed in the chains he had forged.

What tho' over Poland, all blighted and waste,
Barbarians stalk at a despot's behest;
THERE, each rock is an altar, each grave is a shrine,
Where thy votaries shall worship yet, Spirit divine!

SCRAPS.
ORIGINAL AND SELECTED.

LIFE IN A PIG-STY.—Lord Deerhurst's antipathy to soap and water is generally known. One night, during the time that Sophia Debouchette (now Lady Berwick) was living under his protection, his Lordship being rather "Bacchi plenus," was extolling the charms and manners of his mistress to the Club at Whites', and concluded his eulogy with the following trope—"In fact, I live only in Sophia's eyes."—"I don't doubt it," said Lord Alvanley, "for I observed she had a *sty* in them, the last time I saw her."

The Marquis of Hertford recently gave a grand dinner at Pompeii, on the site of the ancient baths. Many of the guests were conveyed thither in one of our omnibuses, containing twenty-five persons. The passage of this stupendous modern machine, followed by several elegant English carriages, along the narrow streets of this antique town, formed a most singular spectacle. An attempt at an excavation was made during the dinner, but was not successful.

LONDON PORTER.—Except in Dublin, this beverage has never been equalled in point of strength and flavour. Imitations have been tried with great exertion and outlay of capital, in different parts of the country, but they can all be detected by their burnt taste, and bear no comparison to the rich, full body of the genuine London porter. This generous liquid, as is well known, is always drunk out of pewter or silver pots, which impart a finer flavour to the mouth of the drinker than if glass or earthenware were used. The reason for this can be scientifically accounted for, by the electro-chemical action which is going on betwixt the acid of the porter and the metal; and, therefore, the popular taste is quite correct in adhering to pewter pots. The Scotch, who import London porter to a large extent, do not seem to be aware of this remarkable fact, as they always drink the liquor from glass tumblers. Between six and seven millions of barrels of porter or strong beer are made annually in England; in 1830, the quantity exported was 74,902 barrels.

ARCTIC LAND EXPEDITION.—We rejoice to learn, that an expedition to the shores of the Polar Seas, for the purpose mentioned in the following statement, is at last finally determined upon—to proceed without delay, under the command of Captain Back, by way of Canada, and, early in the spring, to move towards the territories of the Hudson's Bay Company, who take a warm interest in the success of the enterprise. It is intended that Captain Back, without deviating from the main object of his mission, shall avail himself of every opportunity that may occur to enrich the scientific world, and that, before his return, he will have explored those unknown regions between Point Turnagain, where Captain Franklin finished his journey, and the furthermost point to the west, reached by Captain Parry, and thus wind up the main object of those two expeditions—it being supposed, from the rein deer and musk oxen being found on Melville Island, that the land is either continuous or divided only by narrow straits.

FRIENDLY SOCIETIES.—A statement has been exhibited, showing, in a very striking view, the great benefits and relief which Friendly Societies are calculated to afford at a period of unexampled calamity like the present. Since the cholera appeared at Inverness, the number of deaths applicable to the different societies amounted to 74. The sum of L.5 is allowed by each society to defray the funeral expenses of each person; and when it is taken into consideration that several of the unfortunate sufferers belonged to more than one society, there is here a sum of L.400 applied, in a very short period, to sooth the sorrows of the afflicted; and the relief is afforded at a crisis when its value can be more peculiarly appreciated—when the harrowed feelings of the relatives are gratified by being able to pay the last and most sacred duty to the remains of their friends in decency and propriety. Can we make a more forcible appeal as to the usefulness of such institutions, and to the prudence of the working-classes becoming members of them?

FINANCIAL REFORM.—In order to acquire something like a tolerably accurate understanding of what our Legislators have been doing with our money, it is necessary to go back to some distant period, that we may be able to contrast what our expenditure was with what it now is: The period we shall select is the year 1790; because a report of a Committee of the House of Commons having given an exact account of the expenditure of that year, we shall be safe from error in making use of that account. This account shews that the whole expenditure on the army in that year was L.1,844,153; on the navy, L.2,000,000; on the ordnance, L.375,000; on the national debt, L.10,317,972; and that the total expenditure in 1790, was no more than L.15,969,178. The annual account of the public expenditure laid before the House of Commons this year, shews that it amounted for the year 1832 to L.47,123,298. But to this must be added about L.4,000,000, which is expended in collecting the revenue; making the actual established expenditure of the United Kingdom something more than FIFTY-ONE MILLIONS, in the sixteenth year of profound peace.—*Tait's Magazine*.

THE CHOLERA IN THE UNITED STATES.—At the date of the last accounts from New York, the malady had decreased in virulence in that city; but the deaths and new cases were sufficiently numerous to excite alarm. Even respectable females, when they have occasion to go out, either on business or pleasure, invariably adopt the precaution of displaying a card, which is attached round their necks, with some such directions as the following: "My name is ——; should I be seized with Cholera, do not take me to the hospital, but to my residence, No. —— in —— street."

DR. JOHNSON ON POPULAR AND USEFUL PREACHING.—I talked of preaching and of the great success which those called Methodists have.—Johnson, "Sir, it is owing to their expressing themselves in a plain and familiar manner, which is the only way to do good to the common people, and which clergymen of learning and genius ought to do from a practice of duty, when it is suited to their congregations; a principle for which they will be praised by men of sense. To insist against drunkenness as a crime, because it debases reason, the noblest faculty of man, would be of no service to the common people, but to tell them they may die in a fit of drunkenness, and show them how dreadful that would be cannot fail to make a deep impression. *Sir, when your Scotch clergy give up their homely manner, religion will soon decay in that country.*" Let this observation, as Johnson meant it, be ever remembered.—*Boswell's Johnson*.

BESIDES appearing in WEEKLY NUMBERS, the SCHOOLMASTER is published in MONTHLY PARTS, which, stitched in a neat cover, contain as much letter-press, of good execution, as any of the large Monthly Periodicals: A Table of Contents will be given at the end of the year; when, *at the weekly cost of three-halfpence*, a handsome volume of 832 pages, super-royal size, may be bound up, containing much matter worthy of preservation.

PART II., containing the five September Numbers, with JOHNSTONE'S MONTHLY REGISTER, may be had of all the Booksellers. Price 9d. For the accommodation of weekly readers, the Monthly Register and Cover may be had separately at the different places of sale.

CONTENTS OF NO. XII.

Original Letter of Burns.—Political Martyrs of the end of last century,	177
What have you to do with Politics?	178
Price of Justice,	179
Hydrostatic Bed,	179
Rise, Progress, and Present State of the Secession Church,	180
Portraits by a Lady—taken in the Ventilator of the House of Commons,	182
The Comet—Infectious Character of Superstition,	183
VERSES FOR THE YOUNG,	183
ELEMENTS OF THOUGHT—The Press, &c.	184
COLUMN FOR THE LADIES—Governesses, &c.	184
THE STORY-TELLER—The old White Hat—and the old Grey Mare,	185
Sailors and Marines—Beauties of Flogging,	189
Old Foot-Paths, &c.	190
USEFUL NOTICES—Beer from Sugar, &c.	191
Scraps—Original and Selected,	192

EDINBURGH: Printed by and for JOHN JOHNSTONE, 19, St. James' Square.—Published by JOHN ANDERSON, Jun., Bookseller, 55, North Bridge Street, Edinburgh; by JOHN MACLEOD, and AITKINSON & Co., Booksellers, Glasgow; and sold by all Booksellers and Venders of Cheap Periodicals.

THE Schoolmaster,
AND
EDINBURGH WEEKLY MAGAZINE.

CONDUCTED BY JOHN JOHNSTONE.

THE SCHOOLMASTER IS ABROAD.—LORD BROUGHAM.

No. 13.—VOL. I.   SATURDAY, OCTOBER 27, 1832.   PRICE THREE-HALFPENCE.

ALL-HALLOW EVE.
THE SCOTCH HALLOW E'EN.

ABOUT the time this number of the SCHOOLMASTER comes into the hands of our young readers, preparations will be making, and invitations giving, for the due celebration of the social festivities and ancient mysteries of HALLOW E'EN. On "hauding Hallow E'en" Burns is, and ever will remain classic authority, and Burns, in one shape or other, is to be found in almost every house in the kingdom. All-Hallow Eve is the eve, or *vigil* of *All Saints' Day*— the 1st of November. It is accordingly celebrated on the last day of October. As a church festival, it is said by antiquarians to correspond with the *Ferialia* of the Romans, on which day they sacrificed in honour of the dead, offering up prayers to them, and making oblations. The Church of Rome consecrates it to Saints *en masse*, including all whom the limited number of 365 days cannot comprehend. Bonfires were made on this night in many parts of Scotland, Ireland, and in Wales; but the *Hallow Even blazes* is now nearly fallen into desuetude. From a letter in one of Mr. HONE's most amusing books, it appears that the custom of kindling fires is still observed near Paisley. In the parish of Callander, a Highland border parish, Hallow Even fires were lighted in every hamlet or *toun*, and it is probable the custom still lingers in those districts. When the fire was burnt out, the ashes were swept up into a line, in form of a circle, near the circumference of which a stone was placed for every member of the families connected with the fire; and the stone (or stones) displaced or tumbled over before next morning, foretold the death of the *fey* or doomed person for whom it was placed, before next Hallow Even. In the parish of Logierait, dry heath, broom, and flax-dressings were tied upon a pole, the fagot kindled, and carried round the village by a person running, attended by a crowd of followers. These Hallow Even fagots made a brilliant illumination through the parish in a dark night. Antiquarians derive this custom from the processions of the Romans, and other ancient nations, who bore torches round the tombs of their ancestors. OVID states that when those rites were neglected, the dead left their tombs and went howling about the streets, till the customary honours were paid to their *manes*. From BRAND, one of the most delightful of antiquarian gossips, we learn that,

"On this night young people in the north of England dive for apples, or catch at them, when stuck upon one end of a kind of hanging beam, at the other extremity of which fixed a lighted candle. This they do with their mouths only, their hands being tied behind their backs. From the custom of flinging nuts into the fire, or cracking them with their teeth, it has likewise obtained the name of *nut-crack night*. In an ancient illuminated missal in Mr. Douce's collection, a person is represented balancing himself upon a pole laid across two stools; at the end of the pole is a lighted candle, from which he is endeavouring to light another in his hand, at the risk of tumbling into a tub of water placed under him. A writer, about a century ago, says, 'This is the last day of October, and the birth of this packet is partly owing to the affair of this night. I am alone; but the servants having demanded *apples*, *ale*, and *nuts*, I took the opportunity of running back my own annals of *Allhallows Eve*; for you are to know, my lord, that I have been a mere adept, a most famous artist, both in the college and country, on occasion of *this anile chimerical solemnity*.'[a]

"Pennant says, that the young women in Scotland determine the figure and size of their husbands by *drawing cabbages blind-fold* on Allhallow Even, and, like the English, *fling nuts into the fire*. It is mentioned by Burns, in a note to his poem on 'Hallow E'en,' that 'The first ceremony of Hallow E'en is pulling each a stock or plant of kail. They must go out hand and hand, with eyes shut, and pull the first they meet with. Its being big or little, straight or crooked, is prophetic of the size and shape of the grand object of all their spells—the husband or wife. If any *yird*, or earth, stick to the root, that is *tocher*, or fortune; and the taste of the *custoc*, that is the heart of the stem, is indicative of the natural temper and disposition. Lastly, the stems, or, to give them their ordinary appellation, the *runts*, are placed somewhere above the head of the door; and the Christian names of the people whom chance brings into the house, are, according to the priority of placing the *runts*, the names in question.' It appears that the Welsh have 'a play in which the youth of both sexes seek for an even-leaved sprig of the ash: and the first of either sex that finds one, calls out Cyniver, and is answered by the first of the other that succeeds; and these two, if the omen fails not, are to be joined in wedlock.' †

"Burns says, that 'Burning the nuts is a favourite charm. They name the lad and lass to each particular nut, as they lay them in the fire; and accordingly as they burn quietly together, or start from beside one another, the course and issue of the courtship will be.' It is to be noted, that in Ireland, when the young women would know if their lovers are faithful, they put three nuts upon the bars of the grates, naming the nuts after the lovers. If a nut cracks or jumps, the lover will prove unfaithful; if it begins to blaze or burn, he has a regard for the person making the trial. If the nuts, named after the girl and her lover, burn together, they will be married. This sort of divination is

---
a Life of Harvey, the conjuror. 8vo. 1728.
† Owen's Welsh Dictionary.

also used in some parts of England at this time. Gay mentions it in his 'Spell:'—

> 'Two hazel nuts I threw into the flame,
> And to each nut I gave a sweetheart's name:
> This with *the loudest bounce* me sore amazed,
> That in a *flame of brightest colour* blazed;
> As *blazed the nut, so may thy passion grow*,
> For 'twas thy nut that did so brightly glow!'

"There are some lines by Charles Graydon, Esq.—'On Nuts burning Allhallows Eve.'

> 'These glowing nuts are emblems true
> Of what in human life we view;
> The ill-match'd couple fret and fume,
> And thus, in strife themselves consume;
> Or, from each other wildly start,
> And with a noise for ever part
> But see the happy, happy pair,
> Of genuine love and truth sincere;
> With mutual fondness while they burn,
> Still to each other kindly turn:
> And as the vital sparks decay
> Together gently sink away:
> Till life's fierce ordeal being past,
> Their mingled ashes rest at last,'*

The *blue clew*, the *three dishes*, the *apple ate at the glass*, the *hemp-seed* sawing, the *winning three wechts o' naething*, the *drouking the sark sleeve*, are all familiar spells. The *drapping of the egg* is less practised in the Lowland parts than the Highlands of Scotland; the white of the raw egg is dropt in small quantities into fair water in a glass vessel, when the fantastic floating forms into which it shoots, afford subject of divination. If a single particle of the yolk drop into the glass which is to shadow forth a young maiden's fortune, her fate is as certain as if she had lost the *tap pickle* in drawing the three stalks of oats. For the following selection of Hallow Even customs we are indebted to Mr. HONE's works:—

"At Aberdeen, 'The Midsummer Even Fire, a relic of Druidism, was kindled in some parts of this county; the Hallow Even fire, another relict of Druidism, was kindled in Buchan. Various magic ceremonies were then celebrated to counteract the influence of witches and demons, and to prognosticate to the young their success or disappointment in the matrimonial lottery. These being devoutly finished, the Hallow fire was kindled, and guarded by the male part of the family. Societies were formed, either by pique or humour, to scatter certain fires, and the attack and defence were often conducted with art and fury.' 'But now—the Hallow fire, when kindled, is attended by children only; and the country girl, renouncing the rites of magic, endeavours to enchant her swain by the charms of dress and of industry.'†

"Pennant records, that, in North Wales, 'there is a custom, upon All Saints' Eve, of making a great fire, called Coel Coeth, when every family about an hour in the night, makes a great bonfire in the most conspicuous place near the house; and when the fire is almost extinguished, every one throws a white stone into the ashes, having first marked it, then, having said their prayers, turning round the fire, they go to bed. In the morning, as soon as they are up, they come to search out the stones; and if any one of them is found wanting, they have a notion that the person who threw it in will die before he sees another All Saints' Eve.' They also distribute *soul cakes* on all Souls' Day, at the receiving of which poor people pray to God to bless the next crop of wheat.

"Mr. Owen's account of the Bards, in Sir R. Hoare's 'Itinerary of Archbishop Baldwin through Wales,' says, 'The autumnal fire is still kindled in North Wales, on the eve of the first day of November, and is attended by many ceremonies; such as running through the fire and smoke, each casting a stone into the fire, and all running off at the conclusion to escape from the black short-tailed sow; then supping upon parsnips, nuts, and apples; catching at an apple suspended by a string with the mouth alone, and the same by an apple in a tub of water; each throwing a nut into the fire, and those that burn bright betoken prosperity to the owners through the following year, but those that burn black and crackle denote misfortune. On the following morning the stones are searched for in the fire, and if any be missing they betide ill to those that threw them in.'

"At St. Kilda, on Hallow E'en night, they baked 'a large cake in form of a triangle, furrowed round, and which was to be all eaten that night.'* In England, there are still some parts wherein the grounds are illuminated upon the eve of All Souls, by bearing round them straw, or other fit materials, kindled into a blaze. The ceremony is called *a tinley*, and the Romish opinion among the common people is, that it represents an emblematical lighting of souls out of purgatory.

"The inhabitants of the Isle of Lewis, one of the western islands of Scotland, had an ancient custom, to sacrifice to a sea god, called Shony, at Hallow-tide, in the manner following: the inhabitants round the island came to the church of St. Mulvay, having each man his provision along with him. Every family furnished a peck of malt, and this was brewed into ale. One of their number was picked out to wade into the sea up to the middle; and carrying a cup of ale in his hand, standing still in that posture, cried out with a loud voice, saying, "Shony, I give you this cup of ale, hoping that you'll be so kind as to send us plenty of seaware, for enriching our ground the ensuing year;" and so threw the cup of ale into the sea. This was performed in the night-time. At his return to land, they all went to church, where there was a candle burning on the altar; and then standing silent for a little time, one of them gave a signal, at which the candle was put out, and immediately all of them went to the fields, where they fell a drinking their ale, and spent the remainder of the night in dancing and singing, &c."†

In Ireland, this vigil, in which it is believed the Prince of the Power of the Air, and his minions, have full scope, is observed with nearly the same ceremonies as in Scotland and the north of England. One custom peculiar to the north of Ireland is, for the girl who longs for a glimpse of her predestined partner, to go to some solitary spot by herself, and knitting nine knots on a garter, repeat the while the following spell:—

> "I knit this knot—this knot I knit,
> To see the sight I ne'er saw yet—
> To see my true love in his best array,
> Or the clothes that he wears every day;
> And if his livery I'm to wear,
> And if his children I'm to bear—
> Blithe and merry may he be,
> And may his face be turned to me."

The apparition of course passes the maiden, as in these ruled cases. The only drawback on these old usages was the mortal terror into which they sometimes threw young people, especially the *blue clew*, and the rites practised in solitude. In the southern suburbs of Edinburgh, a girl, a servant in a respectable family, died about twenty-five years ago, in consequence of the agony of fright into which she was thrown by the trick of a mischievous companion.

CURIOUS TRAITS OF FEUDAL MANNERS.

HIGHLAND GRAND VIZIERS.—Under the hereditary jurisdictions, the deputies of the lairds, or *Feudal barons*, the bailies, possessed or assumed delegated authority, of which they often made the most wanton and flagitious use; proving that excessive, and irresponsible *power* is not more dangerous to its unfortunate victims than to the petty or the great tyrant by whom it is exercised. The annals of petty tyranny and cruelty in our own country, if more ob-

---

* Graydon's Collection of Poems. 8vo. Dublin, 1801.
† Sinclair's Stat. Acc. of Scotland.

* Martin's Western Islands. † Ibid.

cure, are not a whit less dark and revolting than the history of despotism on the large scale of a Turkish or Russian despot, before opinion or dread of the bowstring had interposed a restraining power on their actions. The Bailie *More n Strathspey*—or *Big Bailie*—not much more than a century back, hung at pleasure; and, as is not unusual in such cases, took great pleasure in hanging:—so true it is, "that increase of appetite doth grow by what it feeds on;" and his whether for good or evil. On one occasion, the *Big Bailie* hanged two brothers on the same tree. He was, however, surpassed in enormity by another of these Highland janissaries in the same district. Bailie Roy, or the *Red* Bailie, who proceeded with *Jeddart justice*, then the only justice to be obtained, to hang a man, and try him afterwards. The Red Bailie's victim was named Stewart. Those hangings were always attended with the immediate confiscation of goods to the vizier; and indeed this was often the leading object of the execution. Roy once *boiled* the heads of two thieves he had hanged, and afterwards spiked them; and he anticipated the French Terrorists in *Noyades*. Two men he drowned in sacks near the manse of Abernethy, in Strathspey. This vizier founded a family, and purchased an estate with the fruits of his rapine and confiscations. Another of those wretches, *Bailie Bane*, or the *Fair Bailie*, for they were of all complexions, though of one nature, became so detested for his rapacity and cruelty, that the oppressed people drowned him in the Spey, and pretended that he had been thrown into the river from horseback. When affecting, with great sorrow, to search for his body in the Haughs of Cromdale, a man inquired what they sought, and when informed, said, "Turn back, turn back; ye'll find him up the water, like the fiddler's wife. He was ever acting against nature." The viziers, though they had holdings on the estates, had no emoluments save what they were able to extort from the wretched people by confiscations and fines, which they both imposed, and pocketed; they were also entitled to a few days of labour from the tenants or vassals; for they were still in fact vassals. This was called the *Bailie's Darg*,—it was in addition to the laird's dues, and was severely exacted. They were also entitled to a kind of legacy-duty, consisting of the best cow, ox, horse, or other property of which a man died in possession, and which, like the modern legacy-duty, was remorselessly levied from widows and orphans, at the time they most needed solace and assistance.

THE HEIRESS OF BRUX.

SINCE we are noticing feudal manners, we give an instance of the indomitable pride and fierce spirit of revenge which animated our ancestors, which is, we believe, unparalleled. It is given from the traditionary stores of a gentleman, originally of "*the north countrie*," whose reminiscences would be a treasure of Jacobite and popular antiquarian lore:—

Brux is the seat of the ancient Camerons, who were engaged in a quarrel with MUAT, Laird of Abergeldy, who at that time possessed most part of that country which is called Braemar, upon the river Dee. To put an end to their disputes, Cameron, Laird of Brux, and Muat of Abergeldy, agreed to meet at the hill of Drumgaudrum, near the river Don, and to bring twelve horsemen on each side, and there decide their quarrel by the sword. Muat treacherously brought two men on each horse, so that they were two to one. Brux, and all his sons, and most of his party, were killed: on the other side, Muat's two sons, the Laird of Macfadden, and several others, were killed upon the spot, and were all buried there; which place bears the name of Macfadden to this day. Brux left no children but one daughter, named Katherine, under the guardianship of the Earl of Mar, against whom Muat had rebelled, although his vassal. Brux's taking the earl's side was the cause of the quarrel. The young lady made a vow never to marry any but him who would revenge the death of her father. The Lord Forbes had four sons; one of them falling in love with Katherine Cameron, undertook to revenge the death of the Camerons. Muat, hearing of this, sent him a defiance or challenge, to meet him on the 8th of May, at a place called Badenyoan, near the head of Glenbucket. They both kept the appointment; but being afraid of treachery, each brought a great number of their friends and followers along with them. When they met, to prevent more bloodshed, they agreed on a single combat; and both parties solemnly vowed to live in peace with whoever of them should be victorious. But at this place Forbes killed Muat; and here there was a monument set up, which is called Clachmuat, or Muat's stone to this day.

Of this event, tradition gives an account somewhat different, and with additional circumstances, of which the following only are perhaps worthy of notice, viz. That Katherine Cameron, after her father's death, lived under the immediate care or guardianship of her mother, Lady Brux, a woman animated by a spirit suited to the times; and who, exasperated by the treacherous murder of her husband, and successive outrages of the Muat clan, is stated to have made the vow, (ascribed with less probability to the youthful Katherine,) "*That whoever should bring to her Muat's head*, or evidence of having killed him, *should have her daughter and the estate of Brux*." Such a prize, so to be won, could not remain long uncontended for. Robert Forbes, the youngest of Drimminor's sons, a warm admirer of the young lady, challenged Muat, fought, and killed him with his dirk or skien, after a long and desperate contest, as narrated in the poem. Going directly from the field of battle to the house of his fair one, and bearing, no doubt, ample credentials of his zeal and success, Forbes was proceeding to claim the promised reward, and to deprecate the postponement of his happiness to any distant period, when Lady Brux, in a tone and manner sufficiently characteristic of her feelings on the occasion, settled at once all dispute as to the time and preparatory ceremonials of the marriage, by declaring, that "*Kate Cameron should go to bed with Rob Forbes as lang's Muat's blood was reekin' on his gully.*" Of this arrangement, report sayeth, that the gallant Forbes expressed entire approbation, and that his blushing bride did not permit the maiden scruples she was about to make to stand a moment in competition with her filial obedience.

AN OLD ENGLISH BARONET'S OPINION OF MODERN MANNERS.

"ALL is grown pride and poverty, excess and want, show and unsubstantiality. We drive out eight or twelve miles to dinner, when we should be thinking of bed-time; and if I have been shooting in the morning, I live all day in hopes of a disappointment. I visit men and women who care for neither me nor my wife, and whose only thought, from the moment I enter their houses, is to make the greatest display possible; and, to do them justice, this is the exact feeling we have towards them. In my younger days some of my friends thought that I sometimes kept *low* company:—Low company did I? Is it family they alluded to? I am sure I visit more ——— and bastards among this high grade! Or did they mean dunces and fools? I can produce five to one in our privileged order. As for honour and honesty, credit and reputation, I assure you that the intrusion of sycophants and flatterers is so predominant, and the pretensions of upstart professional gentlemen, ashamed of business, trade, and reasonable employ ment, so pressing, that I have greater selection to make than ever I did in my life. Then, during the visiting season, my servants, carriages, and horses, are, from morning till night, ay, and through the night, employed in greater scenes of idleness and demoralization than they ever knew in my very idlest days; when I drove from race course to race course, and drank claret and champagne by the dozen. It cannot last, I plainly see, for some of us are brought to an end year after year. The Rev. Mr. ———, and his wife and family, is just gone off to the continent, while the valuable Rectory goes through a course of sequestration. Mr. M—— has cut down the fine plantation of Oaks, which his grandfather planted, and W——'s race-horses all went to the hammer last week."——This unfortunate baronet had been entrapped into fashionable society by a fine lady wife. She died when he had just full time to understand and despise that utterly worthless and presumptuous state of society, which looks down with superciliousness upon the lower orders. He had found that a "superior style" is only superior show. Characters of wit, he discovered, were very laboured, very uncertain, and yet more wearisome from their sameness. But what proved most offensive to his feelings was to hear upstart great ones talk of "their family and their pedigree." A remark of his will not soon be forgotten in his own neighbourhood. The conversation had continued for two or three hours—of " Who are they ? what are they ?" in reference to the whole circle of the neighbourhood having pretensions to gentility, and all in reference to family consequence and property, when Sir Harry said, " I think a man ought to be stripped of honour as soon as he has lost character. There is not a man in this county can boast higher pedigree than three, one of whom I should little scruple to name a notorious blackleg, the second an arrant swindler, and the third I could put upon trial for his life for forgery. There is a fourth who can trace his pedigree to half the great families in the country, and yet is more infamous than all the rest put together; and it is not a little remarkable that the two proudest people in our neighbourhood are *natural* children. The gentleman is son of a West India planter ; and his lady is the daughter of a celebrated baronet and Mrs. ———, the actress."

FASHIONABLES.

OF all the *castes* into which this country is divided, none is so unhappy as that of the Fashionables, for they alone feel the burden of existence : the other end of society resorts to vice through poverty, the Exclusive to crime from the lack of the power of self-amusement. The extremes meet in the character of their enjoyments, if not in their theatre. A London Exclusive of the present day is pronounced by the Prince Puchler Muskau, an excellent judge—" a bad, flat, dull impression of a *roué* of the Regency and a courtier of Louis the Fifteenth ; both have in common, selfishness, levity, boundless vanity, and an utter want of heart ; both think they can set themselves above every thing by means of contempt, derision, and insolence." Nothing can be more true than this. The class of Fashionables in England are stupid among themselves, and boorish to all others. The Nobodies, we must say, very frequently deserve their contempt, by endeavouring to imitate these odious models. The object of fashionable ambition is always a paltry one: the brilliancy of its votaries consists in a display of some small peculiarity, which mere wealth toils to imitate— some arbitrary disposition of a vehicle or a garment: and in this poor avoidance of the old or the vulgar, they place all their pride, and exhaust all their talents. The principle of exclusion is not inconsistent with enjoyment, if the Exclusives but possessed the social qualities ; but they have neither wit, enthusiasm, imagination, nor learning: the only distinctions they can reach are such as might be attained by stable boys and cabriolet drivers—they consist merely in a violation of all those points of manners and feelings that other classes hold to be respectable. This is an unhappy peculiarity, which, while it separates them from the rest of their countrymen, equally holds them apart from maintaining real fellowship among themselves. They are stars, indeed, but anxiously watching each other's fall: they are atoms of matter brought together by the attraction of cohesion, but rejecting all real union by their principles of repulsion. Among other virtues of the Reform Bill, we anticipate that it will put down the Exclusives and the Fashionable World ; not by interfering with it directly, but by raising the middle classes so far in independence, importance, and virtuous ambition, as to drive the industrious *ennuyés* into their real insignificance. Political power has more to do with the Exclusive principle than has been commonly imagined ; a secret which has, however, struck the German Prince, during his attentive observation of the phenomenon of English society. At present, it is rather equivocal taste to be in the House of Commons —the greater part of that House is pronounced not to be " good society:" wait a while, and there will probably be less "good society" in it than even now ; for, to be a patient and intelligent guardian of the public interests, is no qualification for "good society ;" to be upright, impartial, and persevering in the discharge of duty, implies no pretension to fashion ; nay, a man might possess all the talents and the virtues of the model of a legislator, and yet possess no claim to be any thing but a Nobody.

THE BARN OWL.

AMONGST the numberless verses which might be quoted against the family of the owl, I think I only know of one little ode which expresses any pity for it. Our nurserymaid used to sing it to the tune of the Storm, " Cease, rude Boreas, blust'ring railer." I remember the two first stanzas of it :—

" Once I was a monarch's daughter,
  And sat on a lady's knee ;
But I'm now a nightly rover,
  Banish'd to the ivy-tree.

Crying hoo hoo, hoo hoo, hoo hoo,
  Hoo hoo, hoo, my feet are cold !
Pity me, for here you see me,
  Persecuted, poor, and old."

I beg the reader's pardon for this exordium. I have introduced it, in order to shew how little chance there has been, from days long passed and gone to the present time, of studying the haunts and economy of the owl, because its unmerited bad name has created it a host of foes, and doomed it to destruction from all quarters. Some few, certainly, from time to time, have been kept in cages, and in aviaries. But nature rarely thrives in captivity, and very seldom appears in her true character when she is encumbered with chains, or is to be looked at by the passing crowd through bars of iron. However, the scene is now going to change ; and I trust that the reader will contemplate the owl with more friendly feelings, and under quite different circumstances. Here, no rude schoolboy ever approaches its retreat; and those who once dreaded its diabolical doings are now fully satisfied that it no longer meddles with their destinies, or has any thing to do with the repose of their departed friends. Indeed, human wretches in the shape of body-snatchers, seem here in England to have usurped the office of the owl in our churchyards; " et vendunt tumulis corpora rapta suis." *

Up to the year 1813, the barn owl had a sad time of it at Walton Hall. Its supposed mournful notes alarmed the aged housekeeper. She knew full well what sorrow it had brought into other houses when she was a young woman; and there was enough of mischief in the midnight wintry blast, without having it increased by the dismal screams of something which people knew very little about, and which every body said was far too busy in the churchyard at night-time. Nay, it was a well-known fact, that if any person were sick in the neighbourhood, it would be for ever looking in at the window, and holding a conversation outside with somebody, they did not know whom. The gamekeeper agreed with her in every thing she said on this important subject; and he always stood better in her books when he had managed to shoot a bird of this bad and mischievous family. However, in 1813, on my return from the wilds of Guiana, having suffered myself, and learned mercy, I broke in pieces the code of penal laws which the knavery of the gamekeeper and the lamentable ignorance of the other servants had hitherto put in force, far too successfully, to thin the numbers of this poor, harmless, unsuspecting tribe. On the ruin of the old gateway, against which, tradition says, the waves of the lake have dashed for the better part of a thousand years, I made a place with stone and mortar, about four feet square, and fixed a thick oaken stick firmly into it. Huge masses of ivy now quite cover t. In about a month or so after it was finished, a pair of barn owls came and took up their abode in it. I threatened to strangle the keeper if ever, after this, he molested either the old birds, or their young ones; and I assured the housekeeper that I would take upon myself the whole responsibility of all the sickness, wo, and sorrow that the new tenants might bring into the Hall. She made a low curtsy; as much as to say, "Sir, I fall into your will and pleasure;" but I saw in her eye that she had made up her mind to have to do with things of fearful and portentous shape, and to hear many a midnight wailing in the surrounding woods. I do not think, that up to the day of this old lady's death, which took place in her eighty-fourth year, she ever looked with pleasure or contentment on the barn owl, as it flew round the large sycamore-trees which grow near the old ruined gateway.

When I found that this first settlement on the gateway had succeeded so well, I set about forming other establishments. This year I have had four broods, and I trust that next season I can calculate on having nine. This will be a pretty increase, and it will help to supply the place of those which in this neighbourhood are still unfortunately doomed to death, by the hand of cruelty or superstition. We can now always have a peep at the owls, in their habitation on the old ruined gateway, whenever we choose. Confident of protection, these pretty birds betray no fear when the stranger mounts up to their place of abode. I would here venture a surmise, that the barn owl sleeps standing. Whenever we go to look at it, we invariably see it upon the perch bolt upright, and often with its eyes closed, apparently fast asleep. Buffon and Bewick err (no doubt, unintentionally) when they say that the barn owl snores during its repose. What they took for snoring was the cry of the young birds for food. I had fully satisfied myself on this score some years ago. However, in December, 1823, I was much astonished to hear this same snoring kind of noise, which had been so common in the month of July. On ascending the ruin, I found a brood of young owls in the apartment.

Upon this ruin is placed a perch, about a foot from the hole at which the owls enter. Sometimes, at mid-day,

* And sell bodies torn from their tombs.

when the weather is gloomy, you may see an owl upon it, apparently enjoying the refreshing diurnal breeze. This year (1831) a pair of barn owls hatched their young, on the 7th September, in a sycamore-tree, near the old ruined gateway.

If this useful bird caught its food by day, instead of hunting for it by night, mankind would have ocular demonstrations of its utility in thinning the country of mice, and it would be protected and encouraged everywhere. It would be with us what the ibis was with the Egyptians. When it has young, it will bring a mouse to the nest about every twelve or fifteen minutes. But, in order to have a proper idea of the enormous quantity of mice which this bird destroys, we must examine the pellets which it ejects from its stomach in the place of its retreat. Every pellet contains from four to seven skeletons of mice. In sixteen months from the time that the apartment of the owl on the old gateway was cleaned out, there has been a deposit of above a bushel of pellets.

The barn owl sometimes carries off rats. One evening I was sitting under a shed, and killed a very large rat, as it was coming out of a hole, about ten yards from where I was watching it. I did not go to take it up, hoping to get another shot. As it lay there a barn owl pounced upon it, and flew away with it.

This bird has been known to catch fish. Some years ago, on a fine evening in the month of July, long before it was dark, as I was standing on the middle of the bridge, and minuting the owl by my watch, as she brought mice into her nest, all on a sudden she dropped perpendicularly into the water. Thinking that she had fallen down in epilepsy, my first thoughts were to go and fetch the boat; but before I had well got to the end of the bridge, I saw the owl rise out of the water, with a fish in her claws, and take it to the nest. This fact is mentioned by the late much revered and lamented Mr. Aitkinson, of Leeds, in his " Compendium," in a note, under the signature of W., a friend of his, to whom I had communicated it a few days after I had witnessed it.

I cannot make up my mind to pay any attention to the description of the amours of the owl by a modern writer; at least, the barn owl plays off no buffooneries here, such as those which he describes. An owl is an owl all the world over, whether under the influence of Momus, Venus, or Diana.

When farmers complain that the barn owl destroys the eggs of their pigeon, they lay the saddle on the wrong horse. They ought to put it on the rat. Formerly I could get very few young pigeons, till the rats were excluded effectually from the dove-cot. Since that took place it has produced a great abundance every year, though the barn owls frequent it, and are encouraged all around it. The barn owl merely resorts to it for repose and concealment. If it were really an enemy to the dove-cot, we should see the pigeons in commotion as soon as it begins its evening flight; but the pigeons heed it not; whereas, if the sparrow-hawk or wind-hover should make their appearance, the whole community would be up at once, proof sufficient that the barn owl is not looked upon as a bad, or even a suspicious, character by the inhabitants of the dove-cot.

Till lately, a great and well-known distinction has always been made betwixt the screeching and the hooting of owls. The tawny owl is the only owl which hoots; and when I am in the woods after poachers, about an hour before daybreak, I hear with extreme delight its loud, clear, and sonorous notes, resounding far and near through hill and dale. Very different from these notes is the screech of the barn owl. But Sir William Jardine informs us that this owl hoots; and that he has shot it in the act of hooting. This is stiff authority; and I believe it, because it comes from the pen of Sir William Jardine. Still, however, methinks that it ought to be taken in a somewhat diluted state; we know full well that most extraordinary examples of splendid talents do, from time to time, make their appearance on the world's wide stage. Thus, Franklin brought down fire from the skies:—" Eripuit fulmen cœlo, sceptrumque tyrannis."* Paganini has led all London captive by a single piece of twisted catgut ;—" Tu potes reges comitesque stultos ducere."† Leibnitz tells us of a dog in Germany that could pronounce distinctly thirty words. Goldsmith informs us that he once heard a raven whistle the tune of the "Shamrock" with great distinctness, truth, and humour. With these splendid examples before our eyes, may we not be inclined to suppose that the barn owl which Sir William shot in the absolute act of hooting may have been a gifted bird, of superior parts and knowledge (una de multis,‡ as Horace says of Miss Danaus,) endowed, perhaps, from its early days, with the faculty of hooting, or else skilled in the art by having been taught it by its neighbour the tawny owl? I beg to remark, that though I unhesitatingly grant the faculty of hooting to this one particular individual owl, still I flatly refuse to believe that hooting is common to barn owls in general. Ovid, in his sixth book "Fastorum," pointedly says, that it screeched in his day :—

"Est illis strigibus nomen ; sed nominis hujus
Causa, quod horrendâ stridere nocte solent." ||

The barn owl may be heard shrieking here perpetually on the portico, and in the large sycamore-trees near the house. It shrieks equally when the moon shines and when the night is rough and cloudy ; and he who takes an interest in it may here see the barn owl the night through when there is a moon ; and he may hear it shriek, within a few yards of him, long before dark ; and again, often after daybreak, before it takes its final departure to its wonted resting-place. I am amply repaid for the pains I have taken to protect and encourage the barn owl ; it pays me a hundred fold by the enormous quantity of mice which it destroys throughout the year. The servants now no longer wish to persecute it. Often, on a fine summer's evening, with delight I see the villagers loitering under the sycamore-trees longer than they would otherwise do, to have a peep at the barn owl, as it leaves the ivy-mantled tower : fortunate for it, if, in lieu of exposing itself to danger, by mixing with the world at large, it only knew the advantage of passing its nights at home ; for here

No birds that haunt my valley free
 To slaughter I condemn ;
Taught by the Power that pities me,
 I learn to pity them.

CHARLES WATERTON. §

Walton Hall.

THE STICKET MINISTER.

IN our parish there lived a young lad, a sticket minister, not very alluring in his looks ; indeed, to say the truth, he was by many, on account of them, thought to be not far short of a haverel ; for he was lank and most uncomely, being in-kneed ; but, for all that, the minister said he was a young man of great parts, and had not only a streak of geni, but a vast deal of inordinate erudition. He went commonly by the name of Dominie Quarto ; and it came to pass, that he set his affections on a weel-faured lassie, the daughter of Mrs. Stoups, who keepit the Thistle Inn. In this there was nothing wonderful, for she was a sweet maiden, and nobody ever saw her without wishing her well. But she could not abide the Dominie : and, indeed, it was no wonder, for he certainly was not a man to pleasure a woman's eye. Her affections were settled on a young lad called Jock Sym, a horse-couper, a blithe heartsome young man, of a genteel manner, and in great repute, therefore, among the gentlemen.

He won Mally Stoups' heart ; they were married, and, in the fulness of time thereafter, her pains came on, and I was sent to ease her. She lay in a back room, that looked into their pleasant garden. Half up the lower casement of the window, there was a white muslin curtain, made out of one of her mother's old-fashioned tamboured aprons, drawn across from side to side, for the window had no shutters. It would be only to distress the reader to tell what she suffered. Long she struggled, and weak she grew ; and a sough of her desperate case went up and down the town like the plague that walketh in darkness. Many came to inquire for her, both gentle and semple ; and it was thought that the Dominie would have been in the crowd of callers ; but he came not.

In the midst of her suffering, when I was going about my business in the room, with the afflicted lying-in woman, I happened to give a glint to the window, and startled I was, to see, like a ghost, looking over the white curtain, the melancholious visage of Dominie Quarto, with watery eyes glistening like two stars in the candle light.

I told one of the women who happened to be in the way, to go out to the sorrowful young man, and tell him not to look in at the window ; whereupon she went out, and remonstrated with him for some time. While she was gone, sweet Mally Stoups and her unborn baby were carried away to Abraham's bosom. This was a most unfortunate thing ; and I went out before the straighting-board could be gotten, with a heavy heart, on account of my poor family that might suffer, if I was found guilty of being to blame.

I had not gone beyond the threshold of the back-door that led into the garden, when I discerned a dark figure between me and the westling scad of the setting moon. On going towards it, I was greatly surprised to find the weeping Dominie, who was keeping watch for the event there, and had just heard what had happened, by one of the women telling another.

This symptom of true love and tenderness made me forget my motherly anxieties, and I did all I could to console the poor lad ; but he was not to be comforted, saying, "It was a great trial when it was ordained that she should lie in the arms of Jock Sym, but it's faur waur to think that the kirk-yard hole is to be her bed, and her bridegroom the worm."

Poor forlorn creature, I had not a word to say. Indeed, he made my heart swell in my bosom ; and I could never forget the way in which he grat over my hand, that he took between both of his, as a dear thing, that he was prone to fondle and mourn over.

But his cutting grief did not end that night ; on the Sabbath evening following, as the custom is in our parish, Mrs. Sym was ordained to be interred ; and there was a great gathering of freends and neighbours ; for both she and her gudeman were well thought of. Everybody expected the Dominie would be there, for his faithfulness was spoken of by all pitiful tongues ; but he stayed away for pure grief ; he hid himself from the daylight, and the light of every human eye. In the gloaming, however, after, as the betherel went to ring the eight o'clock bell, he saw the Dominie standing with a downcast look, near the new grave, all which made baith a long and a sad story, for many a day among us : I doubt if it's forgotten yet. As for me, I never thought of it without a pang : but all trades have their troubles ; and the death of a young wife and her unborn baby, in her nineteenth year, is not one of the least that I have had to endure in mine.

But, although I met, like many others, in my outset, both mortifications and difficulties, and what was worse than all, I could not say that I was triumphant in my endeavours : yet, like the Doctors, either good luck or experience made me gradually gather a repute for skill and discernment, insomuch that I became just wonderful for the request I was in. It is therefore needless for me to make a strive for the entertainment of the reader, by rehearsing all the han'lings that I had ; but, as some of them were of a notable kind, I will pass over the generality, and only make Nota-bena here and there of those that were particular, as well as the births of the babies that afterwards came to be something in the world.—*From the Howdie, an Autobiography, given in Tait's Magazine, by John Galt.*

---

* He snatched lightning from heaven, and the sceptre from tyrants.
† Thou canst lead kings and their silly nobles.
‡ One out of many.
|| They are called owls (striges,) because they are accustomed to screech (stridere) by night.
§ The eccentric traveller, sportsman, and naturalist, whose fight with a cayman is so well known.

ONE OF SIR H. DAVY'S EXPERIMENTS.

Mr. Watt's observations on the respiration of diluted hydro-carbonate by man, and the experiments of Dr. Beddoes on the destruction of animals by the same gas, proved that its effects were highly deleterious.

As it destroyed life, apparently by rendering the muscular fibre inirritable, without producing any previous excitement, I was anxious to compare its sensible effects with those of nitrous oxide, which at this time I believed to destroy life by producing the highest possible excitement.

In the first experiment, I breathed for nearly a minute three quarts of *hydro-carbonate*, mingled with nearly two quarts of atmospheric air. It produced a slight giddiness, pain in the head, and a momentary loss of voluntary power; my pulse was rendered much quicker and more feeble. These effects, however, went off in five minutes, and I had no return of giddiness.

Emboldened by this trial, I introduced into a silk bag four quarts of gas nearly pure, which was carefully produced from the decomposition of water by charcoal an hour before, and which had a very strong and disagreeable smell.

My friend, Mr James Tobin, junior, being present, after a forced exhaustion of my lungs, the nose being accurately closed, I made three inspirations and expirations of the hydrocarbonate. The first inspiration produced a sort of numbness and loss of feeling in the chest, and about the pectoral muscles. After the second, I lost all power of perceiving external things, and had no distinct sensation, except that of terrible oppression on the chest. During the third expiration, this feeling subsided, I seemed sinking into annihilation, and had just power enough to cast off the mouthpiece from my unclosed lips.

A short interval must have passed, during which I respired common air, before the objects around me were distinguishable. On recollecting myself, I faintly articulated, "*I do not think I shall die.*" Placing my finger on the wrist, I found my pulse thread-like, and beating with excessive quickness. In less than a minute, I was able to walk, and the painful oppression on the chest directed me to the open air.

After making a few steps, which carried me to the garden, my head became giddy, my knees trembled, and I had just sufficient voluntary power to throw myself on the grass. Here the painful feelings of the chest increased with such violence as to threaten suffocation. At this moment I asked for some nitrous oxide. Mr. Dwyer brought me a mixture of that gas with oxygen, and I breathed it for a minute, and believed myself recovered.

In five minutes the painful feelings began gradually to diminish; in an hour they had nearly disappeared, and I felt only excessive weakness, and a slight swimming of the head. My voice was very feeble and indistinct.

I afterwards walked slowly for half-an-hour with Mr. Tobin, and on my return was so much stronger and better as to believe that the effects of the gas had entirely passed off; though my pulse was 120, and very feeble, I continued without pain for nearly three quarters of an hour, when the giddiness returned with such violence as to oblige me to lie on the bed; it was accompanied with nausea, loss of memory, and deficient sensation.

In about an hour and a half, the giddiness went off, and was succeeded by an excruciating pain in the forehead, and between the eyes, with transient pains in the chest and extremities.

Towards night these affections gradually diminished; and at ten no disagreeable feeling, except weakness, remained.— I slept sound, and awoke in the morning very feeble, and very hungry. No recurrence of the symptoms took place, and I had nearly recovered my strength by the evening.

NOTES ON GERMANY.

At the frontiers of Austria, every one that arrives is scrutinised and searched with great strictness—a prohibited book or a masonic paper is of itself sufficient to lead to arrest and imprisonment. Nothing but an English passport sets aside the rigours and vexatious movements of the police.

Prussia, great and powerful since 1815, divides with Austria the tutelage of Germany. These two principal powers of Germany are the only ones who have refused to their people Constitutional Institutions. From this difference of ideas with regard to government, continual conflicts arise, and the small states which are all constitutional, find themselves placed in a very difficult position, in being obliged to follow the impulse which they receive from the Courts of Vienna and Berlin— such being often in direct opposition to their wants and their interests. The Prince Royal seriously employ shimself in the affairs of government; his anti-constitutional sentiments, which have been publicly avowed upon different occasions, (recently even in the presence of several princes whose territories enjoy constitutions, he drank to the extinction of all constitutions in Germany,) do not presage any near or favourable change for the Prussian states.

The kingdom of Bavaria, the principal constitutional power of Germany, is at this moment in extreme agitation; the storm which everywhere threatens, is on the point of breaking out in the Rhenish provinces, belonging to Bavaria. The present King of Bavaria formerly excited great hopes, but which have not been realised. He was very popular when Prince Royal, and saluted by the unanimous applause of his people when he came to the throne. These brilliant illusions, however, have passed away, and some parts of his private conduct have given great offence. His Bavarian Majesty loves nature and women, and makes frequent journeys to Italy, to visit the Pope and his mistresses, usually returning from these campaigns much fatigued. Meeting by chance with a beautiful English woman, who came to pass the winter at Munich, he became so captivated with her, that, forgetting all sense of propriety, he wished to present her himself to the queen. A scene followed which became a scandal at court, and amongst the public, for the king, in the height of his amorous warmth, persisted in attempting to present Lady E—— to the queen, whilst the latter, actuated by just indignation, quitted the apartment, saying to him, "I was aware long since that you would deceive me as you have deceived your people." It appears, however, that this lesson went for nothing. Lady E—— became the avowed mistress of the king, who went in the spring to do penance for his sins at Rome.

Next in order comes the Prince Elector of Hesse, whose small empire does not reckon more than 500,000 inhabitants. For a long time the daughter of a watchmaker at Berlin, raised to the title of the Countess Reichenbach, has lived publicly with this prince, and has a numerous family by him. The electress was forced to receive her at court with all possible distinction. Several times this unfortunate princess took refuge in a foreign country belonging to the family of the King of Prussia, but the influence of the Cabinet of Berlin succeeded in obliging her husband to take steps to induce her to return home, and she for some time lived at Cassel in good understanding with her rival. The events in France having produced a great agitation in Germany, this prince became frightened; and purchasing considerable property at Frankfort, for his dear countess and her family, he retired thither himself, whilst public opinion openly pronounced against himself and his mistress. The people agreed with the Chamber of Representatives, in refusing their consent to a constitutional prince abandoning his states, and residing in a foreign territory; and he was forced to return home. Not daring to occupy his magnificent palace at Cassel, he chose a small frontier town for his residence, which produced much aggravated discontent in the capital. Seeing that this state of things could not long continue, he handed the reigns of government to the hereditary prince, intending to reside at Montpellier, in France. Scarcely installed in his high functions, the Prince Regent, following the example of his father, purchased the wife of a Prussian officer for 30,000 crowns, gave her the title of Baroness de Schaumberg, and concluded with her a marriage Morganate, in which the female is a sort of privileged concubine.

In Saxony, the old king (who, through his friendship for Napoleon, lost half his territories) promenades the streets of his capital every morning before daylight, repeating his prayers.

The Grand Duke of Hesse Darmstadt passes much of his time in eating and drinking.

The other little sovereigns n Germany possess most of them such small states, that their existence is unknown to the rest of the world, unless some happy chance draws them forth from their profound obscurity. The Prince of Cobourg would never have been known in Great Britain or elsewhere, but for his marriage with a princess of England; nor would the Prince of Hombourg, who reigns over a population of 20,000 and has an army of 200 men, have been distinguished but for his marriage with an English princess.

Animal Life.—Average duration of human life, by an experienced zoologist :—Quadrupeds. The horse, from 8 to 32 years; ox, 20; bull, 15; cow, 23; ass, 33; mule, 18; sheep, 10; ram, 15; dog, 14 to 25; swine, 25; goat, 8; cat, 10.—Birds. Pigeon, 8 years; turtle dove, 35; goose, 28; parrot, from 30 to 100 : raven, 100.—Amphibid. Turtles and tortoises, 50 to 100.

ELEMENTS OF THOUGHT.

WHAT HAVE I TO DO WITH POLITICS?—NOTHING.

From this important question, my countrymen, so weakly and wickedly answered, have arisen all the evils which have afflicted the nation through a long succession of ages. This is the fountain from which not only waters of bitterness, but rivers of blood, have flowed! Did you ever doubt what connexion you had with morals and virtue? And what are politics but that wide system of duties which nation owes to nation. Politics are to nations what morals are to individuals. They have lately, indeed, been called the principal branch of morals—I think they are more: I hold them to be the great trunk of morals, on which all the other duties depend but as branches. It is only upon a strict performance of these duties that you can expect to be prosperous and happy as a people. Now as war can only be just on one side, it must be murder on the other. The good or evil qualities of all actions depend, not on the number or dignity of the agents, but on their tendency to promote the good of mankind. By this standard must equally be tried the actions of the peasant and the prince. In the guilt or innocence of the present war, as we all contribute to carry it on, either by personal service, or the taxes which we pay, the declaration of war by the King has deeply involved us. We are bound, therefore, as moral and accountable agents, to examine the justice of the measure. The means of information are at hand, and let me assure you, that when knowledge is a duty, ignorance is a crime.—*Gerald.**

[This was written in warning at the beginning of the ruinous French war, which ended with the restoration of the now expelled Bourbons, and after the grinding National Debt of Great Britain amounted to sums which may be seen in the following curious calculations]:—On the 5th June, 1811, the debt, funded and unfunded, was L.811,898,811, which is equal to 773,236,267 guineas, which at five dwts. eight grains each guinea, weigh 6312 tons, 11 cwts. three quarters, five pounds, one ounce, six drams avoirdupois. Now suppose a waggon and four horses to extend in length 20 yards, and to carry two and a half tons of the said guineas, the number of teams necessary to carry the whole would extend in length 28 miles and 23 yards. To count the debt in shillings, at the rate of 30s. in a minute, for ten hours a-day and six days a-week, would take 2469 years, 306 days, 17 hours, and 30 minutes. Its height in guineas, supposing twenty to be an inch, would be 610 miles, 339 yards, and 9 inches. And supposing each guinea an inch in diameter, they would extend in a right line 12,203 miles, 150 yards, and 7 inches. Moreover, the said guineas would cover in space 348 acres, 2 roods, and 202 yards; and lastly, in shillings, each an inch in diameter, would cover 7319 acres, one rood, and 34 yards.

The last wars cost Britain not less than L.2,040,000,000 of our money. To aid our conceptions of the vastness of this sum, suppose this money were in gold, and valued at L.5 per ounce, it would weigh about 14,000 tons, which would load, at three tons each, 4800 waggons; and if in silver, at 5s. per ounce, about 76,000 waggons; and allowing 20 yards to a waggon, would reach, in a direct line, about 864 miles. If an ounce of gold can be drawn into a wire of 1000 feet long, the above sum would be sufficient to make a girdle for the whole globe!!!

* Need we say Joseph Gerald the Political Martyr.

CONSCIENCE.

He that hath a scrupulous conscience is like a horse that is not well broken; he starts at every bird that flies out of the hedge. A knowing man will do that which a tender conscienced man dares not do, by reason of his ignorance. The other knows there is no hurt; as a child is afraid to go into the dark when a man is not, because he knows there is no danger. But if one once come to leave that outloose, as to pretend a conscience against law, who knows what inconvenience may follow! For thus, suppose an Anabaptist comes and takes my horse;—I sue him; he tells me he did according to his conscience; his consicence tells him all things are common among the Saints,* what is mine is his, therefore you do ill to make a law that a man who takes another's horse shall be hanged. What can I say to this man? He does according to his conscience. Why is not he as honest a man as he that pretends *a ceremony established by law is against his conscience?* Generally, to pretend conscience against law is dangerous; in some case haply we may. Some men make it a case of conscience, whether a man may have a pigeon-house, because his pigeons eat other folk's corn. But there is no such thing as conscience in the business; the matter is, whether he be a man of such quality, that the state allows him to have a dove-house; if so, there's an end to the business—his pigeons have a right to eat where they please.—*Selden.*

NOT GUILTY.

There is some confusion about this plea, and from conscientious scruples men have refused to employ it. Selden says, "A man may plead *not guilty,* and yet tell no lie;" not that he is conscious of innocence, but that, "by the law no man is bound to accuse himself;" so that when I say *not guilty,* the meaning is, "I am not so foolish as to tell you. If you will bring me to a trial, and have me punished for this which you lay to my charge, prove it against me."

RIGHTS OF CHURCH PROPERTY.

The unwillingness of the monks (or any churchmen) to part with their land, will fall to be just nothing; because they were yielded up to the king by a supreme hand, namely, Parliament. If a king conquer another country, the people are loath to lose their lands; yet no churchman will deny but that the king may give them to whom he pleases. If a Parliament make a law concerning leather, or any other commodity, you or I, for example, are Parliament men; perhaps, in respect to our own private interests, we are against it, yet the major part conclude it; we are then included, and the law is good.—*Selden.*

BISHOPS.

There is no government enjoined by example but by precept; it does not follow that we must have bishops still because we have had them so long. All is as the state pleases.—*Selden.*

Heretofore the nation let the church alone, let them do as they would, because they had something else to think of, viz. wars; but now, in time of peace, we begin to examine all things, and will have nothing; but grow dainty, and wanton—just as in a family, when the heir goes a hunting—he never considers how his meat is drest, but takes a bit and away; but when he stays within, then he grows curious; he does not like this, nor he does not like that; he will have his meat drest his own way; or peradventure, he *will cook it himself.*—*Selden.*

* A wild sect of Anabaptists in Germany held these tenets. There were a few of them in England in the time of Selden.

THE STORY-TELLER.

THE SOLDIER'S RETURN.
ABRIDGED FROM MRS. OPIE.

Simple is the story that I am going to tell, and lowly are the hero and heroines of it; and perhaps, were I to relate it in their humble language, its interest would be much increased: but I dare not do so—lest, while pleasing some, I should displease many: therefore, should my readers experience neither interest nor pleasure in the perusal of this tale, I can only exclaim, " I wish you had heard Mary tell it herself!"

Fanny Hastings was the daughter of a publican in the little town of ———, in South Wales. When she was only eight years old both her parents died, and she became dependent on the kindness of an aunt, and on the labours of her own hands, for support; and she soon found sufficient employment to enable her, with the aid of her relation, not only to maintain herself, but to appear better dressed than many girls whose situation in life was not higher than her own.

Fanny was beautiful; so much so, that her beauty was the subject of conversation, even amongst the genteel circles in ———, and many a youth of the same station with herself was earnest to be her accepted lover; but professions of love she listened to with pleasure from one only.

Lewellyn Morgan, with his father and mother, and his cousin Mary, was her opposite neighbour. His father was a carpenter, his mother took in plain work, and he himself was undecided whether to follow his father's business or seek a different employment,—when he fell in love with our handsome sempstress.

Fanny, whether from coquetry or convenience, always sat by the window at work: it was therefore impossible for her not to observe Lewellyn sometimes,—particularly as he was young, neatly dressed, well made, and as much an object of admiration to the women as she was to the men: besides, his eyes seemed to be often on the watch for hers, and it would have been cruel to disappoint them.

One day his cousin Mary said sarcastically, " That he did nothing but look from the window," and as Lewellyn reddened, his father said, " That girl opposite seems a good industrious girl," and his mother added, " I dare say she will make a good wife."—" She is pretty-looking," faltered Mary. " *Pretty looking!*" cried Lewellyn angrily. " She is an angel."

The young people became acquainted, and the attention of Lewellyn, while Fanny lay sick, so charmed her aunt, that her consent was obtained, and he was an accepted lover, though the marriage was from prudence delayed till Lewellyn should learn his father's trade, which Fanny chose for him. War was declared at this time.

A military spirit pervaded the whole town; the industrious artisan forsook his work-shop to lounge on the parade: here, too, the servant girl showed herself in her Sunday clothes; and even Fanny preferred listening to the military band, and beholding the military array, to a quiet walk in the fields with her lover.

But the sound of martial music was not the only one that reached and delighted her ear. Praises of her beauty ran along the ranks—" A devilish fine girl! who is she?" was audibly whispered by the officers. Some young men, who had in vain sought Fanny's attention when they wore the plain dress of tradesmen, now took pains to attract her eyes by their dexterity in the manual, and by displaying to all possible advantage the brilliancy of their dress, in order, perhaps, to let Fanny feel the value of the prize which she had rejected; while others, not content with exciting her regret for her cruelty to them, were still desirous of gaining her love; and, unawed by the almost fierce looks of Lewellyn, persisted in making way for her in the crowd, that she might hear the band to advantage.

And but too often, Fanny, delighted at the attention paid to her, rewarded it by smiles so gracious, that they conveyed hopes and joy to the bosom of her attendants, and fear and jealousy to that of her lover. Not that Lewellyn was sorry to see the woman of his choice the object of general admiration: on the contrary, he would have felt pleasure in it had not Fanny seemed to enjoy it so much herself; but he saw her eyes sparkle at other praises than his, and he always returned from the parade displeased with Fanny, and dissatisfied with himself.

Still he had not resolution to refuse to accompany her every evening to a scene so fatal to his peace; and if he had, he feared that she might resolve to go thither without him; and he was as wretched as an accepted lover could be, when a day was fixed on for a review of the regulars quartered in the town and its environs, and of the new-raised militia.

" Only think, Lewellyn," said Fanny to her lover; " there is going to be a review!"

" And what then?" replied he in a peevish accent, displeased at the joy that sparkled in her eyes.

" What then!" rejoined the mortified beauty; " only I—I never saw a review in my life."

" And I do not know that it signifies whether you ever see one or no," returned Lewellyn, still more pettishly.

" I am of a different opinion," retorted Fanny; " and if you do not take me to see the review next week, I know who will—that's all:" and away she walked in all the dignity of conscious and offended power.

Nor did she overrate her influence. Lewellyn's jealousy took alarm; he followed her immediately, and with a forced laugh told her that he knew as well as she did who would take her to the review.

" Who?" angrily asked Fanny.

" Myself," replied her humbled swain, " and we will walk together to the heath on which it is to be; it is, you know, only three miles off."

" Walk!" exclaimed Fanny; " walk! and be melted with heat, and our clothes covered with dust when we get there! No, indeed! fine figures we should be."

" I should not like you the worse, Fanny; and I thought you went to see, and not to be seen," said Lewellyn. " However, just as you please; I suppose you have thought of some other way of going."

" O yes, we can borrow your cousin John's cart and horse; Mary can drive me, and you can hire a pony and ride by the side of us."

Lewellyn, with a deep sigh, consented to the proposal, and even assisted Fanny to conquer Mary's aversion to perform her part of the plan.

" I hate war, and all that belongs to it," cried Mary; " believe me, I shall have no pleasure if I go."

" But you will give others pleasure by going," said Lewellyn; and Mary consented directly.

The important day arrived, and Fanny appeared at her aunt's window, ready dressed, long before the hour appointed for them to set off. " How beautiful she looks!" thought Lewellyn, " and how smart she is! too smart for her situation; yet had she been dressed so to please me, I should not have cared for that; but she would not have taken such pains with her dress to please me!"

I doubt Lewellyn was only too much in the right; and that though she looked so handsome that he could not help gazing on her as they went along, at the hazard of riding against posts and carriages, this look had something so sad and reproachful, that Fanny, she knew not why, perhaps wished to avoid it; and when he ventured to say, " You would not have made yourself so smart to walk alone with *me*, Fanny!" a self-accusing blush spread itself over her cheek, and for the first time in her life she wished herself less smart.

Eager, therefore, to change the subject of Lewellyn's thoughts, she asked Mary whence arose her extreme aversion to soldiers and to war.

" I will tell you," said Mary impatiently, " and then I desire you to question me on this subject no more. My father was a soldier, my mother followed him to battle; I was born on a baggage-waggon, bred in the horrors of a camp, and at ten years old I saw my father brought home mangled and dying from the field, while my mother was breathing her last in the camp-fever. I remember it as if it was only yesterday," continued Mary, shuddering and deeply affected; and her volatile companion was awed into silence.

At length they arrived on the review ground; and Lewellyn, afraid lest the horse should be frightened at the firing, made them leave the cart, and then leaning on his arm they proceeded to the front of the ranks. But the crowd was soon so great that Fanny began to find that she was not likely either to see or be seen, and was almost tempted to join Mary in regrets that she had given herself the trouble of coming; when she was seen and recognised by one of her quondam lovers, who, since she had rejected him, had become a sergeant in the militia of the town. Immediately this gallant hero made his way through the crowd; and forcing a poor boy to dismount from a coachbox conveniently situated for overlooking the field, he seized Fanny's unreluctant hand, led her along the ranks, and lifted her to the place, crying out—" Make way for a lady!"

Surprise, and the suddenness of Fanny's removal, prevented Lewellyn's opposing it; but, as soon as surprise gave way to jealousy and resentment, he prepared to follow them. But it was impossible: the review was begun, and Lewellyn could not leave Mary, lest he should expose her to the risk of being run down by the horses, though his own danger he would have disregarded: he was therefore obliged to content himself with watching the conduct of Fanny at a distance, who, placed in a conspicuous situation, and taught by coquetry to make the most of it, attracted and charmed all eyes but those of her lover.

In vain did Fanny cast many a kind glance towards her deserted companions. She received none in return: Mary did not, and Lewellyn would not see them; and the pleasure which she experienced was at length, in spite of the continual attentions of her military beau, completely damped by the expectation of the reproaches which she knew she should receive when she returned to her lover, and which her conscience told her she but too well deserved.

The review ended, and Fanny was reconducted by the young serjeant to the friends whom she had quitted. The reception which she met with I shall leave to my readers to imagine—suffice, that Lewellyn upbraided, that Fanny cried, and Mary mediated, and that they parted the best friends in the world; Lewellyn promising to drink tea at Fanny's aunt's that afternoon, and even to behave cordially to the young serjeant, whom Fanny thought it incumbent on her to ask, in return for his civility.

"But if I come, Fanny, you promise not to make me uncomfortable again by your attentions to him?"

"O yes; I promise faithfully to behave just as you wish me; I will be rude to him if you like it."

"No—I would not have you be absolutely rude, but——"

"But why do you ask him?" said Mary abruptly.

"In return for his civilities," replied Fanny.

"And a pretty return it will be," cried Mary, "if you behave rudely to him; it surely would have been more civil not to have asked him at all."

"Mary is so severe!" retorted Fanny.

"And so wise," said Lewellyn, peevishly—"nothing pleases her."

"I believe, indeed, my temper is altered for the worse lately," answered Mary, bursting into tears. A profound silence ensued, and lasted till they got home:—then Fanny, seconded by Lewellyn, urged Mary with more than common kindness, for her tears had affected them, to be of the party in the evening.

"No," replied Mary;—" I had rather not come—I do not like soldiers; therefore, why should I meet them?" And Fanny, wondering at her want of taste, acceded to the propriety of her not coming; but Lewellyn, while he approved of her determination of staying at home, observed to himself,—" She does not like soldiers!—What a sensible young woman my cousin Mary is!—I wish"— Here he stopped; but the violence with which he struck his stick on the ground, and shut to the door as he entered his own house, were sufficient proofs that the conclusion of his sentence would, if uttered, have had some reference to Fanny's admiration of the very people whom Mary disliked.

Fanny's unhappy admiration of soldier's feathers and red coats had an unhappy influence on her lover, who, in a evil hour, that he might be as captivating to her as was the smart young serjeant, enlisted.

"Now," said he to himself, as he returned home, "she cannot fail of loving me again! But then, to please her, I have assumed a garb hateful to myself and parents. Oh! Fanny, I feel I have purchased your love very dearly!"

As he said this he found himself at his own door. "No, I dare not tell them to-night what I have done!" said he; and with a trembling hand he opened the door of the sitting-room.

"How pale you look!" exclaimed Mary, running to meet him.

"My dear child! you are not well," cried his mother.

"We must send for advice for him," said his father; "the poor lad has looked ill some days, and bad fevers are about. If we should lose you, Lewellyn, what would become of us in our old age?"

Lewellyn tried to speak, but his voice died away; and, leaning on the arm of his father's chair, he sobbed aloud.

Alarmed at his distress, but quite unsuspicious of the cause, his mother hung about his neck; his father walked up and down the room exclaiming, "What can have happened? What can this mean?" and Mary, motionless as a statue, stood gazing on him in silence; when, as he took his handkerchief out of his pocket, he pulled out with it the cockade which he had just received from the recruiting serjeant.

Mary eagerly seized it; and in an instant the truth burst on her mind. "Oh! what does this mean?" cried she in a tone of agony. "How comes this here? Surely, surely, Lewellyn, you have not been so rash as to enlist for a soldier!"

"Is the girl mad!" exclaimed the old man, "to suppose Lewellyn would do what he knew would break my heart?"

Lewellyn hid his face, and again sobbed aloud.

"Would to God I may be wrong!" said Mary, "but I fear"——

"Mary is always full of her fears," said his weeping mother pettishly; and the old man was beginning anew to chide poor Mary, when his son, summoning up all his resolution, faltered out, "Mary is right!—I have enlisted!"

The wretched father tottered into a chair; and, clasping his hands, moved backwards and forwards as he sat, in speechless agony; while the mother threw her apron over her face, and groaned aloud; and Mary in silent grief leaned her head on her hands.

"Oh! that girl! that cursed girl!" at length exclaimed the father. "This is her doing!"

"She knows nothing of it," replied Lewellyn; "and you have no one to blame but me."

"I had rather have to blame any one else," cried his father. "It is a hard thing to have to reproach one's own child, an only child, too. Oh, Lewellyn! we have not deserved this of you; indeed we have not!"

"We will buy him off again!" exclaimed his mother, starting from her chair. "We will spend all our little savings with pleasure to do it!"

"You shall have all mine too," cried Mary; "and Lewellyn will thank us in a short time, whatever he may do now."

"Now, and ever, I shall reject your proposal," he replied.

"My child!" said his father, grasping his hand, and bursting into tears, "do you think I have lived long enough? Do you wish to kill me?"

Lewellyn could not answer; but he threw himself on his neck, and sobbed aloud.

"Have we found our child again?" said his mother, taking his hand tenderly between both hers; and Mary, timidly approaching him, cried—"Dear cousin! why should you be a soldier? If you should be sent abroad, Lewellyn;—if you should be killed, what would become of————?" Here her voice faltered; and, as both his parents at this moment folded their arms round him, Lewellyn's resolution was shaken; and he was listening with complacence to their renewed proposal of purchasing his discharge, when, as he raised his head, he saw Fanny at her window, talking with smiles of complacency and glowing cheeks to a recruiting serjeant; and as she spoke she played with the tassel of his epaulet, and seemed to be admiring the beauty of the uniform.

This sight hurried the unhappy Lewellyn into all his wonted jealousy, and counteracted entirely the pleadings of filial piety in his heart.

"My lot is cast!" he exclaimed, rushing to the door:— "For your sakes, I wish it were a different one: but I am resolved, and nothing can shake my resolution." So saying, he left the house: but he did not go in search of Fanny, who had, he observed, left the window; for he felt dissatisfied both with her and himself, and was at that moment ashamed to prove to her the extent of her influence over him, by telling her that he had become a soldier for her sake. He therefore hastened into the fields, and took a long and solitary ramble, in hopes to compose his feelings, and enable him on his return to meet the just reproaches of his parents with more resolution.

As soon as he thought that his firmness was sufficiently restored, he returned to the town; when, as he approached it, he saw Fanny leaving it in a market-cart driven by a young man. She did not see him; and, overcome by a variety of emotions, he felt unable to call to her loud enough for her to hear him; and, wretched and disappointed, he reached his own house.

His first inquiry was, whether Fanny had called during his absence; and he heard, with anguish, that she had not: and his pride being completely conquered by affection, he went to her aunt's house immediately to know whither she was gone,—and found she was gone to spend two days with a friend of hers in the country.

"And gone without letting me know it, or taking leave of me!" he exclaimed—"Oh, Fanny!"

But Fanny was in this case innocently blamed; and when she heard of the enlistment she was in great distress, especially when told it was to recommend himself to her love.

"To please me!" cried Fanny:—"I solemnly declare that this rash deed was wholly without my knowledge, and quite contrary to my wishes."

"Indeed!" cried both the parents.

"Indeed—so help me God!"

"Then you are willing," said Mary, "no doubt, to use all your influence to prevail on him to let us buy his discharge."

"I am—I am!" returned Fanny in a hurried manner; and the poor old people folded her fondly and gratefully to their bosom.

Fanny now found her voice again, and began to ask several questions concerning the hasty, ill-advised step which her lover had taken. She inquired the name of the regiment; and being told, she eagerly exclaimed—"What! in that regiment!—the uniform is scarlet turned up with deep blue and gold!—Oh, how handsome he will look in his regimentals!" she added, wiping her eyes, and smiling as she spoke.

The poor old man frowned, and turned away; and Mary shook her head: but the mother, with all a mother's vanity, observed—"True, child, he will look handsome, indeed; and more like a captain, I warrant, than many a one that's there!" And Fanny, in the thought of her lover's improved beauty, forgot his absence, and all sense of the danger to which his new profession would expose him.

Mary and Fanny went next day to see a detachment in which Lewellyn marched. As they ascended a hill, a drum and fife were heard.

"Come, Mary, let us run and meet them," cried Fanny, joyfully; but Mary languidly exclaimed, "I can go no further!" and sat down on the ground: and Fanny consoled herself by reflecting that from the hill she could see them pass better than by standing on the level road.

At length Fanny beheld Lewellyn; and in a transport of joy she exclaimed, "See, Mary, there he is! there he is!— Oh how handsome he looks! but I knew he would!"

"But how will he look a year hence?" said Mary, with a sigh.

"How? Why, just the same, to be sure."

"But suppose he should be ordered abroad?" replied Mary.

Fanny started, and turned pale, exclaiming, "Bless me, Mary, you are such a croaker!" She had time for no more —Lewellyn was at the foot of the hill; and Fanny, running down it like lightning, arrived just time enough to clasp her lover's extended hand as he passed, and gaze on him with a look which well rewarded him for all that he had suffered.

"Come, Mary, let us follow them," cried Fanny.

"Presently," she replied, slowly descending the hill.

"You are so slow," said Fanny; " I dare say Lewellyn will get to his father's house before us."

"Before one of us, perhaps."

"Well, that will seem very unkind to him, I am sure."

"No, he will not miss me, I am sure," returned Mary, wiping away a tear; "he did not even see me as he passed; he had no eyes but for you, Fanny." But Fanny was out of hearing before she finished the sentence, and she did not overtake her before she reached the town.

The meeting of the lovers after this, their first separation, was a moment of such true joy to both, that, alive only to the pleasures of affection, they thought not of its pains; and Fanny forgot her anger, Lewellyn his jealousy, while both seemed unconscious that the will of government might, in a few hours, doom them to a long if not an eternal separation.

These fears, however, though strangers to them, were only too present to the minds of the unhappy parents and Mary: when Fanny and Lewellyn, not liking to have their joy damped by the sight of melancholy faces, went out to take a walk; and Fanny, leaning on the arm of her now military lover, led him in triumph, as it were, through the streets of his native town.

When they returned, the father and Mary took Fanny on one side, asked her whether she had begun to persuade Lewellyn to leave the army again: and Fanny, blushing deeply, replied—"No: but that it was time enough yet;" and again she was alive only to the satisfaction of the moment.

Another day passed, and still she was too proud of her lover's appearance as a soldier to endeavour to persuade him to be one no longer; and when spoken to on the subject, she replied, that it would be time enough for him to try to get discharged when he was ordered to a distance, or to go abroad.

"No!" cried Mary indignantly;—"should he be ordered to go abroad, I should despise him if he wished then to be discharged: for, though I value Lewellyn's life, I value his honour more. No; he must gain his discharge now, or never!"

The destiny of Lewellyn was speedily fixed; and when too late, Fanny urged him to get off, though on terms derogatory to his honour, and to which he would not yield.

The hour of his departure now drew nigh. In vain did he endeavour to keep up his spirits, by telling Fanny that he hoped to distinguish himself so much, that he should return a non-commissioned officer at least. His sanguine descriptions caused Fanny to smile, through her tears, with joyful anticipation: but they could not make him smile himself; nor could they call one smile to the pale lip of his cousin Mary. Her grief seemed so deep, so rooted, that Lewellyn felt almost angry with her for feeling more than Fanny did; and sometimes a suspicion that her love for him exceeded the love of a relation darted across his mind, and awakened there no pleasant sensations.

At the moment of his leaving the parental roof, and when his parents, convinced that they should see him no more, had just folded him, in speechless agony, in a last embrace, he wrung Mary's cold hand, and said, pointing to his father and mother—" I bequeath them to your care, Mary."

"That was quite unnecessary," she replied, half reproachfully.

"And Fanny, too," he added, in a fainter voice.

"There was no need of that, either," she returned:—"you love her,—that's enough!"

"Mary, dear Mary!" cried Lewellyn; but she had left the room.

It so happened that a friend of mine was passing a bridge near Lewellyn's native town as the regiment were crossing it, in their way to the place whence they were to embark; and, being obliged to stop to make way for them, his attention was attracted by the violent and audible grief of Fanny, who was walking by the side of Lewellyn; by the settled wo visible in his countenance, and by the still more touching, though quiet, distress expressed by Mary.

"Those two young women are that soldier's sister and wife, I presume!" said my friend to a bystander.

"No, sir;—one is his cousin, and the other his sweetheart," was the answer.

"Oh then, that pretty pale girl, who says nothing, but looks so very sad,—she is his mistress, I conclude?" continued my friend.

"Oh, no, sir,—she is only the cousin!" returned the man.

"I wish she had been the mistress!" observed my friend, "for her grief seems to me to be of the more lasting nature."

Soon did Fanny forget her lover, though at first her grief was violent. Again she was displaying her beautiful face at military parades, and receiving the homage of her numerous admirers: yet she was pleased when letters came from him from Holland. In the course of the winter his father died half-broken hearted, and his widow fell into a kind of harmless insanity, in which she imagined her son was a great man; and every day she would be dressed to go out to meet him returning from battle and conquest. It was only on her death-bed her senses returned; and she blessed the kind and attentive Mary, and with her left a mother's blessing for her son. "Oh! how happy I shall be," said Mary to herself, "to tell him, should he ever return, that they blessed him in their dying moments."

One evening, after they had been dead some months, and when Mary had, as usual, visited their graves to strew them with fresh flowers (as is customary in many parts of Wales,) and weed the little garden which she had planted on them,—instead of returning home she sat herself down on a wooden bench at the entrance of the churchyard, which commanded a view of the town; and as she listened to the distant and varied sounds which reached her ear from the barracks, and a crowded fair about a mile distant —time insensibly stole away, and, lost in her own thoughts, she was not conscious of the approach of a stranger, till he had reached the bench and was preparing to sit down on it.

Mary started;—but, with that untaught courtesy which the benevolent always possess, she made room for the intruder to sit down, by removing to the other side of the seat. Neither of them spoke; and Mary insensibly renewed her meditations. But at length the evident agitation and loud though suppressed sobs of the stranger attracted her attention to him, and excited her compassion. "Poor man!" thought Mary, "perhaps he has been visiting the new-made grave of some dear friend:" and insensibly she turned towards the unhappy stranger, expecting to see him in deep mourning; but he was wrapped up in a great coat that looked like a regimental one. This made Mary's pity even greater than before; for, ever since Lewellyn had enlisted, she had lost her boasted insensibility to soldiers and their concerns.

"He is a soldier, too!" said Mary to herself: "who knows but—?" Here the train of her ideas was suddenly broken; for an audible and violent renewal of the stranger's distress so overset her feelings, already softened by her visit to the grave of her relations and the recollections in which she had been indulging, that she could keep her seat no longer: besides, conscious that true sorrow loves not to be observed, she felt it indelicate to continue there: but, as she slowly withdrew, she could not help saying in a faltering and compassionate tone, "Good evening, sir—and Heaven comfort you!"

At the sound of her voice the stranger started—"'Tis she!—'Tis Mary!" he exclaimed, rushing towards her.

Mary turned about on hearing herself named, and in a voice so dear to her; and in an instant found herself clasped in the arms of Lewellyn.

To describe the incoherence either of grief or joy is impossible: suffice, that Mary was at length able to articulate, "We feared that you were dead!"

"You see that I am not dead," replied Lewellyn; "but I find that others are." Here tears choked his voice; but, recovering himself, he added, pointing to the grave of his parents, "Oh, Mary! that was a sad sight for me!—I have found much sorrow awaiting me."

"You know all, then?" interrupted Mary with quickness.

"I know that I have lost both my parents: and I fear my disobedience—my obstinacy—Tell me—tell me, Mary, did they forgive me, and leave me their blessing? Many, many a pang have I felt when I thought of my ingratitude and disobedience in leaving them; and in all my hardships I have said to myself, Unnatural child! this is no more than you have well deserved."

"Dear, dear Lewellyn!" cried Mary, "do not grieve yourself in this manner.—'If my son should ever return,' they both of them said, and they were loath to believe you would not, 'tell him,' were the words of each of them, 'that I prayed for and blessed him on my death-bed.'"

"Thank God! thank God!" replied Lewellyn: and for a few moments neither he nor Mary could speak. At length Lewellyn said, "Pray, whose pious hand has decked their grave with flowers?"

"I did it," answered Mary; and, as she said this, she thought she saw disappointment in the face of her cousin. But her look was a transient one; for she was careful not to let her eyes dwell on Lewellyn's face, lest she should wound his feelings, as the fate of war had sadly changed him. His forehead was scarred, he wore a black patch on his right cheek, and his left arm was in a sling: besides, fatigue, low living, and imprisonment had made him scarcely recognisable, except by the eye of love and friendship. He had been left for dead on the field of battle; and, when life returned, he found himself in a French hospital, whence he was conveyed to a prison, and in due time was released by a cartel.

"You see I am dreadfully altered," said Lewellyn, observing that Mary watched her opportunity of looking at him—"I dare say you would scarcely have known me?"

"I should know you any where, and in any disguise," said Mary warmly:—"but you seem fatigued: let us go to my little lodging."

"I am faint and weary, indeed," replied he, accepting the arm which Mary offered to him as they walked towards the town: "but I am come home to good nurses, I trust, though one of them is dead" (drawing his hand across his eyes as he said it;) "and my native air and the sight of all I love, will, I doubt not, soon restore me to health."

As he uttered these words he fixed his eyes steadfastly on Mary's face, which she hastily averted, and he felt her arm tremble under his.

"Mary!" exclaimed he, suddenly stopping, "you must guess the question which I am longing to ask, but dare not: —Oh, these horrible forebodings!—Mary, why do you not put an end to this suspense which tortures me?"

"She is well," replied Mary, in a faint voice.

"And not—not married, I hope?"

"Oh! no, no, no—not married," replied Mary.

"Thank God!" exclaimed Lewellyn, and Mary was about to speak, when she was prevented by violent shouts and bursts of laughter from persons approaching them—the path which they were in being immediately across the road which led from the fair.

"Hark! I hear singing," said Lewellyn, his whole frame trembling, "and surely in a voice not unknown to me!"

"Nonsense!—impossible!" replied his agitated companion, violently seizing his arm! "But let us go another way."

"I will go no way but this," said Lewellyn, resolutely; and the voice began again to sing a song which, in happier times, had been often sung by Fanny, and admired by Lewellyn. "I thought so;—it is Fanny who is singing!"

he exclaimed in a tone of suppressed agony.—" What does this mean?—Tell me, Mary, I conjure you!"

"This way,—Come this way," repeated Mary, trying to force him down a different path, but in vain; when, supported under the arms of two drunken soldiers, and more than half intoxicated herself, flushed with intemperance, dressed in the loose and gay attire of a courtezan, and singing with all the violence of wanton mirth, they beheld Fanny! After Lewellyn's departure she had fallen a victim to the flatteries and attentions of an officer, and had at length become a follower of the camp.

At sight of Fanny in this situation, Mary uttered a loud scream; but Lewellyn stood motionless and lifeless as a statue, with his eyes fixed on the still lovely, though degraded form before him. But the scream of Mary had attracted the attention of Fanny; and her eye, quick as lightning, saw and recognised Lewellyn. She also screamed, but it was in the tone of desperation; and rushing forwards, she fell madly laughing on the ground. The soldiers, concluding she fell from excessive mirth, laughed louder than she did; and, in spite of her struggles, conveyed her in their arms up the road that led to the camp. Lewellyn had sprung forward to catch her as she was falling, but Mary had forcibly withheld him—but that was the last effort of expiring energy; with tottering steps, and in silent agony, he accompanied Mary to her lodging, and ere two hours had elapsed, he was raving in the delirium of a fever; and Mary began to fear that the beloved friend whom war had spared to her would have returned only to die the victim of a worthless woman. Day was slowly beginning to dawn, and Lewellyn was fallen into a perturbed slumber, when Mary, as she stood mournfully gazing on his altered features, heard a gentle tap at her window, and, softly approaching it, beheld, with no small emotion, the wretched Fanny herself.

"Go away—go away!" cried Mary in a low voice, putting her lips to the casement.

"I can't go till I have seen him," replied Fanny in a hoarse voice.—"I know he is here—and, for the love of God!" said she, falling on her knees, "let me ask his pardon."

"Impossible!" replied Mary, gently unlocking the door, and closing it after her as she stood at the door.—"He is ill, perhaps dying—the sight of you"—

"Has killed him, no doubt," interrupted Fanny, turning even paler than before, and full of the dreadful irritation consequent on intoxication after its effects have subsided. "But do you think he will not curse me in his last moments, as they say his parents did?"

"Oh, no,—I'm sure he will not."

"Do you think he will pray for me?—Ask him, Mary; ask him to pray for me," she continued with horrible eagerness.

"I will, I will," replied Mary; "but for mercy's sake, go away, lest he wake and know your voice!"

"Well, I will go—I will go. I know I am not worthy to speak either to him or you; but no one is waking but you and me, Mary; so no one sees how you are degraded."

"I did not mean that; I did not indeed," cried Mary, bursting into tears of pity.

We shall not dwell upon the interview of the lost girl with her lover, and the generosity of Mary tried to the uttermost of woman's endurance. But fate removed her miserable rival; who, on leaving Mary's cottage, plunged in despair into a neighbouring stream and was drowned. Nor durst Mary confess to Lewellyn that his worthless mistress had perished by her own deed. He next day insisted upon seeing Fanny, and every day he wondered that she never came.

"I feared, and she feared," replied Mary, blushing, "that her presence might agitate you too much."

"Nonsense," replied Lewellyn, rather pettishly: "it would do me good rather; for in spite of all Mary,—in spite of all, I feel;—I feel that I love her still."

"Indeed!" cried Mary, turning pale.

"Yes," answered Lewellyn, with a deep sigh; "and I am convinced that, as my going away leaving her exposed to temptation was the cause of her guilt, I am bound in conscience to marry her."

"To marry her," exclaimed Mary, while she could not help rejoicing at that moment that Fanny was no more.

"Yes, to marry her!" replied Lewellyn; "you know you yourself imputed all the mischief that has happened, to my going for a soldier."

"Not exactly so," replied Mary: "I imputed it to the war."

"That is much the same thing," retorted Lewellyn hastily; but Mary was of a different opinion. "Therefore," continued Lewellyn, "as I long very much to see her—do, my dear cousin, do go for her this afternoon."

The season of self-command was over. Mary got up; she sat down again; she turned pale, then red; and at last she burst into tears.

"What is the matter?" cried Lewellyn, "what has happened?"

"Fanny—Fanny is ill in bed," faltered out Mary,

"But not dying, I hope?" answered Lewellyn, tottering to a chair.

"Not—not far from it," said Mary, resolved now to tell him the whole truth.

"Let me see her—I will see her," he exclaimed, staggering towards the door.

"It is too late!" cried Mary, forcing him into a chair; "but remember, dearest Lewellyn, that before she died, you had kindly forgiven all her offences towards you."

"She had none to forgive," fiercely replied Lewellyn, remembering at that moment nothing but her merits; and he insisted on seeing her corpse, if she was really dead.

"She is buried, also," replied Mary, almost piqued at this obstinate attachment to an unworthy girl, while her faithful love and modest worth were unregarded; but she soon lost all resentment, in terror and pity at the anguish which now overwhelmed Lewellyn.

At first it showed itself in vehement exclamations and declarations—that she should not die—that she should still be his wife; but at length he sunk into a state of hopeless despondency, and, throwing himself across his bed, for two days all the efforts of Mary were vain to rouse him from his mournful stupor. On the third day he became composed; and taking Mary's hand, he said,

"My dear, good cousin, lead me, pray lead me to her grave."

This request was what Mary had dreaded.

"I—I do not know which it is," replied Mary.

"Then we can inquire," coldly answered Lewellyn.

"No, no,—if you are determined—I think I can find it," said Mary, recollecting that she could show him some other grave for hers.

"I am determined," answered Lewellyn; and with slow steps they set off for the burying-ground.

When there, Mary led him to a grave newly made, but the flowers with which it had been strewed were withered. Lewellyn threw himself across the turf, and darting an angry glance at Mary, said:

"These flowers might have been renewed, I think; however, this spot shall be planted now, as well as strewed:" and Mary did not contradict him.

But, unluckily, at this moment, a woman, whose mother was buried in the grave which Lewellyn mistook for Fanny's, came up to them with fresh flowers to throw on it; and before Mary could prevent her, she demanded what Lewellyn meant by lying on her mother's grave.

Lewellyn, starting up, replied that he thought Fanny Hastings lay buried there.

"She," answered the woman: "no, poor thing! she drowned herself, and is buried in the cross-ways!"

Lewellyn gave a deep groan, and sunk senseless on the ground; nor did he recover till he had been conveyed home and was laid on his bed, his head resting on the arm of Mary.

When he opened his eyes and saw her, he gave her such a look of wo!—and refused for some days all nourishment and all consolation, as he had done before; while Mary, rendered desperate by his obstinate resolution to die, lost all power of exertion; and after one day of great anxiety, when she left him for the night, she felt as if she should never be able to leave her room again.

The next morning, when Lewellyn awoke from his disturbed slumbers, he was surprised not to see Mary watching by his bedside; and though resolved not to eat, he still felt disappointed that his kind nurse was not there to invite him to do so. But hour after hour elapsed, and still no Mary appeared; and Lewellyn's heart died within him, as the probability struck him, that she had at length sunk under the accumulated fatigue and sorrow which he had occasioned her.

The idea was insupportable; he forgot his languid despondence; he forgot regret for the dead Fanny, in fear for the living Mary; and hastily dressing himself, resolved to go in search of her.

Still, respect forbade him to enter her chamber; and having with some difficulty reached the stair-case, he stopped there, irresolute how to proceed. Had he entered her room, he would have seen with some emotion, I trust, what a wretched garret and miserable bed Mary was contented to use, in order to accommodate the ungrateful object of her affection:—but, as I said before, a feeling of delicacy and respect forbade Lewellyn to go further, and he contented himself with calling Mary by her name. Still no Mary answered: again he called, but in vain; for, though Mary did hear him the second time, she was not in a humour to reply.

She had lain awake, revolving in her own mind the whole of her past existence; and she found that her life had been uniformly a life of wearisome exertion, uncheered but by the consciousness of having done her duty; to be sure, that consciousness was a sure blessing, and Mary had found it so; but at this moment, worn down as she was both in body and mind, existence seemed to have lost every charm; and she resolved, like Lewellyn, to lie down and die. Indifferent, therefore, even to Lewellyn himself, she was lying still in her sleepless bed when she heard Lewellyn's voice calling her in an accent of anxiety.

The heart so lately quiet began to beat violently; her imagined indifference immediately vanished; and raising herself up in her bed, she listened eagerly to hear the welcome sound again. "So! he misses me—he wishes for me—he is alarmed for me!" thought Mary; and in another moment she distinctly heard Lewellyn at her door, saying, through the key-hole, "Mary! why, Mary! dear, dear Mary! for mercy's sake speak to me!"

It was the first moment of pleasure that Mary had known for many weeks; and telling him she would be down presently, she hastily dressed herself, and, full of something like renewed hope, joined Lewellyn. But with his fears for Mary's health had subsided his inclination to exertion. She found him as she had left him the night before—stretched on his bed, the picture of wo, and again resolved to refuse all the nourishment which she offered him.

This was more than she could bear with patience. The cheek, so lately flushed with hope, became pale with disappointment; and sinking on the foot of the bed, she exclaimed: "It is over, and the struggle is past; why should I endeavour to keep alive in you, or in myself, an existence painful to us both? Yet, I own it does grieve me, Lewellyn, to see you so very indifferent to me, so very unkind?"

Lewellyn, at these words, raised himself on his elbow, and looked at her with surprise and interest.

"Cruel, cruel Lewellyn!" she continued, rendered regardless of all restraint by despair, "it is not enough, that from my earliest days I have loved, hopelessly loved you, and seen another obtain the love which I would have died to gain? but must I see this happy though guilty rival triumph over me still even in her grave? Must I see you resolve to die with her, rather than live with me?"

Here Mary paused: but Lewellyn's heart being too full to allow him to answer her, she soon continued thus:—

"Dear Mary!" said your parents to me in their last moments, "should our deluded son be still living and ever return to his native town, tell him"———

"Tell him what?" cried Lewellyn, seeing that Mary hesitated.

"Tell him, it was our wish, that he should forget the worthless girl who has forsaken him, (remember, Lewellyn, it was they who called her such names, and not I,) and make you his wife. It is not pretty to praise one's self, I know, Lewelly," continued Mary, blushing, "but I may repeat what they said, surely."

"And what did they say?" asked Lewellyn.

"Why, they said I was a very good girl; and they were sure I should make you happy!"

"Happy!—make me happy!" cried Lewellyn mournfully; "but you are a good girl—a very good girl, Mary!" he added, putting his arm round her waist, and pressing her to him as he spoke.

This circumstance, trival as it was, invigorated the hopes of Mary, and gave her courage to proceed. "Now hear my resolution, Lewellyn!—From my childhood to the present hour, I have lived but for you and your dear unfortunate parents; to them and you—my health, my time, and my strength have been cheerfully devoted; but grief has now nearly exhausted me, and I feel that my power of exertion is nearly over; for I see, that—though I have loved you through all your sickness and your sorrow, and love you as fondly now as if you were still in the pride and bloom of health and youth—I see, wretch that I am! that it is with difficulty you speak kindly to me; and that I am so odious to you at times, that"———

"Odious!—you odious to me!" exclaimed Lewellyn, starting up with unusual animation; "you Mary! my friend! my nurse! my preserver! my all! now"———

"Then promise me not to give way to this deadly sorrow, Lewellyn."

"I will promise you any thing," cried Lewellyn, tenderly.

"For, mark my words, Lewellyn—I will not live to witness your death—I am ill—I am very ill; and unless assured that you will consent to live, I will take no food, no remedies, but give myself up to the languor which is consuming me."

"Mary!—dearest Mary!" cried Lewellyn, catching her fondly to his bosom, "you shall live for my sake, as I will live for yours! We will either live or die together; and from this moment I will shake off this unworthy sorrow."

He said no more: for Mary, more unable to bear joy than sorrow, fainted in his arms, and for some time the terrified Lewellyn feared that she was gone for ever; but she revived at last, and in a few weeks, to the satisfaction of the whole town, to whom Mary was an object both of affection and respect, the lovers were united at the parish church. Not long after, a gentleman, to whom their story was known, put them in possession of a small but comfortable farm on his estate, and Mary shines as much as a wife and mother, as she had before done as a relation and friend.

But the sound of the drum and fife always fades the colour of Mary's cheek; and whenever a recruiting party passes her gate, Mary hastens into a back room till it is past, and Lewellyn runs to the extremity of his fields to avoid it; while Mary, shutting the door after her with violence, exclaims, "I always did, and I always shall hate war, and all that belongs to it; and let who will desire it, —my boys, except in case of an invasion, shall never, never be soldiers."

A clergyman, not quite a hundred miles from this place, preached a most edifying discourse on "Come, and draw water out of the wells of salvation, without money and without price." On the following week some of his parishioners took the liberty of drawing water from a very fine spring-well in the parson's garden, at which the learned divine was not a little nettled. Being reminded by the intruder of his text and sermon, the reverend gentleman replied, "You may draw as much water as ye like from the wells of salvation; but if you come here again, and take my water, I'se send a bullet through you."—*Edin. Paper.*

COLUMN FOR THE LADIES.
MRS. INCHBALD.

WE have been so much pleased with the good sense and high spirit of the subjoined letter, which has accidentally fallen into our way in a pleasing book of theatrical gossip and scraps, published by the survivors of the gentleman to whom the letter is addressed, that we hasten to give it all the publicity in our power. It contains an admirable lesson. Because Mrs. Inchbald did not choose to sacrifice her time and tastes, and expend her money in the way her *friends* thought fit, and chose rather to live to herself and her duties than to their frivolities, they were pleased to call her penurious, and suspect her of being a little mad. Mr. Taylor, one of her friends, ventured to remonstrate, and his epistle called forth her reply.

"My dear sir,—I read your letter with gratitude, because I have had so many proofs of your friendship for me, that I do not once doubt of your kind intentions.

"You have taken the best method possible on such an occasion, not to hurt my spirits; for had you suspected me to be insane, or even nervous, you would have mentioned the subject with more caution, and by so doing, might have given me alarm.

"That the world should say I have lost my senses, I can readily forgive, when I recollect that a few years ago it said the same of Mrs. Siddons.

"I am now fifty-two years old, and yet if I were to dress, paint, and visit, no one would call my understanding in question; or if I were to beg from all my acquaintance a guinea or two, as subscription for a foolish book, no one would accuse me of avarice. But because I choose that retirement suitable to my years, and think it my duty to support two sisters, instead of one servant, I am accused of madness. I might plunge in debt, be confined in prison, a pensioner on 'The Literary Fund,' or be gay as a girl of eighteen, and yet be considered as perfectly in my senses; but because I choose to live in independence, affluence to me, with a mind serene and prospects unclouded, I am supposed to be mad. In making use of the word affluence, I do not mean to exclude some inconveniencies annexed, but this is the case in every state. I wish for more suitable lodgings, but I am unfortunately averse to a street, after living so long in a square; but with all my labour to find one, I cannot fix on a spot such as I wish to make my residence for life, and till I do, and am confined to London, the beautiful view from my present apartment of the Surrey hills and the Thames, invites me to remain here, for I believe that there is neither such fine air nor so fine a prospect in all the town. I am, besides, near my sisters here; and the time when they are not with me is so wholly engrossed in writing, that I want leisure for the convenience of walking out. Retirement in the country would, perhaps, have been more advisable than in London, but my sisters did not like to accompany me, and I did not like to leave them behind. There is, besides, something animating in the reflection, that I am in London though partaking none of its gaieties."

WOMAN.—Woman is a very nice and a very complicated machine. Her springs are infinitely delicate, and differ from those of a man as the work of a repeating watch does from that of a town clock. Look at her body—how delicately formed! Examine her senses—how exquisite and nice!—Observe her understanding, how subtle and acute! But look into her heart—there is the watch work, composed of parts so minute in themselves, and so wonderfully combined, that they must be seen by a microscopic eye to be clearly comprehended. The perception of woman is as quick as lightning. Her penetration is intuition—I had almost said instinct. By a glance of her eye she shall draw a deep and just conclusion. Ask her how she formed it, she cannot answer the question.—As the perception of woman is surprisingly quick, so their soul's imaginations are uncommonly susceptible. Few of them have culture enough to write; but when they do, how lively are their pictures! how animated their descriptions! But if few women write, they all talk! and every man may judge of them in this point, from every circle he goes into. Spirit in conversation depends entirely upon fancy, and women all over the world talk better than men. Have they a character to pourtray, or a figure to describe, they give but three traits of one or the other, and the character is known, or the figure placed before our eyes. Why? From the monument of susceptibility, their imaginations, their fancies receive lively impressions from those principal traits, and they paint those impressions with the same vivacity with which they receive them. Get a woman of fancy warm in conversation, she shall produce a hundred charming images, among which there shall not be one indelicate or coarse. Warm a man on the same subject, he will probably find stronger allusions, but neither be so brilliant nor so chaste.—*Sherlock.*

TO A LADY WITH A VIOLET.
In aspect meek, in dwelling low,
I hide me in the grassy lea;
But twine me round thy modest brow
Lady! the proudest flower I'll be.

PROTESTANT AND CATHOLIC.

WHERE a priest and a poor curate were left to themselves in a remote and poor parish of Ireland, they were often the best friends possible. They were, in fact, forced together by the love of congenial society, and the social propensities of Irishmen. The following is an illustrative instance, and a good story to boot. We find it recorded in a new publication called "Wild Sports of the West," which few would guess to mean Rabbit-chasing and Otter-hunting in the sister island.

"Och, hon!" exclaimed the otter-killer, "isn't it a murder to see the clargy making such fools of themselves now! When I was young, priests and ministers were hand and glove. It seems to me but yesterday, when Father Patt Joyce, the Lord be good to him! lent Mr. Carson a congregation."

"Eh! what, Antony!" said the colonel; "a congregation appears rather an extraordinary article to borrow."

The otter-killer explains the mystery thus:

"We were just as comfortable as we could be, when a currier stops at the door with a letter, which he said was for Mr. Carson. Well, when the minister opens it, he got as white as a sheet, and I thought he would have fainted. Father Patt crossed himself. 'Arrah, Dick,' says he, 'the Lord stand between you and evil! is there any thing wrong?'—'I'm ruined,' says he, 'for some *bad member* has wrote to the bishop, and told him that I have no congregation, because you and I are so intimate; and he's coming down to-morrow with the *dane* to see the state of things. Och, hone!' says he, 'I'm fairly ruined.'—'And is that all that's fretten ye?' says the priest—'Arrah, dear Dick,'—for they called each other by their *Cristen* names,—'is this all? If it's a congregation you want, ye shall have a dacent one to-morrow, and lave that to me ;—and now, we'll take our drink, and not matter the bishop a fig.'

"Well, next day, sure enough, down comes the bishop, and a great retinue along with him; and there was Mr. Carson ready to receive him. 'I hear,' says the bishop, mighty stately, 'that you have no congregation.'—'In faith, your holiness,' says he, 'you'll be soon able to tell that,' —and in he walks him to the church, and there were sitting threescore well-dressed men and women, and all of them as devout as if they were going to be anointed; for that blessed morning, Father Patt whipped mass over before you had time to bless yourself, and the clanest of the flock was before the bishop in the church, and ready for his holiness. To see that all behaved properly, Father Patt had hardly put off the vestment till he slipped on a *cota more*, and there he sat in a back seat like any other of the congregation. I was near the bishop's reverence; he was seated in an arm-chair belonging to the priest—'Come here, Mr Carson,' says he 'some enemy of yours,' says the sweet old gentleman, 'wanted to injure you with me. But I am now fully satisfied.' And turning to the dane, 'By this book!' says he, 'I didn't see a claner congregation this month of Sundays!'"

SCRAPS.
ORIGINAL AND SELECTED.

CONVERSATION OF AUTHORS AND ARTISTS.—Walpole, who had a good deal of experience of them, says, " I have always rather escaped the society of authors. An author talking of his own works, or censuring those of others, is to me a dose of ipecacuanha. I like only a few, who can in company forget their authorship, and remember plain sense. The conversation of artists is still worse. Vanity and envy are the main ingredients. One detests vanity, because it shocks one's own vanity." The same writer gives some good counsel to young authors. "Youth is prone to censure. A young man of genius expects to make a world for himself; as he gets older, he finds he must take it as it is. It is impudent in a young author to make any enemies whatever. He should not attack any living person. Pope was, perhaps, too refined, a jesuit, a professor of authorship; and his arts to establish his reputation were infinite, and sometimes, perhaps, exceeded the bounds of severe integrity. But in this he was an example of prudence, that he wrote no satire till his fortune was made." The advice is good—we cannot so much admire the motive of the course prescribed.

FEMALE QUARRELS.—A gentleman, hearing that two of his female relations had quarrelled, inquired, "Did they call each other ugly?"—" No."—" Or old?"—" No." —" Well, well, I shall soon make them friends."

BISHOP BURNET was a very absent man. It is related, that dining one day with the Duchess of Marlborough, after her husband's disgrace, he compared the great general to Belisarius.—" But then" said the Duchess, " how comes it that such a man was so miserable, and so universally deserted."—" Oh, madam, he *has such a brimstone* of a wife!"

CONTEMPORARY JUDGMENTS.—Burnet speaks of " one Prior," and Whitelocke, of " one Milton, a blind man."— Heath, an obscure chronicler of the civil wars, says, " One Milton, since stricken with blindness, wrote against Salmasius, and composed an impudent and blasphemous book, called Iconoclastes!"

ENCOURAGEMENT TO LITERARY MEN.—One day a Number Publisher of the Row discovered the lodgings of Gibbon the historian, waited on him, and said, "Sir, I am about publishing a History of England, done by several good hands. I understand you have a knack at them there things,—I should be glad to give you every encouragement."—The GREAT author was more offended than enough.

ECONOMY.—" A slight knowledge of human nature will show," says Mr Colquhoun, " that when a man gets on a little in the world he is desirous of getting on a little further." Such is the growth of provident habits, that it has been said, if a journeyman lays by the first five shillings, his fortune is made. Mr. William Hall, who has bestowed great attention on the state of the labouring poor, declares he never knew an instance of one who had saved money coming to the parish. And he adds, moreover, " those individuals who save money are better workmen; if they do not work better, they behave better, and are more respectable; and I would sooner have in my trade a hundred men who save money, than two hundred men who would spend every shilling they get. In proportion as individuals save a little money, their morals are much better; they husband that little, and there is a superior tone given to their morals, and they behave better for knowing they have a little stake in society."

ILLUSTRATION OF THE TRUCK SYSTEM.—The cruelty which is inflicted on the workman by the payment of his wages in goods, is often very severe. The little purchases necessary for the comfort of his wife and children, perhaps the medicines he occasionally requires for them in illness, must all be made through the medium of barter, and he is obliged to waste his time in arranging an exchange, in which the goods which he has been compelled to accept for his labour are invariably taken at a lower price than that at which his master charged them to him. The father of the family perhaps, writhing under the agonies of the toothache, is obliged to make his hasty bargain with the village surgeon, ere he will remove the cause of his pain; or the disconsolate mother is compelled to sacrifice her depreciated goods in exchange for the last receptacle of her departed offspring.—*Babbage's Economy of Manufactures.*

THE SPOONERY.—By what process does a man born with a silver spoon in his mouth,—taught nonsense verses at Eton,—wenching, driving, and the habits of the spendthrift at the university,—learn the condition of the middle and lower classes of society, their wants, their feelings, opinions, and habits? But if chance gives him a glimpse of the circumstances of other ranks of life, made half intelligible to him by the reading of a newspaper or a novel, —by what singular gift of nature does he, whose personal habits are in constant war with business, become possessed of the knowledge of its minute operations? He may understand the law of usury, from his dealings in youth with the Jews; he may not be altogether unacquainted with the law of debtor and creditor, and the doctrine of profits, from having figured in incipient actions, and paid twenty, fifty, or a hundred per cent for long credit. Jurisprudence he may have learnt as a magistrate at the sessions, or a grand-juryman at the assizes: the laws of real property, and the question of the general registry from his attorney, with whom he is deeply mortgaged; the corn-laws from his steward; the poor-laws from his tenants at quarter-day; criminal law from committing poachers: these have been generally the incidental lessons—the casual experiences of a legislator. He started in life flushed with the possession of wealth beyond the powers of his mind to spend usefully, frequented the turf, passed through the gambling house, escaped with a reduced fortune, or else became sordidly poor. In the one case he became sober and wise, and turned his knowledge of life to account by making laws, as if all men were fit for the galleys, irrecoverably vicious, or honest only when they have discovered from the effects of their vices that its seeming is the best policy. In the other case, he presented the *beau idéal* of the place-hunter.—*Westminster Review.*

TO CORRESPONDENTS.

Several communications are in types, but are necessarily delayed for want of room.

The Third Monthly Part of the SCHOOLMASTER will be published on Wednesday the 31st inst., containing the Four September Numbers, and JOHNSTONE'S MONTHLY POLITICAL REGISTER OF NEWS AND SCOTTISH LISTS: Price 8d.

The REGISTER will, in future, like the SCHOOLMASTER, consist of 16 pages, super-royal octavo, and will contain, in addition to the same sort of news given in the first and second numbers, the *Spirit of the London Journals* for the month, &c. &c.

†† The principles of this Monthly Newspaper are decidedly liberal, and thoroughly independent of every party. The great demand for single Numbers of this Register has induced the Editor to double its size and increase the price only one halfpenny.

CONTENTS OF NO. XIII.

All Hallow Eve.—The Scotch Hallow E'en	193
Curious Traits of Feudal Manners	194
An Old English Baronet's Opinion of Modern Manners	195
Fashionables	196
The Barn Owl	196
The Stricket Minister	198
One of Sir H. Davy's Experiments	199
Notes on Germany	197
ELEMENTS OF THOUGHT—What have I to do with Politics? Nothing	200
THE STORY-TELLER.—The Soldier's Return	201
COLUMN FOR THE LADIES.—Mrs. Inchbald, &c.	207
Protestant and Catholic	207
Scraps, Original and Selected	208

EDINBURGH: Printed by and for JOHN JOHNSTONE, 19, St. James's Square.—Published by JOHN ANDERSON, Jun., Bookseller, 55, North Bridge Street, Edinburgh; by JOHN MACLEOD, and ATKINSON & Co., Booksellers, Glasgow; and sold by all Booksellers and Vendors of Cheap Periodicals.

THE Schoolmaster,
AND
EDINBURGH WEEKLY MAGAZINE.

CONDUCTED BY JOHN JOHNSTONE.

THE SCHOOLMASTER IS ABROAD.—LORD BROUGHAM.

No. 14.—Vol. I. SATURDAY, NOVEMBER 3, 1832. Price Three-Halfpence.

PLACES OF PUBLIC WORSHIP IN EDINBURGH.

This article has appeared in the *Chronicle*. I also give it here, as the subject is one of interest, far beyond Edinburgh; many town readers may see the *Schoolmaster*, when they do not see the *Chronicle*.
  J. J.

It may be deemed daring, if not absolutely profane, to say that, in this capital of a Presbyterian country, and in all our great towns, the religious discipline of those who most require instruction is very little cared for, so far as regards facilitating the easy means of attendance on public worship. Two good, or at least fair, discourses are preached in all the stated churches every Sabbath, to all who are able to pay exorbitantly high for seats, and who have decent clothes to appear in them. Although the two new churches projected were built to-morrow, they would be but a drop in the bucket to the wants of this city,—to the most pressing and urgent wants,—those of the stranger, the very young, and the very poor: yet, this is not so much from mere lack of space,— but, of open, free, inviting church accommodation to all who will accept of it. It may be thought too daring to affirm, that, in this city, while the hospitable door of the low tippling-house stands open night and day, those of the churches are rigidly shut against the poor, by pride, and by Mammon. Religion in its modes is become, in this Presbyterian country, as *exclusive* as are fashion and wealth. In our finely decorated temples, there is clearly no place for the humbly-dressed Christian. On liberal Christian principles, this is lamentable enough,—but it were less to be regretted, were more humble places of worship freely and widely opened to him. This, however, in all its bearings, is, perhaps, rather a question for states, and for synods, and assemblies, than for the local authorities. We must, therefore, confine ourselves to Edinburgh, to which there come up every season, for one purpose or other, some thousands of young men, or rather boys, remote from any thing like moral superintendence. They form a mere fraction of our floating population, but a most important part of the men of the world that shall arise a few years hence. Without considerable trouble, which they will not take, and expense, which they will not incur, the doors of every church are shut against them,—for no one will go to church here, that has not a seat;—the door-keepers would soon cure any one of that fancy.—Many hundreds of young women, also, come up every year to service.—They don't know much about taking seats in church; and they cannot, or think they cannot, afford the expense of them; and genteel families now,—that is all families,—would as soon be seen with their servants in their box at the playhouse, as in their pew at church. The consequences are soon seen.—A still more interesting description of persons to our feelings, are the decent poor, driven with their young families from the country parishes and small towns, by misfortune, in search of precarious employment, destitute and miserable, scarcely able to keep a roof over their heads, much less to pay seat-rent,—tossed about from place to place, daily falling back, and growing worse off,—

" The world not their friend, nor the world's law."

The doors of our comfortable churches, and snug meeting-houses, are strictly closed against their ragged penury, should they have sufficient fortitude to shew their wretchedness in our goodly Christian fellowships. Many such persons repair to large towns with good habits; but how are they to retain them, or impart them to their children? In their own villages, their children might have grown up well instructed and respectable;—but what becomes of them among us, where the chief attention they receive is, to be taunted for their residence in the Cowgate or Grassmarket—regions somewhere far beyond the pale of humanity, as it subsists in the comfortable and affluent streets, and a thousand degrees beyond the line of the Christianity of our fine churches.

We have heard of a mission being established in some of the remote half discovered regions, known only to such daring navigators as the police Captain Stuart. It is impossible that any municipality could completely remedy the evils of which we complain, but surely something might be done to prevent their worst consequences. Sometimes, indeed, we have seen a feeble attempt made, which soon languished away.

The extreme poverty, and dense population of the Old Town parishes, place a gulf between the people and the clergyman, which nothing but the zeal of a primitive apostle, or of a modern Catholic priest—if we dare mention so obnoxious a person—could overleap. Now what we would propose is, that there should be small chapels, halls, or school-rooms, where poor neighbourhoods,—the communities of our closes and wynds, that would shrink from our fine churches, as they are at present constituted,—might assemble on Sundays, and where their parish ministers might sometimes meet them, —places of worship which they should have a claim to enter, where the seats would be their own, of right,—connected with their lodging-rooms, for example, or attached in some simple way that might be devised. The regular clergyman never could be able to take care of these auxiliary sanctuaries, but he might frequently visit them ; and in this city he could never want *curates ;* nor would the maintenance of this religious police establishment cost much to each of the Old Town parishes. And if it did, how could a state or municipality expend part of its revenues to better purpose than in making religious and moral discipline what they ought to be—the main object of their sway. It would, to be sure, be better that people of all degrees of rank and fortune would meet together under the same roof of worship. But this, it appears, does not suit our habits ; and what are called *gratis* sittings in the great churches are reprehensible on many accounts. Distinctions,—invidious every where, when people assemble for a common object, are peculiarly so in church. The " Sit thou there, for I am richer," is a principle as injurious to the wealthy man who acts on it, as to the poor man who is insulted by its display. Flesh and blood will rebel, and there is no true wisdom in rousing their corruption, especially in church. Nor do dissenting meeting-houses in the least obviate the necessity of small places of worship for the *very poor.* The congregations attending these have to maintain their own minister ; and though they manage to have their seat-rents much lower than in the Established churches, for which large sums in stipend are raised, the rents are generally far higher than in country parishes and small towns. At any rate, they are not the resort of the *nommade* poor population, for whose wants it is desirable to provide by small auxiliary chapels ; nurseries from which, as they throve, drafts would, from time to time, be made to the regular churches. We must not, we fear, presume to cite with approbation Catholic cities, where the churches stand ever open—where all are entitled to enter the wide area. But there is a medium between this and our custom of selfish exclusion, as there is between the Catholic doctrine of *Confession,* and our system of indifference and non-interference. Because our clergy are not to *confess* their flock, are they never to *converse* with them ?

If there were but one of our fine large churches open to the public at large, to which the young, the stranger, all who chose to enter, should be welcome till it was crowded, to which they might be attracted by talent and character, of how much benefit it might be ? Let us have but one such church, together with a half-dozen small auxiliary chapels, placed in the heart of the poor crowded districts, and the fruits of benevolence, and of true Christian charity, would soon appear. The condition of the sister establishment may make us all think. Upon her the storm has come neither from the south nor the north, neither from bigoted Catholics, nor yet sour Presbyterians. Her deadly and dangerous enemies are those of her own house, the neglected people of her charge, who know nothing about their higher clergy save as wealthy pluralists or sinecurists, and greedy tithe-collectors. Wherever small meeting-houses have been opened in the poorest neighbourhoods of Edinburgh, if there was nothing to pay, save a half-penny at the plate or not at discretion, with a reasonable seat-rent, little congregations have been formed and have soon been crowded, even when the preacher was very inferior to the auxiliaries whom our clergy could find among their unprovided young friends. The extreme care which the Catholic clergy bestow on the instruction of children, is a feature in their discipline deserving of imitation among us. Catholics are not so lazy in their worship ; their service begins at an earlier hour of the morning, and the afternoon is either principally or wholly devoted to the children, who are instructed in presence of their parents ; not by deputy, but by the priest. We may call his wicked pains. Let us take equal pains to better purpose.

A Seat in Church.—A very genteel-looking young man was seen to enter a church in time of service ; he paused at the entrance ; the congregation stared ; he advanced a few steps, and deliberately surveying the whole assembly, commenced a slow march up the broad aisle ; not a pew was opened ; the audience were too busy for civility ; he wheeled, and in the same manner performed a march, stepping as if to " Roslin Castle," or the " Dead March in Saul," and disappeared. A few moments after he re-entered with a huge block upon his shoulders, as heavy as he could well stagger under ; his countenance was immoveable ; again the people stared, half-rose from their seats, with their books in their hands.—At length he placed the block in the very centre of the principal passage, and seated himself upon it. Then, for the first time, the reproach was felt. Every pew door in the church was instantly flung open. But—no the stranger was a gentleman ; he came not there for disturbance ; he moved not ; smiled not ; but preserved the utmost decorum, until the service was concluded, when he shouldered his block, and walked out.

A Frenchman, having a violent pain in the breast and stomach, went to a physician for relief. The doctor inquiring where his trouble lay, the Frenchman, with a dolorous accent, laying his hand on his breast, said, " Vy, sare, I have one very bad pain in my *portmanteau,*" (meaning his *chest.)*

NOTES OF THE MONTH.
NOVEMBER.

> Next was NOVEMBER; the full grown and fat,
> As fed with lard, and that right well might seem;
> For he had been a fatting hogs of late,
> That his brows with sweat did reek and steam.
> *Shepherd's Calendar.*

THIS gloomy month, "when Englishmen hang or drown themselves," was named *wind-monath* by the old English, and also *blod* or *blot-monath*, as in it field fodder and meat for cattle getting scarce, cows, sheep, and pigs were killed, and salted for winter and spring use. Hence in Scotland we have the phrase, "The winter *Mart*." In England, they had Martinmas beef. A goodly crop of puddings, sausages, potted meats, and tripes, are still going at this season in Ireland, the Highlands, and in the primitive parts of England. This is one of the most *domestic* months of the year; one might call it the *fire-side* month. The modern social festivities of the season do not begin for six or seven weeks after its commencement, and it is in town the month of needle-work, reading, and music, in the long evenings;—in the cottage, of the wheel, and the knitting-needles; hoes, and rakes, and shoes are now mended; bee-hives and baskets made. Even the animals now make themselves *snug*, and retire to their hoards in their winter burrows,—repair to their *town-houses*, shall we say. The squirrel, the dormouse, and the bat, are no longer seen abroad. Moles are busy preparing nests for their young of the next spring. Planting is still going forward both in garden and woodland. "The cottager, who puts an elm or ash into his hedge, or an apple-tree into his garden," says some one, " is a patriot in his way. It is an increase of the national wealth, of the best kind." We forget what English gentleman last year planted trees, with his poor neighbours, in commemoration of the Reform Bill. It was a noble idea. TREES have now nearly all shed their leaves. The walnut is the first in succession to drop its foliage; next in order the horse-chestnut, sycamore, lime, ash, elm; and the apple and peach in the gardens. The oak and beech retain their dry russet-coloured leaves till they are pushed off by the young foliage. BIRDS never leave us: The plover is now often heard; and green-finches are seen in flocks; field-fares are appearing, and the robin's plaintive note still comes from the cottage gable, or the mossy pales of the garden.

> "On the haw-clustered thorn, a motley flock,
> Of various plume, and various note,
> Discordant chirp; the linnet and the thrush
> With speckled breast; the blackbird yellow-beaked,
> The goldfinch, field-fare, and the sparrow pert."

FLOWERS.—" This is the time," says Mr. Leigh Hunt, who has written so charmingly of the months, "for domestic cultivators of flowers to be very busy in preparing for those spring and winter ornaments, which used to be thought the work of magic. They may plant hyacinths, dwarf tulips, polyanthus-narcissus, or any other moderately growing bulbous roots, either in water-glasses, or in pots of light dry earth, to flower early in their apartments. If in glasses, the bulb should be just in the water. If in pots, just covered with the earth." This pretty and fanciful species of flower-gardening has been much improved and extended, even in the short period elapsed since Mr. Hunt wrote. By varying the form of the pot, twenty "fantastic tricks" are played with the crocus, and other flowers. The first of the month is All Saints' Day; the 5th that festival of bigotry, the *Gunpowder Plot*, which, however, receives no notice in Scotland, save from Edinburgh Castle. Even that would be more honoured in the breach than the observance. The 9th is the *Lord Mayor's Shew*, now a good deal shorn of its splendours, and somewhat of its "wassail." The 11th, Martinmas term, when the landlord gives a friendly call, and lasses may be seen skimming about, with a band-box under one arm, the other hand keeping their petticoats out of the mud, that they may go *feat* and *trig* to their new homes; a porter or a friend following with " that mystery," the *kist.* The 24th is remembered in England as the anniversary of the Great Storm, which commenced on the 24th Nov. 1703, and raged for three days, committing fearful ravages. The damage in London alone was computed at two millions. About eight thousand vessels were destroyed, or blown away and never more heard of. Innumerable trees were uprooted, in many places. The Eddystone lighthouse was overturned into the sea. Many lives were lost. Some of the events told of the storm in the island of Barbadoes last year appeared incredible; still more incredible is the authenticated fact, of a stone of four hundred weight, near Shaftesbury, being then torn up and carried seven yards by the force of the wind. Queen Anne ordered a National Fast at the time of this storm.

ST. ANDREW'S DAY, 30TH NOV.

St. Andrew, the patron saint of Scotland and of Muscovy, was one of the Apostles. This day is now observed, by his Scottish disciples, on the Ganges, the Mississippi, and the rivers of New Holland. It is also a great day at home, particularly among " the free and accepted masons."

BOOKS OF THE MONTH.

SARRANS' MEMOIR OF LAFAYETTE, and History of the Revolution of the Three Days, is the most important book that has lately appeared. It will be read with great interest by those who like to examine the hidden springs which regulate the movements of great events.

MEMOIRS OF THE DUCHESS OF ABRANTES.—Two more volumes have been published; another volume of the new edition of Byron's works has appeared; and a volume of the FAMILY LIBRARY, forming a history of PETER THE GREAT. The last month has, however, produced little but a few *Annuals;* and for *Perennials*, if we are to have any, we must wait till 1833.

OF PERIODICALS, the *Foreign Quarterly* and *Edinburgh Review*, have appeared. The latter contains several ponderous articles, but sensible and useful, nevertheless; that on Railroads will be read with interest.

BOOK OF BUTTERFLIES.

A very pretty, *cheap* work, highly embellished with coloured butterflies, and the gaudy moths of tropical regions. The *natural history*, or descriptive part, is by Captain BROWN. This will make a delightful present to young people, and is worth a score of the trumpery annuals.

MEMOIR OF SIR WALTER SCOTT; with Critical Notices of his Writings. By David Vedder. Dundee: Allardice.

Remembering the fate of Swift, Pope, Johnson, Byron we were in tribulation lest the death of Sir Walter Scott had called forth about triple the number of biographers and anecdote-mongers. We trust we are quit for our fears; the smaller world of letters has maintained a praiseworthy decorum and delicacy on this subject. Very little *clish-maclaver* has yet been vented—a low word this, we agree with Dr. Jamieson, but an emphatic one. Of the Notices of Sir Walter Scott which have appeared, we consider Mr. Vedder's the most valuable, and for this undeniable reason, that instead of giving us merely the author's opinion, we have the most acute critiques of the *Edinburgh Review*, and of some of our ablest writers, on the works of Scott. The concentration of those scattered lights is highly creditable to the judgment and good taste of Mr. Vedder. These opinions, intermixed with a Narrative of Sir Walter Scott's literary life, form the subject of this cheap memoir, which those who wish to become acquainted with the history of his progress in literature will find a useful acquisition.

LITERARY GEMS. Selected by A. Thomson, Teacher of English, Greenock.

A *nice* little selection, intended, the selector says, for "the use of his pupils," from Mrs. Hemans, Pollok, Bryant, &c. &c. &c. with a *prose* appendix. Unless Mr. Thomson's academy is intended for unfledged poets, his prose should have borne a larger proportion to his verse.

RETROSPECTIONS OF A SEXAGENARIAN; or Latter Struggles in Life.

We have seen with interest correspondent to our personal feelings of respect, and to those entertained by those connected with the publishing trade in Scotland, a work announced under the above title, by Mr. George Miller, late Bookseller in Dunbar. Mr. Miller was, for many years, not only a spirited publisher, but a meritorious writer. All his works we have not seen, but from personal knowledge we are enabled to speak with confidence of some of them. His CHEAP MAGAZINE was the first of the cheap useful works published in Scotland. It appeared about twenty years back, and was as much or more for its day than CHAMBERS' JOURNAL, or JOHNSTONE'S SCHOOLMASTER are now. Mr. Miller's new work is to be published by subscription, and several of the most eminent of the Edinburgh booksellers interest themselves particularly in its success, anxious to show all the attention they can to a worthy member of their profession, in the evening of life, cruelly involved in difficulties by the late mischances of the book trade in London, and through no fault of his own. We believe Messrs. Oliver and Boyd, and Mr. Cadell manage the subscription in Edinburgh; and we cannot doubt but that every Scotch bookseller and individual connected with the press will do what he can to advance it in their different towns. Independently of personal feelings, we have every reason to expect that, from his extent of information and adventures as a publisher, the RETROSPECTIONS of our Scottish Lackington will prove a most amusing work. It will, we understand, contain 400 pages octavo, and be bound in cloth, price eight shillings. It should, we think, have been a half guinea; but half-crowns are, unhappily, become objects of great interest in these days.

SKETCHES OF THE EDINBURGH CLERGY; with Portraits.

This is a handsome volume, got up in the best style, and likely to be highly valued by the friends and parishioners of the different ministers as a pleasing memorial. On fair grounds, no country is more affectionately attached to its ministers than Scotland; and the Edinburgh clergy are understood to be the chosen of the Scottish church. Among the sketches and portraits Sir Henry Moncreiff and Dr. Thomson are included. As a specimen of the work, we give the following interesting notice of

DR. CHALMERS.

"Dr. Chalmers, whose name is entitled to be placed at the head of the Church of Scotland, was born of respectable parents, at the town of Anstruther, in Fife. He received his college education at St. Andrews; and, after having been licensed as a preacher, he officiated, for some time, as assistant to the late minister of Cavers, a parish lying within a few miles of Hawick, in Roxburghshire. He was ordained minister of Kilmany on 12th May, 1803, a parish beautifully situated amid the 'green hills and smiling valleys' of Fife, and in the immediate vicinity of St. Andrews. While here, he, for one season, assisted the late Professor Vilant in teaching the Mathematical Class at the College of St. Andrews, where his talents attracted so much celebrity, that when, in a following session, he commenced a private class of his own, on the same branch of science, the students all flocked to him. He afterwards delivered a course of lectures on chemistry, in which he also excels. Indeed, he had, very early in life, given indication of those superior talents, and that ardent love of science and literature, which have ever marked his career. He made his first appearance as an author, in a pamphlet published at Cupar-Fife, on the Leslie Controversy. It was written in the form of a letter, addressed to Professor Playfair; the *brochure* abounds in talent, wit and genuine humour. It was published anonymously; and, to this day, is not generally known to have been his production. He vindicates in it, very powerfully, the divines of the Church of Scotland, from the imputation of a want of mathematical talent, a reproach which he thought Professor Playfair had thrown upon them. Dr. Chalmers had not then adopted his subsequent views on the subject of pluralities, otherwise he had no reason to regret this his first publication. On the occasion of the vacancy in the Chair of Mathematics in the University of Edinburgh, in 1805, Dr. Chalmers offered himself as a candidate, and, we believe, was not without considerable chance of success: but some of his own nearest relatives felt anxious that he should continue as a minister, and he withdrew his pretensions to the chair, in order to remain in the bosom of that church, of which he was destined one day to be the most distinguished ornament.

"Dr. Chalmers next publication appeared in 1808, and was entitled, 'An Inquiry into the Extent and Stability of National Resources.' In it he endeavours to prove the independence of the country of foreign trade. The work displays talent, and is eloquently written; but his mind now embraced those deep convictions of religious truths which led him to devote himself almost exclusively to his sacred profession. The common statement is, that this happy change took place when engaged in writing the article 'Christianity,' for Brewster's Encyclopædia, which contains an able and original exposition of the evidences of the truth of our religion, and was afterwards published separately. Be this as it may, the result was happy; his zeal, earnestness, and eloquence soon drew on him the public eye, and speedily enthroned him as the first pulpit orator of the age. Latterly, at Kilmany, the people used to flock from Dundee and St. Andrews on the Sabbaths, to hear him preach.

"In 1815, he was called to be minister of the Tron Church of Glasgow, and his name and excellence conferred a new literary celebrity on that commercial city. Besides the ardent direct pursuit of his profession, Dr. Chalmers here embarked keenly, and with indefatigable labour, in plans for the improvement of the education of the poor and though, in the prosecution of these, he had to encounter a vast mass of prejudice, he was eminently successful and accomplished much good for the community of Glasgow. His views on these subjects are fully developed, in a large work he published at this time, entitled the "Christian and Civic Economy of Large Towns;" which, although, from the circumstance of being brought out in a series of numbers, rather diffuse, and interspersed with a most intolerable quantity of foot-notes, very tiresome t the patience of the reader, abounds with many enlightened views, and much valuable matter, regarding the poor laws, and all the other branches of Christian economics. In 1819, Dr Chalmers was translated to the new church and parish of St. John's, where he prosecuted these plans with renewed vigour, till 1823, when he was elected professor of Moral Philosophy in the University of St. Andrews, where he imparted a very different character to this course from the mere worldly cast which it too generally assumes in our universities. While here, he also delivered a separate course of Lectures on Political Economy, as connected with the Moral Philosophy Chair.

"Dr. Chalmers was, more than once, offered an Edinburgh church; but he had long conceived that his widest sphere of usefulness was a Theological Chair. We often used to dread that his valuable life might pass away before an opportunity occurred of his being transferred to the Scottish metropolis; but, at length, in 1828, on the Divinity Chair in the University of Edinburgh becoming vacant, the Magistrates and Council, much to their honour, with one voice, elected Dr. Chalmers. In doing so, they conferred a boon of inestimable value on our national Church, from the ardour, eloquence, and industry he has brought to the important charge, and his deep sense of its great responsibility. Seated in this chair, and with all the ardour of his powerful and energetic mind devoted to the rearing of the future Christian instructors of the land, he may indeed be styled one of the nursing fathers of our Church, and the vast quantum of good that he may thus ultimately accomplish, it is impossible to calculate. His first course more than realized all that his most zealous friends could expect, and he rendered his lectures deeply interesting and stimulating to the students. At one time, the object of the young men seemed to be to evade attendance on the Divinity Lecture, now the difficulty became to get a good place to hear their eloquent instructor. In March, 1832, Dr. Chalmers completed, for the first time, one revolution of his theological cycle, consisting of four different courses of lectures. During the last session, he also delivered, during one day of the week, a series of valuable Lectures on the Importance of Church Establishments. He considers the value of the parochial system as beautifully exemplified in the greater attendance on a *local* than on a *general* Sabbath-school, the process which was first established in Glasgow, and is now pretty widely followed throughout England and Ireland. Church establishments he views as founded on the same principle. He considers that each established *church* throughout the land may be termed a centre of *emanation*, from which Christianity may, with proper zeal, be made to move, by an aggressive and converting operation, on the wide mass of the people, whilst a dissenting *chapel* he views as a centre of *attraction* only for those who are already religiously disposed. He thinks that the population of our large cities has outgrown the provision of ministers and churches, and that the practice of household cultivation, on the part of the clergy, has fallen far too much into desuetude.

"It has often been alleged that the clergy show on all occasions the utmost anxiety to increase their income by any change of place. Dr. Chalmers is one living refutation of this, he having refused the most wealthy living in the Church of Scotland, the West parish of Greenock, which was proffered him recently by the patron.

"Dr. Chalmers has published several volumes of sermons, all of them of a most useful practical tendency. His "Discourses on the Christain Revelation, viewed in connexion with the Modern Astronomy," constitute one of the most splendid productions of his genius, and have had an immense circulation, having gone through eleven editions. His "Sermons on the Application of Christianity to the Commercial and Ordinary Affairs of Life," ought to be in the hands of every person engaged in the business of the world, being of admirable practical utility. Some of his sermons preached on public occasions, are brilliant exhibitions of eloquence and power in pulpit oratory, combined with real usefulness. Dr. Chalmers lately brought out a very interesting and valuable work, "On Political Economy in Connexion with the Moral State and Moral Prospects of Society." This work displays a mind familiar with the *elements* of political science, and which has thought deeply on the subject; while, in the course of it, he has to discuss the most complicated and difficult questions in political economy, the whole structure and process of his argument is to prove, that to rear a well-educated, prudent, virtuous and religious people, habituated to moral restraints, is the true—the only way to accomplish the great objects of political economy. But from this brief notice of Dr. Chalmers' writings, we must return to discuss his character as a minister.

"As a preacher, Dr. Chalmers is altogether unrivalled. The sermon he delivered before the King's Commissioner, in the High Church of Edinburgh, in 1816, perhaps first widely established his fame. His discourse on that occasion comprised the essence of his astronomical sermons, and was probably as magnificent a display of eloquence as was ever heard from the pulpit. The effect produced on the audience will not easily be forgotten by any one who had the gratification of being present.

"From that day crowds followed after him wherever he went; and, to use his own language, he felt the burden of ' a popularity of stare, and pressure, and animal heat.' When in London, Canning, Lord Castlereagh, Lord Eldon, the Duke of Sussex, with several branches of the Royal Family, and many others, whom, the journals remarked, they ' were not accustomed to elbow at a place of public worship,' were found anxiously waiting to obtain admission to hear this modern Massillon. An observation made by Foster, in one of his powerful and original essays, is peculiarly applicable to the talismanic effect of Chalmers eloquence; he observes, that ' real eloquence strikes on your mind with irresistible force, and leaves you not the possibility of asking or thinking whether it be eloquence.'

"Dr. Chalmers is indeed such a preacher as rises up only once in many centuries. Labouring under the disadvantage of a provincial accent and pronunciation, he soon overcomes these, and the stranger hearing him, is speedily made aware that a man of genius and unrivalled eloquence is before him. Even the language of his ordinary prayers betrays him; as for example, when he calls us to remember, ' that every hour that strikes—every morning that dawns—and every evening that darkens around us,' brings us nearer to the end of our earthly pilgrimage.—We know no man whose language in prayer is nearly so impressive, and who so completely lifts the mind from its constant occupation with sublunary things, to the unseen realities of an everlasting world.—He, as it were, draws the mind out of its earthliness to purer and holier regions.

"In passages of solemn religious import, as well as those of deepest pathos, we never heard the orator who could approach him; for though we have had the gratification of hearing the celebrated Robert Hall of Leicester,—and he can be held up as a *perfect model* in writing the English language, which Chalmers cannot,—the two, as mere pulpit orators, cannot exactly be compared,—each was greatest in his own sphere; but though brothers in genius, they were not so in their style of composition.

"Dr. Chalmers is almost the only pulpit orator we ever heard who could preach upwards of an hour without in the least fatiguing the attention of his audience.

"The *frankness* of Dr. Chalmers' eloquence, if we may so designate it, is interesting. He speaks from the heart to the heart. What an ordinary preacher would be afraid to give utterance to, he pours forth with deep and affectionate anxiety to the ears of his audience, and it penetrates to the soul. We can of a truth say of Dr. Chalmers sermons—and it is the strongest criterion of a practical preacher—that we never heard one of them—and we havheard not a few—without having our minds possessed of an anxious desire to become better and holier than before, —and this truly is the best effect of eloquence in a preacher.

"There can be no greater moral and intellectual treat than to hear Dr. Chalmers from the pulpit. His sermons as far transcend those of the mawkish productions to be frequently met with, as does the genius of Milton or Newton surpass that of the common herd of poets and philosophers:

> 'Can earth afford
> Such genuine state, pre-eminence so free,
> As when, arrayed in Christ's authority,
> He from the pulpit lifts his awful hand;
> Conjures, implores, and labours all he can
> For re-subjecting to divine command
> The stubborn spirit of rebellious Man.'

"Owing to his academical duties, Dr. Chalmers has not preached very frequently since he came to Edinburgh; but it is hoped when his different courses of lectures are finally composed, he will more frequently appear in the pulpit. It were to be wished that he would allow himself to become, in Edinburgh, what the famous Kirwan was in Dublin, the preacher for our public charities. Kirwan worked wonders with his audience; but how poor and void of stamina are his discourses compared with those of Dr. Chalmers.

"Dr. Chalmers has some peculiar but enlightened views regarding public charities. These are to be found developed in some able articles on Pauperism he wrote in the *Edinburgh Review* several years ago, in his Christian and Civic Economy of Large Towns, and in his recent work on Political Economy; which opinions, however, need not prevent him advocating the cause of many valuable institutions that exist in Edinburgh, and this he has occasionally done with great success.

"There are two points in Dr. Chalmers' character, which seem chiefly worthy of admiration,—the first is the union of the most profound humility, with the highest genius,—and the other a deeply affectionate interest in the welfare of the human race. These characterize all his writings and actions both as a public and private individual.

"The distinction between Dr. Chalmers and Dr. Andrew Thomson, two of the most celebrated preachers that the Church of Scotland has ever produced, is, that Chalmers, along with great talents, is also a man of original and inventive *genius*; while Thomson, though possessed of powerful talents and indefatigable activity of mind, cannot be designated as a man of genius. The question has often been asked, What is genius? but although it is ethereal, the question has been well answered:—

> ' What is genius ? 'tis a flame
> Kindling all the human frame;
> 'Tis a ray that lights the eye,
> Soft in love, in battle high.
> 'Tis the lightning of the mind,
> Unsubdued and undefined ;
> 'Tis the flood that pours along
> The full clear melody of song ;
> 'Tis the sacred boon of Heaven,
> To its choicest favourites given.
> They who feel can paint it well.
> What is genius ? *Chalmers*, tell !'

"There was great truth in the remark made by the present Lord Advocate Jeffrey—and there could not be a better judge of eloquence—when he first heard Dr. Chalmers, on the occasion of a splendid speech against pluralities, delivered by him in the General Assembly ; that he could not say what it was, but there was something altogether remarkable about that man ; that the effects produced by his eloquence, reminded him more of what he had read of Cicero and Demosthenes than any thing he had ever heard."

SCIENTIFIC NOTICES.
HEAT.

IN No. XI. we intimated to our readers that it is our intention occasionally to devote a column of the *Schoolmaster* to investigation in science, and we shall now, with that view, proceed to explain a few of the properties of *Heat*. The nature or cause of heat, the most extensively diffused and most active agent in nature, is entirely unknown, and likely to remain so; but with many of its properties we are intimately acquainted, and to these only shall we direct the attention of our readers

The great general effect of heat is, that it causes all bodies to which it is applied to expand or increase in size. This law holds, whether the body exists in the solid, fluid, or aëriform state; but this week we shall confine our attention to the expansion of solids. All bodies do not expand in an equal degree by equal additions of heat, but in general seem to do so according to their density. Thus, if we apply equal additions of heat to equal bulks of iron, water, and air, the air will expand more than the water, and the water more than the iron. This probably arises from the particles of dense bodies cohering more firmly together, and presenting greater obstacles to their separation by the heat. We might easily relate various experiments by which the expansion of solids is proved, but it will probably be better understood from examples in which the law is taken advantage of by artisans and others. A blacksmith, in fixing the iron ring on the wheels of carriages, resorts for assistance to the law of expansion. At first he makes it with its diameter less than that of the wheel, and then causes it to increase to the proper size by heating it to a red heat; in this state it is placed on the wheel, and is instantly cooled by dashing cold water upon it; in cooling it contracts to its former size, and thus binds the various parts of the wheel so firmly together, that it will run for years without any other fastening. A singular example of the uses to which a knowledge of the Creator's laws may be put, was given a few years ago in Paris, in the case of the law now under consideration. The walls of a building were observed to bulge out so as to threaten its safety, and it was thought necessary to resort to some measures to prevent its destruction. The following plan was successfully resorted to: In various parts of the side walls holes were made opposite to each other, through which strong iron bars were introduced, so as to connect the two sides of the building; and on the projecting ends of the bars circular plates of metal were screwed close to the wall. Heat being then applied to the bars, they expanded, and consequently projected farther through the walls, which allowed the circular plates, to be screwed farther in; the bars being allowed to cool they contracted to their former length, and pulled the walls along with them. This was repeated until the walls regained their proper position.

The expansion of bodies, from the application of heat, produces effects, in some cases, necessary to be guarded against. It is a source of considerable inconvenience to clock makers. The movements of a clock depending upon the pendulum, whatever disturbs the regularity of its motion, must derange the whole machinery; and as the number of vibrations of the pendulum in a given time depends on its length,—the longer it is vibrating the more slowly, —the clock is found to go slower in warm than in cold weather, from the heat causing the pendulum to expand. Various contrivances have been made, however, to remedy the evil. One remedy, lately attempted, is to make pendulums of pavement stone taken from Sir John Sinclair's quarry. The stones may be distinguished in several streets of the new town of Edinburgh, being dry when the common pavement is damp, especially after frost. It is their close grain, apparently, that makes them expand very little by heat, and contract little by cold, and which thereby fits them for pendulums. We all know how dangerous it is to heat glass too suddenly. Heat, as we shall afterwards see, is diffused through some substances with much greater rapidity than through others. It is slowly diffused through glass, and when we pour hot water into a glass vessel, as a tumbler, the particles of glass contiguous to the water are immediately heated, and consequently they expand; but, as glass conducts heat slowly from one part to another, it is some time till the heat is transmitted to the particles which compose the glass on the outside of the tumbler; they do not therefore expand for some time, and offering a resistance to the expansion of the inner particles, a crack is the consequence. It might be expected from this, that a tumbler made of thin glass would stand sudden alterations of temperature better than one made of thick glass, as the heat will be diffused more rapidly through thin glass, and the expansion consequently will be more uniform, which accordingly is found to be the case.

It may be as well to notice here a singular instance of what appears to be an exception to the law of expansion. We say *appears*, because we have no doubt that, if our knowledge of the laws of Nature was more extended, instead of appearing a solitary exception to a general law, we should see in it a connecting link of the great system of the universe. In cooling, water, according to this law, contracts or decreases in volume; but, when it is cooled down to about 40 deg. Fahrenheit, instead of continuing to contract, it begins to expand, and continues to expand, till it reaches the 32d degree, when it freezes. Ice is, therefore, bulk for bulk, lighter than water, and accordingly it floats on the surface. Now, this is a very curious fact; and although, no doubt, it does appear a complete departure from an established law, we have in it a beautiful example of the benevolent care which the Almighty takes of the safety and comfort of the various inhabitants of the earth. Let us see what would have been the consequence had there been no exception to the law of expansion in this case. Had the water, on arriving within a few degrees of the freezing point, continued to contract, the coldest water, instead of remaining on the surface and freezing there, would have fallen to the bottom, where it would have frozen, and, as the surface of the water would be freely exposed to the cold air, a lake of very considerable depth would have been frozen from top to bottom in the course of a very few days. The consequence would have been, the destruction of the fishes and other inhabitants of the waters; and, instead of our beautiful lakes and rivers, we should have huge masses of ice from January to December, because our warmest summers would be unable to melt them. But, on the other hand, as the Almighty hath decreed that water should expand on approaching to the freezing point, the ice, on being formed, floats on the surface, and, being a bad conductor of heat, it prevents the water underneath from being too rapidly cooled, and, consequently, it requires a long and intense frost to freeze any considerable depth of water. That water expands on freezing may be easily proved:—Fill a bottle full of water, and, having corked it, place it in a freezing mixture of two parts of snow or ice to one of salt, or expose it to the open air in a frosty night, as soon as the water freezes, the bottle will burst. Country people well know the beneficial influence which frost has on rough cloddy land. The water which the clods contain is frozen, and, in freezing, it expands, and thus forces the different parts to fall asunder, like a lime shell when we pour water on it. We shall stop for the present, but by and by we shall treat of the expansion of fluid and aëriform bodies;—of the conduction and radiation of heat, and of the different capacities which different bodies have for heat.

CHILDISH CONCEIT CORRECTED.

I was kneeling one evening on my father's knee, waiting to receive my usual modicum of three roasted chestnuts, when my mother happened to say, "Pray take care of my beautiful goblet, Mr. Harding,—water so hot will break it I fear." My father was mixing his wine with hot water, and he set down the jug till the water would get cooler.

"Such nonsense, mamma," said I, pertly, "how can water, which is *soft*, break glass?" My mother was going away, and did not hear me, but my father looked closely, and, as I fancied, admiringly, at his "clever little Jane."

"Do you think hot water cannot break glass, Jane?"

"Surely not, papa,—how should it stand to reason, that water, which is soft,"—and I triumphantly repeated my former assertion, or, as I thought, rational argument. We were now alone at table. "So I find little Jane does not take things on hearsay,—quite right that," said my father, "she grows a reasoner—wiser than her mother."—"Oh, no, papa, don't say so,—only I am sure water which is soft," &c. &c.

"Suppose we try," said my father; and as I knew my mother was very careful of those richly-cut goblets, which she had lately got in a present from my Aunt Ellen, and often washed and put them away herself, I said I would wash them up for her. Sally, the housemaid, had secretly allowed me to wash china cups, on trial, before now. My own calabash basin was procured; papa gravely assisted me in collecting all the glasses and goblets on the table into it, and over them I directed him to pour the boiling tea-kettle. He warned me to pause—"I might be wrong."—"Oh, no—nonsense!" He poured away. Crack! crack! My heart fluttered. My father looked at me, but I did not now construe his looks into admiration.

The havoc was complete! My eldest sister came in. "All my mother's favourite glasses! ignorant *conceited* child!" My mother came. "The cut wine goblets, mamma," said my sister, "my aunt's present—Jane has broken them all." My mother looked much displeased. "Jane has just learned that there may be truths beyond her comprehension," said my father. "I wish she had made her experiment at a cheaper rate," said my mother; but my father said, "Nothing could be too dear for so good a lesson. Jane had learned one of humility and self-distrust, that would, he hoped, last her for life."

My kind parents never said more to their weeping penitent, though my sisters sometimes, when I was saucy, reminded me of the broken glasses. It needed not; for I never forgot that dreadful, reiterated crack. Several other circumstances occurred about this time, which made me suspect I was not quite the prodigy I had imagined myself.—*Nights of the Round-Table—First Series.*

TO THE NEUTRALS.

I hate and abhor all neutrals. They are a species of hermaphrodite for which both sexes blush. They constitute that abominable gender which no Frenchman or Italian can tolerate—a gender in name only, but not in reality—a thing in *um* or *on*, below the dignity of vegetable life. I never could "*it*" even a child or an idiot

"O thou whom Johnston must abhor,
And Ralph will soon turn to the door,"

List, list, oh list! (I do not mean *in* my regiment, but to my words.)

For the elective franchise you have struggled, petitioned, speechified, written, published, and all but risen in open rebellion; and now that, through exertions unparelleled, you have obtained it, you *decline making use* of the privilege! With all the fickleness of a lover who has obtained the object of his heart's wish, you turn from possession, and neglect the object of your former idolatry!

Is this manly? Is it rational? Is it right?

Manly it cannot be; for it is the cowardly offspring of intimidation—the fruit of a spirit that had rather offend conscience than a party.

Rational it is not; for our reason teaches us to prize objects in proportion to the price of labour and exertion which they have cost.

Right it is not; for it can never be right to yield on *private* grounds that which *conscience* tells us should be exercised for the public good.

What is it, then?

It is cowardly! mean! despicable! and must ultimately subject those who have recourse to it to the curse of the Laodiceans. (Rev. chap. iii. v. 15, 16.)

Is there nothing yet to be done in the great harvest-field of abuse, that you remain idle with the sickle in your hand?

1. Are there no town-councils to rectify? Is the present mode of election the very best and fairest mode possible?

2. Are sinecure offices to be continued, that the minister of the day may command a majority in the House?

3. Is the pension list still to be ornamented with Graces and Right Honourables in petticoats?

4. Are the poor to pay taxes, that hundreds of thousands may be squandered in building up and pulling down—in making sand-hills, in short, with gold dust?

5. Are we to pay 6s. 6d. for a pound of tea, when we might have it for eighteenpence?

6. Is the chain never, and under no circumstances, to be struck from the neck of the slave?

7. Are the laws of the land, civil and criminal, never to be amended?

8. Is one English or Irish non-resident Bishop to be paid L.20,000 per annum *for doing nothing*, whilst fifty efficient curates are starving on a thousandth part of the sum?

ENGLISH MALT.—Thirty millions of bushels of barley are annually converted into malt by the breweries of Great Britain, and upwards of eight millions of barrels of beer (of which more than four-fifths are strong) are brewed annually. This enormous consumption attests the fondness of the people for the beverage of their forefathers.

ELEMENTS OF THOUGHT.

RELIGIOUS TOLERATION.

The argument we have to state is contained in an appeal made by William Penn, the Quaker, the founder of Pensylvania, to the King of Holland:—

"Now, oh prince! give a poor Christian leave to expostulate with thee. Did Christ Jesus, or his holy followers, endeavour, by precept or example, to set up religion with a carnal sword? Called he any troops of men or angels to defend him? Did he encourage Peter to dispute his right with the sword? But did he not say, *Put it up?* Or did he countenance his over-zealous disciples, when they would have had fire from heaven, to destroy those that were not of their mind? No. But did not Christ rebuke them saying, "Ye know not what spirit ye are of?" And if it was neither Christ's spirit, nor their own spirit, that could have fire from heaven, oh! what is that *spirit* that would kindle fire on earth, to destroy such as peaceably dissent upon the account of conscience. Oh king! when did true religion persecute? When did the true church offer violence for religion—were not her weapons prayers, tears, and patience?"

Respect.—It is sometimes unreasonable to look after respect and reverence from servants and inferiors. A great lord and a gentleman talking together, there came a boy by leading a calf. "You shall see me make that boy let go his calf," thinking the boy would take off his hat; but the lad took no notice of him, "Sirrah," says the great man, "do you know me, that you use no reverence?"—"Yes," says the boy, "if your lordship will hold my calf, I will put off my hat."—*Selden.*

MEDICAL SELECTIONS.

Diseases of Tradesmen.—Schultz and Co., tailors of London, employ 334 men. Of these six are above sixty years of age; fourteen about fifty; and the greater number of the remainder about forty; three men of the above six above sixty have distorted spines. They are so subject to anal fistula, that they have a "fistula club." Their most common affections are difficulty of breathing, and dull headache, with giddiness, especially during summer. They attribute their complaints to two causes—one of which is the posture, the body bent for thirteen hours a-day; the other the heat of the shop.—*The Doctor.*

There is, at present, an artist of the Louvre, an eminent historical painter, of the name of Ducornet, who paints with his feet. He was born without arms, of poor parents, at Lille. There are also about the French metropolis a number of beggars, twelve or thirteen of them, at least, all deformed in various ways, and all born at Lille, in certain *dark caverns,* under the fortifications. The effect of these places, from their want of light, producing malformed births, is so notorious, that the magistrates of Lille have issued strict orders to prohibit the poor from taking up their abode in them. It is added, by our correspondent, that he had a conversation with Mr. Edwards on the subject, and that gentleman was greatly struck with the confirmation which the above circumstances afford to his views, stated in his work, "*Sur l'Influence des Agens Physiques sur la Vie.*" Mr. Edwards' experiments of detaining tadpoles in darkness, and thus causing them to grow into gigantic and monstrous *tadpoles,* instead of being transformed into frogs, are well known.—*Medical Gazette.*

USEFUL NOTICES.

Soap.—The word *soap* (*sapo*) occurs first in Pliny. He informs us that it was an invention of the Gauls, who employed it to render their hair shining; that it was a compound of wood ashes and tallow, and there were two kinds of it, *hard* and *soft*, (*spissus et liquidus;*) and that the best kind was made of the ashes of the beech and the fat of goats. Among the Germans it was more employed by the men than the women. It is curious that no allusion whatever is made by Pliny to the use of soap as a detergent; shall we conclude from this that the most important of all the uses of soap was unknown to the ancients? It was employed by the ancients as a pomatum; and during the early part of the government of the emperors, it was imported into Rome from Germany, as a pomatum for the young Roman beaux. Beckmann is of opinion that the Latin word *sapo* is derived from the old German word *sepe,* a word still employed by the common people of Scotland. It is well known that the state of soap depends upon the alkali employed in making it. *Soda* constitutes a *hard* soap, and *potash* a *soft* soap. The ancients being ignorant of the difference between the two alkalies, and using wood ashes in the preparation of it, doubtless formed soft soap. The addition of some common salt, during the boiling of the soap, would convert the soft into hard soap. As Pliny informs us that the ancients were acquainted both with hard and soft soap, it is clear that they must have followed some such process.

The Use of the Berries of the Elder-tree in Manufacturing Spirits.—M. Aloys Wehrle, of Vienna, has found, by a series of experiments, that the berries of the elder-tree produce a much greater quantity of spirit than the best wheat. The spirit is obtained by pressing the berries, and the juice is treated in the same way as the must of the grape, and afterwards distilled. If the results obtained by M. Wehrle are confirmed, it will be an additional motive for cultivating a plant which possesses many other useful qualities.

Gardeners' Calendar, &c. for October.—In this and the three following months dig and trench all vacant ground. Plant early cabbages, where they are intended to come to perfection. About the end of the month plant gooseberry, currant, and raspberry bushes, and the greater part of delicious shrubs. The stage polyanthuses and auriculas should by this time be properly secured from the inclemency of the weather.

THE EVENING WIND.

Spirit that breathest through my lattice—thou
  That cool'st the twilight of the sultry day—
Gratefully flows thy freshness round my brow,
  Thou hast been out upon the deep at play,
Riding all day the wild blue wave till now,
  Roughening their crests, and scattering high their spray,
And swelling the white sail. I welcome thee
To the scorch'd land, thou wanderer of the sea!

Nor I alone: a thousand bosoms round
  Inhale thee in the fulness of delight,
And languid forms rise up, and pulses bound
  Livelier, at coming of the wind of night;
And, languishing to hear thy grateful sound,
  Lies the vast island, stretched beyond the sight.
Go forth into the gathering shade—go forth,
God's blessing breathed upon the fainting earth!

Go, rock the little wood-bird in his nest,
  Curl the still waters, bright with stars, and rouse
The wide old wood from his majestic rest;
  Summoning from the innumerable boughs
The strange, deep harmonies that haunt his breast.
  Pleasant shall be thy way where meekly bows
The shutting flower, and darkling waters pass,
And 'twixt the o'ershadowing branches and the grass.

The faint old man shall lean his silver head
  To feel thee; thou shalt kiss the child asleep,
And dry the moistened curls that overspread
  His temples, while his breathing grows more deep;
And they who stand about the sick man's bed
  Shall joy to listen to the distant sweep,
And softly part his curtains to allow
Thy visit, grateful to his burning brow.

Go; but the circle of eternal change,
  Which is the life of nature, shall restore,
With sounds and scents from all thy range,
  Thee to thy birth-place of the deep once more;
Sweet odours in the sea-air, sweet and strange,
  Shall tell the home-sick mariner of the shore;
And, listening to thy murmur, he shall deem
He hears the rustling leaf and rushing stream.

THE STORY-TELLER.

JOHN KIERNANDER;
OR, THE DECEITFULNESS OF RICHES.

JOHN KIERNANDER was born in 1711, at Akstad, in Sweden. He here received the first rudiments of learning, but completed his education at the university of Upsal. In his twenty-fourth year he became desirous of visiting foreign universities; letters of recommendation and a passport being obtained by the influence of his friends in Stockholm, he journeyed to Halle, in Saxony. He was well received by Professor Augustus Francke, who conferred upon him several appointments. He spent four years; and, having satisfied his youthful curiosity, began to think of returning to Sweden. A circumstance, however, occurred at this time, which changed his purpose, and took him away from his native country, never to return. The Society, instituted in London, for Promoting Christian Knowledge, wrote to Professor Francke, requesting him to recommend a proper person to be sent out as a missionary to Cuddalore. The latter made the proposal to Kiernander, who, after some deliberation, consented. There was evidently a struggle in his mind; for he was an ambitious man; conscious, also, of endowments, both of mind and person, that justified his ambition. The only alternative was to return to his native Akstad, and push his fortune at the university of Upsal. The office of a missionary was, at this time, held in far less estimation than at present; and the influence of religion on the mind could not be feeble, when he decided to choose the former as his portion for life. He was ordained to the ministry, and went to London, whence he sailed for the East.

At Cuddalore he found a congregation, left by Sartorius, now removed to Madras, and he was appointed to be the successor. He was treated with the most polite attention by Admiral Boscawen, and the English settlement of Fort St. David, who having judged it necessary, as a measure of policy, to expel all Popish priests from this part of the Company's territories, put Kiernander into possession of the Portuguese Church. It was solemnly dedicated anew, and from this time the mission at Cuddalore prospered under his care. He seems to have been delighted with the situation and climate, so different from those of his native Akstad; whose barren hills and rocks, and eternal snows, were exchanged for a noble plain, amidst whose wild and glowing vegetation rose the city of Cuddalore. In the first letter to the Society, he writes, "that his prospects were good; that he went out into the villages several times a-week, to make known to the people the truths of Christianity; that his congregation in the town was increased. In the year 1745, its number amounted to near 200 persons, including those who were left by Sartorius, and, in the following year, it received an increase of a hundred and sixty converts." In more than one place, he speaks of the happiness he felt; he had reason to be satisfied; for no mission in India prospered so rapidly at this time as that of Cuddalore. But the hour of trial had not yet come.

He now united himself in marriage to a Miss Wendela Fischer, a lady of some property. Hitherto Augustus Francke had sent him presents—at one time of L.150: the Council of Fort St. David had also been generous and kind: he needed no benefactions now; nor would he receive any. In 1758, the celebrated Count Lally appeared with his forces before the city; it was quickly compelled to surrender, and a general confiscation took place. Kiernander waited on this officer on behalf of the mission, and entreated to be allowed to remain in peace, and continue his office. It was answered that no Protestant minister was required there; that he must instantly leave the city and the church, in the same summary way that he had ejected the Romish minister a few years before. It was a measure of retaliation; Lally spoke politely, but decidedly; yet at the same time offered him a passport to the Danish settlement of Tranquebar. The offer was accepted, and the latter set out on his journey to this city, where he arrived in safety, stripped of all his property, except a few articles of wearing apparel. In the following month, Fort St. David also fell into the hands of the French. In consequence of these events, every prospect of his restoration was at an end, and Kiernander turned his attention toward Bengal.

He left Tranquebar, furnished with ample means by the munificence of the Danes, and arrived in Calcutta, where the celebrated Clive, flushed with his recent victory of Plassey, was pleased with the intention of establishing a mission in the city. It was a strange design for Clive to approve of; but the truth was, Kiernander was a man of polite and insinuating address, and handsome countenance; alike fitted to make his way at the court of a nabob, or in the hamlet of the Hindoo. His portrait, in the old German volume, as well as the painting still preserved in the vestry room of the Calcutta church, by Garbrand, gives a faithful idea of the spirit and character of the man. They are thus sketched by an able hand: "At this period he appeared a man of ardent zeal, of great integrity, with a dauntless courage, and decision of mind." This is a high character, but it is a just one; for his heart was now full of devotion to his cause, and pursued it with fervour and sincerity; his talents and attainments, such as seldom fall to the lot of the missionary, were various and brilliant.

He opened his cause in a dwelling given him by the government. The birth, soon after, of a son, may afford a criterion of the estimation in which he was held at Calcutta; for Clive and Watts, the chief members of the government, stood sponsors, with their ladies, to the infant. In the following year, 175 children were taught in his school, of which number forty were maintained at his own expense. In addition to his many engagements, he preached occasionally at Serampore, where the Danish settlement, then in its infancy, had no chaplain. Three years afterwards he lost his wife, a loss that exercised a dark influence on all his subsequent career. It had been a marriage of affection, not impaired by the bitter vicissitudes of life. Wendela Fischer was a woman of piety, and devoted to her husband; she had borne the wreck of her fortune without complaining, and had journeyed from her home, first to Tranquebar, then to Calcutta, with a mind armed for yet greater reverses. She lived to see her husband admired and esteemed by all, while his religion was stedfast in the midst of many snares. Had she lived, Kiernander had served God with fidelity, and man with usefulness; but when she sunk into a early grave, it was as if his guardian angel had passed away from him.

With such an exterior and manner, the popular preacher need not long remain companionless. About a year afterwards, he married a wealthy widow of Calcutta, a Mrs. Ann Wolley. Now came the love of the world, in full tide, on his heart; the obscure and well-educated Swede, who had tasted of affluence for a short time at Cuddalore, but to be utterly stripped of it again, now saw himself secure. Poverty, like an armed man, would no more claim him for a prey. Is it any wonder that, in the exultation of his heart, he fell into some errors? He raised a handsome tomb over his first wife, in the burial ground to which he had given his own name. And now he mingled with wealthy and well-descended associates; was a favourite guest beneath the roof of the conqueror of Plassey. To his own table numbers came;—were they such as the poor and devoted student of Akstad, the messenger of God to the Hindoo, should have loved? He knew that they were not; but he was carried away by the torrent of example, by the influence of his wife also, who was a young and luxurious woman, and cared little for the souls of the heathen.

The love of one so dowered, so attractive, who lived in splendour, and was courted by the first society in Calcutta, was a subtle and fearful thing. He first assumed great external state in his equipage and mode of living; and displayed the vanity of driving a carriage-and-four through the city. He thus created many enemies, and drew on himself much censure. He now sought some assistance in his ministry, and chose for that purpose two persons, Bento de Silvestre and Manuel da Costa, who had been priests of the church of Rome, but, on their arrival at Calcutta, ha made a public abjuration of the errors of Popery.

Manuel da Costa was a Dominican friar, who, after

spending seven years at Goa, proceeded to Diu, on the coast of Guzerat, invested with the dignity of an inquisitor. Here Da Costa dwelt in sole and absolute authority, and found its exercise sweet. At last he appears to have recoiled from some of the tests, as well as cases of heresy which he was called upon to examine. Being afterwards sent to Siam, he there became acquainted with Antonio Rodriguez, a father of the Jesuits, whose mind had for some time been troubled with doubts as to his own faith. He lent Da Costa a solitary copy of the Bible in Latin; the latter read it with great attention and interest; and after some time procured, among other books, a catechism, published at Tranquebar, which afforded him much light relative to the agreement of the doctrines of the Reformation with the word of God. The two fathers held frequent and fervent conferences together, and balanced, with the keenness and research of able Jesuits, the warring points of the two faiths, till both the reason and the heart yielded. Rodriguez was at last so convinced of the errors of the church of Rome, that he withdrew from her communion, and placed himself under the protection of the Dutch, who at that time had a factory at Siam. He was in consequence excommunicated by his brethren, and an order was received from Goa to deliver him up to the inquisition. This commission, which was addressed to Da Costa, placed him in a very singular position; as an inquisitor, he was commanded to arrest the man who had enlightened his own mind, and deliver him up to a cruel fate. The mandate was peremptory, and he remembered how often and how pitilessly he had condemned many to the torture, or the dungeon, for heresies less light than those of Antonio.

He refused to be the executioner of his friend, and in excuse pleaded the power of the Dutch. Rodriguez soon after fell sick; in his dying moments, the Jesuits visited him, and promised the removal of the sentence of excommunication, and complete absolution and favour, if he would yet return to the bosom of the Church of Rome, and submit to extreme unction. This offer he rejected: the Jesuits, however, buried him with great pomp. Da Costa had now a difficult part to play: he was surrounded with enemies; he strove to conceal the change in his own sentiments; but in spite of all his caution, it was discovered by his brethren. One day, as he lay sick in bed, a friar of the Dominican order, secretly opening his writing table, found a paper, in which were noted many of the errors of the Church of Rome. This manuscript he took with him, together with some of the heretical books. With such evidence in their hands against Da Costa, the Jesuits instantly seized, and sent him on board a vessel bound to Goa. Dreadful fears arose in his mind, for he was no ordinary criminal: he believed in the faith for which he had condemned others to the flames. Rich would be the vengeance, fierce the tortures, which the inquisitors thirsted to exact.

He watched for an opportunity to escape, and one night, when the vessel was becalmed off the shore, contrived, either by bribing some of the crew, or by his own address, to get to land. He made his way along the coast of Coromandel to Tranquebar, where he remained a short time. He next came to Calcutta, and formed an intimacy with Kiernander, whose conversation, full of talent and powerful reasoning, soon decided his choice. He broke through every remaining scruple, and publicly embraced Protestantism. The inquisition soon after sent a Romish priest to Calcutta to menace him, and, if possible, get him once more into their power—well aware that the secrets of their prison-house had been laid open; and that, if he chose, he could make a fearful revelation. But the protection of the English was too powerful to violate: the anathemas of the priest of Goa fell harmless. Kiernander behaved with the kindness of a friend, and took Da Costa and De Silvestre under his own roof. They were of great use to him in his mission, for they were eminently learned men, skilled in many languages, and he delighted in their company.

His residence at Calcutta had strong and various attractions; the assemblage of English in the city was, at this period, less numerous and more select than at present. The city had sprung up with a quick and wanton growth: but a few years before, the ground on which it stood was covered with jungle, where the tiger made his lair. Even now the cry of the jackal, suddenly breaking forth in the night, was heard in the silent streets. Spacious and elegant houses, shrubberies, and lawns, already rose in the suburbs. People of talent, as well as distinction, were perpetually arriving from Europe; the successes of Clive had opened a field of ambition and wealth, which was believed to be boundless. The levees of this man were splendidly attended: native princes dethroned, or candidates for thrones, Mahratta warriors, and the ambassadors of the Emperor Shah Allum, were mingled with civilians, statesmen, and adventurers from England. Into these circles Kiernander sometimes found his way, for Clive was personally attached to him. To a man so well skilled in the Eastern languages, and devoted to their study, Calcutta presented other attractions, in the number of strangers to be met with from all parts of Asia; Chinese, Arabs, Persians, inhabitants of the Eastern Isles, and Jewish merchants. Many of these men found a welcome in the home of the missionary, who passed much of his time, at least all he could spare from his labours, in study with his two companions, De Silvestre and Da Costa. The Arabic, as well as the Hindoo literature, offered an inexhaustible store to his inquiring mind; the priests had passed their whole lives in the country, and were well versed in its manners and customs. Had Kiernander written a detail of his own life, with the fruits of his observations and acquirements, few pieces of biography would have been so instructive, few so full of strange vicissitudes.

This was the golden period of his life: the society of learned men that he loved; admired as a minister, not only by his converts, but by great, distinguished, and intelligent men; a tasteful and luxurious home; a circle of agreeable friends—what had he more to wish for?

He did not at any time neglect the interests of his mission, nor does he appear ever to have deserted its duties; but the subtle influence of his associates had long been fatally playing its part. The Society at home, as well as the missionaries in India, began to see the decline of his fidelity, in his letters, as well as the reports which reached them. The former foresaw the fall, at no distant period, of their able minister: from the latter he sometimes received affectionate, as well as warning letters. But he believed in no fall, and listened to no warning.

So large had been the fortune of his wife, that he was reckoned one of the richest men in Bengal: he was generous to excess, and the poor largely blessed his charities. He built a dwelling-house for two of his assistants, and another for the education of the natives.

In the pauses of his mission, after painfully teaching the native children, going forth to the distant hamlets, or debating with the Brahmins or Moors, he would return to the city, to his affluent dwelling, and take the cool air of the shore in his beautiful equipage. The decline of his religion was perhaps gradual, it might be almost imperceptible, such was the influence of his situation on the soul as well as on the senses; one day holding forth the gospel in some mountain village, where he no doubt spoke sincerely and feelingly, and loved to see the tear flow, and hear the words of conviction; on the following day, preaching before the victor of Plassey, now his intimate friend, and the chief people of the city. Well and eloquently did he speak, for such a minister was rare on the shores of India, and praises quickly followed; sweet, delicious praises, from beautiful lips. His carriage waited at the door of the church; as did many a welcome and invitation, for every home was open to him. They loved the man—and *he* forgot his love to God!

About this period the court of the Emperor Shah Allum, having heard of his reputation, requested from him some copies of the Psalter and New Testament, in the Arabic language. He complied, and had afterwards the satisfaction to hear they were so well received by his majesty's Mullahs, that he was induced to transmit to Allahabad, where the court was then held, all the Arabic Psalters and Testaments in his possession. He now resolved to build a church at his own expense; and, in the month of May, 1767, the foundation of the present mission church at Calcutta was laid. By his unremitting exertions and diligence, it was completed in little more than two years, though the architect died during its progress. In December it was consecrated, and named Beth Tephillah, that is, the house of prayer. The building cost the founder above L.8000 sterling, of which sum, only L.250 had been presented in benefactions. So that after a lapse of the many years from the capture of Calcutta by the English, the first national church was completed at the expense of a stranger and wanderer from Akstad in Sweden. His other buildings for the mission cost L.4000 more. Two years after, Kiernander lost his second wife. She bequeathed her jewels for the benefit of Beth Tephillah, and with the amount their sale produced, he founded a mission school in his own ground behind the church, capable of holding 250 children. It was evident that his wealth was beginning to melt away, or he would hardly have sold the jewels of his wife; yet, it is greatly to his credit, that the object of the sale was so disinterested.

He was now again left alone: he had not loved her like his first wife; they had not passed through the vicissitudes of affluence and poverty together, or proved the scenes of danger and excitement which so cement domestic affection. Yet he deeply felt her loss: she had been ardently attached to him, even to the last; had done the honours of his home, so as to make it attractive to all, for she was a woman of refined manners, and had welcomed him with smiles when he came wearied from the hamlet and the wild. He had seen his table surrounded almost every day by guests, for his style of living was profuse and hospitable.

It is uncertain how long the veil would have rested on his soul; but it was suddenly and rudely torn away. He was seized with blindness; and soon he sat almost solitary in his spacious chambers: his conversation, his vivacity, were no longer the same; nor were his table and wines. A few came to sooth and comfort, but the greater part did not seek the afflicted man. The pleasures of study and learning were also taken from him; all was taken, save the converse of Da Costa and Hanson, but he no longer saw their faces. He at last remembered how far he had wandered from God: O! how welcome would now have been his lost feelings of fervour, of hope, and joy; but they did not come at his call. His sorrow was inexpressibly great, for if there be any situation in which the visitations of mercy and peace are precious, it is amidst the agony of blindness, when the soul is left to struggle alone. It was more than he could bear; and he lifted his humble spirit eagerly to God, resolved to know no rest till " the lost should be found again." His deep repentance, his tears, his unceasing prayers, could not be in vain; and ere long, Kiernander blessed the hand that had chastened him.

His blindness continued four years; at last he consented to submit to the painful operation of couching, which succeeded so well, that he was soon afterwards able to write to the Society in England. The strain of his first letter shews that a stern and decided change had passed on the mind of the once fortunate man. Adversity gathered fast around him. His fortune was now ruined, partly by his former extravagance in living, his generosity of temper, and still more by the neglect of his affairs during his long blindness. He looked abroad on his recovery, as if to begin the world anew with a purer hope and resolve, but found himself impoverished. The seal of the sheriff of Calcutta was affixed to the gates of Beth Tephillah, as a part of the personal estate of the ill-fated and bankrupt missionary. The edifice, however, was redeemed from the desecration which otherwise awaited it, by the munificence of an individual, who paid for it the sum at which it had been appraised, namely, 10,000 rupees. This individual was the late Charles Grant, Esq., the East India director, whose powerful support to Indian missions was ever generously given.

The founder of the edifice, from whatever cause, no longer officiated within its walls. Was it because he was poor—or had lived extravagantly? It was a harsh and pitiless deed. His health soon after became infirm, and he sometimes wandered round the walls, and looked wistfully on them, and thought how it had been with him in former days. Where, now, was the world of admirers and flatterers?—passed away like the moth, when they saw that his resources were at an end. His home, his equipage, his many servants, were all gone. Still he was kindly received at some tables; there were those who felt that they could not utterly forsake the man to whose eloquence they had listened, whom they had loved as a companion, at whose table they had feasted. But he rarely made himself a guest, for he felt that the world was no longer the same to him; that his words were not now listened to with the attention and the applause they were wont to be. He confined himself to a small and retired dwelling. There was a circumstance yet more hard to bear. Another missionary came, entered into his labours, and was chosen to supply his church; and this, Kiernander felt exquisitely.

Soon after this church was enlarged, and he was invited to open the new chancel, in which he administered the sacrament. His authority was passed away; but he said it was a moment of great happiness to his mind. All who were present did not think so; one who had known him in other times, said, " I cannot but lament his destitution in this his hour of sorrow." It was an affecting picture—the declining, grey, and stricken man, giving the holy communion in the chancel of the edifice that he had raised in the hour of his splendour. Around him knelt many of those who had first flattered, and then deserted him; the false friends of his brighter life! And now he resolved to quit a scene that was become too bitter to his memory: he left Calcutta, to offer his services to the Dutch at Chinsura. The sum of forty pounds had been transmitted to him as a present from the Society in England, and enough remained to support him yet longer. But ere he went, he entered the burying-ground called by his own name, to visit once more the graves of his wives; they slept side by side. In the first was the wife of his youth, and his only child; and near her was Anne, his second bride, the proud and richly-dowered woman who had first drawn his heart from God. He sat down beside the graves, and wept bitterly; every object around made the past rush back upon his heart: the church of Beth Tephillah, where his words once fell in power, and his state was glorious; the trees, that stood silent in the evening calm, he had planted till they grew in beauty. And now what had earth for him? had it a home, a friend, a loved one? He went forth, in the eightieth year of his age, to dwell among strangers. If his little girl, who slept with Wendela, had but lived, what a comfort, what a blessing, he thought, would she now be to him: he knelt beside the grave with strong emotion, for he felt so helpless and forsaken, that he clung to each broken reed. O! if that dear, that only child, had lived, she would now have screened her father from the sorrows of the world, and been the companion of his way. He offered up his vows anew to God, and then for ever quitted the scene where he had called others to mercy, and pointed their way to heaven.

He arrived at Chinsura, where his services were instantly accepted, and he was appointed chaplain to that settlement, by the Hon. Mr. Fitsing. His duties as a chaplain were far less laborious than as a missionary. The situation was suited to his age and prospects. The scenery around was of a rich and tranquil character; the Dutch town had quite a national appearance,—small neat houses, with green doors and windows, a pretty little square with grass plots, and promenades shaded by trees. There was a fortified factory' and a gloomy and ancient government-house. The people were in character with the dwellings: mild, plodding, contemplative; they loved, after the business of the day was over, to sit beneath the rows of trees, and smoke and converse. The noble river, Hoogly, flowed in front of the dwellings; its banks were lofty and precipitous, and the sight of the many barks passing to and fro, as well as the incessant bustle and ardour of enterprise, made it pleasant to sit and watch the scene. His duties were confined to the settlement, where their trade made the Dutch reside together: there were no villages or hamlets, where he had to seek the scattered people. The little Lutheran church, in which he performed service twice on the Sabbath, was the only sphere of his exertions. Here he passed several years, still endeavouring to render himself useful, for he kept a school during some days of the week, though he received no salary for it. The people pitied their aged pastor, but, like Dutch traders, their pity did not warm the heart, for they allowed him a very small income, that scarcely raised him above poverty. Their manners were simple, and their converse, as well as souls, centred wholly in their commerce; he found a welcome in their dwellings whenever he chose to enter; but he felt that the society of the phlegmatic and mindless men of Chinsura was a sad contrast to the circles of Calcutta. According to his own confession, he was now brought to a knowledge of himself; it was a knowledge darkly and fearfully purchased!

Chinsura was but thirty miles distant from Calcutta; it was a mere excursion, often taken for pleasure, on the river Hoogly, by the civil as well as military servants of the Company; the route into the interior also lay that way, yet none came to see him, none sent a friendly greeting, or even a message of sympathy to the heart that was bleeding at the unkindness of the world. O, could he have seen some well-known footstep draw nigh his door, or hear one voice of the many that he once loved to hear. He was changed only in outward circumstances; his intellect was as powerful as ever, and his fine and sorrow-stricken countenance, and his conversation full of various knowledge and learning, were strange to meet with in such a place. But his home, whose latch was seldom lifted, the few volumes of his beloved Oriental lore, now his only companions, his thrifty meal, prepared by his own hand—told more indelibly than Persian, Arabian, or even the son of Sirach, could have told, that the human heart is faithless as the wave, even as the passing blast, and that poverty is cruel as the grave.

His great possessions were not utterly passed away; a remnant remained, but it was withheld from him. Part had been laid out in the purchase of houses in Calcutta, in junction with some of his acquaintance, for rents being very high at this period, it was considered a good speculation. He had expended many sums on these dwellings; the speculation did not answer, and they fell, on the failure of his fortunes, into the hands of his associates, who reaped the benefit, while to him it was a total loss. A pittance out of this property, or even of its rents, would have made the exile of Chinsura at ease in his circumstances. Though infirmities were gathering on his frame, he was still able to go forth, at times, into the country around.

The town of Serampore, where he had once laboured, was but a few miles distant, a beautifully clean and quiet little town; and he loved to go there at times, for he found a few to whom he had been useful in his earlier days, who had not forgotten him; they said that they had once been blessed under his ministry, that it had first called them to God. Kiernander was deeply moved at the words that were to him inexpressibly sweet. It was not the voice of the world; it could not be false! There were many lovely spots around the banks of the Hoogly, for they were well cultivated, and laid out in fields and plantations, among which were the ancient woods, as yet unfelled. At a small distance was the French settlement of Chandernagore, to which the victories of Clive had brought decay; all spoke of desolation —large and lofty houses nearly deserted, and warehouses half empty. From the forsaken monastery the priests had taken flight; the scenery around was wild and impressive —silent ghauts, deep and lone ravines. The residence of the former governors, a superb house, was a lesson to put no trust in prosperity; fragments of doors and windows. The roof of what was the music-room, and that of the banqueting room beneath, had fallen in; and the sun-light, falling fiercely on the faded colours on the walls, shewed that they were once decorated with taste. The venerable missionary, on whose head so many storms had beat, now turned his thoughts and desires towards that world, where the heartless and the proud can trouble no more. From this last resting-place he was rudely thrust forth. In 1795, war was declared by the English against the Dutch republic; the settlement at Chinsura was captured, and Kiernander became a prisoner of war; in which character he received from the English Government the pittance of fifty rupees a-month, as a subsistence. He lost his office, and he lost his liberty, even at eighty-six years of age. At last, the English, pitying his age and misfortunes, allowed him to go to Calcutta; he took leave of Chinsura with a faltering step, and a heart almost broken; he had looked upon it as the last asylum on this side the grave, a rest from all his troubles, where he would wait calmly till his hour should come. And now he was to go again to that city of pride and luxury, and seek friends—friends to a poor man bordering on ninety. If Calcutta had such within its bosom, their names should be written in letters of gold. He arrived in the city, and wandered through the streets, and passed by the doors of the rich, the high, and the unhappy, where he was once so welcome. O! when his own home met his eye, what must have been his feelings, where he had lived with the proud and beautiful Anne, in his chambers of luxury? The dwelling was still there, but no one, in the bowed, the humbled, and suffering man, recognized the once admired and beloved Kiernander. The few who would still have soothed his desertion, had gone down to the grave; Clive had perished by his own hand. At last he found a relative of one of his wives, who opened his door to him. In the following spring, when in the eighty-eighth year of his age, rising from his chair too suddenly, he fell, and broke his thigh, and lingered long in agony. If any man had ever cause to pray to be allowed to depart in peace, it was Kiernander. Did no one remember, of the wealthy and the devout, that the noble church in which they weekly worshipped was raised by the man who was lingering, hard by, in torture and desertion. The dwelling in which he was received, had few comforts; for the circumstances of the inmates were narrow, and they had six children: they probably regarded their aged guest as a burden. The Rev. David Brown, the chaplain at Calcutta, and a few others, visited him at times, in order to comfort him with their counsel. But Kiernander had higher comfort: it was not the will of God to give bitterness of heart in the midst of such exquisite misery—his cup was full—and the hand that had so long chastened, now poured into his spirit the richest consolation, the brightest hope. And what counsel could his visitors offer to this man of nearly a century compared to the stores which his strange and chequered life had laid up? Even now, his mind was in all its vigour; it was sad, yet beautiful, to sit at his bed-side, and hear him tell how he had suffered; how he had known all that love, or riches, or learning could give to man—and that now he was going home to his rest.

He spoke also of Akstad, in Sweden, his dear native place! he blessed the hour when he first left it, to labour in the cause of heaven. "My heart is full, but my hand is weak," writes the dying man, in one of his last letters to his distant land, "the world is yet the same; there are many cold friends; others like broken reeds: but God makes the heaviest burden light and easy: I rejoice to see the poor mission prosper; this comforts me amidst all." He then goes on, with great clearness, to depict the then state of India, and predicts, with singular accuracy, the extension of the British power through every part of the empire:— "When I first landed, sixty years ago, there was not any more than a little territory, or small tract of land, of about four or five square English miles, at each settlement of Calcutta, Madras, and Bombay. The time will come, when the whole English nation will unite in a general society to send the gospel to the East Indies. This will give the firmest stability to the British possession in the East." Such were his last thoughts and words: his remains were deposited in the same grave with those of his second wife, Anne: this was strange, for Wendela Fischer had been his first and strongest love, and his only child also slept in her tomb. The funeral procession was slender, that wound its way through the cemetery; through his own cemetery, his own groves of trees! His name is almost forgotten. This is a great and cruel injustice: let his errors, but not his memory, pass away. High talents and endowments are of little avail in a missionary, without consistency of character. But we should not forget that he lavished his wealth in the cause, and impoverished himself to rear a beautiful temple for his fellow Christians: for sixty years he sought the good of others; and founded the mission and the church at Calcutta, where they have since known such power and splendour. After expending twelve thousand pounds on this object, he left it for ever, and wandered to Chinsura, with a pittance of forty pounds, supplied by those he had so benefited. He went with tears, but without complaining, to be a pastor to strangers; It was like the going forth of Lot, when all his possessions had perished; but by Kiernander's side was no companion, no comforter. Let it be remembered, how many he called to knowledge and peace—from how many hearts he drew the sorrows, that were darkly poured into his own!—*Abridged from Carne's Lives of Missionaries.*

SPECTRAL ILLUSION.

THE following is one of the most remarkable of the ghost stories in Sir David Brewster's late book:—On the 30th of December, about four o'clock in the afternoon, Mrs. A. came down stairs into the drawing-room, which she had quitted only a few minutes before, and on entering the room, she saw her husband, as she supposed, standing with his back to the fire. As he had gone out to take a walk about half an hour before, she was surprised to see him there, and asked him why he had returned so soon. The figure looked steadfastly at her, with a serious and thoughtful expression of countenance, but did not speak.—Supposing that his mind was absorbed in thought, she sat down in an arm-chair near the fire, and within two feet at most of the figure, which she still saw standing before her. As its eyes, however, still continued to be fixed upon her, she said, after the lapse of a few minutes, "Why don't you speak, ——?" The figure immediately moved off towards the window at the farther end of the room, with its eyes still gazing on her, and it passed so very close to her in doing so, that she was struck by the circumstance of hearing no step nor sound, nor feeling her clothes brushed against, nor even any agitation in the air. Although she was now convinced that the figure was not her husband, yet she never for a moment supposed that it was any thing supernatural, and was soon convinced that it was a spectral illusion. About a month after this occurrence, Mrs. A., who had taken a somewhat fatiguing drive during the day, was preparing to go to bed, about eleven o'clock at night, and, sitting before the dressing-glass, was occupied in arranging her hair. She was in a listless and drowsy state of mind, but fully awake. When her fingers were in active motion among the papillotes, she was suddenly startled by seeing in the mirror, the figure of a near relation, who was then in Scotland, and in perfect health. The apparition appeared over her left shoulder, and its eyes met hers in the glass. It was enveloped in grave-clothes, closely pinned, as is usual with corpses, round the head, and under the chin, and though the eyes were open, the features were solemn and rigid. The dress was evidently a shroud, as Mrs. A. remarked even the punctured pattern usually worked in a peculiar manner round the edges of that garment. Mrs. A. described herself as at the time sensible of a feeling like what we conceive of fascination, compelling her for a time to gaze on this melancholy apparition, which was as distinct and vivid as any reflected reality could be, the light of the candles upon the dressing-table appearing to shine full upon its face. After a few minutes, she turned round to look for the reality of the form over her shoulder; but it was not visible, and it had also disappeared from the glass when she looked again in that direction. On the 26th of the same month, about two P. M., Mrs. A. was sitting in a chair by the window in the same room with her husband. He heard her exclaim, "What have I seen?" And on looking on her, he observed a strange expression in her eyes and countenance. A carriage and four had appeared to her to be driving up the entrance-road to the house. As it approached, she felt inclined to go up stairs to prepare to receive company; but, as if spell-bound, she was unable to move or speak. The carriage approached, and as it arrived within a few yards of the window, she saw the figures of the postilions and the persons inside take the ghastly appearance of skeletons and other hideous figures. The whole then vanished entirely, when she uttered the above-mentioned exclamation.

EUROPEAN SHEEP.—Nearly every country in Europe has its own race of sheep. Those again are subdivided into peculiar varieties, arising from difference of climate, food, treatment, and intermixture. European sheep vary considerably in size and form; but the most important difference is in the quantity and quality of the wool, it being thin in some, dense in others, coarse or fine, more or less elastic, &c. &c. Of the German sheep there are the following varieties:—The Friesland, about three feet high and four in length, producing a coarse wool about four or five inches long. It yields two lambs in the year, is strong, and endures winter even in the open air. It is found in the marshes of Schleswick near Husum, in Friesland, in the environs of Bremen, in Holland, &c. and if put upon inferior pasture, soon degenerates and becomes smaller. The Eyderstædt, which is somewhat smaller, having long wool on the back, and very short hairs on the belly and thighs. The Suabia, also termed Zaubelschaaf, found in different parts of Suabia and Franconia. It is small, lambs twice yearly, and produces about two pounds of fine wool, like flock silk. It is soon affected by the wet. The Heather sheep, also called Heid-chnucke, one of the smallest kinds, found on the heath of Luneburg, in the environs of Bremen, and the Mark It is commonly horned, with black face and legs, and has a lively, wild disposition. It is clipped twice a-year, yielding each time about a pound and a half of long, coarse wool. This method of twice clipping has been generally adopted in large flocks, amongst sheep bearing a secondary quality of wool. The Spiegelschafe, found in Mecklinburg, Franconia, &c., with a blue woolly ring round the eyes, may be considered a species of German sheep, produced by intermixture. The Polish sheep resembles the German sheep in size and wool. The Danish is distinguished by a smooth head, erect ears, and wild disposition. The wool is coarse, mingled with stiff hairs. The Norwegian is said to be a description of it, but improved by a cross with the English and Spanish. The Swedish, a cross breed of the Spanish, has lately been much improved. It had originally but little wool, and that of a coarse quality. The Belgian, Flemish, and Flanders sheep are nearly five feet in length, and weigh about two cwt. They originally came from the East Indies, and are remarkable for fecundity, producing several lambs in the year. The wool is middling. The Dutch sheep are a species of them. The Hungarian sheep, like the Moldavian, have a very long, coarse and inferior wool, and the flesh is very fat and unpalatable.

CAGED RATS.
By the Author of Corn-Law Rhymes.

YE coop us up, and tax our bread,
   And wonder why we pine;
But ye are fat, and round, and red,
   And filled with tax-bought wine.
Thus twelve rats starve while three rats thrive,
   (Like you on mine and me,)
When fifteen rats are caged alive,
   With food for nine and three.

Haste! havoc's torch begins to glow,
   The ending is begun;
Make haste, destruction thinks ye slow;
   Make haste to be undone!
Why are ye called "My Lord" and "Squire,"
   While fed by mine and me;
And wringing food, and clothes, and fire,
   From bread-taxed misery?
Make haste, slow rogues! *prohibit* trade,
   Prohibit honest gain;
Turn all the good that God hath made
   To fear, and hate, and pain:
Till beggars all, assassins all,
   All cannibals we be,
And death shall have no funeral
   From shipless sea to sea.

PRESENT STATE OF THE SCOTCH TENANTRY.
(Continued from No. 11.)

From the facts we have previously stated in our two former numbers, the inference is obvious, that the greatest distress must necessarily exist among the tenantry, and among those proprietors who have been accustomed to live to the full extent of their incomes during the war. From all the information we can obtain, after extensive inquiries and personal observation, we are convinced we do not exaggerate when we say that two-thirds of the farming capital of Scotland has been lost within the last fifteen years. So little attention has been paid to statistics in this country, that any estimate of the capital, in any employment, must necessarily be vague; but after examining such data as can be easily procured, we think the farming capital of Scotland, in 1813, may be moderately taken at 60 millions sterling, 40 millions of which we conceive has since been lost. To those who have not paid much attention to such subjects, so great a loss may appear incredible; but when it is considered that upwards of 11 years ago, it is proved by the evidence of the numerous witnesses examined before the committee of the House of Commons, that great part of the agricultural capital had *then* been lost, that the soil was rapidly deteriorating from the diminution of the stock of cattle kept on the farms, and that after that period, the value of agricultural produce sunk very considerably, and that there has hardly been a single year in which any profit could have been made, it will appear that the present depression of agriculture has not been exaggerated. The same causes which affect agriculture in England, must affect it in Scotland. Mr. John Ellman, junior, a very intelligent witness, who possessed extensive farms near Lewes, stated, " I am sure, taking the county of Sussex through, one-half of the farming capital is lost, and this is the case in the majority of counties." A writer in the Quarterly Review in 1829, (vol. 37. p. 426,) asserts, " from personal experience, that within 10 years one-fourth of the occupiers of the land in England have been completely ruined, and the remainder have lost a moiety of their property. In Essex, lands which formerly brought three guineas an acre, a very high rent in England, have been offered on a lease of five years without rent, under a restricted system of cultivation, as they have been completely exhausted by letting them for high rents on short leases. From extensive inquiries which we have made in Scotland, we may venture to say, that agriculture has not at any time been in a more depressed state, nor the prospects of landholders and tenants more gloomy. We shall subjoin a few extracts from the communications we have received, and we regret our limits do not permit us to give them at greater length. The first relates to an extensive district in the north, comprehending a large tract of farms, occupied in the rearing of sheep and cattle, as well as some of the best soil in Scotland for the production of wheat. " The state of the tenantry is extremely unprosperous both in corn and pasture farms. Their credit is much lower than at any former period of my recollection; and gloom, anxiety, and discontent, seem to pervade the whole body of the agricultural population." " On pasture lands the arrears are of a very great extent, indeed, amounting in some instances to more than one year's rent, and in other instances, even where abatements have been allowed, to more than two years' rent. This statement applies to the higher, as well as to the lower class of tenants." " Abatements of rent have been very generally, and indeed it may be said, universally demanded, but on corn farms, it is but in few instances they have been allowed." " Most of the landlords are in difficulties and embarrassments." In sheep farms, " abatements have been almost universally granted to the extent of 25 or 30 per cent. of the rents paid five or six years ago, but the tenants are still unable to pay their rents." " Some pasture farms have been let at a reduction of 40 per cent. There is a more than usual number of farms in the market, especially of pasture farms." The ordinary rent of corn land in the district, is 40s. an acre, but the general opinion of intelligent farmers is, that it cannot be cultivated with ordinary profit, if more than 30s. be paid for it. Farms let lately upon a grain rent, have only brought about 30s. " It is only in very few instances extensive improvements are now made by tenants." It is understood that the landlords in general are in difficulties, and some of them under trust. This remark applies to the higher, as well as lower class of proprietors. " The number of youths, children of tacksmen, attending the superior seminaries of education, has greatly diminished,—some boarding schools have ceased to exist. The difficulty of obtaining payment of shop accounts and professional charges has greatly increased. The consumption among the tenantry of tea, sugar, and of all articles which may be deemed luxuries, is falling off. There being little property to dispose of, the drawing of contracts of marriage, or of testaments, has become rare. Exhilarating social amusements are dispensed with. The occupation of the district fiddler or piper is nearly gone."

The next communication is from Perthshire, and applies to a large proportion of that county, including great part of the Carse of Gowrie. " The condition of farms, both of grain and stock farms, is in general very bad. The farms are in most instances rack rented, and as the greater part of the landlords, are, from poverty, unable to give permanent abatements, one set of tenants is generally rouped off, and the land taken by another set, at as high rents." The soil is certainly deteriorating by severe cropping, the best farmers generally agreeing that grain of the weight which formerly grew, is not now produced. The rents are paid with the utmost difficulty, and in all estates of any size, the arrears are heavy. The condition of the landed proprietors, is in general far from good, their estates being in most instances heavily burdened. The condition of proprietors under L.3000 per annum, especially when their estates are entailed, is miserable."— The prospects of landlords and tenants are far from being flattering. In stock farms, the tenants cannot make a living from the very inadequate prices, received from cattle, sheep, and wool. In grain farms, matters are as bad. In 1831, the crop of wheat was barely an average one. In 1827, 28, 29, 30, the wheat crop was a complete failure, chiefly occasioned by the ravages of a grub or worm, and in each of these years, the produce did not exceed 3½ or 4 bolls per acre. In 1830, potatoes were a most abundant crop, and sold from 11s. to 14s. per boll. The consequence of this was, that in 1831, a much larger quantity was planted, and they are now selling at from 4s. to 5s. a boll.

From Roxburghshire it is stated, rents are paid with difficulty. No one is saving money, and the style of living has become very economical? " Abatements have not been given generally within the last five years, though one great proprietor, and one or two smaller proprietors have given abatements. In the former case, 20 per cent. was given on arable farms, 25 on stock." In Fife, the tenantry have been much benefited of late years by the great quantities of potatoes they have sold for the London Market. But, " generally speaking, the tenants are in arrear of rent, and these arrears are in many instances considerable." " The present prices of agricultural produce do not permit the farmers to expend money in improvements, and therefore the soil must be deteriorating."

In East-Lothian we have the authority of a gentleman who possesses an extensive farm, who has been engaged in agriculture in that county for the last thirty years, and who has paid, during that period, the utmost attention to every thing connected with rural affairs, for saying " that agricultural distress exists in that county to an extent never before known." In all cases where the rents of farms let during the war has not been abated 30. per cent, he is of opinion, the rents could only have been paid from the tenant's capital. I have a list of several farms let lately in East Lothian, most of them for rents payable in grain, and converting their grain-rents into money, at the average fiar prices, for the last 10 years; the result is as follows:—A. B. M. let in 1810, and rent converted into grain in 1822. Present rent 44 per cent under that of 1810, and 21 per cent under that of 1822. J. C. let in 1811, at L.1100; now, at L.750; fall, 32 per cent. S. D. let in 1811 at L.6, 11s. per acre; now, at L.4, 11. B, Fall on present rent, compared with that of 1814, 33 per cent. K, fall since 1821, 30 per cent. R, fall in same period, 12 per cent, though the last tenant laid out L.1500. immediately before his removal. We are in possession of a detailed statement, made out by a practical farmer, on whose accuracy we have the utmost reliance, in order to show the value of land in this county, from 1822 to 1832, compared with the value from 1805 to 1815, being the last 10 years of the war. The average value of the grain is taken from the second fiars of the county, for the respective periods, and that of other produce at the ordinary prices. A farm is taken, of 360 Scotch acres, of good land, fully improved, and consisting of equal proportions of clay and turnip soil. The former is supposed to be cropped in a six, and the latter in a four course rotation. The quantity of produce is assumed to have been equal at both periods, and the following are the results:—

	War.	Peace.
Value of produce deducting seed		
Expense of Cultivation	L.3285	L.2227
Rent one quarter of Wheat	1498	1041
Interest of money and profit on tenants. Capital—say L.3600, and for superintending farm.	360	160

It thus appears that even when the rent is paid in grain, and the produce has in every respect been the same, at the two periods, the profits of the tenant have diminished no less than 55 per cent, while the rent has only fallen 31 per cent. It is evident that the cultivation of ground cannot long be carried on with such profits, for they do not amount to the ordinary interest of the capital required. No allowance for the expense of living of the tenant and his family, is made in the statement, at either of the periods. But unfavourable as this view is, the real state of matters is much worse. The rents were not stipulated for in grain during the war, but in money, and no material abatements were given till 1820 or 1822, so that during the period which elapsed from 1814, when the value of agricultural produce fell, till 1820, the tenant was paying the high rent, while receiving the diminished price of produce. After rents were generally reduced, another evil of a most serious nature affected this county, as well as Fife and the Carse of Gowrie, though in these districts not to so great an extent. All the wheat crops from 1825 to 1831, both inclusive, were attacked by a fly which occasioned a decrease in the produce to the extent of thirty-three per cent, and the loss from this cause in a farm of the above description, exceeds L.250 per annum. The reby there has not only been a total loss of the capital expended on the soil, amounting to L.3000, but besides an annual loss of L.90. In these circumstances it is not wonderful that the most gloomy despondency has seized the tenantry. Many have lost all hope of living by their profession, several have emigrated to the continent and to America, and many are preparing to follow them. We believe the emigration would be very general, if the tenantry could get quit of their leases, and recover the capital they have expended on the soil. Improvements by the tenantry are in a great measure at an end. The quantity of lime manufactured in the county, is little more than one-third of what it was 12 years ago. A great number of bankruptcies have taken place, some of them of tenants, who were possessed of many thousand pounds at the end of the war. On one estate purchased 12 or 15 years ago, only one tenant out of 11 who were upon it at the time of the purchase, now remains. All the rest have become bankrupt. The soil is deteriorating from severe cropping, and want of capital, and in many districts of the county, the high farming, for which the county was formerly distinguished, is no longer to be seen.

We are well aware that the distress in this part of Scotland, but more especially in this county, has been attributed, in some measure, to what has been called, the expensive mode of living of the tenantry, and since the high rents formerly given, could not be obtained from the farmers of East Lothian, those from other parts of Scotland have been induced to pay high rents for lands in this county, on the representation or assumption, that by their more economical style of living, they could afford to pay higher rents. But, I believe, the expectations formed on this ground have been completely disappointed. There is no class of the community, who in proportion to their capital, live at so small an expense as the tenantry; and the farmers of East Lothian, Berwickshire, and Roxburghshire, are not an exception from this remark. When a person acquainted only with the inferior districts of Scotland, first goes into those counties, he is no doubt surprised at the appearance of the houses of the tenantry, as well as to observe that they do not themselves personally engage in the labours of the field. But such persons do not consider the very different state of agriculture in these counties from what they have been accustomed to. We have before me the rent roll of an estate in the North of L.25,000 a-year, and there are upwards of six hundred tenants, thus averaging a rent payable, by each, of only L.40. In East Lothian, the land rental of which, in 1811, was L.180,000, there are certainly not 400 tenants, and we have heard them estimated at a much smaller number. Then as to capital, it is held that an arable farm cannot be well cultivated unless the tenant has capital to the amount of L.10 an acre, and as the farms in East Lothian, as well as in Berwickshire and Roxburghshire, consist of from 300 to 500 acres each, many of the tenants holding two and three farms, they ought to possess, and indeed at the end of the war did possess, very large capitals. On farms of such extent it would be absurd for the tenant to engage in labour himself. His time is much more profitably employed in superintending the labour of others. Men with capitals of from L.2,000 to L.10,000 are entitled to live in a decent style, more especially as all of them have received liberal educations, and many of them have been educated, as well as the greater number of those who practise the learned professions. In the above counties, we could point out many tenants paying L.2000 a-year of rent, and a few who pay as much as L.5000. According to the data on which the property tax was levied, these men's profits ought to amount to L.1000 or L.2500 a-year.

Yet we believe that the tenantry in these counties do not generally expend in living, in addition to the pigs, poultry, &c., produced on their farms, more than a sum equal to half the interest of the capital employed in their cultivation."

There is another part of Scotland, into the agricultural state of which it is proper to inquire. We have laid before our readers extracts from communications from the north, east, south, and central parts of the kingdom, let us now turn to the south-west. The following excerpts are from answers to our queries, furnished by a gentleman who has the management of a very extensive district in the stewarty of Kirkcudbright:—" The tenantry both upon tillage and stock farms are struggling with difficulties. Capital is dwindling away, and the tenantry in many instances are not in a situation to do justice to the tillage lands. The rents in 1832 may be considered a third less than 1813. Draining is very much neglected—lime as a manure is used very sparingly; the capital of the tenantry being so much exhausted they have little spare money to expend on manuring with lime, and the land is becoming poorer every repeated rotation. The landed proprietors are in many instances struggling with difficulties."

From all the communications we have received it appears that expensive improvements, or indeed improvements of any kind are not undertaken by the tenantry as formerly. Wedge or tile draining is practised in some districts on wet alluvial soils, but often the tiles are paid for by the landlord. These cost three-fourths of the whole expense. The introduction of bone manure has also a wonderful effect on light soils, and has enabled farmers, having farms of that quality of soil, to pay higher rents than they could otherwise have done. But it has, on the other hand, diminished the value of fine turnip land, and by means of this manure, turnips can be grown on many soils which formerly would not produce them.

SCRAPS.
ORIGINAL AND SELECTED.

JONATHAN'S DESCRIPTION OF A STEAM-BOAT.—It's got a saw-mill on one side, and a grist-mill on t'other, and a blacksmith's shop in the middle, and down cellar there's a tarnation pot boiling all the time.

Ricaut, in his *History of the Turks*, says, " that they so confound chronology and history, as to assert that Job was a judge in the court of King Solomon, and Alexander the Great one of his generals."

INFANT LABOUR.—A certain eccentric Tory member, who, till he obtained a seat in the present Parliament, had never made his appearance in society, dined, last year, in company with Sadler, and several other political personages, at the mansion of Sir Robert Peel. After dinner, as the gentlemen were drinking coffee in the fine picture gallery of the ex-minister, a conversation took place between Sadler and Sir Robert on the subject of the Bill for the Regulation of Infant Labour. Mr. ————, who was standing near, occasionally joining in the discussion, while he contemplated Lawrence's exquisite picture of the infant daughter of his host, (considering, perhaps, that the baronet was lukewarm towards the interests of the manufacturing classes,) suddenly slapped him on the back, and exclaimed, while he pointed to the portrait of little Miss Peel, " Ah! Sir Robert! that little darling *might* have been slaving in the factory you know; 'twas a narrow escape." The amazement of his disconcerted auditors may be easily conjectured.—*Tait's Magazine.*

BARBARISM OF THE CRIMINAL CODE.—I have much to say upon the subject of the recovery of debts in this country—on imprisonment in general; but more particularly on the penal code of Britain. Draco and Co. must have presided when such sanguinary laws were established. Blood, nothing but blood, or " pounds of flesh," are required by this humane people for every offence. Should Hardy (a servant who had stolen some of Mirabeau's linen) be found guilty, he will suffer death—the punishment awarded to the man who has butchered his own mother. Such laws ought to be revised; they are a disgrace to a civilised nation. I have before me a list of crimes —about forty in number—all punishable with death. The laws of the most despotic countries of Europe are merciful if compared with those which are in force here. Every sensible man to whom I have spoken upon this subject entertains a similar opinion; yet no one comes forward to abrogate the obnoxious laws. My excellent friend Romilly tells me, that he has been carefully studying the criminal codes of every nation in Europe. " Ours," he observes, " is the very worst; and, when the plan I have in view is sufficiently matured, I intend not to rest upon my pillow until these laws, worthy of anthropophagi, are for ever abolished."—*Mirabeau's Letters.*

ROYAL APPRECIATION OF GENIUS.—The *Globe* says—" Sir Walter Scott obtained his baronetcy shortly after the accession of George IV., who paid literature the high compliment of bestowing upon one of its principal living ornaments the first creation of title by the monarch."—That is, George IV. paid literature the high compliment of bestowing upon one of its principal ornaments, the title which is the lowest but one in the scale. He might, to be sure, have made him a knight—that would have been lower yet, and lowest; but he was graciously pleased to think the highest genius deserving of a trumpery baronetcy. It is not thus that they honour their tools and panders. The successful direction of force in human butchery, no matter how doubtful or bad the cause, is rewarded with a peerage. The man who has delighted millions existing, and will delight millions yet to be, has the same guerdon as the king's purveyor of gossip, or which any vain booby may purchase for a few hundreds. Jenner, who has prevented more mischief than any king or lord in history ever perpetrated, goes down to a grateful posterity without an addition to his name. It is well that it should be so—royalty has nothing to do with the real services to mankind—let it keep to the rewards of the coarse arts of force, and court parasites, and political prostitutes;—but it is significant to remark how princes do rate the claims of the ornaments or benefactors of the world, when they give them a place in the scale of honours. We have their standard of desert. There is, however, a consistency in it. Kings, who find themselves kings without desert, bestow titles as they have received the power of conferring them. It were a reflection on their own state to distribute titles according to merit, for men's minds would thus be led up to examine the pretensions of the prime pageant. Policy, therefore, directs that the toys should continue to be given to those who could not obtain distinction of any but an infamous kind without them: they are unworthy of men of letters and science, whose honours are in the reverence of mankind, and celebrity in after ages.—*Examiner*.

ROOKS AND CHOLERA.—A curious circumstance is mentioned connected with the appearance of the cholera at Sligo. "In the demesne of the Marquis of Sligo, near Westport House, there is one of the largest rookeries in the west of Ireland. On the first or second day of the appearance of cholera in this place, I was astonished to observe that all the rooks had disappeared; and for three weeks, during which the disease raged violently, those noisy tenants of the trees completely deserted their lofty habitations. In the mean time, the revenue police found immense numbers of them lying dead upon the shore, near Erris, about ten miles distant. Upon the decline of the malady, within the last few days, several of the old birds have again appeared in the neighbourhood of the rookery; but some of them seemed unable, from exhaustion, to reach their nests." A similar departure of the crows and other birds has been observed at the town of Kampen in Holland, and their return when the disease began to abate. If this be not a merely accidental coincidence, it would seem to put the theory of atmospherical influence beyond dispute.

CHRONOMETERS.—Lately terminated the ninth annual trial of skill of the numerous artists employed in the construction of chronometers. The prizes were awarded to three makers in London. The actual error on any of their rates during the year did not amount to one second of time,—a degree of accuracy unprecedented in three chronometers in former trials. So perfectly were they adjusted, that either would have enabled a mariner to navigate a vessel round the world with less than one mile of error in longitude at the close of such voyage.

In the time of the consulate in France, Napoleon, by a word, described the characters of the three consuls. Do you wish to dine badly, go to Le Brun; do you wish to dine well, go to Cambaceres; do you wish to dine rapidly, come to me. Le Brun was a miser, Cambaceres a glutton; and what Bonaparte was all the world knows.—*Le Cercle*.

GOLD.—In Ireland, county of Wicklow, seven miles west of Arklow, about the year 1770, there was an old schoolmaster, who used frequently to entertain his neighbours with accounts of the richness of their valley in gold; and his practice was to go out in the night to search for the treasure. For this he was generally accounted insane. But in some years after, bits of gold were found in a mountain stream, by various persons; and, in 1796, a piece weighing about half an ounce. The news of this having circulated amongst the peasantry, such an infatuation took possession of the minds of the people, that every other sort of employment, save that of acquiring wealth by the short process of picking it up out of the streams, was abandoned; and hundreds of human figures were to be seen bending over the waters, and scrutinizing every object there to be seen. In this way, during six weeks, no less than 800 ounces of gold were found, which sold for L.3, 15s. per ounce, or L.3000. Most of the gold was found in grains; many pieces weighed between two and three ounces; there was one of 5 ounces, and one of 22. It contained about 6 per cent of silver. Government soon undertook the works; but the amount of gold found, while superintended by the appointed directors, was only L.3671. It then appeared that there was no regular vein in the mountain, and that these fragments had probably existed in a part of the mountain which time had mouldered away, and which left its more permanent treasure as the only monument of its ancient existence. The works were at a length discontinued.—*Lardner's Cabinet Cyclopædia*.

A VULGAR FELLOW WHO HAS ACQUIRED GREAT WEALTH BY THE ACCIDENT OF BIRTH OR SITUATION.—We mean commercial accidents of situation, as well as others. In Lancashire, as in other manufacturing districts, men of great wealth, by the possession of a place which, by mere accident, is in the way of a commercial current or demand. These men are generally arrogant and purse-proud in proportion to their ignorance. At a dinner where one of these worthies, an aspirant to public honours, and the holder of an office under the appointment of Lord Melbourne, was present, some one mentioned the names of Homer and Virgil. "Homer and Virgil?" said he; "Homer and Virgil! I never heard the name of that firm before. Is their credit good?"—*Examiner*.

STEAM ENGINE FOR AGRICULTURAL PURPOSES.—At a meeting of the Manchester Agricultural Society, held lately, the model of a steam engine, recently invented by Mr. Gough, of Manchester, applicable to agricultural purposes, was exhibited upon the table. At the close of the proceedings Mr. Gough explained the nature of it, and the objects for which it was intended. The engine was not projected to supersede the labour of men, but to assist and relieve them in the drudgery of their occupation. It was capable of raising water, draining land, washing roots and preparing them for cattle, cleaning of vessels, &c. He had spent much time in attempting to accomplish his object, and after 30 years' trial, had succeeded. It was intended not to exceed five horses' power, and the price would be dependant on the amount of power.

ON LYNDHURST.—"Point d'argent,—point de Suisse."— No hucre—no Lyndhurst—(free translation.)

Lyndhurst will never use his tongue
Unless with cash the Tories deck him;
So, if they wish him to go on,
Their only method is to *cheque* him.

Part III. of the SCHOOLMASTER, containing the four October Numbers, with JOHNSTONE'S POLITICAL REGISTER, may now be had of all the Booksellers and Venders of Cheap Periodicals, price Eightpence.

CONTENTS OF NO. XIV.

Places of Public Worship in Edinburgh............ 209
NOTES OF THE MONTH,............................. 211
BOOKS OF THE MONTH,............................. ib.
Dr Chalmers,.................................... 212
SCIENTIFIC NOTICES,............................. 214
To the Neutrals,................................ 215
ELEMENTS OF THOUGHT,............................ 216
MEDICAL SELECTIONS,............................. ib.
USEFUL NOTICES,................................. ib.
Evening Wind,................................... ib.
THE STORY-TELLER—John Kiernander; or, the Deceitfulness of Riches,............................ 219
Spectral Illusion,.............................. 221
Caged Rats,..................................... 221
Present State of the Scottish Tenantry,......... 222
SCRAPS—Original and Selected,................... 223

EDINBURGH: Printed by and for JOHN JOHNSTONE, 19, St. James's Square.—Published by JOHN ANDERSON, Jun., Bookseller, 55, North Bridge Street, Edinburgh; by JOHN MACLEOD, and ATKINSON & Co., Booksellers, Glasgow; and sold by all Booksellers and Venders of Cheap Periodicals.

THE Schoolmaster,
AND
EDINBURGH WEEKLY MAGAZINE.

CONDUCTED BY JOHN JOHNSTONE.

THE SCHOOLMASTER IS ABROAD.—LORD BROUGHAM.

No. 15.—Vol. I.   SATURDAY, NOVEMBER 10, 1832.   Price Three-Halfpence.

EDUCATION OF THE PEOPLE.

Within the last twenty years there has been much writing, and interminable speculation and discussion on the propriety of the legislature interfering in the education of the working people, on the wisdom of establishments for national education, and also on the danger of giving the labouring classes any knowledge at all, save of their trades, and the sole duty of blind obedience to their civil and spiritual directors. Timid or prejudiced persons could see nothing but revolt in reading, and a general plunder in writing and accounts. Men of better intellects, and more philanthropic natures, took a juster and more enlarged view of the question; and Mr. Brougham, above all other individuals, by his efforts in Parliament and through the press, gave a momentum to the public mind on this important subject which should ever be remembered to his honour. Many good men followed, and co-operated, however they might differ in opinion with the present Lord Chancellor, on the value of some of those objects of which elementary education is but an instrument. The patrons of the Sunday Schools, the Quakers and Phrenologists as societies, and many enlightened individuals from every class, came forward as advocates for the diffusion of knowledge among the people. Education was occasionally made the subject of Parliamentary discussion, and this had its uses, though the legislature did next to nothing. The Lancasterian system arose; the Madras or "Church and King" system followed; Dame Schools, those most useful of all seminaries, where properly managed, were somewhat improved, and a few *Infant Schools* were instituted in the large towns; while, in Sunday Schools, subsidiary to the main object, the general faculties of the scholars were improved by exercise, and a knowledge of reading was either acquired or perfected. And all this was accomplished by the people themselves, without aid or interference from the state, and little indeed from the aristocracy: and in this way, along with sundry concurring and favouring causes, though no general system of education had been adopted for either England or Ireland, nor that existing, extended in Scotland to meet the wants of an increased and impoverished population, a large portion of the people have become "self-taught." They took the matter, which seemed nobody's business, into their own hands, and thus practically solved the difficulty of any government ever permanently or effectually enlightening or ameliorating the condition of a people, save through their own agency. And such, on the subject of education, is the impetus now given to the public mind, that were the working people once set at ease, by the unfettering of trade, and lightening of taxation, it might become a question whether they should not, in general circumstances, be left to that great *Schoolmaster*, the press, with its assistants of Mechanics' institutions, libraries, reading-rooms, and the other machinery of knowledge, which has been carried forward mainly by intelligent artizans themselves. These remarks have been suggested to us by having lately heard of a *Mechanic's Hall of Science*, projected in Manchester some months since by the artizans of that town; which, as we take it, is intended as a joint-stock seminary, managed by the artisans themselves, where every thing shall be taught necessary to the formation of a good man, and a useful citizen, and promotive of individual and social well-being: a system embracing, as we understand it, all a child ought to learn from the period it leaves the infant school till the human being is, as far as school education goes, perfected in intelligence and virtue. The design is worthy of all approbation, and the very idea is proof that education must already have made good progress among those with whom it originated. It shows what is pointed out by many other signs, that the thirst for knowledge among the people was never so strong as now. Nor is it either to shallow or impure sources they repair to allay it. As a sure test of the fitness of the labouring-classes to carry on the work of reformed and extended education which they have happily begun in Manchester, we would invite comparison between the *cheap* publications which circulate and are popular among them, and those which daily issue from the press for the improvement or gratification of the higher orders. Let us run it at all points, of good taste, style, reasoning, moral feeling, sound principle, and we shall then leave the decision to the wildest denouncer of "the plunderers," "the ferocious mob," "the brutal rabble," provided he be a person of any judgment or candour. The husbandry-labourer takes a hundredth share of *Cobbett's Register*,* while his squire orders an entire *John Bull* for his Sunday morning's edification. The working-men read the *Examiner* and *Spectator*. These journals are to be seen in all their reading-rooms; but the higher orders—the educated classes, prefer the slang and filth,—the vulgarity, impudence, and garbage of the Tory Sunday papers, as evidence of their intellectual superiority and refinement. This is tolerably conclusive of the moral state of the respective classes; nor need we push the argument into their weightier literature, where the poor, and the lowest of the middle class, are ministered to by cheap useful publications in *series*, and by *Libraries* written with great talent and ability, while their betters tumble over the leaves of the worst, and, therefore, the most fashionable novels, and the toybooks got up for grown children. But extremes meet; and there is a part—and, we fear, a very large one—of the labouring classes of great towns still as ignorant of all useful and humanizing knowledge as are the very high. Each caste is skilled in the sleight of its own calling, and knows little beyond that. In external shows there may be some difference, but their morals are alike slippery and obtuse, their sensibilities alike blunted, and their general character in all below the mask, tends as certainly to a common centre as that the sporting Duke and the vulgar black-leg rub shoulders, and are "hail! Fellow, well met!" in the gambling house or the race-ground. The very high folks must be left to themselves; but for the kindred division among the low, the unprincipled, shameless, dissolute, idle, and rapacious poor, some organised system of moral training may be necessary.

"In the progress of the division of labour," says Adam Smith, "the employment of the far greater part of those who live by labour, that is, of the great body of the people, comes to be confined to a few very simple operations; frequently to one or two. But the understandings of the greater part of men are necessarily formed by their ordinary employments. The man whose whole life is spent in performing a few simple operations, of which the effects, too, are perhaps always the same, or very nearly the same, has no occasion to exert his understanding, or to exercise his invention in finding out expedients for removing difficulties which never occur. He naturally loses, therefore, the habit of such exertion, and generally becomes as stupid and ignorant as it is possible for a human creature to become. The torpor of his mind renders him not only incapable of judging; and unless *very particular* pains have been taken to render him otherwise, he is equally incapable of defending his country in war, and the uniformity of his life naturally corrupts the courage of his mind, and makes him regard with abhorrence the irregular, uncertain, and adventurous life of a soldier." And the writer proceeds to contrast with this the superior condition of men in a barbarous society, where life is full of vicissitude and interest. His reasoning is worthy of profound attention. "In such societies," he observes, "the varied occupations of every man oblige every man to exert his capacity, and invent expedients for removing difficulties which are continually occurring. Invention is kept alive, and the mind is not suffered to fall into that drowsy stupidity, which, in a civilized society, seems to benumb the understanding of almost all the inferior ranks of people. In those barbarous societies, as they are called, every man is a warrior. Every man, too, is in some measure a statesman, and can form a tolerable judgment concerning the interest of the society, and the conduct of those who govern it. How far their chiefs are good judges in peace, or good leaders in war, is obvious to the observation of almost every single man among them."

The author of the *Wealth of Nations* pursues the parallel between the barbarian and the citizen of a highly civilized state, doomed to spend his existence in moulding a brick or pointing a pin, in the true spirit of Radicalism; and proves the necessity of the State caring for the education of its degraded human machines. With his argument for training all the people to military exercises, thereby rendering only a very small standing army necessary, we shall not now interfere; but we could not conclude the above desultory remarks with any thing more apposite than the conclusion of his reasons for educating *all* the people, and making their education what America, Prussia, France, Sweden, and even Austria have done—the business of the State. It includes his closing remarks on martial training:—

"Even though the martial spirit of the people were of no use towards the defence of the society, yet, to prevent that sort of mental mutilation, deformity, and wretchedness, which cowardice necessarily involves in it, from spreading themselves through the great body of the people, would still deserve the most serious attention of the Government; in the same manner as it would deserve its most serious attention to prevent a leprosy, or other loathsome and offensive disease, though neither mortal nor dangerous, from spreading itself among them, though perhaps no other public good might result from such attention, beside the prevention of so great a public evil. The same thing may be said of the gross ignorance and stupidity, which, in a civilized society, seem so frequently to benumb the understandings of all the inferior ranks of people. A man, without the proper use of the intellectual faculties of a man, is, if possible, more contemptible than even a coward; and seems to be mutilated and deformed in a still more essential part of the character of human nature. Though the State was to derive no advantage from the instruction of the inferior ranks of the people, it would still deserve its attention that they should not be altogether uninstructed. The State, however, derives no inconsiderable advantage from their instruction. The more they are instructed the less liable they are to the delusions of enthusiasm and superstition, which, among ignorant nations, frequently occasion the most dreadful disorders. An instructed and intelligent people, besides, are always more decent and orderly than an ignorant and stupid one."

The rest of the argument has become trite in our day, in which no question has been illustrated with more force and ingenuity than the importance of educating the people. It now remains to act, and the people themselves are acting. Need we say how fervently we hope that the example of the mechanics of Manchester may be followed far and wide; and how cordially we wish success to a design, which, though it should even fail, it is so creditable to have formed.

---

* We have been informed that there are in Sussex and Kent often a hundred readers for one copy of the *Register*.

A CHAPTER FOR MARTINMAS TERM.

MAID SERVANTS.

THOSE who complain of English (and Scotch) servants, do it in ignorance, having none other to compare them with; and it must be remembered that all good and evil is by comparison. I have rambled half over the earth's surface, and beg to assure the good ladies, who labour under the delusion about the badness of servants, (if I may be allowed to parody Alfred Tennyson's beautiful song,) that

"There are no maids like English maids,
Such working maids as they be."

In the United States, good servants may be had, but they must be paid at a much higher rate of wages than in England, and they must be treated much more like human beings. The black slaves of the American continent and isles are not so obedient, so humble, as the free English domestics. The Indians who compose the servants of Peru are virtually, though not legally, slaves; and they are stupid and sullen. In most of the countries of Spanish America, the domestics are divided into two classes, *criadas* and *servientes*. The former are negresses, either slaves or free; they are occupied in coarse labours, such as cookery, &c. The latter are whites in appearance, though from some tinge of black or Indian blood they rank as *mulatas* or *chinas*. With the exception of sitting down to the same table, and intermarrying, they are treated precisely as if they were part of the family, and their duties are confined to the lighter parts of household work, sewing, &c. An English maid-servant going to those countries, as she is of white blood, if she be at all educated, becomes a lady in rank, unless she is obliged to continue a menial, which is rarely the case, especially if she happen to be pretty, for she gets married; but she rarely acquires the grace and sweetness of modulation, in the sound of the voice, peculiar to all Spanish women; and of which the very negresses seem half to partake. In Buenos Ayres, where servants are scarce, I have known a negress hired by an English family in the morning, at the rate of thirty shillings per month, and in the evening present herself in the sitting room, caparisoned in china crape and silk stockings—not to ask leave—but to give notice—that she was going to mass. The English family being greenhorns, refused permission, and quarrelled ere I could interfere. The consequence was, that the dark-skinned lady gave warning, received her day's wages, and quitted her place, all in five minutes. The family grew wiser subsequently. Two ungainly, gawky, boarding-school importations, who arrived at the same town with "Pa," after duly taking lessons in housekeeping under a maiden aunt, were delighted with the idea of keeping Pa's house; and as soon as he got one, they hired a servant, a mulata woman; to whom the first order they gave, in broken Spanish, was—to scour all the floors of the house. The mulata, who had never heard of such doings, was horrified, and flatly refused; the damsels insisted, and the dingy lady quitted her new situation. She spread the report of the strange ways of the strangers far and wide, and not a servant could they get for love or money. Nothing daunted, these lengthy patterns of good householdery resolved to perform the scrubbing in *propria personas*. Aprons were made, and they "downed on their knees" to the task of shaming the handmaidens of Buenos Ayres. The result was, they caught a violent cold each, and after three days' futile labour they discovered, that—tiled floors were better without scrubbing. They also grew wiser in time. There is one remarkable difference between the servants of England and the servants of the Continent, both of Europe and America. The former are for the most part merely hirelings, whose interest, as they themselves conceive, is in direct opposition to that of their employers. The latter are, with few exceptions, attached by a stronger bond than their mere wages, to their masters and mistresses. In many cases they have been known to peril life and limb in their service; and even with slaves this has frequently been the case. Why is this? Because the English treat their servants with all possible hauteur, as if they were not of the same creation as themselves; and endeavour, on all occasions, to draw a line as broad as possible between them. The foreigners, on the contrary, treat their servants as human beings, and there is a great interest mutually felt in each other's affairs. "Keep the servants at a proper distance, my dear," is the lesson of an English mother to her children; and after that, she too frequently leaves her children to be managed and brought up by the despised servants. Unfortunately, too great is the necessity for keeping the children apart from the servants; for the mode in which the latter are treated begets many vices, which would be perpetuated in the children; for nature is fond of types, and readily takes a lesson of evil as well as good. Even external appearance has some effect; and were I the proprietor of a family of children, I should insist on all the nursery maids being as handsome, as well as good, as they could be got. Jealousy, the same passion which impels Mrs. Grundy to keep her servants at a distance, also impels her to select them of the most ugly kind, and, consequently, her children take after them. Poor unfortunate woman! how she suffers for her short-sightedness.—*Junius Redivivus*.

English servants abroad, notwithstanding, the comfor they enjoy, and though travelling as it were *en famille*, must be struck with the ease and familiar footing on which foreigners live with their domestics, compared with the distance and reserve with which they are treated. The housemaid *(la bonne)* sits down in the room, or walks abreast with you in the street; and the valet, who waits behind his master's chair at table, gives monsieur his advice or opinion without being asked for it. We need not wonder at this familiarity and freedom, when we consider that those who allowed it could (formerly, at least, when the custom began) send those who transgressed but in the smallest degree to the Bastile or the galleys at their pleasure. The license was attended with impunity. With us the law leaves less to discretion; and, by interposing a real independence (and plea of right) between the servant and master, does away with the appearance of it on the surface of manners. The insolence and tyranny of the aristocracy fell more on the tradespeople and mechanics, who were attached to them by a semblance of feudal ties. Thus an upstart lady of quality (an imitator of the old school) would not deign to speak to a milliner while fitting on her dress, but gave her orders to her waiting-woman to tell her what to do. Can we wonder at twenty *Reigns of Terror* to efface such a feeling?—*New Monthly Magazine*.

TEMPTATIONS TO WHICH SERVANT GIRLS ARE EXPOSED.—We copy the following observations, written by a lady, and, as we think, of great importance to those who have the well-being of such young persons so much in their power—almost at their mercy:—"Servants have, in common with the rest of the world, the vanities and desires natural to humanity; but while they administer to them in others, they are compelled to control them in themselves. Under such circumstances they do not surely need the aggravation they often meet with from arrogance and irritability. Goaded humanity often bears much ere it falls from virtue; many and bitter are the pangs of hunger often felt before the hand is extended in an act of felony. Many a young and pretty girl tries the effect of a ribbon at her mistress's toilet, and sighs to think how little *she* can command to aid the beauty with which she seeks to charm her lover. Many living in families in which they enjoy plenty, have parents, sisters, brothers, perhaps *children*, wanting the common necessaries of life. None but stoics will deny that these are trials—trials of no common order, and let it not be forgotten, of continual recurrence—the appealing want or wo, the temptations are perpetually present. What then, is there to assure virtue thus vibrating between contending impulses? What but kindness and consideration, which will twine stronger cords around the heart of the dependent than suspicion and penalty ever fabricated to bind the delinquent."

BREVITIES.

For sale, waste paper lying in a loft,
Perceval's speech—*particularly soft!*

THE BAROMETER.

It is a common notion that the indices of the barometer are as easily to be understood, at a glance, as the handle of a clock; and men who do not understand the instrument, or ladies who have a great washing, or a party of pleasure depending upon what they reckon its flattering faithless promise, are often ready to vent their indignation at bad weather by smashing the barometer, and delivering up its maker a sacrifice to that Prince of the Powers of the Air, whose caprices, he seems so ill to understand. About this season, when the weather becomes so fickle, the barometer lies under peculiar odium, but no one stops to enquire whether the instrument suspended in his parlour, be one constructed upon scientific principles, or a bauble, with a gaudy outside to catch the vulgar, and give rise to what learned people call,

VULGAR ERRORS RESPECTING THE BAROMETER.

We shall see what Dr. Lardner says of these mistakes, and of the misleading directions engraved on the hawked cheap instruments.

The barometer has been called a weather-glass. Rules are attempted to be established, by which, from the height of the mercury, the coming state of the weather may be predicted, and we accordingly find the words "Rain," "Fair," "Changeable," "Frost," &c. engraved on the scale attached to common domestic barometers, as if, when the mercury stands at the height marked by these words, the weather is always subject to the vicissitude expressed by them. These marks are, however, entitled to no attention; and it is only surprising to find their use continued in the present times, when knowledge is so widely diffused. They are, in fact, to be ranked scarcely above the *vox stellarum*, or astrological almanack. Two barometers, one near the level of the river Thames, and the other on the heights of Hampstead, will differ by half an inch; the latter being always half an inch lower than the former. If the words, therefore, engraved upon the plates are to be relied on, similar changes of weather could never happen at these two situations. But what is even more absurd, such a scale would inform us that the weather at the foot of a high building, such as St. Paul's, must always be different from the weather at the top of it. It is observed that changes of weather are indicated, *not by the actual height of the mercury, but by its change of height*.—One of the most general, though not absolutely invariable, rules is, that when the mercury is very low, and therefore the atmosphere very light, high winds and storms may be expected. The following rules may generally be relied upon, at least to a certain extent:—1. *Generally the rising of the mercury indicates the approach of fair weather; the falling of it shows the approach of foul weather.* 2. *In sultry weather the fall of the mercury indicates coming thunder. In winter, the rise of the mercury indicates frost. In frost, its fall indicates thaw; and its rise indicates snow.* 3. *Whatever change of weather suddenly follows a change in the barometer may be expected to last but a short time.*—Thus, if fair weather follow immediately the rise of the mercury, there will be very little of it; and, in the same way, if foul weather follow the fall of the mercury, it will last but a short time. 4. If fair weather continue for several days, during which the mercury continually falls, a long continuance of foul weather will probably ensue; and again, if foul weather continue for several days, while the mercury continually rises, a long succession of fair weather will probably succeed. 5. A fluctuating and unsettled state in the mercurial column indicates changeable weather. The domestic barometer would become a much more useful instrument, if, instead of the words usually engraved on the plate, a short list of the best established rules, such as the above, accompanied it, which might be either engraved on the plate, or printed on a card. It would be right, however, to express the rules only with that degree of probability which observation of past phenomena has justified.—There is no rule respecting these effects which will hold good.

THE THERMOMETER.

FAHRENHEIT.—The first who succeeded in constructing thermometers with adequate skill was Fahrenheit. This ingenious man had been a merchant at Dantzic, and through misfortune failed in business; but having a good taste for mechanics, he removed into Holland, and settled as a philosophical instrument maker at Amsterdam. He began with spirit of wine thermometers, which he formed much smaller and neater than had been attempted before. But he soon preferred quick-silver; and having found it to expand from freezing water to blood heat, about 60 parts in 10,000, he assumed the number 64, and obtained the degrees by repeated bisections. In this practice he was confirmed, on observing what he considered as extreme cold, to descend just through half that space, or 32 degrees. From a mixture of water, ice, and sal ammoniac, the scale commenced; 32 degrees were allotted for the interval to ice-water, and 64 more for the ascent to blood heat. But he afterwards enlarged the range, and assumed another point from the limit of boiling water, which he placed at the 212th degree in the mean state of the atmosphere, though liable to some variation from the change of barometric pressure. Such was now his confidence in the delicacy of the construction, that he proposed the thermometer as an instrument for ascertaining the heights of mountains from the depressed temperature of boiling water; a very simple method, which has been lately revived by the Rev. Mr. Wollaston.

MANNERS.—D'Archenholtz, in his *Tableau de l'Angleterre*, asserts that an "Englishman may be discovered anywhere if he be observed at table, because he places his fork upon the left side of his plate; a Frenchman by using the fork alone without the knife; and a German by planting it perpendicularly into his plate; and a Russian by using it as a tooth-pick." Holding the fork is a national custom, and nations are characterized by their peculiarity in the use of the fork at table. Umbrellas, in my youth, were not ordinary things; few but the macaronis of the day, as the dandies were then called, would venture to display them. For a long while it was not usual for men to carry them without incurring the brand of effeminacy, and they were vulgarly considered as the characteristics of a person whom the mob hugely disliked, namely, a mincing Frenchman! At first, a single umbrella seems to have been kept at a coffee-house for some extraordinary occasion—lent as a coach or chair in a heavy shower, but not commonly carried by the walkers. The *Female Tatler* advertises, "the young gentlemen belonging to the custom-house, who, in fear of rain, borrowed the *umbrella* from Wilks' Coffee-house, shall the next time be welcome to the maid's *pattens*." An umbrella, carried by a man, was obviously then considered as extreme effeminacy. As late as in 1778, one John Macdonald, a footman, who has written his own life, informs us, that when he used "a fine silk umbrella, which he had brought from Spain, he could not with any comfort to himself use it; the people calling out, 'Frenchman! why don't you get a coach?'" The fact was that the hackney-coachmen and the chairmen joining with the true *esprit de corps*, were clamorous against this portentous rival. This footman, in 1778, gives us further information. "At this time there were no umbrellas worn in London, except in noblemen's and gentlemen's houses, where there was a large one hung in the hall to hold over a lady or gentleman, if it rained between the door and their carriage." His sister was compelled to quit his arm one day from the abuse he drew down on himself and his umbrella. But he adds, that "he persisted for three months till they took no further notice of this novelty. Foreigners began to use theirs, and then the English. Now it is become a great trade in London." This footman, if he does not arrogate too much to his own confidence, was the first man distinguished by carrying and using a silken umbrella. He is the founder of a most populous school. The state of our population might now in some degree be ascertained by the number of umbrellas.—*New Monthly Magazine.*

MEMORABLE BATTLES.

THE BATTLE OF RONCESVALLES.

The Pyrenees, extending in a continuous line from the Bay of Biscay to the borders of the Mediterranean, rise in a long straight ridge, the superior points of which are but a few yards lower than the summit of Mont Blanc. In the highest part of the chain there are occasional apertures; and from the main body of the mountains, long masses of inferior hills are projected into the plain country on either side, decreasing in height as they proceed, till they become imperceptibly blended with the level ground around. Between these steep natural buttresses, narrow valleys, sometimes spreading out into grand basins, sometimes straitened into defiles of a few yards in width, wind on towards the only passes from one country to another. The roads, skirting along the bases of the hills, which, to the present day, are frequently involved in immense and trackless woods, have always beneath them a mountain torrent, above which they are raised, as on a terrace, upon the top of high and rugged precipices. A thousand difficulties beset the way on every side, and nature has surrounded the path with every means of ambush and concealment. Mounted on heavy horses, and loaded with a complete armour of iron, the soldiers of Charlemagne returned from their victorious expedition into Spain, and entered the gorges of the Pyrenees, without ever dreaming that an enemy beset their footsteps. The monarch himself, with the first division of his host, was suffered to pass unmolested; but when the second body of the Francs, following leisurely at a considerable distance, had entered the wild and narrow valley called the Roseida Vallis, (now Roncesvalles,) the woods and mountains around them suddenly bristled into life, and they were attacked on all sides by the perfidious Gascons, whose light arms, distant arrows, and knowledge of the country, gave them every advantage over their opponents. In tumult and confusion the Francs were driven into the bottom of the pass, embarrassed both by their arms and baggage. The Gascons pressed them on every point, and slaughtered them like a herd of deer, singling them out with their arrows from above, and rolling down the rocks upon their heads. Never wanting in courage, the Francs fought to the last man, and died unconquered. Rolando and his companions, after a thousand deeds of valour, were slain with the rest; and the Gascons, satiated with carnage, and rich in plunder, dispersed among the mountains, leaving Charlemagne to seek for immediate vengeance in vain. The battle must have been fierce and long, and the struggle great, though unequal; for, during the lapse of many centuries, tradition has hung about the spot, and the memory of Rolando and his companions is consecrated in a thousand shapes throughout the country. Part of his armour has there given name to a flower; the stroke of his sword is shown upon the mountains; the tales and superstitions of the district are replete with his exploits and with his fame; and even had not Ariosto, on the slight basis which history affords, raised up the splendid structure of an immortal poem, and dedicated it to the name of Rolando, that name would still have been repeated through all the valleys of the Pyrenees, and ornamented with all the fictions of a thousand years.—*James's History of Charlemagne.*

THE BATTLE OF THERMOPYLÆ.

It was now the dead of night, when the Spartans, headed by Leonidas, marched in a close battalion towards the Persian camp, with resentment heightened by despair. Their fury was terrible, and rendered still more destructive through the defect of barbarian discipline; for the Persians having neither advanced guards, nor a watchword, nor confidence in each other, were incapable of adopting such measures for defence, as the sudden emergency required. Many fell by the Grecian spear, but much greater multitudes by the mistaken rage of their own troops, by whom, in the midst of this blind confusion, they could not be distinguished from enemies. The Greeks, wearied with slaughter, penetrated to the royal pavilion; but there the first alarm of noise had been readily perceived, amidst the profound silence and tranquillity which usually reigned in the tent of Xerxes; the great king had immediately escaped, with his favourite attendants, to the farther extremity of the encampment. Even there, all was tumult, and horror, and despair; the obscurity of night increasing the terror of the Persians, who no longer doubted that the detachment conducted by Epialtes had been betrayed by that perfidious Greek; and that the enemy, reinforced by new numbers, now co-operated with the traitor, and seized the opportunity of assailing their camp, after it had been deprived of the division of Hydarnes, its principal ornament and defence.

The approach of day discovered to the Persians a dreadful scene of carnage; but it also discovered to them, that their fears had multiplied the number of the enemy, who now retreated in close order to the straits of Thermopylæ. Xerxes, stimulated by the fury of revenge, gave orders to pursue them; and his terrified troops were rather driven than led to the attack, by the officers who marched behind the several divisions, and compelled them to advance by menaces, stripes, and blows. The Grecians, animated by their late success, and persuaded that they could not possibly escape death on the arrival of those who approached by way of the mountain, bravely halted in the widest part of the pass, to receive the charge of the enemy. The shock was dreadful, and the battle was maintained on the side of the Greeks with persevering intrepidity and desperate valour. After their spears were blunted or broken, they attacked sword in hand, and their short, but massy and well-tempered weapons, made an incredible havoc. Their progress was marked by a line of blood, when a barbarian dart pierced the heart of Leonidas. The contest was no longer for victory and glory, but for the sacred remains of their king. Four times they dispelled the thickest groups of Persians, but as their unexampled valour was carrying off the inestimable prize, the hostile battalions were seen descending the hill, under the conduct of Epialtes. It was now time to prepare for the last effort of generous despair. With close order and resolute minds, the Greeks, all collected in themselves, retired to the narrowest part of the strait, and took post behind the Phocian wall, on a rising ground, where a lion of stone was afterwards erected in honour of Leonidas. As they performed this movement, fortune, willing to afford every occasion to display their illustrious merit, obliged them to contend at once against open force and secret treachery. The Thebans, whom fear had hitherto restrained from defection, seized the present opportunity to revolt; and approaching the Persians with outstretched arms, declared that they had always been their friends; that *their* republic had sent earth and water, as an acknowledgment of their submission to Xerxes. As they approached to surrender themselves, many perished by the darts of the barbarians; the remainder saved a perishing life, by submitting to eternal infamy. Meanwhile the Lacedæmonians and Thespians were assaulted on all sides. The nearest of the enemy beat down the wall, and entered by the breaches. Their temerity was punished by instant death. In this last struggle every Grecian showed the most heroic courage; yet if we believe the unanimous report of some Thessalians, and others who survived the engagement, the Spartan Dioneces deserved the prize of valour. When it was observed to him, that the Persian arrows were so numerous, that they intercepted the light of the sun, he said it was a favourable circumstance, because the Greeks now fought in the shade. The brothers Alpheus and Maron are likewise particularized for their generous contempt of death, and for their distinguished valour and activity in the service of their country. What these, and other virtues, could accomplish, the Greeks, both as individuals, and in a body, had already performed; but it became impossible for them longer to resist the impetuosity and weight of the darts, and arrows, and other missile weapons, which were continually poured upon them; and they were finally not destroyed or conquered, but buried under a trophy of Persian arms. Two monuments were afterwards erected near the spot where they fell; the inscription of the first announced the valour of a handful of Greeks, who had resisted three millions of barbarians: the second was peculiar to the Spartans, and contained these memorable words: "Go, stranger, and declare to the Lacedæmonians, that we died here in obedience to their divine laws."

THE BATTLE OF MARATHON, AND DEFEAT OF THE PERSIANS.

The continual dread of tyrants had taught the jealous republican of Greece to blend, on every occasion, their civil with their military institutions. Governed by this principle, the Athenians, elected ten generals, who were invested, each in his turn, with the supreme command. This regulation was extremely unfavourable to that unity of design which ought to pervade all the successive operations of an army; an inconvenience which struck the discerning mind of Aristides, who on this occasion displayed the first openings of his illustrious character. The day approaching when it belonged to him to assume the successive command, he generously yielded his authority to the approved valour and experience of Miltiades. The other generals followed this magnanimous example, sacrificing the dictates of private ambition to the interest and glory of their country; and the commander-in-chief thus enjoyed an opportunity of exerting, uncontrolled, the utmost vigour of his genius.

Lest he should be surrounded by a superior force, he chose for his camp the declivity of a hill, distant about a mile from the encampment of the enemy. The intermediate space he caused to be strewed in the night with the branches and trunks of trees, in order to interrupt the motion, and break the order of the Persian cavalry, which, in consequence of this precaution, seemed to have been rendered incapable of acting in the engagement. In the morning his troops were drawn up in battle array, in a long and full line; the bravest of the Athenians on the right, on the left the warriors of Platæa, and in the middle the slaves, who had been admitted on this occasion to the honour of bearing arms. By weakening his centre, the least valuable part, he extended his front equal to that of the enemy; his rear was defended by the hill above mentioned, which, verging round to meet the sea, likewise covered his right; his left was flanked by a lake or marsh. Datis, although he perceived the skilful disposition of the Greeks, was yet too confident in the vast superiority of his numbers to decline the engagement, especially as he now enjoyed an opportunity of deciding the contest before the expected auxiliaries could arrive from Peloponnesus. When the Athenians saw the enemy in motion, they ran down the hill with unusual ardour, to encounter them; a circumstance which proceeded perhaps from their eagerness to engage, but which must have been attended with the good consequence of shortening the time of their exposure to the slings and darts of the barbarians.

The two armies closed; the battle was rather fierce than long. The Persian sword and Scythian hatchet penetrated, or cut down, the centre of the Athenians; but the two wings, which composed the main strength of the Grecian army, broke, routed, and put to flight the corresponding divisions of the enemy. Instead of pursuing the vanquished, they closed the extremities, and attacked the barbarians who had penetrated their centre. The Grecian spear overcame all opposition; the bravest of the Persians perished in the field; the remainder were pursued with great slaughter; and such was their terror and surprise, that they sought for refuge, not in their camp, but in their ships. The banished tyrant of Athens fell in the engagement; two Athenian generals, and about two hundred citizens, were found among the slain; the Persians left six thousand of their best troops in the scene of action. Probably a still greater number were killed in the pursuit. The Greeks followed them to the shore; but the lightness of the barbarian armour favoured their escape. Seven ships were taken; the rest sailed with a favourable gale, doubled the cape of Sunium; and, after a fruitless attempt to surprise the harbour of Athens, returned to the coast of Asia.

THE BATTLE OF BLENHEIM.

It was a summer evening,
　Old Kaspar's work was done!
And he before his cottage door
　Was sitting in the sun.
And by him sported on the green
　His little grand-child Wilhelmine.

She saw her brother Peterkin
　Roll something large and round,
Which he beside the rivulet,
　In playing there, had found;
He came to ask what he had found,
　That was so large, and smooth, and round.

Old Kaspar took it from the boy,
　Who stood expectant by;
And then the old man shook his head,
　And with a natural sigh,
"'Tis some poor fellow's skull," said he,
"Who fell in the great victory.

"I find them in the garden, for
　There's many here about;
And often when I go to plough,
　The ploughshare turns them out;
For many thousand men," said he,
"Were slain in the great victory."

"Now tell us what 'twas all about,"
　Young Peterkin he cries,
And little Wilhelmine looks up
　With wonder-waiting eyes;
"Now tell us all about the war,
And what they killed each other for."

"It was the English," Kaspar cried,
"Who put the French to rout;
But what they killed each other for,
　I could not well make out.
But every body said," quoth he,
"That 'twas a famous victory.

"My father lived at Blenheim then,
　Yon little stream hard by;
They burnt his dwelling to the ground,
　And he was forced to fly;
So with his wife and child he fled,
Nor had he where to rest his head.

"With fire and sword the country round
　Was wasted far and wide,
And many a childing mother then
　And new-born infant died.
But things like that, you know, must be
At every famous victory.

"They say it was a shocking sight
　After the field was won,
For many thousand bodies here
　Lay rotting in the sun;
But things like that, you know, must be
After a famous victory.

"Great praise the Duke of Marlbro' won,
　And our good Prince Eugene."
"Why, 'twas a very wicked thing!"
　Said little Wilhelmine.
"Nay—nay—my little girl," quoth he,
It was a famous victory.

"And every body praised the duke
　Who such a fight did win."
"But what good came of it at last?"
　Quoth little Peterkin.
"Why that I cannot tell," said he,
"But 'twas a famous victory."　　SOUTHEY.

USEFUL AND SCIENTIFIC NOTICES.

EFFECTS OF COMETS.—Between Mars and Jupiter four very small planets have lately been discovered to run their courses. Now, there are several reasons which induce one to admit that these four stars, or three of them at least, at one time formed a single planet, which was split asunder by the shock of a comet; first, their disproportioned smallness in regard to the other bodies of the system; secondly, their moving so closely together; thirdly, their filling up, consistently with a simple proportion, which holds good with all the other planets, a large hiatus; fourthly, the unusually great eccentricity and inclination of their orbits, and particularly of two, Vesta and Pallas, which strongly indicate a violent disturbance; fifthly, their having at one time had a point in space, from which they might all depart as from a common origin; and, lastly, some of them being surrounded with singularly large atmospheres, as if monopolized from the rest, or borrowed from the comet which struck them.—*Standard.*—[Very alarming all this; and undeniably the consequence of the Reform Bill.]

THE COMET.—This anxiously expected visitor was seen by Sir John Herschell early on Monday morning, the 15th; but it is at present too distant and faint to be visible, excepting with very superior instruments. The comet will be nearest the earth about the 22d day, and pass its perihelium on the 27th November.

WOOL.—The wool-growers of Podolia, and the Ukraine, and particularly in the Asiatic province of Astrachan, have a peculiar method of turning wool into fur. The lamb, after a fortnight's growth, is taken from the ewe, nourished with milk and the best herbage, and wrapped up as tight as possible in a linen covering, which is daily moistened with warm water, and is occasionally enlarged as the animal increases in size. In this manner the wool becomes soft and curly, and is by degrees changed into shining and beautiful locks. This is the kind of fur which passes under the name of Astrachan, and is considered on the Continent as the most genteel lining for winter cloaks. Similar trials with German sheep have been attended with the same success. The Saxon breed of sheep have, within the last ten years, superseded the merinos, and their wool is of superior quality.

DISCOVERY SHIPS.—The house of William Brant and Sons, of Archangel, has equipped two ships at its own expense—commanded by officers of the Imperial Navy—to sail on a voyage of discovery to the great gulf of the Icy Sea, between the Government of Archangel and Tobolsk, to explore the entrance of the river Jenisky.

THE ORIGINAL STORY OF BILL JONES.
AS RELATED BY SIR WALTER SCOTT.

THE following story was narrated to me by my friend, Mr. William Clerk, chief clerk to the Jury Court, Edinburgh, when he first learned it, now nearly thirty years ago, from a passenger in the mail coach. With Mr. Clerk's consent, I gave the story at that time to poor Mat Lewis, who published it with a ghost-ballad which he adjusted on the same theme. From the minuteness of the original detail, however, the narrative is better calculated for prose than verse; and more especially, as the friend to whom it was originally communicated, is one of the most accurate, intelligent, and acute persons whom I have known in the course of my life, I am willing to preserve the precise story in this place.

It was about the eventful year 1800, when the Emperor Paul laid his ill-judged embargo on British trade, that my friend Mr. William Clerk, on a journey to London, found himself in company, in the mail coach, with a seafaring man of middle age and respectable appearance, who announced himself as master of a vessel in the Baltic trade, and a sufferer by the embargo. In the course of the desultory conversation which takes place on such occasions, the seaman observed, in compliance with a common superstition, " I wish we may have good luck on our journey—there is a magpie."—" And why should that be unlucky?" said my friend.—" I cannot tell you that," replied the sailor; " but all the world agrees that one magpie bodes bad luck—two are not so bad, but three are the devil. I never saw three magpies but twice, and once I had near lost my vessel, and the second I fell from a horse, and was hurt." This conversation led Mr. Clerk to observe, that he supposed he believed also in ghosts, since he credited such auguries. " And if I do," said the sailor, " I may have my reasons for doing so;" and he spoke this in a deep and serious manner, implying that he felt deeply what he was saying. On being further urged, he confessed that, if he could believe his own eyes, there was one ghost at least which he had seen repeatedly. He then told his story as I now relate it.

Our mariner had, in his youth, gone mate of a slave vessel from Liverpool, of which town he seemed to be a native. The captain of the vessel was a man of a variable temper, sometimes kind and courteous to his men, but subject to fits of humour, dislike, and passion, during which he was very violent, tyrannical, and cruel. He took a particular dislike at one sailor aboard, an elderly man, called Bill Jones, or some other such name. He seldom spoke to this person without threats and abuse, which the old man, with the license which sailors take in merchant vessels, was very apt to return. On one occasion, Bill Jones appeared slow in getting out on the yard to hand a sail. The captain, according to custom, abused the seaman as a lubberly rascal, who got fat by leaving his duty to other people. The man made a saucy answer, almost amounting to mutiny, on which, in a towering passion, the captain ran down to his cabin, and returned with a blunderbuss loaded with slugs, with which he took deliberate aim at the supposed mutineer, fired, and mortally wounded him. The man was handed down from the yard, and stretched on the deck, evidently dying. He fixed his eyes on the captain, and said, " Sir, you have done for me, but *I will never leave you.*" The captain, in return, swore at him for a fat lubber, and said he would have him thrown into the slave-kettle, where they made food for the negroes, and see how much fat he had got. The man died; his body was actually thrown into the slave-kettle, and the narrator observed, with a *naïveté* which confirmed the extent of his own belief in the truth of what he told, " There was not much fat about him after all."

The captain told the crew they must keep absolute silence on the subject of what had passed; and as the mate was not willing to give an explicit and absolute promise, he ordered him to be confined below. After a day or two, he came to the mate, and demanded if he had an intention to deliver him up for trial when the vessel got home. The mate, who was tired of close confinement in that sultry climate, spoke his commander fair, and obtained his liberty. When he mingled among the crew once more, he found them impressed with the idea, not unnatural in their situation, that the ghost of the dead man appeared among them when they had a spell of duty, especially if a sail was to be handed, on which occasion the spectre was sure to be out upon the yard before any of the crew. The narrator had seen this apparition himself repeatedly—he believed the captain saw it also, but he took no notice of it for some time, and the crew, terrified at the violent temper of the man, dared not call his attention to it. Thus, they held on their course homeward, with great fear and anxiety.

At length the captain invited the mate, who was now in a sort of favour, to go down to the cabin and take a glass of grog with him. In this interview, he assumed a very grave and anxious aspect. " I need not tell you, Jack," he said, " what sort of hand we have got on board with us —He told me he would never leave me, and he has kept his word—You only see him now and then, but he is always by my side, and never out of my sight. At this very moment I see him—I am determined to bear it no longer, and I have resolved to leave you."

The mate replied, that his leaving the vessel while out of the sight of any land was impossible. He advised, that if the captain apprehended any bad consequences from what had happened, he should run for the west of France or Ireland, and there go ashore, and leave him, the mate, to carry the vessel into Liverpool. The captain only shook his head gloomily, and reiterated his determination to leave the ship. At this moment, the mate was called to the deck for some purpose or other, and the instant he got up the companion-ladder, he heard a splash in the water, and looking over the ship's side, saw that the captain had thrown himself into the sea from the quarter-galley, and was running astern at the rate of six knots an hour. When just about to sink, he seemed to make a last exertion, sprung half out of the water, and clasped his hands towards the mate, calling, " By ———, Bill is with me now !" and then sunk, to be seen no more.

After hearing this singular story, Mr. Clerk asked some questions about the captain, and whether his companion considered him as at all times rational. The sailor seemed struck with the question, and answered, after a moment's delay, that in general *he conversationed well enough.*

It would have been desirable to have been able to ascertain how far this extraordinary tale was founded on fact; but want of time, and other circumstances, prevented Mr. Clerk from learning the names and dates, that might, to a certain degree, have verified the events. Granting the murder to have taken place, and the tale to have been truly told, there was nothing more likely to arise among the ship's company than the belief in the apparition; as the captain was a man of a passionate and irritable disposition, it was nowise improbable that he, the victim of remorse, should participate in the horrible visions of those less concerned, especially as he was compelled to avoid communicating his sentiments with any one else; and the catastrophe would, in such a case, be but the natural consequence of that superstitious remorse, which has conducted so many criminals to suicide or the gallows. If the fellow-traveller of Mr. Clerk be not allowed this degree of credit, he must at least be admitted to have displayed a singular talent for the composition of the horrible in fiction. The tale, properly detailed, might have made the fortune of a romancer.

ANECDOTE OF SIR WALTER SCOTT.—As Sir Walter was one day returning from Selkirk to Abbotsford, he passed two masons on the road-side, who had been employed in carrying water in a tub, for the purpose of making up lime; the one called out to the other to *whomel* the tub. " Here is half-a-crown for you, my good fellow," said Sir Walter; " *whomel* is the very word I have been in search of for many a long day past."—*Weekly Chronicle.*—[Well did Sir Walter remember the word *whomel*—no man better; but he liked an excuse for offering a poor man a half-crown without hurting his feelings.]

ELEMENTS OF THOUGHT.

HAPPINESS—WELL-BEING.

THE tendency of the present time is strongly set to over-rate the benefits of what is termed civilization. The end is forgotten in the means. There is an everlasting strife and exertion to obtain the means. The days of our youth and our manhood are wasted; and we, in old age, are left to lament that we have lost the time when we might have tasted the pleasures of our life. There is now no repose, no healthy confidence in one's self; our pleasures are the pleasures to be derived from the admiration of others. Unless we can surprise and excite envy in the bosom of our neighbours, we are unhappy. To this end we sacrifice youth, and health, and ease; and when we have attained the object of all our wishes,—when become the admiration and envy of those less successful than ourselves, we sicken at the emptiness of the joy we sought, and die, having discovered that our life has been one long folly. This may be called trite. It is true, however, and at the present time, apposite. If we could be persuaded to seek enjoyment for itself, and not in order to shew relative superiority; if we could be content to be happy, the simple pleasures within the reach of almost every one; pleasures requiring not wealth, and joined with no splendour, pleasures continuous and uncloying, would make our youth, our manhood, and our age alike happy and undisturbed. Philosophy can have no higher object than to create this happy frame of mind.—*Tait's Magazine—Art. Rousseau.*

Our next *quotation* goes deeper into this all-important subject. We must entreat the patience of a few of our readers—though, we trust, of very few of them—for it is the frivolous or thoughtless alone that will not find this a discussion of absorbing interest. It is nothing less than "*Why are we here? What to do? To what destined?*" It is extracted from Mr COMBE'S work on MAN.

If Wisdom and Benevolence have been employed in *constituting* Man, we may expect the arrangements of creation, in regard to him, to be calculated *as a leading object to excite* his various powers, corporeal and mental, *to activity.* This, accordingly, appears to me to be the case; and the fact may be illustrated by a few examples. A certain portion of nervous and muscular energy is infused by nature into the human body every twenty-four hours, and it is delightful to expend this vigour. To provide for its expenditure, the stomach has been constituted so as to require regularly returning supplies of food, which can be obtained only by nervous and muscular exertion; the body has been created destitute of covering, yet standing in need of protection from the elements of heaven; but this can be easily provided by moderate expenditure of corporeal strength. It is delightful to repair exhausted nervous and muscular energy by wholesome aliment; and the digestive organs have been so constituted, as to perform their functions by successive stages, and to afford us frequent opportunities of enjoying the pleasures of eating. In these arrangements, the design of supporting the various systems of the body in activity, for the enjoyment of the individual, is abundantly obvious. A late writer justly remarks, that "a person of feeble texture and indolent habits has the bone smooth, thin, and light; but nature, solicitous for our safety, in a manner which we could not anticipate, combines with the powerful muscular frame a dense and perfect texture of bone, where every spine and tubercle is completely developed." "As the structure of the parts is originally perfected by the action of the vessels, the function or operation of the part is made the stimulus to those vessels. The cuticle on the hand wears away like a glove; but the pressure stimulates the living surface to force successive layers of skin under that which is wearing, or, as anatomists call it, desquamating; by which they mean, that the cuticle does not change at once, but comes off in squamæ or scales."

Directing our attention to the Mind, we discover that Individuality, and the other Perceptive Faculties, desire, as *their* means of enjoyment, to know existence, and to become acquainted with the qualities of external objects; while the Reflecting Faculties desire to know their dependence and relations. "There is something," says an eloquent writer, "positively agreeable to all men, to all, at least, whose nature is not most grovelling and base, in gaining knowledge for its own sake. When you see any thing for the first time, you at once derive some gratification from the sight being new; your attention is awakened, and you desire to know more about it. If it is a piece of workmanship, as an instrument, a machine of any kind, you wish to know how it is made; how it works; and what use it is of. If it is an animal, you desire to know where it comes from; how it lives; what are its dispositions, and, generally, its nature and habits. This desire is felt, too, without at all considering that the machine or the animal may ever be of the least use to yourself practically; for, in all probability, you may never see them again. But you feel a curiosity to learn all about them, *because they are new and unknown to you.* You, accordingly, make inquiries; you *feel a gratification* in getting answers to your questions, that is, *in receiving information,* and in knowing more,—in being better informed than you were before. If you ever happen again to see the same instrument or animal, you find it agreeable to recollect having seen it before, and to think that you know something about it. If you see another instrument or animal, in some respects like, but differing in other particulars, you find it pleasing to *compare them together,* and to note in what they agree, and in what they differ. Now, all this kind of gratification is of a pure and disinterested nature, and has no reference to any of the common purposes of life; yet it is a pleasure—an enjoyment. You are nothing the richer for it; you do not gratify your palate, or any other bodily appetite; and yet it is so pleasing that you would give something out of your pocket to obtain it, and would forego some bodily enjoyment for its sake. The pleasure derived from science is exactly of the like nature, or rather it is the very same."* This is a correct and forcible exposition of the pleasures attending the active exercise of our intellectual faculties.

Supposing the human faculties to have received their present constitution, two arrangements may be fancied as instituted for the gratification of these powers: 1*st,* Infusing into them at birth *intuitive knowledge* of every object which they are fitted ever to comprehend; or, 2*dly,* Constituting them only as *capacities* for gaining knowledge by exercise and application, and surrounding them with objects bearing such relations towards them, that, when observed and attended to, they shall afford them high gratification; and when unobserved and neglected, they shall occasion them uneasiness and pain; and the question occurs, Which mode would be most conducive to enjoyment? The general opinion will be in favour of the first; but the second appears to me to be preferable. If the first meal we had eaten had for ever prevented the recurrence of hunger, it is obvious that all the pleasures of satisfying a healthy appetite would have been then at an end; so that this apparent bounty would have greatly abridged our enjoyment. In like manner, if, our faculties being constituted as at present, intuitive knowledge had been communicated to us, so that, when an hour old, we should have been thoroughly acquainted with every object, quality, and relation that we could ever comprehend, all provision for the sustained activity of many of our faculties would have been done away with. When wealth is acquired, the miser's pleasure in it is diminished. He grasps after *more* with increasing avidity. He is supposed irrational in doing so; but he obeys the instinct of his nature. What he possesses, no longer satisfies Acquisitiveness; it is like food in the stomach, which gave pleasure in eating, and would give pain were it

* Objects, Advantages, and Pleasures of Science, page 1.

withdrawn, but which, when there, is attended with little positive sensation. The miser's pleasure arises from the active state of Acquisitiveness, and only the pursuit and obtaining of *new treasures* can *maintain this state*. The same law is exemplified in the case of Love of Approbation. The gratification which it affords depends on its *active state*, and hence the necessity for *new incense*, and *higher mountings* in the scale of ambition, is constantly experienced by its victims. NAPOLEON, in exile, said, " Let us live upon the past :" but he found this impossible; his predominating desires originated in Ambition and Self-Esteem; and the past did not stimulate these powers, or maintain them in constant activity. In like manner, no musician, artist, poet, or philosopher, would reckon himself happy, however extensive his attainments, if informed, Now you must stop, and live upon the past ; and the reason is still the same. New ideas, and new emotions, best excite and maintain in activity the faculties of the mind, and activity is essential to enjoyment. If these views be correct, the consequences of imbuing the mind with intuitive knowledge, would not have been unquestionably beneficial. The limits of our acquirements would have been reached ; our first step would have been our last; every object would have become old and familiar ; Hope would have had no object of expectation ; Cautiousness no object of fear; Wonder no gratification in novelty; monotony, insipidity, and mental satiety, would apparently have been the lot of Man.

According to the view now advanced, creation in its present form, is more wisely and benevolently adapted to our constitution than if intuitive instruction had been showered on the mind at birth.

THE STORY-TELLER.

GRISELL BAILLIE—A TALE FOR THE YOUNG.
BY MRS. JOHNSTONE.

THE tea-table was cleared. " What diversions of Hollycot to-night ?" said Mrs. Herbert.

" Forest trees, mother, and all about them," cried Sophia.

" About the gipsies if you please, mother," cried Charles. —" where may we read about the gipsies."

" Or about mushrooms. I have not forgot those good little girls we saw this morning, who have the power of doing so much good to their poor mother. When shall I be able to do any thing for you, mamma ?—you who do all for us. Think of that ' respectable child ;'—you called her so, mother, and I never heard you call a little girl so before—earning a whole three shillings in one week !"

" I named her as I thought her, Sophia. She is a respectable child—the *kind*, the *useful* must always be *respectable*, at whatever age, and in whatever rank. But it is not poor children alone—nor is it by money only, that children may be *useful* to their parents and friends. As you have not fixed on the amusement of the evening, I will tell you of Grisell Baillie."

" A real person's story, mother ?"

" Real and true, Sophia."

MEMOIR OF GRISELL BAILLIE.

" Lady Grisell Baillie was the eldest of a very large family. In large families the eldest daughter has often numerous duties: Grisell had her full share of the hardships of seniority, but she gained, as she well deserved, all its honours and privileges. She was born in the reign of Charles II. Her father was Sir Patrick Home, afterwards Earl of Marchmont. His friends, who were virtuous, patriotic men, champions and defenders of liberty and religion, were, about this time, brought into great trouble by their honest principles. When only twelve years of age, Lady Grisell was sent by her father from his country-house to Edinburgh, where his particular friend, Mr. Baillie of Jerviswood, then lay in prison, to try to convey a letter to him containing advice and intelligence, and to bring back news of him to her father. So well did she conduct herself on this mission, that in all the subsequent difficulties and perils of her father, she was trusted with the utmost confidence. Though in years she was still a child, her honourable secrecy, her prudence, her courage, her firmness, and her presence of mind, were worthy of any age. When her father was confined in Dumbarton Castle for his honesty and patriotism, she visited and cheered him with news of his family; and she took many journeys on his account, under the direction of her mother, of which, from her tender years, no one suspected the object. Shortly afterwards, when Sir Patrick, after being released, found it necessary to keep concealed to avoid a fresh imprisonment, and almost certain death, young Grisell was his preserver;—she only, her mother, and a poor village carpenter, in whom they were forced to confide, knew of his place of concealment. The servants were often examined on oath about their master, so that it was impossible to trust any of them ; and very frequent search was made in the house for Sir Patrick, whom the servants believed far distant.

" His real place of concealment was a burial vault under the church of Polwarth,—damp, comfortless, and utterly dark. To this place Jamie Winter, the carpenter—I love to repeat his name, for he was a faithful, friendly man—and Lady Grisell, conveyed a bed and bedding. This vault was a mile distant from Sir Patrick's mansion: but thither his heroic young daughter went every night at midnight to convey him food and drink, and to make his bed ; and by her news of his family, and cheerful and affectionate talk, to beguile his solitude."

Sophia Herbert gazed on her mother, her large brown eyes dilating with affectionate admiration and wonder.

" Lady Grisell was not a coward," mother, said Charles, equally interested.

" Her affection conquered her fears, Charles. Like all young persons reared in Scotland at that time, she had had till then a strong terror of ghosts and churchyards ; but now love for her father made her stumble over the graves every night alone, without fearing any thing, save parties of soldiers in search of him. The minister's dog barked all night long : she was not afraid of the dog, but of discovery. It was necessary that neither the younger children nor the servants should suspect that there was an unseen mouth to be fed, and Grisell was obliged to steal the victuals off her own plate, into her lap, at dinner, to supply her father. Her voracity at table astonished the younger children, who did not perceive how the missing victuals went; and her stratagems to abstract food often occasioned much merriment to her father, in his dark and doleful prison.

" It was at last resolved that a more comfortable place of concealment should, if possible, be procured for Sir Patrick. Grisell kept the key of a low room, in which there was a bed that drew out. She and her condjutor, Jamie Winter, contrived to dig a hole under this bed. They were obliged to work in the night time only, and to carry out the earth between them in a sheet, by a window, into the garden. Lady Grisell scratched at this hole till not a nail was left on her fingers. At his own house the carpenter made a box, which was to fit this hole, and contain bedding, so that Sir Patrick might be concealed here in case of a strict search. It was covered with boards, in which air-holes were bored. But, alas! all poor Grisell's hopes and labours were vain. The ground was so low here, that the hole, so painfully excavated, filled with water; and, to her horror, one day when the upper boards were removed, the box bounded up and floated.

"Her father now resolved to attempt to get abroad, as the alarm of the family was much increased, by hearing from the carrier, that Baillie of Jerviswood, the friend to whom Grisell had conveyed the letter in prison, was, by a most unjust sentence, executed at Edinburgh.

"Ever alert, active, and *useful*, Grisell now worked night and day in altering her father's clothes, so as to disguise his person. He escaped as if by a miracle; and, after many hardships, got to Holland, where he assumed the name of Dr. Wallace, and sent to Scotland for his wife and ten children. Sir Patrick's estates had been forfeited; but his wife, by entreaty, obtained a small pittance to maintain her children; and this was all they had to live upon abroad. Again, the virtues and activity of young Grisell became the support and comfort of her family. She first helped her mother to take the younger children abroad, and then returned alone from Holland to Scotland to conduct over a sick sister, at an age when other girls are scarce permitted to travel alone for thirty miles in a stage-coach. She nursed her sister during a tedious and very bad passage, in which the hardships of these young girls were greatly aggravated by the brutality of the Dutch captain, who eat up their little sea-stores, and suffered them to lie on the bare floor, with a pillow of the books Grisell was carrying over to her father."

The indignation of Charles was excessive at this part of his mother's narrative. His eyes sparkled, and he involuntarily clenched his little fists. "Brute of a Dutch captain!" he cried. "No English sailor, mother, could"——

"And few Dutch, I hope, Charles; but, as you cannot have the pleasure of boxing the Dutch captain, I may go on with my story. It was a dark, wet, stormy night when my heroine and her sister, Julian, landed at Brill. They had to walk to Rotterdam, where Sir Patrick's eldest son, their brother, met them. Poor sickly Julian soon lost her shoes in the mud—as my poor Fanny lost hers to-day—and the heroic Grisell took her sister on her back, and carried her to Rotterdam."

"If I had thought, I am sure I could have carried Fanny a good way to-day on my back," said Sophia.

"And so have been like Lady Grisell Home," said her mother, smiling. "But you had poor Dapple, and old James, and George, all more able, and as willing to carry Fanny. It would not have been like sensible, considerate Lady Grisell, to do a *useless* thing, however kind. Her services were ever as *useful* as they were cheerfully and affectionately bestowed. During the years that the family remained in exile and comparative poverty, she proved the greatest blessing to her parents, and to her brothers and sisters."

"Mother, I fear I shall never be like her," sighed Sophia. "But I may try—you always tell me, mamma, that I may try."

"Certainly, Sophia; and that you may have the clearer an idea of the model you have chosen, I will relate this part of the story of Lady Grisell Baillie, in nearly the very words of her own affectionate daughter.

"Sir Patrick, Lady Grisell's father, I told you, went by the name of Dr. Wallace, for fear of being discovered, though his real rank was well known at the Court of the Prince of Orange. There were at that time many English and Scottish gentlemen, who suffered for their principles, living in exile at the same place, Utrecht. Sir Patrick's family liked to have a good house, and their dwelling was the resort of all adherents of the cause of liberty then in exile. They paid nearly a fourth of their whole income for their house, and so could not afford keeping any servant but a little girl to wash the dishes. 'All the time they were there,' says Lady Grisell's daughter, 'there was not a week my mother did not sit up two nights to do the business that was necessary. She went to the market—went to the mill to have their corn ground, which is the custom with good managers in Holland—dressed the linen—cleaned the house—made ready the dinner—mended the children's stockings and other clothes—made what she could for them, and, in short, did every thing. Her sister, Christian, diverted her father and mother, and the rest who were fond of music—for, out of their small income, they bought a harpsichord for little money. Christian played and sung, and had a great deal of life and humour, but no turn to business; though Lady Grisell had the same qualifications, and liked music as well as her sister, she was content to drudge; and many jokes passed between the sisters about their different occupations. Every morning before six, Grisell lighted the fire in her father's study, then waked him, and got him a warm draught of beer and bitters, which he usually took. Then she dressed the younger children, and brought them to her father, who taught them every thing that was fit for their age. Grisell, when she had a moment's leisure, took a lesson with the rest in French or Dutch, and sometimes found a few minutes for music.

"'I have,' says her daughter Lady Murray, 'now a book of songs of her writing when in Holland. Many of them interrupted, half-writ, and some broke off in the middle of a sentence. She had no less a turn for mirth and society than any of the family when,—mark, Sophia —'*she could come at it without neglecting what she thought more necessary.*'

"Her eldest brother Patrick was about her own age. They had been bred up together; and he was 'her most dearly beloved.' He was admitted a private volunteer in the Prince of Orange's horse-guards, till better fortune came, and it was her pride to have him appear like a gentleman in his dress and linen. The Guards wore point cravats and cuffs, and many a night Grisell sat up to have these in as good order for her brother as those of any richer youth in the place.

"'As,' says her daughter, 'their house was always full of unfortunate banished people, they seldom went to dinner without three, or four, or five of them to share with them. Many a hundred times I have heard her say she could never look back upon their manner of living there without thinking it a miracle. They had no want, but plenty of every thing they desired, and much contentment. She always declared this the most pleasing part of her life, though they were not without their little distresses;

to them they were rather jokes than grievances.'—I am going to tell *you* an anecdote now, Charles," said Mrs. Herbert. "The professors and learned men of the place often came to see Grisell's father. The best entertainment he could give them was a glass of *alabast* beer, which was a better kind of ale than common. One day Sir Patrick sent his little son Andrew, afterwards Lord Kimmerghame, to draw some for them in the cellar. He brought it up with all expedition; but in the other hand the spigot of the barrel. 'Andrew, what is that in your hand?' said his father. When Andrew saw it he ran back with all speed; but, alas! the beer was all run out before he got down. This occasioned much mirth, though perhaps they did not well know where to get more."

"What a good affectionate family," said George Herbert to his mother. "This is the true philosophy of daily life, mother."

"Yes, my dear George; and their *goodness*, their *affectionateness*, their *union* was their dearest happiness—for their prospects at this time were dark enough. They were often reduced to great hardships, by the failure of even the scanty remittances they expected from home. It was the custom in Holland to solicit alms for the poor, by going from house to house with a bell. One evening the bell came to Sir Patrick's door, and there was no money in the house, but a very small coin called an *orkey*, which is about the third of a penny. Every one was so ashamed of the trifle that no one would offer it, till Sir Patrick himself, set them the example of pure and humble charity. —'Well, then, I will go with it,' he said. 'We can do no more than give all we have.'"

"This was like the widow's mite in the gospel, mother," said Sophia.

"It was, my dear, an action done in the same true unaffected spirit of charity. Of Lady Grisell, as of most other ladies, Sophia, the latter end was like the beginning:—she lived to a great age, virtuous and honoured, happy and universally beloved. Some other time I may tell you the rest of her story. She returned to England with her mother and the Princess of Orange, after the Revolution in 1688. Her father was now high in power at Court; and she was offered the place of maid of honour; but she rather chose to go to Scotland with her family. This now, Sophia, was a very young girl whose services were of a higher kind to her family than those that could be paid by the little mushroom-gatherer: for, with equal affection for her parents, she possessed a better education, and far greater power of mind.—A child in years, she almost preserved her father's life, and in so doing re-established the fortunes of her family. She was even instrumental in obtaining the blessings of civil and religious freedom to her country."

"I know one of her songs, mother, made in Holland, I daresay, while she cleaned the house, and dressed the dinner, and did so much," said Sophia.

"Sing it for me,—pray do, Sophia," said Charles.

"I will, Charles,—It says,

'Were na my heart licht I wad dee.'"

"Lightness of heart was, indeed, one of her many admirable qualities. Let me now engrave on your memory some more of her excellencies. Receive some of them as maxims, Sophia. I give them in her daughter's language:—

'Though she had the greatest reason, from the deference always paid to her judgment, to be conceited, she was void of the least self-conceit, and often gave up her own opinion to that of others. If it was to those she loved, she did it from a desire of preferring their pleasure to her own. Of any one I ever knew she was the most entirely void of the least ingredient of selfishness—at all times ever considered herself in the last place, or rather never thought of herself at all. In nothing did the capacity of her mind appear more than in this,—that whatever she did she could apply herself so strongly and thoroughly to it, that a by-stander might imagine that to be her particular attachment. Things of the greatest moment did not make her forget trifles that were fit to be thought of, which she often warned her daughters of,—saying, if neglected, they would become things of moment. She had a power of passing from great things to small ones with a readiness that was surprising; and whatever she did the same character appeared in it,—sprightliness, attention, and good humour. She possessed herself so thoroughly, that I have often heard her say, *she never knew what it was to find herself indisposed to do any thing that she thought was proper to be done*. She was much devoted to piety and the service of God. People who exercise themselves much in this way,' says Lady Murray, 'are often observed to contract a morose way of thinking concerning others, of which my mother had no tincture. Her religion improved her in charity, and patience for other people's failings, and forgiveness of injuries; and no doubt was one great source of that constant cheerfulness for which she was so remarkable. She was always an early riser, and often recommended it to us as the best time to perform our duty either to God or man.'"

"Such a beautiful model, mother—and all *true*," said Sophia.

"That, indeed, gives double value to the lesson—all *true*, Sophia. And what one girl *has been* another *may be*. Lady Grisell Baillie is no specimen of an imaginary perfection. Now you may sing Charles his song, if you please, and then, if we have still leisure, George can, I am sure, treat us with what will delight you, some lines from Mrs. Joanna Baillie's Legend of Lady Grisell Baillie."

"That *will* be delightful," cried Sophia. "I was afraid there was no poetry about her."

"And thought of trying a verse or two yourself, I presume," said George.

"Don't laugh at me, brother; I may try to be a little like her, though, in some small things—May I not, mother?"

"That will be better, Sophia, than trying the verse,—so give us your song."

Sophia's song was not very well sung. It was new to her; but her audience were pleased with the poet, the subject, and the singer; and it was new to them also. She resolved to practice it in the following week. George's reading was much finer. Mrs. Herbert smiled gently as she saw tears rush into the eyes of the young auditors.

"O charming Lady Grisell," cried Sophia—"I hope I shall dream of her all night."

"It will be better to imitate her all day, my dear," said Mrs. Herbert, smiling—"but I don't grudge you a little dream too."—*The Mother's Art of Thinking.* Oliver and Boyd.

SCOTCH VOTERS.
A SKETCH FROM REAL LIFE.

The following sketch, which has just appeared in *Tait's Magazine* for November, is, we fear, "ower true a tale." Any way, it is graphic, and highly amusing; and, as such, we present an abridged edition to our readers.

A sporting gentleman, a good shot, and a good patriot, was lately returning from his hunting lodge among the Grampians, when his vehicle was upset, somewhere, we should imagine, near the place where the hostell of Mr. Ebenezer Cruickshanks flourished under the guardianship of the seven golden candlesticks, and where the march of improvement has now created a thriving market town. While Mr. Strongitharm, the blacksmith, was reducing the compound fractures of the dog-cart, we, says his customer, stood silently watching the labours of him and his attendant Cyclops. The broad and good-natured visage of the smith, that looked as if it had been modelled in black diamond, first began to shine over the anvil, and then, by degrees, it even appeared to ignite by the glow of the fire it was exposed to, until at last it absolutely glowed like a piece of burning charcoal, while he eagerly toiled to accomplish our wishes. As we lounged about the place, yawning, and execrating our ill-luck, our attention was attracted by the appearance of a fat, little, round visaged man, in an apron and sleeves, who entered the smithy, having been driven into it by a sudden and heavy shower of rain; and, after a few of those preliminary nothings which usually serve as preface to a Scotch dialogue between strangers,

"I see you are reformers here, sir," said one of us, pointing to an old Reform Jubilee placard, fragments of which still adhered to the smithy door.

"Ou ay, sir," replied our man; "we're a' stench reformers here. Bless your heart, sir! we had mony a petition here for Reform, baith to the Parliament an' the Lords, an' the King an' a'—an' after the bull passed, od we had a percesshin an' a hantel o' flags—an' a denner, an' speeches that wad na' ha'e disgraced Edinbroch itsell. But here's Maister Messer, the haberdashery merchant, can tell ye far better about it than I can. I'm sayin'—ye can tell the gentleman a' aboot our Reform *Jubile*, Maister Messer," continued he, speaking to a thin, spare, and rather well-dressed man who then entered, puffing and blowing from his anxious haste to escape to a shelter.

"The *Juboli*?" said Mr. Mercer, wiping his bran new blue coat, and his velvet neck, and his gilt buttons very carefully, with a scarlet Menteith-dyed cotton pocket-handkerchief. "Oh yes, Mr. Dallas, I can tell the gentlemen all about the *Juboli*, for you know I had the honour of being one of the *Juboli Comytees*. I assure you, gentlemen, it was got up with the greatest good taste—the flags and devices were all admirable—nothing personally offensive to any one; and as I happened to have the good fortune to have been present at the Juboli in Edinburgh, I was not only enabled to supply all and sundry with the proper ribbons and badges, but I also had it in my power to give many useful hints to the *Comytese*; and although I say it who should not say it, the *Juboli* here was thereby rendered not unworthy of the great victory which Freedom has achieved in Scotland."

"I hope you had a good turn-out of reformers?" said one of us.

"Why, sir, the whole town are reformers here," replied Mr. Mercer; "we set down to dinner about two hundred and fifty persons; and the speeches, toasts, and songs were of the very first description."

"Then Mr. A——, the liberal candidate for these burghs, is sure of his election, so far as this town is concerned," said we, "and Mr. B——, the anti-reform candidate, can have no chance?"

"Not the least chance in the world, sir," replied the haberdasher; "for, as I said before, we are all reformers here."

"Ou ay, that we are!" echoed Mr. Dallas, the grocer, "a' stench reformers."

"Then, sir," said one of us to the last speaker, "I need not ask you whether you are to vote for Mr. A—— or Mr. B——?"

"Troth, sir," replied the grocer, "to tell ye the honest truth, I ha'ena' just made up my mind aboot that pairt o' the story. It's a lang time yet or the yellection, an' I'm thinkin' that I'll just tak' a thocht about it."

"A thought about it, sir!" exclaimed one of us in a tone of undisguised astonishment—"a thought about it! How can you possibly require one single thought, or hesitate one moment in a case where the contest lies between Mr. A——, who has so long advocated the rights of the people, and who has sacrificed his time, and given his labour in the most patriotic and indefatigable manner; all to bring about the accomplishment of that grand work of reform, which, to carry home the matter to yourself, has made *you* a voter for the member of Parliament for this burgh. Why, sir, with the political feelings you have declared you possess, I cannot understand how you could hesitate one moment in your choice between two such candidates as Mr. A—— and Mr. B——!"

"Od, sir, I dinna ken," replied the grocer, "there's a great deal, to be sure, in what you say. But I'm thinkin' I maun just tak' a thocht aboot it."

"He! he! he! Laukerdaisy, such a regular dull one you are, my dear Mr. Dallas!" exclaimed the haberdashery man, with the titter of a man-milliner. "What, man! bless my heart, can't you make up your mind to the right thing at once, without more shilly-shally? Surely you can never go for to think for to vote for such an anti as Mr. B——, you who have signed every reform petition that was sent off from this place? Why, what *are* you thinking on?"

"Od, I tell ye, I maun just tak' a thought about it, Mr. Messer," replied the grocer.

"He! he! he! well, deuce take me if you have not been well nicknamed by the club, *Dull Davy Dallas*," cried the haberdasher; "and if I might be permitted to amend your *nong de garr*, I should propose that instead of *Dull Davy Dallas* it should be *Dull Davy Dowlas!* Ha! Mr. White," continued he, addressing a baker who just then entered, "you're a man of more spirit. I'll be bound you'll act after a more bolder fashion, else I mistake you sadly. You'll give your vote for the right one at once. You'll not hesitate long between Mr. A—— and Mr. B——, I'll warrant me."

"Ou, Mr. A——'s the man for the people's rights, that's true," replied the baker; "and as for the tither chap, it maun be admitted that he has done a' thing that he could to keep them frae us; but ye ken they're baith very good gentlemen, and sae a'm just no thinkin' o' votin' at a'."

"Angels and ministers of grace defend us! here is a determination tenfold more extraordinary than the hesitation of the other gentleman," exclaimed one of us. "Why, sir, what in the world can have brought you, a reformer, to so strange a resolution as this."

"A dinna ken," replied the baker, with some little displeasure in his countenance; a divna see that a'm just obliged to answer that question. The vote, a tak' it, is ma nane; an' a'm thinkin' a man may lawfully do wi' his nane what he likes."

"True, sir," replied one of us, "you have the highest authority for holding such doctrine—even that of an august and noble Duke," and the speaker made a long and eloquent expostulation.

"My eye! there's a speech for you, Master White!" exclaimed the haberdasher, slapping the baker's back, till the twelvemonth's dusting of flour, which had gradually accumulated in his jacket, arose and enveloped us like a mist. "There's a speech for ye, my boy! what say ye to that! Why, that would have done for our last dinner. What say ye to that, I say?"

"Troth, sir, a'll just tell ye the truth," replied the baker: "a ha'e not muckle to say, that's certain; am' there's nae doot muckle gude sense in what this gentleman has said. Weel, indeed, might he speak at dinner or at hustin's aither. But *possitesveley* a wunna vote!"

"Why, what a soft un you are, Mr. White!" exclaimed the haberdasher; "you're one hundred per cent a worse article than Dull David Dowlas here. I tell ye, you are as oft as your own dough! But I am up to the cause of your not voting, Master White. You know that Mr. B—— is son-in-law to the Earl of C——; and the Earl of C——, wonderful to behold! after having, all his life, for his own private purposes, pretended to be the man for the people—so far, indeed, as to have been considered somewhat of a republican in the days of the Reign of Terror in France, at the end of the last century—has now most strangely discovered that his own private purposes require that he should fight like a Turkish Jannissary against freedom wherever it appears. He is the maddest of all the mad antis now going. But, Mr. White, hark in your ear, he takes his household bread from you, and you are afraid to lose his custom. But why don't you act boldly and independently, as I mean to do, and defy the old earl, and the old devil, and all his works? Ah! you are as soft as your own dough, Master White!"

"Sir," said the baker, sulkily, "a'd wish ye to keep in mind, that gif a'm dough, an' soft yenoo, a may grow mair crusty than may please your chafts, if a'm but made het aneuch; sae, a'd advise you to keep your jokes mair till yeresell. A say again what a said afore, an' that is, that *possiteeveley* a wunna vote ava;" and with that Mr. White abruptly left the smithy.

"He's a poor spiritless fellow that," said the haberdasher, after eyeing his retreating steps for some time, till he saw he was effectually out of all hearing. "If all reformers were like him, indeed, what would become of the great cause? Aweel, how goes the county, Farmer Black?" continued he, now addressing a stout young country-looking man, who, at this moment, dismounted at the smithy door to have one of his horse's shoes fastened. "How goes the reform cause in the county? Is the reform candidate, Sir D—— E——, sure of his election?"

"A'm thinkin' he's gey an' shure," replied the farmer shortly.

"I'm sure you wish him well at all events?" said the haberdasher.

"A'm no sayin' but a do," briefly replied Farmer Black.

"Ay, ay," said Mercer, "many's the good bumper of punch that you and I drank together to the glorious cause of reform, on that market day, you remember, when you stopped to take a bit chack of dinner with me, after buying so many gowns, and shawls, and ribbons for your mother and sisters—ay, and maybe for some other lass, too, for aught I know to the contrary. You know you sold your nowt well that day; and I'm bold to say I never beheld a finer show of beauty than your large hay-cart exhibited on the glorious day of the Juboli, standing at the corner of the street; when the old lady and the girls, all dressed in my new gowns and finery, were placed bolt upright in it, thick set together, like so many pots of stock gillyflowers and marygolds, as I passed by you bearing the banner, with the painting of a loom upon it, surmounted by a trifling *jew desprits* of my own."

"The banner was a very bonny flag, Maister Messer," replied the farmer; "an' troth, when a saw ye carrying it, ye pat me in mind o' ane o' ma ain stots routing awa' wi' his tail straight up on end, when the puir beasts are fleggit wi' a flight o' clegs in a het simmer day."

"Aweel, aweel," said the haberdasher, rather dashed by this uncouth simile, and anxious to divert the attention of those present from it, "I am sure you wish the worthy baronet, the representative of the cause of reform, every possible success.

"A'm no saying but a do," replied the farmer.

"Well," said the haberdasher, "he's sure of your vote at any rate, at the very first asking."

"We'll stop a wee till we see how the laird gangs," answered the farmer.

"What has the laird to do with the matter?" demanded the haberdasher. "If you pay him his rent you may laugh at the laird."

"Wha says that a dinna pay him his rent?" said the farmer, looking suspiciously over his shoulder, as he inserted his left toe into the stirrup, and threw his right leg over his beast. "That may a' be true enough that ye say, yet, for a' that, ane may like to bide a wee gliff till ane sees hoo the laird gangs."

"Silly aver!" exclaimed Mercer, after Farmer Black had ridden away, "that fellow has as little sense or spirit as the cart *Bassis* that bears him yonder. Surely, Mr Dallas, you'll be ashamed not to shew more resolution than yon turnip-headed gaby? Come, man, take a swatch from me, and make up your mind to vote, as I mean to do, for Mr A—— and the cause of reform, which we have both stuck to so long."

"Na, na, Maister Messer, we'll no' be so rash.—we'll just tak' a thought about it;" and so, with a civil bow to the party, the grocer departed.

"He! he! he! there goes Dull Davie Dowlas!", exclaimed the haberdasher; "depend upon it his *thought* has been taken already, and he is fairly tied by the leg. The Duke's commissioner has been with him, and deuce another raisin, or fig, or Stilton cheese from his shop will now be eaten within the doors of his Grace's mansion, if he does not give his vote to please the anti-reforming peer! But, let that pass: all men are not made of stuff strong enough to resist such friction as he has been exposed to. Gentlemen, you are strangers here; but I am proud to say, you are no strangers to me; for I had the honour of seeing you both on the hustings in Bruntsfield Links, on the grand day of the *Juboli*, at Edinburgh. You were pointed out to me by a friend as great and well-known reformers, and as able supporters of that valuable, and enlightened, and liberal, and rapidly-rising journal, *Tait's Magazine*; and as such, as I reverenced you then, so I reverence you tenfold more now, that my own ears have heard you utter sentiments such as you have uttered. I see that some accident has happened to your carriage, which, though I regret it on your account, has been a great blessing to me, in giving me the honour of so much of your company and converse; and if I can be of any use to you?"——

The polite invitation was accepted; and, after giving the smith and our own man our final directions, we followed Mr. Mercer through his front and back-shop, into his snug little parlour behind both, where we were introduced to his wife, a smiling, well-favoured, black-eyed *bourgeoise*, to whom he appeared to have been recently united. Wine and cakes being produced, Mercer himself was soon called by his business to the front shop, and we were left in comfortable chit-chat with the lady; who speedily showed herself, like most of the sensible women we have met with, to be a keen reformer.

Whilst thus agreeably engaged, we heard a sound in which the well-practised ear never *can* be deceived; we mean the sound of patrician wheels. The coach of a peer, it is true, has no more wheels than a common stage-coach has; nor has it any more horses. But there is a deep, decorous, dignified roll about such a carriage, that, even when it is hid from our eyes, never fails to conjure up on our retina the fat coachman, or the two splash-looking postilions, and especially the two tall, handsome, lazy, cane-carrying footmen in the rumble behind. It is a sound, very different, indeed, from the rapid rattle, and jingle, and cracking of a mail or other such coach.

"That's the voice of the Countess of C——," whispered Mrs. Mercer to us; "she's a proper anti. I wish my goodman were well quit of her! for, reformer though he be, he has no chance at all with so designing and so persevering a woman as she is; and, depend upon it, she is not begging him into the back-shop that way without some end of her own. Hist! Listen to what they are saying!"

"This way, my lady!—this way!" said the haberdasher.

"Mercer!" drawled out a soft but haughty voice; "I have hitherto been disposed to patronize you; and one of the best proofs of this very good disposition towards you is that which I recently exhibited by bringing my niece, the Marchioness of F—— here, to give you her patronage too. And now, in the same patronising disposition, I come to desire you will give your vote, (for I understand that these levelling times have given you a vote)—I say, I come to desire you will give your vote to my son-in-law Mr. B——, who, notwithstanding all I can say to him, is obstinately determined to contaminate himself among the riff-raff members of that abominable sink, the Reform Parliament."

"Really, my lady," stammered out the haberdasher, after what appeared to us to be a most ominous pause, "I am deeply sensible of your ladyship's patronage, and the patronage of your ladyship's niece. I beg pardon, I mean the patronage of the most noble the Lady Marchioness of F——. I feel all that your ladyship has so eloquently expressed. But, really, my lady, in times like the present, hem!—a-hem!—in times like the present, I say—it is—it is very difficult, indeed, to say what to do."

"What, Mr. Mercer!" exclaimed a new voice, pitched in a much higher key, which our *prologa*, Mrs. Mercer, at once informed us was that of the marchioness; "What, Mr. Mercer! can you have any doubt how to act in a case where the Countess of C——, where *my aunt* the Countess of C—— condescends so far as to advise you?"

"No, no, not exactly doubt, my lady marchioness,—not exactly doubt," replied Mr. Mercer, in a subdued tone, betraying considerable trepidation; and then, after a pause, during which he appeared to have somewhat collected himself, "At all events, I cannot doubt that it must always be my duty to obey the smallest wishes of two ladies of rank, so high and noble, and especially of two such honoured patronesses as the Countess of C—— and the Marchioness of F——. But, really, noble ladies, in these times,—one's country—something must be sacrificed for the good of one's country!"

"A haberdasher talking of his country! There is the march of intellect for you! There is reform with a vengeance! why, I shall next expect to see your man of muslins and of ginghams keep his French cook! Where can such people have learned to talk of their country? But, indeed, when we have such Chancellors and Premiers as Brougham and Grey, who actually talk as if the common herd of the *canaille* were of the same blood, as well as flesh, as we of the Upper House, it is no wonder that we should have a haberdasher giving us a discourse upon his country, as if it were John Kemble himself arisen from the dead to perform the character of Cato of Utica!"

"Let me talk to him, my love!" drawled out the countess. "I shall not waste much time with him, I promise you, though I shall even condescend to reason with him. Mercer! you—are—an—extremely foolish man; a haberdasher, as my niece, Lady F——, says, has no business in the world with his country, except to live in it, and to pay its taxes. He should attend to his muslins, and his silks, and his counter, and all that; but that he should interfere with politics, is a thing absolutely quite shocking. On the contrary, he should always be ready to listen to any lady of quality who deigns to patronize him, as I and my niece, the Marchioness of F——, patronize you, Mercer; to show his gratitude to whom he should always be ready to vote as his patronesses bid him, through thick and through thin; but, as to politics, a haberdasher in a small borough like this should never have any thing to do with politics, and still less with his country. Then say at once that you will vote for my son-in-law, Mr. B——, and don't be so rude—do you hear, Mercer?—as to give me any farther trouble."

"I am sure, my lady," stammered out the haberdasher, "I am sure, my lady,—I—I—I do not know what to say. Your ladyship speaks—both your ladyships speak like members of the House of Com——, I mean of the House of Lords—like Peers of Parliament, I should say. Any thing so eloquent I have never heard in my life before; but, really,—I—I—I do not know what to say."

"But I know what you *must* say," replied the shrill and impetuous marchioness. "You *must* pledge yourself to vote for Mr. B——, and there's an end on't! What, sir, are two women of quality, such as my aunt and myself, to condescend thus to signify their pleasure to such a person as Mr. Mercer, the haberdasher!" ("Proud minx that she is!" was here parenthetically interjected by Mrs. Mercer; "if the fellow has the spirit of a flea, he'll give her his mind.") "Are we, I say, to condescend to lay our commands on any such person as you, and are they to be received with doubt and hesitation? Reptile! if you detain us longer with your doubts, you shall be crushed to the earth like a worm in our path!"

"Hear the vixen!" exclaimed Mrs. Mercer. "If I were he, I would give it to her in the deafest side of her head!"

"Do not permit yourself to be excited thus, my love, by the folly of this weak, silly man," said the drawling countess. "He is a stubborn blockhead, to be sure, as all blockheads are. But I shall never allow such a person as he is, to rob me of my temper. I do not even allow my obstinate poodle to do that; though, it must be confessed, he has more than once tried me pretty severely."

"Ladies, ladies!" exclaimed Mercer, in a perturbed tone that spoke his extreme agitation. "Heaven knows I am the last man in the world that would think—nay, that would dream of offending you, but—but—but, really, what *can* a man do?"

"I say, with all the distinctness of utterance of which I am mistress," continued the countess; "and our family have always been remarkable for distinctness of utterance; and, of all our family, no one has been more remarkable for that quality than myself;—I say, with all the distinctness of utterance of which I am mistress, *give me your promise that you will vote for my son-in-law, Mr. B——*, or I shall not only withdraw from you my patronage, and that of all the members of my family, but the marchioness shall withdraw hers, and we shall blast the reputation of your goods, oppose their introduction by the influence of our superior *ton*, abolish the borough balls; and, finally, bring down a person who was a shopman with the so justly celebrated firm of Dyde and Scribe, to set up under our fostering *surveillance* in opposition to you; and you are, doubtless, sufficiently acquainted with the political economy of this paltry place, to know whether or not it has customers enough to make the new man rich, and to keep you from starving at the same time!"

"Horrible old witch!" muttered Mrs. Mercer; "what a demon she is. Have a care of me! heard ye ever the like of her?"

"A-hem! Your ladyship deals rather hardly with me," said Mercer; "or rather, I should say, you are pleased to, perhaps, just a little disposed to, it may be, to have some amusement at my expense. But—but really, 'pon my honour, I am really much at a loss what to say. But suppose that, just to please you, honourable ladies, I should resolve that I should keep neutral, and not vote at all?"

"What, sir," exclaimed the marchioness, in her highest key, "not vote at all! do you call that pleasing us? By all that is good we shall not bate you one atom of our demands; vote for Mr. B——, and have our patronage; vote for Mr. A——, or remain neuter, and take our heaviest vengeance as your reward. Is that plain and intelligible?"

"Come, come, my love," said the countess, "you are too hasty with this *imbecile*. He is a poor silly creature; but you should remember that our Bible teaches us to have mercy upon the weak. I see that our arguments have at length begun to operate upon him, as the continual dropping of a drop of water is said, by degrees, to perforate the hardest rock; and thus we perceive the powerful effect of sound reason, when properly directed and applied, and conveyed in fitting language. So now, Mercer, call my footman; and, as you show us to the carriage, give me the satisfaction of hearing you say that you have at last come to the determination of supporting my son-in-law Mr. B——. Call my footman, I say; Charles, the man's name is Charles." Here Mrs. Mercer half opened the parlour door, that she might the better hear, and at the same time see the parties, as they moved through the front shop towards the door where the carriage was standing. Mr. Mercer followed the two peeresses, bowing with great humiliation, and pale and trembling like an aspen leaf. "Call Charles, I say!" continued the countess, seating herself in one of the chairs of the front shop. "Charles, where is my book of pledges?"

"Here, my lady."

"Then write down in it that —— Mercer here—your name is Joseph, I believe?"

"No, my lady," replied the subdued haberdasher, in an humble tone, "my name is Dick."

"Ay! ay! true," continued she; "Richard Mercer. Charles, write down that Richard Mercer, (we cannot be too particular in such matters of business,) I say that Richard Mercer, haberdasher and silk merchant, number —— what is your number?"—" Fifteen, my lady."— "That Richard Mercer, haberdasher and silk merchant, dealer in shawls and laces, number fifteen, High Street, pledges himself to qualify and vote for Mr. B——. Ha! let me see it; yes, right enough; that will do. And now, Mr. Mercer, have you any particularly rich lace veils at present? I think you occasionally commission such trifles. Let us see your last parcel; ay, that will do; vastly pretty, indeed! Hum! some of them vulgar enough in pattern, too; but, on the whole, not at all bad for such a shop in a country town. Put the whole parcel into the carriage; I may find use for them all."

"My troth, that is a wholesale bargain, indeed," muttered Mrs. Mercer; "but when shall we see the colour of her ladyship's money?"

Mr. Mercer came sneaking back into the little parlour, and swooped himself down in an easy chair, with a visage sorely humiliated by mortification and chagrin. His lady hardly allowed him to be seated ere she opened upon him.

"Well, Dick, this is a precious business."

But we pass the conjugal dialogue, which ends by Mr. Mercer exclaiming in rage—

"I'll tell ye what it is, Mrs. Mercer," said he, striking the table with his fist, "by the great oath, this is a subject which no woman shall dare to remark upon in my presence; and, damnation, ma'am, my wife shall never speak of it, if she would have her head on the same pillow, or under the same roof with mine, else my name is not Dick Mercer!"

"Mr. Mercer," said we, rising abruptly to take our departure, "we drink to your good health, and many thanks for your polite hospitality. Do not stir, sir; pray do not stir." But the haberdasher did stir, to accompany us to the door, with his habitual professional attention. And oh! what did he behold and hear when he reached it? On the narrow pavement in front of his shop stood a little ring of burghers, among whom we noticed Dull David Dallas the grocer, and the well-powdered Mr. White, the baker; while farmer Black was sitting in his saddle, and leaning over the kennel, listening with eager attention. A shout of laughter was at that moment arising from the group,—in the midst of which one of the haberdasher's shopmen was in the act of finishing a waggish detail of the occurrences which we have so recently narrated.

We returned to Mr. Strongitharm's, just in time to witness another scene, which, after what had passed, was quite refreshing to us, as it will, no doubt, be to our readers. The last touch had been given to our refitted vehicle, and our worthy iron M.D. had received our grateful commendations for his expertness and expedition; when, as we were about to pay him for his very moderate charge, a light barouchette, with four post-horses, and a brace of postilions, drove up to the door of the smithy. On the box in front, was seated Mr. B——, the present and would-be future member for the district of burghs we were then in; and in the interior appeared the heads of two individuals, the one elderly and the other younger. Mr. B—— sprang from the box with great alacrity, and entering the smithy, addressed Mr. Strongitharm with a familiar yet haughty nod.

"You're are a voter, my good fellow, a'n't ye?"

"A believe a wull ha'e a vote, sir, after a ha'e qualifeed," replied the smith, in a plain, simple, yet respectful manner.

"Well, you'll give it to me, wont ye?" said the candidate.

"May a ax wha ye are, sir?" demanded Strongitharm.

"Oh! I'm Mr. B——, you know, who has now represented this district of burghs in Parliament for these eight years back."

"Od, sir, ye mun ha'e been young begun wi' the Parlymentin' business," replied the smith, "but muckle though a ha'e read o' the newspapers, a ha'e never seen o' your doin' ony thing, either for the gude o' the country in general, or for this hamewald pairt o' the warld in parteecler; though they tell me ye ha'e gotten a gude fifteen hunder a-year o' the nation's money; an' for what, a'm sure a kenna."

"That, my good friend, was merely the salary of a laborious office, of which the present men have deprived me," replied the candidate, in a somewhat subdued tone.

"A kenna whaure the labour o't lay than," said the smith, drily; "a can only say, that a dinna think muckle o' laborin' frae sax o'clock till sax o'clock wi' this bit forehammer i' my hand, an' a dinna get the fifteenth part o' that siller for ma pains. They tell me that your warkshop's in Lunnon—an' a'm sure a never saw that the wark o't ever stoppit ye frae saumont-fishing i' the spring; nor frae deuk shootin' i' the loch a' the simmer; nor frae murderin' the poor muirfools nor paitricks, i' the autumn; nor frae ridin' after the fox, a' the rest o' the year. Whaure the labor o't can be than, is mair nor a can find oot. Labor eneuch did you indeed tak' whanever Lord John Russell, or ony o' thae pawtriotic chields, spak aboot reform. Ma certy, whatever sport was in play at the time, ye gaed aff an' left it in an auld hurry. An a' to do what, think ye? By ma soul, for nae ither purpose but to gi'e your silent vote against a' thing that was raisonable; just that you, an' the pairty that gied you that laborious an' ill-paid office o' your's that ye spak o', might haud doon puir fonk's heads, an' prevent sic like as me frae ha'ein' that sma' voice in the nation, to the whilk, a tak' it, common sense wud say that they are fairly enteetled."

"You are a very sensible man, Mr. Strongitharm," said the candidate; "though some of your views are not altogether correct, or quite in harmony with mine. But, however much I may have opposed reform from conscientious motives, I am free to confess, that, since it has now become the law of the land, no one can be more disposed to see that it is fairly administered than I shall be."

"Weel, sir, that may be very true," replied the smith; "but a'm for pitten a chield to the new reform bellyses, wha had some hand in settin' them up, an' wha best kens hoo to work them. In short, sir, to save ye frae blawin' ony mair o' the wund oot o' yours, a maun just honestly tell ye, that a canna' gi'e ma vote to a gentleman, wha, gif he had had his nane wull, wad never ha'e letten me ha'e ony vote to gi'e."

"Then you have been canvassed already by Mr. A——, I suppose," said Mr. B——, in a pettish tone.

"Na, Maister A—— nor nae ane else has been naur me," replied the smith; "ye're the very first that ever spak till me aboot ony siccan a business. But whether Mr. A—— comes till me or no', a mean to gi'e him ma vote, as bein' the best man we can get for our turn; and, gif we can get him to gang to Parliament to do oor wark, a'm thinkin' that oor burghs wull be muckle obliged till him."

"But, Mr. Strongitharm," said the candidate, somewhat moved, "you seem to forget, sir, that although you never saw me before, the whole horses of my stud, hunters, hacks and all, have been shod in your smithy for nearly two years past."

"That may be, sir," coolly replied the smith, "a'm sure I ha'e been very proud o' your custom; an' mair nor that, a'm proud eneuch to believe that your horses were the best shod horses in a' the country side. But what has horseshoein' to do wi' the makin' o' members o' Parliament?".

"Why—hoy—whoy, nothing very directly, indeed," said the candidate, taken a good deal aback by the suddenness of the honest smith's question; "but—but you know it is in my power to send my horses to be shod somewhere else."

"Ou, nae doot o' that, sir!" replied the smith. "Though wi' reverence be it spoken, a canna' just see how siccan a hint as that jumpe very weel wi' your declaration, that nane could be mair disposed than you are to see the Reform Bull fairly administered, noo that it's an ack. But giff you wull be content to ha'e your hunters shod by gleed Wully Robb, puir chield, or even by the bit genty body up the street, that mak's the nice pokers an' tangs, an' nit-crackers, an' nit-mug graters, a ha'e naething for to say against it; an' gif ony o' them, or ony ither man, can shoe ye're hunters as weel as a can do, what for no employ him? But if the truth be, as a jalouse, that a can shoe your horses better than ony ither smith i' this part o' the country side, then, ma opinion just is, that if ye gang elsewhere to fare waur, ye ha'ena just a' that wusdom for your ain interest that fouk gi'e ye credit for."

"Why do you talk so long?" called out one of the personages from the interior of the vehicle, in an impatient tone. "Come away! come away!"

Mr. B—— hastened to the side of the carriage, and after a little private parley, a servant was called to open the door, and to let down the steps; and the indefatigable Mr. B—— returned to the charge, reinforced by the presence of his two friends from the interior.

"Mr. Strongitharm, this is my father-in-law, the earl of C——, and this is my wife's cousin, the Marquis of F——," said the candidate.

"Mr. Strongitharm," said the marquis, with a good-natured, familiar air and manner, "you know that I keep hounds, I believe; that I hunt a pretty wide extent of country; and that not only all my shoeing work is done in your shop, but that I have it in my power to give you, or to take from you, half the shoeing work and farriery business of this county, and those on each side of it. Will you refuse me your vote for my connexion, Mr. B—— ?"

"Mr. Strongitharm," said the earl, taking up the discourse before the smith had time to reply, "you know that I also have some shoeing in my stables, and much smith work a-doing at the castle; all this I have the power of giving or withholding. But there is yet another thing to which I would earnestly call your attention: you hold a farm of three hundred a-year from me; and now, will you refuse me your vote for my son-in-law, Mr. B—— ?"

"Ma lords," replied Mr Strongitharm, apparently now resolved to permit the negotiation to be as little spun out as he possibly could; "as to the horse an' smith part o' your twa speeches, a maun just say to you what a ha'e already said to this gentleman himself, what has the shoein' o' horses and the makin' o' members o' Parliament to do wi' ane anither? Gin ye dinna like to ha'e yer horses shod by me, ye maun just gang elsewhere to ha'e the job dune; an' gin ye find as gude a smith as me, a' that a say is, that a wuse ye baith joy o' him. An' as for the matter o' the farm o' which his lordship, the yearl, spak yenoo, a canna see, for the soul o' me, what that has to do wi' makin' o' a Parliament man, mair nor the shoein' trade. A ha'e gotten a gye stark bargain o' the bit place, but a ha'e a tack o't, an' a'm aye yebble to pay the rent; an' sae a'm thinkin' there's naething left to mak' or mend atween us. But, Lord's sake, sirs! a hinna time to be stannin' haverin' here ony langer: a maun till ma wark as fast's a can; for a daurna leave ma study to gang and catch saumonts, and shoot deuks, as this gentleman can do." And suiting the action to the word, he snatched up the fore-hammer, and began to thunder such a peal upon the anvil as quickly drove the nervous senators of both the Houses to their carriages; and he never stopped his noise till that of their wheels was quite lost in distance.

There was a good-natured waggish leer of comical humour on his face, when he ceased his cannonade of blows, to receive the money which we had all this time been holding in our hands. Before again placing ourselves in our vehicle, we could not resist paying him some compliments on his firm, noble, and straight-forward conduct.

"Fegs, gentlemen, it's a bad account o' human nature," said he, "that ye sould think it wordy while to commend a man for barely doin' that which he would be a rascal for no doin'. But, troth, a maun say that some poor deevils are subjeckit to sair temptations by thae anti fouk, or conservatives, as they are cain' themsells. But, an they dinna let poor fouk alane, to be guided by God and their ain consciences, in the exerceese o' a trust, the whilk they hauld for sae mony ithers beside themsells, a'm muckle mistane gif ballot be na the upshot o'd."

SCRAPS.
ORIGINAL AND SELECTED.

ADVICE OF A PHRENOLOGIST TO ELECTORS.—Flee to the hall of the nearest statuary; entreat him to exhibit to you the bust of the American patriot Franklin; mark well the size and the configuration of that great philanthropist's head; impress upon your minds its great size, and the predominance of its anterior and superior departments over those behind and below, and call to your recollection the unwearied perseverance and industry, the calmness and sagacity, and the strength of mind and aptitude for the practical duties of life which he displayed, and the prodigious impulse which he gave to the cause of civil and religious liberty. Then go forth into the world, and whensoever the wigs are doffed, pick out the man whose head most resembles that of Franklin; for you may rely with confidence, that such a man will "go and do likewise."

A SIMPLE MARRIAGE CEREMONY.—There have been many elaborate works published on the marriage ceremonies of nations, both savage and civilized. I do not, however, remember to have read of any so brief and unceremonious as the following, which I had the opportunity of witnessing when on a visit to a gentleman in Carolina. A fine-looking Negro, and the handsomest mulatto or yellow girl I had ever seen, were the parties who desired to be made one for life. The matter was thus arranged: In the course of our evening walk, my friend, the planter, was sheepishly addressed by the slave in these words:—"Please, massa, me want to marry Riddiky." (This is the "Nigger" for Eurydice.)—"Does Riddiky want to marry you?"—"Yes, massa."—"If you marry her, I won't allow you to run after the other girls on the plantation—you shall live like a decent fellow with your wife."—"Massa, me lub ber, so dat me don't care one dam for de oder gals."—"Marry her then, and be cursed."—"Yes, massa." Washington then gave Riddiky a kiss, and from that day they became man and wife: no other form than that of permission from their owner, thus graciously accorded, being necessary to legalize their union.—*Notes on America.*

TO QUENCH THIRST, pour vinegar into the palms of the hands, snuff it up the nostrils, and wash the hands with it. This will allay the most intense heat.

ADVANTAGES OF CARD PLAYING.—What so truly tells the real disposition and temper of a person as this amusement? Are they inclined to dishonesty, they will cheat; if of a hasty uncontrollable temper, it is almost sure to be shown; if not very scrupulous respecting falsehood or ill-language, here they present themselves unmasked; whilst in almost all other transactions of life those passions are carefully concealed from public view, or glossed over, so as to make them generally palatable to the world.

CONTENTS OF NO. XV.	
EDUCATION OF THE PEOPLE,	225
A Chapter for Martinmas Term,	227
The Barometer—The Thermometer,	228
Memorable Battles,	229
USEFUL AND SCIENTIFIC NOTICES,	230
The Original Story of Bill Jones,	231
ELEMENTS OF THOUGHT—Happiness—Well-being,	232
THE STORY TELLER—Story of Lady Grisell Baillie, 233—Scottish Voters,	236
SCRAPS, Original and Selected,	240

EDINBURGH: Printed by and for JOHN JOHNSTONE, 19, St. James' Square.—Published by JOHN ANDERSON, JUN., Bookseller, 55, North Bridge Street, Edinburgh; by JOHN MACLEOD, and ATKINSON & Co. Booksellers, Glasgow; and sold by all Booksellers and Venders of Cheap Periodicals.

THE Schoolmaster,
AND
EDINBURGH WEEKLY MAGAZINE.

CONDUCTED BY JOHN JOHNSTONE.

THE SCHOOLMASTER IS ABROAD.—LORD BROUGHAM.

No. 16.—Vol. I.   SATURDAY, NOVEMBER 17, 1832.   Price Three-Halfpence.

THE COMMENCEMENT OF THE EDINBURGH YEAR.

> To their high-built airy nests
> See the *rooks* returning home.

The London business year begins in October, and that of high fashion about the end of February. The busy year of Glasgow, Manchester, and Liverpool, either knows no ending, or its periods of leisure depend on causes at work in the uttermost parts of the earth, producing, it may be, its hottest haste in July, and most icy stagnation in January. The Dublin year commences about the same time as that of Edinburgh; with the opening of the Courts. The commencement of the Edinburgh year is, however, manifested by more striking symptoms than that of any other city with which we are acquainted. The University and the Courts of Law extend their crooked ramifications to every corner of Scotland, and the 12th of November brings all to a centre, and puts all in motion. Symptoms of returning life are then apparent in a hundred agreeable ways. Coaches and steamers are arriving every hour, passenger and baggage-laden. The late grass-grown streets kindle to life, and become crowded; and a certain alacrity of movement and look, communicated even to the stationary inhabitants, proclaims the return of the season. The consumption of gas, cigars, mutton-pies, jellies, and newspapers, is doubled in one day. Lodging-boards disappear from the windows, as rig-and-fur hose appear in the streets. The mercers and jewellers hang out their most tempting wares; the Professors re-touch their lectures; the Ministers preach their best sermons; the very ballad-singers and oyster-wives scream and yell with redoubled animation and vigour, and the lubricous commodity of the latter traffickers rises 50 per cent in one night,—thus giving young students a practical and impressive lesson in the principles of political economy, before they have been two days among us. Mr. Murray paints anew his drop scenes, and gets up a new piece; the tobacconists re-blacken the blackamoors, who, in Prince's Street, mount guard over the Havannahs; and new pretty faces are seen beaming from among the high-raised pyramids of sweatmeat jars and jelly-glasses, in all the confectioners' shops. These are but samples of the mighty internal change, of which some flagrant symptoms are always amusingly apparent in the *puff paste-ry* of the North Bridge, where traders of all descriptions conglomerate notices of their wares; and trump and over-trump each other's tricks, to the mighty bewilderment of the innocent, gaping *Hallow Fair* folks.

Here the SCHOOLMASTER ABROAD! peers modestly forth under a flourish of CHAMBERS' JOURNAL, *price only three-halfpence!* and there is—ELEGANCE AND ECONOMY COMBINED—in—SHEEP-SMEARING MATERIALS; A SERMON TO BE PREACHED—BY THE REV.——STATUES ON THE CALTON HILL; NOW EXHIBITING—the CHEAPEST BOOTS AND SHOES IN EDINBURGH; and again—SELLING OFF, AT AND BELOW PRIME COST—HOT TRIPE EVERY NIGHT, PREPARED IN THE GLASGOW WAY—BY ORDER OF THE MAGISTRATES!

But the centre of this complex movement, and of Edinburgh civilization, as well as of some other qualities belonging to an advanced state of society, is unquestionably the *Parliament House*.

> "It was a merry spot in days of yore,
> But something ails it now—the place is haunted,"

by what kind of spirits we are not metaphysicians, nor yet conjurors enough to tell, though the buoyant, the brilliant, the sparkling have certainly evaporated. The dynasty of the Crosbies, Boswells, and Erskines has fallen, never to rise again. Even Scott and Jeffrey are among the things that were. The last spark of the bright wit, which

> "Made a sunshine in that shady place"

the Outer-House—the wit of Henry Erskine, played in a lambent flame for a few seconds round the wig of ——, flashed over the marble features of ——, and—expired for ever. Legal Humour, Fun, and Glee found the climate of the New Town of Edinburgh chill and ungenial; and they died under it, bequeathing the residue of HIGH JINKS to the SPENDTHRIFT CLUB, and their wigs to whoever would pick them up. The consequence has been, that to find any thing about that House worthy of the "amber immortalization" of the SCHOOLMASTER'S pages, we must plod back over some quarter century of tradition, guided by this final scintillation of the wit of the Scotch Bar—

THE DIAMOND BEETLE.*

Notes supposed to have been taken at advising the Action of Defamation and Damages—Alexander Cunningham, Jeweller in Edinburgh, against James Russell, Surgeon there.

LORD PRESIDENT, Sir ISLAY CAMPBELL.—Your Lordships have the petition of Alexander Cunningham against Lord B———'s interlocutor.

It is a case of damages and defamation, for calling the petitioner's Diamond Beetle an Egyptian Louse. You have the Lord Ordinary's distinct interlocutor on pages 29 and 30 of this petition :—" Having considered the condescendence of the pursuer, answers for the defender," and so on, " Finds, in this respect, that it is not alleged that the diamonds on the back of the Diamond Beetle are real diamonds, or any thing but shining spots, such as are found on other Diamond Beetles, and which likewise occur, though in a smaller number, on a great number of other Beetles, somewhat different from the Beetle libelled, similar to which there may be Beetles in Egypt, with shining spots on their backs, which may be termed Lice there, and may be different, not only from the common Louse, but from the Louse mentioned by Moses as one of the plagues of Egypt, which is admitted to be a filthy troublesome Louse, even worse than the said Louse, which is clearly different from the Louse libelled ; but that the other Louse is the same with, or similar to the said Beetle, which is also the same with the other Beetle ; and although different from the said Beetle libelled, yet as the said Beetle is similar to the other Beetle, and the said Louse to the said other Louse libelled, and the other Louse to the other Beetle, which is the same with or similar to the Beetle, which somewhat resembles the Beetle libelled, assoilzies the defender, and finds expenses due."

Say away, my Lords.

Lord MEADOWBANK.—This is a very intricate and puzzling question, my Lord. I have formed no decided opinion ; but at present I am rather inclined to think the interlocutor is right, though not upon the *ratio* assigned in it. It appears to me that there are two points for consideration :—*First*, Whether the words libelled amount to a *convicium*—and, *secondly*, Admitting the *convicium*, whether the pursuer is entitled to found upon it in this action. Now, my Lords, if there be a *convicium* at all, it consists in the *comparatio*, or comparison of the *Scarabæus* or *Beetle*, with the Egyptian *Pediculus* or *Louse*. My first doubt regards this point, but it is not at all founded on what the defender alleges, that there is no such animal as an Egyptian *Pediculus* or *Louse* in *rerum natura* ; for although it does not *actually* exist, it may *possibly* exist, and whether its existence be in *esse vel posse*, is the same thing to this question, provided there be *habiles* for ascertaining what it would be if it did exist. But my doubt is here : How am I to discover what are the *essentia* of any Louse, whether Egyptian or not ? It is very easy to describe its accidents as a naturalist would do—to say that it belongs to the tribe of *asstera*, or that it is a yellow, little, greedy, filthy, despicable reptile ; but we do not learn from this what the *proprium* of the animal is in a logical sense, and still less what its *differentia* are. Notwithstanding these, it is impossible to judge whether there is a *convicium* or not ; for in a case of this kind, which *sequitur naturam delicti*, we must take them *meliore sensu*, and presume the *comparatio* to be in the *melioribus tantum*. And here I beg that parties, and the bar in general——(Interrupted by Lord Hermand—" Your Lordship should address yourself to the chair.") I say,—I beg it may be understood, that I do not rest my opinion on the ground that *veritas convicii excusat*. I am clear that, although this Beetle actually were an Egyptian *Pediculus*, it would afford no relative defence, provided the calling it so were a *convicium*—and there my doubt lies.

With regard to the second point, I am satisfied that the *Scarabæus*, or Beetle itself, has no *persona standi in judicio* ; and therefore the pursuer cannot insist, in the name of the *Scarabæus*, or for his behoof. If the action lie at all, it must be at the instance of the pursuer himself, as the *verus Dominus* of the *Scarabæus*, for being calumniated through the *convicium*, directed primarily against the animal standing in that relation to him. Now, abstracting from the qualification of an actual *dominium*, which is not alleged, I have great doubts whether a mere *convicium* is necessarily transmitted from one object to another, through the relation of a *dominium* subsisting between them ; and if not necessarily transmissible, we must see the principle of its actual transmission here, and that has not yet been pointed out.

Lord HERMAND.—We heard a little ago, my Lord, that there is a difficulty in this case ; but I have not been fortunate enough, for my part, to find out where the difficulty lies. Will any man presume to tell me that a Beetle is not a Beetle, and that a Louse is not a Louse ? I never saw the petitioner's Beetle, and what's more, I don't care whether I ever see it or not ; but I suppose it's like other Beetles, and that's enough for me. But, my Lord, I know the other reptile well—I have seen them, my Lord, ever since I was a child in my mother's arms, and my mind tells me, that nothing but the deepest and blackest malice, rankling in the human breast, could have suggested this comparison, or led any man to form a thought so injurious and insulting. But, my Lord, there's more here than all that, a great deal more ; one could have thought the defender would have gratified his spite to the full, by comparing the Beetle to a common Louse, an animal sufficiently vile and abominable for the purpose of defamation—[shut that door there] ;—but he adds the epithet Egyptian, and I know well what he means by that epithet. He means, my Lord, a Louse that has been fattened in the head of a gipsy or tinker, undisturbed by the comb, and unmolested in the enjoyment of its native filth. He means a Louse ten times larger, and ten times more abominable, than those with which your Lordships and I are familiar. The petitioner asks redress for the injury so atrocious and so aggravated, and as far as my voice goes, he shall not ask it in vain.

Lord CRAIG.—I am of the opinion last delivered. It appears to me to be slanderous and calumnious to compare a Diamond Beetle to the filthy and mischievous animal just libelled. By an Egyptian Louse, I understand one which has been formed in the head of a native Egyptian, a race of men who, after degenerating for many centuries, have sunk, at last, into the abyss of depravity, in consequence of having been subjugated for a time, by the French. I do not find that Turgot, or Condorcet, or the rest of the economists, ever reckon the combing of the head a species of productive labour; and I conclude, therefore, that wherever French principles have been propogated, Lice grow to an immoderate size, especially in a warm climate, like that of Egypt.

I shall only add, that we ought to be sensible of the blessings we enjoy under a free and happy constitution, where Lice and men live under the restraint of equal laws, the only equality that can exist in a well-regulated state.

Lord POLKEMMET.—It should be observed, my Lord, that what is called a Beetle, is a reptile well known in this country. I have seen mony ane o' them in Drumshorlin Muir. It is a little black beastie, about the size o' my thoom nail. The country people ca' them clocks, and I believe they ca' them also Maggy-wi'-the-mony-feet ; but this is not a beast like any Louse that ever I saw, so that, in my opinion, though the defender may have made a blunder, through ignorance, in comparing them, there does not seem to have been any *animus injuriandi*, therefore a'm for refusing the petition, my Lords.

Lord BALMUTO.—A'm for refusing the petition. There's more Lice than Beetles in Fife. They ca' them Beetle-clocks there ; what they ca' a Beetle, is a thing as lang as

---

* This *jeu d'esprit* is understood to be an early production of Mr. Cranstoun, now Lord Corehouse. The allusions are necessarily local, and some of the characters are already beginning to be forgotten even in Scotland. But the wit is as fresh and sparkling as ever.

my arm, thick at the one end, and small at the other. I thought when I read the petition, that the Beetle, or Bittle, had been the thing that the women have when they are washing towels or napery with—things for dadding them with—and I see the petitioner is a jeweller to his trade, and I thought he had ane o' thae Beetles, and set it all round with diamonds, and I thought it a foolish and extravagant idea, and I saw no resemblance it could have to a Louse; but I find I was mistaken, my Lord, and I find it only a Beetle-clock the petitioner has; but my opinion's the same it was before. I say, my Lords, a'm for refusing the petition, I say——

Lord WOODHOUSELEE.—There is a case abridged in the third volume of the Dictionary of Decisions, *Chalmers* against *Douglas*, in which it is found that *veritas convicii excusat*, which may be rendered, not literally, but in a free and spirited manner, according the most approved principles of translation, "the truth of calumny affords a relevant defence." If, therefore, it be the law of Scotland, which I am clearly of opinion it is, that the truth of the calumny affords a relevant defence, and if it be likewise true that the Diamond Beetle is really an Egyptian Louse, I am inclined to conclude, though certainly the case is attended with difficulty, that the defender ought to be assoilzied.—*Refuse.*

Lord Justice-clerk RAE.—I am very well acquainted with the defender in this action, and have respect for him —and esteem him likewise. I know him to be a skilful and expert surgeon, and also a good man; and I would go a great length to serve him, if I had it in my power to do so. But I think on this occasion he has spoken rashly, and, I fear, foolishly and improperly; I hope he had no bad intention—I am sure he had not. But the petitioner (for whom I have likewise a great respect, because I knew his father, who was a very respectable baker in Edinburgh, and supplied my family with bread, and very good bread it was, and for which his accounts were regularly discharged) it seems has a Clock or a Beetle, I think it is called a Diamond Beetle, which he is very fond of, and has a fancy for, and the defender has compared it to a Louse, or a Bug, or a Flea, or something of that kind, with a view to render it despicable or ridiculous, and the petitioner so likewise, as the proprietor or owner thereof. It is said that this beast is a Louse *in fact*, and that the *veritas convicii excusat;* and mention is made of a decision in the case of *Chalmers* against *Douglas.* I have always had a great veneration for the decisions of your Lordships, and, I am sure, will always continue to have while I sit here; but that case was determined by a very small majority, and I have heard your Lordships mention it on various occasions, and you have always desiderated the propriety of it, and, I think, have departed from it in some instances. I remember the circumstances of the case well. Helen Chalmers lived in Musselburgh, and the defender, Mrs. Bailie, lived in Fisherrow, and at that time there was much intercourse between the genteel inhabitants of Fisherrow, and Musselburgh, and Inveresk, and likewise Newbigging, and there were balls, or dances, or assemblies every fortnight, or oftener; and also sometimes, I believe, every week; and there were card parties, assemblies, once a fortnight, or oftener; and the young people danced there also, and others played at cards, and there were various refreshments, such as tea, and coffee, and butter and bread, and, I believe, but I am not sure, porter and negus, and likewise small beer; and it was at one of these assemblies that Mrs. Baillie called Mrs. Chalmers a ——, or an ——, and said she had been lying with Commissioner Cardonald, a gentleman whom I knew very well at one time, and had a great respect for— he is dead many years ago. And Mrs. Chalmers brought an action of defamation before the Commissaries, and it came by advocation into this Court, and your Lordships allowed a proof of the *veritas convicii*, and it lasted a very long time, and in the end answered no good purpose, even to the defender herself, while it did much hurt to the pursuer's character.

I am, therefore, for REFUSING a proof in this case, and I think the petitioner, in this case, and his Beetles, have been slandered, and the petition ought to be seen.

Lord METHVEN.—If I understand this a—a—a—interlocutor, it is not said that the a—a—a—a— Egyptian Lice are Beetles, but that they may be, or a—a—a—a—resemble Beetles.

I am therefore for sending the process to the Ordinary, to ascertain the fact, as I think it depends upon that, whether there be a—a—a—a—*convicium* or not. I think, also, the petitioner should be ordained to a—a—a—produce his Beetle, and the defender an Egyptian Louse or Pediculus, and that he should take a diligence a—a—a— to recover Lice of various kinds, and these may be remitted to Doctor Monro, or Mr Playfair, or to some other naturalist to report upon the subject.—AGREED TO.

FUMIGATION.

Fumigation is practised in various ways, and a great many substances are employed in fumigating processes. Some preparations of mercury have been burned, and patients have been exposed to their fumes, for the purpose of producing on the body the peculiar action of mercury; and fumigation is much employed to destroy the contagious matter of several diseases. One of the most beneficial instances of this, is the employment of the fumes of nitric or muriatic acid to destroy the contagion of fever. This is done by pouring sulphuric acid on saltpetre; the sulphuric acid combines with the potash of the saltpetre, and the nitric acid fumes thoroughly mixing with the air, destroys the contagious matter of which it is the vehicle. The best way to fill the chamber, the ward, or the ship, where contagion is suspected, is to place a number of saucers in different parts of the room, to put saltpetre in each of them, and to pour on the sulphuric acid. The doors and windows should be shut for some time, and then a current of fresh air admitted. Another gas, which has been employed to destroy contagion, is the muriatic acid gas, or vapour from sea-salt. This is to be extracted from sea-salt by nearly the same process, pouring sulphuric acid upon it; the vapour which rises is probably equally effectual, but it is more irritating and offensive to the lungs of those who are exposed to it. Fumigation with sulphur may also be practised. The clothes of those who have been ill of fever should be carefully fumignted, and the walls of their apartment, and the furniture should be completely exposed to the disinfecting vapour. In the small-pox, there is a most peculiar odour in the apartments of the sick, which continues many weeks or months after their recovery; and the contagion of fever, though less obvious to the senses, may reasonably be supposed to lurk as long, if not carefully destroyed. The sprinkling of the sick chamber with heated vinegar, or throwing it upon hot coals, though it may not have the power of destroying contagion, is nevertheless a very good practice, as it encourages ventilation, is refreshing to the sick, and gives confidence to the necessary attendants.

TO MY CARRIER PIGEON.

Come hither, thou beautiful rover,
  Thou wand'rer of earth and of air,
Who hearest the sighs of the lover,
  And bringest him news of his fair;
Oh! perch on my hand, dearest minion,
  And turn up thy bright eye and peck,
With thy love billet under thy pinion,
  And gold circle round thy white neck.

Here is bread of the whitest and sweetest,
  And there is a sip of white wine;
Though thy wing is the lightest and fleetest,
  'Twill be fleeter when nerv'd by the vine;
I have written on rose-scented paper,
  With thy wing quill, a soft billet-doux;
I have melted the wax in Lover's taper,
  'Tis the colour of true hearts—light blue.

I have fasten'd it under thy pinion
  With a blue ribbon round thy soft neck;
So go from me, beautiful minion,
  While the pure ether shews not a speck;
Like a cloud in the dim distance fleeting,
  Like an arrow he hurries away;
And farther and farther retreating,
  He is lost in the clear blue of day.

ON THE MORAL TRAINING OF CHILDREN.
(For the Schoolmaster.)
LETTER II.

When the faculties of the mind begin to open and expand, children are curious and inquisitive. The objects around them affect their senses, and induce them to ask a variety of questions; and it is at this period, principally, that parents, by a simple and affectionate manner of conversing with them, acquire almost unbounded influence over their young minds. But, do not parents, alas! too often neglect to improve this important period by their impatient conduct? At first, indeed, when the little prattlers begin to unfold their ideas, by expressing them in words, we listen eagerly to their simple observations, and are delighted with them; yet it generally happens that, after a while, what had been so delightful and entertaining ceases to be so; when instead of meeting with that encouragement which they ought, in expressing their ideas, they are repulsed for their troublesome talkativeness, or unbecoming presumption. Thus, we not only deter them from opening their minds to us, but also deprive ourselves of the means of affording them that information and instruction which, at their time of life, they so much require; and which it is our duty, as it ought likewise to be our happiness, to communicate.

Children feel severely this change of behaviour towards them; the consequence is, they become shy, silent, and reserved towards their parents, and are induced to associate with those who will be more accommodating to them, such as complaisant servants, from whom it is not to be expected they can derive much improvement. Generally speaking, the ideas of common servants are very limited, often absurd, and even dangerous; while their language is vulgar and their manners coarse. From familiarity with them, therefore, children can derive no advantage; while, by such intercourse they frequently contract awkward habits, and learn ungrammatical and low, if not bad, expressions. It is well if the evil go no further. Too often, alas! is the dreadful contamination of vice communicated from such society, and the young mind polluted by the knowledge of what it ought never to know. Would it not be better still to continue our attentive regard, by listening patiently to what they have to say, and answering their inquiries without suffering even their frivolous prattle to put us out of temper? Very different is this kind of indulgence and encouraging familiarity, from that of gratifying their self-will or unreasonable demands; which is only done by the indulgence of their improper desires, with which every idea of happiness becomes identified, to the exclusion of all concern about the happiness or welfare of others, except so far, indeed, as it may be connected with their own. Thus, selfishness becomes the predominant feature of the character, accompanied with pride, peevishness, and anger, whenever the will is thwarted; and thus, a capricious humour is the unavoidable consequence.

Many are the tyrannical husbands and fathers, and refractory wives and mothers, that have been so formed, by an education in which the will had never been accustomed to be thwarted, or brought into subjection by wholesome correction and reproof in early life. And may we not appeal to those who have lived in a family of spoiled children, that the gratification of the will is uniformly productive of misery, not only to the children themselves, but to all who have any thing to do with them? But whilst we endeavour to avoid all improper indulgence, let us beware of the opposite extreme of over severity. If the first strengthens self-will, and engenders pride and selfishness, the other no less embitters present existence, debases the mind, and strikes at the root of the most valuable social virtues. Where the dread of punishment predominates, the disposition is generally artful; hence, the fear which is thus produced, prompts children not so much to avoid committing faults, as to elude detection by base subterfuges, which still more tend to debase and vitiate the mind.

Correction, when it is necessary, ought rather to be applied to the *mind* than the *body*; so far, at least, as the circumstances will admit. Let it be administered as medicine for the cure of mental disorder; but let children see that it is done with reluctance; let them be convinced that it is necessary, and intended solely for their good. Depriving the offender of something on which he sets a value; withholding our customary marks of affection; putting him into temporary confinement or disgrace; showing him, at the same time, that we are more *afflicted* than *offended* with him for what he has done, will in general have a much better effect than the frequent recurrence to the rod, which only irritates the disposition, without convincing the judgment. If, indeed, the rod should *apparently* effect a cure, it frequently happens that the *will* to do wrong still remains; and, what is worse, the odious and much-to-be-detested spirit of revenge is but too apt to be generated by such a mode of correction.

But, in objection to this, it may be urged, what Solomon says,—"He that spareth the rod hateth his son;" a saying which, it is much to be feared, has, in too many instances, (in consequence of being too literally understood,) been the cause of both parents and others intrusted with the education of children, resorting to corporal punishment much oftener than they ought, or, in all probability, would have done, had they viewed it in a proper light. It is nothing more, indeed, than a strong emblematical figure, implying the necessity of keeping the will under proper subjection; and was never meant to be taken literally, as it stands, any more than a number of other sayings of a similar nature, which, it is manifest, can only be understood in a figurative or emblematical sense. Such, for example, as "Foolishness is bound up in the heart of a child, but the *rod of correction* shall drive it far from him;"—or this, "Withhold not correction from the child; for if thou *beatest him with the rod*, he shall not die. Thou shalt *beat him with the rod*, and shall deliver his soul from hell." Or this, "The *rod and reproof* give wisdom; but a child left to himself bringeth his mother to shame." And so in a variety of other instances, where by "the rod," is not literally meant *the rod*, or corporal punishment, but an early and careful restraint of the will, by whatever means. Other mistakes may be as readily made, as, indeed, many are, by not attending to this figurative mode of expression,—as where it is said "God is angry!" and also "punishes!" which is to be considered not only as peculiar to the sacred writings, but as the best adapted to general comprehension; the Divine Book being read and understood by the simple according to his simplicity, and by the wise according to his wisdom.

Still, it may be asked—"Is corporal punishment to be totally abandoned?" To which we answer,—If it can be wholly dispensed with, so much the better; but when all other means fail, there is then certainly no alternative. In the case of those, however, who have been under proper training from their infancy, the instances in which it would be necessary to resort to the rod, particularly if they are capable of being reasoned with, would be extremely rare. The necessity for it at all, indeed, arises entirely from mismanagement or neglect in their previous moral training. But when it is necessary to inflict correction upon children, never let it be attended by furious looks, or loud tones of voice, nor any other external symptoms of anger and passion, lest it be mistaken for revenge, create mischievous associations, and weaken filial respect and filial affection. Violence will never cure obstinacy; it can only inflame the passionate, and confirm the stubborn. Obstinacy frequently is the offspring of strength of mind and active powers taking a wrong direction. Patience and mildness will have great influence in overcoming obstinacy; for when children find that they cannot provoke to anger, nor vex the temper, they will generally give up the contest. Some children, who seem to manifest the greatest obstinacy, only want to be calmly reasoned with, and to hear an adequate cause assigned why they should act in one manner, and not in another; and when that wish is gratified, they will readily submit. Where such is evidently the disposition, it deserves to be cherished, and not violently repressed; because, when enlightened and properly directed, it may be the parent of unshaken fortitude and virtue.

A very young daughter of a gentleman of high respectability and well-known talents, but who had been mistaken in the mode of managing his child, was committed to the care of a lady, a valued friend of the writer,—who, by those means, has had the satisfaction and happiness of ameliorating many a sullen and obstinate temper, and even of substituting gentleness and pliability for obstinacy and irritability,—with the discouraging declaration, that he feared the case was hopeless—the mental malady incurable. The moral physician, however, after mature examination of the symptoms, discovered the nature of the disease, and applied the proper remedy. Instead of insisting upon blind compliance with commands and rules, she condescended to explain to the thinking, strong-minded girl, the reasons and motives upon which compliance was required, and pointed out its beneficial results. The consequence of which mode of treatment was, that the obstinacy which had resisted the reverence of paternal authority, lonely seclusion, being fed with bread and water, and bodily pain, gave way; and the formerly mutinous girl exclaimed, with some apparent vexation, " I can't think how it is, but Mrs. —— makes me do just what she pleases, in spite of myself!" The perverse child is become an amiable, as well as sensible, well-informed, and steady woman.

When mild but decided measures are pursued in education, young children will seldom need greater punishment than confinement, or being deprived of some amusement or pleasure, to curb their passions. They will probably cry when they are thus treated, but their tears should be disregarded till they are submissive. But they ought never to be confined where there is any danger of their being frightened. Fear, with some children, may be a constitutional defect, but it is more probable to be, in most instances, an acquired one, arising solely from the manner in which they have been treated in infancy. Like other things, it may be early impressed on the mind, which impressions, for the most part, it is difficult to remove in after life, at least so as to be entirely got rid of. For instance, there are many sensible persons who have been slaves all their lives to the fear of darkness, from the circumstance of having, when children, been impressed with it by foolish stories of ghosts and apparitions being seen in the dark, and to which they had attached the idea of fear, thus associating in the mind the idea of fear with that of darkness, so as to make them quite inseparable; and, notwithstanding reason in riper age may have shown them the absurdity of this, still they were incapable of totally overcoming the impression. Hence the propriety of guarding the minds of children from such impressions, by preventing their hearing such ridiculous stories.* Another thing which ought to be equally guarded against in those who have the care of children, is threatening them, in order to prevent their touching what is improper, that *it will bite them!* Or, when they are behaving improperly, to *call for the old man to come down the chimney to take them!* They leave impressions on the mind of a highly injurious nature. If terror be deemed by any as absolutely necessary for the government of children, let it be regarded as a dangerous medicine, which, if administered without the utmost caution, may prove a deadly poison. If frightful objects, which have no real existence, be employed to terrify children into restraint of their feelings, or submission to authority, they will, in course of time, as their minds grow enlightened, discover the falsehood which has been used as a means of managing them; and is it not to be feared, that such a discovery may render the youthful ear deaf to the representations of the beauty and propriety and benefit of truth?

The first and most important lessons for the human mind to learn, are those of self-government, self-denial, and submission to lawful authority. These are lessons which throughout life, they will have to practise. Submission to the will of the Universal Parent,—the righteous and merciful Moral Governor; compliance with the precepts of our holy religion; obedience to the laws of our country; the *partial* sacrifice, at least, of our own individual feelings and conveniences to the common good, regulations, and customs of society. These are duties, upon the fulfilment of which depend, in the highest degree, personal comfort and public welfare. The foundation of such habits and of such principles cannot, therefore, be laid too early. And certainly this can be effected without the instrumentality of terror, and without the risk of generating enfeebling timidity in the breasts of our children.

With these observations, I take my leave for the present, and am, &c.

A FRIEND TO EARLY EDUCATION.
Edinburgh, Nov. 7th, 1832.

*⁂ Letter I. appeared in No. 8.

TO MY CIGAR.

Let others scent the liquid rose,
And perfumes give the pamper'd'nose,*
Be mine, the sweets thy sigh disclose,
   My mild cigar!

When wintry winds the features nip,
What cheers my purple nose and lip,
While gaily o'er the ice I skip?
   My warm cigar!

When yellow fogs obscure the day,
And prowling sharpers prowl for prey,
What lights me through the dubious way?
   My bright cigar!

When night appears with dusky veil,
And Cynthia shows her visage pale,
How fragrantly thy fumes inhale,
   My sweet cigar!

When cares oppress the drooping mind,
And fickle friends are most unkind,
Who constant still remains behind?—
   My true cigar!

Oh! where's the friend who'd cheerfully,
To soothe one pensive hour for me,
Resign his latest breath like thee?
   My kind cigar!

Then come, sweet stranger, come—once more
Go seek again thy native shore—
May soft winds waft thine essence o'er,
   My poor cigar!

Thy spirit's gone, poor fragile thing!
But still thine ashes, mouldering,
To me a valued lesson bring,
   My pale cigar!

Like man's, how soon thy vital spark
Expiring, leaves no other mark
But mould'ring ashes, drear and dark,
   My dead cigar!

And when I watch, with curious eyes,
Thy smoke ascend yon azure skies,
It bids me hope like thee to rise,
   My frail cigar!

---

* "A short time ago, in this neighbourhood, a young girl about seven years of age, whose imagination had been filled with those frightful nursery tales that are conjured up by ignorant servants, and others, to frighten children into obedience, was thrust into a dark closet for some tale she had carried to her parents. The poor thing continued to scream with the most violent apprehension, and when the door was opened to take her from her abode of terror, she was lying on the ground in strong convulsions. The conflict was too powerful for her tender reason, and she now exists one of the most miserable objects of human sympathy. Her parents and friends see their hopes blasted,—their interesting little favourite is now an idiot!"—*Glasgow Chronicle*, March, 1827.

* And 'twixt his finger and his thumb he held
 A pouncet box, which ever and anon
 He gave his nose.—*Hotspur's Fop.*

ELEMENTS OF THOUGHT.

THE SOURCES OF HUMAN HAPPINESS.
BY GEORGE COMBE, ESQ.

Our readers, to go on well, must resume Mr. Combe's thread of reasoning from last number. We repeat the connecting sentence:—

According to the view now advanced, creation, in its present form, is more wisely and benevolently adapted to our constitution than if intuitive instruction had been showered on the mind at birth. By the actual arrangement, numerous noble faculties are bestowed; their objects are presented to them; these objects are naturally endowed with qualities fitted to benefit and delight us, when their uses and proper applications are discovered, and to injure and punish us for our ignorance, when their properties are misunderstood or misapplied; but we are left to find out all these qualities and relations by the exercise of the faculties themselves. In this manner, provision is made for ceaseless activity of the mental powers, and this constitutes the greatest delight. Wheat, for instance, is produced by the earth, and admirably adapted to the nutrition of the body; but it may be rendered more grateful to the organ of taste, more salubrious to the stomach, and more stimulating to the nervous and muscular systems, by being stripped of its external skin, ground into flour, and baked by fire into bread. Now, the Creator obviously pre-arranged all these relations, when he endowed wheat with its properties, and the human body with qualities and functions. In withholding congenial and intuitive knowledge of these qualities and mutual relations, but in bestowing faculties of individuality, form, colouring, weight, constructiveness, &c. fitted to find them out; in rendering the exercise of these faculties agreeable; and in leaving man, in this condition, to proceed for himself,—he appears to me to have conferred on him the highest boon. The earth produces also hemlock and fox-glove; and, by the organic law, those substances, if taken in certain moderate quantities, remove diseases; if in excess, they occasion death; but, again, man's observing faculties are fitted, when applied, under the guidance of cautiousness and reflection, to make this discovery: and he is left to make it in this way, or suffer the consequences of neglect.

Farther, water, when elevated in temperature, becomes steam; and steam expands with prodigious power; this power, confined by muscular energy, exerted on metal, and directed by intellect, is capable of being converted into the steam-engine, the most efficient, yet humble servant of man. All this was clearly pre-arranged by the Creator; and man's faculties were adapted to it: but still we see him left to observe and discover the qualities and relations of water for himself. This duty, however, must be acknowledged as benevolently imposed; the moment we discover that the Creator has made the very exercise of the faculties pleasurable, and arranged external qualities and relations so beneficially, that, when known, they carry a double reward in adding by their positive influence to human gratification.

The knowing faculties, as we have seen, observe the mere external qualities of bodies, and their simpler relations. The reflecting faculties observe relations also, but of a higher order. The former, for example, discover that the soil is clay or gravel; that it is tough or friable; that it is wet, and that excess of water impedes vegetation; that in one season the crop is large, and in the next deficient. The reflecting faculties take cognizance of the *causes* of these phenomena. They discover the *means* by which wet soil may be rendered dry; clay may be pulverised; light soil may be invigorated, and all of them made more productive; also the relationship of particular soils to particular kinds of grain. The inhabitants of a country who exert their knowing faculties in observing the qualities of their soil, their reflecting faculties in discovering its capabilities and relations to water, lime, manures, and the various species of grain, and who put forth their muscular and nervous energies in accordance with the dictates of these powers, receive a rich reward in a climate improved in salubrity, in an abundant supply of food, besides much positive enjoyment attending the exercise of the powers themselves. Those communities, on the other hand, who neglect to use their mental faculties, and muscular and nervous energies, are punished by ague, fever, rheumatism, and a variety of painful affections, arising from damp air; are stinted in food; and, in wet seasons, are brought to the very brink of starvation by total failure of their crops. This punishment is a benevolent admonition from the Creator, that they are neglecting a great duty, and omitting to enjoy a great pleasure; and it will cease as soon as they have fairly redeemed the blessings lost by their negligence, and obeyed the laws of their being.

The winds and waves appear, at first sight, to present insurmountable obstacles to man leaving the island or continent on which he happens to be born, and to his holding intercourse with his fellows in distant climes: But, by observing the relations of water to timber, he is able to construct a ship; by observing the influence of the wind on a physical body placed in a fluid medium, he discovers the use of sails; and, finally, by the application of his faculties, he has found out the expansive quality of steam, and traced its relations until he has produced a machine that enables him almost to set the roaring tempest at defiance, and to sail straight to the stormy north, although its loudest and its fiercest blasts oppose. In these instances we perceive external nature admirably adapted to support the mental faculties in habitual activity, and to reward us for the exercise of them.

It is objected to this argument, that it involves an inconsistency. Ignorance, it is said, of the natural laws is necessary to happiness, in order that the faculties may obtain exercise in discovering them;—nevertheless, happiness is impossible till these laws shall have been discovered and obeyed. Here, then, it is said, ignorance is represented as at once *essential* to, and *incompatible* with, enjoyment. The same objection, however, applies to the case of the bee. Gathering honey is necessary to its enjoyment; yet it cannot subsist and be happy till it has gathered honey, and therefore that act is both essential to, and incompatible with, its gratification. The fallacy lies in losing sight of the natural constitution, both of the bee and of man. While the bee possesses instinctive tendencies to roam about the fields and flowery meadows, and to exert its energies in labour, it is obviously beneficial to it to be furnished with motives and opportunities for doing so; and so it is with man to obtain scope for his bodily and mental powers. Now, gathering knowledge is to the mind of man what gathering honey is to the bee. Apparently with the view of effectually prompting the bee to seek this pleasure, honey is made essential to its subsistence. In like manner, and probably with a similar design, knowledge is made indispensable to human enjoyment. Communicating intuitive knowledge of the natural laws to man, *while his present constitution continues*, would be the exact parallel of gorging the bee with honey in midsummer, when its energies are at their height. When the bee has completed its store, winter benumbs its powers, which resume their vigour only when its stock is exhausted, and spring returns to afford them scope. No torpor resembling that of winter seals up the faculties of the human race; but their ceaseless activity is amply provided for. 1st, The laws of nature, compared with the mind of any individual, are of boundless extent, so that every one may learn something new to the end of the longest life. 2dly, By the actual constitution of man, he must make use of his acquirements habitually, otherwise he will lose them. 3dly, Every individual of the race is born in utter ignorance, and starts from Zero in the scale of knowledge, so that he has the laws to learn for himself.

These circumstances remove the apparent inconsistency. If man had possessed intuitive knowledge of all nature, he could have no scope for exerting his faculties in acquiring knowledge, in preserving it, or in communicating it. The infant would have been as wise as the most reverend sage, and forgetfulness would have been necessarily excluded.

Those who object to these views, imagine that after the human race has acquired knowledge of all the natural laws, if such a result be possible, they *will be in the same condition as if they had been created with intuitive knowledge*; but this does not follow. Although the race should acquire the knowledge supposed, it is not an inevitable consequence that *each individual* will necessarily enjoy it all: which, however, would follow from intuition. The entire soil of Britain belongs to the landed proprietors as a class; but each does not possess it *all*; and hence every one has scope for adding to his territories; with this advantage, however, in favour of knowledge, that the acquisitions of one do not impoverish another. Farther, although the race should have learned all the natural laws, their children would not intuitively inherit their ideas, and hence the activity of every one, as he appears on the stage, would be provided for; whereas, by intuition, every child would be as wise as his grandfather, and parental protection, filial piety, and all the delights that spring from difference in knowledge between youth and age, would be excluded. 1st, *Using* of acquirements is, by the actual state of man, essential to the preservation as well as the enjoyment of them. By intuition all knowledge would be habitually present to the mind without effort or consideration. On the whole, therefore, it appears that man's nature being what it is, the arrangement by which he is endowed with powers to acquire knowledge, but left to find it out for himself, is both wise and benevolent.

It has been asked, " But is there no pleasure in science but that of discovery? Is there none in using the knowledge we have attained? Is there no pleasure in playing at chess after we know the moves?" In answer, I observe, that if we know beforehand all the moves that our antagonist intends to make, and all our own, which must be the case if we know *every thing* by intuition, we shall have no pleasure. The pleasure really consists in discovering the intentions of our antagonist, and in calculating the effects of our own play; a certain degree of ignorance of both of which is indispensable to gratification. In the like manner, it is agreeable first to discover the natural laws, and then to study " the moves" that we ought to make, in consequence of knowing them. So much, then, for the *sources* of human happiness.

In the *second* place, To reap enjoyment in the *greatest quantity*, and to maintain it *most permanently*, the faculties must be gratified *harmoniously*: In other words, if, among the various powers, the *supremacy* belongs to the moral sentiments, then the aim of our habitual conduct must be the attainment of objects suited to gratify them. For example, in pursuing wealth or fame as the leading objects of existence, full gratification is not afforded to Benevolence, Veneration, and Conscientiousness, and, consequently, complete satisfaction cannot be enjoyed; whereas, by seeking knowledge, and dedicating life to the welfare of mankind, and obedience to God, in our several vocations, these faculties will be gratified, and wealth, fame, health, and other advantages, will flow in their train, so that the whole mind will rejoice, and its delights will remain permanent as long as the conduct continues to be in accordance with the supremacy of the moral powers, and laws of external creation.

Thirdly, To place human happiness on a secure basis, the laws of external creation themselves must accord with the dictates of the moral sentiments, and intellect must be fitted to discover the nature and relations of both, and to direct the conduct in coincidence with them.

Much has been written about the extent of human ignorance; but we should discriminate between absolute incapacity to know, and mere want of information, arising from not having used this capacity to its full extent. In regard to the first, or our capacity to know, it appears probable that, in this world, we shall never know the essence, beginning, or end of things; because these are points which we have no faculties calculated to reach. But the same Creator who made the external world constituted our faculties; and if we have sufficient data for inferring that His intention is, that we shall enjoy existence here while preparing for the ulterior ends of our being; and if it be true that we can be happy here only by becoming acquainted with the qualities and modes of action of our own minds and bodies, with the qualities and modes of action of external objects, and with the relations established between them; in short, by becoming thoroughly conversant with those natural laws, which, when observed, are pre-arranged to contribute to our enjoyment, and which, when violated, visit us with suffering, we may safely conclude that our mental capacities are wisely adapted to the attainment of these objects, whenever we shall do our own duty in bringing them to their highest condition of perfection, and in applying them in the best manner.

If we advert for a moment to what we already know, we shall see that this conclusion is supported by high probabilities. Before the mariner's compass and astronomy were discovered, nothing would seem more utterly beyond the reach of the human faculties than traversing the enormous Atlantic or Pacific Oceans; but the moment these discoveries were made, how simple did this feat appear, and how completely within the scope of human ability! But it became so, not by any addition to man's mental capacities, nor by any change in the physical world; but by the easy process of applying individuality, and the other knowing faculties, to observe, causality to reflect, and constructiveness to build; in short, to perform their natural functions. Who that, forty years ago, regarded the small-pox as a scourge, devastating Europe, Asia, Africa, and America, would not have despaired of the human faculties ever discovering an antidote against it? and yet we have lived to see this end accomplished by the simple exercise of Individuality and Reflection, in observing the effects of, and applying, vaccine inoculation. Nothing appears more completely beyond the reach of the human intellect, than the cause of volcanoes and earthquakes; and yet some approach towards its discovery has recently been made.*

Sir Isaac Newton observed, that all bodies which refracted the rays of light were combustible, except one, the diamond, which he found to possess this quality, but which he was not able, by any powers he possessed, to burn. He did not conclude, however, from this, that the diamond was an exception to the uniformity of nature. He inferred, that, as the same Creator made the refracting bodies which he was able to consume, and the diamond, and proceeded by uniform laws, the diamond, would, in all probability, be found to be combustible, and that the reason of its resisting his power, was ignorance on his part of the proper way to produce its conflagration. A century afterwards, chemists made the diamond blaze with as much vivacity as Sir Isaac Newton had done a wax-candle. Let us proceed, then, on an analogous principle. If the intention of our Creator was, that we should enjoy existence while in this world, then He knew what was necessary to enable us to do so; and He will not be found to have failed in conferring on us powers fitted to accomplish His design, provided we do our duty in developing and applying them. The great motive to exertion is the conviction, that increased knowledge will furnish us with increased means of doing good,—with new proofs of benevolence and wisdom in the Great Architect of the Universe.

The human race may be regarded as only in the beginning of its existence. The art of printing is an invention comparatively but of yesterday, and no imagination can yet conceive the effects which it is destined to produce. Phrenology was wanting to give it full efficacy, especially in *moral science*, in which little progress has been made for centuries. Now that this desideratum is supplied, may we not hope that the march of improvement will proceed in a rapidly accelerating ratio?

* *Vide* Cordier, in Edin. New Phil. Journ. No. VIII. page 273.

The following striking lines form the epitaph of a miller in Richmond churchyard. They are traditionally said to have been dreamed by him the night preceding his death:—

Earth walks upon earth, glittering like gold,
Earth turns to earth, sooner than it would,
Earth builds upon earth, cities and towers;
Earth says to earth, all this shall be ours.

COBBETTIANA.

COBBETT'S RECOLLECTIONS.

Forty years ago the education-classes took to the affairs of the nation. We had then a revenue of L.13,000,000 a-year; and I am sure that we do not need more than that to carry on affairs in a time of peace. We had then been at peace about eight years; now we have been so eighteen years, and during all that time, twice every year, either the king or the prince regent has told us there was no prospect of war; and yet we have a standing army of 100,000 men, which, with the dead-weight and all, annually costs more than all the costs of the government at the last peace. Gentlemen, that is one part of the management of this country by the education-classes. Here is another:—During the last forty years they have had our purses at their command; and what with the income-tax, the property-tax, the window-tax, the soap-tax, the malt-tax, the hop-tax, and other taxes almost innumerable, they have taken from us whatever, and as much as they pleased. We are like a parcel of bees; they have left us the hive and the combs, and just honey enough to live through the winter, so that we might work again through the summer and produce just so much more for them. And then they have done what they pleased with our persons—at one time they put red coats upon us, and then they put blue; and they gave us pigtails, and then cut them off; then they put spurs upon us, and ordered mustaches to grow, which they afterwards had shaved off; and then they gave us whiskers, and now they are shaved off. In fact, they have done what they liked with our very souls. And in what condition are we at last? About thirty years ago they changed the currency, which for twelve hundred years had been gold and silver; every man knew the real value of money then, and there was no doubt about it. A man knew that one pound or one shilling was one pound or one shilling; but the education-gentlemen changed it into paper, which they made a legal tender. These wise men, these education-men, have passed no less than sixteen acts to regulate the currency, which before was fixed as the sun or the moon, or as the earth itself. In 1819 they passed an act, which they said was to be *the last*; the vote was unanimous, and they all shouted and huzzaed, because they said they had set the matter at rest for ever. Three years after they changed it again, and in two years and a-half they made another change; and even now they don't know what to do, and actually at this moment, they have a committee sitting upon the question. Some talk of a contraction, and some of an extension of the paper system. The House of Commons consists of 658 of the education of the country. Of these, 31, selected for their double-distilled wisdom, have been sitting for two months to inquire what can be done with the currency. They are like an old turkey hen sitting on addled eggs. They dare not hatch, and they dare not come off their eggs, and so there they sit, but can't hatch.

COBBETT OF HIMSELF.

I am satisfied in my own mind that the regeneration of the political state of the country would not take place, and that instead of regeneration, anarchy and confusion would come, were I not to be in the first reformed Parliament; there being no man in whom the people have that confidence in his judgment that they have in mine, in the proportion of a thousand to one in my favour; that is to say, that there are a thousand men who have great confidence in my judgment, where there is one man who has the same confidence in any body else. I am not pretending that I *possess* this superiority of judgment to this degree, or in any degree at all. In a case like this, your capacity to do good depends almost entirely in the belief of your having that capacity. I have named no man as fit to be a member of Parliament, who has not great capacity of that kind; and I could name others nearer to myself; but here is the singular thing belonging to me,-that I am *known*, more or less, to every rational creature in the kingdom; my enemies are the trumpeters of my talents. All men know that I want nothing for myself or for any body belonging to me. All men are well acquainted with my wonderful capacity to labour, and the still more wonderful extent and variety of my knowledge; and there is this further singularity, which, I believe, was never before the lot of man, that, somehow or other, by means of my travelling all over England, by the means of those prosecutions which I have had to undergo—and which I have undergone with such signal fortitude—by one means or other, it has become written down upon the heart of every working man in England and Scotland, and Ireland too, that I am his sincere, zealous, kind, and compassionate friend. A long undeviating course, a course of thirty-two long years, unbroken by one moment of relaxation in my efforts in behalf of the working-people, has produced this belief, which it is no more possible to root from the minds of the people, than it is possible to root out natural affection from their hearts.

THE IRISH POTATOE.

Next to really good poetry, the execrably bad is to us the most acceptable; and the following piece comes quite *down* to our standard. The author is an Irish gentleman of county Antrim. By an extraordinary anachronism, the verses are said to have been composed while Mr. Cobbett was a corporal in the English militia, and subsequent to his attacks on the potatoes, in his *Register*:—

There's not in the wide world a race that can beat us,
From Canada's cold hills to sultry Japan,
While we fatten and feast on the smiling potatoes,
Of Erin's green valleys, so friendly to man.
It's not an abundance alone, and a plenty,
Of plain simple fare the potatoe supplies,
But milk, beef, and butter, and bacon so dainty;
Hens, ducks, geese, and turkeys, and fine mutton pies.*
  Sweet roots of Erin, we can't live without them;
  No tongue can express their importance to man;
  Poor Corporal Cobbett knows nothing about them—
  We'll boil them and eat them, as long as we can.

On the skirts of our bogs that are covered with rushes,
On the dales that we till with the sweat of our brow,
On the wild mountain's side, cleared of rocks, heath, and bushes,
We plant the kind root with the spade or the plough.
Then comes the south breezes, with soft vernal showers,
To finish the process that man had begun,
With a brilliant succession of sweet-smelling flowers,
Reflecting bright radiance in the rays of the sun.
  Sweet roots of Erin, &c.

The land, too, that's broke, and bro't in by potatoes,
Produces the cream of our northern cheer,
In crops of rich barley, that comfort and cheer us,
With Innishown whisky, and Maghera beer.
Success to the brave boys that plant them and raise them,
To cherish their children, and nourish their wives;
May none of the Corporal's humours e'er seize them,—
To shorten their days or embitter their lives.
  Sweet roots of Erin, we can't live without them;
  No tongue can express their importance to man;
  Poor Corporal Cobbett knows nothing about them—
  We'll boil them and eat them, as long as we can.

* If the poet can assure Mr. Cobbett of this new fact, we could almost undertake that he will give up his hostility to the root of Erin. One day at dinner, in Edinburgh, a gentleman, who helped Mr. Cobbett to a quantity of mashed potatoes to his mutton, smiled as he did so; when Cobbett exclaimed, "That's another of their calumnies—I never said a word against potatoes when there is meat along with them."

Epitaph in French-English for Shenstone, erected at Ermenonville.

    This plainstone
      To William Shenstone.
    In his writings he displayed
      A mind natural;
    At Leasowes he laid
      Arcadian's Greens rural.

This absurdity is reprinted in the *Schoolmaster*, because we see it ascribed to Rousseau. The author was M. Girardin.

THE STORY-TELLER.

WHY do we never give a story told by the most graceful, and, to use a lady's word, *fascinating* of all living story-tellers—Mr. Washington Irving? We shall do so soon; but, prelusive to *The Rose of the Alhambra*, who must tarry one more week, we must give the author's charming description of the scene of his late tales, his

RESIDENCE IN THE ALHAMBRA.

IT is time, he says, that I give some idea of my domestic arrangements in this singular residence. The Royal Palace of the Alhambra is intrusted to the care of a good old maiden dame, called Dona Antonia Molina; but who, according to Spanish custom, goes by the more neighbourly appellation of Tia Antonia (Aunt Antonia.) She maintains the Moorish halls and gardens in order, and shews them to strangers; in consideration of which she is allowed all the perquisites received from visitors, and all the produce of the gardens, excepting, that she is expected to pay an occasional tribute of fruits and flowers to the Governor. Her residence is in a corner of the palace; and her family consists of a nephew and niece, the children of two different brothers. The nephew, Manuel Molina, is a young man of sterling worth, and Spanish gravity. He has served in the armies both in Spain and the West Indies; but is now studying medicine, in hopes of one day or other becoming physician to the fortress, a post worth at least a hundred and forty dollars a-year. As to the niece, she is a plump little black-eyed Andalusian damsel, named Dolores; but who, from her bright looks and cheerful disposition, merits a merrier name. She is the declared heiress of all her aunt's possessions, consisting of certain ruinous tenements in the fortress, yielding a revenue of about one hundred and fifty dollars. I had not been long in the Alhambra, before I discovered that a quiet courtship was going on between the discreet Manuel and his bright-eyed cousin, and that nothing was wanting to enable them to join their hands and expectations, but that he should receive his doctor's diploma, and purchase a dispensation from the Pope, on account of their consanguinity.

With the good dame Antonia I have made a treaty, according to which, she furnishes me with board and lodging; while the merry-hearted little Dolores keeps my apartment in order, and officiates as handmaid at meal-times. I have also at my command a tall, stuttering, yellow-haired lad, named Pepe, who works in the gardens, and would fain have acted as valet; but, in this, he was forestalled by Mateo Ximenes, " the son of the Alhambra!" This alert and officious wight has managed, somehow or other, to stick by me ever since I first encountered him at the outer gate of the fortress, and to weave himself into all my plans, until he has fairly appointed and installed himself my valet, cicerone, guide, guard, and historiographic squire; and I have been obliged to improve the state of his wardrobe, that he may not disgrace his various functions; so that he has cast his old brown mantle, as a snake does his skin, and now appears about the fortress with a smart Andalusian hat and jacket, to his infinite satisfaction, and the great astonishment of his comrades. The chief fault of honest Mateo is an over anxiety to be useful. Conscious of having foisted himself into my employ, and that my simple and quiet habits render his situation a sinecure, he is at his wit's end to devise modes of making himself important to my welfare. I am, in a manner, the victim of his officiousness; I cannot put my foot over the threshold of the palace, to stroll about the fortress, but he is at my elbow, to explain every thing I see; and if I venture to ramble among the surrounding hills, he insists upon attending me as a guard, though I vehemently suspect he would be more apt to trust to the length of his legs than the strength of his arms, in case of an attack. After all, however, the poor fellow is at times an amusing companion; he is simple-minded, and of infinite good-humour, with the loquacity and gossip of a village barber, and knows all the small-talk of the place and its environs; but what he chiefly values himself on, is his stock of local information, having the most marvellous stories to relate of every tower, and vault, and gateway of the fortress, in all of which he places the most implicit faith.

Most of these he has derived, according to his own account, from his grandfather, a little legendary tailor, who lived to the age of nearly a hundred years, during which he made but two migrations beyond the precincts of the fortress. His shop, for the greater part of a century, was the resort of a knot of venerable gossips, where they would pass half the night talking about old times, and the wonderful events and hidden secrets of the place. The whole living, moving, thinking, and acting of this historical little tailor, had thus been bounded by the walls of the Alhambra; within them he had been born, within them he lived, breathed, and had his being; within them he died, and was buried. Fortunately for posterity, his traditionary lore died not with him. The authentic Mateo, when an urchin, used to be an attentive listener to the narratives of his grandfather, and of the gossiping group assembled round the shop-board; and is thus possessed of a stock of valuable knowledge concerning the Alhambra, not to be found in the books, and well worthy the attention of every curious traveller.

Such are the personages that contribute to my domestic comforts in the Alhambra; and I question whether any of the potentates, Moslem or Christian, who have preceded me in the palace, have been waited upon with greater fidelity, or enjoyed a serener sway.

When I rise in the morning, Pepe, the stuttering lad from the gardens, brings me a tribute of fresh-culled flowers, which are afterwards arranged in vases, by the skilful hand of Dolores, who takes a female pride in the decorations of my chamber. My meals are made wherever caprice dictates; sometimes in one of the Moorish halls, sometimes under the arcades of the Court of Lions, surrounded by flowers and fountains; and when I walk out, I am conducted by the assiduous Mateo, to the most romantic retreats of the mountains, and delicious haunts of the adjacent valleys, not one of which but is the scene of some wonderful tale.

Though fond of passing the greater part of my day alone, yet I occasionally repair in the evenings to the little domestic circle of Dona Antonia. This is generally held in an old Moorish chamber, that serves for kitchen as well as hall, a rude fire-place having been made in one corner, the smoke from which has discoloured the walls, and almost obliterated the ancient arabesques. A window, with a balcony overhanging the valley of the Douro, lets in the cool evening breeze; and here I take my frugal supper of fruit and milk, and mingle with the conversation of the family. There is a natural talent of mother wit, as it is called, about the Spaniards, which renders them intellectual and agreeable companions, whatever may be their condition in life, or however imperfect may have been their education; add to this, they are never vulgar; nature has endowed them with an inherent dignity of spirit. The good Tia Antonia is a woman of strong and intelligent, though uncultivated mind; and the bright-eyed Dolores, though she has read but three or four books in the whole course of her life, has an engaging mixture of *naiveté* and good sense, and often surprises me by the pungency of her artless sallies. Sometimes the nephew entertains us by reading some old comedy of Calderon or Lope de Vega, to which he is evidently prompted by a desire to improve, as well as amuse, his cousin Dolores; though, to his great mortification, the little damsel generally falls asleep before the first act is completed. Sometimes Tia Antonia has a little levee of humble friends and dependents, the inhabitants of the adjacent hamlets, or the wives of the invalid soldiers. These look up to her with great deference, as the custodian of the palace, and pay their court to her by bringing the news of the place, or the rumours that may have struggled up from

Granada. In listening to these evening gossipings I have picked up many curious facts, illustrative of the manners of the people and the peculiarities of the neighbourhood. These are simple details of simple pleasures; it is the nature of the place alone that gives them interest and importance. I tread haunted ground, and am surrounded by romantic associations. From earliest boyhood, when, on the banks of the Hudson, I first pored over the pages of an old Spanish story about the wars of Granada, that city has ever been a subject of my waking dreams; and often have I trod in fancy the romantic halls of the Alhambra. Behold for once a day-dream realized; yet I can scarcely credit my senses, or believe that I do indeed inhabit the palace of Boabdil, and look down from its balconies upon chivalric Granada. As I loiter through these Oriental chambers, and hear the murmur of fountains and the song of the nightingale; as I inhale the odour of the rose, and feel the influence of the balmy climate, I am almost tempted to fancy myself in the paradise of Mahomet, and that the plump little Dolores is one of the bright-eyed houris, destined to administer to the happiness of true believers.

BRIEF NOTICE OF OUR LATE ROYAL NEIGHBOUR, CHARLES X.

THIS ill-advised and misguided Prince was born the 9th October, 1757; he was the youngest of the three brothers, who have successively sat upon the throne of France, (with the short interruption of the nominal reign of Louis XVII.) namely, Louis XVI., Monsieur, afterwards Louis XVIII., and the subject of the present article, who was styled the Comte d'Artois, and continued to be so called in general, up to the period of the restoration of the Bourbons, and the enthronement of Louis XVIII., when, according to the formal and ancient usage of the French Court, he was styled Monsieur, being then the next brother of the reigning monarch.

The Comte d'Artois was married on the 17th November, 1773, to the Princess Maria Theresa, daughter of Victor Amadeus, third king of Sardinia, and sister to the consort of Louis XVIII., at which period he was only in the 17th year of his age. By this Princess, who died at Gratz, in Hungary, the 2d June, 1805, he had two children—Louis Antoine, Duc d'Angouleme, born the 6th of August, 1775, who, on his father's accession to the throne, became Dauphin of France, and who married Maria Theresa Charlotte, his first cousin, the only daughter and only surviving child of Louis XVI., but by whom he has no issue; and Henry Charles, Duc de Berri, who married in 1818, Maria Caroline, daughter of Francis I., late King of the two Sicilies, by whom he had two children, viz. Maria Theresa Louisa, (called Mademoiselle,) born 28th September, 1819, and Henry Charles Dieudonne Artois, Duc de Bourdeaux, (a posthumous Prince,) born the 29th September, 1820. The Duc de Berri was mortally wounded by an assassin, in Paris, on the 14th of February, 1820, and died the following morning.

The Comte d'Artois was never favourably spoken of with reference to his domestic relations. On the contrary, he acquired a character for dissipation and extravagance, which rendered him highly unpopular, especially when contrasted with the conduct of Louis XVI. and of Monsieur; for though the unfortunate monarch just mentioned fell a victim to revolutionary fury, his character, as a man, was not only untainted, but was highly estimable. Monsieur, also, (afterwards Louis XVIII.,) though somewhat luxuriously inclined, had conducted himself in a way which secured to him considerable public respect, whilst the ease and affability of his manners contributed to render him highly popular. He was enabled, in consequence, to brave the first storm of the revolution, and it was only when its demagogues hurled their insane fury against the very name of royalty, that he took refuge in flight. The amenity of his manners, and the prudence with which he at times yielded to popular opinion, subsequently served to sustain him firmly upon the throne, till his final summons from this terrestrial scene; and that conduct materially contributed to show by contrast the weakness and folly of his successor, in not adopting the same course of expediency; and still more in setting himself in opposition to the public feeling.

He was the more called upon in prudence to endeavour to conciliate the people, the Comte d'Artois never having been, as just observed, at all popular; a fact of which he must, of course, have been well aware, as he found it necessary, for his own personal safety, to quit France at the outset of the Revolution; and when he subsequently returned he must also have known that he was mainly indebted to his brother, and then Sovereign, for any share of public approbation. The Comte d'Artois, when compelled to quit France, visited the court of his father-in law, the King of Sardinia, at Turin, and subsequently other parts of Europe, but at length sought an asylum in England, where he resided for a considerable period. Becoming deeply involved in pecuniary embarrassments, and some of his creditors being very clamorous and urgent, it was found necessary to assign him, as it were, a refuge; and Holyrood House, Edinburgh, being a privileged place, where the stern ministers of the law could not enter for the purpose of enforcing pecuniary claims, it was fixed upon by the British Government as a residence for the Comte, and some of his family, as he might be there enabled to live without molestation.

In this respect also the characters of the two surviving brothers were strongly contrasted—Louis XVIII. contrived to live at Hartwell, in Buckinghamshire, without being subject to any of the inconveniences just alluded to, and maintaining a character which was always considered highly respectable, whilst his personal conduct conciliated the esteem of all those who approached him, or in any way came in contact with him. The Comte d'Artois, on the other hand, was by no means liked; there was a hauteur in his manner which was not at all pleasing, or calculated to insure him respect or esteem; and his careless and improvident habits, especially situated as he then was, were very ill adapted to raise his character. There was much sympathy in England for Louis XVIII. when residing here; but little or none for his brother, the object of the present article.

The early habits of the Comte d'Artois were very decidedly at variance with that fervour of religion, or rather of *devoteeism* (if such a word may be used) that seems to have seized him in advanced life, and which has been even more injurious to him than his former conduct, *though both decidedly showing the weakness of his mind, or that total want of prudence that unites disregard of expediency, which is an evidence of a deficiency in wisdom, more especially in individuals of high station. For the follies of youth, there is of course an excuse; but for those of age, in the teeth of experience, there is none, except one can be found in imbecility or perverseness of mind.*

It was reserved for the Comte d'Artois, who, previously to the Revolution, (we, of course, mean the old Revolution,) incurred great public odium, by setting himself against the popular feeling, and who mainly contributed, by his conduct, to excite a feeling of dislike towards his whole family, to profit nothing by upwards of forty years' experience, and to pursue a precisely similar course (as to effect,) after being himself, in the order of succession, called to the throne, thereby rendering the French nation so decidedly hostile to his family that they are doomed to another exile, never to return.

The residence of the Comte d'Artois in England, of course, affords but very scanty materials for biography, as there was little or no variety, nor any event of importance to describe. His forced sojourn at Holyrood House was, of necessity, rather monotonous; but, some arrangement having been effected with his creditors, he was subsequently enabled to live at Hartwell, with his brother, Louis XVIII. But here there was very little difference between one day and another, except what was afforded by an occasional journey to London, or to other quarters, and these very rarely. They lived pretty much a retired life, nor could it be otherwise; and indeed, for a considerable period, their prospect with reference to restoration, seemed so shrouded in gloom, that they might have almost calculated upon passing the remainder of their lives in this country.

One of the incidents, however, that occurred, whilst here, the Comte d'Artois, deserves to be recorded, namely, the loss by death of a favourite mistress, as it is said to have altered the frame of his mind, and to have brought on that sort of gloomy moroseness which marked some parts of his subsequent conduct. We can scarcely persuade ourselves of the truth of this statement, it being by no means unfrequent for a weak mind to swerve from one extreme to another—from gaiety, and recklessness, and frivolity, to gloom, and melancholy, and a feeling bordering on despair; but even supposing it to be true, it is only an additional proof of the want of strength of mind, and the absence of that intellectual stamina which befits an individual of high station. It is not the possession of great talents, or splendid attainments, which is requisite, but merely that good sense which enables a personage so situated to do what is right, and proper, and expedient, and thus to secure himself a high place in popular opinion. It was in this respect that the Comte d'Artois, in whatever station, was lamentably deficient, and not possessed of, or contemptuously spurning, that tact of which his brother Louis XVIII. so successfully availed himself. He lost a throne which common prudence might have enabled him to retain and secure for his family.

When the conqueror of great part of Continental Europe was himself in turn conquered, and the pleasing sound of restoration reached the ears of the Bourbons, no time was lost by them in setting out for the promised land, and our late Monarch, then Prince Regent, was foremost on the beach at Dover in loudly cheering Louis XVIII. on his departure for France to take possession of the throne of his ancestors. This restoration took place in 1814.

The Comte d'Artois, then called Monsieur, accompanied his brother, and, of course, as the heir presumptive to the throne, became a personage of high importance; but though exalted at Court, he was by no means popular in the city, or in the country.

Again driven, for a time, from the throne, Louis XVIII. and his family were obliged to take refuge at Lille, in consequence of the return of Bonaparte from Elba. But the latter being compelled to abdicate, in consequence of the splendid victory obtained over him by the Duke of Wellington, at Waterloo, on the 18th of June, 1815, the Bourbons were again restored. Louis XVIII. remained in quiet possession of the throne till his death, on the 16th of September, 1824. He had hoped that the birth of a male heir, in the person of the Prince who was subsequently styled Duc de Bourdeaux, and who received the name of Henry, so popular in France, would have secured the succession in the family of his brother; and there certainly seemed every probability of it; but the extreme folly of that brother was destined to mar the prospect, though he was himself still more deeply interested in securing the succession to his own immediate descendants, than his deceased relative.

In the conduct of the Comte d'Artois, or Monsieur, subsequent to the second restoration, whilst he was the heir presumptive, there was nothing particularly striking or remarkable; but he never enjoyed any popularity at all approaching to that which was conceded to his brother, his sentiments being known too much to approximate to the exploded dogmas of the old regimé, and his manners and deportment, though polite and courteous, betraying evidence of great constraint, and evincing that he was more playing a character which he had assumed, than speaking or acting from the bottom of his heart. Whatever might have been the real sentiments of Louis XVIII. he so effectually disguised them (if they were at all hostile to the existing order of things,) that the people placed confidence in him; but in his brother they never trusted: on the contrary, they always suspected him of being hostile to the new institutions, and their suspicions being confirmed by his ordonnances, they rose as it were en masse, and drove him from the throne. There is little doubt that the Duke of Orleans, (now Louis Philippe I.) had been looked to as the eventual occupant of the throne, in case of the arbitrary conduct of Charles bringing on a crisis; and this may serve to account for the speed and the rapidity with which the new Revolution was effected, its progress and termination having been calculated upon and arranged.

Monsieur, the Comte d'Artois, succeeded his brother as King of France, by the title of Charles X., and made his public entry into Paris on the 27th of September, 1824. Had he then formed a resolution to be in reality a constitutional sovereign, and adhered to it permanently, the greetings of the people with which he was then hailed might have lasted during his life, and all might have been well; but his devotion to priestly influence got the better of whatever sense he had, and thus was gradually brought on the catastrophe. Had he, indeed, at any time, from the period of his accession, to Wednesday the 27th of July when his *ordonnances* were in their effect deluging Paris with blood, shown a *bona fide* intention of governing according to the Charter, and in unison with the principles of rational freedom, he might have preserved the crown upon his head; for even on the day alluded to, had he shown himself, and revoked the fatal *ordonnances*, there is every reason to believe that tranquillity would have been restored, and his reign continued.

But here was evinced the real weakness of his mind.— He had resolved to possess absolute power without having the talent to command the means; and, failing in his attempt, Charles and the crown of France were for ever severed. It would be useless to recount the acts of the short reign of Charles X. (not quite six years), or the measures of his government; matter of recent history, they are subjects of public notoriety. He had to contend with a considerable party hostile to his rule and to his house, but instead of adopting measures of a soothing and conciliatory nature, his conduct was so irritating and exasperating that he alienated many of his friends, and at last converted into enemies very nearly the whole French nation; whilst as his real power decreased he fancied it had become considerably augmented, and thus he became the dupe and the victim of his own delusion.

When his constitutional rule was at an end, and when all that remained—the power of mere physical force—was at its last gasp, he imagined it was great enough to overawe France, and only awoke from his dream when he found himself a fugitive, condemned to hopeless exile.

He had played a desperate game, in which common prudence might have whispered him, that he had every thing to lose, and nothing to gain. He had set his all upon the hazard of a die, without even the chance of a cast in his favour; and when, acting probably under the instigation of evil counsellors, he had thus provoked civil war, and dyed the earth with the blood of the French people, he then, in keeping, as it were, with the terrific sketch he had pourtrayed, endeavoured, as a last resource, to throw the apple of discord among the French people, to prolong civil war, and to cause a prodigal expenditure of the blood of his late subjects, as he seems vainly to have imagined, by abdicating in favour of his grandson, the Duc de Bourdeaux. But his purpose was seen through, and the *ruse* failed. Had he been content with his power as a constitutional king, he might have transmitted it to his grandson in a constitutional manner; but he had himself, like our James II., broken the link of legitimate succession; and, like the convention Parliament of England, the representatives of the French nation determined to fill the vacant throne, without delay, (and delay would have been highly dangerous,) with a Prince of their choice, of the late reigning house.

At the age of 73, Charles X. might have thought himself too old to go upon his travels; and had he only uttered a few words to the purpose, or issued a few short sentences to a similar effect, he might have saved himself the humiliation of a compulsory banishment. It was once said of James II., when in exile in France, and that, too, by an ecclesiastic, " There goes a pious gentleman, who gave up three kingdoms for a mass ;" and something similar may be said of Charles X. Had he attended more to the sound advices of patriotic statesmen, and less to the insidious suggestions of crafty and designing priests, he might still have been King of France.

SOCIAL LIFE IN GLASGOW.
BY JOHN GIBSON LOCKHART, ESQ.

MANY of our readers must have just seen COBBETT'S account of Edinburgh and Glasgow, which stares us in the face in every newspaper, so frequently and familiarly, that we forbear to repeat much of him. Mr. Lockhart's picture of his native city is now comparatively rare, and it was always racy:—

"Mr. ——— asked me to dine with him next day, and appointed me to meet him at the coffeeroom or Exchange, exactly at a quarter before 5 o'clock, from which place he said he would himself conduct me to his residence. My rendezvous is a very large, ill-shaped, low-roofed room, surrounded on all sides with green cane chairs, small tables, and newspapers, and opening by glass folding-doors, upon a paved piazza of some extent. This piazza is, in fact the Exchange, but the business is done in the adjoining room, where all the merchants are to be seen at certain hours of the day, pacing up and down with more or less importance in their strut, according to the situation of their affairs, or the nature of the bargains of the day. I have seldom seen a more amusing medley. Although I had travelled only forty miles from Edinburgh, I could with difficulty persuade myself that I was still in the same kingdom. Such roaring! such cursing! such peals of discord! such laughter! such grotesque attitudes! such arrogance! such vulgar disregard of all courtesy to a stranger! Here was to be seen the counting-house *blood*, dressed in box-coat, Belcher handkerchief, and top-boots, or leather gaiters—discoursing (*Œdepol!*) about brown sugar and genseng! Here was to be seen the counting-house *dandy*, with whalebone stays, stiff neckcloth, surtout, Cossacks, a spur on his heel, a gold-headed cane on his wrist, and a Kent on his head—mincing primly to his brother dandy some question about pullicate handkerchiefs. Here was to be seen the counting-house *bear*, with a grin, and a voice like a glass-blower. Here, above all, was to be seen the Glasgow *litterateur*, striding in his corner, with a pale face and an air of exquisite abstraction, meditating, no doubt, some high paragraph for the *Chronicle*, or perchance, some pamphlet against Dr. Chalmers! Here, in a word, were to be seen abundant varieties of folly and presumption—abundant airs of plebianism—I was now in the coffeeroom of Glasgow.

"My friend soon joined me, and observing, from the appearance of my countenance, that I was contemplating the scene with some disgust, 'My good fellow,' said he, 'you are just like every other well-educated stranger that comes into this town, you cannot endure the first sight of us mercantile whelps. Do not, however, be alarmed; I will not introduce you to any of these cattle at dinner. No, sir, you must know that there *are* a few men of refinement and polite information in this city. I have *warned* two or three of these *raræ aves*, and depend upon it, you shall have a very snug *day's work*. So saying, he took my arm, and observing that five was *just on the chap*, hurried me through several streets and lanes till we arrived in the ———, where his house is situated. His wife was, I perceived, quite the fine lady, and withal a little of the blue-stocking. Hearing that I had just come from Edinburgh, she remarked that Glasgow would certainly be seen to much disadvantage after that elegant city. 'Indeed,' said she, 'a person of taste must of course find many disagreeables connected with a residence in such a town as this; but Mr. ———'s business renders the thing necessary for the present, and one cannot make a silk purse of a sow's ear—he, he, he!' Another lady of the company carried this affectation still further. She pretended to be quite ignorant of Glasgow and its inhabitants, although she had lived among them the greater part of her life—and, by the by, she seemed to be no chicken. I was afterwards told by my friend, the major, that this damsel had in reality sojourned a winter or two at Edinburgh, in the capacity of *flok-spittle*, or *toad-eater*, to a lady of quality, to whom she had rendered herself amusing by a malicious tongue; and that during this short absence she had embraced the opportunity of utterly forgetting every thing about the west country. But there would be no end of it were I to tell you all, &c.

"The dinner was excellent, although calculated apparently for forty people rather than for sixteen, which last number sat down. Capital salmon, and trout, almost as rich as salmon, from one of the lochs—prime mutton from Argyleshire, very small and sweet, and indeed ten times better than half the venison we see in London—veal not superior—beef of the very first order—some excellent fowls in curry—every thing washed down by delicious old West India Madeira, which went like *elixir vitæ* into the recesses of my stomach, somewhat ruffled in consequence of my riotous living at Edinburgh. A single bottle of hock, and another of white hermitage, went round, but I saw plainly that the greater part of the company took them for perry or cider. After dinner, we had two or three bottles of port, which the landlord recommended as being *real stuff*. Abundance of the same Madeira, but, to my sorrow, no claret—the only wine I ever care for more than half-a-dozen glasses of. While the ladies remained in the room there was such a noise and racket of coarse mirth, ill restrained by a few airs of sickly sentiment on the part of the hostess, that I really could not attend to the wine or the dessert; but after a little time, a very broad hint from a fat Falstaff, near the foot of the table, apparently quite a privileged character, thank Heaven! set the ladies out of the room. The moment after which blessed consummation, the butler and footman entered as if by instinct, the one with a huge punch bowl, and the other with, &c.

"A considerable altercation occurred on the entrance of the bowl, the various members of the company civilly entreating each other to officiate, exactly like the "Elders" in Burns' poem of *the Holy Fair*, "bothering from side to side" about the saying of grace. A middle-aged gentleman was at length prevailed upon to draw "the china" before him, and the knowing manner in which he forthwith began to arrange all his materials, impressed me at once with the idea that he was completely master of the noble science of making a bowl. The bowl itself was really a beautiful piece of porcelain. It was what is called *a double bowl*, that is, the coloured surface was cased in another of pure white net-work, through which the red and blue flowers and trees shone out most beautifully. The sugar being melted with a little cold water, the artist squeezed about a dozen lemons through a wooden strainer, and then poured in water enough almost to fill the bowl. In this state the liquor goes by the name of sherbet, and a few of the connoisseurs in his immediate neighbourhood were requested to give their opinion of it—for in the mixing of the sherbet lies, according to the Glasgow creed, at least one-half of the whole battle. This being approved by an audible smack from the lips of the umpires, the rum was added to the beverage, I suppose, in something about the proportion of one to seven. Last of all, the maker cut a few limes, and running each section rapidly round the rim of his bowl, squeezed in enough of this more delicate acid to flavour the whole composition. In this consists the true *tour-de-maitre* of the punch-maker. Upon tasting it, I could not refuse the tribute of my warmest admiration to our accomplished artist—so cool, so balmy, so refreshing a compound of sweets and sours never before descended into my stomach. Had Mahomet, &c.

"The punch being fairly made, the real business of the evening commenced, and, giving its due weight to the balsamic influence of the fluid, I must say that the behaviour of the company was such as to remove almost entirely the prejudices I had conceived in consequence of their first appearance and external manners. In the course of talk, I found that the coarseness which had most offended me was nothing but a kind of waggish disguise, assumed as the covering of minds keenly alive to the ridiculous, and therefore studious to avoid all appearance of finery—an article which they are aware always seems absurd when exhibited by persons of their profession. In short, I was amongst a set of genuinely shrewd, clever, sarcastic fellows, all of them completely *up to trap*—all of them good-natured and friendly in their dispositions—and all of them inclined to take their full share in the laugh against their own peculiarities. Some subjects, besides, of political intent, were introduced and discussed in a tone of great good sense and moderation. As for wit, I must say there was no want of it, in particular from the 'privileged character' I have already noticed. There was a *breadth* and *quaintness* of humour about this gentleman which gave me infinite delight; and, on the whole, I was really much disposed, at the end of the evening (for we never looked near the drawing-room) to congratulate myself as having made a good exchange for the self-sufficient young Whig coxcombs of Edinburgh. Such is the danger of trusting too much to first impressions. The Glasgow people would, in general, do well to assume as their motto, ' Fronti nulla fides ;' and yet there are not a few of them whose faces I should be very sorry to see things different from what they are."—*Peter's Letters.*

PORTRAIT OF AN INTELLIGENT AND VIRTUOUS ARTISAN.
BY ELLIOTT OF SHEFFIELD.

Alas! Miles Gordon ne'er will walk again!
But his poor grandson's footsteps wakes thy tear,
As if indeed thy long-lost friend were near.
Here oft, with fading cheek, and thoughtful brow,
Wanders the youth, town-bred, but desert-born;
Too early taught life's deepening woes to know,
He wakes in sorrow with the weeping morn,
And gives much labour for a little corn.
In smoke and dust, from hopeless day to day,
He sweats to bloat the harpies of the soil,
Who jail no victim, while his pangs can pay
Untaxing rent, and trebly taxing toil,
They make the labour of his hands their spoil,
And grind him fiercely; but he still can get
A crust of *wheaten* bread, despite their frowns;
They have not sent him, like a pauper yet,
For workhouse wages, as they send their clowns;
Such tactics do not answer yet in towns;
Nor have they gorged his soul. Thrall though he be
Of brutes who bite him, while he feeds them, still
He feels his intellectual dignity;
Works hard, reads usefully, with no mean skill
Writes; and can reason well of good and ill.
He hoards his weekly groat. His tear is shed
For sorrows which his hard-worn hand relieves.
Too poor, too proud, too just, too wise to wed,
(For slaves enough already toil for thieves,)
How gratefully his growing mind receives
The food which tyrants struggle to withhold!
Though hourly ills his every sense invade,
Beneath the cloud that o'er his home is rolled,
He yet respects the power which *man* hath made,
Nor loathes the despot-humbling sons of trade.
—But when the silent Sabbath-day arrives,
He seeks the cottage bordering on the moor,
Where his forefathers passed their lowly lives,
Where still his mother dwells, content, though poor,
And ever glad to meet him at the door.
Oh, with what rapture he prepares to fly
From streets and courts, with crime and sorrow strewed,
And bids the mountain lift him to the sky!
How proud to feel his heart not all subdued!
How happy to shake hands with solitude!
Still, Nature, still he loves thy uplands brown,
The rock that o'er his father's freehold towers!
And strangers hurrying through the dingy town,
May know his workshop by its sweet wild-flowers,
Cropped on the Sabbath from the hedge-side bowers.

CRAFTSMEN OF GERMANY.

The different crafts in Germany are incorporations recognised by law, governed by usages of great antiquity, with a fund to defray the corporate expenses; and in each considerable town a house of entertainment is selected as the house of call, or harbor, as it is styled, of each particular craft. Thus we see, in the German towns, a number of taverns indicated by their signs, as the Masons' Harbor, the Blacksmiths' Harbor, &c. No one is allowed to set up as a master workman in any trade, unless he is admitted as a freeman or member of the craft; and such is the stationary condition of most parts of Germany, that no person is admitted as a master workman in any trade, except to supply the place of some one deceased, or retired from business. When such a vacancy occurs, all those desirous of being permitted to fill it present a piece of work, executed as well as they are able to do it, which is called their master-piece, being offered to obtain the place of a master workman. Nominally, the best workman gets the place, but in reality, some kind of favouritism must generally decide it. Thus is every man obliged to submit to all the chances of a popular election whether he shall be allowed to work for his bread; and that, too, in a country where the people are not permitted to have any agency in choosing their rulers. But the restraints on journeymen in that country are still more oppressive. As soon as the years of apprenticeship have expired, the young mechanic is obliged, in the phrase of the country, to *wander* for three years. For this purpose he is furnished, by the master of the craft in which he has served his apprenticeship, with a duly-authenticated *wandering-book*, with which he goes forth to seek employment. In whatever city he arrives, on presenting himself with his credential, at the house of call, or harbor, of the craft in which he has served his time, he is allowed, gratis, a day's food and a night's lodging. If he wishes to get employment in that place, he is assisted in procuring it. If he does not wish to get employment, or fails in the attempt, he must pursue his wandering; and this lasts for three years before he can be anywhere admitted as a master. It is argued, that this system has the advantage of circulating knowledge from place to place, and imparting to the young artizan the fruits of travel and intercourse with the world. But, however beneficial travelling may be, when undertaken by those who have the taste and capacity to profit by it, to compel every young man who has just served out his time to leave his home, in the manner I have described, must bring his habits and morals into peril, and be regarded rather as a hardship than as an advantage. There is no sanctuary of virtue like home.—Many of the German stories, which are of a more homely cast than ours, turn upon the circumstances of the *wanderings* of a young mechanic, who, if he is to turn out well, comes home at the conclusion to his native city, an adept in his trade, and either marries his master's daughter, or some young maiden to whom he had been affianced before he set out on these dangerous travels.

British Benevolence.—The income of the principal Religious Societies supported by voluntary contributions, for the year ending May, 1832, has been as follows :—

British and Foreign Bible Society	£81,700
Wesleyan Methodist Missionary Society	48,200
Church Missionary Society	48,700
London Missionary Society	34,500
London Hibernian Society	9,800
Society for Promoting Christianity among the Jews	11,000
British and Foreign Seamen and Soldiers' Friend Society	5,000
Religious Tract Society	3,300
Irish Evangelical Society	3,000
Home Missionary Society	4,000
Naval and Military Bible Society	2,700
Prayer Book and Homily Society	2,700
British and Foreign School Society	2,500
Continental Society	1,900
Port of London Society	700
Christian Instruction Society	600
Ecclesiastical Knowledge Society	440
Sunday School Society	340
London Itinerant Society	300
Society for the Observance of the Lord's Day	240

The Society for the Propagation of the Gospel in Foreign Parts, the Society for Promoting Religious Knowledge among the Poor, the Baptist Missionary Society, and various other minor institutions, not making up their annual accounts in May, are not included in the above summary. If these were added, the gross amount contributed voluntarily in this country, for the support of religious institutions for general purposes, would exceed L.300,000 annually

COLUMN FOR THE LADIES.

THE SPINNING WHEEL SONG.
BY MISS MITFORD.

Fair Janet sits beside her wheel—
  No maiden better knew
To pile upon the circling reel
  An even thread, and true.
But since for Rob she 'gan to pine,
  She twists her flax in vain;
'Tis now too coarse, and now too fine,
  And now 'tis snapt in twain.

Robin, a bachelor profess'd,
  At love and lovers laughs,
And o'er the bowl, with reckless jest,
  His pretty spinster quaffs;
Then while, all sobbing, Janet cries,
  "She scorns the fickle swain,"
With angry haste her wheel she plies,
  And snaps the thread again!

MY COACH ACQUAINTANCE.

Beautiful girl! although I may never
Behold shining on me again thy fair face:
Though short our acquaintance has been, yet for ever,
Thy form and thy tones in my heart shall have place.

The coach has now stopt—and alas! I must stop, too,
  And the spell thy sweet spirit has cast over mine,
I must tear away—and my trunk from the top, too—
  And start off in a route quite different from thine.

Blest be the fortune that brought us together;
And blest be the showers that drove me inside;
Guard, that's my trunk—that one covered with leather,
And that's my umbrella stuck there by its side.

With all that pass'd by as I've quizz'd and I've shouted,
  Said soft things, and all things I thought would please thee;
Good by; a safe journey—when you think about it,
  O, join with the thought some remembrance of me.
                                C. M.

SHE AND HE;
OR, WHO'S THE DUPE.

She was handsome;
He was tender.
She turning her dark languishing eyes upon him, one day for the space of five minutes,
He said to her, "I love you;"
She replied, "*Je le crois bien, mais que je vous plain.*"
He said to her next day, "I shall die if you do not condescend to love me;"
She answered, "Live on!"
He did live!—
She was more than delighted to have thus restored him to life.
He for a whole fortnight seemed only to prize it, that from henceforth it might be devoted to her.
She fancied, at the end of a month, his gratitude was not quite so warm, and suspected, not without cause, that he had courted new *dangers* elsewhere.
She questioned him of it.
He quite laughed at the notion. Dangers! said he; do you then fancy I run into real ones? Should I have died think you, had you not have loved me? and would you, *par example*, be silly enough to die, if I were *indeed* to leave you?—*Bah!*
She replied not a word—she blushed, then grew pale, and could hardly refrain shedding tears.
He wrote to her saying, "he had altered his mind—it was a thing common enough, and for her part what could *she* do that was better?"
She returned not a line.
He wrote to her again—"I know that you are suffering—I was told of it yesterday—'tis really quite childish (pooh, pooh)—call sense to your aid—I will see you to-morrow."
She could no longer weep now.
He wrote to her once more—"I am convinced you can never exist without loving; but am I the only man in the world?—try to love somebody else, and, prithee! do live."
She reflected upon it for about half a day, and—did live.
Now, gentle reader, and without presumption, let me ask you—"*Who's the Dupe?*"   F. P.

A Good Woman.—Extract from the Statistical Account of the Parish of Whithorn, by the late Dr. Isaac Davidson.—"Mrs Macmillan, widow of Bailie Anthony Macmillan, late of this burgh, died this year (1794) in her hundredth year. She lived in this parish, and near neighbourhood of it, all her life, and was connected with some of the best families of the county. Her age is well authenticated. She left two sons, one of them a present magistrate in the burgh, and two daughters. Upon inquiry, I have found that Mrs Macmillan was blessed with a good natural temper, and was always the friend of peace; that she enjoyed an easy and uniform flow of spirits, and was greatly esteemed by her neighbours as a person of the best moral character. She was remarkable for cleanliness in her person, at her table, and in her house, and to the end of life shewed great attention to her dress. To all her other accomplishments she added those of religion, the duties of which she performed with an attention and zeal highly worthy of imitation. Religion appeared in her with a smiling countenance, guided her honourably through the different stages of life, and ministered to her joy in its evening. Her sense of duty led her to industry; and her religious principles and feelings bestowed upon her contentment, and cheerful trust in God. She lived like a saint, and died like a Christian heroine."

Cobbett on Edinburgh.—I now come back to this delightful and beautiful city. I thought that Bristol, taking in its heights and Clifton and its rocks and river, was the finest city in the world; but it is nothing to Edinburgh, with its castle, its hills, its pretty little seaport, conveniently detached from it, its vale of rich land lying all around, its lofty hills in the background, its views across the Frith. I think little of its streets and its rows of fine houses, though all built of stone, and though every thing in London and Bath is beggary to these; I think nothing of Holyrood House; but I think a great deal of the fine and well-ordered streets of shops; of the regularity which you perceive everywhere in the management of business; and I think still more of the absence of all that foppishness, and that affectation of carelessness, and that insolent assumption of superiority, that you see in almost all the young men that you meet with in the fashionable parts of the great towns in England. I was not disappointed: for I expected to find Edinburgh the finest city in the kingdom. Conversations at Newcastle, and with many Scotch gentlemen for years past, had prepared me for this; but still the reality has greatly surpassed every idea that I had formed about it. The people, however, still exceed the place; here all is civility; you do not meet with rudeness, or even with the want of a disposition to oblige, even in persons in the lowest state of life. A friend took me round the environs of the city; he had a turnpike ticket, received at the first gate, which cleared five or six gates. It was sufficient for him to *tell* the future gate-keepers that he had it. When I saw that, I said to myself, "Nota bene: Gate-keepers take people's word in Scotland; a thing that I have not seen before since I left *Long Island.*"—*Cobbett's Register.*

The Pleasures of Expectation.—A drunken fellow, at a late hour in the night, was sitting in the middle of the Place Vendome. A friend of his happening to pass, recognised him, and said, "Well, what do you do here, why don't you go home?" The drunkard replied, "My good fellow, 'tis just what I want—(hiccup)—but, the place is all going round—(hiccup)—and I'm waiting for my door to go by."

PIGS AND BACON.

We take the following from a letter lately addressed by a gentleman, to the labourers on his brother's estate:—"I have a word or two to say about your pigs, as I expect every one of you to keep one. In the first place, it is very material that the sty be kept quite dry; you must, therefore, always be attentive that the roof of the stye, and see that it does not let in wet. The open part of the stye, where the pig feeds and exercises, should be planked, and sloped sufficiently from the covered part or bed, or all wet to drain away to the dung heap. The stye must be kept clean; it should be cleansed every day. Dry leaves and fern, collected in the autumn, are good substitutes for straw for the bed, when straw is scarce. I would recommend you not to buy in your pig before May, as you would have some difficulty in finding sufficient food for him earlier without going to expense; he should then be not less than six or seven months old. As there is very little common or waste on which your pigs could be turned to graze, you must treasure up all the refuse cabbage leaves, pods of peas and beans, &c., to supply them with sufficient food in the stye during the summer. One long tub you must have, and as soon as you can afford it you should get another, that one may be filling while the other is being emptied; moreover, it is an advantage not to give the wash while it is *fresh*, for pigs are found to thrive better on it when stale. Let the potatoes and carrots intended for the pigs be boiled, and then mashed up with the wash. As soon as the acorns and beech nuts are ripe, set the children to collect them, as they are very nourishing food for pigs. In the beginning of October, you must prepare for fatting, by giving less green food, and more potatoes and carrots, which you will then have in abundance. A pig will require about two bushels of potatoes, and one of carrots or parsnips, boiled, and mixed with the wash every week during this month; but as the appetites of pigs will vary, you must watch them when feeding, and give a little more or less at a meal, taking care not to give at one feed more than they eat up clean. They should be fed three times a-day at the least; I should say four times during November and December, while fatting. During the last week of October, mix about half a peck of barley-meal with the allowance of wash for the week; each of the two first weeks in November, one peck; each of the two last weeks, a peck and a half; the two first weeks in December, two pecks each; the third week, three pecks; and the fourth week, four pecks. It is necessary to be careful in increasing the barley-meal—this must be done gradually in order to prevent surfeit, which will throw the pig back. If your crops of pease should be very abundant, and produce more than you want as a vegetable food, let them ripen well, and put them by for fatting the pigs, to save meal. By the end of December, if you have managed the pig well, he will be fat; if he be not, you must give him a little more time, for he ought to be thoroughly fat before he is killed. I cannot dispose of the pig when killed and burned, better than in the words of Cobbett's 'Cottage Economy.' He proceeds as follows:—'The *inwards* are next taken out, and if the wife be not a slattern, here, in the mere offal—in the mere garbage, there is food, and delicate food, too, for a large family for a week, and hogs' puddings for the children,' &c. 'The butcher, the next day, cuts the hog up, and then the house is filled with meat; souse, griskins, blade bones, thigh-bones, spare ribs, chines, belly-pieces, cheeks, all coming into use, one after the other; and the last of the latter not before the end of about four or five weeks.' 'All the other parts taken away the two sides that remain, and that are called flitches, are to be cured for bacon. They are first rubbed with salt on their insides, or flesh sides, then placed one on the other, the flesh sides uppermost, in a salting trough, which has a gutter round its edges to drain away the brine; for, to have sweet and fine bacon, the flitches must not lie sopping in brine, which gives it a bad taste. Every one knows how different is the taste of fresh dry salt, from that of salt in a dissolved state—the one is savory, the other nauseous; therefore, change the salt often—once in four or five days; let it melt, and sink in, but not lie too long; change the flitches—put that at bottom which was first put on the top; do this a couple of times. As to the time required for making the flitches sufficiently salt, it depends on circumstances—the thickness of the flitch, the state of the weather, the place where the salting is going on. It takes a longer time for a thick than a thin flitch; it takes longer in dry than in damp weather; it takes longer in a dry than a damp place. But, for flitches of a hog of twelve score, in weather not very dry nor very damp, about six weeks may do; and as yours is to be fat, which receives little injury from over-salting, give time enough, for you are to have bacon till Christmas comes again. The place for salting should be cool, and where there is a free circulation of air. Confined air, though cool, will taint meat sooner than the mid-day sun accompanied by a breeze.' The author then directs that the bacon should be smoked, and not dried; that the flitches should be hung up in a chimney, where no rain could fall upon them, and not so near the fire as to melt; that the smoke should proceed from wood fires, not coal. If there be a fire constantly by day, a month would be long enough for the flitches to remain in the chimney; but if not, rather more time must be given, taking care not to leave them long enough to get rusty; that the flitches should be dried to the hardness of a board, but yet not quite dry; that before the bacon is hung up in the chimney, it should be laid on the floor, powdered over pretty thickly with bran, that this should be rubbed on the flesh, and patted well down upon it. The lard must be taken care of, and put away in bladders; mixing a little salt with it will make it keep good for a much longer time. I have been very desirous of collecting for you all the knowledge I could about the pig, for he will furnish you with a great number of good, hearty, and nourishing meals after your day's toil throughout the year; and I hope you will not only attend to all I have written, but collect all the information you can as to the best plan of feeding and management. Never regard a little additional trouble, '*for there are no gains without pains.*'"

SCRAPS.
ORIGINAL AND SELECTED.

SPEED OF THE HORSE.—Common report says that Flying Childers could run a mile in a minute, but there is no authentic record of this. He ran over the Round Course of Newmarket (three miles, six furlongs, and 93 yards) in six minutes and 40 seconds; and the Beacon Course (four miles, one furlong, and 138 yards) in seven minutes and 30 seconds. In 1772 a mile was run by Firetail in one minute and four seconds. In October 1741, at the Curragh Meeting in Ireland, Mr. Wilde engaged to ride 127 miles in nine hours. He performed it in six hours and 21 minutes. He employed ten horses, and allowing for mounting and dismounting, and a moment for refreshment, he rode for six hours at the rate of 20 miles an hour. Mr. Thornhill, in 1745, exceeded this, for he rode from Stilton to London and back, and again to Stilton, being 219 miles, in 11 hours and 34 minutes, which is, after allowing the least possible time for changing horses, 20 miles an hour for 11 hours, and on the turnpike road and uneven ground. Mr. Shaftoe, in 1762, with ten horses, and five of them ridden twice, accomplished fifty miles and a quarter in one hour and forty-nine minutes. In 1763 Mr. Shaftoe won a more extraordinary match. He was to procure a person to ride one hundred miles a-day, on any one horse each day, for twenty-nine days together, and to have any number of horses not exceeding twenty-nine. He accomplished it on fourteen horses; and one day he rode 160 miles on account of the tiring of his first horse. Mr. Hull's Quibbler, however, afforded the most extraordinary instance on record of the stoutness as well as speed of the race-horse. In December 1786, he ran twenty-three miles, round the flat at Newmarket, in fifty-seven minutes and ten seconds.

AMERICAN COURTS OF JUSTICE.—I never went into a court-house in the west, in summer, without observing that the judges and lawyers had their feet invariably placed upon the desks before them, and raised much higher than their heads. This, however, is only in the western county; for in the courts at Orleans, New York, and Philadelphia, the greatest order and regularity is observed. I had been told, that the judges often slept upon the bench; but I must confess, that, although I have entered court-houses at all sessions, during the space of fifteen months, I never saw an instance of it. I have frequently remonstrated with the Americans on the total absence of forms and ceremonies in their courts of justice, and was commonly answered by, "Yes, that may be quite necessary in England, in order to overawe a parcel of ignorant creatures, who have no share in making the laws; but, with us, a man's a man, whether he have a silk gown on or not; and, I guess, he can decide quite as well without a big wig as with one. You see, we have done with wiggery of all kinds, and if one of our judges was to wear such an appendage, he'd be taken for a Merry-andrew, and the court would become a kind of show-box; instead of such arrangements producing, with us, solemnity, they would produce nothing but laughter and the greatest possible irregularity."—*Farrall's Rambles in America.*

THE TREE OF DISSIPATION.
The
sin of
drunkenness
expels reason,
drowns memory,
diminishes strength,
distempers the body,
defaces beauty, corrupts the
blood, inflames the liver, weakens
the brain, turns men into walking
hospitals, causes internal, external, and
incurable wounds; is a witch to the senses, a
devil to the soul, a thief to the pocket,
the beggar's companion, a wife's woe,
and children's sorrow; makes man
become a beast and self-murderer,
who drinks to others' good
health, and robs himself
of his own!
The
root of
all evil is
DRUNKENNESS!!!

NATURAL PROPENSITIES.—There are now living in Sicily, three boys who appear to be gifted with a similar aptitude for mathematical calculations. At the head of the triumvirate stands Vincent Zucchero, to whose extraordinary feats in calculation the public curiosity has of late been repeatedly directed. Two years ago he was ignorant even of his alphabet; but in consequence of the pains taken with him by the Abbé Minardi, who has been engaged as his tutor through the liberal interposition of the Government and Corporation of Palermo, he is at this moment able to read off-hand the most difficult of the Latin and Italian classics, and has given public proofs of the unprecedented extent of his acquirements. Two other boys, by name Ignatius Landolina and Joseph Puglisi, have come forward to enter the lists against him. The former has not reached his tenth year, though he has already attended several public meetings, and resolved some of the most abstruse questions in the highest branches of geometry, which were put to him by Professors Nobili, Scuderi, and Allessi, of the University of Cambria. On these occasions Landolina did not confine himself to a mere dry answer, but assigned the reason for the result; and entered acutely into the metaphysics of the science. The third child, Puglisi, who is about seven years old, afforded no less striking and indisputable proofs of his extraordinary talent in giving off-hand answers to problems which usually require tedious arithmetical calculations. The precocious talents of these three infantine mathematicians would seem to indicate that the spirit of Archimedes still lingers on its native soil.—*From a Sicilian Journal.*

CONTAGION.—Miss Seward relates an extraordinary instance of contagion in one of her letters. The plague raged in 1666 at Eyam in Derbyshire, of which place she was a native, to a great extent. " In the summer of 1757," says Miss S., " five cottagers were digging in the heathy mountain above Eyam, which was the place of graves after the churchyard became too narrow a repository. These men came to something which had the appearance of having once been linen; conscious of their situation they instantly buried it again. In a few days they all sickened of a putrid fever, and three of the five died. The disorder was contagious, and proved mortal to numbers of the inhabitants. My father, who was Canon of Lichfield, resided in that city with his family at the period when the subtle, unextinguished, though much subdued power of the most dreadful of all diseases awakened from the dust in which he had slumbered 91 years.

CANVASSING A HUNDRED YEARS SINCE.—Sir Richard Steele, the celebrated author of the *Tatler*, who represented a borough in 1714, carried his election against a powerful opposition by the laughable expedient of sticking two apples full of guineas; and declaring to the electors, before whom he held them up, that the largest should be the prize of that man whose wife should be the first to bring forth a boy after that day nine months, and that the other would belong to him who should become the father of a girl within the same period. This finesse procured him the interest of the women. One of the borough once made a strenuous effort to procure a resolution, that no man should ever be received as a candidate, who did not offer himself to their consideration, upon the same terms.

Zachariah Macaulay has a servant whom he purchased at Sierra Leone, who affords a very satisfactory proof, that if the mental faculties of the blacks were properly cultivated, they would possess extraordinary reasoning powers. One morning as Cudjoe was lying in bed longer than usual, his master called out to him, and asked him what he was about? " I am doing some head work, massa."—" Head work,—what is that?" asked Zachariah. " Why, massa," continued Cudjoe; " suppose three crow on dat tree, and massa fire, and kill one, how many left?"—" Two, of course," observed Zachariah. " No, massa, wrong dere," replied Cudjoe, showing his teeth, " de other two fly away." [If this anecdote is meant to convey a sneer against the friends of Negroes, it misses the aim. One thing it does effect; it shews what cheerful happy creatures Negroes are when kindly treated.]

THE CUCKOO.—With much deference to the opinion of the learned gentlemen who think proper to reject the testimony of the Scottish peasantry respecting the singular nestling of this bird, we assert, in the most unqualified terms, that it deposits its eggs in the nest of the common tit-lark, or moss-chipper. Had any of the sceptics visited Handax Wood, in the parish of West Calder, during last summer, he might have seen a young cuckoo hatched in the nest of a moss-chipper, and tethered there for several weeks, and all the while fed by the tit-lark, until full grown, when it was carried to Edinburgh by a respectable carter, and sold for eighteenpence.

LIFE AT DERRYNANE.—A person from Kerry, communicates some interesting particulars of the domestic repose of our great Irish giant. He still keeps his fortress in the mountains, where he lives like a patriarch or a Brehon Prince, surrounded by his kindred of all ages and degrees of consanguinity. Fifty persons of both sexes meet around his plentiful board each day, exclusive of the countless retainers in the various departments of serving men and waiting women, dog boys, pipers, boatmen, runners, *shulers*, &c. &c. &c. What with the family and guests above stairs, and the tribes below, the Abbey is seldom *beholding* to fewer than a hundred inmates, who, inhaling " an eager and a *biting* air," some thousand feet above the level of the Atlantic, are every one of them fully qualified to perform their part in the allotted feast.— A Kerry cow *per diem* is moderate store for such a garrison, whose fare is diversified with the delicious mutton of those high regions, brown as venison, and redolent of the sweet heath, as often as they can catch a wether on the mountains. To number the flocks of geese, turkeys, and barndoor fowls, together with the salmons, hares and rabbits, partridges, wild ducks, and plovers, which yield up their happy lives to this perpetual festival *pro bono publico*, would be to lay a burden upon *John Bull's* credulity, which none but an eyewitness should presume to impose. O'Connell partakes freely in the manly sports and exercises of the mountains, and will return to the wordy strife with lungs repaired and strength recruited.

CONTENTS OF NO. XVI.	
The Commencement of the Edinburgh Year	241
The Diamond Beetle	242
Fumigation	243
On the Moral Training of Children	244
To My Cigar	245
ELEMENTS OF THOUGHT—The Sources of Human Happiness	246
Cobbettiana	248
THE STORY-TELLER—Residence in the Alhambra, 249—Brief Notice of Our Late Royal Neighbour, Charles X	250
Social Life in Glasgow	252
Portrait of an Intelligent Artisan	253
Craftsmen in Germany	ib.
COLUMN FOR THE LADIES	254
SCRAPS, Original and Selected	255

EDINBURGH: Printed by and for JOHN JOHNSTONE, 19, St. James's Square.—Published by JOHN ANDERSON, Jun., Bookseller, 55, North Bridge Street, Edinburgh; by JOHN MACLEOD, and ATKINSON & Co., Booksellers, Glasgow; and sold by all Booksellers and Venders of Cheap Periodicals.

THE Schoolmaster,
AND
EDINBURGH WEEKLY MAGAZINE.

CONDUCTED BY JOHN JOHNSTONE.

THE SCHOOLMASTER IS ABROAD.—LORD BROUGHAM.

No. 17.—Vol. I. SATURDAY, NOVEMBER 24, 1832. Price Three-Halfpence.

HOLYDAY RAMBLES.
NO. IV.
THE EILDON HILLS.

As we cannot afford time to creep on at a snail's pace, mile by mile, over the face of Scotland—well-featured, though somewhat high in her cheek-bones—fair, though ferny-tickled, suppose we at once don our seven-league boots, and stride from our old station, the ROMAN CAMP, commanding the Lothians, with

"Fair Fife, and a' the land about it."

even over "moors and mosses many, O," the vale of the Gala, and part of Tweeddale, and take post at or about the next ROMAN STATION, that on the shoulder of the eastern cone or peak of the *Trimontium* of that splendid people; though, we believe, tradition ascribes the cleaving of the Eildon mountain into three conical summits, to the poet and prophet, and Man of Power of this region, Thomas the Rhymer, and thus makes the date of disjunction some twelve hundred years later than the invasion of the Romans. This is an affair which properly belongs to antiquaries—we only aspire to be *guides* to the *Schoolmaster's* pupils. Such of them as, during St. Martin's summer, which extends from this season often on till Christmas, choose to make the perambulation we now trace, had best take the wings of the *Chevy Chace*, any fine morning, and be set down at Melrose Cross, in time to make the ascent with us. If their object be Abbotsford, or a pilgrimage to Dryburgh, they will require more time, and further counselling. The EILDON HILL, and all that it commands, is our present object. But we are not in the least dictatorial: go to Abbotsford first, visit Dryburgh, return by St. Boswells, we care not; provided you start with us from *Melrose Cross* any mild clear day, and at your own hour, (for the affair is not very prodigious,) we promise to guide you well. So up the lane to Dingleton, a cluster of snug *feus*—not quite so picturesque as a Swiss village, though *mountainish*;—and now we cross the burn, and zig-zag up the foot-path till we reach the utmost limit of the arable land, and have our foot on the green springy sward which clothes the Eildon Hills. And here let us make pause the first, and at leisure look round us; for we have long thought that climbing either Scotch mountain or the hill of life, is alike a cheerless, profitless, fagging work, if the climber cannot take leisure to enjoy the extended prospects he has achieved. And now, from our first stage, or breathing place, look round. That snug white house by the burn, and among the trees, is St. Mary's, pretty and fitting name for even a Protestant Nunnery—yet the sisters and novices of St. Mary's, however

"Devout and pure,
Sober, steadfast, and demure,"

are not, so far as ever we heard, "ladies vowed and dedicate" to celibacy. *Au contraire*——but let the gallant yeomen of Tweeddale and Tibbydale* look to this: to them, then, we commit the gentle sisterhood of St. Mary's, and turn to yonder summit rising behind their nunnery, where it is proposed to rear the monument of Sir Walter Scott, intended for his own immediate neighbourhood. The good folks hereabouts feel a natural, and honest pride, even in their vicinity to Abbotsford, and to the immortal dust lately deposited in Dryburgh Abbey; and they are, therefore, proceeding with great zeal in their plan of doing outward homage to their illustrious late neighbour. One of the summits of the mountain we are ascending has been spoken of as the site of this monument, and the idea is too magnificent to be easily abandoned. The majesty of the situation would amply recompense for the rudeness of the structure. A cairn on the top of the Eildon Hills, visible over so much of the ground he has rendered classic, would form, with the true pilgrims of his genius, a much nobler monument to Sir Walter Scott than any little fiddle-faddle nicky-nacky piece of Grecian architecture that could be raised. His genius was lofty, stupendous, massive, simple, and *Gothic;* and such should be his monument,—at least in the heart of his own land.—But let us on.—We have now passed the regions of the plough. The rest of the Eildons are sheep pastures, and, we hope, may remain such till the end of the world. Yonder lies a sheep-fold, about midway up the hill, quiet, and pastoral, and suggestive of every sweet and pastoral image; the bughting hour, "'Tween the gloamin and the mirk," the "Ca'ing the ewes to

---
* Teviotdale, so pronounced in local speech.

the knowes," and, finer still, before daybreak, on the hill-side,

"The lasses a-lilting at the ewes, milking."

This primitive custom has nearly shared the fate of the *quern*, and of our beloved spinning-wheel. All those old habits have been swept away in the march of society, and will soon only live in their few scanty relics, embalmed in the songs, and preserved in the traditionary legends, of the south-land dales. However, our legs and the world are moving in the midst of our lamentation and pensive regrets after what we could scarce wish to see restored; and now we have gained the flat, lying between the main ridges of the hill. Even here the view is fine and expansive; but this is not yet our station of survey. Following the soaring of the old Roman eagle, we shall have an imperial range. We have the choice of three summits. This on the right, the highest; that on the left, next in altitude; the southern peak, the lowest.—We at once choose the loftiest. "There are no gains without pains," as poor Richard says. So set a stout Scotch heart to a steep Scotch hill—and up we go, and make our stand some 1330 feet above where "The boat rocks at the pier of Leith," with a sweep of horizon extending from his Majesty's town of Berwick-upon-Tweed, or the ocean, westward to Ettrick Pen; from the Cheviots to the girdling Frith of Forth, and the dim hills beyond it; while at our feet——But we shall quote the recent words of a local bard:—

"We've all, within our valley to cheer the heart and eye,
Yet when we want to see the world, we climb our mountain high,
And there behold the grandeur of half a kingdom spread;
   And its ground all around
   And its ground all around,
   In its summer beauty clad."

This, of course, refers to the Vale of Melrose, to which one great name has of late years attracted several inhabitants, eminent in literature and science, whose biding-places we shall notice after our grand survey.—Now look eastward, and tell us what you see? Berwick on the verge of the horizon—at a distance, as the crow flies, of 30 miles; but on a clear day distinctly visible. And in the sunned glimpses of the opening skies of this breezy day, one by one, how many storied heights, and memorable and legendary spots are revealed to sight, and revived to memory. Yon little cloud is the smoke of Kelso, and, just nearer, these are the noble woods of *Fleurs* overshadowing the Tweed. Over from them, yet, from this, seeming to approximate Fleurs, these are the romantic and umbrageous crags and heights of Maxwellheuch, and the champaign of opening Teviotdale. Reverting from these, let us course the unseen Tweed upwards, and to us homewards, dwelling in succession on the plantations of Mackerston, and "on Mertoun's woods," as we glance on to the high, square, desolate border Tower of Smailholm, and those eminences beside it, which give the descriptive name of Sandy Knowes to the home of Sir Walter Scott's childhood, and form the scene of the most splendid of his ballads, The Eve of St. John. But of that we dare scarce tell you now. That highest eminence is, he says, still called the *Watchfold*, a frequent name in the olden time; and this height, during the interminable Border wars, was the "eerie beacon hill" of the district—

"When from height to height, the beacons bright
Of the English foeman told."

A half-hour's gaze from the summit of Eildon, on nights like those, might have made a poet. With some reluctance we turn from this point, recommending the reading of Scott's ballads of *Thomas the Rhymer*, and *The Eve of St. John*, as by far the best course of preparation for ascending the Eildon hills.—In the same line of view as Smailholm, but lying nearer us, are the heights and crags of Bemer-side,* clothed with ancient woods and modern plantations, overhanging the Tweed.—— There—mark that craggy bushy bank. At the base of it, the Tweed, making a beautiful sweep, nearly encircles the delicious little vale of Dryburgh, the loveliest spot in the whole course of this march stream of kingdoms. Dryburgh, where "they keep his dust," must be the business of another pilgrimage; nor shall we detain you long on yonder white speck, at this distance not unlike a pipe-stopple, or peppermint lozenge, and yet a colossal statue of Wallace Wight in Roman costume! As we detest all colossal statues, and all masses of marble, metal, or stone, done into monstrosities, in mockery of the human form divine, we cannot except this frail memorial of the good taste of the late Earl of Buchan.† The next

* We are tempted to repeat the prophecy of the Rhymer regarding this old family, for the sake of giving Sir Walter Scott's modern parody on it, as it is the only piece of mirthful innocent malice we ever heard attributed to his guileless muse :—the RHYMER's prophecy runs thus—

"Tide, tide, whate'er betide,
There'll aye be Haigs in Bemerside."

And for five hundred years, it has held, though sometimes in great apparent danger of non-fulfilment, as some time back, when about a dozen daughters were born, before the *heir* made his appearance. Sir Walter's prophecy regards the ancient house of a Scottish Tory baronet, and is equally pithy and comprehensive—

"Befa' befa',' whate'er befa',
There 'ill ye be a gowk in ——— ha?."

† Since we are dealing in notes, we must give another. The above noble Mecænas, in an evil hour, thought, after having raised Washington to a Pantheon of plaster of Paris, of taking the shade of Thomson under his protection. A large party of blues, and belles, and bardlings, were accordingly collected, year after year, far and wide, to assist his Lordship in the apotheosis of the Poet of the Seasons; who, being a man that detested fuss and fudge, had he been able to look up, would assuredly not have thanked them. This annual celebration was again to be held at Ednam, the birth-place of the poet, a sweet spot on the Tweed, and upon his birth-day. Every thing worked well, if not easily. The company assembled—the bust, crowned with bays, was already enshrined behind a curtain, which, at the proper time was slowly to ascend, to slow music, and reveal the divine Thomson, and the classic labours of the Earl. And so it did; and discovered the placid good-humored bard with a black *cuttie* pipe stuck in his mouth! literally a Scotch *cuttie* or Irish *doodhen*. The comic effect of this piece of

widening of the river banks encloses the beautiful Vale of Old Melrose, an ancient site of the first Schoolmasters that came abroad in Scotland, the Culdees. Around this point of the Tweed, mansions and villas, and cots and granges, orchard-slopes, woods, and crags; and swells of arable land, are scattered and clustered, in that charming, picturesque, yet *natural confusion*, which gives so much gusto to landscape. There is Gleidswood; and here, exactly opposite Gleidawood is Ravenswood; and there, the *Leader Water*, the stream of *True Thomas*, having some time since left the *Leader Haughs*, steals through the woods of Drygrange, and falls chiming into the Tweed. But now that cone-like green hill, tapering regularly from its round base to its pyramidal top, seems to attract you. That is *Colding Knowes—The Cowdenknowes* of one of the sweetest of our Scottish pastoral songs. The mansion, at its western base, is one of those lovely places which the lavish charter of imagination instantly appropriates, and never again parts with. But we must, for another week, leave the "Bonny broom" to wave around it uncelebrated. Then we shall return to *True Thomas*, his modern successors in the Vale of Melrose, and the romantic territory not yet surveyed.

CIVILIZATION OF AFRICA.
OLD SPEECHES IN PARLIAMENT.
NO. I.—THE SLAVE-TRADE.

We intend to give a few of these *old* speeches on topics now of interest; and shall set out with Mr. Pitt's speech on the Slave-trade; or, more properly, on the debt of justice Britain owes to Africa.

I rejoice that the debate has taken a turn which contracts the question into such narrow limits. The matter now in dispute is merely as to the time at which the abolition shall take place. I therefore congratulate the House, the country, and the world, that this great point has been gained; that we may now consider this trade as having received its condemnation; that this curse of mankind is seen in its true light; and that the greatest stigma on our national character, which ever yet existed, is about to be removed! Mankind, I trust, are now likely to be delivered from the greatest practical evil that ever afflicted the human race—from the most severe and extensive calamity recorded in the history of the world.

I will now proceed to the civilization of Africa, which, I confess, is very near my heart; and first I will say, that the present deplorable state of that country, especially when we reflect that her chief calamities are to be ascribed to us, calls for our generous aid, rather than justifies any despair, on our part, of her recovery, and still less a repetition of our injuries. On what ground of theory or history do we act, when we suppose that she is never to be reclaimed? There was a time, which it may be now fit to call to remembrance, when human sacrifices, and even this very practice of the Slave-trade, existed in our own island. Slaves, as we may read in Henry's History of Great Britain, were formerly an established article of our exports. "Great numbers," he says, "were exported, like cattle, from the British coast, and were to be seen exposed for sale in the Roman market."—" Adultery, witchcraft, and debt," says the same historian, "were probably some of the chief sources of supplying the Roman market with British slaves—prisoners taken in war were added to the number—there might be also among them some unfortunate gamesters, who, after having lost all their goods, at length staked themselves, their wives, and their children." Now every one of these sources of slavery has been stated to be at this hour a source of slavery in Africa. If these practices, therefore, are to be admitted as proofs of the natural incapacity of its inhabitants, why might they not have been applied to ancient Britain? Why might not, then, some Roman senator, pointing to the British barbarians, have predicted, with equal boldness, that these were a people, who were destined never to be free; who were without the understanding necessary for the attainment of useful arts; depressed by the hand of Nature below the level of the human species; and created to form a supply of slaves for the rest of the world? But happily, since that time, notwithstanding what would then have been the justness of these predictions, we have emerged from barbarism. We are now raised to a situation which exhibits a striking contrast to every circumstance by which a Roman might have characterized us, and by which we now characterize Africa. There is, indeed, one thing wanting to complete the contrast, and to clear us altogether from the imputation of acting even to this hour as barbarians; for we continue to this hour a barbarous traffic in slaves. We continue it even yet, in spite of all our great pretensions. We were once as obscure among the nations of the earth, as savage in our manners, as debased in our morals, as degraded in our understandings, as these unhappy Africans. But in the lapse of a long series of years, by a progression slow, and for a time almost imperceptible, we have become rich in a variety of acquirements. We are favoured above measure in the gifts of providence, we are unrivalled in commerce, pre-eminent in arts, foremost in the pursuits of philosophy and science, and established in all the blessings of civil society: we are in the possession of peace, of liberty, and of happiness: we are under the guidance of a mild and a beneficent religion; and we are protected by impartial laws, and the purest administration of justice: we are living under a system of government which our own happy experience leads us to pronounce the best and wisest, and which has become the admiration of the world. From all these blessings we must for ever have been excluded, had there been any truth in those principles, which some have not hesitated to lay down as applicable to the case of Africa; and we should have been at this moment little superior, either in morals, knowledge, or refinement, to the rude inhabitants of that continent.

If, then, we feel that this perpetual confinement in the fetters of brutal ignorance would have been the greatest calamity which could have befallen us; if we view, with gratitude, the contrast between our present and our former situation; if we shudder to think of the misery which would still have overwhelmed us, had our country continued to the present times, through some cruel policy, to be the

---

burlesque was irresistible. It ought to be told, to scare impertinent people from such outrages in future upon the sacred memory of genius, and from all absurd profanities " in manner of the ancients."

mart for slaves to the more civilized nations of the world,—God forbid that we should any longer subject Africa to the same dreadful scourge, and exclude the sight of knowledge from her coasts, which has reached every other quarter of the globe.

I trust we shall no longer continue this commerce; and that we shall no longer consider ourselves as conferring too great a boon on the natives of Africa in restoring them to the rank of human beings. I trust we shall not think ourselves too liberal, if, by abolishing the Slave-trade, we give them the same common chance of civilization with other parts of the world. If we listen to the voice of reason and duty this night, some of us may live to see a reverse of that picture from which we now turn our eyes with shame. We may live to behold the natives engaged in the calm occupations of industry, and in the pursuit of a just commerce. We may behold the beams of science and philosophy breaking in upon their land, which at some happy period in still later times, may blaze with full lustre; and joining their influence to that of pure religion, may illuminate and invigorate the most distant extremities of that immense continent. Then might we hope, that even Africa (though last of all the quarters of the globe) should enjoy at length, in the evening of her days, those blessings which have descended so plentifully upon us in a much earlier period of the world. Then also would Europe, participating in her improvement and prosperity, receive an ample recompense for the tardy kindness (if kindness it can be called) of no longer hindering her from extricating herself out of the darkness, which, in other more fortunate regions, has been so much more speedily dispelled.

It is in this view—it is as an atonement for our long and cruel injustice towards Africa, that the measure proposed by my honourable friend, Mr. Wilberforce, most forcibly recommends itself to my mind. The great and happy change to be expected in the state of her inhabitants, is, of all the various benefits of the abolition, in my estimation, the most extensive and important. I shall vote against the adjournment; and I shall also oppose every proposition which tends either to prevent, or even to postpone for an hour, the total abolition of the Slave-trade.

POPULAR SCIENCE.

ON THE FORMATION OF DEW.

THE formation of dew is unknown to many; and as some conceive it to emanate from the earth, which is not the case, I will endeavour to explain it, as clearly as possible, by the theory which is generally received.

Heat possesses the well-known property of radiation, which consists in warm bodies throwing off rays of heat in all directions, until they become of the same temperature as the surrounding matter. During the day, the earth becomes heated by the sun, and imparts part of its warmth to the surrounding atmosphere; after the sun sets, the earth, stones, grass, &c., being much warmer than the air, radiate rays of heat, which rays in a cloudy night are reflected back upon the earth by the clouds, and its temperature is reduced little or nothing below that of the air, and no dew is formed; hence you never see dew on the ground after a cloudy night. But when the weather is fine, and the sky quite clear of clouds, the rays of heat having nothing to reflect them, are radiated into vacant space and are lost; the radiation goes on till they become colder than the surrounding air, which always contains a portion of water in the state of vapour, and which, coming in contact with the cold stones, &c., is condensed, and forms water, which is the dew. An experiment illustrative of this in part, is seen every day in bringing a glass of cold water into a warm room; the watery vapour, coming in contact with the cold glass, is condensed, and forms the misty appearance which the glass presents. Some substances radiate heat better than others; thus polished stones and metals, which radiate imperfectly, will be found almost dry on a dewy morning, while in a rough unpolished condition, they will be found drenched with moisture.

DISTANCE OF THE PLANETS.—The method of investigation used to determine the distance of a planet, is the same as that applied to find out the distance of any object within our view upon the earth. Thus, if a ship coasting along the shore, passes any object, such as a lighthouse, if the object lies near her line of course, she very quickly leaves it behind her; but if the object be many miles from her line of course, she appears to be nearly abreast of it, perhaps the whole of the day, although sailing at a rapid rate. This would enable us to judge of the distance, if the diminution of the object in point of size did not also convince us. Now, upon this very fact of principle, united with a discovery of Kepler's, and other information gathered at observations taken during the transit of Venus over the disk of the sun, in 1769 and 1781, do philosophers determine the distances and measure the diameters of the planets. This discovery of Kepler's was, that the squares of the periodical times of the planets are as the cubes of their mean distances from the sun. That is to say, if you multiply the numbers expressing the times of going round, each by itself, the products will be to one another in the proportion of the average distances multiplied each by itself, and that product again by the distance. Thus, if one body take two hours, and is five yards distant, the other, being ten yards distant, will take something less than five hours and forty minutes. Knowing, therefore, the distance of one planet, it is easy to find out the distance of all the rest, because the squares of the periodical times of the planets are as the cubes of their mean distances from the sun.—*The Christian Philosopher.*

DISTANCE OF THE FIXED STARS.—The perfection of astronomical instruments has afforded the prospect of being able to determine the Annual Parallax, and consequently the distance of the fixed stars; but the quantity of deviation is so small as to have hitherto eluded the closest observation. It cannot amount to a single second in the most conspicuous and probably the nearest of the stars. These luminous bodies must, therefore, be more distant, at least two hundred thousand times, than the measure of the diameter of the earth. The light emitted from such neighbouring suns, though it flies with enormous rapidity, must yet travel more than six thousand years before it approaches the confines of our system. But scattered over the immensity of space, there may exist bodies which, by their magnitude and predominant attraction, retain or recall the rays of light, and are lost in solitude and darkness. Had the celerity of the luminous particles not exceeded four hundred miles in a second, we should never have enjoyed the cheering beams of the sun. They would have been arrested in their journey, and drawn back to their source, before they reached the orbit of Mercury. But a star similar to our sun, and having a diameter sixty-three times greater, would entirely overpower the impetus of light.

HOW TO PREVENT GAS EXPLOSIONS.—When a strong smell of gas is perceived, a leakage from some cause must have taken place; and every door and window in the room which may contain it, should be opened, that the mixture of gas and atmospheric air may escape. Neither lighted candle nor any other inflamed substance should be introduced, or allowed to approach the place, until the whole of the mixture of common air and gas is completely expelled, and the room thoroughly ventilated. It cannot be too strongly impressed upon every person who is in the practice of using gas-lights, that the gas is not explosive of itself, in the state the public receive it from the gas-works; and to render it capable of exploding, it requires to be mixed in various proportions, of from five portions of coal gas to twelve of atmospheric air; and when mixed in any of these proportions, it will not explode unless flame come in contact with it. Whenever, therefore, any escape of the gas may be discovered to have taken place, the proper recourse is ventilation without delay, and preventing the introduction of a lighted candle, or any other kind of flame where the circumstance may occur. Proper ventilation, and keeping away flame, will infallibly tend to prevent accidents from explosion. These are facts which every one should know, and then he may use gas-lights not only without apprehension, but with the most perfect satisfaction.

INFLUENCE OF OCCUPATION UPON THE DURATION OF LIFE.

AMONGST men of genius, or those who have distinguished themselves in science or literature, life is, at least in modern times, of rather a short duration. Mr. D'Israeli, in his estimate of the literary character, mentions the excitement which all eminent men are accustomed to feel, and which, by acting physically on the brain, tends naturally to abridge life amongst such persons. But the late Neibhur, the Roman historian, we remember, observes in one of his philosophical chapters, that nothing tends more to longevity, than the contemplation of projects, which one has one's self conceived, in their progress to a successful development. Hence generals, who have retired from the field, after having attained the objects of their warfare according to their wishes, are long-lived—and the historian adduces, as an example of what he says, the case of Camillus. We can ourselves quote many modern instances to confirm this opinion. Marlborough, one of the most fortunate leaders that ever commanded an army, lived rather too long for his own reputation. We sincerely hope that our posterity will not have to repeat the same thing of the Marlborough who succeeded him, and who, under the name of Wellington, carried the glory of the British arms to the ends of the earth. Perhaps it is for a contrary reason that we see so few British statesmen live long in office. Those who lead a party, and are unsuccessful in their plans, die always prematurely. Witness Pitt, Fox, Canning, &c. But the great Bacon died in his 64th year; Newton, at 84; Harvey (the discoverer of the circulation) at 88; Linnæus at 71; Leibnitz at 70; Galileo, 70. On the contrary, Bichat, a modern, died in his 34th year; and Davy, before he reached 60. Amongst 1700 cases of persons in all classes of society, who have reached the age of 100, only one literary man was to be found, and that was Fontenelle. We have before us a list of nearly 300 persons, men and women, in all parts of the United Kingdom, who had attained to a great age (in no instance less than 100) during the term of years, beginning with 1707, and ending in 1823, both included, and we cannot discover throughout the whole catalogue, a single name that has linked itself with an expression or a deed worthy of being remembered for an hour. So true is it, as an illustrious man has profoundly said, and as the only rival of that man's splendid fame which the modern world could produce, has repeated, " The duties of life are more than life." Rather a curious confirmation of Niebhur's doctrine just mentioned, is to be found in the ages of all the successful painters. The Italian artists, with very few exceptions, lived long :—Titian was 96; Spenello was nearly 100; Carlo Cignani, 91; Michael Angelo, 90; Leonardo da Vinci, 75; Calabresi, 86; Claude Lorraine, 82; Carlo Maratta, 88; Tentoretti, 82; Sebastian Ricci, 78; Francesco Albano, 88; Guido, 68; Guercino, 76; John Baptist Crespi, 76; Guiseppe Crespi, 82; Carlo Dolce, 70; Andrew Sacchi, 74; Zucharelli, 86; Vernet, 77; and Schidon, 70.—*Monthly Review.*

CEDAR-TREES.—There are now growing on the grounds at Greenfield Hall, the property of Ralph Richardson, Esq., two cedar-trees, of the immense height of 150 feet; the girth of one is 11 feet, 7 inches, and its branches extend 50 feet; the girth of the other is 8 feet, 7 inches.—*Chester Chronicle.*

A BACHELOR'S COMPLAINT OF THE BEHAVIOUR OF MARRIED PEOPLE.

As a single man, I have spent a good deal of my time in noting down the infirmities of Married People, to console myself for those superior pleasures, which they tell me I have lost by remaining as I am.

I cannot say that the quarrels of men and their wives ever made any great impression upon me, or had much tendency to strengthen in me those anti-social resolutions, which I took up long ago upon more substantial considerations. What oftenest offends me at the houses of married persons where I visit, is an error of quite a different description ;—it is, that they are too loving.

Not too loving neither; that does not explain my meaning. Besides, why should that offend me ? The very act of separating themselves from the rest of the world to have the fuller enjoyment of each other's society, implies that they prefer one another to all the world.

But what I complain of is, that they carry this preference so undisguisedly, they perk it up in the faces of us single people so shamelessly, you cannot be in their company a moment without being made to feel, by some indirect hint or open avowal, that *you* are not the object of this preference. Now there are some things which give no offence, while implied or taken for granted merely ; but expressed, there is much offence in them. If a man were to accost the first homely-featured or plain-dressed young woman of his acquaintance, and tell her, bluntly, that she was not handsome or rich enough for him, and he could not marry her, he would deserve to be kicked for his ill manners ; yet no less is implied in the fact, that having access and opportunity of putting the question to her, he has never yet thought fit to do it. The young woman understands this as clearly as if it were put into words ; but no reasonable young woman would think of making this the ground of a quarrel. Just as little right have a married couple to tell me by speeches, and looks that are scarce less plain than speeches, that I am not the happy man,—the lady's choice. It is enough that I know I am not : I do not want this perpetual reminding.

The display of superior knowledge or riches may be made sufficiently mortifying ; but these admit of a palliative. The knowledge which is brought out to insult me, may accidentally improve me ; and in the rich man's houses and pictures, his parks and gardens, I have a temporary usufruct at least. But the display of married happiness has none of these palliatives : it is throughout pure, unrecompensed, unqualified insult.

Marriage, by its best title, is a monopoly, and not of the least invidious sort. It is the cunning of most possessors of any exclusive privileges to keep their advantage as much out of sight as possible, that their less favoured neighbours, seeing little of the benefit, may the less be disposed to question the right. But these married monopolists thrust the most obnoxious part of their patent into our faces.

Nothing is to me more distasteful than that entire complacency and satisfaction which beam in the countenances of a new-married couple,—in that of the lady particularly : it tells you, that her lot is disposed of in this world; that *you* can have no hopes of her. It is true, I have none ; nor wishes either, perhaps; but this is one of those truths which ought, as I said before, to be taken for granted, not expressed.

The excessive airs which those people give themselves, founded on the ignorance of us unmarried people, would be more offensive if they were less irrational. We will allow them to understand the mysteries belonging to their own craft better than we who have not had the happiness to be made free of the company ; but their arrogance is not content within these limits. If a single person presume to offer his opinion in their presence, though upon the most indifferent subject, he is immediately silenced as an incompetent person. Nay, a young married lady of my acquaintance, who, the best of the jest was, had not changed her condition above a fortnight before, in a question on which I had the misfortune to differ from her, respecting the properest mode of breeding oysters for the London market, had the assurance to ask, with a sneer, how such an old Bachelor as I could pretend to know any thing about such matters.

But what I have spoken of hitherto is nothing to the airs which these creatures give themselves when they come, as they generally do, to have children. When I consider how little of a rarity children are,—that every street and blind alley swarms with them,—that the poorest people commonly have them in most abundance,—that there are few marriages that are not blessed with at least one of these bargains,—how often they turn out ill and defeat the fond hopes of their parents, taking to vicious courses, which end in poverty, disgrace, the gallows, &c., I cannot, for my life, tell what cause for pride there can possibly be in having them. If they are young phœnixes, indeed, that were born but one in a year, there might be a pretext. But when they are so common—

I do not advert to the insolent merit which they assume with their husbands on these occasions. Let them look to that. But why we, who are not their natural-born subjects, should be expected to bring our spices, myrrh, and incense,—our tribute and homage of admiration,—I do not see.

"Like as the arrows in the hand of the giant, even so are the young children:" so says the excellent office in our Prayer-book appointed for the churching of women. "Happy is the man that hath his quiver full of them:" so say I; but then, don't let him discharge his quiver upon us that are weaponless;—let them be arrows, but not to gall and stick us. I have generally observed that these arrows are double-headed; they have two forks, to be sure to hit with one or the other. As for instance, where you come into a house which is full of children, if you happen to take no notice of them (you are thinking of something else, perhaps, and turn a deaf ear to their innocent caresses,) you are set down as untractable, morose, a hater of children. On the other hand, if you find them more than usually engaging,—if you are taken with their pretty manners, and set about in earnest to romp and play with them, some pretext or other is sure to be quickly found for sending them out of the room: they are too noisy or boisterous, or Mr. —— does not like children. With one or other of these forks the arrow is sure to hit you.

I could forgive their jealousy, and dispense with toying with their brats, if it gives them any pain; but I think it unreasonable to be called upon to *love* them, where I see no occasion,—to love a whole family, perhaps, eight, nine, or ten, indiscriminately,—to love all the pretty dears, because children are so engaging.

I know there is a proverb, "Love me, love my dog:" that is not always so very practicable, particularly if the dog be set upon you to tease you or snap at you in sport. But a dog, or a lesser thing,—any inanimate substance, as a keepsake, a watch or a ring, a tree, or the place where we last parted when my friend went away upon a long absence, I can make shift to love, because I love him, and any thing that reminds me of him; provided it be in its nature indifferent, and apt to receive whatever hue fancy can give it. But children have a real character and an essential being of themselves: they are amiable or unamiable *per se*; I must love or hate them as I see cause for either in their qualities. A child's nature is too serious a thing to admit of its being regarded as a mere appendage to another being, and to be loved or hated accordingly: they stand with me upon their own stock, as much as men and women do. O! but you will say, sure it is an attractive age,—there is something in the tender years of infancy that of itself charms us. That is the very reason why I am more nice about them. I know that a sweet child is the sweetest thing in nature, not even excepting the delicate creatures which bear them; but the prettier the kind of a thing is, the more desirable it is that it should be pretty of its kind. One daisy differs not much from another in glory; but a violet should look and smell the daintiest.—I was always rather squeamish in my women and children.

But this is not the worst; one must be admitted into their familiarity at least, before they can complain of inattention. It implies visits and some kind of intercourse. But if the husband be a man with whom you have lived on a friendly footing before marriage,—if you did not come in on the wife's side,—if you did not sneak into the house in her train, but were an old friend in fast habits of intimacy before their courtship was so much as thought on—look about you—your tenure is precarious—before a twelvemonth shall roll over your head, you shall find your old friend gradually grow cool and altered towards you, and at last seek opportunities of breaking with you. I have scarce a married friend of my acquaintance, upon whose firm faith I can rely, whose friendship did not commence *after the period of his marriage*. With some limitations they can endure that: but that the good man should have dared to enter into a solemn league of friendship in which they were not consulted, though it happened before they knew him,—before they that are now man and wife ever met,—this is intolerable to them. Every long friendship, every old authentic intimacy, must be brought into their office to be new stamped with their currency, as a sovereign prince calls in the good old money that was coined in some interregnum before he was born or thought of, to be new marked and minted with the stamp of his authority, before he will let it pass current in the world. You may guess what luck generally befalls such a rusty piece of metal as I am in these *new mintings*.

Innumerable are the ways which they take to insult and worm you out of their husband's confidence. Laughing at all you say with a kind of wonder, as if you were a queer kind of fellow that said good things, *but an oddity*, is one of the ways;—they have a particular kind of *stare* for the purpose;—till at last the husband, who used to defer to your judgment, and would pass over some excrescences of understanding and manner for the sake of a general vein of observation (not quite vulgar) which he perceived in you, begins to suspect whether you are not altogether a humorist,—a fellow well enough to have consorted with in his bachelor days, but not quite so proper to be introduced to ladies. This may be called the staring way, and is that which has oftenest been put in practice against me.

Then there is the exaggerating way, or the way of irony; that is, where they find you an object of especial regard with their husband, who is not so easily to be shaken from the lasting attachment, founded on esteem, which he has conceived towards you; by never-qualified exaggerations, to cry up all that you say or do, till the good man, who understands well enough that it is all done in compliment to him, grows weary of the debt of gratitude which is due to so much candour, and by relaxing a little on his part, and taking down a peg or two in his enthusiasm, sinks at length to that kindly level of moderate esteem, that "decent affection and complacent kindness" towards you, where she herself can join in sympathy with him without much stretch and violence to her sincerity.

Another way (for the ways they have to accomplish so desirable a purpose are infinite) is, with a kind of innocent simplicity, continually to mistake what it was which first made their husband fond of you. If an esteem for something excellent in your moral character was that which riveted the chain which she is to break, upon any imaginary discovery of a want of poignancy in your conversation, she will cry, "I thought, my dear, you described your friend Mr. —— as a great wit." If, on the other hand, it was for some supposed charm in your conversation that he first grew to like you, and was content for this to overlook some trifling irregularities in your moral deportment, upon the first notice of any of these she as readily exclaims, "This, my dear, is your good Mr. ——." One good lady whom I took the liberty of expostulating with for not showing me quite so much respect as I thought due to her husband's old friend, had the candour to confess to me that she had often heard Mr. —— speak of me before marriage, and that she had conceived a great desire to be acquainted with me, but that the sight of me had very much disappointed her expectations; for, from her husband's representations of me, that she had formed a notion that she was to see a fine, tall, officer-like looking man (I use her very words;) the very reverse of which proved to be the truth. This was candid; and I had the civility not to ask her in return, how she came to pitch upon a standard of personal accomplishments for her husband's friends which differed so much from his own: for my friend's dimensions as near as possible approximated to mine; he standing five feet five inches in his shoes, in which I have the advantage of him by about half an inch; and he no more than myself exhibiting any indications of a martial character in his air or countenance.

These are some of the mortifications which I have encountered in the absurd attempt to visit at their houses. To enumerate them all would be a vain endeavour; I shall therefore just glance at the very common impropriety of which married ladies are guilty, of treating us as if we were their husbands, and *vice versa*. I mean, when they use us with familiarity, and their husbands with ceremony. *Testacea*, for instance, kept me the other night two or three hours beyond my usual time of supping, while she was fretting because Mr. ———— did not come home, till the oysters which she had had opened, out of compliment to me, were all spoiled, rather than she would be guilty of the impoliteness of touching one in his absence. This was reversing the point of good manners: for ceremony is an invention to take off the uneasy feeling which we derive from knowing ourselves to be less the objects of love and esteem with a fellow-creature than some other person is. It endeavours to make up, by superior attentions in little points, for that invidious preference which it is forced to deny in the greater. Had *Testacea* kept the oysters back for me, and withstood her husband's importunities to go to supper, she would have acted according to the strict rules of propriety. I know no ceremony that ladies are bound to observe to their husbands, beyond the point of a modest behaviour and decorum: therefore I must protest against the vicarious gluttony of *Cerasia*, who at her own table sent away a dish of morellas, which I was applying to with great good will, to her husband at the other end of the table, and recommended a plate of less extraordinary gooseberries to my unwedded palate in their stead. Neither can I excuse the wanton affront of————

But I am weary of stringing up all my married acquaintance by Roman denominations. Let them amend and change their manners, or I promise to send you the full-length English of their names, to be recorded to the terror of all such desperate offenders in future. Your humble servant,
ELIA.

STATISTICS.

CATTLE AND SHEEP.—A century ago, our cattle, from the inferiority of their food, were not one-half, sometimes even not one-third, of their present weight. It is computed that England and Wales now contain, at least, five million oxen, and a million and a half of horses, of which about a million are used in husbandry, two hundred thousand for pleasure, and three hundred thousand are colts and breeding mares. The number of sheep is about twenty millions, and eight millions lambs. The number of long-wooled sheep is above five millions, their fleeces averaging seven or eight pounds; and of short-wooled sheep fifteen millions, the weight of fleece averaging from three to three and a-half pounds. The whole quantity annually shorn in England is from eighty to eighty-five millions of pounds. The Merino were introduced about the beginning of the present century, and were imported in large numbers after our alliance with Spain, in 1809. The Cachemere goat has lately been introduced into Essex, and is thriving. The great pasturage counties are Leicester, Northampton, Lincoln, and Somerset; and for butter and cheese, Cheshire, Gloucestershire, and Wiltshire. The import of butter and cheese, from foreign countries is checked by duties, but these are important articles of Irish commerce with England.

IRISH TRADE WITH LIVERPOOL.—Some idea of the extent and importance of the trade between Ireland and this port may be formed from the following list of Irish articles imported into Liverpool during the year 1831. It would not be easy to form an accurate estimate of the value of these imports, but it must amount to several millions sterling. It will be seen that the articles exported consist entirely of agricultural produce. Ireland, in fact, seems destined to become the granary of England; and we cannot help hoping that the continually increasing intercourse between the two countries will at last have the effect of raising that rich and beautiful country to its proper rank amongst the nations. The invention of steam has already done more for Ireland than a thousand acts of Parliament; and it must sooner or later, either raise it to the same level as England, or drag down England to the level of Ireland.

Cows	90,715	Lard	4,542 firkins
Horses	276	Butter	5,754 cools
Sheep	134,726	Ditto	258,087 firkins
Mules	243	Ditto	19,217 haid do.
Pigs	156,001	Eggs	2,505 crates
Calves	1,196	Wheat	277,069 quarters
Lambs	25,725	Oats	290,670 do.
Hams and tongues	590 hhds.	Barley	21,328 do.
Bacon	18,090 bales	Rye	423 do.
Pork	14,554 barrels	Beans	8,452 do.
Ditto	936 half do	Peas	1,724 do.
Beef	6,391 tierces	Malt	6,850 do.
Ditto	1,199 barrels	Meal	149,816 loads
Lard	465 tierces	Flour	93,154 sacks

LOCUSTS.

The first record of the ravages of locusts which we find in history, is the account in the Book of Exodus, of their visitation to the land of Egypt. Africa appears to have been generally the quarter of the globe most severely subjected to the inroads of the locust tribe. A law was enacted and enforced, in the territory of Cyrene, according to the account of Pliny, by which the people were obliged to destroy these insects in the egg, in the larva state, and in the image. A similar law prevailed in the island of Lemnos, where each person was forced to furnish annually a certain quantity of locusts. According to Orosius, A.M. 3800, the north of Africa was so infested by them, that every vestige of vegetation vanished from the face of the earth. After this, he adds, that they flew off to sea and were drowned; but their carcases being cast upon shore, emitted a stench equal to what might have been produced by the dead bodies of 100,000 men. We are told by St. Augustine, that a pestilence arising from the same cause, destroyed no less than 890,000 people in the kingdom of Numidia, and many more in the countries along the sea coast.

Blown from that quarter of the globe, the locusts have occasionally visited both Italy and Spain. The former country was severely ravaged by myriads of those desolating intruders in 591 A.C. These were of a larger size than common, as we are informed by Mouffet, who quotes an ancient historian; and from their stench when cast into the sea, caused a plague, which carried off infinite numbers, both of men and cattle. A famine took place in the Venetian territory in 1467, occasioned by the ravages of these insects, in which 30,000 persons are reported to have perished. Mouffet mentions many other instances of the same kind which have taken place in Europe at different periods. They entered Russia in immense divisions, in three different places, in 1600, darkening the air with their numbers, and passed over from there into Poland and Lithuania.

In many parts they lay dead to the depth of four feet. Sometimes they covered the surface of the earth like a dark cloud, loaded the trees, and the destruction which they produced exceeded all calculation. They fall sometimes upon corn, and in three hours will consume an entire field, as happened once in the south of France. When they had finished the corn they extended their devastations to vines, pulse, willows, and in short, to every thing else wearing the shape of vegetation, not excepting even hemp, which was not protected by its bitterness.

In 1748 considerable numbers of locusts visited this country, but luckily they did not propagate, and all soon perished.

COLUMN FOR THE YOUNG.

SIR PHILIP SYDNEY.
BORN 1554—DIED 1586.

Abridged from JOHNSTONE'S *Specimens of the Poets.*

THIS noble soldier and accomplished gentleman was the son of Sir Henry Sydney of Penshurst, in Kent. In his lifetime, Sydney enjoyed a popularity both at home and abroad, which is not easily accounted for, unless we believe what must have been the truth, that by the charm of his manners, and the nobility of his nature, he unconsciously diffused around himself the atmosphere through which his character and actions were viewed; and which gave to a mortal of ordinary proportions the stature and bearing of a hero of the old romance. Sydney is the connecting link between the knight of chivalry and the modern soldier and gentleman,—one of those rare and happy persons who come into the world once in a century to unite the suffrages of mankind in one spontaneous feeling of love and admiration. Though his character was composed of all the elements which constitute a hero and a favourite—bravery, generosity, frankness, courtesy, a noble disinterestedness, and much graceful accomplishment, his person and manners must have created the charm which made him, before the age of thirty-two, the most popular man that ever lived in England.

It was the uniform practice of the age in which he lived, for youths liberally educated to attend both the universities; and Sydney did so before going on his travels. At Paris, he was made a gentleman of the bed-chamber—a mark of high distinction to a young foreigner. He was here seen and admired by Henry IV., then only King of Navarre. "He used him," says Sydney's friend and biographer, Sir Fulke Greville, "like an equal in nature, and fit for friendship with a king." The massacre of the Protestants, which took place during his residence in Paris, disgusted Sydney with France. He went to Frankfort, and at the court of the Emperor distinguished himself by his skill in martial exercises. Printers were at this time among the most learned men; and it is a curious trait of ancient manners to find scholars and foreigners lodged in their houses. At Frankfort, Sydney, lived in the house of Andrew Wechel. Before returning home, he spent a year in Italy, and it is presumed became acquainted with Tasso. On his return he was immediately taken into favour by Queen Elizabeth, who sent him as ambassador to Vienna, with a secret mission to unite the Protestant states of the empire against Spain. Sydney was but a young diplomatist, but he skilfully accomplished this important object; his manliness and candour being found more effective in swaying men's minds, than the subtlety and crooked policy which statesmen of more cunning than wisdom think it needful to employ. He was at this time only about twenty years of age.

Two years afterwards, Sydney was named as a candidate for the throne of Poland; but this proposal, which shews the estimation in which he was held, was crushed by the Queen, both from political and private reasons. "She refused," says the historian, "to farther the advancement, out of the fear that she should lose the jewel of her times."

Sir Philip, having formerly united the Protestant states, was appointed to assist the people of the Netherlands in throwing off the yoke of Spain, and for this purpose he commanded the military force sent from England. He was also made colonel of all the newly-raised Dutch regiments. He was soon joined by Leicester with more troops, and appointed general of horse. On the 22d of September, 1586, in a skirmish near Zutphen, Sydney beat a superior force of the enemy, which he casually encountered, but lost his own life. After his horse had been shot under him he mounted another, and continued to fight till he received his death-wound. The anecdote of his dying moments has been told a thousand times, but will never lose its interest:—While borne off the field, faint with the sick languor which attends the loss of blood, he requested a draught of water; but just as it was put to his lips, seeing a dying soldier beside him look wistfully at it, he put it away, saying, "This man's necessity is yet greater than mine."—He languished till the 15th of October, and died in Holland, whence his body was brought for burial. All England wore mourning for his death, and volumes of poetical laments and elegies were poured forth in all languages.

If not an eminent poet, Sydney was, in the most generous sense, the warm friend and patron of letters. But in literature, as in every other department, his short life was one of bright promise, rather than of wonderful achievement; and perhaps, at the age of thirty-two, the grave never closed over any man who combined such universal accomplishment, with so many amiable qualities, as this darling of the people of England. His learned tutor had recorded on his tomb, that "*he was the tutor of Sir Philip Sydney;*" and his friend Sir Fulke Greville, Lord Brooke, who long survived Sydney, had this inscription put on his monument:—"Fulke Greville, servant of Queen Elizabeth, counsellor to King James, and *friend of Sir Philip Sydney.*" "The life of Sir Philip Sydney," says Mr. Campbell, "was poetry put in action."

INSCRIPTION FOR A TABLET AT PENSHURST, THE BIRTH-PLACE OF SIR PHILIP SYDNEY.

ARE days of old familiar to thy mind,
O Reader? Hast thou let the midnight hour
Pass unperceived, whilst thou in fancy lived
With high-born beauties and enamour'd chiefs,
Sharing their hopes, and with a breathless joy,
Whose expectation touch'd the verge of pain,
Following their dangerous fortunes? If such love
Hath ever thrill'd thy bosom, thou wilt tread,
As with a pilgrim's reverential thoughts,
The groves of Penshurst. SYDNEY here was born,
SYDNEY, than whom no gentler, braver man
His own delightful genius ever feign'd
Illustrating the vales of Arcady
With courteous courage and with loyal love.
Upon his natal day, the acorn here
Was planted. It grew up a stately oak,
And in the beauty of its strength it stood
And flourish'd, when his perishable part
Had moulder'd dust to dust. That stately oak,
Itself hath mouldered now, but SYDNEY'S fame
Endureth in his own immortal works.—SOUTHEY.

Let us explain MR. SOUTHEY'S allusion. An oak was planted at Penshurst on the day of Sydney's birth, which grew to the noble size of twenty-two feet in circumference, and was pulled down, it is said, by mistake. This tree was frequently called the "bare oak," says an English writer on trees. Tradition saith, that when the tenants went to the park gates to meet the Earl of Leicester, they used to adorn their hats with boughs from the Penshurst oak. Within its hollow trunk was a seat which could accommodate five or six persons.

IRISH RELIGION IN AULD LANG SYNE.—"No good will come of it," said the Colonel. "I mind the time in Connaught when no man clearly knew to what religion he belonged; and in one family the boys would go to church and the girls to mass, or may be both would join and go to which ever happened to be nearest. When I entered the militia, I recollect, the first time I was ever detached from headquarters, I went with the company to Portumna. Old Sir Mark Blake, who commanded the regiment, happened to be passing through, and the night before he had a desperate drink with Gen. Loftus at the Castle. When I left Loughrea, I forgot to ascertain where I should bring the men on Sunday, and I thought this a good opportunity to ask the question. I opened his bed-room door softly. 'Sir Mark,' says I, 'where shall I march the men?' 'What kind of day is it?' says he. 'Rather wet,' was my answer. 'It's like the night that preceded it,' said he. 'Upon my conscience, my lad,' he continued, 'my head's not clear enough at present to recollect the exact position of church and chapel; but take them *to the nearest.*' That is what I call," and the Colonel shook his head gravely, "real Christian feeling."—*Wild Sports of the West.*

THE STORY-TELLER.

LEGEND OF THE ROSE OF THE ALHAMBRA.
BY WASHINGTON IRVING.

AMONG those who attended in the train of the monarchs was a favourite page of the Queen, named Ruyz de Alarcon. To say that he was a favourite page of the queen was at once to speak his eulogium; for every one in the suite of the stately Elizabetta was chosen for grace, and beauty, and accomplishments. He was just turned of eighteen, light and lithe of form, and graceful as a young Antinous. To the queen he was all deference and respect; yet he was at heart a roguish stripling, petted and spoiled by the ladies about the court, and experienced in the ways of women far beyond his years.

This loitering page was one morning rambling about the groves of the Generalife, which overlook the grounds of the Alhambra. He had taken with him for his amusement a favourite ger-falcon of the Queen. In the course of his rambles, seeing a bird rising from a thicket, he unhooded the hawk and let him fly. The falcon towered high in the air, made a sweep at his quarry, but missing it, soared away regardless of the calls of the page. The latter followed the truant bird with his eye in its capricious flight, until he saw it alight upon the battlements of a remote and lonely tower in the outer walls of the Alhambra, built on the edge of a ravine that separated the royal fortress from the grounds of the Generalife. It was, in fact, the "Tower of Princesses." The page descended into the ravine and approached the tower, but it had no entrance from the glen, and its lofty height rendered any attempt to scale it fruitless. Seeking one of the gates of the fortress, therefore, he made a wide circuit to that side of the tower facing within the walls. A small garden, enclosed by trellis-work of reeds overhung with myrtle, lay before the tower. Opening a wicket, the page passed between beds of flowers and thickets of roses to the door. It was closed and bolted. A crevice in the door gave him a peep into the interior. There was a small Moorish hall with fretted walls, light marble columns, and an alabaster fountain surrounded with flowers. In the centre hung a gilt cage containing a singing bird; beneath it, on a chair, lay a tortoise-shell cat, among reels of silk and other articles of female labour; and a guitar, decorated with ribands, leaned against the fountain.

Ruyz de Alarcon was struck with these traces of female taste and elegance in a lonely and, as he had supposed, deserted tower. They reminded him of the tales of enchanted halls current in the Alhambra; and the tortoise-shell cat might be some spell-bound princess. He knocked gently at the door; a beautiful face peeped out from a little window above, but was instantly withdrawn. He waited, expecting that the door would be opened, but he waited in vain; no footstep was to be heard within—all was silent. Had his senses deceived him, or was this beautiful apparition the fairy of the tower? He knocked again, and more loudly. After a little while the beaming face once more peeped forth; it was that of a blooming damsel of fifteen. The page immediately doffed his plumed bonnet, and entreated in the most courteous accents to be permitted to ascend the tower in pursuit of his falcon. "I dare not open the door, senor," replied the little damsel, blushing; "my aunt has forbidden it."—"I do beseech you, fair maid; it is the favourite falcon of the Queen: I dare not return to the palace without it."—"Are you, then, one of the cavaliers of the court?"—"I am, fair maid; but I shall lose the Queen's favour and my place, if I lose this hawk."—"Santa Maria! it is against you cavaliers of the court my aunt has charged me especially to bar the door."—"Against wicked cavaliers, doubtless; but I am none of these, but a simple harmless page, who will be ruined and undone if you deny me this small request."

The heart of the little damsel was touched by the distress of the page. It was a thousand pities he should be ruined for the want of so trifling a boon. Surely, too, he could not be one of those dangerous beings whom her aunt had described as a species of cannibal, ever on the prowl to make prey of thoughtless damsels—he was gentle and modest, and stood so entreatingly with cap in hand, and looked so charming. The sly page saw that the garrison began to waver, and redoubled his entreaties in such moving terms, that it was not in the nature of mortal maiden to deny him; so the blushing little warden of the tower descended and opened the door with a trembling hand; and if the page had been charmed by a mere glimpse of her countenance from the window, he was ravished by the full-length portrait now revealed to him. Her Andalusian bodice and trim basquina set off the round but delicate symmetry of her form, which was as yet scarce verging into womanhood. Her glossy hair was parted on her forehead with scrupulous exactness, and decorated with a fresh-plucked rose, according to the universal custom of the country. It is true her complexion was tinged by the ardour of a southern sun, but it served to give richness to the mantling bloom of her cheek, and to heighten the lustre of her melting eyes. Ruyz de Alarcon beheld all this with a single glance, for it became him not to tarry: he merely murmured his acknowledgments, and then bounded lightly up the spiral staircase in quest of his falcon.

He soon returned with the truant bird upon his wrist. The damsel, in the meantime, had seated herself by the fountain in the hall, and was winding silk; but in her agitation she let fall the reel upon the pavement. The page sprang and picked it up, then dropping gracefully on one knee, presented it to her; but seizing the hand extended to receive it, imprinted on it a kiss more fervent and devout than he had ever imprinted on the fair hand of his sovereign. "Ave Maria, senor!" exclaimed the damsel, blushing still deeper with confusion and surprise, for never before had she received such a salutation. The modest page made a thousand apologies, assuring her it was the way at court of expressing the most profound homage and respect. Her anger, if anger she felt, was easily pacified, but her agitation and embarrassment continued; and she sat blushing deeper and deeper, with her eyes cast down upon her work, entangling the silk which she attempted to wind. The cunning page saw the confusion in the opposite camp, and would fain have profited by it; but the fine speeches he would have uttered died upon his lips; his attempts at gallantry were awkward and ineffectual; and to his surprise, the adroit page, who had figured with such grace and effrontery among the most knowing and experienced ladies of the court, found himself awed and abashed in the presence of a simple damsel of fifteen. In fact, the artless maiden, in her own modesty and innocence, had guardians more effectual than the bolts and bars prescribed by her vigilant aunt. Still, where is the female bosom proof against the first whisperings of love. The little damsel, with all her artlessness, instinctively comprehended all that the faltering tongue of the page failed to express; and her heart was fluttered at beholding, for the first time, a lover at her feet —and such a lover!

The diffidence of the page, though genuine, was short-lived, and he was recovering his usual ease and confidence, when a shrill voice was heard at a distance. "My aunt is returning from mass!" cried the damsel, in affright; "I pray you, senor, depart."—"Not until you grant me that rose from your hair as a remembrance." She hastily untwisted the rose from her raven locks; "Take it," cried she, agitated and blushing; "but pray begone." The page took the rose, and at the same time covered with kisses the fair hand that gave it. Then, placing the flower in his bonnet, and taking the falcon upon his wrist, he bounded off through the garden, bearing away with him the heart of the gentle Jacinta. When the vigilant aunt arrived at the tower, she remarked the agitation of her niece, and an air of confusion in the hall; but a word of explanation sufficed.—"A ger-falcon had pursued his prey into the hall."— "Mercy on us! to think of a falcon flying into the tower! Did ever one hear of so saucy a hawk? Why, the very bird in the cage is not safe!"

The vigilant Fredeganda was one of the most wary of ancient spinsters. She had a becoming terror and distrust of what she denominated the "opposite sex," which had gradually increased through a long life of celibacy. Not that the good lady had ever suffered from their wiles, nature having set up a safeguard in her face that forbade all trespass upon her premises; but ladies who have least cause to fear for themselves, are most ready to keep a watch over their more tempting neighbours. The niece was the orphan of an officer who had fallen in the wars. She had been educated in a convent, and had recently been transferred from her sacred asylum to the immediate guardianship of her aunt, under whose overshadowing care she vegetated in obscurity, like an opening rose blooming beneath a brier. Nor indeed is this comparison entirely accidental; for, to tell the truth, her fresh and dawning beauty had caught the public eye, even in her seclusion, and, with that poetical turn common to the people of Andalusia, the peasantry of the neighbourhood had given her the appellation of "the Rose of the Alhambra."

The wary aunt continued to keep a faithful watch over her tempting little niece as long as the court continued at Granada, and flattered herself that her vigilance had been successful. It is true, the good lady was now and then discomposed by the tinkling of guitars and chanting of low ditties from the moonlit groves beneath the tower; but she would exhort her niece to shut her ears against such idle minstrelsy, assuring her that it was one of the arts of the opposite sex, by which simple maids were often lured to their undoing. Alas! what chance with a simple maid has a dry lecture against a moonlight serenade?

At length King Philip cut short his sojourn at Granada, and suddenly departed with all his train. The vigilant Fredeganda watched the royal pageant as it issued forth from the gate of justice, and descended the great avenue leading to the city. When the last banner disappeared from her sight, she returned exulting to her tower, for all her cares were over. To her surprise, a light Arabian steed pawed the ground at the wicket-gate of the garden:—to her horror, she saw through the thicket of roses a youth, in gaily embroidered dress, at the feet of her niece. At the sound of her footsteps he gave a tender adieu, bounded lightly over the barrier of reeds and myrtles, sprang upon his horse, and was out of sight in an instant.

The tender Jacinta, in the agony of her grief, lost all thought of her aunt's displeasure. Throwing herself into her arms, she broke forth into sobs and tears. "Ay di mi!" cried she; "he's gone!—he's gone!—he's gone! and I shall never see him more!"—"Gone!—who is gone?— what youth is that I saw at your feet?"—"A queen's page, aunt, who came to bid me farewell."—"A queen's page, child!" echoed the vigilant Fredeganda faintly; "and when did you become acquainted with a queen's page?"— "The morning the ger-falcon came into the tower. It was the queen's ger-falcon, and he came in pursuit of it."—"Ah silly, silly girl! know that there are no ger-falcons half so dangerous as these young prankling pages, and it is precisely such simple birds as thee that they pounce upon."

The aunt was at first indignant at learning that, in despite of her boasted vigilance, a tender intercourse had been carried on by the youthful lovers, almost beneath her eye; but when she found that her simple-hearted niece, though thus exposed, without the protection of bolt or bar, to all the machinations of the opposite sex, had come forth unsinged from the fiery ordeal, she consoled herself with the persuasion, that it was owing to the chaste and cautious maxims in which she had, as it were, steeped her to the very lips. While the aunt laid this soothing unction to her pride, the niece treasured up the oft-repeated vows of fidelity of the page. But what is the love of restless roving man? A vagrant stream that dallies for a time with each flower upon its bank, then passes on, and leaves them all in tears. Days, weeks, months elapsed, and nothing more was heard of the page. The pomegranate ripened, the vine yielded up its fruit, the autumnal rains descended in torrents from the mountains; the Sierra Nevada became covered with a snowy mantle, and wintry blasts howled through the halls of the Alhambra—still he came not. The winter passed away. Again the genial spring burst forth with song and blossom and balmy zephyr; the snows melted from the mountains, until none remained but on the lofty summits of Nevada, glistening through the sultry summer air. Still nothing was heard of the forgetful page."

Poor Jacinta sits and weeps her time away beside a fountain in the hall.

As the bell in the distant watch-tower of the Alhambra struck the midnight hour, the fountain was agitated; and bubble—bubble—bubble—it tossed about the waters, until a Moorish female rose to view. She was young and beautiful; her dress was rich with jewels, and in her hand she held a silver lute. Jacinta trembled and was faint, but was reassured by the soft and plaintive voice of the apparition, and the sweet expression of her pale, melancholy countenance. "Daughter of mortality," said she, "what aileth thee? Why do thy tears trouble my fountain, and thy sighs and plaints disturb the quiet watches of the night?"—"I weep because of the faithlessness of man, and I bemoan my solitary and forsaken state."— "Take comfort; thy sorrows may yet have an end. Thou beholdest a Moorish princess, who, like thee, was unhappy in her love. A Christian knight, thy ancestor, won my heart, and would have borne me to his native land and to the bosom of his church. I was a convert in my heart, but I lacked courage equal to my faith, and lingered till too late. For this the evil genii are permitted to have power over me, and I remain enchanted in this tower until some pure Christian will deign to break the magic spell. Wilt thou undertake the task?"—"I will," replied the damsel trembling. "Come hither then, and fear not; dip thy hand in the fountain, sprinkle the water over me, and baptise me after the manner of thy faith; so shall the enchantment be dispelled, and my troubled spirit have repose." The damsel advanced with faltering steps, dipped her hand in the fountain, collected water in the palm, and sprinkled it over the pale face of the phantom. The latter smiled with ineffable benignity. She dropped her silver lute at the feet of Jacinta, crossed her white arms upon her bosom, and melted from sight, so that it seemed merely as if a shower of dewdrops had fallen into the fountain. Jacinta retired from the hall filled with awe and wonder. She scarcely closed her eyes that night; but when she awoke at daybreak out of a troubled slumber, the whole appeared to her like a distempered dream. On descending into the hall, however, the truth of the vision was established; for, beside the fountain, she beheld the silver lute glittering in the morning sunshine.

The music of this lute fairly enchants all the hearers, till at length its mistress is sent for to court, to try its influence over the hypochondriac monarch.

At the moment we treat of, however, a freak had come over the mind of this sapient and illustrious Bourbon, that surpassed all former vagaries. After a long spell of imaginary illness, which set all the strains of Farinelli, and the consultations of a whole orchestra of court fiddlers at defiance, the monarch fairly, in idea, gave up the ghost, and considered himself absolutely dead. This would have been harmless enough, and even convenient both to his queen and courtiers, had he been content to remain in the quietude befitting a dead man; but to their annoyance he insisted upon having the funeral ceremonies performed over him, and, to their inexpressible perplexity, began to grow impatient and to revile bitterly at them for negligence and disrespect, in leaving him unburied. What was to be done? To disobey the king's positive commands was monstrous in the eyes of the obsequious courtiers of a punctilious court—but to obey him, and bury him alive, would be downright regicide!

In the midst of this fearful dilemma a rumour reached the court, of the female minstrel who was turning the brains of all Andalusia. The Queen despatched missions in all haste to summon her to St. Ildefonso, where the court at that time resided. Within a few days, as the Queen, with her maids of honour, was walking in those stately gardens, intended, with their avenues, and terraces, and fountains, to eclipse the glories of Versailles, the far-famed minstrel was conducted into her presence. The imperial Elizabetta gazed with surprise at the youthful and unpretending appearance of the little being that had set the world madding. She was in her picturesque Andalusian dress; her silver lute was in her hand, and she stood with modest and downcast eyes, but with a simplicity and freshness of beauty that still bespoke her "The Rose of the Alhambra." As usual, she was accompanied by the ever-vigilant Fredegonda, who gave the whole history of her parentage and descent to the inquiring queen. If the stately Elizabetta had been interested by the appearance of Jacinta, she was still more pleased when she learnt that she was of a meritorious though impoverished line, and that her father had bravely fallen in the service of the crown. "If thy powers equal their renown," said she, "and thou canst cast forth this evil spirit that possesses thy sovereign, thy fortunes shall henceforth be my care, and honours and wealth attend thee."

Impatient to make trial of her skill, she led the way at once to the apartment of the moody monarch. Jacinta followed, with downcast eyes, through files of guards and crowds of courtiers. They arrived at length at a great chamber hung in black. The windows were closed to exclude the light of day; a number of yellow wax tapers in silver sconces diffused a lugubrious light, and dimly revealed the figures of mutes in mourning dresses, and courtiers who glided about with noiseless step and wo-begone visage. On the midst of a funeral bed or bier, his hands folded on his breast, and the tip of his nose just visible, lay extended this would-be-buried monarch. The Queen entered the chamber in silence, and pointing to a footstool in an obscure corner, beckoned to Jacinta to sit down and commence. At first she touched her lute with a faltering hand, but gathering confidence and animation as she proceeded, drew forth such soft aërial harmony, that all present could scarce believe it mortal. As to the monarch, who had already considered himself in the world of spirits, he set it down for some angelic melody, or the music of the spheres. By degrees the theme was varied, and the voice of the minstrel accompanied the instrument. She poured forth one of the legendary ballads, treating of the ancient glories of the Alhambra, and the achievements of the Moors. Her whole soul entered into the theme, for with the recollections of the Alhambra was associated the story of her love. The funeral chamber resounded with the animating strain. It entered into the gloomy heart of the monarch. He raised his head and gazed around: he sat up on his couch; his eye began to kindle; at length, he leaped upon the floor, and called for sword and buckler. The triumph of music, or rather of the enchanted lute, was complete; the demon of melancholy was cast forth, and, as it were, a dead man brought to life. The windows of the apartment were thrown open; the glorious effulgence of Spanish sunshine burst into the late lugubrious chamber; all eyes sought the lovely enchantress; but the lute had fallen from her hand, she had sunk upon the earth, and the next moment was clasped to the bosom of Ruyz de Alarcon.

The nuptials of the happy couple were shortly after celebrated with great splendour; but hold—I hear the reader ask, how did Ruyz de Alarcon account for his long neglect? Oh! that was all owing to the opposition of a proud, pragmatical old father; besides, young people who really like one another, soon come to an amicable understanding, and bury all past grievances when once they meet. But how was the proud pragmatical old father reconciled to the match? Oh! his scruples were easily overcome by a word or two from the Queen, especially as dignities and rewards were showered upon the blooming favourite of royalty. Besides, the lute of Jacinta, you know, possessed a magic power, and could control the most stubborn head and hardest breast. And what came of the enchanted lute? Oh! that is the most curious matter of all, and plainly proves the truth of all this story. That lute remained for some time in the family, but was purloined and carried off, as was supposed, by the great singer Faranelli, in pure jealousy. At his death it passed into other hands in Italy, who were ignorant of its mystic powers, and melting down the silver, transferred the strings to an old Cremona fiddle. The strings still retain something of their magic virtues. A word in the reader's ear, but let it go no further—that fiddle is now bewitching the whole world—it is the fiddle of Paganini!—*Tales of the Alhambra.*

The Rev. George Crabbe, the author of "Phœbe Dawson," and of much beautiful and *true* verse, has been called the poet of the poor, and a *Radical poet*. None has pictured the sins, and sorrows, and sufferings of the poor more truly; and no one has taught them lessons of wisdom in a kindlier spirit. If any thing is wanted to give interest to the tale of Phœbe Dawson, we may notice, that it is said to have been read in MS. by Charles James Fox on his death-bed; admired, we need not say, and marked by his corrections.

PHŒBE DAWSON.

Two summers since, I saw, at Lammas Fair,
The sweetest flower that ever blossom'd there,
When Phœbe Dawson gaily cross'd the Green,
In haste to see, and happy to be seen:
Her air, her manners, all who saw, admired;
Courteous though coy, and gentle though retired;
The joy of youth and health her eyes display'd,
And ease of heart her every look convey'd;
A native skill her simple robes express'd,
As with untutor'd elegance she dress'd:
The lads around admired so fair a sight,
And Phœbe gave, and felt she gave delight.
Admirers soon of every age she gain'd,
Her beauty won them, and her worth retain'd;
Envy itself could no contempt display,
They wish'd her well, whom yet they wish'd away.
Correct in thought, she judged a servant's place
Preserved a rustic beauty from disgrace;
But yet on Sunday-eve, in freedom's hour,
With secret joy she felt that beauty's power,
When some proud bliss upon the heart would steal,
That, poor or rich, a beauty still must feel.—

At length, the youth ordain'd to move her breast,
Before the swains with bolder spirit press'd;
With looks less timid made his passion known,
And pleased by manners most unlike her own;
Loud though in love, and confident though young;
Fierce in his air, and voluble of tongue;
By trade a tailor, though, in scorn of trade,
He served the Squire, and brush'd the coat he made:
Yet now, would Phœbe her consent afford,
Her slave alone, again he'd mount the board;
With her should years of growing love be spent,
And growing wealth:—she sigh'd and look'd consent.

Now, through the lane, up hill, and 'cross the green,
(Seen by but few, and blushing to be seen—
Dejected, thoughtful, anxious, and afraid,)
Led by the lover, walk'd the silent maid:
Slow through the meadows roved they, many a mile,
Toy'd by each bank and trifled at each stile;
Where, as he painted every blissful view,
And highly colour'd what he strongly drew,
The pensive damsel, prone to tender fears,
Dimm'd the false prospect with prophetic tears.—
Thus pass'd th' allotted hours, till lingering late,
The lover loiter'd at the master's gate;
There he pronounced adieu! and yet would stay,
Till chidden—soothed—entreated—forced away;
He would of coldness, though indulged, complain,
And oft retire and oft return again;
When, if his teasing vex'd her gentle mind,
The grief assumed, compell'd her to be kind!
For he would proof of plighted kindness crave,
That she resented first and then forgave,
And to his grief and penance yielded more
Than his presumption had required before.—
Ah! fly temptation, youth; refrain, refrain,
Each yielding maid and each presuming swain!

Lo! now with red rent cloak and bonnet black,
And torn green gown, loose hanging at her back,
One who an infant in her arms sustains,
And seems in patience striving with her pains;
Pinch'd are her looks, as one who pines for bread,
Whose cares are growing and whose hopes are fled;
Pale her parch'd lips, her heavy eyes sunk low,
And tears unnoticed from their channels flow;
Serene her manner, till some sudden pain
Frets the meek soul, and then she's calm again:—
Her broken pitcher to the pool she takes,
And every step with cautious terror makes;
For not alone that infant in her arms,
But nearer cause, her anxious soul alarms.
With water burden'd, then she picks her way,
Slowly and cautious, in the clinging clay;
Till, in mid-green, she trusts a place unsound,
And deeply plunges in th' adhesive ground;
Thence, but with pain, her slender foot she takes,
While hope the mind as strength the frame forsakes:
For when so full the cup of sorrow grows,
Add but a drop, it instantly o'erflows.
And now her path, but not her peace she gains,
Safe from her task, but shivering with her pains;
Her home she reaches, open leaves the door,
And placing first her infant on the floor,
She bares her bosom to the wind, and sits,
And sobbing struggles with the rising fits:
In vain, they come, she feels th' inflating grief,
That shuts the swelling bosom from relief;
That speaks in feeble cries a soul distress'd,
Or the sad laugh that cannot be repress'd.
The neighbour-matron leaves her wheel, and flies
With all the aid her poverty supplies;
Unfee'd, the calls of Nature she obeys,
Not led by profit, nor allured by praise;
And waiting long, till these contentions cease,
She speaks of comfort, and departs in peace.
Friend of distress! the mourner feels thy aid;
She cannot pay thee, but thou wilt be paid.

But who this child of weakness, want, and care?
'Tis Phœbe Dawson, pride of Lammas Fair;
Who took her lover for his sparkling eyes,
Expressions warm, and love-inspiring lies:
Compassion first assail'd her gentle heart,
For all his suffering, all his bosom's smart:
" And then his prayers! they would a savage move,
And win the coldest of the sex to love:"—
But ah! too soon his looks success declared,
Too late her loss the marriage-rite repair'd;
The faithless flatterer then his vows forgot,
A captious tyrant or a noisy sot:
If present, railing, till he saw her pain'd;
If absent, spending what their labours gain'd;
Till that fair form in want and sickness pined,
And hope and comfort fled that gentle mind.
Then fly temptation, youth; resist, refrain!
Nor let me preach for ever and in vain!

How a Barrister may Travel.—It is a well-established rule at the bar, consecrated by old usage, and observed at the present day, that all barristers shall travel the circuit with post-horses, but they may go to sessions by coach. If any member of the bar violates this practice, his brethren refuse to associate with him; or, in other words, he is cut.—*Legal Examiner.*

How to make a Cudgel *par excellence.*—Take a stout elder branch, extract the pith from the hollow part, and insert two eyes of a wolf, three green lizards, seven leaves of yervais, and a parti-coloured stone found in the nest of a lapwing. The wielder of this baton may set thieves and wild beasts at defiance.—See *Thiers' Traité des Superstitions.*

COBBETT THE YOUNGER.

There is a very remarkable resemblance in the style of the younger Cobbett to that of his father, though it wants the vigour of the old Serjeant. We have been much pleased with the following account, which, in a tour through Normandy, he has given of the

FRENCH PRIESTS.

The priests appear to be a very gentle and amiable sort of men. I always pull off my hat to any of them that I meet, and they always return the salutation with great politeness and even humility. They dress, not only while at church, but at all times, in a long sort of coat gown, called a soutane, made of black cloth, and wear the old fashioned cocked-hat. You cannot mistake the country priest in France for any thing other than he is. His devout manner, and the simple and sacred habiliment that he always appears in, make you acquainted with his profession at once. This is not the case with the divines of our country. In the famishing curate we do, to be sure, very often see an example of piety and mildness; but the religious character of the beneficed clergyman is not at all times to be recognised in his manners or in his personal appearance: he, though quite as sincere, no doubt, as these meeker priests in France, is very often admired as the most venturesome rider in the fervour of a fox-chase; as being a "good shot;" as the best hand at a "rubber of whist;" or, the most good-humoured companion, and maker of the best joke over a bottle of wine! I cannot behold the sober and serious deportment of these priests without thinking of a pamphlet, published in London last spring, and written by an Irish squire, giving an account of an Irish Protestant parson's sending a pair of garters to a female of his flock, with a motto, which very few men, except Irish squires, would venture to put into print.

The priests do not lead lazy lives. They visit, and diligently visit every sick person. They are in their churches, on many of the days of every month, soon after daylight. On Sundays they generally say mass three times. They teach all the children their religious duties. For this purpose they have them assembled in the church itself, on certain days, and mostly at a very early hour in the morning, which must have an excellent effect on the morals of the children. There are none of the people too poor to be noticed, and in the kindest manner too, by these priests, who really appear to answer to the appellation of pastor.

Never, while this is the case, will any thing resembling our Methodist meetings rise up here. It is certainly a great feather in the cap of the Catholic Church, that France has returned to her with so much unanimity; and that, too, without any force, without any attempt at force, and without any possible motive in the mass of the people, except that of a belief in the truth of her doctrines. But, as far as I can venture to speak, I must say, that I think that the gentle, the aimable, the kind, the humble, the truly pious conduct of the priests is the great cause of that strong attachment which the Catholics everywhere bear to their church. I give, as it becomes me, this opinion, with great deference to the judgment of the reader; but bare justice to these priests compels me to say, that I see them everywhere held in high esteem, and that they seem to me not to be esteemed beyond their merits. Let the reader suppose an English parson (and there may be such a one in England) abstaining from marriage in order that he may devote his whole time and affection to his flock; let the reader suppose him visiting every sick person in his parish, present at every death in it, comforting the dying, consoling the survivors; let the reader suppose such a parson teaching every child in the parish its religious duties, conversing with each almost daily; let the reader suppose such a parson, and can he suppose that the people of this parish would ever run after a Methodist? The great thing is, however, that the people are more sober, honest, and happy in consequence of having this kind and zealous parson. This is the great thing to think of; and it appears to me, that in this respect, France is at this time in a very excellent state.

CHARACTER OF A PARISH PRIEST.

The late Rev. Charles Wolfe is known chiefly as the author of the nobly simple lines on the death of Sir John Moore, beginning "Not a drum was heard." He deserves to be remembered for much higher merits. We take leave to borrow from ourselves in introducing him to the knowledge of our readers. In "Johnstone's Specimens of the Poets," he is thus spoken of:—

"Wolfe's poetical pieces are few in number, but they are of great excellence, though subordinate to the much loftier qualities of a zeal truly apostolic, and a vigorous and manly intellect, devoted unremittingly to the noblest cause to which the human faculties can be devoted. It was not to crowded cities, nor to fashionable audiences, that Mr. Wolfe dedicated his labours. In a miserable curacy in the province of Armagh he suffered nearly as great privations as a missionary in heathen lands, labouring with zeal, to which he fell an early victim, to promote in all things the spiritual and temporal welfare of the poor people of his extensive parish. In the year 1821, when the typhus fever made such ravages in Ireland, the fatigue which Mr. Wolfe endured in visiting the sick—a duty to which he was peculiarly devoted—and his zeal in administering both to the spiritual and temporal wants of his poor flock, considerably affected his health. His gradual decay became visible to his parishioners, and some of them made affectionate private representations to his relations, who tried to withdraw him from the laborious duties of his parish for the recovery of his health.

"His character as a parish-priest will be contemplated with more delight than his genius as a poet, or his eloquence as a preacher, great as these were. It is thus delineated by a friend:—' As he passed by, all the poor people and children ran to the doors to welcome him, with looks and expressions of the most ardent affection, and with all that wild devotion of gratitude so characteristic of the Irish peasantry. Many fell on their knees, invoking blessings on him, and making the most anxious inquiries about his health. He was sensibly moved by this manifestation of feeling, and met it with all that heartiness of expression, and that affectionate simplicity of manner, which made him as much an object of love as his exalted virtues rendered him an object of respect. The intimate knowledge he seemed to have of all their domestic histories, appeared from the short but significant questions he put to each individual as he hurried along, while at the same time he gave a sketch of the particular characters of several who presented themselves, pointing, with a sigh to one, and to another with looks of satisfaction and fond congratulations. It was indeed impossible to behold a scene like this, which can scarcely be described without the deepest but most pleasing emotions. It seemed to realize the often-imagined picture of a primitive minister of the gospel of Christ living in the hearts of his flock, willing to spend and to be spent upon them, enjoying the happy interchange of mutual affection, and affording a pleasing proof that a faithful and firm discharge of duty, when accompanied by kindly sympathies and gracious manners, can scarcely fail to gain the hearts of the humble ranks of the people.'

"It was with extreme reluctance that Mr. Wolfe, on the entreaty of his friends, left this poor and affectionate people to seek the restoration of his health in the south of France. He made a short recovery, but relapsed on his return to Ireland, and died in 1823, in the 32d year of his age, of deep consumption. What better blessing can be desired for Ireland, than that each of its parishes possessed a Charles Wolfe!"

If this was the best prayer we could breathe for Ireland four years since, how much more fervently is it breathed now, when the actual state of that country is such as almost extinguishes hope. Let us say with an old writer, "God send us more such men, that we may dazzle the eyes of the Papists with the light of Protestant good works."

MARY.
BY CHARLES WOLFE.

If I had thought thou couldst have died,
  I might not weep for thee;
But I forgot, when by thy side,
  That thou couldst mortal be:
It never through my mind had past,
  The time would e'er be o'er,
And I on thee should look my last,
  And thou shouldst smile no more!

And still upon that face I look,
  And think 'twill smile again;
And still the thought I will not brook,
  That I must look in vain!
But when I speak—thou dost not say,
  What thou ne'er left'st unsaid;
And now I feel, as well I may,
  Sweet Mary! thou art dead!

If thou wouldst stay, e'en as thou art,
  All cold and all serene,
I still might press thy silent heart,
  And where thy smiles have been!
While e'en thy chill, bleak corse I have,
  Thou seemest still mine own;
But there I lay thee in thy grave—
  And I am now alone!

THE ORIGINAL JEREMY DIDDLER.
From Taylor's Records.

BIBB, THE ENGRAVER.—How Bibb supported himself, having relinquished engraving, it would be difficult to conceive, if he had not levied taxes upon all whom he knew, insomuch that, besides his title of Count, he acquired that of "Half-crown Bibb," by which appellation he was generally distinguished, and according to a rough, and, perhaps, fanciful estimate, he had borrowed at least L.2000 in half-crowns.

I remember to have met him on the day when the death of Dr. Johnson was announced in the newspapers, and expressed my regret at the loss of so great a man; Bibb interrupted me, and spoke of him as a man of no genius, whose mind contained nothing but the lumber of learning. I was modestly beginning a panegyric upon the doctor, when he again interrupted me with, "Oh! never mind that old blockhead; have you such a thing as ninepence about you?" Luckily for him, I had a little more.

There was something so whimsical in this incident, that I mentioned it to some friends, and that and others of the same kind, doubtless, induced Mr. Kenny to make him the hero of his diverting farce, called "Raising the Wind." Another circumstance of a similar nature was told me by Mr. Morton, whose dramatic works are deservedly popular. He told me that Bibb met him one day after the successful performance of one of his plays, and, concluding that a prosperous author ought to have plenty of cash, commenced his solicitation accordingly, and ventured to ask him for the loan of a whole crown. Morton assured him that he had no more silver than three shillings and sixpence. Bibb readily accepted them, of course, but said on parting, "Remember, I intended to borrow a crown, so you owe me eighteen-pence."

This pitiful creature, Taylor tells us, died on the same night that the farce of *Raising the Wind* was brought out. To him, we presume, we may owe the slang verb *to diddle*, i. e. to cheat out of small sums in a paltry way. Mr. Taylor, who, it will be seen, was a character himself, introduces another family group, which might furnish another slang verb, *to pinchbeck*. In Scotland we have often had families of *Pinchbecks*, one member a Jacobite, another a fierce Whig, with a steady eye to the family interest, and an excellent understanding at bottom. The Pinchbecks, he says, were three brothers. They had invented the metal which went by their name, and to attract public attention they pretended to quarrel, and advertised against each other, all claiming the invention, and proclaiming the superiority of the article in which each of them dealt. They were, however, upon the most amicable footing in reality, and used to meet every night and divide the profits of the day.

DISSENTERS IN ENGLAND.

IN the SCHOOLMASTER, No. 12, we gave an account of the Secession Church of Scotland; which comprehends nearly all the Scottish Dissenters. We are now able, by a statistical summary of 1829, to report on the three great denominations of England, though the number must have increased since then.

	Presby.	Indep.	Bapt.	Total.
In 1812	259	710	582	1,563
In 1827	204	1,205	815	2,212
In 1829	226	1,329	888	2,835

The places of Unitarian worship are calculated at about 300. It is estimated that the English congregations now amount to a MILLION of communicants. A hundred years ago there was not a single Protestant dissenting college, missionary, tract, or Bible Society—scarcely a Sunday school! Dissenting academies are now established throughout the kingdom, supported by munificent endowments, and large annual donations and subscriptions. Many of the young men annually enjoy the advantages of foreign universities. Upwards of L.200,000 a-year is raised by the Protestant dissenters for public institutions connected with the dissemination of religious instruction. It cannot be denied that the education of the bulk of the people originated with the dissenters, and forced the Church, in self-defence, to educate their poor. Most of the great manufactures of the kingdom commenced, and still remain in the hands of the Protestant dissenters; and no small share of the active capital of the country is vested in the same class. They are the leading public men in all our towns—intelligent, public-spirited, active and patriotic. These facts are known to our ministers; but as no cabinet ministers or privy counsellors (except a few Scotch Presbyterians) are dissenters, these facts cannot be too prominently stated, that our rulers may view them *in connexion with the Established Church*. The elements of this vast, increasing, and active influence will soon, if we mistake not, be perceived in active fusion in the reformed House of Commons. The Protestant dissenters will no longer endure the fiscal extortions which tax them for the support of a state religion, that can no longer claim a majority of adherents. Most ardently do we hope that this all-important and pressing subject will receive the early and bold attention of ministers. Such scenes as those enacted at Birmingham demand immediate attention, or the reformers of that town will agitate a second great national question. Church reform *must* demand the *most early* and mature consideration. The monopoly of the Church must follow to the tomb of the Capulets that of the Bank, the East India, and corporate monopolies. Religion suffers under the restrictive system; what the people demand, and will obtain, is a *free trade* in religion, as far as is consistent with existing beneficial institutions. We trust that some measures will be taken to prevent the enforcement of the law against the Birmingham rate-payers. No good can result from coercion. The law will only add "fuel to the fire."

The following passage in Mr. Sharon Turner's History of England, in relation to the contests between the Puritans and Episcopalians, bears strongly on the pending question of Church reform:—"The Commons were not discouraged. They represented again that divers men of Holy Church had not been resident on their livings; and expressly added, that, by this neglect, the people had fallen into Lollardies and heresies, for default of teaching. The government was as unable as unwilling to remedy the evil, and chose therefore to meet this last application by an assertion, that the existing laws were sufficient, if executed, and to join the Church in repressing its opponents. * * * The crown did not choose to be neuter, and leave the church to the only weapons they ought to have used—*reason, law, and wise reformation*. The crown determined to fight the battle for it, and fell with its steadiest supporters.

THE CHURCH AND THE DISSENTERS.
Paragraph from the *St James's Chronicle*, in 1787.

"Some years ago, the Dissenting Ministers applied to

'arliament for relief from subscription to the articles of the Church of England, and were twice refused. But they persevered, and their third application was attended with success. Their petition occasioned several debates in both Houses. In the House of Peers, Lord Lyttleton urged, among other things, in favour of Dissenting Ministers, the manifest integrity and disinterestedness of their conduct. Dr. Drummond, *Archbishop of York*, observed, that they were men of close ambition. Lord Chatham said, " After such proofs of honesty, to suspect men of close ambition, is to judge uncharitably; and whoever brings this charge against them without proof, defames," (here he made a short pause, and the eyes of all were turned to the Archbishop, who made no reply.) Lord Chatham then repeated his words, and added, " The Dissenting Ministers are represented as men of close ambition; my Lords, their ambition is to keep close to the College of Fishermen, not of Cardinals, and to the doctrine of inspired apostles, not to the decrees of interested aspiring Bishops. They contend for a Scriptural creed, a Scriptural worship. We, my Lords, have a Calvinistical creed, a Popish Liturgy, and an Arminian clergy. The Reformation has laid open the Scriptures to all; let not the Bishops shut them again. Laws, in support of ecclesiastical power, are pleaded for, which it would shock humanity to execute. It is, that religious sects have done great mischief when they were not kept under strict restraint. My Lords, history affords no proof that sects have ever been mischievous, when they were not oppressed and persecuted by the ruling Church."

BISHOP BURNET'S ADVICE TO BISHOPS.—I wish the pomp of living and the keeping high tables could be quite taken away; it is great charge, and no very decent one; a great devourer of time; it lets in much promiscuous company and much vain discourse upon you: even civility may carry you too far in a freedom and familiarity that will make you look too like the rest of the world. I hope this is a burden to you; it was, indeed, one of the greatest burdens of my life to see so much time lost—to hear so much idle talk, and to be living in a luxurious waste of that which might have been much better bestowed. I had not strength enough to break through that which custom has imposed on those provided with plentiful bishoprics. I pray God to help you to find a decent way of laying them down.

SIMON PETER'S SHIP.

Simon Peter was the owner
Of a goodly bark, though small;
He to his successors left her
As she stood—a fishing yawl

But so cunning fishers were they,
And so great their booty grew,
That ere long they found, unless they
Should enlarge, 'twould never do.

Hence the boat became a galleon,
Next she to a frigate passed,
Then, with deep mouth'd thunder bellowing,
Bounced a man of war at last.

But, alas! a crazy sheer hulk,
Of each true blue tar the sport,
Now is all you may see of her,
Rotting day by day in port.

Times a thousand she's been keel-hauled
All in vain,—so an't it better
To skuttle her at once, and take to
The good old yawl of Simon Peter.
CURATE.

THE LARCH.—Larch timber was first introduced into this country by the late Duke of Athol. The two first trees of this species implanted by his Grace are still growing at Dunkeld; they have been transferred from the greenhouse to the open air, and are said to be magnificent specimens; although some of their offspring growing in the neighbourhood of Blair, in Scotland, are much more so, having attained the height of 120 feet.

MEDICAL SELECTIONS.
NO. II.

AIR.*

THE researches of modern chemistry have determined that the atmosphere is not a uniform fluid, but a mixture of two principal elastic fluids, with a few others in very minute proportions, and that it holds in solution a varying quantity of watery vapour. The composition of one hundred parts of atmospherical air, freed from all adventitious mixture, is seventy-nine parts of a gas called azote, or nitrogen; and twenty-one parts of another gas, named oxygen gas. Atmospherical air is indispensably necessary for the breathing of animals; and atmospheric air may also be considered as the great supporter of combustion; though inflammable bodies will burn in some other gases, yet these gases are uncommon, except when artificially produced. When, by various methods familiar to chemists, the oxygenous portion of the atmosphere is separated from the azotic, it is found that an animal dies; and a burning body is extinguished in azote: we hence conclude that it is only the oxygenous part of the atmosphere that is fit for the purposes of respiration and combustion. Air is, by these processes, continually becoming more and more unfit for breathing. It is a curious, but difficult subject of investigation, by what means purity is restored to the air, and how it continues to be fit for the respiration of animals, though exposed to many sources of contamination. It is believed, that this is owing to the functions of the leaves of plants. When they are exposed to the bright light of day, they are continually absorbing the carbon of the carbonic acid which exists in the air and water on which they feed, and giving out oxygen gas. By this means the purity of the atmosphere is preserved with wonderfully little variation.

Change of AIR *in apartments necessary.*—Air that has been long unchanged, in which one or more human bodies have been confined, is possessed of qualities highly dangerous and even destructive; as we see in many instances from the fevers and other ailments which arise in jails, ships, and other confined apartments. Hence the necessity and propriety of free ventilation in houses of every description; of daily admitting a thorough current of air into sleeping-rooms, and indeed into every room of the house. From the neglect of this ventilation, arises the dangerous and malignant fevers in the confined and ill-ventilated dwellings in the closes, alleys, and courts of large towns. Since attention has been called to this circumstance, how seldom do we hear of the ship or the jail fevers. Though the fever, which was formerly so fatal in ships and jails, is still lamentably prevalent somewhere or other, and though we still hear of towns or tracts of territory being visited with its depopulating scourge, it is not in ships or jails that it is suspected to take its rise, but in the abodes of slothful and squalid poverty, where no judicious and directing mind enforces the necessity of ventilation and cleanliness.

Even in the apartment where a patient is in bed, the fear of his catching cold should not prevent us from occasionally changing the air of it, by opening the doors and windows for a few minutes at a time, taking care not to expose the sick person to the current of air, but closing the curtains, and using such other precautions as common sense will readily suggest.

Means of purifying the AIR *from Contagion.*—There are various methods practised, to correct the bad air in sick-chambers, and if possible, to destroy its power of producing diseases. Morveau in France made many experiments on the best means of disinfecting the air, and Dr. Thomson, in his Chemistry, gives the result of these experiments. Odorous bodies, as benzoin, aromatic plants, &c. have no effect whatever. There are four substances which have the power of destroying contagious matter and

* *Vide* Hints for Invalids. Schoolmaster, page 61,—East Wind, page 39

of purifying the air, viz. acetic acid, or vinegar, nitric acid, muriatic acid, and chlorine. Acetic acid cannot easily be obtained in sufficient quantity, and in a state of sufficient concentration, to be employed with advantage. Nitric acid may be attended with some inconvenience, because it is almost always contaminated with nitrous gas. Muriatic acid and chlorine are not attended with these inconveniences; the last deserves the preference, because it acts with greater energy and rapidity.

AIR, *considered with reference to the cause, the cure, or the mitigation of diseases.*—Many circumstances connected with air, which chemistry is unable to trace or explain, are much to be attended to in a medical point of view. Under the article AGUE, we have already mentioned the bad air from marshy grounds; and in the article immediately preceding, we have stated the danger of other fevers from the malignant effluvia from animal bodies; we have also to mention that the air seems to carry the infection of other diseases, as small-pox, measles, hooping-cough, scarlet-fever, &c. Some of these contagions, as the small-pox, taint the air with a peculiar disagreeable smell; but in general, the sense perceives nothing different from common air. The air of certain places is justly supposed to have an influence in giving a tendency to certain diseases, or even to bring them on. The croup is frequent in cold damp situations, exposed to the east wind, or near the sea. The sea air is unfavourable in certain states of consumption; or in affections of the breast, which would probably end in that disease. The mild equable air of the country, unloaded with the endless variety of matters mixing with the air in the neighbourhood of large towns, is favourable to recovery from many ailments, as indigestion, dropsy, jaundice, breast complaints, asthmas, the wasting disease of children, as also to that feeble state of constitution which has not received any appropriate name. It is remarkable that some persons in asthma are not better in air which we should think the purest. *Change of air,* even to a worse, has been found of service in hooping-cough; but it is useless to attempt a cure by this at an early period of the disease, as it is hardly possible by any means to prevent it from running on a considerable time. In general, it is hardly worth while to try a change of air, till the cough has continued distinctly at least a month or six weeks, with the back draught.

A good deal of the influence of the air on the skin and lungs must depend on its degree of moisture or dryness. When there is much watery vapour in the air, it is less able to receive more: and the perspirable matter from the skin not being carried off, we shall appear to perspire more, though in reality the perspiration is less. In like manner, the watery vapour which is continually thrown off by the lungs is not carried away fast enough by a heavy moist atmosphere; and in certain diseases of the lungs, in colds, consumptions, asthmas, &c., some patients, according to the quantity of watery vapour or mucous exhaled from the lungs, will be benefited either by dry air or the contrary. It is wrong, therefore, to lay down any general rule about a particular spot or climate, as its good or bad effects will vary according to the state of the disease in each particular patient.—*Macaulay's Medical Dictionary.*

SCRAPS.
Original and Selected.

ANECDOTE OF SIR WALTER SCOTT.—The following anecdote may help to show that Sir Walter had at times a very high opinion of his own dignity. The writer of this had often occasion, in the course of business, to write to him. On one occasion he sent Sir Walter a card, fastened with a wafer. Sir Walter immediately returned it, folded inside out, with a cross at the wafer, and this pithy reply, "I am not a particular man, but I detest wafers."

THE AUTHOR OF THE CORN-LAW RHYMES.—Elliott was born rather more than fifty years since, in a village near the town of Sheffield. There,—we use his own strong words, and none can be found so fit,—he is still "a dealer in steel, working hard every day; literally *labouring* with head and hands, and alas! with my heart too! If you think the steel-trade, in these profitless days, is not a heavy, hard-working trade, come and break out a ton." A man of his knowledge and energy was not likely to remain the mere workman of another. Elliott, though labouring with his hands and head, is his own master, as well as his children's provider. But we must briefly advert to his origin and his youth. His father, a man of education and of great natural humour, was a commercial clerk in an iron establishment, and also a Jacobin,—the name given in those days to the friends of liberty by the artifice of its enemies, and meant to express the last degree of whatever was ruffianly and opprobrious. "He was," his son writes, "a Jacobin, marked as such, and hunted, literally hunted out of society on that account. The yeomanry used to amuse themselves, periodically, by backing their horses through his windows. I," says Elliott, "*I have not forgotten the English Reign of Terror;* there you have the source of my political tendencies." This holds in thousands of instances besides that of Mr. Elliott. The blood of the martyrs of freedom, in the end of the last century, has been the fruitful seed of liberty in this. The children of the persecuted then, are among the most determined of the Radicals now.—*Tait's Edinburgh Magazine.*

CONCISE AND STRIKING.—A woman who lately showed the house and pictures at Easton Newton, near Towcester, the seat of the Earl of Pomfret, expressed herself in these words:—" This picture is Sir Robert Turner; he lived in the country, took care of his estate, built this house and paid for it; managed well, saved money, and died rich. *That* is his son; he was made a Lord, spent his estate, and died a beggar."

INQUESTS EXTRAORDINARY.

Found dead, a rat—no case could sure be harder,
Verdict—Confined a week in Eldon's larder.

Died, Sir Charles Wetherell's laundress, honest Sue,
Verdict—Ennui—so little work to do.—
Figaro in London.

PROLIFIC WALNUT-TREE.—A cottager at Warsop, near Mansfield, has gathered from a walnut-tree in his possession, 60,000 ripe walnuts, allowing, as they are usually sold, six score to the hundred, part of which be sold at one shilling per hundred, and the remainder tenpence; therefore, calculating the whole 60,000 to be sold at tenpence only, the tree produced, at that rate, L.25. It must also be understood, that, in the pickling season, when green, some thousands were also gathered, which are not reckoned in the above calculation.

DOMESTIC YEAST.—Ladies who are in the habit of making domestic bread, cake, &c., are informed, that they can easily manufacture their own yeast, by attending to the following directions: Boil one pound of good flour, a quarter of a pound of brown sugar, and a little salt, in two gallons of water, for one hour. When milk warm, bottle it and cork it close. It will be fit for use in twenty-four hours. One pint of this yeast will make eighteen pounds of bread.

CONTENTS OF NO. XVII.

HOLYDAY RAMBLES, No. IV.—The Eildon Hills.............257
Civilization of Africa..259
POPULAR SCIENCE.—On the Formation of Dew—Fixed Stars, &c..260
A Bachelor's Complaint of the Behaviour of Married People..261
STATISTICS.—Cattle and Sheep—Irish Trade with Liverpool,&c.263
COLUMN FOR THE YOUNG.—Sir Philip Sydney—Inscription for a Tablet at Penshurst, &c...................................264
THE STORY-TELLER—Legend of the Rose of Alhambra, 265—Phœbe Dawson..268
Cobbett the Younger—Character of a Parish Priest...........269
Mary—The Original Jeremy Diddler—Dissenters in England..270
Bishop Burnet's Advice to Bishops—Simon Peter's Ship......271
MEDICAL SELECTIONS.—Air, &c...............................271
SCRAPS, Original and Selected.—Anecdote of Sir Walter Scott, &c. The Author of the Corn Law Rhymes, &c.............272

EDINBURGH: Printed by and for JOHN JOHNSTONE, 19, St. James's Square.—Published by JOHN ANDERSON, Jun., Bookseller, 55, North Bridge Street, Edinburgh; by JOHN MACLEOD, and ATKINSON & Co., Booksellers, Glasgow; and sold by all Booksellers and Venders of Cheap Periodicals.

The Schoolmaster,
AND
EDINBURGH WEEKLY MAGAZINE.

CONDUCTED BY JOHN JOHNSTONE.

THE SCHOOLMASTER IS ABROAD.—LORD BROUGHAM.

No. 18.—Vol. I.   SATURDAY, DECEMBER 1, 1832.   Price Three-Halfpence.

HOLYDAY RAMBLES.
NO. V.
THE EILDON HILLS—*Continued.*

To the *Cowdenknowes* we had last week conducted our dear pupils, ranged lovingly around us, on the highest and western summit of the Eildon Hills. We there saw where the *Leader* fell into "Tweed's fair flood;" let us now trace the *Leader* upwards. That is the smoke of Earlstown, anciently *Erceldoune*, the dwelling of *Thomas the Rhymer;* where the ruins of his tower or castle are still pointed out, with reverence due. In him, as in the mighty men of eld—

——— the honour'd name
Of prophet and of poet was the same.

And though the march of intellect has somewhat diverted the current of legendary education in Scotland, yet we cannot doubt but that every Scottish born child knows of *True Thomas.* We have traced his works and his sayings to the remotest parts of the Highlands. His vaticinations and wonderful performances would fill a volume. Every body knows that his extraordinary powers were derived from the Queen of Fairy Land; to whom he is still a thrall; and that, when he has *dree'd his weird,* he will return to middle earth. Let us hope that the time of the accomplishment of his penance is at hand, for Scotland never had more need of a wise and powerful leader and champion than now. *True Thomas,* by the side of the Lord Advocate, might stead us much in the new Parliament.

Though the name of the Rhymer is diffused over all the legendary traditions of Scotland, it is about the Eildon hills, where he spoke "the word of power," that his fame is concentrated. Every hamlet and brook hereabouts has its couplet, its tale, and story,—nearly as well remembered as those connected with the neighbouring towers of Abbotsford will be, five hundred years hence, unless *Biela* before then give our globe a hitch. The eastern base of the mountain, on which we stand, is the Delphos of Scotland. The *Eildon-tree Stane* stands here a monument, which perpetuates the memory of the *Eildon-tree,* beneath which, like a patriarch of antiquity, the *Rhymer* gave forth his oracular and mysterious sayings and responses. It is neighboured by the *Bogle Burn,* which, for aught we know, may still be haunted by such unearthly visitants as those who attended *True Thomas.*

But turn we from obscure and misty tradition to the living beauty of Teviotdale, lying before us in all its glory, an expanse of twenty miles square, beautifully diversified by knoll and glade, meadow and stream, groves and farm-houses, mansions (not too fine), and all that renders a fair broad Scottish strath delightful. We cannot now stop to reckon up all that Leyden, and Pringle, and many others, have said and sung in its praise. So here —unwire that cork, and in one word—

The lasses of *Tibbydale!*
Echo—The lasses of Tibbydale!

Now recall we our vagrant thoughts, and in all humility look down on Eildon Hall at our feet there, and commanding so glorious a prospect over the vale of the Te'iot. And there beyond it stands Bowden, or Bothie-den, a hamletship as ancient as Melrose Abbey its venerable self. And there is the *Kirk,* and the *Manse,* and there again Moxpople, the residence of the author of *Darnley* and *Richelieu,*—and of *Charlemagne* that is, and *The String of Pearls* that shall be. Have not we, too, dear reader, been stringing pearls—a pleasanter trade than casting them before——; but you know the saying. A little to the south-east of this, you may perceive the village of Newton; and then, nearly opposite Dryburgh *Lessuden,* with its romantic shelving banks hanging over the Tweed, and the famous St. Boswell's Green, of whose caravansaries and great annual sheep fair all the world has heard. Then, again, a little westward, we have the village of Midholm, and Liliesleaf, near which the stream with the tantalizing name of the *Ale Water,* joins the Teviot at Ancrum; beyond are the Minto Hills, the invisible Teviot almost laving their feet; and southward Rubislaw rises majestically from the plain, a noble though somewhat aristocratic-looking mountain, permitting none other to elbow it, though its beacon blazed far and red on the night of the Reform Jubilee. Now we travel on in this direction, till Dunyon Hill looks over Jedburgh, and "the silvan Jed;" and on still, until the lofty range of the Cheviots bounds the southern horizon. There is Cheviot himself, the "monarch of all he surveys"—broad, deep, massy, and even sublime, in his Alpine grandeur. There, again, farther west is Carter Fell, over which the foray often raged into England. We pass the Peniel-heuch, or *Panier-heuch*, where the late Marquis of Lothian has erected a monument to his Grace the Duke of Wellington; considering all such places at present as within the *Debateable Land*. Better do we love to gaze on the conglomerated heights to the southwest, and at the head of Liddesdale; and beyond to those of Dumfries and Galloway, fading into haze. They recall to us Dandy Dinmont's pastoral farm, and his ride homeward from Stagshaw-Bank Fair; and his reception, and the dressing of his wounds, and his gallantry and generosity, and fidelity in friendship. Coming back to the Duke's monument, we recall the battle of *Ancrum Moor*, fought near the Duke's present station, by tactics very different from those which gained Waterloo. There the Douglas (Earl Angus) ranges his spearmen in the flat, to wait the assault of Evers and Latoun, as they hurry down yon height; Norman Leslie and the Fife-men support the Douglas in receiving them, and the tide of battle is stayed; the Scotch becoming in turn the assailants. The scene of battle is at least nine or ten miles from where we stand, the time three hundred years back,—yet gazing on it, and remembering the exclamation of Earl Angus, how livingly it comes before us! A heron, roused by the noise of the conflict, flew from the marsh, and soared away above the combatants. "Oh that my good white hawk were here!" cried the Douglas, "that we might all yoke at once!" But—

"Adieu to bonny Teviotdale,
And Cheviots mountains blue!"

We turn in another direction, and look west over the multitudinous hills of Selkirk and Peebles-shire, pointing out to you the most remarkable peaks and ridges. There is the *Three Brethren Cairn*, rising over the Tweed at Yair, another of the delicious nooks of this river; and there, opposite to Selkirk, is *Peat Law*; and beyond, the broad-backed, elephantine *Minchmuir*, many a rugged, steep defile, and fantastic summit, hid from us, though visible from it, as by the CHEESE-WELL the wayfarer journeys from Yarrow-ford over to Traquair; this *Mons Meg* of the southland mountains occupying the entire space lying between those celebrated places. There, also, is *Newhouse Height*, and "the fair Dodhead," and the hill of Deloraine, and Gilman's Law,—and, rising between the vale of Ettrick and that of Yarrow, *Thirlestane Heights*, and over away those of Buccleuch. And again, in the north-west, *Windlestrae Law*, and the picturesque heights of *Innerleithen*, and those of all Peebles-shire to its northern and western verge. But it is a far cry to Loch Awe, so turn we homeward, to the hills opposite us on the Gala Water, with which we could almost shake hands. And see how fine the opening of the valley of the Gala, and the woods and pastures of Torwoodlee. Lower down is the snug, thriving, spirited town of Galashiels, where stout-hearted reformers to a man, are giving their honest votes to Mr. Pringle of Clifton; not because he is Mr. Pringle of Clifton—for that matter they might like half a dozen other Mr. Pringles quite as well—but because he promises to support the cause of the people, and to be a faithful guardian and representative of their interests. Under the town, the stream of the Gala, which gives name to the most exquisite of the Scottish melodies, falls into the Tweed; and up from it, at the ford, near the confluence, hid from us, but on our side of the river, rises Abbotsford, low in situation relatively, yet standing on a gentle slope, hidden on one side by the peninsulated banks which divide the Tweed and Gala, and on the other by banks and slopes around the mansion itself. From where we stand, it is, as we said, invisible; and, indeed, it is so till one is quite upon it, from all points save the ford below the house. Abbotsford has been called "a romance in stone and lime." It is, however, only a specimen of the modern Gothic romance of architecture. Better far do we like Sir Walter's taste in the real romance—in poesies, legends, humanities, than in constructing castellated buildings. His finest castles, if not in the air, were either in remote distance, or in illimitable space. They were Tullyveolan and Tillietudlem, Ellangowan and Kenilworth. But this was the home of his pride and his affection, and let all look on it with reverence.

Though we cannot from our 'vantage ground see the edifice, the demesne lies under our eye, stretching from *Kaeside*, that house on the ridge among the firs, to the moorland height of *Bowden Muir*, and bounded on the west by that high-lying piece of water which you see shimmering, and which is with much propriety named *Cauldshiels Loch*. As far as the estate extends, it is redeemed from a state of wilderness and barrenness, and abundantly covered with young and thriving plantation. It requires a few generations fully to develop the ideas of a planter and creator of woods. Sir Walter Scott was a greater and more original designer in woods, than in stone, though a little eccentric in both. He followed his own plan in peopling his moors with young vegetable life, and that plan was, to follow Nature as closely as Art ever can do. He planted clumps, masses, grand sweeping lines of waving woods; and scattered groups, groves, and thickets, which will yet tell on these hills; and he built *Modern Gothic*, a Scotch Strawberry Hill. At present, the principal charm of Abbotsford is that it was his abode.

Now, call we home our ranging eyes, and fix them as on a cynosure, as near Abbotsford as possible. Near it, though not under its wing, is *Chiefswood*, a sweet cottage, which has been tenanted by a succession of literary men, and has for some years formed the retreat of the editor of the *Quarterly Review*. There, again, is Huntly Burn. But more inviting than either of these residences, is Darnick, a beautiful old-English-looking village of the days of merry England. Darnick is surrounded and intersected with gardens and orchards—a place of snug white cottages, mossy pales, little wickets, and nice by-paths, with roses, evergreens, and beehives; mossy and herbaceous, teeming with all pleasant sights, and delightful scents, and worthy to have been the "Our Village" of Sir Walter Scott. And why should we forget Gatton-side—that straggling village over from us, yet more rural and picturesque than Darnick, and equally snug? And there is the chain-bridge connecting Gatton-side with Melrose; and to the east of it, Allerslie, the residence of Sir David Brewster, philosopher, or Knight of the Guelphic order, and, we believe, first in the list of that literary and scientific band of knighthood since Sir John Leslie has died without issue. What could have tempted the Lord Chancellor to this preposterous *dubbing*, to which he never would have submitted in his own person, we shall not stop to inquire; but, casting a hasty, sweeping, farewell glance over the northern points of this grand panorama, Lauderdale, and the Lammermuir range, of which, from our old Mid-Lothian Roman Camp, we surveyed the other side, we just nod over to *Friarshall, Langlee*, and the *Pavilion*, and soberly descend to Melrose town, and to the nearer examination of the beautiful ruins of that Abbey on which we have been all day long casting many a furtive glance. It is a clear afternoon, and the moon near the full. Dinner will not occupy many hours; and, while it is preparing, we shall make survey the first. For survey the second, we all know the hour, and the guide too.

> If thou wouldst view fair Melrose aright,
> Go visit it by the pale moonlight;
> For the gay beams of lightsome day
> Gild but to flout the ruins grey.
> When the broken arches are black in night,
> And each shafted oriel glimmers white;
> When the cold light's uncertain shower
> Streams on the ruin'd central tower;
> When buttress and buttress alternately
> Seem framed of ebon and ivory;
> When silver edges the imagery,
> And the scrolls that teach thee to live and die;
> When distant Tweed is heard to rave,
> And the owlet to hoot o'er the dead man's grave,
> Then go—but go alone the while—
> Then view St. David's ruin'd pile;
> And, home returning, soothly swear,
> Was never scene so sad and fair!

ON ITINERATING LIBRARIES.

THE following inquiries were lately made to me respecting the plan of the East Lothian itinerating libraries,—the replies may perhaps suggest some useful information to persons who are disposed to introduce the plan into their neighbourhood. I shall also be happy to give any additional information concerning that economical mode of diffusing knowledge to any person who may wish it.

Q. 1. How many itinerating divisions of fifty volumes would be desirable to form one library?

For the commencement of a system of itinerating libraries, four or five divisions would be a very good beginning, or even fewer. If that number were stationed each for two years in a place, it would be eight or ten years before they went the circuit, and in that time it is probable as many more divisions would be added to the establishment. Ten or twelve divisions could be easily managed by one person, who felt an interest in the plan; and it would be better to divide the labour by different sets all over the country, than to oppress an individual with a large establishment. I prefer the divisions being two years in a place to a shorter period; as at first the lighter and more entertaining reading is chiefly in demand, and were the books changed every year, I should be apprehensive of too strong a taste being formed for amusing works; but when it is stationed for two years, the readers have time to read the more solid and useful books.

Q. 2. At about what expense can each division be procured?

I think a division of fifty volumes bound, or half bound, with book-case, catalogue, labels, advertisements, and issuing book, may be procured for from L.10 to L.12; but the cost will depend very much on the kind of books wanted, and their being recently published. Very good divisions might be selected for from L.8 to L.10. As perhaps the principal hinderance to the introduction of itinerating libraries has been the trouble of setting on foot the first divisions, I would be willing to superintend gratuitously the getting up any number of divisions, with the necessary apparatus, which any individual or society may wish, and to procure, at the wholesale prices, any books they may require.

Q. 3. At about what expense per annum may each division be kept in repair?

If the books are bound, or half bound at first, I suppose five shillings per annum would both keep them in repair and supply any volumes which may be lost, and which it might be difficult to get the reader to replace; if the books are in boards with linen backs, seven or nine shillings a-year will repair and bind them as they require.

Q. 4. How long, with care, may such books last?

Part of our books have been in active circulation for eighteen years, as at the commencement they were used as a Sunday-school library; and forty volumes out of fifty are yet fit for circulation, and will last a few years longer, so that twenty years may be considered the period they will last.

In forming an establishment of itinerating libraries, I would recommend the raising as much money from the friends of the institution, as would purchase four or five divisions to begin with, and that they be placed in different stations, with an intimation that if the books are well read, they will be succeeded by other divisions every second year; that during the first year they will be issued to any person who will pay one penny a-volume for reading it; that in the second year they will be issued gratuitously to any person above twelve years of age, who will take care of them. I consider it of great importance to allow gratuitous reading, as there are many young persons who are not able to pay even a penny a-volume; and others are not willing to pay until a taste for reading is formed in them.

As another means of raising funds and promoting the objects of the institution, I would recommend that, after its commencement, all the new books should be kept for at least one year, for the use of annual subscribers of five shillings, or such other sum as may be thought proper. I adopted this plan in 1822. Previous to that period, the greatest number of our annual subscribers was eight; they now amount to more than one hundred and fifty; and besides adding largely to our funds, this measure has introduced into a considerable number of the most respectable and influential families of the district, a number of religious and useful publications. I have allowed these subscribers the privilege of recommending books, to double the amount of their subscriptions, on condition that they are not, in the opinion of the committee, injurious to the interests of religion or morals; this privilege has been used by them with great discretion, and they have frequently assisted me in procuring very proper books.

In consequence of our having a number of subscribers at the neighbouring towns of Dunbar and North Berwick, new books are purchased with their own subscriptions for the use of these stations; besides which, the new books that have been one year at Haddington, are sent to North Berwick and Dunbar, so as to be double the value of their subscriptions; and the new books which have been at Dunbar and North Berwick, are kept another year for the Haddington subscribers. By this arrangement, all the subscribers have access to many more volumes than their own subscriptions would have purchased. And after this they are formed into divisions for general circulation. In a large town, as Edinburgh or Glasgow, a similar plan might be followed, by placing divisions within the reach of the different squares and streets of the genteel population, many of whom, I am persuaded, would subscribe for the use of the books for the younger branches of their families, as well as for themselves.

As it is of much importance to gratify the annual subscribers with the books they wish to read, as early as possible, in the issuing-book for them, I have adopted the plan of writing the name of the book on the top of the page, and writing the name of the borrower below it, with the date when the volume is issued; and as a volume is frequently called for when some person has it, I also enter the names of the persons who want it, in the same manner; and when it comes in, it is immediately sent to them, and the date is affixed to their name. By this means some volumes are never permitted to stand idle in the book-shelf. The issuing-book for the general readers is more easily kept. The names of the usual readers are arranged alphabetically, and the number of the book is marked opposite their name, and under a column for the month in which they are issued; and when they are returned, the number is merely crossed. It is very useful to call in all the books once a-year for examination, and to get repaired those which require it.

It is not advisable to require any entry money in addition to the first annual subscription, as it is usually a hinderance to new subscribers. When an addition to the catalogue of the new books is printed, which should be once a-year, if it is sent gratuitously to the respectable families in the neighbourhood, it will usually procure more new subscribers than will pay the expense of printing it.

Besides the subscriptions from individuals, we have had occasional donations to the East Lothian Itinerating Libraries from different missionary societies, formed within the district. As the libraries have much of the nature of a Home Missionary institution, there is, perhaps, no plan by which such societies can promote the interests of religion, at so little expense, and in so inoffensive a manner, as by supporting itinerating libraries in their respective districts, by applying a part of their funds to this purpose, and thereby promoting the interests of religion at home. This would ultimately increase their funds for foreign objects, by increasing the number of their subscribers.

Although the principal object of the East Lothian Itinerating Libraries is to promote the interests of religion, we have introduced a number of volumes on all branches of knowledge which we could procure, of a plain and popular nature; and this, I am persuaded, has made the institution much more popular, and also increased the number of religious books which have been read.

Much of the success of such institutions will depend on the zeal of the librarians, and on their acting gratuitously; and also by giving a moderate degree of publicity to the plan, by reports, catalogues, and advertisements.

SAMUEL BROWN.
Manager of the East Lothian Itinerating
Libraries, Haddington.

[This was written some time ago, and Mr. Brown has now, we doubt not, farther progress to report.]

THE QUAKERS AND THE CHURCH.

A BRIEF STATEMENT
Of the Reasons why the Religious Society of Friends object to the Payment of Tithes, and other Demands of an Ecclesiastical Nature.

THE Religious Society of Friends has now existed in this country for nearly two centuries as a distinct Christian community. Amongst other circumstances by which we have been distinguished from our fellow professors of the Christian name, has been an objection, founded on a scruple of conscience, to the payment of tithes, and other demands of an ecclesiastical character. Apprehending that the motives of our conduct herein are not generally well understood, and anxiously desiring also that our own members may be encouraged and strengthened to act consistently with our Christian profession, we think it right, at the present time, briefly to set forth the reasons of our testimony on this important subject.

We have uniformly entertained the belief, on the authority of Holy Scripture, that when, in the fulness of time, according to the all-wise purposes of God, our blessed Lord and Saviour appeared personally upon the earth, He introduced a dispensation pure and spiritual in its character. He taught, by his own holy example and divine precepts, that the ministry of the Gospel is to be without pecuniary remuneration. As the gift is free, the exercise of it is to be free also: the office is to be filled by those only who are called of God by the power of the Holy Spirit; who, in their preaching, as well as in their circumspect lives and conversation, are giving proof of this call. The forced maintenance of the ministers of religion is, in our view, a violation of those great privileges which God, in his wisdom and goodness, bestowed upon the human race, when He sent his Son to redeem the world, and the power of the Holy Spirit, to lead and guide mankind into all truth.

Our blessed Lord put an end to that priesthood, and to all those ceremonial usages connected therewith, which were before divinely ordained under the Law of Moses. The present system of tithes was not in any way instituted by Him, our Holy Head, and High Priest, the great Christian Lawgiver. It had no existence in the purest and earliest ages of the Church, but was gradually introduced, as superstition and apostacy spread over professing Christendom, and was subsequently enforced by legal authority. And it further appears to us, that in this enforcing as due " to God and the Holy Church," a tithe upon the produce of the earth, and upon the increase of the herds of the field, an attempt was made to uphold and perpetuate a Divine institution appointed only for a time, but which was abrogated by the coming in the flesh of the Lord Jesus Christ. The vesting of power by the laws of the land in the king, assisted by his council, whereby articles of belief have been framed for the adoption of his subjects, and under which the support of the teachers of these articles is enforced, is, in our judgment, a procedure at variance with the whole scope and design of the Gospel; and as it violates the rights of private judgment, so it interferes with that responsibility by which man is bound to his Creator.

In accordance with what has been already stated, we of course conscientiously object also to all demands made upon us in lieu of tithes. We likewise object to what are termed Easter-dues, demands originally made by the Church of Rome, but continued in the Protestant Church of England, for services which we cannot receive. We also object to Mortaries, sums applied for and still enforced in some places, as due to the incumbent of a parish on the death of the head of a family. Neither do we find, in the example or precepts of our blessed Lord and his Apostles, any authority for these claims, or others of a kindred nature, which all had their origin in times of the darkness and corruption of the Christian Church. And we further consider, that to be compelled to unite in the support of buildings, where a mode of religious worship is observed in which we cannot conscientiously unite, and in paying for appurtenances attached to that mode of worship from which we alike dissent, is subversive of that freedom which the Gospel of Christ has conferred upon all.

Deeply impressed with a conviction of the truth of these considerations, we have felt it to be a religious duty to refuse active compliance with all ecclesiastical demands which have been made upon us; or to be parties to any compromise whereby the payment of them is to be insured. That this conduct has not arisen from a contumacious spirit, we trust the general character of our proceedings will amply testify. And we trust also that it will be readily admitted, that political considerations have not governed our religious Society, but that we have been actuated by a sincere desire to maintain, in the sight of God and man, a conscientious testimony to the freedom and spirituality of the Gospel of Christ, and thus to promote the enlargement of his kingdom upon earth.

In their support of these views, our pious predecessors underwent many and grievous sufferings, which they bore with Christian meekness and patience.

* * * * * *

Seeing that we have, as a religious society, invariably made, on this subject, an open confession before men, we earnestly desire that we may all steadfastly adhere to the original grounds of our testimony; nor allow ourselves to be led away by any feelings of a party spirit, or suffer any motives of an inferior character to take the place of those which are purely Christian. May none amongst us shrink from the faithful and upright support of our Christian belief, but through the grace of our Lord Jesus Christ, seek after that meek disposition, in which our Society has uniformly thought it right to maintain this testimony, and which we desire may ever characterize us as a body. It becomes us all, when thus conscientiously refusing a compliance with the law of the land, to do it in that peaceable spirit of which our Lord has left us so blessed an example. May we all be concerned, in accordance with the advice of this meeting, given forth in the year 1759, " to demonstrate, by our whole conduct and conversation, that we really suffer for conscience-sake, and keep close to the guidance of that good Spirit, which will preserve in meekness and quiet resignation under every trial. For if resentment should arise against those whom we may look upon as the instruments of our sufferings, it will deprive us of the reward of faithfulness, give just occasion of offence, and bring dishonour to the cause of truth. Cavilling or casting reflections upon any because of our sufferings, doth not become the servants of Christ, whose holy example and footsteps we ought in all things faithfully to follow."

* * * * * *

In conclusion, it is our earnest prayer, that it may please the Supreme Ruler of the Universe to hasten the coming of that period when the light of the glorious Gospel of Christ shall shine forth with unclouded brightness, when righteousness shall cover the earth as the waters cover the sea, and when the kingdoms of this world shall become the kingdoms of our Lord and of his Christ.

Signed, in and on behalf of the yearly meeting, by
SAMUEL TUKE.

USEFUL NOTICES.

BOTANY.—The East India Company have presented to the Linnæan Society their magnificent Herbarium, containing the plants collected between long. 73° to 114° E. and lat. 32° N. to the equator, by Konig, Roxburgh, Ruttler, Russell, Klein, Hamilton, Heyne, Wight, Finlayson, and Wallich. It includes about 1900 genera, more than 8000 species, and amounts in duplicates, to at least 70000 specimens,—the labours of half a century.—For many years a large portion of these vegetable riches were stored on the shelves of the India House, without any one sufficiently conversant in Indian Botany to arrange and render them subservient to the cause of science. On the arrival in this country of Dr. Wallich, the distinguished superintendent of the Company's Garden at Calcutta, in the year 1828,—who brought with him an immense accession to the Herbarium from various parts of India, especially Nepal and the Burmese Empire,—the Court of Directors instructed him to make a catalogue of the aggregate collection, and to distribute duplicate specimens to the more eminent societies and naturalists throughout Europe and America.—This immense labour has occupied Dr. Wallich for the last four years; and it is the chief selection from these various Herbaria, destined for the museum of the India House, which the Court of Directors have, with princely munificence, presented to the Linnæan Society.—The liberality of the East India Company has been duly appreciated throughout the wide circle of science.

METHOD OF PLACING AN OLD PICTURE UPON A NEW CANVASS IN OIL COLOURS.—When your picture has been properly placed, and the old canvass has been removed with due caution, wipe the wrong side of the picture with a fine cloth; when it is dry, place the wrong side upon a light gauze, then give it a coat of Spanish white, take a painted canvass not dry, and place the picture upon this canvass, put it into a press, and when the painting is completely dry, if the operation has been well performed, the painting will be found on the new canvass, and will not be at all influenced by wet weather. Some persons give two coats of Spanish white upon the gauze, leaving the first to dry before the second is given, and it is not till this second is completed that they put the painting upon the canvass.—*Quarterly Review*.

CURIOSITY OF ART.—A very singular, and to the public a yet unknown art was practised a few years since in Paris, by which, impressions of different sizes, either larger or smaller than the original design, were taken from the same copperplate. It would seem, that, according to the ordinary way of printing, it would be impossible to take from a plate an impression smaller or larger than the plate itself; but this has been done by Gonord, a watchmaker in that capital, and it has been ascertained, that, whether the copy be larger or smaller than the plate, it retains all the traces of the original with the nicest accuracy. It is supposed to have been executed in this manner. An impression of the same size as the plate, is taken on the surface of some soft substance, such as the elastic compound of glue and treacle used in conveying landscapes of china ware: this substance is confined in a tube broader at one end than at the other. If a part of the substance be then removed from the narrow end, after the impression has been taken on the surface at the wider end, and the tube be placed with the wider end upwards, the elastic substance will fall, and the printed surface be compressed within a smaller space. The edges of the tube are then cut to a level with the elastic substance, and if the impression upon it be conveyed to paper, the copy will be smaller than the original plate. If we wish to have a copy larger than the original plate, it may be done by removing the substance to a wider tube, in which the printed surface will be made to expand to the requisite dimensions. These, however, are but conjectures, Gonord has hitherto preserved the secret of his process.

A very beautiful mode of representing small branches of the most delicate vegetable productions in bronze has been employed by Mr. Chantrey. A small strip of a fir-tree, a branch of holly, a curled leaf of broccoli, or any other vegetable production, is suspended by one end in a small cylinder of paper, which is placed for support within a similarly formed tin case; the finest river silt, carefully separated from all the coarser particles, and mixed with water so as to have the consistency of cream, is poured into the paper cylinder by small portions at a time, carefully shaking the plant a little after each addition, in order that its leaves may be covered, and that no bubbles of air may be left. The plant and its mould are now allowed to dry, and the yielding nature of the paper allows the loamy coating to shrink from the outside. When this is dry, it is surrounded by a coarser substance; and, finally, we have now the twig with all its leaves imbedded in a perfect mould. This mould is carefully dried, and then gradually heated to a red heat. At the ends of some of the leaves or shoots, wires have been left to afford air-holes by their removal, and in this state of strong ignition a stream of air is directed into the hole formed by the end of the branch. The consequence is, that the wood and leaves which had been turned into charcoal by the fire, are now converted into carbonic acid by the current of air, and after some time the whole of the solid matter of which the plant consisted is completely removed, leaving a hollow mould, bearing on its interior all the minutest traces of its late vegetable occupant. When this process is completed, the mould being still kept at nearly a red heat, receives the fluid metal, which, by its weight, either drives the very small quantity of air, which at that high temperature remains behind, out through the air-holes, or compresses it into the pores of the very porous substance of which the mould is formed.

Dear provisions must produce one of the following effects—they must either lower the condition of the labourer, or raise the rate of wages. Nobody can wish the former result; you must, therefore, wish high wages to be the result of dear corn; but if wages are high, the price of goods must be high; but if the price of goods be high, our manufacturers cannot compete with foreigners; but if they cannot compete with foreigners, our export trade is diminished, and the prosperity of our manufacturing population is undermined; and if their prosperity is undermined, they will consume fewer provisions; the demand for agricultural produce in the manufacturing counties will be restricted; the surplus produce will remain in the hands of the farmer, and the ultimate result will be a fall of rents, occasioned, be it remembered, by an attempt to raise them. Let this sink deep into your minds.—*Lord Milton*.

ON DR. CHALMERS' LATE WORK.

Though apparently desultory, one leading idea pervades Dr. Chalmers' work. He lays it broadly down in the first chapter, that all the miseries that afflict the labouring classes are the result of their own errors and misconduct;—that " there is no possible help for them if they will not help themselves ;" that " it is to a rise and reformation in the habits of our peasantry that we should look for deliverance, and not to the impotent crudities of a speculative legislation." Dr. Chalmers never for an instant loses sight of this principle. It is, in his estimation, the " one thing needful." With it all will be right; without it all will be wrong. Amendment, he contends, can come from no other source.

The error of Dr. Chalmers has arisen from his laying too much stress on the principle of population, as explained by Mr. Malthus. Neither the repeal nor abolition of the most burdensome taxes or regulations, nor the discovery of new machines and processes for reducing the cost of production, can, in his estimation, be of any real service. They may enlarge the field over which population is spread; but it is impossible they should have any considerable or lasting influence over the people. Unless the principle of increase is controlled by the greater prudence of the poor, resulting from their better education, every thing that may be done for them will be as dust in the balance, or will injure rather than improve their situation. " The additional food that may have been created, will be more than overborne in the tide of an increasing population. The only difference will be a greater instead of a smaller number of wretched families—a heavier amount of distress, with less of unbroken ground in reserve for any future enlargements—a society in every way as straitened as before ; in short, a condition of augmented hardship and diminished hope, with all the burden of an expensive and unprofitable scheme to the bargain."—P. 39.

It is obvious, however, that these results can take place only on the supposition that the population is instantaneously, or at least very speedily, adjusted according to variations in the supply of food and other accommodations. But this is very far, indeed, from being the case. It is always an exceedingly difficult matter to change the habits of a people as to marriage. That they are influenced by external circumstances, no one doubts; but there is a *vis inertiæ* to be overcome, that always prevents them from changing to the extent that circumstances change. Suppose that, in consequence of legislative enactments, or of any other cause, wages in Great Britain were generally doubled, nobody believes that this would double the marriages next year; and though it did, the population could not be doubled for very many years; and a period of eighteen or twenty years would have to elapse before the stimulus given by the rise of wages could bring a single labourer into the field. It is clear, therefore, that, during all this lengthened period, the labourers would enjoy an increased command over the necessaries and conveniences of life; their notions as to what was required for their comfortable and decent support, would consequently be raised, and they would acquire those improved tastes and habits that are not the hasty product of a day, a month, or a year, but the late result of a long series of continuous impressions. Did the supply of labour adjust itself, like the supply of most commodities, proportionally to every variation of demand, these results would not follow, and Dr. Chalmers would be right in ridiculing all expectations of " extrinsic assistance." But every one knows that the very reverse is the case—that the population cannot be speedily increased when wages rise; and that time is afforded for the formation of those improved habits that are of such essential importance.

Without undervaluing education, we at the same time contend that extrinsic circumstances have a material and *lasting* influence over the condition of society ; that though " the crudities of speculative legislation" may not raise the " standard of enjoyment," it may be raised by judicious legislative enactments; and that, however well a people may be instructed, their condition is always powerfully influenced by the conduct of their rulers. Were an oppressive tax, or an injudicious law or regulation repealed, Dr. Chalmers would say that the benefit thence resulting must be immaterial; inasmuch as population will forthwith expand to the increased limits of subsistence. Were this true, it would afford a convenient excuse for every species of abuse. Fortunately, however, we do not labour under any such incurable fatality. We are acted upon as well by external circumstances, as by the monitor within. Were a repeal of the corn laws, the introduction of an improved system of cropping, or of some new and more powerful manure, to occasion a fall of twenty or thirty per cent in the price of bread, we doubt very much whether the ratio at which population is at present increasing would be sensibly affected. But supposing it were, *half a century* at least must elapse before wages could be proportionably reduced through such an increase ; and the population being accustomed, during all this interval, to an increased command over the necessaries and enjoyments of human life, would have their " standard of sufficiency" raised, and " would utterly refuse to multiply upon their former diet." *Let us not, therefore, attempt to make the theory of population a scape goat for the errors of blundering legislators.* It is not so mechanical a principle as Dr. Chalmers would seem to suppose. It is influenced, no doubt, by a " moral and Christian education ;" but it is also powerfully influenced by good laws and wise government.—*Edinburgh Review.*

THE DECAY OF GENUINE PSALMODY.

The gradual disuse in the parochial service of those venerable tunes by Purcell, Croft, Jeremiah Clarke, Isaac Smith, Ravenscroft, &c. from which the music of the Church of England, and chiefly, the style of the genuine psalm tune, derives its character, is a source of regret to many judicious organists. In a few of the chapels about the Inns of Court, the old purity of melody and harmony is still preserved ; but in parish churches, where music is exposed to the influence of vulgar tastes, and the organist only holds his place by the tenure of pleasing the majority, there are commonly adopted tunes of the basest and meanest description, which no art of the harmonizer can render tolerable. These tunes have an original taint of vulgarity in the intervals and in the motion of the melody, which no ingenuity can cover, and thus the impressive solemnity which once distinguished the music of the Established Church no longer exists ; and the vocal branch of the service is merged into one " base, common, and popular style." The passion in congregations for singing thirds, or something different from the air of the psalm, is one main cause of the banishment of the old tunes, which, independently of their grave character, do not readily admit of having thirds placed beneath the melody. This conceit of making harmony extempore, each man and woman his and her own part, has reached such a pitch, that it is impossible to be placed in the midst of a church where every one sings, without receiving the most distressing sensations. Notes the most horribly false reach the ear on all sides, and not only when one of the ancient discarded melodies happens to embarrass the congregation, but even in their new especial favourites, whenever the sequence of thirds is interrupted. The organist himself cannot escape, and he is frequently obliged to play more commonplace harmonies than the tune would otherwise suggest, to avoid the clash which a certain chord would make with the sounds emitted by the congregation. His own taste, by perpetually accommodating itself to the ignorance of others, as the least of two evils, becomes insensibly lowered ; and a situation which might afford real pleasure in the discharge of its duties, were the music of the church what it ought to be, is at length associated only with feelings of pain and degradation. Bad voices become neutralized by numbers, and their effect is covered by the organ ; but wrong notes nothing can disguise or render palatable. The evil has arisen from the spread of a superficial knowledge of music, an assumption of superiority to the organist, and a desire to be pleased rather than improved ; and that our statement is not chimerical, attendance at many of our churches will convince the competent hearer.

The old psalm tunes bequeathed to us by our forefathers are so strictly in keeping with the spirit of the church service, and even with the architecture of the buildings, that for their purpose they are unequalled. We are never better acquainted with their value as compositions, than when modern attempts in the same way are brought before us, and which stand in about the same relation to the archetypes of the style, as a new prayer to the collects, or a new church to one of Sir Christopher Wren's. The beauty of the church service consists in its order and regularity, and freedom from innovation. There is no thought of altering the appointed course of morning and evening prayer throughout the year, or the fashion of the steeple, or the chiming of the bells; why should the music of the church (not one of its least important parts) be exposed to change, and made pleasing to the vulgar ear, and conformable to the vulgar taste, rather than to exalt and purify the minds of the congregation? To please (especially bad judges) is, we imagine, not the first object of psalmody. But on this matter every one appears to have a voice, but the man whose decision upon the fit and unfit should be imperative—the organist. The clergyman interferes not, still less the bishop, to protect this officer of the church in the stern and unflinching discharge of his duty; and rather than be at feud with the parish, or expose himself to the numberless ill-offices of spies, he at length reluctantly gives up his own inclination. Hence the departure from the severe simplicity of the old psalm tune, from solemn chords and rich changes of harmony, for the present insipid style of church music; and instead of variety, monotony the most wearisome is the consequence; for nothing is more tedious and samely than the constant march of thirds. But the old tunes, sung alternately by trebles and tenors in unison, and left free for the organist to accompany with such harmonies as his fancy and feeling might suggest, would be productive of the most gratifying variety and the noblest effects. This is one of the most delightful ways in which the organ and voices can be employed, and one by which many verses of the same psalm may be rendered interesting and various. It imposes no restraint upon the accompanyist—it leads to no wrong notes, for the progression is plain and easy. Each of the performers in a London congregation is so engrossed by his own voice that he does not hear his neighbour—this is the reason that the confusion gives him no offence.—*Atlas.*

YEARS OF PESTILENCE AND FAMINE IN SCOTLAND.

One night, in the month of August 1694, a cold east wind, accompanied by a dense sulphurous fog, passed over the country, and the half-filled corn was struck with mildew; it shrunk and whitened in the sun, till the field seemed as if sprinkled with flour; and where the fog had remained longest (for, in some places, it stood up like a chain of hills during the greater part of the night) the more disastrous were its effects. From this unfortunate year until the year 1701 the land seemed as if struck with barrenness; and such was the change in the climate, that the seasons of summer and winter were cold and gloomy in nearly the same degree. The wonted heat of the sun was withholden; the very cattle became stunted and meagre, the moors and thickets were nearly divested of their feathered inhabitants, and scarcely a fly or any other insect was to be seen even in the beginning of autumn. November and December, and, in some places, January and February, became the months of harvest, and labouring people contracted diseases which terminated in death when employed in cutting down the corn among ice and snow. Of the scanty produce of the fields much was left to rot on the ground, and much of what was carried home proved unfit for the sustenance of either man or beast. There is a tradition, that a farmer of Cromarty employed his children, during the whole winter of 1694, in picking out the sounder grains of corn from a blasted heap, the sole product of his farm, to serve for seed in the ensuing spring.

In the meantime the country began to groan under famine. The little portions of meal which were brought to market were invariably disposed of, and at an exorbitant price, before half the people were supplied; and then, says *Walker, there would ensue "a screaming and clapping of hands among the women." "How shall we go home," he has heard them exclaim, "and see our children dying of hunger;—they have had no food for these two days, and we have nothing to give them." There was many "a black and pale face in Scotland;" and many of the labouring poor, ashamed to beg, and too honest to steal, shut themselves up in their comfortless houses, and would sit with their eyes fixed on the floor till their very sight failed them. The savings of the careful and industrious were soon dissipated, and many who were in easy circumstances when the scarcity came on, were sunk in abject poverty ere it had passed away. Human nature is a sad thing when subjected to the test of circumstances so trying. As the famine increased, people came to be so wrapped up in their own sufferings that "wives thought not of their husbands, nor husbands of their wives."

The pestilence which accompanied the terrible visitation, broke out in November, 1694, when many of the people were seized by "strange fevers and sore fluxes of a most infectious nature," which defied the utmost power of medicine. "For the oldest physician," says Walker, "had never seen the like before, and could make no help." In the parish of West Calder, out of nine hundred "examinable persons," three hundred were swept away; and in Liviston, in a village called the Craigs, inhabited by only six or eight families, there were thirty corpses in the space of a few days. In the parish of Resolis, whole villages were depopulated, and the foundations of the houses, for they were never inhabited afterwards, can still be pointed out by old men of the place. So violent were the effects of the disease that people who in the evening were in apparent health, would be found lying dead in their houses next morning, "the head resting on the hand, and the face and arms not unfrequently gnawed by the rats." The living were wearied with burying the dead; bodies were drawn on sledges to the place of interment, and many got neither coffin nor winding sheet. "I was one of four," says the Pedlar, "who carried the corpse of a young woman a mile of way; and when we came to the grave, an honest poor man came and said,—'you must go and help me to bury my son; he has lain dead these two days.' We went, and had two miles to carry the corpse; many neighbours looking on us, but none coming to assist. I was creditably informed," he continues, "that in the north, two sisters on a Monday morning were found carrying their brother on a barrow with bearing ropes, resting themselves many times, and none offering to help them." There is a tradition that in one of the villages of Resolis, the sole survivor was an idiot, and that his mother was the last person who died in it of the disease. He waited beside the corpse for several days, and then taking it up on his shoulders, he carried it to a neighbouring village, and left it standing upright beside a garden wall.—Such were the sufferings of the people of Scotland in the seventeenth century, and such the phenomena of character which these sufferings elicited. We ourselves have seen nearly the same process repeated in the nineteenth, and so invariably fixed are the principles of human nature, and the succession in even the moral world, of cause and effect, that the results have been nearly the same. M.

---

* *David Dean's* friend, Peter Walker, the pedlar, quoted in our 12th number, in the article on the Infectious Nature of Superstition.

CO-OPERATIVE MELODIES.
THE BREAST'S BRIGHTEST GEM.
Air.—"*Hurrah for the Bonnets of Blue.*"
MRS. GRIMSTONE.

Here's wealth for the merchant in mines,
  There's wealth for the student in tomes,
And there's wealth for the Bacchant in wassail and wines
  When in riot and revel he roams:
But the wealth of all wealth is a heart
  By no narrow feeling confin'd,
That looks round the world with a wish to impart
  Its glowings, to gladden mankind.
Then hurrah for the breast's brightest gem,
  That kindles at sympathy's call;
Here's the love and the blessing of all unto them
  Whose hearts hold a blessing for all!

There's pride in the pomp of a throne—
  There's pride in the patriot band—
When they stand in the breach unsustained and alone,
  And strike for their loves and their land:
But there's pride that is purer than this,
  That runs like a rill in the soul,
'Tis a holier pride, for it aims at the bliss,
  Not of one spot of earth, but the whole.
Then hurrah for the breast's brightest gem,
  That kindles at sympathy's call;
Here's the love and the blessing of all unto them
  Whose hearts hold a blessing for all!

ELEMENTS OF THOUGHT.

WORDS IN SEASON FROM NAPOLEON.

If the stability of a Government require a predominant faith, its tranquillity is opposed to a domineering religion.— (Alluding to the *Roman Catholic*.)

There are storms, which are instrumental to the strengthening of a Government in its roots.

The maintenance of the law, in its rules and forms, is the palladium of civil liberty.

The throne is an irresistible magnet; no sooner are we seated upon it, than we are infected with a species of contagion which the best cannot avoid.

The right, which is universally acknowledged amongst all nations, is that of scrupulous reciprocity.

Undisciplined bravery has sometimes succeeded on land; but never at sea.

The crimes of children are, in frequent instances, the fruits of the vicious education they have received from their parents.

How deserving are men of the contempt they inspire? Behold yon resolute republicans! I have but to gild their vestments, and every one of them becomes my servant.

I found a crown lying upon the ground, and stooped to pick it up.

We should never deprive princes of the inheritance of whatever good they do, or whatever eloquence escapes their lips.

Virtue, like all things else, has its limits. Whoever pretends to travel beyond them is most commonly a hypocrite.

My enemies hold rendezvous around my grave; but let him look to it who is last there.

Of Talleyrand he said, "Nothing need create less surprise than his wealth. Talleyrand sells those who buy him."

Of a Russian Count he observed, "I was perfectly aware the youth was a reptile, but I did not think he was a viper."

THE FUTURE PROSPECTS OF EUROPE AND AMERICA.
By JAMES DOUGLAS, ESQ.

THROUGHOUT Europe, there is no less a revolution in the relative position of the nations towards each other, than in the interior condition of each. The French and the Russians have changed situations in the political scale; Petersburgh has become the centre of aggression, and Paris, that of resistance and defence. The invasions which Europe has now to dread are from the north, and the hope of its ultimate freedom rests upon the energy and the prosperity of its southern states. The position of Russia is eminently favourable for successful and limitless encroachment, and possesses within itself ample space for ever-increasing numbers. It has no enemy behind it, to distract its attention or divide its efforts; it has only opposed to it a weak and broken frontier, without any one commanding defence, and with vulnerable points innumerable, from the Baltic to the sea of Japan. The Swedes, the Turks, the Persians, the Turcomans, and the Chinese, are unable to cope with the Russian armies, and must yield at the first shock of the invaders. Austria and Prussia hold their Polish provinces in some measure at the mercy of Russia, and France is the only nation which, single-handed, could afford an adequate resistance. As France has changed from the attitude of aggression to that of defence, England, the supporter of the independence of the Continental nations, becomes the natural ally of France, instead of being its "natural enemy;" and henceforth it is manifestly the interest of this country, that the French should be great, powerful, and free. It is certainly for the advantage of England, that the seat of aggrandizement and danger should be removed from the banks of the Seine to the shores of the Baltic; and an Attila, whose troops are encamped in Poland, and along the frontiers of China, is less to be dreaded than an enemy of inferior power, who has the occupation of Boulogne and Brest. The wide separation of Russia and England, leaves no adjacent field of combat, on which they might measure their forces, and decide the contest; and England, it is now evident, can best preserve the independence and prosperity of Europe by preserving peace; and her surest weapon is the communication of her own knowledge and liberty; before which, barbarism, however potent, must bow, and stirred up by which, vassals, however depressed, will rise up and shake off the yoke. While Britain counterbalances the ascendency of Russia in the west, she will divide with her the supremacy of the east, and have for her share the fairest, if not the most extensive, portion of Asia. They are the two great antagonist powers in the old world, opposite in their nature as in their influence—the one physically, the other morally great—the one at present retarding, the other accelerating, the march of European society; but both ultimately destined to be instruments of political changes, which will give a new face to the institutions of the ancient Continent. As the balance of power is shifting among the nations that compose European confederation, it is changing also in the component parts of each individual state; and the struggle for political liberty is begun, which can only terminate with the general acquisition of free institutions. This tendency to freedom it is every way the interest of Britain to foster and protect. Despotic kings are truly her natural enemies, who must inevitably wish to destroy those institutions which are of so bad example to their own subjects; and it is only from freemen, actuated by a similar spirit, that she can expect cordial sympathy and co-operation.

Freedom, which far more than doubles the force of states, derives a new value from the energy it would communicate to the nations, in resisting the attacks of every aggressor; and the new life and additional permanency it would infuse into the states of the Continent, who require every aid, in their present circumstances, and every amelioration in their condition, to enable them to resist the pressure which they must soon feel, from the vicinity and the growth of the Russian empire.

If the fate of Europe were different from the expectations that are formed of its rising prosperity, and its free and civilized states should fall before a new irruption of barbarians, America would soon fill up the blank, and take the lead in the advancement of society. The enlightened and the brave of the old world would withdraw from the slavery of their native lands, and, with the same ardour, on another side of the globe, would follow the pursuit of truth, and enlarge the boundaries of science. America, no longer receiving the supplies of knowledge from abroad, would commence an original literature, and beginning where the Europeans had ended, would enter a fresh career of improvement, and explore new riches of mind. In less than 25 years the American States double their population, and more than double their resources; and their influence, which is even now felt in Europe, will every year exert a wider sway over the minds of men, and hold out to them a more illustrious example of prosperity and freedom. In little more than a century the United States of America must contain a population ten times greater than has ever yet been animated by the spirit and energy of a free government; and in less than a century and a half, the new world will not be able to contain its inhabitants, but will pour them forth, straitened by their overflowing numbers at home, upon the shores of less civilized nations, till the whole earth is subdued to knowledge, and filled with the abodes of free and civilized men. But the spirit and the imitation of American freedom, will spread still more rapidly and widely than its power. No force can crush the sympathy that already exists, and is continually augmenting, between Europe and the new world. The eyes of the oppressed are even now turning wistfully to the land of freedom, and the kings of the Continent already regard with awe and disquietude the new Rome rising in the west, the fore shadows of whose greatness yet to be are extending dark and heavy over their dominions, and obscuring the lustre of their thrones.

THE STORY-TELLER.

THE PROPS OF THE PULPIT.

Under the above title, your imagination, gentle and intelligent reader, will naturally disport itself amidst the members of our General Assembly. You will think incontinently of our Inglises, our Cookes, our Chalmerses, our Thomsons, or such other Tuscan and Doric pillars upon which the Church visible at present rests; or, in the retirements of former ages, you will discern those mighty shades which have long taken their place with the illustrious departed. Or, perhaps, in the grosser materiality of apprehension, you may even conjure up those beams and pillars on which our pulpits are outwardly and visibly supported. But in all such efforts, you will come wide of the truth, and the "Props of the Pulpit" which are here meant, are nothing more nor less than old men and women who commonly cluster around our parish pulpits, to the exceeding annoyance of the precentor, and the great delight of every efficient and faithful pastor.

It is quite possible that a very useless and inefficient minister may be popular;—the walls of his church may perspire from door to door, and from floor to ceiling, encompassing a dense and gaping multitude, and yet all this while the speaker may be a mere dandy, with a high collar and a white handkerchief, a showy style and a retentive memory. But no such orator will ever clothe his pulpit stair-way with tartan plaids and Shanter bonnets, with clasp-bibles and crooked kents. Till, however, such conquest has been made, and the venerable and pious "Props" I refer to have been attracted into their places, the speaker, though he may tickle the imagination, and gratify the ear of his audience, is yet a great way from utility,—from that true and genuine efficiency, which bespeaks the operation of "Grace," through the instrumentality of our honest, and fervent, and devotional feeling and utterance. Take your summer excursion from "the Mull" to "Pomona," from Ailsa to the Bass, and mark, in your progress, the Sabbath ministrations of every minister in Scotland. Deaf though you were, and altogether incapable of ascertaining from the year the power and value of the respective ministrations, you may gather from the eye alone, from these "Pulpit Props," how the spiritual interests of each parish fare,—whether the incumbent preaches himself or his master, the Gospel or the idle showiness of learning, ingrafted on vanity of worldly wisdom and conceit, gilt and glossed over with a show and a seeming of godliness.

It may be that the church you have visited is not crowded to the door, and that, even amidst a comparatively limited number of hearers, you observe somewhat of an unexcited and inattentive aspect, as if no great expectation had been raised, and no particular exertion had been made to excite it. But if you have the aged and wrinkled faces of threescore and ten immediately fronting you,—if you can mark, while the venerable and venerated man of God is composedly dividing the word of truth, a gradual and a solemn lifting and falling of the hands; if the Bible lies half opened, and dog-leafed *at the text*, in the lap of age, and the eyes of the surrounding "Props" are ever and anon raised in humble acquiescence to the face and the utterance of the pastor, then all is right : such a parish has been blessed in its minister, and such a minister has had, and will have, reason to rejoice in his pastoral labours. I had rather sit under such a ministry, than under all the fiery and scalding droppings from the lamp of the red-hot zealot, or blazing sentimentalist.

Do you observe that figure which occupies the lowest step of the pulpit range? There she sits, with her little orphan grand-daughter at her feet, and there she has sat for many years past : she never desires to ascend higher, or to come into contact and competition with the persons or the privileges of the precentor or bell-man. Her heart is humble, yet it is feelingly alive to any acts of condescension or kindness with which it may be visited. Carefully, as the minister ascends to the pulpit, does she draw in the extremities of her dress, contract her body to leave the requisite breadth of stair-way for the well-known foot, which her very soul embraces in its passing. Her little Nancy, now no longer, through the intervention of female charity, an object of parish relief, sits on her gown tail, looks up the psalms and texts, and occasionally enjoys, with a half-formed smile, the old woman's embarrassment in fixing her *untempled* spectacles firmly and graspingly on her nose. The history of that woman and her orphan ward is interesting, and on another occasion you shall have it; in the meantime, you must be content with a more limited notice of her next neighbour in the order of stair ascent, *videlicet*, Janet Smith.

Janet is a queer body. I have never been able yet to find out with perfect assurance whether Janet is, or is not, truly religious. She is remarkably sagacious, that is certain,—knows the Scriptures better than most clergymen,—and attends most regularly on the ordinances of religion. But then, on the other hand, Janet's voice is loud when a proclamation has been made over her head ; nor are her commentaries always made in perfect charity. To young preachers, or stibblers, as she calls them, she is quite ferocious, cutting them up at the kirk-style, and, indeed, all the way home to her hut in the clachan, at no allowance ; and occasionally, if I am rightly informed, taking a pretty sound and protracted *nap*, even in the midst of my very warmest addresses. For this I ventured, one day lately, to challenge Janet ; contrasting her vigilance and attention, when a young man had officiated, with her supineness and inattention under my own ministrations. " And d'ye no ken the reason o' that, sir," responded Janet, with a look that intimated, in her own language, " that she had not her tale a-seeking ;" " D'ye no ken the reason o' that, sir ?" I immediately acknowledged my ignorance. " Troth, sir," proceeded my instructor, " whan it's yourself that delivers and expounds ' the oracles,' we can a' take a nap wi' safety, for we ken brawly in wha's han's they are. But when a young birkie like *yon* opens, and tries to explain the sacred word, *it tak's us a' to look sharp after him !*" T. G.

[T. G. being interpreted, meaneth Dr. Gillespie, who wrote as above in the *Literary Journal.*]

PADDY FOORHANE'S FRICASSEE.

Paddy Foorhane kept a shebeen house at Barleymount Cross, in which he sold whisky—from which his Majesty did not derive any large portion of his revenues—ale, and provisions. One evening a number of friends, returning from a funeral—all neighbours too—stopt at his house " because they were in grief," to drink a drop. There was Andy Agar, a stout rattling fellow, the natural son of a gentleman residing near there ; Jack Shea, who was afterwards transported for running away with Biddy Lawlor ; Tim Cournane, who, by reason of being on his keeping, was privileged to carry a gun ; Owen Connor, a march-of-intellect man, who wished to enlighten proctors by making them swallow their processes ; and a number of other " good boys." The night began to " rain cats and dogs," and there was no stirring out ; so the cards were called for, a roaring fire was made down, and the whisky and ale began to flow. After due observation, and several experiments, a space large enough for the big table, and free from the drop down, was discovered. Here six persons, including Andy, Jack, Tim—with his gun between his legs—and Owen, sat to play for a pig's head, of which the living owner, in the parlour below, testified, by frequent grunts, his displeasure at this unceremonious disposal of his property. One boy held several splinters to light them, and another was charged with the sole business of making more, and drying them in little bundles at the fire. This, however, did not prevent him from making many sallies to discover the state of the game. A ring, two or three deep, surrounded the players, and in their looks exhibited the most interest. This group formed what might be termed the foreground of the picture. In one corner were squatted five boys and three girls, also playing cards for pins. But notwithstanding the smallness of the stakes, there were innumerable scuffles, and an unceasing clamour kept up, through which the treble of the girls was sure to be heard, and which, every now and then, required curses, loud and deep, from some unfortunate player at the large table, to silence. On the block by the fire sat Paddy himself, convulsing a large audience with laughter at some humorous story, or at one of his own practical jokes, while his wife bustled about, beat the dog, set pieces of plates and keelers to receive the rain wherever it oozed through the thatch, and occasionally stopped, half-provoked and half-admiring, to shake her head at her husband. Card-playing is very thirsty, and the boys were anxious to keep out the wet; so that long before the pig's head was decided, a messenger had been despatched several times to Killarney, a distance of four English miles, for a pint of whisky each time. The ale also went merrily round, until most of the men were quite stupid, their faces swoln, and their eyes red and heavy. The contest at length was decided; but a quarrel about the skill of the respective parties succeeded, and threatened broken heads at one time. Indeed, had Tim been able to effect the purpose at which he diligently laboured, of getting the gun to his shoulder, it is very probable he would have taken ample satisfaction for some dreadful affront offered him by Andy, who, on his part, directed all his discourse to a large wooden gallon at the other end of the table. The imperturbable coolness of his opponent provoked Andy exceedingly. Abuse is bad enough; but contemptuous silence is more than flesh and blood can bear, particularly as he felt that he was running aground fast when he had the whole conversation to himself. He became quite furious, and, after two or three efforts, started up, and made a rush towards his wooden adversary; but the great slipperiness of the ground laid him on the flat of his back. This gave time, so that several interfered, and peace was made; but the harmony of the night was destroyed. At last, Jack Shea swore they must have something to eat; damn him but he was starved with drink, and he must get some rashers somewhere or other. Every one declared the same; and Paddy was ordered to cook some *griskins* forthwith. Paddy was completely nonplussed :—all the provisions were gone, and yet his guests were not to be trifled with. He made a hundred excuses—"'Twas late—'twas dry now—and there was nothing in the house; sure they ate and drank enough." But all in vain. The ould sinner was threatened with instant death if he delayed. So Paddy called a council of war in the parlour, consisting of his wife and himself.

"Agrah, Jillen, what will we do with these? Is there any meat in the tub? Where is the tongue? If it was yours, Jillen, we'd give them enough of it; but I mane the cow's," (aside.)

"Sure the proctors got the tongue ere yesterday, and you know there an't a bit in the tub. Oh the murtherin villains! and I'll engage 'twill be no good for us, after all my white bread and the whisky;—that it may pison 'em."

"Amen! Jillen; but don't curse them. After all, where's the meat? I'm sure that Andy will kill me if we don't make it out any how;—and he hasn't a penny to pay for it. You could drive the mail coach, Jillen, through his breeches pocket without jolting over a ha'penny. Coming, coming; d'ye hear 'em?"

"Oh, they'll murther us. Sure if we had any of the tripe I sent yesterday to the turf-cutters."

"Eh! What's that you say? I declare to God here's Andy getting up. We must do something, *Thonom an Dhiaoul*, I have it. Jillen, run and bring me the leather breeches; run, woman alive. Where's the block and the hatchet! Go up and tell 'em you're putting down the pot."

Jillen pacified the uproar in the kitchen by loud promises, and returned to Paddy. The use of the leather breeches passed her comprehension; but Paddy actually took up the leather breeches, tore away the lining with great care, chopped the leather with the hatchet on the block, and put it into the pot as tripes. Considering the situation in which Andy and his friends were, and the appetite of the Irish peasantry for meat in any shape—"a bone" being their *summum bonum*—the risk was very little. If discovered, however, Paddy's safety was much worse than doubtful as no people in the world have a greater horror of any unusual food. One of the most deadly modes of revenge they can employ, is to give an enemy dog's or cat's flesh; and there have been instances where the persons who have eaten it, on being informed of the fact, have gone mad. But Paddy's habit of practical jokes, from which nothing could wean him, and his anger at their conduct, along with the fear he was in, did not allow him to hesitate a moment. Jillen remonstrated in vain. "Hould your tongue you foolish woman. They're all as blind as the pig there. They'll never find it out. Bad luck to 'em too, my leather breeches, that I gave a pound note and a hog for in Cork. See how nothing else would satisfy 'em!" The meat at length was ready. Paddy drowned it in butter, threw out the potatoes on the table, and served it up smoking hot with the greatest gravity.

"By J——," says Jack Shea, "that's fine stuff. How a man would dig a trench after that."

"I'll take a priest's oath," answered Tim Cohill, the most irritable of men, but whose temper was something softened by the rich steam.

"Yet, Tim, what's a priest's oath? I never heard that."

"Why, sure, every one knows you didn't ever hear of anything of good."

"I say you lie, Tim, you rascal."

Tim was on his legs in a few moments, and a general battle was about to begin, but the appetite was too strong, and the quarrel was settled; Tim having been appeased by being allowed to explain a priest's oath. According to him, a priest's oath was this:—He was surrounded by books, which were gradually piled up until they reached his lips. He then kissed the uppermost, and swore by all to the bottom. As soon as the admiration excited by his explanation, in those who were capable of hearing Tim, had ceased, all fell to work; and certainly, if the tripes had been of ordinary texture, drunk as was the party, they would soon have disappeared. After gnawing at them for some time, "Well," says Owen Conner, "that I mightn't!—but these are the queerest tripes I ever eat. It must be she was very ould."

"By J——," says Andy, taking a piece from his mouth to which he had been paying his addresses for the last half hour, "I'd as soon be eating leather. She was a bull, man; I cant find the soft end at all of it."

"And that's true for you, Andy," said the man of the gun; "and 'tis the greatest shame they hadn't a bull-bait to make him tinder. Paddy, was it from Jack Clifford's bull you got 'em? They'd do for wadding, they're so tough."

"I'll tell you, Tim, where I got them—'twas out of Lord Ramorne's great cow at Cork, the great fat cow that the Lord Mayor bought for the Lord Lieutenant—as a *churp naur hagusheh.*"

"Amen, I pray God! Paddy. Out of Lord Ramorne's cow? near the steeple I suppose. The great cow that couldn't walk with tallow. By ——, these are fine tripes. They'll make a man very strong. Andy, give me two or three *libbhers* more of 'em."

"Well, see that! out of Lord Ramorne's cow; I wonder what they gave her, Paddy. That I mightn't!—but these would eat a pit of potatoes. Any how, they're good for the teeth. Paddy, what's the reason they send all the good mate from Cork to the Blacks.

But before Paddy could answer this question, Andy, who had been endeavouring to help Tim, uttered a loud "*Thonom an dhiaoul!* what's this? Isn't this flannel?" The fact was, he had found a piece of the lining, which Paddy, in his hurry, had not removed, and all was confusion. Every eye was turned to Paddy, but with wonderful quickness he said, "'Tis the book tripe, *agragal*, don't you see," —and actually persuaded them to it.

"Well, any how," says Tim, "it had the taste of wool."

"May this choke me," says Jack Shea, "if I didn't think that 'twas a piece of a leather breeches when I saw Andy *chawing* it."

This was a shot between wind and water to Paddy. His

* May it never come out of his body.

self-possession was nearly altogether lost, and he could do no more than turn it off by a faint laugh. But it jarred most unpleasantly on Andy's nerves. After looking at Paddy for some time with a very ominous look, he said, "*Firroo Pandhrig* of the tricks, if I thought you were going on with any work here, my soul and my guts to the devil if I would not cut you into garters. By the vestment I'd make a *furhurmeen* of you."

"Is it I, Andy? that the hands may fall off me!"

But Tim Cohill made a most seasonable diversion. "Andy, when you die, you'll be the death of one fool, any how. What do you know that wasn't ever in Cork itself about tripes. I never ate such mate in my life: and 'twould be good for every poor man in the County of Kerry if he had a tub of it."

Tim's tone of authority, and the character he had got for learning, silenced every doubt, and all laid siege to the tripes again. But after some time, Andy was observed gazing with the most astonished curiosity into the plate before him. His eyes were rivetted on something; at last he touched it with his knife, and exclaimed, "*Kmhappa dar Dhia!*"*

"What's that you say?" burst from all; and every one rose in the best manner he could, to learn the meaning of the button.

"Oh, the villain of the world!" roared Andy, "I'm pisoned! Where's the pike? For God's sake Jack run for the priest, or I'm a dead man with the breeches. Where is he? D—— yeer bloods won'nt ye catch him, and I pisoned?"

The fact was, Andy had met one of the knee-buttons sewed into a piece of the tripe, and it was impossible for him to fail discovering the cheat. The rage, however, was not confined to Andy. As soon as it was understood what had been done, there was an universal rush for Paddy and Jillen; but Paddy was much too cunning to be caught after the narrow escape he had of it before. The moment after the discovery of the lining that he could do so without suspicion, he stole from the table, left the house, and hid himself. Jillen did the same; and nothing remained for the eaters to vent their rage but by breaking every thing in the cabin, which was done in the utmost fury. Andy, however, continued watching for Paddy with a gun a whole month after. He might be seen prowling along the ditches near the shebeen-house, waiting for a shot at him. Not that he would have scrupled to enter it were he likely to find Paddy there; but the latter was completely on the *shuchraun*, and never visited his cabin except by stealth. It was in one of those visits that Andy hoped to catch him.—*Tait's Magazine.*

[This is the *genuine* Irish story which we promised our readers long ago.]

ODIUM MEDICUM.—The true *Odium Medicum*, says Gregory, in his memorial to the Royal Infirmary, approaches nearer than any thing else known in human nature, to the genuine *Odium Theologicum*. It has even been doubted, by competent judges, which of the two is the worse; for though physicians have never yet carried the joke so far as to burn alive their adversaries whom they could not convert them as Dominican monks and others used to do very successfully with their obstinate opponents; yet there is reason to suspect, that this reserve and delicacy on the part of our faculty has proceeded more from want of power than from want of good-will to the work. It is certain, at least, that, at one time, about two hundred and fifty years ago, in Spain and Portugal, they fairly tried it, and they had well-nigh succeeded in their attempt. There was formerly, in the time of Sydenham, a controversy between those doctors who thought purging good in cases of fever, and those doctors who thought it bad. One of the purging doctors and one of the anti-purgers, meeting at the entry to Sien College, soon came to hard words and from hard words to hard blows; the result of which was, that the purging doctor knocked the other down, and drawing his sword, bid him beg his life. "No, doctor," replied the fallen hero, as he lay sprawling, with the point of his enraged adversary's sword at his throat; "that I will not do, unless you were giving 'me physic.'"—We leave our Edinburgh readers to draw their own conclusions from this text.

* A button, by —.

COLUMN FOR THE LADIES.

AN ESSAY ON FLIRTS.
DEDICATED TO THE LADIES OF EDINBURGH.

FLIRTS are especial favourites of ours, and we hold ourselves bound, as good knights and true, to do battle for their reputation, at all times, and against all comers. Be it understood that we speak now of Flirts in the restricted acceptation of the term, and not of Jilts, who are immoral, nor of Coquettes, who are heartless personages. The true Flirt is quite a different sort of person.

The appellation is the same with that used to designate a certain sudden, but not ungraceful, mode of unfurling a fan; and if we may credit the tradition embodied in one of our most venerable "Joe Millers," there is some mysterious analogy supposed to exist between the character of the motion, and that of the class of the fair sex to whom the name Flirt has been applied.

A Flirt is a girl of more than common beauty, grace, and amiability, just hovering on the verge which separates childhood from womanhood. She is just awakening to a sense of her power, and finds an innocent pleasure in exercising it. The blissful consciousness parts her lips with prouder breath, kindles up her eyes with richer lustre, and gives additional buoyancy and swan-like grace to her motions. She looks for homage at the hands of every man who approaches her, and richly does she repay him with rosy smiles and sparkling glances.

There is no passion in all this. It is the first trembling into conscious existence of that sentiment which will become love in time. It is the heart of woman venturing timidly to inhale imperceptible portions of that atmosphere of devoted affection in which alone she can afterwards breathe and exist. There is nothing of vanity in it, nothing of selfishness. She thinks not of her beauty while thus triumphantly wielding its spell, any more than does that young greyhound fetching his graceful gambols before us. She feels only the delight of exercising a new-born power. She regards not her own indulgence; happy herself, she sees others happy to sun themselves in her smile, and feels yet more happy in consequence. It is the rich gush of young existence that mantles at her heart, and overflows in loveliness. Oh! blame it not, nor regard austerely. Like the first blush of morning, it dies away before we can well note its surpassing beauty, and all that is to succeed of after life is dull and tame in comparison.

That a girl chances to be a Flirt at a certain age, is no proof that she is incapable of enduring affection, but rather the contrary.

Beauty is the exuberance, the fulness, the overflow of nature. And the richer, the more dazzling the beauty at the moment, when, like a butterfly bursting from its hull, the girl passes insensibly into the woman, the more reason there is to expect a ripe store of affection beneath. It is, indeed, warmth of heart alone that can give the finishing grace to the gay and playful creature we have been describing. If there be beauty, and elegance, and sportiveness, and wit at will, and yet the beholder feel himself obliged to confess that there is some charm awanting—he cannot exactly say what, although he feels its absence—he may depend upon it that closer search will show him minute, but sure signs of heartlessness.

A Flirt is, however, a dangerous creature; not that she means any harm, but that she unconsciously and involuntarily turns the heads of all who approach her. Boys she strikes down by dozens, wherever she moves. If, while tripping along the street on a windy day, the increasing vehemence of the blast force her to turn away from it to adjust the set of her bonnet, the sweep of her laughing eye to see whether any one observes, and the ready blush when she marks all eyes turned upon her, make captive at least six juvenile swains. In the turn of a waltz, her aerial gliding (*vera incessu patuit dea*) draws the attention of all. She cannot ask for a glass of lemonade, without making an involuntary conquest. Nay, "tough seniors"— men inured to business—are not safe. They look with complacency on a thing so lovely—with a paternal placid benignity—but longer conversation awakens warmer thoughts, and, in proportion as the infusion of the passion is more difficult into such toil-strung themes, so is its eradication more difficult.

But the danger does not stop here. By a retro-active influence, all this lip and eye homage may well at times turn the head of a giddy and inexperienced girl. This, however, is a danger not to be avoided; and cure we know of none, save a generous, deep-rooted affection, which, sooner or later, is the lot of every true woman. It is beautiful to see the effect of serious love upon the gayest of these creatures!—how completely all their little vanity is melted away by its engrossing warmth. Not that we think love, any more than the feeling we have been describing, an enduring passion. It is only more intense and absorbing. That affection alone is lasting, in which love has, upon further acquaintance, been confirmed by esteem, and which has been heightened by common sympathies, strengthened by the endurance of common trials, rooted for eternity by mutual forbearance. No one, we will be bold to say, has read the romance of Undine without pleasure, and yet we suspect that to the majority of readers (to ourselves we know) its supernatural mysteries constitute the least part of its attraction. The interest centres in Undine. And what is she? A shadowy type of every beautiful and amiable woman, in the successive stages of her mind's development—the Flirt, the Lover, and the Wife.

In our opinion, however, the period of flirtation is of very brief duration. It is (we beg our fair readers not to imagine that any improper insinuation is couched under this simile) an ebullition of momentary excitement, akin to that of the pointer when loosened from his chain on a fine September morning. It excites admiration only so long as it is unconscious. The instant a woman plays off these little airs with foreknowledge and predetermination, their innocence is gone. They are to be reprehended as indications of a designing mind. Their exercise is on a par with the use of cosmetics and dress to repair or conceal the ravages of age. Our fair friend has ceased to be a Flirt, and has become a Coquette.

We have already stated that there exists a distinction between these two characters, and that this distinction is not in favour of the latter. A Coquette may have been, or she may not have been, a Flirt. She is one who envies the success of the other, and seeks to emulate it by acting her character. She is artificial—she has a part to support, and that alone detracts from the worth of any human being. It certainly is our duty to cultivate our powers, even of pleasing, to the utmost, and to check our weaknesses; but this must be done in accordance with the original constitution of our mind: to seek to new-form ourselves according to some favourite model, is to destroy what little good we may have. The Coquette may generally be known by her overacting the character. Her gestures and words come not from the prompting of feeling, they have no internal standard to regulate them; they are false, constrained, or excessive. Her glances are stares, her movements sudden and awkward, her languor overacted. The Flirt attracts us involuntarily, and we feel that this is the case—the Coquette gives us encouragement. Even a sensible man is in danger from the Flirt—the Coquette inspires him with aversion. The victims of the Flirt's charms never complain, for they know her free from any design upon them—the fools who fall into the lures of the Coquette, accuse her, and justly, of heartlessness and vanity.

The Jilt we have called an immoral, we may add, a coarse and vulgar mind. Jilts are of two kinds: those who are incapable of affection, and sell their show of tenderness to the wealthiest; and those who have a sentiment which they call love, but which is transferable at a moment's notice to another. The latter like to indulge in this feeling, but they have no real regard for any one but themselves. They are of those concerning whom it has somewhere been said, that "they love the love, not the lover." In blaming a person of this unamiable class, people are apt to lay much stress upon her inconsistency. This is taking an incorrect view of her character. She cares for nobody but herself, and that attachment knows neither change nor decay.

Having thus done our best to guard our favourites against popular misconstruction, by pointing out the essential difference between them and two other classes with whom they have occasionally been confounded, we proceed to complete our task, by remarking upon one or two inaccuracies in the language of common conversation, which have a tendency to foster misapprehension. We not unfrequently hear people say, that such or such a married woman is a great Flirt, or fond of Flirtation. This is a shocking abuse of the term. A married woman whose deportment bears any likeness to that of a Flirt, must either be one who is possessed of a gay and buoyant temperament, but without heart, and who seeks the pleasure of the moment, careless of every other person's happiness; or she is one who knowingly and wilfully lingers on the frontiers of vice, to indulge herself with the contemplation of its charms—one who wants only courage to be wicked. Had Heaven, for our sins, seen fit to doom us to the married state, we do not know which of these two we should have regarded as the greater curse.

Another strange perversion of language is to speak of male Flirts. Male Jilts there are, and male Coquettes in plenty—with sorrow and shame we make the confession. But a male Flirt would be an anomaly in creation. Nerve, strength, and manly vigour, are the characteristics of our sex, and they at no period unbend into such a happy and graceful unconsciousness as constitutes the Flirt. It is ours to be attracted; when a man sets about to attract, he reverses the order of nature. He acts a part—and he uniformly acts it in a loutish and ungainly style.

Thus we have discharged, however imperfectly, the task we undertook. We rest the defence of Flirts, not upon any desert we suppose to be inherent in them, nor upon any moral value we attribute to them. When young, we loved and admired them, because it is their nature to awaken such feelings. They are as the blossom, delicately expanding amid the freshness and dews of a sunny morning—as the early song of birds, full of flutter and delight—as every thing that is most lovely and evanescent. We commend to the cherishing of future ages these delicate creatures, who, although they were the plague of our youth, have been the objects of tranquil and kindly admiration to our old age. But such commendation is needless, for there is a charm about them which must ever command a willing obedience from all young hearts.—*Edinburgh Literary Journal.*

AN IRISH ELECTION BILL.

A TRUE copy of an account furnished Sir Marcus Somerville by a publican of Trim, after an election:—

To eating sixteen freeholders above stairs, for Sir Marks, at 3s. 3d. a-head, L.2, 12s.

To eating sixteen more below stairs, and two clergymen after supper, L.1, 15s. 9d.

To six beds in one room, and four in the other, at two guineas every bed, three or four in a bed every night, and cheap enough, God knows, L.22, 15s.

To twenty-three horses in the yard all night, at 13d. every one of them, and for a man watching them all night, L.5, 5s.

Breakfast and tea next day for every one of them, and as many as they brought with them, as near as I can guess, L.4, 12s.

For beer, and porter, and punch, for the first day and night, I am not very sure, but I think for the three days and a half of the election, as little as I can call it, and to be very exact, is in all, or thereabouts, as near as I can guess, and not to be too particular, L.79, 15s. 9d.

To shaving, dressing, and cropping the heads off 42 freeholders for Sir Marks, at 13d. every one, cheap enough, L.2, 5s. 6d.

(In the place of Jeremy Carr)
BRIAN GARRATTY.

N.B.—On inquiry it was found that the publican furnished one shoulder of mutton, two barrels of beer, three beds, and a *spacious* back-yard for the horses.

SCOTCH BANKRUPT LAW.

Nothing calls more loudly for amendment than the law regarding mercantile bankrupts, and the whole system of recovering debts, whether by execution against the lands, the moveables, or the person of debtors. Our present sequestration law is made the means of defrauding creditors to a great amount, by the operation of the provisions for the discharge of debtors. To entitle a debtor to his discharge, the consent of four-fifths in number and value of his creditors is required, and to effect a settlement by composition, the majority is increased to nine-tenths. If, in estimating these majorities, the whole creditors of the bankrupt were taken into computation, little harm would arise; but the only creditors who are regarded, are those who have claimed, and have been found entitled to be ranked on the estate. But when the funds of a bankrupt are so nearly exhausted before his failure, that it is doubtful whether they will pay the expenses of the sequestration, very few creditors will be inclined to claim, as they thereby incur the risk of being called on to pay the whole expenses of the sequestration, and of all the proceedings which may arise out of it. When the bankruptcy, therefore, is small, and the funds are inconsiderable, it is always an object to the bankrupt to represent matters in as desperate a light as possible to the body of his creditors, while he procures a few of his own friends to rank on his estate, merely for the purpose of carrying through the sequestration. Before any proceedings have been taken, it is commonly settled who is to be trustee, and the amount of the composition, and the cautioner for it, are commonly fixed on. Calculations regarding the vacations of the Court are at the same time made, that the matter may be carried through without loss of time. At the first meeting of the creditors of the bankrupt, perhaps two or three of his own immediate relations, whose debts may have been created for the purpose, appear, and, after electing one of their own number judicial factor, they authorize him to apply to the court for a personal protection to the bankrupt. The latter, who may have possibly been in the country for a few weeks, to avoid the proceedings of his creditors till matters were brought the proper length, now makes his appearance with his protection in his pocket, and probably carries on his business in the very same manner as he did before the sequestration was applied for. At the next meeting, the factor is appointed trustee; the examinations are afterwards hurried through, and, at the third meeting, a composition is offered, which is unanimously entertained, commissioners are appointed, and, at a subsequent meeting, the composition is approved of, without the slightest investigation being, in some instances, made into the situation of the bankrupt's affairs, or the trustee having ever been in possession of the books or documents of the estate. In this way the bankrupt, in the course of four or five months, and at the expense of from L.80 to L.100, obtains a discharge of all claims against him from the Court of Session, and the debts of his creditors, who have been deterred from claiming in the sequestration, are cut off without their consent. Surely such a system requires amendment. The interests of the creditors deserve at least as much consideration as those of the bankrupt. It may be perfectly right, that one or two perverse creditors should not have it in their power to prevent the settlement of bankruptcies by composition, but care should be taken that all those who are really creditors should not be deterred by any consequences from giving their votes, when so important a measure is to be decided on.

Every honest debtor will call his creditors together when he finds his affairs in a state of irretrievable insolvency; but at present a positive premium is held out to him to go on, if possible, until his funds are utterly exhausted. It will then be easier for him to obtain a discharge than if he could pay a large dividend. Whether it be from this state of our law or not, we cannot say with certainty, but the amount of compositions now generally paid is much less than formerly; and 2s. 6d., 1s., or even 6d. per pound is far from unusual.

Our process for the recovery of debt is also tedious and expensive in an extraordinary degree. If the land is attached, the lapse of several years, and the expenditure of many hundred pounds, are certain before it can be brought to sale. In the execution against moveables, there are many absurd and tedious forms to be observed, and nothing can be more preposterous than that, before a debtor can be imprisoned, on the decree of a Court of Law, two other writs must be obtained, besides their respective warrants, by which much delay, expense, and risk of inaccuracy, and, consequently, of loss, are incurred. A radical reform is imperiously demanded in this branch of our law; but it will never be obtained till the people act as they did in the case of the Reform Bill, and take the matter into their own hands.—*Edinburgh Weekly Chronicle.*

MERCANTILE NAVIES OF FRANCE AND ENGLAND.

In a work lately published in London, entitled, "Statistics of France, by Lewis Goldsmith," we have some information regarding the mercantile navy of France; and it may not be uninteresting to compare its present state with that of Great Britain in the year 1831, the period to which Mr. Goldsmith's statements relate. At the end of the war, the shipping of France was nearly annihilated, while that of Britain was in a more flourishing state than it had been at any former period. In the year 1817, the tonnage of the merchant vessels belonging to Great Britain amounted to 2,397,655 tons, navigated by 152,352 seamen. But a great increase has taken place in the mercantile navy of France since 1815, and she now possesses upwards of 8000 trading vessels of all sorts, the total tonnage of which is 744,000 tons, and the number of sailors employed 57,200. On the 31st December, 1831, there were belonging to the United Kingdom 18,942 registered vessels, admeasuring 2,190,457 tons, manned by 132,200 seamen; and the islands of Guernsey, Jersey, and Man, and the British plantations, possessed 5400 vessels, navigated by 26,222 seamen, and admeasuring 391,507 tons. We thus see the immense superiority of our mercantile navy to that of France, which it exceeds threefold, and how little ground there is for the complaint of the decay of this important branch of our wealth. At the end of the war, we had the carrying trade of nearly the whole of Europe; for the shipping of other states had, in the course of the war, suffered nearly as much as that of France; and although the shipping of the Continental states has increased greatly since the peace, our shipping has decreased in a very inconsiderable degree.

Sir Walter Scott and Mr. Cooper.—[*Loquitur* Hazlitt.]—There are two things I admire in Sir Walter, his capacity and his simplicity; which, indeed, I am apt to think are much the same. The more ideas a man has of other things, the less he is taken up with the idea of himself. Every one gives the same account of the author of Waverley in this respect. When he was in Paris, and went to Galignani's, he sat down in an outer room to look at some book he wanted to see: none of the clerks had the least suspicion who it was: when it was found out, the place was in a commotion. Cooper, the American, was in Paris at the same time: his looks and manners seemed to announce a much greater man. He strutted through the streets with a very consequential air; and in company held up his head, screwed up his features, and placed himself on a sort of pedestal, to be observed and admired, as if he never relaxed in the assumption, nor wished it to be forgotten by others, that he was the American Sir Walter Scott. The real one never troubled himself about the matter. Why should he? He might safely leave that question to others. Indeed, by what I am told, he carries his indifference too far: it amounts to an implied contempt for the public, and *misprision of treason* against the commonwealth of letters. He thinks nothing of his works, although "all Europe rings with them from side to side."

VERSES FOR THE YOUNG.

THE COMMON LOT.

Once, in the flight of ages past,
   There lived a man—and *who* was He?
Mortal! howe'er thy lot be cast,
   That man resembled thee!

Unknown the region of his birth,
   The land in which he died unknown,
His name hath perished from the earth,
   This truth survives alone :—

That joy and grief, and hope and fear,
   Alternate triumphed in his breast;
His bliss and wo, a smile, a tear!—
   Oblivion hides the rest.

The bounding pulse, the languid limb,
   The changing spirit's rise and fall;
We know that these were felt by him,
   For *these* are felt by all.

He suffered—but his pangs are o'er;
   Enjoyed—but his delights are fled;
Had friends—his friends are now no more;
   And foes—his foes are dead.

He loved—but whom he loved, the grave
   Hath lost in its unconscious womb;
Oh, she was fair! but nought could save
   Her beauty from the tomb.

The rolling seasons, day and night,
   Sun, moon, and stars, the earth and main,
Erewhile his portion,—life and light,—
   To him exist—in vain!

He saw whatever thou hast seen;
   Encounter'd all that troubles thee;
He was—whatever thou hast been;
   He is—what thou shalt be!

The clouds and sunbeams o'er his eye
   That once their shade and glory threw,
Have left, in yonder silent sky,
   No vestige where they flew!

The annals of the human race;
   Their ruin since the world began;
Of *Him* afford no other trace
   Than this—*there lived a Man!*
                  JAMES MONTGOMERY.

LINES
ON THE DEATH OF HIS ELDEST SON,
BY THE RIGHT HON. GEORGE CANNING.

Though short thy span, God's unimpeach'd decrees,
Which made that shorten'd span one long disease;
Yet, merciful in *chastening*, gave thee scope
For mild redeeming virtues, faith and hope,
Meek resignation, pious charity.
And since this world was not the world for thee,
Far from thy path removed, with partial care,
Strife, glory, gain, and Pleasure's flowery snare,
Bade earth's temptations pass thee harmless by,
And fix'd on Heaven thine unreverted eye!
Oh! mark'd from birth, and nurtur'd for the skies!
In youth, with more than learning's wisdom wise!
As sainted martyrs, patient to endure!
Simple, as unwean'd infancy, and pure!
Pure from all stain (save that of human clay,
Which Christ's atoning blood hath wash'd away!)
By mortal sufferings now no more oppress'd,
Mount, sinless spirit, to thy destin'd rest!
While I—reversed our nature's kindlier doom—
Pour forth a father's sorrows on thy tomb.

JACK TAYLOR.
A SKETCH FROM THE SPECTATOR.

Everybody knew Jack Taylor, and every body liked him. He was known by the familiar diminutive of his Christian name, on account "of his love of good fellowship and wit," to use Mr. Moore's phrase; and was the associate of some of the brightest men of his time, when "brightness" was the great study and pursuit of the day. Everybody loved Jack Taylor: he was thoroughly harmless; a kind and affectionate creature, with all kinds of light pleasantry fluttering across his butterfly brain. "When *you* do an ill-natured thing," said Sheridan to him, "chaos is come again." And it was true. Through a long life, Jack Taylor was always doing kind little offices, and saying pleasant little speeches. His benefits were necessarily of the small kind, and his wit was not of a high cast; but then, life is composed of small deeds, and filled up with small talk. Jack Taylor was a Tory, but of the very gentlest kind: his politics were rather an affair of feeling than opinion: loyalty seemed to him to imply peace and pleasantness—the reign of the social affections—the triumph of the intellectual enjoyments: the rude and boisterous temperament of a republic would have been fatal to his talents and his pleasures: a man of his calibre would have perished in a political storm. Inasmuch as the strong hand of absolute monarchy, while it quenches the more vigorous efforts of men, favours the exercise of the smaller and more social faculties, he leaned on the idea of a king as on a rock of security. This is the creed of a large mass of citizens, who would gladly purchase the pleasures of settled society by the abandonment of all political influence, which is ignorantly supposed not to affect the private condition of the citizen. As a proof that Mr. Taylor's Toryism was altogether passive, he associated indiscriminately with men of all parties; and as the Opposition of that day was composed of the most brilliant men of the age, he lived even more with them than their antagonists. But Jack Taylor was not a mere fair-weather companion—his good-nature outlasted the storms and vicissitudes of his life: he had a pun always ready over the glass, but then he had a tear for the garret. He never deserted his friends till they were laid in the grave; and this last duty he seems to have taken a sort of melancholy pleasure in performing. It would be curious to know how many funerals good-natured Jack Taylor had attended in the course of his long life. He saw nearly all his old friends out: we meet in these volumes with scarcely a name of living men, with the exception perhaps of a few such Nestorian youths as Lord Eldon and his brother Lord Stowell: but Taylor recollected Thurlow, if not an attorney's clerk, at least a student in the Temple.

Mr. Taylor reminds us a good deal of a Frenchman: he had more mercurial qualities than commonly fall to the lot of our countrymen; he was not ambitious; he was more than ordinarily regardless of the outward circumstances of his friends; he was a worshipper of intellectual superiority; and above all, he was a thoroughly social creature—he lived by constant contact with his like;—and all this is French. He was altogether a citizen, a wanderer among bricks and mortar. He was born at Highgate; and perhaps that was his first and last rural excursion. Soon after his birth, his father, a celebrated oculist, removed to Hatton Garden, where he lived and died: between Hatton Garden and Covent Garden, his son oscillated for upwards of three quarters of a century; and they were probably the greenest places in his recollection, unless perhaps Vauxhall Gardens might put in a claim. We never heard Jack Taylor "babble o' green fields;" though we believe he had repeatedly been to Bagshot, was familiar with Kensington, and used frequently to dine at Bayswater. We say of residents in Paris, they are Parisians: Jack Taylor was not a Cockney, and yet he was a thorough Londonian. His pride was a rencontre of wits at the Turk's Head or elsewhere. At Covent Garden and Drury Lane he was also great, both before and behind the scenes: at the latter place, whenever Shaw, the leader of the band, observed his presence, he would always play a particular concerto between the acts, because he knew it was a favourite: here was distinction!

Then he was the great prologue and epilogue manufacturer of the day: every body came to him for the finishing-stroke, and Jack Taylor never refused anybody any thing: impromptus and epigrams he had equally at the service of his friends: no one in need of verse ever applied to Jack Taylor in vain. His *Monsieur Tonson* is his ground of immortality—a very small spot of Pierian earth, but still large enough for a poet to stand tiptoe on—*stans pede in uno*—making verse at the rate of a line a-second. He was the editor and proprietor of the *Sun* for many years; and in his hands it was seen how very harmless and inoffensive a daily paper might be. Somehow or other, he contrived to get himself ousted by some anonymous scoundrel—so he considers him—a proprietor of one-tenth, and editor by agreement. Taylor was obliged to sell his shares; and after the separation, we believe neither he nor the paper ever prospered.

UNIVERSALITY OF TAXATION.

THE following epigramatic reflections, which have already been published in a hundred different shapes, appeared originally in the *Edinburgh Review*, and are just re-published on a folio sheet, headed with a likeness of the Lord Chancellor. We give them in the order they are printed:—

TAXES
Upon every article that enters into the mouth,
Or covers the back, or is placed under the foot.
TAXES
Upon every thing that is pleasant to see, hear, feel, smell and taste.
TAXES
Upon warmth, light and locomotion.
TAXES
On every thing on earth, and the waters under the earth;
On every thing that comes from abroad, or is grown at home.
TAXES
On the raw material;
TAXES
On every value that is added to it by the industry of man.
TAXES
On the sauce which pampers man's appetite, and the drug which restores him to health;
On the ermine which decorates the judge, and the rope which hangs the criminal;
On the brass nails of the coffin, and the ribands of the bride:
At bed or at board, couchant or levant,
WE MUST PAY.
The schoolboy whips his taxed top;
The beardless youth manages his taxed Horse with a taxed bridle on a taxed road;
And the dying Englishman
Pouring his medicine which has paid 7 per cent,
Into a spoon which has paid 15 per cent, throws himself back upon his chintz bed, which has paid 2½ per cent,
Makes his will on an L.8 stamp,
And expires in the arms of an apothecary,
Who has paid L.100 for the privilege of putting him to death.
His whole property is then taxed from 2 to 10 per cent.
Besides the probate,
Large fees are demanded for burying him in the chancel;
His virtues are handed down to posterity on
Taxed marble;
And he is then gathered to his fathers,
TO BE TAXED NO MORE.

MAGNIFICENT OAK-TREE.—Perhaps the most magnificent oak this country ever produced was lately felled at Tooley, in Leicestershire. It will hardly be credited, but it is nevertheless true, that this tree, when cut down, covered three roods, the ground on which it fell being immediately measured. The quantity of timber which it contained amounted to 1100 solid feet. The butt was about ten feet long, and it had five large branches, one of which contained two hundred solid feet of timber. The tree, when fairly butted, measured at the bottom nine feet in diameter. It produced the enormous quantity of three tons eighteen cwt. of bark. Another striking feature of this most wonderful production of nature is, the quality and beauty of the wood; which is allowed to be superior to any thing of the kind ever seen; it bears a polish equal to the finest mahogany, and the grain is of a most curious and fantastical description. The tree was purchased by Mr. John Thorpe, of Market Bosworth. Nearly the whole of it has been manufactured into various articles of drawing and dining-room furniture, which now occupy the residences of several families of the first respectability in the neighbourhood, where, when standing, it had long been the object of admiration and wonder.

HUMOROUS LETTER OF A HIGHLAND EMIGRANT.

The subjoined letter is said to be genuine—and written from Maryland by a real Donald Macpherson—we do not vouch for it, though Captain Brut does:—

Portobago in *Marilante*, 2 *June* 17—.
Teer Lofen Kynt Fater.

Dis is te lat ye ken, dat I am in quid health, plessed bi Got for dat, houpin te here de lyk frae yu, as I am yer nane sin, I wad a bine ill leart gin I had na latten yu ken tis, be kaptin Rogirs skep da geangs to Innerness, per cunnan I dinna ket sika anither apertunti dis towmen agen. De skep dat I kam in was a lang tym o de see cumin oure heir, but plissit pe Got for a ting wi a keepit our heels unco weel, pat Shonie Magwillivray dat hat ay a sair beet. Dere was saxty o's à kame inte te quintry hel a lit an lim an nane o's à dyit pat Shonie Magwillivray an an otter Ross lad dat kam oure wi's an mai pi dem twa wad a dyit gin tey hed bitten at hame.

Pi mi fait I kanoa komplin for kuming te dis quintry, for mestir Nicols, Lort pliss hem, put mi till a pra mestir, dey ca him Shon Bayne, an hi lifes in Maryland in te rifer Potomak, he nifer gart mi wark ony ting pat fat I lykit mi sel; de meast o' a mi wark is waterin a pra stennt hors, an pringin wyn an pread ut o de seller te mi mestir's tebil.

Sin efer I kam til him I never wantit a pottle o petter ele nor is in à Shon Glass house, for I ay set toun wi de pairns te dennir.

Mi mestir seys til mi, fan I can speek lyke de fouk heir dat I sanna pe pidden di nating pat gar his plackimors wurk, for de *fyt fouk* dinna ise te wurk pat te first yeer aftir dey kum in te de quintry. Tey speek à lyk de sogers in Innerness.

Lofen fater, fan de sarvants hier he deen wi der mestirs, dey grou unco rich, an its ne wonter for day mak a hantil o tombako; an des sivites an apels an de sheries an de pires grou in de wuds wantin tyks apout dem. De swynes te ducks an durkies geangs en de wuds wantin mestirs.

De tombako grous shust lyke de dockins en de bak o de lairts yart an de akeps dey cum fra ilka place an bys dem an gies a hantel o silder an gier for dem.

Mi nane mestir kam til de quintry a sartant an weil I wat hi's nou wort mony a susan punt. Fait ye mey pelieve mi dipirest planter hire lifes amost as weil as de lairt o Collottin. Mai pi fan mi tim is ut I wel kom hem an sie yu pat not for de furst nor de neesst yeir till I gater somting o mi nane, for fan I ha dun wi mi mestir hi maun gi mi a plantashon te set mi up, its de quistium hier in dis quintry; an syn I houp to gar yu trink wyn insteat o tippeni in Innerness.

I wis I hat kum our heir twa or tri yiers seener nor I dit, syn I wad ha kum de seener hame, pat Got pi tanket dat I kam sa seen as I dit.

Gin yu koud sen mi owr be ony o yur Innerness skeps, ony ting te mi, an it war as muckle clays as mak a quelt it wad, mey pi, gar my meister tink te mere o mi. Its trw I ket clays eneu fe him bat oni ting se yu wad luck weel an pony, an ant plese Got gin I life, I sal pey yu pack agen.

Lofen fater, de man dat vryts dis letir for mi is van Shams Macheyne, hi lifes seust a myl fe mi, hi hes pin unko kyn te mi sin efer I kam te de quistrie. Hi wes porn en Petie an kam our a sarfant fe Klesgou an hes peen hes nane man twa yeirs, an has sax plackimors wurkin til him alrety makin tombako ilka tay. Heil win hem, shortly an à te geir dat he hes wun hier an py a LEATS KIP at hem. Luck dat ye duina forket te vryt til mi ay, fan yu ket ony ocashion.

Got Almichte pliss yu Fater an a de leve o de hous, for I hana forkoten nane o yu, nor dinna yu forket mi, for plise Got I sal kum hem wi gier eneuch te di yu à an mi nane sel guid.

I weit yon will be very vokie, fan yu sii yur nane sins fesh agen, for I heive leirt a hantle hevens sin I sau yu an I am unco buick leirt.

A tis is se yur lofen an Opstient Sin,
TONAL MACKAFERSON.

Directed—For James Mackaferson neir te Lairt o Collottin's hous neir Innerness en de Nort o Skotlan.*

---

*. This *jeu d'esprit* has a good deal of humour in it. It is written in the dialect which is spoken on the borders of Murray and Banffshire, the spelling being adapted to the pronunciation of such Highlanders as speak broken English. But it is evidently written by one who did not understand Gaelic; there is not a single idiom of that language in it and the orthography is much too nicely adjusted to be genuine, although the hint may have been taken from an original letter.

THE RABBLE.

How various and innumerable,
Are those that live upon the Rabble!
'Tis they maintain the Church and State,
Employ the priest and magistrate,
Bear all the change of Government,
And pay the public fines and rent;
Defray all taxes and excises,
And impositions of all prices;
Bear all the expense of peace and war,
And pay the pulpit and the bar;
Maintain all character and religions,
And give the pastor's institutions,
(And those who have the greatest flocks,
Are primitive and orthodox;)
Support all schismatics and sects,
And pay them for tormenting texts;
Take all doctrines off their hands,
And pay 'em in good rent and lands;
Discharge all costly offices,
The doctor's and the lawyer's fees,
The hangman's wages and the scores,
Of caterpillars, bawds, and ———;
Discharge all damages and costs,
Of Knights, and Esquires of "The Posts."
All statesmen, cutpurses, and padders,
And pay for all their ropes and ladders;
All pettifoggers, and all sorts
Of markets, churches, and of courts;
All sums of money paid or spent,
With all the charges "*incident.*"

SCRAPS.
ORIGINAL AND SELECTED.

ADVANTAGE OF EVEN A LITTLE KNOWLEDGE.—The mysteries of magnetism should be unfolded to the sailor, above all men, since he is the one, of all others, whose safety depends on its phenomena. He should be told, that on electro-magnetic principles, he would materially influence the march of the needle by wiping the glass which screens it, especially with silk. It is some years ago since a fact was communicated to me, which may be adduced in illustration; it was that of a ship which arrived at Liverpool, after having been for several weeks the sport of winds and waves; the mariner's compass having been washed overboard in a storm, their voyage was dreary and procrastinated, much caution being necessary, and despite of which, their fate, but for a fortuitous circumstance, might have been inevitably sealed. Now, had the simple fact of the extreme ease with which a mariner's needle might be made, been known to any on board, the peril might have been avoided. A sewing needle, or the blade of a penknife, being held in an upright posture, and struck by a hammer, and subsequently floated by cork on water, or suspended by a thread without torsion, would become a magnetic-needle, and point north and south; or the end of a poker held vertically, and passed over its surface from one extreme to the other, would impart magnetism, and which, if the needle be of steele, would be of a permanent character.—*Mechanics' Magazine.*—[The cotsman recently gave an instance where a whole fleet of fishing boats would have been saved, if the fishermen had known the use of the marine barometer.]

THE HORSE-DEALER.

A horse-dealer is a double dealer, for he dealeth more in double meanings than your punster. When he giveth his word, it signifieth little, howbeit it standeth for two significations. He putteth his promises, like his colts, in a brake. Over his mouth, truth, like the turnpike-man, writeth up, No trust. Whenever he speaketh, his spoke hath more turns than the fore-wheel. He telleth lies, not white only or black, but likewise grey, bay, chesnut-brown, cream, and roan—pie-bald and skew-bald. He sweareth as many oaths out of court as any man, and more in; for he will swear two ways about a horse's dam. If, by God's grace, he be something honest, it is only a dapple, for he can be fair and unfair at once. He hath much imagination, for he selleth a complete set of capital harness, of which there be no traces. He advertiseth a coach, warranted on its first wheels, and truly the hind pair are wanting to the bargain. A carriage that hath travelled twenty summers and winters, he describeth well-seasoned. He knocketh down machine-horses that have been knocked up on the road, but is so tender of heart to his animals, that he parteth with none for a fault; 'for,' as he sayeth, 'blindness or lameness be misfortunes.' A nag proper only for dog's meat, he writeth down, but crieth up, 'fit to go to any hounds;' or, as may be, 'would suit a timid gentleman.' String halt he calleth 'grand action,' and kicking, 'lifting the feet well up.' If a mare have the farcical disease, he nameth her 'out of Comedy,' and selleth Blackbird for a racer, because he hath a cunning thrush. Horses that drink only water, he justly warranteth to be 'temperate,' and if dead lame, declareth them 'good in all their paces,' seeing that they can go but one. Roaring he calleth 'sound,' and a steed that high bloweth in running, he compareth to Eclipse, for he outstrippeth the wind. Another might be entered at a steeple chase, for why—he is as fast as a church. Thorough-pin with him is synonymous with 'perfect leg.' If a nag cougheth, 'tis a 'clever hack.' If his knees be fractured, he is 'well broke for a gig or saddle.' If he reareth, he is 'above sixteen hands high.' If he hath drawn a torce in a cart, he is a good fencer. If he biteth, he shows good courage; and he is playful merely, though he should play the devil. If he runneth away, he calleth him 'off the Gretna road, and has been used to carry a lady.' If a cob stumbleth, he considereth him a true goer, and addeth, 'the proprietor parteth from him to go abroad.' Thus, without much profession of religion, yet he is truly Christian-like in practice, for he dealeth not in detraction, and would not disparage the character even of a brute. Like unto love, he is blind unto all blemishes, and seeth only a virtue, meanwhile he gazeth at a vice. He taketh the kick of a nag's hoof like a love-token, saying only, before standers-by, 'Poor fellow, he knoweth me!' and he is content rather to pass as a bad rider, than that the horse should be held restive or over-mettlesome which discharges him from its back. If it hath bitten him beside, and, moreover, bruised his limb against a coach-wheel, then, constantly returning good for evil, he giveth it but the better character, and recommendeth it before all the steeds in the stable. In short, the worse a horse may be, the more he chanteth his praise, like a crow that croweth over Old Ball, whose lot it is on a common to meet with the common lot.—*Hood.*

LUNATICS.—From a report made in 1829, it appears that there was at that time in England, in confinement in public lunatic establishments, 1169 male, and 1314 female lunatics, or idiots; in private lunatic asylums, 1770 males, and 1964 females; in workhouses, &c. 36 males, and 52 females; making, in the whole, 6,325 persons in confinement. The number of individuals in the condition of lunatics, or idiots, who were at large, or with their relations, was 3,029 males, and 3,193 females; making a total of persons at large, of 6,222. The total number of lunatics was 6,806, and of idiots 5,741; making together 12,547 insane persons. To these must be added 1,500 persons belonging either to parishes from which no returns had been made when the lists of the clerks of the peace were made out, or to towns which are counties of themselves, and which are not included in this summary. This addition makes the whole number above 14,000, of whom no fewer than 11,000 are paupers, and maintained at the expense of their respective parishes. Taking the whole of England, the average is one insane person to every 1000 of the population.

CONTENTS OF NO. XVIII.

HOLYDAY RAMBLES, No. V.—The Eildon Hills	274
On Itinerating Libraries	275
The Quakers and the Church	276
USEFUL NOTICES	277
On Dr. Chalmer's Late Work	278
Years of Pestilence and Famine in Scotland	279
ELEMENTS OF THOUGHT.—Words in Season from Napoleon—The Future Prospects of Europe and America	280
THE STORY-TELLER.—Props of the Pulpit—Paddy Foorhane's Fricassee	281
COLUMN FOR THE LADIES.—An Essay on Flirts	283
Scotch Bankrupt Law	284
VERSES FOR THE YOUNG	285
Jack Taylor	ib.
Universality of Taxation	287
Humorous Letter of an Highland Emigrant	ib.
The Rabble	288
SCRAPS, Original and Selected	ib.

EDINBURGH: Printed by and for JOHN JOHNSTONE, 19, St. James's Square.—Published by JOHN ANDERSON, Jun., Bookseller, 55, North Bridge Street, Edinburgh; by JOHN MACLEOD, and ATKINSON & Co., Booksellers, Glasgow; and sold by all Booksellers and Venders of Cheap Periodicals.

THE Schoolmaster,
AND
EDINBURGH WEEKLY MAGAZINE.

CONDUCTED BY JOHN JOHNSTONE.

THE SCHOOLMASTER IS ABROAD.—LORD BROUGHAM.

No. 19.—VOL. I.   SATURDAY, DECEMBER 8, 1832.   PRICE THREE-HALFPENCE

POLITICAL TRUTHS NOT SUFFICIENTLY APPRECIATED.

I. THE degree of the good or evil, and merit or demerit of any act, estimated *in foro humano*, if not *in foro poli*, is precisely in proportion to the extent of the beneficial or injurious effects which do, or may result from its operation on society at large.

II. Hence, those who frame or regulate the institutions, or direct, sway, and influence the conduct and circumstances of society, are more meritorious or more criminal than others, in proportion to the extent of the power which they exercise on the community, and the good or bad consequences which do or may result from it.

III. It is consequently implied, that kings, governors, magistrates, legislators, electors, and other public functionaries and trustees; and also priests, authors, editors, and other public instructors; and, in general, all those who have the power, coercively or influentially, to command direct, or modify the conduct, and alter the circumstances of the various classes, and the general body of society, are, when they transgress the respective moral duties, particularly incumbent on them in their public capacities, more deeply responsible, and more criminal, than others whose power of doing good or evil is more limited. This is true of sins of omission as well as commission.

IV. The KING who wantonly rushes into an unjust and unnecessary aggressive war, is a far greater sinner than the highway robber, who murders him on whose property he seizes. To approve, expressly or tacitly, the conduct of such a king, however successful in conquest, is greatly more criminal than to screen the murdering robber from condign punishment.

V. The GOVERNOR or MAGISTRATE, who perpetrates an act of injustice, is more criminal than the private cheat.

VI. The LEGISLATOR who, wilfully or carelessly, gives his sanction to laws of necessarily evil operation and tendency, and thus gives occasion to the augmentation and extension of sin, is greatly more criminal and sinful than the individual who, in his own person, commits iniquity.

VII. Laws necessarily give extension and intensity to sin.

1. When they deny the liberty of religious belief, and prohibit certain modes of worship, by generating an intolerant, uncharitable, and persecuting spirit,—by encouraging hypocritical conformity as the price of worldly benefit, and by encouraging, in the favoured sect, an insolent spirit of tyrannical domination. Hence proceed " all uncharitableness," and " all deceivableness of unrighteousness."

2. When they impose unnecessary burdens, in order that a few may be unjustly benefited, at the expense of the many;—as when they sanction the maintenance of useless establishments of any description, in order that the useless scions of the aristocracy may be supported, at the expense of the community; and more especially when, for the same unrighteous purpose, they sanction the existence of sinecures, and the payment of unmerited pensions.

3. When they impose partial and unjust restrictions on industry, and sanction monopolies, and confer exclusive privileges, for the exclusive benefit of certain classes, orders, or individuals; or when they impose duties on commodities, for the same iniquitous purpose, and not for the legitimate end of adding to the receipts of the public Fisc. It is obvious to every one of ordinary intelligence, that the CORN LAWS are of this description, and nothing better than a gigantic system of THEFT, iniquitously and sinfully legalized, for the purpose of adding to the wealth and power, and consequently to the injurious and demoralizing influence, of a rapacious, insolent, and tyrannical aristocracy, hostile to the promotion of virtue and the general happiness.

4. When they alleviate the burdens of the rich, and add to the onerosity of those imposed upon, or chiefly affecting the poor. Of this species of iniquity our fiscal code affords numerous examples, especially in those acts which impose duties on consumable commodities.

5. When they interpose obstacles to the speedy, efficient, and economical administration of justice, or commit it to faithless or incompetent functionaries. Of these evils the English code of procedure, and the toleration of such a Magistracy as " the Great Unpaid," afford examples.

All such laws necessarily give confidence and daring to the evil-minded: They generate a rapacious and dishonest spirit, and lead individuals to rely on finesse, manœuvre, and deceitful expedients, rather than on honest, industrious, and righteous conduct.

VIII. The ELECTOR who, wilfully or carelessly, contributes to the choosing of a legislator, who wilfully sanctions, or is incompetent to perceive the evil, or to oppose the enacting, of a bad law, is, so far as his suffrage contributes to the election, responsible for the evil which may ensue from such enactment. He who gives his vote for corrupt purposes, or venal considerations, is a far greater *sinner* than the individual guilty of a breach of private trust. The latter can inflict but an injury of necessarily limited extent: The former may peril the souls, and ruin the worldly circumstances of millions.

The electors who vote for an advocate of the Corn Laws, or other monopolies, or of unnecessary establishments, sinecures, or unmerited pensions, votes for upholding a system of *theft*, on a great scale, which necessarily impoverishes and vitiates the great body of the people.

He who votes for a candidate, who will not pledge himself to use his endeavours to remove such evils, and to repeal the taxes which restrain the diffusion of knowledge, votes in reality for maintaining, as far as possible, the reign of dishonesty and ignorance, and all the evils of which dishonesty and ignorance are necessarily productive: he votes for the extension of poverty and misery, and for maintaining and upholding bad laws, and abuses in the public administration; for giving occasion to disorder and insubordination, and consequently for augmenting and prolonging the duration of the expense of large armies, and other coercive establishments for prolonging the prevalence of public and private immorality; and for maintaining the reign of poverty, misery, and vice, and preventing the extension of the knowledge and influence of true religion.

The elector who votes for an advocate of the West India Slave System, votes for the continuance of the most inhuman oppression; for the prevention of marriage; for the forcible separation of parent and child, and brother and sister; for the counteraction of all the charities of life; for the repression of every laudable motive to industrious exertion; for the upholding of the most debasing superstition; and for the prevention of the spread of Christian truth; for the maintenance among the Colonists of insolence, tyranny, rapacity, vice, and irreligion; and for continuing the imposition on the British people of unjust and onerous burdens, by rendering it necessary to defray the expense of preventing the Negroes from forcibly throwing off the cruel and iniquitous yoke imposed on them.

If any elector, so voting, presume to sit at the Lord's table, and " eat of the bread and drink of the cup," is it uncharitable to say, that there is ground to apprehend that he " eats and drinks damnation to himself?"

IX. The PRIEST who teaches bigotry and intolerance; who restrains free and fair inquiry; who, positively or negatively, supports or defends malificent laws, institutions, or measures; who opposes the progress of useful knowledge; who censures and reproves the poor, but flatters the rich offender; who denounces the minor and private, but who fails publicly to express disapprobation of the greater and public immoralities, is, however correct in his private conduct, an unfaithful servant of his Divine Master. A clergyman is bound, as an *elector*, as well as in his official capacity, to promote the good of mankind. His declining to vote, if not a piece of hypocritical affectation, *ad captandum vulgus*, is a breach of duty, inasmuch as he fails, so far as he is individually able, to promote good or prevent evil.

X. The author, editor, or teacher, who, wilfully or carelessly, propagates falsehood, misrepresents truth, or perverts doctrine, or who leads the multitude astray to do or uphold evil, is the most culpable and pestiferous auxiliary of " the father of lies."

Finally. The individual who, knowingly and wilfully, promotes, directly or indirectly, the enactment or toleration of unjust laws; who supports the power of the advocates of oppression, monopoly, slavery, factitious ignorance, and unequal and unjust taxation; or who interposes obstacles to the promotion " of the greatest possible happiness of the greatest possible number," ought seriously to consider that, for such conduct, he shall have to answer to GOD at the great day of judgment.

November, 1832.   VERAX BOREALIS.

BOOKS OF THE MONTH.

WE have a few new works, and a host of re-prints of good and standard books to report upon. Of the original works, books of amusement form the large majority, though there are some volumes of memoirs and some poetry.

MEMOIRS.

First in our list we place those of Dr. Burney, written by his daughter, Madame D'Arblay, better known as the beloved Miss Burney of many youths of both sexes now fading into age. The author of *Evelina* and *Camilla* we now mean, with whom, if any of our readers have no acquaintance, the sooner they make one the better. The memoirs relate to a period of from forty to sixty years back, when the girlish Miss Burney saw at her mother's tea-table, or around her father's supper-board—"a table of chat, and roast apples and potatoes"—many persons whose names have since been distinguished in the world of letters or science, music or politics; and in the society to which the musical talents of her family, and her own genius and tastes introduced her, we meet some of the fashionable names of that day. The memoirs, in short, place us in London, during what may be called the *Johnsonian* and Thrale and Montague period, and among such persons as Burke, Goldsmith, Reynolds, Barry, Garrick, her own delightful family, and all the clever contemporary characters of that time. And these are not drawn from Madame D'Arblay's fading recollections, but carefully preserved in "a series of Letters from a young Lady," to her friends—that young lady being the author of Evelina. If not a very *useful* book, one of the must-be-boughts, this is a work to borrow, to while away any week of long nights between this and the Ides of March.

As a specimen of the work, we give the first sight of Dr. Johnson. Be it known, that Miss Burney had a mahogany box, with a slit in the top, into which she dropt her off-hand sketches, and its name was Crisp. Daddy *Crisp*, or *Mr. Crisp*, the old familiar and excellent friend of Dr. Burney, and the safe reservoir of his daughter Fanny's remarks on society, and adventures public or domestic. A Daddy Crisp, of whichever sex, is a most useful family appendage, where there are many daughters at the scribbling age. He is a kind of safety-valve to the expanding mind. The free communications to Daddy Crisp are among the most graceful of Miss Burney's writings. They are sparkling with the fresh spirit of youth, full of point, pleasantry, and observation. It is thus she hits off the oft-described sage—and we never saw him externally in what seems a truer light.

" Now, my dear Mr. Crisp, if you like a description of, emotions and sensations—but I know you treat them all as burlesque—so let's proceed.

" Every body rose to do him honour; and he returned the attention with the most formal courtesy. My father then having welcomed him with the warmest respect, whispered to him that music was going forward; which he would not, my father thinks, have found out; and placing him on the best seat vacant, told his daughters to go on with the duet; while Dr. Johnson, intently rolling towards them one eye—for they say he does not see with the other—made a grave nod, and gave a dignified motion with one hand, in silent approvance of the proceeding.

" But now, my dear Mr. Crisp, I am mortified to own, what you, who always smile at my enthusiasm, will hear without caring a straw for—that he is, indeed, very illfavoured! Yet he has naturally a noble figure: tall, stout, grand, and authoritative; but he stoops horribly; his back is quite round: his mouth is continually opening and shutting, as if he were chewing something; he has a singular method of twirling his fingers, and twisting his hands: his vast body is in constant agitation, see-sawing backwards and forwards: his feet are never a moment quiet; and his whole great person looked often as if it were going to roll itself, quite voluntarily, from his chair to the floor. * *

" But you always charge me to write without reserve or reservation, and so I obey as usual. Else, I should be ashamed to acknowledge having remarked such exterior blemishes in so exalted a character.

" His dress, considering the times, and that he had meant to put on all his *best becomes*, for he was engaged to dine with a very fine party at Mrs. Montagu's, was as much out of the common road as his figure. He had a large, full, bushy wig, a snuff-colour coat, with gold buttons, (or, peradventure, brass,) but no ruffles to his doughty fists; and not, I suppose, to be taken for a Blue, though going to the Blue Queen, he had on very coarse black worsted stockings.

" He is shockingly nearsighted; a thousand times more so than either my *padre* or myself. He did not even know Mrs. Thrale, till she held out her hand to him; which she did very engagingly. After the first few minutes, he drew his chair close to the piano-forte, and then bent down his nose quite over the keys, to examine them, and the four hands at work upon them; till poor Hetty and Susan hardly knew how to play on, for fear of touching his phiz; or, which was harder still, how to keep their countenances; and the less, as Mr. Seward, who seems to be very droll and shrewd, and was much diverted, ogled them slyly, with a provoking expression of arch enjoyment of their apprehensions.

" When the duet was finished, my father introduced your Hettina to him, as an old acquaintance, to whom, when she was a little girl, he had presented his Idler.

" His answer to this was imprinting on her pretty face—not a half touch of a courtly salute—but a good, real, substantial, and very loud kiss.

" Every body was obliged to stroke their chins, that they might hide their mouths.

" Beyond this chaste embrace, his attention was not to be drawn off two minutes longer from the books, to which he now strided his way; for we had left the drawing-room for the library, on account of the piano-forte. He pored over them, shelf by shelf, almost brushing them with his eye-lashes from near examination. At last, fixing upon something that happened to hit his fancy, he took it down, and standing aloof from the company, which he seemed clean and clear to forget, he began, without further ceremony, and very composedly, to read to himself, and as intently as if in his own study."

The authoress of *Evelina* is now a very aged woman, which must at once account for, and be the apology of many things in this work which require to be judged with gentleness and indulgence. Madame d'Arblay, from long residence abroad, or her marriage with a foreigner, appears to have forgotten her own language. The style of the memoirs, except in the fresh old letters, is the most stilted and introverted imaginable.

MEMOIR AND CORRESPONDENCE OF THE LATE SIR EDWARD SMITH. *Edited by Lady Smith.*

This is a work which will afford the same kind of quiet satisfaction to the reader, as the above Memoirs of the Burneys mixed with none of the painful feelings with which a great deal of that work must be read. Many of the letters are exceedingly amiable and interesting. The correspondence commences with the appearance of Sir James as a Medical Student, at the Edinburgh University, whither the young man is followed by the affectionate solicitude of his family; and ends but with the close of his prosperous, useful, and strictly honourable life. There is much connected with the scientific pursuits of the subject of these two bulky volumes, which would either prove a dead letter, or irksome to ordinary readers; but the familiar letters of the affectionate son, the assiduous student, the intelligent and liberal traveller, the accomplished scholar, and steady and zealous friend, who, in every relation of life, performs before us so naturally the part of a good and of an admirable man, form the materials of a work such as is not of frequent occurrence. This is a book to borrow by all means. It will be perused with much pleasure by the readers of the past generation, and with great profit, if they are so minded, by those of the present. We have seen no recent work which we would so readily place in the hands of a youth intended for any of the liberal professions, as these memoirs.

MEMOIRS OF SIR DAVID BAIRD.

This is a narrative of Sir David's military exploits in India and the Peninsula. We have had so much campaigning history of late years, that we are become heartily tired of all such affairs. The work will be of interest to military men, and to the personal acquaintances of the gallant officer, whose life afforded no great mark or likelihood for an elaborate memoir.

POETRY.

Several small collections of original poems have appeared, and one poem, which may render memorable the month in which it is at length published,—*The Masque of Anarchy*, by Shelley. It is an occasional piece, written on an event which might have stirred the blood of a snail that had ever crawled on British ground—on the *Manchester Massacre*. It is now published by Mr. Leigh Hunt, with a preface, which forms no small part of the substance of the volume. Mr. Hunt was then Editor of the *Examiner*, and to him the poem was sent by his friend, Mr. Shelley, for publication in that print. It was not prudent to publish it then, for reasons assigned in the preface; but it is believed the time is now arrived which " Mr. Shelley's writings have aided in bringing about—a wiser period." It is noticed by the Editor, and the fact is indeed remarkable, that the advice of submission, or, in the new language, *passive resistance*, given by the poet, is singularly striking as a *political anticipation* of what the Irish and the Political Unions have realized.

The marshalling of the pageant, with which the poem opens—*Murder*, wearing a mask like Castlereagh, and followed by seven blood-hounds, *Fraud*, clothed in Lord Eldon's ermined gown,

" His big tears, for he wept well,
Turning to mill-stones as they fell;"

—all these we pass to come to the counsels, and the admonitory and prophetic passages of the poem. HOPE is here the agent; though at this period of the annals of England

" She looked more like despair,
And she cried out in the air.

"My father *Time* is weak and grey,
With waiting for a better day;
See how idiot-like he stands
Fumbling with his palsied hands!
He has had child after child,
And the dust of death is piled
Over every one but me——"

Hope lays herself down in the street, to be trampled by the horses, and patiently waits the approach of Murder, Fraud, and Anarchy. A dim period of happy change is poetically described, and then these words "of joy and fear," are heard as out of a cloud:—

"Men of England, heirs of glory,
Heroes of unwritten story,
Nurslings of one mighty mother,
Hopes of her, and one another,

"Rise like lions after slumber,
In unvanquishable number;
Shake your chains to earth like dew,
Which in sleep had fallen on you.

"What is Freedom? Ye can tell
That which Slavery is too well,
For its very name has grown
To an echo of your own.

"'Tis to work, and have such pay
As just keeps life from day to day
In your limbs, as in a cell
For the tyrants' use to dwell:

"So that ye for them are made,
Loom, and plough, and sword, and spade,
With or without your own will, bent
To their defence and nourishment.

"'Tis to see your children weak
With their mothers pine and peak,
When the winter winds are bleak:—
They are dying while I speak.

"'Tis to hunger for such diet,
As the rich man in his riot
Casts to the fat dogs that lie
Surfeiting beneath his eye.

"'Tis to let the Ghost of Gold
Take from toil a thousand fold
More than e'er its substance could
In the tyrannies of old:

"*Paper coin*—that forgery
Of the title-deeds, which ye
Hold to something of the worth
Of the inheritance of Earth.

"'Tis to be a slave in soul,
And to hold no strong control
Over your own wills, but be
All that others make of ye.

"And at length, when ye complain,
With a murmur weak and vain,
'Tis to see the tyrant's crew
Ride over your wives and you:
Blood is on the grass like dew.

"Then it is to feel revenge,
Fiercely thirsting to exchange
Blood for blood, and wrong for wrong:
DO NOT THUS, WHEN YE ARE STRONG.

"Birds find rest in narrow nest,
When weary of the winged quest;
Beasts find fare in woody lair,
When storm and snow are in the air;

"Asses, swine, have litter spread,
And with fitting food are fed;
All things have a home, but one—
Thou, oh Englishman, hast none!

"This is slavery:—savage men,
Or wild beasts within a den,
Would endure not as ye do:
But such ills they never knew."

An address to Freedom follows, full of power and spirit; but of that we can only take the concluding stanzas:

"Thou art love—the rich have kiss'd
Thy feet, and like him following Christ,
Give their substance to the free,
And through the rough world follow thee.

"Oh turn their wealth to arms, and make
War for thy beloved sake,
On wealth *and* war and fraud—whence they
Drew the power which is their prey.

"Science, and Poetry, and Thought,
Are thy lamps; they make the lot
Of the dwellers in a cot
So serene they curse it not.

"Spirit, Patience, Gentleness,
All that can adorn and bless,
Art thou: let deeds, not words, express
Thine exceeding loveliness."

And now commence the counsels to *non-resistance*, given by the Spirit or mysterious voice. A vast meeting is to be held on some English plain, the blue sky, and the green earth, and all eternal things witnesses of the solemnity. Thither are to come

"From the corners uttermost
Of the bounds of English coast,—
From ev'ry village, hut, and town,"

all that live to suffer and to labour, with the few in palaces who feel compassion; and here they are to declare that they are free as God had made them, abiding then whatever may arrive.

"Let the tyrants pour around,
With a quick and startling sound,
Like the loosening of a sea,
Troops of armed emblazonry.

"Let the charged artillery drive,
Till the dead air seem alive,
With the clash of clanging wheels,
And the tramp of horses' heels.

"Let the fixed bayonet
Gleam with sharp desire to wet
Its bright point in English blood,
Looking keen, as one for food.

"Let the horsemen's scimitars
Wheel and flash like sphereless stars,
Thirsting to eclipse their burning
In a sea of death and mourning.

"Stand ye calm and resolute,
Like a forest, close and mute,
With folded arms, and looks which are
Weapons of an unvanquished war.

 *   *   *   *   *

"*Let the laws of your own land,*
Good or ill, between ye stand,
Hand to hand, and foot to foot,
Arbiters of the dispute.

"*The old laws of England—they*
Whose reverend heads with age are grey,
Children of a wiser day,
And whose solemn voice must be
Thine own echo—Liberty!

"*On those, who first shall violate*
Such sacred heralds in their state,
Rest the blood that must ensue,
And it will not rest on you.

"And then, if the tyrants dare,
Let them ride among you there;
Slash, and stab, and maim, and hew,
What they like, that let them do.

"With folded arms, and steady eyes,
And little fear, and less surprise,
Look upon them as they slay,
Till their rage has passed away."

These are extraordinary counsellings. We have now to see their issue.

"Then they will return with shame
To the place from which they came;
And the blood thus shed will speak
In hot blushes on their cheek.

"Every woman in the land
Will point at them as they stand.
They will hardly dare to greet
Their acquaintance in the street.

"And the bold true warriors,
Who have hugged danger in the wars,
Will turn to those who should be free,
Ashamed of such base company.

"And that slaughter to the nation
Shall steam up like inspiration,
Eloquent, oracular;
A volcano heard afar.

"And these words shall then become
Like Oppression's thundered doom,
Ringing through each heart and brain,
Heard again—again, again!

"Rise like lions after slumber,
In unvanquishable NUMBER!
Shake your chains to earth like dew,
Which in sleep had fallen on you;
YE ARE MANY,—THEY ARE FEW!"

Thus closes this singular poem. The high pitch of heroic virtue imagined in the great passive sacrifice enjoined, is far beyond the soarings of ordinary poets and patriots! The commentary of Mr. Hunt is rather misplaced by us here, but we must give it. "It advises," he says, "what has since taken place, and what was felt by the grown wisdom of the age, to be the only thing which *could* take place, with effect, as a final rebuke and nullification of the Tories; to wit, a calm, lawful, and inflexible preparation for resistance, in the shape of a protesting multitude—the many against the few—the laborious and the suffering against the spoiled children of Monopoly; Mankind against Tory-kind. * * * There really has been no resistance except by multitudinous protest. The Tories, however desirous they shewed themselves to draw their swords,* did not draw them. The battle was won without a blow."

Mr Hunt mentions, that he first heard from Shelley on the subject of *Reform* in 1811, while the latter was a student at Oxford, and it was on this particular, and, as it has proved, successful means of reform. In 1817, Mr. Shelley published an anonymous pamphlet, proposing to put Reform to the vote throughout the kingdom; and after proposing a meeting of the Friends of Reform, who might carry this plan into execution, he devotes to it L.100, a tenth part of his yearly income, from which he had to support his wife and children, and satisfy, what he terms, "large claims of general justice," "the wants" to wit, as his editor states, "of his friends and the poor." Many of the poems of Shelley give us a higher idea of his powers as a poet—though in this piece there are sublime thoughts—but none of his writings give the same impression of Shelley as the devoted lover of all mankind—a philosophic philanthropist, a man esteemed a visionary because the gross and selfish world was unable to follow his noble conceptions of the destinies of man.

WILD SPORTS OF THE WEST.

A book of agreeable sketches of manners, and descriptions of scenery in the wild and romantic parts of Ireland, interspersed with anecdotes, traditions, natural history, and whatever can make the work pleasant and attractive. And pleasant and attractive it is in no stinted degree. As a specimen of the work we select the following story. It wants but a little touch of the supernatural, to convert the poor seal into an Irish Prince, suffering under the charms of a hag, or the spells of a sorcerer, to make a Fairy Tale. In the *Schoolmaster* it shall answer a two-fold purpose—we call it

A STORY FOR THE YOUNG.

"About forty years ago a young seal was taken in Clew Bay, and domesticated in the kitchen of a gentleman whose house was situated on the sea-shore. It grew apace, became familiar with the servants, and attached to the house and family. Its habits were innocent and gentle, it played with the children, came at its master's call, and, as the old man described him to me, was 'fond as a dog, and playful as a kitten.'

"Daily the seal went out to fish, and, after providing for its own wants, frequently brought in a salmon or turbot to his master. His delight, in summer, was to bask in the sun, and in winter to lie before the fire, or, if permitted, creep into the large oven, which at that time formed the regular appendage of an Irish kitchen.

"For four years the seal had been thus domesticated, when, unfortunately, a disease called in this country *the crippawn*—a kind of paralytic affection of the limbs which generally ends fatally—attacked some black cattle belonging to the master of the house; some died, others became infected, and the customary cure produced by changing them to drier pasture failed. A wise woman was consulted, and the hag assured the credulous owner, that the mortality among his cows was occasioned by his retaining an unclean beast about his habitation—the harmless and amusing seal. It must be made away with directly, or the crippawn would continue, and her charms be unequal to avert the malady. The superstitious wretch consented to the hag's proposal; the seal was put on board a boat, carried out beyond Clare Island, and there committed to the deep, to manage for himself as he best could. The boat returned, the family retired to rest, and next morning a servant awakened her master to tell him that the seal was quietly sleeping in the oven. The poor animal over night came back to his beloved home, crept through an open window, and took possession of his favourite resting-place.

"Next morning another cow was reported to be unwell. The seal must now be finally removed; a Galway fishing-boat was leaving Westport on her return home, and the master undertook to carry off the seal, and not put him overboard until he had gone leagues beyond Innis Boffin. It was done—a day and a night passed—the second evening closed—the servant was raking the fire for the night—something scratched gently at the door—it was of course the house-dog—she opened it, and in came the seal! Wearied with his long and unusual voyage, he testified by a peculiar cry, expressive of pleasure, his delight to find himself at home; then stretching himself before the glowing embers of the hearth, he fell into a deep sleep.

"The master of the house was immediately apprized of this unexpected and unwelcome visit. In the exigency, the beldame was awakened and consulted; she averred that it was always unlucky to kill a seal, but suggested that the animal should be deprived of sight, and a third time carried out to sea. To this hellish proposition the besotted wretch who owned the house consented, and the affectionate and

* "And there will be a dust at Manchester, or elsewhere, and it will be laid in blood," &c. &c.—*Tory Prophecy in Blackwood's Magazine.*

confiding creature was cruelly robbed of sight, on that hearth for which he had resigned his native element! Next morning, writhing in agony, the mutilated seal was embarked, taken outside Clare Island, and for the last time committed to the waves.

"A week passed over, and things became worse instead of better; the cattle of the truculent wretch died fast, and the infernal hag gave him the pleasurable tidings that her arts were useless, and that the destructive visitation upon his cattle exceeded her skill and cure.

"On the eighth night after the seal had been devoted to the Atlantic, it blew tremendously. In the pauses of the storm a wailing noise at times was faintly heard at the door; the servants, who slept in the kitchen, concluded that the *Banshee* came to forewarn them of an approaching death, and buried their heads in the bed-coverings. When morning broke, the door was opened—the seal was there lying dead upon the threshold!"

"Stop, Julius!" I exclaimed, "give me a moment's time to curse all concerned in this barbarism."

"Be patient, Frank," said my cousin, "the *finale* will probably save you that trouble. The skeleton of the once plump animal—for, poor beast, it perished from hunger, being incapacitated from blindness to procure its customary food—was buried in a sandhill, and from that moment misfortunes followed the abettors and perpetrators of this inhuman deed. The detestable hag, who had denounced the inoffensive seal, was, within a twelvemonth, hanged for murdering the illegitimate offspring of her own daughter. Every thing about this devoted house melted away—sheep rotted, cattle died, ' and blighted was the corn.' Of several children none reached maturity, and the savage proprietor survived every thing he loved or cared for. He died *blind* and miserable.

"There is not a stone of that accursed building standing upon another. The property has passed to a family of a different name, and the series of incessant calamity which pursued all concerned in this cruel deed is as romantic as true."

AN IRISH HOUSE.

In the same work we have this charming picture of an Irish home, in the wilder parts of the country.

"I have been here three days, and am as much domesticated in the mansion as my cousin's Newfoundland dog. I know the names and *sobriquet* of the establishment; can discriminate between *Hamish*-a-neilan, (James of the Island,) and Andy-bawn, (Fair Andy;) hold converse with the cook, and am hand and glove with the housemaid. Really I am delighted with the place; every thing is wild, new, and out-of-the-way; but I must describe the *locale* of my kinsman's domicile.

"At the bottom of the narrow creek, you must imagine 'a low snug dwelling, and in good repair.' The foam of the Atlantic breaks sometimes against the windows, while a huge cliff, seaward, defends it from the storm, and on the land side, a sudden hill shelters it from the north wind. Here, when the tempest roars abroad, your friend Laura might venture forth and not endanger a *papilotte*. The bent roof is impervious to the rain:—the rooms are neat, well arranged, and comfortable. In the parlour, if the evening be chilly, a turf fire sparkles on the hearth; and when dried bog-deal is added to the embers, it emits a fragrant and delightful glow, superseding the necessity of candles. The long and measured swell of the Atlantic would almost lull a troubled conscience to repose; and that rural hum, which attends upon the farm-yard, rouses the refreshed sleeper in the morning. In the calm of evening, I hear the shrill cry of the sandlark; and in the early dawn the crowing of the cock grouse. I see the salmon fling themselves over the smooth tide, as they hurry from the sea to reascend their native river; and, while I drink claret that never paid the revenue a farthing, or indulge over that proscribed beverage—the produce and the scourge of this wild district—I trace from the window the outline of a range of hills, where the original red deer of Ireland are still existing. None of your park-fed venison, that tame, spiritle diminutive, which a boy may assassinate with his 'birding-piece,' but the remnant of that noble stock which hunters of other days, *O'Connor the Cus Dhu* (Blackfoot,) and *Cormac Bawn MacTavish*, once delighted in pursuing.

"The offices of this wild dwelling are well adapted to the edifice. In winter, the ponies have their stable; and the kine and sheep a comfortable shed. Nor are the dogs forgotten; a warm and sheltered kennel is fitted up with benches, and well provided with straw. Many a sporting-lodge in England, on which thousands have been expended, lacks the comforts of my kinsman's unpretending cottage. Where are the coachhouses? these, indeed, would be useless appendages; the nearest road on which a wheel could turn, is ten miles distant from the lodge."

LYRIC LEAVES. BY CORNELIUS WEBBE.

This is a collection of short pieces of delightful verse, by an author who, if he seldom rises to the third heaven of imagination, never grovels, and who often pleases in no mean degree. And if to please be the end of poetry, it is here attained.

NEW NOVELS.

The only new novel we have yet seen worthy of attention is ROMANCE in IRELAND. It is a tale of the age of Henry VIII., an historical romance, of which the foundation is the rebellion or insurrection of *Lord Thomas Fitzgerald*. It suggests many painful modern recollections and comparisons. The interest of this tale commences with the first page, and is kept up with great spirit to the close. It teems with striking incident and ready invention, and will, we believe, be read with the true gusto by those who like a work full of action and plot,—we mean, by all who depend on the circulating library for the daily bread of their intellect. This account, we feel, does no justice to this romance, and sorry we are for it. Our limited space permits only an indication of opinion; but, so far as our critical judgment goes, that indication may be safely relied on as a sincere one.

VALPY'S SHAKSPEARE.

A new, handsome, cheap edition of Shakspeare, to be published in monthly volumes, has been announced by Mr. Valpy. The first volumes we have seen. It is of the size and style of Murray's cheap edition of Byron, and is to be completed in 15 volumes. The illustrations are not *originals*, but etchings upon tinted paper, from Boydell's Shakspeare Gallery, which gives assurance of something better than most of the modern illustrations of great writers which we have lately seen.

EDINBURGH CABINET LIBRARY, VOL. X.—TRAVELS AND RESEARCHES OF HUMBOLDT.—By W. Macgillivray, A. M.

A happier subject could not easily be hit upon than this abridgment, which, for this reason alone, independently of other merits, is likely to become one of the most popular volumes of this series. This sum and substance of the works of the greatest of modern travellers, and we may say of all travellers, will form a delightful book to young people, and an attractive introduction to the scientific investigations of Humboldt. Mr. Macgillivray has been successful in presenting his readers with much that is finely descriptive, picturesque, or imaginative in the voluminous writings of his author, either in a condensed form, or in the exact words of the original. In embalming the body he has not suffered the spirit to escape. It is not possible to make a dull or bad book from such materials, yet it is great merit to have made the most of them which the limited space permitted. *This is a book to be bought.* As a specimen of the work, we subjoin this description of

THE CAVE OF GUACHARO.

"The greatest curiosity in the beautiful and salubrious district of Caripe is a cavern inhabited by nocturnal birds, the fat of which is employed in the missions for dressing food. It is named the Cave of Guacharo, and is situated in a valley three leagues distant from the convent. On the 18th of September Humboldt and Bonpland, accompanied by most of the monks and some of the Indians, set out for this aviary, following for an hour and a half a narrow path, leading across a fine plain covered with beautiful turf; then, turning westward along a small river which issues from the cave, they proceeded, during three quarters of an hour, sometimes walking in the water, sometimes on a slippery and miry soil between the torrent and a wall of rocks, until they arrived at the foot of the lofty mountain of Guacharo. Here the torrent ran in a deep ravine, and they went on under a projecting cliff which prevented them from seeing the sky, until at the last turning they came suddenly upon the immense opening of the recess, which is eighty-five feet broad and seventy-seven feet high. The entrance is toward the south, and is formed in the vertical face of a rock, covered with trees of gigantic height, intermixed with numerous species of singular and beautiful plants, some of which hang in festoons over the vault. This luxuriant vegetation is not confined to the exterior of the cave, but appears even in the vestibule, where the travellers were astonished to see heliconias nineteen feet in height, palms, and arborescent arums. They had advanced about four hundred and sixty feet before it became necessary to light their torches, when they heard from afar the hoarse screams of the birds.—The guacharo is the size of a domestic fowl, and has somewhat the appearance of a vulture, with a mouth like that of a goat-sucker. It forms a distinct genus in the order *Passeres*, differing from that just named in having a stronger beak, furnished with two denticulations, though in its manners it bears an affinity to it as well as to the Alpine crow. Its plumage is dark bluish-grey, minutely streaked and spotted with deep brown, the head, wings, and tail being marked with white spots bordered with black. The extent of the wings is three feet and a half. It lives on fruits, but quits the cave only in the evening. The shrill and piercing cries of these birds, assembled in multitudes, are said to form a harsh and disagreeable noise, somewhat resembling that of a rookery. The nests, which the guides showed by means of torches fastened to a long pole, were placed in funnel-shaped holes in the roof. The noise increased as they advanced, the animals being frightened by the numerous lights.—About midsummer every year, the Indians, armed with poles, enter the cave, and destroy the greater part of the nests. Several thousands of young birds are thus killed, and the old ones hover around, uttering frightful cries. Those which are secured in this manner are opened on the spot, to obtain the fat, which exists abundantly in their abdomen, and which is subsequently melted in clay vessels over fires of brushwood. This substance is semifluid, transparent, destitute of smell, and keeps above a year without becoming rancid. At the convent of Caripe it was used in the kitchen of the monks, and our travellers never found that it communicated any disagreeable smell or taste to the food.—The gaucharoes would have been long ago destroyed, had not the superstitious dread of the Indians prevented them from penetrating far into the cavern. It also appears, that birds of the same species dwell in other accessible places in the neighbourhood, and that the great cave is repeopled by colonies from them. The hard and dry fruits which are found in the crops and gizzards of the young ones are considered as an excellent remedy against intermittent fevers, and regularly sent to Cariaco and other parts of the lower districts where such diseases prevail. The travellers followed the banks of the small river which issues from the cavern as far as the mounds of calcareous incrustations permitted them, and afterwards descended into its bed. The cave preserved the same direction, breadth, and height, as at its entrance, to the distance of 1554 feet. The natives having a belief that the souls of their ancestors inhabit its deep recesses, the Indians who accompanied our travellers could hardly be persuaded to venture into it. Shooting at random in the dark, they obtained two specimens of the guacharo. Having proceeded to a certain distance, they came to a mass of stalactite, beyond which the cave became narrower, although it retained its original direction. Here the rivulet had deposited a blackish mould resembling that observed at Muggendorf in Franconia. The seeds, which the birds carry to their young, spring up wherever they are dropped into it; and M. Humboldt and his friend were astonished to find blanched stalks that had attained a height of two feet. As the missionaries were unable to persuade the Indians to advance farther, the party returned. The river, sparkling amid the foliage of the trees, seemed like a distant picture, to which the mouth of the cave formed a frame. Having sat down at the entrance to enjoy a little needful repose, they partook of a repast which the missionaries had prepared, and in due time returned to the convent."

SUNSHINE; OR, LAYS FOR LADIES.

A pretty poetical toy, somewhere between the Hood and Bayly schools. We could swear to having seen some of the airy trifles which compose the slender tome, but cannot tell where. From an Epistle from Madeline, a *prudent* married friend, to "Emma," who has got into a

"Shocking dilemma"—

fallen imprudently in love, we give a few lines:—

"Can you give up your servant and carriage?
Can you live upon love, do you think?
These are joys in perspective in marriage,
When tried, like new friends, they will shrink.

"Could you give up the waltz's soft whirl?
Could you dress in the plainest of ways?
Could you give up your chance of an earl?
Could you give up the flatterer's praise?

"Could you *dine* on the glance of an eye?
Could you live without credit or money?
Could you *tea* on a soft love-sick sigh?
I could not, though lips were of honey.

"Dear love, I implore you to ponder,
To pause ere you settle for life;
Believe me, a moonlight's fair wander,
Is more pleasant befar than when wife."

THE ANNUALS.

We have turned over some of these endless productions, and find them, as was to be expected, wonderfully like their great progenitors. It is conceivable that a person might once for all, make a selection from among them; but that, year after year, any one should heap up indifferent, or, at most, pretty prints, and scraps of the worst literature, is to us marvellous. The *prettiest* of those we have seen is the *Keepsake*, the *best* the *Picturesque Annual*. It really deserves to be bought and treasured up by those who have a taste for forming a collection of prints. Of twenty-six views one half are truly beautiful. They are mostly taken in Germany. There are already published, which we have seen, the *Literary Souvenir*, *New-Year's Gift*, *Friendship's Offering*, *Amulet*, *Juvenile Forget-me-not*, *Comic Offering*, &c. &c. &c. A very *nice* volume might be compiled from among them, not certainly half as good as the collections of reading lessons used in the humblest of our village schools; but *pretty* enough. And is it wonderful that these little seminaries send forth Cobbetts and Clares, and Elliotts, and Burnses, and Howitts, and nearly all the eminent persons we boast; while the regions of the *Annu-*

als give us "seven persons of quality," like those who, Miss Sheridan informs us, have contributed to her *Comic Offering*.

NOTES OF THE MONTH.

DECEMBER.

Season of social mirth! of fireside joys!
I love thy shortened day, when, at its close,
The blazing tapers, on the jovial board
Disperse o'er every care-forgetting face
Their cheering light, and round the bottle glides.
Now far be banished, from our social ring,
The party wrangle fierce, the argument
Deep-learned, metaphysical, and dull;
Oft dropt, as oft again renew'd, endless.
Rather I'd hear stories twice ten times told,
Or vapid joke, filch'd from Joe Miller's page;
Or tale of ghost, hobgoblin dire, or witch.
Grahame.

DECEMBER, the last month of the year, was originally named *Winter-monath* by our Saxon ancestors, though this was changed to *heligh*, or *holy-monath*, on their conversion to Christianity. In it was celebrated the festival of the Scandinavian Jupiter, the deity *Thor*. This was the IOL (or our *Yule*) feast, the holyday season of the northern year. The weather, as in the present year, is often mild in the early part of this month, but liable to sudden variations of temperature. The atmosphere is generally loaded with vapour, and we have often fogs about great towns, and "a *green* (*i.e.* an open, mild) Yule makes a fat kirkyard." It is remarked, that, in this state of the atmosphere, rural sounds are heard at great distances. The pleasantest features of the month we must copy from Mr. Leigh Hunt. Why did he so soon drop, and why never resume his *Literary Pocket-book?* the first, and by how much superior to all the succeeding *Annuals!* "It is," he says, "now complete winter * * * * * The trees look but like skeletons of what they were—

Bare ruin'd choirs, in which the sweet birds sang.

The evergreen trees, with their beautiful cones, such as firs and pines, are now particularly observed and valued. * * * * * But we have flowers as well as leaves in winter-time; besides a few of last month, there are the aconite, and hellebore, two names of very different celebrity; and, in addition to some of the flourishing shrubs, there is the Glastonbury thorn, which puts forth its beauty at Christmas. It is so called, we believe, because the Abbots of the famous monastery at that place first had it in their garden from abroad, and turned its seasonable efflorescence into a miracle." Mr. Hunt might have said much more on December flowers, and shrubs, as every one knows who is familiar with even the most ordinary modern garden. But he *slumps* them all very prettily, roses and evergreens, and passes to more attractive matter. "December has one circumstance in it, which turns it into the merriest month of the year,

CHRISTMAS.

This is the holyday which, for obvious reasons, may be said to have survived all the others; but still it is not kept with any thing like the vigour, perseverance, and elegance of our ancestors. They not only ran Christmas-day, New-Year's Day, and Twelfth Night all into one, but kept the wassail bowl floating the whole time, and earned their right to enjoy it by all sorts of active pleasures." Mr. Hunt must visit Derrynane, or, for change, the Hebrides. The old original Christmas still finds its sanctuary in Kerry and Skye. The wassail bowl* (as some of our readers may know by experience, for it has been a little revived of late) is a composition of spiced wine or ale, with roasted apples put into it, and sometimes eggs. [Here Mr. Hunt is obscure,—one might fancy the eggs were put to float and bob in the bowl like the apples. An Oxford man would have put this more clearly.] —" They also adorned their houses with green boughs, which, it appears from Herrick, was a practice with many throughout the year"—why, so it does from Goldsmith, who might be his great-great-grandson—" box succeeding at Candlemas to the holly, bay, rosemary, and mistletoe of Christmas—yew at Easter to box birch (or the catkins of the palm?) at Whitsuntide to yew, and then bents or oaken boughs." What an evergreen year was that of merry England! "But, again," says Mr. Hunt, "the whole nation was in a ferment at Christmas with the warmth of exercise and their firesides, as they were in May with the new sunshine. The peasants wrestled and sported on the town green, and told tales of an evening; the gentry feasted then, or had music and other elegant pastimes; the Court had the poetical and princely entertainment of masques;" [so, for that part, has it still, and we could tell who are the mummers;] " and all sung, danced, revelled, and enjoyed themselves, and so welcomed the new year like happy and grateful subjects of nature. This is the way to turn winter to summer, and make the world what Heaven has enabled it to be.'

WINTER.

This is the eldest of the seasons: he
Moves not like spring with gradual step, nor grows
From bud to beauty, but with all his snows
Comes down at once in hoar antiquity.
No rains nor loud proclaiming tempests flee
Before him; nor unto his time belong
The suns of summer, nor the charms of song,
That with May's gentle smiles so well agree.
But he, made perfect in his birth-day cloud,
Starts into sudden life with scarce a sound,
And with a tender footstep prints the ground,
As though to cheat man's ear; while yet he stays,
He seems as 'twere to prompt our merriest days,
And bid the dance and joke be long and loud.
Charles Lloyd.

---

* *Wassail-Bowl, a Centre Supper Dish.*—Crumble down as for trifle a nice fresh cake (or use maccaroons or other small biscuit) into a china punch-bowl or deep glass dish. Over this pour some sweet rich wine, as malmsey Madeira, if wanted very rich, but raisin-wine will do. Sweeten this, and pour a well-seasoned rich custard over it. Strew nutmeg and grated sugar over it, and stick it over with sliced blanched almonds. Obs.—This is, in fact, just a rich eating posset. A very good wassail-bowl may be made of mild ale well spiced and sweetened, and a plain rice custard, with few eggs.—*Meg Dods' Cookery.*

THE STORY-TELLER.

FOUR OLD MAIDS.
BY THE AUTHOR OF "ATHERTON," "TRUCKLEBOROUGH HALL," &c.

I LOVE an old maid;—I do not speak of an individual, but of the species,—I use the singular number, as speaking of a singularity in humanity. An old maid is not merely an antiquarian, she is an antiquity; not merely a record of the past, but the very past itself, she has escaped a great change, and sympathizes not in the ordinary mutations of mortality. She inhabits a little eternity of her own. She is Miss from the beginning of the chapter to the end. I do not like to hear her called Mistress, as is sometimes the practice, for that looks and sounds like the resignation of despair, a voluntary extinction of hope. I do not know whether marriages are made in Heaven, some people say that they are, but I am almost sure that old maids are. There is a something about them which is not of the earth earthy. They are Spectators of the world, not Adventurers nor Ramblers; perhaps Guardians, we say nothing of Tatlers. They are evidently predestinated to be what they are. They owe not the singularity of their condition to any lack of beauty, wisdom, wit, or good temper; there is no accounting for it but on the principle of fatality. I have known many old maids, and of them all not one that has not possessed as many good and amiable qualities as ninety and nine out of a hundred of my married acquaintance. Why then are they single? Heaven only knows. It is their fate!

On the left hand of the road between London and Liverpool, there is a village, which, for particular reasons, I shall call Littleton; and I will not so far gratify the curiosity of idle inquirers as to say whether it is nearest to London or to Liverpool, but it is a very pretty village, and let the reader keep a sharp look out for it next time he travels that road. It is situated in a valley, through which runs a tiny rivulet as bright as silver, but hardly wide enough for a trout to turn round in. Over the little stream there is a bridge, which seems to have been built merely out of compliment to the liquid thread, to save it the mortification of being hopped over by every urchin and clodpole in the parish. The church is covered with ivy even half way up the steeple, but the sexton has removed the green intrusion from the face of the clock, which, with its white surface and black figures, looks, at a little distance, like an owl in an ivy bush. A little to the left of the church is the parsonage house, almost smothered with honeysuckles; in front of the house is a grass plot, and up to the door there is what is called a carriage drive; but I never saw a carriage drive up there, for it is so steep that it would require six horses to pull the carriage up, and there is not room enough for more than one. Somewhat farther up the hill which bounds the little valley where the village stands, there is a cottage; the inhabitants of Littleton call it the white cottage. It is merely a small whitewashed house, but as it is occupied by genteelish sort of people, who cannot afford a large house, it is generally called a cottage. All these beautiful and picturesque objects, and a great many more which I have not described, have lost with me their interest. It would make me melancholy to go into that church. The interest which I had in the parsonage house was transferred to the white cottage, and the interest which I had in the white cottage is now removed to the churchyard, and that interest is in four graves that lie parallel to each other, with head-stones of nearly one date. In these four graves lie the remains of four old maids. Poor things! Their remains! Alack, alack, there was not much that remained of them. There was but little left of them to bury. The bearers had but light work. I wondered why they should have four separate graves, and four distinct tomb-stones. The sexton told me that it was their particular desire, in order to make the churchyard look respectable; and they left behind them just sufficient money to pay the undertaker's bills and to erect four grave-stones. I saw these ladies twice, and that at an interval of thirty years. I made one more attempt to see them, and I was more grieved than I could have anticipated, when the neighbours shewed me their newly-closed graves. But no one long pities the dead, and I was, after a while, glad that they had not been long separated. I saw these ladies twice;—and the first time that I saw them, the only doubt was, which of the four would be first married. I should have fallen in love with one of them myself, I do not know which, but I understood that they were all four, more or less, engaged. They were all pretty, they were all sensible, they were all good-humored, and they knew the world, for they had all read Rollin's " Ancient History." They not only had admirers, but two of them even then had serious suitors. The whole village of Littleton, and many other villages in the neighbourhood, rang with the praises of the accomplished and agreeable daughters of the rector; nor were the young ladies dependent for their hopes of husbands merely on their good qualities; they had the reputation of wealth, which reputation I am constrained to say was rather a bubble. The rectory of Littleton was said to be worth a thousand a-year, but it never produced more than six hundred, and the worthy rector was said to be worth ten or twelve thousand pounds. Bless him! he might be *worth* that and a great deal more, but he never possessed so much; the utmost of his private fortune was fifteen hundred pounds in the three per cents. It is enough to designate them by their Christian names. Their good old father used to boast that his daughters had really Christian names. The eldest was Mary, the second Martha, the third Anna, and the youngest Elizabeth. The eldest was, when I first knew them, actually engaged to a young gentleman who had just taken a wrangler's degree at Cambridge, and had gained a prize for a Greek epigram. Such an effort of genius seemed next to miraculous at Littleton, for the people of that village never gain prizes for Greek epigrams. The farmers, who had heard of his success, used to stare at him for a prodigy, and almost wondered that he should walk on two legs, and eat mutton, and say " How do you do?" like the rest of the world. And every body said he was such a nice man. He never skipped irreverently over the river as some young men of his age would do, but always went over the bridge. It was edifying to see how gracefully he handed the young ladies over the said bridge, Mary always the last, though she was the eldest. The young squire of the parish was generally considered as the suitor of the second. The third had many admirers; she was what is called a showy young woman, having a little of the theatrical in her style. She was eloquent, lively, and attitudinizing. She had a most beautiful voice, and her good papa used to say, " My dear Anna, the sound of your voice is very delightful, and it does me good to hear you sing to your own harpsichord, but I wish I could hear you sing at church." Poor man! he did not consider that there was no possibility of hearing any other voice while that of the parish clerk was dinning in his ears. Elizabeth, the youngest, was decidedly the prettiest of the four: sentimentality was her forte, or, more properly speaking, her foible. She sighed much herself, and was the cause of sighing to others. I little thought when I first saw them that I beheld a nest of predestinated old maids; but it was so; and the next time that I saw them they were all living together, spinsters. How I was occupied the next thirty years would be tedious to relate, therefore I pass over that period and come again to Littleton.

Time is like a mischievous urchin that plays sad tricks in our absence, and so disarranges things and persons too, that when we come back again we hardly know where to find them. When I made my second visit to Littleton, the good old rector had been several years in his grave; and when I asked after his daughters, I was told that they were living, and were together, and that they occupied the white cottage. I was rather pleased to hear that they were single, though I was surprised at the information. I knew that I should be well received, that I should not find all their old affections alienated by new ties. I knew that I should not have to encounter the haughty and interrogatory eyes of husbands, that I should not be under the necessity of accommodating myself to new manners. I had indeed some difficulty in making myself known, and still more difficulty in distinguishing the ladies the one from the other, and connecting their present with their past appearance; for Anna's attitudinizing days were over, and Elizabeth had ceased to sigh. But when the recognition had taken place, we were all exceedingly glad to see each other, and we all talked together about every body, and everything at once.

My call at the white cottage was at the latter end of August. The weather was fine, but there had recently been much rain, and there were some few heavy clouds, and some little growling of the wind, like the aspect and tone of an angry schoolmaster who had just given a boy a sound thrashing, and looks as if he were half inclined to give him some more. The cottage was very small, very neat, very light. There was but one parlour, and that was a very pretty one. A small carpet covered the middle of the room; a worked fire-screen stood in one corner; a piece of needle-work, representing Abraham going to sacrifice Isaac, hung opposite to the door; shells, sea-weed, and old china stood on the mantlepiece; an old harpsichord, in a black mahogany case, stretched its leviathan length along one side of the room; six exceedingly heavy and clumsily carved mahogany chairs, with high backs, short legs, and broad square flat seats, any one of which might have accommodated all the four sisters at once, according to their mode of sitting, stood round the room; these chairs, I recollected, had been in the dining-room at the rectory, but then there was a great lubberly cub of a footman to lug them about. The fire-place was particularly neat. It had an old brass fender polished up to the semblance of gold, delineating in its pattern divers birds and beasts, the like of which never entered Noah's ark, but they had a right to go in by sevens, for they were as clean as a penny. The poker looked like a toothpick, the shovel like an old-fashioned salt spoon, and the tongs like a pair of tweezers. The little black stove shone with an icy coldness, as if the maid had been scrubbing it all the morning to keep herself warm; and the cut paper was arranged over the vacant bars with a cruel exactitude that gave no hopes of fire. The ladies themselves looked as cold as the fire-place; and I could hardly help thinking that a stove without a fire, at the cold end of August, looked something like an old maid. The ladies, however, were very chatty, they all spoke together—or nearly so, for when one began the others went on, one after another, in the way and after the manner of a catch, or more accurately speaking, perhaps somewhat in the similitude of a fugue. They talked very loud, and sat very upright, which last circumstance I should have thought very conducive to health, but they were not healthy; the fact is, they lived too sparingly, for their father had left much less than had been expected, and they were obliged to keep up appearances, as they still visited the first families in the neighbourhood. By living together, they had very much assimilated in manners, they all had the same sharp shrill voice, and the same short snappy, not snappish, manner of speaking.

When I called on them I had not dined, but I suppose they had, for they asked me to stay and drink tea with them; though I should have preferred dinner to tea, yet for the sake of such old acquaintance, I was content to let that pass. They pressed me very much to take a glass of wine, and I yielded, but afterwards I repented it. Single elderly ladies are very much imposed on in the article of wine! ill luck to those who cheat them! Then we had tea. I knew the old cups and saucers again, and the little silver tea-pot, and the little silver cream-jug, and the sugar-tongs, made like a pair of scissars; I was glad to see the tea-urn, for it helped to warm the room. The tea made us quite communicative; not that it was strong enough to intoxicate, quite the contrary, it was rather weak. I should also have been glad of some more bread and butter, but they handed me the last piece, and I could not think of taking it, so it went into the kitchen for the maid, and I did not grudge it her, for she seemed by the way to be not much better fed than her mistresses. She was a neat respectable young woman.

After tea we talked again about old times, and I gave several broad hints and intimations that I should like to hear their respective histories; in other words, I wished to know how it was that they had all remained single; for the history of an old maid is the narrative of her escapes from matrimony. My intimation was well received, and my implied request was complied with. Mary, as the eldest, commenced.

"I believe you remember my friend Mr. M———?"

"I do so, and is he living?"

"He is, and still single."

I smiled, and said, "Indeed!" but the lady smiled not.

"Yes," continued the narrator, "he is still living and still single. I have occasionally seen him, but very seldom of late years. You remember, I dare say, what a cheerful companion he was, and how very polite. He was quite of the old school, but that was only as regarded his external manners. In his opinions he partook too much of the new school. He was one of the liberal party at Cambridge; and though he was generally a very serious and good man, he perplexed his head with some strange notions, and when the time came that he should take orders, he declined doing so, on account of some objection which he had to some of the Thirty-nine Articles. Some people have gone so far as to say that he was no better than a Socinian, though I do not believe he was ever so bad as that. Still, however, it would never do for the daughter of a clergyman to marry a man who had any doubts concerning any of the Thirty-nine Articles. We did all in our power to convince him he was wrong, and he did all in his power to convince us that he was right; but it was all to no purpose. Indeed he seemed to consider himself a kind of martyr, only because we talked to him. He argued most ingeniously to shew that exact conformity of opinion was not essential to happiness. But I could not think it correct to marry a man who had any doubts concerning the Articles; for, as my father very justly observed, when a man once begins to doubt, it is impossible to say where it will end. And so the matter went on from year to year, and so it remains still, and so it is likely to remain to the end of the chapter. I will never give up the Thirty-nine Articles."

All the sisters said that she was perfectly right; and then Martha told her story, saying, "It was just about the time that you were visiting Littleton, that Mr. B———, who had long paid me very particular attention, made me an offer. Mr. B——— was not a man of first-rate talents, though he did not want for understanding; he was also tolerably good-humoured, though occasionally subject to fits of violence. His father, however, most strenuously objected to the match, and from being on friendly terms with us he suddenly dropped our acquaintance, and almost persecuted us. My father was a man of high spirit, and could not patiently brook the insults he received, and I have every reason to believe that thereby his days were shortened. In proportion, however, as the elder Mr. B——— opposed our union, the affection of the younger seemed to increase, and he absolutely proposed a marriage in Scotland, but my father would never allow a daughter of his to be married otherwise than by the rites of the Church of England. At length old Mr. B——— died, and then it was thought that we should be married; but it was necessary to wait a decent time after the old gentleman's death, in which interval the young squire, whose attentions had diminished of late, went up to London, where he married a widow with a large fortune. They are now living separately."

"You were faithful to your first loves," I observed.

"But I," said Anna, "have a different story to tell. I had four offers before I was nineteen years of age; and I thought that I was exercising great judgment and discrimination in endeavouring to ascertain which was most worthy of my choice; so I walked, and talked, and sang, and played, and criticised with all in their turn: and before I could make up my mind which to choose, I lost them all, and gained the character of a flirt. It seems very unfortunate that we are placed under the necessity of making that decision which must influence our whole destiny for life, at that very period when we least know what life is."

"It is inexpedient," said I, "to entertain several lovers at once."

"I found it inexpedient," said Elizabeth, "to entertain several lovers in succession. My first lover won my heart by flute-playing. He was a lieutenant in the navy, visiting in the neighbourhood. My father disapproved the connexion, but I said that I could not live without him, and so a consent was extorted; but, alas! my flute-player's ship was ordered to the West Indies, and I heard of him no more. My next lover, who succeeded to the first rather too soon in the opinion of some people, was a medical man, and for a marriage with him a reluctant consent was obtained from my father; but before matters could be arranged, it was found that his business did not answer, and he departed. Another succeeded to the business, and also to my affections, and a third reluctant consent was extorted; but when the young gentleman found that the report of my father's wealth had been exaggerated, he departed also; and in time I grew accustomed to these disappointments, and bore them better than I expected. I might perhaps have had a husband, if I could have lived without a lover."

So ended their sad stories; and after tea we walked into the garden—it was a small garden, with four sides and a circular centre, so small, that as we walked round we were like the names in a round robin, it was difficult to say which was first. I shook hands with them at parting, gently, for fear of hurting them, for their fingers were long, cold, and fleshless. The next time I travelled that way they were all in their graves, and not much colder than when I saw them at the cottage.—*Friendship's Offering.*

CHARLES FRASER FRIZELL, ESQ., OF HARCOURT STREET, DUBLIN.[*]

One of the most extraordinary characters I have ever met with was Mr Fraser Frizell, an Irish barrister. He was much devoted to inquiries regarding education, the state of the poor, and other useful objects; and came to London on purpose to procure such information as the metropolis could furnish regarding them. He happened to call with a letter of introduction to me, just when I was going to sit down to an early dinner, preparatory to a long debate in the House of Commons, and he readily agreed to take a share of it. His conversation was so lively and pleasant, that I felt no wish to exchange it for a dull debate in the House of Commons. Among other things, he said, "We Irish meet with more singular adventures than any other race of men, and, in proof of the assertion, I will tell you a story, which I think will amuse you." In the course of our future correspondence, as will appear from the subjoined letters, I earnestly requested him to send me the story himself, or to procure it from Father O'Leary; but being unsuccessful in those applications, I shall endeavour to make it out the best way I can, from a distant recollection.

THE HISTORY OF DARBY O'SULLIVAN.

Father O'Leary and Captain M'Carty were walking together through the streets of St. Omers, when they came to a house, at the door of which a man was bawling, in the French language, "Walk in, gentlemen, and see the greatest curiosity ever heard of, a Russian bear who can speak, and dance, and sing, and in every respect is as intelligent as a human being. Father O'Leary wished to walk on, but Captain M'Carty insisted on their going in to see so great a curiosity. Upon their entering the apartments where the exhibition was to be seen, they saw, at the bottom of a long room, a great cage, in which a huge bear was reposing. Upon their approaching the cage, the keeper, with a long stick, began to beat the animal, in order to rouse him. Upon his getting up, he commenced speaking some gibberish, which the two visiters immediately knew to be Irish. The keeper then said in French, "Come, Mr. Bear, give these gentlemen a song;" and, to their utter astonishment, he sung an Irish ditty. Father O'Leary immediately said in Irish, "How came you to speak the Irish language?" The astonishment of the bear, on hearing himself addressed in his native tongue, may easily be conceived. He said, "Gentlemen, my name is Darby O'Sullivan. I was born in the county of Kerry. When men were raised for the navy, I became a volunteer, and was put on board a ship of war. We sailed to the coast of Armoric, (Brittany,) and a boat was sent ashore to procure some water and provisions. The people, where we landed, spoke a kind of Irish, and I thought I would be better off among them than on board a ship, where we were not very kindly treated. I ran, therefore, into the country, and came to a little town, where they were very kind to me. I found the cider better than the cider of Kerry, and took my fill of it. I then walked into the country, and I lay down to sleep, and when I awoke, I found myself transformed into a bear."

The keeper was not at all satisfied with what was going forward, and said to the company who had assembled, "Gentlemen, you must now be satisfied of the truth of what I asserted. This bear, in many respects, resembles a human being; but he is tired—we must leave him to his repose." Upon which Captain M'Carty drew his sword, and seizing the man by the collar, he said, "You have been playing some tricks with a countryman of mine, which shall not go unpunished. Instantly open the door of the cage to let him out, otherwise this sword will be buried in your body." The keeper, much terrified, admitted that it was a man in a bear's skin, and gave the following account of the circumstance:—

"My partner and I were exhibiting, in a town in France, a real Russian bear, when he unfortunately became sick, and died. We had the skin taken off, and buried the body; and then resolved to take a walk into the country, to consider what we could do to remedy our misfortune. A short way from the town, we observed a man, lying in a ditch, quite drunk. It accidentally occurred to us, that it would be possible to sew the bear's skin over the man, in the state in which he then was, and to persuade him, when he became sober, that he had been converted into a bear, as a punishment for his drunkenness. We set about it without a moment's delay; and by means of blows, and showing him his figure in a glass, we convinced him that the transformation had actually taken place. The man believes himself to be a bear. He is perfectly reconciled to his fate; and to make him again a man, would do him no good, and would ruin us."

Captain M'Carty immediately replied, "This must not be suffered. I will not permit a countryman of mine to be treated so inhumanly." Scissars were immediately procured, the bear's skin was taken off, and out came a great naked Irishman, who was much delighted with being restored to manhood. Clothes were immediately procured for him, and some money collected for his immediate subsistence; but as he had no means of gaining a livelihood, he resolved to enlist in Captain M'Carty's regiment. It is said, that in the course of the French Revolution, he embraced the cause of liberty, and ultimately rose to a situation of some importance in the armies of the Republic.

A good anecdote is told in the *Court Journal*, of the Duchess de Berri's capture, and told in all simplicity. The wily Neapolitan lady dealt largely in magnificent promises and in small *souvenirs*, knowing the *gullibility* of mankind, and acting accordingly. When she came out of her concealment begrimmed with soot, (the scene should be got up as a spectacle at the Parisian theatres,) she borrowed a handkerchief from one of her captors, in order to wipe her face, and in return, she afterwards presented him with a handsome kerchief. In many instances she cut off locks of her hair, and offered them to those who had rendered her any little services; but there was one sturdy *sansculotte*, who stood out obstinately against Mademoiselle Kersabiec's repeated pressings to accept a locket, containing one of her royal mistress's ringlets. At last, upon importuning him merely to convey it as a *cadeau* to his wife, the republican boor exclaimed,—"Cease your teasing, mademoiselle; and keep the thing for some idiot, who will fall down and worship it." The republican boor! to refuse bartering his honesty, and his love of the peace and happiness of France, for a locket of a Princess's, hair! enough in itself to turn the heads of five hundred boors, and every hair in it worth the lives of as many more. How strangely constructed must the understandings of those persons be calling themselves, *par excellence,* loyal

[*] This extraordinary story is taken from the Reminiscences of Sir John Sinclair.

ELEMENTS OF THOUGHT.

CHANGING SIDES IN POLITICS, OR RELIGION.

It is the trial of a man to see if he will change his side; and if he be so weak as to change once, he will change again. Country fellows have a way to try if a man be weak in the hams, by coming behind him and giving him a blow unawares; and if he bend once, he will bend again. The lords that fall from the king, after they have got estates by base flattery at court, and now pretend conscience, do as a vintner when he first sets up; you may bring your wench to his house, but, when he grows rich, he turns conscientious, and will sell no wine upon the Sabbath-day.—*Selden.*

HUMILITY is a virtue all preach, none practise, and yet every body is content to hear. The master thinks it good doctrine for his servant, the laity for the clergy, and the clergy for the laity. But there is a vicious humility. If a man does not take notice of that excellency and perfection that is in himself, how can he be thankful to God who is the author of all excellency and perfection? Nay, if a man hath too mean an opinion of himself, it will render him unserviceable both to God and man. *Pride* must be allowed to a certain degree, else a man cannot keep up his dignity. In gluttony there must be eating, in drunkenness there must be drinking; it is not the eating nor drinking that is to be blamed, it is the excess. So in pride.

STANDARD OF THINGS.

We measure from ourselves; and, as things are for our use and purpose, so we approve them. Bring a pear to the table that is rotten, and 'tis a fine thing; and yet, I warrant you, the pear thinks as much of itself as the medlar. We measure the excellency of other men by some excellency we conceive to be in ourselves. Nash, a poor poet, seeing an alderman, with his gold chain, upon his great horse, cries in scorn, "Do you see that fellow how big he looks? why, that fellow cannot make a blank verse!"— Nay, we measure the goodness of God from ourselves; we measure his goodness, justice, wisdom, by something we call just, good, wise, in ourselves; and, in so doing, we judge [proportionably to the country fellow in the play, who said, if he were a king he would live like a lord, and have pease and bacon every day, and a whip that cried "slash."

EQUITY—DISCRETIONARY POWER IN JUDGES.

Equity in law is the same that the spirit is in religion, what every one pleases to make it. Sometimes they go according to conscience, sometimes according to law, sometimes according to the rule of court. *Equity is a roguish thing;* for law we have a measure, know what to trust to; *equity* is according to the conscience of him that is Chancellor, and as that is larger or narrower, so is *equity*. 'Tis all one, as if they should make the standard for the measure we call a foot, a Chancellor's foot. What an uncertain measure would this be? One Chancellor has a long foot, another a short foot, a third an indifferent foot.* 'Tis the same thing in the Chancellor's conscience.

CEREMONY keeps up all things; 'tis like a penny vial to a rich spirit, or some distilled water: without it the water were spilt, the spirit lost.

Of all people, women have no reason to cry down ceremony; for they think themselves slighted without it. And were they not used with ceremony, with compliments, and addresses, with legs, and kissing of hands, they were the pitifulest creatures in the world. But yet, methinks, to kiss their hands after their lips, as some do, is like little boys, that, after they eat the apple, fall to the paring, out of a love they have to the apple.—*Selden.*

THE ESTABLISHED CLERGY.

The clergy and laity together are never like to do well; it is as if a man were to make an excellent feast, and should have his apothecary and his physician come into the kitchen; the cooks, if they were let alone, would make excellent meat; but then comes the apothecary, and he puts rhubarb into one sauce, and agaric into another sauce. Chain up the clergy on both sides.—*Selden.*

GOOD SENSE is as different from genius as perception is from invention; yet, though distinct qualities, they frequently exist together. It is altogether opposite to wit, but by no means inconsistent with it. It is not science, for there is such a thing as unlettered good sense; yet, though it is neither wit, learning, nor genius, it is a substitute for each where they do not exist, and the perfection of all where they do.—*Hannah Moore.*

THOUGHTS ON SECONDARY PUNISHMENTS.
BY ARCHBISHOP WHATELY.

FALSE COMPASSION.—In respect to the punishment not only of the supposed insane, and of juvenile delinquents, but of offenders generally, there is afloat in the world much false (not a little of it, I suspect, affected) tenderness. Merely excessive and misplaced compassion is, indeed, an error as much to be respected as any error can be; but when compassion is withheld from the deserving, and bestowed *only* on the undeserving, the error is as odious as it is practically noxious. It seems to me one of the worst and most *barbarian* features of the character of a great part of the nation, that, by the multitude at least, very little sympathy, comparatively, is felt, except for the guilty. The sufferings inflicted by the hand of justice ought, indeed, not to be excessive; that is beyond what the object calls for, and they are at all events to be deplored, since suffering is in itself an evil; but that these should be alone, or chiefly pitied by those who are comparatively callous to the sufferings from lawless outrage, or apprehended outrage, denotes a most disgraceful and a most dangerous state of the public mind. It is said that in Corsica, and in several of the Italian States, while it is hardly possible, by the offer of any amount of pay, to induce a native to accept the office of public executioner, nothing is more easy than to hire, at a moderate price, men who will be ready at their employer's bidding to assassinate any one he may point out. "He who does an injury to one," says the Latin proverb, "threatens it to many." The sense of *insecurity*, produced by every crime that is committed, is by far its worst result; because uneasiness or distress of mind, from perpetual apprehension, though a less evil in each single case than the actual occurrence of what is dreaded, is an evil which extends to many thousand times more. But for this, even the crime of murder would be but a comparatively insignificant evil. For there is hardly any country in which the whole number of persons murdered annually constitutes more than a very trifling portion of the total number of deaths. But the *apprehension* of being murdered—the feeling that one is in continual peril from the hand of the assassin, is one of the most intolerable evils that man can be exposed to. Any one who will but sufficiently reflect on the sleepless and anxious nights, the harassing anxiety, the distressing alarms, the restless and troublesome precautions,—in short, all the evils implied in a feeling of insecurity, which are inflicted on thousands for every crime actually perpetrated, will be convinced that that person is more truly and properly *compassionate* (to wave all other considerations,) who sets himself to devise means for the protection of the unoffending, than he whose

---

* How many inches of difference are there between the foot of Eldon, Lyndhurst, and Brougham? How would the latter have decided many *equity* cases determined by the former—the case of Shelley's children, for example? But, is it not miserable to have the fortune and happiness of men depend on the weak judgment or caprice of any one individual?

kindly feelings are bestowed chiefly on the violators of the law. And yet the former must prepare himself to expect from the unthinking, who are in most places the majority, to be censured as hard-hearted. In pleading the cause of the innocent in opposition to the guilty—in urging the claims to protection of the peaceable and inoffensive citizen against the lawless plunderer or incendiary, and in wishing that honest men may be relieved from the misery of perpetual terror, by transferring that terror to the evil doer, I am sensible that I expose myself (such is the strangely perverted state of many men's feelings) to the charge of inhumanity.

THE PRESS.

A FREE PRESS has, from the very invention of printing up to the present day, been the constant subject of dread, and the object of enmity and persecution, to all tyrants, and their attendant herds of fawners and sycophants—to all, in short, who "hate the light because their deeds are evil."

The efforts of the talented and philanthropic Buckingham, in the East, have been stifled by the aristocratic Directors of an overgrown and bloated monopoly. The efforts of the Constitutionalists in Spain have met the same fate, though from different hands; and most of the principal promoters of the good cause in that country have either perished on the scaffold, or been murdered in cold blood by the soldiers of the " Beloved Ferdinand ;" or are wandering exiles from their homes, considered as traitors and infidels, and, of course, hated as such, by a brutal and ignorant peasantry, the natural effects of their subjection to, and faith in, a bigoted and crafty priesthood. De Wurtz and the patriots of Germany have also been driven into exile, and thrown into dungeons, by a band of petty tyrants, leagued together for their own interests and the common ill.

The tyrants of India, of Spain, and of Germany, knew full well that their deeds could not stand the scrutiny of "knowledge, with her myriad eyes," and that the press was the most efficient disseminator of that knowledge which was to lay open "their secret ways ;" and they did not hesitate to sacrifice the promoters of freedom in their respective dominions, in order that they might continue their system of oppression and misrule. But a day of retribution is at hand. The nations are awakening to a sense of their strength and of their rights. A change has come o'er the spirit of the time; knowledge is overflowing the boundaries attempted to be set to it; and it is worthy of remark, that those who most strenuously, and apparently most successfully, attempted to stem the fertilizing torrent, will be the first to be swept away by its power. The expiry of the East India Charter is at hand, and it is not likely to be renewed. Shall such arbitrary power over the weal or wo of millions be again trusted to the hands of those who have so much abused it? Shall India be again delivered into the hands of that Company

"Whose minions could despise
The heart-wrung anguish of a thousand cries;
Could lock, with impious hands, their teeming store,
While famished nations died along the shore?"

Will Germany longer submit to her present rulers? Shall the land that gave birth to the Fathers of the Reformation—to the men but for whom we might, even now, have been deprived of the blessings of religious freedom—longer lie at the mercy of some petty tyrants, whose education has kept them in ignorance of the interests and feelings of their people, and who bow and cringe at the nod of the more powerful tyrants of Austria and Prussia?

"Shall blind and despot monarchs quell
The land whence Luther sprung;
Where Klopstok hymned, and Korner fell,
And wizard Schiller sung?"

No! Kings must now live for the people—the people will no longer live for them. Over Burns' "wee bit German lairdies" a storm is about to burst, which, to use the words of an eloquent writer, "shall sweep the puny apes of monarchy and their tinsel state from off the land; and, as sure as there is a God in heaven, there are those now alive who will live to see at least the western half of Germany a republic, 'one and indivisible.'" But, to return to our subject, from which we have wandered so far.

No men could better read the signs of the political horizon than Pitt, and the Ministers of his time ; no men sooner perceived the growing influence and ability of the press, and no men likely to be less scrupulous and unhesitating about the means to trammel her growing strength, and avert the coming storm. Pitt, after taxing the light of God's day, appropriately set about taxing the light of knowledge; and the unjust, oppressive, and partial Taxes on Knowledge, were the result of his philanthropic exertions. This is the " Heaven-born statesman"—this the man

"Whose thrilling trump shall rouse the land,
When fraud and danger are at hand."

Not content with thus limiting the extent of the sphere of the press ; and, to the utmost of their power, virtually denying to the poorer and more industrious portion of the community any knowledge of, and the use of any strictures on, the conduct of their rulers, no threats, promises, or gold were spared, to intimidate, cajole, or bribe this formidable enemy to bad government, to turn the remaining portion of its strength to their own uses, and to make it merely the organ and tool of a despotic government. The free utterance of public opinion, through the press, was stopped for a time; but, since then, the desire for knowledge has advanced with unwearied step in spite of all obstacles—

"In vain they trace the wizard ring ;
In vain they limit mind's unwearied spring ;"

and with that desire the power and influence of the press has increased to an amazing extent. The mass of the talent of the country now seeks a vent through the periodical press. It is undeniably the leader of public opinion, and the ablest descanter on public topics. Its title to these distinctions, and the merits of the various leading journals, we reserve for discussion till another opportunity.

[The above is sent us by an anonymous, or rather an initial correspondent. The communication bears certain marks of juvenility, but is, on the whole, conceived in so hopeful a spirit, that we believe our readers will be gratified with the sentiments expressed. Their appearance has another value. There is no doubt that they are the sentiments of millions of growing minds in this country, and in France and Germany. We are all aware of the seed that has been sowing for half a century, and it is curious to watch its germination.]

The subjoined verses—and it would not be excess of praise to call them sublime—were lately composed by *Elliott of Sheffield*, for the printers of that town, when they celebrated the passing of the Reform Bill, and carried a PRINTING PRESS in triumph in the procession of the trades :—

God said, " Let there be light!"
Grim darkness felt His might,
And fled away.
Then startled seas, and mountains cold,
Shone forth all bright in blue and gold,
And cried, " 'Tis day, 'tis day !"

" Hail, holy light !" exclaim'd
The thunderous cloud, that flamed
O'er daisies white ;
And lo ! the rose, in crimson dress'd,
Lean'd sweetly on the lily's breast,
And blushing, murmur'd " Light !"

Then was the lark upborn ;
Then rose the embattled corn ;
Then streams of praise
Flow'd o'er the sunny hills of noon ;
And when night came, the pallid moon
Pour'd forth her pensive lays.

> Lo, heaven's bright bow is glad!
> Lo, trees and flowers all clad
>   In glory, bloom!
> And shall the immortal sons of God
> Be senseless as the trodden clod,
>   And darker than the tomb?
>
> No! By the MIND of Man!
> By the swart ARTISAN!
>   By GOD, our SIRE!
> Our souls have holy light within,
> And every form of grief and sin
>   Shall see and feel its fire.
>
> By earth, and hell, and heaven,
> The shroud of souls is riven;
>   MIND, MIND alone
> Is light, and hope, and life, and power;
> Earth's deepest night, from this blessed hour,
>   The night of minds, is gone.
>
> The second Ark we bring:
> "The Press!" all nations sing;
>   What can they less?
> Oh, pallid want! oh, labour stark!
> Behold we bring the second Ark—
>   The Press! the Press! the Press!

ON THE PURPOSE SERVED IN THE ECONOMY OF NATURE, BY THE EXPANSION OF WATER INTO A STATE OF ICE, AND HOW THIS EXPANSION WHICH IS AN EXCEPTION TO THE LAW OF OTHER BODIES, ILLUSTRATES THE DIVINE WISDOM.

All substances, when heat is thrown into them, become larger in their dimensions in length, breadth, and thickness, and when the heat is again abstracted, a corresponding contraction takes place; from this it has been considered as a law, that bodies become larger by the addition of, and smaller by the abstraction of caloric. One would expect from this, that the greater the quantity of heat you throw into a body, the greater would be its increase of volume, and the more you cooled any substance, the more it would contract in its dimensions. Generally this is the case; but there is one striking exception, which serves a very important purpose in the economy of nature. In speaking of a law of nature, I do not mean any inherent property of matter, but a law stamped on it by the hand of the Deity: Nature of herself could neither make laws nor put them into execution, were it not for a far greater power, namely, "Nature's God."

Water, in being cooled, decreases in volume, until it arrives at the 40th degree of Fahrenheit; when, instead of contracting further, it begins to expand, and continues to do so, until it assumes the solid condition. On the contrary, on adding caloric to ice, instead of expanding, (as, according to the law one would expect,) it actually contracts until it again arrives at the 40th degree of Fahrenheit, where it throws off this peculiar character and follows the usual law.

Had the Deity made no exception to the general law of expansion,—mark the consequences—when the cold weather of winter had set in with its usual attendant frost, the water on the surface of rivers, lakes, &c. would have been cooled, consequently contracted, and of course would have fallen to the bottom, and again another layer would have been cooled and fallen also, and so on until the whole had become one mass of solid ice, which would have proved fatal to the lives of the animals contained in it; man would have been deprived of fish as a constituent of his food, and no traces of their having once existed would be seen, except, perhaps, in the heart of a block of ice, as the bones of the mammoth just now are found in the earth; for suppose that at the beginning of the world they had been created, long ere this their race would have been extinct, the first intense frost after the creation would have finished their brief existence. Navigation could have made no progress, for the quantity of water would be always very small, not more than sufficient to serve the domestic and manufacturing purposes of mankind. Let us suppose that the whole of the rivers, lakes, &c., in the world are in a solid condition in consequence of intense and continued frost, (which we must admit if no exception to the general law had existed,) and that spring is coming when the sun begins to shine longer and more effectual on our earth, a small portion of ice would be dissolved, which would remain on the surface and prevent the sun's rays from acting on the mass, the heat would now be communicated from particle to particle, (in the same manner as in any other solid, for there would be no currents now, as when in the fluid condition,) one circumstance would add to the smallness of the quantity of water dissolved, namely, its being a very imperfect conductor of heat. Now, just suppose summer is at hand, when the sun's rays are very powerful, and man has to hide himself in the shade to escape their scorching influence, and to this add the influence that the sun would have in the months of Autumn, still the quantity melted would be very small. In a state of things as mentioned above, we would see no stately river emerging from a glass-smooth lake, watering and fertilizing the land through which it wound its devious path, until it was swallowed up in the mighty ocean. The ocean herself would stand still, she would now refuse to obey the calls of the moon, as she was wont; angling, and all the other modes of fishing would be unknown as arts; ship-building, as an art, would also be unknown. Numberless, indeed, are the privations that man would be subjected to, too numerous to be mentioned here.

The very circumstance of these being an exception to this law, proves, that the Deity, at the beginning, in arranging matter, and stamping laws thereon according to the purpose of his mighty plan, was not indifferent as to the comfort of the inhabitants of the earth, and did not create, unthinkingly or without a purpose; but, knowing the consequence of every action, he obviated evils by making exceptions to general laws; and there is none that shows the Divine Wisdom more than this exception to the general law of expansion. When, then, we see such an arrangement, so well calculated for our comfort and furtherance in society, can we for a moment stand on as spectators and not join our feeble voices in thanksgiving to the Great God whose infinite foreknowledge saw beforehand how much such a law, without an exception, would annoy us, and removed the cause of annoyance.—[This is another juvenile essay of good promise.]

STANZAS.
BY DAVID VEDDER.

When the orb of morn enlightens
Hill and mountain, mead and dell;
When the dim horizon brightens,
And the serried clouds dispel;
And the sun-flower eastward bending
Its fidelity to prove,—
Be thy gratitude ascending,
Unto Him whose name is love.

When the vesper-star is beaming,
In the coronet of even;
And lake and river gleaming,
With the ruddy hues of heaven;
When a thousand notes are blending
In the forest and the grove,—
Be thy gratitude ascending,
Unto Him whose name is love.

When the stars appear in millions,
In the portals of the west;
Bespangling the pavilions
Where the blessed are at rest;
When the milky way is glowing
In the cope of heaven above,—
Let thy gratitude be flowing,
Unto him whose name is love.

POETRY FOR THE YOUNG.

THE DOVE SENT FORTH FROM THE ARK.

Go! beautiful and gentle Dove,
   And greet the morning ray,
For lo! the sun shines bright above,
   And night and storm are passed away.
No longer drooping here, confined
   In this cold prison, dwell;
Go! free to sunshine, and to wind,
   Sweet bird, go forth, and fare thee well!

Oh! beautiful and gentle Dove,
   Thy welcome sad will be,
When thou shalt hear no voice of love,
   In murmurs from the leafy tree:
Yet freedom, freedom shalt thou find,
   From this cold prison's cell:
Go thou to sunshine, and to wind;
   Sweet bird, go forth, and fare thee well!

MY BIRTHDAY.

" MY birthday!"—what a different sound
   That word had in my youthful ears!
And now, each time the day comes round,
   Less and less white its mark appears!
When first our scanty years are told,
   It seems like pastime to grow old;
And, as Youth counts the shining links,
   That time around him binds so fast,
Pleas'd with the task, he little thinks
   How hard that chain will press at last.
Vain was the man, and false as vain,
   Who said—" were he ordain'd to run
His long career of life again,
   He would do all that he *had* done."
Ah! 'tis not thus the voice, that dwells
   In sober birthdays, speaks to me;
Far otherwise—of time it tells,
   Lavish'd unwisely, carelessly—
Of counsel mock'd—of talents, made
   Haply for high and pure designs,
But oft, like Israel's incense, laid
   Upon unholy, earthly shrines—
Of nursing many a wrong desire—
   Of wandering after Love too far,
And taking every meteor fire,
   That cross'd my pathway, for his star!
All this it tells, and, could I trace
   Th' imperfect picture o'er again,
With power to add, retouch, efface,
   The lights and shades, the joy and pain,
How little of the past would stay!
How quickly all should melt away—

All—but that Freedom of the Mind,
   Which hath been more than wealth to me;
Those friendships, in my boyhood twined,
   And kept till now unchangingly;
And that dear home, that saving Ark,
   Where Love's true light at last I've found,
Cheering within, when all grows dark,
   And comfortless, and stormy round!   MOORE.

SCRAPS.
ORIGINAL AND SELECTED.

JOHNNY NOTIONS, A RUSTIC ESCULAPIUS.—Besides Mr. " Hornbook of the Clachan," every district in Scotland, thirty or forty years ago, had its rural medical practitioner. In thinly-peopled regions, these may still be found, of both sexes, though the surgical department is generally left to the men, while the old ladies are the consulting physicians. There must be great ignorance and presumption among members of this ungraduated faculty; but only the conceit and bigotry of science can deny that these self-educated physicians, like rare self-educated persons in other professions, sometimes discover knowledge and enlightened experience which may put the regularly-trained practitioner to shame. John Williamson, *alias Johnny Notions*, was some twenty years back the practical philosopher of his parish, South and Mid Yell, in Shetland. He practised inoculation with the greatest success, because his practice was guided by sound principles. His most remarkable proceeding was, allowing the small-pox matter to mellow, or meliorate, by long keeping. First procuring the best matter, he kept it for seven or eight years; and *peatreek* dried it. His only healing-plaster was a cabbage-leaf. Johnny Notions, besides his high faculties, was a tailor, joiner, watch-mender, blacksmith, gunsmith, &c. &c.— a most invaluable kind of person in a rude and unaccommodated society, where the Jack-of-all-Trades is supreme.

THE OLDEN TIME.—The stories told of the fine climate of Scotland, cannot be wholly fabulous. In every country parish the old people remember, or were told, of weather so warm, even in May, that the ploughs were unyoked soon after sunrise. Travelling through the meadows in the loans of Fearn, (a parish in Easter Ross,) in some places drops of honey were seen on the dew on the long grass and plantain, sticking to their shoes, as they walked along on a May morning! In other parts their shoes were oiled, as with cream, in going through the meadows. Sweetness and fatness!—These were the times! When a man could buy a pair of shoes or brogues for 10d., and a stone of cheese for the same money! Unfortunately, a famine, or severe scarcity, sometimes visited these Highland Goshens.

OLD RENTS.—Mr. Fordyce of Ardo, who circumnavigated the globe with Anson, when he took possession of his estate, found the *mansion*-house, and forty acres, let for L.3, 6s. 8d. a-year. Wishing to go abroad again, he offered to renew his tenant's lease, and asked if he would give a rent of L.5. " Na, by my faith; God has gi'en me mair wit," replied the Aberdeen man. In a few years afterwards this farm produced a rent of L.1, 5s. an acre!

A HIGHLAND CURE.

A farmer in the Highlands had a very careless servant, and from the artful manner in which he concealed his faults, it was with considerable difficulty, and not till serious losses had ensued, that they could be discovered. One of his chief crimes consisted in his reckless management of the plough. He did not consider it of much importance whether the soil was regularly turned up or not; he thought it enough if he got the surface to bear an even and proper appearance, so as to conceal the blemishes that were below. With this view, when his plough stumbled upon any impediment, or *jumped* over a part of the furrow, which it ought to have turned up, in the next round or *bout* he took care to make the plough run so deep, as to turn up a sufficient quantity of earth, both for the present furrow, and to cover the part he had previously leaped over. This was a very common occurrence with him; and he seemed to exult in the execution of the deception; for on its completion, he was known frequently to exclaim, " That *haps* that." His master had, in consequence, suffered considerable detriment. He had tried every means he could think of for reclaiming his servant from the error of his ways, but all in vain; and at last he resolved to dismiss him. Before putting this *ultimatum* into execution, however, he wished to make trial of an expedient which had not hitherto occurred to him. One day, while the servant was ploughing, and pursuing his usual practice of *happing*, or covering, his master quietly followed him down one of the furrows. He had not proceeded far when several minor *jumps* occurred; at last the raising and downfall of a great quantity of earth, which extended over a large scar, caused the servant to exclaim, with much emphasis,

"That *haps** that." His master immediately seized him by the collar, took his bonnet from his head, and, with a cane, inflicted a smart blow on the cerebellum. The thunderstruck culprit stood amazed, and it was sometime before either opened their lips. At last the master placed the bonnet on the poor fellow's bruised head, and staring him in the face, said, "That *haps* that." This practical lesson had the desired effect, and reclaimed the servant from his besetting sin. V.

ANECDOTE OF THE REV. EBENEZER ERSKINE.—At one time, after travelling, towards the end of the week, from Portmoak to the banks of the Forth, on his way to Edinburgh, he, with several others, was prevented by a storm from crossing that frith. Thus obliged to remain in Fife during the Sabbath, he was employed to preach, it is believed, in Kinghorn. Conformably to his usual practice, he prayed earnestly in the morning for the divine countenance and aid in the work of the day; but suddenly missing his note-book, he knew not what to do. His thoughts, however, were directed to that command, "Thou shalt not kill;" and having studied the subject with as much care as the time would permit, he delivered a short sermon on it in the forenoon after the lecture. Having returned to his lodging, he gave strict injunctions to the servant that no one should be allowed to see him during the interval of worship. A stranger, however, who was also one of the persons detained by the state of the weather, expressed an earnest desire to see the minister; and having with difficulty obtained admittance, appeared much agitated, and asked him, with great eagerness, whether he knew him, or had ever seen or heard of him. On receiving assurance that he was totally unacquainted with his face, character, and history, the gentleman proceeded to state, that his sermon on the sixth commandment had reached his conscience; that he was a *murderer*; that, being the second son of a Highland laird, he had some time before, from base and selfish motives, cruelly suffocated his elder brother, who slept in the same bed with him; and that now he had no peace of mind, and wished to surrender himself to justice, to suffer the punishment due to this horrid and unnatural crime. Mr. Erskine asked him if any other person knew any thing of his guilt. His answer was, that, so far as he was aware, not a single individual had the least suspicion of it; on which the good man exhorted him to be deeply affected with a sense of his atrocious sin, to make an immediate application to the blood of sprinkling, and to bring forth fruits meet for repentance; but, at the same time, since in Providence his crime had hitherto remained a secret, not to disclose it, or give himself up to public justice. The unhappy gentleman embraced this well-intended counsel in all its parts, became truly pious, and maintained a friendly correspondence with this " servant of the Most High God" in future life. It is added, that after he withdrew, the minister had the happiness to recover the manuscript formerly missing; and, in consequence, preached in the afternoon on the topic he had originally in view.

BENEFIT OF STEAM.—A cry is raised by many against the use of Steam, by its doing away in a great measure the working of the handicraft, and being the means of lowering his wages, maintaining that distress must always be in the country so long as machinery is encouraged, and having a desire, when once the new Parliament meets, that some opposition to machinery will take place. The number of horses in Great Britain for which duty was paid in 1821, was 1,780,000; but an allowance may be made as an increase for the last eleven years, so that the number may be estimated at two millions. Now, supposing that one-half of those horses were set aside in consequence of Steam Carriages, what would be the saving in regard of provisions to the population, estimated at fourteen millions? We shall allow, therefore, for one million of horses, one peck of corn to each in twenty-four hours, no doubt, a great many of them do not get so much; but, on the other hand, many of them get a great deal more. At this rate, therefore, the consumpt would be sixty-two thousand five hundred bolls each day, or four hundred and thirty-seven thousand and five hundred bolls each week, or twenty-two millions eight hundred and twelve thousand and five hundred bolls in one year. What a large quantity, say meal for corn, to be used and consumed by the people of Great Britain annually, instead of being used for food to horses alone. As stated above, the population of Great Britain being fourteen millions, the allowance, therefore, of meal to each individual, from one day old and upwards, to that population, would be twenty-six pecks yearly, or one half peck per week. Further, besides corn to the horses, each horse will consume in twenty-four hours—two stone of hay; this is a very moderate allowance. At this rate the number of stones consumed are two millions per day, or fourteen millions per week, or seven hundred and thirty millions yearly. Allowing, therefore, two hundred stones per acre, on an average, to produce the above quantity, the number of acres would amount to three millions six hundred and fifty thousand acres of land. Now these acres planted with potatoes, and supposing the produce to be twenty bolls per acre, the quantity produced would be twenty-three millions of bolls, being upwards of eighty-three pecks yearly, or one peck and a half per week to each individual.—*Glasgow Chronicle*.

ORCHARDS IN SCOTLAND.—Mr. Cobbett, in his account of Scotland, speaking of the orchards on the banks of the Clyde, says, " an orchard is not a mere matter of ornament or of pleasure here, but of prodigious profit; under the apple and pear-trees are gooseberry or currant bushes, very well managed in general; and these orchards very frequently yield more than a hundred pounds sterling in one year from an English acre of land! Like other things, the fruit here has fallen in price since the time of the panic; and therefore the pecuniary produce of orchards, like that of fields and manufactories, has been greatly diminished. But these orchards are always a source of very considerable income. I think that my friend, Mr. M'Gavin, of Hamilton, told me that his orchard, which is less than an English acre, has yielded him eighty pounds a-year clear money; and it is no uncommon thing for the proprietor of ten or a dozen acres to sell the fruit by auction upon the trees, for something approaching a hundred pounds an acre. In our apple counties no man thinks of any thing but fruit to make cider and perry; here the whole is table fruit, and I have never seen so great a variety of fine apples in England, at one time, as I saw on the table of Mr. Hamilton, of Dalzell House."

A HINT TO SCOTTISH GARDENERS.

The different species of apples, which grow in central Russia, were brought from Astrakhan, Persia, and Kabandia. The European kinds are rare. The apple of *Kirsvek*, though very large, is agreeable to the taste. Some of them weigh more than four pounds. The *transparent apple* thrives in the governments of Vladimir and Moscow; it is said to have been imported from China, but many consider it indigenous to the Crimea. It is so permeable to light that the seeds are seen through it.

It is not a little extraordinary that the gardeners of Rostow, in the government of Jaroslavl, *are superior to any in Europe.* Though unaided by the lights of science, and without resources, contending against a rigorous climate, they supply Petersburg and Moscow with all kinds of early vegetables. It is probable that they are the descendants of a foreign colony. The real Russian gives himself little trouble about such pursuits.—*Malte Brun, Vol. 6.*

Have *these* apples ever been grown in Scotland? Have they ever been tried as to their susceptibilities of cultivation in Scotland? If not, why?

TO CORRESPONDENTS.

Several poems and other communications are received, and will be attended to at leisure. We have little space for fugitive poetry.
The letter of R. P. dated Newcastle, is on a subject near our hearts. It will not be forgotten. To unknown friends in various quarters, we beg to make warm acknowledgments. We have also to acknowledge the receipt of several books, some of which came just as this Number was going to press.

CONTENTS OF NO. XIX.

Political Truths	289
Books of the Month	290
Notes of the Month	296
STORY-TELLER	297
ELEMENTS OF THOUGHT	300
The Press	301
Expansion of Water	302
SCRAPS—Original and Selected:—Johnny Notions, &c.	303

EDINBURGH: Printed by and for JOHN JOHNSTONE, 19, St. James's Square.—Published by JOHN ANDERSON, Jun., Bookseller, 55, North Bridge Street, Edinburgh; by JOHN MACLEOD, and ATKINSON & Co., Booksellers, Glasgow; and sold by all Booksellers and Venders of Cheap Periodicals.

* Hides, conceals.

THE Schoolmaster,
AND
EDINBURGH WEEKLY MAGAZINE.

CONDUCTED BY JOHN JOHNSTONE.

THE SCHOOLMASTER IS ABROAD.—LORD BROUGHAM.

No. 20.—Vol. I.   SATURDAY, DECEMBER 15, 1832.   Price Three-Halfpence.

SHE!
A LATE ADVENTURE IN THE QUEENSFERRY COACH.

One very rainy morning, about a month ago, I was bound on that same journey which occasioned such humorous perplexity, and loss of temper to the worthy laird of Monkbarns; but, happier than that flower of antiquaries, had got on, through wet and dry, smoothly, though singly, glasses up, and rain plashing, the length of Drumsheuch, or of what so lately was Drumsheuch, when the stage halted to pick up outsides and insides. The latter were three men, buttoned to the throat, their bundles under their coat-breast, and not exactly of that appearance which could make a stranger be admired at first sight, on 'Change. One of them, to my serious inconvenience, kept bobbing his head out and in at the window, with all the ease of a Frenchman in a French diligence; but with more reason, as was manifested by such loud inquiries to the driver as "Is she a' right, Geordie?—tak' care o' her, man!" It was not till this had been, at least, ten times repeated before we reached the Dean, that my sympathies were touched, or my curiosity excited. Was she his wife? this nameless *She*, his sister, or daughter? and, above all, what kept her up there in a day when "Mine enemy's dog?" &c. &c. I was always o. a metaphysical turn, though my friends may call it curiosity; and, once excited, my mind could find no rest, till about Blinkbonny, I had solved the difficulty to my own satisfaction, by conjecturing that *She* might be constitutionally apt to become sick, travelling inside of a close carriage. Many ladies are so; and though the appearance of her protector forbade the idea of ladyhood on her part, yet I was adept enough to know, that in point of constitutional delicacy, there is often a wonderful resemblance between those widely different species of womankind—a *female* and a *lady*. On we trundled to Mutton-hole, my companions rather chatty; and though the weather scarce permitted us to hear each other, we, nevertheless, talked of the crops, the cholera, and, inspired by our vicinity, reasoned of the Lord Advocate's chances of becoming our member. Our *steady* driver, made the customary halt hereabout, and my opposite neighbour seized the opportunity of banging up the window to satisfy his tender conjugal solicitude. "All right!" was the satisfactory reply of the driver. But could *She* not answer for herself?—Was she deaf, or dumb? More probably, she was only muffled, and wrapped up to defend herself from the rigour of the day. However this might be, no woman had ever been more blessed in the tender solicitude of a husband; for the anxious interest of my fellow-traveller, I now clearly saw, was of a far more intimate and anxious nature, than any that could be inspired either by calm paternal, or steady brotherly affection. "Do ye think She'll no' be the worse of it?" said my uxorious, opposite neighbour, addressing one of his friends, "she'll get an awfu' shake up there; and it's an even-down pour."

"Tuts! de'il a fears o' her," cried the gruff, unpitying fellow; "it's just a bother to travel with you and her, with the work ye make about her." The poor man sighed or hemmed; again turned up his gaze through the dim glass; and as the rain beat harder and harder, stripped off his great-coat, and bawled to the coachman "to wrap that carefully around her." His friends actually sneered at this simple kind action of the honest affectionate man, and thus effectually raised my feelings:—

"Had *she* not better get inside? was my remark, as we reached Barnton gate. The poor man drew in his head, "Lord bless you, Sir; you're very kind, but there is nae room; she would fill a side herself."

"A Stout Gentlewoman," thinks I to myself, internally smiling; "a female Lambert;" and at once dropping the gallant idea of bringing her inside, to my own expulsion, I also popped my head out of the window to have a peep of her goodly person, but was met in the face by a blash of wet, and a waft of the skirts of her joseph, or other frieze riding-gear.

"I'm fear'd she's no half covered, Geordie!" again bawled the husband. "Will ye hand the umbrell' ower her, man," and as much in kindness to the kind-hearted husband as from any gallantry towards "The Stout Gentlewoman," I offered the cloak which lay across my legs. It was most thankfully accepted, and instantly hoisted aloft through the storm as "the gentleman's cloak for her."

For the next mile, I indulged in a thousand vagrant, bachelor fancies, ruminating on the mysteries of conjugal affection; and the many strange vagaries played by the softer passion; which, in the present instance, had led to a mutual and tender attachment between a *sharg* like my little weazened fellow-traveller, and a female of the tremendous dimensions of *She*. Her size was all I had ascertained for certain, and to that I assorted such features and complexion as pleased my own fancy in "a Stout Gentlewoman;" and on what might have been very false premises, and actually turned out so, made up her parcel of perfections in exact opposition or contradiction to those of her helpmate; since he was withered, lean, dry, swivel-eyed, and of parchment hue, *She* must be fair and florid, as well as plump and voluminous. I speculated at my ease on the known admiration of very small men for strappers of the other sex, and framed a feasible theory for this idiosyncrasy of the dwarfed, based on that broad foundation, man's vanity. I recollected, among my personal acquaintance, several instances of little dapper fellows who loved to perk by the side of a prancer of five feet ten at the least; and thus put in a legal claim to sundry inches nature had otherwise denied them. I remembered Captain Weazel and his lady, and internally went over the scene of Burns's " Wee Apollo."

"Her strapping waist and gaucy middle—
He reach'd nae higher—
Had holed his heart through like a riddle,
An' blawn't on fire."

In the midst of these ruminations, and of a thick pelting shower sweeping across the Firth, the coach stopt at the Ha's. My curiosity was now, if not wound up to a high pitch, yet to one as intense as the case admitted. Out leaped my little nimble neighbour, much agitated, as it appeared to me, about how *She* was safely to descend from her altitude, and out leaped I to view the perilous descent, and, perhaps, lend a hand to the accomplishment of what threatened to be a rather difficult achievement. The unfortunate woman, bulky enough in all conscience, lay doubled up across the top of the coach, buried under cloaks and great-coats. One by one they were tossed off by the active Geordie, whose gallantry, I was aware, had been stimulated by the reiterated promise o. a "something," in reward of extraordinary care; and out *She* came!—Yes! there she stood revealed in her full proportions, an enormous—certainly a monstrously overgrown—

BASS FIDDLE!!

SHE was now on her way to Kinross, to a ball, attended by the two humble violins, which my other fellow-travellers had hugged concealed to their bosoms. The fine bowing nose of the one of these artists, and the elongated chin of the other, might have put any reasonable man on the true scent; but *She* had taken full possession of my imagination, and allowed no room for either doubt or inquiry. I laughed outright as I mentioned my mistake

"My wife!" exclaimed the lord of *She*, "Do ye think I would make such a wark about only a wife? *She's* just my ain Bass; and I'll pit her against ony instrument this side of Lon'on. A wife, indeed!—Haud ye the umbrell' ower her head there, Geordie, down to the boat."

I had the pleasure of crossing the ferry with *She*, and seeing her safely landed on the North side.

TRIENNIAL PARLIAMENTS.
OLD SPEECHES IN PARLIAMENT.
NO. II.

SIR JOHN ST. AUBIN'S SPEECH FOP REPEALING THE SEPTENNIAL ACT.

MR. SPEAKER,

The subject matter of this debate is of such importance, that I should be ashamed to return to my electors, without endeavouring, in the best manner I am able, to declare publicly the reasons which induced me to give my most ready assent to this question.

The people have an unquestionable right to frequent new Parliaments, by ancient usage; and this usage has been confirmed by several laws, which have been progressively made by our ancestors, as often as they found it necessary to insist on this essential privilege.

Parliaments were generally annual, but never continued more than three years, till the remarkable reign of Henry the Eighth. He, sir, was a prince of unruly appetites, and of an arbitrary will; he was impatient of every restraint; the laws of God and man fell equally a sacrifice, as they stood in the way of his avarice, or disappointed his ambition. He therefore introduced long Parliaments, because he very well knew, that they would become the proper instruments of both; and what a slavish obedience they paid to all his measures, is sufficiently known.

If we come to the reign of King Charles the First, we must acknowledge him to be a prince of a contrary temper; he had certainly an innate love for religion and virtue. But here lay the misfortune; he was led from his natural disposition by sycophants and flatterers; they advised him to neglect the calling of frequent new Parliaments, and therefore, by not taking the constant sense of his people in what he did, he was worked up into so high a notion of prerogative, that the Commons, in order to restrain it, obtained that independent fatal power, which at last unhappily brought him to his most tragical end, and at the same time subverted the whole constitution. And I hope we shall learn this lesson from it, never to compliment the crown with any new or extravagant powers, nor to deny the people those rights, which, by ancient usage, they are entitled to; but to preserve the just and equal balance, from which they will both derive mutual security, and which, if duly observed, will render our constitution the envy and admiration of all the world.

King Charles the Second naturally took a surfeit of Parliaments in his father's time, and was therefore extremely desirous to lay them aside. But this was a scheme impracticable. However, in effect he did so; for he obtained a Parliament, which, by its long duration, like an army of veterans, became so exactly disciplined to his own measures, that they knew no other command but from that person who gave them their pay.

This was a safe and most ingenious way of enslaving a nation. It was very well known, that arbitrary power, if it was open and avowed, would never prevail here. The people were therefore amused with the specious form of their ancient constitution; it existed, indeed, in their fancy, but, like a mere phantom, had no substance nor reality in it; for the power, the authority, the dignity of Parliaments were wholly lost. This was that remarkable Parliament which so justly obtained the opprobrious name of the PENSION PARLIAMENT; and was the model from which, I believe, some later Parliaments have been exactly copied.

At the time of the Revolution, the people made a fresh claim of their ancient privileges; and as they had so lately experienced the misfortune of long and servile Parliaments, it was then declared that they should be held frequently. But, it seems, their full meaning was not understood by this declaration; and therefore, as in every new settlement the intention of all parties should be specifically manifested, the Parliament never ceased struggling with the Crown, till the triennial law was obtained; the preamble of it is extremely full and strong; and in the body of the bill you will find the word DECLARED before ENACTED, by which I apprehend, that though this law did not immediately take place at the time of the Revolution, it was certainly intended as declaratory of their first meaning, and therefore stands a part of that original contract under which the constitution was then settled. His Majesty's title to the crown is primarily derived from that contract; and if, upon a review, there shall appear to be any deviations from it, we ought to treat them as so many injuries done to that title. And I dare say, that this House, which has gone through so long a series of services to his Majesty, will at last be willing to revert to those original stated measures of government, to renew and strengthen that title.

But, sir, I think the manner in which the septennial law was first introduced, is a very strong reason why it should be repealed. People, in their fears, have very often recourse to desperate expedients, which, if not cancelled in season, will themselves prove fatal to that constitution which they were meant to secure. Such is the nature of the septennial law; it was intended only as a preservative against a temporary inconvenience; the inconvenience is removed, but the mischievous effects still continue; for it not only altered the constitution of Parliaments, but it extended that same Parliament beyond its natural duration; and therefore carries this most unjust implication with it, That you may at any time usurp the most indubitable, the most essential privilege of the people—I mean that of choosing their own representatives. A precedent of such a dangerous consequence, of so fatal a tendency, that I think it would be a reproach to our statute-book, if that law was any longer to subsist, which might record it to posterity.

This is a season of virtue and public spirit. Let us take advantage of it to repeal those laws which infringe our liberties, and introduce such as may restore the vigour of our ancient constitution.

Human nature is so very corrupt, that all obligations lose their force, unless they are frequently renewed. Long Parliaments become, therefore, independent of the people, and when they do so, there always happens a most dangerous dependence elsewhere.

Long Parliaments give the Minister an opportunity of getting acquaintance with members, of practising his several arts to win them into his schemes. This must be the work of time. Corruption is of so base a nature, that at first sight it is extremely shocking; hardly any one has submitted to it at once; his disposition must be previously understood, the particular bait must be found out with which he is to be allured, and after all, it is not without many struggles that he surrenders his virtue. Indeed, there are some, who will at once plunge themselves into any base action; but the generality of mankind are of a more cautious nature, and will proceed only by leisurely degrees. One or two, perhaps, have deserted their colours the first campaign; some have done it a second; but a great many, who have not that eager disposition to vice, will wait till a third.

For this reason, short Parliaments have been less corrupt than long ones; they are observed, like streams of water, always to grow more impure the greater distance they run from the fountain head.

I am aware it may be said, that frequent new Parliaments will produce frequent new expenses; but I think quite the contrary; I am really of opinion, that it will be a proper remedy against the evil of bribery at elections, especially as you have provided so wholesome a law to co-operate upon these occasions.

Bribery at elections, whence did it arise? Not from country gentlemen, for they are sure of being chosen without it; it was, sir, the invention of wicked and corrupt ministers, who have, from time to time, led weak princes into such destructive measures, that they did not dare to rely upon the natural representation of the people. Long Parliaments, sir, first introduced bribery, because they were worth purchasing at any rate. Country gentlemen, who have only their private fortunes to rely upon, and have no mercenary ends to serve, are unable to oppose it, especially if at any time the public treasure shall be unfaithfully squandered away to corrupt their boroughs. Country gentlemen, indeed, may make some weak efforts; but as they generally prove unsuccessful, and the time of a fresh struggle is at so great a distance, they at last grow faint in the dispute, give up their country for lost, and retire in despair. Despair naturally produces indolence, and that is the proper disposition for slavery. Ministers of State understand this very well, and are, therefore, unwilling to awaken the nation out of its lethargy, by frequent elections. They know that the spirit of liberty, like every other virtue of the mind, is to be kept alive only by constant action; that it is impossible to enslave this nation, while it is perpetually upon its guard. —Let country gentlemen then, by having frequent opportunities of exerting themselves, be kept warm and active in their contention for the public good: this will raise that zeal and spirit, which will at last get the better of those undue influences, by which the officers of the crown, though unknown to the several boroughs, have been able to supplant country gentlemen of great characters and fortune, who live in their neighbourhood.—I do not say this upon idle speculation only. I live in a country where it is too well known, and I appeal to many gentlemen in the House, to more out of it, (and who are so for this very reason,) for the truth of my assertion. Sir, it is a sore, which has been long eating into the most vital parts of our constitution, and I hope the time will come when you will probe it to the bottom. For if a minister should ever gain a corrupt familiarity with our boroughs; if he should keep a register of them in his closet, and by sending down his treasury-mandates, should procure a spurious representation of the people, the offspring of his corruption, who will be at all times ready to reconcile and justify the most contradictory measures of his administration, and even to vote every crude indigested dream of their patron into a law; if the maintainance of his power should become the sole object of their attention, and they should be guilty of the most violent breach of Parliamentary trust, by giving the King a discretionary liberty of taxing the people without limitation or control—the last fatal compliment they can pay to the crown:—if this should ever be the unhappy condition of this nation, the people, indeed, may complain; but the doors of that place where their complaints should be heard, will for ever be shut against them.

Our disease, I fear, is of a complicated nature, and I think that this motion is wisely intended to remove the first and principal disorder. Give the people their ancient right of frequent new elections; that will restore the decayed authority of Parliaments, and will put our constitution into a natural condition of working out her own cure.

Sir, upon the whole, I am of opinion, that I cannot express a greater zeal for his Majesty, for the liberties of the people, or the honour and dignity of this House, than by seconding the motion which the honourable gentleman has made you.

MEDICAL SELECTIONS.
NO. III.
INFLUENCE OF DRESS ON THE SKIN.

As life advances, the respiratory and digestive functions become more developed, and play a more conspicuous part in the support of the animal system. In youth, the skin is still delicate in texture, and the seat of extensive exhalation and acute sensation, but it is at the same time more vigorous in constitution than it was in infancy; and the several animal functions being now more equally balanced, it is less susceptible of disorder from external causes, and can endure with impunity changes of temperature, which, either earlier or later in life, would have proved highly injurious. The activity and restless energy of youth keep up a free and equal circulation even to the remotest parts of the body, and this free circulation in its turn maintains an equality of temperature in them all. Cold bathing and lighter clothing may now be resorted to with a rational prospect of advantage; but when, from a weak constitution or unusual susceptibility, the skin is not endowed with sufficient vitality to originate the necessary reaction, which alone renders these safe and proper,—when they produce an abiding sense of chilliness, however slight,—we may rest assured that mischief will inevitably follow at a greater or shorter distance of time. Many young persons of both sexes are in the habit of going about in winter and in cold weather with a dress light and airy enough for a northern summer, and they think it manly and becoming to do so; but those who are not very strongly constituted suffer a severe penalty for their folly. The necessary effect of deficient circulation and vitality in the skin is to throw a disproportionate mass of blood inwards, and when this condition exists, insufficient clothing perpetuates the evil, until internal disease is generated, and health irrecoverably lost. Insufficient clothing not only exposes the wearer to all the risk of sudden changes of temperature, but it is still more dangerous (because in a degree less marked, and therefore less apt to excite attention till the evil be incurred), in that form which, while it is warm enough to guard the body against extreme cold, is inadequate to preserving the skin at its natural heat. Many youths, particularly females and those whose occupations are sedentary, pass days, and weeks, and months without ever experiencing the pleasing glow and warmth of a healthy skin, and are habitually complaining of chilliness of the surface, cold feet, and other symptoms of deficient cutaneous circulation. Their suffering, unfortunately, does not stop here, for the unequal distribution of the blood oppresses the internal organs, and too often, by insensible degrees, lays the foundation of tubercles in the lungs, and other maladies, which show themselves only when arrived at an incurable stage. Young persons of a consumptive habit will generally be found to complain of this increased sensibility to cold, even before they become subject to those slight catarrhal attacks which are so often the immediate precursors, or rather the first stages, of pulmonary consumption. All who value health, and have common sense and resolution, will therefore take warning from signs like these, and never rest till equilibrium of action be restored. For this purpose, warm clothing, exercise in the open air, sponging with vinegar and water, the warm bath, regular friction with a flesh brush or hair glove, and great cleanliness, are excellent means.

But while sufficiency of clothing is attended to, excessive wrapping up must be as as carefully avoided. Warmth ought not to be sought for in clothing alone. The Creator has made exercise essential as a means; and if we neglect this, and seek it in clothing alone, it is at the risk or rather certainty of weakening the body, relaxing the surface, and rendering the system extremely susceptible of injury from the slightest accidental exposures, or variations of temperature and moisture. Many good constitutions are thus ruined, and many nervous and pulmonary complaints brought on, to embitter existence, and to reduce the sufferer to the level of a hot-house plant.

Female dress errs in an another important particular, even when well suited in material and in quantity. From the tightness with which it is made to fit on the upper part of the body, not only is the insensible perspiration injudiciously and hurtfully confined, but that free play between the dress and the skin, which is so beneficial in gently stimulating the latter by friction on every movement of the body, is altogether prevented, and the action of the cutaneous nerves and vessels, and consequently the heat generated, is rendered lower in degree, than would result from the same dress worn more loosely. Every part and every function is thus linked so closely with the rest, that we can neither act wrong as regards one organ without all suffering, nor act right without all sharing in the benefit.

EFFECTS OF COLD FEET AND DAMP.

We can now appreciate the manner in which wet and cold feet are so prolific of internal disease, and the cruelty of fitting up schools and similar places without making adequate provision for the welfare of their young occupants. The circumstances in which wet and cold feet are most apt to cause disease, are where the person remains inactive, and where, consequently, there is nothing to counterbalance the unequal flow of blood which then takes place from the feet and surface towards the internal parts: For it is well known, that a person in ordinary health may walk about or work in the open air with wet feet for hours together without injury, provided he put on dry stockings and shoes immediately on coming home. It is therefore not the mere state of wetness that causes the evil, but the check to perspiration and the unequal distribution of blood to which the accompanying coldness gives rise. Wet and damp are more unwholesome to the feet than to other parts, chiefly because they receive a larger supply of blood to carry on a higher degree of perspiration, and because their distance from the heart or centre of circulation diminishes the force with which this is carried on, and thus leaves them more susceptible of injury from external causes. They are also more exposed in situation than other parts of the skin; but cold or wet applied any where, as to the side, for instance, either by a current of air or by rain, is well known to be pernicious.

USE OF FLANNEL.

The advantages of wearing flannel next the skin are easily explicable on the above principles. Being a bad conductor of heat, flannel prevents that of the animal economy from being quickly dissipated, and protects the body in a considerable degree from the injurious influence of sudden external changes. From its presenting a rough and uneven, though soft surface, to the skin, every movement of the body in labour or in exercise, causes, by the consequent friction, a gentle stimulus to the cutaneous vessels and nerves, which assists their action and maintains their functions in health; and being at the same time of a loose and porous texture, flannel is capable of absorbing the cutaneous exhalations to a larger extent than any other material in common use. In some very delicate constitutions, it proves even too irritating to the skin, but, in such cases, fine fleecy hosiery will in general be easily borne, and will greatly conduce to the preservation of health. Many are in the custom of waiting till winter has fairly set in before beginning to wear flannel. This is a great error in a variable climate like ours, especially when the constitution is not robust. It is during the sudden changes from heat to cold, which are so common in autumn, before the frame has got inured to the reduction of temperature, that protection is most wanted, and flannel is most useful.

VENTILATION.

The exhalation from the skin being so constant and extensive, its bad effects, when confined, suggest another rule of conduct, viz. that of frequently changing and airing the clothing, so as to free it from every impurity. It is an excellent plan, for instance, to wear two sets of flannels, each being worn and aired by turns, on alternate days. The effect is at first scarcely perceptible to the senses, but in the course of time its advantages and comfort become very manifest, as the writer of this has amply experienced. For the same reason, a practice common in Italy merits universal adoption. Instead of making up beds in the morning the moment they are vacated, and while still saturated with the nocturnal exhalations which, before morning, become sensible even to smell in a bed-room, the bed-clothes are thrown over the backs of chairs, the mattresses shaken up, and the windows thrown open for the greater part of the day, so as to secure a thorough and cleansing ventilation. This practice, so consonant to reason, imparts a freshness which is peculiarly grateful and conducive to sleep, and its real value may be inferred from the well-known fact, that the opposite practice carried to extremes, as in the dwellings of the poor, where three or four beds are often huddled up in all their impurities in a small room, is a fruitful source of fever and bad health, even where ventilation during the day and nourishment are not deficient. In the abodes of the poor Irish residing in Edinburgh, we have seen bedding for fourteen persons spread over one floor not exceeding twelve feet square, and when morning came, the beds were huddled above one another to make sitting room during the day, and at night were again laid down, charged with accumulated exhalations. If fever were not to appear in such circumstances, it would be indeed marvellous; and we ought to learn from this, that if the extreme be so injurious, the lesser degree implied in the prevalent practice cannot be wholesome, and ought, therefore, not to be retained, when it can be so easily done away with.

ABLUTION AND BATHING.

Another condition of health in the skin is frequent ablution. The liquid portion of the perspiration, being in the form of vapour, easily passes off with ordinary attention to change of clothing and cleanliness; but its saline and animal elements are in a great measure left behind, and, if not removed by washing or friction, they at last both interrupt perspiration, and irritate the skin. Those who are in the habit of using the flesh-brush daily, are at first surprised at the quantity of white dry scurf which it brings off; and those who take a warm bath for half an hour at long intervals, cannot fail to have noticed the great amount of impurities which it removed, and the feeling of grateful comfort which its use imparts. The warm, tepid, cold, or shower bath, as a means of preserving health, ought to be in as familiar use as a change of apparel, for it is equally a measure of necessary cleanliness. Many, no doubt, neglect this, and enjoy health notwithstanding, but many, very many, suffer from its omission; and even the former would be benefited by it in point of feeling. The perception of this truth is gradually extending, and warm baths are now to be found in fifty places for one in which they could have been obtained twenty years ago. Still, however, we are far behind our continental neighbours in this respect. They justly consider the bath as a necessary of life, while we still regard it as a luxury.

Many entertain a prejudice against the use of the tepid or warm bath, from an apprehension of catching cold after it. This fear is groundless, if ordinary precautions be used; and extensive experience warrants this assertion. Like other good things, it may be abused, or taken at improper times; but, when used judiciously, it will often remove incipient colds, and in severe cases, after the feverish state begins to yield, the bath promotes recovery very much, by equalizing the circulation, and relieving the internal organs, as well as by restoring perspiration. We, therefore, hope to see it speedily rank as an indispensable part of every family establishment.

If the bath cannot be had at all places, soap and water may be obtained every where, and leave no apology for neglect; or, if the constitution be delicate, water and vinegar, or water and salt, used daily, form an excellent and safe means of cleansing and gently stimulating the skin to vigorous and healthy action; and to the invalid, they are highly beneficial, when the nature of the indisposition does not render them improper. A rough, rather coarse, towel is a very useful auxiliary to such ablutions. Few of those who have steadiness enough to keep up the action of the skin by the above means, will ever suffer from colds, sore throats, or such like complaints; while, as a means of restoring health, they are often incalculably serviceable. If one-tenth of the persevering attention and labour bestowed to so much purpose in rubbing down and currying the skins of horses, were bestowed by the human race in keeping themselves in good condition, and a little attention were paid to diet and clothing, colds, nervous diseases, and stomach complaints, would cease to form so large an item in the catalogue of human miseries. But man studies the nature of other animals, and adapts his conduct to their constitution. Himself alone he continues ignorant of, and neglects. He considers himself a rational and immortal being, and therefore not subject to the laws of organization which regulate the functions of the inferior animals; but this conclusion is the result of ignorance and pride, and not a just inference from the premises on which it is pretended to be founded. [From an article on the skin in the Phrenological Journal for December.]

A DECEMBER EVENING WITHIN DOORS.

Picture to yourself, gentle reader, one of those blustering nights, when a boisterous gale from the south-west, with rattling rain, threatens almost the demolition of everything in its way; but add to the scene, a snug and secure cottage in the country, the day closed, the fire blazing, the curtains drawn over the window, a barricadoing of window-shutters, which defy the penetration of Eolus, with all his angry host, the table set for tea, and the hissing urn or kettle scarce heard among the fierce whistling, howling, and roaring, produced alternately, or together, by almost every species of sound that wind can produce in the chimneys and door crannies of the house. There is a feeling of comfort, and a sensibility to the blessings of a good roof over one's head, and a warm and comfortable hearth, while all is tempest without, that produces a peculiar but real source of pleasure. Two or three intelligent friends sitting up over a good fire, and interchanging their thoughts on a thousand subjects of mystery, the stories of ghosts, and the tales of olden times, may perhaps beguile the hours of a stormy night like this, with more satisfaction than they would a midsummer evening.—*Mirror of Months.*

ON ASCERTAINING THE PRICES OF GRAIN, AND STRIKING THE FIARS.

Although the laws regarding the importation and exportation of grain have been a very frequent subject of discussion in Britain for upwards of two centuries, and their regulations have been founded, in a great measure, on the prices of grain in this country, the means for ascertaining these prices are still very imperfect. If we compare the average prices, as set down in documents, which are generally appealed to as authoritative, we find discrepancies which we cannot reconcile; and as there are no means of ascertaining from what causes they arise, our reliance on such documents is necessarily much shaken. The accounts of the prices of middling wheat in Windsor market, as ascertained by the audit books of Eton College, are generally referred to by historians, political economists, and writers on statistics. They have been kept regularly since the year 1646, and they form the record most to be relied on, for the prices of wheat for the latter half of the 16th, and the whole of the 17th century. But if we compare this account with the return of prices laid before Parliament in 1814, by the receiver of corn returns, we will observe very great discrepancies, as will appear from the following list:—

	Price at Windsor.	By Return.
1792	L.2 13 0	L.2 2 11
1800	6 7 0	5 13 7
1805	4 7 10	4 8 0
1809	5 6 0	4 15 7
1811	5 8 0	4 14 6

In comparing the prices of English and Scotch grain, we also find much greater differences than we could previously expect. It was proved, by the evidence of Mr. Turnbull, one of the witnesses examined before the committee of the House of Commons on agriculture in the year 1814, that good Scotch wheat sold in general as high as the average price of English wheat. Thus the average price of the wheat produced on his farm, near Dunbar, for crops 1805, 1812, was 94s., while the average of English wheat for that period was 92s. 7d. Yet, in the return of the average prices of Scotch wheat laid before Parliament, we find the price for 1792, 39s. 4d., for 1800, 91s. 2d., for 1805, 53s. 7d., for 1809, 73s. 7d., for 1811, 78s. 10d. In 1814 the price of English wheat is set down at 74s., while that of Scotch is 96s. 2d. The variations in the price of other kinds of grain are, perhaps, still more remarkable, as will appear from the following table of the price of oats :—

	English average.	Scotch average.
1808	L.1 13 8	L.1 7 1
1809	1 12 8	1 13 10
1810	1 9 4	1 12 1
1812	2 4 0	1 4 6
1814	1 6 6	1 17 9
1817	1 12 1	1 3 8

The prices of barley, pease, &c., vary in the same manner. What we have chiefly in view at present is, to direct the attention of our readers to the anomalies in the fiar prices of grain for Scotland. The purpose of striking the fiars, originally was, in order to ascertain the amount in money of the rents and feu-duties due to the crown, many of which are payable in grain.—Formerly they were struck by the Lords of the Exchequer, from the information received from the sheriffs of the different counties. But about the beginning of the 17th century, the duty was devolved, at least in some of the counties, upon the sheriffs themselves. The sheriff fiars for the county of Haddington are extant since the year 1627, and of the county of Edinburgh from 1640. To regulate the manner of striking the fiars, the Court of Session passed an act of sederunt, on the 21st December, 1723. This act provides that the sheriffs shall, between the 4th and 20th February, yearly, summon before them a competent number of persons who have knowledge and experience of the trade of victual in their bounds, and from these persons they are ordered to choose fifteen, of whom not fewer than eight shall be heritors, as a jury to fix the prices of grain of the preceding crop. Proper witnesses are also to be summoned to give evidence as to the prices of grain, more especially since 1st Nov. preceding, and any person in Court, though not summoned, may offer information to the jury. The jury prepare a verdict setting forth the prices, and the sheriff must, before the 1st March, pronounce his sentence according to the verdict. In this manner the fiar prices for each crop are appointed to be struck. The practice also of ascertaining the prices of the different qualities of grain was ordered to be continued, and to be introduced into the counties where it had not previously been observed. These regulations, seem well adapted to attain the object in view. But it may well be doubted how far the Court of Session had the power to enact them. In many counties little or no attention was paid to the act, and although one or two attempts have been made to set aside the fiars of particular counties, on the ground that they were erroneously struck, these attempts have been unsuccessful.

The object of fixing three fiar prices of each kind of grain, is to distinguish the prices of the different qualities. But the method practised is obviously very rude. To proceed with any degree of accuracy, the quality of the grain should be ascertained before any inquiry is made about the price. But instead of proceeding in this way, no inquiry whatever is made about the quality, which is inferred solely from the price. Now, were the prices of grain for each crop perfectly steady, there would be no great objection to this practice; but as the markets are continually fluctuating, it may, and indeed must happen, that the prices of the first quality of grain are taken into computation to fix the second or third fiars, and the prices of the worst quality to fix the second or first. Suppose, for instance, as happened last year, that the price falls from October until the time of striking the fiars, that the second fiars are fixed at 60s. for wheat, and that the prices at the beginning of the season were 66s., 64s., and 62s. for the three qualities, then the third quality of grain is taken into computation in fixing the price of the first quality, because it is sold above 60s. If, on the other hand, the price of grain rises between September and March, then the prices of the first quality of grain are taken into computation in fixing the fiars of the third quality. Where prices vary much between harvest and the striking of the fiars, it is evident that the mode of proceeding at Haddington makes the first and third fiars utterly fictitious. It would be tedious to examine the mode of proceeding in striking the fiars in other counties; but we may merely point out the discrepancies that exist among the different returns for the same year, which can only arise from different modes of proceeding. Thus it would naturally be expected that the fiars of the county of Edinburgh would be higher than those of other counties, from the great consumption of grain which takes place in the capital; and in point of fact, the prices there are generally higher than in Haddington, by one or two shillings a quarter, on account of the expense of carriage. The East Lothian farmers therefore sell a great part of their crops in Edinburgh, merely on account of the higher price, notwithstanding the distance they must bring their grain. Yet the Edinburgh fiars for the *best* grain are generally lower than those of East Lothian for the *second*. Thus for the years 1827, 1828, 1829, and 1830, the price of the *best* wheat in the county of Edinburgh, as ascertained by the fiars, is 48s. 8d., 76s., 52s. 7d. In the county of Haddington, the *second* fiars for these years were 48s. 11d., 70s. 6d., 55s., 59s. 11d., and the first fiars 4s. or 5s. above these prices. Wheat of as good quality in ordinary years is produced in Fife as in East Lothian, yet a rental of 500 quarters of wheat in the former county, for the three crops 1828-1830, would have produced L.650 less than an equal rental in the latter county, converting the wheat into money at the highest fiars of each county. This is a difference of 15 per cent. In some counties only one fiar price for each kind of grain is struck, in others there are two, in others three. In some, the different species of grain are distinguished as white and red wheat, Angus and potato oats. In the county of Caithness, four species of oats are distinguished. In others the species of the grain is disregarded, but the place where it grows makes a distinction. Thus in Berwickshire we have the Merse grain distinguished from Lammermuir; in Stirlingshire and Clackmananshire we have Kerse barley, Dryfield barley, and Muir barley; in Aberdeenshire and Kincardineshire the only distinction is, "with or without fodder." As a farther source of confusion, the fiars in some of the counties are set down in Imperial bushels; in others in Imperial quarters; in Berwickshire, again, the quantity is four Imperial bushels. In Orkney, the Sheriff makes his return by the Norwegian *meil* and the malt *pundlar*, weights which, for the benefit of the denizens of the south, he explains, contain respectively 177 lb. 12 oz. and 116 lb. 7 oz. We presume the remoteness of the worthy sheriff's jurisdiction has prevented him from learning that some seven years ago an act was passed by the British Parliament, introducing a new measure, and that it is part of his duty to enforce the provisions of that act, and not to give an example of its violation in his own proceedings.

We believe that we have said enough to convince every one that the mode of striking the fiars calls loudly for alteration; but if farther evidence is required, it will only be necessary to refer to the fiar prices of grain for different counties, for the same year, and it will be found that a difference of 10 or 12 per cent in the prices of the same kind and quality of grain is by no means uncommon. Now, this is a serious consideration to many individuals. The whole stipends of the parochial clergy are now modified in grain; and as these stipends are converted, in terms of the 48 Geo. III. chap. 138, at the highest fiars of the county where the parish is situated, it will be found, upon calculation, that of two clergymen having the same stipend in victual, there will be a difference in some instances of 20 per cent. A clergyman is on this account obviously in a much better condition when there are three fiars struck in his county than when there is only one. It is very usual also, to stipulate for rents in grain, the conversion into money taking place at the highest fiars. This is now become a common practice in East Lothian, and in many other districts. Now, an East Lothian farmer, who pays in this manner, will find that by the mode of striking the fiars in that county he pays nearly 10 per cent of rent more than he ought to do, and for twenty years' possession of his farm, he will pay twenty-two years' rent. The difference between a rent paid by the fiars in East Lothian and Fife is still greater.

In order to put an end to the confusion and injustice which exist, one uniform system should be adopted for the whole of Scotland. Why should a clergyman in one county receive one-fifth less stipend than his neighbour in the adjoining county, when it was intended by awarding both the same quantity of victual, to put them on an equal footing? The clergy should be paid as nearly as possible alike where their duties are equal. On this account, as well as for several other reasons, a general average for the whole of Scotland, of the prices of grain, should be annually ascertained and published. By this general average the clergy ought to be paid. It is also expedient to ascertain the average price of the different species, varieties, and qualities of grain; but the present mode is highly objectionable. There appears to be only one mode of proving such prices accurately. This is to distinguish the different species and permanent varieties of grain, as red and white wheat, barley and beer, or bigg, Angus and black oats, and making an average for each species and variety; and further, to distinguish the quality of the grain by the weight. It is well known that the great test of the value of grain is its specific gravity,—the part which yields the flour or meal being much heavier in an equal bulk than the husk or skin. Thus, wheat of a particular species, which weighs 64 lbs. per bushel, is worth several shillings a-quarter more than wheat of the same species which weighs only 60 lbs. per bushel. Unless the weight is given it is impossible to ascertain, without samples, the value of grain of different years, or even of different counties, or, what is generally of more importance, the prices of grain in England and Scotland. Of what value, for instance, is the information that wheat sold in Mark Lane from 50s. to 70s. a-quarter, or how can a corn merchant send grain there with safety, unless he knows what is the current price of the quality of grain he has on hand? The mere quantity, by measurement, of grain is so little relied on, as the means of ascertaining the value, that it is now the practice in Glasgow, as well as in Ireland, and in many districts of England, to sell not by the measure, but by the weight; and undoubtedly weight is, in this instance, a much better criterion of value than measure. But both combined form the only true mode of fixing the value; for a quarter of wheat which weighs 496 lbs. is much more valuable than a larger measure of wheat of the same species, which is precisely the same weight. The introduction of the practice of purchasing grain by weight, however, is leading to much confusion, and which will soon put an end to all the benefit expected from the equalization of weights and measures, for in each town different weights of grain are selling as equivalent to an imperial quarter. This is shown by the following table:—

	Wheat.	Oats.	Barley.
Birmingham	496 lb.	312 lb.	per measure.
Manchester	560	360	480
Glasgow	460	528	640
Malton	560 (per stone of 14 lbs.)	448
Wakefield	480	ditto	504

These weights are reckoned a quarter in the different towns. (Westminster Review, No. 31, p. 70.) If this system is allowed to become general, it will be impossible for any one to say, without a minute calculation, for which he may not always have the data, what is the price of grain in a different part of the country. It humbly appears to us, that all grain should be sold by the imperial quarter, that the species and permanent varieties should be distinguished, and two or three qualities of each species distinguished by the weight. We suggest the following scale for the ordinary white wheat:—

First quality, per imperial bushel, 63 lbs. and upwards.
Second quality, per ditto, between 60 and 63 lbs.
Third quality, per ditto, 60 lbs., and under.

If we had a list of the weights, as well as of the prices of grain, for the last two centuries, it would have been most valuable in shewing the effect of improvements in agriculture, in ameliorating the quality of grain, and it would have enabled us to judge much more accurately, than we can do at present, of the prices at different periods. In a very bad year we would have no grain of the first quality, in a very good year little or none of the third. We would thus see, at a single glance of the table of average prices, the nature of the seasons, in as far as grain was concerned.

The grain consumed in Great Britain and Ireland exceeds, in value, one hundred millions annually. In 1818, we paid more than ten millions to foreigners for grain, and the sums paid during the last year probably exceed seven millions. It is surely of some consequence to ascertain, with some degree of accuracy, the price of a commodity, on which we expend a fourth or a fifth of the value of the total annual produce of the country. It is justly considered an object of importance to observe and register, in every part of the country, the daily and annual fall of rain, even to the hundredth part of an inch. The oscillations of the barometer have been ascertained, for every day, for a century, and they have even been observed for every hour for a whole twelvemonth. The daily, monthly, and yearly temperature of many parts of the country is known with the utmost accuracy, and the information is carefully recorded, and quickly published. These observations have properly engaged the attention of learned societies, and of ingenious individuals; and it would be disgraceful not to be acquainted with the physical condition of our country. But is it not shameful, that no attempt has been made to ascertain the prices of grain with precision? It is an object surely as important, even in a scientific point of view, as the measuring the quantity of rain, the observing of the oscillations of the barometer, or the recording of the variations of the thermometer, for it is of the greatest consequence to the sciences of political economy and agriculture. Besides, until the average prices of grain are more accurately fixed, the merchant must carry on his speculations, in a great measure, in the dark; the landed proprietors, the clergy, and the tenantry, must be continually exposed to injustice in their payments and receipts, and the duties on grain, which often virtually prohibit its importation, cannot be properly ascertained.

THE GOOD OLD TIMES.—The celebrated patriot, Andrew Fletcher of Saltoun, draws the following picture of Scotland in the year 1698—from which it would appear that it was not without reason that King James composed a ballad on " the Gaberlunzie Man," for the beggars were anciently a very formidable race. " There are at this day in Scotland," says Fletcher, " (besides a great many poor families very meanly provided for by the Church boxes, with others, who by living upon bad food fall into various diseases) two hundred thousand people begging from door to door. And though the number of them be double to what it was formerly, by reason of this great distress, yet in all times there have been about one hundred thousand of those vagabonds, who have lived without any regard or subjection either to the laws of the land, or even those of God and nature." These free-and-easy denizens of the soil appear to have occasionally held a sort of wild saturnalia :—" In years of plenty, continues our author, " many thousands of them meet together in the mountains, where they feast and riot for many days; and at country weddings, markets, and burials, and at other the like public occasions, they are to be seen, both men and women, perpetually drunk, cursing, blaspheming, and fighting together." As a remedy to this great mischief, Fletcher proposes, " that every man of a certain estate in the nation should be obliged to take a proportionabl number of those vagabonds, and either employ them in hedging and ditching his grounds, or any other sort of work in town or country." And for example and terror of these formidable " vagabonds," he gravely adds—" Three or four hundred of the most notorious of those villains which we call Jockeys might be presented by the government to the state of Venice, to serve in their gallies against the common enemy of Christendom." This was certainly a radical reform. On perusing the above extracts, it is impossible not to be struck with the contrast which our happy country now presents—her population virtuous and industrious, excelling in all the arts, and her remotest wilds penetrated by that civilization and commerce which have ever been the parents of freedom, peace, and plenty.

A LATE SWISS ADVENTURE.
(For the Schoolmaster.)

My friend pointed out the scene of an adventure of one of his friends, which had nearly proved fatal to him. The Swiss are essentially mountain climbers; armed with a long pole, they dart off wherever the thought strikes them, to climb some point which they perceive, fifty miles off, towering into the third heavens. Of these, Mr. Hutzler is one of the most adventurous. A few years ago he started from Zurich to climb the Titles, and resolved to take the nearest way to it, crossing the Lake of Lucerne, and going over the mountains of Unterwalden in a direction never before attempted. He had a friend with him; and on getting to Unterwalden, he engaged two guides, who engaged to conduct them to the top of the mountain opposite the Titles; but when they got there, they found that there was a precipice of nearly 2000 feet to descend before the foot of their object could be obtained. One of the guides refused to go on. The other, a young man of great strength and desperate courage, made the attempt to descend, and returned to say that he thought he could get down; but if they wished to follow him, they must have good heads. After a consultation of some time, they determined all four to make the attempt. The young man followed, led by his dog, an animal which was renowned for its skill in descending and mounting the most difficult passes, and by the other guide and the amateurs. When he had got 500 feet down, the first guide stopped, as did they all; for they had been labouring with the most painful exertions to descend from one ledge of rock, a few inches wide, to another, until now nothing appeared below but one enormous precipice, nearly perpendicular, of 1500 feet. After a short pause, and seeing the impossibility of retracing their steps, they braced their failing courage, and addressed themselves anew to the task. Their young guide appeared more like a chamois than a man—hanging occasionally by the fingers, and supporting himself on points of rock not half the breadth of his shoe; and he shortly left his friends greatly behind. They heard the dog occasionally whining, as if in distress; but still they toiled on, until they got about half way down, when they heard a rustling noise, joined to the groans of the poor dog, who had lost his footing, and was now scrambling to regain it; but in vain—down, down he went, struggling hard for life, while they eyed him in mute despair. At length, a long-continued howl told them he had cleared the rock, and was descending through the air; they watched his long descent, until the hollow sound of a body falling at an immense distance below, told them all was over. When they turned their eyes on each other, they saw despair and death in each pale countenance; and for a moment hope forsook them. They had a thousand feet of precipice below them, and an equal distance above; their strength and courage were exhausted, and they appeared to give up all hope of life. The young guide was the first to recover; he groaned for the loss of his faithful dog, and set off down the rocks with a speed and desperation which set death and peril at defiance. They looked on, expecting every moment to see him follow the course of his faithful friend; but, to their astonishment, they saw him in a short time seated beside the poor animal on the slope below. This renewed hope within them; and again they started; and, after incredible dangers and difficulties, they all got safely down, and returned thanks to God for their escape. An old guide came up from the other side, and bitterly reproached the young one for his temerity, accusing him of treachery and murder, as no one who regarded the life of himself, or others, would attempt such a precipice. The young one listened in gloomy silence, took up the dead dog, tied him across his shoulders, and, as if in mockery of the old one, took his way up the very path he had descended; and they saw him reach the top in safety.

THE SWISS GIRL.

———— How blest
The Helvetian girl, who daily braves,
In her light skiff, the tossing waves,
And quits the bosom of the deep
Only to climb the rugged steep!
Say whence that modulated shout?
From wood-nymph of Diana's throng?
Or does the greeting to a rout
Of giddy Bacchanals belong?
Jubilant outcry!—rock and glade
Resounded—but the voice obey'd
The voice of an Helvetian maid.

Her beauty dazzles the thick wood;
Her courage animates the flood;
Her step the elastic greensward meets,
Returning unreluctant sweets;
The mountains (as ye heard) rejoice
Aloud, saluted by her voice!
Blythe Paragon of Alpine grace,
Be as thou art; for through thy veins
The blood of heroes runs its race!
WORDSWORTH.

THE BOAR SONG.

Bring me the hunter's goblet deep;
    It holds a flask and more:—
But a single quaff shall drain it off,
    To pledge the mighty Boar!
For to-morrow's field this cup of the Rhine
    Thy prowess shall restore:
Oh! never should less than a flask be thine,
    To pledge the mighty Boar!
(Chorus.)—A flask of wine from the sunny Rhine,
    To pledge the mighty Boar!

We have not chased the coward fox,
    Nor slain the feeble hare:—
A noble prey was our's to-day,
    When the wild swine left his lair.
He fell not by rifle, he fell not by hound,
    Nor by six-foot spear he fell:—
'Twas the hunter's glaive that dealt his wound;
    Be the hunter's song his knell!
(Chorus.)—His pledge be the wine of the sunny Rhine,
    And the hunter's song his knell!

Peril is on the antlered brow,
    While lowered for the fray:
And steady the hand that guides the brand,
    When it strikes the stag at bay.
And the villain wolf has a sharp white fang,
    When he turns on the woodman's edge;
But we honour not his dying pang,
    Nor give him the goblet's pledge.
(Chorus.)—No flask of wine from the sunny Rhine,
    To wolf or stag we pledge!

Nor stalwart arm, nor stedfast heart,
    Are ever needed more
Than when hunters kneel, with levelled steel,
    To receive the rushing Boar.
'Tis thus the serf should crook the knee
    Across his Tyrant's path;
Bending his brow in mockery,
    And pointing his sword in wrath.
(Chorus.)—Then fill the wine from the sunny Rhine,
    To pledge the freeman's wrath!

Speed now! The hunter's feast array!
    Bring on the vanquished Boar!
With vine leaves spread his grisly head,
    The king of the chase before!
To him—he slew the fierce wild swine—
    One princely cup we pour;
And a second from the sunny Rhine,
    We pledge to that mighty Boar!
(Chorus.)—A flask of wine from the sunny Rhine,
    We pledge to that mighty Boar!

Tait's Magazine.

THE STORY-TELLER.

THE TWO SCOTCH WILLIAMS.*
BY MRS. JOHNSTONE.

SOME evenings passed, in which the Stories told around The Round Table were more profitable than generally attractive to part of the juvenile audience. They were stories from Ancient Indian and Egyptian History—of pyramids and pagodas, and of times and people, whose customs, and whose very existence as nations, is long since past, and almost forgotten; and when the ballot fell on the Scottish Boy, Norman Gordon, there was general satisfaction; for they anticipated a Tale of "The North Countrie," a wild legend of ghost, or fay, of Lowland faith and courage, or of Highland chivalry and clanship. The young Scot earnestly whispered Mrs. Herbert, whose gentle manners and maternal kindness had inspired him with confidence, which surmounted his natural and national bashfulness. Her smiles and whispers of approbation, gave him courage to proceed, which he did unceremoniously as follows:—

"To be sure, Miss Sophy, I could tell of ghosts and kelpies, and the Linn of Dee, and a hundred places; but I won't. My story shall be of MEN, and if you shouldn't like it, it does not take long a-telling; or rather I shall read it, like the lazy preachers in my country, who fancy it better to read than make the prose halt. My tale was written out for me by my first tutoress, my Aunt Mary, who was as good an aunt as your aunt Gibbons, Miss Fanny; though instead of Westminister she lived in Old Aberdeen."

The boy was told that no apology was necessary for the sin of reading; and he produced his little MS. book, prefacing his lecture by these words:—"Ladies and Gentlemen of The ROUND TABLE, you are to know that my poor country, Old Scotland, still not wealthy, was, in the higher and inland districts, about the beginning of the last century, very poor indeed. Any one of you would have laughed to see the miserable, black, long cottages, in which those who called themselves, thought themselves, *felt* themselves *gentlemen*, lived at that time:—and now I read."

In one of the most sterile, moorland parishes, a region of heather and moss, in the Upper Ward of Clydesdale, lived an honest, poor couple, who, among several children, had a son, named William, a lively, intelligent, and active boy, whom his mother loved, and the neighbours liked. When William had been at school for about five years, though occasionally away at herding, at peats, or harvest work, his parents, having other children to educate, began to grudge the expenses of William's learning, for what with one branch and another, he cost them nearly two shillings a quarter. It was fortunate that the schoolmaster's conscience compelled him, about this time, to declare, that he could do no more for William. He was *Dux* of the school, read Horace well, and Homer tolerably, and his penmanship was a marvel in the Upper Ward,—which, however, was not saying much. It would be a shame, and a sin, to consign such bright parts and high classical attainments to the plough-tail. William's parents were very willing to believe this; and as an opportunity offered to place him as an apprentice with a small surgeon apothecary,

* NIGHTS OF THE ROUND TABLE. Second Series. Just Published: —OLIVER AND BOYD, Edinburgh; and SIMPKIN AND MARSHALL, London.

a friend of the schoolmaster's, in the city of Glasgow, his whole kindred made a push to raise the supplies necessary to make "Willie a doctor." One aunt gave a pair of home-knit hose perhaps; and a grand-dame a coarse linen shirt or two, with a better one for Sundays; for every grand-dame and matron had, in those simple days, her household stores of linen. The old shoes clouted for common wear, a new pair in the chest, four days of the parish tailor, who, with his apprentice, worked in all the cottages and farm houses at sixpence a-day, completed the equipment of our hero; the tailor displaying some extra flourishes on the rude staple of William's blue coat, as his handywork might haply be seen in so magnificent a place as the Candlerigg of Glasgow. His entire equipment cost the family L.1, 8s.; but it is not every day a son is launched into life, and they were determined to do it respectably: And now the rainy November morning was come when William, mounted behind his father, set out for the capital of the West, boys and girls shouting good wishes after him from the school-house green, and maids and matrons bestowing solemn blessings on "blithe Willie" as he rode past.

Behold him now established with the identical widow, who, twelve years before, had entertained the schoolmaster, when he attended the University, at a pension of four shillings per week; but Willie, as a boy, was received at a more reasonable rate. His board was two shillings and sixpence, of which his master was to pay one-half. His mother's share was to be paid in rural produce, for though neither butter nor meat were very plentiful in the Upper Ward, money was still more scarce. William's heart had never sunk, till next morning that his father, having first shared his porridge and butter-milk, returned thanks after their meal, in what appeared an earnest prayer for the preservation of his boy amid the snares and temptations of life, and for a blessing upon him.

"And mind ye, Willie, to be eident and diligent in your calling; do your master's biddin'; and aboon a' mind that ye have a higher Master, whose will we maun a' strive to fulfil, if we would do weel either here or hereafter. And now, my bairn, mind that if ye do not do weel, there's ane at hame, owre yonder, already thinkin' lang to hear o' ye, whose very heart ye'll break. But, why forsee ill?—to the Lord's keeping I commend ye, and part in peace."

Our William would have said something to comfort and re-assure his father; but excellent and ready as was the natural address of the bright and intelligent boy, he could not at this time articulate one word.

Five years, five busy, short, bright years, passed over young William, every hour improved, and employed either in the study and practice of surgery and pharmacy, in attending his master's shop and patients, or in some way forwarding his general education. The *cadger* from his parish, who weekly visited the Tron—now termed the *Bazaar* I believe—to dispose of his gathered load of eggs and butter, was the general medium of intercourse between William and his family, and the bearer of his mended hose and clean linen, and of those little gifts with which the country matron propitiated the widow who was in place of a mother to her boy. Even one year's residence in a city, which, though an emporium of trade, is also the seat of a University, made a great change on William. When he visited the Upper Ward in the third year of his apprenticeship, his friends had some reason to be proud of

"The Doctor." These important years had made a still greater change on the inner than the outward William. Frugality, diligence, and the love of study, had already gained him distinction. His employer valued him according to his merits, and afforded him every proper indulgence in pursuing his studies. He was now remarked for the frankness and civility of his manners, and known to some of the Professors, who occasionally called in at his master's shop. They recommended him to pupils; and, by teaching what he knew, William acquired the means of learning more. He was able to attend some of the lectures of the College, and, by the time his apprenticeship was concluded, his character for steadiness and ability, and accurate knowledge of all he pretended to know, were so well confirmed, that he readily obtained the appointment of surgeon in a merchant ship trading to the West Indies. His relations now thought his fortune made. William was not quite of this opinion: but he said he had got all he yet deserved,—he must be qualified for more before he got it. In this situation our William made several voyages, and enlarged his knowledge of men and manners, as well as of his profession. But he saw that this was not the place for improvement: and though his appointments were more lucrative than could be hoped for in his own poor country, he resolved to settle in his native district as a rural practitioner. He had saved in his voyages nearly thirty pounds; so before settling down for life he resolved to enlarge his acquaintance with that science in which it was his chief ambition to excel, by a winter's attendance on the medical lecturers of Edinburgh;—some accounts say Glasgow, and that it was not until a later period he was able to receive the instructions of the Edinburgh schools. To chemistry, in particular, a science then comparatively in its infancy, he zealously devoted himself; and the most of his West Indian savings were devoted to the purchase of a small apparatus, which he brought to the country, his chief possession, after a selection of medical books, and a few of general literature. Even thus early William began to study accuracy and elegance in style, and to extend his classic knowledge.

Imagine, now, the pride of William's rustic relations, when he settled at the village of Kirk of Shotts, under the sonorous title of "The Doctor,"—for which he was entirely indebted to the kindness and respect of his compatriots. Fixed in the centre of this bleak moorland district, then proverbial, even in Scotland, for its poverty, our William now began to draw teeth for a groat each, to bleed on the same terms, and sell medicine from his small store in pennyworths. To patients whom he visited all over that region, for fifteen or twenty miles in every direction, his most lucrative visits might bring from 1s. to 1s. 6d.; while three-fourths of them proved, like virtue, their own reward.

William was now twenty-four years of age. His reputation was gradually increasing; so were his practice and his fees. He had performed some notable operations in surgery. The cures he had accomplished were best known to himself, and he was not inclined to boast, not more from modesty and delicacy towards "the Old Doctor," than consciousness of how much he wanted of that perfection of which his profession was capable. About this time, as the season was falling into winter, and his foot-journeys were long, and so fatiguing, that, on returning home to his cottage, he was unable to pursue his studies, our William resolved to buy himself a horse, at Hamilton Fair. None of your "bits of blood," nor in any way remarkable for symmetry, or any fine point whatever, but some hardy brute of a serviceable country nag, which would bear him over the hills and holts of Lanarkshire, and be fitter than Eclipse himself for traversing those wide-spread regions where a good share of William's practice lay; for here mines were now opening, and population gathering. At Hamilton Fair, as William wished to see some friend in that neighbourhood, the purchase was completed, and I think the beast cost the young doctor L.3, 15s., a rather smart price in those days; but there was a bridle to boot, and, borrowing a saddle, William, on his return, cantered over Bothwell Brig on his own horse, with no mean satisfaction. The minister of a parish, about seven miles off, had also been attending Hamilton Fair on some business: and was now jogging on before William. In those days mounted travellers were not so numerous in Lanarkshire as to make introduction a difficult matter; and, besides, Mr. Johnston, being of the number of William's elders and betters, had a right to address him on his own terms. The minister was a very good man: he knew his beadle's child was ill at home of the small-pox; and thus it turned out that the young surgeon of the Kirk of Shotts was invited to halt at the Manse. In those days this could imply nothing less than dinner and a bed. This last civility "The Doctor" was resolved, in his own mind, not to accept; but it was well he had not mentioned his intention, for before the dinner or early supper served up to them was half ended, he began to think that the Minister's small parlour afforded a fully pleasanter prospect than the fairest on that night in the whole fair vale of Clyde. The Minister's daughter had lately returned from a long visit to Glasgow, which she had made to complete her education or finish her manners; and though there was no sign about Miss Johnston of having forgotten the Manse, its duties, and homely pleasures, she possessed an air of ease and refinement, and a degree of spirit, intelligence, and cultivation, which William was not accustomed to meet with every day even in the best "Ha-houses" of the Upper Ward. He accordingly agreed to spend the night where he was, engaged the minister at the canonical game of draughts, was beaten and rebeaten—and being declared stupid, was set down with Bell," as a fitter match, while her reverend papa went forth to commune with one of his elders. Such was the commencement of William's acquaintance with an amiable young woman, whom, as their intimacy improved, he daily more and more admired. Nor did she appear insensible to his merits, even when the whole district declared that it would be but a very poor marriage for Miss Johnston, as, besides her claims of rank, station, and accomplishments, she possessed, in right of her mother, a fortune of six hundred merks, or L.400 sterling. I believe our William thought not much about marriage; nor did he speak of it at all, even when joked by his fair patients on the subject; for, though now mounted, you are not to suppose his toils were at an end, or that he was become a dashing surgeon, comfortably endowed with fees. Very far from it. His meals were still as homely as those of the peasantry about him; and, save for his books and chemical apparatus, there was little to distinguish his dwelling from their cottages. In his appearance there might be more attention to neatness and cleanliness; but his dress was scarcely so good as the Sunday garb of the small lairds' sons. Neither his slender means, his tastes, nor his prospects, allowed of any extravagance. At markets, to which he was often professionally led, the young Doctor passed for a *scrub*; for, instead of a carouse with the better sort of farmers, which the habits of the age sanctioned, he mounted and galloped home, groomed and suppered his own steed, and trimmed his lamp for the indulgence of a few hours of quiet study,—that is, if ever a country surgeon can promise himself one night of quiet. Thus, the only difference between him and the sons of the farmers, who laboured in their own fields, was the immeasurable one of knowledge, hourly increasing, activity of intellect, and superior delicacy and propriety of manners, which naturally flow from the cultivation of literary taste.

In the course of the next season, the young Doctor's nag might be seen fastened to the door-latch of many a Hall-house, and even posted near the dwelling of a laird or two in the Upper Ward. No one partakes more frequently of rural hospitality than that ill-paid *fag*, the country surgeon of Scotland, travel-worn or belated in his attendance at the couch of some miserable and poverty-stricken sufferer,— nor does any one half so well deserve the attentions of hospitality. Many a night must he be knocked up to ride a dozen miles in storm and darkness, to attend a poor sufferer all the night, and then return home to his breakfast.

In this plain hardy fashion, did our William live for about three years, working hard, and recreating himself with study, doing good to many, and rising in favour with all, when an accident occurred which some will call fortunate; but I beg of you not rashly so to name what to an ordinary man could have been attended with no advantage whatever, nor to any man, except one who, like our William, was prepared, by a long course of diligent acquisition, to profit by the good fortune cast in his way. Had he been like ninety-nine youths out of a hundred, into his way it had never fallen. William's reputation had now travelled far abroad, and had even descended to the rich and more populous valley of the Under Ward. He had been heard of at Lanark, was personally known at Dalserf, and named with respect even so far off as Hamilton, as an ingenious, active, steady, obliging, young fellow, who, some of the "auld wives" began to allow, was *skilly* for his years, and who, every body said, "would get on." This was, indeed, the unfailing impression of every one whose opinion was worth minding, received from his steady character, his frank manners, and agreeable conversation. There was the air, the earnest of success about him. He was felt to be a man who must rise—who must, by the force of a natural law, make his way around and upwards: but who among them all, and who less than himself, could have guessed how high in name, how eminent in science and in station, our William was destined to become!—I ought to say was to make himself, for he was the subject of no miracle. But I must come to William's first great adventure. The Duke of Argyle of that period——

"O, I guess it all now," cried Sophia Herbert.

"The Duke was thrown from his horse, I daresay, on these moors, broke his collar bone, and William was called in, and cured him, and his Grace took charge of the Doctor's fortune.

"Quite wrong, Miss Sophia," returned the reader; "His Grace did not give him one sixpence. The Duke of that time,—"

"Of that time!" exclaimed Sophia, "That Duke must have been Jeanie Dean's Duke—our Duke—that we all know."

"And so he was, Sophia," said Mrs. Herbert; "and it is most agreeable to fall in with an old friend on the moors of Lanarkshire, when we least expect it; especially with that frank, good-hearted Scotch nobleman, known to us as the friend of Jeanie Deans; but you must bear in mind that the Scotch Williams are no fictitious beings—they were real living men, of flesh and blood."

This information only whetted the curiosity of the young circle, and Norman was urged to proceed—

The Duke of Argyle of that time was a man of greater scientific attainments than many of his rank. He was an eager agricultural improver, and for this, among other reasons, he was fond of the study of chemistry, in which he dabbled in a gentlemanly way. I have told you that this part of Lanarkshire was beginning to be more and more a mining district. The extensive estates of the Duke in the Highlands were known to abound in minerals; an English Company was then either established, or about to commence the Iron Works at Bunawe. He was at Kirk of Shotts, as he said, looking about him, and required some apparatus, or an acid or alkali, which it was not thought possible to obtain nearer than Glasgow, till a lady—and ladies have quick, as well as kind memories—recollected William; and her husband allowed that he was a clever, steady sort of *chap*, who had made a voyage or two to the Islands, and knew something more of the world than the run of country doctors, though there was little hope that he could serve the present turn. A servant on horseback summoned the Doctor, and his apparatus, to attend his Grace, who at once understood his man. With so much propriety and modesty did William acquit himself in this interview, that the Duke requested he might be asked to repeat his visits. An invitation to dinner followed, and William, by the knowledge and ability he displayed on those mining subjects in which his Grace was interested, created for himself a powerful and generous friend. The approbation of the Duke at once stamped his value, and gave him currency, and the prospect of a higher order of friends and patients than he had yet obtained. After this, he remarked that the mother of Miss Johnston received him on his first call at the Manse rather more graciously. His calls there had not, of late, been frequent; but from about this time the intimacy increased, for William began to find patients down in the richer country, which led him into that neighbourhood, two or three times a-week. About two years after the purchase of his first nag at Hamilton, he was led to think of establishing his head quarters in that pretty town. Several of the more respectable of his patients had recommended, and solicited this change. His friends at the Manse approved; so, after proper consideration, William, seeing he had not much to lose in leaving Kirk of Shotts, and had a fair, and more fertile field before him, moved westward, according to the natural progress of the Arts and Sciences, at the Martinmas term, exactly a century ago, and took up his abode in a better house, in which was one compartment called "the shop," and another, "the study." There was besides a stable, and a kail-yard.

This new establishment might even accommodate a wife —and in spring a wife was brought home to it. Even this step was maturely considered. William's professional engagements had rapidly increased during the winter and spring, and his fees were higher. He now numbered lairds and ladies among his patients, and had accounts amounting to L.1, 5s, and even to L.2, where cases were desperate and tedious. He knew that he often lost money and customers, from having no one save a heedless lad at home to note the orders and calls which came in, while he was galloping through the country. Upon this last prudential argument, the good old people of the Manse yielded; the old lady sighing, and remarking, that "since it must be, it was as well soon as syne." So our William obtained the crowning blessing of his life. His wife's little fortune was useful also. It enabled him to add to his means, and increase the comforts of his family, by farming a small piece of ground; while her connexions brought new friends and new patients. William was now a happy man. He had the neatest, if not the largest house, the handsomest wife, and the highest medical reputation in Hamilton and seven miles round it. At the following Michaelmas, as a mark of respect for his character, he was chosen a member of the council of the burgh, and at the next again, the Provost, though he was still a very young man to have attained such honours. And now respectable neighbours, farmers, and proprietors, pressed their sons upon him as apprentices in surgery and pharmacy. His hands were full of employment, his friends and patients still increasing; and his fame, extending through a wider circle, had now reached Glasgow, where his old master in the Candleriggs, boasted of his former apprentice.

If you suppose that, with this accession of wealth, and honour, and domestic happiness, William was to close his books, and sit down contented, you mistake his character. To increase his knowledge, to excel in his profession, was still, as ever, his fondest ambition. It might have been thought, that with his wife, and children, and friends about him, and with numerous duties, both public and private, his time was fully filled up, and that the social or peaceful night should now have succeeded the busy day. And so it did; and yet William found time to keep pace with the rapidly improving spirit of the age in many things, but especially in all that related to medical science, and his favourite pursuit of chemistry. While every one admired his attainments, he alone was dissatisfied, conscious of the defects of his early medical education, and how much remained to the physician who would press onward in his profession. The smiles of his wife and children could not shake his purposes, or lull him in the dream that he had done enough, while so much lay before him. It would, however, have been most opposite to his character to have neglected his increasing business, and his present duties. His small practice was the means of respectability, and of domestic happiness, and he stuck sedulously to it; looking, meanwhile, cautiously and prudently round, and waiting for the favourable moment no one better knew how to seize and improve. Near William's native parish had lived and flourished, for time immemorial, the family of Long Cawderwude, a race of Lanarkshire dignitaries, who had not, at that time, been much heard of, beyond their own corner of the county, though there, or at least in the parish of Kilbride, they could be traced far beyond the Persecuting Times, and back to the wars of Bruce and Wallace. Though only "small lairds," the Lang Cawderwude family were great folks compared with our William's stock, though I have made the very most that is possible of his ancestry. But education and good conduct level still higher distinctions. The laird of Lang Cawderwude, among a family of ten sons and daughters, had also a William,—our second Scotch William, who was a few years younger than the first. The value of his father's estate might, in those days, be from L.70 to L.80 a-year; and, as was usual, he farmed it himself, and supported his large family on its produce. His father being in the rank of lairds, the second William was not subjected to the indignity of an apprenticeship. He was intended for the Church; and while attending the Glasgow University, he was boarded in a genteeler style than our William, his weekly expenses amounting to almost 6s., besides getting his clean linen, and many little helps from Lang Cawderwude. He had some relatives in a thriving way in Glasgow, and, as a "laird's" son, visited both prosperous citizens and learned professors. When he had attended Glasgow College for five years, his friends were mortified to find that he had no inclination to come out in the Church, and preferred the profession of medicine. Idleness in such a family was out of the question; and when he expressed a wish to become the partner and assistant of our William at Hamilton, they gladly acquiesced, so well established was the character of "The new Doctor," for ability, integrity, and prudence. Similar tastes and pursuits had thrown the young men much together of late; and they promised themselves both pleasure and advantage in a closer connexion. And now, mark the conditions of the compact of these obscure surgeons; the younger William was to be received into the house of the elder to acquire, in the first place, a general knowledge of the routine of actual practice, for it was only by books he yet knew any thing of medicine. The partnership was otherwise entered into with no hope of gain, no speculation of profit—nothing beyond the frugal means of an independent livelihood, and the power of prosecuting their profession in turns, by going alternately to London or Edinburgh in the winter, to attend the medical classes and the hospitals—a singular principle of partnership for two young men to form. Our William's turn, as of right, came first. He left his wife and children, and his practice, to the care of his friend, and in the winter of 1739 repaired to Edinburgh, which at the time boasted of several eminent medical professors. Need I tell you with what assiduity an opportunity was improved, so long waited for, and purchased at so anxious a price, with so many efforts of self-denial. Some of his friends did not scruple to blame him for deserting his practice in this wild way; but, as he had the approbation of the person chiefly interested, his wife, he did not much mind any one else. The second William, left to himself from November till March, worked double tides to keep all right in Hamilton, to attend the shop, and hold the patients together; and he also had his reward, for in the winter of 1740 his turn of study came. He attended the medical classes of Edinburgh; and in spring, with the consent of his partner, went to London to attend such lectures and demonstrations as were fitted to advance his professional knowledge. I mentioned before that he had studied in Glasgow with the reputation of good scholarship. At that time there were in Glasgow two learned printers, brothers, of the name of Foulis, who were connected with scientific and learned men all over Europe. They printed the classics, and all the young students were invited to visit their office, to exercise their critical skill in corrections. For this purpose, it is said, they used to hang up their proof-sheets in the hall of the College, and offer rewards for the discovery of errors. From these gentlemen William of Lang Cawderwude, the Scottish student, obtained a letter of introduction to a very eminent, and also a very rich physician in London. After a trial of his talents and principles, this gentleman received William into his own family, as a professional assistant, and as the tutor of his son. These were brilliant prospects; and our William at Hamilton was too high-minded and too generous to throw any obstacle in the way of his friend's advancement.

The connexion was amicably dissolved, and to their dying day they continued to regard and respect each other, though they never again met. Our London William, so fortunate in his early establishment, we must leave for the present, and keep by our first and favourite hero. He was still provost of his little burgh, and farmer, and surgeon, and student; husband, and father, and friend; and he might have lived and died in the narrow circle of Hamilton a respected man: but a brighter career lay before him, nor was it less happy. Already he had reaped the fruits of his own early planting; but as he had never relaxed in diligent and useful culture, there was still much to gather in.

His grandee neighbour the Duke, who seldom resided at Hamilton Palace, happened once, when there, to be taken suddenly ill; and, on this emergency, the country doctor was sent for, his Grace feeling no reluctance to intrust himself to a practitioner of whom every one spoke so well; and who, instead of the usual conceit of ignorance, had the good sense to attend Monro, even after he was married and in full practice. It is told that William, whose general talents were hardly yet appreciated, not only benefited the Duke as a physician, but delighted him, as a companion full of knowledge and vivacity, as a philosopher and a man of the world, prized the more for being thus found in obscurity. In this year William took out his medical degree at Glasgow, and became entitled to the dignified name long before gratuitously bestowed. He was once more ripe for an access of good fortune—and it came. The lectureship of chemistry in Glasgow was vacant; at the suggestion of the Duke he solicited and obtained a situation which his previous studies had fitted him to fill with honour to himself and advantage to his pupils. He now removed his family to Glasgow. Here he was placed in a light in which he could at last be fairly seen and truly judged. He stood every test, surpassed every expectation, obtained a large and lucrative city practice, eclipsed all his predecessors in the chemical chair, and became, what he always continued to be, the idol of his numerous pupils. He had not held this situation above three years, when a higher became vacant: and without solicitation, William was appointed by the Crown, Regius Professor of Medicine. Universities were now emulous which should obtain so eminent a teacher, so popular a lecturer, so admired a man; and his next step was the Chemical Professorship of Edinburgh, which, from his still increasing reputation for science, he was solicited to fill. In the metropolis of his native country his numerous patients were of the highest classes, and it was said truly, that all his patients became his friends. Step by step he rose to the proudest distinctions in the University. Students flocked from all parts of Europe to his lectures; and his name was now as familiarly known in the colleges, and among the men of science in France and Germany, as it had ever been in the Upper and Lower Wards of Lanarkshire —and how differently appreciated!

Of his merits as a writer on medicine, a lecturer, and practising physician, I am not qualified to speak; but he was the most distinguished man in the University, which was upheld by the lustre of his name. It is understood, that even in this advanced age of discovery and improvement, his reputation still ranks high, nor is it likely to be soon eclipsed. One trait of his character falls within the reach of every understanding—his amiable and generous conduct to his pupils. He had known what it was to struggle with difficulties, and with what may be called poverty; and his sympathies ever flowed freely towards young men of superior talents, placed as he had been in early life. He loved to distinguish them, and to encourage and aid their efforts. He lectured till within a few months of his death, which took place when he had attained the advanced age of seventy-seven, full of years and honours. On his coffin was read the illustrious name of WILLIAM CULLEN.

Having thus disposed of one William, the fortunes of the second may be more rapidly traced. WILLIAM HUNTER of Long Calderwood was the brother of John Hunter, and the uncle of Dr. Matthew Baillie.

"Eminent names these in medical annals" said Mr. Dodsley.

"Brave eaglets from the Scotch nest of Long Calderwood," cried Miss Harding.

"And Joanna, too!" whispered Sophia. "Ay, Joanna Baillie, too—and Mrs. John Hunter. You remember your favourite canzonet in days of *Ancient Melodies*, Mrs. Herbert?"

"'My mother bids me bind my hair,'—to be sure I do:— such a constellation of northern stars! and all clustering about one eminent name—for I derive them all from the little apothecary's shop, and the apprentice in the *Candleriggs*, in preference to the Hall-house of Long Calderwood William the first became the intellectual father of William the second, who again became the parent of John and Matthew. But proceed, Mr. Norman, with the second Hamilton surgeon."

As you know the close of his history already, there can be little interest in following it farther. I shut my book, and tell you, that, after qualifying himself by several years of diligent study and preparation, he commenced a course of lectures on some limited branch of anatomy, with which he was thoroughly acquainted, and succeeded so well, that he was solicited by his pupils to extend his range. He became, as is well known, by slow but sure degrees, the most eminent anatomical lecturer of his time. It is related by a friend, that when, after the first lecture of his second course, he carried home seventy guineas of fees beneath his cloak, he remarked that he never had possessed nearly so much money before; yet he lived to bequeath a museum to the University at which he had studied, which cost L.70,000! with a further donation of L.8000 to keep it up and in order; and obtained the highest honours, if not the highest fame, in his profession. Hunter possessed, in an eminent degree, the virtues usually ascribed to his country. He was economical, cautious, persevering—the same plain, frugal man while associating with the first nobility in England, as he had been in the small shop at Hamilton. He accumulated an immense fortune; but he made noble use of it, in collecting the means of advancing science and perfecting art. I may finish my tale by telling you, that, in his most splendid days, the wealthy, learned, admired, and envied old bachelor always said that the happiest hours of his life had been spent in Hamilton, in the family of WILLIAM CULLEN.

DAN DONNELLY'S TRIP TO PARIS.

"*Alas! poor Yorick.*"

IRELAND's *fisty* champion, Dan Donnelly, as all our readers well know, has been feeding the worms for a few years back upon those very thews and sinews with which he had so pugnaciously snatched the wreath of victory from John Bull for the Emerald Isle. Many of his whims and oddities, however, live in the recollection of his admirers; and occasionally they serve to dispel the gloomy hour at the "Fives Club," when told in Dan's own *nate* style. Indeed there is only one member of the club, at present, who can do justice to "Dan's visit to the Prince *Raigint*;" but there are many who venture to recount his "Trip to Paris," with various shades of success. The following version of it is from the notes of one who assures us that he took it down *verbatim* from Dan's own lips, the last time he told it, which might be about a fortnight before he was finally *floored* by death's unlucky *mauley* :—' Well, boys, I see that you must have from me the full and true account of what came across me the last time I wint to France; so here goes. Now, you don't want to know how I got from this to Dover, nor from Dover to Calis, bekeys ye couldn't be so uncommon ignorant as not to know that I, Dan Donnelly, the re-al champion of ould Ireland, could not be in France without getting there somehow or other, barin I wasn't in it at-all-at-all; so becourse, I'll begin with my journey from Calis, which, by the hoky, I took upon an ould garron of a mare that you wouldn't pick out of the gutter, bad luck to the bit; for, bad cess to the eye, but one she had in her head, and that same was stone blind; and in regard to her legs. there war only three of them worth mentioning, the fourth bein an idle vagabone of a leg that hung flappin about the poor *baste*, an doing more harm nor good. As you may suppose, she had a mighty diverting way of hoppin the road, much like a kangaroo. Howsomdever, 'twas myself that made the crather spin along as if she was starting for the plate, tal we kem to the big city of Paris, for she never cried stop or stay, tal she had me on the tip-top of a place they called the *point of a knife*, as well as I can remembir. ' Och! blur-an-agers,' cried myself, openin wide my two peepers, as if I was roused out of a doze by a bottle-houlder,—' blur-an-agers,' sis I, ' Dan Donnelly, avick, where is it you are, at-all-at-all ?'—' Arrah, where shud ye be, Dan, my darlint,' sis a chap comin up and givin me a *polthouge* out iv pure love, from a *nate* bit of shillelagh as thick as the rowler of a mangle, that made the heart leap in my body, —' where else shud ye be, Dan, my darlint,' sis he, ' bud in the quarest place in the wide world, and that is the City of Paris, my jewel.'—' Why, thin, is that yourself, Tom Mulligan, *ma bouchelaun*, or is it your own brother Jim that's in it ?' sis I. ' Faith, its myself' sis he, ' for Jim is gone to Botany.'—' Glory be to God,' sis I. ' Amen,' sis he. ' But Dan, aroon,' sis he again, ' what the dhoul brought you here among the mounseers ?' —' Is it, what brought me here, Tom, avick,' sis I, ' that you're after axin ?—look at that poor lame baste of a crather,' sis I, ' and you'll see *what* brought me here, God help her, this blessed night.'—' Arrah, blur-an-ounty,' sis Tom, ' is that a raal Irish baste ?'—' Introth she is, every bone in her skin,' sis I ; so wid that, Tom made no more ado, but he runs and claps his two arms round the poor crathur's neck, and hugged her and kissed her, as if she was a natural Christian born, tal myself got ashamed of the dacent people passing by, to be seeing the likes. Well, there's no use in talkin about all that passed tal next day, when Tom hoiks me off to see the Queen of Paris, at a place he called the Pally Royal. Now this same Pally Royal is a big ould building, wid as many windys as Newgate, where people go to see an ould baste, they call the Queen of Paris, maining Louy the Eighteenth. Tom an myself warn't long scrugeing our way up the stairs into the presence-chamber; whin, looking straight forninst me, what shud I see but a big ould woman, sitting upon a bit of red carpet, wid a most beautiful crown upon her sconce, an she all covered over from top to toe wid raal diamonds an emeralds, an bunches of rubies ; and all round about her was stanin heaps of fine ladies and gintlemin. So I whipped off my own caubeen, and made her a low bow; thin wiping my face wid the skirt of my coat—for bad luck to my hankachur, I forgot it at Dover.—' God save all here,' sis I, in raal quality form. And immediately her Majesty called up one of her educongs—some great curnel or giniral, you may be sure—an seys she to him, in a pig's whisper, wid a mighty knowing wink, ' What handsome young fellow, curnel, jewel, is that at the door wiping his face wid tail of his coat ?'—' Och, thin, sure,' sis Tom, makin bould because he understood the Frinch—' och, thin, sure, ma'am,' sis he, ' it's Dan Donnelly, the famous prize champion of both England and Ireland, so renowned in history books.' —' Whithin, by the hoky farmer,' sis the Queen, ' but he's a man that's beyant the common !' So wid that she axed to be introduced to myself in raal quality style, an by coorse, I couldn't have the heart to refuse her. To tell the truth of her, she was mighty polite, intirely, an made myself an Tom stay to dinner wid her ; an in the evenin she axed a power of quality to make up a dance for us, an she led off the first set wid myself. But what bet the world was, that she axed me to dance the Kerry jig upon a trencher ; which, by coorse, I couldn't refuse ; and she tuck such a likin to it that she wanted to make me a *ballet-master*, as I think they called it, to the coort, but I refused the offer, becaise none of the ballets I could remimber war dacint enough to taich the young ladies. Then agin, she med me stan up and take a small twist of handy-gripes wid herself ; an very lucky for her I had the gloves in my pocket, and put them on, or, be the hoky, the first *douse* I gev her in the bread-canister would have knocked a few of her ivories down her throath : ' Stop ! stop ! Dan Donnelly, my jewel,' she roared out, ' that's quite enough !' The poor ould woman was so *struck* wid my performance that she wanted to make a duke of me, but I axed laive to go home first an fight a few battles more, afore I'd give up the BELT. Och ! bethershin ! but it's yourself, Dan Donneily, that might have med your forthin af you had only staid in France an humoured the ould dotin Queen of Paris !"

P. C.

HEAT.
(Continued from page 214.)

BODIES not only expand on the application of heat, but contract on its withdrawal, from which it is evident that they must all, in a natural state, contain a quantity of heat, and that their whole form and appearance must depend on that quantity. Were heat completely withdrawn from the world, its bulk would decrease to an enormous extent. Some have even fancied that the reduction in its size would be so great that it might be placed in a nut shell! On the other hand, were the heat sufficiently increased, the earth and all it contains would be converted into an invisible fluid, and its bulk inconceivably expanded. If we apply heat to a solid body, it expands, and continues to expand till it arrives at a certain temperature, when it undergoes a change, by which its form and properties are totally altered ; it takes the fluid form, and the change is called *liquifaction*. Different bodies require different quantities of heat to effect this change.

When a body changes from the solid to the fluid state, a remarkable circumstance takes place. An enormous quantity of heat is absorbed, which does not increase its sensible temperature in the smallest degree ; the heat which is thus absorbed, is therefore called latent or concealed heat. For example, if we take two basins, and fill one with ice-cold water, and the other with ice and water, and add equal quantities of hot water to each, the temperature of that containing water only will be found to increase by every addition of hot water, but in that containing ice and water, a part of the ice will be melted, but the temperature will not be increased in the smallest degree : nor will it increase till the whole of the ice is melted. The heat which we add enters the ice, and causes it to melt; but being absorbed in the process, it does not increase the warmth of the water. As soon, however, as the ice is all melted, every addition of hot water will cause an increase of temperature. When the fluid again resumes the solid state, as when water becomes ice, the heat which it had absorbed in passing from the solid to the fluid state, is again given out. This absorption of heat in the conversion of a solid into a fluid, its being again set free on the conversion of a fluid into a solid, serves some important purposes in the economy of nature. From this we perceive the cause why ice and snow take so long to melt. As in the conversion of a solid into a fluid, a great quantity of heat is absorbed, a considerable time must elapse ere the requisite quantity of heat can be supplied, to enable ice or snow to become water. The process of melting must therefore go on gradually. Were it not for this, the whole of the ice and snow existing at any one time, would immediately be melted in the change from frost to fresh, and the most dreadful deluges would sweep over the earth, carrying every thing along with them. On the contrary, but for this law, water, on cooling to the freezing point, would instantaneously congeal, to the great inconvenience and destruction of man and other animals. But as fluids in their conversion into solids give out the heat which they had absorbed in passing from the solid to the fluid state, water, in being converted into ice, gives out heat, which lessens the cold, and retards the freezing of the rest of the water; the process of freezing, therefore, goes on gradually.

That fluids expand on the application of heat, may be easily proved. Put some water into a glass tube, marking the height at which the water stands; place it amongst hot water, and the water in the tube will be immediately observed to rise. The most useful purpose to which this law has been applied is that for measuring the temperature or relative quantities of heat existing in bodies. For this purpose what is called a thermometer is used, which is merely a glass tube with a bulb blown at one end, and which is partly filled with some fluid; mercury or quicksilver is generally used. When this instrument is brought in contact with a warm body, the mercury, being heated, expands and rises in the tube. If, on the contrary, it is brought into a colder situation, the mercury parts with some of its heat, and consequently contracts and falls in the tube. Scales are attached to the instrument to tell us the exact height at which the fluid stands in the tube, and the variations which it undergoes. The thermometer principally used in this country is that recommended by Fahrenheit, a Dutchman. Conceiving, erroneously however, that the greatest cold is that produced by two parts of ice and one of salt, he commenced his scale at that point, calling it degree No. 1. The freezing of water takes place, according to his scale, at the 32d, and the boiling of water at the 212th degree.

If we apply heat to a fluid body, it likewise expands, and continues to do so till its temperature is raised to a certain height; in the case of water to 212, when a second change of form and properties takes place. It assumes the form of vapour, which change is called *evaporation*. We have already mentioned that a solid, in its conversion into a fluid, absorbs a great quantity of heat, which does not increase its sensible temperature; and the same occurs when a fluid passes into the aëriform state. A pint of steam, whose temperature, as measured by the thermometer, is 212, will, if mixed with six pints of cold water, raise the temperature of the whole to 212, or the boiling point; thus proving what an immense quantity of latent or concealed heat must have existed in the single pint of steam, and which has been absorbed while passing from the fluid to the aëriform state. But for this law we would in vain attempt to boil water, because, as soon as it arrived at the boiling point, the whole would immediately be converted into steam with a tremendous explosion. But from the quantity of heat absorbed, the process must go on gradually, as the required heat is received from the fire. In India they take advantage of this law for the purpose of cooling their apartments. The rooms are sprinkled with water, which evaporating, absorbs such a quantity of heat as causes a reduction of temperature to the extent of 10 or 15 degrees. When aëriform bodies become fluid, they again give out the heat absorbed while passing from the fluid to the aëriform state. Thus, if we put our hands among common air at 212 degrees, we do so with impunity; but if we place them among steam at the same temperature, they are immediately scalded. The reason is, that the coldness of our hands causes the steam to condense, or become fluid, and its latent heat being set free, it scalds our hands. That aëriform bodies expand on the application of heat, may be proved by filling a bladder half full of air, and holding it near the fire; the air will soon be so expanded that the bladder will be quite filled.

HINTS FOR FARMERS.

FEAR OF OVER-CULTIVATION.—Our excellent friends the farmers must allow us to say, that, like every other class, they are subject to a good many vagaries, which materially affect alike their own prosperity and that of the country at large; and we know that they will feel obliged by an attempt of their well-wisher to lay before them, on sundry points, the results of his own pretty wide experience and tolerably serious meditation. There is not, we venture to allege, one practical mistake productive of so unfortunate consequences to the country in general, and of course especially to the agriculturist, as the prevalent disinclination to cultivate good land to the *full extent* of its productive powers, from the vague fear of *over-cultivating* it. There is never much difficulty in compelling a good farm to return three or four times the *usual crop;* and we have often seen it accomplished,—but when the farmer sees it, he shakes his head, and prophesies *that it will not pay.* Now, as this is an important question, and one which may be easily resolved, we request attention to it for a moment. Suppose the farmer has under his cultivation, land of various qualities—from land which, for an outlay of L.10, produces a return of 10 quarters, to land which, for the same outlay, produces only 3—the intermediate qualities producing returns of 8, 7, 6, 5, &c. In regard of the treatment of this best field, we all know that double the care and expense, or an outlay of L.20, will not produce a return of 20; but if it produces a return of 18, it is plain that the farmer will be as well off by laying it out upon this field, as if he laid out upon it only L.10, and the other L.10 upon the next lowest field capable of returning only 8, —L.20 being in both cases laid out, and the return of 18 being the same. What then is the limit of prudent expense upon this best field? Plainly this:—the farmer ought to go on laying out money in its cultivation—applying to it, as it were, fresh doses of expense, until the last L.10 laid out produced only the additional crop of 3. We have already supposed, that he had land under cultivation capable, on account of its barrenness, of producing only this last return; and as this return must therefore *pay,* his best land will evidently not be sufficiently cultivated until he has so dosed it, that the last outlay shall be compensated by only this same 3. A field of this excellent land may thus be made to produce as much as a whole line of fields from the highest to the lowest degree, were each cultivated but superficially a field which returns 8 in the first instance, as much as all below it; and so on until we descend to the lowest cultivated field which produces 3. These principles are plain and irrefragable, and a very little thought will make them understood. To say that they are generally acted upon, were to say that we have no eyes, for the spots are indeed rare where one-third of that capital is laid out upon a farm, which might be laid out with the ordinary profit. Even at the present rate of profit to the agriculturist, the country might be made at least to treble its produce, and to double its rental; and it is not too much to allege, that of all trades and manufactures, agriculture is that which, in regard of the capital employed in it, is immeasurably behind. And who is to blame? Why is it, that in the present glut of capital, no more is applied to farming? The answer is easy, for the blame rests with the LANDLORD. He, and he alone, by his narrow and blindly selfish policy, has done the evil, and still struggles to perpetuate it. He it is, whose greed of the golden eggs has induced him so nearly to kill the goose. By his senseless and selfish law of hypothec, he has withdrawn his land from the field of free competition, and supplanted the capitalist, by the regardless and half-starved desperado. By his bellowing about the Corn Laws, he has kept the country in a state of suspense, and every market wavering. And by that most admirable malcontrivance, the Entail Law, he has got up the most effective barrier to all improvement ever invented by the wit of man! This system he calls *protecting* agriculture, and it is because of his fears of their innovating upon this system—a system dear to him as the very apple of his eye—that he swears against Reformers and the Reform Bill.—*Fife Herald.*

GOOD NIGHT! GOOD NIGHT!

The sun is sunk, the day is done,
E'en stars are setting one by one,
Nor torch nor taper longer may
Eke out the pleasures of the day;
And since in social glee's despite,
It needs must be—Good Night! Good Night!

The bride into her bower is sent,
And ribald rhyme and jesting spent;
The lover's whispered words and few,
Have bade the bashful maid adieu;
The dancing-floor is silent quite,
No foot bounds there—Good Night! Good Night!

The lady in her curtained bed,
The herdsman in his wattled shed,
The clansmen in the heathered hall—
Sweet sleep be with you, one and all!
We part in hopes of days as bright
As this now gone—Good Night! Good Night!

Joanna Baillie.

SCRAPS.
Original and Selected.
A PLOUGH-DAY—OLD CUSTOMS.

We like all old customs more or less, but especially those which promote good neighbourhood, as the *quiltings* and *huskings* of our descendants in America, and the *plough-day* of the northern parts of Yorkshire, where it is customary to give a tenant, who enters on a new farm, the use of all the ploughs in the country round, to get the ground ready to receive the seed. Eighty ploughs have been at one of these friendly matches. The following preparations were made by a farmer's wife for the entertainment of her husband's assistants, at the close of their day's labour:—Twelve bushels of wheat baked into loaves, and fifty-one rich currant dumplings. Upwards of two hundred pounds of beef, two large hams, fourteen pounds of peas in peas-pudding. Three large Cheshire cheeses, and two Yorkshire cheeses, weighing twenty-eight pounds each, formed the dessert to this national banquet of MERRY ENGLAND; the whole washed down by ninety-nine gallons of ale, and two of rum, for drams. This ploughing feast was given near Guesborough, about twenty years ago. It wanted nothing to make it complete, save the presence of William Cobbett.

EARLY RISING IN WINTER.—A peasant of Nithsdale once expressed to me his horror at braving a winter's morning in very poetical language. "Snow, the inspired man sings, is beautiful in its season. It was nought for him, sitting with his lasses and his wives, to say sae: had he been a dry-stane diker he would have said nae sic thing. As for me, I never see snaw at my window, but I lang to fa' asleep again; and I ne'er wish to step ower the door-stane, till I am sure I can set my foot on the bloom o' three gowans."—*Allan Cunningham's Notes to "Up in the Morning Early."*

Some love the din o' the dancers' feet
To the music leaping rarely;
Some love the kiss and the stolen word
Wi' the lass that loves them dearly;
But I love best the well-made bed,
Spread warm, and feal, and fairly;
For up in the morning's no for me,
Up in the morning early.

ON VEGETABLE STRUCTURE, AND THE BRITISH OAK.—A knowledge of the internal structure of the vegetable body assists greatly in explaining the modifications of its external form. All wood is tubular and cellular, and the different weight, colour, taste, smell, &c. of oak, ebony, poplar, cedar, sandal, and so forth, depend not on the ligneous structure itself, but on the matter the cells contain; for, if ebony be steeped in any fluid which will dissolve the black matter with which its cells are filled, it will become as light and as pale as poplar. But to the example. There are two, if not three species of British oak, (the third species is by some, however, considered only a variety;) one of these alone produces strong and lasting timber fit for naval purposes, i. e. which will endure, unchanged, the transitions from wet to dry, from heat to cold, and remain unhurt between wind and water. This difference depends on the tubes just mentioned conveying to the cells of which the mass of wood consists, a substance different in solubility in the different species; so that, when the timber of the one is wet, part of the inspissated extract is dissolved and borne away; and when this is repeatedly done, the cells become more and more void, and the timber light and spongy, so that, during cold weather, the water within is freezing and becoming expanded, the cells and tubes are ruptured, and consequently more readily let in fresh water and let out the solid matter it dissolves; and these successive crops of icicles soon form chinks and rents, extending for many feet. Now, oak is frequently constructed for in building ships and mill-work, flood-gates, locks, and so forth, merely as oak, and often, either from ignorance or fraud, the perishable timber is purveyed instead of the enduring wood; but a knowledge of vegetable structure can, by the aid of a very simple experiment, easily detect the fallacy or fraud.—*Burnet's Botanical Lecture.*

CONTENTS OF NO. XX.

She—A late Adventure in the Queensferry Coach............305
Triennial Parliaments—Old Speeches on ditto.................306
MEDICAL SELECTIONS—Influence of Dress on the Skin, Effects of Cold Feet and Damp, &c.....................................308
A December Evening within doors..............................309
On Ascertaining the prices of Grain, &c......................310
The Good Old Times..311
A Swiss Adventure—The Swiss Girl—The Boar Song........312
THE STORY TELLER—The Two Scotch Williams.............313
Dan Donnelly's Trip to Paris—Feat..........................316
Hints for Farmers &c...319
Good Night! Good Night!.....................................320
SCRAPS—Original and Selected—Old Customs—Early Rising in Winter—On Vegetable Structure, and the British Oak...320

EDINBURGH: Printed by and for JOHN JOHNSTONE, 19, St. James's Square.—Published by JOHN ANDERSON, Jun., Bookseller, 55, North Bridge Street, Edinburgh; by JOHN MACLEOD, and ATKINSON & Co., Booksellers, Glasgow; and sold by all Booksellers and Venders of Cheap Periodicals.

The Schoolmaster,
AND
EDINBURGH WEEKLY MAGAZINE.

CONDUCTED BY JOHN JOHNSTONE.

THE SCHOOLMASTER IS ABROAD.—LORD BROUGHAM.

No. 21.—Vol. I. SATURDAY, DECEMBER 22, 1832. Price Three-Halfpence.

CHRISTMAS.

England was merry England, when
Old Christmas brought his sports again;
'Twas Christmas broached the mightiest ale,
'Twas Christmas told the merriest tale;
A Christmas gambol oft would cheer
A poor man's heart for half the year.
* * * * *
Nor failed old Scotland to produce,
At such high tide, her savoury goose.

A DELIGHTFUL volume could be collected of what is genial, beautiful, and full of the poetry of real life, written and spoken about this great social festival of the Christian world—this season of merriment that is more heart-felt than boisterous—feasts that are more social than stately, the time of the knitting up of broken attachments, and of the renewal of decaying intimacies; when the friends of youth are affectionately recalled, and old loves freshly remembered. In our own country we have sometimes regretted that the severity of Presbyterian discipline forbids that religion should mingle with, and lend its sanctions to the commemoration of Christmas,—what better preparation could there be for the cheerful, social banquet of the evening, than the temple-service of the morning? And then, what a time for *levelling* sermons from a minister, who feels the spirit, and comprehends the true genius of the Christian system. Sermons which should tell of the common origin, the common lot, and the self-same destinies of men; sharers in a common ruin, and inheritors of the same salvation! How appropriate the commemoration to exhortations to an enlarged and tender charity of mind, to the preservation of the spirit of unity, in the bond of peace, and to the cultivation of the graces and affections enjoined by the divine being, of whom the religious rites of Christmas, are an affecting remembrance. Holding these opinions of the many fine things that have been said, and that might be said of Christmas-tide, we must admire the following Eliaean sketch, connecting cheering faith with cheerful practice:—

"In this spirit our pastor preaches to us always, but most particularly on *Christmas-day*; when he takes occasion to enlarge on the character and views of the divine person who is supposed then to have been born, and sends us home more than usually rejoicing. On the north side of the church at M. are a great many holly trees. It is from these that our dining and bed-rooms are furnished with boughs. Families take it by turns to entertain their friends. They meet early; the beef and pudding are noble; the mince-pies—peculiar; the nuts half playthings and half-eatables; the oranges as cold and acid as they ought to be, furnishing us with a superfluity which we can afford to laugh at; the cakes indestructible; the wassail bowls generous, old English, huge, demanding ladles, threatening overflow as they come in, solid with roasted apples when set down. Towards bed-time you hear of elder-wine, and not seldom of punch. At the manor-house it is pretty much the same as elsewhere. Girls, although they be ladies, are kissed under the mistletoe. If any family among us happen to have hit upon an exquisite brewing, they send some of it round about, the squire's house included; and he does the same by the rest. Riddles, hot-cockles, forfeits, music, dances sudden and not to be suppressed, prevail among great and small; and from two in the day to midnight, M. looks like a deserted place out of doors, but is full of life and merriment within. Playing at knights and ladies last year, a jade of a charming creature must needs send me out for a piece of ice to put in her wine. It was evening and a hard frost. I shall never forget the cold, cutting, dreary, dead look of every thing out of doors, with a wind through the wiry trees, and the snow on the ground, contrasted with the sudden return to warmth, light and joviality.

"I remember we had a discussion that time, as to what was the great point and crowning glory of Christmas. Many were for mince-pie; some for the beef and plum-pudding; more for the wassail-bowl; a maiden lady timidly said, the mistletoe; but we agreed at last, that although all these were prodigious, and some of them exclusively belonging to the season, the *fire* was the great indispensable. Upon which we all turned our faces towards it, and began warming our already scorched hands. A great blazing fire, too big, is the visible heart and soul of Christmas. You may do without beef and plum-pudding; even the absence of mince-pie may be tolerated; there must be a bowl, poetically speaking, but it need not be absolutely wassail. The bowl may give place to the bottle. But a huge, heaped-up, *over* heaped-up, all-attracting fire, with a semicircle of faces about it, is not to be denied us. It is the *lar* and genius of the meeting; the proof positive of the season; the representative of all our warm emotions and bright thoughts; the glorious eye of the room; the inciter to mirth, yet the retainer of order; the amalgamater of the age and sex; the universal relish. Tastes may differ even on a mince-pie; but who gainsays a fire? The absence of other luxuries still leaves you in possession of that; but

> 'Who can hold a fire in his hand
> With thinking on the frostiest twelfth-cake?'

Let me have a dinner of some sort, no matter what, and then give me my fire, and my friends, the humblest glass of wine, and a few penn'orths of chestnuts, and I will still make out my Christmas. What! Have we not Burgundy in our blood? Have we not jokes, laughter, repartee, bright eyes, comedies of other people, and comedies of our own songs, memories, hopes?"

GERMAN CHRISTMAS CUSTOMS—HOUSEHOLD AFFECTION.

Coleridge, in the *Friend*, describes a German CHRISTMAS USAGE, which, to us, appears beautifully characteristic of that domestic and sensible people. The NEW YEAR'S DAY GIFTS of the French, is the same custom modified by the national character of the Gallic race. "The children," says Coleridge, " make little presents to their parents, and to each other, and the parents to their children. For three or four months before Christmas, the girls are all busy, and the boys save up their pocket-money to buy those presents. What the present is to be, is cautiously kept secret; and the girls have a world of contrivances to conceal it—such as working when they are on visits, and the others are not with them—getting up before daylight, &c.; then, on the evening before Christmas-day, one of the parlours is lighted up by the children, into which the parents must not go; a great yew-bough is fastened on the table, at a little distance from the wall. A multitude of little tapers are fixed in the bough. Under this bough the children lay out the presents they mean for their parents, still concealing in their pockets what they intend for each other. Then the parents are introduced, and each presents his little gift; they then bring out the remainder, one by one, from their pockets, and present them with kisses and embraces. Where I witnessed this scene, there were eight or nine children, and the eldest daughter and the mother wept aloud for joy and tenderness, and the tears ran down the face of the father, and he clasped all his children so tight to his breast, it seemed as if he did it to stifle the sob that was rising within it. I was very much affected. The shadow of the bough, and its appendages on the wall, made a pretty picture; and then the raptures of the very little ones, when at last the twigs and their spikes began to take fire, and *snap*. O, it was a delight to them! On the next day, *Christmas-day*, in the great parlour, the parents lay out on a table the presents for the children; a scene of more sober joy succeeds; as on this day the mother says privately to her daughters, and the father to his sons, that which he has observed most praiseworthy, and that which was most faulty in their conduct." So says Coleridge. We recollect some late traveller in Germany, whose name has escaped us, describing the bitter distress of a peasant girl with whom he walked for some time in company, not for her own poverty, but that she should not be able to make Christmas presents to her parents and friends.

FRENCH CHRISTMAS CUSTOM.

At Marseilles, and in many other places in France, on Christmas eve, all of the same blood, residing in the same neighbourhood, are invited to a slight *maigre* supper with the senior of the family; after which the united households go together to midnight mass. Next morning, Christmas, they again repair to the church to mass, from their several dwellings, and when the service is ended, return to the house of the common ancestor, where a joyous feast is prepared, followed by all manner of in-door amusements.

THE COURT OF SINDE.

The silence which reigned within the fort formed a strong contrast to the noise and tumult without. After passing through some narrow streets, which were inhabited only by the immediate retainers of the court, I found myself unexpectedly among a crowd of well-dressed Sindians, in a large open area, the walls of which, on either side, were fancifully decorated with paintings, and the ground covered with variegated carpets. At one end appeared three large arched doors with curtains of green baize, towards one of which I was led by the vizier and another officer; and before I could collect myself from the suddenness of the transition, my boots were taken off, and I stood in presence of the Ameers.

The *coup d'œil* was splendid. I had an opportunity of seeing the whole reigning family at a glance, and I have certainly never witnessed any spectacle which was more gratifying, or approached nearer to the fancies we indulge in childhood, of eastern grandeur. The group formed a semicircle of elegantly attired figures, at the end of a lofty hall spread with Persian carpeting. In the centre were seated the two principal Ameers on their musnud, a slightly elevated cushion of French white satin, beautifully worked with flowers of silk and gold, the corners of which were secured by four massive and highly-chased golden ornaments, resembling pineapples, and, together, with a large velvet pillow behind, covered with rich embroidery, presenting a very grand appearance. On each side, their Highnesses were supported by the members of their family, consisting of their nephews, Meer Sobdar and Mahommed, and the sons of Mourad Ali, Meers Noor Mahommed, and Nusseer Khan. Farther off sat their more distant relations, among whom were Meer Mahmood, their uncle, and his sons Ahmed Khan, and Juhan Khan. Behind stood a crowd of well-dressed attendants, sword and shield bearers to the different princes. To an European, and one accustomed to form his notions of native ceremony by a much humbler standard, it was particularly gratifying to observe the taste displayed in dress, and the attention to cleanliness, in the scene before me. There was no gaudy show of tinsel or scarlet; none of that mixture of gorgeousness and dirt to be seen at the courts of most Hindoo princes, but, on the contrary, a degree of simple and becoming elegance, far surpassing anything of the kind it had ever been my fortune to behold. The Ameers and their attendants were habited nearly alike, in angricas or tunics of fine white muslin, neatly prepared and plaited so as to resemble dimity, with cummerbunds or sashes of silk and gold, wide Turkish trowsers of silk, tied at the ankle, chiefly dark blue, and the Sindian caps I have already described, made of gold brocade, or embroidered velvet. A pair of cashmere shawls of great beauty, generally white, thrown negligently over the arm, and a Persian dagger at the girdle, richly ornamented with diamonds, or precious stones, completed the dress and decoration of each of the princes.

Viewing the family, generally, I could not but admire their manners and deportment, and acknowledge that, in appearance at least, they seemed worthy of the elevation they had gained. The younger Princes, indeed, had an air of dignity and good breeding seldom to be met with, either in the European or native character. The principal Ameers were the least respectable of the party in point of looks; probably from having had less advantages, and more exposure to hardships in early life. They are, in reality, older, but did not appear above the age of fifty, from the very careful manner in which their beards and hair are stained. With one exception, there is little family likeness between them and the younger chiefs, who have inherited from their mothers fair complexions, jet black hair, with long eyelashes and eyebrows.—Meer Nusseer Khan struck me at once as a particularly handsome man.

The general style of the Sinde Court could not fail to excite my admiration, as much as the appearance of the Ameers. All the officers in attendance, judging from their dress and manners, seemed to be of superior rank. There was no crowding for places; the rabble had been shut entirely out of doors; and there was a degree of stillness and solemnity throughout the whole, and an order and decorum in the demeanour of each individual, which, together with the brilliant display I have mentioned, impressed me with a feeling of awe and respect I could not have anticipated. It is scarcely necessary, after what I have described, to say that their Highnesses received me in a state durbar.—The native agent, who had accompanied the two last embassies from our Government, was present, and assured me that the arrangements on this occasion, and the nature of my reception, were very different, indeed, far superior, to any ceremonial he had seen during a residence of twenty years in Sinde.—*Burnet's Visit to Sinde.*

EMIGRATION.

The subjoined letter was written, last spring, by an intelligent gentleman.

Gambier, Ohio, 1832.

DEAR FRIENDS.—Anxious to fulfil my promise, I resume my pen, in order to give you an outline of what I have seen and thought since my last letter: I am encumbered with considerable perplexity, as notwithstanding I have received several requests to proceed with this correspondence, yet I have also received one of a contrary nature from an individual whose approbation I hardly dare endanger. I have hesitated—but being overcome with the paramount obligation to posterity, of making an endeavour to perform the duty of leaving the world a little better than we found it, I will make an effort to give you my feelings and opinions, with candour and mildness. Moreover I would say, to those who may chance to read this, that I came a voluntary exile to this my adopted country—and that before any one has a right to leave his own paternal soil, he has an account to balance with his duties; first to society, and next with his family. If a man has the means of supporting and *properly* educating his children at home, *there* is his post of duty; if a man is single, still more, home is *his* post of duty—he is one of a class whose chief business is to assist in regenerating his country. But if the father of a numerous family has striven, with industry and economy, to provide a frugal maintenance and proper education for his sons and daughters, without success, then surely he is bound in affection and office, if there be a spot on the face of the earth where he can accomplish it, to transplant them, no matter with how many inconveniences to himself.

From this sequestered spot, five miles from the nearest village, and fully occupied with my studies, I fear this letter will be less animating and interesting than if I were travelling and portraying fresh scenery and modern towns. I have taken but one short journey of 45 miles out, and I did enjoy a ride of that distance in a sleigh with two friends, gliding on the surface of the snow at a rapid rate, drawn by a pair of fine horses, the distance easily accomplished from sun-rise to evening, pulling up twice to bait. The country was partially grassed, and villages at eight or ten miles distance; but chiefly over roads cut through apparently endless and impermeable forests, thickdensely thick—with most magnificent timber: oak, black walnut, beech, hickory, &c., from 100 to 120 feet in height. These woods are to be purchased at less than L.1 per acre, ranged now only by wild deer and turkeys, (some of which we saw,) but becoming gradually located, numbers of fresh settlers pouring in every year. The winter, which we have just passed, was acknowledged by all the papers of the Union to have been unusually severe; the thermometer out of doors for one or two mornings was 10° below Zero—on most days several degrees below freezing in my study, until the fire was lighted, when my stove soon brought it up to temperate or summer heat; the ink several times froze in my pen early in the morning before the air felt its influence; the atmosphere almost uniformly bright and clear, and a number of warm days interspersed throughout the season. We did not experience inconvenience from the cold,—not even the children—activity, when out of doors in the lucid atmosphere on the frozen snow, and abundance of fires within, preserved them. The snow is now all gone, and the winter broke up last week, with a great increase of temperature and surcharged electrical air, which passed off by thunder-storm and rain; the frost is out of the ground, and all are buoyant for spring.

I obtained in January five days' leave of absence, and made the journey above noticed to Columbus, the state town, to be present at a sitting of the legislative body, senate, and house of representatives, the former elected biennially, the latter annually, by ballot. Their proceedings, as well those of the court of justice, (which I witnessed,) were conducted with perfect order and decorum, not with the adventitious aid of wigs and robes, or mace-bearers, but in plain clothes, and by the force of reason and propriety. The members of both houses debated extemporaneously and with facility.

Ohio was first settled in 1788. In 1789 it was put under a territorial government, and called the western territory; and in 1802, it was erected into an independent state. Having a population of upwards of 40,000, the territories are admitted as states, electing a governor and legislature—they form a constitution and government of their own, subject to the general confederacy of the Union. There are now 24 states, three territories, and the district of Columbia, which environs the city of Washington, and is under the immediate government of Congress. The territory of Michigan will be admitted into the Union next year, containing now upwards of 31,000; that of Florida, 19,000; and Arkansas, 20,000. Ohio contains, according to the census of last year, 937,670—in 1790, only 3000; the increase during the last ten years being 61 per cent; she is as to population, the fourth state of the Union. The whole population of states and territories is, according to the same document, 12,856,171; an increase of 33 per cent in the same period.

The Government of the United States, at its first institution, established a system of an official census of the inhabitants at regular decimal periods. This was rendered necessary in a primary point of importance, as the apportionment of the representatives from the different states to the general Congress is regulated thereby; the number of inhabitants which are to send a representative is now, on the result of this last census, being fixed by Congress. This number is not yet decided, but will be somewhere between 45, and 48,000. Of course each state sends as many as there are, say 48,000 in its population. I should have said above that the territories are admitted states, when they have the definite number, as above, of the last preceding apportionment, which continues in force until the ensuing census.

Independently of this object, I need not direct your attention to the interest and importance of such documents; their usefulness might be much increased by embracing other subjects, as inhabited houses, houses of public worship, colleges, schools, number of pupils, the resources of the inhabitants in manufactures and agriculture, the number of horses, sheep, &c.

There are in the Union, 59 colleges, 21 theological seminaries, all Protestant, and 5 Catholic, 17 medical schools under the different names of colleges and universities, and nine law schools, 150 Jewish synagogues, 12 Roman Catholic bishops, 12 Protestant Episcopal ditto, and 4 Methodist Episcopal ditto, 9,789 ministers, independent of Roman Catholic or Jewish priests, and a countless number of *common* and private schools. The state of Ohio contains upwards of 24,810,000 acres; and at present it would be an arduous undertaking to get into a western territory as you must traverse the states of Indiana, Illinois, and Missouri, a distance greater than we travelled from New York hence; all three settled since Ohio. One amongst other reasons for turning my attention towards this state, was this, often having read over for the purpose of deciding on the constitutions of *all* the states, I preferred hers. In this country, you are aware every thing must have a constitution, a book club, or an anti-tobacco society, no matter what; if five people unite for any social or useful purpose, they cannot be governed by two or three plain rules, they must have a *constitution.* However, the *constitution of Ohio permits no slavery*, and *admits to the right of suffrage all* male inhabitants above the age of 21. The founders of Ohio saw what all the world now sees, except your aristocracy, that henceforward, if people are to be governed at all, they must be *self-governed.* To this point European nations are marching onward; impediments and resistance they will of course meet with; but the result is certain and irresistible as the progress of time. The means of preserving order in society, which have hitherto been relied on, are growing every day more ineffectual. Mere policy and power, brute force can no longer do it with any prospect of permanency; and nothing can give security to person or property, without which life is a very burden; but by admitting men to participate in the regulations of their own imposts and laws. They have been taught that they have been endowed by their Creator with certain inalienable rights, and that, to secure those rights, Governments are instituted, deriving just powers from the consent of the governed. The only great principles, which can enable men to control themselves, and make it unnecessary for those in power to abridge their rights, so as to give a new power to laws, by making them less necessary, are education and the Gospel. No other causes are adequate to this effect; and it remains with legislators and Christians to do their duty, and apply these renovating principles to the social system, and then such scenes as you had at Bristol will cease to be enacted.

The Governor of Ohio concluded his late address to the State Legislature with the following enlightened and benevolent remarks:—" Having experienced much inconvenience and frequent embarrassment from the want of a more liberal education, I feel more sensibly the great importance of securing to the rising generation the benefits of instruction; and I most earnestly recommend to you, gentlemen, a continuation of those laudable efforts which have hitherto characterised our Legislature for the promotion of education. Our schools and colleges, from that valuable institution the Sunday School, up to those of the highest grade, should always claim the most favourable consideration of our Legislators. A well-educated and religious people only are capable of *self-government*—the greatest temporal blessing which Heaven has bestowed upon man."

An Act was passed to provide for the "support and regulation of common schools," levying a direct tax of "three-fourths of a mite" on the dollar, being 1000th part on the *ad valorem* amount of taxable property. The whole amount of taxes, for 1831, was an average of 62½ cents for every inhabitant, *levied on real property*, but giving the above numerical average. The purposes to which they were applied were "For canal purposes." (The State has two canals, public property, forming an internal artificial navigation of three hundred and seventy-five miles, independent of the Ohio river navigation, extending across the whole of the south and nearly the whole of the eastern boundaries of the state; for steam-boats of the largest size from Pittsburg in Pensylvania to the gulph of Mexico.) " For state purposes, county schools, townships, roads, and other private purposes." This, then, is as far as fiscal circumstances are concerned; we exchange the excise laws and duties—the poor-laws the assessed taxes, the inhabited house duty and window tax, not omitting the tithe and game laws—for 2s. 7¼d.! I will now add a list which I obtained from a gentleman engaged in mercantile pursuits, of the prices in this neighbourhood of labour and produce: common labourers engaged in agricultural employment 33 to 88 cents per day; mechanics and artisans, such as stone cutters, masons, carpenters, and joiners, 60 to 75 cents per day; millers, shoe-makers, smiths, &c. about 60 ditto, Produce; wheat 50 to 75 cents per bushel, of 32lbs.; corn, (maize), rye, buck wheat, and barley, one half the above; oats, and potatoes, 16 to 25 ditto; fresh beef per 100lbs, 2½ to 3 dollars; pork the same; butter and cheese 6 to 10 cents; good cows 10 to 12 dollars; turkeys 25 cents; fowls 8 to 12 a couple; horses 30 to 80 dollars, of course very variable according to age and breed. Land also varies according to location and quality. I this week purchased 136 acres (taking the farm of the Exchange) for L.150, a mile and a half from our College, but being the nearest point that any one can approach, the village and Institution being situated in the centre of a square to the nearest point of which the line extends one mile and a half.

I need not point out to you the proper mode of considering the price of food, &c. with those of labour. Take the very lowest case, the labourer earns, half of a bushel of wheat, or a bushel of barley, or one and a half of potatoes, or quarter of a hundred of beef or pork, a half dozen pounds of cheese, or potatoes, butter, &c. daily. Thus his six days would bring him an ample variety—*as abundance*—and there is ample and abundant employment for all, and more than all.

LORD KENYON.

His dress was the threadbare remains of what might once have been appropriate costume, the sable relics of which frugality had piously preserved. These rare habiliments irresistibly produced a smile at their singularity, from the sterling marks which they bore of studied parsimony and mean economy. The were they daily subjects of joke or comment at the Bar, when the Lord Chief Justice appeared and took his seat on the bench. I happened to be in conversation with Lord (then Mr.) Erskine at Guildhall, before Lord Kenyon arrived there. When he entered the court, Pope's lines in the *Dunciad*, on Settle the poet, came across me, and I quoted them involuntarily—

" Known by the band and suit which Settle wore—
His only suit for twice three years before."

" The period of six years," said Erskine, laughing, " during which that poet had preserved his full-trimmed suit in bloom, seemed to Pope to be the maximum of economy; but it bears no proportion to Kenyon's. I remember the green coat which he now has on for at least a dozen years." He did not exaggerate its claims to antiquity. When I last saw the learned lord, he had been Lord Chief Justice for nearly fourteen years, and his coat seemed to be coeval with his appointment to the office. It must have been originally black; but time had mellowed it down to the appearance of a sober green, which was what Erskine meant by his allusion to its colour.

I have seen him sit at Guildhall, in the month of July, in a pair of black leather breeches; and the exhibition of shoes frequently soled afforded equal proof of the attention which he paid to economy in every article of his dress. His gown was *silk*, but had a better title to that of *everlasting*, from its unchanged length of service. He held a pocket handkerchief to be an unnecessary piece of luxury, and therefore dispensed with the use of one; he found a sufficient substitute in his emunctory powers, which were eminently attractive.

His equipage was in perfect keeping with his personal appearance, and was such as to draw down the gibes of malevolence, the sneer of ill nature, and the regret of those who held him in any respect, while it provoked the ridicule even of them. The carriage which conveyed the Lord Chief Justice and his suite to Westminster Hall, had all the appearance and splendour of one of those hackney coaches which are seen on the stand, with a coronet and supporters, the cast-off carriage of a peer or foreign ambassador. Though the seats were occupied by the Lord Chief Justice himself and his officers, in bags and swords, the eye was involuntarily directed to the panel to look for the number of the coach, as its appearance, and that of the horses which drew it, confirmed the impression that it had been called off the stand. They moved with the most temperate gravity, and seemed to require the frequent infliction of the whip to make them move at all.

That necessary instrument to rouse their latent spirit, was consigned to the unsparing hand of a coachman whose figure and appearance perfectly harmonized with the rest of the appointment. There is an appropriate dress for the different description of servants; and a triangular hat is generally considered part of the costume of a coachman. Whether it was a sacrifice which Lord Kenyon made to fashion, or the vanity of the individual himself which prompted him to adopt it, I will not presume to say but it seemed to both to be necessary that his lordship's coachman should appear with that important symbol of his station. He therefore adopted the appropriate mark of distinction, a three-cornered hat. This appeared to have been effected with great taste, but with the accustomed view to economy. A hat slouched down before, the former ornament of his head, was, by a neat metamorphosis, changed into a cocked one, by turning up the flap, and making it the base of the triangle; and, lest it should prove refractory under its new *regime*, it was kept in its place, and the perpendicular procured, by the aid of a pin. The rest of his dress seemed to be selected from the choicest stores of Monmouth Street, with equal regard to taste and frugality.

Lord Kenyon was a man of religious habits, and properly discountenanced any light allusion, in a speech or conversation, to the Bible, or to the service of the Church. I recollect the ludicrous but unexpected reception which a member of the circuit met with on telling him the following anecdote of Lord Chief Baron Yelverton, of the Court of Exchequer in Ireland; I think it was my excellent and much-lamented friend Nolan, who was a native of that country. He was a man of the purest morals, not wanting in religious feelings, but who did not carry his sentiments of strict discipline as far as the learned lord. He seemed to think that an anecdote of an Irish judge would afford some amusement to the Chief Justice, but he unluckily happened to mistake the character of the tale which suited his taste, and so hit upon one not quite in accordance with his sentiments, on subjects connected with the Church. He addressed himself to Lord Kenyon with the seeming anticipation of the mirthful effect which it would produce, by telling him that Lord Chief Baron Yelverton once went a Lent circuit, and one of the assize towns happened to be where one of his college contemporaries was beneficed. The reverend gentleman, anxious to make a display of his zeal and talents, and at the same time to shew his respect for the Chief Baron, asked permission from the sheriff to preach the assize sermon before the judges, and his request was granted. It was in the month of March, and the weather was intensely cold. The sermon was immensely long, and the Chief Baron most annoyingly chilled. When the service was over, the preacher descended from the pulpit, seemingly highly satisfied with his own performance, came to the judge rubbing his hands, full of the joyful expectation of thanks for his discourse, and gratulation for the excellence of its matter and delivery. "Well, my lord," says he, "how do you like the sermon?" "Wonderfully, my dear friend," replied Yelverton; "it was like 'the peace of God—it passed all understanding;' and, like his mercy, I thought 'it would have endured for ever.'" This jocular narrative was chilled by hearing Lord Kenyon, in an under-tone, pronounce the words "Very immoral."—*From an Article in Fraser's Magazine, entitled "My Contemporaries."*

KING JAMES AND THE WITCHES.

THE general spite of Satan and his adherents was supposed to be especially directed against James, on account of his match with Anne of Denmark—the union of a Protestant princess with a Protestant prince, the King of Scotland, and heir of England, being, it could not be doubted, an event which struck the whole kingdom of darkness with alarm. James was self-gratified by the unusual spirit which he had displayed on his voyage in quest of his bride, and well disposed to fancy that he had performed it in positive opposition, not only to the indirect policy of Elizabeth, but to the malevolent purpose of hell itself. His fleet had been tempest-tost, and he very naturally believed that the Prince of the Powers of the Air had been personally active on the occasion.

The principal person implicated in these heretical and treasonable undertakings, was one Agnes Simpson, or Samson, called the Wise Wife of Keith, and described by Archbishop Spottiswood, not as one of the base or ignorant class of ordinary witches, but a grave matron, composed and deliberate in her answers, which were all to some purpose. This grave dame, from the terms of her indictment, seems to have been a kind of white witch, affecting to cure diseases by words and charms, a dangerous profession, considering the times in which she lived. She was said to be principally engaged in an extensive conspiracy to destroy the fleet of the queen by raising a tempest; and to take the king's life by anointing his linen with poisonous materials, and by constructing figures of clay, to be wasted and tormented after the usual fashion of necromancy.

There was, besides, one Barbara Napier, alias Douglas, a person of some rank; Geillis Duncan, a very active witch, and about thirty other poor creatures of the lowest condition,—among the rest, and doorkeeper to the conclave, a silly old ploughman, called as his nickname Graymeal, who was cuffed by the devil for saying simply, "God bless the King!" When the monarch of Scotland sprung this strong covey of his favourite game, they afforded the Privy Council and him sport for the greatest part of the remaining winter. He attended on the examinations himself, and by one means or other, they were indifferently well dressed to his palate.

Agnes Samson, the grave matron before mentioned, after being an hour tortured by the twisting of a cord around her head, according to the custom of the Buccaneers, confessed that she had consulted with one Richard Grahame concerning the probable length of the king's life, and the means of shortening it. But Satan, to whom they at length resorted for advice, told them in French, respecting King James, *Il est un homme de Dieu*. The poor woman also acknowledged that she had held a meeting with those of her sisterhood, who had charmed a cat by certain spells, having four joints of men knit to its feet, which they threw into the sea to excite a tempest. Another frolic they had, when, like the weird sisters in Macbeth, they embarked in sieves with much mirth and jollity, the Fiend rolling himself before them upon the waves, dimly seen, and resembling a huge haystack in size and appearance. They went on board of a foreign ship richly laden with wines, where, invisible to the crew, they feasted till the sport grew tiresome, and then Satan sunk the vessel and all on board.

Fian, or Cunningham, another of the conspirators, was also visited by the sharpest tortures, ordinary and extraordinary. The nails were torn from his fingers with smiths' pincers; pins were driven into the places which the nails usually defended; his knees were crushed in *the boots*, his finger bones were splintered in the pilniewinks. At length, his constancy, hitherto sustained, as the bystanders supposed, by the help of the devil, was fairly overcome, and he gave an account of a great witch-meeting at North Berwick, where they paced round the church *withershinns*, that is, in reverse of the motion of the sun. Fian then blew into the lock of the church door, whereupon the bolts gave way, the unhallowed crew entered, and their master the devil appeared to his servants in the shape of a black man occupying the pulpit. He was saluted with an "Hail, Master!" but the company were dissatisfied with his not having brought a picture of the king, repeatedly promised, which was to place his majesty at the mercy of this infernal crew. Satan concluded the evening with a divertisement and a dance after his own manner. The former consisted in disinterring a new-buried corpse, and dividing it into fragments among the company, and the ball was maintained by well-nigh two hundred persons, who danced a ring dance, singing this chant—

"Cummer, gang ye before; Cummer, gang ye,
Gif ye will not gang before, Cummers, let me."

After this choral exhibition, the music seems to have been rather imperfect, the number of dancers considered. Geillis Duncan was the only instrumental performer, and she played on a Jew's harp, called in Scotland a *trump*. Dr. Fian, muffled, led the ring, and was highly honoured, generally acting as clerk or recorder.

King James was deeply interested in these mysterious meetings, and took great delight to be present at the examinations of the accused. He sent for Geillis Duncan, and caused her to play before him the same tune to which Satan and his companions led the brawl in North Berwick churchyard.[*] His ears were gratified in another way, for at this meeting it was said the witches demanded of the devil why he did bear such enmity against the king? who returned the flattering answer, that the king was the greatest enemy whom he had in the world.

Almost all these poor wretches were executed, nor did Euphane MacCalzean's station in life save her from the common doom, which was strangling to death, and burning to ashes thereafter. The majority of the jury which tried Barbara Napier, having acquitted her of attendance at the North Berwick meeting, were themselves threatened with a trial for wilful error upon an assize, and could only escape from severe censure and punishment by pleading guilty, and submitting themselves to the king's pleasure. This rigorous and iniquitous conduct shows a sufficient reason why there should be so few acquittals from a charge of witchcraft, where the juries were so much at the mercy of the crown.

It would be disgusting to follow the numerous cases in which the same uniform credulity, the same extorted confessions, the same prejudiced and exaggerated evidence, concluded in the same tragedy at the stake and the pile. The alterations and trenching which lately took place for the purpose of improving the Castlehill of Edinburgh, displayed the ashes of the numbers who had perished in this manner, of whom a large proportion must have been executed between 1590, when the great discovery was made concerning Euphane MacCalzean, and the Wise Wife of Keith, and their accomplices, and the union of the crowns.—*Sir W. Scott.*

[*] The music of this witch tune is unhappily lost. But that of another, believed to have been popular on such occasions, is preserved.
The silly bit chicken, gar cast her a pickle,
And she will grow mickle,
And she will do good.

Entry in the parish register of Glammis, Scotland, June 16, 1676:—"Nae preaching here this Lord's day, the minister being at Gortachy burning a witch."

JOHN CLY THE MILLER.

John Cly, the meal-miller of Tomore, a sturdy, hale, independent-minded old man of 75, has been singularly persecuted by floods, having suffered by that of 1768, and by three or four inundations since, but especially by that of 1768, when his house and mill were carried away, and he was left penniless. He was not a little affected by that calamity which fell upon him, and on no one else; but his indomitable spirit got the better of everything. About seven years ago, he undertook to improve a piece of absolute beach of two acres, entirely covered with enormous stones and gravel. But John knew that a deep rich soil lay below, buried there by the flood of 1768. He removed the stones with immense labour, formed them into a bulwark and enclosure round the field, trenched down the gravel to the depth of four or five feet, and brought up the soil, which afterwards produced most luxuriant crops. His neighbours ridiculed his operations while they were in progress, saying that he would never have a crop there. "Do ye see these ashen-trees?" said John, pointing to some vigorous saplings growing near, "are they no thriving?" It was impossible to deny that they were. "Well," continued John, "if it wunna produce corn, I'll plant it wi' ash-trees, and the laird, at least, will hae the benefit." The fruits of all John's labours were swept away by the direful flood of the 3d of August. But pride of his heart, as this improvement had been, the flood was not able to sweep away his equanimity and philosophy together with his acres. When some one condoled with him on his loss, "I took it frae the Awen," said he, with emphasis, "and let the Awen hae her ain again." And, when a gossiping tailor halted at his door one day, charitably to bewail his loss, he cut him short, by pithily remarking, "Well! if I have lost my croft, I have got a fish-pond in its place, where I can fish independent of any one." After the year 1783, he built his house on a rock, that shewed itself from under the soil at the base of the bank, bounding the glen of the burn. During the late flood, the water was dashing up at his door, and his sister, who is older than he, having expressed great terror, and proposed they should both fly for it; "What's the woman afeard o'?" cried John, impatiently, "hae we not baith the rock o' nature and the Rock of Ages to trust till?—We'll no stir one fit!" John's first exertions after the flood, was to gae down to Ballindalloch, to assist the Laird in his distress. There he worked hard for three days, before Mr. Grant discovered that he had left his own haystack buried to the top in sand, and insisted on his going home to disinter it. When Mr. Grant talked to him of his calamity, "Odd, sir," said he, "I dinna regard this matter hauf sae muckle as I did that slap i' the aughty-three, for then I was, in a manner, a marked man. Noo we're a' sufferin' thegither, an' I'm but neighbour-like." Mr. Grant says that the people of this district bear misfortunes with a wonderful degree of philosophy, arising from the circumstance of their being deeply tinged with the doctrine of predestination. I was much gratified by my interview with honest John Cly. Whilst I was sketching him unperceived, Mr. Grant was doing his best to occupy his attention. "Well, now, John," said Mr. Grant to him, pointing to an apparently impracticable beach of stones a little way up the glen, "if you had improved that piece, as I advised you, it would have been safe still, for you see the burn hasn't touched it at all."—"Na, fegs!" replied John, with a most significant shake of his head, "gin I had gruppit her in wi' the stanes that cam oot o't whaur wad she hae been noo, think ye?—Odd, I kent her ower lang."

There are several tragic scenes of death and danger, and "moving accidents by flood and field," which we should gladly transcribe did our limits permit, but we must content ourselves with one more quotation—a ludicrous account of

WIDOW SHANKS'S ADVENTURES.

The haugh above the bridge of Lower Craigellachie was very much cut up; and the house and nursery at the south end of the arch are gone. The widow of James Shanks, amidst the loss of her furniture, house, and her son's garden-ground, lamented nothing so much as her deceased husband's watch, and his fiddle, on the strings of which hung many a tender recollection. That fiddle, the dulcet strains of which had come over her "like the sweet south breathing upon a bed of violets," stealing the tender affections of her virgin heart, till they all centred on her Orpheus, Mr. James Shanks; that fiddle, to the sprightly notes of which she had so often jerked out her youthful limbs, and whirled round in the wild *pirouette* of the Highland fling, to the animating tune of *Bogan-Lochan*; that fiddle, in fine, which had been the fiddle of her fancy, from the heyday of her youth upwards, "was gone with the water, and was now, for aught she knew to the contrair, in Norrawa or Denmark!" The grief of Mrs. Shanks for the loss of this valued violin was more than I shall attempt to paint. Great artists often envelope the heads of their chief mourners in drapery, from a conscious inability to do justice to the passion, and so must I hide the lachrymose head of Mrs. Shanks. And how indeed shall I describe her joy, some days afterwards, when an idle loon, who had been wandering about the banks of the river "findin' things," as he said himself, appeared before her astonished and delighted eyes, with the identical fiddle in his hands? The yell of Mrs. Shanks was said, by those who heard it, to resemble the wild shriek with which her husband was wont to inspire additional fury into the heels of the dancers, already excited by the power of his wonderful bow hand. She kissed and hugged the fiddle, and, as if its very contact had music in it, she laid hands on the astonished loon, and went a full round of the floor with him, ending with a fling that surprised every one. The fiddle had been found in the neighbourhood of Arndilly, whither it had merrily floated on the bosom of the waves. But what was yet infinitely more extraordinary, the watch, which had hung in a small bag, suspended by a nail to the post of her bed, was found,—watch, bag, post, and all,—near Fochabers, eight or ten miles below, and was safely restored to its overjoyed owner.—*Sir Thomas Dick Lauder's Moray Floods.*

SCENE IN THE BATHS OF LEUK, AMONG THE ALPS.

Bearing in mind the advice of Hippocrates, "Bathe us before eating, and eat not before bathing," about an hour after dinner we went to "do at Rome as Rome does," namely, to immerse ourselves in the warm baths. Equipped in the ample folds of a linen dress, we made our appearance in public—that is to say, in the watery lounge. The scene was as novel as it was, to our unaccustomed eyes, grotesque. Without the slightest blush of indecorum, it was irresistibly ludicrous; and we were constrained to indulge in laughter for some moments before we could calmly scan the individual features of the picture which caused our mirth; we, in our turn, furnished some good-natured amusement to those around us. In the floor of a large furnished apartment were four baths, each about twelve feet square, and three or four feet deep. In these baths reclined groups of ladies and gentlemen, attired in similar dresses to those in which we were habited. Little wooden trays, bearing reticules, work-baskets, &c., and reading-desks, were floating about on the surface of the water. Some of the parties were chatting or telling stories; others singing; and many of the ladies were prettily occupied in some little article of female employment, or wreathing chaplets of half-faded Alpine flowers, the waters rekindling their hues to freshness; but the colours, though bright, were far outshone by the rosy complexions of the fair *employées*, which the effect of the bath heightened into unwonted beauty. On the floor were a few persons conversing with their friends below, and one or two attendants swinging pans of charcoal, to keep the air of the same temperature as the water; while on a platform, above, was a pump, by which fresh water was occasionally supplied to the baths. A few inches from the bottom a ledge runs round the bath, which enables the bather either to be recumbent on the water up to his chin, or to sit upright, in which latter position it reaches only to his neck. There are also moveable seats in the baths. Two passages, into which the water flows, leads from each compartment, and it is the custom for ladies and gentlemen, in proceeding to their respective dressing-rooms, to glide or sail through the door, into this passage, before rising from the water. The dressing-rooms are heated by stoves, and are tolerably comfortable. With regard to the period of time passed in the bath, on their first arrival, half an hour is deemed sufficient; next day, perhaps, an hour; and, in the course of a short time, they are able to bear immersion for nine or ten hours per diem, not only with impunity, but, as they assured me, with signal advantage. The extreme relaxation of the skin which it produces has a marked effect in relieving the complaints that are subjected to its influence. These are principally cutaneous disorders and chronic affections. In England, where warm bathing is not so much a part of domestic luxury as it is in some other countries—I may be allowed to say not so much as, for the good of society, it ough to be—if a physician were to propose to a patient to spend from eight to ten hours a-day for three, or it may be six weeks, in a bath, at 100 degrees, he would probably find his practice less benefited than his patient by the advice. It may indeed be doubted whether an English constitution could bear so exhausting a system, in its full extent, in this climate.—*Aurora Borealis.*

THE DRAMA.

In the forthcoming number of the Westminster Review, there is an excellent paper on Dramatic Literature, in which the causes of its decline in this country are traced to the system of monopoly and censureship, which has long shed its baleful influence over our Drama. The wonder is, not that under the shackles with which it is loaded, our Dramatic Literature is in a declining state, but that it has not been altogether extinguished. The Reviewer remarks, that

"One striking abomination in all monopoly is, that it destroys the natural elasticity of social institutions. To establish a monopoly is to put an infant's foot into a small iron boot:—as the flesh grows the boot pinches. When the evil increases to the magnitude that demands attention, there is a consultation had, how the pain is to be diminished and the iron still kept on. Some say a little hole should be bored about the region of the great toe, others recommend that the iron be ribbed, and others that joints be constructed in the sole, so that the foot shall have a beautiful quasi-natural play. But flinging the iron to the bottom of the sea, and either walking with a free and naked step, or protecting the limb with a covering of pliant leather,—is far too rash and dangerous a measure for safe and prudent characters.

"This iron-binding quality of monopoly has been the grand cause of the complaint and confusion. Had the legitimate drama been left to itself, at this moment we should have abounded both in good plays and good actors. We might possibly have had a Shakespeare in every reign since that of the virgin queen. At any rate, there would have been men who could please their age, and who were as much qualified to satisfy the public taste as any other professors of fine arts or literature.

"When the legitimate drama arose, there was a closer union between poetry and personation than there is now or ever will be again. At that time a drama stood for much more than it does at present; it was novel, poem, and play. Besides, there were few other sources of intellectual entertainment. The play was not merely poem and novel, but it was also review, magazine, voyage and travel. Theology alone divided attention with it in the way of literature. And theology is now-a-days amply represented by 'seriousness,' called in the report 'sectarianism.' So that the drama no longer reigns over a wide domain, but has been, by modern changes, like the German princes, virtually mediatised. Had there been no monopoly, the department of the drama which remains with all its force, viz. personation and exhibition, would have taken more complete possession of the stage than it has done, and in fact been much more developed. Authors and actors having been hampered by their superstitious veneration for the 'legitimate,' have gone upon the old model till they have wearied the public to the uttermost stretch of annoy; while personation and exhibition, taken up as a despised succedaneum for some great unknown, have had to struggle with all kinds of discountenance and discouragement. Thus the drama, like many other things, has fallen between two stools—the old excellence and the new.

"When the drama was the fashionable means of publication of the day, the Bull and the Globe were what the shops of Murray and Colburn are now. Men went there for ideas; there was neither eloquence, scenery, nor dramatic effect. 'Paris,' chalked on a board, served to indicate the capital of France, and a blanket was a sufficient drop-scene. Some personation there doubtless was, and also some elocution, but probably in no very high degree of perfection. The grand object of the audience was the genius of the writer. In a small cabin, crowded with noted persons, where every word was heard as it was deliberately uttered, the play stood or fell by the ideas announced. Now, on the contrary, ideas are sought in books, by the fire-side, or on the sofa, through the medium of the convenient duodecimo. Be it fair or foul, be the reader near or distant from the theatre, be his horses sick or lame, or be he too poor, or too rich, or too great to go to a theatre, the ideas of our modern men of genius are always at his command. In this manner, poetry, and imagination generally, have become surplusage in the drama: and they are consequently oftener left out than recited. Half the 'legitimate drama' is omitted in performance, and only that retained which concerns action. Poetry, luckily, has never been patented; and in consequence, we possess our Miltons, our Popes, our Scotts, and Byrons. The drama, like the peerage, has been handed down in particular lines, till the House of Peers, and the House of Players, have come to be in a similar state of decrepitude.

"Had the legitimate drama been more strictly 'preserved,' the state of things would have been much worse than it is; but monopolies never do all the mischief possible. The very guardians of legitimacy have built houses in which illegitimacy alone could flourish; and the minor theatres being legally excluded from the classical drama, took to what they could get up in compliance with the public taste. The result is, a great deal of splendour in our theatres, fine scene-painting, fine exhibition of all kinds, even to good personal exhibition, that is, personation, play of countenance, action, costume, and all that serves to keep up illusion. The authors have not, however, seconded these efforts; for this reason, that they were aiming at the nominal object of admiration, the legitimate drama,—that is, the drama full of poetry, full of that which told at the Globe and the Bull. The proof of this is in the fact that no tragedy of the legitimate drama, ancient or modern, is ever acted as it is written; half or more is obliged to be left out, because the authors were not thinking of the stage as it is, but as it was. The author of a good play is quite a different person from the author of a good poem; yet it is always expected that a great poet should produce a good play. Acting under this persuasion, Scott, Byron, Moore, and perhaps Campbell, have tried and failed. Whereas, such a writer, or rather doer, as Mr. Jerrold, has carried the whole town before him. If evidence were wanting to prove that the really successful dramatists of the day, are an order of men not characterised by what is ordinarily considered as understanding, appeal might be made to the minutes of examination before the committee. In a direct proportion to their celebrity, are they absurd, illogical, and ridiculous. The players beat the authors in every point of view. The player has been less iron-shod than the author; emancipate the drama, and we shall soon see men who understand their business. There have been good actors under every disadvantage; under obloquy, under monopoly, under the fact of its being an unrequiting profession; *a fortiori*, there will be good actors under a state of things relieved from all these trammels. The very contrary, however, is feared by the greater part of the dramatic witnesses here examined; as in so many other matters it is supposed the cottage cannot stand if the ivy be taken away, though it is proved the parasite entertains moisture, encourages vermin, and in fact is eating into the very elements of strength. Let the profession become remunerative and steady in its demand, and there will be a rush of students towards it; their conduct will be ruled by the regularity of their gains, and the respectability of the class will rise with its responsibility. Actors will no more decrease because of the number of theatres, than corn because of an increase of corn-markets. They might at first, perhaps, be somewhat dispersed; but the corps would be quickly filled up with able volunteers, when placed on a proper footing. It is impudently alleged, that the public will spoil the taste of the actors, if admitted to view them in un-ruined and un-patented abodes. The public, however, has always been a fair judge of merit, and the patentee people have never done more than follow the public's lead, and not always that.

"The case of authors is not less plain. Give them proper remuneration, and relieve them from the idea of perpetually aiming at the legitimate drama, and there will be a conflux of good dramatists in every reign. Give them a law of copyright as in France; so that an author and all his posterity, shall enjoy a small advantage from every representation of his play for an extensive period. Then dramatic authors would be not only men of dramatic genius, but approved citizens of an educated and esteemed class.

THE WAITS.

If there ever be a time in which the floating visions that lie about us, of some dim, pre-existing, happier and purer state of being, seem something more than a dream, it is when one is slowly awakened from a sound, healthful sleep, and languishes, as it were, into blissful life, under the melodies of those relics of the wandering minstrels, and of old manners and pastimes, the *Waits*. But the *Waits* do not restrict their music to the sleeping hours. They are, in most small towns, the voluntary attendants on strangers—presumed bountiful—and on newly-married couples. Christmas, and the New Year is, however, their high-tide. For a few weeks before they humbly request to be "remembered," they parade the streets towards morning; and also for a short time afterwards; thus ushering in, and taking a lingering farewell of the annual season of festivity. No one has looked deeper, and more wisely, into the heart of our old hallowed customs and usages than the poet Wordsworth. The verses addressed to his brother on the *Waits*, are poetry, philosophy, and kindliness combined.

THE CHRISTMAS WAITS.

The Minstrels played their Christmas tune
To-night beneath my cottage eaves;
While, smitten by a lofty moon,
The encircling Laurels, thick with leaves,
Gave back a rich and dazzling sheen,
That overpowered their natural green.

Through hill and valley every breeze
Had sunk to rest with folded wings:
Keen was the air, but could not freeze,
Nor check the music of the strings;
So stout and hardy were the band
That scraped the chords with strenuous hand.

And who but listened?—till was paid
Respect to every inmate's claim;
The greeting given, the music played,
In honour of each household name,
Duly pronounced with lusty call,
And "merry Christmas" wished to all!

O Brother! I revere the choice
That took thee from thy native hills;
And it is given thee to rejoice:
Though public care full often tills
(Heaven only witness of the toil)
A barren and ungrateful soil.

Yet, would that Thou, with me and mine,
Hadst heard this never-failing rite;
And seen on other faces shine
A true revival of the light;
Which Nature, and these rustic Powers,
In simple childhood, spread through ours!

For pleasure hath not ceased to wait
On these expected annual rounds,
Whether the rich man's sumptuous gate
Call forth the unelaborate sounds,
Or they are offered at the door
That guards the lowliest of the poor.

How touching, when at midnight, sweep
Snow-muffled winds, and all is dark,
To hear—and sink again to sleep!
Or at an earlier call, to mark,
By blazing fire, the still suspense
Of self-complacent innocence;

The mutual nod,—the grave disguise
Of hearts with gladness brimming o'er;
And some unbidden tears that rise
For names once heard, and heard no more;
Tears brightened by the serenade
For infant in the cradle laid!

Ah! not for emerald fields alone,
With ambient streams more pure and bright
Than fabled Cytherea's zone
Glittering before the Thunderer's sight,
Is to my heart of hearts endeared,
The ground where we were born and reared?

Hail, ancient Manners! sure defence,
Where they survive, of wholesome laws;
Remnants of love, whose modest sense
Thus into narrow room withdraws;
Hail, Usages of pristine mould,
And ye, that guard them, Mountains old!

Bear with me, Brother! quench the thought
That slights this passion, or condemns;
If thee fond fancy ever brought
From the proud margin of the Thames,
And Lambeth's venerable towers,
To humbler streams, and greener bowers.

Yes, they can make, who fail to find,
Short leisure even in busiest days;
Moments to cast a look behind,
And profit by those kindly rays
That through the clouds do sometimes steal,
And all the far-off Past reveal.

Hence, while the Imperial City's din
Beats frequent on thy satiate ear,
A pleased attention I may win
To agitations less severe,
That neither overwhelm nor cloy,
But fill the hollow vale with joy!

SUPERSTITIONS OF THE WELSH.—The Welsh, speaking generally, are highly superstitious, and, amidst scenery wild and imposing, rigidly tenacious moreover of the traditionary lore inherited from their ancestors—so that their very being is incorporated with divers strange fantasies handed down from father to son, preserved with religious veneration, and influencing their imaginations more or less according to the caprice, the temperament, or the locality of the individual. Like all secluded mountaineers, whose intercourse with the world is limited to a narrow communication necessary for mere existence, they impute natural effects to more than natural causes, and the sunshine and the storm, the whirlwind and the flood, are often attributed to the kind or baneful influence of the good or evil spirit—of the mischievous elf or the good natured fairy. Thus, in the pastoral counties of Carnarvon and Merioneth (and these are now the most secluded districts in the principality,) there is scarcely a glen or a wood, a mountain or a dingle, a rock or a ravine, that has not its due quantity of fairies and spirits; and every nook of this rude upland district, which has hitherto been but little accessible to the innovating approaches of civilization, can boast of no scanty number of supernatural inhabitants.—*Westminster Review.*—Article "Cambrian Superstition."

HIGH-EARED RACE OF MEN.—M. Dureaude Lamalle has made out the strongest evidence in proof of the existence of a distinct variety of the human race, characterized by the position of their ears. Not only, as they are represented in the Memnonium, and other Egyptian statues and coins, were the old Egypto-Caucasians remarkable for their high ears, but in more than forty mummies which were unrolled and examined by M. de Lamalle, at Turin, the auricular foramen, which, drawing a horizontal line, is placed in us on a level with the inferior part of the nose, was in these examples found to be on a level with the middle of the eye. The elevation, as measured, amounted to a full inch and a half. The facial angle was at the same time found equal to that of Europeans, but the temporal region much more depressed than in our variety. Nor does it appear that the high-eared race is extinct; there are instances of it among the people of Upper Egypt at this day; and indeed there is in Paris at present a teacher of Arabic, a Copt of Upper Egypt, who is possessed of this conformation in a most decided degree.—*Medical Gazette.*

THE STORY-TELLER.

LOVE AND AUTHORSHIP.
BY J. SHERIDAN KNOWLES, ESQ.

"Will you remember me, Rosalie?"
"Yes!"
"Will you keep your hand for me for a year?"
"Yes!"
"Will you answer me when I write to you?"
"Yes!"
"One request more—O Rosalie, reflect that my life depends upon your acquiescence—should I succeed, will you marry me in spite of your uncle?"

"Yes!" answered Rosalie. There was no pause—reply followed question, as if it were a dialogue which they had got by heart—and by heart *indeed* they had got it—but I leave you to guess the book they had conned it from.

'Twas in a green lane, on a summer's evening, about nine o'clock, when the west, like a gate of gold, had shut upon the retiring sun, that Rosalie and her lover, hand in hand, walked up and down. His arm was the girdle of her waist; hers formed a collar for his neck, which a knight of the garter—ay, the owner of the sword that dubbed him might have been proud to wear. Their gait was slow, and face was turned to face; near were their lips while they spoke; and much of what they said never came to the ear, though their souls caught up every word of it.

Rosalie was upwards of five years the junior of her lover. She had known him since she was a little girl in her twelfth year. He was almost eighteen then, and when she thought far more about a doll than a husband, he would set her upon his knee, and call her his little wife. One, two, three years passed on, and still, whenever he came from college, and as usual went to pay his first visit at her father's, before he had been five minutes in the parlour, the door was flung open, and in bounded Rosalie, and claimed her accustomed seat. The fact was, till she was fifteen, she was a child of a very slow growth, and looked the girl when many a companion of hers of the same age had begun to appear the woman.

When another vacation, however, came round, and Theodore paid his customary call, and was expecting his little wife as usual, the door opened slowly, and a tall young lady entered, and curtsying, coloured, and walked to a seat next to the lady of the house. The visitor stood up and bowed, and sat down again, without knowing that it was Rosalie.

"Don't you know Rosalie?" exclaimed her father.

"Rosalie!" replied Theodore in an accent of surprise; and approached his little wife of old, who rose and half gave him her hand, and curtsying, coloured again; and sat down again without having interchanged a word with him. No wonder—she was four inches taller than when he had last seen her, and her bulk had expanded correspondingly; while her features, that half a year before gave one the idea of a sylph that would bound after a butterfly, had now mellowed in their expression, into the sentiment, the softness, and the reserve of the woman.

Theodore felt absolutely disappointed. Five minutes before, he was all volubility. No sooner was one question answered than he proposed another—and he had so many capital stories for Rosalie when she came down—and yet, when Rosalie did come down, he sat as though he had not a word to say for himself. In short, every thing and every body in the house seemed to have changed along with its young mistress; he felt no longer at home in it, as he was wont; and in less than a quarter of an hour he made his bow and departed.

Now this was exceedingly strange; for Rosalie, from a pretty little girl, had turned into a lovely young woman. If a heart looked out of her eyes before, a soul looked out of them now; her arm, which formerly the sun had been allowed to salute when he liked, and which used to bear the trace of many a kiss that he had given it, now shone white through a sleeve of muslin, like snow behind a vale of haze; her bosom had enlarged its wavy curve, and leaving her waist little more than the span it used to be, sat proudly heaving above it; and the rest of her form which, only six months ago, looked trim and airy in her short and close-fitting frock, now lengthening and throwing out its flowing line, stood stately in the folds of a long and ample drapery. Yet could not all this make up for the want of the little wife that used to come and take her seat upon Theodore's knee.

To be sure there was another way of accounting for the young man's chagrin. He might have been disappointed that Rosalie, when five feet four, should be a little more reserved than when she was only five feet nothing. Romantic young men, too, are apt to fancy odd things. Theodore was a *very* romantic young man; and having, perhaps, traced for himself the woman in the child—as one will anticipate, in looking at a peach that is just knit, the hue, and form, and flavour of the consummate fruit—he might have set Rosalie down in his mind as his wife in earnest, when he appeared to call her so only in jest.

Such was the case. Theodore never calculated that Rosalie knew nothing about his dreams—that she had no such visions herself; he never anticipated that the frankness of girlhood would vanish, as soon as the diffidence of young womanhood began its blushing reign; the thought never occurred to him that the day would come when Rosalie would scruple to sit on his knee—ay, even though Rosalie should then begin to think upon him, as for many a year before he had thought upon her. He returned from college the fifth time; he found that the woman, which he imagined in a year or two she would become, was surpassed by the woman that she already was; he remarked the withdrawal of confidence, the limitation of familiarity—the penalty which he must inevitably pay for her maturing—and he felt repelled and chilled, and utterly disheartened by it.

For a whole week he never returned to the house. Three days of a second week elapsed, and still he kept away. He had been invited, however, to a ball which was to be given there the day following; and much as he was inclined to absent himself, being a little more inclined to go—he went.

Full three hours was he in the room without once setting his eyes upon Rosalie. He saw her mother and her father, and talked with them; he saw 'squire this, and doctor that, and attorney such a one, and had fifty things to say to each of them; he had eyes and tongue for every body, but Rosalie—not a look, or a word did he exchange with her; yet he was here, and there, and everywhere! In short, he was all communicativeness and vivacity, so that every one remarked how bright he had become since his last visit to college!

At last, however, his fine spirits all at once seemed to forsake him, and he withdrew to the library, which was lighted up for the occasion as an anti-room, and taking a volume out of the bookcase, threw himself into a chair and began to turn over the leaves.

"Have you forgotten your little wife?" said a soft voice near him—'twas Rosalie's—"if you *have*," she added as he started from his seat, "she has not forgotten you."

She wore a carnation in her hair—the hue of the flower was not deeper than that of her cheek, as she stood and extended her hands to Theodore, who, the moment he rose, had held forth both of his.

"Rosalie!"

"Theodore!"—He led her to a sofa, which stood in a recess on the opposite side of the room, and for five minutes not another word did they exchange.

At length she gently withdrew her hand from his—she had suffered him to hold it all that time—"We shall be observed," said she.

"Ah Rosalie," replied he, "nine months since you sat upon my knee, and they observed us, yet you did not mind it!"

"You know I am a woman now," rejoined Rosalie, hanging her head, "and—and—and—will you lead off the next dance with me?" cried she, suddenly changing the subject. "There now; I have asked you," added she, "which is more than you deserve!" Of course Theodore was not at all happy to accept the challenge of the metamorphosed Rosalie.

One might suppose that the young lady's heart was interested, and that Theodore was a far happier man than he imagined himself to be. The fact was neither more nor less. Little Rosalie was proud of being called Theodore's wife, because she heard every body else speak in praise of him. Many a marriageable young lady had she heard declare—not minding to speak before a child—that Theodore was the finest young man in B——; that she hoped Theodore would be at such or such a house where she was going to dine, or spend the evening; nay, that she would like to have a sweetheart like Theodore. Then would Rosalie interpose, and with a saucy toss of her head exclaim, that nobody should have Theodore but Rosalie, for Rosalie was his little wife. 'Twas thus she learned to admire the face and person of Theodore, who more than once paid for her acquired estimation of them; for sometimes before a whole room full of company she would march up to him, and scanning him from head to foot, with folded arms, at length declare aloud, that he *was* the handsomest young man in B——. Then Theodore was so kind to her, and thought so much of any thing she did, and took such notice of her! Often, at a dance, he would make her his partner for the whole evening; and there was Miss Willoughby, perhaps, or Miss Millar, sitting down, either of whom would have given her eyes to stand up if only in a reel with Theodore.

But when the summer of her seventeenth year beheld her bursting into womanhood; when her expanding thoughts, from a bounding, fitful, rill-like current, began to run a deep, a broad, and steady stream; when she found that she was almost arrived at the threshold of the world, and reflected that the step which marks the female's first entrance into it is generally taken in the hand of a partner—the thought of who that partner might be, recalled Theodore to her mind—and her heart fluttered as she asked herself the question—should she ever be indeed his wife?

When, this time, he paid his first visit, Rosalie was as much mortified as he was. Her vexation was increased when she saw that he absented himself; she resolved, if possible, to ascertain the cause; and persuaded her mother to give a ball, and specially invite the young gentleman. He came; she watched him; observed that he neither inquired after her nor sought for her; and marked the excellent terms that he was upon with twenty people, about whom she knew him to be perfectly indifferent. Women have a perception of the workings of the heart, far more quick and subtle than we have. She was convinced that all his fine spirits were forced, that he was acting a part. She suspected that while he appeared to be occupied with every body but Rosalie—Rosalie was the only body that was running in his thoughts. She saw him withdraw to the library; she followed him: found him sitting down with a book in his hand; perceived, from his manner of turning over the leaves, that he was intent on any thing but reading; she was satisfied that he was thinking of nothing but Rosalie. The thought that Rosalie might one day indeed become his wife, now occurred to her for the thousandth time, and a thousand times stronger than ever: a spirit diffused itself through her heart which had never been breathed into it before; and filling it with hope and happiness, and unutterable contentment, irresistibly drew *it* towards him. She approached him, accosted him, and in a moment was seated with him, hand in hand, upon the sofa!

As soon as the dance was done,—" Rosalie," said Theodore, "'tis almost as warm in the air as in the room: will you be afraid to take a turn with me in the garden?"

"I will get my shawl in a minute," said Rosalie, "and meet you there;" and the maiden was there almost as soon as he.

They proceeded arm-in-arm, to the farthest part of the garden; and there they walked up and down without either seeming inclined to speak, as though their hearts could discourse through their hands, which were locked in one another.

"Rosalie!" at last breathed Theodore. "Rosalie!" breathed he a second time, before the expecting girl could summon courage to say "Well?"

"I cannot go home to-night," resumed he, "without speaking to you." Yet Theodore seemed to be in no hurry to speak; for there he stopped, and continued silent so long, that Rosalie began to doubt whether he would open his lips again.

"Had we not better go in?" said Rosalie. "I think I hear them breaking up."

"Not yet," replied Theodore.

"They'll miss us!" said Rosalie.

"What of that?" rejoined Theodore.

"Nay," resumed the maid, "we have remained long enough, and at least allow me to go in."

"Stop but another minute, dear Rosalie!" imploringly exclaimed the youth.

"For what?" was the maid's reply.

"Rosalie," without a pause resumed Theodore, "you used to sit upon my knee, and let me call you wife. Are those times passed for ever? Dear Rosalie! will you never let me take you on my knee and call you wife again?"

"When we have done with our girlhood, we have done with our plays," said Rosalie.

"I do not mean in *play*, dear Rosalie," cried Theodore. "It is not playing at man and wife to walk, as such, out of church. Will you marry me, Rosalie?"

Rosalie was silent.

"Will you marry me?" repeated he.

Not a word would Rosalie speak.

"Hear me!" cried Theodore. "The first day, Rosalie, I took you upon my knee, and called you my wife, jest as it seemed to be, my heart was never more in earnest. That day I wedded you in my soul; for though you were a child I saw the future woman in you, rich in the richest attractions of your sex. Nay, do me justice; recall what you yourself have known of me; inquire of others. To whom did I play the suitor from that day? To none but you, although to you I did not seem to play it. Rosalie! was I not always with you? Recollect now! Did a day pass, when I was at home, without my coming to your father's house? When there were parties there, whom did I sit beside, but you? Whom did I stand behind at the pianoforte, but you? Nay, for a whole night, whom have I danced with, but you? Whatever you might have thought *then*, can you believe *now*, that it was merely a playful child that could so have engrossed me? No, Rosalie! it was the virtuous, generous, lovely, loving woman, that I saw in the playful child. Rosalie! for five years have I loved you, though I never declared it to you till now. Do you think I am worthy of you? Will you give yourself to me? Will you marry me? Will you sit upon my knee again, and let me call you wife?"

Three or four times Rosalie made an effort to speak; but desisted, as if she knew not what to say, or was unable to say what she wished; Theodore still holding her hand. At last, "Ask my father's consent!" she exclaimed, and tried to get away; but before she could effect it, she was clasped to the bosom of Theodore, nor released until the interchange of the first pledge of love had been forced from her bashful lips!——She did not appear that night in the drawing-room again.

Theodore's addresses were sanctioned by the parents of Rosalie. The wedding-day was fixed; it wanted but a fortnight to it, when a malignant fever made its appearance in the town; Rosalie's parents were the first victims. She was left an orphan at eighteen, and her uncle, by the mother's side, who had been nominated her guardian in a will, made several years, having followed his brother-in-law and sister's remains to the grave, took up his residence at B——.

Rosalie's sole consolation now was such as she received from the society of Theodore; but Theodore soon wanted consolation himself. His father was attacked by the fever and died, leaving his affairs, to the astonishment of every one, in a state of the most inextricable embarrassment; for he had been looked upon as one of the wealthiest inhabitants of B——. This was a double blow to Theodore, but he was not aware of the weight of it till, after the interment of his father, he repaired, for the first time, to resume his visits to his Rosalie.

He was stepping up without ceremony to the drawing-room, when the servant begged his pardon for stopping him, telling him at the same time, that he had received instructions from his master to shew Theodore into the parlour when he should call.

"Was Miss Wilford there?"

"No." Theodore was shewn into the parlour. Of all savage brutes, the human brute is the most pernicious and revolting, because he unites to the evil properties of the inferior animal the mental faculties of the superior one; and then he is at large. A vicious-tempered dog you can muzzle and render innocuous; but there is no preventing the human dog that bites from fleshing his tooth; he is sure to have it in somebody. And then the infliction is so immeasurably more severe!—the quick of the mind is so much more sensitive than that of the body! Besides, the savage that runs upon four legs is so inferior in performance to him that walks upon two! 'Tis he that knows how to gnaw! I have often thought it a pity and a sin that the man who plays the dog should be protected from dying the death of one. He should hang, and the other go free.

"Well, young gentleman!" was the salutation which Theodore received when he entered the parlour; and pray what brings you here?"

Theodore was struck dumb; and no wonder.

"Your father, I understand, has died a beggar! Do you think to marry my niece?" If Theodore respired with difficulty before, his breath was utterly taken away at this. He was a young man of spirit, but who can keep up his heart, when his ship, all at once is going down.

The human dog went on. "Young gentleman, I shall be plain with you, for I am a straightforward man; young women should mate with their matches— you are no match for my niece; so a good morning to you!" How more in place to have wished him a good halter! Saying this, the straightforward savage walked out of the room, leaving the door wide open that Theodore might have room for egress; and steadily walked up stairs.

It was several minutes before he could recover his self-recollection. When he did so, he rang the bell.

"Tell your master I wish to speak to him," said Theodore to the servant who answered it. The servant went up stairs after his master, and returned.

"I am sorry, sir," said he, "to be the bearer of such an errand; but my master desires you instantly to quit the house; and has commanded me to tell you he has given me orders not to admit you again."

"I must see Miss Wilford!" exclaimed Theodore.

"You cannot, sir!" respectfully remarked the servant; "for she is locked in her own room; but you can send a message to her," added he in a whisper, "and I will be the bearer of it. There is not a servant in the house, Mr Theodore, but is sorry for you to the soul."

This was so much in season, and was so evidently spoken from the heart, that Theodore could not help catching the honest fellow by the hand. Here the drawing-room bell was rung violently.

"I must go, sir," said the servant; "what message to my mistress?"

"Tell her to give me a meeting, and to apprize me of the time and place," said Theodore; and the next moment the hall-door was shut upon him.

One may easily imagine the state of the young fellow's mind. To be driven with insult and barbarity from the house in which he had been received a thousand times with courtesy and kindness—which he looked upon as his own! Then, what was to be done? Rosalie's uncle, after all, had told him nothing but the truth. His father had died a beggar! Dear as Rosalie was to Theodore, his own pride recoiled at the idea of offering her a hand which was not the master of a shilling! Yet was not Theodore portionless. His education was finished; that term he had completed his collegiate studies. If his father had not left him a fortune, he had provided him with the means of making one himself: at all events, of commanding a competency. He had the credit of being a young man of decided genius too. "I will not offer Rosalie a beggar's hand!" exclaimed Theodore; "I shall ask her to remain true to me for a year; and I'll go up to London, and maintain myself by my pen. It may acquire me fame as well as fortune; and then I may marry Rosalie!"

This was a great deal of work to be done in a year; but if Theodore was not a man of genius, he possessed a mind of that sanguine temperament, which is usually an accompaniment of the richer gift. Before the hour of dinner all his plans were laid, and he was ready to start for London. He waited now for nothing but a message from Rosalie, and as soon as the sweet girl could send it, it came to him. It appointed him to meet her in the green lane after sunset; the sun had scarcely set when he was there, and there, too, was Rosalie. He found that she was Rosalie still. Fate had stripped him of fortune; but she could not persuade Rosalie to refuse him her hand, or her lip; when, half-way down the lane, she heard a light quick step behind her, and, turning, beheld Theodore.

Theodore's wishes, as I stated before, were granted soon as communicated; and now nothing remained but to say good bye, perhaps the hardest thing to two young lovers. Rosalie stood passive in the arms of Theodore, as he took the farewell kiss, which appeared as if it would join his lips to hers for ever, instead of tearing them away. She heard her name called from a short distance, and in a half-suppressed voice; she started, and turned towards the direction whence the pre-concerted warning came; she heard it again; she had stopped till the last moment! She had half-withdrawn herself from Theodore's arms; she looked at him; flung her own around him, and burst into tears upon his neck! In another minute there was nobody in the lane.

London is a glorious place for a man of talent to make his way in—provided he has extraordinary good luck. Nothing but merit can get on there; nothing is sterling that is not of its coinage. Our provincial towns won't believe that gold is gold unless it has been minted in London. There is no trickery there; no treating, no canvassing, no intrigue, no coalition! There, worth has only to shew itself if it wishes to be killed with kindness! London tells the truth! You may swear to what it says, whatsoever may be proved to the contrary. The cause—the cause is every thing in London! Shew but your craft, and straight your brethren come crowding around you, and if they find you worthy, why, you shall be brought into notice, even though they should tell a lie for it and damn you. Never trouble yourself about getting on by interest in London! Get on by yourself. Poets are filled there by merit; or if the man suits not the office, why the office is made to adapt itself to the man, and so there is unity after all! What a happy fellow was Theodore to find himself in such a place as London!

He was certainly happy in one thing; the coach in which he came set him down at a friend's, whose circumstances were narrow, but whose heart was large—a curate of the Church of England. Strange that, with all the appurtenances of hospitality at its command, abundance should allow it to be said, that the kindest welcome which adversity usually meets with, is that which it receives from adversity. If Theodore found that the house was a cold one to what he had been accustomed, the warmth of the greeting made up for it.: "They breakfasted at nine, dined at four, and, if he could sleep upon the sofa, why there was a bed for him!" In a day he was settled, and at his work.

And upon what did Theodore found his hopes of making a fortune, and rising to fame in London? Upon writing a play. At an early period he had discovered, as his friends imagined, a talent for dramatic composition; and having rather sedulously cultivated that branch of literature, he thought that he would now try his hand in one bold effort, the success of which should determine him as to his future course in life. The play was written, presented, and accepted; the performers were ready in their parts; the evening of representation came on, and Theodore, seated in the pit beside his friend, at last, with a throbbing heart, beheld the curtain rise. The first and second acts went off smoothly, and with applause.

Two gentlemen were placed immediately in front of Theodore. "What do you think of it?" said the one to the other.

'Rather tame," was the reply.

"Will it succeed?"

"Doubtful."

The third act, however, decided the fate of the play; the interest of the audience became so intense, that, at one particular stage of the action, numbers in the second and third rows of the side boxes stood up, and the clapping of hands was universal, intermingled with cries of "bravo!" from every part of the theatre. "'Twill do," was now the remark, and Theodore breathed a little more freely than he had done some ten minutes ago. Not to be too tedious, the curtain fell amidst shouts of approbation, unmingled with the slightest demonstration of displeasure, and the author had not twenty friends in the house.

If Theodore did not sleep that night, it was not from inquietude of mind—contentment was his repose. His most sanguine hopes had been surpassed; the fiat of a London audience had stamped him a dramatist; the way to fortune was open and clear, and Rosalie would be his.

Next morning, as soon as breakfast was over, Theodore and his friend repaired to the coffee-room. "We must see what the critics say," remarked the latter. Theodore, with prideful confidence—the offspring of fair success—took up the first morning print that came to his hand. *Theatre Royal* met his eye. "Happy is the successful dramatist!" exclaimed Theodore to himself;" at night he is greeted by the applause of admiring thousands, and in the morning they are repeated, and echoed all over the kingdom through the medium of the press! What will Rosalie say when her eye falls upon this!"—And what would Rosalie say when she read the utter damnation of her lover's drama, which the critic denounced from the beginning to the end, without presenting his readers with a single quotation to justify the severity of his strictures!

"'Tis very odd!" said Theodore.

"'Tis very odd, indeed!" rejoined his friend, repeating his words. "You told me this play was your own, and here I find that you have copied it from half a dozen others that have been founded upon the same story."

"Where?" inquired Theodore, reaching for the paper.

"There!" said his friend, pointing to the paragraph.

"And is this London!" exclaimed Theodore. "I never read a play, nor the line of a play upon the same subject. Why does not the writer prove the plagiarism?"

"Because he does not know whether it is or is not a plagiarism," rejoined the other. "He is aware that several other authors have constructed dramas upon the same passage in history; and—to draw the most charitable inference, for you would not suspect him of telling a deliberate lie—he thinks you have seen them, and have availed yourself of them."

"Is it not the next thing to a falsehood," indignantly exclaimed Theodore, "to advance a charge, of the justness of which you have not assured yourself?"

"I know not that," rejoined his friend; "but it certainly indicates a rather superficial reverence for truth; and a disposition to censure, which excludes from all claim to ingenuousness the individual who indulges it."

"And this will go the round of the whole kingdom?"

"Yes."

"Should I not contradict it?"

"No."

"Why?"

"'Tis beneath you; besides, the stamp of malignancy is so strong upon it, that, except to the utterly ignorant, it is harmless; and even these, when they witness your play themselves, as sometime or another they will, will remember the libel, to the cost of its author and to your advantage. I see you have been almost as hardly treated by this gentleman," continued he, glancing over the paper which Theodore had taken up when he entered the room. "Are you acquainted with any of the gentlemen of the press?"

"No; and is it not therefore strange that I should have enemies among them!"

"Not at all."

"Why?"

"Because you have succeeded. Look over the rest of the journals," continued his friend; "you may find salve, perhaps, for these scratches."

Theodore did so; and in one or two instances salve, indeed, he found; but upon the whole he was in little danger of being spoiled through the praises of the press.

"Why," exclaimed Theodore, "why do not letters enlarge the soul, while they expand the mind? Why do they not make men generous and honest? Why is not every literary man an illustration of Juvenal's axiom?"

"Teach a dog what you may," rejoined his friend, "can you alter his nature, so that the brute shall not predominate?"

"No," replied Theodore.

"You are answered," said his friend.

The play had what is called a run, but not a decided one. Night after night it was received with the same enthusiastic applauses; but the audiences did not increase. It was a victory without the acquisition of spoils or territory.

"What can be the meaning of this?" exclaimed Theodore; "we seem to be moving, and yet do not advance an inch!"

"They should paragraph the play as they do a pantomine," remarked his friend. "But then a pantomine is a expensive thing; they will lay out one thousand pounds upon one, and they must get their money back. The same is the case with their melo-dramas; so, if you want to succeed to the height, as a play-wright, you know what to do."

"What?" inquired Theodore.

"Write melo-dramas and pantomines!"

Six months had now elapsed, and Theodore's purse, with all his success, was rather lighter than when he first pulled it out in London. However, in a week two bills which he had taken from his publisher would fall due, and then he would run down to B——, and perhaps obtain an interview with Rosalie. At the expiration of the week his bills were presented, and dishonoured! He repaired to his publisher's for an explanation—the house had stopped! Poor Theodore: They were in the Gazette that very day! Theodore turned into the first coffee-room to look at a paper; there were, indeed, the names of the firm! "I defy fortune to serve me a scurvier trick!" exclaimed Theodore, the tears half starting into his eyes. He little knew the lady whose ingenuity he was braving.

He looked now at one side of the paper, and now at the other, thinking all the while of nothing but the bills and bankrupts' list. *Splendid Fête at B——* met his eye, and soon his thoughts were occupied with nothing but B——; for there he read that the young lord of the manor, having just come of age, had given a ball and supper, the former of which he opened with the lovely and accomplished Miss Rosalie ——. The grace of the fair couple was expatiated upon; and the editor took occasion to hint, that a pair so formed by nature for each other might probably, before long, take hands in another, a longer, and more momentous dance. What did Theodore think of Fortune now?

"O that it were but a stride to B——!" he exclaimed, as he laid down the paper, and his hand dropped nerveless at his side. He left the coffee-house and dreamed his way back to his friend's. Gigs, carriages, carts rolled by him unheeded; the foot-path was crowded, but he saw not a soul in the street. He was in the ball-room at B——, and looking on while the young lord of the manor handed out Rosalie to lead her down the dance, through every figure of which Theodore followed them with his eyes with scrutinizing glance, scanning the countenance of his mistress. Then the set was over, and he saw them walking arm-in-arm up and down the room; and presently they were dancing again; and now the ball was over, and he followed them to the supper-room, where he saw the young lord of the manor place Rosalie beside him. Then fancy changed the scene from the supper-room to the church, at the altar of which stood Rosalie with her happy rival; and he heard the questions and responses which forge the mystic chain that binds for life; and he saw the ring put on, and heard the blessing which announces that the nuptial sacrament is complete! His hands were clenched; his cheek was in a flame; a wish was rising in his throat—"Good news for you," said some one clapping him on the back; "a letter from Rosalie lies for you at home. Why are you passing the house?" 'Twas his friend.

"A letter from Rosalie!" exclaimed Theodore. Quickly he retraced his steps, and there on his table lay, indeed, the dear missive of his Rosalie.

"Welcome, sweet comforter!" ejaculated Theodore, as he kissed the cyphers which his Rosalie's hand had traced, and the wax which bore the impress of her seal—"Welcome, O welcome! you come in time; you bring an ample solace for disappointment, mortification, poverty—whatever my evil destiny can inflict! You have come to assure me that they cannot deprive me of my Rosalie!"

Bright was his eye, and glistening while he spoke; but when he opened the fair folds that conveyed to him the thoughts of his mistress, its radiancy was gone!

"THEODORE,

"I am aware of the utter frustration of your hopes; I am convinced that at the end of a year you will not be a step nearer to fortune than you are now; why then keep my hand for you? What I say briefly, you will interpret fully. You are now the guardian of my happiness—as such I address you. Thursday—so you consent—will be my wedding-day.

"ROSALIE."

Such was the letter, upon the address and seal of which Theodore had imprinted a score of kisses before he opened it. "Fortune is in the mood," said Theodore with a sigh, so deeply drawn, that any one who had heard it would have imagined he had breathed his spirit out along with it— "Fortune is in the mood, and let her have her humour out! I shall answer the letter; my reply to her shall convey what she desires—nothing more! she is incapable of entering into my feelings, and unworthy of being made acquainted with them; I shall not condescend even to complain."

"ROSALIE,

"You are free!
"THEODORE."

Such was the answer which Theodore despatched to Rosalie. O the enviable restlessness of the mind upon the first shock of thwarted affection! How it turns every way for the solace which it feels it can no more meet with, except in the perfect extinction of consciousness. Find in it an anodyne!—you cannot. A drug may close the eye for a time, but the soul will not sleep a wink; it lies broad awake to agony distinct, palpable, immediate; howsoever memory may be cheated to lose for the present the traces of the cause. Then for the start, the spasm, the groan, which, while the body lies free, attest the presence and activity of the mental rack! Better walk than go to sleep!—A heath, without a soul but yourself upon it!—an ink-black sky, pouring down torrents—wind, lightning, thunder, as though the vault above was crackling and disparting into fragments!—any thing to mount above the pitch of your own solitude, and darkness, and tempest; and overcome them, or attract and divert your contemplation from them, or threaten every moment to put an end to them and you!

Theodore's friend scarcely knew him the next morning. He glanced at him, and took no further notice. 'Twas the best way, though people there are who imagine that it rests with a man in a fever, at his own option to remain in it, or to become convalescent.

Theodore's feelings were more insupportable to him the second day than the first. He went here and there and everywhere; and nowhere could he remain for two minutes at a time at rest. Then he was so abstracted. Crossing a street he was nearly run over by a vehicle and four. This for a moment awakened him. He saw London and B—— upon the panels of the coach. The box seat was empty; he asked if it was engaged. "No." He sprung upon it, and away they drove. "I'll see her once more," exclaimed Theodore, "it can but drive me mad or break my heart."

Within a mile of B—— a splendid barouche passed them. "Whose is that?" inquired Theodore.

"The young lord of the manor," answered the driver. "Did you see the lady in it?"

"No."

"I caught a glimpse of her dress," said the driver. "I'll warrant she is a dashing one! The young squire, they say, has a capital taste!" Theodore looked after the carriage. There was nothing but the road. The vehicle drove at a rapid pace, and was soon out of sight. Theodore's heart turned sick.

The moment the coach stopped he alighted; and with a misgiving mind he stood at the door which had often admitted him to his Rosalie. 'Twas opened by a domestic whom he had never seen before. "Was Miss Wilford within?"—"No."—"When would she return?"—"Never. She had gone that morning to London to be married!" Theodore made no further inquiries, neither did he offer to go, but stood glaring upon the man more like a spectre than a human being. "Any thing more?" said the man, retreating into the house, and gradually closing the door, through which now only a portion of his face could be seen. "Any thing more?" Theodore made no reply; in fact he had lost all consciousness. At last, the shutting of the door, which, half from panic, half from anger, the man pushed violently to, aroused him. "I shall knock at you no more!" said he, and departed, pressing his heart with his hand, and moving his limbs as if he cared not how, or whither they bore him. A gate suddenly stopped his progress; 'twas the entrance to the green lane. He stepped over the stile—she was on the spot where he had parted last from Rosalie—where she had flung her arms about his neck and wept upon it. His heart began to melt, for the first time since he had received her letter: a sense of suffocation came over him, till he felt as if he would choke. The name of Rosalie was on his tongue; twice he attempted to articulate it, but could not. At last it got vent in a convulsive sob, which was followed by a torrent of tears. He threw himself upon the ground—he wept on—he made no effort to check the flood, but let it flow till forgetfulness stopped it.

He rose with a sensation of intense cold. 'Twas morning! He had slept! "Would that he had slept on!" He turned from the sun, as it rose without a cloud, upon the wedding morn of Rosalie. 'Twas Thursday. He repassed the stile; and, in a few minutes, was on his road to London, which he entered about eleven o'clock at night, and straight proceeded to his friend's. They were gone to bed.

"Give me a light," said Theodore, "I'll go to bed."

"Your bed is occupied, Sir," replied the servant.

"Is it?" said Theodore; "Well, I can sleep upon the carpet." He turned into the parlour, drew a chair towards the table, upon which the servant placed a light, and sat down. All was quiet for a time. Presently he heard a foot upon the stair. 'Twas his friend's who was descending, and now entered the parlour.

"I thought you were a-bed," said Theodore.

"So I was," replied his friend, "but hearing your voice in the hall, I rose and came down to you." He drew a chair opposite to Theodore. Both were silent for a time; at length Theodore spoke.

"Rosalie is married," said he.

"I don't believe it."

"She is going to be married to the young lord of the manor."

"I don't believe it."

"She came to town with him yesterday."

"I don't believe it."

Theodore pushed back his chair, and stared at his friend.

"What do you mean?" said Theodore.

"I mean that I entertain some doubts as to the accuracy of your grounds for concluding that Rosalie is inconstant to you."

"Did I not read the proof of it in the public papers?"

"The statement may have been erroneous."

"Did not her own letter assure me of it?"

"You may have misunderstood it."

"I tell you I have been at B——; I have been at her house. I inquired for her, and was told that she had gone up to London to be married! O, my friend," continued he, covering his eyes with his handkerchief, "'tis useless to deceive ourselves. I am a ruined man! You see to what she has reduced me. I shall never be myself again! Myself! I tell you existed in *her* being more than in my own. She was the soul of all I thought, and felt, and did; the primal, vivifying principle! She has murdered me! I breathe, it is true, and the blood is in my veins, and circulates; but every thing else about me is death—hopes! wishes! interests!—there is no pulse, no respiration there! I should not be sorry were there none anywhere else! Feel my hand," added he, reaching his hand across the table, without removing his handkerchief from his eyes; for the sense of his desolation had utterly unmanned him, and his tears continued to flow. "Feel my hand. Does it not burn. A hearty fever, now, would be a friend," continued he, "and I think I have done my best to merit a call from such a visitor. The whole of the night before last I slept out in the open air. Guess where I took my bed. In the green lane—the spot where I parted last from Rosalie!" He felt a tear drop upon the hand which he had extended—the tear was followed by the pressure of a lip. He uncovered his eyes, and turning them in wonderment to look upon his friend—beheld Rosalie sitting opposite to him!

For a moment or two he questioned the evidence of his senses—but soon was he convinced that it was indeed reality; for Rosalie, quitting her seat, approached him, and breathing his name with an accent that infused ecstasy into his soul, threw herself into his arms, that doubtingly opened to receive her.

* * * * *

Looking over her father's papers, Rosalie had found a more recent will, in which her union with Theodore had been fully sanctioned, and he himself constituted her guardian until it should take place. She was aware that his success in London had been doubtful; the generous girl determined that he should no longer be subjected to incertitude and disappointment; and she playfully wrote the letter which was a source of such distraction to her lover. From his answer she saw that he had totally misinterpreted her: she resolved in person to disabuse him of the error; and by offering to become his wife, at once to give him the most convincing proof of her sincerity and constancy. She arrived in London the very day that Theodore arrived in B——. His friend, who had known her from her infancy, received her as his daughter; and he and his wife listened with delight to the unfolding of her plans and intentions, which she freely confided to them. Late they sat up for Theodore that night, and when all hopes of his coming home were abandoned, Rosalie became the occupant of his bed. The next night, in a state of the most distressing anxiety, in consequence of his continued absence, she had just retired to her apartment, when a knock at the street door made her bound from her couch, upon which she had at that moment thrown herself, and presently she heard her lover's voice at the foot of the stair. Scarcely knowing what she did, she attired herself, descended, opened the parlour door unperceived by Theodore, and took the place of their friendly host, who, the moment he saw her, beckoned her, and resigning his chair to her, withdrew.

The next evening a select party were assembled in the curate's little drawing-room, and Theodore and Rosalie were there. The lady of the house motioned the latter to approach her; she rose, and was crossing Theodore, when he caught her by the hand, and drew her upon his knee.

"Theodore!" exclaimed the fair one, colouring.

"My Wife!" was his reply, while he imprinted a kiss upon her lips.

They had been married that morning.

A HINT TO PARENTS.—Depend on it, people's tempers must be corrected while they are children; for not all the good resolutions in the world can enable a man to conquer habits of ill-humour or rage, however he may regret having given way to them.—*Lord Byron.*

SKETCHES OF SOCIETY—BUTCHERS, BAKERS.

NEXT in dignity to the deacons of the trade, are certainly the wives of their electors. They were always a consequential race, in their day and generation; and on that account held in rather slighting respect by the little-less-so-ladies of the burgesses of other trades, who were frequently enraged at the "presumption" of their airs and answers, as they termed it, when these worthy economists sought to cheapen a joint below its market and monopoly value. One, whose offer, or "bode," had been beneath the established ratio of two-thirds of the price demanded, almost set the street on fire, and certainly had nearly brought about a "mutton mob," when impudently told by a "market madam," to go home and boil her cat." They were certainly, it must be admitted, I fear, a pert, but then they were a pretty race—black-eyed—their eyes were all black and roguish; clear-complexioned, rosy-cheeked, tidily made, till they got old and fat, and as trig-ankled queans as ever choused a batchelor buyer into a bad bargain! And then they all dressed with a neatness and showiness that was not limited by considerations of expense or fear of a husband's grumbling at a haberdasher's bill. They were all "comptrollers of the privy purse," and a pound was never missed out of the enormous leather pouches which hung at their sides as they stood at the receipt of custom. There was a substantial richness in every thing they wore, even when in the market. First of all, when there, there was the pretty black velvet bonnet, of the newest pattern, and the highest priced Genoa, tied under the portly-peaked natural, and close to the incipient *double* chin, which good living soon produced among the matrons, and over the frill of a morning cap of the richest lace, and smartest mode, set off with pink ribbons, that sat close to the glossy and well-curled locks of the wearer. Next, there was, in cold weather, one of the husband's most showy silk Barcelona neckerchiefs, of a flaming blue or yellow colour; or in summer there was to be seen a pretty peep of a white neck and bosom, and a string of amber or coral beads, half hid by an abundance of lace, held together by the largest and costliest pebble brooch that could be found. The winter upper garment was always of dark-coloured woollen cloth, made to sit so tight as to show a fine bust, even though a fat one, and a very round, if not very slender waist above the apron string. This last-named girdle suspended no vulgar-looking appendage, but a cloth of the finest diaper, glassed by the mangle till it had a surface whose radiant whiteness every morning it seemed a pity to soil by contact with raw meat. On looking farther down the figure, a glimpse of a bright red flannel petticoat might sometimes be had on a wet day, as the skirts were held up from draggling in the mud—a precaution, it has been hinted, that the use of smart and high clanking pattens rendered somewhat useless—if it were not partly to show the ankle and foot, which lost not their neatness, even when the good things of this life, as how-towdy [a fat fowl, neither hen nor chicken, prepared in a particular way, &c.] had robbed the rest of the figure of all symmetry, save that of the rotund, which were covered with a black stocking "without a brist," and a natty shoe of the highest polish. The hands were always ruddy and fat, and the fingers chained with many rings of massy gold. The pouches I have before spoken of, and only require to mention the multitudinous bunch of keys which hung beside them, to complete the review of the every-day costume of the "guidwives" of the fleshers. Their holyday garb was quite a different thing, however, much more gaudy, much less uniform, and not half so neat. Strong contrasts of glaring colours, superabundance of flounces and trimmings, and profusion of goldsmith's and jeweller's wares, were its characteristics. But I am not good at describing generalities, and *these* are so in all the apings at out-of-the-way grandeur mere wealth indulges in. Their Sunday costume was not theirs alone, it was every rich huxter's wife's; it wanted individuality, and therefore I need not say any thing more about it.

The daughters were gay, glittering, rompish, rosy girls, very anxious to become the wives I have described, and not very long about effecting it. It was an important day their first entrance as matrons among their mothers, and cousins, and aunts, and sisters,—something like a presentation at court, to a girl in high life of the same age, and conducted with almost as much form. Churching was nothing to this ceremonial!

It is time I should now turn to the husbands. Their coats, hats, and aprons I have already noticed. I forgot, however, that the latter had its tuck, as well as the former to cock to one side, equally characteristic. They were a good-humoured, jolly, hard-bargain-making, but honest set of fellows, almost as passionate as their pampered dogs, but nearly as faithful, too. Constant drinkers, without ever being drunk ; incessant wagerers, but never ruined by gambling ; charitable and church-goers, to their own particular chapel—a dissenting one—upon the mere question of the congregation electing the pastor, without being very religious ; and humane enough, as the world goes, to every thing but unruly bullocks, " camstary" sheep, and game cocks. The sport the last-named animals afforded by fighting, was to them " the universal passion," the real undoubted, undebated point of unanimity, and never-failing coincidence of feeling, if not of opinion ; for if that had been unanimous, then there would among them have been no room for bets. Once in their day, they could all handle the " gloves," too ; and were at any time " troublesome customers" in a row, to the watchmen, or other antagonists.

But in this, and canine fighting, and free swearing, they, though tolerable at these, too, were fairly outdone by their own journeymen and apprentices,—if it be right to say that, when they got older, they were surpassed in these accomplishments by those of the classes through whose gradations they had themselves gone. To be sure, such as never got beyond the second stage of the craft, were more daring and reckless in these matters than those who aimed at, or had attained promotion ; for, as I have said, their numbers were replenished almost wholly from among themselves, by the system of constant intermarriages. Such as remained journeymen all their lives, or were driven back to that point by failure in business,—these were the scape-graces of the body generally—the incorrigibles, in short ; but were yet so connected by the ties of relationship or otherwise, with the magnates and masters, that their peccadilloes were regarded with a merciful eye, and looked upon rather as the excesses of a son than of a servant,—so close was the connection between master and man, who generally lived under the same roof. Accordingly, though always boisterous, and often wild, this portion of the little state was seldom criminal, in the Old Bailey sense of the term. The members of it were sad dogs, however—tearing, swearing, swaggering rascals, with a dash of good humour, good nature, and low wit about them. Terrible drinkers, and devils among the girls were they ; but then, with their alliterative brethren the Bakers, they were the first and most fearless at a city fire, if they were the most unruly in a city mob.—Many's the life these two classes of worthies have saved, when the police stood timidly looking on at the burning rafters, and the shrieking wretches beneath them ; and thousands of pounds' worth of property they have rescued for the insurance offices and the non-insured sufferers, with an honesty to both, that would have scorned to pocket so much as a pack of cards, although their own had been even more greasy and old than they were. After a king's birth-night, an illumination, or a riot, the recruiting parties stationed in town, were sure of some dashing and fearless fellows of five feet ten, from these bodies ; and the king never had better or braver soldiers during war. Killing had always been the trade of many of them—fighting the amusement of all —and tramping their daily exercise. To be sure, it was hatches in the one case, and long moorland roads, when sent to bring home their masters' purchases of cattle, in the other ; but both trained the feet to wearisome marches, and the men who would often risk their whole cash on a throw at pitch and toss—their favourite game of chance—were likely to have the true military indifference as to saving money.—*Unpublished.—Author of the Chameleon.*

THE BISHOPS.

The *Dublin Evening Post* thus characterises the Churches of England and Ireland :—

" How comes it to pass, that the Church of England, taken as an aggregate, for there may be, perhaps, some half-a-dozen exceptions, is the most ignorant Church in Europe ? In one word, because she is the richest Church in Europe—and secondly, because learning is not in England the ladder of preferment. It is not denied, however, that there are some able and erudite men on the Episcopal Bench. Dr. Bloomfield, Bishop of London, is profound in the metres of the Greek play-writers—Dr. Maltby has actually superintended the edition of a Greek Prosodial Lexicon. Good men and well skilled in the dithyrambic of Eschylus, but ignorant, as far as the world knows, of Chrysostom or Basil. Dr. Marsh, who has done good service by his clever translation of Michaelis—and, bigoted Armenian as he may be, is more worthy his place on the score of learning, than three-fourths of his brethren. Dr. Copplestone, as liberal as an Oxford divine can be in politics, and that is not much, is, however, a man of considerable rank as a churchman. The Sumners are fortunate and decent, pious, no doubt, and with a reasonable share of the fashionable theology of the day ; Dr. Burgess, who puzzles himself and the learned upon the contested text of the three witnesses, and writes ' stepping stones' to the elements of the Hebrew Grammar—Dr. Brinkley, who owes his elevation in the Church solely to his mathematical knowledge—Doctor Laurence, a really learned linguist and liberal divine, though he voted against Emancipation— and Dr. Whately, the Archbishop of Dublin, an able man, certainly a learned theologian, though he believes in the honesty of Blanco White, a good scholar, and a great proficient in rhetoric, logic, and political economy. These are all the men of any mark or note upon the Bench in England or Ireland. For we suppose Doctor Vanmildert, who is only known by his Bampton lectures, and his edition of Waterland's works—or Dr. Mant, who published some foolish charges, and made some rhyming translations of the Psalms, though a pretty scholar—or Dr. Jebb, though a good man, who has written a pleasing, but superficial book upon Biblical literature—or Dr. Elrington, who has given an edition of Euclid, and a few nopopery pamphlets—or Dr. Phillpotts, who deals so largely in what Lord Durham called pamphleteering slang, and questionable assertions—or a few other right reverend and most reverend doctors, known in the world of letters by the publication of a shilling brochure ;—we suppose, we say, that none of these will be thrust under our noses, as men of learning or hoary divines—as the living lights of the Church, the Latimers, Bulls, Barrowes, and Taylors of modern times. Good men, if you please, decent men, proper men, and as fit timbering for a bishop, though not more fit certainly than the Editor of the *Dublin Evening Post*—but not persons whose names will be remembered thirty years hence. As to the *numerus*—as to the horde of Bishops, *nati consumere fruges*—the Beresfords, Fowlers, Tottenhams, Laws, Alexanders, Howleys, Lindsays— no man can say, with any truth, that they were preferred to the high offices they hold in the Church—to the princely incomes in which they wallow—to the magnificent patronage which the Irish portion of them enjoy—on account either of their superior sanctity or surpassing erudition. They are, generally speaking, ignorant men, versed in the value of Church lands, and in the laws of fines and renewals—learned in rich soups and fine wines, in bullocks and green crops—readers of *Blackwood's Magazine*, the trumpery travels of the day, and Mr. Colburn's Novels ; but utterly deficient in any other attribute, except the faculty of reading parts of the Communion Service almost as well as their chaplains.

" But this deplorable condition of the Anglican Church is deducible principally from its political character—from its close connexion with the state—from its immense riches and their unconscionable distribution. The object of a man with any prospects, as they are called, or with any interest among the political circles in England, when he enters the Church, is *riches*. If he brings talents and decent acquirements to the markets, so much the better ; but these are so far from being necessary, that they are sometimes found to be impediments in a man's progress. Phillpotts was not preferred for his talents as a clergyman, but for being a ready pamphleteer. Law was made a bishop because he was the brother of an able political judge, Ellenborough ; Lindsay, because he was the brother of a Sotch nobleman ; Tottenham, because of his relationship to the house of Ely ; and the Beresfords, because—because they were Beresfords. The higher ranks of the Church, therefore, give a tone to the subordinate classes."

THE POLISH FUGITIVES.
BY THE AUTHOR OF "THE CORN LAW RHYMES."

The day went down in fire,
  The burning ocean o'er;
A son, and grey-hair'd sire,
  Walk'd silent on the shore.

They walk'd, worn gaunt with cares,
  Where land and billow meet—
And of that land was theirs
  The dust upon their feet.

Yet they, erewhile, had lands
  Which plenteous harvests bore;
But spoil'd by Russian bands,
  Their own was theirs no more.

They came to cross the foam,
  And seek beyond the deep,
A happier, safer home,
  A land where sowers reap.

Yet, while the playful gold
  Laugh'd into purply green,
The crimson clouds that roll'd
  The sea and sky between,

The youth his brow uprais'd
  From thoughts of deepest wo,
And on the ocean gazed,
  Like one who fronts a foe.

The sire was calm and mild,
  And brightly shone his eye,
While like a stately child,
  He look'd on sea and sky.

But on his son's lean cheek,
  And in his hands grasp'd hard,
A heart that scorned to break,
  With dreadful feelings warr'd;

For he had left behind
  A wife who dungeon'd lay,
And loath'd the mournful wind,
  That sobb'd—Away, away!

Five boys and girls had he:
  In fetters pined they all;
And when he saw the sea,
  On him he heard them call.

Oh, fiercely he dash'd down
  The tear—that came at length!
Then almost with a frown,
  He prayed to God for strength.

"Hold up!" the father cried,
  "If Poland cannot thrive,
The mother o'er the tide
  May follow with her five.

"But Poland yet shall fling
  Dismay on Poland's foes,
As when the Wizard King[*]
  Aveng'd her ancient woes.

"For soon her cause will be
  Roused Europe's battle cry:
'To perish or be free:
  To conquer or to die!'"

His hands clasp'd o'er his head,
  The sun look'd up for aid;
"So be it, Lord!" he said,
  And still look'd up and pray'd:—

Till from his eyes, like rain,
  When first the black clouds growl,
The agony of pain,
  In tears, gush'd from his soul.

[*] The name which the Turks, in their superstitious dread, gave to the great Sobieski.

SCRAPS.
ORIGINAL AND SELECTED.

GLASS BLOWING.—Among the prizes awarded by the Paris Academy of Sciences, at their last sitting, was the following:—"To Israel Robinet, workman, for the substitution of the action of a machine for that of the human lungs, in glass blowing, 8000 francs. By means of this valuable invention, the health of the glass blower will in future be preserved, and the product of his manufacture greatly improved, both as regards accuracy of form, and the capability of making articles of greater dimensions than was formerly possible."

TEMPERATURE OF ENGLAND.—The mean temperature of London is about two degrees higher than that of the surrounding country; the difference exists chiefly in the night, and is greatest in winter, and least in spring. During the whole year the mean temperature of England does not vary in different years more than four degrees and a half.—*Mechanics' Magazine.*

TEMPERATURE OF SUMMER HEAT.—The last summer was distinguished by an unprecedented regularity of heat. From the register of a clergyman, at Kineton, who kept an account of the weather for many years, it appears that there were, between the first of May and the thirtieth of September, 64 days at and above 70 degrees, and 80 days, at and above 69 degrees. The last week of September was particularly marked by high temperature, the mercury having on the 25th reached 80 in a situation perfectly secluded from solar influence:—a degree which he never before observed at so late a period in the year.

Whitewashing and colouring the inside walls and the ceilings of cottages should not be attempted till they have dried at least a year. If the plaster be of the commonest kind, without a finishing coat of stucco, it is only adapted for water colours, or colours rendered tenacious by glue-paste, or other mucilaginous matter, instead of oil, because of its porosity, which would wholly absorb the oil. The most common colouring for cottage walls is what is technically called lime whiting, which is nothing more than the finest particles of lime or chalk mixed with water, with the addition of a small quantity of size. The colour of this is varied by the addition of the black of charcoal (commonly called blue black, as distinguished from the soot of lamps, which is called lamp-black,) or by yellow ochre, by verdigrise, or any cheap pigment.—*Encyclopædia of Cottage, Villa, and Farm Architecture.*

PARTY MEN.—Fidelity to engagements, due consistency of thought and conduct, respect for the useful institutions of the country, and personal honour, are all sacrificed by the true party man; and there is not a single advantage arrived at through party views which better motives will not secure.—*Westminster Review.*

TO CORRESPONDENTS.

To our Culross Correspondent we can only say, that if the bore of "potchin Bob's" gun contracts on being heated, and expands on being cooled, we are as much puzzled as the "learned dominie," and the "scientific doctor chap" to account for it. The only explanation we can give, is by supposing Bob's gun to have a well developed organ of imitation, which, impelling it to imitate its master, it too has become a "potcher"—a violator of *the laws* of expansion; because we can assure him it is quite different with ordinary guns.

CONTENTS OF NO. XXI.

Christmas	321
German Christmas Customs—Household Affections	322
The Court of Sinde	ib.
Emigration	323
Lord Kenyon	324
King James and the Witches	325
John Cly the Miller—Widow Shanks's Adventures—Scene in the Baths of Leuk	326
The Drama	327
The Waits—Superstitions of the Welsh	328
THE STORY TELLER—Love and Authorship	329
Sketches of Society—Butchers—Bakers	334
The Bishops	335
The Polish Fugitives	336
Scraps, Original and Selected—Glass Blowing—Temperature of England—Party Men, &c.	336

EDINBURGH: Printed by and for JOHN JOHNSTONE, 19, St. James's Square.—Published by JOHN ANDERSON, Jun., Bookseller, 55, North Bridge Street, Edinburgh; by JOHN MACLEOD, and ATKINSON & Co. Booksellers, Glasgow; and sold by all Booksellers and Vendors of Cheap Periodicals.

THE Schoolmaster,
AND
EDINBURGH WEEKLY MAGAZINE.

CONDUCTED BY JOHN JOHNSTONE.

THE SCHOOLMASTER IS ABROAD.—LORD BROUGHAM.

No. 22.—Vol. I.   SATURDAY, DECEMBER 29, 1832.   Price Three-Halfpence.

TO OUR READERS.

With the present year, we close the first volume of the Schoolmaster, to commence 1833 with a new volume. There are several reasons which dictate this arrangement; and the size of the volume, which, with the Political Register, contains above 400 pages, is of itself conclusive. Many of the Subscribers to the *Monthly Parts*, who form a numerous and fast-increasing class of our Readers, have suggested the necessity of half-yearly volumes, from the unwieldy size of a *fire-side* book which would contain, with the Political Register, above 1000 pages.

We cannot close this portion of the Work, without making our respectful acknowledgments to those friends and well-wishers, known or anonymous, who have either directly co-operated in a design, which to them appeared useful and meritorious, or have sent us sometimes useful suggestions, and at others valuable information. The spontaneous testimonies of approbation, received from persons of high moral, literary, and political eminence, have been most cheering and satisfactory; and our reception, by the public at large, has been more liberal and encouraging than we could have reasonably anticipated in a Work begun after the field seemed pre-occupied, where so many had failed, and so few succeeded. As we have employed no clap-trap of any kind, nor bestowed any pains in introducing the Work beyond what is apparent in its internal qualities, there is no assumption in believing that it is for its intrinsic merits the public, but especially the instructed classes, wherever the Schoolmaster has been seen, have at once placed it on a level with the best of the cheap Periodicals; while from the higher cast of its literary selections, and the greater length of the pieces, it is allowed to rank above any literary work hitherto attempted upon the same scale. In now taking leave of our kind and courteous Readers of 1832, we shall only say, that our strenuous efforts will be given to improve the details and arrangement of the Work; and, also, to maintain it in its present creditable position as a cheap *Literary Periodical*, and an *independent Political Register*.

19, St. James's Square,
28th *December* 1832.

*** The Schoolmaster *is regularly stereotyped, and may be had by Booksellers' Monthly Parcels in the different towns, and by Carriers, when ordered, in places where there is no Bookseller.*

The Editor begs once more to apologize to those sending orders for copies of the Schoolmaster *from towns and villages out of the direct line of communication, for seeming inattention to their requests, and suggests to them the propriety of ordering Monthly Parts, which form at once a* Newspaper, *a* Literary Journal, *and a* Review.

ON THE MISMANAGEMENT OF PUBLIC INSTITUTIONS.

The Christmas holidays are a convenient and privileged season for going about to *see sights;* and tens of thousands would avail themselves of such opportunities, save for one small obstruction, the heavy expense attending this rational mode of enjoyment. The narrow exclusive spirit, which shuts the doors of all our national institutions in the face of the public, has long been a reproach to Great Britain among foreigners, and a cause of complaint at home. Let us hope that a better era has arrived, and that the omnipotent spirit of Reform will soon extend to College Libraries and Museums.

The spirit of reformation is extending like the circles on a broken surface of water. Mankind are industriously and steadily repairing the decays of the past; and the *Schoolmaster* cannot deem it irrelevant, at this interesting period, to point out the necessity of repairing some abuses which have too long existed as a reproach to the land. We mean the mismanagement of many of our public institutions and national works, which are shamefully closed against every man who cannot afford to pay for seeing, what is certainly, in a measure, his own. Other nations endeavour to render their capitals the resort of travellers, by admitting strangers to admire and copy whatever of beauty and excellence in the arts they have collected with immeasurable care and expense. The ancient kingdoms of the East possessed this secret of improving their fame. Egypt, for long, was the centre of science. Her magnificent and unrivalled Alexandrine Library, induced philosophers to sojourn in her states: and, when superstition had nearly extinguished the infant struggles of the medical science at Rome, physicians found a stimulus to their exertions in the comparative facility of prosecuting their researches in the cities of Egypt. At one period of the profession, there were only two skeletons in the world.—Yet those two were in Egypt—and to Egypt the students of medicine flocked, from very remote parts of the earth, despite of the formidable obstacles of distance and delay. Italy produced the greatest painters, because her galleries of painting were at their command. And Bonaparte knew, that if once he succeeded in accumulating the pillage of Europe within the walls of the Louvre, he should render Paris the Emporium of the Arts. And yet we, who boast of our encouragement to every liberal pursuit, have, by throwing paltry difficulties in the way, degraded our name to a level with that of the bigoted Spaniard. We have expended the British money in equipping frigates to convey here the mutilated fragments of the statues of Greece ; and, by the conduct of Lord Elgin, have brought down upon our heads the opprobrium and curse of that greatly injured people. The *Elgin Marbles* lie shattered about the court-yard, or bundled up in heaps in the cellars of the British Museum,—Government being unable to grant the money for building a suitable gallery for their reception. And the British Museum is open to the public only three days a-week, during only a part of the year. Westminster Abbey—the monumental home of our warriors and bards—is closed to pilgrims that have journeyed from a distance, to bend at the shrine of most that is revered and sacred in our annals. An Englishman must pay half-a-crown to gaze on the tombs of his sires. The public buildings in London are notoriously known to be barred against those who come not with a silver key, and foreigners depart dissatisfied, and disgusted with our parsimony, and ignorant of the many attractions which, under a worthier administration of these affairs, they might have witnessed with delight. Our libraries, too, instead of being useful and honourable to our name, are the foulest blots of all. Who can gain admittance to the manuscript collections in the British Museum? Not those who can benefit from the classic pages, engulfed there, as in a tomb. Who can say that his studies in our Scottish metropolis, are benefited by the volumes on the shelves of its University? Not the students who pay for its support. Let this reproach be wiped away from us, and instead of our sons spending our money in the celebrated schools abroad, we shall have foreigners crowding for instruction to ours. Let our public edifices be seen, and they shall rapidly increase. Let the heroic child go and kneel at the graves of the illustrious dead—let him decipher the simple tale of their glories sculptured on the marble ; and we shall behold our children as great as our fathers have been !

HEAT.
(Concluded from page 318.)

WE have already, in former Numbers, noticed the remarkable property possessed by heat, of causing bodies to expand. We shall conclude the subject of heat, by making a few observations on the manner in which it is communicated from one body to another. Heat has a constant tendency to diffuse itself, till all bodies become of the same temperature. This is effected in two ways, *by conduction* and by *radiation*. When we place the end of a poker in the fire, the heat is *conducted* from the fire into the poker, and from that part of the poker in contact with the fire to the other parts of it ; which mode of communication is called *conduction*. When, on the other hand, a warm body is suspended in the air, rays of heat are emitted or *radiated* on every side; and in this case the heat is said to be communicated by *radiation*. First, then, of conduction. Bodies possess the power of conducting heat in very different degrees. If we place the end of a poker, or other rod of iron, in the fire, it will speedily become red hot ; and if it be not too long, the heat will soon be conducted to the other end, so as prevent us from laying hold of it. On the contrary, if we put the end of a piece of wood in the fire, it will begin and continue to burn, but the wood a few inches from the flame, will hardly be sensibly heated. Iron, then, is a good, while wood is a bad, conductor of heat. A piece of iron feels much colder to the touch on a cold day than a piece of wood, though both be of the same temperature. This arises from the iron conducting the heat more rapidly out of the hand than the wood. The metals are the best conductors ; and, indeed, as a general rule, the densest bodies are the best conductors. Glass, however, though a dense body, is, as we formerly mentioned, a bad conductor : so is earthen-ware, wool, fur, cotton, and the like substances. Though, at first sight, water appears to be an excellent conductor, it is in reality a very bad one. If we apply heat to the *bottom* of a pan of water, the heat, no doubt, quickly reaches the top ; but it is conveyed in quite a different manner from conduction. When we place a pan of water on the fire, the heat quickly passes into the metal, and from the metal into the water in contact with it ; the water, which is thus heated, expands, becomes bulk for bulk lighter than that above it, and consequently it rises, while the colder water above takes its place ; this, also, in its turn being heated, expands and rises. And thus currents of heated water are constantly ascending, and currents of colder water descending, till the whole is heated to the 212th degree. A different process, however, commences at this point. Water, under the ordinary pressure of the atmosphere, cannot be heated above the 212th degree, as at this point it is converted into steam. The water, which is now at the bottom, does not therefore rise as formerly, but remains at the bottom, where it is converted into steam, which bubbling to the top, constitutes what we call boiling. Heat, therefore, in the case of boiling water, is not conducted from particle to particle, but is conveyed to the top in consequence of the water itself rising. The rapidity with which heat is conveyed from the metal forming the bottom of a vessel in which water is boiling, is very well shewn by the common experiment of taking a boiling kettle from the fire, and placing it on the hand, without being in the slightest degree incommoded. The heat, however, speedily returns when the water ceases to boil, as we soon find, if we continue to hold the kettle in our hand. That water is a bad conductor may be easily proved; if we place a piece of ice at the bottom of a glass-tube, and pour over it a quantity of cold water, we may cause the water to boil a few inches above the ice, and yet the ice will remain unmelted. In this case, the coldest water being already at the bottom, there are no currents; and as the water does not conduct the heat downwards, the ice remains unaffected. Air, also, is a bad conductor; and, indeed, it is supposed, that it is the quantity of air retained in the interstices of cotton, fur, &c. that causes them to conduct heat so slowly. The knowledge of the different conducting powers of bodies has added greatly to the comforts of man, in cold countries especially, where, to preserve life, it is absolutely necessary to employ some means to prevent the heat generated in the body from making its escape too readily. For this purpose, man has selected those substances which do not conduct heat readily, as wool, fur, or cotton. It is a popular notion, that clothes are in themselves actually warmer than our bodies, and that it is by imparting heat that they are effectual in keeping our bodies warm. This, however, is a mistake. Clothes, on the contrary, when first put on, are considerably colder than the bodies; and it is only by preventing the heat generated in our bodies from escaping too easily, that they are of any advantage. A little reflection will soon convince any one of this. It is well known, that a thin covering of snow effectually defends wheat and other winter plants from the effects of frost. It is plain, that in this case, the effect cannot arise from heat being imparted from the snow to the plants. Snow is a bad conductor of heat, and its beneficial influence arises from its preventing the heat which is in the soil from escaping. Again, the *same* substances are used, *to keep bodies both warm and cold.* Thus, in ice-houses, where the object is to keep the place as cool as possible, that the ice may be prevented from melting, the walls are lined with blankets, straw, and the like substances, that the heat during the warm summer weather may be prevented from entering. In like manner, to preserve potatoes from the effects of frost, we place over them a thick covering of earth and straw, which are both bad conductors of heat, and thus prevent the heat in the interior of the *pit* from escaping.

Heat, as we have said, is also communicated by radiation. The heat of the sun is communicated to the earth in this manner. Radiated heat does not at all increase the temperature of the air through which it passes. This is proved, from the well known fact, that, as we ascend in the air, its temperature decreases, though, at the same time, we approach nearer the sun. The rays of heat pass directly from the sun to the earth, where they are absorbed. The air, therefore, in contact with the earth is heated, and consequently expands and rises; and the colder air above taking its place, we have continual currents of warm air ascending, and of cold air descending, which not only prevents impure vitiated air from collecting on the surface of the earth, but prevents it from becoming insupportably hot, which it would soon do were the air stationary. This salubrious exchange of air would not, it is evident, take place, if the air interrupted the rays of heat. Bodies possess the power of radiating heat in different degrees. This property depends, to a great extent, on the nature of the surface; black rough surfaces being the best, and bright shining surfaces the worst radiators. Bodies also differ in their capability of absorbing rays of heat. Those substances which radiate heat readily, also absorb it readily. When, therefore, it is wished to prevent heat from escaping, as in conveying heated air or steam from one apartment to another, as is often done in manufactories, pipes with bright resplendent surfaces ought to be employed, as they do not readily radiate the heat. It is, because black surfaces absorb heat more readily than surfaces of a lighter colour, that white hats are found more comfortable in warm weather than black ones.

Bodies have different capacities for heat. By this we mean, that if equal quantities of heat be added to different bodies, their temperatures will not be equally raised. Thus, the quantity of heat which will raise a pound of quicksilver 28 degrees, will only raise an equal weight of water one degree. Water, therefore, has 28 times the capacity for heat that quicksilver has. Almost every substance differs in its capacity for heat from any other substance. This paper is, however, already much too long; and we must, therefore, conclude. It has been our object merely to excite an interest in the minds of our readers regarding the interesting properties of heat; and those who may wish to pursue the subject a little farther, cannot do better than peruse Nos. 4 and 5 of *The Library of Useful Knowledge*, which are exclusively devoted to the consideration of heat.

Dumoulin, the famous physician, being at the point of death, surrounded by numbers of physicians who were deploring the loss of him, said to them—" Gentlemen, I leave behind me three great physicians." Being pressed to name them by several, each of whom believed himself to be one of the three, he replied, " Water, exercise, and simple food."

SKETCH OF PROFESSOR WILSON.
BY MR. DE QUINCEY.
(In a Letter to an American Gentleman.)

My dear L.—Among the *lions* whom you missed by one accident or another on your late travels in Europe, I observe that you recur to none with so much regret as Professor Wilson; you dwell upon this one disappointment as a personal misfortune; and perhaps with reason; for, in the course of my life, I have met with no man of equally varied accomplishments, or, upon the whole, so well entitled to be ranked with that order of men distinguished by brilliant versatility and ambidexterity—of which order we find such eminent models in Alcibiades, in Cæsar, in Crichton, in that of Servan recorded by Sully, and in one or two Italians. Pity that you had not earlier communicated to me the exact route you were bound to, and the particular succession of your engagements when you visited the English Lakes; since, in that case, my interest with Professor Wilson (supposing always that you had declined to rely upon the better passport of your own merits as a naturalist) would have availed for a greater thing than at that time stood between you and the introduction which you coveted. On the day, or the night rather, when you were at Bowness and Ambleside, I happen to know that Professor Wilson's business was one which might have been executed by proxy, though it could not be delayed; and I also know that, apart from the *general* courtesy of his nature, he would, at all times, have an especial pleasure in waiving a claim of business, for one of science or letters in the person of a foreigner coming from a great distance; and that, in no other instance would he make such a sacrifice so cordially as on behalf of an able naturalist. Perhaps you already know from your countryman Audubon, that the Professor is himself a naturalist, and of original merit; in fact, worth a score of such meagre bookish naturalists, as are formed in museums and by second-hand acts of memory; having (like Audubon) built much of his knowledge upon personal observation. Hence he has two great advantages; one, that his knowledge is accurate in a very unusual degree; and another, that his knowledge, having grown up under the inspiration of a real interest and an unaffected love for its objects—commencing, indeed, at an age when no affectation in matters of that nature could exist—has settled upon those facts and circumstances which have a true philosophical value: habits, predominant affections, the direction of instincts, and the compensatory processes where these happen to be thwarted,—on all such topics he is learned and full; whilst, on the science of measurements and proportions, applied to dorsal-fins and tail-feathers, and on the exact arrangement of colours, &c.—that petty upholstery of nature, on which books are so tedious and elaborate—not uncommonly he is negligent or forgetful. What may have served in later years to quicken and stimulate his knowledge in this field, and, at any rate, greatly to extend it, is the conversation of his youngest brother Mr. James Wilson, who (as *you* know much better than I) is a naturalist *majorum gentium*. He, indeed, whilst a boy of not more than sixteen or seventeen, was in correspondence (I believe) with Montague the Ornithologist; and about the same time had skill enough to pick holes in the coat of Mr. Hüber, the German reformer of our then erroneous science of bees.

You see, therefore, that no possible introduction could have stood you more in stead than your own extensive knowledge of Transatlantic ornithology. Swammerdam passed his life, it is said, in a ditch. *That* was a base, earthly solitude,—and a prison. But you and Audubon have passed *your* lives in the heavenly solitudes of forests and savannahs; and such solitude as this is no prison, but infinite liberty. The knowledge which you have gathered has been answerable to the character of your school; and no sort of knowledge could have secured you a better welcome with Professor Wilson.—Yet, had it been otherwise, I repeat, that my interest (as I flatter myself) would have opened the gates of Elleray to you even at midnight; for I am so old a friend of Mr. Wilson, that I take a pride in supposing myself the oldest; and, barring relations by blood, arrogate the rights of dean in the chapter of his associates; or at least I know of but one person whose title can probably date earlier than mine. About this very month when I am writing, I have known Professor Wilson for a cycle of twenty years and more, which is just half of his life—and also half of mine; for we are almost of equals of the same age: Wilson being born in May, and I in August, of the same memorable year.

My introduction to him—setting apart the introducer himself—was memorable from one sole circumstance—viz. the person of the introducer. William Wordsworth it was, who, in the vale of Grasmere, if it can interest you to know the place, and in the latter end of 1808, if you can be supposed to care about the time, did me the favour of making me known to John Wilson, or as I might say (upon the Scottish fashion of designating men from their territorial pretensions) to Elleray. I remember the whole scene so circumstantially as if it belonged to but yesterday. In the vale of Grasmere,—that peerless little vale which you, and Gray the poet, and so many others have joined in admiring as the very Eden of English beauty, peace, and pastoral solitude,—you may possibly recal, even from that flying glimpse you had of it, a modern house called Allan Bank, standing under a low screen of woody rocks which descend from the hill of Silver How, on the western side of the lake. This house had been then recently built by a worthy merchant of Liverpool; but for some reason of no importance to you and me, not being immediately wanted for the family of the owner, had been let for a term of three years to Mr. Wordsworth. At the time I speak of, both Mr. Coleridge and myself were on a visit to Mr. Wordsworth; and one room on the ground floor, designed for a breakfasting-room, which commands a sublime view of the three mountains, Fairfield—Arthur's Chair—and Seat Sandal (the first of them within about 400 feet of the highest mountains in Great Britain,) was then occupied by Mr. Coleridge as a study. On this particular day, the sun having only just set, it naturally happened that Mr. Coleridge—whose nightly vigils were long—had not yet come down to breakfast; meantime, and until the epoch of the Coleridgian breakfast should arrive, his study was lawfully disposable to profaner uses. Here, therefore, it was, that, opening the door hastily in quest of a book, I found seated, and in earnest conversation, two gentlemen—one of them my host, Mr. Wordsworth, at that time about 37 or 38 years old; the other was a younger man by good 16 or 17 years, in a sailor's dress, manifestly in robust health—*fervidus juventâ*, and wearing upon his countenance a powerful expression of ardour and animated intelligence, mixed with much good nature. "Mr. Wilson of Elleray"—delivered, as the formula of introduction, in the deep tones of Mr. Wordsworth—at once banished the momentary surprise I felt on finding an unknown stranger where I had expected nobody, and substituted a surprise of another kind: I now well understood who it was that I saw: and there was no wonder in his being at Allan Bank, Elleray standing within nine miles; but (as usually happens in such cases,) I felt a shock of surprise on seeing a person so little corresponding to the one I had half unconsciously prefigured.

And here comes the place naturally, if any where, for a description of Mr. Wilson's person and general appearance in carriage, manner, and deportment; and a word or two I shall certainly say on these points, simply because I know that I *must*, else my American friends will complain that I have left out that precise section in my whole account which it is most impossible for them to supply for themselves by any acquaintance with his printed works. Yet suffer me, before I comply with this demand, to enter one word of private protest against the childish (nay, worse than childish —the *Missy*) spirit in which such demands originate. From my very earliest years, that is—the earliest years in which I had any sense of what belongs to true dignity of mind, I declare to you that I have considered the interest which men, grown men, take in the personal appearance of each other, as one of the meanest aspects under which human curiosity commonly presents itself. Certainly I have the same intellectual perception of differences in such things that other men have; but I connect none of the feelings, whether of admiration or contempt—liking or disliking, which are obviously connected with these perceptions by human beings generally. Such words as " commanding appearance," " prepossessing countenance," applied to the figures or faces of the males of the human species, have no meaning in my ears; no man commands me, no man prepossesses me, by any thing in, on, or about his carcass. What care I for any man's legs? I laugh at his ridiculous presumption in conceiting that I shall trouble myself to admire or to respect anything that he can produce in his physics. What! shall I honour Milo for the very qualities which he has in common with the beastly ox he carries—his thews and sinews, his ponderous strength and weight, and the quantity of thumping that his hide will carry? I disclaim and disdain any participation in such green-girl feelings. I admit that the baby feelings I am here condemning are found in connection with the highest intellects; in particular, Mr. Coleridge, for instance, once said to me, as a justifying reason for his dislike of a certain celebrated Scotsman, with an air of infinite disgust—" that ugh! (making a guttural sound as if of execration) he (viz. the said Scotsman) was so chicken-breasted." I have been assured by the way, that Mr. Coleridge was mistaken in the mere matter of fact; but supposing that he were not, what a reason for a philosopher to build a disgust upon! And Mr. Wordsworth, in or about the year 1820, in expressing the extremity of his *Nil admirari* spirit, declared that he would not go ten yards out of his road to see the finest specimen of man (intellectually speaking) that Europe had to show: and so far indeed I do not quarrel with his opinion; but Mr. Wordsworth went on to say that this indifference did *not* extend itself to man considered physically; and that he would still exert himself to a small extent (suppose a mile or so) for the sake of seeing Belzoni. That was the case he instanced; and, as I understood him, not by way of a general illustration for his meaning, but that he really felt an exclusive interest in this particular man's physics. Now, Belzoni was certainly a good tumbler, as I have heard; and hopped well upon one leg, when surmounted and crested by a pyramid of men and boys: and jumped capitally through a hoop; and did all sorts of tricks in all sorts of styles, not at all worse than any monkey, bear, or learned pig, that ever exhibited in Great Britain. And I would myself have given a shilling to have seen him fight with that cursed Turk that assaulted him in the streets of Cairo; and would have given him a crown for catching the circumcised dog by the throat and effectually taking the conceit out of his Mahometan carcass: but then *that* would have been for the spectacle of the passions, which, in such a case, would have been let loose; as to the mere animal Belzoni,—(who after all was not to be compared to Topham the Warwickshire man, that drew back by main force a cart, and its driver and a strong horse,)—as to the mere animal Belzoni, I say, and his bull neck, I would have much preferred to see a real bull or the Darlington ox. The sum of the matter is this: all men, even those who are most manly in their style of thinking and feeling, in many things retain the childishness of their childish years: no man thoroughly weeds himself of all. And this particular mode of childishness is one of the commonest, into which they fall the more readily from the force of sympathy, and because they apprehend no reason for directing any vigilance against it. But I contend that reasonably no feelings of deep interest are justifiable as applied to any point of external form or feature in human beings, unless under two reservations; first, that they shall have reference to women; because women, being lawfully the objects of passions and tender affections, which can have no existence as applied to men, are objects also, rationally and consistently, of all other secondary feelings (such as those derived from their personal appearance) which have any tendency to promote and support the first. Whereas between men the highest mode of intercourse is merely intellectual, which is not of a nature to receive support or strength from any feelings of pleasure or disgust connected with the accidents of external appearance; but exactly in the degree in which these have any influence at all they must warp and disturb by improper biasses; and the single case of exception, where such feelings can be honourable and laudable amongst the males of the human species, is where they regard such deformities as are the known products and expressions of criminal or degrading propensities. All beyond this, I care not by whom countenanced, is infirmity of mind, and would be baseness if it were not excused by imbecility.

Excuse this digression, for which I have a double reason; chiefly I was anxious to put on record my own opinions, and my contempt for men generally in this particular; and here I seemed to have a conspicuous situation for that purpose. Secondly, apart from this purpose of offence, I was at any rate anxious, merely on a defensive principle, to screen myself from the obvious misinterpretation incident to the case; saying any thing minute or in detail upon a man's person, I should necessarily be supposed to do so under the ordinary blind feelings of interest in that subject which govern most people; feelings which I disdain. Now, having said all this, and made my formal protest, *liberavi animam meam*; I revert to my subject, and shall say that word or two which I was obliged to promise you on Professor Wilson's personal appearance.

Figure to yourself, then, a tall man, about six feet high, within half an inch or so, built with tolerable appearance of strength; but at the date of my description (that is, in the very spring-tide and blossom of youth,) wearing, for the predominant character of his person, lightness and agility, or (in our Westmoreland phrase) *lishness*; he seemed framed with an express view to gymnastic exercises of every sort.

"Ἅλμα, ποδωκείην, δίσκον, ἄκοντα, παίς"

In the first of these exercises, indeed, and possibly (but of that I am not equally certain) in the second, I afterwards came to know that he was absolutely unrivalled; and the best leapers at that time in the ring, Richmond the Black and others, on getting " a taste of his quality," under circumstances of considerable disadvantage, [viz. after a walk from Oxford to Moulsey Hurst, which, I believe, is fifty miles,] declined to undertake him. For this exercise he had two remarkable advantages; it is recorded of Sheffield, Duke of Buckingham, that, though otherwise a handsome man, he offended the connoisseurs in statuesque proportions by one eminent defect—perhaps the most obtrusive to which the human figure is liable—viz. a body of length disproportioned to his legs. In Mr. Wilson the proportions were fortunately reversed: a short trunk, and remarkably long legs, gave him one half of his advantages in the noble science of leaping; the other half was afterwards pointed out to me by an accurate critic in these matters as lying in the particular conformation of his foot, the instep of which is arched, and the back of the heel strengthened in so remarkable a way that it would be worth paying a penny or so for a sight of them. It is really laughable to think of the coxcombry which eminent men of letters have displayed in connexion with their powers—real or fancied —in this art. Cardinal du Perron vapoured to the end of his life upon some remarkable leap that he either *had* accomplished, or conceived himself to have accomplished, (not, I presume, in red stockings.) Every 10th page of the Perroniana rings with the echo of this stupendous leap—the length of which, if I remember rightly, is as obviously fabulous as any feat of Don Bellanis of Greece. Des Cartes also had a lurking conceit that, in some unknown place, he had perpetrated a leap that ought to immortalize him; and in one of his letters he repeats and accredits a story of some obscure person's leap, which

" At one light bound high overleaped all bound"

of reasonable credulity. Many other eminent leapers might be cited, Pagan and Christain: but the Cardinal, by his own account, appears to have been the flower of Popish leapers; and, with all deference to his Eminence, upon a better assurance than that, Professor Wilson may be rated, at the time I speak of, as the flower of all Protestant leapers. Not having the Cardinal's foible of connecting any vanity with this little accomplishment, knowing exactly what could, and what could *not* be effected in this department of gymnastics, and speaking with the utmost simplicity and candour of his failures and his successes alike, he might always be relied upon, and his statements were constantly in harmony with any collateral testimony that chance happened to turn up.

Viewed, therefore, by an eye learned in gymnastic proportions, Mr. Wilson presented a somewhat striking figure; and by some people he was pronounced with emphasis a fine-looking young man; but others, who less understood, or less valued these advantages, spoke of him as nothing extraordinary. Still greater division of voices I have heard on his pretensions to be thought handsome. In my opinion, and most certainly in his own, these pretensions were but slender. His complexion was too florid: hair of a hue quite unsuited to that complexion; eyes not good, having no apparent depth, but seeming mere surfaces; and in fine, no one feature that could be called fine, except the lower region of his face, mouth, chin, and the parts adjacent, which were then (and perhaps are now) truly elegant and Ciceronian. Ask in one of your public libraries for that little 4to edition of the Rhetorical works of Cicero, edited by Schutz, (the same who edited Æschylus,) and you will there see (as a frontispiece to the 1st vol.) a reduced whole length of Cicero from the antique; which in the mouth and chin, and indeed generally, if I do not greatly forget, will give you a lively representation of the contour and expression of Professor Wilson's face. Taken as a whole, though not handsome (as I have already said) when viewed in a quiescent state, the head and countenance are massy, dignified, and expressive of tranquil sagacity.

(*To be Continued.*)

MUTINY AT THE NORE.

THE irritated mind of Peters was stimulated to join the disaffected parties. His pride, his superior education, and the acknowledgment among his shipmates that he was an injured man, all conspired to place him in the dangerous situation of ringleader on board of his own ship, the crew of which, although it had not actually joined in the mutiny, now showed open signs of discontent. But the mine was soon exploded by the behaviour of the captain. Alarmed at the mutinous condition of the other ships which were anchored near to him, and the symptoms of dissatisfaction in his own, he proceeded to an act of unjustifiable severity, evidently impelled by fear and not by resolution. He ordered several of the petty officers and leading men of the ship to be thrown into irons, because they were seen to be earnestly talking together on the forecastle,—and recollecting that his conduct towards Peters had been such as to warrant disaffection, he added him to the number. The effect of this injudicious step was immediate. The men came aft in a body on the quarter-deck, and requested to know the grounds upon which Peters and the other men had been placed in confinement; and, perceiving alarm in he countenance of the captain, notwithstanding the resolute bearing of the officers, they insisted upon the immediate release of their shipmates. Thus the first overt act of mutiny was brought on by the misconduct of the captain. The officers expostulated and threatened in vain. Three cheers were called for by a voice in the crowd, and three cheers were immediately given. The marines, who still remained true to their allegiance, had been ordered under arms; the first lieutenant of the ship—for the captain, trembling and confused, stood a mere cipher—gave the order for the ship's company to go down below, threatening to fire upon them if the order was not instantaneously obeyed. The captain of marines brought his men to the "make ready," and they were about to present, when the first lieutenant waved his hand to stop the decided measure, until he had first ascertained how far the mutiny was general. He stepped a few paces forward, and requested that every "blue jacket," who was inclined to remain faithful to his king and country, would walk over from that side of the quarter-deck upon which the ship's company were assembled, to the one which was occupied by the officers and marines. A pause and silence ensued; when, after some pushing and elbowing through the crowd, William Adams, an elderly quartermaster, made his appearance in the front, and passed over to the side where the officers stood, while the hisses of the rest of the ship's company expressed their disapprobation of his conduct. The old man had just reached the other side of the deck, when, turning round like a lion at bay, with one foot on the *comings* of the hatchway, and his arms raised in the air to command attention, he addressed them in these few words: "My lads, I have fought for my king five-and-thirty years, and have been too long in his service to turn a rebel in my old age." Would it be credited that, after the mutiny had been quelled, no representation of this conduct was made to Government by his captain? Yet such was the case, and such was the gratitude of Captain A——— The example shown by Adams was not followed; the ship's crew again cheered, and ran down the hatchways, leaving the officers and marines on deck. They first disarmed the sentry under the half deck, and released the prisoners, and then went forward to consult upon further operations. They were not long in deciding. A boatswain's mate, who was one of the ringleaders, piped, "Stand by hammocks!" The men ran on deck, each seizing a hammock, and jumping with it down below on the main-deck. The object of this manœuvre not being comprehended, they were suffered to execute it without interruption. In a few minutes they sent up the marine, whom they had disarmed when sentry over the prisoners, to state that they wished to speak with the captain and officers, who, after some discussion, agreed that they would descend and hear the proposals which the ship's company should make. Indeed, even with the aid of the marines, many of whom were wavering, resistance would now have been useless, and could only have cost them their lives; for they were surrounded by other ships who had hoisted the flag of insubordination, and whose guns were trained ready to pour in a destructive fire on the least sign of an attempt to purchase their anchor. To the main-deck they consequently repaired. The scene which here presented itself was as striking as it was novel. The after part of the main-deck was occupied by the captain and officers, who had come down with the few marines who still continued stedfast to their duty, and one sailor only, Adams, who had so nobly stated his determination on the quarter-deck. The foremost part of the deck was tenanted by a noisy and tumultuous throng of seamen, whose heads only appeared above a barricade of hammocks, which they had evidently formed across the deck, and out of which, at two embrasures, admirably constructed, two long twenty-four pounders, loaded up to the muzzle with grape and canister shot, were pointed aft in the direction where the officers and marines were standing—a man at the breach of each gun, with a match in his hand, (which he occasionally blew, that the priming powder might be more rapidly ignited,) stood ready for the signal to fire. The captain, aghast at the sight, would have retreated; but the officers, formed of sterner materials, persuaded him to stay, although he shewed such evident signs of fear and perturbation as seriously to injure a cause, in which resolution and presence of mind alone could avail. The mutineers, at the suggestion of Peters, had already sent aft their preliminary proposals, which were, that the officers and marines should surrender up their arms, and consider themselves under an arrest,—intimating, at the same time, that the first step in advance made by any one of their party would be the signal for applying the match to the touchholes of the guns. There was a pause and dead silence, as if it were a calm, although every passion was roused and on the alert, every bosom heaved tumultuously, and every pulse was trebled in its action. The same feeling which so powerfully affects the truant school-boy,—who, aware of his offence, and dreading the punishment in perspective, can scarce enjoy the rapture of momentary emancipation,—acted upon the mutineers, in an increased ratio, proportioned to the magnitude of their stake. Some hearts beat with remembrance of injuries, and hopes of vengeance and retaliation; others with ambition, long dormant, bursting from its concealed recess; and many were actuated by that restlessness which induced them to consider any change to be preferable to the monotony of existence in compulsory servitude. Among the officers, some were oppressed with anxious forebodings of evil,—those peculiar sensations which when death approaches nearly to the outward senses, alarm the heart; others experienced no feeling but that of manly fortitude and determination to die, if necessary, like men; in others, alas!—in which party, small as it was, the captain was pre-eminent—fear and trepidation amounted almost to the loss of reason. Such was the state of the main-deck of the ship at the moment in which we are now describing it to the reader. And yet, in the very centre of all this tumult, there was one who, although not indifferent to the scene around him, felt interested without being anxious—astonished without being alarmed. Between the contending and divided parties stood a little boy, about six years old. He was the perfection of childish beauty; chestnut hair waved in curls on his forehead, health glowed in his rosy cheeks, dimples sported over his face as he altered the expression of his countenance, and his large dark eyes flashed with intelligence and animation. He was dressed in mimic imitation of a man-of-war's-man,—loose trowsers, tightened at the hips, to preclude the necessity of suspenders, and a white duck frock, with long sleeves and blue collar,—while a knife, attached to a lan-yard, was suspended round his neck; a light and narrow-brimed straw hat on his head, completed his attire. At times he looked aft at the officers and marines; at others he turned his eyes forward to the hammocks, behind which the ship's company were assembled. The sight was new to him; but he was already accustomed to reflect much, and to ask few questions. Go to the officers he did not, for the presence of the captain restrained him. Go to the ship's company he could not, for the barricade of hammocks prevented him. There he stood, in wonderment, but not in fear. There was something beautiful and affecting in the situation of the boy; calm, when all around him was anxious tumult; thoughtless, when the brains of others were oppressed with the accumulation of ideas; contented, where all was discontent; peaceful, where each party that he stood between was thirsting for each other's blood:—there he stood, the only happy, the only innocent one, amongst hundreds swayed by jarring interests and contending passions. And yet he was in keeping, although in such strong contrast with the rest of the picture; for where is the instance of the human mind being so thoroughly depraved as not to have one good feeling left? Nothing exists so base and vile as not to have one redeeming quality. There is no poison without some antidote—no precipice, however barren, without some trace of verdure—no desert, however vast, without some spring to refresh the parched traveller, some Oasis, some green spot, which, from its situation, in comparison with surrounding objects, appears almost heavenly;—and thus did the boy look almost angelic, standing as he did between the angry, exasperated parties on the main-deck of the disorganized ship. After some little time, he walked forward, and leant against one of the twenty-four pounders that was pointed out of the embrasure, the muzzle of which was on a level with, and intercepted by, his little head. Adams, the quarter-master, observing the dangerous situation of the child, stepped forward and saved him.

COLUMN FOR THE LADIES.

THE ANNIVERSARY OF A MARRIAGE.
LINES SUPPOSED TO BE ADDRESSED BY A WIFE TO HER HUSBAND.

These verses were written after reading the following extract from the letter of a mother to her son:—" This is our wedding-day. Gratitude to the Giver of all goodness ought to be the predominant feeling of my heart; for during the last seven-and-twenty years of my life, what blessings hath He not bestowed upon me—what kindnesses I have experienced—what smiling, happy faces have cheered my hearth! My mind has wandered, the whole of the day, back to that important morning, when, encircled by friends, I became a happy wife. As vividly as if it were an occurrence of yesterday, it passes before my mental view; but these friends, where are they now? Alas, not one out of four then present is now in being. And when another such period (ay, and a far shorter period) shall have passed away, what other changes will not have taken place!"

Full seven-and-twenty years have roll'd
　Their course o'er Time's swift tide,
Since at the altar I became
　Thy own, thy happy bride.

The anxious father, who consign'd
　His daughter to thy care,
And she who in the bloom of youth,
　With laughing eyes, was there,—

All, all who stood around that shrine,
　Save, dearest, us alone,
Where are their forms, their footsteps now?
　O, whither have they gone?

Their troubles o'er, their cares forgot,
　Life's feverish vision fled,
Unbroken slumber they enjoy
　Among the silent dead.

Come, let us now the blessings own
　Of years together pass'd,
Nor murmur though a cloud hath oft
　The azure sky o'ercast.

How many in their youth have sunk
　In Death's cold arms to sleep,
Or linger in this shifting scene,
　To suffer, writhe, and weep!

How many, girdled round with joys,
　And anxious yet to stay,
All heedless of each sunder'd tie
　The grave hath snatch'd away.

We still survive; each circling year
　Hath crown'd our happy hearth,
With smiling faces, words of love,
　And sounds of cheerful mirth.

The good man's prayer—" Remove from me
　All vanity and lies;
Nor give me poverty, nor yet,
　O Lord, too rich supplies.

" With food convenient feed me, lest
　In fulness I should say,
Who is the Lord? or lest I steal
　Another's goods away."

This virtuous prayer, in wisdom breathed,
　Have we not long enjoy'd?
With food convenient ever fed,
　With luxury uncloy'd.

What though the storm hath sometimes raged,
　And boisterous been the weather,
Hath not each bitter blast but made
　Us closer cling together?

We've reached the summit of the hill,
　Spring gone, and Summer waning:
Without a gloomy, anxious fear,
　We'll tread the steps remaining.

Dear husband, hand in hand we'll go,
　Virtue's fair paths adorning,
So shall the evening of our day
　Be beauteous as the morning.

Though each lov'd form depart, which grew
　To manhood's prime around us,
And on our hearth we sit as lone
　As our glad nuptials found us.

There is a home of peace and rest,
　Where hopes shall bloom—now blighted—
Where the fond circle, broken now,
　In joy shall be united.

ELEMENTS OF THOUGHT.

THE AUTHOR BY PROFESSION.

He lies "stretched upon the rack of restless ecstasy;" he runs the everlasting gauntlet of public opinion. He must write on, and if he had the strength of Hercules, and the wit of Mercury, he must in the end write himself down. He cannot let well done alone. He cannot take his stand on what he has already achieved, and say, "Let it be a durable monument to me and mine, and a covenant between me and the world for ever!" He is called upon for perpetual new exertions, and urged forward by ever-craving necessities. The *wolf* must be kept from the door; the *printer's devil* must not go empty-handed away. He makes a second attempt, and though equal, perhaps, to the first, because it does not excite the same surprise, it falls tame and flat on the public mind. If he pursue the real bent of his genius, he is thought to grow dull and monotonous; or if he vary his style, and try to cater for the capricious appetite of the town, he either escapes by miracle, or breaks down that way amidst the shout of the multitude, and the condolence of friends, to see the idol of the moment pushed from its pedestal, and reduced to its proper level. There is only one living writer who can pass through this ordeal; and if he had barely written half what he has done, his reputation would have been none the less. His inexhaustible facility makes the willing world believe there is not much in it. Still there is no alternative. Popularity, like one of the Danaides, imposes impossible tasks on her votary—to pour water into sieves, to reap the wind. If he does nothing, he is forgotten; if he attempts more than he can perform, he gets laughed at for his pains. He is impelled by circumstances to fresh sacrifice of time, of labour, of self-respect; parts with well-earned fame for a newspaper puff, and sells his birth-right for a mess of pottage. In the meanwhile the public wonder why an author writes so badly and so much. With all his efforts he builds no house, leaves no inheritance, lives from hand to mouth, and, though condemned to daily drudgery for a precarious subsistence, is expected to produce none but works of first-rate genius. No: learning unconsecrated, unincorporated, unendowed, is no match for the importunate demands and thoughtless ingratitude of the reading public.—*Edinburgh Review.*

Men are qualified for civil liberty in exact proportion to their disposition to put moral chains on their own appetites; in proportion as their love to justice is above their rapacity; in proportion as their soundness and sobriety of understanding is above their vanity and presumption; in proportion as they are more disposed to listen to the counsel of the wise and good, in preference to the flattery of knaves. Society cannot exist unless a controlling power upon will and appetite be placed somewhere, and the less of it there is within, the more there must be without. It is ordained in the eternal constitution of things, that men of intemperate minds cannot be free. Their passions forge their fetters.—*Burke.*

HIGH LIVING AND MEAN THINKING.

How much nicer people are in their persons than in their minds. How anxious are they to wear the appearances of wealth and taste in the things of outward shew, while their intellects are all poverty and meanness. See one of the apes of fashion with his coxcombries and ostentations of luxury. His clothes must be made by the best tailor, his horses must be of the best blood, his wines of the finest flavour, his cookery of the highest zest; but his reading is of the poorest frivolities, or of the lowest and most despicable vulgarity. In the enjoyment of the animal senses he is an epicure; but a pig is a clean feeder compared with his mind: and a pig would eat good and bad, sweet and foul alike, but his mind has no taste except for the most worthless garbage. The pig has no discrimination and a great appetite; the mind which we describe has not the apology of voracity; it is satisfied with little, but the little must be of the worst sort, and every thing of a better quality is rejected by it with disgust. If we could see men's minds as we see heir bodies, what a spectacle of nakedness, destitution, deformity, and disease it would be! What hideous dwarfs and cripples! What dirt, and what revolting cravings! and all these in connection with the most exquisite care and pampering of the body. If many a conceited coxcomb could see his own mind, he would see a thing, the like of which is not to be found in the meanest object the world can present. It is not with beggary, in the most degraded state, that it is to be compared, for the beggar has wants, is dissatisfied with his state, has wishes for enjoyments above his lot, but the pauper of intellect is content with his poverty; it is his choice to feed on carrion, he can relish nothing else, he has no desires beyond the filthy fare. Yet he piques himself that he is a superior being; he takes to himself the merit of his tailor, his coachmaker, his upholsterer, his wine merchant, his cook; but if the thing were turned inside out, if that concealed nasty corner, his mind, were exposed to view, how degrading would be the exhibition.

After all our vaunts of the progress of intelligence, the truth yet is, that the minds of the mass of our population, like the bodies of the mass of the Irish nation, are fed on the very lowest kind of food, easy of production in the poorest soils, and affording the slightest nourishment. There is a potatoe diet of the press, which is a positive enemy of improvement; and it is not the labourer and the artizan who sit down content with it, but the gentry, the fashionable, and their host of imitators. In London, every luxury is had or affected to be had for the body, and dunghills yield the banquets for the mind. We often wish that these things could be seen in kind; that the man of professed nicety and taste could see the quality of the stuff with which he regales his mind. The breakfast table is laid out with every delicacy, and on it is a scavenger's cart filled with slabby noisome filth, the collection of the very kennels, the rakings of all the nasty corners; the voluptuary sips his chocolate, daintily picks his French pie, while he fills his mind with that fetid mass, the cookery of the scavengers! How fastidious is the stomach of this man! how unspeakably coarse, and worse than beastly, his intellect! No animal in the creation confines itself to filth only. The appetite for sheer ribaldry is unmatched in the depravities of taste. We lately heard one of the would-be exquisites declare, that the paper of his choice was the most scurrilous, and vulgar withal, of the London weekly papers, and doubtless it was his only reading; and a few minutes afterwards, he expressed his chagrin that some fine people had seen him get into a hackney coach at the door of a theatre! This man had no perception of the shabby way in which he treated his mind. What a loathsome hack vehicle was that, to which, without shame, he committed it! To a just intelligence, how degrading should be accounted such a sign of the poverty of the understanding, or of its preference of the mean and vile! He sighed for the luxury and show of the carriage for his person, but he had no wishes for the mind above the garbage upon which it regaled. In this respect he was destitute of the humblest claims to respect, and yet he was contented. He knew not that his state of intelligence was below beggary; and that, if his fortunes corresponded with his understanding, he would be clothed in the foulest rags, and fed by the sewers. Might it not reasonably be expected that people should take as much pride in the nicety of their minds as in that of their persons? The purity of the mind, the careful preservation of it from the defilement of loose or grovelling thoughts, is surely as much a matter of necessary decency as the cleanliness of the body. The coarse clothing of the person is a badge of poverty: what then should be thought of the coarse entertainment of the imagination? what destitution does it argue? and when it is seen, in connexion with all the luxuries of abundant wealth, how odious is the contest between the superfluities of fortune and the pitiable penury of the understanding! The mansion is spacious and elegantly furnished, but the soul of the occupier is only comparable to its dust-hole, a dark dirty receptacle for the vilest trash and rubbish.—*Tait's Edinburgh Magazine, for January.*

THE STORY-TELLER.

ENGLISH SMUGGLERS.
HARRY WOODRIFF.

The smugglers are the only race of people in this country who have not been at all acted upon by the improvements of society. Everywhere else civilization has been hard at work; scouring through the land with the speed of a twopenny postman,—building schools, breeching Highlanders, and grubbing up the spirit of adventure from the very bosom of rocks and mountains. It has made a smart attack too on the gipsies, but with only a sort of piebald success, robbing the gallows to augment the population of Botany Bay; taking off the edge of their daring, yet by no means lessening their indolence, or their love of petty larceny. But the smuggler,—the sturdy smuggler,—is still the same creature he was fifty years ago, and even allowing him to be a villain,—villain is a hard word,—there is yet something noble in his doings and his sufferings. In fact, the good people of this city know as little about him as they do of Prester John, or the Cham of Tartary. I have some right to speak on the subject, for one part of my early days was spent on the sea-coast, when—to my shame be it spoken.—I preferred the smugglers to my books; and, from many wild pranks, became a favourite among them. There was one outlaw in particular, Harry Woodriff, or Woodrieve, who was much attached to the Master, as they called me, partly, I believe, from the eagerness with which I listened to his tales of himself and his associates, and not a little because he mistook my romantic feelings for courage. Our acquaintance, or rather our intimacy, commenced by my going out with him in a storm, to the relief of a distressed collier, when the chances were twenty to one against our ever returning; but with me it certainly was not courage; there was an exaltation of the spirits more like the effect of wine, as we swept along the waves, that at one moment rose like a mountain, and in the next opened almost to the very sands. I feared no danger, for I *felt* no danger, and there can hardly be courage without the consciousness of peril. But Harry was not the man to look so nicely into things; I had shown no symptoms of fear, and that was enough for him, who held that a stout spirit included all the cardinal virtues: ever after he loved me as a son, and many a tale did I gather from the sturdy smuggler, as he paced up and down the cliff with his glass in his hand, on the look out for what the sea was next to bring him.

It was not, however, of Harry's early stories that I would speak at present, though a time may come for them too, but of our meeting two years ago, when we least expected it, and for an end that thrilled my blood with horror. Remember this is no fiction; here and there some local deviations are introduced, for reasons sufficiently obvious, but the main facts are as true as that the sun is in the heavens.

It was in the autumn of 1820 that my friend, Lieutenant E———, invited me to pass a few weeks with him on the coast where he was stationed on the preventive service,—an invitation that had been too often repeated to be again slighted without offence to honest Frank, whose heart was much better ballasted than his head. Accordingly I set out a little before sunrise, and by six o'clock at night I reached my friend's house. This was a snug cottage, about a hundred yards from a long bed of shingle, which had originally been thrown up there by the sea, and which now served as a defence against its encroachments. As it was impossible to drive the chaise up to the door, I was obliged to get out, and, having paid the post-boy, shouldered my portmanteau, and strode forward lustily to the cottage, where the first thing I heard was the voice of my friend, the Lieutenant, loud in anger on some half dozen subjects, which he contrived to twist together like the different plies of a cable, and of which my absence seemed to be the principal.

"Confound all landlubbers!—Peg, you jade, hand us up the supper.—Kit not cleaned my barkers yet! If I don't give that fellow monkey's allowance—Betsy—What a d—d fool the captain must be to let them smugglers get off—Betsy—Well, well, George—Betsy—D—n it, you're as stupid as the girl. Hand over that bundle of cigars—I tell you what, George,"—

"Well, what will you tell me?" said I, breaking in upon his medley soliloquy.

"George!—glad to see you with all my heart and soul, boy. You're just in time."

"Yes, I smell the supper."

"You shall smell gunpowder, my boy, before you are two day's older. A cargo from Dunkirk—red stern—twelve men and a boy—white gunnell—know all about her—figured on the other side," he added with a knowing wink, at the same time jingling some loose silver in his pocket. "D—n it all, I was afraid you'd be too late for the fun, but here you are, and in good time."

"I can't say I see the fun."

"But you shall, boy; you shall go with us; they fight like devils; no sneakers among them."

I fancy my face testified no great symptoms of delight at the proposed amusement, for the Lieutenant, though not much given to observation, exclaimed quickly, "You're not afraid, lad?"

Still, I rather think, I should have declined this favour, for Frank really meant it as a favour—if his wife had not come in at the critical moment: no man would even seem to be a coward in the presence of a woman, and, before I well knew what I was about, my word was pledged to the business, to the infinite delight of Frank, who thereupon showed me, with great glee, a brace of barkers, as he called them, that Kit was to scour for my especial service. As to any danger I might run, that never once entered into Frank's calculation; he looked on these smuggling frays much as a fox-hunter looks on the chase, in which bruises and broken heads are necessary contingencies, not to be talked of for a moment, and which by no means take away from the pleasure of the pursuit.

Supper over, and the regular allowance of pipes and grog being duly despatched, I was suffered to retire, with a promise from Frank of calling me if there was any stir among the smugglers; a promise that, it may be easily supposed, was altogether unsolicited on my part; indeed, I could have willingly dispensed with his punctuality on this point, but I knew him too well to doubt his keeping his word, and it was now over late to draw back; to bed, therefore, I went, in all that ferment of the spirits, which men of sedentary habits never fail to experience after a day of travel.

It was ten o'clock before I rose from my morning sleep—the only sleep I had enjoyed—and on going down to breakfast, I found that my friend was out, and myself very much in the way of Peggy and her mistress, whose daily occupations were at a stand-still from my laziness. My hostess had involuntarily caught up a broom that had been left by Peggy, and I plainly saw that she was burning to commence a vigorous campaign against the dust and the spiders. In pity, therefore, to her troubles, I swallowed down my breakfast, without, indeed, the least danger to my throat, and posted off in quest of my friend, the Lieutenant, who, she told me, was at the battery, a name by which they had dignified a large mound of earth with two old guns, that might be said to be on half-pay, for though they retained their place, they were never employed. It was not, however, my fate to reach the battery that morning, for I must needs try to make a short cut to my end, by which, as many wise men have done before me, I lost it altogether. The ground, a large tract of open country, was intersected by dykes; the first of these having low banks, and not being very wide, I got over easily enough; the next was too much for me, and I therefore bent my course to a narrower part, which again led me into another difficulty, to be avoided by a similar circuit, and so on, till I was completely entangled. The greater my efforts now, the more they removed me from my object, and, at last, they brought me to a small hollow, partly formed by nature, and partly by the chalk having been originally dug out for the purpose of making lime; three sides of it were perpendicular rocks, with here and there a few broad weeds, not unlike dock leaves, shooting through the interstices; the fourth sloped roughly down to a depth of ninety feet, or perhaps more, and was covered with briers that twined their long thin arms with the high grass, and made the descent a work of toil except by one beaten path. In breadth it was about two hundred feet, in length full twice as many. In the bottom was a cottage and garden as I expected, for I had been used to these artificial glens in Kent, where they are sure to find occupants the moment they are deserted by the chalk-miners. A soil is easily and cheaply formed from the sea-weed, while the exclusion of the wind, and the reflexion of the sun from the chalk, make a shelter for trees and vegetables, which will thrive there much better than on the open downs, exposed as they are to all the bleakness of the weather, and the influence of the salt sea air.

Curiosity led me down into the hollow, where I found the door of the cottage open, and the first object that attracted my attention was a young girl, apparently not more than seventeen years of age: even in a drawing-room, amidst lights and crowds, the enemies to all romance, I should yet have noticed her as something singular; but here, in this wild glen, where the mind was previously prepared, by local circumstances, for the reception of every fanciful impression, I felt as much startled at her presence as if she had been a shadow from the world of spirits. Her form, though extremely elegant in its proportions, seemed as light and airy as if no earth had entered into her composition: her hair curled in jet-black ringlets about a face that was as pale as marble; her eyes were of a deep blue, with an expression that was something akin to madness; and a dark melancholy sate on her forehead, that seemed to fling a shadow over the whole face, and deepen its natural paleness. What rendered her still more striking was the utter discordance of her dress and manners with the luxurious poverty about her, in which wealth and want were strangely blended. A deal table, scored and stained, was waited upon by half a dozen mahogany chairs, of as many fashions as there were chairs; two large silver goblets stood on the same row with a party of coarse white plates, flawed and fractured in every direction; and a Brussels carpet was spread on the floor, though the laths of the ceiling showed through the plaister above, like ribs from the thin sides of poverty. On the mantel-piece, which was tolerably well smoked, was a handsome gold time-keeper, flanked by a whole host of tobacco-pipes in every possible stage, from the black stump to the immaculate whiteness of the perfect tube. Higher up, guns, pistols, and cutlasses were ranged in formidable order, and with the same love of variety, no one weapon had its fellow. I had been too much used to such dwellings in my boyhood not to guess pretty well upon what company I had stumbled, and when a man came out of the inner room, I was prepared to see a smuggler, but not to see Harry Woodriff. It was Harry, however! the identical Harry! —and though full fifteen years had elapsed since we last walked together on the cliffs of Kent, I knew him that instant; it was impossible to mistake that peculiar face; the features were too strongly cast originally to be much affected by time, which, indeed, had only hardened the mould against successive years, and not altered it. His name burst from my lips involuntarily.—"Harry Woodriff!"

"Ay, ay," exclaimed the old man, without the least symptom of recognition,—"What cheer now, messmate?"

"Don't you know me, Harry? Don't you remember your old friend George, and our going off to the brig Sophy?"

"What! the Master?—Sink the customs! you can't be he. George was a little rosy-faced chap, no higher than this table."

"That was fifteen years ago, Harry; and fifteen years will make a difference on your *little rosy-faced chaps, no higher than the table.*"

"Right, messmate;—Sink the customs! and so you are the Master?—D—n you!"—And he grasped me with his iron hand, till my bones cracked again, though without the slightest change of feature on his part, or any symptoms of emotion in his voice.—"Am as glad to see you as though you were an anker of brandy—Nance, girl,"—turning to his daughter, who had hitherto looked on our meeting with silent curiosity,—" Fetch us a drop of the right stuff, and a clean pipe—though, stay, there's plenty of pipes here."

"I don't smoke, Harry, and as to drinking,"—

"You don't drink neither?"

"Not at this hour."

"Why Lunnon has clean spoilt you, Master—you could smoke, and drink, too, for that matter, and without asking whether it was morn or midnight. But you're another guess sort of chap, now. You had better have staid in Kent, Master."

"Why did *you* leave it?"

"Wouldn't do; grew hot as h—ll—sink the customs!"

"I doubt whether you have much mended the matter by coming here."

"Ay, ay; hard times, master, when a poor man can't eat his bread and cheese without fighting for it first.—Not that I much mind that either, if things were a little more on the square, but 'tis d—d hard to fight with a rope round one's neck. It was all fair enough when they looked after the cargo and let the man alone: if they could seize the goods, that was their luck; if we got off, that was ours; and all friends afterwards. But now if they catch you, they haul you off to jail, and if you fight for it, they hang you up as though you were a pirate.—Sink the customs!

"Better take to some other business!"

"Why look ye, lad; I'm hard on sixty, and that's over late to go on a new tack. But here comes Nance with the grog—What's that bottle, girl?"

"Some of the claret that you brought over last week for the innkeeper of ———."

"Avast heaving, Nance—Not that I think the Master would tell tales, but,—draw the cork."

This was more easily said than done, a corkscrew forming no part of Harry's domestic economy, and for a long time Nancy worked at it with a broken fork to very little purpose.

"Hand it over," said Harry, and he gravely knocked off the neck of the bottle.

"There; I've done it—Brave liquor it is too, so help yourself, Master.—Sink the customs! Do you call that helping yourself? Here's a change! You could put your beak deep enough into a pint pot when you were a youngker."

"Let me help you, sir," said Nancy; and she filled up my glass with a grace that certainly did not belong to a smuggler's cottage. I could not keep my eyes off her, and the old man must have read my thoughts; for he spoke as if in answer to them.

"She did not learn it of me, you may be sure, Master; it was all got at Miss Trott's boarding school."

"So, so," thought I—"Another precious instance of parents educating their children above the situation they are to fill in life,—refining them into misery." Something of the same kind was evidently passing through Nancy's mind, for her eyes were suffused with tears, to the sore annoyance of the smuggler, who was dotingly fond of her, notwithstanding his apparent apathy, and who was loved by her in return with no less sincerity.

"What's the matter with you, Nance?—Squalls again? —Is there any thing I can do for you?"

There was a beseeching look in Nancy's eyes, the meaning of which I did not then understand, but which was perfectly intelligible to Harry; for he added, though in his usual even tone,—" That is, any thing but the old story.. Is it a gown you want? Silk? Brussels lace? Only say the word, and it's yours; for not to tell you a lie, Nance, if you wished for all the shells that lie between here and Dunkirk, you should have them or I'd drown for it—Sink the customs!"

And all this he said without the least correspondence of tone, or, indeed, any symptom of feeling, except that he laid one of his huge iron paws on the girl's right shoulder, and gently patted her. Nancy made no answer but by leaning her head on her father's brawny bosom. Following up my first idea of the unfitness of such a situation to a

gan of her habits, I referred her grief to that cause; and under the idea of pleasing her, I ventured to suggest that she would do better by seeking her fortune in the world, and even proferred my assistance. She cut short this proposal, however, with a tone of energy and decision that completely silenced me.

"I shall go nowhere, sir, without my father. Where he is, there his daughter must and shall be."

There was a moment's pause; I was too much confounded by the manner of this address to make any reply: Harry kept on smoking his pipe as if we had been talking of matters that in nowise concerned him, and in a language that he did not understand, while the girl herself seemed to be struggling with some internal resolution. For a few moments she fixed her wild flashing eyes on me with a gaze so keen that it made the blood start up into my cheeks, till at last, as if satisfied with the inquiry, she repeated in a milder tone, "I will not leave my father—Is this a time to leave him?" And she pointed to his grey hairs—"Is this a place? I will not leave him. But oh, sir, if you are his friend, persuade him to quit this life, which must sooner or later end by the waves, or the sword, or the gallows. Persuade him, sir;—'tis a better deed than giving ten alms to the poor, for in that you save the body only, but here you save both soul and body. Persuade him, sir; he shall not want; indeed he shall not: I will work for him, beg for him, steal for him—!"

The poor creature burst into tears, exclaiming, "O father, father!"

"Hey for Dunkirk! No soft water, Nance; you know I can't abide it.—So, hark ye in your ear."

He drew his daughter aside, whispered a few words with his usual imperturbability, and finished by exclaiming aloud, "I will! sink the customs!"

"But will you, indeed?"

"There's my hand to it—smuggler's faith! Will you believe me, now?"

Nancy only answered with a kiss; but there was still a restless expression about her eyes and lips that showed she was far from being satisfied; at the time I attributed it to some lurking distrust of her father's sincerity, for I had no doubt that he had promised her to give up smuggling; shrewd, however, as this guess was, it did not happen to be quite correct, and it was only by combining one fact with another, that I afterwards got at the whole truth. It seems that Harry had risked all he possessed, nearly four hundred pounds, in a single venture to Dunkirk, under the conduct of his son; and his promise to quit the free trade was with express reference to the safe return of his cargo, —a sort of compromise that could not altogether quiet the fears of Nancy. To those who are unacquainted with such scenes it may appear strange that the old man did not rather go out with the boat himself: but the fact is, that in smuggling, as much, if not more, depends on the management by land than by water. Experience has shewn these people that they can put very little confidence in each other; the temptations to betray are much too strong for their slender stock of honesty; and the chiefs, therefore, seldom trust more than one of their associates with the secret of the boat's landing-place, which one the rest follow at a moment's warning, through brake and brier, over moor and mountain, like so many wild-ducks after their leader. Now, Harry thought, and wisely, that such a secret could be trusted to no one so well as to himself, and he had, therefore, sent out his son, a stout able young fellow, who had been brought up to the business from his cradle, while he himself staid behind to look after the landing of the cargo.

It was now nearly two o'clock, the Lieutenant's dinnerhour, and I rose to take my leave, saying, "To-morrow I will be here again."

So saying, I left the glen, and returned to the Lieutenant's; but, notwithstanding my improved knowledge in the geography of these parts, I did not arrive time enough to save my credit with my little fat hostess, whom I found in sad tribulation, fretting and fuming over half-cold fish, fowls done to death, and pudding that was as heavy as lead.

The day passed as might have been expected; my friend, in his capacity of host, toiled like a mill-horse to entertain me, and I, as in duty bound, laboured equally to be entertained, though it was by objects that could have no interest for me whatever. I was dragged successively to see his new cutter, the two old guns, the kennel of his seamen, —I can give it no better name,—and the berth of his Mids, who, according to his idea of things, were lodged like Princes. Their principality, however, did not appear to me a subject for much envy; it consisted of two apartments, one of which was a general bed-room, and the other a general parlour. The floor was sanded, and the white-washed walls were ornamented with a variety of long and short heads, and sundry witty inscriptions, such as "Tom Jenkins is a fool," "Sweet Polly Beaver," "Snug's the word," &c. &c. The windows, indeed, looked out upon the sea; and close under them was a patch of garden, which the Mids, in the lack of better occupation, had surrounded with a wall, formed of rude chalk blocks loosely piled together without cement; under this shelter a few cabbages contrived to run to seed amidst a luxuriant crop of thistles.

Having seen these lions, we returned to tea, and passed the dreary interval between that and supper-time in a water excursion, which only wanted a more congenial companion to have been delightful. I know nothing more annoying to a man of romantic habits than the being linked in with your plain matter-of-fact folks, who have no ideas associated with any subject beyond what are presented to them by the obvious qualities of form and colour. My friend, though an excellent seaman, was precisely one of these; he saw nothing in the ocean but a road for shipping; and as to the sky, I question much whether he ever looked up to it, except to take an observation. Still this water excursion was not without its use; it had whiled away three hours, and that was something; it had procured me an excellent appetite for supper, and that too was not to be slighted; and lastly, the sea-air had so much influence on me, that, when bed-time came, I dropt fast asleep the very moment I laid my head on my pillow. My sleep, however, was any thing but quiet; I dreamt, and my dreams were full of grotesque images, and all more vivid than any I have ever experienced either before or after. The agony was too great for endurance, and I awoke. To my surprise, there stood Frank by my bed-side, a pair of cutlasses under his arm, and a candle in one hand, while with the other he pulled and tugged at me might and main. He had no doubt been the black dog of my dreams, for his fingers were closed on my arm with the gripe of a blacksmith's vice.

"Why, how now, lad? You ate too much of the pork last night." And with that he gave me another shake, as if he meant to shake my arm out of its socket.

"What's the matter? what's the matter?" I exclaimed, for I was not yet quite awake! and black dogs, and Nancies, were making a strange medley of it in my brain.

"There's no time for talking—but clap on your rags as quick as may be." And I set about dressing myself almost mechanically, while he paced up and down the room, as if he had been walking the quarter-deck, whistling a very popular, but not very elegant tune, in all manner of times, now fast, and now slow, according to the rise and fall of his fits of impatience. In a few minutes, the last tie was tied, and the last button buttoned.

"All ready, lad?—Here's your cutlass, then, and your barkers. And now we'll clap on all sails and be up with them in a jiffy."

I was by this time fully awake and conscious of our business, for the night air, that blew on me as I left the cottage, sobered down the fumes of sleep in an instant. The wind was cold and boisterous, rolling the clouds along in dark broken masses over the sky, where neither moon nor stars were shining, but there was a dull grey light that just served to make the darkness visible. Frank was incessantly urging me to speed, though we were going at a brisk rate, and as we went along communicated to me the whole matter, as an additional stimulus to my tardiness. This was precisely what I anticipated; a smuggling boat had long been expected on this very night, according to his information, from the other side of the water; and some fishermen, bribed to his purpose, had kept a sharp look-out from their smack, and had thus been able to give him timely warning of its approach. This story was told with great glee by my friend, but I most honestly confess that "I had no devotion to the business." While all was dark, and still, and nothing announced that the fray was near, and I had reason to believe that it was at least a mile from us, I only felt anxious and bewildered; but when a sudden shout burst on us, followed by a rapid discharge of fire-arms, and the turn of the cliff showed us the battle that moment begun, and not a hundred yards from us, what a change then came over me!— It was not fear, for it had none of the palsy of fear; my hand was firm, and my eye was certain, but it was a most intense consciousness of self and of the present moment. I felt I scarce knew how, nor even at this distance of time can I well make out what were my feelings; to be thus suddenly dragged from warm sleep to deal with blows and death on the midnight shingle, was enough to stupify any man of peaceful habits, and such mine had been for years. At this moment, a voice seemed to whisper close to my ear, "*Mary!*" So perfect was the illusion,—if it was illusion, that I involuntarily echoed "*Mary!*" and looked up for the speaker. Yet no Mary was there—how, indeed, could she be? Still it was her voice; I was neither drunk nor dreaming, nor lunatic, and yet I heard it as clearly as ears could hear it, and at the sound my heart swelled, and I felt that I could dare any thing. In an instant I was in the very midst of the fray, dealing my blows right and left with all the fury of a maniac. As I learnt afterwards, my death had been certain twenty times in the course of the scuffle, if it had not been for Frank, and still more for poor Harry, who was fighting among the smugglers, yet could not forget his young friend, though his hand was against him. Many a blow that was meant for me was parried by their watchfulness; but of all this I knew nothing; when all was over,—and it had scarcely lasted ten minutes,—I had only a confused recollection of having struggled stoutly for life amidst sword-cuts and pistol-shots, and men dropping as if struck by some invisible power. It is difficult to make any body understand this, who never has been in danger, or who has so often faced it that the circumstance has lost its novelty; these are sensations that belong only to the first time of perilling life, and are totally independent of fear or courage; they can not occur a second time.

The fray ended by the seizure of all the goods, the death of five smugglers, and the capture of two, who afterwards contrived to get away. As to the rest, they all escaped, as I then imagined, by favour of the dykes, and their better knowledge of the country, with the exception of one poor wretch, who was desperately wounded; him they bore into a near boat-house, which was nothing more than a rude shed, pitched and tarred, and covered with dry seaweed, as a sort of shelter for the nets and skiffs when not employed. Hither I went with the rest, and looked upon a scene that I shall not easily forget; the poor creature was lying on the ground, pale and dripping with blood; his neckcloth had been taken off, and his clothes were torn to tatters. As the torches glared on his eyes, they seemed blue and glassy, and as if fixed in their sockets; he was evidently dying, and though I had often looked on death in hospitals, I could not stand this sight. The visitations of nature may be even more painful to the sufferer, but there is something soothing in the idea that they are visitations of nature; the sick one is struck by the hand of the Deity himself; he is only undergoing the common doom: but a violent death is always connected with the idea of crime or of unusual suffering; it is an end that might have been avoided; and as I gazed on this poor creature, my very heart was sick; every thing was beginning to swim before me, when I rushed out into the open air, and even there I was forced to lean a few moments for support against the shed.

As I began to breathe more freely in the night-wind, my attention was caught by the sound of voices, and on looking round, I saw on the shingles below, on the other side of the dyke, where the fight had first taken place, a young girl, supporting a wounded smuggler in her arms; it was too dark to distinguish their faces with any degree of precision, but their voices soon betrayed them to me. My blood ran cold as I listened to the following short dialogue, for I was in the shadow and could not be seen by the speakers.

"Sink the customs! It's of no use, Nance; I'm fairly a-ground, and you ha'n't strength enough to shove me off again. So here I must lie, old rotten hull as I am, till they find me, and then I swing for it."

"But try, father, only try; lean on me."

Again she endeavoured to drag or rather support the old man forwards, and her efforts were really wonderful for a creature so slim and lightly formed. She actually succeeded in dragging him up a low bank, and even a few yards beyond it, but there her strength failed; she could go no farther, and it was only by an almost superhuman exertion that she held him from falling.

"It won't do, Nance; this shot in the thigh wont let me move an inch farther—so here I must be caught, and I suppose they'll hang me for being found in arms against the King's officers. Sink the customs! They sha'n't tie a noose about my neck, however. We'll blow up the ship sooner than she shall fall into the hands of the enemy. So give us a kiss, my girl—God bless you. And now—hey for Dunkirk!"

And I saw him hold a pistol to his breast, which Nancy seized with a suppressed scream. Poor thing! her gestures at that moment would have wrung pity from a heart of stone,

"For God's sake, father—for your poor Nancy's sake—there is yet hope. Some of our friends may return before the king's-men leave the boat-house."

"Not much likelihoods of that, Nance: they'll hardly slip their own necks into a halter to save mine."

And I stood listening to all this, like a fool! I must have been bewildered—stunned by what had passed. But I was now awake again, and cursing my own dulness that could waste so many precious moments, I dashed down into the dyke, waded knee-deep through mud and water, and with infinite difficulty clambered up the opposite bank, where I was instantly observed by the old smuggler.

"Sink the customs! They are here, Nance."

In another moment I was at his side, but in that moment the pistol was discharged, and he dropped into my arms mortally wounded, exclaiming :—

"Sink the customs! You are too late to hang me, messmate. Nance, my girl, they cannot say your father was hung; you're a wife now for any man,—the best in the land, let him be who he will.—Sink the customs!"

"'Tis I, Harry,—your friend, George Seymour."

"What, the Master!—Give us your hand, d—n you! —You're a brave lad, Master—fought better than any six of the King's blue jackets, thof it was against myself.— But, Master,—"

He tried to go on, but could not, and was evidently bleeding apace internally, though one little drop of blood upon his lips was the only outward sign of injury.

"Master, you'll think of"—

Again the words were as if stifled in his breast as he pointed with a shivering hand to Nancy. But I replied to the sign, for I understood it well—too well.

"She shall not want a home, Harry, while I have one."

"God bless you, Master. Nancy, my girl, where are you? The night grows so dark, or something is coming over my eyes. Kiss me, Nance."

And Nancy moved towards him with a calmness that was truly frightful. As she stooped to kiss him, something like a smile passed over her blue lips. May I never see such a smile again! In the same moment Harry was slightly convulsed, and with a groan that was scarcely audible he expired in my arms.

By this time, the Lieutenant and his party, who had been alarmed by the report of the pistol, came up to us, and explanations were asked and given in less time than it has taken me to write or my readers to peruse them. Frank carefully minuted down every thing in his pocketbook, and, having given the dead body in charge to a party of his seamen, attempted in his rude way to comfort Nancy. The poor girl, however, was not in a state to need, or listen to, comfort; the blow had stunned her into insensibility, and there she stood a thing of life, but without its functions. After many fruitless attempts at consolation, he exclaimed in a tone that under any other circumstances had been ludicrous,—

"By G—d! the poor thing has gone mad or stupid! I tell you what, George, we'll have her home with us, and put her in Bet's hands; she's a better doctor than half our old women in the navy."

This was no sooner said than done, and without either thanks or opposition from Nancy, who seemed to have lost all powers of volition. The Lieutenant's wife, however, feeling that such a case was something beyond the usual range of her practice, begged the ship-surgeon might be sent for, and willingly sank into the subordinate situation of nurse, to the sore displeasure of Frank, who hated the very sight of a doctor. Yet neither the skill of the one, nor the more than sisterly attention of the other, availed any thing. The morning came, and she was evidently mad; a second, and a third followed, and still she was no better; the idea that her father lived, and was to be hung, had got firm hold of her mind, and nothing could root it out. All we could say was in vain; she brooded on this one thought with a sullen silence, much worse than any violence of frenzy could have been; and I now began to feel myself placed in a most awkward situation by my promise, so unwittingly given, to the father. It could not be expected that Frank would trouble himself many days longer with a maniac, and what was I to do with her? One moment I wished the poor thing might die, and in the next was angry with myself for my selfishness:—then again, I cursed the hour that brought me on such an unlucky visit; when, as if all this was not enough, I was summoned to the coroner's inquest, sitting on the body of Henry Woodriff. I was not surprised at such a call, but it seems I might have spared my wonder; for however the smugglers may perish, this ceremony is never omitted, and the inquest had already sate on the others who were found dead near the beach.

Internally vowing to leave this abominable place within the next four-and-twenty hours, never to return, I set off in obedience to the summons of the law, and found the inquest assembled in the parlour of a little public house, divided only by a field from the village. Here, too, was Frank, with a party of his sailors, either as witnesses, or accessories. The foreman of the inquest was a short, stout man, with a round face, and a short nose turned up as if in scorn of the two thick lips that opened beneath it, and a pair of yellow, flaring eyes, though destitute of all expression. He looked full of the dignity of his office, and as I entered, was in the high tide of discussion with a stout young smuggler, who, by his tone and manner, seemed to care very little for any body present. And he spoke out his mind as plainly as his father would have done, though not quite so cooly.

"Then I'll be d—d if you do. Gentlemen, as you call yourselves, there's ne'er a Crowner of you all shall drive a stake through the old man's corpse, while there's a hand to this body."

"Respect the dignity of the court, young man. Your father being compos, did make away with himself. I take it, gentlemen, the evidence is sufficient to that effect; but we'll presently examine Mr. Seymour—"

"My name is Seymour."

"Pray be seated, Mr. Seymour; I'll speak to you directly.——Your father, I say, being compos, did make away with himself, and the law, in that case made and provided, says"—

"D—n the law. I say, whoever runs a stake through my father's body, I'll send a bullet through his head. So now you all know my mind, and let him try it who likes it."

With this he burst out of the court, to the great dismay of the foreman, who, when he recovered from his surprise, said in a tone of grave importance:

"This is contempt of the court, and must be punished."

The Lieutenant, however, put in his veto; for with all his roughness, he did not want for feeling, and the gallantry of the young smuggler had evidently won his heart.

"Psha! the poor fellow only speaks up for his father, and he has a right to do so."

"Yes, but with your leave, Lieutenant E——,"

"Come, come, Mr. Denton, I know you are too kind-hearted to hurt the lad for such a trifle."

"Trifle! do you call it a trifle to damn the court?"

"Well, call it what you will, but let the poor fellow go scot-free. He has enough of it already, I think; his goods have been taken, his father killed, and his sister is run mad."

"Why, as you say, Lieutenant E——, I am not hard-hearted, and—Oh, Mr. Seymour, I beg your pardon for detaining you. We want your evidence as to this business, merely as a matter of form. You were present when Harry Woodriff shot himself. Administer the oath to Mr. Seymour."

The oath was accordingly administered in due form, and I was reluctantly compelled to tell the whole business, which still farther authorized the little foreman in his darling scheme of burying a man in the meeting of four roads, and driving a stake through his body. I do not believe he was really of a bad disposition, but this ceremony flattered his importance, besides that it gratified the appetite for horror, so common to all vulgar minds. To have been present at such a sight, under any circumstances, would have delighted him, merely as a spectator; but to have it take place under his own auspices, was too great a treat to be given up for any consideration that Frank or myself could offer. In addition to the mere pleasure of the thing itself, his persistency gave him, in his own eyes, all the dignity of a man resolute in the performance of his duty, however unpleasant, and in spite of the most powerful solicitations. We were, therefore, obliged to yield the point, and leave the field to the little foreman, who instantly selected half a dozen stout peasants to keep watch over the body.

In coming out we saw a knot of smugglers in earnest conversation at the end of the street, about fifty yards from us. Among them was young Woodriff, whose gestures spoke pretty plainly that the council was not a peaceful one, and the Lieutenant was not slow in guessing their purpose.

"Do you see them, George? Just as I thought:—they'll have a haul now at the old smuggler's body before night is over, and I'll not stand in their way for any coroner's quest of them all—not I. It's no seaman's duty to look after corpses."

As he said this, we came close upon the little party, who were suddenly silent, eyeing us with looks of scorn and sullen hatred, that made me expect a second fray; Frank, however, was too brave to be quarrelsome.

"You need not scowl so, lads; I have only done my duty, and mayhap I may be sorry to have it to do, but still it was my duty, and I did it, and will do it again, if the same thing happens again. But that's neither here nor there. All I meant to say was, that I shall keep a sharp look-out on the water to-night for any boat that may be coming over, and, in case of the worst, I shall have all hands aboard. So, good-by to you."

"The lieutenant's a brave fellow after all," said one, as we walked off.

"I never thought worse of him," replied young Harry; "but if I find out the scoundrel who first shot my father, b——t my soul, but he's as dead a man as any that lies in the churchyard."

"Come on, George," cried the lieutenant; "if I seem to hear what these fellows say, I must notice it, and I don't wish that, if I can help it—poor devils."

It may be easily supposed, that the day did not pass very pleasantly, with me at least, who was not used to the trade of murder, though on Frank the whole business made very little impression. He was too much accustomed to such things to be much affected by them, for a sailor's life is one of occurrences, while that of a studious man flows on so equally, that a simple thunder-storm is to him a matter of excitement. My brain seemed to reel again, and I was heartily glad when 11 o'clock gave me an excuse for retiring, for I was wearied out, mind and body, and wished for nothing so much as to be alone.

It was a dark and stormy night, though as yet no rain fell; the thunder, too, roared fearfully, and the lightning leapt along the waters, that were almost as black as the clouds above them. I was too weary for sleep, and feeling no inclination to toss about for hours in bed, placed myself at the window to enjoy the sublimity of the tempest. At any other time, this splendid scene would have been delightful to me, but now it awoke none of its usual sympathies; it was in vain that I tried to give myself up to it—my mind was out of tune for such things. Still I sate there, gazing on the sea, when my attention was diverted by a gentle tap at the door, and ere I could well answer, it swung slowly back on its hinges, and Nancy stood before me, with a lamp in one hand, and a large case-knife in the other. I thought she was asleep, for her eyes, though wide open, were fixed; and her voice, when she spoke, was subdued and broken, exactly like one who talks in his slumbers. Something, however, may be attributed to the excited state of my fancy.

"I must pass through your window, it opens upon the lawn—for the front door is locked, and the key taken away by the Lieutenant, who is out at sea to-night on the watch for smugglers."

As she muttered this indistinctly, she glided across the room to the window, and, undoing the button that held it, walked slowly out. Still impressed with the idea of her being asleep, I made no opposition, fearing that she might be seriously affected in health or mind by any sudden attempt to wake her. At the same time I resolved not to lose sight of her lest she should come into peril from the cliffs or the dykes, and accordingly I followed her steps at a short distance till we came to the public house. Late as the hour was, the people had not yet gone to bed, for lights were shining through the kitchen window, and from the room immediately over it came the glimmer of a solitary lamp that stood on a table by the casement. Hitherto Nancy had gone on without taking the least notice of my presence, which had served to confirm me in the idea that she walked in her sleep,—but now she turned round upon me—

"The Lieutenant's wife told me truly; he is here: but not a word; follow me softly,—as though you feared to wake the dead."

I saw now that she was really awake, and my first impulse was either by force or persuasion, to take her back. And yet to what purpose? If her madness should grow violent, I could always overpower her, and at any rate, we were going to, and not from, assistance. I did, therefore, as she bade me, and followed her in silence, while she went cautiously up to the window, and having examined what was passing within with all the deliberate cunning of a maniac, then gently lifted the latch of the door, which opened into a narrow brick passage to the left of the kitchen. At the end of it was a short flight of stairs, and these led us into the room where I had before observed the lamp was burning; in the middle of the chamber was a plain deal coffin on tressels, in which lay the corpse of poor Harry, all but the face covered over with a dirty tablecloth. I now saw plainly that the peasants had held their watch below from pure fear of being in the same room with the dead, and a state of partial intoxication might account for their having left the door open; but to what purpose was this visit of Nancy's? She did not long leave me in doubt.

"Now, Mr. Seymour; you call yourself my father's friend; you have eaten of his bread; will you see him hung like a thief on a gibbet?"

The strangeness of this appeal startled me so that I knew not well what to answer. She repeated the question while her eyes flashed fire.

"Will you see him hung?—hung?—hung?—You understand that word, I suppose."

"My dear Nancy"—

"By God's light, coward, I have a mind to put this knife into you. Don't you see he is their prisoner—in chains? and to-morrow he will be tried and hung. Yes, my poor father will be hung."

And in her changing mood she wept and sobbed like an infant; this, however, did not last long—

"But they shall not—no, they shall not! Here, take this knife; plunge it into him, that they may not take him alive. 'Tis a hard task for a daughter, and since you are here, take it and stab him as he sleeps; mind you do not wake him though; stab home—no half-work—home to the heart; you know where it is; here—here."

She placed my hand upon her heart as if to show me where to strike. I drew back shuddering.

"Coward! but you shall do it; it is a task of your own seeking; you came here of your own free will; I did not ask you to follow me, and you shall do it.

I knew not what to say or do, and for a moment thought of flinging myself upon her to force away the knife, when I heard a scuffle below. A few blows were exchanged, a single pistol-shot discharged, and immediately after was the tramp of feet upon the stairs. Nancy uttered a loud shriek—

"They are here!"

Scarcely were the words uttered than she rushed up to the coffin, and ere I could prevent her, plunged the knife twice or thrice into the dead body. In the same instant the room was filled with smugglers, headed by young Woodriff, who was astonished, as well he might be, at the extraordinary scene before him.

"Mr. Seymour!—Nance too!—Poor girl!—But we have no time for talking, so all hands to work and help bear off the old man to the boat—we'll soon have him in fifty fathoms of water out of the reach of these b———d harpies."

"My father!—You shall not take my father from me!" shrieked the poor maniac.

"Be quiet, Nance!—Gently, lads, down the stair-case—look to our Nance, Mr. Seymour:—gently, lads—I'd sooner knock twenty living men on the head than hear one blow given to a dead one."

So saying, and having again briefly entreated my care of his sister, he followed the corpse out, while the unfortunate maniac, quite contrary to my expectations, made no farther opposition. She leant for a time against the window without speaking a word, and, when I tried to persuade her to return, very calmly replied, "With all my heart. To what purpose should I stay here since they have taken my father from me? They'll hang him now, and I cannot help it."

"My poor girl, your father is dead."

Nancy smiled contemptuously, and, passing her hand across her brow as if exhausted, said, "I am ready to faint; will you be kind enough to fetch me a glass of water."

She did, indeed, seem ready to drop, and I went down into the kitchen to fetch the water. Seven or eight smugglers were there keeping watch over the peasants, and the sentinel, mistaking me for an enemy, levelled his pistol at my head; but the priming flashed in the pan, and before he could repeat the attack, an old man, who had often seen me with Frank, stepped between us just in time to save me by his explanation.

Upon telling him my purpose he directed me to the well in the yard, at the same time putting a lantern into my hand with a caution to "look to the rotting tackling,"—a caution that was not given without good reason, for the wood-work round the well was so decayed that it would scarcely bear the action of the cylinder.

In a few minutes I had drawn up the bucket, and hastened back to Nancy with a jug full of the water. To my great surprise she was gone, and I now saw—too late, indeed—that her request for water was merely a trick to get rid of me, that she might the better escape, though, what her farther object in it might be, I could not possibly divine. It was not long, however, before I learnt this too; for on looking out of the window, I saw her, with the lamp still in her hand, pushing out to sea in a small skiff, that was half afloat, and held only by a thin cable. How she contrived to throw off the rope I know not, but she did contrive it—perhaps she had the knife with her, and cut it. Be this as it may, she was pushing off amidst the breakers that burst about her most tremendously, and kept up a most violent surf for at least half a mile from the shore. Was not this under the idea of rescuing her father?

In an instant I gave the alarm, and the smugglers, leaving the peasants to do their worst, hurried off with me to the beach. Nancy was now about a hundred yards from the shore in the midst of a furious surge, for though it was too dark to see her, the glimmer of the lamp was visible every now and then as the boat rose upon the waters.

" By G—d! it's of no use," said the old smuggler, " No skiff can get through them breakers."

" Well, but she has."

" Not yet, master—see—the light's gone—it's all up with her now."

The light had indeed gone, and not as before to rise again with the rise of the waters. Minute after minute elapsed, and still all was dark upon the waves, and the next morning the corpse of Nancy Woodriff was found on the sands, about half a mile from the place where she had first pushed off amid the breakers. G. S.

THE WITCH DANCE ON THE BROCKEN.

There is a very ancient and favourite tradition in Germany, called, *Der Hexentanz auf dem Brocken*, or " The Witch-dance on the Brocken," which is said to have had its origin in the following circumstances:—Charlemagne had found all his pious endeavours to convert the Saxons ineffectual. The heathens retired before his arms into their woods and fortresses, and, as soon as they found themselves beyond his reach, resumed their horrid rites and devil-worship. To put a stop to these impieties, the Christian emperor stationed guards at the passes of the mountains, when the season of the heathen festivals approached; but the Saxons eluded his soldiers by a very ingenious contrivance. They arrayed themselves in the skins and horns of beasts, and wielding fire-brands and rude clubs, presented themselves in this terrific guise to the guards, who, conceiving them to be so many demons, took to flight, and spread abroad a variety of appalling stories of the spirits which haunted the Brocken, and other inaccessible spots. The Marchen runs as follows:

" Among the Harz mountains there is an exceeding lofty one, which rears its head far above the rest, and overlooks all the country fifteen miles around. It is called the Brocken; but when we talk of the incantations and demon rites which were performed here in heathen times, and are said to be still practised by those wretches who have sold themselves to the Devil, we call it the Blocksberg. Upon its cold and barren summit, which glitters all over with a thousand millions of rock-crystals, the Devil holds an annual festival, on the night between the last day of April and the first of May, well known by the name of Walpurgi's night, to which all the witches and magicians on earth are invited. As soon as midnight has tolled, the guests begin to arrive from all quarters, upon brooms and pitchforks, and giants' bones, and other strange steeds; and the Great Devil himself brings along with him not a few to the entertainment. When all are met, an immense bonfire is lighted up, and a wild dance commences; after which the Devil mounts the Devil-pulpit, and delivers a blasphemous harangue, at the conclusion of which a supper, consisting wholly of sausages, is served up upon the witches altar. The hag who reaches the scene last meets with a dreadful punishment, to serve as a warning to all the rest; for after a warm embrace from the Prince of Darkness, she is suddenly torn in pieces, and her flesh is scattered over the witches' altar. At the first blush of morning the whole assembly disperses. The peasants dwelling in the neighbourhood of the Brocken, on the approach of Walpurgi's night, draw the sign of three crosses on all their doors, being firmly persuaded that it is only by using this precaution they can protect themselves from the bad designs of the unholy assembly."

ECLIPSES IN 1833.—In the ensuing year there will be five eclipses of the two great luminaries, of which one of the sun and three of the moon will be visible. The following are the periods at which it is calculated the eclipses will take place in this latitude. January 6.—The moon will be eclipsed, partly visible here; beginning of the eclipse, thirty-one minutes past six in the morning; end fifty-two minutes past eight. January 20.—The sun will be eclipsed, visible here, at forty-two minutes past nine in the evening. July 1.—The moon will be eclipsed, visible here; beginning of the eclipse, fifty minutes past ten in the evening; end, six minutes past two in the morning of July 2. July 17.—The sun will be eclipsed, visible here; beginning of the eclipse, fifty-six minutes past four in the morning; end, thirty one minutes past six. December 26.—The moon will be totally eclipsed, visible here; beginning of the eclipse, thirty-one minutes past seven in the evening; beginning of total darkness, thirty minutes past nine; end of the eclipse, eight minutes past eleven in the evening.

VERSES FOR THE YOUNG.

We extract from the *Poetical Works of Leigh Hunt* (just published by Moxon) the Father's reflections by the side of his slumbering sick child.

TO T. L. H.,
SIX YEARS OLD, DURING A SICKNESS.

Sleep breathes at last from out thee,
  My little, patient boy;
And balmy rest about thee
  Smooths off the day's annoy.
I sit me down, and think
  Of all thy winning ways;
Yet almost wish, with sudden shrink,
  That I had less to praise.

Thy sidelong pillowed meekness,
  Thy thanks to all that aid,
Thy heart, in pain and weakness,
  Of fancied faults afraid;
The little trembling hand
  That wipes thy quiet tears,
These, these are the things that may demand
  Dread memories for years.

Sorrows I've had, severe ones,
  I will not think of now;
And calmly, midst my dear ones,
  Have wasted with dry brow;
But when thy fingers press
  And pat my stooping head,
I cannot bear the gentleness,—
  The tears are in their bed.

Ah, first-born of thy mother,
  When life and hope were new,
Kind playmate of thy brother,
  Thy sister, father too;
My light, where'er I go,
  My bird, when prison-bound,
My hand in hand companion,—no,
  My prayers shall hold thee round.

To say " He has departed"—
" His voice"—" his face"—is gone;
To feel impatient-hearted,
  Yet feel we must bear on;
Ah, I could not endure
  To whisper of such wo,
Unless I felt this sleep ensure
  That it will not be so.

Yes, still he's fixed, and sleeping!
  This silence too the while—
It's very hush and creeping
  Seem whispering us a smile:
Something divine and dim
  Seems going by one's ear,
Like parting wings of cherubim,
  Who say, " We've finished here!"

THE STIRRUP CUP.

The fashion of compotation described in the text, was still occasionally practised in Scotland, in my youth. A company, after having taken leave of their host, often went to finish the evening at the clachan or village, in "womb of tavern." Their entertainer always accompanied them to take the stirrup-cup, which often occasioned a long and late revel.

The *Poculum Potatorium* of the valiant Baron, his blessed Bear, has a prototype at the fine old Castle of Glammis, so rich in memorials of ancient times; it is a massive beaker of silver, double gilt, moulded into the shape of a lion, and holding about an English pint of wine. The form alludes to the family name of Strathmore, which is Lyon, and, when exhibited, the cup must necessarily be emptied to the Earl's health. The author ought perhaps to be ashamed of recording that he has had the honour of swallowing the contents of the Lion; and the recollection of the feat served to suggest the story of the Bear of Bradwardine. In the family of Scott of Thirlestane (not Thirlestane in the Forest, but the place of the same name in Roxburghshire) was long preserved a cup of the same kind, in the form of a jack-boot. Each guest was obliged to empty this at his departure. If the guest's name was Scott, the necessity was doubly imperative.

When the landlord of an inn presented his guests with *deoch an doruis*, that is, the drink at the door, or the stirrup-cup, the draught was not charged in the reckoning. On this point a learned Bailie of the town of Forfar pronounced a very sound judgment.

A., an Ale-wife in Forfar, had brewed her "peck of malt," and set the liquor out of doors to cool; the cow of B., a neighbour of A., chanced to come by, and seeing the good beverage, was allured to taste it, and finally to drink it up. When A. came to take in her liquor, she found her tub empty, and from the cow's staggering and staring, so as to betray her intemperance, she easily divined the mode in which her "browst" had disappeared. To take vengeance on Crummie's ribs with a stick, was her first effort. The roaring of the cow brought B., her master, who remonstrated with his angry neighbour, and received in reply a demand for the value of the ale which Crummie had drunk up. B. refused payment, and was conveyed before C., the Bailie, or sitting Magistrate. He heard the case patiently; and then demanded of the plaintiff A., whether the cow had sat down to her potation, or taken it standing. The plaintiff answered, she had not seen the deed committed, but she supposed the cow drank the ale while standing on her feet; adding, that had she been near, she would have made her use them to some purpose. The Bailie, on this admission, solemnly adjudged the cow's drink to be *deoch an doruis*—a stirrup-cup, for which no charges could be made, without violating the ancient hospitality of Scotland.—*Sir Walter Scott.*

SCRAPS.
Original and Selected.

MATERNAL AFFECTION.—I observed the motions of a young female, among the shrubs, where grief and sorrow retire to uninterrupted solitude. She was a wife and had lost her first-born. With what care did she replace the old and faded flowers with fresh ones. How lightly did she press her foot on the spade, which she feared to make enter too deeply into the soil. With what care did she use the contents of a small watering-pot, which she took from behind a yew tree; and how lovely, yet how melancholy, her smile at the first shoots of verdure. It was a smile portraying the deep pathos of maternal affection. Three feet of soil seemed not to conceal from her the face of her son. She appeared to look upon him, and hung over his tomb as if it were his cradle. Tender mother! thy babe is asleep, thou smilest upon him, and fearest to awaken him. A stranger to everything around her, and her attention absorbed by fond recollections, she heard not the bustle of the rich man's funeral. Every one else ran to witness this pomp; and each, to save himself trouble, climbed over the graves in his way, sullied with his footsteps the white grave-stones, and made the slight black rails, which form but a feeble rampart to the sepulchres, bend under his weight. The very persons who, but an instant before, had, with religious care, adorned the tomb of a relative or friend, trampled, without pity, upon the freshly turned flower-borders which filial piety had not yet the courage to surround with railings, or threw down the garlands of white flowers which surmounted the monumental inscriptions or adorned the graves. So true is it, that even the cypress of the tomb is sacred for him only by whom it is planted. This heedless profanation is renewed each time that a bier is attended to the last place of its deposit by solemn and ostentatious pomp.—*Cemetiere du Pere la Chaise in Le Livre de Cent-et-Un.*

MENTAL PHYSIC.—I look to tranquillity of mind and patience to contribute as much as anything whatever to the curing diseases. On this principle I account for the circumstance of animals not labouring under illness so long as human beings. Brutes do not think so much as we, nor vex themselves about futurity; but endure their maladies without reflecting on them, and recover from them by the sole means of temperance and repose.—*Sorbiere,* an eminent French physician.

STATISTICS OF SMOKING.—The propensity of smoking is declared by the physicians to be actually one of the most efficient causes of the German tendency to diseases of the lungs. In point of expense, its waste is enormous. In Hamburg alone, 50,000 boxes of cigars have been consumed in a year; each box costing about L.3 sterling, L,150,000 puffed into the air! And it is to be remembered, that even this is but a part of the expense; the cigar adorning the lip only of the better orders, and even among those, only of the young; the mature generally abjuring this small vanity, and blowing away with the mighty meerschaum of their ancestors. This plague, like the Egyptian plague of frogs, is felt every where and in every thing. It poisons the streets, the clubs, and the coffee-houses; furniture, clothes, equipage, and person, are redolent of the abomination. It makes even the dulness of the newspaper doubly narcotic; the napkin on the table tells instantly that native hands have been over it; every eatable and drinkable, all that can be seen, felt, heard, or understood, is saturated with tobacco; the very air we breathe is but a conveyance for this poison into the lungs; and every man, woman, and child, rapidly acquires the complexion of a boiled chicken. From the hour of their waking, if nine-tenths of the population can ever be said to awake at all, to the hour of their lying down, which in innumerable instances the peasantry do in their clothes, the pipe is never out of their mouths; one mighty fumigation reigns, and human nature is smoke-dried by tens of thousands of square miles. But if it be a crime to shorten life, or extinguish faculties, the authority of the chief German physiologists charges this custom with affecting both in a very remarkable degree. They compute, that of twenty deaths of men between eighteen and thirty-five, ten originate in the waste of the constitution by smoking. The universal weakness of the eyes, which makes the Germans *par excellance* a spectacled nation, is probably attributed to the same cause of general nervous debility. Tobacco burns out their blood, their teeth, their eyes, and their brains; turning their flesh into mummies, and their minds into metaphysics.—*Journal of Defence of Hamburgh.*

CONTENTS OF NO. XXII.

Address to our Readers	337
On the Mismanagement of Public Institutions	ib.
Heat.—concluded	338
Sketch of Professor Wilson, by Mr. De Quincey	340
Mutiny at the Nore	342
COLUMN FOR THE LADIES—Anniversary of a Marriage	343
ELEMENTS OF THOUGHT—The Author by Profession—High Living and Mean Thinking	344
THE STORY TELLER—English Smugglers	345
The Witch Dance on the Brocken	351
VERSES FOR THE YOUNG	ib.
The Stirrup Cup	352
SCRAPS—Original and Selected—Maternal Affection—Mental Physic—Statistics of Smoking	ib.

EDINBURGH: Printed by and for JOHN JOHNSTONE, 19, St. James's Square.—Published by JOHN ANDERSON, Jun., Bookseller, 55, North Bridge Street, Edinburgh; by JOHN MACLEOD, and ATKINSON & Co., Booksellers, Glasgow; and sold by all Booksellers and Vendors of Cheap Periodicals.

THE Schoolmaster,
AND
EDINBURGH WEEKLY MAGAZINE.

CONDUCTED BY JOHN JOHNSTONE.

THE SCHOOLMASTER IS ABROAD.—LORD BROUGHAM.

No. 23.—Vol. II. SATURDAY, JANUARY 5, 1833. Price Three-Halfpence.

NOTES OF THE MONTH.

January takes its name from *Janus*, the *double-faced* gate-keeper of the gods, and the presider over the Temple of Peace. It is the coldest month* of the natural, and should be the warmest of the social year. The severity of the weather may be the cause that impels man, bird, and beast, to a closer intimacy in their common defence. In our own country, January is more the prescribed time of festivity than the quiet fire-side months which precede it. The fine, clear, bracing weather makes this a time of keen enjoyment to the pedestrian, and healthfully-minded lover of nature. It is also the very heyday of gregarious and robust games and sports;—cricket and its Highland cousin, the shinny, curling, skaiting, and sliding, lead to the prescribed "Beef and Greens," the whisky-toddy, glees, catches, merry clinches, and filched Joe Millers of the evening. The fineness of the weather leads the ladies abroad, wrapt in red shawls and furs, to witness sports in which, while the grey-haired sire launches his last curling stone, the urchin tempts his first fall on a span-long slide. Pleasant tea-drinking female parties are now hurriedly arranged on the ice; and the ladies left to themselves, quadrille with each other, and regale on the chicken and jellies, and the cake and bun, the relics of the late solemn, high, annual festivals. These are but a handful of the pleasures of January, which, with other riches, brought us a new Waverley novel, for so many years, that we can scarcely yet submit with patience to the privation. There is no season more suitable for long forenoon walks, or in which young people will *see* more, or find more to *observe* in the country. Now is the time to make acquaintance in fields and woods, by pools and streams, with the birds of passage, and water-fowl, and the little trooping birds that congregate till the few genial days usual with us in early February again disperse them. Even the birds that never leave us are now gathered in flocks; the chaffinches and linnets, as well as the field-fares, starlings, and cushats. Besides *coots*, teal, and other wild ducks, one now sees around pools the herons and aquatic birds, driven from the frozen well-heads in the upland marshes by the severity of the frost. The wag-tails, the wrens, the red-breast, and often the king-fisher, and all the little mute song-birds are flying about in every direction in search of food, through the short sun-shine of the winter's day. Birds in cages are now coming into song; and towards the end of the month, the *throstle's* note may occasionally be heard. But the out-door glory of January is the Frost, whose silent breathings, even in a single night, change our English or Scottish neighbourhood to Lapland or Russia. What beautiful, though fantastic and grotesque creations! wilder and more lovely in their jewelled splendour than all the wonders of eastern enchantment—"pearly drops" and "silver plumage," of which it is the pride of art to make, but the faintest imitation. How resplendent a small glade, rich in tall and straggling plants, when struck with frost! But even the commonest field or hedge-row, waxes gorgeous in its winter jewellery. The gemmed, flexile sprays of a single stalk of rye-grass, seem to taste, undebased by sordid associations, worth a prince's ransom.

FROST.

The Frost looked forth, one still clear night,
And he said, " Now I shall be out of sight.
So through the valley and over the height,
   In silence I'll take my way;
I will not go on like that blustering train,
The wind and the snow—the hail and the rain,
Who make so much bustle and noise in vain,
   But I'll be as busy as they."
Then he went to the mountain and powdered its crest,
He climbed up the trees, and their boughs he dressed
With diamonds and pearls, and over the breast
   Of the quivering lake he spread
A coat of mail, that it could not fear
The downward point of many a spear,
That he hung on its margin far and near,
   Where a rock could rear its head.
He went to the windows of those who slept,
And over each pane like a fairy crept,
Wherever he breathed, wherever he stepped,
   By the light of the moon were seen
Most beautiful things. There were flowers and trees,
There were bevies of birds, and swarms of bees—
There were cities, thrones, temples, and towers! and these
   All pictured in silver sheen!

This is but the bright view of the heart of winter, a season which aggravates every misery of

---

* By a series of observations it has been ascertained, that on the average, the coldest day of the year is the 12th of January, or New Year's Day, old style.

the wretched; and, by the cessation of many kinds of labour, becomes a periodical time of distress in most European countries, and, most of all, in our own. And ought this to be? It seems a law of nature in these northern climes that all *land animals* should in winter herd and congregate for mutual aid, and the mitigation of common hardship. The birds fly in flocks, and strange kinds mingle. The very wolves prowl in bands. Among civilized men only, there seems no idea of combination to ward off evil. Well may the poor of wealthy countries envy the dormant animals their snug winter habitations, and stores of provisions. The wise man in the fable became a philosopher from observing and following the instincts of animals; and that would be a foolish squirrel or marmot, which did not store nuts in a plentiful autumn, or make hay when the sun shone, (as marmots literally do,) and thus provide for itself and those of its household. But the sun of labour has been chill, and its fruits scanty of late years in this land; and though kindness, consideration, charity, alms, are all sorry substitutes for what should be the rewards of independent labour, and the accumulations of industry, they are at this season to be encouraged, and even enjoined as duties, by every sanction which gives man a claim on man. He must have a hard heart, an imperfect sense of justice, or a dull imagination, who can at this time of the year sit down night after night in the glow of a good fire, without once thinking of the suffering of tens of thousands of his deserving fellow-creatures, from pinching cold alone; and that is but one evil of those that go in clusters. Let one, in these intensely cold nights, conceive the alternative mentally debated by many a poor mother, of laying out her last few pence on coals or on potatoes; probably ending in dividing the fractions of her purse into the lowest possible values by which *comforts* may be purchased, in a land where coined money is in use. Such difficulties are, we fear, of more frequent occurrence than those by which they are neighboured,—of whether the lady shall give the preference to the opera-house or the private party, or go to both—and whether she shall wear, in this cold weather, her velvet robes, or those of French silk. There is something—there is much, radically, inhumanly, *sinfully* wrong in a social system which we dare to call Christian, and which we pretend is rooted in and buttressed by Christian Institutions.

BOOKS OF THE MONTH.

HOOD'S COMIC ANNUAL

Commences with a *comical* preface, in which the author denies his comic decease, which was more than insinuated by Miss Sheridan. "The lady," he says, "must be content 'to live and let live;' those who have persisted in throwing the pall over me have neither gained their end nor *mine.*" The cuts, though some of them are exceedingly clever, are, as a whole, inferior to those of Miss Sheridan's *Comic Offering,*—the literary contents better. Among the most amusing of the articles is the following letter from *a settler for life in Van Diemen's Land to Mary, at No. 45, Mount Street, Grosvenor Square.*

DEER MARY,

Littel did I Think wen I hadvertized in the Times for anuather Plaice of takeing wan in Van Deimen's Land. But so it his, and hear I am among Kangarooses, and Savidges, and other Forriners. But goverment offering to yung wimin to find them vittles, and drink, and close, and husbands, was turms not to be sneezed at. So i rite to the Outlandish Seckertary, and he was so kind as grant.

Wen this coms to hand, go to No. 22 Pimpernel Plaice, And Mind and go betwext Six and Sevin, For your own sake; cos then the Fammily's having diner. Give my keind love to betty Housmad, and say I am saf of my gurney to forrin Parts, and I hope master as never Mist the wine, and brot them into trubble on My acount. But I did not like to leav for éver and ever without trefting my Frends and feller servents, and drinking to all there fairwells. In my Flury, wen the bell rang, I forgot to take My own Key out of mysis Tekaddy, but I hope sum wan had the thought, and it is good hands, but shall be obleged to no. Lickwise, thro my Lowness of Sperrits, my lox of Hares quit went out of my Hed as was promist to be giv to Gorge, and William, and the too Footmen at the Next dores. But I hope and trust betty pacified 'em with lox of her hone, as begd to be dune wen I rite from dover. O Mary! wen I first see the dover wite cliffs out of site, wat with Squeemishness, and Felings, I all most repentid givin Ingland warning, And had douts if I was goin to better myself. But the Steward was verry kind, tho' I could make him no returns, xcept by Dusting the Ship for him, and helpin to wash up his dishes. Ther was 50 moor young wimmin of us, and, By way of passing our tim, We agreed to tell our Histris of our selves, taken by turns. But they all turned out, Alick! we had all lift on account of Testacious masters, and Crustacious missises, and becos the wurks was too much for our strenths, but betwixt us the reel truths was beeing Flirted with, and unprommist by Perfidious Yung Men. With sich exampls befor there Minds, I wonder sum off them was unprudent enuff to listen to Salers, whom are covered with Pitch, but famus for not stiking to there Wurds. Has for mee, the Mate chos to be verry Partickler wan nite, Setting on a Skane of Rops, but I giv him his Anser, and lucky I did, for Am infourmed he has Got too more Marred wives in a state of Biggamy Thank Goodness wan can marry in New Wurlds without mates. Since I have bean in my Present Sitiation, I have had between too and three hoffers for My hands, and expex them every Day to go to fist-cuffs about Me. This is sumthing lick treetin wimmin as Wimmin ougt to be treetid. Nun of your sarsy Buchers and Backers here as brakes promises like pie-crust, wen it is made Lite and shivvry, And then laffs in your face, and says they can have any Gal round the Square. I don't menshun names, but Eddard as drives the Fancy bred, will no wat I mean. As soon as ever the Botes rode to Land, I don't agrivate the truth to say their was half-a-duzzin Bows a-peace to Hand us out to shoar, and sum go so Far as say they was offered to thro' Speaking Trumpits afore they left the Shipside. Be that as it May or may Not, I am tould We maid a very pritty site, all Wauking too and too in our bridle wite gowands, with the Union Jacks afore us, to Pay humbel Respex to Kornel Arther, who behaved verry jentlemanny, and Complementid us on our Hansome apearences, and Purlitely sed he wisht us All in the United States. Servants mite live Long enuff in Lonnon without Being sich persons of Distinkshun. For my hone Part, cumming ameng Strangers, and Pig in Poken, prudence Dicktated not to be askt out. At the verry furst cumming in, howsummever, All is setlid, and the Match is apruved of by Kornel Arther and the Beightish goverment, who as agreed to giv me away. Thems wat I call honners, as we uaid to say at wist * * * Of course you and betty will xpect me to indulge in Personalities about my intendid, to tell yew wat he is lick. He is not at All lick Eddard as driv the Fancy bred, and Noboddy else. Yew No I wood send yew his pictur, Dun by himself, only it is no more like him than Chork is to Cheese. In spite of the short tim for Luv to take shoots, I am convinst he is verry Passionet. As to his temper, I can't speck As yet, as I have not tride it. O mary! Htel did I think too Munth ago of sendin yew Brid Cake and Weddin favers. Wen I say this, I am only Figgering in speach, for yew Must Not look for sich things from this Part of the wurld. I don't mean this by way of discurridgment; Wat I meen to Say is this, If so be as Young Wimmin prefers a state of Silly Bessy, they had Better remane ware they was Born; but as far as Reel down rite Courting, and no nonsense is concarned, this is the Plaice for my Munny. A Gal has only to cam out hear, and theirs duzness will jump at her lik Cox at Gosherls. It will be a reel kindness to say as mutch to Hannah at 48, and Hester Brown, and Peggy Oldfield, and partickler poor Charlotte. They needn't Fear about being Plane, for you may tell them in this Land Faces don't make stumblin blex, and if the Hole cargo was as uggly as sin, Lots woed git married.

COUNT PECCHIO'S RESIDENCE IN ENGLAND.

THE TOUR OF A GERMAN PRINCE set the fashion of this kind of books. Count Pecchio, an Italian political exile, is a very different man, and far inferior writer and observer; but to atone for this, he is a *true man*. His blunders, which are numerous, form the most amusing part of his travels, and show us the mistakes to which all travellers are liable, English as well as Italian. Some of his innocent surprises are not very creditable to the state of manners and morals in his native state of Piedmont. The Count is the most bland and courteous of travellers. He never wearies in expatiating on the beauty of the ladies, the horses, and the children of England. The farmers' daughters ride like the damsels of old romance—the ladies are neatly dressed when they do not expect company—fathers never quarrel with their sons, and babies never cry, nor children over-eat themselves. " Cowper sees every thing of the colour of roses, and Crabbe every thing with a jaundiced eye." The Count, however, intended to be less universal in his praise, and meant to have devoted a chapter " to the eternally-hysterical, to the tyrants of families, and to those mothers who, anxious to dispose of their wares, aspire only to get their daughters once fairly married, whoever the husband, whether an idiot, a baboon, or a worn-out libertine; but he reflected, " and-resolved to let every man live in his own way." The Count was astonished to find stays still used in sober, sensible England. " The English ladies," he says, " are imprisoned in stays, and in stays so stiff that to embrace them is like embracing an oak. They stand as bolt upright in this cuirass, as our mulberry-trees with wooden fences put round them when they are still tender. This cuirass renders them as stiff and unbending as a hedge-stake, while our ladies are soft and flexible as a silken cord." During his exile, the Count, infinitely to his honour, obtained a subsistence by teaching the Italian language. This, and other modes of introduction, threw open several English houses to him; and he gives the in-door picture rather cleverly, both of the gentry who enjoy all the luxury and refinement of the opulent nobility, and of " the *better* class." His sketch of this class offers a fair and agreeable specimen of a work, which is but the more piquant for its blunders, and cross-readings of English acts and deeds.

AN ENGLISH VILLA.

I was a visit in debt to a widow-lady, mother of two beautiful girls, through an invitation to dinner I had received. This lady's villa is situated in a delicious spot, at the foot of a hill crowned by an old and noble wood, approached by a winding, gently-sloping path across meadows and plantations within the same enclosure. The house is protected from the wind, and from excessive heat; it is not large, in comparison with the immense and useless Italian palaces, but is sufficiently spacious for an English villa, and enjoys a view of a range of hills, irregular in form, clad with trees, and within the space that can be taken in by the eye. The quiet, the mystery of the neighbouring wood, the song of the birds, the flocks feeding in the meadows, all seem to say, " Here reigns love!" What, then, if I add that the two young ladies of the mansion are beautiful, graceful, and courteous, with rosy cheeks, and copious ringlets of flowing hair—

" Whose large blue eyes, fair locks, and snowy hands,
Might shake the saintship of an anchorite?"—BYRON.

Almost every day they ride out alone with their groom, on excursions over the neighbouring country, and are sometimes present for a few moments at a fox-chase, when, at reynard's first breaking cover, the shrill horn and the cry of a hundred panting hounds are heard together, and the red-coated horsemen, leaping hedge and ditch, scour the country at a headlong gallop. They have passed two or three months at Paris, speak of it with enthusiasm, and are eager to return. They speak French, and stammer a little Italian. The piano, the harp, drawing, light reading, the conservatory, and a little flower-garden cultivated with their own hands, divide the time that riding, visiting, balls, invitations, and the annual two-months' visit to London, leave them. I had selected a rainy day, that I might be sure of finding the family at home; but the English ladies pay little regard to the weather. I had not got half across the garden before I perceived the carriage, which was just on the point of setting out. I approach the door,—I am welcomed with a courtesy more than polite. The mother was in the coach, along with the younger daughter, who is also the handsomer of the two. On seeing this, I went through a thousand antics, professed myself *au désespoir, désolé*, &c., and gave in to all the caricature we practise on the Continent. The graceful F——, by way of consoling me, informed me that her sister was at home, and would be very glad to see me. This intimation recalled me to life. I should never have looked for the good fortune of such a passport :—I devoured at a stride the piece of road between me and the house. I knock and re-knock impatiently. A maid-servant opens the door, and invites me to walk into a room on the right. As I had always seen the mistress of the house on the left hand, I did not understand her directions, and entered another room; but the beautiful C—— soon came in, and courteously saluting me, invited me to her own room, her *parlour*. Severe Italian matrons ought here to reflect that the colloquy was between a beautiful young woman and a wandering exile, who leaves no trace of actions, as official persons must do wherever they pass; that I had not concealed the impression made upon me by the lively and sparkling eyes of the beautiful C—— at other times; that in the room—

"Alone we were, and all without suspicion;"

that no guardian, no authorized Cerberus of that garpen of the Hesperides, was in the house; that no one would have dared to enter that *sanctum sanctorum* unless summoned by the bell; that a good fire was burning, that a beautiful silk soffa received an exciting warmth from the chimney ——; yet, instead of the downcast eyes, the mutilated words, the burning blushes in the face, the embarrassment that would accompany such a situation in Italy, there began between us a cheerful and unrestrained conversation, with frank and sparkling eyes, with smiles and merriment. Hunting, the exhibition of pictures, the last new novel, the Parisian opera, and the eternal and the inevitable subject of the English ladies, Lord Byron, passed away two hours' time very pleasantly. Many times did the prohibited fruit, (guarded by the dragon of her own virtue and modesty,) I mean my lovely hostess, offer me something with which I might refresh myself, and many times also entice me to repeat my visits. We were talking before a portrait of his Lordship, which she had copied. She was dressed in green silk, with a border of yellow riband: my mention that the colour was green, will spare me the trouble of telling Italians that C—— had a complexion of perfect whiteness, without which a green dress would have injured her beauty; but where is the lady who does not understand the effect of colour in dress better than Titian himself?—I gaily took my leave, my horse awaited me at the door, and thus I left this most innocent *tête-a-tête*.

These two young ladies were sisters in blood, but not in taste. The younger loved travelling on the Continent, and the theatres and balls of Paris; the elder loved her country and its fogs, above all the romantic scenery of Switzerland, above all the enchantments of Italy. The one played on the piano and the harp; the other gave up music, as she said, with amiable frankness, for want of ear. She told me one day, by way of compliment, that she cultivated Italian as a compensation for music. The elder, instead, contented herself with French. She in her mien was the more reserved and stately; the other, in her motions and her conversation, more winning. Drawing and riding were accomplishments common to both. It seemed as if, like the Roman emperors, who divided the empire between them, they had divided the provinces of amiability; perhaps it was a tacit convention, not to be rivals in matrimony, and to leave those who should offer, some variety in their choice. The second seemed modelled for an Englishman who had travelled on the Continent; the first for one who had never left Old England. Both, however, are amiable, each in her own way; but if I were *condemned* to renounce one of them, I would select her who loves the Continent the most.

BIOGRAPHICAL SKETCHES OF THE REFORM MINISTERS; *With a History of the Passing of the Reform Bills, and a View of Europe at the close of* 1832. By W. Jones.

This may be called the POLITICIAN'S YEAR BOOK; with the further advantage, of placing the political carreer of all the leading members of the Government fairly before us. We are thus enabled to contrast the former professions of such men as Lord Althorp, and Sir John Cam Hobhouse, with their present conduct and recent declarations, and to hold them to their old text. In this view we conceive this work of great value. Things proper to be held in continual remembrance by the nation are here written (not by an adversary) in a book,—and exceedingly well written too. It is fully entitled to the merit of being the most entertaining Annual NATIONAL REGISTER ever published. The lives of Grey, Brougham, Durham, and Russell, are drawn up in the right spirit, and with great care and ability; the portraits are excellent, though some are rather flattering likenesses, and discount a good ten years of the clawings of the tooth of time. This is a book to be bought, by all clubs especially. It places the reader at once abreast with the current of public affairs.

CHILDREN'S BOOKS, AND CHRISTMAS BOOKS.

We confine ourselves to the juvenile literature of Edinburgh and Glasgow. In Edinburgh we have the EXCITEMENT, a judicious selection of entertaining extracts from books of Travels, works on Natural History, and the Periodicals. Fiction is excluded it appears, and yet the book is sufficiently exciting and attractive without its aid.

THE INFANT ANNUAL is a nice fairy quarto, for the nursery shelves; pretty infantine stories, with praise-worthy morals and amiable tendencies; and very pretty, and not garish cuts.

But Glasgow, this year, completely eclipses Edinburgh in the juvenile classics. Besides native productions, America pours out her stores by lapfuls upon Mr. Reid's counter. There is the LITTLE GIRL'S OWN BOOK, and what for not, as well this as the BOY'S OWN, and the YOUNG LADY'S OWN? And there is also a LILLIPUTIAN Code of Politeness, (THE POLITE PRESENT,) and A PRESENT TO A DAUGHTER; and many more, over which, by this time, hundreds of good children are rejoicing, and the fruits of which will be found in their minds and manners, when not a wreck is left behind of the other New Year Day presents, made them by kind friends, whether from the confectioner's or the toy-shop.

THE UNKNOWN POETS OF SCOTLAND.

THIS resurrection, or bringing to light of poets hidden by hard circumstances, but meriting wider fame, is an excellent idea. Besides bringing forward the modest, it will consign some of the modestly assured to their true level. Mr. Campbell, of Leith, who assumes the office of editor, enters upon his, we fear, thankless task, with a becoming spirit, and a proper value for his order; claiming notice for the UNKNOWN POETS as their right, and placing the obligation on the true side, that of the public.

The poets introduced in Part I. are James Forrest, James Home, and James Ballantine; and the *last* is the *first*. Forrest was a poor weaver of Carlops, to whom the poetic spirit, (and the gift was to our thinking granted but in scanty measure,) proved a plague and a curse, if it begot the repining unhappy temper which embittered his humble lot, and shortened his life. There are many nonsensical and mischievous notions abroad about this same poetry; but this is not the place to discuss them. It appears to be expected that poetry, or the power of stringing together a few rhymes, should be meat, drink, and clothing, fire and fending, to "the poet." Even where the faculty really exists, that is, in one case out of five hundred, poetry is not to be blamed for not fulfilling a bargain for which poetry cannot undertake. It may and always ought to make men nobler, purer, and happier beings; but riches or improvement in worldly circumstances are not among its privileges, though they may sometimes accidentally attend the possession of the gift. No great poet ever yet made money by his muse. If Pope be cited as an instance, we say he succeeded by patronage and adroit management; as did Byron, Moore, and Scott, by the most potent power of modern times,— Fashion. If Forrest wished to prosper in the world, he should have invented a shawl border, or improved the machinery of his loom. The verses he has left, though natural and pleasing, scarcely rise to mediocrity, with the exception of a disputed piece; and if " his soul was absorbed by poesy, and his strong, melancholy, manly mind dwelt on it night and day," there has been what men of his calling term " but a short outcome," and little to encourage others to follow his example.

JAMES HOME is a man of more likelihood. He is a sturdy and gallant dyke-builder, who, on Tweedside, as an imitator of Burns, composes and sings his rustic love-lays joyously and tenderly; and, as might be expected, has an immense success among the lasses.

JAMES BALLANTINE, the third James immortalized in Part I., is a house-painter in this city; who wisely shunning all pecuniary or worldly transactions with the Muses, and placing no reliance upon them, brings no idle complaint against their ladyships for being bad payers, nor yet against the world for cruelty and cold-heartedness to the votaries of the Divine Art, provided, we presume, it retains its admiration and its want of house-painting. This is right, manly common sense. Mr. Ballantine wisely makes of the lyre, " a canty whistle with a pleasant sound," to divert his own leisure and amuse his friends, thus turning it to the best possible use in his power. This publication will greatly enlarge the circle of his admirers. The specimens of his humourous or Boswellian verse, are full of life and genuine glee. The piece we give below is of a yet higher order. It unites the finest qualities of the National Muse, pathos and kindliness with easy humour. To us it appears quite charming; and though with some fears for the difficulty of the dialect among our English readers, we adopt it at once into our most select corner—our

VERSES FOR THE YOUNG.
A SON TO HIS MOTHER.

Mine ain wee donsy sonsy minny,
Sae couthy, kindly, cosh, and cannie,
Just sit ye still a wee, an' dinna
  Tent yere ain callant,
But let him sketch your picture in a
  Wee hamely ballant.

There sits thou, on thy creepy stool,
Weel hap't wi' flannen coat and cowl,
While, simmerin' by the chumley jowl,
  Sits thy tea patty;
An' at thy feet, wi' kindly yowl,
  Whurs thy wee catty.

The bluid in thy auld veins is thin,
Sair shrivelled now's thy ance plump skin,
Close to the ribs thou hirsellest in,
  Wi' clocherin' whazle,
Till in thy cutty pipe thou fin'
  A redhet aizle.

Whan sunny simmer comes wi' flowers,
On the door step thou sits for hours,
An' ilka birdie roun' thee cours,
  Cock, hens, an' chickens,
While, wi' an open han', thou showers
  Them walth o' pickings.

An' though thou now art auld an' doited,
Thy back sair bowed, thy pace sair toyted;
I've seen the day thou couldst hae stoyted
  Wi' queenly air,
An' made thy neebour dames sair spited
  At kirk or fair.

On Sunday, whan kirk bells a-jowin'
Set ilka haly heart a-lowin',
Busked brisk an' braw, I've seen thee rowin',
  Fat, fair, an' dumpy,
An' mony a spruce auld bean a-bowin'
  Right straught an' stumpy.

Thou'st been to me, my mair than mither,
Baith faither, mither, a' thegither;
In times o' dearth, thou didna swither
  To scrimp thy coggie,
To schule an' cleed, as weel's anither,
  Thy wee wild roggie.

While manhood's vigour nerves my arm,
While in my breast life's bluid flows warm,
Frae ilka danger, want, or harm,
  I'll keep thee free,
Till death shall break the mystic charm,
  An' close thine ee.

DIARY OF A SPORTING OXONIAN.

Sunday. Waked at eight o'clock by the servant, to tell me the bell was going for prayers—wonder those scoundrels are suffered to make such a noise—tried to sleep again, but could not—sat up and read Hoyle in bed.——Ten, got up and breakfasted.—Charles Racket called to ask me to ride—agreed to ride—agreed to stay till the President was gone to church.——Half after eleven, rode out. Going down the High Street, saw Will Sagely going down to St. Mary's: can't think what people go to church for.——Twelve to two, rode round Burlington Green—met Careless, and a new fresh man, of Trinity—engaged them to dine with me.——Two to three, lounged at the stable—made the fresh man ride over the bale—talked to him about horses—see he knows nothing about the matter—went home and dressed.——Three to eight, dinner and wine—remarkable pleasant evening—sold Racket's stone-horse for him, to Careless's friend, for fifty guineas—certainly break his neck.——Eight to ten, coffeehouse, and lounged in the High Street. Stranger went home to study—afraid he's a bad one. Engaged to hunt to-morrow, and dine with Racket.——Twelve, supped, and went to bed early, in order to get up to-morrow.

Monday. Racket rowed me up at seven o'clock—sleepy and queer, but was forced to get up and make breakfast for him.——Eight to five in the afternoon, hunting—famous run, and killed near Bicester—number of tumbles—fresh man out on Racket's stone-horse—got the devil of a fall in a ditch—horse upon him—but don't know whether he was killed or not.——Five, dressed, and went to dine with Racket.—Dean had crossed his name, and no dinner could be got—went to the Angel and dined. Famous evening till eleven, when the proctors came, and told us to go home to our colleges—went directly the contrary way.——Eleven to one, went down into St. Thomas's and fought a raff.——One, dragged home by somebody, the Lord knows whom, and put to bed.

Tuesday. Very bruised and sore—did not get up till twelve—found an imposition upon my table—*Mem.* to give it the hair-dresser. Did not know what to do with myself; so wrote to my father for money.——Half after one, put on my boots to ride for an hour—met Careless at the stable—rode together—asked me to dine with him, and meet Jack Sedley, who is just returned from Italy.——Two to three, returned home and dressed.——Four to seven, dinner and wine. Jack very pleasant—told good stories—says the Italian women have thick legs, no hunting to be got, and very little wine—wont go there in a hurry.——Seven, went to the stable, and looked into the coffeehouse—very few drunken men, and nothing going forwards. Agreed to play Sedley at billiards—Walker's table engaged, and forced to go to the Blue Posts—lost ten guineas—thought I could have beat him, but the dog has been practising at Spa.——Ten, supper at Careless's—bought Sedley's mare for thirty guineas—thinks he knows nothing of a horse, and believe I have done him—drank a little punch, and went to bed at twelve.

Wednesday. Hunted with the Duke of B.—very long run—rode the new mare—found her sinking, so pulled up in time, and swore I had a shoe lost—to sell her directly—buy no more horses of Sedley—knows more than I thought he did.——Four, returned home; and as I was dressing to dine with Sedley, received a note from some country neighbours of my father's to desire me to dine at the Cross—obliged to send an excuse to Sedley—wanted to put on my cap and gown—not to be found—forced to borrow.——Half after four to ten, at the Cross.——Ten, found it too bad, so got up, and told them it was against the rules of the University to be out later.

Thursday. Breakfasted at the Cross, and walked all the

morning about Oxford with my lions—terrible that work. Lions very troublesome—asked an hundred and fifty silly questions about every thing they saw—wanted me to explain the Latin inscriptions on the monuments of Christ Church chapel—wanted to know how we spent our time—forced to give them a dinner, and, what was worse, to sit with them till six, when I told them I was engaged for the remainder of the evening, and sent them about their business.——Seven, dropped in at Careless's rooms, found him with a large party, all pretty much cut—thought it was a good time to sell him Sedley's mare, but he was not quite drunk enough—made a bet with him, that I trotted my pony from Benson to Oxford within the hour—sure of winning, for I did it the other day in fifty minutes.

Friday. Got up early, and rode my pony a foot pace over to Benson to breakfast—old Shrub at breakfast—told him of the bet, and shewed him the pony—shook his head, and looked cunning when he heard of it—good sign—after breakfast rode the race, and won easy, but could not get any money—forced to take Careless's draft—dare say it is not worth two-pence—great fool to bet with him.—— Twelve to three, lounged at the stable, and cut my black horse's tail—eat soup at Sadler's—walked down the High Street—met Racket, who wanted me to dine with him, but could not, because I was engaged at Sagely's.——Three, dinner at Sagely's—very bad—dined in a cold hall, and could get nothing to eat—wine new—a bad fire—tea-kettle put on at five o'clock—played at whist for sixpences, and no bets—thought I should have gone to sleep—terrible work dining with a studious man.——Eleven, went to bed out of spirits.

Saturday. Ten, breakfasted—took up the last Sporting Magazine—had not read two pages before a dun came—told him I should have some money soon—would not be gone—offered him brandy—was sulky, and would not have any—saw he was going to be savage, so kicked him down stairs, to prevent his being impertinent—thought perhaps I might have more of them, so went to lounge at the stables—pony got a bad cough, and the black horse thrown out two splits—went back to my room in an ill humour, found a letter from my father—no money, and a great deal of advice—wants to know how my last quarter's allowance went—how the devil should I know? He knows I keep no accounts—do think fathers are the greatest *bores* in nature. Very low-spirited and flat all the morning—some thoughts of reforming, but luckily Careless came in to beg me to meet our party at his rooms, so altered my mind—dined with him, and by nine in the evening was very happy.

THE WISDOM OF OUR ANCESTORS.

The practical men among our ancestors left nothing unregulated. The number of dishes each rank were to have on their tables, the quality, nature, and form of their dress, the price of almost every article of food, the entertainments at funerals, baptisms and on other occasions, their arms and armour, their marriages, and even the last habiliments of their dead bodies, were all objects of legislation. Let us follow a man through the Statute Book, in the times of our ancestors. In order to "repress the superfluous expense at baptisms," it was enacted under heavy penalties in 1681, " that besides the parents, children, brothers, and sisters, and those of the family, there shall not be present above four witnesses." Then " Anent the ordouring of everie mannis house" Queen Mary enacted, " that, forsameikle as the Queenis Grace, the Lord Governour, and Lordes of Secret Council havand respect to the great and exorbitant dearth, risen in this realme, of victualles and other stuffe, for the sustentation of mankinde, and dailie increasand, and understandand that the occasion thereof is the cause of the superfluous cheere used commonlie in this realme, alsweill amongst small as well as great men, to the great hurt of the commonweil of the same; and damnage to the body quhilkes makes ane man unable to exercise all leiful and gude warkes necessar and for remeid hereof, and staunching of silk dearth, and exorbitant prices foresaidis, it is devised and ordained that no Archbishop, Bishops, nor Earles, have at his meate but aucht dishes of meate; Nor na Abbot, Lord, Priour, nor Deane, have at his meate but six dishes of meate; nor na baronne nor freeholder have bot four dishes of meate at his messe; nor na burgess nor other substantious man, spiritual nor temporal, sall have at his meate but three dishes, and bot ane kind of meate in everie dish;" and heavy pecuniary penalties were inflicted in case of contravention. Further, King James the sixth, " understanding the great excesse and superfluitis used in bridelles and utheris banquettes amangis the meane subjectes of this realme; alsweill within burgh as to landward, to the inordinate consumption not only of silk stuffs as growes within the realme, but alswa of drogges, confectoures, and spiceries, brocht from the pairties beyond sea, and sauld at deare prices to mony folk that are very unabil to susteine that coaste, for staunching of quhilke abuse, statutest and ordained that na manner of persons his subjectes, being under the degree of prelates, erles, lordis, barounes, landed gentlemen, or otheris, that are worth, and may spend in yearly frie rent twa thousande markes money, or fifty chalders victual, all charges deduced, sall presume to have at their bridelles, or uther banquettes, or at their tables, in daily chere, onie drogges or confectoures brocht from the pairtes beyond sea, and that na banquettes sall be at onie sittings after baptizing of bairnes in time cumming under the pain of twentie pund." And searchers were to be appointed to whom " oppen dures sall be maid of quhatsomever houses they come to search," under heavy penalties. In 1621 it was enacted that no person use any " manner of desert, of wetts and dry confections at banquettings, marriages, baptisms, feastings, or any meales, except the fruites growing in Scotland; as also figs, raisins, plumbdamies, almondes, and other confected fruites, under the pain of a thousand marks, *toties quoties.*"

Dress was another grand object, on which our ancestors exercised their wisdom. " None of our Sovereign Lord's lieges, of whatever quality or degree, were permitted to wear any clothing of gold or silver cloathe, or any gold or silver lace upon their apparels, or any part of their bodies, and no manner of person shall have any apparel of velvet, sattin, or other stuffes of silke, except noblemen, Lords of Parliament, Prelates, his Majesty's Counsellors, Lords of Session, Barrons of quality, having free yearly rent of fourscore chalders victual, or six thousand merks of silver, and the provosts of the principal burrowes within this kingdom, or those that have been provosts, with such also as shall happen to be, or have been provosts, bailies, Deans of Guild," and theasurers within the Town of Edinburgh. It was farther enacted, " that none weare upon their heads buskings or any feathers; and notwithstanding, it is permitted that any person may weare chaines or other goldsmith's worke and having no stones, nor pearles, within the same, that no person weare any pearles nor precious stones, except the persons before privileged." Lawns, Ziffaines, and cambric, were in like manner reserved for the sole use of the higher classes.

The dress of the lower orders was not overlooked. It was ordained, " That no servants, men or women, wear any clothing except those that are made of cloath, fustians, canvass, or stuffes made in the countrie. And that they have no silk upon their cleathes, except silk buttons and button-holes, and silk garters, without pearling or roses ;" but it was declared to be always lawful for them to wear their masters' or mistress's old clothes. The fashion of cloaths was not to be changed either by men or women, under heavy penalties. The husbandmen and labourers of the ground were not to wear any cloathing but gray, white, blue, and selfe black cloth, made in Scotland, and their wives and children were to wear the like, under a penalty of forty pounds.

But still more minute regulations, if possible, are to be found in our Statute-Book. No one was to allow rooks to build in his trees; and if their nests were found at beltane, and the young flown, then the trees were liable to be forfeited to the King, and the owner fined. No man under a baron, or landed man, worth a thousand merks of yearly free rent, was allowed to keep a horse " at the hard meat," from the 15th of May to the 15th of October, and the number to be kept in the intermediate period at hard meat was carefully regulated according to the rank of the party. Foot-ball and golf were prohibited under heavy penalties. " Men of simple estate that should be labourers were required either to have half an ox in the plough, or else delve each day seven foot square." " And each man having a plough of eight oxen was bound to sow yearly at least a firlot of wheat, half a firlot of pease, and fourty beans." Did our limits permit, many other instances of the itch our legislation had in early times to interfere with the private concerns of the subject might be given, but we have cited enough to answer the purpose we had in view. We laugh at such regulations at the present day.

LONDON.

The immediate site of the city of London is about forty-five miles from the sea, westward, in a pleasant and spacious valley, stretching along the banks of the Thames, which river, as it flows through the metropolis, forms a bold curve or crescent. On the northern side, the ground rises with a quick ascent, and then more gradually, but unequally heightens to the north-west and west, which are the most elevated parts. On the south side of the river, the ground is nearly level, and was anciently an entire morass of many miles in extent; this has been reclaimed through the artificial embankment of the river, probably commenced by the Romans, which must have been the work of ages. The average breadth of the river, in this part of its course, is from four to five hundred yards; its general depth at low water, about twelve feet; but at spring tides it rises from ten to twelve feet above that level. The tides used to flow to the distance of fifteen miles above London bridge, but since the alteration at London bridge by the demolition of the old structure, it goes much higher. Considered in the aggregate, London comprises the city and its liberties, with the city and liberties of Westminster, the borough of Southwark, and upwards of thirty of the contiguous villages of Middlesex and Surrey. The extent of this district is, from east to west, or from Poplar to Kensington, near eight miles; its breadth from north to south is very irregular, and may be said to vary from three to four miles. The circumference of this immense congregation of buildings may be estimated at about twenty miles. The metropolis is computed to contain upwards of 60 squares, 12,000 streets, lanes, courts, &c.; and the whole formed by near 300,000 buildings of various descriptions, as public structures, churches, dwelling houses, warehouses, shops, &c. It is a remarkable fact, that vegetation is earlier, by ten days or a fortnight, on the west and south-west sides of the metropolis than at the northern and eastern sides. The more prevalent winds blow from the north-east and south-west; and these, with little variation, occupy about ten or eleven months in the year. The thermometer sometimes rises to above 80 degrees of Fahrenheit's scale, very rarely to 84 degrees; but the common summer heat is from 65 degrees to 75 degrees. In winter it sometimes falls to 15 degrees; but the most common winter heat, when it freezes, is between 20 degrees and 30 degrees; it has been known to fall below the point marked 0, but very rarely; the most frequent, when it does not freeze, is between 40 degrees and 50 deg. The annual temperature of London is 51 deg. 9 min., or in round numbers, 52 deg. The situation of London is so very favourable, that springs, which yield large quantities of water, are found on digging almost every where. In the year 1377, London is said to have contained about 35,000 inhabitants. According to the census of 1801, London, at that time, contained 121,229 houses, inhabited by 216,073 families, making 864,755 persons. In 1811, it had increased to 1,099,104, and in 1821 to 1,225,964 persons. By the last census of 1831, it appears that a still further increase had taken place of no less than 248,105, thus making the present population of the metropolis, 1,474,067. The number of oxen annually consumed in London has been estimated at 110,000, calves 50,000, sheep 500,000, lambs 250,000 hogs and pigs 200,000; besides animals of other kinds. Smithfield is the principal market for the above articles; and the total value of butcher meat sold there annually is stated at L.8,000,000. There are, on an average, annually brought to Billingsgate market 2,500 cargoes of fish, of forty tons each, and about 20,000 tons by land carriage; in the whole 120,000 tons. The annual consumption of wheat, in London, may be averaged at 900,000 quarters, each containing eight Winchester bushels; of porter and ale 2,000,000 barrels, each containing 36 gallons; spirits and compounds 11,000,000 gallons; wines 65,000 pipes; butter 21,000,000 lbs.; and cheese 26,000,000 lbs. The quantity of coals consumed is about 1,200,000 chaldrons, of 36 bushels, or a ton and a half to each children. About 10,000 cows are kept in the vicinity of the metropolis, for supplying the inhabitants with milk, and they are supposed to yield nearly 7,200,000 gallons every year; even this great quantity, however, is considerably increased by the dealers, who adulterate it, by at least one-fourth, with water, before they serve their customers. The Port, as actually occupied by shipping, extends from London bridge to near Deptford, a distance of at least four miles, and is from four to five hundred yards in average breadth.— The number of vessels belonging to this port, in September, 1809, was ascertained, by the official documents laid before Parliament, to be 2,656, carrying 568,262 tons, and 41,402 men. Comparing this number with the number returned in January, 1701-2, the increase will be seen to be astonishing. At that period the vessels amounted only to 560, carrying 84,882 tons, and 10,065 men. The average number of ships in the Thames and docks is 1,100; together with 3,000 barges, employed in lading and unlading them; 2,288 small craft engaged in the inland trade; and 2,000 wherries for the accommodation of passengers; 1,200 revenue officers are constantly on duty in different parts of the river; 4,000 labourers are employed in lading and unlading; and 8,000 watermen navigate the wherries and craft. The household troops, comprising three regiments of foot guards, containing about 7,000 men, including officers, and two regiments of horse guards, consisting of 1,200 men, form the principal military establishment for the metropolis; but none of these troops are permitted to enter the city without especial leave of the Lord Mayor. It is difficult to ascertain the exact number of churches and chapels belonging to the establishment in the metropolis, but it is not far short of 200. The number of religious edifices belonging to the Dissenters in the metropolis is above that number. There are eighty chapels, or places of worship, for the independents, among whom are included the Scotch Presbyterians. The Baptists have nearly fifty chapels; the Methodists, or followers of Whitfield and Wesley, twenty-three; the Unitarians, nine; the Arians, two; the Quakers, six; the Swedenborgians, four; the Huntingtonians, three; the Sandemonians, the Moravians, the New Lights, and the Freethinkers, have one chapel each. In the metropolis, there are six Jewish Synagogues, fifteen Roman Catholic chapels, and nineteen foreign Protestant churches.—*Partington's National Views, and History of London.*

NORMANDY.

Rouen is a noble city. It is situated on one edge of a most delightful valley, and close on the Seine, which river may indeed be said to pass through the city, for on the bank of the river, which is opposite to that on which stands the original city, there is a good deal of building, and much business done in the way of trade. On entering Rouen there appears to be as much life and stir as there is in Paris; the city is just such another place, excepting in respect to size. The looks of the people here, as well as throughout the country parts of Normandy, constitute the most important circumstance in favour of this province. Normandy, excepting in the particular of climate only, says much more for France than all the rest of the country that I have seen. The land is by far the richest, and the best cultivated; the houses (farm-houses, as well as others) are more solid, more clean, in the insides of them, and kept in better general order. The people here, and those belonging to any other province through which I have passed, are as much unlike each other as though they belonged to two different nations. The men in Normandy are larger, better made, and fresher looking. The women are much the prettiest I have seen in France. They wear a cap (amongst the peasantry) that is quite a pattern of neatness. This cap is, in some parts of Normandy, very high in its shape, sometimes as much as thirty inches above the head, and it is so curious in other particulars of its fashion, that I should endeavour to give a more minute description of it, if I were at all conversant in such matters. It is called in France, *le bonnet cauchoix*. The fashion belongs peculiarly to the women of the Pays de Caux, which forms one district of the province of Normandy, and which Rouen stands just upon the borders of. The women of this district, who are called Cauchoises, are universally allowed to be the prettiest in France. On my road from London to Dover, through Kent, I did, however, see more beauty than I have seen in all the other parts of France put together, Paris included. The women that I have seen before I entered this province were not to be compared with those of Normandy, in point of neatness in their dress and general appearance. The Normandy women have a good deal about them which answers the sense of the word "tidy;" a word which has so much significance in our language, and which the French language is a stranger to, and indeed need be a stranger to, as far as relates to the greater part of the people whose habits I have had an opportunity to observe. The faces that appear under the bonnet cauchoix are very pretty. The cheeks of the Normandy women are quite as rosy, though their complexions are not so delicate, as those of English women. There are not, I have noticed, so many black eyes here as I have seen elsewhere in France; but (for I must say it, to be just) there are not so many dirty faces!

There are some manufactories of cotton yarn, and of muslin at this place. The men employed in the factories earn from 25 sous to 3 francs a-day, (2s. 4½d.) which, considering the price of food and raiment, is very high pay.

The giving of credit is much less in fashion in France than in England. Indeed the laws of France discourage it; wisely, in my opinion; but they do it at any rate. Traders must have a license from the government to carry on their trades; but this is not necessary if they do not deal on credit. If they have not the license they cannot be sued for debts contracted in their business, and cannot sue for debts contracted with them by others. If, therefore, they choose to deal solely for ready money, they need no license. The license operates, therefore, as a tax on giving and taking credit. Several persons, with whom I have conversed in France, think this tax a very wise measure; and I have generally found that there is in this country a rooted dislike to adventurous dealings; or, as the cant term is, speculations. This dislike to gambling trade makes commerce less showy, but much more solid.

I cannot look across the channel without contrasting the stir, the bustle, the energetic motions, and the anxious looks that I shall there again behold, with the tranquil and happy carelessness of the scenes that I leave behind me. There seems to be more energy, more force, more human power, existing in one mile of England than in all France. The difference is perfectly surprising; but it by no means follows, that the latter country has not, mile for mile, as much of solid means as the former. — *By Cobbett the younger.*

THE DEATH OF THE OLD YEAR.

From a new Volume, by ALFRED TENNYSON just, published.

Full kneedeep lies the winter snow,
And the winter winds are wearily sighing:
Toll ye the churchbell sad and slow,
And tread softly and speak low,
For the old year lies a-dying.
   Old year, you must not die.
   You came to us so readily,
   You lived with us so steadily;
   Old year, you shall not die.

He lieth still: he doth not move:
He will not see the dawn of day.
He hath no other life above.
He gave me a friend, and a true, truelove,
And the Newyear will take 'em away.
   Old year, you must not go.
   So long as you have been with us,
   Such joy as you have seen with us,
   Old year, you shall not go.

He frothed his bumpers to the brim;
A jollier year we shall not see.
But tho' his eyes are waxing dim,
And tho' his foes speak ill of him,
He was a friend to me.
   Old year, you shall not die.
   We did so laugh and cry with you,
   I've half a mind to die with you,
   Old year, if you must die.

He was full of joke and jest;
But all his merry quips are o'er.
To see him die, across the waste
His son and heir doth ride posthaste;
But he'll be dead before.
   Every one for his own.
   The night is starry and cold, my friend,
   And the Newyear blithe and bold, my friend,
   Comes up to take his own.

How hard he breathes! over the snow
I heard just now the crowing cock.
The shadows flicker to and fro;
The cricket chirps: the light burns low:
'Tis nearly one o'clock.
   Shake hands, before you die.
   Old year, we'll dearly rue for you.
   What is it we can do for you?
   Speak out before you die.

His face is growing sharp and thin.
Alack! our friend is gone.
Close up his eyes: tie up his chin:
Step from the corpse, and let him in,
That standeth there alone,
   And waiteth at the door.
   There's a new foot on the floor, my friend,
   And a new face at the door, my friend,
   A new face at the door.

CONDITION OF BANISHED CONVICTS.

IN one of Miss Martineau's late little books about emigration, we have the condition of felons sent to Botany Bay, Van Diemen's Land, represented in the flattering light, as respects wordly advancement, which seems to have taken possession of all the thieves in the country. A felon brother has made a fortune, and comes in state from Hobart's Town, or Sydney, and takes possession of his purchase—an estate upon which his virtuous brother and sister, who have emigrated, are working as labourers. This is not the only instance in which the writer, looking hastily through the spectacles of books and newspaper reports, which rest on a slender foundation, is drawn to form very erroneous conclusions. The following description is at once more rational and more correct.

NEW SOUTH WALES.

It has been the fashion of England to represent this colony of convicts as the Eldorado of felons—that a rascal is no sooner arrived there than he becomes not only an honest man, but a gentleman; and that fellows, who in London walked up and down with their hands in other people's pockets, may there keep them in their own, with that very comfortable feeling which attends the finding something in them. A colonial newspaper, however, gives us a very different account of the state of affairs, and to undeceive certain speculative philosophers on the subject, we extract the following enumeration of the comforts which await any practical experiments:—

Comfort 1st.—As soon as he lands he is packed off 60, or 70, or 100 miles in the interior, or he is placed in the prisoners' barracks—of which it would be only necessary for any hon. member to see the inside to convince him it was no joke—in either of which cases, if he has brought any trifles with him, he is sure to be relieved of them before the following day. If he does not lose his government clothing, he may consider himself fortunate; should he, however, do so, the following morning he may safely calculate upon

Comfort 2d.—In the shape of 50 lashes, or 10 days' work on the treadmill, or in the chain-gang.

Comfort 3d.—If he be assigned to a master in the town, and happens to take a glass of grog after his long voyage, it is a great chance if he lodge not in the watch-house for the night, and take "fifty" before breakfast in the morning by way of "comfort."

Comfort 4th.—Travelling through a wild forest without knowing his way, and surrounded, perhaps, by the hostile aborigines, who, so sure as they met, would kill him.

Comfort 5th.—Should he lose his way, and escape starvation in the bush, probably a sound flogging for not having arrived sooner at his master's house.

Comfort 6th.—Perpetual work, and no pay; in many cases hard labour, hard living, hard words, and hard usage.

We have hitherto spoken only of the reception met with by a well-disposed prisoner,—one who wishes to reform. A short answer, when spoken to by his master or overseer, or a common soldier, or even a convict constable, is a crime punishable by flogging; getting tipsy places him in the stocks: missing muster may get him flogged, or into the chain-gang, where he works in irons on the roads. Should he commit any second offence, Macquarie Harbour, Port Macquarie, Norfolk Island, or Moreton Bay is his fate; where every rigidity of discipline—nay, sometimes even cruelty—is exercised. The hardest of labour, and but one meal a-day, of the coarsest food, is the lot of the man who goes to a penal settlement. To these places it does not take felony to send a prisoner; many have been removed there for very trivial offences. When men commit murder on purpose to be hanged in preference to bearing the terrors of these places of secondary exile, it cannot be expected that they are in the enjoyment of much "comfort."

THE PRESS IN THE EAST.—There are in Calcutta five daily and eight weekly newspapers, six monthly journals, two quarterlies, and two annuals.

THE STORY-TELLER.

SCOTTISH MANNERS—THE FARMER'S HA' IN A DECEMBER NIGHT.

BY MRS. JOHNSTONE.

In the dark month of December, in or about the year 1798, it chanced that Captain Wolfe Grahame, an officer in one of his Majesty's regiments of horse, then stationed in Ireland, and the Reverend Gideon Haliburton, parson of a small Cameronian congregation about the outskirts of Perthshire, were travelling together towards Gallowayshire, the former to join his regiment, the latter to visit some old friends, and for the arrangement of business connected with his spiritual duties. The association of a young officer of cavalry, and a hill-side preacher, is not among the ordinary relations of social life, even in so primitive a country as Scotland was then: but Wolfe had been the pupil of Mr. Gideon, and was attached, by many early and kind recollections, to his old tutor, who was one of the best men in the world; and circumstances made it desirable that their journey should be made conjointly, since their route lay the same way.

With more management than was perhaps necessary in a country where there was little chance of misconstruing the nature of their connexion, Captain Wolfe Grahame contrived to pilot himself and his companion through the various towns on their route, till on the fourth day they reached "Auld Ayr." They did not, however, at all times travel in company—for Mr. Gideon, with his mare, Jenny Geddes, almost every night diverged into the moors, where some little thatched building, without chimneys, constructed on the model of a farmer's salt-bucket, shewed a Seceder place of worship, and gave hope of a neighbouring cottage equally modest in appearance, inhabited by some one of his truly apostolic brethren. It suited alike ill with Gideon's devotional and parsimonious habits to sojourn in even the humblest places of public entertainment, and would, besides, have been a breach of the customs of his order. When either ecclesiastical or secular business led them from home they had their regular stage-houses; and never was lying palmer or bare-foot friar more welcome at even-tide to the chimney-corner of franklin or yeoman, than was the wandering Cameronian minister to the ingle-neuk of the primitive farmers in the hill-country of the south-west of Scotland. The residences of the regular preachers were necessarily few and far apart; but lay members were, at that time, scattered throughout all those pastoral districts, at easy distances; and some pious and hospitable widow, or wealthy childless couple, had both a comfortable *spence* for the man of God, and a *barn* for the wandering beggar or humble travelling merchant. Even in families less able to exercise hospitality, there was often some "Prophet's Chamber," curiously dove-tailed into a labyrinth of wooden-walled beds, which seldom wanted an occasional occupant. A shed and a little coarse fodder were more grudgingly bestowed upon Jenny Geddes and steeds of her degree, which in those times were as well known on the old drove roads in the southern counties, as are the short-lived horses which draw his Majesty's mail from St. Alban's to London at the present day.

On this kindly footing, Mr. Gideon was spending an evening in a muirland farm-house "behind the hills where Stinchar flows," with a grey-headed elder of his sect; and when he next day, by appointment, met Captain Wolfe Grahame on the coast, it was so late that they entertained some apprehension of reaching their next resting place. There were sickness in the family which the worthy Gideon had visited, and dissensions among the scattered flock; and when the minister let it be understood, that he had been detained by sympathy for the sick and the sorrowful, and in healing divisions and repairing breaches in the Zion of the Stinchar, he seemed to take for granted that no farther apology was necessary. In ordinary circumstances he never prolonged his visits, nor, as the gudewives remarked, "abused discretion." It was generally night-fall before he arrived at his quarters; and by daybreak, with the unbribed assistance of the herd-boy, he and Jenny Geddes were soberly plodding on to their next station.

The friends had already traversed a good part of the interior of Ayrshire. A threatening evening was closing in on a rough gusty day, when they found themselves on the sea-side, but still much farther from their place of destination for the night than the state of the weather made agreeable.—The latter part of their day's journey lay along a bold, wild, and broken line of coast, traversed by a road, leading now around low headlands, then sweeping into bays, and anon winding and climbing round the iron faces of high and rugged promontories. The only thing visible on this road, for many hours, was the Port-Patrick *Fly*, crawling onwards in the distance like the "shard-borne beetle."

The last discovery which Wolfe made before night-fall was unpleasant enough,—a skiff in the offing trimming her sails to meet the gale, and exhibiting marks of distress and alarm.

"We are like to have a wild night, Mr. Gideon," said the young soldier; "I wish to goodness we were at that Cross-gates of Caberax, or whatever you call it. I will insist on your remaining there all night with me, notwithstanding those hospitable friends all along who entertain you every night, I think. You must stay with me, indeed. I am rich, sir,—I have lands and beeves—or I shall have them." This was the light speech which often accompanies a purse as light.

Gideon was accused of parsimonious habits. The phrase was incorrect. That man cannot be called parsimonious who freely spends his whole living. Gideon's was a small one; but his wants were far less, so that he was comparatively a rich man; and, what is more rare, positively thought himself so, when, at the end of the half-year he paid his few debts, and gave to "him that needed" all that remained over, literally laying up his treasure in heaven. With something of the complacence inseparable from the consciousness of possessing property—for he had a guinea and some shillings in his pocket—he replied to Wolfe's proposal of defraying their common travelling charges.

"Na, na! Captain Wolfe, make yourself easy about that, my lad. I'm far frae being a needy man. Did ye no hear of the hunder merks augmentation, man? I never looked for it, I'm sure; but my lot as to temporals has been casten in pleasant places. What wi' ae thing, and what wi' anither; the ruckle of a house, (the Session are to set a man to mend the theek, and have it made warm and water-tight aboon the bed—in summer the holes in the roof were airy and pleasant enough;) the kail-yard, and the gang o' the common muir for Jenny, I cannot call the living o' the Sourholes muckle war, *communibus annis*, put the head o' the sow to the tail o' the grice, than five-and-thretty English punds."

This was whispered—a pause between every emphatic word—in a quite confidential style, Gideon advancing his mouth to the young man's ear, and Jenny kindly laying her long dewy nose on the proud neck of Wolfe's steed, Saladin, a freedom which he scarcely appeared to relish.

"I have a kind people," continued Gideon.—"The gudewives have been on me to take a drop tea-water in my loneliness. Burd 'Lizbeth has given me the trick o' that too—and to be sure I can weel afford it; but for a man like me, Captain Wolfe, to be pettling himsel' up with delicates, while mony a precious saint and puir thing want a meltith o' bare porridge, is no' to be thought of.—Make me worthy o' a' this kindness! and forbid that riches prove a snare to me a second time!"

"No fear of that, sir—I shall be your guarantee," said Grahame.

"I kenna, Captain Wolfe. Let him that thinks he standeth tak' heed. I was laid under sore and dark temptation this very time twalmonth, in the shape of what ye call a *double Joe*. I had never seen coined money o' the splendour and value. It was paid me in the Martlemas half-year's stipend. So I laid by my golden idol i' the kist-coffer, in a horn snuff-mull; and in the very watches of the night, even upon my quiet bed, the demon o' covetousness, Mammon himsel', would put in my head my golden Johannes, and how I could best put it out to usury, and lay anither and anither till't; but I wrestled, and, wi' the help o' the Mighty, prevailed. I trust my bank and coffer will be my breek pouch, or some puir widow wife's meal ark in a' time coming. I'll hae' nae mair locking o' coffers—nae Tubal-Cain wark in my tents."

The good man shut his grey eyes, and appeared engaged for a minute in ejaculatory thanksgiving, for this signal deliverance from the snare of riches, and the power of covetousness. A smile rose on Grahame's lip—a half-heaved sigh chased it away, as he contrasted his own illumination, and the knowledge of good and evil obtained by eating the bitter apples of experience, with the apostolic simplicity of Gideon.

"With your known hospitality," said Wolfe, "I could not have conceived you very rich—so you must indeed allow me"—

"Hospitality! little to brag o' in that way, my lad. To gi'e a meal o' hamely meat, or a brat o' auld duds to a needy fellow-creature that falls in my way, in the name of Him who has given me so largely to enjoy, is but a sma' matter, Captain Wolfe. To be sure my auld garments are, as ye say, nae great shakes."—And he cast his eye on a coat cuff, of which every thread might be counted without the aid of a weaver's magnifying glass.—"But this is my kirk and causey clothes."

"Nay, I rather think I have sometimes seen them very great *shakes*," said Grahame, laughing.

But a pun, however bad or good, fell alike innocuous on honest Gideon, who never had the most glimmering perception of a double meaning in any thing he had heard in his life: so the young man went on.—"I am sure if you are not hospitable, I don't know who is—I have known you keep daft folk, and lamiters, and beggars, about the Sourholes for weeks and months together :—our friend, daft Miss Jacky Pingle, for instance."

"Small thanks to me for that, lad: we were auld stair neighbours, as I have often tauld you, when I was a student; and, when her brain is no a' the higher, she has a sleight wi' her thimble and her sheers that's just wonderfu', the womenfolk tell me, for I'm an ignoramus in needle-work. In that six weeks she last sojourned at the Sourholes, she did as much white seam, and embroidery upon the heels o' my rig-and-fur stockings, as would have cost me twenty-pence sterling to the school-mistress o' Castleburn; so let us ne'er reckon that turn hospitality. We are ready enough to be vain-glorious without calling the keeping of puir Jacky Pingle, (whom never a one would take off my hands neither,) by the name of a grace of deevine injunction, whereby some have entertained angels."

"I certainly do not mistake your keeping poor Miss Jacky for entertaining an angel," said Grahame, laughing again; "but I am sure, as I said, if you are not hospitable I don't know who is. By the way, I know of no word in the English language more abused, or of more ambiguous meaning than this same.—One hears of the hospitality of the feudal chieftain. I beg to place it exactly on the level with that of the modern hospitality of the candidate for parliament;—so much beef and ale,—so many balls and feasts,—for so much reputation to be maintained, or service done or expected.—' The hospitalities of fine people, which we sometimes hear of, are another spurious species of this kindly virtue :—splendid entertainments, a sacrifice to personal vanity, given in ostentation, and received, as they deserve to be, with indifference or scorn, by persons who neither need nor crave kindness nor countenance, though they may lack amusement. In a lower rank, the same feeling of vanity leads another class of persons to *fête* all sorts of people, artists, travellers, recruiting-officers, players, and so forth—the wonderful—the wild! and this, forsooth, must be hospitality! This unfortunate grace has much to answer for, which ought, in all conscience, to be laid elsewhere. No man, Mr. Gideon, was ever yet a martyr to this virtue, if exercised in its pure and simple sense. The entertainer of the desolate and the widow, the sick, the maimed, the blind, he who leads the bashful unfriended stranger to his modest feast, will never, I venture to predict, ruin himself by hospitality; a virtue which, according to some folks, fills half the bankrupt list."

"Verily, there is a smack of rationality in what you say, Captain Wolfe."

"I am sure hospitality, if it has a home on earth, still lingers in Strathorah with you and my uncle," continued Wolfe. "I vow there is more genuine kindness in the dinner he so often gives to these poor devils, the Rookston peripatetic surgeon, scouring our country-side on sixpenny bleedings and shilling blisters, and our nonjuring curate, with his triple duty and quarter pay, than in twenty Lord Mayors' banquets, or letter-of-introduction dinners. I leave him in evil times, Mr. Haliburton; but I trust a blessing will remain on the kind old soul that never once sent a hungry heart from his gate. I am sure if I am not a better man as long as I live for having known you both, I deserve to be hanged."

Upon hearing this suspicious doctrine, savouring, indeed, of ramping prelacy, Gideon girded up his loins for the polemic combat, and was about, at some length, to correct the young soldier's heterodox notions of charity, mercy, and hospitality, when the youth called his attention to the struggling skiff, which a commanding point of the road now enabled them to see clearly. The lazy chill mists, which had all day long hooded the braes, now rolled fast down upon their path. Cape, and island, and promontory, which had all day stretched away in hazy perspective, were, one by one, blotted out; and when the horsemen rounded the shel-

tending angle of a screen of rocks, they were at once exposed to the unmitigated fury of the tempest, which came wildly rushing from the ocean, shaking drizzling vapours from its wings, as they flapped against the splintered cliffs, at whose base the full tide was boiling and lashing. The full moon was drifting on in the heavens through dun and yellow clouds, as if she too had gone astray, and had to maintain the same struggle above which the little vessel held in the weltering tide.—Altogether, the prospect was comfortless and painful.

"We will have a foul night, Mr. Haliburton. The wind has ever some mischief in its head, when it whistles lillibalero at its destructive work in that way. Can you see these poor souls yet?"

Gideon groaned—"Alack no! Those who go down to the sea in ships, and see the wonders of the great deep, have much to thole as well as to see, Captain Wolfe. Let us commit them to Him who sitteth in the floods, and holdeth the winds in the hollow of his hand; who maketh the cloud their tabernacle!—and push on Jenny to Mosskrottles to John Fennick's. He wones in a slack near by the seaside; and we can hing out his lantern to guide the boat off a wanchancy bit down there, that has smashed many a goodly vessel. Profane folk name it the De'il's Saint-becket; and in very deed I never heard it get another name—so what can I ca' it?"

"And very well named too, sir; but as I trust these poor do—— that is souls, will not be laid in his Black Majesty's pickle to night, I shall push on and do what I can with your friends; and you may come up at your leisure with Jenny."

Mightily did Gideon spur not to be left behind in the race of humanity, and often did he apostrophize Jenny Geddes; but before he reached the Caberax, a fire was blazing on the low point, and Grahame stood there directing a group of young fellows, all ready to obey his orders, or, from their superior knowledge of the coast, to suggest better expedients.

Travelling apostles, as well as every other description of traveller, are often, we think, fully as much indebted to the fair, as to the stern sex, for the comfort and kindness o. their reception.

"The best of the board, and the seat by the fire,"

had in Scotland, time immemorial, been the prescriptive right of the "Haly-wark folk;" and, nothing slackened in hospitality, David Fennick and his wife cordially welcomed "the man of God;" and, as he was cold and wet, and could be of no use whatever on the shore, laid hands of violent possession upon him as soon as he proposed going to join the young men. So his clothes were changed for dry and warm garments, and he sat him snugly down in the chimney-nook.

If the evening was rough without, its discomfort served to enhance the cheerful couthiness of the Farmer's Ha'. This kitchen and hall—for it was the common room of the numerous family, and served for all domestic purposes—was a large apartment with strong, rough, stone walls arched by shining smoky rafters, and furnished with a wide, canopied, open chimney. Through its picturesque intricacies a blazing fire filling the cradle-grate, liberally fed from the neighbouring bog, diffused a ruddy lustre, richer and warmer than the costliest blaze ever yet shed through halls of pride, by wax candles or oil gas. A brazen sconce, a few bright copper utensils, and a bink well filled with pewter, did more for the apartment in the way of appropriate decoration than mirrors or pictures could have done. But the Ha' wanted not its pictures. In an antique, carved, oaken settle below the chimney canopy, discoursing with his guest, sat the grey-haired patriarch, clad in homespun mauirland grey, with a softened bearing between the stern old Covenanter and the "monarch of a shed;" regarding with looks of sober kindness, his well-disciplined subjects, busy on all sides of him with their accustomed tasks and duties. Next to him, but lower in place, on a tripod, sat a little decent matron, (a maiden by the way,) his wife's aunt, carding wool to supply the spinning thrift of David's blooming, woman-grown daughter, who merrily turned her wheel, with that subdued hum which was the nearest approach she durst make to profane singing in her father's honoured presence. Sometimes she involuntarily cast backwards a quick and bashful glance if a tirl was heard at the door pin, a movement which as constantly drew upon her the arch eye of a boy, her younger brother, who was stretched before the fire conning his Latin lesson for the next day. A ploughman, nearly as old and grey as his master, was driving hobnails into a clouted shoe; and, a little in the back ground, the herd-boy was twisting a bird's cage of twigs—a little boy, the Benjamin of David's old age, looking on as the wonderful frame grew beneath the cunning right hand of Jock. A squab, four-cornered, ruddy, serving wench pounded away in another corner, mashing a steaming pot of potatoes for the common supper of the family, an allowance which might have fed a whole hill-side congregation; and the gudewife, a comely well-thriven matron, many years younger than her lord, though on hospitable thoughts intent, contrived t ouperintend the whole establishment. A goodly and gracious show of black puddings, hung to be smoked in the chimney, showed that good things were going; for the Mart was lately killed. And while Gideon and his host seated apart—

reasoned high
Of Providence, fore-knowledge, will, and fate,
Fixed fate—

the fate of an eirack* was sealed, perhaps in honour of Captain Grahame.

"My worthy father—ye'll mind him weel, Mr. Gideon,' said the gudewife, "had aye a joke, that there was a natural friendship and couthiness between a black coat and a black puddin'; and ye'se have one to relish the potatoes this night if it were my last." And she cast an eye of pride over her plentiful stores. This was said in the absence of David, who had gone forth to see that the cattle were properly foddered.

David was a good deal of the Milton in his domestic circle. Except towards the darling Benjamin, he was indeed a very strict disciplinarian with all his household. Few external marks of mirth durst be shown in his presence; but when he withdrew to his private out-door devotions, or to his wooden-walled dormitory, there came an hour of juvenile relaxation to the family, at which David winked hard, as every sensible absolute monarch should do, wh wishes to avoid open revolt among his subjects. But peace, and plenty, and goodness were about him; and the whispered gibe of the boys to their sister or to the maid-servant, and the matron's frequent whispered rebuke of—"Will ye no be quiet?—the gudeman will just fell ye!" shewed that

---

* A year old fowl.

genuine gaiety of heart was here, its native spring uninjured, though its expression might be subdued.

While David was occupied in littering his cattle, grumbling a little at the protracted absence of his son and the younger farm-servants, who still fed a bickering fire on the shore, Mr. Gideon strode off in that direction, guided by the signal lights.

The police established along this line of coast at that period, during the Irish insurrection, was, of necessity, extremely vigilant and severe. The pernicious influences of that evil time, which steeled the human breast against its kind, had even extended to this region of tranquillity and comparative safety; and the inhabitants of the Scottish side were disposed to view whatever approached from the opposite coast, with great distrust and unreasonable aversion.

The family of another farmer, who, with David, was joint occupier of this headland moor, were still engaged in the latest harvest-work of a tardy season. During the whole afternoon of this tempestuous day, this farmer had observed the skiff beating about in the bay, and conjectured that it had stolen out from some inlet on the beleaguered coast of Antrim, which perhaps its crew found more perilous than the iron-bound shores of the south-west of Scotland, and that coil of waves, currents, and breakers, amid which they were struggling. The fate of the little vessel had indeed, for some hours back, been the object of eager and agitating interest to the people on the coast. Rebels, murderers, or incendiaries its crew might be—still they were human, and in this hour of mortal peril the claim was felt in all its force. The presence and exertions of Captain Grahame had, moreover, by this time brought humanity into good fashion; and though the discipline of David Fennick's household did not permit his womankind to roam abroad, there were several females standing with the group which Gideon and David joined; and their sympathies were fully awakened, and had the strongest influence on those around them.

"Oh! if they could reach the Cutter—or if the Cutter could reach them!" cried one of the women, who watched the labouring skiff with intense interest, uttering stifled groans as the little storm-tossed speck was seen through the opening spindrift, or swept from view by the swell of the breakers, and expressing renewed hope as the frail thing again rose in sight, and gallantly mounted the ridge of the billow.

"The Cutter!" cried a man of greater information. "That would be gaun between the de'il and the deep sea wi' a witness! 'Od, they may be saying their neck-verse if the Cutter overtake them; and she has been full chase after them since the skiff was first seen aff the Scart's Craig. It's just as weel to be drowned I think, David, at the Almighty's pleasure, as hanged, drawn and quartered by the Government."

"Wo is me! wo is me!" said the female speaker.—"This is nae joking matter. Be they what they will, they are warm flesh and blood like ourselves."

"Ay, and soul and spirit, Euphane!" said David Fennick—"puir, sinfu' perishing souls like *yoursels*, sirs, rocking and reeling on the brink of an eternity, whilk may be as near to us as to them; though there appear to us but a moment's space and a rotten plank, between them and the fierce and fiery indignation which hastens to consume."

"Let us hope better things for them, friend David," said Gideon, "baith for time and for eternity. Is there no balm in Gilead? Is there no Physician there? Is there not hope for the sinner, ay, even were the last sands o' his glass rinnin' low? How shall man, proud worm! limit the dealing of Omnipotence with the immortal spirits He has called into existence?"

Now to David's long ears this sounded very like false doctrine; and he delivered a pious speech, which so stirred the "Old Adam" in the heart of his neighbour-tenant of the Moss, that he exclaimed—"I wad rather hear the sugh o' the south-east win' that's to blaw thae pair battered Irish deevils by the De'ils Saut-backet, than a' the peching and graining e'er was grained on a hill-side."

At this instant a ruffian billow, rushing in with headlong fury, swept the little vessel on, till it almost seemed to touch the firm earth where our anxious group were assembled. The blaze of the fire danced and flared on the foamy crest of the wave and in the faces of the crew, consisting of three men and two females, one of the latter—strange to say!—holding the helm. Words of cheer—of sympathy—of counsel, were eagerly shouted from the land by Grahame and the other young men; and ropes were actively thrown out; but the same tremendous wave which had borne the skiff onward, snatched it back in its fearful recoil, far from sight—for ever from sight, it was feared—and every eye was fixed, and every heart shivered, as a yell rose from some unseen drowning wretch over whom the billows closed for ever. In a few seconds the skiff rose once again into view, but with one man short of its original number. Still the little crew bore them gallantly, with firmness and presence of mind, which gave the spectators something of the wild delight experienced in witnessing some noble pastime, in which ruffian strength is matched against skill, conduct, and energy.

A signal gun was fired from the sea. The flash was seen distinctly; the report came broken and driven about by the wind.

"That's the Cutter still in chase," said David's neighbour. "But the tempest will do their business. I gi'e them up. Come hame, lads, and bring the ropes wi' ye."

"O ye of little faith!" shouted Gideon. Can He that let loose the winds no stay them? Is His arm shortened—is His hand straitened? Did He make the dry land and not the sea also? Is His time not a good time?—is His hand not a gracious hand?—Bide ye still."

Another "ruffian billow" again tossed the skiff up on its foamy mane, and then seemed to gulp it down into its tremendous jaws.

"O, Lord! of thy infinite mercy remember thy puir perishing creatures!" cried Gideon.—"That, neighbours, was a fearfu' whomle!"

"Ay! that jaw gave e'en your faith a belaie, minister," said David's profane neighbour.

Contrary to all expectation, a heavy shower having somewhat beat down the fury of the storm, the little vessel, once more out at sea, was seen to weather the point round which it had all the afternoon been beating. Grahame and Robert Fennick, an intelligent and active young man, David's eldest son, and in reality the most useful person of the rural group, were certain that they had seen, in the bright glimpse of a still-wading moon the shadow of its little mast quivering on the water, and that it had got through the breakers, and past the entrance of that place which Gideon so much disliked to name. Others of the number as confidently predicted the inevitable destination of the boat to be this same *Deil's Saut-Backet*.

Whatever her fate was, he was gone from their sight, and the rain was pouring in torrents, so they dispersed, Mr. Gideon going to his friend's hospitable hearth, and Wolfe Grahame, notwithstanding David's kind if not frank invitation, to the little way-side public-house where he had left his horse.

David's dame had, in the course of her experience, often seen a comfortable supper prove a very agreeable diversion of polemical discourse. Not so on this evening. The argument between the learned patriarchs on the oaken settle in the chimney-neuk, waxed hotter and hotter, and the black pudding, colder and colder, to her secret grief, and at last open discontent; for Mrs. Fennick, though the bosom companion of a self-denying saint, had a housewife's natural pride in her black, and in her white puddings; and Gideon fell considerably in her good graces from his open disrespect to her good things. Had he sojourned but two days longer in her frugal household, he would probably have recovered this lost ground, and gained the more lasting and substantial praise of being "easily shot bye wi' his victuals."—As it was, she cried "Patience!" and turned 'the puddings.

The subject for which her savoury messes were on this night permitted to freeze, was one which, though foreign to our story, afterwards shook the church of Sourholes to its foundation, and involved the latter days of its presiding apostle in much trouble and turmoil.

There was no Cameronian meeting within twenty miles of David Fennick's dwelling of Mossbrettles. The ancient adherents to this *nomsmade* faith, remained at home on Sabbaths and read their bibles, when they could not attend the public worship of their own sect; but the younger members of David's family, had, of late, strayed into the neighbouring parish-church—at first covertly, but now with less care for concealment. There they had, among other defilements, acquired a taste for a sort of church-music, certainly of no very alluring kind, but totally different from that to which their venerable chief had been accustomed. To carry his domestic plagues to the climax, Orpheus, assuming the disguise of a yellow lank weaver from the Riccartown of Kilmarnock, "fashed wi' a stamack complaint," had rambled into the parish, and, in widow Bonalie's public, set up an evening class for teaching this new-fangled palmody. In an evil hour David was teased into granting permission of his children to attend; and now, instead of the old reverend way of twanging out the psalm, line by line, "their rants," David said, "ran straight on, run-line" —thus invading, in fact destroying for ever, his immutable privilege of doling it out line by line, rather than suffer any interruption or suspension of their own "most sweet voices."

The controversy was still novel to Mr. Gideon; and we must do him the justice to say, that, notwithstanding his early prejudices and associations were all on the side of the quaint antique method of chanting the psalms, his naturally candid spirit and sincere understanding rated the subject at its true importance; and David found a much less zealous partisan than he had reckoned upon.—He indeed took but an indifferent part in the afflictions of David.

"Is it not written—there shall be line upon line?" grinned David, the thin white locks that straggled over his pale sunken temples trembling in the eagerness of his controversial zeal.—"What's your opinion of that scripture, minister?"

"And is it not written—'Praise ye *continually*—make a joyful noise?'" said Robert, the smiling champion of St. Cecilia and her new lights.

Gideon was smitten to the heart's core with what he boldly pronounced this Pharisaical Jesuitical wark—"And wo is mine! David," he cried, "to hear this din about robes and phylacteries taking place o' the weightier matters of the law,—and that in a corner of the vineyard ance fair and flourishing. But I'll tell ye, gudeman, what has filled me with shame to hear, and grief, and indignation. In Glasgow yonder, even in kirks pretending to be reformed, bands of singing bairns—they shame not to call them choirs—laddies and lassies lilting away at the praises of their Maker,—and as if it were an auld balland or a ratt-rhyme; and this they call leading the worship of a Presbyterian congregation, in the most hallowed and heaven-like exercise of praise—themselves a' dumb! If we maun ha'e a Popish preluding, take to the kist fu' o' whistles at ance, Robert. Tinkling brass wire and sounding timber boards, have neither hearts to harden nor souls to ensnare, like puir simple bairns."

After delivering his testimony against this enormity, which was at that time quite a recent innovation, Mr. Gideon proceeded, as was his custom wherever he spent the night, to examine the young people and servants of the family, in their attainments in the Assembly's Shorter Catechism, and on their general religious knowledge.—The venerable head of the house had no reason to be ashamed of this exhibition. Whatever were their musical abberrations, they had been trained up in "the way they should go;" and there was good hope that they might never "depart from it." The boy who had conned his Latin lesson by the fire, the embryo preacher, next went over his *penna* and *doceo*, to the infinite delight of his mother. Even stern David grinned complacent, and owned "human lear was nae doubt a mean," and melted into entire delight when his little favourite son, the rosy, smiling, curly-haired Davie, with a good deal of kindly prompting from mother, sister, maiden, and brother, herd, and ploughman, in lisping accents went through his infant manual, and told "Who made him," and "Who redeemed him," very correctly.

"And who was the strongest man, Davie?"

"Samson!" replied Davie. "We ha'e a big grey Samson, the cart aver."

"Very right, Davie," said Gideon.—"And who was the wisest man?"

"Absalom!" cried Davie, undauntedly.

"O fie!" whispered the mother—"So—Sol—o—"

"Solomon!" shouted Davie, triumphantly.

"Very right!"

"And he'll no be four till Candlemas!" whispered the mother, aside.

"And who was the meekest man, Davie?"

"Job."

"Hush, Davie—fie!" cried the sister.

"But it was though—just Moses," cried Davie, dealing her a playful blow, with the petulance of a spoiled, lively, and clever child.

Old David knitted his stern brows over this infant trick of the carnal heart in his beloved child.

"That was na right, my little man," said kind Gideon, in grave rebuke; and Davie looked alarmed, and with some cause. "But we must make a passover; for puir Davie sees his fau't. Think first now—what they call the Gudeman of Mossbrettles, and tell me 'Who was the man according to God's own heart?'"

"Wee Davie's ain Daddy David," cried the cunning and affectionate little rogue, throwing himself into his father's arms; and old David involuntarily kissed his brow, his grey eyes glistening, and after a short fervid clasp, put him hastily away, as if ashamed of this emotion of natural affection.

"Ye think me like auld Eli, minister," said he. And he instantly walked forth to meditate, and question of his own relaxed spirit, and screw up his resolution to chastise wee Davie.

The little victim, when invited to a private conference in his father's dormitory, first had his supper to eat, and then his prayers to say—and, finally, appealed to his mother, who, rebellious as her heart was, durst not for her life have interfered between her stern lord and his just displeasure; so the poor trembler disappeared, Gideon's heart yearning over him. The calm expostulating voice of David was heard for some time, and the low thick sob of Davie,—then rose the voice of one in earnest prayer, and there was a moment's pause, followed by Davie's shrill scream of "Oh! father, father!—reason wi' me, and shew me my error, a wee whilie langer;" but the inexorable scourge descended rapidly, perhaps severely; for David Fennick was no joker in any business to which he seriously thought that duty called him.

Such was the stern discipline of Scotland in those days. A great deal has since been said for and against the use of the rod. We have recorded wee Davie Mossbrettles' opinion, as decidely in favour of *prayer* and *reasoning*, and against stripes.

Davie was put to bed; and David the older again walked out to compose his spirit.

Some pious neighbours had, by this time, come in to gather the manna chance-dropt in this wilderness. Preachers and Probationers were often enough coming to Mossbrettles; but it was not every night that a true-blue unmingled Cameronian minister, of the fame of Mr. Haliburton, tarried there. David, this night, "had gotten a Levite for his priest," and felt his personal consequence augmented accordingly. So he beckoned forward his modest guests to chairs, and stools, and tubs overturned to make seats, with exactly the patronizing feelings of a fine lady, who has caught and lionized a fashionable poet or singer, for the amusement of her friends and the *eclat* of her rout, and of its celebration-paragraph in the Morning Post of the next day. How essentially the same, after all, are the enjoyments of the great human family, however their external manifestations and their moral influences may vary.

The seeds of poetry in Gideon's character, were not unfrequently displayed in his selection of a portion of scripture to be read, or of the psalm to be sung. On this night, from this humble rustic group, a small farmer and a few poor Scottish cotters, from the bosom of the barren moor, there rose to heaven, slowly chanted, line by line, one of the most beautiful lyrics that ever was composed, judging of it merely as a literary composition—the 104th Psalm—the hymn of Universal nature to the Universal Creator! Far higher than this was Gideon's standard of judging of the inspired writings.

A simple, scriptural, earnest, and affectionate prayer, almost as comprehensive as the hymn which had been sung, forgetting no class nor condition of sentient beings—concluded the domestic exercise; and when the group rose from their knees, Robert, David's eldest son, "a noble peasant," grasped the minister's hand and said—

"Your ain, sir, and my father's auld-fashioned sughin' out o' the plaintive *Dundee*, and the noble *Martyrs*, dinnel stronger on the heart-strings after a', than a' their crinkum crankum new tunes."

"Robert, my man, if ye are led to think sae it is weel," replied Gideon. "So grieve not the grey-haired man i' the neuk, whose soul has travailed for the weal o' yours, ay when sweet sleep has sealed your ain eye-lids. Keep ye by these holy harmonies, wi' whilk the wail of the curlew and the plover, and the roar of the linn ha's chimed in yon brave day : yea, the sweet melodies that rose in the night-watches, like myrrh and frankincense, and the rich spices, frae these very moss-hags, and coves, and cleuchs round about us, whither the red arm o' persecution had driven forth the stout true hearts o' covenanted Ayr, and favoured Gallowa'—Ayr, whose plants were as an orchard of pomegranates with pleasant fruits. Alack! that the cankerworm should creep in—that they should either dwine or die!"

This honest ancestral eulogy was highly acceptable to every present ear. But the puddings smoking hot were now served with the mashed potatoes, together with a jorum of stout, home-brewed, harvest ale, of which David partook very sparingly, Robert and Mr. Gideon with greater freedom.—Another hour passed in sober but social talk on public and family affairs. Gideon was pleased to hear that his friend David's "temporals" prospered, and that he was willing and eager to lend his carts, during the winter, to drive stones for the purpose of erecting a meeting-house in the vicinity. The honest man chose a private minute to confess to Gideon his sinful yearnings over the "bairn, wee Davie;" but honest Gideon slurred that offence on the present occasion, and, in spite of the "carts," rather warned his friend against "worldliness," and "covetousness," and "spiritual pride," than any excess of natural tenderness. From these sins David Fennick was certain that he stood wholly clear.

The whole family now retired to rest—to that "quiet sleep" for which Gideon had prayed—that quiet sleep which, in the words of his petition, "is Thy gift to Thy chosen ones!"

And thus was closed the night in a small Scotch FARMER'S HA'!

TRADITION OF THE NORSEMEN.

The Norsemen were the more prone to superstitions, because it was a favourite fancy of theirs that, in many instances, the change from life to death altered the temper of the human spirit from benignant to malevolent; or perhaps, that when the soul left the body, its departure was occasionally supplied by a wicked demon, who took the opportunity to enter and occupy its late habitation.

Upon such a supposition the wild fiction that follows is probably grounded; which, extravagant as it is, possesses something striking to the imagination. Saxo Grammaticus tells us of the fame of two Norse princes or chiefs, who had formed what was called a brotherhood in arms, implying not only the firmest friendship and constant support, during all the adventures which they should undertake in life, but binding them by a solemn compact, that after the death of either, the survivor should descend alive into the sepulchre of his brother-in-arms, and consent to be buried along with him. The task of fulfilling this dreadful compact fell upon Asmund, his companion, Assueit, having been slain in battle. The tomb was formed after the ancient northern custom, in what was called the age of hills,—that is, when it was usual to bury persons of distinguished merit or rank on some conspicuous spot, which was crowned with a mound. With this purpose a deep narrow vault was constructed, to be the apartment of the future tomb over which the sepulchral heap was to be piled. Here they deposited arms, trophies, poured forth, perhaps, the blood of victims, introduced into the tomb the war-horses of the champions, and when these rites had been duly paid, the body of Assueit was placed in the dark and narrow house, while his faithful brother-in-arms entered and sat down by the corpse, without a word or look which testified regret or unwillingness to fulfil his fearful engagement. The soldiers who had witnessed this singular interment of the dead and living, rolled a huge stone to the mouth of the tomb, and piled so much earth and stones above the spot as made a mound visible from a great distance, and then, with loud lamentation for the loss of such undaunted leaders, they dispersed themselves like a flock which has lost its shepherd.

Years passed away after years, and a century had elapsed, ere a noble Swedish rover, bound upon some high adventure, and supported by a gallant band of followers, arrived in the valley which took its name from the tomb of the brethren-in-arms. The story was told to the strangers, whose leader determined on opening the sepulchre, partly because, as already hinted, it was reckoned an heroic action to brave the anger of departed heroes by violating their tombs; partly to attain the arms and swords of proof with which the deceased had done their great actions. He set his soldiers to work, and soon removed the earth and stones from one side of the mound, and laid bare the entrance. But the stoutest of the rovers started back, when, instead of the silence of a tomb, they heard within horrid cries, the clash of swords, the clang of armour, and all the noise of a mortal combat between two furious champions. A young warrior was let down into the profound tomb by a cord, which was drawn up shortly after, in hopes of news from beneath. But when the adventurer descended, some one threw him from the cord, and took his place in the noose. When the rope was pulled up, the soldiers, instead of their companion, beheld Asmund, the survivor of the brethren-in-arms. He rushed into the open air, his sword drawn in his hand, his armour half torn from his body, the left side of his face almost scratched off, as by the talons of some wild beast. He had no sooner appeared in the light of day, than, with the improvisatory poetic talent, which these champions often united with heroic strength and bravery, he poured forth a string of verses containing the history of his hundred years' conflict within the tomb. It seems that no sooner was the sepulchre closed, than the corpse of the slain Assueit arose from the ground, inspired by some ravenous goule, and having first torn to pieces and devoured the horses which had been entombed with them, threw himself upon the companion who had just given him such a sign of devoted friendship, in order to treat him in the same manner. The hero, no way discountenanced by the horrors of his situation, took to his arms, and defended himself manfully against Assueit, or rather against the evil demon who tenanted that champion's body. In this manner the living brother waged a preternatural combat, which had endured during a whole century, when Asmund, at last obtaining the victory, prostrated his enemy, and by driving, as he boasted, of a stake through his body, had finally reduced him to the state of quiet becoming a tenant of the tomb. Having chanted the triumphant account of his contest and victory, this mangled conqueror fell dead before them. The body of Assueit was taken out of the tomb, burnt, and the ashes dispersed to heaven; whilst that of the victor, now lifeless, and without a companion, was deposited there, so that it was hoped his slumbers might remain undisturbed. The precautions taken against Assueit's reviving a second time, remind us of those adopted in the Greek Islands, and in the Turkish provinces, against the Vampire. It affords also a derivation of the ancient English law in case of suicide, when a stake was driven through the body, originally to keep it secure in the tomb.—*Sir Walter Scott.*

COBBETT'S ACCOUNT OF NEW LANARK.

BEING at New Lanark, I was rather curious to know whether there were any reality in what we heard about the effects of the Owen "*feelosophy*," I had always understood that he had been the author of his own great fortune, and the founder of this village; but I found that the establishment had been founded by a Mr. Dale, who had had two or three daughters with great fortunes; that Mr. Owen had got one of these daughters, and one of these fortunes: that Mrs. Owen has been dead for some years; that the concern had long been in other hands; that the only part of it which was ever of his invention, was a large building, in which the "*feelosofical*" working people were intended to eat and drink in common; that they never did this; that there had been a place at some distance from Lanark, fixed upon for the execution of the " Owen Plans;" that a large space had been surrounded with a high stone wall for the purpose; that the scheme had been abandoned; and that the wall had been taken down, and sold as *old stones!* The building, in New Lanark, which Owen had erected for the "*feelosophers*" to carry on their community of eating and drinking, is used as a *school-room*; and here I saw boys in one place, and girls in another place, under masters appointed for the purpose, carrying on what is called "education." There was one boy pointing with a stick to something stuck up upon the wall, and then all the rest of the boys began bawling out what that was. In one large room they were all, *singing out something* at the word of command, just like the tribe of little things in Bolt Court, who there stun the whole neighbourhood with singing "God Save the King," "The Apostles' Creed," and the "Peace Table," and the fellow, who leads the lazy life in the teaching of whom, ought to be sent to raking the kennel, or filling a dung cart. In another great apartment of this house, there were eighteen boys and eighteen girls, the boys dressed in Highland dresses, without shoes on, naked from three inches above the knee, down to the foot, a tartan plaid close round the body, in their shirt sleeves, their shirt collars open, each having a girl by the arm, duly propositioned in point of size, the girls without caps, and without shoes and stockings; and there were these eighteen couples, marching, arm in arm, in regular files, with a look-step, slow march, to the sound of a fiddle, which a fellow, big enough to carry a quarter of wheat, or to dig ten roods of ground in a day, was playing in the corner of the room, with an immense music book lying open before him. There was another man who was commanding officer of the marching couples, who, after having given us a march in quick step as well as slow-step, were disposed off in dancing order, a business that they seemed to perform with great regularity and elegance; and it was quite impossible to see the half-naked lads of twelve or thirteen, putting their arms round the waists of the thinly-clad girls of the same age, without clearly perceiving the manifest tendency of this mode of education, to prevent "premature marriages," and to "check population."

It is difficult to determine, whether, when people are huddled together in this unnatural state, this sort of soldier-like discipline may, or may not, be necessary to effect the purposes of schooling; but I should think it a very strange thing, if a man, calculated to produce effect by his learning, could ever come to perfection from a beginning like this. It is altogether a thing I abhor. I do not say that it may not be useful when people are thus unnaturally congregated; and, above all things, I am not disposed to bestow censure on the *motives* of the parties promoting this mode of education; for the sacrifices which they make, in order to give success to their schemes, clearly prove that their motives are benevolent; but I am not the less convinced that it is a melancholy thing to behold; that it is the reverse of *domestic life*; that it reverses the order of nature; that it makes minds a fiction; and, which is amongst the greatest of its evils, it fashions the rising generation to habits of *implicit submission*, which is only another term for civil and political slavery. However, the consolation is, that it is impossible that it ever should become anything like general in any nation. The order of the world demands that nine-tenths of the people should be employed on, and in the affairs of the land; being so employed, they must be scattered about widely; and there must be homes and domestic life for the far greater part of the rising generation. When men contract a fondness for anything which has a great deal of novelty and of strangeness in it; when they brood over the contemplation of some wonderful discovery which they think they have made; when they suffer it long to absorb all the powers of their minds; when they have been in this state for any considerable length of time, they really become *mad*, as far as relates to the matter which has thus absorbed all their mental faculties; and they think themselves more wise than all the rest of mankind, in exact proportion to the degree of their madness. It is unfortunate enough when follies of this sort lead only to disappointment and ridicule; but the parties become objects of real compassion, when the eccentric folly produces dissipation of fortune, and the ruin of families.

CURE FOR A CRIPPLE.

IT happened on a Sunday evening, about thirty years ago, that two sheep-stealers had meditated an attempt on the flock of a wealthy farmer in the parish of A———, in the west neuk of Fife. The sheep were grazing in a park adjoining the village churchyard, and hard by the public road. The eldest and most experienced of the depredators recommended that only one of them should go in among the sheep, as it would not alarm them so much as two. Accordingly the younger thief was dispatched to bring a sheep, while the other went into the churchyard, and sat down upon a through-stone to amuse himself till his companion returned. Now it so happened that John, the minister's man, had forgot to take home the Bible from the church, after the service of the day was over, which neglect was not perceived until the minister called for the books to perform the duty of family worship, when John was immediately sent to the church for the Bible. John not being possessed of a very daring spirit, and it being a dark winter night, was not very fond of visiting the abodes of the dead at such an hour; but when he arrived at the churchyard gate, and got a glimpse of the man sitting on the through-stone, his hair stood on end, and his fears soon conjured the thief into a demon. Without more ado he wheeled about, and made the best of his way to the manse, where he related his wonderful story, telling them that he saw the devil sitting on a grave breaking dead bones. An old cripple mendicant, who was quartered at the manse during the Sabbath, (for the minister, contrary to the general character of his brethren, was a very charitable man,) heard John telling his appalling story, laughed at him, saying, " if I was as able to gang as you, I would soon bring the Bible."—" Well," says John, " if you will accompany me, I will carry you on my back, and we'll may-be be able to bring the Bible atween us." The beggar agreed, and mounted John accordingly, after he had wrapped himself in his grey plaid. When they came within view of the thief, John would very fain have turned, but the beggar spurred him on, until they came within a very short distance of him, when he, supposing it to be his comrade coming with a sheep on his back, exclaimed, "Is he a fat ane?" John, whose heart was quaking before, on hearing this question put to him, could no longer resist his inclination to turn; he threw the old man off his back, saying, "Be he fat or be he lean, there he is to ye," and run what he was able. The mendicant, finding that he was thus left to his own resources to appease the devil as he could, mastered all his strength; and, strange to tell, his legs that had refused to perform their office for many a long year before, were suddenly strengthened; he soon went past John, and regained the manse before him, and was never lame after.

SCRAPS.

DEATH OF LOGAN THE INDIAN CHIEF.—An old officer of the United States army, who, soon after the close of the revolutionary war, was ordered to make surveys of the country watered by the Alleghany river, informed me that Logan's nephew, a remarkably fine young Indian, dined with him one day in his tent, and that he asked him what became of Logan. I killed him, was the reply. Why did you kill him? The nation ordered it. For what reason? He was too great a man to live: he talked so well, that although the whole nation had intended to put any plan in execution, yet, if Logan did not approve of it, he would soon gain a majority in favour of his opinions. Was he not then generally in the right? Often; but his influence divided the nation too much. Why did they choose you to put him to death? If any one else had done it I certainly would have killed him: I, who am his nephew, shall inherit his greatness. Will they not then kill you also? Yes: and when I become as great a man as Logan (laying his hand on his breast with dignity) I shall be content to die! He added, that he had shot him near the Alleghany river. When informed of the resolution of the council of his nation, Logan stopped his horse, drew himself up in attitude of great dignity, and received the fatal ball without a murmur.—*Vignas's Six Months in America.*

NEGLECTED MERIT.—Robinson Crusoe was hawked about through the trade as a work of neither mark nor likelihood, and at last accepted, as a proof of especial condescension, by an obscure retail bookseller. It is singular, but not the less true, and we leave our readers to draw their own inference from the fact, that almost every book of any pretensions to originality has been similarly neglected. Paradise Lost, with difficulty, found a publisher, while the whole trade vied with each other in their eagerness to procure the works of such dull mechanical writers as Blackmore and Glover; Gulliver's Travels lay ten years in MS. for want of due encouragement from the booksellers; and in our own times, and in a lighter branch of literature, the Miseries of Human Life, and the still more ingenious Rejected Addresses, were refused by the trade with indifference, if not contempt. To crown the list of works thus misunderstood, Sir W. Scott has left it on record, that Waverley was actually declined three several times by the acutest publisher of his day; and at last ushered into the world, after it had lain twelve years unnoticed in its author's desk, with doubt, hesitation, and indifference. *Credite posteri!*—*Monthly Magazine.*

THE DESTRUCTIVE TAXES.—We would destroy, the instant it was possible, the house and window tax, because they are unequal, and the people hate them. We would destroy the malt tax and the hop duty, because they impede the cultivation of the land, and subject tradesmen and farmers to a rigorous and despotic system of excise. We would destroy the tax on soap, because it is a bounty on dirt and disease; as we would destroy the Taxes on Knowledge, because they are bounties on ignorance and error. We would destroy the monopolies of the Bank of England, and of the East India Company, because they tax the whole community for the exclusive benefit of the proprietors of Bank and East India Stock, and subject all commerce to be deranged by the caprice of individuals, against which open and public and general competition is the only sure and certain guarantee. We would destroy the corn laws, because they cheat the farmer with a hope of prices he never realizes, and make him promise a higher rent than he can pay—because they tend to starve the poor and impoverish the opulent manufacturers—and because they do not even benefit those landlords whom they merely flatter with preserving for them a nominal superiority which must come to an end. We would destroy the power of parsons and other justices to interfere with all the pastimes and amusements of the people, because that interference never has been exercised without souring the minds of the people, and making them feel deadly hatred for all those who appear to enjoy pleasures they are not permitted to share. We would destroy every pension not earned by useful public services. We would destroy every public office which is not indispensable for the real service of the public; limiting the whole action of the Government to the one great duty of protecting the property of individuals.—*Brighton Guardian.*

MORAL AND POLITICAL EFFECTS OF RAILWAYS IN ENGLAND.—The moral and political consequences of so great a change in the powers of transition of persons and intelligences from place to place, are not easily calculated. The concentration of mind and exertion which a great metropolis always exhibits, will be extended in a considerable degree to the whole realm. The same effect will be produced as if all distances were lessened in the proportion in which the speed and cheapness of transit are increased. Towns, at present removed some stages from the metropolis, will become its suburbs; others, now at a day's journey, will be removed to its immediate vicinity; business will be carried on with as much ease between them and the metropolis, as it is now between distant points of the metropolis itself. The ordinary habitations of various classes of citizens engaged in active business in the towns, will be at what now are regarded considerable distances from the places of their occupation. The salubrity of cities will thus be increased by superseding the necessity of heaping the inhabitants together, storey upon storey, within a confined space; and by enabling the town population to spread itself over a larger extent of surface, without incurring the inconvenience of distance. Let those who discard speculations like these, as wild and improbable, recur to the state of public opinion at no very remote period, on the subject of steam navigation. Within the memory of persons who have not yet passed the meridian of life, the possibility of traversing by the steam engine the channels and seas that surround and intersect these islands, was regarded as the dream of enthusiasts. Nautical men, and men of science, rejected such speculations with equal incredulity, and with little less than scorn for the understanding of those who could for a moment entertain them. Yet we have witnessed steam-engines traversing, not these channels and seas alone, but sweeping the face of the waters round every coast in Europe, and even ploughing the great oceans of the world. If steam be not used as the only means of connecting the most distant habitable points of our planet, it is not because it is inadequate to the accomplishment of that end, but because local and accidental causes limit the supply of that material, from which, at the present moment, it derives its powers.—*Edinburgh Review.*

CONTENTS OF NO. XXIII.

Notes of the Month	1
Books of the Month	2
VERSES FOR THE YOUNG—A Son to his Mother—Diary of a Sporting Oxonian	5
Wisdom of our Ancestors	6
London—Normandy	7
The Death of the Old Year	8
Condition of Banished Convict	ib.
THE STORY-TELLER.—Scottish Manners—The Farmer's Ha' in a December night	9
Tradition of the Norsemen	14
Cobbett's Account of New Lanark—Cure for a Cripple	15
SCRAPS.—Death of Logan the Indian Chief—Neglected Merit—The Destructive Taxes—Moral and Political effects of Railways in England	16

EDINBURGH: Printed by and for JOHN JOHNSTONE, 19, St. James's Square.—Published by JOHN ANDERSON, Jun., Bookseller, 55, North Bridge Street, Edinburgh; by JOHN MACLEOD, and ATKINSON & Co., Booksellers, Glasgow; and sold by all Booksellers and Venders of Cheap Periodicals.

THE Schoolmaster,
AND EDINBURGH WEEKLY MAGAZINE.

CONDUCTED BY JOHN JOHNSTONE.

THE SCHOOLMASTER IS ABROAD.—LORD BROUGHAM.

No. 24.—Vol. II.   SATURDAY, JANUARY 12, 1833.   Price Three-Halfpence.

FACTORY CHILDREN.

This is not the first time that we have endeavoured, in the pages of the *Schoolmaster*, to draw attention to the miserable condition of the greater number of the children employed in factories. To bring facts under notice, and keep them constantly in view, is, we are persuaded, all that is required to excite interest and sympathy in the public mind, and procure some amelioration of the wretchedness of those unfortunate children. The circumstances brought out in the examinations before the Committee of the House of Commons, exceed any thing we had previously conceived. They speak trumpet-tongued, and any thing we might urge would but weaken the impression they are calculated to produce upon every heart that retains human feeling. By the extracts we give, it will be seen, that the grand objection against legislative interference is nugatory; for it is not the sacred relation of parent and child that would be disturbed or tampered with, but the connexion between the community, and the children thrown upon its funds or its charity. These poor children are generally the offspring of misfortune or vice, to whom early death would appear to be a positive blessing, as the only apparent means of rescuing them from degradation, suffering, and ultimately crime. We blush to say, that the most flagrant instances of this systematic cruelty that have yet transpired, have been traced to Scotland : nor does it mend the matter to find Scottish Members of Parliament (Mr. R. Fergusson, and Mr. Morrison) strenuously opposing the extension of the provisions of Mr. Sadler's Bill to this country, upon the ground, that with us there exists no necessity for legislative interference, so comfortable and happy are all the factory children in Scotland ! This, we hope and believe, was said in ignorance, but it is most culpable ignorance. Our extracts of evidence are confined to-day to the Scotch Mills, and to the testimony of one individual, Alexander Dean, an overseer of a flax mill at Dundee, who has had considerable experience in those scenes of disgusting harshness and cruelty. The first mill he entered was *Duntruin, near Dundee*. He was then thirteen. There they worked not less than 17 hours a-day, exclusive of meals. The master's name was Braid. Four or five orphans, all that were left alive of about 16, supplied by some poor institution in this city, were there employed :—

Usually, for how long a time did they stop ?—I could not say for how long a time ; there were always some of them deserting, and being brought back.

Speaking of those long hours, how were the children kept in the establishment, they having to labour to such an extent as you have described ? They were kept in a constantly standing posture ; no leave was allowed for sitting.

Were they confined to that sort of work ?—Yes, the doors were all locked, both with check and turnkey.

They were locked up while at their labour ?—Yes.

Did they sleep upon the premises ?—Yes, it was upon the very same premises that they slept ; the houses were all connected.

Were those who were immediately under the control of the manager guarded all night ?—Yes ; there were iron-staunched windows, and the master himself, or his son, attended to locking them up at night, whenever they got their suppers ; so that they had no chance of escaping till the morning, when he released them for their next day's employment.

How were they taken care of on the Sundays, then ?—It was always one of the sons that staid at home and guarded them on Sunday ; he would not suffer them to go to Church.

Were the children and young persons kept down to that work by chastisement ?—Yes.

Were they severely chastised ?—Frequently they were ; for the least fault they were struck and abused.

You were speaking about children being prevented from deserting by being locked up ; was it often that children made an attempt to escape ?—Yes, if they got the least opportunity.

Where were the hands that did not sleep in the mill sent at night ?—The houses which the hands slept in were about 50 yards from the mill.

What were they called ?—Bothies.

In any of those Bothies were the boys and girls mixed up indiscriminately at night ?—Yes ; I myself with six boys, was in one apartment, with oldish girls.

What were the ages of those boys so locked up ?—From 14 to 16.

And what were the ages of the females ?—From 12 to 14.

And you state that they were turned indiscriminately into the same Bothy ?—Yes.

And locked up there all night ?—Yes.

He next got into employment at Birdevy Mill, near Dundee, where he was cardwinder, and where he was more humanely treated. The hours were about fourteen, excluding meals. The next mill he went to was Trolick Mill, three miles from Dundee, where the hours of working were also fourteen, excluding meals; amounting altogether to about fifteen hours' confinement. The next place was Mayfield Mill, about four miles and a half from Dundee, where he was a spinner; his treatment there was harsh—sometimes the hours were sixteen:—

What effect upon the children—the female children more especially—has this long standing to their labour any effect?—It has a great effect. I have observed it at the mill: the feet of the girls have swelled so, that they have been ready to take off their shoes.

Does it occasion positive deformity sometimes?—Yes, very often: the girls become in-knee'd and bow-legg'd.

To a considerable extent?—Yes, to a great extent. I know one girl so bow-legg'd that you could put a chair between her legs.

Has it at all affected you?—Yes; I am very much knock knee'd.

Have you seen one of the witnesses in waiting of the name of Openshaw, a boy?—Yes.

Is there any body that you have witnessed in your neighbourhood that is as strikingly deformed as he is?—A great deal more so—one man that is working now at a mill near Brechin, about twenty miles from Dundee, and who is about thirty years of age. This man does not stand, with his deformity, above four feet six inches high; and, had he been grown to his proper height, I think he would have been about five feet eight or nine. He has been in mills since he was five years old, and he is reduced to that state, that he slides about on a stool to do his work; and though he is about 30 years of age, he can now do no more than a girl's work.

The next mill was Strathmartin, distant only half a mile from the former. Fifteen hours, exclusive of meals, the time. But the overseers were jealous of their knowing the time:—

After the overlooker found I was possessed of a watch I had lost the key, and he took the watch and broke it, and gave it me back, and said I had no use for a watch, and chastised me for letting the hands know the time of day.

Here the boys and girls all slept in one apartment, with a small division, about four feet high, between them. After staying a year and a half there, he endeavoured to get some other employment, but was forced to return back to Duntruin Mill as overlooker. There the system, since he had been away from it, was worse:—

At what time of the morning did you have to attend your labour there?—I have been called up by the master, who stood at the door cursing and swearing, at three o'clock in the morning.

How late in the night were you kept at that work?—We were never less than till ten and eleven o'clock at night.

Were the hands principally young ones at that mill?—Yes; there was a great number of them below twelve.

Were they very poor?—Yes, very poor; the poorest of the poor.

Where did they come from?—Some from the poorhouses in Edinburgh.

Were they sent young?—Yes; they came at six and seven years old.

And they were sent for a stated length of time?—Yes.

For a number of years?—Yes; I know some that were engaged for three and four years.

Were those children worked as long as you have been stating?—Yes.

No exceptions in favour of the younger children and the girls?—Not in the least.

Was that excessive working accompanied by excessive beating?—Yes; very frequently they were beaten; children were not able to stand the work; and if they had made the least fault, they were beaten excessively.

Did you ever hear of any one attempting to escape from that mill?—Yes; there were two girls that made their escape from the mill through the roof of the house, and left nearly all their clothes behind them.

No person, says the commentator on this evidence in the *Chronicle*, will have anything to do with any of the unfortunate wretches so reared, for they are quite helpless. If the females, when grown up, are not ugly, they may find relief in prostitution. The flogging or strapping is continual, and when it happens to be extreme, the overseer is fined:

Did you know any individual brought to trial for inflicting the extreme punishment you have described?—I heard of one; there was an overlooker in Mr. Edwards's mill at West End, Dundee, who was brought before the Justice for licking a girl, and on being examined before the Justice he was fined; but the master returned the fine back to the overlooker, and turned away this girl whom he had struck, and also her sister and two other sisters who were connected with her. Mr. Edwards was questioned about it in the *Advertiser* paper, and he refused to answer. The only reply he made was, that he could do anything he liked with his own, though four or five suffered by that transaction of taking the overseer to justice for that bad usage.

This is not a tithe of the evidence. The sittings of the Committee occupied forty days; and though every body knows how the public business is managed through the agency of these sauntering, lounging, dilatory, or, with reverence be it spoken, *humbug* Committees, many facts were brought to light which make one ashamed of their age and their country. The evidence of the medical men examined shows clearly how the manufacturing system must ultimately, and indeed soon affect the whole population of the British isles. We hope we shall hear no more of those wire-drawn principles of political economy which seek to prevent interference, in a case so glaring as is this. If the regulation of slave-labour, and the education and protection of the Africans, are fitting subjects of legislative interference, the state of the more helpless white slaves of the factories is even more pressing. The negro holds over his owner's humanity the bond of self-interest; but the limited period of service of the white, of which the most must be made, as it is soon to terminate, sets the master above this wholesome influence. The whole system of our regulations is one of direct interference with individuals. A man cannot make a bushel of malt, or sell an ounce of tobacco, nor perform the simplest action, without being liable to direct, and often to senseless and irritating interference; but he must not be interrupted or restrained in his systematic torturing and oppressing, for his private gains, miserable and unprotected children, and leaving them depraved and dwarfed in mind and body, a burden and a curse to the community. It is well said by the *Morning Chronicle* that in reading this evidence, one is almost tempted to wish that machinery, and such places as Leeds and Manchester, had never been heard of.

THE BOURGEOIS OF PARIS—A SKETCH.

It is amusing to compare the Parisian *Bourgeois*, not quite a *Badaud*, with the Cockney citizen of London, or with his counterpart in Scotland, Bailie Jarvie or Provost Pawkie. It is in this class that national distinctions are the most strongly marked: and yet differing so widely in important trifles, how closely they approach in every important particular. An Esquimaux or New Zealander could not perceive any difference.

"The bourgeois of Paris is on the wrong side of forty. Before that age, he had lived under the control of his parents; and this, together with the smallness of his income, the long servitude of his education and apprenticeship, his noviciate in the ways of life, his constant exertions in his business, and his daily apprehensions of being unsuccessful in his yet uncertain establishment, had prevented him from before acquiring that air of decision, that confidence in himself, and that freedom of motion, so necessary to one who assumes the rank of a master tradesman in the city. Besides, a bourgeois of Paris must be a teller of good stories:—it is a condition of his existence, a necessity, and fortunately a pleasure to himself. He owes to his family, his friends, and his customers, an account of all that has occurred for at least thirty years past,—not only in his own neighbourhood, but within those walls which encircle his universe, beyond which he sees only foreign countries. If he has nothing to say about the taking of the Bastile, or the events of Fructidor, Thermidor, or Vendimiaire, he enjoys no power, elicits no respect; and as during that agitation of business which divides his whole time with sleep, the bourgeois of Paris cannot read much, he must trust to what he has seen or heard, must store his head with facts resulting from his emotions of each day, and lay in his stock of events whilst he is spending his years.

The bourgeois of Paris is of moderate stature, and decidedly fat. His countenance is generally smiling, and he seems somewhat ambitious of dignity. His whiskers form a slight curve, ending at the corner of his mouth. He is well shaved, and cleanly dressed. His clothes are large and full, without any affectation of those forms which fashion borrows from caprice. Ignorant painters always put an umbrella into his hand;—but this is a mistake suggested by malevolence and party-spirit. The umbrella belongs to small annuitants and clerks in public offices; that is to say, to the imbeciles of the industrious world. The bourgeois of Paris carries a cane to give himself an air of consequence, to drive away dogs, and to chastise saucy boys. But he fears not the weather. If it rains, he calls a coach, as he takes care to inform you beforehand. You must hear a bourgeois of Paris say, "If it rain, I'll call a coach," to be able to appreciate the satisfaction and security with which the improvement in public conveniences fills the heart of a man who is conscious that he can pay for them.

In spite of gibes and taunts, the bourgeois of Paris married young, as his father and mother did before him. At Paris, more than elsewhere, there always exist a swarm of single men who systematically remain so from taste, reason, constitution, and calculation;—a species of Bedouins, who wage war with conjugal happiness, exist by rapine, live in noise, and die in solitude. When young, they are agreeable dancers, dashing gamesters, hawkers of news and of entertaining anecdotes, until they acquire the honour of exciting jealousy;—when old, they are treated without ceremony, and their greatest piece of good fortune is, now and then at the house of an old friend, to sit at a side-table between the two children, in order to avoid at the other table the fatal number of thirteen.

I must now speak of the bourgeois' wife. She never was handsome, and her features want regularity; but every body has agreed to call her pretty. The effect she produced upon the spectators, the day on which she got out of a glass coach before the door of St. Roch's Church, is by no means forgotten. Her form was then more slender, but she was not more blooming than at present: her husband, on the other hand, was young, active, slim, and wore his hair curled. The marriage ceremony was splendid; there was a gold cross, and crimson velvet chairs, purchased by the churchwardens at the sale of some fallen prince! There was likewise a grand dinner at Grignon's, the entrance to which was in those days through a large court-yard. Few Sundays pass without the husband leading the conversation to some reminiscences of this happy day, during which he displays more than ordinary tenderness towards her whom he congratulates himself every hour upon having married. The bourgeois of Paris respects his wife naturally, or rather instinctively; the most refined study could have taught him nothing better.

Certain gossips have asserted, that the wife of the bourgeois was once a coquet, and that finding years grow apace, she had taken precautions not to attain old age without retaining at least one tender recollection. But what matters this to her husband? If it be true, he is not aware of it. His life has not been troubled; nothing in either his comforts or his habits has been interfered with; and he has never ceased for an instant to retail the old jests of the stage against duped husbands. When he comes home he almost always finds his wife in the house. If he be sometimes obliged to wait for her, she always returns loaded with purchases, among which there is generally something for him. She pours out his barley-water when he has a cold, and is silent whenever he speaks. More than all this,—not only is the wife of the bourgeois the mother of his children, but his privy-counsellor in his business, his partner, and his book-keeper. He does nothing without her advice, and she knows the names of his debtors and of his correspondents. When he is in a merry cue he terms her his Minister of the Interior; and if he be in doubt about the spelling of a word, he applies to her, for she is learned, having been educated at a boarding-school.

We now come to the children. I do not well know the name of his daughter;—there are so many pretty names to be found in novels. She has just left boarding-school; she draws and plays upon the piano: in short, she has learned all that is necessary to forget when she marries, and commences the same obscure and simple mode of life as her mother. The son is called Emile, in honour to the memory of Jean-Jacques Rousseau. There are few families in Paris in which an Emile is not to be found, who has been put out to nurse, led about afterwards by a maid, and then sent for education to a school containing two hundred and nineteen other Emiles. The bourgeois' son is gifted by nature, and has not been neglected. He has both facility and intelligence, and is looked upon as likely, by the prizes he will gain at the annual distribution, to do honour to the school to which he belongs. He is therefore caressed and made much of by his masters. All this increases the bourgeois' happiness. With joy and pride he contemplates the child of his love. He lets him talk, and admires the chattering of the infant pedant, whom he is proud of not being able to comprehend; nor does he resume his authority until the rash boy has thrown himself into the arena of politics. The young dog has a penchant for republicanism, and secretly reads the journals of the *mouvement*, just as we children of the Empire used to read Pigault Lebrun's novels. The reign of Terror is, moreover, a fine opportunity for a display of paternal admonition. When the storm is blown over, Emile's prospects are talked of. Since he is a clever boy, he must be a sworn appraiser; but if this cleverness amount to positive talent, why then he must be an attorney;—for each generation of the bourgeoisie seeks to elevate itself one step higher, and that is the reason why the top of the ladder is so encumbered.

I have already hinted at the bourgeois' politics. In the first place, he loves order—he will have order—and he would put every thing out of place to obtain order. Order, as he understands it, is the easy and regular circulation in the streets, of carriages and foot-passengers; the shops displaying their splendid riches on the outside, and the gas which lights them in the evening, throwing the reflection of its light upon the pavement. Give him these things,—and let him not be stopped by any other groups than those which surround ambulating musicians, or contemplate the last agonies of a dog just run over;—let his ears not be assailed by unusual cries, by the dense clamour of a discontented mob;—let him not fear that a lamp will fall at his feet; —let him not hear the crash of breaking windows, the sinister noise of closing shutters, the retreat beaten at an unusual hour, and the precipitous footsteps of horses—and he is satisfied. Give him but this physical tranquillity, and you, who arrogate to yourselves the direction of public opinion—you, who wish to bring him to your way of thinking—you who want his vote at a public meeting, his signature to a petition, or his voice in a judgment—go all of you to him without fear; reason, attack, traduce, abuse; work boldly in overturning principles and slandering reputations :—he will bear all without anger ! If your period be well rounded, he will adopt it; for he also plays the orator. If your epigram be well pointed, he will repeat it at his own table; for he is also fond of a bon-mot. If you bring him news, he will bet against your word; for he religiously believes in everything that is printed. There is no fear of his detecting disorder in a black coat, whose wearer speaks loud, turns a period well, and affects a pensive air. The disorder which he fears, and against which he would go into the streets with his musket and his knapsack, has naked arms, a hoarse voice, breaks open shops, and throws stones at the municipal guard.

Then the bourgeois of Paris is tenacious of political liberty. It is his property, his personal conquest, and it belongs to his creed. The three syllables forming this word bring a smile upon his lips, and throw an air of proud importance over his whole person. If you point out to him any individual as not being desirous of freedom, he will reply, without hesitation, that such individual must be sent to prison. To preserve this precious right, there are no difficulties, no privations, no sacrifices, to which he would not submit. Persuade him that liberty is in danger, and he will immediately forego his dearest interests, quit his simple and industrious mode of life, his business, and his family, and submit to every possible inconvenience, to guard-house duties, and to all the severity of military discipline. He will be the first to insist that the city gates be closed, houses searched, and suspicious individuals apprehended. He knows that liberty cannot defend itself alone; that it requires the assistance of the police, the activity of a Judge of Instruction, and laws of exception which operate with promptitude and vigour, at a distance as well as near. For the sake of liberty, he becomes a gendarme, a police officer—anything, in short, but an informer. For, take notice, that he holds espionage in abhorrence. In the utmost blindness of his zeal, he would let go a Jesuit to run after a *mouchard*.

Amid the various revolutions which have so often changed the name of his street, the scarf of his municipal officer, the colours of the flag waving over the dome of the clock by which he regulates his watch, the postman's cockade, and the armorial bearings over the snuff shops, he has retained a respect for the constituted authorities. He is therefore puzzled when the newspaper he takes in becomes hostile to the existing government; for he has a great esteem for this journal, is one of its oldest subscribers, regularly takes to its office the amount of his patriotic contribution, and is addressed there by his name. The censure of government by this paper makes him uneasy during the whole day. He thinks, however, that Ministers may have been deceived; that the article in his favourite paper will open their eyes to the truth; and, in this hope, he goes to sleep, reconciled to the administration, and to the Prefect of Police, who will perhaps be dismissed the very next day.

The bourgeois of Paris is an elector, and was so before the law which extended the franchise. This last circumstance he always takes care to state. Whenever the Electoral College of his district is convened, he seems to have suddenly grown a foot taller. There is in his look an expression of pride and mistrust. He suspects every one who approaches him of a design upon his vote. But he has raised an impenetrable rampart round his conscience, against which all friendly recommendations, and all the seductions of intrigue strike and rebound without injury. He reads with attention the declaration of each candidate, takes notes for the purpose of comparing their sentiments and promises; which notes he regularly indorses, and places in a box by themselves. On the day of election he retires to his closet, but without his wife, takes out these papers regularly one after another, and reads as follows:—
"No. 1. M. PETER. Independent. Fortune honourably acquired. Ardent zeal for public liberty. Love of order. Engages to accept no office to which a salary is attached. No. 2. M. PAUL. Fortune honourably acquired. Independent. Engages to accept no office to which a salary is attached. Love of order. Ardent zeal for public liberty." And this goes on to No. 13, which is the last, without any other difference than change of expressions. The bourgeois then goes to the preparatory meeting, and returns more in doubt than ever upon whom he shall fix his choice; for the claims of each candidate, which he had considered so fully and clearly made out, had there been terribly shaken. At length the day arrives, and he returns home satisfied; he has maintained his resolution to the last, and voted according to his conscience—for his vote was lost from being not sufficiently specific.

The bourgeois of Paris is likewise a juryman;—this is another act of his political religion. He prepares himself for a due execution of these functions by reading the Gazette des Tribunaux every day for a fortnight before he is to act. Then, behold him in the jury-box fronting the prisoner. On the first day he suspects both the public prosecutor and the president of the court. He leans upon his elbows, that he may not lose a word uttered by the counsel for the defence. He takes compassion upon pickpockets, and acquits, at once, all those whom want has led to the commission of theft. Next day, he is less tender-hearted—less easily moved. On the last day, he has become a judge more inflexible and more severe than those who professionally occupy the judgment-seat, and whose souls are blunted by their daily contemplation of crime and suffering. On returning home at the end of the session, he has a safety-bolt put upon his doors, and discharges his maid-servant. With regard to political offences, however, his feelings are worked upon in an inverse ratio. At first he fancies society shaken to its very foundations by the party violence of a writer, or the temerity of a caricaturist. He soon becomes accustomed to these things, and they then afford him amusement; and, at the end of the session he carries home the libellous caricature to hang it in his dining-room.

The bourgeois of Paris is one of the national guard. There he stands, soul and body, under the uniform of the soldier-citizen. But he is ambitious of rank. He aspires not indeed to that of captain, which of right devolves upon the notary of the neighbourhood;—for a superstition in favour of notaries still exists in certain parts of Paris. Still less does he elevate his views to the higher grades. They belong to individuals whom the law excuses from ordinary service,—to magistrates and deputies. He is content to be sergeant-major, a rank which forms the just medium between command and obedience. The sergeant-major sleeps at home in his own bed, and this is a great point gained. Besides, he finds a pleasure in seeing all his neighbours, receiving their claims, granting them favours, knowing what excuses they send for non-service, and hunting out those who are refractory. Do not laugh at the sergeant-major;—he is a person of importance; and is besides one of the churchwardens of his parish.

In private life, the bourgeois of Paris is an active and intelligent tradesman. He is not, it is true, a man of bright parts, but he has sufficient intellect to show that he is no fool, and that he knows quite as much as his brethren of Bourdeaux or Rouen. He is, moreover, civil, punctual, and of the most rigid honesty. He has some spare time for pleasure; and he enjoys, but in moderation, all those fascinations which attract strangers to Paris. A public festival, in particular, has marvellous charms for him. The most urgent business, nay, every domestic vexation, must give way to a review, a race, a splendid funeral, or a display of fire-works. He finds some attraction even in a religious procession. The noise, the dust, the heat of the weather, the confusion, the blows of the soldiers, the ebb and flow of the crowd as it is driven backwards and forwards—all this is delightful;—it is a subject of conversation and a source of pleasing recollections to the bourgeois of Paris. And how dearly he loves to bestow a great name upon those individuals who pass on horseback with epaulets and crosses. At the last procession, General Lafayette passed before fifty bourgeois who knew him, and yet he did not leave his house on that day. Among the multitude who look upon these solemnities, great personages are multiplied by numerous copies: each of which some one has seen, and pointed out as the original, to his children, who, in their turn, will talk to their children of having seen the great man.

The bourgeois of Paris is also a lover of the fine arts. He has had his portrait painted, which has, moreover, been sent to the exhibition. Who does not recollect, in the exhibition of 1831, at the place where new pictures, enriched with gothic frames, concealed the old works of Rubens, and next to the tigers of Delacroix, the portrait of a national guard, with a flaxen wig, his cap a little on one side, with a laughing, jovial face, which seemed pleased at being painted? This was a bourgeois of Paris. Honour be to the artist; he did full justice to the character of the original. I would tear what I have written, could I but substitute a copy of this picture; it would enable you to understand the bourgeois of Paris at a single glance.

Among the amusements of the burgeois, I must not forget the play,—although it has lost much of its attractions in his eyes since it aimed at producing emotions of a new kind, too strong for his sensibility if they are serious, and too monstrous for his reason to admit if they are only inventions. Do not expect to find him at the Italian Opera;— he never goes there, because he is determined, when he pays, to understand what is sung. He passes with a sigh before the Theatre Français, like a man of the most refined taste and highly cultivated mind. If the Comic Opera were not so often shut up,* it would be his favourite theatre. He goes there with his whole family four times a year, and from the present state of things, this may constitute him an almost regular frequenter of it. When it is closed, he consoles himself with vaudevilles. The plots of the latter are not, he says, very first-rate,—but then they make him laugh, and that is what he wants. The Gymnase alone startles him a little. The characters there are too rich; one might suppose that the revolution had not yet reached the Boulevard Bonne-Nouvelle. You must not now talk to him of melodramas,—formerly so noble, so pathetic, and so popular, when tyrants wore the the knightly costume, with yellow boots and long beards, and spoke in a deep, hoarse tone—when there were abductions of princesses, and captive lords, and dungeons, and gaolers, and children, and miraculous rescues. The melodrama of the present day disgusts him with its rags, it broad truths, and its slang. He leaves its enjoyments to delicate fine ladies, and to fishwomen—to the low vulgar rabble, and to dandies.

His repugnance is not only one of taste, but it has a higher feeling; he is indignant at the immorality of the thing. The bourgeois of Paris prides himself upon being a moral man, and this pretension constitutes one of his titles,—one of his identical peculiarities. By it he places himself in comparison with his superior in rank and condition, and gives the preference to his own merits. When he says, " I am a moral man," it is with the same feeling of pride and self-esteem, that a noble would display in saying, " I am of high lineage,!'—or a banker, in saying, " I am a rich man."

Perhaps you will ask me whether the bourgeois of Paris is a religious man! What a silly question, when you know he was married in church, and had his children christened. He even approves of his wife going to mass on Sundays. He considers it a good example; and if you press him, he will tell you that religion is necessary to keep the vulgar in awe.

Were I to give current to my thoughts, I should never have done with the bourgeois of Paris. But this is my last word. If you seek a specimen of an ardent mind,—young, enthusiastic, impassioned, capable of great exertion in the pursuit of virtue, or of daring courage in the practice of crime; if you seek one of those boldly-drawn figures, stamped with energy of character, which adorn historical pictures of a high order,—look for them elsewhere—any where but in a city of which Julius Cæsar has spoken, which has so many revolutions to tell of, so many names engraved on its monuments one day, and effaced the next; —resort not for such a purpose to a city where man is stifled in a crowd, and worn down by constant friction. If you require only a good, honest, simple, generous, confiding, and hospitable creature, with one of those peaceable and smiling countenances which look well in a family picture, take the bourgeois of Paris. You may safely trust him with your fortune, your honour, or your secret; and may depend upon him for a kind service, whenever it does not interfere with his dinner-hour. Only I would advise you, if you call upon him the day after an insurrection, not to sit down.

WAGES IN ENGLAND IN THE FOURTEENTH CENTURY.

IN the year 1352, 25th of Edward III., wages paid to haymakers was but a 1d. a-day. A mower of meadows 3d. per day, or 5d. an acre. Reapers of corn, in the first week of August, 2d.—in the second, 4d. per day, and so on till the end of August, without meat, drink, or other allowance, finding their own tools. For thrashing a quarter of wheat or rye, 2½d.; a quarter of barley, beans, pease, and oats, 1½d. A master carpenter, 3d. a-day; other carpenter, 2d. per day. A master mason, 4d. per day; other masons, 3d. per day; and their servants, 1½d. per day. Tilers, 3d., and their knaves, 1½d. Thatchers, 3d. per day, their knaves, 1½d. Plasterers, and other workers of mud walls, and their knaves, in the like manner, without meat or drink, and this from Easter to Michaelmas; and from that time less according to the direction of the justices. By the 34th of Edward III., 1361, chief masters of carpenters and masons, 4d. a-day, and the others, 3d. or 2d. as they were worth. By the 13th of Richard II., 1389, the wages of a bailiff of husbandry, 13s. 4d. per year, and his clothing once a-year at most; the master had 10s.; the carter, 10s.; shepherd, 10s.; ox-herd, 6s. 8d.; cow-herd, 6s. 8d.; swineherd, 6s.; a woman labourer, 6s.; a day labourer, 6s.; a driver of plough, 7s. From this time up to the time of 23d of Henry IV., the price of labour was fixed by the justices by proclamation. In 1445, 23d of Henry IV., the wages of a bailiff of husbandry was 23s. 4d. per annum, and clothing of the price of 5s., with meat and drink; chief hind, carter, or shepherd, 20s.; clothing 4s.; common servant of husbandry, 15s.; clothing, 3s. 4d.; woman servant, 10s.; clothing, 4s.; infant under fourteen years, 6s.; clothing, 3s. Freemason or master carpenter, 4d. per day; without meat or drink, 5¾d. Master tiler or slater, mason or mean carpenter, and other artificers concerned in building, 3d. a-day; without meat and drink, 4½d; every other labourer, 2d a-day; without meat or drink, 3½d.; after Michaelmas to abate in proportion. In time of harvest, a mower 4d. a-day; without meat and drink, 6d.; reaper or carter, 3d. a-day; without meat and drink, 5d.; a woman labourer, and other labourers, 2d. a-day; without meat and drink, 4½d. per day. By the 11th of Henry VII., 1496, there was a like rate of wages, only with a little advance; as, for instance, a freemason, master carpenter, rough mason, bricklayer, master tiler, plumber, glazier, carver, joiner, was allowed from Easter to Michaelmas, to take 4d. a-day; without meat and drink, 6d.; from Michaelmas to Easter to abate 1d. A master having under him six men, was allowed a 1d. a-day extra. By the 8th of Henry VIII., 1515, the wages of shipwrights were fixed

---

* A sad fatality seems to pursue this beautiful theatre. What with law proceedings, bankruptcies, and bad management, it can scarcely ever be kept open for six months in succession.—TR.

as follows :—A master ship-carpenter taking the charge of the work, having men under him, 5d. a-day in the summer season, with meat and drink; other ship carpenter, called a hewer, 4d.; an able clincher, 3d.; holder, 2d.; master calker, 4d.; a mean calker, 3d.; a day labourer by the tide, 4d.

ON THE CULTIVATION OF HEMP.

WE spare our readers, or the few among them that can be immediately interested in studying this subject, any long preface on the advantages of growing hemp, a crop suited to pieces of ground which are generally fit for nothing else, and at once describe the process :—The soils most suited to the culture of this plant, are those of the deep, black, putrid, vegetable kind, which are low, and rather inclined to moisture; and those of a deep, mellow, loamy, sandy description. To render the land proper for the reception of the crop, it should be reduced to a fine state of mould, and clear from weeds by repeated ploughings. In many instances, it will require to be dressed with well-rotted manure. The quantity of seed sown per acre, is from two to three bushels; but, as the crops are greatly injured by standing too closely together, two bushels, or at most two bushels and a-half, will be generally found sufficient. In the choice of seed, care should be taken that it is new, and of a good quality, which is known by its feeling heavy in the hand, and being of a bright and shining colour. The best season for sowing it in the southern districts is, as soon as possible, after the frosts are over in April; and, in the more northern districts, towards the close of the same month, or beginning of May. The most general method of sowing it is broadcast, and, afterwards, covering it by slight harrowing; but when the crops are for seed, drilling it in rows, at small distances, may be advantageous. This sort of crop is frequently cultivated on the same piece of ground, for a great number of years, without any other kind intervening; but, in such cases, manure is required in pretty large proportions. It may be also sown after most sorts of grain. When hemp is sown broadcast, it in general requires no after culture; but, when it is drilled, a hoeing or two will be found advantageous. In the culture of this plant, it is particularly necessary that the same piece of land should contain both male and female, of what is sometimes called frimble hemp; the latter contains the seed. When the crop is ripe, which is known by its becoming of a whitish yellow colour, and a few of the leaves beginning to drop from the stems, which happens generally in about thirteen or fourteen weeks from the period of its being sown, it must be pulled up by the roots, in small parcels at a time, by the hand, taking care to shake off the mould well from them before the handfuls are laid down. In some districts, the whole crop is pulled together; while in others, which is the best practice, the crop is pulled at different times, according to its ripeness. When, however, it is intended for seed, it should be suffered to stand till it is perfectly ripe. After the hemp is pulled, it should be set up in small parcels; and, if for seed, the bundles should be tied up in the same manner as corn, till the seed becomes dry and firm; it must then be either thrashed on cloths in the field, or taken home to the barn. The after management of hemp varies greatly in different places; some only dew-ripen or ret it, whilst others water-ret it. The last process is the best and most expeditious; for, by such process, the grassing is not only shortened, but the more expensive ones of breaking, scratching, and bleaching the yarn, are rendered less violent and troublesome. After having undergone these different operations, it is ready for the purpose of the manufacturer. The produce of hemp-crops is extremely variable—the average is, generally, about five hundred-weight per acre. Hemp, from growing to a great height, and being very shady in the leaf, leaves land in a very clean condition; hence it is sometimes sown for the purpose of destroying weeds, and is an excellent preparation for wheat crops.

A PRODIGY IN PAPER.—At the White Hall Mill, in Derbyshire, a sheet of paper was manufactured last year, which measured 13,800 feet in length, four feet in width, and would cover an acre and a half of ground.

CHURCHES FOR THE RICH.

THE subjoined lines were sent us for publication shortly after an article appeared in the *Schoolmaster*, Number 14, upon places of public worship. They are written by a mechanic, who felt what is described, as he had come to town from a rural parish :—

The churches here, like palaces,
  With grandeur strike the eye;
But they are shut against the poor—
  I need not tell you why.

Pride, Pomp, and Luxury are there
  To mar the solemn scene,—
Exclusive Fashion cannot bear
  The vulgar, poor, and mean.

O Worldly Fashion, Wealth, and Pride!
  Ye wield an iron rod,
And drive your humbler brethren forth,
  Even from the House of God!

But Pride shall fall, and Wealth shall fly,
  And Fashion pass away;
And high and low shall level meet,
  Some not far-distant day.

Now spurned from Christian fellowship,
  I sometimes walk abroad,
And in the distant quiet fields,
  I praise and worship God.

Tho' sometimes down my care-worn cheeks
  The burning tears will fall—
Yet for my bless'd Redeemer's sake
  I do forgive them all.

Misfortunes sad caused me to leave
  The vale where I was born,—
And here, in poverty, I bear
  The rich man's haughty scorn.

My memory oft doth backward glance,
  To where, 'midst foliage green,
The simple pastor's modest manse,
  And parish kirk were seen.

A pastor's name he well deserved,—
  The Father of his flock:
The sad he cheer'd, the poor reliev'd,
  From out his slender stock.

Your parsons here   *   *   *   *

Sometimes some fashionable church
  I enter, as by stealth,
And stand afar off, lest my rags
  Defile the garb of wealth.

I hear—but cannot comprehend,
  That which should simple be :—
Your pompous parson's fine discourse
  Is far too high for me.

With learned phrase he but makes dark
  The word that is divine:
For Truth needs no embellishment
  To make it brighter shine.

Your frothy, flowery eloquence,
  No good it doth impart ;—
The sermon, earnest, solemn, plain,
  Sinks deepest in the heart.

Leave off your haughty arrogance,
  Ye scorners of the poor :—
God's Word should be preached *free* to all,
  And *open'd* each church door.

CONSUMPTION OF GAS IN LONDON.—The gas which lights London is calculated to consume 38,000 chaldrons of coals per annum, lighting 62,000 lamps in shops, houses, &c., and 7500 street lamps. In 1830, the gas pipes in and round London were above 1000 miles in length. Gas lights of half an inch in diameter, supply a light equal to 20 candles; of one inch in diameter, equal to 100; two inches, 420; three inches, to 1000.

RELIGIOUS CAMP MEETING IN AMERICA.

The line of tents is pitched; and the religious city grows up in a few hours under the trees, beside the stream. Lamps are hung in lines among the branches; and the effect of their glare upon the surrounding forest is as of magic. The scenery of the most brilliant theatre in the world is a painting only for children compared with it. Meantime the multitudes, with the highest excitement of social feeling, added to the general enthusiasm of expectation, pass from tent to tent, and interchange apostolic greetings and embraces, and talk of the coming solemnities. Their coffee and tea are prepared, and their supper is finished. By this time the moon, for they take thought to appoint the meeting at the proper time of the moon, begins to shew its disk above the dark summits of the mountains; and a few stars are seen glimmering through the intervals of the branches. The whole constitutes a temple worthy of the grandeur of God. An old man, in a dress of the quaintest simplicity, ascends a platform, wipes the dust from his spectacles, and in a voice of suppressed emotion, gives out the hymn, of which the whole assembled multitude can recite the words, and an air in which every voice can join. We should deem poorly of the heart that would not thrill, as the song is heard, like the "sound of many waters," echoing among the hills and mountains. Such are the scenes, the associations, and such the influence of external things upon a nature so "fearfully and wonderfully" constituted as ours, that little effort is necessary on such a theme as religion, urged at such a place, under such circumstances, to fill the heart and the eyes. The hoary orator talks of God, of eternity, a judgment to come, and all that is impressive beyond. He speaks of his "experiences," his toils and travels, his persecutions and welcomes, and how many he has seen in hope, in peace, and triumph, gathered to their fathers; and when he speaks of the short space that remains to him, his only regret is, that he can no more proclaim, in the silence of death, the mercies of his crucified Redeemer.

There is no need of the studied trick of oratory to produce in such a place the deepest movements of the heart. No wonder, as the speaker pauses to dash the gathering moisture from his own eye, that his audience are dissolved in tears, or uttering the exclamations of penitence. Nor is it cause for admiration that many, who poised themselves on an estimation of higher intellect and a nobler insensibility than the crowd, catch the infectious feeling, and become women and children in their turn; and though they "came to mock, remain to pray."

THE MINISTRY IN THE VALLEY OF THE MISSISSIPPI.

There are stationary preachers in the towns, particularly in Ohio. But in the rural congregations through the western country beyond Ohio, it is seldom that a minister is stationary for more than two months. A ministry of a year in one place may be considered beyond the common duration. Nine-tenths of the religious instruction of the country is given by people who itinerate, and who are, with very few exceptions, notwithstanding all that has been said to the contrary, men of great zeal and sanctity. These earnest men, who have little to expect from pecuniary support, and less from the prescribed reverence and influence which can only appertain to a stated ministry, find, at once, that every thing depends upon the cultivation of popular talents. Zeal for the great cause, mixed, perhaps imperceptibly, with a spice of earthly ambition, and the latent emulation and pride of our natures, and other motives, which unconsciously influence, more or less, the most sincere and the most disinterested, the desire of distinction among their contemporaries and their brethern, and a reaching struggle for the fascination of popularity, goad them on to study all the means and arts of winning the people. Travelling from month to month through dark forests, with such ample time and range for deep thought, as they amble slowly on horseback along their peregrinations, the men naturally acquire a pensive and romantic turn of thought and expression, as we think favourable to eloquence. Hence, the preaching is of a highly popular cast, and its first aim is to excite the feelings. Hence, too, excitements, or in religious parlance, "awakenings," are common in all this region. Living remote, and consigned, the greater part of the time, to the musing loneliness of their condition in the square clearing of the forest, or the prairie; when they congregate on these exciting occasions, society itself is a novelty and an excitement. The people are naturally more sensitive and enthusiastic than in the older countries. A man of rude, boisterous, but native eloquence, rises among these children of the forest and simple nature, with his voice pitched upon the tones, and his utterance thrilling with that awful theme, to which each string of the human heart everywhere responds; and while the woods echo his vehement declamations, his audience is alternately dissolved in tears, awed to profound feeling, or falling in spasms. This country opens a boundless theatre for strong, earnest, and unlettered eloquence; and the preacher seldom has extensive influence, or usefulness, who does not possess some touch of this power.—*Flint's History of the Mississippi Valley.*

RANDOM RECORDS OF RETURNS TO PARLIAMENT.

The House of Commons once reformed,
  I hope will be kept clean:
And sure this won't be very hard,
  Its brace of Broughams between.

The House has lost poor Sadler, with
  His twang so methodistical;
But it has gained Jack Gully, with
  His arguments so-phistical!

Why Cobbett for two places stood,
  Surprise need not awaken:
He got elected for *Old-ham,*
  And so has *sav'd his bacon!*

This session will be very fierce,
  May be pronounced before;
One borough is for *Hasting* Warre,
  And one *Devises* Gore!

The rage of the Aristocrats
  Will certainly wax hotter,
To find their benches filled with Clay,
  With Wedgewood, and a Potter.

Though Petersfield Le-Fevre's sent,
  I hope 'twill be but partial:
The Dutch will tremble when they hear
  That Leeds returned a Marshal!

Alas! I fear that the debates
  Will open cease to be:
At least, whatever questions may
  Be under Locke and Key.

St. *Ives* (of course in schedule *B*)
  Has chosen Mr. Halse:
While Brighton confidently trusts
  That Faithful can't prove *false!*

Fearless the Roebuck sent from Bath,
  May raise his noble front;
For Preston wisely has resolved
  That there shall be no Hunt!

The Commons is a *public*-house:
  The reason why, perhaps,
We meet with Whitbread, Burton, and
  With Philpotts and with Tapps!

The house a perfect Pharisee
  Is growing, I'm afraid;
'Tis true enough that it has Neeld,
  But, query, has it Praed?

How pleasant must the landscape be
  Which Hill and Tower have part in;
And where, while here a Heron soars,
  There swiftly skims a Martin!

Long Wellesley has not re-appeared
  (Perhaps because of sickness;)
But what the house has lost in *length,*
  Has been made up in Thickness!

To compliment our sailor King,
  How zealous are the Whigs:
Besides some first-rates, there's a Hoy,
  A Collier, and a Briggs!

Oh! what a motley mass of men
  From these elections spring!
Upon the self-same bench there sit
  A Carter and a King!

ELEMENTS OF THOUGHT.

VALUE OF LITERARY MEN.

As there is no country where money and gentility are so extravagantly valued, so is there none where talent and science are so ridiculously underrated as in England. In France, in Russia, in most of the states of Germany,—(with the exception of these Islands)—we may say throughout the whole of civilized Europe—a man of genius, a man of knowledge, is a recognised power.

The highest honours are awarded—the most distinguished courtesies are paid him. To be even attached to the *clique* of men of letters, is a rank, a passport into all society—a title which is claimed with a certain degree of pride and assurance. Here, to call a man an author, is to treat him with disrespect. He can have no other claim to distinction if he does not ostentatiously put it forth. Horace Walpole exulted in the idea that he was an Honourable; and Gibbon prided himself on being a country gentleman. We ourselves remember a distinguished, and even talented fine lady, calling Washington Irving " the man who writes the books." Graceful affectation! What is the class rising, and that must rise? What is that class which, as our people become a reading people, will be invested with the popular authority? Before whom, and before what, does the bloated arrogance of a purse-proud, pampered aristocracy quail and shrink into utter nothingness at the present moment? Lo! there is the Press! The press—the thousand-tongued—the Briarean-armed press! Every advance which fashionable indolence ventures to make towards literary activity, is a sign that the man of letters is advancing upon my lord.

A new chivalry is in the field. The nobility of knowledge must become the aristocracy of the epoch. The beautiful theory of St. Simon—for so far, if so far only, is it beautiful—that to the superiority of the mind, which elevates and poetizes power, power should and ought to be conferred—is not yet ripe for realization; but, if we know anything of the future, we know that the two great axioms on which society will work out its new changes are,—the diffusion of power with the diffusion of intelligence—the diffusion of property with the diffusion of power.

LITERATURE IN ENGLAND.—In England, literary men, as a body, have few feelings in common with the great mass of the people. Our literature has been and still is essentially aristocratic; they who write seek their chief applause from aristocratic circles, and derive from thence their chief reward; and so long as a low ambition shall influence their minds, so long will they prove the mere servants of a dominant class. But if, in place of money, a fleeting reputation, and an admittance to fashionable circles, the elevated and honest desire of being a nation's instructors, a hope of raising a popular literature, a literature spreading its wide and paramount and beneficial influence among the whole people, had been the ruling spring of action, and the conscious worth of having contributed to such work had been their sole expected reward, then would the literary men of England have taken their fit station among the literary bodies of Europe, and would no longer have been ranked with the footboys and servile hirelings of an arrogant *noblesse.*—*Westminster Review.*

EDUCATION OF THE PEOPLE.

" Knowledge to be useful must be particular: there must be a *bait*, and he who would pursue a difficult, or even a commonly interesting study, must not be distracted in his pursuit. * * * * I can scarce picture to myself a happier being than he who, with single aim and steady purpose, pursues some chosen study till its difficulties become his toys, and his inventive genius forms them into a new structure, inscribing upon it the indelible characters of his future name. Is the superficial gossiping of what is falsely called general knowledge, to be compared with this? And if this same general knowledge be of so little worth, why exhort mechanics to attain it, who have only and barely time for what is useful?

It becomes necessary, then, if a mechanic would derive benefit from his studies, that they should be directed to a subject somewhat abstract or particular. But will he be able to bestow upon it the undivided, undistracted attention required to ensure success? When he arrives at the most interesting and important point, when he may be said to be fluttering with eagerness, and his heart beats as though he beheld a first-love, his time of leisure is expired, and he must either neglect his employment, which is life to his body, or dash aside the gay vision which is life to his soul. But we will even suppose him to have sufficient ability and courage to set aside or resume his studies at will, without pain and without loss; there will yet be a mighty barrier to pass, unconnected with either his moral ability or courage. When he has arrived at the extent of his little library, want spreads a dreary void before him, and he feels its dismal chill just at the point of time when he has obtained a knowledge of his own ignorance. The book upon which his desires and studies hinge is valuable, and out of reach of his purse—it is scarce, and locked up beyond the reach of his interest. How wistfully he looks upon his labours, useful no more, and therefore no longer interesting, because they cannot be brought to a conclusion! And does his ethereal soul condescend to look wistfully, too, upon the station of those above him, and upon the glittering ore that might fill up that same dreary void. Oh! how he feels the depth, the keenness of his curse! Who shall pourtray a want like this? Come, ye poets, with your vivid personifications, depict me the poor student's want! Want of interest, want of purse, want of friends, want of hope—to want which is to starve."

" The child, in his innocent thirst for knowledge, has asked some question out of the line of duty, because reaching beyond the bounds of ignorance. For this he is singled out for punishment—for example; and he meets it as a freeborn child of nature should do, partly with astonishment and partly with scorn. Compare the red glare of the master with the diamond eye of the scholar, as the former raises his brawny arm in the impotent attempt to quench a living soul. Can you doubt the proof of nobility before you, or question for a moment which is the free and which the slave? The spirit of God is said to have brooded upon the face of the waters, when a living creation sprang from the darkness and the deep. Methinks I see the spirit of oppression brooding over that living creation, to darken what it cannot extinguish, to debase what it cannot destroy."

* * * * *

" Your boy carries the alteration in his very looks. That bright inquisitive eye which was so often turned up to yours is now become vacant, and almost soulless; that ear, once open to your gentlest admonition, is now stupified by harsh, unmeaning threats; that head, once erect in its innocent, unconscious liberty, is now inclined to the abasing curve of real or pretended submission. His feelings are changed, his desires and pleasures are inverted. They were formerly *to* his lessons, they are now *from* them. Fear has assumed the place of hope, and sadness that of joy. When you see the force of habit growing on your boy, and the cowering eye of your soul's darling turned to you, too, as if at once to show you what it was become, and to reproach you with having made it so—oh! it would pierce your heart too much! I do not know the enemy I would curse with such a look from his child."

[The above is from an essay written by *Samuel Downing*, a cabinet-maker in London.]

THE STORY-TELLER.

THE ROSE IN JANUARY.—A GERMAN TALE.
INTRODUCTION.

I HAD the good fortune to become acquainted in his old age with the celebrated Wieland, and to be often admitted to his table. It was there that, animated by a flask of Rhenish, he loved to recount the anecdotes of his youth, and with a gaiety and naïveté which rendered them extremely interesting. His age—his learning—his celebrity—no longer threw us to a distance, and we laughed with him as joyously as he himself laughed in relating the little adventure which I now attempt to relate. It had a chief influence on his life, and it was that which he was fondest of retracing, and retraced with most poignancy. I can well remember his very words; but there are still wanting the expression of his fine countenance—his hair white as snow, gracefully curling round his head—his blue eyes, somewhat faded by years, yet still announcing his genius and depth of thought; his brow touched with the lines of reflection, but open, elevated, and of a distinguished character; his smile full of benevolence and candour. "I was handsome enough," he used sometimes to say to us—and no one who looked at him could doubt it; "but I was not amiable, for a *savant* rarely is," he would add laughingly, and this every one doubted; so to prove it, he recounted the little history that follows.

"I was not quite thirty," said he to us, "when I obtained the chair of philosophical professor in this college in the most flattering manner: I need not tell you that my *amour propre* was gratified by a distinction rare enough at my age. I certainly had worked for it formerly; but at the moment it came to me, another species of philosophy occupied me much more deeply, and I would have given more to know what passed in one heart, than to have had power to analyse those of all mankind. I was passionately in love: and you all know, I hope, that when love takes possession of a young head, adieu to every thing else; there is no room for any other thought. My table was covered with folios of all colours, quires of paper of all sizes, journals of all species, catalogues of books, in short, of all that one finds on a professor's table; but of the whole circle of science I had for some time studied only the article *Rose*, whether in the Encyclopedia, the botanical books, or all the gardeners' calendars that I could meet with; you shall learn presently what led me to this study, and why it was that my window was always open, even during the coldest days. All this was connected with the passion by which I was possessed, and which was become my sole and continual thought. I could not well say at this moment how my lectures and courses got on, but this I know, that more than once I have said 'Amelia,' instead of 'philosophy.'

"It was the name of my beauty—in fact, of the beauty of the University, Mademoiselle de Belmont. Her father, a distinguished officer, had died on the field of battle. She occupied with her mother a large and handsome house in the street in which I lived, on the same side, and a few doors distant. This mother, wise and prudent, obliged by circumstances to inhabit a city filled with young students from all parts, and having so charming a daughter, never suffered her a moment from her sight either in or out of doors. But the good lady passionately loved company and cards; and to reconcile her tastes with her duties, she carried Amelia with her to all the assemblies of dowagers, professors' wives, canonesses, &c. &c., where the poor girl *ennuyed* herself to death with hemming or knitting beside her mother's card-table. But you ought to have been informed, that no student, indeed no man under fifty, was admitted. I had then but little chance of conveying my sentiments to Amelia. I am sure, however, that any other than myself would have discovered this chance, but I was a perfect novice in gallantry; and, until the moment when I imbibed this passion from Amelia's beautiful dark eyes, mine having been always fixed upon volumes of Latin, Greek, Hebrew, Chaldaic, &c. &c., understood nothing at all of the language of the heart. It was at an old lady's, to whom I was introduced, that I became acquainted with Amelia; my destiny led me to her house on the evening of her assembly; she received me; I saw Mademoiselle de Belmont, and from that instant her image was engraven in lines of fire on my heart. The mother frowned at the sight of a well-looking young man; but my timid, grave, and perhaps somewhat pedantic air, re-assured her. There were a few other young persons—daughters and nieces of the lady of the mansion; it was summer—they obtained permission to walk in the garden, under the windows of the saloon, and the eyes of their mammas. I followed them; and, without daring to address a word to my fair one, caught each that fell from her lips.

"Her conversation appeared to me as charming as her person; she spoke on different subjects with intelligence above her years. In making some pleasant remarks on the defects of men in general, she observed, that 'what she most dreaded was violence of temper.' Naturally of a calm disposition, I was wishing to boast of it; but not having the courage, I at last entered into her idea, and said so much against passion, that I could not well be suspected of an inclination to it. I was recompensed by an approving smile; it emboldened me, and I began to talk much better than I thought myself capable of doing before so many handsome women. She appeared to listen with pleasure; but when they came to the chapter of fashions, I had no more to say—it was an unknown language; neither did she appear versed in it. Then succeeded observations on the flowers in the garden; I knew little more of this than of the fashions, but I might likewise have my particular taste; and to decide, I waited to learn that of Amelia: she declared for the *Rose*, and grew animated in the eulogy of her chosen flower. From that moment, it became for me the queen of flowers. 'Amelia,' said a pretty, little, laughing *Espiègle*, 'how many of your favourites are condemned to death this winter?' 'Not one,' replied she; 'I renounce them—their education is too troublesome, and too ungrateful a task, and I begin to think I know nothing about it.'

"I assumed sufficient resolution to ask the explanation of this question and answer: she gave it to me. 'You have just learned that I am passionately fond of *Roses*; it is an hereditary taste; my mother is still fonder of them than I am. Since I was able to think of any thing, I have had the greatest wish to offer her a *Rose-tree* in blow (as a new year's gift) on the first of January. I have never succeeded. Every year I have put a quantity of rose-trees into vases; the greater number perished; and I have never been able to offer one rose to my mother.' So little did I know of the culture of flowers, as to be perfectly ignorant that it was possible to have roses in winter; but from the moment I understood that it might be, without a miracle, and that incessant attention only was necessary, I promised myself, that this year the first of January should not pass without Amelia's offering her mother a rose-tree in blow. We returned to the saloon; so close was I on the watch, that I heard her ask my name in a whisper. Her companion answered, 'I know him only by reputation; they say he is an author; and so learned, that he is already a professor.' 'I should never have guessed it,' said Amelia; 'he seems neither vain nor pedantic.' How thankful was I for this reputation. Next morning I went to a gardener, and ordered fifty rose-trees, of different months, to be put in vases. 'It must be singular ill fortune,' thought I, 'if, among this number, one at least does not flower.' On leaving the gardener I went to my bookseller's, purchased some works on flowers, and returned home full of hope. I intended to accompany my rose-tree with a fine letter, in which I should request to be permitted to visit Madame de Belmont, in order to teach her daughter the art of having roses in winter; the agreeable lesson, and the charming scholar, were to me much pleasanter themes than those of my philosophical lectures. I built on all this the prettiest romance possible; my milk-pail had not yet got on so far as *Perette's*; she held it on her head; and my rose was not yet transplanted into its vase; but I saw it all in blow. In the meantime, I was happy only in imagination; I no longer saw Amelia; they ceased to invite me to the dowager parties, and she was not allowed to mix in those of young people. I must then be restricted, until my introducer was in a state of presentation, to seeing her every evening pass by with her mother, as they went to their parties. Happily for me, Madame de Belmont was such a coward in a carriage, that she preferred walking when it was possible. I knew the hour at which they were in the habit of leaving home; I learned to distinguish the sound of the bell of their gate, from that of all the others of the quarter; my window on the ground floor was always open; at the moment I heard their gate unclose, I snatched up some volume, which was often turned upside down, stationed myself at the window, as if profoundly occupied with my study, and thus almost every day saw for an instant the lovely girl, and this instant was sufficient to attach me to her still more deeply. The elegant simplicity of her dress; her rich, dark hair, wreathed round her head, and falling in ringlets on her forehead; her slight and graceful figure—her step at once light and commanding—the fairy foot that the care of guarding the snowy robe rendered visible, inflamed my admiration; while her dignified and composed manner, her attention to her mother, and the affability with which she saluted her inferiors, touched my heart yet more. I began too, to fancy, that, limited as were my opportunities of attracting her notice, I was not entirely indifferent to her. For example, on leaving home, she usually crossed to the opposite side of the street; for had she passed close to my windows, she guessed, that, intently occupied as I chose to appear, I could not well raise my eyes from my book; then as she came near my house, there was always something to say, in rather a louder tone, as 'Take care, mamma; lean heavier on me; do you feel cold?' I then raised my eyes, looked at her, saluted her, and generally encountered the transient glance of my divinity, who, with a blush, lowered her eyes, and returned my salute. The mother, all enveloped in cloaks and hoods, saw nothing. I saw every thing—and surrendered my heart. A slight circumstance augmented my hopes. I had published 'An Abridgement of Practical Philosophy.' It was an extract from my course of lectures—was successful, and the edition was sold. My bookseller, aware that I had some copies remaining, came to beg one for a customer of his, who was extremely anxious to get it; and he named Mademoiselle Amelia de Belmont. I actually blushed with pleasure; to conceal my embarrassment, I laughingly inquired, what could a girl of her age want with so serious a work? 'To read it, sir,—doubtless;' replied the bookseller; 'Mademoiselle Amelia does not resemble the generality of young ladies; she prefers useful to amusing books.' He then mentioned the names of several that he had lately sent to her; and they gave me a high opinion of her taste. 'From her impatience for your book,' added he, 'I can answer for it, that it will be perused with great pleasure; more than ten messages have been sent; at last, I promised it for to-morrow, and I beg of you to enable me to keep my word.' I thrilled with joy, as I gave him the volumes, at the idea that Amelia would read and approve of my sentiments, and that she would learn to know me.

"October arrived, and with it my fifty vases of rose-trees; for which, of course, they made me pay what they chose; and I was as delighted to count them in my room, as a miser would his sacks of gold. They all looked rather languishing, but then it was because they had not yet reconciled themselves to the new earth. I read all that was ever written on the culture of roses, with much more attention than I had formerly read my old philosopers; and I ended as wise I began. I perceived that this science, like all others, has no fixed rules, and that each vaunts his system, and believes it the best. One of my gardener authors would have the rose-trees, as much as possible in the open air; another recommended their being kept close shut up; one ordered constant watering; another absolutely forbade it. 'It is thus with the education of man,' said I, closing the volumes in vexation. 'Always in extremes—always for exclusive systems—let us try the medium between these opposite opinions.' I established a good thermometer in my room; and, according to its indications, I put them outside the windows, or took them in; you may guess that fifty vases, to which I gave this exercise three or four times a day, according to the variations of the atmosphere, did not leave me much idle time; and this was the occupation of a professor of philosophy! Ah! well might they have taken his chair from him, and sent him back to school; to school, a thousand times more childish than the youngest of those pupils to whom I hurried over the customary routine of philosophical lessons; my whole mind was fixed on Amelia and my rose-trees.

"The death of the greater number of my élèves, however, soon lightened my labour; more than half of them never struck root. I flung them into the fire: a fourth part of those that remained, after unfolding some little leaves, stopped there. Several assumed a blackish yellow tint, and gave me hope of beautifying; some flourished surprisingly, but only in leaves; others, to my great joy, were covered with buds; but in a few days they always got that little yellow circle which the gardeners call the collar, and which is to them a mortal malady—their stalks twisted—they drooped—and finally fell, one after the other, to the earth—not a single bud remaining on my poor trees. Thus withered my hopes; and the more care I took of my invalids—the more I hawked them from window to window, the worse they grew. At last, one of them, and but one, promised to reward my trouble—thickly covered with leaves, it formed a handsome bush, from the middle of which sprang out a fine, vigorous branch crowned with six beautiful buds that got no collar—grew, enlarged, and even discovered, through their calices, a slight rose tint. There were still six long weeks before the new year; and, certainly, four, at least, of my precious buds would be blown by that time. Behold me now recompensed for all my pains; hope re-entered my heart, and every moment I looked on my beauteous introducer with complacency.

"On the 27th of November, a day which I can never forget, the sun rose in all its brilliance; I thanked Heaven, and hastened to place my rose-tree, and such of his companions as yet survived, on a peristyle in the court. (I have already mentioned that I lodged on the ground floor.) I watered them, and went, as usual, to give my philosophical lecture. I then dined—drank to the health of my men; and returned to take my station in my window, with a quicker throbbing of the heart.

"Amelia's mother had been slightly indisposed; for eight days she had not left the house, and consequently I had not seen my fair one. On the first morning I had observed the physician going in; uneasy for her, I contrived to cross his way, questioned him, and was comforted. I afterwards learned that the old lady had recovered, and was to make her appearance abroad on this day at a grand gala given by a Baroness, who lived at the end of the street. I was then certain to see Amelia pass by, and eight days of privation had enhanced that thought; I am sure Madame de Belmont did not look to this party with as much impatience as I did. She was always one of the first; it had scarcely struck five, when I heard the bell of her gate. I took up a book,—there was I at my post, and presently I saw Amelia appear, dazzling with dress and beauty, as she gave her arm to her mother; never yet had the brilliancy of her figure so struck me; this time there was no occasion for her to speak to catch my eyes; they were fixed on her, but hers were bent down; however, she guessed that I was there, for she passed slowly to prolong my happiness. I followed her with my gaze, until she entered the house; then only she turned her head for a second; the door was shut, and she disappeared, but remained present to my heart. I could neither close my window, nor cease to look at the Baroness's hotel, as if I could see Amelia through the walls; I remained there till all objects were fading into obscurity—the approach of night, and the frostiness of the air, brought to my recollection that the rose-tree was still on the peristyle; never had it been so precious to me; I hastened to it; and scarcely was I in the anti-chamber, when I heard a singular noise, like that of an animal browsing, and tinkling its bells. I trembled, I flew, and I had the grief to find a sheep quietly fixed beside my rose-trees, of which it was making its evening repast with no slight avidity.

"I caught up the first thing in my way; it was a heavy cane; I wished to drive away the gluttonous beast; alas! it was too late; he had just bitten off the beautiful branch of buds; he swallowed them one after another; and, in spite of the gloom, I could see, half out of his mouth, the finest of them all, which in a moment was champed like the rest. I was neither ill-tempered nor violent; but at this sight I was no longer master of myself. Without well knowing what I did, I discharged a blow of my cane on the animal, and stretched it at my feet. No sooner did I perceive it motionless, than I repented of having killed a creature unconscious of the mischief it had done; was this worthy of the professor of philosophy, the adorer of the gentle Amelia; But thus to eat up my rose-tree, my only hope to get admittance to her! When I thought on its annihilation, I could not consider myself so culpable. However, the night darkened; I heard the old servant crossing the lower passage, and I called her. 'Catherine,' said I 'bring your light; there is mischief here, you left the stable door open, (that of the court was also unclosed,) one of your sheep has been browsing on my rose-trees, and I have punished it.'

"She soon came with the lanthorn in her hand. 'It is not one of our sheep,' said she; 'I have just come from them, the stable gate is shut, and they are all within. Oh, blessed saints! blessed saints! What do I see!'.......... exclaimed she when near, 'it is the pet sheep of our neighbour Mademoiselle Amelia de Belmont. Poor Robin! what bad luck brought you here? Oh! how sorry she will be.' I nearly dropt down beside Robin. 'Of Mademoiselle Amelia?' said I, in a trembling voice, 'has she actually a sheep?' 'Oh! good Lord! no, she has none at this moment—but that which lies there with its four legs up in the air; she loved it as herself; see the collar that she worked for it with her own hands.' I bent to look at it. It was of red leather, ornamented with little bells, and she had embroidered on it in gold thread—'Robin belongs to Amelia de Belmont; she loves him, and begs that he may be restored to her.' 'What will she think of the barbarian who killed him in a fit of passion; the vice that she most detests; she is right, it has been fatal to her. Yet if he should be only stunned by the blow: Catherine! run, ask for some æther, or Eau de Vie, or hartshorn,—run, Catherine, run.'

"Catherine set off; I tried to make it open his mouth; my rose-bud was still between its hermetically-sealed teeth; perhaps the collar pressed it; in fact the throat was swelled. I got it off with difficulty; something fell from it at my feet, which I mechanically took up and put into my pocket without looking at it, so much was I absorbed in anxiety for the resuscitation. I rubbed him with all my strength; I grew more and more impatient for the return of Catherine. She came with a small phial in her hand, calling out in her usual manner, 'Here, sir, here's the medicine. I never opened my mouth about it to Mademoiselle Amelia; I pity her enough without that.'

"'What is all this, Catherine? where have you seen Mademoiselle Amelia? and what is her affliction, if she does not know of her favourite's death?' 'Oh, sir, this is a terrible day for the poor young lady. She was at the end of the street searching for a ring which she had lost, and it was no trifle, but the ring that her dead father had got as a present from the Emperor, and worth, they say, more ducats than I have hairs on my head. Her mother lent it to her to-day for the party; she has lost it, she knows neither how nor where, and never missed it till she drew off her glove at supper. And, poor soul! the glove was on again in a minute, for fear it should be seen that the ring was wanting, and she slipped out to search for it all along the street, but she has found nothing.'

"It struck me, that the substance that had fallen from the sheep's collar had the form of a ring; could it possibly be! I looked at it: and, judge of my joy, it was Madame de Belmont's ring, and really very beautiful and costly. A secret presentiment whispered to me that this was a better means of presentation than the rose-tree. I pressed the precious ring to my heart, and to my lips; assured myself that the sheep was really dead; and, leaving him stretched near the devastated rose-trees, I ran into the street, dismissed those who were seeking in vain, and stationed myself at my door to await the return of my neighbours. I saw from a distance the flambeaux that preceded them, quickly distinguished their voices, and comprehended by them that Amelia had confessed her misfortune. The mother scolded bitterly; the daughter wept, and said, 'Perhaps it may be found.' 'Oh, yes, perhaps,' replied the mother with irritation, 'it is too rich a prize to him who finds it; the Emperor gave it to your deceased father on the field when he saved his life; he set more value on it than on all that he possessed besides, and now you have thus flung it away; but the fault is mine for having trusted you with it. For some time back you have seemed quite bewildered.' I heard all this as I followed at some paces behind them; they reached home, and I had the cruelty to prolong, for some moments more, Amelia's mortification. I intended that the treasure should procure me the entrée of their dwelling, and I waited till they had got up stairs. I then had myself announced as the bearer of good news; I was introduced, and respectfully presented the ring to Madame de Belmont; and how delighted seemed Amelia! and how beautifully she brightened in her joy, not alone that the ring was found, but that I was the finder. She cast herself on her mother's bosom, and turning on me her eyes, humid with tears, though beaming with pleasure, she clasped her hands, exclaiming, 'Oh, sir, what obligation, what gratitude do we not owe to you!'

"'Ah Mademoiselle!' returned I, 'you know not to whom you address the term gratitude.' 'To one who has conferred on me a great pleasure,' said she. 'To one who has caused you a serious pain, to the killer of Robin.'

"'You, sir?—I cannot credit it—why should you do so? you are not cruel.'

"'No, but I am so unfortunate. It was in opening his collar, which I have also brought to you, that your ring fell on the ground—you promised a great recompense to him who should find it. I dare to solicit that recompense; grant me my pardon for Robin's death.'

"'And I, sir, I thank you for it,' exclaimed the mother; 'I never could endure that animal; it took up Amelia's entire time, and wearied me out of all patience with its bleating; if you had not killed it, Heaven knows where it might have carried my diamond. But how did it get entangled in the collar? Amelia, pray explain all this.'

"Amelia's heart was agitated; she was as much grieved that it was I who had killed Robin, as that he was dead— Poor Robin,' said she, drying a tear, 'he was rather too fond of running out; before leaving home I had put on his collar, that he might not be lost—he had always been brought back to me. The ring must have slipped under his collar. I hastily drew on my glove, and never missed it till I was at supper.'

"'What good luck it was that he went straight to this gentleman's,' observed the mother.

"'Yes—for you, said Amelia; he was cruelly received— was it such a crime, sir, to enter your door?'

"'It was night,' I replied; 'I could not distinguish the collar, and I learned, when too late, that the animal belonged to you.',

"'Thank Heaven, then, you did not know it!' cried the mother, ' er where would have been my ring?'

"'It is necessary at least,' said Amelia, with emotion, 'that I should learn how my favourite could have so cruelly chagrined you.'

"'Oh, Mademoiselle, he had devoured my hope, my hope, my happiness, a superb rose-tree about to blow, that I had been long watching, and intended to present—to—to —a person on New Year's Day.' Amelia smiled, blushed, extended her lovely hand towards me, and murmured— 'All is pardoned.' 'If it had eaten up a rose-tree about to blow,' cried out Madame de Belmont, 'it deserved a thousand deaths. I would give twenty sheep for a rose-tree in blow.' 'And I am much mistaken,' said Amelia, with the sweetest naïveté, ' if this very rose-tree was not intended for you.' ' For me! you have lost your senses, child; I have not the honour of knowing the gentleman.' ' But he knows your fondness for roses; I mentioned it one day before him, the only time I ever met him, at Madame de S's. Is it not true, sir, that my unfortunate favourite had eaten up my mother's rose-tree?' I acknowledged it, and I related the course of education of my fifty rose-trees.

"Madame de Belmont laughed heartily, and said 'she owed me a double obligation.' ' Mademoiselle Amelia has given me my recompense for the diamond,' said I to her; ' I claim yours also, madam.' ' Ask, sir,—' ' Permission to pay my respects sometimes to you!' ' Granted,' replied she, gaily; I kissed her hand respectfully, that of her daughter tenderly, and withdrew. But I returned the next day—and every day—I was received with a kindness that each visit increased—I was looked on as one of the family. It was I who now gave my arm to Madame de Belmont to conduct her to the evening parties, she presented me as her friend, and they were no longer dull to her daughter. New Year's Day arrived. I had gone the evening before to a sheepfold in the vicinity to purchase a lamb similar to that I had killed. I collected from the different hot-houses all the flowering rose-trees I could find; the finest of them was for Madam de Belmont; and the roses of the others were wreathed in a garland round the fleecy neck of the lamb. In the evening I went to my neighbours, with my presents. ' Robin and the rose-tree are restored to life,' said I, in offering my homage, which was received with sensibility and gratefulness. ' I also should like to give you a New Year's gift,' said Madame de Belmont to me, ' if I but knew what you would best like.' ' What I best like— ah, if I only dared to tell you.' ' If it should chance now to be my daughter—' I fell at her feet, and so did Amelia. ' Well, said the kind parent, ' there then are your New Year's gifts ready found: Amelia gives you her heart, and I give you her hand.' She took the rose wreath from off the lamb, and twined it round our united hands. And my Amelia,' continued the old professor, as he finished his anecdote, passing an arm round his companion as she sat beside him, ' my Amelia is still to my eyes as beautiful, and to my heart as dear, as on the day when our hands were bound together with a chain of flowers'."

A WINTER SKETCH.—THE CARPENTER'S DAUGHTER.

BY MISS MITFORD.

Next door lives a carpenter "famed ten miles round, and worthy all his fame,"—few cabinet-makers surpass him, with his excellent wife, and their little daughter Lizzy, the plaything and queen of the village, a child three years old according to the register, but six in size, strength, and intellect, in power and in self-will. She manages every body in the place, her schoolmistress included; turns the wheeler's children out of their own little cart, and makes them draw her; seduces cakes and lollipops from the very shop window; makes the lazy carry her, the silent talk to her, the grave romp with her; does any thing she pleases; is absolutely irresistible. Her chief attraction lies in her exceeding power of loving, and her firm reliance on the love and indulgence of others. How impossible it would be to disappoint the dear little girl when she runs to meet you, slides her pretty hand into yours, looks up gladly in your face, and says, "Come!"—You must go; you cannot help it. Another part of her charm is her singular beauty. Together with a good deal of the character of Napoleon, she has something of his square, sturdy, upright form, with the finest limbs in the world, a complexion purely English, a round laughing face, sunburnt and rosy, large merry blue eyes, curling brown hair, and a wonderful play of countenance. She has the imperial attitudes too, and loves to stand with her hands behind her, or folded over her bosom; and sometimes, when she has a little touch of shyness, she clasps them together on the top of her head, pressing down her shining curls, and looking so exquisitely pretty! Yes, Lizzy is queen of the village!

FROST.

January, 23d.—At noon to-day, I and my white greyhound, May-flower, set out for a walk into a very beautiful world,—a sort of silent fairy-land,—a creation of that matchless magician the hoar-frost. There had been just snow enough to cover the earth and all its colours with one sheet of pure and uniform white, and just time enough since the snow had fallen to allow the hedges to be freed of their fleecy load, and clothed with a delicate coating of rime. The atmosphere was deliriously calm; soft, even mild, in spite of the thermometer; no perceptible air, but a stillness that might almost be felt: the sky, rather grey than blue, throwing out in bold relief the snow-covered roofs of our village, and the rimy trees that rise above them, and the sun shining dimly as through a veil, giving a pale fair light, like the moon, only brighter. There was a silence, too, that might become the moon, as we stood at our little gate looking up the quiet street; a sabbath-like pause of work and play, rare on a work-day; nothing was audible but the pleasant hum of frost, that low monotonous sound which is perhaps the nearest approach that life and nature can make to absolute silence. The very waggons, as they come down the hill along the beaten track of crisp yellowish frost-dust, glide along like shadows; even May's bounding footsteps, at her height of glee and of speed, fall like snow upon snow.

But we shall have noise enough presently; May has stopped at Lizzy's door: and Lizzy, as she sat on the window-sill, with her bright rosy face laughing through the casement, has seen her and disappeared. She is coming. No! The key is turning in the door, and sounds of evil omen issue through the key-hole—sturdy "Let me out," and "I will go," mixed with shrill cries on May and on me from Lizzy, piercing through a low continuous harangue, of which the prominent parts are apologies, chilbains, sliding, broken bones, lollypops, rods, and ginger-bread, from Lizzy's careful mother. "Don't scratch the door, May! Don't roar so, my Lizzy! We'll call for you as we come back."—"I'll go now! Let me out! I will go!" are the last words of Miss Lizzy. Mem. Not to spoil that child—if I can help it. But I do think her mother might have let the poor soul walk with us to-day. Nothing worse for children than coddling. Nothing better for chilbains than exercise. Besides, I don't believe she has any; and, as to breaking her bones in sliding, I don't suppose there's a slide on the common. These murmuring cogitations have brought us up the hill, and half-way across the light and airy common, with its bright expanse of snow and its cluster of cottages, whose turf fires send such wreaths of smoke sailing up the air, and diffuse such aromatic fragrance around. And now comes the delightful sound of childish voices, ringing with glee and merriment also from beneath our feet. Ah, Lizzy, your mother was right! They are shouting from that deep irregular pool, all glass now, where, on two long, smooth, liny slides, half-a-dozen ragged urchins are slipping along in tottering triumph. Half-a-dozen steps brings us to the bank right above them. May can hardly resist the temptation of joining her friends; for most of the varlets are of her acquaintance, especially the rogue who leads the slide,—he with the brimless hat, whose bronzed complexion and white flaxen hair, reversing the usual lights and shadows of the human countenance, give so strange and foreign a look to his flat and comic features. This hobgoblin, Jack Rapley by name, is May's great crony; and she stands on the brink of the steep irregular descent, her black eyes fixed full upon him, as if she intended him the favour of jumping on his head. She does; she is down, and upon him: but Jack Rapley is not easily to be knocked off his feet. He saw her coming, and in the moment of her leap sprang dexterously off the slide on the rough ice, steadying himself by the shoulder of the next in the file, which unlucky follower, thus expectedly checked in his career, fell plump backwards, knocking down the rest of the line like a nest of card-houses. There is no harm done; but there they lie roaring, kicking, sprawling, in every attitude of comic distress, whilst Jack Rapley and Mayflower, sole authors of this calamity, stand apart from the throng, fondling and coquetting, and complimenting each other, and very visibly laughing, May in her black eyes, Jack in his wide close-shut mouth, and his whole monkey-face, at their comrades' mischances. I think, Miss May, you may as well come up again, and leave Master Rapley to fight your battles. He'll get out of the scrape. He is a rustic wit—a sort of Robin Goodfellow—the sauciest, idlest, cleverest, best-natured boy in the parish; always foremost in mischief, and always ready to do a good turn. The sages of our village predict sad things of Jack Rapley, so that I am sometimes a little ashamed to confess, before wise people, that I have a lurking predilection for him, (in common with other naughty ones,) and that I like to hear him talk to May almost as well as she does. "Come May!" and up she springs, as light as a bird. The road is gay now; carts and post-chaises, and girls in red cloaks, and, afar off, looking almost like a toy, the coach. It meets us fast and soon. How much happier the walkers look than the riders—especially the frost-bitten gentleman, and the shivering lady with the invisible face, sole passengers of that commodious machine! Hooded, veiled, and bonneted, as she is, one sees from her attitude how miserable she would look uncovered.

Another pond, and another noise of children. More sliding? Oh! no. This is a sport of higher pretension. Our good neighbour, the lieutenant, skaiting, and his own pretty little boys, and two or three other four-year-old elves, standing on the brink in an ecstacy of joy and wonder! Oh, what happy spectators! And what a happy performer! They admiring, he admired, with an ardour and sincerity never excited by all the quadrilles and the spread-eagles of the Seine and the Serpentine. He really skaits well, though, and I am glad I came this way; for, with all the father's feelings sitting gaily at his heart, it must still gratify the pride of skill to have one spectator at that solitary pond who has seen skaiting before.

Now we have reached the trees,—the beautiful trees never so beautiful as to-day. Imagine the effect of a straight and regular double avenue of oaks, nearly a mile long, arching over head, and closing into perspective like the roof and columns of a cathedral, every tree and branch encrusted with the bright and delicate congelation of hoar frost, white and pure as snow, delicate and defined as carved ivory. How beautiful it is, how uniform, how various, how filling, how satiating to the eye and to the mind!—above all, how melancholy! There is a thrilling awfulness, an intense feeling of simple power in that naked and colourless beauty, which falls on the heart like the thought of death —death pure, and glorious, and smiling,—but still death. Sculpture has always the same effect on my imagination, and painting never: Colour is life.—We are now at the end of this magnificent avenue, and at the top of a steep eminence commanding a wide view over four counties—a landscape of snow. A deep lane leads abruptly down the hill; a mere narrow cart-track, sinking between high banks, clothed with fern, and furze, and low broom, crowned with luxuriant hedgerows, and famous for their summer smell of thyme. How lovely these banks are now!—the tall weeds and the gorse fixed and stiffened in the hoar frost, which fringes round the bright prickly holly, the pendant foliage of the bramble, and the deep orange leaves of the pollard oaks! Oh, this is rime in its loveliest form! And there is still a berry here and there on the holly, "blushing in its natural coral" through the delicate tracery; still a stray hip or haw for the birds, who abound here always. The poor birds, how tame they are, how sadly tame! There is the beautiful and rare crested wren, "that shadow of a bird," as White of Selbourne calls it, perched in the middle of the hedge, nestling as it were amongst the cold bare boughs, seeking, poor pretty thing, for the warmth it will not find. And there, farther on, just under the bank, by the slender runlet, which still trickles between its transparent fantastic margin of thin ice, as if it were a thing of life,—there, with a swift scudding motion, flits, in short low flights, the gorgeous kingfisher, its magnificent plumage of scarlet and blue flashing in the sun, like the glories of some tropical bird. He is come for water to this little spring by the hill-side,—water which even his long bill and slender head can hardly reach, so nearly do the fantastic forms of those garland-like icy margins meet over the tiny stream beneath. It is rarely that one sees the shy beauty so close or so long; and it is pleasant to see him in the grace and beauty of his natural liberty, the only way to look at a bird. We used, before we lived in a street, to fix a little board outside the parlour-window, and cover it with bread-crumbs in the hard weather. It was quite delightful to see the pretty things come and feed, to conquer their shyness, and do away their mistrust. First came the more social tribes, "the robin red-breast and the wren," cautiously, suspiciously, picking up a crumb on the wing, with the little keen bright eye fixed on the window; then they would stop for two pecks: then stay till they were satisfied. The shyer birds, tamed by their example, came next; and at last one saucy fellow of a blackbird—a sad glutton, he would clear the board in two minutes—used to tap his yellow bill against the window for more. How we loved the fearless confidence of that fine, frank-hearted creature! And surely he loved us. I wonder the practice is not more general.— "May! May! naughty May!" She has frightened away the kingfisher; and now, in her coaxing penitence, she is covering me with snow.

A SINGULAR STORY.

A chieftain, whose large estates were forfeited in the rebellion of 1715, received at St. Germains, from the confidential agent of a powerful nobleman, intelligence that his grace had obtained a grant of the lands from government, and would make them over to the young heir, on condition of paying an annual feu-duty, and a sum in ready cash, much less than the value of the domains. To restore his hereditary estate to the heir, and to ensure a respectable provision for his lady and ten younger children, the chieftain would have laid down his life with alacrity. He made every possible exertion; all his friends, and even the exiled Prince, contributed in raising the amount demanded. He was known to be a man of scrupulous honour; and when the family regained this estate, they relied upon the lady making remittances to pay the loan by instalments. Securely to convey the ransom of his late property, the chieftain resolved to hazard liberty and life, by venturing to the kingdom from whence he was expatriated. He found means to appoint at Edinburgh a meeting with his lady, directing her to lodge at the house of a clansman, in the Luckenbooths. On arriving there, she would easily comprehend why he recommended a retreat so poor. The lady set out on horseback unattended, leaving her children to the care of her mother-in-law. In those times such a journey was more formidable than now appears an overland progress to India. To the lady it would have cost many fears, even if her palfrey was surrounded by running footmen, as formerly, when feudal state pertained to her husband; but she would not place in competition with her safety, an exemption from danger and discomfort to herself. He had by two days preceded her at Edinburgh, and bore the disguise of an aged mendicant, deaf and dumb. His stature, above the common height, and majestic mien, were humbled to the semblance of bending under a load of years and infirmity; his raven locks, and even his eyebrows, were shaven; his head was enveloped by an old grisly wig and tattered night-cap; the remnant of a handkerchief over his chin hid the sable beard, which, to elude detection, was further covered by a plaster. His garments corresponded to his squalid head-gear. O how unlike the martial leader of devoted bands, from whom she parted in agonies of anxiety, not unrelieved by hope. A daughter of this affectionate pair attempted to give the writer some idea of their meeting, as related by her mother after she became a widow; but language vainly labours to describe transporting joy, soon chastened by sorrow and alarm. We leave to imagination and feeling, a scene exquisitely agitating and pathetic. The chieftain explained his motive for asking the lady to make her abode in a chairman's house. Besides his tried fidelity, the old tenement contained a secret passage for escape, in case of need; and he showed her, behind a screen, hung with wet linens, a door in the panelling, the hinges of which were so oiled, that he could glide away with noiseless movement. If it was his misfortune to be under such necessity, the lady must seem to faint, and throw the screen against the pannels, while he secured the bolt on which depended his evasion, and the chairman had exhausted his skill without being able to cure the creaking it occasioned. The chieftain gave his cash to the lady, urging her not to delay paying the amount to his grace's confidential agent. She complied, but checked all inquiry how the money came to her hands. The rights of the estate were restored to her, and three gentlemen of high respectability affixed their signatures to a bond, promising for the young chief, that whenever he came of age, he would bind himself and his heirs to pay the feu-duty. The records were duly deposited in a public office, and the lady hastened back to her lodgings. The chieftain soon issued from behind the screen, and the lady was minutely detailing how her business had been settled, when stealthy steps in the passage warned the *proscribed* to disappear; and the lady, sinking to the ground, dashed the screen against the pannelling. The common door was locked; but it soon was burst open by a party of soldiers, led by an officer. The lady's swoon was now no counterfeit. A surgeon was called. She revived, and being interrogated, replied no human being was with her. The officer assured her, that he and several of the soldiers saw, through a chink in the door, an old man in close conversation with her. She then confessed that an apparition had endeavoured to persuade her he was commissioned to impart tidings of her husband, but the soldiers interrupted them before the spirit could deliver the subject of his mission. Every part of the house had been searched while the lady lay insensible, and as no discovery ensued, the tale she related passed current at Edinburgh, and spread over the lowlands and highlands. It was not until the lady had a certainty of her husband's decease in a foreign land, that she told her daughters how successfully she had imposed on their enemies; and surely no story of an apparition has been seemingly better attested. B. G.

THE FRIENDLESS ONE.

My mother sleeps i' the cauld, cauld grave;
 I saw her to the kirkyard borne—
My father is streekit by her side,
 An' I am left my lane to mourn!

My brither was drowned i' the deep saut sea—
 He sank wi' his ship in the cauld green wave;
An' my sisters three, that were kind to me,
 Fell ane by ane into the grave.

O was is me! but my heart is lane!
 I'll gang an' I'll seek my father's grave;
I'll lay my head on the flowery sod,
 An' I'll sing me asleep among the lave.

O hearken, O hearken my tale o' wae!
 O bear ye my greetin', ye angels o' air!
O pity, O pity a harmless mane,
 An' bear me awa' frae this world o' care!

O bear me awa' through yon bonny blue sky,
 Where the wee clouds beek in a sorrowless sun;
Where sobbin' an' sighin' are heard nae mair,
 An' a life o' unfadin' glory's begun!

For my kind mother tauld me, afore she dee'd,
 Ere her een turned white, an' cauld grew her hand,
She was leavin' a world o' sin an wae,
 For a sinless, a waeless, a holier land.

O ance was I happy, an' bricht an' blythe,
 As the linty that sang on the flowery lea,
When I was the pride o' my minny that's gane,
 An' my minny that's gane took care o' me.

But my father an' mother have left me now;
 I've seen them a' to the kirkyard borne:
An' friendless, forsaken, forlorn, an' pair,
 I'm left i' the world, my lane to mourn.

Edinburgh, Dec. 2, 1832.   W. D.

TO THE POLE-STAR.
BY MRS. JOHNSTONE.

No gleam is on the roaring wave,
 No Star is in the midnight skies;
The gathering tempests hoarser rave—
 STAR OF THE MARINER, ARISE!
While wild winds blend their melodies,
 To Thee our ardent vows we pour;
O guide us through the pathless seas,
 O guard us from the treacherous shore!

STAR OF THE BRAVE! pale Beauty's eye
 In wild alarm is rais'd to thee;
To thee she breathes the secret sigh,—
 'O save my true love far at sea!
' From rock and shoal my sailor free;
 ' Guide him from whitening waves afar,
' And bring him to his home and me,
 ' And thou shalt be my worshipp'd star!'

BRAVE MARINER! Hebridean seas
 Have rock'd thy bark at summer's e'en;
When soft thou whistling woo'd the breeze,
 And thought on thy young love between;
Or view'd th' appointed margent green,
 And wish'd that pale light would appear,
And called it loveliest star, I ween,
 In all thy northern hemisphere.

STAR OF THE NORTH! where'er he roves,
 To thee he turns in fond review;
Sweet beacon of his early loves,
 First seen 'mid ALBYN's mountains blue;
When life and all its joys were new,
 And love and thou his only guide,
As loud and shrill the night-winds blew,
 And brave he stemm'd Cor'vrekan's tide.

LOVED WANDERER! from thy Highland home,
 Who crossed the deep for Indian gold,
Condemn'd in sunny lands to roam,
 Where nothing but the heart is cold,—
O, well canst thou thy pang unfold,
 When sunk the POLE-STAR down on earth,
Measuring the liquid lapse that roll'd
 Between thee and thy father's hearth.

But cheerly, cheerly, gallant heart!
 Scotland and bliss await thee still;
Well hast thou play'd the manly part,
 Spurning at temporary ill.
Rise! visions of his father's hill,
 And sooth him with the scenes afar;
With lovely hopes his bosom fill,—
 Rise on his soul, thou NORTHERN STAR!

Fond will he watch thee o'er the bow,
 Steal from the blue and billowy main,
And greet thee with the kindly glow,
 That wiles our wanderers back agen,
From golden climes of stranger men,
 From toil, and strife, and grandeur far,
To earn their age in Highland glen,
 Then sleep beneath their NORTHERN STAR!

SAVINGS BANKS.—From a statistical table of the Savings Banks in England, Wales, and Ireland, compiled from the latest official returns, by Mr. Tidd Pratt, it appears that in England and Wales there has taken place, since 1830, a small decrease in the amount (but not in the number) of investments: viz. L.3,597 in England; L.4,047 in Wales, but in Ireland, there has been an increase to the amount of L.122,642.—The total amount of investments is, in England, L.12,916,028;—in Wales, L.349,794;—in Ireland, L.1,046,825. Total, L.14,311,647.—The total number of depositors, exclusive of Friendly and Charitable Societies, is, in England, 374,169; (of whom 297,571 are depositors under L.50)—in Wales, 10,374;—in Ireland, 37,898. Total, 432,441 depositors; being an increase of 13,754. The average amount of each depositor's investment is thirty pounds.

COLUMN FOR THE LADIES.

FRENCH AND ENGLISH WOMEN.

The national portraits we are about to present are attributed to Mirabeau, and internal evidence bears out the statement.

THE FRENCH WOMAN.—When a French lady comes into a room the first thing that strikes you is, that she walks better, has her head and feet better dressed—her clothes better fancied and better put on, than any woman you have ever seen. When she talks, she is the art of pleasing personified. Her eyes, her lips, her words, her gestures, are all prepossessing. Her language is the language of amiableness—her accents are the accents of grace—she embellishes a trifle—interests upon nothing—she softens a contradiction—she takes off the insipidness of a compliment by turning it elegantly—and when she has a mind she sharpens and polishes the point of an epigram better than all the women in the world. Her eyes sparkle with spirit—the most delightful sallies flash from her fancy—in telling a story she is inimitable—the motions of her body, and the accents of her tongue, are equally genteel and easy—an equable flow of sprightliness keeps her constantly good-humoured and cheerful, and the only objects of her life are to please and be pleased. Her vivacity may sometimes approach to folly—but perhaps it is not in her moments of folly that she is at least interesting and agreeable. English women have many points of superiority over the French—the French are superior to them in many others. Here I shall only say, there is a particular idea in which no woman in the world can compare with a French woman—it is in the power *intellectual irritation*. She will draw wit out of a fool. She strikes with such address the chords of self-love, that she gives unexpected vigour and agility to fancy, and electrifies a body that appears non-electric.

ENGLISH WOMEN.—I have mentioned here the women of England, and I have done wrong. I did not intend it when I began the letter. They came into my mind as the *only* women in the world worthy of being compared with those of France. I shall not presume to determine whether in the important article of beauty, form and colour are to be preferred to expression and grace, or whether grace and expression are to be considered preferable to complexion and shape. I shall not examine whether the *piquant* of France is to be thought superior to the *touchant* of England; or whether deep sensibility deserves to be preferred to animation and wit. So important a subject requires a volume. I shall only venture to give a trait. If a goddess could be supposed to be formed, compounded of Juno and Minerva, that goddess would be the emblem of the women of this country [England.] Venus, as she is, with all her amiableness and imperfections, may stand justly enough for an emblem of French women. I have decided the question without intending it, for I have given the perfections to the women of England. One point I had forgotten, and it is a material one. It is not to be disputed on—for what I am going to write is the opinion and sentiment of the universe. The English women are the best wives under Heaven—and shame be on the men who make them bad husbands.

TIGHT LACING.—Tight lacing not only prevents a due development of the muscles by pressure, but, by fixing into one immovable mass the ribs and vertebræ of the back, which, more especially in youth, should have free motion on each other, makes the whole upper part of the body a dead weight on the vertebræ of the loins, which, in consequence, give way to one or other side, and lateral curvature is produced. Not only does tight lacing act directly in this manner, but indirectly it operates in diminishing muscular vigour by impeding respiration. It is well known that muscular power bears a relative proportion to the produce of respiration, animals having the highest development of the respiratory organs, being the most powerful in muscular force. Tight stays compress the ribs together, and prevent the play of the respiratory muscles; when applied during the growth of the body, they prevent the development of the chest, and thus lay the foundation of many pectoral diseases. The female form, at least in youth, requires no artificial aid to improve it. Who would think of putting stays on the Venus de Medicis?—*Beale's Observations on the Spine.*

WINTER FASHIONS.

Plain merinos and washing silks are fashionable in home dress. We observe, however, that merino, even of the very finest kind, is seldom worn but for dishabille. We must except the printed ones, which are sometimes adopted in half dress. The favourite form for plain merino dresses is a body made like that of a habit, with a velvet collar and facings, either black, or to correspond, and sometimes a narrow velvet cuff. The sleeves are tight to the lower part of the arm, but in general the extravagant fulness at top is divided in the middle, so as to form two very large puffs. Washing silk dresses have the body made high in the back of the neck, but rather open on the bosom. The prettiest are those trimmed in the shawl style with velvet; it forms a straight-falling collar behind, slopes down almost to a point on each side of the breast, and, if cut, as is sometimes the case, to resemble frogs, or, as they are fashionably styled *Brandelburge*, has a very dressy look. Caps are very fashionable in home dress; the prettiest are of plain *tulle*, with the trimming of the front turning back as usual at the sides, but partially descending in the centre of the forehead, where it is crossed by a bandeau of ribbon, which terminates in a full knot behind the trimming on one side. A very light knot composed principally of ends is placed on the trimming in front.

Satin is now the material most in favour for matrons in evening dress. A good many gowns have the skirt bordered with a band or rouleau of sable, real or mock, for we perceive that the latter is once more in favour. We have seen, in a few instances that half high bodies crossing in drapery folds before, were bordered with smaller rouleaus, as were also the bottom of sleeves, but velvet is more generally employed. Some dresses that have no trimming round the border have the body decorated with a lappel of the shawl kind, cut round in points, which fall low upon the shoulder, and pass in front under the *ceinture*; they are of the material of the dress, and trimmed with blond lace. This is an elegant style of body, but it displays the bosom so much that a *chemisette* (our mammas called it a tucker) ought to be always worn with it.

There is quite a rage for blond lace caps in evening dress. Berets are fashionable, but not so much so.

We do not forget that our pretty young readers will want ball dresses for this festive season. The materials for these are crape and different kinds of figured gauze. The most elegant are those that have the bodies cut square and low, disposed in full folds across the front, and trimmed with a double fall of blond lace round the back and shoulders. Short sleeves, exceedingly wide, confined to the arm by a narrow satin rouleau, edged with blond lace laid flat. Many of those dresses are made without trimming round the border, others have a light flounce, which is laid on so that the upper edge forms a row of points, to each of which is appended a knot of ribbon, or a sprig of flowers, according to the fancy of the wearer. The head dress must be of hair, in the style we have recently described, adorned with flowers; the most fashionable are larkspurs, dahlias, London pride, pinks, jessamines, and roses.

Fashionable colours are fire colour, dark blue, soot colour, cherry colour, orange; various shades of brown and green. Light colours, as rose, straw colour, &c. &c. are worn in evening dress only, but we also see very full colours adopted in evening dress, particularly by matrons.

WONDERS OF PHILOSOPHY.—The polypus, like the fabled hydra, receives new life from the knife which is lifted to destroy it. The fly-spider lays an egg as large as itself. There are four thousand and forty-one muscles in a caterpillar. Hook discovered fourteen thousand mirrors in the eye of a drone; and to effect the respiration of a carp, thirteen thousand three hundred arteries, vessels, veins, and bones, &c. are necessary. The body of every spider contains four little masses pierced with a multitude of imperceptible holes, each hole permitting the passage of a single thread; all the threads, to the amount of a thousand to each mass, join together, when they come out and make the single thread with which the spider spins its web; so that what we call a spider's thread consists of more than four thousand united. Leuwenhoek, by means of microscopes, observed spiders no larger than a grain of sand, who spun threads so fine that it took four thousand of them to equal in magnitude a single hair.

SAPPING AND MINING.

The Siege of Antwerp has made the above terms of more frequent use than as lovers of peace we admire. But as all kinds of knowledge is valuable, and may be useful, we lay before our readers the following military account of the process technically termed SAPPING:—

There are three or four kinds. That employed by the French has been the plain sap. The sappers are divided into squads of eight. They debouch from the lodgments or approaches, one behind the other, where there is a store of gabions, (cylindrical baskets about three feet high,) and fascines or long faggots. The first man or leader of the sap, pushes before him a gabion stuffed with wool or cotton, shot proof; under cover of this, he places an empty gabion to his right or left, then fills it with earth, digging about eighteen inches deep, assisted by No. 2. This being done, he rolls on his defence and places a second empty gabion, which he fills in like manner. No. 2, deepens the eighteen inches to two feet by three wide. No. 3, deepens this to two feet six, and No. 4, to three feet, always throwing the earth on the gabions, and over the side nearest the defences. Nos. 5, 6, 7, and 8, bring the gabions and fascines from the lodgment, and lay the latter on the top of the former, pegging them down with pickets. Thus, with gabions three feet high, an excavation three feet deep, and fascines or sand bags on the top, a parapet of seven to eight feet is obtained. The interstices between the gabions are filled with earth, short fascines, or sand bags. As the first squad advances they are followed by a second, who improve the work. They again are followed by the working parties, who, being entirely sheltered, complete it, and extend the breadth of the trench to six, ten, or more feet, as may be necessary. This is not a technical description, but it may serve to give some idea of the operation, and show its peril for the sappers, who are, perhaps, working at pistol distance. The leading man is relieved every half hour, each taking the post of danger in his turn. They are paid an extra sum, at so much per toise, and this sum increases in proportion as the sap approaches the crest of the glacis.

The descent into the ditch is not less perilous, and requiring extraordinary precautions. It is of two kinds—by a covered gallery, when the ditch is extremely deep, and a cielcouvert when it is shallow or filled with water. The latter has been adopted at St. Laurent. At the distance of 70 or 80 yards the sappers commence cutting a trench, which gradually descends at the rate of about one foot in four, but this must be regulated by the depth of the ditch. As the excavation proceeds the top is covered with beams, hurdles, and fascines, and the side supported with planks, until it reaches the revetment of the counterscarp. The whole is then widened, strengthened, and improved. The revetment is then knocked in, fascines and sand bags thrown in great quantities into the ditch, so as to form an artificial bottom, or a covered shot-proof raft lowered down and fixed to the revetment of the scalp or wall of the defence. The miner then crosses over, establishes himself in a hole, and prepares the mine.

These operations, however dangerous in appearance, are generally performed with comparatively trifling loss.

SCRAPS.
ORIGINAL AND SELECTED.

CITY OF THE DEAD.—The following striking anecdote is recorded by Lionel Wafer, a surgeon, who sailed with the Buccaneers in the South Sea:—At a solitary place on the Coast of Peru, named Vermejo, the surgeon landed with a party of Buccaneers, and marched, in search of water, four miles up a sandy bay. It was found strewed with the dead bodies of men, women, and children, which, to appearance, seemed as if they had not been a week dead, yet when handled they proved dry, and light as cork or sponge. The Buccaneers were afterwards told by an old Spanish Indian, that in his father's time, the soil here, which now yielded nothing, was well cultivated and fruitful; and the town of *Wormia*, so numerously inhabited with Indians, that they could have handed a fish from hand to hand, till it reached the Incas hand in Peru; but that when the Spaniards laid siege to their city, the Indians, rather than yield to their enemy, dug holes in the sand, and buried themselves alive. The winds had laid bare these self-made graves, and the men lay with their broken bows beside them, and the women with their distaffs and spinning-wheels. Wafer brought away one of those desiccated bodies, that of a boy of ten years, but the superstitious sailors would not permit it to be kept on board.

MANY SLIPS BETWEEN THE CUP AND THE LIP, OR THE LORD CHANCELLOR'S PIE.—Since the elevation of Henry Brougham to the Woolsack, a gentleman in Sheffield, an ardent admirer of his Lordship, has been in the habit of gracing the Noble Lord's table at this season of the year with a Yorkshire pie, in size and contents not unworthy the tables of the Barons of old. This said pie, after being prepared in the first style, and with much taste, containing a goose, a turkey, a hare, a couple of rabbits, brace of partridges, ditto pheasants, ditto grouse, a tongue, &c., was baked by Mr. Walker, in Fargate, where many had the pleasure of looking at the outside, without enjoying what was within. "There's many a slip between the cup and the lip," was most grievously verified in this instance, before the removal of the pie for its final destination. On Saturday morning a servant girl called for it, previous to its being packed for the metropolis; she got it on her head, and whether from the tremendous weight, or the overwhelming flavour of the combustibles, we know not, but unfortunately the Lord Chancellor's pie was upset before she had proceeded many hundred yards, the consequence of which was an immense assemblage of unruly dogs, two of which fought most desperately over the wreck, and otherwise created such a row, that, but for the active exertions of the neighbours, the result might have been very serious. In the meantime one escaped with part of the goose, a second with the turkey, a third with a hare, and so on, till farther dispute was useless. So ended the pie riot, and, we are happy to say, without any bloodshed.

THE BIBLE.—A great religious change is said to be taking place in Germany. The Bible is read with avidity by the Roman Catholics; and the clergy of this religion are, in many parts of the country, making strenuous efforts for the abolition of celibacy, and for liberty to read the Mass in German. In various instances they have turned Protestants, with a great portion of their flocks. But the most important event is the formation of an Anti-Papal Catholic Community at Dresden, which is likely to become the nucleus of a very numerous sect. If we couple this with a growing desire among the Protestants of that country to introduce more ceremonies into their religious worship, a re-union of the two Churches seems not among impossible things.

CONTENTS OF NO. XXIV.

Factory Children 17
The Bourgeois of Paris, a Sketch 19
Wages in England in the Fourteenth Century 21
On the Cultivation of Hemp 22
Churches for the Rich .... ib.
Religious Camp Meeting in America 23
Random Records of Returns to Parliament .... ib.
ELEMENTS OF THOUGHT—Value of Literary Men—Literature in England—Education of the People 24
THE STORY-TELLER—The Rose in January, a German Tale .. 25
A Winter Sketch—The Carpenter's Daughter 27
A Singular Story 29
The Friendless One—The Pole Star, by Mrs Johnstone 30
COLUMN FOR THE LADIES—French and English Women—Tight Lacing 31
Sapping and Mining 32
SCRAPS—City of the Dead, &c. .... ib.

EDINBURGH: Printed by and for JOHN JOHNSTONE, 19, St. James's Square.—Published by JOHN ANDERSON, Jun., Bookseller, 55, North Bridge Street, Edinburgh; by JOHN MACLEOD, and ATKINSON & Co. Booksellers, Glasgow; and sold by all Booksellers and Vendors of Cheap Periodicals.

THE Schoolmaster,
AND
EDINBURGH WEEKLY MAGAZINE.

CONDUCTED BY JOHN JOHNSTONE.

THE SCHOOLMASTER IS ABROAD.—LORD BROUGHAM.

No. 25.—Vol. II. SATURDAY, JANUARY 19, 1833. Price Three-Halfpence.

THE DUTIES OF THE PEOPLE AT THE PRESENT PERIOD.

Although they have been, in a great measure, liberated from the political thraldom in which they were so long and so injuriously compelled to remain, for the purpose of enabling the Aristocracy to enhance its wealth and power, by every legalized expedient of spoliation, the People must not imagine that they have done their duty by obtaining the enactment of the Reform Bills, or by returning to the Parliament, about to assemble, men who were instrumental in getting these bills passed. They must not suppose that this is reform—it is only the instrument by which, if properly exerted, a practical efficient reform is to be obtained: and it must never be forgotten, that it is only by the judicious, steady, persevering exertions of the people themselves, that this instrument can be made to accomplish the great ends for which it was intrusted to them. The duties more particularly incumbent on them, on the eve of the meeting of the first reformed Parliament, are the following :—

DUTIES OF REPRESENTATIVES.

1. To keep constantly and steadily in view, that representatives are sent to Parliament, *not* for the promotion of the particular and exclusive interests of particular individuals, orders, classes, communities, sects, or professions—but for the purpose of ensuring, by the abolition of bad, and the enactment of beneficent laws, " the greatest possible happiness of the greatest possible number" of the *whole* people ; and, therefore,

2. In a spirit of impartiality and philanthropy, to use all the means in their power of acquiring and diffusing an accurate knowledge of the principles of those laws which regulate the acquisition and distribution of public wealth, and of the several classes of circumstances which do, or may affect the welfare of the community: in other words, it is incumbent on every individual, so far as his circumstances allow, to acquire and diffuse a correct knowledge of the principles of political economy and politics ; and consequently,

ABOLITION OF TAXES ON KNOWLEDGE.

3d. To promote petitioning, at as early a period as possible, for the entire abolition of all those taxes which prevent or restrain the diffusion of political and other useful knowledge. These foolish and tyrannical imposts maintain the reign of ignorance, error, and prejudice ; they retard the progress of science and arts, and the improvement of morals ; they consequently prevent the accumulation of wealth, and the amelioration of the circumstances of the people ; and, of course, unnecessarily tend to uphold vice, immorality, and insubordination, and thus to add, unnecessarily and most injuriously, to the expense of military and police establishments, while they render religious and educational institutions much less efficient and beneficial than they would otherwise be. Of imposts of such pestiferous tendency, no *good* government *can* stand in need. It ought never to be forgotten, that it is *not* for the purpose of bringing money into the treasury, but with the diabolic intent of keeping the people in ignorance of their own concerns, and for maintaining abuses and the misgovernment of those who " loved darkness rather than the light, because their deeds were evil," that these taxes were augmented, and have so long, in opposition to the general will, been retained. This was openly and unblushingly avowed in the House of Commons under the Tory regime. Every government, essentially aristocratic and oligarchical, will naturally incline to fetter the press, and seek for plausible pretences for retaining, in part at least, the taxes on paper and advertisements. It has, therefore, been of late hypocritically pretended that these imposts could not, in the actual state of the public finances, be dispensed with ; but were any desire existing among men in power to render the press, as it ought to be, essentially and really free, and usefully efficient, as the Schoolmaster-General of the whole people, an unobjectionable succedaneum could easily be found.—*Vide* next section.

CORN LAWS.

4. Next to the duty of providing for their moral and intellectual, it is incumbent on the people to ensure the supply of their physical wants. The Corn Laws, therefore, which have been enacted not for the purpose of adding to the revenue, nor for affording encouragement or benefit to the actual cultivator of the soil, but merely for the wicked purpose of dishonestly and iniquitously

enhancing the rents of corn lands, for the sole benefit of the owners of such lands, and the clergy, whose incomes are regulated by the price of grain, and plainly also to the detriment of the public fisc, of the owners of pasture lands, of agriculturists of every description, and of all other classes of the community,—*ought not to be any longer tolerated;* and the people, especially in great cities, and in manufacturing towns, ought immediately to denounce them, in strong and plain language, and to petition for their *immediate repeal.* On the particularly injurious tendency and operation of these execrable laws, it is unnecessary, considering how often they have been clearly exposed, to dwell; but it may be mentioned, and ought to be steadily kept in view, that they occasion, according to the moderate calculation of a very cautious and considerate practical financier, an annual loss to this nation of no less than *fifteen millions,* and that, although this large sum is most injuriously extracted from the people, scarcely one million of its amount ever comes to the Exchequer in the shape of duty on foreign corn, and that even but a small proportion of it finds its way into the pockets of the landlords themselves, the rest being as pure loss as if it were sunk in the bottom of the ocean, or consumed in the vomitory of Mount Ætna. It were far better for the people that the landlords should have their incomes enhanced by means of pensions, to the extent of the benefit which they really derive from these laws, than that such a system as the present, of legalized swindling, should be tolerated. In the petitions which have formerly been presented to the burgh-monger Parliaments for their repeal, the injurious effects of these laws were often well pointed out, in a merely economical view; but, *now,* not only should this be done, but their injustice, wickedness, and glaring *dishonesty* and *sinfulness,* should be strongly and solemnly dwelt on, in a manner becoming a moral and religious people, conscious of their responsibility, not merely to their fellow creatures, but to their Omnipotent and All-just Creator. Let any man read seriously and attentively Dr. Dwight's discourse on the eighth commandment, and let him say if, without violating every suggestion of conscience, and disregarding every deduction of reason, he can presume to look with supine indifference on the existence of this grinding, pauperizing instrument of oppression, or fail to bestir himself in relieving his fellow men from its destructive action. It is not meant that foreign corn may not, fairly and properly, be a subject of taxation, when the object is the legitimate one of merely adding to the receipts of the public fisc, and not of giving an undue advantage to a class, who, as mere landlords, contribute little or nothing to the exigencies of the state. Such an impost, if moderate in its rate, say 2s. 6d. or 3s. per quarter, would not, in any considerable degree, enhance the price of grain, and would ensure a handsome addition to the revenue; and thus the taxes on knowledge might be wholly repealed, without diminishing the revenue, or adding to the burdens of the people, while commerce would be encouraged, the rate of profit augmented, the accumulation of capital accelerated, and the poor enabled to live on a more acceptable and nutritious aliment than potatoes. It is much to be deplored that the clergy are remunerated for their services in a manner which makes it their interest to uphold the existing system of iniquity. It is too bad that a clergyman cannot, *with all his heart,* (how could he?) thank the bountiful giver of all good, for an abundant harvest, which may reduce his poor stipend 20 or 30 per cent. No wonder, especially when the actual operation of the law of patronage is considered, that the clergy of the established church are, in general, illiberal anti-reformers'; nor that we have lately seen a parson, as an elector, after uttering a nonsensical Jeremiade on the downfall of the price of corn, wool, and kelp, come forward, in a Highland county, as the proposer of an Ultra-Tory exclusionist, (of whose legislatorial abilities his most partial friends cannot venture to boast,) in opposition to one of the most intelligent and talented men of the age. No wonder that landlords and parsons, and every other profiter by abuse and misrule, should, with such inveterate malignity, decry the study of the all-important science of political economy, and exert all their endeavours to render it a subject of vituperation and ridicule. No wonder that that iniquitous monopolizing triumvirate, Lord Rapax Rackrent, John Company, and Sawney M'Scourger, should co-operate in upholding their respective frauds, in keeping up the price of corn, tea, and sugar, when, in this ungodly work they are assisted by the Right Reverend Father in God, Dr Thomas Tithedraw, Lord Bishop of Pluralstall, and the Reverend Calvin Gatherpecks, minister of Girneldale, without opposition from any other pulpiteer than the Reverend Simon Sectary of Noglebe. The farmers, poor deluded dupes, should at length learn wisdom. They should now be able to perceive that high rents and high profits are incompatible, and should, with fear and trembling, and humble contrition, consider that the great loss of capital, which the corn laws have occasioned to their class, was the just and inevitable punishment of their *sinful* co-operation with their landlords, in the iniquitous spoliation of their fellow subjects. It is now their duty to co-operate with the people, in obtaining the abrogation of these laws; and the people ought, of course, to assist them in obtaining, by law, such equitable deduction of rent as their circumstances require.

ABOLITION OF TITHES.

5. The people, not of England and Ireland only, but those of Scotland also, should early petition for the TOTAL ABOLITION OF TITHES. The Scottish children of the Covenant, the followers of Calvin, and the supporters of the simple forms and institutions of Presbytery, have no interest nor inducement to uphold the prelatic pride, the pluralities, pompous mummeries, or cold inefficient

ormalities, of the proud daughter of the scarlet ame of Babylon; nor are they under any special bligation to submit to the enhancing of the price f their food, merely that Right Reverend Fathers, Venerables, and Reverends, may continue to trouble and annoy the cultivator of the land, and add to the expense of every man's subsistence. If the fox-hunting interest of England *will* maintain a par-oting priesthood, to perpetuate flimsy ceremonial observances, and to keep their boors in ignorant subservient dependence, let the clergy be paid *more Scotice* ; but let not the evils of the tithing system be maintained to impoverish the intelligent and industrious body of dissenters, as well as the admirers of Episcopacy.

EQUAL TAXATION.

6. As it is notorious and undeniable that the greater part of the national burdens is levied from the labourers and industrious portion of the community, and that, in the *ratio* of their abilities, they pay a great deal more to the Exchequer than the landlords and wealthy fundholders, the people should immediately petition for a fair and thorough revision of the fiscal code, and for the repeal or alleviation of the duties on articles of ordinary and general consumption, such as tea, sugar, malt, and soap, and for the imposition, on a gradually ascending scale, of a tax on *Property and Income.*

7. THE PEOPLE OUGHT NOT TO PETITION FOR A REPEAL OF THE ASSESSED TAXES, excepting those on houses and windows, which should be put on a just and rational footing. It would be greatly for the public advantage that *all* taxes were directly assessed. The assessed taxes do not injure the people, otherwise than by their own amount, and the expense of collection ; and it is an advantage that the payment must always be perceived and attended to, because it draws attention to the financial arrangements of government, and leads the payers to check and prevent all unnecessary expenditure. The indirect taxes, on the other hand, cost, in reality, a great deal more than their own amount, and the cost of their collection. Their imposition renders it necessary, that, in every trade affected by them, a much greater amount of capital should be invested than would otherwise be required ; and the profits of the portion of such capital, assigned for the payment of duty, must be added to the price which the consumer has to pay ; and this capital, besides, is locked up, and prevented from being, as it otherwise might be, usefully employed in the production of national wealth. Taxes on consumable commodities are paid without the observation of the consumer. The public expenditure is therefore less regarded than if imposts were directly levied ; and waste and profuse expenditure of the public resources are the natural consequences.

CONCLUSION.

Let the people never forget that many of their representatives have gone to Parliament, not for the purpose of promoting the general good, but to scramble for place, power, and title, and for promoting their own private advantage, or the interest of the particular order or class to which they belong. On such men, however plausible their professions, let no reliance be placed ; and, therefore, let the people be ever watchful of the conduct of their representatives, and openly and manfully expose every demonstration of political iniquity. And let them never cease to petition and remonstrate, until they have achieved the destruction of *sinecures* and *monopolies* of every description, the removal of all *checks and fetters on honest industry*, and the blessing of a cheap and efficient government. To ensure the attainment of these ends, every individual ought to afford to every able and honest journalist, labouring in the people's behalf, as much encouragement as his circumstances allow.

January, 1833. A NORTHERN TRUTH SPEAKER.

ON THE STATE OF FEELING IN A MANUFACTURING TOWN.

[This is part of a letter on a subject of urgent import, addressed, by the author of the " Corn Law Rhymes," to the Editor of the *New Monthly Magazine*.]

There is war in the city of soot. The hand of the workman is lifted against his master, and not in vain, if his intention be to close the butcher's shop. Yet, alas! if the master defeat the workman, the same result is probable; for, while they are injuring each other, a third party, resisted by neither of them, is devouring the substance of both.

" As I am undersold by foreigners," says the employer to the employed, " instead of raising your wages, you should lower them, or you will give my trade to the Germans." " I can but starve, then," replies the workman: " the question is not whether you will lose your trade, for that catastrophe is certain, if we are to pay sevenpence per pound for beef, while our rivals pay only twopence-halfpenny. If I would work for nothing, and give you all my wages, you would tamely suffer the money to be taken from you by the basest of mankind, and be poor still. The real question at issue between us two seems to be, whether I shall starve *after* you lose your trade, or *before* ? Yet why should I starve even then? If your trade go to Germany, I will follow it thither ; and in the meantime, no matter by what means, I will get as high wages as I can, that I may be able to pay for my passage over the herring-pool."

" The Germans," continues the master, " can undersell me forty per cent., and yet obtain twice my profits." " Then they can give twice your wages," answers the workman ; " and the sooner you remove your capital to Germany, and I my skill and labour, the better for us both. It is plain, from your own showing, that if the German workmen are not better paid than I am, the fault rests with themselves ; for their masters can at least afford to give higher wages ; but if there is any truth in your assertions, you will soon be unable to pay any wages at all."

" If you will not work for reasonable wages," resumes the master, " my work shall be done by apprentices." " But," replies the workman, " I will not suffer you to take another apprentice ; no, not one." " Then you are a tyrant," exclaims the master. " The world is full of them," retorts the servant : " it is not the fault of our masters if we have not been brought down to potatoes. How long is it since you sent me to York Castle, merely because I did my best to obtain the fair price for my labour? And do you now blame me for following your example? Curses always come home to roost." " Yes," says the master, " you will find it so."

Now there is no misrepresentation in the statements of the master manufacturer. Every word is true.

The silver-platers of the Continent undersell us twenty

per cent. in price, and fifty in pattern. Still the blind *will* not see.

In another year, perhaps, the merchants of Sheffield will import cutlery from Germany, the German scissors being already fifty per cent. cheaper than ours; for the cutlers of Modlin pay only fifteenpence per stone for bread, while we pay three shillings. Still the blind *will* not see.

The cutlers of Belgium make and sell, for twentypence, a complete set of steel knives and forks, consisting of twenty-four pieces; and the saw-makers of Belgium make and sell, for one shilling and sixpence each, saws equal to ours at nearly twice the price. But then the Belgian artisans and capitalists are not impoverished by act of Parliament. Still the blind *will* not see.

The Russians, in the market of New York, undersell John Barber's razors thirty per cent., Joseph Rodgers and Sons' cutlery forty per cent., and cast cutlery, in general, fifty per cent.; for the Russian workmen, when they buy two pecks of corn, do not lose, or throw away, the price of one peck; in other words, they are not compelled by law to give a shilling for eighteenpence. Still the blind *will* not see.

" Oh, but we shall soon have our bread as cheap as our neighbours." Yes, when our manufactures have left the kingdom,—when we have neither edge-tools, nor saws, nor knives, nor scissors, nor money to give in exchange for bread, we shall have it as cheap as our neighbours have it; for capital will not stay here, for potato-profits, if it can get roast-beef profits elsewhere. *But the blind will then see.* Instead of obtaining, permanently, as they might have done, the fair average price of Europe for their wheat, say forty shillings per quarter, at their doors, they must then be satisfied with two-thirds of that price, say about twenty-four shillings per quarter, at Hamburgh or Amsterdam. Hey, then—but not for a miracle!—let the blind see when it is too late; if they are to be a fate unto themselves; and it is written that they shall break stones on the high roads for subsistence! But how horrifying to our souls, to our bones in the grave, will be the music of their gruntle, then, after receiving eighteenpence for twelve hours' hard labour, they visit the paradise of the market, and there, with their miserable earnings, buy bread—not at thirty-six pence per stone, as their victims do, but at fifteen! " Good bye, fine fellow!" " Who is that vagabond ?" " Lord, sir, he was once a great gentleman, who kept a parson of his own." Well, if the enemy thank God for crime and carnage, may not *we* thank him, if he make themselves his instruments in ridding us of a nuisance—these suicides of their own prosperity, who toil not, neither do they spin? Have they not wickedly and foolishly destroyed more capital, in the memory of one generation, than all the lands of England would sell for at the bread-tax price; and in less than twenty years produced more crime and misery than all other causes in a hundred? This is a subject on which the press has basely, and almost universally, shrunk from the performance of its duty, to the infinite injury of the people, and the now probably inevitable and hopeless ruin of their oppressors, who seem doomed to open their eyes on the edge of a precipice, over which they must plunge headlong. But of all the treason against all, in this matter, that of the Philosophers of Useful Knowledge has the most brass in it. They calmly ask, what the workmen would say if a conspiracy existed to raise the price of beef, butter, bread, and ale? As if *that* conspiracy were not the cause of all our heart-burnings, our agonies, and our despair!

It is frightfully amusing, dismally instructive, to observe the deep hatred, the blasting scorn, with which the working classes of this town, and their betters, as they are called, regard each other. They are all deplorably ignorant on the subjects which most nearly concern them all; but the workmen, I think, are less ignorant than their employers, in spite of the pains which have been, and are taken, by the ultra-pious and intellectual, to keep them in ignorance. Will your readers believe, that the *Westminster Review*—the book most likely to teach our workmen what they most need to know—has been, and is excluded, by an ex press law, from our Mechanics' Library? Such, however, is the fact; the wisest and the best have had their own way, and we are now reaping the consequences. But if our first merchants themselves have yet to learn the alphabet of political economy, can we wonder that rich and poor alike are quarrelling about effects, when they ought to be removing causes?

Nor is it less horribly amusing and instructive to observe, how completely the aristocratic leaven has leavened the whole mass of society here. Even our beggary has its castes. All try to seem rich, that they may not be thought poor; and all, but the tax-fed, are in danger of poverty. Perhaps the most frightful symptom of our social disease is exhibited by the masters who have been workmen, and who exceed in arrogance and insolence, by many degrees, the cab-driving sons of the sons of the dunghill sprung. Next to them, in their vituperation of the poor, are the insolvent—and their name is Legion. There must be some reason why Calamity, like an old woman, lives for ever. Hanging by a hair over the grave dug for Hope, do they vilify the all-plundered poor to conciliate the rich. If so, the flattered and the flatterer are worthy of each other.

" Well, Mister What's-your-name, I hear you still think we must have a free trade or a revolution." " Yes, I do." " But if we have a free trade, what will become of the landlords?" " They never ask what will become of you, if we are not to have a free trade. Why care for people who care for nobody but themselves. Your wheel-barrow is not a coach-and-four; it is the grapery that is in danger, not your grand epergne, plated with sham silver." " Well, but Mr. What's-your-name, how is your trade now?" " Very bad." " Pshaw we never prospered better than at present. Look at that new street! what an income is rising there!" " That income is not rising but sinking. More than one-half of the capital expended there, is already lost for ever, in taxes on wood, bricks, and bread." " Bread! come, that *is* a droll joke! what has bread to do with building? The money, however, must have come from somewhere." " True; but do you know that the poor-rates of England and Wales last year increased eight per cent. on the average? There is not one county upon which to hang a quibble; not one was stationary; in not one was there a decrease; and the increase was greatest in those counties on which depends the prosperity of all the rest. In Warwickshire, the increase was sixteen per cent. —in Lancashire, twenty-two. Does this look like prosperity? A little more such prosperity will close the manufactories from one end of the kingdom to the other; and then your favourite Wetherell will see the difference between a mob that chooses to do evil, and one that cannot avoid doing it." " Well, but Mister What's-your-name, you should not be ungrateful. You see, God has sent his scourge, the cholera among us." A few months since, a very big man, in a certain great house, blamed his Majesty's Ministers for the precautions they took against that disease. Shortly afterwards it arrived at his own door, but it passed on, and entered not; how, then, can it be of God?" " Are famine and bad governments your gods?" " Well, you are a queer fellow, Mr. What's-your-name. But what do you think of your Radicals now? The men are masters." " Yes, sir; but instead of trying to establish low wages, which signify low profits, had you not better try to raise profits by joining with your men, heart and hand, to effect the removal of the great cause of contention?" " What! submit to the beggars? I would starve first." " Now, Mr. Sneak-for-nought, if you were weighed, are you worth three-halfpence? First, let it be possible for you to become rich in England, and then, perhaps you may despise the poor without being ridiculous."

There is one subject on which the great vulgar of this town are nearly unanimous in opinion—I mean the necessity of an issue of small notes. They know nothing about the laws of currency; on the contrary, if put to their choice, they would, I verily believe, choose Pitt's inconvertible ones. We have, however, a few reasoning maniacs, who pretend to know something of the matter, and ho presume to doubt whether Pitt's Bill or Peel's Bill has done most mischief. They audaciously inquire, how it happened that a ministry, advocating the principles of free-trade, interfered with the natural laws of currency, and consequently with the freedom of trade in money? They actually impugn the wisdom of encouraging a huge and mischievous banking establishment, to the injury of all the useful banks in the nation. They stupidly imagine that there is no difference, in principle, between a one-pound note and a five-pound note; and they wonder, with the simplicity of idiocy, why we are compelled to have the note which we do not want, and prevented from having the note which we do want. They innocently ask, why bankers should not be allowed to issue one-pound notes, payable in gold at the counter, and with no other restraint than the mutual watchfulness and jealousy of the respective issuers! When told that if one-pound notes reappear, the gold coins will disappear, they reply, that if so, very few gold coins can be wanted; and that, by an issue of small notes, controlled by no law but the natural law of the case, " one pound might indeed be made to do the work of five." When reminded of the crisis of 1825, they ridiculously assert, that the law alone was the cause of the crisis—that law which sagaciously made one over-grown bank liable to furnish specie for the whole realm, and furnish it in greatest abundance, when directly interested in furnishing none at all. For, they say, if the thousand banks of the empire had each been liable to provide gold (not bank paper) for the payment of its own notes, all the gold wanted would have been found, and no inconvenience whatever would have been sustained by them or the community. When told that theory is but theory, they sneeringly answer, that Watt's steam engine was theory fifty years ago. These fellows, I have little doubt, would rather give a shilling for a peck of good foreign wheat, than thrice that sum for the same quantity and quality grown in their own country. If I were in authority, I would hang every man of them to-morrow. I know, Gentlemen, you do not agree with me on the Currency Question—and perhaps not altogether upon other points—but you will be glad, perhaps, to give insertion to these opinions of the inhabitants of a great manufacturing town. The people to be governed well, must be known well.—I have the honour to be, your most obedient servant,

EBENEZER ELLIOT.

POPULAR ESTIMATION OF GEOLOGY.

St. Fond relates that in Mull, the son of his hospitable landlord, could not make out at all what he might be after " in the hill," whither he carried a small hammer, but declined taking a gun. About twenty years back the late Professor ———, visiting at Donibristle, took a chaise from the North Ferry. On the short drive of three or four miles, his conduct appeared so suspicious to the sapient driver, that he thought it incumbent upon him, as a duty he owed to his lordship, and to a house to which he took so many fares, and from which he received so many horns of ale, to impart his apprehensions to the servants. " I kenna what sort of chap I have brought you the day," said James, as soon as he had got rid of the professor and his portmanteau, " but I ne'er thought to have got him this length. Ye'll need to keep an e'e ower him. We never travelled a quarter of a mile, but I bud stop the chaise, and set him down, when he out wi' a bit little hammer he keeps, and paps at a stane on this side o' the road, and a stane on that side o' the road, and puts them in his pouch!—but at Mr. ——— dyke, I thought he wou'd hae riested a' thegither. He canna be richt—and he's a decent-like, well-put-on man, too." Nor does geology appear to be extending rapidly northward. The subjoined anecdote, which reminds us of the professor's adventure, is given in a late Dundee newspaper. " Nearly the following dialogue took place between a clergyman, in a remote part of Angus, and a parishioner, who was in the habit of letting summer lodgings. After the ordinary inquiries—" Your new lodger seems a quiet man?" " So he seemed at first, Sir, but we're grown doubtfu' that he's no richt."—" No richt, John; not behaving himself, or not paying his accounts?" " Ou no, he's weel aneugh that way—no richt in his mind, I mean. My wife and me notice that he tak's out a hammer wi' him ilka day to the hill, and aye brings hame at night a bit poky fu' o' broken stanes; he bigs them up in an out o' the way corner o' his room, and tak's as muckle care o' a wheen chucky stanes as if they were something o' use. Now I was thinking that he's may-be been no richt, and gotten escaped frae his frien's; so the night, when he was sitting in his room quietly, I just gae the key a thraw that he might nae rin aff, and so cam down to see if you thought we might keep him lockit up till he was cried at all the kirks. Or may-be ye might help us to adverteese him in the papers, to let his friends ken." It is needless to add, that the clergyman advised them just to leave the suspected philosopher to himself, so long as he lived quietly, and paid his bills.

REV. WILLIAM MUIR, D.D.
MINISTER OF ST. STEPHEN'S CHURCH.

Dr. Muir is a native of the west of Scotland; and immediately after being licensed in 1812, while but a very young man, he was at once presented to a city church, the magistrates of Glasgow appointing him to the new parish of St. George's, in the most fashionable part of that city. He was considered at that time decidedly the best and most elegant preacher in Glasgow, though then quite moderate in his religious views. The arrival of Dr. Chalmers of course eclipsed his fame in the public estimation, though not the least with his own congregation, who continued ardently attached to him till deprived of his ministrations by his translation to Edinburgh.

In 1822, Dr. Muir was presented to the parish and church of New Greyfriars, in Edinburgh. Here he greatly surpassed all the expectations that had been formed of him, and drew a crowded audience. He continued minister of this parish till the year 1829, when the magistrates, having erected another handsome church and extensive parish in the New Town, after a good deal of anxious deliberation regarding who was the best minister to appoint to so important and influential a parish, fixed on Dr. Muir, who was accordingly translated to be minister of St. Stephen's. This change was a fortunate one in many respects. Dr. Muir had before this period been severely tried in the furnace of domestic affliction, and his spirits had considerably sunk under it; but here he was a changed man; he was roused to a new and more extended sphere of duty and usefulness, and his animal spirits, as well as mental energy, were greatly improved by the change. Those severe domestic bereavements, which are so heart-rending to our nature, had already proved to him, as they have often proved to thousands, *blessings in disguise*, sent as it were direct from the hand of Providence; and the fruits of them were a meek and sanctified spirit, and a double excitement to the diligent performance of all duty. Whatever his discourses might have been in the earlier part of his career, during his ministry in the parishes of Greyfriars and St. Stephen's they have been decidedly orthodox and evangelical: they are strictly practical and useful; and, from a strong sense of the paramount importance of the labours of the Christian pastor, he evidently bestows the utmost diligence and industry in their preparation. He has been most successful with his congregation: while, on the other hand, they, aware of his great anxiety for their religious welfare, are reciprocally attached to him, though, creditably to themselves, not with that blind devotedness which sometimes leads many well-meaning, but weak-minded people, in a congregation, to make an idol of a favourite minister, forgetting that, excellent though he may be, he is still but a frail and fallible being like themselves.

Dr. Muir's style of composition is very correct and elegant, it abounds in antithesis. His sermons are distinguished by clearness and perspicuity; at the same time his reasoning throughout is so consecutive, as to require a close exercise of the attention. His mind is evidently imbued with a strong view of the selfishness and natural baseness of the world. He is often pointed and severe on the follies and frivolities of the fashionable world, urging his hearers rather to take a deep interest in the things that pertain to *everlasting* life ; to lay up for themselves treasures where neither moth nor rust can corrupt, and where thieves do not break through or steal. He occasionally indulges in a bitter and sarcastic vein of irony against the amazing want of foresight in mankind neglecting this their highest and greatest interest ; and, in alluding to the vanity and deceitfulness of the world, we remember him, in one of his discourses, making the caustic but too true remark, that " the friendship of the world is affectation, heartlessness, and selfish indifference." Strangers hearing Dr. Muir, for the first time, are generally much disappointed, viewing his manner and delivery as artificial. In this they are somewhat mistaken ; for though Dr. Muir, when young, had been anxious to acquire a polished and oratorical delivery, and thus originally formed his present manner, it is now at all events natural to him, and the objection of affectation gives way after hearing him preach two or three times. In his discourses, Dr. Muir takes the interesting view of our connexion with the Deity, of teaching his hearers to look up to Him with *Love*, as children to a parent, who is at once our Creator, Benefactor, and Friend. This is certainly infinitely better, and more scriptural, than what some preachers are apt to inculcate, of regarding the Supreme Being only with fear and terror. In this respect Dr. Muir may be compared with the eloquent American preacher, Channing, though of course at antipodes with him in his Socinian views.

While minister of the parish of New Greyfriars, Dr. Muir personally visited and sought to become acquainted with the lower classes, of whom the parish chiefly consisted ; and he exercised a wholesome and salutary moral and religious influence over them. It may give some idea of the nature of the population he had to visit, when it is mentioned, that there were to be found among them people lending out their children to beggars for sixpence a-day, to aid them in their medicant or worse avocations. In St. Stephen's parish the population is chiefly of the higher and middle classes ; here also he visits his parishioners and congregation ; he attends to placing the children of the poor at school, and holds regular meetings in the church for catechising and instructing the children and adults of the congregation.

Dr. Muir rarely attends meetings of the Presbytery or the General Assembly, having the idea that there are clergymen enough without his aid, to transact the business of the Church Courts, and preferring to hold on the noiseless tenor of his way, without mingling in these scenes.

As regards personal appearance, Dr. Muir's countenance and features are very fine and engaging ; and he is possessed of a well modulated voice, which, added to his excellent style of composition, sincere piety, and private worth, present much of the *beau ideal* of a Christian minister.

Dr. Muir, in 1822, published, as a farewell legacy to his Glasgow congregation, a volume of " Discourses, Explanatory and Critical, on the Epistle of St. Jude ;" and in 1830 he committed to the press his " Sermons on the Characters of the Seven Churches in Asia, described in the Book of Revelation ;" to which were added two excellent sermons on the distinction between secret and revealed things in religion.

The following eloquent passage on the undue love of the world is from one of these discourses :—

" There is an influence arising from the ' evil that is in the world,' which is directly fitted to damp the whole ardour of the religious affections. Even the man who is most solicitous to cherish these affections, knows the disastrous nature of that influence. It casts around him an impure medium, through which he cannot see the spiritual realities, or rightly breathe after them. It operates on him as contagion, from the effects of which he does not soon recover, even when he has escaped its atmosphere. It has enfeebled his desire of Heaven. It has abated his relish for devotion. It has paralyzed his Christian resolution. And, altogether, he feels that when it throws its shadow over him, it has been as the branch of the poisonous tree :—beneath its fatal leaves every flower decays, every plant withers to the root. And if this be felt, even while there is earnestness to maintain against it the ardour of religious sentiment, what must be the consequence of wilfully and eagerly exposing the heart to be acted on by the untoward influence ? Must not the vestiges of religion, which education may have left, be thereby effaced ? Must not every spark of devotional feeling be speedily quenched ? Think what some of the means of cherishing the ardour of religious sentiments are ; and then, mark how opposed to the successful use of these means, are the whole habits of worldliness. Is the serious reading of the Scriptures, for example, essential to maintain in us the very being of religion ? But do we come to the reading of God's word, with the collectedness of mind needful for being improved by the perusal, after having so immersed ourselves in the pursuits of the world as to have yielded the heart alternately to covetousness, and ambition, and sensuality ? On the contrary, what shattered thoughts, what a wandering imagination, what a blinded perception must accompany us, should the force of early custom still bring us to the perusal of the sacred page. Oh, again, is the duty of prayer, the pouring out of the soul at the throne of grace, along with the exercise of self-inquiry and consideration, essential for invigorating in us the principles of religion ? But, in how many of the engagements, in all of the vain pleasures of the world, is there not a direct incompatibility with the devotional frame of mind ! I express what is familiar to the experience of every one of you, on returning from these, when I speak of satiety and dissatisfaction as the attendants on the observances of devotion in which you then try to join. You have come out of a vortex of tumultuary and idle thoughts, after the whirl of which it is not easy to be reduced to sober reflection. You feel that you want the right tone for the exercises of devotion. There is then a chord touched by religion to which nothing in the heart answers. There are then representations unfolded by religion, which are too pure to delight the soul that has been accustoming its vision to the coarse objects of sense and sin. The forms of piety may still be assumed ; but no sentiment of piety glows under them ; and thus, the lukewarmness of the heart to religion is as fatal to moral improvement as the coldness of infidelity itself.

" Be entreated, however, to weigh the whole matter well. You may find, by doing so, that you labour under a mistake as to the importance of the opinion of the world. The terrible thing which, on a general view, bulks so greatly, reduces itself when you proceed to touch it, and examine it, and try it in the scale of truth."—*From Sketches of the Edinburgh Clergy, lately published—a handsome volume, with portraits.*

THE REMARKABLE HISTORY OF SOPHIA DOROTHEA, WIFE OF GEORGE I.

In the state of childhood, when no affection could be formed, or any just notions be conceived, of the nature and obligation of the connubial relation, was Sophia Dorothea obliged to enter into the most serious of all engagements with her first cousin, who was double her own age. Within a year, however, the death of her spouse released her from this preposterous and unnatural tie ; but it was only to consign her over to another, not less inconsistent and oppressive. A widow of ten years old, in one of the most enlightened parts of Europe, conveys an idea so ludicrous, as scarcely to deserve credit, were not the fact upon record. But, what will perhaps appear equally extravagant, is the circumstance, that on the death of the husband of this infant, her father and uncle came to an agreement to unite her in the bonds of marriage to her other cousin, Prince George Lewis of Hanover, then sixteen years of age. It is true the ceremony did not take place at Zell till the 20th of November, 1682, when the bride had completed her sixteenth, and the bridegroom his twenty-second year ; but it is no less certain, that the engagement was made by all the parties, soon after the death of the Prince Augustus Frederick of Wolfenbuttel. In the meantime, Prince George travelled, and made some campaigns; while the bride completed her education, and prepared herself, as well as could be expected for one of her years, for the important duties of a wife and a mother. On the 30th October, 1683, the Princess gave her husband a son, who was named George; and four years afterwards she brought him a daughter, named Sophia Dorothea, who became the wife of Frederick William of Prussia, and mother of Frederick the Great. To account for the distance of time between the births of these children, it must be observed, that Prince George Lewis, soon after his marriage, entered again upon the military career in Hungary, where he commanded the Brunswick troops in the imperial service, and soon after took Neuhausel, and raised the siege of Gran. In 1686, he was at the taking of Buda; in 1689, he was at the capture of Mayence; and the next year he commanded an army of eleven thousand men in the Spanish Netherlands, where, in 1693, he bore a distinguished part in the sanguinary battle of Neerwinden. Soon after this, the Prince returned to Hanover; but within a few months his temper was observed to be much altered, and he either looked upon his wife with an eye of jealousy, or his own affections were estranged from her, and transferred to some other object.

A young German Count, named Philip Christopher Konigsmark, who held the commission of colonel in the Swedish service, happened to be then at Hanover, and upon him the suspicions of the Prince fell, but whether from secret information, or any particular observations of his own, has never been determined. His Highness, however, is said to have entered the bedchamber of Sophia Dorothea so suddenly, that Konigsmark, in his haste to escape, left his hat behind him, which confirmed all that had been surmised of an improper intercourse between him and the Princess, and a separation immediately took place. Another account of a darker hue, which obtained currency, was, that the Prince of Hanover actually found Konigsmark in the room, and in his fury ran him through the body. Though this last story appears to be incorrect in the principal points, certain it is, that the Princess was arrested, and sent off to the castle of Ahlen, where she lingered out a miserable life of two-and-thirty years in close confinement, without a trial, or being allowed to see any of her family.

The fate of the colonel was never exactly known, any farther than that a report of his having died at Hanover, in the month of August, 1694, was transmitted to his friends, who were too much accustomed to such calamities in their family, to make any stir about the affair. That the count came to a violent end, seems to be put beyond all doubt by the manner in which he disappeared; and it is remarkable, that some years ago, when the castle of Zell underwent repair, the skeleton of a man was found beneath one of the floors, which revived the name and story of the unfortunate Konigsmark.

With regard to Sophia Dorothea, her connexions prevented any severer measures from being pursued against her than perpetual confinement; to justify which, a decree was published at Hanover, asserting that circumstances had been produced in evidence before the consistory, of such a nature as warranted the belief that she had been unfaithful to her illustrious husband. The strongest of these circumstances, however, was that of the hat which the Prince found in the room; and the agitation which the discovery naturally produced in her Highness was at once interpreted into a demonstration of conscious guilt. To those who have been accustomed to the consideration of criminal charges, and the minute investigation of evidence, this case will appear more like an occurrence of an iron age, when feudal oppression and military despotism prevailed, than an event of the seventeenth century, in a country boasting of its jurisprudence.

That no proof of adultery was ever brought forward, is certain; and, for the want of it, the parties could not be legally divorced, which they certainly would have been, had evidence existed of the criminality of the Princess. Some there were, even in Hanover, who not only considered Sophia Dorothea as perfectly innocent of what she was accused of, but as being actually made a victim to the prostituted affections of her husband. This opinion may now be adopted, without any hazard of refutation, or of giving offence; for neither before the accession of the Elector of Hanover to the British throne, nor afterwards, when such a proceeding became especially necessary, as a matter affecting the succession, was the conduct of the Duchess brought, as it ought to have been, under judicial investigation. Had Sophia Dorothea been really guilty of an adulterous intercourse with Konigsmark, or any other person, the public interest required a trial; but nothing of the kind ever took place, and the parties remained in the relation of man and wife till the death of the Queen in her prison, at the age of sixty, on the 2d of November, 1726.

It is very extraordinary, and little to the credit of the times, that not the slightest notice was ever taken of the unhappy Sophia by the English Parliament or people, after the arrival of her husband. If she was guilty, a legal divorce ought to have been called for, upon public grounds; and if she was not, the honour of the nation, and the cause of humanity, required her liberation, and an establishment in circumstances suited to her high birth and royal station. Instead of this, though the mother to the heir apparent, and actually Queen of England, she was suffered to linger out her days in a dungeon, while the mistress of her husband shone as a peeress of the first rank at the English court.

One person alone ventured to incur the royal displeasure, by advocating the cause of the afflicted and much injured Sophia Dorothea of Zell. This was the Prince, her son; who was so fully convinced of his mother's innocence, (and he was not ignorant of all that had been alleged against her,) that on many occasions he reproached his father for his injustice towards her, and openly declared his intention of bringing her to England, and acknowledging her as Queen Dowager, in the event of his succeeding to the crown while she was living.

This virtuous resolution he was only prevented from carrying into execution by the death of his unhappy mother, six months before that of her husband. The Prince made several attempts to get access to his imprisoned parent; but all his efforts to accomplish this praiseworthy object proved unavailing, by the vigilance of the guards.

He was so sensibly affected upon this point, that he had the picture of Sophia Dorothea painted in her royal robes, long before he came to the crown; and this portrait he caused to be so placed as to attract the notice of all his visiters, which gave such offence to the King, that he not only declined going himself to see the Prince and Princess, but forbade his courtiers from shewing them that respect. It was also owing to this sentiment of filial regard, that George II., when in a passion, always took off his hat, and kicked it about the floor, without considering the place or the company. Thus it is that early impressions once fixed in the mind, create habits; and circumstances, by an association of ideas with events long since passed away, excite either disagreeable or pleasing emotions. In allusion to this remarkable history, and the effect it had on the mind of the King, Dr. Hoadly, the physician, wrote his comedy of "The Suspicious Husband," the plot of which turns upon an incident similar to that which proved so disastrous to the Princess of Hanover. With this play, George II., who had little taste for the drama, was much delighted.

THE FARMERS' CENTENARY CONTRASTED.
In 1732.
 The MAN to the *Plough;*
 The WIFE to the *Cow;*
 The GIRL to the *Sow;*
 The BOY to the *Mow;*
  And your *Rents will be netted.*
In 1832.
 Best MAN—*Tally-ho!*
 And MISS—*Piano!*
 The WIFE—*Silk and Satin!*
 The BOY—*Greek and Latin!*
  And you'll *all be Gazetted.*

ELEMENTS OF THOUGHT.

SIGNS OF THE TIMES.

The world is in agitation. All kings on earth, whose words were wont to be laws, are troubled. The calm repose of ages, in which thrones and altars were held sacred, has been broken in a moment. Ancient monarchies, which seemed long to defy dissolution and mock at time, pass away like a dream; and the question is not now of the death of a king, or even of the ceasing of one dynasty and the commencement of another, but the whole fabric of government is insecure, the whole frame of society is shaken. Every kingdom, instead of each being knit together and dreaded by surrounding states, is divided against itself, as if dissolution were the sure destiny of them all. A citizen king, the choice of the people, sits upon the throne of the Capets; and, as if the signal had gone throughout the world quick as lightning, nations, instead of progressing slowly to regeneration, start at once into life. And from the banks of the Don to the Tagus, from the shores of the Bosphorus to Lapland; and, wide Europe being too narrow a field for the spirit of change that now ranges simultaneously through the world, from the new states of South America, to the hitherto unchangeable China, skirting Africa, and traversing Asia, to the extremity of the globe on the frozen north, there are signs of change in every country under heaven; and none can tell of what kingdom it may be told in the news of to-morrow, that a revolution has been begun and perfected in a week. Every kingdom seems to wait for its day of revolt or revival; and the only wonder now would be, that any nation should continue much longer what for ages it has been; or that the signs of the times should not every where alike be a striking contrast to those of the past.—*Rev. A. Keith.*

THE FICTION WRITERS, OR MORAL INSTRUCTORS—SIR WALTER SCOTT.

Let our moral philosophers (usefully employed though they be in arranging and digesting the science, and enlightened in modifying, from time to time, the manifestations of its eternal principles)—let our moral philosophers declare whether they expect their digests and expositions to be eagerly listened to by the hundred thousand families, collected, after their daily avocations, under the spell of the northern enchanter; whether they would look for thumbed copies of their writings in workshops or counting-houses, in the saloons of palaces, and under many a pillow in boarding schools. Our Universities may purify morals, and extend their influence as far as they can; their importance in this case runs a chance of being overlooked; for Scott is the president of a college where nations may be numbered for individuals. Our clergy may be, and do all that an established clergy can be and do; yet they will not effect so much as the mighty lay preacher who has gone out on the highways of the world, with cheerfulness in his mien and benignity on his brow; unconcious, perhaps, of the dignity of his office, but as much more powerful in comparison with a stalled priesthood as the troubadour of old—firing hearts wherever he went, with the love of glory—than the vowed monk. Our dissenting preachers may obtain a hold on the hearts of their people, and employ it to good purpose; but they cannot send their voices east and west to wake up the echoes of the world. Let all these classes unite in a missionary scheme, and encompass the globe, and still Scott will teach morals more effectually than them all. They will not find audiences at every turn who will take to heart all they say, and bear it in mind for ever; and if they attempt it now, they will find that Scott has been before them every where. He has preached truth, simplicity, benevolence, and retribution in the spicy bowers of Ceylon, and in the verandahs of Indian bungalowes, and in the perfumed dwellings of Persia, and among groups of settlers at the Cape, and amidst the pinewoods, and savannahs of the western world, and in the vineyards of the Peninsula, and among the ruins of Rome, and the recesses of the Alps, and the hamlets of France, and the cities of Germany, and the palaces of Russian despots, and the homes of Polish patriots. And all this in addition to what has been done in his native kingdom, where he has exalted the tastes, ameliorated the tempers, enriched the associations, and exercised the intellects of millions. This is already done in the short space of eighteen years; a mere span in comparison with the time that it is to be hoped our language and literature will last. We may assume the influence of Scott, as we have described it, to be just beginning its course of a thousand years; and now, what class of moral teachers (except politicians, who are not too ready to regard themselves in this light) will venture to bring their influence into comparison with that of this great lay preacher?—*Achievements of the Genius of Scott.—Tait's Magazine for January.*

PARTIES.

The fact is, that none but aristocratic parties endure. They are like rivers, that sweep in a continued course, more rapid and violent at first, and more large and calm at last, but increasing ever, until they reach the great ocean, where they are destined to disappear. Democratic party, on the contrary, resembles now a huge lake, inundating and overwhelming the whole land; whilst the next season it dries up, disappears, and leaves not even the trace of its channel behind. Look through history. You will see York and Lancaster, Orleans and Burgundy, spill blood, and alternately monopolize influence for centuries; whilst the popular party break forth but in momentary insurrection, quenched soon by the sword and the scaffold. More lately the Puritans were a popular party. They rose in 1640, and were irresistibly triumphant; they placed their chief upon the Stuart's throne. Yet in a short twenty years they were no more. It is said, that the wits and poets of the Restoration put Puritanism to flight by the arrows of their ridicule; but these were spent upon a body already extinct. In 1660, the English people had *sent in their resignation,* to use a phrase of their neighbours, and Charles the Second trod down the upper classes, merely because the lower ones were indifferent. As to Whigs and Tories, those were merely aristocratic parties. A popular one—where is it to be found throughout the last century of our history, except in applauding Sacheverel, and hissing Lord Bute? In 1790, indeed, our people began to awaken to political feeling. Yet how soon were they frightened or lulled. In 1830 they awoke again; and are still awake. But how long will they remain so? Not till 1835, that I venture to prophesy. Radicals, look to it; and although now afloat, look for the time as possibly near, when the tide will ebb, and leave you on the dry sand.

AFFECTATION.

Why, Affectation—why this mock grimace?
Go, silly thing, and hide that simpering face!
Thy lisping prattle and thy mincing gait,
All thy false mimic fooleries I hate;
For thou art Folly's counterfeit, and she,
Who is right foolish, hath the better plea;
Nature's true idiot I prefer to thee!

Why that soft languish?—why that drawling tone?
Art sick?—art sleepy?—Get thee hence—begone!
I laugh at all these pretty baby tears,
Those flutterings, faintings, and unreal fears.

Can they deceive us? can such mummeries move?
Touch us with pity, or inspire with love?
No!—Affectation, vain is all thy art,
Those eyes may wander over every part,
They'll never find a passage to the heart!

RICHARD CUMBERLAND.

Note.—These lines may be recommended to the special attention of certain *would-be-fine* ladies in Scotland, as well as in England. There is no object in nature more ridiculous than an affected woman,—*excepting* an affected man,—compared with either, a monkey is a most respectable and venerable animal,

THE STORY-TELLER.

THE IRISH BESSY BELL AND MARY GRAY.

"Oh! Bessy Bell and Mary Gray,
They were twa bonnie lassies."—*Scotch Ballad.*

These names are perfectly familiar to the inhabitants of the town and neighbourhood of Omagh, in the county Tyrone, and are given to two low mountains, situate on either side of the splendid demesne of Mountjoy Forest. During a late visit to that part of the country, I made it my business to inquire into the origin of these titles, guessing, rightly, that some legend of interest might be found to be connected with them. The result of my investigation I shall now commit to writing, doubting not that the narrative itself, independently of any powers of the narrator, will be found sufficiently engaging to justify me in the attempt. Concerning the date of the events I am about to relate, I have ascertained nothing accurately, further than that they were still fresh in the memory of some of the elders of the district, as either coeval with or shortly preceding their early youth.

Mary Gray and Bessy Bell were two maidens, whose hereditary residences were placed near the foot of the respective mountains which serve to hand down their names to posterity. The former might have had the precedence in years by two summers at the farthest; and while they equalled each other in fascinations and accomplishments of the first order, yet these were in each composed of far different lights and shades, even as their degrees in life were widely removed. Mary's ancestors had long leased the considerable farm which her family now held, and which was justly looked upon as one of the most substantial and thriving in the neighbourhood. Bessy, on the other hand, was highly descended, and connected with many of the leading families around her. Mary's disposition was thoughtful, calm, and imaginative; Bessy's, again, was playful, capricious, and inconsiderate. The one could sit happily for hours, on the summit of her native hills, gazing on the beautiful scenes of lawn and woodland beneath her, and, lulled by the murmur of the river of the valley, conjure up a world of a thousand dreams around her, and trace in admiration the fair handywork of nature. The other, yielding to every passing impulse, fearless of care, and open to enjoyment, was apparently intended to figure only in the more sunny passages of existence, and was herself a potent mistress of the spells of gaiety. Mary's figure was tall, perfect, and commanding, and though her light blue eyes, and auburn tresses, seemed the very emblems of all that was tranquil, yet every fine feature was robed in inexpressible dignity, during her moments of excitement or enthusiasm. It was impossible, on the other hand, to withstand the laughing glances of Bessy's sparkling eyes, set off as they were by a profusion of raven ringlets that clustered down her dimpled cheeks, while her almost fairy form was cast in the finest mould of feminine loveliness.

Such were the two fair creatures whose histories I am about to relate, when the one had reached her twentieth, and the other her eighteenth year; and by what link those histories came to be united, it will be now necessary to explain.

The reader has already, perhaps, felt surprise, that the qualities and attractions I have ascribed to Mary should be found in a farmer's daughter, in a "maiden of low degree." My information, however, accounted readily for the fact. Her family, as I have hinted, had long enjoyed an unusual, and an almost uninterrupted prosperity, and in consequence of singular industry and perseverance on their part—virtues which seldom go without their reward—were conversant with few of the distresses that annoyed and agitated their less-gifted neighbours. Her father, though in other respects a prudent and moderate man, seems to have indulged in overweeningly-ambitious views for his daughter's welfare. Her birth had been soon followed by the loss of an affectionate wife, and he appeared thenceforth to have centred all his warmer feelings in her, whose uncommon beauty, and earlier indications of a superiority of mind, accounted, even in childhood, for all his fond partiality. Thus he was often heard to boast, that "his Mary should be as fine a lady as the best of them;" and with this view he had intrusted her, when but eight years old, to the care of the most fashionable schoolmistress of the metropolis, desiring her to take charge of her until she was as accomplished as unsparing expenditure could make her. Mary was accordingly thrown at once among associates all higher than herself in station and prospects of life; and, save when the honest farmer paid his regular half-yearly visit, she never even saw, for a number of years, any that moved within her own natural sphere.

But while her companions, as I have said, had the superiority in point of rank, she found few to rival her in innate elegance, in graces of person, and in thirst for improvement; and although it must be admitted that the arrival of her unfashionable relative never failed to excite a momentary titter among her playmates, yet it was speedily checked by the recollection of her own unassuming merit and extraordinary good nature, which had won, from the first, the affections of each individual of the little community.

One of these, and inferior only to Mary in acquirements, was the second heroine of my tale; and, strange to say, although as different in tastes as I have described them, they soon formed for each other a fond and faithful attachment. They had been born and nursed amid the same scenes, and it was Mary's greatest delight, during her long exile from the midst of them, to freshen her recollections and multiply her inquiries from her very willing and happier friend, who twice, at least, each year, could draw her information from experience. They were the joint idols of the school, but so far were they either from envying the other's popularity, that they would sit conversing together in some quiet corner on the occasion of many a pastime, when there was the loudest cry for their aid and countenance of the general sports. Thus did each delight in the other's society, the very opposition of their characters enhancing perhaps the charms of intimacy. When Mary sung a pensive melody, Bessy would reply to it in some merry little native air: when Mary's imagination was attracted by the sombre and melancholy, Bessy would discover each lighter sentiment, as if by magic, in their common studies.

Years flitted by, strengthening their attachment as they passed, and Mary was at length delighted by a summons to attend her father on his last expedition homeward. Bessy was to remain one year longer at the academy, and the friends parted with mutual protestations of regard, and threats of almost daily correspondence, which they afterwards put into very accurate execution, to the great pride and pleasure of the farmer, who was gratified by the connexion and intercourse in which his daughter had engaged. Not so with Mr. Bell. Naturally haughty and distant, he listened with little satisfaction to Bessy's account of her great intimacy with one so much her inferior in rank, although accompanied by the most glowing and enthusiastic praise; and when at length the period of her departure from school arrived, and she was to appear as his daughter in society, he sternly interdicted all future intercourse between them. Need I tell of the supplications, of the tears that attended so cruel a disappointment. He was resolute in his severity, and Bessy rode over to make the terrible disclosure, and wept for the last time on the bosom of her devoted and disconsolate friend. It was, indeed, a trying scene—they parted in the deepest affliction.

When poor Mary was left alone, she had time to estimate fully the overpowering loss she had sustained. Even before this sad occasion, indeed immediately on her arrival from school, she had perceived, and almost regretted, the deep mistake her father had committed in giving her an education so completely disproportioned to her rank—an education, which, if it added refinements, yet increased her wants, and unfitted her to take any interest in the pursuits or pleasures of her natural associates and protectors, while the fatal barrier of her birth seemed irrevocably to forbid the acquisition of that place in a higher circle, to which she was both entitled by her accomplishments, and which she could have filled with dignity. Her relations, indeed, had greeted her return with every demonstration of pride and affection, while her father doated on her with the most intense, nay, painful fondness; yet both they and he approached her with an involuntary betrayal of a consciousness of their inferiority, that, to her delicate sensibility, almost destroyed the satisfaction which should naturally be afforded her from the kind interest of kinsfolk, and the warmth of a father's love. Viewing her circumstances, therefore, with discreet and unbiassed penetration, she would have regretted, I say, her adventitious elevation above her fellows, had she not hitherto enjoyed a solace for all distresses in her "sweet communion" with her beloved Bessy, and felt how deep should be her gratitude for being so strangely enabled to preserve an equality and enjoy an interchange of feeling and affection with so much merit and elegance.

Can any wonder, then, that this disappointment preyed heavily on her tender disposition; that she gave herself up for a time to a deep and wearing melancholy, and fancied that she was now left almost alone in the world. It was during the Christmas holidays that the unexpected shock came upon her, which seemed for the moment to stun all her faculties; and the spring had softened into summer, ere her mind regained ought of its natural elasticity. The honest farmer felt deeply affected, and, unable as he was to appreciate her sentiments duly, still endeavoured to sooth her too visible sorrow with unavailing fondness. Fearful of giving offence, by letting him see the inefficiency of his sympathies, she sought rather to retire into solitude; and, as the season advanced, she wandered up the mountain almost daily to some shady spot, and soon forgetting the subject of the book before her, was lost for hours together in her own bitter and crowding thoughts, until the evening's chill, or the gathering gloom, reminded her that it was time to return.

It was on the morning of the 28th of August, that Frederick Montgomery also climbed that mountain, with the eagerness of a sportsman on the first day of the grouse-shooting for the season. As he descended again, it was with no slight astonishment that he perceived, at a little distance, Mary Gray, as it were some fair spirit of the heights, moving slowly and musingly downward towards her father's cottage. It was the thought of a moment to follow cautiously and trace her steps; and at length his inquiries from a labourer in the adjoining field, convinced him that he had discovered her residence. Accordingly he resolved to return the next day to the same ground for sport, trusting to his ingenuity to invent some pretext for gaining admission at Farmer Gray's.

Frederick Montgomery was a stranger in Ireland, and had come down to the neighbourhood to pay, as he had at first intended, but a short visit to a newly-married friend—himself a late settler. Although naturally of a frank and manly disposition, yet the dissipation of an Oxford life, and a subsequent unlimited enjoyment of the pleasures of the Continent during two years, now found him nearly as heartless as he was gay. Early the master of an independent fortune, and gifted with ready and showy talents, he had arrived at perfect self-confidence from his intercourse with the world, and was possessed of an address as insinuating as his person was striking and handsome. It was no wonder then that he boasted of some success with woman, who had been long his favourite study, as her favours were his darling pursuit, and that he now flattered himself with an intimate knowledge of the sex, and believed that he was accomplished in its passions and whims, its oddities and caprice, and every access to its softer feelings.

Such was the person who stopped at Farmer Gray's on the morning of the 21st, under the plausible pretext of remedying some accidental disorder of his gun. While a servant was heating water for that purpose, perhaps it was through some momentary feeling of vanity, that her father requested him to step into Mary's little drawing-room; although the furniture was plain and unpretending, yet it displayed an air of unstudied elegance, that had the power for an instant to change Montgomery's delight into astonishment. Work-boxes, a writing-desk, music and drawing, occupied their various positions through the apartment; a piano-forte lay open, while one or two feminine ornaments had been left in progress on the table. Books of belles-lettres, instruction, and devotion, were arranged in spider-shelves around the walls, and a splendid portrait of their beautiful possessor hung over the mantel-piece. Every thing seemed to acknowledge the governance of a tasteful mistress, though all the occupations whose tokens were thus visible, had been neglected for months previous to the time of which we speak.

Soon mastering his surprise, Montgomery, with admirable tact, displayed his pleasure only so as to flatter the vanity, without exciting the suspicions, of the farmer; and having discovered she had gone abroad for some time, he contrived to carry on so successfully his insidious attacks upon the gratified father, that, won by the courtesy and bearing of his guest, and believing his daughter also might be pleased at the society of one who was evidently so fully accomplished, he invited him to return to his house that evening on his way homeward.

Need I tell the rest? His visits were daily repeated—while his stay with his friend was further protracted, and each morning he started for the mountain with his gun and dogs, long after there had ceased to remain a single feather for his bag. He was a favourite alike with father and daughter, the one he continued to manage as artfully as at their first meeting—the other could not but be taken with a person who possessed so many attractions, taste, talents, and mutiplied, though showy and superficial, reading—who was ready to join in all her studies and amusements—who took such interest in every trifle that engaged her, and carried off all with those delicate and obsequious attentions, which, while they failed not to flatter and delight, could never for a moment appear obtrusive or alarming. They read, they sung, they walked and conversed together; Mary's disappointment at the loss of her friend was soothed, as her place was supplied; nor was she for a long time aware of the potent poison she was imbibing. And, strange to say, although it cannot be denied that his first intentions were of the basest and most infamous order, as his letters to a friend, of that date, attempted not even to disguise, yet the same testimony at a latter period declared him to be caught, as it were, in his own snare, and completely disarmed of his terrible purposes, by the gentle nature and glowing virtues of the fair being they were intended to assail.

Time rolled on, and at length he ventured to speak openly of love and wedlock, and met with a reception, from both father and daughter, as flattering as his pride could desire. He was the first of his sex whom Mary had ever known, and in truth he was a favourable specimen, and it would have been unaccountable if the farmer had not been dazzled at the prospect of such a brilliant alliance. Such was the promise of happiness which enlivened the little party at the cottage; when one noon, in the decline of the season, this young and interesting pair strolled on as they conversed of their prospects far into the enchanting scenery of Mountjoy Forest.

 * * * *

Of the details of that fatal day nothing further was known, than that Mary returned alone, and late in the evening, in a state bordering on frenzy, and never recovered from the shock she had sustained, or regained the peace she had sacrificed. Happily indeed for himself, her father was then absent, and for several days afterwards, and came home to suspect no more from the change in his daughter's spirits, which all her efforts could not conceal, than a mere lover's quarrel, often but the enhancement of lovers' happiness.

Meanwhile, Montgomery appeared early the following morning at the cottage, and from that moment continually besieged the door, begging, supplicating, even fiercely demanding to be admitted, and in vain. A thousand billet-doux, addressed to Mary, he entrusted to her faithful atendant—all, except the first, were immediately returned unopened. He, too, seemed to have become a maniac—his looks and figure were disordered, his words rash and violent, and his voice hoarse and broken.

The farmer's arrival, however, acted like a charm; he seemed to have awaked from a dream, and gained over his feelings so sudden and powerful a mastery, that the poor unsuspecting man was confirmed in the opinion I have mentioned, and pitying his distress, engaged to intercede for him with his daughter. Who will not pause to pity him in the fulfilment of such a task? Whose heart will not bleed for the poor victim whom he solicited? He came back at length, bewildered and displeased at her pertinacity, while she still remained resolute in declining to admit Montgomery in defiance of all importunities.

At length, exhausted and despairing of success, the latter absented himself wholly from the cottage, though he long continued to hover about at some distance, under the vain expectation of accidentally crossing her path. The friend at whose house he was a visiter, and to whom he betrayed no desire to move, though his originally-intended limits were now more than trebled, could not but observe his forlorn and dispirited state of mind, which, indeed, it needed but a glance at his haggard cheek and sunken eye, to ascertain. Too delicate to probe a wound which appeared so deep and irritable, he resorted rather to every kind artifice and design, which might have the effect of reviving and awakening him from the deplorable condition into which his every faculty had fallen. Among the rest, he invited company to his house, and courted the society of all the neighbouring gentry, to whose advances, as a stranger, he had been until now, considered unaccountably distant; and it was in the round of gaiety that ensued, that Montgomery met, for the first time, the former friend of his Mary, who seemed, as it were, the very soul and arbitress of all that was mirthful and happy. Worn and lethargic as he was, he could not help being attracted by such a brilliant display of charms; and his anxious friend was soon delighted to remark, that in her society he appeared to shake off much of the torpor which had so long preyed on him, as the opportunities of meeting her seemed to multiply with an almost fated accuracy.

Surprising and inconsistent, with that morbid and painful state of feelings I have described, as the next passage of his history would appear, let no man, I would say, presume to decide on the hidden motives, the inner workings of a fellow-creature, however open his external conduct to censure or dislike. For myself, I would fain see the sunny side of each fleeting picture, and I am satisfied, with regard to Montgomery, that during the latter part of his intimacy with Mary, he had been perfectly honourable in his intentions, whatever mysterious fatality seemed to have hung over its issue; that his grief and melancholy, when that intimacy was broken off, were equally unaffected; and that it was not owing to heartless indifference, but to natural fickleness and instability, and to the ardent spirits and warm constitution of his youth, that he soon was seen to be inspired with equal devotion to another, and as fair an object.

As for Bessy, she too had recovered from the shock her friendship had sustained, although the latter feeling remained still undiminished; and we have already noticed the number and power of the fascinations which now newly beset her. In a word, Montgomery was formed to be the bane of two gentle creatures, with respect to whom, whether we look to their personal charms, their intellectual attractions, the innocence in which he found them, or their unalterable attachment to each other; it would be difficult to decide which would be the object of the greater interest and admiration.

Yes, is it not, after all, nearly incredible when we recur to the circumstances of this little tale from the commencement, that in the course of four months from the hour when he parted with Mary, her recollection was now almost effaced, at least from the seat of his deeper emotions, and he found himself day after day engaged in attentions as assiduous to another, as he had so lately practised with unwearied zeal towards her? Nor was Bessy long insensible of his addresses, and, though her playful and innocent coquetry left him for a considerable period in doubt as to the state of her feelings towards him; yet, this very coquetry seemed destined to produce a result fatal to herself, as it roused him the more effectually from the languor which had oppressed him, awoke in him an interest and excitement, and elicited numberless fascinations which might have remained unnoticed had her manners been more distant and formal on the one hand, or had she seemed on the other, more easy and open to conquest. As it was, each soon received a sensible impression from the other's attractions, and looked forward with delight from day to day to the renewal of their intercourse. Montgomery, with his usual tact, won the good-will even of the cold Mr. Bell, and began to be looked upon as a constant visiter at his house. His daughter was seldom absent; and, as before, with her early friend, their recreations and pursuits became the same, and as he walked or rode by her side, with admirable versatility of talent he accommodated his thoughts and feelings to hers, and was now as light and gay in his topics of conversation with Bessy, as he had been grave and speculative with Mary.

At length, a lawsuit in which he was engaged, demanded his presence in England within the course of a few days, and he determined, though with considerable compunction, to sound Miss Bell's feelings, and, should he find them propitious, to make an immediate declaration of his own. This important step he reserved for his last day in the country, and on the morning previous engaged to accompany the fair object of his now-undivided passion in her usual ride.

For the first time, and he now remarked it with deep uneasiness, she led the way toward farmer Gray's cottage. Of her former intimacy with his daughter, Montgomery, by some strange chance, had never heard. Each of them perhaps, had thought of it as a painful subject, and one, too sacred, it might be, to be intruded on a stranger's attention. But the reaction of restrained feeling is often more lively than its original force, and on this occasion as the pretty farm-house at the foot of the mountain came suddenly in view, Bessy was as instantaneously overcome, and bursting into tears, "There," she exclaimed, "even there lives one who is dearest to me on earth!"

What? Mary? stammered Montgomery, and, but that his companion was herself so touched at that bitter moment, his guilty confusion could never have passed unobserved. Little did either imagine that the pitiable subject of the thoughts of each, was at that same instant gazing from a shrubbery on the road side, and, after a long wild stare, reeled and fell to the ground!

They had paused for some time involuntarily, Bessy yielding to pathetic and sad remembrances, while Montgomery's heart was nearly rent asunder by a thousand maddening and conflicting emotions; at length they, each as involuntarily, turned their horses' heads, and pursued their way homeward in melancholy and ill-omened silence. He was engaged for the same evening to meet a large party at Mr. Bell's, and it was not until they sat together at dinner that almost a syllable was interchanged between them; even then it cost an effort on both sides. The company observed it, and rallied each on their depression, and Bessy was ere long again the centre and attraction of all cheerfulness. Montgomery still maintained a gloomy taciturnity, for which the frightful convulsions of his mind that morning but too truly accounted. Bessy herself was surprised, when it no longer seemed to originate in compliment to her own feelings; but still following the bent of a fond woman's credulity, she gave it the flattering interpretation of extreme regret at his early intended absence.

The ladies had long retired, and Montgomery had fortified himself with deep and long potations, ere he found it possible to gain even an artificial excitement. Under such influence, he at length appeared in the drawing room, and hastening again to Bessy's side, he lavished on her, to an extravagant excess, all the flattery and compliment of which he was so finished a master. He led her to the piano-forte, hung over her chair, mingled his manly voice with her own sweet thrilling notes, and during each pause whispered in her ear his fixed and unalterable devotion.

They were, after some time, induced by the delighted audience, to attempt a celebrated duet, the most difficult they had yet performed, and peculiarly expressive of tender and impassioned sentiments. It was in the midst of this, and when Montgomery was taking his part with exquisite taste and masterly skill, that a servant slipped into his hand a note which had been just delivered to him. He held it with the air of one totally abstracted in his occupation until it was Bessy's turn to respond, as she did with power equal to his own: then he ventured to snatch one hasty glance at its superscription. It seemed to contain a deadly spell—his very reason appeared to fail him—he staggered to the door, to the astonishment of all present, and seizing his hat, and seeming to fly from their attentions, rushed with the speed of madness to the stable-yard, mounted his saddled horse, and galloped furiously away.

Can it be doubted from whom that communication came? The beautiful characters were but too well known to him, and the words, which he himself read not till the next dawn, were the following:—" Unhappy man! as thou wouldst yet hope for mercy for all thy accumulated guilt, ensnare not by thy wiles another victim, in addition to the lost

MARY.

Often after that night, did Montgomery curse the perfections of the animal which carried him, that he dashed him not to atoms on the rough roads which he passed. On, on he rode, pushing him at the height of his speed, nor pulled a rein till he arrived at Farmer Gray's cottage. It was already an hour past midnight, when he paused, scarce knowing where he was, and having come so far without fixed purpose or intent. All around was calm and quiet, in awful contrast to the tumult that raged within him. The farmer and his household had long retired to rest; yet there was one sleepless being within that heard the horse, and guessed at its rider. It was a moment of fearful excitement, and having almost mechanically led the reeking animal to a stall, he struck his hand against his forehead, and endeavoured to regain the composure which he appeared to have utterly lost. That he soon found was, at the moment, hopeless; and fearful of himself, frantic and distracted as he was, he determined to await the morning ere he sought admission at the cottage. He wandered round the environs of the farm, and as each familiar spot recurred to his eye beneath the clear moonlight, which he had trod so often with the lost, the loving Mary, he imprecated the deepest curses upon his own devoted head. At length the night clouded, as if in unison with his thoughts, the moon disappeared from the heavens, the storm rose apace, the rain descended thick, drifting, and violent. Involuntarily he bared his head and bosom to its assaults, and felt, for the moment, the first relief from frenzy. But in its place came reason, once more calm and cool, and he felt he had but awakened to a clearer sense of his misery. The lightning began to flash, and as its transitory brightness aided the grey glimmering of morning, he traced the expressions of the almost forgotten note. Deadly sickness came over him—a spasmodic shudder—a gravelike chill—and, staggering to a stable door, he sunk senseless beneath his steed upon the straw.

The farmer was, as usual, the first astir, and on going out was surprised to see that door but half-closed. He entered hastily, and was horror-smitten at the spectacle within. There lay Montgomery, as if in the grasp of a cruel and violent death, his throat and breast still bare, his face distorted, his hands clenched, and his hair damp and dishevelled. On closer examination, the farmer was rejoiced to discover that life yet remained: and being somewhat killed in surgery, a power which his retired situation often called into practice—he bore his patient to the cottage, and having bled him freely, used every means to recal the existence which seemed so fast ebbing. Nor were they long without effect; and whilst he bent over him, anxiously watching their progress, and having administered a gentle opiate, laid him in his own bed, and sat him down by the side, he gave up his mind to innumerable conjectures upon the cause which might have reduced Montgomery to such a fearful situation.

His horse might have taken fright, and fled to a haunt once so familiar. He might have been attacked by ruffians, with whom the forest was said occasionally to abound, and fled for protection to his house, whilst the violence of their assaults, or the exhaustion of fatigue, would account for his having been found insensible. These, and a thousand such accidents, his imagination speedily suggested; but they were soon discarded successively, and as it were by instinct; his fears settled finally on the truth—that all he saw was connected, though he guessed not how, with the interests of his beloved daughter.

Instantly he sought her chamber. She heard, with little surprise, that Montgomery was in the house; but was deeply shocked to learn his pitiable condition. She accompanied her father to his bedside, and along with him watched over the wretched being it contained, with a deep intensity of emotion, until a long-drawn sigh and violent contortion at length betokened his reviving senses, and then, in bitterness and misery, she glided back to her own apartment. The farmer, in the meantime, had resumed his painful reverie. During the last three months he had laboured under continual anxiety and doubt, concerning the lovers' unaccountable separation, and had latterly yielded to dark suspicions as to the purity of Montgomery's intentions, whose unworthiness he believed his daughter might have earlier detected, and acted accordingly. Even his present compassion could not prevent their growing form; and it is not then to be wondered at, that when at length the patient opened his eyes, and rolled them wildly round ere he could recollect and account for his present situation, which he finally testified by grasping convulsively the hand of his kind physician, that the latter replied to his wistful look, by saying abruptly,

" Mr. Montgomery, I am a plain-spoken man, and you must not be offended by my asking, what brought you here? or rather, was it to marry my daughter that you came?"

" Marry her!" exclaimed the unhappy young man—" Marry, did you say?—yes, yes I—it was to marry her—and oh! if you have a heart, but prevail on her this hour —to-morrow—or the next day—or when and where she pleases!"

The farmer was at once disarmed of every angry feeling, and all again was the tenderest and most attentive kindness. Finally, he undertook to gain for him an interview with his daughter, and left him for that purpose; while Montgomery, whose powerful constitution had already rallied considerably, made the necessary preparations in case his request should be granted.

And, after a long interval, it was so. Wrought up to the highest pitch of excitement, he received and obeyed the summons—and they met. But alas! how changed was the fair creature before him, from the bright young being he had once known and loved, in the beauty of opening womanhood, in the charms of happy innocence, in the spring-day of health and hope, almost a stranger to care, and possessing within herself a world of fascination, and of peace. Now that cheek was lighted up as brilliantly as ever, but it was hectic flush; that eye was as bright, but with the glare of disease; that brow was as eminently fair, but with the wan pallor of death.

* * * * *

What passed during that sad interview never transpired to any. His voice had been elevated in the various tones of supplication, of passion, and of anguish; even his bitter sobs were heard distinctly through the cottage. She had always spoken in the lowest accents of calm resolution and collected dignity. At length there was a long pause—there was one heart-breaking groan—the door opened, and Montgomery rushed to the stable, and, having thrown himself on his horse, galloped furiously to Omagh, called wildly for a post-chaise, and took the road to Dublin. There were no tidings of him afterward for many a week, save a hasty note to his friend, apologizing for his abrupt departure.

It were idle to detail the innumerable conjectures and rumours in the neighbourhood concerning his strange conduct the preceding evening, and his sudden and mysterious disappearance. Idler far were the hope of describing the woful feelings of the terrified, the forsaken Bessy. She had just learnt what it was to love, and be beloved, when the cup of happiness was dashed from her lips ; she had just felt the full brightness of the vision, when it vanished from her straining gaze.

* * * *

It was in the noon of the 20th August, one year from the day on which he had first seen Mary—and during that short year what misery had he not wrought for himself and others?—that Frederick Montgomery arrived in Omagh, having ridden by easy stages from the metropolis. He was much and visibly changed. His face had lost its former sweet expression, his cheek was pale, his lip colourless, his eye was wilder than before, and his brow wore the ravages of illness, and the traces alike of harrowing affliction and deep despair. What had brought him thither he dared not to ask himself. Could it be to look once more on the waste, the ruin he had made?

He partook of some refreshment, and prepared to resume his lonely way. As he waited the appearance of his horse, the church-bell threw sullenly on the air its awful lament of death. He listened calmly for a moment, then burying his face in his hands, yielded himself up to the succession of bitter emotions that those sounds inspired ; and the groom had summoned him thrice ere he started from his sad reverie. He mounted, rode slowly up the street, and saw the mournful paraphernalia of mortality enter the church-yard as he was about to pass. Under an involuntary impulse he paused, and moved after the sorrowful crowd toward the gate. He thought he heard some whispers of his name in the procession, but was too deeply abstracted to listen with much attention.

At length he reached the gate—there was, immediately within, a newly dug grave, and the coffin was being lowered from the hearse. As he gazed almost unconciously around —suddenly, like the lightning's flash—he caught the chief mourner's eye—that chief mourne rwas Farmer Gray, and in that glance what was there not conveyed ! It seemed to pierce him to the heart, and turning round instantaneously, he fled with the mad speed of the criminal, down the precipitate hill, and whither ?—and wherefore ?

* * * *

That terrible evening, Bessy was sitting in a little arbour which Montgomery's hands and her own had raised in happier days, and she looked on the last beams of the setting sun, and thought how the wit and merriment of which she was then the mistress were now as faint and evanescent as the expiring glories on which she gazed. Then her ideas, as they wandered in a pensive strain, reverted to her happy schooldays, to her beloved companion in them all. Oh ! if she had known that the faithful, the well-remembered, the once-lovely being, was at that very moment being consigned as dust to dust.

Suddenly there was a step—there was a vioce, and in another instant she was folded in the arms of Montgomery ! It was a long—an impassioned, as it had been an involuntary caress. At length it was over, and tears, while they relieved her, prevented her for a while from observing the ghastly, the frantic expression of him who still wildly gazed upon her. But it could not be longer unnoticed, and terrified and horror-struck—" What means that look ?" she exclaimed. " Oh, dearest Frederick, you have never yet recovered from the shock of that awful night," and she burst into a new passion of tears.

" In truth," he replied slowly, and gasping for breath, " in truth it was a fearful shock ; and the next day"—he paused, and added convulsively—" the next day I was to have asked you to marry me. Oh, Bessy ! dearest, best-beloved, would you have been the wife of the ——

" Murderer" he would have added, but he sunk powerless on the ground.

After a considerable interval he revived. A servant was chafing his temples. Bessy stood near, intensely occupied with a paper she held, while her eye glanced from line to line with wild rapidity. It was the manuscript from which some of the leading facts I have related were originally extracted, and as Montgomery started up, and caught the reader's eye, she would have fallen had he not folded her in his arms. He laid her tenderly on the ground—staggered a few yards from the spot—there was the report of a pistol —and all was over. She recovered but too speedily to hear that deadly sound. She rushed to the fatal spot, and threw herself on the bleeding and mangled corpse. At length she was torn away, borne to the house, and laid in her bed under the rage of a delirious fever. Long was her existence hopeless. But joy was in every countenance, when after nineteen days, there was a plain and evident improvement. Then came a few lucid intervals, during which who would not have wept with her ? And then a relapse. And after two months she rose from that bed an unconscious idiot.

It were impossible to describe the emotions with which I listened to this deeply pathetic tale. Two mountains, as I have said, serve to keep up its recollection amidst the scenes of its sad occurrences ; and the weatherwise of the neighbourhood have been often heard to remark, that any menaces from the object of their study, are still earliest indicated by the gloom that gathers around Mary Gray ; while in the darkest hours of the showery season of spring or autumn, if any spot around would seem to indicate a brighter prospect, it is ever the green and sunny summit of Bessy Bell. —*Dublin Magazine.*

AN OLD SCOTTISH TOUN.

CRAWFORD, in the parish of Crawford, afforded, thirty years ago, a good picture of a toun in the intermediate stage between feudalism and the modern degree of civilization. It consisted, or was the centre of above twenty *freedoms*, holden by a certain tenure off the Crawfords and Douglases, the former superiors of the parish and country. Each *freedom* consisted of four or five acres, parcelled out here and there ; as in England, about the the same period, a tenant on a manor, had his wheat soil in one place, his barley field, and ground for peas in another, scattered here and there, a bit of each kind being allotted to equalize the holdings of the different tenants. The proprietors of the *freedoms* of Crawford were named *Lairds*, and their wives *Ladies*. They enjoyed the right of common hill pasture for a certain number of cattle, sheep, and horses. The little statesmen of Westmorland are still in much the same condition. In Crawford, there was an inferior *caste* who only *feud* ground for a hut and a kail-yard. This rural commonwealth was governed by a *Birley*-Court, in which every *Laird* had a vote, or, in his absence, his tenant. The great business of this legislative assembly and executive body, was to settle disputes about the number of animals the several *Lairds* were entitled to graze on the common pasture. Like more celebrated assemblies, it was chiefly remarkable for the noise which attended its deliberations. It was held weekly, and a regular adjournment was made to the village ale-houses, the *Brookses* and *Boodles* of Crawford to wit. Once a-year, about Martinmas, when a cow or a few sheep were sold, each member cleared his annual club-score. The *Lairds* and their tenants were not troublesome, or new fangled about improvements, though, when convenient, they generally threw the dung out of the byres upon the fields ; but if any new-fashioned farmer offered to purchase it,* that was so much money gained, and " a bird in hand was worth two in a bush." The *Lairds* of Crawford were a contrast to the blood-mounted, wine-bibbing gentleman-farmer of a generation later. What a contrast in their habits and modes of cultivation ! The old people spoke of the easy life, and the easy mind of the former times, as making the most striking difference in their condition.

---

* I remember hearing an old farmer tell that the site of a particular cow-house of a farm on the banks of Dollar Burn, was especially valued, some fifty years ago, as it afforded such facility for shovelling off the dung into the rapid rivulet, when it became somewhat more than knee-deep.—*Editor.*

THE LONDON NEWSMAN.

About this season, certain rhyming effusions, leading through a great variety of metres to the same conclusions, draw notice to our news *deliverers*, the boys, or technically, devils of the different newspaper offices. Their duties are light, and their system crude, compared with that of the well-organized newsmen of London. As the anticipated abolition of the *taxes on knowledge*, will at once approximate our system to that of the metropolis, and give rise to a new order in the FOURTH ESTATE, it may be curious to view this branch of the statistics of the press. It is detailed by Mr. Hone, and no better authority could be obtained:—

"All the year round, and every day in the year, the newsman must rise soon after four o'clock, and be at the newspaper offices to procure a few of the first morning papers allotted to him, at extra charges, for particular orders, and despatch them by the 'early coaches.' Afterwards, he has to wait for his share of the 'regular' publication of each paper, and he allots these as well as he can among some of the most urgent of his town orders. The next publication at a later hour is devoted to his remaining customers; and he sends off his boys with different portions according to the supply he successively receives. Notices frequently and necessarily printed in different papers, of the hour of final publication the preceding day, guard the interests of the newspaper proprietors from the sluggishness of the indolent, and quicken the diligent newsman. Yet, however skilful his arrangements may be, they are subject to unlooked-for accidents. The late arrival of foreign journals, a Parliamentary debate unexpectedly protracted, or an article of importance in one paper exclusively, retard the printing and defer the newsman. His patience, well-worn before he get his 'last papers,' must be continued during the whole period he is occupied in delivering them. The sheet is sometimes half snatched before he can draw it from his wrapper; he is often chid for delay when he should have been praised for speed; his excuse, '*All* the papers were *late* this morning,' is better heard than admitted, for neither giver nor receiver has time to parley; and before he gets home to dinner, he hears at one house that 'Master has waited for the paper these two hours;' at another, 'Master's gone out, and says if you can't bring the paper earlier, he won't have it at all;' and some ill-conditioned 'master,' perchance, leaves positive orders, 'Don't take it in, but tell the man to bring the bill, and I'll pay it and have done with him.'

"Besides buyers, every newsman has readers at so much each paper per hour. One class stipulates for a journal always at breakfast; another, that it is to be delivered exactly at such a time; a third, at any time, so that it is left the full hour; and among all of these there are malcontents, who permit nothing of 'time or circumstance' to interfere with their personal convenience. Though the newsman delivers, and allows the use of his paper, and fetches it, for a stipend not half equal to the lowest paid porter's price for letter-carrying in London, yet he finds some, with whom he covenanted, objecting, which it is called for,—' I've not had my breakfast'—' The paper did not come at the proper time'—' I've not had leisure to look at it yet'—' It has not been left an hour'—or any other pretence equally futile or untrue, which, were he to allow, would prevent him from serving his readers in rotation, or at all. If he can get all his morning papers from these customers by four o'clock, he is a happy man.

"Soon after three in the afternoon, the newsman and some of his boys must be at the offices of the evening papers; but before he can obtain his requisite numbers, he must wait till the newsmen of the Royal Exchange have received theirs for the use of the merchants on 'Change. Some of the first he gets are hurried off to coffee-houses and tavern-keepers. When he has procured his full quantity, he supplies the remainder of his town customers. These disposed of, then comes the hasty folding and directing of his reserves for the country, and the forwarding of them to the post office in Lombard Street, or in parcels for the mails, and to other coach offices. The Gazette nights, every Tuesday and Friday, add to his labours—the publication of second and third editions of the evening papers is a super-addition. On what he calls a 'regular day,' he is fortunate if he find himself settled within his own door by seven o'clock, after fifteen hours of running to and fro. It is now only that he can review the business of the day, enter his fresh orders, ascertain how many of each paper he will require on the morrow, arrange his accounts, provide for the money he may have occasion for, eat the only quiet meal he could reckon upon since that of the evening before, and 'steal a few hours from the night' for needful rest, before he rises next morning to a day of the like incessant occupation; and thus from Monday to Saturday he labours every day.

"The newsmen desires no work but his own to 'prove Sunday no Sabbath,' for on him and his brethren devolves the circulation of upwards of fifty thousand Sunday papers in the course of the forenoon. His Sunday dinner is the only meal he can insure with his family, and the short remainder of the day, the only time he can enjoy in their society with certainty, or extract something from, for more serious duties or social converse.

"The newsman's is an out-of-door business at all seasons, and his life is measured out to unceasing toil. In all weathers, hail, rain, wind, and snow, he is daily constrained to the way and the fare of a wayfaringman. He walks, or rather runs, to distribute information concerning all sorts of circumstances and persons, except his own. He is unable to allow himself, or others, time for intimacy; and, therefore, unless he had formed friendships before he took up his servitude, he has not the chance of cultivating them save with persons of the same calling. He may be said to have been divorced, and to live 'separate and apart' from society in general: for, though he mixes with every body, it is only for a few hurried moments, and as strangers do in a crowd.

"The losses and crosses to which newsmen are subject, and the minutiæ of their laborious life, would form an instructive volume. As a class of able men of business, their importance is established by excellent regulations, adapted to their interests and well-being; and their numerous society includes many individuals of high intelligence, integrity, and opulence.

NEW YEAR'S GIFTS.—The custom of New Year's Gifts is very ancient, and was formerly carried to a great extent. The sovereign used to accept gifts from his courtiers and principal favourites, and was also in the habit of making presents to certain individuals; the Prince, however, always taking care that the presents he received greatly exceeded in value those which he gave. It is recorded of Bishop Latimer, that on one occasion he presented to his master Henry VIII., instead of a sum in gold for a New Year's Gift, a New Testament, with the leaf folded down at Hebrews, ch. xiii. v. 4,—on reference to which the King found a text well suited as an admonition to himself. Queen Elizabeth supplied herself with wardrobe and jewels principally from New Year's Gifts. Dr. Drake has given a list of some of these presents; amongst the items we find the following:—" Most of the Peers and Peeresses of the Realm, the Bishops, the Chief Officers of State, her Majesty's Household, even as low as the master of the pantry and head cook, all gave her Majesty a Christmas-box—consisting either of a sum of money, jewels, trinkets, or wearing apparel. The Archbishop of Canterbury usually gave L.40, the Archbishop of York L.30, and the other Prelates from L.10 or L.20. The Peers gave in the same proportion; whilst the Peeresses presented rich gowns, petticoats, shifts, stockings, garters, &c. Her physician presented her with a box of foreign sweetmeats; and from her apothecary she received a box of ginger-candy, and a box of green ginger. Ambrose Lupo gave her a box of lutestrings; and Smith, the royal dustman, presented her Majesty with two bolts of cambric."

COBBETT ON SCOTLAND.

In fulfilment of my promise to my London readers, I have now placed in my shop, at Bolt Court, an assortment of apples, which were grown on the beautiful banks of the Clyde, which, the reader will please to observe, is nearly about the centre of Scotland. These apples were all grown in the orchard of Mr. Hamilton of Dalzell; and, though they have been at Glasgow, at sea, and lying in London unpacked (all put together) ever since the *first of November*, I think they could now challenge Covent Garden! I shall let these apples remain in my shop for eight or ten days, or more; and I have also placed there a Dunlop cheese, Dunlop being a village in Ayrshire famous for making cheese; and, I have no scruple to say that this cheese, which is about half a hundred weight, is, pound for pound equal in quality to any cheese from Cheshire, Gloucestershire, or Wiltshire. There is nothing like seeing things with our own eyes. I cannot bring up Scotland itself, and exhibit it at Bolt Court, but I can exhibit these indubitable proofs of the goodness and productiveness of the soil of that country; and of the virtue and sense of its people I have, in my tour, put upon record proofs enough. As I have, in different numbers of the Register, inserted the greater part of this tour, I now insert the following: the title, dedication, and preface to the volume, which will be published on Thursday next, the 10th inst. And thus I shall, as far as I am able, have done justice to a country and a people, who have been more, and more unjustly, misrepresented than any country and people upon the face of the earth.

* * * *

The motives as to the making of this publication are, to communicate to every body, as far as I am able, correct notions relative to Scotland; its soil; its products; its state, as to the well-being or ill-being of the people; but, above all things, it is my desire to assist in doing justice to the character, political as well as moral, public as well as private, national as well as social, of our brethren in that very much misrepresented part of the kingdom. This is a duty particularly incumbent on me; for, though I never have carried my notions of the sterility and worthlessness of Scotland, and of the niggardly character of its inhabitants, to the extent which many others have; though I have, in reprobating the conduct of the "*booing*" *pro-consular feelosofers*, always made them an exception to the people of Scotland; though I have always done this, still, I could not prevent myself from imbibing, in some degree, the prejudices, which a long train of causes, beginning to operate nearly a thousand years ago, have implanted in the minds of Englishmen; though I had intimately known, for many years, such great numbers of Scotchmen, for whom I had the greatest regard, still the prejudices, the false notions, lay lurking in my mind; and in spite of my desire always to do justice towards everybody, the injustice would slip out, even without my perceiving it. In any other man it would have been of some importance that these erroneous notions should be corrected; but, in me, whose writings I might fairly presume extended to every part of the civilized world, it became of very great importance; and it became my bounden duty to do that justice, which I have endeavoured to do in the following pages; and to make, by a true statement of facts derived from ocular proof, that atonement for past errors which I have in these pages endeavoured to make.

From how many pairs of lips have I heard the exclamation: " Good God! who would have thought that Scotland was such a country! What monstrous lies we have been told about that country and people!" And, which has pleased me exceedingly, not one man have I met with to whom the discovery does not seem to have given delight. If I had before wanted a motive to give further extension to my account of Scotland, these exclamations would have been motive sufficient; for they would have proved, that these same motives demanded that which, by this publication, I am now endeavouring to do. Were it possible that either this statement of motives, or that any part of the work itself, could be, by even the most perverse of human beings, ascribed to any desire on my part to curry favour with the Scotch, or to any selfish desire whatsoever; were this only possible, I am afraid that I should not have had the courage to make this statement; but, as this is completely impossible, I make it as being the just due of the people of Scotland, for whose well-being, whose honour, whose prosperity, whose lasting peace and happiness, I have as great a regard as I have for the well-being, prosperity, and happiness of those who inhabit the spot where I myself was born.

THE WINE TREE.

"'Tis the Vine! 'tis the Vine!" said the cup-loving boy,
 As he saw it spring bright from the earth,
And call'd the young Genii of Wit, Love, and Joy,
 To witness and hallow its birth.
The fruit was full grown; like a ruby it flam'd,
 Till the sun-beam that kiss'd it turn'd pale:
" 'Tis the Vine! 'tis the Vine!" every Spirit exclaim'd,
 " Hail, hail to the Wine-tree, all hail!"

First, fleet as a bird, to the summons Wit flew,
 While a light on the vine-leaves there broke,
In flashes so quick and so brilliant, all knew
 'Twas the light from his lips as he spoke.
" Bright tree! let thy nectar but cheer me," he cried,
 " And the fount of Wit never can fail :"
" 'Tis the Vine! 'tis the Vine!" hills and valleys reply;
 " Hail, hail to the Wine-tree, all hail!"

Next, Love, as he lean'd o'er the plant to admire
 Each tendril and cluster it wore,
From his rosy mouth sent such a breath of desire,
 As made the tree tremble all o'er.
Oh! never did flower of the earth, sea, or sky,
 Such a soul-giving odour inhale :
" 'Tis the Vine! 'tis the Vine!" all re-echo the cry;
 " Hail, hail to the Wine-tree, all hail!"

Last Joy, without whom even Love and Wit die,
 Came to crown the bright hour with his ray;
And scarce had that mirth-waking tree met his eye,
 When a laugh spoke what Joy could not say;
A laugh of the heart, which was echoed around
 Till, like music, it swell'd on the gale;
"'Tis the Vine! 'tis the Vine!" laughing myriads resound;
 " Hail, hail to the Wine tree, all hail!"

[We need scarcely tell that the author of these gay verses is Moore. They are taken from " Evenings in Greece," a musical work, to which he contributes the poetry.

MATTHEWS THE SMUGGLER.

When I found myself in the cabin with the bold outlaw —for Matthews had been legally denounced for many daring and successful contests with the Revenue—I could not but admire the thorough indifference to possible consequences which this singular personage exhibited. He knew that several men of war were at the moment cruising on the station, and that they had been apprised he had sailed from Flushing, and that this coast was the spot selected by the owners to effect the landing—yet he laughed and drank as gaily as I should in a club-house, and despatched the messages which were occasionally brought down with perfect *nonchalance*. He spoke principally of his own exploits; and the scene was admirably in keeping. Around the cabin, muskets, pistols, and blunderbusses were secured in arm-racks, and cutlasses and tomahawks were suspended from the bulk-heads. His had been a wild career; and though not passed the middle age, his life teemed with " perilous adventure." I was so much amused with his varied narratives of brave attempts and desperate successes, that the second hour slipped away before I rose and took my departure. On regaining the deck, the hurry of the business was over. The contraband cargo had been replaced by stone ballast; for, by previous arrangement, each boat brought a quantity of shingle from the beach, and hence the smuggler was already in trim, and ready to stand out to sea. This notorious vessel was considered in size and sailing superior to any of a similar class, and her voyages had been numerous and successful. Her armament was formidable: sixteen heavy carronades were extended along the deck, with two long brass guns of a smaller caliber, and every other appurtenance of war was in perfect efficiency. But the most striking object was her ferocious-looking, but magnificent crew; they seemed only formed for "the battle and the breeze," and well justified their wild commander's boast, "that he could thrash any cruiser of his own size, and land his cargo in six hours afterwards." We left the vessel; and, to judge by the cags and cases stowed away in the gig, my cousin had not been forgotten in the general distribution. The outlaw stood upon a carronade, and waved his hand as we pulled from the ship's side; and in a short time set his head-sails, and stood off to sea with the ebb-tide and a spanking breeze, which carried him out of sight directly. This was fated to be the last landing of the Jane, and the last exploit of her commander —she foundered on her next voyage, and every person on board perished with the vessel.—*Wild Sports of the West.*

THE MONKS OF THE SCREW.

When Lord Avenmore was a young man, better known on the turf than at the bar, he founded a club near Newmarket, called the *Monks of the Screw*; the rules of which he drew up in very quaint and comic Monkish Latin verse. It was on this model that a still more celebrated club of the same name was afterwards established, under his Lordship's auspices, in Dublin. It met on every Sunday during the law terms, in a large house in Kevin's Street, the property of the late Lord Tracton, and now converted into a seneschal's court. The reader may have some idea of the delightful intercourse this society must have afforded, when he learns that Flood, Grattan, Curran, Lord Charlemont, Daly, Bowes, and a host of such men, were amongst its members. Curran was installed Grand Prior of the order, and deputed to compose the charter song. It began thus:—

When St Patrick our order created,
And called us the Monks of the Screw,
Good rules he revealed to our Abbot,
To guide us in what we should do.

But first he replenished his fountain
With liquor the best in the sky,
And he swore, by the word of his saintship,
The fountain should never run dry.

My children, be chaste, till you're tempted;—
While sober, be wise and discreet;—
And humble your bodies with fasting,
Whene'er you've got nothing to eat.

Then be not a glass in the convent,
Except on a festival, found,
And this rule to enforce, I ordain it—
A festival—all the year round.

Saint Patrick, the tutelar idol of the country, was their patron saint; and a statue of him, mitred and crosiered, after having for years consecrated their Monkish revels, was transferred to Curran's convivial sideboard at the Priory. Of the hours passed in this society Curran ever afterwards spoke with enthusiasm. "Those hours," said he, addressing Lord Avenmore on the occasion, as a Judge, and wringing tears from his aged eyes at the recollection, "which we can remember with no other regret than that they can return no more:

"We spent them not in toys, or lust, or wine,
But search of deep philosophy;
Wit, eloquence, and poesy;
Arts which I lov'd, and they, my friend, were thine!"

SCRAPS.
ORIGINAL AND SELECTED.

LOCKS OF HAIR AS KEEPSAKES.
There seems a love in hair, though it be dead;
It is the gentlest, yet the strongest thread
Of our frail plant—a blossom from the tree,
Surviving the proud trunk;—as though it said,
Patience and gentleness is power—in me
Behold affectionate Eternity.

VULGAR ERRORS.—That leases are made for 999 years, because a lease for 1000 years would create a freehold.— That deeds executed on Sunday are void.—That, in order to disinherit an heir-at-law, it is necessary to give him a shilling by the will, for that otherwise he would be entitled to the whole property.—That a funeral passing over any place makes it a public highway.—That the body of a debtor may be taken in execution after his death.—That a man marrying a woman who is in debt, if he take her from the hands of the priest, clothed only in her shift, will not be liable for her engagements.—That those who are born at sea belong to Stepney parish.—That second cousins may not marry, though first cousins may.—That a husband has the power of divorcing his wife, by selling her in open market, with a halter round her neck.—That a woman's marrying a man under the gallows will save him from execution.—That if a criminal has been hung and revives, he cannot afterwards be executed.—That the owners of asses are obliged to crop their ears, lest the length of them should frighten the horses.

TO PRESERVE THE ROOTS OF GERANIUMS IN THE WINTER.—The following method of preserving through the winter the more gross and succulent geraniums, such as the large scarlet, &c. is but little known. On the approach of frost take them out of the ground, in doing which carefully avoid injuring the roots; wash off all the earth, and hang them up to the ceiling of a good under-ground cellar with the roots uppermost. In the spring they will have made some yellowish-green, and unhealthy-looking shoots. When the frosts are over, they are to be replanted, and protected at night, and from cold winds, by mats, or by turning a basket over them until they have resumed their wonted healthy appearance. The above method must prove particularly advantageous to the numerous persons who have not the use of a conservatory, and who happen to think that geraniums never appear so ornamental as when growing in the open ground; and certainly much more beautiful and natural than those long-legged sickly exotics that are frequently seen drawn up in straight lines in a hot-house.

The following is a specimen of Irish logic:—" His landlady was what was termed a 'general dealer,' and, among other things, sold bread and whisky. A customer entered her shop and inquired if she had any thing to eat and drink? 'To be sure,' she replied, 'I have got a thimblefull of the cratur, my darling, that comes only to twopence; and this big little loaf you may have for the same money!' Both twopence? 'Both the same, as I'm a Christian woman, and worth double the sum.' 'Fill the whisky, if you plase.' She did so, and he drank it; then rejoined, 'It comes to twopence, my jewel; I'm not hungry, take back the loaf,' tendering it. 'Yes, honey, but what pays for the whisky?' 'Why the loaf to be sure!' 'But you haven't paid for the loaf.' 'Why you wouldn't have a man pay for a thing he hasn't eat?' A friend going by was called in by the landlady to decide the difficulty, who gave it against her; and from deficiency in her powers of calculation, she permitted the rogue to escape."—*Bernard's Retrospections.*

CONTENTS OF NO. XXV.

The Duties of the People at the Present Period..................33
The State of Feeling in a Manufacturing Town...............35
Popular Estimation of Geology................................37
Reverend William Muir.......................................
The Remarkable History of Sophia Dorothea, Wife of George L...39
ELEMENTS OF THOUGHT—Signs of the Times—The Fiction Writers, or Moral Instructors—Sir Walter Scott—Parties.....46
Affectation...
THE STORY-TELLER—The Irish Bessy Bell and Mary Gray....44
An Old Scottish Town..
The London Newsman...
Cobbett on Scotland...
The Wine Tree—Matthews the Smuggler.........................
The Monks of the Screw.....................................
SCRAPS—Locks of Hair as Keepsakes—To Preserve the Roots of Geraniums in the Winter, &c......................................

EDINBURGH: Printed by and for JOHN JOHNSTONE, 19, St James' Square.—Published by JOHN ANDERSON, Jun., Bookseller, 55, North Bridge Street, Edinburgh; by JOHN MACLEOD, and ATKINSON & Co., Booksellers, Glasgow; and sold by all Booksellers and Venders of Cheap Periodicals.

The Schoolmaster,
AND
EDINBURGH WEEKLY MAGAZINE.

CONDUCTED BY JOHN JOHNSTONE.

THE SCHOOLMASTER IS ABROAD.—LORD BROUGHAM.

No. 26.—Vol. II.   SATURDAY, JANUARY 26, 1833.   Price Three-Halfpence

MR. STUART'S THREE YEARS IN NORTH AMERICA.

This book is likely to attract more general notice, especially in Scotland, than any work which has lately appeared; and this for two reasons; first, it is about that country with which we have so many ties, and upon which the hopes of our suffering population of all classes under the highest, naturally fall back; and secondly, it is written by Mr. Stuart of Dunearn, long a noticeable member of our community, a leading whig, among party whigs, a dashing speculator, a spirited, if not a very calculating agricultural improver, a character in many points formed and fashioned by *war prices*, and the fictitious tide of prosperity which rose so rapidly, ebbed as fast, and left so many traces of misery and ruin on the society over which it swept. Mr. Stuart was also the antagonist of Sir Alexander Boswell, in that unfortunate affair when a "fool-born jest" was most foolishly vindicated, and a contemptible offence atoned by the sacrifice of human life. In this unhappy rencontre Mr. Stuart was, it is said, inextricably involved, and if so, he was certainly more to be pitied than the victim. These circumstances, and the nine days wonderment which arose from his abrupt withdrawal to the United States, have thrown a reflected interest around his book which is not wanted. It may be left to its own fate. Mr Stuart went to America in the summer of 1828, and returned in the spring of 1831. He possessed many of the qualities most requisite to an intelligent and impartial observer. He was of mature age, a man of business and of the world, well acquainted with rural affairs on the grand and expensive style, and withal somewhat of a politician. During his stay he visited nearly every important place in the States, traversing the breadth and length of the land "from Dan to Beersheba" in the humour of finding all fruitful and flourishing, viewing every thing in the fairest light, and putting the best construction upon every occurrence. With such qualifications and dispositions Mr. Stuart collected an immense mass of facts, which he relates in the plain unadorned style of a journalist, leaving the reader to select, compare, weigh, and draw conclusions for himself. His own opinions and impressions are merely stated, never insisted upon.

During his long course of travel he visited schools, colleges, courts of justice, churches of every denomination, proceeded by steam, stage, and on horseback; and faithfully relates all he saw, and much of what he heard, never neglecting what he had for dinner or supper, nor yet what his fare cost, and seldom forgetting to record his assertion of a Briton's right to a single bed, a basin of water, and a clean towel. He is in truth a homely statist, and, we are persuaded, an accurate one; and where his book rises to generalized views, or luxuriates in description, he draws upon higher sources. With all this, and though nothing is idealized or viewed *en beau*, he gives us a most favourable impression of the Americans; at least of the people of the Northern States,—while he only does them justice in a kindly, candid spirit, respecting them (as we do him) too much to think they require glozing and indulgence from a traveller. In towns he is less happy, we think, than in the country; and especially among the new emigrant settlements of the Illinois and Missouri. His account of these fine countries will be read with much interest, and with profit by persons meditating emigration. His description of the southern slave states presents the most horrible and revolting picture we have ever yet seen, of the open profligacy, utter debasement, and moral depravity inseparable from slavery. A selection of Mr. Stuart's anecdotes must put to shame, and for ever strike dumb every one who dare yet raise a voice for a system which to us appears infinitely more brutalizing to the white than to the suffering black population. Of the social habits and domestic character of the Americans, we learn less than we could have wished; for though Mr. Stuart went every where, he has, out of inns and boarding-houses, recorded a few observations. The mental condition of the people of America is best indicated by their political and social state. It is sound, healthful, and happy. We shall begin with the elementary part,—Education, and the provision made for this only sure basis of national prosperity and social well-being.

"On one of the first days I walked out, I was joined by a seafaring person of the name of Sheaffe, with whom I had got acquainted in the course of my walks by the sea side, who lived in the neighbourhood, and had a small boat, and seemed to gain his livelihood by fishing, and ferrying over passengers to and from the island. After congratulating meon my recovery, he asked me if I was not in want of books. He had seen me occasionally bring books from Boston, before I had met with the accident before noticed. He mentioned various historical and philosophical books in his library, which were at my service; and also the London Examiner newspaper for several years. I caught at his offer, when he mentioned the Examiner, having been recently reading the American account of the battles on the Canada frontier in the wars of 1813 and 1814, and being anxious to compare them with the British Gazette accounts. I therefore accepted the Examiner, which he fortunately had at the period I wanted. I doubt whether such an occurrence as this could have happened anywhere else in the world. I found that Mr. Sheaffe, whose house is as humble-looking a wooden cottage as any one in the neighbourhood, had formerly been a seaman in a merchant ship, and had been in England; but the explanation is easy. Education is open to all in this country; and all, or almost all, are educated. It was lately ascertained by reports accurately taken, that, out of a population of about 60,000 persons in the State of Massachusetts, only 400 beyond the age of childhood could not read or write. And more especially, by returns from 131 towns presented to the legislature, that the number of scholars receiving instruction in those towns is 12,393; that the number of persons in those towns, between the ages of fourteen and twenty-one, who are unable to respand write, is fifty-eight; and that in one of those towns, the town of Hancock, there are only three persons unable to read or write,—and those three are mutes. The general plan of Education at the public free schools here is not confined to mere reading, writing, arithmetic, and book-keeping, and the ancient and modern languages; but comprehends grammar, mathematics, navigation, geography, history, logic, political economy, and rhetoric, moral and natural philosophy; these schools being, as stated in the printed regulations, intended to occupy the young people from the age of four to seventeen, and to form a system of education advancing from the lowest to the highest degree of improvement, which can be derived from any literary seminaries inferior to colleges and universities; and to afford a practical and theoretical acquaintance with the various branches of a useful education.

" There are, at present, at Boston, sixty-eight free schools, besides twenty-three Sabbath schools; in all of which the poorest inhabitant of Boston may have his children educated, according to the system of education before specified, from the age of four to seventeen, without any expense whatever. The children of both sexes are freely admitted. The funds for these schools are derived from bequests and donations by individuals, and grants from the legislature and corporations; and enable the trustees, consisting of twelve citizens, annually elected by the inhabitants of each of the twelve wards of the city, with the mayor and eight aldermen, to give the teachers salaries, varying from 2500 to 800 dollars a-year. The assistant teachers have 600 dollars. The trustees elect the teachers, and vote their salaries yearly; and no preference is given on any principles but those of merit and skill. The teachers of the grammar schools must have been educated at college, and must have attained a degree of bachelor of arts. The morning and evening exercises of all the schools, commence with reading the Scriptures. A very strict system of supervision and regulation is established by the trustees.

" No expense whatever is incurred at those schools except for books.

" The richer classes at Boston, formerly, very generally, patronized teachers of private schools, who were paid in the usual way; but they now find that the best teachers are at the head of the public schools, and, in most cases, prefer them,—the children of the highest and lowest rank enjoying the privilege, altogether invaluable in a free state, of being educated together.

" In the adjoining State of Connecticut it has been ascertained by accurate reports, that one-third of the population, of about 275,000, attend the free schools. In the whole of the New England States, the population of which, including Massachusetts and Connecticut, amounts to about two millions, it is unquestionable, that the entire population are educated, that is to say, can read and write, and that the exceptions, which do not at the utmost amount to 2000 persons, are composed of blacks and foreigners.

" The result of the recent inquiry into the state of Education in the State of New York, which adjoins New England, and is almost equal to it in population, and to which I have already alluded, is very much, though not entirely the same. It is proved by actual reports, that 499,434 children, out of a population of one million, nine hundred thousand, were at the same time attending the schools, that is, a fourth part of the whole population. Although the public funds of New York State are great, these schools are not entirely free, but free to all who apply for immunity from payment. The amount of the money paid to the teachers by private persons does not, however, amount to one-third of the whole annual expense, which is some what less than a million of dollars.

" It is not, however, to be inferred, that education at free-schools is so general all over the United States, as in the four millions of inhabitants of New England and the State of New York; but the provision for public schools is admirable in all the populous states, Pensylvania, New Jersey, Maryland, Virginia, &c.; and free education can everywhere be procured, even in the southern states, for whites, on application being made for it. The appropriations of land for schools in the old states were formerly very much confined to the donations of individuals, many of which have now, however, become very valuable; but the appropriations for schools in the new states have been regulated by congress, and their extent is immense. Every township of the new lands is divided into thirty-six sections, each a mile square, and each containing 640 acres. One section of every township is appropriated for schools. In addition to this, great appropriations have been made in Ohio, Tennessee, Kentucky, and others of the western states, for seminaries of 'a higher order, to the extent of about one-fifth of those for schools. The land belonging to public schools in the new states and territories, in which appropriations have been made on the east side of the Mississippi, amounts to about eight millions of acres, and is of course advancing in value as the population increases. The extent of land, which will be appropriated to the same purpose when the land on the western side of the Mississippi is settled, must be prodigious,—at present not capable of being guessed at."

Our next extract must be political: the Ballot is at this moment a topic of universal discussion. Hear Mr. Stuart's report from a land where the ballot has been fully tested.

" It was on the 5th November that I was present at the election at Ballston Spa, held in one of the hotels, about the door of which, twenty or thirty people might be standing. My friend Mr. Brown introduced me, and got me a place at the table. I must confess that I have been seldom more disappointed at a public meeting. The excitement occasioned by the election generally was declared by the newspapers to be far greater than had ever been witnessed since the declartion of indepèrandence in 1776. And at Ballston Spa, any irritation which existed had been increased by an attack made a few days previous to the election by the local press, and by hand-bills, on the moral character of one of the candidates,—a gentleman who had filled a high office in Congress, and who resided in the neighbourhood. I was, therefore, prepared for some fun, for some ebulition of humour, or of sarcastic remark, or dry wit, to which Americans are said to be prone. But all was dumb show, or the next thing to it. The ballot-boxes were placed on a long table, at which half a dozen of the inspectors or canvassers of votes were seated. The voters approached the table by single files. Not a word was spoken. Each voter delivered his list, when he got next to the table to the officers, who called out his name. Any person might object, but the objection was instantly decided on,—the officers having no difficulty, from their knowledge of the township, of the persons residing in it, and to whose testimony reference was instantly made, in determining on the spot, whether the qualification of the voter was or was not sufficient. I need hardly say, that I did not attend this excessively uninteresting sort of meeting for any long time; but I am bound to bear this testimony in its favour, that so quiet a day of election, both without and within doors, I never witnessed either in Scotland or England. I did not see or hear of a drunk person in the street of the village or neighbourhood, nor did I observe any thing extraordinary, except the increased number of carriages or waggons of all kinds, three or four of them drawn by four horses, one by six. We were residing close by the hotel where the election took place, and in the evening the tranquillity was as complete as if no election had occurred.

" The county canvassers for the twenty townships of this county of Saratoga afterwards met, and made up their returns for the county, in all of which, as well as in the whole of the state, the same quietness and perfect order prevailed. The number of votes given in this state for the electors of the president was 276,176, in a population of upwards of 1,800,000; and that this part of the election was most keenly contested, is obvious from the recorded fact, that the majority for Jackson over Adams in this state only amounted to 5,350. The total number of votes given in the presidential election on this occasion was afterwards ascertained to be nearly 1,200,000, in a population of about twelve millions, of which the whole states are composed.

" Thus, in a state far exceeding Scotland in extent, and almost equalling it in population, the votes for the chief magistrate of the United States and his substitute,—for the governor and lieutenant-governor of the state,—for a senator and representatives to Congress,—for three representatives to the State of New York,—for four coroners, a sheriff, and a clerk to the county, were taken,—and the business of the election finished with ease, and with the most perfect order and decorum, in three days. All votes by ballot, which is here considered the only way to obtain independent and unbiassed votes; and if so in this country, how much more in the British islands, where the aristocracy and higher orders are so infinitely more powerful, influential, and numerous. The late eminent Dr. Dwight, President of Yale College in Connecticut describes an election meeting in New England very much as I witnessed it here. After declaring that he had never known a single shilling paid for a vote, he says, ' I have lived long in New England. On the morning of an election day, the electors assemble either in a church or a town-house, in the centre of the township, of which they are inhabitants. The qusiness of the day is sometimes introduced by a sermon, and very often by public prayer. A moderator is chosen. The votes are given in with strict decency, without a single debate, without noise, or disorder, or drink—and with not a little of the sobriety seen in religious assemblies. The meeting is then dissolved; the inhabitants return [quietly to their homes, and have neither battles nor disputes. I do not believe that a single woman, bond or free, ever appeared at an election in New England since the colonization of the country. It would be as much as her character was worth.

" Dr. Dwight's authority, however, is not greater than many others to which I might refer. Chancellor Kent of New York is a person of the greatest respectability as a man, and of the highest character as a lawyer. In his Commentaries, which is quite a standard book, he bears this evidence on the subject of elections: ' The United States, in their improvements upon the rights of representation, may certainly claim pre-eminence over all other governments, ancient and modern. Our elsection are held at stated seasons, established by law. The people vote by ballot in small districts; and public officers preside over the elections, receive the votes, and maintain order and fairness. Though the competition between candidates is generally active, and the zeal of rival parties sufficiently excited, the elections are everywhere conducted with tranquillity.'

" The testimony of Joseph Gerald, a martyr to the sincerity with which he, at a period not so recent, advocated the propriety of resorting to the same form of elections in Great Britain, before biassed judges and a biassed jury, at a time of great political excitement in Scotland, will long be remembered. ' I myself,' he declared, in his speech on his celebrated trial before the Supreme Criminal Court in Scotland, ' resided during four years in a country where every man who paid taxes had a right to vote—I mean the Commonwealth of Pensylvania. I was an eye-witness of many elections which took place in Philadelphia, the capital of the State,—an industrious and populous city; and can safely assert, that no one riot ever ensued.'

"Mr. James Flint, who travelled in the United States about a dozen of years ago, and whose scrupulous correctness of narration is well known to all who know him, in his published letters from America, states his views as to their elections thus:—' A few days ago I witnessed the election of a member of Congress for the State of Indiana. Members for the State Assembly, and county officers, and the votes for the township of Jeffersonville, were taken by ballot in one day. No quarrels or disorder occurred. At Louisville, in Kentucky, the poll wask ept open for three days. The votes were given *viva voce.* I saw three fights in the course of an hour. This method appears to be productive of as much discord here as in England.' With relation to the ballot, I would only further add, that a great point is gained by its celerity, 10,000 votes can easily be taken in five or six hours."

The domestic manners of the Americans are a subject of curiosity among us; and there is now an opportunity of correcting Captain Halls theories, and Mrs. Trollope's *fibberies*, by the correct text of Mr. Stuart. While giving the Americans praise for their unostentatious hospitality, he casts a tender glance back upon the *batterie de cuisine* of Moray Place, and the vintages of its side-board, to the long sumptuous dinners so favourable for conversation, and even for a little gastronomic chat about the wines and viands, instead of the Americans swallowing, smoking, and bolting off to win more dollars. But Mr. Stuart forgets that the frugal simplicity of the American entertainments opens the door to the widest and most frequent hospitality, and includes the women, who are effectually proscribed by our after-dinner convival system. The *tea* the entertainment of ceremony in middle life in America, reminds us of the social suppers of Edinburgh, immortalized by old Creech—which prevailed before we became so ultra- refined and *routish*. " It never," says Jack Cade " was a merry world since gentlefolks came up,"—and gentlefolks are still scarce in America.—We take Mr. Stuart's account of both the easy friendly dinner, and the social *solid* tea.

" The kindness and hospitality of the Americans are quite unostentatious. I write, however, of the mass of the people, and without reference to the small number of people, who consider themselves the great in this country. An invitation to dinner is generally given in such words as these: ' I will be pleased to see you at two oclock.' Frequently no change whatever is made in the dinner, supposing you to accept. Your friend knows that there is always abundance of good food upon his table. That degree of attention is shown to you which a stranger meets with everywhere, in seeing that his plate be filled in the first instance with what he likes, but no pressing or entreaty are used to make him eat or drink more than he likes. If wine is produced, it is left for him to partake of it or not as he chooses. There is hardly ever any talk about the dinner, or the quality of the wine, which you are not provoked to drink by being told how many years it has been in your friend's cellar or to what vintage it belongs.

"It is much more probable that, even amongst the richest classes, excluding always a few who form small coteries in the great towns, or who have been much in England, you will hear little conversation, and that relating more to their professional pursuits, their gains, and their dollars, and their political situations, than to the food they are eating, or the wine they are drinking."

But the *Tea* is the entertainment of ceremony.

"Tea-parties, which are very common in the United States, in some measure make up for what I look upon as the more rational and comfortable conversational dinner of the middling, the best classes of society in Britain. Where those tea-parties take place by invitation, the table is liberally covered, and with a greater number of articles, such as a profusion of cakes of various kinds and preserves. Animal food, too, of some description or other, is almost always produced,—and after the tea or supper is finished, wine of various kinds, nuts, fruit, &c. are placed on the sideboard, or handed round. There is, perhaps, a little more room for conversation at such parties than at British routes; but still I conceive the rational interchange of sentiment which takes place at English dinners, to be, generally speaking, awanting in the meal which is called by the same name in the United States. Let it not, however, be supposed, that I mean to insinuate that at any dinner, public or private, either a stranger or native has any reason to expect an uncivil answer to any conversation which he may address to any one sitting at table; but the custom is so universal in the most populous part of the United States, to leave the table immediately after dinner, to smoke a cigar, and afterwards to return to professional business; that the people generally seem to me to be least inclined for convivial conversation at the very time when we, with better taste, as I think, enjoy it most. I am bound, however, to add, after seeing much more of the United States than I had done when I was making these remarks, that I have been at many tea-parties in various parts of the country where, sitting over our wine after tea, we had the enjoyment of agreeable and instructive conversation for quite as long a time as should ever be devoted to it either in the Old or New World."

The following sketch of a Yankee driver conveys a great deal. We must notice that at first brush, Mr. Stuart had rather *shied* his acute, loquacious and well-informed driver.

"At length we approached the door of our hotel, and all of us felt regret at the idea of so soon being deprived of the agreeable society of our charioteer. As soon as we got out of the carriage, when we were within hearing of each other, I applied for, and had the sanction of my fellow-travellers, to beg him to favour us with his company at dinner, and to take a glass of wine with us. I hastened to the bar-room, where I found him smoking a cigar. I preferred my request in the most civil terms I could think of. He looked at me for a moment, and then expressed great surprise, that a foreigner should have asked his driver to dine with him. I urged our anxiety to have a little more of his agreeable company, and promised that we should endeavour to impart to him all the information we could give, relative to the institutions of our own country, in return for the valuable communications he had made to us. But he finally declined, with perfect civility, though, at the sametime, with that sort of manner which prevented any attempt to press him. 'His family,' he said, 'expected him, and he must go home. Perhaps, sir,' he added, 'you was not aware that the High Sheriff of the County was your driver to-day. We are very neighbourly here. The horses expected for you this morning had not come in, and I could not refuse my neighbour, (mentioning his name,) when he applied to me. I have good horses and would have been sorry to disappoint a stranger.' Having finished his cigar, Mr. Spencer took leave of me with a shake of the hand. We found, on inquiry, that he was a general merchant in the village, and had mills and a store. His neighbours had singled him out,—not on account of his education, which was not superior to that of his fellow-citizens, but on account of his shrewdness and good character,—to make him a justice of peace, which confers the title of judge. As justice of peace, he gave so great satisfaction that they promoted him to be their high sheriff. In the latter capacity he had business this morning to transact at Caldwell, the county town, and where the jail committed to his charge is situated. This explains the anxiety he expressed to be off early. The little boy on the driving seat was the son of a prisoner in the jail, to whom he was carrying linens. *Ne sutor ultra crepidam,* 'let the cobbler stick to his last,' has no part in the republican character of America."

We meant to have given Mr. Stuart's rencontres in the wildernesses and prairies with our country folks, but must defer this till another week,—with much more than we have to say of a book, which will soon be in every one's hands.

STATE OF THE WORKING CLASSES.

DR. CHALMERS' PAMPHLET.

WE were not a little provoked to find the fallacious statements of the last Number of the *Edinburgh Review,* extensively quoted by the country press, as containing a true view "of the vastly improved condition of all classes, *but particularly of labourers,* since the American war, and especially during the present century." Dr Chalmers, in vindication of his own opinions, has taken the field against the Reviewer. His refutation of "the peace peace" or "the peace and prosperity" optimists is triumphant on the point to which alone we can advert. So hear the Rev. Doctor.

"When a writer maintains an untenable position, we generally meet, in the style of exaggeration which he employs, with specially emphatic clauses. The reviewer tells us, "that, instead of being stationary or retrograde, the condition of all classes, but *particularly of the labourers,* has been vastly improved since the American war, and *especially during the present century."* Now, it so happens, that in both the clauses where he has laid the stress of particularity on the one, and of especiality on the other, the emphasis is misplaced. If, by labourers, be meant those to whom the designation purely and properly belongs, who receive wages simply in return for the exertion of their strength, and not because of the power they have of bringing to a dead stand, or state of unproductiveness, the enormous capital of their employers; it will be found, under our exposure of the reviewer's first great error, that their wages lie at the bottom of the scale. And, again, under our exposure of his second great eror, it will be found that a general re-action, in the condition of the working classes, took place about twenty years ago; and that, precisely during the present century, their progress was first arrested, and then turned backwards. He has been unfortunate both in regard to the class of men, and to the period of years, on which he meant to lay the pith of his argument. He made a two-fold selection, for the obvious purpose of enhancing his statement, or the proof by which he was supporting it; and in both he is wrong. We have sometimes to correct a reader for laying the emphasis on wrong words. The reviewer has laid his emphasis on wrong things."

But these are general averments: let us come to particulars.

" Let us return once more to Scotland; and lest the argument, either of special manufactures, or of midway transitions from one state to another, should be alleged, in opposition to all our former instances—we shall now offer a brief view of the circumstances of our agricultural population, at the beginning of this century, and in the present day—assuming that the variation which has taken place in one of its counties, (Peebleshire,) is a fair average specimen of the change, if any, which the condition of our peasantry has undergone, over the whole length and breadth of the land. We, on purpose, keep clear of 1800 and 1801, as having been two years of severe scarcity, amounting to famine; so that the comparison, strictly speaking, is between the rate of wages now, and the mean rate of wages from 1802 to 1812 or 1814.

The wages of married farm-servants—in as far as they are paid in kind, consisting of meal, potatoes, the keep of a cow, and driving of their fuel—have suffered no variation. The money wages at the former period were £16 a year; they are now £10. We are aware that the price of the first necessaries of life has fallen to a greater proportion than this; but the money part of this wages goes to the purchase of second necessaries; and their price has not fallen in so great a proportion. So that the labourers of this description are somewhat worse off at the latter than the former period."

" The wages of unmarried farm-servants were then £18, with their victuals, and are now £12, with victuals; they having suffered a descent too, though less by 13s. 4d. than that of the former class of labourers."

" But there is still another class, of inferior condition to the two former, and who also, as appears from the comparison of their wages at the two distinct periods, have sustained a greater descent than either of them—we mean the day labourers, the job-men of England, or the *orry* men of our own country parishes, employed in the construction and repairs of roads, and all the other varieties of ground labour. About twenty or twenty-four years ago, their allowance was from 10s. to 12s. a week, with victuals, or from 16s. even to 18s. and 20s a week, without victuals. Their allowance at present is 6s. a week with, and 10s. without victuals. But these numbers exhibit in both cases the full summer allowance; and, to estimate their yearly income, we must take into account the reduction of 1s. and 2s. a-week, when the days become shorter, as also the average of about two winter months, when they are totally without employment. A good practical test of the felt straitness in their circumstances, is the extreme fatigue they will undergo at piece-work, when, to eke out a sufficiency for their families, they are known to labour from four in the morning to eight at night; and it is the distinct testimony of the masters who employ them, that this is what these daysmen will do now, and would not have done twenty-five years ago. We might further state, that the services of a man, with two horses and single horse carts, could only be had at that time for 10s. or 12s. a day—but now for 5s. or 6s. 6d. Wrights and masons, in short, all country artisans, with the exception of blacksmiths, have experienced a similar decline in wages; and a decline not countervailed by the greater cheapness of the second, and still greater cheapness of the first necessaries of life. By the general consent of practical and intelligent men, the peasantry of Scotland have not, at this moment, the same command over the various articles which enter substantially into the maintenance of families, that they had during the first ten years of the present century."

" Two causes may be assigned for the glowing exaggerations of the reviewer, respecting the progress which he affirms to have taken place in the economic state of our people. It may be right that we advert, though briefly, to both of them—as they not only seem to have misled him, but are fitted to mislead many others, who are satisfied to make up their minds on a rapid and cursory view of the subject. The sketch which he has drawn of the internal state and history of Scotland, is one of great plausibility—yet it will not be difficult, we are persuaded, to evolve the actual state of the case, the sober reality of the question, from underneath that mantle of speciousness wherewith he hath garnished and overlaid it."

" The first great error of the reviewer, then, lies in this—that he has generalized workmen of all sorts and varieties into but one object of contemplation. He has viewed them only *en masse*, without having adverted to the momentous distinction which obtains between one class of them and another,—between the men, for example, of high wages, in virtue of the control which they have over their employer, because they can at any time bring his large and expensive machinery to a stand; and the men who often have not a third part of the wages of the others, because they possess no such power—as weavers, all whose capital is a handloom, which is their own; or ground labourers, all whose capital is a spade, which is their own also. He reasons, as if the foundation on which society rested, was throughout of homogeneous materials; and then tells us, what a substantial foundation it is, and how it is consolidating every year into greater strength and firmness than before. We reason, as if that foundation was made up of successive strata; and express our apprehension that the lowest stratum of all might become every year more putrid and unsound, and so endanger the stability of the whole fabric. The work recognises a gradation in the branches of regular industry; and takes account of a large and ever-increasing body of supernumeraries at the bottom of the scale. The dashing generality of the reviewer does not admit of such discrimination. It confounds the cotton-spinner of 28s. with the poor weaver of 5s. a week. It takes so distant a view of the object, that it comes not within sight of details and distinctions—though, in the instance on hand, of vital importance to all correct reasoning on the present state and future prospects of society. Like an unobservant by-passer through some plebeian district of a city, who never once dreams of the mighty gradation from the highest to the lowest of its householders—though intermingled with, or even contiguous to each other, the artisan or manufacturing operative, of from 20s. to as much as 50s. a-week, may be found in close juxta-position with the weaver or the labourer, who but realizes an humble fraction of his gains. He overlooks this, and lumps or amalgamates them all, under the one denomination of the common people. And so, whatever comes from that quarter to the savings banks; or whosoever, out of the mighty hosts who congregate there, shall attend a mechanics' institute—he puts it all down to the general, or rather the universal elevation, that has taken place in the habits and comforts of those who overspread the ground-floor or basement of society. It is thus, that, in very proportion to the rapidity, the reckless, but withal confident, rapidity of those slight and transient regards which our reviewer has cast upon the subject—does he overrate, and that prodigiously, not the improvement of the lower, but the improvement of the lowest orders. He exults in the fifteen millions of deposits to the provident banks of the country; but reflects not on that multitude of mere labourers—the hundreds of thousands, who compose a distinct and inferior class, that are every year multiplying upon our hands, and who contribute not so much as one farthing to them. He has not entered at all into the depths or statistics of his subject; he has but looked on the upper surface of it—or, if reasoning on a sort of general average between the most comfortable and the most degraded of the industrious classes, reflects not, that beneath that average there is a gathering mischief, the inevitable tendency of which is to undermine the stablest community on earth, and to bring down the prosperity of all its orders."

Let the *Reviewers, Useful Knowledge* propagators, or any other person or class of persons interested in concealing the truth, do as they will with Dr. Chalmers' economical doctrines, we defy them to impugn these statements.

---

* It is of importance to keep in mind, that the worst paid of our manufacturing labourers in Glasgow are the most numerous. The number of workers, of all ages and both sexes, in the cotton and weaving mills of that city and neighbourhood, was 10,897, in April 1832. We wish that we could state the number of hand-loom weavers at the same period. But as far back as 1820, the number of hand-looms was upwards of eighteen thousand.

PUBLIC CARRIAGES IN BRITAIN.

PROPRIETORS of coaches have at length found out—though they were a long time before they did discover it—that the hay and corn market is not so expensive as the horse market. They have, therefore, one horse in four always at rest; or, in other words, each horse lies still on the fourth day, thus having the advantage of man. In practice, perhaps, no animal toiling for man, solely *for his profit*, leads so easy and so comfortable a life as the English coach-horse; he is sumptuously fed, kindly treated, and if he do suffer a little in his work, he has twenty-three hours in the twenty-four of luxurious ease. He is now almost a stranger to the lash; nor do we ever see him with a broken skin; but we often see him kick up his heels when taken from his coach, after having performed his stage of ten miles in five minutes under the hour. So much for condition. No horse lives so high as a coach-horse. In the language of the road, his stomach is the measure of his corn; he is fed *ad libitum*. The effect of this is visible in two ways; first, it is surprising to see how soon horses gather flesh in this severe work, for there is none more severe while it lasts; and, secondly, proprietors find that good flesh is no obstacle to their speed, but, on the contrary, operates to their advantage. Horses draw by their weight, and not by the force of their muscles, which merely assist the application of their weight: the heavier a horse is, then, the more powerful he is in his harness; in short, it is the weight of the animal which produces the draught, and the play and force of his muscles serve to continue it. Light horses, therefore, how good soever their action, ought not to be put to draw a heavy load, as muscular force cannot act against it for any length of time. The average price of horses for fast coaches may be about £23. Fancy teams, and those working out of London, may be rated considerably higher than this; but taking a hundred miles of ground, well horsed, this is about the mark. The average period of each horse's service does not exceed four years in a fast coach; perhaps scarcely so much; in a slow one we may allow seven; but in both cases we are alluding to horses put to the work at five or six years' old. The price we have named as the average may appear a low one; but blemished horses find their way into coaches, as do those whose tempers are bad; neither is a blind horse, with good courage, altogether objectionable, now the roads are so level.

It may not be uninteresting to the uninitiated to learn how a coach is worked. We will then assume A, B, C, and D enter into a contract to horse a coach eighty miles, each proprietor having twenty miles; in which case he is said to cover both sides of the ground, or to and fro. At the expiration of twenty-eight days, a settlement takes place, and if the gross earnings of the coach should be £10 per mile, there will be £800 to divide between the four proprietors, after the following charges have been deducted, viz. tolls, duty to government, mileage (or hire of the coach to the coach-makers,) two coachmen's wages, porter's wages, rent, or charge of booking-offices at each end, and washing the coaches. These charges may amount to £150, which leaves £650 to keep eighty horses, and to pay the horse-keepers for a period of twenty-eight days; or nearly £160 to each proprietor for the expense of his twenty horses, being £2 per week per horse. Thus it appears that a fast coach, properly appointed, cannot pay, unless its gross receipts amount to £10 per double mile; and that even then the proprietors' profits depend on the luck he has with his stock.

In the present age, the art of mechanism is eminently reduced to the practical purposes of life, and the modern form of the stage-coach seems to have arrived at perfection. It combines prodigious strength with almost incredible lightness, not weighing more than about 18 cwt., and being kept so much nearer the ground than formerly, is of course considerably safer. Accidents, no doubt, occur, and a great many more than meet the public eye; but how should this be otherwise, when we take into account the immense number of coaches on the road, a great portion of which travel through the night, and have all the varieties of our climate to contend with? No one will assert that the proprietors guard against accidents to the utmost of their power; but the great competition they have to encounter is a strong stimulant to their exertions on this score. Indeed, in some respects, the increase of pace has become the traveller's security. Coaches and harness must be of the best quality; horses must be fresh and sound, and coachmen of science and respectability can alone be employed; in fact, to the increased pace of their coaches is the improvement in these men's moral character to be attributed. They have not time now for drinking; and they come in collision with a class of persons superior to those who formerly were stage-coach passengers, by whose example it has been impossible for them not to profit in all respects. A coachman drunk on his box is now a rarity; a coachman quite sober was, even within our memory, still more so.

The worst of accidents, and one which, with the present structure of coaches, can never be entirely provided against, arises from broken axletrees, and the wheels coming off on the road. On the whole, however, travelling by public conveyances was never so secure as it is at the present time. Nothing can be more favourable to it than the build of the modern coaches. The boots being let down between the springs, keep the load, consequently the centre of gravity, low; the wheels of many of them are secured by patent boxes; and in every part of them the best materials are used. The cost of coaches of this description is from £130 to £150, but they are generally hired from the maker at 2½d. to 3d. per mile. Cicero laments the want of post-offices, and well he might. Nothing can excel that department in our country, as it has been long administered by, perhaps, the only universally-approved public servant in our generation, Sir Francis Freeling; but we fear in this, as in more important matters, we are now about to lose sight of the good old rule, of " letting well alone." It is said to be the intention of government to substitute light carriages, with two horses, for the present mail-coaches, drawn by four; but we have many suspicions as to the result of such a change. It is true that persons who horse the mail cry out lustily against the government for not remunerating them better for the increased speed at which they are now required to travel—the maximum price being ten-pence a-mile. The mail-coaches are excellently adapted for quick travelling. When the mail-coach of the present day starts from London for Edinburgh, a man may safely bet a hundred to one that she arrives to her time: but let a light two-horse vehicle set out on the same errand and the betting would strangely alter. It is quite a mistaken notion, that a carriage is less liable to accidents for being light. On the contrary, she is more liable to them than one that is well laden in proportion to her sustaining powers. In the latter case she runs steadily along, and is but little disturbed by any obstacle or jerk she may meet on the road; in the former, she is constantly on "the jump," as coachmen call it, and her iron parts are very liable to snap. Our present mail-coach work reflects the highest credit on the state of our roads, and every thing connected with them. The hills on our great roads are now cut triangular, so that coachmen ascend nearly all of them in a trot. Indeed, coachmen have found out that they are gainers here, as in the trot every horse does his share, whereas, very few teams are all at work together when walking. A wonderful change has taken place in the English coach-horse. Fifty years ago the idea of putting a thorough-bred horse into harness would have been deemed preposterous. In the carriages of our noblemen and gentlemen, the long-tailed black or Cleveland bay—each one remove from the cart horse—was the prevailing sort, and six miles an hour the extent of his pace, and he cost from L.30 to L.50. A few years back a nobleman gave seven hundred guineas for a horse to draw his cabriolet; two hundred guineas is now an every-day price for a horse of this description; and a hundred and fifty guineas for a gentleman's coach-horse. Indeed a pair of handsome coach-horses, fit for London and well broken and bitted, cannot be purchased under two hundred guineas, and even jobmasters often give much more for them to let out to their customers. In harness also, we think we have arrived at perfection, to which the invention of the patent shining leather has mainly contributed. A handsome horse, well harnessed, is a noble sight; and is it not extraordinary, that in no country but England is the art of putting a horse into harness at all understood? Independently of the workmanship of the harness-maker, if our road-horses were put to their coaches in the loose awkward fashion of the Continent, we could never travel at the rate we do. It is the command given over the coach-horse that alone enables us to do it. Our amateur or gentlemen coachmen have done much good: the road would never have been what it now is, but for the encouragement they gave, by their notice and support, to all persons connected with it. Would the Holyhead road have been what it is, had there been no such persons as the honourable Thomas Kennyon, Sir Henry Parnell, and Mr. Maddox? Would the Oxford coachmen have set so good an example to their brethren of " the bench," had there been no such men on the road as Sir Henry Peyton, Lord Clonmell, the late Sir Thomas Mostyn, that Nestor of coachmen, Mr. Annesley, and Mr. Harrison? Would not the unhappy coachman of five-and-twenty years back have gone on wearing out their breeches with the bumping of the coach-box, and their stomachs with brandy, had not Mr. Warde, of Squerries, after many a weary endeavour, persuaded the proprietors to place their boxes upon springs? What would the Devonshire have been, but for the late Sir Charles Bamfylde, Sir John Rogers, Colonel Prouse, Sir Lawrence Palk, and others? Have the advice and the practice of such experienced men as Mr. Charles Buxton, Mr. Henry Villelois, Mr. Okeover, Sir Bellingham Graham, Mr. John Walker, Lord Sefton, Sir Felix Agar, Mr. Ackers, Mr. Maxse, Hon. Fitzroy Stanhope, Colonel Spicer, Colonel Sibthorpe, &c., been thrown away upon persons who looked upon them as protectors? Certainly not. Neither would the improvement in carriages—stage-coaches more especially—have arrived at its present height, but for the attention and suggestions of such persons as we have been speaking of. Gentleman-coaching, however, has received a check, and in more ways than one. "Tampering with the currency," and low prices, have taken off the leaders; and the bars and four-bone whips are hung up for the present—very few four-in-hands being visible. The B. D. C., or Benson Driving Club, which now holds its rendezvous at the Black Dog, Bedfont, is the only survivor of those numerous driving associations whose processions used, some twenty years ago, to be among the most imposing, as well as peculiar spectacles in and about the Metropolis. Hyde Park Corner, on any fine afternoon, in the height of the London season, is more than enough to confound any foreigner, from whatever part of the world he may come. He may there see what no other country under the heavens can show him, and what is more, what no other country ever will show him. Let him only sit on the rail, near our Great Captain's statue, with his watch in his hand, and in the space of two hours he will see a thousand well-appointed equipages pass before him to the mall, in all the pomp of aristocratic pride, and in which the very horses themselves appear to partake. The stream of equipages, of all calibres, barouches, chariots, cabriolets, &c. &c., and almost all got up, as Mr. Robinson's advertisements say, " Regardless of expense," flows on unbroken until it is half-past seven, and people at last begin to think of what they still call dinner. Old Seneca tells us that such a blaze of splendour was once to be seen on the Appian Way. It might be so—it is now to be seen no where but in London.—*Quarterly Review.*

[The *Quarterly* concludes this article with a prophecy, that after the second year of the Reform Bill no such sight of splendour will again be beheld in England. Even for this falling off we shall console ourselves, if " the peasantry" and " coster-mongers" are more tidily fitted in harness, and better mounted on shoe leather.]

MARCH OF STEAM.—The Champlain, a steam boat recently built in America, lately made the voyage from New York to Albany, a distance of 160 miles, in nine hours and 45 minutes, including a loss of time occasioned by fourteen stoppages, reducing the actual time to eight hours and 13 minutes, which gives nearly 20 miles an hour.

GEOLOGY.

AFTER having last week given some account of what Geology is considered in certain quarters, it may not be amiss to tell what it is.

Geology, then, is the science which has for its object the investigation of the nature and constitution of the earth. It therefore presents a wide field. In the remote ages, to which we are wont to look back as the depositories of the rudiments of all our knowledge, it had no existence. In fact, among the Greeks and Romans, Natural History was little better than a collection of old wives' fables. In times not very remote, geology was looked upon merely as a speculative study, which led men to invent poetical theories of the formation of the earth, but took little cognizance of the actual constitution of things. Hence the world-makers of those days, were very little acquainted with the rocks and mountains whose origin and structure they professed to explain; and we will venture to say, most of them were unable to perceive any difference between granite and greywacke. As knowledge increased, the cosmogenies diminished; and at the present day, men examine rocks, and study their relations, collect and describe the fossil remains contained in them, more in the hope that some rational theory of the earth will naturally develop itself from among the accumulated facts which they treasure up, than with any urgent desire to accommodate appearances to a favourite theory. Werner, in respect to the order of the rock formations, and their mineralogical nature; and Cuvier, in respect to the remains of extinct animals contained in them, stand forth among the cultivators of this science, as the great leaders who have directed the motions of numerous followers, zealous and indefatigable in their exertions. To our countryman Hutton, who, it would appear, was more of a world-maker than world-examiner, we are so far indebted, that his adherents, labouring for the purpose of supporting their favourite scheme, increased the knowledge of facts, while the Wernerians, anxious to refute their arguments, also searched every nook and crevice. At present, we have neither Wernerians nor Huttonians. We have a race of genuine geologists; although there are still in all countries, men who cherish peculiar views, and strive to support them. Thus with some, the centre of the earth is red hot, while with others it is a metallic nucleus; some suppose certain strata to have been formed by successive irruptions and retreats of the sea, others attribute their origin to a single deluge. But, be this as it lists, the strata and masses of which the crust of our globe is composed are becoming better known; and from the Himalayan Mountains to Melville Island, there are not wanting investigators of their qualities and relations. Now, what study can be much more interesting than that of the earth on which we tread? Surely, before going to foreign lands for knowledge, we should first make ourselves acquainted with what ? own furnishes:—before launching into the ocean of space, to circumnavigate the wondrous but unapproachable islands floating in it, we should first be familiar with that which forms our home. The uses of geological research need hardly now be insisted upon. As an object of rational inquiry, there is no science more calculated to gratify every intellectual propensity; and with reference to the arts, commerce, and domestic economy, surely the strata from which we obtain our metals, our building-stones, and our fuel, cannot be deemed unworthy of being investigated and known, even by the narrow mind of the artisan and trader. In Scotland, we believe geology occupies a very unimportant place in the system of education. In none of our schools is it taught, and in most of our universities it is sadly neglected. In the metropolis, however, we are more favourably dealt with in this respect; and he who is desirous of being introduced to this important study, possesses the means of gratifying his inclination in the prelections of our celebrated professor of Natural History, and in the inspection of the valuable and extensive collection of rocks and minerals in the museum of the University. People have an idea that science destroys the natural feelings with which men contemplate the objects of nature. No idea can be more false. Is any geologist less sensible of the grandeur of Ben Nevis, because he knows its base to be composed of gneiss and its summit of porphyry? or will he be less impressed by the rugged magnificence of Coruisk, because he perceives that its frightful rocks are composed of hypersthene, and knows the constitution of that atmosphere which bears the clouds in murky masses sullenly along its sublime peaks? We, who understand somewhat of geology, and have waved our bonnet on the proudest summits of the mountain masses of our native land, have never known our enthusiasm borne down by the weight of our science, nor felt our veneration of the author of nature diminished by being permitted to know somewhat of the operations of his wonder-working power. On the contrary, we assert, and will undertake at any time to prove, that the ignorant tourist, whether rhymster or canvass-dauber, or hunter of the picturesque, or to whatever other denomination he belongs, can have but just as little true perception of the sublimities or beauties of nature, as a short-sighted man can have of the shadings of a mountain landscape, as the varied tints of evening creep slowly over it. Let the painter study nature, and he will cease to excite ridicule by his miserable apings of it; let him know that the rock which he has dashed out with his pencil, possesses none of the characteristic features of any rock on this side the moon; that the trees which he has stuck into his landscape he will find in no country of the globe; that the forms of his clouds are not those of the atmosphere of our planet. Let the poet study nature, and he will better succeed in displaying her charms; and let him who fancies every thing of which he is ignorant altogether beneath his notice, learn that, what has exercised the contrivance and wisdom of the divine mind, is well worthy of the exercise of the highest faculties of a far nobler than his puny intellect. Few districts in Britain are much more interesting, in a geological point of view, than that in our own neighbourhood.—*Literary Gazette.*

ELEMENTS OF THOUGHT.

SLAVERY.—A people that pays a poll-tax for the support of slavery is manifestly but a remove from slavery itself; it is therefore nothing surprising, that a government whose basis was the public wrong, should have supported the outposts of slavery in the colonies at all hazards. For all that is thus given to the slave-holders, it is clear the people of England pay twice; once in the loss to the consumers, and once more in the loss to the traders on which the difference in a state of freedom would be spent. It is not a proposition to be minced, but one to be brought forward with the gravity of a theorem in Euclid—that if the West Indies were by a convulsion of nature to sink into the sea, the commercial and political advantages to the British community would be enormous, incalculable; and the gain in a moral and domestic point of view would be that of the cessation of a tribute, in comparison of which any that was ever paid by a nation to a conqueror was honour and positive renown. No man has a right to demand of another that he shall degrade himself by pretending ignorance, that if such a consumption should be in the page of destiny, all the employment to trade, navigation, or manufactures of any kind, which might thereby be caused to cease, would be replaced by a *greater* extent of trade, navigation, or manufactures, arising with the country whose cheaper produce is now prohibited by the delegates of the slave-holders in the House of Commons;—with the single reservation, that places should be lacking in the world from which the same supply would be procured. But this reservation can have no bearing on the effects of removing from us the present slavery-tax on sugar. Either such removal will cause the whole supply of sugar to be increased, or it will not. If it does not, the public will be where it is, and will be under the necessity of giving the same prices for sugars of all kinds as at present; and so the West Indians will go on. The pretence, therefore, that the public would lack a supply of sugar, is only for knaves to frighten children with. The truth is, the government has loved slavery and the support of slave-holders; and for this predilection of the government, we, the slaves at second-hand, must pay.—*Westminster Review.*

THE STORY-TELLER.

WE'LL SEE ABOUT IT.
BY MRS. S. C. HALL.

"WE'LL see about it!"—from that simple sentence has arisen more evil to Ireland, than any person, ignorant of the strange union of impetuosity and procrastination my countrymen exhibit, could well believe. They are sufficiently prompt and energetic where their feelings are concerned, but, in matters of business, they almost invariably perfer *seeing about* to DOING.

I shall not find it difficult to illustrate this observation: —from the many examples of its truth, in high and in low life, I select Philip Garraty.

Philip, and Philip's wife, and Philip's children, and all of the house of Garraty, are employed from morning till night in *seeing about* every thing, and, consequently, in *doing* nothing. There is Philip—a tall, handsome, good-humoured fellow, of about five-and-thirty, with broad, lazy-looking shoulders, and a smile perpetually lurking about his mouth, or in his bright hazel eyes—the picture of indolence and kindly feeling. There he is, leaning over what was once a five-barred gate, and leads to the haggart; his blue worsted stockings full of holes, which the suggan, twisted half way up the well-formed leg, fails to conceal; while his brogues, (to use his own words,) if they do let the water in, let it out again. With what unstudied elegance does he roll that knotted twine and then unrol it; varying his occupation, at times, by kicking the stones that once formed a wall, into the stagnant pool, scarcely large enough for full grown ducks to sail in. But let us first take a survey of the premises. The dwelling-house is a long rambling abode, much larger than the generality of those that fall to the lot of small Irish farmers; but the fact is, that Philip rents one of the most extensive farms in the neighbourhood, and ought to be "well to do in the world." The dwelling looks very comfortless, notwithstanding: part of the thatch is much decayed, and the rank weeds and damp moss nearly cover it; the door posts are only united to the wall by a few scattered portions of clay and stone, and the door itself is hanging but by one hinge, the window frames shake in the passing wind, and some of the compartments are stuffed with the crown of a hat, or a "lock of straw"—very unsightly objects. At the opposite side of the swamp is the haggart gate, where a broken line of alternate palings and wall, exhibit proof that it had formerly been fenced in; the commodious barn is almost roofless, and the other sheds pretty much in the same condition; the pig-stye is deserted by the grubbing lady and her grunting progeny, who are too fond of an occasional repast in the once-cultivated garden to remain in their proper abode; the listless turkeys, and contented half-fatted geese, live at large on the public; but the turkeys, with all their shyness and modesty, have the best of it—for they mount the ill-built stacks, and select the grain, *a plaisir*.

"Give you good morrow, Mr. Philip; we have had showery weather lately." "Och, all manner o' joy to ye, my lady, and sure ye'll walk in, and sit down; my woman will be proud to see ye. I'm sartin we'll have the rain soon agin, for it's every where, like bad luck; and my throat's sore wid hurishing thim pigs out o' the garden—sorra' a thing can I do all day for watching thim." "Why do you not mend the door of the stye?" "True, for ye, Ma'am dear, so I would, if I had the nails—and I've been threatening to step down to Mickey Bow, the smith, to ask him to *see about it*." "I hear you've had a fine crop of wheat, Philip." "Thank God for all things! You may say that; we had, my lady, a fine crop—but I have always the hight of ill-luck somehow; upon my sowkins (and that's the hardest oath I swear) the turkeys have had the most of it; but I mean to *see about* setting it up safe tomorrow." "But Philip, I thought you sold the wheat, standing, to the Steward at the big house." "It was all as one as sould, only it's a bad world, Madam dear, and I've no luck. Says the Stewart to me, says he, I like to do things like a man of business, so, Mister Garraty, just draw up a bit of an agreement, that you deliver over the wheat field to me, on sich a day, standing as it is, for sich a sum, and I'll sign it for ye, and thin there can be no mistake, only let me have it by this day-week. Well, to be sure I came home full o' my good luck, and I tould the wife; and on the strength of it she must have a new gown. And sure, says she, Miss Hennessy is just come from Dublin, wid a shop full o' goods, and on account that she's my brother's sister-in-law's first cousin, she'll let me have the first sight o' the things, and I can take my pick—and ye'll have plinty of time to *see about* the agreement to-morrow. Well, I don't know how it was, but the next day we had no paper, nor ink, nor pens in the house; I meant to send the gossoon to Miss Hennessy's for all—but forgot the pens. So when I was *seeing about* the 'greement, I bethought of the ould gander, and while I was pulling as beautiful a pen as ever ye laid ye'r two eyes upon, out of his wing, he tattered my hand with his bill in sich a manner, that sorra' a pen I could hould for three days. Well, one thing or another put it off for ever so long, and at last I wrote it out like print, and takes it myself to the steward. Good evening to you Mr. Garraty, says he; good evening kindly, sir, says I, and I hope the woman that owns ye, and all ye'er good family's well: all well thank ye, Mr. Garraty, says he; I've got the 'greement here sir, says I, pulling it out as I thought—but behould ye—I only cotcht the paper it was wrapt in, to keep it from the dirt of the tobacco, that was loose in my pocket for want of a box—(saving ye'r presence;) so I turned what little bits o' things I had in it out, and there was a great hole that ye might drive all the parish rats through, at the bottom—which the wife promised to *see about* mending, as good as six months before. Well, I saw the sneer on his ugly mouth (for he's an Englishman,) and I turned it off with a laugh, and said air holes were comfortable in hot weather, and sich like jokes —and that I'd go home and make another 'greement. 'Greement for what? says he, laying down his grate outlandish pipe. Whew! may-be ye don't know, says I. Not I, says he. The wheat field, says I. Why, says he; did'nt I tell you then, that you must bring the 'greement to me by that day-week;—and that was by the same token, (pulling a red memorandum book out of his pocket,) let me see—exactly this day three weeks. Do you think, Mister Garraty, he goes on, that when ye didn't care to look after ye'r own interests, and I offering so fair for the field, I was going to wait upon you? I don't lose my papers in the Irish fashion. Well that last set me up—and so I axed him if it was the pattern of his English breeding, and one word brought on another; and all the blood in my body rushed into my fist—and I had the ill luck to knock him down—and, the coward, what does he do but takes the law o' me—and I was cast—and lost the sale of the wheat—and was ordered to pay ever so much money: well, I didn't care to pay it then, but gave an engagement; and I meant to *see about it*—but forgot: and all in a jiffy, came a thing they call an execution—and to stop the cant, I was forced to borrow money from that tame negur, the exciseman, who'd sell the sowl out of his grandmother for sixpence, (if indeed there ever was a sowl in the family,) and its a terrible case to be paying *interest* for it *still.*

But, Philip, you might give up or dispose of part of your farm. I know you could get a good sum of money for that rich meadow by the river."

" True for ye ma'am dear—and I've been *seeing about it* for a long time—but some how *I have no luck.* Jist as ye came up, I was thinking to myself, that the gale day is passed, and all one as before, sara a pin's worth have I for the rint, and the landlord wants it as bad as I do, though it's a shame to say that of a gintleman; for jist as he was *seeing about* some ould custodium, or something of the sort, that had been hanging over the estate ever since he came to it, the sheriff's officers put *executioners* in the house; and it's very sorrowful for both of us, if I may make bould to say so; for I am sartin he'll be racking me for the money—and indeed the ould huntsman tould me as much—but I must *see about it:* not indeed that it's much good—for I've no luck." " Let me beg of you, Philip, not to take such an idea into your head; do *not lose* a moment; you will be utterly ruined if you do; why not apply to your father-in-law—he is able to assist you; for at present you only suffer from temporary embarrassmnet." " True for ye—that's good advice, my lady; and by the blessing of God I'll *see about it.*" " Then go directly, Philip." " Directly—I can't ma'am dear—on account of the pigs: and sorra a one I have but myself to keep them out of the cabbages; for I let the woman and the grawls go to the pattern at Killaun; it's little pleasure they see, the cratura." " But your wife did not hear the huntsman's story?" " Och, ay did she—but unless she could give him a sheaf o' banks notes, where would be the good of her staying—but I'll *see about it.*" " Immediately then, Philip, think upon the ruin that may come—nay, that *must* come, if you *neglect* this matter: your wife too; your family reduced from comfort to starvation—your home desolate"—" Asy my lady,—don't be after breaking my heart intirely; thank God I have seven as fine flahulugh children as ever peeled pratee, and all under twelve years old; and sure I'd lay down my life tin times over for every one o' them; and to-morrow for sartin—no—to-morrow—the hurling: I can't to-morrow; but the day after, if I'm a living man, *I'll see about it.*"

Poor Philip! his kindly feelings were valueless because of his unfortunate habit. Would that this were the only example I could produce of the ill effects of that dangerous little sentence—" *I'll see about it!*" Oh, that the sons and daughters of the fairest island that ever heaved its green bosom above the surface of the ocean, would arise and *be doing* what is to be done, and never again rest contented with—" SEEING ABOUT IT."

THE RAPIDS.
AN AMERICAN STORY.

"Oh cos, cos, cos, my pretty little cos! that thou didst know how many fathom deep I am n love!"
As You Like It.

MIDNIGHT on board a steam boat, a full moon, and a soft panorama of the shores of the St. Lawrence gliding by like a vision! I thus assume the dramatic prerogative of introducing my readers at once to the scene of my story, and with the same time-saving privilege I introduce my *dramatis personæ*, a gentleman and lady promenading the deck with the slow step so natural on a summer's night, when your company is agreeable.

The lady leaned familiarly on the arm of her companion as they walked to and fro, sometimes looking at the moon, and sometimes at her pretty feet, as they stole out, one after the other, into the moonlight. She was a tall, queenly person, somewhat *embonpoint*, but extremely graceful. Her eye was of a dark blue, shaded with lashes of remarkable length, and her features, though irregular, were expressive of great vivacity, and more than ordinary talent. She wore her hair, which was of a deep chestnut, in the Madoanna style, simply parted, and her dress, throughout, had the chaste elegance of good taste—the *tournure* of fashion without its extravagance.

Her companion was a tall, well-formed young man, very handsome, with a frank and prepossessing expression of countenance, and the fine freedom of step and air, which characterize the well-bred gentleman. He was dressed fashionably, but plainly, and wore whiskers, in compliance with the prevailing mania. His tone was one of rare depth and melody; and as he bent slightly and gracefully to the lady's ear, its low, rich tenderness had the irresistible fascination, for which the human voice is sometimes so remarkable.

It was a beautiful night. The light lay sleeping on the St. Lawrence like a white mist. The boat, on whose deck our acquaintances were promenading, was threading the serpentine channel of the " Thousand Isles," more like winding through a wilderness than following the passage of a great river. The many thousands islands clustered in this part of the St. Lawrence seem to realize the mad girl's dream when she visited the stars, and found them

" —— only green islands, sown thick in the sky."

Nothing can be more like fairy land than sailing among them on a summer's evening. They vary in size, from a quarter of a mile in circumference, to a spot just large enough for one solitary tree, and are at different distances, from a bowshot to a gallant leap from each other. The universal formation is a rock of horizontal stratum, and the river, though spread into a lake by innumerable divisions, is almost embowered by the luxuriant vegetation which covers them. There is everywhere sufficient depth for the boat to run directly alongside, and with the rapidity and quietness of her motion, and the near neighbourhood of the trees, which may almost be touched, the illusion of aerial carriage over land, is, at first, almost perfect. The passage through the more intricate parts of the channel, is, if possible, still more beautiful. You shoot into narrow passes where you could spring on shore on either side, catching, as you advance, hasty views to the right and left, through long vistas of islands; or, running round a projecting point of rock or woodland, open into an apparent lake, and darting rapidly across, seem running right on shore as you enter a narrow strait in pursuit of the covert channel.

It is the finest ground in the world for ' the magic of moonlight.' The water is clear, and on the night we speak of, was a perfect mirror. Every star was repeated. The foliage of the islands was softened into indistinctness, and they lay in the water, with well-defined shadows hanging darkly beneath them, as distinctly as clouds in the sky, and apparently as moveable. In more terrestrial company than the Lady Viola's, our hero might have fancied himself in the regions of upper air; but as he leant over the taffarel, and listened to the sweetest voice that ever melted into moonlight, and watched the shadows of the dipping trees as the approach of the boat broke them, one by one, he would have thought twice before he had said that he was sailing on a fresh water river, in the good steam boat Queenston.

Miss Viola Clay and Mr. Frank Gresham, the hero and heroine of this true story, I should have told you before, were cousins. They had met lately after a separation of many years, and as the lady had in the meantime become the proudest woman in the world, and the gentleman had been abroad and wore whiskers, and had, besides, a cousin's *carte blanche* for his visits, there was reason to believe they would become very well acquainted.

Frank had been at home but a few months when he was invited to join the party with which he was now making the fashionable tour. He had seen Viola every day since his return, and had more to say to her than to all the rest of his relatives together. He would sit for hours with her in the deep recesses of the windows, telling his adventures when abroad. At least, it was so presumed, as he talked all the time, and she was profoundly attentive. It was thought, too, he must have seen some affecting sights, for now and then his descriptions made her sigh audibly, and once the colour was observed to mount to her very temples—doubtless from strong sympathy with some touching distress.

Frank joined the party for the tour, and had, at the time we speak of, been several weeks in their company. They had spent nearly a month among the Lakes, and were now descending by their grand outlet at Montreal. Many a long walk had been taken, and many a romantic scene had been gazed upon during their absence, and the lady had, many a time, wandered away with her cousin, doubtless for the want of a more agreeable companion. She was indefatigable in seeing the celebrated places from every point, and made excursions which the gouty feet of her father, or the etiquette of a stranger's attendance would have forbidden. In these cases Frank's company was evidently a convenience; and over hill and dale, through glen and cavern, he had borne her delicate arm by the precious privilege of cousinship.

There's nothing like a cousin. It is the sweetest relation in human nature. There is no excitement in loving your sister, and courting a lady in the face of a strange family requires the nerve of a martyr; but your dear familiar cousin, with her provoking maidenly reserve, and her bewitching freedoms, and the romping frolics, and the stolen tenderness over the skein of silk that will get tangled—and then the long rides which nobody talks about, and the long *tête-à-têtes* which are nobody's business, and the long letters of which nobody pays the postage—no, there is nothing like a cousin—a young, gay, beautiful witch of a cousin!

Till within a few days Frank had enjoyed a monopoly of the Lady Viola's condescensions; but their party had been increased lately by a young gentleman who introduced himself to papa as the son of an old friend, and proceeded immediately to a degree of especial attention, which relieved our hero exceedingly of his duties.

Mr. Erastus Van Pelt was a tall, thin person, with an aquiline nose, and a forehead that retreated till it was lost in the distance. It was evident at the first glance that he was high *ton*. The authenticity of his style, even on board a steam boat, distanced imitation immeasurably. The angle of his bow had been an indissoluble problem from his *debut* at the dancing school till the present moment, and his quizzing-glass was thrown up to his eye with a grace that would have put Brummel to the blush. From the square toe of his pump to the loop of his gold chain he was a perfect wonder. Every body smiled on Mr. Erastus Van Pelt.

This accomplished gentleman looked with an evil eye on our hero. He had the magnanimity not to cut him outright, as he was the lady's cousin; but tolerated him on the first day with a cold civility, which he intended should amount to a cut on the second. Frank thought him thus far very amusing; but when he came frequently in the way of his attentions to his cousin, and once or twice raised his glass at his remarks, with the uncomprehending ' Sir !' he was observed to stroke his black whiskers with a very ominous impatience. Further acquaintance by no means mended the matter, and Frank's brow grew more and more cloudy. He had already alarmed Mr. Van Pelt with a glance of his eye that could not be mistaken, and anticipated his ' cut direct' by at least some hours, when the Lady Viola took him aside, and bound over his thumb and finger to keep the peace towards the invisible waist of his adversary.

A morning or two after this precaution, the boat was bending in towards a small village which terminates the safe navigation above the rapids of the Split Rock. Coaches were waiting on shore to convey passengers to the next still water, and the mixed population of the little village, attracted by the arrival, was gathered in a picturesque group on the landing. There was the Italian-looking Canadian with his clear olive complexion and open neck, his hat slouched carelessly, and the indispensable red sash hanging from his waist; and the still, statue-like Indian, with the incongruous blanket and belt, hat and moccassin, costume of the border, and the tall, inquisitive-looking Vermontese—all mingled together like the figures of a painter's study.

Miss Clay sat on the deck, surrounded by her party, Frank, at a little distance, stood looking into the water with the grave intentness of a statue, and Mr. Van Pelt levelled his glass at the ' horrid creatures' on shore, and expressed his elegant abhorrence of their *sauvagerie* in a fine spun *falsetto*. As its last thin tone melted, he turned and spoke to the lady with an air evidently more familiar than her dignity for the few first days seemed to have warranted. There was an expression of ill-concealed triumph in his look, and an uncompromised turning of his back on our *penseroso*, which indicated an advance in relative importance; and though Miss Clay went on with the destruction of her card of distances, just as if there was nobody in the world but herself, the conversation was well sustained till the last musical superlative was curtailed by the whisk of the escape valve.

As the boat touched the pier, Frank awoke from his reverie, and announced his intention of taking a boat down the rapids. Viola objected to it at first as a dangerous experiment; but when assured by him that it was perfectly safe, and that the boat, during the whole passage, would be visible from the coach, she opposed it no further. Frank then turned to Mr. Van Pelt, and to her astonishment, politely requested his company. The dandy was thunderstruck. To his comprehension it was like offering him a private interview with a bear. ' No sir,' said he, with a nervous twirl of his glass round his forefinger. Miss Clay, however, insisted on his acceptance of the invitation. The prospect of his company, without the restraint of Frank's presence, and a wish to foster the good feeling from which she thought the offer proceeded, were sufficient reasons for perseverance, and on the ground that his beautiful cap was indispensable to the picturesque effect, she would take no denial. Most reluctantly his consent was at last given, and Frank sprang on shore with an accommodating readiness to find boatmen for the enterprise.

He found his errand a difficult one. The water was uncommonly low, and at such times the rapids are seldom passed, even by the most daring. The old voyageurs received his proposition with shrugs and volumes of *patois*, in which he could only distinguish adjectives of terror. By promises of extravagant remuneration, however, he prevailed on four athletic Canadians to row him to the Coteau du Lac. He then took them aside, and by dint of gesture and bad French, made them comprehend, that he wished to throw his companion into the river. They had no shadow of objection. For a " consideration," they would upset the bateau in a convenient place below the rapids, and insure Mr. Van Pelt's subsequent existence at the forfeiture of the reward. A simultaneous " *Gardes vous!*" was to be the signal for action.

The coaches had already started when Frank again stood on the pier, and were pursuing slowly the beautiful road on the bank of the river. He almost repented his rash determination for a moment, but the succeeding thought was one of pride, and he sprang lightly into the bateau at the '*Allons!*" of the impatient boatmen.

Mr. Van Pelt was already seated, and as they darted rapidly away with the first stroke of the oars, the voyageur at the helm commenced a low recitative. At every alternate line, the others joined in a loud, but not inharmonious chorus, and the strokes were light and deep as the leader indicated, by his tone, the necessity of rapidity or deliberation. In a few minutes they reached the tide, and as the boat swept violently in, the oars were shipped, and the boatmen, crossing themselves and mumbling a prayer to their saint, sat still, and looked anxiously forward. It was evidently much worse than Mr. Van Pelt had anticipated. Frank remarked upon the natural beauties of the river, but he had no eye for scenery. He sat on a low seat, grasping the sides of the boat with a tenacity as unphilosophical as it was out of character for his delicate fingers. The bateau glided like a bird round the island, which divides the river, and, steering for the middle of the stream, was in a moment hurrying with its whole velocity onward. The Split Rock was as yet far below, but the intermediate distance was a succession of rapids, and, though not much dreaded by those accustomed to the navigation, they were to a stranger sufficiently appalling. The river was tossed like a stormy sea, and the large waves, thrown up from the sunken rocks, came rolling back upon the tide, and dashing over the boat, flung her off like a tiny shell. Mr. Van Pelt was in a profuse perspiration. His knees, drawn up to his head by the acute angle of his posture, knocked violently together, and no persuasion could induce him to sit in the depressed stern for the accommodation of the voyageurs. He sat right in the centre of the bateau, and kept his eye on the waves with a manifest distrust of Providence, and an anxiety that betrayed a culpable want of resignation.

The bateau passed the travellers on shore as she neared the rock. Frank waved his handkerchief triumphantly. The water just ahead roared and leaped up in white masses like a thousand monsters; and, at the first violent whirl, he was pulled down by a voyageur, and commanded imperatively to lie still. Another and another shock followed in quick succession, and she was perfectly unmanageable. The helmsman threw himself flat on the bottom. Mr. Van Pelt hid his face in his hands, and crouched beside him. The water dashed in, and the bateau, obeying every impulse, whirled and flung from side to side like a feather. It seemed as if every plunge must be the last. One moment she shivered and stood motionless, struck back by a violent blow, and the next, shot down into an abyss with an arrowy velocity that seemed like instant destruction. Frank shook off the grasp of the voyageur, and holding on to the side, half rose to his feet. " *Gardes vous!*" exclaimed the voyageur; and mistaking the caution for the signal, with a sudden effort he seized Mr. Van Pelt, and, plunging him over the side, leaped in after him. " *Diable!*" muttered the helmsman, as the dandy, with a piercing skriek, sprang half out of the water, and disappeared instantly. But the Split Rock was right beneath the bow, and like a shot arrow the boat sprang through the gorge, and in a moment was gliding among the masses of foam in the smooth water.

They put back immediately, and at a stroke or two against the current, up came the scientific " brutus" of Mr. Van Pelt, quite out of curl, and crested with the foam through which he had emerged to a thinner element. There was no mistaking its identity, and it was rudely seized by the voyageur with a tolerable certainty that the ordinary sequel would follow. All reasoning upon anomalies, however, is uncertain, and, to the terror of the unlettered captor, down went *un gentilhomme*, leaving the envy of the world in his possession. He soon re-appeared, and with his faith in the unity of Monsieur considerably shaken, the voyageur lifted him carefully into the bateau.

My dear reader! were you ever sick? Did you have a sweet cousin, or a young aunt, or any pretty friend who was not your sister or your mother, for a nurse? And do you remember how like an angel's fingers, her small white hand laid on your forehead, and how thrillingly her soft voice spoke low in your ear, and how inquiringly her fair face hung over your pillow? If you have not, and remember no such passages, it were worth half your sound constitution, and half your uninteresting health, and half your long life, to have had that experience. Talk of moonlight in a bower, and poetry in a *boudoir*—there is no atmosphere for love like a sick chamber, and no poetry like the persuasion to your gruel, or the sympathy for your aching head, or your feverish forehead.

Three months after Frank Gresham was taken out of the St. Lawrence, he was sitting in a deep recess with the lady, who, to the astonishment of the whole world, had accepted him as her lover. " Miss Viola Clay," said our hero, with a look of profound resignation, " when will it please you attend to certain responses you wot of?" The answer was in a low sweet tone, inaudible to all save the ear for which it was intended.

JEWS.—A great number of religious Jews in Poland are making preparations for visiting Jerusalem, in the belief that the time predicted by their prophets has nearly arrived, in which they shall be restored to the possession of that country. The Jews generally are, we hear, watching the movements of the Egyptian army with great eagerness, in the belief that some arrangements will be made which will enable them to return to Judea; but this belief has led to actual associations in Poland.

ON THE MORAL TRAINING OF CHILDREN.
(For the Schoolmaster.)
LETTER III.

"That the infant mind," observes the judicious Mrs. Hamilton, "is, at an early period, susceptible of terror, is a discovery unhappily made by every ignorant nurse. This instinct, implanted by the wise Creator as a protection to the helpless state of infancy, is an instrument in the hands of senseless ignorance, too frequently applied to the worst of purposes. It is the first, the constant engine of tyranny. In proportion as it is made to operate, the mind will be debased and enfeebled. Deprived of its power and energy, it will remain the willing slave of sensation. To this calamity many an innocent being is exposed by the the injudicious treatment of the nursery."

Let parents beware of this dangerous rock. Let them be careful that their children be not terrified into the suppression of feeling, or rather into the suppression of the external marks of feeling, by threats of any thing coming to take them away. Let the only fear, used as a compelling motive, be the fear of doing what is wrong, of offending God, of offending their parents and instructors; and even that fear should be applied as a motive, very seldom, and very cautiously. The habit of timidity, degenerating into cowardice, terminates in selfishness. The mind in which this degrading disposition is prevalent, generally becomes absorbed in anxiety for personal, individual safety.

Insincerity and cunning, are also frequently the attendants of a fearful disposition. Timidity, in fact, opens the door to a numerous and mischievous train of false ideas and feelings, which naturally, and almost inevitably produce fatal errors of conduct. If frightful objects, which have no real existence, be employed to terrify children into restraint of their feelings, or submission to authority, they will, in course of time, as their minds grow enlightened, discover the falsehood which has been used as a means of managing them; and is it not to be feared, that such a discovery may render the youthful ear deaf to the representations of the beauty, and propriety, and benefit of truth?

Firmness without anger, without even the faintest appearance of violence; the contriving that some consequence displeasing to the infant mind shall follow acts of resistance and disobedience, and which shall seem to it to be their natural results; the taking care that pleasing consequences shall always attend submission and obedience; these measures will most probably enlist association of ideas [as a powerful auxiliary on the side of duty and happiness.

Let every possible means be used to check the principle of selfishness in children. Let them see their parents, their instructors, ever ready to communicate to others a share of whatever desirable objects they may possess, and preferring the comfort of those they love to their own personal gratification; let them be encouraged and incited, to share with others their food, their playthings, and what must appear to them most valuable; and let some pleasurable result follow such acts.

Selfishness is indeed the predominating or besetting sin of our nature, to which all are more or less hereditarily, or by birth, inclined, according to its predominance with parents. It is therefore an evil which cannot be too early checked in children, otherwise it grows with their growth, and strengthens with their strength; and if they thus live and die without its meeting with a check, they will not only go on, like those before them, to entail the same evil on their offspring, (if they have any,) but they will assuredly plunge their own souls in eternal misery as the unavoidable consequence.

Let us beware of giving children the idea, that they are to engross all attention and all care; that every thing, and every body, should contribute to their amusement. This is often done, unintentionally and unknowingly, by ill-judging and ill-directed fondness in parents, or by friends paying excessive and irrational court to children, in order to flatter their parents. By this most injudicious conduct towards children, the seeds of vanity, of self-will, of interestedness, are sown in the infant mind; there they too quickly take root, grow too rapidly, and soon bear pernicious fruits.

The love of power appears to be natural to the human mind. Its possession is commonly attended by the disposition to exercise it, and by contempt shown towards those who are subjected to it. This disposition evidently leads to tyranny and oppression; and therefore the greatest attention should be given to prevent its growth in the youthful mind. Never should children be permitted to tyrannize over inferiors, and to treat them with contempt. Never should servants be submitted to their caprice and humour. Sometimes, indeed, children experience the abuse of power exercised upon themselves by unnecessary control and vexatious restraint in the nursery. But how often are children trained to despise and ill-treat inferiors! They see them treated as beings of a lower class. They hear commands issued to them in harsh tones and an imperious manner. I have known boys permitted even to strike, and kick, female servants, and servants expected to bow to this infant tyranny. What can be the result of such conduct, but the production of overbearing dispositions, and the spoiling of tempers? Let children, from their earliest years, be taught that servants, and those even in the lowest stations of society, are their fellow-creatures, placed, as well as themselves, where their Heavenly Father hath pleased, in the great chain of beings; and that when they do their duty faithfully and well, they are to be respected and treated kindly, as inferior friends and members of the great family of God. The welfare, happiness, and improvement of servants, ought to be attended to, and all proper means taken to render the condition in which Providence has placed them, as comfortable as is consistent with the proper discharge of their necessary duties.

It is almost impossible to prevent all intercourse between children and servants; is it not, then, a fair object of inquiry, whether it be not worth the time and attention of heads of families to enlighten their servants, to give them good principles, and render them trust-worthy, for their own sakes, and the sakes of their children? If bad masters and mistresses make bad servants, the converse of the proposition is probably true,—good masters and mistresses make good servants.

Every appearance of insincerity, every attempt to deceive, whether made by word or action, should meet with the most marked disapprobation. Such a disposition should be repressed with anxious solicitude, and every circumstance which has any the remotest tendency to form it, every temptation to disguisement, to fraud, to deceit, should be carefully removed.

It has already been remarked, that *fear* leads to insincerity. Let not children be punished for mere accidents; such as breaking china cups, or glasses; or for tearing and inking frocks; but let them be encouraged immediately to run to their parents or guardians, and mention the misfortune which may have happened to them. The lesson of carefulness may be inculcated upon them by showing the waste occasioned by the breaking and destroying of useful things, and the good purposes to which might be applied the money necessary to replace them. If a stronger motive be found necessary, let it be the privation of some pleasure, or the obligation of making good the loss.

If children be deceived by others, they will too soon learn to deceive in turn. Never, therefore, let things be misrepresented to them. If it be not proper for them to receive the information which they require, it is far better to tell them, that it is not fit for them to know, that therefore you do not think it proper to answer their inquiry, than to misrepresent or mistate. Never let them hear the thing that is not, even in jest; never let a falsehood be uttered in their presence. Let them feel the bad effects of lying in being treated with disgrace and contempt. If, unhappily, they are addicted to the wretched habit of lying, enjoin servants and playfellows, in their hearing, to ask them no questions, because they cannot depend upon truth in their answers; and let their assertions, upon indifferent, as well as serious subjects, make no impression. Such treatment will probably be far more efficacious than corporal punishment.

When the propensity to lying is in a child more advanced, perhaps the best method to cure it is, by explaining, in a few forcible words, not only the sin, but the folly of an offence which deprives him who is guilty of it, of our confidence, and debases his character; shew him that in lying he commits a greater crime to hide a smaller one; that he has nothing to hope from telling a falsehood, nor any thing to fear from speaking truth.

Tale-bearing is also a habit attended with degrading and injurious consequences, to which young people in general are but too much addicted, and which seldom fails to produce censoriousness and falsehood. Children should be strictly guarded against it, both by precept and example, and early taught not to speak to the disadvantage of any person.

An early and deep-rooted sense of strict justice, is the proper soil wherein to nourish every moral virtue; and it should therefore be the constant care of parents assiduously to instil this into the tender minds of their children. The feelings of benevolence will never be uniform nor extensive in their operation, unless they are supported by a strong sense of justice. Hence the necessity and propriety of setting before them, on all occasions, both by precept and example, the most scrupulous integrity, liberality, fair-dealing, and honour, consistent with the Divine rule of doing unto others as we would that others should do to us. Far from indulging a smile, therefore, at any instance of selfish dexterity, they should see that we view it with detestation. And as opportunities of inculcating the above rule occur, they ought never to be passed by in silence. As, for instance, when a child has received an act of kindness or generosity, an appeal ought instantly to be made to his feelings, and the duty of contributing, in a similar manner, to the happiness of others, enforced at the moment when the mind is in a proper tone for the exercise of the sympathetic feelings.

To establish an habitual regard to the principles of honesty, a child should not be permitted to pick up the smallest article, without inquiring to whom it belongs. This easy rule, and asking leave before they take any thing, even when very young, will give them a strong sense of the duty of honesty, as enjoined by God,—such, indeed, as may never be effaced. And here, I will just advert to that unjustifiable inquisitiveness that leads to listening at doors, peeping into letters, and other mean devices to gain intelligence, which ought to be strictly prohibited. They should be taught an abhorrence of all indirect means of satisfying their curiosity; and that they ought not even to look at the contents of an open letter without liberty; nor, indeed, of any other writing that does not belong to them.

But above all, particular care should be taken that all those emotions and acts which, in the remotest degree, tend to produce the habit of cruelty or insensibility to the sufferings of others, be most sedulously checked; and every incentive to them, and every possibility of practising them, be removed, as far as authority of parents and heads of families can extend. If passion impel them to strike, to scratch, or to any other open violence against its object, let children feel in themselves the pain occasioned by such acts to the person acted upon. In such cases, perhaps, it would be right and efficacious to follow the *lex talionis*, the law of retribution, and inflict stroke for stroke, and scratch for scratch; that from experience they may learn the unpleasant effects of such indulgence of passion. The first movement may be given to irritable feelings in the minds even of the tenderest infants, by their being taught and encouraged to vent their indignation against persons who control or contradict them in any respect. How often do very young children hear the exclamation from their nurse-maids, and sometimes even from foolish mothers—" Naughty brother, or naughty sister, or cross Sally, beat him! beat her!" I have seen the hand of the baby, as yet incapable of understanding the dangerous exhortation, lifted up by the nurse who was carrying the precious burden, and made to perform the operation of striking. Nay, so far is this mischievous folly carried, that it is not uncommon, when a child has hurt itself by falling, and is expressing its feeling by tears and cries of vexation, to hear the absurd outcry—" Beat the table, or beat the floor, or beat the chair!—naughty table, floor, or chair, to hurt baby!" A more efficacious mode of teaching revenge, and of cherishing irritable emotions could not be devised.

Let children frequently be told what dreadful effects have flowed from ungovernable anger, and what mischief is often committed in the heat and storm of passion; which, afterwards, is followed by bitter sorrow and remorse. Let them be taught never to speak or act while the fervour of passion rages in their bosoms; to be on their guard, and to curb themselves as soon as they feel its glow beginning.

If proper and powerful motives be used, the habit, the important habit of restraining passion, may be formed, and the most irritable temper may be calmed. And surely this is an object worthy of the closest attention, and of the most assiduous exertions of parents.—I am, &c.,

A FRIEND TO EARLY EDUCATION.
Edinburgh, Jan. 17, 1833.

CAPITAL IN TRADE.

The stock possessed by an individual, whether it be of money, or of articles which can be exchanged for money, or for other articles, is called *his capital*. When a man sets up in business, he must possess capital, or credit, or both. If he has made or produced any article himself, the article so produced is his capital. For instance, a farmer may have grown a quantity of hay, which he has to sell; and in that case the hay is capital, as much as any money which he may have in his purse or in a bank; or a watchmaker may have made a watch, and that watch being exchangeable for provisions or clothes, or any thing that he wants, or for money, is also capital. By capital, a man may obtain from another whatever he wants for his own use, or which he intends to sell, if he has something to offer of value equal to that which he desires to purchase. By credit he also obtains what he wants, though generally upon less advantageous terms, because he has no capital immediately to give; he promises to give the capital at some future day. We shall present an example of both modes of dealing. A poor but industrious lad went to a wholesale tea-dealer in London, and said, "If you will trust me with a pound of tea for one day I will bring you the money for it at night, and I can support myself by selling the pound of tea in small quantities." The price of the tea was six shillings; and the dealer having consented, the poor lad went to his neighbours to sell them the tea at sixpence an ounce. There being sixteen ounces in the pound, by disposing of that pound he made a profit of two shillings; that is, he had two shillings clear gain after he had paid for the tea at night; and so, having done the same thing for three days more, and having only spent sixpence each day for his food and lodging, he had six shillings in hand. This money was his capital, and it was no longer necessary for him to buy upon credit; and he went on increasing his capital till he became possessed of more and more capital—whether of tea or money—so that he could afford to take a shop.* He then had to buy scales, and drawers, and counters, and other things, which were necessary for him to use in his trade but not to sell. These things were what men in business call a *fixed* capital; the surplus money or disposable articles which he had gathered together by his industry, were what they call a *floating* capital. The tools of a working man are fixed capital; and if he part with them, he loses some of his power of earning other capital by his labour. Even a savage, who has a hut to live in, and a stock of roots for his food, in the season when the ground produces him nothing, and has lines and hooks to catch fish, and a pot to cook them, has a capital. This is his fixed capital, which he must acquire for his own support; but if he has raised more food than he wants, and has any to exchange for iron, or clothing, with a ship that touches upon his shores, he has a disposable or floating capital. When the people of any country have got together a great many things of value, such as houses and furniture, manufactories and machines, stocks of corn or wine, and other articles of comfort or luxury, then the nation is said to possess capital; it is called a rich nation. England, which has great abundance of every article, for the supply, not only for her own people, but of foreign nations, is therefore called rich; while, on the contrary, such a country as Lapland, in which scarcely food and clothing enough are produced for the rudest wants of the natives, is called poor. But though a nation may be rich, a large number of its people may be poor. There are a great many very poor and wretched persons in the richest nations, because these persons have no capital, and there is not a sufficient demand for their labour. Such an unfortunate state of things, in which the men without capital are desirous to work, but can get no work to do, may arise from many causes; and the best government may be unable to remove the evil. It is the duty, both of governments and of individuals, to labour as much as they can to amend or mitigate this evil. Many men of capital are only possessed of claims upon others; that is, of debts due to them.—Their stock is in the hands of others, to whom they have lent it, upon condition of receiving a payment for it, which is called interest. Thus, if a man lend another a hundred pounds, at five per cent. interest, he receives five pounds for the use of that hundred, or *centum* (a Latin word, meaning hundred, which is shortened into cent.) per annum; that is by the year. The lender does not use his capital himself, but he receives a payment for the use of it; while the borrower, if he trade with it, buys articles which he endeavours to sell at a larger profit than he pays for the money which he has obtained upon credit, and which money is said to be *borrowed* capital. He often acquires profit, by what men in trade call *turning* his capital. For instance, if he borrow L.100 on the first of January, and buy with it a quantity of articles which he sells for L.110 by the 1st of April; and if he does the same over again by the 1st of July, and over again by the first of October, and over again by the 1st of January in the next year, he will have turned his borrowed capital four times in the year, and will have made a profit of thirty-five pounds, over and above the five pounds which he has to pay to the man who has lent him the money. If he is enabled to lay by the thirty-five pounds which he has made as profit, he has so much *clear* capital; but if he has incurred debts equal to, or beyond that sum, he has really no capital at all. Industry and skill will rapidly produce capital; while, on the other hand, idleness and mismanagement will as quickly consume it. We have heard of an elder brother who had a thousand pounds left him by his father, which he locked up in a chest, and spent as he wanted it. In five years all his money was gone, and then he had to sell his furniture to buy food; and when that was all sold he got into debt; and being then poor and idle, he went to gaol, and would have gone to a workhouse but for his younger brother, who had no capital when their father died. He, however, had his industry for his support, and out of that he gradually created capital, went into business, and was prosperous and happy, because he always lived within his means. Men in business, in this, and in all other large commercial countries, are often ruined by what is called *trading beyond their capital*. This they are sometimes enabled to do by the employment of *fictitious* capital; that is, by the issue of more bills or promises to pay money, than they have *real* capital to meet.—*From the Working Man's Companion.*

---

* This happened in London within the last three years.

MY FATHER'S HOME.
From the Chameleon.

Across the troubled Loch I see
   A small white cottage, 'neath a gleam
Of sunlight, resting partially
   On that one spot with fondling beam—
There turn my thoughts where'er I roam—
It is my father's children's home!

Like the chafed wave, 'twixt it and here
   My surging spirit darkly swells;
Yet one bright spot of love will ne'er
   Grow dim beneath its moody spells.
Howe'er the storm cloud o'er me come,
Bright be my father's children's home!

There dwell the sisters dowered with aught
   Of love once warmed a heart now cold;
Which still, for them would think it nought
   To coin its life-drops into gold.
The bright-eyed urchins there, too, roam,
Who glad a gray-haired father's home.

My blessings on the much-loved spot!
   Because I love the dwellers there;
When they are loved not, or forgot,
   Unanswered be my fondest prayer!
Though ne'er within its scope I come,
Heaven shield my father's children's home!

Holy Loch, August 1831.

TO A SLEEPING CHILD.

O sleep, my little infant boy,
    A mother's care shall guard thy bed;
O, once thou wert a father's joy,
    But now, alas! he's cold and dead!

He toiled both night and day for thee;
    But now in vain the tear is shed,
For him who lies beneath the sea—
    Alas! sweet child, thy father's dead!

Then sleep, my little orphan boy;
    Thou'lt never know a father's love—
But still thou art thy mother's joy,
    And his whose spirit soars above!

Great God! my little child protect,
    In the paths of grace to seek thee!
Lord, the little lamb direct
    To obey his shepherd meekly!

And when death's long night is come,
    Heedless let it not o'ertake him—
Bear him to his long loved home,
    And in realms of glory wake him.

TO MY BOOKS.

My faithful monitors! unchanging friends,
    To whom in sorrow, sickness, and despair,
And when, by grief oppressed, my spirit bends
    To earth, with sure reliance I repair,
And solace find, and kindred hearts to share
    And sympathize with feelings, which the cold,
The proud, the selfish, deem it weak to bear;
    Oh! ever let me sweet communion hold
With you, the immortal shades of minds of heavenly
    mould!

A MISER'S OPINION OF BOOKS.—If you wish to know what is desirable and good, you should look abroad among mankind, and see what it is that they desire and pursue. You must not read books my child; books deceive you—your excellent mother read many books, and was misled by them, and talked to me about that which I could not understand. There is a race after honours and riches; all men run that race except the indolent, who are beggars, and the conceited ones misled by books, who generally become beggars in the end. Books and fine talk are the dust which the crafty ones throw into the eyes of their competitors in the race after riches and honour. Look at this great and mighty city, (London,) wherein we live, and mark you how busy it is from morning till night; and for what is all this business—must you read books to know? No, no,—books tell nothing that is true, they mislead, they deceive. When a man has toiled all day long and has gained money, is he not pleased with his gains—does he not count them over carefully and triumphantly? He will not throw his gold into the the street, though books may talk much of the pleasures of generosity. Generosity, my child, is a long word, by means of which crafty people attack our pockets through our pride or superstition; and when they have done so, they laugh at us.—*The Usurer's Daughter.*

SCRAPS.
ORIGINAL AND SELECTED.

COBBETT'S ACCOUNT OF HIS OWN ORATORY.—"Though I never attempt to put forth that sort of stuff which the 'intense' people on the other side of St. George's Channel call 'eloquence,' I bring out strings of very interesting facts; I use pretty powerful arguments; and I hammer them down so closely upon the mind, that they seldom fail to produce a lasting impression."

POMPEII—MOST INTERESTING DISCOVERY.—Our report of the last meeting of the Royal Society of Literature notices a letter of great interest from Sir W. Gell, relative to recent important discoveries at Pompeii. Colonel Robinson, it seems, in boring, as the French do, for Artesian wells, first fell upon a spring resembling the Seidlitz waters, which is already much resorted to, and has performed many cures. But a far more striking discovery ensued—no less than that of the long anticipated Port of Pompeii, with its vessels overthrown upon their sides, and covered and preserved by the eruptive volcanic matter, which has thus anchored them for so many ages. About thirty masts have been found. What a mine of curiosity lies below, to gratify our thirst for knowledge of these remote times!

ANTEDILUVIAN REMAINS.—In the middle of last month, two fishermen, being employed on the banks of the Lippe, near the village of Ahsen, in Westphalia, and at a moment when the water was unprecedentedly low, discovered a heap of bones lying in the bed of the river, and conveyed them ashore. It was a superb and perfect specimen of a mammoth's head, in excellent preservation, and of an unusual size. For instance, the four grinders are from six to nine inches in diameter, and the two tusks, one of which was found adhering to the chin bone, are between three and four feet in length.

METHOD OF QUELLING A RIOT IN THE HIGHLANDS.—The Highlanders, in general, are a very kind, warm-hearted sort of people, and seldom disposed to quarrel, except when affected by the exhalations of the mountain dew. The tranquillity, however, of a certain fiscal was recently disturbed, by one of those brawls that will occur in the best regulated communities. He had been enjoying the society of a friend, and the two had reached that happy point of good fellowship, when parting is the thing farthest from their thoughts—the hearth had just been swept—the subtile flame was blinking through the openings left in the well-built peat cairn; and the ingredients for a fresh jorum were smoking on the table—when "Mary the Maid of the Inn" broke in upon them, and announced, in a lamentable tone, that two men were fighting in Mac——'s, and the fiscal was wanted immediately. The reader, if he has any social feelings about him, may easily imagine how unreasonable a message of this kind was deemed by the worthy official. After scratching his head for sometime, (for who would not consult the *crown* lawyers in such a dilemma,) he turned to Mary, and told her to go Mac——, and tell him "to give the men a gill, provided they gave over fighting!"—"But if they'll no do't, Sir!" said Mary. "In that case," rejoined the fiscal, turning to his toddy, "tell him *to make the rascals fight till I come.*"

SUBSTITUTE FOR PAPER FOR COVERING WALLS.—There is now getting into use, as a substitute for paper for covering the walls of dwelling-houses, a sort of cloth made of cotton wool, pressed by means of calenders, into a flat sheet, resembling, in colour and appearance, a sheet of demy paper, and printed into a variety of suitable patterns. It is very stout, and seems in every way qualified to supersede paper entirely, as it can be produced much cheaper. We understand, that there are very large orders for this sort of cloth.

CONTENTS OF NO. XXVI.	
Mr. Stuart's Three Years in North America	49
State of the Working Classes	52
Public Carriages in Britain	54
Geology	56
ELEMENTS OF THOUGHT—Slavery	ib.
THE STORY-TELLER—We'll See About it—The Rapids	57
Moral Training of Children	61
Capital in Trade	63
My Father's Home	ib.
To a Sleeping Child—To My Books—A Miser's Opinion of Books	64
SCRAPS—Cobbett's Account of his own Oratory—Pompeii—Method of Quelling a Riot in the Highlands	ib.

EDINBURGH: Printed by and for JOHN JOHNSTONE, 19, St. James's Square.—Published by JOHN ANDERSON, Jun., Bookseller, 55, North Bridge Street, Edinburgh; by JOHN MACLEOD, and ATKINSON & Co., Booksellers, Glasgow; and sold by all Booksellers and Venders of Cheap Periodicals.

THE Schoolmaster,
AND
EDINBURGH WEEKLY MAGAZINE.

CONDUCTED BY JOHN JOHNSTONE.

THE SCHOOLMASTER IS ABROAD.—LORD BROUGHAM.

No. 27.—Vol. II.   SATURDAY, FEBRUARY 2, 1833.   Price Three-Halfpence.

MR. STUART'S THREE YEARS IN AMERICA.
(Continued from last Number.)

We promised to give Mr. Stuart's more remarkable rencontres with our countrymen in the course of his travels and now hasten to redeem that pledge. It is like sending a long letter home.

Near Troy, a flourishing town in the State of New York, and not far from Albany, is a hill named Mount Ida. In walking up this eminence, Mr. Stuart stopped at a cottage half-way, and found it occupied by a Scotch family.

"The name of the husband is William Craig, from Lochwinnoch, in Renfrewshire. His wife's name is Robertson. They arrived in the month of May, 1828. Craig was, within a few days after his arrival, engaged by the proprietor of Mount Ida as superintendent of his farm, at 170 dollars a-year, besides a good house, the constant keeping of a cow, vegetables, and potatoes. The proprietor was so much pleased with his management, that, before the crop 1829 was put into the ground, he insisted on Craig's becoming tenant of it, Craig giving the proprietor the usual share of the produce, and the proprietor obliging himself, that if, according to this arrangement, Craig had not 170 dollars a-year, besides the other articles before-mentioned, he would make up the sum to that amount."

In Washington Mr. Stuart met with a gentleman whom it is probable some of our west country readers may still remember.

"On my perambulations in Washington, I observed on a sign-post, 'Kennedy, Theological Bookseller.' Thinking that a theological bookseller was the very person to direct me in what church it was likely I should hear a good sermon on the following day, I entered his store, and we soon recognised each other to be from the same country. I found he was from Paisley. When he was a young man he was attached to those political principles which sent Gerald, Muir, Palmer, &c. to Botany Bay, and which were at that time sufficiently unfashionable. He had been induced to attend the meetings of the Edinburgh Convention, though not a member; but Mr. Kennedy's brother, now a senator in Maryland, was a member of the Convention; and they both thought it prudent, during the reign of terror in Scotland at that period, to emigrate to the United States. Mr. Kennedy had been lately employed by the Government of the United States at Washington in making journeys, with a view to arrangements for the American colony of blacks on the coast of Africa, a very interesting settlement, of which more hereafter."

Mr. Stuart accompanied his countryman to church, and heard a rather flowery sermon by a favourite orator, on which he makes some pertinent remarks. He saw the President Jackson, his seat in no wise distinguished from the other pews. The President bowed at the conclusion of the service to Mr. Kennedy, the old Scotch expatriated jacobin of 1793, and thus the world wags.

Washington appears to abound in Scotsmen. Here we have another:—

"I had not been many days at Washington, when, going accidentally into Mr. Jonathan Elliott's book-store, on the Pennsylvania avenue, I found that he was a Scotsman from Hawick, who had been in America for twenty years. He had originally accompanied Miranda on his famous expedition. He is the author of several literary works. At one time he edited a newspaper here; he is at present engaged in writing a history of Washington, and is a printer as well as bookseller, and of so obliging and hospitable a disposition, that I am sure any of his countrymen who may visit him will have a kind reception. He made me known to several persons whom I wished to see, and accompanied me to some of the public offices, to which I was anxious to get admittance. Mr. Elliot describes Washington as a very cheap place to live at, the neighbouring country abounding in the necessaries of life. Even canvass-back ducks are at present sold at 2s. 6d. a brace.

* * * * *

"Mr. Elliott tells me, that, owing to the cheapness of the necessaries of life, he can amply maintain a family of nine persons, four of whom are servants, (I presume slaves,) and three young people, for, nine dollars a week; he pointed out to me in the Capitol when we were on our way to the library, Litourno's beef-steak and oyster-shop, which is the Bellamy's eating-shop of the American Parliament. Oysters seem to be the favourite lunch of the gentlemen in the forenoon."

At Richmond Mr. Stuart met with a Mr. Forbes, who had left the west of Scotland about thirty years back, and who had been a member of the Legislature of Carolina; and in Charleston he found another countryman, Mr. Ferguson, from Golspie in Sutherland, who was bar-keeper of the hotel where he lodged. It was thus he found him, and the history is valuable, as it shews us the condition of the slaves:—

"On returning to the hotel, I found a gentleman had, in my absence, called for me, and left a note asking me to din with him next day. Having written my answer, accepting the invitation, I went to the bar-room to beg Mr. Street to send it by one of the boys, of whom there were several about the house, but he at once told me that he could not send one of his slaves out of the house. The bar-keeper, Mr Ferguson, from Golspie in Sutherland, North Britain, seeing my dilemma, offered to carry my note, and the landlord consented. Ferguson, however, afterwards told me, that the landlord had been very ill-pleased with him for shewing me so much civility, because he knew that his presence was always necessary in the bar-room. Ferguson, at the same time, told me that the slaves were most cruelly treated in this house, and that they were never allowed to go out of it, because, as soon as they were out of sight, they would infallibly make all the exertion in their power to run away. Next morning, looking from my window an hour before breakfast, I saw Mrs. Street, the landlady, give a young man, a servant, such a blow behind the ear as made him reel, and I afterwards found that it was her daily and hourly practice to beat her servants, male and female, either with her fist, or with a thong made of cow-hide.

* * * * *

"I was placed in a situation at Charleston, which gave me too frequent opportunities to witness the effects of slavery in its most aggravated state. Mrs. Street treated all the servants in the house in the most barbarous manner; and this, although she knew that Stewart, the hotel-keeper here, had lately nearly lost his life by maltreating a slave. He beat his cook, who was a stout fellow, until he could no longer support it. He rose upon his master, and, in his turn gave him such a beating that it had nearly cost him his life; the cook immediately left the house, ran off, and was never afterwards heard of,—it was supposed that he had drowned himself. Not a day, however, passed, without my hearing of Mrs. Street whipping and ill-using her unfortunate slaves. On one occasion, when one of the female slaves had disobliged her, she beat her until her own strength was exhausted, and then insisted on the bar-keeper, Mr. Ferguson, proceeding to inflict the remainder of the punishment. Mrs. Street, in the meantime, took her place in the bar-room. She instructed him to lay on the whip severely in an adjoining room. His nature was repugnant to the execution of the duty which was imposed on him. He gave a wink to the girl who understood it, and bellowed lustily, while he made the whip crack on the walls of the room. Mrs. Street expressed herself to be quite satisfied with the way in which Ferguson had executed her instructions; but, unfortunately for him, his lenity to the girl became known in the house, and the subject of merriment, and was one of the reasons for his dismissal before I left the house;—but I did not know of the most atrocious of all the proceedings of this cruel woman until the very day that I quitted the house. I had put up my clothes in my portmanteau, when I was about to set out, but finding it was rather too full, I had difficulty in getting it closed to allow me to lock it; I therefore told one of the boys to send one of the stoutest of the men to assist me. A great robust fellow soon afterwards appeared, whom I found to be the cook, with tears in his eyes;—I asked him what was the matter? He told me that just at the time when the boy called for him, he had got so sharp a blow on the cheek bone from this devil in petticoats, as had unmanned him for the moment. Upon my expressing commiseration for him, he said he viewed this as nothing, but that he was leading a life of terrible suffering;—that about two years had elapsed since he and his wife, with his two children, had been exposed in the public market at Charleston for sale,—that he had been purchased by Mr. Street,—that his wife and children had been purchased by a different person; and that, though he was living in the same town with them, he never was allowed to see them;—he would be beaten within an ace of his life if he ventured to go to the corner of the street. Whenever the least symptom of rebellion or insubordination appears at Charleston on the part of a slave, the master sends the slave to the gaol, where he is whipped or beaten as the master desires."

In travelling to Mobile, Mr Stuart was driven to Price's Hotel, by Price himself, and in Mrs Price finds a country-woman.

"She had an excellent breakfast prepared. Perceiving, after I had begun breakfast, that she was not partaking, I asked her the reason. She never breakfasted, she said, without her husband, and he was still with the horses. Mrs Price is an Isle of Skye woman, her name Fraser, of the Lovat family, as she told me; but her chief anxiety was to hear particulars as to the family of Macleod of Macleod, respecting which it was luckily in my power in some degree to gratify her. She had lived a long time in South Carolina, but liked Alabama quite as well, if it were not for the want of schools for her children,—the climate was more healthy, and her husband better paid. Captain Hall's Travels had been read in this cabin, and with no small disapprobation. He knew nothing, she said, of American manners."

The Traveller was in great luck this day, if it be true that Scotsmen abroad rejoice to meet each other.

"Lolley had to drive about sixteen miles to Duncan Macmillan's, where we were to remain for the night.—It being dark when we arrived, Duncan himself came out to welcome me, and, as soon as he discovered that I was from Scotland, he gave me his hand; and his pleasure on seeing me was increased, when he found that I could ask him how he was to-day in Gaelic!"

"Duncan came from Argyle when he was very young. He was married to an American woman, whose parents were Scotch; but she, as well as he, can speak Gaelic. He settled in this country about ten years ago, and has seventy acres cleared by his own industry, and a considerable tract of wood-land. He was very inquisitive respecting his native country, but he did not hint at any wish to return to it. He was, he said, under a good government, that did justice to all; and he had many advantages. He never went to market but for coffee. He grew both sugar and cotton on his own plantation; and, being a member of a Temperance Society, he did not taste fermented liquor. Coffee was, he said, the best stimulant, and very good coffee he gave us. The drivers, both Mr Lolley and he who was to be charioteer next morning, were, of course, at supper with us; and I was glad to find, that Mr Macmillan had so much influence with them, as to put an entire stop to their rude, boisterous swearing."

"Mr Macmillan promised me a separate bed-room, and he was as good as his word; but it was a very small apartment, thinly boarded, with hardly any room for a chair or any thing else. He said, however, that he was a man of invention, and, taking his carpenter's tools with him, he in a moment put up pins for a looking-glass and other necessary articles. I was not long in bed when I distinctly heard him, through the thin boarding of the room, engaged in family worship with his family, consisting of his wife and two daughters, who were young women."

In the steam-boat in which our traveller ascended the Mississippi from Natchez, he met with a young man, named Macleod, a blacksmith from Glasgow, "who had been for some years at New Orleans, and whose health has never yet suffered, owing, as he says, to his sobriety and moderation. He admits that he is in a far more comfortable situation here than at home. He receives regularly seventy-five dollars a month, and 100 dollars per month if he remains in the city, which he has hitherto done, during the unhealthy season. He has seen almost all his friends who remained in the city during the unhealthy part of the season die. He was making this trip merely with a view to see the country, and for exercise and health."

All the booksellers seem Scotchmen. At St. Louis, the bookseller, Mr. Palmer, was from Kelso, which he had left in 1801.

Near Jacksonville, in the Illinois county, Mr. Stuart heard of a settler from Scotland, and was told he would be hurt if a Scotsman passed his door without calling; accordingly, on a fine May morning, he made his approach.

"I soon," he says, "reached the farm belonging to Mr. James Kerr, which Mr. Brick had described to me. I found Mr. Kerr out of doors, and he received me with so hearty a welcome, that we were soon acquainted. Mrs. Kerr provided an abundant breakfast, consisting of tea, coffee, eggs, pork-steaks, peach preserves, honey, and various sorts of bread. Mr. Kerr is from South Queensferry, in Scotland, brother-in-law to Mr. Hugh Russell there, and is married to Miss Rowe of Fountain Bridge, near Edinburgh. He was formerly foreman to Mr. Francis Braidwood, a well known upholsterer in Edinburgh. Mr. Braidwood's workmen, about twenty years ago, combined to give up work unless they got higher wages. Mr. Braidwood offered Mr. Kerr higher wages, but he dared not accept the offer, on account of the consequences which he had reason to apprehend from the workmen if he had acted in face of the confederacy. He, therefore, without much consideration, accompanied by a friend of his of the name of George Elder, put his foot in a vessel at Leith bound for North America. When he reached New York, he for some years successfully prosecuted his business of a carpenter and upholsterer,—but it turned out that buildings had been erected too rapidly for the population, and there was a want of employment in his line.

"At that period the New York newspapers were filled with inviting descriptions of settlements in Illinois. He, therefore, came directly here from New York, and procured 500 acres of the very best land in the state, as he thinks, of rich soil, from three to four feet deep. It produces from thirty to forty-five bushels of wheat, and excellent corn and oats in rotation. It would do it injury to give it manure. The land is so easily ploughed, that a two-horse plough ploughs two and a-half acres per day. There is never any want of a market here. Everything is bought by the merchants for New Orleans, or for Galena, where a vast number of workmen are congregated, who are employed in the lead mines on the north-western parts of this state. There is also a considerable demand for cattle for New settlers. Cattle are allowed to run out on the prairie during the whole winter; but Mr. Kerr thinks, that even during the short winter of this country, it would be advisable to have the cattle fed in houses on the prairie, and a sufficiency of grass cut and made into hay in the preceding summer. The cattle on the prairie must, he remarked, have salt at least once a-week. Mr. Kerr, as well as Mrs. Kerr, remarked, that nothing annoyed them so much as the difficulty of getting servants. I have already noticed that Illinois is not a slave-holding state. Indeed, I have seen fewer people of colour since I came into Illinois than in any of the other states of the Union, probably not half-a-dozen altogether. The immigration to Illinois is so great, that the supply of servants has never yet been equal to the demand;—the consequence is obvious, not only that wages are high, but that servants are saucy, and difficult to please. It may, too, be presumed, that many of those servants who have turned out ill in other places, and who, on that account, cannot find situations at home, may be disposed to remove to a country where there is an unusual demand, and where they may readily get employment. In such a mixed population, there must, for some years, be a greater number of worthless persons, and of persons of doubtful character, than in the old-peopled states of North America; but the universal education of the people, wherever the population becomes considerable, will soon banish this temporary state of inconvenience.

"After breakfast, Mrs. Kerr, who had come out with us, put the question plump to me, whether I did not think the view from the door of their house was equal to that from Hopetoun House. In order to render this question, and my answer, at all intelligible, it is necessary to remark, that Hopetoun House is the finest place in the neighbourhood of Mr. Kerr's birth-place, Queensferry,—and that the view from the terrace in front of that house is one of the noblest that can be imagined, commanding the Frith of Forth the whole way to its mouth, with the most beautiful of its banks, and a diversity of ground almost incapable of being described. I could not, therefore, answer Mrs. Kerr's question exactly in the affirmative. I told her that the view which she enjoyed was as fine as that of many of the greatest places in England, but that the presence of the Firth of Forth was necessary before this view could be likened to that from Hopetoun House. Mr. and Mrs. Kerr are advanced in life, and he seems as much satisfied with his situation as it is possible to be. He has not only a beautiful farm, but an excellent well-furnished house, and a good garden and orchards. He considers the situation eminently healthy."

This adventure concludes with advice to emigrants, which we extract:—

"What I would recommend to a stranger emigrating to this country would be, that he should apply at the land-offices at Springfield, or at Vandalia, or at any other of the land-offices, and get the surveyors to show him those situations which they look on as the most desirable, *first*, in point of health; *secondly*, in point of soil; *thirdly*, in being provided with good water, and a sufficient quantity of wood, which is not always the case in the prairie land, and ought most especially to be attended to, strong wooden fences being indispensable; and, *fourthly*, in point of convenience of situation, including the neighbourhood to a town, schools, and churches, and the means of communication by roads and rivers.

"Having got this information, let him lay it before persons of experience in the district or state, such as Mr. Alison or Mr. Kerr, and be much more guided by their advice than by that of the surveyors. The surveyors may be all very good, trust-worthy men, but they may have objects to serve in disposing of this or that tract of land, which a stranger cannot divine."

At Springfield, another town in this fine country, Mr. Stuart met with an emigrant, whose history is worth relating:—

"In walking about the town in the evening, I met Mr. Strawbridge, formerly a farmer in Donegal, in Ireland; a gentleman 75 years old, who brought a family of five children with him to this country twenty years ago, all of whom have done well. He was first settled in the State of Ohio; but hearing of the prodigious fertility of the soil in this part of Illinois, he disposed of 100 acres which he had improved in Ohio, and purchased 640 acres about eight miles to the north-west of Springfield, great part of which he has now improved, and where he also has a mill. His description of his land, and of its produce, was quite equal in point of quality and quantity to that of Mr. Kerr: and he added, that parts of his land had produced forty bushels of wheat to the second crop without sowing. He has advantages, too, in point of situation, by being nearer to the Galena lead mines, to which he last year sold 8000 wooden posts, at three dollars per hundred. No person can be fonder of this country than Mr. Strawbridge. He had been in Scotland; but there was no land in that country to be compared (he said) to that of his farm; and he viewed this district as quite a paradise or garden. Finding him so much disposed to praise, I asked him how he was off for servants. His answer was marked:—'You have hit the nail on the head. It is difficult to get servants here, and more difficult to get good ones.' This difficulty has, I find, been increased of late, in consequence of the number of labourers required at the Galena lead mines."

In the neighbourhood of the late Mr Birkbeck's estates, Mr Stuart has an adventure which places the emigration of respectable farmers in a comfortable light. After noticing the contradictory accounts given of Birkbeck, he says—

"It is, however, sufficiently apparent that Mr Birkbeck was possessed of a very comfortable settlement here, and that his residence and the accommodation afforded, were in substance such as he represented them in his publications. In proceeding from his land towards Albion, I was passing a nice-looking English villa, at the distance of perhaps a hundred yards to the northward, when I found a young man at the plough close to me, in the field in front of the house. I learned from him, on making inquiry, that the place had belonged to Mr Pritchard, a gentleman from England, of the Quaker persuasion; that he was now dead, leaving a widow, a daughter, and two sons, of whom this young man was one. At his request, I went to the house, which is extremely neat, and the view from it quite as delightful as an inland view can be. In short, it is quite a bijou of a place. The situation is considerably higher than the English prairie, great part of which is overlooked,—and the view of hill and dale, of woodland, and of cultivated soil, is as rich and diversified as can well be conceived. Mrs Pritchard told me that all were doing well here, and that, when she saw from the newspapers the sufferings of great part of the population in England, she lamented they did not come here, where all would be well off who could work. Were they thousands, and thousands, and thousands, all would be provided for; and she spoke from experience, having been here for nearly a dozen of years. She added, however, that those settlers were not the most prosperous who had come with their pockets full of money, and had made large purchases of land, and had laid out considerable sums of money in buildings, and in prodigious purchases of cattle, &c. as no adequate return had been obtained for great expenditures; but that every one of the labourers who had come to this country with Mr Birkbeck and Mr Flower, or who had followed them to their settlements, and who had turned out sober and industrious, were now in possession of a plantation of some extent, yielding them a comfortable livelihood. The wages of every one of the labourers was such as to enable them to save a certain sum every year from the period of their arrival, and, in the course of ten or twelve years, they had all scraped together enough of money for the purchase of settlements, on which they were living in comfort, in houses which they had built. They were, in fact, landed proprietors and farmers, living on their own property, and in as respectable a situation as any persons in this country. All had done well who had not begun on too large a scale."

"Mrs Pritchard had shown great taste in cutting trees here and there to obtain the sweetest peeps of the prairie. I hardly remember to have seen a more delightful prospect in any of the fertile valleys in England than from the front of the house."

"Albion is upon Mr Flower's part of the prairie, and was built by him. It was only begun twelve years ago, and contains a town-house, a smithy, three stores, one broad street, with lanes to the prairies and woods, all handsomely laid out, and perhaps more in the substantial English style than I have seen elsewhere in the western country. Mechanics of every necessary description are now resident at Albion."

Mr Stuart says that all Mechanics should take out certificates of character, and illustrates the advice by the following narration:—

"I had not been long at Mr Anderson's when I was applied to by a good-looking young man, from the west of Fifeshire in Scotland, whose name was John Boswell, to give him, or procure for him, a letter of recommendation to a ship-builder in New York. I had never seen him before, so far as I knew; but I had been acquainted with his father, a very respectable person in his line, a farm overseer to the late Mr Mutter of Annfield, near Dunfermline. Boswell's story was this:—He had been bred a ship-carpenter, had married, and was the father of two children. Finding his wages of about 2s. or 2s. 6d. per day insufficient for the maintenance of his family, he commenced being toll-keeper, but did not succeed in his new profession. He had, therefore, brought his wife and children to New York, being possessed only of a small sum of money, and of some furniture, a fowling-piece, &c. He had made application, immediately on his arrival at New York, some weeks previously for employment, but no one would receive him into his ship-building yard, in which there is much valuable property, without attestations of his character for honesty and sobriety. He accidentally heard of my being in the neighbourhood, and applied to me to give him such attestations. Knowing nothing previously of this young man but what I have mentioned, it was impossible for me to comply with his request, but I gave him a letter to a gentleman in the neighbourhood of New York, who might, I thought, be of use to him, stating exactly what I knew of him. Workmen in the ship-building line were at this period plentiful, and months followed before any opening occurred for employing Boswell. In the meantime his finances were exhausted, and he had been obliged to part with some of the property he had brought with him. He was beginning to wish himself well home again when an offer of work was made to him. I happened to be in New York on the very day when this occurred, and remember well the pleasure which beamed in his eyes when he told me of the offer, and asked me what wages he should propose. My advice to him was to leave that matter to his master, after he had been at work a week, and showed what he could do. The next time I saw Boswell he was in the receipt of two dollars a day for ten hours' work, and of as much more at the same rate per hour, if he chose to be longer employed. His gains,—for he told me that he could live at one-half of the expence which it cost him to live in Scotland, although his family here had animal food three times a day,—soon enabled him to have a comfortable well-furnished house, where I again and again saw his family quite happy, and in which he had boarders. I sent for him to Hoboken, where I was then living, two or three days before I left New York, in the month of April 1831, that I might learn if I could be the bearer of any communication to his friends in Scotland. He came over to me in a better suit of clothes on his back and a better umbrella, than, I believe, I myself possessed. He only wished, he said, his friends to know how well settled he now was. He had earned on the preceding day almost as much as he could earn at the same business in Scotland in a week; and he hoped in less than twenty years to make a fortune, and return to Scotland."

"I have mentioned the whole particulars of this case, because it contains information which may be useful to many. I had reason to know, before I left New York, that Boswell was an excellent workman,—industrious, honest, and sober. He told me that he never drank much whisky in his own country, and that he would take far less of it at New York, where, though it was much cheaper, it was of very inferior quality. Certificates of good character are very requisite for all emigrants to the United States, but especially for mechanics and labourers; and they should either be procured from magistrates or from clergymen, no matter to what sect they belong. I need not add, that it is most important to obtain recommendations, where they can be got, to some respectable individual at the port where the emigrants first of all arrive."

With this we must for the present conclude. Our extracts are intended to be useful, to emigrants especially. We might have found many more amusing, but there are none more important.

PERSON AND MANNERS OF COWPER.

Cowper was of the middle stature; he had a fine, open, and expressive countenance, that indicated much thoughtfulness, and almost excessive sensibility. His eyes were more remarkable for the expression of tenderness than of penetration. The general expression of his countenance partook of that sedate cheerfulness, which so strikingly characterizes all his original productions, and which never failed to impart a peculiar charm to his conversation. His limbs were more remarkable for strength than for delicacy of form. He possessed a warm temperament; and he says of himself in a letter to his cousin, Mrs Bodham, dated February 27, 1790, that he was naturally "somewhat irritable;" but, if he was, his religious principle had so subdued that tendency, that a near relation, who was intimately acquainted with him the last ten years of his life, never saw his temper ruffled in a single instance.

His manners were generally somewhat shy and reserved, particularly to strangers; when, however, he was in perfect health, and in such society as was quite congenial to his taste, they were perfectly free and unembarrassed; his conversation was unrestrained and cheerful; and his whole deportment was the most polite and graceful, especially to females, to whom he conducted himself, on all occasions, with the strictest delicacy and propriety.

Much as Cowper was admired by those who knew him only as a writer, or as an occasional correspondent, he was infinitely more esteemed by his more intimate friends; indeed, the more intimately he was known, the more he was beloved and revered. Nor was this affectionate attachment so much the result of his brilliant talents, as it was of the real goodness of his disposition, and gentleness of his conduct.

BIOGRAPHIC SKETCH.

SUSANNA ANNESLEY, THE MOTHER OF JOHN WESLEY.

This admirable woman, the youngest daughter of Dr. Annesley, was born about the year 1670. She possessed a highly improved mind, with a strong and masculine understanding. Though her father was a conscientious *Non-conformist*, he had too much dignity of mind, leaving his religion out of the question, to be a *bigot*. Under the parental roof, and " before she was *thirteen years of age*," say some of her biographers, " she examined, without restraint, the *whole* controversy between the established church and the dissenters."[*] The issue of this examination was, that she renounced her fellowship with the latter, and adopted the *creeds* and *forms* of the Church of England; to which she zealously adhered.

It does not appear that her father threw any obstacles in her way; or that he afterwards disapproved of her marrying a rigid churchman. Nor is it known, after the most extensive search, that the slightest difference ever existed between Dr. Annesley and his son-in-law, or daughter, on the subject. It was about the year 1690 that she became the wife of Mr. Samuel Wesley. The marriage was blessed in all its circumstances; it was contracted in the prime of their youth; it was fruitful, and death did not divide them till they were both full of years. The excellence of Miss Annesley's mind was equal to the eminence of her birth. She was such a helpmate as Mr. Wesley *required*, " and to her," says Dr. Clarke, " under God, the great eminence of the subsequent Wesley family is to be attributed."

As Mr. Wesley's circumstances were narrow, the education of the children fell especially upon Mrs. Wesley, who seems to have possessed every qualification for a public or private teacher. The manner in which she taught her children is remarkable. This she has detailed in a letter to her son *John*, which we shall hereafter insert. She bore *nineteen* children to Mr. Wesley, most of whom lived to be educated; and ten came to man and woman's estate. Her son John mentions the calm serenity with which his mother transacted business, wrote letters, and conversed, surrounded by her *fifteen* children. All these were educated by herself; and as she was a woman that lived by *rule* she arranged everything so exactly, that for each operation she had sufficient time. It appears also, from several private papers, that she had no small share in managing the secular concerns of the rectory. Even the *tithes* and *glebe* were much under her inspection.

About the year 1700, Mrs. Wesley made a resolution to spend one hour *morning* and *evening* in private devotion, in prayer and meditation, and she religiously kept it ever after, unless when sickness, or some urgent call of duty to her family, obliged her to shorten it. If opportunity offered, she spent some time *at noon* in this religious and profitable employment. She generally wrote her thoughts on different subjects at these seasons; and a great many of her meditations have been preserved in her own hand-writing. Though Mrs. Wesley allotted two hours in the day for meditation and prayer in private, no woman was ever more diligent in business, or attentive to family affairs than she was. Remarkable, as before observed, for method and good arrangement, both in her studies and business, she saved much time, and kept her mind free from perplexity. From several things which appear in her papers, it seems that she had acquired some knowledge of the Latin and Greek languages in her youth, though she never made any pretension to it. She had studied human nature well, and knew how to adapt her discourse both to youth and age.

Mrs. Wesley devoted as great a proportion of time as she could, to discourse with each of her children separately every night in the week, upon the duties and hopes of Christianity; and it may readily be believed, that these circumstances of their childhood had no inconsiderable influence upon them in after life, and especially upon her two sons, John and Charles, when they became the founders and directors of a new community in the Christian Church. John's providential deliverance from the *fire* deeply impressed his mother, as it did himself, throughout the whole of his life. Among the private meditations which were found among Mrs. Wesley's papers, was one written long after the event, in which she expressed in prayer her intention to be more particularly careful of the soul of *this child*, which God had so mercifully provided for, that she might instil into him the principles of true religion and virtue ;—" Lord," she said, " give me grace to do it sincerely and prudently, and bless my attempts with good success." The peculiar care which was thus taken of his religious education, the habitual and fervent piety of both his parents, and his own surprising preservation, at an age when he was perfectly capable of remembering all the circumstances, combined to foster in him that disposition which afterwards developed itself with such force, and produced such important effects.

Mrs. Wesley taught her children from their infancy, duty to parents. She had little difficulty in *breaking their wills*, or reducing them to absolute subjection. They were early brought, by rational means, under a mild yoke: they were perfectly obedient to their parents, and were taught to wait their decision in every thing they were to have, or to perform. They were never permitted *to command the servants*. Mrs. Wesley charged the domestics to do nothing for any of her children unless they asked it with *respect*; and the children were duly informed that the servants had such orders. This is the foundation and essence of good breeding. Insolent, impudent, and disagreeable children are to be met with often, because this simple, but important mode of bringing them up is neglected. " Molly, Robert, *be pleased* to do so and so," was the usual method of request both from sons and daughters. They were never permitted to contend with each other; whatever differences arose, their parents were the umpires, and their decision was never disputed. The consequence was, there were few misunderstandings amongst them; and they had the character of being *the most loving family in the county of Lincoln!* But Mrs. Wesley's whole method of bringing up and managing her children, is so amply detailed in a letter to her son *John*, that it would be as great an injustice to *her*, as to the reader, to omit it.

Epworth, July 24th, 1732.

" Dear Son,—According to your desire, I have collected the principal rules I observed in educating my family.

" The children were always put into a regular method of living, in such things as they were capable of, from their birth; as in dressing and undressing, changing their linen, &c. The first quarter commonly passes in sleep. After that they were, if possible, laid into their cradle awake, and rocked to sleep; and so they were kept rocking till it was time for them to awake. This was done to bring them to a regular course of sleeping, which, at first, was three hours in the morning, and three in the afternoon; afterwards two hours, till they needed none at all. When turned a year old (and some before,) they were taught to fear the rod, and to cry *softly*, by which means they escaped much correction which they might otherwise have had; and that most odious noise of the crying of children was rarely heard in the house.

" As soon as they grew pretty strong, they were confined to three meals a-day. At dinner their little table and chairs were set by ours, where they could be overlooked: and they were suffered to eat and drink as much as they would, but *not to call for any thing*. If they wanted aught, they used to whisper to the maid that attended them, who came and spoke to me: and as soon as they could handle a knife and fork, they were set to our table. They were never suffered *to choose their meat:* but always made to eat such things as were provided for the family. Drinking, or eating *between meals* was never allowed, unless in case of sickness, which seldom happened. Nor were they suffered to go into the kitchen to ask any thing of the

---

[*] It seems strange that a girl of *thirteen* years of age should be considered capable of deciding this question, though she might possess, as in the case of Mrs. Wesley, great natural talents.

servants, when they were at meat: if it was known they did so, they were certainly beat, and the servants severely reprimanded. At six, as soon as family prayer was over, they had their supper; at seven the maid washed them, and beginning at the youngest, she undressed and got them all to bed by eight; at which time she left them in their several rooms *awake*, for there was no such thing allowed, in our house, as sitting by a child till it fell asleep. They were so constantly used to eat and drink what was given them, that when any of them were ill, there was no difficulty in making them take the most unpleasant medicine, for they durst not refuse it.

"In order to form the minds of children, the first thing to be done is *to conquer their will*. To inform the understanding is a work of time; and must, with children, proceed by slow degrees, as they are able to bear it : but the subjecting the will is a thing that must be done at once, *and the sooner the better ;* for by neglecting timely correction, they will contract a stubbornness and obstinacy which are hardly ever after conquered, and never without using such severity as would be as painful to me as to the child. In the esteem of the world, they pass for kind and indulgent, whom I call *cruel* parents; who permit their children to get habits which they know must be afterwards broken. When the will of a child is subdued, and it is brought to revere and stand in awe of its parents, then a great many childish follies and inadvertences may be passed by. Some should be overlooked, and others mildly reproved : but no *wilful* transgression ought ever to be forgiven children, without chastisement less or more, as the nature and circumstances of the case may require. I insist upon conquering the will of children betimes, because this is the only strong and rational foundation of a religious education, without which, both precept and example will be ineffectual. But when this is thoroughly done, then a child is capable of being governed by the reason and piety of its parents, till its own understanding comes to maturity, and the principles of religion have taken root in the mind.

"I cannot yet dismiss this subject. As *self-will* is the root of all sin and misery, so whatever cherishes this in children ensures their wretchedness and irreligion: whatever checks and mortifies it, promotes their future happiness and piety. This is still more evident, if we farther consider that religion is nothing else than doing the *will* of God, and not our own; that the one grand impediment to our temporal and eternal happiness being this *self-will*, no indulgence of it can be trivial, no denial unprofitable. Heaven or hell depends on this alone. So that the parent who studies to subdue it in his child, works together with God in the renewing and saving a soul. The parent who indulges it, does the devil's work ; makes religion impracticable, salvation unattainable, and does all that in him lies to damn his child, soul and body, for ever.

"Our children were taught, as soon as they could speak, the Lord's prayer, which they were made to say at *rising* and *bedtime* constantly; to which, as they grew older, were added a short prayer for their parents, and such portion of Scripture, as their memories could bear. They were very early made to distinguish the Sabbath from other days. They were taught to be still at family prayers, and to ask a blessing immediately after meals, which they used to do by *signs*, before they could kneel or speak. They were quickly made to understand that they should have nothing they *cried for*, and instructed to speak respectfully for what they wanted.

"Taking God's name in vain, cursing and swearing, profaneness, obscenity, rude ill-bred names, were never heard among them ; nor were they ever permitted to call each other by their proper names, without the addition of *brother* or *sister*. There was no such thing as loud talking or playing allowed ; but every one was kept close to business for the six hours of school. And it is almost incredible what a child may be taught in a quarter of a year by a vigorous application, if it have but a tolerable capacity, and good health. *Kessy* excepted, all could read better in that time, than most women can do as long as they live.

Rising from their places, or going out of the room, was not permitted, except for good cause ; and running into the yard, garden, or street, without leave, was always considered a capital offence.

"For some years we went on very well. Never were children better disposed to piety, or in more subjection to their parents, till that fatal dispersion of them, after the *fire*, into several families. In those they were left at full liberty to converse with servants, which before they had always been restrained from ; and to run abroad to play with any children good or bad. They soon learned to neglect a strict observance of the Sabbath : and got knowledge of several songs, and bad things, which before they had no notion of. That civil behaviour, which made them admired, when they were at home, by all who saw them, was, in a great measure, lost ; and clownish accent, and many rude ways learnt, which were not reformed, without some difficulty. When the house was rebuilt, and all the children brought home, we entered on a strict reform ; and then we began the custom of singing psalms, at beginning and leaving school, morning and evening. Then also that of a general retirement at five o'clock was entered upon : when the oldest took the youngest that could speak, and the second the next, to whom they read the psalms for the day, and a chapter in the New Testament; as in the morning they were directed to read the psalms, and a chapter in the Old ; after which they went to their private prayers, before they got their breakfast, or came into the family.

There were several by-laws observed among us. I mention them here because I think them useful.

1. It had been observed that cowardice and fear of punishment often lead children into lying ; till they get a custom of it which they cannot leave. To prevent this, a law was made, that whoever was charged with a fault, of which they were guilty, if they would *ingenuously confess it*, and promise to amend, should not be beaten. This rule prevented a great deal of lying.

2. That no sinful action, as lying, *playing at church*, or on the Lord's Day, disobedience, quarrelling, &c., should ever pass unpunished.

3. That no child should ever be chid, or beat *twice* for the same fault ; and that if they amended, they should never be upbraided with it afterwards.

4. That every signal act of obedience, especially when it crossed their own inclinations, should be always commended and frequently rewarded, according to the merits of the case.

5. That if ever any child performed an act of obedience, or did anything with an intention to please, though the performance was not well, yet the obedience and intention should be kindly accepted, and the child, with sweetness, directed how to do better for the future.

6. That *property* be inviolably preserved; and none suffered to invade the property of another in the smallest matter, though it were but of the value of a farthing, or a pin ; which they might not take from the owner without, much less against, his consent. This rule can never be too much inculcated on the minds of children.

7. That promises be strictly observed ; and a gift once bestowed, and the right so passed away from the donor, be not resumed, but left to the disposal of him to whom it was given ; unless it were conditional, and the condition of the obligation not performed.

8. That no girl be taught to work till she can read very well ; and then that she be kept to her work with the same application, and for the same time that she was held to in reading. This rule also much to be observed ; for the putting children to learn sewing before they can read perfectly is the very reason why so few women can read fit to be heard, and never to be well understood."

After such management who can wonder at the rare excellence of the Wesley family ? Mrs. Wesley never considered herself discharged from the care of her children. Into all situations, she followed them with her prayers and counsels: and her sons, even when they became men and scholars, found the utility of her wise and parental instructions. They proposed to her their doubts, and consulted her in all their difficulties.

The following letter to Mr. John Wesley will show what care his excellent mother took of her son's spiritual progress, and of his regular deportment through life.

Jan. 31, 1727.

"———— I am fully persuaded, that the reason why so many seek to enter into the kingdom of heaven, but are not able, is, there is some *Delilah*, some beloved vice, they will not part with; hoping that by a strict observance of their duty in other things, *that* particular fault will be dispensed with. But, alas! they miserably deceive themselves. The way which leads to heaven is so *narrow*, the gate we must enter is so strait, that it will not permit a man to pass with *one* known *unmortified* sin about him. Therefore let every one, in the beginning of their Christian course, weigh what our Lord says, ' for whosoever having put his hand to the plough, and looking back, is not fit for the kingdom of God.'

" I am nothing pleased we advised you to have your *plaid*; though I am that you think it too dear; because I take it to be an indication that you are disposed to *thrift*, which is a rare qualification in a young man who has his fortune to make. Indeed such an one can hardly be too wary, or too careful. I would not recommend taking thought for the morrow any further than is needful for our improvement of present opportunities, in a prudent management of those talents God has committed to our trust: and so far I think it is the duty of all to take thought for the morrow. And I heartily wish you may be well apprized of this while life is young; for

Believe me youth; (for I am read in cases,
And bend beneath the weight of more than fifty years.)

Believe me, dear son, *old age* is the worst time we can choose to mend either our lives or our fortunes. If the foundations of solid piety are not laid betimes in sound principles, and virtuous dispositions; and if we neglect while strength and vigour last to lay up something ere the infirmities of age overtake us, it is a hundred to one that we shall die both poor and wicked.

" Ah! my dear son, did you with me stand on the verge of life, and saw before you a vast expanse, an unlimited duration of being, which you might shortly enter upon, you can't conceive how all the inadvertances, mistakes, and sins of youth, would rise to your view! and how different the sentiments of sensitive pleasures, the desire of sexes, and the pernicious friendships of the world, would be then from what they are now, while health is entire, and seems to promise many years of life."

Mrs. Wesley became a convert to her son John's opinions respecting " the witness of the spirit." He asked Mrs. Wesley whether his father had not the same evidence, and preached it to his people. She replied that he had it himself, and declared a little before his death, he had no darkness nor doubt of his salvation; but that she did not remember to have heard him preach upon it explicitly. Mr. Southey here intimates, that Mrs. Welsey " was then seventy years of age, which induces a reasonable suspicion that her powers of mind had become impaired, or she would not else have supposed that any other faith, or degree o. faith, was necessary, than that in which her husband had lived and died." It is wisely, as well as eloquently said by Dr. Fuller, whose niece married the father of the rector of Epworth as before mentioned; " Of such as deny that we had formerly in our churches all truth necessary to salvation, I ask Joseph's question to his brethren, ' Is your father well? the old man—is he yet alive?' So, how fare the souls of their sires, and the ghosts of their grandfathers? are they yet alive? do they still survive in bliss and happiness? Oh no! they are dead; dead in soul, dead in body, dead temporally, dead eternally; if so be we had not all truth necessary to salvation before their time."

Of the closing scene of Mrs. Wesley's life, her son *John* gives the following account :—" I left Bristol on the evening of Sunday, July 18th, 1742, and on Tuesday came to London. I found my mother on the borders of eternity; but she had no doubts or fears, nor any desire, but as soon as God should call, ' To depart, and be with Christ.' Friday July 23d, about three in the afternoon, I went to see my mother, and found her change was near. I sat down on the bed-side; she was in her last conflict, unable to speak, but I believe quite sensible: her look was calm and serene, and her eyes fixed upwards while we commended her soul to God. From three to four, *the silver cord was loosing and the wheel breaking at the cistern*; and then without any struggle, sigh, or groan, the soul was set at liberty. We stood around the bed, and fulfilled her last request, uttered a little before she lost her speech, ' Children, as soon as I am released, sing a psalm to God.' Her age was 73. Sunday, 1st of August, about five in the afternoon, in the presence of a great number of people, I committed to the earth the body of my mother, to sleep with her fathers. The portion of Scripture from which I afterwards spoke, was, *' And I saw a great white throne, and Him that sat on it, from whose face the earth and the heaven fled away; and there was found no place for them. And I saw the dead, small and great, stand before God; and the books were opened; and another book was opened which is the Book of Life: and the dead were judged out of those things which were written in the books, according to their works.'*—Rev. xx. 11, 12. It was one of the most solemn assemblies I ever saw, or expect to see on this side of eternity.

Mrs. Wesley was interred in *Bunhill-fields* burial ground, where so much precious dust reposes! A plain monumental stone is placed at the head of her grave.

SINGULAR CIRCUMSTANCE.—At the late Meath Assizes, Mr. Wallace, the eminent Barrister, in defending two persons named Reilly and Courtenay, against a charge of conspiracy sworn against them by a Miss Smith, related, in the course of his speech, the following singular circumstance :—" Gentlemen of the Jury,—I implore of you not to place too implicit a confidence in the swearing of any human creature, when placed in a relative position with the person accused by the prisoners. Place not implicit confidence in any human being when brought forward to swear in their own case, where their fortunes, their lives, or their characters, are in jeopardy. There is one circumstance of my life to which I cannot recur without feelings, I may say, of repentance, of pain, and of sorrow, that I find difficult to overcome. When I look back to the circumstances connected with that event, and when I look around here to-day, and see his Lordship on the bench before me, and two poor unfortunate peasants at that bar charged with conspiracy, it brings to my recollection, with all the force of bitter regret, the part I acted on that occasion—an act which I shall repent to the latest hour of my life. I was at one time Counsel on one side, and his Lordship, who is now on that bench before me, was Counsel at the other. A person of high rank and station in life was accused of a horrid crime; a poor peasant was his accuser; he was tried for a conspiracy, and I was retained as Counsel on his behalf. The person accused was no less a personage than a high dignitary of the church. He was of imposing mien and character—he came into Court to support his own case; the Gospels of the Lord God were put into his hands; he raised his eyes to Heaven, to appeal to that God of Truth and Sanctity, whom he was going to blaspheme, that what he was about to swear was true. The solemnity he manifested in taking that oath, which he knew to be false, would induce you to exclaim at once that he was innocent. He took the oath, accompanying it with an appeal to Heaven that he was innocent of the charge imputed to him by the prisoner; yet he swore what was false. I threw up my brief, exclaiming that he who made the charge was a vile conspirator. The unfortunate man was found guilty, and suffered an ignominious punishment.—(Here Mr. Wallace burst into tears, and every individual in the Court was deeply affected.)—Mr. Wallace, after an ineffectual endeavour to overcome his feelings, begged pardon for being so affected, and concluded by giving, with perfect confidence, the case of his clients into their hands." [The above alludes to the Bishop of Clogher, of infamous notoriety.]

THE IDENTICAL LAWRIE TOD.
OR THE WAY TO GET ON.

LAWRIE TOD, as many of our readers may know, is the hero and the name of one of Mr. Galt's novels; but " the identical Lawrie" is a Mr. Thorburn, very much in character resembling his grotesque double, who during the times of political persecution, left Scotland for the United States, under a *fama* of rank Jacobinism. He was seen in New York in 1831, by Mr. Fergusson, whose amusing tour has lately been published, and is thus described " I frequently visited at the *seed-store* of Mr. Thorburn, a character of some celebrity, and of great originality, being, as he informed me, at my first interview, the " *very identical Lawrie Tod*" and that so far as the first volume of that entertaining work goes, Galt had exactly recorded his life and adventures. Besides other sources of enjoyment, Mr. Thorburn is distinguished for a lively and unfailing reliance upon a special over-ruling Providence—not a blind fatalism, but a conviction that in all the crosses of life a blessing will be found by those who faithfully seek it. He detailed many singular instances of this doctrine in his own history, and altogether gratified me much by his acquaintance. His original trade was that of a nail-maker at Dalkeith, and by that alone he looked for a livelihood in the New World. Soon after his arrival, however, this handicraft was annihilated by the introduction of machinery, and poor Thorburn was driven to open a small grocery store for subsistence to *Phemie* and himself. It was his practice to visit the butcher-market at a late hour, that he might pick up a cheap morsel; and observing a man offering plants for sale in pots seemingly like himself rather low in the world, Thorburn accosted him. He proved to be a fellow-countryman, an industrious, but rather unsuccessful market gardener, of the name of Inglis, from Kirkcaldy; and from a sort of commiseration, Thorburn bought a rose-geranium, intending it to ornament his shop. At this time he scarce knew a geranium from a cabbage.* Pleased with his purchase, when he got home he painted the pot a gay green, and placed it in his window. " And now," says he, when he told me the story, with his eyes twinkling, " Mark the kindness of Providence. The day after my geranium appeared in its new pot, a lady happening to drive past, remarked its beauty, and not only bought it at a handsome price, but gave me such orders as enabled me to open a busy trade with poor Inglis. My shop soon became more celebrated for plants than for tea and tobacco; and many inquiries having been made for garden-seed, I procured an assortment, and gradually extended my trade till I reached the possession of the handsome premises and flourishing trade which I now enjoy." To Mr. Fergusson's account of this worthy little man, we may add, that he lately visited his native town, after an absence of nearly forty years, and, with other tokens of welcome, received the honour of a public dinner from his old friends and townsmen.

SUNDAY SCHOOLS IN GLASGOW.—From a paper in this month's *Sunday-School Teacher's Magazine*, we learn, that Glasgow, which contains above 200,000 inhabitants, has about 20 Sabbath-School Associations, 10 of which are parochial, and the others connected with the different religious bodies. The number of schools is about 200, containing about 9000 children, most of them having from 20 to 40 scholars each. The schools are generally open only in the evening, when the teachers spend about two hours with their pupils, which are devoted to the exercises of praise and prayer, hearing the Bible read and explained, and in repeating Scripture lessons and catechising. Reading is rarely taught, except by the Wesleyan Methodists. Some of these schools have itinerating libraries of 20 or 30 volumes each, which are exchanged annually, and given out to the children once a fortnight.

* This, for a native of Dalkeith, the very Scotch Palace of Flora, is impossible—ED.

COLUMN FOR THE LADIES.

FORTUNATE MISTAKE.—When Miss Mellon, the present Duchess of St. Albans was an actress with a company in Staffordshire, a dissolute son of St. Crispin, who had made an impression on the *sole* of our heroine, having privately enlisted in a recruiting party of light horse, on the eve of departure for Liverpool, and thence to Ireland, an elopement was designed by the martial hero, and was discovered in the following curious manner:—Miss Mellon took the part of a chamber-maid one evening in an afterpiece, and had to deliver a letter to her mistress on the stage, for the purpose of a meeting between *supposed* lovers. She had that evening, received a note from her lover, which named an early hour for their meeting and departure. This note and the stage letter were both deposited in her bosom; and in the confusion or hurry on the stage, she gave her own instead of the stage-letter, to her mistress, which was immediately snatched away by the supposed guardian, who was standing behind, and who was personated by a performer of the name of Forrester. Forrester, on opening it, at once saw the contents, which he instantly communicated to the mother and father-in-law of the chambermaid—on this our heroine was put under lock and key, till the departure of the soldier shoemaker. Some time after this Miss Mellon was transplanted from Staffordshire to the boards of Drury Lane, where she was taken by the hand by Sheridan, and subsequently married Mr. Coutts, the rich banker—he died and left her a princely income of L.70,000 a-year, and she has since united her fortune with the young Duke of St. Albans, who is the third Duke in the kingdom, in point of rank, and now enjoys the distinguished title of Duchess.—She is said, by her admirers, to be a most amiable and most charitable woman.

CUPID AND MINERVA.
From Evenings in Greece, by Thomas Moore, Esq., No. II., just published.

As Love, one summer eve, was straying,
  Who should he see at that soft hour,
But young Minerva, gravely playing
  Her flute within an olive bower.
I need not say, 'tis Love's opinion,
  That, grave, or merry, good or ill,
The sex all bow to his dominion,
  As woman will be woman still.

Though seldom yet the boy hath given,
  To learned dames his smiles or sighs,
So handsome Pallas look'd, that even
  Love quite forgot the maid was wise;
Besides, a youth of his discerning
  Knew well that, by a shady rill,
At sunset hour—whate'er her learning—
  A woman will be woman still.

Her flute he praised in terms ecstatic,
  Wishing it dumb—nor cared how soon—
For Wisdom's notes, howe'er chromatic,
  To Love seem always out of tune.
But long as he found face to flatter,
  The nymph found breath to shake and thrill;
As, weak or wise—it doth not matter—
  Woman, at heart, is woman still.

Love changed his plan, with warmth exclaiming,
  " How brilliant was her lips' soft dye!"
And much that flute, the sly rogue, blaming,
  For twisting lips so sweet awry.
The nymph look'd down—beheld her features
  Reflected in the passing rill,
And started, shock'd—for, ah, ye creatures!
  Ev'n when divine, you're woman still.

Quick from the lips it made so odious,
  That graceless flute the Goddess took,
And, while yet fill'd with breath melodious,
  Flung it into the glassy brook;
Where, as its vocal life was fleeting
  Adown the current, faint and shrill,
At distance long 'twas heard repeating,
  " Woman, alas, vain woman still!"

THE STORY-TELLER.

TUBBER DERG;
OR, THE RED WELL.

On the south side of a sloping tract of light ground, lively, warm, and productive, stood a white, moderate-sized farm-house, which, in consequence of its conspicuous situation, was a prominent, and, we may add, a graceful object in the landscape of which it formed a part. The spot whereon it stood was a swelling natural terrace, the soil of which was heavier and richer than that of the adjoining lands. On each side of the house stood a clump of old beeches, the only survivors of that species then remaining in the country. These beeches extended behind the house in a kind of angle, with opening enough at their termination to form a vista, through which its white walls glistened with beautiful effect in the calm splendour of a summer evening. Above the mound on which it stood, rose two steep hills, overgrown with furze and fern, except on their tops, which were clothed with purple heath; they were also covered with patches of broom, and studded with grey rocks, which sometimes rose singly or in larger masses, pointed or rounded into curious and fantastic shapes. Exactly between these hills the sun went down during the month of June, and nothing could be in finer relief than the rocky and picturesque outlines of their sides, as, crowned with thorns and clumps of wild ash, they appeared to overhang the valley whose green foliage was gilded by the sun-beams, which lit up the scene into radiant beauty. The bottom of this natural chasm, which opened against the deep crimson of the evening sky, was nearly upon a level with the house, and completely so with the beeches that surrounded it. Brightly did the sinking sun fall upon their tops, whilst the neat white house below, in their quiet shadow, sent up its wreath of smoke among their branches, itself an emblem of contentment, industry, and innocence. It was, in fact, a lovely situation; perhaps the brighter to me, that its remembrance is associated with days of happiness and freedom from the cares of a world, which, like a distant mountain, darkens as we approach it, and only exhausts us in struggling to climb its rugged and barren paths.

There was to the south-west of this house, another little hazel glen, that ended in a precipice formed by a single rock some thirty feet high, over which tumbled a crystal cascade into a basin worn in its hard bed below. From this basin the stream murmured away through the copsewood, until it joined a larger rivulet that passed, with many a winding, through a fine extent of meadows adjoining it. Across the foot of this glen, and past the door of the house we have described, ran a bridle road, from time immemorial; on which, as the traveller ascended it towards the house, he appeared to track his way in blood, for a chalybeate *spa* arose at its head, oozing out of the earth, and spread itself in a crimson stream over the path in every spot whereon a footmark could be made. From this circumstance it was called Tubber Derg, or the Red Well. In the meadow where the glen terminated, was another spring of delicious crystal; and clearly do I remember the ever-beaten path-way that led to it through the grass, and up the green field which rose in a gentle slope to the happy-looking house of Owen M'Carthy,—for so was the man called who resided under its peaceful roof.

I will not crave your pardon, gentle reader, for dwelling at such length upon a scene so dear to my heart as this, because I write not now, so much for your gratification as my own. Many an eve of gentle May have I pulled the May-gowans which grew about that well, and over that smooth meadow. Often have I raised my voice to its shrillest pitch, that I might hear its echoes rebounding in the bottom of the green and still glen, where silence, so to speak, was deepened by the continuous murmur of the cascade above; and when the cuckoo uttered her first note from among the hawthorns on its side, with what trembling anxiety did I, an urchin of some eight or nine years, look under my right foot, for the white hair, whose charm was such, that by keeping it about me, the first female nam I should hear was destined, I believed in my soul, to be that of my future wife. Sweet was the song of the thrush, and mellow the whistle of the blackbird, as they rose in the stillness of the evening over the " birken shaws" and green dells of this secluded spot of rural beauty. Far, too, could the rich voice of Owen M'Carthy be heard along the hills and meadows, as, with a little chubby urchin at his knee, and another in his arms, he sat on a bench beside his own door, singing the " Trougha," in his native Irish; whilst Kathleen his wife, with her two maids, each crooning a low song, sat before the door, milking the cows, whose sweet breath mingled its perfume with the warm breeze of evening.

Owen M'Carthy was descended from a long line of honest ancestors, whose names had never, within the memory of man, been tarnished by the commission of a mean or disreputable action. They were always a kind-hearted family, but stern and proud in the common intercourse of life. They believed themselves to be, and probably were, a branch of the Mac Carthy More stock; and, although only the possessors of a small farm, it was singular to observe the effect which this conviction produced upon their bearing and manners. To it might, perhaps, be attributed the high and stoical integrity for which they were remarkable. This severity, however, was no proof that they wanted feeling, or were insensible to the misery or sorrows of others: in all the little cares and perplexities that chequered the peaceful neighbourhood in which they lived, they were ever the first to console, or, if necessary, to support a distressed neighbour with the means which God had placed in their possession; for, being industrious, they were seldom poor. Their words were few, but sincere, and generally promised less than the honest hearts that dictated them intended to perform. There is in some persons a hereditary feeling of just principle, the result neither of education, nor of a clear moral sense, but rather a kind of instinctive honesty which descends, like a constitutional bias, from father to son, pervading every member of the family. It is difficult to define this, or to assign its due position in the scale of human virtues. It exists in the midst of the grossest ignorance, and influences the character in the absence of better principles. Such was the impress which marked so strongly the family of which I speak. No one would ever think of imputing a dishonest act to the M'Carthys; nor would any person acquainted with them, hesitate for a moment to consider their word as good as the bond of another. I do not mean to say, however, that their motives of action were not higher than this instinctive honesty; far from it: but I say, that they possessed it *in addition* to a strong feeling of family pride, and a correct knowledge of their moral duties.

I can only take up Owen M'Carthy at that part of the past to which my memory extends. He was then a tall, fine-looking young man; silent, but kind. One of the earliest events within my recollection is his wedding; after that the glimpse of his state and circumstances are imperfect; but, as I grew up, they became more connected, and I am able to remember him the father of four children; an industrious, inoffensive, small farmer, beloved, respected, and honoured. No man could rise, be it ever so early, who would not find Owen up before him; no man could anticipate him in an early crop, and if a widow or a sick acquaintance were unable to get in their harvest, Owen was certain to collect the neighbours to assist them; to be the first there himself, with quiet benevolence, encouraging them to a zealous performance of the friendly task in which they were engaged.

It was, I believe, soon after his marriage, that the lease of the farm held by him expired. Until that time he had been able to live with perfect independence; but even the enormous rise of one pound per acre, though it deprived him in a great degree of his usual comforts, did not sink him below the bare necessaries of life. For some years after that he could still serve a deserving neighbour; and never was the hand of Owen M'Carthy held back from the wants and distresses of those whom he knew to be honest.

* * * * *

Many similar details of Owen M'Carthy's useful life could be given, in which he bore an equally benevolent and Christian part. Poor fellow! he was, ere long, brought low; but to the credit of our peasantry, much as is said about their barbarity, he was treated, when helpless, with gratitude, pity, and kindness.

Until the peace of 1814, Owen's regular and systematic industry enabled him to struggle successfully against a weighty rent and sudden depression in the price of agricultural produce; that is, he was able, by the unremitting toil of a man remarkable alike for an unbending spirit and a vigorous frame of body, to pay his rent with tolerable regularity. It is true, a change began to be visible in his personal appearance, in his farm, in the dress of his children, and in the economy of his household. Improvements which adequate capital would have enabled him to effect, were left either altogether unattempted, or in an imperfect state resembling neglect, though, in reality, the result of poverty. His dress at mass, and in fairs and markets, had, by degrees, lost that air of comfort and warmth which bespeaks the independent farmer. The evidences of embarrassment began to disclose themselves in many small points, inconsiderable, it is true, but not the less significant. His house, in the progress of his declining circumstances, ceased to be annually ornamented by a new coat of whitewash: it soon assumed a faded and yellowish hue, and sparkled not in the setting sun as in the days of Owen's prosperity. It had, in fact, a wasted, unthriving look, like its master; the thatch became black and rotten upon its roof, the chimneys sloped to opposite points, the windows were less neat, and, ultimately, when broken, were patched with a couple of leaves from the children's blotted copy books. His outhouses also began to fail; the neatness of his little farm-yard, and the cleanliness which marked so conspicuously the space fronting his dwelling-house, disappeared in the course of time. Filth began to accumulate where no filth had been;

his garden was not now planted so early, nor with such taste and neatness as before; his crops were later, and less abundant; his haggards neither so full nor so trim as they were wont to be, nor his ditches and enclosures kept in such good repair. His cars, ploughs, and other farming implements, instead of being put under cover, were left exposed to the influence of wind and weather, where they soon became crazy and useless.

Such, however, were only the slighter symptoms of his bootless struggle against the general embarrassment into which the agricultural interests were, year after year, so unhappily sinking.

Had the tendency to general distress among the class to which he belonged become stationary, Owen would have continued, by toil and incessant exertion, to maintain his ground; but, unfortunately, there was no point at which the national depression could then stop. Year after year produced deeper, more extensive, and more complicated misery; and when he hoped that every succeeding season would bring an improvement in the market, he was destined to experience not merely a fresh disappointment, but an unexpected depreciation in the price of his corn, butter, and other disposable commodities.

When a nation is reduced to such a state, no eye but that of God himself can see the appalling wretchedness to which a year of disease and scarcity strikes down the poor and working classes.

Owen, after a long and noble contest for nearly three years, sank, at length, under the united calamities of disease and scarcity. The father of the family was laid low upon the bed of sickness, and those of his little ones who escaped it were almost consumed by famine. This two-fold shock sealed his ruin; his honest heart was crushed—his hardy frame shorn of its strength, and he to whom every neighbour fled as to a friend, now required friendship when the wide-spread poverty of the country rendered its assistance hopeless.

On rising from his bed of sickness, the prospect before him required his utmost fortitude to bear. He was now wasted in energy both of mind and body, reduced to utter poverty, with a large family of children, too young to assist him, without means of retrieving his circumstances, his wife and himself gaunt skeletons, his farm neglected, his house wrecked, and his offices falling to ruin, yet every day bringing the half-year's term nearer! Oh, ye who riot on the miseries of such men—ye who roll round the easy circle of fashionable life, think upon this picture! Ye vile and heartless landlords, who see not, hear not, know not those to whose heart-breaking toil ye owe the only merit ye possess—that of rank in society—come and contemplate this virtuous man, as unfriended, unassisted, and uncheered by those who are bound by a strong moral duty to protect and aid him, he looks shuddering into the dark cheerless future! Is it to be wondered at that he, and such as he, should, in the misery of his despair, join the nightly meetings, be lured to associate himself with the incendiary, or seduced to grasp, in the stupid apathy of wretchedness, the weapon of the murderer? By neglecting the people, by draining them, with merciless rapacity, of the means of life; by goading them on under a cruel system of rack rents, ye become not their natural benefactors, but curses and scourges, nearly as much in reality as ye are in their opinion.

When Owen rose, he was driven by hunger, direct and immediate, to sell his best cow; and having purchased some oatmeal at an enormous price, from a well-known devotee in the parish, who hoarded up this commodity for "dear summer," he laid his plans for the future, with as much judgment as any man could display. One morning after breakfast he addressed his wife as follows:—

"Kathleen, mavourneen, I want to consult wid you bout what we ought to do; things are low wid us, asthore, and except our Heavenly Father puts it into the heart of them I'm goin' to mention, I don't know what we'll do, or what 'ill become of these poor crathurs that's naked and hungry about us. God pity them; they don't know—and maybe that same's some comfort—the hardships that's be-'ore them. Poor crathurs, see how quiet and sorrowful they sit about their little play, passin' the time for themselves as well as they can! Alley, acushla machree, come over to me. Your hair is bright and fair, Alley, and curls so par-tilty that the finest lady in the land might envy it, but, acushla, your colour's gone, your little hands are wasted away, too; that sickness was hard and sore upon you, a colleen machree, and he that 'ud spend his heart's blood for you, darlin', can do nothing to help you!"

He looked at the child as he spoke, and a slight motion in the muscles of his face was barely perceptible; but it passed away, and, after kissing her, he proceeded:—

"Ay, ye crathurs—you and I, Kathleen, could earn our bread for ourselves yet, but these can't do it. This last stroke, darlin', has laid us at the door of both poverty and sickness, but blessed be the Mother of Heaven for it, they're all left wid us; and sure that's a blessin' we've to be thankful for—glory be to God!"

"Ay, poor things, it's well to have them spared, Owen dear; sure I'd rather a thousand times beg from door to door, and have my childher to look at, than be in comfort widout them."

"Kathleen," said he, at length, "in the name of God I'll go; and may his blessin' be about you, asthore machree, and guard you and these darlins till I come back to yees."

Kathleen's faithful heart could bear no more; she laid herself on his bosom—clung to his neck, and, as the parting kiss was given, she wept aloud, and Owen's tears fell silently down his worn cheeks. The children crowded about them in loud wailings; and the grief of this virtuous and afflicted family was of that profound description, which is ever the companion, in such scenes, of pure and genuine love.

"Owen!" she exclaimed—"Owen, a-suilish mahuil agus machree!* I doubt we wor wrong in thinkin' of this journey. How can you, mavourneen, walk all the way to Dublin, and you so worn and weakly wid that sickness, and the bad feedin' both before and since? Och, give it up, achree, and stay wid us—let what will happen. You're not able for sich a journey, indeed you're not. Stay wid me and the childher, Owen; sure we'd be so lonesome widout you—will you, agrah? and the Lord will do for us some other way, maybe."

Owen pressed his faithful wife to his heart, and kissed her chaste lips with a tenderness which the heartless votaries of fashionable life can never know.

"Kathleen, asthore," he replied, in those terms of endearment which flow so tenderly through the language of the people—"sure whin I remember your fair young face—your yellow hair, and the light that was in your eyes,

* Light of my eyes and of my heart.

acushla machree—but that's gone long ago—och, don't ax me to stop. Isn't your lightsome laugh, whin you wor young, in my ears? and your step that 'ud not bend the flower of the field—Kathleen, I can't, indeed I can't bear to think of what you wor, nor of what you are now, when, in the coorse of age and natur, but a small change ought to be upon you! Sure I ought to make every struggle to take you and these sorrowful crathurs out of the state you're in."

The children flocked about them, and joined their entreaties to those of their mother. "Father, don't lave us—we'll be lonesome if you go; and if my mother 'ud get unwell, who'd be to take care of her? Father, don't lave your own 'weeny crathurs,' (a pet name he had for them)—maybe the meal 'ud be eat out before you'd come back; or maybe something 'ud happen you in that strange place."

"Indeed there's truth in what they say, Owen," said the wife: "do be said by your own Kathleen for this time, and don't take sich a long journey upon you. Afther all, maybe, you would'nt see him; sure the nabours will help us, if you could only humble yourself to ax them!"

"Kathleen," said Owen, "when this is past, you'll be glad I went—indeed you will; sure it's only the tindher feelin' of your hearts, darlins. Who knows what the landlord may do when I see himself, and show him these re-nates—every penny paid him by our own family. Let me go, acushla; it does cut me to the heart to laave yees the way yees are in, even for a while; but it's far worse to see your poor wasted faces, widout havin' it in my power to do any thing for yees."

He then kissed them again, one by one; and pressing the affectionate partner of his sorrows to his breaking heart, he bade God bless them, and set out in the twilight of a bitter March morning. He had not gone many yards from the door when little Alley ran after him in tears; he felt her hand upon the skirts of his coat, which she plucked with a smile of affection that neither tears nor sorrow could repress. "Father, kiss me again," said she. He stooped down and kissed her tenderly. The child then ascended a green ditch, and Owen, as he looked back, saw her standing upon it; her fair tresses were tossed by the blast about her face, as with straining eyes she watched him receding from her view. Kathleen and the other children stood at the door, and also with deep sorrow watched his form, until the angle of the bridle road, rendered him no longer visible; after which they returned slowly to the fire and wept bitterly.

We believe no men are capable of bearing greater toil or privation than the Irish. Owen's viaticum was only two or three oaten cakes tied in a little handkerchief, and a few shillings in silver to pay for his bed. With this small stock of food and money, an oaken stick in his hand, and his wife's kerchief tied about his waist, he undertook a journey of one hundred and eighty miles in quest of a landlord who, so far from being acquainted with the distresses of his tenantry, scarcely knew even their names, and not one of them in person.

Our scene now changes to the metropolis. One evening, about half past six o'clock, a toil-worn man turned his steps to a splendid mansion in Mountjoy-square; his appearance was drooping, fatigued, and feeble. As he went along, he examined the numbers on the respective doors, until he reached one—before which he stopped for a moment; he then stepped out upon the street, and looked through the windows, as if willing to ascertain whether there was any chance of his object being attained. Whilst in this situation a carriage rolled rapidly up, and stopped with a sudden check that nearly threw the horses on their haunches. In an instant the thundering knock of the servant intimated the arrival of some person of rank; the hall door was opened, and Owen, availing himself of that opportunity, entered the hall. Such a visitor, however, was too remarkable to escape notice. The hand of the menial was rudely placed against his breast; and as the usual impertinent interrogatories were put to him, the pampered ruffian kept pushing him back, until the afflicted man stood upon the upper step leading to the door.

"For the sake of God, and let me spake but two words to him. I'm his tenant; and I know he's too much of a jintleman to turn away a man that has lived upon his honor's estate—father and son—for upwards of two hundre years. My name's Owen—"

"You can't see him, my good fellow, at this hour. Go to Mr. M——, his Agent: we have company to dinner. He never speaks to a tenant on business; his Agent manages all that. Please, leave the way, here's more company."

As he uttered the last word, he pushed Owen back, who, forgetting that the stairs were behind him, fell—received a severe cut, and was so completely stunned, that he lay senseless and bleeding. Another carriage drove up, as the fellow, now much alarmed, attempted to raise him from the steps, and, by orders of the gentleman who came in it, he was brought into the hall. The circumstance now made some noise. It was whispered about, that one of Mr——'s tenants, a drunken fellow from the country, wanted to break in forcibly to see him; but then it was also asserted, that his skull was broken, and that he lay dead in the hall. Several of the gentlemen above stairs, on hearing that a man had been killed, immediately assembled about him, and by the means of restoratives, he soon recovered, though the blood streamed copiously from the wound in the back of his head.

"Who are you, my good man?" said Mr. S.

Owen looked about him rather vacantly, but soon collected himself, and replied, in a mournful and touching tone of voice—"I am one of your honor's tenants, from Tubber Derg; my name is Owen M'Carthy, your honor, that is, if you be Mr. ———."

"And pray, what brought you to town, M'Carthy?"

"I wanted to make an humble appale to your honor's feelins, in regard of my bit of farm. I and my poor family, your honour, have been broken down by hard times and the sickness of the sason. God knows how *they* are."

"If you wish to speak to me about that, my good man, you must know I refer all these matters to my agent—go to him; he knows them best; and whatever is right and proper to be done for you, he will do it. Sinclair, give him a crown, and send him to the ——— Dispensary to get his head dressed. I say, Carthy, go to my agent; he knows whether your claim is just or not, and will attend to it accordingly."

"Plase your honor, I've been wid him, and he says he can do nothin' whatsomever for me. I went two or three times, and could'nt see him, he was so busy; and when I did get a word or two wid him, he tould me there was more offered for my land than I'm payin'; and that, if I did not pay up, I must be put out—God help me!"

"But I tell you, Carthy, I never interfere between him and my tenants."

"Och, indeed, and it would be well both for your honor's tinants and yourself, if you did, Sir. Your honor ought to know, Sir, more about us, and how we're thrated. I'm an honest man, Sir, and I tell you so for your good."

"And pray, Sir," said the agent, stepping forward, for he had arrived a few minutes before, and heard the last observation of M'Carthy, " pray, how are they treated, you that know so well, and are so honest a man?—As for honesty, you might have referred to me, for that, I think," he added.

"Mr. M———," said Owen, " we're thrated very badly. Sir, you needn't look at me, for I'm not afeerd to spake the thruth; no bullyin', Sir, will make me say any thing in your favour that you don't desarve. You've broken the half of them by severity: you've turned the tenants against yourself and his honor here; and I tell you now, though you're to the fore, that, in the coorse of a short time, there'ill be bad work upon the estate, except his honor here looks into his own affairs, and hears the complaints of the people; look at these resates, yer honor, they'll show you, Sir———."

"Carthy, I can hear no such language against the gentleman to whom I entrust the management of my property; of course I refer the matter solely to him—I can do nothing in it."

"Kathleen, avourneen!" exclaimed the poor man, as he looked up despairingly to heaven—"and ye, poor darlins of my heart! Is this the news I'm to have for yees whin I go home? As you hope for mercy, Sir, don't turn away your ear from my petition, that I'd humbly make to *yourself*. Cowld, and hunger, and hardship are at home before me, yer honor. If you'd be pleased to look at these resates, you'd see that I always paid my rent, and 'twas sickness and the hard times———."

"And your own honesty, industry, and good conduct," said the Agent, giving a dark and malignant sneer at him. "Carthy, it shall be my business to see that you do not spread a bad spirit through the tenantry much longer. Sir, you have heard the fellow's admission. It is an implied threat that he will give us much serious trouble. There is not such another incendiary on your property—not one, upon my honour."

"Sir," said a servant, "dinner is on the table."

"Sinclair," said his landlord, "give him another crown, and tell him to trouble me no more." Saying which, he and the Agent went up to the drawing-room, and, in a moment, Owen saw a large party sweep down stairs, full of glee and vivacity, among whom both himself and his distresses were as completely forgotten as if they had never existed.

He now slowly departed, and knew not whether the house steward had given him money or not, until he felt it in his hand. A cold, sorrowful weight lay upon his heart; the din of the town deadened his affliction into a stupor; but an overwhelming sense of his disappointment, and a conviction of the Agent's diabolical falsehood, entered, like barbed arrows, into his heart.

On leaving the steps, he looked up to Heaven in the distraction of his agonizing thoughts; the clouds were black and lowering; the wind stormy, and as it carried them on its dark wing along the sky, he wished, if it were the will of God, that his head lay in the quiet grave-yard where the ashes of his forefathers reposed in peace. But he again remembered his Kathleen and their children, and the large tears of anguish, deep and bitter, rolled slowly down his cheeks.

We will not trace him into an hospital, whither the wound on his head occasioned him to be sent, but simply state, that, on the second week after this, a man with his head bound in a handkerchief, lame, bent, and evidently labouring under severe illness or great affliction, might be seen toiling slowly up the little hill that commanded a view of Tubber Derg. On reaching the top, he sat down to rest for a few minutes, but his eye was eagerly turned to the house which contained all that was dear to him on this earth. The sun was setting, and shone with half his disk visible, in that dim and cheerless splendour which produces almost in every temperament a feeling of melancholy. His house which, in happier days, formed so beautiful and conspicuous an object in the view, was now, from the darkness of its walls, scarcely discernible. The position of the sun, too, rendered it more difficult to be seen, and Owen, for it was he, shaded his eyes with his hand to survey it more distinctly. Many a harrowing thought and remembrance passed through his mind, as his eye traced its dim outline in the fading light. He had done his duty—he had gone to the fountain-head, with a hope that his simple story of affliction might be heard; but all was fruitless: the only gleam of hope that opened upon their misery had now passed into darkness and despair for ever. He pressed his aching forehead with distraction as he thought of this; then clasped his hands bitterly, and groaned aloud.

At length he rose, and proceeded with great difficulty,

for the short rest had stiffened his weak and fatigued joints. As he approached home his heart sank; and as he ascended the blood-red stream which covered the bridle-way that led to his house, what with fatigue and affliction, his agitation weakened him so much that he stopped, and leaned on his staff several times, that he might take breath.

"It's too dark, maybe, for them to see me, or poor Kathleen would send the darlins to give me the *she dha veha*.* Kathleen, avourneen machree, how my heart beats wid long to see you, asthore, and to see the weeny crathurs——glory be to Him that has left *them* to me—praise and glory to His name!"

He was now within a few perches of the door; but a sudden misgiving shot across his heart when he saw it shut, and no appearance of smoke from the chimney, nor of stir or life about the house. He advanced—

"Mother of glory, what's this!—but, wait, let me rap agin. Kathleen—Kathleen—are you widin, avourneen? Owen—Alley—arn't yees widin, childhre? Alley, sure I'm come back to yees all!" and he rapped more loudly than before. A dark breeze swept through the bushes as he spoke, but no voice nor sound proceeded from the house; all was still as death within. "Alley!" he called once more to his little favourite; "I'm come home wid something for you, asthore; I didn't forget *you*, alanna—I brought it from Dublin all the way—Alley!" but the gloomy murmur of the blast was the only reply.

Perhaps the most intense of all that he knew as misery was that which he then felt; but this state of suspense was soon terminated by the appearance of a neighbour who was passing.

"Why, thin, Owen, but yer welcome home agin, my poor fellow; and I'm sorry that I havn't betther news for you, and so are all of us."

He whom he addressed had almost lost the power of speech:—

"Frank," said he, and he wrung his hand. "What—what? was death among them? for the sake of Heaven spake!"

The severe pressure he received in return ran like a shock of paralysis to his heart. "Owen, you must be a man; every one pities yees, and may the Almighty pity and support yees! She is, indeed, Owen, gone; the weeny fair-haired child, your favourite Alley, is gone. Yesterday she was berrid; and dacently the nabours attinded the place, and sent in, as far as they had it, both mate and dhrink to Kathleen and the other ones. Now, Owen, you've heard it; trust in God, an' be a man."

A deep and convulsive throe shook him to the heart. "Gone!—the fair-haired one!—Alley!—Alley!—the pride of both our hearts; the sweet, the quiet, and the sorrowful child, that seldom played wid the rest, but kept wid mys—! Oh, my darlin', my darlin'!—gone from my eyes for ever! God of glory! won't you support me this night of sorrow and misery! With a sudden yet profound sense of humility, he dropped on his knees at the threshold, and, as the tears rolled down his convulsed cheeks, exclaimed, in a burst of sublime piety, not at all uncommon among our peasantry—" I thank you, O my God! I thank you, an' I put myself an' my weeny ones, my *pastchees boght*, into your hands. I thank you, O God, for what has happened! Keep me up and support me—och, I want it! you loved the weeny one and you took her; she was the light of my eyes and the pulse of my broken heart; but you took her, blessed Father of heaven! an' we can't be angry wid you for so doin! Still if you had spared her—if—if—oh, blessed Father my heart was in the *very* one you took—but I thank you, O God! May she rest in pace, now and for ever, Amin!"

He then rose up, and slowly wiping the tears from his eyes, departed.

"Let me hould your arm, Frank, dear," said he. "I'm weak and tir.d wid a long journey. Och, an' can it be that she's gone, the fair-haired colleen! When I was lavin' home, an' had kissed them all—'twas the first time we ever parted, Kathleen and I, since our marriage—the blessed child came over an' held up her mouth, sayin', 'Kiss me

* A welcome.

agin, father;' an' this was afther herself an' all of them had kissed me afore. But och! och! Blessed Mother, Frank, where's my Kathleen and the rest?—and why are they out of their own poor place?"

"Owen, I tould you a while agone, that you must be a man. I gave you the worst news first, and what's to come doesn't signify much. It was too dear; for if any man could live upon it, you could—you have neither house nor home, Owen, nor land. An ordher came from the Agint—your last cow was taken, so was all you had in the world—hem—barrin' a thrifle. No, bad manners to it—no, you're not widout a home, any way—the family's in my barn, brave and comfortable, compared to what your own house was, that let in the wather through the roof like a sieve; and while the same barn's to the fore, never say you want a home."

"God bless you, Frank, for that goodness to them and me. If you're not rewarded for it here, you will in a betther place. Och, I long to see Kathleen and the childher! But I'm fairly broken down, Frank, and hardly able to mark the ground; and, indeed, no wondher, if you knew but all, still let God's will be done! Poor Kathleen, I must bear up afore her, or she'll break her heart, for I know how she loved the goolden-haired darlin' that's gone from us. Och, and how did she go, Frank, for I left her betther?"

"Why, the poor girsha took a relapse, and wasn't strong enough to bear up against the last attack; but its one comfort to you to know that she's happy."

Owen stood for a moment, and looking solemnly in his neighbour's face, exclaimed, in a deep and exhausted voice,—"Frank!"

"What are you going to say, Owen?"

"The heart widin me's broke—broke!"

The large tears rolled down his weather-beaten cheeks, and he proceeded in silence to the house of his friend. There was, however, a feeling of sorrow in his words and manner which Frank could not withstand. He grasped Owen's hand, and, in a low and broken voice, simply said —" Keep your spirits up—keep them up."

When they came to the barn in which his helpless family had taken up their temporary residence, Owen stood for a moment to collect himself; but he was nervous, and trembled with repressed emotion. They then entered; and Kathleen, on seeing her beloved and affectionate husband, threw herself on his bosom, and for some time felt neither joy nor sorrow—she had swooned. The poor man embraced her with a tenderness at once mournful and deep. The children, on seeing their father safely returned, forgot their recent grief, and clung about him with gladness and delight. In the mean time Kathleen recovered, and Owen for many minutes could not check the loud and clamorous grief—now revived by the presence of her husband—with which the heart-broken and emaciated mother deplored her departed child; and Owen himself on once more looking among the little ones—on seeing her little frock hanging up, and her stool vacant by the fire—on missing her voice, and her blue laughing eyes, and remembering the affectionate manner in which, as with a presentiment of death, she held up her little mouth, and offered the last kiss—he slowly pulled the toys and cakes he had purchased for her out of his pocket, surveyed them for a moment, and then putting his hands on his face, bent his head upon his bosom, and wept with the vehement outpouring of a father's sorrow.

The reader perceives that he was a meek man; that his passions were not dark nor violent; he bore no revenge to those who neglected or injured him, and in this he differed from too many of his countrymen. No; his spirit was broken down with sorrow, and had not room for the fiercer and more destructive passions. His case excited general pity. Whatever his neighbours could do to sooth him, and alleviate his affliction, was done. His farm was not taken; for fearful threats were held out against those who might venture to occupy it. In these threats he had nothing to do; on the contrary, he strongly deprecated them. Their existence, however, was deemed by the agent sufficient to justify him in his callous and malignant severity towards Owen.—*(To be concluded next week.)*

MODERN TRAVELLING.[*]

May we be permitted to make a little demand on our readers' fancy, and suppose it possible, that a worthy old gentleman of this said year—1742—had fallen comfortably asleep à la Dodswell, and never awoke till Monday morning last in Piccadilly? "What coach, your honour?" says a ruffian-looking fellow, much like what he might have been had he lived a hundred years back. "I wish to go home to Exeter," replies the old gentleman, mildly. "Just in time, your honour, here she comes—them there grey horses—where's your luggage?" "Don't be in a hurry," observes the stranger; "that's a gentleman's carriage." "It ain't! I tell you," says the cad, "it's the Comet, and you must be as quick as lightning. *Nolens volens*, the remonstrating old gentleman is shoved into the Comet, by a cad at each elbow, having been three times assured his luggage is in the hind boot, and twice three times denied having ocular demonstration of the fact.

However, he is now seated—and, "What *gentleman* is going to drive us?" is his first question to his fellow-passengers. "He is no gentleman, sir," says a person who sits opposite to him, and who happens to be a proprietor of the coach. "He has been on the Comet ever since she started, and is a very steady young man." "Pardon my ignorance," replies the regenerated; "from the cleanliness of his person, the neatness of his apparel, and the language he made use of, I mistook him for some enthusiastic Bachelor of Arts, wishing to become a charioteer after the manner of the Illustrious Ancients." "You must have been long in foreign parts, sir," observes the proprietor. In five minutes or less, after this parley commenced, the wheels went round, and in another five the coach arrived at Hyde Park gate; but long before it got there, the worthy gentleman of 1742 (set down by his fellow-travellers for either a little cracked, or an emigrant from the Backwoods of America) exclaimed, "What! off the stones already?" "You have never been on the stones," observes his neighbour on his right; "no stones in London, now, sir," "But we are going at a great rate," exclaims again the stranger. "Oh no, sir," says the proprietor "*we never go fast over this stage*. We have time allowed in consequence of being subject to interruptions, and we make it up over the lower ground." Five-and-thirty minutes, however, bring them to the noted town of Brentford. "Hah!" says the old man, becoming young again—"what, no improvement in this filthy place? Is old Brentford still here? a national disgrace!"

In five minutes under the hour the Comet arrives at Hounslow, to the great delight of our friend, who by this time waxed hungry, not having broken his fast before starting. "Just fifty-five minutes and thirty-seven seconds," says he, "from the time we left London!—wonderful travelling, gentlemen, to be sure, but much too fast to be safe. However, thank heaven, we are arrived at a good-looking house; and now, *waiter!* I hope you have got break*f*——." Before the last syllable, however, of the word could be pronounced, the worthy old gentleman's head struck the back of the coach by a jerk, which he could not account for, (the fact was, three of the four fresh horses were bolters,) and the waiter, the inn, and indeed Hounslow itself, disappeared in the twinkling of an eye. Never did such a succession of doors, windows, and window-shutters pass so quickly in his review before—and he hoped they might never do so again. Recovering, however, a little from his surprise—"My dear sir," said he, "you told me we were to change horses at Hounslow?" Surely, they are not so inhuman as to drive these poor animals another stage at this unmerciful rate!" "Change horses, sir! says the proprietor; "why we changed them whilst you were putting on your spectacles, and looking at your watch. Only one minute allowed for it at Hounslow, and it is often done in fifty seconds by those nimble-fingered horse-keepers." "You astonish me—but really I do not like to go so fast." "Oh, sir, we always *spring* them over these six miles. It is what we call *the hospital ground*." This alarming phrase is presently interpreted; it intimates that horses whose "backs are getting down instead of up in their work"—some "that won't hold an ounce down hill, or draw an ounce up"—others "that kick over the pole one day, and over the bars the next," in short all the reprobates, styled in the road slang *bokickers*, are sent to work their six miles—because *here* they have nothing to do but to gallop—not a pebble as big as a nutmeg on the road, and so even, that it would not disturb the equilibrium of a spirit-level.

The coach, however, goes faster and faster over the hospital ground, as the "bokickers" feel their legs, and the collars get warm to their shoulders; and having ten outsides, the luggage of the said ten, and a few extra packages besides on the roof, she rolls rather more than is pleasant, although the centre of gravity is pretty well kept down by four not slender insides, two well-laden boots, and three huge trunks in the *slide*. The gentleman of the last century, however, becomes alarmed;—is sure the horses are running away with the coach—declares he perceives by the shadow, that there is nobody on the box, and can see the reins dangling about the horses' heels. He attempts to look out of the window, but his fellow-traveller dissuades him from doing so:—"You may get a shot in your eye from the wheel. Keep your head in the coach, its all right, depend on't. We always spring 'em over this stage." Persuasion is useless; for the horses increase their speed, and the worthy old gentleman looks out. But what does he see? Death and destruction before his eyes?—No: to his surprise he finds the coachman firm at his post, and in the act of taking a pinch of snuff from the gentleman who sits beside him on the *bench*, his horses going at the rate of three miles in the minute at the time. "But suppose any thing should break, or a linch-pin should give way and let a wheel loose?" is the next appeal to the communicative but not very consoling proprietor. "Nothing can break, sir," is the reply: "all of the very best stuff; axle-trees of the best K. Q. iron, faggotted edgeways, well bedded in the timbers; and as for linch-pins, we have not one about the coach. We use the best patent boxes that are manufactured. In short, sir, you are as safe in it as if you were in your bed." "Bless me," exclaims the old man, "what improvements! And the roads!!!" "They are at perfection," says the proprietor; "no horse walks a yard in this coach between London and Exeter—all trotting ground now." "A little *galloping* ground, I fear," whispers the senior to himself! "But who has effected all this improvement in your paving?" "An American of the name of M'Adam," was the reply—"but coachmen call him the Colossus of Roads. Great things have likewise been done in cutting through hills and altering the course of roads; and it is no uncommon thing now-a-days to see four horses trotting away merrily down hill on that very ground where they formerly were seen walking up hill."

"And pray, my good sir, what sort of horses may you have over the next stage?" "Oh, sir, no more bokickers. It is hilly and severe ground, and requires cattle strong and staid. You'll see four as fine horses put to the coach at Staines as you ever saw in a nobleman's carriage in your life." "Then we shall have no more galloping—no more springing them as you term it?" "Not quite so fast over the next ground," replied the proprietor; "but he will make good play over some part of it; for example, when he gets three parts down a hill he lets them loose, and cheats them out of half the one they have to ascend from the bottom of it. In short, they are half way up it before a horse touches his collar; and we *must* take every advantage with such a fast coach as this, and one that leads so well, or we should never keep our time. We are now to a minute; in fact, the country people no longer look at the *sun* when they want to set their clocks; they look only to the *Comet*. But depend upon it, you are quite safe; we have nothing but first-rate artists on this coach." "Artists! artists!" grumbles the old gentleman, "we had no such term as that."

"I should like to see this *artist* change horses at the next stage," resumes our ancient, "for at the last it had the appearance of magic—' Presto, Jack, and begone!'" "By all means; you will be much gratified. It is done with a

[*] From the liveliest article in the last Quarterly Review.

...ickness and ease almost incredible to any one who has ...ly read or heard of it; but use becomes second nature ...th us. Even in my younger days it was always half-an-...ur's work—sometimes more."

The coach arrives at Staines, and the ancient gentleman ...ts his intentions into effect,—though he was near being ...ain too late; for by the time he could extract his hat from ...e netting that suspended it over his head, the leaders had ...en taken from their bars, and were walking up the yard ...wards their stables. On perceiving a fine, thorough-bred ...orse led towards the coach with a twitch fastened tightly to ...is nose, he exclaims, " Holloa, Mr. Horsekeeper! You ...re going to put an unruly horse in the coach." "What! ...is here on?" growls the man; " the quietest *hanimal* alive, ...r!" as he shoves him to the near side of the pole. At this ...oment, however, the coachman is heard to say, in some-...hat of an under tone, " Mind what you are about, Bob; ...on't let him touch the roller-bolt." In thirty seconds ...ore, they are off—" the staid and steady team," so styled ...y the proprietor in the coach. " Let 'em go, and take care ...f yourselves," says the artist, so soon as he was firmly seated ...pon his box. With this, the near leader rears right on end, ...nd if the rein had not been yielded to him at the instant, he ...vould have fallen backwards on the head of the pole. The ...noment the twitch was taken from the nose of the thor-...ugh-bred near-wheeler, he drew himself back to the extent ...f his pole-chain—his fore-legs stretched out before him—...und then, like a lion loosened from his toil, made a snatch ...t the coach that would have broken two pair of traces of 1742. A steady and good-whipped horse, however, his part-...ner, started the coach himself, with a gentle touch of the thong, and away they went off together. But the thorough-bred one was very far from being comfortable; it was in vain that the coachman tried to sooth him with his voice, or stroked him with the crop of his tool, i. e. *whip*. He drew three parts of the coach, and cantered for the first mile, and when he did settle down to his trot, his snorting could be heard by the passengers, being as much as to say, " I was not born to be a slave." In fact, as the proprietor now observed, " he had been a fair plate horse in his time, but his temper was always queer."

After the first shock was over, the Conservative of the 18th century felt comfortable. The pace was considerably slower than it had been over the last stage, but he was un-conscious of the reason for its being diminished. It was to accommodate the queer temper of the race-horse, who, if he had not been humoured at starting, would never have set-tled down to his trot, but have ruffled all the rest of the team. He was also surprised, if not pleased, at the quick rate at which they were ascending hills which, in his time, he should have been asked by the coachman to have walked up—but his pleasure was short-lived; the third hill they descended, produced a return of his agony. This was what is termed on the road *a long fall of ground*, and the coach rather pressed upon the horses. The temper of the race-horse became exhausted; breaking into a canter, he was of little use as a wheeler, and there was then nothing for it but a gallop. The leaders only wanted the signal; and the point of the thong being thrown lightly over their backs, they were off like an arrow out of a bow: but the rocking of the coach was awful, and more particularly so to the passengers on the roof. Nevertheless, she was not in dan-ger; the master-hand of the artist kept her in a direct line; and, meeting the opposing ground, she *steadied*, and all was right. The newly-awakened gentleman, however, begins to grumble again. " Pray, my good sir," says he anxious-ly—"do use your authority over your coachman, and *insist* upon his putting the drag-chain on the wheel, when descend-ing the next hill." " I have no such authority," replies the proprietor. " It is true, we are now drawn by my horses, but I cannot interfere with the driving of them." " But is he not your servant?" " He is sir, but I con-tract to work the coach so many miles in so many hours, and he engages to drive it, and each is subject to a fine if the time be not kept on the road. On so fast a coach as this, every advantage must be taken, and if we were to drag down such hills as these, we should never reach Exeter to-day."

Our friend, however, will have no more of it. He quits the coach at Bagshot, congratulating himself on the safety of his limbs.

The worthy old gentleman is now shown into a room, and, after warming his hands at the fire, rings the bell for the waiter. A well-dressed person appears, whom he of course takes for the landlord. " Pray, sir," says he, " have you any *slow* coach down this road to-day?" " Why, yes, sir," replies John; " we shall have the Regulator down in an hour." " Just right," said our friend, " it will enable me to break my fast, which I have not done to-day." " Oh, sir," observes John, " these here fast *drags* be the ruin of us. 'Tis all hurry scurry, and no gentleman has time to have nothing on the road. What will you take, sir? Mutton-chops, veal-cutlets, beaf-steaks?"

At the appointed time, the Regulator appears at the door. It is a strong, well-built *drag*, painted what is called choco-late colour; bedaubed all over with gilt letters—a bull's head on the doors, a Saracen's head on the hind boot—and drawn by four strapping horses; but it wants the neatness of the other. The passengers may be, by a shade or two, of a lower order than those who had gone forward with the Comet; nor perhaps is the coachman quite so refined as the one we have just taken leave of. He has not the neat white hat, the clean doeskin gloves, the well-cut trousers, and dapper frock, but still his appearance is re-spectable, and perhaps in the eyes of many, more in char-acter with his calling. Neither has he the agility of the artist on the Comet, for he is nearly double his size; but he is a strong, powerful man, and might be called a pattern card of the heavy coachman of the present day—in other words, a man who drives a coach which carries sixteen passengers instead of fourteen, and is rated at eight miles in the hour instead of ten. " What room in the Regula-tor?" says our friend to the waiter, as he comes to announce its arrival. " Full inside, sir, and in front, but you'll have *the backgammon board* all to yourself, and your luggage is in the hind boot." " Backgammon board! Pray what's that? Do you not mean *the basket?*" " Oh no, sir," says John, smiling—" no such a thing on the road now. It is the hind-dickey, as some call it; where you'll be as com-fortable as possible, and can sit with your back or your face to the coach, or *both*, if you like." " Ah, ah," con-tinues the old gentleman; "something new again, I pre-sume." However, the mystery is cleared up; the ladder is reared to the hind wheel, and the gentleman safely seated on the backgammon board.

Before ascending to his place, our friend has cast his eye on the team that is about to convey him to Hertford bridge, the next stage on the great western road, and he perceives it to be of a different stamp from that which he had seen taken from the coach at Bagshot. It consisted of four moderate-sized horses, full of power, and still fuller of con-dition, but with a fair sprinkling of blood—in short, the eye of a judge would have discovered something about them not very unlike galloping. " All right!" cried the guard, taking his key-bugle in his hand; and they proceeded up the village, at a steady pace, to the tune of " Scots wha hae with Wallace bled," and continued at that pace for the first five miles. " *I am landed*," thinks our friend to himself. Unluckily, however, for the humane and cautious old gen-tlemen, even the Regulator was now to show tricks. Al-though what now is called a slow coach, she is timed at eight miles in the hour through a great extent of country, and must of course make play where she can, being strongly opposed by hills lower down the country, trifling as these hills are, no doubt, to what they once were. The Regu-lator, moreover, loads well, not only with passengers but with luggage; and the last five miles of this stage, called the Hertford-bridge flat, have the reputation of being the best five miles for a coach to be found at this time in Eng-land. The ground is firm, but elastic; the surface undu-lating, and therefore favourable to draught; always dry, not a shrub being near it; nor is there a stone upon it much larger than a marble. These advantages, then, are not lost to the Regulator, or made use of without sore dis-composure to the solitary tenant of her backgammon board.

Any one that has looked into books will very readily account for the lateral motion, or rocking, as it is termed, of a coach, being greatest at the greatest distance from the horses—(as the tail of a paper kite is in motion whilst the body remains at rest)—and more especially when laden as this coach was—the greater part of the weight being forward. The situation of our friend then was once more deplorable. The Regulator takes but twenty-three minutes for those celebrated five miles, which cannot be done without "springing the cattle" now and then; and it was in one of the very best of their gallops of that day, that they were met by the coachman of the Comet, who was returning with his *up* coach. When coming out of rival yards, coachmen never fail to cast an eye to the loading of their opponents on the road, and *now* that of the *natty* Artist of the Comet experienced a high treat. He had a full view of his quondam passenger, and thus described his situation. He was seated with his back to the horses—his arms extended to each extremity of the guard-irons—his teeth set grim as death—his eyes cast down towards the ground, thinking the less he saw of his danger the better. There was what is called a *top heavy-load*—perhaps a ton of luggage on the roof, and, it may be, not *quite* in obedience to the Act of Parliament standard. There were also two horses at wheel whose strides were of rather unequal length, and this operated powerfully on the coach. In short, the lurches of the Regulator were awful at the moment of the Comet passing her. A tyro in mechanics would have exclaimed, "the centre of gravity must be lost, the centrifugal force will have the better of it—*over she must go!*

The centre of gravity having been preserved, the coach arrives safe at Hertford bridge—but the old gentleman has again had enough of it. "I will walk into Devonshire," said he, as he descended from his perilous exaltation. What did that rascally waiter mean by telling me it was a slow coach? and, moreover, look at the luggage on the roof!" "Only regulation height, sir," says the coachman, "we arn't allowed to have it an inch higher:—sorry we can't please you, sir, but we will try and make room for you in front." "*Fronti nulla fides*," mutters the worthy to himself, as he walks tremblingly into the house—adding "I shall not give this fellow a shilling, *he is dangerous*."

The Regulator being off, the waiter is again applied to. "What do you charge per mile posting?" "One and sixpence, sir." Bless me! just double! Let me see,—two hundred miles, at two shillings per mile, postboys, turnpikes, &c. L.20. This will never do. Have you no coach that does not carry luggage on the top?" "Oh yes, sir," replies the waiter, "we shall have one to-night, that is not allowed to carry a band-box on the roof." "That's the coach for me; pray what do you call it?" "The Quicksilver mail, sir; one of the best out of London—Jack White and Tom Brown, pick'd coachmen, over this ground—Jack White down to-night." "Guarded and lighted?" "Both, sir; blunderbusss and pistols in the sword-case; a lamp each side the coach, and one under the footboard—see to pick up a pin in the darkest night of the year." "Very fast?" "Oh no, sir, just keeps time, and that's all." "That's the coach for me, then," repeats our hero; "and I am sure I shall feel at my ease in it. I suppose it is what used to be called the Old Mercury."

Unfortunately, the Devonport (commonly called the Quicksilver mail) is half a mile in the hour faster than most in England, and is, indeed, one of the miracles of the road. Let us, then, picture to ourselves our anti-reformer snugly seated in this mail, on a pitch-dark night in November. It is true she has no luggage on the roof, nor much to incommode her elsewhere, but she is a mile in the hour faster than the Comet, at least three miles quicker than the Regulator; and she performs more than half her journey by lamplight. It is needless to say, then, our senior soon finds out his mistake, but there is no remedy at hand, for it is the dead of night, and all the inns are shut up. He must proceed, or be left behind in a stable. The climax of his misfortunes then approaches. Nature being exhausted, sleep comes to his aid, and he awakes on a stage which is called the fastest on the journey,—it is four miles of ground, and twelve minutes is the time! The old gentleman starts from his seat, having dreamed the horses were running away with the coach, and so, no doubt, they might be. He is, however, determined to convince himself of the fact, though the passengers assure him, "all's right" "Don't put your head out of the window," says one of them, "you will lose your hat to a certainty;" but advice is seldom listened to by a terrified man, and next moment a stentorian voice is heard, crying, "stop coachman, stop—I have lost my hat and wig!" The coachman hears him not—and in another second the broad wheels of a *down* waggon have for ever demolished the lost head-gear. But here we must leave our adventurous Gilpin of 1742. We have taken a great liberty with him, it is true, but we are not without our precedent. One of the best chapters in Livy, contains the history of "an event which never took place." In the full charm of his imagination, the historian brings Alexander into Italy, where he never was in his life, and displays him in his brightest colours. We father our sins then, upon the Patavinian.

SATURDAY EVENING.

BY DR. BOWRING.

The week is past, the Sabbath-dawn comes on.
Rest—rest in peace—thy daily toil is done;
And standing, as thou standest on the brink
Of a new scene of being, calmly think
Of what is gone, is now, and soon shall be,
As one that trembles on Eternity.
For, sure as this now closing week is past,
So sure advancing Time will close my last;
Sure as to-morrow, shall the awful light
Of the eternal morning hail my sight.
 Spirit of good! on this week's verge I stand,
Tracing the guiding influence of thy hand;
That hand, which leads me gently, kindly, still,
Up life's dark, stony, tiresome, thorny hill;
Thou, thou, in every storm has sheltered me
Beneath the wing of thy benignity:—
A thousand graves my footsteps circumvent,
And I exist—thy mercies' monument!
A thousand writhe upon the bed of pain—
I live—and pleasure flows through ev'ry vein.
Want o'er a thousand wretches waves her wand—
I, circled by ten thousand mercies, stand.
How can I praise thee, Father! how express
My debt of reverence and of thankfulness!
A debt that no intelligence can count,
While every moment swells the vast amount.
For the week's duties thou hast given me strength,
And brought me to its peaceful close at length;
And here, my grateful bosom fain would raise,
A fresh memorial to thy glorious praise.

A MAXIM OVERTURNED.

'Tis held that nought's *so light as air*,
 Yet when for *window tax* they levy,
The maxim we refute; and swear
 That *air* thus charg'd comes deuced *heavy*.

CONTENTS OF NO. XXVII.

Mr. Stuart's Three Years in America, (Continued)	65
Person and Manners of Cowper	68
Biographical Sketch—Susanna Annesley, the Mother of John Wesley	69
Singular Circumstance at West Meath Assizes	71
The Identical Lawrie Tod	72
COLUMN FOR THE LADIES—Fortunate Mistake—Cupid and Minerva	ib.
THE STORY-TELLER—Tubber Derg; or, the Red Well	73
Modern Travelling	78
Saturday Evening	80

EDINBURGH: Printed by and for JOHN JOHNSTONE, 19, St. James' Square.—Published by JOHN ANDERSON, Jun., Bookseller, 55, North Bridge Street, Edinburgh; by JOHN MACLEOD, and ATKINSON & Co., Booksellers, Glasgow; and sold by all Booksellers and Venders of Cheap Periodicals.

THE Schoolmaster,
AND EDINBURGH WEEKLY MAGAZINE.

CONDUCTED BY JOHN JOHNSTONE.

THE SCHOOLMASTER IS ABROAD.—LORD BROUGHAM.

No. 28.—Vol. II.   SATURDAY, FEBRUARY 9, 1833.   Price Three-Halfpence.

NOTES OF THE MONTH.

FEBRUARY.

Every month of the year has its peculiar character, and none preserves it more distinctively than February. The weather is generally, in the beginning of the month, blustering and rainy, fully verifying the adage, that

"February fills the dyke
Either with black or white."

In the application of these weather-wise old saws, it should be borne in mind that they suit the old Calendar, which varies about a fortnight from the New Style. This premised, they will be found nearly infallible. By the middle of February, (its commencement by the Old Style,) the weather shews many symptoms of relenting from the rigid severity of mid-winter. The days have greatly lengthened, the morning sun becomes powerful, and though the weather is gusty and rough, often attended with sudden thaws, and short, though heavy falls of snow, the temperature is generally mild. There often also occur a few delicious days of truly vernal mildness. Another ancestral saying teaches us to distrust this premature mildness; and it rarely fails to hold :—

"Candlemas, gin ye be fair,
The half o' the winter 's to come and mair ;
Candlemas, gin ye be foul,
The half o' the winter is gone at Yule."

The English have their own version of the same saying :—

"If Candlemas be fair and bright,
Winter will have another flight."

But whatever be the actual weather, by old Candlemas day, it is visible, by a hundred delightful signs, that nature is once more alive and springing. There is, accordingly, no season in which a rural walk in a proper direction affords more of hopeful enjoyment. To the inhabitants of cities, a walk in a flower nursery-ground is now peculiarly delightful, and one's own small border is never so interesting as when the first pale snow-drop, the deep-golden crocus, the various-coloured hepaticas, and the bloom of the mezereon are our sole treasures—few, but the more fondly noted.

About this season one likes to escape from the monotonous, deep verdure of formal shrubberies, so delightful in winter, to the sheltered *baulks* and *burn-sides*, where the catkins of the *saughs*, and the flower-buds of the alder and hazel begin to peer forth ; and where the blossoming whin regales us with its early perfume, and displays the first wild blossoms of the year. In such situations, and at this time of the year, young people may most fitly be made acquainted with one of the most numerous and lovely classes of plants —the mosses, now in their prime, and often made more exquisitely beautiful by the delicate icy efflorescence which veils them. Reckoning by the Old Style, as we would always be understood to do in noticing the natural appearances of the year, we may mention, that by the 1st, (that is the 12th,) the note of the woodlark is heard ;— ravens have paired, and are building ;—partridges begin to pair ;—the thrush and the chaffinch sing ; —bullfinches re-appear in the orchards ;—sparrows begin to build, and, on a fine day, gnats, and " the gay motes that people the sunbeams," play ; and innumerable insects awaken to happy existence under the budding hedge-rows. Geese now begin to lay, house-pigeons have young broods, the mole,

"The little blackamoor pioneer,
Plodding his way in the darkness drear,"

is as busy under ground, as the myriads of gay ephemeral creatures are full of enjoyment on the surface of the earth.

"It is," says Paley, "a happy world after all—The air, the earth, the water, teem with delighted existence. In a spring noon, or a summer evening, on whichever side I turn my eyes, myriads of happy beings crowd upon my view. "The insect youth are on the wing." Swarms of new-born flies are trying their pinions in the air. Their sportive motions, their wanton mazes, their gratuitous activity, their continual change of place without use or purpose, testify their joy, and the exultation which they feel in their lately-discovered faculties. A bee amongst the flowers in Spring, is one of the most cheerful objects that can be looked upon. Its life appears to be all enjoyment ; so busy, and so pleased ; yet it is only a specimen of insect life, with which, by reason of the animal being half domesticated, we happen to be better acquainted than we are with that of others.

"Other species are *running about*, with an alacrity in their motions, which carries with it every mark of pleasure. Large patches of ground are sometimes half covered with these brisk and sprightly natures. If we look to what the waters produce, shoals of the fry of fish frequent the margins of rivers, of lakes, and of the sea itself. These are so happy, that they know not what to do with themselves Their attitudes, their vivacity, their leaps out of the water, their frolics in it, (which I have noticed a thousand times with equal attention and amusement,) all conduce to show their excess of spirits, and are simply the effects of that excess."

PROCESS OF VEGETATION IN TREES.

Early in February, the influence of the genial weather is perceived in the *ascent of the sap* in trees. This blood of vegetable life now begins to stir in all their ramifications. In Aiken's Natural History of the year we have a minute account of their process, from which the following is in substance taken :—

"The first vital operation in trees, after the frost is moderated, and the earth sufficiently thawed, is the *ascent of the sap*, which is taken up by the small vessels or tubes composing the *inner bark* of the tree, and reaching to the extremity of the fibres at the roots; the water thus taken in by the roots is there mixed with a quantity of sugary matter, and formed into sap, whence it is distributed in great abundance to every bud. The amazing quantity of sweet liquid sap thus provided by nature for the nourishment of some trees, is evident from a general custom in some countries, of *tapping* the birch in the early part of Spring; thus obtaining from each tree a quart or more of liquor, according to its size, which is fermented into a kind of wine. The same method is also practised in hot countries, to procure the favourite liquor of the inhabitants, *palm-wine*; and a similar custom is observed in the northern parts of America, with regard to the sugar-maple, the juice of which, boiled down, yields a rich sugar, each tree affording about three pounds. This great quantity of nourishment causes the bud to swell, to break through its covering, and to spread into blossoms, or lengthen into a shoot bearing leaves. This is the first process, and properly speaking, is all that belongs to the springing or lengthening of trees; and in many plants, particularly those which are annual, or fall every year, there is no other process; the plant sucks in juices from the earth, and in proportion to the quantity of these juices, increases in size: it spreads out its blossoms, perfects its fruit, and, when the ground is incapable, by drought or frost, of yielding any more moisture, or when the vessels of the plant are not able to draw it up, the plant perishes. But in trees, though the beginning and end of the first process are exactly similar to what takes place in vegetables, yet there is a second process, which, at the same time that it adds to their bulk, enables them to endure and go on increasing through many years.

"The second process begins soon after the first, in this way: At the base of the foot-stalk of each leaf, a small bud is gradually formed; but the small vessels of the leaf, having exhausted themselves in forming the bud, are unable to bring it nearer to maturity: in this state it exactly resembles a seed, containing within it the rudiments of vegetation, but without vessels to nourish and enlarge the seed. Being surrounded, however, by sap, like a seed in moist earth, it is in a proper situation for growing; the influence of the sun sets in motion the juices of the bud and of the seed, and the first operation in both of them is to send down oots to a certain depth into the ground, for the purpose of obtaining the necessary moisture. The bud, accordingly, shoots down its roots upon the inner bark of the tree, till they reach the part covered by the earth. Winter now arriving, the cold and want of moisture, owing to the clogged condition of the vessels, cause the fruit and leaves to fall, so that, except the buds with roots, the remainder of the tree, like an annual plant, is entirely dead: the leaves, the flowers and fruit are gone, and what was the inner bark is no longer in its usual state, while the roots of the buds form a new inner bark; and thus the buds with their roots contain all that remains alive of the whole tree. It is owing to this annual renewing of the inner bark, that the tree increases in bulk; and a new coating being added every year, we are hence furnished with an easy and exact method of finding the age of a tree, by counting the number of circles of which the trunk is composed. A tree, therefore, properly speaking, is rather a bundle of a multitude of annual plants, than an individual which lives for many years. The sap in trees always rises as soon as the frost is abated; and if by any means the sap is prevented from ascending at the proper time, the tree infallibly perishes."

OLD HOLYDAYS.

February had its full complement of holydays by the old Calender; and a few still maintain a lingering shorn observance. Mechanics have their CANDLE FEAST, schoolboys Shrove-tide; for though cock-fighting is nearly exploded, happily neither pancakes nor fritters are obsolete. The ladies of Edinburgh still do unconscious homage to the carnival customs, by always holding one of their most splendid assemblies on *Fastern's Eve*; and lovers and friends have St. Valentine's day,—the flower of February days, to describe which aright would occupy our entire pages.

CANDLEMAS DAY.

There is one Scottish custom we would think more honoured in the breach than the observance. By the 2d of February, warning must, by prescribed usage, be given to house proprietors by tenants intending to remove; and till the 25th of May, nearly four months, or a third part of the whole year, our 'dwelling' is liable to the daily and hourly incursions of the curious, and the regular house hirers as well as those wishing to inspect a house on legitimate motives. This is an intolerable nuisance, which should be put under proper regulation in the new police-bill for this city, and reformed throughout all Scotland. In some towns the notice to quit is given so early as Martinmas, so that for half the year one's privacy is apt to be continually invaded if the house remain so long unlet.

BOOKS OF THE MONTH.

THE most important new work within our popular range of literature is *Stuart's Three Years in America*, which we have already introduced to our readers. It is a book to be anxiously borrowed, and bought by those who have plenty of money. It is cheap for its size, but might be diminished in volume without any deterioration of quality.

BIOGRAPHIES.

The last few weeks have produced LIVES of MILTON, COWPER, and of ROBERT HALL. The first is of interest, from giving a fuller account of Milton's prose works than is found in the common biographies. The writer, also, so far as his lights serve, discovers a just appreciation and profound reverence for Milton, the bold questioner, the fearless reasoner, the undaunted reformer, the noblest literary name of England; yet would he fain press the expansive mind of Milton into the service of a sect. The author is, we believe, a Baptist preacher. The new life of Cowper is written by the Rev. Mr. Taylor. It aspires to nothing further than being a careful compilation. It is a handsome volume, such as many people like to see in their parlour collection. A *cheap* life of Cowper, comprehending his correspondence, still remains a *desideratum* in bookmaking, and would require both sound judgment and refined taste.*

The next life, that of Robert Hall of Leicester, is mixed up with his works, which are published under the superintendence of Dr. Olinthus Gregory. Every new fact relating to the manner of life and modes of thinking of a man of great and original mind, is full of interest to all men. But the materials left by Sir James Mackintosh, (the friend of Hall,) whose literary representative Dr. Gregory is, are scanty and meagre, and add not much to our previous stores of information. Mr. Dove, to whom we owe the late cheap Memoir of Marvell, has published a memoir of the Wesley family, but omitting the principal personage, John Wesley, whose life has been so often written. It is a readable enough book of humble pretensions, and contains a great deal of information in short compass.

NEW NOVELS.

THE GHOST-HUNTER, by Mr Banim, forms the first of a new Novelist's Library, intended as an improvement on the Minerva Press and Colburn's fashionable novels, in quality and in cheapness. The idea is good, but it is not well developed. The volumes are too bulky, and the print too small for the skimming and skipping of circulating library readers. Mr Banim is one of the first novelists of his time, and the Ghost-Hunter the best work he has produced since the Nowlans.

TALES OF A CHAPERON, *Edited by Lady Dacre.* These tales are highly *reported* by the London papers: they are said to be written by one of her ladyship's daughters, Mrs. Sullivan. We have not yet seen them; but from the *unsuspected* quarters in which the work is praised, are inclined to believe it must be one of great merit.

AN AMERICAN'S ACCOUNT OF A LEVEE OF THE TIME OF GEORGE IV.

At last I have seen the humours of a levee, which is certainly worth seeing for once, as presenting so remarkable a contrast to the plain simplicity of our own Chief Magistrate, who stands forth as a man among men; " who walks forth without attendants, lives without state, greets his fellow citizens with open hands as his companions and equals; seeks his relaxations from the labours of the cabinet at the domestic hearth; snatches a moment from the hurry of public affairs to superintend the business of his farm, and defrays all the expenses of his high office with a stipend of L.6000 a-year!" How different is the scene at Carlton Palace, with all its pomp and parade of military attendance, and all the glare and frippery of its court costume. I went under the protection of our worthy minister, and it was about two o'clock when we found ourselves in the large ante-room of the palace, which was soon thronged with bishops and judges, generals and admirals, doctors and surgeons, lawyers and authors—all anxious to bask for a moment in the rays of royalty, and catch a passing smile of condescension from the great man. The mob at a levee is much like other mobs, though perhaps less good-humoured and entertaining. After waiting about an hour on the tiptoe of expectation, the folding-doors were at length thrown open, and the mass began to move. Inch by inch we fought our way, till at last I got near enough to command a view of the King. He stood as it were in a door-way, with the whole of his cabinet ministers drawn up in a regular array opposite to him; and the intervening narrow lane, through which two persons could scarcely have passed abreast, just sufficed to let the crowd off. I can compare the scene to nothing so well as to the getting into the pit of a theatre on a full night. The lord in waiting who receives your card, and the king your bow, if one may venture upon so homely a comparison, answered to the check and money takers; the cry of "Get your card ready," would have been as appropriate on one occasion, 'as "Get your money ready," on the other; and the press from behind scarcely allowed time for a moment's pause in the royal presence. The business of presentation was begun and concluded in a moment; the King smiled graciously, saying, "How d'ye do, Mr. Kentucky? I am very glad to see you here,"—and I found myself in the next room before I was well aware that the ceremony had commenced. It was then that a friend who had witnessed the scene, congratulated me upon the gracious reception I had experienced—a fact of which, but for his information, I might have remained in ignorance. The next difficulty was how to get away; for, having no carriage, and having been separated from my ministerial Mentor, I scarcely knew what to do. At last, fiercely cocking my hat on one side, like my namesake Jonathan, of wild memory in his boat scene, I sallied boldly out at the great-gates, and making my way through the crowd, who contented themselves with a few good-humoured jokes at the awkwardness with which I wore my court habiliments, I gained the stand of coaches in Cockspur Street, into one of which I vanished from their gaze. The next day Mr. R―― asked me how I was satisfied with my reception, to which I made a suitable reply of acknowledgment. " Why, yes, indeed," said he, " I think you have reason to be satisfied, for I do not think his Majesty said so much to any one else." I find there is a graduated scale of great exactness, by which these things are measured with the most minute accuracy. " How d'ye do ?" is a gracious reception; but " How d'ye do ? I am very glad to see you here," is the very acmé of condescension and affability.

STATISTICS.

EUROPEAN POPULATION.—A German periodical *(Hesperus)* contains some very fanciful speculations on the causes which affect population, from which we have selected the following particulars :—The increase and decrease of marriages in a country are naturally influenced by great events, such as peace and war, public prosperity and public calamities, famine and disease; but here, we are told, that political feelings exercise an influence. Thus, in Prussia, the number of marriages was greatly increased after the expulsion of the French. During the years 1817, 1818, and 1819, when the political prospects of that country were in their zenith, 1 person was married in 98; in the subsequent years the numbers again fell to 1 in 108, 1 in 111, and 1 in 118. In France, from the year 1815 to 1822, the number of marriages was much less than before the revolution, although the population was greater by several millions. After 1817 the number of annual marriages increased by about 8,000, and continued stationary at that rate till 1821; but in 1822, after the evacuation of the country by foreign troops, the number quickly rose by 20,000, and, in the ensuing year, even by 40,000. But it again declined during the obnoxious administration of Villele, and again increased after the overthrow of his Ministry. Even in Russia, from 70 to 80,000 couples less than usual were married in 1812. The proportions of deaths among children under five years is also remarkable, as it seems to keep pace with the degree of education and comfort of the in-

---

* Since this was in types, we see the very book we want announced as in the press, to form part of the British Library. It is by Dr. Memes, and from his Life of the Empress Josephine, we trust that of Cowper will be all the admirers of the most amiable of the English poets can desire.

habitants. It is smallest in the large towns, and would be smaller still if it were not for those who die in workhouses and hospitals, deserted by their parents. The degree of fertility of marriages seem to vary between 3,590 and 5,590 children to 1000 couples. The author, from an average of more than 77 millions of births, and 17 millions of marriages, all extending over a period of several years, comes to some results, from which we shall extract two or three of the most interesting. To a thousand marriages there were born in the

Kingdom of the Two Sicilies	5,546 children.
In France	4,148
In England	3,565
In Zealand	3,439

the Two Sicilies and Zealand being the extremes. Marriages appear to be less prolific as the countries lie nearer to the north. A fourth point of importance in these investigations is the growing excess of males over females since the general peace, which, if correctly stated, is not a little alarming, and seems to make a periodical return of war an indispensable evil. Thus, in Russia, the increase of males over females in 15 years, was 804,453; in France, 347,254; in Prussia 69,764; in Naples, 25,796; in Bavaria, 8,398; in Bohemia, 69,172; in Sweden, 15,195; in Wirtemberg, 6,877; in Hesse, 3,361; in Nassau, 6,484:—briefly, in a total population of 101,707,212, an excess of 1,356,754 males. If this proportion be applied to all Europe, with a population of 215 millions, the excess of the males would amount, in the same period of peace, to 2,700,000. In the southern provinces of Russia, near the Caucasus, in the two Americas, and at the Cape of Good Hope, the disproportion is still greater.

WEST INDIA COLONIES.

The following estimate of the value of our West India Colonies is taken from the Report of the Select Committee of the House of Lords, recently published:—

BRITISH COLONIES.

Jamaica	...	...	...	£59,125,298
Barbadoes	...	...	...	9,086,630
Antigua	...	...	...	4,364,000
St Christopher	...	...	...	3,783,800
Nevis	...	...	...	1,750,400
Monserrat	...	...	...	1,087,440
Virgin Islands	...	...	...	1,998,400
Grenada	...	...	...	4,994,365
St Vincent	...	...	...	4,006,866
Dominica	...	...	...	3,056,700
Trinidad	...	...	...	4,932,705
Bahamas	...	...	...	2,043,500
Bermudas	...	...	...	1,111,000
Honduras	...	...	...	578,760
				£100,014,864

CEDED COLONIES.

Demerara and Essequibo	...	...	£18,410,480
Berbice	...	...	...	7,415,160
Tobago	...	...	...	2,682,920
St Lucia	...	...	...	2,529,000
				£31,037,560

So the whole amount is no less than £131,052,424

A GHOST STORY.

One of the best authenticated ghost stories which is on record is connected with the Wesley family. It is of goblin Jeffrey, a familiar sprite, who, for more than thirty years, haunted the rectory of Epworth, of which our readers lately heard in the memoir of Mrs Susanna Wesley, the mother of John Wesley, the Founder of Methodism. Sir David Brewster's late amusing work on Natural Magic, and an elaborate article on the Philosophy of Apparitions, in the *Quarterly Review*, have given ghost stories temporary interest. We have read of goblin *Jeffrey* as he is described by Dr. Clarke, but now give him chiefly from Mr. Dove's late ingenious history of the Wesley family.

"About the end of the year 1715, and the beginning of 1716, there were some *noises* heard in the parsonage house at Epworth, so unaccountable, that every person by whom they were heard, believed them to be supernatural. At the latter end of the year 1716, the maid-servant was terrified, by hearing at the dining-room door, several dismal *groans*, as of a person at the point of death. The family gave little heed to her story, and endeavoured to laugh her out of her fears; but a few nights afterwards they began to hear strange *knockings*, usually three or four at a time, in different parts of the house. Every person heard these noises, except Mr Wesley himself; and as, according to vulgar opinion, such sounds are not heard by the individual to whom they forbode evil, they refrained from telling him, lest he should suppose it betokened his own death, as they all indeed apprehended.

"At length, however, these disturbances became so great and frequent, that few or none of the family durst be left alone; and Mrs Wesley thought it better to inform her husband; for it was not possible that the matter could long be concealed from him; and moreover, as she said, she "was minded he should speak to it." These noises were now various, as well as strange; loud rumblings above stairs or below; a clatter among bottles, as if they had all at once been dashed to pieces; footsteps as of a man going up and down stairs at all hours of the night; sounds like that of dancing in an empty room; *gobbling like a turkey-cock*, but most frequently a knocking about the beds at night, and in different parts of the house. Mrs Wesley would at first have persuaded the children and servants, that it was occasioned by *rats* within doors, and mischievous persons without, and her husband had recourse to the same ready solution; or some of his daughters, he supposed, sat up late and made a noise; and a hint, that their *lovers* might have something to do with the mystery, made the young ladies heartily hope their father might soon be convinced that there was more in the matter than he was disposed to believe.

"In this they were not disappointed, for the next evening, a little after midnight, he was awakened by nine loud and distinct knocks, which seemed to be in the next room, with a pause at every third stroke. He arose, and went to see whether he could discern the cause, but he could perceive nothing; still he thought it might be some person out of doors, and relied upon a stout mastiff to rid them of this nuisance. But the dog, which upon the first disturbance had barked violently, was ever afterwards cowed by it, and seeming more terrified than any of the children, came whining to his master and mistress, as if to seek protection in a human presence. And when the man-servant, Robin Brown, took the mastiff at night into his room, to be at once a guard and a companion, so soon as the latch began to jar, as usual, the dog crept into bed, and barked and howled so as to alarm the house.

"The fears of the family for Mr Wesley's life being removed as soon as he had heard the mysterious noises, they began to apprehend that one of the sons had met with a violent death, and more particularly Samuel, the eldest. The father, therefore, one night, after several deep groans had been heard, adjured it to speak if it had power, and tell him why it troubled the house; and upon this three distinct knockings were heard. He then questioned it, if it were Samuel his son, bidding it, if it were, and could not speak, to knock again; but, to his great comfort, there was no farther knocking that night; and when they heard that Samuel and the two boys were safe and well, the visitations of the goblin became rather a matter of curiosity and amusement, than of alarm. Emilia, one of the daughters, gave it the name of old Jeffrey, and by this name he was known as a harmless, though by no means an agreeable, inmate of the parsonage. Jeffrey was not a malicious goblin, but he was easily offended.

"Before Mrs. Wesley was satisfied that there was something supernatural in the noises, she recollected that one of her neighbours had frightened the rats from his dwelling by blowing a horn. The horn therefore was borrowed, and blown stoutly about the house for half a day, greatly against the judgment of one of her daughters, who maintained, that if it were any thing supernatural, it would certainly be very angry, and more troublesome. Her opinion was verified by the event; Jeffrey had never till then begun his operations during the day; but from that time he came by day, as well as by night, and was louder than before. And he never entered Mr Wesley's study, till the owner one day rebuked him sharply, calling him a deaf and dumb devil, and bade him cease to disturb the innocent children, and come to him in his study, if he had any thing to say.

This was a sort of defiance, and Jeffrey took him at his word. No other person in the family ever felt the goblin but Mr. Wesley, who was thrice pushed by it with considerable force. So he relates, and his evidence is clear and distinct. He says also, that once or twice when he spoke to it, he heard two or three feeble squeaks, a little louder than the chirping of a bird, but not like the noise of rats. What is said of an actual appearance is not so well confirmed. Mrs. Wesley thought she saw something run from under the bed, and said it most resembled a badger, but she could not well say of what shape; and the man saw something like a white rabbit, which came from behind the oven with its ears flat upon the neck, and its little scut standing straight up. A shadow may possibly explain the first of these appearances; the other may be imputed to that proneness, which ignorant persons so commonly evince to exaggerate in all uncommon cases.

"These circumstances, therefore, though apparently silly in themselves, in no degree invalidate the other parts of the story, which rest upon the concurrent testimony of many intelligent witnesses. The door was once violently pushed against Emilia, when there was no person on the outside: the latches were frequently lifted up; the windows clattered always before Jeffrey entered a room, and whatever iron or brass was there, was rung and jarred exceedingly. It was observed also, that the wind commonly rose after any of his noises, and increased with it, and whistled loudly around the house. Mr. Wesley's trencher danced one day upon the table, to his no small amazement; and the handle of Robin's hand mill, at another time, was turned round with great swiftness: unluckily Robert had just done grinding: nothing vexed him, he said, " but that the mill was empty; if there had been corn it, Jeffrey might have ground his heart out before he would have disturbed him.

" It was plainly a Jacobite goblin, and seldom suffered Mr. Wesley to pray for the King, and the Prince of Wales, without disturbing the family prayers. Mr. Wesley was sore upon this subject, and became angry, and therefore repeated the prayer. But when Samuel was informed of this, his remark was, ' as to the devil being an enemy to King George, were I the King, I would rather old Nick should be my enemy than my friend.' The children were the only persons who were distressed by these visitations: the manner in which they were affected is remarkable: when the noises began, they appeared to be frightened in their sleep; a sweat came over them, and they panted and trembled till the disturbance was so loud as to awake them. Before the noises ceased, the family had become quite accustomed to them, and were tired of hearing, or speaking on the subject. ' Send me some news,' said one of the sisters to her brother Samuel, ' for we are secluded from the sight, or hearing of any thing, except Jeffrey.'

" There is a letter in existence from Emilia to her brother John, dated 1750, from which, says Dr. Clarke, it appears ' that Jeffrey continued his operations at least thirty-four years after he retired from Epworth.' We shall give an extract from the letter referred to. ' Dear Brother, I want most sadly to see you, and talk hours with you, as in times past. One reason is, that wonderful thing called by us Jeffrey! You won't laugh at me for being superstitious, if I tell you how certainly that something calls on me against any extraordinary new affliction; but so little is known of the invisible world, that I, at least, am not able to judge whether it be a friendly or an evil spirit.'"

FASHION IN ITS LOW PLACES.

This clever *jeu d'esprit* first appeared in an Irish newspaper. It is a felicitous quiz upon the absurdities which are so often served up in the fashionable Morning Prints, and Court Journals.

SPLENDID FETE AT BALLYGROOGAGH.

Ballygroogagh House, the hospitable mansion of Timothy O'Mulligan, and his lady, was, last month, (Nov. 1821,) graced by the most elegant festivities on the happy return of their eldest son from the north of Europe, where he had been *incognito* in the humble guise of a cook to a whaler.

The principal entrance to the house was most handsomely decorated for the occasion; on one side was seen a heap of manure, shaped like an ancient tumulus, and tastefully ornamented with hanging straws, &c.; on the other side appeared a stagnant pool, whose smooth surface was gently moved by a duck and drake, who muddled through it with uncommon vivacity and spirit; in the perspective was seen a venerable turf-kish, around which a pair of trowsers being carelessly thrown, gave a light and graceful finish to the whole scene.

About two o'clock, the approach of company was proclaimed by the distant clatter of wheel-cars; this deep sound, mingled with the finer tones of cur-dogs barking, whipped children crying, &c. produced a full and mellow volume of the most delightful harmony. The first arrival was that of the dowager Mrs. Fluggins, an eminent *accoucheuse*; she was soon followed by the rest of the expected company, who speedily repaired to a grand rustic saloon, the walls of which were painted *à la soot drop*.

Here a rich and finely-flavoured beverage was handed round in noble wooden vases, which the charming hostess, with bewitching simplicity, denominated *broth* in *noggins*. Dinner was shortly afterwards served up; a *plateaus* was dispensed with, but its place was most tastefully supplied by a fine skate, cooked up in the Turkish fashion, with all its tails; near it a quarter of delicate veal, which had breathed its last sigh after an existence of five hours. On the central dish was placed a male bird, which during a life of nine years, had increased to such a size as to excite the admiration of the whole company. There were many other rarities, such as are seldom to be met with at the most sumptuous tables.

After dinner, some original sentiments and well-selected songs were given, a few of which are the following:—

Mr O'Mulligan.—" A speedy rise to the price of pigs."
Song.—" The night that I put the pig under the pot."
Mr O'Loughlin.—" A merry go-round to the foot organ."
Song.—" The weary pound of tow."
Mr M'Dade.—" The weaver's harpsichord."
Song.—" A weaver boy shall be my dear."

When the pleasures of the festive board were concluded, preparations were made for dancing. The orchestra, an unique of the most simple beauty, was an inverted creel, on which a single minstrel sat, the interest of whose appearance was much heightened by the loss of his left eye. Mr Patrick O'Mullaghan, disliking the monotony of the waltz, and the vagaries of a quadrille, opened the ball by dancing a jigg with Miss Judy Higgins; they were soon followed by Master Charley M'Dade, who floated into a reel with Miss Nancy Fluggins. Dancing was kept up until a late hour, and the elegant revellers parted with mutual regret. We subjoin a description of some of the most admired dresses worn on the occasion, which, from their striking costume, will doubtlessly be the standard for fashionable imitation.

LADIES' DRESSES.

Mrs O'Mullaghan—A loose bedgown robe of linsy woolsy, petticoat to match, two-and-sixpenny shawl thrown with graceful negligence over the shoulder; pincushion and scissars suspended by the right side with red tape. Head-dress, dowd and scull cap.

Miss O'Mullaghan—Round gown of striped calico, habit-shirt embroidered *en goble stitch*. Head-dress, bandalettes of scarlet sixpenny ribband.

Miss Nancy O'Mullaghan—A superb old cotton, dyed

blue for the occasion. Head-dress, crooked horn comb, and splendid brass bodkin.

Dowager Mrs Fluggins—Body and train of snuff-coloured stuff, petticoat of deep crimson; the brilliancy of this truly beautiful dress was increased by a pair of large ticken pockets, worn outside of the petticoat. Head-dress, a most valuable antique straw-bonnet.

Miss Fluggins—A light drapery of plain yellow linen over a a prigged cotton-gown, petticoat gracefully sprinkled with pure-coloured spots. Head-dress large velveteen band, with a mother of pearl *button* in front; black worsted stockings, à *la Carraboo.*

GENTLEMEN'S DRESSES.

Mr O'Mullaghan—A wallicoat of white drugget, deep blue inexpressibles—wig unpowdered.

Mr Patrick O'Mullaghan—Jacket and trousers of blue frieze—cravat blue and white handkerchief.

Mr Gulley—A brown jacket, handsomely patched at the elbows with grey cloth—waist chequer. This gentleman's declining to wear shoes, gave a peculiarly cool and easy freedom to his fine figure.

THE PRESS AND THE THEATRES.

A question is gradually growing up between the press and the theatres, which, we suspect, must ultimately be resolved by the public. The free admission of the press—a privilege sanctioned by custom, and producing to the theatres enormous advantages by way of publicity—has been latterly treated, in some few instances, by managers, as if it were held upon good behaviour, and should be considered dependent upon the favourable character of the criticisms. According to this view it is not a privilege existing for the mutual good of the public and the playhouses, but a bribe given by the manager to the dishonest critic.

Suppose this privilege were entirely abolished, and that the newspapers, offended at its withdrawal, were to cease to notice the theatres, what would be the consequence? Why, two-thirds of the play-going people would lose their interest in theatricals; the stimulus that now make the new play and the favourite actor a common type of conversation, would be at an end; and the fame of the stage, and its nightly doings, would be limited to the uncertain, loose, and capricious gossip of private life. All theatrical managers are well assured of the great power of the newspapers in exciting the curiosity of the public, and they know well enough that one paragraph of original commentary is more valuable to them than a hundred advertisements. If they did not feel this, why should they exhibit such anxiety to oblige the very meanest of those hangers-on at newspaper offices, who have impudence enough to assume the airs of responsibility, and are mean enough to accept favours under false pretences? There is, however, no obligation on the part of the newspaper. The obligation lies entirely on the other side. The newspaper can do without the theatre, but the theatre could not maintain itself without the newspaper.

The managers, however, object to unfavourable criticisms. They are well enough satisfied with the good report, but they do not like to take chance for the evil. There is the whole secret; and the soreness they betray where the shoe pinches in reality proves the importance they attach to criticism, even of the poorest order. Why should a manager be so very angry at occasional severities, if he did not feel the weight of their influence?

Mr. Morris, of the Haymarket, withdrew his order in a pet from an evening paper, because it published a critique, the only fault of which, in our estimation was, that it was too lenient. But how did that affect its tranquillity or reputation? Strange as it may appear, this paper is still alive and flourishing. Other papers have been similarly excluded from other houses, on similar grounds; and a few weeks ago the Athenæum was forbidden the squeezing place at Drury Lane because its criticisms were ill-natured, and because the gentleman who was known as its theatrical critic was said to have been heard to hiss a new opera. Upon the latter charge rather than the former, however, the manager finally rested his decision; yet, although the gentleman distinctly denied the assertion and challenged proofs, it does not appear that the decision has been reversed. A gentleman who is understood to have at his control so powerful a medium for the expression of his opinion as the press, ought not to hiss in a theatre. It is indecorous and in bad taste. But the Athenæum denies the charge, and we are bound to believe it, and to look for the reason of its exclusion to the other clause of the indictment.

The Haymarket management is distinguished for its sensitiveness in this way. We were informed by Mr. Morris that we might have orders whenever we would send to him for them. It is unnecessary to add, that we declined to accept as a favour that which, if it be used at all, should be used as an unshackled privilege. Mr. Morris gives very few orders to the newspapers, and is always reducing the number. He is trying an experiment with his theatre similar to that which the Frenchman tried with his horse—when he has just succeeded in bringing it to live without orders, it is not unlikely that its nights will be numbered. Mr. Price once said, that we wanted to drive an actress off his stage, because we did not happen to esteem her talents as highly as his interests required; and he even intimated something about our admission to his theatre. That sort of ill temper is very foolish, because the criticism, if just, must prevail, and, if unjust, it cannot overcome the force of general opinion. At the Surrey, where the value of an order has been very much lessened of late to the critic, they wished us to consent to an occasional "little disappointment" in our admittance, or, in plainer words, they wanted to make our privilege contingent on their good-will! so that one night we should feel ourselves entitled to the *entree*, and the next we should be turned from the doors.

We mention these trifling illustrations of the progress of a question in which the true interests of the drama are concerned, merely to draw attention to the consideration of the subject. If newspapers are to have the free privilege, they should have it clear of all considerations of a personal or interested nature. To hold it as a sort of fee in hand for services to be rendered, would degrade the office of criticism to the level of the auctioneer who puffs the chattels committed to him for sale. No critic whose intellect was superior to that of a puffing auctioneer, or whose descriptive talents were less marvellous, would consent to sell his powers at so small a rate. It would be better to put an end to free admissions at once than to accept them in this slavish spirit. Newspapers that must, of necessity, incur a large expenditure in other departments of taste, would not object to so petty an outlay as this would occasion. But what would be the result? None but the independent papers would take the trouble of noticing the theatres—the confluence of observation would cease; and integrity alone would remain to chronicle the progress of the stage. What an advantage would hereby be gained to the cause of sound criticism—but what a terrible risk it would be to the managers to lose the hope they now repose in timid and friendly journals.—*Atlas.*

BUONAPARTE'S MAY DAYS.

The month of May seems to have been peculiarly inauspicious to this celebrated character; and the day of his Death was the anniversary of several memorable occurrences in his, "strange eventful history." He who impelled his veteran troops to victory with the cry "Behold the sun of Austerlitz!" was "lighted on his way to dusky death," by the last fading beams of the suns of Madrid, of Almeida, and of Elba.

In the year of his own birth and the month of May, his Conqueror, the Duke of Wellington, first drew breath.

In 1799, May 4. He lost Seringapatam. 21. He was defeated at Acre.

1804, May 18. He assumed the title of Emperor of France. This was perhaps his worst political step.

1808, May 2. After massacring the Spaniards at Madrid, he appointed his brother Joseph King of Spain. 5. He issued his mandate to the Queen of Spain to declare her son illegitimate.

1809, May 12. His troops in Portugal, under Soult, were defeated by Sir Arthur Wellesley. 22. He was defeated by the Archduke Charles.

1811, May 5. His army, under Massena, was repulsed at Almeida. 16. His troops, under Soult, were defeated at Albuera.

1812, May 19. The French forces were defeated at Almarez.

1813, May. The like in Saxony, Lutzen. The 20th, at Bautzen. And the 31st, at Wurtschen.

1814, May 5. He was landed at Elba.

1815, May. During his reign of 100 days he was preparing for his final overthrow on the 18th of June at Waterloo.

1821, May 5. He Died at St. Helena.

EFFECTS OF SLOVENLINESS.
COBBETT.

In my English Grammar, I earnestly exhorted my Son, always to write in a plain hand; because if what you write cannot be understood, you write in vain; and, if the meaning be picked out,—that is to say, come at with difficulty—there is a waste of time; and time is property, and, indeed, a part of life itself. The other day, when I first advertised my Trees for sale, I besought gentlemen to write to me in a plain hand; to write the dates and signatures in a plain hand, at any rate. Here was an affair of proper names, both of persons and places; and there was to be a real proceeding of some consequence to be produced by each letter. In such a case, not to write in a plain hand, was, in effect, voluntarily to incur the risk, and the manifest risk, of not receiving that which was written for. Nevertheless, I received some letters which lay unanswered for a good while, owing to the bad hand writing. One I could by no means make out. The name of the writer was plain enough; but the word which was written as the name of the place was, according to the reading of ten different persons, Lancern. We hunted Gazetteer, Book of Roads, and at last came to the conclusion, that it must be some place in Ireland. Very little of this hunting would have taken place, had not the letter contained some Bank Notes. However, in spite of all our efforts to discover what Lancern meant, we were obliged to give the thing up, and to pocket the Bank Notes for our trouble. Yesterday, however, comes, by the two-penny post, a little blotted note, with a signature to it, which appears to be the name of a post-master; this note begins, by saying, "Sir, Mr ———— of Lancing, Sussex." And then the note goes on to say, that this Mr ———— wrote to me some time ago, enclosing a sum of money, and it concludes thus: "the money was put into our box." The devil of any date was there to this note. But the words 'our box,' I discovered that the writer was a post-master. By the sum of money, I knew that this Lancing was the very Lancern that had so plagued and puzzled us. But, upon again hunting through Gazetteer, Book of Roads, Book of Fairs, &c. &c. we can find no such place as Lancing. Happily, however, we had got the County of Sussex. That word, with two s's in the middle, and an x at the end, made us know what county we had got into, at any rate. We then took the Book of Roads, and went to the towns on the cross roads, under the letter L, stopping to read every word opposite the word Sussex. We soon came to the word Launcing! The Gentleman wished to have some Apple-trees, which he can yet have, by mere accident; but nothing like so fine as those would have been which he would have had, if his letter had been dated in a plain manner. I give this as a practical illustration of the mischievous consequences of slovenliness in writing. But, there is another thing to be well considered; and that is, that nobody pays so much attention to a slovenly as to a neat and plain piece of writing. It is an invariable rule with me to fling into the fire at once any blurred or dirty letter that I receive, and every letter that is written across the writing, let such letter come from whom it may. People that write in this manner are idle people. What they put upon paper is unworthy of occupying the time of any persons not like themselves. This seems, at first sight, to be a very trifling matter; but if we duly reflect on it, we shall find it a matter of considerable importance. At any rate, as I am certain that I never in my lifetime sent a slovenly scrawl to any person whatever, I beseech them who do me the honour to write to me, to write in a hand that will not compel me to waste my time, and expose me to the risk of appearing to be guilty of negligence or ill-manners. To young men I would observe, that slovenliness is no mark of gentility; that amongst their most valuable possessions is their time; and I beg them to consider how large a portion of their time is consumed in deciphering even their own bad writing. The hand-writing is, with me, a great thing. I cannot believe that slovenliness of hand-writing can exist without a general slovenliness in the conducting of affairs. Of this, at any rate, I am certain; and that is, that I never should have done a quarter part of what I have done, if to write a plain hand had not been the constant habit of my life. It has cost many thousands of pounds less to print from my manuscript, than it would have cost to print from the manuscript of almost any other man. Then, again, as to time; hundreds upon hundreds of articles written by me, could not have been printed soon enough, if they had been in manuscript like that of writers in general. Habit has made me write fast and plain at the same time; and every man will have the same habit, if he resolutely persevere in writing plain. To write plain is the great thing; writing fast comes of itself.

The Moving Powers.—When Voltaire said, that "a man hanged is good for nothing," this wise aphorism might be very true in his day, but in this country, we have lived to see many changes, which controvert the dicta of philosophers, and confound even the wisdom of Solomon himself. A dead, or hanged man, at this day, becomes at once, " a good subject," not for the King, but the modern Chirons, who mutilate poor mortality when alive, with so much facility and skill, but value it most, when they can mangle it in death, for the relief of the living. " A hanged man" now, what his proportions, his defects, or even his crimes, is worth L.14, or L.15. Very few living subjects, however honest, and *proper* men, would fetch half that sum.—[Voltaire is right again. The value of a hanged man is again, by the operation of the Anatomy Bill, next to nothing.]

Oxalis Crenata; an Improvement on the Potato.—This plant has lately been introduced into this country from S. America, and is likely to be extensively cultivated, as decidedly preferable to the common potato. A root was brought over, in 1830, by Mr. David Douglas, and planted by Mr. Lambert. A few small tubers were exhibited in the Linnæan Society. One of these was planted by Mrs. Hirst, in the garden of Great Roper's Hall, near Brentwood, and has succeeded remarkably well. It was first put into a small pot in the end of April, and in the month of May the pot was placed in the flower garden, and broken, and the parts removed. This precaution appears to have been unnecessary, for it has stood the frost remarkably well, and on the 5th of this month, when it was dug up, the leaves were green. The root planted was about half an ounce in weight, and the roots produced were about ninety in number, in a space not exceeding nine inches in diameter and six inches deep. The aggregate weight was upwards of four pounds. A few of the roots were boiled, and, when eaten, were found to resemble the potato, but were unanimously admitted by all the party to have a more agreeable flavour. Such a result is very promising, and when we consider that the common potato (*Solanum Tuberosum*) was, for a hundred years, confined to gardens, and that its roots were for a long time not larger than beans, and were watery, we may reasonably expect that cultivation may do much to enlarge the size of the roots of the Oxalis, and perhaps improve the flavour beyond what it is at present. It has a fine yellow flower, and is ornamental in the garden. The time of flowering is August.

Uses of the Potato—Salubrity.—Potatoes appear to be particularly useful in the manufacture of bread, by promoting the fermentation of the dough. To effect this they may be introduced among the flour, after being boiled to a mealy state; but the best method is to employ them as a ferment. For two pecks of flour take from 3 lb. to 4 lb. of mealy potatoes, the former quantity will be enough, if it be preferred. Boil them till they will pulp readily through a colander, and when lukewarm add to the pulp *one-fourth* of the barm (*yeast*) which would have been used without potatoes. The pulp, if too dry, should be brought to the consistence of thin paste by addition of milkwarm water, and a table spoonful or two of moist sugar or honey will promote the process; cover the mixture with a plate or cloth, and let it stand near the fire till a strong frothy head arises. This potato yeast should be blended with about a twelfth or sixteenth part of the flour, to work as 'sponge' in the centre of the mass, in order to secure the fermentation of the whole. Some bakers, I have been credibly informed, have given two guineas for a receipt to prepare potato yeast; and it is considered so effectual in promoting fermentation, that the misfortune of a 'sad' (heavy) batch is seldom incurred when it is used. It is said by some who ought to know the fact, that bread, worked with a due proportion of potatoes, is at least two shades whiter in colour, and of much better texture, than when it is wrought with the yeast of beer only; to which it may be added, that the bitter taste frequently communicated by such yeast is wholly obviated, and the ferment can be employed liberally, with almost certainty of a corresponding good result.

COLUMN FOR THE LADIES.

SKETCHES OF NATURAL HISTORY.
THE COQUETTE.

"A *Psyco*logical curiosity."—*D'Israeli, Jun.*

The above-quoted authority proves that the Coquette is of the butterfly species, for, when deprived of its ephemeral blandishments, it appears in its pristine deformity. The insect is of French origin, and although abundant quantities of the animal exist in this country, retains its Gallic cognomen. The only literal translation of its name into English is rendered in the word "Man-trap."

The education of the Coquette is usually derived from boarding-schools, and its sentiment from song-books. It learns precepts of morality from novels, and examples of virtue from waiting-maids; and the only evidence it shows of possessing the power of reasoning is the ingenuity with which it special-pleads out of broken vows. *If* it have a heart, that is like the Public Ledger, "open to all parties and influenced by none."

At Church it ogles under smart bonnets, and attracts general attention from its gaudy attire, while, at the theatre, it becomes the focus of every opera glass, on account of its levity.

This insect is carnivorous, feeding upon the human heart as spiders do upon flies. It spreads the net of insinuation and encouragement, inveigles its victim into the web, and makes a boast and glory of the agonies it may cause.

Its ideas are singularly confused about the monosyllables "Yes," and "No," frequently substituting the one for the other, so that it loses all chances of matrimony, and it is to be anticipated that to this fact and the general contempt into which the race is gradually falling, the Coquette population will decrease in a Malthusian ratio.

Maids and Widows; if you wish to arrive at that "consummation devoutly to be wished," good husbands, eschew coquetry; and ye, O! Wives, who have already got them, be not Coquettes lest they flee from ye!

HINTS FOR WIVES.—Obedience is a very small part of conjugial duty, and, in most cases easily performed. Much of the comfort of the married life depends upon the lady; a great deal more, perhaps, than she is aware of. She scarcely knows her own influence; how much she may do by persuasion—how much by sympathy—how much by unremitted kindness and little attentions. To acquire and retain such influence, she must, however, make her conjugal duties her first object. She must not think that any thing will do for her husband—that any wine is good enough for her husband—that it is not worth while to be agreeable when there is only her husband—that she may close her piano, or lay aside her brush, for why should she play or paint merely to amuse her husband? No, she must consider all these little arts of pleasing chiefly valuable on his account—as means of perpetuating her attractions, and giving permanence to his affection. She must remember that her duty consists not so much in great and solitary acts—in displays of sublime virtues to which she will only be occasionally called; but in trifles—in a cheerful smile, or a minute attention naturally rendered, and proceeding, from a heart full of kindness, and a temper full of amiability.—*Mrs. Sandford's Woman in her Social and Domestic Character.*

WOMAN.

Call woman—angel—goddess—what you will?
 With all that fancy breathes at passion's call,
With all that rapture fondly raves, and still
 That one word, *wife*, outvies, contains them all!
It is a word of music, which can fill
 The soul with melody, when sorrows fall
Round us like darkness, and her heart alone
Is all that fate has left to call our own.

Her bosom is a fount of love that swells,
 Widens, and deepens with its own outpouring;
And like a desert spring, for ever wells
 Around her husband's heart, when cares devouring
Dry up its very blood, and man rebels
 Against his being!—When despair is lowering,
And ills sweep round him, like an angry river,
She is his star, his rock of hope for ever.

Yea, woman only knows what 'tis to mourn,
 She only feels how slow the moments glide,
Ere those her young heart loved in joy return,
 And breathe affection, smiling by her side.
Hers only are the tears that waste and burn—
 The anxious watchings—and affection's tide
That never, never ebbs!—hers are the cares
No ear hath heard, and which no bosom shares.

Cares—like her spirit, delicate as light
 Trembling at early dawn from morning stars.
Cares—all unknown to feeling and to sight
 Of rougher man, whose stormy bosom wars
With every passion in its fiery might,
 Nor deems how look unkind, or absence, jars
Affection's silver chords by woman wove,
Whose soul, whose business, and whose life is *love.*

J. M. W.

[These verses are taken from a neat volume published at Haddington, entitled, AUTUMN LEAVES, and full of pleasing tales, sketches, and verses.]

Why, why, are the Irish a rebellious people? This is a question that must be solved by the Episcopacy of that devoted Country. Why, why, is the produce of the English farmer reduced in value? Let the annexed statement show; let it shew that, to support the Irish Established Church, as well as to maintain the luxuries of *Absentee Landlords*, the poor Irish producer is *obliged to force* a sale in this country, by *underselling* the English farmer.

An Account of Wheat, Barley, Oats and Flour, imported from Foreign Ports, within ten years, from 1821 to 1830; both inclusive.	An Account of Wheat, Barley, Oats, and Flour, imported from Ireland, in the same period:
Qrs.	Qrs.
Wheat 5,073,429	Wheat 3,419,871
Barley 1,558,407	Barley 761,027
Oats 5,212,509	Oats 12,020,258
Total 11,844,345	Ireland 16,201,156
Cwts. of Flour 1,921,066	The World 11,844,345
	4,356,811
	Ireland,
	Cwts. of Flour 4,158,767
	The World 1,921,066
	2,237,701

By which it appears, that *starving* Ireland has exported to Great Britain in ten years, 4,356,811 quarters of corn and 2,137,701 cwts of flour, more than all the other ports of the world!!!!!—*Mark Lane Express.*

THE STORY-TELLER.

TUBBER DERG, OR THE RED WELL.
(Concluded from last Number.)

The misfortunes of Owen and his family were not the consequences of negligence or misconduct on their own part. They struggled long but unavailingly against high rents and low markets; against neglect on the part of the landlord and his agent; against sickness, famine, and death. They had no alternative but to beg or starve. Owen was willing to work, but he could not procure employment, and provided he could, the miserable sum of sixpence a-day, when food was scarce and dear, would not support him, his wife, and six little ones. He became a pauper, therefore, only to avoid starvation.

Heavy and black was his heart, to use the strong expression of the people, on the bitter morning when he set out to encounter the dismal task of seeking alms in order to keep life in himself and his family. The plan was devised on the preceding night; but to no mortal, except his wife, was it communicated. The honest pride of a man whose mind was above committing a mean action, would not permit him to reveal what he considered the first stain that ever was known to rest upon the name of M'Carthy. He therefore sallied out under the beating of the storm, and proceeded, without caring much whither he went, until he got considerably beyond the bounds of his own parish.

In the meantime hunger pressed keenly upon him and them. The day had no appearance of clearing up; the heavy rain and sleet beat into their thin, worn garments, and the clamour of his children for food, began to grow more and more importunate. They came to the shelter of a hedge which enclosed on one side a remote and broken road, along which, in order to avoid the risk of being recognised, they had preferred travelling. Owen stood here for a few minutes to consult with his wife, as to where and when they should "make a beginning;" but on looking round, he found her in tears.

"Kathleen, asthore," said Owen, "I can't bid you not to cry; bear up, acushla machree; bear up: sure, as I said when we came out this mornin', there's a good God above us, that can still turn over the good lafe for us, if we put our hopes in him."

"Owen," said his sinking wife; "it's not altogether bekase we'er brought to this, that I'm cryin. No indeed."

"Thin, what ails you, Kathleen, darlin?"

The wife hesitated, and evaded the question for some time; but at length, upon his pressing her for an answer, with a fresh gush of sorrow, she replied,

"Owen, since you *must* know—och, may God pity us!—since you must know, its wid hunger—*wid hunger!* I kept unknownst, a little bit of bread to give the childre this mornin', an' that was part of it I gave you yesterday early—I'm near two days fastin."

"Kathleen! Kathleen! Och! sure I know your worth, avillish. You were too good a wife, an' too good a mother, amost! God forgive me, Kathleen! I fretted about beggin', dear; but as my Heavenly Father's above me, I'm now happier to beg wid you by my side, nor if I war in the best house in the province widout you! Hould up, avourneen, for a while. Come on, childhre, darlins, an' the first house we meet we'll ax their char———, their assistance. Come on, darlins, all of yees. Why, my heart's asier, so it is. Sure we have your mother, childhre, safe wid us, an' what signifies any thing so long as *she's* left to us."

He then raised his wife tenderly, for she had been compelled to sit from weakness, and they bent their steps to a decent farm-house, that stood a few perches off the road, about a quarter of a mile before them.

As they approached the door, the husband hesitated a moment; his face got paler than usual, and his lip quivered, as he said—"Kathleen—"

"I know what you're goin' to say, Owen. No, acushla, you won't; *I'll* ax it myself."

"Do," said Owen, with difficulty; "I can't do it; but I'll overcome my pride afore long, I hope. It's thryin' to me, Kathleen, an' you know it is—for you know how little I ever expected to be brought to this."

"Husht, avillish! We'll thry, then, in the name o' God."

As she spoke, the children, herself, and her husband, entered, to beg for the first time in their lives a morsel of food. Yes! timidly—with a blush of shame, red even to crimson, upon the pallid features of Kathleen—with grief acute and piercing—they entered the house together.

For some minutes they stood and spoke not. The unhappy woman, unaccustomed to the language of supplication, scarcely knew in what terms to crave assistance. Owen, himself, stood back, uncovered, his fine but much changed features overcast with an expression of deep affliction. Kathleen cast a single glance at him as if for encouragement. Their eyes met; she saw the upright man—the last remnant of the M'Carthy—himself once the friend of the poor, of the unhappy, of the afflicted—standing crushed and broken down by misfortunes which he had not deserved, waiting with patience for a morsel of charity. Owen, too, had *his* remembrances. He recollected the days when he sought and gained the pure and fond affections of his Kathleen; when beauty, and youth, and innocence encircled her with their light and their grace, as she spoke or moved; he saw her a happy wife and mother in her own home, kind and benevolent to all who required her good word or her good office; and now she was homeless. He remembered, too, how she used to plead with himself for the afflicted. It was but a moment; yet when their eyes met, that moment was crowded by remembrances that flashed across their minds with a keen sense of a lot so bitter and wretched as theirs. Kathleen could not speak, although she tried; her sobs denied her utterance; and Owen involuntarily sat upon a chair, and covered his face with his hand.

To an observing eye, it is never difficult to detect the cant of imposture, or to perceive distress when it is real. The good woman of the house, as is usual in Ireland, was in the act of approaching them, unsolicited, with a double handful of meal—that is what the Scotch and northern Irish call a *gowpen*—or as much as both hands locked together can contain—when, noticing their distress, she paused a moment, eyed them more closely, and exclaimed—

"What's this? Why there's something wrong wid you, good people! But first an' foremost take this, in the name an' honour of God."

"May the blessin' of the same Man* rest upon yees!" replied Kathleen. "This is a sorrowful thrial to us; for it's our first day to be upon the world; an' this is the first help of the kind we ever axed for, or ever got; an' indeed now I find we haven't even a place to carry it in. I've no —b—b—cloth, or any thing to hould it."

---

* God is sometimes thus termed in Ireland. By "Man" here is meant person or being. He is also called the "Man above," although this must have been intended for, and often is applied, to Christ only.

"Your first, is it?" said the good woman. "Your first! May the marciful Queen o' Heaven look down upon yees, but it's a bitther day yees war driven out on! Sit down, there, you poor crathur. God pity you, I pray this day, for you *have* a heart-broken look! Sit down awhile, near the fire, you an' the childre! Och, Oh! but it's a thousand pities to see sich fine childre—handsome an good lookin', even as they are, brought to this! Come over, good man; get near the fire, for ye'er wet an' could all of yees. Brian, *ludher* them two lazy thieves o' dogs out o' that. *Eires suas, a wadhee bradadh, agus go mah a shin!*—be off wid yees, ye lazy divil that's not worth you feedin'! Come over, honest man."

Owen and his family were placed near the fire; the poor man's heart was full, and he sighed heavily.

"May he that it plased to thry us," he exclaimed, "reward you for this! We are," he continued, "a poor an' a sufferin' family; but it's the will of God that we should be so, an' sure we can't complain widout committin' sin. All we ax now is, that it may be plasin' to Him that brought us low, to enable us to bear up undher our thrials. We would take it to our choice to beg and be honest, sooner nor to be wealthy an' wicked! We have our failins an' our sins, God help us; but still there's nothin' dark or heavy on our consciences. Glory be to the name o' God for it.

"Throth, I believe you," replied the farmer's wife; "there's thruth an' honesty in your face; one may easily see the remains of dacency about yees all. Musha, throw your little things aside, an' stay where yees are to-day: you can't bring out the childhre undher the teem of rain and sleet that's in it. Wurrah dheelish, but it's the bitther day all out! Faix, Paddy will get a dhrookin, so he will, at that weary fair wid the stirks, poor bouchal—a son of ours that's gone to Ballyboulteen to sell some cattle, an' he'll not be worth three hapuns afore he comes back. I hope he'll have sinse to go into some house, when he's done, an' dhry himself well, any how, besides takin' somethin' to keep out the could. Put by your things, an' don't think of goin' out sich a day."

"We thank you," replied Owen. "Indeed we're glad to stay undher your roof; for, poor things, they're badly able to thravel sich a day—these childhre."

"Musha, yees ate no breakfast, maybe?"

"Owen and his family were silent. The children looked wistfully at their parents, anxious that they should confirm what the good woman, surmised; the father looked again at his famished brood and his sinking wife, and nature overcame him.

"Food did not crass our lips this day," replied Owen; "an' I may say hardly any thing yesterday."

"Oh, blessed Mother! Here, Katty Murray, drop scrubbin' that dresser, an' put down the midlin' pot for stirabout. Be livin' *manim an diouol*, woman alive, handle yourself; you might a had it boilin' by this. God presarve us!—to be two days widout atin! Be the crass, Katty, i you're not alive, I'll give you a douse o' the churnstaff that'll bring the fire to your eyes! Do you hear me?"

"I do hear you, an' did often feel you, too, for fraid hearin' wouldn't do. You think there is no place in the world but your own, I b'lieve. Faix, indeed! Its well come up wid us, to be randied about wid no less a switch than a churnstaff!"

"Is it givin' back talk you are? Bad end to me, if you look crucked but I'll lave you a mark to remimber me by. What woman 'ud put up wid you but myself, you chikasin' flipe? It wasn't to give me your bad tongue I hired you, but to do your business; an' be the crass above us. If you turn your tongue on me again, I'll give you the weight o' the churnstaff. Is it bekase they're poor people that i plased God to bring to this, that you turn up your nose an doin' any thing to sarve them? There's not wather enough there, I say—put in more. What signifies all the stisabout that 'ud make? Put plinty in; it's better always to have too much than too little. Faix, I tell you, you'll want a male's meat an' a night's lodgin' afore you die, if you don't mend your manners."

"Och, musha, the poor girl is doin' her best," observed Kathleen; "an' I'm sure she wouldn't be guilty of usin' pride to the likes of us, or to any one that the Lord has laid his hand upon."

"She had better not, while I'm to the fore," said her mistress. "What is she herself? Sure if it was a sin to be poor, God help the world. No; it's neither a sin nor a shame."

"Thanks be to God, no," said Owen; "it's neither the one nor the other. So long as we keep a fair name, an' a clear conscience, we can't ever say that our case is hard."

After some farther conversation, a comfortable breakfast was prepared for them, of which they partook with an appetite sharpened by their long abstinence from food. Their stay here was particularly fortunate, for as they were certain of a cordial welcome, and an abundance of that which they much wanted—wholesome food—the pressure of immediate distress was removed. They had time to think more accurately upon the little preparations for misery which were necessary, and as the day's leisure was at their disposal, Kathleen's needle and scissars were industriously plied in mending the tattered clothes of her husband and her children, in order to meet the inclemency of the weather.

After being kindly entertained in this hospitable place, the new-made paupers resumed their march.

It is not our intention to trace Owen M'Carthy and his wife through all the variety which a wandering pauper's life affords. He never could reconcile himself to the habits of a mendicant. His honest pride and integrity of heart raised him above it; neither did he sink into the whine and cant of imposture, nor the slang of knavery. No; there was a touch of manly sorrow about him, which neither time, nor familiarity with his degraded mode of life, could take away from him. His usual observation to his wife, and he never made it without a pang of intense bitterness, was—"Kathleen, darlin', it's thrue we have enough to ate an' to dhrink; but *we have no home!—no home!*" To a man like him it was a thought of surpassing bitterness, indeed.

"Ah! Kathleen," he would observe, "if we had but the poorest shed that could be built, provided it was our own, wouldn't we be happy? The bread we ate, avourneen, doesn't do us good. We don't work for it; it's the bread of shame and idleness; and yet it's Owen M'Carthy that ates it! But, avourneen, that's past; an' we'll never see our own home, or our own hearth agin. That's what's cuttin' into my heart, Kathleen. Never!—never!"

Many a trial, too, of another kind was his patience called upon to sustain; particularly from the wealthy and the more elevated in life, when his inexperience as a mendicant led him to solicit their assistance.

"Begone, Sirrah, off my grounds!" one would say. "Why don't you work, you sturdy impostor," another would exclaim, "rather than stroll about lazily, training your brats to the gallows?" "You should be taken up, fellow, as a vagrant," a third would observe; "and if I ever catch you coming up my avenue again, depend upon it, I will slip my dogs at you and your idle spawn."

Owen, on these occasions, turned away in silence: he did not curse them; but the pangs of his honest heart went before Him who will, sooner or later, visit upon the heads of such men their cruel spurning and neglect of the poor.

"Kathleen," he observed to his wife, one day, about a year or more after they had begun to beg; "Kathleen, I have been turnin' it in my mind, that some of these childhre might sthrive to earn their bit an' sup, an' their little coverin' of clo'es, poor things. We might put them to herd cows in the summer, an' the *girshas* to somethin' else in the farmer's houses. What do you think, asthore?"

"For God's sake do, Owen; sure my heart's crushed to see them—my own childhre, that I could lay down my life for—begging from door to door. Och, do something for them that way, Owen, an' you'll relieve the heart that loves them. It's a sore sight to a mother's eye, Owen, to see her childhre beggin' their morsel."

"It is, darlin—it is; we'll hire out the three eldest,—Brian an' Owen, an' Pether, to herd cows; an' we may get Peggy into some farmer's house to do loose jobs an' run of messages. Then we'd have only little Kathleen an' poor Ned along wid us. I'll thry any way, an' if I can get them places, who knows what may happen? I have a plan in my head that I'll tell you, thin."

"Arrah, what is it, Owen jewel? Sure if I know it maybe when I'm sorrowful, that thinkin' of it, an' lookin' forrid to it will make me happier. An' I'm sure, acushla, you would like that."

"But, maybe, Kathleen, if it wouldn't come to pass, that the disappointment 'ud be heavy on you?"

"How could it, Owen? Sure we can't be worse nor we' are, whatever happens?"

"Thrue enough indeed, I forgot that; an' yet we might, Kathleen. Sure we'd be worse, if we or the childhre had bad health."

"God forgive me thin, for what I said! We might be worse. Well, but what is the plan, Owen?"

"Why, when we get the childhre places, I'll sthrive to take a little house, an' work as a cottar. Then, Kathleen, '*we'd have a home of our own.*' I'd work from light to light; I'd work before hours an afther hours; ay, nine days in the week, or we'd be comfortable in our own little home. We might be poor, Kathleen, I know that, an' hard pressed, too; but then, as I said, we'd have our own home, an' our own hearth; our morsel, if it 'ud be homely, would be sweet, for it would be the fruits of our own labour."

"Now, Owen, do you think you could manage to get that?"

"Wait, acushla, till we get the childhre settled. Then I'll thry the other plan, for it's good to thry any thing that could take us out of this disgraceful life."

This humble speculation was a source of great comfort to them. Many a time have they forgotten their sorrows in contemplating the simple picture of their happy little cottage. Kathleen, in particular, drew, with all the vivid colouring of a tender mother, and an affectionate wife, the various sources of comfort and contentment to be found even in a cabin, whose inmates are blessed with a love of independence, industry, and mutual affection.

Owen, in pursuance of his intention, did not neglect, when the proper season arrived, to place out his eldest children among the farmers. The reader need not be told that there was that about him which gained respect. He had, therefore, little trouble in obtaining his wishes on this point, and to his great satisfaction, he saw three of them hired out to earn their own support.

It was now a matter of some difficulty for him to take a cabin and get employment. They had not a single article of furniture, and neither bed nor bedding, with the exception of blankets almost worn past use. He was resolved, however, to give up, at all risks, the life of a mendicant. For this purpose, he and the wife agreed to adopt a plan quite usual in Ireland, under circumstances somewhat different from his: this was, that Kathleen should continue to beg for their support, until the first half-year of their children's service should expire; and in the mean time, that he, if possible, should secure employment for himself. By this means, his earnings, and that of his children, might remain untouched, so that in half a year, he calculated upon being able to furnish a cabin, and proceed, as a cottier, to work for, and support his young children and his wife, who determined, on her part, not to be idle any more than her husband. As the plan was a likely one, and as Owen was bent on earning his bread, rather than be a burthen to others, it is unnecessary to say that it succeeded. In less than a year he found himself once more in a home, and the force of what he felt on sitting, for the first time since his pauperism, at his own hearth, may easily be conceived by the reader. For some years after this, Owen got on slowly enough; his wages as a daily labourer, being so miserable, that it required him to exert every nerve to keep the house over their head. What, however, will not carefulness and a virtuous determination, joined to indefatigable industry, do?

After some time, backed as he was by his wife, and even by his youngest children, he found himself beginning to improve. In the mornings and the evenings he cultivated his garden and his rood of potato ground. He also collected with a wheelbarrow, which he borrowed from an acquaintance, compost from the neighbouring road; scoured an old drain before his door; dug rich earth, and tossed it into the pool of rotten water beside the house, and in fact, adopted several other modes of collecting manure. By this means, he had, each Spring, a large portion of rich stuff on which to plant his potatoes. His landlord permitted him to spread this for planting upon his land; and Owen, ere long, instead of a rood, was able to plant half an acre, and ultimately, an acre of potatoes. The produce of this being more than sufficient for the consumption of his family, he sold the surplus, and with the money gained by the sale, was enabled to sow half an acre of oats, of which, when made into meal, he disposed of the greater share.

Industry is capital; for even when unaided by capital it creates it; whereas, idleness with capital, produces only poverty and ruin.

We cannot follow the gradual rise of this virtuous family by slow and sure degrees; but we will take Owen's return home.

When Owen once more found himself independent and safe, he longed to realize two plans on which he had for some time before been seriously thinking. The first was to visit his former neighbours, that they might at length know that Owen M'Carthy's station in the world was such as became his character. The second was, if possible, to take a farm in his native parish, that he might close his days among the companions of his youth, and the friends of his maturer years. He had, also, another motive; there lay the burying place of the M'Carthys, in which slept the mouldering dust of his own "golden haired" Alley. With them—in his daughter's grave—he intended to sleep his long sleep. Affection for the dead is the memory of the heart. In no other grave-yard could he reconcile it to himself to be buried; to it had all his forefathers been gathered; and though calamity had separated him from the scenes where they had passed through existence, yet he was resolved that death should not deprive him of its last melancholy consolation;—that of reposing with all that remained of the "departed," who had loved him, and whom he had loved. He believed, that to neglect this, would be to abandon a sacred duty, and felt sorrow at the thought of being like an absent guest from the assembly of *his own* dead; for there is a principle of undying hope in the heart, that carries, with bold and beautiful imagery, the realities of life into the silent recesses of death itself.

Having formed the resolution of visiting his old friends at Tubber Derg, he communicated it to Kathleen and his family; his wife received the intelligence with undisguised delight.

"But whin do you mane to go to Tubber Derg, Owen?"

"In the beginnin' of the next week. An' Kathleen, ahagur, if you remember the bitther mornin' we came upon the world—but we'll not be spakin' of that now. I don't like to think of it. Some other time, maybe, when we're settled among our onld friends, I'll mintion it."

"Well, the Lord bliss your endayvours, any how! Och, Owen, do thry an' get us a snug farm somewhere near them. But you didn't answer me about Alley, Owen?"

"Why, you must have your wish, Kathleen; although I intended to keep that place for myself. Still we can sleep one on aich side of her; an' that may be asily done, for our buryin' ground is large: so set your mind at rest on that head. I hope God won't call us till we see our childhre settled dacently in the world. But sure, at all evints, let His blissed will be done!"

"Amin! amin! It's not right of any one to keep their hearts fixed too much upon the world; nor even, they say, upon one's own childhre."

"People may love their childhre as much as as they plase, Kathleen, if they don't let their *grah* for them spoil the crathurs, by givin' them their own will, till they become head-strong an' over-bearin'. Now, let my linen be as white a s bone before Monday, plase goodness; I hope, by that time, that Jack Dogherty will have my new clo'se made; for I intind to go as dacent as ever they seen me in my best days."

"An' so you will, too, avillish. Throth, Owen, it's you that'll be the proud man, steppin' in to them in all your grandeur! Ha, ha, ha! The spirit o' the M'Carthys is in you still, Owen."

Ha, ha, ha! It is, darlin'; it is indeed; an' I'd be sorry it wasn't. I long to see poor Widow Murray. I dunna is her son, Jemmy, married. Who knows, after all we suffered, but I may be able to help her yet?—that is, if she stands in need of it. But, I suppose, her childhre's grown up now, an' able to assist her. Now, Kathleen, mind Monday next; an' have every thing ready. I'll stay a week or so, at the most, an' afther that I'll have news for you about all o' them."

When Monday morning arrived, Owen found himself ready to set out for Tubber Derg. The tailor had not disappointed him; and Kathleen, to do her justice, took care that the proofs of her good housewifery should be apparent in the whiteness of his linen. After breakfast, he dressed himself in all his finery; and it would be difficult to say whether the harmless vanity that peeped out occasionally from his simplicity of character, or the open and undisguised triumph of his faithful wife, whose eye rested on him with pride and affection, was most calculated to produce a smile.

"Now, Kathleen," said he, when preparing for his immediate departure, "I'm thinkin' of what they'll say, when they see me so smooth an' warm lookin'. I'll engage they'll be axin one another, 'Musha, how did Owen M'Carthy get an, at all, to be so well to do in the world, as he appears to be, afther failin' on his ould farm?'"

"Well, but Owen, you know how to manage them."

"Throth, I do that. But there's *one* thing they'll never get out o' me, any way."

"You won't tell *that* to any o' them, Owen?"

"Kathleen, if I thought they only suspected it, I'd never show my face in Tubber Derg agin. I think I could bear to be—an' yet it 'ud be a hard struggle wid me, too—but I *think* I could bear to be buried among black strangers, rather than it should be said, over my grave, among my own, 'there's where Owen M'Carthy lies—who was the only man, of his name, that ever begged his morsel on the king's highway. There he lies, the descindant of the great M'Carthy Mores, an' yet he was a beggar.' I know, Kathleen achora, it's neither a sin nor a shame to ax one's bit from our fellow-creatures, whin fairly brought to it, widout any fault of our own; but still I feel something in me, that can't bear to think of it widout shame an' heaviness of heart."

"Well, it's one comfort, that nobody knows it but our selves. The poor childhre, for their own sakes, won't ever breathe it; so that it's likely the secret 'ill be berried wid us."

* * * * * * * *

The sun had now risen, and as Owen ascended the larger of the two hills which we have mentioned, he stood again to view the scene that stretched beneath him. About an hour before all was still; the whole country lay motionless, as if the land had been a land of the dead. The mountains, in the distance, were covered with the thin mists of morning; the milder and richer parts of the landscape had appeared in that dim grey distinctness which gives to distant objects such a clear outline. With the exception of the blackbird's song, every thing seemed as if stricken into silence; there was not a breeze stirring; both animate and inanimate nature reposed as if in a trance; the very trees appeared asleep, and their leaves motionless, as if they had been of marble. But now the scene was changed. The sun had flung his splendour upon the mountain-tops, from which the mists were tumbling in broken fragments to the vallies between them. A thousand birds poured their songs upon the ear; the breeze was up, and the columns of smoke from the farm-houses and cottages played, as if in frolic, in the air. A white haze was beginning to rise from the meadows; early teams were afoot; and labourers going abroad to their employment. The lakes in the distance shone like mirrors; and the clear springs on the mountain sides glittered in the sun, like gems which the eye could scarcely rest. Life, and light, and motion, appear to be inseparable. The dew of morning upon nature like a brilliant veil, realizing the beautiful image of Horace, as applied to woman :

"Vultus nimium lubricus aspici."

By and by the songs of the early workmen were heard; ture had awoke; and Owen, whose heart was strongly, ough unconsciously, alive to the influence of natural ligion, participated in the general elevation of the hour, id sought, with freshened spirits, the house of his entertainer.

As he entered this hospitable roof, the early industry of his iend's wife presented him with a well-swept hearth and a easant fire, before which had been placed the identical hair that they had appropriated to his own use. Frank as enjoying "a blast o' the pipe," after having risen; to hich luxury the return of Owen gave additional zest and lacidity. In fact, Owen's presence communicated a holiay spirit to the family; a spirit, too, which declined not or a moment during the period of his visit.

Owen, as we said, was prompt in following up his determinations. After breakfast they saw the Agent and his ather, for both lived together. Old Rogerson had been intimately acquainted with the M'Carthys, and, as Frank had inticipated, used his influence with the Agent in procuring or the son of his old friend and acquaintance the farm which he sought.

"Jack," said the old gentleman, "you don't probably know the history and character of the Tubber Derg MacCarthys so well as I do. No man ever required the written bond of a M'Carthy; and it was said of them, and is said still, that the widow and orphan, the poor man or the stranger, never sought their assistance in vain. I, myself, will go security, if necessary, for Owen M'Carthy."

"Sir," replied Owen, "I'm thankful to you; I'm grateful to you. But I wouldn't take the farm, or bid for it at all, unless I could bring forrid enough to stock it as I wish, an' to lay in all that's wantin' to work it well. It 'ud be useless for me to take it—to struggle a year or two —impoverish the land—an' thin run away out of it. No, no; I have what'll put me upon it wid dacency an' comfort."

"Then, since my father has taken such an interest in you, M'Carthy, you must have the farm. We shall get leases prepared, and the business completed, in a few days; for I go to Dublin on this day week. Father, I now remember the character of this family; and I remember, too, the sympathy which was felt for one of them who was harshly ejected, about seventeen or eighteen years ago, out of the lands on which his forefathers had lived, I understand, for centuries."

"I am that man, Sir," returned Owen. "It's too long a story to tell now; but it was only out o' *part* of the lands, Sir, that I was put. What I held was but a poor patch compared to what the family held in my grandfather's time. A great part of it went out of our hands at his death."

"It was very kind of you, Misther Rogerson, to offer to go security for him," said Frank; "but if security was wantin', Sir, I'd not be willin' to let any body but myself back him. I'd go all I'm worth in the world—an', be my sowl, double as much—for the same man."

"I know that, Frank, an' I thank you; but I could put security in Mr. Rogerson's hands here, if it was wanted. Good mornin', an' thank you both, gintlemen. To tell yees the truth," he added, with a smile, "I long to be among my ould friends—manin' the people, an' the hills an' the green fields of Tubber Derg—agin; an', thanks be to Goodness, sure I will soon."

In fact, wherever Owen went, within the bounds of his native parish, his name, to use a significant phrase of the people, was before him. His arrival at Frank Farrel's was now generally known by all his acquaintances, and the numbers who came to see him were almost beyond belief. During the two or three successive days, he went among his old "*croniens*;" and no sooner was his arrival at any particular house intimated, than the neighbours all flocked to him. Sithes were left idle, spades were stuck in the earth, and work neglected for the time being; all crowded about him with a warm and friendly interest, not proceeding from idle curiosity, but from affection and respect for the man.

Owen had no sense of enjoyment when not participated in by his beloved Kathleen. If he felt sorrow, it was less as a personal feeling than as a calamity to her. If he experienced happiness, it was doubly sweet to him as reflected from his Kathleen. All this was mutual between them. Kathleen loved Owen precisely as he loved Kathleen. Nor let our readers suppose, that such characters are not in humble life. It is in humble life, where the springs of feeling are not corrupted by dissimulation and evil knowledge, that the purest, and tenderest, and strongest virtues are to be found.

As Owen approached his home, he could not avoid contrasting the circumstances of his return *now* with those under which, almost broken-hearted after his journey to Dublin, he presented himself to his sorrowing and bereaved wife about sixteen years before. He raised his hat, and thanked God for the success which had, since that period, attended him, and, immediately after his silent thanksgiving, entered the house.

His welcome, our readers may be assured, was tender and affectionate. The whole family gathered about him, and, on his informing them that they were once more about to reside on a farm adjoining to their beloved Tubber Derg, Kathleen's countenance brightened, and the tear of delight gushed to her eyes.

"God be praised, Owen," she exclaimed; "we will have the ould place afore our eyes, an what is betther, we will be near where Alley is lyin'."

There is little more to be said. Sorrow was soon succeeded by cheerfulness and the glow of expected pleasure, which is ever the more delightful as the pleasure is pure. In about a week their old neighbours, with their carts and cars, arrived; and before the day was closed on which Owen removed to his new residence, he found himself once more sitting at his own hearth, among the friends of his youth, and the companions of his maturer years. Ere a twelvemonth elapsed, he had his house perfectly white, and as nearly resembling that of Tubber Derg in its better days as possible. About two years ago we saw him one evening in the month of June, as he sat on a bench beside his door, singing with a happy heart his favourite song of "*Colleen dhas creotha na mo.*" It was about an hour before sunset. The house stood on a gentle eminence, beneath which a sweep of green meadow stretched away to the skirts of Tubber Derg. Around him was a country naturally fertile, and, in spite of the national depression, still beautiful to contemplate. Kathleen and two servant maids were milking, and the whole family were assembled out the door.

"Well, childhre," said the father, "didn't I tell yees the bitther mornin' we left Tubber Derg, not to cry or be disheartened—that 'there was a good God above, who might do somethin' for us yet?' I never *did* give up my trust in Him, an' I never *will*. You see, afther all our little throubles, he has wanst more broug't us together, an' made us happy. Praise an' glory to His name!"

I looked at him as he spoke. He had raised his eyes to heaven, and a gleam of elevated devotion, perhaps worthy of being called sublime, irradiated his features. The sun, too, in setting, fell upon his broad temples and iron-grey locks with a light solemn and religious. The effect to me, who knew his noble character, and all that he had suffered, was as if the eye of God then rested upon the decline of a virtuous man's life with approbation;—as if he had lifted up the glory of his countenance upon him. Would that many of his thoughtless countrymen had been present! They might have blushed for their crimes, and been content to sit and learn wisdom at the feet of Owen M'Carthy.*

FACTORY CHILDREN.

We again present our readers with an extract from that dark record, the forty days' evidence taken before the Committee of the House of Commons, on the condition of the wretched children in the factories. This is a subject of which we shall never lose sight, till the rank offence which cries to Heaven be removed from among us. It matters little whether the bloated idol, fed with infant blood, be Moloch, Juggernaut, or the god of British commercial idolatry, Mammon:—the sin is alike deep, the expiation alike called for. One of the witnesses examined before the Committee, the Rev. Mr. Gordon of Aberdeen, stated, that some years ago, Dr. Chalmers had from the pulpit told the manufacturers of Glasgow, "That they regarded human beings as so many pieces of machinery, the living principle within them as the power which set the machine in motion; and that their sole object was to get out of the machines as much work as possible with the least expense."

RICHARD OASTLER, Esq.—Has seen little boys and girls of ten years old, one in particular, whose forehead was cut open by the thong, whose cheeks and lips were laid open, and whose back was almost covered with black stripes. The same child informed him, that he had been frequently knocked down with the billy-roller, (a heavy rod of from two to three yards long, and two inches in diameter, with an iron pivot at each end, forming part of the machinery,) and that on one occasion he had been hung up by a rope round the body, and almost frightened to death, for the most trivial mistakes in his work. Has seen the bodies of these poor creatures almost broken down, so that they could not walk without assistance, when they have been seventeen or eighteen years of age; some who, after living all their lives in this slavery, were consigned at that age to poor-houses, and not maintained by the masters, for whom they had worked, as would have been the case had they been negro-slaves, but by other people who had reaped no advantage from their labour.

* This story we have abridged from a new work of very great merit, entitled *Traits and Stories of the Irish Peasantry*. The tale we have chosen is one of truth and pathos; others are yet more remarkable for a happy vein of humour. We have seen no work better calculated to make us know and love our fellow-subjects of Ireland; and heartily do we recommend it to such of our readers as draw supplies from circulating libraries. It is worth fifty fashionable novels.

Abraham Whitehead, clothier.—When children, after thirteen, fourteen, fifteen, or sixteen hours of labour, have, in the extremity of their fatigue, fallen into errors and mistakes in piecing, by placing the cording obliquely, has seen the billy-spinner or overlooker take his strap or the billy-roller, and say, "Damn thee! close it little devil, close it!" and then smite the child with the strap or the billy-roller. Some have been beaten so violently that they have lost their lives on such occasions; and even a young girl has had the billy roller jammed quite through her cheek. He has seen the billy-spinner take the billy-roller and rap them on the head, making their heads crack so that you might have heard the blow at the distance of six or eight yards, in spite of the din and rolling of the machinery. Knew a boy of the name of Senior, his school-fellow, who was killed by a blow from the billy-roller. A woman, in Holmforth, was also beaten to death with this instrument; with which the factory children are oftener beaten than with either stick or strap. These beatings usually occurred at the latter end of the day, when the children were sleepy and fatigued. It is a common practice to strike the children with the billy-roller. Hundreds could be brought to swear that the practice was a general one, and that the children so beaten were blind for two or three days. If any attempt is made to punish the overlooker, the children are sure to be discharged. These atrocities took place in Mr. Brown's mill, of Leeds. Has seen children of the age of seven years, going from their homes at five and six, and sometimes four and five, to their mills. Children of this tender age often work till ten on a winter's night. They have no time allowed for breakfast or tea. The forty minutes for dinner is their only time for rest, and then they are often employed in cleaning the machines.

William Kershaw, a clothier.—The pieceners are dreadfully beaten; has been beaten himself with a billy-roller, towards night, when he was particularly drowsy, till he repeatedly vomited blood; was then only eight years old; intreated his mother not to complain, lest he should be further beaten.— This was many years ago; but the children are not better treated now; has two children working at a mill at present; the oldest, when a piecener, has had to stop a day or two at home for three successive weeks, on account of being beaten on the head. Has known the unlimited power of punishment on the part of the overlookers; knew the father and mother of a child who was killed by being beaten on the head with the billy-roller. The children are beaten at all times in the day, for the most trivial mistakes, but the greatest complaints have been at night, when the children are drowsy and fatigued.

John Goodyear, scribble-feeder.—Considers the long hours the cause of the cruelties upon factory children, which are resorted to for the purpose of compelling them to labour beyond their strength. It is a common practice in woollen mills to beat them with a stick, strap, or billy-roller. Had a brother who nearly lost his eye by a blow from one of these instruments. The treatment of children grows more and more inhuman; has seen them a hundred times worse treated of late years than he was when young.

Thomas Bennett, slubber.—He said, with grief, that English children were enslaved worse than the Africans. Complained when working at Mr. Wood's mill, Dewsbury, "that they had not time to eat;" to which Wood replied, "Chew it at your work." Towards the evening, when the children are drowsy, they are apt to get entangled in the machinery. Saw an instance in which the machine caught a girl who had been drowsy, about the middle, bore her to the roof, and when she came down her neck appeared broken. The slubber ran up to her and pulled her neck and sent her to the doctors.

Benjamin Gummersal, piecener.—Has been beaten by the overlooker till black and blue on his face, and has had his ears torn. Became deformed through hard work, and ill treatment; cannot walk at all; is obliged to go up stairs backwards.

Richard Wilson, piecener.—His brother became so deformed that his father was compelled to carry him to the mill. He died at twenty-three. Has seen the children beaten severely towards night.

Benjamin Bradshaw, cloth-dresser, of Holbeck, Leeds.—When children go to work at five in the morning, and remain till ten at night, they become stupified with labour. Has heard, in the room under which he worked, at Mr Rosin's factory, between seven and eight, the cries of children, that would have touched a heart of stone. They were beaten in that mill chiefly with a strap, or leathern belt. His own children have returned home, beaten so severely, that he could not tell the colour of their backs. The girls were treated with the same severity as the boys. He has known a little girl beaten most cruelly for going to the water-closet. He did remonstrate with the master respecting the abuse of his daughter, but instead of discharging the overlooker, the philanthropic individual discharged all his children from his employ. Of seven hundred persons on whom he called to ascertain their sentiments on the factory question, seventeen only could write their own names.

Eliza Marshall.—Worked at Mr. Marshall's flax mill, Waterlane, Leeds, and afterwards at Mr. Warburton's. Became crooked with excessive labour, and went into the Infirmary. Has been beaten, and has seen other children strapped and kicked down. The master was often present and was as bad as the overlooker; they were as frightened when he came as if they were going to be killed. She was so exhausted at night, that she had to be trailed home. Is deformed from excessive labour in a standing position. Had to crawl to bed on her hands and knees.

Abraham Weldam.—Worked at Judson and Brother's mills at Keighley. Considers the lives of factory children one of extraordinary oppression and slavery. In the mill referred to they were chastised and beaten very cruelly at times; the overlooker was a person of very immoral character, a very bad man; he chastised them with any weapon that came at hand. The overlookers are too often in the habit of availing themselves of their controul over the female children for very improper purposes.

Samuel Coulson, tailor, of Stanningley.—His children got to bed about eleven, but were obliged to be up at two to ensure their arriving in time at the mill, thus allowing them only three hours sleep. An accident befel his daughter, who lost one of her fingers, in consequence of the brutal interference of the overlooker, whilst she was at work, in the after part of the day. She was five weeks in the Leeds infirmary, during the whole of which time her wages were stopped. She had not the least assistance from her employer. One of his daughters was beaten until her back was like a jelly. The wounds had to be dressed a fortnight after infliction, "in the way of a poor soldier that has suffered at the halberds."

Hannah Brown.—Worked at nine years of age at Mr. Ackroyd's mill, at Bradford. Has seen the overlooker drag the children about "three or four yards" by the hair of their heads. The master was fully aware the children were thus treated. Has even treated them himself in the manner already described.

Peter Smart, overlooker at Mr. Andrew Smith's mill, Dundee,—was frequently much beaten to keep him up to his labour, often till he was bloody at the mouth and nose. The master was accustomed to beat him as well as the overseer, both with their hands and a leathern strap.

Alexander Dean, overlooker at Dundee.—Was barbarously used by the overseer of Mayfield Mill; was once struck and knocked against the machinery, till he had one of his eyes closed. The instrument with which he was struck was the billy-roller.

Peter Frith, engineer at Winsley.—Was chastised and kicked so severely for being five minutes too late at dinner time on one occasion, (his mother having sent him on an errand,) that his knee was broken in three places. He fell down; but the strap was laid upon him till he arose. He hopped home, leaning on a boy's shoulder.

Eldin Hardgrave.—Grew deformed after he had worked at Mr. Brown's mill, of Leeds. Had worked for seventeen hours a day all the year round; has been discharged for coming to London to give evidence.

Joshua Drake.—The overlooker was accustomed to beat his daughter with a strap, (a heavy thong of leather with a wooden handle,) and sometimes to kick her with his foot. Has seen her arms and neck swelled many times from the beatings she has got.

John Hall, overlooker of Bradford.—Has the names and addresses of two hundred families, who have all deformed children, the whole having been so disabled by the inhuman extent of their labour in tender years at the neighbouring factories.

Joseph Sadler.—The temperature of factories varies; it is 80, 90, 100, and even 110. The temperature of Mr. Marland's mill is about 100; in the dressing rooms, 110. So intense was the application required from the children, that he had frequently seen them exert themselves, with tears in their eyes, and with the most heart-rending entreaties, pray to have their labour alleviated, and to avoid the chastisement that was inevitable. If their food is not brought at the precise moment fixed by factory regulations, they are compelled to go without it. They are often kept a long time without food. It is a common thing to see the children weeping, in consequence of the excessive labour they endure, and their not being able to do the work assigned to them. Has seen terror and apprehension depicted in their countenances when going to work; weeping through the streets is an every day occurrence.

Samuel Smith, Esq. Surgeon of Leeds.—The accidents by machinery are of so fearful a character as to entirely disable the sufferers—Has frequently seen accidents of the most fearful kind that it is possible to conceive. Has seen cases in which the arm has been torn off near the shoulder joint, and the upper extremity chopped into small fragments from the tip of the finger to above the elbow. Has seen every extremity of the body broken. A great number of these accidents might have been prevented by some Act to compel the owners of mills to have such horisontal and upright shafts as revolve with great rapidity in situations where children are placed near them, sheathed and covered with boxes of wood, which might be done at small expense, but is often neglected. Many of these accidents take place when the children are exhausted and sleepy from the long period at which they have continued their labour; they are in that state of lassitude and fatigue that they cannot keep their eyes open, and their fingers are frequently involved in the machinery when they are in that helpless state. Had seen a girl 15 or 16 years of age who was much deformed, and ascertained that she had worked from five in the morning till ten at night, for six months in succession, *without being allowed a single minute for food, rest, or recreation*; she was obliged to take her breakfast, dinner, and tea, as she followed her work. She was a "scribbler" in a flax mill at Holbeck near Leeds.

Reader! bear in mind that the above extracts are taken from *seven hundred closely printed folio pages* of evidence, detailing the most revolting and heart-rending cruelties; and we entirely agree with a London contemporary, "*That if the cruelties herein exposed had been invented by a writer of romance, they would have been considered as outraging probability.*" Can such a system be longer tolerated in a country professing Christianity? Impossible.

TROUBADOURS.

The Norman rhymers appear to have been the genuine descendants of the ancient Scandinavian scalds; they were well known in the northern part of France long before the appearance of the Provençal poets called Troubadours, and Trouvers, that is, Finders, probably from the fertility of their invention. The Troubadours brought with them into the north a new species of language called the Roman language, which in the eleventh and twelfth centuries was commonly used in the southern provinces of France, and there esteemed as the most perfect of any in Europe. It evidently originated from the Latin, and was the parent of the French tongue; and in this language their songs and their poems were composed. These poets were much admired and courted, being, as a very judicious modern writer says, the delight of the brave, and the favourites of the fair; because they celebrated the achievements of the one and the beauties of the other. Even princes became Troubadours, and wrote poems in the Provençal dialect; among others, a monarch of our own country certainly composed verses of this kind. The reader will, I doubt not, readily recollect the common story of Richard I., who, being closely confined in a castle belonging to the Duke of Austria, was discovered by his favourite minstrel Blondel, a celebrated Troubadour, through the means of a poem composed by the poet, in conjunction with his royal master. The story is thus related in a very ancient French author, quoted by Claude Fauchet; Blondel, seeing that his lord did not return, though it was reported that he had passed the sea from Syria, thought that he was taken by his enemies, and probably very evilly entreated; he therefore determined to find him, and for this purpose travelled through many countries without success; at last he came to a small town, near which was a castle belonging to the Duke of Austria; and, having learned from his host that there was a prisoner in the castle who had been confined for upwards of a year, he went thither, and cultivated an acquaintance with the keepers; for a minstrel, says the author, can easily make acquaintance. However, he could not obtain a sight of the prisoner, nor learn his quality; he therefore placed himself near to a window belonging to the tower wherein he was shut up, and sang a few verses of a song which had been composed conjointly by him and his patron. The King, hearing the first part of the song, repeated the second; which convinced the poet, that the prisoner was no other than Richard himself. Hastening, therefore, into England, he acquainted the barons with his adventure, and they, by means of a large sum of money, procured the liberty of the monarch.

THE SWORD DANCE.

There is a dance which was probably in great repute among the Anglo-Saxons, because it was derived from their ancestors, the ancient Germans: it is called the Sword-Dance, and the performance is thus described by Tacitus: "One public diversion was constantly exhibited at all their meetings: young men, who, by frequent exercise, have attained to great perfection in that pastime, strip themselves, and dance among the points of swords and spears with most wonderful agility, and even with the most elegant and graceful motions. They do not perform this dance for hire, but for the entertainment of the spectators, esteeming their applause a sufficient reward. This dance continues to be practised in the northern parts of England about Christmas time, when, says Mr. Brand, "the fool-plough goes about; a pageant that consists of a number of sword-dancers, dragging a plough, with music." The writer then tells us that he had seen this dance performed very frequently, with little or no variation from the ancient method, excepting only that the dancers of the present day, when they have formed their swords into a figure, lay them upon the ground and dance round them.

In the Pirate, Sir Walter Scott gives a picturesque and poetical description of the Sword-Dance, in which the "high-souled Minna Troil figures as in her native element."

COLUMN FOR THE YOUNG.

THE ROYAL GAME OF GOOSE.

This game is little known or practised in Scotland; but we have worse fire-side pastimes, and shall therefore give such a description of it, as may enable any ingenious young persons to play at it. It may be played by two persons; but it will readily admit of many more, and is well calculated to make children ready at reckoning the produce of two given numbers. The table for playing at goose is usually an impression from a copper-plate pasted upon a cartoon about the size of a sheet almanack, and divided into sixty-two small compartments arranged in a spiral form, with a large open space in the midst marked with the number sixty-three; the lesser compartments have singly an appropriate number from one to sixty-two inclusive, beginning at the outmost extremity of the spiral lines. At the commencement of the play, every one of the competitors puts a stake into the space at No. 63. There are also different forfeitures in the course of the game that are added, and the whole belongs to the winner. At No. 5 is a bridge which claims a forfeit at passing; at 19, an alehouse where a forfeit is exacted, and to stop two throws; at 30, a fountain where you pay for washing; at 42, a labyrinth which carries you back to 23; at 52, the prison where you must rest until relieved by another casting the same throw; at 58, the grave whence you begin the game again; and at 61, the goblet where you pay for tasting. The game is played with two dice, and every player throws in his turn as he sits at the table; he must have a counter or some other small mark which he can distinguish from the marks of antagonists, and according to the amount of the two numbers thrown upon the dice he places his mark; that is to say, if he throws a four and a five, which amount to nine, he places his mark at nine upon the table, moving it the next throw as many numbers forward as the dice permit him, and so on until the game be completed, namely, when the number sixty-three is made exactly; all above it the player reckons back, and then throws again in his turn. If the second thrower at the beginning of the game casts the same number as the first, he takes up his piece, and the first player is obliged to begin the game again. If the same thing happens in the middle of the game, the first player goes back to the place the last came from. It is called the game of the goose, because at every fourth and fifth compartment in succession a goose is depicted, and if the cast thrown by the player falls upon a goose, he moves forward double the number of his throw.

SCRAPS.
ORIGINAL AND SELECTED.

NATIONAL CONTRAST.—In a noisy mob, two handsome young women, who were much alarmed, threw themselves into the arms of two gentlemen standing near, for safety; one of the gentlemen, an Irishman, immediately gave her who had flown to him for protection, a hearty embrace, by way, as he said, of encouraging the poor crature. The other, an Englishman, immediately put his hands in his pockets to guard them. Two officers, observing a fine girl in a milliner's shop, the one an Irishman, proposed to go in and buy a watch-ribbon, in order to get a nearer view of her. "Hoot, mon," says his Northern Friend, "there's na occasion to waste *siller*, let us *gang* in and *speer* if she can *gie* us *twa saxpences* for a *shilling*." It is notorious, that in one of the Duke of Marlborough's battles, the Irish brigade, on advancing to the charge, threw away their knapsacks, and every thing which tended to encumber them, all which were carefully picked up by a Scotch regiment that followed to support them. It was a saying of the old Lord Twyrally, at a period when the contests between nations were decided by much smaller numbers than by the immense masses which have taken the field of late years, that to constitute the *beau ideal* of an army, a General should take ten thousand fasting Scotchmen, ten thousand Englishmen after a hearty dinner, and ten thousand Irishmen who have just swallowed their second bottle.

EARLY RISING.—The difference between rising at six, and rising at eight, in the course of forty years, supposing a person to go to bed at the same time he otherwise would, amounts to 29,000 hours, or three years, one hundred and twenty-one days, and sixteen hours; which will afford eight hours a-day for exactly ten years; and is in fact the same as if ten years were added to the period of our lives in which we might command eight hours every day for the cultivation of our minds and the dispatch of business.

THE WINTER GUEST.

I love to listen, when the year grows old
And noisy; like some weak life-wrinkled thing
That vents his splenetic humours, murmuring
At ills he shares in common with the bold.
Then from my quiet room the Winter cold
Is barred out like a thief; but should one bring
A frozen hand, the which December's wing
Hath struck so fiercely, that he scarce can hold
The stiffened finger tow'rd the grate, I lend
A double welcome to the victim, who
Comes shivering, with pale looks, and lips of blue,
And through the snow and splashing rain could walk,
For some few hours of kind and social talk:
And deem him, more than ever, now—my friend.

CONTENTS OF NO. XXVIII.

Notes of the Month—Process of Vegetation in Trees—Old Holidays—Candlemas Day........81
Books of the Month........82
An American's Account of a Levee of the time of George IV....83
Statistics........ib.
Ghost Story........84
Fashion in its Low Places........85
The Press and the Theatres........86
Buonaparte's May Days........ib.
Effects of Slovenliness........87
COLUMN FOR THE LADIES—Sketches of Natural History—The Coquette—Hints for Wives—Woman........88
THE STORY-TELLER—Tubber Derg, or the Red Well, (Concluded).........89
Barbarities of the Factory System........94
COLUMN FOR THE YOUNG—Troubadours—The Sword Dance—The Royal Game of Goose........95
SCRAPS—National Contrast—The Winter Guest........ib.

EDINBURGH: Printed by and for JOHN JOHNSTONE, 19, St. James' Square.—Published by JOHN ANDERSON, Jun., Bookseller, 55, North Bridge Street, Edinburgh; by JOHN MACLEOD, and ATKINSON & Co., Booksellers, Glasgow; and sold by all Booksellers and Vendors of Cheap Periodicals.

THE Schoolmaster,
AND
EDINBURGH WEEKLY MAGAZINE.

CONDUCTED BY JOHN JOHNSTONE.

THE SCHOOLMASTER IS ABROAD.—LORD BROUGHAM.

No. 29.—Vol. II. SATURDAY, FEBRUARY 16, 1833. Price Three-Halfpence·

TEMPERANCE SOCIETIES.

However it may gall our pride, we are shewing good sense in quietly following, in many important points, the example which our rebellious child America is setting us. Temperance Societies, to which we are friendly, were it only as they are an instrument of facilitating rational social intercourse among the people, are the growth of America; where, after a struggle of several years, they are triumphing at last. Whether, relatively, we are a soberer or more intemperate people than the Americans, is not a topic of instructive debate. Both nations are, perhaps, chargeable with excess enough in the use of ardent spirits, but with this differrnce, that the miserable and destitute condition of tens of thousands of our labouring poor, make the ever-ready "dram," the "meat, drink, fire, and fending," a far more powerful temptation than where the more equal distribution of wealth, and the better payment of labour, prevent intemperance from becoming so pernicious in its relative consequences, though equally debasing and demoralizing to its victim. In America, a man may be a considerable drunkard without so certainly inflicting misery and destitution on his family by his selfish and brutalizing appetites: no adequate apology for, but still some palliation of this vice. That the intemperance of the British poor arises in a considerable measure from the privations, and hardships, and absolute destitution to which they are periodically liable, requires no demonstration; and to repeat that drunkeness is but an aggravation of their worst calamities, is one of those unquestionable truisms which carry conviction to the judgment, but, unhappily, almost always fall short of imparting energy to resolution. The comparative temperance and moderation in the use of spirits among the *comfortable* classes, is, of itself, a clear proof, that habits of excess generally arise, either from the pressure of actual distress, or from the precarious and fluctuating gains of labour—from what is overpaid, as certainly as from what is underpaid; both extremes being alike adverse to the formation of steady habits. There are many minor concurring causes to which we cannot now advert. Gin and Gentility, *i. e.* Intemperance and Vanity are the present twin curses of the British people; and both are imputable, in no mean degree, to some of our bad civil and social instituions, and to the abuses of others. Our excise laws, and oppressive system of taxation, have been the fosterers of blear-eyed, bloated Gin; our profuse and profligate expenditure has nursed mincing, pinching, apish Gentility. Which folly is, in its remote consequences, the most pernicious, it is not very easy to decide. We shall afterwards return to them; and, in now introducing our American documents, would only premise that the poor uneducated Scotch or English manufacturer, who

Drinks to forget his griefs and debts;

or, it may be, to deaden the gnawings of hunger, or stifle the shame, and allay the shiverings of nakedness, though often a more degraded being, is also much more an object of compassion and sympathy than the American slave of intemperance; who, well-provided with the means of comfortable existence, may either use spirits, or vinous beverages, at his own discretion, for his personal refreshment, or to heighten the enjoyments of social intercourse. The first document we present is the

MINUTES OF THE GENERAL ASSEMBLY OF THE PRESBYTERIAN CHURCH IN THE UNITED STATES, 1832, ON THE SALE OF ARDENT SPIRITS.

The Pastoral Association, and the General Associations of Massachusetts, and the General Association of Connecticut and Maine, embracing more than five hundred Evangelical ministers of the Gospel, at their last Meeting passed the following resolutions, viz.:—

1. Resolved, that, in the judgment of this Association, the traffic in ardent spirits, as a drink, is an immorality, and ought to be viewed and treated as such throughout the world.

2. Resolved, that this immorality is utterly inconsistent with a profession of the Christian religion, and that those who have the means of understanding its nature and effects, and yet continue to be engaged in it, ought not to be admitted as members of Christian churches.

3. Resolved, that in our view, those members of Christian churches who continue to be engaged in the traffic in ardent spirits as a drink, are violating the principles and requirements of the Christian religion.

Among the means which the Lord has graciously owned and blessed during this year of of jubilee, many of our reports specially commemorate the influence of Temperance Societies. It is now a well-established fact, that the common use of strong drink, however moderate, has been a fatal soul-destroying barrier against the influence of the Gospel.

The cause of Temperance continues to extend and multiply its triumphs, notwithstanding the machinations of Satan, and the madness of the multitudes who are striving to demolish the only barrier which can secure them from destruction. The testimony of our churches as to the signal success which has crowned the efforts of the friends of this cause, the astonishing effect which has thus been produced upon public sentiment, and upon the habits and customs of the higher classes, especially as to the unquestionable connexion between total abstinence from ardent spirits and the success of the Gospel, is of the most decided and gratifying character. The formation of a Temperance Association in each congregation has taken place extensively with the happiest results. While, therefore, in view of these things, the friends of temperance are called upon to thank God, and take courage ; let them remember, that much, very much, remains to be done. Let them not remit their vigilance and activity, for their foes never slumber. All the powers and resources of the kingdom of darkness are vigorously employed in opposition. Much, indeed, has been done, in staying this plague among the more intelligent and elevated orders of society ; but all the energies of Christian benevolence are demanded to stem the torrent which is spreading misery, and guilt, and ruin, through the dwellings of labour and poverty.

A great work is still to be effected in the Church. The sons of Levi must be purified. The accursed thing must be removed from the camp of the Lord. While professing Christians continue to exhibit the baneful example of tasting the drunkard's poison, or, by a sacrilegious traffic, to make it their employment to degrade and destroy their fellow-men ; those who love the Lord must not keep silence, but must lift their warning voice, and use all lawful efforts to remove the withering reproach from the house of God. Let all our congregations become efficient Temperance Associations; let all our ministers and elders be united, consistent, and persevering, in this cause; and we may derive from experience a full persuasion, that the ravages of the direful wo will be arrested ; that the rising race will be rescued from his deadly grasp, and thus a most formidable obstacle to the success of the gospel will at last be removed.

But this is not all. The Government of the UNITED STATES have taken up the cause of temperance, happily having no debt or expenditure requiring that an Excise Revenue should be fed, at whatever expense to the health, morals, and happiness of the people. On the 2d of November last, the American Secretary for the War Department issued the following order, which, perhaps, goes too far ; as so sudden and arbitary a change must provoke men into the temptation of evading it :—" 1. Hereafter, no ardent spirits shall be issued to the troops of the United States as a component part of the ration. 2. No ardent spirits will be introduced into any fort, camp, or garrison of the United States, nor sold by any suttler to the troops, nor will any permit be granted for the purchase of ardent spirits. As a substitution for the ardent spirits, formerly issued, eight pounds of sugar, and four pounds of coffee, will be allowed to every one hundred rations." In the British Navy, coffee has been substituted for *part* of the former allowances of rum ; not at all, we dare say, to the immediate contentment of the seamen ; though there is no doubt that, wherever men can easily obtain regular and sufficient supplies of *warm* comfortable food and clothing, with *hot*, refreshing, and gently-stimulating liquids, like coffee, it will not be difficult, with some attention to the early habits engendered by social northern customs, to conquer intemperance. *Comfort*, in the most extended sense of that word, will prove the most powerful antagonist of intemperance and best auxiliary of the Temperance Societies. Where that is wanting, lecturing will be of small efficacy ; and hence the great success of these associations in America. In this country, the true promoters of temperance should set themselves, in the first place, to improve the condition of the people. Secure to labour its just reward, in a steady and sufficient supply of the necessaries, and a share of the comforts of life, and with the removal of distress and mental anxiety you withdraw from drunkenness its strongest temptation.

COLUMN FOR THE YOUNG.

STORIES OF BIRDS.

THE ROBIN.

Art thou the bird that Man loves best ;
The little bird with the crimson breast ?
Art thou the Thomas of German boors,
And the Peter of Finland, and Russia far inland ?

THERE is a charming little book, containing descriptions and familiar stories about song-birds, and giving lively coloured representations of the more delightful of our common warblers, which we like so much, that we have often, for the sake of our young friends, wished it *cheaper*. It is written, and very delightfully written, by Mr. PATRICK SYME, an artist (we believe) in this city. From it we purpose to tell of the "sweet, social" Robin :—

This delightful little warbler, equally sacred to the cottager's hearth, the farmer's hall, and the squire's mansion, is well known through the popular and piteous story of " *The Children in the Wood*." Its confidence in man has rendered the redbreast a general favourite ; and its familiarity has procured for it, in most countries, a peculiar name ; such as might be given to some welcome annual visitor: with us it is called Robin Redbreast ;—in Germany, Thomas Gierdit ;—in Norway, Peter Ronsmad ;—and in Sweden, Tomi Liden.

The plumage of the redbreast, though harmonious, is plain ; and it is rather remarkable that all our finest songsters have but few showy colours. Though the redbreast is so well known to man, yet naturalists are still doubtful whether to consider it as a migratory or stationary bird. Buffon says, that it migrates singly, not in flocks : many, however, remain with us through the winter ; but these appear, (at least such is our opinion,) to be all males. During severe storms, when the ground is covered with snow, this bird approaches the habitation of man, with a confidence and winning familiarity which always ensure to the tiny stranger kindness and protection. He has been known to come to a window,—to tap, and if it be opened, to enter, to eye the family in a sly manner ; and, if not disturbed, to approach the board, pick up crums, hop round the table, and catch flies, if any remain ; then perch on a chair or window-cornice ; and, finding his situation comfortable, is often seen, in this familiar way, to introduce himself to the family, and to repay, with seeming gratitude, their hospitality, by the melodious warbling of his little throat; and this daily throughout the winter.

We know a gentleman who, last summer, (1822,) caught a young redbreast, one of a brood just flown in his garden. A short time after, the bird was lost, several days elapsed, and robin did not appear; when the gentleman, walking in the garden with a friend, saw a bird of this species, which he thought very like his, hopping among four or five others, that seemed to be all of the same age. He requested his friend not to move, and returned to the house for a few crumbs, which he held in his hand, and calling "*Robie!*" the bird appeared to recognise the name it had been accustomed to, perched upon his finger, and was instantly secured. The bird is now, May, 1823, in full plumage, and singing delightfully; he ranges at liberty through the room; for though he has a large, light, and airy cage, the door of which stands open, he seldom enters it. In the same room is a chaffinch, still more tame than the redbreast; also a titmouse and a mule bird; but the moment they are out of their cages, the redbreast pursues, attacks, and drives them from place to place, so that he remains cock of the room. If his master takes a seed of hemp, and calls "*Robie!*" he instantly flies at it, picks it from between the finger and thumb, darts off, and this so rapidly, that one cannot detect how he extracts the seed. He is a fine healthy bird, in full feather, though only fed on hempseed, loaf-bread, and what flies he can catch, with now and then a spider.

His manner of feeding is rather curious:—a slice of bread is put down, which he pecks at from one point, generally near the centre of the piece, until he has made a hole through it; he then begins at another place, and does the same. He is very inquisitive, and it is amusing to observe him when any thing is brought into the apartment, such as books, paper, &c. At first he advances with great caution; but, finding the object motionless, he ventures nearer, hops round it, but never appears content till he has got upon it, and never quits it unless disturbed, until he has examined it with the eye of a curious inquirer.

One morning, a roll of paper, more than two feet long, being laid on the table, Robie instantly saw it was a new object, flew to it, hopped round and round it several times; and at last, finding it impossible to satisfy himself without a narrower inspection, he hopped in at the one end and out at the other.

We have heard many anecdotes of the redbreast, but what we have mentioned will suffice to show its manners in a state of domestication. This bird may be taught various pretty tricks, and even to articulate words. We know that a lady in Edinburgh possesses one who very distinctly pronounces, "How do ye do?" and several other words. Her method was, early in the morning, before giving it any food, to repeat very often what she wished it to learn.

In a wild state, these birds are very pugnacious. Each cock seems to have certain bounds, which he considers his own, and within which he will allow no other bird of the same species to range. The redbreast builds its nest in different situations according to circumstances: we found one at the edge of a rocky bank near Roslin, but so hid by grass and ivy, that, had it not been for some wild flowers for which we were looking, (the hen sits so very close,) we might never have found it. Last year, (1822,) at Craig-Lockhart, near Edinburgh, we saw a cock-bird rather agitated, with something in its bill; and, thinking the nest might be near, we were anxious to see if they built in so exposed a situation as the way-side. After much trouble, and careful examination of both sides of the road, we at last discovered it by the hen flying out, when we were within a foot of the nest; had she not been on, it was so curiously concealed, we might never have perceived it.

As we are not sure about the propriety of *caging* birds, especially of the species which are so difficult to feed as are Robins, we take leave to pass Mr. SYME's directions for rearing the young, (though we willingly follow his guidance for a quiet peep into the nest,) and come to his description of this *pet* warbler:—

In a garden at Canonmills, for several years, a redbreast, (we believe the same bird,) has built its nest; once in a bower, another time in a laurel close by a wall, and last year artfully hid amongst ivy on the trunk of an old willow-tree. It was found by observing the cock going in with food; and, just as our hand was at the hole which led to the nest, the bird flew boldly down from a tree, and struck at our fingers.

This winter, (1822-3,) the same redbreast watched when the servant went at dusk to shut up a greenhouse in the garden, entered with her, and coming near, pecked the crums which she held to it from her hand,—remained all night, and was ready in the morning for the same fare. When she returned to open the door, he usually came out with her, (unless in very bad weather,) and flew to the garden; and, as she repaired to the house, poured forth a strain of grateful melody: and this he did regularly almost every day during this very severe winter.

OF THE NEST AND EGGS.

The nest is composed of bent, dead leaves, grass-roots, and other fibrous substances, mixed with moss, and lined with thistle-down, hair, and feathers. The eggs, four or five in number, are of an orange-coloured white, freckled, particularly at the large end, with pale orange-red spots, inclining to brown.

TO FIND THE NEST.

It is desirable to know how to look for the nest, it being of consequence to get the birds young, if we wish to tame, or teach them any pretty tricks. When you see a redbreast, observe if it has any thing in its bill: do not frighten it, and it will soon go to the nest; but its instinct is so great that it sometimes flits about before entering the nest: wait therefore until it has gone in and out several times from the same place; when in, steal upon it quickly, otherwise the opportunity may be lost of scaring it, this being the best method of discovering the nest; for, if you do not see the very spot from whence the bird springs, its mossy mansion is so artfully concealed, you may not, after all, be able to find it. The same rule holds for taking the nests of nightingales, wrens, blackcaps, and most of the soft-billed species, which, being the shiest birds, display the greatest ingenuity in concealing their nests. The redbreast builds in April, May, and June, and has sometimes two broods in the year.

DESCRIPTION AND PLUMAGE.

The redbreast is between five and six inches in length, bill slender, and of a horn-colour. Eye black, large, full, and mild, with a small orange-red circle round it. Upper parts of the plumage, viz., head, back, and wings. pale umber-brown inclining to olive, in some lights appearing as if tinged with yellowish-brown. Forehead, throat, and breast, rich orange-red; lower parts, greyish-white, with a mixture of dull cream-yellow; legs, clove-brown, passing into umber-brown; claws black.

The hen is very like the cock; but neither so large or full of spirit, nor so bright in the plumage. To choose a cock-bird, let him be large and sprightly, having a full sparkling eye; the brown on the back, rich, glossy, and dark, and the red on the breast, large and bright; this last is the best criterion to judge by.

The redbreast will learn the notes of other birds; but his own being so fine, it is a pity to spoil it by teaching him to imitate other warblers. His song is rich, full, melodious, melting, and tender; it is very various, at one time having a deep melancholy tone, broken with sprightly turns between; then mellow and plaintive. The spring and autumnal notes are different: in spring his melody is rich, but quick, softly-melting, and dying away in harmonious cadences; in autumn they are plaintive, but still more rich and sweet,—as if he sung the dirge of summer, or wailed the departing year.

SONG.
TO A REDBREAST.

Little bird, with bosom red,
Welcome to my humble shed!
Daily, near my table steal,
While I pick my scanty meal.
Doubt not, little though there be,
But I'll cast a crumb to thee:
Well rewarded, if I spy,
Pleasure in thy glancing eye;
See thee, when thou'st eat thy fill,
Plume thy breast, and wipe thy bill.
Come, my feather'd friend, again!
Well thou knowest the broken pane.
Ask of me thy daily store;
Ever welcome to my door!

COLUMN FOR THE LADIES.

PRINCIPLES OF FEMALE DRESS.

THE philosophy of female dress is a subject that has often engaged the attention of poets, metaphysicians, and artists; hitherto, we are sorry to confess, with little perceptible advantage to its leading principles, whether of *beauty* or *utility*. A fashionable French milliner is still able to put to rout a whole college or academy. One of the most profound modern disquisitions on this interesting subject has proceeded from Mr. Christopher North, who enters elementally into its discussion. His analysis, which we may one day lay before our fair readers, has furnished the leading ideas of the essay subjoined. We need scarce say that it is also the production of a masculine pen.

" The inferior priestess at the altar's side,
Trembling begins the sacred rites of pride."—*Pope*.

A MAN of the name of Thomson, who wrote a poetry-book about the four seasons, which some persons who lived in the eighteenth century are thought to have tried to read, was foolish enough to say or sing somewhere in a story about a country wench called Lavinia, that

———" loveliness
Needs not the foreign aid of ornament,
But is when unadorned adorned the most."

Said Thomson was a sheepish clown of a Scotchman' and therefore knew nothing whatever of the matter. People talk of a ship in full sail, or a waving field of golden grain, but commend us to a beautiful and splendidly dressed woman, entering a ball room, with " grace in all her steps," as the crowning climax of Nature's best and loveliest gifts.

We are inclined to look on dress, of course we speak of ladies' dress, as one of the most beautiful, and, in common life, the most important of the fine arts. We are, therefore, of opinion, that it ought to be uniformly regulated by the principles of true taste. One of the many reasons adduced to prove that there is no fixed standard of beauty, but that whatever appearance is associated in the mind with what is considered dignified and agreeable, is also accounted beautiful, is the obvious one so often remarked, that whatever is fashionable in dress is, for the time, pleasing. Yet, if we examine the dresses of the classic nations, who are still our masters and instructors in all the finer arts, we shall find no instance of any thing that revolts sound taste in their attire, a test from which we fear many of our modern modes would shrink, if subjected to examination two thousand years after their invention.

The greatest beauty in dress is that which is most simple, and at the same time gracefully adapted to exhibit the natural beauty of the female form. This simplicity should be observed even in colour; a profusion of tawdry and glaring colours bespeaks a tasteless and vulgar mind, even if the wearer were a duchess. Colour should also always be adapted to complexion. Ladies with delicate, rosy complexions, bear white and light blue, better than dark colours, while on the contrary, sallow hues of complexion will not bear these colours near them, and imperatively require dark, quiet colours to give them beauty. Yellow is the most trying and dangerous colour of all, and can only be worn by the rich-toned, healthy-looking brunette.

It is difficult to make the bonnet of any shape picturesque or becoming. The hat, with the large leaf and feather, is always so.

Yet the large hat, we fear, might be found inconvenient in a small or close carriage; it would condemn the wearer to solitary imprisonment, or at least prevent her from enjoying (with ease) the society of a *fair* companion, supposing her head-dress to be of equal dimensions. Against this evil we would provide by suggesting a different mode of coiffure for the carriage, from that used in the promenade. What could be more elegant or becoming for the former than an ornamental *cap*, made of some light material, and which might, by lining, be rendered equally warm with the bonnets often worn in summer? A veil, always an elegant and appropriate appendage to female attire, might be thrown over or attached to the cap, and would add much to its graceful appearance. An adoption of this head-dress would avoid the bitter complaints we have so often heard some of our fair friends utter against the narrow doors of their carriages, which, not exceeding half a fathom or so in width, render an awkward lateral mode of ingress indispensable to the fashionable head-piece.

And now for the mode of dressing the hair. We have often observed that ladies, instead of regarding the hair as designed for an ornament to the face, reverse the kind intentions of nature, and consider their foreheads as horticulturalists do the plants constructed for a flower exhibition, namely, as platforms on which to display to the best advantage a goodly array of shining curls, ranged in successive rows, " each above each aspiring," till we are at a loss whether most to admire, the skill of the fair *artiste*, or the beauty of the materials she has had to work upon. Now be it understood, that we wish not to say any thing disrespectful of the said glossy circlets, *au confraire*, we admire them *à merveille*, and think that in themselves they are deserving of all praise, cruel *creve-cœurs* though they be; but we can by no means consent to countenance the undue sacrifices our " fairest of womankind" are willing to make in their behalf; we protest warmly against the total eclipse, or even occultation of the open, ivory forehead, and the delicately arched eyebrow; and we cannot witness the late unwarrantable intrusions upon the softly-rounded cheek, without asserting its rights, and crying aloud for justice. The eyes themselves are scarcely safe from invasion, even in these piping times of peace; and we must entreat the active co-operation of the ladies in averting the threatened evil, and establishing an equitable balance of power between the respective claims of features and tresses, though we have never before ventured to advocate the holy alliance system; and even this we think should rather be considered an instance of *la belle alliance*. Still we should observe that no one uniform mode of dressing the hair can be recommended as superseding all others. In this, as in every other part of the details, each lady must consult the particular style of her own face and figure, and "snatch a grace beyond the reach of art."

Again, as the art of dress is to enable the individual to conceal the defects of nature, as well as to exhibit her beauties to advantage, thin persons should take care, let the fashion be what it may, to dress with a certain fulness of drapery; while, on the other hand, fat or round persons should on no account puff themselves out artificially, unless they wish to appear ludicrous. Thus, the lady with no hips may *bustle*; but if she who has sufficient breadth does so, she will disfigure herself. In like manner, the lady with high, square shoulders should wear sleeves commencing a little below the shoulder; but the lady with a finely formed bust should dress *au naturel*.

Ladies with thick legs or ancles (*soit dit en passant*) should not wear white stockings, but black or dark colours, which, by presenting a smaller mass of light, diminishes the size of objects.

Finally, all monstrosities should be avoided, nothing squeezed or puffed out to extravagance should ever appear. The unnaturally contracted waist, on which so many of the fair sex unfortunately pride themselves, is not less offensive to good taste than injurious to health; and the sufferer who makes such an exhibition has not even the satisfaction of having the sympathy or pity of the spectators to console her for her self-inflicted sufferings.

We should be sorry to see any approach to a quakerish livery, but in the present age of enormity in bustles, and licentiousness in sleeves, something must be done to check the tide of depravity (in taste) which is setting in with so strong a current. The subject is one of far too great importance to be left with any propriety, as it now is, to the silly caprice of milliners and ladies' maids. Ladies! the eyes of Europe are upon you. Vindicate the cause of skirts fashioned for defence or conquest in a manner worthy of yourselves. Forget not that

"True art is Nature to advantage dressed.'

FAREWELL.

BY BISHOP HEBER.

When eyes are beaming
 What never tongue may tell;
When tears are streaming
 From their crystal dell;
When hands are linked that dread to part—
Oh! bitter, bitter is the smart
 Of them that bid farewell.

When hope is chidden
 That fain of bliss would tell
And love forbidden
 In the breast to dwell;
When fettered by a viewless chain,
We turn and gaze, and turn again
Oh! death were mercy to the pain
 Of them that bid farewell.

MARY LINDSAY.

BY JOHN MACDIARMID, ESQ.

DIED at Duncow, in the parish of Kirkmahoe, on the 9th ultimo, Mary Lindsay, at the advanced age of 85. This singular and useful woman, during the long period of threescore years, evinced the most marked and disinterested affection for little children, and voluntarily took upon herself the duties of a protectress. These chosen buds of promise, during their daily attendance at the village school, made greater progress than by the master's lessons, in availing themselves of Mary's goodness of heart; and hence her humble cot became the common depot of plaids, coats, Josephs, and that most necessary and valuable appendage the scrip, stored, we shall say, with a couple of *scones* and a solitary egg—the sweet, though frugal elements of their mid-day refreshment. In an olden pot, of curious dimensions, more than twenty eggs were boiled every day; and not unfrequently the benevolent woman banned the parish hens for not laying them a "wee thouchit bigger."

As property is property, even in an egg, to distinguish each urchin's share in the joint stock, boiling became a matter of no slight difficulty; but Mary's genius was equal to the task. By the application of her finger to the bottom of the pot, and certain other ceremonies not so easily defined, she produced a sort of hieroglyphic mark, which was as final as the court of last resort, although, it must be confessed, nobody knew the key to the cypher but herself. Occasionally certain side-long looks revealed pretty plainly that the gazer would have preferred the biggest egg in the pot to his own; and it was always with reluctance that honest Mary asserted the rights of equity, and insured subordination, by applying, or flourishing vigorously, the *pluff*—a sort of substitute for a pair of bellows. But her strokes fell gentle, "as from parents' hands;" nor did her acts of benevolence end here. When rains flooded the plains, and the burns ran wild on their way to the sea, or when frost and snow crisped every wood and fell, honest Mary was always at her post, displaying her Meg Merrilees-like figure to advantage, in handing the scholars over an intervening stream, often in threes and fours at a time. Indeed, there are persons still living who have been honoured with a seat on Mary's shoulders. Latterly, she was supported almost entirely by what she called " her boys," who are now scattered over various parts of the globe, and all of whom will heave a sigh, or drop a tear, when they learn that their early protectress is no more. One of her protegés requested Mr. Allan to put forth all his strength in painting Mary's picture, no matter at what cost; and the artist produced a correct likeness, which the owner, much to his credit, says he would not barter for the portrait of Mary Queen of Scots. Another friend, in consideration of the miserable hovel in which his early acquaintance wonned, pressed on her acceptance the best of his numerous cottages in Duncow; and the answer he received was quite characteristic —" Na, na, Sir, my mither leeved here, an' de'ed here. I mysel' hae leeved here, an' I'll dee here; and for as little as ye may think o' the bit, I wadna chang'd for the bonniest gilt room in a' Dalswinton."

VERSES FOR THE YOUNG.

A LESSON FOR AN INFANT SCHOOL.

BY J. MONTGOMERY.

Sun, Moon, and Stars, by day and night,
At God's commandment, give us light;
And when we wake, and while we sleep,
Watch over us, like angels, keep.

The bright blue sky above our head,
The soft green earth on which we tread,
The ocean rolling round the land,
Were made by God's almighty hand.

Sweet flowers, that hill and dale adorn,
Fair fruit trees, fields of grass and corn,
The clouds that rise, the showers that fall,
The winds that blow,—God sends them all.

The beasts that graze, with downward eye,
The birds that perch, and sing, and fly,
The fishes, swimming in the sea,
God's creatures are, as well as we.

But us he formed for better things:
As servant of the King of kings;
With lifted hands, and open face,
And thankful hearts, to seek his grace.

Thus God loved man, and more than thus:
He sent his Son to live with us;
And invites us, when we die,
To come and live with him on high.

But we must live to him below:
For none but such to heaven will go;
Lord Jesus, hear our humble prayer,
And lead the little children there.

TRADE WITH THE COUNTRIES ON THE NIGER.*

We arrive now at the important question, what prospects this great interior communication opens to British commerce. Its branches in Africa, since the abolition of that dark one, which Britain has so justly proscribed, have been limited; and high authorities have even doubted if they could admit of any great extension. But it must be observed that the intercourse has hitherto been almost exclusively with the coast; the territory along which is comparatively unproductive, and its inhabitants idle and miserable. It has always been found, in proportion as travellers penetrated inland, that they came to a superior region and people; that, contrary to what takes place in other continents, all the large cities, all the valuable and prosperous branches of industry, were at a distance from the sea. This has been imputed, and not without some reason, to the demoralizing influence of the European slave trade. But there is, besides, a physical cause which must have a powerful influence. A much greater extent of the surface of Africa, than of any other continent, is situated between the tropics, and even immediately under the line. Sterility is there produced by the scorching rays of the sun, to which the coasts, from their low level, are peculiarly liable, and by which many tracts are rendered parched and arid. Others, by the same low situation, are exposed to the inundation of the great rivers, which, swelled by the violent tropical rains, spread often into wide pestilential swamps. But the interior territory becoming always more elevated, enjoys a more temperate climate, and is diversified by hills and mountain ranges, the streams from which supply copious moisture, without deluging the territory with any permanent inundation. The countries rendered accessible by the Niger and its tributaries, are undoubtedly the most productive and industrious in all Africa; and their population, notwithstanding the difficulty of forming any precise estimate, can scarcely be rated at less than twenty-five millions. It seems impossible that British enterprise can find access to such a region, without drawing from it very considerable results. The two questions which call for consideration are—the articles of British produce, for which a vent may be found in this quarter of the world; and the commodities which may be procured in exchange. Under the first head, we may at once refer to that manufacture in which Britain most excels, and has carried to the greatest extent. Cotton fabrics are alone suited to the climate of Central Africa, and, in fact, clothe her entire population. It is true, they are manufactured with skill within the country itself; but the example of India, where Manchester and Paisley have supplanted, in their native seats, the superb muslins and calicoes of Dacca and Masulipatam, leaves little doubt that the less brilliant products of the African loom would be unable to withstand the competition. There is even no need of recurring to so distant an illustration. Manchester clothes Bonny and Eboe at Kiama, more than two hundred miles inland; her robes, of course and gaudy patterns, formed the favourite ornament of the Negro damsels, though their moderate original cost had been raised by a long land-carriage to an almost ruinous height. The navigation of the Niger seems hitherto to have been little instrumental in diffusing commodities through the interior. The communication is almost entirely between city and city; the chief of Damuggo did not know the existence of Eyeo or Youri. It was only at Eggu, the limit of the more improved and industrious districts, that European commodities began to appear. Besides cotton stuffs, arms, it is to be feared, would be a prominent article: but not to mention their use in hunting, perhaps the exchange of the European for the African mode of warfare, would, on the whole, rather advance civilization. Jewels, toys, every gaudy and glittering object, is suited to the rude taste of the African chiefs; and, as they have not yet learned to distinguish the real value of these commodities, high prices might, for some time, be obtained, though experience and competition would doubtless open their eyes. The returns claim our next attention, and form rather a more difficult subject. At the head of the exports we place manufactured cottons, and at the head of the imports we are disposed to place the raw material. This is produced abundantly; and, if we may trust the report of travellers, of excellent quality, over the whole of tropical Africa. European commerce seems never to have reached the cotton-growing districts, which are all considerably in the interior. The demand in Britain is immense, the annual imports being valued at nearly eight million sterling. This demand, too, would be augmented, if Africa, like India and the United States, after supplying the raw material, took back the manufactured produce. Indigo, moreover, the most valuable of dyeing stuffs, and which Britain imports sometimes to the value of L.1,000,000, is produced in these countries plentifully, and, it is said, also of excellent quality. Hides and skins, and some gold, would be the only important additional articles; for palm oil, at present the most extensive one, being produced in the countries near the coast, is probably furnished to the full extent of the demand. After considering what are likely to be the objects of the trade on the Niger, the mode of conducting it presents another question equally important and difficult. The obstacles are indeed such that, according to the ordinary resources of river navigation, they appear altogether insuperable. The pestilential atmosphere along the shores of this delta, and its lower estuaries—the violent and turbulent character of the native tribes, who would doubtless regard the British as rivals and enemies—could scarcely be surmounted, unless by some peculiar agency. This, however, seems to be found in steam, which gives such an entirely new character and power to river navigation. Propelled by it, the vessel could be carried in one day and night from the ocean to the head of the delta, and thus pass swiftly through the region of the pestilence; it could also penetrate, and leave behind it, hostile fleets of armed canoes. Practical skill and experience must decide whether the steam-vessels should be brought direct from England, or be stationed on the coast, where the goods brought out by sailing vessels, could be transferred into them. The first of these plans, if practicable, would avoid the cost of transhipment, and the dangers to health incurred during such an operation on a coast, every spot on which is insalubrious. It may be worth suggesting, whether the Formoso, or Benin branch, might not be the most advantageous for ascending the river. The navigator would thus at once reach the head of the delta, above Kiree, avoiding the dangerous bar at the mouth of the Brass river, and the fierce rivalry of the natives, which would be encountered both there, and still more in the Bonny channel. It may be presumed, however, that the trade can never be carried on with facility, or to any great extent, without a station on the Niger itself, where a depôt of European and African goods could be formed; whence smaller vessels might ascend the inferior rivers, or those parts of the great stream of which the navigation is difficult or obstructed. There would be an obvious convenience in endeavouring to obtain by purchase one of the numerous islands by which the channel is in one place diversified. The only danger might be, of their being rendered unhealthy by a low and damp situation; in which case a salubrious and defensible position might be found on one of the heights by which a great extent of the river course is bordered. It remains only that we inquire what connexion can be traced between these new discoveries, and our previous knowledge of Africa; whether any, and what anticipations have been formed by ancient writers of that lower course of the Niger which has now, for the first time, been navigated by Europeans. These will, we believe, be found extremely limited. Ptolemy, who delineates the river as entirely inland, and without any branch flowing to the southward, evidently had no idea of its termination. The case may be somewhat different with regard to the Arabian writers, who describe their "Nile of the Negroes," as flowing westward, and falling into the Atlantic. We have endeavoured to show, in a former article, (June 1826,) that their settlements were all

* We beg our readers to peruse this in connexion with Mr. Pitt's speech on the civilisation of Africa, in our 17th number.

in the territory now called Houssa; and that their Nile was not the Niger of Park, but a compound of the streams flowing along that plain, particularly the Quartama, or Zirmie. It may be supposed that this last stream, joined to the part of the Niger navigated by Lander, formed their Nile, and that they thus erred only by supposing a tributary to be the main branch. But the great imperfection of their knowledge, is clearly proved by the ignorance of all the details now observed by our traveller; and more particularly by the statement, that from Tocrur (Sockatoo) to Ulil, where the great river fell into the sea, was only eighteen days' journey, which cannot be rated so high as 300 miles; while the real distance to the Gulf of Benin does not fall short of 700. There may, however, be room to believe, that they might receive a general intimation of the termination of the Niger in the Atlantic, and might suppose the remotest city in that direction, of which they obtained distinct intelligence, to be at the point of its entrance; as Sultan Bello supposed Rakah and Fundah to be seaports at the mouth of the river. The name of Youri bears some resemblance to that of Ulil; r and l being readily convertible. But the pits in which the salt of Ulil is said by Edrisi to have been found, and the desert along which it was conveyed, suggest the western salt mines, and seem to prove that Ulil was Walet, and that the Lake Dibbi, in that imperfect state of knowledge, was confounded with the Atlantic. The only writer who discovers a distinct knowledge of any part of the Niger navigated by the present travellers, is Leo Africanus. He describes it as flowing between Guber (which is still well known as a country of Houssa, and appears then to have been its ruling state) and Gago, whose fruitful territory, rude habitations, the innumerable host of the royal wives, and its situation 400 miles south from Timbuctoo, clearly establish to be Eyeo. But he fails altogether to trace it farther, or follow its progress downwards to the Gulf of Benin. On the contrary, he represents it as flowing in a western direction from Timbuctoo to Ghinea, (Jenur,) and thence to the ocean. This impression he evidently derived from the Portuguese, who early began to consider the Senegal and Gambia as the estuaries of the Niger. This last opinion continued to be prevalent among modern Europeans; hence the only attempts made to reach the Niger, were by the English from the Gambia, and the French from the Senegal. They proved abortive; and Delisle and D'Anville obtained positive information, that these rivers had no connexion with the Niger, which rose in the interior, and flowed eastward to Timbuctoo. Yet they never could fully overcome the general prepossession to the contrary, and had, themselves, no correct idea as to its termination. Reichard, a German writer, had the merit of starting, and Mr. M'Queen of warmly supporting the hypothesis, which has now been so happily verified, and affords the main key to the geography of interior Africa. Notwithstanding the great importance of this discovery, it has by no means completed even the outline of our knowledge respecting the central regions of this continent. The Tshadda, with all the countries on its banks, which there is every reason to believe are fertile and populous, remains entirely unexplored. There is a large blank in the course of the Niger between Timbuctoo and Youri. We say nothing of the regions south of the equator, which, unless from the recent observations of M. Donville, are almost entirely untouched by discovery.—*Edinburgh Review.*

LARGE AND SMALL FARMS.

In the Netherlands, and in Switzerland, and in the North of Italy and Tuscany, the most perfect agriculture prevails with small farms. In Flanders, the farmer, like the old English farmer, sits at the table with his servants, and looks carefully into every detail. He is at the same time, according to all accounts, a much better farmer than the English farmer. Radcliff, who was sent by the Farming Society of Ireland to the Netherlands, and published a report on the agriculture of East and West Flanders, in 1819, thus describes the manners of the Flemish farmer and labourer.

"It is a pleasure to observe the laborious industry of the Flemish farmer, recruited by intervals of decent and comfortable refreshment, and not less agreeable to perceive the farm servants treated with kindness and respect. They uniformly dine with the farmer and his family at a clean table cloth, well supplied with spoons, with four pronged forks, and every thing necessary for their convenience. In Flanders, the gentlemen are all farmers, but the farmers do not aspire to be gentlemen, and their servants feel the benefit. They partake with them of a plentiful orderly meal, which varies according to circumstances. * * * The clothing of the peasantry is warm and comfortable—good shoes and stockings, and frequently gaiters of leather or strong linen, which are sold very cheap. * * * Their comfortable supply of linen is remarkable; there are few of the labouring classes without many changes. * * * With respect to the farm house, the exterior is, for the most part, ornamented with creepers or fruit trees, trained against the walls; and within, the neatness which prevails is quite fascinating. Every article of furniture is polished. The service of pewter displays a peculiar brightness, and the tiled floor is purified by frequent ablutions. The cottage of the labourer, though not so well furnished, is, however, as clean; a frequent and periodical use of water and the broom pervades every house, great and small, in the country and in town."

"A large farm requires a large capital. If a man takes a farm which he has not capital to stock sufficiently, whether the farm be large or small, he will labour under difficulties. What is wanted is, not that men without capital shall take farms, (for the mischievous consequence of this is felt in Ireland, where a man without a farthing will take a farm,) but that there should be farms of sizes suited to the capitals by which they can be advantageously cultivated. We believe that after the first great improvements of embanking and draining, &c. have been made in a country, if things were left to their natural course, farms would constantly diminish rather than increase in size. The small farmer can observe all the most improved practices, and he can better attend to minute details,—an immense matter in farming. The difference, too, between the exertions of a hireling and a man who labours for himself, is not to be disregarded. Accordingly, it has been found that, during times of difficulty, the small farmer has struggled through, while the large farmer has sunk, from inability to keep down his expenditure. The small farmer and his family will toil early and late, if necessary, and cheerfully submit to privations, in the hope of better times; but the hireling has no interest in the prosperity of his master, and no motive for encountering privations for the sake of one who, if prosperous, would never bestow a thought on him. The tendency to multiply farms is retarded by the necessity for an outlay on buildings, and still more by the manner in which the poor laws have been abused in a great part of England. The man who cultivates a small possession by his own labour and that of his family, is made to pay the wages of the labourers of the great farmer. In many parishes the rates are as high as thirty shillings a pound, merely through the labourers receiving their wages in the shape of rates. Wherever this system prevails there can be no small farmers. If they were to pay no rent, they would be ruined by the rates. As great farmers hate to have small farms in their neighbourhood, and hate to see labourers possessed of small allotments of land, or any means by which they can escape from absolute dependence, the poor rates were often raised with a view to work the destruction of the small farmers, and the more complete dependence of the labourers.

ABHORRENCE OF WAR.—I wish you joy of the marvellous conclusion of the strange and terrible drama which our eyes have seen opened, and, I trust, finally closed, upon the grand stage of Europe, (date, July 1814.) I used to be fond of war when I was a younger man, and longed heartily to be a soldier; but now, I think there is no prayer in the service with which I could close more earnestly, than "Send peace in our time, good Lord!"—*Walter Scott's Letters.*

ELEMENTS OF THOUGHT.

PATRIOTISM—PHILANTHROPY.
BY DR. CHALMERS.

I now make my appeal to the sensibilities of your heart; and tell me, to whom does the moral feeling within it yield its readiest testimony—to the infidel, who would make this world of ours vanish away into abandonment—or to those angels, who ring throughout all their mansions the hosannas of joy, over every one individual of its repentant population?

And here I cannot omit to take advantage of that opening with which our Saviour has furnished us, by the parables of this chapter,* and by which he admits us into a familiar view of that principle on which the inhabitants of Heaven are so awake to the deliverance and the restoration of our species. To illustrate the difference in the reach of knowledge and of affection, between a man and an angel, let us think of the difference of reach between one man and another. You may often witness a man, who feels neither tenderness nor care beyond the precincts of his own family; but who, on the strength of those instinctive fondnesses which nature has implanted in his bosom, may earn the character of an amiable father, or a kind husband, or a bright example of all that is soft and endearing in the relations of domestic society. Now, conceive him, in addition to all this, to carry his affection abroad, without, at the same time, any abatement of their intensity towards the objects which are at home—that, stepping across the limits of the house he occupies, he takes an interest in the families which are near him—that he lends his services to the town or the district wherein he is placed, and gives up a portion of his time to the thoughtful labours of a humane and public-spirited citizen. By this enlargement in the sphere of his attention, he has extended his reach; and provided he has not done so at the expense of that regard which is due to his family,—a thing which, cramped and confined as we are, we are very apt, in the exercise of our humble faculties, to do—I put it to you, whether, by extending the reach of his views and his affections, he has not extended his worth, and his moral respectability along with it?

But I can conceive a still further enlargement. I can figure to myself a man, whose wakeful sympathy overflows the field of his own immediate neighbourhood—to whom the name of country comes with all the omnipotence of a charm upon his heart, and with all the urgency of a most ighteous and resistless claim upon his services—who never hears the name of Britain sounded in his ears, but it stirs up all his enthusiasm in behalf of the worth and the welfare of its people—who gives himself up, with all the devotedness of a passion, to the best and the purest objects of patriotism—and who, spurning away from him the vulgarities of party ambition, separates his life and his labours to the fine pursuit of augmenting the science, or the virtue, or the substantial prosperity of his nation. Oh! could such a man retain all the tenderness, and fulfil all the duties which home and which neighbourhood require of him, and, at the same time, expatiate in the might of his untried faculties, on so wide a field of benevolent contemplation—would not this extension of reach place him still higher than before, on the scale both of moral and intellectual gradation, and give him a still brighter and more enduring name in the records of human excellence?

And, lastly, I can conceive a still loftier flight of humanity—a man, the aspiring of whose heart for the good of man, knows no limitations—whose longings, and whose conceptions on this subject, overlap all the barriers of geography —who, looking on himself as a brother of the species, links every spare energy which belongs to him, with the cause of its melioration—who can embrace, within the grasp of his ample desires, the whole family of mankind—and who, in obedience to a heaven-born movement of principle within him, separates himself to some big and busy enterprise, which is to tell on the moral destinies of the world. Oh! could such a man mix up the softenings of private virtue, with the habit of so sublime a comprehension—if, amid those magnificent darings of thought and of performance, the mildness of his benignant eye could still continue to cheer the retreat of his family, and to spread the charm and the sacredness of piety among all its members—could he even mingle himself in all the gentleness of a soothed and a smiling heart, with the playfulness of his children—and also find strength to shed the blessings of his presence and his counsel over the vicinity around him,—oh! would not the combination of so much grace with so much loftiness, only serve the more to aggrandize him? Would not the one ingredient of a character so rare, go to illustrate and to magnify the other? And would not you pronounce him to be the fairest specimen of our nature, who could so call out all your *tenderness*, while he challenged and compelled all your *veneration*?

TITHES.—DR. CHALMERS.—"This lingering of an old prejudice in the mind of Luther, because consecrated by antiquity, is a striking example of the tenacity with which such prejudices keep their ground. We are hopeless of any demonstration, however irresistible, having its proper effect, either on the body politic or the body ecclesiastical. I am not nearly so sanguine as I was wont to be, that either of those bodies will save itself from ruin by a timely correction of those abuses, which, if not remedied, will effect its destruction. I am far more afraid that the pauperism of England will shake society to pieces, than that Government will gradually do away with this sore blot on our social system. In like manner, though the subject of Tithes is now, in good earnest, under the notice of Parliament, I fear it may too late to save the Church of Ireland. And it is to be observed, in conformity with the principle before alluded to, that made Government take it up in the decided manner it appears to be doing. It was not at the call of English reasoners, but at the compulsion of Irish pikemen.—How much does the force of expediency, and how little does the force of reason, influence the minds of men!"

[These are the sentiments of Dr Chalmers; and in the spirit of these sentiments, we conceive a frank, open avowal, that the Church of Scotland, in her system of Patronage, her Eldership, and her Discipline, both over pastors and people, is not what she ought to be—what she once was—and may again, by the blessing of God, become,—is alike due to truth and good policy.]

SINBAD THE SAILOR.—At a late meeting of the French Academy of Inscriptions, Baron Walkenaer read a very curious paper on the voyages of Sinbad the Sailor, as detailed in the Arabian Nights. His object was, to ascertain what light these entertaining fictions threw on the geographical knowledge of the Arabians in the time of the Caliph Haroun-al-Raschid; that is to say, the eighth or ninth century of our era. He remarks, that Sinbad rarely mentions the name of more than one or two places in each voyage, and these are usually the principal objects of his expedition; and his details of the natural history and productions of each of them are generally exact; whereas he never names the countries in which the scenes of his extravagant and fictitious adventures are laid, and is silent respecting their productions: whence it is fair to conclude, that this fanciful embroidery has been added as an ornamental appendage to the accounts of real voyages undertaken to and from the city of Bagdad. Thus, the first voyage was to Bijanagur, a city in the Southern part of Hindoostan; the second to the Peninsula of Malacca; the third to the Andaman Islands, and to Sumatra; the fourth to the Pepper Coast of Malabar, the Nicobar Isles, and part of the peninsula of Malacca; the fifth along the Malabar coast, to the Maldive Islands; and the sixth and seventh to Cape Comorin, the southern point of Hindoostan, and thence, by the Gulf of Manaar, to the interior of Ceylon. These appear to have been the principal points of the commercial expeditions of the Arabs at the period alluded to, embracing a space included between 44 and 105 degrees of east longitude, and 33 degrees north, and 5 degrees of south latitude.

---

* Luke xv. 7.

THE STORY TELLER.

FIRST GOING TO CHURCH.
A Tale for the Young.

SUSAN YATES.[*]

I was born and brought up, in a house in which my parents had all their lives resided, which stood in the midst of that lonely tract of land called the Lincolnshire Fens. Few families besides our own lived near the spot, both because it was reckoned unwholesome air, and because its distance from any town or market made it an inconvenient situation. My father was in no very affluent circumstances, and it was a sad necessity which he was put to, of having to go many miles to fetch any thing from the nearest village, which was full seven miles distant, through a sad miry way that at all times made it heavy walking, and after rain almost impassable. But he had no horse or carriage of his own.

The church which belonged to the parish in which our house was situated, stood in this village; and its distance being, as I said before, seven miles from our house, made it quite an impossible thing for my mother or me to think of going to it. Sometimes, indeed, on a fine dry Sunday, my father would rise early, and take a walk to the village, just to see how *goodness thrived*, as he used to say; but he would generally return tired, and the worse for his walk. It is scarcely possible to explain to any one who has not lived in the fens, what difficult and dangerous walking it is. A mile is as good as four, I have heard my father say, in those parts. My mother, who in the early part of her life had lived in a more civilized spot, and had been used to constant church-going, would often lament her situation. It was from her I early imbibed a great curiosity and anxiety to see that thing, which I had heard her call a church, and so often lament that she could never go to. I had seen houses of various structures, and had seen in pictures the shapes of ships and boats, and palaces and temples, but never rightly any thing that could be called a church, or that could satisfy me about its form. Sometimes I thought it must be like our house, and sometimes I fancied it must be more like the house of our neighbour, Mr. Sutton, which was bigger and handsomer than ours. Sometimes I thought it was a great hollow cave, such as I have heard my father say the first inhabitants of the earth dwelt in. Then I thought it was like a waggon, or a cart, and that it must be something movable. The shape of it ran in my mind strangely, and one day I ventured to ask my mother, what was that foolish thing she was always longing to go to, and which she called a church. Was it any thing to eat or drink, or was it only like a great huge plaything, to be seen and stared at? I was not quite five years of age when I made this inquiry.

This question, so oddly put, made my mother smile; but in a little time she put on a more grave look, and informed me, that a church was nothing that I had supposed it, but it was a great building, far greater than any house which I had seen, where men, and women, and children, came together twice a-day on Sundays, to hear the Bible read, and make good resolutions for the week to come. She told me, that the fine music which we sometimes heard in the air, came from the bells of St Mary's Church, and that we never heard it but when the wind was in a particular point. This raised my wonder more than all the rest; for I had somehow conceived that the noise which I heard, was occasioned by birds up in the air, or that it was made by the angels, whom (so ignorant I was till that time) I had always considered to be a sort of birds; for before this time I was totally ignorant of any thing like religion, it being a principle of my father, that young heads should not be told too many things at once, for fear they should get confused ideas and no clear notions of any thing. We had always indeed so far observed Sundays, that no work was done upon that day; and upon that day I wore my best muslin frock, and was not allowed to sing, or to be noisy; but I never understood why that day should differ from any other. We had no public meetings:—indeed the few straggling houses which were near us, would have furnished but a slender congregation; and the loneliness of the place we lived in, instead of making us more sociable, and drawing us closer together, as my mother used to say it ought to have done, seemed to have the effect of making us more distant and averse to society than other people. One or two good neighbours, indeed, we had, but not in number to give me an idea of church attendance.

But now my mother thought it high time to give me some clearer instruction in the main points of religion, and my father came readily into her plan. I was now permitted to sit up half an hour later on a Sunday evening, that I might hear a portion of scripture read, which had always been their custom, though by reason of my tender age, and my father's opinion on the impropriety of children being taught too young, I had never till now been an auditor. I was also taught my prayers.

The clearer my notions on these points became, they only made me more passionately long for the privilege of joining in that social service, from which it seemed that we alone, of all the inhabitants of the land, were debarred; and when the wind was in that point which enabled the sound of the distant bells of St. Mary's to be heard over the great moor which skirted our house, I have stood out in the air to catch the sounds, which I almost devoured; and the tears have come into my eyes, when sometimes they seemed to speak to me almost in articulate sounds, to *come to church*, and because of the great moor which was between me and them I could not come; and the too tender apprehensions of these things have filled me with a religious melancholy. With thoughts like these I entered into my seventh year.

And now the time was come, when the great moor was no longer to separate me from the object of my wishes and of my curiosity. My father having some money left him by the will of a deceased relation, we ventured to set up a sort of a carriage—no very superb one; but in that part of the world it was looked upon with some envy by our poorer neighbours. The first party of pleasure which my father proposed to take in it, was to the village where I had so often wished to go, and my mother and I were to accompany him; for it was very fit, my father observed, that little Susan should go to church, and learn how to behave herself, for we might sometime or other have occasion to live in London, and not always be confined to that out-of-the-way spot.

It was on a Sunday morning that we set out, my little

[*] We cannot tell about the authorship of this very beautiful story. It has been attributed to Elia, and the fine imagination it displays makes this probable.

heart beating with almost breathless expectation. The day was fine, and the roads as good as they ever are in those parts. I was so happy and so proud! I was lost in dreams of what I was going to see. At length the tall steeple of St. Mary's Church came in view. It was pointed out to me by my father, as the place from which that music had come which I had heard over the moor, and had fancied to be angels singing. I was wound up to the highest pitch of delight, at having visibly presented to me the spot from which had proceeded that unknown friendly music; and when it began to peal, just as we approached the village, it seemed to speak, *Susan is come*, as plainly as it used to invite me *to come*, when I heard it over the moor. I pass over our alighting at the house of a relation, and all that passed till I went with my father and mother to church.

St. Mary's Church is a great church for such a small village as it stands in. My father said it had been a cathedral, and that it had once belonged to a monastery, but the monks were all gone. Over the door there was stone work, representing saints and bishops, and here and there, along the sides of the church, there were figures of men's heads, made in a strange grotesque way; I have since seen the same sort of figures in the round tower of the Temple-Church in London. My father said they were very improper ornaments for such a place, and so I now think them; but it seems the people who built these great churches in old times, gave themselves more liberties than they do now; and I remember that when I first saw them, and before my father had made this observation, though they were so ugly and out of shape, and some of them seem to be grinning and distorting their features with pain or with laughter, yet being placed upon a church, to which I had come with such serious thoughts, I could not help thinking they had some serious meaning; and I looked at them with wonder, but without any temptation to laugh. I some how fancied they were the representation of wicked people set up as a warning.

When we got into the church, the service was not begun, and my father kindly took me round, to shew me the monuments, and every thing else remarkable. I remember seeing one of a venerable figure, which my father said had been a judge. The figure was kneeling as if it was alive, before a sort of desk, with a book, I suppose the Bible, lying on it. I somehow fancied the figure had a sort of life in it, it seemed so natural, or that the dead judge that it was done for, said his prayers at it still. This was a silly notion; but I was very young, and had passed my little life in a remote place, where I had never seen any thing nor knew any thing; and the awe which I felt at first being in a church, took from me all power but that of wondering. I did not reason about any thing; I was too young. Now I understand why monuments are put up for the dead, and why the figures which are upon them are described as doing the actions which they did in their lifetimes, and that they are a sort of pictures set up for our instruction. But all was new and surprising to me on that day;—the long windows with little panes, the pillars, the pews made of oak, the little hassocks for the people to kneel on, the form of the pulpit, with the sounding-board over it, gracefully carved in flower-work. To you, who have lived all your lives in populous places, and have been taken to church from the earliest time you can remember, my admiration of these things must appear strangely ignorant. But I was a lonely young creature, that had been brought up in remote places, where there was neither church nor church-going inhabitants. I have since lived in great towns, and seen the ways of churches and of worship, and I am old enough now to distinguish between what is essential in religion, and what is merely formal or ornamental.

When my father had done pointing out to me the things most worthy of notice about the church, the service was almost ready to begin; the parishioners had most of them entered, and taken their seats; and we were shewn into a pew where my mother was already seated. Soon after, the clergyman entered, and the organ began to play what is called the voluntary. I had never seen so many people assembled before. At first I thought that all eyes were upon me, and that because I was a stranger. I was terribly ashamed and confused at first; but my mother helped me to find out the places in the Prayer-book, and being busy about that, took off some of my painful apprehensions. I was no stranger to the order of the service, having often read in the Prayer-book at home; but my thoughts being confused, it puzzled me a little to find out the responses and other things, which I thought I knew so well; but I went through it tolerably well. One thing which has often troubled me since, is, that I am afraid I was too full of myself, and of thinking how happy I was, and what a privilege it was for one that was so young, to join in the service with so many grown people, so that I did not attend enough to the instruction which I might have received. I remember, I foolishly applied every thing that was said to myself, so as it could mean nobody but myself, I was so full of my own thoughts. All that assembly of people, seemed to me as if they were come together only to shew me the way of a church. Not but I received some very affecting impressions from some things which I heard that day; but the standing up and the sitting down of the people; the organ; the singing:—the way of all these things took up more of my attention than was proper; or I thought it did. I believe I behaved better, and was more serious when I went a second time, and a third time; for now we went as a regular thing every Sunday, and continued to do so, till by a still further change for the better in my father's circumstances, we removed to London. Oh! it was a happy day for me my first going to St. Mary's Church: before that day I used to feel like a little outcast in the wilderness, like one that did not belong to the world of Christian people. I have never felt like a little outcast since. But I never can hear the sweet noise of bells, that I don't think of the angels singing, and what poor but pretty thoughts I had of angels in my uninstructed solitude.

THE PONGOS.

The following extraordinary narrative was received by Mr. Hogg, the Ettrick Shepherd, but by what ship, we do not pretend to say.

In my last I related to you all the circumstances of our settlement here, and the prospect that we had of a peaceful and pleasant habitation. In truth, it is a fine country, and inhabited by a fine race of people; for the Kousies, as far as I have seen of them, are a simple and ingenious race; and Captain Johnstone having secured the friendship and protection of their chief, we lived in the most perfect harmony with them, trafficking with them for oxen, for which we gave them iron and copper in exchange, the former being held in high estimation by them. But, alas! Sir, such a fate has befallen to me since I wrote you last, as I am sure never fell to the lot of a human being. And I am now going to relate to you one of those stories which, were it to occur in a romance, would be reckoned quite out of nature, and beyond all the bounds of probability; so true is it that there are many things in heaven and earth that are not dreamed of in our philosophy.

You knew my Agnes from her childhood: you were at our wedding at Beattock, and cannot but remember what an amiable and lovely girl she then was. I thought so, and so did you; at least you said you never had as bonny a bride on your knee. But you will hardly believe that her beauty was then nothing in comparison with what it became afterwards; and when she was going about our new settlement with our little boy in her arms, I have often fancied that I never saw so lovely a human being.

Be that as it may, the chief Karoo came to me one day, with his interpreter, whom he caused to make a long palaver about his power, and dominion, and virtues, and his great desire to do much good. The language of this fellow being a mixture of Kaffre, High Dutch, and English, was peculiarly ludicrous, and most of all so, when he concluded with expressing his lord's desire to have my wife to be his own, and to give me in exchange for her four oxen, the best that I could choose from his herd!

As he made the proposal in presence of my wife, she was so much tickled with the absurdity of the proposed barter, and the manner in which it was expressed, that she laughed immoderately. Karoo, thinking she was delighted with it, eyed her with a look that surpasses all description, caused his interpreter to make another palaver to her concerning all the good things she was to enjoy, one of which was, that she was to ride upon an ox whose horns were tipped with gold. I thanked the great Karoo for his kind intentions, but declared my incapability to part with my wife, for that we were one flesh and blood, and nothing could separate us but death. He could comprehend no such tie as this. All men sold their wives and daughters as they listed, I was told—for that the women were the sole property of the men. He had bought many women from the Tambookies that were virgins, and had never given above two cows for any of them; and because he desired to have my wife, he had offered me as much for her as would purchase four of the best wives in all the two countries, and that therefore I was bound to give her up to him. And when I told him, finally, that nothing on earth could induce me to part with her, he seemed offended, bit his thumb, knitted his brows, and studied long in silence, always casting glances at Agnes, of great pathos and languishment, which were perfectly irresistible, and ultimately he stuck his spear's head in the ground, and offered me ten cows and a bull for my wife, and a choice virgin to boot, when this proffer was likewise declined, he smiled in derision, telling me I was the son of foolishness, and that *he foretold that I should repent it.* Three times he went over this, and then went away in high dudgeon. Will you, Sir, believe, or will any person alive believe, that it was possible I could live to repent this!

My William was at this time about eleven months old, but was still at the breast, as I could never prevail on his lovely mother to wean him; and, at the very time of which I am speaking, our little settlement was invaded one night by a tribe of those large baboons called ourang-outangs, pongos, or wild men of the woods, who did great mischief to our fruits, yams, and carrots. From that time we kept a great number of guns loaded, and set a watch; and at length the depredators were again discovered. We sallied out upon them in a body, not without alarm, for they are powerful and vindictive animals, and our guns were only loaded with common shot. They fled at the first sight of us, and that with such swiftness, that we might as well have tried to catch deer; but we got one close fire at them, and doubtless wounded a number of them, as their course was traced with blood. We pursued them as far as the Keys river, which they swam, and we lost them.

Among all the depredators there was none fell but one youngling, which I lifted in my arms, when it looked so pitifully, and cried so like a child, that my heart bled for it. A large monster, more than six feet high, perceiving that he had lost his cub, returned, brandishing a huge club, and grinning at me. I wanted to restore the abominable brat, for I could not bear the thought of killing it, it was so like a human creature; but before I could do this, several shots had been fired by my companions at the hideous monster, which caused him once more to take to his heels; but, turning oft, as he fled, he made threatening gestures at me. A Kousi servant that we had, finished the cub, and I caused it to buried.

The very morning but one after, Agnes and her black maid were milking our few cows upon the green; I was in the garden, and William was toddling about pulling flowers, when, all at once, the women were alarmed by the sight of a tremendous ourang-outang issuing from our house, which they had just left. They seem to have been struck dumb and senseless with amazement, for not one of them uttered a sound, until the monster, springing forward, in one moment, snatched up the child and made off with him. Instead of coming to me, the women pursued the animal with the child, not knowing, I believe, what they were doing. The fearful shrieks which they uttered alarmed me, and I ran to the milking green, thinking the cows had fallen on the women, as the cattle of that district are ticklish for pushing when any way hurt or irritated. Before I reached the green where the cows stood, the ourang-outang was fully half a mile gone, and only the poor feeble, exhausted women, running after him. For a good while I could not conceive what was the matter, but having my spade in my hand, I followed spontaneously in the same direction. Before I overtook the women, I heard the agonizing cries of my dear boy, my darling William, in the paws of that horrible monster. There is no sensation of which the human heart is capable, that can at all be compared with the horror which at that dreadful moment seized on mine. My sinews lost their tension, and my whole frame became lax and powerless. I believe I ran faster than usual, but then I fell every minute, and as I passed Agnes, she fell into a fit. Kela-kal, the black girl, with an astonishing presence of mind, had gone off at a tangent, without orders, or without being once missed, to warn the rest of the settlers, which she did with all expedition. I pursued on, breathless, and altogether unnerved with agony; but, alas! I rather lost than gained ground.

I think if I had been fairly started, that through desperation I could have overtaken the monster; but the hopelessness of success rendered me feeble. The truth is, that he did not make great speed, not nearly the speed these animals are wont to make, for he was greatly encumbered with the child. You, perhaps, do not understand the nature of these animals—neither do I: but they have this peculiarity, that when they are walking leisurely, or running down hill, they walk upright, like a human being; but when hard-pressed on level ground, or up hill, they use their long arms as fore-legs, and then run with inconceivable swiftness. When flying with their own young, the greater part of them will run nearly twice as fast as an ordinary man, for the cubs cling to them with both feet and hands; but as my poor William shrunk from the monster's touch, he was obliged to embrace him closely with one paw, and run on three, and still in that manner he outran me. O may never earthly parent be engaged in such a heart-rending pursuit! Keeping still his distance before me, he reached the Keys river, and there the last gleam of hope closed on me, for I could not swim, while the ourang-outang, with much acuteness, threw the child across his shoulders, held him by the feet with one paw, and with the other three stemmed the river, though then in flood, with amazing rapidity. It was at this dreadful moment that my beloved babe cast his eyes on me as I ran across the plain towards him, and I saw him holding up his little hands in the midst of the foaming flood, and crying out " Pa! pa! pa!" which he seemed to utter with a sort of desperate joy at seeing me approach.

Alas! that sight was the last, for in two minutes thereafter the monster vanished with my dear child, in the jungles and woods beyond the river, and there my course was stayed; for, to have thrown myself in, would only have been committing suicide, and leaving a destitute widow in a foreign land. I had therefore no other resource but to throw myself down, and pour out my soul in lamentation and prayer to God. From this state of hapless misery I was quickly aroused by the sight of twelve of my countrymen coming full speed across the plain on my track. They were all armed and stripped for the pursuit; and four of them, some of whom you know, Adam Johnstone, Adam Haliday, Peter Carruthers, and Joseph Nicholson, being excellent swimmers, plunged at once into the river, and swam across, though not without both difficulty and danger, and without loss of time continued the pursuit. All pursuit was in vain.

About three months after this sad calamity, one evening, on returning home from my labour, my Agnes was missing, and neither her maid-servant, nor one of all the settlers, could give the least account of her.

I was now determined to attack the native chief, who, I thought, had stolen her. Just when we were on the eve of commencing a war, which must have been ruinous to our settlement, a black servant of Adam Johnstone's came to me, and said that I ought not to fight and kill his good chief, for he had not the white woman. I was astonished, and asked the Kaffre what he meant, when he told me that he himself saw my wife carried across the river by a band of pongos, (ourang-outangs,) but he had always kept it a secret, for fear of giving me distress, as they were too far gone for pursuit, when he beheld them. He said they had her bound, and were carrying her gently on their arms; but she was either dead, or in a swoon, for she was not crying, and her long hair was hanging down.

About the beginning of last year a strange piece of intelligence reached our settlement. It was said that two maids of Kamboo had been out on the mountains of Norroweldt, gathering fruits, where they had seen a pongo taller than any Kousi, and that this pongo had a beautiful white boy with him, for whom he was gathering the choicest fruits, and the boy was gambolling and playing around him, and leaping on his shoulders.

This was a piece of intelligence so extraordinary and so much out of the common course of events, that every one of the settlers agreed that it could not be a forgery, and that it behoved us to look after it immediately. We applied to Karoo for assistance, who had a great number of slaves from that country, much attached to him, who knew the language of the place whither we were going, and all the passes of the country. He complied readily with our request, giving us an able and intelligent guide, with as many of his people as we chose. We raised in all fifty Malays and Kousis; nine British soldiers, and every one of the settlers that could bear arms went with us; so that we had in all nearly an hundred men, the blacks being armed with pikes, and all the rest with swords, guns, and pistols. We journeyed for a whole week, travelling much by night, and resting in the shade by day, and at last we came to the secluded district of which we were in search, and in which we found a temporary village, or camp, of one of those independent inland tribes. They were in great alarm at our approach, and were apparently preparing for a vigorous resistance; but on our guide, who was one of their own tribe, going up to them, and explaining our views, they received us joyfully, and proffered their assistance.

From this people we got the heart-stirring intelligence that a whole colony of pongos had taken possession of that country, and would soon be masters of it all; for that the Great Spirit had sent them a queen from the country beyond the sun, to teach them to speak, and work, and go to war; and that she had the entire power over them, and would not suffer them to hurt any person who did not offer offence to them; that they knew all she said to them, and answered her, and lived in houses, and kindled fires like other people, and likewise fought rank and file; that they had taken one of the maidens of their own tribe to wait upon the queen's child; but because the girl wept, the queen caused them to set her at liberty.

I was now rent between hope and terror—hope that this was my own wife and child, and terror that they would be torn to pieces by the savage monsters, rather than given up. Of this last, the Lockos (the name of this wandering tribe) assured us we needed not to entertain any apprehensions, for that they would every one of them die rather than wrong a hair of their queen's head. But that it behoved us instantly to surround them; for if they once came to understand that we were in pursuit, they would make their escape, and then the whole world would not turn or detain them.

Accordingly, that very night, being joined by the Lockos, we surrounded the colony by an extensive circle, and continued to close as we advanced. By the break of day we had them closely surrounded. The monsters flew to arms at the word of command, nothing daunted, forming a circle round their camp and queen, the strongest of the males being placed outermost and the females inmost; but all armed alike, and all having the same demure and melancholy faces. The circle being so close that I could not see inside, I went with the nine red-coats to the top of a cliff, that in some degree overlooked the encampment, in order that, if my Agnes really was there, she might understand who was near her. Still I could not discover what was within; but I called her name aloud several times, and in about five minutes after that, the whole circle of tremendous brutal warriors flung away their arms and retired backward, leaving an open space for me to approach their queen.

In the most dreadful trepidation I entered between the hideous files, being well guarded by soldiers on either hand, and followed by the rest of the settlers; and there indeed I beheld my wife, my beloved Agnes, standing ready to receive me, with little William in her right hand, and a beautiful chubby daughter in her left, about two years old, and the very image of her mother. Conceive, if you can, Sir, such a meeting! Were there ever a husband and wife met under such circumstances before? Never since the creation of the world! The two children looked healthy and beautiful, with their fur aprons; but it struck me at first that my beloved was much altered; it was only, however, caused by her internal commotion, by feelings which overpowered her grateful heart, against which nature could not bear up; for on my first embrace she fainted in my arms, which kept us all in suspension and confusion for a long space. The children fled from us, crying for their mother, and took shelter with their friends the pongos, who seemed in great amazement, and part of them began to withdraw, as if to hide themselves.

As soon as Agnes was somewhat restored, I proposed that we should withdraw from the camp of her savage colony; but she refused, and told me that it behoved her to part with her protectors on good terms, and that she must depart without any appearance of compulsion, which they might resent; and we actually rested ourselves during the heat of the day in the sheds erected by those savage inhabitants of the forest. My wife went to her hoard of provisions, and distributed to every one of the pongos his share of fruit, succulent herbs, and roots, which they ate with great composure. It was a curious scene, something like what I had seen in a menagerie; and there was my little William, serving out food to the young ourang-outangs, cuffing them, and ordering them, in the broad Annandale dialect, to do this, that, and the other thing; and they were not only obedient, but seemed flattered by his notice and correction. We were then presented with delicious fruits; but I had no heart to partake, being impatient to have my family away from the midst of this brutal society; for, as long as we were there, I could not conceive them safe or fairly in my own power.

Agnes then stood up, and made a speech to her subjects, accompanying her expressions with violent motions and contortions, to make them understand her meaning. They understood it perfectly; for when they heard that she and her children were to leave them, they set up such a jabbering of lamentation as British ears never heard. Many of them came cowering and fawning before her, and she laid her hands on their heads; many, too, of the young ones, came running, and lifting up the children's hands, put them on their own heads. We then formed a close circle round Agnes and the children, to the exclusion of the pongos, that still followed behind, howling and lamenting; and that night we lodged in the camp of the Lockos, placing a triple guard round my family, of which there stood great need. We durst not travel by night; but we contrived two covered hurdles in which we carried Agnes and the children; and for three days a considerable body of the tallest and strongest of the ourang-outangs attended our steps, and some of them came fearlessly every day, as she said, to see if she was well, and if we were not hurting her.

My Agnes's part of the story is the most extraordinary of all. But here I must needs be concise, giving only a short and general outline of her adventures; for, among dumb animals, whose signals and grimaces were so liable to misinterpretation, much must have been left to her own conjecture. The creatures' motives for stealing and detaining her appeared to have been as follows:—

These animals remain always in distinct tribes, and are perfectly subordinate to a chief or ruler, and his secondary chiefs. In their expedition to rob our gardens, they had brought their sovereign's sole heir along with them, as they never leave any of the royal family behind them, for fear of a surprisal. It was this royal cub which we killed; and the queen, his mother, having been distractedly inconsolable for the loss of her darling, the old monarch had set out by night to try, if possible, to recover it; and, on not finding it, he seized on my boy in its place, carried him home in safety to his queen, and gave her to him to nurse! She did so. Yes, she positively did nurse him at her breast for three months, and never child throve better than he did. By that time he was beginning to walk, and aim at speech, by imitating every voice he heard, whether of beast or bird; and it had struck the monsters as a great loss that they had no means of teaching their young sovereign to speak, at which art he seemed so apt. This led to the scheme of stealing his own mother to be his instructor, which they effected in the most masterly style, binding and gagging her in her own house, and carrying her from a populous hamlet in the fair forenoon, without having been discovered. Their expertness, and the rapidity of their motions, Agnes described as inconceivable by those who had never witnessed them. They showed every sort of tenderness and kindness by the way, proffering her plenty of fruit and water; but she gave herself totally up to despair, till behold, she was introduced to her own little William, plump, thriving, and as merry as a cricket, gambolling away among his brutal compeers, for many of whom he had conceived a great affection; but then they far outgrew him, while others as fast overtook him in size.

Agnes immediately took her boy under her tuition, and was soon given to understand that her will was to be the sole law of the community; and all the while that they detained her, they never refused her in aught save to take her home again. Our little daughter she had named Beatrice, after her maternal grandmother. She was born six months and six days after Agnes's abstraction. She spoke highly of the pongos, of their docility, generosity, warmth of affection to their mates and young ones, and of their irresistible strength. She conceived that, however, to have been a tribe greatly superior to all others of the race, for she never could regard them in any other light than as dumb human creatures. I confess that I had the same sort of feeling while in their settlement, for many of the young females in particular were much comelier than negro savages which I have often seen; and they laughed, smiled, and cried very much like human creatures. At my wife's injunctions, or from her example, they all wore aprons; and the females had let the hair of their heads grow long. It was glossy black, and neither curled nor woolly; and, on the whole, I cannot help having a lingering affection for the creatures. They would make the most docile, powerful, and affectionate of all slaves; but they come very soon to their growth, and are but short-lived, in that way approximating to the rest of the brute creation. They live entirely on fruits, roots, and vegetables, and taste no animal food whatever.

I asked Agnes much of the civility of their manner to her, and she always described it as respectful and uniform. For a while she never thought herself quite safe when near the queen; but the dislike of the latter to her arose entirely out of her boundless affection for the boy. No mother could possibly be fonder of her own offspring than this affectionate creature was of William, and she was jealous of his mother for taking him from her, and causing him instantly to be weaned. But then the chief never once left the two queens by themselves; they had always a guard day and night.

I have no objection to the publication of these adventures in Britain, though I know they will not obtain credit; but I should not like that the incidents reached the *Sydney Gazette*, as I intend emigrating to that country as soon as I receive value for the stock I left at the settlements; for I have a feeling that my family is scarcely safe as long as I remain on any part of the coast of Africa. And, for the sake of my rising family, I have an aversion to its being known that they were bred among creatures that must still be conceived to be of the brute creation. Do not write till you hear from me again; and believe me ever your old affectionate friend,—WM. MITCHELL. (Cape of Good Hope, October 1, 1826.—*Altrive Tales.*

CHARACTER OF MR. HUME.

WE select Joseph Hume as the object of this sketch, because we think his character has been more misrepresented and his merits more undervalued, than those of any existing member of the House of Commons;—because he has fought harder, and to more practical purpose, for that consideration which he now enjoys, than any other man we could name; —and because, at this moment, he is really the most important man, out of office, in the British Senate. True, he possesses not one quality calculated for dazzling the crowd;—true, he cannot roar like Hobhouse, draw out a syllogism like Denman, raise a pyramid topped with Latin, like Mackintosh, or break an adversary on the wheel like Brougham;—true, he never delivered a finished oration— nor, perhaps, ever uttered a perfect sentence;—but equally true, he never chose a useless subject on account of its sound, and he never shrunk from what he conceived to be a public duty, on account of the hostility which it stirred up in others, or the labour which it occasioned himself. Upon parade days, he does not rend the air and rattle the benches like some others that we could name; but when these have once let themselves off, they are as inefficient as discharged blunderbusses; they go away, " one to his farm, and another to his merchandise,"—one to his pastime, and another to his private business: while Joseph Hume stands firm at his post, in fair weather or in foul, applauded or deserted. He is a statesman of the Franklin school:—he comes upon his adversaries with the figures of arithmetic, and before their heavy array, the light and gaudy troops of the figures of speech cannot stand for a moment. This has been evinced again and again. All the light missiles of wit, and all the toothed matters of invective, have been literally rained at him from both sides of the House; but he stood, like the tower of Belus amidst the confusion of tongues, or his native hills during a snow storm; he shook not at the noise and the blast; he bore no dint from the flakes; but, waiting his opportunity, he (with the whole strength of his arm, and it is not a weak one) launched at them Cocker's Arithmetic, which very seldom failed to take effect.

When Hume came into Parliament, there were strong prejudices against him. The circumstances of the times identified him with clamouring demagogues, in a manner which he neither desired nor merited; the whig aristocracy kept aloof; and by all their small followers he was held as a man upon whom a joke might always be played off with favour, and the reversionary recompense of a dinner and a compliment. During all this time, however, Joseph Hume was no theoretical dreamer in politics, as little was he a man who sought to overturn the state, the church, or any one branch of either. Educated in a more severe manner, he had none of the ambition or the levity of those who thought to put him down; but he had strong intuitive perceptions of right and wrong; and these he directed, not to what was the most fair and fascinating in theory, but to what was most useful and most within reach in practice. We remember that, about the middle of the first session, the wise ones, who prophesied in the train of their idols on both sides, predicted that next session, he would be lowered; and in a third, he would either be silent or sunk into some little government office; but here he is still, as earnest and as active as ever; and though we agree, that he sometimes speaks when he should be silent, we say, without fearing contradiction, that he is more listened to than ever. We are sure too, that the enlightened members now at the head of the financial and commercial departments of government will admit, and admit without hesitation, that they have profited more, and to better purpose, by Joseph Hume, than by all others on the left hand of the Speaker; and though he generally both argues and divides against them, we find them frequently acting upon his suggestions. Though Hume sits with, and divides with the Old Opposition, we cannot regard him as being one of their *party*. The fact is, that he has formed a party and opposition wholly his own, and were we to apply a distinctive epithet to him and the few who follow his steps—though with less energy and perseverance—we should call them the *Financial* Opposition —the men who work the sledge hammer to ministers in shaping reductions of taxation and expenditure.

For this purpose no man is better fitted than Hume, either in body or in mind; in body he is a perfect colossus in point of strength; and that strength, together with the emperance and regularity of his habits, makes him able to undergo fatigue which would exhaust any other man. Of his mind, firmness and patience are the leading characters; and those characters are so strongly marked in his form and face, that no man who has read the debates, has occasion, upon entering the House of Commons, to ask which is Joseph Hume. You perceive him sitting by his pillar, in a dress equally remarkable for its plainness and its cleanness. There is nothing of the fop or the sloven about him. You never find him lounging; you never hear him laugh; and when he speaks to those about him it is always respecting the business before the House, or the contents of some papers, a pile of which are always beside him. If he be without his hat, you are instantly struck with the appearance of his head. It wants the dazzling eloquence of that of Mr. Canning; it has not the acuteness of that of Huskisson; you seek in vain for the perspicuity of Goderich; and you can mark no trace of the dark-lowering strength of Brougham; but there is in it a firmness of purpose, an inflexibility of temper, and a truth to the end, which accompany not, and perhaps cannot accompany these more splendid qualities. There is no imagination, and neither a beam of wit nor humour; and the power of oratory is entirely lost in the deep retiring of the eyes. But the lower lateral parts of the forehead, and, above all, the firm setting of the nose, and the hard line to which the lips are compressed, tell you that this, and none other that you see in the House must be Joseph Hume. Along with this firmness there is a considerable indication of honesty. You instantly pronounce that the man will neither change a subject nor a mode of treating it, without being in earnest. He rises to speak. His manner is unseemly, his accent strongly and even disagreeably provincial, and his language both inaccurate and inelegant; but still, somehow or other, you find yourself obliged to listen to it; and though he never rounds, and seldom completes a period, he is always intelligible, and very often convincing. No doubt, the constant occurrence of numbers in what he says, and his habit of sometimes mistaking those numbers, make him unpleasant to mere lovers of language; but with those who can judge of things as well as words, he is, though sometimes very tedious, never absolutely tiresome. There, too, the character of such a man as Hume is open to misrepresentation. Of those who attend the House of Commons, so as to be able to form any opinion of the members, there are many who come there as mere loungers, or as the listeners of their favourite orators; and to them the following of Hume through his long and intricate calculations, is a work of aversion. To the intelligent within the House, and the rational without, he, however, appears in a very different point of view. They regard him, as indeed posterity will regard him, as being, though far from the most splendid, one of the most straight-forward, persevering, and useful labourers of the age; and possessing those substantial qualities, he may well leave others to enjoy the show. Indeed, he must so leave them, for he is not at all equal to the field-day parade of the orators—as little as they are equal to his every-day duty.—*Anonymous.*

BLACK HOLE OF CALCUTTA.

The Indian army, in the first occupation of Fort William, did not commit any outrage; but when the nabob entered, accompanied by his general, Meer Jaffier, he sent for Mr Holwell, and burst into violent reproaches at his having attempted to defend the place against the ruler of Bengal. He expressed also the most extreme dissatisfaction at finding in the treasury only the small sum of 50,000 rupees. Yet, after three interviews, he dismissed him with assurances, on the word of a soldier, that no harm should be done to him. Mr. Holwell returned to his companions, and found them surrounded by a strong guard, who led them into a veranda, or arched gallery, constructed to shelter the soldiers from the sun and rain, but which excluded the chambers behind it from light and air. Some quarters of the fort being on fire, they were involved in so thick a smoke as inspired them with the apprehension that a design was formed to suffocate them; but the guard were merely looking out for a proper place of confinement. They pitched upon a chamber employed as the common dungeon of the garrison, called the *black hole* ; it consisted of a space eighteen feet square, with only two small windows barred with iron, opening into the close veranda, and scarcely admitting a breath of air. Into this narrow receptacle, the whole of the officers and troops, 146 in number, were compelled to enter; and, on their venturing to remonstrate, the commander ordered every one who should hesitate to be instantly cut down. Thus were they forcibly thrust into this fearful dungeon, into which the whole number could with difficulty be squeezed; the door was then fast barred from without. Their first impression, on finding themselves thus immured, was the utter impossibility of surviving one night, and the necessity of extricating themselves at whatever cost. The jemautdars, or Indian guards, were walking before the window, and Mr. Holwell seeing one who bore on his face a more than usual expression of humanity, adjured him to procure for them room in which they could breath, assuring him next morning of a reward of 1000 rupees. The man went away—but returned, saying it was impossible. The prisoners, thinking the offer had been too low, tendered 2000 rupees. The man again went,—and returned, saying that the nabob was asleep, and no one durst awake him. The lives of 146 men were nothing in comparison to disturbing for a m-

ment the slumbers of a tyrant. Mr. Holwell has described in detail the horrors of that fatal night, which are scarcely paralleled in the annals of human misery. Every moment added to their distress. All attempts to obtain relief by a change of posture, from the painful pressure to which it gave rise, only aggravated their sufferings. The air soon became pestilential, producing, at every respiration, a feeling of suffocation; the perspiration flowed in streams, and they were tormented with the most burning thirst. Unfortunately, the stations at or near the windows being decidedly the best, the most dreadful struggles were made to reach them. Many of the prisoners being common and foreign soldiers, exempt by this dreadful calamity from all subordination, made an intolerable pressure, and the sufferers, as they grew weaker, began to be squeezed or trampled to death. Loud cries being raised of "water!" the humane jemautdar pushed through the bars several skins filled with that liquid; but this produced only an increase of calamity, through the violent efforts made in order to obtain it. The soldiers without found a savage sport in witnessing these contests, and even brought lights to the windows in order to view them to greater advantage. About eleven, the prisoners began to die fast; six of Mr. Holwell's intimate friends expired at his feet, and were trampled upon by the survivors. Of those still alive, a great proportion were raving or delirious; some uttered incoherent prayers, others the most frightful blasphemies. They endeavoured, by furious invectives, to induce the guards to fire into the prison and end their miseries, but without effect. When day dawned, the few who had not expired were most of them either raving or insensible. In this last state was Mr. Holwell himself, when, about six o'clock, the nabob awoke and inquired for him. On learning the events of the night, he merely sent to ascertain if the English chief yet lived; and being informed that there were appearances as if he might recover, he gave orders to open the fatal door. At that time, of the 146 who had been enclosed, there breathed only twenty-three. Mr. Holwell, being revived by the fresh air, was immediately supported into the presence of the nabob, who, on his beginning the dismal tale, ordered for him a seat and a draught of water, but showed no other mark of sympathy. He immediately commenced a strict interrogatory about the supposed treasure, discrediting extremely the assertion of its non-existence. Being able, however, to learn nothing on this subject, he sent Mr. Holwell, with three other gentlemen, prisoners to Muxadavad. In this voyage they suffered severely, their bodies being covered with boils, that had broken out in consequence of their confinement; to which, however, these eruptions were supposed to afford relief. The other survivors were liberated; while the dead bodies were, without any ceremony, thrown into a ditch.—*Edinburgh Cabinet Library. History of British India.*

VISIT TO A SILK FACTORY.

You will not suppose there was any thing very cheerful or exhilarating in the paradise we had entered. The idea of a mill is the antipathy of this. One perpetual dull, flagging sound pervaded the whole. The walls were bare; the inhabitants were poor. The children in general earned little more than twelve sous in a week; most of the women, and even several of the men, but about one French crown, (two and sixpence English.) We must correct our ideas, and imagine a very sober paradise, before we can think of applying the name to this mansion.

I was most attentive to the employment of the children, who were a pretty equal number of both sexes. There were about twenty on each floor, sixty in all. Their chief business was to attend to the swifts; the usual number being fifty-six, which was assigned to the care of each child. The threads, while the operation of winding was going on, were of course liable to break; and, the moment a thread was broken, the benefit of the swift to which it belonged was at a stand. The affair of the child was, by turning round the swift, to find the end, and then join it to the corresponding end attached to the bobbin. The child was to superintend the progress of these fifty-six threads, to move backward and forward in his little tether of about ten feet, and the moment any accident happened, to repair it. I need not tell you, that I saw no great expressions of cheerfulness in either the elder or the younger inhabitants of these walls: their occupations were too anxious and monotonous—the poor should not be too much elevated, and incited to forget themselves. There was a kind of stupid and hopeless vacancy in every face: this proceeded from the same causes.

Not one of the persons before me exhibited any signs of vigour and robust health. They were all sallow; their muscles flaccid, and their form emaciated. Several of the children appeared to me, judging from their size, to be under four years of age—I never saw such children. Some were not tall enough with their little arms to reach the swift; these had stools which they carried in their hands, and mounted as occasion offered. A few, I observed, had a sort of iron buskins on which they were elevated; and, as the iron was worked thin, they were not extremely unwieldy. Children, before they had learned that firm step with the sole of the natural foot, without which it is impossible ever to be a man, were thus disciplined to totter upon stilts. But this was a new invention, and not yet fully established.

This, or nearly all this, I observed upon my first survey of M. Vaublanc's manufactory. In addition to this, I afterwards found, what you will easily conceive, that it was not without much severity that the children were trained to the regularity I saw. Figure to yourself a child of three or four years of age. The mind of a child is essentially independent; he does not, till he has been formed to it by hard experience, frame to himself the ideas of authority and subjection. When he is rated by his nurse, he expresses his mutinous spirit by piercing cries; when he is first struck by her in anger, he is ready to fall into convulsions of rage: it almost never happens otherwise. It is a long while (unless he is unmercifully treated, indeed,) before a rebuke or a blow produces in him immediate symptoms of submission. Whether, with the philosopher, we choose to regard this as an evidence of our high destination, or with the theologian, cite it as an indication of our universal depravity, and a brand we bear of Adam's transgression, the fact is indisputable. Almost all that any parent requires of a child of three or four years of age, consists in negatives:—stand still: do not go there; do not touch that. He scarcely expects or desires to obtain from him any mechanical attention. Contrast this with the situation of the children I saw: brought to the mill at six in the morning; detained till six at night; and, with the exception of half an hour for breakfast, and an hour at dinner, kept incessantly watchful over the safety and regularity of fifty-six threads continually turning. By my soul, I am ashamed to tell you by what expedients they are brought to this unintermitted vigilance, this dead life, this inactive and torpid industry!

Consider the subject in another light. Liberty is the school of understanding. This is not enough adverted to. Every boy learns more in his hours of play than in his hours of labour. In school he lays in the materials of thinking; but in his sports he actually thinks: he whets his faculties, and he opens his eyes. The child, from the moment of his birth, is an experimental philosopher; he essays his organs and his limbs, and learns the use of he muscles. Every one who will attentively observe him, will find that this is his perpetual employment. But the whole process depends upon liberty. Put him into a mill, and his understanding will improve no more than that of the horse which turns it. I know that it is said that the lower orders of the people have nothing to do with the cultivation of the understanding; though, for my part, I cannot see how they would be the worse for that growth of practical intellect which should enable them to plan and provide, each one for himself, the increase of his conveniences and competence. But be it so! I know that this earth is the great Bridewell of the universe, where spirits descended from heaven are committed to drudgery and hard labour. Yet I should be glad that our children, upon a certain age, were exempt; sufficient is the hardship and subjection of their whole future life; methinks, even Egyptian taskmasters would consent that they should grow up in peace, till they had acquired the strength necessary for substantial service.

Liberty is the parent of strength. Nature teaches the child, by the play of the muscles, and pushing out his limbs in every direction, to give them scope to develope themselves. Hence it is that he is so fond of sports and tricks in the open air, and that these sports and tricks are so beneficial to him. He runs, he vaults, he climbs, he practises exactness of eye and sureness of aim. His limbs grow straight and taper, and his joints well-knit and exigible. The mind of a child is no less vagrant than his steps; it pursues the gossamer, and flies from object to object, lawless and unconfined; and it is equally necessary to the development of his frame, that his thoughts and his body should be free from fetters. But then he cannot earn twelve sous a-week. These children were uncouth and ill-grown in every limb, and were stiff and decrepit in their carriage, so as to seem like old men. At four years of age they could earn salt to their bread; but at forty, if it were possible that they should live so long, they could not earn bread to their salt. They were made sacrifices, while yet tender; and like the kid, spoken of by Moses, were seethed and prepared for the destroyer in their mother's milk. This is the case in no state of society but in manufacturing towns. The children of gipsies and savages have ruddy cheeks and a sturdy form, can run like lapwings, and climb trees with the squirrel."

[At this time, when the condition of the children in the Factories is so powerful a subject of interest to the humane, the above extract from Godwin's Fleetwood, is appropriate.]

SCRAPS.

SAND AS A MANURE.—An elaborate report on this subject has been presented to the French Academy of Sciences. Good arable land is proved to contain four primitive earths, the varied proportions of which form the different qualities of the soil. It appears the silicious principle predominates in good land. M. Chaptal found of it 49 per cent. in the most fertile soil on the banks of the Loire; Davy extracted 60 from the best of the English soils; and Giobert found 79 in the most productive lands near Turin. M. Dutrochet made the experiment of covering with silicious sand previously unproductive land, and obtained, by this means, crops as good as in the most (naturally) fertile soil in the vicinity; and he gives it as his opinion, that its great fertilizing virtue consists in its allowing both water and air to reach and penetrate to the roots of the vegetable, of which they form the two principal elements.

THE WIRE-WORM.—White mustard-seed will protect the grain from the wire-worm; and this fact I have demonstrated perfectly to my own conviction. I first tried the experiment on half an acre, in the centre of a fifty acre field of fallow, which was much subject to the wire-worm. The mustard-seed being carried, the whole field was fallowed for wheat; and the half acre that had been previously cropped with mustard-seed was wholly exempt from the wire-worm—the remainder of the field was much injured. Not only was the half acre thus preserved, but in the spring it was decidedly the most advanced part of the crop; and the prosperous appearance which it presented caused me to repeat the experiment, by sowing three acres more of mustard-seed in the worst part of a field of forty-five acres, also much subject to the wire-worm. The remainder of the field was sown with early frame peas, which, with the mustard-seed, was cleared in the same week. The land was then ploughed for wheat; and I had the pleasure of noticing these three acres to be quite free from the wire-worm, and much superior in other respects to ———— part of the field, which suffered greatly. Thus ———— by these results, I sowed, the next year, a ———— of forty-two acres, which had never repaid me for ———— years, in consequence of nearly every crop being destroyed by the wire-worm; and I am warranted in stating, that not a single wire-worm could be found the following year, and the crop of wheat throughout, which was reaped last harvest, was superior to any which I had grown for twenty-one years.—*Correspondent of the British Farmer's Magazine.*

YOLK OF WOOL.

Until the experiments of that excellent chemist, Vauquelin, were published, the nature of yolk was unknown. He has found it to be an animal soap; and has observed that wool which has remained a long time in its own yolk, swelled up, split, and lost its strength; effects which take place also in too strong soapy water. "If," says M. Vauquelin, 'the water of yolk causes wool to swell, and to split in this manner, is it not possible that this accident may often take place on the backs of the animals, especially during damp warm weather, or when they are shut up in folds, the litter of which is not often enough removed? It may not be impossible also that the acridity of yolk may occasion an irritation in their skin, and prove the cause of some of those maladies to which this organ is subject in these animals, and which must occur chiefly during damp warm weather; fortunately at this season they are occasionally exposed to rains which wash them, and carry off at least a part of this matter. In this respect I am inclined to adopt the opinion of those who think that the washing of sheep, during dry warm weather, may be useful to their health, and to the quality of the wool." Although every respect is due to so good a chemist as M. Vauquelin, he could have formed his opinion of the effect of yolk on the skin of sheep only from analogy. As common soap is often used with success in cleansing the skin, and curing cutaneous disorders, analogy would lead us to expect that yolk, being of the same nature, would be beneficial instead of being injurious. And it is observed, that fine woolled sheep are less subject to diseases of the skin, than those which carry coarse fleeces; the former being well supplied with yolk and oil, and the latter having drier wool and little yolk. M. Vauquelin thinks yolk a naturally perspired matter; but it is more probably a combination of the salt in sweat with the oil of wool.—*Library of Useful Knowledge.*

LEISURE.—Leisure is the noblest wealth; and the habit of employing it well, is the best preparation for a happy and dignified old age. But he who exclusively applies himself to the acquisition of money, shall waste life under the pressure; and, amid the vacuity of mental poverty, shall close his career by an old age of restless imbecility, or of painful insignificance.

CONTENTS OF NO. XXIX.

Temperance Societies.. 97
COLUMN FOR THE YOUNG—Stories of Birds—The Robin........ 98
COLUMN FOR THE LADIES—Exercise—Principles of Female Dress
 —Farewell—Mary Lindsay.. 101
Trade with the Countries on the Niger................................ 102
Large and Small Farms.. 103
Abhorrence of War.. ib.
ELEMENTS OF THOUGHT—Patriotism—Philanthropy............ 104
THE STORY-TELLER—First Going to Church...................... 105
 The Pongos... 106
Character of Mr. Hume... 109
Black Hole of Calcutta.. 110
Visit to a Silk Factory.. 111
SCRAPS—Sand as a Manure—The Wire-worm—Yolk of Wool—
 Leisure... 112

EDINBURGH: Printed by and for JOHN JOHNSTONE, 19, St. James's Square.—Published by JOHN ANDERSON, Jun., Bookseller, 55, North Bridge Street, Edinburgh; by JOHN MACLEOD, and ATKINSON & Co. Booksellers, Glasgow; and sold by all Booksellers and Vendors of Cheap Periodicals.

THE Schoolmaster,
AND EDINBURGH WEEKLY MAGAZINE.

CONDUCTED BY JOHN JOHNSTONE.

THE SCHOOLMASTER IS ABROAD.—LORD BROUGHAM.

No. 30.—Vol. II. SATURDAY, FEBRUARY 23, 1833. Price Three-Halfpence.

HEREDITARY LEGISLATORS.

In a certain kingdom, a wise and just monarch selected one hundred of the cleverest and most conscientious tailors he could find, and ordained that they alone should make clothes for his subjects. His immediate successors imitated his policy, and, from time to time, as the tailors died, appointed others in their room, equally honest and able. So long as this practice continued, the people were well dressed at a moderate price, the tailors were respected for their skill and assiduity, and the monarch was revered for his wisdom. But, in course of time, there arose a king, who, departing from the ways of his predecessors, decreed, that whenever a tailor died, " the heir male of his body lawfully begotten," should become a privileged snip in his stead. Now, it did not always happen that the " heir male" of the deceased tailor had been bred to the tailoring trade; indeed, in most cases, his father had brought him up in idleness, and thus in a few years it came to pass, that the right to make breeches for the nation fell into the hands of men who had never sat upon a shop-board, or flourished a pair of shears. The people, fortunately for themselves, had on hand a stock of good raiment made in the earlier times, and did not for a considerable period require, from " the heirs male of the body," any better kind of work than patching and mending. But at last the national garments began to wear out, and the people were forced to clothe themselves with such things as the bangling offspring of the genuine tailors could produce. Their coats hung about them like hop-sacks, and instead of being, as formerly, the envy and admiration of surrounding nations, they were laughed at for their clumsy attire, and scorned for submitting to the impositions of a handful of botchers. Yet the measure of their misfortune was not full, for another of their kings thought fit, in the exercise of his royal prerogative, to add to the number of hereditary snips. But instead of conferring that honour upon men brought up to the needle, he bestowed it upon butchers, and sausage-makers, and mountebanks, or any one, in short, that he took a particular liking to. The people groaned under this new oppression, but in vain. The law was against them. The king had an undoubted right, in virtue of his prerogative, to order his subjects to wear breeches made by the " heir male" of a sausage-maker, and the heir male of the sausage-maker had an undoubted right, in virtue of his patent, to force the people to wear whatever he chose to invent, and to pay whatever price he thought proper to exact. These hereditary breeches-makers, finding the law upon their side, waxed more lazy and insolent every day, insomuch, that on several important occasions they flatly refused to execute the orders of their customers for new habits, or to obey their instructions for altering old ones. At last the people began to inquire one of another, whether it would not be better that the tailoring trade should be thrown open to the public, so that instead of being compelled by law to deal for clothes with a butcher, or a mountebank, or the heir male of either of these, the nation might be at liberty to employ real tailors, who had served a proper apprenticeship, and who thoroughly understood their business.

The common argument in defence of hereditary peers is, that they operate as a check upon the House of Commons, and ensure an impartial calculation of the effects of every measure proposed by the representatives of the people. Now, admitting for the sake of the argument, that a check upon the proceedings of the popular representatives is, upon the whole, of public advantage, yet it by no means follows, that the salutary degree of control can only be attained through the medium of hereditary peers. It still remains a question, whether the ardour of the Commons might not be moderated, their mistakes corrected, nay, their plans of national improvement facilitated, by a supervising legislative body appointed for life, and founding its claim to that dignity upon acknowledged wisdom and ability, instead of resting it upon the ludicrous basis of the words "heirs male," or, " heirs male of the body," contained in musty pieces of parchment. It is difficult to suppose, that if the title and privileges of a peer were confined to the life of the deserving individual, the business of legislation would be performed in a manner less couducive to the national welfare than in the by-gone times of the constitution. And still more difficult is it to conceive, that a house of peers, so constituted, resting upon the secure rock of personal merit, would appear less respectable in the eyes of the people, or obtain a smaller share of their esteem and veneration, than an assembly brought together without the slightest reference to the moral or intellectual qualifications of its individual members.

There was a time, no doubt, but that was before the Schoolmaster broke loose, when the multitude asked no questions, and believed that, "Noblemen," and "Solomon," were synonyms. But this complimentary delusion has long been vanishing, and recent events have thoroughly dispelled it. Men are now awake to the truth, that what their ancestors transmitted to them as a body of collective wisdom, is, after all, but an assembly of human beings; subject to the same frailties, the same boisterous passions and selfish motives, the same foolish obstinacy and wilful blindness, as any body of men equally numerous, and similarly acted upon by the mighty levers of hope, and fear, and self-interest. The world now discovers, somewhat late in the day, it must be confessed, that wisdom is not the constant concomitant of nobility, nor discretion the inseparable appendage of a dukedom; and although the providential accident of being born of titled parents may still secure heraldic reverence, it is the higher boon of mental power and moral worth, and this alone, that henceforth will command the nobler prize of popular respect. But there are some persons who, without pretending that because a man inherits a title he must inherit sense, would have us believe that hereditary honours exercise a mysterious influence over the minds of their possessors, and, notwithstanding all natural or acquired impediments, qualify them for the arduous duties of the senate or the judgment seat. It is probable that the persons who talk in this way have but a vague idea of the duties of a judge or of a legislator. Their notion of legislation is, perhaps, derived from the newspaper reports of parliamentary proceedings, and thus they naturally conclude that the whole science consists in uttering a few illegal propositions, voting now and then, and once in a session, or so, entering a protest upon the journals of the House. Their idea of the duties of a judge, in the last resort, is, no doubt, the result of their own observations in the House of Lords, where they must frequently have seen the members of that august tribunal sleeping away the hours of noon, amid the arguments and eloquence of counsel at the bar.

That hereditary titles may powerfully contribute to form the habits of judges and legislators such as these, is perhaps nearer the truth than those who make the assertion suspect. But that to talk inconclusively, to say "content," or "non-content," as the case may be, or to sleep comfortably, or yawn listlessly from the beginning to the end of an appeal, are accomplishments sufficient to constitute an efficient legislative body and judicial tribunal, is a proposition rather too monstrous for the needle-eyed scepticism of modern times. The spectators below their Lordships' bar are tempted to ask how it comes to pass that men who blunder in the government of a sentence, should yet be proficient in the government of a nation. And they are lost in all astonishment, when they behold the unlearned son of a chief justice lounge in judgment over a difficult appeal, and, with a yawn, reverse a decree framed by the clear and comprehensive intellect of his learned father.

There are anomalies in the scheme and fabric of our glorious constitution, which, however, harmless or expedient they appeared to the wisdom of our ancestors, may, peradventure, strike the minds of the present generation as too absurd to be successfully defended, and too pernicious to be long endured. But it is not only on public grounds that the system of hereditary honours may be considered objectionable. Such a system seems cruel and unjust towards the very individuals whom it is supposed to consecrate and protect. It labels as a sage and prudent counsellor many an unobtrusive mortal, who is ready frankly to disclaim all pretensions to those Nestorian attributes. It pawns upon the public credulity an assembly purporting to be the concentrated essence of human wisdom, when in truth it is, and from the principle of its constitution ever must be, one of the weakest possible solutions of that rare and invaluable simple. And what is the consequence? The fraud is detected. The innocent assembly, to which the constitution dishonestly ascribes virtues it never did possess, is, by the popular logic, stigmatised as a crowd of impostors. The descendant of a Burleigh is sneered at because he lacks the sagacity of his ancestor, and the imbecile "heir male," of a Chatham or a Somers, is individually contrasted with his prompt and vigorous progenitor. But is it not evident, to every impartial mind, that as peers to whom the titles but not the wisdom of their ancestors descend, are not the architects of their own minds, they are not blamable if they prove unfit for the dignity which devolves upon them? They rather merit our compassion as the victims of a merciless institution which imposes upon them honors nature never intended them to bear, and duties too onerous to be discharged by the efforts of their feeble minds. Nature may have denied them the commonest capacity,—the institution ordains that, whether they have capacity or not, they shall be legislators! Nature may have made them foolish,—unreasonable man demands of them the exercise of wisdom! Did providence dispense to them just sense enough for the humblest occupations of life, the law declares they have genius for the highest! Born with sufficient wit to tend a flock, custom sets them to watch over the safety of millions of human beings! Whether they will or not, they are by their fictitious rank thrust forward into the front of society. It might be asked, even without the implication of satire, why should not any other accident as well as that of birth determine the lot? Why not throw the dice, or draw lots, to ascertain who shall wear a title, and make laws to bind the land? Would the House of Lords consist of a body less wise or less virtuous if the right to sit there depended upon the accidental circumstances of being born at a particular hour, or with eyes of a constitutional colour, or legs of a given length? Instead of the eldest sons of men called "Dukes" or "Marquises" being entitled to frame our laws, why not predestinate to that honour the eldest sons of men with hooked noses or bandy legs? The men with hooked noses would stand quite as good a chance of procreating prudent counsellors, as the men who put "Duke" before their names; and they of the bandy legs might raise a breed of statesmen quite as sensible as the present race of Marquises.

It would be cruel indeed to demand wisdom of any man simply because his father had bow legs, and the height of national folly to set up a class of men as law-makers, because their father's noses were not straight. But it would not be worse than to elevate men, as the peerage now does, for no other reason than that they are the sons of A or B, instead of C or D, to a station, where, if they shew no wisdom, they must provoke contempt. What should we think of a law which forbade us to supply the theatre with actors of obvious merit, and compelled us to fill the *corps dramatique* with none but the children of old performers? What an execrable drama should we have! How the sons of Keeley would mangle Hamlet; and Liston's issue, with the comic visage of their sire, what a jest would they not make of Benedict or Romeo! But wherein are hereditary peers better than hereditary players? The glorious drama of legislation, how is it performed, and by whom? Are the actors selected for their genius? Have they studied their parts long and deeply? Are they masters of the mighty science they profess? No! The truth is known. Like the children of the players, they owe their situation to no real fitness of their own; and, therefore it is we nightly see the noble part of Cicero burlesqued; Solon rants like Cleon; and Demosthenes is perfect only in the stammering.

In the foregoing observations it has been our principal object to attract the attention of our readers towards an institution which, upon account both of the high antiquity of its origin, and the prominent position it occupies in the scheme of our constitution, exercises mighty influence over our social and political character. Hereafter, we may, perhaps, enter into a closer analysis of its merits—to enumerate the benefits it confers, or is supposed to confer, upon the nation at large: and, in the spirit of philosophical candour, to inquire how far its fundamental principle accords with the maxims of the improved science of government, and the superior intelligence of the modern world.

THEORY OF VOLCANOES.

M. GAY-LUSSAC has recently published a memoir on the formation of volcanoes. He inquires into the hypothesis which ascribes combustion on the surface of the earth to the interior being in a state of incandescence. He shows that this supposition cannot account for the lava. The volcanic furnaces must be fed by substances originally foreign to them, and admitted to them only before an eruption. The only foreign substance adequate to the effect is air or water, but the pressure of neither of these could possibly elevate the lava. Besides, this incandescence is itself quite hypothetical; and notwithstanding the observations on the increase of temperature in mines, is regarded as extremely doubtful.

He then considers the theory of Sir H. Davy. The metals which form the alkalies and earths are supposed to lie in a state of purity in the bowels of the globe; and to occasion the volcanic phenomena by uniting with oxygen and forming lava. " There is no difficulty in conceiving that, by their contact with water, they might decompose it, become changed into lava, and produce sufficient heat to account for the greater part of the volcanic phenomena. If water be really the agent which sustains the volcanic fires by means of its oxygen, we must admit, as a necessary and very important consequence, that an enormous quantity of Hydrogen, either free or combined with some other principle, would be disengaged through the craters of volcanoes. Nevertheless, it does not appear that the disengagement of hydrogen is very frequent in volcanoes. Although, during my residence at Naples in 1805, with my friends M. Alexander de Humboldt and M. Leopold de Buch, I witnessed frequent explosions of Vesuvius, which threw up melted lava to the height of more than 200 metres, I never perceived any inflammation of hydrogen. Every explosion was followed by columns (torbillons) of a thick and black smoke, which must have been ignited if they had been composed of Hydrogen, being traversed by bodies heated to a temperature higher than was necessary to cause their inflammation. This smoke, the evident cause of the explosions, contained therefore other fluids than hydrogen. But what was its true nature? If we admit that it is water which furnishes oxygen to volcanoes, it will follow that, as its hydrogen does not disengage itself in a free state, it must enter into some combination. It cannot enter into any compound inflammable by means of heat at its contact with the air; it is, however, very possible that it unites with chlorine to form hydrochloric acid.

The greater number of mountains, when they arose from the heart of the earth, must have left these vast cavities, which would remain empty unless filled by water. I think, however, that De Luc, and many other geologists, have reasoned very erroneously on these cavities, which they imagine stretching out into long galleries, by means of which earthquakes are communicated to a distance.

An earthquake, as Dr. Young has very justly observed, is analogous to a vibration of the air. It is a very strong sonorous undulation, excited in the solid mass of the earth by some commotion which communicates itself with the same rapidity with which sound travels. The astonishing considerations in this great and terrible phenomenon are, the immense extent to which it is felt, the ravages it produces, and the potency of the cause to which it must be attributed. But sufficient attention has not been paid to the ease with which all the particles of a solid mass are agitated. The shock produced by the head of a pin at the one end of a long beam, causes a vibration through all its fibres, and is distinctly transmitted to an attentive ear at the other end. The motion of a carriage on the pavement shakes vast edifices, and communicates itself through considerable masses, as in the deep quarries under Paris. Is it, therefore, so astonishing, that a violent commotion in the bowels of the earth should make it tremble in a radius of many hundreds of leagues? In conformity with the law of the transmission of motion in elastic bodies, the extreme stratum, finding no other strata to which to transmit its motion, makes an effort to detach itself from the agitated mass, in the same manner as in a row of billiard-balls, the first of which is struck in the direction of contact, the last alone detaches itself and receives the motion.

INSCRIPTION ON A BOY'S TOMB-STONE, IN AN IRISH COUNTRY CHURCH-YARD.

A little spirit slumbers here,
Who to one heart was very dear;
Oh! he was more than life or light,
Its thought by day, its dream by night!
The chill winds came—the young flower faded
And died;—the grave its sweetness shaded.
Fair boy! thou shouldst have wept for me,
Not I have had to mourn for thee:
Yet not long shall this sorrowing be,—
Those roses I have planted round,
To deck thy dear and sacred ground,
When spring gales next those roses wave,
They'll blush upon thy mother's grave!

REMARKABLE STORY OF AN AVALANCHE.

On the 19th of March, 1755, a small cluster of houses at a place called Bergemotetto, near Demonte, in the upper valley of Stura, was entirely overwhelmed by two vast bodies of snow that tumbled down from a neighbouring mountain; all the inhabitants were then within doors, except one Joseph Rochia, and his son, a lad of fifteen, who were on the roof of their house, clearing away the snow which had fallen during three days, incessantly. A priest going by to mass, having just before observed a body of snow tumbling from the mountain towards them, had advised them to come down. The man descended with great precipitation, and fled with his son; but scarcely had he gone forty steps, before his son, who followed him, fell down; on which, looking back, he saw his own and his neighbours' houses, in which were twenty-two persons in all, covered with a high mountain of snow. He lifted up his son, and reflecting that his wife, his sister, two children and all his effects were thus buried, he fainted away; but, soon recovering, got safe to his friend's house, at some distance.

Five days afterwards, Joseph, being perfectly recovered, got upon the snow with his son, and two of his wife's brothers, to try if he could find the exact place where his house stood; but, after many openings made in the snow, they could not discover it. The month of April proving hot, and the snow beginning to soften, he again used his utmost endeavours to recover his effects, and to bury, as he thought, the remains of his family. He made new openings, and threw in earth to melt the snow, which on the 24th of April was greatly diminished. He broke through ice six English feet thick with iron bars, thrust down a long pole, and touched the ground; but, evening coming on, he desisted.

His wife's brother, who lived at Demonte, dreamed that night that his sister was still alive, and begged him to help her; the man, affected by his dream, rose early in the morning and went to Bergemotetto, where Joseph was; and, after resting himself a little, went with him to work. Upon opening the snow which covered the house, they in vain searched for the bodies in its ruins; they then sought for the stable, which was about 240 English feet distant, and to their astonishment, heard a cry of "help, my brother." They laboured with all diligence till they made a large opening through which the brother, who had the dream, immediately went down, where the sister, with an agonizing and feeble voice, told him, "I have always trusted in God and you, that you would not forsake me." The other brother and the husband then went down and found, still alive, the wife, about forty-five, the sister, about thirty-five, and a daughter about thirteen years old. These they raised on their shoulders, to men above, who pulled them up, as if from the grave, and carried them to a neighbouring house; they were unable to walk, and so wasted that they appeared like mere skeletons. They were immediately put to bed, and gruel of rye-flour and a little butter was given to recover them. Some days afterwards the intendant went to see them, and found the wife still unable to rise from her bed, or use her feet, from the intense cold she had been in. The sister, whose legs had been bathed with hot wine, could walk with some difficulty. The daughter needed no farther remedies.

On the intendant's interrogating the women, they told him, that on the 19th of March they were in the stable with a boy of six years old, and a girl about thirteen. In the same stable were six goats, one of which, having brought forth two dead kids the night before, they went to carry her a small vessel of rye-flour gruel. There were also an ass and five or six fowls; they were sheltering themselves in a warm corner of the stable till the church-bells should ring, intending to attend the service, but the wife going out of the stable to kindle a fire in the house for her husband, who was cleaning the snow away from the top of it, she perceived an avalanche breaking down towards the east, upon which she ran back into the stable, shut the door, told her sister of it, and, in less than three minutes the mass descended, and they heard the roof break over their heads, and also part of the ceiling. They got into the rack and manger. The manger was under the main prop of the stable, and resisted the weight of the snow above. Their first care was to know what they had to eat: the sister said she had fifteen chestnuts in her pocket; the children said they had breakfasted, and should want no more that day. They remembered that there were thirty or forty cakes in a place near the stable, and endeavoured to get at them, but were not able to penetrate the snow. They called often for help, but received no answer. The sister gave two chestnuts to the wife, and ate two herself, and they drank some snow-water. The ass was restless, and the goat kept bleating for some days, after which they heard no more of them. Two of the goats being left alive, and near the manger, they expected to have young about the middle of April; the other gave milk, and with this they preserved their lives. During all this time they saw not one ray of light, yet for about twenty days they had some notice of night and day, from the crowing of the fowls, till they died.

The second day, when very hungry, they ate all the chestnuts, and drank what milk the goat yielded, being very nearly two pounds a-day at first, but it soon decreased. The third day they attempted again, but in vain, to get at the cakes. They resolved to take all possible care to feed the goats; but just above the manger was a hay-loft, whence, through a hole, the sister pulled down hay into the rack, and gave it to the goat, as long as she could reach it; and then, when it was beyond her reach, the goats climbed upon her shoulder, and reached it themselves. On the sixth day the boy sickened, and six days after desired his mother, who all this time had held him in her lap, to lay him at his length in the manger; she did so, and, taking him by the hand, felt it was cold; she then put her hand to his mouth, and, finding that cold likewise, she gave him a little milk; the boy then cried " O, my father is in the snow! O father, father !"—and then expired.

In the meanwhile the goat's milk diminished daily, and the fowls dying soon after, they could no longer distinguish night from day. Upon the approach of the time when they expected the other goat to kid, they killed her, to save the milk for their own subsistence. This necessity was painful in the extreme, for whenever they called this goat it would come and lick their face and hands. It had given them every day two pounds of milk, and they bore the poor creature great affection.

They said, that, during the entire time of their confinement, hunger gave them but little uneasiness, except for the first five or six days. Their greatest pain was from the extreme coldness of the melted snow-water which fell on them, and from the effluvia of the dead ass, goats, fowls, &c. They likewise suffered great bodily inconvenience from the very uneasy posture they were confined to: for the manger in which they sat, crouching against the wall, was no more than three feet four inches broad. The mother said she had never slept, but the sister and daughter said they had slept as usual. They were buried in the snow for five weeks. The particulars related were obtained and attested on the 16th of May, 1755, by the intendant authorised to take the examination.

TROUT OF LOCH AWE.
BY JAMES WILSON, ESQ.

VERY large trout have been killed in Ullswater, in Cumberland, and still larger in Loch Awe in Argyllshire. The late Mr. Morrison of Glasgow claimed the merit of discovering these fish in the last-named locality, about 40 years ago; and the largest recorded to have been killed there weighed 25 pounds. Mr. Lascelles, a Liverpool gentleman, has also of late years been equally assiduous and successful in their capture; and it appears that any persevering sportsman is almost certain, with the proper tackle, to obtain specimens in Loch Awe of this great fish, weighing from 10 to 20 pounds. The largest we have lately heard of weighed 19¾ pounds. It is said to be by far the most powerful of our fresh-water fishes, exceeding the salmon in actual strength, though not in activity. The most general size caught by trolling, ranges from three to fifteen pounds; beyond that weight they are of uncommon occurrence. If hooked upon tackle of moderate strength, they afford excellent sport; but the general method of fishing for them is almost as well adapted for catching sharks as trout; the angler being apparently more anxious to have it in his power to state that he had caught a fish of such a size, than to enjoy the pleasure of the sport itself. However, to the credit of both parties, it may be stated, that the very strongest tackle is sometimes snapped in two by its first tremendous springs. The ordinary method of fishing for this king of trouts is with a powerful rod, from a boat rowing at the rate of from three to four miles an hour; the lure, a common trout, from three to ten inches in length, baited upon six or eight salmon hooks, tied back to back upon strong gimp, assisted by two swivels, and the wheel-line strong whipcord. Yet all this, in the first impetuous efforts of the fish to regain its liberty, is frequently carried away for ever into the crystal depths of Loch Awe!

When in their highest health and condition, and, indeed, during the whole of the time in which they are not employed in the operation of spawning, these fish will scarcely ever rise at a fly. At these periods, they appear to be almost entirely piscivorous; so, with the exception of night lines, baited also with trout, trolling is the only advisable mode of angling for them. The young, however, rise very freely at ordinary lake-trout flies, and are generally caught in this way, from one to one and a half pound weight. They occur abundantly near the outlet of the lake.

About the middle of August, and during the three following months, the parent fish retire, for the purpose of spawning, to the deep banks of the lake in the neighbourhood of the gorge, and into the gorge of the lake itself, where it empties its immense waters, forming the river Awe. They are said to remain engaged in this operation for two or three months; and at this time their instinctive tendencies are so far changed, that they will rise eagerly at large and gaudily dressed salmon-flies, and may be either angled for from the banks, or trolled with a cross line, where the outlet of the lake is narrow. They do not appear either to ascend the rivers which enter the loch, or to descend the Awe to any extent, though an occasional straggler has been taken some way down the river. Their spawning places are exclusively on the banks, or at the gorge of the loch, and they never attempt to seek the salt water. When in good season, and in their strongest condition, they appear to roam indiscriminately through every part of the loch, though there are certain spots which may be more depended upon than others, and where an experienced angler will have little difficulty in hooking one of these fine fish. To their great strength we may observe that they add unequalled rapacity; and after attaining to the weight of three or four pounds, they appear to feed almost exclusively on smaller fish, and do not spare even their own young. A small trout of this species, not weighing more than 1½ pound, will often dash at a bait not much inferior to itself in size; and instances are recorded of larger fish following with eager eye, and attempting to seize upon others of their own kind after they had been hooked and were in the act of being landed by the angler. It is probable, on account of this strong manifestation of a more than usually predaceous habit, that Sir William Jardine has named the species *Salmo ferox.*

When in perfect season, and full-grown, it is a very handsome fish, though the head is always too large and long to be in accordance with our ideas of perfect symmetry in a trout. The body is deep and thickly formed, and all the members seem conducive to the exercise of great strength. The colours are deep purplish brown on the upper part, changing into reddish gray, and thence into fine orange yellow on the breast and belly. The whole body, when the fish is newly caught, appears as if glazed over with a thin tint of rich lake-colour, which fades away as the fish dies, and so rapidly, that the progressive changes of colour are easily perceived by an attentive eye. The gill-covers are marked with large dark spots; and the whole body is covered with markings of different sizes, and varying in amount in different individuals. In some, these markings are few, scattered, and of a large size; in others, they are thickly set, and of smaller dimensions. Each spot is surrounded by a paler ring, which sometimes assumes a reddish hue; and the spots become more distant from each other as they descend beneath the lateral line. The lower parts of these fish are spotless. All the fins are broad, muscular, and extremely powerful; and it is from the number of their bony rays that the specific characters which distinguish this species from the common trout (*Salmo fario*) are the most easily and accurately evolved.

THE TAILOR AND THE MIDDIES.

SOME people imagine that their sons, if unfit for other professions, will do well enough for the sea. As a warning to them not to assign such a reason before the young gentlemen in the cockpit, we shall quote the following anecdote:—" This reminds me of a tailor at Halifax, who, on being sadly provoked by some of the scampish band amongst us, for not paying his abominably long bills, said, in a rage, in the cockpit before us all, that, after having tried his son in half a dozen professions, without any chance of success, he was now resolved, as a last resource, to make a midshipman of him! This sarcasm was uttered during the short peace of Amiens, when we first visited Halifax; a period when the mids had so little real business to attend to, that they seized eagerly upon any opening for a joke. As soon, therefore, as the tailor had quitted the ship, it was resolved to punish him for his uncourteous speech. It had not escaped the notice of his tormentors, that this vulgar fraction of his species prided himself, in a most especial degree, on the dignity of a very enormous tail or queue, which reached half way down his back; and it was resolved, in secret council, that this appendage should forthwith be docked. Nothing, I must fairly own, could be more treacherous than the means devised to lower the honour and glory of the poor tailor. He was formally invited to dinner with us; and, being well plied with grog, mixed according to the formidable rule for making what is called a Northwester, which prescribes that one half of each glass shall consist of rum, and the other half of rum and water, our poor guest was soon brought under the table. Being then quite incapable of moving, he was lifted in noisy triumph out of the berth, and placed in the tier, across the bends of the small bower cable, where, after many a grunt and groan at the rugged nature of his couch, he at length ell asleep. His beautiful tail, the pride of his life! was presently glued, by means of a lump of pitch, to the strands of the cable; and such was the tenacity of the substance, that in the morning, when, on the daylight gun being fired immediately over his head, poor snip awoke, he could no more detach himself from the spot on which he lay than Lemuel Gulliver in like circumstances. His noddle was still so confused, that he knew not where he lay, nor what held him down. After tugging at his hair for a minute or two, he roared out lustily for help. One of the mids, seized with the brilliant idea of making the tailor the finisher of his own fate, hurried to his assistance, and, handing him a knife, roared out, " by all means to make haste, as the devil had got hold of him by the tail!" The poor tradesman, terrified out of his wits, and in great horror at his mysterious situation, instantly did as he was desired, and cut away lustily, little dreaming that his own rash hand was shearing the highest and most cherished honours of his house! On turning round, he beheld with dismay the ravished locks which, for half a century and more, had been the joint delight of himself and his tender partner Rebecca. As the thought of returning tail-less to his home crossed his half-bewildered brain, he exclaimed, in an agony of spirit, to his malicious tormentors, " Oh, Lord! oh Lord! I am a lost man to my Becky!" The revenge of the malicious middies was now complete; and this expression of being a " lost man to one's Becky" became a by-word in the ship for many years afterwards, to denote the predicament of any one who got into a scrape, and came out of it with loss.—*Hall's Fragments.*

THE YELLOW DOMINO.

In the latter part of the reign of Louis XV. of France the masquerade was an entertainment high in estimation, and was often given at an immense cost on court days and such occasions of rejoicing. As persons of all ranks might gain admission to these spectacles, provided they could afford the purchase of the ticket, very strange rencontres frequently took place at them, and exhibitions almost as curious in the way of disguise or assumption of character. But perhaps the most whimsical among the genuine surprises recorded at any of these spectacles, was that which occurred in Paris the 15th of October, on the day when the Dauphin (son of Louis XV.) attained the age of one-and-twenty.

At this fete, which was of a peculiar glittering character—so much so, that the details of it are given at great length by the historians of the day—the strange demeanour of a man in a yellow domino, early in the evening, excited attention. This mask, who showed nothing remarkable as to figure,—though all rather, and of robust proportion,—seemed to be gifted with an appetite, not merely past human conception, but passing the fancies even of romance.

The dragon of old, who churches ate,
(He used to come on a Sunday,)
Whole congregations were to him,
But a dish of Salmagundi,—

he was a nibbler—a mere fool—to this stranger of the yellow domino. He passed from chamber to chamber—from table to table of refreshments—not tasting but devouring—devastating all before him. At one board, he despatched a fowl, two-thirds of a ham, and half a dozen bottles of champagne; the very next moment he was found seated in another apartment, performing the same feat, with a stomach better than at first. This strange course went on until the company, who at first had been amused by it, became alarmed and tumultuous.

" Is it the same mask—or are there several dressed alike?" demanded an officer of the guards, as the yellow domino rose from a seat opposite to him and quitted the apartment.

" I have seen but one—and, by Heaven! he is here again," exclaimed the party to whom the query is addressed.

The yellow domino spoke not a word, but proceeded straight to the vacant seat which he had just left, and again commenced supping, as though he had fasted for the half of a campaign.

At length the confusion which this proceeding created, became universal; and the cause reached the ears of the Dauphin.

" He is a very fiend, your Highness!" exclaimed an old nobleman—" saving your Highness's presence—or wants but a tail to be so!"

" Say rather he should be a famished poet, by his appearance," replied the Prince, laughing. " But there must be some juggling; he spills all his wine, and hides the provisions under his robe."

Even while they were speaking, the yellow domino entered the room in which they were talking, and, as usual, proceeded to the table of refreshments.

" See here, my Lord," cried one—" I have seen him do this twice !"

" I thrice !"—" I five times !"—" and I fifteen !"

This was too much. The master of the ceremonies was questioned. He knew nothing—and the yellow domino was interrupted as he was carrying a bumper of claret to his lips.

" The Prince's desire is that Monsieur who wears the yellow domino should unmask." The stranger hesitated.

" The command with which his Highness honours Monsieur is perfectly absolute."

Against that which is absolute there is no contending. The yellow man threw off his mask and domino; and proved to be a private trooper of the Irish dragoons!

" And in the name of gluttony, my good friend, (not to ask how you gained admission,) how have you contrived," said the Prince, " to sup to-night so many times ?"

" Sire, I was beginning but to sup, with reverence be it said, when your Royal message interrupted me."

" Beginning!" exclaimed the Dauphin, in amazement, " then what is it I have heard and seen ?—Where are the herds of oxen that have disappeared, and the hampers of burgundy ? I insist upon knowing how this is !"

" It is, Sire," returned the soldier, may it please your Grace, that the troop to which I belong is to-day on guard. We have purchased one ticket among us, and provided this yellow domino, which fits us all. By which means the whole of the front rank, being myself the last man, have supped, if the truth must be told, at discretion! and the leader of the second rank, saving your highness's commands, is now waiting outside the door to take his turn."

TRIMMINGS AND TRAPPINGS OF A MODERN SUCCESSOR OF THE APOSTLES.

Our readers will, we doubt not, be as much edified as we have been, with the items of the inventory of goods lately given in by the Archbishop of Paris, in his claims of damage suffered during the THREE DAYS. It is but a selection we give from a pretty long list.

Monseigneur, then, claims, in the first place, 2,000 francs. For what?—Guess. For valuable manuscript works of the eleventh century?—No, indeed. For a copy, in vellum, of the Decrees of the Council of Trent?—No, not for that. For a copy of the Holy League, signed by the hand of Cardinal Lorraine himself?—No. For the rosary of St Dominque, or a breviary of Father Letellier?—No. For original letters of the wise and excellent Fenelon?—Ah! that must be it. No; it is not that either. Guess again; guess a hundred times; a thousand times. Monseigneur claims—Monseigneur claims—two thousand francs for sweetmeats and preserves! What! two thousand? Why he must have supplied the whole church with sweetmeats. How the pastrycooks and preservers must have worked to enable the suffering Church to claim such damages for the mischief done to its dainties! It is true this includes sugar and coffee; but when we look further into the inventory we find that every thing has its turn. Sometimes one would think it was an account of the posthumous effects of the celebrated Brillat-Savarin; for, in coming to the contents of the cellar, we see three hundred bottles of Cyprus wine of the finest quality, 1,000 francs. At other times we might fancy ourselves in the richest magazines of the most approved seamstress or linen-draper, when we observe the profusion of the ribands and blonds which ornamented the vestments of this minister of the Church. We have three aubes (a priest's garment) made of lawn down to the thighs, and the rest of the finest English lace, (dentelle d'Angleterre,) valued at 4,500 francs; and again, three rochets, ornamented in the same manner, 3,000 francs; and another with ribands, 3,000 francs. We will say nothing more of the lemon and apricot preserves—but the tulle, the lawn, the lace! We stop short for fear of committing an indiscretion; we fear to embroil Monseigneur with the fair sex, if we show what a monopolist of lace, &c., he has been. What scarfs, what veils, what volans, what trimmings, what head-dresses might have been made out of three aubes and five rochets! We select a few more items out of a thousand of like character:—

"A cup and a vessel for holy water, in silver gilt, 600 francs.

"A very fine and large mahogany billiard-table, and appurtenances, the cloth quite new, 1,200 francs.

"A quantity of fine old Bordeaux wine, which orginally cost 1,200 francs, without including the carriage to Paris, or the bottling, 1,200 francs.

"A diamond star, as large as the palm of the hand, 7,200 francs.

"A dress of figured violet silk, 80 francs.

"A black casimir pair of pantaloons, 40 francs.

"A flannel night-gown, 30 francs.

"Six pair of new shoes, 48 francs.

"Portrait of my father, dressed as a Chief of Division, size of life, the frame handsomely carved and gilt, 200 francs.

"A very rich cope of cloth of gold, embroidered in gold, and a raised pattern, with stole, maniple, tassels, &c., in good condition, only used during high mass, 4,500 francs.

"A bonbonniere of large size, made of coral, worked in the Chinese style, representing birds, and bound with gold. A present from the Emperor Napoleon to M. le Duc de V——. The Duchess gave it to me after the death of her husband. (Not valued.)"

Well, Gentlemen, have we not quoted enough? If not, to satisfy you, we will take two more specimens:—

"Full-length portraits of Louis XVIII. and Charles X., 4,000.

"A portrait of the present Archbishop, 4,500 francs."

Monseigneur thus rates himself at a higher price than two Kings put together, and yet these two Kings cost France tolerably dear.

ON TRUE HAPPINESS.

The desire of happiness in general is so natural to us, that all the world are in pursuit of it; all have this one end in view, though they take such different methods to attain it, and are so much divided in their notions of it.

Evil, as evil, can never be chosen; and though evil is often the effect of our own choice, yet we never desire it, but under the appearance of an imaginary good.

Many things we indulge ourselves in may be considered by us as evils, and yet be desirable; but then they are only considered as evils in their effects and consequences, not as evils at present, and attended with immediate misery.

Reason represents things to us, not only as they are at present, but as they are in their whole nature and tendency; passion only regards them in their former light; when this governs us, we are regardless of the future, and are only affected with the present.

It is impossible ever to enjoy ourselves rightly, if our conduct be not such as to preserve the harmony and order of our faculties, and the original frame and constitution of our minds; all true happiness, as all that is truly beautiful can only result from order.

While there is a conflict betwixt the two principles of passion and reason, we must be miserable in proportion to the struggle; and when the victory is gained, and reason so far subdued as seldom to trouble us with its remonstrances, the happiness we have then is not the happiness of our rational nature, but the happiness only of the inferior and sensual part of us, and consequently a very low and imperfect happiness, to what the other would have afforded us.

If we reflect upon any one passion and disposition of mind, abstract from virtue, we shall soon see the disconnexion between that and true solid happiness. It is of the very essence, for instance, of envy to be uneasy and disquieted. Pride meets with provocations and disturbances upon almost every occasion. Covetousness is ever attended with solicitude and anxiety. Ambition has its disappointments to sour us, but never the good fortune to satisfy us; its appetite grows the keener by indulgence, and all we can gratify it with at present serves but the more to inflame its insatiable desires.

The passions, by being too much conversant with earthly objects, can never fix in us a proper composure and acquiescence of mind. Nothing but an indifference to the things of this world, an entire submission to the will of Providence here, and a well-grounded expectation of happiness hereafter, can give us a true satisfactory enjoyment of ourselves. Virtue is the best guard against the many unavoidable evils incident to us; nothing better alleviates the weight of the afflictions, or gives a truer relish of the blessings of human life.

What is without us has not the least connexion with happiness, only so far as the preservation of our lives and health depends upon it. Health of body, though so far necessary that we cannot be perfectly happy without it, is not sufficient to make us happy of itself. Happiness springs immediately from the mind; health is but to be considered as a candidate or circumstance, without which this happiness cannot be tasted pure and unabated.

Virtue is the best preservative of health, as it prescribes temperance, and such a regulation of our passions as is most conducive to the well-being of the animal economy, so that it is, at the same time, the only true happiness of the mind, and the best means of preserving the health of the body.

If our desires are to the things of this world, they are never to be satisfied; if our great view is upon the next, the expectation of them is an infinitely higher satisfaction than the enjoyment of those of the present.

There is no happiness, then, but in a virtuous and self-approving conduct; unless our actions will bear the test of our sober judgments, and reflections upon them, they are not the actions, and consequently not the happiness, of a rational being.—*The Beauties of Franklin.*

PROGRESS OF KNOWLEDGE IN INDIA.

No. 5. of "Periodical Accounts of the Serampore Mission," supplies some interesting intelligence respecting the progress of knowledge in India. It may be proper to mention, that Serampore is a missionary station, about 15 miles North of Calcutta, originally established by the Danes, about 1800. The first newspaper in the vernacular language of Bengal, the *Durpun*, was commenced here in 1818, and was patronized by the Marquis of Hastings, then Governor-General. It is a weekly paper, originally in four, but now in eight pages; and recently, the editor has begun to print it in parallel columns of Bengalee and English, so that it serves as teacher to the natives who wish to learn the latter language. It travels as far as Delhi, 960 miles westward, passing everywhere under a small charge for postage, which in general is about three halfpence, and for the greatest distance, only three-pence. The example set at Serampore was soon followed at Calcutta, where there are now *eight newspapers* in the eastern languages, namely six in Bengalee, and two in Persian. One of these papers is published twice a-week; the other seven, weekly; and the price of the latter is one rupee per month, or two shillings. They contain intelligence respecting the proceedings of the Governor-General, the Supreme Courts, the Police, the Civil and Criminal Courts, and news from Britain, France, and other distant countries, as well as India. In 1825, the subscribers to the six papers were calculated at from 800 to 1000, (Query—to *all* the papers, or to *each?*) and five readers to each paper. Since then they have greatly increased; and from the best information, says the Durpun, in Jan. 1830, "we are led to believe that the number of subscribers to native newspapers has been doubled within the last twelve months." These papers contain intelligence from Europe and other parts of the world, of which a few years ago, the Hindoos did not even know the name. The first work printed in Bengalee for the natives, appeared only sixteen years ago. Since that time, thirty-six other works, great and small, have been published, chiefly, however, upon the Hindoo religion; but as knowledge spreads, the demand for science and literature will arise. Among fourteen publications in English, printed by natives, in English, in 1829, it is curious to find, " Remarks on the Influx of Irish Poor, during the season of Harvest;" "the Early Life of Lord Liverpool;" "A Self-Guide to the English Language, in Bengalee and English," &c. But native efforts now begin to take a higher range. The Durpun states, that an edition of the *Shah Namah*, or great Historical Poem of the Persians, in the original language, was completed by Captain Mahon, in 1829; and printed at the expense of the King of Oude. This poem consists of 110,408 lines, and is therefore about seven times as long as the Iliad. It contains all that remains in the East of the history and antiquities of Persia, from the earliest times to the Mahometan conquest; and served almost solely, we believe, as the basis of Sir John Malcolm's History of Persia. Mill's History of India, we observe, is printing at Serampore, in the Bengalee language. The study of English by the natives has made prodigious progress within these ten years. "It would be easy to point out between one and two hundred native young gentlemen in Calcutta, to whom English is quite as familiar as their own tongue."

RULES FOR SERVANTS.

I. A good character is valuable to every one, but especially to servants; for it is their bread, and without it they cannot be admitted into any creditable family; and happy it is that the best of characters is in every one's power to deserve.

II. Engage yourself cautiously, but stay long in your place, for long service shows worth—as quitting a good place through passion, is a folly which is always lamented of too late.

III. Never undertake any place you are not qualified for; for pretending to what you do not understand, exposes yourself, and, what is still worse, deceives those whom you serve.

IV. Preserve your fidelity; for a faithful servant is a jewel, for whom no encouragement can be too great.

V. Adhere to truth; for falsehood is detestable, and he that tells one lie, must tell twenty more to conceal it.

VI. Be strictly honest; for it is shameful to be thought unworthy of trust.

VII. Be modest in your behaviour; it becomes your station, and is pleasing to your superiors.

VIII. Avoid pert answers; for civil language is cheap, and impertinence provoking.

IX. Be clean in your business; for those who are slovens and sluts, are disrespectful servants.

X. Never tell the affairs of the family you belong to; for that is a sort of treachery, and often makes mischief; but keep their secrets, and have none of your own.

XI. Live friendly with your fellow-servants; for the contrary destroys the peace of the house.

XII. Above all things avoid drunkenness; for that is an inlet to vice, the ruin of your character, and the destruction of your constitution.

XIII. Prefer a peaceful life, with moderate gains, to great advantage and irregularity.

XIV. Save your money; for that will be a friend to you in old age. Be not expensive in dress, nor marry too soon.

XV. Be careful of your master's property; for wastefulness is a sin.

XVI. Never swear; for that is a crime without excuse, as there is no pleasure in it.

XVII. Be always ready to assist a fellow-servant; for good nature gains the love of every one.

XVIII. Never stay when sent on a message; for waiting long is painful to your master, and a quick return shows diligence.

XIX. Rise early; for it it difficult to recover lost time.

XX. The servant that often changes his place, works only to be poor; for "the rolling-stone gathers no moss."

XXI. Be not fond of increasing your acquaintances; for visiting leads you out of your business, robs your master of your time, and often puts you to an expense you cannot afford. And above all things, take care with whom you are acquainted; for persons are generally the better or the worse for the company they keep.

XXII. When out of place, be careful where you lodge; for living in a disreputable house, puts you upon a footing with those that keep it, however innocent you are yourself.

XXIII. Never go out on your own business, without the knowledge of the family, lest in your absence you should be wanted; for "Leave is light," and returning punctually at the time you promise, shows obedience, and is a proof of sobriety.

XXIV. If you are dissatisfied with your place, mention your objections modestly to your master or mistress, and give a fair warning; and do not neglect your business nor behave ill, in order to provoke them to turn you away; for this will be a blemish in your character, which you must always have from the last place you served in.

⁎ *All who pay a due regard to the above precepts, will be happy in themselves, will never want friends, and will always meet with the assistance, protection, and encouragement of the wealthy, the worthy, and the wise.*

The population of the United States, according to the last census, is over twelve millions; and the increase in 1831, including the negroes and the emigrants, exceeded 500,000 souls; so that at the same rate the country might have, in twenty-five years, a population of twenty-five millions. The emigration this year to the ports of the Atlantic has not been so great as the last; but thousands of emigrants have spread from Canada through the States of New York and Ohio, and particularly through the territory of Michigan, which is to be incorporated a State next year.

THE STORY-TELLER.

THE HAUNTED HOUSE.
BY ALLAN CUNNINGHAM.

The great road from England, in former times, skirted the Firth of Solway, pursued its wild and extraordinary way through one of the deepest and most dangerous morasses in Scotland, and, emerging on the Caerlaverock side, conferred on the Kirkgate of the good town of Dumfries the rank and opulence of a chief street. Commanding a view of the winding and beautiful river Nith on one side, and of the green stately hills of Tinwald and Torthorwold on the other, with their numerous villages and decaying castles, this street became the residence of the rich and the far-descended—numbering among its people some of the most ancient and potent names of Nithsdale. The houses had in general something of a regal look—presenting a curious mixture of the Saxon and Grecian architecture, blending whimsically together in one place, or kept separate in all their native purity in another; while others of a different, but no less picturesque character, towered up in peaked and ornamented Norman majesty, with their narrow turret stairs and projecting casements. But I mean not to claim for the Kirkgate the express name of a regular street. Fruit trees frequently throwing their branches, loaded with the finest fruit, far into the way, and in other places antique porchways, shaded deep with yew-tree, took away the reproach of "eternal mortar and stone," and gave the whole a retired and a sylvan look. The presence of an old church, with its thick-piled grave-stones, gave a gravity of deportment to the neighbourhood; the awe inspired by a religious place was visible on the people. There was a seriousness mingled with their mirth; a reverential feeling poured through their legends and their ballads. Their laughter was not so loud, nor their joy so stormy, as that of men in less hallowed places. The maidens danced with something of a chastened step, and sang with a devotional grace. The strings of that merry instrument which bewitched the feet of the wisest men, when placed under the left ear of a Kirkgate musician, emitted sounds so perfectly in unison with devotion, that a gifted elder of the kirk was once known to sanction and honour it, by measuring a step or two to the joyous tune of " An' O to be married an' this be the way." Over the whole street, and far into the town, was breathed much of that meek, austere composure, which the genius of ancient sculptors has shed on their divine performances.

It was pleasant to behold the chief street of this ancient border town in its best days—those times of simplicity and virtue, as one of the town bailies, a barber by trade, remarked, when every woman went with a cushioned brow and curled locks, and all the men flourished in full bottomed wigs. But the demon who presides over the abasement of streets and cities entered into the empty place which the brain of a sheriff ought to have occupied, and the road was compelled to forsake the side of the Solway—the green fields of Caerlaverock, and the ancient Kirkgate,—and approach Dumfries through five miles of swamp, and along a dull, and muddy way, which all travellers have since learned to detest under the name of the *Lochmaben-gate*. From that hour, the glory of the old chief street diminished. The giddy and the gay forsook a place where the chariot of the stranger, with its accompaniment of running lacquies and mounted grooms, was no longer seen; and the ancient inhabitants saw, with sorrow, their numbers gradually lessen, and their favourite street hastening to decay. A new and a meaner race succeeded—the mansions of the Douglasses, the Dalzells, the Maxwells, the Kirkpatricks, and the Herrieses, became the homes of the labouring man, and the mechanic. Tapestried halls, and lordly rooms, were profaned by vulgar feet; and for the sound of the cithern and the rebeck, the dull din of the weaver's loom, and the jarring clamour of the smith's steel hammer, abounded.

With this brief and imperfect notice we shall bid farewell to the ancient splendour of the Kirkgate—it is with its degenerate days that our story has intercourse; and the persons destined to move, and act, and suffer, in our authentic drama, are among the humblest of its inhabitants. The time, too, with which our narrative commences and terminates, is a season somewhat uncongenial for descriptive excursions. A ruinous street and a labouring people, on whom the last night of December is descending in angry winds, and cold sleets and snows, present few attractions to dealers in genteel fictions; and few flowers, either natural or figurative, for embellishing a tale. With all these drawbacks, we have one advantage, which a mind delighting in nature and truth will not willingly forego; the tale, humble and brief as it is, possesses truth beyond all power of impeachment, and follows conscientiously the traditional and accredited narrative, without staying to array it and adorn it in those vain and gaudy embellishments with which fiction seeks to encumber a plain and simple story.

The night which brings in the New Year to the good people of Dumfries, has long been a night of friendly meetings, and social gladness and carousal. The grave and the devout lay aside, for the time, the ordinary vesture of sanctity and religious observance; the sober and self-denying revel among the good things of this life, with a fervour, perhaps augmented by previous penance; and even some of the shining lights of the Scottish Kirk have been observed to let their splendour subside for the evening, that, like the sun, perhaps they might come forth from darkness with an increase of glory. The matron suspends her thrift, and arrays herself in her marriage mantle—the maiden, and the bond-maiden, flaunt and smile, side by side, in ribbons and scarfs, and snooded love-locks, all arranged with a careful and a cunning hand, to assist merry blue or languishing black eyes in making mischief among the hearts of men. Each house smells, from floor to roof, with the good things of this life—the hare caught in her twilight march through the cottager's kaleyard, or the wild duck shot by moonlight, while tasting the green herbage on some lonely stream bank—send up, stewed or roasted, a savour the more gladsome because it comes seldom; while the flavour of smuggled gin and brandy is not the less acceptable, because the dangers of the deep sea, and the terrors on shore of the armed revenue officers, were in the way of its gracing once a-year the humble man's supper board.

Amid the sound of mirth and revelry, and shining of lamps and candles in porch and window, there was one house, covered with humble thatch, and of altogether a modest, or rather mean exterior, which seemed not to sympathize in the joys of the evening. A small and lonely candle twinkled in a small and solitary window; and no sound proceeded from its door, save now and then the moving of the slow and aged feet of the mistress of this rude cottage. As the more roving and regardless youths passed the window, they were observed to lower their voices, regulate their steps, and smooth down their deportment to something approaching to devotional. Within the window sat one who, ungracious in the outward man, and coarse in his apparel, and owner only of a bed-stead and couch, and a few controversial books, was nevertheless a man of note in those days, when things external were of little note in the eyes of a Presbyterian minister. Indeed, had one of the present generation glanced his eye through the coarse green glass of the low-browed window, and seen an old man, whose silver hairs were half concealed by a night-cap, not over pure; whose bent shoulders bore a plaid of homely chequered gray, fastened on the bosom with a wooden skewer, while over his knees lay a large old Bible, clasped with iron, on which his eyes were cast with a searching and a serious glance; our youth of Saxon broad-cloth and French ruffles would have thought of something much more humble than the chief elder of the old kirk of Dumfries. It was, indeed, no other than William Warpentree, one of the burning and shining lights of the Ancient of Days, when serious prayers, and something of a shrewd and proverbial cast of worldly counsel, were not the less esteemed that they pertained to a humble weaver. His consequence, even in this lowly situation, was felt far and wide; of the fair webs which came from the devout man's looms, let the long linsey-woolsey garments of the matrons of Dumfries, even at this day, bear witness—garments which surpass silk in beauty, while many a blythsome bridal and sorrowful burial bore token, in their fine linen vestments, of the skill of William's right hand. Indeed, it was one of the goodman's own practical proverbs, 'that there was more vanity in the bier than the bridal.' Though sufficiently conscious of those gifts, he wished them to be forgotten in the sedate and austere elder of the kirk; and long before the time of our tale, he had become distinguished for the severity of his discipline, and his gifts in kirk controversy.

But the influence of ancient times of relaxation and joy, of which he had been a partaker in his youth, had not wholly ceased; and an observer of human nature might see, that amid all the controversial contemplations in which he seemed involved, the jolly old domestic god of Scottish cheer and moderate hilarity had not yet yielded entire place to the Crumb of Comfort, the Cup of Cold Water to the Parched Spirit, The Afflicted Man's Best Companion, and Boston's Fourfold State. He lifted his eyes from the page, and said, "Marion, even before I proceed to matters of spiritual import, let me know what thou hast prepared for the nourishment of the bodies of those whom we have invited, according to the fashion of our fathers, to sit out the Old Year and welcome in the New. Name me the supper dishes, I pray thee, that I may know if thou hast scorned the Babylonian observances of the sister Church of England in the matter of creature-comforts. What hast thou prepared for supper, I pray thee?—no superstitious meats and drinks, Marion, I hope, but humble and holy, and halesome things, which nourish the body without risk to the soul? I dread, by thy long silence, woman, that thou hast been seeking to pamper the Episcopalian propensities of our appetites by ceremonious and sinful saint-day dishes.

"Ah! William Warpentree," said his douce spouse Marion, covering an old oaken table as she spoke, with a fine-pattern'd table cloth, wove by no other hand than that of the devout owner of the feast himself; "Ah!" said she, "what words have escaped from thy lips—superstitious meats and drinks," said ye? "Na! na! I cared mair for the welfare of the spirit, and the hope to sing hallelujahs in Abram's bosom, as ye say in prayer yoursel'; Ah! Willie, they say, who kenned you in your youth, that ye would sooner gang to Samh's." "Woman, woman," said the douce man, "what say ye to the supper?" "First, then," quoth his spouse, forsaking unwillingly this dazzling road of domestic controversy and strife; "what have ye to say against a dish of collops scored, nicely simmered owre the head amang Spanish onions?" "Spanish onions, woman," said the elder; "I like not the sound." "Sound," said the dame, "would ye lose your supper for a sound? Had they grown in the garden of the Grand Inquisitor, and been sown by some pope or cardinal, then, man, ye might have had your scruples—but they grew in the garden of that upright man, David Bogie; I'll warrant ye'll call the scored collops Episcopalian, since they were cut by a knife of Sheffield steel." "Pass to the other viands and vivers, woman," said the elder. "Gladly will I," said his obedient partner; "the mair gladly because it's a gallant Scottish haggis full, and fat, and fair. Hearken to the ingredients, Willie, and try them by the scrupulous kirk standard of forbidden luxuries. What say you against the crushed heart of the kindly corn—a singed sheep's head—plotted, par-boiled, shorn small, with slice of broiled liver ground to powder, and a dozen of onions sliced like wafers, powdered with pepper, and showered owre with salt; the whole mingled with the fat of the ox, and stowed in a bag as pure as burnbleached linen, and secured with a peg that would make seven spoolpins. I'll warrant it will spout to the rannel-tree when ye stick the knife in it. My certie will't."

At this description of the national dish, the old man displaced the book from his knee, placed his hand on his waistcoat, where time and daily meditation had made some spare cloth, and rising, paced from side to side of his humble abode, with a look of subdued and decent impatience. "I wonder;—wonder is an unwise word," said he, checking himself, "for nought is wonderful, save the divine presence, and the divine works; but what, in the name of warp and waft—a mechanical exclamation of surprise, and therefore not sinful—what can stay Deacon Treddle, my ain dear door neighbour; and what can keep Bailie Burnewin! I hope his prentice boy has not burnt his forge again, and made the douce man swear." "Saul to gudeman, but ye feu ill." "But we have all our times of weakness—even I myself," he muttered, in a low and inaudible tone, "have matters to mourn for as well as the wicked; I have buttered my own breakfast with the butter, which honest men's wives have given me, for anointing their webs. I have worn, but that was in my youth, the snawwhite linen purloined from many customers in hanks and cuts. And I have looked with an unrighteous eye after that dark-eyed and straight-limbed damsel, Mary Macmillan; even I, who rebuked her and counselled her before the session, and made even the anointed minister envy the fluency and scriptural force of my admonishment. But, in gude time, here comes auld Burnewin," and extending his hand as he spoke, it was grasped by a hand protruded from a broad brown mantle, and tinged by exposure at the forge into the hue of a tinker's travelling wallet.

"Whole threads, and a weel-gaun loom to thee, my douce auld fere," said the Bailie, removing a slouched hat as he yoke, and displaying a rough jolly countenance, on which the heat of his smithy fire had inflicted a tinge that would have done honour to Vulcan's forehead hammer man.

"And a hissing welding heat, and an unburnt tow-iron, and ale fizzing and foaming for thee in thy vocation, my old comrade," returned the weaver, in the current language of its friend's trade. "Aha! Marion lass," said the blacksmith, "I have nae forgot that we were once younkers running among the moonlight on the moat-brae—here's a shawl—I wish it silk for thy sake—ye maun wear it for me at Paste and Yule, and the seven trades dance, and other daimen times; and, enveloping the not unwilling shoulders of the matron in his present, he seated himself by the side of a blazing hearth fire, and promising supper board.

It was now eleven o'clock—the reign of the Old Year was within an hour of its close, and the din of the street had subsided, partly from the lateness of the hour, and the fall of a shower of thin and powdery snow which abated a little the darkness of the night. A loud scream, and the sound of something falling, were heard at the end of the little narrow close or street which descended from the old Kirkgate to the residence of the elder. "There's the sound of Deacon Treddle's voice," said Marion, "if ever I heard it in my life; and the cry, too, of sore affliction." Away without bonnet or mantle ran the old friends of the expected deacon; they found him lying with his face to the pavement, his hands clutched like one in agony, while from a shattered punchbowl ran the rich and reeking contents. "As I live by drink, and sometimes bread," said the Bailie, "this is a hapless tumble; I feel the smell of as good brandy punch as ever reeked aneath the nose of the town council—there it runs; water, saith the word, cannot be gathered from the ground, nor brandy punch from the street, saith Bailie Burnewin." "Peace, peace, I pray thee," said the elder; "speak, Thomas Treddle, speak; art thou harmed in spirit, or hurt in body?" "The spirit is running from him," said the son of the forge, in the true spirit of citizenship; "dost thou not feel its fragrance?" "Peace, again I say," enjoined the elder; "I say unto you, something fearful hath happened unto him; he has felt an evil touch, or he has seen some unholy sight: such things have been rife ere now in the land;" and he endeavoured to raise his prostrate friend from the pavement.

"I renounce the sinfulness of long thrums and short ellwands, now and for ever more, Amen!" muttered the overthrown head of the venerable calling of the weavers. "Long thrums and short ellwands," said he of the smithy to him of the loom; "I'll remember his confession, however—there's knavery in all crafts, save mine." "Avaunt avaunt, whither wilt thou carry me!" exclaimed the deacon; "That man hath perfect blessedness, who walketh not astray in counsel of ungodly men. Oh! that I could mind a prayer now, when a prayer might be of service, and no be borne away owre the fiend's left shoulder, like holy Willie gaun hame with a customer's web." "The man's demented," muttered the elder; "possess'd by a demon—fairly possess'd—here, Bailie, bear thou his heels, I'll bear up his head, and let us carry him home, and deliver him up to the admonition of dame Marion." And lifting aloft the weaver as they spoke, away they marched —but not without speech or resistance. "A fiend at my head, and a fiend at my feet! Lost beyond redemption!

Lost beyond redemption! Oh! if I maun be doomed, let me lie in my grave like other sinners, and no be borne away to be picked by the fiend behind the stake and ryse dyke that divides the foul place from purgatory, like a gled picking a cock-bird." Their entrance into the chamber beside dame Marion, seemed at first to augment his terror:—he shut his eyes, and clenched his hands in the resolute agony of despair. "Ah! the black pit, and the burning fire, wi' fiends to torment me in the shape of holy Willie Warpentree and that wicked body Bailie Burnewin A she-fiend, too! Na, then there's nae redemption for me —I'm in the hollowest hell, I'll warrant me!" and half unclosing his eyes, they wandered with something of a half insane and half suspicious scrutiny around the elder's apartment.

At this irreverent allusion to herself and her sex, the yoke-fellow of the elder exclaimed:—"Ungracious and graceless body, I'll she-fiend thee!" and lifting up a spoonful of the fat liquid in which the haggis had been immersed, she threw it fairly in his face. This application was much more effectual than the grave inquiries of her husband; the liquid, too cool to scald, and yet hot enough to make flesh feel, caused him to utter a scream. "Well done, shefiend!" said the blacksmith, "if a woman's wit brings nae a man to his senses, I wot nae what will." The afflicted weaver opened his eyes, exclaimed, "Praise be blest!" leaped to his feet, shouted, "redeemed! redeemed!—won from the clutches of the auld enemy, and set on my feet at the fire-side of my sworn friend, William Warpentree. But, Oh! man, I have got such a fright this blessed evening as will gang wi' me to my grave."

"Fright!" said Marion, "what could have frightened ye in the douce Kirkgate of Dumfries; the kirk at your lug, the kirkyard at your elbow, and the fear o' God afore ye, and a gallant bowl of brandy punch in your hand. I feel the smell of the spilt mercies yet, ye donnered bodie; what fiend made ye coup the creels, and scream yon way?" "Woman, woman," said the elder to his spouse, "bridle thy unruly tongue, and curb thy irreverent speech—this man hath, peradventure, seen something; which he will do well to disburthen his conscience in describing." "I shall make bauld to tell ye," said the deacon of the weavers, "how it happened, and whereabout; but, Oh! man, never let sinful flesh pride itself again in the joys of this world. Who would have thought that a man like me, a bowl of reeking punch in one hand, and buttered short cake in the other; the town clock chapping eleven, a glass in my head, the pavement aneath, and my friend's door open before me, should in ae moment be spoiled and bereaved of all in which he had sinfully prided. Oh! William Warpentree—flesh and blood—flesh and blood." Here he wiped away the moisture of Marion's haggis from his face, muttered, "Grace be near me, I'm barely come to my senses yet— Lord, I'll never forget it—how can I—I'm a doomed creature, that's certain." The elder enjoined him to tell why he was disquieted—the elder's wife desired to know what elf or brownie had scared him out of any little sense he ever laid claim to; while the Bailie declared it would be a droll tale that would recompense him for the privation of the spilt punch.

"Oh! hard, hard! exclaimed the deacon of the weavers; "I maun be frightened out of my senses ae minute with the Packman's ghost, and fairly die in describing it the next." "The Packman's ghost!" exclaimed the three auditors, at once gathering round the affrighted deacon. "Yes! the Packman's ghost," said he; "give me leave to breathe, and I shall tell ye. As I came out to the street, there was a slight fall of snow; the way was as white afore me as a linen web—a light glimmered here and there—the brightest was in the home of Lowrie Linchpin, the Haunted House ye ken; the carle lies in a departing state. As I looked o'er to his window, I thought to myself, the minister or some of the elders will be there, doubtless, and a bonnie death-bed story he'll make on't, if he tells the truth. And then, I stood and thought, may be, on the wild stories the neighbours tell of sights seen at midnight around his house—how he cannot rest in his bed, but converses with his dumb horse to drown darker thoughts; while atween his own house and the stable, the shadowy fingers of an auld Packman are seen plucking at him. A golden pose Auld Linchpin got by nicking the pedlar's thrapple, else there are many liars. There was my douce gudemother, ye mind her weel, Bailie, many a mutchkin of brandy you and auld Brandyburn, and John Borland, and Edgar Wright, and ane I winna name, emptied ahint her hallan. Aweel thae days are gane, and my gudemother too; but mony a time she told me, when she was a tripling of a lassie, that the auld Packman (nae other name had he) was seen coming laden, horse and man, along the lane to the house of Lowrie Linchpin. He was never more seen; but his horse ran masterless about the fields, and mony a ride she, and Peg Lawson, and Nell Thomson had; their daughters are fine madams now, and would nae like to hear that their mothers rode round the town meadows on a stray horse; but it is true that I tell ye."

"And now," said the deacon, "I am come to the present concernment. I stood looking at old Ne'er-do-good's house, and thinking how soon he might be summoned, and what a black account he would render; when lo, and behold! what should I see coming towards me from auld Lowrie's, but a creature,—the queerest creature that een ever saw! I thought I should have sunk where I stood, with dread, and yet the worst had not happened. I could nae for my soul take my een from it, and straight towards me it came. I think I see it yet—the breeks of hodan gray, the Packman plaid, and the Kilmarnock bonnet; the hair of my own head, gray and thin though it be, raised the bonnet from my own brow. Oh! William Warpentree, could I have remembered but three words of thy prayer, which seven times to my knowledge ye have poured out before men who swear by the wolf's head and shuttle in its mouth, I might have come off crouse, perchance, and triumphant. But the world winna credit it.—I tried to pray—I tried to bless myself, I could neither do the one nor the other, and curses and discreditable oaths came to my lips; I shall never dare to sing a psalm, or speak of a thing that's holy again."

The deacon's story had proceeded thus far; Marion had, with a light foot, and a diligent hand, and an ear that drank in every word of the narrative, replenished the table with a noble haggis reeking and rich, and distilling streams of amber from every pore; while, from the collops scored, a smoke thick and savoury ascended; and a table of inferior size exhibited an ancient punch bowl, curiously hooped and clasped, flanked by a brace of gardevines, filled to the corks with choice gin and brandy. Upon the whole looked the elder and Bailie with a strong wish that the deacon's adventure with the pedlar's apparition would come to a close. A hurried foot in the street, and a mighty rap, rap, rap, at the door, equal to the demolishing of any ordinary hinges, accomplished the good man's wish. Ere Marion could say —"Come in,"—in started an ancient Kirkgate dame, her hood awry, and a drinking cup, which her hurry had not hindered her to drain, though she found no leisure to set it down, was still in her right hand. She stood with her lips apart, and pointed towards the haunted house of old Linchpin, half choked with agitation and haste. "The saints be near us, woman; have ye seen a spirit also?" said Bailie Burnewin. "Spirit!" said the dame, an interogatory suggesting words which she could not otherwise find—" ten times worse than a thousand spirits—I would rather face all the shadows of sinners which haunt the earth, than sit five minutes longer by the bedside of auld Lowrie; the fiends have bold of him, there's little doubt of that, for he's talking to them, and bargaining for a cozie seat in the lowing heugh,—its fearful to hear him—and what can have brought the evil spirits around him already,—naebody will dispute possession; and then he thinks the Packman is at his elbow, and begins to speak about the old throat-cutting story: but his wife, a wicked carlin and a stout, lays ever her hand on his mouth and cries out, 'he's raving, sirs, he's raving!'—But I think I'm raving myself. Come away, Elder Warpentree, and try and speak solace to his saul, though it be a rotten and a doomed ane; he may as well gang to hell with the words of salvation sounding in his ear."

Sore groaned the devout man at this ungracious and untimely summons; he looked on the smoking supper-table; he thought on the wretched and the worthless being, for whose soul's welfare he was called to minister by prayer and supplication, and despairing of success in his intercession, he threw himself into a chair, pulled it to the head of the table, laid aside his cap, and spread forth his hands like one ready to bless the savoury morsel before him. The Christian spirit of the messenger, reinforced by strong drink, came down like a whirlwind. "A bonnie elder of God's kirk, indeed, to sit down to his smoking supper, with his full-fed cronies aside him, and leave a poor soul to sink among the fathomless waters of eternity. Had it been a douce and a devout person that was at death's door, the haste might have been less; but a being covered with crimes as with a garment; whose left hand clutched men's gold, and whose right hand wrought murder; it's a burning shame and a crying scandal, not to fly and seek to save, and send him the road of repentance. A bonnie elder, indeed! O my conscience, Sir, if I'm but spared to Sunday—if I stand nae up and proclaim ye for a sensual and selfish man, who shuns the dying man's couch for the sake of a savoury supper, may the holy minister give me a hot face, clad in a penitential garment on the cutty stool." During this outpouring of remonstrance and wrath the good man found leisure for reflection; he rose ere she concluded, assumed his hat and mantle, and saying, "I will go to the couch of this wicked man, but wicked should I be to hold out the hope that an hour of repentance will atone for an age of crime; 'its but casting precious words away, ane might as well try to make damask napery out of sackleth thrums, as make a member for bliss out of such a sinner as Lowrie Linchpin."

When the elder entered the dying man's abode he found him seated in his arm chair, pale and exhausted; his clothes torn to shreds, and his hair (as lintwhite and long, as it had waved over the temples of a saint) scattered about in handfuls; while his wife, a stern and stout old dame, pinioned him down in his seat, and fixed upon him two fierce and threatening eyes, of which he seemed to be in awe. "And what, in the fiend's name, brought auld Wylie Warpentree here at this uncivil hour, when we have more distress than heart can well endure," said she of the Haunted House; "are ye come to steal our purse under the pretence of prayer, like bonnie Elder Haudthegrup? de'el may care if ye were all dancing on the morning air in a St. Johnstone cravat; the land would be well rid of ye." "Woman, woman," said the elder, in a tone of sorrow and Christian submission, "wherefore would ye asperse the servants of Him above; I come not here to take, neither come I hither to steal, but I come to one sick and subdued in spirit, sick even unto death, for the hand of the enemy will soon be upon him. Oh man!" said he, addressing the dying person, "if ye had seven years to live, as ye may have but seven minutes; if your soul was as pure as the unfallen snow, now descending at your window, instead of being stained as with ink, and spotted as with crimson, I say unto you repent, repent; cast thyself in the ashes, groan and spread thy hands, night and morn, and noontide; thy spirit will find it all too little to atone for thy follies, for thy faults, and for——" "Devil! wilt thou talk about the Pedlar also," exclaimed Dame Linchpin, placing her hand, as she spoke, on the mouth of the elder; "it's enough that my own poor old demented husband should upbraid me with planning and plotting on't, without any uncivil tongue. Oh, sirs! but I am a poor broken-hearted mad old woman, and my words should not be minded to my character's harm;" and she covered her face with her hand and wept aloud.

"Ay, ay!" exclaimed her husband, "I'm coming—I'm coming—will ye not indulge me with another little little year—I have much to settle—much to do, and much to say, and I'm not so old—what is seventy and eight?—There's twenty in the parish older, and my limbs are strong and my sight's good—I can see to read the small print Bible without glass, and that's a gallant brag at my time of life. Weel, weel, all flesh is grass, the word says that, and I shall fulfil it—but wherefore am I not to die in my bed like my douce father? ye will never punish an old man like me—its bad for the land when the gallows sees gray hairs. Prove it! who will prove it, I pray thee?—who shall tell that I slew him for his gold?—how my wife plotted his death, and helped me bravely to spill his blood, and rifle his well-filled pack?—Ah! mony a bonnie summer day has she gone gaily to kirk and market with the price of our salvation on her back.—She gave a gallant mantle from the pack to the proud wife of Provost Mucklejohn; the wife's good luck was ended: she gave a plaid to Baillie Proudfoot, and proud was he no longer; he was found drowned in the Nith on the third day: it was nae sonsie to wear the silks and satins, and fine raiment, of which a dead man was the owner. Weel, weel, woman, if ye will tell of me, even tell—all that ye can say is easily summed. Hearken, and I will disclose it myself. He came with his packs and his pillions filled with rich satins, and fine-twined linen, and silver in his pouch, and gold in his purse. I was poor, and my mind was prone to evil." Here he clenched his teeth, wrung his hands fiercely for a moment, his colour changed, his lips quivered, and he said, in a low and determined tone

"I see him, there he sits; there he sits; a thousand and a thousand times have I seen him seated and watching, and he will have me soon: ah, it's he—it's he! My dog Tippler sees him, too, and the creature shivers with fear, for he lapt his blood as it streamed o'er my wife's knuckles upon the floor." The dying man paused again, and he said, "Wife, woman, fiend, why come ye not when I call? Wipe my brow, woman, and clear my een, and let me look on something that seems as a black shadow seated beside me:" and passing his own hand over his eyes, he looked steadfastly on the elder, and uttering a cry of fear, fell back in his chair, and lay, with his palms spread over his face, muttering. "I thought it was something from the other world; and it's ten times worse; an elder of the kirk! an elder of the kirk! He's come to hearken my disordered words; to listen to my ravings, and bear witness against me. Oh, farewell to the fair, and the honest, and the spotless name that my father gave me. The name of my forebears will be put in a prayer, made a proverb in a sermon, and hallowed in a psalm; the auld wives as they go to the kirk will shake their Bibles at the naked walls, and the haunted house, and say blood has been avenged." The shudder of death came upon him; he tried to start from his seat; he held out his hands like one repulsing the approach of an enemy, and uttering a loud groan, expired. "I have been at many a death-bed," said William Warpentree, resuming his seat at his supper-table, and casting a look of sorrow on the diminished haggis—"but I never was at the marrow of this:—and now for the collops scored."—

WILLIAM AND NANCY.

"Bleak was the morn when William left his Nancy,
The fleecy snow frown'd on the whitened shore;
Cold as the fears that chill'd her dreary fancy,
While she her sailor from her bosom tore."

"I've lost one eye, and I've got a timber toe," sung old Joe Jennings, as he swivelled round on his wooden pin, while bustling through the comical Jack-in-the-box gate, at the east end of the Naval Asylum going into Greenwich Park.—

"I've lost one eye and I've got a timber toe."

"And where did you leave your eye, Joe?" "In the Gut of Gibraltar." "Well, Joe, you'll never see double again. Come, let's freshen the nip, my old boy, and spin us a tough yarn. Tell the gemmen about Nancy and her husband; my scuppers run over whenever I think of it." "Why, ay, he shall have it, and do lend me a lift if I should break down, though I don't much fear it. Why, d'ye see, sir, Bill Neville was our messmate, and he used to tell us a little of his history. And so, sir, he was brought up in a country village, and loved his wife when only a little girl; and he went to sea, thinking to make his fortune for her sake. Well, he got to be master of a merchantman, and then they were married. Who can describe the pleasures of that moment when their hands were spliced at the altar, and he hailed her as his own. But he was obliged to sail again. "Oh!" said Nancy, "should you never return, what shall I do? where shall I pass—where end my wretched days!" His heart was too full to speak; one hand clasped in hers, the other pointed to the broad expanse where the noon-day sun was shining with meridian splendour. It had a double meaning—Nancy felt it. Well, sir, eighteen months roll'd away, during which, in due time, Nancy brought into the world a dear pledge of affection—a lovely boy. But oh, the agony of the mother as every day dragged on without intelligence from William! When she looked at the sweet babe—was it indeed fatherless, and she a widow? You'll excuse my stopping, sir, but indeed I cant help it; I've shed tears over it many a time.

"Well, sir, eighteen months was turned, when one morning Nancy rose to pour out her heart before her Maker and weep over her sleeping child. The sun had just risen above the hills, when a noise in the little garden which fronted the cottage alarmed her. She opened the casement, and, putting aside the woodbine, beheld,—delightful, yet, agonizing sight—her dear, her long-mourned William, hand-cuffed between two soldiers, while others, with their side-arms drawn, seemed fearful of losing their prey! His face pale, and his emaciated body worn down with fatigue and sickness, his spirit seemed ready to quit its frail mansion, and was only kept to earth by union with his wife. Nancy forgot all, and clasped him in her arms; but the rattling of the irons pierced her soul. I do not mean to condemn the policy, sir; but 'tis a cruel practice, that of pressing. Ah! I well remember it—though I always served my king, God bless him! Yet I've witnessed many an aching heart, and heard many a groan of agony. But to proceed: William was pressed; Nancy hastened into the cottage, and, wrapping the sleeping babe in its blanket, she prepared to accompany them. Cannot you picture to yourself the first glance which the wretched parent cast upon his child? Oh, it was a sad sweet joy, that wrung the soul! I shall pass by their meeting, their dear delight, their bitter anguish. If you can feel, it is already engraven on your heart. Suffice it to say, William had been shipwrecked on the African coast, and though he had lost the whole of his property, yet heaven had spared his life, and his the only one. Sickness came on him, and but for the humanity of a poor untutored negro, he might have breathed his last. She was black, she was a negro, but God searches the heart. He had procured, with much difficulty, a passage home. The ship arrived; he set out, and walked many a weary mile, led on by love and cheered by hope, till the roof of his cottage appeared in view; with hasty steps he reached the wicket, when—— But I dare not repeat the story. I've told you already he was pressed. Well, he was drafted on board of us, and his dear Nancy permitted to be with him. The evening before the action, she was sitting on the carriage of the bow gun, with her baby cradled in her arms, and William by her side; they were viewing, with admiration and delight, the beauteous scenery displayed by the sinking clouds in a thousand fantastic shapes, tinged with liquid gold streaming from the setting sun, and caressing the little innocent, while all the parent kindled in their hearts. But hark! a hoarse voice is heard from the mast-head—all is hushed. 'Holloo!' said the captain. 'A sail on the larboard bow, sir,' 'What does she look like?' 'I can but just see her sir, but she booms large.' 'Mr. Banks,' said the captain, 'take your glass aloft, and see if you can make out what she is. Call the boatswain, turn the hands up, make sail.' In a moment all was bustle; the topmen were in their station, and every man employed; and in a few minutes every stitch of canvass was stretched upon the yards and booms. The officer that was sent aloft reported it a ship of the line, which looked like a foreigner. Every heart was now elate but Nancy's—it might be an enemy! Oh, that thought was dreadful! And as William conducted her below, the tears chased each other down her pale face, and the heavy sigh burst from her gentle bosom. William mildly reproved her, and again pointing to heaven, flew to his post. The stranger had hauled to the wind, fired a gun, and hoisted French colours. Up went ours with three cheers; and there's seldom a moment of greater pride to a British tar than when he displays the ensign of his country in presence of the enemy. Three cheers resounded through the ship, and broadside upon broadside shook her groaning timbers. Where was Nancy? William was first in every danger. Three times we boarded the foe, but were repulsed. Dreadful grew the scene of blood and horror through the darkening shades of coming night. No one bore tidings of the fight to Nancy, none, save the poor sailor whose shattered limb came to suffer amputation, or the wounded wretch to be dressed, at which she assisted with fortitude. Two hours had passed in this awful suspense and heart-rending anxiety, when a deep groan and piercing shriek from the lower deck convulsed her frame. She knew the voice, and snatching the infant in her arms, rushed to the spot. Soon she found the object of her search: his manly form mangled and shattered; that face, once ruddy with the glow of health, now pale and convulsed; the blood streaming from his side and breast! He saw her too. 'Nancy!' said he, and raising his feeble hand pointed to heaven—it fell—and William was no more! Sinking on the lifeless body of her husband, Nancy fainted with the dear babe still in her arms; when, oh, mysterious Providence! at that very moment—while senseless and inanimate—at that very moment a ball entered through the vessel's side—it pierced her bosom! Need I tell the rest? They were pleasant and lovely in their lives, and in their death they were not divided."—*From Greenwich Hospital, a Series of Naval Sketches.*

COLUMN FOR THE LADIES.

CONDITION OF WOMEN IN ENGLAND AND ITALY CONTRASTED.—GOOD REASONS FOR OLD MAIDENS IN BRITAIN.

THIS is an extract from COUNT PECCHIO'S Work, the "*Serio-Comic Observations of an Italian Exile,*" which we lately noticed among new publications.

"The young women of England, under a stormy and inconstant sky, have hearts and minds peaceful and serene, always equable, and always docile. My amiable countrywomen, under a heaven perpetually smiling, have minds and hearts always in a tempest. The former are educated for quiet and domestic felicity. Every thing conduces to this end,—the order and system of their lives, the simplicity of their food; the climate, compelling them to live in-doors; the silence that reigns within and without their homes; their long residences in the country—all tend to soften or set to sleep their passions. While the latter, animated by the continual sight of the world, stimulated by a thousand objects; now treated tyrannically, now over caressed, and then unreasonably contradicted; carried to the theatres and crowded streets; seem educated to give vent to their passions, brought up only to be haughty and spirited. Hence they are impassioned, greedy of distinction; made more beautiful by the very desire of pleasing, but tormented with a restless rivalry,—unhappy themselves, they too often make all around them so. A true and excellent comparison of the English women and the Italian may be found in the " Corinna," of Madame de Staël. Corinna, all fancy, all impulse, all love of glory, all passion—was unhappy, and would have made her English lover unhappy, had she married him. Lucia, instead, all good sense, sweetness, modesty, and filial affection, was happy in her obscurity, and promised happiness to her husband. Lucia, after spending two hours of the morning in painting a beautiful rose, satisfied and contented, shuts it up in her portfolio. Corinna is dissatisfied and discontented with her talent, unless she declaims a hymn, and receives thunders of applause from thousands of auditors.

Instead of producing extempore poetesses, such as the Bandettinis, the Mazzeis, and the Corillas, is it not better to produce affectionate wives, and sensible mothers of families? Is not the picture of a happy family (Pamela with her children) more touching than that of the coronation of Corilla in the capitol? Italy boasts Nina, Senti, Stampa, Julia Aragons, and many other modern *improvisatrici*; but would it not have tended more to the happiness of its families to have had such women as Miss Edgeworth, Miss Aiken, and Mrs. Hamilton, who have written works for the education of children? Is it better to enjoy a brief youth of tumultuary pleasures, or an entire life full of sweet affections,—the first, like a torrent that dashes triumphantly over the rocks for a space, and then leaves its bed dry and arid,—the second, like a river that flows between humble banks, but flows for ever? To this preachifying of mine, a witty Frenchwoman would reply, that she preferred a life *courte et bonne,* (short and good, that is, brilliant,)—a sober Englishwoman would wish it *long and comfortable,* (that is, serene.)

The young women are accustomed to travelling alone, sometimes in the public carriages, for one or two hundred miles together. The general education of the travellers, —the respect professed by the men towards the fair sex,— the protection that every Englishman is ready to afford them,—and, let it be added, their frozen demeanour and immovable eyes, secure them from the slightest insult or equivocal expression. The fact which the Irish legend relates, that in the olden time, a girl, ornamented with precious jewels, and a beauty still more precious, walked with a gem-decked wand in her hand through all the island, without experiencing either interruption or insult, is an experiment that might be made, or rather, is daily made in England.

Travelling in Ireland, it happened that one of the passengers, who had drunk a little more than he should have done, and could hardly see for the wine he had had, addressed some equivocal words to a lady who sat opposite, who, in reality, was ugly enough to cool the raptures of a Don Juan. Our Lucretia set up a cry of alarm, and the coachman instantly stopped the horses, got down, told the drunken man to get out, and, like a true knight, challenged him to combat—with the fists.

To return,—the young ladies, therefore, in the course of the year, often go to spend some time with their friends or relations in distant parts of the country. By these reciprocal visits, their lives are in no degree changed. As in England they live everywhere in the same way, and time is everywhere equally distributed, the young lady who travels merely makes a change of place, not of habits or occupations; she resumes her work, her reading, in the house of her hosts, as if she were still in the bosom of her own family: not a year passes without one or two of these excursions; and when they are of marriageable age, their relations take them to pass some weeks in London, or Edinburgh. Thus, until the era of marriage, which happens between twenty-two and twenty-five years of age, their life passes in quiet study and amusements; and after marriage, in "pleasing duties," as an amiable English lady told me. It ought not, therefore, to excite surprise that there is in England a prodigious number of *old maids*. As their youth is not a state of slavery, as in other countries, and they enjoy, when marriageable, a liberty of choice, it happens that they are not at all anxious to shake off the maternal yoke to burden themselves with that of a husband; and that they often prefer a state of life a little insipid, and sometimes exposed to derision, to the miseries of an ill-assorted union.

THE LADY'S MAN.

This animal is one of the most useful species of the domestic tribe. He seldom arrives at perfection until the age of 35, when he is usually of short stature, and somewhat bald at the top of the head. He is as active as the monkey, and possesses a similar chatter, commonly denominated "small talk." Like the French poodle, he is perfect in the art of "fetching and carrying;" and may e seen with his canine companion in the society of the fair sex, when all others of the male kind are rightly excluded. To the MAID he is invaluable, no less as a walking-stick in the promenade, than as a convenient partner in the dance. He supplies the place of a play-bill at the theatre; and on account of his acknowledged harmlessness, allows and takes many freedoms; so that a flirtation with *him* is classed among "innocent amusements,"—there being no one instance in the records of Natural History of his ever "pairing."—By the WIFE his services are no less esteemed. He hands the toast at tea—shows off in the science of comparative anatomy at dinner—brews capital lady's punch after supper—and takes the children to see the Christmas pantomimes. At the birth-day juvenile parties, he pares the oranges, performs the principal character in the classical game of "bumble-puppy," and adjusts the machinery of the magic lantern. When an "event" occurs, he stands godfather, and sees home elderly aunts after family tea parties.—But the WIDOW most appreciates the Lady's Man. Does *she* want a new servant? He procures "a two-year's character from the last place." Is *she* curious about the cause of Miss So-and-So's illness? He leaves not an inquiry unasked until the mystery is solved. He receives her dividends at the Bank,—takes the place of "dummy," at whist,— and plays the fiddle at her dances. In short, he all *but* supplies the place of the "dear departed." The sustenance of this animal is derived principally from aliments—tea, candle, negus, &c.; and as he is very abstemious, he generally lives to a good old age, and dies " respected and beloved by a numerous circle of acquaintance," with the satisfactory assurance that his virtues will be immortalized in divers " Stanzas on a departed Friend," and "Sundry Lines on the Death of an esteemed Cousin," in the Lady's Magazine.

Exercises out of doors have again become fashionable among ladies. We have a female system of *Calisthenics* taught in boarding-schools; riding on horseback was never more practised; and every year ladies use their limbs more freely in walking. The study of botany and natural history has led them, of all classes, into the fields, and along the sea-shores. The graceful pastime of archery has once more become a favourite exercise with the higher ranks of females. We still hear of ladies having at least a peep of the hounds, (a fox expired at the feet of Queen Adelaide, the other day,) and the unsuitable diversion of angling is pursued by others.

LADIES' PASTIMES—NEEDLE-WORK.

In the early ages, our fair countrywomen employed a large portion of their time in needle-work and embroidery; and their acquirements in these elegant accomplishments most probably afforded them little leisure for the pursuits of trifling and useless amusements; but though we are not acquainted with the nature of their recreations, there is no reason to suppose that they were unbecoming in themselves, or indulged beyond the bounds of reason or decorum. I have already, on a former occasion, particularly noticed the skilfulness of the Saxon and Norman ladies in handling the needle, embroidering, and working in tapestry; and that their performances were not only held in high estimation at home, but were equally prized upon the Continent, where none were produced that could be placed in competition with them.

DANCING AND CHESS-PLAY.

Dancing was certainly an ancient and favourite pastime with the women of this country; the maidens, even in a state of servitude, claimed, as it were, by established privilege, the license to indulge themselves in this exercise on holydays and public festivals; when it was usually performed in the presence of their masters and mistresses.

In the middle ages, dice, chess, and afterwards tables, and cards, with other sedentary games of chance and skill, were reckoned among the female amusements; and the ladies also frequently joined with the men in such pastimes, as we find it expressly declared in the metrical romance of Ipomydon. The passage alluded to runs thus:—

When they had dyned, as I you saye,
Lordes and ladyes yode to playe;
Some to tables and some to chesse,
With other gamys more or lesse.

In another poem, by Gower, a lover asks his mistress, when she is tired of "dancing and caroling," if she was willing to "play at chesse, or on the dyes to cast a chaunce." Forrest, speaking in praise of Catherine of Arragon, first wife of Henry VIII, says, that when she was young,

With stoole and with needyl she was not to seeke,
And other practiseings for ladyes meete;
To pastyme at tables, tick tack or gleeke,
Cardis and dyce—&c.

LADIES' RECREATIONS IN THE FOURTEENTH CENTURY

The English ladies did not always confine themselves to domestic pastimes; they sometimes participated with the other sex in diversions of a more masculine nature, and engaged with them in the sports of the field. These violent exercises seem to have been rather unfashionable among them in the seventeenth century; for Burton, in his Anatomy of Melancholy, speaks of their pastimes as much better suited to the modesty and softness of the sex. "The woman," says he, "instead of laborious studies, have curious needle-works, cut-works, spinning, bone-lace making, with other pretty devices to adorn houses, cushions, carpets, stool-seats, &c. Not but some of these masculine females have occasionally made their appearance; and at the commencement of the last century, it should seem that they were more commonly seen than in Burton's time, which gave occasion for the following satirical paper in one of the Spectators, written by Addison: "I have," says he, "very frequently the opportunity of seeing a rural Andromache, who came up to town last winter, and is one of the greatest fox-hunters in the country; she talks of hounds and horses, and makes nothing of leaping over a six-bar gate. If a man tells her a waggish story, she gives him a push with her hand in jest, and calls him an impudent dog; and, if her servant neglect his business, threatens to kick him out of the house. I have heard her in her wrath call a substantial tradesman a lousie cur; and I remember one day, when she could not think of the name of a person, she described him, in a large company of men and ladies, as the fellow with the broad shoulders."

SCRAPS.
ORIGINAL AND SELECTED.

ULTIMA DOMUS.

On the gate to the burial vault of the Dukes of Richmond, in their chapel, at Goodwood, is inscribed, "*ultima domus.*" This inscription gives rise to the following impromptu lines:—

Did he who reared this funeral wall,
Not read, or not believe St. Paul;
Who says there is, where'er it stands,
"*Another house,* not made with hands;"
Or may we gather from the words,
That house is not a house of LORDS.

ANCESTOR OF LORD ORMELIE.—About the beginning of last century, a sober and industrious weaver, named Gavin, (no Celt, it is presumed,) lived in a cottage in the parish of Lunan. He had a son, Davy, whom he educated to his own trade, but Davy proved to be "a lazy wenver;" in short, he attended to any thing but his business. At that time the celebrated bay of Lunan was greatly frequented by Dutch smugglers, and it is said that Davy could not resist the temptation of assisting them in their dangerous avocations. Despairing of his well-doing at home, old Gavin determined on sending him abroad "to push his fortune." Davy was accordingly shipped off for Holland, where it is unnecessary to trace the course of his adventures; suffice it to say, that it was fortunate; and, after the lapse of years, the "Lazy Lunan weaver" returned home a rich man, and what is more, with a high and unblemished reputation. He purchased Reamuir, an estate in the adjoining parish of Kennell, and Langton in the Merse." He married "an Earl's daughter;" and David Gavin, Esq. of Langton became the father of the present Marchioness of Braidalbane, and consequently the grandfather of the Earl of Ormelie. Old Gavin was provided for, and was for many years afterwards noted in the parish for wearing a scarlet cloak and a cocked hat. [This story has been told to the imagined disparagement of this patriotic young nobleman. We tell to his praise that there is in his family talent and enterprize, of which, no doubt, he has his share.]

PURE AIR.—Dr. Van Marum, has recently discovered a very simple method, proved by repeated experiments, of preserving the air pure in large halls, theatres, hospitals, &c. The apparatus for this purpose is nothing but a common lamp, made according to Argand's construction, suspended from the roof of the hall, and kept burning, under a funnel, the tube of which rises above the roof without, and is furnished with a ventilator. For his first experiment he filled his laboratory with the smoke of deal shavings. In a few minutes after he lighted his lamp the whole smoke disappeared, and the air was perfectly purified.

STRENGTH OF WINE BOTTLES.—M. Collardeau has constructed a machine for the purpose of trying the strength of wine bottles. It has been presented to the Academy of Sciences, and reported upon by M. Hachette. The apparatus, which is simple, may be well adopted in this country. The bottle to be tried is held by the neck, by means of a lever having three branches, which grasp it below the ring. Being then filled with water, it is connected, by means of pipes, with a forcing-pump—the pipe having a cap furnished with leather, which is firmly held down by the apparatus upon the mouth of the bottle. A pressure-gauge, or manometer, as M. C. calls it, is connected with the water-pipe, and this serves to indicate the precise amount of pressure on the bottle. When a bottle is burst in this way by the hydraulic press, no violent dispersion of its parts takes place, unless, indeed, instead of being entirely filled with water, a portion of air is left in the neck of the bottle. In this way it was ascertained that all brisk or effervescent fluids would require a glass bottle, whose resisting power should not be less than twelve atmospheres, or about 180 lbs. on each inch

TEA PUNCH.—The following receipt for making tea punch is taken from the *Journal des Connoissances Usuelles.* It will be remembered that our late King was very partial to this delicious beverage:—Hyson tea, ¼ lb.; black tea, 4 oz.; boiling water, three gallons; sugar, 16 lb.; old brandy, (*Eau de Vie*) 2¼ gallons; rum, half a gallon; citric acid, and spirit of citron, of each three ounces. The tea is first infused in the water, the citric acid and sugar are then dissolved, and the other ingredients added. We cannot recommend all our readers to adhere to the above quantities, especially at this season. We are happy to assure them, at the same time, that the Journal before named says, that an additional quantity of tea water may be used if indicated by the palate of the *bon vivant.* We take this to be sufficient licence for diminishing the quantity of *Eau de Vie,* which we certainly cannot recommend notwithstanding its attractive designation.

NEW SPECIES OF WHEAT.—A variety of wheat, which does not seem liable to the attack of the wheat-fly, has been accidentally found. It is most prolific, and grows a foot taller than the common wheat. It is awned, and somewhat like the Egyptian, but of a clearer colour, without the protuberances of the latter. If once a supply of this variety for seed be found, the fly will be starved. Of a patch standing in the middle of a field, where every ear of the common wheat was hurt, and the flies were numerous, not an ear was touched, although other bearded varieties suffered.—*Highland Society Transactions.*

CONTENTS OF NO. XXX.

Hereditary Legislators...113
Theory of Volcanoes..115
Remarkable Story of an Avalanche................................116
Trout of Loch Awe...117
The Tailor and the Middies..ib.
The Yellow Domino...118
Trimmings and Trappings of a Modern Successor of the Apostles.119
On True Happiness..ib.
Progress of Knowledge in India....................................120
Rules for Servants...ib.
THE STORY-TELLER—The Haunted House.....................121
William and Nancy..125
COLUMN FOR THE LADIES—Condition of Women in England and Italy Contrasted, &c..126
SCRAPS—Ultima Domus—Ancestor of Lord Ormelie..........128

EDINBURGH: Printed by and for JOHN JOHNSTONE, 19, St. James' Square.—Published by JOHN ANDERSON, Jun., Bookseller, 55, North Bridge Street, Edinburgh; by JOHN MACLEOD, and ATKINSON & Co., Booksellers, Glasgow; and sold by all Booksellers and Venders of Cheap Periodicals

THE Schoolmaster,
AND
EDINBURGH WEEKLY MAGAZINE.

CONDUCTED BY JOHN JOHNSTONE.

THE SCHOOLMASTER IS ABROAD.—LORD BROUGHAM.

No. 31.—Vol. II.   SATURDAY, MARCH 2, 1833.   PRICE THREE-HALFPENCE.

OFFICIAL COSTUMES.
STATE MUMMERY.

OF all the changes which Society is undergoing, none is so rapid in progress as the change of taste. This has proceeded of late with such accelerated velocity, that extremes have met. We have a recent writer, in one of the fashionable periodicals, (the New Monthly,) calling George the Fourth, long known to his subjects as "The first gentleman in Europe," an *Incarnation of vulgarity!* What a phrase! It is certain that the robes and gilt tags, imagined by his "princely taste for magnificence," sold lately for an old song; a bargain even to a country manager as stage properties. And the change has extended, and is descending. Fewer and fewer gazers are every year in attendance on the Lord Mayor's gilt coach; and our own Lord High Commissioner paces up a nearly empty street; the few spectators being more interested in the Bold Dragoons, than the representative of Majesty in the Scottish Kirk. It is time that state ceremonies were renounced when they become a mockery and a jest; and that, in an enlightened age pageants gave place to the simplicity of a higher civilization. We have, in ordinary life, long since laid aside bag-wigs, tawdry lace, and embroidery, and are called upon to follow the same course with tawdry observances, ridiculous pomps and mummeries, and disguisings of the human form. In the first number of Mr. Buckingham's Parliamentary Review, (which, by the way, promises well,) there is an amusing description of the solemn opening of the new Parliament, at which Lord Brougham topped his part. Pity the part, as a mere part, had become obsolete before his Lordship began to star it on those boards. For Bonaparte himself, who has quoted "the late king, my uncle," discovered not a finer genius for the shews of state-craft, when, in the Tuileries, he strictly regulated the imperial court by the rules of the old *régime*, ekeing out his own scanty camp knowledge with the recollections of the superannuated Dowagers of the Faubourg St. Germain, and supplying all deficiencies by his zeal and tact. Unfortunately, not much came of it; the bulk of the nation were of the humour of Hortense, splitting her sides with laughter at the new part every one around her was *mumming* in, and fit to expire outright when inquiries were first addressed to her about her AUGUST MOTHER.—Old Mrs Brougham was in the right; as Henry Brougham, her son, was a great man; and it does pain and mortify those who placed so many hopes in his patriotism and ability, to see him enacting Chrononhotonthologus in state pageants, and reminding Mr. Buckingham, who, we are certain, wishes to think respectfully of him, of a half-mad Levantine consul. If he seemed to submit like a martyr, one might sympathise with him in a matter of state necessity; but he appears to profane spectators to glory in these exhibitions. At the opening of Parliament, Mr. Buckingham relates:—" On the Woolsack sat Lord Brougham, in the centre, having on his right the Marquis of Lansdowne, President of the King's Council, and Earl Grey, First Lord of the Treasury and Prime Minister of State; and, on his left, the Duke of Richmond, Postmaster-General, and Lord Aukland, President of the Board of Trade. One solitary Lord Spiritual, and Right Reverend Father in God, the Bishop of London, occupied the Ministerial side of the House, in the full and flowing costume of his episcopal dignity; and of the Lords Temporal, there were only two at the opening, and one who entered during the proceedings, all of whom sat on the Opposition benches, booted and boa'd, as befitting the wintry weather. The cross-benches were entirely vacant, save and except the seats near the table occupied by the official clerks in their barrister's wigs and gowns, who were to take a part in the sayings, as well as doings of the day.

Of the costume of the learned, noble, and distinguished personages who occupied the woolsack, as his Majesty's Commissioners, it would be difficult for any one, not acquainted with the art of robing, or initiated into the mysteries, which are, no doubt, familiar enough to the keeper of the wardrobe, or groom of the stole, to give an accurate description. Its general effect, however, may be described in one single word—it was *grotesque*. The Lord Chancellor wore his ermined scarlet robe, adown which, on either shoulder, hung the long grey pendant flaps or wings of the judicial wig, not unlike the falling ear-laps of the white or grey elephant of Ava or Siam; and on the extreme point, or crown of the head, just large enough to cover the black patch which distinguishes a serjeant's wig; as though indicating a broken skull was placed a most diminutive and insignificant flat triangular hat, which, not coming down over any part of the block, or having any hold whatever on the rotundity of the seat of intelligence, might be literally called " a skull-cap," though affording so little protection to the small spot it covered, that it might have been blown away by the least breath of wind, or pushed off by the touch of a feather. We remember well, on an occasion of visiting a Levantine consul at Joppa in Palestine, in the year 1816, a tolerably near parallel to this *grotesque* appearance, which is thus described in the volume recording the event:—,' The consul himself soon arrived, and presented one of the most singular mixtures of European and Asiatic costume that we had yet witnessed. His dress consisted of the long robes of the East, surmounted by a powdered bagwig, a cocked-hat, with anchor buttons, and black cockade, and a gold-headed cane, all of the oldest fashion." We thought, at the time, that the figure and costume of this old gentleman were the *most* ridiculous that could be imagined; but we had not then seen a noble Lord presiding on the woolsack as a royal commissioner; and we now give the palm of *grotesqueness* to the Lord High Chancellor of England over the Levantine consul,—the British peer leaving the Asiatic merchant an immeasurable distance behind. We have often heard the people of Yorkshire speak of the curious exhibition of Henry Brougham, the county member, when sworded, hatted, spurred, and mounted, as a knight of the shire in the Castle Yard at York; but it could have been nothing to this appearance of the same person on the woolsack; and both how incomparably less *dignified* than the simple dress and commanding air and manner of the earnest senator in the House of Commons, clothed in all the glory of impassioned eloquence, robed in the majesty of truth, and crowned by the coronet of a free nation's admiration! Oh! dignity! how little are thy true elements appreciated and understood!

" The finest point, however, in the whole scene was this:—When the clerk at the table read over, with deep and solemn tone, the Royal Commission, appointing the noble Lords to act, as he recited the names and titles of the Commissioners, he made a low bow to each, just as the devout idolators of the East bow down at the name of their favourite idol; to which each of the Commissioners responded by taking off his hat, and bowing low in return; not to the clerk, of course, but to the *paper* from which he was reading, just as the Mohammedans shew reverence to their Sultan's firmaun or decree, by bowing before it when they receive it, and putting it to their foreheads in token of respect. We laugh at the Turks for this extreme veneration; but wherein consists the difference between their low bows and our own?

" When the ceremonial had been gone through, the Lord Chancellor addressed the Members of the Commons, who must have been, by this time, duly impressed with the superior dignity of their brother legislators of the Upper House."

Let us hope that one of the very first bills (if bill be necessary) that his Lordship will bring in, may be, one to enable him to doff the beaver-tailed wig, skull-cap, &c., &c., &c. By way of rider, a similar privilege might be secured to our own Lord Advocate, and other minor performers in the State Drama. It is cruel that, when every gentleman's gentleman in the three kingdoms is permitted to wear plain clothes like any other Christain, we should keep our highest official men in their old mountebank liveries. What would an ambassador from Washington think of the scene and costumes described by Mr. Buckingham? Would the admiration of dark *diplomats* for the Queen of his late Majesty Radahma, from Pomaree, or the Sovereign of Ashantee, atone for manly, republican contempt of such fooleries?

ON THE MORAL TRAINING OF CHILDREN.
(For the Schoolmaster.)
LETTER IV.

CHILDREN, from the earliest dawn of reason, should be learning from our *lives*, as well as *conversation*, an esteem for virtue, and a hatred for vice. In their education, our chief object should be, the instilling into them sentiments that are friendly to virtue and true religion; but in order effectually to impress these sentiments on their minds, let us never forget that *example* has a powerful effect. For, while esteem for virtue and piety is professed by *words*, but contradicted by *conduct*, in vain will be the effect of our religious or moral precepts. The experience of mankind in general confirms this; and yet how many cherish the vain idea of effecting wonders with their children, by giving them lessons of virtue, and storing their memories with facts and theories, unaided by example? If we teach them the Love of the Supreme Being with our *lips*, and that of Mammon by our *lives*, we may assure ourselves the latter only will be taught effectually. Parents concerned for the welfare of their children, caution them against anger; yet if they see this passion given way to in the parents, of what effect is precept? Again, we advise them against an avaricious disposition; but if they discover that our prevailing desire is to accumulate wealth, will they be likely to act differently? We teach them the necessity of doing unto others as they would be done unto; and yet, if they detect us conducting ourselves contrary to this rule, will they not learn by our example to do as we do? A mother who is fond of dress and company; whose aim is to attract attention, and outshine her neighbours and friends in the splendour of her furniture, &c., may indeed lecture her children on the necessity of humility, and caution them against the pomps and vanities of this world: such lessons may play upon the ear, but will never sink into the heart, while they are taught by her example, that these very pomps and vanities are the prime end of existence. Parents who are devoted to pleasure and self-indulgence, must expect their children to run the same course.

Some, again, err in pampering and indulging their children in the pleasures of the palate. This mistaken kindness is attended with more danger, perhaps, than they are aware of. It is not only injurious to the health, but also to the mind, by associating the idea of happiness with the gratification of appetite; whence proceeds the degrading habit of self-indulgence in eating and drinking in riper years. All provocatives to eating, should, as much as possible, be kept out of the way of children, but if they unavoidably see and desire them, let gentle, but firm refusal, upon the ground of such viands being pernicious, teach them a lesson of self-command. Appetite should be natural; and if it be so, it will easily be satisfied; wherefore, if children ask for food between the regular meals, the very simplest should be given to them; which, if they really want, they will eat cheerfully. *

Neither let them be indulged in a capricious whimsical taste, with respect to eating and drinking. For which purpose, they should be accustomed to take whatever plain food is deemed suitable for them; and to take it at the regular meal-times of the family, if the meals be not at too long intervals, or at too late an hour in the day. Habit will regulate even the impulses of appetite, and counteract unreasonable antipathies. Thus, by a little attention and prudent management, children may be brought to relish every kind of simple nourishment which may be set before them. For such training, children will, in after-life, thank their parents and teachers.

Children, as soon as they are able to feed themselves, ought always to be admitted to table at meals; and our having company should never prevent it, provided there is room. By this means their manners will be improved, and they will learn from others how to behave, and get over that awkward bashfulness so natural to most of them. We are apt to err, indeed, in not attending sufficiently to bashful children, while the bold and lively are treated with smiles of approbation. Those who are shy and diffident ought to be brought as much into notice as possible: frequently introducing them into the company of engaging friends and acquaintance, will tend greatly to their getting the better of it. The frequent introduction into company, from whose conversation and manners instruction may be derived, is of no small consequence indeed to young people, particularly in keeping them from associating with low companions.

Partiality in parents as to particular children, is another thing which ought carefully to be avoided. Where one or more of the children in a family, are singled out as objects of especial regard, it seldom fails to produce injurious consequences. In the favoured child, it lays the foundation for pride and self-importance. With the others it excites hatred and jealousy, and is the cause of continual dissensions in the family. Whatever may be the motives with parents for partiality, they will undoubtedly have much to answer for the evils which it produces. Concord in a family greatly depends on the parent's management; but it cannot be expected where partiality is shown. That love and harmony may prevail amongst children of the same family, one ought never to be praised at the expense of another. No insidious comparisons must be drawn. Neither should one be allowed to scoff at another who happens to be in disgrace. This practice destroys affection; and gives rise to resentment and retaliation. They should rather be taught to commiserate one another when in disgrace; and not be prevented from interceding in each others' behalf. All teasing derision should be strictly prohibited, as it tends to imbitter the best temper.

When children arrive at an age suitable to have the care of their clothes, and other things, furnish each with a place for their little articles; and being often told it is disgraceful to be disorderly, they will soon adopt the same opinion, and see the propriety, not only as it respects neatness of clothing, but of putting every article they use, when done with it, in its proper place. Thus, regularity will become as easy, and even more agreeable to them, than irregularity. The habit of order and method is important; as the probability is, that, if early taught and prized, it will accompany them through life; and greatly prevent that inconvenience and perplexity which people often experience for want of it in the management of their business.

Do every thing in its proper season; put every thing in its proper place; cleanliness is next to godliness; these are maxims which cannot well be taught too soon, nor inculcated too often, nor impressed too deeply. Regularity in studies, in business, in amusements, is the fosterer of time; nay, it may almost be said that regularity makes time. Without it, how many precious hours are lost in confusion, and in seeking what to do next! Let your children, then, be habituated to regularity, in all their occupations, to do every thing in its due time; and let them be encouraged by your example. They will thank you in after-life for so useful a lesson.

Much time is often lost, likewise, by having to look in one place and another for things that are wanted. Let children, therefore, be trained to replace books, and clothes, and work, and playthings, in their proper situations, that they may be able to lay their hands on those, and other articles, whenever they are called for. Many a master, and especially many a mistress of a family,

---

* Let not children witness any anxiety concerning the niceties of food, nor hear any conversation on the delights of good eating and drinking, nor be rewarded for laudable conduct and exertions by any peculiar delicacies; lest they come to attach high importance to the pleasures of the table, and to the free indulgence of the appetite, and gradually sink into the low and debased character of gluttony.

have lamented the want of this beneficial habit, in themselves, their children, and their servants.

Cleanliness of person, and care of clothes, are habits not to be scorned, as they will have a kindly influence upon health and fortune. The most opulent parent ought not to be ashamed to adopt, in the economical education of his children, the excellent motto, "Waste not, want not." Early habits of care, and an early aversion and contempt of waste and extravagance, may preserve an estate, which, but for such previous training, might be soon lavished away. And, to encourage young people in economy, they should be taught to take a family interest in domestic expenses. Parental reserve in money matters, is impolitic: for as one judiciously observes, "That father who wraps his affairs up in mystery, and who views his child with jealous eyes, as a person who is to *begin to live when himself dies*, will probably make him an enemy, by treating him as such." A frank simplicity, and cordial dependence upon the integrity and sympathy of their children, will be more likely to insure to parents their disinterested friendship. Ignorance is always more to be dreaded than knowledge. Young people who are acquainted with family expenses, and the various wants of a family, will not be so likely to be unreasonable in their own expenditure. And the pleasure of being esteemed and trusted, is early felt, while the consciousness of deserving confidence is delightful to children.

Let children, therefore, gradually learn the use and value of money, that they may be able to manage it to advantage, and to apply it to proper purposes. With respect to girls, this may be greatly aided, by giving them annual allowances, when they are deemed to be of a competent age, to provide for themselves, gloves, ribbons, and other trifling articles of dress. This, by giving them some idea of the expense of dress, may aid in teaching them the important lessons of economy and management. They should be encouraged to save something from this allowance for charitable purposes, that thus frugality and beneficence may be associated. They should also be early admonished, not intentionally to spoil or waste any thing of their own, which may be useful to poor people. They may be taught to take care of shoes and other articles of clothing, when past their use, that they may relieve with them the wants of poor little boys and girls, who have only such charitable supplies to depend on for protection from the cold. Thus, they will learn to save from a principle of benevolence, and not from selfish or sordid motives. Never should children be praised for what is not intrinsically valuable; nor, even for what is actually praise-worthy, should they be immoderately praised. In their presence, let no praise be bestowed upon richness and elegance of dress; upon mere external advantages; upon mere ornamental accomplishments; upon beauty of face or form; upon quickness of speech; upon any advantages not acquired by their own exertions. Praise is pleasing, is fascinating to the heart; and therefore, upon whatsoever it is bestowed, with respect to that, praise creates agreeable associations, which will be useful or pernicious, according to the subjects on which the praise is bestowed. A mistake in this respect may produce lamentable consequences; while praise, judiciously and sparingly given, may prove a powerful and beneficial motive. "Let your little girl," says Mrs. E. Hamilton, "be dressed in new and unusual finery, and brought into company, where every voice shall join in praise of the ornaments with which she is decorated. Observe the satisfaction with which she eyes the pretty shoes, and pretty sash, which are the objects of admiration. The idea of praise may thus be associated with the idea of finery; and thus, no doubt, may the love of finery, and with it pride and vanity, be generated." If, on the contrary, the child be praised for obedience, for readiness to oblige, for diligence, for self-restraint and good temper, pleasing associations will cherish those valuable qualities.

Let parents, therefore, take care that the seeds of pride and vanity be not sown in the minds of their children, by immoderate praise, even when some degree and kind of praise is deserved; by admiration expressed for talents, for external form, or gracefulness of deportment; for finery of dress, of house, of furniture. Self-love, self-satisfaction, are too easily excited, and grow too fast. They are very dangerous guests, and should be brought under strict command, if not expelled, as quickly as possible.

I am, &c.,
A FRIEND TO EARLY EDUCATION.
Edinburgh, Feb. 21st, 1833.

SERVANTS.

RULES FOR SERVANTS formed part of our last publication; not wholly unerring, but generally judicious, and well-considered. The bad qualities of servants have formed a favourite subject of conversation, since Sarah, in a fit of perverseness, turned out the bonds-woman and her son. We fear the censures passed upon this class of persons are often too just; but it is at least equally true, that their worst errors originate in the vices, corruptions, and excessive luxury of society. Among civilized nations, servants are found domestic comforts or plagues, in exact proportion to the state of manners, and to the equality or inequality in the distribution of the wealth of the society. If we may believe report, the worst servants in the world are at present to be found in the great and wealthy families who spend most of their time in London—pampered menials, whose wages and emoluments double or quadruple those of servants in quieter situations. Servants of this cast often understand household business (lying, cunning, and pilfering included) much better than the domestics of respectable families in the middle rank; they only lack fidelity, honesty, affection, gratitude, and respectful attachment. These observations are suggested by a judicious, but somewhat lengthy dissertation upon servants, in the New Monthly Magazine. After dwelling upon the vices and characteristics of servants, the writer thus accounts for some of them:—

"When a slave was deemed not a person, but a thing marketable and transferable, the single principle judged sufficient to regulate the mutual conduct of the master and the domestic was, to command and to obey. It seems still the sole stipulation exacted by the haughty from the menial. But this feudal principle, unalleviated by the just sympathies of domesticity, deprives authority of its grace, and service of its zeal. To be served well, we should be loved a little; the command of an excellent master is even grateful, for the good servant delights to be useful. The slave repines; and such is the domestic destitute of any personal attachment to his master. He listens but to the loss of his freedom in the sound of the "iron tyrant," as once a servant called the summoning bell. Whoever loved the being they feared? Whoever was mindful of the interests of him whose beneficence is only a sacrifice to his pomp? The master dresses and wages highly his pampered train; but this is the calculated cost of state-liveries, of men measured by a standard, for a Hercules in the hall, or an Adonis for the drawing-room; but at those times, when the domestic ceases to be an object in the public eye, he sinks into an object of sordid economy, or of merciless caprice. His personal feelings are recklessly neglected. He sleeps where there is neither light nor air; he is driven when he is already exhausted; he begins the work of midnight, and is confined for hours with men like himself, who fret, repine, and curse. They have their tales to compare together; their unhallowed secrets to disclose. The masters and the mistresses pass by them in review, and little deem they how oft the malignant glance, or the malicious whisper, follow their airy steps. To shorten such tedious hours, the servants familiarize themselves with every vicious indulgence; for even the occupation of such domestics is little more than a dissolute idleness. A cell in Newgate does not always contain more corruptors than a herd of their servants congregated in our winter halls. It is to be lamented, that the modes of fashionable life demand the most terrible sacrifices of the health, the happiness, and the morals of servants. Whoever perceives that he is held in no esteem, stands degraded in his own thoughts. The heart of the simple throbs with this emotion; but it hardens the villain who would rejoice to avenge himself; it makes the artful only the more cunning; it extorts from the sullen a cold unwilling obedience, and it stings even the good-tempered into insolence.

"South, as great a wit as a preacher, has separated, by an awful interval, the superior and the domestic. "A servant dwells remote from all knowledge of his lord's purposes; he lives as a kind of foreigner under the same roof; a domestic, yet a foreigner too." This exhibits a picture of feudal manners, and the title of the master here seems to restrict the observation to the aristocratic order."

The picture of the impudence, insolence, domination, and licentiousness of metropolitan servants, drawn by this writer, is absolutely revolting. We turn from it to the brighter side, remarking, beforehand, that to Switzerland, Germany, and Dalmatia, the writer might have added many untainted districts of England, Scotland, Ireland, and Wales. In the Highlands of Scotland, and in Ireland, servants are often provokingly ignorant of their business, slothful and dilatory; but this is partly chargeable upon their employers: and the absence of this kind of useful knowledge is compensated by qualities of far higher value—the growth of which they owe to the character and condition of their masters. To the instances which the writer in the Magazine brings forward of faithful servitude, sweetened by affection, how many might be added.

"It is in small communities only that we perceive how the affections of the master and the domestic may take root. Look in an ancient retired family, whose servants often have been born under the roof they inhabit, and where the son is serving where the father still serves, and sometimes call the sacred spot of their cradle and their grave, by the proud and endearing term of "Our House." Observe a town of limited extent, where the refined artifices of the metropolis are almost unknown; it is in such place, that the *pater familias* looks on the remoter members moving together with an unity of feeling; it is in such place, that the domestic acts, not oftener prompted by command than by unbidden labours; and such unconstrained service is not like that of those who make a show of their diligence to their masters, which has been emphatically termed 'Eye-service." The passion of domesticity is intense, in proportion to its contraction. In the great capitals of London and Paris it is vague and uncertain; there, mostly, it may be deemed 'Lip-service,' or the art of wheedling;—it is the blaze of kindled straw losing itself in air; but, in a more restricted sphere of domestic life, it is a clear and constant flame, whose fuel never fails.

"It is among the domestic virtues of the middle classes of life, as the residents of an overgrown metropolis would deem those more retired families, that we find the servant a participator in the cares of the household, and an humble associate with the heads of the family. We discover this in whole countries where luxury has not removed the classes of society at too wide distances from each other, to deaden their sympathies. We behold this in agrestic Switzerland, among its villages and its pastures; in France, among its distant provinces; in Italy, in some of its decayed cities; and in Germany, where simple manners, and strong affections mark the inhabitants of certain localities. Holland long preserved its primitive customs; and there the love of order promotes subordination, though its free institutions have softened the distinctions in the ranks of life; and there we find a remarkable evidence of domesticity. It is not unusual in Holland for servants to call their masters uncle, their mistresses aunt, and the children of the family their cousins. These domestics participating in the comforts of the family, become naturalized and domiciliated; and their extraordinary relatives are often adopted by the heart. An heroic effort of these domestics has been recorded; it occurred at the burning of the theatre at Amsterdam, where many rushed into the flames, and nobly perished in the attempt to save their endeared families.

It is in limited communities that the domestic virtues are most intense; all concentrating themselves in their private circles; in such localities there is no public,—no public which extorts so many sacrifices from the individual. Insular situations are usually remarkable for the warm attachment and devoted fidelity of the domestic, and the personal regard of families for their servants. This genuine domesticity is strikingly displayed in the island of Ragusa, on the coast of Dalmatia; for there they provide for the happiness of the humble friends of the house. Boys, at an early age, are received into families, educated in writing, reading, and arithmetic. Some only quit their abode, in which they were almost born, when tempted by the stirring spirit of maritime enterprise. They form a race of men who are much sought after for servants; and, as I have heard, the term applied to them of "Men of the Gulf," is a sure recommendation of the character for unlimited trust, and unwearying zeal.

The mode of providing for the future comforts of their maidens is a little incident in the history of benevolence, which we must regret is only practised in such limited communities. Malte Brun, in his "Annales des Voyages," has painted a scene of this nature which may read like some romance of real life. The girls, after a service of ten years, on one great holyday, an epoch in their lives, receive the ample reward of their good conduct. On that happy day, the mistress, and all friends of the family, prepare for the maiden a sort of dowery or marriage portion. Every friend of the house sends some article; and the mistress notes down the gifts that she may return the same on a similar occasion. The donations consist of silver, of gowns, of handkerchiefs, and other useful articles for a young woman. These tributes of friendship are placed beside a silver basin which contains the annual wages of the servant; her relatives from the country come, accompanied by music, carrying baskets covered with ribbons, and loaded with fruits, and other rural delicacies. They are received by the master himself, who invites them to the feast, where the company assemble, and particularly the ladies. All the presents are reviewed. The servant introduced, kneels to receive the benediction of her mistress, whose grateful task is then to deliver a solemn enumeration of her good qualities; concluding by announcing to the maiden, that having been brought up in the house, if it be her choice to remain, from henceforwards she shall be considered as one of the family. Tears of affection often falling during this beautiful scene of true domesticity, which terminates with a ball for the servants, and another for the superiors. The relatives of the maiden return homewards with their joyous musicians; and, if the maiden perfers her old domestic abode, she receives an increase of wages; and at a succeeding period of six years, another jubilee provides her second good fortune.

Let me tell one more story of the influence of this passion of domesticity in the servant;—its merit equals its novelty. In that inglorious attack on Buenos Ayres, where our brave soldiers were disgraced by a recreant general, the negroes, slaves as they were, joined the inhabitants to expel the invaders. On this signal occasion, the city decreed a public expression of gratitude to the negroes, in a sort of triumph; and, at the same time, awarded the freedom of eighty of their leaders. One of them, having shown his claims to the boon, declaring that to obtain his freedom had all his days formed the proud object of his wishes, his claim was indisputable: yet now, however, to the amazement of the judges, he refused his proffered freedom! The reason he alleged was a singular refinement of heartfelt sensibility:—" My kind mistress," said the negro, " once wealthy, has fallen into misfortunes in her infirm old age. I work to maintain her, and at intervals of leisure, she leans on my arm to take the evening air. I will not be tempted to abandon her, and I renounce the hope of freedom that she may know she possesses a slave who never will quit her side."

Although I have been travelling out of Europe to furnish some striking illustrations of the powerful emotion of domesticity, it is not that we are without instances in the private history of families among ourselves. I have known more than one, where the servant has chosen to live without wages rather than quit the master or mistress in their decayed fortunes; and another where the servant cheerfully worked to support her old lady to her last day.

ON BEES.*

Bees are insects which claim our attention, as not only being interesting and industrious in themselves, but useful and profitable to mankind. Therefore, viewing them as such, I shall endeavour to lay down a few hints to bee-masters which may be of some use, especially to those who are unacquainted with their proper mode of treatment; but at present, I will confine myself to their management during this and the two subsequent months, February, March, and April, reserving their treatment during the other parts of the season to a future period. Towards the latter end of February every hive ought to be lifted from the stool, and its state examined into, both with regard to its provisions, as well as to the number of its inhabitants. If the hive weighs nearly about 20 lbs., it may be safely presumed that they will stand in need of no assistance; and after clearing away from the stool the filth contracted by the bees during the winter, it may be replaced as formerly, plastering up the skirts; but, on the other hand, if the hive should not weigh more than 15 lbs., it ought to be supplied occasionally with a little honey during March and April; and even in May, should the weather prove cold and unfavourable. And when such bad weather occurs, let even those hives who are considered to have plenty of provisions, get an additional supply, as it not only enlivens and exhilarates the bees, but makes them breed much faster than they would otherwise have done. If the weather is mild, bees begin to carry home loads about the end of February or beginning of March; but much depends whether the vegetation in the neighbourhood be early or late. The first day or two, perhaps, only three or four loaded bees may be seen entering the hive; but each day afterwards, if the weather holds good, they will increase more and more. There are some hives at this season of the year, when examined into, found almost utterly deserted of their inhabitants, although pretty well stocked in honey, and the bee-master is at a loss to comprehend the cause; but it is sometimes on account of their having lost the queen; and when this is the case, the bees being unable to breed or replenish their hive with young, consequently go to ruin; and others, by reason of their long confinement, contract disease, become unhealthy, and gradually desert and die away. But many, too many, I fear, perish by famine, that dire disease, which it is in the bee-master's power to avert; but owing to his carelessness and negligence, in not attending to their wants, those which might otherwise have been prospering and flourishing hives, are allowed to perish for lack of food. Particular care should also be taken by bee-masters to confine their bees when snow is on the ground, by fixing in the entry of the hive perforated lead, so that they may have sufficient air, as the sun often tempts them to go abroad, and as soon almost as they alight upon the snow, they are benumbed, and perish in a short time. In these months, too, when little honey can be collected from the plants, bees are apt to rove about, pillaging and plundering weak hives, which are unable to repel them, and if particular care is not instantly taken to despel these robbers, they will soon completely ruin a hive. Whenever the least symptom of robbing appears, which is easily distinguished, as crowds will be seen bustling and fighting at the entry of the hive, and numbers of dead lying before the stool; the robbers ought to be kept off as much as possible until the evening, when, if it be a weak hive, it may be removed to the distance of a mile or so; but if the hive be well stocked with bees, it may be allowed to remain on its entry being lessened, so that no more than one bee can get access at a time; by which means the infested hive may easily repel their invaders. Every hive ought to

* We owe this paper to an anonymous correspondent and think it deserving of extensive publication.

have a narrow entry in the early part of the year, and may be enlarged as the season advances, in proportion to their increase, as warmness is of the utmost advantage to bees at this period, as they will be enabled to bring forward their young brood much faster and earlier.

MEDICAL SELECTIONS.
NO. IV.*
DIET.

Diet may be considered as including all that part of the medical art which gives directions respecting food and drink, whether for the preservation of health, or the cure of diseases. The diet is derived from the animal and vegetable kingdoms, from each of which a numberless variety of articles is procured. By the art of cookery, these are varied and combined in an infinite diversity of ways. It is sufficiently evident, by the structure of the teeth of man, of his stomach and bowels, and of all his organs subservient to digestion, that nature intended him to live on food of both kinds, vegetable and animal; and his limitation or abstinence from the one or the other, is to be regulated solely by his convenience, and by the effect which he finds the different sorts of food to produce on his constitution. Animal food, being already, in a great measure, prepared and rendered similar to our blood, requires less exertion of the digestive powers; but it is found to be heating and stimulating, and hence it should never be used in inflammatory diseases, or made the principal diet in hot climates. Hence the northern nations are benefited by a considerable proportion of animal food, and the nations between the tropics live much on vegetables. There may be certain diseases and habits of body where it may be useful to take a great deal of animal food; but this should be considered as a necessary remedy, and be always under the direction and superintendence of the physician. With respect to the solid or fluid nature of diet, we may remark, that it is necessary to healthy digestion, not only to have a proper quantity of nutritive matter given to the stomach, but that there be a considerable bulk to give that organ a proper degree of distension; it is therefore necessary to add to soups and jellies, some bread and other matter to give them bulk.

Of the Diet *proper for different ages.*—The infant is provided by nature with milk for its nourishment, and farinaceous food may be properly conjoined with it. Little else is required till after the ninth or tenth month. Preparation may now be made for weaning, by giving the child, with his farinacia, a little animal food; as the juices of veal or chicken, or lean beef. If the mother's milk evidently disagrees, and if the farinaceous food produces sourness and flatulence, the nurse must either be changed, or a proportion of animal food, as gravy or beef, must form a great part of the diet. When the teeth have come in, children have a desire for other food, and are pleased to exert their powers on soft bread or a bit of meat; and this may be safely allowed to healthy children. While children are growing, they have very frequent craving for food, and their stomachs have wonderful powers with respect to the quantity they are able to digest. The best proof of the quantity not being excessive, is the growth and healthy appearance of the child, his being lively and active at play soon after his meal, and his sleep being easy and uninterrupted. It may be plausibly urged as the dictate of nature, that we should not hinder children from eating as often as they choose, and at whatever periods. But as the mind and body must be brought under many restraints, if we wish for our off-

* Macauley's Popular Medical Dictionary.

spring either good morals or a good constitution, we are inclined to recommend the early formation of regular habits in the period of taking food. If children are allowed to call for food and drink at every half hour when they are idle, and fancy they want them, a very bad habit of indulgence will be induced; and as we can never be sure of the quantity and kind of the food which they take in, we may expect some morbid changes to take place in the digestive powers. The regulation of the quality of children's food is of the utmost importance. It is there, more than in quantity, that indulgent parents are apt to err. Sweet meats, butter, pastry, high-seasoned dishes, and a great variety of them, ought not to be allowed to children. Their unsophisticated instincts do not desire these things; and if they were carefully kept from them, or resolutely denied them, we should consult at once their health and their character. Water, or occasionally small beer, should be their only drink. A habitual allowance of wine, except as a medicine, should be strictly forbidden; and much more, ardent spirits in every shape. Sauces and condiments should rarely be taken by children and young people.

At a more advanced period, as from eighteen to sixty, if the health be good, there is scarcely any rule to be given for diet, except to enjoin moderation. It has been plausibly enough inculcated, that we should confine ourselves at dinner to one dish only, whether it be of fish or other animal food. Undoubtedly, this is an excellent advice, conducive both to health and temperance, provided a person finds that his digestion goes on properly; but many experience, that their stomachs agree best with some variety in the articles of their food, provided that the quantity taken be not too copious. The drinks that may be used by adults are very numerous; some of them have their advantages, others their inconveniencies. Water, for the healthy and active, is the drink prescribed by nature, and will never injure them; and it is happy for any individual to be quite independent of any other drink. But amid the great variety of other fluids which Providence has bestowed on the industry of man, there are many that agree well both with the palate and the constitution, and which, when not taken in excess, or at improper times, contribute much to his health and comfort. Good small beer is an excellent drink; its slight bitterness assists digestion, it is cooling and antiseptic; and it, in some cases, tends to keep the bowels easy. By those who are troubled with flatulence it should be avoided. Ale and porter are considerably nutritious, and should be avoided by those who are inclined to become corpulent, and who take little exercise. Wine is to be preferred to spirits, even when they are much diluted. Though there is much spirit in some wines, yet they contain extractive matter and mucilage, which hinders the spirit from producing the bad effects which it would do in the same quantity obtained by distillation. Though we cannot wish to encourage the use of ardent spirits, we admit that, with very many persons, they do no harm when taken in small quantity; but the compendious drunkenness which they produce, presents an overpowering temptation, to the vacant and unprincipled mind, to exceed the bounds of moderation; and when these are habitually passed, the character and health may be regarded as being in the most imminent danger. The different kinds of spirits, brandy, rum, gin, &c., agree in their general effects; brandy is best for weak stomachs, and gin for those who require the kidneys to be stimulated; but when those or the neighbouring organs are irritable, gin is better avoided.

In old age, the diet ought to be less heating than in the vigour of life. The quantity of animal food should be diminished, and the stomach should not be overloaded with a variety of high-seasoned food and dressed dishes. Though the relish for wine is less, it should be continued, in moderate quantity, for its cordial effects.

The diet in cold climates should be more generous and nourishing than in warm climates; spices and wines are proper; and in the bleak and mountainous parts of our Caledonian regions, the inhabitants use with impunity a quantity of ardent spirits, which appears enormous to their southern visitants.

Of the Times of taking Food.—The various occupations and circumstances of mankind, render it impossible and useless to lay down any general rules for the periods of taking food. Reason would dictate very different modes and times from those which fashion and custom have prescribed. The hour of rising should be six or seven, and breakfast should be taken about two hours afterwards. With many persons the powers of the constitution are languid and feeble; and even at the end of two hours they have little appetite for breakfast; while others are recruited and invigorated by a moderate meal very soon after rising. The breakfast should be substantial, in proportion to the labour to be undergone during the early part of the day; and in proportion to the time that must elapse before food can again be taken. The best time of taking the principal meal is between one and two; but the necessities of business, and the mandate of fashion, have rendered this impossible for any but the labouring classes; while those employed in all the varieties of mercantile occupations, and who must make their hours to suit the convenience of the higher ranks, are obliged either to fast till four or five o'clock, or be content with a hasty luncheon. Those who have their time more at their own disposal, make their luncheon a plain but copious meal; and in such, it would be a wise plan to dispense with the late dinner altogether. As it is, they either make it a supper, for which it is by far too copious and too stimulating; or if they do not retire to rest five or six hours after dinner, they are over-excited by the wine and stimulants they use, or by the hot and crowded rooms which they frequent: hence the constitution is exhausted, and the orderly and healthful plan of life is totally inverted. Retiring to rest with the stomach loaded with a hearty meal, is a sure way of occasioning feverish restlessness. Copious suppers are therefore to be avoided; and some light food near bed-time is to be preferred.

Consequences of Errors in Diet.—To enumerate all these, would be to give a list of the greater number of diseases which afflict humanity. In early life, the state of the stomach, of the chylopoetic viscera, and of the bowels, is so delicate and easily disordered, that a great proportion of the diseases of children may be traced to errors in their diet. To these we ascribe their green and sour stools, their flatulence and griping pains, their skin-diseases, and sometimes water in the head and convulsions. In more advanced life, irregularities in diet, and habitual indulgence in too much, and too luxurious food and drink, lay the foundation for gout, liver-disease, dropsy, apoplexy, palsy, stomach complaints, and the long train of what are called nervous diseases. Occasional excesses in eating occasion cholic, diarrhoea, sick headach, apoplexy; and a debauch in drinking too often destroys life, or brings on madness.

Of the Diet in Sickness.—The regulation of the diet in disease is a matter of primary importance. In many diseases, health may be restored by abstinence, or a properly regulated diet; and in others, the resources of physic will be unavailing if the diet be not carefully attended to. In fever, there is commonly an aversion to food, which the stomach could not digest, and which would only act injuriously on the system. In many inflammatory diseases, the same salutary instinct occurs: but in some there is no dislike to food; and the friends of the patient, supposing him to be weak, give food or stimulating drinks, with the certainty of aggravating the disease. In the great majority of diseases having febrile symptoms, a spare diet and abstinence from wine, porter, spirits, and the like, are absolutely necessary. In chronic diseases, and those attended with debility, a more generous diet is to be allowed. In stomach complaints, the most important part of the physician's office is to regulate the diet. In the puerperal state, the recovery is essentially aided by avoiding all irregularities in food and drink; while the most dangerous and fatal disorders are brought on by imprudent indulgences. We have given, under the various diseases in different parts of the work, particular directions for diet, in those cases where the consideration of this subject is essential.

Diet of Convalescents.—Great attention is necessary in regulating the diet of those who are recovering from sickness. After a long and debilitating illness, the convalescent's appetite is sometimes keen, and even voracious; but it is highly dangerous to indulge this appetite, or to comply with the kind wishes of his friends, who are desirous to see him quickly restored to health and vigour. The stomach is unable to digest the quantity of food taken, and its over-stimulated powers become exhausted; some other disease, or a relapse of his former one, comes on; and he finds it unsafe to tax nature beyond her strength. A sudden transition from full and luxurious living to great abstinence is not a safe measure. Some have resolutely made the change suddenly and with impunity; but it succeeds better when established habits are not too hastily broken in upon.

On the subject of diet, and especially on provocatives, the moralist has something to say as well as the physician. Industry and temperance have their reward in active vigour, refreshing sleep, and easy digestion; when the stomach is neither overloaded by excess, nor bribed by spices. On the other hand, when the pleasure of eating is made a primary object, and indolence and sensuality neglect the due exercise of the body, the stomach is tardy and irregular in performing its functions; and needs to be solicited by all the arts of the cook, and by condiments, for which all the kingdoms of nature have been ransacked. The powers of digestion are impaired, the body becomes bloated and unhealthy; and diseases of various kinds exact a rigorous compensation for the waste of those resources of the constitution, which have been so improvidently and prematurely expended.

MODERN DICTIONARY.

Distant Relations.—People who imagine they have a claim to rob you if you are rich, and to insult you if you are poor.

Heart.—A rare article, sometimes found in human beings. It is soon, however, destroyed by commerce with the world, or else becomes fatal to its possessor.

Housewifery.—An ancient art, said to have been fashionable among young girls and wives; now entirely out of use, or practised only by the lower orders.

Wealth.—The most respectable quality of man.

Virtue.—An awkward habit of acting differently from other people. A vulgar word. It creates great mirth in fashionable circles.

Honour.—Shooting a friend through the head whom you love, in order to gain the praise of a few others whom you despise and hate.

Marriage.—The gate through which the happy lover leaves his enchanted regions and returns to earth.

Friend.—A person who will not assist you because he knows your love will excuse him.

Wedded Bliss.—A term used by Milton.

Doctor.—A man who kills you to-day, to save you from dying to-morrow.

Lunatic Asylum.—A kind of hospital, where detected lunatics are sent by those who have had the adroitness to conceal their own infirmity.

Water.—A clear fluid, once used as a drink.

Tragedian.—A fellow with a tin pot on his head, who stalks about the stage, and gets into a violent passion so much a night.

Critic.—A large dog, that goes unchained, and barks at every thing he does not comprehend.

Jury.—Twelve prisoners in a box to try one or more at the bar.

Young Attorney.—A useless member of society, who often goes where he has no business to be, because he has no business where he ought to be.

King's Evidence.—A wretch who is pardoned for being baser than his comrades.

Sensibility.—A quality by which its possessor, in attempting to promote the happiness of other people, loses his own.

My Dear.—An expression used by man and wife at the commencement of a quarrel.

THE STORY-TELLER.

"MY PLACE IN THE COUNTRY."

The authoress of the tale which, for the sake of our dear readers, we are about to *condense* by very high pressure, is, of all fashionable novelists, the most fashionable; the writer of MOTHERS and DAUGHTERS, THE FAIR of MAY FAIR, and SKETCHES of FASHION, which last is just published. She is Mrs. Gore, or the Honourable Mrs. Gore, the cleverest delineator and satirist of fashionable follies, and exposer, not of naked fashionable vice, but of the corrupting and the immoral tendencies of fashionable manners, that we know. *Tait's Magazine*, last year, alleged, that her writings were, in tendency, highly *radical*; and the *Westminster Review*, more recently, laughingly accuses her of a secret purpose of bringing the peerage into contempt. In the tale before us, Mrs. Gore does not soar to such high game, but she as surely strikes her quarry. Her moral is, "The curse of every granted prayer." We can go no farther with her work; but, with the following specimen of a specimen, leave our readers to dun the unfortunate keepers of circulating libraries for more: and thus saith Mrs. Gore:—

Mr. MARTINDALE was considered a very fortunate man to return from the Cape of Good Hope with a fortune of ninety thousand pounds, shortly after he had attained the age of forty-four. Ages and their influences are comparative. An individual who, during twenty-two of his four-and-forty years, has scarcely missed as many days of being seen on the pavé of St. James's Street, or in the dust of Hyde Park, —whose visage has been as stationary in the bay window of White's Arthur's, or the Cocoa Tree, as that of the great Saladin over the Saracen's Head coach-office, passes for a middle-aged man, or rather for a man of a certain age: but one who has passed his time in purveying camels for the East India Company in the vicinity of the Himalaya, or planting indigo, or chewing betel in any other oriental settlement, is accounted a young man, should his final settlement with Leadenhall-street be completed within his first half century. Richard Martindale, thanks to currie, magnesia lozenges, and other bilious preventatives, had been so lucky as to lose sight of Table Mountain without the loss of his liver or the reduplication of his spleen;—his fortune was invested in a very safe house;—and on his arrival at Nerot's Hotel from the Downs, he thought himself, and was thought by the waiters, a very important personage. He was not indeed the inheritor of an aristocratic name, but his lineage was respectable and irreproachable; his father having been an eminent physician in the town of Hertford, where his elder brother still practised as the leading attorney. One younger brother was a clergyman; and his two sisters were married to small squires in the neighbourhood of their hereditary homes.

In such a family, secure from all pretension to fashion or distinction, the sum of ninety thousand pounds was as the treasury of the pre-Adamite Sultans! They had been talking for five years past of all Richard would do when he arrived; and now that he was really come, and really pleaded guilty to the possession of a sum so nearly approaching to one hundred thousand pounds, they hardly knew how to make too much of *him*, or too little of themselves. A fortune recently acquired, or still floating, which has not yet been subjected to matter-of-fact calculations respecting interest, investment, and nett produce, always assumes double importance. To say that a man has an income of four thousand a-year, is to say nothing. One set of people regard him as a pauper; another set observe that, with management, he may live handsomely enough; a third declare that he must not attempt to launch out in London society; and the fashionable world vote him admissible only as a giver of moderate dinners, and a proprietor of moderate equipages. But give him boldly out as recently arrived in England with a hundred thousand pounds, and the whole world (with the exception of the mercantile classes) hail him at once as a wealthy man. What may not a man do with a hundred thousand pounds! "No stud,—no service of plate,—no French cook,—no opera box? Shabby fellow!—If a man with a hundred thousand pounds cannot afford to be comfortable, *who* can?" People talk of the earnings of his thirty years' exile—of the whole provision for his future family,—as of a year's income."

Such was the case with Richard Martindale. His elder brother, the A———, but no, he called himself "the Solicitor," had long fixed a greedy eye on a small estate of fifty or sixty acres, adjoining his paddock, in the suburbs of Hertford. "Now Richard is come home," said he, to his smart wife, "I shall get him to manage it for me." The Reverend Jacob, like his namesake, proprietor of twelve blooming children, was no less anxious to build a wing to his parsonage, in order that the fathers of the twelve future tribes might not sleep above three in a bed. "Now Richard is come home," said he to his dowdy wife, "I shall get him to manage it for me." His elder sister, Mrs. Marriott, had an elder son ripe for college; and, in his mother's opinion, needing only that stepping-stone to advancement to reach the highest dignities of church or state. It had long been her ambition to behold him in trencher cap and gown. "Now Richard is come home," said she to her somnolent spouse, "I shall get him to manage it for me." His younger sister, Mrs. Millegan, whose husband, in addition to his own farm, managed the large estates of the Earl of Mowbray, and who was accordingly much noticed by the ladies at Mowbray End, had long been desirous of possessing some sort of carriage, even a pony-cart, in which she could make her appearance there when company was staying in the house, without dust or mud upon her shoes, or traces of plebeian moisture on her brow. "Now Richard is come home," cried she to her three eager daughters, "I shall get him to manage it for me."

Richard, when come home, receives a most fraternal welcome, only it distressed him at first to witness the distress of his kinsfolk.

There could not apparently be four more uncomfortable families than those which had unceasingly favoured him, during his residence among the Hottentots, with glowing pictures of their domestic happiness, and entreaties that he would hasten his return to witness and share it. Their pretensions, however, were far from exorbitant. He was in hopes that five thousand pounds would cover the whole amount of their ambition; and what was five thousand out of ninety?—Within a week, therefore, after his arrival at the dapper residence of his brother Robert, he had promised universal happiness to the family; purchased the Clammer Mill estate; presented to Jacob the fifteen hundred pounds necessary to build and furnish the new wing; settled eighty pounds a year on Richard Marriot; and bestowed on the astonished Mrs. Millegan a handsome chariot and set of horses. He cursed the whole family in short "with many a granted prayer;" and never was a finer or more glowing specimen of the shortsightedness and ingratitude of the human race exhibited, than by the dynasty of Martindale. Having so readily obtained all they asked for, they were now prodigiously vexed they had not asked for more. Bob had little doubt that his dear Richard would have made very little difficulty in adding the Springfield Farm to his purchase; which would, in fact, have made the whole a most complete thing—a most valuable investment—a most saleable property:—while Jacob thought it a great oversight to expend so large a sum as fifteen hundred pounds on a college living, while four thousand would have purchased the advowson of Bramfield, where the parsonage and gardens were calculated for the reception of a large family, (six more sons if he liked), and fit to step into at once, without incurring the perplexities of brick and mortar:—Mrs. Marriot woke her unhappy husband three or four times during his after-dinner doze, to lament that, while she was about it, she had not begged her brother to send Tom to Westminster, as well as Dick to Trinity; and, as to Mrs. Millegan, *she* had an attack of the jaundice in honour of her good fortune. *She*, who had been the most abundantly rewarded of all,—she who had spunged for a pony-cart and obtained a yellow chariot with a light blue bullion hammer-cloth,—*she* was most disappointed,—the most indignant of the whole family;—and knew not whether most to blame, her own improvidence or the injustice of her brother. He was no longer her " dear brother"—no longer even Dick —but merely " Richard Martindale."—Nothing could be more unfair than Richard Martindale's partiality in the family; and to make *her* the sufferer,—his next, and once his *favourite* sister!—she who had been " little Nancy" in his early letters from the Cape;—and who had sent him out year after year, for fifteen seasons, a case of high-dried hams and tongues of her own curing. It was too bad!

Richard Martindale had expended L.2754, 7s. 8d. on the purchase of the Clammer Mill estate;—Richard Martindale had paid in hard cash to his brother Jacob, a sum of L1500;—Richard Martindale had settled on Dick Marriot the interest of L.2,000; while on herself,—on little Nancy, on *poor* little Nancy,—he had bestowed a London built chariot, with a pair of harness and iron-gray horses!—Even allowing for Richard Martindale's absurd ignorance of the value of things, and predisposition to be cheated, the whole gift would not have cost him L.600; and, by a prudent purchaser, might have been secured for L.470. And this was to be *her* portion of his opulence; this her share of the family bounty, amounting in the aggregate to L.6,854, 7s. 8d.!!!

While poor Mrs. M'legan railed at the cruelty of her brother,—her husband and daughters railed at her own bad management; till, in the exuberance of her wrath, she set forth in the town-built chariot aforesaid, with its blue hammer-cloth, to quarrel with her sister Marriot, for having so shamefully overreached " poor Richard." Nay, before the month was over, hard words had passed between Robert Martindale and Jacob; (in whose parish, the momentous farm of Clammer Mill happened to be situated;) and Richard, on his second arrival in Hertfordshire, from Nerot's Hotel, found that those he had left desponding, were grown despairing; and that their complaints were now no longer of their circumstances, but of each other. No two of the four families could meet without bickering; and, in consequence of this novel disunion, it came out that young Dick of Trinity was privately engaged to his cousin Clotilda Martindale, sole heiress to the solicitor, and to Clammer Mill farm; and that the eldest of Jacob's dozen had been writing verses to Miss Helena Millegan, the Mowbray hunter! War was now openly declared among them; and Richard, at length, growing somewhat irritable, began to fancy himself bilious; and having packed himself and his York-tan coloured serving-man (it is impossible to designate him a valet) into a yellow chariot resembling, with the exception of the hammer-cloth, his ill-starred present to the wife of Lord Mowbray's agent, he set off for Cheltenham as fast as four post horses would carry him. If he could not get rid of his indigestion, it would be something to get rid of his family.

Poor Martindale felt as if released from the house of bondage, as he walked jauntily along the Montpelier Parade, arrayed in a new coat, new boots, new gloves, new every thing; betraying in every look and movement the luxurious nabob, intent on his own rejuvenescence, and enchanted with the stir and cheerfulness of an English watering-place.

And if his object in visiting Cheltenham were to recruit his health and spirits, the effort was speedily effectual; for at the close of ten days, he made his way to the spring, not only more spruce and self-complacent than ever, but having a very pretty woman appended to his arm. Discouraged in his attempt to diffuse happiness, and sow contentment in his *own* family, he had conceived a determination to become the founder of a new family, for a renewal of the experiment.

Although forty-four in years, and fifty in complexion, (his face having very much the appearance of a last year's russeting apple,) Richard was by no means an ill-looking man; and, but for a little excess of showiness in his costume, might have passed for a gentlemanly one. Having continued his way to a high appointment at the Cape, he had lived there in the best official society; and was, in fact, a better bred man than either Robert or Jacob, his brethren, who, between themselves, affected to look upon him as a Hottentot. But whether ill-looking, ill-dressed, ill-bred or well, it mattered not. A handsome equipage, and the reports circulated by his York-tan coloured servant, had induced an opinion that he was a man of millions; and it naturally followed, that he soon became an object of universal esteem and admiration.

" We leave it to Mrs. Gore's entire readers to learn how Mary-Matilda, one of the four daughters of Sir John Grinderwell, a Gloucestershire baronet, with a fortune of L.1500, and one sister or two sisters to keep, was wooed, and Richard Martindale wed at Cheltenham; and how the happy pair proceeded on a bridal tour to Wales—" the bride in a white satin hat and ostrich feathers." We just glance at the tail of the honey-moon, where it blends insensibly with what Byron calls the " treacle-moon"—and thus Mrs. Gore gives it:

It would be irrelevant to vary the picture of their pilgrimage, by a hint of all the damp beds, tough beef-steaks, sloe-juice wine, and sloe-leaf tea, they confronted by the way. All these minor miseries served as texts for Richard's protestations to his bride, that

With her conversing, he enjoyed ba d beef,
Sour veal, or musty lamb,—all pleased alike;

while Mary-Matilda maintained, for the first six weeks,

that the tenderness of her dear Richard fully compensated the toughness of the steaks.

At length the November fogs set in. Martindale could no longer travel with the windows down, and was obliged to plead guilty to the twinges of a flying rheumatism. The loving couple having now been acquainted for four months, and united for two, had confided and re-confided to each other (like two benighted princesses meeting in a wood in one of Mademoiselle de Scudéry's novels) all the incidents of their past lives. Mary-Matilda was beginning to yawn wider and oftener than was either becoming or safe, considering the state of the atmosphere; and it was at length agreed between them that, although travelling was a delightful thing, it would be still more delightful to settle in a good warm residence for the winter.

The world was all before them where to choose:—
Richard spoke of Hertfordshire; Mary-Matilda thought of London; but Bath was the place at last. Here Mrs. Martindale, whose fine clothes were now replaced by still finer, and who wore such beautiful pearls and such a quantity of ostrich feathers,—was pronounced to be one of the beauties of Bath, and "quite the woman of fashion." Richard grew more persuaded than ever that he was the luckiest and happiest of men; and Mrs. Millegan (whose daughters had been finished at a Bath boarding-school, and retained several correspondents there) was ready to expire of indignation, on learning in what style her brother lived, and that Mrs. Richard Martindale's ball had been the most splendid of the Circus and the Season. The whole of the Martindale family had, in the first instance, received the announcement of his marriage as a personal injury; and their only comfort was, in pointing out that one of a Baronet's many daughters could not but prove a very unthrifty helpmate.

But all forgave Richard at last, save Mrs. Millegan, alias "little Nancy," who was now a woman of some fifteen stone, and could by no means pardon her brother; and when the newspapers eventually announced that the lady of Richard Martindale, of the Circus, Bath, had given birth to a son and heir, the sole ejaculation of her sisterly tenderness on the occasion, was "Much good may it do him!"

But Bath could not charm for ever. Mary-Matilda was dying to shew her pearls and her baby to her sisters; and to whisper to Harriet and Anne, how strangely Julia, who had done her the sisterly kindness to live with her during the residence at Bath, had been flirting with a militia officer. So off they all set for Exmouth, where the Martindales met the Grinderwells, and lived in lodgings close together, the happiest people in the world. So many young people; so much music; so much riding, driving, and dancing; so many little supper parties; so many large dinner parties at his own house; besides gipseyings, picnics, and other manœuvres invented by Baronets of large family and small fortune; the budding beauties of Master Grinderwell, and the promise of a second olive branch to make glad his heart;—all was auspicious, all was cheering, all was satisfactory!—

"Ay, ay," growled Edward Warton, a cunning old bachelor, who, like his friend, had amassed a considerable fortune on the shores of Table Bay, but was too wise to squander a shilling of it even on himself—"I see you have married half a dozen wives instead of one.—Good look out for old Grinderwell; deuced bad one, I take it, for your weekly bills!—Nunky pays for all, eh, Dick?—Sharp woman, that old mother-in-law!—Sad do, I fear, this match of your's!—Always a sister or two staying in the house, eh, Dick?—Take care they don't eat you out of house and home!—But I forgot; you have got no home, I fancy?—Only a gimcrack lodging-house at a watering-place!"

"I have a very excellent mansion in Bath," said Martindale with indignation, "where I hope you will come and see me—that you may humanize your notions a little respecting my wife and her family."

"Bath!—what a place to live in! a mob of swindlers, dowagers, and decayed spinsters! Bath!—Why not purchase a good substantial country seat at once; which would have given you a stake in the country, and a respectable roof under which to bring up your children, eh, Dick?"

At Exmouth it sometimes occurred to poor Richard, that he was made a butt by the captains of hussars, lancers ragoons, carabineers, fusileers, and fencibles, who lounged, in his house, drank his claret, and flirted with his sisters-in-law. He began to be tired of a round of company, and to long for a quiet study or book-room to spell the newspapers in; and almost regretted that there were still three months unexpired of his year's residence in the Circus. To be sure the waters were supposed to be useful to his rheumatism; and he liked his Whist Club, and found his neighbours, Sir Hookah Smith, and Sir Sangaree Brown, extremely agreeable. But at his time of life (it was the first time he had ever been heard to allude to "his time of life," even in soliloquy) people wanted to be quiet. There was too much bustle at Bath for a man of five-and-forty, worn out by a hot climate.

Nevertheless, when the term of his stay there was on the point of expiring, his resolution to quit was almost shaken by the numerous arguments brought forward by Mary-Matilda for a renewal of the lease.—"She should so much like to be confined again at Bath;—and Ma had promised that Anne and Harriet should come and pass the winter with her!"—This last declaration was decisive. Martindale immediately protested that to prolong their residence at Bath was out of the question; that the air disagreed with him; and after one or two floods of tears, more nearly approaching to hysterics than any thing she had attempted since her scene in the vestry on her wedding-day, Mrs. Richard consented to accompany her lord and master to Nerot's Hotel, till they could procure a suitable residence in town. It was not that she disliked the notion of figuring in London; but she had a shrewd suspicion that, although a somebody at Bath, and a very considerable somebody at Exmouth, she should be a nobody in the metropolis. "Tel brille au second rang qui s'éclipse au premier;" and, after shining as a fixed star in the Circus, it was very hard to dwindle into one of the thousandth magnitude in Baker Street, or Gloucester Place. Unused to London, she was certain she should find it very dull;—nor did her arrival in Clifford Street on a foggy evening in November, tend to brighten her opinions on the subject. It was not till, at the close of a week, she found herself comfortably settled in a handsome house in Harley Street, with an equally handsome establishment, that she began to admit the possibility of living in London.

Richard Martindale was now happier than he had been since the first fortnight of his original arrival at Cheltenham.

In Harley and the half-dozen adjoining streets, he had at least half a dozen oriental acquaintances, with whom he could sit gossipping about things, people, and places,—events past, present, and to come,—wholly uninteresting to the kingdom in general. Instead of one whist club, as at Bath, he had now four; and instead of the captains of hussars, lancers, dragoons, carabineers, fusileers, and fencibles,—he had his friend Ned Warton, besides eight Directors, six Calcutta nabobs, and two yellow Knights Companions who had served with distinction at Bhurtpoor. With the assistance of a speculative agent he still contrived to receive four thousand a-year income from his eighty-five thousand pounds: and, as his brother Robert often observed, "a man might really live like a prince on such a fortune; and do something for his family into the bargain."

In every great metropolis, there must necessarily exist as great a variety of circles and coteries, as of classes in the vegetable or animal creation. It is absurd to attempt the sweeping distinctions of equestrian and pedestrian, patrician and plebeian, in a city numbering a million and a half of inhabitants. Even the minority of the patricians may be subdivided into several classes; and as to the plebeians, Linnæus himself would be puzzled to dispose of the varieties!

Now the coterie to which the Martindales instinctively attached themselves, was of the genus called "dinner-giving people," a large and (as the newspapers say) "influential" body, (chiefly resident in the N.N.W. of London,) who make it the business of their lives to assemble at their tables three or four times a-month sixteen well-dressed individuals, severally possessed of an amount of plate, linen, china, and domestics, equal to their own;—and who, in reward for this mechanical act of hospitality, are entitled to dine on all the other days, in a company equally numerous, and on viands equally delicate. The ambition of displaying at their own board, meat in due season, and fruit out of it,—of obtaining Sir Thomas's opinion that *their* hock is superior to that of Sir Charles, and securing Lady Charlotte's verdict that *their* peaches are three weeks earlier than those of Sir Thomas,—suffices for their happiness; and there is a steadiness of dull decorum about the tribe, an affectation of rationality and "charming people" sort of excellence, essentially different from the sprightliness of ball-haunters, and the brilliancy of genuine fashionables. Fashionables and ball-haunters, of course, occasionally dine out; but they always remain distinct from the lumbering class of regular dinner-giving people.

Mrs. Gore's Martindales were first-rate dinner givers. Not a family in Harley Street "did the thing in better style," and Richard was the happiest of loungers, thus passing his easy life:—

"There was nothing so delightful to him as to saunter into his club, (a club well deserving the name of "The Millionary,") and gossip *tchow tchow* with a knot of other elderly gentlemen of equally gambouged complexion;—to hear and contribute to the last new rumours from Calcutta, Madras, Bombay, Ceylon, the Mauritius, the Cape;—to wonder over old jungle stories, and new romances concerning the cholera;—to elephantize in Asiatic grandiloquence, revel in Asiatic reminiscences, and grow poetical concerning the turbot and lobster-sauce of the preceding day, and the anticipated haunch of the following. And then he loved to wander up and down St. James's Street, linked by either arm to some well-fed, well-dressed, middle-aged, middle-talented man; ready, like himself, to measure inch by inch, with Lilliputian labour, the last arguments of Peel, or the latest eloquence of Brougham; to sneer at Macaulay as a theorist; or break their heads against the cast-iron compactness of an article by Fonblanque; to give their opinions upon all things and all people as lengthily and emphatically as if they were worth listening to; and to take their ease and their ice at Grange's, or their sandwich at the Cocoa Tree. Essentially a good-humoured, happy, and happy-making man, poor Richard Martindale, exulting in comfort at home, and popularity abroad, was one of the most contented and inoffensive among the do-nothings of the west end.

Even his wife,—who, as a very silly woman, with three giggling sisters, four impudent brothers, and a spunging father and mother, might have been expected to form some drawback on his domestic enjoyments,—turned out far better than could have been anticipated; for, following the destinies of her sex, she was fated to behold a *little* Richard Martindale arrive so soon after a little Grinderwell,—a little George so shortly after little Richard,—and a little Clara, Maria, and Sophia, in the three following years, that she had no leisure to do more than sit at the head of Richard's dinner-table, and exhibit her expansive person at a few annual balls in the neighbourhood of Portland Place. Her eldest sister had married the Grinderwell curate; Anne had eloped with an Irish lieutenant of infantry; and Julia had become the wife of a General MacGlashun, chief agent of Bolivar, or prime minister of the Cacique of Poyais, or Chancellor of the Exchequer at Lima, or some such apocryphal dignity, whom she met at Bath, and with whom she shortly afterwards sailed for South America;—but Mrs. Martindale had very little share in promoting either of these three suitable alliances. On her own account, too, she had given up all interest in the attractions of captains of hussars, lancers, or dragoons, carabineers, fusileers, or fencibles; and, following the usual routine of an empty-headed, hollow-hearted woman, had laid aside the coquette to become the dawdle. Although still devoted to dress, her finery was a mere affair of competition with Mrs. Cuffee, or Lady Kedgeree, or Lady Hookah Smith; and the greater part of her time was spent, as a matter of routine, in gossipping with her head nurse or the apothecary. In the autumn, they all went to the sea, for change of air for the children; at Christmas, they either paid a family visit to Grinderwell Hall, or took a course of the Cheltenham waters; but they were always back again in Harley Street by February, to be ready for the east wind, and their favourite Saturday dinner parties. They were regular in their appearance at the gay church of St. Marylebone on Sundays; regular in their drive afterwards in Hyde Park; regular in an annual exhibition at the drawing-rooms; and regular in all the other evolutions of the opulent mediocrasy.

It is not to be supposed but the devil, viewing the paradise Mrs. Gore has pictured, should try to break in; and the temptation came, in right of sex, through Mary Martin. But it is a long story, though the short of it is, that Marriot, junior, who had cost Richard two thousand pounds at Oxford, now married his fair cousin Clotilda, whose fifteen thousand pounds, added to his own fortune, made him a great man in his county, and a somebody even in London, to which he repaired, launched out for a Spring dash, and introduced Clotilda to his aunt Mrs. Richard, who detested them both most cordially.

She had always disliked Mr. Marriot as a presuming consequential young gentleman: and now that he had assumed new dignity, both squirearchical and matrimonial, she prepared herself to dislike him more than ever. She would have borne almost any other relative of her husband's. Poor William, the son of the Rev. Jacob, who was now married to one of his Millegan cousins, and settled as an under master at Charter-House School, was always warmly, though patronizingly, welcomed in Harley Street; but Mr. and Mrs. Marriot, with their bright green carriage, and passion for finery and sight-seeing, were poor Mrs. Richard's aversion; or, as Liston says, "I may say her *favourite* aversion."

Mrs. Marriot daily expecting an invitation to the Harley Street dinner parties, had her wedding dress of Urling's lace, and her new pearls in readiness, but none came; and the Marriots were compelled to be inviters, and afford Mrs. Richard a signal triumph, by the complete failure of Clotilda in dinner-giving.

There was no cucumber for the salmon, although the month of April was half over. The white soup tasted of wash-balls: veal tendrons were made to match with sweetbreads; and the dish of a large boiled turkey was garnished with parsley sufficient to have decorated a jack-in-the-green. An old fashioned blanc-mange was among the sweet dishes of the second course, and altogether the dinner was a contemptible affair;—just such as might have been expected at the table of an attorney's daughter, whose experience did not exceed the apple-tart and custard delicacies of an election supper.

But if, by the supercilious way in which she raised her eye-glass to her eye, to investigate the arrangements of the table, Mrs. Martindale contrived to excite the choler of her niece, Clotilda managed shortly to return the compliment, and with compound interest. She had invited to meet the woman of consequence of her own family, the woman of consequence of her own neighbourhood. The Welbeck Street party consisted, in addition to the four Martindalians, of Mr. Blickling, the county member, and the Hon. Mrs. Blickling his wife; a Mr. and Mrs. Cleverley, of Poplar Grove, in the same neighbourhood; besides two Honourable Mowbrays, a younger Marriot, (a man of wit and fashion about town,) and one or two college friends of the host. In such a circle, the Richard Martindales had very little to say. There was no opportunity for orientalisms from uncle Richard, or nursery anecdotes from his lady; nothing was discussed but the agricultural interests and Hertfordshire topics; and instead of Portland Place balls, Wimpole Street concerts, and the beauties of the new Easter piece, Mr. and Mrs. Richard were compelled to hear of Hatfield, Gorhambury, Panshanger, and the theatricals of the Hoo.

Even when the ladies retreated to the drawing-room and the *partie quarrée* formed by Mrs. Blickling and Mrs. Cleverley on one sofa, and Clotilda and her aunt on the other, commenced the usual tittle-tattle peculiar to such occasions, Mrs. Richard was struck dumb by perceiving that neither of her three companions were in the slightest degree interested, on her account of a family-squabble between her first and second nurses about a dose of rhubarb for her second boy, such as she was in the habit of quoting after dinner at her friend Mrs. Calicut's. Mrs. Blickling had the politeness to cry " indeed !" more than once in the course of her narrative; but it was clear she did not enter into the history with right maternal interest; and like Constance, Mrs. Martindale was tempted to exclaim,

She talks to me, that never had a son.

Mrs. Cleverly and the bride, meanwhile, having none either, turned a decidedly deaf ear to the whole anecdote; and when Mrs. Richard arrived at the close of the tale with it and next day, poor Nurse came to me with tears in her eyes, and told me she should have no objection to stay, provided I made it a rule in my nursery that the under nurse was not to stir the children's tea :" she found that Clotilda and the lady of Poplar Grove were deep in housewifery details of a different nature.

" Oh, yes !" cried Clotilda, who, no longer having the fear of aunt Martindale so strongly before her eyes, had reassumed her loud volubility; "I assure you we have up all our poultry and vegetables from Starling Park. It is really impossible to keep a decent table in London unless one has a Place in the Country."

" I have generally heard," observed Mrs. Richard contemptuously, "that Covent Garden is the best garden in England."

"For those who are accustomed to adulterated London provisions, no doubt it is," retorted her niece; "but when people require things to be pure and wholesome, and in a natural state, there is something so revolting, in the way in which Battersea vegetables are forced, and London poultry fattened."

" Horrible indeed !" exclaimed Mrs. Blickling; "I own I never can prevail on myself to touch that tell-tale colossal asparagus, or those disgustingly bloated fowls. *We* have a cart twice a-week through the season from *our* Place in the Country."

" Mr. Cleverly will eat none but his own mutton," cried the lady of Poplar Grove.

" And I own *I* never fancy any but the Blickling venison !" observed the Member's lady with a grand, parkish sort of air and tone.

" What lovely jonquils !" interpolated Mrs. Richard, anxious to get rid of these details of the buttery hatch. 'And the double violets are really quite luxurious ! How very fragrant !"

" Pray let me offer you a bunch if you are fond of them," cried her niece with patronizing graciousness. " *We* have quantities sent us up from Starling almost every day."

" It is *so* convenient to have one's place within a certain distance of town," said Mrs. Blickling. " When I hear people parading about their estates in Yorkshire or Devonshire, I always recollect the convenience of driving down to peace and tranquillity with as much ease as if we were going to a dejeuner at Wimbledon ! Three hours take us to Blickling. We even have up all our cream for ices, and home-made bread. In short I look upon Blickling as the farm which supplies our table. I should hate a place in one of the remote counties. I hope, however, I am not offending Mrs. Martindale by saying so ?—In what county is Mrs. Martindale's seat ?"

Mary-Matilda, thus interrogated, could not but reply; and though it was with a visage the colour of a stick of red sealing-wax, she managed to make her answer as dignified as periphrasis could render it.

" My father, Sir John Grinderwell, lives in Dorsetshire. At present, Mr. Martindale *has* no country-seat."

The " at present" conveyed of course to the mind of two out of the three ladies, that Mr. Martindale was a landed proprietor in expectancy. Mrs. M. herself was probably in the entail of the Grinderwell estates.

" No country-seat ?—How very tiresome that must be !" drawled Mrs. Cleverley of Poplar Lodge, leaning back on the cushions of the sofa with a singular augmentation of self-importance. " And what *do* you do with yourself at the close of the season ?"

" We generally go the sea," snarled Mrs. Richard; " where, I observe, we meet all our friends who have fine seats of their own, of which they are for the most part horribly tired : so that if Mr. Martindale and myself had any taste for a place in the country during the autumn, we might find hundreds to be let, and the satisfaction of a choice."

" But that is *so* different from a place of one's own !"—ejaculated Clotilda, looking sentimental, and twisting her ermine boa till she pulled off a tail. " I declare I know every bush and briar at Starling ; and there is not a flower in the garden which does not inspire ' thoughts too deep for tears.'"

" Nothing like a place of one's own !" cried Poplar Lodge.

" No,—nothing like a place of one's own !" exclaimed Blickling Hall.

" No,—nothing like a place of one's own !" echoed Starling Park.

" Besides, one cannot hire a place for the Easter holidays, or Whitsuntide, or every now and then when one's children require a week's change of air."

" *We* change the air by going to Brighton," said Mrs. Richard, trying to subdue herself into an air of mildness.".

(*To be continued.*)

SIR WALTER FARQUHAR.
GHOST STORIES.[a]

In early life, years previous to his settling in London, Dr. Farquhar made a temporary sojourn at Torquay, While there, he was summoned professionally to Berry Pomeroy. It is a noble ruin, very much dilapidated and worn away by time; but magnificent even in decay, and an object of interest and attraction to every lover of scenery and antiquity. Here, a massy buttress supports an oak coeval with the castle itself; there, a mouldering turret is clothed with the most luxuriant ivy; while around it sweeps the river proudly, as if it exulted in the contrast of the duration of natural objects with the feebleness, and the frailty, and ephemeral existence of the edifices and efforts of man.

At the time I am speaking of, only one part of it was inhabited. Its occupants were the steward and his wife. The latter was seriously ill, and desired the doctor's advice. Previous to seeing his patient, he was shewn into an apartment, where he waited till the sufferer was apprized of his arrival. It was a large, ill proportioned room. Around it ran pannels, richly carved, of dark oak, which, from time, had assumed the hue of ebony. The only light which it admitted fell through the chequered panes of a gorgeously stained window, on which the arms of the former lords of Berry Pomeroy were richly emblazoned.

In one corner, to the right of the rude fire-place, was a flight of dark oaken steps, forming part of a staircase, leading apparently to some chamber above; and on these stairs the fading gleams of summer's twilight shone strongly.

While Dr. Farquhar wondered, and, if truth be told, chafed at the delay which had been interposed between him and his patient, the door opened, and a female somewhat richly dressed, entered the apartment. He, supposing her

---

[a] From the papers of Whychcotte of St. John's, a clever New Publication.

to be one of the family, advanced to meet her. Unheeding him, she crossed the room with a hurried step, wringing her hands, and exhibiting in her motions the deepest distress. When she reached the foot of the stairs, she paused for an instant, and then began to ascend them with the same hasty step and agitated demeanour. As she reached the highest stair, the light fell strongly on her features, and displayed a countenance,—youthful, indeed, and beautiful,—but in which vice and despair strove for mastery. " If ever human face," to use Sir Walter's own words, " exhibited agony and remorse—if ever eye, that index of the soul, pourtrayed anguish uncheered by hope, and suffering without interval—if ever features betrayed, that within the wearer's bosom there dwelt a hell, the hell of passions that have no room for exercise, and diseases that have no hope of death—those features, and that being, were then present to me."

Before he could make up his mind on the nature of this strange occurrence, he was summoned to the bed-side of his patient. He found the lady so ill as to require his undivided attention, and had no opportunity, and in fact no wish, to ask any questions which bore on a different subject.

But on the following morning, when he repeated his visit, and found the sufferer materially better, he communicated what he had witnessed to the husband, and expressed a wish for some explanation.

The steward's countenance fell during the physician's narrative, and at its close he mournfully ejaculated, " My poor wife! My poor wife!"

" Why, how does this relation affect her ?"

"Much—much," replied the steward, vehemently. " That it should have come to this! I cannot—cannot lose her. You know not," he continued in a milder tone, " the strange, sad history; and—and his lordship is extremely averse to any allusion being ever made to the circumstance, or any importance attached to it; but I must and will out with it. The figure then which you saw, is supposed to represent the daughter of a former baron of Berry Pomeroy, who bore a child to her own father. In that chamber above us, the fruit of their incestuous intercourse was strangled by its guilty mother; and whenever death is about to visit the inmates of the castle she is seen wending her way to the scene of her former crimes, with the frenzied gestures you describe. The day my son was drowned she was observed—and now my wife!"

" I assure you she is better. The most alarming symptoms have given way, and all immediate danger is at an end."

" I have lived in and near the castle thirty years," was the steward's desponding reply; " and never knew the omen fail."

" Arguments on omens are absurd," said the Doctor, rising to take his leave. " A few days, however, will, I trust, verify my prognostics, and see Mrs. S―――― recovered."

They parted mutually dissatisfied. The lady died at noon.

Many years intervened, and brought with them many changes. The Doctor rose rapidly and deservedly into repute; became the favourite physician, and even personal friend of the Regent; was created a baronet, and ranked amongst the highest authorities in the medical world.

When he was in the full zenith of his professional career, a lady called on him to consult him about her sister, whom she described as sinking, oversome, and heart-broken by a supernatural appearance.

" I am aware of the apparent absurdity of the detail I am about to give," the lady began, " but the case will be unintelligible to you, Sir Walter, without it. While residing at Torquay last summer, we drove over one evening to visit the splendid remains of Berry Pomeroy Castle. The steward was very ill at the time, (he died, in fact, while we were going over the ruin,) and there was some difficulty about getting the keys. While my brother and myself went in search of them, my sister was left alone for a few moments, in a large room on the ground floor; and while there—most absurd fancy!—she has persuaded herself she saw a female enter, and pass her in a state of most indescribable distress. This—spectre I suppose I must call her—horribly alarmed her. Its features and gestures have made an impression, she says, which no time can efface. I am well aware of what you will say, that nothing can possibly be more preposterous. We have tried to rally her out of it, but the more heartily we laugh at her folly, the more agitated and excited does she become. In fact, I fear we have aggravated her disorder by the scorn with which we have treated it. For my own part, I am satisfied her impressions are erroneous, and arise entirely from a depraved state of the bodily organs. We wish, however, for your opinion; and are most anxious you should visit her without delay.

" Madam, I will make a point of seeing your sister immediately; but it is no delusion. This I think it proper to state most positively, and previous to any interview. I myself saw the same figure, under somewhat similar circumstances, and about the same hour of the day; and I should decidedly oppose any further raillery or incredulity being expressed on the subject in your sister's presence."

The dialogue that followed is not material. Sir Walter saw the young lady the next day, and after being under his care for a very short period, she recovered.

" Ah! that's all very well," said one of the youngest of the cavillers, as the widow concluded her story; " but I should like to have had the testimony of the young lady herself. The spectre might be accounted for, like that of Lord Grey and the bloody head, on the principles of hallucination. I should wish to have questioned this very sensitive damsel; she might have been a somnambulist, or a simpleton."

" On that subject, put what question you will, it shall be answered. I avow myself to be that sensitive lady, or somnambulist, or simpleton," returned the widow, sharply.

" But what," said our good-natured, hospitable host, wishing to break the awkward pause which this reply had created, " what of Lord Grey and the bloody head ?"

" Simply this. A summer or two ago Earl Grey came down into Devonshire, and fixed his head-quarters at the government house in Devonport. He was declared to be very much out of health, and was indeed afflicted with a most singular disorder; for continually present to his mind's eye was a bloody head. Go where he would, at home or abroad, in solitude or in society, this very revolting spectacle pursued him. The features rigid in death—the lead-like, lifeless eye—the brow convulsed in agony—and the neck, from which drops of gore seemed to trickle—these features form no very agreeable portrait. Such, however, as it was, no art could exclude it from the Earl's presence, and it embittered every moment of his life."

Change of scene was prescribed, and his Lordship came to Devonport; but there his enemy followed him, and confronted him, turn where he would, with its fixed and steady gaze. He then went to Endsleigh Cottage, a beautiful country seat of the Duke of Bedford, near Tavistock. For once he seemed to have distanced his pursuer, and for many days enjoyed the luxury of being *alone*. But to a large dinner party given there, the bloody head came, uninvited, and stationed itself opposite to its old intimate, whom it harrassed and disheartened with its presence, till the companionship became unbearable, and the Earl, abruptly, and in disorder, quitted the table. All this the medical men accounted for on physical grounds, and demonstrated clearly enough to his family, that it arose from hallucination.

COLUMN FOR THE LADIES.
DUTIES OF A WIFE.

It is for the married state that a woman needs the most instruction, and in which she should be most on her guard to maintain her powers of pleasing. No woman can expect to be to her husband all that he fancied her when he was a lover. Men are always doomed to be duped, not so much by the arts of the sex, as by their own imaginations. They are always wooing goddesses, and marrying mere mortals. A woman should therefore ascertain what was the charm that rendered her so fascinating when a girl, and endeavour to keep it up when she has become a wife. One great thing undoubtedly was, the chariness of herself and her conduct, which an unmarried female always observes. She should maintain the same niceness and reserve in her person and habits, and endeavour still to preserve a freshness and virgin delicacy in the eye of her husband. She should remember that the province of woman is to be wooed, not to woo ; to be caressed, not to caress. Man is an ungrateful being in love; bounty loses instead of winning him. The secret of a woman's power does not consist so much in giving, as in withholding. A woman may give up too much even to her husband. It is to a thousand little delicacies of conduct that she must trust to keep alive passion, and to protect herself from that dangerous familiarity, that thorough acquaintance with every weakness and imperfection incident to matrimony. By these means she may still maintain her power, though she has surrendered her person, and may continue the romance of love even beyond the honey-moon.

"She that hath a wise husband," says Jeremy Taylor, "must entice him to an eternal dearness by the veil of modesty, and the grave robes of chastity, the ornament of meekness, and the jewels of faith and charity. She must have no painting but blushings : her brightness must be purity, and she must shine round about with sweetnesses and friendship ; and she shall be pleasant while she lives, and desired when she dies."   IRVING.

She's modest, but not sullen, and loves silence ;
Not that she wants apt words, (for when she speaks,
She inflames love with wonder,) but because
She calls wise silence the soul's harmony.
She's truly chaste ; yet such a foe to coyness,
The poorest call her courteous ; and, which is excellent,
(Though fair and young) she shuns to expose herself
To the opinion of strange eyes. She either seldom
Or never walks abroad but in your company ;
And then with such sweet bashfulness, as if
She were venturing on cracked ice, and takes delight
To step into the print your foot hath made,
And will follow you whole fields ; so she will drive
Tediousness out of time with her sweet character.

FASHIONABLE DANCING.*

Mr. Editor,—I abhor that atrocious and impious doctrine, that France and England are natural enemies, as if God Almighty had made us only to cut one another's throats ; and yet I must say that I hate the French, and hate them, too, for one of their most elegant accomplishments—their inexhaustible genius for dancing. With the fertility of their ballet-masters, I have no quarrel ; let them attitudinize till they have twisted the human form into as many contortions as Fuseli ; let them vary figures and combinations *ad infinitum*, like the kaleidoscope ; let them even appropriate distinct movements to each class of the human and superhuman performers. I admit of the propriety of their celebrated pas called the Gargouillade, which, as a French author informs us, is devoted to the entrée of winds, demons, and elementary spirits, and of whose mode of execution he gravely proceeds to give an elaborate and scientific description. But why must their vagaries quit their proper arena, the stage, and invade our ball rooms and assemblies ? Sir, they have kicked me out of dancing society full twenty years before my time. The first innovation that condemned me to be a spectator where I used to be a not undistinguished performer, was the sickening and rotatory waltz ; of which I never saw the object, unless its votaries meant to form a contrast to the lilies of the valley, "which toil not, neither do they spin." Waving all objections upon the ground of decorum, surely the young men and women of the present age were giddy enough before, without the stimulus of these fantastical gyrations. If a fortune-hunter chooses to single out an heiress, and spin round and round with her, like a billiard-ball, merely to get into her pocket at last, there is at least a definable object in his game ; but that a man should volunteer these painful circumvolutions for pleasure, really seems to be a saltatory suicide. I never saw the figurantes at the Opera, whirling their pirouettes, like whipping-tops, without wishing to be near them with a stout thong-that I might keep up the resemblance! and as to imitating their ungraceful roundabouts, by joining in a waltz, I would rather be a teetotum at once, or one of the front-wheels of Mrs. C——y's carriage. Thanks to the Goddess of Fashion, fickle as she is foolish, our ball-room misses have at length ceased to be twisted and twirled in this unmerciful manner, and our spinning-jennies are again pretty nearly confined to Manchester and Glasgow.

Tired as I was of sitting like a spondee, with my two long feet hanging idle on my hands, (as a noble Viscount would say,) I began now to entertain hopes of again planting my exploded heel upon a chalked board. But, alas ! I was doomed to experience that there are as many disappointments between the toe and the ground, as between the cup and the lip. France, my old enemy, was upon the watch to export a new annoyance : the genius of Quadrille started upon me from amid the roses painted on a ball-room floor, and my discomfited legs were again compelled to resume their inglorious station beneath the benches. I could not put them into a go-cart, and begin all my steps again ; I could not make a toil of a pleasure, rehearse before hand, and study my task by card and compass, merely to make an exhibition of myself at last. It was too like amateur acting ; the constraint of a ballet, without its grace or skill—the exertion of dancing without its hilarity ; and it was moreover, an effort, in which I was sure to be eclipsed by every boarding-school miss or master who would literally learn that by heart, which I, in my distaste to these innovations, could only expect to learn by card.

Oh, for the days that are gone !—the golden age of cocked hats ; the Augustan era of country dance ; the apotheosis of minuet ! One of my nieces played me those exploded tunes a few days ago, and what a flush of rosy recollections did they conjure up ! Their music seemed to penetrate into the quiet caves and grottos of memory, awakening ideas that had long slumbered undisturbed. Methought they issued from their recesses like so many embodied spirits ; and, fastening their flowery wreaths to the spokes of Time's great wheel, they dragged it rapidly backwards, until the days of my youth became evolved before me in all the fidelity and vividness of their first existence. Then did I again behold the rich Miss B——, the sugar baker's daughter, whom my parents invariably urged me to engage for the supper-dances, with many a shrewd hint that a partner at a ball often became a partner for life ; thank heaven, I never danced with her but once, and my mind's eye still beholds her webby feet paddling down the middle, with the floundering porpus-like fling she gave at the end, only accomplished by bearing half her weight upon her partner, and invariably out of tune. She was obtuse in all her perceptions, and essentially vulgar in appearance ; in the consciousness of her wealth, she sometimes strove to look haughty, but her features obstinately refused to assume any expression beyond that of inflexible stupidity. She was too opulent, according to the sapient calculations of the world, to marry any but a rich man ; and she succeeded, at length, in realising her most ambitious dreams. Her husband is a yellow little nabob, rolling in wealth, and half suffocated with bile.

---
* This letter was addressed to the Editor of the New Monthly, some years since, and while Mr. Campbell held that honoured office ; at any rate, it was before the era of Gallopades and the Mazourka.

AN IMPROVED METHOD OF MAKING GOUDA CHEESE.

(A PARTICULARLY GOOD KIND OF DUTCH CHEESE.)

When the milk is all collected, the rennet, which is prepared in the following manner, must be put into it. Six rennets must be taken and cut into small pieces; on these must be poured three kilogrames of water, in which about five kilogrames of kitchen salt have previously been dissolved. It may be proper also to add two ounces of saltpetre, or the salt of nitre, and half a bottle of the vinegar of wine. This mixture must be allowed to remain for about three weeks, when it is put into bottles. The bottles must be corked with great care, the influence of the air being pernicious to the rennet. When the rennet, thus prepared, is poured into the milk, it must be stirred very gently in a plain unpainted wooden trough, without the addition of warm water. It is not advisable to add warm water, unless when the milk comes from very distant pasturage, or when, on account of the coldness of the weather, the heat necessary for promoting the operation of the rennet is wanting. It is, however, still preferable to heat the trough directly by means of fire, as is the custom in Switzerland, where they heat the copper basins employed for this purpose. In those farms, where the pasture is very rich, it is proper to add a little warm water to the milk. Particular care must be taken not to mix portions of milk which have been drawn upon different days, or even at separate hours of the same day, as cheeses made in this manner are always of a very inferior flavour. When, by means of gentle and regular agitation, the different parts of the milk begin to separate, and when the whey is skimmed off, the curd must be kneaded with great care, in order that the large and small particles may not be put together confusedly in the frame, and that they may be as small and as equal in size as possible. The curd must then be wrapped in a thin linen cloth, of a fine but strong texture, and put into the frame. The frames used by M. Van Bell, are different from those usually employed, the sides being vertical. The lids ought to be made to fit exactly. The walls of these frames must be pierced with small holes, through which the whey will exude. If any difficulty be found in taking the cheese from the frame, it will be sufficient to blow into those apertures, as in this way the tension of the air will be removed, and the cheese easily taken out. The frame ought to be placed upon a pedestal, near the press, in order that they may be easily put beneath it. The cheese, with its cloth, ought to be repeatedly returned to the frame, and particularly at the commencement of the pressure. When the cheese is placed under the press, the pressure must at first be light, and afterwards increased by slow degrees. Care must be taken that the pillars of the windlass-press be vertical; and if the lever-press be used, that the pressure may arise exactly on the centre. With regard to the duration of the pressure, M. Van Bell's method differs entirely from that of the English, who leave the cheese under the press for a very long period, sometimes even for three days whereas M. Van Bell does not allow it to remain even so long as is the custom in Holland. It diminishes the duration of the pressure according to the warmth of the temperature, in order that he may be able to put the cheese more speedily into pickle. In truth, nothing produces the putrefaction of the cheese so easily as the acetous fermentation of the milk. Now, it is conceived that this fermentation only increased by allowing the cheese to remain long in the press, especially during warm weather; when, by the method of M. Van Bell, the curd frees it rapidly and effectually from the whey, and the cheese may be sooner put into the pickle, which acts in such a way as to prevent the fermentation. When the cheeses are removed from the pickle, they must be placed upon boards in the usual manner, which is well known to every experimental cheese-maker. M. Van Bell advises the use of pickling-troughs, of a depth sufficient to allow the cheeses to float, in order that the pickle may penetrate them equally on all sides.

INTRODUCTION OF POTATOES INTO IRELAND.—Mr. Tytler in his life of Raleigh, ascribes the introduction of potatoes into Ireland to that illustrious man. He says, "At Youghall, in the county of Cork, of which town he was mayor, and where his house and gardens are still seen, the first potatoes ever planted in Ireland were introduced by Raleigh, who had brought them from Virginia; and he is also said to have been the first propagator of the cherry in that island, which was imported by him from the Canaries. At Lismore, which formed part of the extensive grant made to him by Elizabeth, we find a still more interesting memorial in a Free School which he founded; and the large and beautiful myrtles in his garden at Youghall, some of them twenty feet high, are associated with that love of shrubs and sweet-smelling plants, and that elegance of taste in his rural occupations, which remarkably distinguished him."

MERRILY DANCED THE QUAKER!

A New Song to an Old Tune.

INSCRIBED TO THE ELECTORS OF SOUTH DURHAM:

BY A FRIEND.

'Twas merry, 'twas merry in Darlington,
  The darling town of schism,
What time the battle was fought and won
  With Church-of-Englandism.
From Berwick bounds to thine, Bow-bell!
  From Perth to Pedlar's Acre,
Friends of Reform! the chorus swell—
  Merrily danced the Quaker.

'Twas echoed from Wynyard's * haughty walls,
  And rous'd their Lord in dudgeon—
'Twas echoed from Durham's ghostly stalls,
  And scar'd each cassock'd curmudgeon;
But lordly frown and priestly gown,
  Prelate and prelate-maker,
Couldn't put Pease and Monty down—
  Merrily danced the Quaker.

Merrily dance the Quaker still,
  Through charm'd St. Stephen's portal!
On that dear still sweet shapes of ill
  Oppose th' audacious mortal.
Through cavillings all, that round him fell,
  From trickster and mistake—
Obsolete pests of Church and State—
  Merrily dance the Quaker!

Tait's Magazine for March.

* Lord Londonderry.

CONTENTS OF NO. XXXI.

Official Contents	129
On the Moral Training of Children	130
Geography	132
On Bees	134
Medical Selections, No. IV.—Diet	135
Hebridean Poetry	135
The Story-Teller—My Place in the Country	137
Sir Walter Farquhar, (Ghost Stories)	141
Column for the Ladies—Duties of a Wife—Fashionable Dancing	143
An Improved Method of Making Gouda Cheese	144
Merrily Danced the Quaker	ib.

EDINBURGH: Printed by and for JOHN JOHNSTONE, 19, St. James's Square.—Published by JOHN ANDERSON, Jun., Bookseller, 55, North Bridge Street, Edinburgh; by JOHN MACLEOD, and ATKINSON & Co. Booksellers, Glasgow; and sold by all Booksellers and Venders of Cheap Periodicals.

THE Schoolmaster,
AND
EDINBURGH WEEKLY MAGAZINE.

CONDUCTED BY JOHN JOHNSTONE.

THE SCHOOLMASTER IS ABROAD.—LORD BROUGHAM.

No. 32.—Vol. II.   SATURDAY, MARCH 9, 1833.   Price Three-Halfpence.

NOTES OF THE MONTH.

March derives its name from *Mars*, the God of War. By our Saxon ancestors, before their conversion to Christianity, it was called *Rhedé Monath, i. e.* the *rugged*, or *rough* month. It is in general remarkable for the dry winds and boisterous weather which prepare the soil for the labours of the husbandman, and for receiving the seed; hence the proverb, *A peck of March dust is worth a peck of gold.* Though March is often a cold month in our climate, it is as frequently, (as in the present season, 1833,) distinguished by days of truly "vernal mildness;" and at worst, the air, if cold, is free of damp, bracing and exhilarating; and most inviting to the commencement of out-door exercises, and especially of walking, that best of all modes of *training*. Descriptive of the weather, which is thought seasonable in March, we have another picturesque Scotch proverb, that "*March should come in like the adder's head, and go out like the peacock's tail,*"—stinging in the commencement, and beautiful at the close. In this month the Spring flowers, the fairest of all flowers, appear in the gardens in rich variety; and in the pastures the daisy begins to peer forth. This sweet wilding, which a fair author prettily terms the *Robin* among the flowers, so universally is it beloved, rarely disappears altogether, unless in seasons of great severity; but it is May and June before the profusion of daisies, when their "winking" eyes are broad open at sunny noon, absolutely whiten the "grassy lea." In England, cowslips, butter-cups, and violets,* appear in the meadows, and under the hedge-rows, though with us those beauteous Spring visitants are a full fortnight or three weeks later. Besides the garden flowers enumerated last month, we have, towards the close of this, wall-flowers, and early daffodil, or *Lent lily*,

 That comes before the swallows dares,
 Taking the winds of March, with beauty.

This is the month of those two poetical existences, —the lark and the ploughboy, the one high up in the clear cool sky; the other pacing along the sweet-breathed ridges, each pouring forth his blithe and emulous carol; the whistle of both alike exhilarating, and full of a fresh *Spring* feeling. This is a busy and a happy time with many kinds of birds. The crows are chattering and building; the blackbirds and thrushes are in the heyday of their courtship; and at grey twilight, the saunterer in the field-paths is startled by the call of the partridge, " now here, now there." This, in brief, is a season replete with interest and delight to the lover of nature, whatever be his rank or his pursuits. The ornithologist may now mark the departure of the fieldfare and woodcock for their summer homes in Norway and Sweden; quitting their winter residences with us exactly at the period when our people of fashion seek theirs. He may now hear the goldfinch and the golden-crested wren singing, the ring-dove *cooing*, the pheasant *crowing*, the woodpecker *shrieking;* and the owls, having opened their parliaments and synods, hooting at night, in their unintelligible jargon, to those sages in the hanging wood opposite, who respond in the same grave metaphysical style. The rambling botanist, or rather the lover of plants, has a happier time of it. Every new day adds to his store of pleasures, till by the end of the month, while the flower-borders are in vernal pride, the woods, meadows, and wayside banks yield him treasures of primrose and pansy, cowslip, and crowsfoot, the marsh marygold, and the delicate wood anemone; with arums, periwinkle, chervil, and many more of Flora's hardy-bred imps. About this time the cottage dame has her young broods of ducklings to attend and watch, with hope of profit and certainty of pleasure; and she has often the dove-cote to rifle, with a hand more considerate than the heart is commiserating; as she is happily better acquainted with the price young pigeons bear, than with Shenstone's sentimental ballads. Her husband, after a day spent in field labour, or in tending the new dropt lambs, may now, in an evening, be seen at work for an hour, between twilight and star-light, in their garden plat, putting down cabbage and savoy plants; seizing a fitting evening to sow his kidney beans, peas, and onions; or, if he be a man of horticultural ambition, dabbling in small saladings. Now he also plants a few potatoes for an early crop, to sell to his richer neighbours after his peas; and, when all

---

* The only out-door spot, within the range of Edinburgh pedestrians, where one finds sweet violets in profusion, is (so far as we know) under the walls of Roslin Castle, and scattered over the grassy mound on which that romantic pile stands. Some tasteful hand has, probably, strewed them there.

is over, he rewards the assisting toil of his children, by planting expressly for them a few slips and roots of the commonest but most beautiful flowers; and by digging and trimming the flower-border, neatly hemmed in with box, or thrift, or daisies, or London pride. He begins also to think of his bees; and when he returns at night, the children tell of the frequent bee-journeys on that sunny day, and of the bee visits traced to the neighbouring sallows. To the mechanic, an hour so spent, after a long day at the loom, the *last*, or the forge, is at once health and enjoyment. A garden is also the most potent auxiliary of the Temperance Society that we can imagine. It is the "Schoolmaster abroad," teaching by beautiful and meaning signs, lessons of wisdom and virtue. It is the best club-room of half the year.

Many holydays fall in March. The first is sacred to St. David, the patron saint of Wales, and to his savoury emblem the leek, which, on this anniversary, patriotic natives of the principality were wont to wear in their hats, and may, especially if far from home, still wear. The seventeenth is the yet grander national solemnity of St. Patrick, which, from the castle of Dublin to the lonest cabin in Connemara, is the highest holyday of Ireland, and one which, in conviviality and festivity, far surpasses the duller days of the British saints. On this day the Irishman all over the world may be known by the cross in his hat, formed of "the green immortal shamrock;" and scarcely does he require this national distinction to point out his Celtic origin as quite distinct from that Saxon derivative the Englishman or Scot. This is sufficiently done at all times, but especially on "Patrick's Day," by his air of determined festivity, his franker, or more off-hand manner, and that small dash of swagger which marks the warmer physical temperament, together with his less natural aptitude to forethought and reflection. The *shamrock* is the common white clover or trefoil, though there is reason to believe that this sacred and mystic emblem, which became to the christianized Irish what the mistletoe had been to the Druids, may have originally been that most beautiful plant the the wood sorrel. Both plants possess the tripartite form; and were the *Schoolmaster* a fit personage to engage in antiquarian discussion, many proofs could be brought forward by him to shew that the ancient *shamrock* really was the wood sorrel. The three stalks springing from one root were spiritualized into religious emblems, as they have more recently been made political illustrations. In one of the *Rebel* Songs of ninety-eight, we have the following, among other spirited stanzas, upon Ireland:—

Let her sons like the leaves of her *shamrock* unite,
A partition of sects from one foot-stalk of right,
Drive the demon of discontent back to his den,
And where Britain made slaves there let Erin make men.

Besides natural inclination which goes a good way at all times with Irishmen, the natives allege positive injunction for the jovial observance of their Saint's day. Like Moore's bard, St. Patrick wished no fasting, tears, nor sorrowing to be indulged in, in commemoration of his memory, which shews that he understood the genius of the nation fully better than some modern statesmen. In his last speech handed down by tradition, he recommended his votaries rather to rejoice in the manner of hearty Christians at his departure for a better world than even the Emerald Isle; and the more effectually to fulfill his advice, it was coupled with an injunction to "take a drop of something to drink" in honour of his memory Few Irishmen disobey the dying request of their saint.*

AIR.

The air that encompasses the earth is, from the intimate relation which exists between it and the health of all organized bodies, and from its importance in some of our mechanical operations, an object of singular interest. It is a compound body, being composed of two gases, *oxygen* and *nitrogen*. Oxygen gas, so called from two Greek words signifying *acid* and *generate*, because, when combined with many other substances, acids are generated, is transparent and colourless, and of course invisible. Its distinguishing property is the power of supporting combustion and respiration. A candle, on being placed among this gas, burns with increased splendour; and will, even if extinguished, but with a little redness remaining on the wick, be instantly re-kindled. An animal will live longer in a confined quantity of this gas than in an equal quantity of common air; thus proving its power of supporting respiration. It enters into the composition of many other substances. The properties of nitrogen gas, the other component of air, are very different. If a lighted candle or an animal is placed among this gas, the former is instantly extinguished, the latter immediately dies. These two gases, then, on being mixed in the proportion of 4 of oxygen to 1 of nitrogen, compose common atmospheric air. Though oxygen gas supports respiration, it is not, of itself, well adapted for the support of life, owing to its too powerful stimulating qualities; and it is accordingly mixed with nitrogen, a gas, as we have seen, possessing properties of a negative description; which gases, correcting and modifying the properties of each other, constitute a medium eminently fitted for the support of life—shewing the care and anxiety of the Creator to place the *means* of enjoyment within

---

* A friend of ours in Dublin, was one day, a few years ago, engaging a porter for an office of some trust in his establishment, and plainly put the necessary questions about steadiness, temperance, &c., &c. The candidate for office readily undertook for every day of the year, save Christmas and "Patrick's day." He indeed made it a point of honour and conscience to get drunk upon "Patrick's day;" and he honestly stipulated for the right of doing what he had always done. As the employer was himself an Irishman, though not quite so devoted a votary of the Saint, the declaration was as much a recommendation as an obstacle. The Porter kept both conditions. He was a *steady* man all the year round, but dipped deeply in—"Patrick's pot" on the 17th of March.

our reach. Air, which has been respired or breathed, or in which combustion has taken place, will not answer the same purpose a second time, owing to the oxygen gas having been consumed. Nor, for the same reason, can an animal live in air in which combustion has already taken place; nor will a candle burn in air which has already been respired. If we place a lighted candle on a support in a vessel of water, and invert a jar over it, and thus confine the air it will continue to burn till the oxygen gas is consumed, when it will be extinguished; and, at the same time, water will rise in the jar and occupy the place of the oxygen. If the air that remains in the jar be examined, it will be found to be nitrogen gas only. We all know that an animal placed in a confined quantity of air speedily expires. It continues to live only so long as any oxygen gas remains unconsumed. In this case, however, the *quantity* of air is not lessened, another substance, carbonic acid gas, or the air which escapes from brisk beer, being formed while respiration goes on. Carbonic acid gas is, equally with nitrogen gas, unfit for the support of respiration, of which any one may convince himself by putting his head within a brewer's or distiller's fomenting tun while in active operation. As, in the respiration of animals, oxygen gas is consumed, and carbonic acid gas is formed, the air would soon become very impure were this not provided against by a beautiful provision of nature. Carbonic acid is composed of carbon, or pure charcoal, and oxygen gas; and, as the carbon is necessary for the growth of plants, it is absorbed by their leaves, while they reject the oxygen gas, which is accordingly set free again to purify the atmosphere. The facts here stated shew the necessity of continual ventilation where a number of human beings, or other animals, are collected together; but which, from ignorance or carelessness, is too often neglected. This, however, being a subject of some importance, we shall reserve our remarks for a future number.

CHEMICAL RECREATIONS.

SIMPLE BODIES.—OXYGEN, HYDROGEN, NITROGEN, CARBON, SULPHUR, PHOSPHORUS, THE METALS.

The number of hitherto-undecomposed bodies is *fifty-three*. Four others—light, heat, electricity, and magnetism, called the *imponderable* bodies—have, by some, been added to these; but, as their separate identity has not been clearly ascertained, they are not generally reckoned with the others. The whole of these fifty-three bodies may be *weighed* and *measured*, and hence (in contradistinction to the four bodies just mentioned, which cannot be weighed and measured) they are called *ponderable* bodies. These, in order to facilitate the acquirement of a knowledge of their properties, have been arranged as follows:—

1. Bodies having an immense affinity for the simple bodies of the succeeding two classes; with which bodies they combine, and thereby form substances that are totally different in their properties from the substances of which they are composed:—

1. Oxygen
2. Chlorine
3. Iodine
4. Fluorine

2. Bodies of a non-metallic nature, but inflammable or acidifiable:—

5. Hydrogen }
6. Nitrogen } *Gaseous Bodies.*
7. Carbon } *Fixed and Infusible Solids.*
8. Boron }
9. Sulphur } *Fusible and Volatile Solids.*
10. Phosphorus }

3. Inflammable substances of a metallic nature. This is the most numerous class of simple bodies; the individuals of which it is composed being in number *forty-three*. These substances combine with nearly all the ten bodies named above; but the most important compounds into which they enter, are the bodies formed by their combination with oxygen.

Oxygen is one of the most important agents in nature. Scarcely a process of any description takes place in which it has not a share. In a simple state, it is obtained only in the form of *gas*. It is an exceedingly abundant body; the air of the atmosphere contains one-fifth, and water one-third of its bulk of it. It also exists in most natural products, animal, vegetable, and mineral. *Oxygen gas* is, like common air, colourless, invisible, tasteless, inodorous, and elastic. But it is heavier than common air, in the proportion $11\frac{1}{4}$ to 10. It is a powerful supporter of combustion; that is to say, when any inflamed body, as a lighted taper, is put into it, it burns very vigorously—much more so than if it were put into common air; indeed, it is owing to the oxygen it contains that common air supports combustion at all. Its presence is also essential for the continuance of animal life. We cannot breathe air which has been deprived of its oxygen; and it must be noticed, that an animal lives, and a combustible body burns, much longer in a definite quantity of oxygen gas, than it would in the same quantity of atmospherical air. Hence it is evident, that oxygen is the principle which supports both life and fire. Oxygen is not only found combined in natural bodies, but it can be made, by means of art, to combine with a great variety of substances, with which it forms very peculiar compounds.

Properly speaking, *oxygen gas is not a simple body*: since the gaseous state is not the natural state of oxygen, but is owing to the presence of a peculiar chemical agent, which has been called *caloric*. But as we know of no substances that are *separated* from caloric, it is customary to apply the term simple to such as are combined with caloric only. *Gas* is the name given to all permanently-elastic fluids, both simple and compound, except the atmosphere, to which the term *air* is appropriated. It is necessary to distinguish between *gas* and *vapour*. The latter is elastic and fluid, but not permanently so. The vapour of water, (steam,) upon cooling, becomes a liquid; it is, therefore, not a *gas*, for *gases* are bodies whose aeriform state is permanent.

Hydrogen is only known in the state of *gas*, and is sometimes called *inflammable air*. It is the lightest species of ponderable matter with which we are acquainted; compared to oxygen, its density is as 1 to 16. It is the basis of *water*, from which body only it can be procured. Hydrogen gas, when pure, is possessed of all the physical properties of common air; a slight odour, which it sometimes has, is produced by some substance that is held in solution by it. It does not support combustion, though it is itself one of the most combustible of all bodies; being that which gives the power of burning with flame to all the substances used for the economical production of heat and light. But it only burns in the presence of oxygen.—It is not fit for respiration; for animals which breathe it die almost instantaneously. If pure oxygen and hydrogen gas be mixed together, they remain unaltered; but if a lighted taper be brought into contact with the mixture, it explodes with astonishing violence; and, if the two gaseous bodies have been mixed in certain proportions, the whole is condensed into water; hence we see the origin of the term *hydrogen*, which literally signifies the *water-former*. Hydrogen gas is the substance which, on account of its rarity, is employed to inflate air-balloons.

Nitrogen, called also *azote*, is a gaseous body, rather lighter than common air; of which it forms 4-5th parts in bulk, the remaining 1-5th being oxygen. It is tasteless, inodorous, colourless, and capable of being condensed and dilated. It extinguishes flame, and is fatal to animal life. It combines with oxygen in various proportions, forming compounds which differ greatly in their properties.

One of its most extraordinary compounds is *nitrous oxide*. This gas consists of 36 parts nitrogen and 37 oxygen; and, when inhaled into the lungs, produces an extraordinary elevation of the animal spirits, a propensity to leaping and running, involuntary fits of laughter, &c. This circumstance shows what a variety of delightful or pernicious effects might flow from the slightest change in the constitution of the atmosphere, were the hand of the Almighty to interpose in altering the proportion of its constituent parts; for atmospheric air is composed of 80 parts of nitrogen, and 20 of oxygen, which is not a very different proportion from the above. Another gas, called *nitric oxide*, composed of 56 parts of oxygen, and 44 nitrogen, produces instant suffocation in all animals that attempt to breathe it. One of the most corrosive acids, *aqua fortis*, is composed of 75 parts oxygen, and 25 parts nitrogen; so that we are every moment breathing a certain substance, which, in another combination, would produce the most dreadful pain, and cause our immediate destruction.

Carbon is the name given to the pure inflammable part of *charcoal*, of which substance the diamond is only a variety in a pure crystallized state; for pure charcoal and diamond, when treated in the same manner, produce precisely the same results. Carbon is insoluble in water, and infusable by the most intense heat. Carbon combines with oxygen, and produces a gas called carbonic acid; and, when combined with hydrogen gas, forms carburetted hydrogen gas—the same that is now used to light up shops. Animal and vegetable oils are composed almost entirely of carbon and hydrogen; the difference in their properties resulting chiefly from the variation in the proportions of these two bodies. The same may be observed of gum, sugar, and starch. All these bodies, however, contain oxygen.

Sulphur is a well-known substance, distinguished commonly by the name of brimstone. It is a hard brittle body, of a yellow colour, destitute of smell, and of a weak taste. It is universally diffused in nature; but commonly combined with other bodies. It is insoluble in water; but, if poured into that liquid when liquefied by heat, it retains its softness; and in this state is employed for taking impressions from seals and medals. When exposed to heat in close vessels, it is sublimed or volatilized in the form of very fine powder, called *flower of sulphur*. At a heat of about twice that of boiling water, it takes fire, if in contact with the air, and burns with a flame of a pale blue colour. In this process it dissolves in the oxygen of the atmosphere, and produces an elastic fluid acid. It is a substance of great importance in chemistry and the arts. Oxygen unites with it in four proportions, its compounds forming an interesting series of acids. The compounds of sulphur with metals are called sulphurets. With hydrogen it forms sulphuretted hydrogen gas.

Phosphorus is a semi-transparent yellowish matter, of the consistence of wax. It is procured, in general, by the decomposition of bones. It is so inflammable, that it is set on fire by a heat of about one-third that of boiling water. Indeed, it has a luminous appearance, arising from a slow combustion, at the common temperature of the atmosphere. During its combustion, it emits a dense white smoke which has the smell of garlic, and in the dark is luminous. On account of its very combustible nature, it requires to be handled with great caution. It is a violent poison.

The forty-three *metals* compose the most numerous class of undecompounded chemical bodies, and are distinguished by the following general characters:—They possess a peculiar lustre. They are opaque; they are fusible by heat, and in fusion retain their lustre and opacity. They are excellent conductors of electricity and heat. Many of them may be extended under the hammer, and are called malleable; or under the rolling press, and are called laminable; or drawn into wire, and are called ductile. When exposed, highly-heated, to the action of oxygen, chlorine, or iodine, they take fire, and are converted by the combustion into oxides, chlorides, or iodides,—bodies destitute of lustre and other metallic characteristics. They will combine, in almost any proportion, with each other, when in a state of fusion, and thus form compounds, which are termed alloys, bodies that *retain* the properties of metals. From their brilliancy and opacity, conjointly, they reflect the greater part of the light which falls on their surface; hence they form excellent mirrors. They are very heavy; to this character, however, (though it was till lately considered one of their most prominent features,) there are important exceptions; since metals have been obtained (potassium and sodium, for instance) which are lighter than water.

MRS. ARBUTHNOT, LADY JERSEY, MRS. JORDAN, QUEEN CAROLINE, &c. [a]

"Which is Mrs Arbuthnot?" said an elderly gentleman of the old school, whose bent form and silver locks told a tale of years gone by, to a young aspirant in diplomacy, during an entertainment at Lady Strong's, at Putney; "which is the confidante of Princess Lieven, and the counsellor of the Duke of Wellington? Do I see her in that lovely woman sitting near our host, with that singularly sweet expression and bright laughing eye?"

"No; that is the celebrated beauty, Rosamond Croker, the niece of the sarcastic secretary. The object of your inquiry is nearer home—hush! speak lower—look to the right of Mr. Holmes: see, she is listening with evident satisfaction to the *badinage* of the great captain. With his grizzled hair, hooked nose, and piercing eye, how like an old eagle! Now, now, she looks this way."

"And that is Mrs. Arbuthnot," said the old gentleman, musing. "Those faultless feminine features, and clear pale countenance—"

"Which," interrupted his youthful mentor, "are invariably of the same delicate hue, and at no time—rare instance in a woman of fashion!—masked with rouge. Look at her well; for *she's a woman that has served her country*."

"Her country—how? when? where?"

"Those are questions more easily asked than answered; but as nothing ostensible appears, we must suppose it *to* be in the way of *secret service*. Aid," continued the young diplomatist, "she must have rendered, and of no common description. Otherwise there would never have been granted, under an administration on principle hostile to all extravagance—to unmerited pensions—to every species of expenditure unsanctioned by necessity; under a Premier who pared down the Custom-house clerks without mercy whose watchword was "*economy*," and general order "*retrenchment;*" who spared no salary, and respected no services—a pension of no less than NINE HUNDRED AND THIRTY-EIGHT POUNDS PER ANNUM TO HARRIET ARBUTHNOT.[†]—No, no; rely upon it, her claims upon her country are weighty, and her services in its behalf unimpeachable."

[a] Whychcotte of St. John's
[†] Pensions on Civil List.—England. Harriet Arbuthnot, L.938, 10s. Sir Henry Parnell on Financial Reform, 3d edit. p. 331. To the curious in pensions, the Appendix to this remarkably clever and singularly accurate work will afford some most extraordinary information. It contains many startling facts.

"She is fair," said the old gentleman, "but her predecessor was fairer."

"Her predecessor?"

"Yes; the first Mrs. Arbuthnot was one of the most intellectual, elegant, fascinating women that ever lived. Her daughter, Lady Henry Cholmondeley, in manner resembles her. She accompanied Mr. Arbuthnot in his embassy to Constantinople; and many of his dispatches are indebted for their precision, force, and clearness, to the corrections of her severer taste. Long Wellesley—then an indefatigable student and accomplished man of business, *heu! quantum mutatus ab illo*—was secretary to the embassy; and could bear willing testimony to her delight at the opportunity of enriching her mind with associations acquired from personal observation of a country full of interest, and but little known.

"The last letters that flowed from her polished pen—and those who knew her best will be the first to do justice to the brilliancy of her style, the fidelity and the variety of her descriptive powers—breathed the language of youth and hope; spoke of past pleasures, and anticipated future gratification. The next accounts stated she was no more.

"She died at Pera—died when the sad event was utterly unexpected—died under the hands of "*native talent*," in other words, some Turkish quack undertook her cure, was credited, and confided in—died mourned by the whole embassy, and bewailed by her agonized mother—died, except as far as Mr. Arbuthnot was concerned, in the midst of strangers and alone!

"But now mark," continued the old chronicler, "what trifling events may colour with disaster a whole train of important circumstances.

"About the period of Mrs. Arbuthnot's death, the first memorable investigation was instituted relative to the (then) Princess of Wales. To bear out the charges against this unfortunate woman, the evidence of Mrs. Arbuthnot's mother, Mrs. Lisle,* one of her Royal Highness's ladies in waiting, was peremptorily required. It was given; and was the only deposition which militated materially against the Princess. ' It is the only part of the case,' thus ran her Royal Highness's letter to her Royal father-in-law, ' which I conceive to be in the least against me, or that rests upon a witness at all worthy of your Majesty's credit.' It was, in fact, as I have reason well to know, the sole deposition which distressed the Princess—the solitary testimony which neither the ingenuity of Mr. Perceval could ridicule, nor the arguments of Lord Eldon invalidate. It contained one particular passage, which they both feared would prove fatal in a certain quarter.

" ' Her Royal Highness behaved to him (Captain Manby) only as any woman would who likes FLIRTING. She (Mrs. Lisle) *would not have thought any married woman would have behaved properly, who behaved as Her Royal Highness did to Captain Manby*. She can't say whether the Princess was attached to Captain Manby, only that it WAS FLIRTING CONDUCT.' †

"It was ' this sweeping sentence which went to prove so much,' that the old King was heard more than once to declare, that he ' had tried and tried in vain to banish it from his remembrance.' It was to this statement, short but full of meaning, that the Prince was known again and again to have referred, ' I abandon to the infamy she merits, Lady Douglas; but—but, sire, the evidence of Mrs. Lisle!'

"Now of this evidence of Mrs. Lisle, so important, so unfavourable, and so relied upon, what is the secret history? It is curious, and runs thus:—When Mrs. Lisle received the summons from Lord Chancellor Erskine, acquainting her that her evidence was required before the Commissioners then sitting, she had just perused the melancholy tidings of her daughter's death. If ever mother and child were deeply and devotedly attached,—if ever mother doated upon the external loveliness and mental endowments of an idolized daughter,—if ever daughter reverenced a mother's lofty and unimpeachable character, and remembered with grateful and delighted accuracy a mother's ar-

* Sister to the late Marquis of Cholmondeley.
† Evidence of the Honourable Mrs. Lisle, in the delicate investigation before Earl Spencer and Lord Erskine, &c., &c., in 1805-6.

dent and unceasing love,—these were the sentiments reciprocally entertained by Mrs. Arbuthnot and Mrs. Lisle.

"The agony of the survivor beggared description. She wept in unutterable anguish. ' I cannot appear before the Council! Half frantic and distracted as I am, with my heart swollen almost to bursting by this bitter bereavement, and my thoughts all tending towards my daughter's grave—is it possible I can enter upon a subject which requires such caution, such deliberation, such self-possession, such reflection? For God's sake write, and entreat them to grant me a fortnight's delay.'

"The answer returned was brief and heartless. No delay could be afforded. There was, in fact, little probability of a different reply. The peculiar circumstances of the case—the general excitement throughout the country—the feelings of the parties interested—the anxiety of the reigning monarch—all precluded the possibility of protracted delay.

"But of this Lord Erskine's answer stated nothing. It was couched briefly, peremptorily, harshly. Coarsely was it written, and keenly was it felt.

" ' I have not deserved this,' was Mrs. Lisle's remark to her tried and valued friend Mrs. Forster. ' His Lordship should have known me better. But I go—unfitted, indeed, for the ordeal! I go—and the blame be on those who *dragged* me to their tribunal, if my evidence be tinged by my sorrows.' She went, and her evidence *did* take a tone—a tone of reprehension and severity, from the grief which overwhelmed her. This, her Royal Highness's advisers at once detected, and Mrs. Lisle never denied. ' Thank God this most painful portion of my life is past !' was her hurried exclamation as she quitted the Council Chamber; ' and now,' said she, as she entered her carriage, ' with Courts I have done for ever! This hour I resign my office.'

" ' To the Princess?'

" ' No; *from* the Prince I received my appointment, *to* the Prince will I resign it.'

"In a letter which bore the impress of wounded feelings, and contained touches of the truest pathos—which detailed the painful struggle in her own mind, and, while it paid the deference due to her Prince, kept steadily in view what was due to herself, she entreated permission to lay at H. R. H. feet the appointment which he had formerly conferred upon her in his consort's household. A copy of this affecting communication is yet in existence. *I have one*. He to whom it was addressed was far too generous not to own its justice—had too high a sense of honour not to feel its truth.

" ' I am but too sensible of the difficulties of Mrs. Lisle's situation. They are certainly here very strongly stated. Yet the letter is precisely what a high-spirited and high-principled woman, like Mrs. Lisle, might be supposed to have written; and I entertain for her undiminished respect.' "

"You have called," said the young diplomatist, "the late Queen unfortunate—how is this?"

"I have," said the old man sternly; "and will not recall the epithet. Without passing any opinion on her guilt or her innocence, I term her an unfortunate Princess, because I think few will deny her just claim to that appellation; and that still fewer will assert that she was not, during the greater part of her life, and particularly the closing scenes of it, an object of the sincerest pity. I am old, and, from circumstances and situation, know much of the earlier passages of her married life. I was at Brighton during the first visit of the Princess,—the only period at which she was an inmate of the Pavilion. I was at table on one particular occasion, when Lady Jersey—she has since gone to her account—may she have found mercy with her God!—was sitting at the right hand of the Prince, monopolizing, as usual, his entire and undivided attention. The Princess, who knew little of English manners, and was unguarded in her own, was guilty of some trivial violation of etiquette, which drew down upon her a hasty censure from the Prince, somewhat harshly expressed. The Princess rose, and withdrew in tears. The Prince, who, left to himself, was ever generous and kind-hearted, and who had not calculated that his remark would produce such painful results, rose to follow her. Lady Jersey—what a retrospect a dying hour must have unrolled to the view of that fearful woman!—exclaimed, 'Go, go by all means. Follow her. Sooth her by your submission, and then sue for pardon. Let her see her own power. *She will never abuse it.*' The Prince hesitated—advanced—returned—and, with a smile, resumed his seat. Lady Jersey had triumphed.

"The circumstance was canvassed at Brighton, and commented on. It was mentioned in my hearing, and I called it 'unmanly conduct.' My observation was repeated, and I was dismissed. I was told, 'THAT IN CERTAIN CIRCUMSTANCES NO MAN WAS ALLOWED TO HAVE AN OPINION OF HIS OWN.'

"The Princess was unfortunate in other respects. Dr. Randolph, the Prebendary of Bristol, was appointed to an embassy of a private nature to Germany. Among other commissions, he was charged with letters from the Princess of Wales, which he was directed to deliver personally to the Duchess of Brunswick, and other members of her family. For some reason or other, the Doctor received counter orders, and another gentleman was dispatched to Germany in his stead. Instead of surrendering the Princess's packet to herself in person, he transmitted it to her lady-in-waiting, Lady Jersey, to be by her delivered to her Royal Mistress. The packet was opened—found to contain letters commenting, in ludicrous terms, on various members of her husband's family, and his mother in particular:—these letters were handed over to the parties—and never forgiven. That such communications were highly censurable, indiscreet, and improper, I admit; but what epithet sufficiently strong can be applied to the treachery which could thus way-lay and appropriate them?

"The end of the Countess was singular. During the Queen's trial, and for some years previous to it, she resided at Cheltenham. On the withdrawal of the Bill of Pains and Penalties, she received a round-robin, numerously signed, telling her that her presence was not desired at Cheltenham, and that she would consult both her quiet and her safety, by a speedy retreat. Considerably chagrined at this document, which was powerfully and convincingly written, she asked a leading personage at Cheltenham, whether public opinion there ran so strongly against her as her letter averred. She was told it did; and that the advice given in the round-robin was, in the opinion of her counsellor, judicious and sound.

"'Then I will quit Cheltenham without delay.'

"Whether she did so, and only reached the first stage of her journey; or whether, when all her hasty preparations were completed, she was suddenly taken ill, I am unable to state positively. This I can affirm, that the vexation and annoyance consequent on the round-robin, brought on the illness which rapidly terminated her existence. She died in the same week as the Queen, and their funeral processions passed on the road. Strange that they should thus meet, both silent in death—the injurer and the injured—the oppressor and the victim!

"A more false position can never be assumed, than that happiness and independence, and self-respect, are indigenous within the precincts of a palace. A packet of poor Mrs. Jordan's letters, which I now hold in my hand, will sufficiently disprove it. Two in particular, addressed to her daughter, Mrs. Alsop, though dated from "Bushy House," and franked by a cabinet minister, tell as melancholy a tale of sorrow as language can well express. Kind-hearted, generous woman! her bounty to an unworthy relative, and the base return he made for it, accelerated her end. Henshaw, the stone-mason, and myself, with another Englishman, were all that followed her to her lonely grave in a foreign land."

HOME.

Cling to thy home! If there the meanest shed
Yield thee a hearth and shelter for thine head;
And some poor plot, with vegetables stored,
Be all that pride allots thee for thy board;
Unsavoury bread, and herbs that scattered grow,
Wild o'er the river's brink or mountain's brow:
Yet e'en this cheerless mansion shall provide,
More heart's repose than all the world beside.

COLUMN FOR THE LADIES.
REVOLUTION IN DRESS.

WE seldom notice *modes*, and do not intend to change our plan; but a complete revolution having taken place in female costumes, by an approximation to the taste of our ancestresses, we think it right to notice this *movement* at the centre, which, in about a year or less, will be felt at all the extremities. Our oracle is the *Court Journal*.

In Paris, the revival of long-exploded antiquities is carried to an extravagant length. At evening parties, and balls, ladies have appeared in stiff brocade, of immense patterns, in every colour, intermingled with gold and silver; to all appearance the very identical dresses which figured at the Courts of Louis XIV. and Louis XV. One of these dresses was formed of very thick maroon-coloured satin. The pattern consisted of large serpentine stripes of gold, and each simi-circular interval formed by the waving stripe, was filled up by a bouquet of roses and pinks, embroidered in coloured silk. This certainly had a superb effect, but the eye must become accustomed to these antiquities before they can be admired.

Robes of light texture are no longer considered indispensable for dancing. Ball dresses are now made of moire, satin, and even velvet.

The turban à *la Moabite* is a head dress at present much in favour. Those formed of white gauze, sprigged with gold or silver, are extremely elegant. These turbans may be worn with robes of velvet, satin or gauze; but of course they do not accord with the dresses which are made in imitation of the costumes of the middle ages, the renewal of which appears to be the prevailing taste of the day.

For evening negligé, hats of crape or velvet are much worn. These hats are made with very short wide brims, and are placed very backward on the head. They are trimmed with a single long feather. This sort of head-dress has all the elegance of the beret, with less appearance of full dress.

Boas are now no longer seen in the drawing-room. A scarf alone is admissible in evening dress. Boas, however, have by no means sunk in estimation for promenade dress. No fur has fallen in price this winter, but chinchilla is less in demand than some others.

Short sleeves are now invariably made a double sabot; that is to say, the sleeve is divided into two puffs, the lower one being smaller than that above it, and descending nearly to the elbow. At the bottom of the sleeve is placed a manchette of lace, descending low on the inside of the arm, and raised on the outside, in all respects like those worn by our grandmothers.

The most glaring contrasts of colours are now admissible without incurring the reproach of bad taste. For example it is not unusual to see a blue satin dress trimmed with bows of sans souci, or a lilac dress ornamented with yellow ribbon.

Black lace mantillas are very much worn; but it is necessary to distinguish between the scarf-mantillas, and those which merely form a trimming at the back of the corsage. The latter are also of black lace, but of real lace. This, again, is the revival of a long-exploded fashion.

GERMAN PEASANTRY.

THE greater part of the day at Wabern is one unremitting fugue of cackling, crowing, grunting, lowing, and quacking, beating hemp, thrashing, and if there be any other occupation belonging to a bucolic life, here you have it in full work. Both women and men resume their diurnal task at two o'clock in the morning of summer, and keep it until nightfall. To their laborious habits it must be owing, that the females of the servile order in this country have a breadth of shoulder, extent of thew, and procerity of limb, I would venture to swear, not to be found in any other part of the habitable earth. They really quite outman our sex. In all other animals but the human, the males are, I believe, most usually remarkable for beauty. Here they make good the general analogy. Instead of a "peeping ankle," you have a calf of brawn, in full display, under a petticoat reaching no lower than a little under the knee, whose owner steps along at her ease, a full geometrical yard and a half at a stride. It was, no doubt, women such as these that Cæsar's soldiers had a view of, when his army became panic-struck with the apprehended physical force of this people. But the males are by no means in proportion masculine. The costume of the sex is appropriate. The head is bagged, or trussed, in a sort of night-cap, tied close under the chin, the top of which casing is pursed into a knob stuffed with their hair, and from this a long cue or two of plated tresses depend to the waist, if waist that can be called, which preserves its diameter undiminished one inch from the shoulder to the hip.

NOT YET FIFTEEN.

DURING the worst periods of the French Revolution, it was customary at Lyons, where many victims suffered, to send the condemned to a place named, "the Cave of Death." A lad of fifteen was of the number. His little brother, a child hardly six years old, who had been accustomed to visit him in another prison before trial, no longer finding him there, came to the vault of the Cave of Death, and called to him from the iron grate. His brother heard him and appeared below. The poor child put his little hands between the thick bars to clasp his unseen brother, while the latter, by raising himself on the points of his toes, could just kiss them. "My dear brother," said the child, "art thou going to die, and shall I see thee no more? Why did you not tell them that you are not yet fifteen?" "I did, brother; I said all I could, but they would hear nothing. Carry a kiss to my mother, and try to comfort her; nothing grieves me but that I leave her ill, but don't tell her yet that I am going to die." The child was drowned in tears, his little heart seemed ready to break. "Good bye, brother," he repeated again and again; "but I'm afraid you did not say that you were not yet fifteen." He was at length so suffocated with sobs that he could speak no more, and went away. Every one who passed by, seeing his distress, asked him what was the matter. "'Tis the wicked men that make me cry—they are going to kill my brother, who is so good, and who is not yet fifteen."

THE SAMPHIRE GATHERER.

"—— Below hangs one who gathers samphire,
Dreadful trade!" *Shakspeare.*

THERE are few avocations attendant with so much danger as that of gathering rock samphire, which grows in great plenty along the edges and down the perpendicular side of the cliffs near Rennel's Cave, Glamorganshire. The method employed by the fearless adventurers in their dreadful occupation is simply this:—The samphire gatherer takes with him a stout rope and an iron crow-bar, and proceeds to the cliff, fixing the latter firmly in the earth, at the brow of the rock; and, fastening the former with equal security to the bar, he takes the rope in his hand, and boldly drops over the head of the rock, lowering himself gradually until he reaches the crevice where the samphire is found. Here he loads his basket or bag with the vegetable, and then ascends the rock by means of the rope. Carelessness or casualty, in a calling so perilous as this, will sometimes produce terrible accidents. There is a story related of a poor man of the name of Evans, which is so full of horror, without terminating fatally, that the bare idea of it makes the blood recoil from the heart. It appears that this courageous man was once in good circumstances, but misfortunes had reduced him to the lowest ebb of wretchedness and want. His wife and a family of eight children were crying around him, and he could not endure the thought of his little ones suffering, without making an effort to save them. In a moment of desperation he borrowed the crow-bar and rope of a neighbouring cottager, and proceeding to the extremity of the rock, without one thought of the danger of his undertaking, (never having ventured before,) he fixed the crow-bar, attached the rope to it, and boldly descended the cliff. In the course of a few minutes he reached a ledge which, gradually retiring inwards, stood some feet within the perpendicular, and over which the brow of the rock beetled consequently in the same proportion. Busily employed in gathering the samphire, and attentive only to the object of profit, the rope suddenly dropped from his hand, and after a few oscillations became stationary at the distance of four or five yards from him. Nothing could exceed the horror of his situation; above was a rock of 60 or 70 feet in height, whose projecting brow could defy every attempt of his ascending it, and prevent every effort of others to assist him. Below was a perpendicular descent of 100 feet, terminating by rugged rocks, over which the surge was breaking with dreadful violence. Before was the rope, his only hope of safety, his only hope of return; but hanging at such a tantalizing distance as baffled all expectation of his reaching it. Here therefore he remained, until the piercing cries of his wife and children, who, alarmed at his long absence, had approached the very edge of the cliff, roused him to action. He was young, active, and resolute; with a desperate effort, therefore, he collected all his powers, and springing boldly from the ledge, he threw himself into the dreadful vacuum, and dashed at the suspended rope! The desperate exertion was successful, he caught the cord, and in a short time was once more at the top of the rock. No language can describe the scene which followed—himself, the dear partner of his heart, and his little offspring, were in one moment raised from the lowest depth of misery, to comfort, joy, and happiness.

HEBRIDEAN POETRY.

THERE is a very popular air in the Hebrides, written to the praise and glory of Allan of Muidartach, or Allan of Muidart, a chief of the Clanranald family. The following is a translation of it by a fair friend of mine:—

Come, here's a pledge to young and old!
We quaff the blood-red wine;
A health to Allan Muidart bold,
The dearest love of mine.

CHORUS.

Along, along, then haste along,
For here no more I'll stay;
I'll braid and bind my tresses long,
And o'er the hills away.

When waves blow gurly off the strand,
And none the bark may steer;
The grasp of Allan's strong right hand
Compels her home to veer.
Along, along, &c.

And when to old Kilphedar came
Such troops of damsels gay;
Say, came they there for Allan's fame,
Or came they there to pray?
Along, along, &c.

And when these dames of beauty rare
Were dancing in the hall,
On some were gems and jewels rare,
And cambric coifs on all.
Along, along, then haste along,
For here no more I'll stay;
I'll braid and bind my tresses long,
And o'er the hills away.

WALTER SCOTT.

ELEMENTS OF THOUGHT.

SPRING SOLITUDE.—In solitude, or that deserted state when we are surrounded by human beings, and yet they sympathize not with us, we love the grass, the flowers, the water, and the sky. In the motion of the very leaves of spring, in the blue air, there is found a secret correspondence with our hearts. There is eloquence in the tongueless wind, and a melody in the flowing brooks, and the whistling of the reeds beside them, which, by their inconceivable relation to something within the soul, awaken the spirits to breathless rapture, and bring tears of tenderness to the eyes, like the enthusiasm of patriotic success, or the voice of one beloved singing to you alone. Sterne says, that, if he were in a desert, he would love some cypress. So soon as this want or power is dead, man becomes a living sepulchre of himself, and what yet survives is the mere husk of what he once was.—*Shelley.*

IMPORTANCE OF THE STUDY OF POLITICS TO MINISTERS.
BY THE REV. ROBERT HALL OF LEICESTER.

THERE are but few ministers who have capacity or leisure to become great practical politicians. To explore the intricacies of commercial science, to penetrate the refinements of negotiation, to determine, with certainty and precision, the balance of power, are undertakings, it will be confessed, which lie very remote from the ministerial department; but the *principles* of government, as it is a contrivance for securing the freedom and happiness of men, may be acquired with great ease. These principles our ancestors understood well; and it would be no small shame if, in an age which boasts so much light and improvement as the present, they were less familiar to us. There is no class of men to whom this species of knowledge is so requisite, on many accounts, as dissenting ministers. The jealous policy of the Establishment forbids our youth admission into their celebrated seats of learning; our own seminaries, at least till lately, were almost entirely confined to candidates for the ministry; and as, on both accounts amongst us, the intellectual improvement of our religious teachers rises superior to that of private Christians, in a greater degree than in the national church, the influence of their opinion is wider in proportion. Disclaiming, as they do, all pretensions to dominion, their public character, their professional leisure, the habits of study and composition which they acquire, concur to point them out as the natural guardians, in some measure, of our liberties and rights. Besides, as they are appointed to teach the whole compass of social duty, the mutual obligations of rulers and subjects will, of necessity, fall under their notice; and they cannot explain or enforce the *reasons* of submission, without displaying the *proper end* of government, and the expectations we may naturally form from it; which, when accurately done, will lead into the very depths of political science.

THE STUDY OF THE SCRIPTURES FAVOURABLE TO THE PRINCIPLES OF CIVIL LIBERTY.

THE knowledge and study of the Scriptures, far from favouring the pretensions of despotism, have almost ever diminished it, and been attended with a proportional increase of freedom. The union of the protestant princes preserved the liberties of the Germanic body, when they were in danger of being overwhelmed by the victorious arm of Charles the Fifth; yet a veneration for the Scriptures, at a time when they had almost fallen into oblivion, and an appeal to their decisions in all points, was the grand characteristic of the new religion. If we look into Turkey, we shall find the least of that impatience under restraints, which admirers of despotism lament, of any place in the world, though Paul and his epistles are not much studied there. Hume and Bolingbroke, who were atheists, leaned towards arbitrary power. Owen, Howe, Milton, Baxter, and some of the most devout and venerable characters that ever appeared, were warmly attached to liberty, and held sentiments, on the subject of civil government, free and unfettered.—*Hall.*

To these instances Mr. Hall might have added, the whole reformers of Scotland, from John Knox and the Covenanters to the modern Dissenters.

UNIVERSAL SUFFRAGE AND ANNUAL PARLIAMENTS.

WERE every householder, in town and country, permitted to vote, the number of electors would be so great, that no art or industry would be able to bias their minds, so no sums of money would be sufficient to win their suffrages. The plan which the Duke of Richmond recommended was, if I mistake not, still more comprehensive, including all that were of age, except menial servants. By this means, the different passions and prejudices of men would check each other; the predominance of any particular or local interest would be kept down; and from the whole, there would result that *general impression*, which would convey, with precision, the unbiassed sense of the people. But, besides this, another great improvement, in my opinion, would be to shorten the duration of Parliament, by bringing it back to *one year*. The *Michel Gemote*, or great council of the nation, was appointed by Alfred to meet twice a-year, and by divers ancient statutes after the conquest, the King was bound to summon a Parliament, once a-year or oftener, if need be; when, to remedy the looseness of this latter phrase; by the 16th of Charles the Second, it was enacted, the holding of Parliaments should not be intermitted above three years at most; and, in the first of King William, it is declared, as one of the rights of the people, that, for the redress of grievances, and preserving the laws, Parliaments ought to be held frequently. Parliaments were triennial till the reign of George the First; when, after the rebellion of 1715, the septennial act was passed, under the pretence of diminishing the expense of elections, and preserving the kingdom against the designs of the Pretender. Lord Peterborough observed on that occasion, he was at an utter loss to describe the nature of this prolonged Parliament, unless he were to borrow a phrase from the Athanian creed; for it was "neither created, nor begotten, but proceeding." Without disputing the upright intentions of the authors of this act, it is plain, they might on the same principle have voted themselves perpetual, and their conduct will ever remain a monument of that shortsightedness in politics, which, in providing for the pressure of the moment, puts to hazard the liberty and happiness of future times.—*Works of Hall of Leicester.*

THE SLAVES' ADDRESS TO BRITISH FEMALES.

Natives of a land of glory,
Daughters of the good and brave,
Hear the injured Negro's story,
Hear and help the fetter'd Slave!
Think, how nought but death can sever
Your loved children from your hold;
Still alive, but lost for ever,
Ours are parted, bought, and sold.
Seize, O! seize, the favouring season,
Scorning censure or applause;
Justice, Truth, Religion, Reason,
Are your leaders in our cause.
Follow, faithful, firm, confiding,
Spread our wrongs from shore to shore;
Mercy's God your efforts guiding,
Slavery shall be known no more.

THE STORY-TELLER.

MY PLACE IN THE COUNTRY.
(Continued from last Number.)

Poor Mrs. Richard, from that hour was she haunted by 'A place in the country," and Richard's fate was fixed. His wife did nothing but babble of green fields; and the head nurse saw plainly she had "a longing" for a place in the country; nor could any part of the coast longer satisfy her. From Scarborough to Ilfracombe, nothing would do, and the seven children must die without "a place in the country." Much torture poor Richard endured before he one morning underwent a sudden transformation, while perusing the Morning Post, when he suddenly started up, declaring he was going down to Hertfordshire. Mary-Matilda, who had had several dreadful fits of the sullens, on a proposal of visiting her husband's relations there, was now seized with a fit of jealousy, and how did she know that he was gone into Hertfordshire at all?—How did she know but that the staid and sober Mr. Martindale had received some kind of assignation or appointment through its columns, such as —" * * * 's letter is received; and Rosa will meet him at the time and place appointed, if he can make it convenient to leave town."—

Mary-Matilda hated mysteries. Why had her husband kept so secret his desire of a visit to Hertfordshire? Perhaps he was gone to consult with his brother, the attorney, about some means of getting rid of her, and forming a separate establishment. Perhaps—But why enumerate the vagaries feeding the fancy of a peevish woman, parted for the first time from her husband, without any means of employment for her vacant mind. It was some comfort that she could send for the apothecary; declare herself indisposed; lie on the sofa; take hartshorn; and sentimentalize herself into languour upon a diet of green tea and custard pudding. She was determined that at least, when the truant did think proper to return to the home he had basely abandoned, he should find her looking as pale as the cambric handkerchief she now incessantly applied to her eyes. If she did not favour him with a scene on such an occasion, she might never have another opportunity.

Five tedious days had passed away. Poor Mrs. Richard, having scolded all her children, and as many of her servants as she dared, and being too bent on playing the victimized invalid to admit visitors, was growing very tired of herself and her heroics. At last, on the fifth evening, half famished by her perseverance of sullen abstinence, and satisfied that it was Saturday night, she had no chance of hailing her culprit's marital knock at the door till Monday morning, she suddenly rang the bell, and ordered a supper tray into her dressing-room. When lo! just as she had filled her plate with a provision of cold lamb and sallad, enough to have dined a corporal of dragoons, the door was flung open, and Richard rushed into her arms. The surprise and disappointment were alike overwhelming. She, who had been picturesquifying in her dressing-gown for five long tedious days; who had purchased a new bottle of salts for the occasion; who had rehearsed her shrieks, and prepared her agonizing flood of tears—she to be caught in the fact of a tumbler of Madeira negus, and a fat shoulder of lamb!—It was too ignominious.

"So you are come at last," cried the mortified victim, compelled to wipe her mouth instead of her eyes, as she accepted his warm embrace.

"The business was not settled till six o'clock this evening," cried Richard. "But it is ours, and Heaven send us health to enjoy it."

"I don't understand you?"

"Have you a clean plate there, my dear?" inquired Richard Martindale, seating himself beside her before the fatal tray, having already rung a bell for a further supply of knives and forks. "Do you know I have had no dinner. I was in *such* haste to get up to you, to tell you the news, that I jumped into a post-chaise the moment it was over. How are the children?"

"You will positively drive me distracted. *What* news? —You have told me none."

"Your health, my love. How refreshing is a glass of wine, after a fatiguing day and a dusty drive! I suppose you expected me, as you have prepared supper?—"

"How was I to expect you?—I may think myself lucky that I see you any time within these six weeks. How could I possibly guess when it would suit you to return home?"

"Didn't you receive my letter?—"

"What letter?"—

"By this morning's post?"—

"I have heard nothing of you, Mr Martindale, since you started off on pretence of a visit to your family, nearly a week ago."

"How very extraordinary,—how devilish provoking!" cried Richard, setting down his glass. "I was so very particular about that letter. I inquired so often about the post hour from my brother's clerks. By Jove,—here it is!" —cried he, suddenly detecting the neglected dispatch safe in his waistcoat pocket. "In my hurry, I must have forgotten to put it in the post."

"A very convenient excuse."

"Well, I am not sorry for it. The surprise will be all the greater."

"What surprise?"—

"Nay, since you know nothing about the matter, I shall punish you for that cross face by making you guess."

"You are really too vexatious!—After the week of dreadful suspense I have been passing, to break in upon me in this sudden way, and perplex me with all these mysteries. How am I to know what you mean?"

"My dearest love, do not irritate yourself," said poor Richard, drawing his chair nearer to hers, when he perceived that she was on the verge of a genuine flood of tears. "I will explain the whole business to you from the very beginning."

"No; I don't want to hear a word about it," cried the lady, retreating to the sofa in a magnificent fit of the pouts. "Believe me, I have no curiosity about any of your family affairs. I dare say you and your brothers can manage them very well amongst you without any interference of mine. Doubtless Mr Robert Martindale's professional advice—"

"My dear, dear Mary-Matilda!" exclaimed her husband, somewhat provoked after a long day's fast, to be obliged to procrastinate his cold lamb in honour of her ill-humour. "You *must* be aware that my sole motive in making this purchase is to gratify the desire you have so long expressed of—"

"*What* purchase?" ejaculated the breathless lady, jumping up from her reclining position.

"The Marygold Hill estate, my love. You know how eagerly you have besot me lately for a place in the country."

"You have actually *bought* a place in the country?"

"The papers were signed this afternoon. A great bargain, I am told; but the purchase was a serious affair. Five-and-forty thousand pounds!—But it is the most beautiful thing! All within a ring fence;—a trout stream running through the lawn;—best preserves in the country; —timber magnificent,—gardens superior to those at Grinderwell Hall! The Marriots' place a citizen's villa by comparison!—Drawing room and library opening into a conservatory of rare exotics; saloon forty feet by eighteen. But here is George Robin's advertisement of the place, which originally led me into temptation. Don't you remember how I started in the midst of reading the newspaper that morning at breakfast?—I could not hear or answer a word you said to me, after the notice of sale had caught mine eye."

"My dear, dear Richard!" exclaimed the vanquished lady, holding the crumpled newspaper in one hand, and throwing the other arm round his neck. "Why did you not tell me at once?—"

"I think you must now be satisfied that I have neglected nothing to fulfil your wishes?"

"I never *was* so delighted in my life!—A finer place than Starling Park!—Forty-five thousand pounds!—Saloon, library, conservatory!—Show me the advertisement, Richard; show me the description."

"I can't,—ah,—here it is. 'That unique residence known by the name of MARYGOLD HILL; situate five miles from the stirring little county town of Hertford.'"

"Good Heavens! In Hertfordshire! Just in the midst of all your odious family! How very provoking! I'm sure when I told you that I should like a country seat, I never dreamed that, without consulting *me*, you would think of going and buying a place in Hertfordshire.—I would as soon go to—"

"The devil!" cried the indignant husband; and his new place in the country was the origin of his first serious quarrel with his wife.

Such was the commencement of Mr. and Mrs. Martindale's prospects of rural felicity, and estated grandeur. But at last the ninetieth "loaded wain" had left Harley street; and, with the dislocation of the leg of the magnificent billiard table—a sword-stick poked through a Gainsborough—a nervous fever to Mary-Matilda—sundry fits of rage and profane swearing to Richard—and innumerable casualties with the nurses and small children, Marygold Lodge was made. One season was spent in quarrelling about fixtures, and curing smoky chimneys; but by the next Richard carried on improvements briskly—clearing away evergreens, and felling groves. And now, the first year was gone, and the second tolerably advanced; but the fair proprietress of Marygold Hill could by no means be persuaded to pronounce herself comfortable. A new little marygold was budding; and the fractious invalid could neither bring herself to like the neighbouring apothecary, nor reconcile herself to the loss of Lady Kedgeree's daily calls of inquiry, or her Harley Street neighbour Mrs. Calicut's hourly councils of gossip. Richard Martindale already affected the cockney country gentleman; sported a fustain jacket, leathern gaiters, and a bill-hook; went out before breakfast, spud in hand, to make war upon the thistles and dandelions; and, above all, during the shooting season, was never to be heard of, (except by the distant report of his Manton,) from breakfast till dinner, or, during the hunting season, from breakfast till luncheon. Mary-Matilda consequently found her time hang somewhat heavy on her hands. She was not yet on easy terms with her new neighbours; and her own previous experience of a country life had been made in a house full of giggling sisters, and riotous brothers. But her own girls were too young to giggle—her boys too dull for mischief; and, moreover, a termagant head-nurse, the inseparable prime minister of every silly indolent mother, having more than two thousand a-year, would only allow her the children's company at her own pleasure and convenience. She had no hereditary interests in the condition of the neighbouring poor, or the prosperity of the neighbouring farmers. All were alike strangers; and though the Martindale family were very kind in volunteering visits to Marygold Hill, they always came with prying, investigating, arithmetical looks; Mrs. Robert begging her to take her daughter Marriot's advice in the management of her dairy and housekeeper's accounts; Mrs. Jacob, spunging for cuttings from the greenhouse, or a breed of her choice Dorkings; Mrs. Millegan annihilating the utmost efforts of her fine ladyism by a sketch of the superior splendours of Mowbray End; and Mrs. Marriot, senior, the widow, who was living in a cottage in her son's village, overwhelming her with tracts and controversy. Mrs. Richard was never so ill as after some of these envious, presuming people had been staying at Marygold Hill; and at length, though reluctantly, and with the loneliness of a long winter in perspective, bethought her of renewing her correspondence with her own married sisters. She longed to figure before them in her new dignities of patroness of a village, and proprietress of a country seat; and nothing was more easily arranged.—Mrs. Mac Glashun, who had fancied herself the wife of a Lieutenant-General of Poyais dragoons, now found herself the widow of an ensign of Irish militia, with two young children, whom she was very glad to quarter on the charity of any member of the family willing to provide them with bread and butter; and Harriet, whose union with the Grinderwell curate had caused him to be ejected from his cure, by the rector-nominee of the late Sir John, was now settled with him on a vicarage of forty pounds a-year on the Lincolnshire coast, living on conger eels, and lived upon by the fen-flies. Both, on the first hint of an invitation, hastened eagerly to Marygold Hill; and it was no small affliction to the pride of the arrogant Mrs. Richard Martindale, that Mrs. Trotter made her appearance by the north mail, and Mrs. Mac Glashun and her children by the day coach.

Poor Richard, always kind and well-intentioned, was only the more cordial in his mode of reception, in consideration of their mode of travelling; indeed, he was far better pleased at the idea of having his two sisters-in-law as his inmates, now that they were tamed by misfortune, than during the heyday of their partiality for captains of hussars, dragoons, lancers, carabineers, fusileers, and fencibles. Moreover, if the truth must be told, he was not sorry to have an excuse for occasionally prolonging his day's sports, and taking a bachelor's dinner with the Marriots, Millegan's, Martindales, or his new friend, Jack Cleverley, of Poplar Lodge.

Now this new friend, Jack Cleverley, was, perhaps, of all poor Mrs. Richard's Hertfordshire grievances, the most enormous; being a huge, large-limbed, cheery, back-slapping individual, with the strength, and eke the lungs of an ox; who looked upon the fair and frail sex, (like the mares in his stable, and the cows in his meadow,) as useful animals, created for the service and delectation of mankind. Despising the great lady of Harley Street with all his soul, too lazy to nurse her own children, and too helpless to drive herself round the farm like his own stirring housewife, he was never to be persuaded into the slightest deference towards her nervous headaches; shouting whenever he sat by her at dinner, as if he had been tally-hoing to the hounds, and slamming the doors after him whenever he was staying in the house, as if he were bullying the waiters at a traveller's inn. He was, indeed, a hateful creature in her eyes and ears; talking with his mouth full, wiping it on the table-cloth, breathing like a grampus, and sucking in his tea from the saucer, with the impetus of the famous American whirlpool that swallows up ships of the line. Mary-Matilda's first topic of lamentation, (after listening to Mrs. MacGlashun's moving tale of those Occidental adventures which had terminated with seeing the unhappy Ex-Lieutenant-General hanged higher than Haman, on a Mexican gallows, erected between two cabbage-palm-trees, —and trying to seem interested in poor Mrs. Trotter's description of her little parsonage-garden, with its slimy fen-litches, and fetid exhalations,) was the misfortune of possessing a loud vulgar neighbour like Jack Cleverley, who had no greater satisfaction than in decoying Martindale away from home, brutalizing him with strong ale, and persuading him that it was a mark of manliness to defy the influence of an "affectionate domestic partner." It was in vain that Mrs. MacGlashun described her sufferings when left a nursing mother in a torrid climate;—Mary-Matilda interrupted her to complain that poor little Dick had a chilblain in his little finger, thanks to Martindale's obstinacy in choosing to purchase an estate in a county notoriously the coldest in England; and while Mrs. Trotter was pointing out to her commiseration, that for three years she had been living in a fishing-hamlet, without a neighbour within forty miles, saving the officers of excise, and coast blockade, and their spirituously-inclined consorts, —the lady of Marygold Hill begged to assure her that such a spot was infinitely preferable to a country house, placed under watch and ward of a husband's vulgar family. She appealed to the judgments of both, whether any thing could afford stronger proof of Martindale's want of knowledge of the world, than to sink half his fortune in the purchase of an estate in the only county in England where no extent of landed possessions would obliterate the recollection that, "after all, he was nothing but a second son of old Doctor Martindale of Hertford, who had made money in Indy;"—and to their feelings, as daughters of the house of Grinderwell, on the ignominy of being introduced into the neighbourhood, under the patronage of Richard's eldest brother's wife, (the heiress of a rich brewer,) and to the county in general, per favour of Mrs. Milligan's favour with the great people at Moubray End. Somehow or other, both Julia and Harriet were disposed to harden their hearts towards the picture of their sister's distresses. They, who had been subdued in a rougher school, who had contended with cold and heat, hunger and bereavement, since they flirted at Weymouth, or pouted at Grinderwell House, could not connect the idea of misfortune with the wife of an affectionate husband, the mother of seven fine children, and the owner of a handsome country seat in one of the best counties in England.

Perhaps it was this obduracy which gave them a sinister position in Mrs. Richard Martindale's opinion. Other causes of dissatisfaction soon, however, became apparent. Mary-Matilda had been originally considered by far the prettiest of the four sisters; but now, though the ten years which had passed over her head since the tour into Wales still left her flaxen hair and pink cheeks,—habits of luxurious idleness, and other natural causes had produced an expansion of outline far from conducive to her reputation as a beauty. Her cheeks were bloated, her eyes offuscate; little yellow ringlets hung scantily round the enlarged oval of her rubicund face; and, at eight-and-twenty, she might have passed for the age proverbially connected with the qualification "fat and fair." Mrs. MacGlashun and her sister, on the contrary, attenuated by privations, had preserved their shapes, and therewith that air of gentility with which the choicest costume can never invest a dumpy woman; and no sooner did the good air and good fare of Marygold Hill restore animation to their features, and bloom to their cheeks, than they shone forth as very pretty women, and came to be talked of as Mrs. Richard Martindale's beautiful sisters. The Hon. Mrs. Blickling insisted upon being favoured with their company at a popularity ball, her husband, the member, was giving to the free and independent gentlemen of the county of Herts; and it was indeed wormwood to Mary-Matilda, who had made herself obnoxious in a cheerful social neighbourhood by sticking for precedency as a baronet's daughter, to have her two sisters appear on so ostensible an occasion in dyed silk gowns, as a curate's wife and adventurer's widow; and yet to know that they were fiftyfold as much liked and admired as herself. Now, in London this never could have happened. Her Harley Street friends would never have dreamed of pressing their civilities on a Mrs MacGlashun and a Mrs Trotter, who had no houses of their own in which to requite the obligation; and even had they been capable of such a waste of magnanimity, the general indifference to family connexions prevalent in London society, would have prevented any one from knowing, caring, or commenting upon the relationship, or instituting comparisons between the parties. They had not been established two months at Marygold Hill, before Mary-Matilda wrote to her favourite sister Anne, (the wife of the Irish captain, who was now on half-pay, and settled on a small hereditary estate on the borders of Connemara,) to describe how very troublesome she found those wild heathens, the little MacGlashuns, in her nursery; and how much she was apprehensive that Harriet and Julia, would assume the command of her establishment, and probably give offence in the family and neighbourhood, during her approaching confinement.

There was no resisting this sororal appeal! Mrs. O'Callaghan certainly *had* intended to pass a happy domestic winter in the bogs. But she would not allow poor little Mary-Matilda to be put upon; nobody could say what might be the result of her suffering any annoyance during the ensuing delicate crisis. So, having persuaded Captain O'Callaghan to become her escort, away she went by long sea to London; and, from the Tower Stairs, straight to those of Marygold Hill. The heroine was already in the straw; but her husband (albeit somewhat startled by this third addition to his family circle) gave them a hearty welcome. All colonial people are hospitably inclined; and though he could certainly have dispensed with the Captain's company, against whom, during his courtship of Anne Grinderwell, he had conceived an antipathy, yet will any connexion of his dear Mary-Matilda was welcome. It was still winter. And is it not the custom in Great Britain for people to collect as many as possible of their friends and relations at Christmas, under their roof? Is not hospitality an almost religious duty on the part of the proprietor of a "Place in the Country?"

It was an awful visitation to the irritable nerves of Mrs. Richard Martindale, who, during her annual indispositions, had been accustomed by her kind husband to have things kept so quiet in the house, that the blind mole heard not a foot-fall—when the little MacGlashuns, instigated by uncle O'Callaghan, set up their war-whoops in the hall; or when uncle O'Callaghan himself, after a second bottle of Madeira at luncheon, stumbled along the corridor to the billiard-room, singing "I am the boy for bewitching them," in a tone that would have drowned Jack Cleverley's loudest view halloo! Her head-nurse gave her warning, and even the nursery-maid "warn't going to stay to be made keeper to them two little heathen savages." Forced into a premature assumption of strength and authority, the nervous lady exerted herself to resume her post in the drawing-room :—and then things went worse then ever.

The treacherous Anne had evidently coalesced with Julia and Harriet; and great was the art with which all three prevented their nefarious proceedings from coming under Martindale's observation, by soothing him with their flatteries and pretended regard. It was vain for Mary-Matilda to hint to Mrs. Trotter that her poor husband, doubtless, found his solitary situation in the fens extremely disagreeable; or to Captain and Mrs. O'Callaghan, that the weather was growing delightful for a voyage. They always contrived that the worthy Richard should seize that very opportunity for assuring them that his house was their own; that if Trotter found it dull at Swamperton, he had better join his wife at Marygold Hill; and that the state of Irish affairs was not such as to justify his Connemara brother-in-law in a precipitate return to his Sabine farm. His wife could have found it in her heart to Burke him for his officious hospitality to her encroaching family.

Nor was it only that their innovations produced real inconvenience and annoyance in the establishment; but the Martindale family, living near enough to have an eye upon their proceedings, and enchanted to have an opportunity of paying off to the nabob's wife the innumerable slights and insults with which she had beset them, took care to let her see they were fully aware that her hungry swarm of poor relations had alighted like locusts upon poor Richard's property, to devastate and devour. The elder brother, Robert, had died a few months before; expressly for the purpose, Mrs. Richard thought, of bequeathing sixty thousand pounds to the Marriots, and making Clotilda more vulgar and presumptuous than ever; but the remainder of the Martindale clan (rejoiced to find out, and to show they had found out, that the family of "my father Sir John Grinderwell," with which they had been so frequently twitted, was, in fact a tribe of needy beggars) constantly wrote her word that they would drop in upon her and their brother or uncle Richard, "when her own family had quitted her. They would not think of intruding so long as she had so much good company about her."—Wretches! not one of them but knew she had as much chance of getting rid of her sisters, as of that capital mansion known by the name of Marygold Hill.

Misfortunes now came in battalions upon the unhappy Mrs. Richard. Her Husband's friend, Ned Warton, arrived, and joined O'Callaghan and Jack Cleverley in torturing her delicate sensibilities. She was nearly turned out of her own chamber to accommodate guests, and there found no refuge from shouts of laughter and the fumes of cigars and whisky toddy ascending from the hall, soon warned her that the monster Warton, and the brute O'Callaghan, were colleaguing over their saturnalian orgies; and very probably engaging poor Richard himself in a career of libertinism. "And this," said she, as she wept over a plate of partridge and bread sauce, furtively brought up by her own maid, "*this* is the comfort of having a Place of one's own in the Country!—"

Dick Marriot, to torment his amiable aunt and another lady neighbour, entered into the league offensive of Warton and the gallant O'Callaghan, and undertook to point out to the notice of Mrs. Cleverley the frequency of her dear Jack's visits to Marygold Hill, as connected with the charms and ingenuous sprightliness of the widow MacGlashan; leaving it to the well-known susceptibility of the lady of Poplar Lodge to favour her friend and neighbour Mrs. Martindale, whom she detested as heartily as friends and neighbours in a dull country neighbourhood are compelled to do for want of better employment, with her opinion of the conduct of her sister in encouraging the attentions of a married man ;—and to persuade the poor Jack, that the party at his uncle, Richard Martindale's, could not get on without him, and were much hurt by the infrequency and brevity of his visits. Jack was not the man to resist such an appeal. A house filled with three amateurs of whisky toddy, and three lively chatty women, presented a real attraction; and even Richard Martindale, his friend, was no less surprised than delighted to observe how unreservedly he came among them, and how ready he was for a carouse with the brawling O'Callaghan or his nephew Marriot. Old Warton looked on with his cunning grey and puckered face, and saw, with delight, that a catastrophe was brewing.

Now, Mrs. Richard Martindale, on her inauguration into the circles of the neighbourhood, had not been so inattentive to her own interests as not to secure a partisan; and the same incipient ambition which prevented her from resting on her pillow till she had magnified her own dignity by the acquisition of a place in the country, had secured her choice of the County Member to be her knight and champion. There was something in the solemn dull impracticability of the well-looking, well-conducted Mr. Blickling, which forbade all possibility of scandal;—and it was therefore highly satisfactory to her feelings to rise into the Hertford ball-room on the arm of this mighty dignitary; or to hear the Hertfordshirians from the south-western extremity of the county inquire at the Hatfield Tuesdays, to whom their favourite member was paying such marked attention ?—Mrs. B., like most county members' wives, was too much accustomed to see him bowing and beauing, and philandering, after the fashion of Sir Christopher Hatton with Queen Elizabeth, to take the least note of his proceedings; and Richard was gratified to perceive that his wife, her pearls, and ostrich feathers, were received with becoming attention. Nothing could be further from gallantry than such a liaison. Blickling himself was a man who sometimes "spoke," but never talked. Deeply imbued with a sense of his personal dignity as the representative of the county, and proprietor of one of its finest estates, he considered loquacity derogation: and having made it his maxim that men often repent of saying too much but never of saying too little, was looked upon as one of the most sensible men either in the House or out of it. Thousands of people said "there was no one on whose opinion they relied so much as on that of the Member for Hertfordshire," without perceiving that he was never known to give one, but contented himself with bowing gracefully and assentingly to the expression of their own.

To her growing intimacy with this senatorial tumefaction, the recent occurrences in her family had opposed some obstacles; but now that she was out again, and that the weather permitted her to drive over to Blickling Park, she contrived to make her way there unaccompanied, and to take a long stroll in the shrubberies with a party staying in the house. Satisfied by the profound reverence of the Member's bow, that she was still as great a favourite as ever, Mrs. Martindale no sooner found herself, by one of the turns of the shrubbery, alone upon his arm, than she seized the opportunity to renew all her former declarations of relying solely and singularly upon his guidance in the direction of her own conduct; assuring him that "*his* superior wisdom could alone extricate her from a most unpleasant dilemma. It was impossible to place even Mr. Martindale in her confidence; for the delicate relation in which the offending parties stood towards him, might lead to the most unpleasant results." Mr. Blickling paused, and looked steadfastly and inquiringly at his fair companion, but said nothing. He was very much in the habit of saying nothing.

"During her recent indisposition," she resumed, "the families of the neighbourhood had been so kind as to show a great deal of attention to her sisters. They had been to as many dinner-parties, as many Christmas balls, as if she had not been confined to her room. Mrs. O'Callaghan had been kind enough to stay with her; but Julia and Harriet had been constantly out. Probably he had frequently met them?"

The Member bowed as to the Treasury Bench, but said nothing;—he was very much in the habit of saying nothing.

"All this, she was sorry to admit,—sorry for the sake of her own family, sorry for the sake of a respectable family in the neighbourhood,—had been productive of much mischief!"

Mr. Blickling started and stared. He even spoke; he cried "Indeed!" and much as Kean himself might have ago-ed the word; and when his friend Mrs. Richard Martindale proceeded to unfold to him the agonized apprehensions entertained by Mrs. John Cleverley of Poplar Lodge, and her own terror lest "any thing unpleasant" should happen during her sister's visit at Marygold Hill, he seemed quite as much shocked and alarmed as she could possibly desire. But, although she expressly asked his advice, and in her unwillingness to involve Martindale in a quarrel with his friend Jack, begged to know whether it was not plainly her duty to get rid of the indiscreet Mrs. MacGlashun as quietly as possible, the great man of Blickling Park could not be induced to express a decided opinion. He shook his head, waved his hands, elevated his eyebrows, cleared his voice; and Mary-Matilda finally quitted the shrubbery, under a persuasion that her platonic knight had advised her to do exactly what she had driven over to Blickling determined to effect; viz., to bring matters to a crisis by bringing all the parties concerned publicly together.

To this Mrs. Martindale resolved to give a ball, which, to kill two birds with one stone, was also to be a popularity ball, and to celebrate a christening.

The morning arrived, and the Blicklings (to whom Mrs. Trotter had volunteered to surrender her apartment) arrived also; and while poor Richard paraded the lady round his improvements, and broke her shins over his patent cast-on fences, his wife managed to get the County Member *tête-à-tête* into her book-room to relate to him all that had been going on since she saw him last. They sat opposite each other; Mrs. Richard with compressed lips, looking rigid, stern, and moral;—Blickling like the "Portrait of a Member of Parliament," in the Somerset House exhibition, with his hand picturesquely rested on the writing table, and his legs crossed à la Knight Templar. Whenever Mrs. Martindale terminated a sentence in reprobation of the wickedness of the world, and more especially of married men who run after other men's wives or widows, the senator gravely uncrossed these impressive limbs, and (as if in mute reply to her appeal) re-crossed them in an opposite direction. He was too cautious for words.

"Yes! my dear Mr. Blickling,"—faltered Mary-Matilda in an under-tone; "you will, I am sure, sympathize with my feelings, when I acknowledge I have now more than ever reason to believe that villany has been going on under my roof. The other evening, after dusk, my own maid actually discovered a female in a white dress (it *could* be nobody but the ill-advised Mrs. Mac Glashun) clandestinely receiving a letter over the paling of the shrubbery from a gentleman on horseback, who *could be nobody* but that wretch Cleverley!"—

Mr Blickling replied affirmatively by manœuvring his right leg over his left, and thus altering the balance of his whole attitude.

"Several times lately, the house-dogs have been heard to bark at undue hours; and I have every reason to believe that the alarm was given by these faithful creatures on account of strangers loitering about the premises to favour this vile—this detestable correspondence!"

Her auditor gravely and silently resumed his original position.

"To-night, however, I am determined to be on the alert, and so is poor dear Mrs. Cleverley. They will come early. The guilty parties will not entertain a suspicion that they are watched; and my eyes shall never be off their movements throughout the evening. It is a melancholy thing that the iniquity of mankind should compel one to have recourse to such precautions with one's own sister. But Julia positively persists in denying the charge, that, without procuring distinct proof, I have no excuse for forbidding that vile fellow the house, and preserving the honour of my family."

Again the prim and prudish Blickling executed his favourite evolution; when, startled by a sudden burst of laughter at the bookroom window, both looked up, and perceived the blooming face of the widow MacGlashun laughing under her gipsey-hat; while Ned Warton stood by her side, with a countenance as malignantly significant as that of Vathek's Giaour. Mary-Matilda rose with ineffable dignity; and the County Member again uncrossed his legs, and was on them in a moment.

"Observe, my dear madam, the corrupt condition of modern society," said he sententiously, as he threw open the door into the saloon. "Such is the depraved state of those unfortunate people's minds, that they are putting an evil construction on the innocent friendship existing between a woman so exemplary as you, a man so unsusceptible of immoral impressions as myself. Ah! madam!—ah! Mrs. Richard Martindale!—what is the world coming to!"

The evening arrived—the evening passed;—the eyes of Jack Cleverley's wife and Mrs. MacGlashun's sister were carefully fixed upon the proceedings of the delinquents;—but nothing transpired. The little widow was certainly looking very handsome, and danced beautifully and with great animation; but, as Mr. Blickling observed aside to his fair friend, "If she flirted at all, it was clearly quite as much with that eccentric old humourist, Warton, as with the valiant Jack." The ball passed off, as announced by the Hertford paper next morning, "with unexampled *éclat*." Most of the county grandees were absent from indisposition. Weippert's music was supposed to have gone by the wrong coach, for it never made its appearance. The Argands would not burn. The white soup was sour, and the lobster sallad sweet. Still, for a county-ball, the thing went off tolerably, and Mary-Matilda had the satisfaction, after breakfast next morning, of holding another jeremiad with the Member over the sinfulness of this corrupt generation, and of whispering to him that, notwithstanding all her vigilance of the night before, her own maid had detected the lady and gentleman stealing away together from the ball-room. Mr Blickling shook his head, and was evidently much hurt that so much turpitude should exist under the same roof with himself and his family;—but still he said nothing.

Mrs Richard Martindale dwelt much on this flagrant instance of his hypocrisy, when discussing the subject with her husband a few days afterwards, in consequence of a disgraceful discovery which had set Marygold Hill into consternation, and sent little Mrs Trotter back in disgrace to the fens;—besides very nearly driving the County Member from his seat, both in Herts and the House. Mrs Trotter's had been the white dress in the shrubbery; Mr Blickling's the bay mare that stood so quiet beside the railings of the shrubbery. But Mrs MacGlashun had no leisure to upbraid either of her sisters with the aspersions thrown on her fair fame at Jack Cleverley's expense. Apprehensive of the coming storm and the demur it might occasion in her old beau's intentions, she was already off to Hertford in a post-chaise, with Edward Warton, Esq. and a special license!

"A pretty example have we set in the neighbourhood," faltered poor Mrs Richard, who was confined to her bed with genuine indisposition, occasioned by this double shock. "In London this disgraceful affair would very soon blow over; but I forsee no end to the tittle-tattle it will produce, happening at this season of the year, and at—our Place in the country!"—

What could the Martindales now do but hide their mortification in town. But this was, if possible, worse. They got rid of the O'Callaghans by main force, and after the Captain having made himself comfortable by shooting his brother-in-law's pheasants, drinking toddy, and taming hunters, began to talk of the "paltry upstartness of a place compared with a fine ould ancient castle descending from father to son, from generation to generation.

Worse luck attended Mary-Matilda in town. Her gowns were old-fashioned, Lady Kedgeree had got a new gossip, Mrs Calicut met her, and a law-suit was commenced about a flaw in the title of Marygold Hill. Richard was obliged to commence a brick-work on "our Place in the Country," to secure them from the difficulties into which the purchase had thrown him, while the Marriots got a marble bath in the lady's dressing-room, and trimmed their muslin curtains with red lace. Poor Mrs Richard!

With her own family, meanwhile, Mrs Richard had resigned all intercourse. Sir Joseph Grinderwell affected to resent her negligence as the origin of his sister's indiscretion; and her younger brothers were eating government bread in different parts of the globe;—one as a resident in Newfoundland, one as a consul in Cochin-China, and one thirty feet below the level of the Thames, as clerk in a frog-trap at Somerset House. She had no one to quarrel with, no one to molest;—even the humble Jacob Martindale treated her with that frigid deference which forbids all approach to familiarity; and Mary-Matilda, who had been so lively at Grinderwell House, so merry at Cheltenham, so happy in Wales, so contented at Bath, so dissipated at Weymouth, so courted in Harley Street, discovered, that in the country, to which she had restricted the remainder of her days, she was likely to be dull, dispirited, despised and lonely. It was very little consolation to her to feel that she was proprietress of a place in the country, now that her means no longer permitted her to enliven it with entertainments, fill it with company, and assume a leading part in the neighbourhood. She took it into her head they were designated all over the country as "the Martindales of the Brickfield;" while the more moral circles probably pointed her out to abhorrence, as a member of that obliquitous family which had induced the County Member into backsliding.

"Ah Richard!" she exclaimed, when another winter was about to set in, and they had not so much as the O'Callaghans at their disposal to assist them in making war against the long evenings and snowy mornings, "I shall never forgive you for having made me renounce that comfortable Harley Street house for this desolate place. To live as we did there, forms the utmost limit of my desires;—good establishment, pleasant dinner parties, winter at Brighton, summer at Hastings;—the children always well, the servants always happy;—the Kedgerees, the Calicuts, and poor dear Camphor, the apothecary, within a stone's throw.—It really was madness on your part to set your heart upon a country life. You are not fit for it, my dear, you are really not fit for it.—You cannot do without your club; or your morning's lounge with Sir Hookah Smith, and Sir Brown Kedgeree. I wish to heaven I had been as well aware when you took this place, as I am now, of your inaptitude to rural pleasures; nothing should have induced me to allow you to bury us for life, in order that you might gratify the pride of the Martindale family by purchasing a place in their native country. There are the poor girls who will soon be wanting masters, and who will be brought up mere *Hottentots*, (I beg your pardon,—believe me, I intended no allusion to your early avocations,) and turn out perhaps vulgar fine ladies, like your niece Clotilda."

"Or worse, like *your* two flirting sisters," might have burst from the lips of a man less mildly quiescent than the patient Richard. He, however, contented himself with observing, "Well, my love, we must hope for the best. Your mother may perhaps take it into her head to leave you enough to enable you to make a little visit to town every spring; or perhaps—"

"A letter by express, Sir," said the footman, placing a voluminous dispatch in the hands of Mr. Martindale, and quitting the room.

"What is it, what is it?" cried his wife, breathless with consternation. "Is it any thing about little Grinderwell? —any thing from Eton?"

"No."

"Any thing regarding my sisters?"

"No."

"In a word, are the tidings good or bad?—your banker, your agent?"—

"I hardly know whether to call them good *or* bad," said Richard, much perplexed; "for you women are so confoundedly capricious, that one can never anticipate on what opinion you may finally anchor."

"For Heaven's sake, do not prose so when I am dying with curiosity. Give me the letter!"

"Tell me first," said Martindale, grown cunning with experience, and placing the folded epistle carefully in his pocket, "tell me first, candidly and explicitly, *do* you repent having purchased Marygold Hill; and would you, if you could, return to the freedom of a London life?"

"That I would!"—ejaculated Mrs. Richard, firmly believing such a release to be beyond her husband's power. "If we could but get rid of this estate, I should be the happiest woman in the world."

"I give you joy, then, my dear Mary-Matilda," continued he, drily. "Latitat informs me that we have lost our suit. The title cannot be made good; and, after all, Marygold Hill returns to the possession of its lawful owner. I shall be a loser to the amount of some thousands by the money I have expended on the improvements; in consideration of which, the adverse party have very liberally offered me a long lease of the place on easy terms; and should you feel any reluctance in quitting it—"

"No, no, no!" cried Mrs. Martindale. "Pray let us return to the mode of life for which we were born, and which suits us best. I have had quite enough of Marygold Hill. Believe me, I have lost all predilection for— A PLACE IN THE COUNTRY."

THE WILLOW TREES.

A SKETCH.

"They best can paint them,
Who have felt them most."

THE 8th of July 1824, was a happy day to the young people of B—— Hall, for it was the young heir's thirteenth birth-day; and his sister Sophy and he were to give a ball to their young companions. This ball had been looked forward to with joy by many a one, but by none with such delight as by little Emily, the minister's niece. What was a ball? Would uncle be there? Would aunt Anna? And Frederic was thirteen! How very old! Would she give balls when she was thirteen? With these and such like questions she overwhelmed aunt Anna, and sometimes even her grave uncle William was roused from his studies, by the joyful exclamations of his darling niece. At length the day arrived. Aunt Anna dressed her; and as uncle William lifted her into Sir Henry A——'s carriage, which called to take her to B——, he thought that Lady A——'s French waiting-maid had not made the Misses A—— look half so pretty as his own little Emily. And so thought Frederic;—for, in spite of all Sophy's notions of decorum, he insisted on dancing almost the whole night with Emily, to the utter neglect of Miss Harriet A——'s, as she thought, superior attractions. But she did not mind, not she. What a fool the boy must be! Only think the little minx never got lessons from Monsieur Pironette;—and she told us in the carriage that she had no waiting-maid to dress her hair! It curled itself, and nurse combed it. At last, Miss A——, and her sister and brothers, and all the other guests, went home, except Emily, who was to stay all night at B——. Emily was asleep the moment she laid her head on the pillow. But she dreamed all night of the ball. And Frederic could think of nothing but the blue eyes and curling hair of the minister's little Emily. It was late next morning ere Sophy came to awake her. What would aunt Anna think? She had never slept so long in the morning before. "Perhaps you was never so long up at night before," said Sophy, smiling.

After breakfast, Sophy was busy within doors, but Frederic took Emily to the garden, where they amused themselves with his flowers and his rabbits. Then they went to the river, for Frederic wanted a stick; and when they had cut a bunch of willows, Emily said, "If we were to plant these they would grow beautiful trees, like the one in uncle's shrubbery. It was just a little willow stick, and it has grown a great tree." "Oh! yes," cried Frederic, "I will plant one for you and one for myself, and see how big they shall be when I come home next vacation." Frederic had just planted his willows when a servant came to tell them Mr C―― had called to take Miss Emily home. Emily said good bye to her kind friends at B――, and returned to the Manse with uncle William; and much had she to tell to aunt Anna when she got home, though she said she liked better to play in the garden with Frederic, than to be at the ball. Years passed on, and still Frederic thought there was no one so amiable and so graceful at his birth-day balls as the unaffected Emily. Sometimes, when Frederic's father was shewing his grounds to his visiters, he would point out the thriving young willows, and every body agreed that nothing ever grew so fast as those trees. But Sophy would look slily at Frederic and Emily, and say, "Ah! papa, there is something grows faster." It was exactly eight years after the planting of these trees, when one day Mr B―― was shewing them as usual, and, as usual, every one said nothing ever grew so fast, till Sophy cried, "Ah! papa, there is something grows faster." Emily wondered what Sophy could mean, and so deeply was she taken up with her own thoughts, that she was surprised, on awakening from her reverie, to find the company had left the river and she was alone with Frederic. She wished to follow them, but Frederic had something to say to her. What he said I do not know, but Emily blushed deeply, and whispered something of aunt Anna and my uncle. A few weeks after this there was a small party assembled in the parlour at F―― Manse. Frederic was there—but where was Emily? The door opened, and the minister entered leading in his beloved Emily, now a blushing bride, and gave her to the happy Frederic. Then, with faltering voice and tottering knees, pronounced the nuptial benediction! We shall not tell how lovely the bride looked, or how aunt Anna smiled and wept by turns. But when Mr B―― kissed the forehead of his son's beautiful bride, he said, "Ah! Sophy, now I know what grew faster than the willow trees!!!"   H. R.

CONJUGAL DISCIPLINE.

There flourished in a market-town,
To riches born, to riches grown,
A pair who, free from flagrant strife,
Had reached the middle age of life.
The man was of the gentle kind,
Not ill his person or his mind;
Expert at fishing, and at fowling,
At hunting, racing, or at bowling.
He knew what squire might wish to know, Sir;
But then, hard fate! he was a grocer:
And, spite of all his wife could say,
Would sometimes work, as well as play.
His wife was not unworthy praise,
As women went in former days;
In her own family, so good,
The master managed as he would.
When jars their union discomposed—
Her passion often inward glowed—
Her tongue in anger she would hold,
And rarely condescend to scold;
Her voice not shrill, but rather sweet;
Her conduct virtuous and discreet;
One only failing malice spied,
One only fault, and that was—pride:—
(For country lasses, by the bye,
Can sometimes hold their heads as high,
And be as proud of dower and birth,
As any Princess upon earth.)
One day his business ran so high,
His shop so full of company,
So quick his customer's demands,
He needed more than all his hands;—
Down comes his wife with careless air,
But not to help him—never fear:
Far be from her a thought so mean:
She came to see and to be seen,
Nor e'er intended to do good,
But stand in way of those who would.
While she stands there, a servant comes,
Post haste for spices and for plums,
Who many a mile had home to go:
The grocer peevish 'gan to grow,
To see his dearest loiter so.
Howe'er, he mild accosts her,—"Pray,
Do give your help, or go your way;
Why, otherwise, did you come down?"
She answered only with a frown;
But such a frown as seemed t' express,
Her portion, beauty, and her dress.
"Well, if you will not weigh the ware,
Pray, put it in the basket there."
She turned her back without rejoinder,
And left her spouse to fume behind her.
"Well, now the things are all put in it,
Perhaps you'll be so good as pin it."
When a fourth time her husband spoke,
The dame her sullen silence broke,
In very short, but full reply:—
"I pin your basket! No, not I!"
Enraged, he snatched the footman's stick,
And laid it on her shoulders quick.
Surprised, as never struck before,
And feeling much, but fearing more,
For fear of what might farther come on't,
She pinned the basket in a moment.
Then Tom rode off in merry mood,
And laughed and *tee-hee*'d by the road.
Pleased with the delicate conceit,
To see so fine a lady beat,
He wished the deed at home was done,
And could not help comparison;
For his own mistress was as fine,
As her who suffered discipline;
As proud, as high-born, and as rich,
But not so continent of speech.
At dinner-time, the waggish knave
Was sometimes fleering, then was grave;
Now bites his lips, and quickly after
Bursts out into a peal of laughter.
Quoth Madam, with majestic look,
Who servants' freedom could not brook,
Nor laughter in her presence bear,—
"What ails the saucy fellow there?
What makes the coxcomb giggle so?
Does not the fool his distance know?"
But angry words and looks were vain,
Again he giggled, and again.
The master said,—"Now, Tom, at least,
If you must laugh, pray tell the jest;
That, if 'tis worth our hearing, we
In mirth may bear you company."
Tom up, and told the story roundly,
How a fair dame was cudgelled soundly.
Scarce Madam heard the whole narration,
Until she flew in monstrous passion.

"Was ever anything so base?
A lady strike in market-place!
And was it fitting, pray, that she
Should touch his dirty grocery?
Not pin the basket! beat her for it!
I did not think she would have bore it;
A nasty rogue, a woman strike!
In short, you men are all alike."
Tom now grew merrier, not sadder,
Which made his mistress ten times madder;
Who, starting up, in fury, straight
Vowed she would break the rascal's pate.
Her husband, rising to assuage
The o'erbearing tempest of her rage,
But, as her hand he did not mind,
He caught the rap for Tom designed;
And, not approving of the jest,
Repaid the same with interest.
Tom ran down stairs, as was most fitting
And left his mistress to her beating.
Below stairs was a kitchen-maid,
To whom our hero courtship made.
As cool as you could well desire
For one so conversant with fire,
Says Moll,—"Above stairs, what's the matter;
I never heard so loud a clatter?"
For fear of spoiling his amour, he
Was backward to relate the story.
"I should be sorry, Moll, to see
A difference rise 'tween you and me.
'Tis but a trifle: let it go—
What signifies it you to know?"
"Nay, then I must;" and out it came,
And set her womanhood in flame.
"A trifle!" said she; "Tom, a trifle!
I think my mistress in the right;
With women only cowards fight."
So high at last the contest rose,
From words they quickly came to blows.
The blows so hastily were laid,
The lover and his dear cook-maid,
In spite of all the love they boasted,
Were both confoundedly *rib-roasted.*

It matters not how small the grain,
If but continued be the train.

THE GENTLEMAN.—The term gentlemen is as well known and recognised among highwaymen and pickpockets, as with the highest duke in the land. No doubt, their interpretations of the term do not agree. But if the most generally accepted definition of the term be admitted, that it includes all persons of good education and good manners, I venture to say, without fear of contradiction from any one who has had opportunities of seeing the mass of the population of the United States,—the north and the south, the east and the west—that that great country contains an infinitely greater number of gentlemen than any other country which exists, or ever has existed, on the face of the earth. I am glad to be supported in this opinion by at least one late British traveller in America, Mr. Ferrall, who says, "that all in America are gentlemen."—*Stuart's Three Years in America.*

TO THE LITTLE LADY—THE VOTARY OF HIGH MEN.
Lady, excuse me, but, in my idea,
  Your marriage is extremely indiscreet;
You're but a little biped, while, 'tis clear,
  Your husband runs about upon six feet!
And, I am confident, one moment's thought
  Would have betrayed the folly of the whim;
For its quite evident that you're too short
  A gentlewoman to be-long to him.
Yet, doubtlessly, he holds you very dear;
  And if he does'nt its extremely funny;
For, though you'd twenty thousand pounds a-year,
  You'd still be very little for the money.
And one like him to marry, I declare,
  A little lady, isn't a tall fair!
                                    T. HOOD.

COLUMN FOR THE YOUNG.

"A RIGHTEOUS MAN REGARDETH THE LIFE OF HIS BEAST."

A man of kindness, to his beast is kind;
But brutal actions show a brutal mind.
Remember, He who made *thee,* made the brute—
Who gave *thee* speech and reason, form'd *him* mute.
He can't complain; but God's all-seeing eye
Beholds *thy* cruelty, and hears his cry.
He was designed thy servant, not thy *drudge;*
And *know,* that *his* Creator is *thy Judge.*

THOUGHTLESS CRUELTY.

CHILDREN may often practise the greatest cruelty, to insects in particular, from ignorance of the pain which they inflict. The fault is then more chargeable on those who should have instructed them better, than upon the inconsiderate children. I shall not describe the cruelties often practised on beetles, house-flies, and chafers; but tell a short story which should prove a lesson to mothers, and all who have the charge of young people, as well as to children themselves. Mr. Joseph Strutt, a late celebrated English antiquarian, when a little boy, was one day surprised by his mother, who detested every species of cruelty, "spinning a chafer." He was so much delighted with the "spinning," that is, the torturing struggles of the insect to escape, that he did not perceive her enter the room. When she saw what he was about, without saying a word, she pinched his ear, so smartly, that he cried for mercy. This scene ended, she thus addressed her son, "that insect has its feelings as you have! Do you not see that the swift vibration of its wings are occasioned by the torment it sustains? You have pinched its body without remorse. I have only pinched your ear; and yet you have cried out, as if I had killed you." Young Strutt felt his excellent mother's admonition in its full force, liberated the poor May-fly, and never afterwards impaled another.

TO A HIGHLAND INNKEEPER.

Your salmon are so fat and red,
  Your fowls so thin and blue,
'Tis seen which Providence has fed,
  And which were rear'd by you.
                        Epigrammatist's Annual.

CONTENTS OF NO. XXX.

Notes of the Month...145
Air...145
Chemical Recreations.......................................147
Mrs. Arbuthnot, &c...149
COLUMN FOR THE LADIES—Revolution in Dress.
  German Peasantry—Not yet Fifteen......................150
The Samphire Gatherer......................................151
Hebridian Poetry..ib.
Elements of Thought..152
THE STORY-TELLER—" My Place in the Country"............153
The Willow Trees...155
Conjugal Discipline..158
COLUMN FOR THE YOUNG.—A Righteous Man regardeth the
  Life of his Beast—Thoughtless Cruelty.................160
SCRAPS—The Gentleman—Sonnet, To the Little Lady—To a
  Highland Innkeeper.......................................160

EDINBURGH: Printed by and for JOHN JOHNSTONE, 19, St. James's Square.—Published by JOHN ANDERSON, Jun., Bookseller, 55, North Bridge Street, Edinburgh; by JOHN MACLEOD, and ATKINSON & Co., Booksellers, Glasgow; and sold by all Booksellers and Vendors of Cheap Periodicals.

THE Schoolmaster,
AND
EDINBURGH WEEKLY MAGAZINE.

CONDUCTED BY JOHN JOHNSTONE.

THE SCHOOLMASTER IS ABROAD.—LORD BROUGHAM.

No. 33.—Vol. II.　　SATURDAY, MARCH 16, 1833.　　Price Three-Halfpence.

LEONARD'S VOYAGE TO THE WESTERN COASTS OF AFRICA.

THE SLAVE TRADE AS IT EXISTS.

There is a very general impression abroad in this country, that though the traffic in slaves is still carried on to a certain extent upon the coasts of Africa, it is much circumscribed by the treaties between Great Britain and her allies, and that, at any rate, its attendant horrors are greatly mitigated. This idea, we lament to say, is entirely erroneous; the trade exists at the present moment in full activity; with this difference, that British vessels dare no longer openly engage in it, though British seamen, British colonial merchants, and British capital, all co-operate in the iniquity. And, with this farther difference, that to the wickedness and outrage of the former trade, are now added the pirate's worst vices of license and brutality; and wholesale cruelties more revolting and fiendlike than those which distinguished the traffic in its former open state.

Tait's Magazine, which has been the uncompromising enemy of slavery, has this month brought under our notice a late work which places the trade, as it is carried on at the present moment, in the true light, and shows it to be polluted with more than its original treachery and barbarity. Mr. Leonard, a professional man of good education and talent, sailed lately in the Dryad, a King's ship, appointed to the West-Coast station, for the prevention of the slave trade. Strange things were made known to him, or fell under his notice during his long cruize in 1830-31, and he has performed a duty to God and man in proclaiming them.—The opinion is not peculiar to Mr. Leonard that the French Government, whether the younger or the elder branch of the Bourbons be at its head, has never yet been sincere in wishing to put down the slave trade; for if so, with the cordial concurrence of Britain, nothing could have been easier than to give the purpose efficacy. The treaty with France for the suppression is worse than nugatory. She refuses the right of search conceded by the other states; so that a slaver of any other nation has only to hoist the *tri-color*, and set at nought, and defy, under this guise, all those measures for the protection of the Africans, which the justice and humanity of the British people, and liberal portion of the Legislature, have forced upon the powers of Europe. Mr. Leonard relates twenty instances of the indifference or supineness of the French prevention-ships to their duty; and shows us many of the elusory nature of the provisions of the existing treaties; lax in their letter, and in their spirit a mockery. "No French slave-ship," he says, "can be detained by us, or indeed by ships of war of any nation but their own; and, as the French prevention squadron on the coast of Africa, although nearly as large as ours, possess but little cruising zeal, the trade is carried on, now under the *white flag*, now under the *tri-color*, to an enormous extent. The Portuguese and Spanish slave-dealers, fully aware of their immunity, take advantage of the shelter which it affords, and obtain French papers for the ships they employ in the trade."

Of that trade—that man-abhorred, God-condemned trade, we can only speak in its middle state. We shall neither look back to the brutal violence of deed, the cruel rapacity of motive, which have dragged the miserable Africans from their *homes*; nor forward to the fate which awaits them when the colonial slave-mart shall have severed every tie of kindred, and transferred them to their final house of bondage, and to the legalised lash of the *lawful* proprietor of their flesh and blood; and of all those free energies of body and mind which man claims as the unalienable gift of his Creator, and of which he can no more denude himself, nor be justly deprived, than of his organs and functions of action and thought—than of his life or his immortality. We restrict our view to Mr. Leonard's representations of the intermediate condition of the slaves, in their transfer from their native villages to the islands, and quote by no means the most flagrant cases that he has recorded:—

"18th February. [1831.] His Majesty's brig Plumper arrived to-day from the river Nunez, where she had been despatched in search of a slave vessel, reported to be lying there under Spanish colours. The vessel was found; but she hoisted French colours, and, of course, could not be touched. Several hundred slaves, ready for embarkation, were lodged in a factory, near the spot where she lay, waiting the arrival of a few more, to complete the number she was able to cram into her hold.

"3d March. [1831.] A schooner, under Spanish colours, called the Primeira, arrived here to-day, with three hundred and eleven slaves on board; detained by the Black Joke, tender to this ship, on the 22d ultimo, off Cape Mount, bound from the river Gallinas to the Havanna. From the accounts brought by the captors, there is a very great number of vessels between this and Cape Palmos waiting to take in slaves. The tender, on first seeing the Primeira, fired several blank cartridges to bring her to, but paying no attention to this mild injunction, shot was had recourse to, one of which took effect, killing two of the slaves and the cook of the vessel, and wounding two slaves, the mate, and four of the crew. The slaves consist of one hundred and eleven men, forty-five women, ninety-eight boys, fifty-three girls, and four infants at the breast, one of whom was born since the period of capture, whose mother, unhappy creature, sickly and emaciated, was suckling it on deck, with hardly a rag to cover either herself or her offspring.

"The small space in which these unfortunate beings are huddled together is almost incredible. The schooner is only one hundred and thirty tons burden, and the slave deck only two feet two inches high, so that they can hardly even sit upright. The after part of the deck is occupied by the women and children, separated by a wooden partition from the other slaves. The horrors of this infernal apartment—the want of air—the suffocating heat—the filth—the stench—may be easily imagined; although it is remarked that this ship is one of the cleanest that ever was brought to the colony. The men were bound together in twos, by irons riveted round the ancles. On their arrival these chains were removed, and they appeared much gratified. The countenances of all seemed lighted up with satisfaction at the prospect of being put on shore, towards which they often turned to gaze, with an expression of wonder and impatience. I went on board to visit the wounded. About one half of the boys were circumcised. I could not ascertain that they belonged to a separate tribe, although their general appearance seemed to me slightly different from the rest. Slave vessels, in the rivers adjacent to Sierra Leone, receive considerable assistance in the pursuit of their illicit traffic from some of the merchants of this colony, in the shape of articles of trade and provisions; which trifling circumstance, as it pays well, and is no direct engagement in the slave trade, these peace and farthing individuals may, perhaps, very well reconcile to their consciences. We learn that the Primeira was supplied with bread from a vessel belonging to a merchant of Freetown."

But this bread supply is nothing to what daily passes in a colony maintained by Britain at vast expense of life and money to prevent the slave trade. *Kidnapping* is the constant practice of many of the colonists—*connivance* is a general profession. We give one specimen of the efficacy of the existing treaties. Information was received by the Dryad, that a Spanish brig and schooner, ready to receive slaves on board, was lying in the river Bonny. A tender was despatched to look after them; and mark the result.

"Here are two vessels fitted for the reception of slaves, and anchored at a notorious slave-port, ready to take on board their wretched victims, whenever the number which it is possible to crowd into their holds shall be brought from the interior; and we, although fully aware that they are so fitted, and that such is their intention, cannot legally prevent the inhuman act; when, with the greatest ease imaginable, were the dictates of humanity not obstructed by the cold-blooded arm of the law, our tender or our boats might enter the river, capture, or destroy them, and thereby effectually prevent them from accomplishing their nefarious purpose. But no: the poor Africans must be suffered to be collected together in the "factory," like cattle, until the numerous cargo is completed—we must suffer them to be shipped and subjugated to every horror, and to all the degradation of the slavehold—we must permit, and in a manner countenance a crime which we know is about to be perpetrated of the most diabolical nature, when it might be so easily prevented! Were the commanders of his Majesty's ships, as I have said before, to act otherwise, the most heavy pecuniary penalties would be awarded against them by the law. Therefore, until, as has been already said, the slave trade shall be held, by a law of nations, to be piracy, and until all vessels found fitted for the purpose of carrying it on shall be held to have actually engaged in it, all our efforts to put a stop to this vile traffic must be fruitless."

Mr. Leonard returns again and again to this point.

"The pertinacious determination of the French Government not to grant us the right of search and capture of the numerous vessels we meet with, under the French flag, engaged in this hateful traffic—the extensive annual importation of slaves into the French colonies of Guadaloupe and Martinique, in the face of the established laws, by evident connictation or tacit consent, on the part of the local authorities—the fact of the Portuguese Government agent, at Boa Vista, being openly one of the most extensive slave-dealers on the coast of Africa, and continuing in his illicit course so long unobstructed,—all serve to shew, that these Governments are regardless of their engagements, and have not a genuine desire towards the abolition of negro slavery; but endeavour to screen from merited punishment those unprincipled adventurers, by whom the restrictions of the treaties between these Governments and our own are so flagrantly violated; and it is evident, from the style of our remonstrances, that we cannot command upright dealing, where the interest of these powers is concerned.

"While there are so many facilities afforded to the subjects of these foreign Governments for carrying on this illicit trade, all our single-handed endeavours towards its suppression must prove worse than useless, as will be seen in the sequel. Until it shall be declared piracy by a law of nations, and the equipment of vessels for the slave trade shall be held an actual engagement in it—and until the most cordial union and co-operation, and the most energetic measures are adopted by all civilized nations towards its suppression—and the utmost extent of punishment inflicted on those who bid defiance to the laws enacted against it,—the trade of blood can never be entirely put an end to."

Any one possessed of human feelings, who shall read the extract below, will surely not lack motive to co-operate in atoning for this horrible injustice,—in wiping out this foul blot on European civilization, and on the very name of man. The scene is a Spanish slave brig captured by the Black Joke, an English tender.

"Immediately after the vessel was secured, the living were found sitting on the heads and bodies of the dead and the dying below. Witnessing their distress, the captors poured a large quantity of water into a tub for them to drink out of; but, being unused to such generosity, they merely imagined that their usual scanty daily allowance of half a pint per man was about to be served out; and when given to understand that they might take as much of it, and as often as they felt inclined; they seemed astonished, and rushed in a body, with headlong eagerness, to dip their parched and feverish tongues in the refreshing liquid. Their heads became wedged in the tub, and were with some difficulty got out—not until several were nearly suffocated in its contents. The drops that fell on the deck were lapped and sucked up with a most frightful eagerness. Jugs were also obtained, and the water handed round to them; and in their precipitation and anxiety to obtain relief from the burning thirst which gnawed their vitals, they madly bit the vessels with their teeth, and champed them into atoms. Then, to see the look of gratification—the breathless unwillingness to part with the vessel, from which, by their glistening eyes, they seemed to have drawn such exquisite enjoyment! Only half satisfied, they clung to it, though empty, as if it were more dear to them, and had afforded them more of earthly bliss, than all the nearest and dearest ties of kindred and affection. It was a picture of such utter misery, from without want, more distressing than any one can conceive who has not witnessed the horrors attendant on the slave trade on the coast of Africa, or who has not felt, for many hours, the cravings of a burning thirst under a tropical sun. On their way ashore to this island from the prize—their thirst still unquenched—they lapped the salt water from the boat's side. The sea to them was new, until they tasted all its bitterness; they, no doubt, looked upon it as one of their own expansive fresh water streams, in which they were wont to bathe, or drink with unrestrained freedom and enjoyment. Before they were landed, many of the Africans already liberated at this settlement went on board to see them, and found among them several of their friends and relations. The meeting, as may be supposed, was, for the moment, one of pleasure, but soon changed into pain and grief. Can there be in Britain—the happy and the free—an individual with a heart in his bosom, who will, after this, advocate slavery? A single fact like this overthrows all the plausible sophistry which such an individual may make use of to obtain partisans, besides those who, like himself, are interested in its support. Such converts to the creed of the right of property in human flesh are much misled. They have only shewn to them the bright side of the picture—the comparatively happy (yet truly wretched) condition of the slaves in our West India colonies. They know nothing of the withering horrors daily taking place on the coast of this desolated and unhappy land, from which between sixty or eighty thousand of its poor unoffending children are forcibly abstracted annually—cruelly torn from home, friends, and kindred—from all that can alone make a life of wretchedness tolerable. The Spanish crew, with the exception of a few sent up in the prize to Sierra Leone, were kept prisoners for some time at Fernando Po, but were afterwards sent in the Atholl to the island of Anabona, where they were landed and turned adrift."

One more exhibition of the existing state of the traffic abolished by the British legislature, and by the faith of treaties, and suppressed at a very great annual expense to this distressed country.

"The Black Joke, while cruizing in the Bight of Benin, fell in with and captured, on the 20th of July, the Spanish schooner, Potosi, of ninety-eight tons, twenty-six men, and one hundred and ninety-one slaves on board, from Lagos to Havanna; and, on the 10th September, the two tenders, in company, chased into the river Bonny, and captured the brigs, Rapido and Regulo,—the former of one hundred and seventy-five tons, eight large guns, fifty-six men, and two hundred and four slaves; the latter, one hundred and forty-seven tons, (both Spanish admeasurement,) five large guns, fifty-men, and two slaves; both bound to Cuba. Connected with the capture of these vessels, a circumstance of the most horrid and revolting nature occurred, the relation of which will afford an additional instance of the cruelty and apathy of those who carry on the slave trade,—of the imperfection of the laws enacted for its suppression, as well as of the additional inhumanity entailed upon it by ourselves, as a consequence of the very imperfection of these laws. Both vessels were discovered at the entrance of the Bonny, having just sailed from thence; and, when chased by the tenders, put back, made all sail up the river, and ran on shore. During the chase, they were seen from our vessels to throw their slaves overboard, by twos, shackled together by the ancles, and left in this manner to sink, or swim, as they best could! Men, women, and young children, were seen, in great numbers, struggling in the water, by every one on board of the two tenders; and, dreadful to relate, upwards of a hundred and fifty of these wretched creatures perished in this way, without there being a hand to help them; for they had all disappeared before the tenders reached the spot, excepting two, who were fortunately saved by our boats from the element with which they were struggling. Several managed, with difficulty, as may be supposed, to swim on shore, and many were thrown into large canoes, and in that manner landed, and escaped death; but the multitude of dead bodies cast upon the beach, during the succeeding fortnight, painfully demonstrated that the account given to us, by the natives on the banks of the Bonny, of the extent of the massacre, had been far from exaggerated. The individuals whose lives had been saved by the boats, were two fine intelligent young men, riveted together by the ancles in the manner described. Both of them when recovered, pointed to the Rapido as the vessel from which they were thrown into the water. On board this vessel no slave was found; but her remorseless crew having been seen from both tenders busily engaged in their work of destruction, and as the two poor blacks, who endeavoured to express gratitude for their rescue by every means in their power, asserted, with horror and alarm depicted in every feature, that this was the vessel from which they were thrown, she was taken possession of. On board the Regulo only two hundred and four slaves were found remaining, of about four hundred and fifty."

In one month (October 1830) this active tender boarded five different French slave vessels, on board which were above *sixteen hundred slaves*, from the river Bonny alone. Ten more French vessels were then lying in a neighbouring river ready to take slaves on board. If this is much longer to go on, what becomes of the sincere wish of our own government for the suppression of the trade, admitting the cordiality of Louis Phillipe with the present cabinet, and its wholesome influence in French councils to be any thing more than a name. But one more short quotation and we have done. The censure it conveys need not be confined to the African colonies.

"It has been unfortunate for the improvement of Africa, as well as for the advancement of the interests of our settlements there, that the persons appointed to official situations have very generally made mere jobs of them; and as soon as they have served their end, of pocketing a considerable sum of money, or in some other way furthering their own private views, provided the climate spares their lives, they have scampered off, and left the settlement to the superintendence of other individuals, equally as ignorant and careless of its interests, and equally as solicitous of their own, as their predecessors. And this is one grand reason why I conceive that the natives or permanent residents, such as the Maroons at Sierra Leone, should be appointed, as soon as it can be done, to fill official situations, in preference to the factitious and ephemeral whites."

HOURS OF LABOUR FOR CHILDREN.

This is taken from a pamphlet published in Manchester, intended to shew that the children in the cotton factories are better off than in any other works, as their hours of work are only 69 hours a-week; and that the intended new law should extend to children in all factories. This is quite right.

Hours of Labour of other Trades in which children are employed in conjunction with adults (delivered in, and proved on oath, and inserted in Appendix to that Evidence, No. 34.)

Earthenware and Porcelain—Staffordshire and Derby, 12 to 15 hours daily.

File Cutters—Warrington, 72 hours weekly.

Nail Makers—Birmingham, (Children begin at nine years old) 12 hours daily.

Iron Works, Forges, and Mills—Warwickshire and Staffordshire—(Boys employed at eight years of age) 12 hours daily, and, in alternate weeks, 12 hours nightly.

Iron Founders—Ditto (Ditto) 12 hours daily.

Collieries—Ditto, (Boys begin at eight years old) 12 hours daily, under ground.

Ditto—Lancashire, (Ditto, ditto) 11 hours daily, under ground, 12 and 13 above ground.

Ditto—St. Helen's and Worsely, Girls as well as Boys are employed, ditto, ditto.

Glass Trade—Warwickshire and Staffordshire, Children employed from 9 to 10 years old, 12 hours daily; 12 hours nightly.

Wire Card Makers—Halifax, &c., Employ chiefly children 12 to 13 hours daily.

Watch Makers—Coventry, 12 hours daily in winter, 14 in summer.

Pin Makers—Warrington, Employ younger children than the cotton mills of that place, 14 hours daily.

Needle Makers—Gloucester, 13 hours daily.

Manufacturers of Arms—Birmingham, Children begin from seven to nine years old, 13 hours daily.

Calico Printing—Lancashire, Cheshire, Yorkshire, &c., Boys employed from eight years old and upwards, 12 to 14, 15, and 16 hours daily, sometimes all night.

Worsted Mills—Leeds, 13 hours daily.

Ditto—Halifax, 14 to 15 and 16 hours daily, and sometimes all night.

Ditto—Keighly, some of them all night.

Ditto—Exwick, 12 hours daily.

Ditto—Norwich, Girls begin at 10 years old, 14 hours daily, part of the people all night.

Ditto—Manchester, 14 hours daily.

Flax Mills—Leeds, &c., 13 hours daily.

Ditto—Halifax, 14, 15, and 16 hours daily, several of them all night.

Ditto—Shrewsbury, 71 hours weekly.

Hosiery—Leicester, Boys, girls, women and men employed 12 hours daily in winter, and 13 in summer.

Ditto—Nottingham, 15 hours daily.

Ditto—Mansfield, Employ a great number of children; hours longer than at any cotton mill in that neighbourhood.

Lace Manufactory—Ditto, Children employed as soon as they can use the needle, ditto, ditto.

Ditto—Nottingham, Children employed at seven years old and upwards, 12 hours daily.

Ditto—Tiverton, 14 hours daily.

Silk Mills—Derby, 72 hours weekly.

Ditto—Macclesfield, 76 hours weekly.

Ditto—Nottingham, Children employed at eight years old and upwards, 13 hours daily.

Ditto—Congleton, Employ near 2000 persons, of whom the greater part are children from five years old upwards, 12 hours daily.

Ditto—Stockport, Children as in cotton factories, hours as in cotton factories.

Power-Loom Weaving—Ditto, ditto, ditto, ditto.

Cotton Weavers by hand—Lancashire, Yorkshire, Cheshire, &c., Children at all ages work the same hours as adults, 14 to 16 hours daily.

Draw-Boy Weaving—Paisley, Children from seven years old upwards extensively employed as drawers to weavers, 15 hours daily.

Ditto—Glasgow, In one village, near 1000 children, from 8 to 12 years old, are employed till 11 or 12 at night, or even till one in the morning.

NEW ROUTE TO INDIA.

The project of shortening the communication between Europe and India, by avoiding the circuit of the Cape, has been at all times a favourite subject of theory; but unaccountably (when we consider the practicability of its accomplishment, and the vast results which it would involve) neglected as regards any practical notice. The establishment of a route which should reduce by one-half the long sea-distance by which our vast Indian dependencies are at present reached, would bring with it advantages in which all the European nations would be more or less sharers; but, to Britain, besides the great commercial benefits which the scheme includes, it offers the high political good of drawing more nearly together the remote portions of her scattered empire. Captain Chesney has, it appears, been for some time engaged in ascertaining the feasibility of this project, and surveying and comparing the different routes by which it might be effected. The three lines of communication which have come under his notice are,—that by a canal connecting the Mediterranean with the Red Sea,—that by which the Mediterranean should be connected with the Euphrates,—and a third, suggested by himself, communicating between the Red Sea and the Nile, through the Lake of Menzaleh. It is understood that the Pacha and the Sultan are both friendly to any design which should render the Euphrates navigable; and that river has been sounded by Captain Chesney, undeterred by dangers and difficulties, as far as the town of Bir, full eleven hundred miles up the stream, and to within twenty hours' journey of Aleppo, or fifty of the Gulf of Scanderoon. The reports contain the result of his inquiries, including a fair statement of the difficulties necessary to be overcome, details as to the capabilities and aspect of the country, and the dispositions of its inhabitants, and sketches of the kind of steam-boats which would be necessary for navigating the Euphrates,—the whole accompanied by maps and plans, and forming a highly valuable guide to those who shall come after him in the labours to which they refer. The routes by the Euphrates and the Nile, Captain Chesney states to be both perfectly practicable, but only so for the transport of letters or light goods. They cannot be made sufficiently open for the passage of the stately vessels with which the Company trade to the East. It will be seen, therefore, from the following passage, that his surveys terminate in a recommendation of the ancient plan for connecting the Red Sea with the Mediterranean.

"Any of these routes, however, which may be adopted, will probably only pave the way to the realization of the grand idea, so long indulged in England, and other parts of Europe, of connecting the Mediterranean with the Red Sea; a little time will probably remove the ill-founded apprehension of increasing the height of the former, by the influx of the latter; for, whatever natural causes can be supposed to exist, likely to maintain the Red Sea at a higher level, can hardly fail to influence, equally, the Mediterranean at the distance of little more than one degree; the land, it is true, shelves gradually from the Red Sea to the western shore of the Isthmus, at a mean difference of eighteen feet, according to the French engineers. But it is very questionable whether the sea itself is really higher, communicating, as it does already, with the Mediterranean, round Africa; but, even if it could prove so, an additional inlet will no more increase the height of the latter sea than do the unceasing, and infinitely *more* voluminous ones, pouring in from the Atlantic on one side, and Black Sea on the other; for the surplus is, and equally would be, disposed of by evaporation, when *seemingly* greater, because the influx must be regulated by the quantity of water exhaled; and, I apprehend, can neither be more nor less, when supplied through *one* or *six* inlets; on which principle, the Mediterranean (when it shall communicate) would as readily give to, as receive from the Red Sea; were not the temperature of the latter, and its exhalation, lessened by the cool north winds prevailing during the heat of the year; for which reason, only a moderate current may be expected to run into the Mediterranean; and it is in fact rather to be feared that such an inlet would not give a sufficient body of water to open a noble passage for ships of moderate burden, than that any prejudicial increase should be the consequence, to the shores of the Mediterranean. As to the executive part, there is but one opinion,—there are no serious natural difficulties, not a single mountain intervenes, scarcely what deserves to be called a hillock; and, in a country where labour can be had without limit, and at a rate infinitely below that of any other part of the world, the expense would be a moderate one for a single nation, and scarcely worth dividing between the great kingdoms of Europe, who would be benefited by the measure. Were the Pacha and Sultan to consent, heartily, the former could employ five hundred thousand Arabs on this work, as he did on the Mamoudieh Canal; feeding them out of his stores, so as to put nearly the whole of the contracted sum into his pocket.

Mahomed Ali is fond of speculations, and this would be a grand and beneficial one for the world, as well as a paying one for his coffers."—*United Service Gazette.*

FIRST LINES OF MECHANICS.

EVERY *body* continues in its state of rest, or of uniform motion in a right line, unless compelled to change that state by force impressed upon it. All change of motion is proportioned to the force impressed, and is made in the direction of that force. Action and reaction are always equal and opposite ; or the mutual actions of two bodies are always equal and in contrary directions :—These three general facts are denominated the laws of motion ; they form the axioms in the science of mechanics ; and all the facts and inferences which relate to the motion of bodies presuppose their truth, and are deducible from them.

When a body is simultaneously acted upon by two forces, the one of which would carry it in one direction, and the other in another, it will move in a line betwixt the two. Thus, if a piece of wood be thrown into a river, when the wind blows right across, it will be carried to the other side, but lower down. If the two forces are uniform, the body moves through the diagonal of a parallelogram ; but if only one of the forces is uniform, and the other constantly accelerating or retarding, the body passes through a curve ; thus, when a stone is thrown from the hand, the force impressed upon it tends to make it go on uniformly in the direction given to it ; but, in consequence of the action of gravity, it is drawn more and more from the straight line in which it set off, till it is at last brought to the ground. The two forces here acting upon it make it describe a curve, which is called a parabola. The planets are kept in their orbit by the actions of two forces, the one drawing them to the sun, the other inclining them to fly off at a tangent ; the consequence is, (both forces being constant,) that they revolve in orbits nearly circular.

The *Momentum* of a moving body is its weight combined with the velocity of its motion. Let us take a ball of lead and lay it on the ground, its weight will press on it ; but let us give it velocity also by throwing it on the ground, it will then have momentum, and make a mark. Sand is employed for shooting small birds which it is intended to kill without injuring their plumage ; sand blown by the wind would have no effect. Momentum may be increased by increasing either the velocity or the weight of a body ; and its amount may always be estimated, by multiplying the weight and velocity together. It was on the principle that the momentum of a body is augmented by increasing its velocity, that, in ancient naval battles, the rowers strained with all their might at the onset ; it is on the same principle that a ram, previous to striking, moves a little backward ; and the same principle explains the battering-ram and many other warlike instruments of the ancients.

All bodies near our earth are drawn towards it, and in a direct line towards its centre, by the force of gravity. If, from the top of a high tower or precipice, a stone be dropped, whatever number of feet it falls in the first second, it will fall three times as many in the second, five times as many in the third, seven times as many in the fourth, and so on. It falls, therefore, four times as much in two seconds as it does in one second, nine times as much in three, and sixteen times as much in four seconds. Therefore, to find how far a body falls in any given time, in other words, to find the height of the tower or precipice, multiply the space through which it falls in the first second by the square of the number of seconds. By experiment it is found, that a body falls 16 feet 1 inch in the first second ; in two seconds, therefore, it will fall 64 feet 4 inches ; in three seconds, 144 feet 9 inches, &c. A body rolling down an inclined plane, as the side of a hill, observes the same law— only the distance it rolls the first second depends upon the degree of inclination of the plane.

In retiring from the centre of the earth, gravity decreases as the square of the distance. Thus, a body 4000 miles from the surface of the earth, being twice as far from the centre as it would be at the surface, would weigh only 1-4th of what it usually does ; if 8000 miles from the surface, or three semi-diameters from the centre, it would weigh only 1-9th of what it usually does ; if as far as the moon, or 60 semi-diameters, it would weigh only 1-3600th part. It is impossible to prove *directly,* that the weight of a body is thus diminished by distance from the centre of the earth, as that by which we would compare it must suffer an equal loss by the elevation ; but the pendulum affords the means of proving it indirectly. The vibration of the pendulum depends entirely upon the attraction of the earth ; the smaller, therefore, the attraction is, the less quickly will the pendulum vibrate, and the more slowly will the clock move. At the top of a high mountain, accordingly, a pendulum does not oscillate so fast as on the plain. At the equator, which is farther from the centre than places in the polar regions, the clock moves more slowly than with us. It was this fact observed at Cayenne, which led Newton to suppose that the earth was not perfectly spherical, but flattened towards the poles ; and actual measurement has verified his conjecture.

The *Centre of Gravity* is that part of a body, around which all its parts are so equally balanced, that, if *it* be supported, the whole body will be so too. Take a book, and find by trial under what part the finger must be placed to keep the book from falling ; above that point is the centre of gravity. The centre of gravity always descends first. The cork of a shuttlecock always comes down before the feathers ; and, for this reason, the point of an arrow is made heavier than the other end. A straight line, falling perpendicular to the ground from the centre of gravity, is called the *line of direction.* The broader the base upon which a body rests, the more difficult it will be to overturn it, as it must be moved the more to bring the line of direction beyond the base. A cask is easily rolled along ; a box is moved with difficulty. When a man, in wrestling, is likely to be thrown down, he puts his feet as far asunder as possible. The higher this centre of gravity, the more easily is a body overturned. A coach, empty inside, with passengers and luggage outside, is in more danger, than if there be people inside. In man, the centre of gravity is so situated that the line of direction falls between his feet ; the same in the case of quadrupeds. It is not easy for a dog to stand on his hind-legs, as the centre of gravity lies far forward. Ducks, geese, and swans walk awkwardly for the same reason. In cats and animals that spring upon their prey, the centre of gravity is so situated, that they uniformly fall on their feet.

ROASTING BY GAS.

AN apparatus for roasting meat of every kind by gas, has been recently invented by Mr Hicks, the patentee of the improved iron oven, by which spirit is obtained from the exhalations of fermented bread while baking. This apparatus is so extremely simple and beautiful, that a very few words will suffice to explain it. The gas is admitted to a metallic circle, through a very narrow continuous opening, round the outside of which the gas issues, and forms a ring of blue flame. In the centre, supported by two lateral gas tubes, joined to the circle, is an upright spike, serving as a spit on which the meat to be roasted is stuck. From the centre of the circle, the pipe, which supplies the gas, passes down to the gas main, having a cock, with a regulating lever, by which the gas can be turned on or off, and the degree of flame produced can be regulated with the greatest nicety. The circle is raised a few inches above a bench or table, so as to admit of the introduction of a convex tin dish, furnished with a spout for receiving the dripping, under each spit. From this dish the dripping runs off by the spout, and is collected in any common dish placed under it. Over the bench, at the height of three or four feet, is a projecting boarded canopy or hood, for receiving the heated air and smell from the gas and meat, and conducting them to a flue, so as to prevent them from accumulating in the kitchen. Directly above the gas circle, is a cone of polished copper, suspended by a weight. This cone is two inches wider in diameter at the base than the gas circle, and it has a small orifice at the top. When the operation of roasting is to be performed, all that is necessary is to spit the meat and light the gas, regulating it so as to produce only a blue flame, closely resembling a blue riband round the base of a black turban; and then to bring down the copper cone, until its lower edge is on a level with the base of the gas circle. A vessel to receive the dripping is then placed under the spout of the tin dripping dish, and the process of roasting goes on, without basting, or any other operation whatever being requisite. The heat produced by the gas is radiated from the copper cone on the meat, and, this being done equally on all sides, the latter never requires turning, while, the heat not being so intense as that from an open fire, the meat is neither dried nor burned; and, consequently, does not need basting. It is, in fact, roasted by heated air, but air which is constantly renewed; and, therefore, this operation has no affinity with baking. The time required for roasting in this manner is shorter than that before an open fire, in the proportion of about twelve to fifteen; it requiring fifteen minutes for roasting every pound of meat before an open fire, and only twelve minutes for roasting the same quantity by gas. As the cones are nicely balanced, in the manner of chandeliers suspended from lofty ceilings, the cook, when she wishes to look at the meat, can raise and lower the cone hanging over it, with the greatest ease. The fat drops slowly, and as pure as water, into the dish placed to receive it; and when the period of dressing is nearly completed, it is indicated by the appearance of gravy being mixed with the fat. For different joints, and for fowls of different kinds, and game, there are rims and covers of different sizes; and for a sirloin of beef, the cone approaches to the form of a cylinder with a domical top. The operation, when the meat is once spitted, and the gas properly adjusted, is conducted or rather goes on of itself, with all the quiet precision of a chemical process in a laboratory; and, in short, with so much cleanliness, neatness, and absence of smell and heat, that it would not be offensive in a drawing-room. On the evening of January 5, 1833, we were present, along with a number of gentlemen, in Mr. Hick's kitchen, in Wimpole Street, when a part of a sirloin of beef, a leg of mutton, two fowls, and a pigeon, were roasted in this manner, and afterwards tasted by the company, when they were found to be in all respects equal, if not superior, to meat and fowls roasted in the common way. Mr. Hick's apparatus had only been erected a few weeks, and was, at the time we saw it, not made known to the public. The expense of gas is much less than might be imagined, the effect being produced not so much by intensity of heat as by its concentration. Mr Hicks has found sixteen cubical feet of gas, which cost 2¾d., sufficient for roasting twelve or fourteen pounds of meat; which is considerably less than a farthing per pound. When it is considered that bread is baked and browned at from 280 to 300 degrees of Fahrenheit, and that meat is roasted in bakers' ovens after the bread is removed, the circumstance of gas affording a sufficient degree of heat for roasting will not occasion surprise. We have before described the mode by which boiling and stewing by gas has been for some time practised in Edinburgh; and it is clear that, as roasting can be also effected by it, so may baking. The whole business, therefore, of the preparation of human food, by the application of heat, may be performed by gas, and that with great economy, in all families who roast and bake at home. This is only realizing what was long ago anticipated by the late William Strutt, Esq., of Derby. There can be no doubt that oil, or any liquid fat, burned in the same manner, would effect the same end. How far the art of cooking by gas will be suitable for country inns, may be considered uncertain in the present infancy of the invention; but as, on calculation, it is found in London to be much cheaper than roasting by open fires of coal, and, for small joints, equally cheap with sending meat to be cooked in a baker's oven, it appears highly probable that, wherever gas is used for lighting, it will answer to employ it also for cooking. In cities, which are now generally lighted with gas, it will probably soon effect an important revolution; for, since every house may be supplied with heat by steamer hot water from public companies, domestic fires will become unnecessary; and, as the smoke may be burned in the engines of all manufactories by Witty's furnaces, our atmosphere may be left comparatively pure, and our town architecture be displayed to as great advantage as town architecture now is on the Continent.—*From Loudon's Encyclopædia of Cottage and Villa Architecture.*

OLD CHINA.

I HAVE an almost feminine partiality for old china. When I go to see any great house, I inquire for the china-closet, and next for the picture gallery. I cannot defend the order of preference, but by saying that we have all some taste or other of too ancient a date to admit of our remembering distinctly that it was an acquired one. I can call to mind the first play, and the first exhibition that I was taken to; but I am not conscious of a time when china jars and saucers were introduced into my imagination.

I had no repugnance then—why should I now have?—to those little, lawless, azure-tinctured grotesques, that, under the notion of men and women, float about, uncircumscribed by any element in that world before perspective—a china tea-cup.

I like to see my old friends—whom distance cannot diminish—figuring up in the air, (so they appear to our optics,) yet on *terra firma* still—for so we must, in courtesy interpret that speck of deeper blue, which the decorous artist, to prevent absurdity, has made to spring up beneath their sandals.

I love the men with women's faces, and the women, if possible, with still more womanish expressions.

Here is a young and courtly Mandarin handing tea to a lady from a salver—two miles off. See how distance seems to set off respect! And here the same lady, or another—for likeness is identity on tea-cups—is stepping into a little fairy boat, moored on the hither side of this calm garden river, with a dainty mincing foot, which, in a right angle of incidence, (as angles go in our world,) must infallibly land her in the midst of a flowery mead—a furlong off on the other side of the same strange stream!

Farther on—if far or near can be predicated of their world—see horses, trees, pagodas, dancing the hays.

Here—a cow and rabbit couchant, and co-extensive—so objects show, seen through the lucid atmosphere of fine Cathay.

I was pointing out to my cousin last evening over our Hyson, (which we are old-fashioned enough to drink unmixed still of an afternoon) some of these speciosa miracula upon a set of extraordinary old blue china (a recent purchase) which we were now for the first time using; and could not help remarking, how favourable circumstances had been to us of late years, that we could afford to please the eye sometimes with trifles of this sort—when a passing sentiment seemed to overshade the brows of my companion. I am quick at detecting these summer clouds in Bridget.

"I wish the good old times would come again," she said, "when we were not quite so rich. I do not mean, that I want to be poor; but there was a middle state,"—so she was pleased to ramble on,—"in which I am sure we were a great deal happier. A purchase is but a purchase, now that you have money enough and to spare. Formerly it used to be a triumph. When we coveted a cheap luxury, (and, O! how much ado I had to get you to consent in those times?) we were used to have a debate two or three days before, and to weigh the *for* and *against*, and think what we might spare it out of, and what saving we could hit upon that should be an equivalent. A thing was worth buying then, when we felt the money that we paid for it.

"Do you remember the brown suit which you made to hang upon you, till all your friends cried shame upon you, it grew so threadbare; and all because of that folio Beaumont and Fletcher, which you dragged home late at night from Barker's in Covent Garden? Do you remember how we eyed it for weeks before we could make up our minds to the purchase, and had not come to a determination till it was near ten o'clock of the Saturday night, when you set off from Islington, fearing you should be too late—and

Then the old bookseller, with some grumbling, opened his shop, and, by the twinkling taper, (for he was setting bedwards,) lighted out the relic from his dusty treasures—and when you lugged it home, wishing it were twice as cumbersome—and when you presented it to me—and when we were exploring the perfectness of it—(*collating*, you called it)—and while I was repairing some of the loose leaves with paste, which your impatience would not suffer to be left till daybreak—was there no pleasure in being a poor man? or can those neat black clothes which you wear now, and are so careful to keep brushed, since we have become rich and finical, give you half the honest vanity, with which you flaunted it about in that over-worn suit—your old corbeau—for four or five weeks longer than you should have done, to pacify your conscience for the mighty sum of fifteen—or sixteen shillings was it?—a great affair we thought it then—which you had lavished on the old folio. Now you can afford to buy any book that pleases you, but I do not see that you ever bring me home any nice old purchases now.

"When you came home with twenty apologies for laying out a less number of shillings upon that print after Lionardo, which we christened the 'Lady Blanch;' when you looked at the purchase, and thought of the money—and thought of the money, and looked again at the picture—was there no pleasure in being a poor man? Now, you have nothing to do but to walk into Colnaghi's, and buy a wilderness of Lionardos. Yet do you?

"Then, do you remember our pleasant walks to Enfield, and Potter's bar, and Waltham, when we had a holyday—holydays, and all other fun, are gone, now we are rich—and the little hand-basket in which I used to deposit our day's fare of savoury cold lamb and salad; and how you would pry about at noontide for some decent house, where we might go in, and produce our store—only paying for the ale that you must call for—and speculate upon the looks of the landlady, and whether she was likely to allow us a table-cloth; and wish for such another honest hostess, as Izaak Walton has described many a one on the pleasant banks of the Lea, when he went a-fishing—and sometimes they would prove obliging enough, and sometimes they would look grudgingly upon us—but we had cheerful looks still for one another, and would eat our plain food savourily, scarcely grudging Piscator his Trout Hall? Now, when we go out a day's pleasuring, which is seldom moreover, we *ride* part of the way; and go into a fine inn, and order the best of dinners, never debating the expense; which, after all, never has half the relish of those chance country snaps, when we were at the mercy of uncertain usage, and a precarious welcome.

"You are too proud to see a play anywhere now but in the pit. Do you remember where it was we used to sit, when we saw the battle of Hexham, and the surrender of Calais, and Bannister and Mrs. Bland in the Children in the Wood, when we squeezed out our shillings a-piece to sit three or four times in the season in the one-shilling gallery—where you felt all the time that you ought not to have brought me—and more strongly I felt obligation to you for having brought me—and the pleasure was the better for a little shame; and when the curtain drew up, what cared we for our place in the house, or what mattered it where we were sitting, when our thoughts were with Rosalind in Arden, or with Viola at the Court of Illyria? You used to say, that the gallery was the best place of all for enjoying a play socially—that the relish of such exhibitions must be in proportion to the infrequency of going; that the company we met there, not being in general readers of plays, were obliged to attend the more, and did attend, to what was going on, on the stage—because a word lost would be a chasm, which it was impossible for them to fill up. With such reflections we consoled our pride then—and I appeal to you, whether, as a woman, I met generally with less attention and accommodation, than I have done since in more expensive situations in the house? The getting in indeed, and the crowding up those inconvenient staircases, was bad enough,—but there was still a law of civility to woman, recognised to quite as great an extent as we ever found in the other passages; and how a little difficulty overcome heightened the snug seat, and the play afterwards! Now we can only pay our money, and walk in. You cannot see, you say, in the galleries now. I am sure we saw, and heard too, well enough then—but sight, and all, I think, is gone with our poverty.

"There was pleasure in eating strawberries, before they became quite common—in the first dish of peas, while they were yet dear—to have them for a nice supper, a treat. What treat can we have now? If we were to treat ourselves now—that is, to have dainties a little above our means, it would be selfish and wicked. It is the very little more that we allow ourselves beyond what the actual poor can get at, that makes what I call a treat—when two people living together, as we have done, now and then indulge themselves in a cheap luxury, which both like; while each apologises, and is willing to take both halves of the blame to his single share. I see no harm in people making much of themselves in that sense of the word. It may give them a hint how to make much of others. But now—what I mean by the word we never do make much of ourselves. None but the poor can do it. I do not mean the veriest poor of all, but persons as we were, just above poverty.

"I know what you were going to say, that it is mighty pleasant at the end of the year to make all meet—and much ado we used to have every Thirty-first Night of December to account for our exceedings—many a long face did you make over your puzzled accounts, and in contriving to make it out how we had spent so much—or that we had not spent so much—or that it was impossible we should spend so much next year—and still we found our slender capital decreasing—but then, betwixt ways, and projects, and compromises of one sort or another, and talk of curtailing this charge, and doing without that for the future—and the hope that youth brings, and laughing spirits (in which you were never poor till now,) we pocketed up our loss, and in conclusion, with "lusty brimmers" (as you used to quote it out of *hearty cheerful Mr Cotton*, as you called him) we used to welcome in the "coming guest." Now we have no reckoning at all at the end of the old year,—no flattering promises about the new year doing better for us."

Bridget is so sparing of her speech on most occasions, that when she gets into a rhetorical vein, I am careful how I interrupt it. I could not help, however, smiling at the phantom of wealth which her dear imagination had conjured up out of a clear income of poor ——— hundred pounds a-year. "It is true we were happier when we were poorer, but we were also younger, my cousin. I am afraid we must put up with the excess, for if we were to shake the superflux into the sea, we should not much mend ourselves. That we had much to struggle with, as we grew up together, we have reason to be most thankful. It strengthened, and knit our compact closer. We could never have been what we have been to each other, if we had always the sufficiency which you now complain of. The resisting power—those natural dilations of the youthful spirit, which circumstances cannot straiten—with us are long since passed away. Competence to age is supplementary youth; a sorry supplement indeed, but I fear the best that is to be had. We must ride, where we formerly walked: live better, and lie softer—and shall be wise to do so—than we had means to do in those good old days you speak of. Yet could those days return—could you and I once more walk our thirty miles a-day—could Bannister and Mrs. Bland again be young, and you and I be young to see them—could the good old one-shilling-gallery days return—they are dreams, my cousin, now—but could you and I at this moment, instead of this quiet argument, by our well-carpeted fire-side, sitting on this luxurious sofa—be once more struggling up those inconvenient stair-cases, pushed about, and squeezed, and elbowed by the poorest rabble of poor gallery scramblers—could I once more hear those anxious shrieks of yours—and the delicious *Thank God, we are safe*, which always followed when the topmost stair, conquered, let in the light of the whole cheerful theatre down beneath us—I know not the fathom line that ever touched a descent so deep as I would be willing to bury more wealth in than Crœsus had, or the great Jew R——— is supposed to have, to purchase it. And now do just look at that merry little Chinese waiter holding an umbrella, big enough for a bed-tester, over the head of that pretty insipid half-Madona-ish chit of a lady in that very blue summer house."—*Elia.*

CRITICS OF THE DAILY LONDON PRESS.

From libations enjoyed in the Rainbow, the Mitre, the Red Lion, or the Crown, or one of the other resorts of the reporters, he, the reporter, issues to his important functions; and, upon his state of nerves or temper depends the fate of a sublime tragedy, the reputation of a new actress or vocal aspirant, or the length, accuracy, beauty, or deformity of the speech of a great statesman or Parlinmentary orator—a speech which he has probably conned for days and nights; on which the eyes of his party are intensely fixed, and which is intended to influence the speculations of the merchant, or the political relations of the world. The reporter, strengthened by a repast of Welsh rabbits, or broiled kidneys, and inspired by his favourite potation, criticisms sparkling in his eye, and his soul full of the refinements of taste, and the delicacies of art, goes forth to pronounce whether an opera-dancer possesses the graces of the highest school—whether an actress in genteel comedy have the true *ton* of the highest fashion, such as is witnessed in the drawing-room of the aristocracy—whether a great Italian singer have all the exquisite refinements and nicer delicacies, which nothing can impart but real genius, sublimated by the most finished study of the most exquisite models, under the highest masters. All such points are determined and pronounced upon, *ex cathedra*, by the Aristarchus, albeit he is as ignorant as a horse of the graces; and, as to music, knows not a half note from a natural, or an adagio movement from a jig. We once knew a laughable illustration of this species of newspaper criticism. The proprietor of one of the morning papers became economical, and wished to pick up one or more cheap reporters. He pitched upon a young lad from Ireland, who had just arrived in London to study the law, or rather to gain a livelihood at as little expense of study of any sort as possible. What Doctor Johnson said of French adventurers in London, may truly be applied to all Irish adventurers indiscriminately, and without any risk whatever of doing them injustice :

"All sciences a starving Frenchman knows,
And bid him go to hell—to hell he goes."

An Irishman knows every thing. The poor fellow was a very ingenious specimen of such importations, who, being asked whether he could play the fiddle, instead of answering *yes*, replied with *naïveté*, " I don't know, for I never tried." In the case we allude to, the young gentleman flatly answered,—" And yes, to be sure, now," to whatever he was asked to do. Five guineas a-week was to be given to him; and five guineas a-week to a lad just arrived, at odds with fortune, from a village of one of the western provinces of Ireland, or England either, was an income beyond avarice itself to contemplate. But his place was not to be a sinecure; he was to report in the gallery, and in one of the law courts, to both of which jobs he professed himself perfectly competent. He was asked if he felt himself able to review the theatres, and this function he likewise undertook. " And I suppose you will have no objection," said the employer, " to write us criticisms upon paintings, statuary, and works of art and *vertú*." " None in the least : nothing more easy or *plisant*," replied the youth from the Emerald Isle. At last came the climax of cruel exactions for the five guineas. " Our paper, Sir, makes a great point of the opera and music ; they are more fashionable than plays, and we aim particularly at fashion. Have you any objection to undertake our critiques upon opera and morning concerts, in the season ?" " None in the laist, to be sure, now ; and couldn't I gave them genteelly ?" This was conclusive, and the bargain was struck. It was said of Mirabeau, that, in his distress, he professed his ability to perform any task whatever that was proposed to him, with the promise of a good reward ; and Dumont, his friend, declares, that, had any body asked him to write a Chinese dictionary, he would have undertaken the task. It was the same with this young Irish reporter, this fortunate youth ; and had this learned Theban proprieter suggested to him the composition of a Polyglot Bible, he would have pledged himself to the job without the slightest hesitation. When the gentleman who introduced this universal genius to the proprietor was asked, in secret, whether his young friend, from the unspellable and unpronounceable village of Connaught, understood music; the reply was, " No, indeed ; but I dare say he may have a natural taste." " Does he know any thing whatever of painting ?" " The devil a bit, and how should he ?" " How, then, could he undertake to criticise paintings and works of art ?" " Och, Sir, and an't those things so easily picked up in a big city like London ?" Until the cub's taste and knowledge of art were acquired in the big city, the works of artists, involving their character and support, were to be at the mercy of his caprice and ignorance. When the proprietorship of newspapers falls into the hands of illiterate men, is it to be wondered, that the public are annoyed with the ignorance too often displayed in journals on these subjects ?—*Metropolitan.*

CATALEPSEY.

The following marvellous relation appears in the *Lancet*, seriously :—

" The patient heard no sound, however loud, which reached her by the ears ; but if she was spoken to, even in the lowest whisper, directed on the hollow of the hand, or sole of the foot—on the pit of the stomach, or along the traject of the sympathetic nerve, she heard perfectly the words addressed to her. It was the same if, while speaking to her in a whisper, the speaker applied her hand to any of the places above-mentioned. But, stranger still, she heard also when the person addressing her was only in distant mediate communication with the surface of the body. Amid a crowd of experiments *which leave no doubt of this fact*, it will suffice to mention one in which the chain was of four persons, three of whom held each other's hands, and the fourth communicated with the third by the interposition of a very long wax-taper : the first of the chain, meanwhile, being the only person touching the patient. • •
• • She often, but not always, succeeded in reading words written on paper. Later in the disease this facility became still more prodigiously developed. It sufficed to call her attention to any object placed in her room, or *the next room*, or *in the street*, or *out of the town*, or *even at enormous distances*, to have it described by her as perfectly as if she saw it with her eyes. • • •
The professor subjected her to an anatomical examination, sometimes in Latin, a language of which she was perfectly ignorant ; and sometimes in Italian, but always using scientific nomenclature. He obtained in reply most exact descriptions, in Italian, of the heart and its appendages, the solar plexus, the pancreas, the first vertebræ or atlas, the mastoid opophysis, &c. • • • •
Although she was acquainted only with the four rules of arithmetic, she succeeded, under the cataleptic influence, in extracting several roots of numbers ; amongst others that of the number 4965. However, this experiment was not invariably successful ; she exposed, with much lucidity, several philosophical systems, and discussed others proposed to her. She discovered and described the phases of her own disease. At present the patient is perfectly cured, having had recourse to no remedy whatever ; but the cateleptic access can be now voluntarily reproduced and terminated. She has pointed out means by which analogous phenomena may be occasioned in other persons. The observers propose to make known all these discoveries in a work they are preparing on the subject.

THE STORY-TELLER.

THE YOUNG WIDOW OF BREMEN.

There is a mural monumental tablet, in a common field wall, near a handsome house in the suburbs of Bremen. On one side of the lane in which it stands are the courtyards of some spacious residences, on the other is a walk, leading through some of the prettiest fields near the town.

Two travellers, in the last century, stopped to gaze on this tablet, which appeared to have been very recently erected. It was of very fine execution, and looked fitter for some old church than the place where it stood. The design represented a kneeling female figure, mourning over an urn; in her position and features remorse was mingled with grief. Her eyes were hidden by the hand which supported the weeping head. By the broken sword and entangled balance on which her feet rested, the mourner seemed to personify Justice. No inscription or other guide to the meaning appeared, and our travellers turned eagerly to see if any one were near who could explain what the monument meant, and why it was placed there.

At length an old man, of a sad, but benevolent countenance, came slowly up; and of him they inquired the meaning of this tablet. He sighed deeply, and then bade them sit down beside him on the grass.

You might look long (said the old man after a pause of some minutes) on the crowded ramparts of Bremen, when all the fairest were there, ere your eye rested on a more beautiful face, or a lighter, and more graceful figure, than Mary Von Korper's. Often were her dark eyes beaming, and her little feet seen twinkling, on the favourite resorts of the fair and the gay; and if the stranger asked who she was, whose smile was brightest, and who moved along so trippingly, the answer from all or any of her townsmen would be ever the same, " 'Tis the young Widow of Bremen." And fair—very fair she still was; still looked she younger than many girls under twenty, though she had been the Young Widow of Bremen for seventeen years at least.

She had been married when a mere child; her husband died soon after the birth of his only son, and marriage seemed never to have dimmed the first freshness of her youth and beauty; so that when her son Hermann returned now and then from Jena, where he studied, and when he and his mother walked together, even her near neighbours thought rather of a brother and sister, than of a mother and her son. And he looked rather her older than younger brother, for Hermann, like his father, was of a thoughtful, deeply-channelled cast of features, whilst our widow had the light, sunny glance of a girl. So young, so handsome, and so fond of life and enjoyment, it seemed strange that Mary had never married again. This was not for want of offers. Each suitor, however, met the same cold, civil repulse, and the same answer, in nearly the same words. She said that she could not love him. Indeed the standing jest of her neighbours was, that Mary never looked serious save when refusing an offer.

Up to the period of our narrative, her life during her widowhood had been pure above the breath of scandal; but the same could not wholly be said of her married career. There were queer tales of a young Bavarian officer, whom her husband had found too familiar with his household on his return from a short absence, and whom he drove *an die degens spitze* out of Bremen; for Hermann Von Korper the older, was a man whom few dared to trifle with. But nothing more was ever made of this story than a mere domestic quarrel, and the early unblemished widowhood of Mary banished it from the memories of all save the very old, or the very scandalous.

Our narrative properly begins with the return of young Hermann home in the autumn. He was now eighteen, full of impetuous passions and feelings; just in this point resembling his father, though, when nothing roused him, you would have thought him a quiet, melancholy, low-voiced youth.

The household of Mary Von Korper included a *Verwalter*, or land and house-steward—a sort of confidential manager, raised over all the other servants, and filling, in some sort, the place of master of her establishment. This office had long been filled by one who had entitled himself to the esteem of all the neighbours, and they all sorrowed greatly when old Muller was persuaded by his kind young mistress to better his fortune, by accepting a far higher service which she, unsolicited, procured for him. His place was filled by a wholly different sort of person, and filled so rapidly, that few knew of the change until the stranger was amongst them. Adolphe Brauer was a far younger man than his predecessor, but he was far less liked. Not because he was rude or haughty to the poor; on the contrary, his manners were more than commonly courteous. But all this suavity wanted heartiness and sincerity, and he was feared rather than loved.

I knew the widow's family at this time, and with herself I was always on terms of the most friendly and confidential intercourse. Before this visit, I had been as kindly received by her son as was possible with one of his close and reserved character. Now, however, his manners were more than cold; they were absolutely repulsive.

Meanwhile, rumours began to circulate: first scattered and low-whispered—then more uniform and frequent—louder in voice and bolder in assertion, against the character of my fair neighbour. It was said that the new steward seemed high in his lady's confidence and favour; that he was admitted to many long and close private consultations with her; nay, even that *die junge Wittwe* had been seen leaning on his arm in the open street; and sorely were the antique Misses Keppelcranick, time out of mind, the best modistes in Bremen, scandalized thereat. Out of this same walk had further arisen a most remarkable rencontre which was witnessed by Peter Snick the tailor, who lay *perdu* behind a high wall over which, now and then, he could peep with fear and trembling.

Hermann, who had left his mother's house for the day, but had returned home sooner than he had expected, on turning a corner into the *Bauerstrasse*, met his mother leaning on the arm of Adolphe Brauer, they separated hastily, with fearful looks, the moment they saw him. Hermann merely gave his mother one stern glance; then springing on the steward, he seized him by the throat. Adolphe quailed before his fury; indeed the steward was rather of a crafty nature than of boiling courage; and when his young master flung him from him, and ordered him home, he obeyed without a word. Hermann then, with a proud cold air, took his mother's arm, who looked more dead than alive; and both vanished from the terrified gaze of Peter Snick.

After this the fair widow was not often seen abroad; un-an event occurred which filled the whole neighbourhood with wonder and discussion. The very day when young Hermann should have returned to Jena, Adolphe Brauer vanished as completely as if the earth had gaped and swallowed him. The affrighted widow, on being asked by the servants who waited for the steward's usual household orders, whether she knew what had become of him, merely shook her head and wept. She begged those most in her confidence to avoid mentioning the name of Brauer, for that her son had taken so deep a hatred to him, that the sound of it excited him to phrenzy. Hermann, however, soon made it known that he had sent Adolphe away, and that he would never return. He recalled the late steward, and stayed a day past the time he had intended, to welcome him home. All this time he was unusually merry; and set off for Jena in high spirits.

But a short interval had elapsed ere I remarked, with sorrow, that the widow's health and spirits grew worse from day to day. Whilst I was pondering over the propriety of writing to her son in Jena, an old man arrived suddenly in Bremen, begging to be directed to the widow Von Korper. He said he was Ludwig Brauer, the father of Adolphe her steward, and that he had come all the way from Weimar to see his son. When he heard that Adolphe had departed, some months before, no one knew whether, he displayed the greatest agitation and grief. In the end, a chapter of minute inquiries was addressed to Hermann, the only person of whom intelligence was to be sought; and until the answer could come from Jena, the restless and anxious stranger asked all the neighbours around for news of his son. But Adolphe Brauer was of a distant and reserved disposition, and had mentioned his designs to none. Yet some tidings of him were gleaned; though these were, after all but scanty. Once more had Peter Suick, the tailor, been playing the listener.

None, save himself, had seen Adolphe on the day when he was suddenly missed. But at a very early hour, not long after sunrise, Peter, by some strange chance, happened to be passing the corner of this very wall here, at the back of the Widow Von Korper's residence—a lane very little frequented. Suddenly he came up to young Hermann, who stood in his morning gown and slippers. The young man was in a high fury; one hand grasped the collar of Adolphe Brauer, and the other held a stout oaken cudgel. What more passed, Peter Suick knew not. He feared being punished as an eaves-dropper, and sneaked back silently to Bremen.

Nothing would satisfy old Ludwig, but a visit to the very place where his son had been seen for the last time. Peter led him; and to the astonishment of all present, the old man, in sitting down on a stone, covered by high weeds, to rest, whilst Suick acted over his story on the very spot, found something hidden amongst nettles and dock-weeds. It was a man's hat, crushed and broken, which, by a broad lace he wore, was remembered in a moment to have belonged to Adolphe Brauer!

Business called me to Lubec whilst these strange events were passing; and on my return some months after, I was aghast to learn that Hermann Von Korper was in prison, charged with the murder of Adolphe Brauer, and the concealment of the body. The proof rested principally on their known disagreement—the sudden disappearance of Brauer,—the undenied story of Peter Suick, and the discovery of his hat on the very spot where their last quarrel was supposed to have taken place. The grand difficulty, which no inquiry threw any light upon, was to find how the body had been disposed of. To complete the chain of testimony, an expedient was resorted to which cannot be contemplated without horror. They examined the prisoner by torture. Young Herman was laid upon a low iron bedstead, and his wrists and ancles passed through tight iron rings secured to the four posts. A heavy weight was placed upon his breast. Then the bed was drawn out of the frame by machinery, leaving his body supported by the wrists and ancles alone, and bearing his ponderous load. At first the great muscular force, and symmetry of his frame endured this severe tension, and he suffered apparently but little. Soon, however, his limbs quivered violently; and huge drops started upon his forehead and ran down in a stream to the floor.

Then the judge called aloud, asking him "Whether he would confess where he had hidden the body of Adolphe Brauer, whom he had murdered?" "You may kill me," cried Hermann in a weak voice broken by agony, "but I die innocent, and have told you all the truth." From the strength displayed by the wretched young man, it was thought he had not suffered pain enough to break his obstinacy. Strong levers were applied to the four sides of the bed, by which his limbs were farther strained. Hitherto he had suffered silently; now he scarcely stifled a shriek, and groaned heavily and incessantly. The executioner then brought a second heavy stone, and laid it over the other upon his breast. Human nature gave way: their barbarity had done its worst. He uttered a loud and piercing shriek, and trembled all over so violently, that the joints of his wrists broke. He became quite senseless. His mouth was wetted with a feather, to recal sensation, and the question repeated, but no sign of consciousness was returned. They were forced to end their horrid cruelty—and by many strong stimulants, with difficulty recalled him to life.

He was taken back to his prison, and left all night alone, barely furnished with some liquid to allay his fever, and keep his poor racked frame alive till morning. On the following day he was again brought up for examination. I was present; for I hoped to be able to bring some evidence in his favour; but I was little prepared for the cruel scene which followed. He was brought in, supported by two officers, looking so pale, so anguish-worn, that I could hardly recognize him. When he was brought near the terrible "bed of judgment," and compelled to touch it whilst he answered the questions put to him, his whole frame trembled like a leaf. He returned the answer as before, and passionately called Heaven to witness that he was guiltless of the blood of Adolphe. The judges began to pity him, and obviously believed him innocent, in spite of all appearances to the contrary, when the counsel for old Ludwig Brauer craved leave to examine another who had just arrived in Bremen. As soon as young Von Korper looked on this stranger, he half shouted aloud, and then turned his head away. The witness said his name was Ernest Hertzberg, son of the minister of a Lutheran church in Hamburg. He deposed that he was a fellow-student intimate with young Hermann in Jena; that he had heard the prisoner, on receiving certain letters from Bremen, break out into the most violent and frightful imprecations against Adolphe Brauer, vowing to take his life.

Hermann prayed leave to ask this witness some few questions, when it appeared that they had been rivals for the affections of Sophia Meyer, daughter of the Greek professor at Jena; and that Hermann was the favoured lover; further, that they had fought two separate duels on this quarrel, in both of which young Hortsberg had been worsted. Though these discoveries threw some suspicion over the evidence, yet they seemed important enough to demand a second investigation, by putting "the question"—that is to say, by torture.

Who could paint the looks of young Hermann when this decision was announced, and he was once more asked "What became of Adolphe Brauer?" In a voice that went to my heart, he called Heaven to witness that if he were torn alive joint from joint, he could not tell more than he had already revealed. They made ready again to tie him to the dreadful bed; but when they touched his swollen dislocated wrists, he fairly shrieked aloud, and earnestly called on God for the mercy which man denied. He was bound in the rack; and I had covered my eyes, and was prepared to rush out, for I could bear to see no more, when he called out wildly, that " if they would but untie him, and bring him water, he would confess all." I was thunderstruck on hearing these words, and stood fixed to the spot, looking on him in wonder. He spoke hurriedly and confusedly, and told some tale of his having had a quarrel with Brauer for supplanting his friend, old Muller. He said he made some pretext on that fatal morning for their going out early, to give him an opportunity to commit the murder; that a true account had been given by Peter Snick, soon after whose departure he struck Brauer heavily with a bludgeon, and killed him; that a pedlar happening to pass with a packhorse, he bribed him to take away the body, and that he had never seen the man again, and did not know how he disposed of it; but finding the steward's hat left in the hurry by the pedlar, where it had fallen in the scuffle, he hid it amongst the weeds, just as the old man found it. Having signed this confession, he was taken back to prison.

For some time after he was gone I stood as one stupified; my ears tingled as if I had been hearing the dizzy sounds of a dream, or of delirium. Was young Hermann, then, really a murderer? Impossible! I had known him from a child! But his own confession! I resolved instantly to see him in prison; and though all approach of his friends was denied to him, by a heavy bribe, I obtained, that very morning, admission to his cell.

When I approached the stone on which he lay heavily manacled, and looked on his sickly emaciated features, I could feel only pity for him, and should have stretched out my hand to him had he been guilty of a hundred murders; but he shrunk from me, and hid his face. "You are kind," said he faintly; "but I cannot bear to see you—I am not worthy of the light." "There is forgiveness," I replied, "for all sin which is repented of; and there may have been some palliation for yours—sudden passion—an accidental blow."—He instantly sprung up to the full stretch of his shackles. "You surely cannot think that I killed him?" cried he. "Your own voice said it," I replied. He answered in low and half-choked accents, "God pardon me! What could I do? I should have died beneath their hands. The very sight of that rack maddened me. I could not bear that second torture (holding up his crushed hands.) I said all they wanted, for leave to die in peace; but to stain my fair name—to be beheaded as a murderer—to die with a lie on my lips! God pardon me! My poor, poor mother!"

I now saw the whole truth; and my heart bled with indignation and sorrow. I vowed I would make his innocence appear; it was impossible his judges could be wicked enough to condemn him. He shook his head mournfully, and begged I would comfort his mother.

All my efforts—all that man could do, was vain. His own hand had sealed his fate. He was convicted and executed.

I will hasten over what I cannot bear to think of. He died resigned and firm. Up to the very last moment, he told no one of his real confession to me. But just ere his eyes were bound, he turned to the multitude, and cried, loudly, "That for the sake of his father's name, and his mother, who yet lived, he would not die without raising his voice to declare before God that he died innocent of blood—that in the madness of torture and agony he had confessed to utter falsehoods merely to procure ease, for which he implored Heaven to pardon him! Then he prayed in silence, and waited for the death-blow.

His poor mother pined daily. She could not be prevailed upon to stir into the open air; and if she had now been seen as of old, gliding along the ramparts, few would have recognised in her wasted features the young Widow of Bremen.

There was another sad page in this unhappy story. She received a parcel from Jena, which contained a small box, and a letter from Franz Meyer, the Greek professor. His daughter Sophia was dead; her last care had been to make up this little pacquet—her last request that he would send it when she died, to Mary Von Korper. It contained young Hermann's portrait, and a note from poor Sophia. She said that she sent her lover's picture to the only one now on earth who knew how to love them; and that she prayed with her parting breath, that Heaven might bring her to join them where his innocence would be known to all, as it was now known to them alone.

It was many years before Mary Von Korper crossed her threshold. At last I prevailed on her to walk slowly about the neighbourhood of her house. She seemed slowly sinking into the grave; and her physician told her that exercise was her only chance of life. One morning she expressed a wish to cross some fields at the back of her house, where there was a seat, in a beautiful little woodland, of which she used to be fond. We proceeded onwards; as we slowly passed the corner of this walk here, where the fatal scuffle between Hermann and young Brauer had taken place so long before, I saw an officer standing on this very spot, his arms folded, looking towards us. Mary was then leaning on me, holding her face down; and just before she lifted her head to speak to me, I was shocked to feel how light was her emaciated frame, though I was then bearing her whole weight. As she raised and turned her head, her eyes fell full on the stranger's features: she gave him one wild earnest look, shrieked, and sank lifeless in my arms. The stranger sprang forwards to hold her. "Lay her on the grass," said he, "she has only fainted; run to the house for water, and I will support her."

When I came back she was sitting on the grass, leaning on the stranger, whom she introduced to me as Ernest Von Harstenleit, a friend of her early days, whom she had not seen for a long—long time; the sudden meeting, she said, had been too great a shock for her weak frame. I begged her to let us take her home, that she might rest, and quiet her fevered nerves. We proceeded thither—the stranger and I supporting her between us. When we entered she appeared unable to bear up a moment longer, and called, faintingly, for water. Old Muller, who had watched her return with much anxiety, came himself to attend on her. She looked wildly but significantly at him, and then at me —pointed to the stranger, and gasped out rather than spoke —"Seize him! He is Adolphe; Adolphe, for whom my boy was murdered!" She fainted as the words left her lips, and we were running towards her, when a quick movement of the stranger warned us not to let him escape. The undefined feeling which had made me gaze so earnestly upon him was fully explained. He was, indeed, Adolphe Brauer, for whose supposed murder my poor young friend had been executed! The conspiracy to procure the death of young Hermann, by this false accusation, was clearly brought home to him, and he was executed for it; but the accomplice who had appeared as his father, escaped detection. The poor widow only survived for a few days the shock of this sudden discovery; and from his confession, and her disclosure to me, just before her death, the tissue of this strange and mournful story was made complete.

Ernest Von Harstenleit was the Bavarian officer, of whom mention was made in the beginning of my story. Mary confessed that her husband's suspicions were not groundless. During his absence her heart had been won by the stranger, and when he returned, she had forgotten her duty, and was in Ernest's power. Her husband's fury drove Von Harstenleit ignominiously from the town; and he fled, no one knew whither. During his absence, it appeared by his own confession, that the wretch had employed a woman, since but too notorious throughout Germany, who entered Von Korper's service as cook, merely to poison him.

It was long ere the officer ventured again on the scene; but in his new character of steward he soon regained his ascendancy over the widow, who had no suspicion of his agency in her husband's death. Indeed, I suspect, he was the only man she ever really loved. The fury of young Hermann, who discovered their attachment, drove away the disguised steward; and the scene that ensued, happened just as poor Hermann had confessed, save in the catastrophe.

Burning with hatred, Adolphe fled wounded, and without his hat, which had been struck off in the struggle. He resumed the military dress which he had worn previous to his assuming the disguise of a steward, and Adolphe Brauer was now no more. With the malice of a fiend, Ernest devised the plot, which, by the aid of a suborned villain, brought poor Hermann to the scaffold. He would have remained undetected, had he not madly thought Mary's love would follow him through every depth of crime. No eye but hers could recognize him, and on her he relied undoubtingly.

But though the sanctuary of her affections had been polluted—though even to the last her love remained, and the struggle killed her, Mary Von Korper shrank with horror from the assassin of her son. To clear his memory, she gave up her guilty love; but it was twined in the very heart-strings of her life, and she survived not the sacrifice.

This is the spot (said the poor man, turning to the travellers) where the murder was alleged to have been committed; and here Mary begged me with her last breath to put up this tablet, that the stranger might learn, and the inhabitant never forget, that this history is mournfully true and no idle legend.

FEMALE BLUE BEARDS.

Once in every dozen or twenty years, the public is treated to a fresh hash up of a certain number of marvels. The French papers lately gave the story subjoined, of which we give an earlier, though certainly not the original edition:—

"On Thursday last Mr. M—— (Q. Mirabel) was at Tortoni's eating an ice, when he perceived at the next table a young and elegantly dressed lady, whose brilliant eyes had a power of inflammation so far superior to the cooling effect of the ice, that after interchanging a few glances, he ventured to solicit permission to see her home. She blushed assent, but added that she was cursed with so jealous a husband, that the slightest suspicion of frailty would be fatal to her, and she must therefore assure her new lover's discretion by blinding his eyes and conducting him home in a hackney coach. To this he only objected inasmuch as it would deprive him for a time of the bliss of gazing on his enchantress, and they accordingly entered a coach which happened to be waiting, and after driving a considerable time, arrived at the door of a handsome hotel in a narrow street, where the gallant was unblinded and conducted into a brilliantly lighted saloon. Here an hour had scarcely passed, when the door opened and three gentlemen completely armed entered, and one of them, presenting a pistol to Mr. M.'s breast, with great politeness requested his purse and other valuables. Mr. M. immediately complied with the request, giving up even his silk handkerchief, which was returned to him with a remark, that it might inconvenience him to be deprived of it. A second kindly undid the brace of his shirt to give him air, forgetting, however, to return the four valuable buttons by which it was fastened. During this operation the lady was quietly arranging her curls in a looking glass. Mr. M—— was then conducted down stairs, replaced in the coach with two of the gentlemen, and ultimately left in the middle of the Rue Foues du Temple, without having the least idea where he had passed the night."

The celebrated Madame du Barri, mistress of Louis XV., gives a singular account of a beautiful female with whom, in the earlier part of her career, she became acquainted. This person was a Madame de Mellaniere, who is described as being " tender and loving, with chestnut hair, rosy lips, on which was the most charming smile, and large blue eye, of inexpressible serenity." This beauty, who occupied a genteel apartment in the Marais, Rue Porte Foin, gave herself out as the widow of an officer come to Paris to solicit a pension. Several admirers were attracted by her charms, but Madame du B. observed that she seldom retained one long. The first, a rich Englishman, was suddenly recalled to his own country; the second, a German baron, was compelled to quit Paris by his creditors; the third, a young country gentleman, was carried off by his father for fear of his marrying her. A young Anglo-American, named Brown, was another; when, after a long series of oglings and flirtations, he, too, one evening after supper, declared that he was compelled to set out for St. Petersburg immediately, to arrange some business for his father. This disappointment seemed too severe, and Madame du B. called on her friend the next morning to console her; she was not at home, but her maid-servant, in much agitation, begged her visitor to step in, and informed her of a horrible discovery she had just made.—They proceeded together to the lady's chamber, where, on pushing aside the bed, a trap-door was discovered in the floor. The girl pressed a spring and raised it; an infectious odour proceeded from below, where lay the carcasses of the various lovers of Madame de Mellaniere, who had successively disappeared. The servant, it seems, had made the discovery accidentally only a few minutes before Madame du Barri called. The latter instantly gave information to the Lieutenant de Police who immediately arrested Mr. Brown. Having clapped him into the Bastile to keep him out of harm's way, the house of Me-dame de Meilaniere was invested, and the murderess secured, together with two rascals, her accomplices. All the three, including the "tender, loving" beauty, were executed. As to Mr. Brown, he was set at liberty, with an apology for the "mistake," and "invited" to quit France within eight and forty hours. His escape appears to have been a narrow one; Madame de M. had begged him to accompany her on a tour into Italy, but to prevent scandal, had requested him to pretend that he was leaving Paris on his business. "You can come and sleep here for two or three nights," was added, "and we can commence our journey when we please." It was by the same method that she had ensnared her former lovers, who, coming to stay with her in her apartments, brought with them their jewels, money, bills of exchange, &c., and during the night, slept the sleep from which there was no awaking.—The fair autobiographer, in reflecting on the mild charms of her late friend's exterior, asks herself whether it would not be better upon the whole, if the vices of the heart were always depicted on the countenance, but answers her own question with much naïveté, concluding, that perhaps it is better as it is, since otherwise "there would be so many ugly people in the world."

THE BARBER OF DUNSE.

A clergyman possessing an uncommon share of wit and humour, had occasion to lodge for the night, in company with some friends, at the inn of a town, which, for certain reasons, we shall denominate Dunse. Requiring the services of a barber, he was recommended by the waiter to Walter Dron, who was represented as excellent at cracking a joke, or telling a story. This functionary being forthwith introduced, made such a display of his oral and manual dexterity, as to leave on the mind as well as the body of his customer, a very favourable impression, and induce the latter to invite him to sit down to a friendly glass. The mutual familiarity which the circulation of the bottle produced, served to show off the barber in his happiest mood; and the facetious clergyman, amid the general hilarity, thus addressed him: "Now, Wattie, I engage to give you a guinea, on the following terms,—that you leap backwards and forwards over your chair for the space of half an hour —leisurely, yet regularly—crying out at every leap, 'Here goes I, Wattie Dron, barber of Dunse;'—but that, should you utter anything else during the time, you forfeit the reward." Wattie, though no doubt surprised at the absurdity of the proposal, yet, considering how easily he could earn the guinea, and the improbability that such an opportunity would ever again present itself, agreed to the stipulations. The watch was set, and the barber having stripped off his coat, leaning with one hand on the back of the chair, commenced leaping over the seat, uniformly repeating, in an exulting tone, the words prescribed. After matters had gone on thus smoothly for about five minutes, the clergyman rung the bell, and thus accosted the waiter:—"What is the reason, Sir, you insult me, by sending a mad fellow like that, instead of a proper barber, as you pretended he was?" Barber—(leaping)—"Here goes I, Wattie Dron, barber of Dunse." Waiter—"Oh! Sir, I don't know what is the matter, I never saw him in this way all my life—Mr. Dron, Mr. Dron, what do you mean?" Barber—"Here goes I, Wattie."—Waiter—"Bless me, Mr. Dron, recollect these are gentlemen; how can you make such a fool of yourself?" Barber—"Here goes I—" Landlord—(entering in haste)—"What the Devil, Sir, is all this—the fellow is mad—how dare you, Sir, insult gentlemen in my house by such conduct?" Barber—"Here goes I, Wattie Dron"— Landlord—"I say, Bob, run for his wife, for this can't be put up with—gentlemen, the man is evidently deranged, and I hope you will not let my house be injured in any way by this business." "Here goes—"—(wife pushing in)— "Oh! Wattie, Wattie, what's this that's come ower ye? Do you not ken your ain wife?" Barber—"Here goes I," Wife—(weeping)—"Oh! Wattie, if ye care na for me, mind your bairns at hame, and come awa' wi' me." Barber—"Here goes I, Wat—" The afflicted wife now clasped her husband round the neck, and hung on him so as effectually to arrest his farther progress. Much did poor Wattie struggle to shake off his loving, yet unwelcome spouse, but it was now no "go"—his galloping was at an end. "Confound you for an idiot," he bitterly exclaimed, "I never could win a guinea so easily in my life." It is only necessary to add, that the explanation which immediately followed was much more satisfactory to mine host than to the barber's better half; and that the clergyman restored Wattie to his usual good humour, by generously rewarding his exertions with the well-earned guinea.

The joyfull receiving of JAMES THE SIXT of that Name, King of Scotland, and QUEENE ANNE his Wife, into the Townes of Lyeth and Edenborough the first daie of May last past, 1590. Together with the Triumphs shewed before the Coronation of the said Scottish Queene.

THE King arrived at Lyeth the first day of May, anno 1590, with the Queene his wife and his traine in thirteene shippes, accompanied with Peter Munk, Admirall of Danmarke, one of the Regentes of the King, Steven Brave, a Danish Lorde, and sundry other the Lordes of the same countrey, where at theyr arrival they were welcommed by the Duke of Lennox, the Earle of Bothwell, and sundry other the Scottish Nobility. At their landing, one M. James Elpheston, a Senator of the Colledge of Justice, with a Latine oration welcommed them into the countrey, which done, the King went on to the church of Lyeth, where they had a sermon preached by Maister Patrick Gallowey, in English, importing a thanksgiving for their safe arrivall; and so they departed to their lodging, where they expected the coming in of the rest of the nobility, together with such preparation as was to bee provided in Edenborough and the Abbey of the Holy Roode House.

This performed, and the nobility joyning to the township of Edenborough, they receaved the King and Queene from the town of Lyeth, the King riding before, and the Queene behinde him in her chariot, with her maides of honour of ech side of her Majestie's one. Her chariot was drawne with eight horses, capparisoned in velvet, imbrodered with silver and gold, very rich, her highnesse Maister of her housholde, and other Danish ladies on the one side, and the Lorde Hamilton on the other, together with the rest of the nobility, and after her chariot followed the Lord Chancelour's wife, the Lady Bothwell, and other the ladies, with the burgesses of the towne and others round about her, as of Edinborough, of Lyeth, of Fishrow, of Middleborow, of Preston, of Dalkith, &c., all the inhabitants being in armour, and giving a' volle of shotte to the King and Queene in their passage, in joy of their safe arrivall. In this manner they passed to the Abbey of Holy Roode House, where they remained untill the seventeenth of May, upon which day the Queene was crowned in the said Abbey Church, after the sermon was ended by Maister Robert Bruce and M. David Linsey, with great triumphes. The coronation ended, she was conveide to her chamber, being led by the Lord Chancelour, on the one side and the Embassador of Englande on the other, sixe ladies bearing uppe her trainne, having going before her twelve heraultes in their coates of armes, and sundrye trumpets still sounding. The Earl of Angus bare the sworde of honor, the L. Hamilton the scepter, and the Duke of Lenox the crowne. Thus was that day spent in joy and mirth. Uppon Tuesday the nineteenth of May, her Majesty made her entry into Edinborough in her chariot, with the Lordes and Nobility giving their attendance, among the which there were sixe and thirty Danes on horsebacke with foote clothes, every of them being accompanied with some Scottish Lorde or Knight, and all the ladies following the chariot. At her coming to the south side of the yardes of the Canogit, along the parke wall, being in sight of the Castle, they gave her thence a great volle of shotte, with their banners and auncientes displaied upon the walles. Thence shee came to the West Port, under the which her highnesse staied, and had an oration to welcome her to the towne, uttered in Latine by one Maister John Russell, who was thereto appointed by the towneshippe, whose sonne also being placed uppon the toppe of the Portehead, and was let downe by a devise made in a globe, which being come somewhat over her Majestie's heade, opened at the toppe into foure quarters, where the childe appearing in the resemblance of an angell delivered her the kayes of the towne in silver, which done, the quarters closed, and the globe was taken uppe agayne, so as the childe was no more seen there. She had also a canapie of purple velvet, embrodered with gold, carried over her by sixe ancient townes-men. There were also threescore young men of the towne lyke Moores, and clothed in cloth of silver, with chaines about their neckes, and bracelets about their armes, set with diamonds and other precious stones, verie gorgeous to the eie, who went before the chariot betwixt the horsemen and it, everie one with a white staffe in his hande to keepe off the throng of people, where also rid the Provost and Baileeses of the towne with foote clothes to keepe the people in good order, with most of the inhabitants in their best araie to doe the like. In this order her Grace passed on the Bow-Street, where was erected a table, whereupon stood a globe of the whole worlde, with a boy sitting thereby, who represented the person of a King, and made her an oration, which done, she went up the Bowe, wher were cast forth a number of banqueting dishes as they came by, and comming to the butter trone, there were placed nine maidens bravely arraid in cloth of silver and gold, representing the nine Muses, who sung verie sweete musicke, where a brave youth played upon the organs, which accorded excellentlie with the singing of their psalmes, whereat her Majestie staied awhile, and thence passed downe through the high gate of Edinborough, which was all decked with tapistry from the top to the bottom; at her Graces comming to the Tolboth, there stood on high the foure vertues, as first, Justice with the ballance in one hand, and the sword of justice in the other; then Temperance, having in the one hand a cup of wine, and in the other a cup of water; Prudence, holding in her hand a serpent and a dove, declaring that men ought to be as wise as the serpent to prevent mischief, but as simple as a dove eyther in wrath or malice. The last is Fortitude, who held a broken pillar in her hand, representing the strength of a kingdome.

Thus she passed on to the crosse, upon the toppe whereof she had a psalm sung in verie good musick before her comming to the churche, which done, her Majestie came forth of her chariot, and was conveyed unto S. Giles Church, where she heard a sermon preached by M. Robert Bruce. That ended with praiers for her highnesse, she was conveied againe to her chariot. Against her coming forth, there stood upon the top of the crosse a table covered, whereupon stood cups of gold and silver full of wine, with the Goddesse of Corne and Wine sitting thereat, and the corne on heapes by her, who in Latine cried that there should be plentie thereof in her time, and on the side of the crosse sate the God Bacchus upon a punchion of wine, drinking and casting it up by cups full upon the people, besides other of the townesmen that cast apples and nuts among them, and the crosse itself ranne claret wine upon the caulsway for the royaltie of that daie. Thence her Grace rode downe the gate to the sault trone, whereupon sate all the Kings heretofore of Scotland, one of them lying along at their feete, as if he had bene sick, whom certain souldiers seemed to awake at her Majesties comming: whereupon he arose and made her an oration in Latine. Which ended, she passed down to the neather bow, which was beautified with the marage of a King and his Queene, with all their nobilitie about them, among whom at her highnesse presence there arose a youth who applied the same to the marriage of the King and herselfe, and so blessed that marriage. Which done, there was let downe unto her from the top of the porte in a silke string a box covered with purple velvet, whereupon was embroidered an A. for Anna, (her Majestie's name,) set with diamonds and precious stones, esteemed at twentie thousand crownes, which the townshippe gave for a present to her highnesse; and then, after singing of some psalmes, with verie good musicke, her Grace departed to the Abbey for that night.

SELF-SUPPORTING EDUCATION.

An American publication states, that several flourishing schools have been established in various parts of the United States, in which the pupils have been enabled to defray the entire expense of their sustenance and tuition, by the exertion of a very few hours' manual labour daily. They are founded on the principle " That every lad of ordinary health and capacity, can, if proper facilities are afforded, support himself by manual labour, while attaining his education." The following example are given of the successful application of this principle: " At a flourishing institution in the State of New York, forty students are now receiving their board in exchange for not less than three, nor more than four hours' labour per day; at the Maine Wesleyan Seminary, 130 students generally paid their board by their labour; some all their expenses and others even more than this; while, at the Theological Seminary at Maysville, (East Tennesse,) by the labour of an hour and a half in a day, the expenses of comfortable board are defrayed, and a weekly saving is made by the institution, of one dollar on each labourer!" At Philadelphia there is a chartered school, under the care of the Rev. John Monteith, consisting of thirty-three scholars, (ten of whom are educating for the Gospel ministry,) and who have nearly paid the expense of their board and tuition by their manual labour. Every student is required to spend three or four hours daily in useful labour. The arts in which they have been employed are carpenter work, gardening, and farming. The objects contemplated, and so far attained by the union of manual with mental exertion, are, the establishment of health; the formation of industrious and economical habits; the facility of education afforded to the poor; and the cherishing of a manly independence of feeling. [Of course much, if not the whole of the success, in a pecuniary point of view, which is said to have attended the adoption of this system in America, is owing to the great demand for, and consequent high price of labour in that country. But though we cannot expect the moderate and resistable labour of children to defray the expense of their education in any of the old countries of Europe, it has, for a long time, formed a part of every good theory of education, that the pupils should learn at least some of the useful arts, such as the domestic arts for the females, in which they are, in these manufacturing times woefully deficient.

ELIZABETH'S PROGRESSES.

Raleigh's magnificence in dress was carried to excess, probably as much to gratify Elizabeth, who had a passion for finery, and loved to be surrounded by a brilliant court, as from personal predilection. He wore a suit of silver armour at the tourneys; his sword-hilt and belt were studded with diamonds, pearls, and rubies; his court dress on occasions of state was said to be covered with jewels to the value of L.60,000; and even his shoes glittered with precious stones. It was in this splendid apparel that he waited on his royal mistress as captain of her guard during those visits to the houses of the nobility, known by the name of Progresses. It has been alleged against the queen, that such excursions impoverished the peerage; and, under the pretence of conferring an envied distinction, were really intended to check the overgrown wealth of the aristocracy, whilst they enriched the royal household. But this is considering the matter too deeply. Her object was, in the first instance, to become acquainted with her kingdom, to confirm and increase her popularity by travelling amongst her people, exhibiting her glory to them, accepting with condescension and delight their homage, and repaying it with offices of trust and emolument. When Cecil entertained her at Theobalds in 1591, it was in expectation of being promoted to the secretaryship, though he was then only gratified with the honour of knighthood. When the Earl of Hertford received his royal mistress at Elvetham, the magnificence he displayed was not thought by him too high a price to regain her favour, which had been long withdrawn. It was the age of solemn pageantry and splendid devices. Masques, triumphs, and dramatic exhibitions, which there was a singular combination of Pagan imagery and mythology, with Gothic romances, were the chief amusements of the period. The business, as Bishop Hurd has well described it, was to welcome the queen to the palaces of her nobles, and at the same time to celebrate the glory of her government; and what more elegant way of complimenting a great prince than through the veil of fiction, or how could they better entertain a learned one than by having recourse to the old poetical story? Nor are the masque-makers to be lightly censured for intermixing classical fable with Gothic fancies,—a practice sanctioned by the authority of Chaucer, Spenser, and Milton, and often accomplished with much grace and ingenuity. Elizabeth was in no usual degree acquainted with the writers of Greece and Rome, and well able to appreciate such allusions. She took delight in music, and loved the studied magnificence of those pageants, their intricate mechanism, their lofty conceits, and the incense of high-flown adulation addressed to her. The taste of the gravest men of the times gave a countenance to such pastimes. Sir Thomas Moore did not think it beneath him to compose pageants; and a letter of Lord Bacon is preserved, in which this philosopher appears as the representative of a dozen young gentlemen of Gray's Inn, who declare their willingness to furnish a masque, since the proposal of a joint one by the four inns of court had failed. Some idea of the magnificence of the presents made on such occasions may be formed from an account, in the Sidney Papers, of the queen's dining at Kew, the seat of Sir John Puckering, lord-keeper. "Her entertainment was great and costly. At her first lighting she had a fine fan presented her, with a handle garnished with diamonds. When she was in the middle way between the garden-gate and the house, there came running towards her one with a nosegay in his hand, and delivered it to her with a short, well-penned speech; it had in it a very rich jewel, with pendants of unfurled diamonds, valued at L.400 at least. After dinner, in her private chamber, he gave her a fair pair of virginals, and in her bed-chamber presented her with a fine gown and a jupin, which things were pleasing to her highness; and to grace his lordship the more, she of herself took from him a salt, a spoon, and a fork of fair agate." During her reign, she visited Secretary Cecil at Theobalds twelve times; each of these royal favours cost him from L.2000 to L.3000; nor did she hesitate to remain a month or six weeks, receiving strangers and ambassadors, and entertained as bountifully as if she had been in one of her own palaces.—*Edinburgh Cabinet Library. Life of Sir Walter Raleigh.*

DEATH OF QUEEN ELIZABETH.

BY PATRICK FRASER TYTLER, ESQ.

EARLY in January, 1602, the queen, who for some time had been in a declining state, was seized with a severe cold. She had been forewarned by Dr. Dee, the famous astrologer and mathematician, whom she highly esteemed, to beware of Whitehall, and accordingly removed to Richmond, calling it the "warm box to which she could best trust for sickly old age." The air of the country seemed to revive her, and for some weeks her health improved; but the malady returned at the end of February; and, on the 15th of March, she was so ill that the lords of council were sent for. They found her sunk in a deep melancholy, to which no entreaties could persuade her to take food or medicine. At this sad moment Sir Robert Carey, her was on the borders, to whom she was much attached, arrived; and, though very weak, the queen requested to see him. "I found her," says he, in his Memoirs, "in one of her withdrawing chambers, sitting low upon her cushions. She called me to her; I kist her hand, and told her it was my chiefest happiness to see her in safety and in health, which I hoped might long continue. She took me by the hand and wrung it hard, and said,—'No, Robin; I am not well;' and then discoursed with me of her indisposition, and that her heart had been sad and heavy for ten or twelve days; and in her discourse she fetched not so few as forty or fifty great sighs. I used the best words I could to persuade her from this melancholy humour, but I found it was too deep rooted in her heart, and hardly to be removed."—She soon became obstinately silent; and not only rejected nourishment, but forbore her sleep, refusing to go to bed; being persuaded if she once lay down she should never rise again. The cushions were laid on the floor of her chamber; and there she sat a week, day and night, showing an utter carelessness of all that was passing around her. On the 23d of March, the day before she died, the chief members of her council thought it right to introduce that subject to which the queen had invariably shown a great aversion, the succession to the throne; and their interrogations brought out from the expiring princess a flash of her wonted spirit and severity :—" I told you," said she to the lord-high-admiral, who occupied the right side of the bed, whilst Cecil stood at the foot, " that my seat had been the seat of kings; and I will have no rascal to succeed me! Trouble me no more. He who comes after me must be a king. I will have none but our cousin of Scotland." Soon after this she became speechless, but made signs that her chaplains and the Archbishop of Canterbury should pray with her. Sir Robert Carey, who went into the chamber with them, has left us an affecting account of her behaviour. " I sat upon my knees," says he, " full of tears to see that heavy sight. The bishop kneeled down by her, and examined her first of her faith; and she so punctually answered all his several questions, by lifting up her eyes and holding up her hand, as it was a comfort to all the beholders. Then the good man told her plainly what she was, and what she was to come to; and though she had been long a great queen here upon earth, yet shortly she was to yield an account of her stewardship to the King of kings. He then began to pray, and all who were present joined in the responses; after which, his knees being weary, he blessed her and prepared to depart, when the queen by signs requested him to continue in prayer. Having done so for a considerable time, he once more rose up to depart; but the dying princess again laid her hand upon his, and mutely besought him not to leave her, appearing to have the greatest comfort in his fervent petitions. Soon after she became insensible; and, as it grew late, all left the apartment except the women." She expired about three in the morning on Thursday the 24th of March, in the same chamber where her grandfather Henry VII. breathed his last.—*Edinburgh Cabinet Library, Life of Sir Walter Raleigh.*

GASTRONOMIC PRECEPTS AND ANECDOTES.

VEGETABLES are Policies of Assurance against the fire of the stomach.

Guests, badly arranged at table, lose their value, as ciphers which are placed one after the other, without a figure preceding them.

The Emperor Geta passed three consecutive days at table, whilst a series of courses were brought in whose names began with each letter of the alphabet. The Roman Empire would never have been disturbed, if all the Cæsars had employed their time in occupations as harmless.

Henry VIII., with all his faults, at least deserves well of all good feeders. He respected eating and drinking, and made a baron of a cook who sent him up a mackarel exquisitely boiled.

The Romans would willingly have pardoned Pope Adrian VI., the old preceptor of Charles V., his weak and false policy, but they could not tolerate the infamy of his palate. This Pontiff, says Paulus Jovias, was especially detested, because he was fond of stock-fish.

M. de Chateaubriand has given us a touching description of the effects of the bell which calls the faithful to prayers. This illustrious writer would have perfected his subject, had he added to this eulogium one on the bell which summons us to dinner.

That all o'erpowering, overwhelming knell,
That tocsin of the soul—the DINNER BELL.

Your real gourmand always has his wits about him. One of the right class being invited to dine with a lady, who piqued herself greatly upon etiquette, offered to cut up a couple of patridges. Instead of proceeding to the dissection thereof on the dish, he put them on his own plate. "Pray, Sir, who is to eat your leavings?" inquired the stiff dowager.—"Madam," was the reply, "I do not intend to leave any."

Men of sense never talk of politics at dinner time. It is a bad time to think of governing the state at that particular period when a man is least capable of governing himself.

Breakfast as if you were to have no dinner, and dine as if you had not breakfasted.

A cellar without champagne is a watch without wheels.

A dinner without wine is a magic lantern without a candle.

Count Mirabeau, brother of the celebrated orator of the Constituent Assembly, and so well known as Mirabeau-tonneau, (cask Mirabeau) sent for his valet-de-chambre one morning, and said to him, "You are a faithful servant—very zealous, and I have nothing to say against you, but yet I must dismiss you." "Why, Sir?" was the question. "Because, in spite of our understanding, you get drunk on the same days that I do." "Is that my fault, Count? *You get drunk every day!*" The Count found so much sound argument in this reply, that he kept his valet-de-chambre.

Erasmus very wisely says, in his Eulogium on Folly, "A repast is tasteless, if it be not seasoned with a grain of folly." *Dulce est desipere in loco.*

The nose is the drunkard's compass.

Prince Eugene of Savoy showed vast talent and capabilities at an early age. When only fifteen, Voltaire says, he got drunk every night with Dancourt, and slept with the rest of the family.

Sobriety is the conscience of bad stomachs.

We have volumes of equally apt and true aphorisms and anecdotes, but cannot detail them now; we are summoned to—DINNER.

SCRAPS.

BISHOP PHILPOTTS.—No man ever had more of the courtier in his composition than Dr. Philpotts. He is a clerical Chesterfield. And as to his bows—their profundity, empressement, and frequency—Sir Charles Grandison must have been his model, and Richardson alone could do them! Perhaps his long and close intercourse with Bishop Barrington, himself a finished gentleman, might have contributed to throw that air of overpowering urbanity into his look and language. Of middle stature, with a keen quick eye, ready comprehension of the views of others, and a rapid response to them, he is a thorough man of business. Study, or care, or ambition, has much and deeply furrowed his countenance; but the pliancy of his person equals the pliancy of his politics! Yet he is an able, keen, and persuasive writer. The rectory-house at Stanhope, with its conservatories, hot-walls, and forcing-houses, was built by him. It is worthy of the splendid benefice to which it is attached. In the hall is a fine Roman altar, in perfect preservation, the only appendage of which many of his brethren envy him the possession. It was at Stanhope that his letter to Jeffery, the shortest and smartest of all his pamphlets, was written: the labour, it is affirmed, for he writes rapidly and without effort, of a very few days. Apart from his political transgressions, he has received hard measure from the public press. At Stanhope he preached constantly and earnestly, took his full share of the duty of that populous living, and was ever ready to perform the meanest and most laborious pastoral offices to the humblest of his flock. This point in his character his opponents have carefully kept out of sight, and most unfairly. He was a zealous, indefatigable, and generous parish priest.—*Whyhcotte of St. John's.*

SLAVERY AND CRUELTY.—There was a young Virginian female slave in our boarding-house, employed as a chamber-maid, a cleanly, attentive, quiet, and very regular individual. A Frenchman residing in the house, going in the morning early for water to wash. As the water was not instantly brought to him, he went down the steps and encountered the poor girl, who just then had some other occupation in hand. He struck her immediately with the fist in the face, so that the blood ran from her forehead; the poor creature, roused by this unmerited abuse, put herself on her defence, and caught the Frenchman by the throat. He screamed for help, but no one would interfere. The fellow then ran to his room, gathered his things together, and was about to leave the house. But when our landlady, Madame Hereies, was informed of this, in order to satisfy the wretch, she disgraced herself by having twenty-six lashes inflicted upon the poor girl with a cow-hide, and refined upon her cruelty so much, that she forced the sweetheart of the girl, a young negro slave who waited in the house, to count off the lashes upon her. This Frenchman, a merchant's clerk from Montpelier, was not satisfied with this: he went to the police, lodged a complaint against the girl, had her arrested by two constables, and whipped again by them in his presence. I regret that I did not take a note of this miscreant's name, in order that I might give his disgraceful conduct its merited publicity.—*Stuart's Three Years in America.*

GOOD OLD TIMES.—We often heard of "the good old times." When were these? In Queen Bess's reign—when, to be able to read was so rare an accomplishment that it procured to the greatest criminals "benefit of clergy," namely, impunity from well deserved punishment! When wooden pallets formed the beds of the tenths of the people, and a log of wood their pillow! When their houses had no fire-place —and needed none, fuel being as rare as silk stockings! When a Queen's bed-chamber—even that of the puissant Elizabeth herself—was strewed with fresh rushes daily, in lack of a Kidderminster or Kilmarnock carpet! When, as in the time of her father, bluff Hal, England did not grow a cabbage, turnip, carrot, nor, indeed, any edible root; and Queen Catherine had to send to Flanders for a salad! Pooh! old times, indeed!—Ours are the old rich times. Those were but a beggarly boyhood!—*Chameleon.*

DRINKING SONG OF THE MEN OF BASLE.
Lays and Legends of the Rhine.

[Close by the city of Basle is the field of St. James, where, in the year 1444, a sanguinary battle was fought between sixteen hundred Swiss and thirty thousand French! It lasted ten hours, the French being led by the Dauphin, afterwards Louis XI. The Swiss were not so much vanquished as they were tired with fighting, and exhausted by the number of their adversaries. Out of the sixteen hundred only sixteen survived, who brought the news of the battle to Basle. The French lost six thousand men. On this spot grows a red wine which is called, from this memorable circumstance, " the blood of the Swiss."]

Drink! drink!—the red, red wine
That in the goblet glows,
Is hallow'd by the blood that stained
The ground whereon it grows!
Drink! drink!—there's health and joy
In its foam to the free and the brave;
But 'twould blister up like the elf-king's cup,
The pale lip of the slave!
Drink! drink! and as your hearts
Are warmed by its ruby tide,
Swear to live as free as your Fathers lived,
Or die as your Fathers died!

CONTENTS OF NO. XXXIII.
Leonard's Voyage to the Western Coasts of Africa (Slave Trade)
Hours of Labour for Children
New Route to India
First Lines of Mechanics
Roasting by Gas
Old China
Critics of the Daily London Press
Catalepsey
THE STORY-TELLER—The Young Widow of Bremen
Female Blue Beards
The Barber of Dunse
The Joyfull Receiving of James the Sixt, and Queene Anna
Elizabeth's Progresses
Death of Queen Elizabeth
Gastronomic Precepts and Anecdotes
SCRAPS—Bishop Philpotts—Slavery and Cruelty—Good Old Times—Drinking Song of the Men of Basle

EDINBURGH: Printed by and for JOHN JOHNSTONE, 19, St. James' Square.—Published by JOHN ANDERSON, Jun., Bookseller, 55, North Bridge Street, Edinburgh; by JOHN MACLEOD, and by JAMES & Co., Booksellers, Glasgow; and sold by all Booksellers and Venders of Cheap Periodicals.

THE Schoolmaster,
AND
EDINBURGH WEEKLY MAGAZINE.

CONDUCTED BY JOHN JOHNSTONE.

THE SCHOOLMASTER IS ABROAD.—LORD BROUGHAM.

No. 34.—Vol. II.   SATURDAY, MARCH 23, 1833.   Price Three-Halfpence.

CHURCH ESTABLISHMENTS,
versus,
VOLUNTARY CHURCHES.

" Do you happen to have seen a work lately published by Mrs. Trollope, which gives an account of shocking scenes which have taken place ?" This query was addressed by some Peer, Spiritual or Temporal, to the Reverend Henry Montgomery, a Presbyterian minister in the neighbourhood of Belfast, when he was last year brought over to give evidence before a Committee of the House of Peers on the Irish tithe question. Their lordships spiritual and temporal, endeavoured to sift the dissenting clergyman in various ways, and, in vulgar language, met their match. As the report of this evidence is in very few hands, and interesting and curious in many respects, we purpose to give our readers a few extracts from the testimony of Mr. Montgomery, a clear-headed, self-possessed man, thoroughly conversant with the subjects into which the Peers' Committee, by a trifling divergence from the strict purpose in view, led him. But before coming to his opinion of the superiority of Voluntary Churches, to those Established, we must notice his sympathy with his poor Catholic neighbours.—" When a Roman Catholic," he says, " knows little of the Protestant clergyman, except in the form of the tithe-proctor, or as represented by the tithe-proctor and tithe-agent, or some individual making a demand upon the fruits of his industry, or in the more awful form in which those demands have lately been made by the police and the military in some parts of Ireland, it is almost impossible that there should not be some injury inflicted upon the faith of the church which appears thus to the eyes of the peasant. If we look at the tithe system in its social or in its moral influence, nothing can be more deplorable. Your lordships are aware that for a vast number of years, it has been a source of misery and discord, and has led frequently to the effusion of human blood. I conceive, however, that this is not the greatest evil, after all, though it is one which strikes us as being frightful." And Mr. Montgomery proceeds to describe what he considers yet worse than discord and murder—" The demoralization," namely, "spread through all society by a system of lawlessness, and truly distressing to a christian mind. When men, either from a real or imaginary source of grievances become lawless on one point it is very likely to extend to others. Combinations arising from what many of the people consider a justifiable resistance of tithes are very liable to extend themselves to other points. We find, consequently, the hearts of our peasantry hardened, their religious feelings blunted, and the native social kindness of their hearts destroyed. We know, at least we have reason to fear, that perjury is not considered an enormous crime, when a party-triumph is to accrue. We know that men have been taught, by their resistance to this impost, to glory in crime, and instead of being looked upon as individuals who are justly exposed to the punishment of the law, they are viewed by the people as martyrs in a righteous cause." But laying aside tithes, we proceed to the point in view. Mr. Montgomery stated that without any bitter hostility to the Established Church as an episcopal church, conscientious dissenters are of opinion that *all churches* should be supported by the members of their own communion. " That," he continued, " I can clearly state to your lordships, so far as my knowledge extends, to be a growing feeling in Ireland. I know that it is the feeling of some individuals even of the Establishment themselves. Your lordships may perhaps be aware that a dignitary of the Established Church, the Rev. Dr Hinks, of Killaleagh, once a fellow of Trinity College, and perhaps one of the most learned, able, and conscientious ministers of whom any church could boast, has lately put forth a pamphlet, in which he expresses it as his opinion that the progress of true religion, which he believes to be the Protestant religion as established in this country would be greatly promoted were it altogether unconnected with those temporal sanctions which it now possesses." Mr. Montgomery was asked if he did not think a resident parochial clergyman, calculated to produce a beneficial influence on the habits morals, and improvement of the country, independently of his religious influence over people of his own persuasion.—And at first glance Mr Montgomery admitted that it apparently ought to be so : —but what is the fact ? " If the people perceive that individual living in affluence from the fruits of their industry, whilst he is not discharging any duties to them connected with his clerical profession, it has not the beneficial effect which might be expected. They may, perhaps, look upon him with some degree of envy and jealousy, and the vulgar mind may be disposed to say, "Well, it is hard that this individual should live in splendour from the fruits of my toils and earnings." 'I am persuaded, that instead of producing the moral influence referred to, and which, on the first appearance of the question, would naturally occur to every mind, it has not always, nor generally produced that effect. I am not aware that the clergy are either greatly distinguished for their benevolence or the reverse. I believe that a resident landlord naturally feels a greater interest in the improvement and prosperity of his property than an individual from whose hands the property must naturally in a short time pass away. The hostility in Scotland to the establishment of Episcopacy, as your Lordships are aware, did not arise " so much from the doctrines of the Established Church, as of the system." It is well known that most of the Presbyterian clergy of the north of Ireland receive some small aid from the state; but what they derive in addition from their congregations must vary with the degree of estimation in which their character and services are held; and this, Mr. Montgomery stated, Dissenters held as a happy circumstance; because, in addition to the higher motive that ought to influence a clergyman, he has also this other motive of personal interest to make him industrious and faithful. "I stated," continues the witness, "to the Committee in another place, the fact, that the inroads upon the realms of vice, so far as I am acquainted with the north of Ireland, have not been made by the *endowed clergy* of any church, but by the industrious, energetic clergy of various sectarian denominations who are unendowed. Endowed clergy are too much exalted, perhaps, above the people. It is almost impossible that they should descend into the humble abodes of poverty, and engage in all those offices which are after all so essential " to win men to Christ." Sinners require to be sought in the midst of their poverty, and in the midst of their crimes. I speak of this as no reproach to any body of men; I speak of it as a fact occurring before my open eyes."

When the question was pressed whether the multiplicity of sects might not operate to prevent the support of clergymen without some legal endowment, Mr Montgomery brought forward the triumphant argument of America. " In the United States there was as much zeal for religion, and as much zeal in all societies for the diffusion of the Scriptures, and for the conversion of sinners, as is to be found in any portion of the world. I know that the clergy are supported there in a manner, which I, as a poor dissenter in Ireland, should call munificent, and much more largely indeed than dissenting ministers in the North of Ireland are supported in similar situations." But here the Committee had him, they brought Dr. Binsted against him; that was an authority with which he was not familiar. Captain Basil Hall's Travels he had seen; but Hall's assertions were, to his mind, set aside by that of intelligent individuals who had resided in America for years; and whoseuniversal testimony was, that religion was in a most flourishing condition,—" true religion, in its influence upon the hearts and conduct of men." The members of Committee renewed the charge. " Some districts of America were destitute of Churches, and of all religious principles;" —but Mr. Montgomery was not aware " that the people not having ever had an Established Church, and therefore not having their old habits and prepossessions in favour of religious ordinances, will not originate such institutions themselves; nor yet that the American papers exulted at the prospect open before them, of all religion being abolished." He was aware of no such facts: "I speak," he says, "from having seen the minutes of the General Assembly of the Presbyterian Church, and also of the Associate and Baptist denominations, in which they represent the numerous Churches holding their religious principles as being remarkably flourishing." And now some noble member of the Committee clenched the whole by the question with which we set out. " Do you happen to have seen a work lately published by Mrs. Trollope, which gives an account of some shocking scenes that have taken place? Are you aware that there is a most frightful multiplication of violent enthusiastic sects, which start up in America in one year, and disappear in the next; and that Mr. Binsted, himself an American of great respectability, has stated in the strongest manner the want of some distinct establishment?" —It must have been some right reverend that urged all this. Mr. Montgomery had not seen the book—but he remarked, " that we have had a good deal of fanaticism in our own countries, even with all our wealthy establishment; and that it might be the fanatical clergy had most influence among the women, as this is pretty much the case at home—he had not heard that ministers of religion were treated as an inferior grade by the male population." And now Dr. Chalmers is brought forward as the battle horse of the (certainly reverend) interrogator, in his zeal for establishments; but even against this great authority, Mr. Montgomery stood his ground. He thought the clergy holding the largest emoluments, not those found in the houses of the poor, not the working clergy. "Even where they," he adds, "are resident, I think the humble clergy of all denominations are more useful among the people." So far he admits the principle of Dr. Chalmers, " that if a Church devote itself honestly to Missionary purposes, a greater effect would be produced by the concentration of means, than by desultory efforts.—He could not, however, agree that it would be desirabler for any denomination of dissenters to support an establishment, which should concentrate its efforts to work the destruction of their own principles, at their own cost." Here is an argument against Dr. Chalmers's most substantial reason for an establishment. As a Missionary institution, until there are no diversity of sects, until all hold the same faith, the same objection must remain. How could the Anabaptist, the Quaker, the Presbyterian, approve a concentration of effort upheld by their joint contributions, to overturn the doctrines they hold for truth. "Are you aware," Mr. Montgomery was asked, "that Dr Chalmers considers an Established Church, to be the only political means for the improvement of religion in the country?" "I am not." "Are you aware that, with respect to England, (although he strongly objects to the present tithe system,) he is extremely averse to any proposal that should tend to diminish the *property* of the Established Church? he is of opinion, (putting aside distribution of that property,) that the Church might, with advantage, be put in possession of still more?"—Mr Montgomery did not know that. To another question he answered, " that from what he knew of human nature, ministers *should not be altogether independent of the people*."

The subject of establishments, taking Dr. Chalmers's principle for the basis, was placed in the fairest and most plausible light in the following question. "Supposing that you could rely, humanly speaking, upon the faithfulness of the different ministers of the Established Church, both those who send labourers into the vineyard, and the labourers themselves, do you not conceive that there would be a great advantage in seeing that such a provision should be made for the ministers as would make them independent of the caprice and passions of those they were appointed to teach." The answer was, "That if the whole people were of one opinion, conscientiously and sincerely, the objection to an Establishment, if it were conducted upon the principle of the clergy being a working clergy, would almost entirely cease." This of course embraces an impossibility. It was afterwards, that Mr. Montgomery stated, he did not think it desirable, that the ministers should be altogether independent of the people. And thus, in the Peers' Committee, ended this strange kind of conference, on the relative superiority of Establishments and Voluntary Churches, a question very naturally arising out of that of tithes; the abolition of the one being calculated to give a staggering blow to the other, which it cannot very long survive.

THE BIBLE.

While the general mass of books vary, in their sentiments and character, with the varying habits, opinions, and increasing knowledge of successive ages, and are one after another lost in the revolution of manners, and the flux of time; THE BIBLE seems destined to hold the same language, and present the same aspect to the human heart, till the veil of mortality be rent by the hand of Omnipotence, and the stupendous wonders of eternity laid open to our view.

To a serious contemplative mind, nothing can appear more truly astonishing, than, that a race of creatures, prone to every species of wickedness, and naturally hostile to every thing that is spiritual and holy, through means, which Infinite Wisdom hath planned, and boundless love enforced, become objects of compassion, of mercy, and of favour, to a despised God!* This cheering truth, which enlightens the darkest hours of life, deprives death of its terror, and eternity of its gloom, was dictated by Divinity, and is recorded in the sacred archives of Revelation. In the Inspired Volume we often find Him entering into our confined views, adopting our limited ideas, and clothing the most awful truths, and sublime mysteries, in language at the same time majestic and unadorned. The Being, that spoke the universe into existence, and still continues to support it, by His power,—condescends, in this volume, to impart a portion of His eternal purposes to man, who is no more than a worthless dependent on His bounty; yet, how often do we see this foolish creature, unmindful of the exalted nature of his benefactor, and drawn up to a self-important magnitude in the erring standard of his own conceit, neglecting dictates of the Supreme because they are of easy access—and despising them, because they appear dressed unostentatiously, in the humble guise of human language! That very simplicity, however, which veils their beauties, and conceals their excellence, from the idle and unthinking, is a proof of their divine origin—a demonstration of their intrinsic value. By what other means, than through a medium suited to our nature and faculties, could He have communication with us, the glory of whose presence no mortal can behold " and live?" Had every precept of Revelation been displayed in beams of light, throughout the azure canopy of Heaven; and all the promises breathed melody in every passing breeze, and every threatening rolled around in ceaseless thunder; our minds might have been astonished, but not informed; our hearts perplexed, but not renewed; and our imagination captivated by the charm of endless novelty, but left insensible to the splendours of simple truth. Our senses bewildered by the glare which continually surrounded them, would have allowed us no time to reduce what we saw to practice, or to consider, seriously, the import of what we heard. These senses, therefore, being the medium of all known enjoyment, to be deprived of them would be the depth of wretchedness; and hence, we would have lived in perpetual amazement, and died in the anguish of horror. Occasional revelation, again, through the intervention of subordinate spirits, visions, or, indeed, any other means than those which unerring wisdom has adopted, would leave us to be the continual dupes of idle terrors, ridiculous fancies, and fatal deceits. Here in the Sacred Volume, we have a complete, and unalterable summary of Revelation,—humble in its appearance, but power-

* " He was despised, and we esteemed Him not." Isaiah, liii. 3.

ful, through the Spirit that inspired it, in its operation. Open it, and you will perceive it to be simple; read it, and you will find it possessed of sublimity; study it, and you will feel its energies to be Divine!

> Taught by the Bible, and inspired by faith,
> Frail man can look beyond the vale of death;
> To see, hear, know, the pow'r is to him given,
> All that is dread in hell, or bless'd in heaven.
>
> The Bible sooths us, in the suff'ring hour,
> When naught that pleasure's worshipers call *bliss*,
> Wealth, learning, fame, and dignity, and pow'r,
> Could sooth our pain, or make our sorrows less.
>
> Yes—'tis a source (by bounteous Heaven bestow'd)
> Of joy exhaustless to the human breast,
> Which leads the wand'ring soul from earth to GOD,
> Consoles the griev'd, and bids the weary rest.
>
> The Bible (oft despised, though ev'ry line
> Beams truth immaculate, and love divine)
> Directs our view, this transient scene above,
> Where love inspires an endless song of love!
>
> J. B.

HISTORY OF THE DISCOVERY OF PHRENOLOGY BY DR. GALL OF VIENNA.

Dr. GALL, a physician of Vienna, afterwards resident in Paris,* was the founder of the system. From an early age he was given to observation, and was struck with the fact, that each of his brothers and sisters, companions in play, and schoolfellows, was distinguished from other individuals by some peculiarity of talent or disposition. Some of his schoolmates were characterized by the beauty of their penmanship, some by their success in arithmetic, and others by their talent for acquiring a knowledge of natural history, or languages. The compositions of one were remarkable for elegance; the style of another was stiff and dry; while a third connected his reasonings in the closest manner, and clothed his argument in the most forcible language. Their dispositions were equally different; and this diversity appeared also to determine the direction of their partialities and aversions. Not a few of them manifested a capacity for employments which they were not taught; they cut figures in wood, or delineated them on paper; some devoted their leisure to painting, or the culture of a garden, while their comrades abandoned themselves to noisy games, or traversed the woods to gather flowers, seek for bird-nests, or catch butterflies. In this manner, each individual presented a character peculiar to himself; and Dr. Gall never observed that the individual, who in one year had displayed selfish or knavish dispositions, became in the next a good and faithful friend.

The scholars with whom Dr. Gall had the greatest difficulty in competing, were those who learned by heart with great facility; and such individuals frequently gained from him by their repetitions the places which he had obtained by the merit of his original compositions.

Some years afterwards, having changed his place of residence, he still met individuals endowed with an equally great talent of learning to repeat. He then observed, that his school-fellows, so gifted, possessed prominent eyes, and recollected, that his rivals in the first school had been distinguished by the same peculiarity. When he entered the University he directed his attention, from the first, to the students whose eyes were of this description, and found that they all excelled in getting rapidly by heart, and giving correct recitations, although many of them were by no means distinguished in point of general talent. This observation was recognized also by the other students in the classes; and although the connexion betwixt talent and external sign was not at this time established upon such complete evidence as is requisite for a philosophical conclusion, Dr. Gall could not believe that the coincidence of the two circumstances was entirely accidental. From this period, therefore, he suspected that they stood in an important relation to each other. After much reflection, he conceived that if memory for words was indicated by an external sign, the same might be the case with the other intellectual powers; and, thereafter, all individuals distinguished by any remarkable faculty became the objects of his attention. By degrees, he conceived himself to have found external characteristics, which indicated a decided disposition for Painting, Music, and the Mechanical Arts. He became acquainted also with some individuals remarkable for the determination of their character; and he observed a particular part of their heads to be very largely developed. This fact first suggested to him the idea of looking to the head for signs of the Moral Sentiments. But in making these observations, he never conceived, for a moment, that the skull was the cause of the different talents, as has been erroneously represented; for, from the first, he referred the influence, whatever it was, to the Brain.

In following out, by observations, the principle which accident had thus suggested, he for some time, encountered difficulties of the greatest magnitude. Hitherto he had been altogether ignorant of the opinions of Physiologists touching the brain, and of Metaphysicians respecting the mental faculties. He had simply observed nature. When, however, he began to enlarge his knowledge of books, he found the most extraordinary conflict of opinions every where prevailing, and this, for the moment, made him hesitate about the correctness of his own observations. He found that the moral sentiments had, by an almost general consent, been consigned to the thoracic and abdominal viscera: and that, while Pythagoras, Plato, Galen, Haller, and some other Physiologists, placed the sentient soul or intellectual faculties in the brain, Aristotle placed it in the heart, Van Helmont in the stomach, Des Cartes and his followers in the pineal gland, and Drelincourt and others in the cerebellum.

He observed also, that a great number of Philosophers and Physiologists asserted, that all men are born with equal mental faculties; and that the differences observable among them are owing either to education, or to the accidental circumstances in which they are placed. If differences were accidental, he inferred, that there could be no natural signs of predominating faculties; and consequently that the project of learning, by observation, to distinguish the functions of the different portions of the brain, must be hopeless. This difficulty he combated by the reflection, that his brothers, sisters, and schoolfellows, had all received very nearly the same education, but that he had still observed each of them unfolding a distinct character, over which circumstances appeared to exert only a limited control. He observed, also, that not unfrequently those whose education had been conducted with the greatest care, and on whom the labours of teachers had been most assiduously bestowed, remained far behind their companions in attainments. "Often," says Dr Gall, "we were accused of want of will, or deficiency in zeal; but many of us could not, even with the most ardent desire, followed out by the most obstinate efforts, attain, in some pursuits, even to mediocrity; while in some other points, some of us surpassed our schoolfellows without an effort, and almost, it might be said, without perceiving it ourselves. But, in point of fact, our masters did not appear to attach much faith to the system which taught equality of mental faculties; for they thought themselves entitled to exact more from one scholar, and less from another. They spoke frequently of natural gifts, or of the gifts of God, and consoled their pupils in the words of the Gospel, by assuring them that each would be required to render an account, only in proportion to the gifts which he had received."*

Being convinced by these facts, that there is a natural and constitutional diversity of talents and dispositions, he encountered in books still another obstacle to his success in determining the external signs of the mental powers. He found that, instead of faculties for languages, drawing,

---

* Born at Tiefenbrun, in Suabia, on 9th March 1757, died at Paris, 22d August 1828.

* Preface by Dr. Gall to the "Anatomie, &c. du Cerveau," from which other facts in this work are taken.

distinguishing places, music, and mechanical arts, corresponding to the different talents which he had observed in his schoolfellows, the metaphysicians spoke only of general powers, such as perception, conception, memory, imagination, and judgment; and when he endeavoured to discover external signs in the head, corresponding to these general faculties, or to determine the correctness of the physiological doctrines taught by the authors already mentioned, regarding the seat of the mind, he found perplexities without end, and difficulties insurmountable.

Dr. Gall, therefore, abandoning every theory and preconceived opinion, gave himself up entirely to the observation of nature. Being a friend to Dr. Nord, Physician to a Lunatic Asylum in Vienna, he had opportunities, of which he availed himself, of making observations on the insane. He visited prisons, and resorted to schools; he was introduced to the courts of princes, to colleges, and the seats of justice; and wherever he heard of an individual distinguished in any particular way, either by remarkable endowment or deficiency, he observed and studied the development of his head. In this manner, by an almost imperceptible induction, he at last conceived himself warranted in believing, that particular mental powers are indicated by particular configurations of the head.

Hitherto he had resorted only to physiognomical indications, as a means of discovering the functions of the brain. On reflection, however, he was convinced that Physiology is imperfect when separated from Anatomy. Having observed a woman of fifty-four years of age, who had been afflicted with hydrocephalus from her youth, and who, with a body a little shrunk, possessed a mind as active and intelligent as that of other individuals of her class, Dr. Gall declared his conviction, that the structure of the brain must be different from what was generally conceived,—a remark which Tulpius also had made, on observing a hydrocephalic patient who manifested the mental faculties. He therefore felt the necessity of making anatomical researches into the structure of the brain.

In every instance, when an individual, whose head he had observed while alive, happened to die, he used every means to be permitted to examine the brain, and frequently did so; and found, as a general fact, that, on removal of the skull, the brain, covered by the dura mater, presented a form corresponding to that which the skull had exhibited in life.

The successive steps by which Dr. Gall proceeded in his discoveries, are particularly deserving of attention. He did not, as many have imagined, first dissect the brain, and pretend, by that means, to discover the seats of the mental powers; neither did he, as others have conceived, first map out the skull into various compartments, and assign a faculty to each, according as his imagination led him to conceive the place appropriate to the power. On the contrary, he first observed a concomitance betwixt particular talents and dispositions, and particular forms of the head; he next ascertained, by removal of the skull, that the figure and size of the brain are indicated by these external forms; and it was only after these facts had been determined, that the brain was minutely dissected, and light thrown upon its structure.

At Vienna, in 1796, Dr. Gall, for the first time, delivered lectures on his system.

In 1800, Dr. J. G. Spurzheim† began the study of Phrenology under him, having in that year assisted, for the first time, at one of his lectures. In 1804, he was associated with him in his labours; and, since that period, has not only added many valuable discoveries to those of Dr. Gall, in the anatomy and physiology of the brain, but formed the truths brought to light, by their joint observations, into a beautiful and interesting system of mental philosophy. In Britain, we are indebted chiefly to his personal exertions and printed works for a knowledge of the science.

In the beginning of his inquiries, Dr. Gall did not, and could not, foresee the result to which they would lead, or the relation which each successive fact, as it was discovered, would bear to the whole truths which time and experience might bring into view. He perceived, for instance, that the intensity of the desire for property, bore a relation to the size of one part of the brain; he announced this fact by itself, and called the part the organ of Theft, because he had found it largest in thieves. When he had discovered that the propensity to destroy was in connexion with another part of the brain, he announced this fact also as an isolated truth, and named the part the organ of Murder, because he had found it largest in criminals condemned for that crime. In a similar way, when he had discovered the connexion between the sentiment of Benevolence and another portion of the cerebral mass, he called the part the organ of Benevolence; and so on in regard to the other organs. This mode of proceeding has nothing in common with the formation of a hypothesis; and, so far from a disposition to invent a theory being conspicuous, there appears, in the disjointed items of information which Dr. Gall at first presented to the public, a want of even an ordinary regard for systematic arrangement. His only object seems to have been to furnish a candid and uncoloured statement of the facts in nature which he had observed; leaving their value to be ascertained by time and farther investigation.

As soon, however, as observation had brought to light the great body of the facts, and the functions of the faculties had been contemplated with a philosophical eye, a system of mental philosophy appeared to emanate almost spontaneously from the previous chaos.

When the process of discovery had proceeded a certain length, the facts were found to be connected by relations, which it was impossible sooner to perceive. Hence, at first, the doctrines appeared as a mere rude and undigested mass, of rather unseemly materials; the public mirth was, not unnaturally, excited at the display of organs of Theft, Murder, and Cunning, as they were then named; and a degree of obloquy was brought upon the science, from which it is only now recovering. At this stage the doctrines were merely a species of physiognomy, and the apparent results were neither very prominent nor inviting. When, however, the study had been pursued for years, and the torch of philosophy had been applied to the facts discovered by observation, its real nature, as the science of the human mind, and its high utility, became apparent; and its character and name changed as it advanced. The following observations of Mr. Locke are peculiarly applicable to its history and prospects. "Truth (says he) scarce ever yet carried it by vote any where, at its first appearance. New opinions are always suspected, and usually opposed without any other reason, than because they are not common. But truth, like gold, is not the less so, for being newly brought out of the mine. 'Tis trial and examination must give it price, and not any antique fashion; and, though it be not yet current by the public stamp, yet it may, for all that, be as old as nature, and is certainly not less genuine.

SIERRA LEONE AND ITS CAPITAL, FREETOWN.[a]

FREETOWN and its vicinity, from the anchorage, has a most pleasing appearance, and notwithstanding that its climate is so pernicious to European constitutions, the most prejudiced must grant that the scenery here is magnificently picturesque. The wide confluence of Sierra Leone river with the sea, resembles a smooth and extensive lagoon, bounded on one side by the low, woody Bullom shore, on the other by the verdant and gentle acclivity on which the town is situated, the back ground of which, gradually ascending, terminates in a semicircular range of moderate-sized hills, forming a sort of amphitheatre, decorated with lofty trees and richly-foliated shrubs; while every spot of the ascent, here and there studded with neat country seats, presents to the delighted eye a picture of the most agreeable character. The town covers a large space of ground; its houses appear from the anchorage like so many cottages ornée, elegantly built, and tastefully painted externally, and interspersed with numerous trees; the streets wide, and—which, by the by, is rather ominous than pleasing—covered with grass, through

---

† Born at Longuich, near Treves, on the Moselle, 31st December, 1776.

[a] Leonard's Voyage. Tait, Edinburgh.

which lanes are distinguishable, made by the foot passengers. The huts, scattered about in the suburbs, surrounded with banana, orange, pawpaw, and other fruit trees, put one in mind of the garden summer-houses of the honest Cockney citizens in the neighbourhood of London. But with all that is so pleasing to the eye, it is but a painted sepulchre. It is painful to the imagination to conceive that this very exuberance of vegetation is the remote cause of that great destruction of European life, for which the place is so distinguished—contaminating the surrounding atmosphere with mephitic exhalations by its annual death and putrefaction. On the ridge of an adjacent hill to the westward of the town, is situated a cluster of mud huts, the humble abode of a number of liberated slaves; and still farther to the westward, on the borders of the river, stands another assemblage of mud edifices, similarly inhabited. These villages are called Wilberforce and Murray.

Numbers of boats and canoes, formed of the pullam, a gigantic species of cotton tree, have paddled alongside to-day, full of black washerwomen, liberated slaves, and Kroumen, all noisily talkative; the women well clothed with cotton garments of various hues; the latter free from any such encumberance, excepting a piece of cloth that serves the purpose of the "fig-leaf small clothes of our great progenitor." Some of them, indeed, are *in puris naturalibus*, but the ladies do not appear to be very much shocked at the indecency. Habit is a second nature, it is said, and perhaps blushes are incompatible with a countenance of ebony. They brought for sale bananas, oranges, lemons, and pine apples. The pines, though not so deliciously flavoured as those of English or West India growth, are nevertheless very excellent, and so plentiful, that sixty of them may be had for a dollar, or somewhat less than a penny each.

The fine picturesque appearance which the town assumes from the anchorage is greatly diminished on entering it. It is placed on the side of a hill, situated in the arena, or bosom of the amphitheatre mentioned above. The wooden buildings, with chinks in the walls, and uneven boardings, though they are daubed like the others with colouring matter, and look well at a distance, are only a few degrees superior to the booths of a race-course or a fair; besides, they are not lasting, owing to the destructive incursions of a small and very numerous kind of white ant, which the natives call the "bug-a-bug." The houses are constructed on the principle of free ventilation; most of them being surrounded with covered galleries, open in front, or numerously perforated with jaloused windows, or blinds of wicker work, to exclude the sun and allow the air to permeate. Most of these superior kind of buildings are unconnected with each other, being separated by a colony of small huts, inhabited by people of every shade, from straw-colour to perfect jet, generally maroons. These huts are built of twigs wattled together round poles stuck in the ground; the interstices filled with clay, and the roof four-sided, and thatched with straw or dry grass. Some of them are likewise formed of planks united edgewise, but such belong to certain of the black aristocracy only. The streets of the town are very wide, placed at right angles, and plentifully supplied with grass and rubbish.

Each house has its garden full of fruit trees of various sorts peeping over the roofs and garden walls, reminding one of the green luxuriance of an English village in the month of May. A little higher up the hill, overlooking the town, Fort-Thornton, the citadel or principal fort, is situated, with the military hospital behind,—which, by the by, might be in a much more elevated, and therefore more cheerful, cool, and healthy situation; and on the very summit of the hill stands the new barracks, commodious, clean, and well ventilated. A place more eligible for their erection could not have been found in the whole neighbourhood. The temperature is usually two or three degrees below that of the town, and although the bay should be perfectly calm, there is almost always, in this elevated spot, a light and refreshing breeze. The summit of this hill commands the most superb and agreeable prospect imaginable in every direction but one, where the burying-ground presents itself, and the newly turned up mould which covers the recent victims to fever. The beautiful valley separating this from the semicircular range of woody hills in the back ground, forming a line of demarcation between the vicinity of Freetown and all that may be disagreeable to the eye beyond; the little villas peeping through the woods in rural modesty; the wide spreading town at our feet, embowered in trees; its spacious streets full of moving forms, dark, to be sure, but replete with life and bustle; and the still, expansive estuary, unruffled by a breath, bearing on its smooth surface ships of various size and structure, pilgrim-specks from "regions most remote,"—constitute an assemblage of objects highly pleasing to the eye and gratifying to the imagination." "All the grateful country breathes delight." If we could but add with Gay,

"Here blooming health exerts her gentle reign,"

the agreeable picture would be complete; but, merged in its fatal climate, all the beauties of the country are lost.

Freetown properly consists of several districts connected with each other by intervening huts, of which the residences of our countrymen form a straggling sort of nucleus. The inhabitants are composed, besides Europeans, of Nova Scotia settlers, Maroons from Jamaica, discharged soldiers of the West India regiments and royal African corps, natives, and liberated Africans; and each of these districts receives its name from the principal body of its inhabitants,—such as Settler Town, Maroon Town, Soldier, or Gibraltar Town, Jaloff Town, and so on. The greater number of the respectable inhabitants have low wooden boxes, somewhat resembling pig-styes, placed outside of the doors of their dwelling and storehouses, in which a Krouman or negro keeps watch during the night. These are remarkable objects in the street, and puzzle one not a little to guess their particular use.

Numbers of Foulahs, Serawoolahs, and Mandingoes, tall, slender-made, but athletic, and intelligent looking men, are seen walking, or sitting in groups about the streets, dressed in long loose, coarse blue and white robes, having the arms and legs bare; their heads covered with a small red or white woollen or cotton cap; their hair platted in numerous cords, nearly as thick as the little finger, and hanging round the head; with sandals on their feet; and their arms and necks, and, in some instances, their ancles, loaded with numerous fetishes,—griegris, as they call them, or charms. These are mere scraps of paper, written in Arabic characters, (pieces of the Koran,) and placed in small leather bags or boxes, which are fastened round the arm above the elbow, or round the neck, with straps of the same material, and resembling so many tobacco pouches. They have all muskets, bows, and arrows; some of them long sabres or curved knives, resembling creeses. The Foulahs and Serawoolahs bring gold from the interior in large rough rings, which they barter for articles of dress, gunpowder, &c. The Mandingoes trade chiefly in rice and bullocks.

One thing strikingly remarkable in Freetown, is the total absence of beasts of burden, or carriages of any sort. To be sure, a milch cow is seen here and there grazing in the middle of the street, and a few goats, dogs, pigs, and poultry; and every respectable person keeps his own riding-horse or gig, (in lending which, by the by, they are extremely liberal to visitors;) but with these exceptions, I have never seen a domestic or working animal, or a carriage of any sort. The duties of the camel, horse, ox, mule, and ass, seem to be performed almost entirely by the individual or combined labour of our own species, and chiefly by the Africans recently liberated, who are to be seen in great numbers about the streets, almost in a state of nudity. I observed parties of these men, lately manumitted, dragging huge stones on low-wheeled trucks, for the purpose of building; others arriving from the country in the evening, where they had been at work, clearing the ground, with hoes and pickaxes on their shoulders, all of them seemingly contented with their employment. Besides these men, parties of convicts, in chains, are constantly employed about any public work that may be going on,—black, as well as white men, who have been condemned for offences committed in the colony.

These female Africans all carry their children behind their backs, rolled in the same bodycloth which covers, from the just downwards, their own nakedness. The poor little etch, bound with its face to the back of its mother, and an arm and a leg on each side of her, and both these as well its head exposed to the sun, seems to bear its irksome situation, and all the shaking and rough usage it meets with, most philosophically. The market-place is crowded with berated African females, squatted on the ground, or on mats, with their baskets of fruit, nuts, or Chily peppers, displayed before them, and their naked woolly-headed sable scrubs, released from their dorsal envelope, playing round them, and puckering their little smooth, chubby visages into every form and degree of satisfaction. They sprawl about the narrow lanes through the market, scratching up the mud, and wallowing in it like as many black sucking pigs.

Amidst all the dialects spoken by the various Negro tribes and inhabitants in the colony, English is the language generally understood and made use of, and in every degree of imperfection. Poor Quamino, in giving utterance to our civilized dialect, falls into many diverting errors of style as well as pronunciation; and our countrymen here seem to think that it is necessary he should not improve in this respect, as they all make use of the same defective and incongruous jargon in speaking to every one of dingy exterior, conceiving, no doubt, that the blacks understand better what is said to them when spoken to in their own broken and imperfect English. The following is a specimen of this peculiar *lingua franca* jargon, which I overheard the other day between a European master and his black servant:—

Master. "Why for you no take book to goberna man?"
Man. "Me no get him, sa."
Master. "Yes, you did; you get fum fum palaver plenty."
Man. "Me no like him, sa; me get fum fum palaver plenty too much."

Which means,

"Why did you not deliver that note to the governor?"
"You did not give me any note, sir."
"Yes I did; you shall be punished."
"I would rather not, Sir; for, I have had quite enough of punishment already."

The habitations of the Krou people, Krou Town as it is called, are, in the direction of this spot adjoining Freetown, a complete Indian village; the houses formed, like all the huts in the colony, of clay, twigs, and thatch. These men are an emigrant and industrious race, natives of a part of the Grain Cost, in the neighbourhood of Cape Palmos, about three hundred and fifty or four hundred miles south-east of this, who come here for a few years only—let themselves out for hire to ships or as servants on shore—make a little money—return home again, and are succeeded by some more of their fortune-pushing countrymen. They are, in fact, the Scotsmen of Africa. They are a remarkably strong, active, hardy, and intelligent race of men. Their skin varies from a dark copper colour to black, tattooed about the face, chest and arms. They are distinguished by a tattooed arrow on each temple, with its point to the eye; and almost all of them have the front teeth of the upper jaw filed to a point, or some portion of each tooth removed, according to the fancy of the wearer, or those who begat him, which gives them a savage appearance. Their only article of dress is a piece of printed cotton cloth round the middle. None of them have their wives and families here; these are left at home under the guardianship of their own relations, and the protection of their chief, to whom, on returning home, they always carry a present of cloth, muskets, gunpowder, or some article of dress, as a sort of tribute and acknowledgment for his protection.

Every ship of war on arriving at Freetown, enters a certain number of these Kroumen over and above her compliment, for the purposes of manning her boats when they may be sent on any service where there is likely to be much exposure to the sun or rain, and to the mephitic exhalations from the soil, such as wooding and watering, so that our unassimilated seamen may be subjected as little as possible to the deleterious influence of the climate.

We received upwards of twenty of them on board, chiefly young men, all of them more muscular and athletic, although not generally taller, than our own people; some of them perfect models in point of figure, and possessing features rather more prominent and expressive than the generality of Africans. Nearly all of them had been in the navy before, and, like most other Africans, each has his grigri, or fetish, which is commonly the tooth of some wild animal, fastened round the ancle or wrist. The following are a few of their original proper names, with the laughable and absurd cognomina which they brought with them, among many others of strange and dubious import:—

Namboe	Jack Ropeyarn.
Taboos	Jack Fryingpan.
Yiepam	Great Tom.
Woorawa	Peas Soup.
Blattoo	Will Centipede.
Niaie	Government Packet.

In rowing, they have always a song of some sort or other at command, to which they keep time with the oar, sometimes melodious, but usually harsh and untuneful, having generally for its subject something connected with the ship, or the officers, or the duty that is going on, each chanting a subject in turn, while the rest join in the chorus.

TITHES.—" Tithes," said the Archbishop of Aix, in a whining tone, " that *voluntary* offering of the devout faithful."—" Tithes," interrupted the Duke de la Rochefoucault, in his quiet and modest way, which rendered the trait more piquant, " that *voluntary* offering of the devout faithful, concerning which there are now forty thousand law-suits in the kingdom."—*Recollections of Mirabeau.*

SLAVERY.
A NIGHT SCENE IN AFRICA.

'T was night:—his babes around him lay at rest,
'Their mother slumbered on their father's breast:
A yell of murder rang around their bed;
They woke: their cottage blazed; the victims fled;
Forth sprang the ambush'd ruffians on their prey,
They caught, they bound, they drove them far away.
The white man bought them at the mart of blood;
In pestilential barks they cross'd the flood;
Then were the wretched ones asunder torn,
To distant isles, to separate bondage borne;
Denied, though sought with tears, the sad relief
That misery loves,—the fellowship of grief.
  Lives there a savage ruder than the slave?
—Cruel as death, insatiate as the grave,
False as the winds that round his vessel blow,
Remorseless as the gulf that yawns below,
Is he who toils upon the wafting flood,—
A Christian broker in the trade of blood.
Boisterous in speech, in action prompt and bold,
He buys, he sells,—he steals, he kills, for gold.
At noon, when sky and ocean, calm and clear,
Bend round his bark, one blue unbroken sphere;
When dancing dolphins sparkle through the brine,
And sunbeam circles o'er the waters shine:
He sees no beauty in the heaven serene,
No soul-enchanting sweetness in the scene,
But, darkly scowling at the glorious day,
Curses the winds that loiter on their way.
When swoln with hurricanes the billows rise,
To meet the lightning midway from the skies;
When from the unburthen'd hold his shrieking slaves
Are cast at midnight to the hungry waves;
Not for his victims strangled in the deeps,
Not for his crimes the harden'd pirate weeps,
But, grimly smiling, when the storm is o'er,
Counts his sure gains and hurries back for more.
                                    MONTGOMERY.

ELEMENTS OF THOUGHT.

SOME OF THE EVIL CONSEQUENCES OF CHURCH ESTABLISHMENTS.

HAPPY were it, if Civil Establishments of Religion were *useless* only, instead of being productive of the greatest evils. But when Christianity is established by law, it is requisite to give the preference to some particular system; and as the magistrate is no better judge of religion than others, the chances are as great for his lending his sanction to the false, as to the true. Splendour and emolument must likewise be in some degree attached to the National Church, which are a strong inducement to its ministers to defend it, be it ever so remote from the truth. Thus error becomes permanent; and that set of errors which happens to prevail, when the establishment is formed, continues, in spite of superior light and improvement, to be handed down without alteration from age to age. Hence the disagreement between the public creed of the church, and the private sentiments of its ministers; an evil growing out of the very nature of a hierarchy, and not likely to be remedied before it brings the clerical character into the utmost contempt. Hence the rapid spread of infidelity in various parts of Europe; a natural and never failing consequence of the corrupt alliance between Church and State. Wherever we turn our eyes we shall perceive the depression of religion, in proportion to the elevation of the hierarchy. In France, where the establishment had attained the utmost splendour, piety had utterly decayed; and in Scotland, whose National Church is one of the poorest in the world, a greater sense of religion appears among the inhabitants than in either France or England. It must likewise be plain to every observer, that piety flourishes much more among dissenters, than among the members of any establishment whatever. This progress of things is so natural, that nothing seems wanting in any country to render the thinking part infidels, but a splendid establishment. It will always ultimately debase the clerical character, and perpetuate, both in doctrine and discipline, every error and abuse. Turn a Christian Society into an Established Church, and it is no longer a voluntary assembly for the worship of God; it is a powerful corporation, full of such sentiments and passions as usually distinguish those bodies, a dread of innovation, an attachment to abuses, a propensity to tyranny and oppression. Hence the convulsions that accompany religious reforms, where the truth of the opinions in question is little regarded, amidst the alarm that is felt for the splendour, opulence, and power which they are the means of supporting.

* * * * * * The alliance between Church and State is, in a *political point of view*, extremely suspicious, and much better fitted to the genius of an arbitrary, than a free government. To the former it may yield a powerful support; to the latter it must ever prove dangerous. The spiritual submission it exalts, is unfavourable to mental vigour, and prepares the way for a servile acquiescence in the encroachments of civil authority. This is so correspondent with *facts* that the epithet High Church, when applied to politics, is familiarly used in our language to convey the notion of arbitrary maxims of Government.—*Hall of Leinster.*

TENDENCY OF THE AGE.

THE Tory writers have for some time been prophecying the downfall of poetry, and the annihilation of imagination, and the contraction of all feeling from the doctrines of utilitarianism, and the ascendency of machinery. "They would fain," says Leigh Hunt, in an eloquent passage of the dissertation he has prefixed to his poems, "have persuaded us that the heart, the imagination and flesh and blood of man, were to quit him at the approach of science and utilitarianism, and leave him nothing but his ribs to reckon upon. O believe it not! Count it not feasible, or in nature! The very flowers on the tea-cups, the grace with which a ball of cotton is rolled up, might have shewn the contrary. You must take colour out of the grass first, preference out of the fancy, passion out of the blood. Nay, the more draught the more thirst. The want makes the wish. You may make sects in opinion, and formalize a people for a while, here and there, but you cannot undo human nature. ***** Newton got himself into strange border-lands of dissent. Pascal was a hypochondriacal dreamer. With the growth of this formidable mechanical epoch, which was to take all *dulce* out of the *utile*, we have had the wonderful works of Sir Walter Scott, the criticism of Hazlitt, the imagination of Keats, the tragedy and winged philosophy of Shelley, the passion of Byron, the wit and festivity of Moore, tales and novels endless, and Mr. Wordsworth has become a classic, and the Germans have poured forth every species of romance, and the very French have thought fit to Germanize, and our American brethren have written little but novels and verses, and Sir Humphrey Davy has been dividing his time between coal-mines and fairy-land, (no very remote regions,) and the shop itself and the *Corn Laws* have given us a poet, and Mr. Crabbe has been versifying the Parish Registers; and last, and not least, the Utilitarians themselves are poetical. Dr. Bowring is not satisfied unless we hear of the poetry of Maggyars; and if you want a proper Bacchanalian uproar in a song, you must go to the author of *Headlong Hall*, who will not advance utility itself, unless it be jovial. It is a moot point which he admires most, Bentham or Rossini.

COERCIVE MEASURES.

I HEAR it sometimes asserted, that a steady perseverance in the present measures, and a rigorous punishment of those who oppose them, will, in the course of time infallibly put an end to these disorders. But this, in my opinion, is said without much observation of our present disposition, and without any knowledge at all of the general nature of mankind. If the matter of which this nation is composed be so very fermentable as these gentlemen describe it, leaven will never be wanting to work it up, as long as discontent, revenge, and ambition have existence in the world. Particular punishments are the cure for accidental distempers in the state; they inflame rather than allay those heats which arise from the settled mismanagement of the Government, or from a natural ill disposition in the People. It is of the utmost moment not to make mistakes in the use of strong measures; and firmness is then only a virtue when it accompanies the most perfect wisdom.—*Burke's Thoughts on the Cause of the Present Discontents.*

HYMN
OF THE CONFEDERATE POLES OF LUBLONSEL.
By Mrs Gore.

By each life-pulse warmly beating,—
By each hand in hand we hold,—
By each glance our glances meeting,
Brothers hail! the bell hath tolled!
UNITE! *Be free!*

By yon forest branches waving,—
By yon dread and star-bright spheres,—
By yon waves our pastures laving,—
Brothers kneel! Jehovah hears.
ADORE! Be free!

By our swords, inglorious rusting,
By our land of death and birth,
By our faith, to heaven entrusting
Life, love, honour,—all on earth,—
ARISE! Be free.

THE STORY-TELLER.

THE HARE-HOUND AND THE WITCH.
BY THE O'HARA FAMILY.

Your genuine witches, who

> ———" seemed not creatures of the earth,
> And still were on it;"

withered old women, who united in their persons the decrepitude of age with the most marvellous power of locomotion; half spirits, half mortals; who seemed to live solely for the purpose of paying back to the whole human race the hatred lavished by men, women, and children, on themselves; who could blight the farmer's hope of plenty; cheat his cows of their milk, and his wife of her butter; cause the clouds to gather, and the tempest to scourge the earth; and yet creatures of contrarieties! who, possessed of all this awful power, could not, or would not, redeem themselves from rags, hunger, and misery;—they, your genuine witches, as we have already called them, exist not, alas! at present, in our green island: extinct, though not forgotten, is their race, like that of our noble moose-deer, our formidable wolf, and our as formidable wolf-dog. Degenerate emulators of them, indeed, we still boast; individuals who dip into futurity by the aid of card-cutting or cup-tossing, or who find out stolen property, or vend charms against the peevish malice of the little sprites of the moonbeam; but, compared with their renowned predecessors, these timid assertors of supernatural endowment may be said to disgrace their calling; and, moreover, even they are fast sinking in repute, as well as diminishing in numbers.

But we would attempt to preserve, in the following pages some fit idea of the importance of a true Irish witch of the good olden time. We are aware, that the chief event which must wind up our story—the sudden appearance, namely, of a lost heir—(we have the courage to speak it out so soon) is a threadbare one; it can't be helped, however; and it, at least, is fact, to our own knowledge; although we are not quite as fully accountable for the respectable traditions that surround it with such pleasing wonders as we are about to relate, and which form the real interest of our narration.

On the western coast of Ireland is a certain dangerous bay; into it the broad Atlantic rolls his vast waters. Two leagues inland from its mouth high black cliffs frown over it, at both sides, of which the bases are hollowed into caverns; and when the winds blow angrily—and any wind can effectually visit the open and exposed estuary—tremendous and terrific is the roar, the dash, and the foam, which deafen the ears, and distract the eyes of a spectator. That hapless vessel which, in a storm, cannot avoid an entrance into this merciless turmoil of mad waters, has sealed its doom.

Formerly, a great number of ships, from different countries, used to be dashed to splinters against the iron-bound coast; and a few people conjecture, that the diminution of such terrible accidents, in the present day, is partially owing to some improvement in seamanship, or else to the timely warning now given to distant mariners, by lights erected at the mouth of the bay. But other persons, and by far the greater number in the neighbourhood, think that the comparative paucity of wrecks may more naturally and satisfactorily be accounted for in another way. In fact, there does not now reside, as formerly there did, in an almost unapproachable cavern, high up on the face of one of the black cliffs, " a real witch of the right sort."

Not that her witchship always dwelt in her cave; no, her visits to it were but occasional. Nor did it ever become necessary for her to proclaim her presence on the coast, by exhibiting her person; the results of her close neighbourhood sufficiently " prated of her whereabouts." Farmers' wives toiled in vain at their churns; and when no butter would come, self-evident it was that the witch was at that moment in her cavern, seated on her heels before a vessel of plain water, from which, by drawing a dead man's hand through it, she appropriated the produce of other people's honest labour. Cows suddenly went back in their milk; and then it was known, that, by passing a wheaten straw between her finger and thumb, the witch amply filled her can, while the owner of the beautiful animal uselessly tugged at its udder. Cattle swelled, and died, too; and, once again, every one knew who was in the cave under the cliff; and if none of those events, or similar ones, proved her disagreeable proximity, the direful storms, and the frightful wrecks in the bay abundantly warranted it. Often, amid the bellowing of the tempest she had raised, swelled her shrieking voice; and while the despairing creatures in the doomed vessel topped each short, high, foam-maned billow, which nearer and nearer dashed them on to their dread fate, the terrified watchers on the cliff's brow have heard her devilish laugh, until at last it broke into frenzied loudness, as the ship burst, like a glass bubble, against the sharp rocks under her dwelling-hole.

No one could tell whence she came or whither she went, when, for a time, no longer visible on the coast. Occasionally she was observed in conference with certain notorious smugglers; and the men appeared, it was well known, to petition and bribe her for a fair wind with which to enter the bay, and for a foul one to keep their pursuers out of it. And this was fully proved by the fact, that invariably their light lugger got in, and was safely moored in some little creek, against danger of coming storm; while, the moment the revenue-cutter appeared in the offing, out burst the wildest winds, from the witch's cavern, and up swelled the sea and the bay, in mountain billows; and his Majesty's vessel was sure to be wrecked during the night.

Like all of her sisterhood of that famous period, she could change herself, at pleasure, into various shapes. We give a serious proof of her talent in this respect.

A few miles from the coast which she so despotically ruled, resided a considerable landed proprietor. A great hunter of hares and foxes was he. His wife had just blessed him with an heir to his estate. And the boy was their only child. Of this event, the good squire was not a little proud; for, in case of his not leaving male issue, his property was to pass away to a distant, obscure, and neglected relation, a bone in whose skin its immediate possessor neither loved nor liked; for the heir-presumptive was mean in his habits and associations, uneducated and graceless; and it would be a sad thing to know that the fine old family acres were to go into such hands.

Shortly after his wife's confinement, and while she and her baby were " doing well," the squire, to dissipate the recent anxiety he had suffered, sallied forth for a hunting. His pack of harriers were his attendants on this occasion, for the hare was the object of the day's sport.

And, surely, never had such a hare been followed by dogs, or " sohoed" by mortal lips, as the hare he and his friends and pack started, and hunted, upon that memorable day. From breakfast to dinner time, a sweeping and erratic chace did she lead them all; the dogs at full stretch, and the horses at top speed. Various accidents happened to the sportsmen; one maimed his steed; another fractured his collar-bone; some swamped in bogs; and none, except our good squire and his huntsman, escaped without injury or disaster. But, from starting to pulling up, they gallantly kept at the dogs' tails.

After " an unprecedented run," the hare suddenly scudded towards the cliffs of the bay, immediately over the witch's cavern. The good harriers pursued; and the eager squire did not stay behind them; his huntsman closely following. The hair gained the verge of the cliff. Sheela, the prime bitch of the pack, just had time to close her, make a chop at her, and take a mouthful of flesh from her haunch, before she leaped down the face of almost a precipice. Dogs and horsemen were at a pause; none dared follow her.

In some time, nearly all the other discomfited members of the hunt came up, soiled, wounded, or jaded. They heard of the termination of the chase; and all wondered at the extraordinary freaks of the little animal, which had so distressed and baffled the best harriers and the best hunters in the country, taking men and horses together.

" By ———!" suddenly exclaimed the huntsman, a young fellow of known hardihood of character, swearing a great oath, " I'll tell yez how it is; ye are after hunting the witch o' the cave sthraight undher us! It isn't the first time that creatures like her have made a laugh, in this way, of nearly as good men as we all are, standin' here together.'

Most of his auditors ridiculed the speaker; one or two, however, looked grave: perhaps in patronage of his assertions; perhaps because the pains and aches resulting from their many falls, during the day, lengthened their faces, darkened their brows, and puckered their lips. The huntsman offered, if any one would accompany him on the dangerous enterprize, to scale down the cliff, penetrate the witch's cavern, and prove his saying. One did volunteer to be his companion: an humble friend of his own, forming an individual of the crowd of gaping peasants assembled round the gentlemen hunters.

The adventurers succeeded in reaching and entering the awful cave. Upon their return, over the line of the cliff, they reported that they had found the witch at home, stretched, panting and exhausted, upon some straw, in a dark corner of the cave; that they had dragged her, much against her will (and indeed her screams certainly had reached the squire and his friends above) to the light, at its opening; had, with main force, examined her person; and, sure enough, had found a deficiency of flesh in her haunch, with plainly the marks of Sheela's teeth in and about the wound, from which the blood freshly streamed. To be sure the better-informed of the hearers of this story, or at least a majority of them still laughed at it; but whatever they might think, those to whom the talents and capabilities of witches were better known, firmly believed that the Squire and his companions had hunted all that day, a hare, which was no hare after all; and that the courageous little Sheela had tasted flesh of a forbidden kind.

And happy had it been for the squire and his pet bitch had they proved less eager after their sport. Poor Sheela died in great agonies upon the very night of that day, and her master was doomed to a speedy punishment for his own audacity.

Nothing daunted at the idea of whom he had been hunting, he took the field again a few days after; and now no question could be raised as to the nature of the game he a second time started and pursued. Puss did not, indeed, immediately make for the sea; but this was only a ruse to effect her own malignant purposes. She wanted to get her enemy alone at the edge of the cliff. And for this purpose, her speed and her manners quite outdid those of a former day; so much so, that, in a few hours, even the dare-neck and dare-devil huntsman was thrown out, and returned with a lamed horse and a sprained ankle to the gentlemen who had suffered before him, leaving the squire alone close upon the dogs.

For a considerable time he and his master's friends awaited the re-appearance of the persevering Nimrod. Finally, they repaired to the cliff, which the huntsman had left him speedily approaching. There they found his horse without a rider; but himself they never again beheld. The unbelievers in witchcraft immediately surmised that his highblooded hunter had borne him against his will to the edge of the cliff; had there suddenly started back; and that by the quick and violent action, the unhappy gentleman had been thrown forward out of his saddle, and precipitated from rock to rock hundreds of feet downward. A few who were able for the effort, cautiously descended towards the sea. On their way they discovered their friend's hunting-cap on the sharp pinnacle of a rock; its iron headpiece was stove in; and it became evident that, after having been loosed from its wearer, by the force of the concussion which had fractured it, the squire's body had tumbled still farther downward. They reached the sea's level. His remains were not visible; they must have fallen into the sea, and been floated away by its tide. The witch of the cavern disappeared with her victim,—her victims, we should say; for her vengeance on the squire was not limited to his own destruction. At the story of his shocking death, hastily and injudiciously communicated, his wife, yet enfeebled by her recent confinement, sickened, and in a few days died; nay, nearly within the hour of her departure from this world, her only child, the heir to her husband's estate, disappeared; no one could tell whither, or by what means. Strange enough to say, however, part of the baby's dress was found on the identical pinnacle of rock where his father's hunting-cap had been met with; and in the minds of the educated and wealthy of the neighbourhood, this circumstance started doubts of fair-dealing towards father and child. Suspicion, however, could fasten itself upon no object; and inquiry and investigation did not lead to any solution of the mystery. It need not be added, that by far the greater number of the population of the district smiled at the useless efforts to establish a case of human, that is, ordinarily human agency; or that they went on tranquilly believing that the squire and his family, not forgetting his bitch, had been punished for the mouthful snatched by young Sheela from the haunch of a certain person.

Twenty years after the time of the tragedy we have detailed, our story is resumed. The once indigent and despised relation, of whom mention has before been made, sits at his breakfast-table in the old family house. He is in his forty-fifth year. Like other gentlemen of his day, he carries in his hair the contents of a large potamatum-pot; four tiers of curls rise over his ears; on the top of his head is a huge toupée, and a great queue lolls, like an ox's tongue, between his broad shoulders. On his loose, wide-sleeved, long-skirted, frock-like coat, is a profusion of gold embroidery; a lace cravat calls round his throat; ruffles flaunt over his knuckles; his gaudy waistcoat reaches only to his knees; and satin is his breeches, and silk his hose, and ponderous square silver buckles are in his shoes. So much for the outside of the jocular Squire Hogan. As to his interior pretensions, and, indeed, some of his external ones, too, the least said the soonest mended. He had never been able to raise himself above much of the homely acquisitions of his youth; but though we cannot present to the reader, in his person, a model of the true Irish gentleman of his day, we do introduce him in the character of (to repeat what every one said of him) "as worthy a soul as ever broke the world's bread."

Squire Hogan, upon the morning when we meet him, paid earnest attention to his breakfast. Powdered beef often filled his plate, and as often rapidly disappeared. And yet something seemed to gratify his mental palate as well as his corporeal one. A giuish, self-contented smile played over his round, ruddy face; his small blue eyes glittered; and, to the accompaniment of a short, liquorish laugh, occasionally were drawn up at the corners, as he glanced at his daughter, a good-natured, good-tempered, sensible, and (of course) beautiful girl of nineteen, who sat opposite to him, sipping her coffee, and picking her muffins. And, whenever their eyes met, we'll did Catherine know that the chuckling of her papa had reference to some little triumph which, as he believed, he had cleverly and cunningly achieved over herself. At length the good Squire relaxed in his meal; emptied the silver tankard of October which lay at his hand; leaned back in the chair, and laughingly said—

"By Jove, Kate, my girl, I nicked you there!"

"Indeed, papa, you played me a roguish turn," assented Kate; convinced, from experience, that it was very pleasant to her parent to have the talent of his practical jokes fully admitted.

"Where did I tell you we were driving to, out of Dublin town, eh?"

"You told me, Sir, with as serious a face as you could make, that we were only going to visit a friend a few miles out of Dublin."

"Ho, ho! Good, by Cork! Choice! a capital hoax, as I'm a living sinner! and I told you this confounded lie, with such a serious face, you say?"

"With such a mock-serious face, I meant to say, papa."

"Right, Kate; you are right, beyond yea and nay; a mock-serious face; yes, and there lay the best of it; if I had not been able to keep myself from laughing you might have suspected something; but I was able, as you yourself saw, and as you now don't deny; though, by Jove, Kate, it was enough to make a dead man shout out, seeing you sitting opposite to me, and believing every word I told you!"

"You kept up the farce cleverly, I must, and do admit it, Sir."

"Didn't I, Kate, didn't I? And here we are, this morning, eighty miles from Dublin, in our own house, and taxing no man's hospitality. But devil's in it! there's no fun in playing a good trick on you, Kate."

"Why so, dear papa? am I not as easily blinded as your heart could wish?"

"To be sure you are! What else could you be? I never met man, woman, nor child, that I could not puzzle. That's not the thing at all. No; but succeed as I may with you, 'tis impossible to make you a little cross. Why, if I had a lass of spirit to deal with, there would be no end to her tears, and her pouts, and her petitions, the moment she found that I was whisking her away from her balls, and her dreams, and her beaux, and all the other dear delights of Dublin."

"And I hope that my merry papa does not really wish to have me peevish and short-tempered, even for a greater provocation?"

"Kiss me, Kate, I believe not; and yet I don't know either, by Cork! There would be fun in tormenting you a bit, in a harmless way. But, Kate, can you give a guess why I run away with you in such a devil of a hurry?"

"Let me see, papa. I remember you telling me of some original matches you had on hands before we set out for Dublin. Perhaps you have engaged the two cripples to run a race on their crutches?"

"No; that's put off—ho, ho!"

"Or the two old women to hop against time, carrying weight for age?"

"Ho, ho! wrong again!"

"Probably you have succeeded in making the two schoolmasters promise to fight out their battle of the squares and angles with their respective birches; their scholars standing by to show fair play?"

"Ho, ho, ho! Though that's a matter not to be let out of reach neither."

"Then all my guesses are out, papa."

"I'll help you, then. Tell me, you little baggage, what is it on earth you most wish for?"

"Indeed, my dear papa, I have no particular wish to gratify at the present moment."

"Get out! get out, for a young hypocrite! Kate wouldn't something like a husband be agreeable to you?"

The girl blushed the colour of a certain young gentleman's coat, and drooped her head. Of that certain young gentleman, however, her worthy father knew nothing; at least, in connexion with the present topic.

"Oh, oh! I thought I saw how the land lay."

"Indeed, my dear papa"—

"Say nothing more about it. Leave it all to me, lass. I'll get him for you. None of your half-dead-and-alive fellows, that you could knock down with a tap of your fan; no, he shall be an able, rattling, rollicking chap, able to take your part by land or sea. Did your mother never tell you how I came by her, my girl."

Kate, dispirited by her father's coarse humour, as well as by other things, answered in the negative.

"I'll tell you, then, as truly as if she were alive to hear me. Though as poor as a church mouse at that time, I was a hearty young shaver; ay, as hearty, though not so matured as I am this day; now that I am squire of the town-land, and a justice of the peace, to boot. By the way, I wish they'd make the parish clerk a justice of the peace in my stead; for I hate to be trying to look as grave as a mustard-pot, and as solemn as a wig-block. Well, I was at a Christmas raffle, Kate, and your mother's father was there too; as comical an old boy as you'd wish to know! I had a great regard for him, by Cork! and so, away he and I raffled, and he lost to me every throw, until at last I didn't leave him a stiver. 'All I've won from you, and my watch to boot, against your daughter Nelly!' cries I of a sudden. 'Done!' cries he; 'and we threw again; and he lost, and I won again: and that's the way I get your mother, Kate! And now, do you guess any thing else, I'm going to say about yourself, Kate?"

"Oh, papa, I hope"——

"I know you do hope. Yes, Kate, I am going to provide for you in something like the same way"——

"Now, good heavens, papa!"——

"Don't speak a word more till you hear me out. At the last club dinner in Dublin, Ned O'Brien calls me aside with a face as long as my own when I'm on the bench; and after a long-winded beginning, he prays my interest with you Kate. 'To be sure man,' says I, 'you must have it.' Then, up sneaks George Dempsey, and his business was the same. 'By Cork, I'll court her, in style, for you my boy,' was my word to George. And then, Mick Driscoll takes a turn at me, and begs of me, for the Lord's sake, to listen to him; and I was obliged to listen to him, all about his title-deeds and his pedigree; and he, too, craved my countenance with the prettiest girl, and (what he didn't call you) the richest heiress in the province; and, 'By Jove! I'll do my best for you, Mick,' says I; and Mick nearly pulled the arm out o' my body, shaking my hand; but I'm not done yet. Harry Walshe made his way to me; and the boy to my fancy is Harry Walshe, Kate. 'I am up to the saddle-skirts in love with your beautiful Kate,' says Harry. 'Pull away, my hearty fellow,' answers I; 'never fear, but I'll poll for your election.'"

"My dear papa"——

Let me make an end, as I told you, Kate. Well, after dinner, and the bottle going merrily round, and every one of us right jovial, I rehearsed, for the benefit of the whole company, all the promises I had made, and a high joke it was; and then, 'Here's what I'll do among you all, my good boys,' says I; 'Let every one of Kate's wooers be on the turf the first morning of the next hunting-season, each mounted in his best style; let there be no pull-in from the cover to the death; no baulking or shying, but smooth smack over every thing that offers; and the lad that mounts the brush may come a-courting to my daughter, Kate.' Well, my girl, you'd think they had all lost their wits at this proposal; such joy amongst them, such shouting; many a bottle the rivals emptied, each to his own success; and in ten days from this blessed morning, the match comes off, my girl; and whoever wins, Kate will have a wooer worth throwing a cap at."

Kate remained silent; tears of mortification and disgust, unseen by her father, streaming from her eyes.

"But the cream of the jest I have not told you, Kate. Rattler is in training, privately, the last two months—no one the wiser; and, harkee, Kate! by Cork's own town, I intend to start for you, myself; and the brush I'll wear in my own cap; and then, if I havn't my laugh, right out, why, in that case, 'tis the devil that made little apples!"

And before the sensitive and high-minded, and spirited girl could reply, away went her father to superintend Rattler, greatly chuckling over his scheme; and poor Catherine sat alone to blush and weep at the thought of being made, by her own father, the object of a vulgar and foolish contention.

Other sad thoughts, mingled with her reveries. The unestated military hero, to whom, while in Dublin, she had all but plighted her troth, had promised, in answer to a letter she dispatched to him from the first post where she had halted with her father, on their flight from town, to make his appearance in the country, and try his fortune with the squire; but days had now rolled over, and he came not; neither did he send a line to account for his absence. This was sad mortification to the pure ardency of a first love, in the breast of such a girl as Catherine; particularly when she recollected the most disagreeable predicament in which her father's unthinking folly and indelicacy had placed her.

To be concluded in our next.

LIFE OF AN USURER.
HUGH AUDLEY.

THERE are memoirs of this remarkable man in a rare quarto tract, entitled "The Way to be Rich, according to the practice of the great Audley, who began with two hundred pounds in the year 1605, and died worth four hundred thousand." He died on the 15th of November, 1662, the year wherein the tract was printed.

Hugh Audley was a lawyer, and a great practical philosopher, who concentrated his vigorous faculties in the science of the relative value of money. He flourished through the reigns of James I., Charles I., and held a lucrative office in the "Court of Wards," till that singular court was abolished at the time of the restoration. In his own times he was called "The great Audley," an epithet so often abused, and here applied to the creation of enormous wealth. But there are minds of great capacity, concealed by the nature of their pursuits; and the wealth of Audley may be considered as the cloudy medium through which a bright genius shone, of which, had it been thrown into a nobler sphere of action, the "greatness" would have been less ambiguous.

Audley, as mentioned in the title of his memoir, began with two hundred pounds, and lived to view his mortgages, his statutes, and his judgments so numerous, that it was observed, his papers would have made a good map of England. A contemporary dramatist, who copied from life, has opened the chamber of such an usurer,—perhaps of our Audley—

"Here lay
A manor bound fast in a skin of parchment.
The wax continuing hard, the acres melting;"
Here a sure deed of gift for a market-town,
If not redeem'd this day, which is not in
The unthrift's power; there being scarce one shire
In Wales or England, where my monies are not
Lent out at usury, the certain book
To draw in more—"
Massinger's City Madam.

This genius of thirty per cent. first had proved the decided vigour of his mind, by his enthusiastic devotion to his law studies: deprived of the leisure for study through his busy day, he stole the hours from his late nights and his early mornings; and without the means to procure a law-library, he invented a method to possess one without the cost; as fast as he learned, he taught; and by publishing some useful tracts on temporary occasions, he was enabled to purchase a library. He appears never to have read a book without its furnishing him with some new practical design, and he probably studied too much for his own particular advantage. Such devoted studies was the way to become a Lord Chancellor; but the science of the law was here subordinate to that of a money trader.

When yet but a clerk to the clerk in the Counter, frequent opportunities occurred which Audley knew how to improve. He became a money trader as he had become a law writer, and the fears and follies of mankind were to furnish him with a trading capital. The fertility of his genius appeared in expedients and in quick contrivances. He was sure to be the friend of all men falling out. He took a deep concern in the affairs of his master's clients, and often much more than they were aware of. No man so ready at procuring bail or compounding debts. This was a considerable traffic then, as now. They hired themselves out for bail, swore what was required, and contrived to give false addresses. It seems they dressed themselves out for the occasion: a great seal-ring flamed on the finger, which, however, was pure copper gilt, and they often assumed the name of some person of good credit. Savings, and small presents for gratuitous opinions, often afterwards discovered to be very fallacious ones, enabled him to purchase annuities of easy landholders, with their treble amount secured on their estates. The improvident owners, or the careless heirs, were soon entangled in the usurer's nets; and, after the receipt of a few years, the annuity, by some latent quibble, or some irregularity in the payments, usually ended in Audley's obtaining the treble forfeiture. He could at all times out-knave a knave. One of these incidents has been preserved. A draper, of no honest reputation, being arrested by a merchant for a debt of L.200. Audley bought the debt at L.40, for which the draper immediately offered him L.50. But Audley would not consent, unless the draper indulged a sudden whim of his own: this was a formal contract, that the draper should pay within twenty years, upon twenty certain days, a penny doubled. A knave, in haste to sign, is no calculator? and, as the contemporary dramatist describes one of the arts of those citizens, one part of whose business was

"To swear and break—they all grow rich by breaking—"

the draper eagerly compounded. He afterwards "grew rich." Audley, silently watching his victim, within two years, claims his doubled pennies, every month during twenty months. The pennies had now grown up to pounds. The knave perceived the trick, and preferred paying the forfeiture of his bond for L.500, rather than to receive the visitation of all the little generation of compound interest in the last descendant of L.2000, which would have closed with the draper's shop. The inventive genius of Audley might have illustrated that popular tract of his own times, Peacham's "Worth of a Penny;" a gentleman who, having scarcely one left, consoled himself by detailing the numerous comforts of life it might procure in the days of Charles II.

Such petty enterprises at length assumed a deeper cast of interest. He formed temporary partnerships with the stewards of country gentlemen. They underlet estates which they had to manage; and, anticipating the owner's necessities, the estates, in due time, became cheap purchases for Audley and the stewards. He usually contrived to make the wood pay for the land, which he called "making the feathers pay for the goose." He had, however, such a tenderness of conscience for his victim, that, having plucked the live feathers before he sent the unfledged goose on the common, he would bestow a gratuitous lecture in his own science—teaching the art of making them grow again, by showing how to raise the remaining rents. Audley thus made the tenant furnish at once the means to satisfy his own rapacity, and his employer's necessities. His avarice was not working by a blind, but on an enlightened principle; for he was only enabling the landlord to obtain what the tenant, with due industry, could afford to give. Adam Smith might have delivered himself in the language of old Audley, so just was his standard of the value of rents. "Under an easy landlord," said Audley, "a tenant seldom thrives; contenting himself to make the just measure of his rents, and not labouring for any surplusage of estate. Under a hard one, the tenant revenges himself upon the land, and runs away with the rent. I would raise my rents to the present price of all commodities; for if we should let our lands, as other men have done before us, new other wares daily go on in price, we should fall backward in our estates." These axioms of political economy were discoveries in his day.

Audley knew mankind practically, and struck into their humours with the versatility of genius: ordinarily deep with the grave, he only stung the lighter mind. When a lord, borrowing money, complained to Audley of his exactions, his lordship exclaimed, "What, do you not intend to use a conscience?" "Yes, I intend hereafter to use it. We monied people must balance accounts: if you do not pay me, you cheat me; but, if you do, then I cheat your lordship." Audley's monied conscience balanced the risk of his lordship's honour, against the probability of his own rapacious profits. When he resided in the Temple among those "pullets without feathers," as an old writer describes the brood, the good man would pule out paternal homilies on improvident youth, grieving that they, under pretence of "learning the law, only learnt to be lawless;" and "never knew by their own studies the process of an execution, till it was served on themselves." Nor could he fail in his prophecy; for at the moment that the stoic was enduring their ridicule, his agents were supplying them with the certain means of verifying it; for, as it is quaintly said, he had his decoying as well as his decoying gentlemen.

Audley was a philosophical usurer: he never pressed hard for his debts; like the fowler, he never shook his nets lest he might startle, satisfied to have them, without appearing to hold them. With great fondness he compared his "bonds to infants, which battle best by sleeping." To battle is to be nourished, a term still retained at the University of Oxford. His familiar companions were all subordinate actors in the great piece he was performing; he too had his part in the scene. When not taken by surprise, on his table usually lay opened a great Bible, with Bishop Andrews's folio sermons, which often gave him an oportunity of railing at the covetousness of the clergy! declaring their religion was "a mere preach;" and that "the time would never be well till we had Queen Elizabeth's Protestants again in fashion." He was aware of all the evils arising out of a population beyond the means of subsistence. He dreaded an inundation of men, and considered marriage, with a modern political economist, as very dangerous; bitterly censuring the clergy, whose children, he said, never thrived, and whose widows were left destitute. An apostolical life, according to Audley, required only books, meat, and drink, to be had for fifty pounds a-year! Celibacy, voluntary poverty, and all the mortifications of a primitive Christian, were the virtues practised by this puritan among his money bags.

Yet Audley's was that worldly wisdom which derives all its strength from the weaknesses of mankind. Every thing was to be obtained by stratagem, and it was his maxim, that to grasp our object the faster, we must go a little round about it. His life is said to have been one of intricacies and mysteries, using indirect means in all things; but if he walked in a labyrinth, it was to bewilder others; for the clew was still in his own hand; all he sought was that his designs should not be discovered by his actions. His word, we are told, was his bond; his hour was punctual; and his opinions were compressed and weighty: but if he was true to his bond-word, it was only a part of the system to give facility to the carrying on of his trade, for he was not strict to his honour; the pride of victory, as well as the passion for acquisition, combined in the character of Audley, as in more tremendous conquerors. His partners dreaded the effects of his law library, and usually relinquished a claim rather than stand a suit against a latent quibble. When one menaced him by showing some money bags, which he had resolved to empty in law against him, Audley, then in office in the Court of Wards, with a sarcastic grin, asked, "Whether the bags had any bottom?" "Ay!" replied the exulting possessor, striking them. "In that case I care not," retorted the cynical officer of the Court of Wards; "for in this court I have a constant spring; and I cannot spend in other courts more than I gain in this." He had at once the meanness which would evade the law, and the spirit which could resist it.

The genius of Audley had crept out of the purlieus of Guildhall, and entered the Temple; and having often sauntered at "Powles" down the great promenade which was reserved for "Duke Humphrey and his guests," he would turn into that part called "The Usurer's Alley," to talk with "Thirty in the hundred," and at length was enabled to purchase his office at that remarkable institution, the Court of Wards. The entire fortunes of those whom we now call wards in chancery were in the hands and often submitted to the arts or the tyranny of the officers of this Court.

When Audley was asked the value of this new office, he replied, that "It might be worth some thousands of pounds to him who, after his death, would instantly go to heaven; twice as much to him who would go to purgatory; and nobody knows what to him who would adventure to go to hell." Such was the pious casuistry of a witty usurer. Whether he undertook this last adventure, for his four hundred thousand pounds, how can a sceptical biographer decide! Audley seems ever to have been weak, when temptation was strong.

Some saving qualities, however, were mixed with the vicious ones he liked best. Another passion divided dominion with the sovereign one: Audley's strongest impressions of character were cast in the old law library of his youth, and the pride of legal reputation was not inferior in strength to the rage for money. If in the "Court of Wards" he pounced on encumbrances which lay on estates, and prowled about to discover the craving wants of their owners, it appears that he also received liberal fees from the relatives of young heirs, to protect them from the rapacity of some great persons, but who could not certainly exceed Audley in subtilty. He was an admirable lawyer, for he was not satisfied with *hearing*, but *examining* his clients; which he called "pinching the cause where he considered it was foundered." He made two observations on clients and lawyers; which have not lost their poignancy. "Many clients, in telling their case, rather plead than refute it, so that the advocate heareth not the true state of it, till opened by the adverse party. Some lawyers seem to keep an assurance-office in their chambers, and will warrant any cause brought unto them, knowing if they fail, they lose nothing but what was lost long since,—their credit."

The career of Audley's ambition closed with the extinction of the "Court of Wards," by which he incurred the loss of above L.100,000. On that occasion he observed, that "his ordinary losses were as the shavings of his beard, which only grew the faster by them; but the loss of this place was like the cutting off of a member, which was irrecoverable." The hoary usurer pined at the decline of his genius, discoursed on the vanity of the world, and hinted at retreat. A facetious friend told him a story of an old rat, who having acquainted the young rats that he would at length retire to his hole, desiring none to come near him: their curiosity, after some days, led them to venture to look into the hole; and there they discovered the old rat sitting in the midst of a rich Parmesan cheese. It is probable that the loss of the last L.100,000, disturbed his digestion, for he did not long survive his Court of Wards.

Such was this man, converting wisdom into cunning, invention into trickery, and wit into cynicism. Engaged in no honourable cause, he, however, showed a mind resolved, making plain the crooked and involved path he trode. *Sustine et abstine*, to bear and to forbear, was the great principle of Epictetus, and our monied stoic bore all the contempt and hatred of the living smilingly, while he forbore all the consolations of our common nature to obtain his end. He died in unblest celibacy: And thus he received the curses of the living for his rapine, while the stranger who grasped the million he had raked together, owed him no gratitude at his death.—*D'Israeli.*

EMIGRATION.

THE very favourable accounts which have been received from the agriculturists and others who emigrated to Canada, two or three years ago, from East Lothian and Berwickshire, have excited much attention among the whole agricultural population of these counties. There does not appear to be a single person who has emigrated from the district we have mentioned, who has not succeeded in the most remarkable manner. Farmers, who went out five or six years ago with a few hundred pounds, are now possessed of properties worth nearly as much annually; artisans and mechanics, who had barely the means of defraying the expenses of their passage; and who, had they remained, would never have been able to do more than provide for the day which was passing over them, have become men of capital; the proprietors, in many instances, of considerable farms, and are adding yearly to their wealth. It seems, indeed, of little importance in what line the emigrants have engaged: farmers, mechanics, store-keepers, medical men, have been all successful in an eminent degree. It is not therefore remarkable, in the present depressed state of agriculture, and when the future prospects of the agriculturist, and those depending upon him, are so gloomy, that Canada is looked to as the land of hope and of promise, and that the number of emigrants should increase annually. Nor is it merely the young, who have not hitherto engaged in the business of life, who are preparing to set out. Men advanced in life, who, in many instances, have acquired a competency, are also making arrangements to emigrate with their whole families. Indeed the minds of men are completely unsettled by the favourable accounts which have been received. Canada seems the only subject they think of; and conversation among all ranks is almost confined to emigration. All information regarding it is most eagerly received, and is spread over the country with extraordinary celerity. The great body of the population is evidently considering whether they ought to remain longer at home or not. If matters continue for a very few years in their present state, emigration will take place to a degree hitherto unprecedented, and its effects cannot fail to be felt by the country. That any benefit will arise to those who remain at home, from the emigration, we do not anticipate; for the capital of the country will be diminished by it much more rapidly than the population. Hardly a person leaves the country without some capital; and many of those who set out last year, as well as of those who are now about to emigrate, possess large capitals. The landlords are beginning to take the alarm at seeing many of the best of their tenantry about to transfer their wealth across the Atlantic; but they cannot prevail on themselves to take the only means which is likely to check it—lowering their rents. On the contrary, the farms which have lately been in the market, have uniformly been let to the highest bidder; and as the rents thus obtained are, in some instances, nearly as high as ever, they consider the complaints of their tenants to be without foundation.

While on the subject of emigration, we cannot help remarking how much better it would be to afford facilities to the poor Irish to emigrate, than to tax the people of England and Scotland to keep up a large military force to put them down with the bayonet. Besides an enormous police force, one-third of our army is employed in Ireland. Now, without taking into account the great expense of the non-effective branch of our army, the estimates for the effective branch for the current year, are L.3,555,418, one-third of which is L.1,185,139, being the annual cost of the military alone, employed in keeping down the Irish. Now, if a few of our ships of war were employed as transports, and a small part of the above million expended in the purchase of provisions, thousands of those Irishmen, whose crimes are now so much expatiated on, might be carried out to Canada, where many of them would, undoubtedly, in a few years ecome men of respectability and opulence. To enable them to support themselves in Canada very little assistance would be required. If they sailed early in the season, they would arrive in sufficient time to clear as much ground s would enable them to raise a crop of potatoes; and t would only be necessary to furnish them with a few imple and unexpensive tools for clearing the ground, and or cultivating the potatoes, and to support them until the rop was ripe. We have no doubt, that the sums which are anually expended on soldiers and policemen in Ireland, would provide the means for carrying out half a million of ersons to Canada, and for supporting them as long as would e found necessary. Were such an outlet afforded for the urbulent and starving population, it could hardly fail in roducing the most beneficial effects, not only by removing hose who are the most likely to create disturbances, but, y increasing the wage of labour, and, consequently, the eans of comfortable subsistence to those who remained. Nor would Ireland be the only gainer. The labouring population of Britain, and probably also the classes above hem, are yearly becoming more and more depressed by the onstant emigration of the poorer Irish into this country. That emigration would, by the plan we have proposed be either altogether stopped, or materially checked, and thus he depression of our labouring population would be greatly retarded. It is now full time that some other means than brute force were resorted to for the pacification of Ireland. Such means have been tried for centuries, and the Bill now before Parliament tells us with what success. That the Coercive Bill will have any permanent effect, the most sanguine of its advocates do not pretend; that it will eventually exasperate all the evils which it professes to remedy, s much more probable. After such an outrage on the iberties of Ireland, no one can wonder that the Repeal of he Union, and a separation from a country which rules so despotically, will be eagerly embraced by every Irishman of spirit. That such a repeal, and, as we have always thought, consequent separation will be ruinous to Britain, we cannot hesitate in thinking; and every one, therefore, who has the good of his country at heart, must be desirous of seeing quiet restored to Ireland, not merely for a time, by the rude means of Martial Law, domiciliary visits, and the bayonet, but permanently, by improving the state of her population and by the removal of the evils under which she suffers.

MEDICAL SELECTIONS.

TREATMENT OF BURNS.

There is no part of surgery on which there has been greater difference of opinion, than the treatment of burns; and even the remedies popularly trusted to are very various. It must be admitted, however, that while medical writers have suggested applications, absolutely pernicious in spite of all the plausible theories with which they have recommended them, the remedies known among the people are only more or less salutary; and common sense has preserved them from the improper practice of applying boiling water or turpentine, to an injury requiring to be treated by far gentler means. It is not our intention to enter into any discussion of the comparative merits of the different applications that have been recommended, but simply to state what in general the most judicious practitioners have found to be successful. We shall first suppose that a person has received a pretty extensive scald, and that assistance is promptly at hand. Supposing the skin unbroken, whether blisters are rising or not, we would strenuously recommend the instant application of cold to the injured part. A ready mode of doing this, is by adding one part of vinegar to one part of water, taking a towel, or many folds of soft linen, dipped in this mixture, and keeping it constantly wet to the part, continuing this cooling treatment for a longer or shorter period, according to the continuance or abatement of the pain. We have mentioned vinegar and water, as a good means of applying cold, because, besides its intrinsic excellence, it is generally at hand; but supposing it not to be readily got, we may attempt the same effects by cloths soaked in cold water alone, or spirits and water; always on the supposition that the injury does not destroy the skin, or at most only the outer skin. If there is a deep injury, any acrid substance added to the water, as vinegar or spirits, would be too painful to be borne, and would only add to the irritation; it is, therefore, better to use oily applications, and of these the Carron Oil is one of the most famous. It is made by mixing equal parts of linseed oil and limewater; this is to be plentifully smeared on the place burnt, with a feather or hair pencil, and a single fold of linen placed over it to prevent the access of air. Immediately after the first application of the cooling wash, or oily matter, if the paleness and shivering be great, a full dose of laudanum should be given, proportioned to the age of the patient. During the cure, the diet should be moderate; and no strong drink allowed, except perhaps a little wine and water, or spirits, at first, as a cordial to assist in restoring an equable heat to the system, and puting an end to the depressed and pallid state. In many cases, the application of cold will accomplish the resolution or cure of the burn without further trouble; the skin will not rise in blisters, and at worst the outer skin will dry and peel off. Or supposing blisters have arisen, when the pain has ceased, they may be pricked with a needle, and the fluid allowed to escape, keeping the skin on as long as possible. It may happen that the pain abates and the skin comes off, leaving the part below in a state of ulceration or suppuration; in this case, emollient poultices are to be applied till the suppuration appears inclined to cease, and then the sores are to be dressed with cerate, lard, Goulard's extract, or the like. In the dressing of burns, care must be taken to keep the raw surfaces from contact, to prevent them from growing together. Thus the fingers must all be dressed separately; joints should be extended so as to prevent them from being permanently bent; and the chin must be kept from growing to the breast. It is a disagreeable and frequent characteristic of burns, that they are apt to be accompanied with great rising of proud flesh, and to leave unsightly scars, much above the level of the skin. The rising flesh must be eaten down by blue vitrol, by lunar caustic, or other escharotics; and the new skin kept to its level by proper bandaging and adhesive plaster. When the clothes are set on fire, or when, as too often happens, old persons intoxicated, or incapable of taking care of themselves, fall into the fire, deplorable consequences ensue. Large eschars are formed and drop off, extensive ulceration and exhausting suppuration take place, and death at a longer or shorter period follows. We must dress the sores with all the care and skill possible; and support the strength with bark and wine, and nutritious diet, to give the constitution, if possible, the power of supporting the copious discharge.

A remedy which has in some cases appeared to do good, and has of late been much celebrated, is to apply cotton to extensive burns. The good effects of this are owing to its protecting the tender nervous extremities of the injured part, from the contact of the external air. As formerly hinted, some practitioners have adopted a theory to satisfy themselves about the application of turpentine to burns; but as this practice has not yet made its way beyond the profession, it is unnecessary to caution the general reader against its adoption.

SCRAPS.

ORIGINAL AND SELECTED.

MILTON'S MORNING HAUNTS AND EMPLOYMENTS.

"Those Morning Haunts are where they should be,—at home; not sleeping, or concocting the surfeits of an irregular feast, but up and stirring, in winter often, ere the sound of any bell awake men to labour or to devotion; in summer as oft, with the bird that first arouses, or not much tardier, to read good authors, or cause them to be read, till the attention be weary, or memory have its full fraught; there, with useful and generous labours, preserving the body's health and hardiness, to render lightsome, clear, and not lumpish obedience to the mind, to the cause of religion, and our country's liberty, when it shall require firm hearts in sound bodies, to stand and cover their stations, rather than to see the ruin of our protestation, and the enforcement of a slavish life."

NICK-NAMES.—In the moors of Lancashire, there are numerous instances where wives know their husbands only by their nick-names, and not by their real names; and the custom of giving and adhering to "*noms de guerre*" is so prevalent, that the men do not even know their own names. The Cockey Moor postman lately carried a letter addressed to himself, "James Whitehead," about him for a whole fortnight, without knowing that the letter was for him, or that James Whitehead was his name : instead of "Purring Jim, o' owd Mall o' Tums o' long Ben fowd ;" and great was his astonishment when the wise man of the village, who happened to have been present at his christening, informed him, that, "if he were not mislippent, parsun namt him Jim Whitehead, as his mam stood wi him in ur harms." At the recent County Election, an Entwistle freeholder, who had had his registry attended to by his landlord, was brought to the polling-booth, at Newton, to tender his vote. On being asked his name, he very readily replied, "Mad Bill." He was reminded that this must be his nick-name; he scratched his head, and studied a little, and said, "Aw reckon yo wan't name as is ith' lease?" On being replied to in the affirmative, he scratched his head, Hodge-like, and said, "Hout a bit! Awst think on soon. —Aw think, i' my heart. it's Juan K——, because they sed Squoire ot did um at Bouton, a gud deal o' years sin, wurt same name os me." The next query was—"Where do you reside?" The answer was—"Entwas.." The clerk, being nonplussed, gently inquired, "How is it spelled?" The voter replied "Aw'm no great skollard, but aw believes it begins e——n——t, ent; but as for ' twssl,' it's more than aw con manage; so yo mun just put doawn that os youn o' moind."

LIVERPOOL AND MANCHESTER RAILWAY.—Notwithstanding the injury which the pecuniary interests of the concern sustained by the prevalence of the cholera during the two best months of the year, July and August, which occasioned a diminution in the number of passengers as compared with the preceding half year, to the extent of nearly 74,000 persons, yet this loss was in some degree made up by the increase of business in the conveyance of merchandise, and a decrease in the general expense of management. The total number of passengers conveyed by the railway from the 1st of July to the 31st of December 1832, was 182,823, and the merchandise, during the same period, amounted to 86,642 tons, independently of the coal that was also carried during the same period. The gross receipts of the half year amounted to L.80,901, of which L.43,120 was for passengers, and L.37,781 for goods; the expenses were L.48,278, (of which one item alone, for the repairs of the locomotive engines, amounted to L.12,646,) leaving a profit for the six months of L.32,623; to this sum should be added the balance in the hands of the treasurer for the preceding half year of L.1538—total L.34,161. This profit enables the company to make a dividend of L.4, 4s. per share, to be paid on the 5th of next month, and leaves a surplus of L.693.

FINERY.—There is nothing more vulgar among the sins of social life than what is termed *finery*. It is, in fact, a distinguishing mark of *absence* of caste; for what can a person, *really* distinguished by birth or merit, gain by presumptuous disparagement of the rest of the human race? It is the policy of the eminent to *elevate* the claims of those beneath them, in order that, by raising the standard of comparison, their own superiority may attain yet higher distinction; and the moment a man or woman affects to be *fine*—to shrink from contact with any but the elect, and to raise a glass of inquiry to the unknown physiognomies of plebeian life, it is to be inferred that "something is rotten in the state of Denmark;" that so studious an arrangement of the folds of the velvet mantle and ermined robe, purports the concealment of some gash or blemish beneath, known only to the wearer.—*Mrs. Gore.*

THE MINSTREL.

Keen blaws the wind o'er Donocht Head,
  The snaw drives smelly through the dale,
The gaberlunzie tirls at my sneck,
  And shivering tells his woeful tale.
"Cauld is the night; O, let me in,
  And dinna let your minstrel fa';
And dinna let his winding sheet
  Be naething but a wreath o' snaw.

"Full ninety summers have I seen,
  And piped whar gorcocks whirring flew;
And mony a day ye've danced, I ween,
  To lilts that frae my drone I blew."

My Eppie waked, and soon she cried,
  "Get up, gudeman, an' let him in;
For weel ye ken the winter night
  Seemed short when he began his din."

My Eppie's voice—O, wow, it's sweet!
  E'en though she banns and scolds a wee;
But when its tuned to pity's tale,
  O, haith, its doubly sweet to me!

"Come ben, auld carle, I'll stir my fire,
  And gar it bleeze a bonny flame.
Your blude is thin; ye've tint the gate;
  Ye should na stray sae far frae hame."

"Nae hame have I," the Minstrel said,
  Since faction overturned my ha';
And, weeping at the eve of life,
  I wander through a wreath o' snaw."

This touching ballad was published anonymously in a Newcastle newspaper, and attributed to Burns, who was then writing. He said to a friend that it was not his; but that "he would give ten guineas that it were." The name of the author was Pickering.

CONTENTS OF NO. XXXIV.

Church Establishments *versus* Voluntary Churches	177
The Bible	179
History of the Discovery of Phrenology	180
Sierra Leone and its Capital, Freetown	181
Tithes	183
Slavery, (a Night Scene in Africa)	ib.
Elements of Thought—Some of the Evil Consequences of Church Establishments—Tendency of the Age—Corrective Measures	184
Hymn of the Confederate Poles of Lublonski	ib.
The Story-Teller—The Harehound and the Witch	185
Life of an Usurer, (Hugh Audley)	188
Emigration	190
Medical Selections—Treatment of Burns	191
Scraps—Milton's Morning Haunts and Employments—Nick-Names—Liverpool and Manchester Railway—Finery—The Minstrel	192

Edinburgh: Printed by and for John Johnstone, 19, St. James's Square.—Published by John Anderson, Jun., Bookseller, 55, North Bridge Street, Edinburgh; by John Macleod, and Atkinson & Co., Booksellers, Glasgow; and sold by all Booksellers and Venders of Cheap Periodicals.

THE Schoolmaster,
AND EDINBURGH WEEKLY MAGAZINE.

CONDUCTED BY JOHN JOHNSTONE.

THE SCHOOLMASTER IS ABROAD.—LORD BROUGHAM.

No. 35.—Vol. II.   SATURDAY, MARCH 30, 1833.   Price Three-Halfpence.

AIR—RESPIRATION.

In a former number we explained the composition of air,* and we shall now make a few remarks explanatory of the objects of respiration, and of the evil effects of breathing impure air. Healthy food, of whatever kind, is converted by the action of the digestive apparatus into a milky-like fluid termed *chyle*, which is taken up by numerous vessels opening into the intestines, and by them conveyed to a vein near the heart, where it mixes with the blood returning from the various parts of the body. The whole now enters the right side of the heart, from whence it is forced into blood vessels, by which it is conveyed to the lungs; continuing its course, it passes from the lungs back again to the left side of the heart. Here it is again forced into blood vessels, through which it passes to every, even the minutest part of the body; at the extremities of these vessels it enters the veins through which it again returns to the right side of the heart. The vessels which convey the blood *from* the heart are termed *arteries*, those which return it are called *veins*. The blood is injected into the arteries by the contractions of the heart; and though the arteries, by their contractions, also assist the motion of the blood, yet it is found that the contractions of the heart correspond with those of the arteries; and thus, by placing the hand on an artery even at the extremity of the body, we can tell how often the heart contracts; this is, in fact, the pulse. In healthy people the heart contracts about seventy times in a minute. These contractions go on unceasingly from birth to death; and it is calculated that the whole blood passes through the heart every three minutes. The objects of the circulation are most important. The particles which compose the body are continually changing; new particles taking the place of old. Every new formation, whether it be of bone, muscle, nerve, &c., is derived from the blood. It is necessary, then, to provide for this continual waste, or change, by supplying every part with healthy blood, that none may languish for want of nourishment—and such is the purpose of the circulation. We have, however, spoken of a double circulation; of one when the blood goes from the right side of the heart through the lungs, and back again to the left side of the heart; and of another, where the blood passes from the left side of the heart to the various parts of the body, and returns through the veins to the right side of the heart. The first, or the circulation through the lungs, is named the *pulmonic*—the last, or that through the body, the *systemic* circulation. The objects of these circulations are entirely different, though both are, of course, conducive to the same end—the support of life. We have already explained the purposes of the systemic, and shall now explain those of the pulmonic circulation. After passing through the arteries, and serving the purposes of nourishment, the properties of the blood are no longer the same;—it is now not fit for the nourishment of the body, and is returned through the veins to the right side of the heart. Here commences the pulmonic circulation. In passing through the lungs, the blood undergoes an important change; a change on which the existence of the animal depends. The lungs is a substance composed almost entirely of blood vessels, which are filled with the circulating blood; and of air cells, supplied with air by the process of respiration. While flowing through the lungs, the carbon of the blood combines with the oxygen of the air, and forms carbonic acid gas, or that kind of air which escapes from fermenting liquors, which, along with the nitrogen of the air, is expelled from the lungs by expiration, while, by inspiration, fresh air immediately succeeds, which, also acting on the blood, undergoes a like change, and is also in its turn expired. The blood, in its passage through the lungs, is changed from a dark, to a bright red colour. It has, in fact, been renovated, fitted once more for the systemic circulation, and for the nourishment of the various parts. Accordingly, it passes on to the left side of the heart, there to commence the circulation through the body. We have thus then, described the purposes of the two circulations: the one is to provide for the waste which is at all times proceeding; the other is for purifying and renewing the properties of the blood, which it has lost while administering to the nourishment of the body, and also for converting *chyle* into proper blood.

* The proportions of the gases were accidentally reversed; they are four of nitrogen to one of oxygen.

These explanations, imperfect though they be, will enable our readers to perceive the vast importance of attending to the state of air where a number of individuals are collected. Air which has already been respired cannot, of course, answer that purpose a second time, because the oxygen, the principle of the air which purifies and renovates the blood, has already been consumed. If care, therefore, be not taken to change the air, if ventilation be not attended to, the room will soon be filled with nitrogen gas, the other component of air, and with carbonic acid gas, the product of respiration, and evil consequences will immediately follow. An animal kept in a confined quantity of air speedily dies. Our readers will recollect the account we lately gave of the lamentable death of 123 persons out of 146 who were confined but for a few hours in a dungeon in Calcutta, where the ventilation was insufficient to provide fresh air for so many individuals. We need not, however, multiply examples—the principle in every case is the same. Though these facts have been long known, any thing like a proper attention to ventilation is, to this day, very much neglected, which we can attribute to nothing but the grossest ignorance on the part of the public generally. Indeed, one great division of the public is so exclusively occupied with more engrossing pursuits—some in money-making, others in the gratification of their vanity and other lower feelings, that they have no time to attend to their mental and bodily comfort; while the other great division has not hitherto possessed, nor does it yet possess the means of gaining the requisite information, far less of putting this information into practice. Thus we daily meet in large numbers in churches and other assemblies, for the most part with closed doors and windows; we sleep in small, close rooms, carefully surrounded with curtains, as if we regarded the approach of fresh air with horror. We have no doubt that much of the bodily and mental debility under which our manufacturers labour, is to be attributed to imperfect ventilation; and certainly, whatever objections may be urged to a legislative interference with the hours of labour, there can be none to adopt some means of compelling the manufacturers to ventilate their factories in an efficient manner. The houses of the labourers are, in general, ill provided with the means of ventilation, their windows being fixed, while, from their smallness, it is peculiarly necessary. This was, however, remedied in some parts of the country, on the late alarm of cholera. Those disgusting manufactories of carbonic gas, or non-respirable air, dunghills—because this gas rises in great quantity from fermenting dung—were also removed from the doors, though in some places they are already beginning to creep back. We are sometimes inclined to bless the cholera, owing to the favourable impulse it gave to the mind of the public.

MODERN GALLANTRY.

I shall believe in it, when the Dorimants in humbler life, who would be thought, in their way, notable adepts in this refinement, shall act upon it in places where they are not known, or think themselves not observed—when I shall see the traveller for some rich tradesman, part with his admired box coat, to spread it over the defenceless shoulders of the poor woman, who is passing to her parish on the roof of the same stage-coach with him, drenched in the rain—when I shall no longer see a woman standing up in a pit of a London theatre, till she is sick and faint with the exertion, with men about her, seated at their ease, and jeering at her distress; till one, that seems to have more manners or conscience than the rest, significantly declares, "she should be welcome to his seat, if she were a little younger and handsomer." Place this dapper warehouseman, or that rider, in a circle of their own female acquaintance, and you shall confess you have not seen a politer-bred man in Lothbury.

Lastly, I shall begin to believe that there is some such principle, influencing our conduct, when more than one half of the drudgery and coarse servitude of the world cease to be performed by women.

Until that day comes, I shall never believe this boasted point to be any thing more than a conventional fiction; a pageant got up between the sexes, in a certain rank, and at a certain time of life, in which both find their account equally.

I shall be even disposed to rank it among the salutary fictions of life, when in polite circles I shall see the same attentions paid to age as to youth, to homely features as to handsome, to coarse complexions as to clear—to the woman, as she is a woman, not as she is a beauty, a fortune, or a title.

I shall believe it to be something more than a name, when a well-dressed gentleman in a well-dressed company, can advert to the topic of *female old age* without exciting, and intending to excite a sneer:—when the phrases, "antiquated virginity," and such a one has "overstaid her market," pronounced in good company, shall raise immediate offence in man, or woman, that shall hear them spoken.

Joseph Plaice, of Bread-Street Hill, merchant, and one of the Directors of the South Sea company—the same to whom Edwards, the Shakspeare commentator, has addressed a fine sonnet—was the only pattern of consistent gallantry I have met with. He took me under his shelter at an early age, and bestowed some pains upon me. I owe to his precepts and example whatever there is of the man of business (and that is not much) in my composition. It was not his fault that I did not profit more. Though bred a Presbyterian, and brought up a merchant, he was the finest gentleman of his time. He had not one system of attention to females in the drawing room, and *another* in the shop or at the stall. I do not mean that he made no distinction. But he never lost sight of sex, or overlooked it in the casualties of a disadvantageous situation. I have seen him stand bare-headed—smile, if you please—to a poor servant girl, while she has been inquiring of him the way to some street—in such a posture of unforced civility, as neither to embarrass her in the acceptance, nor himself in the offer of it. He was no dangler, in the common acceptation of the word, after women: but he reverenced and upheld, in every form in which it came before him, womanhood. I have seen him—nay smile not—tenderly escorting a market-woman, whom he had encountered in a shower, exalting his umbrella over her poor basket of fruit, that it might receive no damage, with as much carefulness as if she had been a Countess. To the reverend form of Female Eld he would yield the wall (though it were to an ancient beggar-woman) with more ceremony than we can afford to show our grandams. He was the Preux Chevalier of Age; the Sir Calidore, or Sir Tristan, to those who have no Calidores or Tristans to defend them. The roses, that had long faded thence, still bloomed for him in those withered and yellow cheeks.

He was never married, but in his youth he paid his addresses to the beautiful Susan Winstanley, old Winstanley's daughter of Clapton—who dying in the early days of their courtship confirmed to him the resolution of perpetual batchelorship. It was during their short courtship, he told me, that he had been one day treating his mistress with a profusion of civil speeches—the common gallantries, to which kind of thing she had hitherto manifested no repugnance, but in this instance with no effect. He could not obtain from her a decent acknowledgment in return. She rather seemed to resent his compliments. He could not set it down to caprice, for the lady had always shewn herself above that littleness. When he ventured on the following day, finding her a little better-humoured, to expostulate with her on her coldness of yesterday, she confessed, with her usual frankness, that she had no sort of dislike to his attentions; that she could even endure some high-flown compliments; that a young woman placed in her situation had a right to expect all sort of civil things said to her; that she hoped, she could digest a dose of adulation, short of insincerity, with as little injury to her humility as most young women: but that, a little before he had commenced his compliments, she had overheard him by accident, in rather rough language, rating a young woman, who had not brought home his cravats quite to the appointed time; and she thought to herself, "As I am Miss Susan Winstanley, and a young lady, a reputed beauty, and known to be a fortune, I can have my choice of the finest speeches from the mouth of this very fine gentleman who is courting me, but if I had been poor Mary Such-a-one, (naming the milliner,) and had failed of bringing home the cravats at the appointed hour, though perhaps I had sat up half the night to forward them, what sort of compliments should I have received then? And my woman's pride came to my assistance; and I thought, that if it were only to do *me* honour, a female, like myself, might have received handsomer usage: and I was determined not to accept any fine speeches, to the compromise of that sex, the belonging to which was, after all, my strongest claim and title to them."

I think the lady discovered both generosity, and a just way of thinking, in this rebuke which she gave her lover; and I have sometimes imagined, that the uncommon strain of courtesy, which through life regulated the actions and behaviour of my friend towards all of womankind indiscriminately, owed its happy origin to this seasonable lesson from the lips of his lamented mistress.

I wish the whole female world would entertain the same notion of these things, that Miss Winstanley showed. Then we should see something of the spirit of consistent gallantry; and no longer witness the anomaly of the same man, a pattern of true politeness to a wife, of cold contempt or rudeness to a sister—the idolater of his female mistress—the disparager and despiser of his no less female aunt, or unfortunate, still female, maiden cousin. Just so much respect as a woman derogates from her own sex, in whatever condition placed—her handmaid, or dependant—she deserves to have diminished from herself on that score; and probably will feel the diminution, when youth, and beauty, and advantages, not inseparable from sex, shall lose of their attraction. What a woman should demand of a man, in courtship, or after it, is first, respect for her as she is a woman; and next to that, to be respected by him above all other women. But let her stand upon her female character, as upon a foundation; and let the attentions, incident to individual preference, be so many pretty additaments, and ornaments, as many, and as fanciful, as you please, to that main structure. Let her first lesson be, with sweet Susan Winstanley, to *reverence her sex.*

ELIA.

GERMAN MANNERS.*

They manage their hospitalities incomparably better than we do—no *stuck out* drawing room parties, solemnly convened, awaiting a nocturnal summons to dine, and simpering out the interval in a martyrdom of formal talk;—no playing at ladies and gentlemen in their Sunday clothes. Refection and sociability are the true objects of a German repast. Your digestion is not taxed with any rules or observances that can in the slightest degree discompose the process. Even your lion of a talker, for effect sake, would be a sort of monster, whose best things would pass completely unheeded.

The German has diurnally four regular meals—breakfast at eight, dinner at one, an evening repast at four, and coffee and supper at nine. His symposiums are moderate. If we condemn such *gourmands*, assuredly in England we have not much to boast on the score of abstinence, with our eggs, tea, and cold meat for breakfast, a lunch (itself no despicable dinner) at two or three o'clock, the grand evening cram at seven, besides a supplementary complement of tea and coffee, and, until Abernethy's book appeared, a supper. Yet there are few liver cases in Germany. The people of all conditions are well nourished and portly, and in possession of a stock of health and strength not to be accomplished among us by all our might of mutton and blue pill, of which latter they know no more than they do of our bile and blue devils.

But notwithstanding the absence of blue devils, it should seem that they possess an invincible dulness, which to a traveller, must be a bore of the first order. In proof of this charge, Sir Arthur quotes Madame de Staël's opinion in support of his own:—" In Germany," says this queen of the blues, "they don't know how to express their thoughts in conversation; and very few persons, even among the most distinguished, are in the habit of asking and answering questions; so that there is hardly any thing that can deserve to be called society.

" I myself might have as easily drawn living water out of the obdurate flint without the wand of Moses, as by any device got them into a *fluent* humour. Information was to be dug out by dint of distressing labour; the *testa tedesca* to be worked like a pump, which, if you would have a flow at all, you must keep perpetually feeding. Pleasantry, or any approach to it, is quite exotic. I have now been here several months, and if my affidavit were required to the fact, I hardly think I could honestly charge my conscience with ever having seen a German laugh, with three exceptions, the two already mentioned at Marburg, and the third, the basso at my quartett, who used, when any thing tickled his fancy, to explode into a sort of epileptic chuckle, and then tenor and secondo would stare at him with more than common seriousness."

German Barons are, as is well known, a vastly plentiful race; and no wonder, seeing that " the title is purchasable at Wurtemburg for an old song." On this point Sir Arthur, waxing somewhat satirical, says, " Though Darmstadt absolutely swarms with the gaudy herd of cordons and stars, yet there are but very few nobility of ancient family. A *von* is a diurnally negociable affair, and orders of various kinds are conferred without any specification of services or desert. All the sons of a baron are barons, *et qui nascentur ab illis*, just as all the sons of an ass are asses to the thousandth generation. A sensible German gave me a rule to go by, in estimating the genuine worth of the baronial genus; and that is, if a man calls himself Baron you may *suspect* him; if only Mr. you may *respect* him."

RICHES OF PARLIAMENTARY CANDIDATES,—CAUSES OF THE CONTEMPT SHEWN TO " LANDLESS MEN."

The *Westminster Review*, in taking up our admired Andrew Marvell, our *beau ideal* of a Member of Parliament, (See *Schoolmaster*, 2d No.) makes the following remarks on Marvell:—" History does not state that the friends of tyranny and corruption raised any objection to Marvell as a Parliamentary candidate, on the score of his poverty. But they are now become bolder; and the struggle of party, which is at present going on, affords an opportunity for the discussion of an important question to the welfare of the community. The *gravamen* of the charge raised by one of the contending parties against the other, is that of not being rich, or, as some of the most violent express it, of being beggars,—the world being too far advanced to pay much attention to the cries of heresy and blasphemy,

* From an account of Sir Arthur Faulkner's Work on Germany.

which are become tolerably threadbare since the days when they assumed the sound of 'Crucify him! Crucify him!' Now this charge of poverty involves matters of so much importance, that the question becomes one not of individual or temporary interest, but a question of principle, involving the consideration of interests as enduring and universal as man. The present is the first time that the charge of not being rich has been openly brought against Parliamentary candidates; and is also the first time, at least since the days of Andrew Marvell, that candidates had come forward to offer themselves to the people's choice, resting their pretensions solely on their intrinsic merit,—to wit, on their capacity, their honesty, and their knowledge. Where has this heavy charge, this grave accusation, lain so long concealed? The truth is, there was no guilt in being poor, till poor men stood forth the champions of the poor. Where was the accusation when Burke, and Sheridan, and Canning, and Huskisson, and Mr. Praed, and Mr. Wrangham, and men of that class came forward as candidates? Neither the monied nor the landed interest conceived itself to be in danger, or raised any hue and cry then. The people of England now stand in the place of the individuals who brought into Parliament the gentlemen named above; and the moment they begin to exercise their privilege, the 'men of property' raise a howl as loud as if their souls, which are their money bags, were ravaged from them. Expand your sordid souls, and conceive that independence has nothing to do with wealth,—that a man is independent, not in proportion as he has many possessions, but as he has few wants. Does not all history, all experience, go to convince you of the falsehood of your position? Would all the riches in the world have purchased a Socrates or a Bentham? Would the riches of the universe have satisfied a Charles Stuart, or a George Guelph, or formed one atom of security for their political good conduct? As is the model, so are the copies; as is the master, so are the followers. The vulgar admirers of a Guelph and a Stuart may be expected to labour under some difficulty in the conception, that there are men who would dine with more satisfaction at the simple board of Marvell than at the '*regales dupes*' of a Charles or a George,—men who could live, happy and contented, without gorgeous palaces, coroneted trappings, gilded lacqueys, and jewelled harlots. But though such qualities are rare, they are to be found; and the education necessary to form them has not entirely, with Astræa, deserted the earth. Now, it may be asked of any person of sense, whether it is most likely that a man who, though he has little, has what he wants, would, for the sake of making some addition to his income, sell the power of being useful, not only to the present race of his countrymen, but to the men of all countries, and of every time,—or that a man who has much more, should do the same, for the purpose of gratifying his irregular desires. For the man who has once so sold himself, is sold for ever. He has irrevocably sullied the purity of a patriot's honour. There is a stain upon the brightness of his name, which the tide of ages could not wash out. Those men must have a strange idea, not only of the morality, but of the intellect, of a philosophic Radical like Marvell, if they imagine him such a dolt as to sacrifice so much for so little; as to exchange a greater happiness for one so palpably, so immeasurably less."

MEMBERS OF PARLIAMENT may be, not inaptly, compared to coveys of partridges. In the early part of the season the birds are tame, and shots easily obtained. So Members at the commencement of the Session, are exceedingly courteous, affable, and easy of access. As the season proceeds the birds get wilder, stronger on the wing, and shots are much more difficult. So Members, who now, feel the daily, and almost hourly, annoyance of enclosure lawyers, rail-road lawyers, and turnpike-road lawyers, get more shy; they fear to present themselves at the front windows of their club-houses—sometimes change their lodgings, and get to the House through back ways and alleys, and are not easily caught by their pursuers. Towards the end of the season the birds are perfectly wild—soon a double-barrel Manton becomes perfectly useless. In like manner the Members, as the Session closes, avoid the private Bill-mongers with the utmost anxiety, exerting as much ingenuity to get rid of them as some have done to avoid a Sheriff's officer previous to their election. Burke replied to some one who asked his support to a private Bill, "That his *Injustice* was engaged."

THE FRENCH MOLL FLAGONS, OR VIVANDIÈRES.— A class of persons attached to the French army deserve especial mention. These were the *vivandières* or licensed suttler-women, of whom a certain number is attached to every regiment, in the proportion of four per battalion. They receive lodgment in barracks, and rations in the field. They wear, for the most part, a peculiar costume, have a *plaque*, or tin on the arm, denoting their number and the corps to which they belong, and have the exclusive privilege of selling spirits to the troops or battalion to which they are attached. Their dress was generally a glazed hat, a blue petticoat with a tri-coloured border, and red or *garance* military trousers, boots, a short cloak, and a keg slung round the shoulder, with a small basket containing one or two glasses, and a few loaves. Wherever the fire was the hottest, there they were to be seen; and it was singular to see the prevailing passion of gain, not only leading these heroines into the most dangerous positions, but to observe them utterly forgetful of the showers of grape and projectiles that, to use the expression of one of them, "fell like plums" around, alone intent on receiving their small change, or rating some debtor who had neglected to pay his score. Whilst, however, the matter of business was always kept in sight, they were not without frequently exhibiting instances of nobler sentiments. Their devotion and attention to the wounded, and the readiness with which they exposed themselves in the cause of humanity were as remarkable as praiseworthy. One amongst them was particularly cited. She was a young woman of rather prepossessing appearance, and peculiar for the neatness of her dress. Her courage and disregard of self were so striking, that she was not only cited by the whole army, and the subject of conversation to strangers, but she was thought worthy of being noticed in general orders. She was thus spoken of by Marshal Gerard, in his order of the day. "Antoinette Moran, cantinière of the 25th line, affords daily proofs of her courage and devotion; she rescued a wounded miner, who had fallen into the ditch, from under the enemy's fire. She had already had her hat perforated by a ball, in assisting a wounded man: and, amidst a shower of shells and bullets, she brought a bearer to carry off another. She deserves the gratitude of the army." During the subsequent reviews at Valenciennes, the celebrated cantinière was presented to the king, when she received a gold medal of 1,000 francs value, and a pension of 250 francs per annum. Accustomed as the British officers are to the dry and laconic style of our own general orders, where individual traits of courage, especially those performed by men below the rank of field officers, rarely find place, to notice the conduct of a woman may appear puerile. But the policy of such proceedings cannot be denied, and may safely be adopted by us who have no decoration for junior officers, and no provision for such soldiers as may particularly distinguish themselves. * * * In our army a single medal is distributed—not to record the valour of the men, but to commemorate the notoriety of the event. Honours of a similar nature are distributed; but when do they reach the breast of the subaltern, non-commissioned officer? * * * The concussion of air (from a bomb) was so great, that the lights were extinguished, and the gallery being filled with smoke and left in utter darkness, officers and men at the bottom supposed the roof had given way, and that they were buried; and, as the lateral gallery was not yet completely opened, there was no escape on that side. After a few moments' anxious suspense they were reassured by hearing the voice of a *vivandière*, who, though a second bomb followed close on the heels of the first, killing two and wounding three men, with the utmost coolness, walking down, and calling to one of the miners said, "Here's your dram, but you must drink from your hand, for the cursed shell has broken my glasses."—

A SMUGGLER'S TALE.

Upon the eastern coast of Suffolk, stands upon a high cliff, the village of Pakefield. It was formerly the haunt of many a bold and adventurous smuggler, and even in recent times, an occasional freak of that description took place, and the church itself has been the depository of "a run." In the broad face of day, a short time ago, a vessel was seen in the offing standing in for town, with a flag flying half-mast high, and shortly afterwards brought up in "Abraham's Bosom." A boat made the beach from her soon after; out jumped the crew with faces as long as handspikes, full of grief and woe. They inquired for the clergyman, and stated they had an old man, the father of the captain, who had died on board, and having great respect for him when living, they had been very unwilling to consign his remains to the "watery deep," but had determined to keep him, if possible, till they touched the land, in order to give him Christian burial. They were shewn the way to the parson's, where they succeeded in making good their tale, and exciting his commiseration for their pious feeling. The parson kindly complied with their wishes—had a coffin knocked together, and given to the crew, who hastened off with it to their ship. At the time appointed for the interment, the boat returned with the remains of their lamented and still dearly-respected shipmate. Six brawny Pakefield boys carried the coffin, followed by the weeping Nereides. To Kirdey Church they bent their way, but many were the restings which they made, for they bore a "deadly weight." At last they reached the church-yard, where his Reverence, the "cunning man," awaited his charge, but he expressed a desire to see the body. This was somewhat of a poser—the crew became more violent in their grief; but one, more alive to the living than the rest, and who bore his grief with becoming manliness, assured the clergyman that it would be very dangerous to open it—indeed, if they did, not one would be able to escape from the effect it would produce; and he, for one, would withdraw to a distance. The tears of our "weeping beauty" prevailed, and the coffin was consigned to its grave, and the service commenced with due solemnity, till the clergyman read "He heapeth up riches, and cannot tell who shall gather them,"—when the crew stared at each other.—"Be not deceived"—they looked around. "In the twinkling of an eye the *dead* shall be raised," exclaimed the clergyman—the crew tittered, and the parson stopped surprised; but went through the service. The ceremony ended, the clergyman retired, and the mourners, with solemn steps and downcast looks, went down to their ship. All was quiet—the grey mist of evening fell—the morning chased away the hours of night, and discovered that the vessel had sailed; but that was not all.—The grave had been opened, the *dead raised*, and the coffin, with L.1,100 worth of silk goods, carried off.

HAZLITT'S DEATH-BED.

The late William Hazlitt was hailed at the commencement of his term of authorship as a star. Vast things were predicted of him; and he, looking at the flattering picture, promised a happy voyage through life; but how soon was the scene changed! His determined bent of thought having been ascertained to be on the popular side, he was soon marked down as a fit object for legal calumny—the fitter because the more conspicuous. I use the term legal calumny with the intention of distinguishing that sort of wrong from illegal calumny, or libel. To say he was an infidel, that his associates were the same, to assail the integrity of his opinions and the motives from which he supported them, were the lightest missiles hurled at him by his enemies. Would he had lived to see his principles triumphant! The harassing nature of his occupation, the periodical supply of a certain quantum of copy, at length produced its effect. Those alone who are doomed to the same drudgery can appreciate my simile when I liken the press to "the horseleech, which cries give! give!" and this eternal cry, together with the application of stimuli to enable him to supply the demand, brought on that depravation of the stomach which is the usual effect of such a course of life. Reluctantly, nay, tremblingly, do I lift the veil which now hangs over the death-bed of poor Hazlitt. Imagine this highly-gifted man stretched on a couch in the back room of a second floor, his only child, and Martha, his faithful companion and friend, watching over him. Others were not deficient in their attentions and in providing the means of existence for him; for know, reader, that the death-bed of this author was not distinguished by the circumstance of his possessing wherewithal to support life when exertion was not in his power. It seems that some sudden turn of memory caused a pang in the dying man's bosom, and calling to one, whom I shall conceal under the name of Basilius; (to the gentleman thus designed, poor Hazlitt was already under obligations,) he gently said: "Basilius, stoop down, and let me talk to you." Basilius, crouching by the bedside.—"What can I do for you, my dear Hazlitt?" Hazlitt.—"Rid me of a pang." Basilius.—"Willingly, dear friend." Hazlitt.—"Lend me forty pounds?"—Basilius.—"Forty pounds! Dear Hazlitt, what can you want with forty pounds?" Hazlitt.—"Lend me forty pounds." Basilius.—"Do not talk so, my dear Hazlitt. You cannot want forty pounds." Hazlitt.—"I know—I know, Basilius what I ask. Lend it me—lend it me—I want it. 'Twill ease my mind—I want it. Lend it me: and think Basilius, think what the world will say when it is known that you lent a dying man forty pounds without a hope of being re-paid." The argument of Hazlitt did *not* prevail. Very shortly after he said to Martha, (whose attendance was constant,) "Martin, come here." Martin approached. Hazlitt,—"Martin, I want you to write a letter for me (starting up with energy.) Swear you will do it!" Martin went through the ceremony of an oath. Hazlitt.—"Now write, 'Dear Sir, I am at the last gasp; pray send me a hundred pounds, yours truly, Wm. Hazlitt.'"—It was written. Hazlitt.—"Now fold the letter." Martin folded it. Hazlitt.—"Write: 'To Francis Jeffrey, Esq. Edinburgh.'" Martha superscribed the letter. Hazlitt.—"Now I am satisfied." Martin.—"Shall I not put in a word, Hazlitt, explaining who wrote it?" Hazlitt, starting up.—"Swear, Martin, you won't do so; swear you'll send it as to it." Martin sent the letter; Hazlitt died very soon after; and on the day subsequent to his death, a letter from Jeffrey arrived with an enclosure of fifty pounds. Hone called on the previous day: he met a physician who had attended Hazlitt, at the door about to depart. "How is your patient, Sir?" inquired Hone. "'Tis all over," replied the medical man. "Clinically speaking, he ought to have died two days ago; he seemed to live, during the last eight-and-forty hours, purely in obedience to his own will." A third person, who had just come up, here observed, "He was waiting, perhaps, until return of post, for Jeffrey's reply. What he could have wanted with *that forty pounds*, is a perfect mystery." A few months before, Hone had met Hazlitt in the street, and kindly inquired as to his health and circumstances. Both were bad. "You are aware," said Hazlitt, "of some of my difficulties (those dreadful bills—those back accounts)—but no human being knows ALL. I have carried a volcano in my bosom up and down Paternoster-row, for a good two hours and a half. Even now I struggle—struggle mortally to quench—to quell it—but I can't. It's pent up throes and agonies, I fear, will break out—*Can you lend me* A SHILLING? I have been WITHOUT FOOD THESE TWO DAYS!" To state what Hone felt; and did, on hearing this, would be needless.

[The above appears in the *Monthly Magazine*. It is evidently a piece of exaggeration based on truth. All men are more or less false to themselves—literary men more than all.]

SLAVERY.

EXTRACT OF AN ADDRESS OF THE QUAKERS TO THEIR CHRISTIAN BRETHREN.

"THE present circumstances of the slaves, and of the free people of colour in the British colonies, the troubles in the Mauritius, the insurrections in Jamaica, and the religious persecutions which have followed, are momentous signs of the times as regards the continuance of slavery. Contemplating these events, and the increased interest for the oppressed, which so manifestly pervades every class of society in this land, the time is surely arrived when all should co-operate in Christian endeavours wholly and speedily to remove this national sin. When a people have become enlightened on the enormity of a crime, the guilt of continuing that crime is aggravated. Ignorance of the real character and tendency of slavery can no longer be pleaded. Warning has, of later times, succeeded warning with portentous rapidity. Divine revelation teaches us, and the history of mankind exemplifies the truth, that the retributive justice of the Most High does fall on individuals and on nations, when they wilfully continue in their guilt, and take not heed to the solemn warnings conveyed in the exercise of his over-ruling providence.

Now is our time:—protraction accumulates the guilt. It is fearful to look at the present state of society in the Colonies; it is still more fearful to look *forward*. As we believe that the continuance of slavery is an offence in the sight of God, so we also believe, that, if from a conviction of its sinfulness, in repentance towards God, we put away this evil from before him, he will graciously turn unto us and bless us—that if laws for its immediate and entire extinction, accompanied by judicious and equitable provisions, are forthwith made, our Heavenly Father will prosper this work of mercy. And we further believe, that by the substitution of the paternal care of the Government in the place of the arbitrary power and authority of the master, the peace of society will be secured, and the comfort, the happiness, and the prosperity of all be greatly promoted.

In conclusion, it is our earnest prayer that it may please Almighty God to continue to regard this kingdom for good; and to direct its councils in this and other acts of justice and mercy, so as to promote his glory in the harmony of his rational creation.

Signed in and on behalf of a meeting representing the religious Society of Friends in the intervals of its yearly meeting.

London, the 4th of the 1st month.

DIVINE RETRIBUTION FOR THE SIN OF SLAVERY.[*]—The West Indies are an example that the laws of God are never neglected with impunity, and that no lasting prosperity can be based upon injustice and human misery. Whether we look to the wretched slaves, the bankrupt planters, or their creditors, the merchants, who lend out their money upon usury, in vain sought to be wrung out of the tears and blood of wretched men; or to that portion of the British army, which, to the disgrace of this country, forms the only solid support of a system as impolitic as it is unjust,—we everywhere behold the curse of an avenging God pressing heavily upon the abettors of this slavish tyranny, which is without its equal in atrocity either in ancient or modern times. The command of God to the parents of the human race, to replenish the earth and possess it, which has overcome all other preventive checks to population, disease, misery, and vice, is yet found too weak to resist the overwhelming evils of Colonial Slavery. The ill-gotten treasure of the planter is his gang of slaves, and these slaves are perishing under the lash of their short-sighted oppressors. While the West Indians are dispeopling of their inhabitants, their fertile soil itself is stricken with an increasing barrenness,—the necessary effect of slave cultivation. Britain, in addition to a new load of guilt, has a new load of taxes, in the shape of bounties and preferences, to the inhumanity and folly of employing slave instead of free labour; and its commerce is restricted, and its workmen unemployed, in order that the planters may continue to extort labour by the cart-whip, instead of paying the labourer his justly-merited wages. If there is a spot in existence (except the regions of eternal punishment) where all things are contrary to the mind and laws of God, we must certainly find it in the West Indies, where property is robbery; labour, tyrannous exaction; law, merciless oppression; governors, murderers and men-stealers; and where all things are conducted, not according to the maxims of a wise and holy Being, but according to the devices of the enemy of human happiness,—the envier, in his own abyss of misery, of all prosperity: and who, in the triumph of evil over good in the West Indies, glories that he has still unlimited power in one corner of the world, though even there, while one well-wisher to humanity remains on earth, neither he nor his adherents can hope any longer to keep "his goods in peace."

BOOK STALLS—LOVE OF BOOKS.

THERE is a class of street-readers whom I can never contemplate without affection—the poor gentry, who, not having wherewithal to buy or hire a book, filch a little learning at the open stalls—the owner, with his hard eye, casting envious looks at them all the while, and wondering when they will have done. Venturing tenderly, page after page, expecting every moment when he shall interpose his edict, and yet, unable to deny themselves the gratification, they "snatch a fearful joy." Martin B——, in this way, by daily fragments, got through two volumes of Clarissa; when the stall-keeper damped his laudable ambition, by asking him (it was in his younger days) whether he meant to purchase the work? M—— declares, that under no circumstance of his life did he ever peruse a book with half the satisfaction which he took in those uneasy snatches. A quaint poetess of our day has moralized upon this subject in two very touching but homely stanzas:—

" I saw a boy with eager eye
Open a book upon a stall,
And read, as he'd devour it all:
Which when the stall-man did espy,
Soon to the boy I heard him call,—
" You, Sir! you never buy a book;
Therefore on one you shall not look!"
The boy passed slowly on, and, with a sigh,
He wished he never had been taught to read,
Then of the old churl's books he should have had no need.

Of sufferings the poor have many,
Which never can the rich annoy:
I soon perceiv'd another boy,
Who look'd as if he'd not had any
Food for that day at least—enjoy
The sight of cold meat in a tavern larder.
This boy's case, then, thought I, is rather harder;
Thus hungry, longing, without a penny,
Beholding choice of dainty-dressed meat;
No wonder if he wish he ne'er had learn'd to eat
Last Essays of Elia.

UGLINESS.—Perhaps no lady was ever better reconciled to positive ugliness in her own person than the Duchess of Orleans, the mother of the Regent d'Orleans who governed France during the minority of Louis XV. Thus she speaks of her own appearance and manners :—" From my earliest years, I was aware how ordinary my appearance was, and did not like that people should look to me attentively. I never paid any attention to dress, because diamonds and dress were sure to attract attention. My husband, on the other hand, loved to cover himself with jewels, and was well satisfied at my dislike of them, as it saved all disputes for the possession of them. On great days he used to make me rouge, which I did greatly against my will, as I hate everything that incommodes me. One day I made the Countess Soissons laugh heartily. She asked me why I never turned my head whenever I passed before a mirror—every body else did? I answered, because I had too much self-love to bear the sight of my own ugliness. I must have been *very ugly* in my youth. I had no sort of features; with little twinkling eyes, a short snub nose, and long thick lips, the whole of my physiognomy was far from attractive. My face was large, with fat cheeks, and yet my figure was short and stumpy; in short, I was a very homely sort of person. Except for the goodness of my disposition, no one would have endured

[*] From a pamphlet by James Douglas, Esq. of Cavers, just published.

me. It was impossible to discover any thing like intelligence in my eyes, except with a microscope. Perhaps there was not on the face of the earth such another pair of ugly hands as mine. The king often told me so, and set me laughing about it; for as I was quite sure of being very ugly, I made up my mind to be the very first to laugh at it. This succeeded very well, though I must confess it furnished me with a good stock of materials for laughter. My temperament is naturally rather melancholy, and when any thing distresses me, my left side swells up as if it were filled with water. I hate to be in bed, and the moment I wake I rise immediately. As for breakfast, I take it very seldom, and then have nothing but bread and butter. Chocolate, coffee, tea, and all other foreign drugs, I detest. My habits are completely German, and nothing suits me in the eating and drinking way which is not conformable to our old customs. I cannot eat soup unless it is mixed up with milk, beer, or wine; and as for gravy broth, it is abominable; it always makes me so ill, that nothing but sausages and ham can put my stomach to rights again."

THE HIGHLAND HOMES OF SCOTLAND.

The Highland Homes of Scotland,
  O, they are dear to me!
Though poor and humble to the eye,
  There dwell the bold and free.
I see them on the mountain's side,
  Where rocks above them frown;
While, from their doors, how beautiful
  The green strath stretches down!
I see them scattered o'er the heath,
  And by the woodland shade,
Where many a kind heart glows beneath
  Old Albyn's chequered plaid!
What though wise Heaven has here denied
  The myrtle and the vine,
Though round the rude and humble porch
  No clustering roses twine;
The mountain ash and dark green pine
  Spring from the fissured rock;
Emblems of Highland hardihood,
  They bide each tempest's shock.
Pure as the spotless lily,
  Behold the mountain maid!
And modest as the violet,
  Within the greenwood shade!
What though no foreign glittering toys,
  Her faultless form adorn,
Amid her raven ringlets glows
  The wild rose from the thorn.
The hue of health and innocence
  Is blooming on her cheeks;
And every glance of her dark eye
  A guileless heart bespeaks.
Now see the active Highland youth,
  So full of game and glee;
The bounding roe in greenwood glade
  Is not more fleet and free!
Sprung from the sires, in days of yore,
  Who Rome's proud arms repelled,
And those who, in a later day,
  Made Gallia's squadrons yield;
Should war e'er call him from his home,
  He'll act a warrior's part;
For faith and dauntless courage dwell,
  With mercy, in his heart.
Dear is to him his Highland home,
  'Mid scenes sublime and wild—
With every torrent, rock, and hill,
  Familiar since a child!
Each blast that whistles round the eaves,
  And every storm that blows,
Makes him more thankful for the lythe*
  His Highland Home bestows!

                    W. C.

* Lythe—shelter.

GEORGE MILLIGAN.*
"A wise, good man, contented to be poor."

GEORGE MILLIGAN, long a farm-servant, and latterly the most celebrated thatcher and thrasher in the whole district, died at the Glen Mill, on the 21st ult., in the 89th year of his age. He was born in Lochrutton, in 1748, but removed about the age of manhood to the parish of Terregles, where he resided more than sixty years. His cottage stood by the side of a wood, within hearing of a murmuring stream; and not even the small birds, or the rooks themselves, darting from the highest bough to arrest the dewworm in his evanescent course, could be more regular in their hours of labour, recreation and rest, than the subject of this brief memoir. At Terraughty, where he worked for many years, the sound of his flail was the first thing that intimated to other portions of the household that it was time to rise; and wherever he went, his movements were regulated with all the accuracy of the clock itself. He wore the same watch for more than sixty years, never forgot to wind it up, and never had occasion to replace the original glass,—a circumstance he sometimes mentioned while recommending carefulness and economy to others, neither was he ever touched with liquor, known to utter an oath, or wittingly commit a breach of the truth. His piety was remarkable, free from ostentation and unnecessary austerity; and for many years he visited the poor and sick, praying with them, and administering spiritual consolation. The pastor of the parish felt the value of his services, and during the funeral ceremony paid a merited tribute of respect to his memory. Frequently the deceased said, "I was trained to live well in my youth, and that makes me a fresh auld man the day." His wedding garments he retained to the last, though his wife had long predeceased him, and his cravat was put into the coffin, according to the custom of the olden time. Their fashion was most peculiar; and as often as "Patie and Roger" was enacted by amateurs for the benefit of the poor, recourse was had to the wardrobe of honest George Milligan. Humble as his station in life was, he adorned it by the sterling worth and integrity of his character; and we may quote, in his case, the words which Mr. Murdoch, the instructor of Burn's, so happily applied to the poet's father; "O for a world of men of such dispositions! I have often wished for the good of mankind, that it was as customary to honour and perpetuate the memory of those who excel in moral rectitude, as it is to extol what are called heroic actions; then would the mausoleum of the friend of my youth overtop and surpass most of those we see in Westminster Abbey."

CONFESSION OF AN IRISH PEASANT.—Luke M. Geogham being at confession, owned, among other things, that he had stolen a pig from Tim Carrol. The Priest told him he must make restitution. Luke could'nt—how could he, when he had eaten it long ago? Then he must give Tim one of his own. No; Luke didn't like that—it wouldn't satisfy his conscience—it wouldn't be the downright identical pig he stole. Well, the Priest said, if he wouldn't, he'd rue it, for that the *corpus delictum*, Tim's pig, would be brought forward against him at his final reckoning. "You don't mane that, father?" Indeed but the father did. "And, may be, Tim himself will be there too?" "Most certainly." "Och, then, why bother about the trifle *this* side the grave? If Tim's there, and the pig's there, sure I can make restitution to him *then*, you know."—*Monthly Magazine.*

AN IMPOSSIBILITY.—Two barristers, of the names of Doyle and Yelverton, were constantly quarrelling before the bench. One day the dispute arose so high that the incensed Doyle knocked down his adversary, exclaiming vehemently, "You scoundrel, I'll make you behave like a gentleman!" The other, smarting under the blow as he lay on the ground, energetically replied, "No, never! I defy you. *You cannot do it, Sir.*"—*New York Mirror.*

* We have got this extract without a name, but intrinsic evidence makes us unhesitatingly attribute it to the Editor of the Dumfries Courier.

ELEMENTS OF THOUGHT.

STUDY.

"STUDY is a weariness without exercise, a labourious sitting still, that racks the inward and destroys the outward man; that sacrifices health to conceit, and clothes the soul with the spoils of the body." So says South; but in the 19th century, we have reversed all that. Study is prosecuted to clothe the body with the spoils of the mind. The scabbard is now more than the sword. South's is a hard fate for the student. "Nature," he says, "allows a man a great freedom; and never gave an appetite but to be instrumental of enjoyment, nor made a desire but in order to the pleasure of its satisfaction." Mr. Combe could not have stated this better; but then comes the draw-back. "He that will increase knowledge must be content not to enjoy, and not only to cut off the extravagance of luxury, but also to deny the lawful demands of convenience, to forswear delight, and look upon pleasure as his mortal enemy." South should have said what the world calls pleasure; for we have a notion, that what is named *study*, or the passionate pursuit of knowledge may often be among the most intoxicating of pleasures. The most absorbing it unquestionably is. Yet there is truth mixed with the error of South's querulous statement. The student "must call that study which is indeed confinement; he must converse with solitude; walk, eat, and sleep thinking; read volumes, devour the choicest authors, and, like Pharoah's kine, after he has devoured all, look lean and meagre. He must be willing to be sickly, weak, consumptive; even to forget when he is hungry; and to digest nothing but what he reads. He must read much and perhaps meet little; turn over much trash for one grain of truth; study antiquity, till he feels the effects of it; and, like the cock in the fable, seek pearls in a dunghill." Here South is wrong; the cock did not seek pearls in the dunghill; but he found one; and then said a grain of barley would have been better for him. Seekers who prefer glittering but useless pearls to nutritious grains, must look for the fate of South's unlucky student.

CATHOLIC CHURCH PROPERTY.

IN the hands of the clergy of the Catholic Church, wheresoever they were, the property called the church property was looked upon as a trust; and whether it was divided in the proportions mentioned in the tripartite division, or whether divided otherwise, the obligation existed everywhere of dividing it amongst the poor, and applying it for the building and repairing of churches, and conducting public worship, and furnishing to themselves only a becoming support. This discipline prevailed wherever the Catholic Church existed, and prevails to this day. * * * The uniform doctrine of the Catholic Church is, that the clergyman can have no property in the fruits of the ecclesiastical benefice; that all that is lawful for him to do is to take from it what is necessary for his competent support; and that the residue he is bound to apply to the relief of the poor, and the promotion of works of piety and charity.—*From Dr. Doyle's Evidence before the Peers' Committee on Tithes.*

[Though we fear the clergyman might sometimes, nay very often, abuse this discretionary power, and take the lion's share in the division, we are bound to admire the principle.]

THE DOCTRINE OF LAWFUL RESISTANCE.

THE common notion is, that the Catholic prelates and clergy, hold as principles, *passive obedience and non-resistance.* Whatever they may have done, they now leave this to High Church-men. Let us see how Dr. Doyle, the titular Bishop of Kildare, unravels this ticklish doctrine, in his evidence before the Peers on the state of tithes in Ireland. "I find in the country a number of persons subject to tithe law, namely the Society of Friends, who, through a conscientious feeling, do not pay tithes; they suffer distress to be levied, and sale to be made; and they are not blamed. Now, if I adopt their conduct, and act in like manner, why should that be culpable in me which is blameless in them? To be sure, in pursuing that peaceable and orderly line of conduct evils may result; but has any right ever been pursued, in any state, that did not bring those who sought to enforce the right into collision with those who support the wrong; and out of such collisions how many crimes have sprung; yet will any man impute those crimes to him who pursues a just course; and not rather to those who oppose obstacles to the fulfilment of the end of justice." Dr. Doyle was asked if this did not bring it to the assertion of the right of every individual to judge for himself, and act upon that judgment, whether the law is or is not to be obeyed. The answer is admirably reasoned. "I would ask, what is the universal judgment made up of but the judgment of individuals; and if the greater number of individuals in a state view the matter as I do, where is the illegality or immorality of them in forming an opinion, and acting on that opinion in a manner not to be condemned by the law. I think, if abuses exist in a state, if individuals were bound to captivate their judgments to the obedience of the authority which supports these abuses, we never could have any reform whatever in the country; and we would not only have passive obedience established upon the broadest and firmest basis, but something worse than the divine right of Kings; for we would have a divine right of abuse. In the name of the Lord! what improvement has ever happened in this country that has not been effected by men pursuing justice in opposition to the law? I know of none. The whole despotism of James was all according to law; even in the case of the ship-money the Judges decided in his favour. If you come to the Revolution of 1688, that was clearly against law, and yet it is the foundation of our happiness as a nation. If we come to Catholic Emancipation, it was pursued for fifty years by the Protestants and Catholics in Ireland, and also in this country; and how many crimes were committed on account of the opposition given to it; numberless collisions, hatreds, and suspicions, and even bloodshed, in many instances. To come to a later event, is not the constitution of the House of Commons legal? No man will deny that it is; yet the King and the Government, pursuing a reformation of that House, so protected by law, gives rise to the riots at Bristol and Nottingham, will any man impute these riots, and the bloodshed that occurred, to Government? So that, if we are prevented from pursuing the recovery of a right, because, in pursuing that right, evils may arise, we must abandon ourselves to utter despotism; and your Lordships will not succeed with me, and, I believe, not with the public in general, in so captivating their understandings to the letter of the law, as to preclude them from pursuing what they think is right."

COMBINATIONS AGAINST IMPOSTS—PASSIVE RESISTANCE.—Dr. Doyle was asked, if giving advice how to avoid paying tithes, and yet not violating law, did not tend to produce combinations: "Let it be so," was his reply, "I do not see any inconvenience that will follow my admitting the thing to its full extent. I should be glad to see the whole population of Ireland combined in one effort to withhold the payment of tithe in money. The combination I look for is a combination which the law has not defined to be illegal; namely, an uniform resolution by the people not to pay the tithe in kind, but to let their goods be distrained. I do not know that any law makes that illegal. I should be extremely glad that the whole population of Ireland, as one man, should adopt it." Dr. Doyle was asked this singular question: "Do you not apprehend that a combination to defeat a legal claim, even by the use of legal means, is in itself illegal?" "I think the combination should be rather designated as one to do that which was legal, than a combination to defeat a legal claim. This was a common law offence; but a common law offence can never be committed by a whole people. When it becomes the cause of a nation, it cannot be a common law offence."

THE STORY TELLER.

THE HARE-HOUND AND THE WITCH.
BY THE O'HARA FAMILY.
From Tait's Edinburgh Magazine.
(Concluded from our last.)

THE morning of the hunt drew near, and still her lover was absent and silent. The match had become the talk of the whole country. With great difficulty and perseverance, Catherine succeeded in bringing her father's mind to contemplate her position, in something of a vein of seriousness. He could not, indeed, "for the life of him," surmise why she seemed so earnest and afflicted. But he did see and comprehend that she was really unhappy; and the best that he could think of, to cheer her, he said and swore. He would break his neck with pleasure, and to a dead certainty, rather than not bring home the brush, and fling it into her lap. And when Kate's fears, at this solemn declaration, took, naturally, another turn, the honest Squire was again at a loss to account for her tears, her clinging, though gentle embraces, and "her tantrums." He bawled right out, in utter mystification, at her entreaties that, come what might, he would not join the hunt; and, in fact, upon the appointed morning, away he rode towards the fox-cover, mounted on his crack hunter, Morgan Rattler, as full of buoyancy, and vigour, and solicitude, as the youngest of the competitors he expected to meet.

Great shouts rent the skies, as, one by one, the candidates for the gentle Catherine arrived at the appointed ground. Their horses, as well as themselves, were examined by curious and critical eyes, and heavy bets were laid upon the issue of the day's chase. The Squire, without communicating to any of his rivals his intention to hunt for his daughter himself, had contrived that his own fox-hounds should be in requisition; because he well knew that Morgan Rattler would do surpassing wonders on their tails.

The ruler of the hounds was the same who had held that situation under the former owner of Squire Hogan's estate. In his youth, twenty years previously, we have noticed him as a daring fellow; we should have added that he used to be as remarkable for his boisterous good spirits as for his reckless intrepidity. Now, however, at five-and-forty, mirth, and even outward dash of every kind, had disappeared from his character. His face was forbidding; his words were few; he never laughed, he never smiled; and, altogether, people regarded him as a dogged and disagreeable man. But enough of our huntsman for the present.

The day promised to be most favourable for the remarkable chase it was to witness.

"A southerly wind, and a cloudy sky,
Proclaimed a hunting morning."

The ground was in prime order; the horses were full of vigour and spirit, after their long training; and, except the huntsman's, (and he comes in again sooner than we foresaw,) every face beamed with joyous animation. In fact, upon this day, he was making himself particularly offensive; quarrelling unnecessarily with his hounds; sulkily refusing to take any advice or opinions (commands were out of the question) concerning his treatment of them; and giving short answers, and looking "as black as thunder."

"What is the matter with you, Daniel?" questioned the Squire.

"I have no fancy for the work to-day," answered the huntsman.

"Why so, man? what is all this about?"

"It was this day twenty years that my ould masther followed the witch down the rocks into the sey; and I was dreaming last night that he and I were hunting here, again, together, and that he drew me down the same lip afore him."

"Hutt, tut, you fool! there's no witch to hunt now, you know."

"I know no such thing. You hav'n't heard that she is in her cave again?"

"Pho, no; and 'tis impossible."

"It is not impossible! 'tis thrue. Let little Tony take my place to-day; for I tell you twice once, I don't like the work."

"Brother, Daniel. This day, of all days, I can't, and I wont spare you. Draw on the dogs; come, stir! see to your business."

With mutterings and growlings, Daniel proceeded to obey. He cast the dogs into the cover. For some time they drew through it in silence. Presently some yelpings were heard; then the leader of the pack sent forth his most melodious note; dogs and men took it up; the fox broke cover; away after him stretched the eager hounds, and, close upon them, the no less eager huntsmen.

The Squire stood still a moment, willing to let the foremost and most headlong candidates for his daughter's favour blow their horses a little before he would himself push forward. While thus manœuvering, "Whom have we here?" he asked of the person nearest to him. His inquiry was directed to a strange huntsman who had just then appeared on the ground, no one could tell whence.

"By the good day!" exclaimed the person addressed, "that's Jack Hogan who fell over the cliff, this day twenty years!"

"Nonsense, nonsense," said the Squire. The stranger turned round his head, as if he could have heard these words though he was at a good distance.

"'Tis he, man! just as he looked the last day he hunted! his very dress! see how different from ours; and his black horse. I'd know horse and rider among a million! By all that's good, it is himself!"

The horses of the Squire and of his neighbour, a man of fifty, who thus spoke, would brook no further delay; and their riders were compelled to loosen their reins, and allow them to spring onward.

Daniel, the black-browed huntsman, was at this moment immediately next the hounds. Two or three of the rivals of fair Catherine's love rode within a little distance of him. The new-comer loitered behind the last of the candidates; of course, the Squire and his friend now pressed him hard. Suddenly his coal-black horse, seemingly without an effort, and certainly independently of one from his master, cleared the ground between him and Daniel. The huntsman turned in his saddle, fixed an appalled look at his follower, uttered a wild cry, and desperately dashed his spurs into the sides of his steed. The stranger, still seemingly unexcited, as also appeared his horse, stuck so close to Daniel's crupper, that he could have put his hands upon it.

All swore that the fox outstripped the wind in swiftness. The hounds did their very best, and more than they had ever done before, to keep near to him. Each huntsman, including even our honest Squire, spared not whip and spur to rival them; but the huntsman first, and the stranger at his horse's tail, were the only persons who succeeded in the achievement.

Vain was the endeavour to come up with those two. And every now and then, Black Daniel would glare behind him into the face of his pursuer, and with a new shout of horror, re-urge his hunter to greater speed; and still, and still, although the stranger sat tranquilly in his saddle, Daniel could not gain a stirrup's-length a-head of him. Over hill and valley, over ditch and hedge, over bog and stream, they swept, or plunged, or leaped, or scrambled, or swam, close upon the dogs, as if life were of no value; or as if they were carried, eddied forward, with supernatural speed, and in superhuman daring. Onward, onward they swept, scarce seeming to touch the earth, until at length only three other horsemen were able to keep them even in distant view. And soon after, those three became two; and, again, but one followed remotely in their track; and this one was our excellent friend Squire Hogan.

The sea-cliffs came in view! and straight towards them did the mad chase now turn. In amazement, if not in terror, the Squire pulled up his horse on a rising ground, and stood still to note its further progress. He saw the panting fox make for the dangerous place over the cliff's brow. For an instant he saw him on its very line. The next, he disappeared towards the sea. At his brush came the hounds and down they plunged also. The rival horsemen followed, and they, too, were in a second, lost to view. A woman suddenly started up over the perilous pass, gazed below, and then sprang, as if into the air.

The mysterious fate of his predecessor fully occurred to our Squire; and he sensibly vowed to himself that, "By Cork! the faggot of a witch should never tempt him to leave the world by the same road." He also brought to mind the huntsman's words that morning; and a struggle arose between his reason and superstitious propensities, as to whether or no the man's dream had been verified.

While thus mentally engaged, one of the baffled aspirants for Catherine's hand came up, himself and his horse soiled and jaded. Another and another followed, until almost all the members of the day's hunt surrounded Squire Hogan. He recited to them what he had witnessed. Greatly excited, some of them dismounted, and, under the care of an experienced guide, descended the cliff.

They found that the bewitched hounds, and their bewitched followers, need not, as the Squire had supposed, have jumped direct from the land into the sea; inasmuch as they might have turned, obliquely, into a narrow, rocky ravine. Down this pass, however, it seemed impossible that horses of mortal mould could have found a footing. The explorers themselves were obliged to follow their guide very cautiously; as well to avoid tumbling downward, as to save their heads from the loose stones and fragments or rocks, which almost every step displaced and set in motion.

After having proceeded a little way, they caught, far below them, a glimpse of the dogs, whose cry came up to them, mingled with the roar and chafe of the waters of the sea. Shortly after, they saw the huntsman still closely pressed by the stranger. The next moment, dogs, horses, and riders were lost to view, behind a curve of the tortuous and stony course of the ravine, all hurrying onward and downward with whirlwind speed, as if to bury themselves in the waves of the ocean.

Our adventurers, persevering in their descent, suddenly turned a projecting rock, and came in view of a strip of strand, running, promontory-like, into the sea; this they soon gained. Daniel, the huntsman, lay on his back upon it; his horse not to be seen. His dogs were squatted around him, each holding a fragment of bone between his teeth. The stranger sat still in his saddle, as if intensely observing the prostrate man. The woman who had appeared to Squire Hogan on the cliff's brow, stood on a rock amid the shallow breakers which rippled over the edges of the neck of strand.

As the explorers approached this group, the unknown horseman glanced towards them, took off his cap, waved it, and said, "Let no man claim Catherine Hogan's hand till I come to woo it. I have hunted for her; won her; and she is mine."

Those of Catherine's lovers who heard this speech were not chicken-hearted fellows. They resolved to ascertain who was the dictatorial speaker. Their friend, Squire Hogan, appeared in view, having nearly completed, at his cautious leisure, the descent to the sea's level, after them; and they first approached him, momentarily turning their backs on the object of their interest, for the purpose of consulting him, and enlisting him in a common plan of operations. After some discourse with the good Squire, and when he and they would have confronted the unknown horseman, no human form but that of sulky Daniel was visible on the patch of strand; and there he lay, stretched at his length, and still apparently insensible.

To him their attention became directed. They found him covered with blood, and seemingly a corpse. His dogs continued to couch around him, holding bones between their grinning teeth; and they snarled fiercely when the new comers approached them.

"By the blessed light!", exclaimed the Squire, " this is part of a man's skull that Ranger has his teeth through!"

"It is," answered Harry Walshe; "and not one of the dogs but holds a human bone between his jaws!"

The prostrate huntsman opened his eyes, and glared fearfully around him.

"What has happened to you, Daniel?" questioned the Squire.

Daniel's head turned in the direction of the voice; and he seemed to recognise the speaker.

"Is he gone?" he asked faintly.

"Is who gone? for whom do you inquire?"

"The masther's sperit—the sperit of the murthered man—the man that I murthered and buried in the sand, twenty years ago!"

Amid exclamations of surprise and horror from all who heard him, the huntsman gained, for a moment, more perfect power of observation. He looked from one to another of the group around him; then most ghastlily at the dogs; and then, closing his eyes, and shuddering, continued to speak in snatches.

"Ay, and it was a cruel murther. I have never slept a night's sleep since I did it. And every dog of the pack brought me one of his bones to-day. I will hide it no longer! I will own it to the world, and suffer for it. His sperit drove me before him to the spot where I had buried his broken body, afther I tumbled him over the cliff—yes, buried it, as deep as I could dig. Twenty years passed away, and he came to chase me to his unblessed grave; and at the sight of it, my horse tossed me out of my saddle, and my own accursed bones are broken this day, and so I have half my punishment. Did I see the witch near me, here, a while ago? I did; an' the wathers o' the sey gave her up, alive, to be a witness against me. For, when I was burying him, this day twenty years, I spied her watching me; and I ran afther her, and seized her, and pitched her far into the waves; but now she is come to hang me. Let her. I will tell all—all—of my own accord; I will; and swing high for the deed."

He was conveyed to the Squire's house; and in his presence, and that of other magistrates, made a more ample confession. He had been tempted to commit the murder under the following circumstances:—

The mother of his old master received under her protection a friendless and pennyless orphan girl of low birth. The young huntsman loved her to distraction; and his ardours were seemingly returned, until the Squire, then a minor, became his successful rival, seducing, under a promise of marriage, at his mother's death, his fickle mistress. Rage, hatred, loathing, took possession of Daniel's heart; he could have beaten out the brains of his young master with the loaded end of his hunting whip; and his amiable feelings were not added to, when, upon a day that he was expostulating alone, with the estranged object of his affections, the Squire suddenly rushed upon him, snatched that identical whip from his own hands, and energetically laid it across his own shoulders.

The Squire's mother died. The Squire cast off his mistress, and married a wealthy wife. It was now the turn of the depraved, bad-hearted, and forsaken girl, to look for her revenge. Upon certain conditions, she offered herself, " soul and body," and without the trouble of a marriage, to her old lover. Daniel's eager passion for her, and his deep detestation of her undoer, had scarce abated. He felt sorely tempted, but hesitated. The girl threw herself in his way, from time to time; reffred him; and in almost a year subsequent to the first attempt to make him a murderer, he was one, nay, a double one; for, a few days after he had dragged his master off his horse, and hurled him down the cliff, he placed in his tempter's arms, on the understanding that she was to destroy it, the only child of his victim. But, even in the disappointment of his feverish dream of passion, he had a foretaste of the punishment due to his crime. From the moment he committed to her the helpless infant she so much detested, he had never seen the authoress of his ruin; and his belief was, that, after having murdered " the child of days," she had put an end to her own existence.

A few hours following his confession the huntsman died.

Whether or no the gentle Catherine shared the popular belief that she had been hunted for, and won by, and was doomed to become a spectre's bride, is not clearly ascertainable. True it is, that her cheek faded, that her eyes grew dull, and that the smile of contented pleasure forsook her moistly-red lip, now no longer red nor moist. But these changes may as well be accounted for on less supernatural grounds. Her military adorer still continued absent and silent: he who had so often vowed himself away into wordless sighs, nay, tears, under the big effort to define how much he loved her, and whose only hesitation to declare himself to her father, had always assumed the shape of a fear of being regarded as a speculating fortune hunter; when, at a glance, it could be ascertained that he was almost an unfriended adventurer, courting the hand of a wealthy heiress.

As to good Squire Hogan, he contrived, or, perhaps, rather tried to laugh at the whole thing; vaguely calling it a very good hoax; " a choice one, by Jove!" just to save himself the trouble of trying to unravel it; or else to hide his half-felt ignorance on the subject. Meantime he got some cause to laugh a little less than usual. Ejectments were served upon his estate, in the name of the lost son of the man whom he had succeeded in it. And Squire Hogan only strove to laugh the more; and to affect that he considered the claim as an uncommonly good attempt at " a capital hoax!" practised upon him by some unknown persons whom, on some past occasion, he must have outwitted " gloriously;" but it was a poor attempt at mirth, and he saw that Catherine, as well as himself, felt that it was.

In fact, he spent many hours alone, mourning for his beloved child, and taxing his brains to shield her from probable and verging misfortune. And a brilliant thought came into his head.

Would it not be a happy, as well as an exceedingly clever thing, to dispose of Catherine, before the trial at law, grounded upon the ejectments, should commence, and while the matter was little suspected, to one or other of her ardent admirers at the club-dinner in Dublin; to in fact, Ned O'Brien, or George Dempsey, or Mick Driscoll; or, above all, to Harry Walshe? And the wise father made the attempt, duly, four times in succession; and learned, thereby, that the serving of the ejectments was more generally known than he had imagined.

Still he tried to laugh, however; until one morning, when his boisterousness ended in sudden tears, as he cast his head on Catherine's shoulder, and said:—"Oh, Kate, Kate! what is to become of *you* ?—I think I can bear poverty,—but you!"

" My dear father do not be cast down," answered Catherine; " I can earn money, in many ways, for us both, if good people will give me employment."

" And you are going a-working to support your father Kate?" He left the room sobbing. His tears affected Catherine to the quick. Other sad and bitter recollections swelled her sorrow into a flood. She could now account for the persevering neglect of her lover, and her tenderly-beloved, upon no other grounds than those of her approaching poverty. Oh, that was a heart-cutting thought!

The day upon which the poor Squire must necessarily start from the country to attend the trial in Dublin, arrived; and he commenced his journey with another magnificent conception in his head; to eke out which, he carried in his pocket, without her knowledge, a miniature of his daughter Catherine. And with this miniature, and a note, expressive of his willingness to compromise the matter by a marriage, he called on the new claimant for his squireship, the evening of his arrival in the metropolis. But, having retired to his own town-house long before he could have thought it possible that his note had received a leisurely reading, he received back the miniature with a technical epistle from his rival's attorney, stating that no compromise could be entered into; that the heir-at-law was determined to accept nothing which the law should not decide to be his right; and, adding, that any attempts to see the young gentleman must prove unavailing, while they would be felt to be intrusive; inasmuch as, in cautious provision against a failure in his attempt to establish his claim, he had invariably concealed his person even from his legal advisers.

This was the first really serious blow our Squire had received. Hitherto he had courageously depended on his own innate cleverness to outwit the coming storm; now, within a few hours of the trial which was to determine his fate, he acknowledged himself without a resource or an expedient beyond patience to attend to the grave proceeding, sit it out, and endeavour to comprehend it.

To beguile the remainder of his sad evening, after receiving the attorney's communication, he repaired to his club-room. He found himself out there. Issuing, in no pleasant mood, into the streets, he encountered, by lamp-light, an individual in a red coat whom he had hitherto considered rather as a deferential hanger-on than as an acquaintance to boast of. Now, at least, by unbending himself, he need not fear a repulse; so, he warmly stretched out both his hands, he received a very distant bow of recognition, and was left alone under a lamp-post.

"By Cork!" said the Squire, with a bitter laugh, "the puppy officer thinks I am turned upside-down in the world already!"

The cause came on. Our good friend's eyes were riveted on every person who uttered a word, upon one side or the other. The usual jollity of his countenance changed into the most painful expression of anxiety; and when any thing witty was said by one of his Majesty's counsel, learned in the law, at which others laughed, his efforts to second them were miserable to behold. And although it was a bitter cold day, the Squire constantly wiped the perspiration from his forehead and face; chewing, between whiles, a scrap of a quill which he had almost unconsciously picked off his seat.

The depositions, on his death-bed, of Daniel the huntsman, were tendered against him. They established the fact of the wretched self-accuser having kidnapped the heir of his then master, and handed the infant to his partner in crime. And the first living witness who appeared on the table, was that witch, supposed to have been long dead, even by Daniel himself. She swore that she had intended to destroy the babe; that, however, having got it into her arms, she relented of her purpose, and gave it, with a bribe, to a strange woman, in a distant district, to expose for her on the high road. Next came the woman alluded to, and she proved that she had followed the directions of her employer, and afterwards watched, unseen, until an elderly lady of her neighbourhood, passing by with a servant, picked up the little unfortunate. And, lastly, the aforesaid elderly lady, who, by the way, had endured some little scandal, at the time, for her act of Christian charity, corroborated this person's testimony; and further deposed that she had carefully brought up, on limited means, until the day she procured him a commission in his Majesty's service, the plantiff in the case at issue. Not a title of evidence, in contradiction to that stated, was offered by the defendant; and the only link of the chain of proof submitted by the heir-at-law, which the Squire's counsel energetically sought to cut through, was that created by the first witness. On her cross-examination, it was ingeniously attempted to be impressed on the minds of the jury, that no reliance could be placed upon the oath of a depraved creature like her; that she had really made away with the infant, according to her original intention; and that the one she had offered for exposure, must have been her own, the result of her acquaintance with the son of her benevolent and ill-requited Protectress. But, without pausing upon details, we shall only say, that during the trial, some confirmatory evidence of the truth of the miserable woman's assertion was supplied; and that, in fact, without hesitation, the jury found for the plaintiff.

Squire Hogan's look of consternation, when he heard the verdict, was pitiable. For a moment he bent down his head and wiped his forehead with his moist handkerchief. Then, with a wretched leer distorting his haggard countenance, he started up, and, muttering indistinctly, bowed low to the judge, the jury, the bar, the public, all; as if he would humbly acknowledge the superiority of every human being. After this, forgetting his hat, he was hurrying away; some one placed it in hand; he bowed lowly, and smiled again; and, finally, forgetting the necessity to remain uncovered, he pressed it hard over his eyes and left the court; carrying with him the sincere, and, in some instances, the tearful sympathy of the spectators.

As fast as horses could gallop with him, he left Dublin, a few moments following.

"By Cork, Kate"——he began, laughing, as his daughter, upon his arrival at the house which used to be his home, hurried to meet him: but he could not carry on the farce; his throat was full and choking; and suddenly throwing himself upon his child's neck, he sobbed aloud.

She understood him, but said nothing; she only kissed his cheeks and pressed his hands, keeping down all show of her own grief and alarm.——Woman! in such a situation, you can do this: man cannot: it is above the paltry selfishness of his nature.

He rallied, and tried to take up his absurd jeering tone, but soon tripped in it a second time.

"Ay, Kate, by the good old Jove, I'm a poorer man than the day I raffled for your mother: and you must work, sure enough, to try and keep a little bread with us. If there's any thing you think I can turn my hand to, only say the word, and you'll see I'll not be idle, my poor girl."

He entered into the details of his misfortunes and mortifications. Among other things, he mentioned the slight of "the puppy officer;" and neither his wonder nor his curiosity was excited, when, now for the first time, Catherine burst into tears.

It shows much good sense to take my Lady Law at her word. Fortune is fickle, but law is fickleness; the principle itself. And so seemed to argue the successful young aspirant to the Squire's estate. While yet only expatiating on his past misfortunes, our worthy friend received a note which informed him that, in a quarter of an hour, an authorized agent would arrive to take possession of the house and lands; and father and daughter had not recovered from the shock this gave them, when the agent was announced and entered the room where they sat. Catherine turned away her face: she could not look at him.

"Possession of every thing in the house too?" asked the trembling Squire.—"Every thing you say?"—"Every thing," answered the agent; who was no man's agent but his own, after all. Catherine started at his voice.—"Yes, every thing; even of the angel that makes this house a heaven."——He advanced to her side. She turned to him—shrieked—laughed—and lay insensible in his arms. 'Twas the Squire's "puppy officer" in the first place; Catherine's faithful adorer, in the second place; the plantiff in the late action, in the third place; and the triumphant hunter for his mistress' hand, in the fourth place. Surely, dear fair readers, he had a claim on her. "Yes—if he account for

COLUMN FOR THE LADIES.

COURTSHIP AND MARRIAGE IN THE UNITED STATES.

The place in which American society appears to the greatest advantage is Washington, during the winter. In summer the city is almost deserted; it is then inhabited principally by the members of government, and those connected with the government establishments. But the first Monday in December of every year, is the day fixed for the assembling of Congress. As the time approaches, the senators and representatives arrive in crowds, accompanied by their families, and followed by shoals of solicitors, and people having business with Congress. The city seems full instantaneously. The ministers and diplomatic body give entertainments; the members of Congress give dinners in return; if the day passes in the whirl of business, the night is borne away by that of pleasure. The president holds a levee once a week; that is to say, one evening in the week he opens his house to all those who desire to pay him a visit. Nothing can be more simple than the etiquette of the head of the Government. The concourse of visitors is the only thing which distinguishes these assemblages from those of any other individual.

The conditions of life being perfectly equal in America, parents have nothing to oppose to the choice their daughters may make of a husband. Thus it is a received maxim throughout the Union, that this choice only concerns young ladies, and it is therefore for them to be prudent enough not to enter into engagements unworthy of their hands. But it would be considered almost as an act of indiscretion on the part of the parents to wish to influence their choice. Nothing in the world can be so happy as the situation of an American young lady from fifteen to twenty-five, particularly if she is pretty, as almost all are, and has some fortune. She finds herself the centre of general admiration and homage; her life passes in holidays and pleasures; she is a stranger to contradiction, still more to refusals. She has only to choose, among a hundred adorers, the one she thinks most likely to ensure her future happiness; for here every body marries, and every body is happy in marriage. This state of "belle," as it is called, is too attractive to make young ladies consent to quit it too soon; accordingly, it is not, in general, until after rejecting many offers, and when they perceive that their charms are beginning to lose something of their empire, that they conclude by choosing a liege lord. It is to Washington, in particular, that the fine women of all the States come to shine; a sort of female congress, in which the charms of every part of the Union are represented. An ardent deputy from the south is captivated by the modest charms of a beauty from the east; while a damsel from Carolina rejects the overtures of a senator from the north. All, however, are not rejected, for at the end of every session a certain number of marriages is declared; they serve to strengthen further the Union of the States, and multiply the ties which unite all parts of this great whole in an indissoluble manner.

Once married, the young lady entirely changes her habits. Farewell gaiety and frivolity. She is not less happy, but her happiness is of a serious character; she becomes a mother, is employed in her household, becomes quite the centre of domestic affections, and enjoys the esteem of all who know and surround her. Society everywhere in the United States may be considered, therefore, as divided into two very distinct classes: that of unmarried persons of both sexes, whose principal occupation is courtship, and the finding a suitable companion with whom to make the voyage of life; the other of people who have already made that choice. You see in the corner of a drawing-room, people of the latter class forming groups among themselves, and talking politics or business: they will hardly address a word to the young girls who flutter around them, unless it be to joke them upon the success of some coquettish frolic; the mothers are in another corner, chatting together about their domestic matters, and receiving interested attentions from the admirers of their daughters. But for these, and the young men, a ball-room is a real field of battle. They boast among themselves of the number of declarations made, and refusals given, in the course of the evening: a thousand little coquetries are played off to draw a young man to declare himself, only to have the pleasure of refusing him afterwards. All these little tricks and skirmishes are perfectly innocent, for such is the general purity of morals that no inconvenience is ever the result of them.—*Letters of Achille Murat.*

Very young ladies cannot be said to have any conversation. Experience, knowledge of society, acquirements gradually and imperceptibly accumulated, are requisite before a person can be properly said to converse. Our heroine, at seventeen, was a creature rather to look at than to listen to. * * * * The female character is, from its attributes, peculiarly under the control of circumstances, and the influence of other and stronger natures. There cannot be a more momentous condition than that of a young woman under twenty. A fool may win her admiration, and her character becomes, for a time at least, frivolous. Many a noble spirit in woman has been checked by an ill-placed first affection; but if she be fortunate enough to place an early dependence upon a worthy object, the tenor of her life is determined. It is observable, that in youth women cannot understand friendship towards men. Girls never stop at that point. There is always a tinge of love in their sentiments towards intimate associates in the other sex. Hence the dangerous ascendency acquired by their male instructors, and by other less attractive and less meritorious individuals, over women who have been delicately nurtured.—*Constance.*

TO ROSALIE.
BY THE AUTHOR OF "THE VILLAGE POORHOUSE."

There is a quiet cot, its walls are white
And covered o'er with foliage green and deep,
And round the casement clustering wall-flowers creep,
And, in link'd arches, o'er the porch unite.
Retired and calm that humble hut is placed
In a warm valley,—and the smoke upcurls,
From the near village in fantastic whirls,
Above the sheltering trees. Embowered and graced
By their rich covering, stands that modest dome;
The light gate closed before it, and all round
The gravell'd path, pinks, daisies, deck the ground;—
That simple cot is mine,—my bosom's home,
My heart's own resting-place, for ever fair,
For thou, my Rosalie, art smiling there!

I look into the past! and see thee there,
Laughing, yet chastened in thy young heart's glee:
And o'er that brow, unshadowed yet by care,
The rich brown tresses, clustering wild and free;
Thy bosom heaving with delicious sighs
That speak of aught but sorrow,—and thy cheek,
Flushing with unknown fancies,—and thine eyes
Speaking more tenderly than words can speak—
Thou lov'st me!
    And within those eyes I gaze,
Bright with the pure soul's brightness; and thy smile
Reproves in vain—and only tempts—the praise
Of lips, by smiling made more sweet the while!
And there thou standest with that glistening eye,
Blushing in youth's first love, my Rosalie!
I see thee, Rosalie!—thy charms the same,
But mellow'd and more lovely;—on thy knee
A fair-haired infant laughs with childish glee,
Or clings around thy neck to lisp thy name!
Still art thou beautiful; and as thy head
Is bent to kiss its cheek, thy tresses brown,
Floating in wavy ringlets loosely down,
O'er the fair features of the child are spread,
Which sleeps within their shadow.—
      At thy feet
Stands the light cradle, and I see thee place
Thy slumbering babe within it, and thy face
Grows bright as listening to its breathings sweet,
Thou gazest on its rest so soft and mild,
And callest on thy God to guard thy child!

KINGS AND COURTIERS.*

At length the King (who calls himself 'Tom Standey, or Scandey') came on board, in a canoe, which shewed no superiority over the others in point of size or ornament. His Majesty was a tall, thin personage, considerably on the wrong side of fifty. He was dressed in the cast off garments of some merchant skipper, viz. an old black beaver, blue coat, duck trowsers, reaching scarcely to the middle of his leg, cotton stockings, that might once have been white and sound, but were now rather dingy, like his skin, and full of holes, with shoes of a most ponderous construction. He was distinguished from the canaille in the other canoes by a coarse cotton umbrella, of English manufacture, and was accompanied by only one attendant, who seemed to stick always close to the old gentleman, and gave himself out to be 'Cocoa Jack,' the King's Physician [The Sir William Knighton of Anoboes?] This man of influence, while he basked in the smiles of royalty, afforded, even in savage life, an admirable specimen of the fawning, courtly sycophant. While he enjoyed his share of the good things, he seemed to have little regard for the feelings of his humbler brethren in the canoes, to whom he evinced a rooted antipathy, urging the weak old gentleman to thrust them out of his way, and to offer them other indignities in his passage alongside. The canoe-men seemed to burn with indignation; but their murmurs were scarcely listened to, although the frown of ineffable contempt met the pampered favourite on every side. His Majesty was ushered into the Commodore's cabin, where, after speedily discussing, with the assistance of his henchman, two or three bottles of wine, he was presented with a shirt, a dressing-gown, and a green night-cap, all of which he donned instantly, stripping to the buff, for that purpose, in the presence of every one, without the slightest ceremony. We afterwards introduced him to the gun-room, but had good reason to repent of our complaisance. As long as there was any thing to drink, he did not evince the slightest inclination to budge one inch, and we were at length obliged, very unceremoniously, to hand him over the side, pretty nearly as drunk as a lord, to use a commoner's expression.

Some hours after King Tom left the ship, a few of us went on shore, and looked round the village. As there was a heavy surf on the sandy beach, we landed on some rocks to the right of the town, which form a sort of natural pier, and got on *terra firma* without the slightest difficulty. By his umbrella, [the oriflamme of King Tom] which he always had expanded for distinction's sake, whether the sun was bright or clouded, whether it was noon or night, we observed his Majesty in the midst of a dense multitude of his black and ragged subjects, approaching to meet us. Before we had gone far, we were surrounded by at least fifteen hundred persons, men, women, and children, dressed every one according to his own fashion, in the cast off clothes of their civilized visitors. The poorer sort, however, and the women, had only the usual rag round the middle, and the children were perfectly naked. Here was one fellow with a tattered dress coat, and no other habiliment but the above-mentioned rag, or duty—there another whose sole garment consisted of a cloak of shreds and patches, which, from its 'cut,' must have once seen better company—and yonder a party of 'bloods,' I suppose, by their dress being different from that of the more sober part of the community, consisting of inexpressibles only, but arranged in the most novel and fanciful manner, the legs being tied round the loins, and the waist and hinder parts of the garment hanging down before. His Majesty, expecting a few presents, received us very graciously, and conducted us—surrounded, and half choked in the clouds of dust raised by all the subjects living in the vicinity of his court, collectively—to his royal residence, a wretched hovel, differing in no respect from the other huts in the village, where we were regaled with palm wine. A rude table was placed under the still ruder verandah of boughs before his door, and three or four chairs, of a construction

---

* Leonard's Voyage.

quite unique, were placed round this for our party. A dirty cloth was then laid, which had once apparently been a sheet, appertaining, perhaps, to the bed linen of some drunken skipper, and on this were placed two or three jugs and a tumbler, which one might conclude, from their appearance, had never been washed since they became the property of these unsophisticated aedi. These were filled with the fermented juice of the palm, and we necessarily partook of it, his Majesty setting us an excellent example, by quaffing a copious draught, and nodding us a welcome, with regal condescension; while his subjects in myriads surrounded the verandah, within three feet of us, shouldering each other and almost suffocating us with heat, dust, and the peculiar offensive odour proceeding from their filthy carcases, and stunning us with the incessant, loud, and discordant clatter of their tongues. They seemed to pay very little deference to the kingly authority.

The only revenue which this chief, president, or king, or whatever else he may be called, receives, arises from the presents made to him by those vessels which, like ourselves, happen to touch here for refreshments; it being an invariable practice throughout the whole coast of Africa to give the chief personage a 'dash' on arriving and taking leave; and as this is the only means the king of this island has of acquiring riches, it is wisely provided, that no single individual of the community shall grow too opulent, lest he also grow supercilious, and despise his poorer countrymen; but that all may have an equal chance of profiting by what fortune may throw in their way. The presents from ten vessels are therefore considered by the community to be quite a large enough share of the loaves and fishes, for one individual, and on the departure of the tenth he is superseded; consequently there is no zeal wanting on his part in soliciting gifts, and making the most of the present opportunity of adding to his revenue. The importunities of his Majesty King Tom were, in consequence, most troublesome, and his impudence and assurance were occasionally most diverting.

IMPROVED STEAM ENGINE.

A LECTURE was lately delivered at the Mechanics' Institution by Mr. Hemming, for the purpose of explaining some most important improvements lately introduced into the construction of the steam engine by Mr. Hall. These improvements may be reckoned five in number. The first relates to the piston, the preservation of the packing of which is effected for many years, and the consequent expense, labour, and interruption of re-packing avoided. This advantage is obtained by causing the steam to operate as an adjusting spring against the packing, and consequently to act as accurately after being used for years as it does at the commencement. It is well known that hemp, cotton, or other vegetable packing, in common pistons, becomes very imperfect, and allows the steam to escape long before re-packing becomes absolutely necessary. This first improvement, Mr. Hemming characterised as the most important of the whole, describing it as "self-compensating packing." The second improvement relates to the valve. The advantage gained in this respect was described to be, that the steam is effectually secured by the facing of the working face of the sliding frame with steel plates and hemp or cotton packing, and by the compensating nature of the seat-plate on which the sliding frame works. By this means, the durability of the valve is greatly increased, and its becoming untrue by friction and unequal expansion (allowing a consequent loss of steam) are prevented.

The third advantage secured by Mr. Hall's ingenuity relates to the lubrication of steam-engines. The friction of the piston, both in the working cylinder and air-pump, is nearly annihilated, as well as that of the valves and piston-rods; whereby a great saving of power is effected, and the cylinders and other parts of the engine are preserved. The escape of steam by the working piston and valves is effectually prevented by the uniform and plentiful flow of oil, a stratum of which is formed and constantly floats on the upper side of the piston, hermetically sealing any passage between it and the side of the cylinder.

This the lecturer described as the second improvement, in point of importance, which Mr. Hall has effected in the steam engine. By the uniform and continued injection, he observed, of an ample stream of oil, or other lubricating matter, into the pipe which conveys the steam from the boiler to the working cylinder, and the recovery of the lubricating matter after it has passed through the engine, to repeat the operation, the quantity of oil which would otherwise be expended in one day, will last for years. The fourth improvement relates to the condensation and the supplying of water to boilers. By means of this the power required to pump the injecting water out of a vacuum is saved, for the air-pump is of much less than the usual size; the introduction of air into the condenser (which is in combination with injection-water, and materially injures a vacuum) is also avoided, as well as the pumping of it out of the condenser along with the injection-water. The injury done to the air-pump, &c., by water impregnated with saline matters, and other extraneous substances, is prevented. The destruction of the boilers and the slow generation of steam, consequent upon the deposition of such extraneous matters, is effectually avoided; and it was stated that a new engine, with Mr. Hall's improvements, will remain perfect, and not require the expense of repairs for an exceedingly greater number of years than any engine upon the old principles. The lecturer observed, that the means adopted for supplying the necessary quantity of distilled water, to replace any waste that may take place, is the insertion within the boiler of a small vessel containing the water for distillation; for although the temperature of boiling water only is applied to it, the requisite quantity of distilled water, or even more, will be produced. The fifth improvement relates to the consumption of fuel; and this, indeed, may be considered as the result of the preceding advantages. These several points were illustrated by a small model engine, which worked with the most beautiful precision and accuracy. Attached to this miniature engine was an ingenious model of a loom, also the invention of Mr. Hall, for the manufacture of lace; the different threads of which were directed over burning gas in order to free them from the superfluous film. The theatre was excessively crowded, and the lecture, which was listened to with the utmost attention, greeted at its close with the loudest demonstrations of applause.

PEAS.

THE following communication on the relative qualities of peas, may be useful at the present season; it is taken from the Gardener's Magazine for October last:—*On Bishop's Dwarf Pea, as compared with other early Peas.*—By Mr. Anthony Adamson, in a Letter to Mr. John Gibson.

SIR,—I return you, with this, one quart and three quarters of Bishop's early dwarf peas. They have been saved from the sowings of those I received from you upon experiment, and for which I feel much obliged. I think it due to you, to send you the result of the experience which I have had in comparing Bishop's pea with other varieties mentioned below, all of which were sown on the same day, viz., the 5th April, 1861. Bishop's pea came into full pod on the 2d of July, i. e., in 88 days: the early frame in 140 days; Knight's dwarf marrow in 146 days; and the Spanish dwarf in 150 days. Thus there was a space of 53 days in favour of Bishop's pea over every other variety, even the early frame. The produce of Bishop's pea is fully double that of the frame, and quite equal in flavour when taken early; the pods are short, but abundantly numerous; and, being dwarfs, their blossoms form a most elegant border. The seed from them is most easily saved, even from sowings made on the 4th of June. They require only short sticks, about one foot from the ground; as an early variety, they are of first-rate excellence. This pea was raised originally from an impregnated blossom of the Spanish dwarf. By the way, the Spanish Dwarf is an excellent pea, but not early; and if compared with Knight's dwarf marrow, sinks into insignificance. There was never such a pea for the marrow flavour known before, as Knight's marrow. Its faults are, its not being early, and the great difficulty of saving its seed in this climate; besides, it cannot be prudently sown early, because of its tenderness of stalks. It is, however, of inestimable value, and might do well if raised in a moderate hot-bed, and transplanted as soon as the frosts were over; or if it were protected with straw ropes, or thick spray pea sticks. Knight's marrow pea is entitled to stand highly prized, from its great delicacy and flavour, and from the difficulty of saving its seed; and, Bishop's pea has the same claim, as one of the most productive and early varieties; but I must observe that Bishop's pea, of all others, is most benefited by a liberal manuring of old hot-bed dung. But though Bishop's pea is so well deserving of praise as an early pea, it has little merit as a late pea, except as to the producing plenty of seed. Knight's marrow deserves a high price, for flavour produce, and difficulty of saving the seed.

PRACTICAL REMEDY FOR THE DRY ROT.—Everybody has heard of the havoc which has been effected in some of our most valuable shipping, and of the destructive process which has rendered the work of the architect vain in some of our noblest edifices. To discover a remedy, or a preventive rather, of this insidious power—the dry rot—has long been a problem. It is now, however, we think, we may venture to be sanguine about it—found: corrosive sublimate is that remedy. The preservative powers of this substance have long been known to anatomists, curators of museums, and others interested in an acquaintance with antiseptics. It occurred to Sir H. Davy, some years ago, when applied for a recipe to check the approaches of the book-worm in the magnificent library at Althorp, to suggest corrosive sublimate; but he was induced to abandon the idea, from a supposition that a poisonous atmosphere would attend on the volumes which should be charged with this active mercurial. Dr. Faraday confesses that it was he himself who influenced Sir Humphrey in coming to such a conclusion; but the result of his researches since that time, and particularly within the last two or three years, warrants him in stating now the contrary. Organic matters treated with corrosive sublimate form with it a chymical compound, and contract none of its noxious qualities. It is on this principle that Dr. Faraday is enabled to show, and indeed may be said to have succeeded in proving, that timber which has been steeped for a time in a saturated solution of the sublimate, becomes indestructible, and affords that which has been so long a desideratum in the building of our wooden walls. The lecturer detailed the various experiments which have been made on this subject at Woolwich, under the sanction of the Lords of the Admiralty; and in every instance wherein the results have been examined, (for some of them are yet undergoing the test of time,) it appears they have been eminently marked with success. Pieces of the same wood, some saturated, and some left untouched, have been exposed to the same influence, when the latter have turned out to be utterly devoured with the rot, the former remaining perfectly sound. The saturated and the unprepared pieces have even been mortised into each other, when the dry rot has eaten the latter to the boundary line, and stopped there. The same thing occurred with pieces of cotton canvass; those washed in the solution remaining uninfluenced by the rot, while those not so protected perish. A Mr. Kyan, we understand, is the inventor of the remedy.—*Medical Gazette.*

SCRAPS.

THE COST OF BUILDING LONDON BRIDGE.—The particulars of the money raised and expended on account of this great undertaking have been published, including the approaches to it on both sides of the water. The difference between the cost and the estimate is stated at L.40,000; the whole amount raised for that purpose was L.1,458,311, 8s. 11¾d., and the cost of the bridge and approaches, law expenses, &c., L.1,426,145, 3s. 3d. leaving a balance in hand of L.32,166, 5s. 8½d.

ANDREW WILSON.—The following is copied literally from the burial yard register of Pathhead:—"The corpse of Andrew Wilson, baker, son to Andrew Wilson, baker and inn-dweller in Dunnikeer, (Qui mortuet .... Edinburgum,) was interred the 5th April, 1736 years, lying in the grave of William Paterson and Euphan Beveridge;— the grave 2 feet and ¼ wide, 7 feet long." This is the Andrew Wilson who was executed at Edinburgh at the time of Porteous's mob, as described by Sir W. Scott in his tale of the Heart of Mid Lothian, and who, when he was conducted to church the Sunday previous to his execution, guarded by three soldiers, held them all three fast, one in each hand, the other by his teeth, till his fellow-prisoner, designated in the novel by the name of Geordie Robertson, made his escape. An old inhabitant of Pathhead was heard to declare, that he saw Wilson's bones disinterred on occasion of the grave being re-opened, and could not but remark the firmness of their texture and uncommon size.

PHILOSOPHY OF A FAN.—To explain the apparent contradiction implied in the fact that the use of a fan produces a sensation of coldness, even though the air which it agitates is not in any degree altered in temperature, it is necessary to consider that the air which surrounds us is generally at a lower temperature than that of the body. If the air be calm and still, the particles which are in immediate contact with the skin acquire the temperature of the skin itself, and having a sort of molecular attraction, they adhere to the skin in the same manner as particles of air are found to adhere to the surface of glass in philosophical experiments. Thus sticking to the skin, they form a sort of warm covering for it, and speedily acquire its temperature. The fan, however, by the agitation which it produces, continually expels the particles thus in contact with the skin, and brings new particles into that situation. Each particle of air, as it strikes the skin, takes heat from it by contact, and, being driven off, carries that heat with it, thus producing a constant sensation of refreshing coolness. Now, from this reasoning, it would follow, that if we were placed in a room in which the atmosphere has a higher temperature than 96 degrees, the use of a fan would have exactly opposite effects; and, instead of cooling, would aggravate the effects of heat; and such would, in fact, take place. A succession of hot particles would therefore be driven against the skin, while the particles which would be cooled by the skin itself would be constantly removed.—*Lardner on Heat—Cabinet Cyclopedia.*

CONTENTS OF NO. XXXIV.

Air—Respiration	193
Modern Galloway, by ELIA	194
German Manners	195
Riches of Parliamentary Candidates—Reasons of the contempt shown for "Landless Men"	ib.
The French Moll Flagons, or Vivandieres	196
A Smuggler's Tale	197
Hazlitt's Death-bed	ib.
Slavery	ib.
Book stalls—Love of Books	198
Ugliness	ib.
The Highland Homes of Scotland	199
George Milligan	ib.
ELEMENTS OF THOUGHT—Study—Catholic Church Property—The Doctrine of Lawful Resistance—Passive Resistance	200
THE STORY-TELLER—The Harehound and the Witch (continued)	201
COLUMN FOR THE LADIES—Courtship and Marriage in the United States	205
To Rosalie—by the Author of the Village Poorhouse	206
Kings and Courtiers	ib.
SCIENTIFIC NOTICES.—Improved Steam Engine—Peas	207
Practical Remedy for the Dry Rot	208
SCRAPS.—The Cost of Building London Bridge—Andrew Wilson—Philosophy of a Fan	ib.

EDINBURGH: Printed by and for JOHN JOHNSTONE, 19, St. James's Square.—Published by JOHN ANDERSON, Jun., Bookseller, 55, North Bridge Street, Edinburgh; by JOHN MACLEOD, and ATKINSON & Co. Booksellers, Glasgow; and sold by all Booksellers and Venders of Cheap Periodicals.

THE Schoolmaster,
AND
EDINBURGH WEEKLY MAGAZINE.
CONDUCTED BY JOHN JOHNSTONE.

THE SCHOOLMASTER IS ABROAD.—LORD BROUGHAM.

No. 36.—Vol. II.   SATURDAY, APRIL 6, 1833.   Price Three-halfpence.

ON THE MORAL TRAINING OF CHILDREN.
(For the Schoolmaster.)
LETTER V.

The late admirable writer Mrs. E. Hamilton, in her LETTERS ON THE ELEMENTARY PRINCIPLES OF EDUCATION, makes the following just remark, to account for her examining the affections, before she treats of the principles of the cultivation of the understanding :—

" Desires and aversions are the springs of human conduct, because their influence commences in some degree with our existence. In the production of our intellectual faculties, nature operates by a slow and gradual process. When her wise regulations are attended to, and not counteracted by our officious folly, one faculty attains sufficient vigour before another is produced to assist in its development. But desire and aversion, which may be termed the germ of the passions, appear in the infancy of life, and show symptoms of strength and vigour, at a period when the higher intellectual faculties are yet feeble and imperfect. Hence the necessity of paying an early and unceasing attention to every circumstance which tends to call forth those active powers, which, without such superintendence, may become instrumental to the misery of the possessor."

Another excellent writer (the late Dr. Estlin of Bristol, in his Lectures on Moral Philosophy) also remarks, that,—" As soon as the mind has acquired any notion of good or evil, by grateful or uneasy sensations of any kind, there naturally arise certain motions of the will, namely, desire of what is good, and aversion from what is evil. For there constantly appears in every being, a fixed propensity to desire its own happiness, and whatever seems to be the means of procuring it; and to avoid those things which would render it miserable. Besides these two primary motions of the will, desire and aversion, there are two others commonly ascribed to it, joy and sorrow. The former desire and aversion, have a reference to what is future; the latter, joy and sorrow, to what is past and present. So that when good to be obtained is in view, there arises desire; when evil is to be repelled, aversion : when good is actually obtained or evil avoided, arises joy ; when good is lost, or evil has befallen us, sorrow. But besides these calm motions or affections of the mind, and the stable desire of happiness, which employ our reason for their conductor, there are also others of a different nature :—

" Certain vehement, turbulent impulses, which, upon some occasions, agitate the mind, and hurry it on, with blind inconsiderate force, to actions and pursuits, or to efforts exerted about such things, as we have never deliberately determined to be of consequence to happiness or misery. These turbulent passions, which are generally foes to mental peace, are reducible to the four classes above mentioned. Such as impel towards some apparent *good*, are called passionate *desires ;* such as tend to ward off some supposed evil, are called *aversions* or *fears ;* such as arise from the obtainment of what was desired, as a good, or the avoiding of what was feared as evil, are turbulent *joys ;* and such as arise from the loss of supposed good, or the suffering of supposed evil, are termed *sorrows.*"

From these reasonings it appears that the prime duty of parents and teachers, towards the children who are intrusted to their care by the universal father, is to regulate those affections of desire and aversion which are awakened so early in the human mind ; to prevent the formation of improper associations of ideas ; and to induce the habit of self-command and restraint. By the association of ideas is meant, that some ideas are so closely connected, either by natural correspondence, or by habit, or by fortuitous circumstances, that, when one idea arises in the mind, it shall introduce its associate idea, and to separate them, is a very difficult task. Thus, if we have suffered severe pain in any particular place, ill treatment from any particular person, or great loss from any particular circumstance ; let us find ourselves again in that place in which we endured the pain, and surrounded by the same external objects ; let the same person who injured us re-appear ; let us be once more involved in the very circumstances which were the immediate occasion of our loss, and the same sensations of uneasiness and aversion will recur. And, in like manner, if we be placed a second time in scenes in which we had formerly experienced emotions of pleasure, the same pleasurable feelings will again be awakened.

"A man receives a sensible injury from another," says the illustrious reasoner, Locke; "he thinks on that man and that action, over and over again; and by ruminating strongly, or much in his mind, he so cements those two ideas together, that he makes them almost one. He never can think on that man, but the pain and displeasure he suffered come into his mind with it, so that he scarcely distinguishes them, but has as much aversion for the one as the other. Thus, hatreds are often produced from slight occasions, and quarrels are spread and continued in the world."

These associations, when suffered to take root, are frequently, we may indeed say, generally, so tenacious as never to be completely rooted out, even by good sense and acquired knowledge. Let parents and tutors of children, therefore, take heed that disagreeable repulsive ideas be not associated, in their infants, with circumstances and objects, they must frequently meet in the common course of things; nor with employments in which they will be called to engage, nor with duties they will be required to fulfil in after life.

This is an object which requires great care and attention.

Ideas of ghosts, of supernatural appearances, of mysterious dangers, associated with the idea of darkness, awakened in the mind of the infant, by tales of terror and superstition told in the nursery, have often rendered the man a slave through life to fears of the imagination; and even when growing strength of intellect, and wise instruction, have banished the belief in apparitions, the impression has continued ineffaceable. Let children, then, be early familiarized to darkness, and be taught, by example and experience, that no danger attends the absence of light, but that of hurting themselves by striking against some hard or pointed substance, a danger which may be avoided by some little precaution.

Parents and teachers should take especial care, that repulsive associations do not attend the means of acquiring knowledge. If more be expected of children than what is just and reasonable; if lessons be given them, too long, or too difficult; if they be required to attend to studies, subjects, and books, above their capacities; if they be expected to keep up painful application; and if they be deprived of those hours of bodily exercise, which are necessary to refresh the mind and recruit the spirits, such unpleasant ideas will be associated with learning, as may form an insuperable obstacle to their progress in the path of science, when they advance in years. Such association has excited in many minds a dislike of books, and of the other means of intellectual improvement, which has grown into settled aversion to all mental application.

A public lecturer once declared, that he never opened a Latin grammar, or a grammar of any language, without an involuntary shudder, because he had been oppressed with that species of learning when he was a school-boy. And still more careful should parents and instructors be not to permit any circumstances to intermingle with moral and religious instruction, which might cause either of those most important of all subjects to be attended with unpleasant associations.

Let not virtue, morality, religion, be presented to children in an unamiable point of view, as hard and severe, as frowning upon innocent enjoyments, as contracting the circles of human pleasures, lest unfavourable impressions be made upon their minds, which may operate as slow but fatal poison. Let children, on the contrary, be led to behold virtue, morality, and religion, as all lovely in their natural charms, as their best friends, as enhancing every true delight; that thus pleasurable associations may aid in conducting them to the path of happiness, and to life everlasting.

Let parents beware of uniting disagreeable associations, with the observance of the Sabbath, by rendering it austere and gloomy, by stripping it of all innocent occupation, by overpowering the attention of children on that day of rest, with too large portions of moral and religious instruction. By such injudicious zeal, well intended but not according to knowledge, many a youthful mind has been led to dread the return of that holy day; and when the curb of parental authority has been loosened, has flown to the other extreme, namely, its utter neglect. Let parents take care also, that disagreeable ideas be not associated in the minds of their children, with family worship, by making it tiresome by length, or by having it at improper seasons. Let not the interference of parental or superintending authority be too apparent, or too frequent, or exerted upon trifling occasions; lest, by disagreeable association, it become disgusting to children, and terminate in absolute contempt and aversion. Let not even affection manifest itself in officious care, in unreasonable and excessive anxiety; lest, becoming burdensome, and an obstacle in the way of enjoyment and exertion, it excite, in the mind of its object, repelling ideas, and, by being associated with them, produce irritation and fretfulness, instead of gratitude and love.

Antipathies the most absurd and unreasonable to animals perfectly innocent, and to other objects, on account of form and colour, are frequently seen in grown persons, who, thereby are rendered ridiculous to others, and uncomfortable to themselves. These antipathies are not natural, they are created in children by the force of example; care, therefore, should be taken to prevent this evil, for an evil it certainly is, because all unnecessary fear is an evil.

Children may be taught to view, with delighted curiosity, spiders skilfully constructing their webs, and earwigs with their shining cases of wings; and their attention may be gradually led from them to their Great Maker. But if they hear those around them screaming, "Oh, the nasty, ugly creatures!" and see their mothers, or other friends, shrinking back, shuddering with real or affected terror, they will catch the infection, and habit will soon confirm the same false feelings.

Let parents, then, carefully watch over the earliest operations of mind in their children; and if they discern any of those antipathies, erroneously styled natural, forming or formed, let them endeavour instantly to counteract the impressions, by destroying the association of pain or disgust which excited them. Inform your children of the good effects those animals may produce; such as destroying others whose excessive multiplication might prove prejudicial, or who are, in some respects, noxious, or devouring substances which might prove detrimental to the health of man, were they left to putrefaction. Convince them that even those which have the power of inflicting pain, by bites or stings, are necessary and beneficial parts of the grand and wise economy of Nature, which the benevolent Maker of all things has established.

But antipathies may not only be early formed in the minds of children, against certain animals of the inferior orders; they may be directed, by ignorant prejudice, against the opinions, and even against the persons of those fellow-men, who differ from generally received notions, or from those of their parents and friends. Such antipathies should be sedulously repressed, or rather prevented, by preventing the youthful mind from associating the idea of evil with difference of opinion; by pointing out pious and learned men, virtuous, benevolent, and amiable characters, of totally different sentiments and sects. To preclude the formation of such prejudices, is of no small importance; because they lead to bigotry, to ill-will, to all antichristian feelings, and finally to hatred and persecution. Such antipathies, founded upon the associations of evil with differences of political and religious faith, have been fruitful sources of bad passions, of angry feelings, of inhuman actions, of deadly and cruel oppression.

Prejudices friendly to virtue, and to religion in general, and hostile to vice, are the only prejudices which may be permitted and cherished with safety. All other prejudices are, in some respect or other, unfavourable to the culture of the mental faculties, and of the moral feelings.

Let children be accustomed from earliest childhood to take a care and interest in the affairs and happiness of others. They should be taught to consider how their little pursuits and arrangements may conduce to the pleasure and gratification of their playmates, as well as their own; and thus may be formed, in early life, the germ of that benevolence, which will increase as they grow up, and become universal philanthropy. Children should be made to feel for every thing that has life, and to take delight in imparting pleasure, even to the most insignificant of percipient beings. Let them be instructed to consider every creature as the creature of God; and in the happiness of every creature to find an addition to their own. Let them be taught to view with pleasure the vast variety of animals, enjoying their respective powers and happy in their several ways. Let the delightful spectacle of the benevolence of the Creator, displayed in the animate world, be pointed out to their observation; and here let them be trained to feast their eyes and their hearts. This will be the most efficacious method of giving the soul genuine sensibility, of rendering it all alive to feelings of true sympathy. To rejoice with those who rejoice, and to weep with those who weep, is one of the noblest, most improving exercises of the human mind. From such dispositions will flow condescension, courteousness, affability. If such sentiments rule in the souls of children, they will show no overbearing haughtiness, no insulting contempt of inferiors; they will use no harsh, commanding language towards servants, nor expect them to attend their nod, and study to humour their caprices.

Let children be trained to be actively charitable. Let them be conducted to the humblest hut of poverty, that they may witness the difficulties with which the poor have to struggle. Let them be taught to cheer the spirits of the afflicted, and to soften the pains of sickness, by condolence and gentle offices of love. Let them feel the pleasure of relieving or mitigating distress, out of their own means, and by denying themselves some of their usual gratifications and amusements; and let them know, that such sacrifices give additional satisfaction in their practice, besides being, from the exercise of self-denial, the more acceptable to God. Let them, therefore, see objects of compassion, of pity, of charity, that those amiable feelings may be excited in their hearts, that they may have opportunities of exercising them, and that they may taste the delicious satisfaction of doing good. But this should be done under prudent direction. They should be taught gradually to discriminate between worthy and unworthy objects, and not to be impelled by blind generosity, lest, as they advance in life, they meet with fraud and imposition, and their benevolent feelings be shocked and blunted.

By such methods, with such care and attention, should parents labour to exclude from the minds of their children all unfavourable, prejudicial, associations; all improper desires; all evil propensities; indulgence of appetite; pride of rank or wealth; vanity of dress, person, or talents; selfishness; self-will; obstinacy; impatience of restraint; insincerity; dissimulation; cunning; and every species and degree of falsehood. Thus should they endeavour to cherish in the hearts of their children all the amiable, benevolent affections; love to God, to their parents, to their relatives and friends, to all mankind; religious principles and feelings; compassion; condolence; mercy; pity; courteousness; regard for the happiness of all creatures; active self-denying charity. These are seeds of the best, the most precious kinds, which, if sown in the infant mind, will, by the blessing of God, take root, grow up, blossom in heavenly fragrance and beauty, and produce the fruits of virtue, of usefulness, of felicity. I am, &c.

A FRIEND TO EARLY EDUCATION.

COLUMN FOR THE LADIES.

EDUCATION OF INFANCY.

THE BODILY SENSES.*

Few people think that the management of very young babes has any thing to do with their future dispositions and characters; yet I believe it has more influence than can easily be calculated. One writer on education even ventures to say, that the heaviness of the Dutch and the vivacity of the French are owing to the different manner in which infants are treated in these two countries.

The Dutch keep their children in a state of repose, always rocking, or jogging them; the French are perpetually tossing them about, and showing them lively tricks. I think a medium between these two extremes would be the most favourable to a child's health and faculties.

An infant is, for a while, totally ignorant of the use of the senses with which he is endowed. At first, he does not see objects; and when he sees them, he does not know that he can touch them. "He is obliged to serve an apprenticeship to the five senses," and at every step he needs assistance in learning his trade. Any one can see that assistance tends to quicken the faculties, by observing how much faster a babe improves, when daily surrounded by little brothers and sisters.

But in trying to excite an infant's attention, care should be taken not to confuse and distract him. His mind, like his body, is weak, and requires to have but little sustenance at a time, and to have it often. Gentleness, patience, and love, are almost every thing in education; especially to those helpless little creatures, who have entered into a world where every thing is new and strange to them. Gentleness is a sort of mild atmosphere; and it enters into a child's soul, like the sunshine into the rose-bud, slowly but surely expanding it into beauty and vigour.

All loud noises and violent motions should be avoided. They pain an infant's senses, and distract his faculties. I have seen impatient nurses thrust a glaring candle before the eyes of a fretful babe, or drum violently on the table, or rock the cradle like an earthquake. These things may stop a child's cries for a short time, because the pain they occasion his senses, draws his attention from the pain which first induced him to cry; but they do not comfort or sooth him. As soon as he recovers from the distraction they have occasioned, he will probably cry again, and even louder than before. Besides the pain given to his mind, violent measures are dangerous to the bodily senses. Deafness and weakness of eye-sight may no doubt often be attributed to such causes as I have mentioned; and physicians are agreed that the dropsy on the brain is frequently produced by violent rocking.

Unless a child's cries are occasioned by sharp bodily pain, they may usually be pacified by some pleasing object, such as stroking a kitten, or patting the dog; and if their tears are really occasioned by acute pain, is it not cruel to add another suffering, by stunning them with noise, or blinding them with light?

Attention should be early aroused by presenting attractive objects—things of bright and beautiful colours, but not glaring—and sounds pleasant and soft to the ear. When you have succeeded in attracting a babe's attention to any object, it is well to let him examine it just as long as he chooses. Every time he turns it over, drops it, and takes it up again, he adds something to the little stock of his scanty experience. When his powers of attention are wearied, he will soon enough shew it by his actions. A multitude of new playthings, crowded upon him one after another, only serve to confuse him. He does not learn so much, because he has not time to get acquainted with the properties of any one of them. Having had his little mind excited by a new object, he should be left in quiet, to toss and turn, and jingle it, to his heart's content. If he look up in the midst of his play, a smile should always be ready for him, that he may feel protected and happy in the atmosphere of love.

It is important that children, even when babes, should never be spectators of anger, or any evil passion. They come to us from heaven, with their little souls full of innocence and peace; and, as far as possible, a mother's influence should not interfere with the influence of angels.

The first and most important thing, in order to effect this, is, that the mother should keep her own spirit in tranquillity and purity; for it is beyond all doubt that the state of a mother affects her child. There are many proofs that it is true, both with regard to mind and body. A mere babe will grieve and sob at the expression of distress on a mother's countenance; he cannot possibly *know* what that expression means, but he *feels* that it is something painful—his mother's state affects him.

Effects on the bodily constitution will be more readily believed than effects on the mind, because the most thoughtless can see the one, and they cannot *see* the other. Children have died in convulsions, in consequence of a mother nursing, while under the influence of violent passion or emotion; and who can tell how much *moral* evil may be traced to the states of mind indulged by a mother, while tending the precious little being, who receives every thing from her?

Therefore the first rule, and the most important of all in education, is, that a mother should govern her own feelings and keep her heart and conscience pure.

The next most important thing appears to me to be, that a mother should, as far as other duties will permit, take the entire care of her own child. I am aware that people of moderate fortune cannot attend exclusively to an infant. Other cares claim a share of attention, and sisters or domestics must be intrusted; but where this must necessarily be the case, the infant should, as much as possible, feel its mother's guardianship. If in the same room, a smile, or a look of fondness, should now and then be bestowed upon him; and if in an adjoining room, some of the endearing appellations to which he has been accustomed, should once in a while meet his ear; the knowledge that his natural protector and best friend is near, will give him a feeling of safety and protection alike conducive to his happiness and beneficial to his temper.

You may say, perhaps, that a mother's instinct teaches fondness, and there is no need of urging that point; but the difficulty is, mothers are sometimes fond by fits and starts: —they frequently follow impulse, not principle. Perhaps the cares of the world vex or discourage you,—and you do not, as usual, smile upon your babe when he looks up earnestly in your face—or you are a little impatient at his fretfulness. Those who know your inquietudes may easily excuse this; but what does the innocent being before you know of toil and trouble? And why should you distract his pure nature by the evils you have received from a vexatious world? It does you no good, and it injures him.

Do you say it is impossible always to govern one's feelings? There is one method, a never-failing one—prayer. It consoles and strengthens the wounded heart, and tranquillizes the stormy passions. You will say, perhaps, that you have not leisure to pray every time your temper is provoked, or your heart is grieved. It requires no time—the inward ejaculation of "Lord, help me to overcome this temptation," may be made in any place, and amid any employments; and if uttered in humble sincerity, the voice that said to the raging waters, "Peace! Be still!" will restore quiet to your troubled soul.

As the first step in education, I have recommended gentle, but constant efforts to attract the attention, and improve the bodily senses. I would here suggest the importance of preserving the organs of those senses in full vigour. For instance, the cradle should be so placed that the face of the infant may be in the shade. A stream of light is dangerous to his delicate organs of vision; and if it be allowed to come in at one side, he may turn his eyes, in the effort to watch it. Glaring red curtains and brilliantly striped Venetian carpeting are bad things in a nursery, for similar reasons.

---

* From the Mother's Book, a sensible little Volume, by an American Lady, republished in Glasgow.

THE YOUNG ACTRESS.

Barbara S——.

On the noon of the 14th of November, 1743 or 4, I forget which it was, just as the clock had struck one, Barbara S——, with her accustomed punctuality, ascended the long rambling staircase, with awkward interposed landing-places, which led to the office, or rather a sort of box with a desk in it, whereat sat the then Treasurer of (what few of our readers may remember) the old Bath Theatre. All over the island it was the custom, and remains so I believe to this day, for the players to receive their weekly stipend on the Saturday. It was not much that Barbara had to claim.

This little maid had just entered her eleventh year; but her important station at the theatre, as it seemed to her, with the benefits which she felt to accrue from her pious application of her small earnings, had given an air of womanhood to her steps and to her behaviour. You would have taken her to have been five years at least older.

Till latterly she had merely been employed in choruses, or where children were wanted to fill up the scene. But the manager, observing a diligence and adroitness in her above her age, had for some few months past intrusted to her the performance of whole parts. You may guess the self-consequence of the promoted Barbara. She had already drawn tears in young Arthur; had rallied Richard with infantine petulance in the Duke of York; and in her turn had rebuked that petulance when she was Prince of Wales. She would have done the elder child in Morton's pathetic after-piece to the life; but as yet the "Children in the Wood" was not.

Long after this little girl was grown an aged woman, I have seen some of these small parts, each making two or three pages at most, copied out in the rudest hand of the then prompter, who doubtless transcribed a little more carefully and fairly for the grown-up tragedy ladies of the establishment. But such as they were, blotted and scrawled, as for a child's use, she kept them all; and in the zenith of her after reputation it was a delightful sight to behold them bound up in costliest Morocco, each single—each small part making a *book*—with fine clasps, gilt-splashed, &c. She had conscientiously kept them as they had been delivered to her; not a blot had been effaced or tampered with. They were precious to her for their affecting remembrancings. They were her principia, her rudiments; the elementary atoms; the little steps by which she pressed forward to perfection. "What," she would say, "could India rubber, or a pumice stone, have done for these darlings?"

I am in no hurry to begin my story—indeed I have little or none to tell—so I will just mention an observation of hers connected with that interesting time.

Not long before she died I had been discoursing with her on the quantity of real present emotion, which a great tragic performer experiences during acting. I ventured to think, that though in the first instance such players must have possessed the feelings which they so powerfully called up in others; yet, by frequent repetition, those feelings must become deadened in a great measure, and the performer trust to the memory of past emotion, rather than express a present one. She indignantly repelled the notion, that, with a truly great tragedian, the operation, by which such effects were produced upon an audience, could ever degrade itself into what was purely mechanical. With much delicacy, avoiding to instance in her *self*-experience, she told me, that so long ago as when she used to play the part of the Little Son to Mrs. Porter's Isabella, (I think it was,) when that impressive actress had been bending over her in some heart-rending colloquy, she has felt real hot tears come trickling from her, which (to use her powerful expression) have perfectly scalded her back.

I am not quite so sure that it was Mrs. Porter; but it was some great actress of that day. The name is indifferent; but the fact of the scalding tears I most distinctly remember.

* * * *

As I was about to say—at the desk of the then treasurer of the old Bath theatre—not Diamond's—presented herself the little Barbara S——.

The parents of Barbara had been in reputable circumstances. The father had practised, I believe, as an apothecary in the town. But his practice, from causes which I feel my own infirmity too sensibly that way to arraign—or perhaps from that pure infelicity which accompanies some people in their walk through life, and which it is impossible to lay at the door of imprudence—was now reduced to nothing. They were in fact in the very teeth of starvation, when the manager, who knew and respected them in better days, took the little Barbara into his company.

At the period I commenced with, her slender earnings were the sole support of the family, including two younger sisters. I must throw a veil over some mortifying circumstances. Enough to say, that her Saturday's pittance was the only chance of a Sunday's (generally their only) meal of meat.

One thing I will only mention, that in some child's part, where, in her theatrical character, she was to sup off a roast fowl (O joy to Barbara!) some comic actor, who was for the night caterer for this dainty—in the misguided humour of his part, threw over the dish such a quantity of salt, (O grief and pain of heart to Barbara!) that when she crammed a portion of it into her mouth, she was obliged sputteringly to reject it; and what with shame of her ill acted part, and pain of real appetite at missing such a dainty, her little heart sobbed almost to breaking, till a flood of tears, which the well-fed spectators were totally unable to comprehend, mercifully relieved her.

This was the little starved, meritorious maid, who stood before old Ravenscroft the treasurer, for her Saturday's payment.

Ravenscroft was a man, I have heard many old theatrical people beside herself say, of all men least calculated for a treasurer. He had no head for accounts, paid away at random, kept scarce any books, and summing up at the week's end, if he found himself a pound or so deficient, blest himself that it was no worse.

Now Barbara's weekly stipend was a bare half-guinea. By mistake he popped into her hand a—whole one.

Barbara tripped away.

She was entirely unconscious at first of the mistake: God knows, Ravenscroft would never have discovered it.

But when she had gone down to the first of those uncouth landing-places, she became sensible of an unusual weight of metal pressing her little hand.

Now mark the dilemma.

She was by nature a good child. From her parents and those about her, she had imbibed no contrary influence. But then they had taught her nothing. Poor men's smoky cabins are not always porticoes of moral philosophy. This little maid had no instinct to evil; but then she might be said to have no fixed principle. She had heard honesty commended, but never dreamed of its application to herself. She thought of it as something which concerned grown-up people—men and women. She had never known temptation, or thought of preparing resistance against it.

Her first impulse was to go back to the old treasurer, and explain to him his blunder. He was already so confused with age, besides a natural want of punctuality, that she would have had some difficulty in making him understand it. She saw *that* in an instant. And then it was such a bit of money! and then the image of a larger allowance of butcher's meat on their table next day came across her, till her little eyes glistened, and her mouth moistened. But then Mr. Ravenscroft had always been so good-natured, had stood her friend behind the scenes, and even recommended her promotion to some of her little parts. But again the old man was reputed to be worth a world of money. He was supposed to have fifty pounds a-year clear of the theatre. And then came staring upon her the figures of her little stockingless and shoeless sisters. And when she looked at her own neat white cotton stockings, which her situation at the theatre had made it indispensable for her mother to provide for her, with hard straining and pinching from the family stock, and thought how glad she should be to cover their poor feet with the same—and how then they could accompany her to rehearsals, which they had hitherto been precluded from doing, by reason of their unfashionable attire,—in these thoughts she reached the second landing-place—the second, I mean from the top—for there was still another to traverse.

Now virtue support Barbara!

And that never-failing friend did step in—for at that moment a strength not her own, I have heard her say, was revealed to her—a reason above reasoning—and without her own agency, as it seemed (for she never felt her feet to move) she found herself transported back to the individual desk she had just quitted, and her hand in the old hand of Ravenscroft, who in silence took back the refunded treasure, and who had been sitting (good man) insensible to the lapse of minutes, which to her were anxious ages; and from that moment a deep peace fell upon her heart, and she knew the quality of honesty.

A year or two's unrepining application to her profession, brightened up the feet, and the prospects of her little sisters, set the whole family upon their legs again, and released her from the difficulty of discussing moral dogmas upon a landing-place.

I have heard her say, that it was a surprise, not much short of mortification to her, to see the coolness with which the old man pocketed the difference, which had caused her such mortal throes.—*Last Essays of Elia.*

USEFUL KNOWLEDGE.*

SUMMER AND WINTER CLOTHING.—If several pieces of cloth, of the same size and quality, but of different colours, black, blue, green, yellow, and white, be thrown on the surface of snow in clear daylight, but especially in sunshine, it will be found that the black cloth will quickly melt the snow beneath it, and sink downwards. The blue will do the same, but less rapidly; the green still less so; the yellow slightly; and the white not at all. We see, therefore, that the warmth or coolness of clothing depends as well on its colour as its quality. A white dress, or one of a light colour, will always be cooler than one of the same quality of a dark colour; and especially so in clear weather, when there is much sunshine. A white and light colour reflects heat copiously, and absorbs little; while a black and dark colour absorbs copiously, and reflects little. From this we see that experience has supplied the place of science in directing the choice of clothing. The use of light colours always prevails in summer, and that of dark colours in winter.

COLD FROM DAMP CLOTHES.—If the clothes which cover the body are damp, the moisture which they contain has a tendency to evaporate, by the heat communicated to it by the body. The heat absorbed in the evaporation of the moisture contained in clothes, must be, in part, supplied by the body, and will have a tendency to reduce the temperature of the body in an undue degree, and thereby to produce cold. The effect of violent labour, or exercise, is to cause the body to generate heat much faster than it would do in a state of rest. Hence we see why, when the clothes have been rendered wet by rain or by perspiration, the taking of cold may be avoided, by keeping the body in a state of exercise, or labour, until the clothes can be changed, or till they dry on the person; for in this case, the heat carried off by the moisture in evaporating, is amply supplied by the redundant heat generated by labour, or exercise.

DAMP BEDS.—The object of bed-clothes being to check the escape of heat from the body, so as to supply at night that warmth which may be obtained by exercise or labour during the day, this end is not only defeated, but the contrary effect produced, when the clothes by which the body is surrounded contain moisture in them. The heat supplied by the body is immediately absorbed by this moisture, and passes off in vapour; and this effect would continue until the clothes were actually dried by the heat of the body.

A damp bed may be frequently detected by the use of a warming-pan. The introduction of the hot metal causes the moisture of the bed-clothes to be immediately converted into steam, which issues at the open space in which the warming-pan is introduced. When the warming-pan is withdrawn, this vapour is again partially condensed, and deposited on the surface of the sheets. If the hands be introduced between the sheets, the dampness will then be distinctly felt—a film of water being in fact deposited on their surface.

DANGER OF DRYING CLOTHES IN AN INHABITED ROOM.—The danger of leaving clothes to dry in an inhabited apartment, and more especially in a sleeping-room, will be readily understood. The evaporation which takes place in the process of drying, causes an absorption of heat, and produces a corresponding depression of temperature in the apartment.

HEAT AND LIGHT.—Innumerable operations of nature proceed as regularly, and as effectually, in the absence of light, as when it is present. The want of that sense which it is designed to affect in the animal economy, in no degree impairs the other powers of the body; nor in man does such a defect interfere in any way with the faculties of the mind. Light is, so to speak, an article rather of luxury than of positive necessity. Nature supplies it, therefore, not in an unlimited abundance, nor at all times and places, but rather with that thrift and economy which she is wont to observe in dispensing the objects of our pleasures, compared with those which are necessary to our being; but heat, on the contrary, she has yielded in the most unbounded plenteousness. Heat is everywhere present. Every object that exists, contains it in quantity without known limit. The most inert and rude masses are pregnant with it. Whatever we see, hear, smell, taste, or feel, is full of it. To its influence is due that endless variety of forms which are spread over and beautify the surface of the globe. Land, water, air, could not for a single instant exist as they do, in its absence; all would suddenly fall into one rude formless mass—solid and impenetrable. The air of heaven, hardening into a crust, would envelop the globe, and crush, within an everlasting tomb, all that it contains. Heat is the parent and the nurse of the endless beauties of organization,—the mineral, the vegetable, the animal kingdom, are its offspring. Every natural structure is either immediately produced by its agency, maintained by its influence, or intimately dependent on it. Withdraw heat, and instantly all life, motion, form, and beauty, will cease to exist, and it may be literally said, "Chaos has come again."

DUTCH SERVANTS AND NOBLES.

DUTCH servants are the greatest thieves in Christendom. Even their masters do not scruple to tell you that thieving is a part of a servant's perquisite, which he, therefore, no doubt, makes a chief consideration in his calculation of the value of any given family he engages with. A gullible, rich, easy-tempered lodger must, of course, very much dispose him to abate his demand for wages. But it is thieving of a peculiar kind,—sly, nimble pilfering, under a mask of the most guileless simplicity, without any of the glorious risks of robbing upon a daring scale. They will open your buffet and nibble at a cake, or empty an unperceived portion of your wine or liqueur. But every thing is done *tout doucement.* The following extract from a friend's letter is illustrative:—"One day," says he, "my servant suspected that a larger portion of sweetmeats had been abstracted; but as he was in possession of the key of the buffet, his misgivings acquired no force. It occurred to me at last, that the housemaid who swept the apartments (she was the only servant who had access beside my own) might have another key. To ascertain the fact, a trap was set by placing an empty wine-bottle in such a situation, that when the door of the buffet should open, the bottle, by one of the most in-

* Compiled from Dr. Lardner's last volume.

evitable of necessities, must tumble and be shivered to pieces. A whole day elapsed, and the bottle remained in *situ*. The morning came, and with it came Molly into the rooms to dust, about the time when her appropriations were suspected to commence. I lay in the adjoining apartment, eagerly awake to every stir and movement of her operations. The window, I observed, she carefully shut. Her dustings were, on former occasions, usually over about eight o'clock. Half-past eight arrived, but all was quiet, and my patience, nearly exhausted, had given place to self-reproach for indulging what might, after all, be only an ungenerous suspicion. The thing was given up in despair, and I turned to compose myself to sleep. Crash went the apparatus of the thief-trap, accompanied with a scream, so loud that it might be heard in the street. I jumped out of bed. Lo! Molly on bended knee, with hands and eyes uplifted, and the bottle smashed, and multiplying and reflecting the evidence of her guilt in a thousand fragments. She cried and sobbed, and made the most dolorous noise that Dutch can be imagined capable of, but, excepting what might be inferred from the pathetic tone of the cadence, the appeal was all lost upon me. For the same reason, my rebuke must have been lost upon her, if I had attempted it; so that she got off better than I intended, certainly much better than she deserved. I should have informed her master of the particulars, but I knew it would lead to no result, save that, perhaps, of getting the girl removed, and a worse in her place. Besides, it was far from clear that the master might not himself be a sleeping partner in the proceeding."

A common *ruse* is to hide a thing until it is missed: if not missed, it is so much clear gain. Should the thief be taxed and pushed hard, seeing no way of escape, he will affect to make a most eager and prying search into every hole and corner of your apartments, which, however, will end in nothing, unless you rise in your tone, or begin to talk about the police, when the missing article is sure sooner or later to come forth, the affected discovery most probably backed by indignant expressions of rage, for neither Cæsar nor his wife, on these occasions, will be suspected.

Next to their love of money, there is no Dutch passion more dominant than the pride of birth. To impute to their grandees a pedigree much later than the flood, of which their country exhibits such unequivocal marks, were positive scandal. But to speak the fact, they hold a very lofty head on the score of ancestry; and yet is their nobility, compared with their despised Belgian neighbours, only as the cheese of the spring to the rottenness of ripe decay. Their aristocracy are the veriest quintessence of ultraism, and in every way worthy to companion with their hopeful prototypes of Austria and Russia. In conversing on politics, there was an insufferable hauteur whenever they touched upon any subject connected with popular rights. Occasions of this kind not seldom occurred to me pending the discussions on the Reform Bill. Nothing gave me more delight than in these discussions to let them hear a little of our English notions, when I seldom failed to set the bile of the most phlegmatic listener in a ferment. "You are a Whig, I suppose?" said a lady, with whom I had been conversing at a soirée about the barbarities of the Russians to the Poles, eyeing me certainly with not the most feminine softness. "And can I do better, Madam," said I, "than follow the example of my own most excellent sovereign?" This was an *argumentum ad verecundiam*, especially as she had just been enlarging on the many virtues of her own monarch, she seemed no way prepared to gainsay. Still, the venomous expression of her countenance remained unabated, leaving not the smallest doubt in my mind, that her tongue would have done it ample justice, if the rules of good breeding in her own house had not interposed in my favour.—*From Sir Arthur Brooke Faulkener's Visit to the Low Countries.*

CURIOUS PENMANSHIP—GASTROGRAPHY.

WHEN I was in the city of Lyons, in the spring of 1819 I went out in the evening of my arrival to take a walk, and to look at the site and the buildings[*] of a city so famous for its manufactures, and its superiority in *dying in bright and permanent colours*.[†] Near the hotel I observed an elderly Frenchman sitting in the street at a small writing-desk, and several people gathered round him. I joined the circle, and found the man engaged in writing in a very extraordinary manner. To a belt firmly fastened round his waist, there was attached a socket with a pen in it projecting forwards. This pen, by a motion of his trunk, he dipped into the ink-stand before him, and then proceeded to write upon the sheet of paper fixed to the desk. To describe his manner of writing, I have taken the liberty of coining a new Greco-English word, viz., *Gastrography*. By certain movements of his trunk and belly he directed the pen upon the paper so as to write quite evenly, and to form all his letters and words quite regularly. The writing was beautiful in the French character. I paid him for a specimen of his penmanship. I gave this to a friend. I regret that I did not keep it as a rare curiosity, for I believe it is now lost. Instead of saying of this man, that he wrote a "good hand," we should say that he wrote a "good belly."

G.

FOUR-AND-TWENTY FIDDLERS.

THERE is a Comic English Song beginning—"Four-and-twenty fiddlers all in a row," &c. *Why*, "four-and-twenty," (or twenty-four) fiddlers? Is the *public* aware of the origin of this number of fiddlers? No! Very well, then we shall tell the public all about it.

Once upon a time, during the reign of Catherine de Medicis in France, a violin-player, named Baltazarini, *with his band of violin-players*, was sent to her from Piedmont. He received from her certain musical and *official* situations. His ingenuity in contriving magnificent "Balets" (Ballets,) &c., for the Court, drew upon his fortunate head other honours and emoluments. The extravagance of Henry III. in these shows and musical mummeries, &c., was so great as to milk his subjects nearly dry.

Well, these fiddlers remained in glory; and some of them died out, and were replaced by others; and, at last, there was a body of these fiddlers constituted as "les vingt-quatre violons du Roi," some time about the end of 16th, or the beginning of the 17th century.

These twenty-four fiddlers were *officers* of the king, and were obliged to play every Thursday and Sunday at the king's dinner, and at all the balls and ballets given by order of his Majesty. The expense of *one* of these extravagant *fêtes* given by Henry III., on the marriage of the Duc de Joyeuse to Mademoiselle de Vaudemont, in 1581, is estimated at L.250,000 sterling!!!

Is our patient public satisfied? We think so! The "Four-and-twenty fiddlers, all in a row," instead of being "all *down* below!" as the song says, are now *shown up*, all in a row! Why, Paganini was (is) nothing to this, for he is no *courtier*; he exists upon *popular* support! What says our patient public to that?

---

[*] The lofty houses in Lyons, of five and six storeys, looking gloomy enough in the narrow streets and even on the side next the river, put an Edinburgh man in mind of the "Lands" in the old town of "Auld Reikie."

[†] British Silk-dyers and others would do well, now-a-days, to inquire into the peculiar nature of the *water* at Lyons, and other circumstances, so as to enable them to dye their goods as brightly and as permanently. "La teinture de Lyons," has been celebrated for centuries. The advanced state of chemical knowledge, &c., ought to help such inquiries. *Verbum sapienti*. A word to the wise

ELEMENTS OF THOUGHT.

MINISTERS.—There are a generation which measure their time not so much by the revolution of the sun as by the revolutions of power. There are two eras particularly marked in their calendar; the one the period they are in the ministry, and the other when they are out, which have a very different effect on their sentiments and reasoning. Their course commences in the character of friends to the people, whose grievances they display in all the colours of variegated diction; but the moment they step over the threshold of St. James's, they behold every thing in a new light, the taxes seem lessened, the people rise from their depression, the nation flourishes in peace and plenty, and every attempt at improvement is like heightening the beauties of paradise, or mending the air of elysium.—*Hall of Leicester.*

FACTIONS IN ENGLAND.—After the manner of the ancient factions, we hear much in England of the Bedford party, and the Rockingham party, and the Portland party, when it would puzzle the wisest man to point out their political distinction. The useful jealousy of the separate orders is extinct, being all melted down into one mass of corruption. The House of Commons looks with no jealousy on the House of Lords, nor the House of Lords on the House of Commons. The struggle in both is maintained by the ambition of powerful individuals and families, between whom the kingdom is thrown as the prize; and the moment they unite, they perpetuate its subjection, and divide its spoils.—*Hall of Leicester.*

It is a fine remark of Rousseau's, that the best of us differ from others in fewer particulars than we agree with them in. The difference between a tall and a short man is only a few inches, whereas they are both several feet high. So a wise and learned man knows many things, of which the vulgar are ignorant!—but there is still a greater number of things, the knowledge of which they share in common with him.—*Hazlitt.*

NATURAL CONNEXION BETWEEN THE FEELINGS AND THE INTELLECT.

IN morality and philanthropy, original thought is often the result of strong feeling. Necessity is the mother of that invention which has selfish for its prænomen. There is an invention, which affiliates itself on sympathy. However anatomy may reverse the relative position, the heart is as a heaven to the head; and emotion is the angel that comes and troubles the thick stagnation of the thinking pool, and gives it the power of healing. When the evils which press upon the feebler portions of humanity can make themselves understood and felt by the stronger, the discovery of the remedy, and its application, is drawing nigh. This is better than the sentimentality of a sighing heart. It is turning emotion to good account. Tears, like other water, should not run to waste. The moralist should be like the practical engineer, who, if he finds a full flowing stream, gives a blessing on its beauty, and then puts up a corn or a cotton-mill.—*Monthly Repository.*

Economy is the parent of liberty and ease.—*Swift.*

THE ROBBERS OF TANTALLON.*

TANTALLON is the name of an old castle, situated "near to that place where the sea rock, immense, amazing Bass, looks o'er a fertile land." It was built, as tradition says, to repel the invasion of the Danes, and has been for many ages in ruins; nor was it supposed capable of being inhabited by human beings, until about twenty years ago, when a lawless band of robbers who at that time infested the eastern coast of Scotland, and were prowling among its dilapidated walls to elude the public gaze, discovered a kind of subterraneous passage, which winded with a gentle declivity to the ground floor of the building, and ended in the midst of several vaulted apartments. Here they at once determined to construct a retreat, as it afforded not only a commodious depot for their spoils, but also a secure hiding-place in case of danger. They accordingly set to work, and fitted up their new habitation in a tolerably comfortable manner; secreted and secured the entrance so well that an occasional visiter might pass by it without observation. They then concentrated in it all the plunder they had concealed in other parts of the country; and thus the venerable walls of Tantallon were so far perverted from their original purpose, that, instead of being a defence, they were tenanted by a troop of marauders, who carried on an extensive and systematic work of spoliation throughout the land. As Tantallon was now head-quarters, they lived longer and oftener there than at any other place; and so cautiously did they conduct themselves, that although they were often seen in the villages around, not the most distant suspicion was entertained, either of their habitation or profession. When their stock of provisions became scanty, they set out on a new crusade of depredation, always leaving one of the number as guardian of the fortress. How long they lived in this manner at Tantallon is not certain; and they might have kept their quarters a great deal longer, had it not been for the indiscretion of him who was left as warder of the castle on one of their foraging excursions. This man was a most devoted worshipper of the jolly god; and one day, having remained rather long at his devoirs, he got himself what a sailor would call "half seas over;" and being somewhat merry inclined, he went and thrust his head through a small window in the wall, towards two women who were employed weeding corn in an adjoining field. When they looked at him, he distorted his face like the clown in a pantomime; and having on his head a nightcap he made a singularly grotesque appearance. At a sight so unusual the women stared with amazement; nor did they recover from their fright until the robber (who perhaps thought, by this time, that his imprudence had carried him too far) withdrew from the window. They then went home immediately, and related to their master what a curious being they had seen looking through one of the windows of Tantallon; but from only seeing what they supposed to be its head, they could not specify its shape or determine whether it was human or supernatural. The farmer, who was a bold athletic man, instantly collected a number of his men, who armed themselves with pitchforks and such rustic weapons as the place afforded, and himself, accoutred with his yeomanry sword and pistols, marched at their head, resolved to besiege the nondescript in his castle, and force him to capitulate, if he would not surrender at discretion. When they arrived at Tantallon the women pointed out the place where they saw him. After a long search they discovered the secret entrance; but the robber, who was aware of what was going forward, and fear of discovery having taken the place of inebriety, had obstructed their way with every thing in his power, so that it was not till after an obstinate struggle that they reached the interior and captured the enemy. And now it was that they understood the nature of his employment, and the extent to which it had been carried. Here were found clothes of every description and quality; meat also of every kind, and a number of live poultry, that they could have fresh at pleasure. Their cellar was stocked with the choicest wines and spirits, both foreign and British; they had also a good collection of plate and other valuables, from which it appeared that they had lived in a splendid and luxurious manner. A warrant was immediately obtained for the commitment of the robber; several of the others were apprehended soon after, tried and transported for life. And thus was Tantallon again bereft of inhabitants, and its grey walls left to moulder in peace beneath the silent but sure decaying hand of time.

* For the truth of the above story, which is from a correspondent, we do not vouch.

THE STORY-TELLER.
A PARISIAN GOSSIPPING.

You wish to know something of the manners of the French; not of the very high in rank, who have not much, language apart, to distinguish them from those of the same rank in London, Vienna, or St. Petersburgh; but of the French people, *en masse*, the middle classes in particular. You go to Paris by land and water; see a few of the sights; eat of a few of the dishes; languish under fatigue, or fume with passion; and return, thanking heaven you are once more in a land where English is spoken freely, and coal burned in large quantities; and though you may thenceforth occasionally adventure on " They order these things better in France," you are in reality as ignorant of French character and manners as before you packed your valise. You try books of travel, and learn at second hand, through a dim misty medium, what you may have already seen. This is not very satisfactory; and now we beg to recommend our method of learning something of French society. It is by the perusal of those lively gossipping works of fiction which we level to ordinary life; the JEAN* of C. Paul de Kock, for example, from which we take the birth and christening of the hero; premising that, after the perusal, something must be known of the inside of Parisian dwellings; of the amiable manner in which female servants live with their mistresses; the invariable good-humour and politeness which accompany the familiar intercourse of neighbours, and obtain a relish of the humours of our " natural enemy."

M. Francis Durand, herbalist, in the Rue St. Paul, was a man of about forty years of age, who stuck close to his business as much from taste as from its having proved a lucrative concern: he flattered himself there was not a botanist in Paris could compete with him in the knowledge of herbs, and of course he felt very indignant when he was called a seedsman, as he sometimes was, by people who ought to have known better. He had been in bed since eleven o'clock, according to his invariable custom, which he had never broken, even on the day of his marriage; and M. Francis Durand had been twelve years united in holy matrimony with Miss Felicia Legros, daughter of a cloth-merchant in the city.

M. Durand, then, was in bed, and alone, for a reason you shall soon know. M. Durand slept soundly, because his deep knowledge of simples did not so far excite his mind as to interfere with his repose. His maid, Catherine, had been for some time shaking his arm, and bawling in his ear, before he opened his eyes, and, raising his head from the pillow, asked, " What do you want? What's the matter? eh, Catherine?"

" What's the matter, Sir? Why, have not I been telling you for the last quarter of an hour that my mistress is in great pain—that she is getting worse and worse, and that, in a very short time, the business will all be over."

M. Durand raised himself on his elbow, pushed his nightcap back on his head, and gazing with a vacant countenance on his maid—" Why, what's the matter with my wife?"

" Matter with your wife!" screamed Catherine, again shaking the drowsy herbalist; " why, don't you recollect the situation of my mistress?—that she expects every moment to———"

* This work is just translated under the title of the *Modern Cymon*. The translation is executed with much spirit.

" Ah, parbleu! that's true," said M. Durand, rousing himself; " my dream had made me forget every thing. I dreamt I was in a field picking sorrel, when, all at once ———"

" Upon my word, a pretty time to be telling dreams! I tell you my mistress is very ill. Run, fetch the doctor and nurse. You know Madame Moka, Rue Nonaindieres? Make haste, Sir, whilst I return to my mistress, who ought not to be left alone."

So saying, she quitted the little closet where M. Durand had been sleeping, in the expectancy of that event with which he had just been made acquainted. This loft served as a store, and the walls were furnished with shelves, loaded with plants and roots, whilst others were hung to dry on cords, which were suspended from the roof in every direction. Under these aromatics M. Durand found a temporary couch, so that when he got out of bed, he might have been mistaken for a hortus siccus.

" Well, well, Catherine, I'll go, I'll run," said the herbalist yawning; but all at once it occurred to him, how odd it was his wife should be taken ill at night, when he had settled in his own mind that she would be delivered in the day time—" but I suppose," thought he, " a man may be very easily mistaken in affairs of this kind."

In trying to recollect his dream, M. Durand's head fell on the pillow, his eyes closed, and he was soon snoring again, no doubt with the view of dreaming out his dream.

Catherine had returned to her mistress, whom she found still suffering, and fretting herself at the non-arrival of the accoucheur, whom she was persuaded would never come in time. Madame Durand was the more uneasy, as, though approaching to her thirty-fifth year, she had never been a mother, though most ardently desiring that event.

" Well, Catherine," she exclaimed, as her maid returned.

" My master slept as if he was deaf; but I awoke him at last. He has run off for the nurse and midwife."

" Ah! I hope he will make haste. Oh! how I suffer! But then what pleasure I shall feel in embracing my own child!"

" Ah, to be sure, yes, after twelve years' marriage—time was slipping away. I am sure it will be a boy. I have betted an ounce of snuff with Madame Moka, who says it will be a girl."

" Ah! boy or girl, I shall love them equally well."

" I have a great mind to call our neighbour, Madame Ledoux."

" Oh, presently, Catherine; but I have not heard the street door shut; are you sure your master is gone?"

" Why he ought to be by this time in the Rue St. Nonaindieres."

" Go see, Catherine."

The servant, by way of satisfying her mistress, returned to the garret, and, long before she reached the bed, was saluted by the strong steady snoring of M. Durand. Catherine was a bouncing lively girl of about twenty-eight years of age; having lived as a faithful servant eight years in the family, she occasionally took a little liberty with her master. She felt very angry on finding him again asleep, and immediately seized on the warm blankets, under which the poor herbalist had ensconced himself, and threw them on the floor. It was the month of March, and very cold, and Catherine thought with justice, that the nipping air would most effectually arouse her master. This operation disclosed M. Durand in an extremely simple dress; but in cases of emergency, age or sex should no longer be thought of.

Catherine's plan succeeded. M. Durand felt the keen wind blowing on him, and turned and turned again, without getting at all the warmer. At length he opened his heavy eyes, and was not a little surprised at finding the servant at his bed side, and himself so totally devoid of covering.

"What's the matter, Catherine?" said M. Durand gravely, trying to pull down the tail of an extremely scanty shirt.

"What, Sir! is it possible that you have gone to sleep again, after my telling you that Madame was so ill, and when we thought you had gone for the midwife and nurse?"

"Ah, my God, you are right, Catherine; it was that made me dream I was at a baptism."

"Well Sir, but the child must be born before it is baptized."

"That's true; but how the devil came I in *naturalibus*?"

"Come, come, I will not leave the room again till I see you out. Here are your stockings and your pantaloons."

"Well, then, Catherine, since you are not afraid of my dressing before you—"

"Afraid, indeed! a pretty thing to be afraid, when Madame is so ill!"

M. Durand made up his mind to get out of bed, and throwing off his night-cap, disclosed a round grey head, red cheeks, a bottle nose, and little grey eyes; all this supported by a body neither small nor large, neither fat nor thin, made one of those kind of men so often seen, and of whom it is impossible to form any opinion till you hear them speak.

"Here's your waistcoat."

"It's dreadfully cold to night, Catherine!"

"Come, Sir, make haste; here's your cravat—"

"And my garters, Catherine, you did not give me them."

"Gracious me, can't you go without garters at this time of night?"

"Stay, I see one near the strawberry-plants, *fraga fragorum*. Provided the accoucheur is at home—"

"Here, Sir, here is your coat."

"Stay a moment, Catherine, my cravat."

"Ah, Sir, if you don't make a little more haste—"

"My hat, then—Oh, how cold it is to night!"

"Run, Sir, run; that will warm you."

"I will put this warm handkerchief round my neck; and then,—Catherine, mind that parcel of sage, *salvia salviæ*, which has fallen from the shelf."

By way of reply, Catherine pushed her master out of the room, ran down the stairs before him, opened the back-door into the alley, and shut it in M. Durand's face, just as he had turned round to retrace his steps to his room for his pocket-handkerchief, which he had forgotten.

Satisfied that her master was gone at last, Catherine ran to call Madame Ledoux, who lodged on the second floor, and when she had awakened her, she returned to her mistress.

Madame Ledoux was the widow of a bailiff, an upholsterer, and a stationer; she had had by her three husbands fourteen children, of whom six were married, and settled in the world; nevertheless, she was only forty-nine years old, a tall thin woman, stiff and unbending in her person, with a well-curled wig, and a stiffly starched collar most regularly plaited. No wonder then she was well satisfied with her own appearance, and gave the world to understand she had repeatedly refused a fourth husband; and when a woman has had fourteen children, her opinion, in similar cases, ought to have great weight. Thus Madame Ledoux, who flattered herself that, in case of necessity, she could act as midwife, was by no means disturbed by Catherine's summons; it was a pleasure to her to witness the entry into the world of a little innocent; and, as all women have not this taste, when such an event was about to take place in the neighbourhood, it was rare indeed that the parties interested did not apply to the widow of the stationer, the upholsterer, and bailiff. At Catherine's first summons, she replied, "Here I am, I'll follow you; I'll just put on my gown and go down." And in fact the servant had scarce entered her mistress's chamber, when the door again opened and they saw Madame Ledoux, who, with the candle in her hand, her immense height—white dressing-gown, and cap stuck on the top of her head, would have made an excellent ghost in an old castle.

"Well, neighbour, has the time arrived."

"Oh, yes, Madame Ledoux; I believe this time there can be no mistake," replied Madame Durand.

"So much the better, neighbour: night is a better time to be ill than the day, there is less noise to annoy you. I had my first three—my fifth, and my last four in the night."

"And the accoucheur—the nurse,—not one is here!"

"Well, and what then? An't I with you? and an't I worth them all? My eighth child—it was a boy,—he who died of a bilious fever; great pity,—for he was a fine child, with a Grecian nose: he was by the upholsterer. I was alone, just as you are now, neighbour. I had sent away my servant the evening before, because she robbed me; and my husband was travelling, and far away. Well, I was not frightened, but made all my little arrangements———"

"Catherine, is not M. Durand returned yet?"

"Returned," said Catherine; "oh, no, Madame, he could not have returned yet—but I told him to run very fast."

M. Durand had been gone nearly three quarters of an hour, and no one appeared—yet the accoucheur and nurse lived at no great distance. Madame D. and Catherine had lost all patience, whilst Madame Ledoux endeavoured to tranquillize them.

When he had gone about a hundred yards, the herbalist recollected that he had not asked whether he was to call the accoucheur or nurse first. He stopped, and was half disposed to turn back, when he reflected, that the accoucheur ought certainly to be called first; so turning towards the Rue St. Antoine, muttering to himself, he said, "Confound it, how cold it is! and Catherine would not give me time to look for my garters; if my stockings come down I shall never escape the rheumatism. I'll take pretty good care never to have a child again—that is to say, to be born in the winter. To be turned out alone in the street in the middle of the night!—I ought to have routed out my friend Bellequeue, as he is godfather—it was almost as much his business as mine; a godfather is nearly the same as a father. And there was a woman robbed only eight days ago, in Rue Petit Musc; but they will be deucedly clever if they rob me, for I have nothing to be robbed of, not even a watch. But here is the Rue St. Antoine: how different a street looks in the night from the day; I hardly know one house from another. Hem! hem!—I have caught cold already. When I get home, I will take an infusion of violets with some orange-leaves in it—*malus aurea*."

Talking to himself in this way, M. Durand traversed

hat part of the Rue St. Antoine where the moon shone,—keeping a most respectful distance from the darkened side. A few steps nearer, and the herbalist would have gained the accoucheur's abode, which he could already see, although it was the shaded side, which not a little discomfited him; but, on throwing a fearful glance across, he was horrified by the apparition of a man standing exactly opposite the house he wished to enter. The herbalist came to a dead stop, then took two or three steps, feeling for his pocket handkerchief, no longer recollecting that he had left it at home. He then wiped the cold sweat from his forehead with the handkerchief he had tied round his neck, and stood with his eyes fixed on the man whom he perceived through the darkness. "There's some one there: a man, perhaps two. It's so dark there's no telling; but he is not here for nothing. What man is it?—if it was a question of simples, now, I could tell about them and their properties. Confound the man!—exactly in front of the Doctor's house. I am unarmed—that infernal Catherine hurried me so. What shall I do? I believe I had better go first to Madame Moka; I can come back here, and by that time, perhaps the man will be gone. It is very odd, it is not near so cold as it was."

We cannot give M. Durand's adventure with a drunken workman, who has lost his money in the gutter, in attempting to count his wages. He finds the doctor called out—not at home; and in terror of the drunken man, whom he takes for a ghost or a robber, and raises the hue and cry, as he runs home, while twenty windows are opened, people bawling—

"But what's the matter? what ails you? is there a house on fire?"

"Help! help! at my house—herbalist—Rue St. Paul."

M. Durand could say no more; he saw the dreaded stranger was nearing him, and darting down the street as fast as he could run, he turned and doubled, till, without well knowing how, he reached his door, and opening it with a latch-key which Catherine had slipped into his pocket, he hurried into his alley with all the feelings of a man who had just had an escape for his life.

Madame Durand's sufferings had increased. Hearing the door of the alley shut violently, she cried, "Here they are at last!" But M. Durand entered alone, pale, horror-struck, and his forehead bathed in sweat, with his stockings over his heels. He sank exhausted into a chair.

"Ah, my dear, you have run fast," said Madame Durand, who had a minute's respite from pain.

"Yes—yes—I did run certainly," said M. Durand, casting a wild look round, as if not quite sure that he was even now in safety.

"Nevertheless we thought the time long enough," said Madame Ledoux.

"And I, too; do you think I was very comfortable in the streets?"

"The accoucheur—is he coming, my dear?"

"Yes, yes, every body is coming; I did my best—"

"But what's the matter, Sir?" said Catherine; "you look as if you had seen something."

"Eh! seen something! I was attacked by a robber—two or three robbers. They followed me a considerable time; and if I had not had strength enough—to run away—it was all over with me."

"Oh, my poor husband!"

"I assure you, Madame, this child has cost me not a little—"

"Ah, neighbour, that's exactly the way with my thirteenth. My husband, the stationer, went out just as you did, to call the accoucheur. We lived at that time in Rue des Lions, and you know it is not in the very best neighbourhood: it was about three o'clock; the night dark as pitch; and I recollect it had rained all the evening. In turning the corner of the Rue des Lions, my husband heard footsteps. Fortunately, I had made him take his——"

"Oh!" cried Madame Durand, "Ah, there, it is returned again."

"Who's returned?" said the herbalist, starting up and looking behind him.

"Faith Sir," said Catherine, "here's my mistress, as bad as possible, and no signs of any accoucheur!"

Just then, a violent knocking was heard at the door of the alley. The servant hastened down, without waiting for a light; she ran and opened the door, calling to the persons in the street, "Come in, come in! follow me: you are just in time!" and poor Catherine was again at her mistress's bed-side in an instant.

"Oh, Madame!" she cried, "here they are all come;" and as she spoke the steps of several people were heard on the stairs. The door was thrown open violently, and a corporal at the head of four soldiers, entered the room, crying out, "Where are the robbers?"

At that very instant of time the crisis had arrived, and Madame Durand ushered a boy into the world, which Madame Ledoux received in her arms saying, "He will be just as strong as my fourteenth."

M. Durand sank back into his chair, as he gazed on the soldiers with lack-lustre eyes, muttering, "Gentlemen, it is a boy!"

"It is a boy!" repeated Catherine. And the corporal, turning round to his men, who were all lost in astonishment, re-echoed, "Ah! it is a boy."

After the first moments of grief and joy, which the presence of the new-born had occasioned, who had come into the world graced by the presence of a corporal and four soldiers, each began to eye his neighbour, and to ask an explanation of this curious scene.

"Well, my brave fellow," cried the corporal, "I suppose it was as witness to the birth of your son that you sent for us?"

"My dear, what are you thinking of?" said Madame Durand.

"To bring a regiment of soldiers here!" muttered Catherine.

"For certain," said Madame Ledoux, "I have had fourteen myself, and have seen upwards of one hundred born; but this is the most military lying-in I ever witnessed."

M. Durand, who had by this time recovered from his fright and surprise, said, "I never required your services, gentlemen; and I have no conception what brought you hither."

"We came here by desire of two young men of Rue Nonaindieres, who ran to our guard-house and begged us to go as quickly as possible to the herbalist's in Rue St. Paul, who had awakened the whole street by his cries for help: that's what brought us here my good man."

M. Durand bit his lips at this recital, and Catherine turned her head away to prevent laughing in her master's face. Madame Ledoux exclaimed, "There is some mistake —you seem to have alarmed the neighbourhood unawares."

M. Durand pretended not to be able to understand how the mistake could have arisen, and whilst they were discussing the point, they heard the shrill voice of Madame Moka, who cried, "Hold a light! Catherine, here's the Doctor!"

"High time, indeed;" said Madame Ledoux.

The accoucheur and nurse in fact, arrived the day after the fair; and the nurse would not have come at all, but that she had heard M. Durand's house was on fire. The first thing was to get rid of the soldiers; but as they were present at the birth of his son, M. Durand would not allow them to go away without drinking his health.

Catherine was therefore desired to take them into the shop, and to give each of them a dram. M. Durand followed, in order to give them their choice of a little violet or linden-water, but they one and all professed to be quite satisfied with brandy.

"To the health of the new-born," said the corporal, emptying his glass; the soldiers followed the example of their leader.

M. Durand bent his head, and swallowed a large glass of sugared water, saying, "To the health of my young son— *primogenitus*."

"To the health of the little Primogenitus!" cried the corporal, thinking that was the child's name.

Catherine clapped her hands; "Ah, he will be a fine fellow," said she, "already to have his health drank by soldiers!"

The corporal twisted his moustaches and vouchsafed a gracious smile to Catherine.

"And my mistress! won't you drink her health also?" said she.

"Well recollected, my girl," replied the corporal, holding out his little glass; "it would be a thousand pities to forget the mamma."

M. Durand mixed another glass of water and sugar, whilst Catherine filled the glasses of the soldiers, who, with one voice, drank, "to the health of the lady in the straw."

"To my wife's health—*mea uxor!*" said M. Durand, clearing off his glass.

"My poor dear mistress!" said Catherine, "what she has suffered!"

"I think," said the corporal, turning to his men, "we should be wrong to forget the papa."

"Certainty, certainly;" replied the soldiers, holding out their glasses immediately to Catherine, whilst the herbalist prepared for a third mixture of sugar and water.

"Comrades, the papa's health!" cried the corporal, holding up his glass; the soldiers did the same.

M. Durand made a point of hob-nobbing with them, and bowing profoundly, he said, "Gentlemen, here's my health—*suum cuique*. I drink your toast with the greatest pleasure."

The soldiers were getting quite at home, and seemed to be ready to drink the health of any other relation or friend of the family; but M. Durand, who could scarcely get down his last glass of sugar and water, affected to believe they were pressed for time, and opening the door, bowed them into the street.

By this time all was quiet in the sick-room: the Doctor had given his directions; the nurse had taken her post; Catherine had kissed the infant, and laid it by its mother's side; who found, in the assurance of that fact, a full compensation for all her sufferings. Madame Ledoux had retired to her own room, and M. Durand, after kissing his wife on the forehead, returned to his bed saying "This has been a trying night to my wife and me."

It was hardly six in the morning, when a little man was seen ringing at the herbalist's door. This little gentleman, who was in dressing-gown and slippers, and wore no hat, had his hair powdered and frizzed as if dressed for a ball: two large curls hung over each ear, and his hair behind was gathered into a pigtail, which, though short, was very thick; and being tied round with a black ribbon, played gracefully from side to side of his neck. True, it was no longer the fashion to wear powder and pomatum; but the gentleman we have been describing had his reasons for continuing the powder: he was a hair-dresser and wig-maker, and had been heard to declare, that the political changes in Europe had been many and great; but that nothing would ever induce him to cut off his tail.

M. Bellequeue, the name of the hair-dresser, (and well named he was,) was thirty-six years of age; his face round and fresh; his nose, although rather large, not ill made; his eyes, although rather small, sparkled like two diamonds; his mouth, perhaps too open, disclosed extremely good teeth; joined to which his eyebrows were black, his cheeks rosy, his waist small, and his legs well made: it is no wonder, then, that with pleasing manners, M. Bellequeue had the reputation in the neighbourhood of being an extremely well-bred man, a great admirer of the fair sex and credit for dressing hair with as much taste as any one even in the Palais Royal.

Catherine opened the door, when M. Bellequeue ran in, saying, "Well, my dear, so all is over! all is well. I have just met the doctor at one of my customers."

"Yes, M. Bellequeue, all is over, thank God! My poor mistress! what she has suffered!"

"And we have a boy!"

"Yes, Sir; a thumping boy, who is as handsome—"

"Who is he like, Catherine?"

"Egad, Sir, it is hard to say yet; though I think he is rather more like mistress."

"So much the better, for Durand is no great beauty. I shall be delighted to see this child, for I feel as if——I am to be his godfather."

"Yes, Sir; but you can't see him yet, for he is on my mistress's bed, who I should think, is still asleep; for we have had a busy night of it. What do you think of my master's bringing the patrol here?"

"Bah! soldiers!"

"Yes, Sir; and with their bayonets fixed!"

"Why, what the devil could Durand have been thinking of? And good breeding! for one should never forget one's manners with the ladies. Catherine, I must begin the day well by kissing you."

"Oh, Sir!"

M. Bellequeue kissed Catherine on both cheeks; then stepping softly up to the loft, he found M. Durand dressing himself. "Good day, my dear Durand. Well, we are papas now."

"Yes, my dear M. Bellequeue, we are."

"I wish you joy most sincerely, my friend."

"Thank you, thank you. I know, M. Bellequeue, the sincere attachment which you have to all my family. For which reason both my wife and I are determined to make you godfather to our child, in preference to some near relations who might expect that compliment. But a friend before all the world."

"Believe me, my dear Durand, I estimate your attention as I ought. I will be a second father to your son, and trust that he will always consider me as such. By the by who is to be my gossip?"

"An aunt of my wife's."

"How old may she be?"

"I should think about fifty-five—an extremely respectable woman."

Bellequeue made a wry face, muttering to himself, "Two ounces of comfits will do."

M. Durand, as he finished dressing, related the strange events of the night.

"You should have called on me," said the hair-dresser, "and I would have gone with you. You know that I am a smart blade. I would have taken my sword-cane with me, and we would have settled these rascals. What is that you are drinking?"

"Some linseed tea; to prevent any ill consequences from the shock of last night. I intended to have taken something vulnerary, but as I did not fall——"

"Eh—I think I hear some one crying."

"Ah! no doubt it is the little stranger. He has done nothing else all night."

"What a fine mellow voice he has. I must go and kiss him—no doubt his crying has awakened his mamma."

M. Bellequeue dragged the herbalist after him to the lady's room, who was sitting up in bed, already dressed in a very pretty morning cap; for once out of pain, a woman's first thought is to look well.

Madame Durand smiled graciously on the perruquier, who stepped on tiptoe to the bed-side, where the nurse presented him the child, saying, "What a handsome fellow he is." Bellequeue kissed the child affectionately, and hung over him in the most languishing manner; whilst M. Durand, peeping over his shoulder, and looking at the child, said, "He has my chin to a nicety, and the shape of his head is exactly the same."

"Ye-e-s," said Bellequeue, "I think there is a kind of a something. When is he to be baptized?"

"To-morrow, gossip, if you please."

"How—if I please, my pretty gossip? don't you know I am always ready."

"Write at once to the nurse, M. Durand. You know St. Germain."

"St. Germain-en-laye, is not it?"

"Yes, my dear, en-laye, and take care you do not forget to write to our friends and relations. You know, I made out a list."

"Yes, Madame: how shall I get through all this? My dear M. Bellequeue, could you spare me a moment to help me with these letters?"

"Willingly: it is still early, and the fashionable ladies whom I have to dress won't be up yet a while."

"Come down to my desk." M. Durand led the way to his shop. Bellequeue kissed the lady in the straw, and looked all the godfather at the child, and then followed the herbalist, as usual, on the points of his toes, a habit he had long ago contracted, in picking his way through the dirty streets, from one customer's house to another.

The herbalist scratched his head and bit the top of his pen, saying, "How shall we phrase these letters? You see, this being a first child, I have no practice. If it were a prescription for a sedative or aperient draught, I should be quite up to it."

"Oh, then, you are a bit of a doctor, are you?" said Bellequeue, sitting down opposite him.

"Why, I am thoroughly acquainted with simples. I have botanized at Pentin, St. Denis, Fontenay, Sèvres. When I walk in the country I stop at every step—I look in every corner."

"You must have seen, then, some very strange things—but, we are forgetting my godson. You must write a circular that will do for all."

"Ah! exactly so, a circular."

"Although I am a bachelor, I assure you, I have often helped a husband. One always begins in this way—' I have the honour to inform you.' "

"Ah, exactly so, I only wanted a beginning."

M. Durand took a sheet of paper, and wrote, "I have the honour to inform you—that my wife is delivered of her first——" "Will that do?"

"Very well," said Bellequeue; "go on."

"The infant is a boy."

"Extremely well turned."

"The infant is a thriving child—and all the family are quite well."—"I think that says every thing, does not it?"

"The very thing! could not be better. Here, I will make some copies for you."

This important business settled, Bellequeue left Durand, promising to call again in the course of the day; and as the christening of to-morrow must necessarily be followed by a family dinner, the herbalist's household were put in requisition to celebrate, in a fitting manner, the birth of his son and heir.

M. Durand, nailed to his counter, began already to think of what he should make his son; and, whilst dispensing camomile and poppy-seed, saw him in his mind's eye invested with an advocate's gown, or bedizened in the uniform of a colonel. Madame Durand pictured to herself her child old enough to give her his arm, and to accompany her in her walks. Her son would be handsome, well-made, witty. She saw all this whilst looking on the little doll that could scarcely open its eyes. She laid plans—plans: who does not? But those of a mother are very pleasing, and at least are not always traced in sand.

Bellequeue returned in the afternoon. M. Durand had run up for a moment to his wife, and they were puzzling themselves what name to give the child, when the godfather arrived just in time to settle the question.

"What do you call yourself, my dear Bellequeue?" said the herbalist.

"What do I call myself!"

"Yes, gossip; what is your Christian name," said the lady. We were thinking of a pretty name for my son."

"My dear gossip, my name is Jean Bellequeue, at your service."

"Only Jean!"

After a long discussion on names, Durand wishing for something Latin and learned, JEAN is fixed upon, and the christening day arrives.

After a night which would have passed very quietly had the little stranger been silent, which he did not find it convenient to be, as he cried for five consecutive hours, the baptismal morn appeared, accompanied with a pleasant small rain, or rather hail, for it froze as it fell, and rendered the streets extremely slippery. Fortunately the nurse arrived safe. She was a ruddy country woman of four-and-twenty, whose husband let out asses to the inhabitants of St. Germains, whilst his wife disposed of something better to the little one's of the metropolis. When Madame Ledoux saw her, she said she was as like as two peas to the nurse of her twelfth, the child of the stationer.

The party most interested in this affair, was probably equally well pleased with his nurse, for he darted with eagerness at what she offered to him, and, pressing with his little hands the bosom which promised to supply his every want, fixed himself for an hour, without its being possible to move him from his quarters. The nurse wanted to return the same day, but Madame Durand could not bring herself to part so soon from her son, and it was decided that Susan should stay over the christening, and go back the next day.

M. Durand dressed himself in black from head to foot, thinking that, in this costume, he had very much the appearance of a physician. The relatives invited to the ceremony arrived in due time. First the aunt, Madame Grosbleu, who kissed her niece, and begged her acceptance of a little christening cap, which was trimmed with fine lace, and then attempted to take her little godson, who, so far from meeting her half way, cried and kicked with all his force.

"What a lovely child! he is your very image, my dear Felicite."

She was soon followed by M. and Madame Renard, bonnet-makers in the Rue du Temple, and cousins of M. Durand. M. Renard had intended to show that he was piqued at not having been chosen for godfather; but his wife had made him sensible that there was a certain expense saved, to say nothing of birth-days, Christmas-days, &c., anniversaries on which a godfather was sure to have a visit from his affectionate godchild. M. Renard admitted that a godson was an indirect tax on one's purse, and dismissing his ill-humour, determined to make himself as agreeable as possible. Then came M. Fourreau and his sister, Mademoiselle Aglae. He was a saddler of the Rue St. Avoie, and a relation of Madame Durand. He was a man who filled his chair at table most respectably, but who was perfectly ignorant of every thing unconnected with his business. Mademoiselle Aglae Fourreau was on the verge of her thirtieth year, and had not yet met with an admirer of serious intentions. Naturally very lively, she affected a childish giddiness, which did not become her, for we readily pardon that at eighteen, which is quite unbearable at eight-and-twenty. She spoke in such a mincing tone as to produce a very monotonous effect, and tittered not only at every thing that was said to her, but also when she spoke herself, no matter what the subject might be. In a word, Mademoiselle Aglae had been rather well looking at eighteen, and would have been generally considered so even now, could she have learnt to laugh a little less.

Two neighbours, one of whom, always ailing, and ever taking M. Durand's prescriptions, was one of his best customers, and the other an everlasting domino-player, completed the party who had met together on this auspicious occasion, and joined in the cuckoo note of "what a beautiful child!" "what a strong fellow!" "what fine eyes!" To each of these exclamations, M. Durand made a profound bow; whilst, with a knowing look, he said, "I have not done much in this way, but when I set about it in earnest ——!"

M. Endolori, the hypochondriac, whispered the herbalist, "Have you given him an infusion?"

"Who?"

"Your child."

"I wished him to take a decoction of pellitory *Helxine*, a capital thing for the bowels; but the nurse pretended it would be too strong—these women will never hear any thing new. But this morning, whilst my wife was asleep, and the nurse at breakfast, I washed his face all over with elder water, *sambuceus*, an admirable cosmetic. See how clear the skin looks already."

"Very true, one would think his cheeks were varnished."

Just then Madame Ledoux, in full dress, ran into the room crying out as loud as possible, "What a crowd there is in the room! why you have no brains, to get about a sick person in this way—and then asking her questions when she ought not to speak a word. Well, neighbour, how do you feel? what sort of a night have you had? not got over your fatigue yet, I'll engage? and the child—let me see the child—how he smells of elder-water! What, has he had anything the matter with his eyes?"

"No," said M. Durand; "it is only a little experiment, a little preventive, that I have used."

"What! Monsieur," said Madame Durand, "have you been washing this little love in elder water? I never heard of such a thing."

"I assure you, Madame, it is all for his good—I am well acquainted with the virtues of simples."

"Well, Sir, do what you please with your simples, but I beg you will leave my son alone."

"I have had fourteen, and never used elder-water with one of them. My husband, the bailiff, made my first drink a little wine, which set him coughing and almost choaked him. At the birth of my seventh, my husband, the cabinet maker, bathed the child with brandy, as he said, to stretch his joints, and the poor thing died humpbacked. My thirteenth, by the stationer, was born with very weak eyes. We had cataplasms and I know not what to put to them, and he was blind for life. So much for experiments. But every body seems to be come. What are we waiting for?"

"The godfather, my dear friend."

"Ah, that's true; I forgot the godfather."

"And my cousin, M. Mistigris, the professor of dancing—I should be sorry indeed, if he did not come—such a pleasant man, and so obliging—his kit always at the service of his friends—and he plays country dances so beautifully, with such taste and such style."

"Ah, yes—hah, hah, hah! how funny!" said Mademoiselle Aglae, laughing with all her might.

"Madame Ledoux replied, "I think I have heard him play in your shop; he seemed a most capital stick—I thought you had at least four blind fiddlers with you."

"I think the violin is apt to make one nervous," said M. Endolori to M. Durand.

"Yes, replied the herbalist; "but you should take a few pinches of mint, *mentha menthea*, a fine anti-spasmodic."

A little man, four feet seven inches high at most, here entered the room, with the lightness of a zephyr, and placed himself at the bedside in a graceful *mouvement en avant*. In this aerial entrée, it was easy to recognize M. Mistigris, the professor of dancing, who, although forty years old, seemed scarcely to touch the ground; his legs were in continual motion—his whole appearance betrayed his profession, and stamped him as a man who thought of nothing but pirouettes.

"We were speaking of you my dear cousin," said Madame Durand, holding out her hand to M. Mistigris, who kissed it, while standing on one leg. "I was afraid you were not coming."

"You know I promised to be here at twelve, and here I am. I had some lessons to give which made me rather late. Besides, the streets are very dangerous; I saw more than one person upset. Good day, Durand; where is the child?"

"Here," said Madame Moka.

"What do you think of him, cousin?" said Madame Durand.

"Oh, there is no judging of him in that way; let me see his legs."

"Impossible just now; he is dressed for the christening."

"If I saw his legs, I could tell you exactly what sort of a man he will make. You may depend, cousin, it is from the legs alone that you can form a correct opinion. A large or small calf—well or ill turned—are the unfailing proofs of wit and ability."

"Hah, hah!" said Mademoiselle Aglae Fourreau; "who ever heard of wit in the calf?"

"Every thing is there, Mademoiselle, even the soul."

"As for the soul, cousin," said the herbalist gravely, "Hippocrates conceives the seat of it to be in the left ventricle of the heart; Erasistratus, in the membrane of the brain; and Strabo, between the eye-brows."

"Well, if these gentlemen think the soul dwells in the stomach, in the brain, or between the eye-brows, I think I have just as much right to place it in the calf—every one has his system."

"Again, gentlemen," said Madame Ledoux, at the pitch of her voice, in order to drown the others. "I tell you, you make too much noise, you speak too loud, you will give my neighbour a headache, and a fever, just as I had with my sixth, the child of the cabinet-maker."——"Ah! here is the godfather."

At this announcement all was quiet; for every one was anxious to know who had been judged worthy of this honour, and to see the presents he had brought. M. Bellequeue presented himself, dressed in a blue frock coat, with buttons shining like gold; a white silk waistcoat and black breeches; and it may be well to note that such things as breeches were worn in 1805, the epoch at which the events took place which we have the honour to relate. Bellequeue, whose hair was dressed with more than ordinary care, held his three-cornered hat in his hand, under each arm boxes of comfits, two little parcels tied up with favours, ung by his fingers, and a handsome boquet was fastened to one of the boxes. The godfather, although a little embarrassed with his load, entered the room with that peculiarly grave air, often affected by those who are fearful of cutting rather a ridiculous figure, and by which none but a fool is deceived. But he soon felt himself at home, and had a smile for every one. Stepping lightly towards the invalid he presented her with four boxes tied with blue favours, and a little parcel containing four pair of gloves.

"I knew you would do something, foolish," said Mme. Durand, throwing a soft look on the hair-dresser; who drew from his right pocket two little pots of *confiture de Bar*, and presented them, saying, "this is for the stomach."

"What, more! Upon my word I am quite ashamed."

"And this for the chest," said Bellequeue, drawing from his left pocket a pint bottle of Schubac.

"Ah, this is too much."

"Here is your gossip, my dear Bellequeue," said the herbalist, introducing Mme. Grosbleu, who made a low curtsey. He then begged the godmother's acceptance of four boxes which he had made up his mind to buy, as well as a packet of gloves. But whilst Mme. Grosbleu was occupied with her presents, Bellequeue found means to approach Mme. Durand and whispered her, "Hers are Grenoble, but yours are Parisian gloves; your comfits are *à la Vanille*, and you have plenty of pistachio, whilst she has nothing but common nuts."

Mme. Durand replied to all this by a tender look, and a soft squeeze of the hand.

"By the by, my dear aunt, what is your Christian name?" said she.

"Jane, my dear friend; don't you recollect I was always called Jenny."

"It follows, then," said Bellequeue, "as a matter of course, that our godson's name must be Jean; however, if the mother wishes a second name——"

"Well, then, let it be Stanislas—that is a very pretty name, Jean Stanislas—but it must be time to be going."

"The two hackney coaches are at the door," said Catherine.

(We omit the church ceremonial, and come to the feast.)

It was near three o'clock, and the breakfast, or rather dinner, was laid out in the chamber of the invalid, who would by no means consent that the feast should take place in another room. Catherine had out-done herself, and the savoury smell of the first course promised most favourably. Madame Durand had fixed the seats; and not particularly wishing that Bellequeue should sit by Mademoiselle Aglae she placed him between the godmother and Madame Renard. Mademoiselle Fourreau had no resource but to laugh with M. Endolori and the domino-player, who was as gay as a double-six.

During the first course there was nothing to be heard but the rattling of the knives and forks, relieved by the noise of M. Mistigris's feet, who was practising steps under the table all the time he was eating. At the second course they found time to talk, and the conversation became general; and whilst discussing the herbalist's old Burgundy, they universally agreed as to the beauty of the new-born; and the virtuous character he was sure to prove, if he followed the good example set him by his parents. Mademoiselle Aglae tittered at M. Endolori's soft speeches, which chiefly consisted of recommendations not to eat anchovies, and to be careful of the mushrooms which flavoured some of the dishes. As for Bellequeue, he eat and drank almost as much as Madame Moka, who cleared her plate with admirable dexterity. Madame Ledoux eat but little, and continued talking of the children of her three husbands, the bailiff, the cabinet-maker, and the stationer; to all of which M. Renard smiled and listened with an air of the greatest interest. Madame Renard was silent, and busily calculated the probable cost of the dinner. M. Fourreau gorged, and drank, and filled again. To the domino-player nothing came amiss. M. Durand impatiently awaited the appearance of a dish of eggs, *à la neige*, into which, whilst Catherine's back was turned, he had thrown an infusion of simples, which, according to him, would impart a most excellent flavour. The eggs, *à la neige*, were at length served up. The herbalist said nothing, but smiled when he saw the surprise which the taste excited in his guests, who looked at each other inquiringly.

"I will tell you what it is," said M. Durand; "for I think you will puzzle a long time before you find it out. It is a selection of simples exceedingly purifying for the blood, and at the same time particularly aromatic, from which I have distilled an extract, which I secretly mixed with these eggs, in order to give you an agreeable surprise. I am certain that even at court they have never eaten any thing like this. How delicious! is it not?"

The guests looked at each other, and muttering "Yee-e-s" —"rather strange"—"a very particular taste."

"Oh, I knew what I was about; the more you eat, the better you will like it."

"It's very odd," said Bellequeue, "I cannot get on with it at all."—

"Nor I," said M. Mistigris, throwing an *antrechat* under the table, by which means his left leg came on the right of Madame Renard, who did not know what to make of this, being about the fiftieth she had received since the appearance of the soup. The other guests availed themselves of the example of Bellequeue, and left their eggs *à la neige* unfinished, except M. Endolori, who hearing that it was a purifier of the blood, sent his plate a second, and even a third time; as the herbalist assured him that it was a sure preventive for many maladies.

Fortunately, M. Durand had made no experiments on the dessert, and his *entremets aux simples* was forgotten in drinking the health of the new-born and his parents. The Champagne sparkled in the glasses, and Mademoiselle Aglae laughed like a fool, because the cork struck Madame Renard on the nose. Bellequeue refilled the glasses.

"What will you do with my godson?" said Madame Grosbleu; "have you already been scheming for him, my dear Felicité?"

"I should wish him, above all things, to be a handsome young man, my dear aunt. As to his employment, we shall observe his bent."

"The principal thing is to have him taught early to dance," said M. Mistigris; "that is the way to develop both body and mind."

"Let them make a brave soldier of my godson," said Bellequeue, who had seen service, and always spoke with pleasure of his campaigns—"Eh! that is the way to push him forwards; he should enter the service at eighteen, and I will bet that before twenty he will be a captain."

"Ah, M. Bellequeue, would you kill my son?"

"No, my dear gossip; but I say the army is the best profession nowadays."

"I should like my son to be a man of science," said M. Durand. "When he is four or five years old, I shall take him to botanize with me. Once well acquainted with simples, and the business is done."

"Buy a box of dominos for him," said the neighbour, "nothing will so soon teach him to reckon."

M. Endolori had said nothing for some time. He kept twisting about on his chair, became pale, and every now and then made a wry face, as if the *entremets aux simples* did anything but agree with him.

In the meantime, as they could not make little Jean a hero, nor a man of science, M. Bellequeue proposed a general bumper to his health. M. Endolori filled not, but whispered a few words in the ear of the herbalist.

"A sure proof that it agrees with you."

M. Endolori, not wishing to exhibit these proofs to the company, gave a ghastly look in reply, and hurried out of the room, bent almost double. Nevertheless the gaiety increased. Bellequeue sang, Mistigris capered about the room, and Mademoiselle Aglae laughed at every thing. Madame Durand at length admitted, that she felt a little tired, which was a hint for the breaking up of the party.

The guests made their adieus, and retired through the shop, where M. Mistigris proposed to dance a gavotte with Mademoiselle Fourreau. But as it was very cold, every one preferred returning home. M. Endolori, who just then re-appeared, and seemed to walk with considerable pain, begged M. Durand to give him his arm as far as his own door. The herbalist saw his neighbour home, assuring him that he would feel all the better the next day, and returned to seek repose whilst devising means to give his son a love of botany.

SCRAPS.

THE OBJECTS OF AMBITION.

THE ambitious lawyer sidling towards the woolsack,—the ambitious politician, dreaming of the treasury and its premiership,—the ambitious physician, looking forward to the presidency of his college,—the ambitious colonel of dragoons, fighting his way to a baton, through volumes of smoke and dust,—the ambitious author, scrawling *his*, through volumes of " sound and fury signifying nothing," —are in fact less actuated by lust of the empty distinctions of life, than by regard to its loaves and fishes. One is perhaps enamoured of a well appointed equipage, and urges on his own industry by visions of chariots and horsemen, running footmen, and outriders. Another is prone to sensual luxury, and his finest speeches are concocted with the *fumet* of a good dinner fragrant in his nostrils,—advocating the abolition of the slave trade till half the nation are in tears, only for love of a second course. A third man is covetous of a couple of yards of tabby ribbon,—red, blue, or green, according to his nation and language, calling or profession; —and perils his life or reputation with a view to their attainment. A fourth is fonder of the apostrophe of " my Lord," than of the mere " Sir," implying nothing of right or title over the apostrophizer;—or his wife has a predilection for walking out of a room two feet in advance of her country neighbour Mrs. Thomson,—or his sons want to make their honourable way to Almack's under cover of his new Peerage.—*Mrs. Gore's Sketch Book of Fashion.*

PULPIT PLEASANTRY.

PEOPLE now-a-days would be shocked to hear from the pulpit the droll things which in times past used to be uttered by preachers of all denominations; yet it may be doubted whether the congregations, now so nice of ear, are a jot more cleanly in the mind than in past times. In the reign of Anne, there was a minster named Burgess, who always attracted crowded audiences: he was a man of learning and virtue, as well as a humourist. Here is a specimen of his way;—" If " (he said, when speaking of the robe of righteousness) " any of you would have a cheap suit, you will go to Monmouth Street; if a suit for life, you will go to the Court of Chancery; but if you wish for a suit that will last to eternity, you must go to Christ, and put on his robe of righteousness."

THE CHANCELLOR IN A WATCH-HOUSE.—Among the many incidents which occur in my reminiscences of Brougham in those halcyon days, I may mention one. A party of us had supped at the rooms of a Dr. Parry, the brother of the circumnavigator. After supper, as we were crossing the South Bridge, we chanced to be witnesses of a very disgraceful scene—a mob of idle scoundrels (most of them bakers) beating an unfortunate woman with brutal ferocity. It was impossible to stand by and not make some attempt towards her deliverance. The tumult, in place of abating by our interference, grew frightful. All the watchmen within hail were about our ears in an instant, and, in return for our chivalry, lodged us all fast in the watch-house. The chancellor probably never found himself in a position less congenial to his taste and habits; but, even here, a mind so avaricious of knowledge was not to be unemployed. Among our associates in this vile prison, which was filled with the refuse of both sexes, an old soldier sat cowering over the embers of a fire that " taught light to counterfeit a gloom." He had campaigned in the American war; and with this hero our embryo candidate for the woolsack picked up an acquaintance, and continued during the whole space of our durance, extracting all he could on the favourite theme of his martial exploits. The names of the several officers under whom he served, the amount of the forces opposed to each other in particular engagements, the scenes of battles, position of the combatants, skill of the manœuvres, advantages, reverses, in short, every thing that was likely or not likely to come within the veteran's ken, was asked and responded to. So passed our night, until it pleased Aurora to leave her saffron couch, when, through Brougham's interference, we were set at large by a sort of general gaol delivery, by an order from the police magistrate, on the condition that, if required, we should be ready to make our appearance at the sessions—a condition which, as we had been guilty of neither blood nor battery, was not likely very seriously to damp the joy of our liberation.—*Sir Brooke Faulkner's Visit to Germany.*

MASTERS AND SERVANTS.—I myself possess but little knowledge of what is called the great folks; but when I am in want of information respecting the history or character of a particular family, instead of consulting *Debrett's Peerage*, I invariably sojourn to one of these tavern parlours, take my cigar, and make myself at home with the company—then mention in some way the Duke of —— or my Lord of ——, &c., &c., and immediately a half-dozen well-dressed men start on a colloquial race of the family genealogy, from the first young lord, down to the last marriage of the beautiful grand-daughter into the family of the Duke of ——, including all their lives, characters, and behaviour—always dwelling with marked emphasis, and lengthening their tale on those members of the family, who have been remarkable for their great goodness or rascality. These are the epithets they commonly use whilst scanning the merits of our proud aristocracy. The quality of goodness, as they use the term, is applied to the extravagant and thoughtless, who quietly suffer themselves to be pigeoned; and there have been instances of servants having met with so much superlative goodness in masters, as to have done the trick (made their fortunes) in from two to four years. By the rascals, they mean the masters who are famed for their meanness, and who are stingy and niggardly, to a degree of detestation; that is, in whose service they can barely be supplied with food and clothes, with scanty wages and no vails.—*From an Article in Fraser's Magazine.*

BLOTTING PAPER.—Blotting paper betrays secrets. Nothing astonished a foreign diplomatist more, some years since, than finding it used in the bureau of one of our then Cabinet Ministers.

CONTENTS OF NO. XXXVI.
On the Moral Training of Children......................... 209
COLUMN FOR THE LADIES—Education of Infancy............ 212
The Young Actress... 213
Useful Knowledge.. 214
Dutch Masters and Servants................................ ib.
Curious Penmanship (Gastrography)........................ 215
Four-and-Twenty Fiddlers.................................. ib.
ELEMENTS OF THOUGHT—Ministers—Factions in England—
  Natural Connexion between the Feelings and the Intellect 216
The Robbers of Tantallon.................................. ib.
THE STORY-TELLER—A Parisian Gossipping................ 217
SCRAPS—The Objects of Ambition; Pulpit Pleasantry; The
  Chancellor in a Watch-house; Masters and Servants;
  Blotting Paper.. 224

EDINBURGH: Printed by and for JOHN JOHNSTONE, 19, St. James's Square.—Published by JOHN ANDERSON, Jun., Bookseller, 55, North Bridge Street, Edinburgh; by JOHN MACLEOD, and ATKINSON & Co., Booksellers, Glasgow; and sold by all Booksellers and Venders of Cheap Periodicals.

THE Schoolmaster,

AND
EDINBURGH WEEKLY MAGAZINE.

CONDUCTED BY JOHN JOHNSTONE.

THE SCHOOLMASTER IS ABROAD.—LORD BROUGHAM.

No. 37.—Vol. II.　　SATURDAY, APRIL 13, 1833.　　Price Three-halfpence.

LOTTERIES.

"*Hæ nugæ seria ducentur mala.*"

In the present age, confessedly one of improvement, when "*the Schoolmaster is abroad,*" and consuetude affords no plea for abuse, but every thing is canvassed on its real merits, and rigidly submitted to the tests of truth and reason, it is not a little strange, that the votaries of fickle Fortune should have entered so little into the spirit of such an æra. Far from profiting by the increased opportunities of acquiring knowledge, and deriving practical benefit therefrom, her followers display now, not less arrogance and presumption than their fellow worshippers of former times. And of the various forms in which a blind reliance in Fortune presents itself, there is none more ludicrously absurd, or, at the present time, more deserving of rebuke, than that of Lottery. Without now considering the moral effects which the species of gambling, known by that name, must necessarily give rise to, we shall endeavour to acquaint our readers with its principles and management, and thence attempt to deduce the ignorance or consummate folly of its numerous patronizers.

Many readers, no doubt, are already conversant with the origin of Lotteries; but, for the sake of those who are not so, we shall say a few words on the subject. As early as the commencement of the sixteenth century, speculations of this description were not uncommon in this country. Plate, jewels, and other valuables, for the most part, were the articles so disposed of. The plan seems to have been borrowed from the Venetians, and to have prospered well for the projectors. So numerous at last did the fraudulent practices immediately allied to the system become, and so ruinous were their effects upon industry and morality, that, in the reign of Queen Anne, we find them suppressed by Government, "as nuisances to the public." For the several last centuries, however, they have been made sources of revenue, by most of the States of Europe. In Great Britain, it was customary for Ministers to calculate upon a large sum annually to be raised in this manner; till, in the year 1826, all Lotteries (*unless specially* authorized,—*eroh pudor*) were declared illegal, by an act of the Legislature. In France, Sweden, and frequently in Germany, they are still continued, to the reproach of their respective governments. The mode in which these transactions are conducted may be easily illustrated. Suppose the projectors wished to realize a profit of £5000, the Lottery, in such a case, might probably be divided into 1500 shares or tickets, at £10 each, amounting in all to £15,000. From this sum, £10,000 would be portioned into prizes of different amount, leaving to the projectors a profit of £5000, after disposing of all the shares to a contractor for £15,000. The contractor again disposes of these 1500 shares, through inferior agents, at a large profit; and, as often happens, the ticket which, in the fair estimation of chances, and in such a Lottery as now sketched, is worth only £6, 13s. 4d., is retailed to an infatuated public *at an advance of two hundred per cent.!* Shares are often subdivided, into one-half, one-fourth, one-eighth, and one-sixteenth parts; and the trouble attendant on this forms an excuse for an increase of price. In such a lottery as we have supposed, it must be evident, that the chances of loss are nearly doubly greater than the chances of gain. If one individual were to adventure upon all the shares, it is indubitable he would be a loser of £5000, even presuming the contractor were to have no gain. From which it directly follows, that the more tickets purchased the nearer you approach the certainty of loss. Were the amount of prizes equally divided into 1500 portions, there would then be only a dividend of £6, 13s. 4d. to each shareholder; consequently the loss of each will be greater or less, in proportion to the difference betwixt that sum and the purchase money. Some persons, in order (as they think) to have a better chance for a large prize, purchase a number of small shares. Nothing can be more erroneous than the principle here proceeded on; for, in the event of a prize being drawn, so much the smaller sum comes to his share. Let the wiseacre venture on one-sixteenth of every ticket, and leaving out of account the advance for subdivision, he is in the same situation, though to a smaller extent, as the individual above alluded to, who purchases every ticket.

The majority of those who have sufficient spare cash for the purchase of a lottery-ticket, may reasonably be supposed capable of performing the calculation requisite for discovering the profit which accrues to the projector. In the face, then, of the plainest demonstration of nearly certain loss, it is indeed a subject of wonder, that so much infatuation is to this hour displayed by those who, in ordinary matters, are shrewd and prudent. He who stakes his money on the casting of a die, acts a more reasonable part than the shareholder in a lottery. To the former, in all likelihood, the chances of loss or gain are equally balanced; while, to the latter, we have shewn, the chances of loss greatly preponderate. The purchaser of a lottery-ticket is equally culpable, in a moral point of view, with a gambler; but the imprudence of the former is far more deserving of censure. That overweening self-confidence in our own good *luck*, so common to human nature, and the ill-grounded hope of procuring, without exertion, some one of the large prizes, would seem, though no doubt fallacious, the only ground on which lotteries are encouraged; so much so, that the success of these speculations, unless influenced by other circumstances, has been remarked invariably to depend on the artful distribution of the prizes. It has uniformly happened, that lotteries in which the prizes were very numerous, but consequently of proportionally small sums, though on a much fairer scale, have never succeeded so well as those of a less equitable description where the prizes were few and of large amount. "Some one must have the £20,000, or £30,000 prize," is an every day remark; "and why shouldn't it fall to me as well as to any one else? You know I'm always lucky, and, moreover, I've a strong *presentiment* that Fortune will not now forsake me." Such reasoning, if to call it so be not an abuse of words, is of a piece with the pompous advertisements which make known to the public "the success of Mr. Such-a-thing in selling prizes, which," says the barefaced puffer, "*is too well known to require comment.*" All are invited, after the most liberal fashion, to repair to the *Lucky* Office of Agent ———, where fortunes are dispensed through excess of generosity!!! What says our poet?

"It's a wonder the very great prizes
He sells he don't keep to himself;
But respect for the public so rises
In his breast, he foregoes all the pelf!"

The world never yet saw a perfectly fair lottery; that is to say, one in which the amount of prizes was equal to the sum total derived from their sale; nor can we reasonably expect such a lottery ever to be drawn. The projector must reap some advantage in return for his labour and expense; and though that labour and expense be entirely misspent, and productive of no benefit to the vast majority of participators, still they must pay the forfeit of their folly.

Hitherto, we have confined our remarks to the *unreasonableness* of supporting Lotteries. Let us now shortly consider their moral influence. As tending to create a spirit of restless discontent with the regular means of acquiring wealth, and to distract the mind from industrious labour, a greater evil of the kind can scarcely exist. Avarice, idleness, and dissipation are thereby excited; and the disappointment which in most cases must follow, not unfrequently drives their victim to despair. The peace of mind of which an adventurer in a lottery is deprived, for several months previous to the date of drawing, is extremely inimical to steady exertion. His mind, occupied in forming visionary conceptions of the anticipated fortune about to befall him, becomes languid and unsettled. Business is neglected; and for business habits, which are lost, a reckless taste for games of hazard is not unlikely contracted. Absorbed in dreams of ideal prosperity, upon the confidence of an uncertainty, he borrows money, with the expectation of repaying it from the proceeds of a prize, and is only awakened to the weakness of his conduct by the unwelcome intelligence of having drawn a blank. Remorse and discontent either force him to a continuation in the system, or unfit him for the plodding ways of his former life. Happy if, pursuing a different course since the fondly cherished delusion has vanished, he betake himself to honourable toil, and vow determined enmity to the inveiglements of Fortune for the future. But how seldom are we gratified by so wise a determination being acted on? Too often gambling has its commencement in small beginnings:—it is an eating canker which insidiously diffuses its baneful and progressive influence throughout every portion of the body.—But let it be supposed that a prize of large amount is drawn. What satisfaction or self-complacency can a virtuous mind derive from pocketing thousands known to be wrung by chicanery and deceit from unsuspecting victims? To an honest and reflecting man, the conviction of his prosperity having been dependant on the misery and disappointment of others, would be far from affording joy; and, of a truth it may be said, with the feelings of him who rejoices in success, virtue must withhold all sympathy. The wealth which is acquired by industrious application, is far more highly prized, is productive of a goodly satisfaction, and is ever more judiciously expended, than the ill-acquired gains of chance. For the most part, these are dissipated within a short period of their acquirement, and their late ill-fated possessor is left a poorer and less useful member of society than, had he persisted in his former pursuits, he would eventually have found himself. This is familiarly illustrated by Miss Edgeworth, in one of her Moral Tales upon the subject, to which we would refer such readers as may not have perused it. It is one of the most interesting that has proceeded from her popular pen. The moral of the tale tends to inculcate the ruinous effects of Lotteries upon public morals, and the truth of the remark, that those who, by self-interested jobbers, are vauntingly heralded "Fortunate Holders," are, alas! but too often, *unfortunately fortunate.*

To some it may appear that we have overdrawn, or greatly exaggerated the fatal consequences of public Lotteries. It is far from so;—in every particular, melancholy to say, we are borne out by facts. The mischief is far from ideal; and though timeserving senators have affected, and still continue to ffect, ignorance of its debasing tendencies, and, careless of public morality, fraudulently tax their country in this underhand manner, still the moral degradation attendant on the system is glaring and enormous. Sceptics to the justice of these remarks, may, if leisure permit, turn to the report of a Select Committee of the House of Commons, appointed 27th August, 1808) for inquiring into the manner of conducting Lotteries at that period, and the effects they had upon the country. Their scepticism, on the examination of that paper, will be instantly removed. What a heart-rending spectacle of misery and vice is there exposed to our pity and reprobation. What transactions of nefarious baseness are there brought to light, through the evidence of the witnesses connected with the Metropolitan Police. Some idea of the enormous profits of the contractors and agents to the State Lotteries may hence be formed, from the declaration, upon oath, of one of the most extensive London Lottery Office Keepers, that *for every £600,000 gained to the State by Lottery, the people were fleeced of £1,275,000* !!! So thoroughly convinced was the Committee of 1808, of the radically vicious foundation and tendency of raising money by Lottery, that their report explicitly declared, that under no system of regulations which might be devised, could Parliament possibly adopt it, as an efficient source of revenue, and at the same time divest it of the evils and calamities of which it had proved so baneful a source; that no mode of raising money was so burdensome, so pernicious, and so unproductive; that in no species of gambling with which they were acquainted, were the chances so great against the adventurer; and in none was the infatuation more powerful, lasting, and destructive. After perusing the report referred to, authenticated, as it is, by the honest admissions of the principal Lottery agents themselves, it is impossible but to feel and to express unmingled sorrow at the re-appearance of the nuisance. Despite the fearful recital of crime, which the document contains, and which is distinctly traced to its origin in Lotteries, Scotland is disgraced by being first to revive the opprobrious system of exaction. Let our readers—let the public—but especially let the people of Scotland remember, that in abetting such a scheme, they foster a viper destructive of prudence and industry, which, when mature in growth, may prove subversive of our national character. D.

FERDUSI, THE PERSIAN POET.

The following sketch of the life of Ferdusi is extracted from a review of a work by Dr J. A. Vuller, in a German publication, (the *Literatur-Blatt:*

The immortal poet of the Shah nameh was born in the fourth century, at Thus, in Khorasan, of poor parents; but on account of some wrong done him by the governor of the province, he left his native town and betook himself to the capital. When here, he made many ineffectual attempts to before him; but while engaged in this vain attempt, the stock of provisions on which he had hitherto subsisted came to an end, and he began to make verses from sheer necessity. The great talent displayed in these essays gained him the favour of an eminent Court poet, to whom the Sultan had intrusted the task of celebrating in song the early history of Persia; and this poet transferred to Ferdusi the arduous but honourable office. The Sultan was prejudiced against him, on account of his being a native of the heretical city of Thus, and, for some time, would not hear of his substitution. Ferdusi, however, did not allow this circumstance to disturb him; but, absorbed in the magnitude of his undertaking, and supported by a consciousness of his own power, he began and finished his task, to his eternal glory.

The Sultan now rewarded him by a present of sixty thousand pieces of silver, viz. one for every verse. Ferdusi accepted this gift, although he knew well that, in comparison with his achievement, it was small indeed. After receiving the money, he went into the Bazaar to take a bath, and before leaving the place he expended the whole sum;—he paid for the bath 20,000 pieces, the same sum for a glass of Tukka, and the remaining 20,000 he gave to the poor. After this he concealed himself in Chasna, and, by a stratagem, succeeded in obtaining from the Sultan's library the copy of his poem, and in the volume he wrote a satire upon Mahmud himself, from which we extract three verses: " Thirty years have I toiled with this poem, in the hope that a crown and a treasure would have been my reward. Were this king descended from kings, he would have adorned my head with a golden diadem.—Since, in his origin nobility was unknown, may his name be unknown in the line of heroes." He fled, and eluded the pursuit of the Sultan by the assistance of his countrymen, by whom he was beloved. Long after this, it happened that the Sultan was in embarrassed circumstances, and asking advice from one of his councillors, he was answered by a verse from the poem of Ferdusi, exactly fitted to the present emergency. At these words, Mahmud was penetrated with a sense of his injustice, and instantly made inquiry as to the present circumstances of Ferdusi. Meimendi seized this opportunity, and informed him that Ferdusi lived in retirement and in poverty in his native town of Thus. The Sultan was deeply moved at this recital, and ordered twelve camels, loaded with indigo, to be instantly despatched as a present to the poet. As the camels with their loads entered the Rudvor gate of the city of Thus, the corpse of Ferdusi was borne out at the gate of Risan! X. X.

The guilt of all aristocracies has consisted not so much in their original acquisition of power as in their perseverance in retaining it; so that what was innocent or even reasonable at the begining, has become in later times atrocious injustice; as if a parent in his dotage should claim the same authority over his son in the vigour of manhood, which formerly, in the maturity of his own faculties, he had exercised naturally and profitably over the infancy of his child.

LADY GRANGE.

The extraordinary case of Mrs. Erskine, known by the title of Lady Grange, excited great curiosity about ninety years ago; and it is yet very interesting on account of the mystery which attends it, and its apparent connexion with the plots of those who were concerned in the rebellions which broke out in the years 1715 and 1745.

Mrs. Erskine's maiden name was Rachel Chiesly. She was a daughter of Chiesly of Dalry, who shot the Lord President, Sir George Lockhart, in revenge for deciding against him a law-suit, which had been referred to his Lordship, and another of the judges, as arbiters. She was a beautiful woman, but of a very violent temper. It was reported that Erskine of Grange (a brother of the Earl of Mar) had seduced her, and that she compelled him to marry her, by threatening his life, and reminding him that she was Chiesly's daughter.

Mr. Erskine's character is represented as having been by no means amiable. He was dissipated, restless, and intriguing; and was supposed to be concerned in some of the measures preparatory and subsequent to the rebellion in 1715, of which his wife was in the secret. His frequent journeys to London, and some of his amours there, gave her so much uneasiness that she threatened to inform Government of all she knew, unless he consented to give up plotting, and live quietly at home. He did not choose to comply with these terms; and he formed a plan, by which she was violently seized in her own house, and dragged away. It is a remarkable circumstance that, notwithstanding the noise which this barbarous and tyrannical act occasioned, no means were taken to bring the perpetrators to justice, though some of them were well known.

Grange had the address to persuade the public and his connexions, that his wife was a mad woman, who had frequently attempted his life, and that confinement was absolutely necessary. He used to show a razor, which he said, he had taken from under her pillow. She had two sons grown to manhood at the time she was carried off, and it was suspected, that either one or both consented to it. Her daughter, by Mr. Erskine of Grange, was married to the Earl of Kintore. None of her relatives ever made the smallest stir about the matter. The fate of Lady Grange, after her seizure, has hitherto remained uncertain, except that it was known she had been carried to St. Kilda. There is, however, a MS. which throws much light on this transaction. This manuscript is a copy of another, partly written for Lady Grange, by the minister of St. Kilda, and partly by herself. It was found among the papers of a gentleman who flourished at the time of the transaction to which it refers, and who never would have put into his repository anything of the kind which was not authentic. Indeed, the internal evidence it bears, proves the authenticity of the narrative almost beyond question. During my inquiries in regard to this extraordinary transaction, I learned the existence of several documents which confirmed the story as narrated in the manuscript; and also that some original letters of Lady Grange, which had found their way from St. Kilda, had been recently in the hands of a bookseller in Edinburgh, from whom they had been purchased for the purpose of destroying them. It is not surprising that the descendants of the parties concerned should feel a desire to bury the story in oblivion, on account of the conduct which the narrative displays. But in matters of history, especially when the dispositions and manners of a people become interesting, private feelings must be disregarded. Nothing has yet appeared which exhibits in a stronger light than the following narrative, the ferocity not only of the Highland clans, but of a portion of their southern neighbours; and it is valuable, in so far as it proves the long duration of barbarism, and assists us to appreciate the astonishing rapidity with which civilization has proceeded in Scotland, and more particularly in the Highlands. Many of my name were concerned in the rebellions which agitated Scotland during the first half of the 18th century; and many may have been guilty of actions equally atrocious with that of which I now give you the details; yet I thankfulness for having lived to see the effects of the enlightened policy of Chatham, and that policy followed up by the liberality of the Government towards the most remote districts of the Empire, in opening up a country hitherto inaccessible, by roads and bridges, executed under the direction of the most able engineers. Now for the narrative.

"*January* 21, 1741.

"I, the unfortunate wife of Mr. James Erskine, of Grange. That, after I had lived twenty-five years in great love and peace, he, all of a sudden, took a dislike to my person, and such a hatred that he could not live with me, nor so much as to stay in his house; and desired me to subscribe a separation during his pleasure, which I thought was contrary to my vows before God; and that I dearly loved my husband. Both his friends and mine own were at a great deal of pains to persuade me, but I absolutely refused to subscribe it. At last, after much threatening, he got me out of the house; and I designed at that time to go straight to London; but some of my friends thought his temper might alter, and gave me your house to stay in, it being a little without the town, I desiring to live retired. After having lived some months there, I came into Edinburgh, and I took a chamber in a private house near to my Lord's lodgings, that I might have the pleasure to see the house he was in, and to see him and my children when going out; and I made his relations and mine own speak to him, and was always in hopes that God would shew him his sin of putting away his wife contrary to the laws of God and man; and this was no secret, for the President of the Session, and some of the Lords, the solicitor, and some of the advocates and ministers of Edinburgh, knew all this to be truth. When I lost all hopes, then I resolved to go to London, and live with some of my friends, and make myself as easy as I could without. Having paid a part of my coach hire, and taken leave of my friends and the ministers, two days before I should have gone away, upon the 22d, 1732, after eleven o'clock at night, it being the Saturday evening, the house belonging to one Margaret M'Lean, a Highland woman, she put the few she had in her house to bed, which were two Highland women, and a little servant maid, an hour and half before ordinary. I had no servant with me in that house, but a chambermaid, and whether she was upon that plot, or whether the mistress put her out of the way, I know not; there came two men to the door, saying they had a letter for my lady, and the mistress of the house brought them to my room door, and then rushed in some Highlandmen, whom I had seen frequently attending my Lord Lovat, and, if I well remember, had his livery upon them, who threw me down upon the floor in the most barbarous manner, and I cried out murder, murder. Then they stopt my mouth, and dang out several of my teeth, and I bled; and abused my face in the most pitifully with their hard, rude hands, till there was no skin left on my face all below my eyes; for I was always putting out the clothes as fast as they put in, being on the floor at the time; and I defended myself with my hands, and beat with my heels upon the loft, in hopes the people below would hear me. And then a near cousin of my Lord Lovat's looked in at the door, and gave directions to cover my head, and tye down my hands with a cloth; they had wrestled so long with me, that it was all that I could breathe; and then they carried me down stairs, as if they had a corpse. I heard many voices about me; being blindfolded, I could not discover who they were. They had a chair at the stair foot, which they put me in; and there was a man in the chair who took me on his knee, and I made all the struggle I could; but he held me fast in his arms, and hindered me to put my hands to my mouth, which I attempted to do, being tied down. The chair carried me off very fast, and took me without the ports; and when they opened the chair, and taken the cloth off my head, to let me get air, I perceived, it being clear moonlight, that I was a little way from the Mutters Hill,* and that the man on whose knee I sat was one Alexander Foster of Carnbonny, who had there six or seven horses and men with him, who said all these were his servants, though I knew some of them to be my Lord Lovat's servants who rode along; one of them was called Alexander Frazer, and the other James Frazer, and his groom, whose name I know not. These were the names they gave them; but whether they were their proper names I know not.

"Another that rode along was Andrew Leishman, a tenant in West Pomeise, which belongs to Mr. Stewart, and had been tenant there these twenty-six years. I heard another of the horse was a young gentleman, my Lord Lovat's cousin; I heard so; but did not see him, for he kept out of my sight. Before they set me on horse, I shewed him all the linens about my face were covered with blood, and that they had torn all the clothes upon my head, and torn out some of my hair, and blind-folded me; but the joggling of the horse shuffled up the clothes off my eyes, so that I saw what way they rode with me, straight by the long way. I saw that I was at the back of the castle. They took me the straightest way to Lithgow; and it was a very frosty, cold, and bitter night. I took stitches in my side, sitting in a constrained posture, and I begged Mr. Foster to allow me to light a little till I was eased of my pains. Mr. Foster cried to Sandy Frazer to stop my mouth again; for it was he that stopt my mouth when I was in my own room, and called me a damned bitch, that he would break my neck, if I did not hold my peace; was he venturing his life for me? He took me a little beyond Lithgow. When he saw that day was approaching, he took me into a house which belongs to John Macleod, who is an advocate, whose servant had known of my coming, and met me with candles in their hands, at the far end of the entry, and brought me into a very good room, and fire in, so that they knew of my coming. I saw no servants in the house but two men and a woman, and told them whose wife I was, and that I was stolen; and he presently took me up stairs to a very good bed-room, which had a fire in, and good linens in the bed, which I looked to, and found Mr. Macleod's name on them. They kept me there all day, and would not allow a woman to come up into the room, but set Sandy Frazer with me all day; for which reason I would not throw off my clothes, for as wearied and cold as I was, Frazer was barbarous and cruel.

"When it was night, about seven, he told me I had some more miles to ride; and he took me down stairs by force, and tied me on to the horse, as I was the night before. He rode straight to Falkirk, and we met none on the way; it being the Sabbath night, which I thought very misfortunate, or else I would have cried out for help. He rode away by the south side of Falkirk, and through the Torewood, which way I knew all, having travelled it before. Some little after we left the Torewood, he rode a way which I knew not; and I was very weary, it being a bitter night. He said he was taking me to his own house, but did not tell me its name, and thought all along I did not know whom he was, a cloth being tied to his face, that I might not perceive it; and he brought me straight to Wester Pomeise, where he was a factor for Mr. Stewart, who married to Brisbane of Bishopstown's sister. He took me in through a large vault, and then into a room of the vault, the windows of the room being nailed with thick boards, and no light in the room; but in a little closet, a little slit, where a man could hardly put in his hand, less than the thieves' hole in Edinburgh, and a very old ugly bed, without a roof, a timber chair, with the half of the bottom in it; and there I was kept a close prisoner for thirteen or fourteen weeks, not having liberty as much as to go without doors; and two doors locked on me, cross bars on the outside. The servant that waited on me there, was an old gardener and his wife that he had provided, who had a meal garden in Stirling. His name is George Ross, and his wife's name Agnes Watt. He lived in Stirling many years, and had two sons and a daughter, who was frequently with their father and saw me.

"Andrew Leishman, mentioned before, brought what meat and drink I needed, and all other provisions, such as coal and candle. He went always to Mr. Foster, got directions about it. His wife served me in what things she could do about me. They have three daughters which his wife had born, and his eldest son, William Leishman. They kept me so long close prisoner that it endangered my health, and I grew sick, and Andrew told Mr. Foster that they would allow me to go out, and that he would not have a hand in my death; and then I was allowed to go to the high rooms, and to go to the court to get air, much against Mr. Foster's will.

"The gardener was kept there for a scoury to dress the garden and the trees. Sandy Frazer was left with me the first three days, and then James Frazer was sent out to wait of me; for he would not trust me to the gardener; and he kept the key in his own custody day and night. My Lord Lovat came frequently through Stirling to Mr. Foster, his house being within a mile of it; and Mr. Foster went out and met him, to concert matters about me; and James Frazer, who waited of me, went with him. I was kept prisoner there till the 12th of August, and then Peter Frazer, my lord's page, came and staid till the 13th. Mr. Frazer came up then, and three Highlandmen with him, and took me out of the room by force; James and Peter Frazer carried me out, and set me on a horse behind the Captain. It was about ten o'clock at night, and carried me along by Stirling Bridge, and after that I knew no more of the way. It was moonlight, and they rode till it was near day, and then took me into ———— house. The Captain, Mr. Foster, went to the room with me, and sat a little with me, and never came near me after that. He gave the charge of me to one who called himself Alexander Grant, but I believe he feigned his name; he rode with me out of Pomeise that night's journey; Andrew Leishman, and Peter and James Frazer were the rest of the company that rode, and a man who was our guide, called himself Macdonald, and told me he was born at Glengarry's. Always, when they took me out of any place, they did by force, and I bad them consider what they were doing, in taking me away against my will. Whenever it was night, they sat me on a horse behind Grant, who was nothing but a silly fellow, and he could ride before me; and then they set my Lord Lovat's footman, James Frazer, before me, and tied me to him, that I might not leap off; and rode all night with me, and brought me into General Wade's new way, I knew not how far in the Highlands. Whenever it was day, they took me to a house, and kept me there all day, and when it was night set me on a horse by force. And always, when we came by houses, I attempted to speak; then they offered to stop my mouth. We rode all night, and again morning, with great difficulty, they found a barn to put me in; there they kept me all day, and it being far in the Highlands, by four in the afternoon, they set me on a horse again, and rode all night.

"Again, Saturday, they brought me to a ————. Mr. Foster, though he came not near me, always rode behind or before, and lodged always in the same place I lodged. Upon Saturday, I saw him take horse, and his man with him. I lookt out of a hole, and saw him. Again night, they set me on a horse again, and carried me amongst the Highland hills, and rode till it was near morning, and laid me down on the grass, being very weary, and they rode all the Sabbath; the side of a hill, and the way was so bad, that it was not rideable, for they carried me in their arms; we were as an open ship all that night, and the day the waters were so high, that we could not cross till it was near night; then they got me on horse, and carried me to a place called Miltown, when preparations were made for me, that being the 28th day of the month. I was never in bed all the time since we came from Pomeise. With their rude hands they had hurt one of my breasts. I was kept there sixteen days, and all the company left me but James Watson's lad. This was on my Lord Lovat's ground. They called the man of the house Andrew Frazer. Grant came on the ———— of September, and set me on horse by force at night, and put me in a boat, which was in a loch about a mile from Miltown. They crossed the loch with me, and James Frazer left me there, some nights without, and some nights in byres.

"After we crossed the loch, and again the ninth of the

month, at the evening, we came to a loch-side on Glengarry's ground. I should have been taken to Scot's house,* brother to the Laird of Glengarry, but they altered their minds, and ordered him to come to Lochnirr,† and wait for me on the tenth of the month, on the break of day, for fear of their being seen, for they were always in terror. They dragged me by force, and I cried bitterly out; they were all Highlanders, and nobody understood me; and took me into a shop of which Alexander Macdonald was master, who is a tenant in an island called Hesker, belonging to Sir Alexander Macdonald, who told me he had been at Scot's house, and seen my Lord Lovat's cousin, formerly mentioned; he was ordered to take me home to his own isle, and keep me there till further orders. I told him I was stolen out of Edinburgh, and brought there by force, and that it was contrary to the laws what they were doing. He answered that he would not keep me or any other against their will, except Sir Alexander Macdonald were in the affair. How far Sir Alexander is concerned in this I am not certain; but the man being poor and greedy of money, made him go beyond his own light. We lay long in the loch for want of wind, and young Scot's son and his father's brother, came into the sloop, the time that the sloop lay in the loch. They came with design to see me, but not to relieve me. We came not out of the loch till the 19th day of the month, and the ———— Macdonald, another son of Scot's, came with the sloop, and had a long conversation with Alexander Macdonald. We were storm-stayed by the way, and we were in hazard of being lost before we came to Hesker, which was a poor miserable island. Upon the 30th day of the month we came there. That day we came out of the loch, there came in a son of Dornick's called John Macleod, and William Toling, who lives on Macleod's ground, who before was merchant at Inverness, and Rory Macdonald, brother to Castletown, and they all understanding the language, I told them all my misfortunes; and William Toling said he was at Edinburgh the time I was stolen, and promised me he would tell Renkiller where I was to be taken. I was in the island of Hesker ten months before I got bread, and suffered much cold and hunger, and many hardships and barbarous usage. I was in that strait almost, I wanted stockings, shoes, and many other necessaries. And Macdonald said he had no orders to give me any meat but what they eated themselves; but had no orders for clothes. After I was near a year in his custody, he said he would go and tell them from whom he got me, that he thought it was a sin to keep me, and that he would let me away, and that he had writ twice or thrice about what necessaries I wanted, but got no answer. When he came back, he said he had seen Sir Alexander Macdonald, and said to him it was a sin and shame to keep me, for that he would keep me no longer. Sir Alexander said, that he was sorry that he had meddled in such an affair, and did not know how to get out of it, but discharged him to let me go till further orders. Alexander said he was bidden treat me harshly, and do nothing but what was his pleasure, and to cross me in every thing. Though he got me bread, yet I was much more hardly dealt with than he had done the first year; and I thought it hard enough when he was in Skye, at Sir Alexander's, he told me he saw Alexander Mackenzie, of Delvin's two brothers. I well remember they are called Kenneth and John Mackenzies; and he pretended he told them that he had me in custody, for he made it no secret. I often begged him to allow me to write to my friends the time I was with him, and then I would be relieved, for he said he was discharged to let me write, or tell me the place of the world I was in. I was many months there before I knew whose ground I was on. I often begged him to tell the minister, who was one Mr. John Maclean, and the name of his parish is the Weist, which is in the middle of the long island, and bordering on Clanronald's ground. I desired him to come and see me, and pray for this distress of my family. Mr. Macdonald told me he answered, it was his duty to pray for every body in distress; but if he could not come and see me, he had but an eight-mile ferry to cross. But whether Alexander told him I was there, cannot be positive or sure.

"In May, 1734, Sir Alexander Macdonald came to the Weist, to set his land, and sent word to Alexander I was to be taken away from him very soon, and that he would allow no more board for me; therefore, he should let me go with the first that came for me. It was but a small island, none in it but cottars and his servants. Upon the 14th day of June, there came a sloop to the Hesker, with John Macleod, tenant to the Laird of Macleod, in a place which they call Northtown, in the parish of Harrioch, and brought a letter to Alexander. He showed me the letter to give up the cargo that was in his hands. The day before he got the letter, he had been at the Captain of Clanronald's house, and had met with my Lord Lovat's cousin there, the Captain being married to his sister. William and his man were very rude to me, and hurt me very sore in the taking me away. Alexander told me he knew not where I was going to, and John Macleod said he was taking me to the Orkney islands. The galley belonged to himself, but his brother Norman Macleod was manager of it. He was in such terror that it should be known that I was in his custody, that he ———— now all his men. When I came to the island, I found it as I heard of it, a very desolate island, but nobody in it but natives of the place. John and his brother stayed a few days in the place, and by no means would confess from whom he had got me, but I found out; what hand the Laird of Macleod had in it I am not sure. He left me in a very miserable condition, but had no provision for me but what the island afforded; and nobody to wait on me, that understood me, but one ill-natured man, who understood a little English, and explained to others what I wanted; and he was not only ill-natured, but half-witted, and one day drew out his dirk to kill me.

"After being some time in this island, God in his good providence, who in all my distress has taken care of me, for which I have great reason to bless and praise him, where I found God much present with me for as desolate as it is, comforting me, and supporting me in my long and heavy trial, a minister and his wife came to the island, to whom I am exceeding much obliged; and if it had not been for the care that he and she took, I had died of want of meat, for there were no provisions sent me, but two pecks of flour, and what the place can afford, such as milk and a little barley knocked, and that forced from them by threatenings; for the people are very poor and much oppressed. I have nobody to serve me but a little Highland girl;* and the minister and his wife must explain to her. He is a sincere and a devout man, and very painful, and what time he can spare from his business, he is so good as to come to see me. I am not sure whose hands this may come to, but if I be dead, I beg my friends may be kind to reward this minister and his wife, for he hath helped to preserve my life, and made it comfortable the time I lived. John Macleod, above named, is tenant of this island.† I got the minister persuaded to write the account of the way I was stolen, and by whom, that he might acquaint my friends. He would not give me a pen to write to any of them, but said that he would do all for me in his power. When he went from this island, he resolved to go to Edinburgh, but he would not venture to carry this paper with him. But I gave him a bill on you, and two other of my friends, that they might know where I was: but his life being threatened, he left this island, and he was after hindered, either to go to Edinburgh, or to write to anybody about me. Since he came back to this island, he sent me word by his wife, that he had burnt the bills I had given him; he is in such fear of his life and his uncles. Some other of the ministers were angry at him for the care and concern he had taken of me. He bade his wife get this paper from me that he might destroy it, that it might never come to light as written by him. Since I could not get paper to write so full an account as this, I thought it no sin to deceive her, and I burnt

---

* Macdonald of Scot's house.
† Probably Lochbourn.

* This person was alive in North Uist, in 1817, at the advanced age of 90 years. She was seen by Mr. Campbell, author of Albyn's Anthology, who lately travelled into the remote parts of Scotland, in search of ancient music.
† Mrs. Erskine's own hand begins at "I got."

two papers before her, and bade her tell the minister now to be easy. I am not sure who of my kin and friends is dead, or who is alive; but I beg whosoever hands this comes first to, to cause write it once in a fair hand, and to shew it to all my friends."

The following notices are written at the end of the narrative.

" Grant had his felows.

" Scoto's wife, aunt to Roderick Macleod, his father's sister.

" There sprang a leek in the sloop, we were in great danger.

" One of Lord Lovat's lyes which he said to John Macleod, the young man of Dynwick, that I was going to kill my husband—you know that a lye.

" Sir Alexander Macdonald, at any time he wrote about me, the name he gave me was Carup.

" I hear that Alexander Macdonald is in the Hesker, is dead. His wife is since married to Logan Macdonald, her tenant to Clanranold. She knows it was Lord Lovat and Roderick Macleod that stole me.

" The minister's dame saw me taken out of Mrs. Margaret Macleod's house, by Roderick Macleod—and he told Lady Macleod, he said——"

This Roderick Macleod was Macleod of Muiravonside, who, it was well known, acted the principal part in the barbarous scene described by the sufferer.

From the above curious document, it appears that Lady Grange was at St. Kilda's nine years after she was taken from Edinburgh. When the author of the notice which precedes the narrative, was at St. Kilda, in the year 1800, he was informed by an old man, who remembered having seen Lady Grange, that she had been seven or eight years in that island. On making inquiry respecting what happened afterwards to this ill-fated woman, he was informed by a gentleman in Skye, that, in consequence of a dread of discovery, she had been removed to Assint, (the western district of Sutherland,) and from thence to Skye, where she died.

THAT WE SHOULD RISE WITH THE LARK.

At what precise minute that little airy musician doffs his night gear, and prepares to tune up his unseasonable matins, we are not naturalists enough to determine. But for a mere human gentleman—that has no orchestra business to call him from his warm bed to such preposterous exercises—we take ten, or half after ten, (eleven, of course, during this Christmas solstice,) to be the very earliest hour, at which he can begin to think of abandoning his pillow. To think of it, we say; for to do it in earnest, requires another half hour's good consideration. Not but there are pretty sun-risings, as we are told, and such like gauds, abroad in the world, in summer time especially, some hours before what we have assigned; which a gentleman may see, as they say, only for getting up. But, having been tempted once or twice, in earlier life, to assist at those ceremonies, we confess our curiosity abated. We are no longer ambitious of being the sun's courtiers, to attend at his morning levees. We hold the good hours of the dawn too sacred to waste them upon such observances; which have in them, besides, something Pagan and Persic. To say truth, we never anticipated our usual hour, or got up with the sun (as 'tis called) to go a journey, or upon a foolish whole day's pleasuring, but we suffered for it all the long hours after in listlessness and headaches: Nature herself sufficiently declared her sense of our presumption, in aspiring to regulate our frail walking courses by the measures of that celestial and sleepless traveller. We deny not that there is something sprightly and vigorous, at the outset especially, in these break-of-day excursions. It is flattering to get the start of a lazy world; to conquer death by proxy in his image. But the seeds of sleep and mortality are in us; and we pay usually in strange qualms, before night falls, the penalty of the unnatural inversion. Therefore, while the busy part of mankind are fast huddling on their clothes, or are already up and about their occupations, content to have swallowed their sleep by wholesale, we choose to linger a-bed, and digest our dreams. It is the very time to recombine the wandering images, which night, in a confused mass, presented; to snatch them from forgetfulness; to shape, and mould them. Some people have no good of their dreams. Like fast feeders, they gulp them too grossly to taste them curiously. We love to chew the cud of a foregone vision; to collect the scattered rays of a brighter phantasm, or act over again, with firmer nerves, the sadder nocturnal tragedies; to drag into day-light a struggling and half-vanishing night-mare; to handle and examine the terrors, or the airy solaces. We have too much respect for these spiritual communications, to let them go so lightly. We are not so stupid, or so careless, as that Imperial forgetter of his dreams, that we should need a seer to remind us of the form of them. They seem to us to have as much significance as our waking concerns; or rather to import us more nearly, as more nearly we approach, by years, to the shadowy world whither we are hastening. We have shaken hands with the world's business; we have done with it; we have discharged ourself of it. Why should we get up? we have neither suit to solicit, nor affairs to manage. The drama has shut in upon us at the fourth act. We have nothing here to expect, but in a short time a sick bed, and a dismissal. We delight to anticipate death by such shadows as night affords. We are already half acquainted with ghosts. We were never much in the world. Disappointment early struck a dark veil between us and his dazzling illusions. Our spirits showed grey before our hairs. The mighty changes of the world already appear as but the vain stuff out of which dramas are composed. We have asked no more of life than what the mimic images in play-houses present us with. Even those types have waxed fainter. Our clock appears to have struck. We are superannuated. In this dearth of mundane satisfaction, we contract politic alliances with shadows. It is good to have friends at court. The abstract media of dreams seem no ill introduction to that spiritual presence, upon which, in no long time, we expect to be thrown. We are trying to know a little of the usages of that colony; to learn the language, and the faces we shall meet with there, that we may be the less awkward at our first coming among them. We willingly call a phantom our fellow, as knowing we shall soon be of their dark companionship. Therefore, we cherish dreams. We try to spell in them the alphabet of the invisible world; and think we know already, how it shall be with us. Those uncouth shapes, which, while we clung to flesh and blood, affrighted us, have become familiar. We feel attenuated into their meagre essences, and have given the hand of half-way approach to incorporeal being. We once thought life to be something; but it has unaccountably fallen from us before its time. Therefore we choose to daily with visions. The sun has no purposes of ours to light us to. Why should we get up?—*Elia.*

FRUIT OF CHURCH OF ENGLAND ESTABLISHMENTS.

The exactions of tithes and Church rates from the Irish Roman Catholics, for the support of a host of Church-of-England bishops and pluralists, has at length irritated, almost to madness, the wretched and starving population of Ireland.

The same effect was formerly produced on the Scottish people by the forced establishment of the Church of England bishops, and form of worship in Scotland. During the reigns of Charles the Second and James the Second, (the favourite monarchs of the Tories,) the great body of the Scottish nation suffered a most merciless persecution, instigated and conducted by the Anglican bishops and their curates. Under the direction of these Episcopal priests, the soldiers lived at free quarter on all the Presbyterians who were slack in their attendance on the celebration of the liturgy. At the instigation of the English curates, who acted as spies and informers against their parishioners, the soldiers, without any form of law, inflicted torture and death on all persons, young and old, who were suspected of joining in the worship of God under Presbyterian ministers.

The tortures inflicted by command of these priests of the Church of England on the people of Scotland, even on women and children, were as atrocious as those of the Spanish Inquisition; and the number of persons put to death for refusing to conform to the Episcopal worship and liturgy, was at least five hundred times greater than that of all the martyrs in the previous persecutions by the Papists in the whole of Great Britain.

By the Revolution in 1688, the Scotch people were freed from the dead weight of a Church of England Establishment, and its idle, pampered, and persecuting bishops and priests; and, in place of Episcopacy, Presbytery, which was the religious profession of the majority of the people, became the Established Church.

The Scottish Revolution Parliament passed an Act, declaring all the sentences of death and confiscation against the patriots, which had been pronounced during the persecution, to have been unjust; and stigmatized the execution of these sentences of death as bloody murders committed under form of law. By this Act of Parliament, the Tory nobles in Scotland, and among others the Duke of Gordon, were compelled to restore the confiscated estates of their murdered victims, of which they had obtained grants from the Crown as a reward for their zeal and services in the cause of despotism and persecution.

Ireland is now in the situation in which Scotland was when subjected to the forced establishment of the Church of England. The adherents of that greedy and persecuting church do not amount to one-sixteenth part of the population of Ireland. But then they form the body of the aristocracy; and aristocracy has always been a monster, ready to devour, or to sacrifice even its own children.

To lessen the number of Irish bishops, and particularly of such bishops as the notorious Bishop of Clogher, is but a palliative of injustice and robbery. The whole system is so contrary to justice and honesty, and even decency, that it ought to be totally abolished in Ireland, as it most justly has been abolished in Scotland.

PEEP AT THE AGITATOR AND HIS MASTER.

I BECAME acquainted with an interesting character under O'Connell's roof; an eminent leader, too, among the Catholic party—much like a steam-boiler; not the less "agitatious," because he works under cover. I had caught a glimpse of this gentleman and his "robe de chambre" as I crossed O'Connell's threshold; 'twas Father L'Estrange, a friar; no less a personage, than the liberator's ghostly confessor. It is he, who has the equivocal merit of being the real contriver and main-spring of the ci-devant Catholic Association; it is he who cunningly devised its *negative* powers of action,—gave it sure and swift-footed, yet noiseless and unseen energy, and employed it as an instrument for organizing the popular mind to his momentous purposes. He is, indeed, one of the earliest fathers of the great revolution which is passing under our eyes at the present hour; a revolution, which marches onwards by the activity of men's minds in contradistinction to the physical appliance of their hands and arms, and relies for its aliment and progress on the press and public oratory. This L'Estrange is a man of immovable cold-bloodedness, and, every inch of him, a professed secretary of the *philosophical* school. His manners bespeak him the perfect man of the world; he has been employed on every sort of mission in every quarter of Europe, has studied his fellows in all their moods and shades, and endeavours to conceal the sharpness of his cunning beneath a mask of polished softness. He is, in short, the *beau ideal* of one of Loyola's captains.

Our friend, O'Connell, being busy, I accompanied the friar in an early visit to a desert island, to which the ebbing tide gave us access across the dry bed of the ocean. Here we strayed among the actual ruins of the ancient abbey of Derrynane: for the agitator's mansion forms nothing more than an appendix to them. It is his intention to restore them to their pristine splendour; but this, I heard, was dependent on the golden consummation of certain *political dreams*. On our return, we found O'Connell, like an old Irish chieftain, standing on the terrace before his house, and surrounded by groups of his vassals and others, who were awaiting his instructions, or listening to his verdict on some rural squabble. He is both counsel and attorney, and, consequently, never at a loss; moreover, his decisions are a thousand times more positive, and not a jot less sacred with his auditory, than the Pythian's say. We betide the sceptic that should dream of recourse to an appeal against them; for I doubt, whether the Holy Father himself would dare measure weapons with him here, on the score of infallibility. Lawsuits, indeed, have been banished in his dominions: and this, with regard not merely to his own tenantry, but, as I was assured, to the whole neighbourhood. I was naturally astonished to find both worthies, in a religious point of view, untainted with any stain of bigotry, so far as outward appearance went: nay, it would seem, as if they had discovered the art of amalgamating fire and water,—for they professed the most enlightened and tolerant of opinions, in the very same breath, with which they made profession of the most immaculate *Roman Catholicism!*—(*From Original Notes by a foreign Nobleman.*)

WASHINGTON AND MAJOR ANDRÉ.—It became known, long after Major André's death, that General Washington had been most anxious to save him. First of all he offered to the British general to save him upon his delivering up General Arnold. But this offer being rejected, he attempted to get Arnold into his power by stratagem, determined, if it succeeded, to save the life of André. He communicated his views to a single confidential officer, Major Lee, commanding a corps of cavalry. Having sent for Lee, he told him his object was to have Arnold brought off from New York, where he then was, that he might, by getting him, save André. He made this communication (be said) in the expectation that Lee had in his corps individuals capable and willing to undertake so hazardous an enterprise. Accordingly, Sergeant Champe was the person fixed on, a man of tried courage and inflexible perseverance. Champe, having agreed to make the attempt, set off as soon as the necessary instructions were prepared for him, and, after encountering difficulties and dangers of no ordinary kind, succeeded in reaching New York. Every arrangement for the abduction was completed, when Arnold was ordered to remove his quarters, and it became impossible to carry the design into execution. Major Lee, in his memoirs, gives more interesting details relative to Champe's mission. André was the author of a satirical poem, called " The Cow Chase," which was published at New York, written on the failure of an expedition of General Wayne, for the purpose of collecting cattle. In one part of it he thus alludes to Wayne—

" The Congress dollars, and his prog,
  His military speeches,
  His corn-stalk whisky for his grog,
  Black stockings and blue breeches."

He concludes by observing that it is not safe for him to proceed farther—

" Lest the same warrior, Drover Wayne,
  Should catch and—hang the poet !"

Major André, in the end, happened to be actually delivered up to the division of the American army under Wayne!—*Stuart's Three Years in North America.*

DESTRUCTION OF CHILDREN.—Few persons, not familiar with the diseases of children, can have any just conception of the extent of the practice which now prevails, among the lower order of monthly nurses, of giving spirits and opiates to children. A poor woman, the wife of a labourer, lately informed me, that out of ten of her children, who were born healthy, nine had died under the age of three years, and most of them under two months; and that, by the advice of her nurse, she had given spirits to them all before they were a week old. Another poor woman had twins, who were healthy until they were three months old, when, being obliged to work daily for her subsistence, she endeavoured to procure herself rest during the night by giving them an opiate at bed-time. The consequence was such as might have been foreseen; the poor infants immediately became ill from it, and in the course of a few weeks literally perished from its effects.—*Dr. Ayre on Disorders of the Liver.*

THE STORY-TELLER.

THE PASIEKA; OR, BEE FARM.

From Polish Tales, by Mrs. Gore, an admirable work, recently published by Saunders and Otley, of which we shall give a Review in an early Number of the Schoolmaster.

"She is dying,—I am sure she is dying!"—murmured little Benisia to her sister Dzidzilia, as they stood hand in hand beside an anxious group, composed of their mother, aunt, and one or two peasant women belonging to the Pasieka, or Bee Farm of Zwieta, in the heart of Samogitia.

"Hush! Benisia; look at Aunt Anulka's grave face!—There is no hope!"

"What are they doing, Dzidzilia? You are taller, and can see all that is going on."

"My mother is carefully administering a few drops of miod. But she shakes her head. The cordial is too late!"

"Jesus Marya!—and so gay only yesterday morning: who would have thought it!—What will become of the young ones! the most industrious mother of the whole Pasieka!"

"See, see, sister,—Aunt Anulka has tears in her eyes!——The poor soul has breathed her last."

And so mournful a murmur of lamentation burst from the little group, that none but a true-born Zmujdsin would have been led to suspect that this excess of sympathy was lavished on the queen-bee, or, as they are termed in Poland, Matka, or mother-bee of a hive; which, having come to mischance, was expiring under the aid of the most experienced doctresses of the Pasieka. But with the pristine, pious, and honest-hearted people of Zmujdz, the bees, the chief source of their wealth and prosperity, have obtained a sanctity exceeding even that of the redbreast in our own country. To put a bee wantonly to death is regarded as a sin;—to neglect their health and comfort as a fault;—and the result of the superstitious veneration with which the bee farmers watch over their hives is rewarded by an excess of tameness, and a degree of mutual understanding, such as these winged usurers rarely exhibit in other countries. Instances of familiarity and anecdotes of instinct are cited round the hearth, by the Samogitians, incontestably authenticated, but bordering on the marvellous.

The province of Zmujdz, or Samogitia, is perhaps the only one in Poland, or even in Europe, where ignorance and superstition, in their grossest form, have wrought no evil on the moral character of the people; and whether attributable to the bounty of nature, which has blessed them with ample competence, without the enervating means of luxury—or to the protecting influence of the Pantheon of household divinities, so vaunted by the Samogitians of old, certain it is that they retain the purity and simplicity of the antique time, and live for the worship and service of God,—contented,—laborious,—virtuous,—cheerful;—ignorant alike of the corruptions generated by populous cities, and the vices and struggles of surrounding nations; nay, almost beyond the influence of the political misfortunes of their own.

Clothed with luxuriant woods, fed by a thousand fertilizing streams, and presenting a rich and diversified surface, Samogitia is parcelled into commodious farms rather than divided among a few insatiate magnats, as in the adjoining province of Lithuania. The few nobles who possess territories in the province are men unconnected with the Court, and resident on their estates; and the traveller arriving in this favoured nook of Sarmatia, and admiring at once the culture of the country, and the jovial and open countenances of the inhabitants, involuntarily reverts to the age of gold; and, with the exception that the expansive figures of the fat good-humoured Samogitians resemble as little as possible the nymphs and swains of Thessaly, might be tempted to exclaim,—

> Queste son le contrade
> Si chiare un tempo, e queste son le selve
> Ove 'l prisco valor visse, e moria.
> In quest' angolo sol del ferreo mondo
> Cred 'io che ricovrasse il secol d'oro,
> Quando fuggia le scelerate genti.
> Qui non veduta altrove
> Liberta moderata, e senza invidia
> Fiorir si vide in dolce sicurezza.
> Non custodita; e in disarmata pace,
> Cingea popolo inerme,
> Un muro d' innocenza e di virtute.*

On the banks of a rapid brook, skirting extensive woodlands, in one of the most favoured districts of the province, stood the Pasieka of Zwieta; a farm which had descended to the good Jakob Bremglicz, its present proprietor, from a race of ancestors tracing the legendary yeomanship of the family to the illustrious reign of Sigismund Augustus.—He was a worthy, warm-hearted man;—comely, healthy, wealthy, and even *wise*, according to the highest acceptation of the term; for he knew the path of duty, and walked in it humbly and stedfastly. But this was the limit of his knowledge. The schools now established in Samogitia had not come into operation in time to include the good Jakob among their neophites; and notwithstanding his privilege of crying "Veto," in the senate as loudly as a Radziwil or a Sapieha; notwithstanding his goodly pastures, nobly timbered woods, and high account in the neighbourhood, his smattering of scholarship endowed him with little reading and less penmanship. Yet small as was this advance in civilization, it sufficed to render him the intellectual president of the simple rural population among which he lived and prospered; whose veneration was lavished upon Jakob and his wife Jozefa, (or, as she was termed by the custom of the province, Jakubowa, or Madam Jakob)—as upon the wisest, virtuousest, discreetest, best, and even happiest couple in the district!

Of their three children, Dzidzilia, the eldest daughter, was already in her seventeenth year; while Benisia and her brother Janek were children of nine and ten, and still under the vigilant tutorage of their aunt Anulka, the sister of Jakob; a spinster whose early education in the Ursuline convent at the neighbouring town of Rosienie, caused her to be venerated among the Bee Farmers as a semi-saint, and full and perfect philosopher. Even Jakubowa, the most expert housewife of the neighbourhood,—whose bees produced the finest honey, whose spinning the finest yarn, whose bleaching the whitest linen, and whose Dereniak, Lipiec, Wisniak, Maliniak, and every other variety of Samogitian mead had been pronounced by the illustrious Count Plater to be the purest in the province,—looked up to her sister Anulka, the reader of pious books, the inditer of the family correspondence, and Chancellor of the Exchequer to the Pasieka,—as to the great Kopernic, disguised under the Koszula and veil of a Smujdziuka!

Under these distinctions, sister Anulka was by no means proud. Her disposition was as sweet as the miod or honey turned to such good account under her presidency; and had any healing or peace-making been required in a family, where, by the blessing of Heaven, all was gentleness, hap-

* Guarini.

piness, and love, the mild spinster was the very person to have smoothed down irritation and softened asperities.

But at the Pasieka of Zwieta nothing of the kind existed! —The farm flourished; the children flourished; the bees flourished; while the neighbours applauded, and the parents gave thanks to Providence, with smiles on their rubicund faces, and tears in their clear blue eyes. The rich incense of the bee-garden formed a fragrant atmosphere round their dwelling; and the hives that rose like golden globes in the stages of the hive shed, and the wild swarms cultivated as stock, in the woodlands of the farm, seemed to rejoice in contributing to the stores of the happy family. Sometimes, indeed, late in the autumn, the bears were known to come down from the Lithuanian forests, and pillage the wild honey-combs they had been anxiously watching through the summer; or the spider would make its invidious way into the hives; or the moth deposit her baleful eggs among the combs. But these were minor grievances;—and the effigies of the Holy Marya, and St. Jozef with his branch of lilies, erected over the gateway of the Pasieka were greeted morning and evening with tokens of Praise and thankfulness.

Such was the happy family united in the bee-garden, deploring the misadventure of one of their winged favourites; when their lamentations were suddenly interrupted by a clear, strong, cheerful voice from without the paling.

"What—what has happened?" cried the intruder; and instead of waiting a reply, a fine young man bounded over the fence—without much regard to the beds of thyme, mignionet, marjoram, and annis, among which he alighted, and made his way towards the little sorrowful group.

"She is dead, Ludwyk!"—murmured Aunt Anulka, perceiving that the eyes of the intruder were fixed upon the motionless body of the bee.

"Fetch me quick a plantain leaf, Maruchna!" cried he, tapping the shoulder of an aged woman, the domestic nurse of the farm.

"Go thou, Benisia, child," growled the old lady, apparently impatient of his authority.

And in a few moments the little insect, relieved from the oppressive heat of the touch and breathing of her attendants, stretched her contracted legs,—rolled heavily on her side,—and uttered the faint murmuring so long listened for in vain.

"Look at the raggedness of her wings! The pszczoleczka* has been injured by a bird," said Ludwyk, in reply to the admiring congratulations of his companions.

"Boh!" cried Maruchna morosely. "The strife of the hive nearest the roof of yonder shed, tells another story. A strange matka has intruded into the Roy Pszczo; there has been a fight, and the poor soul was overmatched. 'Tis well that the Jegomosc Jakob returns to-night from Wilna, —for since he has gone away, methinks, every thing has gone wrong at the Pasieka."

This last ejaculation, directed by a glance of her deep-set eye towards the skilful young bee-doctor, bore an especial reference to Ludwyk's introduction into the family at Zwieta. It was not indeed till the departure of Jakob into Lithuania for the fulfilment of his contract of flax from the preceding lint harvest, that the stranger had made his appearance in Samogitia. The object of his sojourn there was even yet a mystery; and in the eyes of the mistrustful

*Diminutive of endearment for pszczoła, or bee.

Maruchna, a mystery of sinister import. The mind of the old woman was, in fact, super-abundantly imbued with the superstitions of her native province. In addition to the zeal with which she paid her devotions to every saintly image or Christian shrine suspended among the oak-trees of the neighbouring woodlands, (a remnant probably of the ancient Herulian rites which apportioned a presiding divinity to every tree, plant, and flower,) she persisted in her yearly sacrifice to Waisgantho, the god of the flax-fields, and other deities of equally minute capacity. It was Maruchna who still insisted on the necessity of propitiating Peroun, the god of thunder, whenever the forked lightning menaced the bark roofs of Zwieta; it was Maruchna who persisted in spreading annually, in the adjoining forest, the banquet of dainties intended to appease the manes of the dead!

Now among other superstitions expunged when the victories of the Teutonic Knights overthrew, in the sixteenth century, the heathen altars of Samogitia, was the worship of the Givoite, or sacred serpents, which infest its spreading forests; and towards which, the lapse of three ages has scarcely availed to obliterate the bigoted reverence of the peasants. It is esteemed superlatively unlucky to destroy the large wood-snakes which feed upon the wild honey. And as it chanced that the incident which introduced young Ludwyk to the esteem of Jakubowa, was the hardihood with which he had rescued her little Janek from the coil of one of these legendary divinities, the stranger had been marked, from the moment of crossing the threshold of Zwieta, with the reprobation of its ancient sybil!

"He is no Samogitian born, who would venture to bruise the head of one of the wily watchers of the wood!" had been her private insinuation to Aunt Anulka; who, discerning no evil in any created thing, could neither be moved to chime in with her invectives, nor to applaud the extermination of the serpent.

"The time will come when you will see the thing as I do," persisted the nurse; "for although this busy doer of nothings may affect to come probing the earth here, and smashing a pebble stone there, as if he would not let the all-wise Creator keep a single mystery to Himself, I misdoubt me that other causes may be found for his wanderings than the love of stocks and stones, or the prying into chalk-pits."

"What mischief should there be in the youth?"—replied Anulka, turning her spindle with a degree of rapidity forming a miraculous contrast to the slow progress of her conclusions. "He saved the little Janek from a strait which, if in truth no peril, was still a parlous fright;"——

"Thereby misleading the lad into irreverence towards the customs of his forefathers," insinuated Maruchna.

"And he has instructed my sister and myself in the mystery of nature which so often causes us to find our bees dead or dying at the bottom of the tulip-cups;"——

"Thereby inducing you to root up the choicest bed of tulips between this and Memel!" continued the sybil.

"He has kindly instigated to Grzegorz, the Pasiecznik, the advantage of making merchandize of the medicinable flies that gather upon our ash-trees;"——

"Thereby withdrawing his time and notice from the lint-crops," grumbled the old lady.

"And he has bestowed upon my niece, Dzidzilia," continued the spinster, directing a smile of implication towards

he nurse, " a chaplet of Lithuanian amber, such as might
it the devotions of Queen Hedwig of blessed memory!"

" Thereby," cried Maruchna, roused by the insinuation
to her utmost pitch of displeasure, " putting nonsense into
the young girl's head, during the absence of the Jegomosc.
The saints be praised, my good master will be amongst us
anon;—and all this new-fangledness sent flying forth at the
chimney vent. Swift to come,—swift to go!—Master
Ludwyk's footing at Zwieta may be a trifle less sure than
he dreams of!"——

It was not likely that the worthy Jakubowa should allow
the Boerhaave of the Ul to depart dry-lipped from her premises. Ludwyk was now invited in; and pledged in a
cup of Lipiec that would have done honour to the far-famed
mead-vats of Kowno;—thrice sacred to the Lithuanians, as
producing the favourite beverage of Kosciuszko.

" I was about to inquire," said the young man in a hesitating tone, " whether any of you would accompany me
over the hill towards Rosienie?—Grzegorz the Pasiecznik
has been telling me of a stratum of clay above the brook-
lands, where fossil shells are found."

" *Any* of us?—*All* of us, did time allow," cried Jakubowa,
heartily; " for it lies hard by the ford which Jakob will
cross, if God pleases, this very afternoon on his way homeward to Zwieta. As it is, Janek will gladly away with
you—(eh! lad?)—and Benisia,—if you care to be troubled
with a baggage who taxes your time to carry her over the
brooks and dykes.—But for me, you must fain excuse me.
I have still the buckwheat to sift and the manna to seethe
for the supper furmenty. For you are to know, friend
Ludwyk,'tis a custom of old esteem at Zwieta, that Jakob,
—on returning home from his flint-sale and bringing me
from Wilna a luck-penny or new tunic-stuff,—shall find
a bowl of choice furmenty simmering for his supper."——

" And Dzidzilia?"—hesitated Ludwyk, who, notwithstanding his short intimacy with the family at Zwieta, was
already familiar with the episode of the manna-gruel and
tunic-stuff. " Has your daughter work in hand;—or
———"

" How say you, lass?"—cried the kind, cordial mother.
" Is the manna turned dry for me upon the sieve;—and
will you away with Ludwyk over the fields to meet your
father?"——

" If you desire it, mother," said the fair girl with a
blush emulating the crimson ensign of her native country.

" If *I*?—nay—'tis as *you* wish!" cried Jakubowa, making her way towards the kitchen in pursuance of her dutiful preparations for the arrival of the Jegomosc.

And Dzidzilia, readily accepting the sanction of her mother, was about to array herself in the flowing veil forming
part of the singular costume of a Samogitian peasant, when
Aunt Anulka (at the instigation of the severe Maruchna)
came forward with an intimation that the assistance of her
pretty niece was indispensable to herself, to set the bleach-
green in order previous to the arrival of the Dzierzawca.*

Howbeit, heavily disappointed by this arrangement, young
Ludwyk was obliged to put a gracious face upon the matter; and to accept the company of the children as cheerfully
as though it formed the real motive of his invitation. He
had been earnestly bent indeed, upon obtaining a private
interview with the bright-eyed Dzidzilia, previous to the
return of her father;—but was too young a lover, and too

* A farmer or Dzierzawca, is called Jégomosc by the peasants.

true a lover, to venture on opposing the fiat of the virgin-
president of the Pasieka; more especially when it was
backed by the menacing aspect of the old nurse, peeping
over the shoulder of Anulka. Jakubowa had already engaged him to return at supper-time, and take a share in the
family-festival; and he trusted to the star which prospers
the plottings of lovers to obtain for him, in some interval
of the feast, a few minutes explanatory conversation with
the beauty of the Pasieka. Meanwhile, the sweet farewell
glance and still sweeter farewell smile directed towards him
by Dzidzilia, as he crossed the threshold with Janek and
Benisia, and their favourite dog sporting around them,
afforded almost a sufficient balm for his mortification.

And yet, on emerging from the porch of Zwieta, the
luxuriant fragrance of the lime-trees (to whose blossoms
the Lipiec of the Pasieka was indebted for the superior
whiteness of its honey,) appeared so soothing,—and the
freshness of the evening air so inspiriting, that he was half
inclined to return to the farm, and strive to move the acquiescence of Aunt Anulka.—

" No, no!—let us hasten across the hills!" cried little
Benisia, leaping on before, with an energy that defied all
hope of a retrograde movement.

" On——on——on!"—shouted her brother Janek; and both
were soon out of hearing on the pathway traversing the vast
fields of buckwheat perfuming the mellifluous lands of
Zwieta;—making to themselves panpipes of the hemlock-
stems, or crowning each other with garlands of wild poppy.

It was a delicious evening. A sprinkling of rain had
fallen in the morning, the last drops of which a gentle
breeze was drying upon the lime-leaves; a breeze that ever
and anon swept upward along the slopes, as though to reap
the exhaling sweetness of the earth and its blossoms. Even
while watching the career of the sportive boy and girl, as
they chased each other along the hand-bridge of the streamlet threading the valley;—even while listening to the
creaking wain, (which with its harness of plaited bark and
linchpins and joists of mountain ash, presented so primeval
an object while jolting along the rude harvest road;)—even
when soothed, after its discordant rumble, by the mellow
even-song of the blackbirds perched on some stunted oak
amid the streaming effulgence of the evening sun,—Ludwyk
could not but admit that the weather was heavenly,—the
sylvan scenery enchanting,—although the company of his
lovely Dzidzilia, enhanced not its manifold delights. He
seemed to tread on air. Nature was happy around him,—
his heart was happy within him;—happy with the consciousness of worth,—happy with the inward-beaming sunshine of content!—

At the auspicious age of three-and-twenty, Ludwyk was
still somewhat of an enthusiast. In Warsaw, his spirit
might have been tamed down into soberness by the conven-
tions of society or the practicality of business. But un-
versed in the usances of cities,—like an insulated tree
watered by the rain, fanned by the winds, and warmed by
the beams of Heaven,—the generic characteristics of his
nature were still distinctly prominent. Impetuous, sanguine, impatient of injustice,—his pride lay in defiance to
the oppressor;—his happiness in the goodwill of his fellow-
creatures;—his trust—in the strength of the Omnipotent!

But notwithstanding its engrossing devotion to the cause
of the injured, the heart of the young Bee-healer was now
enthralled by a person by no means to be included in the

class of victims. Dzidzilia Bremglicz was not only fair and young, and wealthy after her degree, but blest in the especial regard of the district, the fond affection of her parents, and the doating and triumphant partiality of the aunt and nurse under whose eyes she had grown up as a wonder of perfection. The Samogitian maiden had never heard a harsh word,—never seen an angry countenance,—never experienced a sorrow,—never shed a tear, unless in compassion to the wants or woes of some poorer neighbour. And then her features were so delicate, her smile so radiant, her voice so joy-bespeaking!—No wonder that Ludwyk pondered over her perfections during his ramble with a beating heart ;—and resolved to ask her in marriage of her father as early as decency would permit, after the Dzierzawca's return. Nay,—he was even engaged in composing his demand after the most approved courtesies of Samogitia, when a loud outcry from little Benisia disturbed him from his reverie; and he beheld his charge, Janek, the pride of Jakubowa and of the Pasieka, mounting the trunk of a hoary mountain-ash in search of the pendent nest of the Remisz or Lithuanian titmouse!

Poor Ludwyk might be pardoned for exclaiming somewhat vociferously against the ornithological pursuits of the young adventurer in a tone of authority and reprehension, savouring of the future brother-in-law. But his anger was of brief endurance; and the happy thoughts of the young lover soon shaped themselves to one of the popular carols of his native province.

LITHUANIAN CHANT.

'Tis morning,—ho!—O'er wilds and woods
Shine out thou gladness-bringing Sun!—
Leap, leap for joy, ye sparkling floods!
Breathe warbling groves, your orison.
'Tis morn!

'Tis noonday,—ho!—Sweet incense fling,
Rose!—from thy censer's treasuries;—
Skim o'er the pool, ye light of wing,
Ope, daisied meads, your thousand eyes—
'Tis noon!—

'Tis evening,—ho!—Turn, meek-eyed herds
Turn gathering flocks unto your fold;
Home, to your nests, ye wandering birds,
The West pours down its molten gold.—
'Tis eve!—

'Tis nightfall—ho!—Keep, starry sky,
Stern watch upon the stealthy earth!
Sing chirping crickets, merrily;
Crackle bright brands upon the hearth,—
'Tis night!—

'Tis midnight,—ho!—On flail-worn floor,
Ye mice, your thriftless orgies keep;
Blink watchful owl!—Our tasks are o'er,
The weary household sinks to sleep.—
God guard our rest!

Could the high-spirited Ludwyk have conjectured, as he stood musing, lover-like, by many a spreading tree; or smiling in vague but happy self-abstraction as he glanced downward from the hill to the valley,—wherein the solitary vulture sat perched upon his insulated barrier-stone like a warning effigy of rapine,—could he have dreamed, during that cheering summer walk, what mischief was plotting against his peace under the mossy roof of the Pasieka, he would most assuredly have preferred remaining at Zwieta to assist in the seething of the manna, and to keep watch against his enemies.

Scarcely had Dzidzilia quitted the house, after his departure, on her errand to the bleaching ground, when she observed the venerable figure of Maruchna stumping, stick in hand, toward her;—and as the decrepitude of the old aunt, upon whose knees Jakob, albeit a man in years, had himself been reared and nurtured, prevented her in general from extending her perambulations further than the musky paths of the Pszczolarnia,—the gentle girl retraced her steps to lend the support of her arm to the old woman in reverence of whom she had been reared.

"Rest we here!" cried Maruchna, staying the steps of her fair conductress, as they reached a spreading lime tree,—the pride of the Pasieka,—whose shapely cone of purest green adorned the entrance to the bleaching-ground. "Rest we here, nursling!—There are no eaves-droppers under the linden but our trusty bees, who are neither tatlers nor talebearers;—or at worst, a brood of green-finches nestling in their callow down. Rest we here, Dzidzilia!" And seating herself on a rude log-bench, constructed by Jakob himself in his days of his courtship to Jozefa,—she motioned to their daughter to take place beside her.

"Aunt Anulka," remonstrated Dzidzilia, intimidated by the austere countenance bent upon her by the sybil, "bad me use my utmost haste in gathering in the webs, lest———"

"And I," interrupted Maruchna, "bid thee eschew haste, and listen leisurely to my words!"

Nor did the damsel hesitate in her obedience. There was something in the white hair and furrowed face of the ancient of days, which mingled a degree of awe with the affection testified towards her by her master's children. To Dzidzilia Bremglicz's eye, accustomed only to sights of joy and looks of love, the terrific sublimity of eternity was typified by the venerable age of her father's nurse. She was the only thing connected with a past century in the household of Zwieta;—all else was in its prime,—all else bright and flourishing!

A silence of several minutes followed her choice of a resting-place; and never before had Jakubowa's daughter noted with impatience the whirring murmur indicative of the banqueting hour of the pensioners of Aunt Anulka's hives. It seemed as though the bloom-charged branches over-head were alive with bees! Yet when she raised her eyes towards the roofing of pale emerald, it was rather to avoid the scrutinizing glances of Maruchna, which she fancied were fixed upon her face, than in reverence to the little votive altar, appended there in sanctification by the hands of Grzegorz, the pious Pszczelnik, or bee-tender of the Pasieka.

"You are sorrowful, good mother," cried the young girl, at length, perceiving that tears were gathering in the eyes of the nurse, as she sat contemplating the eldest-born of her master's house.

"No!"

"Sick then?"—still interrogated Dzidzilia.

"Still less!"

"What ails you then, dear, good Marysia?"—cried the daughter of Jakob, still more and more alarmed.

"Nothing, child!—'Tis *you* who are ailing—'tis *you* who will soon be sorrowful!—A cup of bitterness is in store for you, Dzidzileczka; and the old woman [would this put away the draught, or pour it forth in libation to the evil ones."

"Leave we the world of spirits and libations!" cried Dzidzilia, fully on her guard against that abundant chapter

Maruchna's eloquence;—"and tell me explicitly your fears, and gently your instructions."

"Can I speak gently of that which concerns the ruin of my master's house?" cried Maruchna. "I behold you on the brink of perdition; and must hold you back from the abyss, even though my grasp be rude as the iron gauntlet of Lesko the warrior. I have a greivious tale to tell. Listen and be admonished!"

"Of all the hirelings of Zwieta, my Dzidzilia,—(as the reverence of my masters is a token,) I alone am no bondswoman of the land.—Yet the whole generation now flourishing around me at the Pasieka,—your father, with his noonday manhood,—Anulka, the kind aunt,—yourself—the younglings,—*all* were swathed by my hands, and tended in innocent helplessness upon my knees.—I love you all, for dearly did I dote upon your father's infancy;—I doted upon your father's infancy, for I had nothing else to love! —I had been a wife,—a happy wife;—I had been a mother, —a joyous, triumphant mother:—but that was past. All were gone—all withered; I was alone,—oh! how bitterly, bitterly alone!

"My father, like our own good Jakob, was a flourishing farmer on the Polesian frontier of Lithuania, of good credit, and such fame for honesty and worth as caused the hand of his daughter to be sought of many suitors; his daughter *Marysia*,—for no peevishness of humour had then obtained for the free-hearted girl of the Niemen the accusing name of Maruchna. But to me, their various suits were a matter of mere importunity; for, from my earliest years, my heart was pledged to one whose qualities were so great and noble, that nothing,—no! not even my parent's malediction,— could move me to deplore that Pawel was of ignoble birth, and son to a serf of Derenczyn. His father, it is true, had prospered; and rented extensive lands of the house of Sapieha, to which his own and his children's service was due in perpetual villanage. For however well endowed with worldly belongings, Pawel was in truth a slave—a denizen; —and his children must perforce be born in bondage!

"' But 'tis not this alone that moves my interdiction,' cried my father, when I ventured to frustrate a more prosperous marriage, urged upon me by his will, by a confession of my attachment. ' There is that in the young man's blood which would make a wretch of my Marysia.—Mark you not the sign of the Plica-stricken upon him and all his race?' I shuddered, Dzidzilia! for that word was indeed a word of warning! ' Yes!' continued my father, ' Pawel is come of parents whose industry and integrity may have effaced all blemish of their birth: and it were as well to deny the honour of the Burgher of Krakow, as of Pietrus, the father of your lover. But 'tis now thirty years, Marysia, since my eyes have kept watch over the doings of his house. Three of his goodly sons has that fearful malady laid in the grave; the fourth is a raving lunatic in the hospital of the Camaldolite convent at Minsk. Shall I give my daughter to the fifth?'

"' It may indeed be thus, father!' I replied. But my Pawel is free of foot as free of heart. The blood dances lightly in *his* veins, and he, at least, is exempt from the frightful contamination that besets his race. Who so active in the round of the Kruciszczy, when at eve we dance under the linden trees? For three successive winters has he won the premium as largest owner of wolf skins deposited in the mayorality of Minsk. And did he not preserve your own life, father, by mere vigour of arm, when, but a season ago, you joined the bear hunters of the Niemen?'

"' To what avail,' cried my father, ' seek you to gainsay my words; which nought but parental love arrays in judgment against your choice? Pawel is all that is good, brave, generous, handsome! But I would not wittingly tell over a daughter's dowry to the son of a slave; and never, were he thrice ennobled, and willing to accept her dowerless, would I bestow the hand of my Marysia on one within whose polluted veins rankles the filthy poison of the Plica!'"

" And upon this declaration you were obedient, and gave up your lover?" inquired the pretty Dzidzilia bending her eager eyes upon those of the venerable sybil.

"No!" replied Maruchna in a low hoarse voice. " I was over bold in defying the vengeance of God. For the following year, having lost my kind father, instead of marking double reverence to the words of his lips when those lips were cold in the grave, I turned aside from the desolate home where I was now an orphan, and became the wife of Pawel!"

"But you were happy, dearest Maruchna?" cried Dzidzilia, her feelings deeply interested by a tale of love and wilful wedlock.

"Happy?"—reiterated the old woman with fervour. "Why is there no brighter word in the mouths of men, to designate the joy of those who, loving long and long estranged, are at length united for eternity in the blessed marriage bond? Every thing was rapture around us! The skies, the earth, the very household duties which elsewhere had seemed irksome, were a delight when ministered to the service of my husband. Happy?—What could surpass the happiness of being *his*; of finding him ever near me,—with love upon his lips and transport in his eyes? Yet something *did* surpass it; for soon I was fated to hold a babe of Pawel's within my arms, my husband's very self in smile and features; and while listening to his sportive declaration that it resembled only me, to bend my ear to the gentle murmurings of the fondled one;—faint, low, plaintive, love-stirring! *Happy?* All-righteous God, what earthly happiness could out-measure mine?"

Dzidzilia now drooped her gentle head on the bosom of the nurse. She wished that Maruchna might not see her weeping at the touching holiness of such a picture.

"The aged father of my husband died, ere I again became a mother," said Maruchna, labouring to assume a calmer demeanour. " And now, we were rich indeed. The old man had a lease of especial favour from Prince Sapieha, of the forest of Szczoth, with its beaver-dams and rights of manorage; even where the weeping pine abounds, and the largest and clearest masses of Lithuanian amber are dug up from the sand. Our commerce prospered, we had a dwelling in a wild fast by the river side, with a hamlet as of our own around us. Every thing was within those walls that could make glad the heart of man. Pawel was cheerful, laborious, forbearing; our hirelings duteous, our trade thriving, our babes, (there were three now rolling on the moss beside our forest door,) our babes beauteous as the imaged cherubim of heaven! All three were alike fair, alike gracious; but it was the sport of Pawel to excite my mother's wrath by accusing me of partial favour towards the second,—my little Jozia;—with her plaintive voice as of the calling quail,—her curls of golden brown floating over her graceful shoulders,—and her mild blue eyes that beamed as with the emanating spirit of God!—A moment!"

—faltered the aged woman, pressing her hands upon her breast. "I must gather breath to speak of all this."

"Let me forestal the relation, dearest Maruchna!" cried her nursling, willing to spare her the pang of farther explanation. "The Almighty who dealt forth of old his judgments upon the patriarch whose flocks were fairest and whose offspring loveliest, smote *you* also with the chastening of his hand! I see it all."

"No! *none* can see it as I saw it!" faltered the nurse. "None can see, with the agony of my own watching, the change that came over the fair face of my cherished one! The burning forehead, the pallid cheeks, the blackened lips. 'Tis the Plica!' cried my unfortunate Pawel when he heard the sweet voice of his child crying aloud upon us for aid and soothing. And I would not believe it—and in my horror, I cursed him for the word!—And even when those bright brown curls grew dim and clammy, and hung together and clung together, I would not own that it was disease that matted them in frightful entanglement; but smoothed them, and smoothed them, as was my wont; and kissed the pale cheeks of the sufferer, and said she would be better anon. At length, maddened with the agony of watching the dishevelment of those lovely locks, I shore them closely off, and flung them upon the blazing logs! Dzidzilia, there was blood upon the steel as I laid it aside. Dzidzilia!—within a week from that act of rashness, my gracious babe was in her grave! And for one bitter moment I was glad when the earth closed over the loathsomeness of my fondling! But soon, very soon, I would have uprooted the sod to gaze upon her disfigured face, and press to my lips,—to my heart of hearts,—all that remained of her I loved with such overweening tenderness!

"Then remembered I my father's curse! For I knew that the fatal infection must be in the veins of my surviving children, of my Pawel himself, and that a destiny was upon our little household. I dared no longer lift my eyes upon them, lest I should descry the fatal sign upon their brows. I dared not wander forth with them into the sunshine, lest peradventure its fervours might stimulate the latent poison. If the rain rained, I dreaded its humid exhalations; if the wind blew, I closed up with moss every cranny of our dwelling. I could not sleep by night for creeping to the cradle of my boys and feeling that their little hands lay calm and feverless on the coverlid. I could not rest by day, for stealing out to the cottages of the peasants, and questioning them of their own experience, and of the signs and symptoms of the malady: till the thought of the new-formed nail, and new-springing hair, and scarified flesh, became as tokens of horror to my mind! I saw them before me when I waked; I dreamed of them in my dreams by night!"

Dzidzilia started, and gazed inquiringly into the face of Maruchna; who, without notice of her agitation, speedily resumed. "My terrors, dearest, were not premature. Both sickened—both died! Pawel (the gay-hearted one who so much resembled his father)—perished first,—in fearful and bitter anguish. Franciszek, the little one, the youngest born, of slow and gradual suffering, as if pining for the playmates who were gone before. *Three* babes! Dzidzilia Bremglicz! three glorious, lovely, loving babes, all taken from a heart overflowing with mother's love, to be thurst into darkness beneath our forest turf!—I was hopeless!— dared not speak my grief to my husband, lest he should hold it in reproach, or imbibe injurious alarm on his own behalf. I dared not complain, I dared not even weep. I could only pray,—pray,—pray;—clasp my hands in heart-broken fervour and supplication, and trust that the earnest voice from the wilderness would reach the pitying ear of the Almighty!

"But that merciless ear was closed against my entreating; and the hand of the avenger was against me. The worst was yet to come!—Pawel, conscious of the fate that waited him, and dreading the contagion his touch might convey, now tarried hour after hour, day after day, from the desolate dwelling of his wife;—he would no longer hold my hand in his;—he would not even press his arm around me when we wept together upon the grave of our children!—He shuddered whenever I approached him; and oh! what glaring looks of tenderness and horror contended in his eyes, when he fixed them upon me as the first pains of the pestilence assailed him; the heavy brow, the burning hand, the bewildered brain!—Yes!—dearest, yes!—with *him* the Plica took its deadliest shape; and the howlings of a lunatic were soon heard in our happy dwelling. Two years did I watch by him;—even when the gyves were upon him,—and——but why should I thus agonize your gentle nature?—He, too, died;—and dying heirless, the laws of the land awarded to the lord of the soil all that the industry of his bondsman had amassed. A desolate widow, I was turned forth into the world. A distant kinsman at Rosienie afforded me a refuge;—and it was there, sweet, I became the hireling of your grandsire, and took the new-born Jakob tenderly into my arms, as a remembrancer of the precious ones that had been wrested from them."

"One word, Maruchna!" faintly ejaculated Dzidzilia Bremglicz, without venturing to raise her face from the bosom of the nurse. "On Ludwyk's hands the nails are springing newly;—on Ludwyk's head the locks are of recent growth;—on Ludwyk's cheek there is a wide and fearful scar——"

"My poor child!" replied the monitress, "your fears forestal my warning.—'Tis even as you dread.—The young stranger has been, and will be again, a victim to the loathsome Plica. A fearful infection already riots in the veins of him you love!"

(*To be continued.*)

CENTENARY OF THE BIRTH OF DR. PRIESTLEY.—On Monday the 100th anniversary of the birth-day of Dr Priestley was celebrated by a dinner at the Freemasons' Tavern. Between 150 and 200 gentlemen sat down to table comprising some of the most eminent scientific characters in the metropolis. Dr. Babington presided. He proposed "The memory of Dr Priestley," upon whom he pronounced a brief eulogy.—Professor Daubeny bore testimony to the importance of the discoveries of Dr Priestley, more especially that which showed the carbonic acid gas, so prevalent in animals, was also the food and pabulum of plants.—Professor Cumming regretted those disgraceful proceedings by which Dr Priestley had been driven away from this country, and congratulated the company that they lived to an age when such occurrences would be scarcely credited. (Cheers.) He beheld before him men of different religious and political opinions, but all were united in the endeavour to do honour to a man who was unhonoured in his age and his country. (Applause.) Mr Lubbock, Mr Faraday, Mr J. Taylor, concurred in expressing their admiration of the talents and respect for the memory of Dr Priestley.

COLUMN FOR THE LADIES.

MRS. HEMANS.

Some writer has remarked, with equal force and beauty, that, "by a visit to those places which we know to have been the haunt of genius, we are more affected than when we hear of their actions, or read their works. And this remark is founded on a thorough knowledge of human nature. The room where Newton was born at Wynford—and the chamber in which Shakspeare saw the light on Avon—the churchyard where Gray wrote his Elegy—and the study where Johnson penned his immortal Rasselas—must always possess a spell for those to whom learning and genius are dear. And such was the feeling with which I gazed on the cottage of the poetess at Rhyader. The situation is pretty and picturesque. The view, at once rich in the foreground, and romantic in the distance, is precisely that on which a mind, so exquisitely alive to the charms of nature, would delight to repose. Of the interior, I will only say (for the home of such a woman is hallowed ground and its secrets should not be delivered over to the vulgar gaze of the public eye) that it is plentifully adorned with that best furniture—books; and is rich in those little embellishments which a woman's ingenuity can so readily supply, and a woman's taste can best arrange. By a commonplace observer Mrs. Hemans would be considered an interesting, rather than a beautiful woman. And yet hers is beauty of the highest class. It depends neither on feature nor complexion. It is that which lasts the longest, and over which time has so little power—the beauty of the soul. The intellect which lights up that pale and placid countenance, bestows on it a life and loveliness, a grandeur and a majesty, to which no complexion, however brilliant, no features, however faultless, can aspire. The expression of the countenance, when in repose, is deeply melancholy. That dark, soft, sad eye, tells a tale of past sorrow and suffering. But the expression about the mouth, when speaking, is frank, and singularly winning; and in conversation on any favourite topic, her eye lights up with living lustre. At these moments, she bears no faint resemblance to Pasta. —*Whyohotte of St. John's*.

CAROLINE.

Auburn are the locks thou bearest,
   Gentle Caroline;
Golden are the locks thou wearest,
   Fawn-like Caroline;
And thy voice is as a lute,
   Touch'd by a gentle maiden;
And thy cheek is like ripe fruit,
   Sweet, and blossom-laden;
   Gentle Caroline!
Wherefore are thy lips so red,
   Sylph-like Caroline?
And thy locks flow down thy head
   Like the twisted vine?
If love be not within thy heart,
   Earth is not meant for thee;
And I not made for earth if thou,
   Sweetest, love not me,
   Sylph-like Caroline!

CHRISTIAN NAMES OF WOMEN.
TO EDITH S——

In Christian world Mary the garland wears!
Rebecca sweetens on a Hebrew's ear;
Quakers for pure Priscilla are more clear;
And the light Gaul by amorous Ninon swears.
Among the lesser lights how Lucy shines!
What air of fragrance Rosamond throws round!
How like a hymn doth sweet Cecilia sound!
Of Marthas and of Abigails, few lines
Have bragg'd in verse. Of coarsest household stuff
Should homely Joan be fashioned. But can
You Barbara resist, or Marian!
And is not Clare for love excuse enough?
Yet, by my faith in numbers, I profess,
These all, than Saxon Edith, please me less.
Athenæum.   C. LAMB.

SCIENTIFIC NOTICES.

STEAM ENGINES.—Steam engines were introduced about 130 years ago, and continued upon the atmospheric construction for about fifty years. From the joint experiments of Messrs. Watt and Bolton, and the principle miners, the best of those engines, in 1778, raised 2,000 gallons from a depth of 348 feet, for every bushel of coals used. An ordinary man, working with a good pump, will raise 1,000 gallons from the same depth in a day. In 1829, the best engine in Cornwall did *ten times* the work of those in 1778, or each bushel of coals raised 20,006 gallons of water. In 1829, therefore, one bushel of coals did the wages of twenty men, or of four horses for one whole day. The rearing of men, or of horses, bears as great a proportion to the whole of their labour, as the cost of steam engines does to that which they can do; therefore, a bushel of coals, by the steam engine, buys as much labour as the wages of twenty men, or the keep of four horses. A bushel of coals (which is about three quarters of a hundred weight, at 20s. a ton) costs 9d., in the coal districts; in the places where the price is highest, it will not cost more than 1s. 9d., and the cost of coal, for the whole engines, may be, therefore, taken at the average of 1s. 3d., while the men, at 1s. 3d. a day would cost 24s. Men, therefore, could not compete with steam engines if their wages exceeded 4d. in the week, or three farthings for each day's hard work of ten hours. If they worked at a rate like this, they would be worse off than were the Indians of South America. If the men did work as cheaply as the engines, the coals would not be consumed as extensively as machinery enables them to be consumed. The consumption of coals has increased much more rapidly than the increase of the population. In the time of Charles the II. 200,000 chaldrons were annually consumed in London. At the present time, above a million and a half chaldrons are consumed. It has been calculated that each person in London, in 1801, used a chaldron of coals in a year, and that now a chaldron and one-sixth is used by each person. The competition of capital and improved machinery have made coals cheaper.

HYDRO-OXYGEN MICROSCOPE.—The great defect in the Solar Microscope is, that its effectiveness depends wholly upon the unclouded presence of the sun. Its operations, the result of refraction, are suspended whenever it is deprived of the full potency of the solar beams. In our climate, therefore, but especially in winter, it can be resorted to but seldom, and never with perfect satisfaction. To obviate this inconvenience, the aid of oxygen and hydrogen gas has been resorted to, and their united stream being directed against a piece of lime, produces a light of such vivid force as effectually answers all the purposes of strong illumination. We need not refer to the wonderful magnifying power of the solar microscope. Most of our readers must ere this be familiar with it. Suffice it to say that it can in truth represent objects five hundred thousand times larger in size than they really are. Thus the pores of the slenderest twig, and the fibres of the most delicate leaf, expand into coarse net-work. The external integuments of a fly's eyes, filled with thousands of lenses, appear in the dimensions of a lady's veil—that gentleman yclept the flea swells into six feet—worms seem like boa constrictors, while the population of a drop of goodly ditch water present such shapes as Teniers should have seen before he pencilled the grotesque monsters who troubled the solitude of St. Anthony. The hydro-oxygen microscope, we need scarcely, remark promises to do much more for mankind than to gratify his curiosity. It will prove an important assistant in the investigation of physical science.

SYMPATHY OF MOTION.—It has been found, that in a watchmaker's shop, the time-pieces or clocks, connected with the same wall or shelf, have such sympathetic effect in keeping time, that they stop those which beat in irregular time; and if any are at rest, set agoing those which beat accurately.—*Gardiner's Music of Nature.*

SCRAPS.

EDUCATION IN IRELAND.

In favour of mere learning the poor Catholics of Ireland have made prodigious exertions, such as would not pass for credible, were not the facts attested by those who were unwilling witnesses. By data furnished in 1827, we have in round numbers, the following:—

SCHOLARS IN IRELAND.

		Paid for their Schooling.	Free.
Protestants,	90,000	56,000	44,000
Catholics,	400,000	320,000	80,000

It is hence obvious, that about half the Protestant children are free, while not above one-fifth of the Catholics are so. Here, however, is the willingness proved, notwithstanding their well-known comparative weakness in means, which should have ensured them fairness, if not indulgence, in the distribution of the public funds for education.—*A Cry to Ireland.*

BARBARITY OF BIRD CATCHING.—The summer bird catchers are the most barbarous, who entrap only singing birds, and take them without regard to their having young, which may perish by their absence, or to that harsh change from the enjoyment of summer sunshine and pleasures, to the captivity of a cage. When I see their nests spread in the field, I wish them all manner of villanous ill luck, and I never omit a favourable opportunity of deranging or destroying lime twigs when they fall in my way; none of our customs mark our selfishness more than keeping singing birds in perpetual confinement, making the pleasure of our ears their misfortune, and that sweet gift which God has given them, wherewith to make themselves happy, and the country delightful, the curse of their lives. This practice is detestable, doubly so, in the capture of migratory birds, who have not merely the common love of liberty, but the instinct of migration to struggle with, and it may be safely asserted, that out of every ten nightingales so caught, nine pine away and die.

A SYNONYMY.—At the Liverpool Quarter Sessions, the other day, an action of trover was brought for the recovery of a cart of very little value, the delivery of which to the plaintiff, as the alleged purchaser, had been refused by the defendant; and it was quite certain that the trial of the question would cost many times the worth of the article. In the course of the proceedings the following dialogue occurred:—Counsel—Then you went and demanded the cart from the defendant? Witness—Na, indeed. He said the plaintiff might go to hell for it, or he might go to the devil for it; I don't exactly recollect which of the words he used. The Recorder—But it meant, in point of fact, that he might "go to law for it," I suppose.—(Loud laughter.)—*Macclesfield Courier.*

THE ENGLISH PEASANT.

BY WILLIAM HOWITT.

"The condition of the West Indian slave is much better and happier than that of the English peasantry."—*Common Assertion.*

THE land for me! the land for me!
Where every living soul is free;
Where winter may come, where storms may rave,
But the tyrant dare not bring his slave.

I should hate to dwell in a summer land,
Where flowers spring up on every hand,
Where the breeze is glad, the heavens are fair,
And the taint of blood is everywhere.

I saw a peasant sit at his door,
When his weekly toil in the fields was o'er;
He sat on the bench his grandsire made,
He sat in his father's walnut shade.

'Twas the golden hour of an April morn,
Lightly the lark sprung from the corn,
The blossoming trees shone purely white,
And the young leaves quivered in the light.

The Sabbath bells, with a holy glee,
Were ringing o'er woodland, heath, and lea;
'Twas a season whose living influence ran
Through air, through earth, and the heart of man.

No feeble joy was that peasant's lot,
As his children gambolled before his cot,
And archly mimicked the toils and cares
Which coming life shall make truly theirs.

But their mother, with breakfast call, anon
Came forth, and their merry masque was gone;
'Twas a beautiful sight, as meekly still
They sat in their joy on the cottage sill.

And is this the man, thou vaunting knave,
Thou hast dared to compare with the weeping slave?
Away! find one slave in the world to cope
With him in his heart, his home, and his hope.

He is not in thy lands of sin and pain,
Scared with the lash, and cramped with the chain;
In thy burning clime, where the heart is cold,
And man, like the beast, is bought and sold.

He is not in the East in his gorgeous halls,
Where the servile crowd before him falls,
Till the bowstring comes in an hour of wrath,
And he vanishes from the tyrant's path.

But oh! thou slanderer false and vile,
Dare but to cross that garden stile,
Dare but to touch that lowly thatch,
Dare but to force that peasant's latch;

And thy craven soul shall wildly quake,
And the thunder peal that deed shall wake,
And myriad tongues of fire shall sound,
As if every stone cried from the ground.

The indignant thrill like flame shall spread,
Till the isle itself rock 'neath thy tread,
And a voice from the people, peer, and throne,
Ring in thine ears, "Atone! atone!"

For Freedom here is common guest,
In princely hall, in peasant's rest;
The palace is filled with her living light,
And she watches the hamlet day and night.

Then the land for me! the land for me!
Where every living soul is free;
Where winter may come, where storms may rave,
But the tyrant dare not bring his slave.

TO CORRESPONDENTS.

In answer to several applications, we beg to mention that some of the early numbers of the *Political Register* are out of print, and of course we cannot furnish them without incurring a heavy expense. The *Register* is not stereotyped like the *Schoolmaster*, but we keep each number in types for a month, to accommodate such of our weekly subscribers as wish to procure it, to bind up with the *Schoolmaster*.

CONTENTS OF NO. XXXVII.

Lotteries,	225
Ferdusi, the Persian Poet,	227
Lady Grange,	229
That we should rise with the Lark,	231
Fruit of Church of England Establishments,	ib.
Peep at the Agitator and his Master,	232
Washington and Major Andre,	ib.
THE STORY-TELLER—The Panicks; or, Bee Farm,	233
COLUMN FOR THE LADIES—Mrs. Hemans—Christian names of Women,	235
SCIENTIFIC NOTICES—Steam Engines—Hydro-Oxygen Microscope,	ib.
SCRAPS,	240
The English Peasant,	ib.

EDINBURGH: Printed by and for JOHN JOHNSTONE, 19, St. James' Square.—Published by JOHN ANDERSON, Jun., Bookseller, 55, North Bridge Street, Edinburgh; by JOHN MACLEOD, and Atkinson & Co. Booksellers, Glasgow; and sold by all Booksellers and Vendors of Cheap Periodicals.

THE Schoolmaster,
AND
EDINBURGH WEEKLY MAGAZINE.

CONDUCTED BY JOHN JOHNSTONE.

THE SCHOOLMASTER IS ABROAD.—LORD BROUGHAM.

No. 38.—VOL. II.　　SATURDAY, APRIL 20, 1833.　　PRICE THREE-HALFPENCE.

HINTS FOR CONVERSATION.

IN this paper I shall give hints for subjects of conversation, and directions as to the manner of treating them. The first and most obvious topic is the *weather*, and a strict investigation of the state of the atmosphere. For this purpose I would advise every gentleman to keep a barometer in his room, and a thermometer to a northern exposure, that he may be able with accuracy to determine the exact state of the air; this will shew his attention to a subject of such great importance, and general use in conversation. The advantages arising from this topic are incalculable; it furnishes a gentleman with an opportunity of displaying his discernment, and giving a great deal of useful information, such as, when a great-coat ought to be worn, or an additional pair of stockings put on; when a store of liquorice or sugar-candy ought to be provided; or if it might be proper to take a glass of tody before going to bed—when a dram should be taken to keep one warm, or a little spirits and water to keep one cool. This subject ought always to be treated with great gravity, and a few epithets occasionally bestowed upon the day. It may be observed, that it is devilish hot, or d—'d cold; this gives it an elegant turn, and relieves it from being entirely a dry disquisition. From the weather, the transition is easy and natural to the state of the *health*, which ought never to be neglected, especially if the person we meet happens to be looking ill; he should be particularly informed of this circumstance, and warmly reminded to take more care of himself; this shows our friendship for him. He should be minutely questioned about the nature of his distemper; and should he answer, as some people have a trick of, that he is very well, insist upon it that he is not, and that you never saw him looking worse; this will probably lead him to give a full account of the matter, and afford you an opportunity of giving him a cure. I have known a gentleman get twenty infallible cures for a cold in a morning, by the attention of his friends in this respect. Should you be questioned about your health, give a full account of all the troubles you may have had for a fortnight or a month past at least, how you got them, and how you got rid of them; this is highly entertaining, and may be of much use; in return you will probably receive an account of every person of your acquaintance who may have had the same disorder, by which means you may excite and bestow sympathy, which, according to Dr. Adam Smith, is one of the most amiable feelings of the human mind. As the sublime, however, shows a greater degree of genius than the tender, and as terror, according to Blair and to Burke, is a requisite in the sublime, I would advise, especially if ladies be present, that a Radical Rebellion in Ireland, if possible, be introduced, and often recurred to; thus as the penetrating *Faber*,

"One of these learned philologists, who trace
A panting syllable, through time and space,
Start it at home, and hunt it in the dark,
To Gaul, to Greece, and into Noah's ark,"
　　　　　　　　　　　COWPER,

presses every word into his service that has one letter of similitude; I would advise every observation whatever to be made, to bear upon this subject. Is it remarked that the weather is boisterous? "It would be a bad day to flee if the Radicals were rising." Is it foggy? "The Radicals will have fine opportunity for drilling in this weather." Is the dinner ill cooked? "We'll perhaps be glad of such as this when the Radicals come." The other excellencies of this subject are, that it changes every day, and gives scope to the imagination, and possesses that obscurity which is also necessary in the sublime. The *Yeomanry* necessarily follow; if any be present, the conversation of course turns upon uniforms and military evolutions; the language upon this topic ought to be as technical as possible, intermingled with frequent apostrophes to the devil in favour of O'Connell and Cobbett; the reviews, drills, &c. &c. will easily furnish one half-hour's conversation. The pikemen may be here introduced with advantage, and a dissertation upon the Macedonian phalanx thrust in with great effect. *Dinner* furnishes a noble subject, as it affords to all present an excellent opportunity of descanting upon cookery, which I have often heard done much to my edification, for whole hours together, and thereby have been saved the necessity of studying the excellent publication of Mistress Margaret Dods, upon that subject, which however I would earnestly recommend to every gentleman's perusal who would wish to take a part in this most indispensable subject. Having at learned length discussed those topics which I have merely suggested, *Character* should immediately be brought upon the carpet; though this be a prerogative of the tea-table, yet it is not peculiarly so, and may be elegantly introduced in the form of an anecdote, and come in like a tart at the close of the dinner. As *de mortuis nil nisi bonum* is a justly exploded maxim, so a similar line of conduct ought to be held with regard to the absent: of what use are the failings of friends, if not to afford instruction? For which cause these should always be particularly pointed out; and this is always attended with the greatest advantage when the person is absent, because greater freedom is used, and consequently more instruction obtained; and the larger the company in which this is done the better, as it stands a greater chance of being more beneficial.

So much with regard to topics in which both sexes are concerned; but it would be unpardonable not to offer a few hints for the particular improvement of the fair sex. I would recommend to them *dress*, the fashions, the characters, politeness, and prices of all the haberdashers about town; particular details, how Mrs. ―― becomes her pelisse, and how Miss ―― looks in her Indian shawl, and how Mr. ―― wears his ――. Here the making of matches should commence, and every couple that are at all acquainted should be paired with due expedition. I have heard of marriages actually taking rise from this laudable practice. The married ladies should enlarge upon the advantages of *matrimony*, and particularize distinctly all the peculiarities of their husbands; upon which side he likes to lie in the night-time, and whether he snores; when he rises in the morning, and how long he takes to dress; how many clothes he dirties during the week; what seat he usually sits on, and how he likes his dinner cooked; what dishes he is fond of, and how thick his shoes are in the soles. After husbands, then the *servants* should come in; how difficult it is to find a good one, and how many you have had since you were married. The faults of servants is a fine topic; I have known it serve for a whole evening's entertainment; more especially, how much they are given to *wastery*; how many candle-ends have been found in the dresser drawer, and how much butter thrown among the ashes, and what a quantity of coals are made use of in the year; always concluding with such a sentence as the following, that "servants are enough to ruin any body;" or, "servants are a perfect pest;" or, that they require to be strictly looked after; which serves like a truism at the tail of a sermon, by way of a practical improvement of the subject. As the first dawnings of intellect are extremely interesting to the philosophic mind, and as Locke, in his essay, seems to have felt the want of facts upon this subject, I would merely hint to mothers, that they should be as full as possible in their details of the first prattlings of their *infants;* what word they first uttered, what curious questions they ask, especially when they begin to get their 'echism; how droll they are, and what funny tricks they have played. If is a pity that such a fund of instruction and amusement should be kept entirely between husband and wife. There is only one hint more, which I shall presume to give the fair sex, and that is, that upon no occasion should they allow the smallest quarter to *the frail sisterhood*. Men consider this as the most unequivocal mark of virtue, and when they see ladies *outrageously chaste*, never infer that *disgust* is the consequence of disappointment. When virgins advance in years, they should be careful to enumerate, as frequently as possible, the conquests they have made, and the lovers they have slighted in their youth: this gives them a degree of respectability. Should any scholastic *Bore* unhappily introduce a literary subject, his mouth should be immediately closed with the merits of a fur tippet; should he persist, ask him whether the military cap or velvet bonnet is most likely to prevail during the winter; and depend upon it, he will not get in another word during the evening. I shall now proceed to *the ornamental* parts of speech, which I would recommend to the particular notice of those who wish to make themselves agreeable. *Expletives*, if well introduced, are among the greatest beauties of conversational eloquence. Those most generally in repute are apostrophes and imprecations; and they are sanctioned by the most genteel societies and classical authorities. Bless me! Devil take him! Good heavens! and Good gracious! are a few of the elementary and most simple ones; but a little observation will easily enable the learner to excel these, and a little practice to throw them in with a good grace. The above are merely a few, which ladies, and those who possess a degree of bashfulness (which is ever an enemy to excellence) usually employ; I have known a whole sentence of expletives introduced at a time, which adds astonishingly to the beauty of conversation. To quote these is needless, as they may be heard in any number, in walking along Prince's Street or the Bridges. Demosthenes and Cicero used imprecations at great length; and hence the superiority of their eloquence over all modern attempts in this way. There is another beauty which has been too much considered as the peculiar property of travellers, and which has given their conversation immense advantage over that of such as never roamed from home; I mean the free use of *the metaphor*. I am afraid the public cannot show cause why this privilege should not be extended; for my own part, I consider nothing so, "stale, flat, and unprofitable," as a mere detail of *facts;* this gives no opportunity for displaying genius; it shows no ingenuity; mere correctness is the strongest proof a person can give of mediocrity. Genius carries the rapt astonished hearer beyond the feeble bounds of probability; and if this can be done in the common intercourse of life, so much the more ingenuity is displayed. In reciting conversation, therefore, a person should consider not merely what has been said, but what *might have been* said; this was the plan pursued by Thucydides and Livy, and has given their histories so much celebrity; and I see no reason why people may not speak as well as write in the name of others. In all these little recitals, a person should introduce himself as frequently as possible. One is so apt to be overlooked in a large company, that this is absolutely necessary if he wishes for distinction. *Great* acquaintances, such as my friend Lord ———, or my brother the Major, are also great ornaments in a story. *Learned words*, too, are a vast embellishment; tall handsome words in a sentence, like grenadiers in a regiment, give it a fine appearance; it is of little consequence how they are introduced, if there. *Punning* is an astonishing beauty; the more distant the allusion, the more interesting; I would not give a straw for a pun which any body might understand. This beauty has one recommendation, *i. e.* it is easily attainable. The *innuendo* is a species of the above, and possesses the qualification of giving ladies an excuse for blushing, and gentlemen an opportunity of observing that the blush is not entirely an ornament of the old school, which they might otherwise be apt to imagine. As agitation prevents the vast mass of fluids which surround this globe from stagnation and putrefaction, so a little contradiction prevents conversation from suffering a similar fate; and if a gentleman can get out of temper easily, it adds greatly to the entertainment. A stamp with the foot, or a knock on the table, though it does not make so deep an impression as a rhetorical flourish on the countenance of your opponent, yet frequently produces an admirable effect. Indeed gesticulation is, as Dr. Blair has well expressed it, natural eloquence. I am sorry Mr. Thelwall has not favoured the public with his eloquent and erudite lectures upon ORGANIC ACTION, as these would have enabled me to be more full upon this part of the subject; and I shall merely suggest a few attitudes, as the last beauty of conversation, which may in part make up the loss to the public. In recitation, if you are near the person you address, the most elegant attitude certainly is, to stare in his face; though sometimes it is graceful to turn away your head, and speak to the door or the fire-place; catching hold at the same time of his button-hole; if not, the arms should be placed *akimbo*, and, to prevent uniformity, the neckcloth may be occasionally tucked up. In declamation, a slap upon the forehead, a twirl with a stick, the arms extended, a pocket handkerchief, are all requisites, and may be applied according to the nature of the subject. The ladies can lift up both hands very prettily, ay, and both eyes too.

If you speak to an inferior never deign to look at him; it is low, and he is a fool if he expects it; always in this case, throw your eyes, your head, and even your whole body, in a different direction; turning round on the heel, presenting your back, and speaking like Hotspur, "indifferently," are to be recommended. In talking to the ladies, be sure you put yourself in such an attitude as may best show the elegant symmetry of your limbs, the fitness of your dress, the ring on your finger and the neck-pin in your *Dicky*. By stretching your leg and complaining of rheumatism, an opportunity will be had of exhibiting the elegance of the net-work in the ancle of your silk hose. After these have been exhibited, you may look at your watch; by this means your *Cairngorum* seal will likely have its share of compliment. But there is one most important circumstance to be attended to all the while, and this is the change of the voice; it would be highly rude and brutish to address a delicate lady in the same rough common accents which are used in speaking to a he-creature; no; you must simper and lisp, and bring your voice as near as possible to the delicate key of the lady's tones.

The above are only a few of the many hints which might be suggested; nothing but an imperious sense of the duty I owe to the public could have forced me thus to venture upon this important topic; my hints indeed are but crude, while the subject is capable of the most fertile and varied illustration.

> But great perfections are like heaven,
> Too rich a present to be given;
> Nor are such master-strokes of beauty,
> To be perform'd without hard duty.

SOCIETY IN NORTH AMERICA.
(From a Moral and Political Sketch of the United States of North America, by Achille Murat.)

IF, in the United States, the government is established upon a principle altogether new and unknown, at least in its application—that of the sovereignty of the people, in the strictest sense of the word,—so also society and the relations of individuals towards each other are based on a footing not less new; namely, competition. There is no sort of aristocracy of birth; fortune gives no rights, but to the physical advantages it may purchase; but talent and merit see no bounds to their reasonable ambition. Every body in our republican system is rigorously classed according to his capacity. You are about to conclude we are St. Simonians; —no, my friend, do not mistake me. Can you suppose that I, a white man and free, am going to submit my reason to that of any of my equals? Do you think that I will go and ask some buffoon to class me, when I am sure of conquering by myself that station, whatever it may be, to which I am entitled in the scale of beings? Do you think that I will go and acknowledge the Pere Infinatin, or any other quack to whom he may delegate his functions? I, who am dependent on nobody, and free as the air I breathe? Quite the reverse: the St. Simonian system and the American system are the two extremes of the diameter of human thought. The one is based upon an absolute subjection, a slavery much stronger than has ever existed, since it extends even to the mind, and if we are to believe certain reports, perhaps slanderous, even over the most sacred affections; the other, on the contrary, is founded on the principle of the most absolute liberty: independence is its result. The one will protect me against all dangers, real or imaginary, and force me to be happy, in its own way, even against my will; the other launches me, young and hardy, upon the waves of life, to sport as I please, extricate myself from difficulties as I can, and be happy or perish in my own way; for it is very certain that without losing my identity I cannot be so in that of another. Competition,—that is the secret of the American system; every thing is to be won by competition: fortune, power, love, riches, all these objects of desire are attainable; it is for the most skilful to go in pursuit of them. Just as in the old fairy tales, those enchanted princesses are defended by dragons, vultures, roaring lions, but still more, by rivals who crowd the same path, and who will not be sparing of a kick to assist you in tumbling down. Fortunately, however, in our land of plenty, the princesses to conquer and deliver are sufficiently numerous to content all valiant knights, and even many of their squires; so that the combat is not so desperate as it might be supposed. There is room for every one at the banquet of life; and what is more, the table has no upper end, no seat distinguished by a canopy.

All men are born equal in rights and in chances of success; for if, on the one hand, fortune gives advantages to some; on the other, she withholds the spur of necessity, and thus greatly slackens their energy. All have equal chances of attaining every thing. The rich fool will not be less a fool, and cannot, but with difficulty, maintain his fortune against the attempts of the man of parts impelled by necessity. The man once engaged in any career cannot stop an instant, nor relax in his exertions, without being immediately passed by young rivals whose very names were unknown the day before. This continual competition, this perpetual struggle of all against all, maintains a society in a state of activity which has the happiest results. Whatever may be the pursuit followed, every one is wholly dependent upon public opinion. This it is which reigns despotically, and "classes" each according to his works, with strict disinterestedness and unerring judgment. But, in order that public opinion may be duly enlightened, the utmost publicity is necessary; therefore nothing is neglected in the United States to effect that object in every possible manner. The press is entirely free. The publication of newspapers and their circulation, so far from being shackled by duties, securities, and stamps, or being restricted by the post, is encouraged as much as possible. Consequently newspapers multiply. Every town or village has at least one; and every shade of opinion, however slight, is sure of having its interpreter. Every thing is known, every thing is discussed, every thing is explained, and the sole means in the United States of not being discovered is to have no mystery. Guided by a light so sure, the people form their judgments, and are never deceived in their verdict.

I am not inclined here to defend the American periodical press. There are hardly four or five good papers in the crowd; the rest copy these, and shew very little delicacy in the means of which they avail themselves to support their opinions. But their virulence acts as an antidote to itself; and besides, a personality never remains without an answer, so that the deplorable spirit which animates them, produces no effect upon ears accustomed to hear the reproaches put forth by opposite parties. At the time of the contested election between Adams and Jackson, the newspapers of the two parties assumed so virulent a tone, and published so many calumnies, that it was truly disgusting to look into them. Whoever believed them, might have sincerely commiserated the fate of the nation, obliged to choose between two such scoundrels as the candidates were respectively represented to be by journals of the opposite parties. It is proper to be just, however; the great difficulty met with in the United States, in the elections, is how to select among many persons of equal merit. The nation advances calmly in prosperity, without any of those concussions which give occasion to the display of talents of a superior order. It certainly possesses people of the first merit, and abundance of them, but it is almost impossible for them, in the present state of peace and tranquillity, to attain their proper elevation, above the rank of merit immediately inferior to them. The less, therefore, the difference is between two candidates, the more must it be exaggerated by the papers of their respective parties, who in that perform the office of repeating circles. The difference is so small that it would pass unperceived, if it was not multiplied some thousands of times.

One of the most remarkable effects of this publicity is the interest which every one takes in the politics of the day; an interest which produces a sameness in conversation, in whatever society you may happen to fall. The hackney-coachman talking at the corner of the streets with a porter; the lawyer, the planter, the preacher, dining together with a rich tradesman, all speak of the same thing. The next election, the measure now being proposed, whether in Congress or in the state legislature, or at the last lawsuit which attracted the crowd, form the subject of conversation; it is treated differently in the different circles, but still it is always the same subject; and it is equally well understood by all classes, for the newspapers are read by every body.

It is easy to see that when there reigns in a country such an unanimity of opinions, such a similarity of intellectual tastes and occupations, the differences among the classes which compose society are entirely chimerical. I do not mean to say that there are not in the United States several circles of society, that cannot be otherwise in any polished society; but I do mean to say, that the limits which divide them are so delicate, that they melt into each other; and that, if there are many circles, there are neither casts nor ranks.

The American is mild, polite, but proud, as it befits a freeman to be; he does not pretend to any superiority, but he will in no respect submit to be treated as an inferior. Every one considers that he carries on a trade, that he may live; and far from coveting idleness, he despises it, he thinks all honest trades equal in dignity; although requiring, as they do, different degrees of talent, he sees no injustice in their being unequally recompensed. The servant of a lawyer or a physician, for instance, perceives no material difference between himself and his employer, (for the word master is only used by people of colour.) One brushes clothes, the other pleads causes, or feels pulses, or preaches, or judges, or makes laws, or governs—and all for money. There is not so much difference; each tries to do his duty in the best way he can. Thus the domestic will be very attentive and submissive. Whenever his situation no longer suits him, he will leave his master; and in no case will he suffer on his part either insult or violence. Let him fall ill, or have a lawsuit, and he will give his custom to his master, pay him like any body else, and consider himself *quoad*, as having changed characters with him.

This spirit of independence forms the grand distinctive character between the English and American manners; for outwardly and physically they are much alike. If, for example, you go into what those who compose it call the first society of New York, this circle is composed of tradesmen newly arrived at the summit of Fortune's wheel, where it is very doubtful if they long remain. They take advantage of their fleeting days of prosperity to show off as much luxury and folly as their situation will permit them. All who have made a voyage to Europe, try to ape the exclusive manners of which they have been the victims on the other side of the Atlantic; affect to value every thing foreign, and consider America as a barbarous country, where nothing elegant has ever been invented,—not even the gallopade and gigot sleeves. The first European swindler, who takes the trouble to pass himself off for a Duke or a Marquis, is sure to carry away all their suffrages, until it pleases him to join thereto their purses. Men of this stamp will pretend not to trouble themselves about politics, or at least not to talk about them; for it is a subject so vulgar and so unfashionable . . . in London! They try to imitate the perfect nullity of conversation in that city, and in general, assisted by their natural resources, they succeed pretty well.

But apart from this society is that formed by the merchants, shipowners, lawyers, physicians, and magistrates of the city. This is truly American; they do not amuse themselves by apeing European manners; among them, conversation is solid and instructive, and turns upon business and the politics of the day. Society in New York is perhaps more tinged with European manners than in other of the great towns in the United States; and that is very natural, if we consider the immense number of foreigners who reside there. It is the city which has most theatres, (for it has no less than five,) and it has had even an opera and a *corps de ballet*. There is more dissipation and more foolish expenses in it than in any other place. The principal street, the Broadway, gives a striking impression of America to the European on his landing. After Regent Street, in London, it is the finest street I know. The wide pavements, with their elegant shops, are, at certain hours of the day, crowded with all the fashion of the place. All the pretty women go there to take a turn, and there the fine gentlemen are eager to meet them. The fareigner reading his newspaper, in the large parlour of the city hotel, sees all the *beau monde* defile before him.

Society in Philadelphia is much more quiet: the Quakers are a happy people, who give a look of repose to all the city. Here there is no noise as in New York; the carriages are much fewer; the streets being so clean there is no occasion for them. All the streets are alike; none, therefore, serves as a general promenade like the Broadway of New York. Chestnut Street, however, is the best built, and there the fashionable people come to take their lounge. The library of Messrs. Carey and Lea is the place where you must take your station towards noon, to see this street in all its lustre. The society of Philadelphia is much more enlightened than that of New York; the professors of the university give the tone, which communicates to it, perhaps, a slight degree, almost imperceptible, however, of pedantry. The winter parties are meetings of learned and literary people, including also citizens in any way distinguished: they are always open to foreigners, properly introduced. Ladies are never present. The meetings are held on appointed days at the houses of different persons in rotation: science, literature, the fine arts, and politics form the subjects of conversation, and in general much intelligence and urbanity are displayed. They are always terminated by a supper, and are calculated to give foreigners a high idea of the intellectual resources of that city.

But it is to Charleston that he should go to enjoy American society in all its luxury. There the various circles, composed of planters, lawyers, and physicians, form the most agreeable society I have ever known. The manners of the south have a perfect elegance; the mind is highly cultivated; and conversation turns upon an infinite variety of subjects with spirit, grace, and facility. The affectation of frivolity, or of foreign manners, is as completely banished as pedantry and religious hypocrisy; everything is intellectual, moral, and rational. Charleston is the ordinary residence of many of the most distinguished statesmen of the Union, who are always willing to explain their views to their fellow-citizens. Alas! why can I not recall the delightful hours I have passed in that society, without being reminded of the loss of that friend in whose hospitable residence I first knew it. He is no more; and Charleston has lost, for me, one of its greatest attractions.

The society of Richmond greatly resembles that of Charleston, and is as agreeable. In Virginia, good society is spread more generally over the whole surface of the State than it is anywhere else, owing to the want of a large capital, which always serves to attract it, and gives the tone exclusively. Virginian hospitality is proverbial, and with great justice.

New Orleans forms a perfect contrast to all the other cities: here there is no intellectual conversation, no instruction; there are but three booksellers in a city of sixty thousand souls, and yet even their warehouses are composed of the refuse of the filthiest productions of French literature. But if there is no conversation, there are eating, playing, dancing, and making love in abundance. An institution peculiar to this city, are the quarteron balls, where the free women of colour are alone admitted to the honour of dancing with their lords the whites; for the men of colour are most strictly excluded from them. It is truly a magical spectacle to see some hundreds of women, all very pretty, and well dressed, and of every shade, from that of cream coffee, to the most delicate white, assembled in superb saloons, to display their mercenary charms. The most respectable people frequent these balls, which are quite public, and where everything invariably passes with the greatest decorum. The gaming-houses are also very numerous in New Orleans, and have ruined many of the young people of Kentucky come to pass their carnival in this Babylon of the west.

SHELL-FISH.

" In shelly armour wrapt, the lobsters seek
Safe shelter in some bay, or winding creek;
The rocky ebasms the dusky natives cleave,
Tenacious hold, nor will the dwelling leave."

If the wonderful productions we have just been contemplating, may be considered as part of the connecting link betwixt the vegetable and animal kingdoms, the lowest gradation of this species may be accounted that which unites the animal to the fossil class; but what a prodigious variety of these exist, from the humble Oyster, which vegetates in its shell, to the ponderous Tortoise that grazes the aquatic meadow, (a) or the wondrous Lobster that shoots with rapidity across the gulf. (b)

The distinguishing appendage of this class, and that from which they derive their name, is the hard crustaceous covering in which their bodies are enveloped, and how admirably fitted are they by this natural bulwark for that particular station in which providence has placed them; for how could such soft and tender bodies have been otherwise defended and protected from injury among the many rugged and uneven masses where their habitations are assigned, and how could they escape from their numerous enemies had they not the power of withdrawing and shutting themselves up, on the approach of danger, within their shelly covering. But, besides this, there are several things remarkable in each individual species of this order, which demonstrates the whole to be fitted in the best possible manner for their various situations, habits, and propensities, and to be the workmanship of the same Being, whose wisdom and goodness are so conspicuously displayed in his other works.

The Limpet, stationed as a sentinel on the top of the rock, and oft exposed to the mid-day's heat when the tide is out, as well as to the continual tossings and agitations of its waves when it is covered, is safely lodged in a little cone, impervious to the most penetrating rays of the sun, and so firmly cemented to the rock by means of the broad muscular surface he presents, that neither storm or tempest can prevail to loosen his grasp, or make him relinquish his firm hold. The Muscle is not provided by nature with such a strong and firm sheet-anchor, but she is taught to supply the defect by art, and to spin to herself cables, by which she can be moored in security to her favourite spot. (c) The Periwinkle does not attach itself so firmly as either of these, nor has she the means or the power to do so; but her stony habitation is almost proof against accident, and she can roll about in safety, hermetically sealed up under her scaly covering. The Cockle burrows deep in the sand or mud, and its edges are notched, in order to enable it to clasp more firmly together. The Nautilus, which can exist either as a diver or swimmer, and lives sometimes at the bottom, sometimes on the surface of the ocean, has a power of contracting and drawing itself into its shell when it has occasion to descend to the bottom, and of unfolding and expanding its oars and sails, when it has an inclination to sport on the surface. The Cutler, or Razor Fish, never creeps but penetrates perpendicularly into the sand; and how nicely is its long and slender shell formed for this purpose. The Crab is provided with claws and feet for scrambling about, but amongst such rugged precipices, and with so many enemies to encounter, it must often be at the expense of a limb; and, lo! it is endowed with the singular property of shaking off and reproducing a new one at pleasure. (d) The Lobster is admirably formed for either running or swimming, and can bound with such a spring to her hole in the rock when frightened, that she enters it with velocity through an opening barely sufficient, to appearance, for her body to pass;—and the Pholas, though not furnished with an instrument apparently calculated for boring and scooping out stones, is endowed with such a fund of patient perseverance, that it is enabled to penetrate into these callous substances by the application of a fleshy member, resembling a tongue. (e)

The instinctive sagacity of the crustaceous tribe also claims our attention. We have already remarked, that the little Nautilus is furnished with an apparatus for either diving or swimming. But who taught the Nautilus to sail? and yet, without the instinctive knowledge how to make use of them, of what use would be either her sails or oars; these, however, are not given her in vain, for she evinces a knowledge in the art of navigation which is supposed to have been copied by some of the early mariners; and the example she affords has been held out by the poet as still deserving imitation:—

" Learn of the little Nautilus to sail,
Spread the thin oar, and catch the driving gale." (f)

Sea Tortoises, without any teacher but nature, are instinctively taught to lay their eggs on the sea-shore, and cover them with sand; and no sooner are the young hatched and fitted for their journey, than they leave the place of their nativity, and run towards that element which providence has destined for their abode; so that the poet may well say:—

" Reason progressive—instinct is complete;
Swift instinct leaps—slow reason feebly climbs.
Brutes soon their zenith reach; their little all
Flows in at once; in ages they no more
Could know, or do, or covet, or enjoy."

When the young Lobsters leave the parent, they betake themselves to hiding-places in the smallest clifts of the rocks; but no sooner do they find themselves incrusted with a firm shell, than they sally out in quest of plunder. When the time of moulting, or changing the shell draws on, this animal again betakes itself to a retired situation, where it remains in security during its defenceless state; (g) no sooner, however, does it find itself covered with its new suit of armour, than it appears again on the stage, lively and active as before. The common Crabs herd together in distinct tribes, and keep their separate haunts. (h) The Soldier Crab is not provided by nature with a shell attached to his body, but she has inspired him with instinctive sagacity to take up his abode in the first empty one he can lay hold of, suitable to his purpose, and to change it for another when it grows incommodious; (i) and the Land Crabs of the West Indies, (which also may be counted among the natives of the deep) are represented as living in a kind of orderly society, and regularly once a-year marching down from the mountains to the sea, in spite of every intervening obstacle, in order to deposit their spawn; and after the little creatures are hatched under the sand, they also are observed at regularly quitting the shore in crowds, and slowly travelling up towards the mountains. (k)

When the Tellina has occasion to move, she puts herself into a certain position, which occasions her to spring out with considerable force to a distance. When the SeaHop finds herself deserted by the tide, it jerks itself forward by opening and shutting its shell in a singular manner! When the Razor Shell-fish, finds itself deceived by the fisherman, when he decoys it from its subterraneous habitation by a sprinkling of salt, and has time to retreat, no such attempt will succeed a second time! When part of the legs of the Sea Hedge-hog are at work carrying him forward, the horns that are nearest in that direction are busily employed in making soundings or feeling the way. The Muscle, when she has commenced spinning her cable, will make trial of a thread by drawing it out strongly towards her, before she proceeds to stretch out a second! The Limpet, when she has occasion to unmoor, finds means to disengage herself without any great effort, and to move from her place by the same muscle by which she adhered so firmly to her anchorage. Even oysters are said not to be destitute of the power and the instinctive sagacity to turn themselves round when thrown irregularly into a vessel of water, so that the concave shells may remain downmost, in order to retain their favourite liquor.

USES OF SHELL-FISH.

From the number of animals which prey upon insects, it was inferred, that the principal object the Creator had in view in the formation of these, was the subsistence of many of the larger orders of creatures; so, from the numerous herds of shell-fish, which (in a great degree resemble insects) and everywhere abound among the beds of the ocean, and the extraordinary digestive faculties of the many tribes, we have reason to conclude, that the former were principally intended and brought into existence for food to the latter. (l) I shall, however, mention a few particulars in which the crustaceous tribes may also be said to be otherwise serviceable.

The Hawk's-bill Turtle is valued on account of its shell, from whence our most beautiful snuff-boxes and other trinkets are said to be formed. (m) The Green Turtle, as a wholesome and highly delicious food, has become such a valuable article in commerce, that our West India vessels are now generally fitted up with conveniencies for importing them alive. The Land Crab (which is also a native of the deep) is said to be regarded as a delicacy in Jamaica; and it is even asserted, that the slaves are often entirely fed upon them. Among the shell-fish on the Waterford coast, the Murex, which gave the Tyrian purple, is said to exist. I need not mention of what estimation the Lobster, the Crab, and other shell-fish are held among ourselves, and the delicacy of flavour which makes the Oyster prized as an article of food. (n) In the Oyster also is found that beautiful substance called Mother of Pearl.

(a) The great Mediterranean Turtle is the largest of any known species. One of these was caught in 1729, at the mouth of the Loire, said to be nearly eight feet in length, and two over!

(b) THE WONDROUS LOBSTER.—The lobster, indeed, may be well styled wondrous. According to Sturm, it is one of the most extraordinary creatures that exists. An animal, (observes this writer,) whose skin is a shell, and which it casts off every year, to clothe itself with new armour. An animal, whose flesh is in its tail and legs, and whose hair is in the inside of its breast; whose stomach is in its head; and which is changed every year for a new one, and which new one begins by consuming the old. An animal which carries its eggs within its body, till they become fruitful and then carries them outwardly under its tail. An animal which can throw off its legs when they become troublesome, and can replace them with others; and lastly, an animal whose eyes are placed in moveable horns. So singular a creature will long remain a mystery to the human mind. It affords new subject, however, to acknowledge and adore the power and wisdom of the Creator.

(c) The sea has its spinners as well as the land; and, if the common muscles may be compared to the caterpillers, the Pinnæ Marinæ, which are a larger species, may be likened to the spiders.

(d) Nature has given this singular power to these creatures for the preservation of their lives, in their frequent quarrels. In these one crab lays hold of the claw of another, and crushes it so, that it would bleed to death, had it not the power of giving up the limb in the strange manner described by naturalists. If one of the outer joints of a small leg be bruised, and the creature be laid on its back, it shews uneasiness at first, by moving it about, afterwards it holds it quite still, in a direct and natural position, without touching any part of the body, or of the other legs with it. Then, on a sudden, with a gentle crack, the wounded part of the leg drops off; the effect will be the same with the great leg, only it is thrown off with greater violence. Having got clear of the injured part, a mucus now overspreads the wound, which presently stops the bleeding; and a small leg is by degrees produced, which gradually attains the size of the former.

Lobsters have also the power of reproducing an injured leg; and this accounts for them being so often found with limbs of unequal sizes—the small leg must be a new one, which has not attained its full growth.

(e) With this soft and yielding instrument, the indefatigable and persevering Pholas perforates marble and the hardest stones; and when small and naked, it has effected an entrance; it then enjoys a life of security and ease, existing upon sea water that enters at the aperture, and increasing its habitation as it increases in size.

(f) The natural sagacity of the Nautilus, in the use of his instruments of motion, is thus beautifully delineated by the descriptive pen of Hervey. "The dexterous inhabitant (whose shell forms a natural boat) unfurls a membrane to the wind, which serves him instead of a sail. He extends also a couple of arms, with which, as with two slender oars, he rows himself along. When he is disposed to dive, he strikes sail; and without any apprehension of being drowned, sinks to the bottom. When the weather is calm, and he has an inclination to see the world, to take his pleasure, he mounts to the surface; and, self-taught in the art of navigation, performs his voyage without either chart or compass; is himself the vessel, the rigging, and the pilot."

When the sea is calm, numbers of these animals are said to be seen sailing on its surface; but at the approach of a storm, they fold in their legs, and swallowing as much water as will enable them to sink, they plunge to the bottom, where they no doubt remain in a place of security during the raging of the tempest, and when they wish to rise, they void this abundant water, and so decreasing their specific gravity, quickly ascend to the top, where, by means of their tails answering the purpose of helms, they can steer themselves about in any direction.

(g) After losing the shell, (which both crabs and lobsters do annually,) and before a new one is formed, the animal is in a very naked and defenceless state, exposed to the dog-fish, and a multitude of other depredators. In this situation they do not, however, long continue; for the new covering is formed, and completely hardened, in little more than forty-eight hours.

(h) This has been tried by marking a crab, carrying it two or three miles, and leaving it among other crabs. The crab has afterwards found its way home, and been caught in its old abode.

(i) When it has overgrown, or otherwise has occasion to change the shell, the little soldier is seen busily parading the shore, but still dragging its old habitation along, unwilling to part with one, until it has found another shell more convenient for its purpose. It is seen stopping at one shell, turning it, then going on to another, looking at it a while, then slipping its tail from the old habitation to try on the new. This is sometimes found to be more inconvenient, in which case, it quickly returns to its old shell, and goes in quest of another more roomy and commodious. But it is not till after many trials and frequent combats, that the soldier sometimes finds himself completely equipped; for there are frequent contests betwixt two of this species, for some well-looking and commodious shell; and it is from this circumstance, perhaps, the soldier crab derives its name. When two of them meet with the same object, each strives to take possession; they strike with their claws; they bite each other till the weakest is obliged to yield. It is then the victor takes possession, and parades in his new conquest, backwards and forwards upon the strand before his envious antagonist.

(k) These creatures commence their expedition in the months of April and May. At that time the whole ground is covered with this numerous band of adventurers. The sea is the place of their destination, and to that they direct their march. No geometrician could send them by a shorter course. They never turn aside to the right or to the left, if they can possibly avoid it, whatever obstacles intervene. If they meet with a house, they will attempt to scale the walls, in order to keep their ranks, and if the country be intersected by rivers, they wind along the course of the stream. They are commonly divided into three battalions, of which the first consists of the strongest and boldest males, that, like pioneers, march forward to clear the route, and face the greatest dangers. They are often obliged to halt for want of rain. The main body is composed of females, which never leave the mountains till the rain is set in, and then descend in regular order, in columns of fifty paces broad, and three miles deep, and so close, that they almost cover the ground. Three or four days after this, the rear-guard follows, a straggling and undisciplined tribe, consisting of males and females; but neither so robust, nor so numerous as the former. The night is their chief time of proceeding, but if it rains by day, they do not fail to profit by the occasion. When they are terrified, they march back in a disorderly manner, holding up their nippers, with which they sometimes tear off a piece of the flesh of an assailant, and leave the weapon where they inflicted the wound. They even try to intimidate their enemies, by clattering their nippers together, which, considering their number, must have a powerful effect. When they have arrived at the shore, which sometimes takes them three months, they prepare to cast their spawn, by eagerly going to the edge of the water, and letting it wash several times over their bodies. At the expiration of some days, spent on the land, after this washing, they again seek the shore, and shaking off the spawn into the water, leave it there. The sea, to a great distance is black with the eggs, and shoals of hungry fish attend, and devour a considerable quantity of them; those that escape are hatched under the sand; and soon after millions at a time of these little crabs, are seen quitting the shore, and making their way slowly to the mountains.

The Bahama, and other American islands, produce land crabs in great abundance, where they burrow in pairs in the earth.

(l) The digestive faculties of fishes are so extraordinary, that their stomachs are said to have a power of softening the most callous shells.

(m) Tortoise-shell is formed into ornamental articles, by first steeping it in boiling water, till it has acquired a proper softness, and immediately afterwards committed to the pressure of a strong metallic mould of the form required; and when it is necessary to join the pieces, so as to form a large extent, the edges of the pieces are first scraped, or thinned, and being laid over each other during their heated state, are committed to a strong press, by which means they are effectually joined, or agglutinated. These are the methods also, by which the various ornaments of gold, silver, &c., are fixed to tortoise-shell.

(n) A species, called Rock Oysters, are frequently seen as large as a plate; and those which are caught on the coast of Coromandel, are said to be of so great a size, that one of them will serve several men for a meal; but they have not so delicate a flavour as those of the smaller kind.

INTERESTING REFLECTION.—We do not see nature from merely looking at it. We fancy that we see the whole of any object that is before us, because we know no more of it than we see. The rest escapes us, as a matter of course; and we easily conclude, that the idea in our minds, and the image in nature, are one and the same. But in fact we only see a very small part of nature, and make an imperfect abstraction of the infinite number of particulars which are always to be found in it, as well as we can. Some do this with more or less accuracy than others, according to habit or natural genius. A painter, for instance, who has been working on a face for several days, still finds out something new in it which he did not notice before, and which he endeavours to give, in order to make his copy more perfect, which shews how little an ordinary and unpractised eye can be supposed to comprehend the whole at a single glance. A young artist, when he first begins to study from nature, soon makes an end of his sketch, because he sees only a general outline, and certain gross distinctions and masses. As he proceeds, a new field opens to him,—differences crowd upon differences; and as his perceptions grow more refined, he could employ whole days in working upon a single part, without satisfying himself at last. No painter, after a life devoted to the art, and the greatest care and length of time given to a single study of a head, or other object, ever succeeded in it to his wish, or did not leave something to be done. The greatest artists that have ever appeared are those who have been able to embody some one view or aspect of nature, and no more. Thus Titian was famous for colouring; Raphael for drawing; Correggio for the gradations; Rembrandt for the extremes of light and shade. The combined genius and powers of observation of all the great artists in the world would not be sufficient to convey the whole of what is contained in any one object in nature; and yet the most vulgar spectator thinks he sees the whole of what is before him, at once, and without any trouble at all.—*Hazlitt.*

ON A MOTHER'S TOMB-STONE, IN THE BURIAL GROUND OF ST. LOUIS, PARIS.

MOTHER—sweet mother,—thou can'st never know
   That yearly, thus, I deck thy mossy bed
With the first roses of the Spring that blow,
   And tears of fond affection shed.

Mother—sweet mother,—though I knew thee not,
   I feel that one I love is buried here;
And though this grave by others is forgot,
   To me it shall through life be dear—most dear.

Ah! who that gazes on the lights of life—
   Man in his might, and woman in her bloom—
Can think that, after some brief years of strife,
   We sink for ever in the silent tomb.

Shall fears of senseless slumber then enthral
   The soul, when death dissolves the form we see—
O never, never,—for our spirits shall
   Burst then their bonds, and from earth's follies flee.

THE DAISY.

NOT worlds on worlds, in phalanx deep,
   Need we to prove a God is here;
The Daisy, fresh from Winter's sleep,
   Tells of his hand in lines as clear.

For who but he who arch'd the skies,
   And pours the Day-spring's living flood
Wondrous alike in all he tries,
   Could rear the Daisy's purple bud?

Mould its green cup, its wiry stem;
   Its fringed border nicely spin;
And cut the gold-embossed gem
   That, set in silver, gleams within?—

And fling it unrestrain'd and free,
   O'er hill and dale and desert sod,
That man, where'er he walks, may see
   In every step, the stamp of God.
                 Dr. Mason Good.

USEFUL NOTICES.

GARDENING.—THE CISALPINE STRAWBERRY.—Cobbett, speaking of this strawberry says:—This strawberry, unlike all others that I ever heard of, produces its like from the seed; is raised with the greatest facility, bears more abundantly, and keeps bearing until the hard frosts come. The seeds are so small, that a little pinch of them, between the finger and the thumb, is sufficient for a very large garden; and the method of raising the plant is this; about the first week of February, or it may be a little later; fill with fine earth, to within about an inch of the top, a flower-pot from 12 or 18 inches over; take the little pinch of seed and scatter it very thinly over the top of the earth; then put some very fine earth over the seed a quarter of an inch thick, or rather less. Set the pot in a green-house, or in the window of any room where the sun comes, and give water very carefully and very gently, as occasion may require. When the warm weather comes, the pot should be set out of doors, in a warm place, where there is no heavy rain; and should be taken in at night, if there be any fear of frost. Towards the end of April, the pot may be set out of doors altogether; and small as the plants of it shall be, they will be fit to be planted out into the open ground by the middle, or towards the latter end of May. Then dig a piece of ground deep, and make it extremely fine upon the top, and put out the little plants in rows two feet apart, and two feet apart in the row; for, though not bigger than a thread, each plant will multiply itself into a considerable tuft before the middle of July; and then they will begin to bear, and will keep on bearing as long as the hard frosts keep away. The very runners which proceed from those plants will take root, blow, and have ripe fruit, during the first Autumn. When the bearing is over, cut off all the runners, clear the ground close up to the tufts, and let the tufts remain to bear another year, when their produce is prodigious. But then you must grub them up; for they so multiply their offsets, and cover the ground with their roots, that they almost cease to bear if they remain longer. So that you must have a new plantation from seed every year; and the seed you may sow yourself, by squeezing the pulp of dead-ripe strawberries in water, which sends the seed to the bottom of the water, you skim off the pulp, and drain away the water, then turn the seed out in the sun to dry, and then put it up and preserve it for sowing in the winter. There is a red sort and a white sort, which you may keep separate, or sow them and plant them promiscuously.—*Cobbett's Register.*

THE CHINESE METHOD OF PROPAGATING FRUIT-TREES BY ABSCISSION.—The Chinese, instead of raising fruit-trees from seeds or from grafts, as is the custom in Europe, have adopted the following method of increasing them. They select a tree of that species which they wish to propagate, and fix upon such a branch as will least injure or disfigure the tree by its removal. Round the branch, and as near as they can conveniently to its junction with the trunk, they wind a rope, made of straw, besmeared with cow-dung, until a ball is formed five or six times the diameter of the branch. This is intended as a bed, into which the young ones may shoot. Having performed this part of the operation, they immediately, under the ball, divide the bark down to the wood, for nearly two-thirds of the circumference of the branch. A cocoa-nut-shell, or small pot, is then hung over the ball, with a hole in its bottom, so small that, water put in, it will only fall in drops; by this the rope is continually kept moist. During three succeeding weeks, nothing further is required, except to supply the vessel with water. At the expiration of that period, one-third of the remaining bark is cut off, and the former incision is carried considerably deeper into the wood, as by this time it is expected that some roots have struck into the rope, and are giving their assistance in support of the branch. After a similar period the operation is repeated, and in about two months from the commencement of the process, the roots may generally be seen intersecting each other on the surface of the ball; which is a sign that they are sufficiently advanced to admit of the separation of the branch from the tree. This is best done by sawing it off at the incision; care must be taken that the rope, which, by this time is nearly rotten, is not shaken off by the motion. The branch is then planted as a young tree. It appears probable that to succeed with this operation in Europe, a longer period would be necessary, vegetation being much slower in Europe than in India, where I made most of my experiments. I am, however, of opinion, from some trials which I have lately made on cherry-trees, that an additional month would be adequate to make up for the difference of climate. The advantages to be derived from this method are, that a further growth of three or four years is sufficient, when the branches are of a considerable size, to bring them on their full bearing state, whereas, even in India, eight or ten years are necessary with most kinds of fruit-trees, if raised from the seed. When I was at Prince of Wales's Island, I had an opportunity of seeing this proved by experiment. Some orange trees had been raised by a gentleman, from seed sown in 1786, which had not borne fruit in 1795, while branches taken off in the Chinese mode in 1791, had produced two plentiful crops. Whether forest trees may be propagated in Europe, in the same manner, I have not had sufficient experience to determine. I have observed that the roots from a branch under the process of abscission, were uniformly much longer in shooting into the rope, when the tree was in leaf, than the contrary; hence the spring season seems the most proper for performing this operation.—*Horticultural Register.*

HINTS TO HOUSEWIVES.—Vessels intended to contain a liquid at a high temperature, and keep that liquid as long as possible at the highest temperature, should be constructed of materials which are the worst radiators of heat. Thus, tea-urns and tea-pots are best adapted for their purpose when constructed of polished metal, and worst when constructed of black porcelain. A black porcelain tea-pot is the worst conceivable material for that vessel; for both its material and colour are good radiators of heat, and the liquid contained in it cools with all possible rapidity. On the other hand, a bright metal tea-pot is adapted for the purpose, because it is the worst radiator of heat, and therefore cools as slowly as possible. A polished silver or brass tea-urn is better adapted to retain the heat of the water than one of a dull brown colour, such as is commonly used. A tin tea-kettle retains the heat of the water boiled in it more effectually, if it be kept clean and polished, than if it be allowed to collect the smoke and soot, to which it is exposed from the action of the fire. When coated with this, its surface becomes rough and black, and is a powerful radiator of heat. A set of polished fire-irons may remain for a long time in front of a hot fire, without receiving from it any increase of temperature beyond that of the chamber, because the heat radiated by the fire is all reflected by the polished surface of the irons, and none of it is absorbed; but, if a set of rough unpolished irons were similarly placed, they would become speedily hot, so that they could not be used without inconvenience. The polish of the fire-irons is, therefore, not merely a matter of ornament, but of use and convenience. The rough, unpolished poker, sometimes used in a kitchen, becomes speedily so hot that it cannot be held without pain. A close stove, intended to warm an apartment, should not have a polished surface, for in that case it is one of the worst radiators of heat, and nothing could be contrived more unfit for the purpose to which it is applied. On the other hand, a rough unpolished surface of cast-iron, is favourable to radiation, and a fire in such a stove will always produce a most powerful effect.

WOMEN, says Defoe, in my observation of them, have little or no difference, but as they are or are not distinguished by education. Tempers, indeed, may in some degree influence them, but the main distinguishing part is their breeding. The whole sex are generally quick and sharp: you rarely see them lumpish and heavy when they are children, as boys will often be. If a woman be well-bred, and taught the proper management of her natural wit, she proves generally very sensible and retentive; and a woman of sense and manners is the finest and most delicate part of God's creation.

THE STORY TELLER.

THE PASIEKA; OR, BEE FARM.
(Concluded from our last.)

MEANWHILE a scene of very different import was passing in the farm. Instead of fording the brook where his girl and boy were watching for him, while the light-hearted Ludwyk busied himself in snaring cray-fish, as a tribute to the well-known predilections of Aunt Anulka, Jakob had taken the path to Zwieta which led him longest through his thriving pastures. Even while his daughter wept beneath the lime tree of the bleaching-ground, he dismounted from his horse at the gate;—and, surprising his good housewife in the busiest of her labours, clasped her heartily in his arms and saluted her on either cheek.

"I need not ask if all be well," cried he, clasping his worthy Jakubowa by the hand. "Those happy looks are as good as a gazette of the doings of Zwieta. I read them at a glance. My boy and girls are well,—my sister is well;—the knaves are diligent,—the crops thriving,—the bees prospering,—and my furmenty brewing on the stove."

"All, all, and more!" cried the comely Jakubowa, flinging aside her apron of service, and smoothing back her flaxen tresses, while she smiled archly into her husband's face. "We have a stranger among us, Jakob; a likely youth, who at our first meeting won to my very heart to welcome him to the farm, by slaying the largest wood-snake ever seen at Zwieta, (its skin hangs in the granary!) upon which the disobedient urchin Janek had incautiously set his foot!"

"That was a thing of no good omen!" said the farmer, gravely. "But how call you the youth,—and whence comes he,—and what does he in Samogitia?"

"He is named Ludwyk," replied Jakubowa, smiling still more archly than before; "and unless I am much mistaken we shall one day have to call him—son-in-law!"

"Aha!" cried Jakob, still more gravely. "I hope that notion has not gained ground in the family?" Dzidzilia is a mere child; and unfit to go forth from her mother's eye."

"And what was her mother, think you, when she went forth from the roof of her parents, to become wife to Jakob Bremglicz? A year and four months younger,—if there be truth in the world!"

"Nevertheless, my Josefa displayed such early sageness and discretion."

"Not more so than our own good girl!"

"I then, at least, evinced such steady prudence, and skill of culture-craft, and——"

"Not more so, I warrant him, than our gallant Ludwyk!"

"Well,—well,—give not too rapid credence to the merits of a stranger. Every new Soloducha kettle has a gloss of its own that wears off after nearer service. We must know more of a lad than that he can bruise the head of a wood-snake, ere we give him our daughter. And now, my woman, a cup of Anulka's balmy Wisniak, for I thirst after my sultry ride; and must take a passing peep at the Pszczólarnia, stable and granary, pen, sty, and cote, ere we settle down for our evening love-meal, to hear and say all that has been said and done since last we parted."

And having summoned the kind sister to bear her share in the joy of his return, and taking from her hands a sparkling goblet of Wisniak, or wild-cherry mead, perfuming the chamber like the blossoms of the heliotrope, Jakob made his way to the office to confer with Grzegorz, touching heifers added to his herds, and lambs sold from his flocks, and yeanling calves, and tenders from the Jewish woolstaplers of Rosienie for the fleeces of his last shearing. But although a man of humane and patient nature, it moved him almost to irritation that every reply elicited by his interrogations was connected remotely or immediately with the name of the young stranger. Master Ludwyk had counselled this,—Master Ludwyk had counselled that; and above all, Master Ludwyk had delivered certain criticisms upon the ill-economy of the Pasieka,—poor Jakob's pet department in his farm of Zwieta.

"I was about to ask the good master's permission," insinuated Grzegorz, with whom Ludwyk was a first favourite and unimpugnable authority,—"to root away the unprofitable hedge of roses with which the Bee Garden is fenced; and substitute in its stead an espalier of gooseberry bushes. There is stock of gooseberry plants to be begged or bought at the physic garden of Rosienie; and Master Ludwyk protests that a damask rose, however sweet of perfume, holds its honey too deeply guarded from the seeking of the bees; —whereas—'tis plain as the hand of my body,—that the flower of the gooseberry,—the earliest of the spring, yields——"

"Boh!—Away with these fancies of bookmakers!" cried the farmer. "Have I coined money, as it were, for twenty years past from my Pszczolarnia, to be lessoned in my old age by a meddling, ignorant boy? This Ludwyk may be a clever lad; but let him exercise his wits elsewhere than in the homestead of Zwieta!"

A cloud upon the brow of Jakob was a thing as transitory as the snow-flake which for a moment chills the bright and leaping waters of some gladsome stream. The sound of the farm, where all was in neatest trim and happiest progress, restored him to his usual complacency. And when he had been seated for ten minutes on his favourite bench beside the bee-house, and made his usual signals, and found his winged favourites slowly recognising their master, deserting the beds of centaury, savoury, and lemon-thyme, to settle upon the sleeve of his zupan, there was not in the whole province of Samogitia a more contented man than Bremglicz, the bee-farmer. Even when, on his return to the farm, Janek and Benisia, clinging to his knees, reproached him amid all their kisses for having abandoned the ford-road, and he beheld the tall, easy, smiling stranger who had borne them company standing familiarly by his hearthstone, his anger was so far from regaining ascendency in his mind, that he extended both hands towards the invader of the Pasieka, with the habitual hospitality of a Zmujdzin. They looked steadily each in the other's face, for a minute's space, and the recognisance was mutually satisfactory. The fine, open, guileless, manly face of the farmer bespoke the confidence of his guest; the noble brow, and finely expressive mouth of the stranger overthrew all the growing prejudices of Jakob Bremglicz.

"Where is my girl,—and where my good Maryeta," cried he, relinquishing the young man's hand, as his family circle gathered busily around them. But though Ludwyk would fain have reiterated the inquiry of—"Where is my Dzidzilia?"—he was discreet enough to draw aside, that he might not overhear the reply of the partial mother, whose frank —————, on the matter of his unacknowledged affection for her daughter, had already brought him, more than once, to shame.

"The girl hangs back!" whispered Jakubowa, laying her soft round hand on her husband's shoulder, "fearing, perhaps, that the heightened bloom upon her cheek and the brightened glance within her eyes would reveal her secret to her father."

But at that moment the door of the inner chamber opened; and Dzidzilia, affecting to uphold the tottering steps of the nurse, but in reality leaning heavily on the old woman for support, advanced towards her father.

"How is this?" whispered Jakob drawing his wife aside. "Talk you of colour heightened, or of glances brightened?—I see nothing but a forced and ghastly smile upon her sweet face; and her braided hair, howbeit, as lint-white as your own, shows dark beside the whiteness of her cheeks!"

"Mere maiden fear!" replied Jakubowa, too happy and too innocent for idle apprehensions of evil. "The girl is fearful that the father she loves may think lightly of the lover she loves. Tut,—Jakob—man!—is it so long since you were yourself a suitor, that you forget the flitting of these summer clouds?—Tut, Jakob! Pledge the poor lad in a draught of hydromel;—and you will bring a blush to the cheek of your child as bright and deep as ever you brought to the cheeks of her mother."

And tapping him fondly on the shoulder, the goodwife went forth to preside over the final seasoning of the furmenty, and aid sister Anulka in the serving and disposing of the festal supper-table.

The toils of the day were over. Every Kmiec of Zwiets, rejoicing in the return of his master, had appeared on the threshold of the door, to speak a heartful salutation, and win a word of kindness in return. The huge watch-dogs of the Pasieka were dozing by the kitchen-fire till the hour of human rest should render their vigilance availing. The ————— of the Bee Garden was at rest; and a heavy dew, stooping the downy leaves of the lavender, rosemary, and ————— bushes, refreshed the beds of thyme and basil for their mellifluous incense of the morrow. The casements of the chamber, wherein sat the family of Jakob Bramglicz at their innocent revels, were thrown open that the moon might smile in upon their sports, and the fragrance of the limes, honeysuckles, and herbs of the Bee Garden perfume their humble feast.

"And you have simply and surely brought us nought from Wilna?" cried little Janek, nestling closer to his father's chair; when, the bowl of furmenty and other substantial dishes being removed, a huge platter of wood strawberries, yellow-tinged and musky, was set upon the cloth of Zwiets-spun damask.

"Wait, boy,—wait patiently till the monthly waggon reaches Rosienie," cried his father; "and you shall see hornbooks, quittances, grammars, and what not; and a mighty rod withal, for Aunt Anulka to uphold their instructions."

"We know better, father,—we know better!" cried both children at once. "So do you ever mock us!—You have at this moment a travel-token for each of us in your pocket!"

And, after a moment's rallying with their curiosity, Jakob was persuaded to draw forth from his vest an etui of implements of housewifery, bearing on its silver lid the initials of his wife;—a newly published compendium of domestic economy, a tribute for Anulka; a chaplet of Swedish coral, from the blessed shrine of Czenstohowa, for his old Marysia; and, for his pretty Dzidzilia, a rich forehead-plating, with its chain of pearls and gold.

"It might fit a bride!" whispered Jakubowa, smiling as she appended the costly gift to the fair brow of her child, —"courage, sweetest, and it will grace one yet!"

"And what for us, father? and what for us?" cried the disappointed children.

"You promised me a box of dominos," cried Janek.

"And me an ebony spindle, and——"

"Peace—peace—peace!" cried Jakob in pretended anger. "Think you I ride backward and forward between Zwiets and the lint-market of Wilna, for no better purpose than to make myself pedlar and packman to a tribe of craving brats?—Go to! I have brought you that which is lighter of porterage."

"What,—what?" exclaimed the eager boy.

"A tale, by word of mouth."

"A tale!" reiterated the disappointed Benisia. "Aunt Anulka will spin us tales from now to Hallowmas, without travelling to Wilna in search of them."

"Since we can have nought else," interrupted Janek, "let us rest content with that. My father is not apt to be a teller of tales: his story should needs be something uncommon."

"'Tis some whim-wham of new forms of husbandry," said Aunt Anulka, contemptuously.

"No!"

"'Tis some harangue upon the fashions introduced at Wilna, by the new governor and his lady," cried Jakubowa.

"Wrong, again!"

"'Tis a tale of knights and giants!" said the boy.

"'Tis a tale of saints and angels!" added the little girl.

"'Tis a legend of the household gods!" muttered Maruchna.

"No!" replied Jakob, chuckling as he marked the eagerness his mystery had created. "To all and each,—no! 'Tis a tale that illustrates the barbarity of our enemies of the Wolga;—and does honour to Polanders and Poland!"

"Let us hear it;—speak—speak—speak!" cried the voices of all present.

"First let me put about the flask towards my friend and guest!" cried Jakob, glancing towards Ludwyk, whose eyes were fixed in sympathy and alarm upon the pale and bewildered face of his Dzidzilia,—who sat between Marrucha and her aunt, shrinking from endurance of her trial in presence of one whom she loved so well, and had so stoutly promised to forget!

"Drink, Ludwyk!" cried the Dzierzawca. "Health and happiness to your lady-love!"

And the young man mechanically raised the glass to his lips; his whole soul engrossed by the sudden change of Dzidzilia's aspect and demeanour. She might be ill,—but why even in illness thus cold and careless towards him?

"And now then, father!" exclaimed the children, drawing towards his knees; in the hope that his tale would contain at least a bloody battle, if not a murder or a ghost.

"All ready?" inquired the farmer, looking round, and

perceiving the Pasiecznik and one or two of his domestic serfs loitering about the door. "In! Grzegorz,—in all of you, and listen;—for there is profit, if not pleasure in the story I am about to narrate.

"You may remember, Jakubowa!" said he, turning with affectionate deference towards his wife, as he spoke, "that, on my last visit to Wilna, there had been a rising amongst the people against their Russian masters,—a struggle of some dozen weeks betwixt the peasants and the soldiery; ending, as such struggles mostly do, in double injury to the injured, and double ascendency to the ascendant. A single regiment took part with the insurgents: a brave one, and a winner of high renown in the fatal field of Raszyn; but so far rash and wrong in the present quarrel, that it broke an oath of fealty and idly dared the vengeance of an oppressor. At that period I quitted Wilna as hastily as my merchantry would permit; for I was loath to witness the chastisement of those in whose cause my heart was warm; and even accelerated my journey lest I should be a dweller in a city where Christian blood was outpouring, and the retribution of a jealous God wantonly evoked."

"I do remember, father!" interrupted the young heir of Zwieta, "that you chid me for questioning you of the executions, and the knoutings, and the banishments into Siberia; and bade me consider with other eyes than those of a gaping wonderer, the sufferings of men who suffered in the cause of their country."

"A good lad—a good lad—to keep a year's mindfulness of his father's lesson!" ejaculated the fond mother, heaping a pile of hautbois on his plate.

"But although the insurrection was after a sort suppressed, and though the students, and burghers, and others implicated in the outbreak were in the safe keeping of the dungeons of their Muscovite masters, this one regiment still held out; and, better skilled than the lumbering Kozacks in the mires, mosses, and morasses of the country, still kept at bay the Russian troops; dodged them from forest to marsh,—from marsh to dyke-drain; and reduced them at length to insulting disadvantage. "The peasants of the country, favouring their dispositions, provided forage and provisionment. No need of commissariat, no need of farriers,—horses, rations, and even clothing were thrust upon their acceptance. The women stitched for them,—the men slaved for them,—the hands and hearts of the people were with their banner!"

"Brave hearts!—true hands!"—cried the boy, clapping his hands with enthusiasm. And Jakob pushing the flask again towards Ludwyk pledged him a health to the heroism of the heir of the family.

"This universal zeal and sympathy did but, as you may think, stir up the black and bitter blood of the vindictive Russians. Wherever they came, there were curses, and pleas of drought, dearth, and famine against all largesse of contribution. And when at length the snows of winter set in, and the soldiers were kept out in cantonments, in chase of the rebels, they swore a deadly vow, that they would celebrate with libations of blood the day of their eventual triumph. Still the patriots defied their menaces, and still the peasantry supported the resistance of the patriots."

Jakob Bremglicz was now waxing angry, that, in the midst of all the enthusiastic ejaculations of his family and household, Ludwyk, the stranger remained so coldly silent. "The lad is pondering upon his love," thought the Dzierzawca—"Nevertheless, it were better that his country kept the uppermost place."

"And these brave men—do they still resist?" inquired Aunt Annika, wondering whether she could by any means contrive to despatch unguents and vulneraries to the wounded.

"No, sister,—the Almighty, for his own good purpose, willed their defeat;" replied Bremglicz. "Cut off from their supplies, exhausted by privation, wearied by watchfulness—there came at length a desperate skirmish, when the cry for quarter was raised in vain; and a scattered remnant of the gallant squadron remained captive in the hands of the Philistines."

"Alas, alas!" moaned the little circle round the table of Jacob Bremglicz; and from a distance the peasants echoed that melancholy cry.

"Among these was the Colonel of the regiment," continued Jakob. "A grey-haired man, who had fought with Dombrowski; on whose breast was the badge of honour—on whose brow a still more honourable scar. And they doomed him to die like a dog. In the after calm of victory, when the strife was done, and its bloody record wiped from their savage hands, the Muscovites brought him forth, (handbound and footbound, lest, single-handed, the valour of a Polander should prove too much for their craven souls,) to be piked and mangled by their murderous bayonets."*

A deep groan burst forth on all sides round the narrator.

"Now the scene of this vile exploit," resumed Bremglicz, with kindling eyes, "was most auspiciously selected. The skirmish which gave conquest to their hands had chanced within a verst or so of a country seat belonging the Syndic of Wilna; and beneath the very walls of his garden was the brave man dragged forth to die. But there was an eye upon the wicked movements of the Russians."

"The eye of Jehovah!" ejaculated his wife.

"The eye of Auxteia-vis-gist!" muttered Maruchna, reverting to her Runic superstitions.

"The eye of a mere mortal; but, by divine emotion, quite as much to the purpose," rejoined Jakob. "The house was tenanted by a younger son of the Syndic; a student of high repute in the University of Wilna; who, having been convicted in the recent insurgency, had been smuggled, per favour of his father's office, out of the city, and concealed in this secluded spot. The youth, like other lads of spirit, expert and eager in the chase, was impatiently watching the departure of the soldiery to go forth birding after the snowhens;† when, having mounted guard behind the wall of the garden, he beheld the gallant old soldier led forth to slaughter. 'Twas but a moment of horror—the next was for action. Gun in hand he climbed the wall; rushed through the circle of military, and threw his arm round the veteran. 'My gun is double loaded,' cried the young hero; and the first man who dares approach, I shoot and level him to the earth.' 'Do ye flinch, knaves?' cried the Russian commandant. 'Seize them both; tear them limb from limb!' 'Say but that word again,' shouted the young student, raising his piece to his shoulder, 'and 'tis thy last you ever utter in this world!—Heaven!—Upon him! —Strike him down!' cried the Muscovite. 'What! fifty

---

* A similar scene, occurring under the same circumstances, was described to me by a Polish gentleman of high reputation, an eye witness of the fact.

† The Salaguhr, or snow-hen, a sort of ptarmigan.

of ye, and shrink from a boy without a twelvemonth's growth of beard upon his chin? The gauntlet and the knout may bring my corps to better discipline.' And on this menace, some ten among the slaves advanced with bayonets and swords, to hack the old soldier into pieces! But the word of command was dearly atoned; even before the brave old Polander lay gashed and bleeding under their feet,—the Russian commander was smitten into the dust by the steady aim of the valiant son of Syndic of Wilna!"

"And they murdered him?" cried every voice present. "The gallant youth!—the brave youth!—A Trepka—a Sobieski!—a Kosciusko!"

"Lithe of limb, and versed in the shaping of every bush and hedge-row," continued Jakob, "he burst from them, though stabbed by many bayonets; and took refuge in a hut or lodge of the grounds, to which the miscreants, having surrounded it with brushwood, instantly set fire. But their Commandant lay dead:—they lacked farther instructions;—many had no good will for the murderous task assigned them; and, in fine, the peasants of the Syndic having warning of what was passing, and loyal to their brave young master, drove them from the field."

"And the youth—the good youth?"—cried his impatient auditors.

"Wounded, stunned, senseless, and scorched to the very marrow of his young bones,—he was extricated from the smoking pile!"

"To die?"—murmured the gentle Dzidzilia, clasping her hands. "An evil fate is over the destinies of the heroes of Poland."

"No,—not to die," interrupted Jakob;—"but to suffer agonies in a cause which even his prowess could not render triumphant. Slowly recovering, his father's interest would not have availed to save his forfeited life, but that he had been surreptitiously conveyed from the country."

"Heaven is gracious!—Praise be to the virgin of virgins!" cried the eager listeners.

"In Wilna, as you may guess, the name of this boy-patriot is worshipped as that of the first of heroes;—and for my own part," continued Jakob, brushing his hand hastily over his eyes, "I would give half my substance—not to be Syndic of Wilna, but to call the noble one my son!"

"Delay not then the concession!" cried Ludwyk, having risen from his seat, and throwing himself upon the neck of Birkngttcz. "Give me your daughter and your blessing; and my wounds, my sufferings, my banishments, are a thousand-fold overpaid!"

"And you reviled those honourable scars as tokens of the Plica-sticken!" whispered Dzidzilia reproachfully to Maruchna.

"Why did he slay the wood-serpent!" grumbled the old woman. "That one misdeed misled me!"

But Dzidzilia had no further leisure for reproaches; she was required by her father to kneel down and receive his benediction of betrothment, hand in hand with Ludwyk; and by her mother to be kissed and wept over and congratulated, as the plighted love of the champion of little Janek, —the bride of the patriotic defender of the liberties of Poland! At that moment not one among them had a thought for the temporal dignities of the son of the Right Honourable the Syndic of the city of Wilna!

"Heir to a Kasztellan and chief magistrate!" cried old Jakob,—having, with Anulka's aid and at Ludwyk's suggestion, decyphered the letter of paternal sanction which Ludwyk's visit to the post office of Rosienie, had that very evening secured.

"A distinguished student of the learned University!" exclaimed Aunt Anulka, bestowing upon her niece the kiss of peace.

"And the best snarer of cray-fish and netter of quails in the country?"—vociferated Janek and Benisia, flinging themselves into the arms of their new brother.

"And so let me even accomplish my own prophecy!" cried Jakubowa, encircling the lovely brows of her daughter with her head-gear of pearls. "Said I not that the Dzierzawca's city-token would well become a bride?"

"God is good!" murmured Maruchna, devoutly crossing herself in joyful recognisance of the prosperous fortunes of her nursling. "The duteous daughter will make a happy wife."

"Push aside the tables!" cried Jakob clapping his hands. "Tap me a hogshead of Lipiec, and call in the knaves and wenches. Grzegorz, man!—fetch thy dulcimer, and give us our Mazurek. Sister Anulka,—wife,—Marzanna, Malgorzata,—Janowa,—your voices—your voices to the burden!"

And while Ludwyk and his pretty bride stood whispering at the window (discussing perhaps the culture of the Bee Garden on which they were gazing) the happy household of the Pasieka raised the chorus of the National Mazurka; while the floors of Zwieta echoed under the ringing heels of the dancers to the following popular strain:—

MAZUREK.

Form the gay Mazurka's round,—
Damsel, come!—thy hand—Ah! no—
Both hands,—then,—and with a bound
O'er the corded lists we go!
Hop!—hop!—and spring for ever,—
All is mirth and gratulation;—
Those who love or dance should never
Pause for idle cogitation.

Still thy lightsome footsteps prancing,
Mock the flow of tender tears;—
Better far a week of dancing,
Thats an hour of hopes and fears.
Hop!—hop!—and spring for ever;—
All is mirth and gratulation;—
Those who love or dance, should never
Pause for idle cogitation.

When the sparks are flashing brightly,
From my iron heels comprest;—
When my love flies round me lightly,
Oh! what transport warms my breast!
Hop!—hop!—and spring for ever,—
All is mirth and gratulation;—
Those who love or dance, should never
Pause for idle cogitation.

And when sunn'd beneath her glances,
Round her form my fond arms cling;—
Then oh! that's the dance of dances,—
A Mazurka for a king!—
Hop!—hop!—and spring for ever,—
All is mirth and gratulation;
Those who love or dance should never
Pause for idle cogitation.

A gentleman recently travelling near Huddersfield, called out to a boy, "Where does this road go to, my lad?" "I do not know," said the boy, "where it goes to, but it is always here when I come by."

ASSASSINATION OF MARAT BY CHARLOTTE CORDAY.

I HAD scarcely pronounced the name of Marat, when the porter said, "It is here, Sir." It was, no doubt, at the door of this dark lodge that Charlotte Corday said, "Is the Citizen Marat at home?" And the porter, seeing this beautiful and dignified girl, with a smile upon her countenance, suspected nothing. How indeed could he associate the idea of a murder with that of a lovely woman, whose large black eyes displayed a humid and intellectual brilliancy; whose elegant and fully-developed figure, exquisitely fair complexion, and pearly teeth, seen under the voluptuous fulness of her half-closed lips, would have melted a savage? How could he associate a concealed poinard with drapery which flowed, without concealing the most perfect harmony of contour?—how trace a sanguinary design in that face so lovely, so noble, and so calm, whose only expression seemed the timidity of chaste and virtuous affection. On that day, no doubt, her toilet displayed a sort of simple and sublime coquetry. It was necessary that she should captivate the good opinion of those who were to admit her. She knew, likewise, that such a murder is not perpetrated a second time; that her life would fall a sacrifice to the deed. She knew that she was committing a generous suicide in favour of reason and justice; that she should be arrested the instant the deed was performed, for she determined to make no attempt to escape. She could not forget that a woman's dress, even the most important actions of her life, represents in some degree, her habitual ideas and opinions. Oh, now beautiful she looked! Her glossy hair was tied with a wide green ribbon, and around her lovely neck flowed undulating curls. And then her forehead of animated white, that modest air, and those lips!—who could have anticipated that her delicate hand was about to be stained with blood? . . . . . On the 13th of July she went to the Palais National, and bought a sharp-pointed table-knife, with a black sheath. On her return home she put into her pocket her baptismal register, and an address to the French people . . . . . . She knew that she should leave the place to which she was going, only to be thrown into a dungeon, condemned a few hours after, and then placed in that fatal cart which was daily dragged to the Greve, the Place de Revolution, elsewhere and everywhere! She had provided against all contingencies. Marat was ill, and she was refused admittance. But she wrote him a note, stating that she had just arrived from Caen, and was able to render an important service to the country. In the evening, at five o'clock, she returned. The housekeeper still refused her admittance; but Marat being in the bath, and hearing the voice of a young girl, ordered that she should come in. "This is the closet," said the servant; "the bath was there, just opposite the window." I understood the whole action as well as if it had occurred in my presence. The three rooms are so small, that an instant sufficed to cross them. I could fancy I saw the whole scene pass before my eyes. "Marat," exclaimed I, "had a handkerchief round his head; his right hand was out of the water, and he used as a writing-table a board placed across the bath. Charlotte, from the closeness of the bath, nearly touched him." "The paper hangings are not now the same," said the servant; "those which then covered the walls were taken down a few months since. They were large twisted pillars drawn upon a white ground." "She was there," continued I; Marat questioned her, and inquired the names of the refugees of Calvados; she dictated to him, and he wrote. "It is well," said he, "they shall all go to the guillotine. This was the last threat he uttered. She drew from its sheath the knife concealed in her bosom, and plunged it in his heart?—"Help!" cried he, "help, my dear friend! I am murdered." "And Charlotte," resumed the servant, "putting her hand to her hair, crossed the second room, and seated herself in the ante-chamber, there, near that window. This was told me by an eye-witness to the murder. A commissionaire who had been folding up copies of L'Ami du Peuple, knocked her down with a chair. She rose and claimed the protection of the Members of the Section, all of whom were struck with her beauty. Danton arrived and applied to her the most disgraceful epithets. Charlotte opposed to his abuse an animated though cold disdain. She was dragged into the room which opened into the street." It was this moment that M. Sheffer has so judiciously selected for his picture; but from this room the bath in which Marat lay could not be seen. What matters this to the artist? Genius can lay upon walls. It was in this apartment that she was examined by the Conventionalists Chabot and Drouet; their report is authentic testimony, and both declared their astonishment at the answers of the young girl, who seemed to speak with a prophetic voice. The coach in which she came was still at the door. She descended to the street, escorted by the Commissioners and gendarmes of the Convention. On her appearance, the populace uttered cries and execrations that would have terrified the stoutest heart. She turned pale—she dreaded being torn in pieces by these wretches. She, poor girl, had anticipated a less horrible death. But, in the summer of life, beautiful and admirable as she was, to be insulted, trampled under foot, dragged half alive through the filth of the kennel, torn in pieces with hooks dripping with gore, and stabbed with pikes; to lift up her bruised head—one so lovely, now defaced and hideous—and implore, as an act of clemency, the *coup de grace*, either delayed or given by an unskilful hand; her last struggles amid curses and imprecations; no hope of a tomb, not even a coffin! her limbs torn asunder and dispersed—as had occurred in the September in the preceding year. All this harrowed up her very soul. For an instant such a death threatened her. But Drouet thundered out to the tumultuous and exasperated mob—"In the name of the law." In an instant the cries ceased, the crowd opened, and the coach slowly proceeded . . . There is no tablet inscribed to the memory of Charlotte Corday, nor is it known to what earth her remains were consigned.

THE REV. ROBERT HALL.

Mr. Hall was the great pillar and ornament of the Baptist denomination; and all who admire the spectacle of talent of the loftiest description, engaged in the sacred cause of doing good, will deplore the sudden extinction of so bright a luminary. His was of the highest order of cultivated intellect. He was by no means one of those who bigotedly decry the blending of literary taste with spiritual pursuits and enjoyments. He fed his intellectual faculties with the richest supplies of ancient and modern literature; and, within a few months of his death, was re-perusing at hours of leisure, the tragedies of Euripides. Of Greek literature in general, he was particularly fond. The tragedians, Homer and Plato, were his favourites; these, together with the works of Virgil, Milton, and Burke, were the chief sources of his pure and classical eloquence. His works are, it is to be feared, too few to preserve a reputation which might have built itself an imperishable fortress. But Mr. Hall was indolent, and some strong external motive was required to force his intellectual machinery into operation. He was also, we should say, too modest; he shrank from observation; and was by no means "ambitious of having," as he used to say, when solicited to write more, "all the world laughing at him." Those amazing efforts of sacred oratory, to the splendid display of which Lord Brougham, Sir James Mackintosh, Sir Thomas Denman, and Mr. Canning, and other not less distinguished men, have listened with delight, were deemed by himself undeserving of permanent record; and whoever of the noblest discourses that ever "breathed and burned", on the lips of mortal, shall at last find their way before the public, we shall be indebted more to the private solicitude of friends, or perhaps of interested individuals, than to the care of the high-minded orator himself. A third cause of the fewness of Mr. Hall's publications was, the heavy bodily afflictions to which he was subject for several years previous to the close of his life. A dreadful disease of the spine frequently incapacitated him from every kind of exertion, mental and bodily; and rendered him, for many hours together, the victim of the most excruciating agonies. Throughout these severe sufferings, he was calm and tranquil in the highest degree, affording a most emphatic example of the power of religion to support the mind, when the heart and flesh fail. While a young man, Mr. Hall published his first work, "An Apology for the Freedom of the Press," a masterly work, written in a style of the purest argumentative eloquence, and fervid with the spirit of freedom. Some time after appeared his sermon on Modern Infidelity, indisputably the first work of its kind in the language, adorned with all the graces of finished composition, and displaying the mighty powers of a master of reasoning. His Sermon on the Death of the Princess Charlotte is without a rival. Amongst the numbers delivered on that melancholy occasion, and to those who would see noble ideas wedded to noble diction, the eloquence of thought fitly enshrined amidst all the "glories and beauties" of impassioned language, we would strongly recommend the perusal of Mr. Hall's Sermons on War; and of the last twenty pages of the "Thoughts on the Present Crisis," we have much doubt if there are twenty consecutive pages comparable with these in the prose works of any other English writer.—*New Monthly.*

AFTER their disgraceful retreat at the battle of Preston, Cope's dragoons were anything but a popular regiment; they were frequently stigmatized, and exposed to much bitter sarcasm and raillery. Once, when quartered in a town on the eastern coast of Scotland, both officers and men were sadly annoyed by Adam S—— of ——, a person, at that time, well known in the district alluded to. His appearance and manners were in accordance with the age in which he lived. He was a robust, homely, "out spoken" man—an adept at leaping, running, and such exercises—and possessed much real, pungent wit, which was willingly and unsparingly employed against this regiment, which had always been the object of the laird's particular dislike and contempt. At length, his lampoons became so frequent and touchy, that one of the officers determined to challenge the offender; and, by this method, at once to vindicate the honour of the corps, and put an end to all further annoyance from such a quarter. Accordingly, a brother officer was despatched with the challenge. The laird espying a red-coat approach his mansion, guessed right well his intent, but determined on granting him admittance. He was forthwith ushered into *the presence*, and formally communicated what he had been charged with. Adam heard him to an end, and agreed to accept the challenge, on the condition that they should "fecht wi' swurds, as pistols were kittle things." This was acceded to; and the time and place of meeting determined on—a hill at some distance. True to their engagement, came the challenger and his second, and with them a surgeon; and no less punctual came the party challenged, accompanied by a six feet farmer, whom he had pressed into the service. The swords were measured, and other necessary preliminaries adjusted with great nicety. "Now," said the laird to his opponent, "are ye ready?" He was replied to in the affirmative. "Weel, lad, keep a gude look out, for ye see, I intend fechting you the day as ye did the Hielandmen at Preston; and ye ken hoo that was." "Sir, explain yourself," retorted the officer. "Catch me if ye can, man!" shouted Adam; and giving a not very delicate pat i' the mouth in token of defiance, he bounded off, and was out of sight in a moment, closely followed by his long-legged second, to the no small astonishment of the two dragoons, and disappointment of the expectant surgeon.

THE minister of a country town was solicited by a parishioner to administer the ordinance of baptism to his child. It had always been the practice of the divine, before complying with such a request, to put a few questions to the applicant regarding the nature of the rite. On this occasion, the usual interrogatories were gone into with all solemnity on the part of the minister, and answered by the parishioner with much confidence, and not a little self-appreciation. But the catechist, not entertaining the same opinion as the catechised, came to this conclusion—" Really, Saunders, after a', I dinna think ye're fit to haud up the bairn." "What d'ye say, Sir?" exclaimed his visiter. "I'm sayin', Saunders, that I dinna think ye're fit to haud it up." "Fit to haud it up! 'Od saves, I could fling't ower the kirk!"

PARTIALITY FOR SCOTSMEN.—If the press is ever unanimous, it is in favour of some Scotsman: Does he publish a book?—there is a reverberating echo of praise like the notes of a trumpet in the Lakes of Killarney: His exploits in any other way are equally sure of fame. Scotland, in comparison of this country, is in all respects contemptible; and yet we would challenge any list of names, containing those of beneficial postholders, beneficial whether for honour, for profit, or patronage, and sure we are there would be found a majority of Scotsmen. In the army—that is to say, an arduous as well as honourable service—the Irish come in for a fair share. In the colonies, where money is to be made, the preference of Scotsmen is a most notorious joke. With regard to the press of London, from causes that might be explained, it could, we think, be proved, that it is governed three parts by Scotland. This does not mean that the editors are three parts Scotsmen, but many more than the mere editors have powerful influence in a paper; there are sub-editors and other subordinates, who, in their own departments, are supreme. In the London press, what is not Scottish, with a few remarkable exceptions, is Irish: So much from the fourth estate. Few persons will venture to dive into the mysteries of these matters; for he might share the fate of the bear in the fable, who put his rude paw into the hornet's nest.—*New Monthly Magazine.*

THE IRISH GENTRY AND THE IRISH POOR.—The classes of society in Ireland are ill arranged. There is a wide hiatus between the gentry and the labouring class, for the class of small farmers, which constitute the tenantry of the country, cannot be ranked much above those who labour for their daily subsistence. The class of farmers in England and Scotland, which forms the pride and the strength of Britain, is unknown in Ireland. Until such a class is created by some means, there is little hope of the improvement in agriculture of that country. As society is there at present constituted, the nobility and gentry can live in apparent splendour, while their tenantry, the farmers, as they are called, eke out an existence more pitiable than the class who labour for hire. A bond of sympathy is wanting betwixt them, and, whilst the connecting link is supplied, a reciprocal desire of mutual support, arising from an assimilation of interest, cannot be expected to exist among so widely separated classes of community.—*Quarterly Journal of Agriculture.*

SKETCH OF AN IRISH PEASANT.—Observe the half-clad peasant, breasting the storm with wiry sinews, his ragged coat streaming in the wind, travelling to some neighbouring market with a load on his shoulders. This load is a web of linen cloth, for which, should he be fortunate enough, he may obtain from 6d. to 10d. a yard. And this trifling sum is all that this man obtains for a yard of cloth, after having grown his own flax, on land for which he must pay from thirty to eighty shillings per acre,—after the labour attending the pulling, watering, drying, crigging, dressing, spinning, weaving, and taking to market. Then with the proceeds of the sale of this cloth, together with the sale of his corn—for these men generally rent three or four acres of ground—he contrives to pay his rent; while himself and family live on rather drag out a miserable existence, entirely on potatoes; for his ducks and fowls, geese and turkeys, are all brought to market to enable him to purchase something to cover his nakedness with; nor will his utmost exertions enable him to procure better fare.—*Loudon's Gardener's Magazine.*

ANECDOTE OF THOMAS CLARKSON, ESQ.—We extract the following account of an attempt to kill Mr. Clarkson, one of the earliest and most zealous friends of the injured sons of Africa, from *The Tourist, or, Sketch Book of the Times*, a weekly periodical, which constantly advocates the abolition of slavery, and is also, in other respects, a valuable publication:—" I was one day on the pier-head at Liverpool, with many others, looking at some little boats below at the time of a heavy gale. Several persons, probably out of curiosity, were hastening thither. I had seen all I intended to see, and was departing, when I noticed eight or nine persons making towards me. I was then only about eight or nine yards from the precipice of the pier, but going from it. I expected that they would have divided to let me through them; instead of which, they closed upon me, and bore me back. I was borne within a yard of the precipice, when I discovered my danger; and perceiving among them the murderer of Peter Green, and two others who had insulted me at the King's Arms, it instantly struck me that they had a design to throw me over the pier-head; which they might have done at this time, and yet have pleaded that I had been killed by accident. There was not a moment to lose. Vigorous on account of the danger, I darted forward. One of them, against whom I pushed myself, fell down. Their ranks were broken, and I escaped, not without blows, amidst their imprecations and abuse."

ANECDOTE OF ANDREW MARVELL.—The borough of Hull, in the reign of Charles II., chose Andrew Marvell, a young gentleman of little or no fortune, and maintained him in London for the service of the public. His understanding, integrity, and spirit, were dreadful to the then infamous administration. Persuaded that he would be theirs for proper asking, they sent his old school-fellow, the Lord Treasurer Danby, to renew acquaintance with him in his garret. At parting, the Lord Treasurer, out of pure affection, slipped into his hand £1000, and then went to his chariot. Marvell looking at the paper calls after the Treasurer, "My Lord, I request another moment." They went up again to the garret, and Jack, the servant boy, was called. "Jack, child, what had I for dinner yesterday?" "Don't you remember, Sir? You had the little shoulder of mutton that you ordered me to bring from a woman in the market." "Very right, child—What have I for dinner to-day?" "Don't you know, Sir, that you bid me lay by the blade-bone to broil?" "'Tis so; very right, child; go away. My Lord, do you hear that? Andrew Marvell's dinner is provided; there's your piece of paper, I want it not. I know the sort of kindness you intended. I live here to serve my constituents; the ministry may seek men for their purpose; I am not one."

TALLEYRAND.—A sententious manner, frigid politeness, and an air of observation, formed an impenetrable shield round his diplomatic character. When among his intimate friends he was quite a different being. He was particularly fond of social conversation, which he usually prolonged to a very late hour. Familiar, affectionate, and attentive to the means of pleasing, he yielded to a species of intellectual epicurism, and became amusing, that he might be himself amused. He is the author of the bon-mot quoted somewhere by Champfort, where Rulhière said: "I know not why I am called a wicked man; and I never, in the whole course of my life, committed but one act of wickedness."—The Bishop of Autun immediately exclaimed, with his full sonorous voice, and significant manner, "But when will this act be at an end?" One evening, at whist, while he was in London, a lady of sixty was mentioned as just having married a footman. Several expressed their surprise at such a choice. "When you are nine," said the bishop of Autun, "you do not count honours." His manner of life, telling is peculiarly graceful, and he is a model of good taste in conversation. Indolent, voluptuous, born to wealth and grandeur, he had yet, during his early accustomed himself to a life of privation; and he liberally shared with his friends the only resources he had left, arising from the sale of the wreck of his superb library, which fetched a very low price, because even in London, party-spirit prevented a competition of purchasers.—*Dumont's Recollections of Mirabeau.*

ANECDOTE OF THE IRISH NORTHERN CIRCUIT.—The father of the bar was engaged to defend a prisoner of equal purity of character and spotless integrity with my "gentle-handed" client. The prosecutor was a steady old northern, whose dim eyes and grey locks told the close of three-score years and ten, but whose honest indignation against the innovations of knavery and theft supplied him with all the vehemence of youthful ardour. " My good man," said his lordship, " take the crier's rod, and see if you can point out the person who lightened your pocket; begin now up here, and look all around the court," said the learned judge, pointing up at the head of the seat occupied by the bar. The old gentleman looked steadily and cautiously down the seat; at length, with the fixed and motionless glare of the rattlesnake, placed himself opposite the worthy father, and laying the rod upon his hoary locks, exclaimed, " I'm thinking that's the chap!—eh, hould on a wee bit; 'come up Jack," he shouts, turning round to his son, who was amongst the crowd, " come up, mon, and gie's a hann to thrapple the rubber (robber.") Judicial gravity could not withstand this; it was truly electric. " Very likely, my good man," said his lordship, " that white headed man may have got some of your money in his pocket; but will you swear that he's the lad that robbed you?"—" Well, in troth, I'm no joost directly positive sure, but he's grey, and like the chap that I gruppit by the cuff of the neck anyhow." " Why, man," said his lordship, " that's the prisoner's counsel." " Och, I kenn'd bravely," replies my old friend, " he was yin o' a bad crap; he maun hae a lang-shanked ladle that sups kale with the diel."—*Dublin University Magazine.*

THE LATE DR. ADAM CLARKE.—A correspondent inquires whether the late Dr. Adam Clarke adhered to the last to the opinion he expressed respecting the probability of animals being recompensed in a future state for the unmerited sufferings they endure in this? Our correspondent has addressed the inquiry to us, in consequence of having perused the introductory chapter of the *Melange*, in which the learned and pious Doctor's theory on this subject is noticed and commented upon. In answer to this correspondent, all we can say is, that we never heard that Dr. Clarke had ever repudiated his own doctrine on this subject; and we know that many persons of unaffected piety have held the same opinion,—opinions from which nothing but good effects can result. " The dumb animals"—in the words of the preface to the *Melange*, " are the work of the same God who created man; and who shall presume to say that the author of nature, who has called them into life, may not perpetuate their existence after their earthly career?"

A MORE THAN SPARTAN BREVITY OF SPEECH.—It is one thing to write a good speech and another to speak one. This fact was illustrated some years since in a neighbouring county, in which a regiment of yeomanry cavalry had resolved on presenting their Colonel with a splendid silver porter jug, through the hands of the Adjutant. The day of review came on, when the present was to be made. The Colonel had got a hint, and had prepared a splendid oration to return thanks to The Adjutant's presentation speech, was to be unsurpassable; the troops were drawn out in line, all eyes were turned towards the Adjutant, as he advanced before the soldiers, holding the glittering gift in his hand, and the Colonel waiting to hear the address of the giver. All ears were intent to hear the speech and reply. Alas! memory in both individuals had proved a treacherous guardian of their sentences. The Adjutant approached, extended his hand, presenting the donation, but all his speech was—" Colonel, there's the jug!" and what was the equally obliging officer's reply?—" Ay, is that the jug?"

SCRAPS.

IRISH LANDED PROPERTY.—We have a striking illustration of the extent to which Irish estates are *dipped*, in the evidence of Mr. Mahony, before the tithe committee. According to a return from the Registrar's office, the mortgages in the three last years were L.932,350: that is, this was the aggregate amount of such of them as had the consideration money marked on the memorials; but as there were 341 which had no indication of the amount of the consideration money, the real aggregate total must be above the sum stated, and may, according to Mr. Mahony's calculation, be estimated at least at a million. Besides mortgages, there were transactions of enormous magnitude in bonds and judgments. In the three Courts of King's Bench, Common Pleas, and Exchequer, 17,336 original judgments were entered on cognovit (that is upon bonds with warrant of attorney;) 3,776 judgments were revived; and 1,465 judgments re-docketed, all of which represent a penal sum of L.24,156,856, or an actual debt of L.12,304,372, besides interest. Adding to this the amount of the mortgages, we have a total debt recorded, within the last three years, of L.13,546,602, nine-tenths of which, as Mr. Mahony justly supposes, affect landed property alone. The average annual increase of debt, within the period specified, is L.4,515,534, and the value of all the landed property of Ireland is not estimated by Mr. Griffith, the engineer, at more than L.12,715,578.—*Dublin Evening Post.*

STERNE'S DAUGHTER—Sterne's daughter had been baited incessantly about her religious opinions by a young man, a commonplace puppy, the son, or the nephew, or the brother, I declare I can't say which, for I never thought the fact worth ascertaining, of one of the prebends of Durham. She had listened to his *niaiseries* with exemplary patience for several days, when on a sudden it seemed to occur to her, that even to forbearance there are limits. He resumed the attack this morning, with—" Mrs ——, what made you sceptical?"

"The lives," said she, " of the Dean and Chapter of Durham."

The laugh went against him. Instead of readily joining in it, and treating the matter as a merry jest, a burst of merriment ensued on his rejoining, aside—a most vehement aside it was—with an air of desperate pique, "I hate your clever women, they are all such d——'d fools."

EDUCATION IN IRELAND.—There has been no want either of Acts of Parliament, or grants of money, to make Ireland both wealthy and wise. The treasury has been taxed; the purses of the English, who, though a money-loving, are a kind-hearted people, have bled freely; sermons have been preached in cathedrals and conventicles; the widow has given her mite, and the child its allowance; and yet, every two or three years, we are sickened with the same ghastly tale of famine. Again, for the remedy of Irish ignorance, society upon society has been constituted, thousands after thousands have been subscribed by individuals; successive administrations in the greatest financial straits have liberally voted the public money, and the tightest economists have hardly objected to the disbursement. Schools have risen in all quarters, and schoolmasters are almost as numerous as authors; and yet the same complaint continues—the Irish are perishing for want of instruction. At length the Government take the matter into their own hands. They resolve that the education for which the nation are to pay, shall be a national education; that the funds appropriated to the purpose shall be vested in responsible hands; and that they shall be rendered beneficial to all who need and desire to avail themselves of the boon. What has followed? Feeble, wavering support from half friends, and clamorous opposition from Tories and Demagogues, a union such as hath not been seen since the Pharisees and the Herodians took counsel together.—*Yorkshire Mon. Mag. of Education.*

In the anti-titheism of the mob, I beheld a venture introducing to anti-rental doctrine; and this latter opening upon an area for tumultuous and anti-property and anti-rank contention; though, in the demolition of rank and opulence, the constitution that supported them must come down, overwhelming in its fall the interests of those persons who rashly pulled it to the ground.—*Baron Smith's Charge.*

HOWARD, THE PHILANTHROPIST.—The energy of his determination was so great, that if, instead of being habitual, it had been shown only for a short time on particular occasions, it would have appeared a vehement impetuosity: but by being unintermitted, it had an equability of manner which scarcely appeared to exceed the tone of a calm constancy, it was so totally the reverse of anything like turbulence or agitation. It was the calmness of an intensity kept uniform by the nature of the human mind forbidding it to be more, and by the character of the individual forbidding it to be less. The habitual passion of his mind was a pitch of excitement and impulsion, almost equal to the temporary extremes and paroxysms of common minds; as a great river, in its customary state, is equal to a small or moderate one when swollen to a torrent.—*Foster on Decision of Character.*

BARKING OF DOGS, THE RESULT OF CIVILISATION.—Dogs in a state of nature never bark; they simply whine, howl, and growl; this explosive noise is only found among those which are domesticated. Sonnini speaks of the shepherd's dogs in the wilds of Egypt as not having this faculty; and Columbus found the dogs which he had previously carried to America, to have lost their propensity to barking.

BEAR-CATCHING.—The inhabitants of the mountainous parts of Siberia fasten a very heavy block to a rope that terminates at the other end with a loop. This is laid near a steep precipice, in the path in which the bear is accustomed to go. On getting his neck into the noose, and finding himself impeded by the log, he takes it up in a rage, and, to free himself from it, throws it down the precipice; it naturally pulls the bear after it, and he is killed by the fall. Should this, however, accidentally not prove the case, he drags the block again up the mountain, and reiterates his efforts with increasing fury, till he either sinks exhausted to the ground, or ends his life by a decisive plunge.—*Cabinet of Arts.*

PUNISHMENT OF CHILDREN.—Never let a child be punished for an action which he does not know to be a fault. Never let the punishment be calculated to degrade him in the view of others, for it will then infallibly harden his heart. Never let a child be punished till he has offended in the same way the third time. Never punish him without being sure he has committed the fault in question. And let the punishment you intend to inflict be well considered, and when the proper occasion comes, rigorously inflicted.—*Christian's Penny Magazine.*

CONTENTS OF NO. XXXVIII.

Hints for Conversation.....................................281
Society in North America..................................282
Shell-Fish..285
Interesting Reflection....................................287
On a Mother's Tomb-stone..................................ib.
The Daisy...ib.
USEFUL NOTICES—Gardening; The Chinese Method of Propagating Fruit Trees by Abscission; Hints to Housewives..289
THE STORY TELLER—The Pasieka; or, Bee Farm—concluded..290
Assassination of Marat by Charlotte Corday................293
The Rev. Robert Hall.....................................
Anecdotes, &c..294, 295
SCRAPS—Original and Selected.............................296

EDINBURGH: Printed by and for JOHN JOHNSTONE, 19, St James' Square.—Published by JOHN ANDERSON, Jun., Bookseller, 55, North Bridge Street, Edinburgh; by JOHN MACLEOD, and ATKINSON & Co., Booksellers, Glasgow; and sold by all Booksellers, and Venders of Cheap Periodicals.

THE Schoolmaster,
AND
EDINBURGH WEEKLY MAGAZINE.
CONDUCTED BY JOHN JOHNSTONE.

THE SCHOOLMASTER IS ABROAD.—LORD BROUGHAM.

No. 39.—Vol. II. SATURDAY, APRIL 27, 1833. Price Three-halfpence.

CURSORY REMARKS ON IRELAND.

In August last we visited Belfast, Newry, Drogheda, Dublin, Kildare, Rosscrea, Limerick, Charleville, Buttevant, Mallow, Cork, Fermoy, Clonmel, Kilkenny, Carlow, and Dublin again, and returned by Slane and Ardee to Belfast. The stage-coaches are admirable, drawn by high-mettled horses, which require to be held at the stages to prevent them running away; and while held, not unfrequently leap over the traces from impatience to get off. The drivers are well-dressed, spirited, yet cautious men; the roads are, in general, as good as highways not Macadamised can be made; the country is uncommonly fertile, and extensively cultivated; the inns are in general good, and the charges moderate; so that, altogether, travelling in Ireland is commodious, rapid, and highly interesting.

The accounts generally given of the misery of the Irish peasantry are below rather than above the truth. In Belfast, and the neighbourhood, the people have the Scotch head, and manifest the corresponding talents and dispositions;—there, order, industry, and comfort, abound. After passing the Newry mountains, however, thirty miles south of Belfast, wretchedness begins, and has no termination, except in the towns, till it reaches the sea. The habitations of the lower orders are cottages of mud or stone, without windows and chimneys; straw serves for a bed, and stones for seats; a pot to boil potatoes, and a coarse brown jug to hold water, complete the articles of household furniture. Many individuals are in perfect tatters; and those who are better clad can boast only of a great-coat, with one or two necks, worn over a collection of rags. Under the burning sun of August, thousands were seen loitering on the roads, or before the cottage doors, with these heavy great-coats. At the plough they wear the great-coat; labourers mixing lime are burdened with it, and, under the encumbrance, tuck up its skirts. At the church and in the market-place the people are clad in great-coats. In short, Ireland is the great-coated nation. On asking an explanation, we were told that the men have almost no employment, and no food except potatoes, and, in consequence of the want of excitement, feel cold at all seasons of the year, so that a great-coat is thus a prime necessary of life.

The cottages abound to a degree that to us was inconceivable till we had observed it. In many places, and particularly between Limerick and Cork, one or more is to be met with every five hundred yards along the road, and they are to be seen extending, in dense profusion on every side, as far as the eye can reach. The fields are divided into patches of two or three acres, and two or three fields constitute a farm. The wretched cultivators plant one acre or more of their possessions with potatoes, and sow the remainder with wheat and oats. The produce of the latter they deliver in kind to the Protestant clergyman and landlord's factor, and are well contented to be permitted to reserve the potatoes as their own. We saw scarcely any corn in stack in the open country. The advanced season of the year, just before harvest, might account for this to a great extent; but we were informed that, owing to the system just described, comparatively few stacks are to be seen at any period.

Huts and palaces are almost the only habitations met with in the open country. In some districts nearly all the houses which may have served proprietors with incomes under L.1000 a-year, or tenants of 300 or 400 acres, have been burned down, and present to the traveller walls without roofs, while the winds of heaven are heard sweeping through the windows. The palaces belong to bishops, or proprietors, whose revenues enable them to maintain a retinue fit to constitute a garrison. Every twenty or thirty miles a great fabric is seen rising, huge and massive, in the horizon. As you approach it, it turns out to be barracks as large as an extensive square in a great city, walled all round; and, besides, every village has its outpost of soldiers. In the small towns alone, which are very numerous, is there any population of the middle rank to be found.

We travelled from Dublin to Limerick with a very intelligent merchant, who exports rags and feathers from that city. This trade brings him into close contact with the people. Last winter, he said, the fever-hospitals, and all other places that could be commanded, were crowded with patients, and still the calls for succour were loud and incessant. He collected L.9 in his own circle, and went among the poor to see how it could be best applied; he laid it all out in purchasing straw, (which is there very cheap,) and was not able to provide a bed of this material for all the cottagers who were sick of fever and destitute even of straw to lie on. Some of his customers confessed openly, that they had been concerned in the conflagrations which then every night occurred; and one said, "Last week we buried two-and-twenty men shot in these attempts; and many a widow sits with a tear in her eye that must not be shed, and many a mother laments her son in grief that must not be expressed;—complaint would betray the living, *and the dead are more fortunate than they.*"—About twenty miles east of Limerick, we passed a group of cottages. It rained fast; and across the corner of one of them, the walls of which were raised only about four feet high, and which had as yet no roof, we saw some branches of trees stretched, and a rude kind of thatching with turf and rushes attempted over them. The space covered did not exceed a triangle of six feet in the sides. It contained a woman sick of fever, who was deposited there by the inmates of her own cottage to avoid contagion; and this was a common practice and a wise one. A collection was made for her among the passengers in the coach.

In the towns, the number of wretches flying in rags is appalling: and yet, in spite of all this external appearance of misery, the Irishman is a gay, light-hearted being.

This population is pretty generally instructed in letters. A gentleman, who had been employed by government in investigations in the county of Tipperary, stated, that, eighteen years ago, not one in ten of the lower orders could read or write his name, but that now the proportions are reversed. He discharged the same duties last year, and spoke from observation in both instances. We saw many schools held in huts such as already described; the children sitting in crowds on the floor, and employed with books and slates. Hedge-schools also were occasionally met with; children were collected on the road-side, under the lee of a high wall, or the shelter of a thick plantation, and there were taught to read.

Idleness prevails in Ireland to an extent that is inconceivable, not from want of will to labour, but of work to perform. Every little farm is overstocked with hands, and there is no employment for those who wish to let their labour to hire. The millions of starving tenants with whom the soil groans have no capital; and hence there are no tradesmen. The cartwright's shop and the blacksmith's forge, the shoemaker's and the tailor's shops, are not met with every two or three miles, as in the sister kingdoms. The Irish drive sledges of the rudest fabric; dig potatoes with a spade nine inches long, three inches broad, and five feet long in the handle, which is used without stooping, and rarely needs repair; and for raiment they import the cast rags of England, and go without shoes. An Irish town on a market-day presents a spectacle truly deplorable. The articles exposed for sale are tin-pots, and the coarsest crockery-ware; and the country population bring nothing to sell but yarn, and loiter about famished and wan, like ghosts on the Stygian shore.

Until we saw the condition of the peasantry, we could not understand the motives of their conflagrations; *but then these became too evident.* Every part of the soil is possessed and over-peopled; a tenant ejected cannot plant a foot on an inch of ground without dispossessing others as poor as himself, and cannot obtain employment as a servant for hire. Losing his farm, therefore, is like an excommunication from existence. If a landlord turn out a tenant, and a *neighbour* take the ground, this is a mere shifting of possession; a farm is left vacant by the removal, and the community is nothing the worse; but if a stranger is introduced, the previous tenant is thrust abroad on a country in which there is no room for him to exist. He is sometimes induced to offer an exorbitant rent for another person's possession, and thus the misery is more widely diffused. The overwhelming calamity produced by the settlement of a stranger, especially if he possesses capital, takes extensive farms, and dispossesses twenty or thirty families, may be easily conceived. It is the experience of this evil that has generated the Rockite system. Notice is given to a new-comer to quit his possession, which, if not complied with, is followed up by his murder, and the destruction of his property. To curb this system, soldiers are stationed in the villages; single houses even are hired in the country, and converted into military stations; an armed police patroles the highways during night; and under the insurrection-act it is a transportable offence to be abroad after eight o'clock in the evening. These causes co-operating, produce a state of society which banishes the proprietors of the soil, renders property insecure, prevents the introduction of capital and manufactures, and seems to threaten perpetual misery and degradation to the country. In England and Scotland, every corner of the land is teeming with new houses and nascent manufactories. The north of Ireland partakes in this demonstration of prosperity; but after passing the Newry mountains, in all the remainder of our tour, we saw extremely few tenements exclusive of mud-cottages, in the course of erection.

We were present at the assizes in Cork. *In forty minutes we saw two men tried and sentenced to transportation; a woman to long imprisonment; and a man to death, —all separate cases, and after proof led; some of them under the insurrection-act, on the evidence of one witness.* The complaint was loud everywhere, that neither civil nor criminal law, in the spirit of justice, existed. Nobody blamed the higher judges; but Catholics and enlightened Protestants concurred in ascribing this evil to the exacerbation of feeling existing in the minds of inferior magistrates and juries. Protestants and Catholics regard each other with deadly and enduring hatred; and the class from which jurors are selected is that which suffers most frequently and most severely from the outrages of the lower orders. Rage, therefore, begets a presumption of guilt, and the moral sentiments and kindly affections have been so benumbed by the recurrence of crime, condemnation, and punishment, that the life of a fellow-creature is disposed of with indecent haste and palpable indifference. The officers or macers of Scotch criminal courts create disturbance by calling "Silence!" to the auditory. In Cork they manage this matter better; they write "*Silence,*" in large letters on a piece of pasteboard, stick it into the cleft-end of a long white rod, and wave it in the face of any one whose voice is heard rising above a whisper. If this does not produce quiescence, the admonition is enforced by a rap on the head with the rod.

In some places, where extensive proprietors are resident, great exertions are used to introduce industry and regular habits. In the neighbourhood of Limerick we saw women, whose attire scarcely sufficed the purpose of decency, sewing fine linen, and others busily employed at the spinning-wheel. The great obstacle to the success of these benevolent endeavours is the want of consumption. The people have no money, and nobody requires their labour; they have therefore nothing to offer in exchange for the necessaries, much less the comforts and elegancies of life; and hence these schemes are prosecuted at a loss, and soon exhaust the funds destined for their support.

These are the manifestations; and our Phrenological readers will naturally desire to know what is the development of brain that produces them. *

---

* For this development we must refer to Phrenological Journal No. VI. The above is understood to have been written by Mr. George Combe, to a friend during a tour in Ireland, in 1828.

STATE OF IRELAND.—The following is from "Traits and Stories of the Irish Peasantry:"—

Any person conversant with the Irish people must frenently have heard such dialogues as the following, during he application of a beggar for alms :—

Mendicant—We're axin your charity, for God's sake!

Poor Tenant—Whethen for His sake you would get , poor crathur, if we had it ; but it's not widin the four orners of the house. It 'ud be well for us if we had now ll we gave away in charity durin' the whole year; we rouldn't have to be buyn' for ourselves at three prices. Vhy don't you go up to the Big House? They're rich an an afford it.

Mendicant, (with a shrug, which sets all his coats and ags in motion)—Och! och! The Big House inagh! Musha, o you want me, an' the childhre here, to be torn to pieces rid the dogs? or lashed wid a whip by one o' the sarrints? No, no, avourneen (with a hopeless shake of the ead.) That 'ud be a blue look-up, like a clear even.

Poor Tenant.—Thin, indeed, we haven't it to help on now, poor man. We're buyn' ourselves.

Mendicant.—Thin, throth, that's lucky, so it is! I've a purty a grain o' male here, as you'd wish to thicken rather wid, that I sthruv to get together in hopes to be ble to buy a quarther o' tobaccy, along wid a pair o' new ades an' a scapular for myself. I'm suspicious that there's bout a stone ov it altogether. You can have it anundher he market price, for I'm frettin' at not havin' the scapular n me. Sure the Lord will sind me an' the childhre a bit n' sup some way else—glory to his name!—besides a lock ' praties in the corner o' the bag here, that'll do us for this ay, any way.

The bargain is immediately struck, and the poor tenant glad to purchase, even from a beggar, his stone of meal, n consequence of getting it a few pence under market price. Such scenes as this, which are of frequent occurrence in the country parts of Ireland, need no comment.

This, certainly, is not a state of things which should be ermitted to exist. It is an indelible disgrace to the legislaure so long to have neglected the paupers of Ireland. Is it to e thought of with common patience, that a person rolling in vealth shall feed upon his turtle, his venison, and his costly uxuries of every description, for which he will not scruple o pay the highest price—that this heartless and selfish nan, whether he reside at home or abroad, shall thus unonscionably pamper himself with viands purchased by the eople, and yet not contribute to their miseries, when overty, sickness, or age, throws them upon the scanty suport of casual charity.

DEMORALIZATION OF SLAVERY AND ITS BARBARITIES.

IN a pamphlet, entitled *Three Months in Jamaica*, published by Hatchard, a shocking account is given of West Indian profligacies and barbarities. The author, Mr. Whiteley, states that he went out (seeking the employnent of book or storekeeper) with favourable notions of he condition of the slaves. He was well acquainted with he state of the factory children, and conceived their lot o be worse than that of the negroes; he had soon reason o alter his opinion.

"I proceeded on horseback to New Ground Estate. On my way thither I saw much majestic and beautiful cenery, and enjoyed the prospect exceedingly, until I ame in sight of a gang of negroes at work. Most of hem were females; and they were superintended by a driver, with his cart-whip in his hand. Just as I rode ast, the driver cracked the whip, and cried out— "Work! vork!" They were manuring the canes, and carrying he manure in baskets on their heads. It appeared to ne disgustingly dirty work; for the moisture from the nanure was dripping through the baskets, and running lown the bodies of the negroes. This sight annoyed me onsiderably, and raised some doubts as to the preferable ondition of West India slaves to factory children.

The enchanting scenery and beautiful humming birds no longer amused me; and the thundering crack of the cartwhip, sounding in my ears as I rode along, excited feelings of a very unpleasing description. On reaching the estate I was received in the most friendly manner by the overseer, and entertained with West Indian hospitality. This gentleman, after some inquiries as to the state of things in England, began to enlarge on the comfortable condition of the slaves; and pointing to some negro coopers who were working in the yard, asked if I could perceive any difference between the condition of these slaves and that of English labourers. I owned I could not; they seemed to work with great regularity and apparent good humour. Immediately afterwards the overseer called out in a very authoritative tone, "Blow shell." A large conch shell was then blown by one of the domestic slaves, and in a few minutes four negro drivers made their appearance in front of the house, accompanied by six common negroes. The drivers had each a long staff in his hand, and a large cart-whip coiled round his shoulders. They appeared to be very stout athletic men. They stood before the hall doors, and the overseer put on his hat and went out to them, while I sat at the open window and observed the scene which followed, having been informed that the other six negroes were to be punished. * * * *

The first was a man of about 35 years of age. He was what is called a pen-keeper, or cattle herd; and his offence was having suffered a mule to go astray. At the command of the overseer he proceeded to strip off part of his clothes, and laid himself flat on his belly, his back and buttocks being uncovered. One of the drivers then commenced flogging him with the cart-whip. This whip is about ten feet long, with a short stout handle, and is an instrument of terrible power. It is whirled by the operator round his head, and then brought down with a rapid motion of the arm upon the recumbent victim causing the blood to spring at every stroke. When I saw this spectacle, now for the first time exhibited before my eyes, with all its revolting accompaniments, and saw the degraded and mangled victim writhing and groaning under the infliction, I felt horror-struck. I trembled, and turned sick ; but being determined to see the whole to an end, I kept my station at the window. The sufferer, writhing like a wounded worm, every time the lash cut across his body cried out "Lord! Lord! Lord!" When he had received about 20 lashes, the driver stopped to pull up the poor man's shirt (or rather smock frock), which had worked down upon his galled posteriors. The sufferer then cried, " Think me no man? think me no man?" By that exclamation I understood him to say, " Think you I have not the feelings of a man?" The flogging was instantly recommenced and continued ; the negro continuing to cry " Lord ! Lord! Lord !" till 39 lashes had been inflicted. When the man rose up from the ground, I perceived the blood oozing out from the lacerated and tumefied parts where he had been flogged ; and he appeared greatly exhausted. But he was instantly ordered off to his usual occupation. The next was a young man apparently about 18 or 19 years of age. He was forced to uncover himself and lie down in the same mode as the former, and was held down by the hands and feet by four slaves, one of whom was a young man who was himself to be flogged next. This latter was a mulatto— the offspring, as I understood, of some European formerly on the estate by a negro woman, and consequently born to slavery. These two youths were flogged exactly in the mode already described, and writhed and groaned under the lash, as if enduring great agony. The mulatto bled most, and appeared to suffer most acutely. They received each 39 lashes. Their offence was some deficiency in the performance of the task prescribed to them. They were both ordered to join their gang as usual in the afternoon at cane-cutting.—Two young women of about the same age were, one after the other, then laid down and held by four men, their back parts most indecently uncovered, and 39 lashes of the blood-stained whip inflicted upon each poor creature's posteriors. Their

---

* This pamphlet is selling at one penny in England. We wish thousands of it were sent here.

exclamations likewise was "Lord! Lord! Lord!" They seemed also to suffer acutely, and were apparently a good deal lacerated. Another woman (the sixth offender) was also laid down and uncovered for the lash; but at the intercession of one of the drivers she was reprieved. The offence of these three women was similar to that of the two young men—some defalcation in the amount of labour. The overseer stood by and witnessed the whole of this cruel operation, with as much seeming indifference as if he had been paying them their wages. * * *

* * * I resided on New Ground estate, from the time of my arrival in the beginning of September, and exclusive of some occasional absences, altogether fully seven weeks; and during that period I witnessed with my own eyes the *regular* flogging of upwards of 20 negroes (277 on the estate.) I heard also of many other negroes being flogged by order of the overseer and book-keepers in the field, while I resided on the plantation, besides the cases which came under my own personal observation. Neither do I include in this account the slighter floggings inflicted by the drivers in superintending the working gangs, which I shall notice afterwards. * * * * * I shall mention only two other cases which particularly excited my sympathy; for, after a few weeks, although my moral abhorrence of slavery continued to increase, my sensibility to the sight of physical suffering was so greatly abated, that a common flogging no longer affected me to the very painful degree that I at first experienced. The first of these two cases was that of a married woman, the mother of several children. She was brought up to the overseer's door one morning; and one of the drivers who came with her accused her of having stolen a fowl. Some feathers, said to have been found in her hut, were exhibited as evidence of her guilt. The overseer asked her if she would pay for the fowl. She said something in reply, which I did not clearly understand. The question was repeated, and a similar reply again given. The overseer then said, "Put her down." On this the woman set up a shriek, and rent the air with her cries of terror. Her countenance grew quite ghastly, and her lips became pale and livid. I was close to her, and particularly noticed her remarkable aspect and expression of countenance. The overseer swore fearfully, and repeated his order—"Put her down!" The woman then craved permission to tie some covering round her nakedness, which she was allowed to do. She was then extended on the ground, and held down by two negroes. Her gown and shift were literally torn from her back, and, thus brutally exposed, she was subjected to the cart-whip. The punishment inflicted on this poor creature was inhumanly severe. She was a woman somewhat plump in her person, and the whip being wielded with great vigour, every stroke cut deep into the flesh. She writhed and twisted her body violently under the infliction—moaning loudly, but uttering no exclamation in words, except once when she cried out, entreating that her nakedness (her parts of shame) might not be indecently exposed,—appearing to suffer, from matronly modesty, even more acutely on account of her indecent exposure than the cruel laceration of her body. But the overseer only noticed her appeal by a brutal reply, (too gross to be repeated,) and the flogging continued. Disgusted as I was, I witnessed the whole to a close. I numbered the lashes, stroke by stroke, and counted *fifty*,—thus exceeding by eleven the number allowed by the colonial law to be inflicted at the arbitrary will of the master or manager. This was the only occasion on which I saw the legal number of 39 lashes exceeded, but I never knew the overseer or head book-keeper give less than 39. This poor victim was shockingly lacerated. When permitted to rise, she again shrieked violently. The overseer swore roughly, and threatened, if she was not quiet, to put her down again. He then ordered her to be taken to the hot-house or hospital, and put in the stocks. She was to be confined in the stocks for several nights, while she worked in the yard during the day at light work. She was too severely mangled to be able to go to the field for some days. This flogging took place on the 27th of September.—The flogging of an old man, about 60 years of age, is the last case I shall mention. He was the third driver upon the estate—there being five altogether, whose sole employment was literally, *driving,* or coercing by the whip, the negro population to labour. With this old man I had had some conversation, and felt particularly interested in him, for his silvery locks and something in his aspect reminded me powerfully of my aged father, whom I left in England. He had been upon the estate a great number of years. He told me that not one of the negroes belonging to the gang he wrought in when he first came to New Ground was now alive. He came up to the overseer's door at shell-blow one day, and gave in, as is the practice, on a tally or bit of notched stick, his account of the half day's work of the gang he superintended. The overseer was dissatisfied —said it was insufficient—and ordered him to get a flogging. The old man said, "Well, Busha, one could have done no better had you been standing by." Then, groaning deeply, he laid down his staff and whip, unloosed his clothes, and lay quietly down to be flogged without being held. One of the other drivers, who had been called forward, appeared very reluctant to perform the office; but on the overseer swearing a rough oath or two, he proceeded to inflict the usual punishment of 39 lashes. The old man, looking up in the overseer's face imploringly, cried out after every stroke for several minutes, "Busha! Busha! Busha!" but seeing no signs of relenting, he ceased to call on him, expressing his feelings only by groans. I was deeply affected by the sight, and felt at the moment that these groans were an awful appeal to the judgment seat of Him who heareth the cry of the oppressed. When the punishment was over, and the poor man arose, the other drivers looked at each other and shook their heads, but uttered not a word. They dared not.

The horror with which Mr. Whiteley viewed these scenes, and the fact of his being a sectarian (a Methodist) soon subjected him to persecution. A friend warned him, that it was necessary to his safety to renounce any appearance of sectarianism, and enrol himself a member of the Colonial Church Union; for the Established Church is the shibboleth of tyranny in those as well as in other parts; whence it is, we suppose, that the Bishops, as Lord Eldon remarked in justification of the practice, have never raised their voices against the wickedness of slavery. Mr. Whiteley not complying with this advice, the intention to tar and feather him was formally communicated by a deputation from the St. Ann's Colonial Church Union. His alleged offences were the mention of the name of God, especially to negroes, inquisitiveness as to crimes and punishments, and preaching to the slaves, which last charge he denies. In little more than three months he was obliged to quit the island. Mr. Whiteley mentions the case of negroes who were punished for praying!

EDUCATION IN AMERICA.

"There are at present at Boston (says Mr. Stuart) sixty-eight free Schools, besides twenty-three Sabbath schools, in all of which the poorest inhabitant of Boston may have his children educated, from the age of four to seventeen, without any expense whatever. The children of both sexes are freely admitted. The funds for these schools are derived from bequests and donations, and grants from the Legislature and Corporations, and enable the trustees, consisting of twelve citizens annually elected by each of the twelve wards of the city, with the Mayor and eight Aldermen, to give the teachers salaries, varying from 2500 to 800 dollars a-year. The assistant teachers have 600 dollars. A very strict system of supervision and regulation is established by the trustees. No expense whatever is incurred at these schools for the children except for books. The richer classes at Boston formerly very generally patronized teachers of private schools who were paid in the usual way, but they now find that the best teachers are at the head of the public schools, and in most cases prefer them; the children of the highest and lowest rank enjoy the privilege, altogether invaluable in a free state, of being educated together."

Here is a passage which some folks in Scotland would do well to ponder over. How different are their usages from those of the New Englanders? In every squire's family here, a tutor—paid partly in cash and partly in a promise of church preferment,—is retained for the express purpose of keeping the sprouts of aristocracy free from plebeian contamination;—and if they are sent to a public school, it is still under the inspection of the same mentor, and the seminary chosen is usually that Eton of Scotland, the Edinburgh New Academy. From such a course of tuition, what fruits can be expected but an inordinate stock of selfishness, pride, and conceit, that render their possessors, in after life, offensive or ridiculous to the inferior classes of society? Even in our burgh towns, where a desire to ape the great is but too prevalent, we find the local exclusives, with the means of excellent education at their doors, sending off their children to distant schools, for no other discoverable reason than to keep them away from the ordinary children of the place. The good example of the Americans apart,—we are much mistaken if political causes be not now at work which will break this pragmatical system of education to pieces; and, by a more promiscuous mixing up of the youth of all classes, give birth to those early associations which form the only true and enduring cement among the diversified orders of a free country.

Nor is the course of instruction in the New England schools so stinted and meagre as it is in our deservedly praised parochial schools of Scotland. Mr. Stuart thus describes it—

"The general plan of education at the public free schools here is not confined to mere reading, writing, arithmetic and book-keeping, and the ancient and modern languages; but comprehends grammar, mathematics, navigation, geography, history, logic, moral and natural philosophy; these schools being, as stated in their printed regulations, intended to occupy the young people from the age of four to seventeen, and to form a system of education advancing from the lowest to the highest degree of improvement which can be derived from any literary seminaries inferior to Colleges and Universities, and to afford a practical and theoretical acquaintance with the various branches of a useful education."

Mr. Stuart follows up his account of the New England schools with a few general notices.

"It is not however, to be inferred that education at free schools is so general all over the United States as in the four millions of inhabitants of New England and the State of New York; but the provision for public schools is admirable in all the populous States,—Pennsylvania, New Jersey, Maryland, Virginia, &c.; and free education can any where be procured, even in the southern States, for whites, on application being made for it. The appropriations of land for schools in the old States were formerly very much confined to the donations of individuals, many of which have now, however, become valuable; but the appropriations for schools in the new States have been regulated by Congress, and their extent is immense. Every township of the new lands is divided into thirty-six sections, each a mile square, and each containing 640 acres. One section of every township is appropriated for schools. In addition to this, great appropriations have been made in Ohio, Tennessee, Kentucky, and other of the western States for seminaries of a higher order, to the extent of about one-fifth of those for schools. The land belonging to public schools in the new states and territories, in which appropriations have been made on the east side of the Mississippi amounts to about eight millions of acres, and is of course advancing in value as the population increases. The extent of land which will be appropriated to the same purpose when the land on the western side of the Mississippi is settled must be prodigious,—at present not capable of being guessed at."

The reflections which Mr. Stuart makes on the subject we have been treating of, are too judicious to be omitted.

"It presents views not unworthy of notice, especially if the order and decorum which distinguish the people of the United States, and the total absence, in that country, of those whom, in Britain, are designated as the rabble or the mob, are to be ascribed to the general education of the people. All ranks are educated in those parts of the United States where there is any thing like a crowded population. Their example proves that there is no risk in bestowing the right to vote in elections on all persons not incapacitated by crime, who have been well educated."

And why has not Britain long ere now seen to the education of the great mass of her population? In the United States, a country yet in its infancy, the matter has ever been one of main concernment. In many parts of Germany, State schools are found in every district, and the attendance even rendered compulsory. Communal schools have now been established in France, and parochial ones, though ill-endowed and faultily organized, have long existed in Scotland. We do not require to look far to discover the cause of this gross omission on the part of our rulers. The past government of the country has not been paternal, but oligarchical,—its policy was to aggrandize the few, and to neglect the many. The axiom of knowledge being power, was never lost sight of by the dominant faction, whose uniform object has been to keep the mass of the people in as ignorant and debased a state as possible. Hence the little favour shewn to the Scotch parochial schools; hence the withholding of the like establishments from England and Ireland; hence the taxes on knowledge and other restrictions on the press; hence a brutalizing criminal code; hence dear justice; hence flogging in the army; hence the game laws,—and hence many other enactments and usages which will melt before the popular breath of a Reformed Parliament, as the noxious vapours of the night are dispelled by the beams of the sun.

The United States are amply supplied with Universities for the higher branches of study,—of which, Yale College in Connecticut, and Cambridge, near Boston, both visited by Mr. Stuart, are the most distinguished.

LORD BROUGHAM has moved for certain returns respecting national education. He states, that the endowed and other schools are not equal to more than the instruction of one-fifteenth part of the population, and mentions that, "In one of the largest goals in this country, out of 400 prisoners there were 200 utterly incapable of reading, and 50 more could only tell their alphabets, without being able to read even the shortest words. He hoped that some plan, founded on rational principles, could be devised to improve this condition of things."

THE MINERS OF BOIS-MONZIL.
AN AFFECTING AND AUTHENTIC NARRATIVE, BY AN EYE-WITNESS.

On Tuesday, February 22, a violent detonation was suddenly heard in the coal-mine of Bois-Monzil, belonging to M. Robinot. The waters from the old works rushed impetuously along the new galleries. "The waters, the waters!" such was the cry that resounded from the affrighted workmen throughout the mine. Only ten miners out of twenty-six were able to reach the entrance. One of them brought off in his arms, a boy eleven years old, whom he thus saved from certain death; another, impelled by the air and the water, to a considerable distance, could scarcely credit his escape, from such imminent danger; a third rushed forward with his sack full of coals on his shoulders, which, in his fright, he had never thought of throwing down.

The disastrous news, that sixteen workmen had perished in the mine of M. Robinot, was soon circulated in the town of St. Etienne.* It was regarded as one of those fatal and deplorable events, unfortunately, too common in that neighbourhood, and on the ensuing Thursday it was no

* St. Etienne, a manufacturing town for hardware, and ribbands, with a population of 100,000 souls; the Birmingham and Coventry of France. It is situated on the banks of the Loire.

longer talked of. Politics, and the state of parties in Paris, exclusively occupied the public attention.

The engineers of the mines, however, and some of their pupils, who, on the first alarm, had hastened to the spot, still remained there, continuing their indefatigable endeavours to discover the miners who were missing. Nothing that mechanical science, manual labour, and perseverance, prompted by humanity, could perform, was left undone.

Thirty hours had already elapsed since the fatal accident, when two workmen announced the discovery of a jacket and some provisions belonging to the miners. The engineers immediately essayed to penetrate into the galleries where these objects had been found, which they accomplished with much difficulty, by crawling on their hands and feet. In vain they repeatedly called aloud; no voice, save the echo of their own, answered from those narrow and gloomy vaults. It then occurred to them to strike with their pick-axes against the roof of the mine. Still the same uncheering silence !...Listen! yes! the sounds are answered by similar blows !—Every heart beats, every pulse quickens, every breath is contracted ;—yet, perhaps, it is but an illusion of their wishes—or, perhaps, some deceitful echo ......They again strike the vaulted roof.—There is no longer any doubt.—The same number of strokes is returned. No words can paint the varied feelings that pervaded every heart! It was (to use the expression of a person present) a veritable delirium of joy, of fear, and of hope.

Without losing an instant, the engineers ordered a hole to be bored in the direction of the galleries where the miners were presumed to be; at the same time they directed, on another point, the formation of an inclined well, for the purpose of communicating with them.

Two of the engineer's pupils were now despatched to the mayor of St. Etienne, to procure a couple of fire-pumps, which they conducted back to the mine, accompanied by two firemen. In the ardour of youthful humanity, those young men imagined that the deliverance of the miners was but the affair of a few hours; and, wishing to prepare an "agreeable surprise" for the friends of the supposed victims, they gave strict injunctions at the mayoralty to keep the object of their expedition a profound secret.

Notwithstanding the untiring efforts made to place these pumps in the mine, it was found impossible. Either they were upon a plane too much inclined to admit of their playing with facility, or the water was too muddy to be received up the pipes; they were therefore abandoned. In the meantime, the attempts made to reach the miners by sounding, or by the inclined well, seemed to present insurmountable difficulties. The distance to them was unknown: the sound of their blows on the roof, far from offering a certain criterion, or, at least, a probable one, seemed each time to excite fresh doubts; in short, the rock which it was necessary to pierce was equally hard and thick, and the gunpowder unceasingly used to perforate it, made but a hopeless progress. The consequent anxiety that reigned in the mine may be easily conceived. Each of the party, in his turn, offered his suggestions, sometimes of hope, sometimes of apprehension, and the whole felt oppressed by that vague suspense, which is, perhaps, more painful to support, than the direst certainty. The strokes of the unfortunate miners continued to reply to theirs, which added to their agitation, from the fear of not being able to afford them effectual help. They almost thought that in such a painful moment, their situation was more distressing than those they sought to save, as the latter were, at any rate sustained by hope.

While most of the party were thus perplexed by a crowd of disquieting ideas, produced by the distressing nature o the event itself, and by their protracted stay in a mine where the few solitary lamps scarcely rendered "darkness visible," the workmen continued their labours with redoubled ardour; some of them were hewing to pieces blocks of the rock, which fell slowly, and with much difficulty; others were actively employed in boring the hole before named, whilst some of the engineer's apprentices sought to discover new galleries, either by creeping on "all fours," or by penetrating through perilous and narrow crevices and cefts of the rock.

In the midst of their corporeal and mental labours, their attention was suddenly excited from another painful source. The wives of the hapless miners had heard that all hope was not extinct. They hastened to the spot: with heart-rending cries, and through tears, alternately of despair and hope, they exclaimed, "Are they *all* there ? " Where is the father of my children ? Is *he* amongst them, or has he been swallowed up by the waters ?"

At the bottom of the mine, close to the water-reservoir, a consultation was held on the plan to be pursued. Engineers, pupils, workmen, all agreed that the only prospect of success consisted in exhausting the water, which was already sensibly diminished, by the sole working of the steam-pump; the other pumps produced little or no effect, notwithstanding the vigorous efforts employed to render them serviceable. Somebody then proposed remedying the failure of these pumps by *une chaine a bras*, viz. by forming a line, and passing buckets from one to the other; this method was adopted, and several of the pupils proceeded with all speed to St. Etienne. It was midnight. The *générale* was beat in two quarters of the town only. The Hotel de Ville was assigned as the place of rendezvous. On the first alarm a great number of persons hurried to the town-hall, imagining a fire had broken out, but on ascertaining the real cause, several of them returned home, apparently unmoved. Yet these very same persons, whose supposed apathy had excited both surprise and indignation, quickly reappeared on the scene, dressed in the uniform of the National Guard. So powerful is the magic influence of organized masses, marching under the orders of a chief, and stimulated by *l'esprit de corps*.

It was truly admirable to see with what address and rapidity, the three or four hundred men, who had hastened to Bois-Monzil, passed and repassed the buckets, by forming a chain to the bottom of the mine. But their generous efforts became too fatiguing to last long. Imagine a subterranean badly lighted, where they were obliged to maintain themselves in a rapid descent, in a stooping posture, to avoid striking their heads against the roof of the vault, and, most of the time, up to the middle in the water, which was dripping from every side; some idea may then be formed of their painful situation. They were relieved from this laborious duty by the *Garde Nationale* of St. Etienne, whose zeal and enthusiasm exceeded all praise. But a more precious reinforcement was at hand: the workmen from the adjacent mines now arrived in great numbers. From their skill and experience every thing might be expected; if they failed there was no further hope.

The *chaine a bras* was again renewed by companies of the National Guard, relieved every two hours, who, at respective distances, held the lights, and under whose orders they acted. It was a cheering spectacle to behold citizens of all ranks engaged in one of the noblest offices of humanity, under the direction of poor colliers.

The immense advantages of the organization of the National Guard, were never more strikingly exemplified than on this occasion. Without them there would have been no means or possibility of uniting together an entire population; of leading the people from a distance of more than three miles night and day, so as to insure a regular and continued service; all would have been trouble and confusion. With them, on the contrary, every thing was ready, and in motion, at the voice of a single chief; and the whole was conducted with such precision and regularity as had never, on similar occasions, been witnessed before.

The road from St. Etienne to Bois-Monzil, exhibited a scene of the most animated kind. In the midst of the motley and moving multitude, the National Guards were seen hurrying to and fro; *chasseurs*, grenadiers, cavalry, and artillerymen, all clothed in their rich new costume, as on a field day. Some of the crowd were singing *la Parisienne*, others were lamenting, praying, hoping, despairing, and by "fits and starts," abandoning themselves to those opposite extravagancies of sentiment so peculiarly characteristic of a French population. When night drew her sable curtains around, the *picturesque* of the scene was still more heightened. Fresh bands of miners, conducted by their respective chiefs, coming in from every side; their sooty visages lighted up by glaring torches; National Guards arriving from different parts of the country, to join their comrades of St. Etienne; farmers and peasants, on horseback and a-foot, hastening to offer their humane aid; sentinels posted—muskets piled—watch-fires blazing, and, in short, the *tout ensemble* rendered the approaches of Bois-Monzil, like a *bivouac* on the eve of an expected battle; happily, however, the object of these brave men was to preserve life, and not to destroy it. It is but just to render homage here to the worthy *curé* of St. Villars, who, in his simple clerical dress, mingled everywhere with the anxious throng, exhorting and encouraging them in "their good work," both by precept and example:

"He had no bigot's pride—no sectary's whim;
"Christian and countryman were all to him."

On the Saturday the *chaîne à bras* was discontinued, as the engineers had now brought the pumps effectually to work. Suddenly a cry of joy was echoed from mouth to mouth: "They are saved! they are saved! six of them are freed from their subterraneous prison! shouted a person at the entrance of the mine. The rumour was instantly repeated along the crowd, and a horseman set off at full speed for St. Etienne, with the gratifying news; another followed and confirmed the report of his predecessor. The whole town was in motion, and all classes seemed to partake of the general joy, with a feeling as if each person had been individually interested. In the exuberance of their delight they were already deliberating on the subject of a *fête*, to celebrate the happy event, when a third horseman arrived. The multitude thronged round him expecting a more ample confirmation of the welcome tidings. But their joy was soon turned to sorrow, when they were informed that nothing had yet been discovered, save the dead bodies of two unfortunate men, who, together, had left eleven children to lament their untimely fate.

On Sunday, the workmen continued their labour with equal zeal and uncertainty as before. A sort of inquietude and hopelessness, however, occasionally pervaded their minds, which may be easily accounted for, from the hitherto fruitless result of their fatiguing researches. Discussions now took place on what was to be done; differences of opinion arose on the various plans proposed, and, in the meantime, the sounds of the hapless victims, from the recesses of the rocky cavern, continued to be distinctly audible. Every moment the embarrassment and difficulties of the workmen increased. The flinty rock seemed to grow more impenetrable; their tools either broke, or became so fixed in the stone, that it was frequently impossible to regain them. The water filtered from all parts, through the narrow gallery they were perforating, and they even began to apprehend another irruption.

Such was the state of things on the Monday morning, when, at four o'clock, an astounding noise was heard, which re-echoed throughout the whole extent of the mine. A general panic seized on every one; it was thought that the waters had forced a new issue. A rapid and confused flight took place; but, luckily, their fears were soon allayed on perceiving that it was only an immense mass of rock, detached from the mine, which had fallen into a draining-well. This false alarm, however, operated in a discouraging manner, on the minds of the workmen; and it required some management to bring them back to their respective stations, and to revive that ardour and constancy, which they had, hitherto, so admirably displayed.

They had scarcely renewed their endeavours to bore through the rock, when suddenly one of them felt the instrument drawn from his hands, by the poor imprisoned miners. It was indeed, to them, *the instrument of deliverance* from their cruel situation. Singular to relate, their first request was neither for food nor drink, but for *light*, as if they were more eager to make use of their eyes, than to satisfy the pressing wants of appetite! It was now ascertained that eight of the sufferers still survived; and this time an authentic account of the happy discovery was despatched to St. Etienne, where it excited the most enthusiastic demonstrations of sympathy and gladness. But there is no pleasure unmixed with alloy; no general happiness unaccompanied by particular exceptions. Amongst the workmen, was the father of one of the men who had disappeared in the mine. His paternal feelings seemed to have endowed him with superhuman strength. Night and day he never quitted his work but for a few minutes, to return to it with redoubled ardour: one sole, absorbing thought, occupied his whole soul; the idea that his son, his *only* son, was with those who were heard from within. In vain he was solicited to retire; in vain they strove to force him from labours too fatiguing for his age. "My son is amongst them," said he; "I hear him; nothing shall prevent my hastening his release;" and, from time to time, he called on his son, in accents that tore the hearts of the bystanders. It was from his hand that the instrument had been drawn. His first question was, "My child?" Like Apelles, let me throw a veil over a father's grief.—His Antoine was no more; he had been drowned!

For four days several medical men were constantly on the spot, to contribute all the succours that humanity, skill, and science could afford. It was they who introduced, through the hole, broth and soup, by means of long tin tubes, which had been carefully prepared beforehand. The poor captives distributed it with the most scrupulous attention, *first to the oldest and weakest of their companions*, for, notwithstanding their dreadful situation, the spirit of concord and charity had never ceased for a single moment, to preside amongst them. The man who was appointed by the others to communicate with, and answer the questions of their deliverers, displayed, in all his replies, a gaiety quite in keeping with the French character. On being asked what day he thought it was, and on being informed that it was Monday instead of Sunday, as he had supposed, "Ah!" said he, "I ought to have known that; as we yesterday indulged ourselves freely in drinking——water." Strange that a man should have the heart to joke, who had been thus "cabin'd, cribb'd, confin'd" during five days, destitute of food, deprived of air, agitated by suspense, and in jeopardy of perishing by the most horrible of all deaths!

There still remained full sixteen feet of solid rock between the two anxious parties; but the workmen's labours were now, if possible, redoubled by the certainty of complete success. At intervals, light nourishment, in regulated quantities, continued to be passed to the miners; this, however, they soon rejected, expressing but one desire, that their friends would *make haste*. Their strength began to fail them; their respiration became more and more difficult; their utterance grew feebler and fainter; and towards six o'clock in the evening, the last words that could be distinguished, were—"Brothers make haste!"

The general anxiety was now wound up to the highest pitch; it was, perhaps, the most trying crisis yet experienced since the commencement of these benevolent labours; at length the moment of deliverance was, all at once, announced, and at ten o'clock it was accomplished. One by one they appeared, like spectres, gliding along the gallery which had just been completed; their weak, and agitated forms supported by the engineers, on whom they cast their feeble eyes, filled with astonishment, yet beaming with gratitude. Accompanied by the doctors, they all, with one single exception, ascended to the entrance of the mine, without aid; such was their eagerness again to inhale the pure air of liberty. From the mouth of the mine to the temporary residence allotted them, the whole way was illuminated. The engineers, pupils, and the workmen, with the National Guard under arms, were drawn up in two lines to form a passage; and, thus, in the midst of a religious silence, did these poor fellows traverse an attentive and sympathizing crowd, who, as they passed along, inclined their heads, as a sort of respect and honour to their sufferings.

Such are the affecting particulars of an event, during the whole of which, every kind of business was suspended at St. Etienne; an event which exhibited the entire population of a large town, forming, as it were, but one heart, entertaining but one thought, imbued with but one feeling, for the god-like purpose of saving the lives of eight poor obscure individuals. Christians, men of all countries, whenever and wherever suffering humanity claims your aid,—*Go ye and do likewise!*

THREE ARGUMENTS

IN FAVOUR OF A REPEAL OF THE TAXES ON KNOWLEDGE, BY LORD BROUGHAM.

" WHY," asks Lord Brougham, in his pamphlet on the education of the people, published in 1825, " Why should not *political*, as well as other works, be published in a cheap form and in numbers?" We echo the question with all the voice we can give to it—why should not political knowledge be as widely and cheaply diffused as scientific knowledge?

" *Honest Althorp*, tell us why?"

Neither of the Chancellors answer this question; but if neither of them give a reason why it should not, the Lord Chancellor gives many a good reason, in his pamphlet aforesaid, why it should; and these we proceed to quote:—

ARGUMENT 1.—*Cheap political knowledge should be widely disseminated, because it would conduce to the welfare and interests of the people:*—

" That history, the nature of the constitution, the doctrines of political economy, may safely be disseminated in this shape, no man now-a-days will be hardy enough to deny. Popular tracts, indeed, on the latter subject, ought to be much more extensively circulated for the good of the working classes as well as of their superiors. The interests of both are deeply concerned in sounder views being taught them; I can hardly imagine, for example, a greater service being rendered to the men, than expounding to them the true principles and mutual relations of population and wages; and both they and their masters will assuredly experience the effects of the prevailing ignorance upon such questions, as soon as any interruption shall happen in the commercial prosperity of the country, if indeed, the present course of things, daily tending to lower wages as well as profits, and set the two classes in opposition to each other, shall not of itself bring on a crisis. To allow, or rather to induce the people to take part in these discussions, is, therefore, not merely safe, but most wholesome for the community; and yet, some points connected with them, are matter of pretty warm contention in the present times; but these may be freely handled, it seems, with safety; indeed, unless they are so handled, such subjects cannot be discussed at all."

ARGUMENT 2.—*Cheap political knowledge should be widely disseminated, because it is not only safe but beneficial:*—

" It is highly useful to the community, that the true principles of the constitution, ecclesiastical and civil, should be well understood by every man who lives under it. The great interests of civil and religious liberty are mightily promoted by such wholesome instruction; but the good order of society gains to the full as much by it. The peace of the country, and the stability of the government, could not be more effectually secured than by the universal diffusion of this kind of knowledge. The abuses which through time have crept into the practice of the constitution, the errors committed in its administration, and the improvement which a change of circumstances require, even in its principles, may most fitly be expounded in the same manner. And if any man, or set of men, deny the existence of such abuses, see no error in the conduct of those who administer the Government, and regard all innovation upon its principles as pernicious, they may propagate their doctrines through the like channels. Cheap works being furnished, the choice of them may be left to the reader. Assuredly a country which tolerates every kind, even the most unmeasured of daily and weekly discussion in the newspapers, can have nothing to dread from the diffusion of political doctrines, in a form less desultory, and more likely to make them be both well weighed at the time, and reserved for repeated perusal."

ARGUMENT 3.—*Cheap political knowledge should be widely disseminated, because it would be fatal to tyranny and misrule:*—

" To tyrants, indeed, and bad rulers, the progress of knowledge among the mass of mankind is a just object of terror; it is fatal to them and their designs; they know this by unerring instinct, and unceasingly they dread the light. But they will find it more easy to curse than to extinguish. It is spreading in spite of them, even in those countries where arbitrary power deems itself most secure; and in England, any attempt to check its progress would only bring about the sudden destruction of him who should be insane enough to make it."

Such are the arguments of Lord Brougham in favour of a repeal of the taxes on knowledge. We trust that his philosophy will

" Propagate its kind where'er it may;"

and that his associates in the Ministry will not be among the last to derive benefit from it.[*]

VERSES FOR THE YOUNG.

HYMN FOR THE SONS OF THE CLERGY.

BY MRS. GRANT OF LAGGAN.

How blest those olive plants that grow
  Beneath the altar's sacred shade,
Where streams of fresh instruction flow,
  And Comfort's humble board is spread.

'Twas thus the swallow rear'd her young,
  Secure within the house of GOD,
Of whom the Royal Prophet sung,
  When banish'd from that blest abode.

When, like the swallow's tender brood,
  They leave the kind paternal dome,
On weary wing to seek their food,
  Or find in other climes a home.

Where'er they roam, where'er they rest,
  Through all the varied scenes of life,
Whether with tranquil plenty blest,
  Or doom'd to share the deadly strife.

Still may the streams of grace divine,
  Glide softly near their devious way;
And faith's fair light serenely shine,
  To change their darkness into day.

Still may they with fraternal love,
  Each other's shield and aid become;
And while through distant realms they rove,
  Remember still their childhood's home;

The simple life, the frugal fare,
  The kind parental counsels given,
The tender love, the pious care,
  That early winged their hopes to heaven.

And when the evening shades decline,
  And when life's toilsome task is o'er,
May they each earthly wish resign,
  And holier, happier climes explore.

And when the faithful shepherds view
  Each ransom'd flock around them spread,
How will they bless the plants that grew
  Beneath the altar's sacred shade!

---

[*] We printed some of these extracts in the first No. of the *Schoolmaster*. If any one wish to know why we do so again, let him search Lord Althorp's Budget.

THE STORY-TELLER.

THE KING OF THE PEAK, A DERBYSHIRE TALE.
BY ALLAN CUNNINGHAM.

It happened on a summer evening, when I was a boy, that several curious old people had seated themselves on a little round knoll near the gate of Haddon Hall; and their talk was of the Vernons, the Cavendishes, the Manners, and many old names once renowned in Derbyshire. I had fastened myself to the apron-string of a venerable dame, at whose girdle hung a mighty iron key, which commanded the entrance of the hall; her name was Dolly Foljambe; and she boasted her descent from an ancient red-cross knight of that name, whose alabaster figure, in mail, may be found in Bakewell church. This high origin, which, on consulting family history, I find had not the concurrence of clergy, seemed not an idle vanity of the humble portress; she had the straight frame, and rigid, demure, and even warlike cast of face, which alabaster still retains of her ancestor; and had she laid herself by his side, she might have passed muster, with an ordinary antiquarian, for a coeval figure. At our feet the river Wye ran winding and deep; at our side rose the hall, huge and grey; and the rough heathy hills, renowned in Druidic, and Roman, and Saxon, and Norman story, bounded our wish for distant prospects, and gave us the mansion of the Vernons for our contemplation, clear of all meaner encumbrances of landscape.

"Ah! dame Foljambe," said an old husbandman, whose hair was whitened by acquaintance with seventy winters; "it's a sore and a sad sight, to look at that fair tower, and see no smoke ascending. I remember it in a brighter day, when many a fair face gazed out at the windows, and many a gallant form appeared at the gate. Then were the days when the husbandman could live—could whistle as he sowed; dance and sing as he reaped; and could pay his rent in fatted oxen to my lord, and in fatted fowls to my lady. Ah! dame Foljambe, we remember when men could cast their lines in the Wye; could feast on the red deer and the fallow deer, on the plover and the ptarmigan; had right of the common for their flocks, of the flood for their nets, and of the air for their harquebuss. Ah! dame, old England is no more the old England it was, than that hall,—dark and silent and desolate—is the proud hall that held Sir George Vernon, the King of the Peak, and his two lovely daughters, Margaret and Dora. Those were days, dame; those were days." And, as he ceased, he looked up to the tower, with an eye of sorrow, and shook and smoothed down his white hairs.

"I tell thee," replied the ancient portress, sorely moved in mind, between present duty and service to the noble owner of Haddon, and her lingering affection for the good old times, of which memory shapes so many paradises, "I tell thee, the tower looks as high and as lordly as ever; and there is something about its silent porch, and its crumbling turrets, which gives it a deeper hold of our affections, than if an hundred knights even now came prancing forth at its porch, with trumpets blowing, and banners displayed."

"Ah! dame Foljambe," said the husbandman; "yon deer now bounding so blithely down the old chase, with his horny head held high, and an eye that seems to make nought of mountain and vale; it is a fair creature. Look at him! see how he cools his feet in the Wye, surveys his shadow in the stream, and now he contemplates his native hills again. So! away he goes, and we gaze after him, and admire his speed and his beauty. But were the hounds at his flanks, and the bullets in his side, and the swords of the hunters bared for the brittling; ah! dame, we should change our cheer: we should think that such shapely limbs, and such stately antlers, might have reigned in wood and on hill for many summers. Even so we think of that stately old hall, and lament its destruction."

"Dame Foljambe thinks not so deeply on the matter," said a rustic; "she thinks, the less the hall fire, the less is the chance of the hall being consumed; the less the company, the longer will the old hall floor last, which she sweeps so clean, telling so many stories of the tree that made it;—that the seven Virtues in the tapestry would do well in avoiding wild company; and that the lass with the long shanks, Diana, and her nymphs, will hunt more to her fancy on her dusty acre of old arras, than in the dubious society of the lords and the heroes of the court gazette. Moreover, the key at her girdle is the commission by which she is keeper of this cast-off and moth-eaten garment of the noble name of Manners; and think ye that she holds that power lightly, which makes her governess of ten thousand bats and owls, and gives her the awful responsibility of an armoury containing almost an entire harquebuss, the remains of a pair of boots, and the relic of a buff jerkin?"

What answer to this unceremonious attack on ancient things committed to her keeping, the portress might have made, I had not an opportunity to learn.

"I marvel much," said the hoary portress, "at the idle love for strange and incredible stories which possesses, as with a demon, the peasants of this district. Not only have they given a saint, with a shirt of hair-cloth and a scourge, to every cavern; and a druid with his golden sickle and his mistletoe to every circle of shapeless stones; but they have made the Vernons, the Cavendishes, the Cockaynes, and the Foljambes, erect, on every wild place, crosses or altars of atonement for crimes which they never committed; unless fighting ankle-deep in heathen blood, for the recovery of Jerusalem and the holy Sepulchre, required such outlandish penance. They cast, too, a supernatural light round the commonest story; if you credit them, the ancient chapel bell of Haddon, safely lodged on the floor for a century, is carried to the top of the turret, and, touched by some invisible hand, is made to toll forth midnight notes of dolour and woe, when any misfortune is about to befall the noble family of Rutland. They tell you, too, that wailings, of no earthly voice, are heard around the decayed towers, and along the garden terraces, on the festival night of the saint who presided of old over the fortunes of the name of Vernon. And no longer agone than yesterday, old Edgar Ferrars assured me that he had nearly as good as seen the apparition of the King of the Peak himself, mounted on his visionary steed, and, with imaginary horn, and hound, and halloo, pursuing a spectre stag over the wild chace of Haddon. Nay, so far has vulgar credulity and assurance gone, that the great garden entrance, called the Knight's porch, through which Dora Vernon descended step by step among her twenty attendant maidens, all rustling in embroidered silks, and shining and sparkling, like a winter sky, in diamonds, and such like costly stones—to welcome her noble bridegroom, Lord John Manners, who came cap in hand with his company of gallant gentlemen—"

"Nay, now, dame Foljambe," interrupted the husbandman, "all this is fine enough, and lordly too, I'll warrant; but thou must not apparel a plain old tale in the embroidered raiment of thy own brain, nor adorn it in the precious stones of thy own fancy. Dora Vernon was a lovely lass, and as proud as she was lovely; she bore her head high, dame; and well she might, for she was a gallant Knight's daughter; and lords and dukes, and what not, have descended from her. But for all that, I cannot forget that she ran away in the middle of a moonlight night, with young Lord John Manners, and no other attendant than her own sweet self. Ay, dame, and for the diamonds, and what not, which thy story showers on her locks and her garments, she tied up her berry brown locks in a menial's cap, and ran away in a mantle of Bakewell brown, three yards for a groat. Ay, dame, and instead of going out regularly by the door, she leaped out of the window; more by token she left one of her silver heeled-slippers fastened in the grating, and the place has ever since been called the Lady's Leap. And, now dame, I will tell thee the story in my own and my father's way: The last of the name of Vernon was renowned far and wide for the hospitality and magnificence of his house, for the splendour of his retinue, and more for the beauty of his daughters, Margaret and Dorothy. This is speaking in thy own manner, dame Foljambe; but truth's truth. He was much given to hunting and hawking, and jousting with lances either blunt or sharp; and though a harquebuss generally was found in the hand of the gallant hunters of that time, the year of grace 1560, Sir George Vernon despised that foreign weapon; and well he might, for he bent the strongest bow, and shot the surest shaft, of any man in England. His chace-dogs, too, were all of the most expert and famous kinds—his falcons had the fairest and most certain flight; and though he had seen foreign lands, he chiefly prided himself in maintaining unimpaired the old baronial grandeur of his house. I have heard my grandsire say, how his great grandsire told him, that the like of the Knight of Haddon, for a stately form, and a noble, free, and natural grace of manner, was not to be seen in court or camp. He was hailed, in common tale, and in minstrel song, by the name of the KING OF THE PEAK; and it is said, his handsome person and witchery of tongue chiefly prevented his mistress, good Queen Bess, from abridging his provincial designation with the headsman's axe.

"It happened in the fifth year of the reign of his young and sovereign mistress, that a great hunting festival was held at Haddon, where all the beauty and high blood of Derbyshire assembled. Lords of distant counties came; for to bend a bow, or brittle the deer, under the eye of Sir George Vernon, was an honour sought for by many. Over the chase of Haddon, over the hill of Stanton, over Bakewell-edge, over Chatsworth hill and Hardwicke plain, and beneath the ancient Castle of Bolsover, as far as the edge of the forest of old Sherwood, were the sounds of harquebuss and bowstring heard, and the cry of dogs and the cheering of men. The brown-mouthed and white-footed dogs of Derbyshire were there among the foremost; the snow-white hound and the coal-black, from the Scottish Border and bonny Westmoreland, preserved or augmented their ancient fame; nor were the dappled hounds of old Godfrey Foljambe, of Bakewell Lank, far from the throat of the red deer when they turned at bay, and gored horses and riders. The great hall floor of Haddon was soon covered with the produce of wood and wild.

"Nor were the preparations for feasting this noble hunting party unworthy the reputation for solid hospitality which characterised the ancient King of the Peak. Minstrels had come from distant parts, as far even as the Scottish Border; bold, free-spoken, rude, rough-witted men; for the selvage of the web,' says the northern proverb, ' is 'aye the coarsest cloth.' But in the larder the skill of man was chiefly employed, and a thousand rarities were prepared for pleasing the eye and appeasing the appetite. In the kitchen, with its huge chimneys and prodigious spits, the menial maidens were flooded nigh ankle deep in the richness of roasted oxen and deer; and along the passage, communicating with the hall of state, men might have slided along, because of the fat droppings of that prodigious feast, like a slider on the frozen Wye. The kitchen tables, of solid plank, groaned and yielded beneath the roasted beeves and the spitted deer; while a stream of rich smoke, massy and slow, and savoury, sallied out at the grated windows, and sailed round the mansion, like a mist exhaled by the influence of the moon. I tell thee, dame Foljambe, I call those the golden days of old England.

"But I wish you had seen the hall prepared for this princely feast. The floor, of hard and solid stone, was strewn deep with rushes and fern; and there lay the dogs of the chase in couples, their mouths still red with the blood of stags, and panting yet from the fervour and length of their pursuit. All the lower end of the hall, where the floor subsided a step, was spread a table for the stewards and other chiefs over the menials. There sat the keeper of the bows, the warder of the chase, and the head falconer, together with many others of lower degree, but mighty men among the retainers of the noble name of Vernon. Over their heads were hung the horns of stags, the tusks of boars, the skulls of the enormous bisons, and the foreheads of foxes. Nor were there wanting trophies, where the contest had been more bloody and obstinate—banners and shields, and helmets, won in the Civil, and Scottish, and Crusading wars, together with many strange weapons of annoyance, or defence, borne in the Norwegian and Saxon broils. Beside them were hung rude paintings of the most renowned of these rustic heroes, all in the picturesque habiliments of the times. Horns, and harquebusses, and swords, and bows, and buff coats, and caps, were thrown in negligent groups all about the floor, while their owners sat in expectation of an immediate and ample feast, which they hoped to wash down with floods of that salutary beverage, the brown blood of barley.

"At the upper end of the hall, where the floor was elevated exactly as much in respect, as it was lowered in submission at the other, there the table for feasting the nobles stood; and well was it worthy of its station. It was one solid plank of white sycamore, shaped from the entire shaft of an enormous tree, and supported on squat columns of oak, ornamented with the arms of the Vernons, and grooved into the stone floor, beyond all chance of being upset by human powers. Benches of wood, curiously carved, and covered, in times of more than ordinary ceremony, with cushions of embroidered velvet, surrounded this ample table; while, in the recess behind, appeared a curious work in arms, consisting of festivals, and processions, and bridals, executed from the ancient poets; and for the more staid and grave, a more devout hand had wrought some scenes from the controversial fathers and the monkish legends of the ancient church. The former employed the white hands of Dora Vernon herself; while the latter were the labours of her sister Margaret, who was of a serious turn, and never happened to be so far in love as to leap from a window.

"Suppose the table filled about with the gallants of the chase and many fair ladies, while at the head sat the King of the Peak himself, his beard descending to his broad girdle, his own natural hair of dark brown—blessings on the head that keeps God's own covering on it, and scorns the curled inventions of man—falling in thick masses on his broad, manly shoulders. Nor silver, nor gold wore he; the natural nobleness of his looks maintained his rank and pre-eminence among men; the step of Sir George Vernon was one that many imitated, but few could attain—at once manly and graceful. I have heard it said, that he carried privately in his bosom a small rosary of precious metal, in which his favourite daughter Dora had entwined one of her mother's tresses. The ewer-bearers entered with silver basins full of water; the element came pure and returned red; for the hands of the guests were stained with the blood of the chase. The attendant minstrels vowed, that no hands so shapely, nor fingers so taper, and long, and white, and round, as those of the Knight of Haddon, were that day dipped in water.

"There is wondrous little pleasure in describing a feast of which we have not partaken; so pass we on to the time when the fair dames retired, and the red wine in cups of gold, and the ale in silver flagons, shone and sparkled as they passed from hand to lip beneath the blaze of seven massy lamps. The knights toasted their mistresses, the retainers told their exploits, and the minstrels with harp and tongue made music and song abound. The gentles struck their drinking vessels on the table till they rang again; the menials stamped with the heels of their ponderous boots on the solid floor; while the hounds, imagining they heard the call to the chase, leaped up, and bayed in hoarse but appropriate chorus.

"The ladies now reappeared, in the side galleries, and overlooked the scene of festivity below. The loveliest of many counties were there; but the fairest was a young maid of middle size, in a dress disencumbered of ornament, and possessed of one of those free and graceful forms which may be met with in other counties, but for which our own Derbyshire alone is famous. Those who admired the grace of her person were no less charmed with her simplicity and natural meekness of deportment. Nature did much for her, and art strove in vain to rival her with others; while health, that handmaid of beauty, supplied her eye and her cheek with the purest light and the freshest roses. Her short and rosy upper-lip was slightly curled, with as much of maiden sanctity, perhaps, as pride; her white high forehead was shaded with locks of sunny brown, while her large and dark hazel eyes beamed with free and unaffected modesty. Those who observed her close, might see her eyes, as she glanced about, sparkling for a moment with other lights, but scarce less holy, than those of devotion and awe. Of all the knights present, it was impossible to say, who inspired her with those love-fits of flushing joy and delirious agitation; each hoped himself the happy person; for none could look on Dora Vernon without awe and love. She leaned her white bosom, shining through the veil which shaded it, near one of the minstrels harps; and looking round on the presence, her eyes grew brighter as she looked; at least so vowed the knights, and so sang the minstrel.

"All the knights arose when Dora Vernon appeared. 'Fill all your wine-cups, knights,' said Sir Lucas Peverel. 'Fill them to the brim,' said Sir Henry Avenel. 'And drain them out, were they deeper than the Wye,' said Sir Godfrey Gernon. 'To the health of the Princess of the Peak,' said Sir Ralph Cavendish. 'To the health of Dora Vernon,' said Sir Hugh de Wodensley; 'beauty is above titles, she is the loveliest maiden a knight ever looked on, with the sweetest name too.' 'And yet, Sir Knight,' said Peverel, filling his cup, 'I know one who thinks so humbly of the fair name of Vernon, as to wish it charmed into that of De Wodensley.' 'He is not master of a spell so profound,' said Avenel. ['And yet he is master of his sword,' answered De Wodensley, with a darkening brow. 'I counsel him to keep it in its sheath,' said Cavendish, 'lest it prove a wayward servant.' 'I will prove its service on thy bosom where and when thou wilt, Lord of Chatsworth, said De Wodensley. 'Lord of Darley,' answered Cavendish, 'it is a tempting moonlight, but there is a charm over Haddon to-night, it would be unseemly to dispel. To-morrow, I meet Lord John Manners to try whose hawk has the fairer flight, and whose love the whiter hand. That can be soon seen; for who has so fair a hand as the love of young Rutland? I shall be found by Durwood-Tor, when the sun is three hours up, with my sword drawn —there's my hand on't, De Wodensley;' and he wrung the knight's hand till the blood seemed starting from beneath his finger nails.

"'By the saints, Sir Knights,' said Sir Godfrey Gernon, 'you may as well beard one another about the love of "some bright particular star and think to wed it," as the wild wizard of Warwick says, as quarrel about this unattainable love. Hearken, minstrels; while we drain our cups to this beauteous lass, sing some of you a kindly love-strain, wondrously mirthful and melancholy. Here's a cup of Rhenish, and a good gold Harry in the bottom on't, for the minstrel who pleases me.' The minstrels laid their hands on the strings, and a sound was heard like the swarming of bees before summer thunder. 'Sir Knight, said one, 'I will sing ye, Cannie Johnie Armstrong with all the seventeen variations.' 'He was hanged for cattle stealing,' answered the knight. 'I'll have none of him.' 'What say you to Dick of the Cow, or the Harper of Lochmaben?' said another, with something of a tone of diffidence. 'What! you northern knaves, can you sing of nothing but thievery and jail-breaking?' 'Perhaps your knightship,' humbly suggested a third, 'may have a turn for the supernatural, and I'm thinking the Fairy Legend of young Tamlane is just the thing that suits your fancy.' 'I like the naïveté of the young lady very much,' answered the knight, 'but the fair dames of Derbyshire prize the charms of lovers with flesh and blood, before the gayest Elfin-knight that ever ran a course from Carlisle to Caerlaverock.'—'What would your worship say to William of Cloudesley?' said a Cumberland minstrel, 'or to the Friar of Orders Grey?' said a harper from the halls of the Percys.

"'Minstrels,' said Sir Ralph Cavendish, the invention of sweet and gentle poesy is dead among you. Every churl in the Peak can chant us these beautiful but common ditties. Have you nothing new for the honour of the sacred calling of verse, and the beauty of Dora Vernon? Fellow—harper,—what's your name? you with the long hair and the green mantle,' said the knight, beckoning to a young minstrel who sat with his harp held before him, and his face half buried in his mantle's fold; 'come, touch your strings and sing; I'll wager my gold-hilted sword against that peasant feather in thy cap, that thou hast a new and a gallant strain; for I have seen thee measure more than once the form of fair Dora Vernon with a ballad-maker's eye.—Sing, man, sing.'

"The young minstrel, as he bowed his head to this singular mode of quest, blushed from brow to bosom; nor were the face and neck of Dora Vernon without an acknowledgment of how deeply she sympathized in his embarrassment. A finer instrument, a truer hand, or a more sweet and manly voice, hardly ever united to lend grace to rhyme.

THE MINSTREL'S SONG.

Last night a proud page came to me;
Sir Knight, he said, I greet you free;
The moon is up at midnight hour,
All mute and lonely is the bower;
To rouse the deer, my lord is gone,
And his fair daughter's all alone,
As lily fair, and as sweet to see,—
Arise, Sir Knight, and follow me.

The stars stream'd out, the new-woke moon,
O'er Chatsworth hill gleam'd brightly down,
And my love's cheeks, half-seen, half-hid,
With love and joy blush'd deeply red:
Short was our time, and chaste our bliss,
A whisper'd vow and a gentle kiss;
And one of those long looks, which earth
With all its glory is not worth.

The stars beam'd lovelier from the sky,
The smiling brook flow'd gentlier by;
Life, fly thou on; I'll mind that hour
Of sacred love in greenwood bower;
Let seas between us swell and sound,
Still at her name my heart shall bound;
Her name—which like a spell I'll keep,
To sooth me and to charm my sleep.

"'Fellow,' said Sir Ralph Cavendish, 'thou hast not shamed my belief of thy skill; keep that piece of gold, and drink thy cup of wine in quiet, to the health of the lass who inspired thy strain, be she lordly, or be she low.' The minstrel seated himself, and the interrupted mirth re-commenced, which was not long to continue. When the minstrel began to sing, the King of the Peak fixed his large and searching eyes on his person, with a scrutiny from which nothing could escape, and which called a flush of apprehension to the face of his daughter Dora. Something like a cloud came upon his brow at the first verse, which, darkening down through the second, became as dark as a December night at the close of the third, when rising, and motioning Sir Ralph Cavendish to follow, he retired into the recess of the southern window.

"'Sir Knight,' said the lord of Haddon, 'thou art the sworn friend of John Manners, and well thou knowest what his presumption dares at, and what are the letts between him and me. *Cavendo tutus!* ponder on thy own motto well.—'Let seas between us swell and sound :'—let his song be prophetic, for Derbyshire,—for England has no river deep enough and broad enough to preserve him from a father's sword, whose peace he seeks to wound.' 'Knight of Haddon,' said Sir Ralph, 'John Manners is indeed my friend; and the friend of a Cavendish can be no mean person; a braver and a better spirit never aspired after beauty.' 'Sir Knight,' said the King of the Peak, 'I court no man's counsel; hearken to my words. Look at the moon's shadow on Haddon dial; there it is beside the casement; the shadow falls short of twelve. If it darkens the midnight hour, and John Manners be found here, he shall be cast fettered, neck and heel, into the deepest dungeon of Haddon.'

"All this passed not unobserved of Dora Vernon, whose fears and affections divined immediate mischief from the calm speech and darkened brow of her father. Her heart sank within her when he beckoned her to withdraw; she followed him into the great tapestried room. 'My daughter,—my love, Dora,' said the not idle fears of a father, 'wine has done more than its usual good office with the wits of our guests to-night; they look on thee with bolder eyes, and speak of thee with a bolder tongue, than a father can wish. Retire, therefore, to thy chamber. One of thy wisest attendants shall be thy companion.— Adieu, my love, till sunrise!' He kissed her white temples and white brow; and Dora clung to his neck, and sobbed in his bosom;—while the secret of her heart rose near her lips. He returned to his guests, and mirth and music, and the march of the wine-cup, recommenced with a vigour which promised reparation for the late intermission.

"The chamber, or rather temporary prison, of Dora Vernon, was nigh the cross-bow room, and had a window which looked out on the terraced garden, and the extensive chase towards the hill of Haddon. All that side of the hall lay in deep shadow, and the moon, sunk to the very summit of the western heath, threw a level and a farewell beam over river and tower. The young lady of Haddon seated herself in the recessed window, and lent her ear to every sound, and her eye to every shadow that flitted over the garden and chase. Her attendant maiden—shrewd, demure, and suspicious, of the ripe age of thirty—yet of a merry pleasant look, which had its admirers—sat watching every motion with the eye of an owl.

"It was past midnight, when a foot came gliding along the passage, and a finger gave three slight scratches on the door of the chamber. The maid went out, and after a brief conference suddenly returned, red with blushes from ear to ear. 'Oh, my lady!' said the trusty maiden,—'oh, my sweet young lady,—here's that poor young lad—ye know his name—who gave me three yards of crimson ribbon, to trim my peach-bloom mantle, last Bakewell fair.— An honester or a kinder heart never kept a promise; and yet I may not give him the meeting. Oh, my young lady, my sweet young lady, my beautiful young lady, could you not stay here for half an hour by yourself?' Ere her young mistress could answer, the notice of the lover's presence was renewed. The maiden again went—whispers were heard—and the audible salutation of lips; she again returned more resolute than ever to oblige her lover. 'Oh, my lady—my young lady; if ye ever hope to prosper in true love yourself—spare me but one half hour with this harmless kind lad. He has come seven long miles to see my fair face, he says;—and, oh, my lady, he has a handsome face of his own.— Oh, never let it be said that Dora Vernon sundered true lovers!—but I see consent written in your own lovely face—so I shall run—and, oh, my lady, take care of your own sweet handsome self, when your faithful Nan's away.' And the maiden retired with her lover.

"It was half an hour after midnight, when one of the keepers of the chase, as he lay beneath a holly bush listening, with a prolonged groan, to the audible voice of revelry in the hall, from which his duty had lately excluded him, happened to observe two forms approaching; one of low stature, a light step, and muffled in a common mantle:— the other with the air, and in the dress, of a forester—a sword at his side, and pistols in his belt. The ale and the wine had invaded the keeper's brain, and impaired his sight; yet he roused himself up with a hiccup and a 'hillloah,' and 'where go ye, my masters?' The lesser form whispered to the other—who immediately said, 'Jasper Jugg, is this you? Heaven be praised I have found you so soon;—here's that north country pedlar, with his beads and blue ribbon—he has come and whistled out pretty Nan Malkin, the lady's favourite, and the lord's trusty maid.' I left them under the terrace, and came to tell you.'

"The enraged keeper scarce heard this account of the faithlessness of his love to an end,—he started off with the swiftness of one of the deer which he watched, making the boughs crash, as he forced his way through bush and glade direct for the hall, vowing desertion to the girl, and destruction to the pedlar. 'Let us hasten our steps, my love,' said the lesser figure, in a sweet voice; and unmantling as she spoke, turned back, to the towers of Haddon, the fairest face that ever left them—the face of Dora Vernon herself. 'My men and my horses are nigh, my love,' said the taller figure; and taking a silver call from his pocket, he imitated the sharp shrill cry of the plover; then turning round he stood and gazed to Haddon, scarcely darkened by the setting of the moon, for the festal lights flashed from turret and casement, and the sound of mirth and revelry rang with augmenting din. 'Ah, fair and stately Haddon,' said Lord John Manners, 'little dost thou know, thou hast lost thy jewel from thy brow—else thy lights would be dimmed, thy mirth would turn to wailing, and swords would be flashing from thy portals in all the haste of hot pursuit. Farewell, for a while, fair tower, farewell for a while. I shall return, and bless the time I harped among thy menials and sang of my love—and charmed her out of thy little chamber window.' Several armed men now came suddenly down from the hill of Haddon, horses richly caparisoned were brought from among the trees of the chase, and the ancestors of the present family of Rutland sought shelter, for a time, in a distant land, from the wrath of the King of the Peak."

BIOGRAPHICAL SKETCH OF THE LATE REV. ROWLAND HILL.

It is our melancholy task to record in our present paper, the decease of that truly venerable Christian pastor, the Rev. Rowland Hill, which took place on Thursday evening, the 11th instant, at his house in Blackfriars-road, after an illness of about a week. Mr. Hill was born in August 1744. He was the son of Sir Rowland Hill, Bart., of Hawkestone, an ancient and highly respectable Shropshire family. His elder brother, Sir Richard Hill, for several sessions sat in the House of Commons as member for the county. He was a man of distinguished piety, benevolence, and eccentricity, and was the author of a tract, entitled *Pietas Oxoniensis*, in defence of the young men who were expelled from the University of Oxford in 1766, for praying, and expounding the Scriptures. This has given rise to the erroneous notion that Mr. Rowland Hill was one of the number. The present Lord Hill, Commander-in-Chief of his Majesty's Forces, is nephew to the venerable personage who is the subject of this brief memorial.

Mr. Hill was educated at Eton College, whence he was removed to St. John's College, Cambridge, where he took the degree of M.A. with some degree of *eclat*. Before he was of age to take orders, he occasionally preached at the Tabernacle, and at the Tottenham-court-road Chapel, which threw some impediment in the way of his receiving ordination. The Bishop of Bath and Wells was at length induced to admit him to a deacon's orders, which was the highest step he was permitted to attain in the hierarchy. Mr. Hill was however, always tenacious of his clerical character, regarding himself as an Episcopal clergyman. One of the first public occasions upon which he distinguished himself, was in delivering a funeral oration on the death of Mr. Toplady, who had forbidden a funeral sermon to be preached on the occasion, and who, moreover, had expressed his disapprobation of some of Mr. Hill's uncanonical proceedings, although his young friend stood high in his esteem. In 1783, Mr. Hill laid the first stone of Surrey Chapel, which was opened in 1784; but, although he was usually considered as the pastor, preaching there constantly during the winter, the chapel was not licensed as under his pastoral care. He generally spent a considerable portion of the summer in visiting various parts of the United Kingdom, preaching in places of worship of every denomination which would admit of his services, and occasionally preaching in the open air. The remainder of the summer he usually passed at Wotton-under-Edge, Gloucestershire, where he had a house and a chapel. About the time that he opened Surrey Chapel, he married Miss Mary Tudway, sister of Clement Tudway, Esq., M.P., for Wells, by whom he had no issue. Mrs. Hill, died a few years ago.

Few ministers of the Gospel have had to bear the scornful brunt of opposition, to contend against religious animosity, and to bear on through good report and evil report, through so long and and active a career as Mr. Hill. Few have challenged the encounter so boldly, or sustained it so single-handed. The independent and ambiguous ecclesiastical position which he assumed, as theoretically a Churchman and practically a Dissenter,—a Dissenter within the Church, a Churchman among Dissenters,—necessarily involved him, especially in the early part of his career, in continual polemic skirmishing. His very catholicism sometimes put on an aggressive form; for of nothing was he so intolerant as of sectarianism. But while he thus made himself many opponents, his blameless character precluded his having any personal enemies. The sarcastic or censorious polemic was forgotten in the warm-hearted philanthropist, the indefatigable evangelist, the consistent saint. In Mr. Hill, no ordinary degree of natural shrewdness was combined with an unsuspecting and guileless mind. This sometimes laid him open to imposition. Deep and accurate as was his acquaintance with human nature, he was not always quick-sighted in reading its appearance in the individual. He understood the heart better than the moral physiognomy of character; and thus his shrewdness did not preserve him altogether from forming mistaken estimates. His generous benevolence was a distinguishing trait of his character; and he seemed to have the power of inspiring his flock with the same spirit. On two occasions on which collections were made in the churches and chapels throughout the kingdom, (the Patriotic Fund at Lloyds, and the subscription for the relief of the German sufferers,) the collections at Surrey Chapel are recorded to have been the largest raised at any one place. The sum annually raised for charitable and religious institutions at Surrey Chapel, has been from £1,500 to £2,000. As a preacher, Mr. Hill was extremely unequal, as well as systematically unmethodical; generally rambling, but pithy, often throwing out the most striking remarks, and sometimes interspersing touches of genuine pathos, amid much that bordered upon the ludicrous. But even in his most grotesque sallies, there was a redeeming simplicity of purpose and seriousness of intention. You felt that the preacher did not mean to trifle; that there was no attempt at display, no unhallowed familiarity in his feelings, or want of reverence to sacred things. In his more private expository exercises, he was generally grave and edifying, with fewer inequalities, and often highly impressive.—*Patriot*.

THE SALMON.

We learn from the *Scotsman*, that of late years Dr. Knox has paid much attention to the natural history of the salmon and herring; and the following is given as the substance of several papers, which the Doctor has read before the Royal Society:—

"The deposition of the ova or eggs of the salmon under the gravel of mountain-streams,—its long confinement in that situation,—its growth into a fish about an inch in length,—its ascent through the gravel, and rapid growth whilst in the rivers—he carefully watched, and observed personally. Twenty weeks was the period from the time of deposition to their bursting the shell. For nine days longer they continue under the gravel as fishes, drawing their nourishment from the yolk of the egg, which is, of course, attached to them by the umbilical vessels, or more properly by the omphalo mesenteric vessels. During this period they do not eat or grow much, but, without doubt, acquire strength. When the yolk on which they have been feeding becomes nearly exhausted, they rise from their sandy and gravelly bed, making their way to the surface, through a thickness varying from one foot to two; and at last gain their new habitation in the waters. Dr. Knox had not opportunities of observing the fry immediately after their coming into the river, but in ten days they may be caught in the river very considerably grown, and in twenty days have attained a length varying from eight to nine inches. An extensive personal inquiry shewed that they are never the prey of the trout, and a more limited one renders it doubtful if they can become the prey of kelt or spawned salmon on its return to the ocean. It is probably to avoid the effects of severe frosts that the salmon selects the beds of the running streams as the spot for the favourable deposition of the ova. The beds of rivers, he conjectures, must vary in temperature somewhat, and the author supposes that extreme frosts are less likely to reach the gravel under the stream than under the pool. Whether this, together with other circumstances, may lead the salmon to prefer the soil below the stream to that below the pool, he does not pretend to decide, but frequent experiments have convinced him that the opinions of Sir Humphrey Davy, Jacobi, and others—opinions which maintain that the gravel is selected by the salmon on the ground of the better aëration of the ova, have no real foundation whatever.

The food of the fry has been determined precisely, and their whole habits, by repeated anatomical examinations made by himself; and he has left as little as possible for conjecture on any of these points, in so far as regards the anatomical and physiological parts of the inquiry. The facts next brought out regard the hybernation of salmon and trout. This led to an investigation of the par, and of the original type of the trout species. The inquiries into the history of the par was attended with more difficulty than any other part of the inquiry; and all he pretends at present to advance is, that the par is male and female, and that it does not grow either into a trout or a salmon. The hybernation of the trout, and the curious circumstance of its burying itself under the gravel during winter, can scarcely be questioned. The salmon seems to hybernate somewhat in certain seasons. A great number of salmon and trout do not enter into the spawning condition, and consequently may be got in first rate order as food, at any time, provided they have the means of subsistance. Now, this the salmon can always get at in the ocean, which is his true feeding ground. He cannot get food in rivers, of the kind he desires, if he be a true salmon. The salmon-trout, on the contrary, even at the mouth of rivers, will take to the fry of other fishes, to worms; and, in rivers themselves, he will feed on the *larvæ* of insects, insects themselves; and in short, on the ordinary food of trouts. He is a coarse feeding fish, seldom good as an article of food, and only at that time when feeding on the true salmon food of the ocean. At other times he is coarse and without value; maintaining, however, it is true, his weight in rivers tolerably well. The true salmon, on the other hand, prefers a peculiar kind of food, the ova of the echinodermata, and takes with great reluctance any other kind of food. Hence, the moment he enters rivers, having abandoned his natural feeding ground, he deteriorates constantly, refuses all kind of food, loses weight and flavor and gets, in short, entirely out of order; nor can he ever recover from this state till he has visited the feeding ground in the ocean.

THE HERRING.

As to food, whilst feeding on the incredibly minute entomostraceous animals which form his food, and which it more especially affects, the condition of the herring is excellent, rendering it an extremely desirable food for man. In this state the stomach seems as if almost altogether empty, though at the moment full of minute animals, to be discovered only by the microscope, and on which the animal has been feeding. The intestines, also, seem as if empty; the tunics of the whole digestive canal are fine and semi-transparent, and as free of intestinal and putrescent debris found in the stomach and intestines of animals, as if the herring actually fed on nothing but air and water. Nevertheless, the intestines are full of the remains of the entomostracea, but these give rise to no putrescence. Whilst thus fed, the herring is in the very highest condition, and is scarcely inferior to any fish. When he approaches the shores, thus quitting the proper feeding ground, he, like the herling, takes to other and coarser food: his condition alters, and his flesh becomes soft and tasteless; the stomach and intestines are found loaded with putrescent remains, and, gutted or ungutted, this fish prepared, could never be brought into the market as equal to the product of the Dutch fisheries. The examination of the reports of the British fisheries, and of the efforts made by them to force upon foreign markets the ill-conditioned herrings caught on the British coasts, and to bring them into competition with the finely assorted and carefully prepared products of the Dutch deep-sea fisheries, affords matter for much serious reflection. The Trustees for the fisheries took up a theory which rested upon no proper foundation whatever, viz., that the difference of the product of the fisheries consisted in the mode of preparation, and that this depended on the Dutch gutting the herring previous to salting or curing. Dr. Knox found that this had no foundation whatever, and states his readiness to prove that the highest bounties imaginable on British herring, and the imposing restrictions, amounting nearly to prohibitions against the entry of Dutch herrings into our West India colonies, and into Britain, will never improve the British fisheries, but will be attended with an effect diametrically opposite. It was somewhat consolatory to know, in a national point of view, that for want of knowledge, the French followed pretty nearly our own plan, and by means of duties, restrictions, and bounties, contrived to import into their West India possessions, cured fish, totally unfit for the use of man, and which were thrown into the sea. The importation of bad British herrings into our colonies, and into Germany, differed in this respect, that from the former foreign herrings could be prohibited from competition, by heavy duties. Since the period of James I. to the present day this seems to have been the mode adopted to force the consumption of British products. Dr. Knox thinks he is able to point out a better mode for the attaining this very desirable object, by means of knowledge of a strictly scientific kind, regarding the natural objects to be legislated upon, which can never be attained through the evidence of persons whose modes of life, habits of thought, motives, and interests, at once render them hostile to truth, and unfit for the investigation of scientific objects.

MEANS OF PREVENTING GLASS FROM CRACKING BY HEAT.—Mr. Steele, of this place, has communicated to us that he has ascertained that by making with a diamond a slight cut from the top to the bottom of the convex side of glass used for lamps, it is prevented from cracking, notwithstanding the heat to which it is exposed. The incision affords room for the expansion produced by the heat; and the glass, after it is cool, returns to its original shape, with only a scratch where the cut is made.

SIR CAHIR O'DOHERTY.

The rock of Doune, or, as it was originally called, the rock of Kilmacrenan, is famous as being the place where the chieftains of Tyrconnel were inaugurated by the Abbots of Kilmacrenan; and also as being where the fierce Sir Cahir O'Doherty closed his life, in the reign of James I.

The plantation of Ulster had not as yet taken place; but already many Scots had settled themselves along the rich alluvial lands that border the Loughs Foyle and Swilly; and it was Sir Cahir's most desired end and aim to extirpate these intruders. He was the Scotchman's curse and scourge. One of these Scots had settled in the valley of the Lennon; Rory O'Donnell, the Queen's Earl of Tyrconnel, had given him part of that fertile valley— and he there built his bawn. But Sir Cahir, in the midst of night, and Sandy Ramsay's absence, attacked his enclosure, drove off his cattle, slaughtered his wife and children, and left his pleasant homestead a heap of smoking ruins.

The Scot, on his return home, saw himself bereaved, left desolate in a foreign land, without property, kindred, or home; nothing his, but his true gun and dirk. He knew that five hundred marks was the reward offered by the Lord Deputy for Sir Cahir's head. With a heart maddened by revenge, with hope resting on the promised reward, he retired to the wooded hills that run parallel to the Hill of Doune; there, under covert of a rock, his gun resting on the withered branch of a stunted oak, he waited day by day, with all the patience and expectancy of a tiger in his lair. Sir Cahir was a man to be marked in a thousand; he was the loftiest and proudest in his bearing of any man in the Province of Ulster; his Spanish hat with the heron's plume was too often the terror of his enemies—the rallying point of his friends, not to bespeak the O'Doherty; even the high breastwork of loose stones, added to the natural defences of the rock, could not hide the chieftain from observation.

On Holy Thursday, as Sir Cahir rested on the eastern face of the rock looking towards the Abbey of Kilmacrenan, expecting a friar to come from his favoured foundation of St. Columbkil, to shrive him, and celebrate mass; and, as he was chatting to his men beside him, the Scotchman applied the fire to his levelled matchlock, and, before the report began to roll its echoes through the woods and hills, the ball had passed through Sir Cahir's forehead, and he lay lifeless on the ramparts. His followers were panic-struck; they thought that the rising of the Scotch and English was upon them, and, deserting the lifeless body of their leader, they dispersed through the mountains. In the meanwhile, the Scotchman approached the rock; he saw his followers flee. He soon severed the head from the body, and wrapping it in his plaid, off he set in the direction of Dublin. He travelled all that day, and at night took shelter in a cabin belonging to one Terence O'Gallagher, situated at one of the fords of the river Finn. Here Ramsay sought a night's lodging, which Irishmen never refuse; and, partaking of an oaten cake and some sweet milk, he went to rest, with Sir Cahir's head under his own as a pillow. The Scotchman slept sound, and Terence was up at break of day. He saw blood oozing out through the plaid that served as his guest's pillow, and suspected all was not right; so, slitting the tartan plaid, he saw the hair and head of a man. Slowly drawing it out, he recognized features well known to every man in Tyrconnel; they were Sir Cahir's. Terence knew as well as any man that there was a price set on this very head,—a price abundant to make his fortune,—a price he was now resolved to try and gain. So off Terence started, and the broad Tyrone was almost crossed by O'Gallagher before the Scotchman awoke to resume his journey. The story is still told with triumph through the country, how the Irishman, without the treason, reaped the reward of Sir Cahir's death.

UNITARIANISM IN ENGLAND.

From a calculation made upon returns printed in the *Unitarian Chronicle* for September, October, and November last, it appears that there are in England about 200 congregations (Presbyterians, General Baptist, &c.) of Unitarian, *alias* Socinian principles. Of these, 180 never exceed 250 hearers, and the average is below 100; 20 consist of between 250 and 500 hearers; and about four may sometimes approach towards 1000 or 1200 hearers. The Unitarian chapel at Birmingham is stated to be attended by about 1100. Finsbury Chapel, London, (W. J. Fox,) has about 700. Hackney Chapel, (R. Aspland,) 500. Nottingham, (B. Carpenter,) 500. Bridport, (R. Cree,) 500. Newcastle, (W. Turner,) 500. Chorobent, Lancashire, (B. Davis,) 500. Bolton, (F. Baker,) 400. Leicester, (C. Berry,) 400. Essex Street, London, (T. Madge,) 350. With the exception of these and a few others, the congregations of this sect present only skeleton regiments. " To Unitarians," says a writer in the *Monthly Repository*, " a Bristol or a Manchester audience is magnificent! But let those half-dozen flourishing congregations be deemed of as highly as we will, still *six* prosperous societies, out of some three hundred, is a small proportion. Of our knowledge, we can speak of some *scores* that scarcely show signs of life. The number of hearers in them will not average more than *thirty*. Few beings are more to be pitied than a Unitarian minister placed in one of these societies." This writer, himself a Unitarian, while bearing evidence to the dying state of the greater part of the congregations, appears to overrate their total number. From 220 to 230 must be, we are persuaded, the utmost number, and the total number of hearers cannot exceed 12,000, or at most, 15,000. The orthodox dissenting congregations of the three denominations exceed 2,200 in England alone; and the aggregate of attendants is estimated at nearly a million. The total number of dissenting congregations of every Protestant denomination in England and Wales, is upwards of 7,500. Such is the proportion which Unitarianism bears to Evangelical dissent.

SIR HUMPHREY DAVY'S CORRESPONDENCE.

I hardly know what to say to you concerning your plans of studying chemistry. Chemistry is the science of the minutest forms of nature, and your peculiar science is the enunciation of the great parts of the Great Being—human society—or man. The two sciences have no connexion. The little, the obscure, and the unknown ought not, perhaps, ever to be the subjects of speculation for the moral philosopher, and all chemical subjects are of this kind.

Chemistry spoils me—perhaps will destroy me—as a metaphysician. When I ought to be generalizing concerning wholes, I find myself endeavouring to divide and to find parts.

It may be worth your while to amuse yourself with chemistry; but it is not worth your while to study it as a science. You have nobler pursuits. Any man can be a chemist. One of the most celebrated chemists in town is one of the most stupid fellows I ever met with. All his powers seem to be seated in his hands and eyes. Not one of a million can be a poet-philosopher; for I persist in giving you this title.

Why then should you employ the instruments of the meaner arts in acting upon mankind, when the great, the wonderful instrument of language connected with feeling is all your own. Use it. Hasten to act upon the deformed being—civil society. Be the kindler of the flames that are to destroy the unintelligible. Make its ashes the receptacles of the germ of pure and simple truth. Be the father of the language of life.

I am alternately experimenting and idling; sometimes full of energy, and smeared with dirt and quicksilver—at other times dreaming beneath a great rock hanging over the dell of the Avon; a dell which is beautiful, because Nature is not murdered, or even wounded in it, by the savage hands of man.

SCIENTIFIC NOTICES.

THE WONDERS OF PHYSICS.

WHAT mere assertion will make any man believe that in one second of time, in one beat of the pendulum of a clock, a ray of light travels over 192,000 miles, and would therefore perform the tour of the world in about the same time that it requires to wink with our eyelids, and in much less than a swift runner occupies in taking a single stride? What mortal can be made to believe, without demonstration, that the sun is almost a million times larger than the earth? and that, although so remote from us, that a cannon ball shot directly towards it, and maintaining its full speed, would be twenty years in reaching it, it yet affects the earth by its attraction in an inappreciable instant of time?—Who would not ask for demonstration, when told that a gnat's wing, in its ordinary flight, beats many hundred times in a second? or that there exist animated and regularly organized beings, many thousands of whose bodies laid close together would not extend an inch? But what are these to the astonishing truths which modern optical inquiries have disclosed, which teach us that every point of a medium through which a ray of light passes is affected with a succession of periodical movements, regularly recurring at equal intervals, no less than 500 millions of millions of times in a single second! that it is by such movements, communicated to the nerves of our eyes, that we see—nay, more, that it is the difference in the frequency of their recurrence which affects us with the sense of the diversity of colour; that, for instance, in acquiring the sensation of redness our eyes are affected 482 millions of millions of times; of yellowness, 542 millions of millions of times; and of violet, 707 millions of times per second? Do not such things sound more like the ravings of madmen, than the sober conclusions of people in their waking senses? They are, nevertheless, conclusions to which any one may most certainly arrive, who will only be at the trouble of examining the chain of reasoning by which they have been obtained.

BLASTING ROCKS UNDER WATER BY MEANS OF THE DIVING BELL.—Three men are employed in the diving bell; one holds the jumper, or boring iron, which he keeps constantly turning; the other two strike alternately quick smart strokes with hammers. When the hole is bored of the requisite depth, a tin cartridge filled with gunpowder, about two inches diameter and a foot in length, is inserted, and sand placed above it. To the top of the cartridge a tin pipe is soldered, having a brass screw at the upper end. The diving bell is then raised up slowly, and additional tin pipes with brass screws are attached until the pipes are about two feet above the surface. The man who is to fire the charge is placed in a boat close to the tube, to the top of which a piece of cord is attached, which he holds in his left hand. Having in the boat a brazier, with small pieces of iron red hot, he drops one of them down the tube, this immediately ignites the powder, and blows up the rock. A small part of the tube next the cartridge is destroyed; but the greater part which is held by the cord, is reserved for future service. The workmen in the boat experience no shock, the only effect is a violent ebullition of the water arising from the explosion; but those who stand on the shore, and upon any part of the rock connected with those blowing up, feel a very strong concussion. The only difference between the mode of blasting rock at Howth and at Plymouth is, that at the latter place they connect the tin pipes by a cement of white lead. A certain depth of water is necessary for safety, which should not be less than from 8 to 10 feet.—*Repertory of Patent Inventions.*

WHAT ARE COALS?—Among the results of geological changes, those of vegetable bodies, or remains turned into (from *fossus*, Latin, dug out of the earth), are not the least interesting. Thus, coals are fossils produced from trees which have been overwhelmed by the earth, and subject to certain influences, which philosophy has hitherto been perplexed in satisfactorily defining. That wood may be converted into coal is acknowledged, yet men do not so well agree in their explanation of the process by which the change is effected. Any person who has not considered the subject, will probably ask what resemblance does coal bear to wood? a ready answer to which may be given in the concise definition of Dr. Ure; "Coal is in fact to vegetable matter, what adipocire is to animal matter, a complete chemical change, in which the fibrous structure disappears."

THE NEW FULMINATING SILVER.—The Royal Dublin Society lately published a paper by Professor Davy, "On a new acid (the fulminic) and its combinations." While examining these substances, he discovered a new fulminating silver, having the common properties of Howard's compound, but distinguished from it by spontaneously exploding in chlorine gas. A single grain of this fulminate is sufficient to produce about 100 separate explosions in this gas, and about 1000 explosions may be produced in about half ounce phial of the gas. The fulminate is instantly exploded when dropped into mixtures of gases containing 1-100 of chlorine gas. Hence it is a delicate test of the presence of this gas, and will probably admit of application as a substitute for the fulminating compounds at present used in the percussion locks of guns.

PITT.—Pitt was a tall thin man, of a fair skin, and with rather an effeminate gait. He had light-coloured hair, and grey, watery eyes, and a projecting sharp-pointed nose a little turned up. His forehead, in the part nearest to his eyebrows, came far out, as may be seen in his statues and busts; and to those who are observers of human face, gave the notion of his being a man of the greatest possible clearness of thought, and firmness of character; and such he proved himself on every occasion. His manner of speaking in the House (and I seldom heard him except in Parliament) was very lordly and commanding; he generally stretched forth his right arm to its utmost length, kept his left hand on his hip, or on the table near which he usually stood, and his feet at a proper distance from each other, and spoke deliberately, like a person reading from a well-written book, and in a voice as loud and deep almost as a bell.—*Piozziana.*

CONTENTS OF NO. XXXIX.

Cursory Remarks on Ireland	257
State of Ireland	29
Demoralization of Slavery and its Barbarities	ib.
Education in America	30
The Miners of Bois-Monzil	263
Three Arguments in Favour of a Repeal of the Taxes on Knowledge, by Lord Brougham	265
VERSES FOR THE YOUNG.—Hymn for the Sons of the Clergy	ib.
THE STORY-TELLER.—The King of the Peak, a Derbyshire Tale, By Allan Cunningham	
Biographical Sketch of the late Sir Rowland Hill	29
The Salmon	270
The Herring	ib.
Sir Cahir O'Doherty	271
Unitarianism in England	
Sir Humphrey Davy's Correspondence	
SCIENTIFIC NOTICES.—The Wonders of Physics;—Blasting Rocks under Water by means of the Diving Bell; &c.	272

EDINBURGH: Printed by and for JOHN JOHNSTONE, 19, St. James' Square.—Published by JOHN ANDERSON, Jun. Bookseller, 55, North Bridge Street, Edinburgh; by JOHN MACLEOD, and ATKINSON & CO. Booksellers, Glasgow; and sold by all Booksellers and Vendors of Cheap Periodicals.

THE Schoolmaster, AND EDINBURGH WEEKLY MAGAZINE.

CONDUCTED BY JOHN JOHNSTONE.

THE SCHOOLMASTER IS ABROAD.—LORD BROUGHAM.

No. 40.—Vol. II.　　SATURDAY, MAY 4, 1833.　　Price Three-halfpence.

ON BEES.
(Continued from No. 31.)

About the middle of May when the of Bees in a hive come to be pretty numerous, the consumption of honey within is much greater than in any of the preceding months. Consequently, should cold, misty, or cloudy weather occur, light hives will run a great hazard of perishing by famine. Particular attention ought, therefore, to be paid to Bees at this season by supplying them, as I formerly directed, with some honey when the weather is unfavourable. But, on the other hand, should the weather in this month prove mild and serene, the Bees will procure plenty of honey and farina in the fields, as the flowering plants are now becoming plenteous. They have the furze, a very early flowering plant which continues long in blossom, and from which they collect abundance of farina; also the garden and wild mustard, the yellow gowans and hawthorn, and, towards the latter end of May, there are the broom, and the balmy plane-tree, both of which are extremely grateful to Bees, as they afford them abundance of provision, and also fruit trees of various descriptions. Then, in June, come the white clover, a flower which Bees very much resort to, and which yields them the finest of honey, and numerous other plants and flowers which wise nature lavishes with a prodigal hand on these industrious insects, furnishing them with abundance of honey and wax in their different seasons. Now, the entries of the strong hives should be considerably enlarged, both to allow the Bees freedom to work, as well as sufficient air. Bees seldom begin to swarm before the beginning of June. The symptoms which are shewn by them before swarming are of so various and uncertain a nature that it is almost impossible to determine the exact time when a hive is ready to swarm; although a person well skilled in Bee-husbandry may form a tolerably correct idea of the time when a hive will throw a swarm. The following observations, however, may tend to throw some light upon the subject. When the number of Bees in a hive increases fast they begin to water or sweat. This water, which is the exhalations occasioned by their warmth, is of an insipid taste, and is observed in the morning upon the stool before the entry of the Hive, but, when the Bees get very numerous, this water is dried up by the still greater increase of that heat. Then, in June, when the Bees in a hive begin to be very crowded, so that they come out and hang in clusters on the front, or about the entry of the hive, and if, previous to this, drones were observed amongst them, they ought to be carefully watched every fine day from nine or ten o'clock, A. M., until three or four P. M., as a swarm may be expected very soon if the weather holds good. There are some hives, in which, instead of the Bees hanging in clusters about the entry of the hive, they spread themselves on the stool for three or four days before swarming, and great bustling will be observed about the entry of the hive; but if they do not swarm in the course of a week after this symptom is observed, they generally begin to cluster together as in the former case, and continue, perhaps, in this way, for several weeks before swarming. There are other hives, although comparatively few in number, that swarm without showing any outward or visible appearance, such as clustering about the entry, or front of the hive; but although they do not show any signs of this description, yet they will be observed to reel every fine day, which reeling is occasioned by a great number of Bees flying about, and making a confused motion before the entry of the hive. Therefore, when any of the foregoing symptoms are observed, it is an indication that the Bees are making preparations for swarming, and accordingly ought to be attentively watched every fine day during the whole of the swarming season. During the time a hive is swarming the utmost silence ought to be observed, and the Bees not interfered with until they alight and are fairly settled on some bush, when, if possible, let the swarm be immediately brought to the ground, laid carefully on a sheet or other cloth, and a hive placed over it, resting the edges of the hive on two or three small knobs of wood, so as to prevent the Bees from being crushed, and also to afford them sufficient room to go up into the hive. Then let the hive be well screened from the rays of the sun, and watched closely until the heat of the day is past. As, sometimes, the Bees, after continuing two or three hours in the hive, will rise and return to the mother hive again, or perhaps fly away altogether to some place previously fixed on, such as a dead hive which may have been left standing in any apiary near by, a trunk of a tree, or any other building wherein they can conveniently work. But if the Bees be contented with their new habitation, they will go up into the hive very fast, and fall to work almost immediately. In the evening the hive may be removed wherever it is intended to be placed, and covered over with straw or turf. Before Bees swarm a second or third time, they do not hang out in clusters about the entry of the hive, or spread themselves on the stool as before first swarming, but come off without any ceremony, and in weather which is by no means very favourable. Yet the signs which late swarms show are much more certain than those observed before first swarming. By listening attentively in the evening at a hive about eight, ten, or twelve days after the first swarm has gone off, peculiar sounds will be heard which may be compared, says one, to a chicken peeping when it has lost its mother. It sounds, as it were, peep, peep, peep, pronounced a dozen or twenty times successively with one breath, at one time in a shrill, and at another in a more hoarse tone, which at different times stops and begins again, and continues in this way for two or three nights before swarming. These different sounds are probably occassioned by there being more than one Queen ready to go off with a second swarm. The first night that these sounds are heard, they are less frequent and not so loud as the night previous to swarming. The second or third day after these peculiar sounds are heard, a swarm may be depended on if the weather holds in any degree favourable. If there be a third swarm, it never exceeds three or four days after the second, but in general it is so small that it would be better if it had not come off at all; and even should there be a third swarm, it ought to be put back again to the mother hive, as it is far better to have one really good hive than two bad ones. When two hives in an apiary happen to swarm at the same time they will run a great hazard of uniting together. As it is impossible to prevent the Bees from joining in such circumstances, let the Bees, as soon as they alight on any bush, be divided in the best possible mannner, and each division laid on a cloth with a hive placed over it. Convey one of these divisions a good distance off from the other, cover it pretty closely with a cloth as also the other division. If there be a Queen in each, the Bees will in a short time be perfectly contented, but if any of the divisions be observed to be in a very restless and agitated state running up and down the hive in the utmost confusion; in that case let the other division be carefully searched, and one of the Queens taken from it, and presented to the other division in the disordered state, which will in a short time be the means of appeasing the Bees; and although they may treat the Queen a little harshly at first, yet they will soon be reconciled to each other, and the Bees, in a short time afterwards, will fall to work as if nothing had happened them. But as this process is sometimes attended with no little perseverance and trouble, in procuring the Queen out of such a great mass of Bees, it ought not to be attempted but by a person thoroughly experienced in Bee-husbandry.

EXAMINATION OF THE ACCUSED.

"It is the delight of lawyers to go on plodding in paths which reason has never visited, or, having visited, has deserted."—BENTHAM.

THE practice which the Lord Mayor has adopted of examining prisoners, is approved by all persons not bigoted to custom, or the dupes of maxims which lawyers have invented for the benefit of their craft. The wisdom of Solomon has never been the wisdom of our law. The idea of confronting and examining the parties fills them with horror—it is so short a cut to the truth. Sportsman's law and Lawyer's law are precisely of the same nature; both are designed not for the seizure but the pursuit. The interest of the public is simply the detection of the culprit; the interest of the lawyer is to make that detection as roundabout and difficult as possible, for in unravelling the perplexity consists his craft. The hunter gives fair play, or law, as it is most appropriately called, to the fox, because it is not the capture of the fox that he desires or cares about, but solely the pleasure of the run; the lawyer demands fair play for the rogue, because it is not the detection that he desires or cares about, but solely the profit of the prosecution, and if the rogue escapes, he makes more business for the profession. The sportsman cries shame on him who shoots the hare squatting in her form; the lawyer cries shame on him who leads a prisoner into a betrayal of himself. What does the public want but the detection? What does the lawyer want but the pursuit, and to make the detection as difficult as possible? The discovery of the truth is the first business of justice, and the law rejects the truth which a man states against himself; and what better evidence can be had? what evidence proceeding from such certain knowledge? what evidence so clear of the suspicion of malice or adverse prejudice? When you get it, it is by virtue of the subtilty of truth which will not be suppressed—which will out in spite of all artifices for concealment. But it is called *humane* not to allow the prisoner to convict himself—that this dogma should have been invented by lawyers, to whose interest it serves, in no degree surprises; but that it should have been received by the public, against whose interest it works, is an amazing instance of gullibility. The humane rule which will not allow a villain to convict himself of villany, suffers the villain to go free and prey upon society. Is this humanity? Acquit erroneously, observes Bentham, a man guilty of crime, you sacrifice the property or the lives of all those whom destiny has marked out for victims to his future enterprises. Are the innocent to be thus exposed, that the guilty may be preserved from the mortification of convicting themselves out of their own mouths? Never could this absurd dogma have obtained footing, but for the undue severity of punishments, which creates sympathy with criminals, and disposes people to see, not without satisfaction, their chances of escape multiplied.

To Sir Peter Laurie, who has with equal sense and courage broken through the absurd custom, and adopted the natural method of procedure recommended by Bentham, (in all probability without being aware of the authority for his deviation from the crooked way of law into the broad path of reason,) very high praise is due. The city may reckon this example of its Magistracy among its truest honours.—*Examiner.*

WEALTH OF CANDIDATES.

From an Article on the Life of Andrew Marvell, in the Westminster Review.

HISTORY does not state that the friends of tyranny and corruption raised any objection to Marvell as a parliamentary candidate on the score of his poverty. But they are now become bolder; and the struggle of party which is at present going on, affords an opportunity for the discussion of an important question to the welfare of the community. The gravamen of the charge raised by one of the contending parties against the other, is that of not being rich, or, as some of the most violent express it, of being beggars;—the world being so far advanced to pay much attention to the cries of heresy and blasphemy, which are become tolerably threadbare since the days when they assumed the sound of "Crucify him! Crucify him!" Now this charge of poverty involves matters of so much importance, that the question becomes one not of individual or temporary interest, but a question of principle, involving the consideration of interests as enduring and universal as man. The present is the first time that the charge of not being rich has been openly brought against parliamentary candidates; and is also the first time, at least since the days of Andrew Marvell, that candidates had come forward, to offer themselves to the people's choice, resting their pretensions solely on their intrinsic merit—to wit, on their capacity, their honesty, and their knowledge. Where has this heavy charge, this grave accusation, lain so long concealed? The truth is, there was no guilt in being poor, till poor men stood forth the champions of the poor. Where was the accusation when Burke, and Sheridan, and Canning, and Huskisson, and Mr. Praed, and Mr. Wringham, and men of that class came forward as candidates? Neither the monied nor the landed interest conceived itself to be in danger, or raised any hue and cry then. The people of England now stand in the place of the individuals who brought into parliament the gentlemen named above; and the moment they begin to exercise their privilege, the "men of property" raise a howl as loud as if their souls, which are their money bags, were ravished from them. Expand your sordid souls, and conceive that independence has nothing to do with wealth; —that a man is independent, not in proportion as he has many possessions, but as he has few wants. Does not all history, all experience, go to convince you of the falsehood of your position? Would all the riches in the world have purchased a Socrates or a Bentham? Would the riches of the universe have satisfied a Charles Stuart or a George Guelph, or formed one atom of security for their political good conduct? As is the model, so are the copies; as is the master, so are the followers. The vulgar admirers of a Guelph and a Stuart may be expected to labour under some difficulty in the conception, that there are men who would dine with more satisfaction at the simple board of Marvell than at the "*regales dapes*" of a Charles or a George:— men who could live, happy and contented, without gorgeous palaces, coroneted trappings, gilded lacqueys, and jewelled harlots, but though such qualities are rare, they are to be found, and the education necessary to form them has not entirely, with Astræa, deserted the earth. Now it may be asked of any person of sense, whether it is most likely that a man who, though he has little has what he wants, would, for the sake of making some addition to his income, sell the power of being useful, not only to the present race of his countrymen, but to the men of all countries and of every time,—or that a man who has much more, should do the same for the purpose of gratifying his irregular desires. For the man who has once so sold himself, is sold for ever. He has irrevocably sullied the purity of a patriot's honour. There is a stain upon the brightness of his name, which the tide of ages could not wash out. Those men must have a strange idea, not only of the morality but of the intellect, of a philosophic Radical like Marvell, if they imagine him such a dolt as to sacrifice so much for so little, as to exchange a greater happiness for one so palpably, so immeasurably less.

EMIGRATION TO CANADA.

FROM all the accounts we receive, it appears that Emigration to Canada is likely to be carried to a much greater extent this season than in any preceding year. The accounts which have been received from those who have formerly emigrated are very favourable; and the depressed state of agriculture which has been getting from bad to worse, ever since the peace, seems to have deprived the agriculturists even of the hope of more favourable times. Some of the English and Irish land-proprietors are, we are happy to observe, assisting the poorest of their tenantry to emigrate—an example which is well deserving of imitation. In East Lothian and Berwickshire we understand that emigration is almost the only subject of conversation, and nothing but the difficulty of getting rid of leases, and raising the necessary funds prevent a very large proportion of the farmers from leaving the country. The emigrants this year are of the most respectable class; and many of them are possessed of large sums of money. It appears from the English and Irish provincial papers, that the number of emigrants from England and Ireland is also very great. In the Londonderry Journal of the 16th ultimo, we observed twenty-nine vessels advertised to sail in less than a month, from that port to the British North American possessions, New York, and Philadelphia, and vessels sail almost daily from Liverpool to the same destination.

In a former number we gave some information to intending emigrants, and we may also give them the following cautions. At Liverpool, and very probably at other places the guards and the coachmen of some coaches seem to be in league with certain passenger-brokers, who are not over scrupulous when they get an ignorant countryman into their hands. Intending emigrants should apply, immediately on their arrival in town, to the respectable passenger-brokers, who will take care that they are embarked on board of good vessels, and on reasonable terms. Let them, above all, avoid making acquaintance with men about the docks, many of whom are swindlers. Another caution is contained in a Letter from the Ettrick Shepherd, which he lately addressed to an Edinburgh Paper. He enjoins emigrants not to "pay one farthing of earnest money on booking their names at the various agents of each ship. Let them enter their names as passengers where they will, but never pay a sixpence until they are on board, and have received their berths. I received a letter from Quebec last year, from a friend who had just landed there on his way to Upper Canada, desiring me to charge any of his friends, or my own, who come out this year, to pay no earnest-money. And I think you will allow that this tale warrants this caution. An American Company advertised a ship to sail about the end of May. They had agents over all the country, both in Scotland and England, who took in all that offered, and charged earnest-money for all, to the amount of 5s. a head, or L.1, 1s. for a family. What was the consequence? The ship was only registered for eighty passengers, so the first eighty that arrived were received on board, and the vessel set sail. Upwards of three hundred arrived from all quarters, these were handed over, partly to an English ship lying at Maryport, and the rest to a large American lying at Whitehaven. This last party, in which were several of my intimate friends and relations, had to board themselves there for a month before the vessel sailed. The American Captain then took them on board at the fare formerly stipulated, but every one lost their *arrals*, or earnest-money; and my friend avers, that what with board before sailing, and the loss of their former payments, that poor company of industrious emigrants lost upwards of L.100.'" No one should go to Canada who has not L.300, or upwards, unless he is prepared to be industrious and work hard; and if he is of dissipated and immoral habits, he will find himself in a worse situation than in this country. It is a bad place for all who have been accustomed to lead a lazy luxurious life, even though possessed of capital, unless it is to be employed in some kind of business; for although the interest of money is high, clothes are very dear, provisions not cheap, and the wages of servants, artizans, and labourers of all descriptions, much higher than in this country. Several thousand pensioners, who sold their pensions and emigrated within these last two years, have, from want of industrious habits, suffered the greatest misery. A Report, by the Emigration Committee of Quebec, as to their situation, states, that they must have brought with them, or received here since they arrived, probably about L.10,000; and, we believe, that few will assert that they are not now, in general, in a worse condition than they could have possibly been at home. But it is not necessary that the emigrant, to enable him to succeed in Canada, should be acquainted with agriculture. The method of cultivating the land is so different from that followed in Britain, that the knowledge of the system of agriculture in use in this country is comparatively of little value. A Scotch agriculturist has no knowledge of the clearing of land as practised in Upper Canada, or of the cultivation of Indian corn and pumpkins, two of the most valuable crops cultivated in that country. With sobriety, industry, and perseverance, every one who can use his hands may insure success; without these qualities he can no more expect to succeed in Canada than he can in Britain. We have some farther remarks to make on the subject of emigration to Canada; but we shall, at present, conclude with the following Extract of a Letter from an Officer's Widow, dated Township of Orillia, near Lake Simcoe, Upper Canada, 25th January 1833:—

"About two months ago, the Indians took it into their heads to complain to the Governor, that the white people occupied too many of the houses, and they insisted on all of them leaving the village of the Narrows. We had just engaged two men to chop five acres, and we got them to put up a shanty on our own lot, which they did in a few days, and we entered it when the snow was knee deep. I considered it a great hardship to be dislodged from the village, fearing the winter in a shanty in the woods, but I have regretted ever since that it did not happen sooner, as I am much more comfortable in every respect. It is only a temporary and rough log hut, such as all the families in these townships who came out last spring are living in, until their houses are ready—but we have made it warm and comfortable. We have plenty of water and fuel, and are secured from the cold by these majestic woods; and for the delighted feeling of independence! to look around and say this is all your own; no landlord, coal merchant, or shopkeeper dunning you for money—no fear of any thing disagreeable. The heart is light, knowing that in a year or two, with a little money, common prudence, and industry, one may enjoy every comfort any reasonable person would desire. We have fairly commenced our operations, and the trees are falling around us. Our choppers are young Scotch Highlanders, from a township on the opposite side of the lake, where they are numerous. They have been eleven years in the country, and are well acquainted with all the usual operations, and are civil, decent men. The plan followed by settlers is, to contract with a person to chop, that is, to cut down the trees, hew them into lengths 12 feet long, and pile all the tops into heaps, ready for burning, for seven dollars (30s.) an acre, they finding themselves in provisions. This is done during winter. You again contract, that in the end of April they log and clear the land—that is, draw the logs together with oxen, burn them, fence, harrow, and sow the ground, for from seven or eight dollars per acre. We have got nearly five acres chopped, and intend to get other five acres done. These men (their fathers being masons and carpenters) are to have the contract for our house, which will cost about L.25. except, perhaps, the partitions, which require well-seasoned wood—but I think it will include the whole. The situation must be fixed on, and the timber cut in March or April; and perhaps the shell put up, but nothing more done till after seed time. We shall have Indian corn, potatoes, turnips, pease, oats and pumpkins, but no wheat, till the autumn, as spring wheat does not thrive so well. We must have a yoke of oxen, two cows, pigs and poultry as soon as vegetation appears, for they cost neither trouble nor expense, except to cut down a basswood tree that the cattle may eat the tops, and treat them with a little salt. It is astonishing to see how simply every thing animate and inanimate, is managed in this country. Every thing is made of wood; all is done with the axe—a different weapon, however, from the English axe. One hundred pounds would cover the above, but would not admit of more improvements. The average expense of land till you receive your crop, is L.4. 10s. to L.5, per acre, when you hire labourers to clear it; but every one here says, the first crop of Fall wheat will more than repay the outlay. We have this yet to prove; all that I can say is, that I am more and more satisfied with my plan, but it must be understood, that it requires at least L.300 to enable a genteel *family* to come out; L.100 for outfit and passage, L.100 to reach the ground and live a year, and L.100 to carry through the operations to build a house, clear the land, reap a crop, and pay the first instalment of the price of the land. There is not a settler here who is well-inclined, active, and respectable in his conduct, who would wish to return to Great Britain with much greater advantages. Persons too refined, as lawyers, &c., would do no good; nor doctors, for the people, are very healthy. Industrious mechanics, particularly shoemakers, would be a treasure. Shoes we are much in want of. Even these for women cost 10s. per pair.

"We have had a most delightful winter, except for a few days. We have felt no cold though up to the knees in snow. The woods are warm, and there is no wind. Every thing is dry; the snow may be knocked about like dust. I wander about in the woods with nothing on but what I have in the house; but this winter I understand has been very favourable. I am afraid all the best government land here is taken up, and the company's land has risen to 10s., and 12s. 6d., currency, per acre, according to quality. There is plenty of pine-land vacant, but nobody likes it. Several townships, however, are to be settled this year not far from here, in which there is plenty of good land."

THE following extracts are from letters from persons who have, within these few years, gone from England to settle in Upper Canada. The first is dated "January 16, 1833, St. Thomas, Talbot Road, Upper Canada." St. Thomas is a village, about 150 miles from York:—

"Wheat harvest is over, I never saw finer crops. We had three acres of wheat, three of oats and pease; and next year we shall have more than double that quantity. As we increase our tillage, so we increase our stock. We milk three cows, and are rearing three calves. Last winter was a very long one, but I did not suffer more from the cold than at home. We kept large fires day and night. The snow was on the ground from the middle of November to the beginning of April; but never more than 18 inches thick. We fed the cattle on the tops of trees, of which they are very fond, particularly of young beech, elm, maple, and bass wood. We have plenty of sugar maple here. We made about 200 cwt. of beautiful sugar. We tapped about 100 trees with an inch augur, and with a shoot carried the sap which flowed out into small troughs; and, after boiling the sap, in about ten days we had the sugar as good as we could wish. I wish I had come over 30 years ago. Although we are 700 miles back in the woods, there is no want of any thing. If the people are industrious, we are sure to do well; for *there is no tithe*, and very little taxes. We have not paid any yet; and Dodd, for 375 acres of land, has only paid six shillings. We have six large stores in the village, that will take all corn, oats, and pork, paying half in cash, and the other half in such articles as you may require from the Store."

The following is given as a list of the prices of provisions, reckoning the sovereign at 38s. New York currency; so that the amount in English money would be but little more than half set down here:—

"Wheat, 8s., corn and oats, 4s., potatoes, 3s., pease, 4s. per bushel. Beef, mutton, and veal, 5d. per lb. Beer and Cider, 1s. per quart, whisky, ditto; rum, 2s. 6d. best French Brandy, 8s., Hollands, 6s. Cider however will in a year or two be very low, as almost every farmer has planted an orchard, and the trees grow twice as fast here as they do at home, and bear most excellent fruit. I never enjoyed my health so well as home as I do here, and mother has not been stronger these 20 years than she is at present. We are very busy now in burning the trees we have cut down, to prepare the ground for wheat. We take but little trouble with our breech after the logs are burnt, we do not plough the ground the first year. We w one bushel of wheat and drag it in, and we get better crops than you do with all your trouble of ploughing and dressing. They sow in general six pecks of oats per acre, and they are as thick at harvest as yours of five bushels an acre sowing. Our pease produce better crops than yours, and I think both our green and dry of better quality than yours in England. We don't plough down the potatoes, but put four close together and draw a little earth over them with a hoe about the size of a mole hill, leaving the hills three or four feet apart, and thus we get good crops. We make our own candles and soap, as it is necessary to do every thing one can for ones self in a country where labour is so high—a labouring man will not work on a farm for less than 6s. per day, a carpenter or mason, 12s. a day (currency.) The reason of this is, that as soon as they have saved a few dollars, they become landed proprietors, by purchasing one hundred acres of land at 2½ dollars an acre, paying one quarter down, and the rest in small instalments, which allow them eight or nine years to complete their purchase, paying 7 per cent., however, for interest.

"*Postscript.*—I wrote the above last fall; since then 2000 emigrants have come out. We have had no winter. Christmas has been as mild as May. We have paid no taxes yet, but I had notice yesterday, and Joseph took his rifle and went out by the corn rick, and shot a wild turkey, and sold it for five shillings, and that paid our taxes at once."

Among the miscellaneous information of this letter, we learn that there are two newspapers in this village, so that the emigrants get all the news of "*home*" in five or six weeks after date; they have four doctors, who, however, have not work enough for one, as there is little doing in the village, except in the obstetric department of the art, and this is chiefly managed by the matrons.

The second letter is dated,
Peterborough, Newcastle District,
Upper Canada, 22d January, 1833.

"Another description of settler is that individual who possesses means, having L.300 or L.400, and a large family. At home the amount is considered *quite sufficient*. Now, let us see how it can be best appropriated. We must, in order to come to a close calculation, name the extent of his family,—say, a man, his wife, and five children. Suppose the children are not of a *working age*. The expense of fitting himself out, and that which is incurred by reaching the upper province, will dip deep into one hundred pounds. However, it brings him to the town or village which is *nearest* to the land that he may purchase. This will not be at a less distance than from 15 to 20 miles of the aforesaid town or village; otherwise, the price will increase from 5s. per acre to 20s. or 30s. After several expensive trips into the Bush, (for he is compelled to take a guide with him at 7s. 6d. per day,) this excursion will, as it must be made on foot, occupy the best part of a week, and he may think himself *fortunate* if he succeeds in making his selection, without further loss of time, trouble, and expense.

	£	s.	d.
However, let us commence with this charge...	4	0	0
200 acres of land at 5s. per acre is £50 in four instalments. First instalment..............	12	10	0
Expense in conveying his family to his land...	5	0	0
His next proceeding is contracting for the clearing of ten acres, whereon to build his house, and commence his farm. This will be	35	0	0
Building his house or shanty.....................	30	0	0
It will be necessary to lay in flour and pork, for one year..	50	0	0
Having now got up his house, and ten acres cleared, he crops it, with potatoes, Indian corn, pumpkins, grass seed, and what will make fodder for his cow and oxen; by the next year he purchases them, and during the growth of them, he is compelled to hire a man to assist him in chopping down, logging, and burning five acres more. One year's hire for this man and his keep, cannot be less than...........................	46	0	0
He now buys his cow and a yoke of oxen, say	20	0	0
He must build a barn; otherwise his produce is not safe...	20	0	0
	L.222	10	0
Remaining payments to be paid in course of three years, and interest...........................	37	10	0
Currency............	L.260	0	0

I have surmised he has his furniture, &c.; he has consumed two hundred and sixty pounds, and he has forty pounds left, which is to serve him in addition to what he may grow. Not having hands enough to clear more than five acres in each year, unless he increases his annual expense by hiring men—say, at the end of four years he has thirty acres cleared, twenty of which he has under wheat. The average crops upon fresh cleared land being twenty-five bushels to the acre; this, if taken to market, will produce four shillings per bushel. The remaining ten acres must be kept for spring crops, grass, &c.; as in all probability his stock has increased. It will be necessary to mention, that the whole of these calculations are made in currency, our adventurers means are somewhat greater than might appear at first view."

JOURNAL OF A SCIENTIFIC LADY,
ADDRESSED TO A FRIEND IN EDINBURGH.

AH! my dearest Anna; you, who are still enjoying, at the College, the lecture of the most elegant of all Professors; you, who thrice a-week witness his ingenious experiments; you, who perhaps at this moment are inhaling the *gas of nitrous oxide*, or *gas of Paradise*; how do I envy your sensations and associations. Most joyfully do I sit down to perform my promise of noting an account of my journey to Rothsay; not to indulge in the frivolous tittle-tattle to which many of our sex are addicted, but to attempt a *scientific* journal worthy of our studies.

Nothing occurred on the road worthy of mentioning; the indications of the barometer, the mean temperature of the thermometer, and the contents of the pluviometer, will be found in the table we have agreed to interchange weekly. The day after our arrival, we dined with our friends the S———s, where we had the scapula of the ovis, or shoulder of mutton, with a sauce of macerated cæpe; two birds of the gallinaceous tribe, served with sysimbriam, or water-cresses, and the customary vegetables, brassica, lactura, and spinacia, through none of which the *aqueous fluid* had been sufficiently allowed to percolate. There was also soup, which retained so considerable a portion of *caloric* that it scalded my *palati epidermis*; and the *piper nigrim*, or black pepper, with which it was seasoned, occasioned an unpleasant titillation in the whole *oral region*. In the afternoon the water in the kettle not having been raised to 212° Fahrenheit, or the point at which evaporation takes place, the *thea viridis*, or green tea, formed an imperfect solution, in which state I believe its diaphoretic qualities are injurious. Mrs. S——— declared that she never drank any thing but the *simple* element; but I informed her if she meant *water*, it was not a simple element, but composed of oxygen and hydrogen; and I availed myself of this opportunity to instruct her that the *atmospheric* air is also a mixture, containing about 73 parts of azotic, and 27 of oxygen *gas*; at which the ignorant creature only exclaimed, " Well, I have myself seen a good many red *gashes* across the sky, particularly at sun-set." But, my dearest Anna, I may confess to you, that I am more and more horrified at the sad blunders of mamma, who has not, like us, received the advantages of a *scientific education*; and yet she will every now and then catch a word which she fancies she understands, and betrays the most pitiable ignorance. When I was describing a *resinous matter*, obtained by *precipitation*, she shook her head and exclaimed, " Impossible, child; nothing is ever gotten by precipitation; your poor father was ever telling you not to do things in such a hurry." And once, when Professor Jameson shewed me a lump of *mineral earth*, I inquired whether it was friable; she ejaculated, " Friable, you simpleton: no, nor boilable either; why it is not good to eat." These are but a few specimens of her lamentable ignorance; in point of acute misapprehension, she exceeds Mrs. Malaprop herself; and you cannot conceive the painful humiliation I am continually subjected to by such exposures. As to experiments, I have not yet ventured on many; for having occasioned, a small solution of continuity in the skin of my forefinger, by an accidental incision, I have been obliged to apply a styptic, secured by a ligature; by placing some butter, however, in a temperature of 96, I succeeded in reducing it to a state of diliquescence, and by the usual refrigerating process, I believe I should have converted it into a gelatine, but that it refused to coagulate, doubtless owing to some fault in the apparatus. You are aware that a phosphorescent light emanates from some species of fish in an incipient state of putrefaction, to which has been attributed the irridescent appearance of the sea at certain seasons. To illustrate this curious property, I hoarded a mackarel in a closet for several days; and it was already beginning to be most interestingly luminous, when mamma who had for some days been complaining of a horrid stench in the house, discovered my hidden treasure, and ordered it to be thrown on the dunghill, observing, she expected sooner or later, to be poisoned by my nasty nonsense; but mamma has no *nose* for experimental philosophy; no more have I, you will say, for yesterday, as I was walking with a *prism* before my eyes, comparing the different rays of the *spectrum* with the Newtonian theory, I came full bump against an open door, which drove the sharp edge of the glass against the cartilaginous projection of the nose, occasioning much sternutation and a considerable discharge of blood from the nasal emanatories. By nitrate of silver I have also formed some chrystals of Diana, and I have been eminently successful in making detonating powder; although the last explosion happening to occur just as our neighbour James Heaviside was reading of the tremendous thunderbolt that fell in the gentleman's garden at Alloa, he took it for granted he was visited by a similar phenomenon, and in the apprehension shuffled down stairs on his nether extremity (being prevented from walking by the gout) ejaculating all the way, "Lord have mercy upon us." Upon learning the cause of his alarm, he declared the blue-stocking hussey (meaning me) ought to be sent to the tread-mill, and mamma says I shall be indicted for a nuisance. I have done nothing yet in botany; the extreme cold of the early season makes it impossible to find plants, having only picked up a few specimens of the bellis order, "polygamia superflua," vulgo the daisy. And now, my dearest Anna, adieu. You will receive this by my cousin George, who goes to Edinburgh to-morrow; but as the youth is of the *bashful* species, I fear, in spite of my lecture, he will commit it to the penny post, not having the honour of your acquaintance. Once more adieu, and believe me ever yours most truly. *

H. C.

INTERESTING CASE OF SOMNOLENCY.

Samuel Chilton, an inhabitant of the village of Tinsbury, near Bath, was a labourer of a robust habit of body, though not corpulent, and had reached the 25th year of his age. When apparently in perfect health, he fell into a profound sleep on the 13th May, 1694, and every method which was tried to rouse him proved unsuccessful. His mother ascribed his conduct to sullenness of temper; and dreading that he would die of hunger, placed within his reach bread and cheese, and small beer; and though no person ever saw him eat or drink during a whole month, yet the food set before him was daily consumed. At the end of a month, he rose of his own accord, put on his clothes, and resumed his usual labours in the field.

After a lapse of nearly two years, namely, on the 9th of April, 1696, he was overtaken with excessive sleep. He was now bled, blistered, cupped, and scarified, and the most irritating medicines applied externally; but they were unable to rouse or even to irritate him, and during a fortnight he was never seen to open his eyes. He ate, however, as before, of the food which was placed near him, and performed the other functions which were required; but no person ever saw any of those acts, though he was sometimes found fast asleep with his mouth full of food. In this condition he lay *ten* weeks.

* The above is, we presume, written in ridicule of the attempts lately made to give women a better and more useful education. It is "silly sooth," and so perfectly harmless, that we re-publish it without the least apprehension of mischief. It will scarce even create a laugh.

A singular change in his constitution now took place. He lost entirely the power of eating; his jaws were so and his teeth so closely clenched, that every attempt to force open his mouth with instruments failed. Having accidentally observed an opening in his teeth, made by the action of the tobacco-pipe, and usual with great smoken, they succeeded in pouring some tent wine into his throat through a quill. During *forty-six* days, he subsisted on about three pints or two quarts of tent; and during all that period he had no alvine evacuation.

At the end of *seventeen* weeks, viz., about the 7th of August, he awoke, dressed himself, and walked about the room, being perfectly unconscious that he had slept more than one night. Nothing, indeed, could make him believe that he had slept so long, till, upon going to the fields, he saw crops of barley and oats ready for the sickle, which he remembered were only sown when he last visited them.

Although his flesh was somewhat diminished by so long a fast, yet he was said to look brisker than he had ever done before. He felt no inconvenience whatever from his long confinement, and he had not the smallest recollection of any thing that had happened. He accordingly entered again upon his rural occupations, and continued to enjoy good health till the morning of the 17th of August, 1697, when he experienced a coldness and shivering in his back; and, after vomiting once or twice, he again fell into his former state of somnolency.

Dr. William Oliver, to whom we owe the preservation of these remarkable facts, happened to be at Bath, and hearing of so singular a case, set out, on the 23d of August, to inquire into its history. On his arrival at Tinsbury, he found Chilton asleep, with bread and cheese, and a cup of beer, placed on a stool within his reach. His pulse was regular, though a little too strong, and his respiration free. He was in "a breathing sweat," with an agreeable warmth over his body. Dr. Oliver bawled into his ear, pulled his shoulders, pinched his nose, stopped his mouth and nose together; but, notwithstanding this rude treatment he evinced no indications of sensibility. Impressed with the belief that the whole was "a cheat," Dr. Oliver lifted up his eyelids and found the eyeballs drawn up under his brows, and perfectly motionless. He held a phial containing spirit of *sal ammoniac* under one nostril a considerable time; but though the doctor could not bear it for a moment under his own nose without making his eyes water, the sleeping patient was insensible to its pungency. The ammoniacal spirit was then thrown up his nostrils, to the amount of about half an ounce; but though it was "as strong almost as fire itself," it only made the patient's eyelids shiver and tremble, and his nose run.

Thus baffled in every attempt to rouse him, our ruthless doctor crammed the same nostril with the powder of *white* hellebore; and finding this equally inactive, he was perfectly convinced that no imposter could have remained insensible to such applications, and that Chilton was really overpowered with sleep.

In the state in which Dr. Oliver left him, various gentlemen from Bath went to see him; but his mother would not permit the repetition of any experiments.

On the 2d of September, Mr. Woolmer, an experienced apothecary, went to see him, and finding his pulse pretty high, he took fourteen ounces of blood from his arm; but neither at the opening of the vein, nor during the flow of the blood, did he make the smallest movement.

In consequence of his mother removing to another house, Chilton was carried down stairs when in this fit of somnolency. His head accidentally struck against a stone, and received such a severe blow, that it was much cut; but he gave no indications whatever of having felt the blow. Dr. Oliver again visited him in his new house; and, after trying again some of his former stimulants, he saw a gentleman who accompanied him "run a large pin into the arm of Chilton to the very bone, without his being sensible of it. During the whole of this long fit he was never seen to eat or drink, though generally once a-day, or sometimes once in two days, the food which stood by him had disappeared.

Such was the condition of our patient till the 19th November, when his mother having heard a noise, ran up to his room and found him eating. Upon asking him how he was, he replied, "Very well, thank God." She then asked him whether he liked bread and butter or bread and cheese best. He answered, bread and cheese. She immediately left the room to convey the agreeable intelligence to his brother; but upon their return to the bed-room, they found him as fast asleep as ever, and incapable of being roused by any of the means which they applied.

From this time his sleep seems to have been less profound; for though he continued in a state of somnolency till the end of January, or the beginning of February, yet he seemed to hear when they called him by his name; and though he was incapable of returning an answer, yet they considered him as sensible to what said. His eyes were less closely shut, and frequent tremors were seen in his eyelids. About the beginning of February, Chilton awoke in perfect health, having no recollection whatever of any thing that had happened to him during his long sleep. The only complaint he made was, that the cold pinched him more than usual. He returned, accordingly, to his labours in the field, and, so far as we can learn, he was not again attacked with this singular disease.

DR. PRIESTLEY.—A numerous and highly respectable meeting of nearly two hundred gentlemen of Birmingham and its vicinity, was lately held to celebrate by a public dinner the hundredth anniversary of the birth of Dr. Priestley. The Reverend John Corrie, President of the Birmingham Philosophical Society, was in the Chair. Several excellent speeches were made by the Chairman, and the other Dissenting ministers of Birmingham and the neighbouring towns. The great change in the feelings of the people since the time of the Church-and-King riots which drove Priestley across the Atlantic, was especially pointed out; and the late meeting in London, held for the purpose of doing honour to his scientific acquirements and discoveries, and which was attended by so many eminent men of science, was adduced as a gratifying proof of the increasing liberality of the age. The memory of Priestley was drunk in silence; and Mr. Joseph Parkes, in returning thanks, paid a just and warm tribute to his virtues as a public and private man. He said that

"The purity of Dr. Priestley's personal character and his private virtues were never even questioned by a virulent press, or the tongue of slander. He was indebted to his own single exertions, unaided by factitious circumstances of birth and fortune, for his distinguished literary eminence and scientific reputation. To use the language of the Roman, Dr. Priestley was 'born of himself,' and could boast no aristocratic lineage—he was essentially a self-educated man, who had derived no advantages from academical education. His own zealous love of truth and science raised him to celebrity. Mr. Corrie, and the recent meeting of the first men of science in London, had done ample justice to his promotion of science and philosophy. Mr. Parkes would not involve the unanimity of the meeting by any ill-timed or illiberal allusion to Dr. Priestley's particular political or religious opinions; but it was due to that illustrious man to say, that truth was the great and single object of all his intellectual exertions—that the freedom of discussion and opinion which he claimed for himself he desired to extend to all mankind—and that he boldly maintained civil and religious liberty, in the most unrestricted sense, to be the right of all men in all countries. The war of opinion which burst out on the first French Revolution involved the characters of many great public men in temporary prejudice and persecution, but the political opinions of Dr. Priestley were now the practical views of the present generation; and to him was especially due the merit of exciting public attention to the injustice of the civil disabilities of the Protestant Dissenters, now so happily erased from the Statute-book of England.

The memory of the Reverend Robert Hall was drank in the course of the evening; and the Reverend Mr. Berry, who spoke to the toast, as a friend of Mr. Hall, related the following anecdote of that eminent man.

"Travelling with the venerable and learned Andrew Fuller in a coach from Bristol to London, the conversation turned on political topics. Mr. Hall was told that there was a probability of speedily obtaining a Reformed Parliament; on which he said, 'Sir, I should think nothing of walking a thousand miles barefoot, to be beheaded at the end of my journey, if so desirable an end could be accomplished.' (*Cheers.*) To which Mr. Fuller humorously replied I think Brother Hall, you would walk mighty slow.'"

THE TRUE POET.

I AM a Poet of right sort;
My works are works indeed;
The brightest fancy's best effort
Infinitely exceed.
I hate your lazy sullen shade,
Nor flimsy paper use;
Nor do I know that phantom jade
Vain poets call the Muse.
The sunny field is my delight,
Where labour is no toil :
From dawn to dark, there pleas'd I write
Along the fertile soil.
Two doughty mares my muses are;
The plough it is my quill ;
Each step's a word ; my line a fur;
The couplet is a drill.
My ridges, too, they that are skill'd,
For stanzas much extol them :
Scots acres fifty, fairly till'd,
I count a noble volume.
Manuring is my preface good ;
My argument is sowing ;
And harrowing, though rough and rude,
Is lines both full and flowing.
And thus complete in each respect,
The Press I then invite,
Whose glowing colours, type correct,
Impress supreme delight.
Three brothers, of divine descent,
That surnamed Seasons are,
Do honour me my works to print :
Who with them can compare ?
First, coming Spring, with ink of dew,
The embryo letters moulds ;
And, clad in green, the gayest line,
Both blade and ear unfolds.
With golden type and sweaty brows,
Then Summer does succeed,
Till plump and hard the pickle grows,
And no bad usage dread.
With harden'd hand and eager look,
Now Autumn owns his care ;
For sheet and quire, by sheaf and stook,
Throws off the copies fair ;
And plies his work with quick dispatch,
Till every thing's complete :
And sure, bound up with rape and thack,
Each ruck 's a copy neat.
And now my critics, flail and mill,
While thundering at your duties,
Your thumping wit and pondering skill,
Discover only beauties.
A quick demand I'm sure to have ;
My works suit every taste :
Each year a new edition craves—
Their fame and profit last—
My readers, with me, vow I'm right—
We seek no other song,
But still pursue, with new delight,
What health and life prolong.

A PLOUGHMAN.

[The above sturdy verses were lately sent to the *Schoolmaster*. We publish them not without certain misgivings of their being original ; but if this suspicion be erroneous, we beg the poet to construe our doubts into compliments to his vigour and originality.]

SCIENTIFIC NOTICES.

CAUTION TO ALL WHO VALUE THEIR EYES.

THE first thing to be attended to is a careful regulation of the use of the eyes, in regard to the length of time, as far as this is practicable; entire disuse of them suddenly would be almost injurious as a continued straining of them beyond their capabilities. They should, therefore, be variously employed, as much as this can be done, not applying them too long, or too intently, to the same object, but relieving them by change of scene and diversity of occupation. Another means that will be found to be beneficial, and to help the eyes where much relaxation cannot be obtained, consists in shutting them now and then while at work, going into the air, looking out of a window, especially if there are trees or verdure within sight. This interval of rest, though only of a few minutes' continuance, will be found greatly to relieve the eyes, and enable them to resume their employment with comparative pleasure. A third caution is, that those who are conscious from experience, that their sight has been weakened by its severe and protracted exercise, or arising from any other cause, should carefully avoid all attention to minute objects, or such business or study as requires close application to the visual faculty immediately on rising; and the less it is taxed for a while after eating, or by candle light, the better. The fourth means I have already recommended, viz., bathing the eyes frequently through the day, with cold water. Though the effect of this simple remedy may, for a time, be hardly perceptible, yet, if duly persevered in, I can vouch for its producing the happiest results. So long as there is no actual disease in the eyes, only cold water should be used—and this, applied in the gentlest manner, will soon become sufficiently tepid for all the ends of utility and comfort.—*Curtis on the Eye.*

OPTICAL WONDERS.—People laugh at the story of Argus with a hundred eyes; but what was even Argus to some insects? The cornea of insects seems cut into a number of little planes or facets, like the facets of a diamond, presenting the appearance of net-work, and each of these facets is supposed to possess the power and properties of an eye. Lewenhoeck counted in the cornea of a beetle 3,181 of these facets, of a horse-fly 8,000, and of the grey drone fly 14,000.

CREAM AND BUTTER.—If we are to believe the following notice, our Highland Society, as an *economical* Board, is beat hollow. We are told, for we have not seen the publication, that the *Repertory of Patent Inventions*, contains a notice of a novel and ingenious method of obtaining cream from milk, founded upon the system acted upon in Devonshire, for obtaining what is called "clotted" or "clouted cream," and which is well known to many to be very delicious. Mr. Carter, of Nottingham Lodge, near Eltham, Kent, the originator of the new process, gives, in the *Repertory*, a description of the machine which he constructed, and by which he obtained from four gallons of milk, in twenty-four hours, four and a half pints of clotted cream, which, after churning only fifteen minutes, gave forty ounces of butter, being an increase over the ordinary method of 12¼ per. cent. in cream, and upwards of 11 per cent. in butter. If this be so, our dairy farmers should look to it.

ZINC MILK-PAILS.—Among the patents recently taken out in America one is for a process for extracting cream from milk by the use of zinc. It is said that if zinc be put into the milk-pan, or the milk be put into a vessel made of that substance, the same quantity of milk will yield a greater quantity of cream or butter.

EASY MODE OF FINE EDGING RAZORS.—On the rough side of a strap of leather, or on the undressed calf-skin binding of a book, rub a piece of tin, or a common pewter spoon, for half a minute, or till the leather become glossy with the metal. If the razor be passed over this leather about half a dozen times, it will acquire a finer edge than by any other method.

THE MODERN BROWNIE; OR, THE LITTLE MAN WI' THE BRAID BANNET.

IN a Scottish provincial paper, we learn that this "wee, wee, man" was last seen between Dumblane and Stirling. It is, however, well known, that he waylays travellers on almost every cross-road in the three kingdoms. His appearance near Stirling is described as follows:—We understand, that of late much has been reported in the district to which it refers, regarding the felonious exploits of a certain personage on the public road betwixt Stirling and Dumblane, familiarly termed "the Little Mannie wi' the braid bannet," owing to his antique and uniform appearance to the several wights benighted by the way, and who had been relieved of the burden of their *orra pennies* by his nefarious acts in the vicinity of the Bridge of Allan. One fact deserves to be mentioned:—Late in the evening of Wednesday se'ennight, a rather errant and wayward knight of the shuttle arrived at his humble domicile in Dumblane from Stirling, in a piteous plight. He stated to his wife that he had been robbed of his all, with the exception of a few coppers, near Lecrop Bridge, by a "little auld man wi' a braid bannet," and thanked his stars that his *swab and life* were not also away. The poor wight being all bespattered with mud, and several parts of his body bearing the marks of contusion, his better half credited his story, but rallied him next morning rather sharply on his permitting "a little auld mannie wi' a *braid* bannet to tak' his siller," seeing that he himself was *young*, and a "big and buirdly *chiel*;" besides his *hat* would resist a blow better than a *bannet*, however *braid* that bannet might be. All this was well enough at his own fireside; but the fool must tell all *to his* acquaintances, with exaggerated particulars of the robbery. The "wives o' Dumblane," however, wished not to see " pair Michael" too severely handled by his companions out of doors, and excused his cowardice on this occasion, by observing that better men than he, to their certain knowledge, have been robbed of more than 5s. by "THE Little *Auld* Mannie wi' the *braid bannet*," betwixt Stirling and Dunblane. Now, good courteous reader, you no doubt desire to know something more, of this extraordinary "Little Mannie." Be assured then that he has the power, and has often exercised it, of knocking a man down, without ever laying hands upon him—and that there is some truth in the remarks made by an old toper of the "auncient citie" to his rib, that this wonderful "Little Mannie" was the least of all his tribe. "But what is he like, Tam?" inquired the wife impatiently.—"Why, Jenny," he replied, " if ye maun ken, of a' the things in the warld, he's likest to a gill stoup."

LADY LOUISA'S COW.—During the last war, when that truly worthy General, Lord John Lennox, was Governor of Plymouth, he gave strict orders that the green in front of the Government-house should not be trespassed upon, and the sentry had orders not to allow any one to walk on it, or any cattle to graze, except Lady Louisa's favourite little Alderney cow. Shortly after, the lady of the Port-Admiral going to call at the Government-house, was crossing the green, when the sentry stopped her Ladyship, who remarked to him, that perhaps he was not aware that she was the Admiral's Lady. "I don't care, Ma'am, who you be," said the man, " or if you be the Admiral's *Lady* or his *Wife*, you must stop, for I know you are not Lady Louisa's Alderney Cow.'

THE STORY-TELLER.

GEORGE MASON.

LIFE IN THE NEW SETTLEMENTS OF AMERICA.

PEOPLE cannot at present be satiated with information specting the condition of the settlers in the western territory of the United States. The American story we have give contains a fair picture of some of the hardships to hich emigrants are exposed, from climate, and the want population, and a neighbourhood. The tale is, besides teresting and pleasing, and the most unexceptionable. It ay help to form an emigrant's Guide, or at least give useul hints.

In the autumn of 1816, the Rev. Mr. Mason arrived towards sun-set at a settlement, eight miles south of the Iron anks, in what is commonly called the Jackson Purchase, n the Lower Mississippi. The family had emigrated from lew England, and consisted of this gentleman, a man of ignified appearance, though indicating fatigue and feeble ealth, and turned of forty; his lady, with a complexion riginally fair, but now browned by the suns of a long ourney of sixteen hundred miles, in the warmest days of utumn, and with an expression of great sweetness, though louded by care and sorrow; and five children, four sons, nd a daughter. George, the hero of this tale, was a fair lue-eyed boy, of about fourteen; Lizzy, a pretty little irl of twelve, with bright black eyes, and glossy ringlets f black hair curling in her neck. Her shrinking and imid manners were the consequence of the retirement in which she had lived, and of the fears inspired by the rough people amongst whom they had been travelling. Henry, Thomas, and William, were ten, eight, and four years old. It was altogether a group, in which the parents excited uncommon interest, and the children were lovely beyond what I shall attempt to describe, because I would avoid expresions that might be deemed extravagant. Still less can I paint that mingled dignity and lowliness, which is apt to mark the countenances and manners of our western ministers, who constitute the connecting link between the rich and the poor: their education, and the respect paid to their profession, placing them upon a level with the rich; and the scantiness of their subsistence, placing them upon a level with the poor. It was obvious, from their fatigued and weather-beaten appearance, that they had travelled a long way. A slight inspection of their dress, and the hired waggon that had brought them and their baggage from the banks of the Mississippi, where they had, that morning, disembarked from a flat boat, manifested that one of their trials had been the want of sufficient money to bring them comfortably over such a long way, by such a tedious and expensive route. There was a shyness about them, too, which marked that the outlandish aspect of the planters, who stood staring at the new comers, made a disagreeable impression on them. Real dignity, however, is an internal thing, independent of dress and equipage. A family could not have been reared, as these had been, where self-respect had been inculcated every day and every hour, both by precept and example, without showing the influence of this discipline, be their dress and appearance in other respects as they might. There was a look of decency, and an indescribable, but easy-felt manner, perceptible in every individual of this family, which manifested, at a glance, that it was the family of a gentleman. It repressed the rude curiosity of two or three tall planters habited in deer-skin shirts, with fringed epaulets of leather on their shoulders, a knit sash, of red green and blue about their waists, buck-skin pantaloons and mocassins, a rifle on their shoulders, five or six dogs attending each of them, and a dozen ragged, listless negroes behind them. There was much rough, but well-intended complimenting and offers of aid, on the part of those who had come down to welcome the new settlers to their cabin in the woods. It might have been welcome after a little time, but at present, the dim shades of twilight gathering over the boundless woods, the savage aspect of these huntsmen and their negroes, even the joyous evening yell of the hounds, the unwonted and strange terms of welcome, the foreign look of every thing about them; all this was of a character to inspire dismay and home-sickness, in the hearts of people lately transferred from a pleasant New-England village. Weary, and but slenderly furnished with the simplest means of subsistence, whether they looked round them upon the new society, in the midst of which their lot was cast; upon the dark and sterile woods whose leaves were falling about them; or into the roofless and floored cabin, where they were to shelter for the night—the whole scene was desolate and chilling. In such circumstances as these, God is a shade, a shelter, and a high tower of defence. The younger children had wept with weariness, thrown themselves upon a blanket, and were asleep under the open sky. The neighbours saw that the strangers were weary, and wished to be by themselves. They had considerately provided plenty of provisions, spread bear-skins for them in the interior of the cabin, and left a black woman to cook supper and breakfast for them. In that mild season and cloudless weather, there was nothing formidable to them in the idea of leaving the family to repose on bear-skins under the canopy of heaven. One after another, with the significant western salutation, " I wish you well," left the travellers to themselves. The little children were too soundly asleep to be awakened to supper. The parents, George, and Eliza, eat that which was provided for them by the black woman, and soon forgot their cares, and slept as soundly as if they had been stretched upon beds of down in a palace.

Mr. Mason had purchased, on report only, and without having seen it, this unfinished log-house in the midst of a "clearing" of three acres, cut out of the forest eight miles from the river. The nearest habitation was distant two miles. Beyond that there was a considerable settlement recently established. Some of the planters were comparatively opulent, and had a considerable number of slaves.

A bright morning sun, slanting its beams through the forest, at this season delightfully rich with all the varied colours of autumn; a plentiful breakfast, provided for the family before they were awake, by the black woman, and to which she awakened them; the keen appetite of the children, refreshed by their sleep; the air, prospects, and cheerful sounds of the morning, rendered the scene before them as different from that of the preceding evening as can be imagined. Every member of the family was exhilarated; and the whole conversation was, how they should render the habitation comfortable, and lay in a sufficient quantity of provisions for the approaching winter. Immediately after breakfast, at the departure of the black woman, the father was seen in company with George, making mortar from the clay, and exerting himself to fill up the intervals between the logs, (in the language of the country, "*daubing*" the house,) and by all the common expedients of the country, to render the habitations a warm and secure shelter from the frosts and rains of the approaching winter. Though his neighbours were rough, some of them were kind in their way, and they came and aided him. He saw in their mode of managing the business, that there is a dexterity to be acquired only by practice, and that they knew better than he how to "*daub*" and "*chink*" a log cabin. In a couple of days, which fortunately continued fair, the house had a roof, which would turn the rain, though the covering was of cypress "*splits*," secured in their places by logs, laid at right angles over them, and a chimney which did not smoke, although it was made of "*clefts*," plastered with clay mortar; the intervals between the logs were tightly closed with *chinking*, well covered with the same material. A partition of small and straight timbers, with an opening cut through one end for a door, divided the area of the cabin into two rooms, one of which contained one, and the other two husk mattresses. The neighbours assisted him to raise another smaller cabin, in the language of the country a "*log-pen*," covered and "daubed" in the same manner, but without a chimney: and here was another mattress on which George and Henry slept. These mattresses, thanks to the cheapness of bleached cottons in America, had an appearance of coolness, and neatness, which spread a charm round the precinct of the rustic, but clean cabin. Mr. Mason was obliged to employ some part of the small sum of money that remained to him after defraying the expense of their long journey and which he reserved for the most pressing emergencies, in purchasing a supply of winter provision. These consisted of the substantial materials of a west-countryman's fare—corn, bacon, and sweet potatoes. Such are the appointments with which a hundred thousand families have commenced in the Western settlements, and with which they have probably been more contented and happy than their descendants will be when dwelling in spacious mansions.

When the white frosts of November rendered an evening fire necessary, when a bright one was kindled on their broad clay hearth; when the "*puncheon*," shutters,—for glass had they none,—had excluded the uncertain light, and the chill air of evening; when the table made with an adze from white poplar *clefts*, was spread before this fire; when the repast of smoking corn-loaf, sweet potatoes, and fried bacon, was arranged on it; when the fragrant tea was added in remembrance of New England, for they still retained a few pounds brought all the way from that country; and when the whole was seasoned by cheerful conversation, and that appetite which is felt in such cabins, and by industrious back-woodsmen in the highest perfection,—the guests at this humble feast had no need to envy the best-fed alderman of London. A brilliant blaze, kindled with dry wood, enlightened the whole interior of this fresh looking, rough-cast, timbered apartment. Their faithful dog, Rover, who had followed them all the way from their late home, and who was now doubly dear to them, sat beside the table, looking earnestly upon its contents, apparently as hungry and as happy as the children, wagging his tail, and occasionally uttering a yelp of joy to fill up the pauses of cheerful conversation. The prolonged and distant howl of the wolves, the ludicrous, and almost terrific noises of a hundred owls, the scream of other nocturnal animals, the measured creaking of the crickets and *catadeds*, and the gathering roar of autumnal winds along the forest, only sweetened a sense of present protection to the children, and rendered the brightness of the scene within more delightful by contrast with the savage and boundless forest without. I have never passed, and I never expect to pass, happier hours than I have spent in such a cabin. It has seemed to me that a back-woodsman's cabin, just risen in the forest, rendered happy by innocence, competence, contentment, and gratitude to the Supreme Being, concentrates affection, and produces some singular associations of contrast, that render it the chosen and hallowed abode of that unassuming, simple happiness, which is the most durable and satisfying that we can feel here below. I have delightful remembrances of my long sojourn in such places; and as they return to my thoughts, I earnestly invoke the blessing of God upon their inhabitants.

The children were delighted with these first essays of the life of a back-woodsman. A circumstance contributed to heighten the charm. The sixth day after their arrival, a deer strayed so near the cabin, that George shot it from the door. The same day the father and son, in exploring the grounds directly about them, with the view of commencing a clearing, started a bear from the cane-brake. He retreated slowly and growling from their path; and made his retreat upon a prodigious sycamore. A passing neighbour came to the place. Two or three dogs surrounded the tree, and made the woods ring with their cries, which indicated to a knowing huntsman, that fear was mingled with their joy. A few rifle-shots brought the animal to the ground. There was something less wounding to their feelings in the slaughter of such a ferocious beast, than in that of an inoffensive deer. Apart from the spirit-stirring sport of bringing down a monstrous fat bear, the meat, which is excellent and easily preserved, was a matter of no small consideration to a family like this. Even the skin is an important item in the arrangement of a back-wood cabin. The hunting of the day furnished ample materials for pleasant evening conversation and amusement. Tender pieces of venison and bear's meat smoked upon the table. The success of that day seemed to promise, that there would be no danger of want of meat, while they possessed a rifle, powder, and lead. The black eyes of Eliza glistened with intense interest, as she contemplated, with a shudder, the terrible claws and teeth of the savage animal, observing, that much as she longed to gather the wild-flowers, she should always tremble to go into the woods where such beasts were common. George exulted, in the spirit of a little Nimrod, as he related the circumstances of bringing down the bear, to his younger brothers, who had not been permitted to be present. The only misfortune of this pleasant little circle was, that there were generally two or three speakers at a time. One practised in the study of canine physiognomy would have read the satisfaction expressed even in Rover's countenance, as he sat with his eyes fixed on George, evidently listening with all his ears, and perhaps regretting the want of speech that prevented him from giving his opinion of the bear-hunt. Even Mr. Mason turned a countenance brightening from its usual languid expression of sickness and fatigue on Mrs. Mason, who, it would appear had been averse to this emigration. "Eliza," said he, "are you sorry now, that we have brought our little ones here?" Mrs. Mason admitted that the first samples of their new way of life were more pleasant than she had anticipated.

It is unnecessary, and would be tedious to explain at length the causes of Mr. Mason's removal from New England, to the banks of the Mississippi. It will suffice to say, that both he and his wife had been reared delicately. His salary as a minister was very small, and his family increased too rapidly for his means. His parish refused to augment his stipend, he consequently resigned his office, and resolved to seek his fortune in the western country. His wife at first argued against a plan which appeared attended with so much difficulty and risk, but she loved and respected her husband, and she ceased to oppose his wishes.

The children, their eyes swollen with weeping, were packed along with Mrs. Mason and the bulky baggage, into a two-horse waggon.

In due time, and with the common experience of sweet and bitter things, they had toiled over the last of the Alleghany mountains; had descended to the Ohio; had sold their waggon and horses; had purchased a flat boat, and were floating down the beautiful Ohio, which happened this autumn to be in an uncommonly favourable state for boating. They had admired the forest, the valley, the "bluffs," and the incipient towns and villages as they alternated on its long course; had encountered the sweeping and turbid current of the Mississippi; had disembarked at the Iron Banks, and hired a waggon to carry them out to the settlement, where, as we have seen, Mr. Mason had purchased the cabin and the clearing already mentioned.

As they became better acquainted with the settlers, they found them illiterate and rude. The most distinguished amongst them professed no superiority over the rest, but what they derived from their wealth; some possessing, beside a number of slaves, a drove of horses and four-wheeled carriages, which they honoured with the name of coaches. The Masons soon discovered that there were disagreeable people elsewhere as well as in New England; but their general circumstances were so pleasant and novel during the winter that succeeded their arrival, that Mr. Mason pronounced himself as well satisfied with his new condition as he had anticipated. Young George became a hunter of considerable expertness. Whenever they chose, by rambling a few hours, they could bring home wild ducks, squirrels, opossums, and rabbits. The coffee and tea which they had brought with them, it is true, were soon exhausted; the want, at first, from the power of habit, was felt as a painful privation. The milk of a couple of cows which they had purchased, supplied, however, a more healthful and nutritive substitute, if not so pleasant to them as that which they had been compelled to renounce, since they could not afford to recruit their stock. When the weather or other circumstances forbade his working abroad, Mr. Mason found sufficient occupation for his leisure hours in reading the few books he had brought with him, and in instructing the children.

In his own family, as a substitute for public worship on the Sabbath, he adopted a private course of worship, blending interest and amusement with religious instruction. Prayers, instructions, select readings from the Scriptures, tales calculated to excite moral reflections and benevolent feelings, first by the father, then by the mother, and the children in succession. Their understandings were exercised by questions. Their hearts were improved by representations of the beauty of humility and kindness, contrasted with the baseness and self-torment of pride, and the bad passions that follow in its train. One grand aim in this worship, was to represent the Almighty in that amiable character in which He shows himself in his words and in his works; and sedulously to shield their minds from any ideas of his being and providence, but those of mercy, love, justice, goodness, and truth. It closed with a kind of court of inquiry. The general tenor of the children's deportment, words and actions, during the past week, underwent a solemn review. The facts were proved; the character and tendency of the actions pointed out; the source whence they had arisen explained; and, if matter of reprehension existed, what ought to have been said or done in the case declared; and, finally, praise and blame were distributed according to the merits of the actions.

When these services were concluded, and the ardour of the sun quenched by his descent behind the forests, they walked together into the woods and clearings. Every object in these walks was at once a source of instruction and amusement, and a theme whence Mr. Mason did not fail to deduce new proofs of the wisdom, mercy, and power of God. The moss, or the evergreen at the foot of the sycamore; the paroquets settling on their branches to feed; the partridge flitting on their path; the eagle screaming in the blue sky, far above the summits of these trees; the carrion vultures sailing round, and at times, to the eye, seeming to lie still in the air, as they scented intensely, in the heights of the firmament, for their appropriate food; the squirrels skipping, and performing gambols indescribable, or sitting with their tails elevated over their heads, and curling gracefully back, nibbling the wild fruits; the rabbits starting from the cane-brake; the endless variety of trees and shrubs around them; the prodigious grape-vines climbing to the highest tops; the violets, even now, at the end of autumn, close on the heels of winter, starting into bloom; the diversified seed-capsules of flowers that had already come to maturity; the various starry forms of the gossamer down of seeds, sailing slowly in the breeze; in fine, every object which they met, was sufficient to excite the attention and interest of the family, and furnish a theme for a lecture on natural history, or a warm and heartfelt sermon on the goodness and wisdom of the Creator. It is thus that minds rightly trained every where find amusement and instruction.

Yet, though they had these delightful Sabbath walks in the woods; though it was a source of constant delight and amusement to the parents to answer the thousand questions of their children, raised by the novelty of the objects in their walks; though the illusive veil which imagination spreads over an unexplored region, still rested upon the country,— we must not infer that they were all the time happy, and had not a mixture of bitter, with their pleasant things. It belongs to earth to have this mixture, and our friends were not exempt from the portion of man every where under the sun. On their return from such walks, there was no tea and coffee to cheer them. The children were nearly barefoot, while the creole children of the settlement, when they met them, would hold up their red morocco shoes, as if to provoke painful comparisons. They now began to discover that if there were jealousies, divisions, and burnings in New England, the same evil existed here in an aggravated form. To meet these evils they had, besides religion, one grand resource. Would that every family had the same! Nearly one half of the misery of this earth proceeds from disunion and selfishness in families. The voice of wrangling, dispute, and separate interests, is heard in the family dwelling. Good angels scatter not their blessings in such habitations. Such was not the log cabin.

Their evening union was one of peace, love, and joy. Every one, even the youngest boy, scarcely five years old, brought kindness and good feeling to the common stock. The bright evening fire was kindled: the Bible was read: they prayed together; and each of these affectionate inmates loved the other as he loved his own soul. This mutual affection showed in every word and action. When the members of a family really love one another, this is food and raiment, and society and cheerfulness, and every thing. To such a family external sorrows are like weights pressing upon an arch, the strength of which increases with the amount of pressure applied. But when to poverty and trouble, and sickness, are added selfishness, disputing, and quarrelling within, I know not how the members of such a family can sustain life.

With this resource, the winter wore away comfortably and pleasantly, notwithstanding their passing disquietudes and vexations. On every fine sunshiny day, Mr. Mason was employed with young George, before the sunbeams had dissolved the frost, *girdling* the trees. The latter had his little axe and grubbing hoe, cutting down the smaller trees, delighted with the mellow appearance, and the healthy smell of the virgin mould. A hundred times his delight was excited by seeing the grey and black squirrels skip away from the trees which he began to fell. The paroquets in their splendid livery of green and gold were fluttering about the sycamores, raising their shrill scream, as disagreeable as their plumage is brilliant; and seemed to be scolding at these meddlers in their empire. The red-birds, springing away from the briar copse, which he began to disturb with his grubbing hoe; the powerful mocking-bird, seated at its leisure on a dead branch, and pouring its gay song, and imitating every noise that was heard; the loud and joyous bark of their favourite dog, as he was pursuing his own sport beside them, digging for an opossum; the morning crow of the cock; the distant cry of the hounds in the settlement, ringing through the forests; the morning mists lying like the finest drapery of muslin, spread over the tops of the trees; these, and a thousand mingled and joyous cries of animals in the woods, filled his young heart with joy, and often arrested his axe and his hoe. In such pursuits passed away the morning till breakfast.

When the labour of clearing was resumed after breakfast, the mother and Eliza came out, attended by the younger children, and looked on the work as they sat on the logs already cut. A falling tree was a grand object to them. Henry, now a stout boy of ten, had already obtained permission to take his share in these labours. Not unfrequently the whole group would suspend their toils, and laugh to watch him tugging at the branch of a shrub, catching by its points upon others, and pulling him back, delighted to see his little cheeks flush with exultation and exercise, and note the promise of future perseverance in the efforts which he made, until he had overcome the resistance and added it to the pile.

After sunset it was a high treat to the children to fire the huge piles of dry bushes and logs, heaped for burning, and to see the flames rising above the tops of the highest trees, enlightening every object around, and disturbing the owls and roosting birds from their retreats. The noise of the bursting cane-stalks was like the report of a thousand guns, and they called these nightly fires their celebrations. Not but there were also discouragements and difficulties in this work of clearing. Mr. Mason was both unused to labour and feeble in health. To cut down a single Mississippi sycamore of the large size, required three days of his best exertions. Of course he was compelled to let all the largest trees to stand in his clearing, only deadening them by girdling. How it grieved him to see his rich and level field marred in its appearance, by a hundred huge standing dead trees, and the broken limbs and branches, which the wind was constantly detaching from them. It was trying to his temper, too, to have one of his rude neighbour planters (for since the Mason family had ceased to be a novelty, they experienced a sensible diminution in the kindness with which the other settlers had received them) surveying his work with affected pity, expressed in conversation something like this:—" Why, Doctor, if you do not get a greater force, you will have a field hardly large enough for a '*truck patch*.' One of my negroes would cut many more trees in a day, than you will in a month. Doctor, you must have some negroes." But he took especial care not to offer the services of his.

But the severest of the whole was splitting rails. This was a task absolutely beyond the strength of young George. The kind hearted boy was assiduous to hand the wedges and the maul to his exhausted father. In this most laborious business there is a dexterity only to be acquired by practice. Many a tree, cut down with great labour, would not split at all. It was long before Mr. Mason, with his utmost exertions, could make five-and-twenty in a day. It did not mend the matter to be told, by those who looked on his work, that one hundred and fifty a-day was the regular task of each of their negroes. At night Mr. Mason's hands were one blister. Poor George could count his blisters, too. Mrs. Mason bound up their sore hands, and turned away her face to conceal her tears. The severe toil caused Mr. Mason rheumatic pains and sleepless nights. He found, moreover, when stormy weather confined him to the house, that a body full of the pains of exhausting labour unfitted him for mental exertion. But neither the voice of complaining or of dejection was heard; for in this cabin there was union, mutual love, confidence in God, and the hope of immortality.

The middle of March approached, and in this climate it is the dawn of spring. The wilderness began to be gay; the rose-bud in a thousand places was one compact tuft of peach-blow flowers; the umbrella tops of the dog-woods were covered with the large blossoms of brilliant white; at every step the feet trampled on clusters of violets; the swelling buds and the half-formed leaves diffused on every side the delicious perfume of spring. The labours of Mr. Mason had been slow and painful, but they had been constant and persevering. A little every day produces a great result. In four months the clearing was increased from six to nine acres, which were well fenced, and fit for planting. The surface of the soil was black, rich, and perfectly pliable. It was a pleasant novelty to him to plant corn without ploughing, and among thick deadened trees, reaching almost to the clouds. The field was laid out in rows in right lines, by taking sight from one tree to another. The father went before making a hole for the corn with his hoe. George followed, dropping the corn into the hole, and covering it with his. Eliza, with her face shaded by her large sun-bonnet, and Henry with his broad-leafed straw-hat, with little bags pinned to their sides, walked beside George and their father. They carried beans, the seed of pumpkins, squashes, cucumbers, and the different kinds of melons, to hand to each, where a place offered that seemed suitable to these seeds. A garden, or as the people call it, a *truck-patch*, was also prepared, and sowed and planted with such seeds and vegetables as their more considerate neighbours had taught them were congenial to the soil and climate.

The violent thunder-storms of that country and season were at first a source of alarm to the family. They trembled as they heard the thunder echoing through the forests, and saw the lightning firing the high dead trees. They soon perceived that the thunderbolts fell harmless to the earth. Their ears became accustomed to the crash, and the beautiful mornings that followed, hailed by all the birds of spring, and embalming the air with the mingled odours of the forest, more than compensated for the passing terrors of the night. There are a few lovers of nature who will be able to comprehend the enjoyment of this family on visiting the field the first sabbath after the crops had come fully up. It is a delightful spectacle to one that has eyes and a heart. It was the promise of future support to those who had nothing else on which to depend; of subsistence and comfort to all they loved on earth. It was cultivated vegetation sprung up on the wild soil, where nothing but weeds and bushes had flourished from the creation. I enter into their delight, as their eyes caught the straight stems of the corn, rising in lines that already marked the rows with a vigour of vegetation and depth of verdure which they had never seen corn wear before. Parents and children gazed with unsated eagerness upon the melons and cucumbers, starting up with leaves broader and fresher than any they had ever beheld in New England. There they had required great care in preparing the hills, and laborious attention to the kind and amount of manure; here, they were barely deposited in the virgin soil. There, in March, the ground was still covered with snow; here, these vegetables had already thrown out their second leaves. The inspection of the sweet-potato patch, which was large, and the hills of which had been prepared with great care, was a source of still more gratifying curiosity. Our emigrants were all fond of this vegetable, and had never seen it growing. It was therefore with the highest gratification that they watched the unfolding stem, and the first development of the leaves of this beautiful creeper.

The season was favourable, and their crops came forward to their utmost hopes. To watch it daily advance was a constant source of amusement. But the sad leaven of sorrow remained at the bottom of their cup. The great heats of the climate began to make themselves felt early in April. The lassitude that ensued was a new sensation to this family, and at first not unpleasant. But the increase of this lassitude, as the season and the heat advanced, became a source of apprehension to Mr. Mason. Half an hour's labour in the field, after the sun was up, completely drenched him in perspiration, and left him powerless to renew his work, until he had rested an hour upon his mattress. His inward apprehension was, " If such be the effect of an April sun, what will be that of July and August?"

Midsummer already furnished their table with green corn and the common vegetables of the season in ample abundance; but their joy in the prospect of their crops was damped by observing, that as the summer heats advanced the health of Mr. Mason more visibly sunk under the influence of the season. He could no longer labour abroad more than an hour in the day, and that in the morning before the sun was above the trees.

The heavy dews, which lay like rain upon the leaves of the corn and the rank weeds, were found scarcely less noxious to his health when he was drenched by them, than the heats of the sun. Young George, fully comprehending the case, laboured from morning till night to spare his father, and to keep down the weeds. It discouraged him to see that more grew up in a night, than he could cut down in a day.

In attempting to work with his son in the sweet-potato patch, in the middle of July, under the influence of a powerful sun, Mr. Mason experienced a *coup de soleil*, and was assisted to his bed by the united exertions of his wife and children. During three hours, he was not expected to survive from one minute to another. I do not design to describe the agony of his family. He who knows how they loved one another can imagine it. There are events whose suddenness throw the mind into a kind of stupefaction, and it was only when Mr. Mason exhibited signs of being out of immediate danger, that tears were shed by those who watched over him. Mr. Mason died, exhorting his family never to despair, and the duties of a father to the orphan flock devolved upon George.

I should be glad to give the reader as distinct an image as I have myself of this rustic funeral in the Mississippi forest. I see the two solitary cabins standing in the midst of the corn, which overtopped the smaller cabin. I see the high and zig-zag fence, ten rails high, that surrounds the field, and the hewn " puncheon" steps in the form of crosses, by which the people passed over the fence into the enclosure; the smooth and beaten footpath amidst the weeds, that leads through the corn-field to the cabins. I see the dead trees throwing aloft their naked stems from amidst the corn. I mark the square and compact enclosure of the deep green forest, which limits the prospect to the summits of the cornstalks, the forest, and the sky. A path is cut through the corn a few feet wide to a large sycamore, left in its full verdure in one corner of the field, where Mr. Mason used to repose with George when he was weary, and where he had expressed a wish, during his sickness, that he might be buried. Under that tree is the open grave. Before the door of the cabin, and shaded by the western slope of the sun behind it, is the unpainted coffin, only wanting the covering plank. In it is the lifeless body of the pastor, the cheek, blanched to the colour of the bands about the neck, and contrasting so strongly with the full and flowing black silk robe, in which, in the far country of his birth, he had been accustomed to go up to the house of the Lord. I see the white mothers, their children, and a considerable number of blacks who had been permitted to attend the funeral, in consideration of the service which was to be performed by one of their number. I see the tall and swarthy planters, with the stern authority and rude despotism, which they exercise over their slaves, and their conscious feeling of their standing and importance, impressed upon their countenances. I see the pale faces of the little group of mourners, struggling hard with nature against lamentation and tears. They could not have, and they needed not, the expensive and sable trappings which custom has required for the show of grief. Their faded and mended dresses were in perfect keeping with the despondency in their countenances, and their forlorn and desolate prospects.

The assembled group was summoned to prayer. The black, who officiated, was dressed, by the contributions of his fellow-servants of the whole settlement, in a garb as nearly like that of the methodist ministers, who were in the habit of preaching in the settlement, as the case would admit. The position was to him one of novelty and awe. His honest and simple heart was affected with the extreme distress of the mourners. He began, at first, in awkward and unsuccessful attempts to imitate the language and manner of educated ministers. He soon felt the hopelessness of the effort, and poured out the simple, earnest effusions of real prayer, in language not less impressive from being uttered in the dialect of a negro. He dissolved into tears from his own earnestness; and, while the honest and sable faces of his fellow-slaves were bathed in tears, the contagion of sympathy extended through the audience, producing a general burst of grief. I should despair of being able to catch the living peculiarities and dialect of the discourse, or exhortation, which followed. Nevertheless, I shall attempt an outline of the beginning, which may fairly serve as a sample of the rest:—

"White Massas and people, please to hark and hear the poor words of Pompey. Great God let white men bring poor Pompey over the sea, and make him work hard in field. Great God good, when he seem hard with us. He send good men to turn Pompey's heart, and make him Christian. Strange things God work. Here Massa Mason, great Yankee preacher, know all tongues, read all books, wear the grand gown you see there in coffin, preach in big meeting. He come way off here to Massaseepa to die,—die in the woods. Nobody pray over him but poor Pompey. Well, me think all one thing for God. Me feel here when me die, me go to Heaven. God no turn me out cause me no got book learning. Massa Mason he die, he go to Heaven. Oh! Lord God, touch Pompey's lips, that he speak a word in season to poor Missis and the dear children. Oh! Missis, you see Heaven, you no want him back. No sin, no labour, no tears."

And the poor earnest slave proceeded to pour forth from the fulness of his heart all the motives of resignation, patience, and hope, that his retentive memory enabled him to utter. The audience melted anew into tears. When the service was finished, he recited in his peculiar accent and dialect those beautiful verses of a funeral hymn, which he had so often heard repeated as to have committed it to memory:—

"Those eyes he seldom could close,
By sorrow forbidden to sleep," &c.

I have never heard voices so sweet as those of some black women on such occasions. The thrilling tones will remain on my memory as long as I live. To me, too, there is something very affecting in that sacred music in which the whole congregation unite. Every one joined in this hymn, and it seemed to be a general wail sent up from the woods to Heaven.

When the hymn was ended, the man whose business it was to direct the ceremony, proposed to those who wished to take a last look at the deceased to come forward. It is the common custom in that country for widows, who affect refinement, to shut themselves up in retirement from the funeral solemnities of their husbands. But not so did Mrs. Mason. She walked firmly to the coffin side, and all her children came with her. They looked long at the pale and care-worn, but peaceful countenance, of the being who had been, next to God, their stay and dependence. At a signal from the same man, the lid was placed on the coffin and nailed down. Twelve of the principal planters were the bearers. The mourners walked directly behind the coffin, and the whole mass of people followed through the corn-field. The coffin was let down with cords into the grave, and the fresh black soil heaped upon it. According to the custom of that region, each one present took up a handful of earth, and threw it into the grave. A couple of stakes were planted, one at the head and the other at the foot; the neighbours dispersed to their several abodes; and the widow and her children returned to their desolate dwelling. A season was claimed by natural grief, but the family did not give themselves up to despair.

I do not purpose very particularly to narrate the subsequent fortunes of this family, any further than as their circumstances are calculated to develop the character and conduct of George. It is only necessary to say, that, for the present, the family were amply supplied with corn, and the common vegetables from their field, which nature had been beneficent in ripening for them, during their utmost distress. They might, therefore, behold the approach of winter without any immediate apprehension of starving. But people may suffer, and suffer acutely from poverty, after the fear of the immediate want of food is removed.

The clothes which they brought with them from New England were wearing out, and they had no means of replacing them. The deer-skin dresses, so common in a country, were still more expensive to purchase, than the cheap domestic articles. Either were alike beyond the means, which, as regarded money, were entirely exhausted by the sickness of Mr. Mason. There are many ways and expedients in such cases, to which back-wood's people are accustomed, which the Masons had yet to learn. The decent habits of the mother had hitherto kept the clothes of her children whole, by patching and darning. But this could not be possible much longer. There are severe frosts even in that fine climate; and five children could not be always confined to the narrow precincts of a log-house. In the bright and delightful frosty mornings of December, it is natural that children should feel the cheering elasticity and invigorating influence of the frosts as other animals. They soon, like the domestic fowls and animals, became accustomed to running abroad unshod. But when they returned from their excursions, to hover round the fire, their feet red, inflamed, and smarting to agony with the reaction of the fire, the tender mother felt the inflammation as keenly as though it had been in her own heart. Her own sufferings of the same sort were as nothing in the comparison.

Whenever the question of the future course of the family was in discussion, and the question of " What were they to do?" followed by gloom and despondency, George failed not to recall to them his father's last declaration: " That God never forsakes them who do not forsake themselves."

"They were in good health," he said, "and in a country where sustenance was easy to be procured; and, if they could only hit upon the right way, some one might surely be devised, in which they might become independent of every body, and take care of themselves." The grand object of all their conversations was to find this way.

Few if any of my young friends can have any idea of the heart-wearing study of this family, to find some track, by following which, they might obtain sufficient money to clothe themselves, and pay the doctor's bill and taxes. Destitute as they were, these bills were presented, and payment pressed with persevering importunity. In discoursing every evening upon this matter, Mrs. Mason, George and Lizzy, were of course chief speakers, though Henry, Thomas, and even little William, often made their speech and threw their light upon the subject. If the reader would not feel a smile out of place in the circle of this afflicted family, he could not have restrained one at hearing some of the propositions of the junior branches of the family counsel. Henry proposed the mystery of bird-catching, and sending cages of mocking-birds, red-birds, paroquets, and turtle-doves, to New Orleans for sale. Thomas was for applying their exertions to the gathering reed-canes, and sending them to the northern manufacturers for weaver's sleys. George had high hopes from a chemical composition for ink and blacking, which he expected to complete from the vegetables of the country. Mrs. Mason and Lizzy limited their projects to the tried and simple experiment of raising cotton, and spinning night and day to clothe themselves, and manufacture a little surplus for sale. A thousand inconveniences attended every experiment, as preliminary difficulties equally insuperable appended to another. Night after night, and week after week wore away in unprofitable speculations. The party generally retired from the evening fire to their beds, their brains dry and exhausted by useless searching for some practicable project, and their hearts sunk with the discouraging impression, that nothing was before them but the same hopeless poverty.

But when their supper of milk, corn-bread, and sweet potatoes was finished, and they were again assembled about the evening fire, the repetition of Mr. Mason's maxim, " never despair," like a voice from Heaven, renewed their courage and strength for a new discussion of their prospects. Success, as it ought, ultimately attended their counsels; but we must defer the remainder of the history till next week. (*To be Continued.*)

THE BIBLE.

A NATION must be truly blessed if it were governed by no other laws than those of this Blessed Book. It is so complete a system, that nothing can be added to it, or taken from it; it contains every thing needful to be known or done; it affords a copy for a king, and a rule for a subject; it gives instruction and counsel to a senate; authority and direction for a magistrate: it cautions a witness; requires an impartial verdict of a jury; and furnishes the judge with his sentence: it sets the husband as lord of the household, and the wife as mistress of the table; tells *him* how to rule, and *her* how to manage. It entails honour to parents, and enjoins obedience to children: It prescribes and limits the sway of the sovereign, the rule of the ruler, and authority of the master; commands the subjects to honour, and the servants to obey; and promises the blessing and protection of its AUTHOR to all that walk by its rules. It gives directions for weddings and for burials; it promises food and raiment, and limits the use of both: It points out a faithful and an eternal Guardian to the departing husband and father; tells him with whom to leave his fatherless children, and in whom his widow is to trust, and promises a father to the former, and a husband to the latter: It teaches a man how to set his house in order, and how to make his will: it appoints a dowry for the wife, and entails the right of the first-born; and shews how the youngest branches shall be left: It defends the rights of all, and reveals vengeance to every defaulter, over-reacher, and oppressor. It is the *first* book, the *best* book, and the *oldest* book, in all the world: It contains the choicest matter, gives the best instruction, and affords the greatest pleasure and satisfaction that ever was revealed. It contains the best laws, and profoundest mysteries that ever were penned: It brings the best tidings, and affords the best of comfort to the inquiring and disconsolate: It exhibits life and immortality, and shews the way to everlasting glory. It is a brief recital of all that is past, and a certain prediction of all that is to come. It settles all matters in debate, resolves all doubts, and eases the mind and conscience of all their scruples: It reveals the only living and true GOD, and shews the way to him; and sets aside all other gods, and describes the vanity of them, and of all that trust in them. In short, it is a book of laws to shew right and wrong; a book of wisdom, that condemns all folly, and makes the foolish wise; a book of truth, that detects all lies, and confutes all errors; and a book of life, and shews the way from everlasting death. It is the most compendious book in all the world; the most authentic and the most entertaining history that ever was published: It contains the most ancient antiquities, strange events, wonderful occurences, heroic deeds, unparalleled wars. It describes the celestial, terrestrial, and infernal worlds; and the origin of the angelic myriads, human tribes, and infernal legions. It will instruct the most accomplished mechanic, and the profoundest artist: it well teach the best rhetorician, and exercise every power of the most skilful arithmetician; puzzle the wisest anatomist, and exercise the nicest critic. It corrects the vain philosopher, and guides the wise astronomer; it exposes the subtile sophist, and makes diviners mad. It is a complete code of laws, a perfect body of divinity, an unequalled narrative; a book of lives, a book of travels, and a book of voyages. It is the best covenant that ever was agreed on, the best deed that ever was sealed, the best evidence that ever was produced, the best will that ever was made, and the best testament that ever was signed. To understand it, is to be wise indeed; to be ignorant of it, is to be destitute of wisdom. It is the king's best copy, the magistrate's best rule, the housewife's best guide, the servant's best directory, and the young man's best companion. It is the school-boy's spelling book, and the learned man's masterpiece: it contains a choice grammar for a novice, and a profound mystery for a sage: it is the ignorant man's dictionary, and the wise man's directory: It affords knowledge of witty inventions for the ingenious, and dark sayings for the grave; and it is its own interpreter. It encourages the wise, the warrior, the racer, and the overcomer; and promises an eternal reward to the excellent, the conqueror, the winner, the prevalent. And that which crowns all is, that the Author is without partiality, and without hypocrisy, " In him is no variableness, nor shadow of turning."

In this small piece, we have a pleasing Portrait of the CHRISTIAN RELIGION. It is not known by whom it was drawn; but so many useful remarks, comprised in so narrow a compass, and expressed with ease and simplicity, cannot fail producing some good effects upon the mind of every real christain. If the philosophers of Greece and Rome made it their great object to explain and thought their time well employed in inculcating the tenets of the several sects to which they were attached, can it be thought unworthy the attention, or beneath the dignity of a lover of the Bible, to commend, explain, and inculcate the tenets of his Religion?—Reader, value your *Bible*.

MAY.

MAY, sweet May, again is come,
May, that frees the land from gloom;
Children, children, up, and see
All her stores of jollity!
On the laughing hedge-row's side,
She hath spread her treasures wide,—
She is in the green wood shade,
Where the nightingale hath made
Every branch, and every tree,—
Ring with her sweet melody,—
Hill and dale are May's own treasures;
Youths rejoice! In sportive measures
   Sing ye! join the chorus gay,
   Hail this merry, merry May!

Up then, children, we will go,
Where the blooming roses grow,
In a joyful company;
We the bursting flowers will see;
Up! your festal dress prepare!
Where gay hearts are meeting there;
May hath pleasures most inviting,
Heart, and sight, and ear delighting;
Listen to the bird's sweet song,
Hark! how soft it floats along;
Courtly dames! our pleasures share,
Never saw I May so fair:
Therefore, dancing will we go;
Youths rejoice! the flowerets blow!
   Sing ye! join the chorus gay,
   Hail this merry, merry May.

These verses are by a German *Minnesinger* of the twelfth century, and are translated by Mr. T. Roscoe.

SCRAPS.

LESSON TO LAWYERS.—An important jury trial took place in Edinburgh a number of years ago. The subject at issue was a property of considerable value in a northern parish; and the question on which the whole turned was the state of the intellect of the person who had disposed of it. A great many witnesses were examined on either side, and among the rest a shrewd old man, a cattle-dealer, who was chiefly versant in the language he was in the daily habit of hearing. Mr. Jeffrey.—" I am given to understand that you have been long intimately acquainted with the late Mr. Badenach, and I wish you to state to the Court what was the estimate you formed of his intellectual character." Witness.—" I kent the man brawly, but never heard ony thing till his character. To be sure he seldom gaed to the kirk." Mr. Jeffrey.—" It is not his moral character I wish to know about, but I do wish to know, and I insist on your stating, whether or not you consider the late Mr. Badenach a gentleman of peculiar quick parts or otherwise." Witness.—" What's your wull, Sir?" Mr. Jeffrey.—" Did you think Mr. Badenach *compos mentis?*" Witness.—" Compass mentus!" Mr. Jeffrey.—" In other words, did you consider Mr Badenach's mental faculties to be on a par with those of the generality of other men, or otherwise?" Witness.—" A man of faculties and otherwise!" Mr. Jeffrey.—" Why, my Lord, I can make nothing of this witness." Mr Cockburn—" My Lord, my learned brother is himself in fault. I shall examine this witness myself." " Weel, Saunders," said he, in a most familiar manner, at the same time handing the witness a snuff-box to give him a snuff, " hae ye been ony thing lang acquainted wi' Badenach?" " Ever since he was the hieht o' my knee," was his ready reply. " Did ye think," says Mr. Cockburn, giving the witness a significant look, " that there was ony thing intill the creature?" Witness.—" Troth man, no that muckle, nae mair indeed than the spune stappet intill him." Mr. Cockburn—" Could he have been trusted to sell cattle in the market?" Witness.—" The body couldna hae been lippent wi' the selling o' a calf. Ony flesher's bairn might hae cheated him." Mr Cockburn.—" The witness may retire, I have no more questions to put to him."

THE COMPLETE LETTER WRITER.—The following curious epistle was despatched not many months since to a medical gentleman residing in the neighbourhood of Old Romney :—" Cir, yole oblige me if youle kom and see me, I have a bad kowd, am hill in my bow hills, and have lost my happy tight. Your sarvt R. Stace."

A HAPPY RETORT.—The obscurity of Lord Tenterden's birth is well known; but he had too much good sense to feel any false shame on that account. We have heard it related of him, that when, at an early period of his professional career, a brother barrister with whom he happened to have a quarrel, had the bad taste to twit him on his origin; his manly and severe answer was, " Yes, Sir, I am the son of a barber; if you had been the son of a barber, you would have been a barber yourself."

SLAVES.—The manner of purchasing slaves is thus described in the plain and unaffected narrative of a German merchant :—The girls were introduced to me one after another. A Circassian maiden, eighteen years old, was the first who presented herself; she was well dressed, and her face was covered with a veil. She advanced towards me, bowed down, and kissed my hand. By order of her master she walked backwards and forwards to show her shape and the easiness of her gait and carriage. When she took off her veil, she displayed a bust of the most attractive beauty; she rubbed her cheeks with a wet napkin to prove she had not used art to heighten her complexion, and she opened her inviting lips to show a set of teeth of pearly whiteness. I was permitted to feel her pulse, that I might be convinced of the good state of her health and constitution. The price of this beautiful girl was four thousand piastres.—*Murray's Byron.*

Why is a man's nose always in the middle of his face? D'ye give it up?—Because it's the scenter. (centre!)

IRISH PHRASES OF AFFECTION AND GOOD-W... There is no country in which the phrases of good-... affection are so strong as in Ireland. The Irish... actually flows with the milk and honey of love and fr... ship. Sweet and palatable is it to the other sex, and... can Paddy, with his deluding ways, administer it to th... at the top of his mellifluous tongue, as a dove feeds i... young, or as a kind mother her babe, shaping with her... pretty mouth every morsel of the delicate viands befor... goes into that of the infant. In this manner does Pat... seated behind a ditch, of a bright Sunday, when he o... to be at Mass, feed up some innocent girl, not with " i... music," but with sweet words; for nothing more... or melting than his brogue ever dissolved a female hear... What language has a phrase equal in beauty and tender... to *cushla ma chree—the pulse of my heart?* Can it b... paralleled in the whole range of all that are, ever wer... ever will be spoken, for music, sweetness, and a knowle... of anatomy? Another expression of peculiar force is re... *ma chree*—or, son of my heart. This is not only eleg... but affectionate, beyond almost any other phrase excep... foregoing. It is in a sense somewhat different from tha... which the philosophical poet has used it, a beautiful c... ment upon the sentiment of " the child's the father of... man," uttered by the great, we might almost say the g... rious Wordsworth.—A third phrase peculiar to love an... affection, is " *Manim asthee hu*—or, my soul's within... Every person acquainted with languages knows how m... an idiom suffers by a literal translation. How beautif... then, how tender and powerful, must those short exp... sions be, uttered, too, with a fervour of manner peculi... a deeply feeling people, when, even after a literal transl... tion, they carry so much of their tenderness and ener... into a language whose genius is cold when compared to... glowing beauty of the Irish.

EDINBURGH CHESS CLUB.—A notice in the *Monthly Magazine* for April, speaks of this Society as follows:— " The Edinburgh Club is a highly respectable body, consisting of seventy-five members, of whom Mr. Donalds... the chieftain; next in rank are Messrs. Crawford and M... ray—*cum multis aliis*, whom the trump of fame has... heralded so loudly. They meet for the present in a boa... ing-house in St. Andrew Square, but this arrangeme... is, I believe, only temporary. Their rules of play a... the same as in the London Club; in both, the mode o... election is by ballot, and visiters must be introduced by... member; there is an exception in Edinburgh on this... point in favour of officers of the garrison or of ships... war in the roads. The club meets every week-day fr... eleven to eleven; it has been established about ten yea... Soon after its formation, a Dr. Berry presented it with... medal to be worn by the best player—a proud distinctio... the eye of a chess-worshipper, far superior to the badg... Waterloo, or the decoration of *the three days.*"

CONTENTS OF NO. XL.

On Bees (continued from No. 31.)	
Examination of the Accused	
Wealth of Candidates	
Emigration to Canada	
Journal of a Scientific Lady	
Interesting Case of Somnolency	
Dr. Priestley	
The True Poet	
SCIENTIFIC NOTICES—Caution to all who value their Eyes—Optical wonders—Cream and Butter—Zinc Milk Pail	
The Modern Brownie; or the Little Man wi' the Braid Bannet	
THE STORY-TELLER—George Mason	
The Bible	
May	
SCRAPS—Lesson to Lawyers—Complete Letter Writer—A Happy Retort—Irish Phrases of Affection, &c.	

EDINBURGH : Printed by and for JOHN JOHNSTONE, ... Square.—Published by JOHN ANDERSON, Jun., Booksell... Bridge Street, Edinburgh; by JOHN MACLEOD, and A... Co., Booksellers, Glasgow; and sold by all Booksellers an... of Cheap Periodicals.

THE Schoolmaster,
AND EDINBURGH WEEKLY MAGAZINE.

CONDUCTED BY JOHN JOHNSTONE.

THE SCHOOLMASTER IS ABROAD.—LORD BROUGHAM.

No. 41.—Vol. II.   SATURDAY, MAY 11, 1833.   Price Three-Halfpence.

ON THE MORAL TRAINING OF CHILDREN.

(For the Schoolmaster.)

LETTER VI.

The idea of a Supreme Intelligence, the creator and preserver of all things; the disposer of all events; the ever-present moral governor and judge of all accountable beings; the constant inspector of every heart,—is the foundation of all right feeling, and of all good action. Let this idea, then, be given to children as soon as their tender minds can admit it. Let it be arrayed in the most attractive colours. Let it be surrounded by a crowd of pleasing associations.

The human mind is capable of receiving the idea of a GREAT and GOOD God sooner than many writers have been willing to admit. Some have thought that this idea should not be attempted to be imparted until all the mental powers be completely expanded, and called into action. Others have deemed it wiser not to impart it at all, but to leave the youthful mind to make the discovery itself. To comprehend the nature and attributes of the great First Cause, is, indeed, far above the capacity of children; it likewise is beyond the grasp of the human intellect in its fullest vigour; it is beyond the capability of the most exalted intelligence. "Who can by searching find out God; who can find out the Almighty to perfection?" But some ideas, influential ideas, of the incomprehensible, all-comprehending Deity, may be communicated, even to young children, in some degree, and in a certain manner, which may have a powerful influence, both on their present and future life.

To tell inquiring children that God made the things with which they are most familiar, exactly in the same state and form in which they behold them, might confuse their thoughts, and lead them astray. But most of those things may be easily and naturally traced to God, *ultimately.* For example,—

A father asks his little boy, "Who made the coat which I wear?"

"The tailor made it."

"He did so; for he cut out the pieces of which it is composed from a very large piece of cloth, and fitted and sewed them together. But who made the tailor himself?"

"God."

"Who made the cloth?"

"Men, whose business it is to make cloth by a machine, called a loom, and by an operation called weaving."

"But of what is the cloth made?"

"Of a substance called wool."

"Whence do they get the thing called wool?"

"It grows on the backs of sheep."

"Who makes it grow there?"

"God."

"Who made this table?"

"The cabinet-maker."

"Of what is it made?"

"Of wood."

"What is the wood?"

"Part of a tree named an oak."

"Who made the tree?"

"A man planted a kind of nut called an acorn, which is the seed of the oak-tree, and the tree grew up from that."

"But who made it grow?"

"God."

"All the men in the world together could not make a sheep, nor wool, nor an acorn, nor an oak-tree. Therefore there must be a Being more powerful and wiser than all men, and that Being is God."

Thus, there is no need at all of telling the child that God made the coat and the table. This would only puzzle the child, as he would probably know that Mr. A. was the immediate maker of the coat, and Mr. B. of the table.

In this manner all the productions of human art and labour may be referred to the Deity; and such reasoning appears to be level with the capacity of a child beginning to observe and to ask questions. With respect to the grand objects of nature, he might be informed that God made *them,* just as he sees them; because he would not imagine that men could possibly have formed the sun, the moon, the stars, the mountains, the seas, and so on. By such means may some idea of God be conveyed to the minds of young children. The sooner this is done the better, that the most important of all ideas may take root in the mind early, and grow with it as it grows. With this idea may be easily associated that of goodness, of kindness. For, *if* God be the *author* of all the conveniences and comforts of life, then He is their giver likewise, and consequently He must be good and bountiful.

To associate these ideas in the minds of children, is of the utmost moment, as this will habituate them to regard God as their protector, their best friend, and benefactor; and will thus gradually and naturally introduce love for Him, trust in Him, desire of pleasing and serving Him, into the soul, and establish them there as perpetual inmates. Blessed, and blessing inmates will they prove,—enlightening, purifying, cheering, invigorating the mind,—steering steadily through life,—sustaining in the hour of death,—and conducting safely to a new and more exalted state of existence.

Let parents take heed that they do not deprive their children of this most precious blessing, by introducing the idea of God into their minds, so as to produce associations of terror and aversion, instead of confidence and love. The sensible and pious female writer, to whom I have already alluded more than once, says upon this subject—" By pious, but ill-judging parents, the idea of the Deity is introduced to the imagination of infants, accompanied by exactly similar impressions to those which were conjured up by the name of some terrific, imaginary being. Their kind heavenly Father is made to appear to them in the light of an invisible, but avenging tyrant, whose service is perfect bondage. That hatred of sin, which springs from the perfections of the moral attributes of the Deity, is prematurely presented to their minds, at a period when they are yet incapable of perceiving abstract truths. The impression that is, by this means, made upon their senses, is, however, sufficiently deep to remain permanent. The associations thus produced must surely be those of aversion. Would good people permit their zeal to be under the dominion of their judgment,—would they pay some attention to the progress of minds, and observe the slow and gradual progress of nature in the development of the faculties, they would not idly attempt to explain to children subjects of abstract speculation, at a period when, at best, it can have no other effect than to leave upon their minds impressions of weariness and wonder."

If parents, therefore, wish that the celestial plants of piety and religion should be rooted in the hearts of their children, let them be careful to give them, early in life, the idea of a supreme Lord of all, and to let that idea be connected with the most pleasing associations. Let the idea of almighty power be united with the ideas of infinite knowledge, wisdom, benevolence, bounty, and mercy. If God and religion be presented to the infant mind, as surrounded with gloom, as clothed in severity, as dressed in frowns, as tremendously awful and threatening,—such representations will, assuredly, awaken terror and aversion, not confidence and love; and most probably will end in not only breaking such a heavy yoke of bondage, but also in completely throwing off the curb of restraint.

How readily will they, to whom, in the days of infancy, religion was rendered an oppressive burden, when they attain to the season of youth, listen to the song of the siren, Pleasure—to the ensnaring sophistry of infidelity! They will probably disengage themselves from the beneficial influences of true religion, while they may still remain under the tyranny of slavish fear and superstitious dread.

Let us be solicitous to connect in the minds of our children, *indissolubly* to connect, the ideas of God, religion, and virtue, with those of enjoyment and happiness; and the idea of vice, with that of misery. Let us take care that their first impressions concerning those most momentous objects be cheerful, agreeable, encouraging. Then will there be every reason to hope that those principles of true wisdom will be so deeply planted in their hearts, as to stand firm against the attempts of scepticism, the temptations of prosperity, the trials of adversity. Let, then, the idea of God—whose high and holy name is JESUS CHRIST*—the bestower of good, be intermingled with all the pleasures, the comforts, the enjoyments of children, —with every thing which affords them delight. Let them be taught thus to feel and reason: " Our parents and friends provide for us food, and clothing, and habitation, and amusements, and give us knowledge and instruction; but it is God who enables them to do so, and therefore it is God who, in fact, affords us all those good things."

These ideas of the Divine Being may be communicated much more easily, and far more impressively, from the lips of parents who sedulously embrace every opportunity of conveying them which may arise in their daily intercourse with their children, than by formal lessons and catechisms, in learning which they too often learn only words, and the labour of committing which to memory hazards the excitement of disgust, and sentiments unfavourable to the formation of the religious frame and temper. Children may gently, gradually, and pleasingly, be led " through nature, up to nature's God." Every object of the creation, especially the more grand and beautiful objects, which raise delight and admiration, may be made subservient to this purpose. The power, the wisdom, the goodness of God, may be pointed out, as apparent on all sides; and pleasurable ideas may naturally be united with those displays.

If the Divine Being be thus represented to the infant mind, then may his omnipresence be made a source of joy, of trust, of confidence; as well as of reverence, awe, self-command, obedience, and regard for sincerity. The idea of the constant presence of a God who loveth truth, peace, kindness, and purity, should be early and deeply infixed in the heart, as it will probably prove the powerful friend and supporter of virtue in after-life. The idea of the constant presence of God, as a benefactor, a father, a protector, ever ready

---
* " For in Him dwelleth all the fulness of the Godhead bodily," Col. ii. 9.

to hear and bless those who heartily love and uniformly obey him, should be indelibly impressed upon the soul; as it will prove an unfailing source of consolation, strength, and fortitude, a preservative against all groundless terrors and alarms.

As the intellectual faculties expand and strengthen, the moral attributes of the Eternal may be unfolded to their view; His justice, His holiness, His mercy, His unfailing loving-kindness, as being all exercised in His Government of the world, and the providential care which He extends to all creatures.

The pleasing association supposed to be previously formed in the youthful mind, will facilitate the admission of these ideas, and render them more acceptable. Hence we may proceed to conduct our children to the sublime truths of revealed religion; the rational, grand and delightful representations it gives of the Almighty; the paternal character which it assigns Him in conjunction with that of Creator, of Redeemer, of Preserver, of Ruler, and of Judge; the present state of man, as his infancy of being; the certainty of another very different and far more exalted state, for which we are now to prepare, and in which our powers and our felicity will advance to their maturity. These views and principles will be potent aids in the formation and cultivation of all amiable, generous, noble dispositions.

"The power of the affections," says the amiable authoress of Elementary Principles of Education, "in influencing our opinions is obvious to common observation. Where the associations of religion have produced secret antipathy and disgust, the powerful principle of self-love may be considered as enlisted on the side of infidelity. The very contrary of this must be the case, where all the affections of love, esteem, and complacency, have been engaged on the side of religion. Those who have been taught to view the wonders of creation as the work of Divine wisdom, and to enjoy every blessing of existence as the gift of infinite goodness, will embrace, without repugnance, the doctrines of Christianity. These, as the capacity unfolds, ought to be presented in the simplest forms, divested as much as possible of all scholastic terms, and all incomprehensible articles of belief, however we may ourselves venerate and respect them. A knowledge of the Scriptures I look upon as a very essential part of religious education; but to render this knowledge useful, it is not sufficient that their contents be impressed on the memory; the lessons they contain must reach the heart. Where the knowledge of Scripture is forced upon children as a task, where they are compelled to recite long portions of it from memory, in the same manner as they decline nouns and conjugate verbs, the passages learned may be retained by the memory, but we may reasonably doubt whether they will ever impress the heart."

The same enlightened writer gives the following directions for introducing children to the study of the Holy Scriptures. They are so judicious, that no apology need be offered for adding them to the many quotations already taken from her excellent work:—

"The first step towards inspiring your children with a veneration for the Sacred Writings, and with a desire of knowing something of their contents, must be the observations they will naturally and voluntarily make upon your own frequent perusal of them. While they see other books read and dismissed, and the Bible alone remaining the constant companion of your serious hours, the subject of your daily and delightful meditation, they will associate the idea of superior excellence with the Bible, before they are able to read. But, on the contrary, if they see it only brought out upon a tedious and gloomy Sunday, and then read as a duty, merely, and a task, the prepossession that will take place in disfavour of its contents, will probably never be eradicated.

"As soon as a child can read so well as to be able to understand something of what it reads, its imagination and curiosity ought to be excited by the mention of some passages in the Old Testament, which are most likely to amuse and gratify the fancy; these, afterwards, as a favour, it ought to be permitted to read. By a repetition of this, as often as occasion offers, a pretty accurate knowledge of the Old Testament history will be acquired, and acquired at a period when the purity of the mind is incapable of being soiled by an account of manners, which, though suitable to ancient simplicity, appear gross to modern refinement; but which will pass unnoticed, where no train of ideas upon improper subjects has been previously fixed in the mind, so as to be called up by the perusal. As the understanding opens to the perception of moral truth, the sublimer doctrines, events, and examples of virtue contained in the New Testament, should, in the same manner, be impressed upon the heart, at such times and seasons as the impression is likely to be most favourably received."

"The counsels of religion," says the venerable and pious Bishop Taylor, "are not to be applied to the distempers of the soul, as men take hellebore; but they must dwell together with the spirit of a man, and be twisted about his understanding for ever. They must be used like nourishment, not like a single medicine, and upon the actual pressure of a present necessity. For counsels and wise discourses applied to an actual distemper, at the best, are but like strong smells to an epileptic person; they may sometimes raise him, but they never cure him."

Instruction upon religious subjects should be administered, as daily bread, in such portions as the appetite calls for and nature can digest; and not as a nauseous medicine, which children must be forced to take for the good of their souls.

I am, &c.

A FRIEND TO EARLY EDUCATION.

ENGLISH MAY-GAMES.*

"On the calends or first of May," says Bourne, "commonly called May-day, the juvenile part of both sexes were wont to rise a little after midnight and walk to some neighbouring wood, accompanied with music and blowing of horns, where they break down branches from the trees, and adorn them with nosegays and crowns of flowers; when this is done, they return with their booty homewards about the rising of the sun, and make their doors and windows to triumph with their flowery spoils; and the after part of the day is chiefly spent in dancing round a tall pole, which is called a May-pole; and being placed in a convenient part of the village, stands there, as it were, consecrated to the Goddess of Flowers, without the least violation being offered to it in the whole circle of the year."

This custom, no doubt, is a relic of one more ancient, practised by the Heathens, who observed the last four days in April, and the first of May, in honour of the goddess Flora. An old Romish calendar, cited by Mr. Brand, says, on the 30th of April, the boys go out to seek May-trees, "Maii arbores a pueris exquiruntur." Some consider the May-pole as a relic of Druidism; but I cannot find any solid foundation for such an opinion.

It should be observed, that the May-games were not always celebrated upon the first day of the month; and to this we may add the following extract from Stow: "In the month of May the citizens of London of all estates, generally in every parish, and in some instances two or three parishes joining together, had their several Mayings, and did fetch their May-poles with divers warlike shows; with good archers, morrice-dancers, and other devices for pastime, all day long; and towards evening they had stage-plays and bonfires in the streets. These great Mayings and May-games were made by the governors and masters of the city, together with the triumphant setting up of the great shaft or principal may-pole in Cornhill before the parish church of Saint Andrew," which was thence called Saint Andrew Undershaft.

No doubt the May-games are of long standing, though the time of their institution cannot be traced. Mention is made of the May-pole at Cornhill, in a poem called the "Chaunce of the Dice," attributed to Chaucer. In the time of Stow, who died in 1605, they were not conducted with so great splendour as they had been formerly, owing to a dangerous riot which took place upon May-day 1517, in the ninth year of Henry VIII., on which occasion several foreigners were slain, and two of the ringleaders of the disturbance were hanged.

Stow has passed unnoticed the manner in which the May-poles were usually decorated; this deficiency I shall supply from Philip Stubs, a contemporary writer, one who saw these pastimes in a very different point of view, and some may think his invectives are more severe than just; however, I am afraid the conclusion of them, though perhaps much exaggerated, is not altogether without foundation. He writes thus: "Against Maie-day, Whitsunday, or some other time of the year, every parish, towne, or village, assemble themselves, both men, women, and children; and either all together, or dividing themselves into companies, they goe some to the woods and groves, some to the hills and mountaines, some to one place, some to another, where they spend all the night in pleasant pastimes, and in the morning they return, bringing with them birche boughes and branches of trees to deck their assemblies withal. But their chiefest jewel they bring from thence is the Maie-pole, which they bring home with great veneration, as thus— they have twentie or fourtie yoake of oxen, every oxe having a sweete nosegaie of flowers tied to the tip of his hornes, and these oxen drawe home the May-poale, their stinking idol rather, which they covered all over with flowers and hearbes, bound round with strings from the top to the bottome, and sometimes it was painted with variable colours, having two or three hundred men, women, and children following it with great devotion. And thus equipped it was reared with handkerchiefes and flagges streaming on the top, they strawe the ground round about it, they bind green boughs about it, they set up summer halles, bowers and arbours hard by it, and then fall they to banqueting and feasting, to leaping and daunceing about it, as the heathen people did at the dedication of their idols. I have heard it crediblie reported, by men of great gravity, credite, and reputation, that of fourtie, threescore, or an hundred maides going to the wood, there have scarcely the third part of them returned home again as they went."

In the churchwarden's account for the parish of St Helen's in Abingdon, Berks, dated 1566, the ninth of Elizabeth, is the following article: "Payde for setting up Robin Hoode's bower, eighteenpence;" that is, a bower for the reception of the fictitious Robin Hood and his company, belonging to the May-day pageant.

THE LORD AND LADY OF THE MAY.

It seems to have been the constant custom, at the celebration of the May-games, to elect a Lord and Lady of the May, who probably presided over the sports. On the thirtieth of May, 1557, in the fourth year of Queen Mary, "was a goodly May-game in Fenchurch-street, with drums, and guns, and pikes; and with the nine worthies who rode, and each of them made his speech, there was also a morrice-dance, and an elephant and castle, and the Lord and Lady of the May appearing to make up the show." We also read that the Lord of the May, and no doubt his Lady also, was decorated with scarfs, ribands, and other fineries. Hence, in the comedy called "The Knight of the Burning Pestle," written by Beaumont and Fletcher in 1611, a citizen, addressing himself to the other actors, says, "Let Ralph come out on May-day in the morning, and speak upon a conduit, with all his scarfs about him, and his feathers, and his rings, and his knacks, as Lord of the May." His request is complied with, and Ralph appears upon the stage in the assumed character, where he makes his speech, beginning in this manner:

With gilded staff and crossed scarf, the May Lord here I stand.

The citizen is supposed to be a spectator, and Ralph is his apprentice, but permitted by him to play in the piece.

At the commencement of the sixteenth century, or perhaps still earlier, the ancient stories of Robin Hood and his frolicsome companions seem to have been new-modelled, and divided into separate ballads, which much increased their popularity; for this reason it was customary to personify this famous outlaw, with several of his most noted associates, and add them to the pageantry of the May-games. He presided as Lord of the May; and a female, or rather, perhaps, a man habited like a female, called the Maid Marian, his faithful mistress, was the Lady of the May. His companions were distinguished by the title of "Robin Hood's Men," and were also equipped in appropriate dresses; their coats, hoods, and hose were generally green. Henry VIII., in the first year of his reign, one morning, by way of pastime, came suddenly into the chamber where the queen and her ladies were sitting. He was attended by twelve noblemen, all apparelled in short coats of Kentish kendal, with hoods and hosen of the same; each of them had his bow, with arrows, and a sword, and a buckler, "like outlawes, or Robyn Hode's men." The queen, it seems, at first was somewhat affrighted by their appearance, of which she was not the least apprised. This gay troop performed several dances, and then departed.

Bishop Latimer, in a sermon which he preached before king Edward VI., relates the following anecdote, which proves the great popularity of the May pageants: "Coming," says he, "to a certain town on a holiday to preach, I found the church door fast locked. I tarryed there half-an-houre and more, and at last the key was found, and one of the parish comes to me and sayes, Syr, this is a busy day with us, we cannot hear you; it is Robin Hoode's day; the parish are gone abroad to gather for Robin Hood; I pray you let them not. I was fayne, therefore, to give place to Robin Hood. I thought my rochet would have been regarded; but it would not serve, it was faine to give place to Robin Hood's men." In Garrick's Collection of Old Plays

---
* Strutt's Sports and Pastimes of the People of England.

is one entitled, "A new Playe of Robyn Hoode, for to be played in the May-games, very pleasaunt and full of Pastyme," printed at London by William Copland, black letter, without date. This play consists of short dialogues between Robyn Hode, Lytell John, Fryer Tucke, a potter's boy, and the potter. Robyn fights with the friar, who afterwards becomes his chaplain; he also breaks the boy's pots, and commits several other absurdities. The language of the piece is extremely low, and full of ribaldry.

MAY MILK-MAIDS.

"It is at this time," that is, in May, says the author of one of the papers in the Spectator, "we see the brisk young wenches, in the country parishes, dancing round the Maypole. It is likewise on the first day of this month that we see the ruddy milk-maid exerting herself in a most sprightly manner under a pyramid of silver tankards, and like the virgin Tarpeia, oppressed by the costly ornaments which her benefactors lay upon her. These decorations of silver cups, tankards, and salvers, were borrowed for the purpose, and hung round the milk-pails, with the addition of flowers and ribands, which the maidens carried upon their heads when they went to the houses of their customers, and danced in order to obtain a small gratuity from each of them. In a set of prints called Tempest's Cryes of London, there is one called the merry milk-maid's, whose proper name was Kate Smith. She is dancing with the milk-pail decorated as above mentioned, upon her head. Of late years the plate, with the other decorations, were placed in a pyramidical form, and carried by two chairmen upon a wooden horse. The maidens walked before it, and performed the dance without any encumbrance. I really cannot discover what analogy the silver tankards and salvers can have to the business of the milk-maids. I have seen them act with much more propriety upon this occasion, when in place of these superfluous ornaments they substituted a cow. The animal had her horns gilt, and was nearly covered with ribands of various colours, formed into bows and roses, and interspersed with green oaken leaves and bunches of flowers.

THE RURAL POPULATION.
By Mr. Macdiarmid of the Dumfries Courier.

For a number of years there has been little variation in the wages of rural labour; and here we cannot help glancing at the steadiness that distinguishes the agricultural from the manufacturing districts. How often, within the last eighteen years, have the public read, with pain and commiseration, of the appalling distress that had overtaken the hand-loom weavers—the depression of the silk, the glove, the lace, the stocking, and other trades. Repeatedly the town and the crowded mart have been convulsed and well nigh shaken to their centre, while the country remained perfectly tranquil; the farmers might be suffering from bad years and the more limited demand which distress generates, but the condition of their labourers remained nearly the same—a very beautiful state of things, which acts as a corrective to many evils and makes us cherish more fondly the aphorism of the poet—

"And a bold peasantry, their country's pride,
When once destroyed, can never be supplied."

Nor is this idle speculation. We have at this moment before us an official account of the Fiars prices of the county of Wigton for the last eight years. Wigtonshire is divided into two districts—the upper and lower; and in both, the jurymen and witnesses that fix the fiars prices, determine also the wages of labour. This is an excellent system, the advantages of which we have more than once pointed out while recommending its adoption in other quarters. But the Act anent fiar-rents, minister's stipend, and schoolmaster's salary, is silent as regards the wages of labour; and it is unfortunately true that the majority of men are slow to move in any thing out of the ordinary track of business. The relative value of remuneration lies at the very root of political science; and where the machinery is so simple, it is strange that the Sheriffs and Fiscals of every county in Scotland should grudge the labour of putting a few additional questions to the jurymen and witnesses assembled once a-year for a special purpose, the legitimate depositories of both kinds of knowledge. In examining the document alluded to, we find that wheat, in the year 1824, cost £2, 17s. 6d. per quarter; barley very nearly the same; common oats £1, 8s.; and oatmeal £1, 12s. 8d. per 280 lbs. avoirdupois. Every year since, the prices of grain have varied considerably, sometimes mounting and sometimes falling; and so late as last year are given as follows:—wheat £2, 15s. 4d.; barley £1, 7s.; common oats £1, 9s. 8½d.; and meal £1, 3s. 8d.; which since the introduction of the new weights and measures in 1826, is now calculated by 289 imperial lbs.; and by eight imperial bushels. During the same period that is from 1824 to 1832 the variations in the rate of wages have been exceedingly trifling, namely— for day-labourers 1s. 4d. in summer, and 1s. 2d. to 1s. 1d. in winter. In 1826 a farm servant, living in the house, got £10, 4s.; in 1827 £10, 10s.; in 1828 £11; in 1829 £10, 10s.; in 1830 £11; in 1831 £11; and in 1832 £12 per half-year. In 1829-30, the wages of a cottar were £25; in 1831 they mounted to £26; and in 1832 fell to £25. These are rather striking results, which contrast singularly with the statements made by Mr. Attwood, and seem to strengthen the position we have often assumed, that after allowing for the seasons of prosperity that occasionally dawn on the manufacturing districts, the balance of happiness is in favour of what the old Scots Acts call the "poor tillers of the soil," and that the agricultural, beyond all other classes, give steadiness and stability to the social machine. An isolated, is generally a virtuous population; and those who rarely meet in numbers, excepting at church, or at fairs once or twice a-year, escape many temptations which beset the paths of those who congregate in masses every day in the year, and partake by the force of circumstances of that species of denizenship which Rousseau likened to dwelling in tents of sin. There are five millions of sheep in Scotland, and from two to three thousand shepherds, all of whom we firmly believe are happier among their mountains than a monarch is on his throne. In summer particularly, their labours are light excepting at stated seasons; payment in kind gives them an interest in the flocks they tend; in good years their wages may be £40, under all circumstances they are allowed a cow's grass; and if an unmarried shepherd lodge with them, they are permitted to keep two; the kine have an extensive gang, crop herbs as well as grass, and every body knows that a shepherd's butter is better than his master's in the valley, and brings a higher price in the market. The family rear poultry and pigs, and manufacture butter and cheese; wool is spun and carded, to be woven into plaiding and other articles; potatoes are planted and peats cast; the garden yields its tribute of herbs and even fruit; and whether in summer, when to be abroad is a privilege, or in winter, when the "carey" indicates a storm, none save those who have seen and shared it, can appreciate justly the happiness which obtains in a shepherd's *sheiling*—the door barred upon frosty winds, the ingle blazing, and the hirsels, from their position on the weather-side of the hill, secure against the keenest drifts that may blow. The intelligence and urbanity of these men are proverbial; they not only read, but, what is better, reflect; and we know no class that can so well be designated gentlemen by nature, and moralists by habit. In directing attention to the true state of the Scottish peasantry, we are far from denying that great distress exists in towns; that land is too high rented in many instances; that numbers of farmers make a bare living of it; that agricultural capital is not improving; that even proprietors feel the pressure of the times; and that the capitalist's, or money lender's, is the most thriving of all trades. At the same time, were some bold and healing measure adopted, such as a properly graduated property tax, as a substitute for the burdens which press so severely upon industry, and bind, as Lord Althorp once said, commerce to the earth, so far from despairing of the fortunes of our country, we would say that matters might again come round, and predict the probability, in the course of twenty years or less, of a new and better era dawning on the weary destinies of Britain.

SLAVERY NECESSARILY A SYSTEM OF CRUELTY.
BY JAMES DOUGLAS, ESQ. OF CAVERS.

Slavery must be a system of cruelty and terror; there fear, not hope,—pain, not profit,—are the only inducements to labour. The most benevolent man on earth, whose head teems with projects for ameliorating the condition of slavery, must at last have recourse to the whip. There is no alternative between freedom and the lash. Man cannot act without a motive. The slave can have no motive but fear. And the sense of terror would soon become extinct, if it were not for the frequent repetition of pain. It is useless to censure individuals,—it is the system itself which is pitiless. But if, even under the most benevolent taskmaster, the horrors of slavery cannot be greatly alleviated, but only plausibly disguised, how deep must be the atrocities of this inhuman system, when, in addition to its natural horrors, is added the gloom of those supernumerary evils which every baneful passion can inflict! when avarice and cruelty, like the defied fiends of Milton, Mammon and Moloch, have come to torture the human race before the time, and are joined by a third demon, "Lust hard by Hate."

In the West Indies all things are reversed,—women and men are less considered than "horses and mares." "According to the Barbadoes legislature," says Lord Brougham, "any slaves guilty of quarrelling, or swearing, or drunkenness, or riding faster than a walk, or cruelly beating any horse, mare, &c., or of any disorderly conduct," shall receive, at the discretion of a magistrate, not more than thirty-nine stripes. Here we see profanity and cruelty are reserved as the peculiar prerogative of the whites. The whites, with the tender mercies of fiends, are humane towards beasts, in order that they may be bestially cruel towards men.

But the slaves are claimed as the property of their owners. "Man can have no property in man." The very claim to such a property strikes at the root of all property whatsoever. God is the proprietor of all things, because he is the Creator of all things. Labour stamps a right of property upon the objects on which it is exercised, because it creates the value. God having only given the raw elements, and having appointed that the art and labour of man should work them into their useful applications, has thus given to man a right of proprietorship, by making him a fellow-worker with himself. God creates, and man forms. But no man can assert a right of property in the involuntary labour of other men, without vitiating the title on which all his own property rests. By such a claim he shakes the foundation upon which civil society is built, and introduces a universal system of robbery and wrong. Man can have no property in man. The slave-holders are therefore men-stealers; for wrong, by repetition, can never become right, but, by continuance, is only a more intolerable and excessive wrong. We are aware that the hereditary arbiters of right and wrong, the Peers of Britain, in several instances, derive no inconsiderable portion of their income from the involuntary labour of slaves; but their eminence and their privileges cannot alter the nature of things. They are involved in the same guilt with every kidnapper who carries a human prey from the coast of Africa; nor will their titles or privileges exempt them, more than other slave-holders, from the indelible brand of being stealers of men. It is one of the dark stains of Britain, that there are men around the throne, not distantly connected with Majesty itself, who must be called upon to advise upon the great subject of Colonial Slavery, and who yet can give no impartial advice, because the luxury with which they are surrounded is in no small degree procured by the sufferings of their slaves,—men, whose delicacies and refinements have all the stain of blood upon them, and whose voluptuous repose is purchased by the groans and tears, and by the often sleepless, and always unrequited, labour of human beings, whom they persevere in holding in the most iniquitous thraldom.

INQUIRY INTO THE RIGHT OF PROPERTY IN SLAVES.

It would be well if the proprietors of slaves (as they call themselves) would fix the period at which this pretended property began. The Africans, when evening closed around their native village, were happy and free. Did the slave-dealers acquire a right over them by burning that village, slaughtering a portion of its inhabitants, and dragging away the still more wretched residue to a hopeless captivity? Or, if it be owned that the manacles which were placed upon their limbs could not efface the natural and inherent freedom of the mind, nor wrong, merely because it was excessive and intolerable, be changed into right, shall we only date the period of the loss of liberty to the African from the moment when he no longer trode his native soil? Is this ruffian-right of property established, when the trader has packed his cargo of human beings into less room than would be allowed for so many coffins, scarcely affording them so much food as will keep them alive, and condemning them to endure all the miseries of want of air and water, so that two-thirds of their original number often perish on their passage; and the few who have survived this horrid treatment, when a slave-ship arrives in port, have been seen to rush upon deck like so many maniacs, lolling out their parched tongues with eager desire to obtain a drop of water to quench their thirst? If atrocities like these constitute a right of property for the man-stealer, it is such a property as Burke might claim in the victims whom he massacred and sold for anatomical purposes; and the circumstance of the miserable Africans being sold *alive* does not alter the nature of the claim, though it much increases the amount of sufferings inflicted. If such be the right of property in the trader, what better title can he transfer to the planter who purchases his human cargo, even though there be exacted from the latest purchaser the trebly advanced price, the *blood-money*, which must cover the loss of their companions? And does the planter improve and confirm his supposed right in his purchased victims, when he urges them to unremitting toil by the cart-whip, and withholds not only the wages due to labour, but all the civil rights and privileges of man?

Upon which link in this chain of iniquity will the slave-holder establish his claim to this species of property, and pronounce it sacred and inviolable?

It has been said, that slavery existed in Africa before Europe was guilty of the traffic of slaves. And this is true. Where, indeed, has slavery not existed,—what nation under the whole heavens has not been polluted in some former age with the tears and groans of slaves? This proceeds from the miserable condition of our fallen nature, and those wars and fightings which have been ever occasioned by the fierce and unruly passions of men. Slavery, in the early ages of the world, was a necessary evil, so far as war was a necessary evil; it was the only method of disposing of the prisoners reserved from the sword. It was an improvement upon the former method of warfare, since it arose from sparing the lives of the vanquished. Strictly speaking, it was not slavery, in the first instance: it was a voluntary compact, by which he who surrendered himself to the victor, surrendered his liberty as a ransom for his forfeited life. West Indian slavery has no such excuse to plead: it has been well ascertained that many of the barbarous wars that rent the interior of Africa, and desolated her villages, were kindled for the express purpose of supplying the European slave-market while the slave-trade flourished.

CONDITION OF SLAVES AMONG THE JEWS.

Again, slavery as it existed in the early ages, though always an evil, cannot be put in comparison with the barbarities of the colonial system. The case of Abraham, as it affords the earliest authentic example of slavery, shews likewise how very mild that slavery was, so as to be improperly designated by the same term which is applied to the victims of West Indian avarice and folly. The servants of Abraham, though bought with his money, might more properly be termed Abraham's family; they differed little from a clan under their patriarchal head. If Abraham had no son, one of his slaves was considered as his heir. There is no mention of stripes or of forced labour. Neither could any of their tasks be considered even as severe, for Abraham and Sarah performed the same works as their servants! The obedience of Abraham's servants was a willing obedience, for they were trained to war, and had weapons in their hands, and Abraham could only coerce them by the authority of his character, and by their devotion to him. The master and the slave fed on the same food, led the same life, observed the same rites, and worshipped the same God. And as they were the family of Abraham in the lifetime of the patriarch, so they were identified with his descendants; for no distinction is observable among the Edomites between the direct descendants of Esau and the children of those men whom Abraham bought with his money, trained to the services of peace and of war, and instructed in his own pure religion. The same noble feelings which made Abraham prefer to be the father of his people rather than the tyrant of his slaves, led Job, whom we consider to be his illustrious, and not very remote, descendant, to express himself so beautifully in regard to those whom God had made dependent upon his protection and care: " If I did despise the cause of my man-servant, or of my maid-servant, when they contended with me, what then shall I do when God riseth up? And when he visiteth, what shall I answer him? Did not he that made me in the womb make him? And did not one fashion us in the womb?"—" If my land cry against me, or that the furrows likewise thereof complain; if I have eaten the fruits thereof without money, or have caused the owners thereof to lose their life: Let thistles grow instead of wheat, and cockle instead of barley. The words of Job are ended."

But again, it is argued from the Bible by the slave-owners —who, alas! seldom quote the Bible to a better purpose— that slavery is permitted, if not sanctioned, in Scripture, not only by the example of the Patriarchs, but by the Mosaic precepts.

The truth, however, is, that the Bible does not sanction slavery; it only sanctions its mitigations and restrictions. The legislation of Moses on this head, goes to this one point —not to establish slavery, but to temper it, and, in many instances, to terminate it. God, by the hands of Moses, gave such a constitution to the Israelites, that even the most mitigated form of slavery could exist to no extent amongst them. By this constitution, after having once settled in Canaan, they were disqualified from carrying on offensive wars, till the changes in their government that occurred about the time of David, and had, consequently, no prisoners of war to dispose of as bondmen; and, by the agrarian law of Israel, slavery was rendered altogether unprofitable; for who in his own hereditary garden would employ the wasteful labour of the slave, when with ease he could cultivate his own estate by his own free, intelligent, and productive efforts? Slavery can only be profitable in an ill-peopled country, and in a new soil; but Canaan, before the Israelites entered it, was already fertile by artificial means, and, both before and after its conquest by Joshua, was crowded with population. The slave-owners appeal to the Bible when it suits their purpose so to do; but they would not, we presume, wish the laws of Israel revived, by which it was decreed, that "he that stealeth a man, and selleth him, or if he be found in his hand, he shall surely be put to death." And if Revelation has not abolished slavery positively in direct terms, it has done so in effect, commanding every man to love his neighbour as himself.

The injustice, then, of the West Indian system is manifest from this,—that man, by right, can have no property in man: but the whole West Indian system is founded on a property in man; hence, with them, wrong must be right, and right wrong. The order of nature is perpetually reversed—the rule of eternal justice for ever violated. What is praised in Britain is execrated in the West Indies;—what is here the object of reward, is there the subject of punishment. The very laws themselves are the worst part of the system, being a violation of all law. There the innocent become the victims, and the criminals are the judges and the legislators. Tyrants alone talk of liberty and independence, and those who have the hearts of Tell and of Bruce, must either live branded as slaves, or be massacred like dogs. In Britain all presumptions are in favour of liberty,—in the West Indies of slavery. Whoever touches the soil of Britain is free; whatever Black, without the require certificates, touches the soil of the West Indian Islands, is, according to the proper form, seized, put into " the cage," advertised ten days, and, " if no owner or claimant appear," is sold to pay the expenses; so that, if he has no master upon his arrival, he is sure by this admirable process to find one sooner or later.

GRAFTED FRUITS, &c.

An opinion has taken root not only among gardeners, but also among botanists of high name, that grafted fruits continue during their whole existence in some way dependent upon their parent stock. If the ancestral tree fall into old age and dotage, the young grafts which were taken from it in its vigour, sympathize with its infirmities, and decay with its decay, in spite of all the efforts of the stock on which they have been grafted, to administer nourishment. The old tree, and the transferred graft, are, according to this theory, still as much the same individual as if they grew from the same root; and the connexion of the graft with another stock, is only an accident, which enables it to spread to a greater size; but which no more gives it power to live beyond the age of its parent, than the support of a shred of cloth which allows its branches to extend farther on the walls, can enable these to live after they have been cut asunder from the stem. To the advocates of this theory, we beg to recommend the following observations, extracted from a paper on the subject by Dr. Fleming of Flisk:—

" We are as yet but imperfectly acquainted with the natural term of life of our fruit-trees, which outlive us by many centuries, and cannot, with any degree of propriety, refer the decay of such plants to a cause, which the want of records, and our own limited existence, prevent us from comprehending. But we may adopt the cautious plan of reasoning from what we do know, respecting things analogous, which are yet obscure. There are many herbaceous plants, as the Scarlet Lychnis, the *annual* stems of which may be converted into *extensions*, capable of living *many years*, and giving rise to annual roots and stems like the stock from which it was taken. Cuttings from the wallflower, a plant limited in its duration to two or three years, may, by cuttings, have existence prolonged; nay, the very branch, which would have flowered and died in the course of a few months, may be made to strike root and flower, year after year, when the stock whence it was taken shall have closed its natural term of life. Even the leaf of a potato may outlive the stem, and be kept alive until the following spring. Not only may the stems and branches of plants be made to outlive the natural term of life of the stock with which they were connected, but the roots may likewise be made to prolong their functions. Thus I have kept a plant of oats alive for *four years*, simply by preventing it from producing flowering stems; and the common bean, if subjected to similar treatment, may exhibit a similar longevity. The natural term of life of the osier, in this country certainly very limited, is far exceeded by those *extensions*, everywhere propagated for hoops and basket-work. The gooseberry has been considered as subject to this sympathetic law, and many meritorious efforts have been made to raise healthy plants from seed, to supply the place of those destined soon to perish, or which have already exhibited symptoms of decay. But the extent of the useful term of the life of this plant may probably be underrated. In the garden at Pitlithie, in the parish of Leuchars, Fife, the seat of Thomas Lawson, Esq., there is a gooseberry of the ironmonger kind, still in vigour, which was planted in 1760, the fruit on which, two years ago, exceeded twenty Scotch pints.

" The potato, it is well known, is subject to disease in its present condition, by which the success of its cultivation is greatly retarded. It has been asserted that the term of life of the parent stocks having arrived, the extensions can no longer be propagated with advantage; that though a change of soil may for a time retard the tendency to dissolution, renovation can only be effected successfully by raising new plants from seed. It is known to all who have cultivated potatoes to any extent, that a *change of seed*, from a high, cold, and moist district, to a lower, warmer, and drier one, is attended with important advantages. The crop is more productive, and the disease termed the curl in a great measure disappears. But the following fact will demonstrate that the potato may be cultivated long, by extension in the same soil, and without change of seed; and neither disease to any uncommon degree be generated, nor any symptom announcing approaching dissolution.

"When, in 1812, I came to reside in the manse here, I was much pleased with the appearance and excellent quality of a large, bent, depressed kidney potato, cultivated by my neighbour, the late Mr. James Sime, tenant in Wester Flisk. He told me, that, thirty years before that period, he brought the seed with him from a farm he previously occupied, about five miles to the eastward; and during the whole intervening period he had annually planted the potatoes in the fields in the immediate neighbourhood, without change. In the spring of 1813, I got a supply for my own use, and from that period to the present I have continued to cultivate the roots, equally without change. In size and quality I have never seen better, nor any equally good. The soil on which this variety of potato has been cultivated, in this immediate neighbourhood, and *by extensions from the same stock*, during the period of forty-five years, is a stiff clay, with a close, tilly bottom, and varying from 150 above, nearly, to the level of the sea, and on the margin of the estuary of the Tay.

"Before concluding these hurried observations, I beg distinctly to state, that I by no means deny the existence of those symptoms of decay which certain kinds of fruit-trees or other cultivated vegetables exhibit. I consider it probable that the causes of this decay may yet be traced to the kind of culture, or the constitutional habits of the plants which have been extended. At least it would be safer to refer such calamities to causes yet to be developed, than to the operation of a law, which does not act where its manifestations ought to be displayed, and where they could be easily detected; but which is supposed to act where its limits are removed from our present powers of investigation, and which will require the lapse of ages before its foundation can be established on the basis of sound induction."

THE LUXURY OF LEATHER BREECHES.—We remember the time when the young officers of the Guards used to mount guard in superlatively tight leathers; and the operation necessary to a smart appearance was then so painful and laborious, that in no cause but that of fashion would these gentlemen, so particularly addicted to the study of their own ease, have subjected themselves to it. To get into a well-made pair of leathers was the business of about two-hours, with the aid of two able-bodied servants, and certain mechanical appliances to boot. The waist-band of the pantaloons being held open by the assistants, the officer was dropped into them, and sunk by his own weight as far as the extreme tightness of the leathers would permit; he then kicked and plunged for a season, (suspended by the waist-band, as aforesaid,) until he had made as much way as could be effected by this process, and his strength was pretty nearly exhausted. All that kicking and plunging on his part, and jerking on that of the servants could do, having been accomplished, he was carried out, (still by the waist-band,) and set astride of the bannisters, where, with ordinary industry and perseverance, he could, in about an hour's time, force his legs down into their appointed places of confinement. The earnestness with which this operation was carried on, contrasted with the attitude of the party, had a very ludicrous effect. With the introduction of trousers these pains and troubles went out; but stays, which were at first worn by the dandies with their cossacks, furnished a continuation to the afflictions of the flesh.—*Atlas.*

"What are you threshing that poor boy for?" said somebody to a sweep of some 12 years of age, who was laying it on thick upon one much younger. "Vy, 'cause he insulted me: he called me a *Tory*," was the reply of the "son of the clergy."—"Vell," cried the other, still holding up his little fists in the attitude of defence, as the tears washed two white streaks down his sable cheeks, "he fust called me a *Vig*, Sir."

A DUET.

PARISH PAUPER.
WHEN large of me my mother lay,
And father swore he'd never pay,
Who kindly let him run away?
      The Parish.

Who pitied mother's sad mishap,
And gave her pay to give me pap,
And nurse me in her own dear lap?
      The Parish.

STATE PAUPER.
When I was born the third of three
As jolly lads as you might see,
Who paid the expense of rearing me?
      The People.

Who bonfires made, and made a fuss
Uproarious and riotous,
And wish'd my mother more of us?
      The People.

BOTH.
When I was come to boy's degree,
Who didn't know what to do with me,
So rigg'd and sent me off to sea?
     { *The Parish.*
     { *The People.*

When war was up, and Boney down,
And I came back to London town,
Who tipp'd me handsome—with a crown?
     { *The Parish.*
     { *The People.*

For several little slips of grace
That happen'd in my younger days,
I wonder who the piper pays?
     { *The Parish.*
     { *The People.*

And, now that I've a lawful wife,
Who makes us lead, with little strife,
A pretty comfortable life?
     { *The Parish.*
     { *The People.*

Who knows our means are very small,
And wont refuse us when we call,
And never wants no work at all?
     { *The Parish.*
     { *The People.*

PARISH PAUPER.
Who pays our house-rent every year,
And keeps us rates and taxes clear?
Who buys us gin? who buys us beer?
      The Parish.

When sleeves or shoes are worse for wear,
And toes or elbows getting bare,
Who furnishes another pair?
      The Parish.

STATE PAUPER.
Who gives us tax-free houses fine,
And finds us wherewithal to dine
On turtle and on Bourdeaux wine?
      The People.

Should phaetons be worse for wear,
Or parks and temples want repair,
Who suffers when we take the air?
      The People.

BOTH.
My Parish } how I love that name!
My People }
Thro' grief, thro' joy, thro' praise, thro' blame,
To me they ever were the same
     Kind { *Parish!*
       { *People!*

And when I'm dead, as die I must,
And these *poor* bones return to dust,
Ah! who will bury me? I trust,
     { *The Parish!*
Examiner.   { *The People!*

THE STORY-TELLER.

GEORGE MASON;

OR, LIFE IN THE WESTERN TERRITORY.

(Concluded.)

THE postmaster, on the bank of the river, had noticed George, and had inquired into the circumstances and character of the family. He was a man that had both an understanding and a heart. While Mrs. Mason and her children were wearying themselves in fruitless attempts to invent some kind of pursuit in which to employ their industry, he had more than once been occupied in the benevolent desire to be useful to them. As a foretaste of good will to them, he was in the habit of sending George the newspapers and pamphlets that came to his office, after he had perused them. These were beneficial to them in a hundred ways. In an imperfect way they supplied the want of books. They learned from them the events, passions, and employments of the great world without their forests. The thousand projects and discoveries of manufacturing inventiveness were brought to their view. They could trace the range of other minds in the same inquiries which themselves were pursuing with so much interest. Among other inventions in manufactures, they noted, with keen interest, that the town from which they had emigrated had become famous for the manufacture of a new kind of grass bonnets, in imitation of Leghorn straw. A premium of fifty dollars had been obtained by a school-mate of Lizzy's for a bonnet of this kind, which had sold for thirty dollars beside—eighty dollars for a single bonnet, and that made by a girl, neither older, nor more ingenious, than herself! In fact, the whole family, from constantly seeing the manufactures going on about them while in New England, had become familiar with all the mysteries of cutting, bleaching, and platting straw, and with every stage of the operation, from the cutting the grain to arranging the artificial flowers on the finished bonnet. From a dissertation upon the kind of grass used in this manufacture, George was confident that it was none other than the identical crab-grass which was such an abundant and troublesome inmate in their corn-fields. So impatient were they all to satisfy themselves upon this point, that, immediately after reading the article in question, George and Henry sallied out with a light at ten o'clock at night, to gather some of the crab-grass, and to satisfy themselves as to its capabilities for the manufacture. The grass was still unharmed by the frost, though so late in the season, and Mrs. Mason and Lizzy found it to succeed as an experiment beyond their most sanguine expectations. They retired to rest, full of cheerful and golden dreams; even Lizzy dreaming that the children were all clothed in new suits, with shoes and stockings, and that she and her mother were once more fine.

This was a project for immediate and earnest trial. Sufficient quantities of the grass were collected from the corn-field. George and his brothers concluded to try their skill upon the coarser manufacture of Vevay straw hats for gentlemen, of which some for domestic use were already made in the settlement. In the newspapers, too, were minute dissertations on rearing silk worms, and on the making of silk. The woods about them abounded in mulberry-trees, and there were acres covered with young and thriving ones, such as were represented to be in the right stage, to furnish tender leaves for feeding the silk-worm. Eggs for rearing the worms were offered gratuitously, to encourage this species of industry. Behold the promise of pleasant, practical, and profitable labour, both for winter and summer.

The trials and efforts of Mrs. Mason and her daughter were commenced with the morning light, and scarcely relinquished until midnight. It is true, they did not succeed to their satisfaction at once; but active and ingenious people, who are in earnest, and determined not to be discouraged, seldom fail in such efforts, and soon improve upon their first attempts. Courage, patience, industry, and perseverance, conquer all difficulties in practice. The inexperienced manufacturers made many mistakes at first, and their progress was slow. But in the course of the winter, the mother and daughter finished two grass bonnets, of which the first might be said to be very tolerable, and the second, even beautiful, in comparison with Leghorn straw. George and his brothers, in the same interval, had completed eight gentlemen's straw hats, which were considered merchantable; besides one of a less perfect workmanship, the fruit of their first essays and experiments, for each of themselves. The last half-dozen were wrought with considerable ingenuity and neatness.

In the same period, they had made considerable preparation for the manufacture of silk, in which they were favoured by their friend, the postmaster, who not only furnished them with all his printed instructions in relation to this business, but franked their letters requesting eggs, and they had the pleasure of learning that their requests were granted, and that the eggs were forwarded according to their desire.

March came again; the brooks were once more tufted with the beautiful blossoms of the meadow-pink, and the woods rendered gay by the opening flowers of the red-bud. These pleasant harbingers of spring admonished them to begin their preparations for subsistence through the coming year. It was necessary that the field should be ploughed this season. The frank deportment and the persevering industry of George had so far won upon the good feelings of the planters about them, that two of the richest offered to send their slaves and teams to plough it for him. This was regarded in the family as a benefit from heaven; for they could not expect a second crop without ploughing; neither had they been able to devise any means of getting it done. They were inspired with new courage, and the circumstance was regarded as an omen of future good fortune.

How in every difficulty did these poor things miss their departed guide and support! And when any thing occurred to brighten their prospects, how they missed the kind and cheerful partaker in their joys!

The grand obstacle overcome, it was proposed that, before planting, George and Henry should carry the fruits of their winter's industry to the village on the banks for sale, at the time when they were advertised by the papers that a steam-boat would arrive there from New Orleans. It seemed the only chance that offered for a market for their hats and bonnets. They had made some attempts to sell these articles to their neighbours. They had even offered the last bonnet for the ploughing of their field: but such is the effect of prejudice, that these men found the bonnets and hats mean and coarse, compared with much meaner and coarser ones brought from their stores. An impartial eye could have seen at once the superiority of our friends' manufactures; but these had been made at home and under their eyes, and by a destitute family with patched garments and bare feet. Those that they fetched from the stores were far-fetched and dear-bought. People are too often apt to undervalue what grows up under their eyes. Of all this Mrs. Mason was fully aware. Highly as she thought of George, and highly as he really deserved to be thought of, she was aware that he must be an inexperienced trader—that his market was an unpromising one—and she allowed herself to indulge very slender hopes from the proposed excursion to the river. But there was not a shoe or stocking amongst them. Notwithstanding her's and Lizzy's patient patching and mending, their clothes were verging to that state of raggedness when patching and mending would do no more. As the mother made the last arrangements for the departure of the boys, it was with many prayers and tears. Nevertheless the grand maxim of her husband, "Never despair," came to her thoughts, as though it were his spirit hovering near to cheer them. Her last and best exertions were to render the lads as neat and decent in their appearance as circumstances would permit. But though their dress was so patched, and seemed that the original colour could hardly be discerned, it was still manifest that they were the children of a mother who had been used to comfort and respectable society. After giving them all the counsels suggested by maternal apprehension and forecast; after long and laborious dictation of what was to be said and done in various supposed cases; she packed up the merchandise in two bundles, in the only two decent handkerchiefs she had left, the larger to be carried by George, and the smaller by Henry. She kissed them both, suppressed her starting tears, and trusting the return purchases, if they should sell the hats, entirely to the judgment of George, and to his knowledge of what they needed most, she sent them forth.

It was a beautiful March morning when they started, and the swelling buds of the spice-wood filled the air with aromatic fragrance. Wherever they crossed a run with a southern exposure, they saw the delicious meadow-pink and the red-bud in flower. The beauty of the day, and that inexplicable spirit of freshness and joy to the whole creation, which spring diffuses over earth and through air, and with which it fills every thing that has life with gaiety and song; the canopy of branches in the grand forest through which they passed, just beginning to be tinged with countless points of green; every object in their way was calculated to cheer our youthful travellers. They, too, were full of the freshness and buoyancy of youthful existence, and the sweet illusions of hope were diffused over their minds.

When they were a little rested, they rose, and resumed their march, whistling and singing, until they arrived at the river. The steam-boat had just fired its guns, and swept to the bank in all the pageantry of flags and music, as they arrived. It may be imagined what an imposing spectacle it presented to boys, who, for so many months, had seen nothing but log-cabins and trees. Hundreds of waggish boatmen were cutting their jokes and plying for employment on the deck and in their boats along-side. Seventy-five or eighty gaily dressed cabin-passengers sprang ashore as soon as the plank was put out. A trading boat was moored a few rods above them. George considered this as a good omen. The people in these boats are known to be traffickers, who deal in every thing. Besides, it was to remain there two days, whereas the steam-boat was only to take in wood and a few passengers, and would depart in two hours; of course, the first trading essay of the two boys would be made upon the steamer. It will be seen that it was but an unpromising business for two ragged boys to carry such articles as hats and bonnets on board such a vessel, returning from New Orleans, crowded with passengers, some of them dandies, some of them belles, many of them empty, heartless, and unfeeling, most of them in a careless, selfish frame of mind, and scarcely one of them disposed to offer a fair chance to the speculation of our poor little merchants. True, they were boys with fine handsome faces, and decent manners, and keen observers might easily have noted that they were not common boys. But who, of the idle, self-conceited men and women on board this steamboat, greedy only for some kind of heartless amusement, would inspect them closely enough to look beyond their first appearance and their rags? Besides, all that could be supposed capable of such a purchase, had been to the great mart of finery, New Orleans, and would little think of supplying themselves, with any thing that they had overlooked there, in such a place as this. All these thoughts were sufficiently obvious, even to the inexperience of George. His heart palpitated; his mouth was dry; and, as he gave his hand to his brother Henry to lead him along the plank on board the steam-boat, his very hand trembled, and was covered with a cold sweat. Never had the poor boy more urgent occasion for his father's maxim, "Never despair." He made a vigorous effort to conquer his feelings, and walked up to a tall gentleman with an air of patronage and authority, who seemed to be intimate with some of the ladies.

"Will you please to buy one of our hats or bonnets, Sir?" said the boy.

The gentleman answered carelessly, but not unkindly, "My boys, I have no need of either." But as if struck with the singularity of the offer of such articles in such a place—"Let us look at them, though," he continued, "what kind of hats and bonnets do you make here?"

To have an opportunity to display his articles was an unexpected advantage, and no small point gained. So he very modestly undid his handkerchiefs, and spread his hats before the gentleman. "Come and look, ladies," he said. "Why, they are really fine. It would be curious to have come all the way from New Orleans, to buy bonnets at the Iron Banks! Who made these articles, boys?" he continued, handling them rather roughly.

"My mother and myself," answered George. "Please not to rumple them, Sir."

By this time a circle was formed round the boys and their merchandise. Some of the ladies showed their wit at laughing at the idea of bonnets being made at such an outlandish place. Another took one of them, and screwed it sideways on her head, giving herself a great many of what she thought pretty airs, in order to attract the attention of the gentleman, and to make him laugh. George felt every ill-natured remark upon his hats and bonnets as he would have felt an insult upon his mother, and every rude pull upon them as though it were upon his heart-strings. His temper, for he was a high-spirited boy, was fifty times ready to burst forth. But he saw that all depended upon his self-command; so he swallowed the angry words that were ready to be spoken, and attempted to conceal the palpitations of his heart as they agitated his tattered jacket, and bade himself be calm. Some tumbled over his hats, remarking that they showed an astonishing ingenuity, and

gan to ask questions about a family that could originate ich manufactures in such a place. To all these questions eorge, and even Henry, had such modest, prompt, and roper answers, that persons of much thought and feeling ould naturally have been roused to interest in them. But unfortunately these people, like many others equally shallow, preferred to show their own wit and talent at ridicule ather than exercise consideration and benevolence to little upers like these. There was, in particular, a forward ung lady, with a fine complexion, who was pretty, conited, and vain, the belle and wit of her circle when at me; she was, moreover, wealthy, and dressed as fine as lours, ribands, and lace, could make her. She made ch ridiculous efforts to squeeze the handsomest bonnet over a huge combs upon her head, that Henry could not help ying out in terror, that "she would spoil the bonnet." lady of more amiable character, and more consideration, w and pitied the distress of the boy, and begged her, if e did not wish to purchase it, at least to return it uninred. The young lady coloured at this rebuke, and gave e bonnet back to George, comparing it, however, with her vn Leghorn, bedizzened with flowers, but really of a very ferior texture. "You see, my boy," said she, holding out r own beside his, "that I can hardly want to buy such a ing as this. Still, as you seem to be poor, I will give you lf a dollar.". At the same time she offered him one from r splendid purse. Half dollars had been rare visitants ith George, and he thought how much it would purchase r his mother. A glow passed over his cheek; he knew t whether what he felt was pride, resentment, or proper irit. He was not even sure whether he ought or ought t to accept the money. But he answered promptly, Thank you Ma'am; I should be glad to sell, but I did t come to beg. As you do not find my bonnets worth ying, I will go." An answer so proper from a boy so ung, and so dressed, produced an instant and unexpected pression. It did the business for George. It aroused tention, and created instant sympathy. The considerate dy, who had spoken before, whispered a person who med to be her brother, and a momentary conversation sued between the ladies and gentlemen in general. The ntleman came forward, and asked George the prices of s bonnets and hats. "Six dollars for the one, and four r the other; and seventy-five cents for each of the hats;" as the answer. The gentleman remarked, as one who s a judge, that the best bonnet was a fine one, and ought sell for more than six dollars. He proposed to buy it, d dispose of it by lottery, to which the company assented general acclamation. He paid George six dollars, and ok the bonnet. The example was contagious. All at ce, it was discovered that the men's hats were light and e for the approaching summer. The story of the cleverss of the poor boys ran through the crowd, and in a few inutes George had sold five of his hats.
There still remained one bonnet and two hats. The boys d now acquired confidence from success, and they walked the stream a few paces, to where the trading-boat was ored. The two partners who managed it, probably took em to be boys bringing eggs on board for sale. One of em held out his hand, to lead them aboard.
"What do you ask for your eggs?" was the question.
"We have none to sell," answered George; "but an itation Leghorn bonnet, and a couple of gentlemen's straw ts."

The traders were shrewd fellows from Connecticut, whose business on the river, as they phrased it with the true northern accent, was "trading and trafficking," and to whom no article of barter came amiss. Like the people in the steam boat, their curiosity was excited by having such articles offered there, in a region where they had been accustomed to suppose nothing was manufactured. These knowing traders examined the articles with seeming carelessness, but the character and circumstances of the boys in a moment learned that they were Yankees, and perceived that they offered their articles cheap. They ascertained, too, at once that they had money, which they wished to expend in purchases. Such an opportunity to "trade and traffick" was not to be lost.

The sight of so many goods, arranged for show and effect, and with many a gaudy article on the external part of the shelves to strike the eye, could not fail to arrest the admiration of the boys from the woods. Henry held up his hands, exclaiming: "Oh! brother, brother! what would I give to carry home some of these fine things to mother and the children! Dear George, you *must* buy some of these things for them.

After a little pretended difficulty about the price, the traders purchased the remaining bonnet and hats. But it was part of the contract that the boys were to receive their pay in goods, and moreover, to expend their money in purchases there, they engaging to furnish every article as cheap as it could be bought at the stores. Sorry I am to say, that George, with all his natural cleverness and quickness, had better have thrown his articles into the river, than have dealt with this trader. But *one* was endowed with a heart and a conscience. The artless story of the boys had moved his pity and his feelings. He was determined that no advantage should be taken of their youth and inexperience. He called his partner aside, and told him as much. The younger of the traders remonstrated, but, being the inferior partner, was obliged to yield, while the elder dealt with them. The whole amount of the purchase was to be sixteen dollars. The trader made many considerate and kind inquiries, with a sincere view to inform himself what they most needed at home. It was a business of extreme perplexity with George to decide between conflicting claims in their purchases. He went on shore with Henry to consult with him on points that he was reluctant to mention before the traders. After all, it would have occupied all day to fix on the specific articles to purchase, had it not been necessary that he should decide in season to return home that night. The important selections at length, after much doubt and solicitude and aided by the honest and more decided judgment of the trader, were made. They consisted of patterns for a chintz dress for the mother and daughter, a pair of shoes for each of the children. Two dollars that remained were bestowed in coffee and sugar, luxuries that had not been tasted in the family since the first month after their arrival in the country. The trader had not only given them the full value of their money and articles, but had generously allowed them more, and in the noble spirit of saving their feelings, and wishing them to receive it, not as a gift, but as a purchase. The whole amount, when done up in a bundle, was no inconsiderable package, and constituted a burden too heavy for their strength and the distance they had to travel that night. Fortunately, a neighbour from the settlement was at the river, carrying out a load of articles in his horse-waggon to the settlement. He offered to take their package, and even themselves back again. But, as his waggon was heavily loaded, and inconvenient, and uncomfortable as a vehicle, they thankfully accepted the offer for the transport of their package, preferring themselves to return on foot, as they came.

This matter arranged, away marched the boys for home, with hearts as light as a feather. It was cheering to hear their young voices echoing in songs through the woods, as they walked briskly forward. The still dusk of a March sunset overtook them before they reached home. It happened in this case, as it always happens, that too high a flood of joy is succeeded in the mind by an ebb of sadness. The solemn sensations of decaying light in the forests, weariness, and the reaction of feelings that had been too highly excited, drew from Henry, with a long sigh, as they rested for a moment, this remark: "Dear George, it takes away all my gladness in carrying our fine things home, to think that my poor dear father is gone, never to come back. Oh! I would give all this world that he were only alive and well; what we have got would render him so happy! Oh! how glad he would be to see that we are able to make ourselves comfortable, and able to take care of ourselves. I shall never see him more, and I care nothing about all we have bought."

As this thought came over him, in all its bitterness, his surcharged heart found vent to its feeling in a burst of crying. George was not a little proud of his reputation for philosophy, but he had been brooding in his mind over the same gloomy train of remembrance; and this ill-timed remark of his brother's, the echo of his own thoughts, so nearly vanquished him, that he was obliged to turn away to conceal the tears that were forming in his own eyes. While they were thus crying in company, their neighbour's waggon came up with them. His company, and the view of their package, introduced a new train of thought. They were still two miles from home, and as the waggon parted from their path there, and took another direction, it became necessary that they should take their package themselves. It was heavy; but it was a precious burthen, and they wiped their eyes, as George resumed it. In this way they arrived in view of the house. The sweet low voices of the mother and daughter were heard, singing the evening hymn. They distinctly heard the burthen of the closing stanza,

"Oh! guide the dear ones safely home."

Rover received them with caresses at the door. The two boys threw down their package as they entered, and, rushing to the arms of their mother, made no effort to restrain their tears of joy. They both sobbed together, "Father, dear father, if you were only here!" But the tears and kisses, and embraces, that followed, were only those of tenderness and joy. They all agreed, that if his spirit could be among them, it would be to chide them for any other feelings than those of gladness on this occasion.

And now, after half an hour spent in this way, came on, of course, the happy business of unrolling the goods, and displaying their purchases. My readers may have seen a lady dressed for a ball, they may have seen a dandy sport a new suit of clothes in an entire new fashion; but I question if they have ever seen or heard of a more real, heartfelt, honest exultation of joy, than that of this family.

To make the dresses was now the work of Mrs. Mason and Lizzy. Privation rendered this occupation a perfect pastime. The boys, meanwhile, were in the field, busily employed in planting, and delighted, on their return from work, to watch the progress of the important operation within the hut. The needle-workers, too, often came out to observe the diligent labourers in the field. During this inspection, you might have seen George in all the dignity of head workman and overseer, directing Henry to straighten the rows, and Thomas to take some kernels from the hill, or add them as he saw the case require. These subalterns also had a pleasure in manifesting, under the eye of their mother, their prompt obedience.

The imagination of the reader may easily supply the detail of a considerable interval of time that ensued, marked with no incident but the rejoicings of the first Sunday after the boys' return, in which the family assembled for their customary prayers in entire new dresses from head to foot.

The field was planted, and the corn waved in its beauty. The showers descended, and they were again cheered with the prospect of an ample harvest. The materials for the labours of the winter were prepared, as they were matured for gathering. It was a delightful employment for them to tend their silk-worms; for this season they calculated upon little more than an experiment. But they contemplated, with untiring pleasure, the manifestations of the wisdom and contrivance of God, in the labours of these humble animals. They admired the beauty of the little silken world in which they enclosed themselves, and saw, in the increase of their stock, and the extension of their occupations, the promise not only of pleasant employment, but a adding to their means of support. One of their most important arrangements was, before evening prayer, to settle the business of the succeeding day, and parcel out the amount of time that should be appropriated to each duty. This appreciation of time, this wise and settled distribution of it beforehand, redeems half a life. By rising an hour earlier than other people, and by drawing on the evening an hour later, by which two hours are gained each day; by having all the employments of the day, and the length of time to be devoted to each, they gained altogether at least four hours a-day upon the most industrious of their neighbours.

Yet, with their utmost industry, the evils of poverty pressed hard upon them. Their sugar and coffee were soon expended, and the privations rendered more disagreeable from the inclination for such luxuries having been rekindled, and the habit renewed by this transient indulgence. This, perhaps, was the least well-judged of George's purchases. Yet it must be said in his favour, that he had not so much the gratification of his own palate in view when he bought them, as the idea of procuring a treat for his mother. A single dress for each of them rendered the want of a change more striking and painful. The doctor's bill and the tax bill were presented anew, with the remark, that "people ought to pay their debts before they make themselves fine."

The spring and the summer passed away calmly, and without other incidents than those everywhere brought about by the progress of time. Their days glided by in their quick innocent employments. Every day added to the strength of the children and to their knowledge, as far as their mother and their own observations, directed by her, could instruct them. Every day developed the energy

mness, and forethought of George. Their silk was laid for future winding. An abundant supply of crab-grass, for the manufacture of the coming winter, was provided. At this period of hope and cheerful anticipation, an event befell them of which they had been forewarned, but which it fell upon them like a thunder-stroke. They had been told, that they must expect the sickness of *acclimation*, called " *seasoning*," in the phrase of the country. They had been too busy, too much occupied, and too deep in their schemes for the future, to think of sickness till it came.

The corn had just began to whiten on the ears, and the intense heats of summer to soften into the milder temperature of autumn, when, one morning, Mrs. Mason felt a chill, which compelled her to go to bed. Her lips and hands had the customary livid appearance. She had hardly lain down, before the three younger children came in from the field, all attacked in the same way. They, too, laid themselves down in their beds. The fits of chill in each were most severe, from Mrs. Mason to her youngest boy. Their teeth chattered, and a kind of low moaning noise, accompanied by violent and spasmodic shaking. Each was under the influence of a delirious excitement, and the cry of " *drink! drink!*" was uttered with the eagerness of a traveller expiring with thirst on the parched sands of a desert. A couple of hours passed in this way, when they dozed for a few moments, and then roused up, with cheeks crimsoned with fever, and another kind of delirium, attended with new tones and accents of distress. Lizzy and George were continually carrying the water-gourds, first to one, and then to another. The patients seized the vessel with a convulsive grasp, and held it so long that one would have thought that they would have suffocated themselves by the eagerness and duration of their drinking. This paroxysm lasted somewhat longer than the former, and, when it had passed, a few moments of agony succeeded; then the sweat began to start, slowly at first, and without much sensation of relief. But soon it burst from every pore, and dropped from each particular tress of hair. This immediately brought calmness and relief, and a delightful languor, which they only know who have felt it, attended by such soothing and tranquillizing sensations, as we may suppose to belong to the spirit of the just, after the last struggles of escape from the prison of the flesh.

But though relieved, they were so weak that they were unable to rise from their beds. A thick fog arose above the tops of the trees, and the sun went down in utter darkness. What a night for this family, of which only two of the children were able to walk from bed to bed of the sick! Lizzy was, as may be supposed from her age, subdued and pale as death. George felt that the grand trial of his fortitude was come. He repeated his father's maxim, as he kindled the evening light; told them, in the common proverb of the West, that " *The darkest hour in the night was just before morning;*" talked with them calmly of this sickness as the common course of things in this country; and remarked that, though distressing to endure, they ought all to be thankful; that it was by no means a dangerous disorder, and prophesied that they would all soon be well of this " *seasoning*," and find it to be the harbinger of new good fortune.

Still he was aware, that in such violent attacks, something must be done to arrest the fury of the disease. He consulted none but his sister: he made every necessary arrangement within the limits of their slender means, to meet the renewal of the paroxysm, which, he was aware, the patients must expect again on the morrow; (for he had often heard a description of the disorder;) and he was away, before daybreak, on the road to the river to fetch the doctor. There was now no brother Henry to accompany him, whose prattle might serve to beguile him on the way. The day was sultry, and the subject of his meditations dreary and full of gloom. But courage and affection achieve wonders. He reached the river early in the day. The doctor could not accompany him back as he had hoped, but promised, (as is customary in that climate, and at that season, to avoid heat and flies, and to save time,) that he would start for the log-cabin of the sick family at midnight. George was on his return by ten in the morning. He had already accomplished half his distance home, when he felt himself suddenly seized with a chill. So violent was the attack that he found himself obliged to stop and sit down. Fortunately the disease had attacked him on the bank of a rivulet, and at the ford. He crawled on his hands and knees through the mud, and bending over the water, drank as long as he could hold his breath. A momentary sense of relief caused an impulse of courage to flash through his frame, and he thought that he should be able to resume his journey. He waded through the ford, and staggered a few steps. All would not do. Every thing flashed before his eyes in long and flaky streams of green and yellow light, succeeded by darkness. His head swam, and thick pantings oppressed his bosom. The poor fellow fell, but fortunately on the moss at the foot of a sycamore. It was some minutes before consciousness returned; and, as he felt as he had never felt before, and perceived that he was covered with a cold clammy sweat, his first idea was that the hand of death was upon him. Even then, the noble lad thought only of the poor sufferers at home, looking in vain through the evening and night for his return. It was long before he could gather strength to repeat his adage, and resume his courage. He settled himself as comfortably as he could on the moss, and in a position as convenient as might be to crawl to the stream. It was a thought sufficiently gloomy, it must be admitted, for such a lad to contemplate his probable chance of expiring there in the woods, unattended and alone, and, perhaps, be devoured by panthers or wolves, even before the death of nature had taken place; and leave the sufferers at home entirely forlorn. But he said, " *Our Father, who art in heaven!*" and he prayed first for those at home, and then for himself, and laid himself down to await the disposal of Providence. His paroxysm was increased by fatigue, and the want of a bed, and the comforts which even his home would have afforded. He was afflicted with partial delirium and devouring thirst. He fell into a profound sleep. The angels of God not only guarded this pale and exhausted lad from the wolves, but inspired pleasant dreams into his innocent bosom. He fancied that he had just returned home. His mother and the children were recovered, and were about him with kisses and caresses. Water seemed to be handed to him, and, in his eagerness to grasp the gourd and bring it to his lips, he awoke himself from his dream, just as he heard the distant trampling of the doctor approaching on horse-back.

It might have startled another to have been thus called

upon, as he passed, by a feeble human voice imploring aid at that hour and in that place. But the doctor was a man of temperament such as not to find miracles in incidents wide from the common, and, when he learned the state of the case, it was nothing strange to find a sick lad on the way, who had just passed the paroxysm of the ague. He made some difficulty about taking him up behind him, remarking, that he seemed very comfortably situated, and that he could notify his mother to have him sent for in the morning. Poor George had to exert himself to the utmost to be taken up. But he succeeded at length, and was carried home.

When George returned, he found that Lizzy, towards night, had likewise been attacked, and that the family had suffered inexpressibly for want of water. But they were still alive, and the sight of him and the doctor revived their spirits. The doctor prescribed as he thought the case required; and I am sorry to add, that it appeared to him to call for cheap medicines. He was a man who made most exertions for those who pay best. Physicians, generally, are kind men, and there are few who would thus have left a helpless family in the woods, with the nearest neighbour distant two miles, and each member so sick as to be unable to go to the spring and bring a gourd of water for the rest, without having attempted an arrangement to procure some one to nurse them. But this doctor had a thick head and an unfeeling heart. He daily saw much misery and sickness of the same sort, and he thought very little upon the scene before him, except that it afforded him little immediate prospect of a bill. He thought in this case, I rather imagine, if he thought at all upon the subject, that men were made to be sick, take pills, and pay the doctor; and, as this family could not to do the last, he felt it right to hurry away to those patients who could. Be that as it may, he left the family, in which no one was able to walk to the spring, to shift for themselves. They had all taken medicine, and this had produced an exacerbation of the morning attack. It was distressing to hear their groans during the paroxysm, and their incessant cries for drink. However, Mrs. Mason and George might be able to sustain the agony of thirst in silence, it was an effort of self-restraint not to be expected of the rest.

For aught that appears, they might all have expired together, without any relief, had not Providence, in its own merciful way, sent them aid. Pompey, the old slave who had officiated at the funeral of Mr. Mason, had been on an errand to the river, and had returned that way. Hearing the groans within, he was induced to stop, and enter the cabin. What a scene was before him! There was none to bring them water to quench their burning thirst. His kind heart was affected. He repaired to the spring for a couple of gourds full of water, and gave them drink. He opened the shutters, to ventilate the room. He cut green boughs, and put them in the windows, to keep out the sun, and admit the coolness of the air. He grated the tender corn of the half-ripe ears, and made them gruel. He made their beds, and assisted them from one to the other while he did it. In short, he did every thing which a diligent and affectionate nurse could do, with the means of the house, and then fell on his knees beside their beds, and prayed with them. Nor was his prayer less effectual above, or less cheering and consoling to the patients, because it was uttered in the broken accents of an African dialect. He then sat by them, and talked to them in his good-natured and affectionate way, bidding them take courage, and promising that he would hurry home, and ask leave of his master to return and watch with them. And as he was old, and, as he said, of little account in the field, he had no doubt that his master would allow him to come back and stay with them. He added—" Me cure heap people of the ague. Me know six times more about him than the doctors. Me come and cure you all."

A solemn conversation between the mother and the children on their beds ensued. The two younger children were wild with delirium of fever; Henry, Lizzy, and the mother, were in utter despondency; and certainly few prospects on earth can be imagined more gloomy than theirs. The only article in the cabin for sustenance was corn-meal, and the alternative before them seemed only that of perishing of sickness or hunger. George, though the sickest of the whole, held fast to his grand maxim. He declared an undoubting confidence that all things would yet go well with them. He exhorted them to consider how mercifully God had dealt with them in many respects already. From their rich experience of the Divine mercy in time past, he called on them to take courage for the future. None but people so situated know what invigorating refreshment arises to cheer despondency, and banish despair, from one such firm and undoubting prophet of good. In due time Pompey came. The kind-hearted and considerate slave had perceived their condition. From the stores of his fellow-servants he brought a little sugar and tea. Of his master he had begged powder and shot. He killed several squirrels and partridges in an hour's hunt. With these and grated corn, he prepared a nutritive and rich soup. He then went along the " run," and gathered *eupatorium perfoliatum*, or thorough-wort. He gave to each a cup of the infusion of these leaves, a grand remedy among the slaves in such cases, and perhaps the best that can be given. The medicine operated at once powerfully and gently, and when the fever and the effect of the medicine were passed, a devouring appetite returned. Their fear and dejection were dispelled, and the kind black fellow was in the midst of them, a sort of ministering angel, and enjoying their thankfulness and their hopes, with all the sympathy of his affectionate nature. He prayed with them again in the earnest language of thanksgiving and praise, and he sang his own wild hymns as a part of the worship. Nor did he take his sleep on his blanket beside them on the floor until he had ascertained that all his patients were asleep.

Next day, it is true, their fever returned, but with symptoms of abated violence, and an hour later in the day. The same medicine and the same diet was repeated, and with the same effect. The duration of the fever was short, and the attack of this day comparatively mild. On the third day of his attendance, instead of the infusion of thorough-wort, he gave an infusion of dog-wood, wild-cherry, and yellow poplar bark. On the fourth day, nothing remained of the sickness but a kind of pleasing languor, and Pompey pronounced the fever " broken," assuring them that all that was now necessary was to use great caution to prevent relapse, or, in his phrase, " getting it again."

They were now able once more to help each other. Leaving them materials for soup, and killing them abundance of small wild game, obtained in those woods with little trouble, he left them with tears and " blessings of them that were ready to perish," as his reward. As they shook hands at parting, George gave him his promise, if ever he was able, as he hoped one day to be, to purchase him, and give him his freedom. In a few days the family were perfectly recovered, and able to resume their usual routine of cheerful occupation and industry.

By the kindness of their neighbour, the postmaster, George soon after this obtained the place of clerk to the captain of one of the large steam-boats that navigate the Mississippi.

It is unnecessary to relate all the conversations which took place before George's final departure between him and the different members of his family. He was the only one of their number who had yet developed strength of character, and the mother and the children leaned upon him not only for support, but to resolve their doubts, and to decide their plans. Meanwhile Mrs. Mason had faithfully investigated, from all the sources within her reach, the dangers of the river, and had heard, with all its exaggerations, of every accident that had ever happened to a steam-boat on the Mississippi or Ohio. She learned all she could gather about storms and "*snaggs*," and more than all, the dreadful death of scalding by the bursting of the boiler.

Neither was George idle on his part. He had expended the advanced twenty dollars for the comfort of the family during his absence. Henry was of sufficient age to take his place in the charge of the field, and the stewardship of their little concern of silk, the bonnet manufactory, and their other humble affairs. Many and solemn charges did he give him. The main points were stated in writing, that they might not be forgotten when he was gone. It was an affecting charge on both sides; and when Henry received this responsibility, he gave a promise as solemn that he would strive faithfully to discharge its duties.

George was turned of eighteen when he was thus turned upon the world. He was dressed decently, thanks to the aid of his friend the postmaster, but in the most plain and quaker-like style. A small handkerchief-bundle, containing his shirts and a bible, constituted all his baggage. He stole away before the family had risen in the morning, to avoid the agony of those partings which make a separation so distressing. The deepest emotions excited on such occasions, are not always those that show themselves in words or tears. When he had taken the last look of mother, sister, and brothers, and their humble cabin, which together made that dear and sacred word *home*,—a word which means more to a good mind and heart than almost any other in our language,—he turned round before he crossed the stile which led out of the field, and gave the dear spot a benediction that rose to the Almighty from a pious child, an affectionate brother, and a pure heart. "God keep you," said he, "and watch over your innocent slumbers! For me, though now a wanderer in the wide world, I will think of you, and the thoughts shall be as a talisman to shield me against temptations. I will think of the pale face of my mother. I will think of the last look of my father. I will think of Lizzy and my dear brothers."

By perseverance and unfailing good conduct, George, in the course of a few years, rose to be captain of a steam-boat, and became a great man in the estimation of the settlement he had left. With his assistance, and their own industry, the family in the cabin, who always watched on the beach when his boat was to pass, were reared and educated; and, in process of time, he removed them to a pleasant and populous village on the Ohio, where George spent the hot months with them, during which his boat was laid up. To this new residence the voyage was delightful to Mrs. Mason and her family.

Every thing conspired to render it a charming voyage. The season was the pleasantest in the year, that is to say, spring; and that season is no where more delightful than on the shores of the Ohio. A large portion of the passengers were of the most respectable class, and many of them very agreeable. The boat was in fine order. The river was full to the brim. The vernal gales were breathing their sweetest influence from the south. The verdure of the forests, as far as they could be seen from the boat, had that depth and grandeur which are peculiar to the lower course of the Ohio and Mississippi. With the exception of two or three solitary " bluffs" on the Mississippi, the children had but once seen hills since they had lived in the country. The first bluffs that are seen in ascending the Ohio are singularly magnificent and grand. There is deep water, directly on the verge of the shore, at the foot of these bluffs. They have a nobleness of rounding, and a whimsical variety of summits, which I want words to describe. The boat sweeps along at their base, and early in the afternoon is completely in the shade. Oftentimes these bluffs appear as if they would roll down upon the boat, and dam up the beautiful river. I have never seen spring more charming, and I have never known existence more enjoyable, than in sitting on the guard of the boat, in mild weather, in the spring, after the sun has sunk behind these noble hills. At this season, on pleasant evenings, there is an ineffable softness and mildness in the temperature, and a balmy fragrance in the atmosphere. There is not, I think, a more beautiful shrub in nature than the red-bud in full blossom. It is a perfect tuft of peach-blossom flowers, and they make such a show on the precipitous declivities of these " bluffs," strung one above the other—and diffused on every side through the forest, that, taken into the eye along with the splendid white flowers of the dog-wood, the wilderness at this season may literally be said to blossom. A hundred romantic stories told by the boatmen, about the " house of nature," " the cave in the rock," the residence of robbers, and their exploits of blood, and the attacks of the Indians in former days, concur to make this scenery impressive and interesting beyond most others in the country.

Mrs. Mason spent this first evening sitting on the guards of the boat, as it was gliding swiftly along, in the shade of the lofty and flowering " bluffs," on the north bank of the Ohio. She sat on a cushioned settee, with her two younger children on her right hand, and Lizzy and Henry on her left. George coming backwards and forwards to join in their conversation, as often as his avocations as Captain permitted. The scene was full of sublimity and repose; and the shrubs, the flowers, the cliffs, the trees, the sky, and the columns of smoke spouted up from the tubes of the furnace, were beautifully painted in the water, as the boat seemed to fly over the painting, and yet to transport it as it went. The children expressed their untrained admiration by interjections—" Oh! how beautiful!"—" Only look here!"—" Look there!" was echoed from one to the other. The mother enjoyed the scene with the calm and pleasing silence of contemplation, and communion with the Author of this beautiful nature. Half way up the cliffs the birds were singing their vesper hymns, undisturbed by the uproar of the passing boat.

On arriving at their destination the children were forthwith put to school. From August until October the steamboat was laid up, and George spent all this happy interval with his mother. In his next trip to the Iron Banks, he performed his promise to Pompey, the kind slave, by purchasing him from his master, and setting him free. But the poor black's grateful heart bound him to Mrs. Mason and her family for the remainder of his life.

My dear youthful reader, whenever you are in any way tempted to discouragement in any of your engagements, remember the old maxim, that "the darkest time in the night is just before day." Exert yourself in hope. Be industrious, diligent, and innocent. Trust in God. Never despond; and assume the genuine American motto, "Don't give up the ship."

TRADE WITH CHINA.

It has long been the opinion of those best acquainted with the Chinese, and with their eagerness to make money, that the exclusion of Europeans from all the ports of the celestial empire, with the exception of Canton, was much more the fault of the East India Company than of the Chinese themselves. The following intelligence from the *Singapore Chronicle* will show how well founded this opinion is:—
"The intelligence from Canton received at Singapore came down to the 3d of November, and was of some interest in a commercial point of view, it appearing, from the report of some vessels appointed to ascertain the fact, that a reasonable prospect existed of opening a beneficial trade with the Chinese ports to the eastward, notwithstanding the imperial prohibition against it. A report, at some length, had been published of the voyage of the Amherst, sent out by Mr. Majoribanks, the late head of the English factory at Canton, to ascertain the disposition of the natives along the coast. In the course of the voyage it was ascertained that the Chinese generally were anxious to cultivate friendship and to trade; the local mandarins, for the most part, not at all averse to second the efforts of the foreigners, though more solicitous about maintaining their rank, than desirous of temporary gain; but the supreme government is decidedly hostile to any such attempts. At the same time it was found that none of the local squadrons in the harbour were able to drive away one well-armed merchant-ship. Great jealousy existed almost universally of the privileges enjoyed by Canton, which give to that port virtually the monopoly of the whole trade of the empire with foreigners. This information, now that the period for opening the trade is so near at hand, will not fail to be truly appreciated."
If any thing connected with the East India Company's commercial policy could be considered strange, it would be strange that they should have traded two hundred years with China without making this discovery. We have not the least doubt that in five years from this time, we shall see ships sail from Liverpool for ports in the Yellow Sea, and even in the islands of Japan, of which we do not at present know the name.

The first English ships reached China in the year 1634; and at length, in 1834, the trade will be thrown open. The commerce of the most numerous, the most industrious, and the richest people of Asia, will therefore have been bound in the fetters of monopoly for exactly two centuries, in so far as England is concerned. How singular, that the greatest commercial nation in the world, and the nation which, after all, best understands the true principles of commercial policy, should be the last to abandon so prodigious a nuisance as the China monopoly! It would be impossible to form an exact estimate of the evils and losses which the country has sustained from our perseverence in this folly; but the reader may arrive at a tolerable notion of it, by considering, that in the fifty years which have elapsed since the Commutation Act, the people of this country will have paid to the East India Company, for the single article of tea, beyond what the tea might have been had for in a free market, a sum equal, with simple interest, to at least a hundred millions sterling,—or what would have paid one-eighth part of the National Debt. During the same time, without reckoning interest, the people have paid as taxes to the Crown, on this department of commerce, about 120 millions sterling.

SCRAPS.

TRAP FOR A PUN.—Dr. Parr being on a visit at a friend's house in Grosvenor Square, and a warm bath having, at his request, been prepared for him, his attention was directed to two bells in the room, one of which, he was told, was for *hot*, and the other for *cold* water, Mr. ——— had, however, given orders, that, upon the ringing of either bells, a fresh supply of *hot* water should be poured in. Parr, when in the bath, thinking it too warm, immediately rang what he had been told was the cold water bell, and waited for a minute or two, expecting the heat to diminish. Finding, to his great surprise, the water hotter than before, and thinking that he had pulled the wrong bell, he rang the other as hard as possible. But this only increased the evil, by producing a reinforcement of hot water; until at length the heat became so intolerable, that he jumped out of the bath in a passion, exclaiming, "Good God, do they mean to boil me?"—"No, Doctor," said Mr. ———, who was listening on the side of the door, "I only intended that you should be *par-boiled*."—*New Monthly Magazine.*

NOLLEKINS, the celebrated sculptor, could never be made to comprehend the distinctions of rank, or even of persons. He would go up to the Duke of York or the Prince of Wales (in spite of warning,) take them familiarly by the button, like common acquaintance, ask them how their father did, and expressed great pleasure at hearing he was well, saying, "When he is gone, we shall never get such another." He once, when the old King was sitting to him for his bust, fairly stuck a pair of compasses into his nose, to measure the distance from the upper lip to the forehead, as if he had been measuring a block of marble. His late Majesty laughed heartily at this, and was amused to find that there was a person in the world ignorant of that vast interval which separated him from every other man.—*Cambridge Chronicle.*

CELIBACY.—It is a miserable lot. It is a branchless tree growing up to decay, without a limb to shelter its trunk from the storms of existence.

Lord Mayors, a few centuries ago, must have been considered terrible fellows, when an assemblage of *three* of them was looked upon as an omen of the most dreadful import. We find in an old northern perdiction of the fifteenth century that such a combination portended evils to the country of the most awful character. It is said—

"When London sees *three* Lord Mayors,
Let England for troubles prepare;
For in that year, on mischief bent,
The Devil will stalk through Kent,*
And the men of the West and North,
To the battle field will go forth;
And the raven of war will be fed,
For the living can't bury the dead."

* Was he not *Swinging* it there very lately?

CONTENTS OF NO. XIV.

On the Moral Training of Children	289
English May-Games	291
The Rural Population	293
Slavery Necessarily a System of Cruelty	294
Grafted Fruits, &c.	295
A Dust	295
The Luxury of Leather Breeches	ib.
THE STORY-TELLER—George Mason; or, Life in the Western Territory	297
Trade with China	304
SCRAPS—Trap for a Pun, &c.	ib.

EDINBURGH: Printed by and for JOHN JOHNSTONE, 19, St. James's Square.—Published by JOHN ANDERSON, Jun., Bookseller, 55, North Bridge Street, Edinburgh; by JOHN MACLEOD, and ATKINSON & Co. Booksellers, Glasgow; and sold by all Booksellers and Venders of Cheap Periodicals.

The Schoolmaster,
AND
EDINBURGH WEEKLY MAGAZINE.
CONDUCTED BY JOHN JOHNSTONE.

THE SCHOOLMASTER IS ABROAD.—LORD BROUGHAM.

No. 42.—Vol. II. SATURDAY, MAY 18, 1833. Price Three-Halfpence

TECHNICALITIES OF THE DUELLO.

Duelling is about done. So long as this custom was only impious, immoral, and semi-barbarous, there was small hope of it being abandoned; but it has for some time been waxing *vulgar*, and is now getting so ridiculous, or ludicrous, that for one duel that is seriously talked of a score are the subject of outrageous laughter. These are fatal symptoms. Unless a man is killed, it is now impossible to preserve a serious face in hearing of the challenge, the acceptance, and fierce rencontre. No one now profits by duels save the caricaturists and paragraph-mongers. For a long time tailors, men-milliners, and young clerks, having more of the fear of commonsense before their eyes than " the better classes," abstained from a practice, most wretched and sinful, if earnest,—and if, as in ninety-nine cases out of a hundred, half or whole make-believe, as purely ludicrous. But since they have mingled in the high mysteries of the Duello, it has waxed into contempt. An affair of honour is now at best an affair of words —at worst an affair of utter folly. In the United Service Journal, a high and competent authority, being both Tory and Military, we find the following rules of procedure laid down for the conduct of a Duel—it being understood that the affair may originate in anything or nothing:—

" The message having been carried by a friend, the seconds are appointed. They are immediately to put themselves in communication with each other, and from that moment are not to have any direct parlance with each other's principals. The principals are in the hands of the seconds. The seconds are to appoint the place and time of meeting, which must be subject to no change after the principals are informed of them, unless the seconds think proper to alter either to prevent interruption. So soon as the time and place shall be appointed, the seconds will select the spot, taking notice that there shall be as little advantage as possible on either side in the position of the ground—twelve paces making the extremities. The seconds will toss up for ends, and the principals will be placed accordingly. The pistols having been loaded by the seconds, in presence of each other, the brace will be separately given by them to the principals. The principals will stand right hand to right hand, each with the pistol cocked. This being done, the seconds will move wide off the centre, where, on arriving, they will stand together. One of the seconds, previously appointed with the knowledge of the principals, will give the word " ready," upon which the principals will each bring their pistols to the " present." The same second will then give the word " fire." The seconds will be at liberty to cry " stop," in the event of either of the parties not having fired directly after the word " fire." Either of the parties firing after this word " stop," must be liable to the consequences before a court of law. In the event of the party who has offended or provoked the challenge not returning the fire, or firing in the air—this is to be considered as an apology, and the challenger's second must be satisfied, unless a blow, or any such violent insult may have been the cause of the challenge. If neither of the parties be killed, or so severely wounded as to prevent further proceedings, the second of the principal who considered himself aggrieved, or who sent the challenge, will be asked whether he is satisfied; if he should be, the affair ceases; if he should not be, the second of the adversary will be asked whether, after his principal having received the fire of the other whom he has offended or aggrieved, he will acknowledge it, so as to render further proceedings unnecessary—the affair may then be arranged by the seconds. Should the intervention of the seconds be without success, a second round is to be fired with the other brace of pistols—the same words being given, but by the other second. If a blow should have passed, which can hardly be supposed between officers, the second of the party who struck the blow must consent that his principal shall be fired at so long as the second of the party struck shall think proper, unless a written apology is made by the offending party. The evading the operation of the civil law, in fatal cases, must be left entirely to the judgment of the parties concerned; but in the event of the duel being fatal to either party, it is the first duty of the seconds to proceed immediately together, and make written note of the proceedings of the whole transaction, which should be signed by both of them, each keeping a copy."

After the promulgation of this pandects, no one can be held excusable who misconducts himself in the Duello, whether as principal or second.

LETTER FROM ITALY.
TERMINATION OF THE HOLY YEAR AT ROME—PILGRIMS—CLOSING OF THE HOLY GATE BY THE POPE—CHRISTMAS CEREMONIES—EXHIBITION OF THE INFANT JESUS—PAPAL BENEDICTION AT ST. PETER'S—LESSON OF HUMILITY TO PROTESTANTS.

Rome, December 28, 1826.

It may not be unacceptable to you to learn how the Holy year, or year of jubilee, so celebrated throughout all catholic countries, has terminated in the metropolis of the catholic world. I have witnessed the ceremonial of closing the holy gate, which, though not the grandest, is one of the rarest ceremonies of the Roman church, not having taken place for half a century past; and I now sit down to give you a few particulars concerning it, to which I shall add some account of the usual Christmas ceremonies in this city.

The year of jubilee, intended, I believe, on its original institution, to be held once in a century, having been found to promote the interests of the church, as well as to afford pecuniary advantage to the papal government, has, in more modern times, been renewed every quarter of a century; and it was not held in the year 1800, only because war, and the will of the French, who then held the control in Italy, prevented it. In this year, usually called the holy year, the pope gives a general invitation to the sons of the church in all countries, to make a pilgrimage to the seat of their spiritual head, promising absolution of sins and extraordinary indulgences to those who shall visit certain churches, and perform certain ceremonies within the year. Such an invitation, given (as you may remember it was) with affectionate earnestness and solemnity, by one who is held to be infallible, and addressed to those who look upon such performances as a sure means of obtaining favour in the sight of heaven, could not fail to produce a considerable effect; and, accordingly, the number of pilgrims who have arrived during the year 1825 at Rome, though not wonderful when the population of the catholic countries is considered, and though much inferior, I understand, to the number in former holy years, produces no small stir in this capital. The vast majority of them seem, from their dress, to be peasants and Italians, with a large admixture of priests and monks, but there are also numbers from Germany, Spain, and even Ireland, and there are priests from every quarter of the globe. The places to be visited were the cathedral churches (*basiliche*) of St. Peter's, St. John Lateran, Santa Maria Maggiore, and Santa Maria Trastevere; at all which there are holy gates only opened during the holy year, and to be entered by none but pilgrims. I have never gone to any of these churches without seeing pilgrims entering on their knees, worshipping before the shrines and attending the confessionals; they also ascend on their knees the *Scala Santa*, (holy staircase,) a flight of twenty-eight marble steps, said to have belonged to the house of Pilate, and to have been ascended and descended by Christ. In walking about the streets I have continually encountered parties of pilgrims, male and female, usually dressed in the bright colours worn in the southern parts of Europe, with tattered sandals, long staff, scallop shell on their breasts, and scrip over their shoulder, slowly pacing from one church to another, and devoutly muttering or reading their prayers.

The pilgrims are entertained during three days at the public expense, and at dinner they are waited upon by individuals in the middle and upper ranks of society who also wash their feet before the meal. The nobles and princesses of Rome, as well as the cardinals and bishops, frequently assist on these occasions. I went on the last evening of this entertainment to see the pilgrims at dinner, and saw the men, but was not allowed to enter the halls where the women dined. Several large halls were repeatedly filled and emptied by the pilgrims, and I was informed that on the preceding day no less than 9,747 persons had been fed. The fare was somewhat meagre, being on a Friday, but the food appeared good of its kind, and abundant; it consisted of bread, fish, soup, eggs, sallads, cheese, wine, and fruit, and sausages are added on other days. The waiters were not numerous, and I think there were none of rank, except the Bishop of Aleppo.

The termination of the holy year is marked by the closing of the holy gates at the churches, which is performed with great pomp and ceremony on Christmas eve. The Pope himself officiates at St Peter's, and cardinal legates at the other churches. His Holiness having been of late most seriously indisposed, and being in such a state of health that it is thought he cannot live long, there had been considerable doubt whether he would be able to appear in public; but this was in a great measure removed by his appearance on the preceding Sunday in St Peter's, during the ceremony of canonizing a saint.[*] The holy gate is one of the five gates communicating from the grand vestibule to the interior of the church, and which correspond with the five external gates of the building; it is the one to the right as you enter, and it is always, except in holy years, made up with brick and covered with a curtain on which is a large cross worked in gold. The ceremony of closing it takes place in the vestibule, which, being four hundred and thirty-six feet long, thirty-seven wide, and sixty-two high, affords accommodation for a large number of spectators. In the portico, unequalled for its magnificence as well as for its dimensions, and now richly adorned with crimson bordered with gold, was placed the papal chair, covered with white silk and golden flowers, and having a canopy of crimson. It was elevated on several steps with the back to the church, a few yards from the holy gate, and opposite to it was erected a gallery running the whole length of the portico, intended for the accommodation of ladies, who were, however, nearly excluded from sight by a kind of lattice-work. Underneath the gallery was a division intended for the gentlemen, and there were other compartments appropriated to the ambassadors, and the religious orders; a large space around the papal chair was left to be occupied by the cardinals, bishops, and other members of the procession, as well as by a few of the pope's guards. Half the portico was left for the crowd, and it would easily accommodate several thousand persons. It was required that every individual admitted into the galleries, and other compartments near the pope, should be provided with a ticket from a member of the Government or a representative of some foreign power, and should be dressed either in black or in uniform. A large proportion of the privileged spectators were English, who, from their numbers and wealth, and I think, I may add from their commanding appearance, always receive the highest honour and distinction, on public occasions, at Rome, and in every part of Italy. Even I have often found myself here to be a "*gran Signor Inglese;*" and, therefore, invested with my greatness, and provided with what is at least equally necessary when you have to do with Swiss guards—a ticket from the British Consul, I went and placed myself nearly opposite his Holiness. The galleries were full to overflowing at two o'clock, though the ceremony did not take place till four; and long before the latter hour the other compartments were filled with ambassadors, nobles, jesuits, dominicans, and capuchins. In private boxes were the dowager Queen of Sardinia, the Duke and Duchess of Lucca, and some other members of the royal families, but they also were latticed off like so many nuns.

The first ceremony of the day was the performance of vespers by the cardinals in the Sistine chapel; and a short time after this was over, the procession was formed to usher in his holiness. We first saw issuing through the holy gate a long train of priests bearing large wax candles; they were followed by numerous dignitaries, according to their rank, in their sweeping sacerdotal robes, and amongst them, by far the most conspicuous, were two Armenian bishops, wearing crowns richly adorned with jewels; next succeeded the cardinals, nearly forty in number, in scarlet robes, of which the trains were carried by attendants, with ermine capes, and plain white mitres. Lastly, bearing, like all the rest, an enormous candle, advanced the pontiff, wearing a mitre of gold brocade and an ample white stole, loaded with gold, and clasped over the breast with an ornament representing the keys of St. Peter; slowly moving through the ranged file of cardinals, amidst the blaze of the candles, the sound of martial music, and the peals of all the bells in the city, he ascended the steps of the chair and took his seat. All eyes were anxiously bent upon him, and I believe it was the general impression that he appeared pale and feeble. He sat looking deliberately round for about two minutes, and his physiognomy, though not striking, gave me the idea of a man of some character and energy. He then rose, and advanced to a table placed near the holy gate where, his mitre being removed, as well as the mitres of the cardinals, he read a short prayer, and swung to and fro the vessel containing incense. After this, having put on an apron edged with lace, he took three gilded bricks, and a golden trowel, and blessed them, and, on his knees laid the bricks with mortar, at the same time pronouncing a prayer, which being done, he was conducted back to his chair, and

---

[*] The venerable Father Angelo, of Acri, in the kingdom of Naples, a capuchin missionary, who died in the year 1739. The *Diario di Roma* of November 23, 1825, contains an account of three miracles having been proved before the pope and the congregation of sacred rites to have been performed by the images and relics of this saint after his death; and, in consequence of this proof, the beatification of the monk was decreed and solemnized.

the mitre replaced on his head. Other bricks, covered with silver, were laid by the grand penitentiary and four other dignitaries, and then the curtain, bearing the golden cross, was drawn, the rest of the brick work being left to secular hands. A service, composed for these great occasions, was then chanted and read by the pope, who stood uncovered, the cardinals and the band of singers joining in the responses; his voice was uncertain and tremulous, though he exerted himself to chant distinctly. For a few moments he knelt down, and, at the same time, the military, the cardinals, the priests of every order, and all the spectators near him, except us heretics, sunk on their knees. The service being concluded, he stretched out his hands and made the sign of the cross to the multitude, who again knelt. The whole ceremony lasted about half an hour, when his holiness retired to the vatican by the great staircase, amidst the beat of drums and the pealing of cannon from the castle of St. Angelo. And thus terminated the year of jubilee.

Christmas day is ushered in with splendid religious ceremonies in many of the Churches of Rome. A midnight mass is performed in St. Peter's, and several other churches, amongst which, the one most visited on account of the magnificence and brilliant illumination, is the French church of St. Louis. I went there at half-past eleven o'clock, and found the building, which is rather small, but decorated with a profusion of rich marbles, one blaze of light from five hundred wax candles, placed above and around the altar. Several priests were engaged in performing mass, but the chanting was not remarkably good, and the organ, like all that I have heard in Italy, was exceedingly poor. After staying upwards of half an hour, I quitted the stifling crowd that filled the church, and retired to my hotel.

I issued forth again, however, at half-past four in the morning, to see an exhibition which is made at one of the first cathedrals in Rome, St. Mary the Greater (better known, perhaps, even in England, by the Italian name of *Santa Maria Maggiore*), of the infant Jesus in the cradle. The splendid edifice was brilliantly illuminated and crowded to excess: a large body of priests, richly arrayed, with a mitred bishop at their head, were engaged in performing mass. When this was over, they moved in procession to one of the chapels at the side of the nave, which, from the lights, the marbles, the paintings, and the gilded and jewelled altar, presented a gorgeous spectacle. Hence they shortly issued and made a procession round the church, bearing the crucifix, and a large vase of glass, about the size of a cradle, which had on its cover the golden image of a child, and contained also a representation of a new-born infant, in wax. Returning to the chapel, the priests commenced another mass. With some difficulty we got admission to the chapel, a cordon of soldiers being drawn round the entrance, and the multitude pressing to see through the open gates the exhibition within. We found, under the altar-piece, a representation of the birth of Christ, consisting of statues, &c., in some material as white as alabaster: the infant was seen lying in the manger, with rays of gold round its head, and two oxen feeding near it. On one side the virgin mother, with clasped hands, was worshipping the child; and, on the opposite side, was another figure in the same attitude. But what surprised me most was, to hear occasionally, a short, plaintive cry, evidently proceeding from that part of the chapel where the child was, and so exactly resembling the cry of an infant, that I supposed there must be a living child in the place. I was confirmed in the opinion of those around me, as to the quarter from which the cry proceeded, and I can therefore only conjecture that it was a contrivance of the priests, to impress more vividly upon the minds of the multitude the scene which they wished to represent. If all the spectators had been children, it might have answered the end proposed, but surely, to persons of mature age, this puppet-show mimicry must appear calculated to attach degrading and ridiculous associations to sacred events. I was in company with two English catholic ladies at this spectacle, and one of them said after it was over—" Well, I own, though I am a catholic, I don't like these ceremonies; they may do very well for persons in this country; but to us sober English they appear ridiculous." I would say, however, from all that I have seen and heard, that they won't do even for Italians much longer, and that there is scarcely an individual in this country, above the most illiterate and credulous vulgar, who does not inwardly despise them.

I was very differently impressed by the ceremony of the papal benediction, a few hours after. We went, at eleven o'clock, to the Sistine chapel in the vatican, where we found the cardinals performing mass; the singers in this chapel, which is the pope's own chapel, and, on several accounts, the most celebrated in Rome, chanted remarkably well; they are accounted the finest performers of sacred music in the world; but I confess I was more engaged in looking at the *Last Judgment*, and the frescos of Michael Angelo, which I now saw for the first time, than in listening to what I could not understand. When the service was concluded, the old cardinals walked in procession past us, and proceeded to the balcony where the pope was to give his benediction; I particularly noticed Cardinal Fesch, the uncle of Napoleon, a fresh-looking little man of sixty-three, with a good countenance, but without resemblance to his imperial nephew, or anything striking in his features. When the cardinals had passed, we hurried through the court of the vatican, and took our places in a gallery erected over one of the sides of the rectilinear place in front of St. Peter's. You are aware that the vatican palace communicates with St. Peter's, and in front of the church extends an area, compared with which all the places I have seen shrink into insignificance. That part nearest the church is rectilinear, and is nearly four hundred feet each way: beyond it, inclosed by enormous colonnades, four pillars deep, and surmounted by a hundred and ninety-two colossal statues, is a still larger oval piazza, in the midst of which is a lofty Egyptian obelisk, flanked by two noble fountains. It is only on such occasions as these that you can really feel the magnitude and grandeur of the church and its piazza: every part of the architecture is so well proportioned, that when the area is empty, you cannot persuade yourself of its actual dimensions; when, on the contrary, it is covered with human beings, you learn to appreciate its magnitude from their diminutiveness, and from the multitudes it contains. The magnificent flights of steps stretching nearly the whole breadth of the piazza, were covered with spectators, and in front of them a large space was kept open by two regiments of soldiers, outside of whom was also a great throng; perhaps forty thousand persons might be present, but I believe the area, if closely packed, would contain twenty times that number. The place whence the benediction is pronounced, and where the cardinals had already stationed themselves, is an open window over the centre gate of the church, with a projecting balcony, now adorned with crimson cloth. Till I saw this window filled with the priests, I could form no idea of the size of the building; we were stationed in a gallery, which, on any other day, I should have thought exceedingly near the balcony, but which I now found so distant as to render our hearing anything that passed quite hopeless. However we saw perfectly; and, to render the scene more lively and impressive, the sun, which had been obscured in the morning, shone forth in unclouded splendour. We had waited some time, when, on a signal, the military band struck up, and all eyes were instantly fixed on the balcony; the cardinals opened in the midst, and two large fans of ostrich feathers were borne forwards, immediately behind which appeared the pontiff, seated in his chair, carried on the shoulders of men invisible to us. He wore the same rich garment as on the previous day, but had now the tiara, or triple crown, instead of the mitre, and it is difficult to conceive the noble effect of these flowing robes and this lofty diadem. One of the cardinals then read the solemn prayer of the high-priest to heaven, for a blessing on the people, and the remission of their sins; he invoked the Redeemer, the Virgin, the Archangel Michael, the Evangelists, and the Apostles; and, at the concluding sentence, the pope rose from his chair, made a cross to the multitude as each person of the Trinity was named, then stretched his hands towards Heaven, as if to draw down its benediction on the kneeling thousands, and finally, as he resumed his seat, clasped his arms fervently upon his breast. The tall and venerable figure of the pontiff, supported, we saw not how, over the heads of the cardinals, and so high above all the multitude,—his dignified attitude, which told us what we were too distant to hear,—the wrapt silence which prevailed around, the humble posture of the soldiers and the multitude, apparently actuated by one feeling of awe,—the solemnity of the appeal from one who claims the sovereignty over the church on earth to his heavenly master for a blessing on the whole world,—all combined to make this the most sublime and touching ceremony I ever witnessed. Its effect was that of an unearthly vision, and we were ready to exclaim—"how awful is this place!" This was not my feeling alone—the impression was universal; the protestants almost longed to be catholics, and many of the catholics were melted in tears.

The pope was borne out in the same manner as he had entered, and amidst peals of cannon from the castle of St. Angelo. Immediately on his retiring, all our heresy was confirmed afresh, for the cardinals threw down indulgences amongst the people, which there was a most violent and indecent scuffle to secure. The preposterous farce filled us with sorrow and indignation, and even provoked us to think that much of the surprising effect of the previous ceremony was owing to politic contrivance.

The firing of cannon continued for some time; the multitude gradually dispersed; the files of soldiers were drawn off; the cardinals drove away in their splendid coaches;—and we—we protestants, retired from this scene of unequalled magnificence, went out of the city gates, and mounted up into a garret* to perform our devotions, not ashamed, I hope, of our numbers, or of our religion, but having received a seasonable lesson of humility.

No protestant can travel through catholic countries without frequently receiving lessons of humility and liberality. He sees many things which he is compelled to disapprove, and he expresses himself strongly, as, perhaps, I have done, in reprobation of them. But it is useful, if not agreeable, for him to find, that all mankind do not entertain exactly the same opinions and prejudices as are cherished by himself, his neighbours, and his country; on the contrary, that the religion which he has, from his infancy, seen held up to all honour and to unquestioning allegiance at home, is despised abroad; and that a religion, which he has always contemned, is regarded by whole nations with humble reverence. The stately cathedral, the proud hierarchy, the royal protection, the magisterial attendance, and the full congregation of the people are with *him* no longer; but he must seek out the plain chapel, the obscure priest, the small and humble audience, and worship God, if he can, from conscience and not from custom. To some men this must occasion a sad disturbance of their ideas. They have believed, with all the confidence of ignorance, that what everybody said must be right, and have imagined that *everybody* meant the inhabitants of their parish, or, in the wider sense, the people of their country, and they have thought that any one who differed from this general sense, must do it from mere perverseness, and must deserve punishment. Now, when such persons enter the cathedrals of catholic countries, and above all those of Rome, where they find themselves in a miserable minority, and summarily condemned as heretics, they must feel exceedingly embarrassed by the novel circumstances. Nor can they account for the mystery, by setting down all who differ from them as ignorant and vulgar, for the catholic religion has, for many ages, comprehended kings, nobles, men of genius, and the larger part of the civilized world amongst its votaries. If, then, they should attribute the errors of catholics to the invincible power of early prejudice, they may, perhaps, stumble upon the thought, that they themselves are not exempt from prejudice, and may, by possibility, be labouring under its influences. These considerations should unsettle no man's faith, but should teach him to examine well into the grounds of it, and to commit his conscience to no keeping but his own. Seeing the infirmity of human reason, he should be humble in the maintainance of his own opinions, and liberal towards the opinions of others. He should revolt from the idea of compelling any man to change his views, or punishing him, in the slightest degree, for maintaining them. He should be jealous of the excitements of any established clergy towards intolerance, for he finds that every established clergy, though of the most opposite tenets, is intolerant, and, from interested motives, even more than from prejudice—intolerant, too, just in proportion as they are interested. He should seek for the recognition of universal religious liberty, that conscience may be unfettered, that judgment may be free, that an open field may be left for truth to fight her own battles against every form of error. He should promote liberality abroad by setting the example of it at home. He should uniformly act upon the sage counsel of Gamaliel—"Refrain from these men, and let them alone: for if this counsel, or this work be of men, it will come to naught; but if it be of God, ye cannot overthrow it; lest haply ye be found even to fight against God."

NOTES ON THE ISLAND OF TAHITI, AND ON THE SANDWICH ISLANDS, SOUTHERN PACIFIC OCEAN.
BY GEORGE BENNET, M.R.C.S. &c.

It was on the 29th of September, 1829, at 6 A.M. that the towering mountains of this modern Cythera became visible, bearing N. ¼ E. by compass, at the distance of about 40 miles; by 6 P.M. we were off the eastern extremity of the island, the appearance of this part of the island was mountainous, woody, and, as the sun sank behind the mountains, a glare of light was thrown over portions of the romantic dells, which had a beautiful effect. At daylight of the 30th, we bore up for Point Venus, were boarded by a native pilot, and anchored in Taone harbour at 7 A.M. It was not long since that Captain Laws, in H.M.S. Satellite, had visited the island, established port regulations, and given the Tahitans a flag, which was usually hoisted every Sunday, on a small islet situated in the centre of Papiété harbour.

Soon after anchoring, I accompanied my friend Mr. S. P. Henry to his residence at Mairipéhé, which was situated on the south side of the island, distant about forty miles from our anchorage; we proceeded by water, passing Papiété bay, which has a beautifully picturesque appearance; we passed also Motuveoio Point, and at 1 P.M. arrived at the Missionary station at Bunaawia, and were kindly received by Mr. Darling, the missionary on that station. The land on the west side of the island had an arid appearance from a long drought having been experienced. Resuming our voyage from this place, we found the navigation very bad; the tide falling, the rocks and shoals impeded our progress. We passed a place named Tarévareva, which was pointed out as memorable from the last battle having been fought there, between the Christians led on by Pomaré and the Idolaters, which terminated in favour of the former: at this place were two elegant groups of aito trees (*casuarina equisetifolia*.) The island of Eimeo or Morra was very distinctly seen, not being more than 15 miles distant from this part of Tahiti: this island is included under the Tahitan government. About midnight we landed at Papara, (20 miles distant from Bunaawia), not being able from the intricacy of the navigation to proceed further that night, being however only five miles distant from Mairipéhé; we slept at a house of Tati, the chief of Papara.

At daylight of the following morning (1st October) we proceeded and arrived at Mairipéhé in about two hours; the appearance of this part of the island was verdant and beautiful, more rain having fallen at this than other parts of the island. The appearance of the country was fertile; nature appears to have been very bountiful, but art has done but little for the country; cultivation was very limited. On the 3d of October, I visited, in company with Mr. Henry, the mission station at Tiarei. The portion of

---

* The English chapel is a room on the third or fourth storey of a house just outside the *Porta del Populo*; a soldier is stationed at the entrance, I have been told, for the purpose of preventing any but English attending.

country over which we passed was very picturesque; numerous rivers, but of small size, discharge themselves into the sea, and we had to pass several before we had proceeded a distance of two miles. After riding on the sea beach for the distance of about 10 miles, we arrived at Taravao harbour, over which we were obliged to swim the horses, and pass over ourselves in a canoe. At this place the scenery was beautiful, and what was termed the isthmus, was for the most part flat, but covered by a profusion of flowering shrubs and plants; a verdant hill of moderate height rose at one part of the isthmus, and the view was terminated in the distance by the lofty mountains of Taiarabu. This place would be valuable for a settlement, having a good harbour for shipping, and excellent land calculated for the cultivation of the sugar-cane.

Horses have been imported from South America, but riding on the island is frequently unpleasant from a deficiency of good roads, which are now however in progress of formation. We arrived at Tiarei about 11 P.M., where we were kindly received by Mr. Henry, the missionary on the station. At Tiarei I was introduced to the chiefs Paofai and Hitoti, who appeared very intelligent men. The population of the island has been stated to me as consisting of 7,000 persons.

The musical instruments now remaining among the natives, were the Vivo or nasal flute, and the Hio or reed pipes; the former were of bamboo, and have a pleasing but monotonous sound: the latter were usually played in concert, and were not inharmonious.

On the 11th of October I visited Matavai bay. The recollections of this place from its frequent description, and the numerous scenes which have occurred, and are related by our circumnavigators, excited much interest, when I stood on " One-tree hill," and viewed the scene in the distance, which may be felt but not described. The view from " One-tree Hill" was beautiful, consisting of the fertile valley of Matavai, the village of Hapape, in the bay, which was distinctly seen, and the surf breaking on the " Dolphin rock," or more correctly reef. It was on this reef that Wallis's ship struck; it recalled to my recollection the scenes and incidents he had described. Here also Cook anchored, and a low point seen in the distance was that to which he gave the name of Point Venus; and on this hill a column ought to be erected, commemorating the discoveries of that great circumnavigator. On descending into the valley, we arrived at a place where the first residences of the missionaries were pointed out to me, near which grew some large orange and lemon trees, as also a tamarind tree which had been planted by them. The place where the King's house stood during the visit that Cook made to this island, was also shewn me; several houses had been erected on this spot since that time, as the materials of which the dwellings are constructed, are very perishable.

On my return from Matavai, I observed at Papaoa or Pare the residence of the Queen Pomare, (who was at this time absent on a visit to the Leeward Islands;) near it is a long thatched building, where " the Parliament" assembles to make or revise the laws, &c. &c. Not far from the royal residence was a small house, whitewashed, with Venetian windows painted of a black colour: this was the tomb of Pomari the late king, and also his son who died young; the coffin of the late king had been placed on stools in this dwelling, the natives not liking to have it placed underground; there were several contrary statements given to me respecting the remains being still there. Some said, that being decayed, the bones were buried; others stated, that they had been taken away to another island, and kept secret in whatever place they had been deposited, so that on the event of a war the bones of the king might not be captured; this is a remnant of old superstitions. Near the spot was a place in which numerous tamanu trees (*calophyllum inophyllum*) grew; this spot had formerly been the site of a large morae, where the kings were elected, &c.

We left Tahiti at daylight of the 17th of October, 1829, and about 2 P.M. we were off the island of Eimeo, when I accompanied Mr. Simpson, a most intelligent missionary, and the Commander, to land on the island. This island has a mountainous but romantic appearance; the towering rocks were of various fantastic forms, some having the appearance of ruined castles. We had a good view *en passant* of Talu harbour in which Cook anchored, and arrived at Mr. Simpson's residence at Papetoai soon after dark. This island, from the parts I visited, has a fertile appearance; and cattle introduced by the missionaries were now abundant both at this island and Tahiti, from which excellent milk and butter, as also good beef can be procured. At this island I saw a misshapen native dwarf, of about four feet in height. He reminded me of the " Black Dwarf" of Sir Walter Scott, his arms were long, head large, legs short, &c. He was employed in tolling the church-bell.

On the 14th November, 1829, the dark towering volcanic mountains of the island of Hawai were seen bearing W. by S. at a distance of 40 miles; on the 15th we passed Maui, Morokai, and other islands forming the group; on the 16th at daylight, we were off Diamond Hill, (Island Oahu,) which is a high conical hill, having a crater on the summit, and forms the west point of Waititi bay; we had been aided during the night by a strong westerly current, setting about two or three miles an hour. The Island had, about this part, a dry, barren appearance, occasioned by a long drought. We passed the bay and village of Waititi, at which the native houses were intermingled with cocoa-nut trees, and about nine A.M., the pilot, Adams, came on board, and as we neared the harbour and town of Honoruru, (which was seen crowded with shipping,) the British Consul, R. Charlton Esq., and C. Jones, Esq., the American consul, came on board; when off the harbour, boats from the whale and other ships came off and towed us in. We fortunately entered before the breeze set out, which would otherwise have obliged us to anchor in the outer roads, which is considered unsafe.

The town of Honoruru is of some extent, but the streets are irregular, the scattered style of native towns not having yet given place to the European; the greatest part of the dwellings are in the native style, and have not an unapt resemblance to haystacks, being covered with a kind of grass called pide, and sometimes the edges are decorated with a black ridge, formed from fern leaves, dyed of a black colour by being steeped in taro mud, which is a revival of an old native custom; there are, however, several fine buildings belonging to European and American residents.

The natives of both sexes adopt, some the European style of dress, others the native, and some a dress in which both are mingled; the native females decorate their heads with wreaths of flowers, giving a preference to flowers of a yellow colour, which have a neat and elegant appearance, displaying that taste in the arrangement, in which the female sex, in every part of the world, whether among civilized or uncivilized nations, excel; these ornaments are called lei, and the yellow flowers of the rima (*sida sp.*) or the nohu (*tribulus sp.*) are much used for the purpose. Among those of high rank, these ornaments are formed of red and yellow feathers.

On the 21st of November, I visited the beautiful valley of Nuanu, in company with Mr. Wilson, from it the view of Honoruru and the shipping in the harbour was very fine; the lofty towering hills were verdant; taro plantations, irrigated by small rivulets of water, were numerous, and occasionally a few native habitations, near which the plantain tree spread its broad foliage, diversified the scene. The *acacia falcata*, or koa of the natives, was abundant in different stages of growth, displaying the curious change of foliage peculiar to the acacia tribe. After riding for some distance up the valley, we arrived at the country residence of Boki, the governor of Oahu, who was residing there for change of air; after having an interview, we proceeded. The valley increasing in beauty and luxuriance of vegetation as we proceeded; on reaching the Pare or precipice, the view of the valley below, named Kolou, interspersed with small verdant hills, was very picturesque. It is said that over this pare Tameahmeah drove a chief and his party when he conquered the island; and human bones, it was also stated, could still be found in the valley, being the remains of those who perished on that occasion: a steep pathway wound down from the height on which we stood into the valley. On our return from our agreeable excursion, the report of cannon announced the arrival of a ship of war; it proved to be the United Service ship, Vincennes, Captain Finch, from Hawai, returning with the king and suite. In the evening I accompanied the British consul on board, and was politely received by the officers; the Vincennes was a fine ship, in excellent order, mounting 24 guns of heavy metal for her class, (medium 24 lbs.) and had a crew of 210 men.

A subsequent journey up the beautiful valley of Manoa was delightful. Although not equal in extent to Nuanu, it surpassed it in beauty; the sun shone bright, but was not oppressive; the hills were verdant, and numbers of a species of hawk moth (*sphinx pungens*) flitted about like the puny humming-bird, thrusting its proboscis into every flower to extract the nectar; plantations of taro and sugar-cane were numerous, and the latter being in full flower had a splendid appearance, as the silvery flowers waved to the passing breeze. The summit of the valley terminated in a dense vegetation, among which the apu or *cibotium chamissoi*, and mau or *sadeleria oyatheoides ferns* were abundant, and the declivities of the hills were adorned by the whitened foliage of the *aleurites triloba* or candle nut-tree. On the 2d of December I rode towards Diamond Hill; the evening was very fine and clear; a few cocoa-nut trees (particularly about Waititi) mingled with the native habitations, but did not seem to be much valued by the natives; the tou or kou tree (*cordia orientalis*) was also abundant. Near Diamond Hill is the remains of a morae, or, as called by the natives of this group, the heiau; it was now in ruins; it did not appear originally to have been of much extent. On its ruinous walls grew several small kou trees, covered with a profusion of orange-coloured blossoms.

The natives carry about for sale calabashes, neatly painted; they are sold at low prices, and called huawai. The native mats are manufactured from the fara or *pandanus*; the finer kind are made from a species of rush, one of which is of small size, but has the culms of a red colour, which are dried, and worked tastefully into the mats of the best kind, and are ornamental. This kind of rush is named by the natives makaroa. There is a rush of a large size, called akakai, used by the coopers of the whale ships, and by the natives in the manufacture of a coarser kind of matting.

The bodies of the late king and queen are supposed to be removed from Hawai, that island being the usual burial-place of the royal family. I could obtain no further information respecting their place of removal; it appeared to be preserved with secrecy. The only answer I received was, that the house having fallen down, the bodies had been removed.

On the 8th of December I accompanied the British consul on a visit to Wymea, situated about 45 miles distant from the town of Honoruru. Between Honoruru and the Pearl River we passed a salt pond; it has no visible outlet, and is situated about a quarter of a mile from the sea-coast. It has the appearance of an old volcanic crater. It yields a quantity of excellent crystallized salt, and, during dry weather, the pond is covered with a saline incrustation. Not far distant from it is a high hill, called Mouna Roa, and a pond of fresh water. The salt pond was stated to be unfathomable.

We rode on for some time, the scenery occasionally diversified by taro plantations, the taro being the most cultivated vegetable at these islands, which may be accounted for by the great consumption of the favourite poë which is made from the taro root. Then the Pearl river appeared in view, its appearance, whether at a distance or near approach, was very picturesque and beautiful; this, although termed a river, is, more properly speaking, an arm of the sea, forming an extensive harbour, of a very picturesque appearance, being studded with numerous low verdant islands, and several small rivers empty themselves into it; the depth of water in the harbour is sufficient in almost any part for a ship of the line; the only impediment to this harbour is a bar at the entrance, which, however, from being old coral-rock, might be removed; that being effected, it would be a superior harbour to that of Honoruru, not only in point of size, but from the great advantage it would possess over it in situation, permitting ships to enter or take their departure with the trade-wind. About dusk we arrived at Eva or Wyeva, where, after taking refreshment, we retired to rest, sleeping on the cool mats of the country so agreeable in a sultry climate, and with our coverlet of native cloth. The usual beds of the chiefs in this country are mats piled to about the height of two feet from the ground.

On the dawn of the following day (the 9th) we resumed our journey over a long extent of elevated plains, of which the soil was fertile, but now lying waste, covered by dried grass and a few plants and shrubs, calculated to form an excellent pasturage for innumerable herds of cattle; the distant view was high-wooded hills forming a fine background to the landscape. After some hours' ride, during which we had to cross some deep ravines, we arrived at Wyrua, (wy, water, rua, two, from two rivers passing near it,) and took breakfast at the house of an Englishman named Thomas, who had a neat habitation, about which in a plantation grew taro, breadfruit-trees, and several large trees of the *Eugenia malaccensis*, called by the natives ohia, and which were loaded with ripe fruit; this man held the tenure of the land under one of the chiefs, and he complained of the oppression he experienced. From his account it appears that the holders of land have to give half their produce to the chiefs, and as much more as the chiefs demand; they can also be called upon to serve the chief in any of his war expeditions, and if they refuse, the tenure of the land is lost. The increasing desire of the chiefs for luxuries causes the holders of lands to suffer much oppression, it was a subject of general complaint during the time that I visited these islands; the provisions brought into the markets pay to the government half of the price for which they are sold, which necessarily raised the price. At the village of Wyrua we met Kaliakanoa, wife of the chief Hiva, hiva, (hiva, hiva, signifies crazy; this personage was formerly high-priest to the old king Temermea,) who accompanied us to Wymea, situated at a distance of about two miles from Wyrua. Wymea is a small village, at the time of my visit thinly inhabited, in consequence of most of the inhabitants being in the mountains collecting sandal wood; during which time they build houses in the mountains, where they reside until having collected the quantity of wood required they return to their village; it is situated in a valley close to the sea-shore; the coast at this period was covered by a heavy surf, but at times it was stated there was merely a ripple, so that a boat could land in safety; behind the village were lofty hills. Wymea bay opposite the village has good anchorage, but is very exposed. It was in this bay that the Dædalus store-ship anchored, which was commanded by Lieutenant Hurgest; the spot was pointed out to me where Lieutenant Hurgest and Mr. Gooch were seated when the attack was first made on them with stones by the natives; they fled across a narrow river, and were finally killed a short distance up the valley, and some marines also who were with them. The principal chief who killed them was named Uehu; they were formerly considered a more savage race at this island than at any other of the group. The narrative of the above unfortunate circumstance is related in Vancouver's Voyage. We left Wymea on the 11th, and arrived at Honoruru in the evening, enjoying the diversified scenery of Pearl River again on our return. Turkeys have been introduced from America, and thrive well at these islands, (although geese and ducks have not yet succeeded,) and are sold at from two and a half to four dollars each; goats are numerous, and are taken as stock by shipping, and are sold at from one to three dollars each.

The winter season at these islands is said to be usually as hot as the summer; the reason assigned for which was, that the north-east trade-wind blew with more constancy during the summer than the winter months, and rendered the atmosphere more cool during the preceding months. The females of these islands are not generally handsome; and when dressed in the native style, which is oriental in its character, appear to more advantage than when dressed in a mingled costume of native and European; the head and neck is generally decked with the lei, which being either of the golden flowers of the rima or nohu, or of red and yellow feathers, are displayed advantageously over their dark hair and necks: the native dress among the *fair sex* consists of the paii, which is several folds of either the native or European cloth, and resembles [the komboi of Ceylon, or the cumberbund of India; over the shoulder the tié is worn, it is spacious, and frequently thrown over the head, like the chadda of India; the chief ladies have adopted a dress (after the European fashion) of black silk, and it is a colour highly esteemed among them. The chief ladies are corpulent, and consequently destitute of any beauty or grace of figure. The leis are formed of feathers procured from a bird, called by the natives oo, the small yellow feathers under the wing being used for that purpose; these feathers are also used in making the aahu, or feathered cloaks, as also the aumanu, or tippets, and in the decoration of the mai-i-ore, or helmets; the black feathers of the oo are used for making the kairi, or fly-wisks; the inside of the feathered cloaks, on which the feathers are placed, is formed of a fine net-work, called aupene, made from the inner bark of the orena, a species of *urtica*. The red feathers procured from a small bird called tivi is also used in the lei, and there is another bird from which a smaller bright yellow feather is procured; it is called mamu by the natives, and is very rare.

The tapa, or native cloth used for the pau, is painted in an infinite variety of patterns, several apparently in imitation of those of our cotton prints, so much so that at a distance it was difficult to distinguish whether the dress was of native or European manufacture; the native cloth is now principally made at the island of Hawai.

A few strawberries and oranges have been grown on the elevated land at some parts of Hawai, but they have not yet succeeded at Oahu; the oranges at the islands of Tauai and Hawai were excellent, and trees thrive better at those islands than at any other of the group.

We sailed from Oahu at daylight on the 26th of January, 1830, and on the 28th were off Wymea, island of Tauai; landing was difficult on account of the surf, and it is frequently impracticable. The village of Wymea was pleasantly situated on the borders of a sandy beach, and near it a small river flows, discharging itself into the sea, but appears to be only navigable at a short distance for canoes. On the opposite side, on a rocky ascent, a fort is situated, which was constructed after scientific principles; this was explained by its being an abortive attempt of the Russians to form a settlement on the island; the natives' alarm, however, was excited in time, and the fort was taken by them; it was mounted with a few ships' carronades, swivels, &c. The appearance of this village from the ship was picturesque, the land gradually ascending behind; the soil appears to be a red clay—the chief or governor of the island is named Kakioeva. On ascending the elevated ground behind the village, on one side appeared a beautiful valley abounding in taro plantations, laid out with much neatness and regularity, having numerous cocoa-nut and plantain trees planted on the banks. The hills about the village were uncultivated, the valleys, among all the islands of the group, being the only places usually under cultivation. Some of the native women, I observed, wore bonnets manufactured from the very young leaves of the cocoa palm, and they had a neat appearance, but do not equal the bonnets made by the females of the Society Islands from the prepared stalks of the pia, or arrow-root plant (*tacca pinnatifida*.) In the evening we took our departure from the island.

The following very interesting piece of advice was lately given by the housekeeper of a maiden lady of thirty, who at last had some thoughts of entering into holy bonds:—" Take my advice, and never marry, Ma'am, take care how you lay down master and get up dame. I married a cross man of a husband, and the very first week of our marriage, Ma'am, he snapped me because I put my cold feet to his'n. You don't know men, Ma'am, so well as I do."

MEDICAL SELECTIONS.

No. VI. DISLOCATION.

WHEN the articular surfaces of bones are forced out of their proper place, the accident is termed a *dislocation* or *luxation*. The loose joints which admit of motion in every direction, as the shoulder-joint, and the hip-joint, are those which are most frequently dislocated; while those which move like a hinge, as the knee-joint and elbow, are more rarely dislocated, and require an unusual degree of violence to accomplish it. Dislocation may be complete, as when the articulating surfaces are quite separated; or incomplete, when a part still remains in contact with its neighbouring bone. The dislocation of the round-headed bones may take place in every direction, that is, they may be pushed backward, forward, upward, downward, or in any part of the circumference. The other kinds of joints are capable of dislocation only backward, forward, and to either side. When a dislocated bone has been restored to its place, it is said to be *reduced*; and the ease with which this is accomplished depends much on the length of time which has elapsed since the accident. When bones have been out of their place for a few days, their reduction becomes very difficult; and when the time is very long, it is impossible. The soft parts and the bone accommodate themselves to the altered position. In several cases, the opening in the capsular ligament becomes closed, and will not allow the bone to return into its place; or adhesions may be formed between the bones and the place to which it has come. For this reason, when a person has had the misfortune to dislocate a joint, he should immediately apply for assistance to have it reduced if possible, before swelling and inflammation of the parts, or any other untoward consequence, render reduction difficult or impossible. In cases of very great external violence, it sometimes happens that not only is the joint luxated, but an external wound is inflicted, by which the danger and severity of the symptoms are exceedingly increased; and, in some cases, so great is the danger of a wounded joint, and of the air getting admission into its cavity, that immediate amputation of the limb is advisable.

A bone is known to be dislocated by there being a loss of the usual motion in the joint, by the limb being altered in its length, or distorted; by there being great pain in the surrounding parts, and this pain increased on motion or pressure. The head of the dislocated bone is sometimes distinctly felt in a wrong place, and a vacuity or depression is perceived where there ought to be a fulness.

The causes of dislocation are either internal or external. The internal causes are, diseases of the joint or its appendages, relaxation of the ligaments, palsy of the muscles, any morbid affection that destroys the cartilages, the ligaments, or articular cavities. A white swelling sometimes partially dislocates the knee; and scrofulous disease of the hip-joint is the cause of dislocation there. External causes of dislocation are such as blows, falls, violent wrenches or twists, and the like. Dislocations from the last set of causes are more easily reduced than others.

Treatment.—The treatment of dislocations, though a branch of surgery requiring great skill and dexterity as well as anatomical science, has very frequently been in the hands of those who had no pretensions to either, and who were possessed only of brute strength, or of a certain knack, empirically acquired, of which they knew not the mechanism nor the reason. " Many people (says Mr. Pott) regard bone-setting, as it is called, as no matter of science; as a thing which the most ignorant farrier may, with the utmost ease, become soon and perfectly master of; nay, that he may receive it from his father and family as a kind of heritage." In the former practice of surgery, too much was expected from mere force, either of the human arm alone, or assisted by machinery; and too little was allowed to the powers of nature, which might be brought into action by proper knowledge of the muscles which favour or oppose the reduction. The muscles which move the joints in a sound state, do not lose their power when the joint is luxated; but, on the contrary, are often spasmodically affected, and draw the bone out of the direction most favourable for its reduction. It becomes, therefore, a matter of accurate consideration, what muscles are likely to oppose the reduction of a joint; and these muscles will vary according to the direction in which the bone is luxated. In the writings of Mr. Pott are some of the best and most judicious observations on dislocations; and much of what follows is extracted from that eminent surgical author. Although a joint may have been luxated by means of considerable violence, it can by no means follow that the same degree of violence is necessary for its reduction. When a joint has been luxated, at least one of the bones is kept in that unnatural situation by the action of some of the muscular parts in connexion with it. We cannot know whether the ligaments of the joints are broken or not, and this circumstance need not influence our methods for reduction. All the force used in reducing a luxated bone, be it more or less, be it by hands, towels, ligatures, or machines, ought always to be applied to the other extremity of the said bone, and, as much as possible, to that only. In the reduction of the shoulder and hip-joint, the whole body should be kept as steady as possible. In order to make use of an extending force with all possible advantage, and to excite thereby the least pain and inconvenience, it is necessary that all parts serving to the motion of the dislocated joint, or in any degree connected with it, be put into such a state as to give the smallest possible degree of resistance. In the reduction of such joints as consist of a round head, moving in a socket, no attempt ought to be made for replacing the head, until it has, by extension, been brought forth from the place where it is, and nearly to a level with the socket. All that the surgeon has to do, is to bring it to such level; the muscles attached to the bone will do the rest for him, and that whether he will or not. Whatever kind or degree of force may be found necessary for the reduction of a luxated joint, that force must be employed gradually; the lesser degree must always be first tried, and it must be increased by degrees. They who have not made the experiment, will not believe to how great a degree a gradually increased extension may be carried without any injury to the parts extended, whereas great force exerted hastily, is productive of very terrible and lasting mischief. Extension may either be made by means of assistants, who are to take hold of napkins or sheets, put round the part at which it is judged proper to make the extension, or else a multiplied pulley may be used. The first is the preferable method. The extension should always be first made in the same direction into which the dislocated bone is thrown; but in proportion as the muscles yield, the bone is to be gradually brought back into its natural position. The extension will prove quite unavailing, unless the bone, with which the dislocated head is naturally articulated, be kept motionless by counter-extension, or a force at least equal to the other but made in a contrary direction. When the attempts at reduction fail, the want of success is sometimes owing to the extension not being powerful enough, and to the great muscular strength of the patient, whose muscles counteract all the efforts to replace the bone. In the latter case, the warm bath, bleeding, and other means of relaxation are to be employed; and some have even recommended intoxication; but though a drunken man is sometimes quite incapable of resisting any force applied to him, the propriety of this is very questionable, as the same effect may be produced by more scientific and less immoral means. Long-continued, unremitting, gradual extension, will at last weary out the most powerful muscles; and this practice is the most to be recommended. A dislocation is known to be reduced by the limb recovering its natural length, shape, and direction, and by the patient being able to perform certain motions, which he could not do when the bone was out of its place. There is a great and sudden diminution of pain; and sometimes the bone is heard to give a loud crack when going into its natural position.

After the reduction of a dislocated bone is effected, care must be taken to prevent a recurrence of the accident, by retaining the limb steady by appropriate bandages, which should be put as far as possible from the centre of motion. To the ankle and the wrist, splints may sometimes be necessary. After luxations of the shoulder-joint, the arm is to be kept in a sling. If there is any appearance of inflammation or swelling taking place from the accident, or from the force employed in reduction, a cold lotion is to be kept to the place, and even leeches may be necessary, with a saline purgative. The patient must for some time be cautious in using the limb.

Compound luxations are those which are attended with a wound communicating with the cavities of the injured joints. These injuries are often attended with very great danger, and much skill and judgment are required to decide upon the treatment immediately after the accident. So much injury may be done, that any attempt to cure it would soon be frustrated by violent fever, gangrene, and death; all of which may be prevented by the amputation of the limb. At the same time, it is to be remarked, that by proper care and judicious treatment, many apparently untoward cases may do well. The reduction of compound dislocations must be effected as gently and as quickly as possible. The wound is to be cleared from dirt or any extraneous matter, and its lips are to be brought together by adhesive plaster. The limb is to be bound with the proper splints and bandages, and to be kept cool by refrigerant lotions; and if there is much constitutional excitement, bleeding, large and general, is to be put in practice; and internal means are to be used for the diminution and cure of feverish symptoms, should any such present themselves. Saline draughts and antimonial medicines must be resorted to, and purgatives also, provided they do not subject the patient to too much motion of the injured part. If the febrile symptoms abate, and the local inflammation does not run to any great extent, we may hope that the injury is to pass over without bad consequences; but the reverse may happen, violent inflammation may attack the joint, and be followed by suppuration, and all the dangers and debilitating symptoms of hectic fever. While these continue it would be dangerous to attempt amputation; but we must wait till these symptoms abate, and then give the patient the only chance of saving his life. Having made these general observations on dislocations, and shown the principles on which they should be treated, it can hardly be considered necessary or proper, in a popular work, to enter on the minute details of the symptoms and cure of every particular dislocation. For these we must refer to books of Surgery.

Dislocations or fractures of the limbs of infants sometimes happen in delivery. They ought never to be concealed or neglected, but the proper measures should be taken for their replacement and cure.

IRELAND.

Land of beauty, land of sadness,
Land whose lyre is turned to madness,
Why that throb of deep emotion,
Felt o'er valley, mount, and ocean?
Why that look of wordless anguish?
Why that strain, whose echoes languish?
Land of beauty, doth thy spirit
Some undying wound inherit?
Land of sadness! beams of glory
Lit thy times of ancient story—
When freedom wove a wreath of honour,
Round the brow of bold O'Connor.
Athunree! dark hour of sorrow!
Night of blood, thou had'st no morrow.
Thou did'st bind the chain of slavery
Round the nerveless hand of bravery;
Thou did'st still the high-toned bosom,
Thou did'st blight green Erin's blossom!

G. P.

THE STORY-TELLER.

WHAT EVERYBODY SAYS MUST BE TRUE.

A TALE.

So thought Mrs. Leger; but so thought not her son Leslie. Mrs. St. Leger had long been a rich widow, and consequently had long been what a woman seldom is—her own mistress. She had learned with her catechism to have due reverence for all those "in authority over her." The only person in authority over her for years had been herself; therefore for her own judgments and opinions upon all subjects, she entertained the greatest deference. Her parents had been of the stern school, of the last age; she had sacrificed her best affections to obey their wishes, and formed a worldly marriage, which had made her miserable. Yet while she exulted in her own exemplary conduct, she never, even in thought, murmured at the tyranny of those who had obtained for her the thorny diadem that recompensed her filial martyrdom; on the contrary, they were her parents, and therefore *their* conduct was a model for all parental proceedings. It is true, that in her own proper person she eschewed tyranny; for, from the time he could lisp "mamma," to the (in him very precocious) epoch when he could distinctly and emphatically pronounce the words "*I will*," and "*I wont*," she had never thwarted the lightest wish of her only son, who was at the same time her only idol; for which reason she concluded herself to be the most devoted of mothers, and conceived herself justly entitled to a double, and more implicit share of obedience from her son, whenever he should arrive at the epoch of human life, at which, of all others, people have the best right to judge for themselves. But *she* had married against her inclination to obey her parents; how much more, then, ought he to do so to gratify the most indulgent of mothers! Yet if one had hinted to Mrs. St. Leger that he was unreasonable in any thing, she would have stared in unfeigned astonishment; for she would instantly recollect how much more reasonable and less *exigeante* she was than her parents had been. Moreover, like all persons who live totally out of it, she piqued herself on great knowledge of the world. A love of solitude was the idiosyncrasy of her whole family; and the worst of indulging in solitude is, that we are apt to get a trick of wearing our virtues wrong side out, and where caution would be quite a sufficient defence against the monster, the world, (whom, as we rarely see, but live quite near enough for neighbourly feuds, we must conclude to be our enemy,) we are not content with arming ourselves with its extremity—suspicion. We may seclude ourselves with economy, but the odds are, we emerge with avarice. Solitude is a soil in which few feelings grow, but errors—those spring up into excess. All who indulge it grow a little mad. But to our story. Mrs. St. Leger, notwithstanding her solitary faults, was an excellent woman, kind at heart, and faultless in intention, and often would have been the very first to have appreciated and admired certain qualities had she happened to find them in any other individuals than those she especially disliked. Of her son she had, perhaps, more reason to be proud than fond. Not that he lacked any of the virtues that beget esteem, or the good qualities which can alone create or retain genuine affection; nor did he want those thousand little nameless failings, which rescue very gifted persons from the chilling heights on which they would otherwise be placed above their fellows—failings which, in those we love, give us additional cause to love them, because they give us something to forgive; and there is a pertinacity in human affection which clings more closely to all for which it has in any degree suffered. But nature is a niggard, and while she lavishes with one hand, is sure to hold back something with the other. She had given to Leslie St. Leger a handsome person, a keen wit, and a strong, penetrative, and generous mind; but she or education, or both combined, had bestowed upon him a rash, self-willed, and obstinate disposition.

"Every body says so, therefore it must be true," said Mrs. St. Leger to Mrs. Brambleton, (a toady in every thing but salary and suavity,) as her son Leslie entered the breakfast room.

"And what is it that is so true because every body says so?" inquired he, with a smile.

"Why, my dear, that the house which Mr. Manningfield has just bought in Whitehall smokes most abominably, or else he would not have got it so cheap."

"I only know," said Leslie, "that all the time Lord Leitrim lived in it, which has been for the last thirty years, he declares he has never known a single room in it to smoke once."

"Of course he would say so," snapped Mrs. Brambleton, "when he wanted to sell it. Some chicken, Mr. St. Leger? Really you eat nothing. I should think you were in love, only Mrs. St. Leger tells me she cannot get you to go into society at all since you returned from abroad."

"My dear mother, I don't know what you call going out, but Heaven and myself only know what I have endured, in the way of dancing and dinnering, from my arrival here; or, as the newspaper would phrase it, how largely I have tasted of 'British hospitality,' a hospitality, forsooth, which marvellously resembles that fountain at Smyrna, of which no man can partake without its being *expected* that he should take away a wife from the place; for hospitality, in this country, is chiefly confined to fathers of families labouring under an accumulation of daughters, all and each ready to fall to the lot of the first man who can give them 'a local habitation and a name.'"

"My dear Leslie, young men get up such strange notions on the continent, and learn so soon to undervalue the true and solid blessings of an English fireside: it is really quite shocking. Where abroad will you meet with such a family as the Jernynghams?"

"Where, indeed, thank God!" cried Leslie.

"Emmeline Jernyngham—such a sweet, retiring, lady-like, unobtrusive girl, and so pretty!"

"Sweet, retiring, and unobtrusive! *C'est a dire, gauche comme une vache Espagnole, et bornée comme une bosquet à l'opera*; and as for beauty, that of Ætna,—ice for the basis and fire for the summit; her hair is positively *couleur feu d'enfer*."

Poor Mrs. St. Leger lifted up her hands and eyes in astonishment at her graceless son's cavalier treatment of her panegyric. She had known the well-regulated times when a parent's opinion was indisputable, and when people read, heard, dreamed of nothing else but "the wisdom of our ancestors;" but she had lived to see the inauspicious day when she was afraid to provoke contradiction from her own son, and when it was a hundred to one but that very book she opened, from the pompous and Johnsonian-looking quarto down to the dandified and finikin duodecimo, or even the penny *canaille* of the paper democracy, would have for its opening sentence some "grievous grievance" saddled upon the "ignorance of our progenitors," ancestors being by far too aristocratic a term for the phenomena of the present age to use even figuratively. Mrs. St. Leger wisely forebore a reply, but, like a true woman, continued, expatiating upon the same text.

"And Lady Jernyngham is such a sweet woman—so much Christian charity and forbearance! I never heard her speak ill of any one, even if they are ever so bad. It was only the other night, at her sisters, Mrs. Humdrum's, that I heard her palliating, in the most amiable manner, the vices of that young profligate, Lord Rentall."

"Oh!" cried the incorrigible Leslie, "she would no doubt have done the same by his Satanic Majesty, were he about town in guise of a bachelor elder-brothership, and likely to ask for either of her daughters; and then, notwithstanding her exemplary maternalism, I would stake Miss Fanny to a hackney coach-horse, that she would have let the d——l take either of them, and then have said in her most purring and conciliating voice, that the d——l is often painted blacker than he is."

"I hear St. George Erpingham is very much in love with Emmaline," persevered Mrs. St. Leger.

"Heavens, what a fool that man is!" said Mrs. Brambleton. By cramming his little, narrow, dark, crooked, antediluvian mind with a few modern chimeras, which he picks up, like his furniture, and jumbles incongruously and heterogeneously together, he thinks to pass for a wondrously clever person, especially as he is hugely sceptical upon all mysteries, except his own importance, and that of his Yorkshire Siberia; and to these he pays the homage of a most idolatrous worship, after the fashion of the aboriginal priests of Isis, who always selected for their individual Latria an idol that never received the reverence of others."

"Ah, my dear Mrs. Brambleton, I fear this is all the good the 'march of intellect' is likely to do."

"*March* of intellect! my dear Madam, I begin to think that is past, and that it must now be the *April* of intellect, one meets so many fools."

"Pray, Mrs. Brambleton," asked Leslie (very *apropos de botte*, as his mother thought,) "did you ever happen to meet a Miss Fielding?" Mrs. Brambleton put her head on one side, and leaned her cheek upon her hand to consider, for she was of that genus of ancient ladies, who pride themselves upon the diffusion of useful knowledge to all, and therefore, could ill brook being thought ignorant either about persons or things. "Why, let me see: ye—s; you mean a little, odd-looking, dark girl, with a profusion of long black ringlets, like a *Pont Neuf* poodle *coiffée* for sale, don't you?"

"No, I mean a tall, fair girl, with blue eyes, and golden hair."

"Oh! the daughter of that odd Mrs. Fielding, that has such strange opinions upon all subjects; and the daughter is, I believe, as odd and as disagreeable as the mother."

"I have heard," said Mrs. Leger, in a deprecating tone, "that she is a most undutiful daughter, and that she gives herself such tremendous airs, and that she never will appear to any of her mother's guests, and is in every way thoroughly unamiable."

"And I have heard," said Leslie, somewhat more warmly than the occasion appeared to demand, "that her mother's guests are persons of such strange opinions, and of such equivocal character, that you, my dear mother, would be the very first person to condemn any girl for voluntarily associating with them."

"I dare say," growled Mrs. Brambleton, "she only avoids their society to annoy her mother, and not out of any sense of propriety."

"And I understand she is exceedingly satirical—a quality, to say the least of it, very unbecoming in any young woman," said Mrs. St. Leger.

"Oh! horribly ill-natured," responded Mrs. Brambleton, with a sneer that displayed her very sable teeth, which, at that moment, Leslie thought the venom of her tongue must have turned black.

Mrs. St. Leger began to feel a vague, though faint and ill-defined alarm, at the unwonted warmth of her son's championship in behalf of Florence Fielding; and finding that he was not to be moved by the *niaiseries* of English modesty and vacuity, she thought she would see what wit and wealth would do; and although, before she named Miss Marsham, she herself felt it was hardly fair to accuse Miss Fielding of satire, while she called Miss Marsham's undisguised and unprovoked ill-nature *wit*—yet Miss Marsham was an heiress, while Florence Fielding had not a shilling—and, therefore, had no right to a sense of the ridiculous, even upon the most trifling and external points. Having arrived at this conclusion, she commenced her operations with,

"Pray, my dear Leslie, tell me. Miss Marsham dined at Lord Audicy's yesterday: don't you think her a most charming, agreeable person?—and so *very* clever and witty?"

"Oh!" cried Leslie, putting both hands before her eyes, "name her not; she is my favourite aversion; there is genuine unsophisticated ill-nature, if you will; and as to wit— If she had any pretensions to it, it must, indeed, be that she 'builds her fame upon the ruins of another's name:' and then her loud laugh, and her extraordinary plainness, which would make any man afraid to marry her, unless she could prove that she had taken out a patent for it, so as to confine it exclusively to herself; and with the eternal diamond *Ferroniere*, she is, indeed, 'like the toad, ugly and venomous, which yet wears a precious jewel in its head.'

"It is a strange anomaly in English society," continued Leslie, "where persons are certainly much more personally and rancorously ill-natured than in any other, that the only species of ill-nature never tolerated or forgiven, is that which is at all accompanied by wit. In England, people might write and speak libels for ever, provided they avoided epigrams. The retailers of scandal, the assassins of reputation, who merely circulate the leaden lie in all its unwrought dulness, are never shunned as a pest, or denounced as dangerous; but let them omit half the malice, and only substitute wit for the remaining quantum, and they will soon be dreaded as though they were walking cholera. A friend of mine (lucky fellow!) was once avoided for a whole season at Florence by all the English, for having happened to remark of one of his compatriots, who appeared at a ball with one of those turbans of the old English breed, (now happily extinct,) composed of white muslin handkerchiefs and red scarfs, that she looked like a Chinuck Tartar returning from the wars, with his headgear garnished by the bleached bones of his enemies. Strange, strange contradiction! that a nation which excels more than any other in the talent of being able to eat mutton

..., should not be able to forgive those who 'cut blocks with a razor!'"

A few days after the above conversation, Leslie requested an audience with his mother in her dressing-room, where she generally was to be found alone for some three hours after breakfast, unenvironed by the eternal Mrs. Bramble-ton; and he did then and there, after much hesitation, circumlocution, and ineffectual attempts at lessening the shock, coldly ask her consent to marry Miss Fielding!

Poor Mrs. St. Leger! Had he asked her consent to cut his throat, she could not have looked more aghast, or felt more heart-stricken, than she did. Leslie kept his eyes fixed as attentively on that part of the carpet immediately under them, as though he had been taking an inventory of the stitches or forming a synopsis of the colours. The "Morning Post" dropped from Mrs. St. Leger's little, aristocratic, thin, white hand, which seemed within the last minute to have grown thinner and whiter. She leaned, or rather sank back, in her bergere—she looked at her son for some seconds with as much intensity of despair, as though the grave, or the perdition beyond it, had yawned before him. At length a pale smile cast a faint gleam over her countenance, which had been actually palsied with horror, and she said, "Oh, no, no! Surely, Leslie, I might have known you were jesting."

Long and bitter was the scene which ensued. Leslie defended and eulogised Florence Fielding with all the eloquence of a lover. Mrs. St. Leger warned him, and inveighed against her with all that sophistry of parental devotion which convinces itself the more that it fails in convincing others—that the happiness of her child alone actuated her—that she was totally unbiassed by any other or more worldly motive—she even went so far as to say (what parents generally do on such occasions) that it is not money, it was not rank, she wished for her son—it was only happiness; and even had he preferred any one more portionless, and less well born than Miss Fielding—provided she had been in herself amiable and likely to make him happy—she would have willingly consented; but the daughter of such a woman! brought up as she had been! what could he expect? In vain Leslie pleaded that Florence's mother had never liked her, and that on no one subject had they an opinion in common; in vain he brought innumerable instances to prove how much affection for the individual influences our adoption of the individual's opinions—how almost impossible it is for us to think those wrong in any thing who are never wrong to us—and how nearly equally impossible it is to think those right in any thing who are never just or kind towards ourselves; thus it is that affection ever makes the very failings and even vices of those we love a haven to run into, while dislike to the object makes us light up the very same vices, as a beacon to be shunned; in vain Leslie told of the many good traits he had noted in Florence's character—in vain he urged his mother to know before she condemned her. As for her good qualities, Mrs. St. Leger was convinced they only existed in his imagination—and as for knowing her, he was quite a sufficient proof of her art, without another member of his family being subjected to it. She was *convinced*, too, that she did not care one straw for him; for in her was that strange anomaly (that exists in most parents' minds) which, while it made her think her son more loveable, more amiable, more beautiful, more clever, and more attractive than any one else ever was, or ever will be, would not allow her to believe that any body *could* love, admire, or appreciate him but herself. Her pet scheme about him and Miss Jernyngham was at an end, for that morning's paper had announced her marriage with Sir George Erpingham; so Mrs. St. Leger was going to close this painful conference with a sigh and a hope, that "her dear Leslie, to whom she had always given credit for sense beyond his years, would take some time to consider before he sealed his misery for life, by marrying a woman who, everybody said, had not a good quality, and who, to say the least of her, she was certain, would run away from him at the end of six months."

A year elapsed after this conversation, during which time Leslie St. Leger vainly contrived to gain his mother's consent to his marriage—and by the end of that time he contrived (by arguments best known to himself) to persuade Florence to become his wife without it, and consequently against her own conviction of right. The day of their marriage Mrs. St. Leger gave a large dinner-party—certainly not to celebrate the event, but chiefly to show the world in general, and her son in particular, that from that time he was as nothing to her—and that she would henceforth take refuge in crowds, which she had hitherto shunned, and seek in the many, all that she persisted in thinking she had *now* lost in the one. The dinner passed off as English set-dinners usually do, which for the most part seem modelled on the plan of the banquets of the old Florentine painters, who, Vassart tells, used, even with their confections, desserts, and ambrosial wines, to introduce the most appalling skeletons, spectres, and images from the infernal regions; for at the dinner in question, fire, robberies, murders, and diseases, and elopements, were duly discussed.

About four years after her marriage, as Florence was sitting alone one evening, during one of the frequent absences of her husband, who was then in Leicestershire, busy about his election, a servant entered, and said, "Ma'am, Mrs. Charlton is below, and wishes to speak to you."

"Who is Mrs. Charlton?" asked Florence.

"Mrs. St. Leger's housekeeper, Ma'am."

"Let her come up, said Florence, trembling violently, as a vague idea that her husband was in some danger, flitted across her; for his mother had persisted in not seeing her since her marriage, and therefore she could not suppose it was any message from her. Mrs. Charlton at length came curtseying into the room—the very incarnation of an apology for having intruded upon her at all, much less at so unseasonable an hour—" but, Ma'am, Mrs. Leger is so *dangerously ill*, and Mrs. Lewyn (that is her maid, Ma'am) being in the fever, too, Ma'am, and therefore, as the saying is, of no use, Ma'am—and my own poor girl being seized not an hour ago—(and one must look to one's own, Ma'am) —and a nurse not to be had to-night for love or money —and Dr. B—— saying as *Missis* might not live through the night, if so be she was not properly 'tended— and Master Leslie—I beg pardon Ma'am—Mr. St. Leger being out of town—and hearing you was such a good lady, I thought I would venter to call, thinking as you might be able to get a nurse, Ma'am—and that—then Mr. Leslie need not to be written to, as he is so busy about his 'lection—and as I know he loves his mother dearly, it would sadly vex him, as his interest like would pull one way, and his duty, Ma'am, another!"

"You did quite right, Mrs. Charlton, not to write and alarm Mrs. St. Leger," said Florence, "and I hope Mrs.

St. Leger will be quite well before he even hears that she has been ill. I will endeavour to send a nurse to Grosvenor Street in less than half an hour. I suppose you are going back there immediately?"

"Oh, dear no, Ma'am, I am going on to my poor girl, who is lying so *dangerously hill in Igh Obern*—and that's chiefly what made me come to you, Ma'am, as I could not stay and do for *Missis* myself, poor dear lady!"

No sooner had the worthy Mrs. Charlton departed on her maternal mission to *Igh Obern*, than Florence repaired to her own room, put on a morning cap, poke bonnet, and *babtiste* dress, and then, under a strict injunction of secrecy, confided to her astonished abigail her intention of herself going to nurse Mrs. St. Leger. The maid could not suppress her surprise and horror. "What! at this time of night, Ma'am?"—"That is the very reason; for no one else can be got." "And the typhus fever and all! Dear, dear, Ma'am, if you should catch it, and die of it, and all, before Mr. St. Leger returns, what would he say?"

"And if his mother should die through my selfish fears, because I was afraid to go near her, Gerald, what would he say then?"

"I don't know, Ma'am, what *he* would say; but I should say," cried the the woman somewhat pertly, but still more indignantly, " that if it had been you, she would have let you die before *she* would have gone to *you*."

Florence arrived in Grosvenor Street as fast as fear and anxiety could take her. For four nights, and four days, which the darkness of a sick room made like night, she watched by the bed-side of Mrs. St. Leger. Never did nurse tread so noiselessly, never did leech administer his anodynes so carefully;—and never did a mother smooth the pillow of a sick child more tenderly than did Florence that of her mother-in-law; and though, in the ravings of the poor sufferer, she often heard her own name coupled with epithets of reproach and aversion, yet this was more than atoned for by the unbounded affection for her son, which, even on the brink of the grave, Mrs. St. Leger evinced was her ruling passion; and Florence actually loved her for not thinking that she herself was good enough for him. The worst of her trials, in her new capacity, was the incessant praises of Dr. B———, his endless inquiries as to the hospitals she had attended! his surprise at her youthful and anti-professional appearance, and his reiterated promises of patronage and recommendation! On the evening of the fifth day Mrs. St. Leger was pronounced out of danger. The fever had quite left her; and she was profuse in her thanks to Dr. B——— for his unremitting attention, of which she said she had a confused but strong impression.

"Not at all, Madam, not at all," said the Doctor, "it is to this young woman you are indebted, for never did I see so indefatigable a nurse; she has not left you night or day these five days, and many a thing has she anticipated, which I was not here to order; yet which, nevertheless, was of more importance than medicine itself."

"Come hither child," said Mrs. St. Leger, putting aside the curtain, " as far as money can repay your services, you shall not find me ungrateful; but you look very young for a nurse, and rather of a different rank of life, too; but how long have you been a nurse? and where did Dr. B——— hear of you?"

"I am not a nurse, Madam," said Florence, blushing and stammering, "and it was not Dr. B———, but Mrs. Charlton who found me out, for her own daughter being ill she was obliged to go to her, and, as it was late at night, she could not get any body else, I came, and thought I might be able to nurse you, if I was wakeful and careful."

"And God knows you have been both," cried Dr. B———

"And I shall not forget either," said Mrs. St. Leger: and then added with a sigh, " but Leslie—has he not been here? Surely if he can think of anything but his wife, he might have come when I was so ill."

"Oh for that matter," said the Dr., Mrs. Charlton and I held a Cabinet council, and as he was electioneering, we determined not to harass him by letting him know of your illness till you were out of all danger; but I wrote to him yesterday, and should not be surprised if he were here tonight; he could not be here before—do you think he could Mrs. Charlton?" addressing the housekeeper, who had returned that morning, and now came into the room with some arrowroot.

"Oh dear, no, Sir, by no manner o' means."

Mrs. St. Leger seemed appeased at this, but could not retreat without aiming one more shaft at Florence. "I think Mrs. Leslie St. Leger, in common respect, putting humanity out of the question, might have sent to inquire after me."

"Mrs. Leslie St. Leger *has* inquired after you four or five times a-day Ma'am," said the housekeeper, darting a look at Florence's crimson cheek, as she thus pointedly alluded to her almost hourly inquiries in her capacity of nurse; the good woman stirred the arrowroot somewhat more vehemently than it seemed to require; and Mrs. St. Leger turned to Dr. B——— with a sigh of resignation at her son's wife having for once actually done what she said she ought to do —and inquired if there was any news?

"No, nothing, except that Lady Erpingham has gone off with Lord Rentall."

"Lady Erpingham! and left her two children?—you amaze me!" said Mrs. St. Leger, sinking back upon her pillow, as if she had been electrified.

"Humph!" quoth the Doctor, "she was much too automaton a personage for me to be surprised at anything she did; but it is a common error to mistake vacuity for virtue, and ignorance for innocence. Why, here is Mr. St. Leger, I have no doubt," cried the Doctor, as a carriage stopped at the door. In another minute a step was heard upon the stairs, Florence attempted a precipitate escape into the dressing-room, but was detained by Mrs. St. Leger, laying her hand upon her arm, and ordering her not to go. In another instant Leslie was in the room, and at his mother's bed-side; he did not see his wife in his anxiety to see his mother, and poor Florence had fainted for fear of the *denouement* that must inevitably take place. Dr. B——— put out his arm to prevent her falling to the ground. Mrs. Charlton ran for some water. Leslie turned to see what was the cause of the commotion—he saw a woman lying across the bed with her face downward. As he helped to raise her, the dim light of a solitary candle gleamed upon her face, and he beheld his wife to all appearance dead. "Good God! Florence, my own Florence! how came you here? and they have murdered you!" cried Leslie, franticly:— "will no one save her?" continued he, " send—go—bring a physician—every physician—bring them all."

"Gently, Sir," said the Doctor, "she will recover soon, if you do not all crowd round her, and keep the air from her."

"On your peril do not trifle with me," said Leslie, looking wildly on his wife's wasted form, and the wan cheek, where want of sleep, and so many nights and days of watching had wrought a change that appeared fearful in his eyes:— "you think she *will* recover?"

"She *is* recovering," said Dr. B———, dashing a tear from the corner of his eye, for he now began to comprehend the whole scene, and how Florence had been so good a nurse, although she had *not* walked the hospitals.

"Mother, mother," said Leslie, willing to grasp at hope from every one, do you think she will recover?"

"I do, Leslie," said Mrs. St. Leger, bursting into tears, as she placed Florence's cold hand in Leslie's burning palm, and pressed them both within her own—"and I do think, although *everybody does not say so*, that she is an angel."

—*New Monthly Magazine.*

CURIOUS ANECDOTE OF NAPOLEON AND ISABEY THE PAINTER.

FROM THE M.S. JOURNAL OF A DISTINGUISHED FOREIGNER.

I CALLED one morning on Isabey, to see his fine collection of portraits, which have now, in a great measure, become historical. I found him in his *atelier*, working upon that splendid picture which is destined to connect the name of the artist with most of the distinguished characters of his day.[*] In a moment I found myself surrounded by the almost living likenesses of all the celebrated men and beautiful women, at that time assembled in Vienna. I saw the portrait of young Napoleon, which Isabey was just finishing, when I first met him at Schœnbrunn; also a likeness of the Prince de Ligne, animated by all the fine expression of the original, and a full-length of Napoleon himself walking in the gardens of Malmaison. "Then he really had the habit of walking with his arms cross in this manner?" said I. "Unquestionably," replied Isabey; "and that, together with his other remarkable habit of stooping his head, at one time well nigh proved very fatal to me. During the Consulate, I had been dining one day with some of Bonaparte's young aides-de-camp at Malmaison. After dinner we went out on the lawn fronting the Château, to play at leap-frog; you know that was a favourite college game of ours. I had leaped over the heads of several of my companions, when a little further on, beneath an avenue of trees, I saw another apparently waiting for me in the requisite position. Thinking I had not yet completed my task, I ran forward, but unfortunately missed my mark, springing only to the height of his neck, I knocked him down, and we both rolled along the ground to the distance of at least ten yards. What was my horror on discovering that the victim of my unlucky blunder was no other than Bonaparte himself! At that period he had not even dreamed of the possibility of a fall; and this first lesson was naturally calculated to rouse his indignation in the utmost degree. Foaming with rage, he rose and drew his sword, and, had I not proved myself a better runner than a leaper, I have no doubt but he would soon have made an end of me. He pursued me as far as the ditch, which I speedily cleared, and, fortunately for me, he did not think fit to follow my example. I proceeded straight to Paris, and so great was my alarm, that I scarcely ventured to look behind me until I reached the gates of the Tuileries. I immediately ascended to Madame Bonaparte's apartments, for the persons of the household were accustomed to admit me at all times. On seeing my agitation, Josephine at first concluded that I was the bearer of some fatal news. I related my adventure, which, in spite of my distress, appeared to her so irresistibly comic, that she burst into a fit of laughter. When her merriment had somewhat subsided, she promised, with her natural kindness of heart, to intercede with the Consul in my behalf. But knowing her husband's irascible temper, she advised me to keep out of the way until she should have an opportunity of appeasing him, which to her was no very difficult task, for at that time Napoleon loved her most tenderly. Indeed, her angelic disposition always gave her a most powerful ascendency over him, and she was frequently the means of averting those acts of violence, to which his ungovernable temper would otherwise have driven him.

"On my return home, I found lying on my table an order not to appear again at the Tuileries; and it was during my temporary retirement, that I finished the portrait you were just now looking at. Madame Bonaparte, on presenting it to the Consul, obtained my pardon, and my recall to court. The first time Bonaparte saw me after this affair, was in Josephine's apartments, and stepping up to me good-naturedly, he patted me on the cheek, saying, 'Really, Sir, if people will play tricks, they ought at least to do them cleverly.'—'*Mon Dieu!*' said Josephine, laughing, 'if you had seen his look of terror, when he first presented himself to me, you would have thought him sufficiently punished for his intended feat of agility.'"

[*] This picture is now almost generally known, through the medium of the engraving. It represents the Hall of the Congress, at the moment when the Duke of Wellington was introduced by Prince Metternich.

Isabey related this anecdote with all his peculiar animation and drollery; and he accompanied the story with such expressive gestures and attitudes, that he seemed to bring the whole scene visibly before me. I could imagine I saw Napoleon prostrate on the ground, and then rising to vent his rage, like angry Jupiter hurling his thunderbolts.

FAMILY DIGNITY.

THE Welsh, like their Celtic brethren in the Highlands, are remarkably tenacious of the honours of clanship and primogeniture. We are not certain that the chief of Glengarry himself would, in the circumstances which follow, have refused hospitality to the laird of Clanranald, although he had denied the former the coveted title of the Lord of the Isles:—

Mr. Proger of Werndee, riding one evening from Monmouth, with a friend who was on a visit to him, a heavy rain came on, and they turned their horses a little out of the road towards Perthyer. "My cousin Powell," said Mr. Proger, "will, I am sure, be ready to give us a night's lodging." At Perthyer all was still, the family were a-bed. Mr. Proger shouted aloud under his cousin Powell's chamber window. Mr. Powell soon heard him, and putting his head out, inquired, "In the name of wonder what means all this noise? Who is there?" "It is only your cousin Proger of Werndee, who is come to your hospitable door for shelter from the inclemency of the weather; and hopes you will be so kind as to give him, and a friend of his, a night's lodging." "What, is it you, cousin Proger? You and your friend shall be instantly admitted; but upon one condition, namely, that you will admit now, and never hereafter dispute that I am the head of your family." "What was that you said?" replied Mr. Proger. "Why, I say that if you expect to pass the night in my house, you must admit that I am the head of your family." "No, Sir, I will never admit that—were it to rain swords and daggers, I would ride through them this night to Werndee, sooner than let down the consequence of my family by submitting to such an ignominious condition. Come up, Bald! come up!" "Stop a moment, cousin Proger; have you not often admitted that the first Earl of Pembroke (of the name of Herbert) was a younger son of Perthyer; and will you set yourself up above the Earls of Pembroke?" "True it is I must give place to the Earl of Pembroke, because he is a Peer of the realm; but still, though a Peer, he is of the youngest branch of my family, being descended from the fourth son of Werndee, who was your ancestor, and settled at Perthyer, whereas I am descended from the eldest son. Indeed my cousin Jones of Lanarth is a branch of the family elder than you are, and yet he never disputes my being the head of the family." "Well, cousin Proger, I have nothing more to say; good night to you." "Stop a moment, Mr. Powell," cried the stranger, "you see how it pours; do let *me* in at least; *I* will not dispute with you about our families." "Pray, Sir, what is your name, and where do you come from?" "My name is so and so, and I come from such a county." "A Saxon, of course; it would indeed be very curious, Sir, were I to dispute with a Saxon about family. No, Sir, you must suffer for the obstinacy of your friend; so good night to you both."—*Williams's Monmouth.*

IMPERISHABLE NATURE OF SILK.—Some years ago, the sexton of the parish of Falkirk, in Stirlingshire, upon opening a grave in the church-yard, found a riband wrapped about the bone of an arm, and which, being washed, was found to be entire, and to have suffered no injury, although it had lain for more than eight years in the earth, and had been in contact with a body which had passed through every stage of putrefaction, until it was reduced to its kindred dust.

EPISTOLARY CONDENSATION; OR COMING TO THE POINT.—Copy of a tradesman's letter to a debtor:—"Sir —If you will favour me with the amount of my bill, you will oblige *me* :—if not, I must oblige *you*."

REMARKABLE ACCOUNT OF A BATTLE BETWEEN TWO SNAKES.

From Letters from an American Farmer, by MR. J. HECTOR ST. JOHN.

As I was one day sitting solitary and pensive in my arbour, my attention was engaged by a strange sort of rustling noise at some paces distance. I looked all around, without distinguishing any thing, until I climbed one of my great hemp stalks; when, to my astonishment, I beheld two snakes of considerable length, the one pursuing the other with great celerity through a hemp stubble-field. The aggressor was of the black kind, six feet long; the fugitive was a water snake, nearly of equal dimensions. They soon met, and in the fury of their first encounter, they appeared in an instant firmly twisted together; and whilst their united tails beat the ground, they tried with open jaws to lacerate each other. What a fell aspect did they present! Their heads were compressed to a very small size; their eyes flashed fire; and after this conflict had lasted about five minutes, the second found means to disengage itself from the first, and hurried toward the ditch. Its antagonist instantly assumed a new posture, and, half creeping, and half erect, with a majestic mien, overtook and attacked the other again, which placed itself in the same attitude, and prepared to resist. The scene was uncommon and beautiful; for, thus opposed, they fought with their jaws, biting each other with the utmost rage; but notwithstanding this appearance of mutual courage and fury, the water snake still seemed desirous of retreating toward the ditch, its natural element. This was no sooner perceived by the keen-eyed black one, than, twisting its tail twice round a stalk of hemp, and seizing its adversary by the throat, not by means of its jaws, but by twisting its own neck twice round that of the water-snake, it pulled the latter back from the ditch. To prevent a defeat, the water-snake took hold likewise of a stalk on the bank, and by the acquisition of that point of resistance became a match for its fierce antagonist. Strange was this to behold; two great snakes, strongly adhering to the ground, fastened together, by means of the writhings which lashed them to each other, and stretched at their full length, they pulled, but pulled in vain; and, in the moments of greatest exertions, that part of their bodies which was entwined, seemed extremely small, while the rest appeared inflated, and now and then convulsed with strong undulations, rapidly following each other. Their eyes seemed on fire, and ready to start out of their heads; at one time the conflict seemed decided; the water snake bent itself into two great folds, and by that operation rendered the other more than commonly outstretched; the next minute the new struggles of the black one gained an unexpected superiority; it acquired two great folds likewise, which necessarily extended the body of its adversary in proportion as it had contracted its own. These efforts were alternate; victory seemed doubtful, inclining sometimes to the one side, and sometimes to the other: until at last the stalk, to which the black snake was fastened, suddenly gave way, and in consequence of this accident they both plunged into the ditch. The water did not extinguish their vindictive rage; for by their agitations I could trace, though not distinguish, their mutual attacks. They soon re-appeared on the surface, twisted together, as in their first onset but the black snake seemed to retain its wonted superiority, for its head was exactly fixed above that of the other, which it incessantly pressed down under the water, until it was stifled and sunk. The victor no sooner perceived its enemy incapable of farther resistance, than, abandoning it to the current, it returned on shore, and disappeared.

THE POST OFFICE TAX.

This must be considered either a tax on commerce, or a tax on the pleasure of familiar correspondence: and strange it is, that the public voice has not been raised, long ere this, for nearly its entire abrogation. In nine cases out of ten—perhaps forty-nine out of fifty—it amounts to an entire prohibition of one of the enjoyments most congenial with the best feelings of humanity—the pleasure of communication with relatives or friends, near and dear; from whom circumstances of necessity, or of duty, has compelled a separation. How often are the tender sympathies of nature, or of affection, left to wither and die, because prudence prohibits the sacrifice of frequent postage from the little hard-won earnings of humble life; the young woman who has left home for service—or the young man who has left a widowed mother—or an aged pair; in rural life, where they have few necessaries, but no more;—and he or she, who could save ten shillings in a half-year, and would rejoice in adding to the comforts of declining age, must even be forbidden the pleasure of mutual correspondence, except at an expense which would absorb their whole savings—a few postages to and fro, in the course of half-a-year, would; and then, if they should venture to drop a line by a friend, they are liable to be mulcted in the penalty of £5 for defrauding the post office! But, no; home is forgotten, and the youthful friend together, with whom a kindred correspondence might, in other respects, that is, with easy postage, have been maintained and cherished till it produced the best of consequences. Think again of the labourer or the peasant, not to speak of the widow, whose son has gone, like many more, to America, to seek a better country, but perhaps to meet with disappointment and delay; he knows what it must cost his parent to relieve his letter when it arrives, and therefore he does not write, till many months have gone by—his letter arrives; his father's last week's wages is gone; the letter lies in the post office till the return of pay day, and with pleasure the parent parts with a portion of his little all, to secure the precious packet; which, but for this impolitic tax, he would have received at a moderate rate. But the man of business must have his letters, and that whether his profits are great or small, and not unlikely his letters will be more numerous, if his business has been depressed, and he has entertained the laudable desire to extend it, or to seek new customers; his orders are small and frequent, consequently, his postages are frequent, and, perhaps, when he balances at the year's end, he finds that his business has been charged more through this impolitic tax than the whole amount of his net profits. Still business must be done, and letters must be had; but when it is considered that nearly the whole of this tax is a tax upon trade, and that it next to effectually operates as a prohibition to friendly and social correspondence; the impolicy of the weighty tax on letters must be considered a real grievance, and one to which the attention of our new Parliament should be especially and immediately called

A FAIR AND HAPPY MILKMAID.

A FAIR and happy milkmaid is a country wench, that is so far from making herself beautiful by art, that one look of hers is able to put all *face-physic* out of countenance. She knows a fair look is but a dumb orator to commend virtue; therefore minds it not. All her excellencies stand in her so silently, as if they had stolen upon her without her knowledge. The lining of her apparel, which is herself, is far better than outsides of tissue; for though she be not arrayed in the spoil of the silk-worm, she is decked in innocence, a far better wearing. She doth not, with lying long a-bed, spoil both her complexion and conditions;—nature hath taught her too immoderate sleep is rust to the soul—she rises, therefore, with chanticleer, her dame's clock, and at night makes the lamb her curfew. In milking a cow, and straining the teats through her fingers, it seems that so sweet a milk-press makes the milk whiter or sweeter; for never came almond-glare or aromatic ointment on her palm, to taint it. The golden ears of corn fall and kiss her feet when she reaps them, as if they wished to be bound and led prisoners by the same hand that felled them. Her breath is her own, which scents all the year long of June, like a new-made hay-cock. She makes her hands hard with labour, and her heart soft with pity; and when winter evenings fall early, sitting at her merry wheel, she sings defiance to the giddy wheel of fortune. She doth all things with so sweet a grace, it seems ignorance will not suffer her to do it ill, being her mind is to do well. She bestows her year's wages at next fair and in choosing her garments courts no bravery in the world like decency. The garden and bee-hive are all her physic and surgery, and she lives the longer for it. She dares go alone and unfold the sheep in the night, and fears no manner of ill, because she means none; yet, to say truth, she is never alone, but is still accompanied with old songs, honest thoughts, and prayers, but short ones—yet they have their efficacy in that they are not palled by ensuing idle cogitations. Lastly, her dreams are so pure, that she dares tell them—only a Friday's dream is all her superstition; that she conceals for fear of anger.—Thus lives she, and all her care is, she may die in the spring-time, to have store of flowers stuck upon her winding-sheet."

THE SILK MANUFACTURE.

Though to ourselves "familiar as household words," the nature and origin of silk were but obscurely, if at all, known in ancient times; and in the days of Aurelian it was valued at its weight in gold. This is probably owing to the mode in which the material was procured by the merchants of Alexandria, who had no direct intercourse with China, the only country in which the silk-worm was then reared. Though the manufactures of silk were lauded in terms of the highest admiration both by Greek and Roman authors, they were in frequent use for several centuries before any certain knowledge was obtained either of the countries from which the material was derived, or of the means by which it was produced. By some it was supposed to be a fine down, adhering to the leaves of trees or flowers; by others it was regarded as a delicate kind of wool or cotton; and even those who had some idea of its insect-origin were incorrectly informed of the mode of its formation. The court of the Greek emperors, which surpassed even that of the Asiatic sovereigns in splendour and magnificence, became profuse in its display of this costly luxury; but as the Persians, from the advantages which their local situation gave them over the merchants from the Arabian Gulf, were enabled to supplant them in all those marts of India to which silk was brought by sea from the East, and as they had it in their power to cut off the caravans which travelled by land to China through their own northern provinces, Constantinople thus became dependent on a rival power for an article which its sumptuous nobles deemed essential to the enjoyment of refined life. Of course the Persians, with the accustomed and long-continued rapacity of monopolists, raised the price to an exorbitant height, and many attempts were made by Justinian to free his subjects from such exaction. An accidental circumstance is said to have accomplished what the wisdom of the great legislator was unable to achieve. Two Persian monks who had been employed as missionaries in one of the Christian churches established in India, had penetrated into the country of the Seres, that is, to China, where they observed the natural operations of the silk-worm, and acquired a knowledge of the arts of man in working up its produce into so many rich and costly fabrics. The love of lucre, mingled perhaps with a feeling of indignation that so valuable a branch of commerce should be enjoyed by unbelieving nations, induced them to repair to Constantinople, where they explained to the Emperor the true origin of silk, and the various modes by which it was prepared and manufactured. Encouraged by the most liberal promises, they undertook to transport a sufficient supply of these extraordinary worms to Constantinople, which they effected by conveying the eggs in the interior of a hollow cane. They were hatched, it is said, by the heat of a dunghill, and the larvæ were fed with the leaves of wild mulberry. They worked, underwent their accustomed metamorphosis, and multiplied according to use and wont; and, in the course of time, have become extensively cultivated throughout all the southern countries of our continent,—thus effecting an important change in the commercial relations which had so long existed between Europe and the East. It is curious to consider how the breeding of a few millions of caterpillars should occasion such a disparity in the circumstances of different tribes of the human race. When the wife and empress of Aurelian was refused a garment of silk on account of its extreme costliness, the most ordinary classes of the Chinese were clad in that material from top to toe; and although among ourselves week-day and holiday are now alike profaned by uncouth forms, whose vast circumference is clothed " in silk attire," yet our own James VI. was forced to borrow a pair of silken hose from the Earl of Mar, that his state and bearing might be more effective in the presence of the ambassador of England; " for ye would not, sure, that your king should appear as a scrub before strangers." King Henry VIII. was the first of the English sovereigns who wore silk stockings.—*Edinburgh Cabinet Library, India.*

THE BLIND BEGGAR OF BAGNOLET.

Of late I met, at Bagnolet,
  A grey-beard with a constant smile;
Blind, from the wars he came away,
  And poor, he begs, and sings the while;
He turns his viol, to repeat,
" 'Tis Pleasure's children I entreat,
    Ah! give a trifle, give, I pray,—
And all are prompt to give and greet,—
    Ah! give a trifle, give, I pray,
    To the blind man of Bagnolet!"

A little damsel guides his way,
  And when a joyous crowd he nears,
At revel on the green, he'll say,
  " Like you, *I* danced in former years!
Young men, who press, with rapturous air,
The yielded hand of many a fair,
    Ah! give a trifle, give, I pray;
In youth, I did not oft despair,
    Ah! give a trifle, give, I pray,
    To the blind man of Bagnolet!"

Where revellers in the bower carouse,
  He says, " Remember, as ye pour,
That here the sunniest year allows
  No vintage-gleanings to the poor!
Glad souls, whose merry faces shine
O'er beakers filled with aged wine—
    Ah! give a trifle, give, I pray,
The sourest draught's a treat in mine.
    Ah! give a trifle, give, I pray,
    To the blind man of Bagnolet!"

Where, drinking deep, a soldier-band,
  In chorus shout their amorous lays,
And ring the glass from hand to hand,
  To pledge the feats of other days,—
He says, " By memory stirr'd to tears,
Enjoy what Friendship's charm endears—
    Ah! give a trifle, give, I pray,
Like you, *I* carried arms for years!
    Ah! give a trifle, give, I pray,
    To the blind man of Bagnolet!"

In fine, we're bound in truth to state,
  In quest of alms, 'tis said, he's seen
More rarely at the church's gate,
  Than near the tavern on the green:
With all whom Pleasure's garlands bind
The beggar and his rote I find,—
    " Ah! give a trifle, give, I pray,
Enjoyment makes the heart so kind!
    Ah! give a trifle, give, I pray,
    To the blind man of Bagnolet!"

Tait's Magazine.

---

* We take this from an old writer recommended by William Hazlitt.

SCRAPS.

FANCY versus REALITY.—Few people properly estimate the power of poetry. We eat, drink, and sleep, under illusions for which we are indebted to the fictions of poets. Who disputes the good cheer of old times? Who doubts the genial breath of spring? Who does not imagine it to be a fine thing to read books in the open air, or under a greenwood shade? Whose imagination does not kindle at the idea of beholding Rome, the Eternal City? Who does not revel in the idea of a vintage in the south of France? And yet the truth! Food was scarcer, and fare much harder in the good old times than the poorest of us would relish. Spring demands a great-coat, and carries consumption on its easterly wings. The leaves of your book can never be kept down in the open air, nor your attention confined—a garret and a chair and table are less poetical, but more practical. Old Rome, to the unprejudiced eye, is a mere heap of broken bricks and battered stones; and a vintage is a very dirty, dull, and laborious thing. Vines, too, which the untravelled Englishman, misled by poetical description, imagines to hang in graceful festoons on the laughing bank of a mountain side, or to invite him with their rich and tempting bunches from luxurious trellis-work, by the margin of gaily-flowing streamlets, by no means correspond with his expectations. The formal rows of dwarfish plants twining round a moderate pea-stick in a manner not half so picturesque as the raspberries of our gardens, he can scarcely believe to be the vineyards of Burgundy; and the grapes, little dirty dull bunches of large black currants, infinitely inferior both in size and flavour to those of our hot-houses, are tasted, and turned, and picked, and looked at, and tasted again with an air of unhappy incredulity. All travellers, one after the other, have gone with the same expectations, and have been successively disappointed; and yet poetry maintains her spell over our senses.

THE LAW OF LIBEL!—We remember once to have been present at a controversy on this subject between two very able arguers. One of the parties was proceeding to justify, with great ingenuity, the justice of the maxim, "The greater the truth the greater the libel," when the other sharply replied, in the form of an impromptu,

If the greater the truth be the greater the libel,
Permit me to ask what becomes of the Bible?

This was certainly a poser. No sophistry can extricate any one, professing a particle of belief in Christianity, from the meshes of this interrogatory couplet. When our Saviour called, and justly called, the Pharisees or Jewish saints of his day "vipers, whited sepulchres, generation of hell," and moreover accused them of leading the people astray by their gross perversions of the law of Moses, he was eminently guilty of "*scandalum magnatum*." He was manifestly a criminal by that law of libel which the canting hypocrites of the present day defend, on the score, forsooth, of "preserving the sacredness of private character!" Godwin, in his "Political Justice," has well remarked, that "the mind spontaneously shrinks from instituting a prosecution for libel;" and though we are of opinion that any one who can be clearly proved in court to have written or printed deliberate calumnies on private character, should be legally punished—since, without moral character, life should always be regarded as insupportable—we think that on that very account no person who may be *truly* arraigned by the press for individual or political profligacy, should be allowed to extract money from the editor of a paper, by the way of healing an incurable reputation with a golden plaster! We have been led into these remarks by the annexed observations from Chief Justice Doherty, on a recent libel prosecution between the proprietors of two Belfast journals, the *Guardian* and the *Northern Whig*. His Lordship said, "he had never understood that character *could* be freed from any imputation by a criminal prosecution for libel!" After this declaration from such an unexpected quarter, we have only to exclaim with the Indian Rajah, "What can *we* say more?"—*The Dublin Evening Freeman*.

AN ODD FISH.—In Larimer's Cyclopædia is recorded the following strange circumstance recorded by the old Chroniclers, and not questioned:—Some fishermen of Orford caught in their nets what the chroniclers call a fish, but which they describe as "resembling in shape a wild or savage man; he was naked, and in all his limbs and members resembling the right proportion of a man; he had hairs also on the usual parts of his body, albeit that the crown of his head was bald; his beard was long and rugged, and his breast hairy." The fishermen presented him to Sir Bartholomew de Glanville, who had then the keeping of Orford Castle. When meat was set before him, he greedily devoured it; and he ate fish, whether raw or boiled, only pressing in his hands those that were raw, till he had squeezed out the moisture. "He would get him to his couch at the setting of the sun, and rise again at the rising of the same. He would not, or could not, utter any speech; although, to try him, they hung him up by the heels, and miserably tormented him." His after-usage must have been exceedingly kind, and he must have been of a most forgiving temper not to resent this cruelty; for it seems that he was well reconciled to living ashore. One day they took him to the haven, and, enclosing a part of it with their strong nets, to prevent, as they thought, his escape, they let him take the water for his diversion. He presently dived under the nets, rose beyond them, sported about as if mocking at his keepers, and then, of his own accord, returned to them, and remained their guest about two months longer; then, being weary of a land life, he took an opportunity of stealing to sea. Strange as this story is, and incredible as it will be deemed by most readers, it is inserted here, because there is complete evidence that a similar circumstance occurred in the latter part of the seventeenth century, on the coast of Spain, with this remarkable difference, that the man who had there chosen an aquatic life, was recognised, and the history of his disappearance known at the place where he was supposed to have been drowned in bathing; he was carried back to his mother's house, remained there nine years, and then took again to the water.

CONVICTS.—The expenses of the convict establishment in England, from January 1 to June 30, 1832, was 34,168*l*. 18s. 2d., and the total earnings 23,287*l*. 9s. The expense of the Bermuda establishment for the half-year ending Dec. 31, 1831, was 9472*l*. 13s. 9d.; earnings of the convicts, 13,564*l*. 4s. On the first of Jan. 1832, there were 4139 prisoners on board the hulks in England, since which there have been received at the several depots 4712, including 85 from Bermuda. Of these 3877 have been transported to New South Wales and Van Diemen's Land; 120 to Bermuda; 600 discharged by pardon and expiration of sentence; 4 escaped; 262 died (of which 110 from cholera;) and 3898 remained in the hulks in England January 1833. For the last half-year the expenses in England were 34,811*l*. 9d.; the earnings 25,366*l*. 18s. 6d. For the first half-year of 1832, the expense at Bermuda was 8764*l*. 14s. 4d.; the earnings 13,043*l*.

CONTENTS OF NO. XLII.

Technicalities of the Duello	305
Letter from Italy	ib.
Notes on the Sandwich Islands	308
MEDICAL SELECTIONS, No. VI.—Dislocation	311
Ireland, a Poem	312
THE STORY-TELLER—What everybody says must be true	313
Curious Anecdote of Napoleon and Isabey the Painter	317
Family Dignity	ib.
Remarkable Account of a Battle between two Snakes	318
The Post Office Tax	ib.
A Fair and Happy Milkmaid	ib.
The Silk Manufacture	319
The Blind Beggar of Bagnolet	ib.
SCRAPS—Fancy versus Reality—The Law of Libel—An Odd Fish—Convicts	ib.

EDINBURGH: Printed by and for JOHN JOHNSTONE, 19, St. James' Square.—Published by JOHN ANDERSON, JUN., Bookseller, 55, North Bridge Street, Edinburgh; by JOHN MACLEOD, and ATKINSON & Co., Booksellers, Glasgow; and sold by all Booksellers and Venders of Cheap Periodicals

The Schoolmaster,
AND
EDINBURGH WEEKLY MAGAZINE.

CONDUCTED BY JOHN JOHNSTONE.

THE SCHOOLMASTER IS ABROAD.—LORD BROUGHAM.

No. 43—Vol. II.   SATURDAY, MAY 25, 1833.   Price Three-Halfpence

SLAVERY REPORT.

How is it that whenever people hear of a Parliamentary Commission, or a Committee of the House of Lords, the idea is immediately suggested of a piece of machinery set agoing to elude, or at least delay, a demand for justice? The humane demand that young children shall not be worked to death, or not be kept above ten hours out of the twenty-four, at hard duty in the unwholesome atmosphere of a factory, was, we should have thought, not so very unreasonable. The desire that some slender means of subsistence should be secured to the famishing, and consequently infuriated people of Ireland, from the soil which they cultivate, was nothing so wonderful in its nature that solemn inquiry must first be instituted into facts that stare every one in the face; but, above all, we had, in fifty years of horrible experience, acquired as much information on the evils and enormities of slavery, and the condition of the negro population in our Colonies, as might have sanctioned legislation on this subject, without much longer delay. But here again it was necessary or expedient to interpose a committee, and, to mend the matter, a committee of the Lords. The evidence elicited is precisely of the nature which previous experience led us to anticipate. It is reported in a goodly volume, containing many new, but no strange facts. Unhappily, the atrocities and horrors of the slave islands are but too familiarly known to be longer startling. The first witness examined was one equally entitled to take precedence from high rank, and the official station he had held for eighteen years, as Governor of Jamaica. This was the Duke of Manchester, who almost admits that he knows very little about the acts and events of his own long administration; but, at the same time, is perfectly confident that the treatment of the slaves is humane and excellent, their food and clothing abundant, their labours light and considerate, their cabins so many black paradises, and their situation altogether far superior to that of the greater part of the labourers of this country. This assurance, so often, and so pertinaciously and *impudently* made, if it be good for anything, furnishes the strongest argument for rebellion at home, that reason or manliness could listen to. If it be indeed true that the social condition of the workmen of Britain and Ireland is worse than that of the negroes in the West India Islands, why, then, by the memory of the Past, and the hopes of the Future, let them instantly arise and change and better it. Worse, more degraded, it cannot be. It will, however, take a few more witnesses, ducal and reverend, to persuade us of the truth of this favourite assertion of the planters; for, we grieve to say, there are witnesses in favour of slavery even among the Protestant Established Clergy. The Rev. J. Curtin of Antigua, who has nineteen slaves of his own, believes the negroes the happiest race in the world! their proprietors the most generous and civilized of mankind. We can spare room for only a few instances of the beatitudes of the slaves. What thinks the reader of the following suggestion for an improved whip? "Mr. Edmund Sharp thinks that switches, which *draw blood*, but do not *leave marks*," might be substituted for the cart-whip. This substitution of the frying-pan for the fire is strongly illustrative of plantation humanity. Against the worst accounts that we obtain of the slave states of America, and we do not conceive those lately given by Mr. Stewart one whit exaggerated, we have to set the fact that the slaves there increase their numbers; while, in our islands, with all the motives to maintain the breed given by the abolition of the direct traffic, and the difficulty of finding a supply, the negro population decreases. One of the witnesses, the Rev. John Barry,

"Is of opinion, that the slave population decreases from causes connected with slavery; one of these, he believes to be excessive punishment, which is sometimes so severe as to occasion death. He detailed several cases of oppression arising out of the power possessed by masters and overseers to oblige female slaves to submit to their desires. Once, when travelling, he was arrested by the shrieks of a woman, who was undergoing punishment with the cat. She was raised from the ground, on which she had been extended, on his coming up, and sent to her work; but she was unable to stand upright, so severely had she been punished. An old lady in Spanish Town, on being requested to allow one of her slaves to meet in religious society, replied, "I certainly cannot allow her to pray; she is young, and I must keep her to breed." William Taylor, Esq. states, that he has known eighteen lashes (inflicted on a young girl) cause a degree of suffering that was dreadful, and called for notice; but the law having allowed thirty-nine, the parties who sought redress were completely baffled. The overseer set them all at defiance, by simply pointing to the statute; the spirit of which, by-the-by, is evaded by a subsequent switching, as will appear from the following statement of the Reverend Peter Duncan.

"'A negro was laid down to be flogged almost under my window, when I resided at Morant Bay—at least at no great distance. His master went to the workhouse; he came back with the supervisor, and four workhouse negroes came along with the master and supervisor; two of them had whips. The negro man was laid down; two of the negroes held him down, one at the feet, and the other by the hands; and the negroes who had the whips went one to each side of the man thus laid down and stripped. I counted either thirty-nine or forty lashes; that was with a cart-whip—I mean what is called a cart-whip.' This was in 1821. 'The negro man received thirty-nine or forty lashes with the whip. I observed that they still kept him down, while the two men, the negroes who had been flogging him, went some little distance, and came back with tamarind switches—they are hard and flexible almost as wire—and then they began upon him again, to flog him with those tamarind switches. I did not count the strokes they gave with the switches; but to the best of my knowledge they were as many as had been given before. I observed, when the former lashes were inflicted, the slave never uttered any thing more than a deep groan; but, when he came to be flogged with the tamarind switches, he shrieked most dismally. His flesh was first lacerated with the whip, and then those small switches gave him great pain. I would observe this is a very common course in Jamaica; after they have received thirty-nine or forty lashes with the whip, then to use the tamarind switches; the common expression is, *beating out the bruised blood*.'"

"On being asked if he had ever known an instance of *a hole being dug to enable the driver to place a negro woman that was pregnant in the hole to flog her?*—Mr. Taylor replied, 'Yes; I was told that by the head driver of Papine; in one instance he had himself inflicted the punishment. The woman was pregnant, and he told his story very clearly. There was an excavation made, and she was placed in it, and he flogged her with a whip, and afterwards, Mr. Taylor thought, with the ebony switch. After giving them the thirty-nine, they switch them.'"

"The Reverend Peter Duncan says, In the year 1823 I knew of a slave driver having to flog *his mother*. In the year 1827 or 1828 I knew of a married negress having been flogged in the presence of her fellow slaves, and I believe her husband too. I asked her what had kept her from the chapel. She said, she had been severely flogged; she looked very ill; she was scarcely able to walk. I said 'What have you done?' She said she had done nothing, but her overseer had wished her to come and sleep with him. She said, 'No, Massa; I am a married woman, and I was married in the Church of England, on the Parade at Kingston, and I cannot do any thing of the kind.' Other negroes told me that they were present at a part of this conversation, and saw Ann flogged, avowedly for that reason, and among the rest her husband; she was very severely flogged; I was told she got about fifty lashes, and was then put into the stocks. *After she had remained in the stocks two or three days,* the overseer asked her whether she would come and sleep with him yet. She said, 'No; she was ready to do her master's duty, but could not do any thing of that sort.' He brought three or four others, and pointed her out by way of scorn, and said, 'This is a holy woman—this is a married woman; she cannot come and sleep with me, because she is a Methodist, and has been married in the Church of England.' There were a considerable number of negroes with her at the time I saw her, who were witnesses to the whole, or part of these facts. Though I do not at present recollect any other such flagrant instance of cruelty as that, it was no uncommon thing to me to hear that the young female slaves had been flogged because they would not comply with those wishes of their overseers."

Those who do not believe that the speediest end which can be put to this system is the best, would not believe, though one rose from the dead.

DR. BIRKBECK.[*]

THE father of Dr. Birkbeck was a merchant and banker at Settle, a small town in the West Riding of Yorkshire. His family was large, and he was the youngest son. He was born in the year 1776. He discovered, even before he went to school, a strong attachment to mechanical pursuits. A cotton-mill in the neighbourhood of Settle attracted his attention, and its machinery excited his admiration to such a degree, that he was anxious to be employed among the working children of the place, that he might constantly watch its movements, and render himself familiar with its more minute and complex parts. The shops in the town in which articles of mechanism were made, also drew his early attention, and rendered him ambitious to handle whatever tools lay within his reach for the same purpose. Of these things, in the childhood of ordinary men, we should take no notice; but in the early days of one so anxious, amidst the pressing duties of a learned profession, to promote the humbler pursuits of mechanical science among his ingenious and industrious countrymen, they claim at least a simple mention.

At eight years of age he was sent to a school at Newton, a village on the borders of Lancashire, at which he remained about six years, and where he acquired, in addition to the full amount of a common education, the rudiments of classical knowledge. At fourteen his father placed him under the care of a gentleman, whose instructions determined the scientific partialities and pursuits of young Birkbeck. This gentleman was Mr. Dawson, of Sedburg, well known as one of the first mathematicians of his day. In addition to the scientific advantages to be derived from such an instructor, young Birkbeck enjoyed considerable opportunities of acquiring classical knowledge, by a residence in the house of a learned relation, Mr. Foster, of Hebblethwaite-hall. It was at this auspicious period, and with these valuable resources opened before him, that our industrious subject laid the foundation of those mathematical and literary acquirements which he has since matured, and applied to such diffusive and beneficial purposes. It has often and justly been remarked, that they who are most eager for the early attainment of knowledge, are generally most ready in after life to communicate it; while, from the zeal of an individual to enlighten his fellow-creatures, may generally be inferred the earnestness of his own mind when young to acquire illumination and enlargement. These remarks were never more verified than in the example before us.

Already we can imagine those of our readers who know what the staple profession of Dr. Birkbeck is, to be anxious also to know how his mechanical and mathematical genius came to reconcile itself to the studies necessary to constitute a physician. We will not say "an enemy did this," because the Doctor himself always ranked the individual who caused it among his choicest friends. It was the late Dr. Garnett, who had also been a pupil of Mr. Dawson, and with whom young Birkbeck became intimately acquainted soon after his return to his native town. It is not easy in every place to turn the best mechanical genius and the most promising attainments in general science to a profitable account; nor is it desirable that young men, of the most commendable habits of research and industry, should be allowed to proceed in an irregular and indefinite course. Considerations like these might weigh with the friends of Mr. Birkbeck, and induce them to advise and him to adopt a profession somewhat at variance with the early bent of his mind.

But, however the purpose of making him a physician was first formed, it was confirmed and brought into action by the influence of Dr. Garnett. With him Mr. B. spent some time, during which the Doctor was engaged in the analysis of mineral waters, and in the publication of his "Treatise on the Waters of Harrowgate." From his house in that village, Mr B. proceeded to Leeds, for the purpose of acquiring a knowledge of pharmacy. Here he

[*] This gentleman may be termed the founder of the Mechanics' Institution; and to this circumstance, rather than the attainments in science by which he is distinguished, has he become an object of interest with the public.

remained a short time with Dr. Logan, during which he had frequent opportunities of witnessing the practice of that gentleman and Dr. Hird in the Leeds Infirmary. Mr. B. was little more than eighteen when he left Leeds for Edinburgh, whither he repaired to prosecute a plan of study, which Dr. Garnett had marked out, and strongly recommended. That judicious friend also advised him, on arriving in the Scottish metropolis, to unite himself with the Royal Medical Society, which he did as early as possible, much earlier than he was qualified to take any active share in the proceedings of that institution.

Deeming it likely to be of considerable advantage, Mr. Birkbeck, before he became of age, spent one whole winter in London. Science was still his object, not pleasure: upon the gaieties and fascinations of the great city he turned his back without difficulty and without regret; while his time was actively occupied in augmenting the knowledge likely to raise him to some eminence and utility in the profession he had chosen. For this purpose he entered the school of the late Dr. Baillie, and then commenced a friendship with that estimable man and excellent physician which terminated only with his life. Anatomy was his chief study in this school, and dissection consequently his chief practice; but from these he was able to secure intervals of his time, which he devoted chiefly to an attendance on the chemical lectures of Dr. Pearson, and the more celebrated lectures of Dr. Fordyce on the practice of physic.

His honours, in recompense of past industry, and the encouragement of future labours, now commenced. He returned to Edinburgh with more ardour in his purposes and pursuits than ever; and his fellow-students soon perceived that he had not visited London in vain. Jealous as the Scottish Professors were of the fame of their own city, they, too, were constrained to acknowledge the rapid advances which Mr. B. had made in his studies, and the propriety of his taking a more active part among their pupils than before. Such was the estimation in which his talents were held, that while only twenty, he was raised to the chairs of the Society for Natural History, and the Royal Medical Society, by the unanimous suffrage of their members.

In the summer of 1797, a new source of instruction and interest was opened before him, of which he availed himself with characteristic eagerness. We allude to Professor Robison's Lectures on Natural Philosophy. The renown of the lecturer as a profound mathematician, drew around him a large and respectable audience, among whom the Professor was particularly attracted and gratified by the attention of Mr. Birkbeck. In a very short time he requested his acceptance of a ticket of free admission, and was ever afterwards attached to him with the cordiality of a chief and devoted friend. Dr. John Thomson, Professor of Military Surgery in the University of Edinburgh, and Mr. John Allen, the celebrated lecturer on the Animal Economy, and now Master of Dulwich College, also became the warm friends of Mr. Birkbeck about this time, and contributed in no small degree to augment his stores of knowledge, and to strengthen his ardent mind for fresh pursuits of science and usefulness.

We have now reached the third winter of Mr Birkbeck's residence in Edinburgh, during which he acted as clinical clerk of Dr. Rutherford. This office at first appears too self-denying and retired to afford the least encouragement to a mind like Mr. B.'s; but he appears to have considered it one of the greatest advantages of his early life; not only as it brought him into intimate association and friendship with a man of such distinction and worth, but also as it afforded him a valuable opportunity of acquiring the practical knowledge of which he stood much in need. Added to these important advantages, the formation of the Academy of Physics, at this time, though it did not long continue, introduced him to the friendship of several individuals of celebrity; among whom were Drs. Brown and Leyden; the late Mr. Horner, Professor Wallace, and Henry Brougham. In another year, we find him elected, for the second time, President of the Royal Medical Society—a circumstance of rare occurrence, and therefore of the greater honour. At the close of the Session of this year, 1798, Mr. Birkbeck underwent the customary examination for taking his first medical degree, and was freely admitted to the honour, having previously delivered and published a Dissertation on Blood.

Very soon after his graduation, Dr. Birkbeck quitted Edinburgh for his native country: and on his way he spent a few days with a friend at Peebles. About this time his valuable friend Dr. Garnett was appointed Professor of Natural Philosophy in the Royal Institution of London, and lost no time in nominating him to succeed to the chair of a kindred office, which the Doctor had previously held at Glasgow. Intelligence to this effect reached him while at the house of his friend at Peebles; and though it could not fail to afford him high gratification, his first impressions were unfavourable to the acceptance of the proffered honour. He had, it seems, intended to enter on a course of medical practice, in some suitable and promising situation; while his early age appeared to restrain his anticipation of any important official appointment. Very little consideration on his part, and advice on the part of his friends, was, however, necessary to place the whole subject in directly a contrary light—to render his early age a reason for abstaining for the present from settled regular practice, and for availing himself of so favourable an opportunity as that which the removal of Dr. Garnett presented, to acquire additional preparatory knowledge. He therefore prepared his testimonials, secured the votes of a large number of the Glasgow Trustees; and, in a few weeks, commenced a course of lectures on Natural and Experimental Philosophy, and the more interesting parts of Chemistry.

This important change in his prospects and pursuits took place in the latter end of the year 1799, and contributed, perhaps, more than any other event in his life, to confirm his attachment to experiments in mechanical science.

Retiring for a short vacation to his native country, he thence issued a prospectus of the lectures he proposed delivering to the "Mechanics' Class" in the following session. When the business of the session commenced, he sent circular letters to the various manufactories in Glasgow, requesting lists of the more sober and intelligent workmen in each, with an offer of tickets of admission. The first effect of this liberal communication was an audience of seventy-five mechanics. The next lecture—so deep was the impression on their minds—was attended by two hundred. Three hundred were present at the third lecture, and five hundred at the fourth.

Several interesting circumstances connected with these lectures deserve special notice, as they illustrate the gratitude and intelligence of individuals of the audience, as well as the impressive and useful tendency of the lectures themselves. One attendant communicated to the lecturer a new plan for an air-pump—a second sent him a novel method for determining the sun's distance—and the whole united in the purchase of a handsome silver cup, on which an appropriate device and inscription were engraved, and which was delivered to Dr. Birkbeck, on the termination of the course, by Mr. Robertson, a mechanic of eminence, in the name of the whole body. During two more sessions the Doctor continued his lectures to this worthy class of men, and received from them testimonies of their gratitude and esteem, upon which he must often look with delight far exceeding the most costly gifts of those "who distribute from their abundance, not always from their hearts."

We next find Dr. Birkbeck lecturing to the inhabitants of Birmingham, Hull, and Liverpool.

These numerous professional engagements, involving, as they must have done, studies and labours which few have strength or spirits to undergo, did not entirely detach the thoughts of Dr. Birkbeck from the charms of society, and the anticipations of domestic bliss. In the spring of 1805, he married the youngest daughter of Sampson Lloyd, Esq. of Farm, near Birmingham. A union, every way gratifying to all parties concerned, of course turned the Doctor's attention to measures preparatory to settling in the practice of his chief profession. He settled in London under circumstances of great promise, which did not disappoint him.

His connexion enlarged to as wide an extent as his necessities or his wishes required, and his course would have been remarkably prosperous and gratifying—perhaps too much so for imperfect humanity—but for the unexpected and almost overwhelming loss of one of the best of wives. Mrs. Birkbeck died in a few days after the birth of a son, and in less than two years after her auspicious marriage. Ten years elapsed before the Doctor resolved upon supplying this affecting domestic vacancy: then, however, he took for his second wife the youngest daughter of Henry Gardner Esq. of Liverpool.

He had not been settled in London many months before he was elected one of the Presidents of the Physical Society of Guy's Hospital, an office to which he has been annually re-elected from that period to the present. In less than two years after his establishment in the metropolis, he was appointed Physician to the General Dispensary in Aldersgate Street, in which station he continues to the present day. His active mind was enabled for some time to add to these multiplied engagements considerable attention to the "London Medical Review," a work published quarterly, and extending to two volumes.

The London Institution was the next new scene of Dr. Birkbeck's labours. In 1820 he delighted and instructed prodigious assemblies by a course of lectures on Natural and Experimental Philosophy. Three years afterwards he delivered a shorter course on the History of the Atmosphere; and in the next year after that, a still shorter but remarkably interesting course on Terrestial Magnetism. The whole of these courses were delivered gratuitously.

The distance of London from Glasgow had prevented the frequent intercourse with his old friends in the latter city, which Dr. Birkbeck had wished to carry on; which led, in the course of years, to the suspicion that he and his labours were almost forgotten. In this, however, he judged wrongly of a class of men who have proved themselves not less grateful than teachable and industrious. A letter in the *Morning Chronicle* early in 1822, dated from Glasgow, convinced him of his error; and, in the following year, a letter from his successor, Doctor Ure, convinced him that he was more than remembered by his northern pupils. This letter communicated a series of resolutions much to the Doctor's honour and gratification. One of them determined on an address, to be signed by the members, and which was transmitted to the Doctor with the signatures of upwards of four hundred mechanics of the city.

Having this casually mentioned this admirable publication, it will be proper, especially as this is the appropriate place in our narative, to mention the influence which it had in first attracting the attention of Dr. Birkbeck to the mechanics of London, and at length deciding him upon promoting the formation of the London Mechanics' Institution. Of this society Dr. Birkbeck has, from the first, been President—actually as well as nominally President; and should Divine Providence spare his life a few years longer, he will doubtless see tokens of success resulting from his unwearied labours far surpassing the anticipations even of his own ardent and sanguine spirit.

TURKISH LADIES.—Singular as it may appear to those who imagine there is no wisdom except in books, the Turkish ladies are remarkable for the strength and acuteness of their understandings, for their sagacity; and for that scrupulous delicacy which makes the want of education disappear. Their air and manner are noble, and their conversation full of charms. Such is the uniform testimony of those Christian ladies who have visited the harems; and an author, well entitled to credit, remarks in corroboration—"I have myself been in the company of ladies of all conditions, at the houses of the ministers of government, noblemen and magistrates; and I have been surprised at the purity of their language, the easy flow of their elocution, the refinement and delicacy of their thoughts, and the grace and simplicity visible in their whole conversation." Polygamy, the bugbear which terrifies Europeans, is not common in Turkey. Few Mohammedans have two wives; and four, the number permitted by law, are scarcely ever seen in the same mansion.

THE AUTOBIOGRAPHY OF A GREENWICH OUT-PENSIONER.

LIKE the godess Venus, I am extra parokial in my birth, as I first sea lite at sea one dark nite in the Bay of Biskey, lat. 45° 12'; nor., long 5° 16' 32" wes from Lunnun. I was suckled at Brest, and larned redin an riting off my ole granmother, who kep a smal skool at Wapping, where I got many a good wapping myself. Ask for speling I never *cud doo it*, for a spel seamed to hang uver me; and in regard of somes, I was cast down, wenevar I tried to cast up.

As soon as I was ole anuf I run away from my granmother, and tuk a trip to Newcassle in the Lilly wite, a wether befen ole colier; but I had to walk all the way bak, askin charity off every body I met, who told me if ide go an throw myself on my parish, I shoud get releaf direcly—wich was a tail, alass, too true! When my granmother first see me she tuk me for a sperret; but as soon as she fond I wus nothing but flesh and blud (and rite hwel ov that) she set too and licked me with her Cain as long as she was Able. I found she had dun skool an tuk to sowing, from wich she reaped verry litel arvest. We lived pretty comfortable for some time, tho I wus alwys ancorin after the sea, and got menny a good box on the hear for swimin my spoon in my tea, or sailing my new hat on the duk pond.

As war soon broke out in Ameryca, I determined to go and defend my country in furren parts, and aplied for a birth aboard the Charity, tho not first-rate. The captain said he liked my looks, and ast me if I wood stand fire, to wich I said I cood, uponwich he appointed me Cook's assistant, and told me to mind and not capsize the buter boat. As I hod no objeckshuns to larn navygashun in all its branshes, in case of being cast on a disolvate iland, and hopin to have a opertunity of signalising myself wen we cum among the niggers, I made no words, but said I wood go round the world with Cook; tho, to confess, if it had been left to me, I should never have chose pethooks in preference to hangers. Nothink partickler ocurd during the passage xept one day Cook skalded his foot verry bad, by putin his petty toes splash into a sanspan of bilin water. Wen we come to Amerryca, in cours I was verry much sirprised; indeed it was quite a New World to me, and so larg that Great briton is quite smal in comparysen. The niggers are funny chaps, and often set me a niggerin agen my wil. As for the happyriginals, as the captin caled em, we never got near anuf; but I see an old sailer as had been took prisoner fourteen ears among the fethered tribes, and he says they are sad skiny chaps to look at, as they always *Hide* their nakedness with the skins of wild whimails.

But I am not goin to rite the whole of my boyegraphy, with all the partickler events as they ocured eventually throw my life, tho I cood fil a hole log book with adventures such as noddy wood beleave to be in a marinars compass. I shall say nothink of the strange countrys I have seen, where the fish are covered with fethers the same as birds are bear, and fli wislinin about, and roost in branshes of trees made ov stone, all groin under water. Nor I when mens hun the six ole mer maids as I seened afternoon drinkin tea ov china, sweatened with moist sugar; nor the birds of Paradice flighin about a desert iland in the Sue sea, and the too naked figgers in the same place, wich I suppose was *A dam* and *Heave*. Nayther shal I so much as hint about the wonders I see in the *Nor*, were avry day in the weak is six months long, and sunshine all the while, wich I use to think it was nothink but moonshine. But I can't help notising one thing, wich is that among all the strang and savage nashuns I have seen, not one ov em speak inglish but all frensh. Allso about the Antippordese, wich I dount beleave there is no such peple; for wen I was at Hamam they told me they was in New Zeland, and wen I was in New Zeland they told me they was in Ingland. Also in Chines Tartary they said they was in Pattagony, and wen I ast about em in Pattagony they told me they was in Chines Tartary. So that I am come to this conclusion, I dont beleave they arnt no where at all.

likewise the vast number of pickle herrins I have seen swimin about, so thick as to make shole water in the deepest parts of the oshun. Nor furthermore, of Wales, both North and South, with bones so long and so thik as wood do to put in the stays of a ship; nor wat I observed in Greenland were evry think is quite wite; nor in the Wite sea, wich is quite green. Allso the same or all unnatural fenominous, such as water spouts, red snow, flighin Duchmen, wich our captin always said was nothink but sperrets and water; in addition to wich, I have often ear speak ov the iland off our one coast where the arms ov the natives is nothink but legs.

I shall now beg leaf to give my genteel reder a set down in the midel of the Paysifick oshun, in the year anno domino 79. Evry body must remember the takein of the seven gunboats off Dominnica, in wich I first signalised myself, being then cockswain on bord the George, a 74, which I had entered in 75. Soon after this, as we was crewsin off the coat of Amerryca, we fell in with a frensh line a battle, to wich we gey chase, and had a verry long run. We several times like to Mist her on account of the Fog; dublin Cape Horn, on wich old god Holeas was blowing with all his mite; and running out into the Pasyfick determined for bloody war. At last she brought too, and showed us har teeth; upon wich we returned the compliment, and gave her a taste of our guns, wich, as we fight for freedom, we loaded with chain shot. The fire was hot, as is usually the case when you are too nere, and numbers of the enemy was seen lyin ded in their shrouds, wile many of our own men was obliged to lay down their harms, rite and left, and others hadent a leg to stand on. We was now yard harm and yard harm, broadsite to broadsite, no quarters bein giving; but, the both kep fitin like furies, nayther of us seemed inclined to strike. Our stud sales stud a verry litel wile, and our stay sales dident stay much longer. In fact, all our sales were under distress of rents; our main top was flotin on the top of the main, and our missen mast was missen soon after. But there was one consolashon in all our trouble—the enemy was wors off than us. Graplin hiarns was now fixt by both partys, and no sooner was the links aplied to the vessels than they was discovered to be on fire. Our force at this time was verry weak, not being above forty strong, and the guns were verry warm in the caus that they wood no longer wait for the word of command, but went off afore they were pinted. Our prospecs at this moment was sublime in the extream, the smoke bein so thik that you coodent see your hand before you, and I only wish that Mister Stand feald (if he cud Stand fire) had been there with his paint cans, &c., to make a drawn batel of it, or mister Dibdin to rite a song about it, afore that took place wich I am goin to relate.

Whiz—fiz—whack—crack—bang—whang—flash—crash—splash—dash! This is the only idear I can giv you of the seen that felowd, wich was the too ships blowin one another up ski hi, ane leaving only me and another chap quite non cumpass, without any binicle to steer by, or any vessel to steer. I soon found my companion was French bilt, and accordin I hailed him in his own langwidge, wich proved after to be a terrible oth, upon which mountseer looked as bitter as Gaul, and returned my bad langwidge in verry good Inglish. This I considered as a signal for acshun, and tho I wood willingly have pleded a prior ingagement, I cood not submit to have it gave out that I had gave in; so, pickin up a spar, a large colecshon of wich was lying round, and the enemy doin the same, we set too sparin as hard as we cood. Mountseer had the best of it at first, as he was in a biger pashun than me, but as soon as he feeh me a good nock on the hed, my blud was up directly; upon wich I imediately gave him a nock over, wich soon made him neck under. I forgot to say how we kep afloat all this time, wich was threw part ov the George rex, my meemate having got hold ov a companion, and me being mounted on the top ov a wale. I had no sooner scouted my prisloner by tighing his hans behind him, than I dident no what to do with him; but as fate wood have it, a vessel just then have in site, wich proved to be Inglish, takein in water at June Ferdinando, and having herd reports ov our ingagement, come out to assist us. In coury, they soon tuk us on bord, an furnished us with grog and fresh regin, being both verry wet an verry dri.

My redir, I dar say, is perty wel tird by this—if he arnt I am, an consequenshaley shal put off the futur for the present: hopein in rememberance ov my poor old granmother, he will excuse my bad Inglish and worse Polish. If he wants to no more, I beg leaf to say I now keep the Bear at Greenwich; where, if he will do me the honer to cum, I hope he wil not fal out with my bruin.—*Metropolitan.*

CURIOUS EXPERIMENT ON A RATTLESNAKE

The following curious facts respecting the rattlesnake are from a letter of Judge Samuel Woodruff, to Professor Silliman, in the last number of the *American Journal of Science.* Some time in the month of August, I went with Mr. T. Kirtland and Dr. C. Dutton, then residing at Poland, to the Mahoning, for the purpose of shooting deer, at a place where they were in the habit of coming to the river, to feed on the moss attached to the stones in the shoal water. We took our watch station on an elevated part of the bank, fifteen or twenty yards from the edge of the water. About an hour after we commenced our watch, instead of a deer we discovered a rattlesnake, which, as it appeared, had left his den, in the rocks beneath us, and was advancing across a smooth, narrow sand beach towards the water. Upon hearing our voices, or from some other cause, he stopped, and lay stretched out with his head near the water. It occurred to me that an opportunity now offered to try the virtues of the white-ash leaves. Requesting the gentlemen to keep in my absence a watch over our object, I went immediately in search of the leaves, and on a piece of low ground, thirty or forty rods back from the river, I soon found, and by the aid of my hunting knife, procured a small white-ash sapling, eight or ten feet in length; and with a view to make the experiment more satisfactory, I cut another sapling of the sugar maple, and with these *wands* returned to the scene of action. In order to cut off a retreat to his den, I approached the snake in his rear. As soon as I came within about seven or eight feet of him, he quickly threw his body into a coil, elevated his head eight or ten inches, and brandishing his tongue, "gave note of preparation" for combat. I first presented him the white ash, placing the leaves upon his body. He instantly dropped his head to the ground, unfolded his coil, rolled over upon his back, writhed and twisted his whole body into every form but that of a coil, and appeared to be in great anguish. Satisfied with the trial thus far made, I laid by the white ash. The rattlesnake immediately righted, and placed himself in the same menacing attitude as before described. I now presented him the sugar maple. He lanced in a moment, striking his head into a tuft of the leaves, "with all the malice of the under fiends," and the next moment coiled and lanced again, darting his whole length at each effort with the swiftness of an arrow. After repeating this several times, I again changed his *fare,* and presented him the white ash. He immediately *doused his peak,* stretched himself on his back in the same manner as at first application. It was then proposed to try what effect might be produced upon his temper and courage by a little flogging with the white ash. This was administered; but instead of arousing him to resentment, it served only to increase his troubles. As the flogging grew more severe, the snake frequently struck his head into the sand as far as he could thrust it, seeming desirous to bore his way into the earth and rid himself of his unwelcome visiters. Being now convinced that the experiment was a satisfactory one, and fairly conducted on both sides, we deemed it unnecessary to take his life after he had contributed so much to gratify our curiosity; and so we took our leave of the rattlesnake, with feelings as friendly at least as those with which we commenced our acquaintance with him, and left him to return at leisure to his den.

THE WALHAM WAG.
(From the Diary of a Joke-Hunter.)

* * INQUIRED for the queerest coachman. Mat said that Walham Jem was the rummest kiddy on the road, barring Duck-nosed Dick. "But the latter warment," added Mat, "arn't so conversable: that's Jem a-coming up—he with the blue muzzle and white hat, what looks so wicked—him there what's all clothes and hands—barring his face. I had occasion to tip him a dig in the ogle t'other day, and you see, master, he an't struck my colours yet."

Jem now approached—"Fulham, Sir?" said he, "a box vacant." Agreed to ride by his side, and in rather more than ten minutes we started. Over the stones conversation was out of the question, but the moment we got on the road we had a "talk" to the following effect:—

"Bad black eye that of your's, Jem—how did you get it?"—"I was trying to wink, Sir."—"Your near horse is lame in the off fore-foot, Jem."—"High grand-actioned horse that! Lamed himself last night by striking his toe against his upper teeth. Been a charger!"—"The other's lame, too."—"Yes; he trod upon a *frog*—poor thing!"—"How he whistles!"—"Ah: he's invaluable, Sir. Got a *thrush* in each foot."—"What time will you reach Fulham?"—"I shall draw the *boot* of my wehicle on the *foot* of the bridge precisely at eleven."—"Why, you're a punster, I perceive!"—"No; I'am a Chelseaman—birth, parentage, and education."—"Write a good hand?"—"Not at all—I was born a *pen-shunner*—close by the college; but for all that I can make my mark to a receipt for any amount."

"Twig this here old gentleman—'Fulham, Sir?'—I only says that to plague him. He's a rare-admiral. *Rear* indeed, and can't ride a rocking horse! He won't travel with me."—"How have you offended him?"—"Why, one night when he got to his door, being a mighty uppish sort of a cove, he would'nt lean on my arm; which the step was broken, and down he fell flat upon the porch.—'Why, admiral,' says I, 'you've *struck your flag!'"*—"So you lost your passenger by your joke?"—"Joke—I can't see no joke in it."—"Then you don't know what a joke is."—"Don't I? Only look at this lady with a little boy in her arms, what's a coming—now, this is what I calls a joke.—'Beg your pardon, Ma'am, there's the child's shoe—on it's foot!' Did you twig how flustrated she was—and how she looked about her; and how, when I said 'on it's foot,' she half frowned, half laughed, and went off blushing, giggling, and biting her lip, and away I went laughing like Winkin?"

"Who was Winkin, Jem?"—"A printer's apprentice, what run away with little 'Gin and Bitters,' Mather Waterton's bar-maid at the Red Cow. There goes Miss Evelina Thingumbob—the female swell—she's cut me for a downright good honest akshun. In course, Sir, you can't be so hignorant as not to know that *bustle* is *tin*, which means money. Very well. One day I sets her down at the bottom of Bond Street, and arter she'd paid me—while I was putting up the steps—I sees a farthing on the flags; so thinking in course it was her property, I runs arter her, calling out, ' Hallo, Ma'am—you've dropped your *bustle!'* Wi' that she puts down one hand just under her waist in front, and t'other like lightning behind, where, in some out-and-out swell ladies, there's an opening to the pocket,—which, what with nutmegs, nutmeg graters, the cupboard keys, and so forth, makes them stick out so in that department. 'Good God!' says she, 'my bustle!' and she'd have fainted if I had'nt showed her the farthing. You'd hardly believe it, may be; but as sure as I'm here sitting, she slapped my face and won't never ride wi' me since."

"Allow me to tell you that it was a joke, Jem."—"No such thing, Sir, axing your pardon: this is a joke, as you shall see. There's Mr. Burchell's man, and Colonel MacLeod's man, both blackey-moors, standing at ther masters' garden gates, and looking down the road as if they were awaiting for the milkman or summat, while all the time the lazy wagabones is doing nothing but dawdling to see my coach pass. Now you'll please to notice how I'll make 'em front about. The nearest, this here chap to the left, is Mr. Burchell's Pompey. 'I say, Inky-face.' Did you see how he turned? Now for the other. 'Hollo! Alabaster, what's lignum whitey?' There, he knows his name, because for why; Alabaster and Inky-face is all one, black and white being the same thing. Some people call me 'Gipsey,' because I'm brownish; and others know me by the name of 'Lilly white,' for the same reason."

"But dash my rags, if here an't some o' the royal family; notice the coachman." This gentleman was *worthy of* notice; his livery-coat was intensely scarlet, his complexion crimson, his eye lurid and bloodshot. My companion halloed to him in stentorian tones as the two vehicles passed each other. "Why, coachee, you look as if you had been put in a smith's forge, and blowed red-hot."

"Jem, I must ride with you again; set me down at the top of Fulham town." "Thank ye, Sir; but afore we reaches the corner, talking of jokes, I'll make bold to tell you the best joke I knows. One night, 'twas my last journey, I'd just stepped into Jerman Street to get a go of Kennet ale to wash down my wittles, while my wehicle was at the cellar, when, as I was coming back, I puts up my foot on a stone what propt a post in St. James's Street, to tie my shoe. Well, it so happened, that just then, some nobleman, who'd lost all he had, as I should think, at one of the club-houses, comes along—choke full of fury, without having nobody to abuse—when he sees me bent double with my back towards him. So—mind me, we'd no acquaintance, it was the first time we met—he takes a bit of a run, and gives me a kick behind what sends me bang into the middle of the road, saying, says he, 'D—n you! you're *always* tying that shoe !'—"Well! and what did you do?"—"I laughed fit to split my sides; for thinks I, he's lost his *tin*; and supposing I'd been regularly *cleaned out* at a club-house, and set eyes on a coachman, what I'd never seen afore, a-tying his shoe under a lamp-post, should have made so free as to kick him into the middle of the road, saying, says I, 'D—n you, you're *always* tying that shoe of your's.' —Now that to my fancy, is a joke."—*Monthly Magazine.*

EPICEDIUM.

WRITTEN ON THE DEATH OF A SISTER.[*]

By James Lawson.

Gone, gone! dead and gone!
To the churchyard dank and lone.
It seems to me as yesterday
That she, who now is silent clay,
  Was in heart the lightest,
  And in eye the brightest;
  Was in step the fleetest,
  And in voice the sweetest;
Health was upon her young cheek blooming,
And flowers were in her path perfuming;
Her presence was a dream of bliss,
Her smile a ray of loveliness,
The Graces held with her their reign,
While pleasure sported in the train,
And all of bright, and pure, and fair,
To praise or prize was mingled there.
Where now are music, mirth, and flowers?
And where the dearest one of ours?
  Gone, gone! dead and gone!
  To the churchyard dank and lone.

Although it was as yesterday,
'Twas in my own loved isle, away
A thousand leagues beyond the sea,
That she appeared all this to me—
I did not hear her latest sigh,
Nor soothed a pang, nor closed an eye;
Received no blessing, heard no prayer,
Saw not her grave, nor mourners there

---

[*] These tender and affecting verses were written in the United States, where the author is the editor of a newspaper, and transmitted to "HOME."

Unconscious I of grief or fear,
Of corse or knell, or pall or bier—
Of mourners' grief, and friends' despair—
I could not know—I was not there.
The stars that hid their fires from them,
To me decked nature's diadem;
Each cherished thing beneath their light
Was fair and lovely to my sight:
But soon, too soon, the tidings came,
For ear to hear, or lip to name—
For where was she, who, by my side,
Had bloomed, with me and mine the pride?

 Gone, gone! dead and gone!
 To the churchyard, dank and lone.

They tell how gently passed her breath,
How beautiful she lay in death;
That while around her all were weeping,
They could not deem but she was sleeping;
Yet soon the cold, the pallid look
And form, her lovely features took:
The fixed eye, the marble brow,
The lips so pale and breathless now;
All on their hearts were sadly stealing,
To wake the lone and dreary feeling,
That she, so long and dearly cherished,
Had, like the summer roses perished.
As perfume oft survives the flowers,
Remembrance only lives of ours—

 Gone, gone! dead and gone!
 To the churchyard, dank and lone.

Now soon the gentle zephyrs winging,
On ladened pinions perfume bringing,
Will waft again the breath of flowers,
And fragrancy of summer bowers;
And soon will blithe-voiced maidens stray
By ripened meads of wave-like hay;
Soon by the fields of brairding grain
The husbandman will smile again;
Soon will the shepherd's pipe prevail,
To glad his flocks on hill and dale;
And soon the note of mavis sounding,
When morn o'er eastern hill is bounding;
Soon will awake the blackbird's song,
When twilight would the day prolong;
Soon all that grow, or live, or breathe,
Will smile the balmy skies beneath;
But, though come zephyrs, songs, and flowers,
O, where will be the pride of ours?

 Gone, gone! dead and gone;
 To the church-yard, dank and lone.

VULGAR IDEA OF THE FRENCH REVOLUTION.—There is nothing more disgraceful to Englishmen than their utter ignorance, not only of the causes and effects, but of the very events, the story, of the French Revolution. With the majority of them, even of those among them who read and think, the conception they have of that great event is all comprehended in a dim but horrible vision of mobs, and massacres, and revolutionary tribunals, and guillotines, and fishwomen, and heads carried on pikes, *noyades*, and *fusillades*, and one Robespierre, a most sanguinary monster. What the Tory prints choose to tell them of this most interesting period in modern history, so much they know, and nothing more; that is, enough to raise in their minds an intense yet indefinite horror of French reforms and reformers. *Now*, however, when they have ceased to tremble for themselves, and to start from their sleep at the terrific idea of the landing of French jacobins, or a rising of English ones, to confiscate their property and cut their throats, they can perhaps bear to look at the subject without horror; and we exhort them to buy and read Mignet's work, that they may know in what light the Revolution is regarded by the nation which saw and felt it, which endured its evils, and is now enjoying its benefits.—*Westminster Review, No. X.*

SKILL OF HORSE JOCKEYS.

GREAT interests are committed to the skill, and *honour* of Jockeys. The duties of an eminent counsel are, in a pecuniary view, rarely of more importance. Tens of thousands, and the reputation of racers and their owners, depend upon their knowledge, presence of mind and resource. "It is," says a competent authority, "the first duty of a Jockey to win, and not *to do more than win.*"—Were he to win with apparent ease, this would prove a bar in the way of new bets, and lessen the chances of profit of his employer. This we imagine the main reason why he must not do more than win. Half a neck is sufficient where his antagonist is exhausted, and as much judgment is shown in avoiding useless exertion as in making that which is sufficient. The best and most expert jockeys, such as Robinson and Chifney, avoid the use of the whip, if possible. Boys more readily resort to it, and thereby sometimes lose a race, that might otherwise have been won. When a race horse is in the fullest exercise of his power, and doing his best, the blow of a whip will sometimes make him wince and shrink—he will, as it were, tuck up his flanks to escape from the blow, and, in raising his legs higher up, lose ground instead of stretching himself forth over a larger surface. In this way considerable space may be lost, when nothing is wanting but a quiet steady hand, and a forbearance from the use of the whip. A curious example of this occurred a few years ago at Doncaster, in the celebrated race between Matilda and Mameluke. The latter was of a hot and violent temper, and being irritated by several false starts, not only lost considerable ground, but a great deal of his strength, at the outset of the race. Robinson was riding Matilda, and saw Chifney on Mameluke pass every horse in succession, till he came up with Matilda. At that moment he calculated Mameluke's strength with such nicety, that he was convinced he could not maintain the effort he was then making.—He permitted Chifney, therefore, to reach him, and even to be a little ahead of him, and so far from whipping Matilda, actually gave her a kind of check. That check, that slightest imaginable pull, strengthened Matilda, and, by assisting her to draw her breath, enabled her to give those tremendous springs by which she recovered her ground, headed Mameluke, and won the race for her owner, Mr. Petrie. It was in this race that a Scotch gentleman, who had won seventeen thousand pounds by the issue, went up to Robinson in the joy of the moment, and gave him a thousand pounds as a present. Gully, the owner of Mameluke, is said to have lost forty thousand pounds on the occasion, every sixpence of which was punctually and honourably paid. Mr. Gully maintained a fair character till he got into the "Honourable House," and it is to be expected that he may retain it there.

THE DUELLO.—The following remarks are a suitable sequence to the observation upon the *duello* in the last number of this publication. They were made by Mr. Guthrie in his clinical lecture at the Westminister Hospital,—" I do not know," he said, "whether it is advisable to recommend, with *Sir Lucius O' Trigger* in *The Rivals*, that gentlemen should stand fair to the front, in duelling, and be shot clean through one side of the body, instead of making as small as possible an edge, by standing sideways, and running the risk of being certainly killed by the ball penetrating both sides; but this I do know, that there is neither charity nor humanity in the manner of choosing the pistols at present adopted. The balls are so small, that the hole they make is always a source of inconvenience in the cure; and the quantity of powder is also so small, that it will not send a ball clean through a moderately thick gentleman; it therefore sticks in some place where it should not, to the extreme disadvantage of the patient, and to the great annoyance of the surgeon. These things really should be altered, with the present diffusion of knowledge."

ELEMENTS OF THOUGHT.

THE BRITISH CONSTITUTION.

THE theory of the constitution, in the most important particulars, is a satire on the practice. The theory provides the responsibility of ministers as a check to the execution of ill designs; but in reality we behold the basest of the tribe retreat from the ruin of their country, loaded with honour and with spoils. Theory tells us the Parliament is free and independent; experience will correct the mistake by showing its subservience to the crown. We learn, from the first, that the Legislature is chosen by the unbiassed voice of all who can be supposed to have a will of their own; we learn, from the last, the pretended electors are but a handful of the people, who are never less at their own disposal than in the business of election. The theory holds out equal benefits to all, and equal liberty, without any other distinction than that of a good or bad subject: its practice brands with prescription and disgrace a numerous class of inhabitants on account of their religion. In theory, the several orders of the State are a check on each other; but corruption has oiled the wheels of that machinery, harmonized its motions, and enabled it to bear, with united pressure, on the happiness of the people.—*Hall of Leicester.*

TRUTH, PROGRESSION OF OPINION.

IF truth were in all its characters well defined, and i power were unrestricted, there would then be no room for opinion. The perfect delineation of truth, when once viewed, would be perfectly reflected to the mind, and knowledge, therefore, would be accurate. But to man, in this his first and lower state of being, the mysteries of eternal truth are but partially unveiled; and the capacity to comprehend what is revealed is neither perfect, nor even in its imperfect state, fully or at once bestowed. For not only is there a cloud mercifully interposed to obscure the lustre of that glory, whose brightness would consume the intellectual sight, but there are also mists of earthly error, which confuse and distort the view of what we are permitted to behold. The faculties, too, by which we are enabled to study and learn the lineaments of truth, are themselves capable of increase, and subject to diminution. Knowledge is to be gained by gradual acquirement, and power increased by continued exercise. And as this state of progression cannot, while life endures, arrive at an impassible limit, it follows that our conceptions will be continually undergoing modification, and that, if we are sincere and earnest in our inquiries, doubt and error will gradually disappear; that fresh and purer light will irradiate the mind; that we shall be daily rejoicing in the opening beauties of a less limited intellectual prospect, and, by tracing the analogies more fully displayed in this wider and clearer view, and beholding the order and the harmony that reign in all the words and works of Him who is Truth itself, shall pass, with rapidly-increasing flight, from doubt and opinion, to faith and knowledge, on whose untiring pinions we shall at last be borne to perfect and unclouded wisdom.

FREEDOM OF THE PRESS.

THE liberty of the press is the true measure of the liberty of the people. The one cannot be attacked without injury to the other. Our thoughts ought to be perfectly free; to bridle them, or stifle them in their sanctuary, is the crime of lese humanity. What can I call my own, if my thoughts are not mine?—*Mercier.*

COUNT OXENSTIERN, the Chancellor of Sweden, was a person of the first quality, rank, and abilities, in his own country, and whose share and success not only in the chief ministry of affairs there, but in the greatest negotiations of Europe, during his time, rendered him no less considerable abroad. After all his knowledge and honours, being visited, in his retreat from public business, by Commissioner Whitlock, our ambassador to Queen Christina, at the close of their conversation, he said to the ambassador:—

"I, Sir, have seen much, and enjoyed much of this world; but I never knew how to live till now. I thank my good God, who has given me time to know *Him* and likewise *myself.* All the comfort I take, and which is more than the whole world can give, is the knowledge of God's love in my heart, and reading of this Blessed Book,"—laying his hand on the Bible.—"You are now, Sir," (continued he) "in the prime of your age, and vigour, and in great favour and business; but this will all leave you, and you will one day, better understand and relish what I say to you. Then you will find that there is more wisdom, truth, comfort, and pleasure, in retiring and turning your heart from the world, in the good spirit of God, and in reading His Sacred Word, than in all the courts and all the favours of princes.

SUNDAY AMUSEMENTS.—In an old magazine, printed about the year 1789, the writer, speaking of the persons whose habit it was to resort to the various tea-gardens near London, on a Sunday, calculates them to amount to 200,000. Of these, he considers that not one would go away without having spent half-a-crown, and, consequently, the sum of L.25,000 would have been spent in the course of the day: twenty-five thousand multiplied by the number of Sundays in a year, gives, as the annual consumption of that day of rest, the immense sum of L.1,300,000. The writer calculates the returning situation of these persons as follows:—Sober, 50,000; in high glee, 90,000; drunkish, 30,000; staggering tipsy, 10,000; muzzy, 15,000; dead drunk, 5,000.—Total, 200,000.

ANECDOTE OF GALT.—It is very well known among the friends of this amusing writer, that he has availed himself, in some of his graphic delineations of Scottish character, of many little incidents which have occurred within his own domestic circle—and, in particular, that he has been greatly indebted for a number of the choicest idioms, peculiar to the language used by a certain class in Scotland, to his mother, who is considered among her neighbours as a "gaucy, auld farrand, gash gudewife." Mrs. Galt who, no doubt, feels much pride of heart on account of the literary character of her son, is nevertheless, at times, piqued when she finds allusions made, and phrases used, the origin of which she is too familiar with not to know the source from whence they are derived. On a visit which our author some time ago paid to the place of his nativity, the old lady thought proper to take him to task for certain liberties which she conceived he had taken with matters connected with the family, and after administering what she, no doubt, considered to be a very becoming reprimand—she took down from a cupboard a little, old fashioned, antique-looking teapot, with whose appearance she knew her son had been intimately acquainted since his childhood, and thus addressed him—"Now, John Galt, I've just been telling ye that you've middled a great deal owre muckle wi' the things about this house; and there's a wee tea pat that you've seen as often as there's teeth in your head, and as I hae it a great respect for the bit pat, I'm just gawn to be sa plain as I am pleasant wi' ye, and tell ye, that if ye say a single word about the pat, in ony o' your books, ye maun expect to get ony thing in this house when ye come back, but a pouket lug, and that I'll no craw in youth ony o men." John has, as yet, been "biddable," and said nothing about the "bit pat."

THE STORY-TELLER.

THE SEVEN DAUGHTERS OF THE RECTOR OF EPWORTH.

In a former number of the *Schoolmaster* we gave some account of the mother of John and Charles Wesley, and of a family that may be truly termed *illustrious*. To-day we follow up that notice by a sketch of the various, and, in some respects, singular fortunes of the daughters, educated upon that strict system which Mrs. Wesley details in the letter to her son, John, the founder of Methodism, for which we refer to page 69, of the present volume. Our history is principally taken from Dove's late excellent Memoir of the Wesley family.

EMILIA, afterwards Mrs. Harper, appears to have been the eldest of the seven surviving daughters of the Rector of Epworth. She is reported to have been the favourite of her mother, (though some accounts state this of *Patty*,) and to have had good strong sense, much wit, a prodigious memory, and a talent for poetry. She was a good classical scholar, and wrote a beautiful hand. She married an apothecary at Epworth, of the name of Harper, who left her a young widow. What proportion the intellect of Mr. Harper bore to that of his wife, we know not; but in politics they were ill suited, as he was a violent Whig, and she an unbending Tory.

It appears from the education given to Miss Emilia, and some of her other sisters, that their parents designed them for governesses. About the year 1730, Emilia became a teacher at the boarding school of a Mrs. Taylor, in Lincoln, where, though she had the whole care of the school, she was not well-used, and worse paid. Having borne this usage as long as reason would dictate forbearance, she laid the case before her brothers, with a resolution to begin a school on her own account at Gainsborough. She had their approbation, gave Mrs. Taylor warning, and went to Gainsborough, where she continued at least till 1735, as she was there at the time of her father's death. With her Mrs. Wesley appears to have sojourned a while, before she went to live with her sons John and Charles; where, free from cares and worldly anxieties, with which she had long been unavoidably encumbered, she spent the evening of her life in comparative ease and comfort. We learn several particulars respecting Mrs. Harper from a letter she wrote to her brother John, when she had resolved upon going to Gainsborough.

"DEAR BROTHER,

"Your last letter comforted and settled my mind wonderfully. O! continue to talk to me of the reasonableness of resignation to the Divine Will, to enable me to bear cheerfully the ills of life, the lot appointed me; and never to suffer grief so far to prevail, as to injure my health, or long to cloud the natural cheerfulness of my temper. I had writ long since, but had a mind to see first how my small affairs would be settled; and now can assure you that, at Lady-day, I leave Lincoln certainly. You were of opinion that my leaving Mrs. Taylor would not only prove prejudicial to her affairs, (and so far all the town agrees with you,) but would be a great affliction to her. I own I thought so, too: but we both were a little mistaken. She received the news of my going with an indifference I did not expect. Never was such a teacher, as I may justly say I have been, so foolishly lost, or so unnecessarily disobliged. Had she paid my last year's wages but the day before Martinmas, I still had staid: instead of that, she has received £120 within these three months, and yet never would spare one six or seven pounds for me, which I am sure no teacher will ever bear. She fancies I never knew of any money she received; when, alas! she can never have one five pounds but I know of it. I have so satisfied brother Sam, he wishes me good success at Gainsborough, and says he can no longer oppose my resolution: which pleases me much, for I would gladly live civilly with him, and friendly with you.

"I have a fairer prospect at Gainsborough than I could have hoped for; my greatest difficulty will be want of money at my first entrance. I shall furnish my school with canvass, worsted, silks, &c., though I am much afraid of being dipt in debt at first: but God's will be done. Troubles of that kind are what I have been used to. Will you lend me the other £3 which you designed for me at Lady-day; it would help me much: you will if you can, I am sure,—for so would I do by you. I am half starved with cold, which hinders me from writing longer. Emery is no better. Mrs. Taylor and Kitty give their service. Pray send soon to me. Kez is gone home for good and all. I am knitting brother Charles a fine purse;—give my love to him.

"I am, dear brother,

"Your loving sister and constant friend,

"EMILIA HARPER."

Mrs. Harper is represented as a fine woman; of a noble yet affable countenance, and of a kind and affectionate disposition, as appears by a poem addressed to her by her sister, Mrs. Wright, before her marriage, of which we give a stanza or two.

> True wit and sprightly genius shine
> In every turn, in every line:
> To these, O skilful nine annex
> The native sweetness of my sex;
> And that peculiar talent let me shew
> Which Providence doth oft bestow
> On spirits that are *high*, with fortunes that are *low*.
>
> Thy virtues and thy graces all,
> How simple, free, and natural!
> Thy graceful form with pleasure I survey;
> It charms the eye,—the heart, away.—
> Malicious fortune did repine,
> To grant her gifts to worth like thine!
>
> To all thy outward majesty and grace,
> To all the blooming features of thy face,
> To all the heavenly sweetness of thy mind,
> A noble, generous, equal soul is joined,
> By reason polished, and by arts refined,
> Thy even steady eye can see
> Dame fortune smile, or frown at thee;
> At every varied change can say, it moves not me!
>
> Fortune has fixed thee in a place
> Debarred of wisdom, wit, and grace.
> High births and virtue equally they scorn,
> As asses dull, on dunghills born:
> Impervious as the stones, their heads are found;
> Their rage and hatred steadfast as the ground.
> With these unpolished wights thy youthful days
> Glide *slow* and *dull*, and nature's lamp decays;
> Oh! what a lamp is hid, 'mid such a sordid race!

Mrs. Harper was left without property: but in her widowhood for many years, she was maintained entirely by her brothers, and lived at the preacher's house adjoining the chapel, in West Street, Seven Dials, London. She terminated her earthly existence at a very advanced age, about the year 1772. That her mind was highly cultivated, and her taste exquisite, appears from the following assertion of her brother, John:—"My sister, Harper, was the best reader of Milton I ever heard."

MARY, afterwards Mrs. Whitelamb, was the second of the grown-up daughters of the Rector of Epworth. Through affliction, and probably some mismanagement in her nurse, she became considerably deformed in body: and her growth in consequence was much stinted, and her health injured; but all written and oral testimony concur in the statement, that her face was exquisitely beautiful, and was a fair and legible index to her mind. Her humble, obliging, and even disposition, made her the favourite and delight of the whole family. Her brothers, John and Charles, frequently spoke of her with the most tender respect; and her sister, Mrs. Wright, (no mean judge of character,) mentions her as one of the most exalted of human characters. She married, with the approbation of the family, Mr. John Whitelamb. He was the son of parents at that time in very low circumstances, and was put to a charity school at Wroote. He suffered many privations in order to acquire a sufficiency of learning to pass through the University and obtain orders. It is in reference to this that Mrs. Wesley calls him "poor starveling Johnny." So low were his circumstances that he could not purchase himself a gown when ordained. Mr. John Wesley, writing to his brother Samuel in 1732, says, "John Whitelamb wants a *gown* much: I am not rich enough to buy him one at present. If you are willing my twenty shillings should go towards that, I will add ten more to make up the price of a new one." In every respect, the Wesleys divided with him, according to their power: and by his humble and upright conduct in the early part of his life, he repaid their kindness. When he got orders, Mr. Wesley made him his curate in Wroote; and having engaged Miss Mary's affections, they were married, and Mr. Wesley gave up to him the living at Wroote. Her sister, Wright, the most interesting of the Wesley family, composed some lines to her memory, which contain an affecting allusion to her own fate.

"If blissful spirits condescend to know,
And hover round what once they loved below;
Maria! gentlest excellence! attend
To her, who glories to have called thee *friend*!
Remove in merit, tho' allied in blood,
Unworthy I, and thou divinely good!
* * * * *
With business and devotion never cloyed,
No moment of thy life pass'd unemployed;
Well-natured mirth, matured discretion joined,
Constant attendants of the virtuous mind.
From earliest dawn of youth, in thee well known,
The saint sublime and finished Christian shone.
Yet would not grace one grain of pride allow,
Or cry, 'Stand off, I'm holier than thou.'
A worth so singular since time began,
But once surpassed, and He was more than *man*.
When deep immers'd in grief beyond redress,
And friends and kindred heightened by distress,
And with relentless efforts made me prove
Pain, grief, despair, and *wedlock without love*;
My soft Maria could alone dissent,
O'erlook'd the fatal vow, and mourn'd the punishment!
Condoled the ill, admitting no relief,
With such infinitude of pitying grief,
That all who could not my *demerit* see,
Mistook her wond'rous love for *worth* in me.

ANNE, afterwards Mrs. Lambert, was married to a gentleman of the name of John Lambert, a land-surveyor in Epworth, of whom and their children, if they had any, we know nothing. Mr. and Mrs. Lambert are probably the persons meant by Mr. John Wesley in his Journal, under date Tuesday, June 8, 1742, where he says:—"I walked to Hibaldstone, about ten miles from Epworth, to see my brother and sister;" but he mentions no name. On Mrs. Lambert's marriage, her brother Samuel presented to her the following verses:—

No fiction fine shall guide my hand,
But artless truth the verse supply;
Which all with ease may understand,
But none be able to deny.

Nor, sister, take the care amiss,
Which I, in giving rules, employ
To point the likeliest way to bliss,
To cause, as well as wish, you joy.

Let love your reason never blind,
To dream of paradise below;
For sorrows must attend mankind,
And pain, and weariness, and wo!

Though still from mutual love, relief
In all conditions may be found,
It cures at once the common grief,
And softens the severest wound.

Through diligence, and well-earned gain,
In growing plenty may you live!
And each in piety obtain
Repose that riches cannot give!

If children e'er should bless the bed,
O! rather let them infants die,
Than live to grieve the hoary head,
And make the aged father sigh!

Still duteous, let them ne'er conspire
To make their parents disagree;
No *son* be rival to his *sire*,
No *daughter* more beloved than *thee*!

Let them be humble, pious, wise,
Nor higher station wish to know;
Since only those deserve to rise,
Who live contented to be *low*.

Firm let the husband's empire stand,
With easy but unquestioned sway;
May HE have *kindness* to command,
And THOU the *bravery to obey*.

Long may he give thee comfort, long
As the frail knot of life shall hold!
More than a *father* when thou'rt young,
More than a *son* when waxing *old*.

The greatest earthly pleasure try,
Allowed by Providence divine;
Be still a *husband*, blest as I,
And *thou* a wife as good as *mine*!

There is much good sense and suitable advice in these verses; and they give an additional testimony to the domestic happiness of their author. "I wish," says Dr. Clarke, "they were in the hands of every newly married couple in the kingdom."

SUSANNA, afterwards Mrs. Ellison, was born about the year 1701. She is reported to have been good-natured, very facetious, but a little romantic. She married Richard Ellison, Esq., a gentleman of good family, who had a respectable establishment. But though she bore him several children, the marriage, like some others in the Wesley family, was not a happy one. She possessed a mind naturally strong, which was much improved by a good education. His mind was common, coarse, uncultivated, and too much inclined to despotic sway, which prevented conjugal happiness. Unfitness of minds more than circumstances, is what in general mars the marriage union. Where minds are united, means of happiness and contentment are ever within reach.

What little domestic happiness they had, was not only interrupted, but finally destroyed, by a fire which took place in their dwelling-house. What the cause of this fire was, is not known: but after it took place, Mrs. Ellison would never again live with her husband! She went to London, and hid herself among some of her children, who were established there, and received also considerable helps from her brother John, who, after the death of his brother, Samuel, became the common almoner of the family. Mr. Ellison used many means to get his wife to return; but she utterly refused either to see him, or to have any further intercourse with him. As he knew her affectionate disposition, in order to bring her down into the country, he advertised an account of his death! When this met her eye, she immediately set off for Lincolnshire, to pay the last tribute of respect to his remains: but when she found him still alive and well, she returned, and no persuasion could induce her to live with him. It does not appear that she communicated to any person the cause of her aversion; and after this lapse of time it is in vain to pursue it by conjecture.

MEHETABEL, afterwards Mrs. Wright, (called also Hetty, and, by her brother, Samuel, sometimes Kitty,) gave, from infancy, such proofs of strong mental powers, as led her parents to cultivate them with the utmost care. These exertions were crowned with success; for at the early age of eight years, she made such proficiency in the learned languages, that she could read the Greek text. She appears to have been the most eminently gifted of the female branches of the Wesley family. She had a fine talent for poetry, and availed herself of the rich, sweet and pensive warblings of her lyre, to sooth her spirit under the pressure of deep and accumulated calamity. At the tale of her afflictions every feeling heart must sigh. Religion was the balm which allayed her anguish; and the sorrows of the moment, now enhance her eternal joy. From her childhood she was gay and sprightly; full of mirth, good humour, and keen wit. She appears to have had many suitors; but they were generally of the thoughtless class, and ill suited to make her either happy or useful, in a matrimonial life.

To some of those proposed matches, in early life, the following lines allude, which were found in her father's handwriting, and marked by Mr. John Wesley "Hetty's letter to her Mother."—

"DEAR MOTHER,

"You were once in the ew'n,
As by us cakes is plainly shewn,
Who else had ne'er come after.
Pray speak a word in time of need,
And with my sour-look'd father plead
For your distressed daughter."

In the spring freshness of youth and hope, her affections were engaged by one who, in point of abilities and situation might have been a suitable husband; some circumstances, however, caused a disagreement with her father. This interference did not move *Hetty*. She refused to give her lover up; and had he been faithful to her, the connexion, in all probability, would have issued in marriage; but whether he was offended with the opposition he met with, or it proceeded from fickleness, is not known. He, however, remitted his assiduities, and at last abandoned *a woman who would have been an honour to the first man in the land.* The matter thus terminating, *Hetty* committed a fatal error, which many woman have done in their just, but blind resentment,—she married the first person who offered. This was a man of the name of Wright, in no desirable rank in life, of coarse mind and manners, inferior to herself in education and intellect, and every way unworthy of a woman, whose equal in all things it would have been difficult to find; for her person was more than commonly pleasing, her disposition gentle and affectionate, her principles those which arm the heart either for prosperous or adverse fortune, her talents remarkable, and her attainments beyond what are ordinarily permitted to women, even those who are the most highly educated. Duty in her had produced so much affection towards the miserable creature whom she had made her husband, that the brutal profligacy of his conduct almost broke her heart. He did not know the value of the woman he had espoused! He associated with low, dissolute company, spent his evenings from home, and became a confirmed drunkard. This marriage is supposed to have taken place at the end of the year 1725. Mary, of all her sisters, had the courage to counsel her not to marry him.

A perplexed and thorny path appears to have been the general lot of the sensible and pious daughters of the Rector of Epworth. They were for the most part unsuitably, and therefore unhappily, married. At a time when Mrs Wright believed and hoped that she should soon be at peace in the grave, she composed this Epitaph for herself:—

"Destined, while living, to sustain
An equal share of grief and pain;
All various ills of human race
Within this breast had once a place.
Without complaint, she learn'd to bear,
A living death, a long despair;
Till hard oppressed by adverse fate,
O'ercharged, she sunk beneath the weight;
And to this peaceful tomb retired,
So much esteem'd, so long desired.
The painful mortal conflict's o'er;
A broken heart can bleed no more."

From that illness, however, she recovered, so far as to linger on for many years, living to find in religion the consolation she needed, and which nothing else can bestow. That she was almost *compelled* by her *father* to marry Wright, appears evident from the following letter:—

"July 3, 1729.

"HONOURED SIR,

"Though I was glad, on any terms, of the favour of a line from you; yet I was concerned at your displeasure on account of the unfortunate paragraph, which you are pleased to say was meant for the *flower* of my letter, but which was in reality the only thing I disliked in it before it went. I wish it had not gone, since I perceive it gave you some uneasiness.

"But since what I said occasioned some queries, which I should be glad to speak freely about, were I sure that the least I could say would not grieve or offend you, or were I so happy as to think like you in everything; I earnestly beg that the little I shall say may not be offensive to you, since I promise to be as little witty as possible, though I can't help saying, you only accuse me of being too much so; especially these late years past I have been pretty free from that scandal.

"You ask me 'what hurt matrimony has done me?' and 'whether I had always so frightful an idea of it as I have now?' Home questions indeed! and I once more beg of you not to be offended at the *least* I can say to them, if I say any thing.

"I had not always such notions of wedlock as now; but thought where there was a mutual affection and desire of pleasing, something near an equality of mind and person; either earthly or heavenly wisdom, and any thing to keep love within between a young couple, there was a *possibility* of happiness in a married state: but *where* all, or *most* of *these, are wanting,* I ever thought people could not marry without sinning against God and themselves. I could say much more; but would rather eternally stifle my sentiments than have the torment of thinking they agree not with yours. You are so good to my spouse and me, as to say, 'you shall always think yourself obliged to him for his civilities to me.' I hope he will always continue to use me better than I merit from him in one respect.

"I think exactly the same of *my marriage* as I did before it happened; but *though I would have given at least one of my eyes for the liberty of throwing myself at your feet before I was married at all;* yet since it is past, and matrimonial grievances are usually *irreparable,* I hope you will condescend to be so far of my opinion, as to own,—that since upon some accounts I am happier than I deserve, *it is best to say little of things quite past remedy;* and endeavour, as I really do, to make myself more and more contented, though things may not be to my wish."

* * * * *

Wright had an establishment in Frith Street, Soho, London, where he carried on the business of *plumbing* and *glasing*, and had lead works connected with it. His employment greatly injured his own health, and materially affected that of Mrs. Wright. They had several children, all of whom died young; and it was their mother's opinion that the effluvia from the lead-works was the cause of their death.

We extract the following from a MS. letter of Mr. William Duncombe, to Mrs. Elizabeth Carter, inserted in "*Brydges' Censura Literaria,*" Vol. vii. p. 277. It speaks better of Wright than he deserved.

"You desire some account of Mrs. Wright. She was sister to Samuel, John, and Charles Wesley. The first was an Usher at Westminster, and died master of Tiverton School in Devonshire. John and Charles are eminent preachers among the Methodists. Her father was a clergyman, and author of a poem called *The Life of Christ.* It is a pious book, but bears no character as a *Poem.* But we have a volume of poems by Samuel Wesley, jun., which are ingenious and entertaining. He had an excellent knack of telling a tale in verse. I suppose you must have seen them.

"Mr. Highmore, who knew Mrs. Wright when young, told me that she was very handsome. When I saw her she was in a languishing way, and had no remains of beauty, except a lively piercing eye. She was very unfortunate, as you will find by her poems, which are written with great delicacy; but so tender and affecting, they can scarcely be read without tears. She had an uncle, a surgeon, with whom she was a favourite. In her bloom, he used to take her with him to Bath, Tunbridge, &c.; and she has done justice to his memory in an excellent poem.

"Mr. Wright, her husband, is my plumber, and lives in this street; an honest, laborious man, but by no means a fit husband for such a woman. He was but a journeyman when she married him; but set up with the fortune left her by her uncle. Mrs. Wright has been dead about two years. On my asking if she had any child living, she replied, 'I have had several, but the *white hand* killed them all!' She had just come from Bristol and was very weak. 'How, madam,' said I, 'could you bear the fatigue of so long a journey?' 'We had a coach of our own,' said she, 'and took short stages; besides, I had the *King* with me!' 'The King; I suppose you mean a person whose name is King.'—'No; I mean my brother, *the King of the Methodists!*' This looked like a piece of lunacy.

"She told me that she had long ardently wished for death; 'and the rather,' said she, 'because we, the methodists, always die *in transports of joy!*' I am told that she wrote some hymns for the methodists, but have not seen any of them.

"It affected me to view the ruin of so fine a frame; so I made her only three or four visits. Mr. Wright told me she had burned many poems, and given some to a beloved sister, which he could never recover. As many as he could procure, he gave me. I will send them to you speedily.

"I went one day with Wright to hear Mr. Charles Wesley preach. I find his business is only with the *heart* and *affections.* As to the understanding, that must shift for itself. Most of our *clergy* are in the contrary extreme, and apply themselves only to the *head*. To be sure they take us all for stoics; and think that, like a young lady of your acquaintance, we have no passions.

"W. Duncombe."

"20th Nov. 1752."

The following beautiful lines by Mrs. Wright, seem to have been a mere *extempore* effusion, poured out from the fulness of her heart on the occasion, and sharpened with the keen anguish of distress.

A MOTHER'S ADDRESS TO HER DYING INFANT.

Tender softness! infant mild!
Perfect, purest, brightest child!
Transient lustre! beauteous clay!
Smiling wonder of a day!
Ere the last convulsive start
Rends thy unresisting heart;
Ere the long enduring swoon
Weigh thy precious eyelids down;
Ah! regard a mother's moan,
Anguish deeper than my own.

Fairest eyes, whose dawning light
Late, with rapture, blest my sight,
Ere your orbs extinguish'd be,
Bend their trembling beams on me!
Drooping sweetness! ve dant flower!
Blooming, withering in an hour!
Ere thy gentle breast sustains
Latest, fiercest, mortal pains,
Hear a suppliant! let me be
Partner in thy destiny!
That whene'er the fatal cloud
Must thy radiant temples shroud;
When deadly damps, impending now,
Shall hover round thy destin d brow,
Diffusive may their influence be,
And with the *blossom* blast the *tree*.

This was composed during her confinement, and written from her mouth by her husband, who sent it to Mr. John Wesley. The original letter sent with these verses was in Dr. Clarke's possession, who says, "it is a curiosity of its kind; and one proof amongst many, of the total unfitness of such a slender, and uncultivated mind, to match with one of the highest ornaments of her sex. I shall give it entire in its own *orthography*, in order to vindicate the complaints of this forlorn woman, who was forced to accept in marriage the *rude* hand which wrote it. It is like the ancient Hebrew, all without points."

"To the Reverend Mr. John Wesley, Fellow in Christ Church College, Oxon.

"DEAR BRO:

"This Comes to Let you know that my wife is brought to bed and is in a hopeful way of Doing well but the Dear child Died—the Third day after it was born—which has been of great concerne to me and my wife She Joyns With me In Love to your Selfe and Bro : Charles

"From Your Loveing Bro:

"to Comnd—WM. WRIGHT."

"PS. I've sen you Sum Verses that my wife maid of Dear Lamb Let me hear from one or both of you as Soon as you Think Conveniant."

Mrs. Wright wrote much beautiful poetry, but could never be prevailed upon to collect and give her poems to the public. It is said that she gave them at her death to one of her sisters. Many have been published in different collections. Some may be found in the Poetical Register, the Christian Magazine, the Arminian Magazine, and in the different lives of her brothers, John and Charles. Most of the poems were written under strong mental depression.

She was visited by her brother Charles in her last illness. He says in his journal :—"I prayed by my sister, Wright, a gracious, trembling soul; a bruised reed which the Lord will not break." She died March 21, 1751; and Mr. Charles Wesley preached her funeral sermon from these words,—"Thy sun shall no more go down, neither shall thy moon withdraw itself, for the Lord shall be thine everlasting light, and the days of thy mourning shall be ended." Mrs. Wright was described to Dr. Clarke, by one who knew her, as "an elegant woman, with great refinement of manners."

She was reported to be her mother's favourite. Mr. Charles expressed his "wonder, that so wise a woman as his mother could give way to such a partiality." Many years after, when this saying was mentioned to Mrs. Hall, she replied, "what was called partiality, was what they might all have enjoyed if they had wished it; which was to sit in my mother's chamber when disengaged; and listen to her conversation." "What was called partiality to *Patty*," says Dr. Clarke, "was the indulgence of a propensity to store her mind with the observations of a parent, whose mode of thinking was not common, and whose conversation was peculiarly interesting; and it would have been cruelty to have chased away a little one, who preferred her mother's society to recreation."

Mrs. Wesley's opinion of the strong characteristic steadiness of Martha will appear from the following incident. One day, when she entered the nursery, all the children, Patty excepted, (who was ever sedate and reflecting,) were in high glee and frolic, as they ought to be, their mother said, but not rebukingly, "You will all be more serious one day." Martha lifting up her head, immediately asked, "shall I be more serious, Ma'am?" "No," replied the mother. The truth appears to be, that the partiality was on the part of the child. *Patty* loved the mother, and wished to listen to her discourse, by which she increased her fund of knowledge: a propensity which was very properly indulged." To her brother *John* she was uncommonly attached. They had the same features as exactly as if cast in the same mould; added to a great similarity of disposition. Even their *handwriting* was so much alike that one might be easily mistaken for the other.

But there is one part of *Martha's* character which has been strongly censured—her conduct in reference to her marriage. Whilst she was at her uncle's house in London, she received the addresses of a gentleman of the name of Hall, who was one of Mr. Wesley's pupils at Lincoln College. He possessed an agreeable person, considerable talents, and manners which were in a high degree prepossessing, to those who did not see beneath the surface. Mr. John Wesley was much attached to him; he thought him humble, and teachable, and in all manner of conversation holy and unblameable. There were indeed parts of his conduct which might have led a wary man to suspect either his sanity, or his sincerity; but the tutor was too sincere himself, and too enthusiastic, to entertain the suspicion which some of his extravagances might justly have excited. Samuel formed a truer judgment. "I never liked the man," says he, "from the first time I saw him. His *smoothness* did not suit my *roughness*. He appeared always to dread me as a wit and a jester: this with me is a sure sign of guilt and hypocrisy. He never could meet my eye in full light. Conscious that there was something foul at the bottom, he was afraid that I should see it, if I looked keenly into his eye." John, however, took him to his bosom.

In Hall's addresses to Martha, there is no doubt he was sincere; and in order to secure her, he took the expedient which was frequently practiced in those days, to *betroth* her to himself. All this was done without the knowledge of her parents, or her brothers, for some time. He afterwards accompanied John and Charles to Epworth, and there he saw her sister Kezzia, became enamoured of *her*, obtained her consent to marry him, and was on the point of leading poor unconscious Kezzia to the altar, affirming vehemently that "the thing was of God; that he was certain it was his will; God had revealed to him that he must marry, and that Kezzia was the very person." The family was justly alarmed at his conduct; in vain they questioned him on the reason of this change, when, to the utter astonishment of all parties, in a *few days* Hall changed his mind again, and pretending, with blasphemous effrontery, that the Almighty had changed His; declared that a second *revelation* had countermanded the first, and instructed him to marry not Kezzia, but her sister Martha. The family, and especially the brothers, felt indignant at this infamous proposal.

Martha appears at that time to have been in London, when Hall went down into Lincolnshire; and knew nothing of the transaction with Kezzia at Epworth till a considerable time after it took place. When she found how matters stood, she wrote to her mother, and laid open the whole business; who, on this explanation, wrote her full consent, assuring Martha, " that if she had obtained the consent of her uncle, there was no obstacle."

Dr. Clarke, who labours hard to vindicate Mrs. Hall in this matter, says, " Kezzia, on hearing the true relation, cordially renounced all claim to Hall; and, from every thing I have been able to learn, she sat as indifferent to him as if no such transaction had ever existed. Her uncle, Matthew, with whom Patty lived, was so satisfied with her conduct and the match, that he gave her L.500 on her marriage, and his testimony of 'her dutiful and grateful conduct during the whole time she had resided in his house.' Kezzia also gave her consent by choosing to live with Mr. and Mrs. Hall after their marriage, though she had a pressing invitation to reside with her brother Samuel; and her brother John was to have furnished L.50 per annum to cover her expenses. The true state of the case was for some years unknown to her brothers; and Mr. John Wesley, in a letter to Hall, dated Dec. 2, 1747, charges him ' with having stolen Kezzia from the God of her youth; that in consequence she refused to be comforted, fell into a lingering illness, which terminated in her death; but her blood still cried unto God from the earth against him, and that surely it was upon his head.' That this was Mr. Wesley's impression I well know; but it is not strictly correct. I have the almost dying assertions of Mrs. Hall, delivered to her beloved niece, Miss Wesley, and by her handed in writing to me, that the facts of the case were as stated above."

Opposed to this opinion, however, we have the testimony of Mr. Moore, who was intimately acquainted with Mrs. Hall. He says that " Mrs. Hall did not speak of her marriage quite as the respectable biographer of her family does. She was convinced for many years, that her brothers were so far right, that for *both* sisters to have refused him, after he had manifested such a want of principle and honour, would have been *the more excellent way*."

Till this time John Wesley believed that Hall was, " without question, filled with faith, and the love of God; so that in *all England* he knew not his fellow. He thought him a pattern of lowliness, meekness, seriousness, and continual advertance to the presence of God; and, above all, of self-denial of every kind, and of suffering all things with joyfulness." But afterwards he found " there was a worm at the root of the gourd." Hall began to teach that there was " no resurrection of the body, no general judgment, no hell, no worm that never dieth, no fire that never shall be quenched." Mr. J. Wesley, in the course of his travelling, came to Hall's house, near Salisbury, and was let in, though orders had been given that he should not be admitted. Hall left the room as soon as he entered, sent a message to him that he must quit the house, and presently turned his wife out of doors. Having now thrown off all restraint, and all regard to decency, he publicly and privately recommended polygamy, as conformable to nature, *preached* in its defence, and practised as he preached. Soon he laid aside all pretensions to religion, professed himself an infidel, and led, for many years, the life of an adventurer and a profligate, at home and abroad; acting sometimes as a physician, sometimes as a priest, or figured away with his sword, cane, and scarlet cloak; assuming any character, according to his humour, or the convenience of the day. Hall passed from change to change, till at last he gloried in his shame, and became a proverb of reproach,—

" The vilest husband, and the worst of men."

He would talk, with apparent ease, to his chaste wife concerning his concubines! He would tell her, that she was his *carnal* wife, but they his *spiritual* wives! for he had taught them to despise all sober, scriptural religion, and to talk as corruptly as himself. At length he broke all bounds, and retired to the West Indies, taking his chief favourite with him. She was a remarkable woman; and appears to have had more personal courage than her wretched paramour. In an assault upon the house in which they lived, by a black banditti, she seized a large pewter vessel, and standing at the turning of the stairs which led to their apartment, she *knocked the assailants down* in succession, as they approached, and maintained the post till succour arrived, and dispersed the villains. Hall continued his connexion with this wretched woman till she died, and then returned to England, weak, and in some degree humbled, and was afterwards seen officiating in a church in London, where, not long before his death, he delivered, with great energy, an extempore discourse, which a gentleman who heard it, says was inimitably pathetic. Mrs. Hall, bound, as she most conscientiously thought herself, by her original vows, showed him every kind of charitable attention till his death, which took place at Bristol, January 6, 1776. He exclaimed, in his last hours, " I have injured an angel! an angel that never reproached me!" Mr. John Wesley gives the following account of the closing scene :—" I came to Bristol just in time enough not to see, but to bury poor Mr. Hall, my brother-in-law, who died on Wednesday morning, I trust in peace, for God had given him deep repentance. Such another monument of Divine mercy, considering how low he had fallen, and from what heights of holiness, I have not seen, no not in seventy years. I had designed to have visited him in the morning, but he did not stay for my coming. It is enough, if, after all his wanderings, we meet again in Abraham's bosom."

We shall now consider Mrs. Hall's behaviour as a *wife*, to one of the worst and most unkind of husbands. " I will adduce an instance," says Dr. Clarke, " recorded by witnesses on the spot, and corroborated by herself, on being questioned as to its truth. When they lived at Fullarton, near Salisbury, where Hall was the curate, she had taken a young woman into the house as a seamstress, whom he seduced: these were the beginnings of his ways. Mrs. Hall being quite unsuspicious, was utterly ignorant of any improper attachment between her husband and the girl.

" Finding the time of the young woman's travail drawing near, *he* feigned a call to London on some important business, and departed. Soon after his departure the girl fell into labour. Mrs. Hall, one of the most feeling and considerate of women on such occasions, ordered her servants to go instantly for a doctor. They all refused; and when she had remonstrated with them on their inhumanity, they completed her surprise by informing her that the girl, (to whom they gave any thing but her *own name*,) was *in labour*, through her criminal connexion with Mr. Hall, and that they all knew her guilt long before. She heard, without betraying any emotion, what she had not before even suspected, and repeated her commands for assistance. They, full of indignation at the unfortunate creature, and strangely inhuman, absolutely refused to obey; on which Mrs. Hall immediately went out herself, and brought in a midwife; called on a neighbour; divided the only six pounds she had in the house, and deposited *five* with her, who was astonished at her conduct; enjoined kind treatment, and no reproaches; and then set off for London, found her husband, related in her own mild manner the circumstances, told him what she had done, and prevailed upon him to return to Salisbury as soon as the young woman could be removed from the house. He thought the conduct of his wife not only Christian, but heroic; and was for a time suitably affected by it; but having embraced the doctrine of polygamy, his reformation was but of short continuance. Mr. Hall was guilty of many similar infidelities; and after being the father of *ten children* by his wife, *nine* of whom lie buried at Salisbury, he abandoned his family, and went off to the West Indies with one of his mistresses. Notwithstanding all this treatment, Mrs. Hall was never heard to speak of him but with kindness. She often expressed wonder that women should profess to love their husbands, and yet dwell upon their *faults*, or indeed upon those of their friends. She was never known to speak evil of any person."

When Mr. Charles Wesley asked her " how she could give money," as previously related, " to her husband's concubine?" she answered, " I knew I could obtain what I wanted from many; but she, poor hapless creature! could not; many thinking it meritorious to abandon her to the distress which she had brought upon herself. Pity is due to the wicked; the good claim esteem; besides, I did not act as a *woman*, but as a Christian."

Mrs. Hall frequently visited Dr. Samuel Johnson, (at his own particular request,) who always treated her with high respect. The injuries she had sustained, and the manner in which she had borne them, could not but excite the esteem and pity of such a mind as his. He wished her very much to become an inmate of his house; and she would have done so, had she not feared to provoke the *jealousy* of two females already there, Mrs. Williams and Mrs. Desmoulins. She ventured to tell him the reason, and he felt its cogency. It is no wonder that Dr. Johnson valued her conversation. In many cases it supplied the absence of books; her memory was a repository of the most striking events of past centuries; and she had the best parts of all our poets by heart. She delighted in *literary* discussions, and moral argumentations; not for *display*, but for the exercise of her mental faculties, and to increase her fund of useful knowledge; and she bore opposition with the same composure which regulated all the other parts of her conduct. Of *wit*, she used to say, she was the only one of the family who did not possess it; and Mr. Charles Wesley remarks, that his "sister Patty was too *wise* to be *witty*." Yet she was very capable of *acute remark*; and once, at Dr. Johnson's house, when he was on a grave discussion, she made a remark which turned the laugh against the doctor, in which he cordially joined, feeling its propriety and force. "It excited her surprise," says Dr. Clarke, " that women should dispute the *authority* which God gives the husband over the wife." "It is," said she, so clearly expressed in scripture that one would suppose such wives never read their Bibles: and those women who contest this point should not marry." Her mother seems to have been of the same opinion, though she evidently possessed what is called a *great spirit*. "Vixen and unruly wives," continues Dr. Clarke, " did not relish Mrs. Hall's sentiments on this subject, and her *example* they could never forgive."

In a conversation, there was a remark made, that the public voice was the voice of God, universally recognised, whence the proverb, " Vox populi, vox Dei." This Mrs. Hall strenuously contested; and said the " public voice," in Pilate's court, was " Crucify him! Crucify him!"

She had a great dread of melancholy subjects. " Those persons," she maintained, " could not have real feeling, who could delight to see, or to hear details of misery they could not relieve, or descriptions of cruelty which they could not punish." Nor did she like to speak of death: it was heaven, the society of the blessed, and the deliverance of the happy spirit from this tabernacle of clay, (not the pangs of separation, of which she always expressed a fear,) on which she delighted to dwell. She could not behold a corpse, " because," said she, " it is beholding Sin sitting upon his throne."

There were few persons of whom she had not something good to say; and if their faults were glaring, she would plead the influence of circumstances, education, or sudden temptation, to which all imprisoned in a tenement of clay are liable, and by which their actions are often influenced: yet she was no apologist for bad principles; for she thought with an old puritan, that a fault in an individual was like a fever; but a bad principle resembled a plague, spreading desolation and death over the community. Few persons feel as they should do for transgression, when it is the effect of sudden temptation.

" Of her sufferings," says Dr. Clarke, " she spoke so little, that they could not be learned from herself. I could only get acquainted with those I knew from other branches of the family. Her blessings and the advantages she enjoyed, she was continually recounting. ' Evil,' she used to say, ' was not kept from me; but evil has been kept from harming me.' Though she had a small property of her own, yet she was principally dependent on the bounty of her brothers, after her husband had deserted her; and here was a striking illustration of the remark, that ' in noble natures benefits do not diminish love on either side.' She left to her niece, whom she dearly loved, and who well knew how to prize so valuable a woman, the little remains of her fortune, who in vain urged her to sink it on her own life, in order to procure her a few more comforts."

Her niece, Miss Wesley, was with her in her last moments. Mrs. Hall had no disease, but a mere decay of nature. She spoke of her dissolution with the same tranquillity with which she spoke of everything else. A little before her departure, she called Miss Wesley to her bedside, and said, " I have now a sensation which convinces me my departure is near—the heart-strings seem gently, but entirely loosened." Miss Wesley asked her if she was in pain? " No," said she, " but a new feeling." Just before she closed her eyes, she bade her niece come near,—she pressed her hand and said, " I have the assurance for which I have long prayed—shout!" and then expired. Thus her noble and happy spirit passed into the hands of her Redeemer on the 12th July, 1791, a few months after the death of her brother, John, with whom she is interred in the same vault. She was the last survivor of the original Wesley family.

We shall conclude this account with a few words extracted from her niece Miss Wesley's description of her:— " Mrs. Hall's trials were peculiar. Wounded in her affections in the tenderest part,—deserted by the husband she much loved,—bereaved of her ten children,—reduced from ample competency to a narrow income,—yet no complaint was ever heard from her lips! Her serenity was undisturbed, and her peace beyond the reach of calamity." Active virtues command applause—they are apparent to every eye; but the passive are only known to Him by whom they are registered on high, where the *silent* sufferer shall meet a full reward.

KEZZIA WESLEY, called, in the family papers, Kezzy and Kez, appears to have been the youngest daughter. About 1730, Miss Kezzy became a teacher in a boarding school, at Lincoln. She possessed very delicate health through life, which prevented her from improving a mind that seems to have been capable of high cultivation. She wrote a peculiarly neat and beautiful hand, even more so than her sister Emilia. Her brother John frequently gave her directions both for the improvement of her mind, and increase in true religion. To a letter of this description she thus replies:—

"*Lincoln, July* 8, 1731.
" DEAR BROTHER,

" I should have writ sooner had not business, and indisposition of body prevented me. Indeed sister *Pat*'s going to London shocked me a little, because it was unexpected; and perhaps may have been the cause of my ill health for the last fortnight. It would not have had so great an effect upon my mind if I had known it before: but it is over now—

' The past as nothing we esteem ;
And pain, like pleasure, is a dream.'

" I could like to read all the books you mention, if it were in my power to buy them; but as it is not at present, nor have I any acquaintances of whom I can borrow them, I must make myself easy, if I can; but I had rather you had not told me of them. *Here* I have time in the morning, three or four hours, but want books; at *home* I had books, but not time. I wish you would send me the questions you speak of, and I would read them. Perhaps they may be of use to me in learning *contentment*, for I have long been endeavouring to practice it.

" I should be glad if you would say a little to sister Emily on the same subject. I can't persuade her to the contrary, because I am so much addicted to the same failing myself."

Miss Kezzy was to have been married to a gentleman who paid his addresses to her when she resided with her sister Hall, near Salisbury, but death prevented the union. It appears that her brother Charles was present when she died. Of her closing scene, he gives the following account to his brother John:—" Yesterday morning, (March the 9th, 1741,) sister Kezzy died in the Lord Jesus. He finished his work, and cut it short in mercy. Without pain or trouble, she commended her spirit into the hands of Jesus, and fell asleep."

SCIENTIFIC NOTICES.

PHILOSOPHY OF THE ATMOSPHERE.

The most inattentive observer of nature must have been frequently struck with the ever-varying phenomena of the lower heavens. At one time, the surrounding air is still, giving no symptom of its existence; at another, the tempestuous hurricane carries desolation in its progress, and again sinks into the gentle breeze, playing among our floral beauties, or scarcely stirring the leaves of the forest. In some places the mariner reckons with confidence upon the assistance of the winds; whilst in others he knows not at what moment he may meet the gathering storm, or from which quarter the gale will be let loose upon his adventurous bark. The inhabitants of tropical countries, who dwell near the shore, have the admirable advantage of the refreshing sea-breeze by day, and the warmer land breeze at night; whilst the mountaineer has every variety of climate by ascending or descending; at the foot, the torrid heat might swelter, at the same time that the mountain's summit is hooded in eternal snow. Our own country furnishes an interesting variety in the surrounding atmosphere. We have the bright sunshine shooting through a beautiful transparent air, warming or exhilarating all animated nature; and we have the foggy gloom, which relaxes even the strongest mind with lassitude. Sometimes the clouds sail high, and in all their tinted splendour give a beauty and interest to the surrounding depths of ether;—now, they gather and sink in masses through which the sun's light can hardly struggle;—after a hot day has parched the soil, and the vegetable creation droops with thirst, the aqueous vapour, as the "gentle dew of heaven," descends to refresh and invigorate; and in the growing Spring-time the rain-shower falls to nourish what is intended as food for man and beast. In winter, too, the snow forms a warm clothing for the young shoots and plants, to protect them from the biting frost. Then we have the beautiful and sublime phenomena of the aurora, the lightning flash, and the meteors. The grand causes of the general phenomena of the atmosphere appear to be gravity, permanent elasticity, solar heat, diurnal rotations of the earth, evaporation and precipitation of water. The weight of the air pressing upon any given extent of surface varies according to its elevation above the level of the ocean. As we ascend through the air its weight is lessened by that portion which is left below. This simple truth was suggested by the fine genius of Pascal, as a convincing proof of the gravity of the air. It is not, however, of equal density at all elevations; if it were, the mercury would sink in proportion to the height above the level of the sea. It has been ascertained that the mercury falls about one-tenth of an inch in every 87 feet of air upwards, and, accordingly, this rule has been applied with great success in determining elevations within moderate limits. In very lofty ascents, however, it requires an attention to the changes of the density of the mercury and of the air by heat and cold, and, above all, the changes of the density of the air from its elasticity, to ascertain the exact truth.

Equal weights of air may be supposed to form stratas, which increase in thickness from below upwards; because, as we ascend, the weight of the superior air becomes less, and allows its elasticity to expand it in proportion. This was illustrated by placing a small bladder half filled with air in the receiver of the air-pump; when the pressure of the air was removed, the confined air expanded, till the bladder appeared quite full. The same would occur had the bladder been taken to the upper regions of the atmosphere. Hence, then, an important consequence of elasticity is, that the air decreases in density in proportion to its elevation above the surface of the ocean. For a similar reason the aëronauts only partially fill their balloons with gas, to allow of its expansion in ascending through the air, otherwise the unresisted spring of the swelling contents would rend open their silken walls.

ECLIPSES, still to take place in the present year.—July 1. The moon will be eclipsed, visible here; beginning of the eclipse, fifty minutes past ten in the evening; end, six minutes past two in the morning of July 2.—July 17. The sun will be eclipsed, visible here; beginning of the eclipse, fifty-six minutes past four in the morning; end, thirty-one minutes past six.—December 26. The moon will be totally eclipsed; beginning of the eclipse, thirty-one minutes past seven in the evening; beginning of total darkness, thirty minutes past nine; end of the eclipse, eight minutes past eleven in the evening.

PRECAUTIONS IN THE MANAGEMENT OF GAS-LIGHTS.—(From a useful work called *Practical observations on Gas-Lighting.* By J. O. N. Rutter.)—Children should never be permitted to touch the stop-cocks nor any other part of gas-fittings, nor should servants be too much depended on, until it is ascertained they fully understand turning the gas off and on; and they must be very dull, indeed, if they cannot comprehend that process in less than a week. It is a safe plan to turn off the main-cock at night; but when gas is kept burning in a bedroom or nursery, of course that is impracticable. The pressure, however, on the fittings, generally, might be diminished by turning off so much of the main-cock as only to allow sufficient gas to enter by it for one or two burners, as may be required.—It is important that attention should be paid to the quantity of gas admitted to the burners, as may be required.—Whenever there is any smoke or other effluvia arising from well-purified gas, it implies unnecessary waste, and is the result of ignorance or of carelessness. If the escape of the gas at the stop-cock be properly regulated, the whole of it enters into combustion and the products pass off in a state of vapour. On the principle of economy, therefore, as well as of comfort and cleanliness, it is desirable to attend to this particular. An accidental escape of gas, whether it arise from a fractured service-pipe, an imperfect joint, or a stop-cock carelessly left open, can scarcely pass unnoticed for many minutes, excepting it be in a cellar or closet from which fresh air is carefully excluded. If the escape occur in a room which is ever so imperfectly ventilated, either by a window, a grating, or a chimney, some time will elapse before the air becomes sufficiently vitiated by the gas to render the mixture explosive. Whenever an escape is indicated by a strong smell of gas in any part of the house, the first thing that should be done is to open the doors and windows, so as to pass a current of air through all the suspected apartments. The main-cock should be turned off as speedily as possible; but if it be in a cellar, or other confined situation, on no account should it be approached with a lighted candle or lamp, nor indeed with a flame of any kind. As a measure of prudence, it would be advisable, under the peculiar circumstances we have described, not to take a light into any part of the house until it has been well ventilated. It is best to be on the safe side, and to be too careful rather than too negligent.

A NEW METHOD OF PRESERVING IRON WORK FROM RUST, communicated by M. Paymen to the French Institute, consists in plunging the pieces to be preserved in a mixture of one part concentrated solution of Impure soda, (soda of commerce,) and three parts water. Pieces of iron left for three months in this liquid had lost neither weight nor polish; whilst similar pieces immersed for five days in the simple water were covered with rust.

COLUMN FOR THE LADIES.

"The virgin, virgin violet!"—BYRON.

ALTHOUGH this favourite little flower has given its name to one of the primitive colours, we must not imagine that the violet is always of a violet hue; it is often blue, purple, lilac, or white. The *viola tricolor* indeed is partly yellow, but then in common life this is called a heart's-ease; botanically speaking, however, it is a violet. The flowers were formerly considered pectoral; *i. e.* useful in diseases of the chest; but the supposed virtues of the whole class of pectoral medicines have vanished before the severe medical criticism of the last fifty years; and at the present day the petals of the violet are never prescribed by educated practitioners. The root of the violet, however, is an emetic, and may be useful as a domestic remedy in country practice. The dose is forty grains. The infusion of violets is one of the most delicate tests of the presence of acids and alkalies; the former changes its colour to red, the latter to green. According to Lightfoot, the Highland ladies of former times used the violet as a cosmetic, the old Gaelic receipt being "Annoint thy face with goat's milk in which violets have been infused, and there is not a young prince upon earth who will not be charmed with thy beauty."

A YOUNG MAIDEN'S LOGIC.

A Puritanical preacher was one day struck with surprise at beholding a beautiful set of curls on the head of a lovely maid, a member of his class, whose hair had been usually very plain. "Ah! Eliza," said he, "you should not waste your precious time in curling your hair; if God intended it to be curled, He would have curled it for you." "Indeed," said the witty maid, "I must differ from you. When I was an infant He curled it for me, but now I am grown up, He thinks I am able to do it myself."

COBBETT AND THE LADIES.—I have received as a present from the women of Bury, in Lancashire, a circular plumcake, nearly a yard in diameter. I am very much obliged to them for it, as a mark of their esteem; and, particularly, when they tell me, that they intend it to show their gratitude for what they are pleased to call my exertions in behalf of the working people; but, there is another, and a far greater pleasure that they may be able to give me, namely, to prevail upon their husbands, at the next election, to send Mr. Edmund Grundy to sit by my side.—*Cobbett's Register.*

ORCHARDS IN SCOTLAND.—Mr. Cobbett, in his account of Scotland, speaking of the orchards on the banks of the Clyde, says "an orchard is not a mere matter of ornament or of pleasure here, but of prodigious profit; under the apple and pear trees are gooseberry or currant bushes, very well managed in general; and these orchards very frequently yield more than a hundred pounds sterling in one year from an English acre of land! Like other things, the fruit here has fallen in price since the time of the panic; and therefore the pecuniary produce of orchards, like that of fields and manufactories, has been greatly diminished. But these orchards are always a source of very considerable income. I think that my friend Mr. M'Gavin of Hamilton, told me that his orchard, which is less than an English acre, has yielded him eighty pounds a-year clear money; and it is no uncommon thing for the proprietor of ten or a dozen acres to sell the fruit by auction upon the trees, for something approaching a hundred pounds an acre. In our apple counties no man thinks of any thing but fruit to make cider and perry; here the whole is table fruit, and I have never seen so great a variety of fine apples in England, at one time, as I saw on the table of Mr. Hamilton of Dalzell House."

SCRAPS.

EFFECT OF HIGH SALARIES.—On the accession of George II. the queen consort, Caroline, made a visit to the Royal Observatory; being pleased with every thing she saw, and understanding the smallness of the astronomer's salary, (£100 per annum,) her Majesty very graciously said she would speak to the King to have it increased; to which Dr. Halley, alarmed, replied,—"Pray, your Majesty, do no such thing; for, should the salary be increased, it might become an object of emolument to place there some unqualified needy dependant to the ruin of the institution."

THE PRESS OF THE THIEVES AND THE ARISTOCRATS COMPARED.—There are papers written for the pot-houses, and papers written for the fashionables, and their legions of servile imitators; and it is an indisputable fact, that the pot-house papers are, in style, matter, and decorum, superior to the fashionable. The paper which, in evidence before a Committee of the House of Commons, was stated to be the favourite paper of the thieves, is more respectable in every point of morals and intelligence than the paper which is peculiarly patronized by the clergy and the aristocracy.—*Tait's Magazine.*

EXPEDITION IN SEARCH OF CAPT. ROSS.—Captain Back and his party have arrived at New York, on their route in search of Captain Ross. At a *déjeuné à la fourchette*, given by the British Consul there, Captain Back explained the plan of his expedition to a number of distinguished individuals there assembled. The party, it appears, intended at once proceeding to the Great Slave Lake, and instead of penetrating to the Arctic Sea by either of the former routes of the Coppermine or Mackenzie River, would pursue a more easterly track. The country beyond the lake is unknown to European travellers, but the Indians describe a large stream called the Thloocke-chok, or Great Fish River, which flows due north, or nearly so, and discharges itself into the sea about the 100th meridian. By this river the party intended to proceed, and sail from its mouth in search of the navigators. The distance from the mouth to the Prince Regent's Inlet is computed at 300 miles, but Captain Back intended to shape his course to Point Turnagain, the sea of his former exertions, unless he should find a point of land described by the Indians running a long distance to the north, in which case he would proceed at once to Regent's Inlet. Should no trace of Captain Ross be found at Cape Turnagain, the barks would be launched on the Arctic Sea for the spot where the Fury was lost.

Slavery, ... 321
Dr. Birkbeck, ... 322
Turkish Ladies, ... 344
Autobiography of a Greenwich Out-Pensioner, ... Ib.
Curious Experiment on a Rattlesnake, ... 325
Walham Wag, ... 326
POETRY—Epicedium, ... Ib.
Vulgar Idea of the French Revolution, ... 327
Skill of Horse Jockeys, ... Ib.
The Duello, ... Ib.
ELEMENTS OF THOUGHT—The British Constitution—Truth—Progression of Opinion—Freedom of the Press........ 328
The Bible—Sunday Amusements—Anecdote of Galt........ Ib.
THE STORY-TELLER—The Seven Daughters of the Rector of Epworth, ... 329
SCIENTIFIC NOTICES—Philosophy of the Atmosphere—Eclipses during the present Year—Recreations in the management of Gas—Method of preventing Iron-Work from Rust, ... 335
COLUMN FOR THE LADIES—"The virgin, virgin violet"—Young Maiden's Logic—Mr. Cobbett and the Ladies 336
Orchards in Scotland, ... Ib.
SCRAPS—Effect of High Salaries—The Press of the Thieves and the Aristocrats compared—Expedition in Search of Captain Ross .... Ib.

EDINBURGH: Printed by and for JOHN JOHNSTONE, 19, St. James' Square.—Published by JOHN ANDERSON, Jun., Bookseller, 55, North Bridge Street, Edinburgh; by JOHN MACLEOD, and ATKINSON & Co., Booksellers, Glasgow; and sold by all Booksellers and Venders of Cheap Periodicals.

THE Schoolmaster,
AND
EDINBURGH WEEKLY MAGAZINE.
CONDUCTED BY JOHN JOHNSTONE.

THE SCHOOLMASTER IS ABROAD.—LORD BROUGHAM.

No. 44.—Vol. II. SATURDAY, JUNE 1, 1833. PRICE THREE-HALFPENCE.

THE FEMALES OF THE FASHIONABLE WORLD.

FAR and near rings the loud shout of freedom, and the clang of the bursting fetters of bondsmen resolving to be free. Great moral truths are now stirring to the very depths of society, and half the world is plunged in the sea of politics, setting at naught all antique precedents, and looking only to the utility of those things which are to come. And this is well. But it would be still better, if those engaged would reflect, that as that which is taken by the sword may be retaken by the sword, even so that which is won by the spirit-stirring excitement of political agitation, may be again lost in the revulsion, when the spirit shall be laid in slumber, or an excitement of a new kind shall prevail. Only by laying a firm ground-work of just public opinion, can the causes of future strife be entirely removed; but to the very root of the evil, few have yet adverted. Well-intentioned men have frequently said, "Give us the boys to educate, and we care not what you may do with the men." There is a deeper depth than this. A philosopher would say, "Give me the women to educate, and the whole world shall be fashioned after the pattern I may lay down." The philosopher of old, when the father told him that he could buy a slave for the price he required for teaching his child, replied, "Do so, and you will then possess two slaves!" Even thus is it with our women. We make of them bond-slaves, and with their milk they breathe the self-same spirit into our children. The influence of women, attractive women,—and a large portion of the English women are attractive—is all but boundless; be they slaves or companions, sensual toys or reasoning friends, their influence is still exerted either for good or for evil. The child that is born takes the mould of its mother, in mind as in body, and she can model the infant hero, or form the plastic and emasculate slave with equal facility, according to the bent of her own disposition; and the impression thus given is lasting. Can it be expected, that the imperfect model should give forth a perfect cast?

Whatever be the rank of our females, whether high or low, they are, with few exceptions, as much slaves as the inmates of a Turkish haram, though after a different fashion. The difference between the classes here is, that the poor man seeks an efficient working-slave, the rich man, an agreeable and well-taught haram slave. The man in middling circumstances endeavours, if possible, to combine both. In this classification I do not include the cases of reasoning and delightful mutual affection, which of course, are to be found in all classes, where human nature has not been corrupted by bad teaching; but, alas! these cases are as nothing in the great mass. What is the education of the women of the higher classes? Does it not consist almost entirely in what are called accomplishments, i.e. singing, and music, and dancing, and dressing, and a peculiar carriage and capacity for gesticulation, whereby to excite the senses, and attract the notice of those of the male sex who are deemed sufficiently wealthy, or sufficiently noble, to be worth looking after as husbands? Do they, for the most part, add to these qualities any others, save the parrot-acquirement of three or four languages, for the purpose of misusing them in speech, the capacity of working at certain useless toys, and the knowledge of the regular routine of fashionable business, which all fashionable people undergo—the breakfasts and dinners, and balls and suppers, and the proper time to go out of town and the proper time to return? Are they ever instructed in useful knowledge; are their minds trained; is their judgment in any way exercised or enlarged, to enable them to distinguish between good and evil, between virtue and vice? Are they not taught to make the *expedient* the ready substitute for the *right*? And when what is called their "education" is ended, or when they are what is called "finished" —alas! how true is that word—what then remains for them? Are they not led out like "lambs to the slaughter;" are they not put up for sale at the fashionable shambles, where they are "brought out" to be disposed of to the highest bidder, with more real coarseness, though disguised under the veil of hypocrisy, than it is the lot of female servants to undergo at a statute fair? Are their feelings ever consulted, their likings or dislikings? Are they not bidden to sit, and to walk, and to recline, in those modes which are most likely to attract the eyes of the chapmen, just as a horse is put through its paces? May they speak ere they are spoken to, and are they not required to overcome every feeling of repugnance, when a likely bidder appears to make his offers? Are they not studiously instructed that marriage is not an affair of love, or affection, or judgment, but merely a matter of bargain and sale, for the purpose of securing as much of wealth, or station, or both, as they can possibly achieve? Are not the whole arrangements made with diplomatic caution, and is not a half-concluded bargain frequently broken off, in consequence of a better offer? What is the female in all this better than an eastern slave? What is she better than the female who sat by the way-side and received the gifts of Judah? Wherein does she differ from the hirelings who infest the street-corners to entrap the unwary? Nay, she is worse than they, for in most instances they have been betrayed in the days of inexperience, by the influence of passion or affection, and the harshness of the world, shewn to a fault, has driven them onwards to a crime. But the female of rank or "respectability," as it is termed, is trained to undergo in her youth a species of prostitution which is sanctioned by law. Disguise it as we will, under the fine sounding names of "honourable alliance," "excellent match," and other specious terms which have been invented to make interest look like affection, the marriage which is entered into by a female for the consideration of wealth or station, is at best but prostitution clothed in the robes of sanctity. And what is the usual result? After a few weeks have elapsed, the haram-master is tired of his new toy, and wanders forth to seek fresh excitement, leaving his victim to her own sad thoughts, and the full consciousness that there exist desirable things, which neither wealth nor station can purchase. Thus abandoned, she is marked out as a prey by the designing, and an insidious lover reaps the harvest of affection, which her master could not purchase with her person. Perchance a discovery takes place, and the poor victim becomes one of the Pariahs offered up at the shrine of the Moloch of pseudo-civilization. Or, the treacherous lover, tired and sated like her legitimate master, abandons her, and another, and yet another succeeds, till her heart becomes hardened, and selfish sensuality utterly destroys the remnants of affection. To such a woman are children born, and one after another they are consigned to the hands of hirelings for their nutriment, and the first germs of the awakening mental perceptions are warped by the blighting coarseness of those who serve, with the disgusting sycophancy of selfish interest, a race of beings whom they in secret hate, because they are by them treated as animals of an inferior class. The after bringing-up is of the same nature, the judgement is never trained, the better feelings are never brought forth, the sensual appetites alone are pampered, and the most abhorrent selfishness becomes the distinguishing attribute of the race. Have I overdrawn the picture? Let the "hereditary legislators" speak! Where amongst them shall be found even a single individual on whom peculiar circumstances have not operated; where amongst them shall be found a single individual imbued with the principles of justice, or beneficence, or patriotism? What is their justice, or what rather is by them substituted for justice, save judicial ferocity towards the poor and ignorant? What is their beneficence, save the winter dole of soup and blankets to those whom their unjust laws have made poor? And what is their patriotism, save their readiness to oppress other countries for military aggrandizement, even as they have oppressed their own for the sake of plunder? And what is the fate of the female children, save to run through the same misery-giving routine that their mothers have done? Would all this be, were the mothers really educated as useful members of society, were their powers of thinking brought forth, and their reasoning faculties cultivated, so that the qualities of their minds might be more attractive than the beauty of their persons, were they trained to possess resources in their own minds, and were their taste cultivated, so that they could yield a harvest of intellectual pleasure to those around them, and more especially to their children? It was a Cornelia who gave birth to the Gracchi; an Agrippina produced only a Nero.—*Junius Redivivus.*

KIND INQUIRY.—A physician, residing on the coast of Hampshire, begins an advertisement by stating that he "would wish to meet with a young gentleman labouring under ill health." The gods keep us from meeting with this physician.

NARRATIVE OF THE WRECK OF THE ISABELLA, OFF EASTBOURNE.
BY ONE OF THE PASSENGERS.

[WE confess to a strong liking for perilous adventures by sea; especially when, amidst the most appalling danger, there are exhibited calm courage, unshaken fortitude, self-possession, presence of mind, ingenuity and readiness of resource, high generosity; and, with reliance on Providence, resignation to its will. Of these qualities, less or more is seen in every disastrous sea-adventure. We give the following narrative from such claims on our attention.]

Eastbourne, March 15.

THIS wreck is still visible; she was a fine ship, and offers an awful evidence of the power of nature over the noblest works of art. My heart still sickens with dismay at the recollection of the dreadful trials I have passed through. I have not before had health and strength enough to give you an outline of the particulars, and even now I tremble as they pass in review before me.

All our valuable furniture, plate, books, manuscripts, outfit, and necessaries, had been put on board the *Isabella*, in the docks, when she dropped down to Gravesend, where I joined her on the evening of Saturday the 16th of February, with my wife and three children, a girl of 18 months, and two boys of four and six years. We were opposed by contrary winds, and put our pilot on shore to our great concern, on Monday evening. On Tuesday, the wind freshened into a gale; and that dreadful aggravating sickness usually attending these scenes dispossessed my wife and myself of all energy and strength. The wind was now directly against us, and every hour increased its fearful power; but our Captain, Wildgoose, commanding a very fine ship, of 340 tons, full of intrepidity and confidence, determined to proceed, although he left behind a fleet of perhaps 100 sail. As night closed the tempest raged yet more fearfully. Our gallant ship was but as a feather on the wave's surface, and all was fearfully dark as any night in the black catalogue of tempests; the wind right a-head; yet there was equal peril now in advancing or receding; the Captain, however, gave his orders with as much precision as if he were exhibiting in a state pageant. The loud voice of the speaking-trumpet was the only sound that could be heard amid the wild roar of contending elements. No one had talked of danger; but Mrs. L——, with inquiring looks, had observed she thought it might not be prudent to undress, but to lie down in her day clothes—our dear infants at this time enjoying their usual slumbers, happily unconscious of their real condition, and seemingly gathering strength for the dreadfully impending trial. Between three and four o'clock, our Captain entered the cabin; he spoke little. I saw the distressed workings of his manly mind, too big with thought for idle utterance, and one or two questions constituted all the interruptions I offered. He took brandy and water, threw off his saturated dress, and having got a little in dry clothes, retired.

From this time the ship seemed to me to labour and strain more than before, and the hurricane to drive and lay down the ship lower on her side; but as the captain was taking rest, I had fancied more security, and had laid myself down on the floor of the cabin in the hope of getting also some repose. I had been lying there, I suppose, thirty minutes, when I thought I heard or felt the keel of the ship drag. I had been to this time sick to death. I was exhausted and listless, and almost lifeless, when the dreadful suspicion and announcement of "shore" alarmed me; I was ill no more. I jumped out, and was rushing through the cabin to mention my fears, when the ship beat twice on the rock, and I heard the cry of "The ship has struck!" I called the captain. The dreadful shock, and the loud cries of alarm, combined to summon all on deck, excepting the ladies and the poor children, who had been roused at first by the general crash, and these I would not allow to leave their berths lest they might interrupt the exertions made above. Here, indeed, was redoubled energy. The

was unshipped when we first struck, and was abandoned. Now was the loud cry for the speaking trumpet, now for the hatchet, which for a time could not be found; and what a hatchet when found! Never did I see a more diminutive, ill-conditioned, useless article. I asked if there were no guns to fire signals of distress? No guns. No rockets to let off to acquaint the coast-guard with our condition? No rockets. It was evident that our captain had been, as Napoleon said of Massena, a spoiled child of fortune! Always happy and successful in his adventures, his voyages deservedly fortunate, had superseded all contemplation of disaster. Every effort was now made, by manœuvring the sails, to force us once more to sea, and made in vain; we were constrained to wait until daylight enabled us to appreciate our real situation and condition, and procure for us from the shore the necessary assistance.

It is difficult to judge of distance on water, but I believe we lay nearly half a mile from the beach. Every succeeding wave raised the ship several feet, and, subsiding, we beat with tremendous violence on the rock. An immense quantity of bricks had been shipped in lieu of ballast; between these and the rock, the ship's bottom might represent the metal works between the anvil and the hammer, and strange indeed it would have been had it not severely suffered. Every wave was a fearful mountain, while the hurricane momentarily threatened to shiver us into atoms. Such a storm has not been felt on these shores during the last fifty years. As the ungoverned state of the rudder was now breaking up all within its range, the binnacles were removed below for security, and the rudder lashed to the boom; but these cords were soon rent asunder like threads. After lying here in "darkness visible" for nearly two hours, sometimes hoping we saw boats approaching to our assistance, sometimes fancying lights as signals, the dawn at length assured us we were descried from the shore, where we saw a general activity corresponding to the peril of our unhappy condition. Not a boat could, however, venture to put out through the frightful surf, and I own I saw little hope of relief while the elements continued their frightful ravages. The shore was now lined with spectators, but their probable sympathies could avail us nothing. While this was our condition without, within the ship all was devastation. At each new concussion something was strained and gave way. Bedsteads, lamps, tables, and trunks, were falling or hurled from side to side with frightful noise, which made the females believe, in spite of our assurances, the ship was breaking up. But now beamed suddenly forth, in our extremity, the dawn of our deliverance. We had watched a team labouring along the shingle conveying away to windward a boat. It was launched, and in the same moment manned. It was the Godlike life-boat, equipped with the most intrepid crew that ever deserved their country's gratitude. In half an hour of unequalled struggles they were alongside, and boarded us, and now, indeed, I saw countenances where the glad gleam of joy endeavoured to penetrate through a mass of suffering and despair; but we had scarcely interchanged congratulations when I was told the boat had left the ship. I could not believe it. I ran aloft and found it true. I felt I had now a duty to perform to my family, and I asked the captain if the boat were dismissed, what would be his plan? I represented that as our rudder was useless, he could have no command of the ship if she floated with the coming flood, and if her bottom was pierced, of which there could be no doubt, we must expect that if she dipped into deep water, she would fill and go down, and all would inevitably perish; that it would be impossible, in her present crippled state, to work her into any port, and I submitted, therefore, that our safety should be consulted above all things. Our captain firmly answered, our safety was his principal duty, and first care; that I might rely on him that he would not hazard our safety; and that if the ship were not in a condition to leave the shore, he would not attempt it. I own I returned to my family with a heavy heart to announce the fearful experiment.

The flood-tide was coming in, and the trumpet of our gallant captain was again in full activity. After many mighty workings, an awful blast drove us over the reef, and hurried us to sea. Hope beamed again, but it was found that the ship had made five feet of water in ten minutes. The signal of distress was hoisted, and every possible effort made to put the ship's head to the shore; but without the assistance of her rudder she was wholly unmanageable, and very soon became water-logged. I now caught the captain's eye; he motioned to me, and on reaching him, gave me the dreadful intelligence that the ship was sinking, and I must prepare Mrs. L—— and my children for any event! I asked how long she might be before she went down? He said, "Some time yet." Without making any communication, I conveyed my family on deck, and watched the progress the ship visibly made in sinking. Efforts were yet made to put the ship about, but they were made in vain.

Happily for our safety, the life-boat, better acquainted with the distressing features of disaster, had kept hovering around. I had grieved at its dismissal, but now suddenly heard it hailing the captain to let go the remaining anchor. After dragging a little, he held on, and threw round her stern; but we were water logged, and made little progress. We were so low now, that every wave rolled in on one side and discharged itself on the other. It now became a question of our returning proximity to the shoal, whether I should carry up my wife and children and lash them separately to some material of buoyancy, and throw them over to the charge of the life-boat, which dared not approach us. We had thrown out a line to the boat, but it had quickly snapped, and we threw others, in the hope of keeping them at a short distance. We were now in extremes; and, as it appeared we must in a few seconds go down, I was preparing cords for the safety of my family, when a squall a hundred times more frightful than any that had yet assailed us, gave hopes, and the crew cried out, "Now—now the masts must go." But still they stood, to our great danger and annoyance. The ship had, however, felt the impulse received from the last blast, and been impelled forward; and I saw some men clasping their hands, and looking to heaven with great emotion. Simultaneously with this movement, the bowsprit turned up her nose to the gale, and now a shock succeeded which gave the glad auspicious tidings of shore. The last nearly-overwhelming gale had lifted us forward, and proved our deliverance; and now the exertions of the crew of the life-boat were increased tenfold, and they were quickly under our stern. Our captain with intrepidity worthy of any period, lashing himself for security, jumped over the ship's side, and though overwhelmed by every wave, called aloud for the children first. I had taken them below, lest the fall of the masts should injure them; I flew down, and in an instant my eldest son was in his arms. The life-boat was now riding on the brink of the wave, and now was lost in the abyss; but as she was descending, my son was caught by the heel, and, swinging round a part of a circle, as the captain loosed his arm, was caught head downwards by a dozen eager arms raised for his safety. The second boy met with more facility, and the infant was thrown and caught, when the whole crew, with generous sympathy, cried out—"Now the mother." The mother soon embraced her infants, and seemed to us protected by these our worldly saviours from destruction. The other females were then handed down, with a youth of fourteen; and I next followed in agonizing anxiety to share with those I felt dearer to me than life, the yet remaining perils.

Lifted sometimes mountains high, sometimes hidden from all view in the depths into which we descended, we reached the shore amid deafening cheers from a thousand heroes to whom danger was familiar, and who rushed into the surf, braving all its perils for our security. The boat was soon lightened, when a tremendous wave dashed against it, and threw me into the raging surf. I was soon rescued; and as I was shaking the water from my clothes, my hand was grasped by my dear Tom, who, looking anxiously in my face, inquired, "Shall we all live now, papa?" I must pause.

A cart was in waiting to convey those who required aid to the small alehouse adjoining, where rustic clothing was soon exchanged for those garments long saturated with brine. The captain and crew were left on the wreck with one passenger, and two hours elapsed before the boat could succeed in extricating these from the dangers assailing them. For a considerable period the sea had been covered with floating packages, carried by the storm and tide many miles along the beach, and these, generally, rendered utterly useless: but at nightfall began the active work of plunder, and that which had resisted other violence, was soon conveyed away from observation. P. T. L.

P.S. Perhaps I ought to add, that nearly every shred I embarked with, including watches, plate, trinkets, &c., are irrecoverably lost.

NARRATIVE OF JOHN WILLIAMS,
ONE OF THE PERSONS WHO WERE BURIED ALIVE IN THE RUINS OF THE BRUNSWICK THEATRE.

[Taken down from his conversation.]

In the beginning of last autumn, I was sent to London on some matters of business, by my father, Mr. Williams, the building-surveyor of Chester, who is also known to the literary world by his "Remarks" on some of the architectural antiquities of that city. I carried letters of introduction to Mr. Nash, to Mr. Rickman of the House of Commons, and to another member of Parliament, whose name I do not wish to mention. The last gentleman invited me to his house, overwhelmed me with professions of esteem, and quite turned my head with his offers of services. When the business which had called me to town was finished, I wrote to my father of the new prospects that had been opened to me, and, in contempt of his advice and injunctions, determined on remaining in London to follow out a career so much better adapted to my talents than that of a provincial builder. An open quarrel with my family was the consequence, but I took no trouble to appease their anger, being convinced that a very short time would prove the wisdom of my conduct, and enable me to demand, rather than solicit forgiveness.

Two months passed away in expectation. My money was spent, and the people at my lodgings began to abate in their civility, when I thought it necessary to bring my patron to the point. I called at his house for that purpose, and found him just stepping into a post-chaise. He seemed as glad to see me as ever, but, of course, had little time for conversation. When he had fairly seated himself in the vehicle, and, in my despair, I had ventured to ask, how long he meant to be absent from town, shaking me cordially by the hand, he informed me that, if there were a call of the House, he might be obliged to return in the course of the session, but that, at all events, he would have the pleasure of seeing me this time next year. I do not remember the carriage driving off, but the passers-by, stopping to look at me, as I stood like a statue on the flags, recalled me to myself, and I went home to my lodgings.

It would be disgusting to pursue, step by step, the path of my decline, which was now fearfully precipitous. From the parlour I sank to the tap-room—from the society of masters to that of journeymen—from the shabby surtout to the tattered jacket. My place of refuge was in Barlow Court, a narrow lane in the neighbourhood of Wells Street, and having some slight knowledge of the upholstery and cabinet-making businesss. I received employment accidentally in fitting up the Brunswick Theatre.

My earnings were very small, but I contrived to cheat my hunger out of sufficient to enable me to drown, almost every night, in intoxication, the sense of my degradation and my despair.

The theatre was at length opened, although the internal work was not all finished. I was in attendance at the fatal rehearsal of the 28th of February, in the course of my duty. As I was passing across the stage, I was arrested by the voice of a new actress—a voice that had lingered in my ear in spite of every thing. The earnestness of my gaze was observed by one of my fellow-workmen, who informed me that the lady whom I seemed to admire so much was Mrs. ——, Mrs ——! She was married! I forgot at the moment my situation, my dress, the proprieties of time and place, and I rushed forward to demand from her own lips a confirmation or a denial of the truth of what I had heard. That motion saved my life. There was heard at the instant a sound which I cannot describe by crash, or roar, or any other imitative word in the language; it was not loud —nor shrill—nor hollow: perhaps its associations in my memory with what followed may have fixed its peculiar character in my mind—but I can only describe it to the imagination by likening it to one's conception of the harsh, grating, sullen, yet abrupt noise of the grave stone when it shall be suddenly raised from its sandy, clammy bed at the sounding of the last trumpet. One of the actors rushed across the stage, and darted out by the side-door. Of the rest, those who were speaking stopped in the middle of a word; the hand raised in mimic passion was not dropped; the moving crowd of human beings stood still, as if by one impulse; there was a pause of two or three seconds. Some, whose mind was more present, raised their eyes to the roof; but the rest were motionless, even in the vagrant organs of vision, and stood mute and still like a gallery of statues. I cannot even attempt to describe the sound which awoke the scene from its appearance of death, only to give it the reality. I would liken it to thunder, if you could mingle the idea of the explosion without that of its effects,—or to the rush of a mighty torrent, if you could fancy amalgamated, as it were, in its roar, the typical voices of pain, and horror, and confusion, and struggling, and death. I staggered back, and nearly fell into an abyss that was cloven into the floor by a fragment of the iron roof on the very spot where I had stood but a moment before. While rushing up the side of the newly formed precipice to regain my footing, by the single terrified glance I had time and light to cast behind, I saw that the iron and wood were wet with blood and brains and the other horrible mysteries of a man's inner body, and that the "living soul" I had just talked to was not to be recognised by the sight as having ever borne the external characteristics of a human being.

The light was suddenly shut out—and yet so slowly as to inflict upon my sight that which will ever stand between it and the sun. Fragment after fragment rushed furiously from the roof, but yet so thickly intermingled that I cannot at this moment say whether or not the mass of roof was disunited at all in its descent. Then the bursting of the walls—the grating of the stones and the bricks as they were ground into powder—the rending of the planks and wooden partitions—the hissing sound of the lamps and brass-work—the damp crush of human bodies—and the yells of mortal agony from a hundred hearts, which seemed wilder and stronger even than the inanimate sounds that had called them into being—to choke, conquer, and silence them for ever.

All was dark. A weight was upon my shoulders which an Atlas could not have moved; my left leg was between two planks, and, as I discovered by feeling with my hand before the pain announced it, it was broken and distorted: the side outline of the narrow chamber in which I sat would have nearly described a right-angled triangle, the hypothenuse leaning on my back; above I could extend my hand to its full length without obstacle, but the aperture could not have admitted any thing thicker than the arm: before me was a wall apparently of solid iron, and below, and at the sides, the surface, consisting of iron, brick, stones, and wood, was broken into narrow interstices.

When the united sounds I have described had subsided into a distant hum, a single voice rose upon my ear; it was the voice of the lady mentioned above; it was one wild, shrill, unbroken scream. I do not know how long it lasted; I do not even know whether it was a human voice at all; it did not stop for breath; its way was not impeded like that of the rest, by the intervention of the ruins; minute after minute it continued, and every minute it became wilder and shriller, piercing like an arrow through my head and heart, till my tortured senses found temporary relief in insensibility.

My fainting-fit probably lasted a considerable time; for, when I recovered, it was long before I could understand my situation, or recall any thing that had happened to my memory. At length, piece by piece, the truth came before me, and I could feel the cold sweat trickling down my brow. The voice I had heard existed probably only in imagination, for it was now silent. A low deep sound was humming in my ears, which I could at length distinguish to be the simultaneous groans of human beings, separated from me either by distance or some thick and deadening barrier. My ear endeavoured in vain to divide it into its component parts, and to recognise the voices of those I knew; and there was something more horrible in this vague mysterious monotony than if it had been distinctly fraught with the dying accents of the one I loved best on earth. I felt as if my lot must be bitterer than that of the rest. I was alone—I was cut off even from communion of suffering; while they, I imagined, were together, and in the sound of one another's voices, and the touch, even, of one another's clothes, received some relief from the idea of total abandonment, of agony unimagined and unshared.

My senses, I believe, began to totter; for I complained aloud of my lonely fate: I knew that I was behaving absurdly, but I could not help it; I beat the iron walls of my dungeon with my clenched hands till they were wet with blood, and shrieked aloud with a voice rendered terrific by the fury of despair. The voices of the rest appeared to be startled into silence at the sound—or perhaps it fell upon their ears like a cry of comfort and hope, an answer to their groans from the surface of the earth. After a pause, I heard another dull, heavy sound, like that produced by a muffled drum; it was, in reality, a drum, and probably beat by one of the band, as a more powerful means of awakening attention than his own voice. The sound, in such circumstances, was inexpressibly awful; and when the hand that smote the instrument in so unaccustomed a scene wandered by habit into a regular tune, my sensations were exaggerated into a species of horror which I can liken only to that which might be supposed to visit a religious mind on witnessing some shocking and blasphemous impiety.

It may seem a species of insanity to mention it; but when the roll of the drum and the sound of human voices had ceased, and after I had been left for a considerable time, as it were, to myself, even in these circumstances of terror, and loneliness, and mystery, I possessed a species of knowledge, which the denizens of the surface would have deemed equally useless and unattainable to those underground:—I knew the hour of the night. Like the idiot who mimicked, at the proper intervals, the audible measurement of time, after the clock was removed which had taught him the practice, my inclination for drinking had been converted by habit into an almost unconquerable passion, and returned at the accustomed time of its gratification. In spite of surrounding circumstances, I fancied myself in the midst of my dissolute companions, in the scene of our coarse and vulgar revels; I drank, but without being filled; I became drunken with imagination; and the close and poisonous atmosphere, which before had been burthened with my groans, now rung with songs, and laughter, and imprecations. This state of unnatural excitement passed away, but the reaction which took place exhibited all the symptoms that attend the awakening of the young and inexperienced drunkard. With headache, sickness, faintness, fear, foreboding, repentance,—I awoke, in " an horror of great darkness."

Then the ideas, wholesome in themselves, but which in such circumstances are felt like daggers, crowded round my burthened and wearied heart. My father—my family—my arrogance—my ingratitude—my dishonesty—my misspent time—my forgotten duties—my blasphemed and unregarded God! I buried my face in my hands, but I could not hide them from my soul. Slowly and sternly they passed before me; but the last idea swallowed up its precursors; and with a start and a shudder, I found myself trembling on the verge of eternity—on the very steps of the judgment-seat, entering into the presence of the awful and eternal Judge.

It will be esteemed an example of the bathos when I mention next my hunger and thirst, and say that these passions of the perishing body almost neutralized the effect of the above sentiments of my immortal soul. Hunger, indeed, may be borne, at least to the extent it was my lot to endure it; but thirst is truly a chastisement " of scorpions."

I have not described my feelings; I have simply catalogued, and in a very incomplete manner, their proximate causes. I sunk by degrees into a sort of stupor, from which I was awakened by the light of heaven streaming full in my face, through an aperture made in the ruins by my deliverers. The apparent apathy, or, as some term it, philosophy, which I displayed, has been attributed to wrong causes. The truth is, that although at first my body was awoke, my mind was almost wholly insensible; it recovered its consciousness by very slow degrees, and it was not until I was left alone at night, that I became completely sensible of my deliverance.

This young man ultimately recovered.

THE BLACK DEATH IN THE FOURTEENTH CENTURY.

From the German of I. F. C. Hecker, M.D.—Translated by G. B. Babington, M.D.—London.

THE peculiar views and opinions advanced in this work, we shall leave to be discussed by our medical journals—we refer to it as an interesting and curious history of the greatest natural calamity on record—for the minute and authentic particulars it contains of that pestilence which, in the fourteenth century, spread desolation over the earth from China to Greenland, and which, it is believed, destroyed at least one-fourth of the population of the whole world, visiting England, indeed, with such peculiar severity, that nine-tenths of the people perished; certainly the general mortality must have been awful when, from the most credible accounts, it would appear that 100,000 died in London alone, and 51,100 in Norwich. Of its ravages in some continental cities, the particulars are here collected from the contemporary historians. At Florence there died certainly not less than 60,000*—Venice 100,000—in Marseilles, in one month, 16,003—in Sienna, 70,000—in Paris, 50,000—in Avignon, 66,000. But we shall now extract from the work some account of its desolating career :—

" Cairo lost daily, when the plague was raging with its greatest violence, from ten to fifteen thousand, being as many as, in modern times, great plagues have carried off during their whole course. In China, more than thirteen millions are said to have died; and this is in correspondence with the certainly exaggerated accounts from the rest of Asia. India was depopulated. Tartary, the Tartar kingdom of Kaptschak, Mesopotamia, Syria, Armenia, were covered with dead bodies, the Kurds fled in vain to the mountains. In Carmania and Cæsarea, none were left alive. On the roads, in the camps, in the caravansaries, unburied bodies alone were seen. In Aleppo five hundred died daily; 22,000 people, and most of the animals, were carried off in Caza within six weeks. Cyprus lost almost all its inhabitants; and ships without crews were often seen in the Mediterranean, as afterwards in the North Sea, driving about, and spreading the plague wherever they went on shore. It was reported to Pope Clement, at Avignon, that throughout the East, probably with the exception of China, 23,840,000 had fallen victims to the plague.

" Merchants, whose earnings and possessions were unbounded, coldly and willingly renounced their earthly goods. They carried their treasures to monasteries and churches, and laid them at the foot of the altar; but gold had no charms for the monks, for it brought them death. They shut their gates; yet still it was cast to them over the convent walls. People would brook no impediment to the last pious work, to which they were driven by despair. When the plague ceased, men thought they were still wandering among the dead, so appalling was the living aspect of the survivors, in consequence of the anxiety they

---

* According to Boccacio, 100,000; according to Matt. Villani, three out of five.

had undergone, and the unavoidable infection of the air. Many other cities probably presented a similar appearance; and it is ascertained that a great number of small country towns and villages which have been estimated, and not too highly, at 200, were bereft of all their inhabitants.

"In many places in France not more than two out of twenty of the inhabitants were left alive, and the capital felt the fury of the plague, alike in the palace and cot.

"The church-yards were unable to contain the dead, and many houses, left without inhabitants, fell to ruins.

"In Avignon, the Pope found it necessary to consecrate the Rhone, that the bodies might be thrown into the river without delay; as the church-yards would no longer hold them; so likewise in all populous cities, extraordinary measures were adopted in order speedily to dispose of the dead. In Vienna, where for some time twelve hundred inhabitants died daily, the interment of corpses in the church-yards, and within the churches, was forthwith prohibited, and the dead were then arranged in layers by thousands, in six large pits outside the city, as had already been done in Cairo and Paris.

"In many places it was rumoured that plague patients were buried alive, as may sometimes happen through senseless alarm and indecent haste; and thus the horror of the distressed people was everywhere increased. In Erfurt, after the church-yard was filled, twelve thousand corpses were thrown into eleven great pits; and the like might, more or less exactly, be stated with respect to all the larger cities. Funeral ceremonies, the last consolation of the survivors, were everywhere impracticable.

"In all Germany, according to a probable calculation, there seems to have died only 1,244,434 inhabitants; this country, however, was more spared than others: Italy, on the contrary, was most severely visited. It is said to have lost half its inhabitants; and this account is rendered credible from the immense losses of individual cities and provinces; for in Sardinia, and Corsica, according to the account of the distinguished Florentine, John Villani, who was himself carried off by the Black Plague, scarcely a third part of the population remained alive; and it is related of the Venetians, that they engaged ships at a high rate to retreat to the islands; so that after the plague had carried off three-fourths of her inhabitants, that proud city was left forlorn and desolate. In Padua, after the cessation of the plague, two-thirds of the inhabitants were wanting; and in Florence it was prohibited to publish the numbers of the dead, and to toll the bells at their funerals, in order that the living might not abandon themselves to despair."

Dr. Hecker seems inclined to attribute this fatal pestilence to the great revolutions in the organism of the earth, which preceded its appearance. Dr. Babington, however, well observes, "to assume causes of whose existence we have no proof, in order to account for effects, which, after all, they do not explain, is making no real advance in knowledge—still, I regard the author's opinions, illustrated as they are by a series of interesting facts diligently collected from authentic sources, as, at least, worthy of examination before we reject them; and valuable, as furnishing extensive data on which to build new theories." We intend to confine ourselves to recording the facts so collected.

"From China to the Atlantic, the foundations of the earth were shaken—throughout Asia and Europe the atmosphere was in commotion, and endangered, by its baneful influence, both vegetable and animal life.

"The series of these great events began in the year 1333, fifteen years before the plague broke out in Europe; they first appeared in China. Here a parching drought, accompanied by famine, commenced in the tract of country, watered by the rivers Kiang and Hoai. This was followed by such violent torrents of rain, in and about Kingsai, at that time the capital of the Empire, that, according to tradition, more than four hundred thousand people perished in these great floods. Finally the mountain Tsincheou fell in, and vast clefts were formed in the earth.

A few months afterwards an earthquake followed, at and near Kingsai; and, subsequent to the falling in of the mountains of Ki-ming-chan, a lake was formed of more than a hundred leagues in circumference, where, again, thousands found their grave. In Hou-koung and Ho-nan, a drought prevailed for five months; and innumerable swarms of locusts destroyed the vegetation; while famine and pestilence, as usual, followed in their train. Connected accounts of the condition of Europe before this great catastrophe, are not to be expected from the writers of the fourteenth century. It is remarkable, however, that simultaneously with a drought and renewed floods in China, in 1336, many uncommon atmospheric phenomena, and in the winter frequent thunder storms were observed in the north of France, and so early as the eventful year of 1333, an eruption of Etna took place.

"In 1333, Kingsai was visited by an earthquake of ten days' duration; at the same time France suffered from a failure in the harvest; and, thenceforth, till the year 1342, there was in China a constant succession of inundations, earthquakes, and famines. In the same year great floods occurred in the vicinity of the Rhine and France, which could not be attributed to rain alone, for, everywhere, even on the tops of the mountains, springs were seen to burst forth, and dry tracts were laid under water in an inexplicable manner.

"The signs of terrestrial commotions commenced in Europe in the year 1348.

"On the island of Cyprus, the plague from the East had already broken out; when an earthquake shook the foundations of the island, and was accompanied by so frightful a hurricane, that the sea overflowed, the ships were dashed to pieces on the rocks, and few outlived the terrific event, whereby this fertile and blooming island was converted into a desert. Before the earthquake a pestiferous wind spread so poisonous an odour, that many, being overpowered by it, fell down suddenly, and expired in dreadful agonies.

"Pursuing the course of these grand revolutions further, we find notice of an unexampled earthquake, which, on the 25th of January, 1318, shook Greece, Italy, and the neighbouring countries.—Naples, Rome, Pisa, Bologna, Padua, Venice, and many other cities suffered considerably; whole villages were swallowed up. Castles, houses, and churches were overthrown, and hundreds of people were buried beneath the ruins. In Carinthia, thirty villages, together with all the churches, were demolished; more than a thousand corpses were drawn out of the rubbish; the city of Villach was so completely destroyed, that very few of its inhabitants were saved; and when the earth ceased to tremble, it was found that mountains had been removed from their positions, and that many hamlets were left in ruins.

"These destructive earthquakes extended as far as the neighbourhood of Basle, and recurred until the year 1360, throughout Germany, France, Silesia, Poland, England, and Denmark, and much farther north."

Having thus briefly referred to the natural phenomena which preceded this frightful pestilence, Dr. Hecker adverts to the moral consequences which followed. The fears, the mental agonies of the people, of course influenced them according to their several natures. "An awful sense of contrition seized Christians of every communion; they resolved to awake from their vices, to make restitution for past offences, before they were summoned hence—to seek reconciliation with their Maker, and to avert, by self-chastisement, the punishment due to their former sins."

The Brotherhood of the Flagellants, which first consisted chiefly of persons of the lower classes was now increased by many nobles and Ecclesiastics.—" They marched through the cities, in well-organized processions, with leaders and singers;—their heads covered as far as the eyes; their look fixed on the ground, accompanied by every token of the deepest contrition and mourning. They were robed in sombre garments, with red crosses on the breast, back, and cap, and bore triple scourges, tied in three or four knots, in which points of iron were fixed. Tapers and magnificent banners of velvet and cloth of gold were carried before them;

whenever they made their appearance, they were welcomed by the ringing of the bells; and the people flocked from all quarters to listen to their hymns, and to witness their penance, with devotion and tears."

But the most astounding and dreadful consequence was the persecution of the Jews, who were accused of having caused the calamity by poisoning the springs and wells, and infecting the air:—

"The persecution of the Jews commenced in September and October, 1348, at Chillon, on the Lake of Geneva, where the first criminal proceedings were instituted against them, after they had long before been accused by the people of poisoning the wells; similar scenes followed in Bern and Freyburg, in Jan., 1349.
      *   *   *   *

"Already, in the autumn of 1348, a dreadful panic, caused by the supposed poisoning, seized all nations; and in Germany especially, the springs and wells were built over, that nobody might drink of them, or employ the water in culinary purposes; and for a long time, the inhabitants of numerous towns and villages, used only river and rain water. The city gates were also guarded with the strictest caution—only confidential persons were admitted; and if medicine, or any other article which might be supposed to be poisonous, was found in the possession of a stranger—and it was natural that some should have these things by them for private use—they were forced to swallow a portion of it. By this trying state of privation, distrust, and suspicion, the hatred against the supposed poisoners became greatly increased, and often broke out in popular commotions, which only still further infuriated the wildest passions. The noble and the mean fearlessly bound themselves by an oath, to extirpate the Jews by fire and sword. Few places can be mentioned where these unfortunate people were not regarded as outlaws—martyred and burnt. Solemn summonses were issued from Bern to the towns of Basle, Freyburg in the Breisgau, and Strasburg, to pursue the Jews as poisoners. The Burgomasters and Senators, indeed, opposed this requisition; but in Basle the populace obliged them to bind themselves by an oath to burn the Jews, and to forbid persons of that community from entering their city for the space of two hundred years. Upon this, all the Jews in Basle, whose number could not be inconsiderable were enclosed in a wooden building, constructed for the purpose, and burnt, together with it, upon the mere outcry of the people, without sentence or trial, which, indeed, would have availed them nothing. Soon after, the same thing took place at Freyburg.   *   *   *   Wherever the Jews were not burnt, they were at least banished; and so, being compelled to wander about, they fell into the hands of the country people, who, without humanity, and regardless of all laws, persecuted them with fire and sword. At Spires, the Jews, driven to despair, assembled at their own habitations, which they set on fire, and thus consumed themselves with their families. The few that remained, were forced to submit to baptism; while the dead bodies of the murdered, which lay about the streets, were put into empty wine casks, and rolled into the Rhine, lest they should infect the air. The mob was forbidden to enter the ruins of the habitations that were burnt in the Jewish quarter—for the senate itself caused search to be made for the treasure, which is said to have been very considerable. At Strasburg, two thousand Jews were burnt alive in their own burial-ground, where a large scaffold had been erected; a few who promised to embrace Christianity were spared, and their children taken from the pile. The youth and beauty of several females also excited some commiseration; and they were snatched from death against their will; many, however, who forcibly made their escape from the flames, were murdered in the streets.

A SURE METHOD OF PREVENTING FIELD-MICE FROM UPROOTING AND DESTROYING GARDEN PEASE.—Sow all borders about an inch thick with coal-cinders. After this you will find no trace of these animals; and the cinders have the effect of producing more abundant crops and finer pease.

SUNDAY IN LONDON.

Illustrated in Fourteen Cuts, by GEORGE CRUICKSHANK, and a Few Words by a Friend of his; with a Copy of Sir ANDREW AGNEW's Bill.

THE fourteen *cuts*—for such in reality they are—settle the whole matter. They are indeed perilous gashes, and put Sir Andrew and his bill past hope of surgery. Our modern Hogarth divides the metropolitan public into three orders—to wit, the "Higher Orders," the "Middle Orders," and the "Lower Orders," agreeably to the classification of the Political Economists; and in order that all things may "be done decently and in order," the Sunday is also divided into portions. Beginning with the first portion and the first order, you are let into the mysteries of the King's Theatre, at the last hour of Saturday night, where are thousands of the chosen of the land—the Peers—brave Peers of England, pillars of the State!—the legislators, who curb and curtail the Sunday pleasures and recreations of the Lower Orders—the *veritable crème du bon ton*. Here we find them, tier over tier, "with feathered spinsters, and thrice-feathered wives," dispensing small talk until the clock strikes twelve; and then the first hour of Sunday, the "Advent of the Sabbath of the Lord," is twirled in by the pirouette of the dancer, and loud bravos for that damsel on the stage who dare lift her leg the highest, or can spin the longest upon one toe! Can there be a more intellectual and appropriate mode of beginning "to observe the Sabbath?" Them we see *the ladies, par excellence*, jostling with thieves and prostitutes, amidst bawling and cursing, and the clashing of carriages, and having been led to their vehicles scamper along, their snorting steeds striking fire out of the flinty pavement as they dash over it.—" Lord Thingemmy's *buggy* stops the way!" roar the cads. " Have any of you d————d fellows seen my *devil*?" lisps my Lord. " Yer honner, he's jest gaun a little ways round the canner for summat shaut—oh, here he comes, *as right as a trivet*—jump up, my Lord." My Lord jumps up, and having d————d his devil a bit, away he rattles to ———— *Hell*, with many another high-couraged Honourable and Right Honourable:—he there continues to get through the greater portion of the Sunday morning, and all his loose cash at least. Then, the fact of these *Hells* being allowed to be kept open at all hours, day and night, Sunday and week-day, is contrasted with the case of the poor pot-house keeper, who suffers a couple of cobblers to play a game of shove-halfpenny for a pint of porter, and is pounced upon, and fined L.5 for his *immorality!* Then the Middle Classes begin the Sunday in imitation of the Higher Orders, but after an humbler fashion, commencing with the theatres. The Sunday of the Lower Orders follows in due course, and originates with the public-house *pay table* on Saturday night; where the spigot is running until the first or second hour of Sunday morning, by which contrivance one-half of the labourer's pittance is wasted, and the whole of his health. Of the Pay Table there is an inimitable sketch, equal in design to some of Wilkie's best productions. Here we have the three Orders, all excellently well fitted for a "proper observance of the remainder of the Sabbath." The Sunday Market,—the Military marching to Divine Service, to an opera tune, followed by the thieves and loose women, and the unwashed from the Gin Temples;—the Gin Temple turn-out at Church time;—Interior of a Bishop's Kitchen, "The Servants Within our Gates;"—the fat housekeeper in the square receiving the ices, confectionary, and turbot, during divine service, while a pompous serjeant of the New Police is putting some poor emaciated orange-women to the rout for vending their fruit at the same time!—" Thou shalt do no manner of work—thou, nor thy *cattle*," represents a Dignitary of the Church—a slender, venerable gentleman in black, with a buzz wig, stepping out of an elegant carriage, with the step of a dancing master, the horses piping hot, while the beadle and churchwardens are paying their obsequious duty at the outward door of the Temple:—" *Miserable* Sinners!" depicts some well-fed fashionable company, seated in their carpeted and nicely cushioned pews, making this humble acknowledgment. If these be *miserable sinners*, what must those be on the hard seats and cold pavement of the middle aisle? —Then we are presented with a sketch of the Higher Orders promenading, and riding, and driving in Hyde Park; —Sunday *Soirée Musicale* in St. James's Square, gives another edifying glance at people of condition;—Sunday Ruralizing affords a view of the Lower Orders, gathered together " a-recreating" themselves on a Sunday in the fields between Primrose-hill and Highgate, exhibiting mechanics and others with their better halves toiling up the hill, some dragged-looking, over-worked artisans, dragging a chaise after them full of squalid children, while here and there, interspersed among the crowd, are abundance of peripatetic pastry cooks and confectioners, winding in and out with " Hot kidney pudd'ns!"—" Hot mutton pies, and no *vel* uns —all hot !"— " Brandy balls !"— " Cock-tail !"—" Hot *sassengers*—all hot !"—" *Tauss* an win 'em !—*Tauss* an win !" The humorous pencil with which all these subjects are pourtrayed by Mr. Cruickshank places the Pharisaical attempt to legislate against the pleasures and pastimes of the humbler classes in a more forcible light than could have been produced by the most talented invective.

PROGRESS OF ARTS AND INVENTIONS.

TRIUMPH OF STEAM.—An omnibus, *worked by steam*, has begun to ply between Paddington and the Royal Exchange London. It carries fourteen passengers; and is so constructed, that it can stop to take up, or let out passengers, at a moment's notice, and that, too, without the machine receiving that sudden check or impetus which takes place in the stopping or starting of a carriage drawn by horses. Coke is used; and therefore there is no inconvenience resulting from the smoke of the furnace. The success of this undertaking at once settles the point of steam carriages being capable to be employed on ordinary roads; for here we have a steam coach, of handsome form, threading its way, with ease and safety, through the vast crowds that throng the streets of London, at the rate of ten miles an hour, and over roughly-paved streets. It is one of the most successful efforts connected with the application of steam.

The Repertory of Patent Inventions for May, contains the specifications of two new patents, the one is that of Gibbs and Applegarth's improvements on steam carriages, the other is that of Trevithick's improvements on the steam engine, and in the application of steam power to navigation and locomotion. What Mr Trevithick claims as his invention is this:—

Firstly, the interposing between the boiler and the working cylinder of the steam engine, a long many-curved heated pipe, through which the steam is forced to pass with great rapidity, without being permitted to come in direct contact with water, by which arrangement the steam is made to absorb additional heat, and, at the same time, allowed to expand itself into a greater volume. Secondly, placing the working cylinder of the engine within such part of the flue or chimney as shall insure the cylinder to be kept hotter than the steam used in it, by which means the expanding of the steam is still farther promoted. Thirdly, propelling a navigable vessel by the force of the recoil, produced from water received, with a moderate degree of velocity, into a receptacle near within the stern, in the direction of the course of the vessel, and ejected with great velocity in a direction opposite to that course, the velocity of the jet being at least double the required speed of the vessel to be propelled. Fourthly, applying a boiler combined with a steam-expanding apparatus, as before described, instead of a boiler alone, to a locomotive engine, whereby the power of the steam is applied after the steam has undergone the expanding process; and whereby a diminution is effected in the weight of the boiler, and in the weight and consumption of water and fuel.

Accounts are given of the following patents, viz.:—

Palmer, for improvements in making candles, candlesticks, &c.; Swan, for certain improvements in brewing; Durrant, for an improved method of securing and preserving printed, written, or plain papers, &c., so as to be readily accessible; Lutton's, for improvements in easy-chairs; Halloway, for a wing-gudgeon valve for steam-engines; Sawyer, for a machine for cleansing paper pulp; Quimby, for an improvement in the truss for vessels; Urquhart, for an improvement in setting the teeth of mill saws; Camel, for an improvement in the duster for cleaning rags; and Brown, for an improvement in the construction of the dry dock.

Besides these, a list of 13 new patents is given, taken out for an improvement in the manufacture of wrought-iron chains, applicable to various purposes; certain improvements in machinery for making nails; certain improvements in machinery, to be worked by steam or other power, applicable to raising water, and to other purposes; improvements in producing leather from hides and skins; an improved process for generating heat, applicable to the heating of boilers and retorts, and to other purposes for which heat is required; an improved apparatus or machine for cutting files and rasps; a machine or apparatus for preventing accidents with carriages in descending hills, or in other perilous situations; an improved button; improvements in the means, apparatus, and machinery for exhibiting scenery paintings, or certain descriptions of pictures; an engine for producing motive power, whereby a greater quantity of power is obtained from a given quantity of fuel than heretofore; certain improvements in looms or machinery for weaving fabrics; certain improvements in machinery for cutting marble and other stones, and cutting or forming mouldings in grooves thereon; improvements in certain machinery for manufacturing lace, commonly called bobbin-net lace.

BRICK-MAKING BY MACHINERY INSTEAD OF BY HAND.—We thank a correspondent for the description he has sent us of Nash's Patent Brick Machine, although the terms in which we may speak of its merits may not altogether come up to our or his wishes. We have no doubt that the machine fully answers its intended purpose, and that it will produce from eight to sixteen thousand bricks in a day; but in the present state of society its very excellence in superseding human labour, is the principal objection we have to offer to its introduction. If the people of this country were one large family, united by one common interest, every invention for facilitating human labour would be hailed as an unmixed good, as it would add to the common stock of the necessaries and comforts of life, and allow each individual of the community more leisure than he previously possessed for recreation, mental or bodily. Mr. Owen's plan aimed at the realization of such a community, but with whatever success the attempt might be attended on a small scale, it requires all the enthusiasm of a partisan to expect to see such a state of fellowship extended to a nation. The great evil of which the people of this country so justly complain, is the want of full and regular employment, and this evil has unquestionably been aggravated by the substitution of machinery for human hands. Mr. Macculloch, and some other political economists, tell us that those members of the community who are deprived of their ordinary occupation by the introduction of machinery, may turn to something else; but in many cases the proposed alteration is little more than mockery, a mere figure of speech. There are few trades more humble or laborious than that of the brick-maker; and if he is driven from his station by machinery, what is he to do? If he apply for spade-work, or for employment as a porter, he will find that the labour market is already overstocked; that there are, if we may use a vulgar but significant phrase, " more pigs than teats." In this predicament he and his family may starve or become paupers; and instead of spending eighteen shillings or a pound, the amount of his wages weekly, with his neighbours, the baker, the butcher, grocer, tailor, shoemaker, &c. he becomes burthensome and useless to the community, in order that men may procure their bricks a few shillings a thousand cheaper than they could previously to the discovery. In the present condition of British society every improvement, therefore, that has for its object the superseding of human labour, especially that of the humblest description, instead of being a positive good, as it ought to be, becomes a positive evil.—*English Paper.*

THE STORY-TELLER.

CONSUMPTION.

WILL my young friends forgive me, if, under the character of a fictitious story, I should in reality preach them a sermon; and that on the gravest of all possible subjects —on the subject of death?

We learn, from an immense number of the publications of the present day, how the righteous pass away from works to rewards; and, from the public papers, how the murderer and malefactor expire on the scaffold; but there is an extent of intermediate space filled up by those of whose fate we know comparatively nothing; those who act, unheeded, their little part upon the stage of life, then die, and are forgotten.

It is from this class of beings that I have selected the individual who is to furnish to the attentive reader food for serious reflection during the perusal of a few dull pages, in order that we may lift the veil by which the moral secrets of the fashionable and well-bred may be concealed from vulgar observation, and see for once how an amiable and very beautiful young lady may die.

There lived, in a certain large city, a family of the name of Eskdale, consisting of a highly respectable gentleman, his lady, and three daughters. To describe them individually would be a waste of words and patience, they were so much like half the people one meets and visits with. One thing, however, ought to be remarked about this family, though by no means peculiar to them, that, while living in a populous city, where the loud death-bell was often heard to toll, and where as often a solemn funeral was seen to pass along the streets; yet, for themselves, they never thought of death. It is true they had been made acquainted with some instances of fatality within their own sphere of observation; for once their white muslin dresses came home from the washerwoman's uncrimped, because, as she said, her youngest daughter then lay a corpse in the house; and their old footman, Thomas Bell, died in the workhouse the day before the five shillings which they sent him reached his necessities. And, in high life, too, had they not known it? Had they not all worn fashionable mourning for their most revered monarch, King George the Third? And had they not lost a maiden aunt? And were not the fountains of their grief staid by a legacy of six thousand pounds? Yes,—they remembered all these things, and yet they looked upon death only as a frightful and far-off monster, who might never come to them; so they lighted up their drawing-room, and let down the rich damask curtains, and drew in the card-tables, and never thought of death. Perhaps, one reason might be, they had never known sickness. It is true, the mother sometimes presented, at the breakfast table, a countenance pale and cloudy as a morning in November, but the evening party always found her adorned with ready smiles, and new-made blushes;—smiles that betrayed no meaning, and blushes that told no tale but one.

Ellen Eskdale, the youngest of the three fair sisters, was, at this time, making her first appearance in the fashionable world. She had grown prodigiously during her last year at school, and now, though a little in danger of becoming too stout, was as lovely a young creature, both in form and face, as you could well behold.

"A little in danger of growing too stout," has a very serious sound to a young lady, and yet it was much whispered among Ellen's friends, that, in a few years, she would be monstrous. The gentlemen thought otherwise, and swore it was all envy, for they could not see a fault in Ellen Eskdale, and perhaps she did not see many in herself; for she had ears to bear all that love and flattery could offer, and eyes to see, when gazing in the tall mirror, that love had hardly been too partial, or flattery too profuse. Though trained, and pushed, and bribed forward, in all the accomplishments of the age, Ellen's chief excellence was in music; and never did she look more beautiful than when her light and ivory fingers touched the harp; for then a rich mass of sunny hair fell over her cheek and forehead, often thrown back with girlish carelessness, when she forgot herself in any of her favourite airs.

Could the bright eye, the blooming cheek, or the polished forehead—could all, or any of the attributes of beauty, support us in the hour of trial, or cheer us on the bed of sickness, they would then be worth cherishing and mourning for; but there must be something else, my young friends, to render the pilgrimage of life a path of pleasantness and peace. Rich as you may be, the grave has closed over the possessor of greater wealth than yours. Fair as you may be, the worm has fed upon a cheek as lovely. Young as you may be, death has laid his icy hand upon those who had not numbered half your years. But, as this is not the style of preaching which I have the talent, or you the patience to pursue, we will, if you please, return again to the family of the Eskdales; not as we first beheld them, but after a summer had passed away; and the assemblies, the concerts, the plays, and the parties of another winter had commenced.

Ellen was still the centre of attraction, and still she was not wholly sophisticated, but would sometimes look, and speak, as if at the bottom of her heart there were left some latent feeling, that struggled to be free from the yoke of fashion—that rose in fruitless efforts to assert itself no longer the slave, but the minister of pleasure.

These ebullitions of feeling, however, came like angel visits; and, when they did come, they were so faint, so ill-defined, and generally so mixed up with various and contending emotions, that no one knew from whence they flowed, whether from heaven, or earth; no—not even the fair possessor herself; only the ladies wondered at these times how so young a girl could venture to talk sentiment; still more, how she could make it answer, when they had so long talked it in vain; and, at the same time, the gentlemen would begin to doubt whether they might not do worse than make serious proposals to Ellen Eskdale.

Miss Eskdale, the oldest sister, had been striving for the last five years, to attain that footing in society, which had been awarded to Ellen, apparently, without any effort of her own. In loveliness, her own face would not stand the test of a comparison with her sister's; and in accomplishments, she was far behind her; so taking to herself another standing, or rather, hanging her orb in another sphere, she determined that their rays should never intercept each other, and having failed to be a beauty, Miss Eskdale became a blue; and corresponded with (at least wrote to) great authors, and patronized poor ones, and held in her charmed possession the first manuscript copies of half the bright effusions that annually come forth, to delight or disappoint the expectant winter circle.

Of the second sister, it could not well be said that she had ever been guilty of any aim at all, and, therefore, feeling no less in her sister's gain, she would often kindly, and almost affectionately, fall in with her wild fancies, when Ellen's exuberance of spirits exacted from others a somewhat unreasonable submission to her own whims and follies.

Gay evening parties came and went; and who was happier than Ellen Eskdale?

Of all the young gentlemen who flocked to her father's house, there was none more constant in his visits, more attractive in his person, or more pointed in his attentions, than Harry Wentworth, a young man of enviable fortune, just whiling away the winter months, before commencing his travels on the continent.

It was, for a long time, matter of doubt with the two elder sisters, which of the three could possibly be the object of attraction, but the whole secret had been revealed to Ellen during a long moonlight walk by the side of the river, late in the autumn, when a party of pleasure had been formed to visit the ruins of a castle, situated some miles up the stream. Ellen had always been afraid of water, and Wentworth was happy to be her escort on the shore. The dew was falling heavily, the grass was thick and long, and Ellen found a more dangerous enemy than she had feared: for she dated from this night the commencement of a thick and frequent cough, which was, at times, exceedingly troublesome. But it was surprising how little she thought or cared about the cough; for, on this night, her lover had declared himself, and though she had insisted that nothing should be said on the subject, as she was quite too young to think seriously of such a thing, she had kindly promised that she would try to think of it; and there is every reason to believe that it did really occur to her thoughts almost as often as her lover himself could desire. There was such unspeakable satisfaction in knowing that the very man, whom her sisters were trying every art to fascinate, was secretly and surely devoted to her. He was so handsome, too—so gay—so fearless—so playful in his disposition—and in everything so much like herself— Oh! it was worth all the world to hear the whispers of Harry Wentworth, when he tried, amongst the crowd, to catch her attention for a moment, while she would pass on with affected carelessness, not unfrequently returning to assure herself of the reality.

"What is all this harangue about?" said she to her lover, after they had listened, for a few moments, to a little party of grave personages, gathered round Miss Eskdale.

"Your sister," replied he, "is edifying her friends on the subject of suicide; she is telling them the nature of different poisons, and what is the readiest mode of quitting the world."

"Oh! that does not concern me," said Ellen, "for I shall never be tired of living; shall you Harry?"

"Not if you will promise to live with me."

"Now, tell me the truth for once," said she, looking up into his face,—"the truth, and nothing but the truth; for, mind you, I have a charm by which I know a falsehood, and you have told me a great many of late; tell me then, truly, whether you could live without me?"

Wentworth paused for a moment, and then coolly answered—"I think I could."

Ellen had been gazing on his face with the sweet confidence of a child, and, perhaps, it was the steady look of her clear and cloudless eyes which, somehow or other, had impelled him, almost unconsciously, to speak what she had demanded, the whole truth; which he did at once, boldly, and thought no more about it; but, had he been a nice observer of woman's character, he would have seen that the ready smile of expectation had passed away from Ellen's lips,—that the blush had faded from her cheek,—and that, though she instantly took up a new point, and began to expatiate upon its beauties with rapturous enthusiasm, she bent down her head lower than was necessary, that her thick falling ringlets might conceal her altered countenance, while she wiped from her eye the first tear that Harry Wentworth had ever made her shed.

It might be that he did not know the degree of feeling of which Ellen was capable; or that, in his own heart, there was no such deep and hidden fountain; for he never dreamed that he had given pain, and would almost rather have wept himself, than that eyes so beautiful should have been dimmed with tears. It was, however, but a light and passing cloud, and those eyes again beamed forth in all their wonted brightness; music and dancing drowned the evening in noise and confusion, and all was sunshine and glad summer beneath the roof of Mr. Eskdale, in spite of the wintry blast that howled without.

"What can be the matter with Ellen Eskdale?" said a lady to her companion, one evening, as they returned home from the play.

"Oh, in love, to be sure," was the reply; for her companion was a gentleman.

"She need not pine away for that," said the lady, "for Wentworth seems as much in love as she does. She must be ill; that cold of hers lasts so long. Did you not observe, the other day, at Mrs. Beverley's, how she leaned upon the harp, and how dreadfully worn-out she looked, after the first dance?"

"As for the leaning upon the harp," replied he of the charitable sex, "it was to show off her figure; and young ladies always look languid, when they can, to excite interest."

"Well," continued the lady, "these beauties never last. I wish poor Mrs. Eskdale may not lose her daughter yet."

It was true enough: Ellen was now often so weary that she could hardly walk up stairs, when the family retired to rest; and in the morning there was a cold glassy look about her eyes, that might well have startled the fears of a more anxious and experienced parent; and her mother did at last begin to think something must be the matter; for Ellen could not sing as she was wont; the highest tones of her voice were almost entirely gone, and she seldom got through a piece of music without a violent fit of coughing.

"Poor girl! she has quite outgrown her strength," said the mother; "she must have tonics." So Ellen tried tonics, and her cough was worse than ever; but it was not before she was obliged to give up dancing, too, that the family had recourse to medical advice.

"A slight pulmonary affection," said the doctor; and he rubbed his hands, for he saw before him a good winter's work.

Some persons, on looking back, would have been alarmed to see how much had been given up during the last few weeks; but Ellen only laughed, and told Wentworth she was growing quite a saint; and that, after Christmas, she would put on a plain cap, and go and sit with sister Cartwright, at her class-meetings.

All could have been borne; her bad nights, her cough, her weakness,—and all borne cheerfully; but now the ill-natured old doctor forbade her going out, except in the middle of the day, and when the weather was mildest. Her evenings must be spent at home, quietly, and without any excitement. If the family would stay with her, and Harry Wentworth, and two or three others would come, it might be endured; but sometimes she was left entirely alone; and, worst of all, had run through the last volume of the last novel before they returned. On Sunday, however, she had them all safely enough, and Wentworth, too, and a merry evening they managed to pass together; for they had everybody to describe, and to mimic; and when Ellen had their follies second-hand, it was almost as entertaining as if she had seen them herself. But even these amusements began to pall upon her; and sometimes, when they looked round for her ready laugh, she had turned away her face, and was quite unable to laugh at all.

Oh, the emptiness of folly, when mortal sickness falls upon the heart!

It was at the close of one of these Sabbath evenings, when her sister and Wentworth had been unusually animated, that Ellen suddenly burst into tears, and left the room.

"What is the matter with that silly girl?" said Miss Eskdale; "she grows so fretful, there is no such thing as pleasing her."

"No," said her sister Mary, "you should not say so; Ellen was never fretful, but her spirits are so weak now, that the least thing overpowers her;" and so saying, Mary followed her up stairs.

It was well that she did; for the poor girl, having at last given full vent to her feelings, in a violent fit of hysterics, the rupture of a blood-vessel was the natural and fearful consequence.

From this time, Ellen never spent the night alone; Marston, a middle-aged woman, who had been in the family for many years, had a bed placed beside her, and she was reduced to the necessity of being in all respects an invalid.

Still there seemed to be no immediate danger. It was a case which needed care and quiet. Marston was an excellent nurse, and the kindest creature in the world; so there was no need to sit much with Ellen, especially as the dear girl was not allowed to converse; and thus she was left, hour after hour, to muse in solitude; for those who were nearest and dearest to her, knew, not that love that will steal into the darkened chamber, and watch by the bedside of a beloved object, not only enduring, but choosing that faithful vigil, before all the pleasures of the world—that soul-felt and expressive stillness, when affection, like the evening dew, sheds her silent influence on the drooping soul.

There was no immediate danger:—Ellen's excellent constitution rallied again, and she was able, once more, with the help of Marston, to pace slowly to and fro in her room, casting many a wistful glance at the dull window, that looked out upon a square of formal garden, where the shrubs were matted up, and here and there a wasted drift of dirty snow told of a chilly and humid atmosphere, with all its melancholy accompaniments. Ellen gazed, and gazed, till she was wearied out; and then she turned within, and opened her box of trinkets, which had pleased her so often; but now they failed in producing any other effect than a slight touch of pain—it might be a faint apprehension that what had been would never be again, which had well nigh brought the tears into her eyes; so she asked Marston for her music; but music, without either voice or instrument, is the dullest thing in the world, and this failed her, too. What could she do? Swallow her sleeping draught two hours before the time, and beg of Marston to assist her into bed, for she was weary of herself, and everything beside.

In a few days, however, Ellen had so far recovered as to regain the wonted tone of her mind, and with this transient and delusive convalescence, came busy, thoughts of that world in, which she had been so bright a star,—that ungrateful world, that never missed nor mourned her waning light.

As soon as her strength would permit, she amused herself with looking through her wardrobe. One by one, her rich dresses were unfolded; the dressmaker was called in, to alter them to her present shape; and ah! it was like a mockery of the grave, to see her tall thin figure, decked out in the vestments of fashion, and folly, and to hear her difficult and laborious breathings, and the short quick cough that perpetually interrupted her directions, as she told how the trimmings, the fullness, and the folds, were to be so placed, as to conceal the alteration in her wasted person.

Oh! it needs religion to wean us from the things of earth!

There is nothing like a return to the domestic scenes, and pursuits of a family, for giving spirits to an invalid; and Ellen, when released from the prison of her own room really fancied she was gaining strength. With her returning spirits, the hopes of the family returned, and with their hopes, the longing to be again in the world, just to tell Lady B. that dear Ellen was recovering; and then the party at Sir Robert Long's, could they refuse that, now that Pa and Sir Robert had had a difference about their game; it would look as if the ladies of the family wished to keep it up—no, they must go, and not one of them only, but all. Marston would sit with Ellen; so they dressed themselves, and kissed her very kindly, and left her; and she sat for a long time listening to the sound of the carriages, as they rolled along the street, each conveying its rich freight to the door of the wealthy Baronet.

It so happened, on that day, that Wentworth had not been invited, and hearing that his mistress was again visible, and having nothing else to do, he went and knocked at that busy door, that was for ever turning on its hinges. Oh, how well did Ellen know his step, as he lightly skipped up the stairs! she tried to meet him at the door of the drawing-room: but her breath failed her, and she could only look a welcome kinder than words.

When her lover first beheld her, he started back; for there is a disease which makes rapid inroads upon beauty, in the course of a few days, without the sufferer being aware of any change; but he soon recovered himself, and began to apologize for his long absence, by a thousand excuses, which Ellen often interrupted by her exclamations of pleasure, that he had come at last, and so opportunely.

"I began to think that you would never come again, it is so long since you have been here. Oh, I am so glad to see you, it is so dull shut up here alone, when they all leave me; but come, sit down, and be as happy as you can, and tell me all that you have seen and heard since we last met; but do not make me laugh, for I have a wretched feeling here," (laying her hand upon her breast,) " and laughing hurts me worse than anything;" so they sat down together, and fixed their eyes upon the fire, and were both silent for a long time.

"Did you ever see any one in a consumption?" was the first question which Ellen asked; and her lover started, for he had been thinking of the very same thing.

"No, I never did, and hope I never shall; your illness is not consumption, dear Ellen; it is not, it shall not be."

"Then what can be the meaning of all this fever; and why cannot I get rid of this horrid cough; I strive against it, indeed I do; and sometimes I think it is all fancy, I feel so well; but oh! Harry Wentworth, if it should be!" And she fixed her eyes upon him, with such an expression of wild and convulsive agony, that he almost shrank away.

Wentworth was not entirely a stranger to the thought of death, but he had only thought of dying as a man, or a soldier, in the cause of honour, or on the field of battle: the certain symptoms of a lingering and fatal malady had never before been present to his observation; and now, when he looked upon the being he had regarded as least mortal, and met the glaring of the hollow eye, and saw the falling away of the fair cheek, the wasting of the once rounded lips, and felt the earnest pressure of the thin and feverish hand, his spirits failed within him; for it was beyond what his imagination had ever pictured, what his fortitude was able to endure, and he felt that he had no consolation to offer in such an hour as this.

It is true he loved her—but how? Not as a fellow-pilgrim through a vale of tears, journeying on towards a better land:—not as a creature of high hopes and capabilities, whose talents are to be matured, and whose good feelings strengthened into principle. He loved her as man too often loves woman, for the sake of her bright eyes, her shining hair, and the symmetry of a graceful and elastic figure. He loved her as a fair and charmed creature, who was to be exclusively his own—to minister to his gratification, to sooth him when weary, and to supply fresh stimulus to his tastes, when sated with fruition. How then should he find consolation for such an hour as this! He could only fold to his bosom this frail and fading beauty—kiss off the falling tears—and tell her, that she would not, could not die.

Oh! it needs religion to reconcile us to the thought of death!

After this distressing interview, Wentworth had no disposition to come again; and, if he had, it would probably have been in vain, for the poor invalid was very soon confined to her own room, and strictly forbid to see any one, except her own family, who now were all sufficiently concerned at the sad change, and would probably have made any sacrifice of their wonted amusements to save her.

Mrs. Eskdale was by no means an unfeeling woman, though her fears had been late in taking alarm; but now she felt, in its full force, how much dearer to her was the life of her child, than all her wealth, her rich furniture, and her fashionable guests.

But what could she do? The ablest physicians were consulted, and there was no hope;—her child must die! Regardless of the wonted placidity of her countenance, she wandered from one stately room to another, by habit adjusting all the little ornaments which had been misplaced, without knowing what she did; and often both she and her daughters stole, on tiptoe, into the sick room, asking the inexhaustible question, Did Ellen want anything? but never staying long beside her; for the stillness was intolerable to them, and they knew not what to say,—Marston was an excellent nurse, and Ellen wanted nothing. Poor child! she wanted that best of friends, a friend who will kindly and candidly tell her the truth; for though she knew that she was daily giving up one thing after another, and gradually losing ground, such is the deceitful nature of this disease, that she did not feel at all certain that it would terminate in death. Her physician was the only person who thought of revealing the awful truth, and a consultation was held on the subject, to consider whether it should be done, and how.

"It may be right," said one, "but I could not tell her for the world;" and another, and another, excused herself until, at last, the lot fell upon the physician, a man who had neither wife nor child, nor knew any thing of the sensibilities of woman's heart; so he took up his cane, and went straight into the sick-room, and sat down by the bedside.

"It has been thought right, Ma'am," said he, and he cleared his voice; "it has been thought right, by your family, to depute me to be the bearer of unwelcome information;" and he paused again, for Ellen turned away her head. "I doubt not, Ma'am, you understand my meaning;—all has been done that medical skill affords, but there are diseases which baffle the art of the physician; something, however, may yet be done to alleviate suffering; and allow me to assure you, Ma'am, that nothing shall be omitted on my part."

Ellen gave no sign of intelligence, either by word or motion. She had by this time buried her face in the pillow, so that, if he had said more, she would not have heard it; and the physician, with the satisfaction of having discharged his duty, rose, and gravely and quietly took his leave.

Indeed, every one in the house seemed to think they were doing their duty. Pills were compounded, physicians were fee'd, parties were given up, bells were muffled, and knockers wrapped in leather,—what more could they do? Nurses were hired, receipts were borrowed, and fruits of every description were purchased at any cost,—they could do nothing more! and still the poor girl lay stretched upon her uneasy bed, her face turned towards the pillow to hide the profuse perspiration that stood in pearly drops upon her forehead, and the still more copious flow of burning tears, which gave some evidence to the beholder of the uncontrollable agony within.

They could, indeed, do nothing more; for death had set his seal upon that beautiful form, and she was sinking into the fathomless depths of eternity—passing away, in the pride and the promise of her youth, from all its glory, and from all its exquisite enjoyments; while those who had cherished her infancy, and exulted in her ripened years; who knew that they were rearing an immortal fabric to stand for ever, a witness of their faithfulness or their neglect, looked upon their miserable child, and wrung their helpless hands, and mingled their melancholy wailings with hers; but no one pointed out a ray of hope, or spoke one word of comfort, or even thought of the blessed Saviour, who walked upon the troubled waters in the majesty of his benignant love. Trembling, fearful, hopeless, she was about to be pushed off from the frail bark of mortality; and where now were all the energies of that strong and buoyant heart? Hope, that burns brightest in the youthful bosom—hope, that too often deceives us in the intricate wilderness of life, but is ever ready to stand forth in undeniable reality on the brink of the grave—where was Ellen's hope? Weeping over the ruins of her own "fantastic realm," and faith, her sober sister, came not in that hour of need,—and why? because she had been sought only to give stability to idle professions, and vain promises, and giddy smiles, and had never been solicited to preside over her own peculiar province, the life, the duties, and the death-bed of the Christian.

The medicine, which was sent that afternoon, soothed the patient into a long slumber, from which she awoke considerably refreshed, and sat up, as usual, during part of the evening; indeed she felt so well as almost to question the doctor's infallibility, and could not help asking Marston if she thought there was really no hope.

"Oh! yes, Ma'am; a great deal of hope when the warm weather comes."

"Warm weather! how you talk, woman! it is now the depth of winter, and the spring cannot come for months yet; but oh! I dare not think about the spring;" and she fell into a long fit of childish weeping, partly the effect of the opiate she had taken. "Marston," said she, as soon as she regained some degree of self-command, "I wish you would tell Mr. Wentworth what the doctor thinks; but stay, give me paper, I will write;—no, I cannot guide the pen; do steal out, and ask to see him yourself, and tell him he must come once again. I will send for him when I am at the best, for I would not for the world distress him, poor fellow." So, one evening, when she felt able to bear it, he was sent for and came with Marston into the room where Ellen lay, stretched out upon a sofa, which had been placed beside the fire for her accommodation, when weary of her bed.

Poor girl! she had felt strong enough before her lover came, but now, when he walked silently up to her, and affectionately took her hand,—but most of all, when she heard again the well-remembered tones of his rich and manly voice, it seemed as if the ties that bound her to the world were drawn about her with fresh power, and, in that moment, she tasted the full bitterness of death.

Wentworth asked a few kind questions, and that was all, for he had not a single word of comfort to offer, and there was a choking in his throat, which almost forbade him to say anything.

Ellen all the while lay still and motionless; she did not raise her eyes, nor speak one word; yet the lids were not so closely shut, but that one big tear after another stole from beneath the long silken lashes, and wandered unheeded down her hollow cheek, where a single bright spot of burning crimson told its fearful tale.

It is impossible to say how long this painful silence might have lasted, had not the door opened and Marston beckoned Wentworth out.

"You will be so good as to remember, Sir," said she, "that I have strict orders not to admit any one; I should, therefore thank you to leave us as soon as possible."

When Wentworth returned, he gently took up Ellen's long, thin hand, that lay stretched out as pure, and almost as lifeless, as marble, and said, in a quiet voice, that he feared it was time for him to leave her. Then, and not till then, she raised her eyes, and looked full into his face.

There is an expression in the eye that is lighted up by the fever of consumption, which those who have not seen it never can imagine, and which those who have seen it never can forget. It was in vain that the poor sufferer struggled to speak. Her lips quivered, but she had no words to express the anguish of her soul. Wentworth stooped down, that his ear might catch the sound, if there were any; and, with the hand that was disengaged, she raised from his brow the thick curls of raven hair, and then gently circling his neck with her slender arm, drew him still nearer, and pressed upon his forehead her farewell kiss; saying, at the same time, in a low whisper, " It is the last!"

And this was all; and he, who had so loved her in this world, parted with her on the brink of another; left her at the gates of death, without one word about eternity to cheer her on her awful way.

Here let us draw a veil over the closing scene. He to whom time has no limits—to whom opportunity gives no advantage—to whom all things are possible, is, doubtless, able to carry on his own work of preparation in the soul, even when the sufferer dies and makes no sign.

It is the task of the writer to describe, as well as feeble powers are able to describe, the external evidence of that struggle, which must naturally attend the dissolution of the earthly tenement, to those who have not insured a place in any higher habitation.

The heart alone knoweth its own bitterness, and the heart alone beareth witness, with anguish unutterable, to that which is in reality the sting of death—the victory of the grave.

In a few days the public papers announced the death of Ellen, youngest daughter of Charles Eskdale, Esq., and all the ceremony of preparation for the deepest grief went on in the still busy family.

On the sixth day after this melancholy event, Wentworth found himself, to his great surprise, still thinking of Ellen. It was true and faithful, and looked well not to forget her; but to bear about with him continually the remembrance of her loveliness, and his own loss, was a weakness of which he had not conceived himself capable; so he filled another bumper of champagne, and determined to be wiser. He had that day dined alone at his own table, and now sat gazing, without a wish, at the rich dessert that was spread before him—not only without a wish, but without a definite idea, for he drank deeply, with a determination to drown reflection, and now the lights were dancing before him with a dizzy glare, and half-imagined images flitted by, in quick succession, amongst which the pale and lifeless form of Ellen returned too often, until at last, by one of those unaccountable operations of the human mind, by which we sometimes feel impelled to do that which is most revolting to our feelings, he started from his seat, and determined that he would go and look upon the dead body. This resolution, once formed, was soon acted upon, for he had neither power nor patience to think, and in a few minutes he entered the hall of Mr. Eskdale, and called for Marston.

She came, and neither of them spoke, for Wentworth pointed to the stairs, and the woman, taking up a tall candle, walked silently before him, until they stopped at the door of what was once Ellen's chamber. The door was locked, and Marston tried to turn the key without making any noise, as if afraid to wake the slumberer within. They entered—four wax candles, that stood burning night and day, two at each end of the coffin, gave a pale and solemn light to the chilly aspect of the room. Over the coffin there had been carefully drawn a cover of white muslin, which Marston slowly folded down as soon as Wentworth drew near; and he stood gazing on the lifeless figure, with the bewildered astonishment of one who has but a partial apprehension of some great and awful calamity.

The soft tresses of silky hair that were wont to wave and glitter in the light, agitated by the quick and playful movements of her who was so proud to wear them, were now combed out and laid in bands upon the forehead, as smooth and close as if no breath or motion had ever stirred them. The eyes, from which the very soul of merriment had once beamed forth, were now for ever folded under their snowy lids, and the long lashes fell with a deep shadow on the cheek—the hollow cheek, for which health, and youth, and beauty had once contended, as for a treasure that was peculiarly their own,—and then the mouth—where now was the exquisite play of the lips, that would puzzle the beholder with such rapid expression of mingled emotions—of pride—of laughter—of contempt—until all were lost in a smile, so beaming with the best affections of the soul, that those who felt its sweetness were apt to forget everything beside? Those lips were now drawn out into long purple lines, between which the white teeth were visible; and the chin, and the nose, too, had become so pointed and prominent, that those who had well known Ellen Eskdale might now have looked upon, without recognising, her face. And yet, in spite of all these fearful changes, there was beauty still—that beauty which every heart can feel, but which no words can describe—the beauty of eternal stillness—the beauty of death!

Wentworth gazed, and gazed, and neither he nor his companion spoke one word, until at last he lifted his rosy fingers, warm with the circling blood of life, and touched the cheek!" The chill of horror that instantly ran through his veins, brought back his scattered senses, to suffer with redoubled intensity of feeling. He had pictured to himself, before he came, the eye, the lips, the forehead, the whole countenance; but the solid marble feeling, the cold resistance of that cheek, whose yielding softness he had known so well, was what no one had ever described to him—what he had never dreamed of.

That chilling touch had, in one instant, dispersed all his imaginary fortitude, and he stood beside the coffin, pale as its own lifeless occupant; weak, and trembling as a child.

How dark and dreary was that long night to Harry Wentworth. Sleep came not to draw her misty curtain between him and the distressing realities of life—the still more terrible realities of death. If for one moment he closed his eyes in forgetfulness, the next they were wide open, vainly endeavouring to pierce into the abyss of darkness; and whenever he turned his face towards the vacant pillow, his distempered imagination presented a long white figure, stretched beside him, with Ellen's eyes, just as he had seen them in their last interview, fixed full upon his countenance, while every time his hand touched the cold bed-clothes, the remembrance of that icy cheek came back to him, bringing its own deathly chillness to his bursting heart.

At five o'clock on the following morning, the household of Harry Wentworth were alarmed by the ringing of their master's bell.

"It must be as I thought," said the old house-keeper, "he is breaking his heart for that dear young lady,"—and recollecting the efficacy of hartshorn in many former cases, when her own heart was broken, and well knowing that neither her master nor John would be able to find the nostrum, she took up the light, kept always burning in her room, and proceeded to the landing of the stairs, where she could distinctly hear the conversation which took place between the master and his man.

"Sir," said John, "the roan has never eaten a handful of corn since the trotting match on Weston common."

"Then take Ronald; I don't care which, only mind you are there in time to let him breathe before we start. The hounds meet at Bexley. I shall breakfast at the Grange, and see that you are ready for me. But stop—give me a light, for this room is darker than —"

"Break his heart!" said the housekeeper, and she turned again into her own chamber, where she was soon asleep in her own bed.

It was a noble and heart stirring sight to those who care for such things, to see young Wentworth that day on his black hunter—a furious and high-mettled animal, that few could manage; but it was the pride of his rider that he could manage anything—could bring anything into subjection. He forgot that little field of action, his own heart, and those eternal enemies, his own wild passions, and his own stubborn will. In fact he forgot everything for a few hours at least, for the frost was all gone—the scent lay well—the ground was in the best possible condition, and Ronald outdid himself, to say nothing of the merits of the poor fox, who died like a Briton.

There was excitement in the chase that day, enough to wean a heart like Wentworth's from every thought of sorrow; and if, sometimes, the image of his lost treasure would present itself unbidden, it only served as a stimulus to fresh action—to urge his horse to a more desperate leap.

Thus passed those hours of boisterous hilarity, and forgetfulness of care. But moments of enjoyment must have a crisis, and mornings of felicity an afternoon.

He was issuing from a by-lane, which led out by a sudden angle into the great public road, when in an instant, his philosophy and himself had well-nigh been dismounted, by Ronald giving a tremendous start; and Wentworth started, too; for, by that turn in the road, they had come at once upon the sight and sound of the quick stroke of a spade, upon the fresh earth of a new-made grave, in a little church-yard, that was separated by a high and thin hedge from the public road. The funeral procession was all gone—the clergyman had left the church—the clerk had just locked the door, and was carrying home the keys, and a troop of merry children were enjoying their last gambol amongst the graves, before the sexton should finish his work and turn them out of their favourite play-ground.

"That's a cold lodging," said Wentworth, as soon as he recovered himself; while he pushed up his horse's head a near as he could bring it to the part of the hedge, behind where the sexton stood. "That's a cold lodging for somebody, my good fellow; for whom are you doing that kind service?"

"Sir," said the man, looking up, and resting one hand upon the spade, while with the other he slowly raised his hat; "who lays here, did you mean, Sir?—It's a Miss Eskdale—there's a monument in that church to old Sir Jonas Eskdale, and the family has buried here ever since his time."

Before the old man had finished speaking, Wentworth was again proceeding slowly on his way; but his head was now bent forward, and strongly, and violently, yet without aim, or object, his hands were clenching the reins of his bridle.

For some time he pursued his way more like a statue than a living man, when another start of his horse induced him to look up, and he saw that he was falling in with a long line of mourning coaches; and now he could hear the hollow rumbling of the hearse, as it passed under the arch of the ancient gateway, and, when he looked down the first street into the city, its glimmering lights were intercepted at intervals by the nodding of the heavy plumes.

Wentworth would have given much, could he have entered by some other road, for to say nothing of his own internal struggle, he felt, in this rencontre, the want of the decency of external mourning.

In his scarlet coat, he had unwittingly joined the funeral procession, and his sleek and high mettled hunter was proudly rearing and prancing beside the hearse, which had just conveyed Ellen to her grave.

Before he could reach his own door, it was necessary to pass the house of Mr. Eskdale.

He looked up to the windows—the drawing-room was again lighted, and the shadows of female figures flitted to and fro.

Ah! how well could Wentworth picture to his mind the scene within. The blazing fire of a winter's evening—the many lights of paler lustre—the thick folds of damask curtains—the crimson furniture, that gave a glow of warmth and comfort to all around—the soft and flowery carpets, and the rich sofas inviting to luxurious repose. He thought of all these, and then of that little church-yard, where the night was closing in, unheeded, and that solitary grave, on which a still and steady rain was falling, unfelt; and then, for the first time, the full conviction took possession of his soul, that Ellen was indeed no more—that through the whole of his after-life he should never gaze upon her face again. There might, and he believed there would, be much to cheer and animate him on his future course, but Ellen would not be near to share it. Creatures as bright and beautiful might minister to his gratification—music might sooth him on his way; but Ellen's harp, and the far sweeter tones of Ellen's voice, would be for ever mute.

Wentworth passed on—his heart was not broken—he rushed with fresh ardour into the vortex of dissipation—he drank deeply of the cup of pleasure; but sometimes, before the cup was tasted, there would arise thoughts that were almost intolerable, of that dismal church-yard, the hearse, the coffin, and the worms.

Oh! it needs religion to reconcile us even to the earthly part of death.

Of the family of the Eskdales, it is not necessary to say more than that, at the expiration of the usual time for seclusion, they entered the church, in which they maintained a warm and comfortable seat, dressed in a full costume of fashionable mourning; that many times, during that day's service, the mother's face was shrouded in a white and delicately scented cambric handkerchief; and that once or twice, when the daughters lifted up their blue eyes, they were seen to be suffused with tears.

* From Pictures of Private Life by Sarah Stickney, a highly interesting volumes of Tales, lately published.

TIGRE-TER.

TIGRE is the name of a province in Abyssinia. In Volume XII. of the *Edinburgh Cabinet Library* (Nubia and Abyssinia), which is just published, we find the following marvellous relation of a singular kind of nervous malady to which females are especially liable. We should like to hear what medical men think of this local disease. One of the most annoying of the Abyssinian superstitions is the belief or affectation of being possessed with a certain kind of evil spirit, which cannot be expelled in any other way than by music and dancing. This complaint is called *tigré-ter*, and is more common among women than among men. It seizes the body as if with a violent fever, then turns to a lingering sickness, which, unless the proper remedy can be procured, often reduces the patient to the greatest extremity. During the paroxysm, the speech is changed to a kind of stammering, which no one can understand but those who have been afflicted with the same disorder. When the relatives find the malady established, they join together to defray the expenses of curing it; the first step towards which is to procure the assistance of a learned doctor or priest, who reads the gospel of St. John, and drenches the sufferer with cold water for the space of seven days—an application that very often proves fatal. A more effectual remedy is found to consist in a band of trumpeters, drummers, and fifers, a full supply of liquor, and an assemblage of juvenile personages to enjoy these means of hilarity. Pearce once saw a young woman who had the misfortune to be afflicted with this disorder, and, as she was the wife of an intimate friend, he visited her very frequently. Her voice was so much affected that she could not be understood by her nearest relations; and it was observed that the sight of a book or a priest threw her into great agony, during which, a torrent of tears, like blood mingled with water, flowed from her eyes. After allowing her to linger three months in this miserable condition, the husband resolved to employ the wonted remedy, however expensive and inconvenient to him. For this purpose he collected a band of music, and likewise borrowed from all his neighbours their silver ornaments, with which to load her arms, legs, and neck. The evening this singular experiment was tried, our countryman attended to give his assistance. About two minutes after the trumpets commenced, he observed her shoulders begin to move, and soon afterwards, her head and breast, and in less than a quarter of an hour, she sat up on the couch. The wild look she had, though she occasionally smiled, made him withdraw to a greater distance, being alarmed to see a person reduced almost to a skeleton exert such strength; her head, neck, shoulders, hands, and feet, all moved to the sound of the instruments, and in this manner she proceeded for some time, till at length she started up, and stood on the floor. Afterwards she began to dance and to jump about, and at last as the music and noise of the singers increased, she often sprang three feet from the ground. When the band slackened, she appeared quite out of temper, but when it became louder she smiled and was delighted. During this violent exercise she never shewed the least symptom of being tired, though the musicians were thoroughly exhausted; and whenever they stopped to take a little rest, she manifested signs of the utmost discontent and impatience. Next day, according to the prescribed method in the cure of this disorder, she was taken to the market-place, where several jars of maize were provided for the respective performers. When the crowd had assembled, and the music was ready, she advanced into the centre, where she began to dance and throw herself into the maddest postures imaginable, and continued to exert herself in the same manner throughout the whole day. Towards evening she was seen to drop the silver ornaments from her neck, arms, and legs, one at a time, so that in the course of three hours she had stripped herself of every article. As the sun went down she made a start with such swiftness that the fastest runner could not keep pace with her; and when at the distance of about two hundred yards, she fell to the ground on a sudden as if she had been shot. Soon afterwards a young man fired a matchlock over her body, struck her on the back with the side of his large knife, and asked her name, to which she answered as when in possession of her senses; a sure proof that the cure was accomplished, for during this malady those afflicted with it never answer to their Christian name. She was now taken up in a very weak condition, and carried home; and a priest came and baptised her again, as if she had just come into the world or assumed a new nature. Mr. Pearce had soon afterwards a less agreeable opportunity of becoming acquainted with the characteristics of this strange disease. His own wife was seized with some of the most alarming symptoms; but having a strong suspicion that this ailment sprang from the weak minds of women, who were gratified with the display, the rich dresses, and music, which accompany the cure, he determined not to yield to her fancy. He thought the application of a whip might be attended with a good effect, and actually had recourse to a few strokes when there was no one present to witness the proceeding. But what was his surprise when, instead of profiting by his skill, she appeared like a corpse, her joints stiffened, and life seemed to become extinct. Alarmed and grieved at the want of success, he immediately consented to pay for the band, the drink, and the other apparatus used in similar cases; and the result proved a complete reward for his connubial affection. "One day," says he, "I went privately with a companion to see my wife dance, and kept at a short distance, as I was ashamed to go near the crowd. On looking steadfastly upon her, while dancing and jumping, more like a deer than a human being, I said that it was certainly not my wife; at which my companion burst into a fit of laughter, from which he could scarcely refrain all the way home."

DESCRIPTION OF DUBLIN.
By an American Tourist.

THIS city presents the most extraordinary contrast of poverty and magnificence to be met with in Europe. As you approach it you find the suburbs composed of hovels, the sides of which are partly stone and partly earth, the roofs of turf, the entrances about four feet and a half high, and the whole dimensions of each not exceeding twelve or fourteen feet square. These miserable caves may or may not have a hole for a window, and an aperture on the top to let out the smoke, if the luxury of fire can be afforded. Around the door the dirty children are huddled—not one-half are decently clad; some of them still evince notions of civilization by slinking into the house, or turning their bare parts against the wall. I see hundreds whose whole dress, consisting of a mass of rags, of all colours and all sorts of fabrics, will not furnish one piece of cloth eight inches square; and these tatters seem to be sewed together only to prevent them deserting each other. Having passed the suburbs, the dwellings improve; and, on reaching Sackville Street, you imagine yourself in one of the finest cities in Europe. In walking over the city, the late Parliament House, (now the Bank,) the Exchange, the quay along the Liffey, and several of the public squares, excites the stranger's admiration. There is no part of London which can compare with the centre of Dublin in beauty or magnificence. But in turning the eye from the architectural splendour which surrounds him, upon the crowds which flow along the streets, the stranger will be struck with the motley nature of the throng. Here is a lass almost buoyant with satin and feathers; there is a trembling girl of eighteen, purple from cold, shrinking from shame, and drawing around her the poor rags, which with all her care, scarce cover her body; here is an *Exquisite*, perfuming the air as he passes, with rings on his fingers, diamonds on his brooch, and a gemmed quizzing-glass at his side; there is an honest fellow who cannot afford a hat, whose feet, summer or winter, know not the luxury of shoe or stocking, and whose whole wardrobe, consisting of but two articles, viz. a tattered jacket, and about half a pair of small clothes; and, not to multiply pictures, while the Lieutenant dashes by in a coach and four, the stranger gazes at the gallant and costly pageant, while he empties his pockets to satisfy the throng of beggars who pray him, in the name of God, to give them a penny.

SCRAPS.

DUELLING.—Every petty quarrel must nowadays be decided in the field. All ranks fight. It seems as if a military mania pervaded every class of men. The hero of Waterloo *fought*, and many dared to infringe the laws. Two writers' clerks lately exchanged a challenge and acceptance. A country distiller and grocer, not above thirty miles from the metropolis, did the same;—one only, however, went to the field; and not finding his antagonist there, fired off his pistol at a passing wood-pigeon, and returned in triumph. Two poulterers exchanged shots last week,—quarriers have been heard talking of throwing *squibs* at one another out of their match-powder; nay, the very coal-heavers, over their cups, have been heard to boast that they can defy the police, by *measuring off* in their subterranean dens. In short, the word DUEL is now perfectly understood by every urchin at school; and is as often in their mouths as "household words." And how can it be otherwise, since not a week passes but the columns of the public papers are bloated with the foul stain of *honourable murder*. The ancient Greeks and Romans never fought duels—among them, single combat was never practised, except between rival princes, with a view to prevent a greater effusion of blood; and this only against the enemies of their country. The story of T. Pulfio and L. Varenus, in Cæsar's Commentaries, is familiar to every scholar. But the following anecdote will do more than a thousand sage advices to show the light in which one of the bravest men that ever lived viewed this *fashionable, gentleman-like, honourable* mode of deciding quarrels, and acquiring the reputation of brave.—A young booby of an officer, having just joined at headquarters, was informed by some of his messmates, that if he did not signalize himself, by fighting some man of known courage, he would soon be despised in the regiment. On his way to Antwerp, where the corps was lying, he had the good fortune to travel in company with the celebrated Duke of Guise, who, with his usual benevolence, offered to take care of him whither they were going, which he accordingly did, and then took leave of him. The raw soldier told his gasconading brethren, that he knew no one but Colonel Guise; and to him he was indebted for many personal civilities. That made no difference, they said, in these cases; the colonel was the fittest man in the world, as every body knew his bravery. The young officer soon afterwards met the colonel, walking up and down in the coffee-house, and in a half-hesitating manner began to tell him how much he had been obliged to him, and how sensible he was of his kindness. "Sir," replied Guise, "I have done my duty by you, and no more." "But, colonel," added the other, faultering, "I am told that I must fight some gentleman of known courage, and who has killed several persons; and that nobody——" "Oh, Sir," replied the colonel, "your friends do me too much honour; but there is a gentleman," showing him a fierce-looking, black fellow, who was sitting at one of the tables, "who has killed half the regiment." Upon this, the tyro approached the man of death, and proceeded to tell him that he was well informed of his bravery, and for that reason he must fight him. "Who, me, Sir?" replied the gentleman; "why, I am *an apothecary*." The sum of the whole, then, is, that every man will find, if he takes pains to examine into the grounds of dispute, that he might have avoided them without the smallest injury to his reputation; for it is always some silly display, either of anity or pride, that gives occasion to duels.

MANLY AMUSEMENTS.—THE MOUSE AND TIGER.— Captain Hall, in his "Fragments of Voyages and Travels," relates, with proper glee, the following anecdote of a tiger kept at the British residency in India, and whose dinner was a sheep every day:—"But what annoyed him far more than our poking him up with a stick, or tantalizing him with shins of beef or legs of mutton, was introducing a mouse into his cage. No fine lady ever exhibited more terror at the sight of a spider than this magnificent royal tiger betrayed on seeing a mouse. Our mischievous plan was to tie the little animal by a string to the end of a long pole, and thrust it close to the tiger's nose. The moment he saw it he leaped to the opposite side, and when the mouse was made to run near him, he jammed himself into a corner, and stood trembling and roaring in such an ecstacy of fear, that we were always obliged to desist from sheer pity to the poor brute. Sometimes we insisted on his passing over the spot where the unconscious little mouse ran backwards and forwards. For a long time, however, we could not get him to move, till at length, I believe, by the help of a squib, we obliged him to start; but instead of pacing leisurely across his den, or making a detour to avoid the object of his alarm, he generally took a kind of flying leap, so high as nearly to bring his back in contact with the roof of his cage."

ANECDOTE OF SIR WALTER SCOTT.—In the fervour of his manly anxiety to fulfil his pecuniary engagements, he considered each hour mispent which did not directly contribute to the accomplishment of that noble end. At last, the eager desire to work himself out of debt seemed to have become a sort of fascination which he could not resist. One day, Dr. Abercrombie, of Edinburgh, (than whom none more ably "minister to the mind diseased") urged upon him the necessity of greater moderation in his mental labours: "Sir Walter," said the kind physician, "you must not write so constantly; really, Sir, you must not work." "I tell you what it is, doctor," said the Author of Waverley. "Molly, when she puts the kettle on, might just as well say, 'Kettle—kettle, don't boil.'"

HALF-AND-HALF.—A wag, on being told that the Chancellor of the Exchequer had taken off half of the duty on soap, observed, that one step had been taken towards improving the people; and we should no longer hear the phrase "*unwashed* artificers" applied to the "lower orders," who would, in future, be termed "*half-washed* artificers." This is not so good as the chimney-sweep in a northern town, who shewed one half of his sooty face clean, and pleaded for the other that the duty was but half taken off.

DEPARTURE OF A STEAM-BOAT FOR BOMBAY.—Let our readers fancy (which they easily will do, if they have any imagination) that they see the steam-boat making its way out of the harbour of Falmouth, with a crowd of passengers on deck. In the front stand a bevy of pretty girls, who have failed in their matrimonial speculations in this over-peopled country, have wisely determined to export themselves, while they are still marriageable, to regions where Parson Malthus was never heard of; close to them, and acting as their comforters, are grouped a dozen young fellows, half school-boys and half men, in the regimentals of the Hon. Company's army, going to seek their fortunes in the field of battle, and probably to perish in the swamps of Ava, the jungles of Bengal, or on the burning plains of Delhi; a little in the rear stand a group of more prudent followers of fortune, who, preferring solid pay to empty praise, are proceeding to India as civil servants of the company; scattered about on the deck stand merchants, agents, and clerks, drawn to the East, by the hope of gain; two or three ramblers by profession, made up the complement of passengers; whilst in the midst of the parting scene the captain gives his orders, which are shouted from mouth to mouth—the paddles revolve rapidly—the vessel gains the channel—and in a few hours the white cliffs of Old England vanish, it may be, for ever, from the view.—*Liverpool Times.*

CONTENTS.

The Females of the Fashionable World,	337
Narrative of the Wreck of the Isabella,	338
Narrative of John Williams,	339
The Black Death in the Fourteenth Century,	341
Sunday in London,	343
PROGRESS OF ARTS AND INVENTIONS,	344
THE STORY-TELLER—Consumption,	345
Tigre-Ter,	351
Description of Dublin,	ib.
SCRAPS.—Duelling—Manly Amusements—Anecdote of Sir Walter Scott—Half-and-Half—What's in a Name, &c.	352

EDINBURGH: Printed by and for JOHN JOHNSTONE, 19, St. James' Square.—Published by JOHN ANDERSON, Jun., Bookseller, 55, North Bridge Street, Edinburgh; by JOHN MACLEOD, and ATKINSON & CO. Booksellers, Glasgow; and sold by all Booksellers and Vendors of Cheap Periodicals.

THE Schoolmaster,
AND
EDINBURGH WEEKLY MAGAZINE.

CONDUCTED BY JOHN JOHNSTONE.

THE SCHOOLMASTER IS ABROAD.—LORD BROUGHAM.

No. 45.—Vol. II.   SATURDAY, JUNE 8, 1833.   Price Three-Halfpence.

HOLIDAY RAMBLES, No. V.
INCHKEITH.

Were you ever on the Island of Inchkeith? If not, avail yourself of the very first opportunity that offers for such an excursion, and be assured that you will be gratified with as fine a panoramic view as can possibly be seen in any part of the world, and that both in reference to the internal and external scenery.

Set off to Newhaven, then, on the first fine calm day, (the latter quality not the least important, as you will afterwards learn;) engage a boat, and if a steam boat can be got, so much the better, and sail away to the pleasant isle. You may land either on the south or north side, as may suit your convenience, or according to the direction of the wind, there being eligible landing places on both sides; but the boatmen sway you to bear for the nearest, and they are in general to be depended on. You glide smoothly along, admiring the delightful picture spread out in every direction, so that, turn your eyes to whichever quarter you may, all is charming, varied, beautiful.

Now we shall suppose you have reached the island, and have entered a fine creek at the south-west corner, and almost immediately under the highest part of it, on which the lighthouse is erected. "But what, in the name of all that is marvellous, are we to be about here?" you will exclaim; "the rocks all around are apparently perpendicular precipices, sixty feet in height; are we to be drawn up by block and tackle to yon dizzy altitude? Stop, boatmen, we are far enough into this iron-bound inlet—put the boat back immediately." "Bide awee, Sir, if you please," quoth the boatmen; "we didna come a' this way to put back so soon,—you will get ashore directly." "And where are we to go after? Is our excursion to be round the base of the precipitous basaltic walls?" "I never heard the Climpers get that name afore," says the Newhaven man with a grin; "but, howsomdever, I'll pilot you up to the lighthouse." The boat now touches the rocks, and you reluctantly step upon a ledge of them; but still you cannot discover how you are to scale the height. On you walk in the wake of the boatman, however, and anon you perceive a ravine, up which is a zigzag beaten path, which you ascend, till you emerge into a beautiful verdant valley. Along the bottom of this valley you proceed, till about the middle of it, where you observe another cleft in the rocks, up which your road continues in a direction at right angles with that of the former. You continue to ascend till you get to the top of those very precipices, which, a little before, you imagined to be inaccessible from this side of the island.

It is now that the external view gradually opens on you. There lie the shores of the three Lothians, stretched at your feet like a beautiful carpet, richly embellished with all the radiant hues of summer, and far surpassing anything that has ever come from the pencil of the artist. In the eastern horizon you have the ever-pleasing, never tiring sea, sprinkled with sails of all shapes and sizes, with the island of May on the one side, and the Bass Rock on the other, both pleasing objects—yet how different in their appearance! There, too, stands North-Berwick Law, and, farther on, the Soutra and Lammermuir range of hills, which you had a nearer view of last year during your railway jaunt; yet from this point they look even loftier than they did then. There is our "own romantic town," which is easily distinguished by its classic hills and eminences,—and see how proudly Arthur's Seat rears his head. Did you ever admire his fine form half so much while strolling at his foot, or climbing his sides? We are sure you never did. Why, even the Calton Hill, "the modern Acropolis," looks infinitely more interesting than when viewed from Prince's Street; and you may discern there the twelve pillars raised as a Monument of our National Pride and Poverty. The Pentland Hills, rising in their grandeur behind the town, throw the Castle Hill, Corstorphine, and other eminences into the shade. But to the west the scene is beautiful in the extreme. There, at your feet, is the Roadstead of the aristocratic port of Leith, in which are about a score of the wooden palaces of Britain, preparing to set off to every quarter of the habitable globe; farther away, the clear mirror-like water is dotted with numerous sweet little islands, among which are Inchmickery, Inchgarvie, Cramond,—we cannot recollect the half of their names,—while the southern shore is studded with gentlemen's houses, some of them stretching, you would think, into the very sea; and over the high land at Queensferry the Castle of Stirling may be observed merging into the clouds. But we cannot stop at this point any longer, or we will not have seen all the beauties in and around Inchkeith, in a fortnight; so come along:—see here is the south entrance to the lighthouse enclosed grounds; and as we are sure of a cordial welcome from Mr. B., who superintends the light, do not let us linger here any longer.

You must make a considerable detour after entering the enclosure, before you come to the main building or tower, where the light is exhibited, but then your every step affords additional pleasure from the scenery around you. And now you are at the door of the lighthouse, you receive a kind invitation to enter, while you almost believe that there is to be to-day an inspection by the Commissioners for the Northern Lights,—every thing around appears so clean and neat. You immediately ascend to the upper part of the tower—and then what a strange room you enter into, the top and walls of which form one complete window. In the centre stands what at first sight may be taken for a table clock, which is enclosed in a glass case, so as to afford a view of the whole interior machinery, now in motion, as it indeed must be day and night; the only difference being that you are lighted by the rays of the glorious sun, whereas at night these argand lamps, and beautifully burnished reflectors, are made to revolve, so as to cast ever and anon their light afar over the deep, to guide the way-worn mariner in his obscure tract, and direct his course on entering the Firth. From the side of this room a door opens to a balcony on the outside, and you may walk round the building, and enjoy such a view as can nowhere be surpassed for loveliness; the place, too, is so safe that ladies may walk round it without fear or trembling. This is a spot from which Mr. Marshall, or some other of our panoramic painters, should take one of their pictures; and a very splendid one it would be, if executed with any spirit, and one that would no doubt very soon repay the artist for his labour.

The spectator, on the outside of the light-room, has, in looking down the Firth, a first-rate sea view. There, in the distance, to your left, is the isle of May, the reflection of the sun on the glass of the lighthouse of which dazzles your eyes, even at this distance, and you can see the sheep browsing close by the lighthouse. On the right stands out the Bass Rock, frowning defiance on every ship that passes, while the vessels move on like living creatures, proud in their strength. There you have the land on the north side from the East Neuk to the western part of Fife, the Ochil Hills bounding the view in that direction, though there appear more distant hills overtopping these, until they are lost in the clouds, from which, indeed, they are not easily distinguishable. Immediately opposite to you, in the fine sandy bay, stands the thriving town of Kirkaldy, which, from your present situation, appears to merit the epithet *lang*, as with it the Wemyss, Dysart, and Kinghorn, blend finely into one continuous range of a busy, stirring population; while the same may be said of Burntisland, Aberdour, and Inverkeithing, to the west. In short, the whole coast of Fife is instinct with life; the background affording a delightful diversity of hill and dale, the hills not too numerous; and, in the extreme distance, the Grampians may be discerned, towering aloft in their misty grandeur. On this spot the topographer might enjoy a bird's-eye view of one of the finest portions of Scotland, a living map of the country being, as it were, laid down before him, and it is such a one as all must admire, and which an enthusiastic artist would luxuriate on for months together.

But we have spent so much time looking at distant objects, that we must descend and take a hurried ramble through the island, or it will be late ere we reach Auld Reekie again. The keen sea breeze, and the unwonted exercise, however, have sharpened the appetite; and, as our host has invited us to rest ourselves in the room under that in which we have enjoyed so much pleasure during the last two hours, we may as well try to allay the unpleasant sensation about the region of the stomach with what we have brought with us. We shall suppose all the replenishing of the inner man over, including a glass or two to qualify the substantial meal we have made; and out we sally to roam over the island, on the highest part of which, as formerly mentioned, the lighthouse stands. As we descend the path on the north side, cast your eyes to the west: down in the valley bounded by that bluff, you see the keeper has a spot of promising vegetables that will supply the pot during the year; and there is an enclosed park that would afford a good bite to a cow and a few sheep during the summer at least, though in the winter they could only "chew the cud of sweet and bitter reflection" in this place. After descending for a short space, you get to a level the greatest in extent in the island, where, we believe, the sports of the Celtic Society are held, when they take their summer jaunt to Inchkeith; and below this, just at the foot of this perpendicular precipice, is the north landing place, which you may reach by winding your way a little to the east. The whole coast of this side of the island is strewn with rocks, some only covered, and others shewing their heads above the water, while the tide is foaming and boiling among them with great noise. Farther east you see a deep ravine with precipitous banks on both sides, where, although at present dry at bottom, you can easily perceive traces of the ravages made by the sea during some tremendous storm, which occurred at no very distant date; the sides of the ravine are here and there torn, and large openings formed, which, if there is a spice of romance in your composition, you will, of course, call "caverns vast." As we are neither mineralogists nor geologists we will not descend, but hurry on to the eastern extremity of the island, which is the narrowest part; and, as you eave fully a mile to walk from this spot ere you reach the extreme east, you had better move on, for you will find it attended with more labour and time than walking the same distance over a Macadamized road in the neighbourhood of a town. While you are travelling along, however, you may as well cast your eyes about you, for though you thought you saw everything worth seeing from the dizzy height of the balcony around the light-room, yet you will find yourself mistaken; besides, the greater distance, or some other cause, makes even the objects you formerly saw wear a different aspect, now you are on *terra firma*. Every step you take the scene changes, and every change is, like the figures of the kaleidoscope, if possible more beautiful than the one preceding.

We have been viewing the north, or Fife coast, in going east, so you may as well keep up to the rising ground in returning, and then we have the south coast in view all the way. The reader may now be as tired as the travellers, and will, no doubt, hail with pleasure the south entrance to the lighthouse grounds, the spot we formerly set out from. We now bid adieu to the pleasant isle, embark again in the boat, reach Newhaven, and get home delighted and fatigued with the day's excursion.

If it should come to blow a gale while you are on the island, you need not be surprised if you have to take up your quarters in the lighthouse for a night, as such has happened before to parties of pleasure visiting the island. About eight years ago a party were detained in the hospitable little mansion of the lightkeeper from Friday till the Monday following, ere they got back to their friends. However, this is but a trifling inconvenience, in comparison to the unpleasant predicament in which a friend and a companion found themselves placed some thirty years ago. The two youths, who were both very ardent sportsmen, and considered good shots, got a boat from Leith harbour, and set off early in the morning for the purpose of shooting rabbits, at that time in great abundance on the island of Inchkeith. They had scarcely reached the island when it came on a strong gale, which shortly afterwards increased to a hurricane. They proceeded with their sport, notwithstanding, and soon killed a number of rabbits; but the boat, during the time, having broken from her moorings, and drifted to sea, their anxiety for game quickly changed to anxiety for their personal safety. There was at that time no lighthouse or building of any description on the island, and never having anticipated detention there, they had taken no provisions with them; but necessity and a keen appetite sharpened their wits, and they collected some drift wood on the shore, with which, aided by their gun and powder, they made a fire, roasted some of the rabbits, and made a hearty meal. At sunset they took shelter in one of the caves in the island, where they slept soundly, expecting to be picked up by some vessel next day, and by that means get home. The next day, however, brought them no relief, the wind continuing as violent as ever; they had therefore to kindle their fire again, repeat their repast of rabbits' flesh, ardently wishing for the accompanying luxury of a stale biscuit, or a crust of bread, and in the evening were compelled again to betake themselves to the cave for their repose. In this manner they passed the second day and night; and it was late in the afternoon of the third day ere the wind abated, when they were picked up by a man-of-war's boat, the crew of which observed them in passing, and were landed in Leith in a very exhausted state. Their friends and acquaintances having given them up as lost, the boat in which they left the harbour having been cast ashore at Fisherrow, their joy at their return may be easily imagined.

There are, however, no dangers of this description to be encountered nowadays—no hair-breadth escapes to be feared in an excursion to Inchkeith; with the exception of the remote chance of a short detention in comfortable quarters, all is as safe as a journey by the railway or any other land conveyance.

COMMERCIAL THIEVES.

In a book, entitled, "A Caution to Merchants, Traders, &c., &c., against Impositions of different kinds," we have the following singular scenes unfolded. Who could imagine so much roguery possible in the cautious and well-governed city of Edinburgh. The work is said to be intended for private circulation only, though we believe our readers will agree with us in thinking this portion of it deserves all manner of publicity. But where is the use of concealing the names of the parties? The very least punishment a fraudulent trader or undoubted swindler deserves is exposure.

An account of Mr. ——— a London Distiller and Rectifier, well known in Scotland by the name " Mr. Patent Schiedam."

A few years ago there appeared in Scotland a person from London, who represented himself to be a scientific rectifier and one who had learned the distiller's art in Holland. This said personage having visited Scotland for the express purpose of becoming acquainted with our distillers and rectifiers, was at no loss for want of an introduction, he being in possession of a secret which served as his passport. In the course of his Scottish journey, of distilled rectified calling, he waited upon a rectifier, a friend of mine, stated that the purport of his visit was to teach Scotch rectifiers the art of making Hollands upon the principle practised in the celebrated distillery of Schiedam. The Scotch rectifier on this occasion, although, no doubt, anxious to possess a secret which might be the means of securing to him a fortune, had no notion of paying away his cash for fair promises. He, however, having ascertained Patent Schiedam's terms, stated, that if an article, upon experiment, was made to rival the famous Schiedam, the premium asked would then be taken into consideration. To this proposal Mr. Patent Schiedam agreed, and being allowed to use the still-house of the Scotch rectifier, in due time made the gin-experimental. My friend, the rectifier, invited a few of his intimate acquaintances to dine at his house, along with Mr. Patent Schiedam. After dinner the gin-experimental was produced, and the company were requested to pass judgment on the super-excellent new distilled Schiedam. The verdict returned was guilty, and the gin-experimental being thus condemned, because of its infra excellence, accounts for my friend, the Scotch rectifier, declining to avail himself of the instructions offered to him by Mr. Patent Schiedam.

Shortly after this experimental failure, Mr. Patent Schiedam returned to London, and, as fate would have it, one of the presons who dined with him in the house of the Scotch rectifier, visited London in the way of business, nearly about the same time. This said person was a wine and spirit merchant, and having by chance met with Mr. Patent Schiedam on the streets of London, they recognised each other. In the course of conversation, the Scotchman told the London rectifier that his principal errand in London was to look out for a reputable agent to sell his Scotch whisky, which he meant to send to London. Mr. Patent Schiedam immediately replied to the Scotchman, "I am in the employ of the greatest London rectifier, who is vastly rich, and has made a fortune of my services alone; and thus, of course, I am well acquainted with the London spirit trade."

The Scotchman, taking it for granted that his "ain gude luck wad ne'er forsake him," concluded that he had now met the man for his purpose, and hesitated not to treat Mr. Patent Schiedam to a good dinner, and plenty to drink. Whilst the decanter passed freely betwixt the parties, the Scotchman proposed the agency for his whisky to Patent Schiedam; but Patent Schiedam being a rogue, more than cent. per cent. overproof, declined accepting the offered agency; pretended that nothing but a multiplicity of already entered-into engagements prevented him undertaking the commission; and, by way of shewing his willingness to serve his new acquaintance, promised to introduce him to another gentleman still better qualified to do justice to so important an undertaking.

The Scotch Merchant introduced to Mr. ———, a London Commission Agent; or, the Rogue his own Trumpeter.

The day after Patent Schiedam had honoured the Scotchman with his presence at dinner, he called upon the said Scotchman, and introduced him to his friend the commission agent. The agent spoke much in his own behalf; entered into a lengthened narrative of his success in forcing sales; and, in fine, acted the part of his own trumpeter so well, that the Scotch merchant began to think it might be as well to sell out and out, instead of consigning his whisky on commission. The London agent declared that it was equally the same to him whether he was, to purchase the whisky, or to receive it in charge on commission. The Scotch merchant, therefore, offered to sell a few puncheons by way of a beginning; and, at last, after much ado about nothing, concluded a bargain for one puncheon, by way of sample. The terms of payment came next to be adjusted. The Scotch merchant stated, that as only one puncheon was to be forwarded, and particularly, as it was the first business transaction, he of course, expected to be paid ready money. The London agent had no notion of ready-money buying, and, by way of evading such a make-sure merchant, at once declared that his practice was to treat all his mercantile connexions upon the broad basis of impartiality; and that, therefore, as he was only possessed of a limited capital, it would be both absurd and unjust for him to pretend to pay ready money for any of his purchases. The said agent proposed, in lieu of cash payment, a bill at three months, for aqua, and duties thereon. The Scotch merchant agreed to the proposed arrangement, provided respectable references could be granted. Mr. Patent Schiedam immediately volunteered his services, and promised to furnish the very best of references; namely, the house by which he himself was employed. The Scotchman expressed his satisfaction with the reference fixed upon, and accompanied Mr. Schiedam to a brewery, belonging to the aforementioned Mr. ——— the great London rectifier.

The Scotch Merchant introduced to Mr. ———, "The great London Distiller, Brewer, and Rectifier."

Mr. Schiedam having conducted the Scotch merchant to a brewery about two miles distant from the city, and, upon their arriving there, not finding the great L—, D—, B— and R—, he next conducted the Scotchman to a counting-house in Red Lion Square, and there he introduced him to the great wealthy man. This noted distiller, brewer, and rectifier, took much pains to persuade the Scotch merchant that he was a man of great importance; swore that had it not been for the faithful services of Patent Schiedam, and those of his friend, the Commission Agent, he would have been a ruined man, through the failure of worthless blackguards. By way of example, he stated to the Scotch merchant that he had been in partnership with said merchant's countryman, Robert More, late distiller of Underwood, who, the d——d scoundrel, had swindled him out of ten thousand pounds. The Scotch merchant naturally concluded that this London distiller, brewer, and rectifier, must in reality have been possessed of much wealth, if, after sustaining many losses, equal in extent to the one said to have been sustained through the failure of More, he was still able to carry on trade. However, the Scotchman, after ruminating a little, brought to his own recollection a report which passed current in the country, namely, that Robert More was a very speculative and unfortunate man; that, in order to keep up his credit as long as possible, he purchased, at the regular London mart, patent bills of exchange; and that, in order to realise cash to honour said bills as they became due, he forwarded goods to the care of the parties who furnished him with such bills, which parties allowed the bills to be returned dishonoured; and, at the same time, made a claim upon More's estate to the amount of these accommodation bills, they having, latterly, received in exchange for the patent currency, the said Robert More's own acceptances. Although the Scotch merchant only considered the report of Mr. More's trafficking with patent London currency as being an ill-natured and ill-founded one, yet he considered it necessary to make some inquiry concerning the respectability of this great man who had given Mr. Schiedam and the Commission Agent such excellent characters. In the course of research and investigation, he discovered that this great London distiller had never been known to have been in partnership with Mr. More; but it appeared that the firm or firms of this wonderful distilling, brewing, and rectifying copartnery, had at last been pointed out to the Scotch merchant in a private list at No. 76, Cornhill. This convinced the Scotchman that all was not right, and, therefore, he lost no time in sending notice to his intended agent that, after mature deliberation, he had come to the resolution of not forwarding the whisky, unless the sum was to be paid in ready money.

The Scotch merchant, without fixing any agent for selling his whisky, left London; but upon his arrival in Scotland, found the following letter waiting him, the style of which cannot but be admired.

Letter 1st from the London Commission Agent to the Scotch Merchant; or a Swindler's Sincerity.

"London, 22d November, 1830.

"SIR,—Mr. 'Schiedam' called upon me the other day and showed me a note, in which he is informed, that you are not sufficiently acquainted with my circumstances to enter into any arrangement respecting the whisky and ale commission. I must confess I was surprised, as, at our second interview you appeared to be satisfied, and booked my order for the puncheon of whisky, which, likewise, in your note you decline to execute. *My maxim thus far in business has been open sincerity;* sometimes I have found this (as in the present instance) to operate against me; but, in the long run, I have no doubt I shall find 'honesty to be the best policy.' I acknowledged to you that my capital was small; that I had been but a short time in business. This I told you without asking. If you had put any questions to me you thought proper, I should not have had any occasion to conceal the truth from you; but, as you had seen Mr. ———, 'the great London distiller, brewer, and rectifier,' I concluded you had received all the information you wished, otherwise I should have been more communicative, and perhaps, by so doing, have been still farther from your confidence; but, *to cut the matter short*, it is not convenient to pay for the whisky, until the latter end of January next, and I want the spirits before Christmas; but, if you choose to execute the orders which I wish, to make you secure, Mr. D—n T—s, ———, Bow Road, will back the bill, which you may make at two months, if you will divide the threepence. You may inquire respecting this gentleman of Mr. B——y, ————; or of Mr. B——n, ————, my solicitor; and, if you think well of the commission, the same gentleman will be bound for the sum of two or three hundred pounds, that my transactions with you shall be correct. Waiting your reply, I am, Sir, yours truly, W— T—."

The above letter, from its pretensions to candour and honesty, together with the kind of references given, and securities offered, satisfied the Scotch merchant that he had acted wisely in declining the London Agent's order, and caused him take no notice of the post office communication. The London Commission Agent, after three weeks' daily expectation of hearing from the Scotch merchant, began to suspect that the whisky-man was not to be easily victimised; and that, therefore, it would be better to make a second attack on the Scotch rectifier.

Letter 1st from the London Commission Agent to the Scotch Rectifier; or a Swindler's Responsibility.

" *Minories, London, 12th January, 1831.*

"Sir,—My friend, Mr. ————, alias 'Mr. Patent Schiedam,' has informed me, that when you were in London he had some conversation with you respecting sending Edinburgh ale to this market, and pointing me out as a person qualified to act as your agent. I have been sometime engaged in the spirit trade, and my connexion lies among old established and respectable houses; and, upon making inquiries, I have no doubt that if I command a good article in Scotch ale, at the regular market price, I could dispose of a considerable quantity. I learn from Mr. Schiedam that you are not a brewer, but that you could readily furnish me with the article through some of your friends, provided a proper understanding was entered into between us as to the mode of delivery and terms of payment. If an arrangement is concluded, I should propose it to be upon the basis of *mutual advantage and mutual responsibility;* but I should not dispose of ale where I hesitated in sending spirits, let our agreement be upon what principle it might. Mr. Patent Schiedam likewise told me that you have it in contemplation to work the Patent for the production of rye spirit; if you should do so, I have every reason to think that I could get rid of some quantity of it amongst the London rectifiers, if the price was near to that of the raw grain spirit. I may observe, that if you think well of my proposal, I have premises in a good situation, and well adapted for the ale trade, and can give you substantial security for the honourable and honest exercise of any trust that may be reposed in me. In the meantime, if you think proper, and are writing to Mr. ————, alias 'the great London distiller, brewer, and rectifier,' you can inquire of him respecting myself, and likewise respecting D——n T——s, ———— Place, Bow Road, the gentleman who would be my security if necessary. Respecting Mr. T——s, you can likewise inquire of Mr. B——n, ———— Inn, my solicitor. Waiting your reply, I am, Sir, your humble servant, W— T—."

From the foregoing letters, it would appear, that although the Scotch rectifier did not purchase from Mr. Schiedam the gin-distilling art, he must have parted with him on friendly terms; accordingly, on looking over the records of the society to which I belong, I found the original manuscript of the following letter.

Letter 1st from Mr. Patent Schiedam, to Mr. ————, the Scotch Rectifier; or a Swindler's Specifications and Patents.

" *London, 28th Oct. 1830.*

"Sir,—Owing to very contrary winds, I only arrived here on Tuesday, since when I have seen Mr. ————, the great London distiller, &c., who informs me that in consequence of the increase of his business, since the opening of the beer trade, he has been prevented replying to the letter which I wrote him, respecting his forwarding for your inspection extracts or specifications of the patents which he holds for the production of rye spirits. He informs me that he intends to write his solicitor, Mr. ————, by this post, to whose care the patents will be forwarded by Saturday's steam-vessel.

"Should you still have a desire to add the manufacturing of this spirit to your present business, I feel satisfied from the conversation that I have had with some of the rectifiers here, since I returned, and to whom I have shewn the sample of the Hollands I made at your works, that there would be a very considerable demand for it in this market, as the flavour of what I made for you is preferred in preference to what I have made for them, either from English spirit or common grain.

"When you have made the necessary arrangements, I will be glad to hear from you, and will cheerfully forward for you, under cover, my receipt, enclosed to my 'law agent,' whom I will leave to fix what remuneration ought to pass between us for it. You may either address to me here, or to the care of Mr. B————, alias the 'Great London Distiller, Brewer, and Rectifier.' I am, Sir, your very obedient servant, 'S———— J————,' alias 'Patent Schiedam.'"

The Scotch rectifier having returned no answer to this letter of Patent Schiedam, renders the letters from the London Commission Agent, to the Scotch merchant and Scotch rectifier, to be productions from a suspicious quarter, and I having been consulted on the contents of the London letters, as a member of a society for the Protection of Trade, gave it as my opinion that the said letters came from a gang of London swindlers. I advised the Scotch merchant and Scotch rectifier to keep clear of the parties. I have now to warn the allies of the Friends of Commerce, that the common enemy is again abroad under new colours.

(*To be continued.*)

THE INFLUENZA.

THE alarmists have begun to raise the most absurd and groundless apprehensions in the public mind, on the subject of the present epidemic, and we hear of maladies of all kinds and of all colours that are to follow it, but especially of the "white plague," which is at once the newest and most dreaded. We are told that this visitation is to come from the east, in the track of the influenza. Now we have received very recent medical journals from Berlin, and we have examined those of Paris, into which news relating to such matters is always speedily copied, but in neither have we been able to find anything to justify the coming of any pestilence; on the contrary, the only form of disease of any considerable prevalence seems to be the *grippe*, or influenza, such as we now have among us, and occasional cases of cholera and dysentery. But again, we are told that the records of past epidemics show that visitations of plague and other malignant diseases have been generally preceded by influenza. We take leave to deny this. Influenza, exactly such as the present, has been known almost as long as we have any medical records; it was particularly prevalent in the sixteenth and eighteenth centuries, but was scarcely heard of in the seventeenth; thus it has traversed Europe in 1510, 1557, 1564, 1580, and 1591: then we lose it till 1675, but have it again in 1709, 1732-3, 1743, 1762, 1767, 1775, and 1781-2. The 17th century (in the course of which influenza appeared only once) was remarkable not only for the "great plague" of London, but for three other of the most formidable epidemics ever witnessed in this country. As to the rest, so far as regards the metropolis, the influenza has been "plague" enough, without looking for another; it has been a hundred-fold more prevalent than cholera was, and we are inclined to believe has proved fatal within the last fortnight to a greater number of persons than that disease carried off in London within an equal period. Certainly this holds good with respect to the upper and middle classes of society, among whom a large number of aged persons have fallen victims to it. The increased mortality of the metropolis during the present epidemic, is strikingly exemplified by the weekly accounts of the burials; that ending April 16, exhibits an increase over the preceding of 266; that ending April 23, another increase upon the above of 209; that of May 1, a farther increase of 165—making the entire increase in the number of funerals last week equal to 640, and this, too, within the limits of the bills of mortality. The epidemic is now, however, rapidly on the decline, though a considerable number of relapses have occurred, and many continue to linger under its effects.—*Medical Gazette.*

ELEMENTS OF THOUGHT.

EDUCATION—THE FORMATION OF HABIT.
Abridged from Bishop Butler.

The constitution of human creatures (and indeed of all creatures which come under our notice) is such, as that they are capable of naturally becoming qualified for states of life, for which they were once wholly unqualified.

We find *ourselves*, in particular, endowed with capacities, not only of perceiving ideas, and of knowledge, or perceiving truth, but also of storing up our ideas and knowledge by memory. We are capable, not only of acting, and of having different momentary impressions made upon us; but of getting a new facility in any kind of action; and of settled alterations in our temper or character. The power of the two last is the power of habits; but neither the perception of ideas, nor knowledge of any sort, are habits; though absolutely necessary to the forming of them. However, apprehension, reason, memory, which are the capacities of acquiring knowledge, are greatly improved by exercise.

There are habits of perception, and habits of action. An instance of the former is our constant and even involuntary readiness in correcting the impressions of our sight concerning magnitudes and distances, so as to substitute judgment in the room of sensation imperceptibly to ourselves. And it seems as if all other associations of ideas, not naturally connected, might be called passive habits; as properly as our readiness in understanding languages upon sight, or hearing of words. And our readiness in speaking or writing them is an instance of the latter, of active habits.

For distinctness, we may consider habits as belonging to the body, or the mind; and the latter will be explained by the former.

Under the former are comprehended all bodily activities or motions, whether graceful or unbecoming, which are owing to use: under the latter, general habits of life and conduct; such as those of obedience and submission to authority, or to any particular person; those of veracity, justice, and charity; those of attention, industry, self-government, envy, revenge.

Habits of this latter kind seem produced by repeated acts, as well as the former. And in like manner, as habits belonging to the body are produced by external acts; so habits of the mind are produced by the exertion of inward practical principles, that is, by carrying them into act, or acting upon them; the principles of obedience, of veracity, justice, and charity. Nor can those habits be formed by any external course of action, otherwise than as it proceeds from these principles: because it is only these inward principles exerted, which are strictly acts of obedience, of veracity, of justice, and of charity. So likewise habits of attention, industry, self-government, are in the same manner acquired by exercise; and habits of envy and revenge by indulgence, whether in outward act, or in thought and intention; which is inward act, for such intention is an act. Resolutions also to do well are properly acts. And endeavouring to enforce upon our own minds a practical sense of virtue, or to beget in others that practical sense of it, which a man really has himself, is a virtuous act. All these, therefore, may and will contribute toward forming good habits.

But going over the theory of virtue in one's thoughts, talking well, and drawing fine pictures of it; this is so far from necessarily or certainly conducing to form an habit of it, in him who thus employs himself, that it may harden the mind in a contrary course, and render it gradually more insensible; that is, may form an habit of insensibility to all moral considerations. For, from our very faculty of habits, passive impressions, by being repeated, grow weaker. Thoughts, by often passing through the mind, are felt less sensibly; being accustomed to danger begets intrepidity, that is to say, lessens fear; to distress, lessens the passion of pity; to instances of other's mortality, lessens the sensible apprehension of our own.

And from these two observations together—that practical habits are formed and strengthened by repeated acts, and that passive impressions grow weaker by being repeated upon us—it must follow, that active habits may be gradually forming and strengthening, by a course of acting upon such and such motives and excitements, whilst these motives and excitements themselves are, by proportionable degrees, growing less sensible, are continually less and less sensibly felt, even as the active habits strengthen.

Experience confirms this; for active principles, at the very time that they are less lively in perception than they were, are found to be, somehow, wrought more thoroughly into the temper and character, and become more effectual in influencing our practice. The three things first mentioned may afford instances of it. Perception of danger is a natural excitement of passive fear and active caution; and by being inured to danger, habits of the latter are gradually wrought, at the same time that the former gradually lessens. Perception of distress in others, is a natural excitement, passively to pity, and actively to relieve it; but let a man set himself to attend to, inquire out, and relieve distressed persons, and he cannot but grow less and less sensibly affected with the various miseries of life, with which he must become acquainted; when, yet, at the same time, benevolence, considered not as a passion, but as a practical principle of action, will strengthen; and whilst, he passively compassionates the distressed less, he will acquire a greater aptitude actively to assist and befriend them. So also, at the same time, that the daily instances of men's dying around us give us daily a less sensible passive feeling or apprehension of our own mortality, such instances greatly contribute to the strengthening a practical regard to it in serious men, to forming an habit of acting with a constant view to it. And this seems again further to show, that passive impressions made upon our minds by admonition, experience, example, though they may have a remote efficacy, and a very great one, towards forming active habits, yet can have this efficacy no otherwise than by inducing us to such a course of action; and that it is not being affected so and so, but acting, which forms those habits; only it must be always remembered, that real endeavours to enforce good impressions upon ourselves, are a species of virtuous action. Nor do we know how far it is possible, in the nature of things, that effects should be wrought in us at once, equivalent to habits, *i. e.* what is wrought by use and exercise. However the thing insisted upon is, not what may be possible, but what is in fact the appointment of nature: which is, that active habits are to be formed by exercise. Their progress may be so gradual, as to be imperceptible of its steps. It may be hard to explain the faculty by which we are capable of habits throughout its several parts; and to trace it up to its original, so as to distinguish it from all others in our mind; and it seems as if contrary effects were to be ascribed to it. But the thing in general, that our nature is formed to yield, in in such manner as this, to use and enjoying, is matter of certain experience.

Thus, by accustoming ourselves to any course of action, we get an aptness to go on, a facility, readiness, and often pleasure in it. And a new character, in several respects, may be formed; and many habitudes of life, not given by nature, but which nature directs us to acquire.

Nature does in no wise qualify us wholly, much less at once, for a mature state of life. Even maturity of understanding and bodily strength, are not only arrived to gradually, but are also very much owing to the continued exercise of our powers of body and mind, from infancy. But if we suppose a person brought into the world with both these in maturity, as far as this is conceivable; he would plainly at first be as unqualified for the human life of mature age, as an idiot. He would be in a manner distracted with astonishment, and apprehension, and curiosity, and suspense: nor can one guess how long it would be before he would be familiarized to himself and the objects about him, enough even to set himself to anything. It may be questioned, too, whether the natural information of his sight and hearing, would be of any manner of use to him in acting, before experience. And it seems that men would be strangely head strong and self-willed, and disposed to exert themselves with an impetuosity, which would render society insupportable, and the living in it impracticable, were it not for some acquired moderation and self-government, some aptitude and readiness in restraining themselves, and concealing their sense of things. Want of everything of this kind which is learnt, would render a man as incapable of society, as want of language would; or as his natural ignorance of any of the particular employments of life would render him incapable of providing himself with the common conveniences, or supplying the necessary wants of it. In these respects, and probably in many more, of which we have no particular notion, mankind is left by nature, an unformed, unfinished creature; utterly deficient and unqualified, before the acquirement of knowledge, experience, and habits, for that mature state of life which was the end of his creation, considering him as related only to this world.

But then, as Nature has endowed us with a power of supplying those deficiences, by acquiring knowledge, experience, and habits; so, likewise, we are placed in a condition in infancy, childhood, and youth, fitted for it; fitted for our acquiring these qualifications of all sorts which we stand in need of in mature age. Hence, children, from their very birth, are daily growing acquainted with the objects about them, with the scene in which they are placed and to have a future part; and learning somewhat or other necessary to the performance of it. The subordinations to which they are accustomed in domestic life, teach them self-government in common behaviour abroad, and prepare them for subjection and obedience to civil authority. What passes before their eyes, and daily happens to them, gives them experience, caution against treachery and deceit, together with numberless little rules of action and conduct, which we could not live without, and which are learnt so insensibly and so perfectly, as to be mistaken perhaps for instinct; though they are the effect of long experience and exercise; as much so as language, or knowledge in particular business, or the qualifications and behaviour belonging to the several ranks and professions.

Thus the beginning of our days is adapted to be, and is, a state of education in the theory and practice of mature life. We are much assisted in it by example, instruction, and the care of others; but a great deal is left to ourselves to do. And of this, as part is easily done, and of course, so part requires diligence and care, the voluntary foregoing many things which we desire, and setting ourselves to what we should have no inclination to, but for the necessity or expedience of it. For, that labour and industry, which the station of so many absolutely requires, they would be greatly unqualified for in maturity; as those in other stations would be, for any other sorts of application, if both were not accustomed to them in their youth. And according as persons behave themselves in the general education which all go through, and in the particular ones adapted to particular employments, their character is formed, and made appear; they recommend themselves more or less, and are capable of, and placed in, different stations in the society of mankind.

The former part of life then, is to be considered as an important opportunity which Nature puts into our hands; and which, when lost, is not to be recovered. And our being placed in a state of discipline throughout this life, for another world, is a providential disposition of things, exactly of the same kind as our being placed in a state of discipline during childhood, for mature age. Our condition in both respects is uniform and of a piece, and comprehended under one and the same general law of Nature.

CAN any man, possessing a moderate degree of commonsense, not see with a glance, that if butter, bread, cheese, calicoes, woollens, &c., &c., &c., can now be bought at half the price they could formerly, and that the amount of the salaries of the servants of Government, its pensioners and its annuities remain the same, that those classes get twice as much of the produce of the labouring classes; that, in fact, they are as well off as if the people had said, we will double your salaries, pensions, &c., but prices shall not be altered. A sapient senator said, prices have fallen from facility of production; this should be for the advantage of the producers, I should think, and would have been so had not Parliament diminished the facility of producing money, instead of increasing the facility of producing that also, so that it might keep pace with every thing else. Do not supply and demand regulate markets? This admitted, is it not evident, that if the quantity of the medium of exchange either diminishes, or remains even stationary, whilst the quantities of every thing else increase, that the medium rises, or, what is the same thing, every thing else falls, and thus the Government employs, from top to bottom, pensioners to prey upon the producing classes, and exact from them what ought to have been the reward of their invention and increased toil.

EXERCISE, COURAGE, AND RECREATION.

THE exercise which I commend first, is the exact use of their weapon, to guard, and to strike safely with edge or point; this will keep them healthy, nimble, strong, and well in breath; it is also the likeliest means to make them grow large and tall, and to inspire them with a gallant and fearless courage, which being tempered with seasonable lectures and precepts to them of true fortitude and patience, will turn into a native and heroic valour, and make them hate the *cowardice of doing wrong.* The interim of unsweating themselves regularly, and convenient rest before meat, may both with profit and delight be taken up in recreating and composing their travailed spirits with the solemn and divine harmonies of music heard or learned; either whilst the skilful organist plies his grave and fancied descent in lofty fugues, or, the whole symphony with artful and unimaginable touches adorn and grace the well studied chords of some choice composer; sometimes the lute or soft organ stop waiting on elegant voices, either to religious, martial, or civil ditties; which, if wise men and prophets be not extremely out, have a great power over dispositions and manners, to smooth and make them gentle from rustic harshness and distempered passions.—*Milton.*

THE CAUSE OF BAD GOVERNMENT.

THE immediate cause of all the mischief of misrule is, that the men acting as the representatives of the people have a private and sinister interest, and sufficient power to gratify that interest, producing a constant sacrifice of the interest of the people. The secondary cause of the mischief—the cause of this immediate cause—is this, that these same agents are in one case unduly independent, in another unduly dependent. They are independent of their principals—the people; and dependent upon the Conservator-General, by whose corruptive influence the above-mentioned sacrifice is produced.—*Bentham.*

A NOBLE RESOURCE IN PAINFUL MOMENTS.

WHENSOEVER thou wilt rejoice thyself, call to mind the several gifts and virtues of them whom thou dost daily converse with; as, for example, the industry of the one, and the modesty of another, the liberality of a third, of another some other thing. For nothing can so much rejoice thee as the resemblances and parallels of several virtues, visible and eminent in the dispositions of those who live with thee; especially when all at once, as near as may be, they present themselves unto thee. See, therefore, that thou have them always in a readiness.—*Meditations of Marcus Aurelius Antoninus.*

SLUMBER.

(FROM THE SPANISH.)

FLOW, softly flow, thou murmuring stream!
  Beside my Lady's bower;
And do not mar her spirit's dream,
  In this delightful hour.

But, gently rippling, greet her ear
  With sounds that lull the soul,
As near the bower, all bright and clear,
  Thy beauteous billows roll.

Blow, softly blow, thou balmy air!
  Beside my Lady's bower;
The rudest winds would hush, to spare
  So soft and fair a flower!

Breathe gently o'er her rosy cheek
  Thy mildest, purest balm;
But heed, lest thou a slumber break
  So beautiful and calm.

FIRST ENGLISH DEED.—The earliest instance yet known of the English tongue being used in a deed, is that of the indenture between the Abbot, and Convent of Whitby, and Robert, the son of John Bustard, dated at York, in the year 1343.

A MOST REMARKABLE MAY IN PERTH.—An old chronicle of the affairs of Perth, speaking of the year 1630, says,—" In this May were five Setterdays, five Mondays, twa changes in the mone, twa eclipses of the sone, ane uther of the mone, all in our horizone."

COLUMN FOR THE LADIES.

BLACK EYES AND BLUE.

BLACK eyes most dazzle at a ball;
Blue eyes most please at evening fall.
Black a conquest soonest gain;
The blue a conquest most retain;
The black bespeak a lively heart,
Whose soft emotions soon depart;
The blue a steadier flame betray,
That burns and lives beyond a day.
The black my features best disclose;
In blue my feelings all repose.
Then let each reign without control;
The black all mind, the blue all soul.

MR. MOORE'S NEW WORK.

FROM one of the Homilies of St. Chrysostom, who, it is known, particularly distinguished himself by his severe strictures on the gay dresses of the Constantinopolitan ladies, the following specimen of his style of rebuke, on such subjects, is selected, and thus translated by Moore, in his new work, "*Travels of an Irish Gentleman, in search of a Religion.*"

Why come ye to the place of prayer,
  With jewels in your braided hair?
And wherefore is the House of God
  By glittering feet profanely trod,
As if, vain things, ye came to keep
  Some festival, and not to weep?—
Oh! prostrate weep before that Lord
  Of earth and heaven, of life and death,
Who blights the fairest with a word,
  And blasts the mightiest with a breath!

Go—'tis not thus, in proud array,
Such sinful souls should dare to pray.
Vainly to anger'd Heaven ye raise
Luxurious hands where diamonds blaze;
And she who comes in broider'd veil
To weep her frailty, STILL is frail.

We must give another specimen of this work—it is the pathetic remonstrance addressed by St. Basil to a Fallen Virgin, (of which Fenelon has said, "*on ne peut rien voir de plus eloquent.*") It abounds with passages to which, though in the form of prose, such poetry as the following does but inadequate justice:—

ST. BASIL TO A FALLEN VIRGIN.

Remember now that virgin choir
  Who loved thee, lost one, as thou art,
Before the world's profane desire
  Had warm'd thine eye, and chill'd thy heart.

Recall their looks, so brightly calm,
  Around the lighted shrine at even,
When, mingling in the vesper psalm,
  Thy spirit seem'd to sigh for heaven.

Remember, too, the tranquil sleep
  That o'er thy lonely pillow stole,
While thou hast pray'd that God would keep
  From every harm thy virgin soul.

Where is it now—that innocent
  And happy time; where is it gone?
Those light repasts, where young Content
  And Temperance stood smiling on;

The maiden step, the seemly dress,
  In which thou went'st along so meek;
The blush that, at a look, or less,
  Came o'er the paleness of thy cheek;

Alas, alas, that paleness, too,
  That bloodless purity of brow,
More touching than the rosiest hue
  On beauty's cheek—where it now?

THE STORY-TELLER.

A TALE OF NINETY-EIGHT.

Those who have been so fortunate as to have passed a few summer months in the barony of Forth, enjoying the hospitalities of its kind-hearted and primitive inhabitants—roving through its blossomed bean fields—wandering along its indented coast—tracing the remains of the Dane and Norman; or, what is still more delightful, viewing its neat farm-houses, with their orchards, bee-gardens, and all those evidences of rural comfort, that remove so effectually from the mind every idea of toil and poverty, and admiring the fair blue-eyed girls, whose taste and industry have so largely contributed to the embellishment of their happy homes, must often turn with pleasure to the beautiful pictures of Nature in her happiest aspect, which those scenes have impressed on their memory.

During the unfortunate year of 1798, the ravages of death and ruin that desolated this unhappy country, were deeply felt in this quarter, hitherto so distinguished for peace and good order; and many traces of this disastrous period may be found there even at this day.

Few may pass the lands of R———— without remarking a tall blackened gable, rising like a gloomy shadow, which no sunbeam brightens; the offices once attached to it have been long since levelled; the plough has passed over the orchard and enclosures by which it was surrounded, and nothing is left but this solitary wall, to mark that a dwelling had formerly been there. This now deserted spot had been, for a century at least, the residence of a family named Redmond, who held a lease of the townland attached to it, on such terms as left to the lord of the soil little from this part of his estate, beyond the honour of signing a receipt and paying the quit-rent. We cannot say what advance the younger branches of this family might have made towards fortune or beggary, when they left the paternal roof and entered the high-ways of the world; but, we can safely state, that the heirs of R————, one after another, held pretty much the same course; contenting themselves to live in peace and abundance, and practice all the unpretending virtues of benevolence and hospitality without impairing, in any great degree, or in the least improving their inheritance. Their lot was a happy one, but there is no condition exempt from some crosses. The repose of the good people of R———— was often disturbed by a rivalry, and consequent jealousy, that existed between them and the Barrys, a neighbouring family much in their own circumstances. We are seldom at a loss for a cause to keep up the quarrel that originates in vanity; with these good folks, some point of precedence, that a council of all the old gossips in the parish could alone settle—the cut of a coat, the colour of a ribbon, the slightest movement in private or public, that seemed to imply an assumption of superiority by one party, was sure to provoke the hostility of the other. But love, who in general delights so much in mischief, often, to do him justice, proved a pacificator between those worthy people; he blinded the young to the faults and follies which their parents had been so quick-sighted in discovering; while they saw, with approving eyes, the thousand agreeable qualities possessed by each other—so that the fond and indulgent father and mother were now more than once driven to the extremity of sacrificing some darling prejudice to the happiness of a darling child; and thus the feuds of the Barrys and Redmonds, like the sorrows and trials of many a gentle heroine ended in a wedding.

Towards the year of 1798, the interests of these rival houses, that had been long gradually uniting, were about to be blended for ever by the union of the heir of the Barrys, and the daughter and only child of Philip Redmond, of R————. Philip Redmond had been long a widower, all his affections and cares were centred in this daughter; feeling his health declining rapidly, he rejoiced that she should be so well settled before he left the world; and well he might, for never were there a pair better formed for the happiness of each other. The stranger who might have met them in their evening rambles through the rich and fruitful fields, or wandering along the sea-shore, by which the farm of R———— was situated, could not pass them by with indifference—could not forget for a time the expression of rapture that lighted up the fine manly countenance of Lambert Barry, as he listened to the unconscious bursts of feeling, or the playful sallies of the beautiful girl that hung on his arm; while his fancy coloured, with the warm hues of love and hope, the years of bliss that seemed brightening before them: but coming events cast their shadows on the path of the happy couple. Societies of the United Irishmen were at this period formed in every part of the country, and Lambert Barry became a member of that body long before he was aware of the consequence to which that step would lead. This circumstance made no change in his habits or temper for a time, for his mind was too much occupied with rational plans of happiness to indulge in the speculations with which others of the fraternity which he had joined, amused their imaginations; but he was brave and high spirited, impatient of injury and insult, and loved his country too well, not to be driven to desperation by the little tyrants who seemed to be turned loose on her, for the purpose of goading her people to madness. His sound judgment and good sense might have saved him notwithstanding, had there been any fair field left open for the exercise of them; but he was exposed to the machinations of a secret enemy, who knew the dangers by which he was surrounded, and resolved he should not escape from them. This was a young man of rather a good personal appearance, and considerable pretensions for his sphere in life; the son of a thriving farmer in the neighbourhood named Ganly, who well knew how to avail himself of all the advantages possessed by a loyal Protestant in those days. This youth hated Lambert Barry, who was wholly unconscious of ever having done him the slightest injury, with all the rancour of one whose heart is corroded with envy, and burning to revenge the fancied slights and insults of those whom they are forced to acknowledge their superiors.

The marriage of Lambert and Mary, which had been long settled on, was to have taken place in the spring of the year before mentioned, but was postponed to the following autumn, in consequence of the death of a near relation to one of the parties; in the meantime, the outrages committed by the armed Orangemen on the people, drove the latter into open rebellion, and long before the time arrived at which Lambert was to have led his betrothed bride to the altar, he found himself an exile from his home, an outlaw on the hills, the leader of a wild and infuriated band, formed, for the most part, of men who had been driven from their blazing homes and ruined families—men, whose watchword was vengeance on their persecutors—a vengeance they too often wreaked on the innocent, without measure or mercy.

It would be impossible to describe the feelings of Lambert, when he reflected on the happiness from which he had been torn, and the hopeless and desperate situation in which he was placed; alternately excited almost to madness by the reckless spirit, and daring valour of the men he led, and sickened with the horrors he was obliged to witness, and could not prevent, he was dragged on from scene to scene, until the defeat of his brave but undisciplined band, at the memorable battle of Ross, relieved him from the galling station he had filled, and left him at liberty to choose his own path.

About a week after this dearly purchased victory over the rebel forces, which filled the surrounding country with grief and dismay, Mary Redmond left the side of her father, whose feeble constitution was now completely broken down by the disappointment of his hopes, and the continual alarms with which he had been harassed since the breaking out of the insurrection, and walked into the fields to breathe the air, or rather to give vent to the feelings with which her heart was bursting; for she had heard no account of Lambert since the battle, and judged that he had fallen.

The beauty of the surrounding landscape, as it shone in the yellow beams of the setting sun, had something of repose in its aspect, that might well have soothed a weary or wounded heart; but to poor Mary the view of it was agony; she covered her eyes—pressed her hand on her burning brow, as if to shut it out from her sight, and paused for some time; then starting, seemingly roused by the breaking of the waves on the beach that lay but a short distance from the spot where she stood, with a hurried step pursued her course in that direction. Passing the cabin of one of her father's labourers, who had followed the rebel standard, she saw his aged mother standing in the little yard before it, anxiously watching the setting sun, while the prattle of a fine boy, about four years old, that was clinging to her side, seemed to awaken the emotions of grief and tenderness that were visible on her countenance. Mary approached her, well knowing the source of her inquietude; her son had not returned from the battle, nor had she heard any tidings of him since that fatal day; the poor woman on seeing her burst into tears, exclaiming, "Miss Mary, my jewel, what brings you to this desolate spot?" "Have you heard any news, Ally?" said Mary, in a faint voice.

"Ay, news enough, my darlint," the old woman replied, wringing her hands, "but little to comfort me: I hear the story of death and destruction in every mouth, and my boy comes not to his sorrowful mother." While she was speaking, the wife of her son entered the yard, with the wild and disordered look and manner of one rendered almost frantic by grief and terror.

"You have heard of him, Anty," cried the old woman; "I see the dark sorrow in your brow—spake, girl, spake, —tell his ould mother where she may find her boy's grave."

"His grave is a deep one, I fear, mother honey," replied the afflicted wife. "Tom Murphy, who run home first to tell 'em he was alive, saw him at the river's brink, by the side of Lambert, in the thickest of the fight; but never heard of him or seen him since."

On hearing this intelligence, Mary uttered a piercing cry, and would have fallen to the ground, if Anty Hayes had not caught her in her arms and supported her. Whilst the women were using all their simple skill to restore her, the boy thinking Mary was dying, and terrified by the altered and distracted looks of his mother and grandmother, run towards the little garden adjoining the cabin, screaming violently, and heedless of the calls of his mother to him to return and be quiet.

At length she was obliged to leave Mary, who was now slowly reviving, to the care of her mother-in-law, and follow her refractory boy; as she approached the little enclosure into which he had taken flight, she thought she heard the sound of a well-known voice; she started, and paused an instant to listen; the screams of the child had sunk to a whimpering tone: some person appeared to be soothing him; she advanced with a beating heart, entered the little garden, and, to her unspeakable surprise and joy, found her child in the arms of his father. Gazing on him for a time, as if she had doubted the evidence of her senses, she then rushed forward, and throwing herself on his neck, could only say—"It's you, you then, your own-self, and you still live?"

"I b'lieve I do, Anty, my darlint," replied Hayes; "but no one can tell how long he'll have that story to tell in these times; if I stopped long here, I'd have a short reckoning of it; there's a sharp look-out for me hereabouts, and for others, too, of more consequence than I am; so bring me to my mother, if there's no stranger within: and do you, Anty, jewel, run to the big house as fast as your legs can carry you, and give this scrap of a note to Miss Mary."

"Miss Mary, is here in the cabin, poor thing; but tell me, Billy, have you any news of Mr. Lambert?"

"Come, come, I can't stay here to tell you," said Hayes, making a few rapid strides in the direction of the cabin, and muttering to himself as he went.

"Billy, dear," said his wife, following him, "for the love of heaven don't attempt to go in on them of a suddent, or you'll kill them; the life is hardly in Miss Mary, for she thinks its all over with Mr. Lambert, and your mother is half light wid throuble for you."

"Well, here's the man that can cure 'em both; but how is the poor masther, Anty?"

"Ah, poorly enough, Billy, honey; its only the shadow of him that's in it," said Anty; "these cruel times have kilt him."

"They've kilt many a brave man," said Hayes, mournfully; "but never a kinder one than my poor, poor masther; but let me see Miss Mary; run in, Anty, tell 'em I'm comin, if you like—but be quick."

Hayes gave little time to his wife to prepare his mother and Mary for his appearance; she had scarcely finished the usual preface of, "Oh! well to be sure, and now don't be frightened at what I'm goin to tell ye," when he cut her short in her narrative, by presenting himself before them.

"My son, my son," were the only words his mother had power to articulate on seeing him, while Mary remained motionless with astonishment.

"Don't cry, mother, honey," said Hayes, "you see I'm alive still; but, to keep myself so, I must be goin quickly from this, or I might soon have unwelcome company wid me; but cheer up, be of good heart, all may be well yet— there's a boat on the beach that will soon carry me out of danger, and there's one in that boat, Miss Mary, who ventures his life to see you once more."

"Who, Mr. Barry?" said Mary eagerly; "he is safe, then?"

"Not altogether safe," said Hayes; "but if you'd have him so, you'd best come with me and advise him to lay this place without delay, for I've rason to think his enemies are not far off."

"I will go to him, then," said Mary; "lead the way, Hayes, without further loss of time, and you, Anty, come with us, that you may accompany me home."

Before leaving his cabin, Hayes turned to his mother, who had sat down in silent sorrow beside her cheerless hearth; and his stout heart melted within him as he placed his boy on her knee, and bent down to receive her blessing, and perhaps her last farewell; but recovering himself in an instant, he rushed out, followed by Mary and his wife, and a few minutes' walk brought them in view of the boat.

"Go now, Miss," said Hayes, "spake to Mr. Lambert; it will give him new life to see you; it may be the saving of him. Anty and I will remain here until you come back; and make haste, Miss, dear, the time is slipping over us very fast."

Mary approached the boat, against which Lambert was leaning, pale, haggard, and only sustained from sinking under the toil he had endured, by a spirit of desperation. The darkness of the hour could not conceal from her the change in his countenance; she clasped the hand he extended to receive her, and wept passionately. Lambert drew her gently to him, and rested her head on his bosom;—the horrors he had so lately witnessed, the dangers he had passed, all he had yet to apprehend, were forgotten in that moment of brief, but exquisite happiness, as, gazing on his betrothed bride, he surrendered his whole soul to the charm her pure and devoted attachment breathed over it.

Mary soon roused him from this dream. "It is not thus, Lambert," she said, "we should waste the few minutes that are left us. I know the dangers by which you are surrounded; tell me then quickly what are your plans for the future—whither do you go, and where or when may we hope to meet again?"

"Heaven alone can tell, my dearest Mary," said Lambert, "for I must fly this country without delay—a gibbet or grave is all that now remains in poor Ireland for me.— I am almost hunted down.—That cold-blooded assassin, Ganly, who, I suppose, is calculating on the confiscation of my property, and his ruffian gang, are on my track wherever I turn; I should have been long since their prey, if another of my neighbours, honest John Smith, who belongs to this troop, and who, though obliged "to herd with tigers," has not lost the feelings of a man, had not contrived to warn me of their designs against me. Poor faithful Hayes, who has risked his life a hundred times to save mine, saw him this morning; I was then lying concealed a few miles from hence, near the sea-shore, waiting for a boat to bring me hither, as I could find no safe path by land. He sent me word not to attempt landing here, as it was suspected that I was somewhere in this neighbourhood—that my enemies kept a close eye on this quarter—that he knew not how soon the party would be out to search it, and that he feared much their fury would be turned against your father. But his warning was vain; I would die a thousand deaths rather than leave the country without seeing you, and putting you on your guard against the dangers that threaten you. You have friends among the Protestant gentry, who possess sufficient authority to be able to control those wretches; lose no time, then, in applying to them for protection. I expect to be able to be concealed in a cavern, well known to me, of one of the Saltee Islands, until the pursuit cools a little; and then, with the assistance of Hayes, to procure a boat and escape to France, from which place I intend to embark for America, to try my fortune in the new world."

"Then fly from hence," interrupted Mary, "without a moment's delay; I shall do all you have desired me; save yourself, and we may yet be happy."

She had scarcely finished these words, when they heard a loud shout in the direction of Hayes' cabin, which was answered by another from a different quarter.

Ere the unfortunate pair could stir from the spot, or utter a word, Hayes darted from the bank where he was standing, and began to push the boat out to sea, exclaiming, "There, now, Misther Lambert, there, now; afther all we waited for them—they are scattered right and left over the town. Come, Sir, come put your hand to the boat, and let's take the only road that's ready for us."

"Fly, Lambert, fly from this fatal spot," cried Mary in an agony of terror. "Heavens, do you fold your arms and remain immoveable, and your pursuers at your back! Will you have me see you murdered before my eyes?"

"I cannot leave you, Mary," said Lambert, "to the mercy of those ruffians, though I shall die at your feet; you cannot now return to your father's house in safety."

"You are mad, you are mad!" cried Mary wildly, "Dear, dear Lambert," she then added in a supplicating tone, "have pity, have mercy on me, and save yourself."

As she thus spoke, she grasped his arm with all her force, as if to urge him into the boat which was waiting for him. At this moment, the voices of some persons approaching the strand were distinctly heard. Lambert, roused by the pressing danger, recovered in an instant his wonted energy. Taking Mary, who was now rendered passive by terror, in his arms, he placed her in the boat, jumped in after her, and seizing an oar, aided so powerfully the efforts of Hayes, that in a few moments, and before Mary could utter a word, the little skiff was dancing on the waves, concealed from those on the beach by the shade of night.

"My father, my poor father!" were the first words pronounced by Mary, "to leave him at such a time,—he ignorant of my fate, too;—it will kill him! I am worse than the wretches who are now surrounding his house."

"Be calm, Mary, my love," said Lambert in a firm tone, "your absence at this hour may be well for you both; sanguinary as they are, they will not attempt to offer violence to your father in his present state of health. I do not mean to carry you to the island; we shall keep near the shore, and when all is quiet there, we shall land, and leave you at Hayes' cabin, where you may be sheltered for the night, if you cannot return home with safety."

"An its there you'd be welcome, Miss, said Hayes, "for there's them sitting sorrowful enough in that poor hut that would shelter you in their hearts within."

As he spoke, he directed his eyes towards where it stood, when, to his unutterable horror, he beheld a burst of smoke and flame rising from its roof. He groaned heavily, and dropped his oar on the edge of the boat. Lambert, unable to comfort him, watched the progress of the fire in silence, while Mary, bewildered with terror, clung to his arm.

The materials of the roof being dry and decayed, it was quickly consumed; as it fell in, the flickering flame rose, and sunk for a short time; then expired, and all was dark again.

"Now Heaven look down on my poor houseless family to-night," said Hayes, "and grant that the fury of those orange thieves may end with our poor cabin; but come, let's row for life, Misther Lambert, till I lave you safe on the island, and come back to see what is become of them."

"In the depth of your affliction, my poor fellow," said Lambert, "you still think of my safety. But I must be silent, for the arm that would avenge your wrongs is now powerless."

Without saying more, they rowed briskly towards the island. Already they were nearly under the shadow of the steep and rugged cliffs with which it is in a manner embattled. Hayes stopped the strokes of his oar, and touching the arm of Lambert, pointed in the direction of the island, asking him if he saw anything? Lambert cast a piercing look through the gloom: then hastily exclaimed—"Your eyes have not deceived you, Hayes. that is a Revenue Cutter you see yonder; she is cruizing round the island—to approach nearer to it would be certain destruction to us; we must make to shore again. Hunted by sea and land— 'tis too much! But courage! we have weathered a worse storm before now. Why do you tremble so, Mary, my love? Cheer up; this is only a retreat from danger. If you knew all I have braved and overcome, you would not fear for me now." But Mary, unable to reply, covered her face with her hands, and letting her head sink on her bosom, abandoned herself to the gloomy reflections the events of the evening inspired. She was roused from this reverie by the sudden starting of Lambert. Nervously alive to every sound and motion, she immediately raised her head, and looking towards the land, she beheld the sky reddened with the flames that ascended in huge volumes from the roof of her father's house. Shrieking wildly, she started from her seat, and in the frenzy of the moment would have plunged into the sea, if she had not been restrained by Lambert. He attempted to calm her, but all his efforts to that effect were vain!—"Bring me to my father, bring me to my father—living or dead, let me see him again;" were the only answers she returned to his soothing. As they approached the shore, he vainly implored her to remain with him, and not attempt landing until Hayes should go and seek some intelligence of her father's situation. She would not hear him, but as soon as the boat was moored, tore herself from his arms and jumped on shore. Lambert, when he could not restrain her, followed; and addressed her once more in a subdued though determined tone, besought her, if she had still any regard for his life, to be calm,—for if I cannot, he said, prevent you from rushing on destruction, I will at least follow you wherever you go.

"This is cruel, Lambert," said Mary, bursting into tears, "do you think I wish to lead you to death?—Leave me I beseech you; I am now calm; my brain no longer burns; I shall go quietly to seek my father—but go I will, if I were even surrounded by the fiends themselves."

"An if there are worse than fiends," said Hayes, "the Lord have mercy on us—amen. But come, Miss Mary, jewel, don't be so hasty; listen to reason, and be guided by those that loves you. Look at me that have cause to run mad! where is she that was the light of my heart—my own Anty? where is my poor grey-haired mother—and where the child that used to run and welcome me at the cabin door? All on the wide world this night; and yet ye see I'm sayin nothin, though the heart within me is goin to shivers. Come, then, he continued, let us leave this wild strand for the shelter of a hedge, and then we'll see what's to be done. Stay abit—like enough all is quiet about the walls of the poor cabin now, for there's no more to be done there; it is the safest place we can go to for a while." As the way that led to this now desolate spot, was the direct path to the house of H——, Mary offered no opposition to Hayes' proposal, and they all proceeded towards it in silence. On entering the little yard before it, they were startled by the glare of some burning brands that were heaped together at little distance from the black and smouldering ruins of the cabin; but their fears were quickly removed, when they distinguished, by the red light of the fire beside which she sat, the form of Hayes' mother, wrapt in her cloak, rocking to and fro, as she watched over her little grandson, who quietly slept in her arms. Her son approached her, and tapping her on the shoulder, asked her in a voice choked with grief and apprehension—"Where is Anty."

The old woman raised her head, and gazing on him for some minutes, exclaimed, "is it you, my son; or has this terrible night turned my head: do I dhrame?"

"No, mother, you do not dhrame," replied Hayes, "it is myself that's in it; but where is she?"

"She is safe and well; but what brings you to this dismal spot, when I thought you safe at sea?"

"Anty is safe and well, you say: no matter then about me. But where is she? Why does she lave you here alone?"

"She's gone to the big house, to see what they are goin to do wid the poor masther."

"With my father! They are going to murder him, then?" cried Mary, who had come near enough to hear what the old woman said. "The stranger flies to him, and I am lingering here." So saying, she disengaged herself from the arm of Lambert—darted off with the speed of lightning, and, regardless of every obstacle that impeded her course, in a few moments stood in the light of her burning dwelling, before which she saw her father placed on his knees, as if ready for execution, surrounded by a circle of men, whose fierce and savage looks, strongly marked by the red beams of the conflagration, formed a striking contrast to the pale, mild, and resigned countenance of their victim. She rushed forward towards the place where he knelt. Those about him involuntarily made way for her, and in a moment she was clasped in his arms, where she remained until the heroes, who had been surprised by her sudden appearance, and awed by the energy of her manner, recovered themselves, and found tongue to address her.

"Come, tell us, my bird," said one tall, gaunt ruffian, whose fiendish grin seemed to mock all her feelings and affections, "where have you been flying at this late hour? what news have you brought from the hills and groves? Eh, Ganly, my boy, don't you think the buck of the parish may be caught afore mornin yet? Come, my pet," he continued, laying his hand rudely on the shoulder of Mary, "tell us, as you love your father, where you have been takin your evening's walk, and who was your company?"

Mary shook off the ruffian's hand, and slowly rising, placed herself by her father, whose feeble hand, as if it could still protect her, she firmly grasped. The fever of her mind was now gone, and she clearly saw the dangers that threatened her on all sides. The fire that so lately sparkled in her eyes, was quenched, and the flush of her cheek had given place to the ashy hue of death. Yet, weak girl as she was, a close observer might have discovered resolution on her raised brow, and something of defiance in her compressed lips.

"Now to business, boys," says the wretch who had just addressed her; "I knew I'd bring her to kindness. Put the questions to her: I knew she'd be a good girl, and save her father."

Here Ganly, the sworn enemy of Lambert Barry, the most important personage of the body, and the prime mover of the present expedition, now came forward, and took the examination of Mary on himself.

"Miss Redmond," said the villain, in a civil tone, "it grieves me much that my duty has obliged me to come to your father's house in this manner: but positive informations have been given to us, that Lambert Barry was concealed here. We have come in search of him, with directions to spare no one who would screen him from justice. Your father must know something of him, but will tell us nothing; so we must obey our orders if you do not be more wise, and speak the truth."

"You wrong my father," said Mary; "wrong him most cruelly. I will swear to you he has never seen or heard from Mr. Barry since the fatal day he first left his home."

"Will you swear the same for yourself?"

"No; I have seen him."

"Where is he now?"

"Far beyond your reach. He has left this country for ever."

"When did he leave it."

"This very evening. Your shouts, as you surrounded his place, were the last sounds he heard as he left the shore."

"And where is he bound for?"

"The first land to which the winds and waves may carry him."

"The revenue cutter, my lads," roared out one of the party; "do you forget she's on the look out? Her men won't sleep on her decks: I'll go bail they will save the gentleman from the dangers of a long voyage in an open boat."

Ganly heeded not the fellow that had thus interrupted his examination. He only thought of the escape of Lambert from his grasp; for there was something in the manner in which Mary had given her testimony, that placed it beyond all doubt. He remained for a time silent, as if weighing the various circumstances of the case: while the paleness of his usually unchanging countenance—the quiver of his lip, and more than all, the fierce expression of his eyes, too plainly showed the disappointment and rage that were working at his heart.

This short pause was interrupted by the oaths and vociferations of some of the lowest of the *loyal* body, who, after having secured to themselves a handsome share of plunder, had been trying the quality of some liquors they had rescued from the flames. One of these fellows now reeled forward towards the place where his superiors seemed to be assembled in council. "How now, my masthers," shouted he, "ant the business over yet? D'ye want a hand? Clear the way, then, and I'll soon send his Papish sowl aflight;" and as he spoke, the miscreant actually levelled his musket, with the intention of firing on the old man, who was still kneeling, but was prevented by one of his companions, who saw the shot might have taken down one of his brethren instead of the poor Papist, so incapable was the fellow of seeing what he was doing.

Mary when she saw the movements of this fellow, and heard his language, uttered a piercing shriek, and threw herself before her father, who fell forward. She stooped to support him, and sunk to the ground under his weight; but recovering herself in an instant, she raised his head, placed it on her knee, and wiped the cold dew from his brow. The spasm that had convulsed his features passed away; he seemed to revive; his lips moved, as if he wished to speak; his eyes opened, and fixed with an intense gaze on his beloved child—then closed for ever! The tumultuous agitations of that night had been too much for his broken spirit and enfeebled frame.

Those around him—the very men that caused his death, were shocked by the manner of it. Had he fallen by their hands, all feeling of remorse or pity would have been lost in the excitement which the shedding of blood produces on such ferocious spirits. But expiring as he did, in the arms of his child, awakened all that was human in their nature, as they stood gazing on the sad spectacle.

Their attention, however, was soon engaged by another object. It was Lambert Barry, who rushed forward, without seeming to notice them, and flung himself on his knees beside the body of his old friend, grasped his cold hand, and endeavoured to sooth the agonized feelings of Mary, with that tone of sincere sympathy and affection, that reaches the heart in the lowest depths of misery to which it may be sunk.

The state of Lambert's feelings from the moment Mary left him could not be well conceived. His first impulse was to follow her, but a moment's reflection showed him the madness of such a proceeding. It could only aggravate the horrors of her situation.

While he was yet undecided as to what course he ought to pursue, Anty Hayes, who had followed the yeomen up to the house of R——, to watch their proceedings there, seeing Mary arrive, knew her husband must be nigh, came to where she had left his mother, guessing he might be there.

She described to Lambert the manner in which Mary had thrown herself into the arms of her father; expressed a hope that she would be able to save his life; and advised him to quit the place without delay, as it was for him, to use her own expression, "they were roaring like lions."

Lambert listened to her account, and resolved not to leave the place, come what might. He had even the intention of surrendering himself, in hopes his doing so might appease their fury. Partly with this intention, after charging Hayes to remain with his wife and mother until he should return, he approached the house of R——, screening himself from observation behind a thick hedge. He stopped at a point near enough to hear distinctly the different sounds that proceeded from it. Whilst stationed here, deliberating on what step he had better take, the shriek of Mary pierced through his brain, and without farther consideration he rushed to her side.

His enemies soon lost every feeling of remorse and shame in the triumph of seeing him thus in their power. They gathered round him, as if they feared he would sink through the earth, and again elude their grasp; and regardless of the sad office in which he was engaged, after a short space of time they loudly called on him to surrender. Without deigning to answer this summons, he rose, and drew a pistol from his breast, then waved his hand for silence, that he might name the conditions on which he would become their prisioner.

At this critical moment, one of the magistrates of the neighbourhood entered the yard, followed by a company of regular soldiers, with their captain at their head. Mr. L—— was a man of justice and humanity. He had always felt the most friendly regard for the family of R——, and was resolved, should the furious spirit of the times be turned against them, to do all in his power to protect them.

It was late in the evening when Smith, friend of Lambert Barry, who so often warned him of his danger, gave notice to Mr. L—— that part of his troop had sallied out to search the premises of Mr. Redmond for the rebel Barry, who, they asserted, was concealed somewhere about them.

Mr. L——, well knowing the *worthies* that were abroad and fearing the result of their visit to his friend, hastened to procure a body of soldiers, without whose aid he knew all his efforts to restrain them would have been unavailing, and follow them without delay. Unfortunately, he had found some difficulty in getting out the soldiers, so that before he was able to reach R——, the destruction was nearly complete. When he saw that he was too late, and beheld the scene of ruin that presented itself, he groaned, and wrung his hands in a paroxysm of rage and grief, in which Captain Waller, the officer that accompanied him, so sincerely sympathized, that he cursed in his heart the laws that restrained him from ordering his men to fire on the perpetrators of such crimes.

Mr. L—— ordered the heroes of the night, in a voice that made them quail, to stand aside, as he approached the body of his deceased friend, over which he bent, without being able to utter a single word; but taking the hand of Mary, he wept plentifully. After having thus testified his sincere sympathy in the poor girl's misfortunes, he expressed, in the liveliest manner, his regret for what had befallen her, and assured her he would do all in his power to protect her property, and provide for her future safety. Then turning to Lambert, who, on seeing Mary under safe and honourable protection, patiently awaited his fate. He told him, in a severe tone, he was their prisoner. "Unfortunate young man," he added, "what brought you here?"

"My cry," replied Mary, with energy, roused by the danger of Lambert; "he came here to throw himself between me and those murderers, to die for me. Save him, kind Mr. L——; as there is mercy in your heart, spare him."

"Be calm, my poor girl," said Mr. L——; "he must now submit to the law. But he shall have justice, and mercy, too, if it can be obtained. I know the honour and humanity of Captain Waller, the gentleman in whose charge I now place him; and I think I can answer for him exercising his interest and influence in his favour, as it may be consistent with his duty."

After leaving some soldiers with Mr. L―― to protect the property that had escaped the flames, Captain Waller put himself at the head of the remainder of his men, and marched off with his prisoner; while the yeomen slunk away, cursing Mr. L―― in their heart, and vowing to denounce him as a rebel.

The neighbours of R―― seeing the yeomen dispersed, flocked to unite their efforts to those of Mr L――, to console poor Mary, and render her all the offices of friendship and kindness in their power to bestow.

Lambert Barry, immediately after being lodged in the jail of Wexford, was seized with a violent fever, chiefly brought on by the toil and agitation he had suffered; this circumstance operated greatly in his favour, as it gave time to his friends to examine his case, and use their interest in his behalf. Several respectable Protestants came forward on his trial, who all bore the most honourable testimony to his forbearance and humanity, whilst leading the rebels; and the number of families he had saved from their fury. In consideration of his clemency he was pardoned, on condition of leaving the country for ever.

Lambert did not go alone into exile; his betrothed bride became his wife—sold out her property, and accompanied him to America: where they became prosperous settlers; and never forgot the pleasant fields of barony Forth; nor ever ceased to execrate the system of tyranny and misrule, that had driven them from the scenes of their youth, to seek an asylum in a foreign land.

SOLDIERS.

MEHEMET ALI, the Regenerator of Egypt, is said to be one of the most enlightened princes of the age, and the most able and beloved of military leaders, adored by the troops, and so forth. The truth is, all military service is nearly alike, and few men, who could avoid it, would ever voluntarily enter any army. If it were otherwise, even in the well-paid British service, then are the Sergeant Kites exaggerated characters. Although they were, it cannot be denied that when men are balloted for the militia, the easiest of all military service, every pretext is employed to avoid going out. Human vanity is completely subdued; and men proclaim aloud their physical infirmities and defects, and put in pleas of exemption, on the score of deafness, shortsight, a squint, or a halt, that would never otherwise have been heard of. The conqueror of the Turks has not been able to conquer this disinclination among his subjects; and the following extract from one of his general orders shews us the exact nature of the war, and the character of Ali, that modern specimen of a Prince who has so far outstripped his country and his age:—

"With respect to the men whom *we take* for the service of our *victorious war* department, some draw their teeth, some blind themselves, and others maim themselves on their way to us. Send, then, *before an hour elapses*, all the men wanting, provided they be able-bodied and healthy, and when thou dost expedite them, let each know that he must not maim himself, because I will take from the family of every such offender, men in his place, and he who has maimed himself shall be sent to the galleys all his life."

Here is a Prince for you!

MILKING.—My father had a cow which could draw her own milk. She was no doubt delighted with the flavour of it, for she practised the sucking of herself every day. She grew quite plump, and was a subject of wonder at the small quantity of milk she yielded, and at her sleek appearance. She was detected one day in the very act, after which a wood collar was suspended round her neck, which prevented her continuing it. She afterwards gave more milk, but decreased in fatness. Such cows are best fitted for Canadian pastures, when disposed to take holyday in he woods.—*Fidler's Observations.*

DR. PRIESTLEY'S OPINION OF HIGH LIFE.

REFLECTING on the time that I spent with Lord Shelburne, being as a guest in the family, I can truly say, that I was not at all fascinated with that mode of life. Instead of looking back upon it with regret, one of the greatest subjects of my present thankfulness is the change of that situation for the one in which I am now placed; and yet I was far from being unhappy there, much less so than those who are born to such a state, and pass all their lives in it. These are generally unhappy from the want of necessary employment; on which account chiefly there appears to be much more happiness in the middle classes of life who are above the fear of want, and yet have a sufficient motive for a constant exertion of their faculties; and who have always some other object besides amusement.

I used to make no scruple of maintaining, that there is not only most virtue, and most happiness, but even most true politeness in the middle classes of life. For in proportion as men pass more of their time in the society of their equals, they get a better established habit of governing their tempers; they attend more to the feelings of others, and are more disposed to accommodate themselves to them. On the other hand, the passions of persons in higher life, having been less controlled, are more apt to be inflamed; the idea of their rank and superiority to others seldom quits them; and though they are in the habit of concealing their feelings, and disguising their passions, it is not always so well done but that persons of ordinary discernment may perceive what they inwardly suffer. On this account they are really entitled to compassion, it being the almost unavoidable consequence of their education and mode of life. But when the mind is not hurt in such a situation, when a person born to affluence can lose sight of himself, and truly feel and act for others, the character is so godlike, as shews that this inequality of condition is not without its use. Like the general discipline of life, it is for the present lost on the great mass, but on a few it produces what no other state of things could do.

AN EFFECT OF POVERTY.

AMONGST the poor, refined love can scarcely exist at all; the passion must become a more sensual impulse, in many cases scarcely more delicate than that of the lower animals; in some instances more disgusting, as those who are acquainted with the manufacturing towns, where huddled heaps of human beings earn low wages, will readily testify. There is perhaps scarcely anything which has so great a tendency to refine the tastes of human beings, as the capacity for love. In proportion as people recede from this, they become savages, for love is known to exist in its most perfect state, in countries of the highest civilization; I mean real civilization, not her bastard sister, luxury. It would, therefore, be a duty incumbent on all good and wise governments, to promote such physical arrangements amongst the people, as might beget a taste for refinement. At present there is no hope.—*Junius Redivivus.*

JUNIUS REDIVIVUS should have limited his affirmation to the manufacturing poor. Does he know anything of the authorship of the older Scotch ballads? Has he ever heard of the songs of the poor peasant, Burns; or of the shepherd, Hogg; or the stone-mason, Allan Cunningham—or the thousand nameless writers of love verses which are now existing among the very poorest labourers and common mechanics? Has he never read the poem containing these lines:—

"If Heaven a draught of heavenly pleasure spare,
One cordial in this melancholy vale"—

But if his statement be well-founded, let the manufacturing system bear the blame. Poverty has nothing to suffer of reproach, if unallied with other causes.

BALSAM OF MECCA.

THE balessan, balm, or balsam of Mecca (*Balsamodendron Opobalsamum,*) belonging to the family *Burseraceæ*, is a native of the eastern coast of Abyssinia, especially at Azab, and as far as the strait of Bab el Maudeb. Bruce says, it is a small tree above fourteen feet high, with scraggy branches and flattened top, like those which are exposed to the seaside blasts; the appearance is consequently stunted, and the leaves are besides small and few. He supposes that it was transplanted to Arabia, and there cultivated at a very early period. This was the *Balsamum Judaicum*, or Balm of Gilead of antiquity and of the Sacred Writings, it being supposed at one time to be produced only in Judea. It seems, however, to have disappeared from that country, and the supply to have proceeded from Arabia. Many fables are connected with it. Tacitus says, that the tree was so averse from iron that it trembled when a knife was laid near it, and it was thought the incision should be made with an instrument of ivory, glass, or stone. Bruce was told by Sidi Ali Tarnboloussi that " the plant was no part of the creation of God in the six days, but that in the last of three very bloody battles which Mahomet fought with the noble Arabs of Harb, and his kinsmen the Beni Koreish, then pagans, at Beder Hunein, Mahomet prayed to God, and a grove of balsam trees grew up from the blood of the slain upon the field of battle; and that with the balsam which flowed from them he touched the wounds even of those that were dead, and all those predestinated to be good Mussulmans afterwards immediately came to life." An equally marvellous legend is the Arabic fable respecting El Wah, a shrub or tree not unlike our hawthorn in form and flower. From the wood of this tree they believe that Moses' rod was made when he sweetened the waters of Marah; and they say also, that by means of a rod of the same wood, Kaleb Ibn el Waalid, the great destroyer of Christians, sweetened the waters at El Wah, —the Oasis Parva, of the ancients,—which were once bitter, and that he bestowed upon the place the name borne by the wonder-working plant. To return to the balsam-tree; the mode of obtaining it remains to be described. This, according to Bruce, is done by making incisions in the trunk at a particular season of the year, and receiving the fluid that issues from the wounds into small earthen bottles, the produce of every day being collected and poured into a larger bottle, which is kept closely corked. When first obtained, it is, says Bruce, "of a light yellow colour, apparently turbid, in which there is a whitish cast, which I apprehend arises from the globules of air that pervade the whole of it in its first state of fermentation; it then appears very light upon shaking. As it settles and cools it turns clear and loses that milkiness which it first had. It has then the colour of honey, and appears more fixed and heavy. The smell at first is violent, and strongly pungent, giving a sensation to the brain like that of volatile salts when rashly drawn up by an incautious person. This lasts in proportion to its freshness; for being neglected, and the bottle uncorked, it quickly loses this quality, as it probably will at last by age, whatever care is taken of it." The natives of the East use it medicinally in complaints of the stomach and bowels, as well as a preservative against the plague; but its chief value in the eyes of Oriental ladies lies in its virtue as a cosmetic,—although, as in the case of most other cosmetics, its effects are purely imaginary. Lady Mary Wortley Montague ascertained that it was in request by the ladies of the Seraglio at Constantinople; but having tried it on her own person found it exceedingly irritating to the skin. Much of the virtue attributed to it depends on the costliness of the material.—*Edinburgh Cabinet Library, Nubia and Abyssinia.*

" You saved my life on one occasion," said a beggar to a captain under whom he had served. " Saved your life!" replied the officer; "do you think that I am a doctor?" " No," answered the man; " but I served under you in the battle of ——; and when you ran away, I followed, and thus my life was preserved."

HOW TO DETECT MR. MACAULAY'S WRITINGS.

THE Member for Leeds is known to be a great writer in the *Edinburgh Review*, and an occasional contributor to other periodicals. A writer in a London Magazine says, he may be at once detected by his standing illustration of the foul Duessa:—

" Some painters," says the magazine writer, " write their names on their pictures; others use a mark, or symbol, which serves quite as well as the signature to identify their works. In like manner some magazine men sign their names to their contributions; others (for the most part without intending it, be it confessed) use a sign which is quite as distinct as the painter's. A friend of mine who diversifies his graver pursuits by writing facetious poetry and funny prose, never yet indited an article without talking of blowing either his own nose, or somebody else's nose. Well, then, a nose is his sign. But what is Macaulay's sign? Duessa, the enchantress of the Red Cross Knight. In every production of his that I have ever read, from the first that gained him any note to the last he has acknowledged, I find this same Duessa. In his gorgeous paper upon Milton, published in 1825, I can well remember that he tells us, certain illusions had cast over the minds of the royalists a spell potent as Duessa's, which made them, like the Red Cross Knight, imagine they were doing battle for a ladye-fair, when, in fact, they were fighting in behalf of a foul sorceress! And again, in 1832, I see in this paper on *Dumont's Mirabeau*:—' During two generations, France was ruled by men, who, with all the vices of Louis XIV., had none of the art by which that magnificent prince passed off his vices for virtues. The people had now to see tyranny naked. That foul Duessa was stripped of her gorgeous ornaments. She had always been hideous; but a strange enchantment had made her fair and glorious in the eyes of her willing slaves. The spell was now broken, the deformity was made manifest; and the lovers, lately so happy and so proud, turned away loathing and horror-struck.' Whenever I detect Duessa in any article cast in that mould of style and thought which belongs to Macaulay, I feel justified in declaring positively that the paper in which the foul enchantress shews is indubitably his!"

Now, it is unfortunate that this writer has let the cat out of the bag; for if Mr. Macaulay had really been trafficking so long and steadfastly with the enchantress, we fear that, after this, he will carefully avoid all allusion to her: and how are we to detect him then? However it may be done, we trust it will not be by the rule to know an old Whig—a man, viz., who says directly the reverse of everything he has been saying all his life.

FAREWELL.

Farewell! farewell! these accents chill
    Fall heavy on my ear;
Yet why?—Since thou to me must still
    Be nothing, far or near.

Though to each other we are now
    No more than formal friends;
Still, sadder feelings cloud my brow—
    Regret with parting blends.

Farewell! farewell! be thine each joy
    The happiest,—wisest cull
From out the mass of sad alloy,
    Of which our lot is full!

Though Time around my feelings cast
    His all-subduing spell,
Each fond remembrance of the past
    Shall wake the wish—Farewell!

R. D. D.

WHAT'S IN A NAME?—It is odd enough that a sheep when dead should turn into mutton, all but its head; for while we ask for a leg or a shoulder of mutton, we never ask for a mutton's head. But there is a fruit which changes its name still oftener. Grapes are so called, when fresh; raisins when dried, and plums when in a pudding.

SCIENTIFIC NOTICES.

NEW PRINTING MACHINE.

Mr. J. KITCHEN, Reporter of the *Newcastle Journal*, has invented a printing press, which, from all we hear of it, bids fair to revolutionize this department of the art—it bears no analogy, even in appearance, to any machine for the purpose hitherto known. The *form* can be fixed in its place in a single moment, and will, when adjusted, *remain stationary* until the work is finished. Complete facilities are given for regulating the power, and the quantity of ink, or for *overlaying or obtaining register.* The same machine will be equally applicable for the smallest job or the largest sheet; it will be perfectly under control, and only require *one man* during the process of printing; or where great speed is wanted, and the work is heavy, a man and a *fly boy*, whilst it can be sold for the same price as the common press ! Mr. Kitchen is now employed in the application to his invention of a clock-work movement, so that the machine may keep a *register* of its own work, and will thus act as a check upon waste of paper or idleness in the absence of the employer or overseer.—[We give this as we get it. It may be like ninety-nine announcements out of the hundred, premature; but this does not lessen our confidence in the march of improvement.]

MODE OF FIXING AND VARNISHING DRAWINGS.

To fix pencil or chalk drawings, they should be washed in water, in which a small quantity of isinglass has been dissolved. Any colourless glue will be available. Skimmed milk is used for the same purpose by some, but isinglass is preferable. To varnish the same drawings, after having fixed and thoroughly dried them, pass on them a coat of Spa, or colourless spirit varnish; and, when perfectly dry, a second. These two will be sufficient. The isinglass water must be applied lightly, and never put twice over the same spot, until the first coat be dry, otherwise the drawing will become smeary. Care also must be taken to clear the drawing from every particle of dust before commencing the operation, and to preserve it from the same afterwards, till it be quite dry; otherwise, in the former case, it will be cloudy and smutty, and, in the latter, the particles will so adhere as never to be removed. Finally, the brushes must be perfectly clean. A better plan of passing over the isinglass wash than by means of the brush, is, to pour it into a flat vessel, such as a dish, and insert the drawing into the composition, laying the paper flat immediately afterwards. This will preclude the chance of its becoming smeared, which, in the case of drawings of considerable vigour in touch, or of powerful shading, will occasionally happen to the most cautious user of the brush. —*Repertory of Patent Inventions.*

IMPORTANT OBSERVATIONS ON THE HYGROMETRIC WATER CONTAINED IN FLOUR.

Most important researches have recently been carried on by M. M. Payen and Persoz, on the several points in the chemical history of bread, flour and grain. Their observations are not yet published in detail, but we select the following as being one of the very highest commercial dietetic importance. They have found that 100 parts of flour, sold as dry, and imparting no moist stain to blotting-paper, contain, under atmospheric circumstances, 19 per cent. of water, and but 80 of dry or nutritive matter; that flour exposed to moist air contains as much as 23 per cent. water; that the finest flour employed by the bakers, contains 16 per cent. under ordinary circumstances. In summer these proportions of water are reduced, but they are remarkably increased in moist weather. Thus the quantity of flour which by weight, at the rate of 5 per cent. of water, would produce 150lbs. of bread, will produce but 127¾lbs., when the same weight of flour is purchased in long continued wet weather. The price of flour should consequently in all seasons be based on the true quantity of dry matter it contains, and which a simple and rapidly performed experiment would exactly indicate. Thus, by placing 100 grains of flour on a plate, and heating this on a vessel of boiling water for one hour, the loss sustained will denote the precise quantity of water mixed with the flour.

SCRAPS.

HUMANITY.—A single trait of this divine principle has often gained a hero greater honour and applause than the most brilliant and dazzling achievements. Indeed it may be said to hold the first rank among the moral virtues, and to give a lustre to all the rest. In a military man, but especially in a victorious commander, it is charming. Marlborough and Wellington were both great generals; the former, in addition to his knowledge of the art of war, possessed all the graces, and felt for all mankind; the latter is composed of " sterner stuff"—uncompromising—unrelenting. The following anecdote raises the character of the former to the climax of earthly fame. Immediately after the battle of Blenheim, when victory had declared in favour of the British arms, the Duke observing a soldier leaning pensively on the butt of his firelock, thus accosted him : " Why so sad, my friend, after so glorious a victory ?" " It may be glorious," replied the brave fellow ; " but I am thinking that all the blood I have spilt to day has only earned me *fourpence.*" To the immortal honour of the Duke, let it be recorded, that when he turned aside, a tear was observed to fall from his cheek.

THE ODD FAMILY.—In the reign of William the Third there lived in Ipswich, in Suffolk, a family which, from the number of peculiarities belonging to it, was distinguished by the name of the *Odd Family*. Every event, whether good or bad, happened to this family on an odd day of the month, and every one of them had something odd in his or her person, manner, and behaviour; the very letters in their Christian names always happened to be an odd number. The husband's name was Peter, and the wife's Rabah; they had seven children, all boys,—viz. Solomon, Roger, James, Matthew, Jonas, David, and Ezekiel. The husband had but one leg, his wife but one arm. Solomon was born blind of the left eye, and Roger lost his right eye by an accident; James had his left ear pulled off by a boy in a quarrel, and Matthew was born with only three fingers on his right hand; Jonas had a stump foot, and David was hump-backed; all these, except David, were remarkably short, while Ezekiel was six feet two inches high at the age of nineteen; the stump-footed Jonas and the hump-backed David got wives of fortune, but no girls would listen to the addresses of the rest. The husband's hair was as black as jet, and the wife's remarkably white; yet every one of the children's was red. The husband had the peculiar misfortune of falling into a deep saw-pit, where he was starved to death, in the year 1701, and his wife, refusing all kinds of sustenance, died in five days after him. In the year 1703, Ezekiel enlisted as a grenadier; and, although he was afterwards wounded in twenty-three places, he recovered. Then Roger, James, Matthew, Jonas, and David, died at different places on the same day, in 1713; and Solomon and Ezekiel were drowned together in crossing the Thames, in the year 1723.

CONTENTS OF NO. XLV.

HOLIDAY RAMBLES, No. V.—Inchkeith,	353
Commercial Thieves,	355
The Influenza,	357
ELEMENTS OF THOUGHT—Education—The Formation of Habit—Exercise, Courage, and Recreation—The Causes of Bad Government—A Noble Resource in Painful Moments,	359
Slumber.—First English Deed.—Wonderful May in Perth,	360
COLUMN FOR THE LADIES—Black Eyes and Blue—Mr. Moore's New Work,	ib.
THE STORY-TELLER—A Tale of Ninety-Eight,	361
Soldiers.— Milking,	366
Dr. Priestley's Opinion of High Life.—An Effect of Poverty,	ib.
Basim of Mecca,	367
How to Detect Mr. Macaulay's Writing,	ib.
Farewell,	ib.
SCIENTIFIC NOTICES—New Printing Machine—Mode of Fixing and Varnishing Drawings—Important Observations on the Hygrometric Water contained in Flour,	368
SCRAPS—Humanity—The Odd Family,	ib.

EDINBURGH : Printed by and for JOHN JOHNSTONE, Square.—Published by JOHN ANDERSON, Jun., Bookseller, Bridge Street, Edinburgh ; by JOHN MACLEOD, and ATKINSON & Co. Booksellers, Glasgow ; and sold by all Booksellers and Venders of Cheap Periodicals.

THE Schoolmaster,
AND
EDINBURGH WEEKLY MAGAZINE.
CONDUCTED BY JOHN JOHNSTONE.

THE SCHOOLMASTER IS ABROAD.—LORD BROUGHAM.

No. 46.—Vol. II.   SATURDAY, JUNE 15, 1833.   Price Three-Halfpence.

AUTHENTIC LETTERS FROM CANADA.

It will we fear, be a long while before authentic information from Emigrants to America, ceases to be interesting to millions ill at ease at home, and anxious yet afraid to follow in a track which they are assured, if pursued with judgment and energy, will ultimately lead to independence and peace of mind, in the secure and comfortable means of plentiful subsistence, and the settlement of children. The Letters under consideration are of an original and interesting kind. They are written by the members of two Irish family groups that emigrated, the one in 1827, and the other last year. Both consist of persons of intelligence and education, moving in what are considered the refined classes of society. They are directly from Ireland, and their respective heads are clergymen. The Rev. Mr. Magrath, formerly a Rector in the diocese of Ferns, went out with his wife, sons, daughter, nephew, servants—nine persons in all. Of the numerous family of the Rev. Mr. Radcliff, thirteen individuals, sons, daughters-in-law, grandchildren, &c., went out last year, after having obtained all the information possible from their friends the Magraths. The writer of the Magrath family is Mr. Thomas Magrath, who obtained an appointment from the Governor, as an agent for superintending the settlement of emigrants. This situation gave him many facilities for acquiring useful and accurate information, which he transmitted in the close of 1830, and the beginning of 1831, to the Rev. Mr. Radcliff for the guidance of his family. The letters, which are just published in Dublin, are edited by this gentleman; they will be read with interest, and with advantage by persons of the same class, who are still anxiously ruminating the mighty question, "To go, or not to go?" They will prove of less utility to the labouring classes, save in setting them right on the point of the enormously high rate of wages, held out in some flattering accounts of Canada. This is a cruel exaggeration, which has betrayed many into temporary distress, and raised the most fallacious expectations. Mr. Thomas Magrath is a lively, intelligent Irishman, suiting to the education and habits of a gentleman of "The Old Country," the temper and energy necessary to success in the new Land of Promise. We shall quote him freely. Though, on subsequent experience, he strongly advises emigrants to proceed to Canada by New York, and up the Hudson, he and his friends nine in all, embarked at Liverpool, in a Whitehaven vessel, paying L.50 among them, and finding their own provisions. The captain, who was only going to Quebec, (for a cargo we presume,) was bound to send them free to Montreal with their luggage. Their provisions cost L.20; their farther expenses in Montreal, and in going up the St. Lawrence to Prescott, lodgings, carriage of luggage, &c., &c., with an allowance to convey them to the final point of settlement, was, in all, L.135, or L.15 a-head. They had above seven tons of luggage. Mr. Magrath's directions as to the quality and quantity of provisions, tools, seeds, clothing, &c., &c., are judicious and minute, and apply to single men, as well as to families; though he strongly recommends all men to come out married, provided they can meet with "cheerful, accommodating, and economizing lasses, with a little of the *needful*," and, we presume, as few boarding school accomplishments as possible—*raising* a loaf, or making a pumpkin pie, being far more valued in the *bush* than the *pretty*, or even the fine arts. The articles, besides, tools (which every man must handle who would live in comfort in a new settlement,) which Mr. Magrath directs to be purchased, come to about L.26, in addition to the ordinary wardrobe and equipage usually possessed by British gentlemen— as gun, pistols, dressing-case, &c., &c. He thinks, however, that *money* is the best commodity a man can bring. No *single* gentleman should lay in his own ship provisions, as he cannot superintend the cooking and economy of them; and all should go by *New York*. To that port there are passages to be obtained at all prices, and with every varying degree of accommodation; and once there a man may get to York—the central point with all new settlers who wish for land in Upper Canada—for L.5, 4s., and by a delightful route. Magrath gives all the reasons for and against settling at once in *the bush*, that is, on wild land, or for purchasing a half cleared estate. The choice must often be determined by the circumstances of the intending settlers. The Radcliffs, as we shall see, bought wild land; the Magraths, at coming out, instead of accepting of a large grant in an unsettled district, preferred to purchase within 18 miles of York, the capital of Upper Canada.

"Having purchased our lot of seven hundred acres from Government, for fifteen hundred and seventy dollars, (about 1,325 British,) my father, during the period of his residence in York, sent my brothers and myself to erect a log-house on our farm, of which we all took possession immediately after its completion; and when fairly lodged in that, we undertook the building of our present residence, which is a frame-house.

"This dwelling is 44 feet by 33, containing three storeys; *that* under ground is 12 feet high, and built with stone and lime.

"The mode of forming such a house is as follows:—

"A framer, on receiving the dimensions and plan, cuts out the mortices and prepares the frame. A *Bee*, which means an assemblage of the neighbours, is then called; and a person well skilled in the business, and termed a *Boss*, takes the leadership of the active party, who, with the mere mechanical aid of a *following*, or *raising* pole, gradually elevates the mighty bents, until the tenants (connected with each other by tie beams,) drop into their mortices in the sill, to which, as well as to each other, they are immediately afterwards secured by pins, and in a few hours the skeleton of the house, with its rafters, &c. is ready for shingles and clap boards.

"It will appear strange to you that a house could be covered in before the sides are finished; and still more so, that the cellar, or basement storey should not be excavated, nor the foundation-walls built up to the sill, until the upper works were completed; but such was our course of proceeding.

"At the raising of my father's house, seventy kind neighbours assisted, and worked extremely hard for an entire day, without any recompense whatever, except a plentiful dinner *al fresco*.

"In a few months my brothers and I, who are tolerably handy, with the aid of two carpenters, had the *inside* finished; and we have now been nearly three years inhabiting a truly comfortable house, quite in the home fashion, except that it has the advantage of a verandah, (not very common in Ireland,) on three sides, (supported by pillars and secured by railing,) into which we can walk from our bed-rooms, and enjoy the delightful air of the summer and autumn mornings.

"This verandah is 12 feet in breadth. We pass our leisure hours in it during the fine weather, choosing the shady and sheltered side, according to the sun, or wind; and frequently sitting there with candles until bed-time; with the occasional annoyance, however, of the troublesome moskitoes;—but where can we expect to find perfect enjoyment?

"When we had completed the house, we raised a barn, sixty feet by thirty-six, and eighteen feet in height, with an ice-house, root-house, and summer dairy beneath it, which cost us, in cash for hired labour, only twelve dollars to a framer, and the price of some nails, worth about 2s. 10d.

"We had a second *Bee* for the raising of this, which was effected in five hours, and on this occasion were able to supply our obliging neighbours, who again volunteered their valuable services, with an abundant dinner and supper in the dwelling-house; and to gratify them with a little music.

"The floor of this barn would surprise you; it is supported by twenty-three beams of wood, eighteen inches square—with two courses of three-inch plank over them. There is in fact as much timber in the floor alone, as would cost *you* more than a hundred pounds.

"With us it is a *cheap* commodity, and it is less expensive to draw and use it in great bulk, than to send it to the saw mill to be reduced to smaller scantlings. The cause of the double flooring of thick plank is that (the timber being fresh) the grain, which would be lost through the opening joints of a single floor may be saved, by having those joints covered by a second tier of boards.

"My two brothers, James and Charles, unassisted, cut eighteen thousand shingles for the roof, and laid them on, besides siding and flooring the barn. No idle hours here!

"Before the house was ready for our reception, we had cleared twenty* acres of the land for wheat, and during the successive operations of brushing, chopping, logging, burning and fencing—my father was obliged to hire workmen.

"The land has a miserable appearance when first cleared, the surface and stumps being as black as fire can render them, and these latter standing three feet high, to facilitate their being drawn out by two yoke of oxen when their roots decay, which does not take effect for seven or eight years, (according to the kind of timber) and is more tedious if the land be laid down for grass.

"Our first agricultural proceedings are as rude and simple as can well be imagined. A triangular harrow, the teeth of which weigh 7 lbs. each, is dragged over the newly prepared ground; its irregular and jumping passage over the roots and loose vegetable earth, scatters the ashes of the burned timber over the entire surface; the wheat is then sown, about one bushel to the acre, and another scrape of the harrow completes the process.

"On some portion of his land thus cleared, the new settler plants potatoes, turnips, pumpkins, and Indian corn, merely laying the seed upon the ground, and, with a hoe, scratching a sufficient portion of earth and ashes to cover it—a luxuriant crop generally succeeds; (in this district) from twenty to thirty bushels of wheat per acre. The land is sown with Timothy grass and clover in the following spring, while the snow is on the ground, that it may be easily ascertained whether the seed is sown correctly.

"After wheat no other crop is taken (generally speaking) except hay, until after the removal of the roots, when the ploughs can work.

"The weight of hay seldom exceeds two tons per acre, because mowing on such land, is a work of difficulty; with all our care we leave much of it uncut, and frequently break our scythes.

"To reduce the expense in harvest time, we use cradle scythes to cut *all* the grain, although they do not make quite as clean work as the sickles.

"A good cradler will take down from two to three acres of wheat in a day. Gleaning is not worth the attention of even a child; the scattered grains go to the sustenance of the wild pigeons of which the flocks are sometimes *miles* in length.

"It is an advantageous circumstance for the clearing of this country, that the settler finds it his advantage to bring in fresh land every year. Some emigrants, who are without capital or assistance, exhaust their first clearance; and others prepare their land by *girdling*† the trees, which, though it kills them, and allows vegetation under and around them, is an injudicious mode, as they frequently fall either on the fences or on the crops, or, what is worse, on the cattle, and occasion annual and often very inconvenient labour to remove them.

"We had a very spirited manager for the Canada company in this neighbourhood—Mr. Galt—whose various publications bear strong evidence of his literary powers, and whose foresight and perseverance, acting upon a great scale, would eventually have produced a wonderful improvement, in advancing the most important interests of this country.

"The London merchants, however, composing the Canada company, did not approve of the expenditure of too much of their cash on general improvements, without an *immediate* return, and recalled him, placing in his room the Hon. William Allen, and Messrs. Thomas Mercer Jones and Dunlop, better known by the name of Tiger Dunlop—the last, though not least, of whom is Warden of the woods and forests—all excellent and honourable men, who will conscientiously do their duty, and may, perhaps, eventually reap the advantage of Mr. Galt's wisdom and exertions.

"An *individual* emigrant must expend capital and toil before he can have an overplus for market, why then should

---

* They have subsequently cleared about 20 acres every year, and now have for cropping 150 acres.

† This is done by cutting through the bark in rings, by which the communication of the sap being interrupted—the trunk perishes.

immediate profit be expected by the company from a *number* of colonists, within a shorter period."

In reply to a remark of the Rev. Mr. Radcliff, Mr. Magrath writes,

" It is true that every one who comes here, feels, at the outset, the difficulties of his new and trying circumstances; even the lowest peasant, on first entering his shanty, laments the loneliness of his situation, and experiences a sinking of the heart, and a longing after his potatoes and buttermilk at *home ;* but as his comforts increase, he becomes reconciled to his lot ; finding himself independent, he becomes happy, and experimentally learns that this is really a Paradise to *him.*

" Land is often managed on shares here, from want of money to pay for labour. The man who has land and seed, leaves the management of them to the labourer, who takes half the produce, and draws the rest into the barn of the proprietor. If we want timber sawed, we take the logs to the mill, and have them cut to any scantling we require, leaving one half for payment.

" In the same way, if we want wool made into cloth, it is sent to the mill, where it is carded into rolls for a certain share or portion, spun for another, and afterwards woven for a third ; the want of money rendering all this traffic, and sometimes interchange of commodities, in primeval simplicity, essentially necessary to the settler's wants and comforts.

" We have no walls to our gardens, because there are no *stones*, and, if there were, building would be too expensive.

" Melons, cucumbers, and pumpkins, grow freely and very abundantly in the open air, and require less attention than any crop we have. We preserved a barrel of cucumbers last year, and kept them in salt and water, pickling them in vinegar occasionally, as they were required either by our servants or ourselves.

" Many of your garden plants grow wild here, tiger lilies, magnificent turncap and scarlet lilies, ladies' slippers, columbine, marygolds, and various others ; but strange to say, I have not seen in Canada the daisy, the holly, or the ivy, and the hawthorn very rarely ; it is quite a garden shrub. I have planted three thousand trees, and a great variety of evergreens to conceal our offices, and for ornament : for in truth the trees about us of natural growth are far from pleasing in their appearance, their closeness preventing the lateral furnishing of the branches, so essential to beauty.

" Our house stands in the garden, with a circular paling at one end to fence off the yard and offices. The poultry plague us a good deal in spring, by scratching up the seeds. In the severity of winter their claws are, in many cases, frostnipped, and our seed beds become more secure ; a good farm yard and a busy barn door are the best remedies. Many of the domestic fowl totally lose their toes in winter, and consequently become harmless in the gardens ; they are pitiable objects, when rambling about on their stumps, and we sometimes, in the excess of good-natured feeling, wish them their full complement of pedal members, even at the expense of our seeds.

" When we first came here, our hands were soft and delicate, as those of a lady, from being unused to laborious occupation, but seeing every one around us employed at manual works—magistrates, senators, counsellors and colonels, without any feeling of degradation, we fairly set to, in the spirit of emulative industry, and have already exhibited pretty fair specimens of our efforts in clearing land, and afterwards ploughing it.

" My brother Charles can take, what is termed here, a great *gap* out of a field of corn, with a cradle scythe ; he and his brother James once cut down two acres of rye before dinner.

" The latter makes all the waggons, sleighs, harrows, &c., and when I am not superintending the emigrant settlements, my time, at home, is occupied in shoeing horses, making gates, fences, chimney-pieces, and furniture. Indeed my mechanical labours are so multifarious that I can hardly enumerate them, but you may form some idea of their versatility, when I tell you that I made an ivory tooth for a very nice girl, and an *iron* one for the harrow, within the same day.

" My younger brother lends a hand at every thing, from a duet on the piano-forte to the threshing of a sheaf of corn ; and, believe me, we are neither degraded in our own estimation, nor in that of the most elevated of our acquaintances, by thus earning the bread of independence ; nor are we without our full share of amusement, which is much more grateful than can be imagined by those, whose days are spent in idleness or vanity.

" We have frequently occupied the morning at work in a *potato field,* and passed the evening most agreeably in the *ball* room at York !!!

" What would *Mrs. Grundy* say to that ?"

Mr Magrath writes most animatedly and knowingly on the subject of Canadian Field Sports, if *Field* they may be called ; and, we are told, meditates a volume upon the sports and scenery of that fine country. Canada may truly be called a sporting country. The sylvan pastimes of our gentle huntsmen at home, are but child's play to those of the hardy hunters and fishers of the primeval forests, and broad lakes, and infinite creeks of Canada.

Of the Radcliff family, the principal Letter-Writer is a Lady ; Mrs. William Radcliff whose lively descriptions convey only too vivid an idea of the miseries of a long sea voyage to delicate females. She, however, gives excellent hints to those who may follow her track in similar circumstances, without all " the appliances" of a *liner*, as the splendid New York and Liverpool Packets are named. She recommends, above all things necessary to the comfort of female passengers, a filtering machine ; which we should think a most useful article to settlers ; and a liberal store of bottled ale and porter. For a month this poor lady had been tortured with the parching thirst of sea-sickness, and disgusted with the nauseous water of the ship ; and she enforces her counsel to *malt* liberally with the observation, that " the more delicate the ladies who may have occasion to avail themselves of it, the more applicable the recommendation." The prepared bottled milk which they carried out, soon became good for nothing to sea-sick people. Mrs. Radcliff's travelling distresses increase as she approaches her forest home. The family party and several friends of the same rank, who came out intending to settle near them, landed when cholera was still raging in Upper Canada. Some of them became sick, and a child died of the pestilence. One of the brothers pressed forward, and selected land. The Radcliff settlement is in Adelaide township, London district.

" The choice of my lots," says Mr. William Magrath, writing to his father, " I left to my brother, not being able to go myself. He has succeeded to admiration, for himself, for me, and for some friends in the same township.

" I have, for the present, bought four hundred acres for two hundred pounds, land of superior quality, in the Huron tract, London district, township Adelaide, named after the Queen, within twenty miles of Lake Huron, and thirty of Lake Erie.

" As to people of moderate capital, (say from five to eight hundred pounds,) purchasing *desirable* land anywhere but in the absolute forest, is out of the question. So that, having been informed by a kind friend of the prime quality of that we have purchased, and, my brother and his companions, who went to view it, having approved of it very much, our lots are all chosen there; and, as far as I can learn, we have every reason to be satisfied.

"Improved farms have risen to a price that no common capital can compass.* Even in our remote district, it is thought that land will be of three-fold value in two or three years. Therefore, if A——r, or any of our friends, decide upon coming out, and wish to be near us, they should write at once, that we may secure the lots in time; for the townships are filled up almost as fast as they are surveyed.

"Our divisions adjoin that which is laid out for the town. When that comes to be built, (and it is said it will be completed in three years,) the value of our property will obviously be enhanced.

"Our fellow-travellers, Phillips and Groom, have settled themselves beside us.

"The former, as resident physician, has got the grant of a town lot to build on.

"How lucky to have such a man in the midst of us.

"All the spare cash I had, I have vested in bank stock, in the bank of Upper Canada. It is a decided fact that this stock pays regularly twelve per cent., and is as safe as in the Bank of England.

"Government are the holders, as I am informed, of one-third of the entire, and I am well assured that capital may be vested with perfect safety in this fund.

"No *individual* is permitted to invest more than one thousand pounds, that *many* may partake of the advantage.

"The influx of emigrants to our province of Upper Canada has been such, that in the last year the population is said to have increased one-fourth; and in this season, fully as much is expected. This affects the resources of the country in various ways, particularly as to the facility of disposing of farming produce; and also, as to the banking interests, of which I have been speaking. As I am informed, and indeed read in the public prints, that so numerous have been the arrivals of settlers, with considerable capital, that within a year three hundred thousand sovereigns have been deposited in the bank of Upper Canada.

"My deposit was in gold, and I received four shillings exchange on each sovereign.

"Bank stock has this year paid sixteen per cent., never less than twelve; the legal interest is but eight; but on the last dividend there was a bonus of eight more, in consequence of the country rising into such rapid prosperity. So that I request you to get our friend and kinsman to call in any money that I can command, and to send it me forthwith. Double interest in Ireland may be a very bad thing; but, being well secured, is quite the reverse here.†

"I can tell you nothing of the country, as I have been shut up for a month in this unhealthy town; where, however, the markets, being nearly on a par with ours, speak well for farming profits, though consumers (as *we* are now) may feel the inconvenience.

Beef, mutton, and pork,   5d. per lb.
Butter,   11d. do.
Bread dearer than at home.

"In fact, every thing is dear, as the province cannot supply itself, and is obliged to import from the States.

"The farmers here have no difficulty in finding a market for their corn. For all that we can grow, these ten years to come, we shall have a ready sale at our door.

"The number of emigrants going up each year, will take away all that can be spared at a full price.

"All the old people say, that the country raises more now in one year, than it did before in fifty. Upon the whole, then, I cannot see any risk the prudent and industrious farmer can be subject to, who pays no rent, has plenty to subsist him, with a ready market, and good price for the overplus.

"Amongst some agreeable acquaintances I have made, is Dr. Gwynn, come to settle at York, in the medical department. He was introduced to me by a letter from our worthy friend and relative, S—— G——. We have become very intimate; he is an excellent fellow, and accompanied me on a trip to Niagara, from whence we returned yesterday."

It is to Mrs. Radcliff we must refer for the mode of approach to the family head-quarters, and for a sketch of American manners.

"We were comfortably entertained at Burford, and though much fatigued, set forward next morning by break of day for the next tavern, Putham, I think, a distance of forty miles, in the very waggon which had brought our friends there sometime before. This was driven by the owner, Mr. Lyster, a very conversable and well informed person, for his rank in life; but all here considered themselves gentlemen and ladies—and this man, who, I must admit, was not troublesome or forward in his conversation, breakfasted and dined at table with us, without compunction or apology.

"The farther we proceeded up the country, the more we were gratified by the scenery. The birds, too, are very beautiful; the blue jay and woodpecker, especially—the wild flowers were in greater variety here, than at any other stage of the journey—the whole country abounds in sunflowers of gigantic size,—there are wild grapes also, which don't ripen till they get frost—and partridges without number—when you whistle, they stop to listen, and are shot. This came under my own eye.

"I was much amused at seeing William shaking hands most heartily on the road with a man from whom he was buying a pair of oxen. On inquiry, he proved to be a parishioner of yours, my dear Mr. R., many years ago, at Lisandill. He asked about you most affectionately, and was delighted to see one of the name.

"We proceeded next day to Delaware, twenty miles, in the same conveyance, which was tolerably easy, having the seats slung from the sides, in lieu of springs, and covered with Buffalo skins, (which are called blankets,) very handsome, soft, and comfortable.

"The horses were excellent, and we were tempted to purchase the entire equipage, for 160 dollars.

"At Delaware we came up with our party; found them all in good health, and enjoyed, with them, an agreeable day. They went forward to Colonel Mount's, at Caradoc, the Government agent for the western district, a most kind and attentive gentleman. We took up our abode at a farmer's, near Delaware, while our house was building; and passed six weeks there, very well accommodated, and abundantly supplied, on the most reasonable terms. For the whole family, (six in number, great and small,) we paid six dollars a-week, and had a private sitting-room—never dining with the family of the house, which was thought very strange, nor suffering our servants to dine with us, which was considered still more extraordinary. This was a log-house, the first I had been in—very comfortably fitted up, and in some respects thought preferable to a frame-house, as being warmer in winter, and cooler in summer, from the greater thickness of the walls. The objectionable point is, that as the timber seasons, the logs settle, but not equably, by which the doors and windows are set awry.

"Nevertheless, I am quite content with ours, which is of black ash, a timber not so liable to shrink as maple and bass wood, of which they are generally constructed. The farmer's sons generally supplied the dinner tables—their own, with black squirrels—ours, with chickens, both shot by themselves. These, with bacon, venison, &c., constituted a plentiful larder. Most of the necessaries of life can be had for the trouble of providing them, and many of the luxuries at the cheapest rate.

"I preserved some wild plums with maple sugar, which was better than that we bought. We had water melons in great profusion; and, when one year settled, we can have what we please; it is, indeed, the country of abundance. For the lower classes, in every respect, it presents a most inviting scene of plenty and independence; whilst those who have been educated otherwise, cannot but feel the want of

---

* On this subject, it may be perceived, opinions vary. The settler must decide for himself.

† 100 Sovereigns at 4s per exchange, are equal to L.120. This vested in Bank Stock, at 12 per cent., yields interest, L.14, 8s., per British L.100.

refinement, which generally prevails, and which it will require ages to correct; the palliative is to be sought in the manners and enjoyment of one's own domestic circle, nor need *they* much compassion, who, like us, have been fortunate enough to settle with so many agreeable friends around us.

"Whilst in the farm-house, it was my amusement to study the manners of the people, which confirm the foregoing remarks.

"They call every one *lazy* that does not engage in some manual work—and their dialect and mode of expression are quite amusing—on asking one of the girls, whether the Indians were cross when they indulge in any excess?' *Well*,' said she, (for they commence every sentence with *this* word,) —'they are *pretty ugly*.'

"The mistress of the house, bringing in breakfast, says, 'Well, I guess the tea looks black—but my husband thought it *dreadful good*.'

"I asked her how we were to feed our cows in winter, to make them give milk?

"'Well, *slop your cows*.'—And 'How am I to get them to come home from the wood?' 'Well *salt your cows*, and they'll come home.'

"'Is your dairy much under ground?'—'Well, considerable.'

"This dialogue affords a specimen of the comfortable and affluent in this class—who received us as lodgers, at the urgent request of Colonel Mount; not wishing to be put to any inconvenience, and at the same time not *willing* to decline the *remuneration*.

"On asking one of the daughters whether 'they ever saw a clergyman or preacher?' she answered, 'Well, *preachers*, once in a while; and then they *sing so*, really I am sometimes in roars of laughter at them.'

"I have now only to recount the miseries of my day's journey from the farm-house to Adelaide—where our mansion not being perfectly ready, Dr. Phillips proposed that we should occupy his, which was sooner built.

"How any unfortunate female carrying an infant in her arms, could have passed the tremendous road we were reduced to on this occasion, is almost miraculous. In my long journey from the coast, I had suffered many hardships in travelling, and many barbarous roads that I thought could not be exceeded in badness and danger; but all was smooth and agreeable, when compared with this last day. It did not happen so with our friends who went six weeks before us—but in that long interval the rain fell, and the floods had risen—and the road which *they* had travelled without much difficulty, being for us perfectly impassable, the woods were our only resource. Through these we had to cut our way—and to travel in a waggon drawn by one horse, the second being too spirited for the intricacy of the dangerous passes.

"We fortunately met upon the way one of Colonel Mount's overseers, who sent a man with an axe to assist us; William, who had one of his own, went forward to clear the way, and our northern servant, Sandy, led the waggon.

"All this we could have borne, but for the innumerable creeks, or streams which crossed our way; and were it not for a party of men sent to our relief, we could never have compassed such repeated obstructions. They made themselves useful, indeed indispensably so, by cutting down trees for temporary bridges, which we were to pass over in the best manner we were able:—conceive, my dear Mr. R. my walking over deep creeks, upon two long and small trees thrown across, which, however, with good assistance, I effected; but how the horses and waggon were made to manage it, I am unable to describe; certainly the horses here are wonderful animals—highly trained, and if you let them go ahead, they will bring you up heights that would amaze you. At one place, I shut my eyes and gave myself up as lost: this was a deep creek with very high banks on either side—our descent was so rapid as nearly to throw us forward on the horse, whilst the sudden rise at the opposite side, was as likely to shoot us out behind the waggon; on opening my eyes, I perceived William and his man in extreme terror lest we should fall back; but by encouraging the poor horse, he brought us up in safety. At another place we were obliged to cross one of those dangerous bridges on foot, and to walk a great distance, mounting over trunks of immense trees which lay across, whilst the waggon was sent through the wood, with twenty men to clear the way—after this, so great was my fatigue, I passed over fallen trees of great size without leaving the waggon; and had I preferred doing so, the want of time would have prevented me. The day was closing fast, half an hour's delay would have doomed us to the forest for the night—fortunately we escaped this disagreeable alternative, and upon reaching the line of road, fancied all our difficulties over—alas! it was *but* fancy. The road was flooded, and full of mud-holes; the horse up to his haunches in water, and wretched Sandy walking through it all. So dark had it become, I passed my own house without being able to see it, and, a little farther on, was hospitably received in that of Dr. Phillips.

"I can never be sufficiently thankful to a kind Providence, for protecting us through so many difficulties, and bringing us to the termination of our long and weary journey, without accident or suffering, except from excessive fatigue.

"Having given you a detail, which may appear sufficient to deter all female emigrants from so distant a settlement, it is but fair that I should explain how others may avoid the inconveniences which we experienced.

"This is to be done by emigrating at an early season, and by not wasting time when they land. They will then find the roads in passable order; and may have some provisions growing, and their houses comfortable, before the summer is past. We were too late all through, and feel the inconvenience of it.

"The log-house we now inhabit, till our own is ready, was the first completed in the township—if that can be called *complete*, which, on our arrival, consisted of but one room on the ground floor, and one in the upper storey.

"The owner, in politeness to us, went *up stairs*,—that is, *up the ladder, to sleep!!*—leaving us a room 24 feet by 16, the full dimensions of the house, with our cooking stove, and its various appendages, at one end, and his own Franklin stove at the other. A partition was soon formed for my convenience, and very snug we felt ourselves; though, in the unfinished state of the edifice, we could see the light through many apertures.

"I conclude this letter from *my own house*, of which we took possession yesterday.

"It is considered the handsomest in the township; being 46 feet in front, and 16 feet deep, in the clear;—but when finished next spring, by an addition in the rear, will consist of parlour and drawing-room, 16 feet square each; hall, kitchen, and five bed-chambers. The two stacks of chimneys, now of mud, but hereafter to be of brick, going up through the centre of the building, afford the means of warm presses and commodious closets. The roof is formed on Cantalivers, very unexpensive here, which gives the whole a gay appearance. The entire cost, L.60. This may be a good hint for some of our friends.

"We had a large and merry party to breakfast this morning. I enjoyed it, as the forerunner of an agreeable society, fast forming about us."

We should have wished much for another of this lady's agreeable epistles after her first winter in the wilds was over, but for that we wait. Up to January, the winter was one of remarkable mildness for the country, which proved inconvenient to the settlers in one respect, as they could not get their goods—their British comforts and elegancies *sleighed* on to the settlement, and thus wanted many accommodations that would have been doubly valued in the wilderness. Our next quotation must be from a letter written by Mr. Thomas Radcliff, to his father, which contains some useful information.

"The despondency we suffered at having our dear little girl taken off in a few hours by that fatal pestilence, and our anxiety for the safety of the other children, caused our difficulties, and privations, in settling, to be doubly felt. We are now, thank God, in perfect health, our spirits beginning to revive, and absolutely enjoying, if not a luxurious, at least a comfortable residence in *our own log-house*—the timbers of which, about three months ago, displayed their leafy honours in the wild forest. It consists of a cellar, three rooms, and a small store-room, in the principal storey, and two bed-rooms in the roof, or *ruff*, as the Canadians term it. The *edifice* is thirty feet by twenty-five, from out to out. For the five rooms, we have three flues, and two stoves, and mean to be very snug and warm. When perfectly finished, the whole expenditure will be about L.30, Halifax currency, or L.25 British.

"I have discovered limestone, which my Connaughtman, (an excellent servant,) has contrived to burn in sufficient quantity for building the stack of chimneys, and plastering the interior of the house, all which he has been handy enough to accomplish; and it may answer very well for some little time, till I can build a frame-house, of greater dimensions, which I mean to do. But I am most anxious that you should know how this said mansion is situated In order to this, I must give you some idea of the land itself.

"My lot is beautifully undulated. A creek or small river winding nearly through its entire length, between rich *flats*, as they are here called, is bounded on each side, at some distance, by high banks, upon which I am leaving a belt of ornamental timber, which swells with the form of the hills, and is, in general, about one hundred yards in depth. Between those banks and the river, all trees are to be removed, except a few maples.

"At a short distance from the site of the town, the right bank takes a bend, as it were, across the flats, and on that my house is placed, commanding from its windows a second smaller stream, with rising ground beyond, and a handsome point of land, embellished by a considerable clump of the best trees. The quality of the timber denotes the richness of the soil. Ours consists of maple, beech, butternut, elm, white ash, hornbeam, a sprinkling of oak, and some cherry and bass wood; all indicating a prime soil, and with great correctness, as I find it to be, in surface, five inches of black vegetable mould, over a few inches of clay loam, with a substratum of strong clay—and almost all my land, of this description, is an extended level of wheat soil, without the least unevenness. The knowing ones who have seen it, say it will give wheat for ever; and speak of fifty bushels to the statute acre. This I think scarcely possible, as I saw a standing crop, which I thought much better than any about you, and which the Fingallians would say, was '*the load of the earth*,' yet I am told it produced but forty bushels; but this is a wonderful return, upon the small acre, particularly when you consider that the stumps, after clearing, occupy nearly one-fourth of the ground.

"To so *handsome* an establishment, it is necessary to have a suitable approach. I have laid one out with some taste, useless, however, to man or beast, till the snow comes —now knee deep, of glutinous mud, that would slip off your Wellingtons like a boot-jack. This is one of our miseries, and must be that of all new settlers for a short time. We are in daily expectation of this much wished-for frost and snow. These last three days have given some menace, (*promise*, I should say,) of its setting in. A great part of my furniture which lies at Kettle Creek, must remain there till the sleighs can work. The waggon and oxen would be swamped at present in the sloughs and mud-holes.

"It snows lightly at this moment; and I have every hope that I may have tables and chairs for a party of nineteen, to dine under this roof, this day fortnight, being Christmas Day. Here we think nothing of the expense, the larder is so cheaply and abundantly supplied. We are much worse off, however, than we shall be next year, venison being our chief article of consumption—brought to our door at one halfpenny a pound. We have occasionally beef, (not the best,) with mutton and fowls; potatoes bad, and dear.

"I bought a young milch cow and a calf for twenty-four dollars—she gives a good supply of milk and cream—butter from 7½d. to 9d., per lb. I was taught to think that all cattle would be well subsisted in the woods. In summer they certainly will thrive, even to good condition—not so in winter. My teams of oxen are making the experiment; but if they did not get bran mashes, they would have a poor chance of seeing another summer. The first year is, to all settlers, and to all animals under their care, the most trying and inconvenient; I mean with those who settle in the Bush. The second year brings with it, its produce, its plenty, and its comforts.

"Till this last week, the weather has been delightful. I have been occupied in getting as many acres as I can cleared and prepared for cropping. Sixteen are already under operation, which will make a good open about the house. If I can get choppers in time, I will finish a good many more. The best management, in these new townships, is, to clear as much as possible in the first few years, while you have a sure market on the spot.

"The task price is very moderate for such heavy work. My brother and I, have set ours at L.1, 3s., per acre; the brushwood to be collected and piled, and the logs cut to the proper lengths. It will fall to ourselves to collect the logs, and to burn all; but this, where we have our own oxen, will pay well by the ashes, which are very profitable."

There are one or two letters, probably of Dublin manufacture, purporting to be written by Bridget Lacy, a charity girl, serving maid to the Radcliffs, which are not quite equal to those of Winifred Jenkins, and which throw an air of doubt and absurdity over the book. The Editor indeed says, the name of the fair writer is a fictitious one, but he should also have mentioned that the epistles themselves are arrant fictions; nor do they at all harmonize with the spirit or the serious purpose of a volume, which we conceive an important addition to the late numerous works upon Canada. The emigrants though of a genteel class and dearly loving "ould Ireland," seem to have found it perhaps too *hot*, and certainly much too poor to hold them, as men and women bred and educated as ladies and gentlemen expect to be maintained themselves, and to leave their children. They, accordingly, after due inquiry and deliberation, formed the sensible resolution of transferring themselves, before they had run down to the last guinea, to a land where there were no large landed absentees, and still abundant elbow-room for active, intelligent, persevering, and *industrious gentlemen*; though possessed of no more capital than, in our *wealthy* community of paupers and aristocrats, would be considered adequate for one or two years' maintenance of a respectable family. Conceive the misery of a fashionable family doomed to live upon from L.500 to L.800 a-year! Yet this is the sum of capital required by the class of persons, to whom these letters will be useful. For this is not exactly a poor man's book; though from it he may learn in time, that wages in Canada are principally increased by harder work and longer hours than at home. The labourer is, however, undeniably much better fed; and he has the strong and cheering inducement to exertion, that the possession of a few pounds, will enable him to become himself an independent land proprietor, when his labours will be all for himself. He may work on in the animating belief that his sinews are and his sweat poured forth for the exclusive advantage of his children. The facility of obtaining safe and profitable employment for children, is of itself motive sufficient to encourage the poor man to brave the unavoidable hardships of emigration. According to these letters, the wages of a good general farm servant, is about L.25, a year, with ample food. A maid-servant receives from L.5, to L.4, in the new settlements; but a good female servant will probably get more. The labour of both sexes is hard and constant; as baking, brewing, sugar-making, candle and soap-making, ashes burning, and the manufacture of coarse cloth, raising flax, &c., &c., are all household employments. The new Canadian settlers have not yet reached minute division of labour. We shall conclude these extracts with part of a letter from Mr. William Radcliff, to a friend in Dublin. It is to our mind very natural, and charmingly Irish.

"Let no one persuade you against bringing out your dogs; they would be invaluable. I have not been able to see, or hear of a good one in this country. A flock of about thirty turkeys came round the house last week; my man fired at them, and, like sportsmen that you and I have met, boasted that he had knocked as much feathers out of one of them, as *would make a good pillow*, but the *larder* fared nothing the better. They are very numerous, but very wary—and run faster than an Indian. If you were with me we could shoot more game in a day than a good horse could carry home. When I can spare time to go out, I can, without failure, bring back one, two, or three deer, any day please. They are in hundreds in the lands all round, and nothing can be more certain than the Calderwood rifle, which I brought from home. It has obtained a great character here, from my having tried it at a mark, against an Indian chief, whom I beat unmercifully.

"I have already cleared five acres, and by February, thirty are to be completed for me, and an equal number for my brother, at L.1, 8s. per acre, for brushing, piling ready to burn, chopping, and cutting into lengths. The drawing together, and burning, to be executed by ourselves. The workmen demanded much more, and had not we been a full party with a little steadiness, and some money stirring among us, they would have beaten us out, whereas we are now victorious, and the defeated party, perfectly contented, in the expectation of touching a little hard cash, of which they have very little, and are passionately fond. I could never have imagined that the axe could be used with such dexterity; I realy think that two Canadians would clear all Gerardstown in a fortnight; they would take but two blows to every tree in the plantations.

"Desire all friends who come out to bring delft, but not glass—as the latter is as cheap here, as the former is extravagant in price—also, hardware of the necessary kinds, and spades and shovels, which are ill constructed in this country,—but, above all, a hay-knife. Here they cut their hay with an axe, and, I may say, do almost every thing with that *universal* implement.

"I have bought a waggon and pair of horses; one of them a choice saddle horse, fully equal to my weight, which however is much decreased. He cost me a hundred dollars, and such a one would bring a hundred pounds with you. They are very good here, and very cheap.

"Now, my dear A. as to advising you whether to come out or not, as I promised to do, I can safely say, from all that I have seen and heard, that if you can contrive to reach my house, with five hundred pounds in your pocket, you may, with your present experience, ensure yourself a certain and gentlemanlike independence.

"Think what an advantage you would have over me, who have spent a little fortune in bringing out a family, and in the delays and heavy cost of their voyage, journey, lodgings, residence in towns, and charges at taverns and elsewhere, till nearly the present date, when we are at length settled, but not unexpensively, till next year, when the produce of the farm will begin to tell; whereas you, who are a single man, can apply all your time, and energy, and money to settling yourself prudently and comfortably, and make us happy by remaining with us till you do so. I only fear that if you do not come soon, you will not be able to find land near us, so fast are the lots disposed of. You need have no scruple about adding to our establishment, if you can live on venison and many other good things that cost but little. My cellar also defies you. I have a very snug one, moderately stocked with choice Teneriffe at 7s. the gallon, Brandy at 10s., Rum at 4s. 6d., and Whisky (very good) at 1s. 8d. No locks or bolts here, which is rather new to me. The Canadians never steal, but are sharp enough, and will take advantage when they can.

"I have now told you many of the favourable circumstances of the country, which are decidedly very great; still, however, an *Irish* day of recollection, sinking the spirits down, down! will occur; and sometimes, notwithstanding the outrages and the murders, the politics, and the poverty of that unhappy country, I would give all I am worth to be walking beside you, shooting the Enfield bottoms, as in those happy days we have spent together; again, these feelings vanish, when I look at my rich land, unencumbered by rent or taxes, and ask myself, if I *were* back again, how could I command such certain independence.

"If I had my friends all here, I should be the happiest man breathing.

"I inspect my choppers, and am much interested. They say here, that once we see the crops growing, we shall never think of home again; but this is a bold assertion.

"I do not feel at home here yet. My former life, my sea voyage, and travelling some seven hundred miles through a new country, appear more like a dream than reality; my very existence in these drowsy woods appears doubtful, till I rouse myself by thinking on my College friends, my hunting days, the animating hounds, the green open fields, and the scarlet coats.

* * * * *

"What I have still to say may be comprised in a nutshell; come by New York, don't loiter on the road to waste your money; bring out rape-seed, hay-seeds, garden-seeds, especially those of culinary and aromatic herbs, and sail in April, if you can.

It would be cruel to doubt the powers of the Calderwood rifle; though, we could advise no Scotch or English emigrant, to trust his family provision in his first year or any future year, to the "bringing back" even "one deer a-day." These are the sweets, not the *utilities*, of the long hard life of endeavour, which must precede the beatitudes of the emigrant of moderate capital. At Adelaide, a church is to be built, and a log schoolhouse was to be erected immediately. Mr. Thomas Radcliff gives his father an account of the state of religion in the province. The number of Methodist Missionaries is considerable.

"Wherever a settlement is formed, there they are to be found. Many of them are excellent men, and all of them are really or apparently zealous; and from all I can hear they have done infinitely more among the *Indians* in promoting a knowledge of Christianity, than our clergymen have been able, or anxious to effect. I know that there exists, at this moment, a demand, (in mercantile phraseology,) for thirty, or forty Church of England clergymen.

"If care be taken to select able, zealous and active men, the happiest results will follow; but if a swarm of *Drones* be sent among us, attracted merely by the temporal advantages of a settlement, without higher motives and anxieties, the degradation of *our* religion and the general contempt of inefficient ministers, must be anticipated.

"But I much fear that the government of the parent

country has let the time pass by, when good might have been effected through the instrumentality of our clergy. The Methodist dissenters have obtained an ascendency over our infant population. Their habits of domiciliary visitation, their acquaintance with the tastes and peculiarities of the Canadians, their readiness to take long and fatiguing rides, in the discharge of their self-imposed labours, render them formidable rivals to our more *easy-going* clergy.

"I repeat, that it is of the utmost importance to send us men of *character* and high religious attainments, deeply convinced of the responsibility attached to their calling, and determined that every other pursuit, and care, shall be secondary to the great purpose, for which they are designed, and to which they should be principally devoted."

Other observations are made by this gentleman which we cannot so entirely approve. It is evident that the good example of the United States, in which provision is always made for education, is not lost upon the Canadian Government.

PRECAUTIONS TO BE USED DURING A THUNDER STORM.

It is still to be regretted that, notwithstanding the discoveries of modern philosophy respecting the electric fluid, and the laws of its operation, no *thunderguard* has yet been invented which, in all situations, whether in the house, in the street, in the open field, in a carriage, or on horseback, shall serve as a complete protection from the ravages of lightning. Till some contrivance of this kind be effected, it is probable that the human race will still be occasionally subjected to accidents from electrical storms. Such accidents are more numerous and fatal, even in our temperate climate, than is generally imagined. From an induction of a variety of facts of this kind, as stated in the public papers and other periodical works, in the year 1811, the author ascertained that more than twenty persons were killed by lightning, (or at the rate of a thousand persons every fifty years,) during the summer months of that year within the limits of our island ; besides the violent shocks experienced by others, which did not immediately prove fatal, and the damage occasioned to sheep and cattle, and to public and private edifices ; and it is worthy of notice, that most of the individuals who were killed by the lightning had either taken shelter under trees, or were in situations adjacent to bells or bell-wires. The experience of succeeding years proves that a similar number of disasters of this kind annually take place. It is, however, more than probable, that at least half the number of accidents arising from the same cause might have been averted, had the nature of lightning, and the laws which regulate its movements, been generally known. Seldom a year passes but we are informed by the public prints of some person or other having been killed by lightning, when taking shelter under a large tree,—of whole families having been struck down when crowding around a fire-place, during a thunder storm,—of one person having been struck when standing beside a bell-wire, and another while standing under a bell connected with the wire, or under a lustre hanging from the ceiling.

There can be little doubt that a considerable number of such accidents would have been prevented had the following facts respecting the nature of lightning been extensively known :—That lightning is a fluid of the same nature, and is directed in its motions by the same laws which regulate the motions of the electric fluid in our common electrical machines ;—that it is attracted and conducted by trees, water, moisture, flame, and all kinds of metallic substances ;—that it is most disposed to strike high and pointed objects ; and that, therefore, it must be dangerous to remain connected with or in the immediate neighbourhood of such objects when a thunder-cloud is passing near the earth.

Hence the following precautionary maxims have been deduced, by attending to which the personal accidents arising from thunder-storms might be, in a great measure, prevented. In the open air, during a storm, rivers, pools, and every mass of water, even the streamlets arising from a recent shower, should be avoided, because water being an excellent conductor, might determine the course of an electrical discharge towards a person in contact with it, or in its immediate neighbourhood. All high trees and similar elevated conductors, should also be avoided, as they are in more danger of being struck than objects on the ground ; and, therefore, a person in contact with them exposes himself to imminent danger, should the course of the lightning lie in that direction. But, to take our station at the distance of thirty or forty paces from such objects, or, at such a distance as may prevent us from being injured by the splinters of wood, should the tree be struck, is more secure than even in the midst of an open plain. Persons in a house not provided with thunder-rods, should avoid sitting near a chimney or fire-place, whether there be a fire in the grate or not. For when there is a fire in the grate, the flue contains the following conductors,—flame, smoke, rarified air, and soot. Even when there is no fire, the soot with which the flue is lined, is a conductor ; and, from the superior height of the chimney-shaft above every other part of the building, it is more liable than any other part of the house to be struck with lightning. In a house, too, gilt mirrors or picture frames, lustres or burning candles, bell-wires, and all metallic substances, should be carefully avoided, as they afford so many points of attraction, which might determine the course of an electric discharge. The safest position is in the middle of the room, if not near a lustre a bell, or any thing hanging from the ceiling ; and if we place the chair on which we sit on a bed or mattress, almost every possible danger may be avoided.* Such are a few maxims easy to be recollected and put in practice, by attending to which, not a few accidents from electrical explosions might be averted.

USEFUL HINTS AND RECEIPTS FOR WARM WEATHER.

CHEAP COOLING BEVERAGES.—The water in which cucumbers is cooked may have any cucumber parings or scrape put to it, and be boiled up, strained, and sweetened for a cooling draught. Water with melon the same.—*Cook and Housewife's Manual.*

RHUBARB or rhubarb stems yield, at this season, far more acid juice than it is desirable to have in tarts, pies, or stews of this useful spring vegetable. Drain off what is considered superfluous when stewing the stems, preparatory to making your pie, sweeten this, and keep the syrup to mix with water for a refreshing summer drink, which costs nothing save the sugar. The drink is exceedingly pleasant, and, I should presume, perfectly wholesome ; but, perhaps, some of the *Schoolmaster's* medical friends may inform him on the latter subject.

BLOSSOM OF THE LIME TREE.—I send you another receipt which, though unknown in this country, is of value. The present favourable season promises an abundant crop of this valuable production of nature's laboratory, of which, in France, every family endeavours to keep a store for the purpose of making an infusion, which is administered with great success in cases of colds or feverishness, in which it has a most agreeable and soothing effect. The process of gathering and preserving it is very simple. When the blossom is mature, it should be gathered from the trees, and spread out on linen sheets in the sun until perfectly dry ; a portion of the young and tender leaves of the tree are sometimes plucked and dried along with the blossom ; it may be kept in linen or paper bags. To make the infusion, a large handful of the dried flowers is put into a teapot, and treated as tea, which being sweetened with a little honey or sugar, is taken hot on going to rest.

* It has been generally thought that the cellar is the most secure situation during a thunder storm ; but this is true only in certain cases. When the lightning proceeds from the clouds, it is unquestionably the most secure position ; but in the case of a thunderstorm, if, upon the lightning proceeds from the earth, it is less secure than the higher parts of the building.—*Dick's Diffusion of Knowledge.*

THE STORY-TELLER.

A PASSAGE IN THE LIFE OF SIR H. DE GREY.
BY MRS. S. C. HALL.

Before young ladies had become the scientific and rational beings they are supposed to be in the present day, and before gentlemen deemed it necessary (as a *dernier resort* to keep their intellectual superiority, I suppose) to discard good manners by being *clubbish*, political, and argumentative when in their presence; in the olden times, I say—the times of stiff satins and high-heeled shoes—Lady Olivia Bulwer was considered a perfect pearl—a peerless union of loves, graces, and virtues; such a being as poets dream of; yet in reality a woman, a very woman! possessing all those dear delightful little whims and peculiarities of the sex, which, however much they may be found fault with, constitute, after all, the half of woman's charms. Nobody who knows any thing of human nature will dispute this. Look as grave as you will about it, it is no less true. Let a woman be gentle, affectionate, generous, and sincere—let her, above all, have a warm and tender heart; but if she mean either to please in society, or to cage (*not net*) a heart into herself for life, let her be a little fond of tormenting, and studiously avoid sameness; suiting herself with lady-like demeanour to the society she joins, and yet enlivening withal by sprightliness and good temper. A little gravity—even a pretty pout—is a pleasing variety; but the former must never be of long continuance, nor the latter deepen into a frown.

It is credibly asserted that Lady Olivia Bulwer never frowned; and I can believe it, gazing upon her picture as I do now; that noble brow looks as if formed for heaven's own light to rest upon; and the clear blue eye tells of more feeling—ay, and more intellect also—than one would suppose could consistently associate with her laughter-loving mouth. How nobly that gallant hawk sits upon her wrist! But this is nought. It behoves me to tell how, in the end of the month of May, that fair lady leant her head upon her hand, in her own favourite bower, before which sloped a green lawn, studded, according to the fashion of the day, with divers yew trees, cut into the semblance of peacocks, monkeys, and other animals. Beside her sat her youthful cousin, the Lady Janet Melbourne, a gentle girl, who had hardly numbered eighteen summers, and looked upon her kinswoman—who, truth to say, was about five-and-twenty—with mingled reverence and affection. Their conversation proceeded as follows:—

"When you urge me to marry, Janet," said the Lady Olivia, "you speak even as an inexperienced girl; and yet I must, I suppose, sooner or later, resign my liberty to some lordly man, who will not thank me when the deed is done. My estates are more than I can manage; and methinks that attention to matters of pounds, shillings, and pence, almost unsexes a woman; certes, it destroys the finer feelings of her heart, and leaves her what Iago sneered at—a great mathematician!"

"Cousin, cousin," interrupted Janet, "you shall not so slander yourself in my presence: but, indeed, 'tis hard to choose from among so many gallant cavaliers as wait your pleasure. Let us canvass their claims to your affections. What say you to the good Colonel Kinlock, with his crab-tree emblem and his noble plaid? I pray you be merry, cousin. I will not say a word of Sir Huon de— There, do not look angry, but tell me how you are affected to Kinlock?"

Lady Olivia smiled; and then resuming an air of even more than her usual gaiety, replied, "Would'st have me marry mere kail-broee and haggis? His face and his pedigree are both too long for Olivia Bulwer."

"What think ye, then, of the young Irish Peer?" persisted Janet; "the gay young Irish Peer?"

"What! he of the long-tailed family! scores of distant cousins—dozens of near relations—ever so many fathers and mothers—O's and bogs—feasts and fasts—saints and sinners—pride and poverty! I will sing you their delicious melodies, an' ye will; but affirm truly to you, my own Janet, that I will never be led to the altar by a compound of shillelahs, shamrocks, and whisky."

Janet laughingly continued: "Perhaps you will not be so severe to your own countryman; him whom I call the second Falstaff?"

"Now out upon thee for a saucy minx!" retorted the lady. "What! the knight of the beetle brow and enormous rotundity, whose eyes wander unceasingly over the crowded board, seeking what they may devour, even while the mouth is employed discussing the contents of a well-filled trencher! The very king of turtle! the lord of venison! the emperor of high feeding! He told me the other day that I did not look well crammed. Heard ye ever the like? to mention him *to me*——"

"Hush, Olivia!" exclaimed the younger lady. "See through yon trees. There are three gentlemen coming this way. If their wit keep pace with their speed, methinks they might soon win a woman's heart. By their dress I can tell them to be, the Baron of Burlybrook, the young poet of Upton Lea, and the gentle Sir Huon de Grey—all suitors for your fair hand, I suppose."

Lady Olivia shook her head, and, after a pause, replied:— "I love to tease that young poet; but, indeed, teasing a poet does not give one, even moderately skilled in the art, much trouble, nature having bestowed upon him a double portion of nerves and spleen; consequently you have only to work upon his infirmities; to cough, or gently sneeze, when he condemns you to a listener's task—or shrug, or move your chair, or pet your dog; when he expects congratulation loud and lengthened, just seem oblivious, smile, and say, ' Surely in some quaint book I read that tale;' or, —but Janet, here they come *en masse*; and, by the mass, a goodly looking trio!"

The gentlemen entered the presence with courtly grace, and were received with the courtesy which a well-born gentlewoman never fails to bestow even upon disagreeable guests. I trow, however, they were not *all* disagreeable; for a colour mounted to the lady's brow, lofty as it was, as Sir Huon de Grey, bending lowly on one knee, touched the fingers of her embroidered glove respectfully with his lips. A gentleman, to my taste, never appears to such advantage as upon one knee, in the attitude which Chalon and Leslie alone can paint. It would be much better than the cut-and-dry bow, or attempt at it, which they make now-a-days, when removing that ugly composition of felt or beaver from their odd-looking cropt heads: it would, I think, be better, and more graceful, at all events, whenever they entered into a lady's presence, to prostrate themselves, as in duty bound. I wish the king would be graciously pleased to bring it into fashion. When he does, I am certain it will be universally adopted. For my own part, I conceive it the very height of ill-breeding for a man to treat a woman as his equal. Sir Huon de Grey was a true-born gentleman, and perhaps too proud of being so; he had known the Lady Olivia for many years, and, it was conjectured, loved her;—nay, it was even said, she loved him, although he had never declared his passion;—but be that as it may, he never flattered her vanity, nor praised her follies; he seemed to regard her more as a brother does a sister, and even calmly looked on the attentions paid by other lovers to the richly-dowered lady. Many called him fool for this, but he heeded it not. At this meeting, however, there was a marked difference in his manner—an agitation, an earnestness, that the ladies could not account for. The Baron of Burlybrook at length spoke; and while twisting the long feather of his velvet hat carefully around his finger by way of pastime, commenced thus:—

"My friend of Upton Lea—for friends we are, despite the honourable rivalship which the love (" adoration" interrupted the poet) of you has occasioned—has penned some verses to your beauty, and, if it would pleasure you to hear them, will read them now. I cannot woo in verse; yet we both pray you to decide our fate this day, as our affection can no longer brook the delay with which we have been tortured."

"Worshipping, as we do!" concluded the poetaster, unfolding the perfumed paper, from which he read the following lines:—

"Hail, woman, hail! the star of hope, whose rays
Gild both the morn and evening of our days,
Shining and smiling on each path we tread,
Through which in peace and calm our feet are led—
Bright'ning each hour with joys that ever last,
And shedding still a perfume o'er the past;
All that is lovely, all that's fair, is thine;
Bright while it rises, dear to its decline!

"Oh, woman! woman!—soul of love and truth!
Joy of our manhood, transport of our youth!
The only hope when pleasures fade away,
And still the same, at morn, at noon, at even!
A star of bliss—to light the way to heaven!"

"I pray thee peace!" said the Lady Olivia, laughing. "Dost think, good Sir Poet, that we do not know our excellences already! Entertain us with a song that is new, if it please ye—not with such a strain as that."

"Your attention for one moment," interrupted Sir Huon, advancing from a recess in the arbour, from whence he had marked the group—"Gentlemen, I never presumed once to cross your suit; whatever my feelings were, I restrained them within my own breast. Lady Olivia, I was a penny-less Knight, and too proud to trust to a lady's purse for wealth;—but times are changed: within a week I have been left a splendid fortune, which, together with a heart that has long been yours, I now tender to you openly."

Lady Olivia looked astonished, gratified, and confused. She could not reply, but sat, the colour now advancing, now fading from her cheek, when Lady Janet, with woman's ready wit, exclaimed, "Let me decide, let *me* answer for my cousin. Thus, then, gentlemen:—the Lady Olivia cannot marry you all three, that is certain. Seeing, then, that such is the case, she is willing to give you all the same chance of obtaining her hand."

"Janet! Janet!" interrupted Lady Olivia.

"Hush! do I not know best? be quiet!" continued the lively girl, as she pressed her rosy fingers to the lady's lips; then, in her cousin's ear, she whispered one or two gentle words, so softly that they could not be heard even by Sir Huon. Lady Olivia bowed her head, and Janet proceeded.

"Gentles three, proceed to the bottom of the lawn, and choose, from out the parterre, each a flower. He who brings here Lady Olivia Bulwer's favourite of the garden shall have her hand,—is it not so, cousin?"

Olivia again bowed her head.

"Tarry, tarry!" said the Baron of Burlybrook, in his usual gruff voice, "What mummery is this! How are we to know but you or her ladyship may elect her favourite flower on the instant?—Lady Janet Melbourne, I am an Englishman."

"It little needed your telling it, Sir; for no other would be guilty of the rudeness of supposing a lady would change her emblem for the sake of a man. Hie! and do my bidding."

"It pleaseth me much," said the poet; "and I will gladly submit to such a test, if those gentlemen will also."

"I consent," replied Sir Huon de Grey.

"How can I be assured as to the emblem," persisted the burly Baron.

"Out, infidel!" laughed lady Janet; "but I can assure you a wreathe of her favourite flower is painted on the first page of her private tablets, which the eye of man has never yet rested on."

"Enough," growled forth the Baron, as with the poet of Upton Lea, and Sir Huon de Grey, he departed.

"Are you certain that he *cannot* mistake?" said Lady Olivia, as she watched their receding figures.

"Quite, quite!" replied the Lady Janet. "Once, when speaking of your taste, I told him; and his smiles convinced me he has not forgotten; besides I made a V with my fingers; and after that, you know——"

"Ay, girl, how my heart beats!—dear Huon!—And yet it is but half a triumph: I should have liked better, if his love had conquered his pride."

"You would not have respected him so much, though; and is not that necessary for love's existence?—But come, are you not grateful to me for getting you breathing time? The power of speech had left you. Good, my cousin, I would not be in love for the world! As I live they are coming, but each has encompassed his flower in a broad green leaf of the giant peony, fearful lest the sun should tinge its beauty!"

It was a quaint sight to behold the three cavaliers present, on bended knee, to that stately lady, the flowers which were to decide their fate. The lady spoke at first in a faltering, but afterwards in a firm, voice. "'Tis beautiful and fragrant," said she to the poet, as he proffered her a white and fresh blown lily; "but mark, it is cold and stately, devoid of feeling; yet it opens its chalice with proud heartlessness to the flirting butterfly, as well as to the industrious bee, which proves it to be as undiscriminating as it is vain: moreover, even now the canker shelters 'neath its shade: 'tis not my favourite.

"Most noble Baron, thy rose is glorious. I have seldom seen so glowing or so beautiful a flower:—but it is gaudy, and courts observation—it receives alike the homage of the wise and foolish, and bestows its perfume on every zephyr that flirts amid its leaves; it may be called the emblem of voluptuousness, and so it cannot be fit for a lady's bosom."

The colour on her cheek, as she extended her taper fingers to take the simple offering (it was but a deep-blue violet) of

Sir Huon de Grey, blushed to the deepest crimson—and the delicate flower trembled on its stem. There was perfect stillness for a moment, which afforded time to the Lady Janet to draw forth from a silver net, that hung upon her cousin's arm, the envied tablets; at her touch they expanded, and on the first page was a violet wreath, encircling the pretty motto of

"*Il faut me chercher.*"

Sir Huon repeated, in a voice which, however delightfully it sounded upon the ear of Lady Olivia, appeared (as Lady Janet afterwards declared) " queer and nervous enough at the time," these old lines—

" Violet is for faithfulness,
Which in me shall abide;
Hoping likewise that from your heart
You will not let it slide."

What did Lady Olivia say? Nothing—positively nothing. She blushed, as I have before stated—she let her hand drop into that of Sir Huon—and then (it is really melancholy to think what fools women, and sensible women, too, make of themselves,) she burst into tears. The Baron of Burlybrook started and stormed; and on the instant offered his hand to the Lady Janet Melbourne, who laughed him to scorn. It is said that the poet forswore the sex—for a time, at all events: certainly the following lines were found dangling on the bough of a rose-tree, which breathed a very different spirit from his former enamoured stanzas.

" Vainly the muse her favoured son inspires,
In vain elicits the poetic spark;
If fancy breathe not on the latent fires,
The light is gone—the glow of thought is dark.

" What power the gift to mortal eyes shall give,
In woman's soul such innocence to see?
In fancy's bower such virtues *seem* to live;
Then vice in masque is perfect purity.

" Then hear me, Fancy, from this weary earth,
Where fickle woman is a feeble flower,
That fate decrees, e'en from its hapless birth,
Shall blossom, droop, and perish in an hour."

" Oh, most lame and impotent conclusion!" exclaimed the Lady Janet, laughing—I hope my readers will not say the same!

THE COPPER-LEG CONSPIRACY.—We have been more amused by the following ingenious piece of roguery, than anything of the kind that has occurred for a long while. The scene was the neighbourhood of Canterbury, where an old woman was lately rescued from the police by a man with a wooden leg. This fellow was met at Harbledown last Saturday by two of the city police, when he unbuckled his leg, and ran with it under his arm, showing as nimble a pair of heels as ever helped a rogue to turn his back upon the gallows. Finding his pursuers gaining upon him, however, and having good reasons for not wishing to be taken (if taken at all) with *that particular leg* in his possession, he practised the same trick upon the constables that Hippomanes did upon Atalanta, not indeed by dropping golden apples, but by dropping his leg. The bait took. The constables stopped to pick up the leg, and were so amazed, that while *they* stood staring and wondering, *he* continued running and laughing, till he was fairly out of sight; and he has never been heard of since. The leg, having been examined, was found to be hollow, and filled with all sorts of combustibles, detonating balls, &c.; and, in consequence of information received by the Magistrates, a *depot* of copper legs (resembled in every respect the one described) has been seized at Copperhaus Sole, in Kent; and it is said that the confederacy of the *Copper Legs* are trained, organized, and bound by illegal oaths, in the same manner as the *White Feet!*

COMMERCIAL THIEVES.

(*Concluded.*)

Letter 1st from the Old London Commission Agent, with a new name, to Messrs. ———— ————, Scotch Ale Brewers; or the Offer of a Swindler's Services.

" Cornhill, London 24th September, 1832.

" GENTLEMEN,—I am induced to trouble you with the offer of my services as agent for the sale of your ale, from having been in treaty with Mr. ————, of Musty Hall Brewery, who was on the point of engaging with me, but the pressure of the season obliging him to depart for Scotland, on Wednesday last, induced him to close with another. I am so convinced of the desire Mr. ———— had to obtain my services, which he preferred over those of 100 competitors, that I have no hesitation in referring to him for his opinion, and even recommendation, having now perfected securities to the amount of L.1,000, which were not ready when he left town.

" In consequence of this disappointment, I called upon Mr. C————, of ———— Wharf, and it is from the probability that I may suit you, that he has permitted me to use his name in making this application. I have no doubt that I could at first dispose of forty or fifty barrels a-week after a short trial; but I by no means confine my views to that, having the best grounded expectation, from the success that has attended Messrs. Coldstream and Co., with the first of whom I am acquainted, that I can do as much as they can do, from 4,000 to 5,000 barrels per annum, when I have been as long in the business. Should this proposal be worthy of your consideration, I will be happy to receive your idea as to terms; or I will send you those proposed by Mr. ————, of Musty Hall Brewery, with which I am perfectly satisfied, and which Mr. C———— thinks fair on both sides. The references I shall give you for my respectability, integrity, and perseverance, are Messrs. ————, my bankers, also my intimate friend C———— J————, Esq., M. P., and many other gentlemen, equally respectable, who have known me for upwards of twenty years.

" It would be my endeavour, and, in a great degree, my pride, *apart from any consideration of gain,* if I should enter into an engagement with you, to promote your interest in every possible manner, and in no degree to be outdone by any other agent. After making those due allowances for a commencement, in a market already, in a great degree, pre-occupied, and the disadvantages to which every new article is at first necessarily exposed, I am, gentlemen, &c. ' W—— W—— A——,' *alias* the ' Old Commission Agent with a new name."

The ale brewers to whom this more than unexpected offer of services was made, being intimately connected with the Scotch merchant, handed over to him their London letter; and he, having asked and obtained permission to be the answerer of said letter, wrote as follows:—

Letter 1st from the Scotch Merchant to his old acquaintance the London Agent, who had changed his name in expectation of procuring a commission.

" Scotland, 27th September, 1832.

" To W—— W—— A——

" SIR,—Your letter of the 24th instant, addressed to my young friends the Brewers, has been duly received; and they authorize me to acquaint you, that, as the quality of their ale is fine, they have hitherto had, at home, a sufficient demand for all they can make, and therefore, have no intention of extending their business to London this season.

" The only way you could make a beginning with my young friends would be in the shape of a regular sale, to a moderate extent, allowing you a discount from the price charged equal to a guarantee commission; and this, perhaps, might lead to a more extensive connexion.

" If your connexion in London lies amongst the spirit trade, I would be glad to know upon what terms you could undertake to sell spirits for us upon commission. Since whisky was allowed to be exported to England, we, that is the house with which I am connected, have been accustomed to ship extensively to the northern counties of England, and have long had a desire to extend our business to London, where, we understand, a taste for the finest qualities of West Highland whisky is now springing up. By a judicious admixture of the different spirits made in the small distilleries distributed over the West Highlands, we are confident of producing a quality greatly exceeding anything which has yet appeared in London, where a numerous class of Scotch gentlemen would be glad to procure a genuine supply of their own native mountain dew. You would, therefore, oblige us by stating the terms upon which you would undertake to introduce such an article amongst your numerous customers. I am, &c.

"Scotch Merchant."

The Scotch merchant being somewhat on his guard against the tricks of London agents, and half suspecting that the person who had begun a correspondence with the young ale brewers, was no other than the agent recommended to himself by Patent Schiedam, was determined to be on the outlook, and to be guided by the advice of the members of a society for the protection of trade, who had done so much to punish fraudulent delinquents. I, the writer of this narrative, being the member just alluded to, encouraged the Scotch merchant to continue his investigation, and in due course I was intrusted with the keeping of another London letter.

Letter 2d from the London Commission Agent, under a changed name, to the Scotch Merchant and Scotch Ale Brewers; or a Swindler's Whisky Commission.

"London, 4th October, 1832.

"To Mr. ―――, Scotch Merchant.

"Sir,—I have to acknowledge the receipt of your favour of the 24th ultimo, and to inform you that, in the interval between its receipt and the one to which it is a reply, I had formed an agency for the sale of British brandy with Messrs. S― and W―, chiefly with a view of obtaining their friendly introduction for the sale of Scotch ale to some of their numerous connexions, which, I understand, exceed 3,000 in number. I intend to combine ale, brandy, and whisky, which are very successfully united in the establishments east and west of the Royal Exchange. It is my intention to obtain cellarage, and a small counting-house, if possible, in the most striking and eligible situation in the city; and if I succeed in obtaining it, I shall have a greater advantage of publicity than any other house can possess; but I am happy to say that I shall neither depend on that nor on my own connexion, which is very respectable and extensive, but greatly on the kind introduction of Mr. C―――, who informs me he is three or four times a-week applied to for an introduction to good whisky. He will be happy to favour me with a recommendation on future occasions, as, from long experience, he knows who is safe to be trusted. I consider this an invaluable assistance, which must lead, when once fairly established, to the most favourable connexion in London; but, I presume, the best Highland whisky will come too high for the trade, and that a second, or even a third quality will be requisite. If I confine myself exclusively to the sale of yours, which I have no objections to, I have no objections to purchase it; but not being able to judge of quality at this distance, shall confine myself to your proposition of the terms under which I could effect sales for you. I will engage to sell your spirit, of whatever quality, at the price you may affix to it, for 4s. per gallon, you paying all charges, duty, and running all risks of shipments, and bad debts, and remit you monthly all receipts; or I shall be happy to hear a proposition from yourself, being willing to place our connexion on a basis that shall give satisfaction to both parties. I trouble you with a letter on the other side, to Messrs. ―――, Scotch ale brewers, and remain your very obedient servant,

"W― W― A―"

"Finch Lane, 4th October, 1832.

"To Messrs. ―――, 'Scotch Ale Brewers.'

"Gentlemen,—I have been favoured with your sentiments, through the communication of Mr. ―――, 'The Scotch Merchant,' and shall be very happy to form a connexion for the purchase of your ale, which I am glad to hear is of such an excellent quality. As your supply will be limited, I shall decline the services of a person who has been many years in the trade, and whom I only intended to engage to make it more advantageous to the brewer, and shall confine myself to the supply of my own connexion, which at present is small.* Should I require more than you can conveniently supply, I must obtain it of some other house; but I do not doubt that your means of production will keep pace with my moderate wants. The system of purchase, by the London houses, is adopted, I believe, but I know it is the arrangement of Messrs. Younger and Brown, as I have learnt from their respective agents. If you can favour me with a small cask as a sample of your 60s., which is the quality most in request, I shall be better able to know to what extent I shall require a supply, and do me the favour of stating the terms on which you are willing to dispose of it. I am, gentlemen, your very obedient servant,

"W― W― A―"

From the style of the letters intrusted to my care by the Scotch merchant, I was convinced that his suspicions were well grounded, and that his new London correspondent was in reality none other than his old acquaintance the London agent, under a changed name. The circumstance of this agent of many names, charging 4s. per gallon commission, proved that he was altogether ignorant respecting the whisky trade, and that it was possession of the goods, under false pretences, he had in view. I, as a member of a society formed for the express purpose of protecting the fair trader, candidly told the Scotch merchant that his correspondent, W― T―, and W― W― A―, was, in my opinion, one and one person, and belonged to a fraternity of fraudulent traders, who have long infested the country, and been but too successful in their numerous attempts to get goods under an almost innumerable variety of false pretences. I advised the Scotch merchant to cease corresponding with such vagabonds; and I am persuaded he would have followed my advice, had not the party sent one of their secret agents for Scotland to the very counting-house of my friend the merchant, who has furnished me with the following particulars.

An account of a Co-Partner-Seeking Advertiser; or the Whisky Ale-Tun Seasoner.

About the middle of November, 1832, there came one day to our counting-house a strange gentleman, who inquired if we had any grain whisky for sale, and what would be the lowest cash price. A sample of whisky was shown to the stranger, and the price asked was a low one. The stranger said, that although the price might be a low one for the quality of the spirit, it was too high for the purpose to which he intended to apply the spirit; that he was Mr. ―――, of the ――― Brewery, and that he wanted the whisky for seasoning musty ale-tuns. I told him that I considered this an expensive mode of seasoning tuns; that I had a friend a brewer, and that, if it was of any consequence to him, I would ask my friend's opinion as to the best mode of seasoning musty tuns. The Whisky Ale-Tun Seasoner replied, "I feel much obliged to you, Sir; but as I have already tried all the usual methods and cannot succeed, I am resolved to try whisky, as I have been told that it is the only remaining chance for sweetening the casks which have stood long unused in the ――― Brewery." Believing that the stranger was what he represented himself to be, I offered to inquire whether a cheaper article of whisky could not be procured, as quality was no object. The Tun Seasoner agreed to call again on the morrow. When my friend, the brewer, came to dinner, I stated to him that I had had in the forenoon a visit from a neighbour brewer wishing to buy a quantity of grain whisky for the purpose of seasoning tuns. My friend replied, "A pretty brewer he must be; for, in the first place, the whisky will cost more than the value of the tuns; and, in the next place, were he to attempt seasoning his tuns with whisky, it would at once check fermentation and spoil the ale." This made me doubt if all was right, and my suspicions were confirmed by the following protestation of

―――――――
* A swindler as well as a liar requires a good memory; for, in the previous letter, we find this very agent declaring his connexion to be very respectable and extensive.

trade warning, which was handed to me in the course of the evening:—"*Take care of the man with whiskers for two puncheons grain, in case he rub you against the grain.*"—"*Bailie F——.*" I at once recollected that the Tun Seasoner answered the cautionary description, and it immediately flashed upon my mind that he was the person to whom the change-name London Commission Agent referred my young friends, the Scotch Ale brewers, and that he, therefore, was in some way or other connected with the same gang of London swindlers.

The Tun Seasoner, punctual to a minute, came again on the morrow to ascertain what I had been able to do for him in the way of low-priced whisky. I told him that I had met, up to that time, found leisure to make further inquiries; but rather than disappoint him would, as he was to pay me ready money, give two puncheons of what I had on hand at the lowest market price. The Tun Seasoner declined purchasing with ready money, under pretence that he still considered the price too high. I then embraced the opportunity of asking the Tun Seasoner if he knew the Change-Name London Commission Agent, and the houses referred to in said Agent's letters; at the same time I shewed him the letter in which reference was made to himself. Upon looking at the letter, he said that he knew but little of Mr. W—— W—— A——, the London agent; that W—— W—— A—— was one of those out of about 150 more who had applied to him when in London in answer to an advertisement for an agent to sell his ale; that, as far as he had seen of W—— W—— A——, he thought highly of him as an agent; that he also knew the houses to whom reference had been made to be respectable, but that, to tell the truth, he was not quite satisfied with the securities offered for intromissions, and that, if I intended to employ Mr. W—— W—— A—— as an agent, I should be careful as to the security received, as there was much deception playing off in London in these times. I was now satisfied in my own mind that the Tun Seasoner was no better than he should be, himself, and therefore resolved to watch his movements.

The Tun Seasoner proved to be an Agent and Copartner of the Grand London Association of Fraudulent Traders, and detected carrying on the trade of Changing Name and Residence in Scotland.

Determined to find out the character and history of the Tun Seasoner, I commenced my inquiries at the people who live in the immediate neighbourhood of the —— Brewery, and discovered that although said brewery would be high enough rented at L.100 per annum, the Tun Seasoner had taken a lease of it at the extravagant rent of L.265 per annum. I was also informed that the Tun Seasoner had taken this brewery for the avowed purpose of brewing ale for the London market; that upon taking possession of the premises, he immediately commenced repairs, as if he intended to lose no time in setting the work a-going upon a large scale, although, up to this present moment, the end of October, 1832, he has laid in no stock of barley or other material from which ale could be brewed. This situation of the Tun Seasoner's affairs did not tally with the statement given in W—— W—— A——'s letter dated the 24th September, 1832, for in that letter it is expressly stated that the pressure of the season obliged the Tun Seasoner to leave London for Scotland before W—— W—— A—— had time to perfect his securities. I further learned that whilst the Tun Seasoner pretended to be fitting up the brewery, he actually pulled down the utensils which belonged to the proprietor, and disposed of them as old material at an undervalue. I continued my observations and inquiries, and—mark my astonishment,—when, upon comparing notes with my friend, the Protection-of-Trade man, this said Tun Seasoner turned out to be none other than a secret agent of a gang of London swindlers, and which agent, from his nefarious transactions through Scotland a few years ago, was known amongst a considerable portion of respectable traders by the name of the Straw-Bill Circulator, and Partner Victimiser. I now thought it high time to put bankers on their guard, and when I waited upon several for the purpose of warning them against the tricks of the Tun Seasoner, I found that he had actually waited upon them all, under various pretences, presenting for discount bills regularly drawn upon, and accepted by London firms, purporting to be of great respectability. I also discovered that the Tun Seasoner, in order to induce one banker to cash his London Bills, offered to lodge in his hands a bond for L.2,000, by way of security, and that that bond was signed by an M.P.

Continuing my look-out after the Partner Victimiser and Straw-Bill Circulator, *alias* the Tun Seasoner, I discovered, that after making various unsuccessful attempts to procure spirits on credit, he at last had succeeded in obtaining two puncheons of grain whisky from a respectable mercantile house, and that he had agreed to give 6d. per gallon more than I offered him whisky at. I also discovered that the Tun Seasoner had induced this respectable house to credit him, through a reference to a person whom he was on terms of receiving as a partner in the Musty Tun Brewery, and which person had likewise been deceived, along with many others, in consequence of an advertisement which appeared some time ago, headed, "*Partner Wanted in a Brewery, where the profits will be guaranteed at 50 per cent.*" I now thought of the warning given by Friends of Commerce against such gulling advertisements, and became more and more watchful of the movements and actions of the Tun Seasoner.

Shortly after the purchase, the Tun Seasoner returned to the house from whom he had purchased, presented a sample of their own whisky discoloured, as if it had actually been used for ale-tun seasoning, and wished to know if they could dispose of it again, as he would let them have it at an undervalue. The unsuspecting house being by this time apprized of their danger, began to look about them, and soon ascertained that their new customer had been offering to sell the whisky to different spirit-dealers at 1s. 10d. below the purchase price, and not discoloured, but pure as delivered to himself. They further ascertained that the identical whisky had been handed over to an unfortunate tradesman who had turned clamorous, in lieu of money due for work done at the Musty Tun Brewery.

The duped firm being now satisfied that they had been swindled out of their two puncheons of whisky by the Tun Seasoner, procured a Sheriff's warrant to apprehend him; but he being, through the watchfulness of intimate associates, apprized of the duped firm's intention towards him, left his dwelling, Musty Hall, took up his head-quarters at one of the principal inns in Scotland, and, had it not been for his audacity in dining publicly at the traveller's table, he might have eluded the search after his person. However, as fate would have it, there dined one day at said traveller's table, a gentleman to whom the Tun Seasoner was known by the name of the Partner Victimiser, and Straw-Bill Agent; and the aforesaid gentleman and I having, a few days before, compared notes, and come to the conclusion that the Partner Victimiser and the Tun Seasoner was the self-same person, carrying on the additional trade of changing name and residence in Scotland, he, the aforesaid gentleman, forwarded to me, by a private hand, the following intimation:—

"——Hotel, 7 o'clock evening.

"Mr. B——— to Mr. ———, the Scotch Merchant.

"If you have any thing to say to the Tun Seasoner, he will be found taking his wine at the traveller's table, ——— Hotel, where he is lodging."

I forwarded this intimation to the duped firm, who lost no time in communicating with the sheriff's officers; but, before the officers could reach the hotel, Mr. Tun Seasoner had taken leg-bail, leaving nothing behind him but his unpaid bill, for board, lodging, wine, &c. The principal partner of the double-puncheon-robbed firm now declared, that he was sure the name of the arch-swindler was not Tun Seasoner, but Straw-Bill Agent, or Partner Victimiser, and that, indeed, he could be no other person than that very rogue, who a few years ago insinuated himself into the good graces of a most respectable gentleman in Scotland, whom he ultimately ruined. I assured the puncheon-robbed merchant that he was right in his conjectures: that the rascal who had robbed him so artfully, after ruining the person already spoken of, and carrying on, successfully, various other swindling practices, left Scotland for Hamburgh, from whence he returned to London; and, after an absence of a few years from Scotland, he had lately come back to carry on his nefarious trade amongst us. I also informed the puncheon-robbed merchant that I was on the outlook as well as he was, and that, in order to discover the chain of connexion betwixt the London Swindlers, and their agents in Scotland, I corresponded with several persons, both in England and Scotland.

The remaining links of this chain we must defer for the present. Again we would say, what is the use of mystifying about the real names of the parties, if the editor of "THE CAUTION" is sure of the facts.

THE COURT OF LONDON.

MR. RUSH, who was the American ambassador here twenty years ago, has published a narrative of his residence, drawn from his journal. It is not the kind of book one would have expected from the Envoy of the great Republic of the West. Mr. Rush dives less deeply into the heart of our society than even the German Prince; or if he saw more, he tells less. The manner in which very great people dine is a subject of infinite concernment to very small people. Mr. Rush's account of a diplomatic dinner, if less amusing than some of those that we find in the Fashionable Novels, is at least a more correct description of a dull and heavy affair.

"January 20, 1818.—Dined at Lord Castlereagh's. The company consisted of Lord and Lady Castlereagh, the Earl of Westmoreland, Lord Melville, Lord Mulgrave, Mr. Wellesley Pole, the Duke of Wellington, Lord Burghersh, the Ambassador of France and his Marchioness, the Austrian Ambassador, the Portuguese Ambassador and his Countess, the Minister Plenipotentiary from Bavaria, the Marquis Grimaldi of Sardinia, and a few others. Of the foregoing, some were strangers, to whom, as to myself, it was a first dinner.

"The invitation was for seven o'clock. Our names were announced by servants in the hall, and on the landings. The company had chiefly assembled when we arrived. All were in full black, under the Court mourning for the Princess Charlotte. I am wrong—one lady was in white satin! It would have been painfully embarrassing, but that her union of ease and dignity enabled her, after the first suffusion, to turn her misfortune into a grace. Salutations were in subdued tones, but cordial, and the hand given. Introductions took place at convenient moments. Before eight, dinner was announced. The dining-room was on the floor with the drawing-rooms. As we entered it through a doorway surrounded by a hanging curtain that drew aside, the effect was beautiful. A profusion of light fell upon the cloth, and as every thing else was of silver, the dishes covered, and wines hidden in ranges of silver coolers, the whole had an aspect of pure white. Lord Castlereagh sat at the head. On his right was the lady of the French Ambassador, with whom, in going in, he had led the way. Lady Castlereagh was on the side, half way down. On her left, was the Duke of Wellington, with whom she came in. Between the Duke and the Earl of Westmoreland, was my wife, who came in upon the arm of the latter. Opposite was the lady of the Portuguese Ambassador. She entered with the French Ambassador, and sat next to him. I was between Lords Melville and Mulgrave. The former gratified me by the manner in which he spoke of the United States; the latter by what he said of President Monroe, who was Minister in England when he was Secretary for Foreign Affairs. He had ever found him, he said, conciliatory in business, while steadfast in his duty. Being near to these two noblemen in coming in, I paused to give place, having understood that Cabinet Ministers preceded Ministers Plenipotentiary on these occasions; but they declined it, and I went first; Lord Melville remarking, "We are at home." There were twelve servants; the superior ones not in livery.

"The general topics related to France and French society. The foreigners spoke English; nevertheless, the conversation was nearly all in French. This was not only the case when the English addressed the foreigners but in speaking to each other. Before dinner, I had observed in the drawing-room, books lying about. As many as I glanced at were French. I thought of the days of Charles the Second when the tastes of the English all ran upon the models of France. Here, at the house of an English minister of state, French literature, the French language, French topics were all about me; I add, French entrées, French wines! I was unwilling to believe that the parallel to the days of Charles the Second held throughout. By my longer residence in England I discovered, that the enlightened classes were more ready to copy from the French what they thought good, than the same classes in France to copy from England. As regards language, the difference is striking. There is scarcely a well-educated person in England who does not speak French, whilst thousands among the best educated in France are ignorant of English. In the competition between these great nations, this gives England an advantage. It is no answer that French is the language of intercourse in Europe: the Frenchman may repose upon this, for not acquiring the English; but it cannot take from Englishmen the advantage of being at home in both tongues. Equally have the English the advantage in travel. They go in great numbers to France; while few of the French, comparatively speaking, visit England."

To this we must add a dinner at Mr. Bentham's, at which, in those days, the Lord Chancellor was proud to make one. The part he acted, and the impression he made, are quite characteristic of Rush and of Brougham.

"I was driven nearly three miles through streets for the most part long and wide, until I passed Westminster Abbey. Thereabouts things changed. The streets grew narrow. Houses seemed falling down with age. The crowds were as thick, but not as good-looking, as about Cornhill and the Poultry. In a little while I reached the purlieus of Queen Square Place. The farther I advanced, the more confined was the space. At length, turning through a gateway, the passage was so narrow that I thought the wheels would have grazed. It was a kind of blind-alley, the end of which widened into a small, neat court-yard. There by itself stood Mr. Bentham's house. Shrubbery graced its area, and flowers its window-sills. It was like an oasis in the desert. Its name is the Hermitage.

"Entering, he received me with the simplicity of a philosopher. I should have taken him for seventy or upwards. Everything inside of the house was orderly. The furniture seemed to have been unmoved since the days of his fathers, for I learned that it was a patrimony. A parlour, library, and dining-room, made up the suite of apartments. In each was a piano, the eccentric master of the whole being fond of music as the recreation of his literary hours. It was an unique, romantic little homestead. Walking with him into his garden, I found it dark with the shade of ancient trees. They formed a barrier against all intrusion. In one part was a high, dead wall, the back of a neighbour's house. It was dark and almost mouldering with time. In that house, he informed me, Milton had lived. Perceiving that I took an interest in hearing it, he soon afterwards obtained a relic, and sent it to me. It was an old carved baluster, from the staircase, which there was reason to think the hand of the great bard had often grasped —so said the note that accompanied the relic.

"The company was small, but choice. Mr. Brougham, Sir Samuel Romilly, Mr. Mill, author of the well-known work on India, M. Dumont, the learned Genevan, once the associate of Mirabeau, were all who sat down to table. Mr. Bentham did not talk much. He had a benevolence of manner suited to the philanthropy of his mind. He seemed to be thinking only of the convenience and pleasure of his guests, not as a rule of artificial breeding, as from Chesterfield or Madame Genlis, but from innate feeling. Bold as are his opinions in his works, here he was wholly unobtrusive of theories that might not have commanded the assent of all present. Something else was remarkable. When he did converse, it was in simple language, a contrast to his later writings, where an involved style, and the use of new or unusual words are drawbacks upon the speculations of a genius original and profound, but with the faults of solitude. Yet some of his earlier productions are distinguished by classical terseness.

"Mr. Brougham talked with rapidity and energy. There was a quickness in his bodily movements indicative of the quickness of his thoughts. He shewed in conversation the universality and discipline that he exhibits in Parliament and the Courts of Law. The affairs of South America, English authors, Johnson, Pope, Swift, Milton, Dryden, Addison, (the criticisms of the last on Paradise Lost he thought poor things,) anecdotes of the living judges of England, of Lord Chancellors, living and dead; the errors in Burrow's Reports—not always those of the reporter, he said; the Universities of Oxford and Cambridge, the Constitution of the United States;—these were topics that he touched with the promptitude and power of a master. He quoted from the ancient classics and poets of modern Italy, (the latter in the original also,) not with the ostentation of scholarship, which he is above, but as if they came out whether he would or no, amidst the multitude of his ideas and illustrations. He handled nothing at length, but with a happy brevity—the rarest art in conversation when loaded with matter like his. Sometimes he despatched a subject in a parenthesis, sometimes by a word that told like a blow. Not long after this, my first meeting with him, one of his friends informed me that a gentleman whose son was about to study law, asked him what books he ought to read. 'Tell him to begin with Demosthenes and Dante.' —'What, to make a lawyer?' said the father.—'Yes,' he replied, 'and if you don't take, we won't argue about it.' Mr. Mill, M. Dumont, and Sir Samuel Romilly did their parts in keeping up the ball of conversation. Sheridan being spoken of, Sir Samuel Romilly, who had often heard him in the House of Commons, said that nothing could be more marked than the difference between the parts of his speeches previously written out, and the extemporaneous parts. The audience could discover in a moment when he fell into the latter. 'It was well known,' he added, 'that all the highly wrought passages in his speeches on Hastings' impeachment were prepared beforehand, and committed to memory.'

"After we rose from table, Mr. Bentham sought conversation with me about the United States. 'Keep your salaries low,' said he; 'it is one of the secrets of the success of your Government. But what is this,' he inquired, 'called a board of Navy Commissioners, that you have lately set up? I don't understand it.' I explained it to him. 'I can't say that I like it,' he replied; 'the simplicity of your public departments has heretofore been one of their recommendations, but *boards* make *screens*; if anything goes wrong, you don't know where to find the offender: it was the board that did it, not one of the members, always the *board*, the board!'"

THE GERMAN STUDENT'S DRINKING SONG.

Fill up!
Let joy and mirth abound,
And send the sparkling glasses round.
Fill up!
Fill up!
Who cares for sorrow now,
Cheer up my friend,—ne'er cloud thy brow.
Fill up!
Fill up!
Let canting hypocrites
Bepraise the life of anchorites
Fill up!
Fill up!
And while the glass we quaff,
Loud let us revel, sing, and laugh.
Fill up!

RECEIPT FOR THE DESTRUCTION OF CATERPILLARS.

Mr. Schoolmaster,—I understand that you wish to be useful in a homely way, as well as to be learned, witty, instructive, entertaining, and useful on the great scale; all of which I allow you to be. There is no doubt that many of your numerous readers may, like myself, have a few gooseberry and currant bushes in their small garden plat, in which, like myself, they may take as much pride as " my Lord" can do in his shrubberies and vineries. In this genial May, the May of the poets, and of the gardeners too, bushes of this kind looked remarkably luxuriant and healthy; but for all that the spoiler has appeared. To prevent and arrest his progress, all useless and straggling branches should be regularly cut away at the proper season, and the roots freed of all weeds, to admit of a free circulation of air. In the end of November, or before midwinter, throw a shovel-full, or two or three, of quick-lime, in powder, into the heart of each bush that has been infected; and if one is infected in a garden all generally suffer. The lime must completely cover the branches nine or ten inches above the surface of the earth. Early in May, when the caterpillar begins its ravages, examine the bushes while the dew lies upon them, and destroy the caterpillar fly, which is easily known, whenever it appears. I shall now copy my own instructor and authority, literally, for the advantage of all your horticultural readers:—

"The caterpillar fly is easily known, being a little less, and darker in colour than a common dung fly, and so sluggish that it is easily destroyed.

"A little attention to the bushes at this time, will also discover the young caterpillar as soon as the egg is hatched, and when it begins its first depredations. The fly on the gooseberry, deposits from ten to twelve eggs on the under side of the leaf, and on the currant bush, from fifteen to twenty. The eggs run along the vein of the leaf, and as soon as the insects quicken, while they are scarcely visible to the eye, they puncture the leaves with small holes, according to the number of eggs on each leaf. A boy, with a little practice, will clear a hundred bushes of such leaves in four hours. They are generally found towards the bottom of the bush, and are easily seen by opening the branches on every side. The first leaf is consumed in a few days, and the progress of the destruction is upwards, the caterpillars dividing their forces as they ascend. If the leaf is not taken off, the veins of it, after the web is consumed, are seen in a withered state, and then, though with more trouble the caterpillars ought to be taken off the leaves above where they are found to be lodged. This should never be delayed beyond the eighth day; and though the labour, by neglecting to take off the punctured leaf, be increased, yet it is still easy, compared to what must be done after the leaves of the bush are half consumed, and the caterpillars from many neglected leaves are spread over the whole bush.

"The eggs are deposited at different times, and therefore it is necessary that the punctured leaves should be attended to once a-week till the season is over.

"I am certain, from the experience of many years, that these simple means, if resorted to in time, and observed with care, will be a sufficient protection against this noxious insect; and in the years when there was the greatest danger, I have had a full crop of gooseberries, when the bushes in my neighbourhood were entirely destroyed."

I shall conclude with a French receipt for the destruction of caterpillars. It is taken from a periodical publication on economics, entitled *Connaissances Usuelles*.

"Caterpillars, at certain periods of the year, and frequently during the day, are found upon the small branches of the trees, towards the extremities. The manner of destroying them is as follows:—Take a pocket-pistol, the mouth of which is widened like that of a blunderbuss; half load this with powder only, and fire it off at the distance of a foot; this will completely destroy all within its reach, without in the least injuring the most delicate buds. The nests of these insects, however elevated, may be destroyed in this manner, by fixing the pistol upon a pole."

Our Scotch plan, detailed above, is surely better than this pop-gun system.

SCRAPS.

MAGNIFICENT CHESS PLAYING.—We have somewhere read that Frederick the Great, or Frederick the I. of Prussia, played chess with soldiers, some of whom were knights, Bishops, Rooks, &c.—that this game was performed in a large saloon paved in chequers, which the prince might overlook. Even this regal pastime is outdone by the Chinese, of the order of Rothschild, and Baring, who will be the true princes of the Earth, in Asia as in Europe, so long as Mammon remains its Deity. Our account is taken from the *Canton Register*, which states: "It is well known that the provinces of Shense and Shanse contain some of the most opulent men in China. The natives say they have money heaped up like mountains; and the chief money lenders in Canton are from these provinces. During the last years of the late Emperor Kea-King, a rich widow of the name of Chun, of the district of Tae-yuen-foo, had a son who went all lengths in luxury and extravagance. Among other idle pursuits, he was a great chess-player. But chess, on a piece of board or paper, as the Chinese have it, is a very meagre though interesting game. Master Chun conceived a new idea: he got a large room painted as a chess board, with tables for himself and friend on opposite sides. For chess men, he purchased a set of female slaves, dressed them up in various colours, and made them perform, by a signal, the duty of knights, pawns, horses, kings, queens, castles, &c. This high chess player saved himself the trouble of moving the pieces. At a given signal the pieces taken made their exit at the door. Of these proceedings the Emperor got some intelligence, and, probably, offended by a rich subject outdoing him in luxury, he affected to be horribly offended (his own habits gave the lie to this) at the idea of bringing slaves to perform the office of chess-men! He fined master Chun 3,000,000 of taels, and transported him to the Black Dragon River for life; telling him, at the same time, that he ought to be infinitely grateful that his "brain cup"* (or head) was not separated from his shoulders.

THE DEVIL AND THE LAWYERS.—It is believed that there is a certain intimacy carried on between the inhabitants of *Inns of Court* and his *Satanic Majesty*. When the various *volunteer corps* were formed, each was distinguished by some appropriate appellation: the residents in one parish were called the St. James's, of another parish, the St. Pancras'; and in various places were called the Queen's Own Regiment, the Duke of Cumberland's Own Regiment, and so on. Shortly after sprang up the "*Temple Corps*." When the modest title they had assumed pleased not the public, they, accordingly, received another additional name, by which they are *universally known*, viz., the *Devil's Own Regiment*. How this is, the following anecdote will explain:—

THE LAWYERS' PATRON.—St. Evona, a lawyer of Britain, went to Rome to entreat the Pope to give the *lawyers a patron*; the Pope replied, that he knew of no saint not disposed of to some other profession. His holiness proposed, however, to St. Evona, that he should go round the church of *San Giovanni di Laterano* blindfold, and after saying a certain number of Ave Marias, the first saint he laid hold of should be his patron. This the good lawyer undertook, and at the end of his Ave Marias, stopped at the altar of St. Michael, where he laid hold, not of the saint, but unfortunately of the *Devil* under the saint's feet, crying out, "*This is our Saint, let him be our patron!*"

* *Scottice, Harn-pan.*

THE POLISH EAGLE.

"Whither, O whither, proud bird,
  Is thy trackless wandering?
Dashing aside the waves of light,
  With thy free, glorious wing?

"Say—hast thou swept the hoarsy arch
  That bounds the wave's commotion?
Hath thy unchained, unbounded march
  Been o'er the pride of Ocean?

"'Mid Blanc's eternal crest of snow,
  Is thy cold, viewless dwelling?
Or is it where, 'mid glooms below,
  Proud Gunga's waves are welling?"

"I've crossed the wave in calm and   ath,
  My flight is far and lonely,
From where the winding-sheet of death
  Is weve for freedom only.

"I leave the hallowed dwelling-place
  Of bosoms bold and fiery;
'Mid Poland's wastes of war and chase
  Is my romantic eyry.

"When Kosciusko's plume afar
  In freedom's van was streaming,
My crest was Poland's guiding star
  On her proud banner beaming.

"When Lithuania's dirge was sung,
  And cold each patriot's pillow,—
In desert hall when the sword was hung,
  I braved the dark blue billow.

"Adieu, brave land! thy heart is still!
  An upas wreath's around thee!
Yet once more let thy proud heart thrill,
  And break the spell that's bound thee.

"Then, Poland, when thou spurn'st the chain,
  Though unactified and regal,
O, I will sweep thy skies again—
  Thy own Majestic eagle!"   G. P.

TO CORRESPONDENTS.

WE cannot be every week noticing correspondents. Once for all we beg of them to remember that the *Schoolmaster* is not a local publication, but one that circulates over all Scotland, and also in England and Ireland; and that Londoners care little for Edinburgh or Glasgow jokes, and very little indeed for Scottish poetry; while, on the other hand, Scotch folks are indifferent to Dublin news, or funny stories of priests; and also to anecdotes of Cockneys. Our poetical friends, we beg to thank, while we entreat their patience. One and all must appear "on Saturday first!" but they forget that this publication is not a newspaper, and is prepared and circulated, perhaps, before their communications are received. The late month of MAY has been so genial and favourable to the Muses, that we have now accumulated more verse, good, bad, and indifferent, than would fill a volume of this publication. It is delightful to find poetical talent, and its attendant humanising influences so widely diffused; though, we suspect, it will often be best employed in contributing to the solitary enjoyment of the pleasure, and when exercised independently of appearances on "Saturday first," or any other Saturday. We have also to acknowledge many prose communications of merit, some of which will appear at the proper time; for all our pupils are expected to be docile, patient, and reasonable.

☞ If our compliance with the request of C. M. could forward his object, we should promptly attend to it. Will he send his address, and more information, to the Schoolmaster Office, 19, St. James's Square?

CONTENTS OF NO. XLVI.

Authentic Letters from Canada, ...
Precautions to be used during a Thunder Storm, ...
Useful Hints and Receipts for Warm Weather, ...
THE STORY-TELLER—A Passage in the Life of Sir H. du Grey,
The Copper-Leg Conspiracy, ...
Commercial Thieves, ...
The Court of London, ...
The German Student's Drinking Song, ...
Receipt for the Destruction of Caterpillars, ...
SCRAPS.—Magnificent Chess Playing.—The Devil and the Lawyers.—The Lawyers' Patron, ...
The Polish Eagle, ...
To Correspondents, ...

EDINBURGH: Printed by and for JOHN JOHNSTONE, 19, St. James's Square.—Published by JOHN ANDERSON, Jun., Bookseller, Bridge Street, Edinburgh; by JOHN MACLEOD, and D. ROBERTSON, Booksellers, Glasgow; and sold by all Booksellers and Vendors of Cheap Periodicals.

THE Schoolmaster,
AND
EDINBURGH WEEKLY MAGAZINE.
CONDUCTED BY JOHN JOHNSTONE.

THE SCHOOLMASTER IS ABROAD.—LORD BROUGHAM.

No. 47.—Vol. II.   SATURDAY, JUNE 22, 1833.   Price Three-halfpence.

OLD SCOTCH HOLIDAYS.

The fairs and holidays which were formerly observed in Scotland, are now fast sinking into oblivion. Such of them as were observed for merely superstitious reasons, have gradually been neglected from the increasing knowledge of the country; and agriculture and commerce leave no time for such as were devoted to idleness and mirth alone. Before the Reformation, the observance of rites and ceremonies formed a principal part of the *business* of the people. With this business, however, they contrived to mingle much frolic and revelry. But our peasantry have no longer this pretext for relaxation and amusement; and fairs are now the only holidays for the agricultural classes of the community, and meetings for political purposes are the holidays of tradesmen. Different trades have, indeed, the days of their particular saints set apart as holidays still. Even these, however, are beginning in most places to wear out, and most of the days whose return was once the signal for idleness, and merriment, and joy, are now only to be distinguished from the other days of the year by the dead letter of an almanack; and few of the rising generation know them but by name. It may not be uninteresting, therefore, to some of our readers, to learn something of these holidays, and of a few of the superstitions connected with them.

Christmas, or *Yule-day*, had formerly a celebrity which, within the last twenty or thirty years, has almost dwindled into oblivion. On Christmas-eve, better known by the name of Yule-e'en, the *gudewife* was busily employed in baking her Yule bread, and if a bannock fell asunder, after being put to the fire, it was an omen that she would never see another Yule. Young men, and sometimes women, went through the villages in masquerade, (commonly termed *gysarts*,) carrying a besom, sweeping in the floor of every house they entered, and singing Christmas carols, sometimes accompanied with a violin or a bagpipe.

"On the farmer's kitchen fire was to be seen
The muckle pat, that seads the whey, put on;"

in which was a large joint of beef for o-morrow's breakfast; for, "from the cottar to the laird," every one had *fat brose* on Yule-day morning, after which all were at liberty to go where they pleased; the day was a kind of Saturnalia, on which the most rigorous master relinquished his claim to the service of his domestics. The females visited their friends, and the young men generally met at some rendezvous, to try their skill as marksmen at a wad-shooting, that is, firing with ball at a mark, for small prizes of black-smith or joiner work. These were paid for by the contributions of the candidates, (each laying down his two-pence or three-pence,) and carried off by him who hit nearest the mark. This is a manly, rational exercise, and ought to meet national encouragement. The policy of our ancestors endeavoured to promote the skill of the peasantry in archery, by bow-butts, &c.; but, independently of its importance in a political point of view, it is at all events preferable to pugilism or bull-baiting. When darkness prevented the continuance of shooting, a raffle in the ale-house generally followed, while cards and hard drinking closed the scene.

On this day friends and neighbours feasted together, for all labour, except such as was altogether unavoidable, was totally suspended. No mechanic or artisan would have wrought at his ordinary employment on that day. I have often heard it stoutly maintained, that the domestic bees sing in their hives on Yule-e'en, in a manner quite different from what they do on any previous or subsequent night.

Every body knows, that when Presbyterianism was fixed as the national religion in Scotland, Episcopacy was held as an abomination by the first settled Presbyterian clergymen, who were zealous against every thing connected with, or in any degree similar to the rites of their sister church.

Yule-day was dear to the Scottish peasantry, and equally obnoxious to the Presbyterian clergy, among whom was a Mr. Goodsir, minister of Monikie, who made it a rule to go over as much of his parish as possible on that day, that he might detect his parishioners in any superstitious observances. Upon a visitation of this kind, he entered the village of Guildy, and inspected every house, to see whether the people were at their ordinary employments, or if they were cooking a better dinner than usual. One old wife, whose pat was playing brown over the fire, saw him coming through her kail-yard. She had just time to lift off the pot, but in her agitation could find no better place to hide it than below her bed-cover; this accomplished, she had got seated at her spinning-wheel by the time that his reverence entered, who paid her some compliments upon her conduct, contrasting it with that of some of her neighbours, who shewed less disposition to comply with the austerity of his injunctions. Maggy, in her solicitude to escape detection, overshot her own mark, for she echoed her minister's remarks so zealously, that he felt a pleasure in prolonging his stay; but unfortunately for both, during the bitter censure of those who offered unrighteous sacrifice, or still "longed for the flesh-pots of

Egypt," Maggy's pot set fire to the bed-clothes, and the smoke came curling over the minister's shoulders. Maggy started up, flew to the bed, and, in her hurry to remove the clothes, overset the tell-tale pot, splashing Mr. Goodsir's legs with the hot and fat broth, &c. The consequence may easily be conjectured :—Maggy's conduct was reported to the elder of the quarter,—she became the laughing-stock of her neighbours, and had further to do public penance before the congregation, for the complicated crimes of heresy and hypocrisy.

In relating that all ranks breakfasted on brose on Yuleday morning, it appears also worthy of recording, that till within the last forty years, it was the custom, at a nobleman's seat in this county, for a quantity of brose to be made on Yule-day morning, sufficient to breakfast " man, wife, and wean," of his tenantry, if they chose to attend. The hospitable board was spread in the great hall, and if the company was not very select, it was always sufficiently numerous, while beef and good ale crowned their repast.

On *New Year's-Day* morning, no one would go to ask a light from their neighbour ; it was considered as unlucky to the person from whom such a favour was requested, to carry fire out of the house on this day. It was also considered improper to enter a neighbour's house emptyhanded. The practice so prevalent in large towns, of running about with the whisky bottle was unknown ; but neighbours commonly ate and drank together of a more simple, and less pernicious beverage. The first Monday of the year, reckoning by old style, is still termed *Handsel Monday*, and was formerly also kept as a holiday. It is still the practice for the scholars to carry a small pecuniary present to their teacher on that morning. However well intended this might have been at its commencement, it ought to be done away; it produces jealousies and envyings among the pupils, and it is also derogatory to the dignity of the schoolmaster, as it bears the appearance of an eleemosynary contribution ; and where he has many pupils from the poorer classes, he can hardly fail to reflect, that the donation which he receives is probably wrung from them by a struggle between dignity of mind and indigence. I some time ago observed an advertisement from a school, where it was announced, that the *handsel* must not be below five shillings: This is well so far, but it completely takes away the apparent kindness of a gift when a *minimum* is fixed, and in this case it may be said, in the nervous language of Crabbe, that

" Strong compulsion plucks the scrap from pride."

Would it not be better to change the name, abolish the mode of payment, and add it to the school fees?

When I was a boy, *St. Valentine's Eve* was set apart for drawing the names of lads and lasses by lot, and valentines, of various forms, in rude and artless rhymes, were often sent by the adoring swain to the object of his affection; but the practice appears now to be forgotten.

Shrovetide, better known by the name of *Fasten's E'en*, is only remarkable for cock-fighting. Formerly, at every parish school a cock fight was held, where the master received a few pence as the entry-money of every cock ; all the cravens who would not strike three strokes were also considered his property ; the poor boys whose parents had no cocks were obliged to beg or borrow, for they must be like their neighbours. As the sports of the day often concluded in the ale-house, high words, and even blows were sometimes the consequence. This is certainly a practice most improper for seminaries, where the ductile mind ought to be taught the principles of benevolence and mercy. Indeed, we can hardly conceive anything more absurd or preposterous than a parent or teacher laying down precepts for his children, which he so directly counteracts by the barbarous example which he thus sets before them. It is to the credit of the age, that many schoolmasters have now abolished the practice.

In some quarters of this county, it is still common for the scholars, on Candlemas day, to carry each a large candle to school, range them on their tables, light them for a few minutes, then put them out and leave them for the master.

Pasch Sunday, (vulg. Peace Sunday,) is still noticed by the children playing with eggs dyed of various colours,— a custom of great antiquity, and by no means confined to Britain, or even to Europe.

On Palm Sunday, I have seen the children gathering the catkins of the different species of willow, &c. of which they attempted to twine garlands in honour of the day.

The new term of Whitsunday, (known here by the appellation of the " *Rood-day*,") was formerly reckoned a most important and dangerous day ; for witches and wylie (cunning) wives were believed to have more power that day, than on any other in the year; as their incantations were more easily performed, and their spells far more difficult to counteract. The scum of a spring well procured on that morning before sunrise, was considered as possessing magical virtues; and those suspected of witchcraft were often watched, lest they should obtain this potent liquid, and apply it to unhallowed purposes. This was also the day on which they attempted to take the milk from their neighbours' cows, not by milking, but by magical incantations, by which they acquire possession of the milk for the season. The belief of this practice is still prevalent among some old ignorant people, and I have seen several wives in great vexation and agitation of mind, because their *cow's milk was taken.* According to the superstitious credulity of the people, there are certain ways of effecting this ; the most common is, for the witch to collect a certain quantity of hair from the tail of every cow of whose milk she wishes to get possession ; of this hair she then twists a rope, on which she casts a knot for every cow of whose hair it is composed ; she then walks backward across the entrance of every cow-house where any of her victims are lodged, dragging the rope after her, and muttering some unhallowed and unlawful incantation, and the feat is accomplished. Some cows of uncommon sagacity, are believed to have the faculty of discovering by instinct when this magical rite is performing, even although the byre door be shut; in that case, the cow lows, and the spell is ineffectual. I have heard a wife maintain, that she would know the low of a cow upon this occasion, as it was a cry of pain, different from any other. To counteract the wiles of these modern daughters of Satan, the most common counter-spell is, to lay a twig of Rowan-tree, (mountain ash,) bound round with a scarlet thread, across the byre door on the inside. The children here have a common proverb, that

" Rowan tree, and a red thread,
Makes the witches tyne (lose) their speed."

Or, fix a stalk of clover (trefoil) with *four* leaves to the stall of the animal. These are talismans of such anti-magical virtues, as completely to defy the devil and all his imps. Another mode is, to take the gudeman's breeches and put them upon the cow's horns, a horn in each leg; and the animal, when set loose, will run straight to the door of the enchantress. I know a family where this exorcism was performed, not more than seven years ago; but, as might be expected, no discovery was made of the witch, nor did the cow recover her milk. It is also believed, that if the cow is sold, the spell is dissolved.

Early on the Rood-day morning, witches hold their unhallowed orgies in the shape of hares; and I have known people who would have trembled with terror, had an animal of that species crossed their path on that day. Witches are supposed to have a peculiar attachment to the form of a hare, and it is believed that they get what is called a *brief* from their infernal master, against lead; hence, if attempted to be shot, it must be with something else. I think I have in my possession a magazine published at Dundee, (if I recollect aright,) about the year 1775 or 1776, in which, among his articles of domestic intelligence, the Editor very gravely relates, as an event that had recently happened,—that a gentleman went out a-hunting, and in the parks of Clessington, scarcely a mile from the town, shot and wounded a hare, which escaped through a hedge, or over a wall; the sportsman followed, and upon coming to the spot where he expected to find the hare, he discovered—an old woman breathing her last!

The belief in fairies was once very general here, and many remarkable stories could be told concerning them, such as their interference with the utensils and labours of the peasantry during the night. My antiquated chronicler Lizzie R———, assured me that, when about sixteen years of age, she was servant to a weaver, one of whose young men being anxious to finish a piece of cloth in his loom, he fixed upon rising very early on a winter morning, and had engaged her, by the promise of a pecuniary recompense, to rise at the same time, and wind pirns for him. She awoke during the night, and heard the pirn-wheel driving furiously. Imagining that she had slept too long, she put on her clothes in great haste, (the wheel still sounding in her ears,) entered the shop by an inner door, and found all dark; upon uttering some exclamation, the wheel immediately stood still. All this I believe the credulous woman would have sworn before a magistrate. Relations of hers still more wonderful I forbear to relate.

Fairies, although, in some of the instances exhibited, guilty of gross infractions upon the rights and comforts of domestic life, were not in general dreaded or hated in the same degree as witches. These were revengeful, malignant, and never exerted their supernatural powers except for a bad purpose; while the former were supposed to delight in merry and fantastic tricks; such as hiding keys, loosing cattle from their stalls, pinching the housemaids in their sleep, or sometimes tickling them, so as totally to prevent their repose, &c.; and upon many occasions they got credit for supplying bread to the hungry, and other benevolent actions.

Witches, on the contrary, stole property, produced sickness and death; raised storms and tempests; deprived some of their virility, and others of their senses. It is not yet long ago, since many were of opinion, that they took horses from the stable, and rode them during the night; and I have repeatedly heard it affirmed, that the horses so treated were easily known in the morning, as they were always found in a state of profuse perspiration, jaded, and quite fatigued. I have seen in a stable a stone which is often to be found by the sea-side, or on the banks of rivers, with one or more natural holes through it, hung up by a string above the horses, to prevent the witches from having power over them. Yea, it was at one period currently believed, that they would seize men against whom they had any grudge; maltreat them by sousing them in rivers, &c., and then, carrying them through the air to a great distance, leave them in some unknown and desert place, half dead with terror and fatigue, to find their way home as they best could; and I have heard men named, who were oftener than once treated in this manner.

Water-kelpie, or, as he is termed by Home, "the angry spirit of the waters," was a bogle of great celebrity in this county, and the terrors of his name have scarcely yet vanished. I have repeatedly been told of a stone of very large dimensions, that has been upon the bank of a rivulet for time immemorial, and was one morning found on the opposite side; this was reported as one of Kelpie's feats, which were commonly of a more dangerous kind; for he was a malignant sprite, and generally appeared on the banks of rivers, like a little black horse, when the fords were impassable, alluring strangers to mount him for the benefit of crossing, when he was always certain to throw them into the water, vanishing with a wild, *unearthly* laugh.

The church of St. Vigeans, about a mile north of Arbroath, stands upon the top of a romantic and very precipitous knoll, in the midst of a fine valley. This edifice is of considerable antiquity, and the vulgar had a current tradition, that the knoll on which it stands is artificial, being raised over the centre of a loch or small lake: That both the materials for constructing the knoll, and the stones for building the church, were brought from a distance by Water-kelpie, guided by a man who had the address to clap his own horse's branks on the head of the sprite, which gives him who does so, the complete command over this demon while the branks remain on him: That in consequence of the great fatigue he had undergone, he denounced bitter and dreadful vengeance against the parishioners of St. Vigeans. Sometime after this, a prediction came forth, that the minister who should officiate there at a given period, described in a mystical manner, would commit suicide; after which, the first time that the sacrament of the Lord's Supper was celebrated in the church, the whole fabric and its congregation were to sink into the lake during the service of the first table.

However strange it may appear, it is certain that, about the beginning of last century, the incumbent, whose name (if my memory be correct) was Mr. Henderson, did commit suicide. This part of the prediction being fulfilled, the people believed implicitly that the rest would be accomplished; in consequence of which, the sacrament was not administered for several years, until the next incumbent at last resolved upon the full discharge of his duty, and of encouraging his congregation both by precept and example. The usual preparation, according to the form of the Church of Scotland, was gone about with more than ordinary solemnity:—the hallowed day arrived, the minister proceeded in the previous part of the service, having the assistance of several clerical brethren; but it was with great difficulty that they could persuade the people to come forward, or sit down at the holy table. At length they prevailed upon a certain number to take their places; while the greater part of the congregation withdrew from the church, and seated themselves on an eminence at some distance, expecting to see the church sink into the lake. The service was concluded, and nothing happened; consequently the apprehensions of the people were banished. This is a strong and authentic instance of popular credulity.

There was another being of whom I have often heard in my early days; and I still recollect, that the relation of his feats, and the descriptions of his different appearances, produced a degree of horror in my mind, that all the spirits who composed the train of hobgoblins could not inspire. His name was *Shelly-coat*; I was never able to comprehend his character. Of fairies, witches, &c., I believed that I had a proper conception. I imagined their forms, and could, in some degree, conceive the boundaries of their power; but Shelly-coat, like Milton's Satan among the other fallen spirits, towered proudly eminent. I was taught to believe his form gigantic, but indefinable; and his powers almost infinite: his strength was always commensurate to what he undertook, and his swiftness that of a spirit; he delighted only in horrible deeds and devastations; blood and massacre marked his progress. He was clothed in a coat of shells, the rustling of which appalled the stoutest heart; when his hellish work was finished, he stripped off his coat, and deposited it below a rock, which defied mortal strength to move it; after which he continued invisible, until he again resumed his dress for a repetition of his infernal purposes.

Such were the ideas impressed upon my infant mind of this monstrous and mysterious being, of whom I have never been able to obtain any information. The only recollection that I just now have of this character being noticed in our popular poems, is the line of Ramsay, "she fled as frae a *shelly-coated* cow." I wish some of your correspondents acquainted with the superstitions of our country, would favour your readers with an illustration of this strange character, with some account of his origin, and supposed place of residence.

Hallowe'en is famous in Angus, as the season when the fates are propitious in disclosing the future destiny of such young men and maids as perform the necessary rites; but these have been so faithfully and humorously described by the immortal Burns, that it would be gross presumption to offer an enumeration.

I may take this opportunity of mentioning a few *freits* and prejudices formerly credited, and still partially acted upon.

The death-watch, death-drop, and death-stroke, are all previous signals of approaching dissolution. Within these last twenty years, I have heard a house carpenter affirm, that on the night previous to a coffin being ordered from him, he hardly ever failed to hear the noise of saws, planes, &c. in his shop, giving "dreadful note of preparation." Before the death of a friend, his or her *wraith* appears clad in white; will glide along the room, and suddenly vanish.

When the tallow at a lighted candle melts, and again freezes, curling over like a ribbon, (an effect which a particular current of air will produce,) it is a dead *speal*, and the person to whom it is opposite shall die first of the company. If a person is sick, and a magpie rests on the roof of the house, it is a sure sign of death. The cock crowing at an unseasonable hour is very uncouthy; a phrase for which we have not a correct and equally expressive English synonyme; it implies dreary, an unknown something, to agitate and alarm the mind. It is also believed that the feathers of wild fowl in a pillow under the head of a dying person, will prevent the approach of death, and protract the sufferings of the patient; for this cause I have known the pillows removed. Should a horse stumble when riding for a mid-wife, it is a bad omen for either mother or child. Salt spilt on the table prognosticates evil; but this is common to England,—see Gay's Fables. If a bride or bridegroom's wedding shirt is stolen, it is a sure indication that one of the parties will violate the marriage vow; any of the rest of the clothes stolen is reckoned bad luck.

Many people are still afraid of what they term an evil-eye; and I have known several old women accused of this, when butter would not make, or when different other operations failed of success. Such poor old creatures are always deemed unlucky to meet in a morning, or when one is setting off upon a journey; the best way to counteract their malign influence, is to address them before they speak to you. Some people are reckoned lucky as a first-foot, and others the contrary. Good and bad hansel at the New-year, or at the commencement of a sale, is still believed in by the common people.

It is still a received opinion, that the last three days of March, old style, (termed the Borrowing Days,) indicate the weather for the ensuing season: if they are boisterous and stormy, the season will be propitious; if they are fine weather, a bad season is expected.

In this quarter, the following rhymes are proverbial:—

"If Candlemas day be wet an' foul,
The half o' winter's gane at Yule;
If Candlemas day be fair an' clear,
The half o' winter's to gang—an' mair."

There are certain stones to be found in the earth which are lucky to build in the wall of a house; and others the reverse.

When a boy, I was well acquainted with an old man, who most tenaciously held and acted upon this opinion. Some of his young and roguish neighbours, taking advantage of his superstitious notions, procured a large stone of the unlucky species, (for he had taught them to distinguish them,) and laid it at his door during the night. They watched in the morning, and saw the poor man carry the stone to a considerable distance, and deposit it on a cairn. His tormentors had it again at his door next morning; again he carried it with much labour to a greater distance, and digging a hole, buried it in the earth. A third time it met him on his threshold in the morning, when, with great perturbation of mind, and fatigue of body, he carried it still farther off, and deposited it in a mill-dam, where his persecutors allowed it to remain.

Among the prejudices or antipathies still entertained by the common people, there is one which seems to be handed down from parent to child with unabated virulence: it is against that beautiful and innocent bird, the yellow-hammer; whose nest is destroyed wherever it is discovered. The children appear to have a savage delight in torturing the unfledged younglings. They have a doggrel stanza which, being currently repeated, has doomed this hapless bird, by its vulgar name, to cruelty and infamy.

> "Half a paddock, half a toad,
> Half a yellow-yaldrin;
> Gets a drap of the devil's blood
> Ilka May mornin'."

Perhaps some of your readers may be able to communicate, through the medium of your Magazine, from whence this prejudice has originated. It has been already observed, that the Magpie is reckoned ominous; this bird, and also the stone-chaffer, (vulgarly the clochrate,) are generally the objects of vengeance and dislike among the vulgar. The toad, and land-lizard, (vulgarly the ask,) are also doomed to instant death whenever they appear; the lizard, particularly, seems to excite a kind of horror the moment it is observed; and I have seen a man stop on a journey and collect stones to kill this poor reptile, when he discovered it crawling in his path; if he did not kill it at the first stroke he had to find another stone, and so on till it was despatched, for he would not again touch the stone that had come in contact with so horrible an antagonist.

Spells, charms, and talismans, are still in repute among some old people, as preventatives or cures for diseases, particularly the toothache, and intermittent fever, known here by the appellation of the ague, and trembling fever. Happily for the inhabitants, this painful and lingering disease is now almost banished, except in some low and marshy situations; although there are people still alive, who recollect the time when a farmer in this quarter of the country would not have engaged a servant unless he had previously had the ague; so prevalent was this disorder about the month of May, when the labours of a farm-servant were particularly wanted.

It may be remarked, that the opinions imbibed, and the practices adopted in early life, are not easily changed, especially if they have the sanction of our ancestors. A striking instance of this occurred not many years ago. An old man, who had only one cow, which was the principal support of his family, found one morning that his valuable animal was stolen; his grief was excessive, and his family were in deep dejection, as they were totally unable to purchase another. A few of his kind and more opulent neighbours, pitying the distress of the family, contributed a sum adequate, purchased another cow, and sent her to the poor man; two or three of them also waited upon him, and at parting, enjoined him to get a lock and key to his byre-door, to prevent a repetition of the same misfortune; when they received the following reply :—"Na, na, Sirs! I'm nae doubt obliged to you for the cow,—but, to put a lock upo' my byre-door!—I'll do nae sic a thing—my father never had ane upo' his, a' his days,—an' it's now o'er far afternoon wi' me, to begin an' fallow new fashions!"

SCALE OF MARRIAGES.—A calculator has made out the following estimates of the chances of matrimony a girl has at the different periods of her life. Out of a thousand women, 32 are married between 14 and 15; 101 between 16 and 17; 219 between 18 and 19; 233 between 20 and 21; 165 between 22 and 23; 102 between 24 and 25; 60 between 26 and 27; 45 between 28 and 29; 18 between 30 and 31; 14 between 32 and 33; 8 between 34 and 35; 2 between 36 and 37; and one between 38 and 39. To judge by this table, a lady of 30 years would have only 28 chances of getting married out of 1000; when passed 40, the chances are far less.

EXTERNAL COMFORT, AND DOMESTIC ACCOMMODATION OF THE PEOPLE.

A BENEVOLENT, and on many points an enlightened writer, Mr. Dick, the author of the "*Christian Philosopher*," and other books of highly useful tendency, in a recent work upon the general diffusion of knowledge, enumerates many of the most obvious late improvements in roads, travelling conveyances, houses, churches, manufactories, steam vessels, &c., &c., but he does not, like some of his fellow-labourers, stop there. He admits that much remains to be done; and that with the progress of the arts, and the extension of manufactures, the comforts of the people have not kept pace, nor their millennium begun.

"Much," he owns, " is still wanting to complete the enjoyments of the lower ranks of society. In the *country*, many of them live in the most wretched hovels, open to the wind and rain, without a separate apartment to which an individual may retire for any mental exercise; in *towns*, a whole family is frequently crowded into a single apartment in a narrow lane, surrounded with filth and noxious exhalations, and where the light of day is scarcely visible. In such habitations, where the kitchen, parlour, and bed-closet are all comprised in one narrow apartment, it is next to impossible for a man to improve his mind by reading or reflection, amidst the gloom of twilight, the noise of children, and the preparation of victuals, even although he felt an ardent desire for intellectual enjoyment. Hence the temptation to which such persons are exposed to seek enjoyment in wandering through the streets, in frequenting the ale-house, or in lounging at the fire-side in mental inactivity. In order that the labourer may be stimulated to the cultivation of his mental powers, he must be furnished with those domestic conveniences requisite for attaining this object. He must be paid such wages as will enable him to procure such conveniences, and the means of instruction, otherwise it is next thing to an insult to exhort him to prosecute the path of science. *The long hours of labour, and the paltry remuneration which the labourer receives in many of our spinning-mills and other manufactories, so long as such domestic slavery and avaricious practices continue, form an insurmountable barrier to the general diffusion of knowledge.*

"But were the minds of the lower orders imbued with a certain portion of useful science, and did they possess such a competency as every human being ought to enjoy, their knowledge would lead them to habits of *diligence* and *economy*. In most instances it will be found, that ignorance is the fruitful source of indolence, waste, and extravagance; and that abject poverty is the result of a want of discrimination and proper arrangement in the management of domestic affairs. Now, the habits of application which the acquisition of knowledge necessarily produces, would naturally be carried into the various departments of labour peculiar to their stations, and prevent that laziness and inattention which is too common among the working classes, and which not unfrequently lead to poverty and disgrace. Their knowledge of the nature of heat, combustion, atmospheric air, and combustible substances, would lead them to a proper economy in the use of fuel; and their acquaintance with the truths of chemistry, on which the art of rational cookery is founded, would lead them to *an economical practice in the preparation of victuals*, and teach them to extract from every substance all its nutritious qualities, and to impart a proper relish to every dish they prepare; for want of which knowledge and attention, the natural substances intended for the sustenance of man will not go half their length in the hands of some as they do under the judicious management of others. Their knowledge of the structure and functions of the animal system, of the regimen which ought to be attended to in order to health and vigour, of the causes which produce obstructed perspiration, of the means by which pestilential effluvia and infectious diseases are propagated, and of the disasters to which the human frame is liable

certain situations, would tend to prevent many of those diseases and fatal accidents to which ignorance and inattention have exposed so many of our fellow-men. For want of attending to such precautions in these respects, as knowledge would have suggested, thousands of families have been plunged into wretchedness and ruin, which all their future exertions were inadequate to remove. As the son of Sirach has well observed, " Better is the poor being sound and strong in constitution, than a rich man that is afflicted in his body. Health and good estate of body are above all gold; there are no riches above a sound body, and no joy above the joy of the heart."

As slovenliness and filth are generally the characteristics of ignorance and vulgarity, so an attention to cleanliness is one of the distinguishing features of cultivated minds. Cleanliness is conducive to health and virtuous activity, but uncleanliness is prejudicial to both. Keeping the body clean is of great importance, since more than the one-half of what we eat and drink is evacuated by perspiration; and if the skin is not kept clean the pores are stopped, and perspiration consequently prevented, to the great injury of health. It is highly necessary to the health and cheerfulness of children; for where it is neglected, they grow pale, meagre, and squalid, and subject to several loathsome and troublesome diseases. Washing the hands, face, mouth, and feet, and occasionally the whole body, conduces to health, strength, and ease, and tends to prevent colds, rheumatism, cramps, the palsy, the itch, the toothache, and many other maladies. Attention to cleanliness of body would also lead to cleanliness in regard to clothes, victuals, apartments, beds and furniture. A knowledge of the nature of the mephitic gases, of the necessity of pure atmospheric air to health and vigour, and of the means by which infection is produced and communicated, would lead persons to see the propriety of frequently opening doors and windows to dissipate corrupted air, and to admit the refreshing breeze, of sweeping cobwebs from the corners and ceiling of the room, and of removing dust, straw, or filth of any kind which is offensive to the smell, and in which infection might be deposited. By such attention, fevers and other malignant disorders might be prevented; vigour, health, and serenity promoted, and the whole dwelling and its inmates present an air of cheerfulness and comfort, and become the seat of domestic felicity.

Again, scientific knowledge would display itself among the lower orders, in the tasteful decoration of their houses and garden plots. The study of botany and horticulture would teach them to select the most beautiful flowers, shrubs, and evergreens; to arrange their plots with neatness and taste, and to improve their kitchen-garden to the best advantage, so as to render it productive for the pleasure and sustenance of their families. A genius for mechanical operations, which almost every person may acquire, would lead them to invent a variety of decorations, and to devise many contrivances for the purpose of conveniency, and for keeping every thing in its proper place and order—which never enter into the conceptions of rude and vulgar minds. Were such dispositions and mental activity generally prevalent, the circumstances which lead to poverty, beggary, and drunkennness, would be in a great measure removed, and home would always be resorted to as a place of comfort and enjoyment.

Again, the study of science and art would incline the lower classes to enter into the spirit of every new improvement, and to give their assistance in carrying it forward. The want of taste and of mental activity, and the spirit of selfishness which at present prevails among the mass of mankind, prevent the accomplishment of a variety of schemes which might tend to promote the conveniences and comforts of general society. For example; many of our villages which might otherwise present the appearance of neatness and comfort, are almost impassable, especially in the winter season, and during rainy weather, on account of the badness of roads and the want of foot-paths. At almost every step you encounter a pool, a heap of rubbish, or a dunghill, and in many places feel as if you were walking in a quagmire. In some villages, otherwise well planned, the streets present a grotesque appearance of sandy hillocks and mounds, and pools of stagnant water scattered in every direction, with scarcely the vestige of a pathway to guide the steps of the passenger. In winter, the traveller, in passing along, is bespattered with mire and dirt, and in summer, he can only drag heavily on, while his feet at every step sink into soft and parched sand. Now, such is the apathy and indifference that prevail among many villagers as to improvements in these respects, that although the contribution of a single shilling, or of half a day's labour might, in some instances, accomplish the requisite improvements, they will stand aloof from such operations with a sullen obstinacy, and even glory in being the means of preventing them. Nay, such is the selfishness of many individuals, that they will not remove nuisances even from the front of their own dwellings, because it might at the same time promote the convenience of the public at large. In large towns, likewise, many narrow lanes are rendered filthy, gloomy, and unwholesome by the avarice of landlords, and the obstinate and boorish manners of their tenants, and improvements prevented which would tend to the health and comfort of the inhabitants. But as knowledge tends to liberalize the mind, to subdue the principle of selfishness, and to produce a relish for cleanliness and comfort, when it is more generally diffused, we may expect that such improvements as those to which I allude, will be carried forward with spirit and alacrity. There would not be the smallest difficulty in accomplishing every object of this kind, and every other improvement conducive to the pleasure and comfort of the social state, provided the majority of a community were cheerfully to come forward with their assistance and contributions, however small, and to act with concord and harmony. A whole community or nation acting in unison, and every one contributing according to his ability, would accomplish wonders in relation to the improvement of towns, villages, and hamlets, and of everything that regards the comfort of civil and domestic society.

In short, were knowledge generally diffused, and art uniformly directed by the principles of science, new and interesting plans would be formed, new improvements set on foot, new comforts enjoyed, and a new lustre would appear on the face of nature, and on the state of general society. Numerous conveniences, decorations, and useful establishments never yet attempted, would soon be realized. Houses on neat and commodious plans, in airy situations, and furnished with every requisite accommodation, would be reared for the use of the peasant and mechanic; schools on spacious plans for the promotion of useful knowledge would be erected in every village and hamlet, and in every quarter of a city where they were found expedient; asylums would be built for the reception of the friendless poor, whether young or old; manufactories established for supplying employment to every class of labourers and artisans, and lecture-rooms prepared, furnished with requisite apparatus, to which they might resort for improvement in science. Roads would be cut in all convenient directions, diversified with rural decorations, hedge-rows, and shady bowers,—foot-paths, broad and smooth, would accompany them in all their windings, and gas-lamps, erected at every half-mile's distance, would variegate the rural scene and cheer the shades of night. Narrow lanes in cities would be either widened or their houses demolished; streets on broad and spacious plans would be built, the smoke of steam-engines consumed, nuisances removed, and cleanliness and comfort attended to in every arrangement. Cheerfulness and activity would everywhere prevail, and the idler, the vagrant, and the beggar would disappear from society. All these operations and improvements, and hundreds more, could easily be accomplished, were the minds of the great body of the community *thoroughly enlightened and moralized*, and every individual, whether rich or poor, who contributed to bring them into effect, would participate in the general enjoyment. And what an interesting picture would be presented to every benevolent mind, to behold the great body of mankind raised from a state of moral and physical degradation to the dignity of their rational natures, and to the enjoyment of the bounties of their Creator!—to behold the country diversified with the neat and cleanly dwellings of the industrious labourer,—the rural scene, during the day, adorned with seminaries, manufactories, asylums, stately edifices, gardens, fruitful fields and romantic bowers, and during night, bespangled in all directions with variegated lamps, forming a counterpart, as it were, to the lights which adorn the canopy of heaven! Such are only a few specimens of the improvements which art, directed by science and morality, could easily accomplish."

Most benevolently reasoned! but when will these things be done? Who will commence the career of improvement? What signs of daybreak are in the heavens?—scarcely the faintest streak.

NATURAL HISTORY.

HYENAS of Abyssinia.—These animals generally inhabit caverns and other rocky places, from whence they issue under cover of the night to prowl for food. They are gregarious, not so much from any social principle, as from a greediness of disposition, and a gluttonous instinct, which induce many to assemble even over a scanty and insufficient prey. They are said to devour the bodies which they find in cemeteries, and to disinter such as are hastily or imperfectly inumed. There seems, indeed, to be a peculiar gloominess and malignity of disposition in the aspect of the hyena, and its manners in a state of captivity are savage and untractable. Like every other animal, however, it is perfectly capable of being tamed. A contradictory feature has been observed in its natural instincts. About Mount Libanus, in the north of Asia, and the vicinity of Algiers, the hyenas, according to Bruce, live mostly upon large succulent bulbous roots, especially those of the fritillaria, &c.; and he informs us that he has known large patches of the fields turned up by them in their search for onions and other plants. He adds, that these were chosen with such care, that after having been peeled, if any small decayed spot became perceptible, they were left upon the ground. In Abyssinia, however, and many other countries, their habits are certainly decidedly carnivorous,—yet the same courage, or at least fierceness, which an animal diet usually produces does not so obviously manifest itself in this species. In Barbary, according to Bruce, the Moors in the daytime seize the hyena by the ears and drag him along, without his resenting that ignominious treatment otherwise than by attempting to draw himself back; and the hunters, when his cave is large enough to give them entrance, take a torch in their hands, and advance straight towards him, pretending at the same time to fascinate him by a senseless jargon. The creature is astounded by the noise and glare, and allowing a blanket to be thrown over him, is thus dragged out. Bruce locked up a goat, a kid, and a lamb, all day with a Barbary hyena which had fasted, and he found the intended victims in the evening alive and uninjured. He repeated the experiment, however, on another occasion, during the night, with a young ass, a goat and a fox, and next morning he was astonished to find the whole of them not only killed, but actually devoured, with the exception of some of the ass's bones!—The general size of the stripped hyena is that of a large dog. Bruce regarded the Abyssinian species as distinct from those described as natives of other parts of Africa, but recent observation has failed to confirm that impression of the Scottish traveller. This species was known to the ancients, and was exhibited at Rome for the first time in the reign of Gordian. One which died a few years ago in Paris was of an irritable and dissatisfied disposition, and had eaten away in its impatience all the toes of its hind-legs.—Nubia and Abyssinia.

PAPYRUS.—The papyrus of the ancients, the CYPERUS PAPYRUS of botanists, is a graceful marsh plant, twelve or fifteen feet in height. The roots creep extensively and throw up numerous stems sheathed at the base by a few sword-shaped leaves, and terminated with large and elegant umbels of flowers. The paper of antiquity was prepared from the inner portion of the stem; and, on the authority of Pliny, the best and most beautiful paper was made out of the very heart of the substance of the stem, and was composed of three layers arranged in parallel and transverse rows and submitted to heavy pressure. A kind of size seems also to have been used, which glued the parts together and rendered the spongy texture fitter for the reception of writing. To be of good quality this paper was required to be fine, compact, white, and smooth. Several coarser kinds were made. It would appear from the same author, that the Egyptians formerly applied the plant to many purposes. " The inhabitants of Egypt do use the root instead of wood, not for fuel only, but also to make thereof sundry vessels and utensils in an house. The very bodie and pole of the papyr itselfe serveth very well to twist and weave therewith little boats, and the rinds thereof be good to make saile-clothes, curtains, mats, and coverlets, clothes also for hangings, and ropes. Nay, they use to chew and eat it both raw and sodden: but they swallow the juice only down the throat and spit out the grosse substance." As for the flower, it served no other purpose than for " chaplets to adorn the images of the gods." At one time the papyrus was in general request not only in Egypt but in other countries. Under the Ptolemies the books of the great Alexandrian library were copied on this paper; but when Eumenes, king of Pergamus, began to establish a rival library, a mean jealousy controlled the dissemination of knowledge and forbade the exportation of papyrus. Parchment came into more general use soon afterwards, and is said to have derived its Latin name *pergamenea* from the city of Pergamus, where it was substituted for the papyrus, which was no longer to be obtained.

INSTINCT OF BIRDS OF PASSAGE.—A curious instance is related in the *Philosophical Transactions*, illustrative of that wonderful, incomprehensible faculty which enables the migratory birds, on their return to this country from foreign climates, to find their way, year after year, to the identical arm-houses from which they had migrated. Several swifts were marked by taking off two claws from the foot, and the same birds were found to return to their former haunts for seven successive years. The following paragraph on the same subject appeared in the recent London journals:—" During last summer an inhabitant of Waldmuenchen, in Bavaria, caught a house-swallow, which had returned to the same nest for four successive seasons, and fastened a slight gold ring, bearing his initials (I. G. N.) round his neck. On the 12th of April last the wanderer arrived from his winter quarters with a second ring, as well as the former one, round his neck; it was also of gold, and had some Arabic letters upon it."

THE MAMMOTH OF FLOWERS.—The plant called krubut, or great flower of Sumatra, is a most extraordinary vegetable prodigy: the breadth of a single full-grown flower exceeds three feet, and the petals or blossom leaves are of a sub-rotund shape, and measure twelve inches each from the base to the apex, and it is about a foot from the insertion of one petal to the opposite one. That part which is considered the nectarium, situated in the centre of the flower, would hold twelve pints of water. The pistils which are abortive, are as large as cows' horns, and the weight of the whole is estimated at about fifteen pounds.

THE TRUE BALM.

ADAPTED FROM AN OLD POET.

If torn from all we hold most dear,
  The tedious moments slowly roll,
Can music's tenderest accents cheer
  The silent grief that melts the soul?

Or can the poets' boasted art
  To breasts that feel corroding care,
The healing balm of peace impart,
  And pluck the thorn engender'd there?

Ah, no! in vain the verse may flow,
  In vain the softest strain begin,
The only balm to sooth our wo
  And calm our grief is—BEST LOCHRIN.

COLUMN FOR THE LADIES.

FREE TRADE—A SCOTCH D'EON.

ABOUT twelve or fourteen years back, a female, whose sex had long been suspected, was discovered in the person of a plasterer in Glasgow, who every day pursued *his* calling, in the most steady and regular way. Her history is curious; but before going into it, we would briefly inquire why, among all the advocates of *Free Trade*, no one thinks of throwing open the many species of mechanical art, for which they are fit, to women? The occupations by which they can earn their bread are limited to the hardest and foulest kinds of drudgery, or to a few light employments generally depending on *fashion*, and liable to continual fluctuations and depression.

HELEN OLIVER,

Our heroine, belonged originally to Saltcoats. When her sex was discovered, she had for upwards of four years worn the dress, and worked at the trade of a man. She took the name of a brother, John Oliver. About two years before her transformation, she was a maid-servant in a farm house in West Kilbride; a particular intimacy took place between her and a person in a neighbouring house, who officiated as ploughman. Being frequently seen walking together in quiet and sequestered places, they were regarded as lovers: ultimately, however, this "ploughman" turned out to be also a female; and it is believed by Helen's relatives and acquaintances, that it was the arguments of this personage which induced her to abandon the female dress and duties. One Sunday, while in her parent's house at Saltcoats, she requested her mother to give her, her "wee cutty pipe," and she would give her two new ones in exchange. To this unusual demand the mother, after some questions, consented; and Helen immediately afterwards began to write a letter, which, in answer to an inquiry from her parent, she said was to inform the people in Greenock, to whom she was hired as a servant, that she would not be with them for some time, for several reasons she then alleged. Early on the following morning, Helen helped herself to a complete suit of her brother's clothes and disappeared, without giving the least intimation of her future prospects, or where she intended to fix her residence. Dressed in her new attire, she reached the house of a cousin in Glasgow on the same day. Her relative was not sufficiently intimate with the person of the fair impostor to detect the fraud. Never doubting in the least that she was "the real John Oliver," among other inquiries for absent relatives, "sister Helen" was not forgotten. A plasterer stopt at the time in her cousin's house, and she resolved to learn that business. Accordingly she went for a trial to a person in the Calton; but having fallen out with her master, she left the town. She then went to Paisley, where she wrought for about three months, and she was next employed for about half-a-year in Johnstone. There, either for amusement, or to prevent suspicion, and insure concealment, she courted a young woman, and absolutely carried the joke so far as to induce the girl to leave her service to be married. [This was going rather far.] Travelling one night between Johnstone and Paisley, she was accosted by a lad from Saltcoats, who was intimate with her person, parents, and history; and in consequence she removed to Kilmarnock, where she remained six months. Besides the places already mentioned, she has been in Lanark and Edinburgh, working always at the plastering, except a short time she was employed by a Glasgow flesher. A variety of circumstances have frequently impelled this rustic D'Eon to change not only her master and house of residence, but also the town in which she was comfortably employed, particularly as she was often or rather almost obliged to board and share her lodgings with some neighbour workman, and though for obvious reasons she seldom detailed more of her previous history than mentioned the towns she had visited and the masters she had served, yet some sagacious females have been known to declare that "Johnny must have been a sodger or a tailor," because "when he likes himsel' he can brawly clout his breeks, darn his stockings, mak' his ain meat, and wash his ain claise." At the beginning of February last, Helen applied for employment to a master plasterer in Hutchesontown. She said she was seventeen years of age, and stated that she and a sister were left orphans at an early age; urged her forlorn condition, and that having already had some practice, she was very anxious to be bound an apprentice, that she might obtain an ample knowledge of the business. Eventually she was employed, and though she had the appearance of a little man, she was in reality a tall woman, being about five feet four inches high. By no means shy of a lift, times without number she has carried the heavy hod full of lime for the Irish labourer in attendance. Steady, diligent, and quiet, she gave her master every satisfaction, who considering her rather a delicate boy, feelingly kept her at light ornamental work, and paid her 7s. a-week. Sometime since a workman was employed by the same master, to whom Helen was intimately known. The master having learned the fact of the case, placed her apart at work from the men, and took a favourable opportunity to speak with her. She indignantly denied her metamorphosis, offered to produce letters from her sister, declared that she was a free-mason and besides had been a flesher, a drummer in the Greenock volunteers, and made a number of statements with a view to escape detection. One day, an Irishman, with characteristic confidence, sprang upon the heroine, hugged her like a brother bruin, and cried in his genuine Dic, "Johnny, they tell me you're a woman, and dang it, I am to know, for I love a purty girl." The agile female extracted herself in an instant, and with a powerful kick drove him from her; at the same time exclaiming, with an oath, she would soon convince him she was not a woman. Ultimately, however, the truth was wrung from her, and she consequently left the town. She writes a good hand, and previous to her departure, she addressed a letter to her master, in which she bade him farewell, and requested him not to make much talk about H. Oliver.

What has since become of Helen John we have not heard; but it is likely that some of our readers may be able to give us the conclusion or progress of her history.

LOVE AT FIRST SIGHT, AND A LOVE LETTER.

THE following is from a Van Diemen's Land paper, *The Colonist.*—Friday, August 24, 1832:—*A Police Incident.*—Last week, a damsel was brought to the police office, charged with putting one Mrs. Norah Mulgan in bodily fear. Prisoner pleaded guilty, but begged that the offence might be passed over, as she had received an offer of marriage from a *gentleman*, who, in all probability would turn her off, were she to be punished, and he to discover her disgrace. To prove her veracity she produced the following epistle from her enamoured swain:—"My dear angel, this comes with a pound of sausages, which I hope will find you in good health, as it leaves me at present. I seed you last Sunday for the first time, since which I haven't had no peace for thinking of your dear self; therefore will take it as a great favour if you will marr me as early as possible, as I can earn by my profession a excellent livelihood; I was rat-catcher and sow-gelder to the late Duke of York; I bleed horses, cures the choleric morbus, and all other dumb animals, and have received a good hedication: the childres we shall have will get air learning free gratis. I have been schoolmaster in Mr.——'s family for the last fortnight, and have already teach'd the eldest boy jography and the manufacture of ginger beer; and as for the second un, have made him the most best gunmaker and rethmeticker of all the lads I ever teached; so as see I have every chance of prospering; I have bought a ng and a pair of blankets. I have written to the govern for his permission, and requested the clergyman to hre us asked in church; he appears to be a very nice sober man; I wanted him to go and have half a pint of rum, bu he was too bashful. Please send me an answer post paid.—remain my dear angel your true love."

THE STORY TELLER.

THE TEN YEARS OF SILVIO PELLICO.

This most interesting narrative is written by the sufferer himself, an Italian gentleman; a poet, known to Europe as the author of *Francesca dai Rimini*; a patriot, a man of the purest character and the most amiable dispositions, who became the victim of Austrian tyranny. He was a native of Turin, where he lived, when he drew upon himself the suspicions, and the cruel revenge of that vile government which has usurped the domination of Italy. His first imprisonment was under the burning leads of Venice. The original sentence was death, but he was informed that the Emperor had graciously mitigated it to fifteen years' imprisonment in the fortress of Spielburg, in Moravia, with hard labour, chains on the feet, the bare floor for a bed, and scanty and miserable food. Such are the tender mercies of paternal monarchs, to men whose only fault is love of their native country, and the desire of its independence, and whose sole offence was becoming members of a secret political society. His friend, Maroncelli the poet, was the sharer of this remorseless punishment. Maroncelli's period of condemnation was twenty years. On their way to their prison, the German, as well as the Italian villagers, shewed the greatest sympathy with their fate.

"How grateful (says Pellico) I felt to all; how sweet is the sympathy of our fellow-creatures—how delightful to love them. This mitigated the rancour I had felt towards those whom I had called my enemies. Who knows, thought I, if I could see them more narrowly—if they could but see me, we might feel ourselves compelled mutually to pity—to love each other."

On the 10th April, 1822, they reached the fortress of Spielburg. They were immediately thrown into a damp, unwholesome dungeon, and subjected to confinement as rigorous as could be imposed on the most atrocious felons. Several Italian gentlemen, confined for like offences in this horrible prison, died under their sufferings. Pellico applied to the head gaoler for some few comforts to relieve the distress of their subterranean cell. He was an old soldier, and, under a rough exterior, a man of humane and gentle feelings.

"It is the Emperor's concern, I must obey—you have fever enough to kill a horse—but you cannot have a mattress till the physician comes to order it." At last the physician comes, orders the mattress, and a change to the floor above, but the Governor of the province has also to be applied to, before the indulgence can be granted. The prison dress is, however, put on him—a harlequin hat and a rough shirt, with chains to the feet. As the smith fastened on the latter, "I might have been saved the trouble—he has not two months to live"—he observed to the gaoler in German. "Would it were so," exclaimed Pellico, who to his surprise understood him.

The rules of the prison were harshness itself—the officials ran the greatest risk if they attempted to mitigate them: Pellico could not swallow the black bread, but he dared not for his gaoler's sake accept the bit of white loaf, surreptitiously put into his hands, least the sentinels should find it out. One evening he heard an Italian song from the adjoining cell—he sprang from the mattress—"Who are you, unfortunate man? *I* am Silvio Pellico." "Silvio," said the neighbour, "I know you not by sight, but I have loved you long. Come, let us to the window, and talk in spite of the gaolers." It was the young Count Oroboni, imprisoned on a charge similar to his own. The sentinels soon overheard and suppressed this; but by whispering, and by watching the rounds, they held much sweet converse. They never saw each other, but their friendship was soon endearing—they comforted each other, relating the story of their lives, and dilating on religious topics, and Pellico was delighted to derive lessons of resignation and Christian charity from the tone in which this youth of twenty would talk of his sorrows and his oppressors.

Months passed away. Both the friends felt their health declining—one evening Oroboni said, "My friend, the day is not far off when one of us two will be no longer able to come to the window. Let us be prepared, the one to die—the other to survive his friend." His lungs afterwards became affected—he felt his time would be short, and would often grieve aloud that his remains would moulder in Germany, far from the sunny skies of his own dear Italy. In June 1823, his spirit was released. The sentinel said to Pellico, his last words were: "I pardon from my heart all my enemies." The old gaoler next falls ill. "We inquired after him," says Pellico, "with the anxiety of children; and when he got a little better, and could walk under our windows, we hailed him, and he would look up with a melancholy smile and say to the sentinel,—'These are my sons.' Poor old man! what grief it gave me to see him tottering feebly along, without being able to offer him the support of my arm." He shortly died.

Years passed on: Maroncelli was still kept in the subterranean cell. His close confinement and fetters had caused a swelling of the knee joint. He was permitted to share Pellico's upper cell, and as he grew worse, his chain was removed:—various applications were tried in vain.

"How much," says his loving companion, "did I suffer for him—to see him wasting under such cruel tortures—to feel certain that the knee would never be healed—to perceive that the patient himself thought death more probable than recovery, and with all this to be obliged every instant to admire his courage and serenity. He could no longer digest nor sleep—he grew frightfully wasted; he often fainted, yet he would even endeavour to encourage me. After nine months a consultation was allowed. The chief physician came—approved of what had been done and disappeared. A moment after the sub-attendant entered to say 'The chief physician did not like to explain himself in your presence.' 'What would he recommend?' asked the sufferer. 'Amputation, Signor! Weak as you are, will you run the risk? We will send word immediately to Vienna, and the moment the permission is obtained—' 'What! is a permission necessary?' 'Yes, Signor.'

"In eight days the warrant arrived,—the patient was carried into a larger room. He asked me to follow him. 'I may die,' said he, 'under the operation; let me do so in the arms of a friend.' I was permitted to be with him. The confessor came in, and administered the sacrament to the sufferer. The surgeon had not yet arrived. Maroncelli employed the interval in singing a hymn. At last they came—one our household barber-surgeon, who officiated as of right; the other an *elevé* of the school of Vienna. The patient was seated on the bedside, with his legs hanging down, while I supported him. The old surgeon cut away all round to the depth of an inch, then drew up the skin, which had been cut, and continued to cut through the muscles. The blood flowed in torrents. At last came the sawing of the bone; Maroncelli never uttered a cry. When he saw them carry away the leg, which had been cut off, he gave it one melancholy look, then turning to the surgeon who had operated, he said—'You have rid me of an enemy, and I have no means of recompensing you.' There was a rose standing in a glass near the window; 'May I request you to bring me that rose?' said he. I took it to him, and he presented it to the surgeon saying—'I have nothing else to present you in token of my gratitude.' The surgeon took the rose, and, as he did so, let fall a tear."

In forty days his cure was complete, and, with wooden stump and crutches, he accompanied Pellico back again to their old prison.

On Sunday, Aug. 1, 1630, Pellico completed ten years of his imprisonment. At noon the Inspector of Police summoned them to his presence to announce that the Emperor had cut short the term of their imprisonment. One would suppose this would have thrown them into transports of joy;—yet it was not so. Instantly their hearts reverted to their relatives, of whom they had heard nothing; their joy was neutralized. Tedious forms and a journey to Vienna were necessary to their complete release. The evening of the 17th September Pellico reached his own Turin a free man!

"Who can attempt to describe the consolation of heart I received," says he, "when I again saw father, mother, and brothers. My dear sister joined, as soon as possible, our happy group. Restored to these five objects of my tenderest affection, I was,—I am, the most enviable of mortals. Then for all these past sorrows and present happiness blessed be that Providence in whose hands men and events are but wonderful instruments for the promotion of his all-wise and beneficent ends."

Amen! responds every British heart.

These interesting memoirs, which have just been reprinted in Paris and London, are prohibited in Italy and in the Austrian States.

VENTRILOQUISM.

THE tricks and impositions practised by ventriloquists furnish many curious narratives. By this art, certain persons can so modify their voice as to make it appear to the audience to proceed from any distance, and in any direction, and by this means impostors have sometimes accomplished their nefarious designs, of which the following are instances:—

Louis Brahant, a dexterous ventriloquist, valet de chambre to Francis I., had fallen desperately in love with a young, handsome, and rich heiress; but was rejected by the parents as an unsuitable match for their daughter, on account of the lowness of his circumstances. The young lady's father dying, he made a visit to the widow, who was totally ignorant of his singular talent. Suddenly, on his first appearance, in open day, in her own house, and in the presence of several persons who were with her, she heard herself accosted in a voice perfectly resembling that of her dead husband, and which seemed to proceed from above, exclaiming, "Give my daughter in marriage to Louis Brahant. He is a man of great fortune and of an excellent character. I now suffer the inexpressible torments of purgatory for having refused her to him. If you obey this admonition I shall soon be delivered from this place of torment. You will at the same time provide a worthy husband for your daughter, and procure everlasting repose to the soul of your poor husband." The widow could not for a moment resist this dreadful summons, which had not the most distant appearance of proceeding from Louis Brahant, whose countenance exhibited no visible change, and whose lips were close and motionless during the delivery of it. Accordingly, she consented immediately to receive him for her son-in-law. Louis's finances, however, were in a very low situation, and the formalities attending the marriage-contract rendered it necessary for him to exhibit some show of riches, and not to give the ghost the lie direct. He, accordingly, went to work on a fresh subject, one Cornu, an old and rich banker at Lyons, who had accumulated immense wealth by usury and extortion, and was known to be haunted by remorse of conscience, on account of the manner in which he had acquired it. Having contracted an intimate acquaintance with this man, he, one day, while they were sitting together in the usurer's little back parlour, artfully turned the conversation on religious subjects, on demons, and spectres, the pains of purgatory, and the torments of hell. During an interval of silence between them, a voice was heard, which, to the astonished banker, seemed to be that of his deceased father, complaining, as in the former case, of his dreadful situation in purgatory, and calling upon him to deliver him instantly from thence, by putting into the hands of Louis Brahant, then with him, a large sum for the redemption of Christians then in slavery with the Turks; threatening him, at the same time, with eternal damnation, if he did not take this method to expiate, likewise, his own sins. Louis Brahant, of course, affected a due degree of astonishment on the occasion; and further promoted the deception by acknowledging his having devoted himself to the prosecution of the charitable design imputed to him by the ghost. An old usurer is naturally suspicious. Accordingly, the wary banker made a second appointment with the ghost's delegate for the next day; and, to render any design of imposing upon him utterly abortive, took him into the open fields, where not a house or a tree, or even a bush, or a pit were in sight, capable of screening any supposed confederate. This extraordinary caution excited the ventriloquist to exert all the powers of his art. Wherever the banker conducted him, at every step, his ears were saluted on all sides with the complaints, and groans, not only of his father, but of all his deceased relations, imploring him for the love of God, and in the name of every saint in the calendar, to have mercy on his own soul and theirs, by effectually seconding with his purse the intentions of his worthy companion. Cornu could no longer resist the voice of heaven, and, accordingly, carried his guest home with him, and paid him down ten thousand crowns; with which the honest ventriloquist returned to Paris, and married his mistress. The catastrophe was fatal. The secret was afterwards blown, and reached the usurer's ears, who was so much affected by the loss of his money, and the mortifying railleries of his neighbours, that he took to his bed and died.

Another trick of a similar kind was played off about sixty or seventy years ago, on a whole community, by another French ventriloquist. "M. St. Gill, the ventriloquist, and his intimate friend, returning home, from a place whither his business had carried him, sought for shelter from an approaching thunder-storm in a neighbouring convent. Finding the whole community in mourning, he inquired the cause, and was told that one of the body had died lately, who was the ornament and delight of the whole society. To pass away the time, he walked into the church, attended by some of the religious, who showed him the tomb of their deceased brother, and spoke feelingly of the scanty honours they had bestowed on his memory. Suddenly a voice was heard, apparently proceeding from the roof of the choir, lamenting the situation of the defunct in purgatory, and reproaching the brotherhood with their lukewarmness and want of zeal on his account. The friars, as soon as their astonishment gave them power to speak, consulted together, and agreed to acquaint the rest of the community with this singular event, so interesting to the whole society. M. St. Gill, who wished to carry on the joke a little farther, dissuaded them from taking this step, telling them that they would be treated by their absent brethren as a set of fools and visionaries. He recommended to them, however, the immediately calling the whole community into the church, where the ghost of their departed brother might probably reiterate his complaints. Accordingly, all the friars, novices, lay-brothers and even the domestics of the convent, were immediately summoned and called together. In a short time the voice from the roof renewed its lamentations and reproaches, and the whole convent fell on their faces, and vowed a solemn reparation. As a first step, they chanted a *De profundis* in a full choir; during the intervals of which the ghost occasionally expressed the comfort he received from their pious exercises and ejaculations on his behalf. When all was over, the prior entered into a serious conversation with M. St. Gill; and, on the strength of what had just passed, sagaciously inveighed against the absurd incredulity of our modern sceptics and pretended philosophers, on the article of ghosts or apparitions. M. St. Gill thought it high time to disabuse the good fathers. This purpose, however, he found it extremely difficult to effect, till he had prevailed upon them to return with him into the church, and there be witnesses of the manner in which he had conducted this ludicrous deception." Had not the ventriloquist, in this case, explained the cause of the deception, a whole body of men might have sworn, with a good conscience, that they had heard the ghost of a departed brother address them again and again in a supernatural voice.

HOUSEHOLD OF THE TYROLESE PEASANT.

The peasant of the Upper Tyrol seldom possesses more than supplies the wants of his family; a cow, a pig or two, are the whole of his live stock; and all the land which he possesses beyond what suffices for the support of these, produces Indian corn, and a few vegetables, and sometimes a little flax; these crops being no more than sufficient for the support of his family. The Tyrolean peasant, therefore, though in one sense independent, treading, and labouring his own soil, and eating the produce of his own industry, is yet poor; and lives worse than a day-labourer in many other countries. His family is nourished almost solely upon Indian corn, and milk; and it must be admitted, that with small properties like those in the valley of the Inn, no other produce could be half so serviceable. This plant is indeed the staff of life here, and is prized by the inhabitants, as it deserves. Three times a-day, soup made of Indian corn and milk, is served at the table of the Tyrolean peasant; and this, with bread, sometimes entirely of Indian corn, but most commonly with one-third, or one-fourth part of wheat, forms his whole diet. I have frequently, in the course of a walk, while residing at Inspruck, entered the houses of the peasantry, and tasted both the soup and the bread. To those who are fond of a milk diet, the soup would not be found disagreeable; and the bread appeared to me good, precisely in proportion to the quantity of wheat that was mixed with the Indian corn. It is never used half-and-half in the Tyrol. This would be too expensive; for very little wheat is grown in the valley of the Inn—none in the upper part of it, and that which is brought to the Inspruck market, must be received either from Trent, and the Italian frontier, or from Bavaria.

However tastes may differ as to the palatableness of an Indian-corn diet, the fine athletic peasantry of the Tyrol, sufficiently attest its wholesome and nutritious qualities. Indeed, I have generally seen a robust peasantry in those countries in which Indian corn forms a large portion of their subsistence. The people of Languedoc and Bearn, are stronger than those of central and northern France; and the Biscayans, who eat more Indian corn than any other kind of bread, are greatly superior in strength to the Castilians. In the Tyrol, Indian corn is used in other ways than as an article of diet: the surplus, if any there be, finds a ready market for horses' food; and the husks and sheaths are used in stuffing mattresses; and also as a substitute for firewood. As much flax is generally grown by the Tyrolean peasant as suffices for the wants of his family, and for employment during the winter.

The cultivation of Indian corn has made some noise in England; and has excited some interest, owing to the idea, that its cultivation would ameliorate the condition of the lower classes; and there have been, in fact, two parties in this matter;—one asserting its great advantages, and its adaptation to the climate of England; and the other denying both. I am no agriculturist, and am able only to state facts. As for the advantages of the cultivation of Indian corn, I can only say, that throughout the valley of the Inn, it is considered the most useful and the surest produce; and that the peasantry who live upon it, are the finest peasantry in Europe; and with respect to its fitness for the climate of England, I would only observe, that the climate of the Upper Tyrol is most uncertain. Its centre is two thousand feet above the level of the sea; and its winters are extremely severe; and although from its more southern latitude than England, the heats of summer are great, the summer is late, as some proof of which, I may state, that near the end of June, I was under the necessity of having a stove lighted in the hotel at Inspruck. I do not know how these facts bear upon the probable success of Indian corn in England; but if Indian corn be supposed to require a milder climate than that of England, I think the success of Indian corn in the Upper Tyrol, proves this to be an error. The same fruits that come to perfection in the southern parts of England, will not ripen in the valley of the Inn.

Although the properties of the peasantry of the Upper Tyrol be in general limited, this is of course not universal; some are in such circumstances as to be called opulent among their neighbours; though in richer countries, such opulence would be considered but an indifferent competency. A peasant whose possessions are worth fifteen thousand florins (£1750) is rich; and one possessing the half of this sum, is in easy circumstances. Such peasants and their families, do not, of course, live upon Indian corn,—though this forms, in all families, one important article of diet. The lower order of peasants never eat meat excepting on feast-days,—and bacon only on great feasts.

In all countries—even in those where the great bulk are proprietors, there are of necessity some hewers of wood, and drawers of water. In this part of the Tyrol, these are miserably off. The usual wages of labour do not exceed, for a man, fourpence half-penny per day,—with maintenance; and a woman seldom receives more than one penny half-penny, or two-pence. This is a wretched state of things, but fortunately the class of day, labourers is small. The necessaries of life are not, indeed, dear. Meat usually sells at 4d. or 4½d. per lb. of 21 oz. which is not more than 2¾d. for 16 oz.; butter costs 9d. for 21 oz., or 6½d. per lb.; bread of Indian corn is extremely cheap. Fruit, vegetables, and wine, are all dear; for the valley of the Inn produces none of the latter, and little of the two former,—most of which are brought from Botzen; but these are articles with which the poor may dispense. Fish, and most kinds of game, are plentiful and cheap.

The wages of a man-servant in the Tyrol (and this applies to the country generally) are about L.5. The wages of a female servant, about L.3."

I have already spoken of the dress of the women; but here, in the lower Innthal, it becomes more and more preposterous. In the Tyrol, vanity does not appear to be exercised on the same object as elsewhere. A handsome leg,—or at least, a pretty ancle, is generally looked upon as not the least contemptible of female charms; but in the Tyrol it is otherwise; stockings—thick woollen stockings, are three times the length of the leg: and are therefore allowed to gather themselves in enormous folds, and plaits, that render the ankle as thick as a moderate waist in Paris or elsewhere. It may be, indeed, that they look upon a charm as more a charm, the more it is concealed. There is a limit, however, to this principle. I ought to mention, that the older the women are, they have the greater number of petticoats. The hostess and her daughter permitted me to satisfy my curiosity as to the number and quality of theirs. The mother, who was about fifty years of age had nine; the eldest daughter, who looked almost thirty, but who assured me she was not yet twenty-three, wore six,—and the younger,—a girl of eighteen or nineteen, was contented with one less. All of these were of a woollen stuff, thicker in its texture than moderately thick flannel. The younger of the damsels was also prevailed upon to draw her stocking tight; but she was shocked at the display; and immediately reinstated the leg in its Tyrolean privileges. I do assure my fair readers, however, that had the leg so essonced in woollen, been fitted with an elastic silk stocking, it might have excited the envy of some of them.—*Inglis's Travels in the Tyrol.*

THE DWELLING OF HOFER.

From Meran, the road ascends the right bank of the stream, leaving the castle of the Tyrol on the left hand. At first, the valley is narrow, but gradually widens, though never losing the character of an upland valley. Cottages and hamlets are scattered, but thinly scattered, here and there; little rivulets tumble into the Passeyer, leaping from the adjoining steeps; and many gentle and beautiful scenes open among the slopes and dells that form the valley. Four hours' walk, with many rests by the river side, and upon the stones that lay in its bed, brought me within sight of the house of Andrew Hofer. The brawling Passeyer, full o. large stones, runs past the house at the foot of a little stone wall raised to protect it against torrents; a few trees grow round the house, and, on either side, are seen mountains, their lower acclivities enclosed, and bearing a little corn and a small church, with a green spire, stands upon a neighbouring knoll. The house itself is no way remark able; like most other houses in this part of the Tyrol, the entry to it is by a wooden stair outside, which leads to a little balcony. Several targets, perforated in many places near the centre, were fixed to the wall, evidences of Hofer's prowess in marksmanship. In the house, which is, and ever has been an inn, I resolved to spend the night.

I had finished a rural meal on the balcony, when four peasants of the neighbourhood walked in, to refresh themselves with a little wine, and possibly to see the stranger. They were fine looking, and intelligent men; and spoke without much reserve about the state of the Tyrol, and the patriot who had owned a home in that valley. One of them, a man about fifty years old, had known Hofer well, and had attended his obsequies; and when he said that the Austrian authorities, professing a reverence for him, had attended the procession, he spat with violence on the ground, to express contempt of the hypocrisy: he represented Hofer as a sturdy broad-shouldered man; with a high and capacious brow; eyes a little sunken: and an honest expression of countenance: he wore mustachios, and a beard,—why the latter, I was not able to learn. We shared amongst us several bottles of tolerable wine; and drank to the memory of Hofer, and to better times.

It was dusk when the party broke up; and I accompanied one of the number to his house, about a mile farther up the valley; here we repeated our toast; and in the old fashion, he accompanied me half-way back. "We can never be otherwise than we are," said he, "unless France stretches her hand to us." It was a quiet and calm scene as I strolled leisurely back to the house of Hofer: there was only the noise of the stream, which guided me safely to my quarters. —*Ibid.*

BRIEF HISTORY OF THE ESTABLISHED CHURCH OF ENGLAND.

UPON a text furnished by the *Quarterly Review*, which states that "*the Established Church is the greatest of all our blessings,*" Mr. ENSOR, after making some pungent commentaries on the text, gives the following *precis* of the history of this greatest of our blessings:—

Its present excellence is not inferior to its reverential antiquity. It may be dated from the day that Constantine, who was hailed Emperor by the British legions, saw the cross in the clouds with the inscription,—"By this sign you shall conquer." Charlemagne, another conqueror, took religion under his special protection; but it was through our own conqueror, William the Norman, that the Church reached its palmy state. Then, of 60,215 knights' fees into which England was divided, 28,015 were granted to the Church and the vassals of the spiritual brethren:—and they proceeded accumulating till they had nearly obtained, what St. Augustin says is the right of the saints—the property of the nation. At this period the country became distressed— there was a difficulty to meet the expenditure; and, in 1412, the Commons, who had been required to grant supplies proposed that the King should seize all the temporalities of the Church, and employ them as a perpetual fund for the exigencies of the State. The Archbishop of Canterbury replied, that the clergy prayed day and night for the prosperity of the State. The speaker smiled, and said that was a slender supply. In the eleventh of the same King, the Commons again attacked the opulent Church, and they proposed that, instead of the bishops, &c., 16,000 parish priests should be substituted at a moderate stipend. This was accompanied with a request that the statutes against the Lollards should be mitigated. The King was angry, and to prove his respect for the Church, he, during the Session of Parliament, ordered a Lollard to be burned, as lately anti-tithe gentry were prosecuted and imprisoned in Ireland. Indeed it shewed great reserve in his Majesty to have made a single sacrifice. The Lollards were in truth heretics and traitors: no uncommon combination where the sacred union of Church and State is complete. They preceded the Puritans, and were a sort of great-grandfathers of the Presbyterians, a most ungentlemanly sect according to Charles II.,

the finest gentleman of his age. Thus, however, by the Lollards the rent was first made, and thence the alien priories, which had been occasionally seized by Edward the First, Second, and Third, were dissolved by the second of Henry V., and vested in the Crown. After came, but at a long interval, Luther's heresy—his order was overlooked— and Henry VIII., *defensor fidei*,—who loved virgin wives like a Jew, and married them like a Mahometan—halved the reformation proposed in Parliament in Henry VI.'s reign, playing Filch with the temporalities of the Church. How Cranmer, while he rejoiced at the Reformation, lamented that the property of the Catholic Church did not descend entire to the holy men of his tribe; he asserted as Messrs. Lefroy and Shaw in our days, that ecclesiastical properties should be reserved for ecclesiastical purposes. This was the cause of the poverty of the Church of England—for all things are comparative.—Some think the Church is rich. The Rev. Francis Wrangham asserts, "that the opulence of the Church is a misnomer." The Rev. Daniel Lysons is most pathetic on the same point, asserting "that most of them (the Bishoprics) and even the most plentiful, are now scarcely answerable to the burdens that attend them." What a state is this for the bishops, whom Laud, with his usual discretion, declared to be *jure divino*; though Prettyman, Bishop of Lincoln, does, in his *Elements of Christian Theology*, rather reduce their divinity, as he says, in speaking of the difference of bishops and priests, "a point which can be decided only by the ancient ecclesiastical writers." However that may be, bishops are bishops, and no one can doubt, for the *Quarterly Review* give it their high sanction, "that the Protestant Reformed Church of England, is the best constituted that this world has ever seen." (No. xxiii. p. 190.) So say I, saving and excepting the Protestant Established Church of Ireland; yet is this Church poorer than the English—and a writer in a magazine of this month talks of the destitution of the Irish Church, as if the clergy were like the priests of Boudha, who entirely depend on alms. And yet this Milesian contributor of Irish articles to the Scotch periodical, possesses a greater income as Protestant parson, than the primate of that religion enjoys, which he renounced. The Irish Protestant clergy are poor. The primate has only L.15,000, and his successor is to be reduced to L.10,000 a-year net revenue. This is poverty, but I repeat not lamentable destitution! and as to the clergy in this diocese of Armagh, very few have so little as L.400 a-year, and some receive as much as L.2500 a-year. They should have more, of course, and yet they, in fact, seized the first-fruits to their own use; they obtained the Composition Act—an Act so beneficial for the clergy that it is to be adopted for the English Church. They, indeed, complain that the landlords may obtain 15 per cent., from their tithes, yet they who do not concur in this arrangement are regarded askance, by some parsons at least. By it the landlord becomes virtually tithe-proctor, and security for the payment in money of L.85 in every L.100. The parson, in consequence, must be paid L.85, though the landlord should not receive L.1 of his rent. The parson should be paid, I admit, the full L.100; yet still L.85, without vexation, or expense in collection, or losses by various circumstances in one sum, is not a mortal stripping of the clergy. With respect to the Church of England, in England, all is fair sailing. By some unaccountable cause the dissenters increased in England till they doubled the amount of the members of the Established Church. In Queen Anne's time there was a parliamentary vote to build 50 churches; only 11 were built; had the other 39 been erected, who could say what would have been the result. The want was obvious; for, as the Rev. Mr. Yates wrote, "no less than 977,000 souls are shut out from the common pastoral offices of the national religion within the small circle of ten miles round London." To remedy this, the Minister proposed, in March 1818, a grant of L.1,000,000, to build churches in England. Then was the era, or influenza of church-building, for Clarke mentions the rage of the Government of Sweden for building churches. (Scandinavia, p. 461.) Further, large sums were granted to propagate the Established Church in the Colonies; but what was still more interesting to the Establishment, there were annual grants of L.100,000, to the English clergy. In 1809, Mr. Baring resisted the grant, saying, " There was no part of the civilized world in which so large a portion of the produce of the earth and the industry of the inhabitants were appropriated to the use of the clergy, as in this country. The money thus voted every year was laid out in stock, so that the clergy had not only a tenth of the produce of the land, but they also derived profit as stockholders." The grant passed by a majority of 94 to 20. These were the halcyon days of the Church. Then the Church prayed for George III., in a first and a second edition of a prayer, both issued on the same day, the 25th of May, 1804, (prayer is better than sleep, says the Koran,) as they had prayed on the 18th of February in the same year, for his Majesty afflicted, according to them, for the wickedness of his people, and whom they called the *nursing father of the Church:* a rhetorical expression, yet not contrary to nature, as Humboldt mentions an authenticated account of a man, who, during the illness of his wife, suckled his child for four months. George III. was not particular in this respect, for Denham rhymed truly :—

Our monarchs were acknowledged here,
That they their churches' nursing-fathers were.

They gave and they took, " like the sweet south, that breathes upon a bank of violets, stealing and giving odour."

And they have nursed the Irish Church; and it is nursing with a vengeance. Tithe, which was proclaimed to be extinguished, has been levied in the Protestant county of Armagh by police, headed by magistrates specially commanded to do so—magistrates, who employ paid agents to receive their own rents. The commission under the Church Temporalities' Bill, has obtained a fresh infusion of episcopacy; nor can any act of the commissioners be valid without the signature of one ecclesiastic. Ten bishops are to be abstracted, but twelve are to remain. On what principle are so many reserved? Two bishops in the English Church (the best possible church) manage the affairs of 2200 parishes, and these two bishoprics contain 3,000,000 of Protestants; all Ireland does not number half a million of Protestants of the Established Church. By a simple rule of arithmetic, if two bishops suffice for 3,000,000, one-third of one bishop would suffice for half a million; we could, therefore, without hating bishops as the Biscayans or the Cameronians, do very well without one entire bishop, according to the scale of duties and of the flocks of the bishops of York and Chester. One-third of a bishop might be converted into a four months' visit in the year by some Welsh bishop, or, what would be better perhaps, by William Ward, who would thus be indemnified for the loss of Sodor, which was lost to the bishopric of Man, when that island was conquered by the English.

ORIGIN OF ENGLISH NONCONFORMITY.

It was about this time (the reign of Edward VI.) that the distinction between *conformist* and *nonconformist* took its rise, owing to a difference of opinion amongst the clergy on the subjects of habits and ceremonies, the former readily and unscrupulously submitting to whatever forms and ceremonies might be imposed by authority; the latter (amongst whom were some of the best and holiest of the British reformers) objecting strenuously to many of the rites and garments which had been derived from Rome, and which contributed to perpetuate a spirit of idolatry and superstition amongst the people. Dr. Hooper, a man of eminent zeal, learning, and piety, along with many other worthy and conscientious ministers, deemed these canonical habits altogether inconsistent with the simplicity of Christian worship, and decidedly resisted their imposition. This excellent man having been appointed to the bishopric of Gloucester, declined it for two reasons; first, the form of the oath of supremacy, which he called foul and impious, and which required him to swear " by God, by the Saints, and by the Holy Ghost." He considered that God only ought to be appealed to in an oath, since He only knows the thoughts of men; and the excellent and amiable young king, being convinced of this, struck out the words with his own pen. But Hooper's second scruple about the habits was not so easily overcome. He contended that they had no sanction in scripture; that they were the inventions of antichrist, in the most corrupt ages; that they had been abused to superstition and idolatry; and consequently to retain them was to agree with antichrist, to mislead the people, and to oppose the simplicity of the religion of Christ. The king and council seemed disposed to concede the point; but several of the bishops vehemently opposed. With a most strange perverseness, they would not allow him to decline either the habits or the bishopric. Sincere as was his *nolo episcopari*,[*] they resolutely refused his plea, in spite of himself he must be a bishop; and he must be consecrated to the office in the habits which the law imposed, and which he regarded with loathing and abhorrence. To force his compliance, he was served with an order in council, first to silence him, and then to confine him to his own house, but he was afterwards imprisoned for several months in the Fleet. The difficulty was at length got rid of by a slight compromise. We have detailed this circumstance at greater length than so brief and compressed a narrative might seem to allow, for the purpose of showing our young readers how early and how vigorously the spirit of Protestant nonconformity began to work, and that it was in point of fact coeval with the existence of the church of England herself—that they began to exist and to act almost together. It will shew also how inconsistent were the practices of the rulers of the reformed church with their own professed principles. To justify their separation from Rome, they pleaded the sufficiency of the holy scriptures as the rule of faith, and the right of private judgment in the concerns of religion; but when they came to shape and organize their own church, and to legislate for its constitution, orders, and services, they admitted other laws and authorities than the word of God, and they allowed no liberty of thinking and acting to those who differed from them, but insisted upon a passive obedience and an absolute uniformity. In the reign of Queen Elizabeth, this tyrannical and domineering spirit was pushed to still greater lengths, and made fearful havoc amongst those who scrupled compliance with any of the forms which the Queen and her advisers thought proper to introduce. They whose consciences were tender, and who wished for further reformation, were nicknamed *Puritans*; and though they were amongst the best, the ablest, and most learned men, and the most powerful preachers of those times, yet because they could not submit to popish habits and ceremonies, nor take oaths which they deemed unlawful, and subversive of the authority and power of Christ, as the Head of the Church, they were not suffered to hold their livings, and were harrassed with every species of persecution. Year by year, great numbers of them were deprived. Some left the kingdom; others retired into private life; and many were received by the nobility and gentry, who favoured their opinions, and valued their learning and piety, into their houses, in the capacity of chaplains and tutors. But there were also many who did not break off from the church, who held private associations, and met frequently for the purpose of concerting measures to effect a further reform, and to restore the discipline of the first ages. In all such movements as these, our readers may perceive the stirring impulse of that spirit which gives the character to Protestant dissent, and which spurns at all human impositions in the concerns of a divine religion, and recognises no other authority than that of Christ himself in his own church, and no other rule for his government than the holy scriptures, which contain " the law of his house."—*Protestant Magazine.*

HIGHLAND INDORSATION.—The following words were actually written upon a bill some time ago, at Oban, by a person belonging to one of the isles:—" Pay the within to the bearer; and if you fail to do so, may the L—— have mercy on your bones, for I will have none. JOHN MCLEAN."

---

[*] The words put into the mouth of the person to be consecrated, and which mean, " I have no wish, or I am unwilling, to be made a bishop."

YOUNG NICK AND THE BOSUN.

When Lord Durham went out on the secret or humbug mission to Russia last year, it may be remembered that a fulsome account of the visit made by the Emperor to the officers of the Talavera appeared in the London papers, to the disgust of almost every one that read it. Nicholas, who like his predecessor Alexander is a great pretender to religion, nay, we believe, to Christianity—yes, to Christianity!—the cruel extirpator of the Poles! among his other pious declarations and fulsome flatteries, informed the crew, who, we suspect, very nearly made fools of themselves, that he prayed for their brave Sailor King every night! One of the crew of the Talavera, or some one for him, sent the following amusing letter to the *Times*, as a true statement and running commentary, on "t'other swab's yarn of a swab."

H. M. Ship Talavera, off Plymouth, Aug. 17, 1832.

Mr. Editor,—I makes so bold as to trouble you with these here pothooks and hangers o' mine, 'cause me and my messmates is given for to understand as you're a real trump, and does the thing what's right, without caring a —— for nobody. Now if so be as you're that there sort o' chap,—why then you don't want no palaver; and so here I goes at once to the pint.

You must know that as soon as we got in this here latitude, off comes the bum-boat; and Bumboat Bet—who's always been mighty civil to me ever since I pressed her lubberly husband (what had the luck to have his head blowed off in his country's sarvice afore he'd been at sea three weeks)—hands up to me a Lunnun newspaper. The old girl takes that there way o' showing her gratitude to me, 'cause she knows the ship's company looks up to Ben Bowling for all the news—as well them as can't, as them as won't read them there printed logs as you chaps in Lunnun keep about every thing in the whole universal world.

Well, I unfurls the log, and the very first thing as I claps my precious eyes upon was a gallows long yarn about the Emp'ror o' Rushy and we o' the Talavera; and shiver my timbers if I shall ever forget it—no, not if I live as long as the *Wandering Jew* of you landsmen, or the *Flying Dutchman* as haunts us sailors. It struck me all of a heap like—and well it might,—for I'll take my fidavy that I looks upon that there rigmarole as a disgrace to the British navy, and a downright insult to the crew o' the Talavera. My eyes!—If you had but a' seen what a rag it put all my messmates into! Howsumdever, they all pulled together, and agreed, that, seeing as how I was the best scholar among 'em, I should tip you a yarn in the name o' the ship's company—just for to shew that we arn't such a set o' —— spooneys as that there lying log makes out.

Concerning o' that there swab as wrote t'other yarn, I shall only say as how I considers such a snivelling son of a gun as beneath the notice o' Ben Bowling,—unless so be the Captain should order him what he desarves,—which, according to my reckoning, is a round dozen at least; and if the Captain does,—my precious eyes!—how I shall bless the wind that blowed me into the birth of Bosun to the Talavera. I'm pretty sartin, though, he'll turn out to be none of our crew. Perhaps it was one of those land lubbers we took out to wait on the embassy,—or a marine may be,—one o' the young 'uns. I'd hardly believe the First Lord of the Admiralty himself, if he told me that any British seaman would go for to disgrace the sarvice in such a way as that there. But he be ——; he arn't worth talking about.

Well, then, now for my yarn about this here Emp'ror o' Rushy, and the Talavera.

There can't be no manner o' doubt that the Rushy Old Nick, as my messmates call him, did come aboard to look at the Talavera; and —— odd it would have been if he had'nt, considering the difference between she and the craft what his Board o' Admiralty turns out. The swab as wrote t'other yarn makes a fuss about Old Nick drinking "the King's health," and saying "God save the King;" but I'll just ask you whether that there was any more nor manners in Nick, considering as how he was lushing at his Majesty's expense, on board one of his Majesty's ships? Sartinly not; but I suppose the swab arn't been used to people as knows what manners is. There was a —— sight o' palaver between Nick and the Captain, which I did'nt pay no attention to, though I stuck quite close to 'em, as I considered I was obligated in duty for to do. And 'cause why? Why 'cause I did'nt think as how a chap, whose family afore him, as well as himself, had been so long in the habit o' prigging from their neighbours the very ground they walked upon, was very likely to have heard o' such a thing as the 8th commandment. So, as you may suppose, I kept a —— sharp look-out arter him.

I'm very sorry to say the swab's right when he says that Nick would shake hands with all the officers,—from the Captain down to the Mids.; and when I saw that there sort o' grappling going on, I thought upon the poor murdered Poles, and thank'd my luck I was no officer, but only a Bosun. I should as soon ha' thought o' tippling my daddle to his namesake,—I meant t'other old Nick, what cruises about in the latitude of Davy's locker.

Well, you see, as we'd shew'd Nick all he wanted to see—and as he couldn't be such a fool as not to know well enough, that his craft warn't worth looking at arter our's—why he couldn't well do no less than give us a sight o' some sort or other, if it was only by way of swap in good manners. This was how he come for to shew us them there lobsters of his going through their *devilutions*, as the swab who wrote t'other yarn calls 'em. I was as much gravelled as the swab at that there gimcrackery, and so I can't tell no more than him how the lobsters did it. Don't go for to suppose though, as how I was such a —— spooney as to be humbugged like the swab, when them there *knoutty* slaves in uniform called Old Nick "*father,*" and said "*we'll live and die for you.*" No, no. Do you think all that there warn't down upon their orders?—do you think the drill sergeant had'nt told 'em to make that there speech for some —— fool in our company, to carry home with him and tell to the marines? Lord love you,—there was no more earnest in it than in anything you ever seed from the one-shilling gallery in a play-house. None but the swab was gammoned by that there clumsy tack. I'll warrant.

Concerning Old Nick going to prayers in that there sort of a way, as the swab describes—why, that there's a serious subject, and so now just look you, friend, while I takes in a reef or two, and scuds along steady. The swab takes Ben Bowling a little out of his latitude in all that there fine spatter of his about the priest, and the altar, and "tears a glistening," and the "beggars description;" so for fear I should make a false report about his craft, and what sail she carries, I'll just make so bold as to scatch you out his own very words:—

" The Emperor alighted from his carriage with his head uncovered, and the priest stood forward and offered up to God the evening prayer, which was responded by the assembled thousands. Need a British sailor blush to acknowledged that he was affected, even to tears, at such a scene? No! I saw the tears glistening in the eyes of more than one of my brother officers; and I gloried to see, that though they could not join in the language, yet they joined in spirit in the worship of the king of kings, the one God and Father of us all. I assure you the effect was so grand, so awful! so sublime! that it beggars description." * * *

Now I arn't neither a Jew, nor a Heathen, nor a Turk, nor no other Dissenter whatsumdever, but a rale right arnest Church-of-England man, as our chaplin is ready to sartify,—and a good Christian, too, I hope, though I never sailed along o' Admiral Gambier (*nor never wants*) nor never piped all hands to morning sarvace on board the floating chapel off Wapping (*nor never will.*) But what I says is this here—namely,—that that there patter of the swab don't do him no credit as a Christian or a British seaman; and if he means to say as how any of our crew joined in the prayer, why we denies it plump. I don't blush to own that

I was very near piping my eye at this here part of the concarn; but 'cause why? 'cause when I looked round me at all them there thousands o' soldiers, the poor Poles came into my mind again: and when I thought o' them, I couldn't help recollecting how cruelly they'd been sarved out, and how their wives and young 'uns has been clapped into limbo, or sent to the Rushy Bot'ny-bay in Siberia, by that there very chap as was then axing mercy for himself, though, like a pirate as he is, he never show'd no mercy to them there poor creatura. These here were the things as was running in my head, and instead o' keeping a look-out arter what the swab says was so grand, and all the rest on it, why I was saying to myself, says I, " Ben Bowling, Ben, my boy, how much would you take to stand in the shoes o' that there Emp'ror?" " Not all the gould o' the Ingies," says I,—ay, and I say it again now, and all my messmates say ditto to it—and we means it.

Now, this here's the plain truth o' all that there yarn, what some snivelling swab has been pitching so strong in the log as Bum-boat Bet brought us; and what we just axes o' you is to shore this here yarn o' mine into *your* log; 'cause, you see, as there's been a swab fool enough to write t'other yarn, me and my messmates begins for to think as how some o' you poor simple landsmen may believe that a crew of British seamen have been humbugged into taking a liking for such a land shark as that there Rushy Old Nick. Bah! the swab might as well ha' said that every man in the ship had married a she bear, and desarted into the Rushy sarvice. I don't think Marm Bruin or the Rushy sarvice would have any great catch if the swab was to do both;—but the sooner he does, the more agreeable it will be to the crew of the Talavera, and particularly to your humble sarvant at command,

BEN BOWLING.
Bosun of H. M. S. Talavera.

P.S. My messmates and I consider as how our Captain Brown ought to take up this here mater; 'cause, if what the swab says of him is the rale truth, why, blow me tight, it Captain arn't *done* Brown. Howsumdever, that there's the Captain's look out.

. We have sent Mr. Bowling's letter to " *Susan* " as directed; and put the order for the shag and pigtail into the two-penny post.—*Times.*

SINGULAR SUPERSTITION.

In Dr. Russell's Nubia and Abyssinia, we find an account of the following superstition, which the author, with great probability, imputes to the true cause,—a juggle kept up by cunning, interested craftsmen, to preserve their lucrative mystery from interlopers:—" Of the superstitions of the Abyssinians none is more remarkable than the prejudice which expels from society, and even from the holy sacrament, all men who work in iron or pottery. One reason for this strange aversion is, that such artisans are considered even by their nearest neighbours as possessing the supernatural power of changing themselves into hyenas and other ravenous beasts. All convulsions or hysterical disorders which are as common in Abyssinia as in other parts of the world, are attributed to the evil eye of these unfortunate workmen. They are known by the name of *Buda*; and many marvellous exploits are attributed to them, not only by the vulgar, but even by individuals of superior intelligence. Though excluded from the more sacred rites of Christianity, they still profess great respect for religion, and are not surpassed by any of their countrymen in the strictness with which they keep Lent and the other stated fasts. Pearce readily acknowledges his inability to trace this whimsical notion to any plausible source. Mr. Coffin, who was in the country at the same time, and who appears to have enjoyed the gift of deeper reflection than his comrade, is equally puzzled, and regards some of the facts which came immediately under his own knowledge as almost inexplicable. The Budas are distinguished, it seems, from other classes by a peculiarly formed gold ring, worn by the whole race, and which kind of ring he declares he has frequently seen in the ears of hyenas that have been shot, caught in traps, or speared by himself; but in what way these ornaments came to be so strangely applied, he declares that, after taking considerable pains to investigate the subject, he had been utterly unable to discover. Besides the power that these persons are supposed to have of transforming themselves into wild animals, they are imagined, as we have already stated, to possess the still more dangerous attribute of inflicting disease by directing a malign look towards their victim. So fully convinced, too, are the Abyssinians that these unhappy blacksmiths are in the habit of rifling the graves in their character of hyenas, that no one will venture to eat what is called *quanter*, or dried meat, in their houses, though they have not the smallest repugnance to sit down with them to a repast of *raw flesh*, where the killing of the cow or sheep before their eyes dissipates at once the horrible illusion. Mr. Coffin relates a story respecting one of these Budas, the circumstance of which fell under his own observation. It happened that among his servants he had hired an individual of this gifted class, who, one evening when it was still perfectly light, came to request leave of absence till the next morning. His petition was immediately granted, and the young man withdrew; but scarcely had the master turned round to his other servants, when some of them called out, pointing in the direction the Buda had taken, " Look! look! he is turning himself into a hyena!" Mr. Coffin instantly looked round, and though he certainly did not witness the transformation, the youth had vanished, and he saw a large hyena running off at the distance of about a hundred paces. This happened in an open plain, where there was not a bush or tree to intercept the view. The absentee returned in the morning, and was attacked by his companions on the subject of his metamorphosis, which, according to the usual practice of his brethren, he rather affected to countenance than to deny. From the latter circumstance it has been inferred that the belief in this most extravagant superstition is, owing to some motive or other, encouraged by the Budas themselves. The trades they follow are the most lucrative in the country; and as these are exclusively in the hands of particular families, in whom the right of exercising them descends from father to son, it is not improbable that, in order to prevent all competition, they may choose to envelop their persons and their craft in a certain degree of mystery. With this view, it may be presumed, they place the ornaments described above in the ears either of such young hyenas as they may happen to catch, or of old ones, which are frequently entrapped, and then dismiss them to the wilderness with their newly-acquired embellishments. This idea was stated to Mr. Coffin, who thought the conjecture more than probable, and promised on his return to the country to do all in his power to ascertain the fact. He remarked at the same time, that he had never seen a very young hyena with the gold ring in its ear.

Church Reform with a Vengeance.—The following ludicrous, at the same time scandalous scene was enacted in the church at Tarbes, in the Hautes Pyrennees, a few weeks ago. The late bishop, from some cause, interdicted the entrance into the cathedral of an elderly priest named Claverie, who, however, was much beloved by the people, or probably by the ancient devout ladies of the place, to whom the disgrace of their favourite pastor was a great mortification. On the death of the bishop it was hoped he would be restored to his functions, but the chapter thought fit to continue his exclusion from the sacred offices. This over-excited the zeal of his female admirers, and one day, after vespers, the doors of the church were suddenly closed, and the disappointed devotees fell upon the canons, grand vicars, and other ecclesiastics, beat them with their umbrellas, rolled them upon the ground, tore their vestments from their shoulders, and then turned them out bareheaded, and almost devoid of decent covering, to make the best of their way home. The victorious Amazons then affixed a placard on the church door declaring they would acknowledge no one for their pastor but their beloved curé Claverie.

SCRAPS.

A WORD IN SEASON.—People, though hot themselves, forget how much more hot their suffering furred or feathered friends must be in dry, sultry weather. Let your dog or dogs have free access to water, and opportunities of swimming in the sea, lake, streams, or pools. They may at least have air and dew in almost every situation. Let your horse have plenty of water, and the frequent means, with your help, of moistening his mouth. Do not expose birds in cages to the sun without a shade over the cage of baize or fresh turf, or green branches, or the fresh weeds run to seed, which birds delight to pick. Nor should you forget your fishes kept in glasses. The former animals are called " dumb creatures," yet they may make loud intimations of distress. The latter are the " mute creation," and thus more helpless when subjected to man's immediate control.

FOX HUNTING.

FORTY men in scarlet coats, with the button of the club, and forty hounds are matched against one fox. It is not a fair fight—the proposed victim derives no advantages from his superiority in prowess, over any one of his pursuers, human or quadrupedal. He can save his life alone by speed, or cunning. The human portion of his enemies incur no risk of being tickled by his glibsome tooth—they war on him on horses sixteen hands high. They have "taken the field" to see the fun—not to join in the strife. They stand aloof, and yell, while their four-footed ministers, by force of superior numbers slaughter the enemy. They have not the plea of necessity—their dinners are ordered—they don't hunt him to eat him—their sublime ambition is—to obtain his *brush*. The savages of America scalp their victims—those of this country are content with tails. Imagine for a moment, how pathetically honourable gentlemen would protest against a similar course, were it possible, being taken against themselves. What would Captain Berkeley say, if, while prowling peaceably near his noble friend's residence in the sister country, he were to be held hotly in chase by an imported pack of gigantic Pongos, Chimpansés, and orang-outangs, followed by fifty giraffes and emus, as enthusiastic spectators of his agony and bootless speed! What consolation would it be to him, that, in an account of the recreation, all proper honours would be awarded to his exertions to get off—that (shifting the scene with Shaksperian celerity, to allow us the benefit of an extent or two in point) among the exalted portion of his pursuers—the Giraffes and Emus, " bellows to mend was the order of the day;" that " he crossed the road near Tetbury, and sinking the wind through Cherrington Park, was headed near Hampton; being thus obliged to vary his direction to Cowcomb, he took a peep at Lord Bathurst's woods; and after having occasioned the most beautiful hunting ever heard of—gratifying at once the oldest and the best—he was run into and killed at Charford—thereby making good his distance of sixteen miles,—that the fair Diana in the hunt, who has honoured every cover in the county with her smiles—our amiable and accomplished townswoman, Mrs John Co d—accepted his brush?" What would Captain Berkeley think of this? Let him bless his stars—if he should have any—that Providence has made him a Member of Parliament, and not a fox.—*Monthly Mag.*

ANTICIPATIONS OF STEAM-CARRIAGES ON RAILWAYS. —Speaking of the railroads for small coal-carriages, in the neighbourhood of our coal-mines and foundries, Southey, in his Letters of Don Manuel Espriella, written in the year 1807, says,—" It has been recommended by speculative men that they should be universally introduced; and a hope is held out that some future time this will be done, and all carriages drawn along by the action of steam-engines, erected at proper distances. If this be at present one of the dreams of philosophy, it is a philosophy by which trade and manufactures would be benefited, and money saved; and the dream therefore may probably one day be accomplished."

VERSES TO A LONELY LOCH IN THE HIGHLANDS.

Lone lake among the mountains,
  Soft gleaming on my sight,
Thou type of peace and gentleness,
  I hail thee with delight.

I love that placid beauty,
  So pure, so bright and still,—
From every airt the wind can blow
  Thou hast a sheltering hill.—

Sweet lake! thou'rt Nature's mirror,—
  The sky, the hills and trees
Are shadowed on thy bosom
  Unruffled by a breeze.

I see the fish disporting
  Amid thy waters clear;
But the heron and the otter
  Are the only fishers here.

Yon castle by thine outlet,
  Fast mouldering to decay,
Shows how the feeble works of man
  Pass silently away!

Man's boasted works soon perish—
  The wonders of his hand;
But the mighty works of Nature
  Imperishable stand.

Still from thy depths of crystal
  The river on doth flow,
And the hills are round thee as they stood
  A thousand years ago!

And from the scene around thee,
  Tho' barren, rude, and stern,
The unsophisticated heart,
  A moral here may learn.

And other eyes shall view thee,
  And thy mild beauty own,
When I am with my fathers,
  To rest eternal gone.

W. G.

CONTENTS OF NO. XLVIII.

Old Scottish Holidays,
External Comfort and Domestic Accommodation of the People
Natural History,
The True Balm,
COLUMN FOR THE LADIES.—Free Trade—A Scotch D'un.
  Helen Oliver. Love at First Sight; and a Love Letter,
THE STORY TELLER.—The Ten Years of Silvio Pellico,
Ventriloquism,
Household of the Tyrolese Peasant,
The Dwelling of Hofer,
Brief History of the Established Church of England,
Origin of English Nonconformity,
Young Nick and the Bosun,
Church Reform with a Vengeance,
Singular Superstition,
SCRAPS.—A Word in Season—Anticipations of Steam Carriages and Railways—Verses to a Lonely Loch in the Highlands.

EDINBURGH: Printed by and for JOHN JOHNSTONE, Square.—Published by JOHN ANDERSON, Jun., Bridge Street, Edinburgh; by JOHN MACLEOD, Booksellers, Glasgow; and sold by all Booksellers and Cheap Periodicals.

THE Schoolmaster,

AND
EDINBURGH WEEKLY MAGAZINE.
CONDUCTED BY JOHN JOHNSTONE.

THE SCHOOLMASTER IS ABROAD.—LORD BROUGHAM.

No. 48.—Vol. II.   SATURDAY, JUNE 29, 1833.   Price Three-Halfpence.

TO THE READERS OF THE SCHOOLMASTER.
NEW SERIES.

This Number of The Schoolmaster completes the Second Volume, which, with the Political Register, consists of 516 pages. It concludes the work as a Weekly Series.

In making our acknowledgments for the kindness and encouragement with which The Schoolmaster has been received, we beg to announce an important alteration in the mode of publication, which has been adopted after mature consideration of what is best calculated to make a work of this nature of the greatest utility and permanent interest.

The Schoolmaster will henceforth appear as a Monthly Periodical only, and under the more direct name of JOHNSTONE'S EDINBURGH MAGAZINE. The first Number, for August, will appear upon the 31st July, and will be sold at Eightpence. Considering the size and quality of the Paper, and the quantity of Letterpress contained in each Number, it will be found the cheapest Monthly Magazine that has ever appeared in Britain.

Johnstone's Edinburgh Magazine will regularly appear in all the towns of Scotland, England, and Ireland upon the same day as the other Magazines; and at the price of *Eightpence*, will contain nearly as much letterpress as the Three-Shillings-and-Sixpence Magazines. It is intended to supply, as far as is compatible with the limits of such a work, a Magazine and Review, with a Register of Public Events and Remarkable Domestic Occurrences; Lists of Births, Marriages, and Deaths, &c. &c. One reason for the change, is the belief that these objects may be better effected in a Monthly work, which admits of greater scope in balancing and arrangement, than in detached sheets appearing weekly. But the most powerful motive is the decided preference which the public have shown to The Schoolmaster in *Monthly Parts*, and the certainty that we could make these Parts better were they published as a Monthly Periodical.

Without the prospect of larger sales than any monthly periodical has ever yet obtained, it would have been rash and ill-advised to hazard this important change in the form of publication. But having explained the motives which induce the alteration, we throw ourselves with confidence upon the intelligence and kindness of all who, valuing useful and humanising knowledge, wish to encourage the diffusion of cheap literature.

We have watched "the stream of tendency," and boldly launch our bark upon the headlong current, only entreating the good offices of the friendly bystanders, in helping us off the Shoals, and keeping us steady while we shoot the first Rapids. We hope to obtain as Monthly Subscribers for Johnstone's Edinburgh Magazine, all those who have hitherto been weekly purchasers of our Schoolmaster; and trust that the nature of our undertaking, and the character and standing it has already attained, will secure for the New Series of The Schoolmaster the patronage of those who agree with us in the estimate formed of the advantages of which a Monthly Work is susceptible when compared with a Weekly Sheet. These advantages will, however, be of no avail without corresponding zeal, ability, and industry in improving them. We desire rather to be tried by performance, than credited on professions.

Johnstone's Edinburgh Magazine will be published by Mr William Tait, Bookseller, 78, Prince's Street, by whom all Booksellers and dealers in the country will be supplied with the utmost punctuality, in the same parcels which convey his own Magazine.—The Booksellers in Edinburgh may be supplied with this work, either by Mr Tait, 78, Prince's Street, or by Mr John Anderson, Jun., 55, North Bridge Street.

⁎ *Prospectuses* of Johnstone's Edinburgh Magazine will be issued immediately, giving a detailed view of the plan of the work.

19, St. James's Square, 29th June, 1833.

BANKRUPTS.

The whole system of the bankrupt laws is framed with a lenity which, contemplating only the honest bankrupt, is abused in the most scandalous manner by the fraudulent. We believe it to be a fully ascertained fact, that one-half of the bankruptcies are fraudulent. There are, of course, shades of fraud, from the wholesale robber of the public, who makes himself a bankrupt for the direct purpose of conveying away the property of his creditors, and enabling himself to start breast-high in the world again, down to the petty-larceny bankrupt, who secretes but a portion of the property of others, and in the general wreck makes a privy purse for himself. But, if the sternest hand of the law grasped the majority of bankrupts, it would do good national service. As the matter now stands, the commissioners may have been harsh beyond the general custom. But where is the tradesman who seems to be the worse for his bankruptcy? In a multitude of instances bankruptcy is clearly the high road to fortune. The merchant whom we saw in the Gazette yesterday, we see to-morrow in a showy establishment, perhaps with a villa, certainly with a gig, and probably a barouche, or probably a couple of them. He has slipped through the fingers of the law, that ought to have been round his neck; and he has now nothing to do but to reinforce his servants' hall, order in his pipe of wine, and throw open his doors in ———— Place, or ———— Square, to his wife's select party of five hundred friends. His next step is a borough; or, if he feel popularly inclined, a canvass for the county. We then find him flourishing for a year or two in directorships, the management of companies, the proprietorship of canals, and the projectorship of every new-fangled contrivance for the robbery of every man who is silly enough to confide in him. Then comes the crush again. The man of plums and prosperity again sinks into the Gazette, again comes out of it clear as the new-born babe, again sets up the counting-house, the curricle, the villa, and leads a life of impudent defiance of the common honesty of mankind, and insolent indulgence in every luxury that fraud can supply; until the bloated feeder on public credulity and legal weakness goes in pomp to a grave, to which he ought to have been ushered by the gallows.

Of the many and endless ways in which fraudulent traders prey upon the public. The following is a relation of one, we believe, very frequently practised. It is retailed in a Periodical work:—"A firm in the Manchester line, which had made some money, (I will not say how,) resided next door to a large carpet warehouse, the proprietor of which offered the trade and premises to his neighbours for a certain sum. They in consequence entered into a negotiation for the sale and purchase of the same. The firm, which was situated not far from Bow Church, suggested, that as the carpet dealer had a good trade and credit, (although on the eve of showing embarrassment to his creditors,) he should make a journey among the carpet manufacturers, and purchase as largely as he could, and fill the warehouse with goods, which they (the firm) would take, after deducting twenty per cent. from the invoice prices, together with the other goods on the premises at the same rate; reminding the carpet warehouseman, that, as his circumstances would constrain him to make a compromise with his creditors, the ready cash which would be paid by them would enable him to offer prompt payment of a small dividend—an offer more likely to be acceded to by his creditors, than a larger composition in prospective. By this arrangement the firm realized upwards of 1700*l*., the carpet-man paid 5s. in the pound to his creditors, and thus both parties were gainers, at the expense of honest men." This statement, which is founded on facts, needs no comment.

This is only one sample of many others of daily occurrence in our virtuous metropolis. Abuses of every description, when about to be exposed, meet with opposition. The principals in this transaction, aware of my knowledge of their proceedings, in this and many similar doings, have had the audacity to threaten any who may cause the *exposé*. As this is not a place to indulge in digression, all I shall say for the present is, that every thing on city business will be out in due time. I should have stated, that an eminent silversmith had some participation in this nefarious transaction, and that the Manchester warehousemen are at this moment prosperously carrying on their trade, on the premises of the carpet-dealer so *respectably obtained*. How is it that these receivers of stolen goods are not *more exposed*? Is it because they all become rich, and, by the modern gauge of respectability, are influential, and company for gentlemen?

' Men are what they name not to themselves,
And trust not to each other.' "

THE AMERICAN INDIANS IN CANADA—MISSIONARY LABOURS.

MR. MAGRATH, to whose letters from Canada we alluded in a late number, has given a very pleasing and full account of an Indian village of the Mississaguas, which will, we think, interest our readers.

"The village," he says, "consists, as well as I recollect, of twenty-four houses, inhabited by about two hundred and thirty individuals. It is situated on a high bank of the river Credit, where what is termed the *Pond* of that river begins.

"On the flat immediately below the present village, the Mississagua Indians, and other tribes, were in the habit of encamping for the purpose of salmon-fishing, during the season.

"Their camp, at that time, presented the most heterogeneous mass of dirty wigwams, surrounded by heaps of fish bones, offals of deer, and putrid filth of every description. How different is its *present* appearance! laid out in beautiful enclosures, well cultivated by their own hands, and having borne, in the last harvest, the finest crop of Indian corn ever raised in this country. It is gratifying to perceive that, instead of the drunken and savage brawls which disgraced even their beastly orgies, happiness and peace have sprung up among them; good order, sobriety, and cleanliness in house and person. I think I hear you say,—how was this surprising change effected? I answer, by the Methodist clergy. Although I do not agree with them in politics, or as to church government, it is but fair to allow them every credit for their zealous exertions amongst the Indians, which have been most successful in several instances, as well at Rice Lake and Simcoe Settlements, as here.

"In passing through our village at an early hour, I have often heard the morning hymn sung by an Indian family, in a manner that would surprise a European, and with greater sweetness than in many churches. Their demeanour is moral, their attendance at divine worship regular, and their observance of the church service grave and attentive.

"There are three chiefs resident in the village—Lawyer, Crane, and Jones.—My friend, Lawyer, is certainly a very intelligent and clever fellow, but in council they complain of his being sometimes a little *long-winded*. Crane is a fine specimen of a true Indian. He stands six feet four inches in height, with a lofty carriage that would do credit to a guardsman, and 'fearlessly looks heaven in the face.'

"Mr. Jones, happening to dine with us in company with some friends, surprised the new comers of the party, by the perfect ease, and unembarrassed manners, with which he acquitted himself in all the modern attentions of the table, conversing naturally with both ladies and gentlemen, on light or graver subjects, with equal address.

"They were also struck with his dress, the full costume of an Indian chief—a coat (made in form of a shirt) of deer skin, dressed in the Indian method without the hair, of a golden colour, and as soft as glove leather.

"On the front, and behind the shoulders, are lappets ten inches deep, beautifully punched in various patterns, like coarse lace or net-work—all seams (instead of being sewed) fastened with narrow stripes of skin cut into fringe for that purpose.

"The head dress—a valuable silk, or fine cotton handkerchief, in turban form; worn by some tribes with feathers. Leggins, reaching to the hip, and ornamented on the sides, serve as trousers. Mocassins, curiously ornamented with porcupine quills, complete the drawing-room habit; whilst the tomahawk, scalping knife, tobacco pouch, and rifle, equip the Indian for the woods. As he becomes civilized silver ornaments, previously worn in profusion, are laid aside, and the European dress of his white brother is adopted.

"I have frequently met John Brandt, the Mohawk chief, at the Government house, and in the first circles. He attends all our assemblies, and dances quadrilles much better than many of Garboi's pupils. His manners are perfectly those of a gentleman, and our ladies have no objection to 'trip it on the light fantastic toe,' with a thoroughbred Indian chief.

"John Brandt was returned as member for his county, to the last parliament, and made some excellent speeches in the house; but, on a petition, lost his seat, by some trifling informality in the Election.*

"As amongst the 'untutored' Indians are to be found all the worst traits of uncivilized life; so are there to be met, especially among the chiefs, noble specimens of dignified and rational character; and those that I have mentioned are not singular in this respect.

"But whoever desires the true and characteristic picture of the Indian, must read the inimitable portraitures of Cooper in his unrivalled novels. The accuracy of their delineation I had the means of putting to the test.

"On a hunting excursion through the woods for some weeks, with two Indians who carried my baggage, and a few others who joined me, happening to have 'The last of the Mohicans' in my pack, I read extracts to my party at night, around the fire; and the astonishment they expressed at a white man being able to describe their native scenes and characters so precisely, was a greater compliment to the talented author than any I can pay him; for the Indian seldom forgoes his self-possession, or evinces feelings of pleasure or pain by words or gesture. On this occasion they were highly pleased, and expressed themselves so. One night, when encamped on the shore of Lake Huron, our *literary* party was interrupted by the sound of many paddles, and we soon discovered that some new arrival had taken place. On going out, I perceived eleven canoes discharging their crews opposite our encampment. In less than twenty minutes there were fires blazing in all directions, and the cooking going on as if they had been there as many weeks. Shortly after, two chiefs came forward, shook hands with me in the free and friendly manner an Indian generally does, and, at my request, supped with me. They had come to that part of the lake to take white fish, which is the best fish; and, there, most abundant.

"Next morning I had a noble dish sent me as a present, by the Chief, Wagna; and, on his signifying that they would take to the fishing-ground at noon, I purchased one of their bark canoes and paddles, for five dollars, and joined the *Fleet*.

"Will you believe it? I never passed a more agreeable time in my life, than when surrounded by this party, at times 150 in number; nearly one hundred miles from any settlement, and I myself the only white man (not *very white* either) in the entire camp. My tent was pitched on a green bank, about twenty yards from the wigwams, with its door to the lake, into which I plunged every morning from my bed, and either joined my companions during the day, in hauling the net; or, taking my rifle to a deer pass, never failed of sport, as some obliging Indians were always ready to surround a portion of the bush, and drive the game in the direction where I stood. This was generally at the entrance of the valley; and, with two or three good marksmen below me, we seldom returned *lightly* laden. I always beat the Indians at a running shot, at which they are not expert; but, whatever might be our individual success, all we shot went into the general stock; and, whether I went out or not, my table, or rather my mat, was regularly furnished with fish, duck, or venison, in profusion. With what pleasure I look forward to another such excursion! At night the shore was brilliant with the fishing lights in the canoes; and I had to walk but twenty paces into mine, to enjoy as fine sport as the most enthusiastic fisherman could desire.

"After a residence of six weeks with my red brothers, I prepared to return homeward, and felt much regret at parting from them, so marked was their kindness to me, and so good-natured their attention. When I fixed the day, every one had something to give; and had I accepted half what they presented, two canoes would have been insufficient to carry away the provisions. I embarked at five in the morning. When three miles distant from shore, the sudden swell of the lake, and black appearance of the sky foreboding storm, I directed the men at the paddles to turn back, and, before we had got within a mile of shore, the waves (as is often the case in those lakes) running mountain high, we made every possible exertion, but very little way.

"The wind was right ahead, the canoe small, and freighted with six persons—but she rode it like a duck. We at length reached the land, nearly exhausted, and I was welcomed back with as much cordiality as if my absence had been for weeks instead of hours. Had we not returned we must have been inevitably lost; in a short time, however, I was safely lodged again in my old quarters.

"About dusk, a canoe, with two squaws on board, was observed struggling to make the shore. On inquiry, I found they belonged to our camp, had been about a mile along the coast, for some fish which had been left behind, and were blown out as they were rounding a head-land close to us. We could observe them throwing out the fish, and the group on shore had hopes of their arriving in safety; none, however, attempted to go to their assistance, knowing that, in such a gale, both canoes would be endangered, as, by a sudden collision they would be upset or staved to pieces; they, nevertheless, looked on with deep anxiety, when, as the little vessel was on the summit of a wave, the foremost paddle snapt close to the hand of the squaw that plied it, and disappeared. She lay down in the canoe, and her comrade could do no more than prevent it from turning. In a moment a canoe was launched by two men, one of them the husband of her who still worked that which was in distress; they were making some progress to her relief, when it became so dark that we lost sight of both. The shouts of the two men to discover where the canoe lay were feebly answered by the unhappy women, and then all was still.

"I had a fire lighted on the beach, as a beacon to direct them, in the excessive darkness of the night.—The group around it formed the finest subject for a painter that can be imagined.—There we stood, about eighty in number, gazing at the flame, blown by the wind in all directions, the light thrown strongly, but fitfully, on the features and figures of the Indians, but not a word was spoken—at length the grating sound of paddles reached our ears; the light of the immense fire flashed on the approaching canoe, and the persons it contained—the two enterprizing men, accompanied by *one female!*—Poor Segenauck,—the wife of an attached husband, who hoped and tried to save her, —was no more!

"They landed—not a question was asked—all retired to their wigwams in solemn silence. In a few minutes I was alone.

"The manly and dignified manner in which this melancholy occurrence was received—the solemn, but silent tribute of regret paid by all to the memory of one of their tribe thus suddenly called away, gave me a still more favourable impression of my Indian companions, and sent me to bed, with the storm in my ears, and its fatal result occupying my waking and sleeping thoughts till morning.—I learned, then, from Segenauck's husband, that as soon as the canoes came near each other, the squaw at the head, taking hold of the gunwale of that in which he was, cautiously stept in, forgetting, in the hurry and danger of the moment, to keep hold of that she had left, which, losing the weight in front, rose at once out of the water, was blown round and upset, without a possibility, on his part, of saving his unfortunate helpmate.

"The storm ceased in the night; the morning was very fine. I left the camp at break-of-day, and was soon out of sight of my kind and hospitable companions. I quitted them with a degree of regret, in which, I have since found, I was not singular. In Moore's Life of Lord Edward Fitzgerald, we find that unfortunate nobleman expressing himself to the same effect; and I have heard many say, that those who were long in the habit of Indian society, were generally fascinated by it."

---

* This chief is since dead.

GHOSTS BY WAGGERY.

Dr. Plot, in his Natural History of Oxfordshire, relates a marvellous story of a ghost which Sir Walter Scott has employed in one of his romances. Soon after the murder of King Charles I. a commission was appointed to survey the King's house at Woodstock, with the manor, park, woods, and other demesnes belonging to that manor. One Collins, under a feigned name, hired himself as secretary to the commissioners, who, upon the 13th October, 1649, met, and took up their residence in the King's own rooms. His Majesty's bed-chamber they made their kitchen, the council-hall their pantry, and the presence-chamber was the place where they met for the despatch of business. His Majesty's dining-room they made their wood-yard, and stored it with the wood of the famous royal oak from the High Park, which, that nothing might be left with the name of King about it, they had dug up by the roots, and split and bundled up into faggots for their firing. Things being thus prepared, they sat on the 16th for the despatch of business; and, in the midst of their first debate, there entered a large *black dog* (as they thought) which made a dreadful howling, overturned two or three of their chairs, and then crept under a bed and vanished. This gave them the greater surprise, as the doors were kept constantly locked, so that no real dog could get in or out. The next day their surprise was increased, when sitting at dinner in a lower room, they heard plainly the noise of persons walking over their heads, though they well knew the doors were all locked, and there could be nobody there. Presently after, they heard also all the wood of the King's oak brought by parcels from the dining-room, and thrown with great violence into the presence-chamber, as also all the chairs, stools, tables, and other furniture forcibly hurled about the room; their papers, containing the minutes of their transactions, were torn, and the ink-glass broken. When all this noise had ceased, Giles Sharp, their secretary, proposed to enter first into these rooms; and, in presence o. the commissioners, from whom he received the key, he opened the doors, and found the wood spread about the room, the chairs tossed about and broken, the papers torn, but not the least track of any human creature, nor the least reason to suspect one, as the doors were all fast, and the keys in the custody of the commissioners. It was therefore unanimously agreed that the power that did this mischief must have entered at the key-hole. The night following, Sharp, the secretary, with two of the commissioners' servants, as they were in bed in the same room, which room was contiguous to that where the commissioners lay, had their beds' feet lifted up so much higher than their heads, that they expected to have their necks broken, and then they were let fall at once with so much violence as shook the whole house, and more than ever terrified the commissioners. On the night of the 19th, as they were all in bed n the same room for greater safety, and lights burning by them, the candles in an instant went out with a sulphurous smell, and that moment many trenchers of wood were hurled about the room, which next morning were found to be the same their honours had eaten out of the day before, which were all removed from the pantry, though not a lock was found opened in the whole house. The next night they fared still worse; the candles went out as before, the curtains of their honours' beds were rattled to and fro with great violence, they received many cruel blows and bruises by eight great pewter dishes, and a number of wooden trenchers being thrown on their beds, which, being heaved off, were heard rolling about the room, though in the morning none of these were to be seen.

The next night the keeper of the king's house and his dog lay in the commissioners' room, and then they had no disturbance. But on the night of the 22d, though the dog lay in the room as before, yet the candles went out, a number of brickbats fell from the chimney into the room, the dog howled piteously, their bed-clothes were all stripped off, and their terror increased. On the 24th they thought all the wood of the king's oak was violently thrown down by their bed-sides; they counted 64 billets that fell, and some hit and shook the beds in which they lay; but in the morning none was found there, nor had the door been opened where the billet-wood was kept. The next night the candles were put out, the curtains rattled, and a dreadful crack like thunder was heard; and one of the servants running in haste, thinking his master was killed, found three dozen of trenchers laid smoothly under the quilt by him. But all this was nothing to what succeeded afterwards. The 29th, about midnight, the candles went out, something walked majestically through the room, and opened and shut the windows; great stones were thrown violently into the room, some of which fell on the beds, others on the floor; and at about a quarter after one, a noise was heard as of forty cannon discharged together, and again repeated at about eight minutes' interval. This alarmed and raised all the neighbourhood, who coming into their honours' room, gathered up the great stones, fourscore in number, and laid them by in the corner of a field, where, in Dr. Plot's time, they were to be seen. This noise, like the discharge of cannon, was heard over the country for several miles round. During these noises the commissioners and their servants gave one another over for lost, and cried out for help; and Giles Sharp, snatching up a sword, had well nigh killed one of their honours, mistaking him for the spirit, as he came in his shirt from his own room to theirs. While they were together the noise was continued, and part of the tiling of the house was stripped off, and all the windows of an upper room were taken away with it. On the 30th, at midnight, something walked into the chamber treading like a bear; it walked many times about, then threw the warming-pan violently on the floor; at the same time a large quantity of broken glass, accompanied with great stones and horse bones, came pouring into the room with uncommon force. On the 1st of November the most dreadful scene of all ensued. Candles in every part of the room were lighted up, and a great fire made; at midnight, the candles all yet burning, a noise like the bursting of a cannon was heard in the room, and the burning billets were tossed about by it even into their honours' beds, who called Giles and his companions to their relief, otherwise the house had been burnt to the ground; about an hour after the candles went out as usual, the crack as of many cannon was heard, and many pailfuls of green stinking water were thrown upon their honours' beds, great stones were also thrown in as before, the bed-curtains and bedsteads torn and broken, the windows shattered, and the whole neighbourhood alarmed with the most dreadful noises; nay, the very rabbit-stealers, that were abroad that night in the warren, were so terrified that they fled for fear, and left their ferrets behind them. One of their honours this night spoke, and, *in the name of God, asked what it was, and why it disturbed them so?* No answer was given to this; but the noise ceased for a while, when the spirit came again; and, as they all agreed, *brought with it seven devils worse than itself.* One of the servants now lighted a large candle, and set it in the doorway between the two chambers, to see what passed; and as he watched it, he plainly saw a hoof striking the candle and candlestick into the middle of the room, and afterwards, making three scrapes over the snuff, scraped it out. Upon this the same person was so bold as to draw a sword, but he had scarce got it out when he felt another invisible hand holding it too, and pulling it from him, and at length prevailing, struck him so violently on the head with the pummel, that he fell down for dead with the blow. At this instant was heard another burst like the discharge of the broadside of a ship of war, and at the interval of a minute or two between each, no less than nineteen such discharges. These shook the house so violently that they expected every moment it would fall upon their heads. The neighbours being all alarmed, flocked to the house in great numbers, and all joined in prayer and psalm-singing; during which the noise continued in the other rooms, and the discharge of cannons was heard as from without, though no visible agent was seen to discharge them. But what was the most alarming of all, and put an end to their proceedings effectually, happened the next day, as they were all at dinner, when a paper, in which they had signed a mutual agreement to reserve a part of the premises out of the general survey, and afterwards to share it equally among themselves, (which paper they had hid for the present, under the earth in a pot in one corner of the room, and in which an orange tree grew,) was consumed in a wonderful manner by the earth's taking fire with which the pot was filled, and burning violently with a blue flame, and an intolerable stench, so that they were all driven out of the house, to which they could never be again prevailed upon to return.

PICTURE OF A LONDON QUARTER AND MORAL EDUCATION OF THE PEOPLE.

THE *Morning Chronicle* should take away its old motto about holding up a mirror of fashion, and exhibiting the "body of the time, its form and pressure," from the top of the Court Circular, and place it over the Police Reports. There is no such exact records of the true state of our population as the moving drama of Bow Street. Sir Frederick Roe's theatre is a more accurate mirror of the age than the patent one hard by. Foreigners who are just now coming over in shoals, all intent upon circulating in the higher regions of society, would learn far more of England from the police-offices than Almack's or the Duke of Devonshire's. The view is certainly not quite so flattering; on the contrary, it exhibits our masses in a very painful state of degradation. But to know the truth is the first step to a cure, and to attempt to hide the fact is the folly which Horace condemns—that of concealing a cancerous shame. We are speaking not merely of the crime of the metropolis, but its vice: it is not merely robbery and violence which come before the magistrate, but domestic broils, quarrels, drunkenness, &c. &c., in the course of which is displayed incidentally the moral condition of the party concerned. Poverty has much to do with the aggravation of the evil, but it is scarcely at the bottom of it. Immorality of every description makes even competency miserable. We observe that among the lower classes of the town—the inhabitants of those quarters where what are called respectable people never set foot, but by the merest accident—parties living together are very commonly not married, and have no shame on the subject; that both sexes indulge in porter and gin to the very extent of their means, usually spending the greater part of their casual earnings in one long debauch,—out of this state arise quarrels, bruises, and fights, not a tithe of which ever appear at the offices. While such scenes are going on in one apartment of the house, perhaps the cellar, the rest of the building is occupied with the thief and the prostitute, a domestic pair, or the old hag of a receiver of stolen goods, and perhaps opposite to her some dealer in flash paper or counterfeit coin. Mixed up with these is probably the hard-working lady's shoemaker, or the poor man's cobbler with his wife, and perhaps a family of eight or ten children playing up and down the stairs with the promiscuous progeny of the neighbourhood. The street itself—and of such there are many hundreds—is one rag fair. The receivers of stolen goods expose bottles and old clothes; the rubbish shop placards "Dripping bought here," as a trap to cookmaids; the cobbler protrudes from his cellar huge draymen's shoes; the green-grocer exhibits his cabbages and potatoes; the middle of the street is occupied with ragged brats at play, pregnant women with arms a-kimbo, and in high disputation, with, perhaps, some half-a-dozen fellows in their shirt-sleeves and pipes in their mouths, gazing listlessly from the various glassless windows above them. The corner of this precious retreat is sure to have a substantial gin-shop at its corner; and its well-worn swinging doors betray the constancy of its custom. Lower down in the street is the flash-house—the snug public, where crimes are concocted and concealed. In such holes as these, also, are the academies of theft, where burglary is taught on scientific principles—where effigies, hung with wires and bells, are put up to exemplify the practice of pocket-picking.

Before the committee of the House of Commons, a convict was examined; among other questions (and the whole evidence is very curious) he was asked—

"Did you ever hear the prisoners at the Hulks speak of the places of resort in London—their flash-houses?"—"Yes; I have heard them speak of the Cross-Keys, in Belton Street. There is a terrible flash-house in our neighbourhood."

"Where is that?"—"That is the Cock, in the corner of Cock Court; and the worst house going is the Shades, for thieves. I have heard them talk on board the Hulks, and in Newgate, too, about the Shades, dividing their spoils there of a night."

"Where is the Shades?"—"In the Strand, against Waterloo Bridge. You can go down there at twelve o'clock at night, and stay there all the next day, if you like. There are men and women and girls, and all down there, and they go out thieving. I have heard them say, 'We went out some days, and made L.9 or L.10, and then went down there, and called for pints of gin, and regulated our money there.'"

"The Shades, you say, is in the Strand, against Waterloo Bridge?"—"Yes; you can see Waterloo Bridge as you stand in the Shades; it is like a bar that you go in at—something like the front of the Adelphi, and you go down stairs; —there is a cellar under ground,—a very large place, I have heard some of them say,—and there is dancing, and singing, and dominoes, and cards played there."

It may surprise many that places of this description are found to exist in the very centre of our wealth, and comfort, and respectability; but the fact is, people are blind to that which has long existed before their eyes. The streets, courts, alleys, lanes—such as we have given a general description of above—are at the back-doors of the best houses in town; they crowd the neighbourhood of streets of the greatest thoroughfare. Many who read what has been said above will fancy that we are speaking of some modern Alsatia—the Petticoat Lane of Whitechapel, the Rosemary Lane of the Minories, or the Seven Dials of sevenfold infamy; if we had done so, it would have been bad enough, for all these places, St Giles's to boot, are in the heart of London; but more unsuspected places than these are worse—both the north and south sides of the Strand and Fleet Street, for instance, are doubly lined with infamy.

But there is something still more shocking than the existence of the mere holes and corners of thieves and prostitutes in the heart of London. It is this—that the abodes of the industrious and the quasi-honest are mixed up with them, and that without pain to either party. On the same staircase dwells the drayman and the burglar; their children play together, and their quasi-wives interchange their hospitalities and their conversation. In such quarters it is as little a disgrace to be a robber as it was in the time of Homer. When a man is apprehended, he "gets into trouble," and a sympathy for him spreads. The drayman, the waterman, the cab-driver, the shoemaker, is not a robber, because he is in work. The boundaries of morality amongst this large class are utterly confounded; at this present moment the only moral distinction they make is that of rich and poor. Perhaps this great and overgrown city contains within its bosom a quarter of a million of such *doctrinaires*. As long as all is quiet, they go on sprawling in their own mud; if, however, times of a hot turbulence were to break out, the sections of St Antoine never poured forth such a race of monsters—monsters, we mean, of a bad education. Is nothing to be done for the suppression of crime—for the separation of the habitual honest and the habitual dishonest—for the moral education of the people?—*New Monthly Magazine.*

KING JAMES'S CLASP KNIFE.—The word "Jockteleg," which is still Scotch for a clasp knife, was of unknown etymology till a knife was found with the inscription, "Jacques de Liege," who was a famous cutler, and supplied Scotland with clasp knifes. It is said of James VI., that to puzzle his courtiers in England, he one day said to his stable boy!—"Callan, ha'e, there's thretty pennies, gae wa' and buy me a jockteleg; an' gin ye byd, I'll gang to the bougars o' the house, an' tak' a cabar and reesle your riggin wi' 't." That is, "Boy! here is thirty pence, go and buy me a clasp knife; and if you delay, I shall go to the roof of the house, and take a rafter and thrash your back with it."—*Jamieson's Dict. in Voce.*

USEFUL NOTICES.

IMPROVEMENT OF HEATH LAND AND CULTIVATION OF POTATOES.

Waste lands are admirably adapted to the growth of potatoes. The east side of Dilhornheath was cultivated with potatoes after the heath and gorse had rotted, and being mixed with lime and compost, the crop of potatoes was so abundant as to admit many waggon loads being sent in the winter into the vicinity of the potteries, about six miles from Dilhorn, which afforded a seasonable supply to many thousand manufacturers. The quantity was not only immense, but the quality of potatoes was in so high repute, that the Dilhorn potatoes produced 2d. per bushel above the market price. Many instances have occurred of great success in raising potatoes on waste land, but the shortest way is to pare and burn. Two day-labourers gave a guinea for an acre of waste land to plant with potatoes; they pared and burnt it by moonlight after their daily labour, spread the ashes, and paid for ploughing them in; the crop proved so good, and the price of potatoes so high, that they shared L.40 between them, besides receiving a sufficient quantity of potatoes for their families. A peat bog on waste land was drained, then pared and burnt; the ashes immediately regularly spread, and the land ploughed in twelve-furrow ridges (it could not be ploughed in narrow ones from toughness;) the furrows were hacked and levelled with heavy hoes, then planted across the ridges with potatoes in rows, and, owing to the large quantity of ashes, produced an abundant crop. The land afterwards produced, the two next years, two very strong crops of oats in succession; it was then well limed, and clean fallowed, and is now a good meadow.—*Pitt's History of Staffordshire.*

A Simple and Useful Invention.—" A blacksmith of this city, named Pontisick, has, to the great comfort of his neighbours, especially the rich, successfully practised a very simple contrivance to diminish, in a remarkable degree, the loud noise caused by the percussion of the hammer on the anvil. It is merely to suspend a piece of iron chain to one of the horns of the anvil, which carries off a great portion of the acute sound usually produced. Sig. Gaudenzio Vicinia, of Asso, in the province of Como, has, however, introduced an improvement on this contrivance, by the addition of a spring fixed in the basis of the anvil, which, keeping the chain stretched, diminishes the sound in a much greater degree; and it is equally easy to remove the ring of the chain from the horn of the anvil, if needful by a mere blow of the hammer."—Milan, 20th Feb.

EARLY DAYS OF LORD BROUGHAM.

In 1805, Brougham, Eyre, and myself found ourselves the tenants of two contiguous lodgings, in Craven Street, where the same intercourse was kept up until the divergence of our several pursuits partially interrupted, and, finally, suspended it. Cobbett, I think, on one occasion, took it into his head to pack Brougham, and a whole party of Edinburgh reviewers, as adventurers, in the same bottom of a Berwick smack, for London. Whether the fact be so or not, that mode of travelling was, certainly, no disgrace then, any more than it is now. Some of the first families in Scotland thought it no degradation, even in those steamless times, to prefer it to their private carriage. Brougham was then distinguished for the same gift of sarcasm which has since made him the terror of the senate; yet he was one of the best-humoured fellows breathing, full of fun and frolic. He has been blamed, in Parliament, for the malignant abuse of his power; and, it must be owned, the excesses into which conscious superiority have now and then led him, were often in a very equivocal state. But what was he to do with so useful a gift? It was his main weapon, offensive and defensive. Had he laid it aside, his victories, though equally assured, would perhaps have been long delayed, and harder earned. When all argument had failed, how often have we seen him escape from defeat, by the aid of this ready and unsparing auxiliary! To turn the laugh against an adversary, was itself a victory. Whether he succeeded or failed in his logic, the witnesses of the contest were equally impresse with the superior power of the nimble tactitian. In his youth, as at the present day, the encyclopædic range of his information left him without a competitor. His industry knew no bounds, and his mind was as versatile in its power of alternate application and relaxation, as, at other times, remarkable for an untiring perseverance.—*Sir Arthur Brookes Faulkner.*

Reward of Authors.—Byron's poems produced upwards of fifteen thousand pounds. A prudent man would have turned them to still better account. Surely, one thousand pounds per annum produced in the time which the composition occupied can scarcely be ill-usage on the part of the public. How many authors are there of infinitely greater national utility whose works would not have kept them from starving! Mr. Bentham, to wit. The writings of Walter Scott are not of one-hundreth part of importance of the writings of Mr. Bentham, yet how highly have they been paid! The public is willing to pay more for amusement than for instruction. The principal value of the works of Scott is, that they have helped, as beautiful pictures, to humanize the people, and have enticed many to read who otherwise would have shunned books. But of sound morality there is scarce a jot to be found in the whole collection. It was not to be expected. The mind of Scott was warped in early youth, and it could not be expected that wisdom would be the result. But, notwithstanding the large sums of money which were paid for his copyrights, Scott lived in difficulties and died in debt. Why was this? The sin which besets most authors beset him also. He deemed that ostentation was dignity, and he wasted his means before he had earned them. The desire to vie with the feudal puppets whom he worshipped led him into expenses which his means would not warrant, and he paid the penalty by dying before his natural period, tortured in mind, and overwrought in body. But let it never be forgotten, that he acted the part of an honest man in striving to redeem his errors and to accomplish the payment of his debts. The principle of moral honesty was strong within him, and has shed a halo round his memory which will not lightly pass away. It were well if his fate might prove a beacon to those who might come after him. But it is the part of the public to enforce the penalty, by witholding their countenance from those who possessing the talents necessary to elevate the perceptions of their fellows, only hold forth the example of moral degradation.—*Foss's Repository.*

EXTRAORDINARY SURGICAL OPERATION.

The most surprising and most honourable operation of surgery ever performed, is, without any contradiction that executed by M. Richerand, by taking away a part of the ribs and of the pleura. The patient was himself a medical man, and not ignorant of the danger he ran in this operation being had recourse to, but he also knew that his disorder was otherwise incurable. He was attacked with a cancer on the internal surface of the ribs and of the pleura, which continually produced enormous fungosities, that had been in vain attempted to be repressed by the actual cautery. As soon as he had made the opening, the air rushing into the chest occasioned the first day great suffering and distressing shortness of breath; the surgeon could touch and see the heart through the pericardium, which was as transparent as glass, and could assure himself of the total insensibility of both. Much serous fluid flowed from the wound, as long as it remained open, but it filled up slowly by means of adhesion of the lung with the pericardium. And the fleshy granulations that were formed in it. At length the patient got so well, that on the 27th day after the operation, he could not resist the desire of going to the Medical School to see the fragments of the ribs that had been taken from him, and in three or four days afterwards he returned home, and went about his ordinary business.—The success of M. Richerand is the more important because it will authorize in other cases, enterprizes which, according to received opinions, would appear impossible; and we shall be less afraid of penetrating into the interior of the chest. M. Richerand even hopes, that by opening the pericardium itself, and using proper injections, we may cure a disease that has hitherto been always fatal, the dropsy of that cavity.—*Thomson's Annals.*

MEDICAL SELECTIONS.
No. VII.

ESTIMATE OF DIFFERENT DESCRIPTIONS OF FOOD IN REGARD TO NUTRIMENT.

BEEF and mutton possess more nutritient properties than any other kind of meat, particularly the prime parts. Pork ranks next to beef and mutton, as it regards usefulness; although there are few persons who can digest it. There is the same objection to veal, notwithstanding it is a very lean kind of meat, and does not offend the stomach on the score of richness; but to render it palatable, it is always obliged to be overdone.

As to dried meat, of whatever kind it may be, we must regard it as of little or no use in contributing to our nourishment. To persons who are subject to indigestion, salt and dried meat is highly improper; yet we often find persons whetting a bad appetite with a slice of ham, which if it do not digest properly, must render the case worse subsequently; sausages of every kind are liable to the same objections, but especially those which are dried, such as Bologna sausages. This last article of luxury is of all others the most difficult to be solved by the stomach.

Poultry stands next to flesh among our edible articles, but is less easy of digestion, particularly geese and ducks. People after eating goose, frequently take a glass of brandy to assist digestion; this is a habit that ought to be deprecated, as it has a tendency to induce too great action on the part of the stomach, which weakens it subsequently. Wild fowls are particularly well fitted for debilitated stomachs; they are more nutritious than the domestic kinds.

The first of vegetable food is wheaten bread, when made of the best flour; it is well termed the "staff of life," for it imparts almost as much nourishing matter as meat, and has this advantage over the other—when disease attacks the system it does not augment heat.

The vegetable that comes nearest to bread, in point of utility, is the potato; that extensively-useful root abounds with nutritious matter, and is capable not only of sustaining life, but of imparting to the body great vigour and robustness, even under great bodily exertion. To prove this, we need only look to Ireland, where a great portion of people live exclusively upon it the greatest part of the year. Potatoes are well fitted for persons who have a weak digestion, provided they be of the best quality, i. e. mealy.

Soups and broths to debilitated stomachs, prove very detrimental. The best mode then of taking this kind of diet, is to soak toast or stale bread in it until it be absorbed. Dyspeptics should avoid soups or broths on every occasion.

Beef-tea has long been held as the most eligible spoon diet for the sick, provided the stomach be not called upon to digest it without its being previously soaked in bread. Persons, however, who suffer by indigestion, should be careful not to live too much on slop diet.

Spirituous liquors possess no property of imparting strength to our system, except it be that transitory feeling of vigour which they give to the nerves. It may be sometimes observed, that the beer-bibber grows stout from his beverage, and this is certainly the case, but it is not the result of healthy action in the system; for out of this corpulency disease frequently arises. The reason why a person gets fat with porter-drinking is this: the sedative property of hops, and the employment, perhaps, of deleterious drugs, causes the blood to flow through the veins with less velocity, which gives it a disposition to form fat; but we generally find that persons so bloated are subject to several dangerous diseases.

But the practice of taking drams after dinner should never be indulged in, as it has a tendency to produce an incurable weakness of stomach.

Every kind of wine labours under the same objection as the most common fermented liquors, for they all have a disposition to turn acid on the stomach. Foreign wines, indeed, have a less tendency to do so, but still all kinds of wine are improper in every stage of indigestion, and unless they can be abstained from, there can be no prospect of cure held out. The best beverage is either spring or distilled water.

Cheese, although extracted from milk, possesses a very little nutritient principle. There is a popular error prevalent with respect to this article of food, that ought to be corrected. Butter, which is produced from the same material, is not half so objectionable; as, when it is eaten in moderation, it is both easily digested and nourishing.

All kinds of pudding are more or less difficult to digest, and especially those which are made of flour and suet; or which consist of batter; in short, things of this kind should never be eaten by persons who are subject to indigestion. All pottages are likewise unfit for weak stomachs, and principally gruel. But the habitual use of gruel operates in a way that few would imagine; it produces eruptions on the skin, which nearly resembles itch.

Tea has been deprecated by some writers, and to the use of it is ascribed the prevalence of stomach complaints; but a beverage cannot be so detrimental when it yields such refreshment. It is of great consequence to drink unadulterated teas, for the things that are sometimes mixed with them, will certainly disorder the stomach.

There is an opinion prevalent, that eating "a little and often," is the best mode of bringing a stomach into tone, and of imparting nourishment; but this is quite a popular error; nothing is more likely to derange that organ than calling it into action so often; in short, the practice would impair the best digestion.

Various are the sauces and pickles which epicurism hath invented for the purpose of giving zest to an already pampered appetite. Most of these are incompatible with healthy digestion. Dyspeptics should confine themselves to the two most universal sauces in this country, viz., mustard and salt; the latter of these is a valuable assistant to the stomach when it is masticated with the food.

Dyspeptics should take every meal very deliberately, for fast eating will frequently bring on an oppression of the stomach after it.

One of the principal means of preserving health, is sound and refreshing sleep. A bad night's rest is sometimes produced by the bed-room not being properly ventilated during the day, especially if there has not been a fire kept in it. Beds should also be well-aired, and not be made up too soon. Some people sleep too much, which is productive of bad consequences in dyspeptic cases.

Walking is most beneficial to the system; it should be daily taken, to the extent of at least two miles, and even more. Carriage exercise is but a poor substitute. Riding on horseback is nearly as good as foot exercise.—*Medical Adviser.*

EFFECTS OF DIFFERENT TEMPERATURES UPON THE BODY, AND UPON HEALTH.

WHEN the air is warm and dry it excites a most agreeable sensation in the lungs, and in every part of the body. It increases the power or function of every organ, and health is perfect; this is observed in a dry spring after a cold and moist winter; but when the weather is intensely hot, and persons exposed to the burning sun in the tropics, they often drop dead suddenly from apoplexy; this has happened even in France and Spain during very hot summers. All the functions, as breathing, digestion, &c., are diminished and oppressed. There is danger of mortification of wounds and ulcers, bowel complaints, fever, hysteria, epilepsy, &c. Persons labouring under consumption have been advised to live in warm climates; but many physicians suppose that the acceleration of the breathing and pulse caused by the hot air in summer, only hurry the sufferers to a more speedy death. The change of habitation from a cold climate to a warm one in winter is highly advisable, though it is now believed that the southern coasts of this country are as eligible as foreign climes for our consumptive patients.—A cold and moist atmosphere produces debilitating effects on man and animals; a cold and dry air is not so injurious; it braces the nerves and is favourable to health, although it sometimes induces determinations of blood to the head, chest, and abdomen, and causes inflammations in the organs of their cavities.—*Ten Minutes' Advice on Coughs and Colds.*

REMEDIES FOR CONSUMPTION.

Mr. Murray in his work on consumption says,—" We need scarcely enumerate the multiplicity of remedies and medicines employed in this complaint, as all have disappeared like 'wave succeeding wave.' Some of them have been of a very extraordinary kind, such as vipers' broth and snails, livefrogs also have been allowed to pop down the throat—Salvadore's method seems to have attracted greater attention than it deserves. He directed his patients to climb an eminence quickly till they were out of breath and bathed in sweat, and then increase it before a large fire, change their clothes, and live on meat and wine. Gregory prescribed Spanish liquorice in the form of pills. Hoffman wrote a volume on the virtues of asses' milk; even riding on this special animal has been supposed curative. A cow's shed has also been proposed as a proper place of repose for the consumptive. The vapour of tar and prussic acid have all been tried in vain, and digitalis or foxglove has been employed with very questionable success. Dr. Fothergill's opinion, as a forlorn hope, was 'country air, with rest, asses' milk, and riding daily.' We believe Dr. Bacon exhibited minute doses of ipecacuanha, sufficient to excite nausea; and among the patients in the Vallois, according to Dr. Tissot, warm baths have been frequently resorted to; some pass the greater part of their time in the water. At Baden, Dr. Marcard has seen invalids sit, four or five hours in the bath, and the patient sit up to the chin in water. The most recent plans and proposals we have heard of are those of Dr. Myddleton, of Exeter, who employs mixed powders in a box, the chief ingredients of which we understood to be hemlock. A circular having a rotary motion, as in the blooming of cucumbers, by turning a winch, volatalizes, or temporarily suspends these powders in the atmosphere; this is done with a view to encrust the lungs. We have heard, however, of no instance of cure. We know nothing of Mr. St. John Long's practice, which has been severely criticised and ridiculed. The *lobelia inflata* is said, however, to be his remedy. This plant is stated in the 'Flora Americana' to be common in the woods of America. Dr. Cotteran has invented an apparatus for conveying the vapour of chloride of lime into the lungs, acting as a kind of inhaler. The well-known effect of chlorides on morbidly-affected parts, and the expectoration of tubercles detached by its influence in certain recent experiments, promise some interesting results in this disease. The committees of the Royal Academies of Science and of Medicine have made a favourable report of it. Sir Charles Scudamore has also announced a work on the efficacy of chlorine, iodine, &c., in consumption. We first promulgated, at this Surry Institution, in 1818, the probability of aërial chlorine proving curative in pulmonary consumption." This is all that is at present known on the subject of cure; but Mr. Murray thus sums up the measures of precaution against the attacks of this dreadful disease: these are, " Early rising, free perspiration, a pure atmosphere, and agreeable temperature; light food and of easy digestion, gentle exercise, warm clothing to prevent the effects of sudden alteration of temperature, and condensation of perspiration on the skin,—these will generally prove effectual."

ALLITERATION — THE BATTLE OF THE PIGS.—A Latin poem was published at Niverstadt in 1669, consisting of three hundred and two hexameter lines, comprising one thousand five hundred words, which, with the title-page, author's name, &c., began every one with the letter P. It is called " Pugna porcorum, per Petrum Porcinum, paraclesis pro potatore." It takes for its motto—

" Perlege porcorum pulcherrima prœlia, Potor,
    Potando poteris placidam proferre poesin."

It commenced with the line—

" Plaudite porcelli, porcorum pigra propago."

The whole is correct Latin, the verse perfect in its quantities, and the fable conducted on the best rules of Aristotle. It is, perhaps, the greatest literary curiosity in existence.

ALPINE STRAWBERRIES.—By picking off their first and second show of flower stems, their bearing season will be delayed till August, and continue through the two following months.

COLUMN FOR THE LADIES.

PRAISE OF WOMEN,

BY RANDOLPH, AN OLD POET.

He is a parricide to his mother's name,
And with an impious hand murders her fame,
That wrongs the praise of women; that dares write
Libels on saints, or with foul ink requite
The milk they lent us. Better sex! command
To your defence my more religious hand,
At word, or pen. Yours was the nobler birth,
For you of man were made, man but of earth—
The son of dust: and though your sin did breed
His fall, again you raised him in your seed.
Adam in sleep a gainful loss sustained,
That for one rib a better self regained;
Who, had he not your blest creation seen,
An anchorite in paradise had been.
Why in this work did the creation rest,
But that eternal Providence thought you best
Of all his six days' labour? Beasts should do
Homage to man, but man should wait on you.
You are of comelier sight, of daintier touch,
A tender flesh, a colour bright, and such
As Parians see in marble; skin more fair,
More glorious head, and far more glorious hair;
Eyes full of grace and quickness, purer roses
Blush in your cheeks, a milder white composes
Your stately fronts; your breath, more sweet than his,
Breathes spice, and nectar drops at every kiss.
Your skins are smooth; bristles on theirs do grow
Like quills of porcupine, rough wools doth flow
O'er all their faces; you approach more near
The form of angels,—they like beasts appear.
If then in bodies where the souls do dwell,
You better us, do then our souls excel?
No; we in souls equal perfection see,
There can in them nor male nor female be.
Boast we of knowledge? you have more than we;
You were the first ventured to pluck the tree;
And that more rhetoric in your tongues doth lie,
Let him dispute against that dares deny
Your least commands, and not persuaded be,
With Samson's strength and David's piety,
To be your willing captive. Virtue, sure,
Were blind as fortune, should she choose the poor
Rough cottage, man, to live in, and despise
To dwell in you, the stately edifice.
Thus you are proved the better sex, and we
Must all repent that, in our pedigree,
We choose the father's name, where, should we take
The mother's, a more honoured blood, 't would make
Our generation safe and certain be,
And I'd believe some faith in heraldry.
Thus, perfect creatures! if detraction rise
Against your sex, dispute but with your eyes,
Your hand, your lip, your brow,—there will be sent
So subtle and so strong an argument,
Will teach the stoic his affection, too,
And call the cynic from his tub to woo.
Thus mustering up your beauteous troops, go on,
The fairest is the valiant Amazon.

THE STORY TELLER.

DUNCAN AND HIS DOG.

BY THE ETTRICK SHEPHERD.

DUNCAN CAMPBELL came from the Highlands, when six years of age, to live with an old maiden aunt in Edinburgh, and attend the school. His mother was dead; but his father had supplied her place, by marrying his house keeper. Duncan did not trouble himself about these matters, nor indeed about any other matters, save a black foal of his father's, and a large sagacious colley, named Oscar which belonged to one of the shepherds. There being no other boy save Duncan about the house, Oscar and he were constant companions—with his garter tied round Oscar's neck, and a piece of deal tied to his big bushy tail, Duncan would often lead him about the green, pleased with the idea that he was conducting a horse and cart. Oscar submitted to all this with great cheerfulness, but whenever Duncan mounted in order to ride on him, he found means instantly to unhorse him, either by galloping, or rolling himself on the green. When Duncan threatened him, he looked submissive and licked his face and hands; when he corrected him with the whip, he cowered at his feet;—matters were soon made up. Oscar would lodge nowhere during the night but at the door of the room where his young friend slept, and wo be to the man or woman who ventured to enter it at untimely hours.

When Duncan left his native home he thought not of his father, nor any of the servants. He was fond of the ride and some supposed that he even scarcely thought of the black foal; but when he saw Oscar standing looking him ruefully in the face, the tears immediately blinded both his eyes. He caught him around the neck, hugged and kissed him. "Good-by, Oscar," said he blubbering; "good-by, God bless you, my bonny Oscar." Duncan mounted before a servant, and rode away. Oscar still followed at a distance, until he reached the top of the hill; he then sat down and howled. Duncan cried till his little heart was like to burst. —"What ails you?" said the servant. "I will never see my poor honest Oscar again," said Duncan.

Duncan staid a year in Edinburgh, but he did not make great progress in learning. He did not approve highly of attending the school, and his aunt was too indulgent to compel his attendance. She grew extremely ill one day,—the maids attended her closely, and never regarded Duncan He was an additional charge to them; and they never loved him, but used him harshly. It was now with great difficulty that he could obtain either meat or drink. In a few days after his aunt was taken ill she died.—All was in confusion, and poor Duncan was like to perish with hunger;—he could find no person in the house, but hearing a noise in his aunt's chamber he went in; and beheld them dressing the corpse of his kind relation;—it was enough. Duncan was horrified beyond what mortal breast was able to endure; he hasted down the stair, and ran along the High Street, and South Bridge, as fast as his feet could carry him, crying incessantly all the way. He would not have entered that house again if the world had been offered him as a reward. Some people stopped him, in order to ask what was the matter; but he could only answer them by exclaiming, "O! dear! O! dear!" and, struggling till he got free, held on his course; careless whither he went, provided he got far enough from the horrid scene he had so lately witnessed. Some have supposed, and I believe Duncan has been heard to confess, that he then imagined he was running straight for the Highlands, but mistook the direction. However that was, he continued his course until he came to a place where two ways met, a little south of Grange Toll. Here he sat down, and his frenzied passion subsided into a soft melancholy;—he cried no more, but sighed excessively; fixed his eyes on the ground, and made some strokes in the dust with his finger.

A sight just then appeared, which somewhat cheered, or at least interested his heavy and forlorn heart,—it was a large drove of Highland cattle. They were the only acquaintances that Duncan had seen for a twelvemonth, and a tender feeling of joy, mixed with regret, thrilled his heart at the sight of their white horns and broad dew-laps. As the van passed him, he thought their looks were particularly gruff and sullen; he soon perceived the cause :—they were all in the hands of Englishmen; poor exiles, like himself, going far away to be killed and eaten, and would never see the Highland hills again!

When they were all gone by, Duncan looked after them, and wept anew; but his attention was suddenly called away to something that softly touched his feet. He looked hastily about—it was a poor, hungry, lame dog, squatted on the ground, licking his feet, and manifesting the most extravagant joy. Gracious heaven! it was his own beloved and faithful Oscar! starved, emaciated, and so crippled that he was scarcely able to walk! He was now doomed to be the slave of a Yorkshire peasant, (who it seems had either bought or stolen him at Falkirk,) the generosity and benevolence of whose feelings, were as inferior to those of Oscar, as Oscar was inferior to him in strength and power. It is impossible to conceive a more tender meeting than this was, but Duncan soon observed that hunger and misery were painted in his friend's looks, which again pierced his heart with feelings unfelt before. I have not a crumb to give you my poor Oscar! said he, I have not a crumb to eat myself, but I am not so ill as you are. The peasant whistled aloud,—Oscar well knew the sound, and clinging to the boy's bosom, leaned his head upon his thigh, and looked in his face, as if saying, "O Duncan! protect me from yon ruffian." The whistle was repeated, accompanied by a loud and surly call; Oscar trembled, but fearing to disobey, he limped away reluctantly after his unfeeling master, who, observing him to linger and look back, imagined he wanted to effect his escape, and came running back to meet him. Oscar cowered to the earth in the most submissive and imploring manner, but the peasant laid hold of him by the ear, and, uttering many imprecations, struck him with a thick staff till he lay senseless at his feet.

Every possible circumstance seemed combined to wound the feelings of poor Duncan, but this unmerited barbarity shocked him most of all. He hastened to the scene of action, weeping bitterly, and telling the man that he was a cruel brute, and that if ever he himself grew a big man he would certainly kill him. He held up his favourite's head that he might recover his breath, and the man, knowing that he could do little without his dog, waited patiently to see what would be the issue. The animal recovered, and stammered away at the heels of his tyrant without daring to look behind him. Duncan stood still, but kept his eyes eagerly fixed upon Oscar, and the farther he went from him, the more strong his desire grew to follow him. He looked the other way, but all there was to him a blank,—he had no desire to stand where he was, so he followed Oscar and the drove of cattle.

The cattle were weary and went slowly, and Duncan, getting a little goad in his hand, assisted the men greatly in driving them. One of the drivers gave him a penny, another gave him twopence; and the lad who had the charge of the drove, observing how active and pliable he was, and how far he had accompanied him on the way, gave him sixpence; this was a treasure to Duncan, who being extremely hungry, bought three penny rolls as he passed through a town; one of these he ate himself another he gave to Oscar, and the third he carried below his arm in case of farther necessity. He drove on all the day, and at night the cattle rested upon a height, which, by his description, seems to have been that between Gala Water and Middleton. Duncan went off at a side, in company with Oscar, to eat his roll, and taking shelter behind an old earthen wall, they shared their dry meal most lovingly between them. Ere it was quite finished, Duncan, being fatigued, dropped into a profound sleep, out of which he did not awake until the next morning was far advanced. Englishmen cattle, and Oscar, all were gone! Duncan found himself alone on a wild height, in what country or kingdom he knew not. He sat for some time in a callous stupor, rubbing his eyes and scratching his head; but quite irresolute what was farther necessary for him to do, until he was agreeably surprised by the arrival of Oscar, who (though he had gone at his master's call in the morning,) had found means to escape and seek the retreat of his young friend and benefactor. Duncan, without reflecting on the consequences, rejoiced in the event, and thought of nothing else than furthering his escape from the ruthless tyrant who now claimed him. For this purpose he conceived it would be best to leave the road, and accordingly he crossed it, in order to go over a waste moor to the westward. He had not got forty paces from the road, until he beheld the enraged Englishman running towards him without his coat, and having his staff heaved over his shoulder, Duncan's heart fainted within him, knowing it was all over with Oscar, and most likely with himself. The peasant seemed not to have observed them, as he was running and rather looking the other way; and as Duncan quickly lost sight of him in a hollow place that lay between them, he crept into a bush of heath and took Oscar in his bosom. The heath was so long, that it almost closed above them. The man had observed from whence the dog started in the morning, and hastened to the place, expecting to find him with the sleeping boy beyond the old earthen dike. He found the nest but the birds were flown;—he called aloud,—Oscar trembled and clung to Duncan's breast. Duncan peeped from his purple covert like a heath cock on his native waste, and again beheld the ruffian coming straight towards them, with his staff still heaved, and fury in his looks. When he came within a few yards he stood still and bellowed out, "Oscar, yho, yho!" Oscar quaked, and crept still closer to Duncan's breast; Duncan almost sunk in the earth. "D—n him," said the Englishman, "if I had a hold of him I should make both him and the little thievish rascal dear at a small price; they cannot be far gone,—I think I hear them." He then stood listening, but at that instant a farmer came up on horseback, and having heard him call, asked if he had lost his dog? the peasant answered in the affirmative, and added, that a blackguard boy had stolen him. The farmer said that he met a boy with a dog about a mile forward; during this dialogue the farmer's dog came up to Duncan's den,—smelled upon him, then upon Oscar,—cocked his tail,—walked round them growling, and then behaved in a very improper and uncivil manner to Duncan, who took all patiently, uncertain whether he was yet discovered. But so intent was the fellow upon the farmer's intelligence that he took no notice of the discovery made by the dog, but ran off without looking over his shoulder.

Duncan felt this a deliverance so great that all his other distresses vanished; and as soon as the man was out of his sight, he arose from his covert, and ran over the moor, and ere it was long came to a shepherd's house, where he got some whey and bread for his breakfast, which he thought the best meat he had ever tasted, yet shared it with Oscar.

Though I had his history from his own mouth, yet there is a space here which it is impossible to relate with any degree of distinctness or interest. He was a vagabond boy, without any fixed habitation, and wandered about Herriot moor, from one farm-house to another, for the space of a year; staying from one to twenty nights in each house according as he found the people kind to him. He seldom resented any indignity offered to himself, but whoever insulted Oscar, or offered any observations on the impropriety of their friendship, lost Duncan's company the next morning. He staid several months at a place called Dewar, which he said was haunted by the ghost of a piper. That piper had been murdered there many years before, in a manner somewhat mysterious, or at least unaccountable; and there was scarcely a night on which he was not supposed either to be seen or heard about the house. Duncan slept in the cow-house, and was terribly harassed by the piper;—he often heard him scratching about the rafters, and sometimes he would groan like a man dying, or a cow that was choked in the band; but at length he saw him at his side one night, which so discomposed him that he was obliged to leave the place, after being ill for many days. I shall give this story in Duncan's own words, which I have often heard him repeat without any variation.

"I had been driving some young cattle to the heights of Willenslee,—it grew late before I got home. I was thinking, and thinking, how cruel it was to kill the poor piper! to cut out his tongue, and stab him in the back! I thought it was no wonder that his ghost took it extremely ill; when all on a sudden I perceived a light before me.—I thought the wand in my hand was all on fire, and threw it away; but I perceived the light glide slowly by my right foot, and burn behind me. I was nothing afraid, and turned about to look at the light, and there I saw the piper, who was standing hard at my back, and when I turned round he looked me in the face. 'What was he like, Duncan?' He was like a dead body! but I got a short view of him; for that moment all grew dark around me as a pit. I tried to run, but sunk powerless to the earth, and lay in a kind of dream, I do not know how long. When I came to myself, I got up, and endeavoured to run, but fell to the ground every two steps. I was not a hundred yards from the house, and I am sure I fell upwards of an hundred times. Next day I was in a high fever,—the servants made me a little bed in the kitchen, to which I was confined by illness many days, during which time I suffered the most dreadful agonies by night, always imagining the piper to be standing over me on the one side or the other. As soon as I was able to walk I left Dewar, and for a long time durst neither sleep alone during the night, nor stay by myself in the daytime."

The superstitious ideas impressed upon Duncan's mind by this unfortunate encounter with the ghost of the piper, seems never to have been eradicated; a strong instance of the power of early impressions; and a warning how much caution is necessary in modelling the conceptions of the young and tender mind, for of all men I ever knew, he is the most afraid of meeting with apparitions. So deeply is his imagination tainted with this startling illusion, that even the calm disquisitions of reason have proved quite inadequate to the task of dispelling it. Whenever it wears late, he is always upon the look out for these ideal beings, keeping a jealous eye upon every bush and brake, in case they should be lurking behind them, ready to fly out and surprise him every moment; and the approach of a person in the dark, or any sudden noise, always puts him past speaking for some time.

After leaving Dewar, he again wandered about for a few weeks, and it appears that his youth, beauty, and peculiarly destitute situation, together with his friendship for his faithful Oscar, had interested the most part of the country people in his behalf, for he was generally treated with kindness. He knew his father's name and the name of his house, but as none of the people he visited had ever before heard of either the one or the other, they gave themselves no trouble about the matter.

He staid nearly two years in a place he called Cowhaur, till a wretch with whom he slept, struck and abused him one day. Duncan in a rage flew to the loft and cut all his Sunday hat, shoes, and coat to pieces; and not daring to abide the consequences, decamped that night.

He wandered about for some time longer among the farmers of Tweed and Yarrow; but this life was now become exceedingly disagreeable to him; he durst not sleep by himself, and the servants did not always choose that a vagrant boy and his great dog should sleep with them.

It was on a rainy night at the close of harvest that Duncan came to my father's house. I remember all the circumstances as well as the transactions of yesterday. The whole of his clothing consisted only of one black coat, which, having been made for a full-grown man, hung fairly to his heels; the hair of his head was rough, curled, and weather-beaten —but his face was ruddy and beautiful, bespeaking a healthy body and a sensible feeling heart. Oscar was still nearly as big as himself, had the colour of a fox, with a white stripe down his face, and a ring of the same colour around his neck, and was the most beautiful cur I have ever seen.— My heart was knit to Duncan at the first sight, and I wept for joy when I saw my parents so kind to him. My mother, in particular, could scarcely do anything else than converse with Duncan for several days. I was always of the party, and listened with wonder and admiration; but often have these adventures been repeated to me. My parents, who soon seemed to feel the same concern for him as if he had been their own son, clothed him in blue drugget, and bought him a smart little Highland bonnet, in which dress he looked so charming, that I would not let them have peace until I got one of the same. Indeed, all that Duncan said or did was to me a pattern, for I loved him as my own life. I was, at my own request, which he persuaded me to urge, permitted to be his bed-fellow; and many a happy night and day did I spend with Duncan and Oscar.

As far as I remember we felt no privation of any kind, and would have been completely happy if it had not been for the fear of spirits. When the conversation chanced to turn upon the Piper of Dewar, the Maid of Plora, or the Pedlar of Thirlstane-mill, often have we lain with the bedclothes drawn over our heads until nearly suffocated. We loved the fairies and the brownies, and even felt a little partiality for the mermaids, on account of their beauty and charming songs; we were a little jealous of the water-kelpies, and always kept aloof from the frightsome pools. We hated the devil most heartily, but we were not much afraid of him—but a ghost! oh dreadful! the names, ghost, spirit, or apparition, sounded in our ears like the knell of destruction, and our hearts sunk within us as if pierced by the cold icy shaft of death. Duncan herded my father's cows all the summer—so did I; we could not live asunder. We grew fishers so expert, that the speckled trout, with all his art, could not elude our machinations; we forced him from his watery cove, admired the beautiful shades and purple drops that were painted on his sleek sides, and forthwith added him to our number without reluctance. We assailed the habitation of the wild bee, and rifled all her accumulated sweets, though not without encountering the most determined resistance. My father's meadows abounded with hives, they were almost in every swath—in every hillock. When the swarm was large, they would beat us off day after day; in all these desperate engagements Oscar came to our assistance, and, provided that none of the enemies made a lodgment in his lower defiles, he was always the last combatant of our party on the field. I do not remember of ever being so much diverted by any scene I ever witnessed, or laughing as immoderately as I have done at seeing Oscar involved in a moving cloud of wild-bees—wheeling—snapping on all sides, and shaking his ears incessantly.

The sagacity which this animal possessed is almost incredible, while his undaunted spirit and generosity it would do honour to every servant of our own species to copy. Twice did he save his master's life: at one time when attacked by a furious bull, and at another time when he fell from behind my father off a horse into a flooded river. Oscar had just swimmed across, but instantly plunged in a second time to his master's rescue. He first got hold of his bonnet, but that coming off he quitted it, and again catching him by the coat, brought him to the side where my father reached him. He waked Duncan at a certain hour every morning, and would frequently turn the cows of his own will when he observed them wrong. If Duncan dropped his knife, or any other small article, he would fetch it along in his mouth, and if sent back for a lost thing, would infallibly find it. When sixteen years of age, after being unwell for several days, he died one night below his master's bed. On the evening before, when Duncan came in from the plough, he came from his hiding-place, wagged his tail, licked Duncan's hand, and returned to his death-bed. Duncan and I lamented him with unfeigned sorrow, buried him below the old rowan-tree at the back of my father's garden, placing a square stone at his head, which was still standing the last time I was there. With great labour we composed an epitaph between us, which was once carved on that stone: the metre was good, but the stone was so hard, and the engraving so faint, that the characters, like those of our early joys, are long ago defaced and extinct.

Often have I heard my mother relate with enthusiasm, the manner in which she and my father first discovered the dawnings of goodness and facility of conception in Duncan's mind, though I confess, dearly as I loved him, these circumstances escaped my observation. It was my father's invariable custom to pray with the family every night before they retired to rest; to thank the Almighty for his kindness to them during the bygone day; and to beg his protection through the dark and silent watches of the night. I need not inform any of the readers of this paper that that amiable (and now too much [neglected and despised) duty, consisted in singing a few stanzas of a psalm, in which all the family joined their voices with my father's, so that the double octaves of the various ages and sexes swelled the simple concert. He then read a chapter from the Bible, going straight on from beginning to end of the scriptures. The prayer concluded the devotions of each evening, in which the downfall of Antichrist was always strenuously urged, the ministers of the gospel remembered, nor was any friend or neighbour in distress forgot.

The servants of a family have, in general, liberty either to wait the evening prayers, or retire to bed as they affect; but no consideration whatever could induce Duncan to go one night to rest without the prayers, even though both wet and weary, and entreated by my parents to retire for fear of catching cold. It seems that I had been of a more complaisant disposition, for I was never very hard to prevail with in this respect; nay, my mother used to say that I was extremely apt to take a pain about my heart at that time of the night, and was of course frequently obliged to betake me to the bed before the worship commenced. It might be owing to this that Duncan's emotions on these occasions escaped my notice. He sung a treble to the old church tunes most sweetly, for he had a melodious voice, and when my father read the chapter, if it was in any of the historical parts of scripture, he would lean upon the table, and look him in the face, swallowing ever sentence with the utmost avidity. At one time, as my father read the 45th chapter of Genesis, he wept so bitterly that at the end my father paused and asked what ailed him? Duncan told him that he did not know.

At another time, the year following, my father, in the course of his evening devotions, had reached the 19th chapter of the book of Judges; when he began reading it, Duncan was seated on the other side of the house, but ere it was half done he had stole close up to my father's elbow. "Consider of it, take advice, and speak your minds," said my father, and closed the book. "Go on, go on, if you please, Sir," said Duncan; "go on, and let us hear what they said about it." My father looked sternly in Duncan's face, but seeing him abashed on his hasty breach of decency, without uttering a word he again opened the Bible and read the 20th chapter throughout notwithstanding of its great length. Next day Duncan was walking about with the Bible below his arm, begging of everybody to read it to him again and again. This incident produced a conversation between my parents on the expenses and utility of education; the consequence of which was, that the week following Duncan and I were sent to the parish school, and began at the same instant to the study of that most important and fundamental branch of literature, the A, B, C; but my sister Mary, who was older than me, was already an accurate and elegant reader.

This reminds me of another anecdote of Duncan, with regard to family worship, which I have often heard related, and which I myself may well remember. My father happening to be absent over night at a fair, when the usual time of worship arrived, my mother desired a lad, one of the servants, to act as chaplain for that night; the lad declined it, and slunk away to his bed. My mother testified her regret that we should all be obliged to go prayerless to our beds for that night, observing that she did not remember the time when it had so happened before. Duncan said he thought we might contrive to manage it amongst us, and instantly proposed to sing the psalm and pray, if Mary would read the chapter. To this my mother with some hesitation agreed, observing, that if he prayed as he could, with a pure heart, his prayer had as good a chance of being accepted as some others that were *better worded*. Duncan could not then read, but having learned several psalms from Mary by rote, he caused her seek out the place, and sung the 23d psalm from end to end, with great sweetness and decency. Mary read a chapter in the New Testament, and then (my mother having a child on her knee) we three kneeled in a row, when Duncan prayed thus :—" O Lord, be thou our God, our guide, and our guard unto death, and through death." That was a sentence my father often used in his prayer; Duncan had laid hold of it, and my mother began to think that he had often prayed previous to that time. "O Lord, thou"———— continued Duncan, but his matter was exhausted; a long long pause ensued, which I at length broke by bursting into a loud fit of laughter. Duncan rose hastily, and without once holding up his head, went crying to his bed; and as I continued to indulge in laughter, my mother for my irreverend behaviour, struck me across the shoulders with the tongs; our evening devotions terminated exceedingly ill, I went crying to my bed after Duncan, even louder than he, and abusing him for his *useless prayer*, for which I had been nearly felled.

By the time that we were recalled from school to herd the cows next summer, we could both read the bible with considerable facility, but Duncan far excelled me in perspicacity, and so fond was he of reading bible history, that the reading of it was now our constant amusement. Often has Mary, and he, and I, lain under the same plaid by the side of the corn or meadow, and read chapter about on the bible for hours together, weeping over the failings and fall of good men, and wondering at the inconceivable might of the heroes of antiquity. Never was man so delighted as Duncan was when he came to the history of Samson, and afterwards of David and Goliath; he could not be satisfied until he had read it to every individual with whom he was acquainted, judging it to be as new and as interesting to every one, as it was to himself. I have seen him standing by the girls as they were milking the cows, reading to them the feats of Samson, and, in short, harassing every man and woman about the hamlet for audience. On Sundays my parents accompanied us to the fields, and joined in our delightful exercise.

Time passed away, and so also did our youthful delights! but other cares and other pleasures awaited us. As we advanced in years and strength, we quitted the herding, and bore a hand in the labours of the farm. Mary, too, was often our assistant. She and Duncan were nearly of an age—he was tall, comely, and affable; and if Mary was not the prettiest girl in the parish, at least Duncan and I believed her to be so, which, with us, amounted to the same thing. We often compared the other girls in the parish with one another, as to their beauty and accomplishments, but to think of comparing any of them with Mary, was entirely out of the question. She was indeed the emblem of truth, simplicity and innocence, and if there were few more beautiful, there were still fewer so good and amiable; but still as she advanced in years, she grew fonder and fonder of being near Duncan; and, by the time she was nineteen, was so deeply in love that it affected her manner, her spirits, and her health. At one time she was gay and frisky as a kitten; she would dance, sing, and laugh violently at the most trivial incidents. At other times she was silent and sad, while a languishing softness overspread her features, and added greatly to her charms. The passion was undoubtedly mutual between them; but Duncan, either from a sense of honour, or some other cause, never declared himself farther on the subject than by the most respectful attention, and tender assiduities. Hope and fear thus alternately swayed the heart of poor Mary, and produced in her deportment that variety of affections which could not fail of rendering the sentiments of her artless bosom legible to the eye of experience.

In this state matters stood, when an incident occurred which deranged our social happiness at once, and the time arrived, when the kindest and most affectionate little social band of friends, that ever panted to meet the wishes of each other, were obliged to part.

About 40 years ago the flocks of southern sheep, which have since that period depopulated the Highlands, had not found their way over the Grampian mountains; and the native flocks of that sequestered country were so scanty, that it was found necessary to transport small quantities of wool annually to the north, to furnish materials for clothing the inhabitants. During two months of each summer, the hill countries of the Lowlands were inundated by hundreds of women from the Highlands, who bartered small articles of dress, and of domestic import, for wool: these were known by the appellation of *norlan' netties*, and few nights passed, during the wool season, that some of them were not lodged at my father's house. It was from two of these that Duncan learned one day who and what he was; that he was the laird of Glenegle's only son and heir, and that a large sum had been offered to any that could discover him. My parents certainly rejoiced in Duncan's good fortune, yet they were disconsolate at parting with him, for he had long ago become to them as a son of their own; and, I seriously believe, that, from the day they first met, to that on which the two *norlan' netties* came to our house, they never once entertained the idea of parting. For my part, I wished that the netties had never been born, or that they had staid at their own home, for the thoughts of being separated from my dear friend, made me sick at heart. All our feelings were, however, nothing, when compared with those of my dear sister Mary. From the day that the two women left our house, she was no more seen to smile; she had never yet divulged the sentiments of her heart to any one, and imagined her love for Duncan a profound secret—no,

"She never told her love;
But let concealment, like a worm i' the bud,
Feed on her damask cheek:—she pined in thought;
And, with a green and yellow melancholy,
She sat, like patience on a monument,
Smiling at grief."

Our social glee and cheerfulness were now completely clouded; we sat down to our meals, and rose from them in silence. Of the few observations that passed, every one seemed the progeny of embarrassment and discontent, and our general remarks were strained and cold. One day at dinner, after a long and sullen pause, my father said, "I hope you do not intend to leave us very soon, Duncan?" "I am thinking of going away to-morrow, Sir," said Duncan. The knife fell from my mother's hand;—she looked him steadily in the face for the space of a minute. "Duncan," said she, her voice faultering, and the tears dropping from her eyes,—" Duncan, I never durst ask you before, but I hope you will not leave us altogether." Duncan thrust the plate from before him into the middle of the table—took up a book that lay on the window, and looked over the pages.—Mary left the room.—No answer was returned, nor any further inquiry made; and our little party broke up in silence.

When we met again in the evening we were still all sullen. My mother tried to speak of indifferent things, but it was apparent that her thoughts had no share in the words that dropped from her tongue. My father at last said, "You will soon forget us, Duncan, but there are some among us who will not so soon forget you." Mary again left the room, and silence ensued, until the family were called together for evening worship. There was one sentence in my father's prayer that night which I think I yet remember word for word. It may appear of little importance to those who are nowise interested, but it affected us deeply, and left not a dry cheek in the family. It run thus: —" We are an unworthy little flock, thou seest here kneeling before thee, our God; but few as we are, it is probable we shall never all kneel again together before thee in this world. We have long lived together in peace and happiness, and hoped to have lived so much longer; but since it is thy will that we part, enable us to submit to thy will with firmness, and though thou scatter us to the four winds of heaven, may thy almighty arm still be about us for good; and grant that we may all meet hereafter, in another and a better world!"

The next morning, after a restless night, Duncan rose early, put on his best suit, and packed up some little articles to carry with him. I lay panting and trembling, but pretended to be fast asleep. When he was ready to depart, he took his bundle below his arm, came up to the side of the bed, and listened if I was sleeping. He then stood long hesitating, looking wistfully to the door, and then to me alternately; and I saw him three or four times wipe his eyes. At length he shook me gently by the shoulder, and asked if I was awake? I feigned to start, and answered as if half asleep. "I must bid you farewell," said he, groping to get hold of my hand. "Will you not breakfast with us, Duncan?" said I. "No," said he, "I am thinking that it is best to steal away, for it will break my heart to take leave of your parents and—" "And who, Duncan?" said I. "And you," said he. "Indeed, but it is not best, Duncan," said I; "we will all breakfast together for the last time, and then take a formal and kind leave of each other." We did breakfast together, and, as the conversation turned on former days, it became highly interesting to us all. When my father had returned thanks to heaven for our meal, we knew what was coming, and began to look at each other. Duncan rose, and after we had all loaded him with our blessings and warmest wishes, he embraced my parents and me. He turned about. His eyes said plainly, there is somebody still wanting, but his heart was so full he could not speak.

"What is become of Mary?" said my father. Mary was gone! We searched the house, the garden, and the houses of all the cottagers, but she was nowhere to be found. Poor lovelorn, forsaken Mary! She had hid herself in the ancient yew that grows in front of the old ruin, that she might see her lover depart, without being herself seen, and might indulge in all the luxury of wo. Poor, tender-hearted Mary! how often have I heard her sigh, and seen her eyes red with weeping; while the smile that played on her languid features, when ought was mentioned to Duncan's recommendation, would have melted a heart of adamant.

I must pass over Duncan's journey to the north Highlands for want of room, but on the evening of the sixth day after leaving my father's house, he reached the mansion-house of Glenegle, which stands in a little beautiful woody strath, commanding a view of the Deu-Caledonian Sea, and part of the Hebrides. Every avenue, tree, and rock was yet familiar to Duncan's recollection, and the feelings of his sensible heart, on approaching the abode of his father, whom he had long scarcely thought of, can only be conceived by a heart like his own. He had, without discovering himself, learned from a peasant that his father was still alive, but that he had never overcome the loss of his son, for whom he lamented every day: that his wife and daughter lorded it over him, holding his pleasure at nought, and rendering his age extremely unhappy: that they had expelled all his old vassals and farmers, and introduced the lady's vulgar presumptuous relations, who neither paid him rents, honour, nor obedience.

Old Glenegle was taking his evening walk on the road by which Duncan descended the strath to his dwelling. He was pondering on his misfortunes, and did not even deign to lift his eyes as the young stranger approached, but seemed counting the number of marks which the horses' hoofs had made on the way. "Good e'en to you, Sir," said Duncan. The old man started, and stared him in the face, but with a look so unsteady and harassed that he seemed incapable of distinguishing any lineament or feature of it. "Good e'en, good e'en," said he, wiped his brow with his arm, and passed by. What there was in the voice that struck him so forcibly it is hard to say. Nature is powerful. Duncan could not think of ought to detain him, and being desirous of seeing how matters went on about the house, thought it best to remain some days in cog. He went into the fore-kitchen, conversed freely with the servants, and soon saw his stepmother and sister appear. The former had all the insolence and ignorant pride of vulgarity raised to wealth and eminence; the other seemed naturally of an amiable disposition, but was entirely ruled by her mother, who taught her to disdain her father, all his relations, and whomsoever he loved. On that same evening he came into the kitchen where she then was chatting with Duncan, to whom she seemed attached at first sight. "Lexy, my dear," said he, "did you see my spectacles?" "Yes," said she, "I saw them on your nose to-day at breakfast." "Well, but I have lost them since," said he. "You may take up the next you find," said she. "I wish they may never be more seen." The servants laughed. "I might well have known what information I would get of you," said he, regretfully. "How can you speak in such a style to your father, my dear lady," said Duncan. "If I were here I would place you where you should learn better manners. It ill becomes so pretty a young lady to address an old father thus." "He!" said she, "who minds him! he's a dotard,—an old whining, complaining creature,—worse than a child." "But consider his years, my dear," said Duncan; "and, besides, he may have met with crosses and losses sufficient to sour the temper of a younger man. You should, at all events, pity and reverence, but never despise your father." The old lady now joined them. "You have yet heard nothing, young man," said the old laird, "if you saw how my heart is sometimes wrung! Yes, I have had losses, indeed!" "Your losses?" said his spouse; "no, you have never had any losses that did not in the end turn out a vast profit." "Do you then account the loss of a loving wife and a son nothing?" said he. "But have you not got a loving wife and a daughter in their room, you old ungrateful being?" returned she; "the one will not waste your fortune as a prodigal son would have done, and the other will take care of both you and that, when you can no longer do either. The loss of your son, indeed!—it was the greatest blessing you could have received." "Unfeeling woman!" said he, "but Heaven may yet restore that son to protect the grey hairs of his old father from insult, and lay his head in an honoured grave." The old man's spirits were quite gone—he cried like a child—his lady mimicked him—his daughter pulled his wig, and the servants raised a horse laugh. "Inhuman wretches!" said Duncan, starting up, and pushing them aside, "thus to mock the feelings of an old man, even though he were not the lord and master of you all; but take notice—the individual among you all that dares to offer such another insult to him, I'll roast on that fire." The old man clung to him, and looked him ruefully in the face. "You impudent, beggarly vagabond!" said the lady, "do you know to whom you speak?—servants turn that wretch out of the house, and hunt him with all the dogs in the kennel." —"Softly, softly, good lady," said Duncan, "take care that I do not turn you out of the house."—"Alas! good youth," said the old laird, "you little know what you are about; for mercy's sake forbear! you are brewing vengeance both for yourself and me."—"Fear not," said Duncan, "I will protect you with my life."—"Pray, may I ask you what is your name?" said the old man, still looking earnestly at him.—"That you may," replied Duncan, "no man has so good a right to ask anything of me as you have, I am Duncan Campbell, your own long lost son." "M—m—m— my son!" exclaimed the old man, and sunk back on a seat with a convulsive moan. Duncan held him in his arms—he soon recovered, and asked many incoherent questions, looked at the two moles on his right leg—kissed him, and then wept on his bosom for joy. "Oh, God of Heaven," said he, "it is long since I could thank thee heartily for anything; now I do thank thee, indeed, for I have found my son! my dear son!"

Contrary to what might have been expected, Duncan's pretty only sister Alexia, rejoiced most of all in his discovery. She was almost wild with joy at finding such a brother—the old lady, her mother, was said to have wept bitterly in private, but knowing that Duncan would be her master, she behaved to him with civility and respect. Everything was committed to his management, and he soon discovered that, besides a good clear estate, his father's personal funds were very large. The halls and cottages of Glenegle were filled with feasting, joy and gladness.

It was not so at my father's house, misfortunes seldom come singly. Scarcely had our feelings overcome the shock which they received by the loss of our beloved Duncan, when a more terrible misfortune overtook us. My father, by the monstrous ingratitude of a friend whom he trusted, lost at once the greatest part of his hard-earned fortune. The blow came unexpectedly, and distracted his personal affairs to such a degree, that an arrangement seemed almost totally irrecoverable. He struggled on with securities for several months, but perceiving that he was drawing his real friends into danger, by their signing of bonds which he might never be able to redeem, he lost heart entirely, and yielded to the torrent. Mary's mind seemed to gain fresh energy every day. The activity and diligence which she evinced in managing the affairs of the farm, and even in giving advice with regard to other matters, was quite incredible;—often have I thought what a treasure that inestimable girl would have been to an industrious man whom she loved. All our efforts availed nothing; my father received letters of horning on bills to a large amount, and we expected every day that he would be taken from us and dragged to a prison.

We were all sitting in our little room one day, consulting what was best to be done—we could decide upon nothing, for our case was desperate. We were fallen into a kind of stupor, but the window being up, a sight appeared that quickly thrilled every heart with the keenest sensations of anguish: two men came riding sharply up by the back of the old schoolhouse. "Yonder are the lawyers now," said my mother, "what shall we do?" We hurried to the window, and all of us soon discerned that they were no other than the officers of justice. My mother entreated of my father to escape and hide himself until this first storm was overblown, but he would in nowise consent, assuring us that he had done nothing of which he was ashamed, and that he was determined to meet every one face to face, and let them do their worst; so finding all our entreaties vain, we could do nothing but sit down and weep. At length we heard the noise of their horses at the door. "You had better take the men's horses, James," said my father, "as there is no other man at hand." "We will stay till they rap, if you please," said I. The cautious officer did not however rap, but, afraid lest his debtor should make his escape, he jumped lightly from his horse, and hastened into the house. When we heard him open the outer door, and his footsteps approaching along the entry, our hearts fainted within us—he opened the door and stepped into the room—it was Duncan!—our own dearly beloved Duncan. The women uttered an involuntary scream of surprise,—but my father ran and got hold of one hand, and I of the other,—my mother, too, soon had him in her arms; but our embrace was short, for his eyes fixed on poor sweet Mary, who stood trembling with joy and wonder in a corner of the room, changing her colour every moment. He snatched her up in his arms and kissed her lips, and ere ever she was aware, her pretty arms had encircled his neck. "O, my dear Mary," said he, "my heart has been ill at ease since I left you, but I durst not then tell you a word of my mind, for I little knew how I was to find affairs in the place where I was going; but, ah! you little elusive rogue, you owe me another for the one you cheated me out of;" so saying, he pressed his lips again to hers, and then led her to a seat. Duncan then recounted all his adventures to us, with every circumstance of his good fortune,—our hearts were uplifted almost past bearing—all our own cares and sorrows were now forgotten, and we were once more the happiest little group that ever perhaps sat together. Before the cloth was laid for dinner, Mary ran out to put on her white gown, and comb her yellow hair, but was surprised at meeting with a smart young gentleman in the kitchen, with a scarlet neck on his coat, and a gold-laced hat. Mary, having never seen so fine a gentleman, made him a low curtsey, and offered to conduct him to the room; but he smiled, and told her he was the squire's servant. We had all of us forgot to ask for the gentleman that came with Duncan.

Duncan and Mary walked for two hours in the garden that evening. We did not know what passed between them, but the next day he asked her in marriage of my parents; and never will I forget the supreme happiness and gratitude that beamed in every face on that happy occasion. I need not tell my readers that my father's affairs were soon retrieved, or that I accompanied my dear Mary a bride to the Highlands, and had the satisfaction of saluting her as Mrs. Campbell, and lady of Glenegle.

CHEAP NEWSPAPERS.—In the State of New York, there are about 234 newspapers. In the city of New York alone, there are 51 papers, of all kinds; 11 of these are published daily, ten twice a-week, 24 weekly, 5 once a-fortnight, and one monthly. The number of papers printed in the city, in one year, is 9,536,000; in the whole State, 14,536,000. In Great Britain and Ireland, there are only 334 newspapers, of which 17 are daily papers; 13 in London, and 4 in Dublin. Scotland, with all its wealth and intelligence, has not one daily paper. The total amount of the circulation of these papers, is estimated at 27,827,000, with a population of 23 millions. In the whole United States of America, with a population of 10 millions, there are about 800 newspapers, and the total circulation is 64,000,000; thus establishing the fact, that the United States have five newspapers for its population, in proportion to one in the British isles. A newspaper, about the usual size, costs little more than one-sixth of the amount which the stamp-duty, and duties on paper, compel us to charge. There is not, in consequence of this, any portion of the population of the United States, to which newspapers do not find access. There is no book so cheap as a newspaper. Being new every day or week, it excites to a habit of reading, and affords an easy and agreeable mode of acquiring knowledge, so essential to the welfare of the individual and community. It causes an hour to be spent pleasantly, and oftentimes profitably, which might otherwise have been wasted in idleness and dissipation. Of this description of literature, the Americans have the full benefit. In this country the taxes prohibits the introduction of newspapers to the great mass of the population, and the poor are left without being much acquainted with the circumstances which occasion the gradations of rank and inequality of fortune,—the circumstances which at times elevate or depress the state of wages, with many other things connected with their interests. If the poorer classes of the population enjoyed the same advantages of information which those in a higher sphere possess, they would make known their wants by peaceable and constitutional means, instead of the blinded influence of physical power. In America, the working classes have Journals of their own, which represent their wants and desires. In this country the great majority of this class are excluded from benefits which would undoubtedly tend to improve their moral condition, and do away with those demoralizing habits which frequently give place to hours of listless vacancy. Were the tax *entirely* removed from newspapers, we would soon witness the salutary effects which would follow such an arrangement, exemplified in the morals, and advancing intelligence of the people.

SCRAPS.

ORIGIN OF CARDS.—About the year 1390, cards are said to have been invented, to divert Charles IV., then King of France, who had fallen into a melancholy disposition. About the same time is found in the account-book of the King's cofferer, the following charge for a pack of painted leaves, bought for the King's amusement—3 livres. Printing and stamping being not then discovered, the cards were painted, which made them dearer.

Of their designs—the inventor proposed by the figures of the four suits (or colours) to represent the four classes of men in the kingdom. By the Cæsars (Hearts) are meant the *gens de chœur*—choirmen or ecclesiastics. The nobility, or prime military parts of the kingdom, are represented by the ends or points of lances or pikes, (and our ignorance induced us to call them Spades.) By Diamonds are designed the merchants and tradesmen. Treste, or the trefoil-leaf, or clover-grass, (corruptly called Clubs,) alludes to the husbandmen and peasants.

The "History of the four Kings," which the French, in drollery, sometimes call "the cards," is that of David, Alexander, Cæsar, and Charles—names which were, and still are on the French cards. These respective names represent the four celebrated monarchies of the Jews, Greeks, Romans, and Franks, under Charlemagne.—By the Queens, are intended Argine, Esther, Judith, and Pallas, (names retained in the French cards,) typical of birth, piety, fortitude, and wisdom—the qualification residing in each person.—By the Knaves, were designed the servants of knights, (for knave originally meant only a servant; and in an old translation of the Bible, Paul is called the knave of Christ. Others fancy that the knights themselves were designed by those cards, because Hogier and Lahires, two names on the French cards, were famous knights at the time cards were invented.

A GHOST STORY—PROFESSOR JUNKER.—The Professor was in the habit of sleeping next to the place in which he kept his subjects, and one night hearing a noise in that room, and supposing that the cats or mice had got at the bodies, he rose from bed, and, directed by the noise, advanced to the further end of the apartment, where, to his inexpressible horror, he beheld a naked man standing with his back to the wall! His eyes glared, and were widely opened, and his distended nostrils and convulsed features so alarmed the Professor, that he frankly confessed he was so terrified that he retired, with his face to the figure, which followed him to his bed room; but unfortunately in stepping into the chamber, his foot slipped, he fell down, and the candle was extinguished! He crept, however, as quietly and quickly into bed as possible, but was very soon disturbed by the figure pulling at the bed-clothes, and at length seizing his feet, implored him, as the executioner, to spare his life. The Professor, after a few moments' reflection, recollected that one of the subjects which had been brought into the rooms during the day was a man who had been hanged, immediately rose, and, procuring a candle, put those remedies in requisition which are deemed necessary in such cases. The man was perfectly restored to life; but Junker knew not what to do with him as he could not procure a passport, and no one was allowed to pass through the gates without one. However, with some little difficulty, he contrived to get him out of town, and giving him such a sum as his means permitted, wished him farewell, and returned back. Many years afterwards the Professor had some business which took him to Hamburgh, and one day while standing on the Exchange, a very respectable looking man addressed him by name, and inquired if he remembered him? He replied that a man in his public capacity could not recollect all the persons who might be introduced to him—but that it was more than likely they had met before. The stranger then led him aside, and told him he was the person he had many years ago in Halle; that on leaving him he had m his way to Hamburgh, where, by frugality and indu he had amassed a considerable fortune. He then invi the Professor home with him; treated him sumptuous and dying soon after this, bequeathed all his wealth to J ker. We quote this anecdote from memory, as we do remember the work in which we read it, but know we correct in the outline, however deficient in detail. Professor used to tell the story himself, but not until a the death of the man.

A DINNER AT HAVANNAH.—The charge for din was one dollar, for which abundant fare was provided, clusive of French claret. Soups, solids, and dessert w placed on the table at once; the dishes were crowded on another, and on the ringing of the bell the company hasti took their seats, and made a vigorous onslaught. Every o plunged his fork into the dish he liked best; and there w such a scramble, such a clatter of knives and plates, that reminded me of Dugald Dalgetty laying in his provent f three days. Such a quantity of oil and grease, to say n thing of garlic, is used in Spanish cookery, that I real could not "play the knife and fork" that my appeti prompted me to do, but contrived to allay the cravings hunger with coffee and bread at the end of the feast. Th company consisted of Spaniards, Germans, Frenchmen, Ru sians, and English, captains of ships; it was a strange medle both as to language and manners. Most of the guests ha the air of desperadoes and adventurers, and they seeme very indifferent to common courtesy in their behaviour to each other: thus, at these houses, it is no uncommon thing to see joints of meat and glasses flying across the table, and violent quarrels ending in blows. Sometimes they commence in this way: a skipper asks for an omelet opposite to him; a negro runs round to fetch it; in conveying it to the sailor he is stopped half-way by another gentleman, who coolly seizes the dish, cuts the omelet in two, takes half himself, and gives the other half to a friend next him; the disappointed skipper vents his rage by uttering a hearty curse, and sends his glass at the head of the gentleman who had taken "the bread out of his mouth."—*Alexander's Transatlantic Sketches.*

CLERICAL COMPLIMENT IN GERMANY.—The marriage ceremony was just concluded, and the reverend priest enjoined the bride and bridegroom to think solemnly of the engagement they had contracted. "It is true," he added, "that few marriages promise more substantial happiness than yours. Men commonly are "influenced on such occasions, by either *beauty*, *wealth*, or *youth*,—things, in their essence, vain and frivolous; but he whom you have now taken as a husband was evidently unbiassed by any of those *paltry considerations*, and—" (here the *modest* bride, overcome by so much flattery, fainted away.)

To the Readers of the Schoolmaster	401
The American Indians in Canada—Missionary labours	402
Ghosts by Waggery	404
Picture of a London Quarter, and Moral Education of the People	405
King James's Clasp Knife	ib.
USEFUL NOTICES—Improvement of Heath land, and Cultivation of Potatoes—Simple and Useful Invention	406
Early Days of Lord Brougham—Reward of Authors—Extraordinary Surgical Operation	ib.
MEDICAL SELECTIONS—Estimate of different descriptions of Food in regard to Nutriment—Effects of different temperatures upon the Body and upon Health—Remedies for Consumption	407
COLUMN FOR THE LADIES—Praise of Women	408
THE STORY-TELLER—Duncan and his Dog	408
Cheap Newspapers	415
SCRAPS—Origin of Cards—A Ghost Story—A Dinner at Havannah—Clerical Compliment in Germany	416

EDINBURGH: Printed by and for JOHN JOHNSTONE, 19, St. James's Square.—Published by JOHN ANDERSON, Jun., Bookseller, 55, North Bridge Street, Edinburgh; by JOHN MACLEOD, and ATKINSON & Co. Booksellers, Glasgow; and sold by all Booksellers and Vendors of Cheap Periodicals.

Lightning Source UK Ltd.
Milton Keynes UK
UKOW05f0256111115

262444UK00001B/36/P